P9-CJH-934

Catalog of the Genera of Recent Fishes

Catalog of the Genera of Recent Fishes

William N. Eschmeyer

Published by
California Academy of Sciences

San Francisco

1990

Published by the California Academy of Sciences

Library of Congress Catalog Card Number 90-082789
ISBN 0-940228-23-8

Catalog of the Genera of Recent Fishes

William N. Eschmeyer

Department of Ichthyology, California Academy of Sciences, San Francisco, California 94118

Contents

PROGRAMMERS: Barbara Weitbrecht and David Boughton

INTRODUCTION

William N. Eschmeyer

The audience needing information about fishes is broader today than ever. It includes evolutionary and environmental biologists concerned with biodiversity, fishery biologists, ecologists, and even administrators and legislators. There is no up-to-date worldwide summary of the knowledge of the kinds of fishes, and one must rely on regional works and on abstracting services such as *Zoological Record* and *Biological Abstracts*. These and similar services provide an ongoing review of the increase in knowledge. Computer searches for cumulative information (by taxa and key words) are becoming available, but the changing nature of taxonomic classifications and scientific names sometimes makes it impossible to know under which specific, generic, or even family names one will find pertinent information. For fishes, there are important regional summaries for some areas, such as North America, Europe, and many marine areas, but such summaries are lacking for major geographic regions of the world, such as the fresh-waters of South America and Asia. The building of large computer databases should facilitate the availability and usefulness of taxonomic information. The present Catalog is reproduced from a larger database project for fishes underway at the California Academy of Sciences. Even though some information is lacking for some genera and nomenclatural problems remain, it was considered timely to publish this Catalog to bring the available information on genera of fishes up to date. Genus-group names described prior to 1 January 1990 are included.

It is hoped that the present summary of the genera and subgenera of fishes will serve several audiences. The broad audience consists mostly of non-specialists needing information about fishes. For them, this summary may be useful in providing a guide to recent literature treating the various genera and subgenera. For fish systematists, a special effort was directed toward making this Catalog accurate with regard to spellings, type species, and nomenclatural particulars such as availability, date of publication, and authorship; it is hoped that it will be a valuable reference for those workers. Other zoological taxonomists may use the catalog to avoid creating new genus-group names that are already used in fishes, or to solve homonymy problems. Appendix A provides an interpretation of the Code of Zoological Nomenclature as it applies to genus-group names (with examples from fishes), and this may prove of interest to other taxonomists.

Preparation of the Catalog

In late 1984, the first genus record was begun in a database maintained at the California Academy of Sciences. A request to the National Science Foundation for support to build databases for fishes was made, and a two-year project to treat the genera of fishes was funded. Subsequent support was provided to proof and improve the database of genera and to begin building databases for the approximately 55,000 named species and subspecies of fishes, as well as genera based on fossils, family-group names of fishes, and the corresponding bibliography.

The database for genera was built from several sources. About half of the computer records were started from Jordan's (1917-23) *Genera of Fishes*; new genera proposed since 1920 were added from the Zoological Record. Cards maintained at the University of Michigan for post-Jordan genera were compared with information in the database. Next, all genera treated in Fowler's *Fishes of the World* (see below) were compared with information in the database, as were genera in Zoological Record from 1920 back to its beginning in 1864. Information in the database was then compared to generic treatments in monographs and large general works, including Norman's *Draft Synopsis* [Norman 1966], *Smith's Sea Fishes* [Smith & Heemstra 1986], CLOFNAM [Hureau & Monod 1973], CLOFRES [Dor 1984], CLOFFA [Daget et al. 1984, 1986], *Zoological Catalogue of Australia* (v. 7) [Paxton et al. 1989], and other sources, such as Golvan's (1962 [ref. 13459]) list of genera. As the genera records were being created, the corresponding literature was entered in the references database. By this time, many discrepancies, errors in current literature, and potential nomenclatural problems were identified. It became obvious that the best course would be to attempt to examine all original descriptions; this process was begun in late 1986. At the same time, an attempt was made to provide the current status of each genus, using recent references. We began the project using dBase III® software and later updated to Foxbase®. Xerox® Ventura Publisher 2.0® was used to assemble camera-ready copy.

Probably the most useful source in preparing the Catalog was Henry W. Fowler's *Fishes of the World*. Fowler was a bibliophile, known for his extensive synonymies and literature summaries. Fairly late in his long career at the Academy of Natural Sciences of Philadelphia, he began a project summarizing names of all Recent and fossil fishes, including taxa at all levels. He ended active work on this project in the middle 1950s. Over the period 1964 to 1977 the first portions of the manuscript were published in parts by the Taiwan Museum in their Quarterly Journal. Fowler became incapacitated in 1962 and died in 1965, and much of the typescript was not seen by him before being published. Most of the work of assembling, typing, and editing was done by Venia T. Phillips, and later by Judy Silver, from Fowler's handwritten notes on slips of paper. By 1977, nearly 2000 printed pages had been published (see Fowler 1964-1977 references in the Literature Cited). The published portions contained many errors, and correspondence (in archives at the Academy of Natural Sciences) between Philadelphia and Taiwan indicated that the Philadelphia Academy did not wish to have more of the manuscript published (see also Copeia 1977 (no. 4):811). After inquiries to the Academy of Natural Sciences, and with assistance from Eugenia Böhlke (and William Smith-Vaniz and William Saul), the remaining portions of the manuscript were located and made available to me. This consisted of nearly 4000 typed pages and two boxes of folders containing handwritten entries for the remaining groups (only the plectognath section was missing). Each generic entry was checked against information in the database. Although the work contained many errors, they were not crucial for our purposes—nearly all genera were spelled correctly, dates were normally accurate, and errors in citations were mostly obvious ones. The unpublished typed manuscript had fewer errors than the published portions, as many errors in the published parts seemingly were introduced in typesetting. From Fowler's manuscript we located some genera that only he found, noted earlier publications of genera, and located many discrepancies between information already in the database and Fowler's findings.

Fowler's contemporary and equal as a bibliophile was the late Gilbert P. Whitley. Whitley (1966 [ref. 12521]) stated his intention to publish a *Genera of Fishes*. Through correspondence with John Paxton at the Australian Museum, I was able to examine sample portions of notebooks maintained by Whitley, but his notebooks consisted only of a list of genus name, author, and date in alphabetical order. This list was not useful in the present project, because by the time it was examined, the genera database was more complete and contained more information than Whitley's list.

Also transferred from the Academy of Natural Sciences of Philadelphia for use on this project was a card catalog of genera and species prepared by Henry Fowler. Most cards appear to be prepared directly from original descriptions. The cards treat taxa only to about 1905, but they were very useful in solving some date problems, in finding the earliest reference to original descriptions, and in obtaining dates and pages for the citation to type species.

Organization of the Catalog

The Catalog is divided into three major parts: I. Genus-Group Names, II. Names in a Classification, and III. Literature Cited. These are followed by a glossary and two appendices. Since genera are arranged alphabetically in Part I, no index to them is provided.

Part I. Genera of Recent Fishes

Part I consists of all genus-group names (genera and subgenera—and referred to collectively as "genera" in the Catalog), arranged alphabetically. Reeve M. Bailey, who helped prepare this part, provided xeroxes of cards recording genus-group names maintained by the Fish Division of the Museum of Zoology, University of Michigan; he assisted with the proofing of some original descriptions of genera, and with analysis of specific nomenclatural or date problems; and he was responsible for the assignment of gender for most taxa.

The following items are treated:

Name. The genus-group name as first proposed. The original spelling is used except where mandatory changes are necessary, such as changing *Lucio-Perca* to *Lucioperca.*

Subgenus of. When the name was proposed as a subgeneric one, the genus of which it was a subgenus, or qualifying "section," is given in parentheses.

Author. The author of the new name is given next—qualified as necessary by "in" statements, such as Cuvier in Cuvier & Valenciennes, or "ex," meaning from, such as Lacepède (ex Commerson). Authorship is discussed in Appendix A.

Date. The year of publication of the name is provided.

Page. Usually only one page is cited—the page on which the main generic description begins (not necessarily the page on which the genus is first mentioned). When more than one page is given, the genus may appear in a key, for example, and be followed later in the text by additional information. In some early works, where a generic description may not have been given, several pages that concern publication of the name may be cited. Pages in brackets are those assigned in an unpaginated work or in a separate in which pagination differs from that in the original publication.

Reference Number. The reference number enclosed in brackets corresponds to the number given in the Literature Cited section (Part III).

Gender. When given, the abbreviations are as follows: Masc. = masculine, Fem. = feminine, Neut. = neuter.

Type Species, Author, Date, Page. The original genus of the type species, the specific name, author, date, and page are given next. Mandatory corrections to species names have been made. Occasionally a second species is indicated in parentheses, and the use of this convention may have several meanings (usually amplified in the remarks section). The species in parentheses is typically the senior objective synonym, especially when the author of the genus provided a new (unneeded) name for the older species name. In other cases the author of the new genus or subgenus may attribute authorship of the type species not to the original author of the species but to some later author; normally the original author of the species is given (regardless of the species authorship attributed by the author of the genus), but there are some statements such as, "Type species *Alpha beta* of Jones (= *Gamma delta* Smith 1945)." When an author makes an equivalent type designation statement—i.e., type is so- and-so = so-and-so, amplification is given in the remarks. The use of parentheses does **not** show subjective taxonomic decisions involving the status of the type species; only objective synonyms are dealt with.

Text Remarks. Remarks, given next, cover such items as the method of type designation, the subsequent designator, comments on preoccupation, misspellings, emendations, and other pertinent remarks.

a. Method of Type Designation. First is given the method by which the type species was established (fixed). This subject, which is discussed in some detail in Appendix A, seems to cause current workers many problems. Although "type by original designation" takes precedence over other designations, a distinction is made between "original designation (also monotypic)" and "original designation"; the former insures that the likelihood of the name having a different type is remote; the latter means there was more than one originally included available species treated as valid. Other amplification is sometimes given, e.g., "Type by monotypy (also by use of *typus*)," but in these instances the use of *typus* or similar denotation is a form of indication that comes into play only when other designations do not take precedence, and when there are two or more originally included species in the taxon. When the type species is designated after the original description, amplification is provided, such as a citation to the subsequent designation.

b. SECONDARY APPEARANCES. If the genus appeared in a second work at or near the time of the first appearance, a citation to this second work is provided. It was not uncommon in the early literature for an author to publish a new genus description in more than one place.

c. PREOCCUPIED NAMES. Names that are unavailable because of previous use are preoccupied. To be sure that a genus name of fishes is in fact preoccupied—for example in insects—would require going to the original description of the insect name and confirming the original spelling, date, availability, and other details. Preoccupied names in fishes were verified, but names preoccupied in other groups were not.

d. MISSPELLINGS AND EMENDATIONS. Misspellings that are included are ones made by the original author in later papers, or made in Jordan's *Genera of Fishes*, in the *Zoological Record* the first time the genus was listed there, in major treatments (such as monographs), or in references used to document the status of the genus. Many other misspellings were not included. Emendations require careful study; some were evaluated as to whether they were justified emendations or unjustified ones (or merely misspellings). In those not so evaluated, the expression "Spelled..." is often used to show that the investigation was not made.

e. OTHER REMARKS. Such items as action by the International Commission on Zoological Nomenclature (ICZN), nomenclatural remarks, and other comments are included next.

f. STATUS. When given, the status of the nominal genus is provided next under each name. Citations documenting the status include the author, date, page, and the reference number. When a page is not given, the entire article typically deals with only that taxon. For example, under *Brochis*, the citation "Nijssen & Isbrücker 1983 [ref. 5387]" is found; reference 5387 treats only the genus *Brochis*. When a page is given, it refers to one pertinent page in which the status of the taxon is discussed, although the taxon may be mentioned on other pages in the same article; for genera that are junior synonyms the page given usually refers to the page on which a generic synonymy occurs.

The status of some genera is not provided. Some of these taxa are old synonyms not mentioned in current literature, whereas others have just not been treated recently. In some cases, the status has been obtained by looking for the placement of the type species in current genera, even though the genus in question is not mentioned; these are qualified with statements like, "Synonym of ... (Paxton et al. 1989:470 [ref. 12442] based on placement of type species)." I have not followed aquarium literature, and certain geographic areas have received little attention, or pertinent literature is not readily available to me (especially freshwaters of South America and Asia). The cutoff date for status references is essentially the end of 1989, with only a few publications after 1 January 1990 included.

In general, only literature from the last 15-20 years has been used to document status, although some earlier monographs have been included, especially when that monograph is the only thorough treatment available that mentions the taxon. In some current systematic papers, authors tend to omit old synonyms. My aim in documenting the current status of taxa was not to provide extensive synonymies, but to be able to give one or a few recent references that can serve as an entry or source to other literature treating the taxon. Some widespread marine genera have a number of references provided, but it was decided to retain these, rather than eliminating references where there were more than a specific number of them.

g. FAMILY/SUBFAMILY. At the end of each account the family and subfamily (if used) in which the genus has been placed in Part II is provided. Names that are not placed in the classification appear at the end of Part II as "Unplaced Genera."

Part II. Genera in a Classification

The genera and subgenera of Recent fishes are listed in a framework of orders, families and subfamilies (with occasional use of suborders). In some groups, subfamilies are not used, although they may be used in current literature; these include some small families with only a few genera, but also some large families, such as the Cyprinidae, where some "specialized" subfamilies could be recognized, but the family as a whole has not been divided into subfamilies on which there is general agreement. My aim was to present a classification that reflects as nearly as possible current use. The classification portion, however, was secondary to the goal of compiling Part I. Unfortunately, at this time in ichthyology there is no generally accepted classification, and many workers are actively involved in research on higher-category taxa. Cladistic studies of the same groups by different workers often result in different hypotheses of relationships (for example see "Papers on the Systematics of Gadiform fishes," Cohen 1989 [ref. 13632]). The classification used here follows Nelson (1984 [ref. 13596]) for many categories, with some modification based on findings in more recent studies, especially those reported in the "Ahlstrom volume," 1984 [Special Publication no. 1, American Society of Ichthyologists and Herpetologists]. The classification of Anguilliformes follows the treatment in *Fishes of the Western North Atlantic* (see Böhlke 1989 [ref. 13282]). Fink (1985 [ref. 5171]) in a cladistic study of stomiiform fishes, combined several families in a proposed hypothesis of relationships that differs substantially from that in current use; I have not followed his suggestions because they have not yet been adopted in current literature. The composition of some families follows those used in Smiths' Sea Fishes (see Smith and Heemstra 1986 [ref. 5715]). The relationships and limits of the families of the large suborder Percoidei are uncertain, and many genera are treated as incertae sedis in the suborder (following Johnson 1984 [ref. 9681]). In many cases, information on the placement of a genus is mentioned under that genus in Part I; or the composition of a taxon or the classification followed for a subfamily or family is given under the account of the type genus in Part I. Dr. Bailey prefers a classification different than the one used here; his views of classification are better reflected in Robins et al. (In press, 1 and 2).

Synonyms of family group names usually are not provided, and the index to family names presented at the end of Part II includes only those mentioned in Part II. However, it is possible to determine the current placement of a family or subfamily that is not specifically included in Part II by using Part I of this work. For example, in the literature one may encounter a family name that is not included in the Catalog. Since family group names are based on a stem-genus (by dropping the terminal letter or letters and adding -idae for a family or -inae for a subfamily), one may look up the genus in Part I, go to the end of its account, and find where that family is now placed.

Family-group names used in the classification follow current use. Some problems involving family-group names in fishes include currently used family names that are not the oldest for the family and should be replaced by the older names (unless a case can be presented to retain the younger name); also some family names are being misspelled in the current literature. In some cases, two spellings are used (such as Engraulidae or the more correctly formed Engraulididae). Most of these result from an article by Steyskal 1980 [ref. 14191] calling attention to incorrectly formed family group names; to make many of them grammatically correct an extra syllable "id" (ididae) is needed. The ICZN in the interest of stability has already ruled on one family-group name in fishes, picking the shortened form, and a second is under consideration. Wheeler (1990 [ref. 14274]) lists many of these names and suggests a committee to help settle them at one time rather than approach the ICZN on a case by case basis; see also Robins et al. 1980:4 [ref. 7111] and Géry 1989 [ref. 13422]. In Part II, I list the shortened form for most of these families and sometimes include the longer form in parentheses, except for names based on the suffixes *-aspis* and *-lepis* (because they are common in fossil fishes, with fossil family names based on them being in the correct form).

Most family-name problems are not addressed directly in the Catalog, but some comments regarding family-group names are mentioned under their type genera (e.g., see *Phosichthys* and *Bovicthys*). A few genera are not placed within families in the classification. Some are based on mythical specimens, or are indeterminable, or they are names only (without a description); many of these are unavailable names. They appear at the end of Part II in a category of unplaced genera. Other genera that are identifiable only to order or suborder are listed under those taxa within the classification.

Part III. Literature Cited

This section includes all literature cited. Some additional references may be included when they complete a series in which only some works in that series are actually cited in Part I. Citations are given for original generic descriptions but are not given for type species, except as those species appeared in a work that contained a new genus-group name or was used as a reference documenting status.

AUTHOR. Author's initials are given, and to obtain a date-ordered printout, these have been standardized. For example, Gill published as T. Gill, T. N. Gill, and Theodore Gill, and these are treated as authored by T. N. Gill, although both initials may not appear in some of his publications. If an author's name normally has a diacritical mark, it is added to all citations of that author, for example Géry has published both as Gery and Géry. We were unable to provide certain diacritical marks for some languages, such as Rumanian. Chinese names are given as they might be in an English language journal; typically there is a family name plus two given names, and the two given names are often written together or hyphenated; Wu is given here as H.-W. Wu although in the actual article his name may be given as Wu Hsienwen, Wu Hsien-Wen, H.-w. Wu, H.-W. Wu, or H. W. Wu.

All names with "de" are entered in one form; de Buen, for example, published as Buen and as de Buen. Some cross-referencing of names is provided.

DATE OF PUBLICATION. Information on the month or month and day of publication when available or researched is given in parentheses following the year of publication. The references in the Literature Cited are ordered only by year, not by date of publication within a year.

REFERENCE NUMBER. Each reference has a unique reference number, and this is given next in brackets. The number corresponds to the entry of that reference in a larger database of references maintained at the California Academy of Sciences. A unique number is used instead of "a, b, c, etc." that one might find in a smaller bibliography. The unique numbers were an aid in proofing original descriptions of genera; the genera were printed out by reference number and citation. The use of reference numbers in Part 1 also allows an on-line database user to record the references (by number) that he or she is interested in examining, and then ask for a printout of those references by number.

TITLE. The title of the article is given as published with the article; not the title as given, for example, in a table of contents (which sometimes differs). Scientific names are italicized even though, because of constraints in type style, they may not have been so treated in the title as published. Titles in Russian, Japanese, and Chinese are given in English.

BOOK AND JOURNAL CITATIONS. Journal abbreviations in general follow the BioSciences Information Service "Serial Sources for the BIOSIS Data Base, volume 1984." We have composed comparable abbreviated journal titles for old, discontinued journals not treated in that BIOSIS List. We capitalize the first letter of all nouns and adjectives, so we give, for example, "Proc. Acad. Nat. Sci. Phila." rather than "Proc. Acad. nat. Sci. Phila." To aid in finding literature, we designate volume ("v."), number (no.), part (pt), or other amplification, but usually if a foreign word (e.g., tome, fascicle) corresponds to an English word, we give the English equivalent abbreviation. This is followed by the inclusive pages of the work and plates if any.

REMARKS. Information in brackets includes the original language of the article if not clear from the title, sources for information on dates of publication, or dates of appearance of parts of the work if it was published in sections. The entry "Not seen." at the end of a reference indicates that the work or article has not yet been examined.

Glossary and Abbreviations.

This section explains the words and abbreviations used in Part I and in Appendix A. The definitions are not necessarily the same as, or as precise as, those appearing in the Glossary of the *International Code of Zoological Nomenclature*. Most are further defined and discussed in Appendix A.

Appendix A. Genera of Recent Fishes and the International Code of Zoological Nomenclature

In preparing Part I, it was necessary to refer to and interpret the various articles and subsections of the *Code of Zoological Nomenclature*. This appendix provides an interpretation, with examples, that served as the basis for nomenclatural decisions in Part I. In cases where Dr. Bailey and I differed on interpretation, the decision used was mine.

Appendix B. Opinions and Other Actions of the International Commission Involving Fishes

This appendix includes those Opinions and other actions taken by the International Commission on Zoological Nomenclature that involve fish taxa. Opinions, Directions, and presence of names on Official Lists or Indexes as cited in Part I of the Catalog are listed in this Appendix. Actions taken by the ICZN through June 1990 are included.

ACKNOWLEDGMENTS

A computer project like this one could not have been done without programmers. I was fortunate to work with two able and innovative computer programmers and biologists: Barbara Weitbrecht through 1988, followed by David Boughton. Alan Leviton, the Academy's "computer person," and Richard Robertson, Precision Software Products, also were very helpful with computer aspects of the project. Mysi Dang Hoang and Yves Barbero assisted with the final printouts of text. Richard Thunes was the broker for printing. The project also could not have been done without support from the National Science Foundation, and I am grateful to James C. Tyler for funding the initial grant (NSF BSR 8416085) and to James Edwards for the second award (NSF 8801702).

Others at the California Academy of Sciences who assisted were librarian technician Patti Shea-Diner and, for data input, Frances Bertetta, Pamela Donegan, Jon Fong, Melissa Gibbs, Lezlie Skeetz, and Geraldine Stockfleth. Others at the Academy who assisted in a number of ways, including finding new descriptions of genera, helping with references, and especially in providing encouragement were Frank Almeda, Eric Anderson, David Catania, Lillian Dempster, W. I. Follett, Jon Fong, Roy Eisenhardt, Terry Gosliner, Mysi Dang Hoang, Tomio Iwamoto, David Kavanaugh, John McCosker, Lynne Parenti, Pearl Sonoda, Tyson Roberts, Frank Talbot, and Jens Vindum.

Original literature needed to proof the original descriptions came from several sources. The Department of Ichthyology library at the Academy, including the important David Starr Jordan and Stanford reprint library, the reprint libraries of George S. Myers and W. I. Follett, and my own library combined contained about 75% of the literature used. The main library at the California Academy of Sciences was used extensively, and James O'Brien, Patti Shea-Diner, Pearl Sonoda, and Lillian Dempster were the major retrievers of references from this source. I thank Tom Moritz, head librarian, for his assistance and interest in the project; also especially Brian Lym, who researched and secured many interlibrary loans, and to James Jackson, Doris Cantou, Anne Malley, Richard Pallowick, and Lesley Segedy of the library staff. Visits by me to other libraries and persons assisting included The Australian Museum, Sydney (John Paxton, Tony Gill, Mark McGrouther), the Academy of Natural Sciences of Philadelphia (William Smith-Vaniz, Eugenia Böhlke, William Saul, Carol Spawn, Marsha Gross, and especially William Giglioli), and the Smithsonian Institution (Richard Vari, David Steere, Jr.). Warren Burgess and Maurice Kottelat provided important literature. I also wish to acknowledge the many ichthyologists who exchanged or sent reprints, and the librarians who assisted with interlibrary loans.

I am grateful to Joseph T. Gregory, University of California, Berkeley, who is preparing with me a database on genera of fishes based on fossils. We had many discussions that were helpful in the preparation of the present Catalog.

Margaret Hinson and Cheryl Zello helped with preparation of generic reference cards at Michigan from the Zoological Record, and Robert Miller added some names to the card system at Ann Arbor. The Horace H. Rackham School of Graduate Studies of the University of Michigan provided the initial funding for the card system maintained at Michigan.

Through the efforts of Eugenia Böhlke at Philadelphia, I was able to obtain a copy of Fowler's manuscript for the unpublished portions of his "Fishes of the World." Also from Philadelphia, it was arranged through William Smith-Vaniz that Fowler's file cards of taxa of genera and species (up to about 1905) were transferred to the California Academy of Sciences.

Don E. McAllister, National Museums of Canada, contemporaneously was building a computer database of genera and species of Recent fishes, and he and I had many useful discussions about the present project. He also sent various printouts from his database, and comparison resulted in location of some missed genera. The International Commission on Zoological Nomenclature, through the executive secretary P. K. Tubbs, gave permission to quote extensively from the Code in Appendix A.

A number of persons aided in the preparation of generic accounts or in the placement of genera in the classification, or they provided assistance in the development of the classification used in Part II, or assisted by providing literature or other advice. For this kindness the following are thanked: Eric Anderson, Gloria Arratia, Marian Bailey, Marie-Louise Bauchot, Robert Behnke, David Bellwood, Stanley Blum, Eugenia Böhlke, Margaret Bradbury, Paulo Buckup, Warren Burgess, H. Don Cameron, Peter Castle, Ted Cavender, Miles Coburn, Daniel Cohen, Brian Dyer, William and Sara Fink, Carl Ferraris, Jr., W. I. Follett, Harvey Garber, Tony Gill, William Gosline, Dannie Hensley, Douglas Hoese, Tomio Iwamoto, Ann Jensen, G. David Johnson, Patricia Kailola, Robert Lavenberg, Robert Lea, Richard Longmore, John Lundberg, John McCosker, G. F. Mees, Thomas Munro, Douglas Nelson, Audrey Newman, Wayne Palsson, Lynne Parenti, John Paxton, Theodore Pietsch, Stuart Poss, John Randall, Tyson Roberts, Richard and Cathy Robins, David G.

Smith, Gerald R. Smith, William Smith-Vaniz, Victor Springer, Kenneth Tighe, James Tyler, Dan Walton, Stanley Weitzman, Jeffrey Williams, Peter Whitehead, Richard Vari. Maurice Kottelat generously reviewed major sections of part II and noted omissions and errors. I also wish to thank my children Lisa, David and Lanea Eschmeyer. Finally, although the final product has mistakes, it has far fewer than it would have had without comments from reviewers. Wojciech Pulawski painstakingly reviewed Appendix A. Paul Eschmeyer edited early drafts of Appendix A and the Introduction. Tomio Iwamoto assisted with editing and provided advice on style matters. The Academy's Publications Committee sought a critique of the overall work from five ichthyologists with extensive experience in publishing and editing ichthyological papers. The comments made by them were provided to me; for their important suggestions I thank Bruce Collette, Phillip Heemstra, John Paxton (including comments from Douglas Hoese), Richard Robins, and William Smith-Vaniz.

PART I

GENERA OF RECENT FISHES

William N. Eschmeyer and Reeve M. Bailey

Abalistes Jordan & Seale 1906:175, 364 [ref. 2497]. Masc. *Leiurus macrophthalmus* Swainson 1839:326. Type by being a replacement name. Replacement for *Leiurus* (subgenus of *Capriscus*) Swainson 1839, preoccupied by Swainson 1839:242 in fishes. Valid (Matsuura 1980:39 [ref. 6943], Tyler 1980:121 [ref. 4477], Arai 1983:199 [ref. 14249], Matsuura in Masuda et al. 1984:358 [ref. 6441], Smith & Heemstra 1986:877 [ref. 5714]). Balistidae.

Abantennarius Schultz 1957:(55) 66 [ref. 3969]. Masc. *Antennarius duescus* Snyder 1904:537. Type by original designation. Synonym of *Antennarius* Daudin 1816 (Pietsch 1984:34 [ref. 5380]). Antennariidae.

Abbottina Jordan & Fowler 1903:835 [ref. 2463]. Fem. *Abbottina psegma* Jordan & Fowler 1903:835. Type by original designation (also monotypic). Valid (Banarescu & Nalbant 1973:235 [ref. 173], Lu, Luo & Chen 1977:516 [ref. 13495], Sawada in Masuda et al. 1984:56 [ref. 6441], Hosoya 1986:488 [ref. 6155], Chen & Li in Chu & Chen 1989:111 [ref. 13584]). Cyprinidae.

Abcichthys Whitley 1927:304 [ref. 4662]. Masc. *Liocranium praepositum* Ogilby 1903:25. Type by being a replacement name. Unneeded replacement for *Liocranium* Ogilby 1903 [possibly 1904], not preoccupied by *Liocranum*. Misspelled *Abeichthys* by McCulloch 1929:390 [ref. 2948]. Scorpaenidae: Tetraroginae.

Abeichthys (subgenus of *Cheilopogon*) Parin 1961:171 [ref. 3362]. Masc. *Exocoetus agoo* Temminck & Schlegel 1846:247. Type by original designation (also monotypic). Not *Abeichthys* McCulloch, a misspelling of *Abcichthys*. Exocoetidae.

Abeona Girard 1855:322 [ref. 1820]. Fem. *Abeona trowbridgii* Girard 1854:152. Type by monotypy. Synonym of *Micrometrus* Gibbons (May) 1854 (Tarp 1952:81 [ref. 12250]). Embiotocidae.

Ablabys Kaup 1873:80 [ref. 2585]. *Apistus taenianotus* Cuvier 1829:404. Type by subsequent designation. Type designated by Whitley 1966:233 [ref. 12521]. Valid (Washington et al. 1984:440 [ref. 13660], Poss 1986:479 [ref. 6296], Paxton et al. 1989:439 [ref. 12442]). Scorpaenidae: Tetraroginae.

Ablennes (subgenus of *Tylosurus*) Jordan & Fordice 1887:342, 345 [ref. 2456]. *Belone hians* Valenciennes in Cuvier & Valenciennes 1846:432. Type by original designation (also monotypic). Misspelled *Athlennes* by Jordan & Fordice when proposed; corrected by ICZN (Opinion 41). Valid (Yoshino in Masuda et al. 1984:78 [ref. 6441], Collette et al. 1984:336 [ref. 11422], Paxton et al. 1989:341 [ref. 12442]). Belonidae.

Aboma Jordan & Starks in Jordan 1895:497 [ref. 2394]. Fem. *Aboma etheostoma* Jordan & Starks in Jordan 1895:497. Type by original designation, also monotypic; two additional species questionably referred to genus. Gobiidae.

Aborichthys Chaudhuri 1913:244 [ref. 819]. Masc. *Aborichthys kempi* Chaudhuri 1913:245. Type by monotypy. Synonym of *Noemacheilus* Kuhl & van Hasselt 1823, but as a valid subgenus (Menon 1987:183 [ref. 14149]); valid genus (Jayaram 1981:145 [ref. 6497], Kottelat 1990:18 [ref. 14137]). Balitoridae: Nemacheilinae.

Abramidopsis Siebold 1863:133, 387 [ref. 4021]. Fem. *Abramis leuckartii* Heckel 1836:229. Type by monotypy. Thought to be a hybrid of *Abramis* and *Rutilus* (Jordan 1919:328 [ref. 4904]). Cyprinidae.

Abramis Cuvier 1816:194 [ref. 993]. Fem. *Cyprinus brama* Linnaeus 1758:328. Type by subsequent designation. Earliest subsequent designation not located. Valid (Howes 1981:46 [ref. 14200], Bogutskaya 1987:936 [ref. 13521]). Cyprinidae.

Abramites Fowler 1906:331 [ref. 1373]. Masc. *Leporinus hypselonotus* Günther 1868:480. Type by original designation (also monotypic). Valid (Géry 1977:175 [ref. 1597], Winterbottom 1980:2 [ref. 4755], Vari & Williams 1987 [ref. 5980], see also Géry et al. 1987:398 [ref. 6001]). Curimatidae: Anostominae.

Abramocephalus Steindachner 1869:302 [ref. 4217]. Masc. *Abramocephalus microlepis* Steindachner 1869:302. Type by monotypy. Synonym of *Hypophthalmichthys* Bleeker 1859 (Howes 1981:45 [ref. 14200]). Cyprinidae.

Abranches Smith 1947:813 [ref. 4073]. *Abranches pinto* Smith 1947:813. Type by original designation (also monotypic). Synonym of *Gobiopsis* Steindachner 1860 (Lachner & McKinney 1978:10 [ref. 6603]). Gobiidae.

Abron Gistel 1848:X [ref. 1822]. *Silurus lima* Bloch & Schneider 1801:384. Type by being a replacement name. Replacement for *Platystoma* Valenciennes [= Agassiz 1829], preoccupied by Meigen 1803 in Diptera. Pimelodidae.

Abrostomus Smith 1841:Pl. 12 [ref. 4035]. Masc. *Abrostomus umbratus* Smith 1841:Pl. 12. Type by subsequent designation. Type designated by Bleeker 1863:193 [ref. 397] or 1863:25 [ref. 4859]. *Habrostomus* Agassiz 1846:1 [ref. 64] is an unjustified emendation. Synonym of *Labeo* Cuvier 1816 (Lévêque & Daget 1984:305 [ref. 6186]). Cyprinidae.

Abryois Jordan & Snyder 1902:486 [ref. 2516]. *Abryois azumae* Jordan & Snyder 1902:486. Type by original designation (also monotypic). Synonym of *Pholidapus* Bean & Bean 1896 (Shiogaki 1984 [ref. 5309]). Stichaeidae.

Absalom Whitley 1937:133 [ref. 4689]. *Caranx radiatus* Macleay 1881:537. Type by original designation (also monotypic). Synonym of *Pantolabus* Whitley 1931 (Laroche et al. 1984:513 [ref. 13525]). Carangidae.

Abudefduf (subgenus of *Chaetodon*) Forsskål 1775:xiii, 59 [ref. 1351]. Masc. *Chaetodon sordidus* Forsskål 1775:62. Type by subsequent designation. Type usually stated as determined through vernacular abu-defduf on p. xiii as *Chaetodon sordidus*, but Code does not provide for this; Fowler (MS) says Bleeker 1877:91 [ref. 452] designated *saxatilis* as type, but Bleeker was listing the type for *Glyphidodon*. Earliest technical designation of *sordidus* as type not researched. Valid (Allen 1975:110 [ref. 97], Shen & Chan 1979:37 [ref. 6944], Yoshino in Masuda et al. 1984:196 [ref. 6441], Allen 1986:671 [ref. 5631]). Pomacentridae.

Abuhamrur (subgenus of *Sciaena*) Forsskål 1775:44 [ref. 1351]. *Sciaena hamrur* Forsskål 1775:45. Appeared as Abu hamrur, a subgroup of *Sciaena* and tied to the species *Sciaena hamrur*. Not available; regarded as non-latinized Arabic name (see Jordan 1917:33-34 [ref. 2407]). In the synonymy of *Priacanthus* Oken 1817. Priacanthidae.

Abyssicola Goode & Bean 1896:417 [ref. 1848]. Masc. *Macrurus macrochir* Günther 1877:438. Type by monotypy. Synonym of *Caelorinchus* Giorna 1809 (Marshall 1973:293 [ref. 7194], Marshall & Iwamoto 1973:538 [ref. 6966]); valid (Okamura in Masuda et al. 1984:96 [ref. 6441]). Macrouridae: Macrourinae.

Abyssobrotula Nielsen 1977:41 [ref. 3198]. Fem. *Abyssobrotula galatheae* Nielsen 1977:42. Type by original designation (also monotypic). Valid (Cohen & Nielsen 1978:24 [ref. 881], Hureau & Nielsen 1981:6 [ref. 5438]). Ophidiidae: Neobythitinae.

Abyssocottus Berg 1906:908 [ref. 265]. Masc. *Abyssocottus korotneffi* Berg 1906:908. Type by original designation. Valid (Sideleva 1982:30 [ref. 14469], Washington et al. 1984:443 [ref. 13660], Yabe 1985:123 [ref. 11522]). Cottocomephoridae.

Abythites Nielsen & Cohen 1973:82 [ref. 3200]. Masc. *Bythites lepidogenys* Smith & Radcliffe 1913:172. Type by original designation (also monotypic). Valid (Cohen & Nielsen 1978:45 [ref. 881], Machida in Masuda et al. 1984:101 [ref. 6441]). Bythitidae: Bythitinae.

Acahara Jordan & Hubbs 1925:177 [ref. 2486]. Fem. *Leuciscus semotilus* Jordan & Starks 1905:199. Type by original designation. Jordan & Hubbs refer to an earlier "List of Fresh-water Fishes of Korea" by Mori (Howes 1985:67 dates to 1930) in which this name was first used [not located]. Questionably a synonym of *Phoxinus* Rafinesque 1820 (Howes 1985:66 [ref. 5274]). Cyprinidae.

Acanestrinia (subgenus of *Cobitis*) Bacescu 1962:435 [ref. 6454]. Fem. *Cobitis elongata* Heckel & Kner 1858. Type by original designation (also monotypic). Cobitidae: Cobitinae.

Acanthalburnus Berg 1916:299 [ref. 277]. Masc. *Alburnus punctulatus* Kessler 1877:159. Type by monotypy. Valid (Bogutskaya 1987:936 [ref. 13521]). Cyprinidae.

Acanthaluteres Bleeker 1865:100 [ref. 416]. *Aleuterius paragaudatus* Richardson 1840:28. Type by original designation (also monotypic). Also in Bleeker 1866:13 [ref. 417]. Valid (Tyler 1980:176 [ref. 4477]). Monacanthidae.

Acanthaphritis Günther 1880:43 [ref. 2011]. Fem. *Acanthaphritis grandisquamis* Günther 1880:43. Type by monotypy. Misspelled *Acanthaphrites* in Zoological Record for 1880 and by authors. Valid (Nelson 1982:7 [ref. 5469]). Percophidae: Hemerocoetinae.

Acanthapogon Fowler 1938:197 [ref. 1428]. Masc. *Acanthapogon vanderbilti* Fowler 1938:198. Type by original designation (also monotypic). Synonym of *Gymnapogon* Regan 1905 (Fraser 1972:32 [ref. 5195]). Apogonidae.

Acantharchus Gill 1864:92 [ref. 1706]. Masc. *Centrarchus pomotis* Baird 1855:325. Type by original designation (also monotypic). Misspelled *Acantharcus* by Bean 1880:97 [ref. 6452]. Valid (Cashner, Burr & Rogers 1989 [ref. 13576]). Centrarchidae.

Acanthemblemaria Metzelaar 1919:159 [ref. 2982]. Fem. *Acanthemblemaria spinosa* Metzelaar 1919:159. Type by monotypy. Also appeared as new in Metzelaar 1922:141 [ref. 5741]. Valid (Stephens 1963:27 [ref. 4270], Smith-Vaniz & Palacio 1974 [ref. 7151], Greenfield & Johnson 1981:51 [ref. 5580], Acero P. 1984 [ref. 5534], Rosenblatt & McCosker 1988 [ref. 6383], Johnson & Brothers 1989 [ref. 13532]). Chaenopsidae.

Acanthenchelys Norman 1922:296 [ref. 3211]. Fem. *Acanthenchelys spinicauda* Norman 1922:296. Type by subsequent designation. Type designated by Jordan 1923:133 [ref. 2421] with author of type wrongly as Regan. Synonym of *Ophichthus* Ahl 1789 (Blache et al. 1973:247 [ref. 7185], McCosker 1977:80 [ref. 6836], McCosker et al. 1989:379 [ref. 13288]). Ophichthidae: Ophichthinae.

Acanthias Bonaparte 1846:15 [ref. 519]. Masc. *Squalus acanthias* Linnaeus 1758:233. Type by absolute tautonymy of included junior synonym. Same as *Acanthias* Risso, but Risso not cited by Bonaparte. Objective synonym of *Squalus* Linnaeus 1758. Squalidae.

Acanthias Leach 1818:62 [ref. 12565]. Masc. *Squalus acanthias* Linnaeus 1758:233. Brief description; one unavailable species *antiquorum* mentioned on p. 64. Addition of available species not researched. Type as given by Compagno. Objective synonym of *Squalus* Linnaeus 1758 (see Compagno 1984:109 [ref. 6474]). Squalidae.

Acanthias Risso 1826:131 [ref. 3757]. Masc. *Squalus acanthias* Linnaeus 1758:233. Type by being a replacement name. Apparently an unneeded replacement for *Squalus* Linnaeus; *A. vulgaris* Risso is an unneeded substitute for the species *S. acanthias* Linnaeus. Objective synonym of *Squalus* Linnaeus 1758 (Krefft & Tortonese 1973:37 [ref. 7165], Compagno 1984:109 [ref. 6474]). Squalidae.

Acanthicus Agassiz in Spix & Agassiz 1829:2 [ref. 13]. Masc. *Acanthicus hystrix* Agassiz in Spix & Agassiz 1829:3. Type by monotypy. Authorship follows that suggested by Kottelat 1988:78 [ref. 13380]. Valid (Isbrücker 1980:75 [ref. 2303], Isbrücker & Nijssen 1988 [ref. 7320], Burgess 1989:437 [ref. 12860]). Loricariidae.

Acanthidium Lowe 1839:91 [ref. 2829]. Neut. *Acanthidium pusillum* Lowe 1839:91. Type by subsequent designation. Type designated by Jordan & Evermann 1896:55 [ref. 2443] and Goode & Bean 1896:10 [ref. 1848]. Misspelled *Acanthidim* in Zoological Record for 1903. Synonym of *Etmopterus* Rafinesque 1810 (Krefft & Tortonese 1973:42 [ref. 7165], Compagno 1984:69 [ref. 6474]). Squalidae.

Acanthinion Lacepède 1802:499, 500 [ref. 4929]. Neut. *Chaetodon rhomboides* Bloch 1787:100. Type by subsequent designation. Type designated by Jordan & Evermann 1896:939 [ref. 2443]. *Acanthinium* Agassiz 1846:2 [ref. 64] is an unjustified emendation. Synonym of *Trachinotus* Lacepède 1801 (Daget & Smith-Vaniz 1986:319 [ref. 6207]). Carangidae.

Acanthistius Gill 1862:236 [ref. 1664]. Masc. *Plectropoma serratum* Cuvier in Cuvier & Valenciennes 1828:399. Type by monotypy. Valid (Hutchins 1981 [ref. 5583], Hutchins & Kuiter 1982 [ref. 5373], Kendall 1984:500 [ref. 13663], Nakamura in Nakamura et al. 1986:196 [ref. 14235], Heemstra & Randall 1986:510 [ref. 5667], Paxton et al. 1989:489 [ref. 12442]). Serranidae: Serraninae.

Acanthobrama Heckel 1843:1033 [ref. 2066]. Fem. *Acanthobrama marmid* Heckel 1843:1075. Type by subsequent designation. Type designated by Bleeker 1863:31 [ref. 4859] and 1863:210 [ref. 397]. The spelling *Trachibrama* (p. 1033) is a lapsus (see Krupp & Schneider 1989:354 [ref. 13651]). Synonym of *Rutilus* Rafinesque 1820 (Howes 1981:45 [ref. 14200]); valid (Yang 1964:132 [ref. 13500], Goren, Fishelson & Trewavas 1973 [ref. 1853], Coad 1984 [ref. 5347], Li 1986 [ref. 6154], Krupp & Schneider 1989:354 [ref. 13651]). Cyprinidae.

Acanthocaulus Waite 1900:206 [ref. 4558]. Masc. *Prionurus microlepidotus* Lacepède 1804:(205) 211. Type by being a replacement name. Unneeded replacement for *Prionurus* Lacepède 1804, apparently not preoccupied by Ehrenberg 1829. Objective synonym of *Prionurus* Lacepède 1804 (Randall 1955:362 [ref. 13648]). Acanthuridae.

Acanthocephalus Döderlein in Steindachner & Döderlein 1883:237 [ref. 4246]. Masc. *Doederleinia orientalis* Steindachner in Steindachner & Döderlein 1883:237. Type by monotypy. Not available, name noted in passing in synonymy of *Doderleinia*; not subsequently made available; also preoccupied. Acropomatidae.

Acanthocepola Bleeker 1874:369 [ref. 435]. Fem. *Cepola krusensternii* Schlegel in Temminck & Schlegel 1845:130. Type by original designation (also monotypic). Valid (Araga in Masuda et al. 1984:201 [ref. 6441], Smith-Vaniz 1986:727 [ref. 5718], Mok 1988:507 [ref. 12752]). Cepolidae.

Acanthochaenus Gill 1884:433 [ref. 1728]. Masc. *Acanthochaenus luetkenii* Gill 1884:433. Type by monotypy. Species originally spelled *lütkenii*, change to *luetkenii* is mandatory. Valid (Nielsen 1973:347 [ref. 6885], Ebeling & Weed 1973:419 [ref. 6898], Maul in Whitehead et al. 1986:766 [ref. 13676], Heemstra 1986:431 [ref. 5660]). Stephanoberycidae.

Acanthochaetodon Bleeker 1876:308 [ref. 448]. Masc. *Holacanthus annularis* Bloch 1787:114. Type by original designation (also monotypic in ref. 448). Also in Bleeker 1876:Pls. 365, 367, 370, 372 [ref. 6835] (earliest not established). Synonym of *Holacanthus* Lacepède 1802. Pomacanthidae.

Acanthocharax Eigenmann 1912:258, 404 [ref. 1227]. Masc. *Acanthocharax microlepis* Eigenmann 1912:405. Type by original designation (also monotypic). Valid (Géry 1977:310 [ref. 1597]). Characidae.

Acanthochromis Gill 1863:214 [ref. 1684]. Masc. *Dascyllus polyacanthus* Bleeker 1855:503. Type by original designation (also monotypic). See also *Actinochromis* Bleeker 1877. Valid (Allen 1975:66 [ref. 97], Richards & Leis 1984:544 [ref. 13668]). Pomacentridae.

Acanthocirrhitus Fowler 1938:50 [ref. 1426]. Masc. *Cirrhites oxycephalus* Bleeker 1855:408. Type by original designation (also monotypic). Synonym of *Cirrhitichthys* Bleeker 1857. Cirrhitidae.

Acanthocleithron Nichols & Griscom 1917:720 [ref. 3185]. Neut. *Acanthocleithron chapini* Nichols & Griscom 1917:721. Type by monotypy. Valid (Gosse 1986:105 [ref. 6194], Burgess 1989:197 [ref. 12860]). Mochokidae.

Acanthoclinus Jenyns 1841:91 [ref. 2344]. Masc. *Acanthoclinus fuscus* Jenyns 1841:92. Type by original designation (also monotypic, second species questionably included). Valid (Hardy 1985:360 [ref. 5184]). Acanthoclinidae.

Acanthoclinus Mocquard 1885:18 [ref. 3033]. Masc. *Acanthoclinus chaperi* Mocquard 1885:19. Type by original designation (also monotypic). Preoccupied by Jenyns 1841 in fishes, replaced by *Paraclinus* Mocquard 1888. Objective synonym of *Paraclinus* Mocquard 1888 (Clark Hubbs 1952:65 [ref. 2252]). Labrisomidae.

Acanthocobitis Peters 1861:712 [ref. 3451]. Fem. *Acanthocobitis longipinnis* Peters 1861:712. Type by monotypy. Synonym of *Noemacheilus* Kuhl Kuhl & van Hasselt 1823, but as a valid subgenus (Banarescu & Nalbant 1968:332 [ref. 6554], Jayaram 1981:158 [ref. 6497], Menon 1987:140 [ref. 14149]); valid genus (Kottelat 1989:12 [ref. 13605], Kottelat 1990:18 [ref. 14137]). Balitoridae: Nemacheilinae.

Acanthocottus Girard 1850:185 [ref. 1814]. Masc. *Cottus groenlandicus* Cuvier in Cuvier & Valenciennes 1829:156. Type by subsequent designation. Type apparently designated by Sauvage 1878:137 [not researched] and by Jordan & Evermann 1898:1970 [ref. 2444]. Synonym of *Myoxocephalus* Tilesius 1811 (Neyelov 1973:597 [ref. 7219], Neyelov 1979:120 [ref. 3152]). Cottidae.

Acanthocybium Gill 1862:125 [ref. 1659]. Neut. *Cybium sara* Lay & Bennett 1839:63. Type by original designation (also monotypic). Valid (Postel 1972:474 [ref. 7208], Collette & Nauen 1983:25 [ref. 5375], Collette et al. 1984:600 [ref. 11421], Nakamura in Masuda et al. 1984:225 [ref. 6441], Collette 1986:832 [ref. 5647], Johnson 1986:34 [ref. 5676]). Scombridae.

Acanthodemus Marschall (ex Castelnau) 1873:63 [ref. 6455]. Masc. *Hypostomus aurantiacus* Castelnau 1855:43. Type by subsequent designation. Appeared first in French only as "Acanthodémes" in Castelnau 1855:43 [ref. 766] as a subgroup of *Hypostomus*; latinized by Marschall 1873:63 as above. Earliest type designation found is by Jordan 1919:264 [ref. 2410]; technical first addition of species not researched. Loricariidae.

Acanthodes Fourmanoir & Crosnier 1964:23 [ref. 5568]. Masc. *Acanthodes fragilis* Fourmanoir & Crosnier 1964:23. Type by monotypy. Not available, genus not defined and perhaps not intended as a new genus. Based on a scorpionfish with a malformed dorsal fin. Name preoccupied. *Yacius* Whitley 1970 is an unneeded replacement. Scorpaenidae: Scorpaeninae.

Acanthodoras Bleeker 1862:5 [ref. 393]. Masc. *Silurus cataphractus* Linnaeus 1758:307. Type by original designation (also monotypic). Valid (Burgess 1989:223 [ref. 12860]). Doradidae.

Acanthognathus Duncker 1912:228 [ref. 1156]. Masc. *Syngnathus dactylophorus* Bleeker 1853:506. Type by original designation, also monotypic (only one named species included). Preoccupied by Mayr 1887 in Hymenoptera, replaced by *Dunckerocampus* Whitley 1933. Synonym of *Doryrhamphus* Kaup 1856 (Dawson 1985:58 [ref. 6541]). Syngnathidae: Syngnathinae.

Acanthogobio Herzenstein 1892:228 [ref. 5037]. Masc. *Acanthogobio guentheri* Herzenstein 1892:228. Type by monotypy. Valid (Banarescu & Nalbant 1973:173 [ref. 173], Lu, Luo & Chen 1977:453 [ref. 13495]). Cyprinidae.

Acanthogobius Gill 1859:145 [ref. 1762]. Masc. *Gobius flavimanus* Temminck & Schlegel 1845:141. Type by monotypy. Valid (Akihito in Masuda et al. 1984:278 [ref. 6441], Birdsong et al. 1988:183, 184 [ref. 7303]). Gobiidae.

Acanthogonia (subgenus of *Paraplesiops*) Ogilby 1918:45 [ref. 3298]. Fem. *Paraplesiops poweri* Ogilby 1907:17. Type by subsequent designation. Type designated by McCulloch 1929 [ref. 2948]. Misspelled *Acanthagonia* by Jordan 1920:564 [ref. 4905]. Synonym of *Paraplesiops* Bleeker 1875 (Hoese & Kuiter 1984:9 [ref. 5300]). Plesiopidae.

Acantholabrus Valenciennes in Cuvier & Valenciennes 1839:242 [ref. 1007]. Masc. *Lutjanus exoletus* (not of Linnaeus) Risso 1810:263 (= *Lutjanus palloni* Risso 1810:263). Type by subsequent designation. Type apparently designated by Bonaparte 1841:puntata 156, fasc. 30. Valid (Bauchot & Quignard 1973:429 [ref. 7204], Quignard & Pras in Whitehead et al. 1986:920 [ref. 13676]). Labridae.

Acantholatris Gill 1862:119 [ref. 1658]. *Chaetodon monodactylus* Carmichael 1818:300. Type by original designation (also monotypic). Cheilodactylidae.

Acantholebius Gill 1861:166 [ref. 1775]. Masc. *Chiropsis nebu-*

losus Girard 1858:45. Type by monotypy. Synonym of *Hexagrammos* Steller 1809. Hexagrammidae: Hexagramminae.

Acantholepis Krøyer 1846:98 [ref. 2693]. Fem. *Argentina silus* Ascanius 1763:24. Type by monotypy. Objective synonym of *Silus* Reinhardt 1833; synonym of *Argentina* Linnaeus 1758 (Cohen 1973:152 [ref. 6589]). Argentinidae.

Acantholingua Hadzisce 1960:47 [ref. 13406]. Fem. *Salmo ohridanus* Steindachner 1892:132. Also appeared in Hadzisce 1961 [ref. 13566] as a subgenus of *Salmo* [was to have appeared before ref. 13406]. Apparently not available from Hadzisce; two included species, neither designated as type (but article not fully translated). Synonym of *Salmo* Linnaeus 1758, but as a valid subgenus (Behnke 1969:11 [ref. 250], Kendall & Behnke 1984:144 [ref. 13638]). Salmonidae: Salmoninae.

Acantholiparis Gilbert & Burke 1912:83 [ref. 1634]. Masc. *Acantholiparis opercularis* Gilbert & Burke 1912:83. Type by original designation (also monotypic). Probably valid (Stearley, pers. comm., June 1990). Valid (Stein 1978:35 [ref. 4203]); synonym of *Paraliparis* Collett 1878 (Kido 1988:230 [ref. 12287]). Cyclopteridae: Liparinae.

Acantholumpenus Makushok 1958:87 [ref. 2878]. Masc. *Lumpenus mackayi* Gilbert 1896:450. Type by original designation. Type given by author as, "*Lumpenus mackayi* Gilbert = *Lumpenus fowleri* Jordan et Snyder = *Blennius anguillaris* Pallas." Valid (Amaoka & Miki in Masuda et al. 1984:301 [ref. 6441], Miki et al. 1987:131 [ref. 6704]). Stichaeidae.

Acanthonotus Bloch & Schneider 1801:390 [ref. 471]. Masc. *Notacanthus nasus* Bloch 1795:113. Type by monotypy. Apparently an unneeded name change for *Notacanthus* Bloch 1788; *Notacanthus* not cited. Objective synonym of *Notacanthus* Bloch 1788 (Wheeler 1973:256 [ref. 7190]). Notacanthidae.

Acanthonotus Gray 1830:Pl. 85 (v. 1) [ref. 1878]. Masc. *Acanthonotus hardwickii* Gray 1830:8. Type by monotypy. Also appeared in Gray 1831:8 [ref. 1879]. Apparently not preoccupied by Cuvier 1800 (nomen nudum) but preoccupied by Goldfuss 1809 in Mammalia. Synonym of *Ailia* Gray 1830. Schilbeidae.

Acanthonotus Tickell in Day 1888:807 [ref. 1082]. Masc. *Acanthonotus argenteus* Tickell in Day 1888:807. Type by monotypy. Preoccupied by Goldfuss 1809 in Mammalia and by Gray 1830 in fishes; replaced by *Matsya* Day 1889. Sometimes cited with Day as author. Synonym of *Mystacoleucus* Günther 1868 (Chu & Kottelat 1989:1 [ref. 12575], Roberts 1989:45 [ref. 6439]). Cyprinidae.

Acanthonus Günther 1878:22 [ref. 2010]. Masc. *Acanthonus armatus* Günther 1878:23. Type by monotypy. Valid (Cohen & Nielsen 1978:18 [ref. 881], Machida in Masuda et al. 1984:99 [ref. 6441]). Ophidiidae: Neobythitinae.

Acanthopagrus (subgenus of *Chrysophrys*) Peters 1855:242 [ref. 13448]. Masc. *Chrysophris vagus* Peters 1852:681. Type by monotypy. Appeared as "64, *Chrysophrys (Acanthopagrus) vagus* Pet." in the Arch. Naturgesch., v. 21:242 and not on the corresponding p. 435 in ref. 3449 (see note under ref. 3449). Valid (Akazaki in Masuda et al. 1984:178 [ref. 6441], Smith & Smith 1986:581 [ref. 5710], Bauchot & Skelton 1986:331 [ref. 6210]). Sparidae.

Acanthopegasus McCulloch 1915:106 [ref. 2941]. Masc. *Pegasus lancifer* Kaup 1861:116. Type by original designation (also monotypic). Synonym of *Pegasus* Linnaeus 1758 (Palsson & Pietsch 1989:18 [ref. 13536]). Pegasidae.

Acanthoperca Castelnau 1878:44 [ref. 762]. Fem. *Acanthoperca gulliveri* Castelnau 1878:45. Type by monotypy. Synonym of *Parambassis* Bleeker 1874 (Roberts 1989:161 [ref. 6439]). Ambassidae.

Acanthophacelus Eigenmann 1907:426 [ref. 1219]. Masc. *Poecilia reticulata* Peters 1859:412. Type by original designation (also monotypic). Synonym of *Poecilia* Bloch & Schneider 1801 (Rosen & Bailey 1963:44 [ref. 7067]). Poeciliidae.

Acanthophthalmus see *Acantophthalmus*. Cobitidae: Cobitinae.

Acanthoplesiops Regan 1912:266 [ref. 3646]. Masc. *Acanthoclinus indicus* Day 1888:264. Type by monotypy. Valid (Hayashi in Masuda et al. 1984:142 [ref. 6441], Hardy 1985:381 [ref. 5184], Smith 1986:541 [ref. 5712]). Acanthoclinidae.

Acanthoplichthys Fowler 1943:72 [ref. 1441]. Masc. *Acanthoplichthys pectoralis* Fowler 1943:72. Type by original designation (also monotypic). Hoplichthyidae.

Acanthopodus Lacepède 1802:558 [ref. 4929]. Masc. *Chaetodon argenteus* Linnaeus 1758:272. Type by subsequent designation. Earliest type designation found is by Jordan 1917:64 [ref. 2407]. *Acanthopus* Agassiz 1846:3 [ref. 64] is an unjustified emendation. Synonym of *Monodactylus* Lacepède 1801 (Desoutter 1986:338 [ref. 6212]). Monodactylidae.

Acanthopolyipnus (subgenus of *Polyipnus*) Fowler 1934:257 [ref. 1416]. Masc. *Polyipnus fraseri* Fowler 1934:257. Type by original designation (also monotypic). Sternoptychidae: Sternoptychinae.

Acanthopoma Lütken 1892:57 [ref. 2857]. Neut. *Acanthopoma annectens* Lütken 1892:57. Type by monotypy. Valid (Burgess 1989:324 [ref. 12860]). Trichomycteridae.

Acanthopsetta Schmidt 1904:237 [ref. 3946]. Fem. *Acanthopsetta nadeshnyi* Schmidt 1904:237. Type by monotypy. Appeared first as name only in Schmidt 1903:521 [ref. 3945]. Valid (Norman 1934:303 [ref. 6893], Ahlstrom et al. 1984:643 [ref. 13641], Sakamoto 1984 [ref. 5273], Sakamoto in Masuda et al. 1984:351 [ref. 6441]). Pleuronectidae: Pleuronectinae.

Acanthopsis Agassiz 1832:134 [ref. 5111]. Fem. *Acanthopsis angustus* Agassiz 1835:Pl. 50. Type by subsequent monotypy. See discussion of type species as given by Kottelat 1987:372-373 [ref. 5962]. Type by subsequent monotypy, established in Agassiz 1835:Pl. 50 [ref. 13390]. Type not *Cobitis taenia* Linnaeus 1758 as given by Jordan 1919:180 [ref. 2410]. Synonym of *Cobitis* Linnaeus (authors). Possibly not a cobitid based on change of type to a fossil species (see Kottelat 1987:372 [ref. 5962]). Cobitidae: Cobitinae.

Acanthopsoides Fowler 1934:103 [ref. 1417]. Masc. *Acanthopsoides gracilis* Fowler 1934:103. Type by original designation (also monotypic). Valid (Nalbant 1963:365 [ref. 3140], Sawada 1982:201 [ref. 14111], Kottelat 1985:267 [ref. 11441], Kottelat 1989:13 [ref. 13605], Roberts 1989:94 [ref. 6439]). Cobitidae: Cobitinae.

Acanthopus Oken 1816:122 [ref. 6406]. On Official Index (genera), published in a rejected work; homonym of *Acanthopus* Klug 1801 (Opinion 417, Direction 37). Unplaced genera.

Acanthorhinus (subgenus of *Squalus*) Blainville 1816:121 [ref. 306]. Masc. *Squalus acanthias* Linnaeus 1758:233. Type by subsequent designation. Type designated by Bory de Saint-Vincent, v. 1, 1822:41 [ref. 3853] (see Whitley 1935:137 [ref. 6396]). Objective synonym of *Squalus* Linnaeus (Krefft & Tortonese 1973:37 [ref. 7165], Compagno 1984:109 [ref. 6474]). Squalidae.

Acanthorhodeus Bleeker 1871:40 [ref. 6421]. Masc. *Acanthor-*

hodeus macropterus Bleeker 1871:40. Type by subsequent designation. Apparently appeared first as name only in Bleeker 1870:253 [ref. 429]. Description and several species appeared as above, without type designation. Type apparently first designated by Jordan 1919:355 [ref. 4904]. Valid (Wu 1964:211 [ref. 13503], Kottelat 1989:6 [ref. 13605]); synonym of *Acheilognathus* Bleeker 1859 (Arai & Akai 1988:205 [ref. 6999], Chen & Li in Chu & Chen 1989:128 [ref. 13584]). Cyprinidae.

Acanthorutilus Berg 1912:42, 81 [ref. 5874]. Masc. *Oreoleuciscus dsapchynensis* Warpachowsky 1889. Type by original designation (also monotypic). Cyprinidae.

Acanthosoma DeKay 1842:330 [ref. 1098]. Neut. *Diodon carinatus* Mitchill 1825. Type by monotypy. Synonym of *Mola* Koelreuter 1770 (Fraser-Brunner 1943:8 [ref. 1495]). Molidae.

Acanthosphex Fowler 1938:86 [ref. 1426]. Masc. *Prosopodasys leurynnis* Jordan & Seale 1905:525. Type by original designation (also monotypic). Valid (Poss & Eschmeyer 1978:404 [ref. 6387], Washington et al. 1984:440 [ref. 13660]). Aploactinidae.

Acanthostedion Fowler 1943:75 [ref. 1441]. Neut. *Acanthostedion rugosum* Fowler 1943:76. Type by original designation (also monotypic). Triglidae: Peristediinae.

Acanthostelgis Fowler 1958:16 [ref. 1470]. Fem. *Agonus vulsus* Jordan & Gilbert 1880:330. Type by being a replacement name. Unneeded replacement for *Stelgis* Cramer 1895, preoccupied by Pomel 1872 in sponges, earlier replaced by *Ganoideus* Whitley 1950. Synonym of *Agonopsis* Gill 1861 (Lea & Dempster 1982:250 [ref. 14236]). Agonidae.

Acanthostethus Herre 1939:142 [ref. 2129]. Masc. *Gulaphallus falcifer* Manacop 1936:375. Type by original designation (also monotypic). Preoccupied by Smith 1869 in Hymenoptera, replaced by *Manacopus* Herre 1940. Synonym of *Gulaphallus* Herre 1925 (Parenti 1989:274 [ref. 13486]). Phallostethidae.

Acanthostracion (subgenus of *Ostracion*) Bleeker 1865:Pls. 202-204 [ref. 416]. Neut. *Ostracion quadricornis* Linnaeus 1758:331. Appeared first in Pls. 202-204 (in pt. 17, 8 Feb. 1865) [corresponding text (p. 28) appeared in pt. 19]. Also in Bleeker 1866:15 [ref. 417]. *O. quadricornis*, designated type by Bleeker (p. 28), was not figured. If relative dates are correct, then type species will change (designation not researched). Synonym of *Lactophrys* Swainson 1839 (Robins et al. 1980:66 [ref. 7111]); valid (Tyler 1980:239 [ref. 4477], Arai 1983:203 [ref. 14249], Smith 1986:891 [ref. 5712]). Ostraciidae: Ostraciinae.

Acanthotaurichthys (subgenus of *Hemitaurichthys*) Burgess 1978:218 [ref. 700]. Masc. *Hemitaurichthys multispinus* Randall 1975:19. Type by original designation (also monotypic). Type species given as Burgess and Randall and described as new on Burgess p. 218, but species described in 1975 by Randall alone. Synonym of *Hemitaurichthys* Bleeker 1876, but as a valid subgenus (Maugé & Bauchot 1984:462 [ref. 6614]). Chaetodontidae.

Acanthothrissa Gras 1961:401 [ref. 1876]. Fem. *Acanthothrissa palimptera* Gras 1961:402. Type by monotypy. Synonym of *Denticeps* Clausen 1959 (Greenwood 1965 [ref. 5765], Daget 1984:40 [ref. 6170]). Denticipitidae.

Acanthurus (subgenus of *Chaetodon*) Forsskål 1775:59 [ref. 1351]. Masc. *Chaetodon sohal* Forsskål 1775:63. Type by subsequent designation. Type designated by Jordan 1917:33 [ref. 2407] but earlier designation may be located; Fowler (MS) says *hepatus* Linnaeus designated by Desmarest 1874:240 [not investigated]. *Acanthura* is a misspelling. Valid (Desoutter 1973:455 [ref. 7203], Leis & Richards 1984:548 [ref. 13669], Kishimoto in Masuda et al. 1984:230 [ref. 6441], Randall 1986:812 [ref. 5706], Allen & Ayling 1987 [ref. 13388], Tyler et al. 1989:37 [ref. 13460]). Acanthuridae.

Acanthus Bloch 1795:105 [ref. 464]. Masc. *Acanthurus velifer* Bloch 1795:106. Type by monotypy. Apparently just a typesetting error for *Acanthurus* as used by Bloch on p. 106 and not an original description. Would predate *Zebrasoma* Swainson 1839 if *Acanthus* is regarded as a new name. Acanthuridae.

Acantoderma Cantraine 1835:24 [ref. 7207]. Neut. *Acantoderma temminckii* Cantraine 1837. Type by monotypy. Appeared first as above in notice of manuscript; perhaps without differentiating characters; species only as "...et il dédie l'espèce type à M. Temminck ..." Appeared in more detail in Cantraine 1837 [ref. 716] where species was named [ref. not seen]. Synonym of *Ruvettus* Cocco 1829. Gempylidae.

Acantophthalmus van Hasselt 1823:132 [ref. 4513]. Masc. *Cobitis taenia* Linnaeus 1758:303. Type by monotypy. Spelled *Acantophthalmus* in 1823, *Acanthophthalmus* in French version (= van Hasselt 1824:377 [ref. 5104]). Code requires use of original spelling. Type by monotypy, 3 more included species not available (Kottelat 1987:371 [ref. 5962]). Objective synonym of *Cobitis* Linnaeus 1758 by action of ICZN (Opinion 1500). Treated as valid with type as *A. fasciatus* (Jayaram 1981:179 [ref. 6497], Sawada 1982:202 [ref. 14111] and Roberts 1989:95 [ref. 6439] as *Acantophthalmus*). Cobitidae: Cobitinae.

Acantopsis van Hasselt 1823:133 [ref. 5963]. Fem. *Acantopsis dialuzona* van Hasselt 1823:133. Type by monotypy. Spelled *Acantopsis* in 1823 and *Acanthopsis* in French version (= van Hasselt 1824:376, 377 [ref. 5104]); Code requires use of original spelling. Valid (Kottelat 1985:267 [ref. 11441], Roberts 1989:99 [ref. 6439], Kottelat 1989:13 [ref. 13605]). Cobitidae: Cobitinae.

Acapoeta Cockerell 1910:149 [ref. 869]. Fem. *Capoeta tanganicae* Boulenger 1900:478. Type by original designation (also monotypic). Valid (Lévêque & Daget 1984:217 [ref. 6186]). Cyprinidae.

Acara Heckel 1840:338 [ref. 2064]. Fem. *Acara crassispinis* Heckel 1840:357. Type by subsequent designation. Type apparently first restricted by Gill 1858:19 [ref. 1750] (see Eigenmann 1910:470-471 [ref. 1224]). Synonym of *Astronotus* Swainson 1839 (Kullander 1986:60 [ref. 12439]). Cichlidae.

Acaramus Rafinesque 1815:86 [ref. 3584]. Masc. Not available; name only. Unplaced genera.

Acarana Gray 1833:Pl. 98 (v. 2) [ref. 1878]. Fem. *Ostracion auritus* Shaw 1798. Type by monotypy. Spelled *Acerana* on legend, *Acarana* on Pl. 98, *Acarana* on Sawyer's legend page (1953:55 [ref. 6842]). Spelled *Aracana* by Gray 1838:110 [ref. 1884]. *Acarana* probably is the correct original spelling. Possibly based on a misidentified type species. Regarded as valid but with spelling *Aracana*; see account of *Aracana*. Ostraciidae: Aracaninae.

Acarauna Catesby 1771:31 [ref. 774]. Not available, published in a rejected work on Official Index (Opinion 89, Opinion 259). Unplaced genera.

Acarauna Sevastianoff 1802:357, 364 [ref. 4011]. *Acarauna longirostris* Sevastianoff 1802:363. Type by monotypy. Apparently a synonym of *Gomphosus* Lacepède 1801. Labridae.

Acarichthys Eigenmann 1912:483, 500 [ref. 1227]. Masc. *Acara heckelii* Müller & Troschel in Schomburgk 1849:624. Type by original designation (also monotypic). Valid (Kullander 1980:23 [ref. 5526], Kullander 1986:134 [ref. 12439]). Cichlidae.

Acaronia Myers 1940:170 [ref. 3117]. Fem. *Acara nassa* Heckel 1840:353. Type by being a replacement name. Replacement for *Acaropsis* Steindachner 1875, preoccupied by Moquin-Tandon 1863 in Arachnida. Valid (Kullander 1986:78 [ref. 12439]). Cichlidae.

Acaropsis (subgenus of *Acara*) Steindachner 1875:80 [ref. 4220]. Fem. *Acara nassa* Heckel 1840:353. Type by monotypy. Preoccupied by Moquin-Tandon 1863 in Arachnida, replaced by *Acaronia* Myers 1940. Objective synonym of *Acaronia* Myers 1940 (Kullander 1986:78 [ref. 12439]). Cichlidae.

Acedia (subgenus of *Symphurus*) Jordan 1888:321, 327 [ref. 2482]. Fem. *Aphoristia nebulosa* Goode & Bean 1883:192. Type by original designation (also monotypic). Synonym of *Symphurus* Rafinesque 1810. Cynoglossidae: Symphurinae.

Acentrachme Gill 1862:234 [ref. 1663]. *Amphisile scutata* of Cuvier (= *Centriscus scutatus* Linnaeus 1758:336). Type by monotypy. Objective synonym of *Centriscus* Linnaeus 1758. Centriscidae: Centriscinae.

Acentrogobius Bleeker 1874:321 [ref. 437]. Masc. *Gobius chlorostigma* Bleeker 1849:27. Type by original designation (also monotypic). Valid (Yanagisawa 1978:313 [ref. 7028], Akihito in Masuda et al. 1984:249 [ref. 6441], Hoese 1986:777 [ref. 5670], Maugé 1986:358 [ref. 6218], Birdsong et al. 1988:192 [ref. 7303], Kottelat 1989:18 [ref. 13605]). Gobiidae.

Acentrolophus Nardo 1827:11 or 28 or 62 [ref. 3146]. Masc. *Perca nigra* Gmelin 1789:132. Original not seen; appeared at least twice in 1827; above taken in part from Haedrich. Type *Perca nigra* by being a replacement name, not *Acentrolophus maculatus* Nardo. Unneeded replacement for *Centrolophus* Lacepède 1802. Also in Isis, v. 20:478. Objective synonym of *Centrolophus* Lacepède 1802 (Haedrich 1967:62 [ref. 5357], Haedrich 1973:559 [ref. 7216]). Centrolophidae.

Acentronichthys Eigenmann & Eigenmann 1889:28 [ref. 1253]. Masc. *Acentronichthys leptos* Eigenmann & Eigenmann 1889:29. Type by original designation (also monotypic). Synonym of *Heptapterus* Bleeker 1858 (Mees 1974:177 [ref. 2969], Buckup 1988:644 [ref. 6635]); valid (see Stewart 1986:668 [ref. 5211]). Pimelodidae.

Acentronura (subgenus of *Hippocampus*) Kaup 1853:230 [ref. 2569]. Fem. *Hippocampus gracilissimus* Temminck & Schlegel 1850:274. Type by monotypy. Valid (Dawson 1984 [ref. 5276], Araga in Masuda et al. 1984:89 [ref. 6441], Dawson 1985:15 [ref. 6541], Dawson 1986:446 [ref. 5650], Paxton et al. 1989:412 [ref. 12442]). Syngnathidae: Syngnathinae.

Acentrophryne Regan 1926:23 [ref. 3679]. Fem. *Acentrophryne longidens* Regan 1926:23. Type by monotypy. Valid (Pietsch & Lavenberg 1980 [ref. 6913]). Linophrynidae.

Aceratias Brauer 1902:296 [ref. 631]. Masc. *Aceratias macrorhinus* Brauer 1902:296. Type by subsequent designation. Type apparently designated first by Jordan 1920:497 [ref. 4905]. Based on larval males. Synonym of *Linophryne* Collett 1886. Linophrynidae.

Acerina Cuvier 1816:283 [ref. 993]. Fem. *Perca acerina* Cuvier 1816 (= *Perca cernua* Linnaeus 1758:294). Type by absolute tautonymy. See Whitley 1935:138 [ref. 6396] for comments regarding type species. Synonym of *Gymnocephalus* Bloch 1793 (Collette & Banarescu 1977:1453 [ref. 5845]). Percidae.

Acerina Güldenstädt 1774:455 [ref. 1955]. Fem. *Acerina babir* Güldenstädt 1772:456 (= *Perca cernua* Linnaeus 1758:294). Type by monotypy. Jordan 1917:32 [ref. 2407] lists type as *kabir* Güldenstädt = *cernua* Linnaeus. Collette 1963:617 [ref. 6459] indicated that he could find no *kabir* mentioned by Güldenstädt and indicated he merely described *Perca acerina* and compared it with *Perca cernua*. The title indicates that Güldenstädt was describing a genus and on p. 456 he mentions *babir* russice salutatur *acerina. Cernua* autem... Article needs translation; name probably available. Percidae.

Acestra Bonaparte (ex Jardine) 1846:91 [ref. 519]. Fem. *Syngnathus aequoreus* Linnaeus 1758:337. Apparently not available, name published in synonymy of *Syngnathus* and *Nerophis*, and apparently not subsequently used as a valid name or senior homonym; type above as given by Fowler (MS). Synonym of *Nerophis* Rafinesque 1810. Syngnathidae: Syngnathinae.

Acestra Kner 1853:93 [ref. 2627]. Fem. *Acestra acus* Kner 1853:93. Type by subsequent designation. Type designated by Bleeker 1862:4 [ref. 393] and 1863:82 [ref. 401]. Preoccupied by Bonaparte 1846 in fishes and by Dallas 1852 in Hemiptera; replaced by *Farlowella* Eigenmann & Eigenmann 1889. Objective synonym of *Farlowella* Eigenmann & Eigenmann 1889 (Isbrücker 1980:96 [ref. 2303]). Loricariidae.

Acestridium Haseman 1911:319 [ref. 2047]. Neut. *Acestridium discus* Haseman 1911:319. Type by monotypy. Valid (Isbrücker 1980:102 [ref. 2303], Burgess 1989:441 [ref. 12860]). Loricariidae.

Acestrocephalus Eigenmann 1910:447 [ref. 1224]. Masc. *Xiphorhamphus anomalus* Steindachner 1880:84. Type by original designation (also monotypic). Valid (Menezes 1976:37 [ref. 7073] in subfamily Cynopotaminae, Menezes 1977 [ref. 7070]); synonym of *Cynopotamus* Valenciennes 1849, as a valid subgenus (Géry 1977:307 [ref. 1597]). Characidae.

Acestrorhamphus Eigenmann & Kennedy 1903:527 [ref. 1260]. Masc. *Hydrocyon hepsetus* Cuvier 1816:313. Type by monotypy. Also appeared in Eigenmann 1903 (Dec.):146 [ref. 1218]. Synonym of *Oligosarcus* Günther 1864, as a valid subgenus (Géry 1977:326 [ref. 1597]). Characidae.

Acestrorhynchus Eigenmann & Kennedy 1903:527 [ref. 1260]. Masc. *Salmo falcatus* Bloch 1794:120. Type by being a replacement name. Replacement for *Xiphorhynchus* Agassiz 1829, preoccupied by Swainson 1827 in Aves; also replaces *Xiphorhamphus* Müller & Troschel 1845, preoccupied by Blyth 1843 in Aves. Also in Eigenmann 1903 (Dec.):146 [ref. 1218]. Valid (Géry 1977:326 [ref. 1597], Vari 1983:5 [ref. 5419]). Characidae.

Acharnes Müller & Troschel 1848:622 [ref. 3072]. *Acharnes speciosus* Müller & Troschel 1848. Type by monotypy. Synonym of *Cichla* Bloch & Schneider 1801 (Kullander 1986:50 [ref. 12439], Kullander & Nijssen 1989:5 [ref. 14136]). Cichlidae.

Acheilognathus Bleeker 1859:427 [ref. 370]. Masc. *Acheilognathus melanogaster* Bleeker 1860:92. Type by subsequent monotypy. Apparently appeared first in key, without species. One species added by Bleeker 1859:259 [ref. 371] (five added by Bleeker 1860:225 [ref. 380]). *Achilognathus* Günther 1868:276 [ref. 1990] is an unjustified emendation. Valid (Wu 1964:207 [ref. 13503], Sawada in Masuda et al. 1984:54 [ref. 6441], Arai & Akai 1988 [ref. 6999], Chen & Li in Chu & Chen 1989:128 [ref. 13584]). Cyprinidae.

Achiroides Bleeker 1851:262 [ref. 325]. Masc. *Plagusia melanorhynchus* Bleeker 1851:15. Type by monotypy. Apparently appeared first as *Achiroïdes melanorhynchus* Blkr. = *Plagusia melanorhynchus* Blkr." Species described earlier in same journal as

P. melanorhynchus (also spelled *melanorhijnchus*). Diagnosis provided in Bleeker 1851:404 [ref. 6831] in same journal with second species *leucorhynchos* added. Valid (Kottelat 1989:20 [ref. 13605], Roberts 1989:183 [ref. 6439]). Soleidae.

Achirophichthys Bleeker 1864:35, 39 [ref. 4860]. Masc. *Achirophichthys typus* Bleeker 1864:39. Type by original designation (also by monotypy and use of *typus*). Misspelled *Achirophthichthys* in Zoological Record for 1864. *Auchenichthys* Kaup in Duméril 1856:198 [ref. 1154] apparently the same but not available. Also in Bleeker 1865:41 [ref. 408]. Valid (McCosker 1977:65 [ref. 6836]). Ophichthidae: Ophichthinae.

Achiropsetta Norman 1930:361 [ref. 3219]. Fem. *Achiropsetta tricholepis* Norman 1930:362. Type by original designation (also monotypic). Valid (Norman 1934:248 [ref. 6893]); synonym of *Mancopsetta* Gill 1920 (Hensley 1986:860 [ref. 5669], Hensley 1986:941 [ref. 6326]); valid (Evseenko 1987 [ref. 9289]). Achiropsettidae.

Achiropsis (subgenus of *Solea*) Steindachner 1876:158 [ref. 4225]. Fem. *Solea (Achiropsis) nattereri* Steindachner 1876:158. Type by monotypy. Achiridae.

Achirostomias (subgenus of *Eustomias*) Regan & Trewavas 1930:72, 94 [ref. 3681]. Masc. *Eustomias lipochirus* Regan & Trewavas 1930:95. Type by original designation. Synonym of *Eustomias* Vaillant 1888 (Gibbs in Morrow & Gibbs 1964:377 [ref. 6962], Morrow 1973:137 [ref. 7175]). Melanostomiidae.

Achirus Lacepède 1802:658 [ref. 4929]. Masc. *Pleuronectes achirus* Linnaeus 1758:268. Type by absolute tautonymy. *Pleuronectes achirus* Linnaeus was treated in the synonymy of *Achirus fasciatus* Lacepède 1802, but apparently *fasciatus* Lacepède is not the same as *achirus* Linnaeus and belongs in the genus *Trinectes*. Valid (Robins et al. 1980:65 [ref. 7111]). Achiridae.

Achlyopa Whitley 1947:150 [ref. 4708]. Fem. *Synaptura nigra* Macleay 1881:49. Type by original designation. Not technically a replacement name for *Euryglossa* Kaup 1858, preoccupied by Smith 1853 in Insecta. Misspelled *Achylopa* in Zoological Record for 1947. Valid (Chapleau & Keast 1988:2799 [ref. 12625]). Soleidae.

Achoerodus Gill 1863:222 [ref. 1685]. Masc. *Labrus gouldii* Richardson 1843:353. Type by original designation (also monotypic). Labridae.

Acinacea Bory de Saint-Vincent 1804:93 [ref. 6460]. Fem. *Acinacea notha* Bory de Saint-Vincent 1804:93. Type by monotypy. Suppressed (for priority) by ICZN, on Official Index (Opinion 487) to preserve *Gempylus* Cuvier 1829; *Acinaces* Agassiz 1846:4 [ref. 64] suppressed for both priority and homonomy and placed on Official Index. Original not seen. In the synonymy of *Gempylus* Cuvier 1829 (Parin & Bekker 1973:457 [ref. 7206]). Gempylidae.

Acipenser Linnaeus 1758:237 [ref. 2787]. Masc. *Acipenser sturio* Linnaeus 1758:237. Type by Linnaean tautonymy. Spelled *Accipenser* by authors. On Official List (Opinion 77, Direction 56); *Acipenses* Linck 1790 placed on Official Index. *Acipenseres* used by Heckel & Kner 1856:336 [ref. 2078]. Valid (Svetovidov 1973:82 [ref. 7169], Svetovidov in Whitehead et al. 1984:220 [ref. 13675], Nakaya in Masuda et al. 1984:18 [ref. 6441]). Acipenseridae: Acipenserinae.

Acipenses Linck 1790:37 [ref. 4985]. On Official Index, incorrect subsequent spelling of *Acipenser* Linnaeus 1758 (Opinion 77, Direction 56). Acipenseridae: Acipenserinae.

Acmonotus Philippi 1896:382 [ref. 3465]. Masc. *Acmonotus chilensis* Philippi 1896:383. Type by monotypy. Preoccupied by McLachlan 1871 in Neuroptera; apparently not replaced. Synonym of *Leptonotus* Kaup 1853 (Fritzsche 1980:190 [ref. 1511], Dawson 1982:40 [ref. 6764], Dawson 1985:111 [ref. 6541]). Syngnathidae: Syngnathinae.

Acnodon Eigenmann 1903:147 [ref. 1218]. Masc. *Myleus oligacanthus* Müller & Troschel 1844:98. Type by original designation (also monotypic). Valid (Géry 1976:50 [ref. 14199], Géry 1977:275 [ref. 1597]). Characidae: Serrasalminae.

Acomus Girard 1856:173 [ref. 1810]. Masc. *Catostomus forsterianus* Richardson 1823:720 (= *Cyprinus catostomus* Forster 1773;158). Type by subsequent designation. Type apparently first designated by Bleeker 1863:189 [ref. 397] or 1863:23 [ref. 4859]. Preoccupied by Reichenbach 1852 in Aves; apparently not replaced. Synonym of *Catostomus* Lesueur 1817. Catostomidae.

Aconichthys Waite 1916:30 [ref. 4568]. Masc. *Aconichthys harrissoni* Waite 1916:30. Type by monotypy. Bathydraconidae.

Acoura Swainson 1839:310 [ref. 4303]. Fem. *Acoura obscura* Swainson 1839:310 (= *Cobitis savona* Hamilton 1822:357, 394). Type by subsequent designation. Type designated by Swain 1882:281 [ref. 5966]. Spelled *Acourus* on p. 190 and 436. *Acura* Agassiz 1846:5 [ref. 64] is an unjustified emendation. Swainson's *obscura* an unneeded replacement for *savona* Hamilton. Synonym of *Schistura* McClelland 1839 (Banarescu & Nalbant 1968:333 [ref. 6554], Kottelat 1990:21 [ref. 14137]). Balitoridae: Nemacheilinae.

Acourus [ref. 4303]. see *Acoura*. Balitoridae: Nemacheilinae.

Acra (subgenus of *Gymnostomus*) Bleeker 1860:225, 230 [ref. 380]. *Cyprinus acra* Hamilton 1822:284. Type by absolute tautonymy, fifteen included species; type not *Chondrostoma syriacum* Valenciennes as designated by Bleeker 1863:197 [ref. 397] or 1863:26 [ref. 4859]. Cyprinidae.

Acreichthys (subgenus of *Pervagor*) Fraser-Brunner 1941:183 [ref. 1494]. Masc. *Balistes tomentosus* Linnaeus 1758:328. Type by original designation (also monotypic). Valid (Matsuura 1979:164 [ref. 7019], Tyler & Lange 1982 [ref. 5509], Arai 1983:199 [ref. 14249], Matsuura in Masuda et al. 1984:359 [ref. 6441]). Monacanthidae.

Acrobrycon Eigenmann & Pearson in Pearson 1924:44 [ref. 3396]. Masc. *Tetragonopterus ipanquianus* Cope 1878:44. Type by original designation (also monotypic). Valid (Géry 1977:358 [ref. 1597], Weitzman & S. Fink 1985:1 et seq. [ref. 5203], Weitzman et al. 1988:383 [ref. 13557]). Characidae: Glandulocaudinae.

Acrocheilichthys See *Sarcocheilichthys*. Cyprinidae.

Acrocheilus Agassiz 1855:96 [ref. 71]. Masc. *Acrocheilus alutaceus* Agassiz & Pickering in Agassiz 1855:99. Type by original designation (also monotypic). Cyprinidae.

Acrochordonichthys Bleeker 1858:204, 209, 221 [ref. 365]. Masc. *Acrochordonichthys platycephalus* Bleeker 1858:224. Type by subsequent designation. Also on p. 27 et seq. Type designated by Bleeker 1862:13 [ref. 393] and 1863:105 [ref. 401]. Valid (Burgess 1989:119 [ref. 12860], Kottelat 1989:14 [ref. 13605], Roberts 1989:137 [ref. 6439]). Akysidae.

Acromycter Smith & Kanazawa 1977:541 [ref. 4036]. Masc. *Ariosoma perturbator* Parr 1932:31. Type by original designation. Valid (Smith & Leiby 1980 [ref. 6930], Asano in Masuda et al. 1984:28 [ref. 6441], Smith 1989:554 [ref. 13285]). Congridae:

Congrinae.

Acronurus Gronow in Gray 1854:190 [ref. 1911]. Masc. *Acronurus fuscus* Gronow in Gray 1854:191 (= *Teuthis hepatus* Linnaeus 1766:507). Type by subsequent designation. Earliest type designation not researched; three included species. Synonym of *Acanthurus* Forsskål 1775 (Randall 1955:364 [ref. 13648]). Acanthuridae.

Acronurus Günther (ex Gronow) 1861:345 [ref. 1964]. Masc. *Acanthurus argenteus* Quoy & Gaimard 1825:372. Type by subsequent designation. Type designated by Jordan 1919:307 [ref. 4904]. Synonym of *Acanthurus* Forsskål 1775. Acanthuridae.

Acroperca Myers 1933:76 [ref. 3106]. Fem. *Siniperca roulei* Wu 1930:54. Type by original designation (also monotypic). Valid (Zhou et al. 1986:966 [ref. 6332]). Percichthyidae.

Acropoecilia (subgenus of *Poecilia*) Hilgendorf 1889:52 [ref. 2164]. Fem. *Poecilia tridens* Hilgendorf 1889:52. Type by monotypy. Synonym of *Poecilia* Bloch & Schneider 1801 (Rosen & Bailey 1963:44 [ref. 7067]). Poeciliidae.

Acropoma Temminck & Schlegel 1843:31 [ref. 4371]. Neut. *Acropoma japonicum* Günther 1859:368. Original description without named species; one species added and type fixed by subsequent monotypy by Günther 1859:250 [ref. 1961]. Valid (Johnson 1984:464 [ref. 9681], Katayama in Masuda et al. 1984:124 [ref. 6441], Heemstra 1986:561 [ref. 5660], Fourmanoir 1988 [ref. 6870], Paxton et al. 1989:510 [ref. 12442]). Acropomatidae.

Acrossocheilus Oshima 1919:206 [ref. 3312]. Masc. *Gymnostomus formosanus* Regan 1908:149. Type by original designation (also monotypic). Misspelled *Acrossochilus* by Jordan 1920:570 [ref. 4905]. Valid (Wu et al. 1977:273 [ref. 4807], Jayaram 1981:122 [ref. 6497] as *Accrossocheilus*, Kottelat 1985:260 [ref. 11441], Chu & Cui in Chu & Chen 1989:203 [ref. 13584]). Cyprinidae.

Acroteriobatus (subgenus of *Rhinobatus [Rhinobatos]*) Giltay 1929:26 [ref. 5065]. Masc. *Rhinobatos (Syrrhina) annulatus* Smith 1841:116. Type by subsequent designation. Type apparently designated first by Fowler 1969:141 [ref. 6832]. Synonym of *Rhinobatos* Linck 1790. Rhinobatidae: Rhinobatinae.

Acrotus Bean 1888:631 [ref. 227]. Masc. *Acrotus willoughbyi* Bean 1888:631. Type by monotypy. Synonym of *Icosteus* Lockington 1880. Icosteidae.

Acteis Jordan 1904:543 [ref. 2400]. Masc. *Malococtenus moorei* Evermann & Marsh 1900:309. Type by original designation. Synonym of *Labrisomus* Swainson (Springer 1958:439 [ref. 10210]). Labrisomidae.

Actenolepis Dybowski 1872:210 [ref. 1170]. Fem. *Actenolepis ditmarii* Dybowski 1872:210. Type by monotypy. Synonym of *Siniperca* Gill 1862. Percoidei.

Actinicola (subgenus of *Amphiprion*) Fowler 1904:533 [ref. 1367]. Masc. *Lutjanus percula* Lacepède 1802:239, 240. Type by original designation (also monotypic). Synonym of *Amphiprion* Bloch & Schneider 1801. Pomacentridae.

Actinoberyx Roule 1923:1027 [ref. 3821]. Masc. *Actinoberyx jugeati* Roule 1923:1027. Type by monotypy. Synonym of *Beryx* Cuvier 1829 (Nielsen 1973:337 [ref. 6885], Woods & Sonoda 1973:282 [ref. 6899], Maul in Whitehead et al. 1986:740 [ref. 13676], Heemstra 1986:409 [ref. 5660]). Berycidae.

Actinochir Gill 1864:190, 193 [ref. 1700]. Fem. *Liparis tunicata* of Krøyer 1862 (= *Liparis major* Gill 1864:193). Type by original designation. Proposed somewhat conditionally (p. 190), but available (conditional proposal before 1961). Synonym of *Liparis* Scopoli 1777 (Lindberg 1973:609 [ref. 7220], Kido 1988:165 [ref. 12287]). Cyclopteridae: Liparinae.

Actinochromis Bleeker 1877:5, 6, 142, 166 [ref. 454]. Masc. *Heliastes lividus* Klunzinger 1872:36. Type by original designation (also monotypic). Spelled *Acanthochromis* on pp. 5-6 (not of Gill, see p. 151), corrected to *Actinochromis* in "Corrigenda et Addenda" on p. 166. Synonym of *Parma* Günther 1862 (Allen & Hoese 1975:263 [ref. 7097]). Pomacentridae.

Actinogobius Bleeker 1874:319 [ref. 437]. Masc. *Gobius ommaturus* Richardson 1845:146. Type by original designation (also monotypic). Synonym of *Synechogobius* Gill 1863. Gobiidae.

Aculeola de Buen 1959:180 [ref. 697]. Fem. *Aculeola nigra* de Buen 1959:180. Type by original designation (also monotypic). Valid (Burgess & Springer 1986:189 [ref. 6149]). Squalidae.

Acus Catesby 1771:30 [ref. 774]. Not available; published in a rejected work on Official Index (Opinion 89, Opinion 259). Lepisosteidae.

Acus Müller 1766:141 [ref. 3055]. Not available, published in a rejected work on Official Index (Opinion 701). In the synonymy of *Syngnathus* Linnaeus 1758. Syngnathidae: Syngnathinae.

Acus Müller [P. L. S.] 1774:341, suppl. p. 7 [ref. 6461]. *Esox belone* Linnaeus 1761:126. Above from Fowler (MS), original not examined. In the synonymy of *Belone* Cuvier 1816 according to Fowler. Belonidae.

Acus Plumier in Lacepède 1803:327 (footnote) [ref. 4930]. Fem. Apparently not available; Plumier manuscript name mentioned in passing under *Sphyraena chinensis*. See remarks under Opinion 89 in Appendix B. In the synonymy of *Sphyraena* Röse 1793. Sphyraenidae.

Acus (subgenus of *Syngnathus*) Swainson (ex Willoughby) 1839:195, 333 [ref. 4303]. Fem. *Syngnathus aequoreus* Linnaeus 1758:337. Type by subsequent designation. Apparently not preoccupied by *Acus* Plumier in Lacepède 1803 in fishes (not available); not replaced. Type perhaps designated first by Jordan 1919:205 [ref. 2410]. Synonym of *Nerophis* Rafinesque 1810. Syngnathidae: Syngnathinae.

Acus Valmont de Bomare 1791 [ref. 4508]. Fem. Original not seen. Not available, published in a rejected work on Official Index (Opinion 89, Direction 32). In the synonymy of *Syngnathus* Linnaeus 1758. Syngnathidae: Syngnathinae.

Acuticurimata Fowler 1941:166 [ref. 1437]. Fem. *Curimatus macrops* Eigenmann & Eigenmann 1889:429. Type by original designation (also monotypic). Synonym of *Curimata* Bosc 1817 (Vari 1989:6 [ref. 9189], Vari 1989:21 [ref. 13506]). Curimatidae: Curimatinae.

Acutomentum Eigenmann & Beeson 1893:669 [ref. 1212]. Neut. *Sebastodes ovalis* Ayres 1862:209. Type by original designation. Synonym of *Sebastes* Cuvier 1829. Scorpaenidae: Sebastinae.

Acyrtops Schultz 1951:244 [ref. 3968]. Masc. *Gobiesox (Rimicola) beryllinus* Hildebrand & Ginsburg 1927:213. Type by original designation (also monotypic). Valid (Briggs 1955:73 [ref. 637]). Gobiesocidae: Gobiesocinae.

Acyrtus Schultz 1944:56 [ref. 3961]. Masc. *Sicyases rubiginosus* Poey 1868:391. Type by original designation (also monotypic). Valid (Briggs 1955:125 [ref. 637], Allen [L. G.] 1984:629 [ref. 13673] as *Acrytops*). Gobiesocidae: Gobiesocinae.

Adamacypris (subgenus of *Barbus*) Fowler 1934:125 [ref. 1417]. Fem. *Puntius proctozysron* Bleeker 1865:200. Type by original designation. Objective synonym of *Puntioplites* Smith 1929 (Roberts 1989:59 [ref. 6439]). Cyprinidae.

Adamas Huber 1979:6 [ref. 2269]. Masc. *Adamas formosus* Huber 1979:6. Type by monotypy. Also appeared in Huber 1979 [ref. 2270]. Valid (Parenti 1981:479 [ref. 7066], Wildekamp et al. 1986:195 [ref. 6198]). Aplocheilidae: Aplocheilinae.

Adamasoma (subgenus of *Rhombosolea*) Whitley & Phillipps 1939:231 [ref. 4737]. Neut. *Rhombosolea retiaria* Hutton 1874:107. Type by original designation. Pleuronectidae: Rhombosoleinae.

Adelosebastes Eschmeyer, Abe & Nakano 1979:78 [ref. 1275]. Masc. *Adelosebastes latens* Eschmeyer, Abe & Nakano 1979:80. Type by original designation. Valid (Kanayama 1981:124 [ref. 5539], Washington et al. 1984:440 [ref. 13660], Amaoka in Masuda et al. 1984:315 [ref. 6441]). Scorpaenidae: Sebastolobinae.

Adenapogon McCulloch 1921:132 [ref. 2945]. Masc. *Adenapogon roseigaster* Ramsay & Ogilby 1887:1101. Type by original designation (also monotypic). Synonym of *Siphamia* Weber 1909 (Fraser 1972:14 [ref. 5195]). Apogonidae.

Adenops Schultz 1948:(14) 34 [ref. 3966]. Masc. *Adenops analis* Schultz 1948:34. Type by original designation. Synonym of *Membras* Bonaparte 1836 (Chernoff 1986:239 [ref. 5847]). Atherinidae: Menidiinae.

Adinia Girard 1859:117 [ref. 1821]. Fem. *Adinia multifasciata* Girard 1859:118. Type by monotypy. Valid (Parenti 1981:498 [ref. 7066]). Cyprinodontidae: Fundulinae.

Adiniops (subgenus of *Fundulus*) Myers 1924:6 [ref. 3091]. Masc. *Fundulus guentheri* Pfeffer 1893:167. Type by original designation. Synonym of *Nothobranchius* Peters 1868 (Parenti 1981:479 [ref. 7066], Wildekamp et al. 1986:263 [ref. 6198]). Aplocheilidae: Aplocheilinae.

Adioryx Starks 1908:614 [ref. 4196]. Masc. *Holocentrum suborbitale* Gill 1864:86. Type by original designation (also monotypic). Correct spelling for genus of type species is *Holocentrus*. Valid (Woods & Sonoda 1973:349 [ref. 6899]); synonym of *Sargocentron* Fowler 1904 (Matsuura & Shimizu 1982 [ref. 5503], Randall & Heemstra 1985:5 [ref. 5144], Randall & Heemstra 1986:417 [ref. 5707]). Holocentridae.

Adiposia Annandale & Hora 1920:182 [ref. 128]. Fem. *Nemachilus macmahoni* Chaudhuri 1909:341. Type by original designation. Synonym of *Paracobitis* Bleeker 1863 (Kottelat 1990:20 [ref. 14137]). Balitoridae: Nemacheilinae.

Adonis Gronow in Gray 1854:93 [ref. 1911]. Masc. *Adonis pavoninus* Gronow in Gray 1854:93 (= *Blennius ocellaris* Linnaeus 1758:256). Type by subsequent designation. Six included species, subsequent designation not researched. Objective synonym of *Blennius* Linnaeus 1758 (Bath 1973:519 [ref. 7212]). Blenniidae.

Adontosternarchus Ellis in Eigenmann 1912:424 (in key) [ref. 1227]. Masc. *Sternarchus sachsi* Peters 1877:473. Type by subsequent monotypy (Ellis 1913:155 [ref. 1271]). Appeared first in Eigenmann 1912:424 (in key) [ref. 1227] without species; more fully described in Ellis 1913:155, with one species. Valid (Mago-Leccia et al. 1985 [ref. 5732]). Gymnotidae: Apteronotinae.

Adrianichthys Weber 1913:204 [ref. 4601]. Masc. *Adrianichthys kruyti* Weber 1913:205. Type by monotypy. Valid. Adrianichthyidae: Adrianichthyinae.

Adventor (subgenus of *Membracidichthys*) Whitley 1952:27 [ref. 4716]. Masc. *Membracidichthys (Adventor) elongatus* Whitley 1952:27. Type by original designation (also monotypic). Valid (Poss & Eschmeyer 1978:404 [ref. 6387], Washington et al. 1984:440 [ref. 13660], Paxton et al. 1989:459 [ref. 12442]). Aploactinidae.

Aegaeonichthys Clarke 1878:245 [ref. 841]. Masc. *Aegaeonichthys appelii* Clarke 1878:245. Type by monotypy. Original typescript somewhat unclear, possibly *Aegoeonichthys* rather than *Aegaeonichthys*. Species spelled *appelii* once in text and *appellii* once on plate; named after Mr. Appel, so *appelii* is correct. Synonym of *Himantolophus* Reinhardt 1837 (Bertelsen & Krefft 1988:35 [ref. 6615] as *Aegeonichthys*). Himantolophidae.

Aeglefinus Malm 1877:106, 481 [ref. 2881]. Masc. *Aeglefinus linnei* Malm 1877:481 (= *Gadus aeglefinus* Linnaeus 1758:251). Type by monotypy. Malm's *A. linnei* is an unneeded replacement for *G. aeglefinus* Linnaeus. Synonym of *Melanogrammus* Gill 1862 (Svetovidov 1973:306 [ref. 7169]). Gadidae.

Aelurichthys see *Ailurichthys*. Ariidae.

Aemasia Jordan & Snyder 1901:883 [ref. 2508]. Fem. *Aemasia lichenosa* Jordan & Snyder 1901:883. Type by original designation (also monotypic). Synonym of *Lycodontis* McClelland 1844 (Blache et al. 1973:225 [ref. 7185]). Synonym of *Enchelycore* Kaup 1856 (Böhlke et al. 1989:134 [ref. 13286]). Muraenidae: Muraeninae.

Aeoliscus Jordan & Starks 1902:71 [ref. 2525]. Masc. *Amphisile strigata* Günther 1861:528. Type by original designation. Valid (Araga in Masuda et al. 1984:85 [ref. 6441], Heemstra 1986:461 [ref. 5660], Paxton et al. 1989:410 [ref. 12442]). Centriscidae: Centriscinae.

Aequidens (subgenus of *Astronotus*) Eigenmann & Bray 1894:616 [ref. 1248]. Masc. *Acara tetramerus* Heckel 1840:341. Type by monotypy in subgenus. Valid (Kullander 1986:338 [ref. 12439], Kullander & Nijssen 1989:134 [ref. 14136]). Cichlidae.

Aequidens (subgenus of *Tetragonopterus*) Steindachner 1915:34 [ref. 4244]. Masc. *Tetragonopterus (Aequidens) fasslii* Steindachner 1915:34. Type by monotypy. Preoccupied by Eigenmann & Bray 1894 in fishes, replaced by *Evenichthys* Whitley 1935. "Misprint for *Astyanax*" written in separate at the California Academy of Sciences, and this plus style (see new subgenus *Pseudepapterus*) suggests that the name was in error and not intended as an original description. Characidae.

Aeschrichthys Macleay 1883:5 [ref. 2871]. Masc. *Aeschrichthys goldiei* Macleay 1883:5. Type by monotypy. Mugilidae.

Aeschynichthys Ogilby 1907:25 [ref. 3283]. Masc. *Diceratias bispinosus* Günther 1887:53. Type by being a replacement name. Unneeded replacement for *Diceratias* Günther 1887, not preoccupied by *Diceratia* in Mollusca. Diceratiidae.

Aesopia Kaup 1858:97 [ref. 2578]. Fem. *Aesopia cornuta* Kaup 1858:98. Type by subsequent designation. Type designated by Günther 1862:487 [ref. 1970]. Valid (Ochiai in Masuda et al. 1984:355 [ref. 6441], Heemstra & Gon 1986:869 [ref. 5665]). Soleidae.

Aetapcus (subgenus of *Pataecus*) Scott 1936:124 [ref. 3993]. Masc. *Pataecus maculatus* Günther 1861:292. Type by original designation. Valid (Washington et al. 1984:440 [ref. 13660], Paxton et al. 1989:462 [ref. 12442]). Pataecidae.

Aethaloperca (subgenus of *Bodianus*) Fowler 1904:522 [ref. 1367]. Fem. *Perca rogaa* Forsskål 1775:38. Type by original designation (also monotypic). Valid (Katayama in Masuda et al. 1984:127 [ref. 6441], Heemstra & Randall 1986:516 [ref. 5667], Smith-Vaniz et al. 1988:11 [ref. 9299], Paxton et al. 1989:489 [ref. 12442]). Serranidae: Epinephelinae.

Aethiomastacembelus Travers 1988:256 [ref. 6869]. Masc. *Mastacembelus marchei* Sauvage 1879. Type by original designation. Mastacembelidae.

Aethoprora Goode & Bean 1896:86 [ref. 1848]. Fem. *Nyctophus metopoclampus* Cocco 1829:144. Type by subsequent designation. Type designated by Jordan 1920:467 [ref. 4905]. Synonym of *Diaphus* Eigenmann & Eigenmann 1890 (Nafpaktitis 1968:22 [ref. 6979], Krefft & Bekker 1973:176 [ref. 7181], Paxton 1979:7 [ref. 6440]). Myctophidae.

Aethotaxis DeWitt 1962:828 [ref. 1123]. Fem. *Aethotaxis mitopteryx* DeWitt 1962:829. Type by original designation (also monotypic). Valid (Stevens et al. 1984:563 [ref. 13633], Andersen 1984:25 [ref. 13369]). Nototheniidae.

Aetiasis Barnard 1937:59 [ref. 197]. *Aetiasis cantharoides* Barnard 1937:60. Type by monotypy. Synonym of *Paracaesio* Bleeker 1875 (Allen 1985:130 [ref. 6843]). Lutjanidae.

Aetobatus (subgenus of *Raia [Raja]*) Blainville 1816:112 [= 120] [ref. 306]. Masc. *Raja aquila* Linnaeus 1758:232. Type by subsequent designation. *Aetobatis* and *Aetobates* of authors are incorrect subsequent spellings. Type usually given as *narinari* designated by Müller & Henle 1838 (e.g. Jordan 1917:95 [ref. 2407]), but Whitley 1935:137 [ref. 6396] found *aquila* Linnaeus, designated by Bory de Saint-Vincent, v. 1, 1822:129 [ref. 3853]. Valid (Nakaya in Masuda et al. 1984:16 [ref. 6441], Compagno 1986:132 [ref. 5648], Cappetta 1987:170 [ref. 6348], Paxton et al. 1989:49 [ref. 12442]). Myliobatidae.

Aetomylaeus Garman 1908:252 [ref. 1543]. Masc. *Myliobatus maculatus* Gray 1832:101. Type by original designation. Misspelled *Aetomyleus* in Zoological Record for 1908. Correct spelling for genus of type species is *Myliobatis*. Valid (Nakaya in Masuda et al. 1984:16 [ref. 6441], Cappetta 1987:171 [ref. 6348]). Myliobatidae.

Aetoplatea Valenciennes in Müller & Henle 1841:175 [ref. 3069]. Fem. *Aetoplatea tentaculata* Valenciennes in Müller & Henle 1841:175. Type by monotypy. *Aetoplatia* Agassiz 1846:10 [ref. 64] and of Scudder 1882:8 [ref. 6462] is an unjustified emendation. Synonym of *Gymnura* van Hasselt 1823 (Cappetta 1987:165 [ref. 6348]). Gymnuridae.

Afromastacembelus Travers 1984:145 [ref. 5147]. Masc. *Mastacembelus tanganicae* Günther 1893:629. Type by original designation. Valid (Travers et al. 1986:415 [ref. 6221], Roberts & Travers 1986 [ref. 6759]); synonym of *Caecomastacembelus* Poll 1958 (Travers 1988 [ref. 6869]). Mastacembelidae.

Afronandus Meinken 1955:59 [ref. 2971]. Masc. *Nandopsis sheljuzhkoi* Meinken 1954:28. Type by being a replacement name. Replacement for *Nandopsis* Meinken 1954, preoccupied by Gill 1862 in fishes. Valid (Thys van den Audenaerde & Breine 1986:342 [ref. 6214]). Nandidae: Nandinae.

Afropuntio Karaman 1971:190 [ref. 2560]. *Barbus pobequini* Pellegrin 1911:187. Type by original designation (also monotypic). Synonym of *Barbus* Cuvier & Cloquet 1816 (Lévêque & Daget 1984:219 [ref. 6186]). Cyprinidae.

Afroscion Trewavas 1977:337 [ref. 4459]. Masc. *Argyrosomus thorpei* Smith 1977:562. Type by original designation (also monotypic). Synonym of *Argyrosomus* De la Pylaie 1835 (Sasaki & Kailola 1988:263 [ref. 12553]). Sciaenidae.

Agalaxis (subgenus of *Galaxias*) Scott 1936:105 [ref. 3994]. Masc. *Cobitis zebrata* Castelnau 1861:56. Type by original designation (also monotypic). Name is an anogram of *Galaxias* and regarded as masculine. Synonym of *Galaxias* Cuvier 1816 (McDowall 1984:126 [ref. 6178]). Galaxiidae: Galaxiinae.

Agamyxis Cope 1878:699 [ref. 945]. *Doras pectinifrons* Cope 1870:568. Apparently appeared as name only in list of Siluridae and unavailable; Fowler (MS) says genus refers to *Doras pectiniforms* Cope 1870:568; subsequent availability not researched but name is in current use. Valid (Burgess 1989:223 [ref. 12860]). Doradidae.

Ageneiogarra (subgenus of *Garra*) Garman 1912:114 [ref. 1544]. Fem. *Garra imberba* Garman 1912:114. Type by monotypy. Synonym of *Garra* Hamilton 1822 (Karaman 1971:232 [ref. 2560], Wu et al. 1977:372 [ref. 4807], Lévêque & Daget 1984:301 [ref. 6186]). Cyprinidae.

Ageneiosus Lacepède 1803:132 [ref. 4930]. Masc. *Ageneiosus armatus* Lacepède 1803:132. Type by subsequent designation. Type validly designated first by Eigenmann & Eigenmann 1890:299 [ref. 12251]. Spelled *Ageneios*, *Ageniosus* and *Ageneirosus* by early authors. *Agenius* Agassiz 1846:11 [ref. 64] is an unjustified emendation. Valid (Burgess 1989:286 [ref. 12860]). Ageneiosidae.

Agenigobio Sauvage 1878:87 [ref. 3878]. Masc. *Agenigobio halsoueti* Sauvage 1878:87. Type by monotypy. Synonym of *Ochetobius* Günther 1868 (Chu 1935:33 [ref. 832], Yang & Hwang 1964:44 [ref. 13497], Chen & Li in Chu & Chen 1989:43 [ref. 13584]). Cyprinidae.

Agenor Castelnau 1879:371 [ref. 764]. Masc. *Agenor modestus* Castelnau 1879:371. Type by monotypy. Synonym of *Scorpis* Valenciennes 1832. Kyphosidae: Scorpidinae.

Aglyptosternon Bleeker 1862:12 [ref. 393]. Neut. *Silurus cous* Linnaeus 1766:504. Type by original designation (also monotypic). Misspelled *Aclyptosteron* in Day 1877:499 [ref. 4886] and unjustifiably emended to *Enclyptosternum* by Günther 1864:183 [ref. 1974]. Synonym of *Glyptothorax* Blyth 1860 (Li 1986:522 [ref. 6132]). Sisoridae.

Agmus Eigenmann 1910:379 [ref. 1224]. Masc. *Bunocephalus scabriceps* Eigenmann & Eigenmann 1889:49. Type by original designation (also monotypic). Full description appeared in Eigenmann 1912:128 [ref. 1227], but available from Eigenmann 1910 by name plus one available species. Synonym of *Bunocephalichthys* Bleeker 1858 (Mees 1988:89 [ref. 6401]); valid (Burgess 1989:303 [ref. 12860]). Aspredinidae: Bunocephalinae.

Agnathomyzon Gracianov 1906:18 [ref. 1870]. Masc. *Petromyzon wagneri* Kessler 1870:207, 302. Type by monotypy. Original not seen. Objective synonym of *Caspiomyzon* Berg 1906 (Sept. 1906); date for Gracianov is Dec. 1906 (Hubbs & Potter 1971:43 [ref. 13397]). Petromyzontidae: Petromyzontinae.

Agnus Günther 1860:229 [ref. 1963]. Masc. *Uranoscopus anoplos* Valenciennes in Cuvier & Valenciennes 1831:493. Type by monotypy. Preoccupied by Burmeister 1847 in Coleoptera. Objective synonym of *Astroscopus* Brevoort 1860 (Mees 1960:47 [ref. 11931], Pietsch 1989:297 [ref. 12541]). Uranoscopidae.

Agoniates Müller & Troschel 1845:19 [ref. 3071]. Masc. *Agoniates halecinus* Müller & Troschel 1845:20, 33. Type by monotypy. Also appeared as new in Müller & Troschel 1848:636 [ref. 3072]. Valid (Géry 1977:298 [ref. 1597]). Characidae.

Agonocottus Pavlenko 1910:23 [ref. 3393]. Masc. *Agonocottus cataphractus* Pavlenko 1910:23. Type by monotypy. Synonym of *Icelus* Krøyer 1845 (Nelson 1984:19 [ref. 5391]). Cottidae.

Agonomalus Guichenot 1866:254 [ref. 1947]. Fem. *Aspidophorus proboscidalis* Valenciennes 1858:1040. Type by monotypy. Valid

(Washington et al. 1984:442 [ref. 13660], Kanayama in Masuda et al. 1984:331 [ref. 6441], Yabe 1985:123 [ref. 11522], Maeda & Amaoka 1988:65 [ref. 12616]). Agonidae.

Agonopsis Gill 1861:167 [ref. 1775]. Fem. *Aspidophorus chiloensis* Jenyns 1840:30. Type by original designation (also monotypic). Valid (Washington et al. 1984:442 [ref. 13660], Yabe 1985:123 [ref. 11522]). Agonidae.

Agonostomus Bennett 1832:166 [ref. 4944]. Masc. *Agonostomus telfairii* Bennett 1832:166. Type by monotypy. Unjustifiably emended to *Agonostoma* by Günther 1861:461 [ref. 1964]. Valid (Thomson 1986:344 [ref. 6215]). Mugilidae.

Agonus Bloch & Schneider 1801:(xxx) 104 [ref. 471]. Masc. *Cottus cataphractus* Linnaeus 1758:264. Type by subsequent designation. Four included species, first subsequent designation found that of Gill 1861:167 [ref. 1775]. Valid (Lindberg 1973:605 [ref. 7220], Washington et al. 1984:442 [ref. 13660], Yabe 1985:123 [ref. 11522], Andriashev in Whitehead et al. 1986:1265 [ref. 13677]). Agonidae.

Agosia Girard 1856:186 [ref. 1810]. Fem. *Agosia chrysogaster* Girard 1857:187. Type by subsequent designation. Type designated by Jordan & Gilbert 1877:91 [ref. 4907]. Valid. Cyprinidae.

Agrammobarbus (subgenus of *Barbus*) Pellegrin 1935:382 [ref. 5041]. Masc. *Barbus apleurogramma* Boulenger 1911:136. Type by original designation (also monotypic). Perhaps also appeared in Pellegrin 1933:107, with *barbaulti* Pellégrin as type [not researched]. Synonym of *Barbus* Cuvier & Cloquet 1816 (Lévêque & Daget 1984:218 [ref. 6186]). Cyprinidae.

Agrammus Günther 1860:94 [ref. 1963]. Masc. *Agrammus schlegelii* Günther 1860:94 (= *Labrax agrammus* Temminck & Schlegel 1843:56). Type by monotypy; species needlessly renamed *Agrammus schlegelii* by Günther. Hexagrammidae: Hexagramminae.

Agrioposphyraena (subgenus of *Sphyraena*) Fowler 1903:749 [ref. 1361]. Fem. *Esox barracuda* Walbaum 1792:94. Type by original designation (also monotypic). Misspelled *Agriosphyraena* by Jordan 1920:502 [ref. 4905]. Synonym of *Sphyraena* Klein 1778 (de Sylva 1975:76 [ref. 6302], Daget 1986:350 [ref. 6203]); as a subgenus (de Sylva 1984:534 [ref. 13666]). Sphyraenidae.

Agriopus Cuvier in Cuvier & Valenciennes 1829:380 [ref. 998]. Masc. *Blennius torvus* Walbaum 1792:187. Type by subsequent designation. Appeared first as "Les Agriopes" in Cuvier (Mar.) 1829:168 [ref. 995], latinized as above and species added. Type designated by Bleeker 1876:8 [ref. 12248] and 1876:300 [ref. 450]. Synonym of *Congiopodus* Perry 1811. Congiopodidae.

Agripopa Whitley 1928:296 [ref. 4663]. Fem. *Onychognathus cautus* Troschel 1866:231. Type by being a replacement name. Replacement for *Onychognathus* Troschel 1866, preoccupied by Hartlaub 1859 in Aves. Pomacentridae.

Agrostichthys Phillipps 1924:539 [ref. 3466]. Masc. *Regalecus parkeri* Benham 1904:198. Type by monotypy. Valid (Olney 1984:369 [ref. 13656], Heemstra 1986:403 [ref. 5660], Paxton et al. 1989:401 [ref. 12442]). Regalecidae.

Aguarunichthys Stewart 1986:662 [ref. 5211]. Masc. *Aguarunichthys torosus* Stewart 1986:663. Type by original designation (also monotypic). Valid (Burgess 1989:282 [ref. 12860]). Pimelodidae.

Agunia Fowler 1946:207 [ref. 1456]. Fem. *Agunia quindecimfasciata* Fowler 1946:207. Type by original designation (also monotypic). Synonym of *Kelloggella* Jordan & Seale 1905 (Hoese 1975:474 [ref. 5294]). Gobiidae.

Ahlia Jordan & Davis 1891:639 [ref. 2437]. Fem. *Myrophis egmontis* Jordan 1889:44. Type by original designation (also monotypic). Valid (McCosker et al. 1989:272 [ref. 13288]). Ophichthidae: Myrophinae.

Ahliesaurus Bertelsen, Krefft & Marshall 1976:21 [ref. 289]. Masc. *Ahliesaurus berryi* Bertelsen, Krefft & Marshall 1976:22. Type by original designation. Valid (Krefft in Whitehead et al. 1984:422 [ref. 13675], Okiyama 1984:207 [ref. 13644], Fujii in Masuda et al. 1984:64 [ref. 6441], Krefft 1986:268 [ref. 5684]). Notosudidae.

Ahynnodontophis Fowler 1912:25 [ref. 1385]. Masc. *Gymnothorax stigmanotus* Fowler 1912:26. Type by original designation (also monotypic). Synonym of *Lycodontis* McClelland 1844 (Blache et al. 1973:225 [ref. 7185]). Synonym of *Gymnothorax* Bloch 1795 (Böhlke et al. 1989:145 [ref. 13286]). Muraenidae: Muraeninae.

Aiakas Gosztonyi 1977:198 [ref. 6103]. *Aiakas kreffti* Gosztonyi 1977:199. Type by original designation (also monotypic). Valid (Anderson 1984:578 [ref. 13634]). Zoarcidae.

Aida Castelnau 1875:10 [ref. 768]. Fem. *Aida inornata* Castelnau 1875:11. Type by monotypy. Synonym of *Melanotaenia* Gill 1862 (Allen 1980:474 [ref. 99], Allen & Cross 1982:44 [ref. 6251]). Atherinidae: Melanotaeniinae.

Aidablennius Whitley 1947:150 [ref. 4708]. Masc. *Blennius sphynx* Valenciennes in Cuvier & Valenciennes 1836:226. Type by original designation (also monotypic). Synonym of *Blennius* Linnaeus 1758 (Bath 1973:519 [ref. 7212]); valid (Bath 1977:176 [ref. 208], Zander in Whitehead et al. 1986:1096 [ref. 13677]). Blenniidae.

Aidaprora Whitley 1935:224 [ref. 4683]. Fem. *Aidaprora carteri* Whitley 1935:224. Type by original designation (also monotypic). Synonym of *Melanotaenia* Gill 1862 (Allen 1980:474 [ref. 99], Allen & Cross 1982:44 [ref. 6251] but as *Aidapora*). Atherinidae: Melanotaeniinae.

Ailia (subgenus of *Malapterus*) Gray 1830:Pl. 85 (v. 1) [ref. 1878]. Fem. *Malapterus (Ailia) bengalensis* Gray 1830:Pl. 85. Type by monotypy. Also appeared in Gray 1831:8 [ref. 1879] as a new genus. Valid (Jayaram 1977:12 [ref. 7006], Jayaram 1981:212 [ref. 6497], Burgess 1989:98 [ref. 12860]). Schilbeidae.

Ailiichthys Day 1872:712 [ref. 1079]. Masc. *Ailiichthys punctata* Day 1872:713. Type by monotypy. Synonym of *Ailia* Gray 1830 (Jayaram 1977:12 [ref. 7006] and Jayaram 1981:212 [ref. 6497] as *Ailichthys*, Burgess 1989:98 [ref. 12860]). Schilbeidae.

Ailurichthys Baird & Girard 1854:26 [ref. 168]. Masc. *Silurus marinus* Mitchill 1815:433. Type by subsequent designation. Type designated by Jordan & Evermann 1896:116 [ref. 2443]. Spelled *Aelurichthys* by Gill 1863:172 [ref. 1681]. Synonym of *Bagre* Cloquet 1816 (Robins et al. 1980:28 [ref. 7111] based on placement of type species). Ariidae.

Ainocottus Jordan & Starks 1904:283 [ref. 2528]. Masc. *Ainocottus ensiger* Jordan & Starks 1904:283. Type by original designation (also monotypic). Synonym of *Myoxocephalus* Tilesius 1811 (Neyelov 1979:120 [ref. 3152]). Cottidae.

Ainosus Jordan & Snyder 1901:109 [ref. 2509]. Masc. *Gobius geneionema* Hilgendorf 1879:108. Type by original designation (also monotypic). Synonym of *Sagamia* Jordan & Snyder 1901. Gobiidae.

Aioliops Rennis & Hoese 1987:70 [ref. 6602]. Masc. *Aioliops tetrophthalmus* Rennis & Hoese 1987:79. Type by original designation. Microdesmidae: Ptereleotrinae.

Akamefugu (subgenus of *Fugu*) Abe 1954:122 [ref. 5]. Masc. *Tetrodon chrysops* Hilgendorf 1879:80. Type by original designation (also monotypic). Synonym of *Takifugu* Abe 1949 (Masuda et al. 1984:364 [ref. 6441] based on placement of type). Tetraodontidae.

Akarotaxis DeWitt & Hureau 1979:784 [ref. 1125]. Fem. *Bathydraco nudiceps* Waite 1916:27. Type by original designation (also monotypic). Valid (Stevens et al. 1984:563 [ref. 13633], Voskoboinikova 1988:45 [ref. 12756]). Bathydraconidae.

Akysis Bleeker 1858:204, 234 [ref. 365]. Masc. *Pimelodus variegatus* Bleeker 1846:177. Type by monotypy. Valid (Jayaram 1977:30 [ref. 7006], Jayaram 1981:229 [ref. 6497], Kottelat 1985:271 [ref. 11441], Burgess 1989:119 [ref. 12860], Kottelat 1989:14 [ref. 13605], Roberts 1989:138 [ref. 6439]). Akysidae.

Alabes Cloquet 1816:99 [ref. 852]. Fem. *Alabes cuvieri* Vaillant 1905:149. Type by subsequent monotypy according to Springer & Fraser 1976:1 [ref. 7086]. Misspelled *Alabis* and *Alaebes* by Swainson 1838 [ref. 4302]. See also Whitley 1935:136 [ref. 6396]. Valid (Springer & Fraser 1976 [ref. 7086] as specialized gobiesocid genus, Scott 1976:163 [ref. 7055]). Gobiesocidae: Cheilobranchinae.

Alaeops Jordan & Starks 1904:623 [ref. 2526]. Masc. *Alaeops plinthus* Jordan & Starks 1904:623. Type by original designation (also monotypic). Synonym of *Poecilopsetta* Günther 1880 (Norman 1934:387 [ref. 6893]). Pleuronectidae: Poecilopsettinae.

Alausa Valenciennes in Cuvier & Valenciennes 1847:389 [ref. 1012]. Fem. *Alausa vulgaris* Valenciennes in Cuvier & Valenciennes 1847:391 (= *Clupea alosa* Linnaeus 1758:318). Apparently a misspelling of, or unjustified emendation of *Alosa* Linck 1790 (see Whitehead 1967:77 [ref. 6464]). Synonym of *Alosa* Linck 1790 (Svetovidov 1973:105 [ref. 7169], Whitehead 1985:191 [ref. 5141]). Clupeidae.

Alausella Gill 1861:36 [ref. 1767]. Fem. *Clupea parvula* Mitchill 1814:21. Type by original designation (also monotypic). Synonym of *Alosa* Linck 1790 (Whitehead 1985:191 [ref. 5141]). Clupeidae.

Alazon Gistel 1848:X [ref. 1822]. Masc. *Poecilia vivipara* Bloch & Schneider 1801:86. Type by being a replacement name. Unneeded replacement for *Poecilia* Bloch & Schneider 1801, not preoccupied by *Poecilus* in Coleoptera. Synonym of *Poecilia* Bloch & Schneider 1801 (Rosen & Bailey 1963:44 [ref. 7067]). Poeciliidae.

Albacora Jordan 1888:180 [ref. 2389]. Fem. *Scomber thynnus* Linnaeus 1758:297. Type by being a replacement name. Unneeded replacement for *Thynnus* Cuvier 1816, preoccupied by Fabricius 1775 in Hymenoptera but earlier replaced by *Thunnus* South 1845. Synonym of *Thunnus* South 1845 (Gibbs & Collette 1967:97 [ref. 13640], Postel 1973:467 [ref. 7208]). Scombridae.

Albatrossia Jordan & Gilbert in Jordan & Evermann 1898:2563, 2573 [ref. 2445]. Fem. *Macrourus (Malacocephalus) pectoralis* Gilbert 1891:563. Type by original designation (also monotypic). Authorship should be Jordan & Gilbert in Jordan & Evermann as evidenced by synonymy on p. 2574 and subsequent publication by Jordan & Gilbert 1898 [ref. 1793]. Synonym of *Coryphaenoides* Gunner 1761 (Marshall 1973:294 [ref. 7194]); valid (Iwamoto & Sazonov 1988:39 [6228]). Macrouridae: Macrourinae.

Albula Bloch & Schneider (ex Gronow) 1801:432 [ref. 471]. Fem. *Albula conorynchus* Bloch & Schneider 1801:432. Type by monotypy. Objective synonym of *Albula* Scopoli 1777. Albulidae: Albulinae.

Albula Catesby 1771:6 [ref. 774]. Fem. Not available, published in a rejected work on Official Index (Opinion 89, Opinion 259). In the synonymy of *Mugil* Linnaeus 1758. Mugilidae.

Albula Gronow 1763:102 [ref. 1910]. Fem. Not available, published in a rejected work on Official Index (Opinion 261); see Whitehead 1986:215 [ref. 5733]. Albulidae: Albulinae.

Albula Osbeck 1762:309 [ref. 3311]. Fem. *Albula chinensis* Osbeck 1762:309. Not available; apparently published in a work that was not consistently binominal, but not on Official Index; based on Osbeck 1757. In the synonymy of *Salanx* Cuvier 1816. Salangidae.

Albula Scopoli (ex Gronow) 1777:450 [ref. 3990]. Fem. *Esox vulpes* Linnaeus 1758:313. Early nomenclatural history confused; this authorship the valid one for the bonefish genus (see Whitehead 1986 [ref. 5733]). Valid (Uyeno in Masuda et al. 1984:21 [ref. 6441], Smith 1986:157 [ref. 5712], Paxton et al. 1989:106 [ref. 12442], Smith 1989:970 [ref. 13285]). Albulidae: Albulinae.

Albulichthys Bleeker 1859:430 [ref. 370]. Masc. *Systomus albuloides* Bleeker 1855:425. Type by subsequent monotypy. Apparently appeared first in key, without species. One species included by Bleeker 1859:153 [ref. 371] and 1860:175, 305-307 [ref. 380]. Type apparently not *Rohteichthys microlepis* Bleeker as designated by Bleeker 1863:27 [ref. 4859]. Valid (Wu et al. 1977:270 [ref. 4807], Kottelat 1985:260 [ref. 11441], Kottelat 1985:956 [ref. 5288], Kottelat 1989:6 [ref. 13605], Roberts 1989:27 [ref. 6439]). Cyprinidae.

Alburnellus Girard 1856:193 [ref. 1810]. Masc. *Alburnus dilectus* Girard 1856:193. Type by subsequent designation. Genus name proposed conditionally, but available (conditional proposal before 1961). Type designated by Jordan & Gilbert 1877:91 [ref. 4907]. Synonym of *Notropis* Rafinesque 1818 (Gilbert 1978:15 [ref. 7042]). Cyprinidae.

Alburnoides Jeitteles 1861:325 [ref. 2339]. Masc. *Alburnus maculatus* Kessler 1859:535. Type by monotypy. Valid (Bogutskaya 1987:936 [ref. 13521]). Cyprinidae.

Alburnops Girard 1856:194 [ref. 1810]. Masc. *Alburnops blennius* Girard 1856:194. Type by subsequent designation. Type designated by Jordan & Gilbert 1877:91 [ref. 4907]. Synonym of *Notropis* Rafinesque 1818, but as a valid subgenus (Gilbert 1978:15 [ref. 7042], Mayden 1989:41 [ref. 12555]). Cyprinidae.

Alburnus Catesby 1771:12 [ref. 774]. Masc. Not available, published in a rejected work on Official Index (Opinion 89, Opinion 259). Sciaenidae.

Alburnus Rafinesque 1820:236 [ref. 7310]. Masc. *Cyprinus alburnus* Linnaeus 1758:325. Genus proposed for European species, but no species mentioned; first addition of species not researched. Also appeared in Rafinesque 1820:46 (Dec.) [ref. 3592]. Valid (Bogutskaya 1987:936 [ref. 13521]). Cyprinidae.

Alcichthys Jordan & Starks 1904:301 [ref. 2528]. Masc. *Centridermichthys alcicornis* Herzenstein 1892:115. Type by original designation (also monotypic). Valid (Washington et al. 1984:442 [ref. 13660], Yabe in Masuda et al. 1984:329 [ref. 6441], Yabe 1985:111 [ref. 11522]). Cottidae.

Alcidea Jordan & Evermann 1898:1880, 1886 [ref. 2444]. Fem. *Paricelinus thoburni* Gilbert 1896:432. Type by original designation (also monotypic). Synonym of *Paricelinus* Eigenmann & Eigenmann 1889 (Bolin 1944:11 [ref. 6379]). Cottidae.

Alcockella (subgenus of *Narcetes*) Fowler 1934:255 [ref. 1416]. Fem. *Narcetes garmani* Fowler 1934:255. Type by original designation (also monotypic). Alepocephalidae.

Alcockia Goode & Bean 1896:329 [ref. 1848]. Fem. *Porogadus rostratus* Günther 1887:113. Type by monotypy. Valid (Cohen & Nielsen 1978:25 [ref. 881]). Ophidiidae: Neobythitinae.

Alcockidia Gilbert 1905:586 [ref. 1631]. Fem. *Gavialiceps microps* Alcock (ex Wood-Mason) 1889:461. Type by monotypy. See account of *Gavialiceps*. Synonym of *Serrivomer* Gill 1883 (Bauchot & Saldanha 1973:229 [ref. 7186], Tighe 1989:617 [ref. 13291]). Serrivomeridae.

Alcolapia Thys van den Audenaerde 1970:290, 291 [ref. 12518]. Fem. Not available, name only; as a subgroup of *Sarotherodon (Oreochromis)*. Cichlidae.

Aldrichetta Whitley 1945:19 [ref. 4707]. Fem. *Mugil forsteri* Valenciennes in Cuvier & Valenciennes 1836:141. Type by original designation (also monotypic). Mugilidae.

Aldrovandia Goode & Bean 1896:129, 132 [ref. 1848]. Fem. *Halosaurus rostratus* Günther 1878:251. Type by original designation. Valid (Harrisson 1973:255 [ref. 7189], Uyeno in Masuda et al. 1984:32 [ref. 6441], Sulak in Whitehead et al. 1986:593 [ref. 13676], Sulak 1986:196 [ref. 5720], Paxton et al. 1989:147 [ref. 12442]). Halosauridae.

Alectis Rafinesque 1815:84 [ref. 3584]. Masc. *Gallus virescens* Lacepède 1802:583. Type by being a replacement name. As "*Alectis* R. [Rafinesque] *Gallus* Lac. [Lacepède]." An available replacement name for *Gallus* Lacepède 1802, preoccupied by Linnaeus 1758 in Aves. Valid (Gushiken in Masuda et al. 1984:157 [ref. 6441], Smith-Vaniz 1984:524 [ref. 13664], Smith-Vaniz 1986:640 [ref. 5718], Daget & Smith-Vaniz 1986:308 [ref. 6207], Gushiken 1988:443 [ref. 6697], Paxton et al. 1989:573 [ref. 12442]). Carangidae.

Alectrias Jordan & Evermann 1898:2869 [ref. 2445]. Masc. *Blennius alectrolophus* Pallas 1811:174. Type by original designation (also monotypic). Valid (Amaoka & Miki in Masuda et al. 1984:301 [ref. 6441], Shiogaki 1985 [ref. 5199], Miki et al. 1987:11 [ref. 12551]). Stichaeidae.

Alectridium Gilbert & Burke 1912:87 [ref. 1634]. Neut. *Alectridium aurantiacum* Gilbert & Burke 1912:87. Type by original designation (also monotypic). Valid (Miki et al. 1987:11 [ref. 12551]). Stichaeidae.

Aledon Castelnau 1861:76 [ref. 767]. *Aledon storeri* Castelnau 1861:76. Type by subsequent designation. Earliest type designation found that of Jordan & Evermann 1898:1753 [ref. 2444]. Synonym of *Mola* Koelreuter 1770 (Fraser-Brunner 1943:8 [ref. 1495]). Molidae.

Alepes (subgenus of *Trachinus*) Swainson 1839:176, 248 [ref. 4303]. Fem. *Trachinus (Alepes) melanoptera* Swainson 1839:248. Type by monotypy. *Alepis* Agassiz 1846:14 [ref. 64] is an unjustified emendation. Valid (Smith-Vaniz 1984:524 [ref. 13664], Gushiken in Masuda et al. 1984:155 [ref. 6441], Smith-Vaniz 1986:641 [ref. 5718], Gushiken 1988:443 [ref. 6697], Paxton et al. 1989:574 [ref. 12442]). Carangidae.

Alepichthys Facciolà 1882:166 [ref. 1291]. Masc. *Alepichthys argyrogaster* Facciolà 1882:167. Type by monotypy. Family placement not determined, in Evermannellidae according to Fowler 1974:735[ref. 7156], not treated in Hureau & Monod 1973 [ref. 6590]. Alepisauroidei.

Alepideleotris Herre 1935:413 [ref. 2109]. Fem. *Alepideleotris tigris* Herre 1935:413. Type by original designation (also monotypic). Synonym of *Eleotrica* Ginsburg 1933. Gobiidae.

Alepidichthys Torres-Orozco & Castro-Aguirre 1982:38 [ref. 5384]. Masc. *Alepidichthys paradoxa* Torres-Orozco & Castro-Aguirre 1982:38. Type by original designation (also monotypic). Probably a synonym of *Psenes* Valenciennes 1833 (see author's addendum, back of p. 45). Nomeidae.

Alepidogobius Bleeker 1874:310 [ref. 437]. Masc. *Gobiosoma fasciatum* Playfair 1866:72. Type by original designation (also monotypic). Gobiidae.

Alepidomus Hubbs 1944:7 [ref. 2249]. Masc. *Atherina evermanni* Eigenmann 1903:222. Type by original designation (also monotypic). Atherinidae: Atherininae.

Alepisaurus Lowe 1833:104 [ref. 2825]. Masc. *Alepisaurus ferox* Lowe 1833:104. Type by monotypy. *Alepidosaurus* Agassiz 1846:14 [ref. 64] is an unjustified emendation, and used by Günther 1860:353 [ref. 1963]. Valid (Maul 1973:201 [ref. 7171], Post in Whitehead et al. 1984:494 [ref. 13675], Okiyama 1984:207 [ref. 13644], Fujii in Masuda et al. 1984:77 [ref. 6441], Heemstra & Smith 1986:280 [ref. 5668], Paxton et al. 1989:251 [ref. 12442]). Alepisauridae.

Alepocephalus Risso 1820:270 [ref. 3756]. Masc. *Alepocephalus rostratus* Risso 1820:271. Type by monotypy. *Alepidocephalus* Agassiz 1846:14 [ref. 64] is an unjustified emendation. Valid (Krefft 1973:86 [ref. 7166], Markle & Quéro in Whitehead et al. 1984:228 [ref. 13675], Amaoka in Masuda et al. 1984:42 [ref. 6441], Markle 1986:219 [ref. 5687], Paxton et al. 1989:209 [ref. 12442]). Alepocephalidae.

Aleposomus Gill 1884:433 [ref. 1728]. Masc. *Aleposomus copei* Gill 1884:433. Type by monotypy. Roule 1915:46 [ref. 12566] redefined the genus based on Brauer 1906 and excluded Gill's type species; Roule's treatment apparently can qualify as a genus description, but *Aleposomus* Roule is preoccupied by Gill's use of the name. Synonym of *Xenodermichthys* Günther 1878 (Krefft 1973:92 [ref. 7166]). Alepocephalidae.

Aleposomus Roule (ex Brauer) 1915:46 [ref. 12566]. Masc. *Xenodermichthys guentheri* Alcock 1892. Roule retained Gill's name *Aleposomus* but changed definition to exclude Gill's type species; perhaps can be regarded as a genus on its own, with Roule as author (but preoccupied by Gill's use of name). Type above as given by Norman (MS); subsequent designation not researched. Alepocephalidae.

Alertichthys Moreland 1960:241 [ref. 3041]. Masc. *Alertichthys blacki* Moreland 1960:243. Type by original designation (also monotypic). Valid (Paulin & Moreland 1979:601 [ref. 6915], Washington et al. 1984:440 [ref. 13660]). Congiopodidae.

Alestes Müller & Troschel 1844:88 [ref. 3070]. Masc. *Characinus niloticus* Geoffroy St. Hilaire 1809:Pl. 4. Type by subsequent designation. Earliest type designation not researched; type above as given by Jordan 1919:221 [ref. 2410]. Valid (Géry 1977:19 [ref. 1597], Paugy 1984:140 [ref. 6183]). Alestiidae.

Alestiops (subgenus of *Alestes*) Hoedeman 1951:3 [ref. 2178]. Masc. *Alestes tanganicae* Hoedeman 1951:3. Not available from Hoedeman 1951—no fixation of type species after 1930 (Art. 13b). Earliest available publication apparently by Fowler 1975:73 [ref. 9331], where citation to Hoedeman is given and a type (as a subspecies) is designated. Author would be Fowler and date 1975. Synonym of *Alestes* Müller & Troschel 1844 (Paugy 1984:140 [ref. 6183]). Alestiidae.

Alestobrycon Hoedeman 1951:3 [ref. 2178]. Masc. *Alestes intermedius* Boulenger 1903:22. Type by original designation. Type designation by placing type species in parentheses. Synonym of *Alestes* Müller & Troschel 1844 (Paugy 1984:140 [ref. 6183]). Alestiidae.

Alestogrammus (subgenus of *Phenacogrammus*) Hoedeman

1956:559 [ref. 6184]. Masc. *Alestes abeli* Fowler 1936:255. Type by original designation. Appeared first in Hoedeman 1951:7 [ref. 2178] as a subgenus of *Alestopetersius* but not available; three included species but no type established (Art. 13b). Apparently dates to Hoedeman as above (not seen). Synonym of *Bathyaethiops* Fowler 1949 (Paugy 1984:163 [ref. 6183]). Alestiidae.

Alestopetersiini Hoedeman 1951:5 [ref. 2178]. Appeared in key as "...genus *Alestopetersiini* (new name)," but it is clear from key that this was intended as a new subtribe and not a new genus. Alestiidae.

Alestopetersius Hoedeman 1951:6 (in key) [ref. 2178]. Masc. *Petersius hilgendorfi* Boulenger 1899:91. Type by monotypy. Paugy 1984:140 [ref. 6183] says dates to Hoedeman 1956 [ref. 6184], but probably can date to 1951 based on organization of key and Art. 68d(i); all other species but one assigned to other subgenera. Synonym of *Hemigrammopetersius* Pellegrin 1926 (Géry 1977:42 [ref. 1597]); valid (Poll 1967:77 [ref. 3529], Paugy 1984:140 [ref. 6183]). Alestiidae.

Aleuteres see *Alutera*. Monacanthidae.

Aleuterius see *Alutera*. Monacanthidae.

Alexeterion Vaillant 1888:282 [ref. 4496]. Neut. *Alexeterion parfaiti* Vaillant 1888:283. Type by monotypy. Synonym of *Barathronus* Goode & Bean 1886 (Nielsen 1969:28 [ref. 3195], Nielsen 1973:555 [ref. 6885]); valid (Cohen & Nielsen 1978:62 [ref. 881]). Aphyonidae.

Alexurus Jordan 1895:511 [ref. 2394]. Masc. *Alexurus armiger* Jordan 1895:511. Type by original designation (also monotypic). Synonym of *Erotelis* Poey 1860. Eleotridae.

Alfaro Meek 1912:72 [ref. 2960]. Masc. *Alfaro acutiventralis* Meek 1912:72. Type by monotypy. Valid (Rosen & Bailey 1963:42 [ref. 7067], Parenti & Rauchenberger 1989:6 [ref. 13538]). Poeciliidae.

Algansea Girard 1856:182 [ref. 1810]. Fem. *Leuciscus tincella* Valenciennes in Cuvier & Valenciennes 1854:323. Type by subsequent designation. Type apparently first designated by Bleeker 1863:207 [ref. 397] and 1863:30 [ref. 4859]. Valid (Barbour & Miller 1978 [ref. 7033]). Cyprinidae.

Algoa Castelnau 1861:69 [ref. 767]. *Algoa viridis* Castelnau 1861:69. Type by monotypy. Gadidae.

Algoma Girard 1856:180 [ref. 1810]. Fem. *Algoma amara* Girard 1856:181. Type by subsequent designation. Type designated by Bleeker 1863:29 [ref. 4859] and 1863:206 [ref. 397]. Cyprinidae.

Allabenchelys Boulenger 1902:234 [ref. 569]. Fem. *Allabenchelys longicauda* Boulenger 1902:234. Type by monotypy. Valid (Poll 1977:146 [ref. 3533]). Clariidae.

Allanetta Whitley 1943:132, 135 [ref. 4702]. Fem. *Atherina mugiloides* McCulloch 1913:47. Type by original designation (also monotypic). Valid (Patten & Ivantsoff 1983:330 [ref. 5424], Paxton et al. 1989:354 [ref. 12442], White et al. 1984:360 [ref. 13655]; near *Craterocephalus* McCulloch 1912 (Ivantsoff 1986:383 [ref. 6292]); synonym of *Craterocephalus* (Crowley & Ivantsoff 1988:167 [ref. 12286]). Atherinidae: Atherininae.

Allartedius Hubbs 1926:8 [ref. 6069]. Masc. *Allartedius corallinus* Hubbs 1926:8. Type by original designation (also monotypic). Synonym of *Artedius* Girard 1856 (Bolin 1944:53 [ref. 6379], Begle 1989:646 [ref. 12739]). Cottidae.

Allector Heller & Snodgrass 1903:228 [ref. 2089]. Masc. *Allector cheloniae* Heller & Snodgrass 1903:228. Type by monotypy. Family placement uncertain. Linophrynidae.

Allenichthys Pietsch 1984:38 [ref. 5380]. Masc. *Echinophryne glauerti* Whitley 1944:272. Type by original designation (also monotypic). Valid (Paxton et al. 1989:277 [ref. 12442]). Antennariidae.

Allenina Fernández-Yépez 1948:39 [ref. 1316]. Fem. *Curimata murieli* Allen in Eigenmann & Allen 1942:298. Type by original designation. Synonym of *Curimata* Bosc 1817 (Vari 1989:6 [ref. 9189], Vari 1989:21 [ref. 13506]). Curimatidae: Curimatinae.

Allinectes (subgenus of *Careproctus*) Jordan & Evermann 1898:2866 [ref. 2445]. Masc. *Careproctus ectenes* Gilbert 1895:442. Type by being a replacement name. Replacement for *Allurus* Jordan & Evermann 1896, preoccupied by Forster 1862 in Hymenoptera and by Eisen 1874 in worms. Synonym of *Careproctus* Krøyer 1862 (Kido 1988:193 [ref. 12287] as *Allinectis*). Cyclopteridae: Liparinae.

Allips McCosker 1972:116 [ref. 2932]. Masc. *Allips concolor* McCosker 1972:117. Type by original designation (also monotypic). Valid (McCosker 1977:70 [ref. 6836], McCosker et al. 1989:298 [ref. 13288]). Ophichthidae: Ophichthinae.

Alloblennius Smith-Vaniz & Springer 1971:10 [ref. 4145]. Masc. *Rhabdoblennius pictus* Lotan 1970:376. Type by original designation. Valid (Bath 1983:76 [ref. 5393], Springer 1986:743 [ref. 5719]). Blenniidae.

Allochela (subgenus of *Chela*) Silas 1958:64, 87 [ref. 4026]. Fem. *Chela (Allochela) fasciata* Silas 1958:87. Type by original designation. Synonym of *Chela* Hamilton 1822 (Roberts 1989:31 [ref. 6439]). Cyprinidae.

Allochir (subgenus of *Careproctus*) Jordan & Evermann 1896:452 [ref. 2442]. Fem. *Careproctus melanurus* Gilbert 1891:560. Type by original designation (also monotypic). Synonym of *Careproctus* Krøyer 1862 (Kido 1988:193 [ref. 12287]). Cyclopteridae: Liparinae.

Allochromis Greenwood 1980:57 [ref. 1899]. Masc. *Haplochromis welcommei* Greenwood 1966:309. Type by original designation (also monotypic). Cichlidae.

Alloclinus Hubbs 1927:351 [ref. 2236]. Masc. *Starksia holderi* Lauderbach in Jordan & Starks 1907:73. Type by original designation (also monotypic). Valid (Clark Hubbs 1952:96 [ref. 2252]). Labrisomidae.

Alloconger Jordan & Hubbs 1925:192, 195 [ref. 2486]. Masc. *Leptocephalus flavirostris* Snyder 1908:93. Type by original designation (also monotypic). Synonym of *Ariosoma* Swainson 1838 (Smith 1989:492 [ref. 13285]). Congridae: Bathymyrinae.

Allocottus Hubbs 1926:14 [ref. 2235]. Masc. *Oligocottus embryum* Jordan & Starks 1895:808. Type by original designation (also monotypic). Synonym of *Clinocottus* Gill 1861 (Bolin 1944:76 [ref. 6379]). Cottidae.

Allocyttus McCulloch 1914:114 [ref. 2940]. Masc. *Allocyttus propinquus* McCulloch 1914:116. Type by original designation (also monotypic). Type designated as "*Cyttosoma verrucosum*, Gilchrist, var. *propinquus*, var. nov.; based on Art. 61d, the type should be referred to as *Allocyttus propinquus* McCulloch. Valid (Machida in Masuda et al. 1984:118 [ref. 6441], Karrer 1986:438 [ref. 5680], James et al. 1988:314 [ref. 6639], Paxton et al. 1989:392 [ref. 12442]). Oreosomatidae.

Allodanio (subgenus of *Danio*) Smith 1945:96, 97 [ref. 4056]. Masc. *Danio (Allodanio) ponticulus* Smith 1945:100. Type by original designation (also monotypic). Synonym of *Barilius* Hamilton 1822 (Roberts 1989:30 [ref. 6439]). Cyprinidae.

Allodontichthys Hubbs & Turner 1939:49 [ref. 2265]. Masc.

Zoogoneticus zonistius Hubbs 1932:69. Type by original designation (also monotypic). Valid (Miller & Uyeno 1980 [ref. 5576], Uyeno et al. 1983:501 [ref. 6818], Rauchenberger 1988 [ref. 6411]). Goodeidae.

Allodontium Howell Rivero & Rivas 1944:9, 17 [ref. 7312]. Neut. *Heterandria cubensis* Eigenmann 1904:227. Type by original designation (also monotypic). Synonym of *Girardinus* Poey 1854 (Rosen & Bailey 1963:109 [ref. 7067]). Poeciliidae.

Alloelops (subgenus of *Elops*) Nybelin 1979:20 [ref. 3239]. Masc. *Elops lacerta* Valenciennes in Cuvier & Valenciennes 1846:217. Type by original designation (also monotypic). Elopidae.

Allogambusia Hubbs 1924:8 [ref. 2231]. Fem. *Gambusia tridentiger* Garman 1895:89. Type by original designation. Synonym of *Neoheterandria* Henn 1916 (Rosen & Bailey 1963:126 [ref. 7067]). Poeciliidae.

Allogobius Waite 1904:176 [ref. 4561]. Masc. *Allogobius viridis* Waite 1904:177. Type by original designation (also monotypic). Type designated on p. 139. Synonym of *Eviota* Jenkins 1903 (Lachner & Karnella 1980:12 [ref. 6916]). Gobiidae.

Alloheterandria Hubbs 1924:9 [ref. 2231]. Fem. *Gambusia nigroventralis* Eigenmann & Henn 1912:26. Type by original designation. Synonym of *Priapichthys* Regan 1913 (Rosen & Bailey 1963:120 [ref. 7067]). Poeciliidae.

Allohistium (subgenus of *Etheostoma*) Bailey in Bailey & Gosline 1955:6 [ref. 6833]. Neut. *Etheostoma cinerea* Storer 1845:49. Type by original designation (also monotypic). Synonym of *Etheostoma* Rafinesque 1819, but as a valid subgenus (Collette & Banarescu 1977:1455 [ref. 5845], Page 1981:31 [ref. 3347], Bailey & Etnier 1988:12 [ref. 6873]). Percidae.

Allolepis Jordan & Hubbs 1925:322 [ref. 2486]. Fem. *Allolepis hollandi* Jordan & Hubbs 1925:323. Type by original designation (also monotypic). Valid (Toyoshima in Masuda et al. 1984:308 [ref. 6441]). Zoarcidae.

Allolumpenus Hubbs & Schultz 1932:321 [ref. 2261]. Masc. *Allolumpenus hypochromus* Hubbs & Schultz 1932:4. Type by original designation (also monotypic). Valid. Stichaeidae.

Allomastax (subgenus of *Atherinella*) Chernoff 1986:243 [ref. 5847]. Fem. *Melaniris sardina* Meek 1907:114. Type by original designation. Atherinidae: Menidiinae.

Allomeiacanthus (subgenus of *Meiacanthus*) Smith-Vaniz 1976:87 [ref. 4144]. Masc. *Meiacanthus (Allomeiacanthus) ditrema* Smith-Vaniz 1976:87. Type by original designation (also monotypic). Blenniidae.

Allomicrodesmus Schultz in Schultz et al. 1966:12 [ref. 5366]. Masc. *Allomicrodesmus dorotheae* Schultz 1966:12. Type by original designation (also monotypic). Valid, in Xenisthmidae (Springer 1988:530 [ref. 6683]). Xenisthmidae.

Allomonacanthus (subgenus of *Navodon*) Fraser-Brunner 1941:185 [ref. 1494]. Masc. *Monacanthus convexirostris* Günther 1870:248. Type by original designation. Balistidae.

Allomycter Guitart 1972:1 [ref. 1954]. Masc. *Allomycter dissutus* Guitart 1972:2. Type by monotypy. Synonym of *Mustelus* Linck 1790 (Compagno 1984:397 [ref. 6846], Compagno 1988:219 [ref. 13488]). Triakidae: Triakinae.

Allomycterus McCulloch 1921:141 [ref. 2945]. Masc. *Diodon jaculiferus* Cuvier 1818:130. Type by original designation (also monotypic). Synonym of *Dicotylichthys* Kaup 1855, but as a valid subgenus (Fraser-Brunner 1943:17 [ref. 1495]); valid genus (Leis 1984:448 [ref. 13659]). Diodontidae.

Alloophorus Hubbs & Turner 1939:40 [ref. 2265]. Masc. *Fundulus robustus* Bean 1892:285. Type by original designation (also monotypic). Name appeared first in Turner 1937:507 et seq. [ref. 6400], without clear differentiating characters. Valid (Uyeno et al. 1983:501 [ref. 6818]). Goodeidae.

Allophallus Hubbs 1936:232 [ref. 2247]. Masc. *Allophallus kidderi* Hubbs 1936:236. Type by original designation (also monotypic). Preoccupied by Dziedzicki 1923 in Diptera, replaced by *Carlhubbsia* Whitley 1951. Objective synonym of *Carlhubbsia* Whitley 1951 (Rosen & Bailey 1959:3 [ref. 12020], Rosen & Bailey 1963:114 [ref. 7067]). Poeciliidae.

Allopholis Yatsu 1981:178 [ref. 4814]. Fem. *Centronotus laetus* Cope 1873:27. Type by original designation. Valid (Yatsu 1985:281 [ref. 5149]). Pholidae.

Allopoecilia Hubbs 1924:11 [ref. 2231]. Fem. *Girardinus caucanus* Steindachner 1880:87. Type by original designation (also monotypic). Synonym of *Poecilia* Bloch & Schneider 1801 (Rosen & Bailey 1963:45 [ref. 7067]). Poeciliidae.

Alloricuzenius (subgenus of *Ricuzenius*) Matsubara & Iwai 1951:87 [ref. 2909]. Masc. *Ricuzenius toyamensis* Matsubara & Iwai 1951:87. Type by original designation (also monotypic). Cottidae.

Allosebastes Hubbs 1951:129 [ref. 2251]. Masc. *Sebastichthys sinensis* Gilbert 1890:81. Type by original designation (also monotypic). Synonym of *Sebastes* Cuvier 1829. Scorpaenidae: Sebastinae.

Allosmerus Hubbs 1925:53 [ref. 2232]. Masc. *Osmerus attenuatus* Lockington 1881:66. Type by original designation (also monotypic). Osmeridae.

Allosomus (subgenus of *Argyrosomus*) Jordan 1878:361 [ref. 2376]. Masc. *Salmo (Coregonus) tullibee* Richardson 1836:201. Type by monotypy. Synonym of *Coegonus* Linnaeus 1758. Salmonidae: Coregoninae.

Allotaius Whitley 1937:139 [ref. 4689]. Masc. *Dentex spariformis* Ogilby 1910:91. Type by original designation (also monotypic). Sparidae.

Allothunnus Serventy 1948:132 [ref. 4008]. Masc. *Allothunnus fallai* Serventy 1948:132. Type by monotypy. Valid (Collette & Nauen 1983:26 [ref. 5375], Collette et al. 1984:600 [ref. 11421], Collette 1986:832 [ref. 5647]). Scombridae.

Allotis Hubbs in Ortenburger & Hubbs 1926:139 [ref. 3306]. Fem. *Bryttus humilis* Girard 1858:201. Type by original designation (also monotypic). Synonym of *Lepomis* Rafinesque 1819 (see Bailey in Böhlke 1984:38 [ref. 13621]). Centrarchidae.

Allotoca Hubbs & Turner 1939:55 [ref. 2265]. Fem. *Fundulus dugesii* Bean 1887:373. Type by original designation (also monotypic). Name appeared first in Turner 1937:498 et seq. [ref. 6400], without clear differentiating characters. Valid (Smith & Miller 1980 [ref. 6906], Uyeno et al. 1983:501 [ref. 6818], Smith & Miller 1987 [ref. 6773]). Goodeidae.

Allouarnia (subgenus of *Synodus*) Whitley 1937:219 [ref. 4690]. Fem. *Synodus sageneus* Waite 1905:58. Type by original designation (also monotypic). Synonym of *Synodus* Scopoli 1777 (Anderson et al. 1966:47 [ref. 6977]). Synodontidae: Synodontinae.

Allurus (subgenus of *Careproctus*) Jordan & Evermann 1896:452 [ref. 2442]. Masc. *Careproctus ectenes* Gilbert 1896:442. Type by original designation (also monotypic). Preoccupied by Forester 1862 in Hymenoptera and by Eisen 1874 in worms, replaced by *Allinectes* Jordan & Evermann 1898. Synonym of *Careproctus* Krøyer 1862 (Kido 1988:193 [ref. 12287]). Cyclopteridae:

Liparinae.

Alopecias Müller & Henle 1837:114 [ref. 3067]. Masc. *Squalus vulpes* Gmelin 1789:1496. Type by monotypy. Also in Müller & Henle 1838:84 [ref. 3068] and 1839:74 [ref. 3069]. Apparently an unjustified emendation of and objective synonym of *Alopias* Rafinesque 1810, *Alopias* cited by Müller & Henle. Synonym of *Alopias* Rafinesque 1810 (Springer 1973:17 [ref. 7162], Compagno 1984:229 [ref. 6474]). Alopiidae.

Alopecula Valenciennes in Moreau 1881:319, 320 (v. 1) [ref. 3040]. Fem. Not available; Valenciennes manuscript name published in synonymy of *Thalassinus* Moreau, and apparently never made available by subsequent use as a valid name or senior homonym. Carcharhinidae.

Alopias Rafinesque 1810:12 [ref. 3594]. Masc. *Alopias macrourus* Rafinesque 1810:12. Type by monotypy. Misspellings include *Alopius* and *Alopes*. Valid (Springer 1973:17 [ref. 7162], Quéro in Whitehead et al. 1984:91 [ref. 13675], Compagno 1984:229 [ref. 6474], Nakaya in Masuda et al. 1984:7 [ref. 6441], Bass 1986:101 [ref. 5635], Cappetta 1987:105 [ref. 6348], Paxton et al. 1989:69 [ref. 12442]). Alopiidae.

Aloricatogobius Munro 1964:179 [ref. 3058]. Masc. *Glossogobius asaro* Whitley 1959:318. Type by original designation (also monotypic). Gobiidae.

Alosa Linck 1790:35 [ref. 4985]. Fem. *Clupea alosa* Linnaeus 1758:318. Type apparently by subsequent absolute tautonymy; no species initially mentioned, species added by Cuvier 1829:319 (see Whitehead 1967:77 [ref. 6464]). Valid (Svetovidov 1973:105 [ref. 7169], Poll et al. 1984:41 [ref. 6172], Grande 1985:249 [ref. 6466]). Clupeidae.

Alpharaia (subgenus of *Raja*) Leigh-Sharpe 1924:567, 568 [ref. 5748]. Fem. *Raja circularis* Couch 1838:53. Type by original designation (also monotypic). As a "pseudogenus" of *Raia* [=*Raja*]. Not available [Art. 1b(6)], used as an artificial category (see Leigh-Sharpe 1928 [ref. 6152] and Appendix A). In the synonymy of *Raja* Linnaeus 1758. Rajidae.

Alphascyllium (subgenus of *Scyllium*) Leigh-Sharpe 1926:322 [ref. 5627]. Neut. *Squalus canicula* Linnaeus 1758:234. Type by original designation. As a "pseudogenus" of *Scyllium*. Not available [Art. 1b (6)], used as an artificial category (see Leigh-Sharpe 1928 [ref. 6152]). In the synonymy of *Scyliorhinus* Blainville 1816 (Compagno 1984:355 [ref. 6846], Compagno 1988:119 [ref. 13488]). Scyliorhinidae.

Alphestes Bloch & Schneider 1801:236 [ref. 471]. *Epinephelus afer* Bloch 1793:12. Type by subsequent designation. Type designated by Jordan & Swain 1884:394 [ref. 9337] and by Eigenmann 1890:349 [ref. 2440] subgenus of *Epinephelus* Bloch 1793 (Smith 1971:162 [ref. 14102], Kendall 1984:500 [ref. 13663]). Serranidae: Epinephelinae.

Alpismaris Risso 1826:458 [ref. 3757]. Fem. *Alpismaris risso* Risso 1826:458 (= *Stolephorus risso* Risso 1810:342). Type by subsequent designation. Type designated by Jordan 1917:120 [ref. 2407]. Synonym of *Synodus* Scopoli 1777 in family Synodontidae (Anderson et al. 1966:47 [ref. 6977], Nielsen 1973:161 [ref. 6885]). Doubtfully a synonym of *Aphanius* Nardo 1827 in Cyprinodontidae (Wildekamp et al. 1986:165 [ref. 6198]). Cyprinodontidae: Cyprinodontinae.

Alpismaris (subgenus of *Engraulis*) Swainson 1838:90 [ref. 4302]. Fem. Not available, name only. In the synonymy of *Engraulis* Cuvier 1816 (Whitehead et al. 1988:311 [ref. 5725]). Engraulidae.

Alticops Smith 1948:340 [ref. 4074]. Masc. *Salarias periophthalmus* Valenciennes in Cuvier & Valenciennes 1836:311. Type by original designation. Synonym of *Istiblennius* Whitley 1943 (Smith-Vaniz & Springer 1971:25 [ref. 4145], Bath 1986:356 [ref. 6217]). Blenniidae.

Alticorpus Stauffer & McKaye 1988:442 [ref. 6412]. Neut. *Alticorpus mentale* Stauffer & McKaye 1988:442. Type by original designation. Valid (Eccles & Trewavas 1989:151 [ref. 13547]). Cichlidae.

Alticus Lacepède (ex Commerson) 1800:479 (footnote) [ref. 2709]. Masc. *Blennius saliens* Lacepède) 1800:479. Type by monotypy. Name published in synonymy of *Blennius saliens*, but available because of later use (possibly by Bleeker 1869:234 [ref. 426], Jordan & Seale 1906:421 [ref. 2497] and others (Art. 11e). An alternative view is that *Alticus* was part of a polynomial and not available (genus would then date to Valenciennes); see remarks under Opinion 89 in Appendix B. Valid (Smith-Vaniz & Springer 1971:14 [ref. 4145], Yoshino in Masuda et al. 1984:300 [ref. 6441], Bath 1986:354 [6217]). Blenniidae.

Alticus Valenciennes (ex Commerson) in Cuvier & Valenciennes 1836 [ref. 1005]. Masc. *Salarias alticus* Valenciennes (ex Commerson) in Cuvier & Valenciennes 1836. Name first published in synonymy; genus and species quoted from Commerson manuscript, but made available back to this date by later use (Art. 11e) of Schultz and Chapman in Schultz et al. 1960:366 [ref. 3972]. If *Alticus* Lacepède is regarded as unavailable, then the genus *Alticus* would be cited as Valenciennes 1836. See remarks under Opinion 89 in Appendix B. Blenniidae.

Altigena (subgenus of *Osteochilus*) Lin 1933:341, 342 [ref. 5932]. Fem. *Varicorhinus discognathoides* Nichols & Pope 1927:360. Apparently not available from Lin 1933; proposed for four species without designation of type after 1930 (Art. 13b). Apparently can date to Burton 1934 in the Zoological Record for 1933, Pisces p. 49; see Art. 13b in Appendix A. In the synonymy of *Sinilabeo* Rendahl 1932 (Wu et al. 1977:333 [ref. 4807]). Cyprinidae.

Altiserranus Whitley 1947:150 [ref. 4708]. Masc. *Serranus jayakari* Boulenger 1889:237. Type by original designation (also monotypic). Synonym of *Epinephelus* Bloch 1793 (Randall et al. 1989:414 [ref. 12737]). Serranidae: Epinephelinae.

Altolamprologus Poll 1986:66 [ref. 6136]. Masc. *Lamprologus compressiceps* Boulenger 1898:494. Type by original designation. Cichlidae.

Altona Kaup in Duméril 1856:201 [ref. 1154]. Not available, no description or indication; in list of genera and species as "*Altona rostrata*." Presumed to refer to *Gymnotus rostratus* Linnaeus and therefore in synonymy of *Rhamphichthys* Müller & Troschel 1849. Gymnotidae: Rhamphichthyinae.

Alutera Oken (ex Cuvier) 1817:1183 [ref. 3303]. Fem. *Balistes monoceros* Linnaeus 1758:327. Based on "Les Alutères" Cuvier 1816, but latinized first by Cloquet as *Aluterus*. See also Whitley 1935:136 [ref. 6396]. Junior objective synonym of *Aluterus* Cloquet (Dec.) 1816. Monacanthidae.

Aluterus Cloquet 1816:135 [ref. 852]. Masc. *Balistes monoceros* Linnaeus 1758:327. Type by subsequent designation. Type designated by Jordan 1917:98 [ref. 2407]. Based on "Les Alutères" Cuvier 1816, first latinized by Cloquet (Dec.) 1816. Misspelled *Aleuteres*, *Alutarius*, *Aleisterius*; see also *Alutera* Oken 1817. Valid (Matsuura 1979:165 [ref. 7019], Tyler 1980:178 [ref. 4477] and Arai 1983:199 [ref. 14249] as *Alutera*, Matsuura in Masuda et al.

1984:361 [ref. 6441] and Hutchins 1986:883 [ref. 5673] as *Aluterus*). Monacanthidae.

Alvarius Girard 1859:101 [ref. 1821]. Masc. *Alvarius lateralis* Girard 1859:101. Type by monotypy. Synonym of *Gobiomorus* Lacepède 1800 (Bailey & Richards 1963 [ref. 6029]). Eleotridae.

Alvordius Girard 1859:68 [ref. 1821]. Masc. *Alvordius maculatus* Girard 1859:68. Type by monotypy. Synonym of *Percina* Haldeman 1842, but as a valid subgenus (Page 1974:83 [ref. 3346], Collette & Banarescu 1977:1454 [ref. 5845], Mayden & Page 1979 [ref. 6989], Beckham 1980 [ref. 5464]). Percidae.

Alysia Lowe 1839:87 [ref. 2829]. Fem. *Alysia loricata* Lowe 1839:87. Type by monotypy. Preoccupied by Latreille 1804 in Hymenoptera; replaced by *Gonichthys* Gistel 1850. Objective synonym of *Gonichthys* Gistel 1850 (Krefft & Bekker 1973:182 [ref. 7181], Paxton 1979:11 [ref. 6440]). Myctophidae.

Amacrodon Regan & Trewavas 1932:91 [ref. 3682]. Masc. *Thaumatichthys binghami* Parr 1927:25. Type by monotypy. Synonym of *Thaumatichthys* Smith & Radcliffe 1912 (Bertelsen & Struhsaker 1977:35 [ref. 5331]). Thaumatichthyidae.

Amanses Gray 1835:Pl. 98 (v. 2) [ref. 1878]. *Amanses hystrix* Gray 1835. Type by monotypy. Valid (Randall 1964:333 [ref. 3148], Matsuura 1979:165 [ref. 7019], Tyler 1980:176 [ref. 4477], Arai 1983:199 [ref. 14249], Aboussouan & Leis 1984:452 [ref. 13661], Matsuura in Masuda et al. 1984:360 [ref. 6441], Hutchins 1986:883 [ref. 5673]). Monacanthidae.

Amaralia Fowler 1954:40 [ref. 1465]. Fem. *Bunocephalus hypsiurus* Kner 1855:28. Type by original designation (also monotypic). Objective synonym of *Bunocephalus* Kner 1855 (following Mees 1988:89 [ref. 6401]). Valid (Burgess 1989:303 [ref. 12860]). Aspredinidae: Bunocephalinae.

Amarginops Nichols & Griscom 1917:713 [ref. 3185]. Masc. *Amarginops platus* Nichols & Griscom 1917:713. Type by monotypy. Valid (Risch 1986:2 [ref. 6190], Burgess 1989:68 [ref. 12860]). Bagridae.

Amarsipus Haedrich 1969:8 [ref. 2028]. *Amarsipus carlsbergi* Haedrich 1969:8. Type by original designation (also monotypic). Valid (Aboussouan 1983:19 [ref. 12850], Horn 1984:628 [ref. 13637], Haedrich 1986:842 [ref. 5659]). Amarsipidae.

Amate Jordan & Starks 1906:228 [ref. 2532]. Fem. *Achirus japonicus* Schlegel in Temminck & Schlegel 1846:186. Type by original designation (also monotypic). Synonym of *Heteromycteris* Kaup 1858 (Desoutter 1986:430 [ref. 6212]). Soleidae.

Amazonsprattus Roberts 1984:317 [ref. 5829]. Masc. *Amazonsprattus scintilla* Roberts 1984:318. Type by original designation (also monotypic). Valid as an engraulid (Whitehead et al. 1988:393 [ref. 5725]). Engraulidae.

Ambassis Cuvier in Cuvier & Valenciennes 1828:175 [ref. 997]. Fem. *Centropomus ambassis* Lacepède 1802:252. Type by absolute tautonymy. Spelled *Ambassus* by Swainson 1839:(18, 168) 200 [ref. 4303]. *Ambasis* Agassiz 1846:16 [ref. 64] is an unjustified emendation. Valid (Hayashi in Masuda et al. 1984:123 [ref. 6441], Heemstra & Martin 1986:507 [ref. 6298], Paxton et al. 1989:484 [ref. 12442], Kottelat 1989:17 [ref. 13605]). Ambassidae.

Amblodon Rafinesque 1819:421 [ref. 3590]. Masc. *Amblodon bubalus* Rafinesque 1819:421. Type by subsequent designation. Type designated by Jordan & Evermann 1896:163 [ref. 2443]. Rafinesque (1819:372 [ref. 7308]) equated *Amblodon* with *Aplodinotus* based on erroneous description of dentition in *Amblodon*, but switched *bubalus* (type of *Amblodon*) to a new name *Ictiobus* (1820:55 [ref. 3592]) (see Bailey & Eschmeyer 1988 [ref. 6624]). *Amblyodon* Agassiz 1846:16 [ref. 64] is an unjustified emendation. *Amblodon* was suppressed (for priority) in favor of *Ictiobus* (Opinion 1582). Catostomidae.

Ambloplites Rafinesque 1820:53 [ref. 7305]. Masc. *Lepomis ictheloides* Rafinesque 1820:52. Type by monotypy. Also appeared in Rafinesque 1820:33 (Dec.) [ref. 3592]. *Amblyoplites* Agassiz 1846:16 [ref. 64] is an unjustified emendation. Valid (Cashner & Jenkins 1982 [ref. 5463]). Centrarchidae.

Amblyapistus Bleeker 1876:297 [ref. 450]. Masc. *Apistus taenianotus* Cuvier in Cuvier & Valenciennes 1828:168. Type by original designation (also monotypic). Valid (Nakabo in Masuda et al. 1984:319 [ref. 6441]); synonym of *Ablabys* Kaup 1873 (Poss 1986:479 [ref. 6296]). Scorpaenidae: Tetraroginae.

Amblycentrus Goren 1979:22 [ref. 1852]. Masc. *Biat magnusi* Klausewitz 1968:13. Type by original designation. Synonym of *Amblygobius* Bleeker 1874. Gobiidae.

Amblyceps Blyth 1858:281 [ref. 476]. Neut. *Amblyceps caecutiens* Blyth 1858:282. Type by monotypy. Valid (Jayaram 1977:28 [ref. 7006] and Jayaram 1981:227 [ref. 6497] with type as *Pimelodus mangois* Hamilton, Kottelat 1985:271 [ref. 11441], Burgess 1989:108 [ref. 12860], Kottelat 1989:14 [ref. 13605]). Amblycipitidae.

Amblychaeturichthys Bleeker 1874:324 [ref. 437]. Masc. *Chaeturichthys hexanema* Bleeker 1853:(16) 43. Type by original designation (also monotypic). Apparently misspelled *Amblychaeturichthus* on p. 324, as above on p. 292, 299. Synonym of *Chaeturichthys* Richardson 1844 (Hoese, pers. comm.); valid (Akihito in Masuda et al. 1984:279 [ref. 6441], Birdsong et al. 1988:184 [ref. 7303]). Gobiidae.

Amblycirrhitus Gill 1862:105 [ref. 1658]. Masc. *Cirrhites fasciatus* Cuvier in Cuvier & Valenciennes 1829:76. Type by original designation (also monotypic). Correct spelling for genus of type species is *Cirrhitus*. Valid (Araga in Masuda et al. 1984:199 [ref. 6441], Randall 1986:664 [ref. 5706], Donaldson 1986:624 [ref. 6317]). Cirrhitidae.

Amblydoras Bleeker 1862:6 [ref. 393]. Masc. *Doras affinis* Kner 1855:121. Type by original designation (also monotypic). Valid (Burgess 1989:223 [ref. 12860]). Doradidae.

Amblyeleotris Bleeker 1874:373 [ref. 436]. Fem. *Eleotris periophthalmus* Bleeker 1852:477. Type by original designation (also monotypic). Valid (Yanagisawa 1976 [ref. 7088], Polunin & Lubbock 1977:92 [ref. 3540], Yanagisawa 1978:298 [ref. 7028], Akihito & Meguro 1983:347 [ref. 5301], Akihito in Masuda et al. 1984:255 [ref. 6441], Hoese 1986:777 [ref. 5670], Birdsong et al. 1988:192 [ref. 7303]). Gobiidae.

Amblygaster Bleeker 1849:73 [ref. 316]. Fem. *Amblygaster clupeoides* Bleeker 1849:73. Type by monotypy. Synonym of *Sardinella* Valenciennes 1847 (Svetovidov 1973:103 [ref. 7169]); valid (Yoshino in Masuda et al. 1984:19 [ref. 6441], Grande 1985:249 [ref. 6466], Whitehead 1985:86 [ref. 5141], Paxton et al. 1989:152 [ref. 12442]). Clupeidae.

Amblyglyphidodon (subgenus of *Glyphidodon*) Bleeker 1877:92, 94 [ref. 454]. Masc. *Glyphisodon aureus* Cuvier (ex Kuhl & van Hasselt) in Cuvier & Valenciennes 1830:479. Type by original designation. Also appeared in Bleeker 1877:40 [ref. 453] [earliest of two publications not researched]. Valid (Shen & Chan 1979:62 [ref. 6944], Yoshino et al. 1983 [ref. 5730], Yoshino in Masuda et al. 1984:197 [ref. 6441]). Pomacentridae.

Amblygobius Bleeker 1874:322 [ref. 437]. Masc. *Gobius sphynx* Valenciennes in Cuvier & Valenciennes 1837:93. Type by original designation (also monotypic). Valid (Akihito in Masuda et al. 1984:25 [ref. 6441], Hoese 1986:778 [ref. 5670], Maugé 1986:359 [ref. 6218], Birdsong et al. 1988:192 [ref. 7303]). Gobiidae.

Amblyopsis DeKay 1842:187 [ref. 1098]. Fem. *Amblyopsis spelaeus* DeKay 1842:187. Type by monotypy. Valid. Amblyopsidae.

Amblyopus Valenciennes in Cuvier & Valenciennes 1837:157 [ref. 1006]. Masc. *Taenioides hermannii* Lacepède 1800:532. Type by being a replacement name [or by subsequent designation]. Regarded as an unneeded substitute for *Taenioides* Lacepède 1800. Lacepède spelled the species as *hermannii* in a footnote; Valenciennes used the spelling *Hermannianus* based on *Taenioïde Hermannien*, Lacepède's vernacular. Valenciennes included additional species; he felt Lacepède's definition was incomplete. Objective synonym of *Taenioides* Lacepède 1800 (Maugé 1986:385 [ref. 6218]). Gobiidae.

Amblyotrypauchen Hora 1924:160 [ref. 2205]. Masc. *Amblyotrypauchen fraseri* Hora 1924:160. Type by monotypy. Valid (Birdsong et al. 1988:197 [ref. 7303]). Gobiidae.

Amblypharyngodon Bleeker 1859:433 [ref. 370]. Masc. *Cyprinus mola* Hamilton 1882:334, 392. Type by being a replacement name. Apparently appeared first in key, without species. Two species included by Bleeker 1859:260 [ref. 371]. Based on "*Amblypharyngodon* Blkr = *Mola* Heck." and discussion by Bleeker 1860:409-410 [ref. 380], regarded here as a replacement name (*C. mola* also designated type by Bleeker 1863:202 [ref. 397] and 1863:28 [ref. 4859]). Valid (Jayaram 1981:86 [ref. 6497], Kottelat 1989:6 [ref. 13605]). Cyprinidae.

Amblypomacentrus Bleeker 1877:68 [ref. 454]. Masc. *Pomacentrus breviceps* Schlegel & Müller 1844:23. Type by subsequent designation. Type designated by Jordan 1919:387 [ref. 4904]. Also appeared in Bleeker 1877:39 [ref. 453], and if this predates ref. 454 then type is by monotypy. Valid (Allen 1975:123 [ref. 97]). Pomacentridae.

Amblyraja Malm 1877:120, 607 [ref. 2881]. Fem. *Raja radiata* Donovan 1808:Pl. 114. Type by subsequent designation. Misspelled once as *Amblyraya* by Malm (p. 607). Type designated by Jordan 1919:391 [ref. 4904]. Synonym of *Raja* Linnaeus 1758, but as a valid subgenus (Stehmann 1973:61 [ref. 7168], Ishihara & Ishiyama 1986:273 [ref. 5142], Ishihara 1987:277 [ref. 6264]). Rajidae.

Amblyrhynchichthys Bleeker 1859:430 [ref. 370]. Masc. *Barbus truncatus* Bleeker 1851:32. Type by subsequent monotypy. Apparently appeared first in key, without included species. One species included by Bleeker 1859:153 [ref. 371] and 1860:275, 302-305 [ref. 380]. Valid (Kottelat 1985:260 [ref. 11441], Roberts 1989:28 [ref. 6439]). Cyprinidae.

Amblyrhynchote Bibron in Duméril 1855:279 [ref. 297]. Masc. *Tetrodon honckenii* Bloch 1785:133. Appeared as non-latinized "Amblyrhynchote" (unavailable); see next entry. In the synonymy of *Amblyrhynchotes* Troschel 1856. Tetraodontidae.

Amblyrhynchotes Troschel (ex Bibron) 1856:88 [ref. 12559]. Fem. *Tetraodon honckenii* Bloch 1785:133. Appeared as "Amblyrhynchote" Bibron in Duméril 1855:279 [ref. 297]; latinized by Troschel (also Hollard 1857:319 [ref. 2186] as *Amblyrhynchotus*). Addition of species and type designation not researched; type from Fraser-Brunner 1943:11 [ref. 1495]. Valid, varied author/spelling (Tyler 1980:341 [ref. 4477], Arai 1983:207 [ref. 14249], Hardy 1984:33 [ref. 5182], Matsuura in Masuda et al. 1984:364 [ref. 6441], Smith & Heemstra 1986:895 [ref. 5714]). Tetraodontidae.

Amblyscion Gill 1863:165 [ref. 1681]. Masc. *Amblyscion argenteus* Gill 1863:165. Type by monotypy. Synonym of *Larimus* Cuvier 1830 (Chao 1978:31 [ref. 6983]). Sciaenidae.

Amblystilbe Fowler 1940:85 [ref. 1436]. Fem. *Amblystilbe howesi* Fowler 1940:85. Type by original designation (also monotypic). Synonym of *Prodontocharax* Eigenmann & Pearson 1924 (Géry 1977:590 [ref. 1597], Böhlke 1984:48 [ref. 13621]). Characidae.

Amblytoxotes Bleeker 1876:311 [ref. 448]. Fem. *Toxotes squamosus* Hutton 1875:313. Type by original designation (also monotypic). Synonym of *Brama* Bloch & Schneider 1801 (Mead 1972:25 [ref. 6976], Mead 1973:386 [ref. 7199]). Bramidae.

Ameca Miller & Fitzsimmons 1971:3 [ref. 3019]. Fem. *Ameca splendens* Miller & Fitzsimmons 1971:3. Type by original designation (also monotypic). Valid (Uyeno et al. 1983:503 [ref. 6818]). Goodeidae.

Ameiurus (subgenus of *Ictalurus*) Rafinesque 1820:359 [ref. 7311]. Masc. *Silurus lividus* Rafinesque 1820:51. Type designated by ICZN (Opinion 1584). Also in Rafinesque 1820:65 (Dec.) [ref. 3592]. *Amiurus* Agassiz 1846:17 [ref. 64] is an unjustified emendation. On Official List (Opinion 1584). Valid (see Bailey & Robins 1988 [ref. 6626]). Ictaluridae.

Amentum Whitley 1940:403 [ref. 4699]. Neut. *Stolephorus commersonii* Lacepède 1803:381. Type by original designation (also monotypic). Objective synonym of *Stolephorus* Lacepède 1803 (Whitehead et al. 1988:401 [ref. 5725]). Engraulidae.

Amia Browne 1789:442 [ref. 669]. Fem. Not available, published in a rejected work on Official Index (Opinion 89). Megalopidae.

Amia Gronow 1763:80 [ref. 1910]. Fem. Not available, published in a rejected work on Official Index (Opinion 261). In the synonymy of *Apogon* Lacepède 1801 (Tortonese 1973:365 [ref. 7192]). Apogonidae.

Amia Gronow in Gray 1854:173 [ref. 1911]. Fem. *Amia percaeformis* Gronow in Gray 1854:173. Type by monotypy. Preoccupied by *Amia* Linnaeus 1766 in fishes; *Gronovichthys* Whitley 1929 is a replacement for *Amia* of Meuschen (1781, index to Gronow 1763) and Gray 1854. Synonym of *Apogon* Lacepède 1801 (Fraser 1972:17 [ref. 5195]). Apogonidae.

Amia Linnaeus 1766:500 [ref. 2786]. Fem. *Amia calva* Linnaeus 1766:500. Type by monotypy. Valid (Patterson & Longbottom 1989 [ref. 13507]. Amiidae.

Amiatus Rafinesque 1815:89 [ref. 3584]. Fem. *Amia calva* Linnaeus 1766:500. Type by being a replacement name. As "*Amiatus* R. [Rafinesque] *Amia* L. [Linnaeus]." An available replacement name (unneeded) for *Amia* Linnaeus 1766 based on Rafinesque style in this work. In the synonymy of *Amia* Linnaeus 1766. Amiidae.

Amiichthys Poey in Jordan 1887:586 [ref. 2388]. Masc. *Amiichthys diapterus* Poey 1868:305. Type by monotypy. Description of species appeared in Poey 1868:305 [ref. 3505] without a genus as, "Familia.... ? and Genus ...? *diapterus* Poey.—479." For technical reasons, perhaps the species name should date to Poey in Jordan 1886 when it became a binominal name (and with reference to a previous description); see Appendix A. Name apparently not in current literature. Apogonidae.

Amioides Smith & Radcliffe in Radcliffe 1912:439 [ref. 3576]. Masc. *Amia (Amioides) grossidens* Smith & Radcliffe in Radcliffe 1912:440. Type by monotypy. Apogonidae.

Amitra Goode 1881:477, 478 [ref. 1833]. Fem. *Amitra liparina* Goode 1881:477, 478. Type by monotypy. Not preoccupied by *Amitrus* in Coleoptera, *Monomitra* Goode 1883 is an unneeded replacement. Synonym of *Paraliparis* Collett 1878 (Stein 1978:37 [ref. 4203], Andriashev 1986:14 [ref. 12760], Kido 1988:230 [ref. 12287]). Cyclopteridae: Liparinae.

Amitrichthys (subgenus of *Paraliparis*) Jordan & Evermann 1896: 453 [ref. 2442]. Masc. *Paraliparis cephalus* Gilbert 1891:561. Type by original designation. Synonym of *Paraliparis* Collett 1878 (Andriashev 1986:14 [ref. 12760], Kido 1988:230 [ref. 12287]). Cyclopteridae: Liparinae.

Amiurus see *Ameiurus*. Ictaluridae.

Ammocoetus Duméril (ex d'Hallois) 1812:16 [ref. 1153]. Masc. *Petromyzon branchialis* Linnaeus 1758:130. Type by subsequent designation. If above is first appearance, then type is *Petromyzon rouge* Lacepède, the only species mentioned. Type as *branchialis* designated by Jordan & Gilbert 1883:9 [ref. 2476]. Also spelled *Ammocoetes* (dating to Duméril in Cuvier 1816). Synonym of *Petromyzon* Linnaeus 1758. Petromyzontidae: Petromyzontinae.

Ammocrypta Jordan 1877:5 [ref. 2374]. Fem. *Ammocrypta beanii* Jordan 1877:5. Type by monotypy. Valid (Williams 1975 [ref. 7402], Collette & Banarescu 1977:1455 [ref. 5845], Page 1981:28 [ref. 3347]). Percidae.

Ammocryptocharax Weitzman & Kanazawa 1976:326 [ref. 4619]. Masc. *Ammocryptocharax elegans* Weitzman & Kanazawa 1976:331. Type by original designation. Valid. Characidae: Characidiinae.

Ammodytes Linnaeus 1758:247 [ref. 2787]. Masc. *Ammodytes tobianus* Linnaeus 1758:247. Type by monotypy. On Official List (Opinion 75). Valid (Wheeler 1973:446 [ref. 7190], Stevens et al. 1984:574 [ref. 13671], Ida in Masuda et al. 1984:222 [ref. 6441], Reay in Whitehead et al. 1986:946 [ref. 13676], Winters & Dalley 1988 [ref. 12881]). Ammodytidae.

Ammodytoides Duncker & Mohr 1939:23 [ref. 1158]. Masc. *Bleekeria vaga* McCulloch & Waite 1916:447. Type by monotypy. Ammodytidae.

Ammopleurops Günther 1862:490 [ref. 1969]. Masc. *Plagusia lactea* Bonaparte 1833:5. Type by monotypy. Synonym of *Symphurus* Rafinesque 1810 (Torchio 1973:635 [ref. 6892]). Cynoglossidae: Symphurinae.

Ammotretis Günther 1862:458 [ref. 1969]. Masc. *Ammotretis rostratus* Günther 1862:458. Type by monotypy. Valid (Norman 1934:419 [ref. 6893], Scott 1981:146 [ref. 5533], Ahlstrom et al. 1984:643 [ref. 13641], Sakamoto 1984 [ref. 5273]). Pleuronectidae: Rhombosoleinae.

Amneris Whitley 1935:37 [ref. 4685]. Fem. *Nematocentris rubrostriatus* Ramsay & Ogilby 1886:14. Type by monotypy. Synonym of *Melanotaenia* Gill 1862 (Allen 1980:474 [ref. 99], Allen & Cross 1982:44 [ref. 6251]). Atherinidae: Melanotaeniinae.

Amniataba Whitley 1943:183 [ref. 4703]. Fem. *Therapon [Terapon] percoides* Günther 1864:374. Type by original designation. Synonym of *Terapon* Cuvier 1816 (Mees & Kailola 1977:32 [ref. 5183]); valid (Vari 1978:238 [ref. 4514], Paxton et al. 1989:531 [ref. 12442]). Terapontidae.

Amora see *Anaora*. Callionymidae.

Amorphocephalus Bowdich 1825:xii, 238 [ref. 590]. Masc. *Amorphocephalus granulatus* Bowdich 1825:235. Type by monotypy. Also involves fig. 36 opposite p. 238 in conjunction with p. xii. Synonym of *Xyrichtys* Cuvier 1814 (Bauchot & Quignard 1973:442 [ref. 7204]). Labridae.

Amoya Herre 1927:225 [ref. 2104]. Fem. *Gobius brevirostris* Günther 1861:41. Type by original designation (also monotypic). Valid (Hoese 1986:778 [ref. 5670], Birdsong et al. 1988:192 [ref. 7303]). Gobiidae.

Amphacanthus Bloch & Schneider 1801:206 [ref. 471]. Masc. *Chaetodon guttatus* Bloch 1787:55. Type by subsequent designation. Type apparently designated by Desmarest 1874:240 [not seen], but see Whitley 1935:138 [ref. 6396] who says Desmarest designated *javus* as type. Misspelled *Amphacantus* by Cuvier 1816:330 [ref. 993]. Synonym of *Siganus* Forsskål 1775 (Tortonese 1973:456 [ref. 7192]). Siganidae.

Ampheces (subgenus of *Anampses*) Jordan & Snyder 1902:628 [ref. 2514]. *Anampses geographicus* Valenciennes in Cuvier & Valenciennes 1839:10. Type by original designation (also monotypic). Objective synonym of *Pseudanampses* Bleeker 1862. Labridae.

Amphelikturus Parr 1930:31 [ref. 3370]. Masc. *Amphelikturus brachyrhynchus* Parr 1930:32. Type by original designation. Valid (Dawson 1982:10 [ref. 6764]); synonym of *Acentronura* Kaup 1853 (Dawson 1985:15 [ref. 6541]), as a valid subgenus (Dawson 1986:447 [ref. 5650]). Syngnathidae: Syngnathinae.

Amphibichthys Hogg 1841:361, 362 [ref. 2183]. Masc. *Lepidosiren paradoxa* Fitzinger 1837:379. Type by being a replacement name. Unneeded replacement for and objective synonym of *Lepidosiren* Fitzinger 1837, which Hogg felt was inappropriate. Lepidosirenidae: Lepidosireninae.

Amphichaetodon Burgess 1978:286 [ref. 700]. Masc. *Amphichaetodon melbae* Burgess & Caldwell in Burgess 1978:291. Type by original designation. Synonym of *Johnrandallia* Nalbant 1974 (Maugé & Bauchot 1984:463 [ref. 6614]); valid (Nalbant 1986:169 [ref. 6135]). Chaetodontidae.

Amphichthys Swainson 1839:184, 282 [ref. 4303]. Masc. *Amphichthys rubigenes* Swainson 1839:282. Type by monotypy. Species called *Batrachus rubigenis* in Appendix, p. 414; we treat species description as occurring on p. 282 with genus and species as above. Valid (Greenfield & Greenfield 1973:562 [ref. 7128], Shimizu in Uyeno et al. 1983:239 [ref. 14275]). Batrachoididae.

Amphigonopterus Hubbs 1918:13 [ref. 2227]. Masc. *Abeona aurora* Jordan & Gilbert 1880:299, 300. Type by original designation (also monotypic). Synonym of *Micrometrus* Gibbons 1854. Embiotocidae.

Amphilius (subgenus of *Pimelodus*) Günther 1864:115, 134 [ref. 1974]. Masc. *Pimelodus platychir* Günther 1864:134. Type by monotypy. Described in key (p. 115) as section of *Pimelodus* with 1 species on p. 134. Valid (Skelton & Teugels 1986:54 [ref. 6192], Teugels et al. 1987 [ref. 6346], Burgess 1989:113 [ref. 12860]). Amphiliidae.

Amphilophus Agassiz 1859:408 [ref. 74]. Masc. *Amphilophus froebelii* Agassiz 1859:408. Type by monotypy. Cichlidae.

Amphiodon Rafinesque 1819:421 [ref. 3590]. Masc. *Amphiodon alveoides* Rafinesque 1819:421. Type by monotypy. Appeared as a subgenus of *Hyodon* [=*Hiodon*] in Rafinesque 1820:173 (Apr.)[ref. 7309] and 1820:41 (Dec.) [ref. 3592]. Synonym of *Hiodon* Lesueur 1818. Hiodontidae.

Amphipnous Müller 1841:246 [ref. 3061]. *Unibranchapertura cuchia* Hamilton 1822:16, 263. Type by monotypy. Objective synonym of *Cuchia* Hamilton 1831. Synonym of *Monopterus* Lacepède 1800 (Rosen & Greenwood 1976:56 [ref. 7094], Daget 1986:291 [ref. 6203]). Synbranchidae.

Amphiprion Bloch & Schneider 1801:200 [ref. 471]. Masc. *Lutjanus ephippium* Bloch 1790:121. Type by subsequent designation. Type designated by Griffith 1834:160 [ref. 1908]. Spelled *Amphiprionum* by Bosc 1816:469 [ref. 5126]. Valid (Allen 1975:50 [ref. 97], Richards & Leis 1984:544 [ref. 13668], Ida in Masuda et al. 1984:191 [ref. 6441], Allen 1986:672 [ref. 5631]). Pomacentridae.

Amphiprionichthys Bleeker 1855:172 [ref. 347]. Masc. *Amphiprionichthys apistus* Bleeker 1855:173. Type by monotypy. Misspelled *Amphprionichthys* by Bleeker on p. 172, correctly as *Amphiprionichthys* (pp. 169, 173). Synonym of *Caracanthus* Krøyer 1845. Caracanthidae.

Amphiscarus Swainson 1839:172, 227 [ref. 4303]. Masc. *Siganus fuscus* Griffith 1834:Pl. 35. Type by monotypy. [Footnote given by Swainson 1839:227 [ref. 4303] does not apply to *Amphiscarus*]. Synonym of *Siganus* Forsskål 1775. Siganidae.

Amphisile Cuvier 1816:350 [ref. 993]. *Centriscus scutatus* Linnaeus 1758:336. Type by subsequent designation. Earliest type designation not researched. Spelled *Amphistyle*, *Amphisilis*, *Amphycile* and *Amphisyle* in early literature; also *Amphisilen* Klein 1775. Objective synonym of *Centriscus* Linnaeus 1758. Centriscidae: Centriscinae.

Amphisilen Klein 1775:280 [ref. 2618]. Not available, published in a work that does not conform to the principle of binominal nomenclature. In the synonymy of *Centriscus* Linnaeus 1758. Centriscidae: Centriscinae.

Amphistichus Agassiz 1854:367 [ref. 70]. Masc. *Amphistichus argenteus* Agassiz 1854:367. Type by monotypy. Misspelled *Amphisticus* in early literature. Published May 1854, predating *Mytilophagus* Gibbons, July 1854. Valid (Tarp 1952:39 [ref. 12250]). Embiotocidae.

Amphitherapon Whitley 1943:183 [ref. 4703]. Masc. *Datnia? caudavittata* Richardson 1845:24. Type by original designation (also monotypic). Synonym of *Amniataba* Whitley 1943 (Vari 1978:238 [ref. 4514]). Synonym of *Terapon* Cuvier 1816 (Mees & Kailola 1977:32 [ref. 5183]). Terapontidae.

Amphotistius (subgenus of *Dasybatus*) Garman 1913:375, 392 [ref. 1545]. *Trygon sabina* Lesueur 1824:109. Type by original designation. Valid (Paxton et al. 1989:41 [ref. 12442]). Dasyatidae.

Amplolabrius Lin 1933:81 [ref. 2782]. Masc. *Amplolabrius mirus* Lin 1933:82. Type by original designation (also monotypic). Synonym of *Semilabeo* Peters 1880 (Chu & Cui in Chu & Chen 1989:238 [ref. 13584]). Cyprinidae.

Amplova Jordan & Seale 1925:31 [ref. 2499]. Fem. *Anchovia brevirostra* Meek & Hildebrand 1923:198. Type by original designation (also monotypic). Synonym of *Anchoviella* Fowler 1911 (Whitehead et al. 1988:323 [ref. 5725]). Engraulidae.

Anabarilius (subgenus of *Barilius*) Cockerell 1923:532 [ref. 13498]. Masc. *Barilius andersoni* Regan 1904:416. Type by original designation. As (p. 532) "A really distinct subgenus or genus..." Treated as a subgenus on legend to Pl. 18. Valid (Yih & Wu 1964:71 [ref. 13499], Chen in Chu & Chen 1989:56 [ref. 13584]). Cyprinidae.

Anabas Cloquet (ex Cuvier) 1816:35 [ref. 12560]. Masc. *Perca scandens* Daldorf 1797:62. Type by monotypy. Cuvier 1816:339 [ref. 993] has only "Les Anabas" and mentions "*Perca scandens* Daldorf. *Anthias testudineus* Bl. 322." Apparently dates to Cloquet 1816:35 as above (else to Oken 1817:1782 [1182]). See also Whitley 1935:136 [ref. 6396]. Misspelled *Anabus* by Swainson 1839:237 [ref. 4303]. Valid (Jayaram 1981:378 [ref. 6497], Kottelat 1985:275 [ref. 11441], Kottelat 1989:19 [ref. 13605], Roberts 1989:171 [ref. 6439] credited to Cuvier). Anabantidae.

Anableps Bloch (ex Gronow) 1794:7 [ref. 463]. Fem. *Anableps tetrophthalmus* Bloch 1794 (= *Cobitis anableps* Linnaeus 1758: 303). Type by monotypy. Objective synonym and junior homonym of *Anableps* Scopoli 1777. Anablepidae: Anablepinae.

Anableps Gronow 1763:117 [ref. 1910]. Fem. Not available, published in a rejected work on Official Index (Opinion 261). In the synonymy of *Anableps* Scopoli 1777. Anablepidae: Anablepinae.

Anableps Scopoli (ex Gronow) 1777:450 [ref. 3990]. Fem. *Cobitis anableps* Linnaeus 1758:303. Described first without species; first addition of species not researched. Type possibly by subsequent absolute tautonymy. Valid (Parenti 1981:501 [ref. 7066]). Anablepidae: Anablepinae.

Anacanthobatis von Bonde & Swart 1923:errata [18] [ref. 522]. Fem. *Anacanthobatis marmoratus* von Bonde & Swart 1923:18. Type by subsequent designation. Appeared as *Liobatis* but corrected in printed errata sheet (affixed to separates) to *Anacanthobatis*. Two included species; earliest type restriction not researched. Valid (Nakaya in Masuda et al. 1984:15 [ref. 6441], Hulley 1986:127 [ref. 5672], Ishihara & Ishiyama 1986:270 [ref. 5142], Shen 1986:106 [ref. 6381], Séret 1986:317 [ref. 6753]). Anacanthobatidae.

Anacanthus Cuvier (ex Ehrenberg) 1829:400 [ref. 995]. Masc. Appeared only as "Les Anacanthes" with mention of "*Raia orbicularis* B.Schn." (species apparently never described); Jordan (1917:131 [ref. 2407]) gives type as *Raja uarnak* Forsskål. Subsequent latinization not researched. In the synonymy of *Dasyatis* Rafinesque 1810. Dasyatidae.

Anacanthus Ehrenberg in Van der Hoeven 1833:179 [ref. 5061]. Masc. *Raja africana* Bloch & Schneider 1801:307. Preoccupied by Cuvier (ex Ehrenberg) 1829, replaced by *Rhachinotus* Cantor 1849. Original not examined. Synonym of *Urogymnus* Müller & Henle 1837. Dasyatidae.

Anacanthus Gray 1830:Pl. 84 (v. 1) [ref. 1878]. Masc. *Anacanthus barbatus* Gray 1830:Pl. 84. Type by monotypy. Also in Gray 1831:8 [ref. 1879]. Valid (Aboussouan & Leis 1984:452 [ref. 13661]). Monacanthidae.

Anacanthus Minding 1832:117 [ref. 3022]. Masc. *Silurus electricus* Gmelin 1789:1354. Type by monotypy. Preoccupied by Cuvier 1829 in fishes. Synonym of *Malapterurus* Lacepède 1803. Malapteruridae.

Anacyrtus Günther 1864:345 [ref. 1974]. Masc. *Salmo gibbosus* Linnaeus 1758:311. Type by being a replacement name. Replacement for *Epicyrtus* Müller & Troschel 1844, preoccupied by Dejean 1833 in Coleoptera. Objective synonym of *Charax* Scopoli 1777. Characidae.

Anadoras Eigenmann 1925:305, 327 [ref. 1244]. Masc. *Doras grypus* Cope 1872:270. Type by original designation. Valid (Burgess 1989:224 [ref. 12860]). Doradidae.

Anaecypris Collares-Pereira 1983:2 [ref. 6668]. Fem. *Phoxinus hispanicus* Steindachner 1866:268. Type by original designation (also monotypic). Cyprinidae.

Anago Jordan & Hubbs 1925:191, 193 [ref. 2486]. Masc. *Conger anago* Temminck & Schlegel 1846:259. Type by original designation (also monotypic and by absolute tautonymy). Valid (Asano in Masuda et al. 1984:27 [ref. 6441]); synonym of *Ariosoma* Swainson 1838 (Smith 1989:492 [ref. 13285]). Congridae:

Bathymyrinae.

Analithis Gistel 1848:X [ref. 1822]. *Platyrhina sinensis* Bloch & Schneider 1801:352. Type by being a replacement name. Unneeded replacement for *Platyrhina* Müller & Henle 1838, not preoccupied by *Platyrhinus* Clairville-Schellenberg 1798. *Analithes* is a misspelling. On Official Index (Opinion 345). Objective synonym of *Platyrhina* Müller & Henle 1838 (Cappetta 1987:139 [ref. 6348]). Platyrhinidae.

Anampses Quoy & Gaimard (ex Cuvier) 1824:276 [ref. 3574]. Masc. *Anampses cuvier* Quoy & Gaimard 1824:276. Type by monotypy. Misspelled *Anampsis* by Swainson 1839:173, 233 [ref. 4303]. Valid (Araga in Masuda et al. 1984:204 [ref. 6441], Randall 1986: 685 [ref. 5706]). Labridae.

Anaora Gray 1835:Pl. 90 (v. 2) [ref. 1878]. Fem. *Anaora tentaculata* Gray 1835:Pl. 90. Type by monotypy. As *Amora* on plate examined, as *Anaora* in list of figures; Jordan 1919:179 [ref. 2410] regarded *Amora* as a misspelling; Sawyer 1953:54 [ref. 6842] lists only *Amora*. In footnote to list of plates (1835) it is stated, "In some copies a few of the names on the Plates are incorrectly printed but these are corrected in this list..." That list uses *Anaora*. Valid (Fricke 1982:57 [ref. 5432], Nakabo 1982:108 [ref. 3139], Nakabo in Masuda et al. 1984:345 [ref. 6441]). Callionymidae.

Anaoroides (subgenus of *Synchiropus*) Fricke 1981:149 [ref. 1499]. Masc. *Synchiropus zamboanganus* Seale 1910:540. Type by original designation (also monotypic). Synonym of *Synchiropus* Gill 1860, but a valid subgenus (Fricke 1982:78 [ref. 5432]). Callionymidae.

Anarchias Jordan & Starks in Jordan & Seale 1906:204 [ref. 2497]. Masc. *Anarchias allardicei* Jordan & Starks in Jordan & Seale 1906:204. Type by original designation. Valid (Blache et al. 1973:226 [ref. 7185], Hatooka in Masuda et al. 1984:26 [ref. 6441], Bauchot in Whitehead et al. 1986:537 [ref. 13676], Castle & McCosker 1986:166 [ref. 5645], Paxton et al. 1989:126 [ref. 12442], Böhlke et al. 1989:117 [ref. 13286]). Muraenidae: Uropterygiinae.

Anarchopterus Hubbs 1935:1 [ref. 2245]. Masc. *Siphostoma crinigerum* Bean & Dresel 1884:99. Type by original designation (also monotypic). Valid (Dawson 1982:33 [ref. 6764]). Syngnathidae: Syngnathinae.

Anarhichas Linnaeus 1758:247 [ref. 2787]. Masc. *Anarhichas lupus* Linnaeus 1758:247. Type by monotypy. On Official List (Direction 56). Variously misspelled, or unjustifiably emended, in early literature as *Anarichas, Anarchias, Anarchichas, Annarhichas, Anarrhichas*. *Anarhicas* Latreille 1804 on Official Index (Direction 56). Valid (Barsukov 1973:528 [ref. 7213], Amaoka in Masuda et al. 1984:304 [ref. 6441], Barsukov in Whitehead et al. 1986:1113 [ref. 13677]). Anarhichadidae.

Anarmostus Putnam (ex Scutter) 1863:12 [ref. 3567]. Masc. *Diabasis flavolineatus* Desmarest 1823:35. Type by subsequent designation. Two included species, earliest type designation not researched. Preoccupied by Loew 1860 in Diptera, apparently not replaced. Synonym of *Haemulon* Cuvier 1829. Haemulidae.

Anarrhichas see *Anarhichas*. Anarhichadidae.

Anarrhichthys Ayres 1855:[31] [ref. 13428]. Masc. *Anarrhichthys ocellatus* Ayres 1855:[31]. Type by monotypy. Read at the meeting of 26 Feb. 1855; appeared first in "The Pacific" newspaper, v. 4 (13), 2 March 1855, then in the Proceedings, p. 32 [ref. 159]. Valid. Anarhichadidae.

Anarrichas see *Anarhichas*. Anarhichadidae.

Anathyridium (subgenus of *Baeostoma*) Chabanaud 1928:21 [ref. 783]. Neut. *Solea gronovii* Günther 1862:472. Type by subsequent designation. Earliest type designation not researched. Achiridae.

Anatirostrum Iljin 1930:19, 31, 48 [ref. 2297]. Neut. *Benthophilus profundorum* Berg 1927:355. Type by original designation (also monotypic). Valid. Gobiidae.

Anatolichthys Kosswig & Sözer 1945:77 [ref. 2664]. Masc. *Anatolichthys splendens* Kosswig & Sözer 1945:77. Type by monotypy. Synonym of *Kosswigichthys* Sözer 1942 (Parenti 1981:524 [ref. 7066]). Cyprinodontidae: Cyprinodontinae.

Ancharius Steindachner 1881:251 [ref. 4230]. Masc. *Ancharius fuscus* Steindachner 1881:251. Type by monotypy. Valid (Taylor 1986:153 [ref. 6195]). Ariidae.

Anchenionchus see *Auchenionchus*. Labrisomidae.

Ancherythroculter Yih & Wu 1964:106 [ref. 13499]. Masc. *Chanodichthys kurematsui* Kimura 1934. Type by original designation. Cyprinidae.

Anchichoerops Barnard 1927:746 [ref. 194]. Masc. *Choerops natalensis* Gilchrist & Thompson 1909:259. Type by monotypy. Valid (Randall 1986:686 [ref. 5706]). Labridae.

Anchisomus Richardson (ex Kaup) 1854:156 [ref. 3746]. Masc. *Tetraodon spengleri* Bloch 1782:135. Type by subsequent designation. Type designated first by Jordan 1919:261 [ref. 2410] according to Su et al. 1986:102. Objective synonym of *Spheroides* (Shipp 1974:34 [ref. 7147], Su et al. 1986:102 [ref. 12582]; see also account of *Spheroides*). Tetraodontidae.

Anchoa (subgenus of *Anchoviella*) Jordan & Evermann 1927:501 [ref. 2453]. Fem. *Engraulis compressus* Girard 1858:336. Type by original designation (also monotypic). Valid (Grande 1985:245 [ref. 6466], G. Nelson 1986 [ref. 5735], Whitehead et al. 1988:339 [ref. 5725]). Engraulidae.

Anchovia Jordan & Evermann in Jordan 1895:411 [ref. 2394]. Fem. *Engraulis macrolepidota* Kner & Steindachner 1865:21. Type by monotypy. Genus described more fully in Jordan & Evermann 1896:449 [ref. 2443]. Valid (Grande 1985:245 [ref. 6466], Whitehead et al. 1988:377 [ref. 5725]). Engraulidae.

Anchovicypris (subgenus of *Engraulicypris*) Fowler 1936:294 [ref. 1424]. Fem. *Engraulicypris congicus* Nichols & Griscom 1917: 703. Type by original designation. Synonym of *Chelaethiops* Boulenger 1899 (Lévêque & Daget 1984:299 [ref. 6186]). Cyprinidae.

Anchoviella (subgenus of *Anchoa*) Fowler 1911:211 [ref. 1382]. Fem. *Engraulis perfasciatus* Poey 1860:313. Type by original designation. Valid (Grande 1985:245 [ref. 6466], Whitehead et al. 1988 [ref. 5725]). Engraulidae.

Anchovietta (subgenus of *Anchoa*) Nelson 1986:895 [ref. 5735]. Fem. *Stolephorus naso* Gilbert & Pierson in Jordan & Evermann 1898:2813. Type by original designation. Engraulidae.

Ancistrus Kner 1854:272 [ref. 2628]. Masc. *Hypostomus cirrhosus* Valenciennes in Cuvier & Valenciennes 1840:511. Type by subsequent designation. Type designated by Bleeker 1862:2 [ref. 393]. Valid (Isbrücker 1980:65 [ref. 2303], Heitmans et al. 1983 [ref. 5278], Reis 1987:81 [ref. 6263], Burgess 1989:436 [ref. 12860], Muller 1989 [ref. 13512], Malabarba 1989:148 [ref. 14217]). Loricariidae.

Ancylodon Oken (ex Cuvier) 1817:1182 [ref. 3303]. Masc. *Lonchurus ancylodon* Bloch & Schneider 1801:102. Type apparently by subsequent absolute tautonymy. Based on "Les Ancylodons" Cuvier 1816:299 [ref. 993] (see Gill 1903:966 [ref. 5768]). Spelled *Ancylodonus* by Jarocki 1822:234 [ref. 4984]; misspelled

Anclyodon by Jordan 1917:104 [ref. 2407]. Preoccupied by Illiger 1811 in mammals, replaced by *Macrodon* Schinz 1822 and *Normalus* Gistel 1848. Possibly dates to Bosc 1816:497 (see Bauchot & Desoutter 1987:3 [ref. 6382]). In the synonymy of *Macrodon* Schinz 1822. Sciaenidae.

Ancylopsetta Gill 1864:224 [ref. 5773]. Fem. *Ancylopsetta quadrocellatus* Gill 1864:224. Type by monotypy. Valid (Norman 1934:124 [ref. 6893], Matsuura in Uyeno et al. 1983:457 [ref. 14275], Ahlstrom et al. 1984:640 [ref. 13641]). Paralichthyidae.

Andameleotris (subgenus of *Amblyeleotris*) Herre 1939:346 [ref. 2127]. Fem. *Amblyeleotris (Andameleotris) raoi* Herre 1939:346. Type by monotypy. Synonym of *Parioglossus* Regan 1912 (Rennis & Hoese 1985:172 [ref. 5859]). Microdesmidae: Ptereleotrinae.

Andamia Blyth 1858:270 [ref. 476]. Fem. *Andamia expansa* Blyth 1858:271. Type by monotypy. Valid (Smith-Vaniz & Springer 1971:16 [ref. 4145], Yoshino in Masuda et al. 1984:300 [ref. 6441]). Blenniidae.

Andersonia Boulenger 1900:528 [ref. 554]. Fem. *Andersonia leptura* Boulenger 1900:529. Type by monotypy. Valid (Skelton & Teugels 1986:59 [ref. 6192], Burgess 1989:114 [ref. 12860]). Amphiliidae.

Andracanthus Longley 1927:222 [ref. 5630]. Masc. *Clinus ocellatus* Steindachner 1876:230. Type by original designation. Synonym of *Starksia* Jordan & Evermann 1896 (Rosenblatt & Taylor 1971:452 [ref. 3811]). Labrisomidae.

Andreasenius (subgenus of *Procatopus*) Clausen 1959:264 [ref. 843]. Masc. *Procatopus aberrans* Ahl 1927:80. Type by original designation. Synonym of *Procatopus* Boulenger 1904 (Parenti 1981:511 [ref. 7066], Wildekamp et al. 1986:193 [ref. 6198]). Cyprinodontidae: Aplocheilichthyinae.

Andriashevia Fedorov & Neyelov 1978:952 [ref. 1312]. Fem. *Andriashevia aptera* Fedorov & Neyelov 1978:953. Type by original designation (also monotypic). Valid (Anderson 1984:578 [ref. 13634], Fedorov & Sheiko 1988 [ref. 12755]). Zoarcidae.

Anduzedoras Fernández-Yépez 1968:28 [ref. 1325]. Masc. *Anduzedoras arleoi* Fernández-Yépez 1968:28. Type by original designation. Valid (Burgess 1989:223 [ref. 12860]). Doradidae.

Anema Günther 1860:226, 230 [ref. 1963]. Neut. *Uranoscopus lebeck* Bloch & Schneider 1801:47. Type by subsequent designation. Three included species; Jordan 1919:296 [ref. 2410] wrongly lists *anoplus* as type (that species placed by Günther in *Agnus*). Apparently earliest type designation is by Mees 1960:47 [ref. 11931]; *lebek* treated in synonymy of *Uranoscopus inermis* by Günther. See also *Synnema* Haast 1873. Objective synonym *Ichthyscopus* Swainson 1839 (Mees 1960:47 [ref. 11931], Pietsch 1989:297 [ref. 12541]). Uranoscopidae.

Anemanotus (subgenus of *Ailurichthys*) Fowler 1944:171 [ref. 1448]. Masc. *Ailurichthys panamensis* Gill 1863:172. Type by original designation (also monotypic). Ariidae.

Anematichthys (subgenus of *Cyclocheilichthys*) Bleeker 1859:149 [ref. 371]. Masc. *Barbus apogon* Valenciennes in Cuvier & Valenciennes 1842:299. Type by subsequent designation. Apparently appeared first as name only in Bleeker 1859:431 [ref. 370] and dates to Bleeker 1859 as above, possibly to 1860:2 [ref. 376] or 1860:279, 363 [ref. 380]. Type designated first by Bleeker 1863:199 [ref. 397] or 1863:27 [ref. 4859] but if 1860:2 [ref. 376] was first, then type is by monotypy. Synonym of *Cyclocheilichthys* Bleeker 1859 (Roberts 1989:33 [ref. 6439]). Cyprinidae.

Anemoces Jordan 1929:156 [ref. 6443]. *Ulocentra gilberti* Evermann & Thoburn in Jordan & Evermann 1896:1049. Type by original designation (also monotypic). Synonym of subgenus *Cottogaster* Putnam 1863 of genus *Percina* Haldeman 1842 (Collette & Banarescu 1977:1455 [ref. 5845]). Percidae.

Anemura (subgenus of *Dentex*) Fowler 1904:527 [ref. 1367]. Fem. *Dentex (Synagris) notatus* Day 1870:884. Type by original designation (also monotypic). Synonym of *Nemipterus* Swainson 1839. Nemipteridae.

Anepistomon Gistel 1848:IX [ref. 1822]. Neut. *Leptorhynchus capensis* Smith 1840:Pl. 6. Type by being a replacement name. Replacement for *Leptorhynchus* Smith 1840, preoccupied by Clift 1828 in Reptilia, Du Bus 1835 and Ménetriés 1835 in Aves. Synonym of *Ophisurus* Lacepède 1800 (Blache et al. 1973:249 [ref. 7185], McCosker 1977:82 [ref. 6836]). Ophichthidae: Ophichthinae.

Angelichthys Jordan & Evermann 1896:420 [ref. 2442]. Masc. *Chaetodon ciliaris* Linnaeus 1758:276. Type by original designation. Synonym of *Holacanthus* Lacepède 1802. Pomacanthidae.

Angola Myers 1928:7 [ref. 3099]. Fem. *Xenopom(at)ichthys ansorgii* Boulenger 1910:542. Type by original designation (also monotypic). Synonym of *Kneria* Steindachner 1866 (Poll 1984:129 [ref. 6180]). Kneriidae.

Anguilla Schrank 1798:304, 307 [ref. 6444]. Fem. *Muraena anguilla* Linnaeus 1758:245. Type apparently by absolute tautonymy, original not examined. Apparently appeared first as name only in Thunberg 1795 [not researched]. Schrank as author predates Shaw 1803. Valid (Blache et al. 1973:220 [ref. 7185], Asano in Masuda et al. 1984:21 [ref. 6441], Bauchot in Whitehead et al. 1986:535 [ref. 13676], Castle 1986:160 [ref. 5644], Kottelat 1989:4 [ref. 13605], Paxton et al. 1989:122 [ref. 12442], Smith 1989:32 [ref. 13285]). Anguillidae.

Anguillichthys Mowbray in Breder 1927:10 [ref. 635]. Masc. *Anguillichthys bahamensis* Mowbray in Breder 1927:10. Type by monotypy. Synonym of *Moringua* Gray 1831 (Smith 1989:65 [ref. 13285]). Moringuidae.

Anguilloclarias (subgenus of *Clarias*) Teugels 1982:13 [ref. 6670]. Masc. *Clarias theodorae* Weber 1897:150. Type by original designation. Also appeared in Teugels 1982:738 [ref. 4377]. Synonym of *Clarias* Scopoli 1777 (Teugels 1986:69 [ref. 6193]). Clariidae.

Anguisurus Kaup 1856:50 [ref. 2572]. Masc. *Anguisurus punctulatus* Kaup 1856:50. Type by monotypy. Also in Kaup 1856:24 [ref. 2573] and with genus and species as name only in Kaup in Duméril 1856:199 [ref. 1154]. Synonym of *Lamnostoma* Kaup 1856 (McCosker 1977:68 [ref. 6836]). Ophichthidae: Ophichthinae.

Aniculerosa Whitley 1933:101 [ref. 4677]. Fem. *Aniculerosa taprobanensis* Whitley 1933:101. Type by original designation (also monotypic). Synonym of *Paraploactis* Bleeker 1865 (Poss & Eschmeyer 1978:405 [ref. 6387]). Aploactinidae.

Anisarchus Gill 1864:210 [ref. 1702]. Masc. *Clinus medius* Reinhardt 1838:114, 121, 194. Type by monotypy. Valid (Makushok 1973:538 [ref. 6889], Amaoka & Miki in Masuda et al. 1984:301 [ref. 6441], Makushok in Whitehead et al. 1986:1127 [ref. 13677], Miki et al. 1987:131 [ref. 6704]). Stichaeidae.

Anisitsia Eigenmann & Kennedy in Eigenmann 1903:144 [ref. 1218]. Fem. *Anodus notatus* Schomburgk 1841:218. Type by original designation (also monotypic). Synonym of *Hemiodus* Müller 1842 (Roberts 1974:432 [ref. 6872], Géry 1977:198 [ref. 1597]). Hemiodontidae: Hemiodontinae.

Anisocentrus Regan 1914:281 [ref. 3660]. Masc. *Nematocentris rubrostriatus* Ramsay & Ogilby 1886:14. Type by monotypy. Synonym of *Melanotaenia* Gill 1862 (Allen 1980:474 [ref. 99], Allen & Cross 1982:44 [ref. 6251]). Atherinidae: Melanotaeniinae.

Anisochaetodon (subgenus of *Chaetodon*) Klunzinger 1884:54 [ref. 2625]. Masc. *Chaetodon auriga* Forsskål 1775:xii, 60. Type by subsequent designation. Type designated by Jordan 1920:429 [ref. 4905]. Objective synonym of *Linophora* Kaup 1860. Synonym of *Chaetodon* Linnaeus 1758, subgenus *Rabdophorus* Swainson 1839 (Burgess 1978:578 [ref. 700]). Chaetodontidae.

Anisochirus (subgenus of *Synaptura*) Günther 1862:480, 486 [ref. 1969]. Masc. *Synaptura panoides* Bleeker 1851:440. Type by subsequent designation. Described in key (p. 480) as section of *Synaptura* with 2 species (p. 486). Type designated by Jordan 1919:319 [ref. 4904]. *Chabanaudetta* Whitley 1931 is an unneeded replacement. Soleidae.

Anisochromis Smith 1954:298 [ref. 4092]. Masc. *Anisochromis kenyae* Smith 1954:300. Type by original designation (also monotypic). Valid (Springer et al. 1977 [ref. 5510], Smith 1986:539 [ref. 5712]). Pseudochromidae: Anisochrominae.

Anisotremus Gill 1861:32 [ref. 1766]. Masc. *Sparus virginicus* Linnaeus 1758:281. Type by monotypy. Valid (Johnson 1980:11 [ref. 13553], Matsuura in Uyeno et al. 1983:352 [ref. 14275]). Haemulidae.

Annamia Hora 1932:306 [ref. 2208]. Fem. *Parhomaloptera normani* Hora 1930:584. Type by original designation (also monotypic). Valid (Silas 1953:221 [ref. 4024], Sawada 1982:205 [ref. 14111], Kottelat 1985:267 [ref. 11441], Kottelat 1989:12 [ref. 13605]). Balitoridae: Balitorinae.

Anodontiglanis Rendahl 1922:168 [ref. 3701]. Masc. *Anodontiglanis dahli* Rendahl 1922:169. Type by original designation (also monotypic). Misspelled *Anodontoglanis* in Zoological Record for 1922 and by Jordan 1923:index [p. 749 of reprint edition]. Valid (Burgess 1989:180 [ref. 12860] as *Anodontoglanis*, Paxton et al. 1989:222 [ref. 12442]). Plotosidae.

Anodontostoma Bleeker 1849:15 [ref. 320]. Neut. *Anodontostoma hasseltii* Bleeker 1849:15. Type by monotypy. Valid (Grande 1985:248 [ref. 6466], Whitehead 1985:252 [ref. 5141], Kottelat 1989:4 [ref. 13605], Paxton et al. 1989:152 [ref. 12442]). Clupeidae.

Anodontus Cervigón 1961:119 [ref. 777]. Masc. *Anodontus mauritanicus* Cervigón 1961:119. Type by monotypy. Synonym of *Guentherus* Osório 1917 (Bussing & López 1977:181 [ref. 7001]). Ateleopodidae.

Anodus Agassiz in Spix & Agassiz 1829:57, 60 [ref. 13]. Masc. *Anodus elongatus* Agassiz in Spix & Agassiz 1829:61. Type by subsequent designation. Type designated by Eigenmann & Eigenmann 1889:410 [ref. 1254]. See Kottelat 1988:78 [ref. 13380]. Valid but with authorship as Cuvier 1829 (see account of *Anodus* Cuvier 1829). Hemiodontidae: Hemiodontinae.

Anodus Cuvier 1829:309, footnote [ref. 995]. Masc. *Anodus elongatus* Agassiz in Spix & Agassiz 1829:61. Type by subsequent designation. Kottelat 1988:78, 83 [ref. 13380] regards as available from Cuvier, accepting the type designation of Eigenmann & Eigenmann for *Anodus* Spix [= Agassiz] as designating a type for *Anodus* Cuvier, and that is incorrect. Cuvier's earlier account is brief, but sufficient to make available, with no included species. Technical addition of species and type designation apparently can date to Kottelat 1988:78 (earlier designation not researched). Should be treated as valid. Hemiodontidae: Hemiodontinae.

Anogramma Ogilby 1899:175 [ref. 3279]. Neut. *Callanthias allporti* Günther 1876:390. Type by monotypy. Spelled *Anagramma* by authors. Synonym of *Callanthias* Lowe 1839. Callanthiidae.

Anomalochromis Greenwood 1985:259 [ref. 4951]. Masc. *Paretroplus thomasi* Boulenger 1915:204. Type by original designation (also monotypic). Cichlidae.

Anomalodon Bowdich 1825:xii, 237 [ref. 590]. Masc. *Anomalodon incisus* Bowdich 1825:237. Type by monotypy. Also involves fig. 51 opposite p. 123 in conjunction with p. xii. Synonym of *Pomadasys* Lacepède 1802 (Roux 1973:391 [ref. 7200], Roux 1986:328 [ref. 6209]). Haemulidae.

Anomalophryne Regan & Trewavas 1932:112 [ref. 3682]. Fem. *Haplophryne hudsonius* Beebe 1929:21. Type by monotypy. Ceratioidei.

Anomalops Kner 1868:26 [ref. 6074]. Masc. *Anomalops graeffei* Kner 1868:26. Type by monotypy. Also appeared as new in Kner 1868:294 [ref. 2646]. *Anomalopsis* Lee 1980 is a misspelling. Valid (Shimizu in Masuda et al. 1984:109 [ref. 6441], McCosker & Rosenblatt 1987:158 [ref. 6707], Johnson & Rosenblatt 1988 [ref. 6682], Paxton et al. 1989:368 [ref. 12442]). Anomalopidae.

Anomalopterichthys Whitley 1940:242 [ref. 4660]. Masc. *Anomalopterus pinguis* Vaillant 1886:1239. Type by being a replacement name. Replacement for *Anomalopterus* Vaillant 1886, preoccupied by Gray 1855 in Aves. Valid (Krefft 1973:87 [ref. 7166]). Alepocephalidae.

Anomalopterus Vaillant 1886:1239 [ref. 4494]. Masc. *Anomalopterus pinguis* Vaillant 1886:1239. Type by monotypy. Preoccupied by Gray 1855 in Aves, replaced by *Anomalopterichthys* Whitley 1940. Objective synonym of *Anomalopterichthys* Whitley 1940 (Krefft 1973:87 [ref. 7166]). Alepocephalidae.

Anomiolepis Gill 1861:82 [ref. 1771]. Fem. Based on an unnamed Chinese species allied to *Corvina tridentifer* Richardson but without small teeth in upper jaw. Apparently not available for lack of addition of an available species. Sciaenidae.

Anommatophasma Mees 1962:27 [ref. 2966]. Neut. *Anommatophasma candidum* Mees 1962:27. Type by original designation (also monotypic). Synonym of *Ophisternon* McClelland 1844 (Rosen & Greenwood 1976:50 [ref. 7094] and Daget 1986:291 [ref. 6203] but misspelled *Anomatophasma*). Synbranchidae.

Anoplagonus Gill 1861:167 [ref. 1775]. Masc. *Aspidophoroides inermis* Günther 1860:524. Type by monotypy. Valid (Washington et al. 1984:442 [ref. 13660], Kanayama in Masuda et al. 1984:333 [ref. 6441], Yabe 1985:123 [ref. 11522], Maeda & Amaoka 1988:117 [ref. 12616]). Agonidae.

Anoplarchus Gill 1861:261 [ref. 1777]. Masc. *Anoplarchus purpurescens* Gill 1861:262. Type by original designation (also monotypic). Valid (Miki et al. 1987:10 [ref. 12551]). Stichaeidae.

Anopleutropius Vaillant 1893:198 [ref. 4486]. Masc. *Anopleutropius henrici* Vaillant 1893:199. Type by monotypy. Placement in the Siluridae follows Kottelat (pers. comm.). Siluridae.

Anoplocapros (subgenus of *Acerana*) Kaup 1855:220 [ref. 2571]. Masc. *Ostracion lenticularis* Richardson 1841:21. Type by subsequent designation. Type designated by Bleeker 1865:28 [ref. 416]. Valid (Tyler 1980:205 [ref. 4477], Winterbottom & Tyler 1983:902 [ref. 5320]). Ostraciidae: Aracaninae.

Anoplogaster Günther 1859:12 [ref. 1961]. Fem. *Hoplostethus cornutus* Valenciennes in Cuvier & Valenciennes 1833:470. Type by monotypy. Valid (Nielsen 1973:348 [ref. 6885], Woods & Sonoda

1973:387 [ref. 6899], Shimizu in Masuda et al. 1984:109 [ref. 6441], Post in Whitehead et al. 1986:767 [ref. 13676], Hulley 1986:415 [ref. 5672], Paxton et al. 1989:369 [ref. 12442]). Anoplogastridae.

Anoplopoma Ayres 1859:27 [ref. 155]. Neut. *Anoplopoma merlangus* Ayres 1859:27. Type by monotypy. Valid (Washington et al. 1984:442 [ref. 13660], Amaoka in Masuda et al. 1984:320 [ref. 6441]). Anoplopomatidae.

Anoplopterus Pfeffer 1889:15 [ref. 3460]. Masc. *Anoplopterus uranoscopus* Pfeffer 1889:16. Type by monotypy. Synonym of *Amphilius* Günther 1864 (Skelton & Teugels 1986:54 [ref. 6192]). Amphiliidae.

Anoplus Temminck & Schlegel 1842:17 [ref. 4370]. Masc. *Anoplus banjos* Richardson 1846:236. Type by subsequent designation. Appeared originally without species, type designated by Bleeker 1876:277 in providing a replacement name. Preoccupied by Schoenherr 1826 in Coleoptera, not preoccupied by Dejean 1821 (nomen nudum). Synonym of *Banjos* Bleeker 1876. Banjosidae.

Anopsus Rafinesque 1815:93 [ref. 3584]. Masc. *Muraenoblenna olivacea* Lacepède 1803:652. Type by being a replacement name. As "*Anopsus* R. [Rafinesque] *Murenoblenna* [sic] Raf." An available replacement name for *Muraenoblenna* Rafinesque 1803 based on style in this work. *Anopsis* Agassiz 1846:25 [ref. 64] is an unjustified emendation. Synonym of *Myxine* Linnaeus 1758 (Fowler 1964:48 [ref. 7160]). Myxinidae: Myxininae.

Anoptichthys Hubbs & Innes 1936:3 [ref. 2256]. Masc. *Anoptichthys jordani* Hubbs & Innes 1936:5. Type by original designation (also monotypic). Synonym of *Astyanax* Baird & Girard 1854 (see Géry 1977:418 [ref. 1597]). Characidae.

Anosmius (subgenus of *Tetraodon*) Peters 1855:462 [ref. 3449]. Masc. *Tetraodon (Anosmius) taeniatus* Peters 1855:462. Type by subsequent designation. Earliest type designation found that of Jordan 1919:266 [ref. 2410]. Synonym of *Canthigaster* Swainson 1839 (Allen & Randall 1977:478 [ref. 6714]). Tetraodontidae.

Anostoma van Hasselt in Bleeker 1859:82 [ref. 371]. Neut. *Panchax pictum* Valenciennes in Cuvier & Valenciennes 1846:385. Type by monotypy. Apparently not available, name in synonymy; apparently never subsequently made available; type as listed by Fowler (MS). In the synonymy of *Betta* Bleeker 1850. Belontiidae.

Anostomoides Pellegrin 1909:346 [ref. 3423]. Masc. *Anostomoides atrianalis* Pellegrin 1909:346. Type by monotypy. Valid (Géry 1977:178 [ref. 1597], Winterbottom 1980:2 [ref. 4755]). Curimatidae: Anostominae.

Anostomos Gronow 1763:122 [ref. 1910]. Not available, published in a rejected work on Official Index (Opinion 261). Curimatidae: Anostominae.

Anostomus Cuvier (ex Gronow) 1816:165 [ref. 993]. Masc. *Salmo anostomus* Linnaeus 1758:312. Type by monotypy (also by absolute tautonymy). Same as *Anostomus* Scopoli 1777 but described independently. Objective synonym and homonym of *Anostomus* Scopoli 1777. Curimatidae: Anostominae.

Anostomus Scopoli (ex Gronow) 1777:451 [ref. 3990]. Masc. *Salmo anostomus* Linnaeus 1758:312. Appeared first without species; first addition of species not researched. *Anostoma* is a misspelling or unjustified emendation. Apparently *Anastomus* Minding 1832 [ref. 3022] refers to this taxon as does *Anostomus* Cuvier 1816. Valid (Géry 1977:178 [ref. 1597], Winterbottom 1980:9 [ref. 4755], Vari 1983:5 [ref. 5419]). Curimatidae: /ano stominae..

Anotopterus Zugmayer 1911:13 [ref. 6161]. Masc. *Anotopterus pharao* Zugmayer 1911:13. Type by monotypy. Also appeared in Zugmayer 1911 (Dec.):138 [ref. 4846]. Valid (Maul 1973:211 [ref. 7171], Post in Whitehead et al. 1984:509 [ref. 13675], Okiyama 1984:207 [ref. 13644], Fujii in Masuda et al. 1984:77 [ref. 6441], Hulley 1986:278 [ref. 5672]). Anotopteridae.

Anoxypristis White & Moy-Thomas 1941:397 [ref. 4652]. Fem. *Pristis cuspidatus* Latham 1794:279. Type by being a replacement name. Replacement for *Oxypristis* Hoffman 1912, preoccupied by Signoret 1861 in Hemiptera. Valid (Compagno 1986:110 [ref. 5648], Cappetta 1987:157 [ref. 6348], Paxton et al. 1989:58 [ref. 12442]). Pristidae.

Ansorgia Boulenger 1912:17 [ref. 581]. Fem. *Ansorgia vittata* Boulenger 1912:17. Type by monotypy. Preoccupied by Warren 1899 in Lepidoptera; replaced by *Ansorgiichthys* Whitley 1935. Synonym of *Eutropiellus* Nichols & La Monte 1933 (Myers 1938:98 [ref. 3116], De Vos 1986:36 [ref. 6191]). Schilbeidae.

Ansorgiichthys Whitley 1935:249 [ref. 4683]. Masc. *Ansorgia vittata* Boulenger 1912:17. Type by being a replacement name. Replacement for *Ansorgia* Boulenger 1912, preoccupied by Warren 1899 in Lepidoptera. Synonym of *Eutropiellus* Nichols & La Monte 1933 (De Vos 1986:36 [ref. 6191]). Schilbeidae.

Antacea Bory de Saint-Vincent 1822:410 [ref. 3853]. Fem. *Acipenser schypa* Güldenstädt 1772:533. As *Antacei*, a group within *Acipenser* as used by Heckel & Kner 1858:346 [ref. 2078]. Original not seen. Synonym of *Acipenser* Linnaeus 1758. Acipenseridae: Acipenserinae.

Antaceus Heckel & Fitzinger 1836:269, 293 [ref. 2077]. Masc. *Acipenser schypa* Güldenstädt 1772:533. Original not seen. Spelled *Antacei* by Dybowski 1874:393 [ref. 1172]. Synonym of *Acipenser* Linnaeus 1758. Acipenseridae: Acipenserinae.

Anteliochimaera Tanaka 1909:7 [ref. 4322]. Fem. *Anteliochimaera chaetirhamphus* Tanaka 1909:7. Type by original designation (also monotypic). Misspelled *Antiliochimaera* in Zoological Record for 1909. Synonym of *Harriotta* Goode & Bean 1895. Rhinochimaeridae.

Antennablennius (subgenus of *Blennius*) Fowler 1931:245 [ref. 1409]. Masc. *Blennius hypenetes* Klunzinger 1871:492. Type by original designation (also monotypic). Valid (Bath 1983 [ref. 5393], Springer 1986:743 [ref. 5719]). Blenniidae.

Antennarius Commerson in Lacepède 1798:327 (footnote) [ref. 2708]. Masc. *Lophius commersonianus* Lacepède in Jordan 1917:69. Validated by ICZN Opinion 24 (in 1910), but then suspended by Opinion 89 (1925). See discussion under Opinion 89 in Appendix B. More research is need on the authorship of *Antennarius*. In the synonymy of *Antennarius* Daudin 1816 (Pietsch 1984:33 [ref. 5380]). Antennariidae.

Antennarius Cuvier (ex Commerson) 1816:310 [ref. 993]. Masc. *Lophius commersonii* Shaw 1804:387. Type by subsequent designation. Type designated by Jordan 1917:104 [ref. 2407]; designation of *Antennarius princeps* Commerson by Gill 1863:90 [ref. 1680] should be investigated. Synonym of *Antennarius* Daudin 1816 (Oct.), Cuvier is Dec. 1816 (see Pietsch 1984:33 [ref. 5380]). Antennariidae.

Antennarius Daudin 1816:193 [ref. 6445]. Masc. *Lophius chironectes* Lacepède (ex Commerson) 1798:325. Type by subsequent designation. Type designated by Bleeker 1865:5 [ref. 416]. Type above assumes species can in fact date to Lacepède 1798. *Antennaria* is a misspelling. Valid (Pietsch 1984:33 [ref. 5380], Araga in

Masuda et al. 1984:103 [ref. 6441], Pietsch 1986:366 [ref. 5704], Pietsch in Whitehead et al. 1986:1364 [ref. 13677], Paxton et al. 1989:277 [ref. 12442]). Antennariidae.

Antennatus Schultz 1957:(57) 80 [ref. 3969]. Masc. *Antennarius strigatus* Gill 1863:92. Type by original designation. Valid (Pietsch 1984:36 [ref. 5380]). Antennariidae.

Anthea Catesby 1771:25 [ref. 774]. Fem. Not available, published in a rejected work on Official Index (Opinion 89, Opinion 259). Lutjanidae.

Anthias Bloch 1792:97 [ref. 470]. Masc. *Labrus anthias* Linnaeus 1758:282. Type by absolute tautonymy. *Anthias sacer* Bloch 1792:99 is an unneeded replacement for *L. anthias* Linnaeus. *Aylopon* Rafinesque 1810 is an unneeded replacement, *Anthias* not preoccupied by *Anthia* Weber 1801 in Coleoptera. *Anthias* Bonaparte 1839:166 [ref. 4978] also involved. Valid (Tortonese 1973:356 [ref. 7192], Anderson & Heemstra 1980 [ref. 5434], Randall 1983 [ref. 6022], Heemstra & Randall 1986:511 [ref. 5667], Katayama & Amaoka 1986 [ref. 6680], Paxton et al. 1989:501 [ref. 12442]). Serranidae: Anthiinae.

Anthiasicus Ginsburg 1952:91 [ref. 1805]. Masc. *Anthiasicus leptus* Ginsburg 1952:91. Type by original designation (also monotypic). Serranidae: Anthiinae.

Anthiiblennius (subgenus of *Ecsenius*) Starck 1969:1 [ref. 4192]. Masc. *Ecsenius (Anthiiblennius) midas* Starck 1969:2. Type by original designation (also monotypic). Synonym of *Ecsenius* McCulloch 1923 (Smith-Vaniz & Springer 1971:22 [ref. 4145], Springer 1988 [ref. 6804]). Blenniidae.

Anticitharus Günther 1880:47 [ref. 2011]. Masc. *Anticitharus polyspilus* Günther 1880:48. Type by monotypy. Synonym of *Arnoglossus* Bleeker 1862 (Norman 1934:173 [ref. 6893]). Bothidae: Bothinae.

Antigonia Lowe 1843:85 [ref. 2832]. Fem. *Antigonia capros* Lowe 1843:86. Type by monotypy. Valid (Krefft 1973:353 [ref. 7166], Machida in Masuda et al. 1984:117 [ref. 6441], Quéro in Whitehead et al. 1986:777 [ref. 13676], Parin & Borodulina 1986 [ref. 6005], Heemstra 1986:506 [ref. 5660], Zehren 1987 [ref. 6060], Paxton et al. 1989:394 [ref. 12442]). Caproidae.

Antimora (subgenus of *Haloporphyrus*) Günther 1878:18 [ref. 2010]. Fem. *Haloporphyrus (Antimora) rostratus* Günther 1878:18. Type by original designation (also monotypic). Valid (Cohen 1973:322 [ref. 6589], Small 1981 [ref. 5546], Paulin 1983:110 [ref. 5459], Okamura in Masuda et al. 1984:90 [ref. 6441], Fahay & Markle 1984:266 [ref. 13653], Cohen in Whitehead et al. 1986:713 [ref. 13676], Cohen 1986:326 [ref. 5646], Paxton et al. 1989:298 [ref. 12442]). Moridae.

Antipodocottus Bolin 1952:431 [ref. 511]. Masc. *Antipodocottus galatheae* Bolin 1952:432. Type by original designation (also monotypic). Valid (Washington et al. 1984:442 [ref. 13660], Fricke & Brunken 1984 [ref. 5262]), Nelson 1985 [ref. 5155], Paxton et al. 1989:477 [ref. 12442]). Cottidae.

Antobrantia Pinto 1970:13 [ref. 3482]. Fem. *Antobrantia ribeiroi* Pinto 1970:13. Type by original designation (also monotypic). Synonym of *Ophichthus* Ahl 1789 (McCosker 1977:80 [ref. 6836], Böhlke & Menezes 1977:786 [ref. 5524], McCosker et al. 1989:379 [ref. 13288]). Ophichthidae: Ophichthinae.

Antonichthys Bauchot & Blanc 1961:50 [ref. 210]. Masc. *Antonichthys wetmorelloides* Bauchot & Blanc 1961:50. Type by monotypy. Original authors on p. 50a (Corrigendum) synonymized their genus *Antonichthys* with *Doratonotus* Günther 1862. Labridae.

Antonogadus Wheeler 1969:265 [ref. 6834]. Masc. *Motella macrophthalma* Günther 1867:290. Type by monotypy. Valid (Svetovidov 1973:317 [ref. 7169], Svetovidov in Whitehead et al. 1986:695 [ref. 13676]); synonym of *Gaidropsarus* Rafinesque 1810 (Cohen & Russo 1979:100 [ref. 6975], Svetovidov 1986 [ref. 8033]). Lotidae.

Antu (subgenus of *Clupea*) de Buen 1958:87 [ref. 695]. *Clupea fuegensis* Jenyns 1842:133. Type by original designation. Synonym of *Sprattus* Girgensohn 1846 (Whitehead 1985:45 [ref. 5141], Whitehead, Smith & Robertson 1985:263 [ref. 6542]). Clupeidae.

Anyperistius Ogilby 1908:3, 11 [ref. 3285]. Masc. *Anyperistius perugiae* Ogilby 1908:11. Type by original designation (also monotypic). Spelled two ways by Ogilby 1908, *Anyperistius* on p. 3, once on p. 11, p. 12 (footnote), and p. 39 (index); *Anyperisteus* with main genus heading on p. 11; the latter regarded as in error. Synonym of *Tandanus* Mitchell 1838. Plotosidae.

Anyperodon Günther 1859:95 [ref. 1961]. Masc. *Serranus leucogrammicus* Valenciennes in Cuvier & Valenciennes 1828:347. Type by monotypy. Unjustifiably emended to *Anhyperodon* by Boulenger 1895:269 [ref. 537]. Valid (Kendall 1984:500 [ref. 13663], Katayama in Masuda et al. 1984:129 [ref. 6441], Heemstra & Randall 1986:516 [ref. 5667], Paxton et al. 1989:489 [ref. 12442]). Serranidae: Epinephelinae.

Aodon Lacepède 1798:297 [ref. 2708]. Masc. *Squalus massasa* Forsskål 1775:x. Type by subsequent designation. Type designated by Jordan & Evermann 1896:91 [ref. 2443]. Available as above (with 3 species). *Anodon* Agassiz 1846:24, 27 [ref. 64] is an unjustified emendation. See also Whitley 1936:165 [ref. 6075]. Mobulidae.

Aoria Jordan 1919:341 [ref. 2413]. Fem. *Bagrus lamarrii* Valenciennes in Cuvier & Valenciennes 1840:407. Type by being a replacement name. Replacement for *Macrones* Duméril 1856, preoccupied by Newman 1841 in Coleoptera. *Aoria* itself preoccupied by Baly 1863 in Coleoptera and replaced by *Aorichthys* Wu 1939 and by *Macronichthys* White & Moy-Thomas 1940. Synonym of *Mystus* Scopoli 1777 (Roberts 1989:120 [ref. 6439]). Bagridae.

Aorichthys Wu 1939:131 [ref. 4805]. Masc. *Bagrus lamarrii* Valenciennes in Cuvier & Valenciennes 1840:302. Type by being a replacement name. Replacement for *Aoria* Jordan 1919, preoccupied by Baly 1863 in Coleoptera. *Aoria* itself a replacement for *Macrones* Duméril 1856. Objective synonym of *Sperata* Holly 1939, apparently a slightly earlier replacement for *Macrones*. Valid (Jayaram 1977:38 [ref. 7005] and Jayaram 1981:204 [ref. 6497] but with type as *Pimelodus aor* Hamilton); synonym of *Mystus* Scopoli 1777 (Burgess 1989:70 [ref. 12860], Roberts 1989:120 [ref. 6439]). Bagridae.

Aotea Phillipps 1926:533 [ref. 6447]. Fem. *Aotea acus* Phillipps 1926:534. Type by monotypy. Synonym of *Muraenichthys* Bleeker 1853 (Castle 1976:365 [ref. 11394], McCosker 1977:58 [ref. 6836] with question, McCosker et al. 1989:256 [ref. 13288]). Ophichthidae: Myrophinae.

Aoyagichthys (subgenus of *Paratrigla*) Whitley 1958:46 [ref. 4728]. Masc. *Trigla vanessa* Richardson 1839:97. Type by original designation (also monotypic). Synonym of *Lepidotrigla* Günther 1860 (Richards & Saksena 1977:209 [ref. 5285]). Triglidae: Triglinae.

Apagesoma Carter 1983:94 [ref. 5165]. Neut. *Apagesoma edentatum* Carter 1983:95. Type by original designation. Valid (Anderson et al. 1985 [ref. 5164]). Ophidiidae: Neobythitinae.

Apareiodon Eigenmann 1916:71 [ref. 1234]. Masc. *Parodon piracicabae* Eigenmann in Eigenmann & Ogle 1907:6. Type by original designation. Synonym of *Parodon* Valenciennes 1849, but as a valid subgenus (Géry 1977:206 [ref. 1597]); valid genus (Roberts 1974:433 [ref. 6872], Géry et al. 1987:408 [ref. 6001]). Hemiodontidae: Parodontinae.

Aparrius Jordan & Richardson 1908:278 [ref. 2492]. Masc. *Gobius acutipinnis* Valenciennes in Cuvier & Valenciennes 1837:80. Type by original designation (also monotypic). Synonym of *Oligolepis* Bleeker 1874 (Maugé 1986:377 [ref. 6218]). Gobiidae.

Apeches Gistel 1848:IX [ref. 1822]. *Johnius carutta* Bloch 1793:133. Type by being a replacement name. Unneeded replacement for *Johnius* Bloch 1793, *Johnius* regarded as an objectionable personal name (see Jordan 1919:338 [ref. 2409]). Objective synonym of *Johnius* Bloch 1793 (Trewavas 1977:406 [ref. 4459]). Sciaenidae.

Apeltes DeKay 1842:67 [ref. 1098]. Masc. *Gasterosteus quadracus* Mitchill 1815:430. Type by original designation. Valid. Gasterosteidae: Gasterosteinae.

Apepton Gistel 1848:IX [ref. 1822]. *Lepadogaster piger* Nardo 1827:9. Type by being a replacement name. Unneeded replacement for "*Gouana*" [sic for *Gouania*] Nardo (species *Lepadogaster piger*), a personal name (see Jordan 1919:236 [ref. 2409]). Type as given by Briggs 1973:653, but Briggs gives type for *Gouania* as *G. prototypus*. Synonym of *Gouania* Nardo 1833 (Briggs 1955:23 [ref. 637], Briggs 1973:653 [ref. 7222]). Gobiesocidae: Gobiesocinae.

Aper Lacepède (ex Plumier) 1803:162, footnote [ref. 4930]. Masc. Not available; Plumier manuscript name mentioned in passing under *Sparus abildgaardi* (see remarks under Opinion 88 in Appendix B). Scaridae: Scarinae.

Aperioptus Richardson 1848:27 [ref. 3744]. Masc. *Aperioptus pictorius* Richardson 1848:27. Type by monotypy. Unidentifiable (Roberts 1972:2 [ref. 12567]). Cypriniformes.

Aphanacanthus Troschel (ex Bibron) 1856:88 [ref. 12559]. Masc. Appeared first as *Aphanacanthe* Bibron in Duméril 1855:278 [ref. 297] without description; latinized by Troschel 1856 as above, also by Hollard 1857:319 [ref. 2186]. First technical addition of species not researched; Jordan 1919:263 [ref. 2410] lists type as *Tetraodon reticulatus* Bibron, but that species apparently never validated; genus itself perhaps unavailable for lack of description. Tetraodontidae.

Aphaniops Hoedeman 1951:2 [ref. 2177]. Masc. *Lebias dispar* Rüppell 1828:66. Type by original designation (also monotypic). Synonym of *Aphanius* Nardo 1827 (Tortonese 1973:270 [ref. 7192], Parenti 1981:521 [ref. 7066], Wildekamp et al. 1986:165 [ref. 6198], Krupp & Schneider 1989:388 [ref. 13651]). Cyprinodontidae: Cyprinodontinae.

Aphanius Nardo 1827:17, 23 [ref. 3146]. Masc. *Aphanius nanus* Nardo 1827:17, 23. Type by subsequent designation. Original not seen. Perhaps more than one publication or a separate is involved; pages sometimes given as 34 and 39-40. Also in Isis, v. 20:482 (seen). Type designated by Jordan 1917:121 [ref. 2407]. Valid (Tortonese 1973:270 [ref. 7192], Parenti 1981:521 [ref. 7066], Tortonese in Whitehead et al. 1986:623 [ref. 13676], Wildekamp et al. 1986:165 [ref. 6198], Coad 1988 [ref. 11814], Krupp & Schneider 1989:388 [ref. 13651]). Cyprinodontidae: Cyprinodontinae.

Aphanopus Lowe 1839:79 [ref. 2829]. Masc. *Aphanopus carbo* Lowe 1839:79. Type by monotypy. Valid (Parin 1983 [ref. 5304], Collette et al. 1984:600 [ref. 11421], Nakamura in Masuda et al. 1984:227 [ref. 6441], Parin in Whitehead et al. 1986:977 [ref. 13676], Nakamura 1986:829 [ref. 5696]). Trichiuridae: Aphanopodinae.

Aphanotorulus Isbrücker & Nijssen 1983:105 [ref. 5389]. Masc. *Aphanotorulus frankei* Isbrücker & Nijssen 1983:108. Type by original designation (also monotypic). Valid (Burgess 1989:430 [ref. 12860]). Loricariidae.

Aphareus Cuvier in Cuvier & Valenciennes 1830:485 [ref. 996]. Masc. *Aphareus caerulescens* Cuvier in Cuvier & Valenciennes 1830:487. Type by subsequent designation. Type designated by Jordan, Tanaka & Snyder 1913:165 [ref. 6448]. Valid (Johnson 1980:9 [ref. 13553], Yoshino in Masuda et al. 1984:167 [ref. 6441], Allen 1985:18 [ref. 6843], Anderson 1986:572 [ref. 5634], Akazaki & Iwatsuki 1986 [ref. 6316]). Lutjanidae.

Aphia Risso 1826:287 [ref. 3757]. Fem. *Aphia meridionalis* Risso 1826:288 (=*Atherina minuta* Risso 1810:340). Type by monotypy. *Aphya* Agassiz 1846:28 [ref. 64] is an unjustified emendation. Originally thought to be an atherinid. Valid (Miller 1973:489 [ref. 6888]), Miller in Whitehead et al. 1986:1023 [ref. 13677], Maugé 1986:360 [ref. 6218], Birdsong et al. 1988:202 [ref. 7303]). Gobiidae.

Aphobus Gistel 1848:XI [ref. 1822]. Masc. *Trachidermis fasciatus* Heckel 1840:168. Type by being a replacement name. Unneeded replacement for *Trachydermis* [Heckel 1840], not preoccupied by *Trachyderma*; correct original spelling was *Trachidermis*. Cottidae.

Aphododerus see *Aphredoderus*. Aphredoderidae.

Aphoristia Kaup 1858:106 [ref. 2579]. Fem. *Achirus ornatus* Lacepède 1802:659, 663. Type by monotypy. Synonym of *Symphurus* Rafinesque 1810. Cynoglossidae: Symphurinae.

Aphos Hubbs & Schultz 1939:476 [ref. 2263]. Masc. *Batrachus porosus* Valenciennes in Cuvier & Valenciennes 1837:506. Type by original designation (also monotypic). Valid (Nakamura in Nakamura et al. 1986:154 [ref. 14235], see Walker & Rosenblatt 1988:888 [ref. 9284], Pequeño 1989:41 [ref. 14125]). Batrachoididae.

Aphredoderus Lesueur in Cuvier & Valenciennes 1833:445 [ref. 1002]. Masc. *Aphredoderus gibbosus* Lesueur in Cuvier & Valenciennes 1833:448. Type by monotypy. Misspellings in early literature include *Aphrodederus*, *Aspredoderus*, *Aphododerus*, and *Aphododirus*. Aphredoderidae.

Aphritis Valenciennes in Cuvier & Valenciennes 1831:483 [ref. 1000]. Fem. *Aphritis urvillii* Valenciennes in Cuvier & Valenciennes 1831:484. Type by monotypy. Preoccupied by Latreille 1804 in Diptera, replaced by *Phricus* Berg 1895. Synonym of *Pseudaphritis* Castelnau 1872 (Scott 1982:202 [ref. 5472]). Bovichtidae.

Aphthalmichthys Kaup 1856:68 [ref. 2572]. Masc. *Aphthalmichthys javanicus* Kaup 1856:105. Type by monotypy. Also in Kaup 1856:105 [ref. 2573] and as name only (*Aphthalmoichthys*) in Kaup in Duméril 1856: 200 [ref. 1154]. Synonym of *Moringua* Gray 1831 (Smith 1989:65 [ref. 13285]). Moringuidae.

Aphthalmoichthys Kaup in Duméril 1856:200 [ref. 1154]. Masc. Not available, appeared as *Aphthalmoichthys javanicus* in list of genera and species taken from Kaup manuscript, without description or indication. Correctly as *Aphthalmichthys* Kaup 1856:68

[ref. 2572]. Moringuidae.

Aphyobranchius (subgenus of *Nothobranchius*) Wildekamp 1977: 326 [ref. 6449]. Masc. *Nothobranchius janpapi* Wildekamp 1977:326. Type by original designation (also monotypic). Synonym of *Nothobranchius* Peters 1868 (Parenti 1981:480 [ref. 7066], Wildekamp et al. 1986:263 [ref. 6198]). Aplocheilidae: Aplocheilinae.

Aphyocharacidium Géry 1960:24 [ref. 1605]. Neut. *Odontostilbe melandetus* Eigenmann 1912:312. Type by original designation (also monotypic). Valid (Géry 1977:591 [ref. 1597]). Characidae.

Aphyocharax Günther 1868:480 [ref. 1992]. Masc. *Aphyocharax pusillus* Günther 1868:480. Type by monotypy. Also published in Günther (Sept.) 1868:245; 1868:480 is June. Spelled *Aphiocharax* by Eigenmann & Eigenmann 1891:55 [ref. 12252]. Valid (Géry 1977:350 [ref. 1597]). Characidae.

Aphyocheirodon Eigenmann 1915:58 [ref. 1231]. Masc. *Aphyocheirodon hemigrammus* Eigenmann 1915:59. Type by original designation (also monotypic). Characidae.

Aphyocyprioides Tang 1942:162 [ref. 4335]. Masc. *Aphyocyprioides typus* Tang 1942:163. Type by original designation (also by monotypy and use of *typus*). Misspelled *Aphyocyproides* in Zoological Record for 1943. Cyprinidae.

Aphyocypris Günther 1868:201 [ref. 1990]. Fem. *Aphyocypris chinensis* Günther 1868:201. Type by monotypy. Valid (Yang & Hwang 1964:14 [ref. 13497], Sawada in Masuda et al. 1984:57 [ref. 6441], Kuang in Chu & Chen 1989:35 [ref. 13584]). Cyprinidae.

Aphyodite Eigenmann 1912:255, 314 [ref. 1227]. *Aphyodite grammica* Eigenmann 1912:314. Type by original designation (also monotypic). Valid (Géry 1977:586 [ref. 1597]). Characidae.

Aphyogobius Whitley 1931:334 [ref. 4672]. Masc. *Gobius albus* Parnell 1838:248. Type by being a replacement name. Replacement for *Latrunculus* Günther 1861, preoccupied by Gray 1847 in Mollusca. Synonym of *Aphia* Risso 1826 (Miller 1973:489 [ref. 6888]). Gobiidae.

Aphyonus Günther 1878:22 [ref. 2010]. Masc. *Aphyonus gelatinosus* Günther 1878:22. Type by monotypy. Valid (Nielsen 1969:13 [ref. 3195], Cohen & Nielsen 1978:61 [ref. 881], Nielsen in Whitehead et al. 1986:1167 [ref. 13677], Nielsen 1986:356 [ref. 5699], Paxton et al. 1989:318 [ref. 12442]). Aphyonidae.

Aphyoplatys Clausen 1967:32 [ref. 5926]. *Epiplatys duboisi* Poll 1952:298. Type by original designation (also monotypic). Synonym of *Epiplatys* Gill 1862, but as a valid subgenus (Parenti 1981:475 [ref. 7066]); valid genus (Wildekamp et al. 1986:196 [ref. 6198]). Aplocheilidae: Aplocheilinae.

Aphyosemion Myers 1924:2 [ref. 3091]. Neut. *Aphyosemion castaneum* Myers 1924:2. Type by original designation. Valid (Parenti 1981:476 [ref. 7066], Huber 1978 [ref. 6070], Wildekamp et al. 1986:196 [ref. 6198]). Aplocheilidae: Aplocheilinae.

Apistes Cuvier in Cuvier & Valenciennes 1829:391 [ref. 998]. Masc. Appeared first in Cuvier (Mar.) 1829:167 [ref. 995] as "Les Apistes"; *Ap. alatus* in footnote (p. 167) apparently not sufficient for latinization as *Apistes* or *Apistus*; latinized by Cuvier in Cuvier & Valenciennes (Nov. 1829) as *Apistus*, with Apistes as above a French vernacular name. In the synonymy of *Apistus* Cuvier 1829. Scorpaenidae: Apistinae.

Apistogramma Regan 1913:282 [ref. 3655]. Neut. *Mesops taeniatus* Günther 1862:312. Type by being a replacement name. Replacement for *Heterogramma* Regan 1906, preoccupied by Guenée 1854 [not investigated, but see Kullander 1980:22 [ref. 5536]]. Valid (Kullander 1980 [ref. 5526], Kullander 1986:155 [ref. 12439], Kullander 1987 [ref. 9163], Kullander & Staeck 1988 [ref. 6866], Kullander & Nijssen 1989:74 [ref. 14136]). Cichlidae.

Apistogrammoides Meinken 1965:48 [ref. 2972]. Masc. *Apistogrammoides pucallpaensis* Meinken 1965:48. Type by original designation. Valid (Kullander 1986:194 [ref. 12439]). Cichlidae.

Apistoloricaria Isbrücker & Nijssen 1986:103 [ref. 5212]. Fem. *Apistoloricaria condei* Isbrücker & Nijssen 1986:103. Type by original designation (also monotypic). Valid (Nijssen & Isbrücker 1988 [ref. 7322], Burgess 1989:444 [ref. 12860]). Loricariidae.

Apistops Ogilby 1911:36, 54 [ref. 3290]. Masc. *Apistus caloundra* De Vis 1886:145. Type by monotypy. Valid (Paxton et al. 1989:439 [ref. 12442]). Scorpaenidae: Apistinae.

Apistus Cuvier in Cuvier & Valenciennes 1829:391 [ref. 998]. Masc. *Apistus alatus* Cuvier in Cuvier & Valenciennes 1829:392. Type by subsequent designation. Type designated by Bleeker 1876:4 [ref. 12248] and Bleeker 1876:296 [ref. 450]. See also *Apistes*. Valid (Shimizu in Masuda et al. 1984:317 [ref. 6441], Washington et al. 1984:440 [ref. 13660], Eschmeyer 1986:464 [ref. 5652]). Scorpaenidae: Apistinae.

Aplatophis Böhlke 1956:1 [ref. 596]. Masc. *Aplatophis chauliodus* Böhlke 1956:3. Type by original designation (also monotypic). Valid (McCosker 1977:74 [ref. 6836], McCosker et al. 1989:354 [ref. 13288]). Ophichthidae: Ophichthinae.

Aplesion (subgenus of *Etheostoma*) Rafinesque 1820:56 [ref. 7305]. Neut. *Etheostoma calliura* Rafinesque 1820:56. Type by subsequent designation. Also appeared in Rafinesque 1820:36 (Dec.) [ref. 3592]. Type designated by Jordan & Gilbert 1877:86 [ref. 4907]. Synonym of *Micropterus* Lacepède 1802 (Hubbs & Bailey 1940:13 [ref. 12253]). Centrarchidae.

Apletodon Briggs 1955:25 [ref. 637]. Masc. *Lepadogaster microcephalus* Brook 1889:166. Type by original designation. On Official List (Opinion 638). Valid (Briggs 1973:651 [ref. 7222], Briggs in Whitehead et al. 1986:1352 [ref. 13677], Briggs 1986:378 [ref. 5643], Allen [L. G.] 1984:629 [ref. 13673]). Gobiesocidae: Gobiesocinae.

Aplites (subgenus of *Lepomis*) Rafinesque 1820:50 [ref. 7305]. Masc. *Lepomis pallida* Rafinesque 1820:50. Type by subsequent designation. Type designated by Jordan & Gilbert 1877:86 [ref. 4907]. Also appeared in Rafinesque 1820:30 (Dec.) [ref. 3592]. Type not *Labrus palladus* Mitchill 1814. *Hoplites* Agassiz 1846:185 [ref. 64] is an unjustified emendation and put on Official Index (Opinion 353). Synonym of *Micropterus* Lacepède 1802 (Hubbs & Bailey 1940:13 [ref. 12253]). Centrarchidae.

Aploactis Temminck & Schlegel 1843:51 [ref. 4371]. Fem. *Leptosynanceia (Aploactis) aspera* Richardson 1844:72. Original description without species; one species added and type fixed by subsequent monotypy by Richardson 1844:72 [ref. 3739]. *Haploactis* Agassiz 1846:29, 172 [ref. 64] is an unjustified emendation. Valid (Poss & Eschmeyer 1978:404 [ref. 6387], Washington et al. 1984:440 [ref. 13660], Nakabo in Masuda et al. 1984: 319 [ref. 6441], Paxton et al. 1989:459 [ref. 12442]). Aploactinidae.

Aploactisoma Castelnau 1872:244 [ref. 757]. Neut. *Aploactisoma schomburgki* Castelnau 1872:244. Type by monotypy. Misspelled or unjustifiably emended to *Haploactisoma* by authors. Valid (Scott 1976:205 [ref. 7055], Washington et al. 1984:440 [ref. 13660], Paxton et al. 1989:459 [ref. 12442]). Aploactinidae.

Aploactoides Fowler 1938:88 [ref. 1426]. Masc. *Aploactoides* *philippinus* Fowler 1938:88. Type by original designation (also monotypic). Synonym of *Erisphex* Jordan & Starks 1904 (Poss & Eschmeyer 1978:404 [ref. 6387]). Aploactinidae.

Aplocentrus Rafinesque 1819:419 [ref. 3590]. Masc. *Aplocentrus calliops* Rafinesque 1819:420. Type by monotypy. Apparently a mythical genus, based on an Audubon drawing. Percidae.

Aplocheilichthys Bleeker 1863:116 [ref. 395]. Masc. *Aplocheilichthys typus* Bleeker 1863:116. Article not translated; type apparently by use of *typus*. Unjustifiably emended to *Haplochilichthys* by Garman 1895:156 and early authors. Valid (Parenti 1981:507 [ref. 7066] with type as *spilauchena*). Cyprinodontidae: Aplocheilichthyinae.

Aplocheilus (subgenus of *Paecilia (sic)*) McClelland 1839:301, 426 [ref. 2923]. Masc. *Aplocheilus chrysostigmus* McClelland 1839:426. Type by subsequent designation. Type designated by Bleeker 1864:140 [ref. 4859]. Also in McClelland 1939:944 [ref. 2924] without species. Spelled *Aplochelus* by McClelland on p. 261. *Haplochilus* Agassiz 1846:29, 172 [ref. 64] is an unjustified emendation. Valid (Jayaram 1981:294 [ref. 6497], Parenti 1981:471 [ref. 7066] with type as *Esox panchax*, Kottelat 1985:272 [ref. 11441], Kottelat 1989:16 [ref. 13605]). Aplocheilidae: Aplocheilinae.

Aplochiton Jenyns 1842:130 [ref. 2344]. Masc. *Aplochiton zebra* Jenyns 1842:131. Type by subsequent designation. Type designated by Eigenmann 1910:462 [ref. 1224]. *Haplochiton* Agassiz 1846:29, 172 [ref. 64] is an unjustified emendation. Valid (McDowall 1984:151 [ref. 11850], McDowall & Nakaya 1987 [ref. 6701], McDowall & Nakaya 1988 [ref. 6237]). Galaxiidae: Aplochitoninae.

Aplodactylus Valenciennes in Cuvier & Valenciennes 1832:476 [ref. 1000]. Masc. *Aplodactylus punctatus* Valenciennes in Cuvier & Valenciennes 1832:477. Type by monotypy. *Haplodactylus* Agassiz 1846:29, 172 [ref. 64] is an unjustified emendation. Valid. Aplodactylidae.

Aplodinotus Rafinesque 1819:418 [ref. 3590]. Masc. *Aplodinotus grunniens* Rafinesque 1819:419. Type by original designation (also monotypic). Unjustifiably emended to *Haploidonotus* by Gill 1861:101 [ref. 1773]. Valid. Sciaenidae.

Aplodon Thominot (ex Duméril) 1883:141 [ref. 4386]. Masc. *Aplodon margaritiferum* Duméril in Thominot 1883:141. Type by subsequent designation. Type apparently first designated by Jordan 1919:426 [ref. 4905]. Unjustifiably emended to *Haplodon* by authors. Synonym of *Girella* Gray 1835. Kyphosidae: Girellinae.

Aplurus Lowe 1838:180 [ref. 2831]. Masc. *Tetragonurus simplex* Lowe 1833:143. Type by monotypy. Synonym of *Ruvettus* Cocco 1829 (Parin & Bekker 1973:460 [ref. 7206]). Gempylidae.

Apocope Cope 1872:472 [ref. 923]. Fem. *Apocope carringtonii* Cope 1872:472. Type by subsequent designation. Type designated by Jordan & Gilbert 1877:94 [ref. 4907]. Synonym of *Rhinichthys* Agassiz 1849. Cyprinidae.

Apocryptes Osbeck 1762:130 [ref. 3311]. Masc. *Apocryptes chinensis* Osbeck 1762. Not available, apparently published in a non-binomial work but not on Official Index; based on Osbeck 1757, reprinted in 1762. Gobiidae.

Apocryptes Valenciennes in Cuvier & Valenciennes 1837:143 [ref. 1006]. Masc. *Gobius bato* Hamilton 1822:40. Type by subsequent designation. Type designated by Bleeker 1874:327 [ref. 437]. Valid (Birdsong et al. 1988:195 [ref. 7303], Murdy 1989:5 [ref. 13628]). Gobiidae.

Apocryptichthys Day 1876:302 [ref. 1081]. Masc. *Apocryptes cantoris* Day 1870:693. Type by monotypy. Synonym of *Scartelaos* Swainson 1839 (Murdy 1989:10 [ref. 13628]), with specimen in Pl. 17 a synonym of *Oxyderces* Eydoux & Souleyet 1850. Gobiidae.

Apocryptodon Bleeker 1874:327 [ref. 437]. Masc. *Apocryptes madurensis* Bleeker 1849:35. Type by original designation (also monotypic). Valid (Akihito in Masuda et al. 1984:286 [ref. 6441], Birdsong et al. 1988:195 [ref. 7303], Murdy 1989:9 [ref. 13628]). Gobiidae.

Apodastyanax Fowler 1911:422 [ref. 1383]. Masc. *Apodastyanax stewardsoni* Fowler 1911:422. Type by original designation (also monotypic). Synonym of *Ctenobrycon* Eigenmann 1908. Characidae.

Apodichthys Girard 1854:150 [ref. 5769]. Masc. *Apodichthys flavidus* Girard 1854:150. Type by subsequent designation. Type designated by Jordan & Evermann 1898:2411 [ref. 2445]. Valid (Yatsu 1981:182 [ref. 4814]). Pholidae.

Apodocreedia de Beaufort 1948:476 [ref. 240]. Fem. *Apodocreedia vanderhorsti* de Beaufort 1948:476. Type by original designation (also monotypic). Valid (Nelson 1986:736 [ref. 5698]). Creediidae.

Apodoglanis Fowler 1905:463 [ref. 1370]. Masc. *Apodoglanis furnessi* Fowler 1905:463. Type by original designation (also monotypic). Synonym of *Silurus* Linnaeus 1758 (Haig 1952:97 [ref. 12607]). Siluridae.

Apodolycus Andriashev 1979:29 [ref. 120]. Masc. *Apodolycus hureaui* Andriashev 1979:30. Type by original designation (also monotypic). Synonym of *Lycenchelys* Gill 1884 (Anderson 1988:87 [ref. 7304]). Zoarcidae.

Apodontis Bennett 1832:169 [ref. 4944]. *Apolectus immunis* Bennett 1831:146. Type by being a replacement name. Replacement for and objective synonym of *Apolectus* Bennett 1831. Synonym of *Scomberomorus* Lacepède 1801 (Collette & Russo 1984:611 [ref. 5221]). Scombridae.

Apogon Lacepède 1801:411 [ref. 2710]. Masc. *Apogon ruber* Lacepède 1801:412 (= *Mullus imberbis* Linnaeus 1758:300). Type by monotypy. Valid (Tortonese 1973:365 [ref. 7192], Fraser 1972:17 [ref. 5195], Hayashi in Masuda et al. 1984:145 [ref. 6441], Gon 1986:547 [ref. 5657], Paxton et al. 1989:545 [ref. 12442]). Apogonidae.

Apogonichthyoides Smith 1949:209 [ref. 5846]. Masc. *Amia uninotata* Smith & Radcliffe in Radcliffe 1912:436. Type by original designation (also monotypic). Synonym of *Apogon* Lacepède 1801 (Tortonese 1973:365 [ref. 7192]), subgenus *Nectamia* Jordan 1917 (Fraser 1972:17, 19 [ref. 5195]). Apogonidae.

Apogonichthys Bleeker 1854:321 [ref. 343]. Masc. *Apogonichthys perdix* Bleeker 1854:321. Type by monotypy. Valid (Fraser 1972:9 [ref. 5195], Hayashi in Masuda et al. 1984:144 [ref. 6441], Gon 1986:553 [ref. 5657], Paxton et al. 1989:551 [ref. 12442]). Apogonidae.

Apogonoides Bleeker 1849:70, 71 [ref. 316]. Masc. *Apogonoides macassariensis* Bleeker 1849:71. Type by monotypy. Status uncertain, species regarded as a nomen dubium (Fraser 1972:5 [ref. 5195]). Apogonidae.

Apogonops Ogilby 1896:23 [ref. 3269]. Masc. *Apogonops anomalus* Ogilby 1896:24. Type by monotypy. Placement uncertain (Fraser 1972:42 [ref. 5195]). Valid in Acropomatidae (Johnson 1984:464 [ref. 9681]); valid in Percichthyidae (Tominaga 1986:595 [ref. 6315], Paxton et al. 1989:510 [ref. 12442]). Acropomatidae.

Apolectus Bennett 1831:146 [ref. 5778]. Masc. *Apolectus immunis*

Bennett 1831:146. Type by subsequent designation. Apparently two included species, *Scomber maculatus* Mitchill and *A. immunis* Bennett; earliest subsequent designation not researched; type above as given by Jordan. Predates *Apolectus* Cuvier 1832. Synonym of *Scomberomorus* Lacepède 1801 (Postel 1973:473 [ref. 7208], Collette & Russo 1984:611 [ref. 5221]). Scombridae.

Apolectus Cuvier in Cuvier & Valenciennes 1832:438 [ref. 1000]. Masc. *Apolectus stromateus* Cuvier in Cuvier & Valenciennes 1832:439. Type by monotypy. Preoccupied by Bennett 1831 in fishes. Valid (Witzell 1978 [ref. 6802]); synonym of *Parastromateus* Bleeker 1865 (Smith-Vaniz 1984:530 [ref. 13664], Smith-Vaniz 1986:653 [ref. 5718]). Carangidae.

Apolemichthys (subgenus of *Holacanthus*) Fraser-Brunner 1933:579 [ref. 671]. Masc. *Holacanthus trimaculatus* Lacepède in Cuvier & Valenciennes 1831:196. Not available from 1933, no type designated or indicated after 1930 and 3 included species (Art. 13b). The genus can date to 1934 with author as Burton as published in the Zoological Record for 1834 (see Art. 13b in Appendix A). Valid (Heemstra 1984 [ref. 5298], Araga in Masuda et al. 1984:188 [ref. 6441], Smith & Heemstra 1986:624 [ref. 5714]). Pomacanthidae.

Apolinarella Fernández-Yépez 1948:22 [ref. 1316]. Fem. *Curimatus meyeri* Steindachner 1882:176. Type by original designation. Synonym of *Curimatella* Eigenmann & Eigenmann 1889 (Vari 1989:6 [ref. 9189]). Curimatidae: Curimatinae.

Apollonia Iljin 1927:133 [ref. 5613]. Fem. *Gobius melanostomus* Pallas 1811:151, 160. Type by monotypy. Synonym of *Neogobius* Iljin 1927 (Miller 1973:502 [ref. 6888]). Gobiidae.

Apomatoceros Eigenmann 1922:113 [ref. 1242]. *Apomatoceros alleni* Eigenmann 1922:113. Type by monotypy. Valid (Burgess 1989:324 [ref. 12860]). Trichomycteridae.

Apomotis (subgenus of *Lepomis*) Rafinesque 1819:420 [ref. 3590]. Fem. *Lepomis cyanellus* Rafinesque 1819:420. Type by monotypy based on information in description (also designated by Jordan 1877:35 [ref. 2374] and Jordan & Gilbert 1877:85 [ref. 4907]). Synonym of *Lepomis* Rafinesque 1819. Centrarchidae.

Apopterygion Kuiter 1986:90 [ref. 6026]. Neut. *Apopterygion alta* Kuiter 1986:90. Type by original designation (also monotypic). Valid (see Hardy 1987:266 [ref. 5960]). Tripterygiidae.

Aporops Schultz 1943:112 [ref. 3957]. Masc. *Aporops bilinearis* Schultz 1943:112. Type by original designation (also monotypic). Valid (Kendall 1984:501 [ref. 13663], Hayashi in Masuda et al. 1984:140 [ref. 6441], Smith 1986:541 [ref. 5712], Paxton et al. 1989:523 [ref. 12442] in Pseudogrammatidae). Serranidae: Grammistinae.

Apostata Heckel in Canestrini 1860:309 [ref. 712]. Masc. *Apostata calcarifer* Heckel in Canestrini 1860:309. Canestrini indicates that *A. calcarifer* may be identifiable with *Perca plumieri* Cuvier & Valenciennes; this is indefinite, so type is by monotypy. Synonym of *Conodon* Cuvier 1830. Haemulidae.

Aposturisoma Isbrücker, Britski, Nijssen & Ortega 1983:34 [ref. 5388]. Neut. *Aposturisoma myriodon* Isbrücker, Britski, Nijssen & Ortega 1983:35. Type by original designation (also monotypic). Valid (Burgess 1989:440 [ref. 12860]). Loricariidae.

Apporetochaetodon (subgenus of *Chaetodon*) Maugé & Bauchot 1984:171 [ref. 6614]. Masc. *Chaetodon nigropunctatus* Sauvage 1880:222. Type by original designation (also monotypic). Chaetodontidae.

Aprion (subgenus of *Carcharias*) Müller & Henle 1839:31 [ref. 3069]. Masc. *Carcharias (Aprion) isodon* Valenciennes in Müller & Henle 1838:32. Type by subsequent designation. Earliest type designation not researched; three included species in 1839:31. Preoccupied by Valenciennes 1830 in fishes, replaced by *Aprionodon* Gill 1861. Synonym of *Carcharhinus* Blainville 1816 (Compagno 1984:449 [ref. 6846], Cappetta 1987:121 [ref. 6348], Compagno 1988:307 [ref. 13488]). Carcharhinidae.

Aprion Valenciennes in Cuvier & Valenciennes 1830:543 [ref. 996]. Masc. *Aprion virescens* Valenciennes in Cuvier & Valenciennes 1830:544. Type by monotypy. Valid (Johnson 1980:9 [ref. 13553], Yoshino in Masuda et al. 1984:167 [ref. 6441], Allen 1985:20 [ref. 6843], Anderson 1986:573 [ref. 5634], Akazaki & Iwatsuki 1986 [ref. 6316]). Lutjanidae.

Aprionichthys Kaup 1858:104 [ref. 2578]. Masc. *Aprionichthys dumerili* Kaup 1858:104. Type by monotypy. Valid (Chapleau & Keast 1988:2799 [ref. 12625] as *Apionichthys*). Achiridae.

Aprionodon Gill 1861:59 [ref. 1766]. Masc. *Aprionodon punctatus* Gill 1861:59. Type by monotypy. Also in Gill 1862:411 [ref. 4910]. Synonym of *Carcharhinus* Blainville 1816 (Compagno 1973:23 [ref. 7163], Compagno 1984:449 [ref. 6846], Garrick 1985:1 [ref. 5654], Cappetta 1987:121 [ref. 6348], Compagno 1988:307 [ref. 13488]). Carcharhinidae.

Apristurus Garman 1913:96 [ref. 1545]. Masc. *Scylliorhinus indicus* Brauer 1906:8. Type by original designation. Compagno 1984:345 [ref. 6846] and 1988:164 [ref. 13488] believes that *Pentanchus* Smith & Radcliffe 1912 may be a senior synonym of *Apristurus*. Correct spelling for genus of type species is *Scyliorhinus*. Valid (Springer 1973:20 [ref. 7162], Nakaya 1975:22 [ref. 7083], Springer 1979:11 [ref. 4175], Compagno 1984:257 [ref. 6846], Bass 1986:88 [ref. 5635], Nakaya 1986 [ref. 6323], Nakaya 1988 [ref. 6696], Nakaya 1988 [ref. 6855], Compagno 1988:163 [ref. 13488]). Scyliorhinidae.

Aprodon Gilbert 1890:106 [ref. 1623]. Masc. *Aprodon corteziana* Gilbert 1890:107. Type by original designation (also monotypic). Valid (Toyoshima 1985:237 [ref. 5722]). Zoarcidae.

Aprognathodon Böhlke 1967:99 [ref. 602]. Masc. *Aprognathodon platyventris* Böhlke 1967:100. Type by original designation (also monotypic). Valid (McCosker 1977:62 [ref. 6836], Leiby 1984:401 [ref. 12859], McCosker et al. 1989:300 [ref. 13288]). Ophichthidae: Ophichthinae.

Aprolepis Hubbs 1921:1 [ref. 2229]. Fem. *Aprolepis barbarae* Hubbs 1921:2. Type by original designation (also monotypic). Synonym of *Gillichthys* Cooper 1863. Gobiidae.

Apsetta Kyle 1901:986 [ref. 2704]. Fem. *Apsetta thompsoni* Kyle 1901:986. Type by monotypy. Synonym of *Rhombosolea* Günther 1862 (Norman 1934:429 [ref. 6893]). Pleuronectidae: Rhombosoleinae.

Apseudobranchus Gill 1862:18 [ref. 1657]. Masc. *Otolithus toeroe* Cuvier in Cuvier & Valenciennes 1830:72. Type by original designation (also monotypic). Correct spelling for genus of type species is *Otolithes*. Synonym of *Cynoscion* Gill 1861 (Chao 1978:34 [ref. 6983]). Sciaenidae.

Apsicephalus Hollard 1857:324, 327 [ref. 2186]. Masc. *Tetraodon laevigatus* Linnaeus 1766:410. Type by monotypy. Proposed as a genus (p. 327) for seven genera or subgenera of Bibron (see p. 324), apparently only species mentioned is in caption to Pl. 5, and this is regarded as type by monotypy (type not *T. fluviatilis* as given by Jordan 1919:275). Tetraodontidae.

Apsilus Valenciennes in Cuvier & Valenciennes 1830:548 [ref. 996]. Masc. *Apsilus fuscus* Valenciennes in Cuvier & Valenciennes

1830:549. Type by monotypy. Valid (Johnson 1980:10 [ref. 13553], Allen 1985:21 [ref. 6843], Akazaki & Iwatsuki 1986 [ref. 6316]). Lutjanidae.

Apterichthys Kaup in Duméril 1856:201 [ref. 1154]. Masc. Not available, name only without description or indication as "*Apterichthys caecus*" in list of genera and species taken from Kaup manuscript. Apparently intended for *Apterichtus*. This spelling used by Bleeker 1864:36 [ref. 4860]. Ophichthidae: Ophichthinae.

Apterichtus Duméril 1806:112, 331 [ref. 1151]. Masc. *Muraena caeca* Linnaeus 1758:254. Type by being a replacement name. Replacement for *Caecilia* Lacepède 1800, preoccupied. As *Aptérichthe* Duméril on p. 112, but latinized on p. 331. Spelled *Apterichtes* and *Apterichthys* by authors. Valid (Blache et al. 1973:248 [ref. 7185], McCosker 1977:65 [ref. 6836], Bauchot in Whitehead et al. 1986:578 [ref. 13676], McCosker & Castle 1986:177 [ref. 5690], McCosker et al. 1989:317 [ref. 13288]). Ophichthidae: Ophichthinae.

Apterigia Basilewski 1852:247 [ref. 200]. Fem. *Apterigia saccogularis* Basilewski 1852:247. Type by subsequent designation. Type designated by Jordan 1919:263 [ref. 2410]. Synonym of *Monopterus* Lacepède 1800 (Rosen & Greenwood 1976:56 [ref. 7094], Daget 1986:291 [ref. 6203]). Synbranchidae.

Apterogasterus De la Pylaie 1835:532a [ref. 1086]. Masc. *Apterogasterus rostellatus* De la Pylaie 1835:532a. Type by monotypy. Original not seen; above from Jordan and Fowler. Clupeidae.

Apteronotus Lacepède 1800:208 [ref. 2709]. Masc. *Apteronotus passan* Lacepède 1800:209. Type by monotypy. Valid (Mago-Leccia 1978:14 [ref. 5489]). Gymnotidae: Apteronotinae.

Apterurus Rafinesque 1810:48, 62 [ref. 3595]. Masc. *Apterurus fabronii* Rafinesque 1810:48 (= *Raia fabroniana* Lacepède 1800:111). Type by monotypy. Synonym of *Mobula* Rafinesque 1810 (Krefft & Stehmann 1973:77 [ref. 7167], Cappetta 1987:177 [ref. 6348]). Mobulidae.

Apterygia Gray 1835:Pl. 92 (v. 2) [ref. 1878]. Fem. *Apterygia ramcarata* Gray 1835:Pl. 92. Type by monotypy. Synonym of *Raconda* Gray 1831 (Whitehead 1985:302 [ref. 5141]). Clupeidae.

Apterygocampus Weber 1913:115 [ref. 4602]. Masc. *Apterygocampus epinnulatus* Weber 1913:116. Type by monotypy. Valid (Dawson & Allen 1978:402 [ref. 1073], Dawson 1985:19 [ref. 6541]). Syngnathidae: Syngnathinae.

Apterygopectus Ojeda R. 1978:3 [ref. 3301]. *Apterygopectus avilesi* Ojeda R. 1978:5. Type by original designation (also monotypic). Synonym of *Mancopsetta* Gill 1881 (Hensley 1986:860 [ref. 5669], Hensley 1986:941 [ref. 6326]). Achiropsettidae.

Aptocyclus De la Pylaie 1835:529 [ref. 1086]. Masc. *Cyclogasterus [sic] ventricosus* Pallas 1769:15. Original not seen. Valid (Kido in Masuda et al. 1984:337 [ref. 6441]). Cyclopteridae: Cyclopterinae.

Apturus Rafinesque 1815:93 [ref. 3584]. Not available, name only; for a ray. Torpediniformes.

Aptychotrema Norman 1926:977 [ref. 3215]. Neut. *Rhinobatus (Syrrhina) bougainvillii* Valenciennes in Müller & Henle 1841:117. Type by subsequent designation. Earliest subsequent type designation not researched; possibly first designated by Sére and McEachran 1986:5 [ref. 9312]. Valid (Paxton et al. 1989:52 [ref. 12442]). Rhinobatidae: Rhinobatinae.

Apua Blyth 1860:169 [ref. 477]. Fem. *Apua fusca* Blyth 1860:169. Type by monotypy. Regarded by Kottelat 1987:371 [ref. 5962] as a simultaneous objective synonym of *Pangio* Blyth 1860, and as first reviser he selected *Pangio* over *Apua*. See also *Acantophthalmus* van Hasselt 1823. Cobitidae: Cobitinae.

Apuredoras Fernández-Yépez 1950:195 [ref. 1321]. Masc. *Apuredoras rivasi* Fernández-Yépez 1950:195. Type by original designation (also monotypic). Valid (Burgess 1989:225 [ref. 12860]). Doradidae.

Aracana (subgenus of *Ostracion*) Gray 1838:110 [ref. 1884]. Fem. Dates to Gray 1833 [ref. 1878] as *Acarana*. In 1838 there were 5 included species; type designated by Bleeker 1866:15 [ref. 417] if needed. Above spelling is apparently an incorrect subsequent spelling of *Acarana* and not a new genus name. Treated as valid with this spelling (Tyler 1980:205 [ref. 4477], Winterbottom & Tyler 1983:902 [ref. 5320], Arai 1983:202 [ref. 14249]). Ostraciidae: Aracaninae.

Aracanostracion Smith 1949:354 [ref. 4078]. Neut. *Aracanostracion rosapinto* Smith 1949:355. Type by original designation (also monotypic). Synonym of *Kentrocapros* Kaup 1855 (Matsuura & Yamakawa 1982:40 [ref. 5504], Winterbottom & Tyler 1983:902 [ref. 5320]). Ostraciidae: Aracaninae.

Araias Jordan & Starks 1904:624 [ref. 2526]. Masc. *Araias ariommus* Jordan & Starks 1904:624. Type by monotypy. Synonym of *Dexistes* Jordan & Starks 1904 (Norman 1934:347 [ref. 6893]). Pleuronectidae: Pleuronectinae.

Araiophos Grey 1961:463 [ref. 1905]. Masc. *Araiophos gracilis* Grey 1961:465. Type by original designation (also monotypic). Valid (Weitzman 1974:472 [ref. 5174], Ahlstrom et al. 1984:185 [ref. 13643], Weitzman 1986:254 [ref. 6287]). Sternoptychidae: Maurolicinae.

Aramaca (subgenus of *Citharichthys*) Jordan & Goss in Jordan 1885:921 [133] [ref. 2385]. Fem. *Hemirhombus paetulus* Bean in Jordan & Gilbert 1882:304. Type by original designation. Synonym of *Syacium* Ranzani 1842 (Norman 1934:129 [ref. 6893]). Paralichthyidae.

Arapaima Müller 1843:326 [ref. 3063]. Fem. *Sudis gigas* Schinz in Cuvier 1822:305. Type by being a replacement name. Replacement for *Sudis* Cuvier. On Official List (Opinion 1132). Valid. Osteoglossidae: Heterotidinae.

Arbaciosa Jordan & Evermann in Jordan 1896:230 [ref. 2395]. Fem. *Gobiesox humeralis* Gilbert 1890:95. Type by original designation. Synonym of *Tomicodon* Brisout de Barneville 1846 (Briggs 1955:57 [ref. 637]). Gobiesocidae: Gobiesocinae.

Archaeomyripristis (subgenus of *Myripristis*) Greenfield 1974:17 [ref. 7142]. Fem. *Myripristis trachyacron* Bleeker 1863:24. Type by original designation. Appeared first in Greenfield 1966 (abstract, name only [ref. 1890]). Holocentridae.

Archamia Gill 1863:81 [ref. 1679]. Fem. *Apogon bleekeri* Günther 1859:245. Type by original designation, Gill's style of including type in parentheses in key (also monotypic). Valid (Fraser 1972:25 [ref. 5195], Hayashi in Masuda et al. 1984:149 [ref. 6441], Gon 1986:554 [ref. 5657], Paxton et al. 1989:551 [ref. 12442]). Apogonidae.

Archaulus Gilbert & Burke 1912:36 [ref. 1634]. Masc. *Archaulus biseriatus* Gilbert & Burke 1912:36. Type by original designation (also monotypic). Valid (Washington et al. 1984:442 [ref. 13660]). Cottidae.

Archeria Nichols 1949:5 [ref. 3182]. Fem. *Archeria jamesonoides* Nichols 1949:6. Type by monotypy. Synonym of *Hephaestus* De Vis 1884 (Vari 1978:280 [ref. 4514]). Terapontidae.

Archerichthys (subgenus of *Leiopotherapon*) Whitley 1951:398 [ref. 4715]. Masc. *Archeria jamesonoides* Nichols 1949:6. Type by being a replacement name. Replacement for *Archeria* Nichols 1949, preoccupied by Case 1915 in reptiles. Synonym of *Hephaestus* De Vis 1884 (Vari 1978:280 [ref. 4514]). Terapontidae.

Archiaphyosemion (subgenus of *Aphyosemion*) Radda 1977:214 [ref. 3580]. Neut. *Aphyosemion guineense* Daget 1954:300. Type by original designation. Synonym of *Aphyosemion* Myers 1924 (Wildekamp et al. 1986:197 [ref. 6198]), but as a valid subgenus (Parenti 1981:477 [ref. 7066]). Aplocheilidae: Aplocheilinae.

Archicheir Eigenmann 1909:46 [ref. 1222]. Fem. *Archicheir minutus* Eigenmann 1909:46. Type by monotypy. Synonym of *Nannostomus* Günther 1872 (Weitzman & Cobb 1975:3 [ref. 7134]). Lebiasinidae: Pyrrhulininae.

Archistes Jordan & Gilbert in Jordan & Evermann 1898:1881, 1900 [ref. 2444]. Masc. *Archistes plumarius* Jordan & Gilbert in Jordan & Evermann 1898:1900. Type by original designation (also monotypic). Also in Jordan & Gilbert 1899:454 [ref. 2478]. Valid (Washington et al. 1984:442 [ref. 13660]). Cottidae.

Archocentrus (subgenus of *Heros*) Gill 1877:186 [ref. 1714]. Masc. *Heros centrarchus* Gill & Bransford 1877:185. Type by monotypy. Cichlidae.

Archolaemus Korringa 1970:267 [ref. 2662]. Masc. *Archolaemus blax* Korringa 1970:268. Type by original designation (also monotypic). Valid (see Mago-Leccia 1978:14 [ref. 5489]). Gymnotidae: Sternopyginae.

Archomenidia Jordan & Hubbs 1919:54 [ref. 2485]. Fem. *Atherinichthys sallei* Regan 1903:60. Type by original designation (also monotypic). Valid (Chernoff 1981 [ref. 6824], Chernoff & Miller 1982 [ref. 8494]); synonym of *Atherinella* Steindachner 1875 (Chernoff 1986:240 [ref. 5847]). Atherinidae: Menidiinae.

Archoperca (subgenus of *Mycteroperca*) Jordan & Evermann 1896:1169, 1171 [ref. 2443]. Fem. *Mycteroperca boulengeri* Jordan & Starks in Jordan 1895:445. Type by original designation (also monotypic). Synonym of *Mycteroperca* Gill 1862 (Smith 1971:171 [ref. 14102], Randall et al. 1989:414 [ref. 12737]). Serranidae: Epinephelinae.

Archoplites Gill 1861:165 [ref. 1775]. Masc. *Ambloplites interruptus* Girard 1854:129. Type by monotypy. Valid. Centrarchidae.

Archosargus Gill 1865:266 [ref. 1707]. Masc. *Sparus probatocephalus* Walbaum 1792:295. Type by monotypy. Valid. Sparidae.

Archoscion Gill 1862:18 [ref. 1657]. Masc. *Otolithus analis* Jenyns 1842:164. Type by original designation (also monotypic). Correct spelling for genus of type species is *Otolithes*. Synonym of *Cynoscion* Gill 1861 (Chao 1978:34 [ref. 6983]). Sciaenidae.

Arcos Schultz 1944:71 [ref. 3961]. Masc. *Gobiesox erythrops* Gilbert 1882:360. Type by original designation. Valid (Briggs 1955:81 [ref. 637]). Gobiesocidae: Gobiesocinae.

Arctogadus Drjagin 1932:151 [ref. 1140]. Masc. *Arctogadus borisovi* Drjagin 1932:151. Type by original designation. Valid (Svetovidov 1973:304 [ref. 7169], Fahay & Markle 1984:266 [ref. 13653], Svetovidov in Whitehead et al. 1986:682 [ref. 13676]). Gadidae.

Arctoraja (subgenus of *Breviraja*) Ishiyama 1958:337 [ref. 2308]. Fem. *Raja smirnovi* Soldatov & Pavlenko 1915:162. Type by original designation. Rajidae.

Arctoscopus Jordan & Evermann 1896:464 [ref. 2442]. Masc. *Trichodon japonicus* Steindachner 1881:182. Type by original designation (also monotypic). Valid (Amaoka in Masuda et al. 1984:221 [ref. 6441]). Trichodontidae.

Arctozenus Gill 1864:188 [ref. 1699]. Masc. *Paralepis borealis* Reinhardt 1832:115. Type by original designation (also monotypic). Post 1973:208 suggests in his synonymy that this genus is based on a misidentified type species, with Gill referring to *borealis* of Krøyer in Gaimard (not of Reinhardt). Misspelled *Actozenus* in Zoological Record for 1864. Valid (Post 1973:208 [ref. 7182], Post 1987:79 [ref. 6225]). Paralepididae.

Ardeapiscis Whitley 1931:314 [ref. 4672]. Masc. *Hemirhamphus welsbyi* Ogilby 1908:91. Type by original designation (also monotypic). Correct spelling for genus of type species is *Hemiramphus*. Synonym of *Hemiramphus* Cuvier 1816 (Parin et al. 1980:111 [ref. 6895]). Hemiramphidae.

Arelia Kaup 1858:107 [ref. 2579]. Fem. *Pleuronectes arel* Bloch & Schneider 1801:159. Type by subsequent designation. Earliest subsequent designation not researched; *aral* listed as type by Jordan 1919:282 [ref. 2410]. Synonym of *Cynoglossus* Hamilton 1822 (Menon 1977:16 [ref. 7071], Desoutter 1986:432 [ref. 6212]); valid (Ochiai in Masuda et al. 1984:355 [ref. 6441]). Cynoglossidae: Cynoglossinae.

Areliscus Jordan & Snyder 1900:380 [ref. 2502]. Masc. *Cynoglossus joyneri* Günther 1878:486. Type by monotypy. Synonym of *Cynoglossus* Hamilton 1822 (Menon 1977:16 [ref. 7071], Desoutter 1986:432 [ref. 6212]). Cynoglossidae: Cynoglossinae.

Arengus Cornide 1788:91 [ref. 5057]. *Arengus minor* Cornide 1788:91. Type by monotypy. Not available, published in a rejected work (Opinion 799); in synonymy of *Sardina* Antipa 1904; name on Official Index. Clupeidae.

Arenichthys Beebe & Tee-Van 1938:301 [ref. 249]. Masc. *Arenichthys apterus* Beebe 1938:301. Type by original designation (also monotypic). Synonym of *Chlopsis* Rafinesque 1810 (Smith 1989:92 [ref. 13285]). Chlopsidae.

Arenigobius Whitley 1930:122 [ref. 4669]. Masc. *Gobius bifrenatus* Kner 1865:177. Type by original designation. Valid (Scott 1976:191 [ref. 7055]); synonym of *Gobionellus* Girard 1858 (Maugé 1986 [ref. 6218]), but see *Ctenogobius*. Gobiidae.

Argentina Linnaeus 1758:315 [ref. 2787]. Fem. *Argentina sphyraena* Linnaeus 1758:315. Type by monotypy. Valid (Cohen 1973:152 [ref. 6589], Cohen in Whitehead et al. 1984:387 [ref. 13675], Ahlstrom et al. 1984:156 [ref. 13627], Uyeno in Masuda et al. 1984:40 [ref. 6441], Cohen 1986:215 [ref. 5646], Paxton et al. 1989:166 [ref. 12442]). Argentinidae.

Arges Valenciennes in Cuvier & Valenciennes 1840:333 [ref. 1008]. Masc. *Arges sabalo* Valenciennes in Cuvier & Valenciennes 1840:335. Type by monotypy. Preoccupied by Goldfuss 1839 in Trilobites and by de Haan 1833 in Crustacea. Astroblepidae.

Argo Döderlein in Steindachner & Döderlein 1883:242, P. 7 [ref. 4246]. *Argo steindachneri* Döderlein in Steindachner & Döderlein 1884:174. Type by monotypy. Appeared first in figure caption to Pl. 7; appeared as name in synonymy of *Brama longipinnis* in Steindachner & Döderlein 1884:174-175 [ref. 4247]). Apparently preoccupied by Herrmannsen 1846 in Mollusca, perhaps also by Bohadsch 1761 in Mollusca [not researched]. Synonym of *Taractichthys* Mead & Maul 1958 (Mead 1972:83 [ref. 6976], Mead 1973:397 [ref. 7199]). Bramidae.

Argonectes Böhlke & Myers 1956:2 [ref. 608]. Masc. *Argonectes scapularis* Böhlke & Myers 1956:2. Type by original designation. Valid (Roberts 1974:432 [ref. 6872], Géry 1977:198 [ref. 1597]). Hemiodontidae: Hemiodontinae.

Argopleura (subgenus of *Bryconamericus*) Eigenmann 1913:10 [ref. 1229]. Fem. *Bryconamericus magdalenensis* Eigenmann 1913:14.

Type by original designation. Valid (Géry 1977:358 [ref. 1597], Weitzman & S. Fink 1985:1 et seq. [ref. 5203]). Characidae: Glandulocaudinae.

Argoraja (subgenus of *Pavoraja*) Whitley 1940:190 [ref. 4700]. Fem. *Raja polyommata* Ogilby 1910:86. Type by original designation (also monotypic). Synonym of *Raja* Linnaeus 1758. Rajidae.

Argyctius Rafinesque 1810:55 [ref. 3594]. Masc. *Argyctius quadrimaculatus* Rafinesque 1810:55. Type by monotypy. Synonym of *Trachipterus* Goüan 1770 (Palmer 1973:330 [ref. 7195], Scott 1983:172 [ref. 5346]). Trachipteridae.

Argylepes (subgenus of *Siganus*) Swainson 1839:247 [ref. 4303]. Fem. *Siganus (Argylepes) indica* Swainson 1839:247. Type by monotypy. Misspelled *Argyrlepes* by Jordan 1919:200 [ref. 2410]. *Argyrolepis* Agassiz 1846:33 [ref. 64] is an unjustified emendation. Synonym of *Leiognathus* Lacepède 1802. Leiognathidae.

Argyrea DeKay 1842:141 [ref. 1098]. Fem. *Atherina notata* Mitchill 1815:446. Type apparently by subsequent designation. Name mentioned (to include several American species) but not adopted by DeKay; unclear from text if all species mentioned would belong to *Argyrea*. Preoccupied by Billberg 1820 in Lepidoptera, apparently not replaced. Synonym of *Menidia* Bonaparte 1836. Atherinidae: Menidiinae.

Argyreiosus Lacepède 1802:566 [ref. 4929]. Masc. *Zeus vomer* Linnaeus 1758:286. Type by monotypy. Spelled *Argyreios*, *Argyreyosus*, *Argyriosus* and *Argyregosus* in early literature. Synonym of *Selene* Lacepède 1802 (see Opinion 569). Carangidae.

Argyreus Heckel 1843:1040 [ref. 2066]. Masc. *Cyprinus atronasus* Mitchill 1815:460. Type by subsequent designation. Type designated by Bleeker 1863:31 [ref. 4859] and 1863:209 [ref. 397]. Preoccupied by Scopoli 1777 in Lepidoptera, not replaced. Synonym of *Rhinichthys* Agassiz 1849. Cyprinidae.

Argyripnus Gilbert & Cramer 1897:414 [ref. 1635]. Masc. *Argyripnus ephippiatus* Gilbert & Cramer 1897:414. Type by monotypy. Valid (Witzell 1973:115 [ref. 7172], Weitzman 1974:472 [ref. 5174], Badcock in Whitehead et al. 1984:303 [ref. 13675], Ahlstrom et al. 1984:185 [ref. 13643], Weitzman 1986:254 [ref. 6287], Paxton et al. 1989:190 [ref. 12442]). Sternoptychidae: Maurolicinae.

Argyrocottus Herzenstein 1892:219 [ref. 5037]. Masc. *Argyrocottus zanderi* Herzenstein 1892:219. Type by monotypy. Valid (Neyelov 1979:115, 141 [ref. 3152], Washington et al. 1984:442 [ref. 13660], Yabe in Masuda et al. 1984:327 [ref. 6441], Yabe 1985:111 [ref. 11522]). Cottidae.

Argyropelecus Cocco 1829:146 [ref. 857]. Masc. *Argyropelecus hemigymnus* Cocco 1829:146. Type by monotypy. Species originally as *emigymnus*; usually written *hemigymnus*. Valid (Baird 1973:123 [ref. 7173], Weitzman 1974:472 [ref. 5174], Badcock in Whitehead et al. 1984:304 [ref. 13675], Ahlstrom et al. 1984:185 [ref. 13643], Fujii in Masuda et al. 1984:48 [ref. 6441], Baird 1986:255 [ref. 6288], Paxton et al. 1989:191 [ref. 12442]). Sternoptychidae: Sternoptychinae.

Argyrops (subgenus of *Chrysophrys*) Swainson 1839:171, 221 [ref. 4303]. Masc. *Sparus spinifer* Forsskål 1775:32. Type by monotypy. Valid (Akazaki in Masuda et al. 1984:177 [ref. 6441], Smith & Smith 1986:581 [ref. 5710]). Sparidae.

Argyrosomus Agassiz 1850:339 [ref. 66]. Masc. *Salmo clupeaformis* Mitchill 1818:321. Type by subsequent designation. Earliest type designation not researched. Possibly based on a misidentification. Preoccupied by De la Pylaie 1835 in fishes. Synonym of *Coregonus* Linnaeus 1758. Salmonidae: Coregoninae.

Argyrosomus De la Pylaie 1835:532 [ref. 1086]. Masc. *Argyrosomus procerus* De la Pylaie 1835:532 (= *Cheilodipterus aquila* Lacepède 1803:684.). Type by monotypy. Original not seen. On Official List (Opinion 988). Valid (Trewavas 1973:397 [ref. 7201], Trewavas 1977:322 [ref. 4459], Okamura in Masuda et al. 1984:162 [ref. 6441], Daget & Trewavas 1986:333 [ref. 6211], Heemstra 1986:616 [ref. 5660]). Sciaenidae.

Argyrotaenia Gill 1861:40 [ref. 1766]. Fem. *Ammodytes vittatus* DeKay 1842:317. Type by monotypy. Synonym of *Ammodytes* Linnaeus 1758. Ammodytidae.

Argyrozona (subgenus of *Polysteganus*) Smith 1938:300 [ref. 4067]. Fem. *Dentex argyrozona* Valenciennes in Cuvier & Valenciennes 1830:235. Type by monotypy (also by absolute tautonymy). Valid (Smith & Smith 1986:582 [ref.5710]). Sparidae.

Arhynchobatis Waite 1909:150 [ref. 4564]. Fem. *Arhynchobatis asperrimus* Waite 1909:150. Type by monotypy. Rajidae.

Ariodes (subgenus of *Bagrus*) Müller & Troschel 1849:9 [ref. 3073]. Masc. *Bagrus (Ariodes) arenarius* Müller & Troschel 1849. Type by subsequent designation. Type designated by Bleeker 1862:8 [ref. 393] and 1863:91 [ref. 401]. Valid (Taylor 1986:212 [ref. 6282]). Ariidae.

Ariomma Jordan & Snyder 1904:942 [ref. 2518]. Neut. *Ariomma lurida* Jordan & Snyder 1904:943. Type by original designation (also monotypic). Valid (Haedrich 1967:90 [ref. 5357], Aboussouan 1983:3 [ref. 12850], Karrer 1984 [ref. 12817], Horn 1984:628 [ref. 13637], Nakabo in Masuda et al. 1984:235 [ref. 6441], Haedrich 1986:847 [ref. 5659], Ajiad & Mahasneh 1986 [ref. 6760]). Ariommatidae.

Ariopsis Gill 1861:56 [ref. 1766]. Fem. *Arius milberti* Valenciennes in Cuvier & Valenciennes 1840:74. Type by monotypy. Ariidae.

Ariosoma Swainson 1838:220 [ref. 4302]. Neut. *Ophisoma acuta* Swainson 1839:396. Type by subsequent designation. Appeared first without included species, renamed *Ophisoma* by Swainson 1839:334 [ref. 4303] with 2 included species. Type apparenty designated first by Bleeker 1864:20 [ref. 4860] through *Ophisoma* (Art. 67(h)). Valid (Blache et al. 1973:240 [ref. 7185], Karrer 1982:11 [ref. 5679], Asano in Masuda et al. 1984:27 [ref. 6441], Bauchot & Saldanha in Whitehead et al. 1986:567 [ref. 13676], Castle 1986:162 [ref. 5644], Smith 1989:491 [ref. 13285]). Congridae: Bathymyrinae.

Ariscopus Jordan & Snyder 1902:479 [ref. 2513]. Masc. *Ariscopus iburius* Jordan & Snyder 1902:479. Type by original designation (also monotypic). Valid (Mees 1960:47 [ref. 11931]); synonym of *Gnathagnus* Gill 1861 (Pietsch 1989:294 [ref. 12541], Kishimoto 1989:303 [ref. 13562]). Uranoscopidae.

Aristeus Castelnau 1878:141 [ref. 763]. Masc. *Aristeus fitzroyensis* Castelnau 1878:141. Type by subsequent designation. Type designated by Jordan & Hubbs 1919:24 [ref. 2485]. Preoccupied by Duvernoy 1840 in Crustacea, replaced by *Rhombatractus* Gill 1894. Synonym of *Melanotaenia* Gill 1862 (Allen 1980:474 [ref. 99], Allen & Cross 1982:44 [ref. 6251]). Atherinidae: Melanotaeniinae.

Aristichthys Oshima 1919:246 [ref. 3312]. Masc. *Leuciscus nobilis* Richardson (ex Gray) 1844:140. Type by original designation (also monotypic). Synonym of *Hypophthalmichthys* Bleeker 1859 (Howes 1981:45 [ref. 14200]); valid (Yang 1964:223 [ref. 13500], Sawada in Masuda et al. 1984:58 [ref. 6441], Bogutskaya 1987:936

[ref. 13521], Bogutskaya 1988:108 [ref. 12754], Chen & Li in Chu & Chen 1989:98 [ref. 13584]). Cyprinidae.

Aristochromis Trewavas 1935:(69) 117 [ref. 4451]. Masc. *Aristochromis christyi* Trewavas 1935:117. Type by monotypy. Valid (Ribbink et al. 1983:244 [ref. 13555], Eccles & Trewavas 1989:264 [ref. 13547]). Cichlidae.

Aristommata Holmberg 1893:95 [ref. 5977]. Fem. *Aristommata inexpectata* Holmberg 1893:96. Type by monotypy. Appeared first in Holmberg 1893:95 [ref. 2193] as name only at end of article preceding Holmberg 1893:96 [ref. 5977]. Misspelled *Aristomata* by Eigenmann 1910:412 [ref. 1224]. Valid (Isbrücker 1980:87 [ref. 2303]). Loricariidae.

Aristostomias Zugmayer 1913:1 [ref. 5032]. Masc. *Aristostomias grimaldii* Zugmayer 1913:1. Type by monotypy. Also as Zugmayer 1940:201 [ref. 4849]. Valid (Morrow 1964:531 [ref. 6958], Goodyear 1973:142 [ref. 7176], Kawaguchi & Moser 1984:171 [ref. 13642], Gibbs in Whitehead et al. 1984:367 [ref. 13675], Fujii in Masuda et al. 1984:53 [ref. 6441], Fink 1985:11 [ref. 5171], Goodyear & Gibbs 1986:235 [ref. 5658]). Malacosteidae.

Arius Valenciennes in Cuvier & Valenciennes 1840:53 [ref. 1008]. Masc. *Pimelodus arius* Hamilton 1822:170, 376. Type by absolute tautonymy. Valid (Sawada in Masuda et al. 1984:60 [ref. 6441], Taylor 1986:153 [ref. 6195], Kailola 1986 [ref. 6312], Burgess 1989:168 [ref. 12860], Paxton et al. 1989:218 [ref. 12442], Kottelat 1989:15 [ref. 13605], Roberts 1989:110 [ref. 6439]). Ariidae.

Arizonichthys Nichols 1940:1 [ref. 3181]. Masc. *Arizonichthys psammophilus* Nichols 1940:1. Type by monotypy. Synonym of *Poeciliopsis* Regan 1913. Poeciliidae.

Arlina Girard 1859:64 [ref. 1821]. Fem. *Arlina effulgens* Girard 1859:64. Type by monotypy. Synonym of subgenus *Boleosoma* DeKay 1842 of genus *Etheostoma* Rafinesque 1819 (Collette & Banarescu 1977:1456 [ref. 5845]). Percidae.

Armatogobio Taranetz 1937:113, 115 [ref. 4340]. Masc. *Saurogobio dabryi* Bleeker 1937:113. Type by original designation (also monotypic). Synonym of *Saurogobio* Bleeker 1870 (Banarescu & Nalbant 1973:283 [ref. 173]). Cyprinidae.

Arndha Deraniyagala 1931:132 [ref. 1116]. Fem. *Gymnothorax zebra* Shaw 1797:Pl. 322. Type by original designation (also monotypic). Muraenidae: Muraeninae.

Arnillo Jordan, Evermann & Tanaka 1927:668 [ref. 2454]. *Arnillo auricilla* Jordan, Evermann & Tanaka 1927:668. Type by original designation (also monotypic). Synonym of *Pristipomoides* Bleeker 1852 (Allen 1985:141 [ref. 6843], Akazaki & Okazaki 1987:326 [ref. 6699]). Lutjanidae.

Arnion Gistel 1848:X [ref. 1822]. Neut. *Mugil cephalus* Linnaeus 1758:316. Type by being a replacement name. Unneeded and unexplained replacement for *Mugil* Linnaeus 1758. Mugilidae.

Arnoglossus Bleeker 1862:427 [ref. 388]. Masc. *Pleuronectes arnoglossus* Bloch & Schneider 1801:157. Type by monotypy (also by absolute tautonymy). Valid (Norman 1934:173 [ref. 6893], Amaoka 1969:185 [ref. 105], Nielsen 1973:621 [ref. 6885], Ahlstrom et al. 1984:642 [ref. 13641], Amaoka in Masuda et al. 1984:349 [ref. 6441], Nielsen in Whitehead et al. 1986:1294 [ref. 13677], Hensley 1986:855 [ref. 5669], Hensley 1986:941 [ref. 6326]). Bothidae: Bothinae.

Arnoldichthys Myers 1926:174 [ref. 3095]. Masc. *Petersius spilopterus* Boulenger 1909:239. Type by original designation (also monotypic). Valid (Poll 1967:65 [ref. 3529], Géry 1977:50 [ref. 1597], Paugy 1984:162 [ref. 6183]). Alestiidae.

Arothron (subgenus of *Tetrodon [=Tetraodon]*) Müller 1841:252 [ref. 3061]. *Arothron testudinarius* Müller 1841:252. Type by monotypy. Possibly appeared in Müller 1839 (Abh. Akad. Wiss. Berlin, p. 196) (see Leis & Bauchot 1984:85 [ref. 12539]). Apparently valid (see Matsuura & Toda 1981 [ref. 5537]); valid (Tyler 1980:341 [ref. 4477], Arai 1983:207 [ref. 14249], Matsuura in Masuda et al. 1984:364 [ref. 6441], Randall 1985 [ref. 6719], Smith & Heemstra 1986:896 [ref. 5714]). Tetraodontidae.

Arotrolepis Fraser-Brunner 1941:184 [ref. 1494]. Fem. *Monacanthus sulcatus* Hollard 1854. Type by original designation. Valid (Matsuura 1979:164 [ref. 7019], Tyler 1980:183 [ref. 4477], Arai 1983:199 [ref. 14249]). Monacanthidae.

Arrhamphus Günther 1866:276 [ref. 1983]. Masc. *Arrhamphus sclerolepis* Günther 1866:277. Type by monotypy. Valid (Parin et al. 1980:94 [ref. 6895], Collette et al. 1984:352 [ref. 11422], Paxton et al. 1989:336 [ref. 12442]). Hemiramphidae.

Arripis Jenyns 1840:13 [ref. 2344]. Fem. *Centropristes georgianus* Valenciennes in Cuvier & Valenciennes 1831:338. Type by monotypy, second species doubtfully included; type also designated by Richardson 1842:120 [ref. 12568]. Correct spelling for genus of type species is *Centropristis*. Valid. Arripidae.

Artedidraco Lönnberg 1905:39 [ref. 2839]. Masc. *Artedidraco mirus* Lönnberg 1905:40. Type by original designation (also monotypic). Valid (Eakin 1981:138 [ref. 14216], Stevens et al. 1984:563 [ref. 13633]). Harpagiferidae.

Artediellichthys (subgenus of *Artediellus*) Taranetz 1941:434 [ref. 5535]. Masc. *Artediellina nigripinnis* Schmidt 1937:563. Type by subsequent monotypy. Needs more work; no species included in 1941:434. Valid (Neyelov 1979:116, 159 [ref. 3152]). Cottidae.

Artediellina Taranetz 1937:117 Fem. *Artediellus antilope* Schmidt 1937:564. Type by monotypy. Original not examined. Valid (Neyelov 1979:116 [ref. 3152]). Cottidae.

Artediellscus Fedorov 1973:20, 41 [ref. 5567]. Masc. *Artedielliscus aleutianus* Nyelov 1973. Not available. Appeared in list as *Artedielliscus aleutianus* Nyelov gen. et sp. n. on pp. 20 and 41. Also in Fedorov 1973:64 [ref. 5567] as name only in list. Apparently never published in an available way; not mentioned by Neelov 1979 [ref. 3152]. In list (Washington et al. 1984:442 [ref. 13660]). Cottidae.

Artedielloides Soldatov 1922:352 [ref. 4160]. Masc. *Artedielloides auriculatus* Soldatov 1922:353. Type by original designation (also monotypic). Valid (Neyelov 1979:116, 159 [ref. 3152]). Cottidae.

Artediellops (subgenus of *Artediellus*) Neelov 1979:88, 155 [ref. 3152]. Masc. *Artediellus dydymovi* Soldatov 1915. Type by original designation. Synonym of *Artediellus* Jordan 1887, but as a valid subgenus (Nelson 1986:34 [ref. 5808]). Cottidae.

Artediellus Jordan 1885:898 [110] [ref. 2385]. Masc. *Cottus uncinatus* Reinhardt in Orsted 1835. Type by original designation (also monotypic). Proposed as a genus or subgenus, but treated as a genus. Valid (Neyelov 1973:593 [ref. 7219], Neyelov 1979:116, 153 [ref. 3152], Washington et al. 1984:442 [ref. 13660], Yabe in Masuda et al. 1984:327 [ref. 6441], Yabe 1985:111 [ref. 11522], Fedorov in Whitehead et al. 1986:1244 [ref. 13677], Nelson 1986 [ref. 5808]). Cottidae.

Artedius Girard 1856:134 [ref. 1809]. Masc. *Scorpaenichthys lateralis* Girard 1854:145. Type by subsequent designation. Type designated by Jordan & Evermann 1896:1902 [ref. 2444]. Valid (Bolin 1944:41, 53 [ref. 6379], Washington et al. 1984:442 [ref. 13660], Yabe 1985:111 [ref. 11522], Washington 1986 [ref. 5202],

Begle 1989 [ref. 12739]). Cottidae.

Arthrophallus (subgenus of *Gambusia*) Hubbs 1926:25, 38 [ref. 2233]. Masc. *Heterandria patruelis* Baird & Girard 1854:390. Type by original designation (also monotypic). Synonym of *Gambusia* Poey 1854 (Rosen & Bailey 1963:90 [ref. 7067]), as a valid subgenus (Rivas 1963:333 [ref. 3761], Parenti & Rauchenberger 1989:9 [ref. 13538]). Poeciliidae.

Artisia de Beaufort 1939:17 [ref. 237]. Fem. *Artisia festiva* de Beaufort 1939:17. Type by monotypy. Labridae.

Aruma (subgenus of *Gobiosoma*) Ginsburg 1933:16 [ref. 1800]. *Gobiosoma occidentale* Ginsburg 1933:16. Type by original designation. Misspelled *Amma* in Zoological Record for 1933. Valid (Birdsong et al. 1988:189 [ref. 7303]). Gobiidae.

Arusetta (subgenus of *Heteropyge*) Fraser-Brunner 1933:572 [ref. 671]. Fem. *Chaetodon asfur* Forsskål 1775:61. Type by monotypy. Pomacanthidae.

Asarcenchelys McCosker 1985:12 [ref. 5238]. Fem. *Asarcenchelys longimanus* McCosker 1985:12. Type by original designation (also monotypic). Valid (McCosker et al. 1989:276 [ref. 13288]). Ophichthidae: Myrophinae.

Ascelichthys Jordan & Gilbert 1880:264 [ref. 2367]. Masc. *Ascelichthys rhodorus* Jordan & Gilbert 1880:264. Type by monotypy. Valid (Bolin 1944:88 [ref. 6379], Washington et al. 1984:442 [ref. 13660], Yabe 1985:111 [ref. 11522]). Cottidae.

Ascomana Castle 1967:5 [ref. 770]. *Ascomana eximia* Castle 1967:7. Type by original designation (also monotypic). Based on leptocephalus larva. Of uncertain relationships (Smith 1989:981 [ref. 13285]). Synonym of *Coloconger* Alcock 1889 (Castle, pers. comm.). Colocongridae.

Asellus Minding 1832:83 [ref. 3022]. Masc. Name apparently not in current literature. Three included species (*merlangus*, *carbonarius*, and *polacchius*). Moridae.

Asellus Plumier in Lacepède 1800:589 (footnote) [ref. 2709]. Masc. Not available, name mentioned in passing in synonymy without description. See also remarks on footnotes in Lacepède under Opinion 89 in Appendix B. Eleotridae.

Asellus Valenciennes in Webb & Berthelot 1838:Pl. 14 [ref. 4502]. Masc. *Asellus canariensis* Valenciennes 1838:Pl. 14. Type by monotypy. In text in 1843:76, plate in 1838. Preoccupied by G. St. Hilaire 1762 in Crustacea (not Plumier in Lacepède 1800 in fishes, not available); according to Fowler (MS): "replaced by *Cerdo* Gistel 1848:VIII" sic Neave 1939:644 [ref. 12569]. Synonym of *Mora* Risso 1826. Moridae.

Asemichthys Gilbert 1912:215 [ref. 9276]. Masc. *Asemichthys taylori* Gilbert 1912:215. Type by original designation (also monotypic). Misspelled *Asematichthys* by Jordan, Evermann & Clark 1930:390 [ref. 6476]. Synonym of *Radulinus* Gilbert 1891 (Eschmeyer & Herald 1983:181 [ref. 9277]; valid (Washington et al. 1984:442 [ref. 13660], Yabe 1985:111 [ref. 11522]). Cottidae.

Aseraggodes Kaup 1858:103 [ref. 2578]. Masc. *Aseraggodes guttulatus* Kaup 1858. Type by subsequent designation. Earliest subsequent designation found is by Jordan 1919:282 [ref. 2410]. Misspelled *Aserragodes* in literature. Valid (Ochiai in Masuda et al. 1984:354 [ref. 6441], Randall & Meléndez C. 1987 [ref. 9173], Chapleau & Keast 1988:2799 [ref. 12625]). Soleidae.

Asiphonichthys Cope 1894:67 [ref. 966]. Masc. *Asiphonichthys stenopterus* Cope 1894:67. Type by monotypy. Synonym of *Charax* Scopoli 1777 (Géry 1977:310 [ref. 1597], Malabarba 1989:132 [ref. 14217] based on placement of type species). Characidae.

Askoldia Pavlenko 1910:50 [ref. 3393]. Fem. *Askoldia variegata* Pavlenko 1910:50. Type by monotypy. Valid (Amaoka & Miki in Masuda et al. 1984:301 [ref. 6441] as *Ascoldia*). Pholidae.

Aspasma Jordan & Fowler 1902:414 [ref. 2458]. *Lepadogaster minimus* Döderlein 1887:270. Type by original designation. Valid (Allen [L. G.] 1984:629 [ref. 13673], Yoshino in Masuda et al. 1984:341 [ref. 6441], Briggs 1955:135 [ref. 637]). Gobiesocidae: Gobiesocinae.

Aspasmichthys Briggs 1955:133 [ref. 637]. Masc. *Aspasma ciconiae* Jordan & Fowler 1902:415. Type by original designation (also monotypic). Valid (Allen [L. G.] 1984:629 [ref. 13673], Yoshino in Masuda et al. 1984:341 [ref. 6441]). Gobiesocidae: Gobiesocinae.

Aspasmodes Smith 1957:397 [ref. 4116]. Masc. *Aspasmodes briggsi* Smith 1957:398. Type by original designation (also monotypic). Gobiesocidae: Gobiesocinae.

Aspasmogaster Waite 1907:315 [ref. 4563]. Fem. *Crepidogaster tasmaniensis* Günther 1861:507. Type by being a replacement name. Replacement for *Crepidogaster* Günther 1861, preoccupied by Boheman 1848 in Coleoptera. Misspelled *Aspasmagaster* by Jordan 1920:526 [ref. 4905]. Valid (Briggs 1955:49 [ref. 637], Scott 1976:182 [ref. 7055], Hutchins 1984 [ref. 5230]). Gobiesocidae: Gobiesocinae.

Asper Schaeffer 1761:59 [ref. 3910]. Masc. Not available, published in a rejected work on Official Index (Opinion 345). Original not examined. In the synonymy of *Zingel* Cloquet 1817 (Collette & Banarescu 1977:1459 [ref. 5845]). Percidae.

Asperapogon Smith 1961:375, 384 [ref. 4128]. Masc. *Asperapogon rubellus* Smith 1961:384. Type by original designation (also monotypic). Apogonidae.

Aspericorvina (subgenus of *Johnius*) Fowler 1934:153 [ref. 1417]. Fem. *Johnius melanobrachium* Fowler 1934:154. Type by original designation. Valid (Trewavas 1977:368 [ref. 4459], Kottelat 1989:17 [ref. 13605]). Sciaenidae.

Asperina Ostroumoff 1896:30 [ref. 3320]. Fem. *Asperina improvisa* Ostroumoff 1896:30. Type by monotypy. Synonym of *Umbrina* Cuvier 1816 (Trewavas 1973:399 [ref. 7201], Trewavas 1977:278 [ref. 4459]). Sciaenidae.

Asperulus Gill (ex Klein) 1861:46 [ref. 1768]. Masc. *Perca zingel* Linnaeus 1766:482. No description or species mentioned; refers to *Asperulus* of Klein. Subsequent use of name not researched. Type above as given by Jordan 1919:303 [ref. 4904]. In the synonymy of *Zingel* Cloquet 1817 (Collette & Banarescu 1977:1459 [ref. 5845]). Percidae.

Asperulus Klein 1776:686 [ref. 4919]. Masc. Not available, published in a work that does not conform to the principle of binominal nomenclature. In the synonymy of *Zingel* Cloquet 1817. Percidae.

Asperulus Schaeffer 1761:58 [ref. 3910]. Masc. Not available, published in a non-binominal work (Opinion 345). Original not examined. In the synonym of *Zingel* Cloquet 1817 (Collette & Banarescu 1977:1459 [ref. 5845]). Percidae.

Aspicottus Girard 1854:130 [ref. 1817]. Masc. *Aspicottus bison* Girard 1854:130. Type by subsequent designation. Type designated by Jordan & Evermann 1898:1937 [ref. 2444]. Misspelled *Aspidocottus* by Bleeker 1859:xxiv [ref. 371]. Synonym of *Enophrys* Swainson 1839 (Bolin 1944:90 [ref. 6379]); valid (Neyelov 1979:115, 147 [ref. 3152]). Cottidae.

Aspidobagrus Bleeker 1862:9 [ref. 393]. Masc. *Bagrus gulio*

Hamilton 1822:201, 379. Type by original designation (also monotypic). Apparently dates to p. 9 in part 6 (26 Nov. 1862), Pl. 74 and text p. 59 published in part 7 (27 Jan. 1863). Also appeared as name only in Bleeker 1862:392 [ref. 391]. Synonym of *Mystus* Scopoli 1777 (Roberts 1989:120 [ref. 6439]). Bagridae.

Aspidontus Cuvier in Quoy & Gaimard 1834:719 [ref. 3573]. Masc. *Aspidontus taeniatus* Quoy & Gaimard 1834:719. Type by monotypy. Valid (Smith-Vaniz 1976:53 [ref. 4144], Yoshino in Masuda et al. 1984:297 [ref. 6441], Springer 1986:743 [ref. 5719], Smith-Vaniz 1987:3 [ref. 6404]). Blenniidae.

Aspidoparia Heckel 1847:186 [ref. 2068]. Fem. *Aspidoparia sardina* Heckel 1847:186. Type by subsequent designation. Original not seen, possibly dates to 1843. Type designated by Bleeker 1863:197 [ref. 397] and 1863:26 [ref. 4859]. Valid (Jayaram 1981:85 [ref. 6497], Kottelat 1989:6 [ref. 13605], Kuang in Chu & Chen 1989:33 [ref. 13584]). Cyprinidae.

Aspidophilus Koumans 1931:147 [ref. 5623]. Masc. A "museum name" included in synonymy of *Benthophilus* Eichwald 1931; no description; apparently never made available. Gobiidae.

Aspidophoroides Lacepède 1801:227 [ref. 2710]. Masc. *Aspidophoroides tranquebar* Lacepède 1801:227, 228 (= *Cottus monopterygius* Bloch 1786:156). Type by monotypy. Valid (Washington et al. 1984:442 [ref. 13660], Kanayama in Masuda et al. 1984:333 [ref. 6441], Yabe 1985:123 [ref. 11522], Maeda & Amaoka 1988:112 [ref. 12616]). Agonidae.

Aspidophorus Lacepède 1801:221 [ref. 2710]. Masc. *Cottus cataphractus* Linnaeus 1758:264. Type by subsequent designation. Apparently *Aspidephorus* Minding 1832:105 is an incorrect subsequent spelling. Type designated by Bory de Saint-Vincent, v. 2, 1822:27 [ref. 3853] (see Whitley 1935:137 [ref. 6396]). Lacepède included *cataphractus* in synonymy of his *A. armatus*. Synonym of *Agonus* Bloch & Schneider 1801 (Lindberg 1973:605 [ref. 7220]). Agonidae.

Aspidoras Ihering 1907:30, 31 [ref. 2294]. Masc. *Aspidoras rochai* Ihering 1907:30, 31. Type by original designation (also monotypic). Valid (Gosline 1940:9 [ref. 6489], Nijssen & Isbrücker 1976 [ref. 7077], Nijssen & Isbrücker 1980 [ref. 6921], Burgess 1989: 364 [ref. 12860]). Callichthyidae.

Aspilurochaetodon (subgenus of *Rabdophorus*) Maugé & Bauchot 1984:469 [ref. 6614]. Masc. *Chaetodon selene* Bleeker 1853:76. Type by original designation. Chaetodontidae.

Aspiobarbus Berg 1932 Masc. Unable to locate original; Karaman included in synonymy of *Barbus* but provided no details. Not in Fowler manuscript. Synonym of *Barbus* Cuvier & Cloquet 1816 (Karaman 1971:192 [ref. 2560]). Cyprinidae.

Aspiolucius Berg 1907:326, 327 [ref. 268]. Masc. *Aspius esocinus* Kessler 1874:28. Type by monotypy. Valid (Bogutskaya 1987:936 [ref. 13521]). Cyprinidae.

Aspiopsis Zugmayer 1912:682 [ref. 4847]. Fem. *Aspiopsis merzbacheri* Zugmayer 1912:682. Type by monotypy. Cyprinidae..

Aspiorhynchus Kessler 1879:289, 291 [ref. 2598]. Masc. *Aspio rhynchus przewalskii* Kessler 1879:291. Type by original designation (also monotypic). Spelled *Aspiorrhynchus* and *Aspiorrhyncho* by Nikolskii 1897:346 [ref. 3201]. Valid (Tsao 1964:167 [ref. 13501], Wu 1987:47 [ref. 12822]). Cyprinidae.

Aspiostoma Nikolskii 1897:345 [ref. 3201]. Neut. *Aspiostoma zarudnyi* Nikolskii 1897:346. Type by monotypy. Possibly preoccupied by Martens 1869 in Mollusca, an emendation of *Pyrostoma* Vest 1867. Synonym of *Schizothorax* Heckel 1838, subgenus *Schizopyge* Heckel 1843 (Tsao 1964:150 [ref. 13501], Mo in Chu & Chen 1989:287 [ref. 13584]). Cyprinidae.

Aspiscis Whitley 1930:251 [ref. 4670]. Masc. *Apogon savayensis* Günther 1871:656. Type by original designation (also monotypic). Synonym of *Apogon* Lacepède 1801, subgenus *Nectamia* Jordan 1917 (Fraser 1972:17-18 [ref. 5195] but spelled *Aspiscus*). Apogonidae.

Aspistor Jordan & Evermann 1898:2763 [ref. 2445]. Masc. *Arius luniscutis* Valenciennes in Cuvier & Valenciennes 1839:458. Type by original designation (also monotypic). Ariidae.

Aspisurus Lacepède 1802:556 [ref. 4929]. Masc. *Chaetodon sohar* Forsskål 1775:xiii, 63. Type by monotypy. Synonym of *Acanthurus* Forsskål 1775 (Randall 1955:363 [ref. 13648]). Acanthuridae.

Aspitrigla (subgenus of *Trigla*) Fowler 1925:5 [ref. 1401]. Fem. *Trigla cuculus* Linnaeus 1758:301. Type by original designation (also monotypic). Valid (Blanc & Hureau 1973:587 [ref. 7218], Hureau in Whitehead et al. 1986:1231 [ref. 13677]). Triglidae: Triglinae.

Aspiurochilus (subgenus of *Lepidaplois*) Fowler 1956:176 [ref. 1469]. Masc. *Crenilabrus stejnegeri* Ishikawa 1904:12. Type by original designation (also monotypic). Labridae.

Aspius Agassiz 1832:132, 134 [ref. 5111]. Masc. *Cyprinus aspius* Linnaeus 1758:395. Type by absolute tautonymy. Appears to date to Agassiz 1832 as above with species as (p. 132), "...und *Aspius [as a species], Alburnus, bipunctatus*, etc. als Genus *Aspius* Ag..." and (p. 134) "...Aus dem Genus *Aspius*: eine Art *A. gracilis* Ag., mit *bipunctatus* verwandt." Also in Agassiz 1835:38 [ref. 22]. Valid (Yang & Hwang 1964:19 [ref. 13497], Bogutskaya 1987:936 [ref. 13521]). Cyprinidae.

Aspredinichthys Bleeker 1858:328, 329 [ref. 365]. Masc. *Aspredo tibicen* Temminck in Cuvier & Valenciennes 1840:438. Type by monotypy. Valid (Mees 1987:188 [ref. 11510], Burgess 1989:304 [ref. 12860]). Aspredinidae: Aspredininae.

Aspredo Gronow 1763:102 [ref. 1910]. Not available, published in a rejected work on Official Index (Opinion 261). Aspredinidae: Aspredininae.

Aspredo Scopoli (ex Gronow) 1777:453 [ref. 3990]. *Silurus aspredo* Linnaeus 1758:304. Appeared without species; first inclusion of species under name attributed to Scopoli not researched. Fowler (MS) lists the type as *Silurus batrachus* Linnaeus as designated by Eigenmann 1910:380 [ref. 1224] for *Aspredo* Bleeker. Mees 1987:183 [ref. 11510] indicates type is by subsequent designation of Fowler 1954:39 [our ref. 1465]. Not *Aspredo* Swainson 1838. Valid (Mees 1987:183 [ref. 11510], Burgess 1989:304 [ref. 12860]). Aspredinidae: Aspredininae.

Aspredo Swainson 1838:332 [ref. 4302]. *Aspredo gronovii* Swainson 1838:332. Type by monotypy. Preoccupied by *Aspredo* Scopoli 1777. Synonym of *Bunocephalichthys* Bleeker 1858 (Mees 1988:89 [ref. 6401]). Aspredinidae: Bunocephalinae.

Aspro Commerson in Lacepède 1802:273 (footnote) [ref. 4929]. Apparently not available, name mentioned in passing under *Centropomus ambassis*. See remarks under Opinion 89 in Appendix B. Not *Aspro* Cuvier 1828. In the synonymy of *Cheilodipterus* Lacepède 1801 (Fraser 1972:16 [ref. 5195]). Apogonidae.

Aspro Cuvier in Cuvier & Valenciennes 1828:188 [ref. 997]. *Perca asper* Linnaeus 1758:290. Type by subsequent designation. Type designated by Jordan 1917:124 [ref. 2407]. Not preoccupied by Commerson in Lacepède 1802 in fishes (not available). Synonym of *Zingel* Cloquet 1817 (Collette & Banarescu 1977:1459 [ref. 5845]). Percidae.

Asprocottus Berg 1906:907 [ref. 265]. Masc. *Asprocottus herzensteini* Berg 1906:907. Type by monotypy. Valid (Washington et al. 1984:443 [ref. 13660], Yabe 1985:123 [ref. 11522]). Cottocomephoridae.

Asproperca Heckel in Canestrini 1860:311 [ref. 712]. Fem. *Pileoma zebra* Agassiz 1850:308. Type by monotypy. Synonym of subgenus *Percina* of genus *Percina* Haldeman 1842 (Collette & Banarescu 1977:1455 [ref. 5845]). Percidae.

Asprotilapia Boulenger 1901:5 [ref. 5758]. Fem. *Asprotilapia leptura* Boulenger 1901:5. Type by monotypy. Appeared first in Boulenger 1901 (Jan.) [ref. 5758], also in Boulenger 1901 (Oct.) [ref. 556]). Valid (Liem 1981:192 [ref. 6897], Poll 1986:104 [ref. 6136]). Cichlidae.

Asquamiceps Zugmayer 1911:2 [ref. 6161]. Neut. *Asquamiceps velaris* Zugmayer 1911:2. Type by monotypy. Also appeared in Zugmayer 1911 (Dec.):10 [ref. 4846]. Valid (Krefft 1973:88 [ref. 7166], Markle 1980 [ref. 6077], Markle & Quéro in Whitehead et al. 1984:233 [ref. 13675], Markle 1986:219 [ref. 5687], Paxton et al. 1989:210 [ref. 12442]). Alepocephalidae.

Asra Iljin 1941:385, 388 [ref. 2298]. Fem. *Asra turcomanus* Iljin 1941:385, 388. Type by monotypy. Author as Ilyin [= Iljin]. Valid (Hoese, pers. comm.). Gobiidae.

Assessor Whitley 1935:231 [ref. 4683]. Masc. *Assessor macneilli* Whitley 1935:231. Type by original designation (also monotypic). Valid (Hoese & Kuiter 1984:8 [ref. 5300], Hayashi in Masuda et al. 1984:141 [ref. 6441], Paxton et al. 1989:524 [ref. 12442]). Plesiopidae.

Assiculus Richardson 1846:492 [ref. 3743]. Masc. *Assiculus punctatus* Richardson 1846:494. Type by monotypy. As a genus, but "... ichthyologists may consider *Assiculus*, either as a proper generic form, or as merely a subgenus or subdivision of *Pseudochromis* ..." Synonym of *Pseudochromis* Rüppell 1835. Pseudochromidae: Pseudochrominae.

Assurger Whitley 1933:84 [ref. 4677]. Masc. *Evoxymetopon anzac* Alexander 1917:104. Type by original designation (also monotypic). Valid (Collette et al. 1984:600 [ref. 11421], Nakamura in Masuda et al. 1984:228 [ref. 6441]). Trichiuridae: Lepidopinae.

Astatheros (subgenus of *Cichlasoma*) Pellegrin 1904:203 [ref. 3419]. Neut. *Heros (Cichlasoma) heterodontus* Vaillant & Pellegrin 1902:86. Type by monotypy. Misspelled *Astotheros* by Eigenmann 1910:475 [ref. 1224]. Cichlidae.

Astatichthys Vaillant 1873:106 [ref. 4492]. Masc. *Etheostoma caerulea* Storer 1856:47. Type by subsequent designation. Type designated by Jordan & Gilbert 1877:95 [ref. 4907]. Synonym of *Etheostoma* Rafinesque 1819 (Collette & Banarescu 1977:1456 [ref. 5845]). Percidae.

Astatoreochromis Pellegrin 1904:384 [ref. 3419]. Masc. *Astatoreochromis alluaudi* Pellegrin 1904:385. Type by monotypy. Valid (Bailey & Stewart 1977:2 [ref. 7230], Poll 1986:41 [ref. 6136]). Cichlidae.

Astatotilapia Pellegrin 1904:(164) 299 [ref. 3419]. Fem. *Labrus desfontainii* Lacepède 1802:54, 160. Type by subsequent designation. Earliest type designation not yet located, 3 included species. Species originally spelled *desfontainii* (p. 54) and *desfontaines* (p. 160), the latter emended to *desfontainesi* by Pellegrin; *desfontainii* regarded as correct. Valid (Greenwood 1980:6 [ref. 1899], Ribbink et al. 1983:245 [ref. 13555] with wrong author, Poll 1986:40 [ref. 6136], Krupp & Schneider 1989:393 [ref. 13651]). Cichlidae.

Astemomycterus Guichenot 1860:525 [ref. 1941]. Masc. *Trichomycterus pusillus* Castelnau 1855:50. Type by original designation (also monotypic). Trichomycteridae.

Asternopteryx Günther (ex Rüppell) 1861:288 [ref. 1964]. Fem. *Asternopteryx gunnelliformis* Rüppell in Günther 1861:288. Type by monotypy. Not available; name in synonymy. Apparently never subsequently made available. In the synonymy of *Pholis* Scopoli 1777 (Yatsu 1981:169 [ref. 4814], Makushok in Whitehead et al. 1986:1124 [ref. 13677]). Pholidae.

Asternotremia Nelson in Jordan 1877:51 [ref. 2374]. Fem. *Sternotremia isolepis* Nelson 1876:39. Unjustified emendation of *Sternotremia* Nelson 1876. Synonym of *Aphredoderus* Lesueur 1833. Aphredoderidae.

Asterophysus Kner 1858:402 [ref. 2630]. Masc. *Asterophysus batrachus* Kner 1858:403. Type by monotypy. Misspelled *Astrophysus* in literature. Valid (Burgess 1989:242 [ref. 12860], Curran 1989 [ref. 12547]). Auchenipteridae.

Asterorhombus Tanaka 1915:567 [ref. 4324]. Masc. *Asterorhombus stellifer* Tanaka 1915:567. Type by monotypy. Valid (Amaoka 1969:174 [ref. 105], Ahlstrom et al. 1984:642 [ref. 13641], Amaoka in Masuda et al. 1984:349 [ref. 6441], Hensley 1986:855 [ref. 5669], Hensley 1986:941 [ref. 6326]). Bothidae: Bothinae.

Asterotheca Gilbert 1915:343 [ref. 1632]. Fem. *Xenochirus pentacanthus* Gilbert 1890:91. Type by original designation. Valid (Yabe 1985:123 [ref. 11522]). Agonidae.

Asterropteryx Rüppell 1830:138 [ref. 3843]. Fem. *Asterropteryx semipunctatus* Rüppell 1830:138. Type by monotypy. Valid (Hayashi in Masuda et al. 1984:241 [ref. 6441], Hoese 1986:779 [ref. 5670], Birdsong et al. 1988:192 [ref. 7303]). Gobiidae.

Asthenomacrurus Sazonov & Shcherbachev 1982:708 [ref. 3908]. Masc. *Asthenomacrurus victoris* Sazonov & Shcherbachev 1982:709. Type by original designation. Valid (Paxton et al. 1989:324 [ref. 12442]). Macrouridae: Macrourinae.

Asthenurus Tickell 1865:32 [ref. 4405]. Masc. *Asthenurus atripinnis* Tickell 1865:32. Type by monotypy. Synonym of *Bregmaceros* Thompson 1840. Bregmacerotidae.

Astrabe Jordan & Snyder 1901:119 [ref. 2509]. Fem. *Astrabe lactisella* Jordan & Snyder 1901:119. Type by original designation (also monotypic). Valid (Akihito in Masuda et al. 1984:281 [ref. 6441], Akihito & Meguro 1988 [ref. 6694], Birdsong et al. 1988:183, 185 [ref. 7303]). Gobiidae.

Astrape Müller & Henle 1837:117 [ref. 3067]. Fem. *Raja capensis* Gmelin 1789:1512. Type by subsequent designation. Included species in 1837:117 as "*Astrape* M. u. H. (*T. capensis* und *dipterygia* aut. [= Bloch & Schneider 1801])." Also in Müller & Henle 1841:130 [ref. 3069] with same included species. Type perhaps not designated until Jordan 1919:193 [ref. 2410]. Objective synonym of *Narke* Kaup 1826. Narkidae.

Astrapogon (subgenus of *Apogon*) Fowler 1907:527 [ref. 1375]. Masc. *Apogonichthys stellatus* Cope 1869:400. Type by original designation (also monotypic). Valid (Fraser 1972:13 [ref. 5195]). Apogonidae.

Astroblepus Humboldt 1805:19 [ref. 2278]. Masc. *Astroblepus grixalvii* Humboldt 1805:19. Type by monotypy. Spelled *Astroblepes* by Swainson 1838:322, et. seq. [ref. 4302] and 1839:189, 308 [ref. 4303]. Original not seen. Valid (Burgess 1989:449 [ref. 12860]). Astroblepidae.

Astrocanthus Swainson 1839:331 [ref. 4303]. Masc. *Lophius stel-*

latus Vahl 1797:214. Type by monotypy. Synonym of *Halieutaea* Valenciennes 1837. Ogcocephalidae.

Astroconger Jordan & Hubbs 1925:194 [ref. 2486]. Masc. *Anguilla myriaster* Brevoort 1856:282. Type by original designation (also monotypic). Synonym of *Conger* Oken 1817 (Blache et al. 1973:239 [ref. 7185], Smith 1989:513 [ref. 13285]). Congridae: Congrinae.

Astrocottus Bolin 1936:330 [ref. 504]. Masc. *Astrocottus leprops* Bolin 1936:331. Type by original designation (also monotypic). Valid (Washington et al. 1984:442 [ref. 13660], Yabe in Masuda et al. 1984:325 [ref. 6441], Yabe 1985:111 [ref. 11522]). Cottidae.

Astrodermus Cuvier (ex Bonnelli) 1829:216 [ref. 995]. Masc. *Astrodermus guttatus* Cuvier (ex Bonnelli) 1829:216. Type by monotypy. Spelled *Astrodermes* by Swainson 1839:79 [ref. 4303] (ex Bonnelli), *Astroderma* by Lowe 1843:83 [ref. 2832], *Astrodermis* by Swainson 1839:440 [ref.4303]. Synonym of *Luvarus* Rafinesque 1810 (Topp 1973:476 [ref. 7209]). Luvaridae.

Astrodoras Bleeker 1862:5 [ref. 393]. Masc. *Doras asterifrons* Heckel in Kner 1855:123. Type by original designation (also monotypic). Valid (Burgess 1989:224 [ref. 12860]). Doradidae.

Astrolytes Jordan & Starks 1895:807 [ref. 2522]. Masc. *Artedius fenestralis* Jordan & Gilbert 1882:973. Type by original designation (also monotypic). Synonym of *Artedius* Girard 1856 (Bolin 1944:48 [ref. 6379], Begle 1989:646 [ref. 12739]). Cottidae.

Astronesthes Richardson 1845:97 [ref. 3739]. Fem. *Astronesthes nigra* Richardson 1845:97. Type by monotypy. Valid (Gibbs 1964: 313 [ref. 6960], Gibbs & Morrow 1973:126 [ref. 7174], Gibbs in Whitehead et al. 1984:326 [ref. 13675], Fujii in Masuda et al. 1984:49 [ref. 6441], Fink 1985:11 [ref. 5171], Gibbs 1986:231 [ref. 5655], Gibbs & McKinney 1988 [ref. 6628], Paxton et al. 1989:194 [ref. 12442]). Astronesthidae.

Astronotus (subgenus of *Crenilabrus*) Swainson 1839:173, 229 [ref. 4303]. Masc. *Lobotes ocellatus* Agassiz in Spix & Agassiz 1829: 129. Type by monotypy. Valid (Kullander 1986:60 [ref. 12439]). Cichlidae.

Astroscopus Brevoort in Gill 1860:20 [ref. 1763]. Masc. *Uranoscopus anoplos* Valenciennes in Cuvier & Valenciennes 1831:493. Type by subsequent designation. Two included species; earliest type designation not researched. Valid (Mees 1960:47 [ref. 11931], Inada in Nakamura et al. 1986:262 [ref. 14235], Pietsch 1989:297 [ref. 12541]). Uranoscopidae.

Astyanacinus Eigenmann 1907:769 [ref. 1220]. Masc. *Tetragonopterus moorii* Boulenger 1892:11. Type by original designation (also monotypic). Spelled *Astycinus* by Jordan 1920:522 [ref. 4905] and *Astyacinus* by Neave 1939:337 [ref. 12569]. Valid (Géry 1977:415 [ref. 1597]). Characidae.

Astyanax Baird & Girard 1854:26 [ref. 168]. Masc. *Astyanax argentatus* Baird & Girard 1854:27. Type by monotypy. Valid (Géry 1977:418 [ref. 1597], Weitzman [M.] & Vari 1986 [ref. 5979], Géry et al. 1988:9 [ref. 6408], Malabarba 1989:128 [ref. 14217]). Characidae.

Asymbolus (subgenus of *Scyliorhinus*) Whitley 1939:229 [ref. 4695]. Masc. *Scyllium anale* Ogilby 1885:445. Type by original designation (also monotypic). Valid (Springer 1979:30 [ref. 4175], Compagno 1984:289 [ref. 6846], Compagno 1988:127 [ref. 13488], Paxton et al. 1989:71 [ref. 12442]). Scyliorhinidae.

Asymmetrurus Clark & Ben-Tuvia 1973:68 [ref. 838]. Masc. *Hoplolatilus oreni* Clark & Ben-Tuvia 1973:68. Not available; two included species without type designation after 1930 (Art. 13b). Apparently made available by Dooley 1978:13, 62-64 [ref. 5499], who provides a description and type designation, as a subgenus of *Hoplolatilus*; if Dooley was first, then the genus dates to Dooley 1978 with type as above. Synonym of *Hoplolatilus* Günther 1887, but a valid subgenus (Randall & Dooley 1974:458 [ref. 5336]). Malacanthidae: Latilinae.

Ataeniobius Hubbs & Turner 1939:39 [ref. 2265]. Masc. *Goodea toweri* Meek 1904:138. Type by original designation (also monotypic). Name appeared first in Turner 1937:510 et seq. [ref. 6400], without clear differentiating characters. Valid (Parenti 1981:519 [ref. 7066], Uyeno et al. 1983:503 [ref. 6818]). Goodeidae.

Atahua Phillipps 1941:243 [ref. 3467]. *Atahua clarki* Phillipps 1941:244. Type by monotypy. Mullidae.

Ataxolepis Myers & Freihofer 1966:197 [ref. 3088]. Fem. *Ataxolepis apus* Myers & Freihofer 1966:197. Type by original designation (also monotypic). Megalomycteridae.

Ateleobrachium Gilbert & Burke 1912:94 [ref. 1634]. Neut. *Ateleobrachium pterotum* Gilbert & Burke 1912:94. Type by original designation (also monotypic). Synonym of *Coryphaenoides* Gunner 1765 (Marshall 1973:295 [ref. 7194], Marshall & Iwamoto 1973:565 [ref. 6966]). Macrouridae: Macrourinae.

Ateleopus Temminck & Schlegel 1846:255 [ref. 4374]. Masc. *Ateleopus japonicus* Bleeker 1853:19. Type by subsequent monotypy. Appeared first without species. One species added by Bleeker 1853:19 [ref. 340]. *Podateles* Boulenger 1902 is an unneeded replacement, not preoccupied by *Atelopus* Dumeril & Bibron 1841 in Reptilia or by *Ateleopus* Agassiz 1846:39 [ref. 64], an unjustified emendation of an amphibian genus probably published after Temminck & Schlegel (Whitley 1976:46 [ref. 4735]). Valid (Mochizuki in Masuda et al. 1984:115 [ref. 6441], Smith 1986:404 [ref. 5712], Paxton et al. 1989:403 [ref. 12442]). Ateleopodidae.

Atelomycterus Garman 1913:100 [ref. 1545]. Masc. *Scyllium marmoratum* Bennett 1830:693. Type by monotypy. Valid (Springer 1979:32 [ref. 4175], Compagno 1984:292 [ref. 6846], Compagno 1988:100 [ref. 13488], Paxton et al. 1989:72 [ref. 12442]). Scyliorhinidae.

Atelurus Duméril 1870:584 [ref. 1147]. Masc. *Atelurus germani* Duméril 1870:584. Type by monotypy. Synonym of *Acentronura* Kaup 1853 (Dawson 1985:15 [ref. 6541]). Syngnathidae: Syngnathinae.

Athaena Castelnau 1861:72 [ref. 767]. Fem. *Athaena fasciata* Castelnau 1861:72. Type by monotypy. Synonym of *Chorisochismus* Brisout de Barneville 1846 (Briggs 1955:39 [ref. 637]). Gobiesocidae: Gobiesocinae.

Atheresthes Jordan & Gilbert 1880:51 [ref. 2366]. Fem. *Platysomatichthys stomias* Jordan & Gilbert 1880:301. Type by original designation (also monotypic). Valid (Norman 1934:286 [ref. 6893], Ahlstrom et al. 1984:643 [ref. 13641], Sakamoto 1984 [ref. 5273], Sakamoto in Masuda et al. 1984:351 [ref. 6441]). Pleuronectidae: Pleuronectinae.

Atherina Linnaeus 1758:315 [ref. 2787]. Fem. *Atherina hepsetus* Linnaeus 1758:315. Type by monotypy. On Official List (Opinion 75). Valid (Kiener & Spillmann 1973:576 [ref. 7217], White et al. 1984:360 [ref. 13655], Ivantsoff 1986:382 [ref. 6292], Quignard & Pras in Whitehead et al. 1986:1207 [ref. 13677], Maugé 1986:277 [ref. 6218]). Atherinidae: Atherininae.

Atherinason Whitley 1934:242 [ref. 4680]. *Atherina dannevigi* McCulloch 1911:31. Type by monotypy. Valid (White et al. 1984:360 [ref. 13655], Pavlov et al. 1988:392 [ref. 12285], Paxton et al.

1989:355 [ref. 12442]). Atherinidae: Atherininae.

Atherinella Steindachner 1875:477 [ref. 4222]. Fem. *Atherinella panamensis* Steindachner 1875:477. Type by monotypy. Valid (Chernoff 1986:240 [ref. 5847], Chernoff 1986 [ref. 5848]). Atherinidae: Menidiinae.

Atherinichthys Bleeker 1853:40 [ref. 340]. Masc. *Atherina humboldtiana* Valenciennes in Cuvier & Valenciennes 1835:479. Type by subsequent designation. Spelled initially *Atherinichthijs*, correctly latinized as *Atherinichthys*. Earliest subsequent designation not researched. Synonym of *Chirostoma* Swainson 1839. Atherinidae: Menidiinae.

Atherinoides Bleeker 1853:40 [ref. 340]. Masc. *Atherina vomerina* Valenciennes in Cuvier & Valenciennes 1835:357. Type by monotypy. Synonym of *Chirostoma* Swainson 1839. Atherinidae: Menidiinae.

Atherinomorus (subgenus of *Atherina*) Fowler 1903:730 [ref. 1362]. Masc. *Atherina laticeps* Poey 1861:265. Type by original designation (also monotypic). Valid (Whitehead & Ivantsoff 1983:361 [ref. 5418], White et al. 1984:360 [ref. 13655], Yoshino in Masuda et al. 1984:119 [ref. 6441], Quignard & Pras in Whitehead et al. 1986:1209 [ref. 13677], Ivantsoff 1986:382 [ref. 6292], Paxton et al. 1989:355 [ref. 12442]). Atherinidae: Atherininae.

Atherinops (subgenus of *Atherinichthys*) Steindachner 1875:89 [ref. 4223]. Masc. *Atherinopsis affinis* Ayres 1860:73. Type by monotypy. Valid (White et al. 1984:360 [ref. 13655], White 1985: 16 [ref. 13551], Crabtree 1987:861 [ref. 6771]). Atherinidae: Atherinopsinae.

Atherinopsis Girard 1854:134 [ref. 1817]. Fem. *Atherinopsis californiensis* Girard 1854:134. Type by monotypy. Valid (White et al. 1984:360 [ref. 13655], White 1985:17 [ref. 13551], Crabtree 1987: 861 [ref. 6771]). Atherinidae: Atherinopsinae.

Atherinosoma Castelnau 1872:138 [ref. 757]. Neut. *Atherinosoma vorax* Castelnau 1872:138. Type by monotypy. Valid (Prince et al. 1982:64 [ref. 5417], White et al. 1984:360 [ref. 13655], Pavlov et al. 1988:392 [ref. 12285], Paxton et al. 1989:356 [ref. 12442]). Atherinidae: Atherininae.

Atherion Jordan & Starks 1901:203 [ref. 2524]. Neut. *Atherion elymus* Jordan & Starks 1901:203. Type by monotypy. Valid (White et al. 1984:360 [ref. 13655], Yoshino in Masuda et al. 1984:119 [ref. 6441], Ivantsoff 1986:383 [ref. 6292], Paxton et al. 1989:357 [ref. 12442]). Atherinidae: Atherioninae.

Atherodus (subgenus of *Ventrifossa*) Gilbert & Hubbs 1920:544, 545 [ref. 1638]. Masc. *Optonurus atherodon* Gilbert & Cramer 1897: 431. Type by original designation (also monotypic). Valid. Macrouridae: Macrourinae.

Atherthyrina Fowler 1958:16 [ref. 1470]. Fem. *Thyrina evermanni* Jordan & Culver in Jordan 1895:419. Type by being a replacement name. Replacement for *Thyrina* Jordan & Culver 1895, preoccupied by Poujade 1886 in Lepidoptera. Synonym of *Atherinella* Steindachner 1875. Atherinidae: Menidiinae.

Athlennes (subgenus of *Tylosurus*) Jordan & Fordice 1887:342, 345 [ref. 2456]. Not available; an incorrect original spelling. See *Ablennes* Jordan & Fordice 1887 and Opinion 41 in Appendix B. Belonidae.

Atimostoma Smith 1845:Pl. 24 [ref. 4035]. Neut. *Atimostoma capensis* Smith 1845:Pl. 24. Type by monotypy. Synonym of *Cubiceps* Lowe 1843 (Haedrich 1967:78 [ref. 5357]). Nomeidae.

Atinga Le Danois 1954:2356 [ref. 6451]. Fem. *Diodon atringa* Linnaeus 1758:334. Type by monotypy; one species but four subspecies; type is the nominate subspecies. Le Danois apparently misspelled Linnaeus' species as *atinga*. See also Leis & Bauchot 1984:85 [ref. 12539]. Also Appendix A. Diodontidae.

Atlantoraja (subgenus of *Raja*) Menni 1972:167 [ref. 2979]. Fem. *Raja cyclophora* Regan 1903:60. Type by original designation. Rajidae.

Atomaster Eigenmann & Myers 1927:565 [ref. 1262]. Masc. *Atomaster velox* Eigenmann & Myers 1927:565. Type by monotypy. Probably a synonym of *Bivibranchia* Eigenmann 1912 (Roberts 1974:412 [ref. 6872]); valid (Géry 1977:199 [ref. 1597]; synonym of *Bivibranchia* (Vari 1985:512 [ref. 5270]). Hemiodontidae: Hemiodontinae.

Atopichthys Garman 1899:326 [ref. 1540]. Masc. *Atopichthys esunculus* Garman 1899:327. Type by subsequent designation. Type designated by Jordan 1920:486 [ref. 4905]. Used in the sense of a genus by Garman as a temporary catchall for unplaced larval eels, some now reassigned (see Raju 1985 [ref. 5287]). Synonym of *Albula* Scopoli 1777 (Whitehead 1986:216 [ref. 5733]). Albulidae: Albulinae.

Atopocheilichthys Boulenger 1915:40 [ref. 584]. Masc. Not available, name published in synonymy; perhaps a mistake for *Aplocheilichthys* Bleeker 1863. Cyprinodontidae: Aplocheilichthyinae.

Atopochilus Sauvage 1879:96 [ref. 3881]. Masc. *Atopochilus savorgnani* Sauvage 1879:97. Type by monotypy. Valid (Gosse 1986:105 [ref. 6194], Burgess 1989:198 [ref. 12860], Roberts 1989:164 [ref. 13302]). Mochokidae.

Atopoclinus Vaillant 1894:73 [ref. 4488]. Masc. *Atopoclinus ringens* Vaillant 1894:74. Type by monotypy. Synonym of *Plagiotremus* Gill 1865 (Smith-Vaniz 1976:108 [ref. 4144]). Blenniidae.

Atopocottus Bolin 1936:30 [ref. 505]. Masc. *Atopocottus tribranchius* Bolin 1936:30. Type by original designation (also monotypic). Valid (Yabe in Masuda et al. 1984:329 [ref. 6441], Nelson 1985 [ref. 5155]). Cottidae.

Atopomesus Myers 1927:112 [ref. 3096]. Masc. *Atopomesus pachyodus* Myers 1927:112. Type by original designation (also monotypic). Valid (Géry 1977:587 [ref. 1597]). Characidae.

Atopomycterus Bleeker (ex Verreaux) 1865:49 [ref. 416]. Masc. *Atopomycterus diversispinis* Bleeker (ex Verreaux) 1865 (= *Dicotylichthys punctulatus* Kaup 1855:230). Type designated by Bleeker as *A. diversispinis*, but that species appeared as name only and not available; subsequent addition of species and type designation not researched; Leis & Bauchot 1984:85 [ref. 12539] say Bleeker's species is equal to *D. punctulatus* Kaup. Diodontidae.

Atractodenchelys Robins & Robins 1970:296 [ref. 3783]. Fem. *Atractodenchelys phrix* Robins & Robins 1970:297. Type by original designation (also monotypic). Valid (Robins & Robins 1976:250 [ref. 3784], Robins & Robins 1989:240 [ref. 13287]). Synaphobranchidae: Ilyophinae.

Atractoperca Gill 1861:164 [ref. 1775]. Fem. *Labrax clathratus* Girard 1854:143. Type by monotypy. Synonym of *Paralabrax* Girard 1856. Serranidae: Serraninae.

Atractophorus Gilchrist 1922:48 [ref. 1648]. Masc. *Atractophorus armatus* Gilchrist 1922:48. Type by monotypy. Spelled *Actractophorus* once by Gilchrist on p. 48, *Atractophorus* with main heading and on p. 42. Synonym of *Centrophorus* Müller & Henle 1837 (Krefft & Tortonese 1973:38 [ref. 7165], Compagno 1984:35 [ref. 6474], Bass et al. 1986:49 [ref. 5636], Cappetta 1987:53 [ref.

6348]). Squalidae.

Atractoscion Gill 1862:18 [ref. 1657]. Masc. *Otolithus aequidens* Cuvier in Cuvier & Valenciennes 1830:66. Type by original designation (also monotypic). Correct spelling for genus of type species is *Otolithes*. Valid (Trewavas 1977:282 [ref. 4459], Heemstra 1986:617 [ref. 5660]). Sciaenidae.

Atractosteus (subgenus of *Lepisosteus*) Rafinesque 1820:171 [ref. 7306]. Masc. *Lepisosteus (Atractosteus) ferox* Rafinesque 1820:171. Type by monotypy. Also in Rafinesque 1820:75 (Dec.) [ref. 3592], Synonym of *Lepisosteus* Lacepède 1803 (Suttkus 1963:69 [ref. 7110]); valid (Wiley 1976:61 [ref. 7091]); or as a valid subgenus of *Lepisosteus* (e.g. Robins et al. 1980:70 [ref. 7111]). Lepisosteidae.

Atrilinea Chu 1935:10 [ref. 832]. Fem. *Barilius chenchiwei* Chu 1931:33. Type by original designation (also monotypic). Valid (Yang & Hwang 1964:50 [ref. 13497]). Cyprinidae.

Atrobucca Chu, Lo & Wu 1963:64, 93 [ref. 833]. Fem. *Sciaena nibe* Jordan & Thompson 1911:258. Type by original designation (also monotypic). Valid (Trewavas 1977:339 [ref. 4459], Okamura in Masuda et al. 1984:162 [ref. 6441], Heemstra 1986:617 [ref. 5660], Sasaki & Kailola 1988 [ref. 12553]). Sciaenidae.

Atrophacanthus Fraser-Brunner 1950:1 [ref. 1497]. Masc. *Atrophacanthus danae* Fraser-Brunner 1950:1. Type by monotypy. Valid (Tyler 1968:163 [ref. 6438], Tyler 1980:56 [ref. 4477], Aboussouan & Leis 1984:452 [ref. 13661], Matsuura in Masuda et al. 1984:357 [ref. 6441], Tyler 1986:888 [ref. 5723]). Triacanthodidae.

Atropus Oken (ex Cuvier) 1817:1182 [ref. 3303]. Masc. *Brama atropos* Bloch & Schneider 1801:98. Type by monotypy. Based on "Les Atropus" Cuvier 1816:324 [ref. 993] (see Gill 1903:966 [ref. 5768]). See also Whitley 1935:136 [ref. 6396] for possible earlier date [not investigated]. Valid (Smith-Vaniz 1984:524 [ref. 13664], Gushiken in Masuda et al. 1984:157 [ref. 6441], Kijima et al. 1986:841 [ref. 6320], Gushiken 1988:443 [ref. 6697]). Carangidae.

Atrosalarias Whitley 1933:93 [ref. 4677]. Masc. *Salarias phaiosoma* Bleeker 1855:306, 317. Type by original designation (also monotypic). Valid (Smith-Vaniz & Springer 1971:18 [ref. 4145], Yoshino in Masuda et al. 1984:298 [ref. 6441]). Blenniidae.

Attilus Gistel 1848:109 [ref. 1822]. Masc. *Sciaena cirrosa* Linnaeus 1758:289. Type by being a replacement name. Apparently an unneeded replacement for *Umbrina* Cuvier 1816. Objective synonym of *Umbrina* Cuvier 1816 (Trewavas 1973:399 [ref. 7201], Trewavas 1977:278 [ref. 4459], Chao 1978:29 [ref. 6983]). Sciaenidae.

Atule Jordan & Jordan 1922:38 [ref. 2487]. *Caranx affinis* Rüppell 1836:49. Type by original designation. Synonym of *Selar* Bleeker 1851 (Hureau & Tortonese 1973:379 [ref. 7198]; valid (Smith-Vaniz 1984:524 [ref. 13664], Gushiken in Masuda et al. 1984:155 [ref. 6441], Smith-Vaniz 1986:641 [ref. 5718], Daget & Smith-Vaniz 1986:309 [ref. 6207], Gushiken 1988:443 [ref. 6697], Paxton et al. 1989:574 [ref. 12442]). Carangidae.

Atulonotus Smith 1955:174 [ref. 4100]. Masc. *Priodon hexacanthus* Bleeker 1855:421. Type by original designation. Acanthuridae.

Atuona Herre 1935:428 [ref. 2109]. Fem. *Atuona tricuspidata* Herre 1935:429. Type by original designation (also monotypic). Synonym of *Kelloggella* Jordan & Seale 1905 (Hoese 1975:474 [ref. 5294]). Gobiidae.

Aturius Dubalen 1878:157 [ref. 1141]. Masc. *Aturius dufourii* Dubalen 1878:603. Type by monotypy. Original not seen. Synonym of *Leuciscus* Cuvier 1816. Cyprinidae.

Atypichthys Günther 1862:510 [ref. 1969]. Masc. *Atypus strigatus* Günther 1860:64. Type by being a replacement name. Replacement for *Atypus* Günther 1860, preoccupied by Latreille 1804 in Arachnida. Valid (Scott 1976:173 [ref. 7055]). Kyphosidae: Microcanthinae.

Atyposoma Boulenger 1899:379 [ref. 551]. Neut. *Atyposoma gurneyi* Boulenger 1899:379. Type by monotypy. Synonym of *Parascorpis* Bleeker 1875 (Heemstra 1986:602 [ref. 5660] based on placement of type species). Parascorpididae.

Atypus Günther 1860:64 [ref. 1963]. Masc. *Atypus strigatus* Günther 1860:64. Type by monotypy. Preoccupied by Latreille 1804 in Arachnida, replaced by and objective synonym of *Atypichthys* Günther 1862. Kyphosidae: Scorpidinae.

Auchenalepoceps (subgenus of *Xenodermichthys*) Fowler 1943:53 [ref. 1441]. Neut. *Xenodermichthys funebris* Fowler 1943:54. Type by original designation. Alepocephalidae.

Auchenaspis Bleeker 1858:198, 205, 208 [ref. 365]. Fem. *Pimelodus biscutatus* Geoffroy St. Hilaire 1809:Pl. 14. Type by subsequent designation. Type designated by Bleeker 1862:12 [ref. 393] and 1863:101 [ref. 401]. Preoccupied by Egerton 1857 in fossil fishes, replaced by *Auchenoglanis* Günther 1865. Objective synonym of *Auchenoglanis* Günther 1865 (Risch 1986:2 [ref. 6190]). Bagridae.

Auchenichthys Kaup in Duméril 1856:198 [ref. 1154]. Masc. *Auchenichthys typus* Kaup in Duméril 1856:198. Not available; name only as "*Auchenichthys typus*" in list of genera and species taken from Kaup manuscript. Later named *Achirophichthys* by Bleeker 1864. Ophichthidae: Ophichthinae.

Auchenionchus Gill 1860:103 [ref. 1765]. Masc. *Clinus variolosus* Valenciennes in Cuvier & Valenciennes 1836:281. Type by original designation (also monotypic). Originally as *Anchenionchus*, but that spelling regarded as in error for *Auchenionchus* (see Stephens & Springer 1974:11 [ref. 7149]). Valid, as *Auchenionchus* (Stephens & Springer 1974:11 [ref. 7149]). Labrisomidae.

Auchenipterichthys Bleeker 1862:7 [ref. 393]. Masc. *Auchenipterus thoracatus* Kner 1858:425. Type by original designation (also monotypic). Valid (Mees 1974:33 [ref. 2969], Burgess 1989:241 [ref. 12860], Curran 1989 [ref. 12547]). Auchenipteridae.

Auchenipterus Valenciennes in Cuvier & Valenciennes 1840:207 [ref. 1008]. Masc. *Hypophthalmus nuchalis* Agassiz in Spix & Agassiz 1829:17. Type by subsequent designation. Type designated by Bleeker 1862:15 [ref. 393] and 1863:109 [ref. 401]. Unjustifiably emended to *Auchenopterus* by Agassiz 1846:40 [ref. 64], not *Auchenopterus* Günther 1861. Valid (Mees 1974:16 [ref. 2969], Burgess 1989:241 [ref. 12860], Curran 1989 [ref. 12547]). Auchenipteridae.

Auchenistius Evermann & Marsh 1900:359 [ref. 1283]. Masc. *Auchenistius stahli* Evermann & Marsh 1900:359. Type by original designation (also monotypic). Valid (Clark Hubbs 1952:65 [ref. 2252]); synonym of *Stathmonotus* Bean 1885 (Springer 1955:74 [ref. 10208]). Labrisomidae.

Auchenoceros Günther 1889:24 [ref. 2017]. Masc. *Calloptilum punctatum* Hutton 1873:267. Type by being a replacement name. Replacement for *Calloptilum* Hutton 1873, preoccupied by Richardson 1845 in fishes. Valid (Paulin 1983:103 [ref. 5459], Fahay & Markle 1984:266 [ref. 13653]). Moridae.

Auchenoglanis Günther 1865:165 [ref. 1980]. Masc. *Pimelodus biscutatus* Geoffroy St. Hilaire 1809:Pl. 14. Type by being a replacement name. Replacement for *Auchenaspis* Bleeker 1858, preoccupied by Egerton 1857 in fossil fishes. Valid (Risch 1986:2 [ref. 6190], Risch 1987:33 [ref. 6751], Burgess 1989:71 [ref. 12860]). Bagridae.

Auchenopterus Günther 1861:275 [ref. 1964]. Masc. *Auchenopterus monophthalmus* Günther 1861:275. Type by monotypy, second species doubtfully included. Not preoccupied by *Auchenipterus* Valenciennes 1840 but preoccupied by *Auchenopterus* Agassiz 1846, an unjustified emendation of Valenciennes' genus. *Cremnobates* Günther 1861 and *Cremnotekla* Whitley 1940 are replacements. Synonym of *Paraclinus* Mocquard 1888 (Clark Hubbs 1952:65 [ref. 2252]). Labrisomidae.

Auctospina Eigenmann & Beeson 1893:670 [ref. 1212]. Fem. *Sebastes auriculatus* Girard 1854:131, 146. Type by original designation. Synonym of *Sebastes* Cuvier 1829. Scorpaenidae: Sebastinae.

Aulacocephalus Temminck & Schlegel 1842:15 [ref. 4370]. Masc. *Aulacocephalus temmincki* Bleeker 1854:12. Type by subsequent monotypy. Original description without species; one species added by Bleeker 1854:12 [ref. 357]. Valid (Katayama in Masuda et al. 1984:139 [ref. 6441], Randall 1986:537 [ref. 5706], Paxton et al. 1989:516 [ref. 12442]). Serranidae: Grammistinae.

Aulastomatomorpha Alcock 1890:307 [ref. 83]. Fem. *Aulastomatomorpha phospherops* Alcock 1890:307. Type by monotypy. Spelled *Aulastomorpha* by Alcock 1899:178 [ref. 5114]. Alepocephalidae.

Aulichthys Brevoort in Gill 1862:234 [ref. 1663]. Masc. *Aulichthys japonicus* Brevoort in Gill 1862:235. Type by monotypy. Valid (Ida in Masuda et al. 1984:83 [ref. 6441]). Gasterosteidae: Aulorhynchinae.

Auliscops Peters 1866:510 [ref. 3439]. Masc. *Auliscops spinescens* Peters 1866:510. Type by monotypy. Synonym of *Aulorhynchus* Gill 1861. Gasterosteidae: Aulorhynchinae.

Aulixidens Böhlke 1952:775 [ref. 592]. Masc. *Aulixidens eugeniae* Böhlke 1952:775. Type by original designation (also monotypic). Characidae.

Aulohalaelurus (subgenus of *Halaelurus*) Fowler 1934:237 [ref. 1416]. Masc. *Catulus labiosus* Waite 1905:57. Type by original designation (also monotypic). Valid (Springer 1979:35 [ref. 4175], Compagno 1984:294 [ref. 6846], Compagno 1988:103 [ref. 13488], Paxton et al. 1989:72 [ref. 12442]). Scyliorhinidae.

Aulohoplostethus (subgenus of *Hoplostethus*) Fowler 1938:37 [ref. 1426]. Masc. *Hoplostethus metallicus* Fowler 1938:37. Type by original designation (also monotypic). Synonym of *Hoplostethus* Cuvier 1829, but as a valid subgenus (Kotlyar 1986:137 [ref. 6004]). Trachichthyidae.

Aulonocara Regan 1922:726 [ref. 3673]. Neut. *Aulonocara nyassae* Regan 1922:727. Type by monotypy. Valid (Ribbink et al. 1983:245 [ref. 13555], Trewavas 1984 [ref. 5302], Tawil & Allgayer 1987 [ref. 6745], Eccles & Trewavas 1989:138 [ref. 13547]). Cichlidae.

Aulonocranus Regan 1920:47 [ref. 3669]. Masc. *Paratilapia dewindti* Boulenger 1899:88. Type by original designation (also monotypic). Valid (Poll 1986:105 [ref. 6136]). Cichlidae.

Aulopareia Smith 1945:534 [ref. 4056]. Fem. *Aulopareia janetae* Smith 1945:535. Type by original designation (also monotypic). Valid (Birdsong et al. 1988:192 [ref. 7303]). Gobiidae.

Aulophallus Hubbs 1926:64, 69 [ref. 2233]. Masc. *Poecilia elongata* Günther 1866:342. Type by original designation. Synonym of *Poeciliopsis* Regan 1913, but as a valid subgenus (Rosen & Bailey 1963:131, 139 [ref. 7067], Parenti & Rauchenberger 1989:9 [ref. 13538]). Poeciliidae.

Aulopus Cloquet (ex Cuvier) 1816:128 [ref. 852]. Masc. *Salmo filamentosus* Bloch 1791:424. Type by monotypy. See Whitley 1935:136 [ref. 6396]. Valid (Nielsen 1973:160 [ref. 6885], Sulak 1977:53 [ref. 4299], Sulak in Whitehead et al. 1984:403 [ref. 13675], Okiyama 1984:207 [ref. 13644], Yamakawa in Masuda et al. 1984:60 [ref. 6441], Paxton et al. 1989:227 [ref. 12442], Parin & Kotlyar 1989:407 [ref. 12748]). Aulopidae.

Aulopus Cuvier 1816:170 [ref. 993]. Masc. *Salmo filamentosus* Bloch 1791:424. Type by monotypy. Objective synonym of *Aulopus* Cloquet (Oct.) 1816, Cuvier is Dec. 1816. Aulopidae.

Aulopyge Heckel 1841:384 [ref. 2065]. Fem. *Aulopyge huegelii* Heckel 1841:73. Type by monotypy. Needs more research. As above without named species. Fowler cites earliest as Heckel 1841:73 (Amt. Ber. Vers. Deutsch. Nat. und Aerzte [not seen]). Also appeared in Heckel 1842:523 [see under ref. 2065] and Heckel 1843:1021 [ref. 2066]. Valid (Karaman 1971:191 [ref. 2560]). Cyprinidae.

Aulorhynchus Gill 1861:169 [ref. 1776]. Masc. *Aulorhynchus flavidus* Gill 1861:169. Type by monotypy. Valid (Fritzsche 1984 [ref. 13658]). Gasterosteidae: Aulorhynchinae.

Aulostomus Lacepède 1803:356 [ref. 4930]. Masc. *Fistularia chinensis* Linnaeus 1766:515. Type by monotypy. Spelled *Aulo stoma* by Dumèril 1806 [ref. 1151] and authors. Valid (Wheeler 1973:272 [ref. 7190], Araga in Masuda et al. 1984:84 [ref. 6441], Heemstra 1986:444 [ref. 5660], Paxton et al. 1989:404 [ref. 12442]). Aulostomidae.

Aulotrachichthys (subgenus of *Paratrachichthys*) Fowler 1938:40 [ref. 1426]. Masc. *Paratrachichthys latus* Fowler 1938:40. Type by original designation. Valid (Paxton et al. 1989:365 [ref. 12442]). Trachichthyidae.

Aulus Commerson in Lacepède 1803:350 (footnote) [ref. 4930]. Masc. Not available, Commerson manuscript name mentioned in passing under *Fistularia petimba*. Commerson names in footnotes in this volume placed on Official Index of Rejected Works; see remarks under Opinion 89 in Appendix B. In the synonymy of *Fistularia* Linnaeus 1758. Fistulariidae.

Aurata Catesby 1771:16 [ref. 774]. Fem. Not available, published in a rejected work on Official Index (Opinion 89, Opinion 259). In the synonymy of *Calamus* Swainson 1839 (Jordan 1917:30 [ref. 2407]). Sparidae.

Aurata Oken (ex Cuvier) 1817:1183 [ref. 3303]. Fem. *Sparus aurata* Linnaeus 1758:277. Based on "Les Daurades" of Cuvier 1816:272 [ref. 993] (see Gill 1903:966 [ref. 5768]). First technical addition of species and type designation not researched. Objective synonym of *Sparus* Linnaeus 1758 (Tortonese 1973:405 [ref. 7192]). Sparidae.

Aurata Risso 1826:355 [ref. 3757]. Fem. *Aurata semilunata* Risso 1826:355. Type by monotypy. Sparidae.

Aurigequula (subgenus of *Leiognathus*) Fowler 1918:17 [ref. 1396]. Fem. *Leiognathus fasciatus* Lacepède 1803:460. Type by original designation (also monotypic). Synonym of *Leiognathus* Lacepède 1802 (James 1978:141 [ref. 5317]). Leiognathidae.

Aurigobius (subgenus of *Ctenogobius*) Whitley 1959:317 [ref. 4729]. Masc. *Ctenogobius (Aurigobius) auriga* Whitley 1959:317. Type by original designation (also monotypic). Synonym of *Favonigobius* Whitley 1930 (Hoese, pers. comm.). Gobiidae.

Aurion Waite 1916:63 [ref. 4568]. Neut. *Aurion effulgens* Waite 1916:64. Type by monotypy. Bovichtidae.

Ausonia Risso 1826:341 [ref. 3757]. Fem. *Ausonia cuvieri* Risso 1826:342. Type by monotypy. Synonym of *Luvarus* Rafinesque 1810 (Topp 1973:476 [ref. 7209]). Luvaridae.

Australaphia Whitley 1936:48 [ref. 4687]. Fem. *Australaphia annona* Whitley 1936:49. Type by original designation (also monotypic). Described as a gobiid, synonym of apogonid genus *Gymnapogon* Regan 1905 (Fraser 1972:31 [ref. 5195], Paxton et al. 1989:555 [ref. 12442]). Apogonidae.

Australuzza Whitley 1947:136 [ref. 4708]. *Sphyraena novaehollandiae* Günther 1860:335. Type by original designation (also monotypic). *Austroluzza* is a misspelling. Synonym of *Sphyraena* Klein 1778 (de Sylva 1975:76 [ref. 6302], Daget 1986:350 [ref. 6203]); as a subgenus (de Sylva 1984:534 [ref. 13666]). Sphyraenidae.

Austranchovia Whitley 1931:311 [ref. 4672]. Fem. *Atherina australis* Shaw 1790:296. Type by original designation (also monotypic). Synonym of *Engraulis* Cuvier 1816 (Whitehead et al. 1988 [ref. 5725]). Engraulidae.

Austroatherina Marrero 1950:113 [ref. 5939]. Fem. *Atherina incisa* Jenyns 1842:79. Type by subsequent designation. Not available from Marrero 1950 —three included species and no designation of type after 1930. Doubtfully a synonym of *Odontesthes* Evermann & Kendall 1906 (White 1985:18 [ref. 13551]). Atherinidae: Atherinopsinae.

Austrobatrachus Smith 1949:423 [ref. 5846]. Masc. *Pseudobatrachus foedus* Smith 1947:820. Type by original designation (also monotypic). Valid (Hutchins 1986:358 [ref. 5673]). Batrachoididae.

Austroberyx McCulloch 1911:39 [ref. 2936]. Masc. *Beryx affinus* Günther 1859:13. Type by original designation. Synonym of *Centroberyx* Gill 1862 (Scott 1981:115 [ref. 5533]). Berycidae.

Austrochanda Whitley 1935:357 [ref. 4684]. Fem. *Pseudoambassis macleayi* Castelnau 1878:43. Type by being a replacement name. Unneeded replacement for *Pseudoambassis* Castelnau, not preoccupied by *Pseudambassis* Bleeker in fishes. Ambassidae.

Austrocobitis Ogilby 1899:158 [ref. 3279]. Fem. *Mesites attenuatus* Jenyns 1842:121. Type by being a replacement name. Replacement for *Mesites* Jenyns 1842, preoccupied by Schoenherr 1838 in Coleoptera. Synonym of *Galaxias* Cuvier 1816 (McDowall & Frankenberg 1981:455 [ref. 5500], McDowall 1984:126 [ref. 6178]). Galaxiidae: Galaxiinae.

Austrofundulus Myers 1932:159 [ref. 3103]. Masc. *Austrofundulus transilis* Myers 1932:160. Type by original designation (also monotypic). Valid (Taphorn & Thomerson 1978 [ref. 4337], Parenti 1981:487 [ref. 7066]). Aplocheilidae: Rivulinae.

Austroglanis Skelton, Risch & de Vos 1984:361 [ref. 5835]. Masc. *Gephyroglanis sclateri* Boulenger 1901:228. Type by original designation. Valid (Risch 1986:8 [ref. 6190], Burgess 1989:68 [ref. 12860]). Bagridae.

Austroglossus Regan 1920:217 [ref. 3671]. Masc. *Synaptura pectoralis* Kaup 1858:96. Type by original designation (also monotypic). Valid (Heemstra & Gon 1986:869 [ref. 5665]). Soleidae.

Austrogobio (subgenus of *Carassiops*) Ogilby 1898:784, 788 [ref. 3278]. Masc. *Carassiops (Austrogobio) galii* Ogilby 1898:788. Type by original designation (also monotypic). Synonym of *Hypseleotris* Gill 1863 (Hoese, pers. comm.). Eleotridae.

Austrogobius de Buen 1950:122 [ref. 13462]. Masc. *Gobiosoma parri* Ginsburg 1933:44. Type by monotypy. Also in de Buen 1951:64 [ref. 693]. Gobiidae.

Austrolabrus Steindachner 1884:1100 [ref. 4234]. Masc. *Labrichthys maculatus* Macleay 1881. Type by monotypy. Valid (Russell 1988:40 [ref. 12549]). Labridae.

Austrolethops Whitley 1935:243 [ref. 4683]. Masc. *Austrolethops wardi* Whitley 1935:243. Type by original designation (also monotypic). Valid (Hoese 1986:779 [ref. 5670], Birdsong et al. 1988:192 [ref. 7303]). Gobiidae.

Austrolycichthys Regan 1913:244 [ref. 3651]. Masc. *Lycodes brachycephalus* Pappenheim 1912:179. Type by subsequent designation. Type designated by Jordan 1920:550 [ref. 4905]. Valid (Anderson 1984:578 [ref. 13634], Pequeño 1989:49 [ref. 14125]); synonym of *Pachycara* Zugmayer 1911 (Anderson 1988:74 [ref. 7304], Anderson 1989:223 [ref. 13487]). Zoarcidae.

Austrolycus Regan 1913:245 [ref. 3651]. Masc. *Austrolycus depressiceps* Regan 1913:245. Type by subsequent designation. Type designated by Jordan 1920:550 [ref. 4905]. Valid (Gosztonyi 1977:200 [ref. 6103], Nakamura in Nakamura et al. 1986:234 [ref. 14235], Pequeño 1986:441 [ref. 6718], Pequeño 1989:48 [ref. 14125]). Zoarcidae.

Austromenidia Hubbs 1918:307 [ref. 2226]. Fem. *Basilichthys regillus* Abbott 1899:339. Type by original designation. Synonym of *Odontesthes* Evermann & Kendall 1906 (White 1985:17 [ref. 13551]). Atherinidae: Atherinopsinae.

Austronibea Trewavas 1977:361, 373 [ref. 4459]. Fem. *Austronibea oedogenys* Trewavas 1977:374. Type by original designation (also monotypic). Sciaenidae.

Austroperca Hubbs 1936:1 [ref. 2246]. Fem. *Etheostoma australe* Jordan 1884:362. Type by being a replacement name. Takes same type species as *Torrentaria*, not *Diplesion fasciata* Girard as designated by Hubbs. Replacement for *Torrentaria* Jordan & Evermann 1896, preoccupied by Hodgson in Gray 1863 in Aves. Synonym of *Etheostoma* Rafinesque 1819, but as a valid subgenus (Collette & Banarescu 1977:1456 [ref. 5845]); in the subgenus *Oligocephalus* Girard 1859 (Bailey & Etnier 1988:25 [ref. 6873]). Percidae.

Austrophycis Ogilby 1897:90 [ref. 3272]. Fem. *Austrophycis megalops* Ogilby 1897:91. Type by monotypy. Valid (Paulin 1983:101 [ref. 5459], Nakamura in Nakamura et al. 1986:108 [ref. 14235], Paxton et al. 1989:299 [ref. 12442]). Moridae.

Austrosparus Smith 1938:241 [ref. 4067]. Masc. *Chrysophrys globiceps* Valenciennes in Cuvier & Valenciennes 1830:100. Type by original designation. Synonym of *Rhabdosargus* Fowler 1933 (Smith 1979:702 [ref. 6940], Smith & Smith 1986:592 [ref. 5710], Bauchot & Skelton 1986:332 [ref. 6210]). Sparidae.

Austrotirus (subgenus of *Synodus*) Whitley 1937:219 [ref. 4690]. Masc. *Synodus similis* McCulloch 1921:167. Type by original designation. Synonym of *Synodus* Scopoli 1777 (Anderson et al. 1966:47 [ref. 6977]). Synodontidae: Synodontinae.

Autanadoras Fernández-Yépez 1950:8 [ref. 1323]. Masc. *Autanadoras milesi* Fernández-Yépez 1950:8. Type by original designation (also monotypic). Valid (Burgess 1989:223 [ref. 12860] as *Autanodoras*). Doradidae.

Autanichthys Fernández-Yépez 1950:11 [ref. 1323]. Masc. *Autanichthys giacopinii* Fernández-Yépez 1950:12. Type by original designation (also monotypic). Mention (Géry 1977:438

[ref. 1597]). Characidae.

Autisthes De Vis 1884:398 [ref. 1090]. *Autisthes argenteus* De Vis 1884:398. Type by monotypy. Synonym of *Terapon* Cuvier 1816 (Vari 1978:254 [ref. 4514], Vari 1986:304 [ref. 6205], but misspelled *Authistes* both times, see also Mees & Kailola 1977:32 [ref. 5183]). Terapontidae.

Auxis Cuvier 1829:199 [ref. 995]. Fem. *Scomber rochei* Risso 1810:165. *Scomber bisus* Rafinesque apparently treated as a synonym of *rochei*, therefore type by monotypy; type also designated by Gill 1862:125 [ref. 1659]. Valid (Postel 1973:470 [ref. 7208], Collette & Nauen 1983:27 [ref. 5375], Collette et al. 1984:600 [ref. 11421], Nakamura in Masuda et al. 1984:225 [ref. 6441], Collette 1986:832 [ref. 5647]). Scombridae.

Averruncus Jordan & Starks 1895:821 [ref. 2522]. Masc. *Averruncus emmelane* Jordan & Starks 1895:821. Type by original designation (also monotypic). Synonym of *Agonopsis* Gill 1861. Agonidae.

Avocettina Jordan & Davis 1891:655 [ref. 2437]. Fem. *Nemichthys infans* Günther 1878:251. Type by original designation. Apparently not preoccupied by *Avocettinus* Mulsant & Verreaux 1866 in Aves; *Borodinula* Whitley 1931 is an unneeded replacement. Valid (Asano in Masuda et al. 1984:22 [ref. 6441], Nielsen in Whitehead et al. 1986:551 [ref. 13676], Castle 1986:193 [ref. 5644], Paxton et al. 1989:134 [ref. 12442], Smith & Nielsen 1989:447 [ref. 13290]). Nemichthyidae.

Avocettinops Roule & Bertin 1924:63 [ref. 3828]. Masc. *Avocettinops schmidti* Roule & Bertin 1924:63. Type by monotypy. Also appeared as new in Roule & Bertin 1929:30 [ref. 3829] but clearly dates to 1924. Valid (Smith & Nielsen 1976:4 [ref. 7084], Smith & Nielsen 1989:447 [ref. 13290]). Nemichthyidae.

Awaous Steindachner 1860:289 [ref. 4205]. Masc. See *Awaous* Valenciennes 1837. Synonym of *Chonophorus* Poey 1860 (Maugé 1986:363 [ref. 6218]). See remark on dates under *Chonophorus*. Gobiidae.

Awaous (subgenus of *Gobius*) Valenciennes in Cuvier & Valenciennes 1837:97 [ref. 1006]. Masc. *Gobius ocellaris* Broussonet 1782:Fig. 142. Type by subsequent designation. If regarded as a subgenus, then authorship and type are as above. If regarded as used in a vernacular sense, then name dates to Steindachner 1860:289 [ref. 4205]. Type apparently designated first by Koumans 1931:83 [ref. 5623]. Valid (Hayashi in Masuda et al. 1984:263 [ref. 6441], Hoese 1986:779 [ref. 5670], Birdsong et al. 1988:198 [ref. 7303]). As a synonym of *Chonophorus* Poey 1860 (Maugé 1986:363 [ref. 6218] who dated to Steindachner 1860). Gobiidae.

Axelrodia Géry 1965:31 [ref. 1584]. Fem. *Axelrodia fowleri* Géry 1965:33. Type by original designation (also monotypic). See also Géry 1966:111 [ref. 1587]. Valid (Géry 1977:602 [ref. 1597]). Characidae.

Axineceps (subgenus of *Polysteganus*) Smith 1938:301 [ref. 4067]. Neut. *Dentex praeorbitalis* Günther 1859:368. Type by monotypy. Synonym of *Polysteganus* Klunzinger 1870. Sparidae.

Axinurus Cuvier 1829:225 [ref. 995]. Masc. *Axinurus thynnoides* Cuvier 1829:225. Type by monotypy. Synonym of *Naso* Lacepède 1801 (Randall 1955:361 [ref. 13648]). Acanthuridae.

Axoclinus Fowler 1944:288 [ref. 1448]. Masc. *Axoclinus lucillae* Fowler 1944:288. Type by original designation (also monotypic). Synonym of *Enneanectes* Jordan & Evermann 1895 (see Böhlke 1984:61 [ref. 13621]). Tripterygiidae.

Axyrias Starks 1896:554 [ref. 4195]. Masc. *Axyrias harringtoni* Starks 1896:554. Type by monotypy. Synonym of *Artedius* Girard 1856 (Bolin 1944:45 [ref. 6379], Begle 1989:646 [ref. 12739]). Cottidae.

Aygula Rafinesque 1815:87 [ref. 3584]. Fem. *Coris aygula* Lacepède 1801:96. Type by being a replacement name. As "*Aygula* R. [Rafinesque] *Coris* Lac. [Lacepède]. An available replacement name (unneeded) for and objective synonym of *Coris* Cuvier 1801. Labridae.

Aylopon Rafinesque 1810:52 [ref. 3594]. Neut. *Labrus anthias* Linnaeus 1758:282. Type by being a replacement name. As "*Aylopon* R. *Anthias* Bl.," meaning *Aylopon* Rafinesque for *Anthias* Bloch. An available unneeded replacement for *Anthias* Bloch 1792, not preoccupied by *Anthia* Weber 1801 in Coleoptera. Objective synonym of *Anthias* Bloch 1792 (Anderson & Heemstra 1980:73 [ref. 5434]). Serranidae: Anthiinae.

Ayresia Cooper 1863:73 [ref. 905]. Fem. *Ayresia punctipinnis* Cooper 1863:73. Type by monotypy. Synonym of *Chromis* Cuvier 1814. Pomacentridae.

Azevia Jordan in Jordan & Goss 1889:271 [ref. 2482]. Fem. *Citharichthys panamensis* Steindachner 1875:62. Type by original designation (also monotypic). Synonym of *Cyclopsetta* Gill 1889 (Norman 1934:134 [ref. 6893]). Paralichthyidae.

Azteca (subgenus of *Notropis*) Jordan & Evermann 1896:254, 258 [ref. 2443]. Fem. *Codoma vittata* Girard 1856:195 (= *Notropis aztecus* Woolman 1894:63). Type by original designation (also monotypic). Preoccupied by Forel 1878 in Hymenoptera, replaced by *Aztecula* Jordan & Evermann 1898. Synonym of *Notropis* Rafinesque 1818, subgenus *Aztecula* Jordan & Evermann 1898 (Gilbert 1978:16 [ref. 7042]). Cyprinidae.

Aztecula Jordan & Evermann 1898:2799 [ref. 2445]. Fem. *Notropis vittata* Girard 1856:195 (= *Notropis azetucus* Woolman 1894:63). Type by being a replacement name. Replacement for *Azteca* Jordan & Evermann 1896, preoccupied by Forel 1878 in Hymenoptera. Synonym of *Notropis* Rafinesque 1818, but as a valid subgenus (Gilbert 1978:16 [ref. 7042]). Cyprinidae.

Azuma Jordan & Snyder 1902:463 [ref. 2516]. *Azuma emmnion* Jordan & Snyder 1902:463. Type by original designation (also monotypic). Pholidae.

Azurella Jordan 1919:341 [ref. 2413]. Fem. *Pomacentrus bairdii* Gill 1862:149. Type by original designation (also monotypic). Pomacentridae.

Azurina Jordan & McGregor in Jordan & Evermann 1898:1544 [ref. 2444]. Fem. *Azurina hirundo* Jordan & McGregor in Jordan & Evermann 1898:1544. Type by original designation (also monotypic). Also appeared in Jordan & McGregor 1899:281 [ref. 2488]. Pomacentridae.

Azygopterus Andriashev & Makushok 1955:50 [ref. 6465]. Masc. *Azygopterus corallinus* Andriashev & Makushok 1955:50. Type by original designation (also monotypic). Stichaeidae.

Azygopus Norman 1926:261 [ref. 3216]. Masc. *Azygopus pinnifasciatus* Norman 1926:262. Type by monotypy. Valid (Norman 1934:416 [ref. 6893], Ahlstrom et al. 1984:643 [ref. 13641], Sakamoto 1984 [ref. 5273]). Pleuronectidae: Rhombosoleinae.

Babka Iljin 1927:132 [ref. 5613]. *Gobius gymnotrachelus* Kessler 1857:464. Type by original designation. Synonym of *Neogobius* Iljin 1927 (Miller 1973:501 [ref. 6888]). Gobiidae.

Bachmannia Nani in Szidat & Nani 1951:336 [ref. 5955]. Fem. *Basilichthys smitti* Lahille 1929:336. Type by original designation (also monotypic). Preoccupied by *Bachmannia* Dolgophol de Saez 1945 in fossil fishes; apparently not replaced. Synonym of *Odontesthes* Evermann & Kendall 1906 (Dyer, pers. comm.). Atherinidae: Atherinopsinae.

Badis Bleeker 1853:106 [ref. 341]. *Labrus buchanani* Bleeker 1853:107 (= *Labrus badis* Hamilton 1822:70, 368). Type by absolute tautonymy of senior objective synonym (*L. badis* needlessly renamed *buchanani* by Bleeker), but perhaps type is *buchanani* by monotypy (not translated). Valid (Jayaram 1981:334 [ref. 6497], Kottelat 1989:18 [ref. 13605]. Nandidae: Badinae.

Bagarius Bleeker 1853:121 [ref. 341]. Masc. *Pimelodus bagarius* Hamilton 1822:186, 378. Type by monotypy (also by absolute tautonymy). Valid (Jayaram 1981:237 [ref. 6497], Roberts 1983 [ref. 6816], Kottelat 1985:270 [ref. 11441], Burgess 1989:133 [ref. 12860], Kottelat 1989:15 [ref. 13605], Roberts 1989:133 [ref. 6439]). Sisoridae.

Bagre Catesby 1771:23 [ref. 774]. Masc. Not available, published in a rejected work on Official Index (Opinion 89, Opinion 259). Ictaluridae.

Bagre Cloquet 1816:52 [ref. 852]. Masc. *Silurus bagre* Linnaeus 1766:505. Type by absolute tautonymy. Based on "Les Bagres" Cuvier 1816:204 [ref. 993]. Predates *Bagre* Oken 1817. On Official List (Opinion 1402). Valid (Burgess 1989:167 [ref. 12860]). Ariidae.

Bagrichthys Bleeker 1858:59, 130 [ref. 365]. Masc. *Bagrus hyselopterus* Bleeker 1852:588. Type by monotypy. Also mentioned on pp. 27, 64. Valid (Jayaram 1968:377 [ref. 5615], Burgess 1989:71 [ref. 12860], Roberts 1989:111 [ref. 6439]). Bagridae.

Bagroides Bleeker 1851:204 [ref. 329]. Masc. *Bagroides melapterus* Bleeker 1851:204. Type by monotypy. Type species subsequently spelled *melanopterus* by Bleeker. Valid (Jayaram 1968:373 [ref. 5615], Kottelat 1985:270 [ref. 11441], Burgess 1989:71 [ref. 12860], Kottelat 1989:13 [ref. 13605], Roberts 1989:115 [ref. 6439]). Bagridae.

Bagropsis Lütken 1874:32 [ref. 2855]. Fem. *Bagropsis reinhardti* Lütken 1874:32. Type by monotypy. Misspelled *Bacropsis* in Zoological Record for 1873. Valid (Burgess 1989:281 [ref. 12860]). Pimelodidae.

Bagrus Bosc 1816:147 [ref. 5126]. Masc. *Silurus bajad* Forsskål 1775:66. Type by subsequent designation. Type designated by Bailey & Stewart 1983:168 [ref. 5242]. On Official List (Opinion 1402). Valid (Risch 1986:9 [ref. 6190], Burgess 1989:69 [ref. 12860]). Bagridae.

Bahaba (subgenus of *Otolithes*) Herre 1935:603 [ref. 2110]. Fem. *Otolithes (Bahaba) lini* Herre 1935:603. Type by original designation (also monotypic). Valid (Trewavas 1977:285 [ref. 4459], Jayaram 1981:330 [ref. 6497], Kottelat 1989:17 [ref. 13605]). Sciaenidae.

Baicalocottus Berg 1903:100 [ref. 263]. Masc. *Cottus grewingkii* Dybowski 1874:384. Type by original designation. Synonym of *Cottocomephorus* Pellegrin 1900. Cottocomephoridae.

Baileychromis Poll 1986:134 [ref. 6136]. Masc. *Leptochromis centropomoides* Bailey & Stewart 1977:13. Type by original designation (also monotypic). Cichlidae.

Baillonus Rafinesque 1815:85 [ref. 3584]. *Caesiomorus baillonii* Lacepède 1801:93. Type by being a replacement name. As "*Baillonus* R. [Rafinesque] *Caesiomorus* Lac. [Lacepède]." Name only but an available (unneeded) replacement for *Caesiomorus* Lacepède 1801. Synonym of *Trachinotus* Lacepède 1801 (Daget & Smith-Vaniz 1986:319 [ref. 6207]). Carangidae.

Baiodon Agassiz 1859:408 [ref. 74]. Masc. *Baiodon fasciatus* Agassiz 1859:408. Type by monotypy. Essentially without description [further use of name not researched]. Cichlidae.

Baione DeKay 1842:244 [ref. 1098]. *Baione fontinalis* DeKay 1842:244. Type by monotypy. Synonym of *Salvelinus* Richardson 1836, but as a valid subgenus (Kendall & Behnke 1984:144 [ref. 13638]). Salmonidae: Salmoninae.

Baiostoma Bean in Goode & Bean 1882:413 [ref. 1840]. Neut. *Baiostoma brachialis* Bean in Goode & Bean 1882:413. Type by monotypy. Achiridae.

Bairdiella Gill 1861:33 [ref. 1766]. Fem. *Bodianus argyroleucus* Mitchill 1815:417. Type by monotypy. Valid (Chao 1978:38 [ref. 6983]). Sciaenidae.

Bajacalifornia Townsend & Nichols 1925:8 [ref. 4420]. Fem. *Bajacalifornia burragei* Townsend & Nichols 1925:8. Type by monotypy. Valid (Krefft 1973:88 [ref. 7166], Markle & Quéro in Whitehead et al. 1984:233 [ref. 13675], Amaoka in Masuda et al. 1984:43 [ref. 6441], Markle & Krefft 1985 [ref. 6789], Markle 1986:219 [ref. 5687], Sazonov 1989 [ref. 14118]). Alepocephalidae.

Balantiocheilos Bleeker 1859:430 [ref. 370]. Masc. *Barbus melanopterus* Bleeker 1850:11. Type by subsequent monotypy. Appeared first in key, without included species. One species in Bleeker 1859:149 [ref. 371] and 1859:102 [ref. 369]. Subsequently spelled *Balantiocheilus* and *Balantiochilus* by Bleeker. Valid (Wu et al. 1977:331 [ref. 4807], Kottelat 1985:260 [ref. 11441] and Chu & Cui in Chu & Chen 1989:147 [ref. 13584] as *Balantiocheilus*, Chu & Kottelat 1989:4 [ref. 12575], Kottelat 1989:6 [ref. 13605], Roberts 1989:29 [ref. 6439]). Cyprinidae.

Balistapus Tilesius 1820:302 [ref. 4407]. Masc. *Balistapus capistratus* Tilesius 1820:306, 309. Type by monotypy. Valid (Matsuura 1980:52 [ref. 6943], Tyler 1980:121 [ref. 4477], Arai 1983:199 [ref. 14249], Aboussouan & Leis 1984:452 [ref. 13661], Matsuura in Masuda et al. 1984:358 [ref. 6441], Smith & Heemstra 1986:877 [ref. 5714]). Balistidae.

Balistes Linnaeus 1758:327 [ref. 2787]. Masc. *Balistes vetula* Linnaeus 1758:329. Type by subsequent designation. Type designated by Bleeker 1865:98 [ref. 416] and 1866:10 [ref. 417]. Valid (Torchio 1973:641 [ref. 6892], Tyler 1980:121 [ref. 4477], Arai 1983:199 [ref. 14249], Aboussouan & Leis 1984:452 [ref. 13661], Tortonese in Whitehead et al. 1986:1335 [ref. 13677], Smith & Heemstra 1986:877 [ref. 5714]). Balistidae.

Balistoides Fraser-Brunner 1935:659, 662 [ref. 1489]. Masc. *Balistes viridescens* Bloch & Schneider 1801:477. Type by original designation. Valid (Matsuura 1980:44 [ref. 6943], Tyler 1980:121 [ref. 4477], Arai 1983:199 [ref. 14249], Matsuura in Masuda et al. 1984:357 [ref. 6441], Smith & Heemstra 1986:878 [ref. 5714]). Balistidae.

Balitora Gray 1830:Pl. 88 (v. 1) [ref. 1878]. Fem. *Balitora brucei* Gray 1830:Pl. 88. Type by monotypy. Kottelat 1988 [ref. 13379] and 1989 [ref. 13605] regards Balitoridae Swainson 1839 as the valid name for the family, predating Homalopteridae Bleeker 1859. Valid (Silas 1953:205 [ref. 4024], Menon et al. 1978 [ref. 6801], Chen 1878:335 [ref. 6900], Jayaram 1981:143 [ref. 6497], Sawada 1982:204 [ref. 14111], Kottelat 1985:267 [ref. 11441], Menon 1987:228 [ref. 14149], Kottelat 1988 [ref. 13379], Kottelat & Chu 1988:188 [ref. 13491], Kottelat 1989:12 [ref. 13605]). Balitoridae: Balitorinae.

Balitoropsis Smith 1945:278 [ref. 4056]. Fem. *Balitoropsis bartschi* Smith 1945:279. Type by original designation (also monotypic). Valid (Silas 1953:208 [ref. 4024], Chen 1978:333 [ref. 6900], Sawada 1982:204 [ref. 14111]). Synonym of *Homaloptera* (Kottelat & Chu 1988:106 [ref. 12840]). Balitoridae: Balitorinae.

Ballerus Heckel 1843:1033 [ref. 2066]. *Cyprinus ballerus* Linnaeus 1758:327. Type by monotypy (also by absolute tautonymy). Synonym of *Abramis* Cuvier 1816 (Howes 1981:46 [ref. 14200]). Cyprinidae.

Balsadichthys Hubbs 1926:19 [ref. 2233]. Masc. *Goodea whitei* Meek 1904:137. Type by original designation (also monotypic). Synonym of *Ilyodon* Eigenmann 1907 (Miller & Fitzsimons 1971:10 [ref. 3019]). Goodeidae.

Bambradon Jordan & Richardson 1908:643 [ref. 2491]. *Bembras laevis* Nyström 1887:26. Type by original designation (also monotypic). Valid (Washington et al. 1984:441 [ref. 13660] as *Bembradon*). Bembridae.

Bandichthys (subgenus of *Melanostigma*) Parin 1979:167, 170 [ref. 3363]. Masc. *Melanostigma (Bandichthys) vitiazi* Parin 1979:167. Type by original designation (also monotypic). Zoarcidae.

Bangana (subgenus of *Cyprinus*) Hamilton 1822:277, 385 [ref. 2031]. *Cyprinus dero* Hamilton 1822:277, 385. Type by subsequent designation. Type designated by Jordan 1917:155 [ref. 2407]. Valid (Kottelat 1985:260 [ref. 11441], Kottelat 1989:6 [ref. 13605]). Cyprinidae.

Banjos Bleeker 1876:277 [ref. 447]. *Banjos banjos* Richardson 1846:236. Type by being a replacement name. We regard as a replacement name for *Anoplus* Temminck & Schlegel 1842 based on style of Bleeker 1876; *Anoplus* preoccupied by Schönherr 1826 in Coleoptera. Valid (Akazaki in Masuda et al. 1984:174 [ref. 6441], Paxton et al. 1989:538 [ref. 12442]). Banjosidae.

Barathrites Zugmayer 1911:11 [ref. 6161]. Masc. *Barathrites iris* Zugmayer 1911:11. Type by monotypy. Also appeared in Zugmayer 1911 (Dec.):132 [ref. 4846]. Valid (Nielsen 1973:549 [ref. 6885], Cohen & Nielsen 1978:25 [ref. 881], Anderson et al. 1985 [ref. 5164], Nielsen in Whitehead et al. 1986:1159 [ref. 13677]). Ophidiidae: Neobythitinae.

Barathrodemus Goode & Bean 1883:200 [ref. 1838]. Masc. *Barathrodemus manatinus* Goode & Bean 1883:200. Type by original designation (also monotypic). Valid (Cohen & Nielsen 1978:25 [ref. 881], Carter & Musick 1985 [ref. 6791]). Ophidiidae: Neobythitinae.

Barathronus Goode & Bean 1886:164 [ref. 1844]. Fem. *Barathronus bicolor* Goode & Bean 1886:164. Type by monotypy. Valid (Nielsen 1973:555 [ref. 6885], Cohen & Nielsen 1978:61 [ref. 881], Nielsen 1984 [ref. 5286], Nielsen & Machida 1985 [ref. 5222], Nielsen in Whitehead et al. 1986:1168 [ref. 13677], Nielsen 1986:357 [ref. 5699], Paxton et al. 1989:318 [ref. 12442]). Aphyonidae.

Barbantus Parr 1951:18 [ref. 3380]. *Bathytroctes curvifrons* Roule & Angel 1931:6. Type by original designation (also monotypic). Valid (Krefft 1973:95 [ref. 7166], Quéro et al. in Whitehead et al. 1984:258 [ref. 13675], Sazonov 1986 [ref. 6003]). Platytroctidae.

Barbatogobius Koumans 1941:241 [ref. 2677]. Masc. *Barbatogobius asanai* Koumans 1941:242. Type by original designation (also monotypic). Synonym of *Gobiopsis* Steindachner 1860 (Lachner & McKinney 1978:10 [ref. 6603]). Gobiidae.

Barbatula Linck 1790:38 [ref. 4985]. Fem. *Cobitis barbatula* Linnaeus 1758:303. Type by absolute tautonymy. See Kottelat 1990:18 [ref. 14137] for remarks on type and availability. Valid (Kottelat 1990:18 [ref. 14137]). Balitoridae: Nemacheilinae.

Barbellion Whitley 1931:334 [ref. 4672]. Neut. *Barynotus lagensis* Günther 1868:61. Type by being a replacement name. Replacement for *Barynotus* Günther 1868, preoccupied by Germar 1817 in Coleoptera. Cyprinidae.

Barbichthys Bleeker 1859:424 [ref. 370]. Masc. *Barbus laevis* Valenciennes in Cuvier & Valenciennes 1842:192. Apparently appeared first in key, without species. One valid species included by Bleeker 1859:147 [ref. 371] and 1860:115, 208 [ref. 380]. Type by subsequent monotypy. Valid (Kottelat 1985:260 [ref. 11441], Kottelat 1989:6 [ref. 13605], Roberts 1989:29 [ref. 6439]). Cyprinidae.

Barbodes (subgenus of *Systomus*) Bleeker 1860:275, 313 [ref. 380]. Masc. *Systomus (Barbodes) belinka* Bleeker 1860:321. Type by subsequent designation. Apparently appeared first as name only in Bleeker 1859:431 [ref. 370]. Dates to Bleeker 1860 as above or to 1860:2 [ref. 376], if the latter then *belinka* is not type; type designated by Bleeker 1863:27 [ref. 4859] or 1863:200 [ref. 397]. Valid (Wu et al. 1977:234 [ref. 4807], Chen & Chu 1985:82 [ref. 5250], Chu & Cui in Chu & Chen 1989:180 [ref. 13584], Kottelat 1989:6 [ref. 13605]); synonym of *Puntius* Hamilton 1822 (Roberts 1989:60 [ref. 6439]). Cyprinidae.

Barbodon Dybowski 1872:216 [ref. 1170]. Masc. *Barbodon lacustris* Dybowski 1872:216. Type by monotypy. Synonym of *Sarcocheilichthys* Bleeker 1859 (Banarescu & Nalbant 1973:39 [ref. 173], Lu, Luo & Chen 1977:467 [ref. 13495]). Cyprinidae.

Barboides Brüning 1929:759 [ref. 6187]. Masc. *Barboides gracilis* Brüning 1929:759. Type by monotypy. Valid (Lévêque & Daget 1984:217 [ref. 6186]). Cyprinidae.

Barbopsis Caporiacco 1926:23 [ref. 720]. Fem. *Barbopsis devecchii* Caporiacco 1926:24. Type by original designation (also monotypic). Valid (Lévêque & Daget 1984:218 [ref. 6186]). Cyprinidae.

Barbourichthys Chabanaud 1934:388 [ref. 790]. Masc. *Barbourichthys zanzibaricus* Chabanaud 1934:388. Type by monotypy. Soleidae.

Barbourisia Parr 1945:128 [ref. 3377]. Fem. *Barbourisia rufa* Parr 1945:128. Type by monotypy. Valid (Amaoka in Masuda et al. 1984:115 [ref. 6441], Paxton & Bray 1986:433 [ref. 5703], Lea 1987 [ref. 6376], Paxton et al. 1989:383 [ref. 12442]). Barbourisiidae.

Barbucca Roberts 1989:100 [ref. 6439]. Fem. *Barbucca diabolica* Roberts 1989:100. Type by original designation (also monotypic). Valid (Kottelat 1990:19 [ref. 14137]). Balitoridae: Nemacheilinae.

Barbuliceps Chan 1966:4 [ref. 807]. Neut. *Barbuliceps tuberculatus* Chan 1966:5. Type by original designation (also monotypic). Chan (p. 4) lists type as *B. tubercularis* sp. nov., but otherwise spelled the species *tuberculatus*; *tubercularis* is an obvious lapsus, but Cohen (1974:446 [ref. 7157]) serves as first reviser if needed. Synonym of *Saccogaster* Alcock 1889 (Cohen 1972:446 [ref. 7157], Cohen & Nielsen 1978:50 [ref. 881]). Bythitidae: Bythitinae.

Barbulifer Eigenmann & Eigenmann 1888:70 [ref. 1250]. Masc. *Barbulifer papillosus* Eigenmann & Eigenmann 1888:70. Type by subsequent designation. Type apparently first designated by Jordan & Evermann 1896:461 [ref. 2442], not *Gobiosoma ceuthaecum* as given by Jordan 1920:440 [ref. 4905]. Valid (Hoese & Larson 1985 [ref. 6787], Birdsong et al. 1988:189 [ref. 7303]). Gobiidae.

Barbuligobius Lachner & McKinney 1974:871 [ref. 2547]. Masc. *Barbuligobius boehlkei* Lachner & McKinney 1974:871. Type by original designation (also monotypic). Valid (Yoshino in Masuda et al. 1984:264 [ref. 6441], Birdsong et al. 1988:192 [ref. 7303]). Gobiidae.

Barbupeneus Whitley 1931:317 [ref. 4672]. Masc. *Upeneus signatus* Günther 1867:59. Type by original designation (also monotypic). Synonym of *Parupeneus* Bleeker 1863 or *Mullus* Linnaeus 1758. Mullidae.

Barbus Cuvier & Cloquet 1816:4 [ref. 993]. Masc. *Cyprinus barbus* Linnaeus 1758:320. Type by absolute tautonymy. Fowler (MS) attributes (probably correctly) to Cuvier & Cloquet (Dict. Nat., ed. 2, v. 4, suppl.) as prior to Cuvier 1816. Valid (Karaman 1971:192 [ref. 2560], Lévêque & Daget 1984:218 [ref. 6186], Kottelat 1985:260 [ref. 11441], Lévêque et al. 1988 [ref. 6865], Skelton 1988:294 [ref. 7302], Lévêque 1989 [ref. 12829], Lévêque 1989 [ref. 13471], Krupp & Schneider 1989:359 [ref. 13651]). Cyprinidae.

Barchatus Smith 1952:332 [ref. 4084]. *Batrachus cirrhosus* Klunzinger 1870:500. Type by original designation (also monotypic). Batrachoididae.

Barffianus Curtiss 1844:13 [ref. 12574]. Masc. *Barffianus naneae* Curtiss 1844:13. Type by monotypy. Original not seen; above from Fowler (MS). Synonym of *Synanceia* Bloch & Schneider 1801. Scorpaenidae: Synanceiinae.

Barilius (subgenus of *Cyprinus*) Hamilton 1822:266, 384 [ref. 2031]. Masc. *Cyprinus barila* Hamilton 1822:267, 384. Type by subsequent designation. Type designated by Bleeker 1863:203 [ref. 397], 1863:263 [ref. 403] and 1863:28 [ref. 4859]. Valid (Jayaram 1981:87 [ref. 6497], Roberts 1989:30 [ref. 6439], Kuang in Chu & Chen 1989:19 [ref. 13584], Kottelat 1989:6 [ref. 13605]). Cyprinidae.

Bario Myers 1940:35 [ref. 3118]. *Tetragonopterus steindachneri* Eigenmann 1893:53. Type by being a replacement name. Replacement for *Entomolepis* Eigenmann 1917, preoccupied by Brady 1889 in Crustacea. Valid (Géry 1977:454 [ref. 1597]). Characidae.

Barnardichthys Chabanaud 1927:3 [ref. 781]. Masc. *Solea fulvomarginata* Gilchrist 1904:13. Type by original designation (also monotypic). Synonym of *Solea* Quensel 1806 (Heemstra & Gon 1986:873 [ref. 5665] based on placement of type species). Soleidae.

Barombia Trewavas 1962:184 [ref. 4456]. Fem. *Barombia maclareni* Trewavas 1962:184. Type by original designation (also monotypic). Apparently preoccupied by Karsch 1891 in Orthoptera and by Jacoby 1903 in Coleoptera (see Whitley 1976:46 [ref. 4735]). Cichlidae.

Barrosia Smith 1952:147 [ref. 4083]. Fem. *Barrosia barrosi* Smith 1952:149. Type by original designation. Predates *Barrosia* Villers (June) 1952 in Hemiptera, Smith was Feb. 1952 (see Whitley 1965:25 [ref. 4733]). Plesiopidae.

Bartramiolus Fowler 1945:253 [ref. 1453]. Masc. *Ambloplites ariommus* Viosca 1936:37. Type by original designation (also monotypic). Synonym of *Ambloplites* Rafinesque 1820. Centrarchidae.

Bartschina (subgenus of *Dampieria*) Fowler 1931:5, 18 [ref. 1407]. Fem. *Dampieria bitaeniata* Fowler 1931:18. Type by original designation (also monotypic). Synonym of *Pseudochromis* Rüppell 1835. Pseudochromidae: Pseudochrominae.

Baryancistrus Rapp Py-Daniel 1989:245 [ref. 13470]. Masc. *Hypostomus niveatus* Castelnau 1855:43. Type by original designation (also monotypic, one species mentioned). Both new genera in this work were proposed as (p. 235), "...herein preliminary established." Regarded as available, not falling under Art. 15 (taxa proposed conditionally after 1961 are unavailable; see Appendix A). Loricariidae.

Barynotus Günther 1868:61 [ref. 1990]. Masc. *Barynotus lagensis* Günther 1868:61. Type by subsequent designation. Type designated by Jordan 1919:351 [ref. 4904]. Preoccupied by Germar 1817 in Coleoptera; replaced by and objective synonym of *Barbellion* Whitley 1931. Cyprinidae.

Bascanichthys Jordan & Davis 1891:621 [ref. 2437]. Masc. *Caecula bascanium* Jordan 1885:48. Type by original designation. Valid (McCosker 1977:70 [ref. 6836], McCosker & Castle 1986: 177 [ref. 5690], McCosker et al. 1989:329 [ref. 13288]). Ophichthidae: Ophichthinae.

Bascanius Schiødte 1868:274 [ref. 3927]. Masc. *Bascanius taedifer* Schiødte 1868:274. Type by monotypy. Based on a larva. On p. 382 as appeared in Ann. Mag. Nat. Hist. (see under ref. 3927). Synonym of *Arnoglossus* Bleeker 1862 (Norman 1934:173 [ref. 6893], Nielsen 1973:621 [ref. 6885]). Bothidae: Bothinae.

Basilichthys Girard 1855:198 [ref. 1819]. Masc. *Atherina microlepidota* Jenyns 1842:78. Type by subsequent designation. Type apparently first designated by Fowler 1903:734 [ref. 1362]. Valid (White 1985:17 [ref. 13551], Crabtree 1987:860 [ref. 6771]). Atherinidae: Atherinopsinae.

Basilisciscartes (subgenus of *Salarias*) Fowler 1939:2 [ref. 1430]. Masc. *Blennius saliens* Forster 1788:343. Type by original designation (also monotypic). Synonym of *Alticus* Commerson 1800 (Smith-Vaniz & Springer 1971:14 [ref. 4145], Bath 1986:355 [ref. 6217]). Blenniidae.

Bassanago Whitley 1948:71 [ref. 4710]. Masc. *Bassanago bulbiceps* Whitley 1948:71. Type by original designation (also monotypic). Valid (Castle 1986:162 [ref. 5644], Paxton et al. 1989:140 [ref. 12442], Smith 1989:512, 533 [ref. 13285]). Congridae: Congrinae.

Bassetina Whitley 1941:30 [ref. 4701]. Fem. *Caranx hullianus* McCulloch 1909:319. Type by being a replacement name. Replacement for *Zamora* Whitley 1931, preoccupied by Roewer 1928 in Arachnida. Synonym of *Uraspis* Bleeker 1855 (Smith-Vaniz, pers. comm.). Carangidae.

Bassobythites Brauer 1906:307 [ref. 632]. Masc. *Bassobythites brunswigi* Brauer 1906:307. Type by monotypy. Valid (Cohen & Nielsen 1978:26 [ref. 881]). Ophidiidae: Neobythitinae.

Bassogigas Goode & Bean (ex Gill) 1896:328 [ref. 1848]. *Bassogigas gillii* Goode & Bean 1896:328. Type by monotypy. Goode & Bean give Gill as author, but it is unclear if Gill was responsible for the description; current workers attribute to Goode & Bean. Valid (Nielsen 1973:549 [ref. 6885], Cohen & Nielsen 1978:26 [ref. 881], Nielsen 1980:17 [ref. 6926], Nielsen & Cohen 1986:345 [ref. 5700]). Ophidiidae: Neobythitinae.

Bassozetus Gill 1883:259 [ref. 1724]. *Bassozetus normalis* Gill 1883:259. Type by monotypy. Valid (Cohen & Nielsen 1978:27 [ref. 881], Anderson et al. 1985 [ref. 5164], Nielsen & Cohen 1986:345 [ref. 5700], Machida & Tachibana 1986 [ref. 6620], Machida 1989 [ref. 13417]). Ophidiidae: Neobythitinae.

Batanga Herre 1946:121 [ref. 2142]. Fem. *Eleotris lebretonis* Steindachner 1870:947. Type by original designation (also monotypic). Species often misspelled *lebretoni*. Valid (Maugé 1986:389 [ref.

6218], Birdsong et al. 1988:181 [ref. 7303]). Eleotridae.

Batasio Blyth 1860:149 [ref. 477]. *Batasio buchanani* Blyth 1860:150 (= *Pimelodus batasio* Hamilton 1822:179, 377). Type by original designation. Type designated as "*B. Buchanani*, nobis; *Pimelodus batasio*, B.H." Blyth needlessly renamed *batasio* as *buchanani*. Valid (Jayaram 1977:16 [ref. 7005], Jayaram 1977 [ref. 7007], Jayaram 1981:190 [ref. 6497], Burgess 1989:70 [ref. 12860], Kottelat 1989:13 [ref. 13605]). Bagridae.

Bathophilus Giglioli 1882:199 [ref. 1620]. Masc. *Bathophilus nigerrimus* Giglioli 1882:199. Type by original designation (also monotypic). Description brief, but probably sufficient [in 1882] to allow dating of name to 1882:199; more fully described in Giglioli & Issel 1884:261 [ref. 5325]. Spelled *Bathyophilus* by Jordan 1920:423 [ref. 4505] and others. Valid (Morrow in Morrow & Gibbs 1964:456 [ref. 6962], Morrow 1973:135 [ref. 7175], Fujii in Masuda et al. 1984:52 [ref. 6441], Fink 1985:11 [ref. 5171], Gibbs 1986:237 [ref. 5655], Swinney 1988 [ref. 13445], Paxton et al. 1989:198 [ref. 12442]). Melanostomiidae.

Bathophilus Miles 1942:57 [ref. 12429]. Masc. *Pygidium totae* Miles 1942:57. Type by monotypy. Preoccupied by Giglioli 1882 in fishes, replaced by *Bathypygidium* Whitley 1947. Trichomycteridae.

Bathyaethiops Fowler 1949:247 [ref. 1461]. Masc. *Bathyaethiops greeni* Fowler 1949:247. Type by original designation (also monotypic). Valid (Poll 1967:72 [ref. 3529], Paugy 1984:163 [ref. 6183]). Alestiidae.

Bathyagonus Gilbert 1890:89 [ref. 1623]. Masc. *Bathyagonus nigripinnis* Gilbert 1890:89. Type by original designation (also monotypic). Valid (Washington et al. 1984:442 [ref. 13660], Yabe 1985:123 [ref. 11522]). Agonidae.

Bathyalopex (subgenus of *Chimaera*) Collett 1904:5 [ref. 9338]. Fem. *Chimaera (Bathyalopex) mirabilis* Collett 1904:5. Type by monotypy. Synonym of *Hydrolagus* Gill 1862 (Krefft 1973:79 [ref. 7166]). Chimaeridae.

Bathyanthias Günther 1880:6 [ref. 2011]. Masc. *Bathyanthias roseus* Günther 1880:6. Type by monotypy. Tentative synonym of *Pikea* Steindachner 1874 (Robins 1967:593 [ref. 3786]). Serranidae: Liopropomatinae.

Bathyaploactis Whitley 1933:102 [ref. 4677]. Fem. *Bathyaploactis curtisensis* Whitley 1933:103. Type by original designation (one species, two subspecies). Misspelled *Bathaploactis* in Zoological Record for 1933. Valid (Poss & Eschmeyer 1978:404 [ref. 6387], Washington et al. 1984:440 [ref. 13660], Paxton et al. 1989:460 [ref. 12442]). Aploactinidae.

Bathybagrus Bailey & Stewart 1984:8 [ref. 5232]. Masc. *Bathybagrus tetranema* Bailey & Stewart 1984:11. Type by original designation (also monotypic). Valid (Risch 1986:13 [ref. 6190], Burgess 1989:69 [ref. 12860]). Bagridae.

Bathybates Boulenger 1898:15 [ref. 547]. Masc. *Bathybates ferox* Boulenger 1898:15. Type by monotypy. Valid (Poll 1986:125 [ref. 6136]). Cichlidae.

Bathybatrachus Gilchrist & von Bonde 1924:21 [ref. 1649]. Masc. *Bathybatrachus albolineatus* Gilchrist & von Bonde 1924:21. Type by monotypy. Considered a nomen dubium by Hutchins 1986:358 [ref. 5673]. Batrachoididae.

Bathyblennius Bath 1977:177 [ref. 208]. Masc. *Blennius antholops* Springer & Smith-Vaniz 1970:217. Type by original designation (also monotypic). Blenniidae.

Bathycallionymus Nakabo 1982:86 [ref. 3139]. Masc. *Callionymus kaianus* Günther 1880:44. Type by original designation. Synonym of *Callionymus* Linnaeus 1758 (Fricke 1982:58 [ref. 5432]); valid (Houde 1984:637 [ref. 13674], Nakabo in Masuda et al. 1984:343 [ref. 6441]). Callionymidae.

Bathyceratias Beebe 1934:191 [ref. 247]. Masc. *Bathyceratias trilychnus* Beebe 1934:191. Type by monotypy. Apparently available, no specific article in Code makes it unavailable; described from observations from a bathysphere. Status uncertain. Ceratioidei.

Bathychaunax Caruso 1989:156 [ref. 9287]. Masc. *Chaunax coloratus* Garman 1899:83. Type by original designation. Valid (Caruso 1989:155 [ref. 9287], Caruso 1989 [ref. 14230]). Chaunacidae.

Bathyclarias Jackson 1959:112 [ref. 2312]. Masc. *Clarias longibarbis* Worthington 1933:309. Type by original designation. Synonym of *Dinotopterus* Boulenger 1906 (Teugels 1986:95 [ref. 6193]). Clariidae.

Bathyclupea Alcock 1891:130 [ref. 87]. Fem. *Bathyclupea hoskynii* Alcock 1891:131. Type by monotypy. Valid (Dick 1974 [ref. 7044], Shimizu in Uyeno et al. 1983:384 [ref. 14275], Heemstra 1986:669 [ref. 5660]). Bathyclupeidae.

Bathycongrus Ogilby 1898:292 [ref. 3276]. Masc. *Congromuraena (sic) nasica* Alcock 1893:183. Type by original designation. Valid (Smith 1989:512 [ref. 13285]). Congridae: Congrinae.

Bathycygnus (subgenus of *Bathypterois*) Sulak 1977:75, 94 [ref. 4299]. Masc. *Bathypterois longipes* Günther 1878:184. Type by original designation. Synonym of *Bathypterois* Günther 1878, but as a valid subgenus (Sulak & Shcherbachev 1988 [ref. 6677]). Chlorophthalmidae: Ipnopinae.

Bathydraco Günther 1878:18 [ref. 2010]. Masc. *Bathydraco antarcticus* Günther 1878:18. Type by monotypy. Valid (Stevens et al. 1984:563 [ref. 13633], DeWitt 1985 [ref. 5161], Voskoboinikova 1988:45 [ref. 12756]). Bathydraconidae.

Bathyembryx Beebe 1934:190 [ref. 247]. Masc. *Bathyembryx istiophasma* Beebe 1934:190. Type by monotypy. Apparently available as no article in the Code specifically makes it unavailable; described from observations from a bathysphere. Status uncertain. Stomiidae.

Bathygadus Günther 1878:23 [ref. 2010]. Masc. *Bathygadus cottoides* Günther 1878:23. Type by monotypy. Valid (Marshall 1973:288 [ref. 7194], Marshall 1973:287 [ref. 7194], Marshall & Iwamoto 1973:525 [ref. 6963], Fahay & Markle 1984:274 [ref. 13653], Okamura in Masuda et al. 1984:93 [ref. 6441], Geistdoerfer in Whitehead et al. 1986:645 [ref. 13676], Iwamoto 1986:331 [ref. 5674], Paxton et al. 1989:324 [ref. 12442]). Macrouridae: Bathygadinae.

Bathygobius Bleeker 1878:54 [ref. 456]. Masc. *Gobius nebulopunctatus* Valenciennes in Cuvier & Valenciennes 1837:58. Type by subsequent designation. Type apparently first designated by Jordan 1919:393 [ref. 4904], not *G. petrophilus* Bleeker 1863 [but needs further investigation]. Valid (Miller 1973:515 [ref. 6888], Akihito & Meguro 1980 [ref. 6920], Akihito in Masuda et al. 1984:272 [ref. 6441], Maugé 1986:360 [ref. 6218], Hoese 1986:780 [ref. 5670], Goren 1988 [ref. 6612], Birdsong et al. 1988:184, 186 [ref. 7303]). Gobiidae.

Bathylaco Goode & Bean 1896:57 [ref. 1848]. *Bathylaco nigricans* Goode & Bean 1896:57. Type by monotypy. Valid (Nielsen 1973:85 [ref. 6885], Iwamoto et al. 1976 [ref. 7089], Markle & Quéro in Whitehead et al. 1984:234 [ref. 13675], Markle 1986:220

[ref. 5687]). Alepocephalidae.

Bathylagichthys Kobyliansky 1986:48 [ref. 6002]. Masc. *Bathylagus longipinnis* Kobyliansky 1985:52. Type by original designation. Bathylagidae.

Bathylagoides (subgenus of *Bathylagus*) Whitley 1951:61 [ref. 4711]. Masc. *Bathylagus argyrogaster* Norman 1930:273. Type by original designation (also monotypic). Valid (Kobyliansky 1986:44 [ref. 6002]). Bathylagidae.

Bathylagus Günther 1878:248 [ref. 2010]. Masc. *Bathylagus arcticus* Günther 1878:248. Type by subsequent designation. Type designated by Jordan and Evermann 1896:295 [ref. 2442] — valid under Art. 69(a)(iv); Follett & Cohen 1958 [ref. 12570] argue that *atlanticus* should be type. Valid (Cohen 1973:155 [ref. 6589], Cohen in Whitehead et al. 1984:392 [ref. 13675], Uyeno in Masuda et al. 1984:41 [ref. 6441], Ahlstrom et al. 1984:156 [ref. 13627], Cohen 1986:216 [ref. 5646], Kobyliansky 1986:38 [ref. 6002], Gon 1987 [ref. 6268], Paxton et al. 1989:168 [ref. 12442]). Bathylagidae.

Bathyleptus Walters 1961:315 [ref. 4578]. Masc. *Bathyleptus lisae* Walters 1961:316. Type by original designation. Giganturidae.

Bathylychnops Cohen 1958:48 [ref. 877]. Masc. *Bathylychnops exilis* Cohen 1958:50. Type by original designation (also monotypic). Valid (Cohen 1973:156 [ref. 6589], Cohen in Whitehead et al. 1984:395 [ref. 13675], Ahlstrom et al. 1984:156 [ref. 13627], Fujii in Masuda et al. 1984:42 [ref. 6441]). Opisthoproctidae.

Bathylychnus Brauer 1902:289 [ref. 631]. Masc. *Bathylychnus cyaneus* Brauer 1902:289. Type by monotypy. Synonym of *Astronesthes* Richardson 1845 (Gibbs 1964:313 [ref. 6960]). Astronesthidae.

Bathymacrops Gilchrist 1922:53 [ref. 1648]. Masc. *Bathymacrops macrolepis* Gilchrist 1922:53. Type by monotypy. Synonym of *Nansenia* Jordan & Evermann 1896. Microstomatidae.

Bathymaster Cope 1873:31 [ref. 929]. Masc. *Bathymaster signatus* Cope 1873:31. Type by monotypy. Valid (Amaoka in Masuda et al. 1984:289 [ref. 6441]). Bathymasteridae.

Bathymicrops Hjort & Koefoed in Murray & Hjort 1912:88, 416 [ref. 6969]. Masc. *Bathymicrops regis* Hjort & Koefoed in Murray & Hjort 1912:88, 416. Type by monotypy. Also in Koefoed 1927:64 [ref. 2650]. Valid (Nielsen 1973:166 [ref. 6885], Sulak 1977:53 [ref. 4299], Sulak in Whitehead et al. 1984:414 [ref. 13675], Okiyama 1984:207 [ref. 13644], Sulak 1986:261 [ref. 5720], Merrett & Nielsen 1987 [ref. 6058]). Chlorophthalmidae: Ipnopinae.

Bathymyrus Alcock 1889:305 [ref. 84]. Masc. *Bathymyrus echinorhynchus* Alcock 1889:305. Type by monotypy. Valid (Castle 1986:163 [ref. 5644], Smith 1989:490 [ref. 13285]). Congridae: Bathymyrinae.

Bathymyzon (subgenus of *Petromyzon*) Gill 1883:254 [ref. 1724]. Masc. *Petromyzon (Bathymyzon) bairdii* Gill 1883:254. Type by monotypy. Synonym of *Petromyzon* Linnaeus 1758 (Hubbs & Potter 1971:42 [ref. 13397], Vladykov 1973:2 [ref. 7159]). Petromyzontidae: Petromyzontinae.

Bathynectes Günther 1878:20 [ref. 2010]. Masc. *Bathynectes laticeps* Günther 1878:20. Type by subsequent designation. Type designated by Jordan 1919:394 [ref. 4904]. Preoccupied by Stimpson 1871 in Crustacea, replaced by *Bathyonus* Goode & Bean 1885. On Official Index (Direction 37). Synonym of *Mixonus* Günther 1887 (Nielsen 1973:551 [ref. 6885]). In the synonymy of *Bathyonus* Goode & Bean 1885 (Cohen & Nielsen 1978:27 [ref. 881]). Ophidiidae: Neobythitinae.

Bathyonus Goode & Bean 1885:603 [ref. 1842]. *Bathynectes laticeps* Günther 1878:20. Type by being a replacement name. Replacement for *Bathynectes* Günther 1878, preoccupied by Stimpson 1871 in Crustacea. Valid (Cohen & Nielsen 1978:27 [ref. 881], Nielsen in Whitehead et al. 1986:1159 [ref. 13677]). Ophidiidae: Neobythitinae.

Bathyophis Günther 1878:181 [ref. 2010]. Masc. *Bathyophis ferox* Günther 1878:181. Type by monotypy. Synonym of *Idiacanthus* Peters 1877 (Gibbs 1964:513 [ref. 6961], Krueger 1973:144 [ref. 7177]). Idiacanthidae.

Bathypercis Alcock 1893:177 [ref. 89]. Fem. *Bathypercis platyrhynchus* Alcock 1893:178. Type by monotypy. Percophidae: Bembropinae.

Bathyphasma Gilbert 1896:447 [ref. 1628]. Neut. *Bathyphasma ovigerum* Gilbert 1896:448. Type by monotypy. Synonym of *Careproctus* Krøyer 1862 (Stein 1978:10 [ref. 4203], Kido 1988:192 [ref. 12287]). Cyclopteridae: Liparinae.

Bathyphylax Myers 1934:10 [ref. 3107]. Masc. *Bathyphylax bombifrons* Myers 1934:10. Type by original designation (also monotypic). Valid (Tyler 1968:175 [ref. 6438], Tyler 1980:56 [ref. 4477], Tyler 1983:1 [ref. 5293], Tyler 1986:888 [ref. 5723]). Triacanthodidae.

Bathyprion Marshall 1966:4 [ref. 2894]. Masc. *Bathyprion danae* Marshall 1966:4. Type by original designation (also monotypic). Sometimes placed in its own family or subfamily. Valid (Krefft 1973:94 [ref. 7166], Markle & Quéro in Whitehead et al. 1984:235 [ref. 13675], Anderson et al. 1985 [ref. 5164], Markle 1986:220 [ref. 5687]). Alepocephalidae.

Bathypropteron (subgenus of *Rouleina*) Fowler 1934:256 [ref. 1416]. *Aleposomus nudus* Brauer 1906:22. Type by original designation. Alepocephalidae.

Bathypterois Günther 1878:183 [ref. 2010]. *Bathypterois longifilis* Günther 1878:183. Type by subsequent designation. Type designated by Jordan 1919:395 [ref. 4904]. Spelled *Brachypterois* by Jordan & Seale 1906:189 [ref. 2497]. Valid (Nielsen 1973:164 [ref. 6885], Sulak 1977 [ref. 4299], Sulak in Whitehead et al. 1984:414 [ref. 13675], Okiyama 1984:207 [ref. 13644], Okamura in Masuda et al. 1984:63 [ref. 6441], Sulak 1986:262 [ref. 5720], Merrett & Nielsen 1987 [ref. 6058], Sulak & Shcherbachev 1988 [ref. 6677], Paxton et al. 1989:235 [ref. 12442]). Chlorophthalmidae: Ipnopinae.

Bathyraja (subgenus of *Breviraja*) Ishiyama 1958:325 [ref. 2308]. Fem. *Raja isotrachys* Günther 1877:434. Type by original designation. Valid (Ishiyama & Hubbs 1968 [ref. 2309], Stehmann 1973:68 [ref. 7168], Ishiyama & Ishihara 1977 [ref. 5401], Nakaya in Masuda et al. 1984:13 [ref. 6441], Ishihara & Ishiyama 1985 [ref. 5799], Hulley 1986:115 [ref. 5672], Stehmann 1986 [ref. 6151]). Rajidae.

Bathysaurops Fowler 1938:31 [ref. 1426]. Masc. *Bathysaurops malayanus* Fowler 1938:32. Type by original designation (also monotypic). Synonym of *Bathysauropsis* Regan 1911 (Sulak 1977:53 [ref. 4299]). Chlorophthalmidae: Ipnopinae.

Bathysauropsis Regan 1911:126 [ref. 3639]. Fem. *Chlorophthalmus gracilis* Günther 1878:182. Type by monotypy. Valid (Sulak 1977:53 [ref. 4299], Okiyama 1984:207 [ref. 13644], Okamura in Masuda et al. 1984:62 [ref. 6441], Sulak 1986:264 [ref. 5720], Hartel & Stiassny 1986:10 [ref. 5471], Merrett & Nielsen 1987 [ref. 6058], Paxton et al. 1989:231 [ref. 12442]). Chlorophthalmidae: Chlorophthalminae.

Bathysaurus Günther 1878:181 [ref. 2010]. Masc. *Bathysaurus ferox* Günther 1878:182. Type by subsequent designation. Type designated by Jordan & Evermann 1896:539 [ref. 2443]. Valid (Nielsen 1973:163 [ref. 6885], Sulak 1977:53 [ref. 4299], Sulak in Whitehead et al. 1984:405 [ref. 13675], Okiyama 1984:207 [ref. 13644], Fujii in Masuda et al. 1984:61 [ref. 6441], Cressey 1986:270 [ref. 6289], Paxton et al. 1989:241 [ref. 12442]). Synodontidae: Bathysaurinae.

Bathysebastes Döderlein in Steindachner & Döderlein 1884:207 [ref. 4248]. Masc. *Bathysebastes albescens* Döderlein in Steindachner & Döderlein 1884:207. Type by monotypy. Synonym of *Setarches* Johnson 1862:355 (Eschmeyer & Collette 1966:355 [ref. 6485]). Scorpaenidae: Setarchinae.

Bathyseriola Alcock 1890:202 [ref. 82]. Fem. *Bathyseriola cyanea* Alcock 1890:202. Type by monotypy. Synonym of *Psenopsis* Gill 1862 (Haedrich 1967:72 [ref. 5357]). Centrolophidae.

Bathysidus Beebe 1934:192 [ref. 247]. Masc. *Bathysidus pentagrammus* Beebe 1934:192. Type by monotypy. Apparently available, with no Article in Code excluding; based on observation from bathysphere. Status uncertain, see Hubbs 1935:105 [ref. 6467]. Unplaced genera.

Bathysolea (subgenus of *Solea*) Roule 1916:28 [ref. 3818]. Fem. *Bathysolea albida* Roule 1916:28. Type by subsequent designation. Torchio (1973:630) dates to Roule 1916 in Bull. Mus. Natn. Hist. Nat. v. 22:10. Roule 1916:28 dates to 20 May with two included species; type apparently first designated by Jordan 1920:560 [ref. 4905], not *Solea profundicola* Vaillant 1888 (if 1916:28 was earlier). Valid (Torchio 1973:630 [ref. 6892] with type as *profundicola*, Quéro et al. in Whitehead et al. 1986:1309 [ref. 13677]). Soleidae.

Bathysphaera Beebe 1932:175 [ref. 5015]. Fem. *Bathysphaera intacta* Beebe 1932:175. Type by monotypy. Apparently available; description based on observations from a bathysphere. No Article of the Code precludes availability. Morrow in Morrow & Gibbs 1964:510 [ref. 6962] treat as incertae sedis in the family Melanostomiatidae [= Melanostomiidae]. Melanostomiidae.

Bathysphyraenops Parr 1933:28 [ref. 3373]. Masc. *Bathysphyraenops simplex* Parr 1933:29. Type by original designation (also monotypic). Placement follows Johnson 1984:465 [ref. 9681]. Valid (Fraser 1972:41 [ref. 5195], Mouchizuki in Masuda et al. 1984:125 [ref. 6441] in Percichthyidae). Percoidei.

Bathystethus Gill 1893:123 [ref. 1736]. Masc. *Cichla cultrata* Bloch & Schneider 1801:343. Type by being a replacement name. Replacement for *Platystethus* Günther 1860, preoccupied by Mannerheim 1831 in Coleoptera. Valid (Paxton et al. 1989:567 [ref. 12442]). Kyphosidae: Scorpidinae.

Bathystoma Fitzinger 1873:152, 168 [ref. 1337]. Neut. *Squalius microlepis* Heckel 1843:1041. Type by subsequent designation. Type apparently first designated by Jordan 1919:369 [ref. 4904]. Preoccupied by Scudder in Putnam 1863 in fishes; apparently not replaced. Synonym of *Leuciscus* Cuvier 1816. Cyprinidae.

Bathystoma Scudder in Putnam 1863:12 [ref. 3567]. Neut. *Haemulon jeniguano* Poey 1861:183. Type by subsequent designation. Earliest type designation not researched. Synonym of *Haemulon* Cuvier 1829. Haemulidae.

Bathystorreus Howell Rivero 1934:69 [ref. 3766]. Masc. *Benthocometes claudei* Torre 1910:81. Type by original designation (also monotypic). Synonym of *Oligopus* Risso 1810 (Cohen 1964:3 [ref. 6891], Cohen & Nielsen 1978:49 [ref. 881]), but see account of *Oligopus* Risso 1810. Bythitidae: Bythitinae.

Bathysudis (subgenus of *Paralepis*) Parr 1928:41, 42 [ref. 3368]. Fem. *Paralepis speciosus* Bellotti 1878:54, 57. Type by monotypy. Synonym of *Paralepis* Cuvier 1816 (Post 1973:203 [ref. 7182]). Paralepididae.

Bathythrissa Günther 1877:443 [ref. 2009]. Fem. *Bathythrissa dorsalis* Günther 1877:443. Type by monotypy. Junior synonym of *Pterothrissus* Hilgendorf (3 Sept. 1877); *Bathythrissa* dates to Nov. 1877. Albulidae: Pterothrissinae.

Bathytoshia Whitley 1933:61 [ref. 4677]. Fem. *Dasyatis thetidis* Ogilby 1899:46. Type by original designation (also monotypic). Second species doubtfully included. Synonym of *Dasyatis* Rafinesque 1810. Dasyatidae.

Bathytroctes Günther 1878:249 [ref. 2010]. Masc. *Bathytroctes microlepis* Günther 1878:249. Type by subsequent designation. Type apparently first designated by Jordan 1919:395 [ref. 4904]; Goode & Bean 1896:40 [ref. 1848] wrongly designated *B. macrolepis* Günther, a species not described until 1887. Valid (Markle & Quéro in Whitehead et al. 1984:236 [ref. 13675], Markle 1986:220 [ref. 5687]). Alepocephalidae.

Bathytyphlops Nybelin 1957:258, 260 [ref. 3235]. Masc. *Bathymicrops sewelli* Norman 1939:26. Type by original designation (also monotypic). Valid (Nielsen 1973:166 [ref. 6885], Sulak 1977:53 [ref. 4299], Sulak in Whitehead et al. 1984:419 [ref. 13675], Okiyama 1984:207 [ref. 13644], Sulak 1986:264 [ref. 5720], Merrett & Nielsen 1987 [ref. 6058]). Chlorophthalmidae: Ipnopinae.

Bathyuroconger (subgenus of *Uroconger*) Fowler 1934:273 [ref. 1416]. Masc. *Uroconger braueri* Weber & de Beaufort 1916:266. Type by original designation (also monotypic). Valid (Blache & Bauchot 1976:405 [ref. 305], Karrer 1982:36 [ref. 5679], Machida in Masuda et al. 1984:28 [ref. 6441], Castle 1986:163 [ref. 5644], Smith 1989:541 [ref. 13285]). Congridae: Congrinae.

Batis Bonaparte 1838:204 [ref. 4979]. Fem. *Raja radula* Delaroche 1809:321. Type by original designation (see p. 2 of separate; also monotypic). Preoccupied by Boie 1833 in Aves. Synonym of *Raja* Linnaeus 1758 (Stehmann 1973:58 [ref. 7168]). Rajidae.

Batman Whitley 1956:36 [ref. 4726]. Masc. *Batman insignitus* Whitley 1956:36. Type by original designation (also monotypic). Synonym of *Cryptocentrus* Valenciennes (ex Ehrenberg) 1837 (Hoese & Allen 1977:205 [ref. 2179]). Gobiidae.

Batracheleotris Fowler 1938:129 [ref. 1426]. Fem. *Eleotris sclateri* Steindachner 1880:157. Type by original designation (also monotypic). Only one definitely included species. Objective synonym of *Metagobius* Whitley 1930. Synonym of *Callogobius* Bleeker 1874. Gobiidae.

Batrachichthys Agassiz 1846 see *Batrictius* Rafinesque 1815. Batrachoididae.

Batrachocephalus Bleeker 1846:176 [ref. 5872]. Masc. *Batrachocephalus ageneiosus* Bleeker 1846:176 (= *Ageneiosus mino* Hamilton 1822:159, 375). Type by monotypy. Bleeker's *B. ageneiosus* is an unneeded substitute for *A. mino* Hamilton 1822. Valid (Jayaram & Dhanz 1979:49 [ref. 6800], Jayaram 1981:277 [ref. 6497], Kottelat 1985:271 [ref. 11441], Burgess 1989:167 [ref. 12860], Kottelat 1989:15 [ref. 13605]). Ariidae.

Batrachocottus Berg 1903:108 [ref. 263]. Masc. *Cottus baikalensis* Dybowski 1874:384. Type by original designation (also monotypic). Valid (Sideleva 1982:28 [ref. 14469], Washington et al. 1984:443 [ref. 13660]). Cottocomephoridae.

Batrachoides Lacepède 1800:451 [ref. 2709]. Masc. *Batrachoides tau* Lacepède 1800:451. Type by subsequent designation. Type designated by Jordan & Evermann 1896:466 [ref. 2442]. Synonym of *Halobatrachus* Ogilby 1908 (Monod 1973:657 [ref. 7193]); valid (Collette & Russo 1981 [ref. 5575]). Batrachoididae.

Batrachomoeus Ogilby 1908:46, 54 [ref. 3284]. Masc. *Batrachomoeus broadbenti* Ogilby 1908:49. Type by subsequent designation. Type apparently first designated by Jordan 1920:529 [ref. 4905]. Typsetting of dipthong "ae" or "oe" in chomaeus or chomoeus difficult to determine, spelled with oe by current authors. Appeared first as name only in Annual Report authored by Ogilby in 1907 (see Hutchins). Valid (Hutchins 1976:19 [ref. 6971], Hutchins 1981 [ref. 6830], Paxton et al. 1989:271 [ref. 12442]). Batrachoididae.

Batrachops Bibron in Duméril 1855:280 [ref. 297]. Masc. *Tetraodon psittacus* Bloch & Schneider 1801:505. Type by monotypy. Preoccupied by Heckel 1840 in fishes, replaced by *Colomesus* Gill 1884. Objective synonym of *Colomesus* Gill 1884 (Shipp 1974:108 [ref. 7147]). Tetraodontidae.

Batrachops Heckel 1840:432 [ref. 2064]. Masc. *Batrachops reticulatus* Heckel 1840:433. Type by subsequent designation. Type designated by Eigenmann & Bray 1894:620 [ref. 1248]. Synonym of *Crenicichla* Heckel 1840 (Kullander 1986:82 [ref. 12439], Kullander & Nijssen 1989:207 [ref. 14136]). Cichlidae.

Batrachopus Goldfuss 1820:110 [ref. 1829]. Masc. *Lophius commersonianus* Lacepède. Type by being a replacement name. Replacement for *Chironectes* Cuvier [= Rafinesque 1814], preoccupied by Illiger 1911 in Mammalia. Type species not researched. Synonym of *Histrio* Fischer 1813 (Monod & Le Danois 1973:659 [ref. 7223], Pietsch 1984:37 [ref. 5380]). Antennariidae.

Batrachus Bloch & Schneider 1801:42 (xxvi) [ref. 471]. Masc. *Batrachus surinamensis* Bloch & Schneider 1801:43. Type by subsequent designation. Type apparently first designated by Jordan 1917:57 [ref. 2407]. Synonym of *Holobatrachus* Ogilby 1908 (Monod 1973:657 [ref. 7193]). Synonym of *Batrachoides* Lacepède 1800 (Collette & Russo 1981:198 [ref. 5575]). Batrachoididae.

Batrachus Klein 1776:202 [ref. 4919]. Masc. Not available, published in a work that does not conform to the principle of binominal nomenclature. In the synonymy of *Lophius* Linnaeus 1758 (Monod & Le Danois 1973:659 [ref. 7223]). Lophiidae.

Batracocephalus Hollberg 1819:39 [ref. 6468]. Masc. *Blennius raninus* Linnaeus 1758:258. Type by monotypy. Synonym of *Raniceps* Oken 1817 (Svetovidov 1973:315 [ref. 7169]). Lotidae.

Batrichthys Smith 1934:98 [ref. 4064]. Masc. *Batrichthys albofasciatus* Smith 1934:99. Type by original designation. Valid (Hutchins 1986:359 [ref. 5673]). Batrachoididae.

Batrictius Rafinesque 1815:82 [ref. 3584]. Masc. Not available; name only and apparently an incorrect subsequent spelling of *Batrachoides* Lacepède 1800. *Batrachichthys* Agassiz 1846:44 [ref. 64] is an unjustified emendation. In the synonymy of *Batrachoides* Lacepède 1800 (Collette & Russo 1981:198 [ref. 5575]). Batrachoididae.

Batrochoglanis Gill 1858:389 [29] [ref. 1750]. Masc. *Pimelodus raninus* Valenciennes in Cuvier & Valenciennes 1840:157. Type by original designation. Spelled *Batrochoglanis* in original (twice) and in separate [p. 29]. *Batrachoglanis* (e.g. as used by Bleeker 1862:11 [ref. 393] and Jordan 1919:281 [ref. 2410]) is an incorrect subsequent spelling. Objective synonym of *Pseudopimelodus* Bleeker 1858 (Mees 1974:187 [ref. 2969]). Pimelodidae.

Bauchotia Nalbant 1965:585 [ref. 3141]. Fem. *Chaetodon marcellae* Poll 1950:2. Type by original designation. Synonym of subgenus *Prognathodes* Gill 1862 of genus *Chaetodon* Linnaeus 1758 (Burgess 1978:314 [ref. 700]). Synonym of *Prognathodes* Gill 1862 (Maugé & Bauchot 1984:464 [ref. 6614]); as a valid subgenus (Nalbant 1986:168 [ref. 6135]). Chaetodontidae.

Bayonia Boulenger 1911:70 [ref. 580]. Fem. *Bayonia xenodonta* Boulenger 1911:70. Type by monotypy. Apparently preoccupied by Bocage 1865 [not researched]. Synonym of *Macropleurodus* Regan 1922 (Greenwood 1956:299 [ref. 1894]). Cichlidae.

Bdellorhynchus Jordan & Tanaka 1927:391 [ref. 2537]. Masc. *Mastacembelus maculatus* Cuvier (ex Reinhardt) in Cuvier & Valenciennes 1832:461. Type by original designation (also monotypic). Synonym of *Mastacembelus* Scopoli 1777 (Sufi 1956:105 [ref. 12498], Roberts 1989:180 [ref. 6439]). Mastacembelidae.

Bdellostoma Müller 1836:79 [ref. 3060]. Neut. *Bdellostoma hexatrema* Müller 1836:79. Type by subsequent designation. Earliest type designation not researched. Synonym of *Eptatretus* Cloquet 1819. Myxinidae: Eptatretinae.

Beanea Steindachner 1902:337 [ref. 4239]. Fem. *Beanea trivittata* Steindachner 1902:337. Type by monotypy. Genus named for "Ichthyologen Dr. Beane in Washington," but that was T. H. Bean; *Beania* would have been more correctly formed. On Official Index (Opinion 1481). In the synonymy of *Siphamia* Weber 1909 after suppression of *Beanea* for purposes of priority (Opinion 1481). Apogonidae.

Beaufortella Chabanaud 1943:291 [ref. 799]. Fem. *Aserragodes abnormis* Weber & de Beaufort 1929:163. Type by original designation (also monotypic). Correct spelling for genus of type species is *Aseraggodes*. Soleidae.

Beaufortia Hora 1932:318 [ref. 2208]. Fem. *Gastromyzon leveretti* Nichols & Pope 1927:340. Type by original designation. Valid (Silas 1953:234 [ref. 4024], Chen 1980:112 [ref. 6901], Sawada 1982:205 [ref. 14111]). Balitoridae: Balitorinae.

Bedotia Regan 1903:416 [ref. 3620]. Fem. *Bedotia madagascariensis* Regan 1903:416. Type by monotypy. Valid (White et al. 1984:360 [ref. 13655], Maugé 1986:277 [ref. 6218]). Atherinidae: Bedotiinae.

Bedula Gray 1835:Pl. 88 (v. 2) [ref. 1878]. *Bedula nebulosus* Gray 1835:88. Type by monotypy. Synonym of *Nandus* Valenciennes 1831 (Roberts 1989:164 [ref. 6439]). Nandidae: Nandinae.

Beirabarbus Herre 1936:99 [ref. 2112]. Masc. *Beirabarbus palustris* Herre 1936:100. Type by original designation (also monotypic). Synonym of *Enteromius* Cope 1867 (Karaman 1971:189 [ref. 2560]). Synonym of *Barbus* Cuvier & Cloquet 1816 (Lévêque & Daget 1984:219 [ref. 6186]). Cyprinidae.

Beliops Hardy 1985:378 [ref. 5184]. Masc. *Beliops xanthokrossos* Hardy 1985:378. Type by original designation (also monotypic). Valid (Paxton et al. 1989:528 [ref. 12442]). Acanthoclinidae.

Bellapiscis Hardy 1987:259 [ref. 5960]. Masc. *Tripterygium medium* Günther 1861:278. Type by original designation. Correct spelling for genus of type species is *Tripterygion*. Tripterygiidae.

Bellator Jordan & Evermann 1896:488 [ref. 2442]. Masc. *Prionotus militaris* Goode & Bean 1896:464. Type by original designation (also monotypic). Valid (Uyeno & Sato in Uyeno et al. 1983:441 [ref. 14275]). Triglidae: Triglinae.

Belligobio Jordan & Hubbs 1925:172 [ref. 2486]. Masc. *Belligobio eristigma* Jordan & Hubbs 1925:173. Type by original designation (also monotypic). Valid subgenus of *Hemibarbus* Bleeker 1859 (Banarescu & Nalbant 1973:183 [ref. 173]); valid (Lu, Luo & Chen 1977:459 [ref. 13495]). Cyprinidae.

Bellocia Parr 1951:6, 12 [ref. 3380]. Fem. *Bellocia vaillanti* Parr 1951:12. Type by original designation (also monotypic). Valid (Krefft 1973:88 [ref. 7166], Markle & Quéro in Whitehead et al. 1984:237 [ref. 13675]). Alepocephalidae.

Bellottia Giglioli 1883:399 [ref. 1619]. Fem. *Bellottia apoda* Giglioli 1883:399. Type by monotypy. Valid (Nielsen 1973:549 [ref. 6885], Cohen & Nielsen 1978:45 [ref. 881], Papaconstantinou 1984 [ref. 12847], Nielsen in Whitehead et al. 1986:1153 [ref. 13677]). Bythitidae: Bythitinae.

Belobranchus Bleeker 1856:300 [ref. 355]. Masc. *Eleotris belobrancha* Valenciennes in Cuvier & Valenciennes 1837:243. Bleeker 1874:304 [ref. 437] says type is *Belobranchus quoyi* Bleeker; type possibly designated on p. 300 (not translated). Valid (Birdsong et al. 1988:181 [ref. 7303]). Eleotridae.

Belochromis Fowler 1944:333 [ref. 1448]. Masc. *Azurina eupalama* Heller & Snodgrass 1903:198. Type by original designation (also monotypic). Pomacentridae.

Belodontichthys Bleeker 1858:255, 256, 266 [ref. 365]. Masc. *Belodontichthys macrochir* Bleeker 1858:266. Type by monotypy. Valid (Haig 1952:65 [ref. 12607], Kottelat 1985:268 [ref. 11441], Burgess 1989:85 [ref. 12860], Kottelat 1989:14 [ref. 13605], Roberts 1989:144[ref. 6439]). Siluridae.

Beloholocentrus Fowler 1944:100 [ref. 1448]. Masc. *Beloholocentrus atractus* Fowler 1944:101. Type by original designation (also monotypic). Synonym of *Holocentrus* Scopoli 1777 (see Böhlke 1984:113 [ref. 13621]). Holocentridae.

Belone Cuvier 1816:185 [ref. 993]. Fem. *Esox belone* Linnaeus 1761:126. Type by monotypy (also by absolute tautonymy). Spelled *Belona* by Lesueur 1821:124 [not researched]. On Official List (Opinion 225). *Belone* Oken 1816 suppressed; placed on Official Index (Opinion 225). Valid (Parin 1973:258 [ref. 7191], Collette et al. 1984:336 [ref. 11422], Collette & Parin in Whitehead et al. 1986:605 [ref. 13676]). Belonidae.

Belone Oken 1816:102 [ref. 6406]. Fem. On Official Index, published in a rejected work (Opinion 417, Opinion 225). Unplaced genera.

Belonepterygion McCulloch 1915:51 [ref. 2943]. Neut. *Acanthoclinus fasciolatus* Ogilby 1889:63. Type by original designation (also monotypic). Valid (Hardy 1985:375 [ref. 5184], Paxton et al. 1989:528 [ref. 12442]). Acanthoclinidae.

Belonesox Kner 1860:419, 422 [ref. 2632]. Masc. *Belonesox belizanus* Kner 1860:419. Type by monotypy. Valid (Rosen & Bailey 1963:107 [ref. 7067], Parenti & Rauchenberger 1989:9 [ref. 13538]). Poeciliidae.

Belonichthys Peters 1868:147 [ref. 7935]. Masc. *Syngnathus zambezensis* Peters 1855:465. Type by monotypy. Also appeared in Peters 1868:108 [ref. 3440] [above apparently earliest but not researched]. Synonym of *Microphis* Kaup 1853, but as a valid subgenus (Dawson 1984:136 [ref. 5879], Dawson 1985:128 [ref. 6541], Dawson 1986:284 [ref. 6201]). Syngnathidae: Syngnathinae.

Belonion Collette 1966:7 [ref. 892]. Neut. *Belonion apodion* Collette 1966:12. Type by original designation. Valid (Collette et al. 1984:352 [ref. 11422]). Belonidae.

Belonocharax Fowler 1907:464 [ref. 1374]. Masc. *Belonocharax beani* Fowler 1907:464. Type by original designation (also monotypic). Synonym of *Ctenolucius* Gill 1861. Ctenoluciidae.

Belonoglanis Boulenger 1902:50 [ref. 562]. Masc. *Belonoglanis tenuis* Boulenger 1902:50. Type by monotypy. Valid (Skelton & Teugels 1986:60 [ref. 6192], Burgess 1989:114 [ref. 12860]). Amphiliidae.

Belonoperca Fowler & Bean 1930:175, 181 [ref. 1477]. Fem. *Belonoperca chabanaudi* Fowler & Bean 1930:182. Type by original designation (also monotypic). Valid (Randall et al. 1980 [ref. 6923], Katayama in Masuda et al. 1984:133 [ref. 6441], Randall 1986:537 [ref. 5706], Paxton et al. 1989:516 [ref. 12442]). Serranidae: Grammistinae.

Belonophago Giltay 1929:272 [ref. 1795]. *Belonophago hutsebouti* Giltay 1929:273. Type by original designation (also monotypic). Valid (Géry 1977:94 [ref. 1597], Vari 1979:340 [ref. 5490], Daget & Gosse 1984:184 [ref. 6185]). Citharinidae: Distichodontinae.

Belonopsis Brandt 1854:175 [ref. 617]. Fem. *Leptorhynchus leuchtenbergi* Lowe 1852:252. Type by being a replacement name. Replacement for *Leptorhynchus* Lowe 1852, preoccupied by Clift 1828 in Reptilia, Du Bus 1835 and Ménétries 1835 in Aves, and Smith 1840 in fishes. Synonym of *Nemichthys* Richardson 1848 (Larsen 1973:231 [ref. 7187], Smith & Nielsen 1989:452 [ref. 13290]). Nemichthyidae.

Belonopterois Roule 1916:13 [ref. 3818]. *Belonopterois viridensis* Roule 1916:13. Type by monotypy. Synonym of subgenus *Benthosaurus* Goode & Bean 1886, genus *Bathypterois* Günther 1868 (Sulak 1977:76 [ref. 4299]). Chlorophthalmidae: Ipnopinae.

Belontia Myers 1923:63 [ref. 3089]. Fem. *Polyacanthus hasselti* Cuvier in Cuvier & Valenciennes 1831:353. Type by original designation. Valid (Kottelat 1989:19 [ref. 13605], Roberts 1989: 171 [ref. 6439]). Belontiidae.

Belophlox Fowler 1947:1 [ref. 1457]. Fem. *Belophlox mariae* Fowler 1947:2. Type by original designation (also monotypic). Synonym of *Etheostoma* Rafinesque 1819, but as a valid subgenus (Page 1981:37 [ref. 3347], Bailey & Etnier 1988:26 [ref. 6873]). Percidae.

Bembradium Gilbert 1905:637 [ref. 1631]. Neut. *Bembradium roseum* Gilbert 1905:637. Type by original designation (also monotypic). Valid (Washington et al. 1984:441 [ref. 13660], Ochiai in Masuda et al. 1984:321 [ref. 6441]). Bembridae.

Bembras Cuvier in Cuvier & Valenciennes 1829:282 [ref. 998]. Fem. *Bembras japonicus* Cuvier in Cuvier & Valenciennes 1829:282. Type by monotypy. Valid (Knapp 1979:52 [ref. 14196], Washington et al. 1984:441 [ref. 13660], Paxton et al. 1989:466 [ref. 12442]). Bembridae.

Bembrops Steindachner 1876:211 [ref. 4225]. Masc. *Bembrops caudimacula* Steindachner 1876:212. Type by monotypy. Valid (Nelson 1978 [ref. 7023], Okamura in Masuda et al. 1984:289 [ref. 6441], Heemstra & Nelson 1986:738 [ref. 6304]). Percophidae: Bembropinae.

Bendilisis (subgenus of *Opsarius*) Bleeker 1860:431 [ref. 370]. *Cyprinus bendilisis* Hamilton 1822:345. Type by monotypy (also absolute tautonymy). Appeared first as name only in Bleeker 1859:436 [ref. 370]. Two species included in subgenus by Bleeker 1860:289, 431 [ref. 380]. Synonym of *Barilius* Hamilton 1822 (Roberts 1989:30 [ref. 6439] and Kuang in Chu & Chen 1989:19 [ref. 13584] as *Bendelisis*). Cyprinidae.

Bengalichthys Annandale 1909:47 [ref. 126]. Masc. *Bengalichthys impennis* Annandale 1909:48. Type by monotypy. Narkidae.

Bengana (subgenus of *Cyprinus*) Gray 1832:Pl. 97 (v. 2) [ref. 1878].

Cyprinus falcata Gray 1832. Type by monotypy. Also appeared on Pl. 96 (of vol. 2) with spelling *Bengala* on plate examined (at least some plates apparently hand lettered). Plate 96 was issued in 1834 (see Sawyer 1953:54 [ref. 6842]). Jordan 1917:139 [ref. 2407] and 1919:179 [ref. 2410] spells as *Bengala*. Species misspelled *falcala* on plate examined. *Bengana* is correct original spelling. Cyprinidae.

Bennettia (subgenus of *Lutianus*) Fowler 1904:524 [ref. 1367]. Fem. *Anthias johnii* Bloch 1792:113. Type by original designation (also monotypic). Synonym of *Lutjanus* Bloch 1790 (Allen 1985:33 [ref. 6843], Allen & Talbot 1985:8 [ref. 6491]). Lutjanidae.

Bentenia Jordan & Snyder 1901:306 [ref. 2506]. Fem. *Bentenia aesticola* Jordan & Snyder 1901:306. Type by monotypy. Synonym of *Pteraclis* Gronow 1772 (Mead 1973:388 [ref. 7199]). Bramidae.

Benthalbella Zugmayer 1911:14 [ref. 6161]. Fem. *Benthalbella infans* Zugmayer 1911:14. Type by monotypy. Also appeared in Zugmayer 1911 (Dec.):140 [ref. 4846]. Valid (Maul 1973:199 [ref. 7171], Johnson 1974:61 [ref. 7050], Iwami & Abe 1980 [ref. 6894], Johnson 1982:154 [ref. 5519], Johnson in Whitehead et al. 1984:485 [ref. 13675], Fujii in Masuda et al. 1984:63 [ref. 6441], Johnson 1986:265 [ref. 5677], Paxton et al. 1989:233 [ref. 12442]). Scopelarchidae.

Benthenchelys Fowler 1934:267 [ref. 1416]. Fem. *Benthenchelys cartieri* Fowler 1934:269. Type by original designation (also monotypic). Valid (Castle 1972 [ref. 6968], McCosker 1977:57 [ref. 6836], McCosker et al. 1989:271 [ref. 13288]). Ophichthidae: Myrophinae.

Benthobatis Alcock 1898:144 [ref. 92]. Fem. *Benthobatis moresbyi* Alcock 1898:145. Type by monotypy. Valid (Fechhelm & McEachran 1984 [ref. 5227]). Narkidae.

Benthochromis Poll 1986:141 [ref. 6136]. Masc. *Haplotaxodon tricoti* Poll 1948:19. Type by original designation. Cichlidae.

Benthocometes Goode & Bean 1896:327 [ref. 1848]. Masc. *Neobythites robustus* Goode & Bean 1883:161. Type by subsequent designation. Type designated by Jordan & Evermann 1896:2514 [ref. 2445]. Valid (Nielsen 1973:550 [ref. 6885], Cohen & Nielsen 1978:28 [ref. 881], Nielsen in Whitehead et al. 1986:1160 [ref. 13677], Nielsen & Evseenko 1989 [ref. 12830]). Ophidiidae: Neobythitinae.

Benthodesmus Goode & Bean 1882:380 [ref. 1839]. Masc. *Lepidopus elongatus* Clarke 1879:294. Type by original designation (also monotypic). Type designated on p. 381. Valid (Collette et al. 1984:600 [ref. 11421], Nakamura in Masuda et al. 1984:227 [ref. 6441], Parin in Whitehead et al. 1986:977 [ref. 13676], Nakamura 1986:829 [ref. 5696]). Trichiuridae: Aphanopodinae.

Benthophiloides Beling & Iljin 1927:309, 324 [ref. 7211]. Masc. *Benthophiloides brauneri* Beling & Iljin 1927:309. Type by monotypy. Also appeared in Iljin 1927:129, 131 [ref. 5613], earliest not established. Valid (Miller 1973:490 [ref. 6888], Miller in Whitehead et al. 1986:1024 [ref. 13677]). Gobiidae.

Benthophilus Eichwald 1831:77 [ref. 5562]. Masc. *Gobius macrocephalus* Pallas 1787:52. Type by monotypy. Original not seen. Spelled *Bentophilus* by Eichwald in 1838. Valid (Miller 1973:490 [ref. 6888], Miller in Whitehead et al. 1986:1025 [ref. 13677]). Gobiidae.

Benthosaurus Goode & Bean 1886:168 [ref. 1844]. Masc. *Benthosaurus grallator* Goode & Bean 1886:168. Type by monotypy. Synonym of *Bathypterois* Günther 1878 (Nielsen 1973:165 [ref. 6885], Sulak 1977:53 [ref. 4299]). Chlorophthalmidae: Ipnopinae.

Benthoscopus Longley & Hildebrand 1940:264 [ref. 2822]. Masc. *Benthoscopus laticeps* Longley & Hildebrand 1940:264. Type by monotypy. Authorship attributed to both authors, not Longley alone (see note by Hildebrand on p. 267). Synonym of *Gnathagnus* Gill 1861 (Mees 1960:47 [ref. 11931], Pietsch 1989:294 [ref. 12541], Kishimoto 1989:303 [ref. 13562]). Uranoscopidae.

Benthosema Goode & Bean 1896:75 [ref. 1848]. Neut. *Salmo muelleri* Gmelin 1789:1378. Type by original designation. Type given as *Salmo muelleri* Gmelin = *Scopelus glacialis* Reinhardt 1837 as identified by Lütken. Valid (Krefft & Bekker 1973:172 [ref. 7181], Paxton 1979:6 [ref. 6440], Hulley in Whitehead et al. 1984:432 [ref. 13675], Moser et al. 1984:219 [ref. 13645], Fujii in Masuda et al. 1984:65 [ref. 6441], Hulley 1986:285 [ref. 5672], Paxton et al. 1989:254 [ref. 12442]). Myctophidae.

Benthosphyraena Cockerell 1919:172 [ref. 872]. Fem. *Alepocephalus macropterus* Vaillant 1888:150. Type by monotypy. Perhaps not intended as a new genus but unclear from text; original description consists only of: "*Benthosphyraena macroptera* also referred to the Alepocephalidae, has small round scales wholly unlike those of *Alepocephalus*." Alepocephalidae.

Bentuviaichthys Smith 1961:412 [ref. 4128]. Masc. *Bentuviaichthys nigrimentum* Smith 1961:412. Type by original designation (also monotypic). Synonym of *Rhabdamia* Weber 1909, but as a valid subgenus (Fraser 1972:28 [ref. 5195]). Apogonidae.

Bergeniana (subgenus of *Lycodes*) Popov 1931:140 [ref. 5702]. Fem. *Lycodes uschakovi* Popov 1931:141. Synonym of *Lycodes* Reinhardt 1831 (McAllister et al. 1981 [ref. 5431], Toyoshima 1985:180 [ref. 5722]). Zoarcidae.

Bergia Steindachner 1891:173 [ref. 12571]. Fem. *Bergia altipinnis* Steindachner 1891:173. Type by monotypy. Also appeared as Steindachner 1891:365 [ref. 4236]. Preoccupied by Duchassaing & Michelotti 1861 in Coleoptera and by Scott 1881 in Hemiptera; apparently not replaced. Synonym of *Pseudocorynopoma* Perugia (30 Apr.) 1891 and of *Chalcinopelecus* Holmberg (June) 1891; *Bergia* dates to 9 July 1891 according to Fowler 1975:184 [ref. 9333]). Characidae.

Bergiaria Eigenmann & Norris 1901:272 [ref. 1265]. Fem. *Pimelodus westermanni* Reinhardt 1874:32. Type by being a replacement name. Replacement for *Bergiella* Eigenmann & Norris 1900, preoccupied by Baker 1897 in Hymenoptera. Valid (Burgess 1989:281 [ref. 12860]). Pimelodidae.

Bergiella Eigenmann & Norris 1900:355 [ref. 1264]. Fem. *Pimelodus westermanni* Reinhardt 1874:32. Type by original designation (also monotypic). Preoccupied by Baker 1897 in Hymenoptera, replaced by *Bergiaria* Eigenmann & Norris 1901. Pimelodidae.

Beridia Castelnau 1878:229 [ref. 761]. Fem. *Beridia flava* Castelnau 1878:229. Type by monotypy. Spelled *Baridia* by Castelnau on legend for Pl. 2. Synonym of *Gnathanacanthus* Bleeker 1855 (Scott 1986:53 [ref. 5807], Paxton et al. 1989:464 [ref. 12442]). Gnathanacanthidae.

Bermudichthys Nichols 1920:62 [ref. 3173]. Masc. *Bermudichthys subfurcatus* Nichols 1920:62. Type by original designation (also monotypic). Synonym of *Thalassoma* Swainson 1839 (Collette 1962:442 [ref. 4554]). Labridae.

Bero Jordan & Starks 1904:317 [ref. 2528]. *Centridermichthys elegans* Steindachner 1881:85. Type by original designation (also monotypic). Valid (Washington et al. 1984:442 [ref. 13660], Yabe in Masuda et al. 1984:329 [ref. 6441], Yabe 1985:111 [ref. 11522]). Cottidae.

Berowra Whitley 1928:224 [ref. 4661]. *Gobius lidwilli* McCulloch 1917:185. Type by original designation (also monotypic). Synonym of *Pandaka* Herre 1927 (Miller 1987:701 [ref. 6336]). Gobiidae.

Bertella Pietsch 1973:193 [ref. 3472]. Fem. *Bertella idiomorpha* Pietsch 1973:194. Type by original designation (also monotypic). Not preoccupied by *Bertella* Paetel 1875, an incorrect subsequent spelling of *Berthella* Blainville 1842 in Mollusca (see Whitley 1976:46 [ref. 4735]). Valid (Pietsch 1974:33 [ref. 5332], Amaoka in Masuda et al. 1984:106 [ref. 6441]). Oneirodidae.

Bertelsenna Whitley 1954:30 [ref. 4721]. Fem. *Dolopichthys gladisfenae* Beebe 1832:86. Type by being a replacement name. Unneeded replacement for *Spiniphryne* Bertelsen 1951, not preoccupied by *Spinophrynus* Koch 1951 in Coleoptera. Objective synonym of *Spiniphryne* Bertelsen 1951 (Bertelsen & Pietsch 1975:7 [ref. 7062]). Oneirodidae.

Bertinichthys Whitley 1953:133 [ref. 4718]. Masc. *Barbus lorteti* Sauvage 1862:165. Type by being a replacement name. Unneeded replacement for *Bertinius* Fang 1943, not preoccupied by *Bertinia* Jousseaume 1883 in Mollusca. Synonym of *Barbus* Cuvier & Cloquet 1816 (Krupp 1985:67 [ref. 6403], Krupp & Schneider 1989:359 [ref. 13651]). Cyprinidae.

Bertinius Fang 1943:400 [ref. 1306]. Masc. *Barbus lorteti* Sauvage 1862:165. Type by original designation (also monotypic). *Bertinichthys* Whitley 1953 is an unneeded replacement, *Bertinius* not preoccupied. Synonym of *Barbus* Cuvier & Cloquet 1816 (Krupp 1985:67 [ref. 6403], Krupp & Schneider 1989:359 [ref. 13651]). Cyprinidae.

Bertinulus Whitley 1948:73 [ref. 4710]. Masc. *Oxystomus hyalinus* Rafinesque 1810:49, 62. Type by being a replacement name. Not a serrivomerid (Tighe 1989:618 [ref. 13291]). Ophichthidae: Ophichthinae.

Bertoniolus Fowler 1918:141 [ref. 1395]. Masc. *Bertoniolus paraguayensis* Fowler 1918:141. Type by original designation (also monotypic). Synonym of *Astyanax* Baird & Girard 1854 (see Böhlke 1984:52 [ref. 13621]). Characidae.

Beryx Cuvier 1829:151 [ref. 995]. Masc. *Beryx decadactylus* Cuvier in Cuvier & Valenciennes 1829:222. Type by subsequent designation. Cuvier 1829 published Mar. 1829, with two species that were not yet available but described in Cuvier & Valenciennes Apr. 1829. Type apparently designated first by Fowler 1911:173 [ref. 6398]. Valid (Nielsen 1973:337 [ref. 6885], Woods & Sonoda 1973:282 [ref. 6899], Scott 1981: 112 [ref. 5533], Shimizu in Masuda et al. 1984:108 [ref. 6441], Maul in Whitehead et al. 1986:740 [ref. 13676], Heemstra 1986:409 [ref. 5660], Paxton et al. 1989:374 [ref. 12442]). Berycidae.

Besnardia Lahille 1913:1 [ref. 2712]. Fem. *Besnardia gyrinops* Lahille 1913:3. Type by monotypy. Synonym of *Neophrynichthys* Günther 1876 (Nelson 1977:486 [ref. 7034]). Status uncertain (Nelson 1982:1499 [ref. 5470]). Psychrolutidae.

Betaraia (subgenus of *Raja*) Leigh-Sharpe 1924:567, 568 [ref. 5748]. Fem. *Raja clavata* Linnaeus 1758:232. Type by original designation. As a "pseudogenus" of *Raia* [=*Raja*]. Not available [Art. 1b (6)], used as an artificial category (see Leigh-Sharpe 1928 [ref. 6152]). Same as *Amblyraja* Malm 1877 and *Hieroptera* Fleming 1841. In the synonymy of *Raja* Linnaeus 1758 (Stehmann 1973:58 [ref. 7168]). Rajidae.

Betascyllium (subgenus of *Scyllium*) Leigh-Sharpe 1926:325 [ref. 5627]. Neut. *Squalus catulus* Linnaeus 1758:234. Type by original designation. As a "pseudogenus" of *Scyllium*. Not available [Art. 1b (6)], used as an artificial category (see Leigh-Sharpe 1928 [ref. 6152]). In the synonymy of *Scyliorhinus* Blainville 1816 (Compagno 1988:120 [ref. 13488]). Scyliorhinidae.

Betta Bleeker 1850:12 [ref. 323]. Fem. *Betta trifasciata* Bleeker 1850:12. Type by monotypy. Valid (Kottelat 1985:275 [ref. 11441], Kottelat 1989:19 [ref. 13605], Roberts 1989:171 [ref. 6439], Schaller & Kottelat 1989 [ref. 13604]). Belontiidae.

Bhanotia Hora 1926:463 [ref. 2207]. Fem. *Corythoichthys corrugatus* Weber 1913:112. Type by original designation. Valid (Dawson 1978 [ref. 7025], Dawson 1985:20 [ref. 6541]). Syngnathidae: Syngnathinae.

Bhanotichthys Parr 1930:27, 29 [ref. 3370]. Masc. *Syngnathus fasciatus* Gray 1830. Type by original designation. Type designated on p. 29. Objective synonym of *Corythoichthys* Kaup 1853 (Dawson 1977:297 [ref. 7048], Dawson 1985:36 [ref. 6541]). Syngnathidae: Syngnathinae.

Bhavania Hora 1920:202 [ref. 2200]. Fem. *Platycara australis* Jerdon 1848. Type by subsequent designation. Two included species, type perhaps first designated by Silas 1953:183 [ref. 4024]. Spelled *Blavania* by Jordan 1923:145 [ref. 2421]. Valid (Silas 1953:183 [ref. 4024], Jayaram 1981:141 [ref. 6497], Sawada 1982:205 [ref. 14111], Menon 1987:233 [ref. 14149]). Balitoridae: Balitorinae.

Biat Seale 1910:532 [ref. 4000]. Fem. *Biat luzonica* Seale 1910:532. Type by original designation (also monotypic). Synonym of *Amblyeleotris* Bleeker 1874 (Hoese, pers. comm.). Gobiidae.

Bibronia Cocco 1844:25 [ref. 866]. Fem. *Bibronia liculata* Cocco 1844:26. Type by monotypy. Originally species as *liculata*; later spelled *ligulata* [see under ref. 866], which would be the correct spelling (Tom Munro, pers. comm.). Synonym of *Symphurus* Rafinesque 1810 (Torchio 1973:635 [ref. 6892]). Cynoglossidae: Symphurinae.

Bicanestrinia (subgenus of *Cobitis*) Bacescu 1962:436 [ref. 6454]. Fem. *Cobitis simplicispina* Hanko 1924. Type by original designation. Cobitidae: Cobitinae.

Bicuspidatus de Buen 1926:87 [ref. 5054]. As a "grupo" for 1 species of *Callionymus*. Not available on basis of Art. 1b(6) [see de Buen's definition of "grupo" on p. 11]; see Appendix A. Callionymidae.

Bidenichthys Barnard 1934:232 [ref. 195]. Masc. *Bidenichthys capensis* Barnard 1934:234. Type by monotypy. Valid (Cohen & Nielsen 1978:53 [ref. 881], Cohen 1986:354 [ref. 5646]). Bythitidae: Brosmophycinae.

Bidyanus Whitley 1943:182 [ref. 4703]. Masc. *Acerina (Cernua) bidyana* Mitchell 1838:95. Type by original designation (also monotypic). Synonym of *Terapon* Cuvier 1816 (Mees & Kailola 1977:32 [ref. 5183]); valid (Vari 1978:297 [ref. 4514], Paxton et al. 1989:532 [ref. 12442]). Terapontidae.

Bigener Hutchins 1977:14 [ref. 2283]. *Aluterius ? brownii* Richardson 1848:68. Type by original designation (also monotypic). Correct spelling for genus of type species is *Aluterus*. Monacanthidae.

Bikinigobius Herre 1953:186 [ref. 2143]. Masc. *Bikinigobius welanderi* Herre 1953:186. Type by original designation (also monotypic). Synonym of *Istigobius* Whitley 1932 (Murdy & Hoese 1985:5 [ref. 5237]). Gobiidae.

Bilabria Schmidt 1936:98 [ref. 3942]. Fem. *Lycenchelys ornatus*

Soldatov 1922:162. Type by monotypy. Valid (Anderson 1984:578 [ref. 13634], Toyoshima in Masuda et al. 1984:306 [ref. 6441]). Zoarcidae.

Binghamia Parr 1937:7, 22 [ref. 3376]. Fem. *Binghamia microphos* Parr 1937:22. Type by monotypy, second species doubtfully included. Preoccupied by Tutt 1908 in Lepidoptera, replaced by *Binghamichthys* Whitley 1941. Alepocephalidae.

Binghamichthys Whitley 1941:4 [ref. 4701]. Masc. *Binghamia microphus* Parr 1937:22. Type by being a replacement name. Replacement for *Binghamia* Parr 1937, preoccupied by Tutt 1908 in Lepidoptera. Alepocephalidae.

Biotodoma Eigenmann & Kennedy 1903:533 [ref. 1260]. Neut. *Geophagus cupido* Heckel 1840:399. Type by being a replacement name. Replacement for *Mesops* Günther 1862, apparently preoccupied by Billberg 1820 in Coleoptera and by Audinet-Serville 1831 [details not researched]. Valid (Gosse 1975:98 [ref. 7029], Kullander 1980:23 [ref. 5526], Kullander 1986:128 [ref. 12439]). Cichlidae.

Biotoecus Eigenmann & Kennedy 1903:533 [ref. 1260]. Masc. *Saraca opercularis* Steindachner 1875:125. Type by being a replacement name. Replacement for *Saraca* Steindachner 1875, preoccupied by Walker 1865 in Lepidoptera. The "oe" or "ae" dipthong is difficult to read, apparently "oe" as used in current literature. Misspelled *Biotaecus* by Jordan 1920:502 [ref. 4905]. Valid (Kullander 1980:23 [ref. 5526]). Cichlidae.

Bipennata de Buen 1926:76 [ref. 5054]. As a "grupo" for 1 species of *Cristiceps*. Not available on basis of Art. 1b(6) [see de Buen's definition of "grupo" on p. 11]; see Appendix A. Blenniidae.

Bipinnula Jordan & Evermann 1896:877, 878 [ref. 2443]. Fem. *Thyrsitops violaceus* Bean 1887:513. Type by original designation (also monotypic). Included by proofing error, was to have been *Escolar* as given by Jordan & Evermann in Goode & Bean 1896 (23 Aug.) [ref. 1848]. Objective synonym of *Escolar*; synonym of *Nesiarchus* Johnson 1862 (Parin & Bekker 1973:459 [ref. 7206], Nakamura et al. 1981 [ref. 5477]). Gempylidae.

Biradiostomias (subgenus of *Eustomias*) Gomon & Gibbs 1985:2 [ref. 5268]. Masc. *Eustomias brevibarbatus* Parr 1927:68. Type by original designation. Melanostomiidae.

Bitricarinata Fernández-Yépez 1948:64 [ref. 1316]. Fem. *Curimatus schomburgkii* Günther 1864:291. Type by original designation. Synonym of *Curimata* Bosc 1817 (Vari 1989:6 [ref. 9189], Vari 1989:21 [ref. 13506]). Curimatidae: Curimatinae.

Bivibranchia Eigenmann 1912:253, 258 [ref. 1227]. Fem. *Bivibranchia proctractila* Eigenmann 1912:259. Type by monotypy. Valid (Roberts 1974:432 [ref. 6872], Géry 1977:199 [ref. 1597], Vari 1983:5 [ref. 5419], Vari 1985 [ref. 5270], Vari & Goulding 1985 [ref. 5200]). Hemiodontidae: Hemiodontinae.

Biwia Jordan & Fowler 1903:838 [ref. 2463]. Fem. *Pseudogobio zezera* Ishikawa 1895:127. Type by original designation (also monotypic). Valid (Banarescu & Nalbant 1973:242 [ref. 173], Sawada in Masuda et al. 1984:56 [ref. 6441], Hosoya 1986:488 [ref. 6155]). Cyprinidae.

Blachea Karrer & Smith 1980:642 [ref. 2566]. Fem. *Blachea xenobranchialis* Karrer & Smith 1980:643. Type by original designation (also monotypic). Valid (Karrer 1982:37 [ref. 5679], Paxton et al. 1989:140 [ref. 12442], Smith 1989:480 [ref. 13285] mentioned in passing). Congridae: Congrinae.

Blakea Steindachner 1876:196 [ref. 4225]. Fem. *Myxodes elegans* Cooper 1864:109. Type by monotypy. Preoccupied by Grote 1875 in Lepidoptera. Objective synonym of *Gibbonsia* Cooper 1864 (Clark Hubbs 1952:116 [ref. 2252]). Clinidae.

Blanchardia Castelnau 1875:47 [ref. 768]. Fem. *Blanchardia maculata* Castelnau 1875:47. Type by monotypy. Synonym of *Notograptus* Günther 1867. Notograptidae.

Blandowskiella Iredale & Whitley 1932:95 [ref. 2299]. Fem. *Pseudoambassis macleayi* Castelnau 1878:43. Type by being a replacement name. Apparently an unneeded replacement for *Pseudoambassis* Castelnau 1878, not preoccupied by *Pseudambassis* Bleeker. Synonym of *Ambassis* Cuvier 1828 (Paxton et al. 1989:485 [ref. 12442] based on placement of type species). Ambassidae.

Blandowskius Whitley 1931:329 [ref. 4672]. Masc. *Blandowskius bucephalus* Whitley 1931:329. Type by original designation (also monotypic). Valid (Tyler 1980:183 [ref. 4477]). Monacanthidae.

Bleeckeria Castelnau 1873:14 [ref. 759]. Fem. *Bleeckeria catafracta* Castelnau 1873:14. Type by monotypy. If *Bleeckeria* (before May 1873) is named for Bleeker, then the genus was misspelled and is preoccupied by *Bleekeria* Günther 1862. In the synonymy of *Paraplesiops* Bleeker 1875 (Hoese & Kuiter 1984:9 [ref. 5300]). Plesiopidae.

Bleekeria Günther 1862:387 [ref. 1969]. Fem. *Bleekeria kallolepis* Günther 1862:387. Type by monotypy. Valid (Stevens et al. 1984:574 [ref. 13671], Heemstra 1986:769 [ref. 5660]). Ammodytidae.

Blennechis Valenciennes in Cuvier & Valenciennes 1836:279 [ref. 1005]. Masc. *Blennechis filamentosus* Valenciennes in Cuvier & Valenciennes 1836:280. Type by subsequent designation. Type designated by Jordan & Seale 1906:431 [ref. 2497]. Misspelled *Blennichus* by Swainson 1839:79 [ref. 4303]. Synonym of *Aspidontus* Cuvier 1834 (Smith-Vaniz 1976:53 [ref. 4144]). Blenniidae.

Blennicottus Gill 1861:166 [ref. 1775]. Masc. *Oligocottus globiceps* Girard 1858:58. Type by monotypy. Synonym of *Clinocottus* Gill 1861 (Bolin 1944:76 [ref. 6379]). Cottidae.

Blenniculus Facciolà 1911:286 [ref. 7188]. Masc. *Blennius variabilis* Rafinesque 1810:29. Apparently an overlooked name. Available; based upon the species described with the name of "*Blennius variabilis* da Rafinesque e di *Blennius argenteus* da Risso" — regarded as one species with a synonym, so type by monotypy. Apparently an objective synonym of *Clinitrachus* Swainson 1839 based on treatment of *variabilis* and *argenteus* by Wheeler 1973:530 [ref. 7190]. Clinidae.

Blenniella Reid 1943:383 [ref. 3686]. Fem. *Blenniella rhessodon* Reid 1943:383. Type by original designation (also monotypic). Synonym of *Istiblennius* Whitley 1943 (Smith-Vaniz & Springer 1971:24 [ref. 4145], Bath 1986:356 [ref. 6217]). Blenniidae.

Blennioclinus Gill 1860:103 [ref. 1765]. Masc. *Clinus brachycephalus* Valenciennes in Cuvier & Valenciennes 1836:371. Type by original designation (also monotypic). Valid (Smith 1986:759 [ref. 5712]). Clinidae.

Blenniolus (subgenus of *Hypsoblennius*) Jordan & Evermann 1898:2386, 2390 [ref. 2445]. Masc. *Blennius brevipinnis* Günther 1861:226. Type by original designation (also monotypic). Synonym of *Hypsoblennius* Gill 1861 (Bath 1977:186 [ref. 208]). Blenniidae.

Blenniomimus Smith 1946:539 [ref. 4072]. Masc. *Clinus taurus* Gilchrist & Thompson 1908:126. Type by original designation. Synonym of *Clinus* Cuvier 1816 (Bennett 1983 [ref. 5299], Smith

1986:761 [ref. 5712]). Clinidae.

Blenniophidium Boulenger 1893:583 [ref. 534]. Neut. *Blenniophidium petropauli* Boulenger 1893:584. Type by monotypy. Pholidae.

Blenniops Nilsson 1855:184 [ref. 3205]. Masc. *Blennius galerita* of Nilsson (not of Linnaeus) 1766. Type by monotypy. Apparently based on a misidentified type species, see Makushok 1973 [ref. 6889]. Synonym of *Chirolophis* Swainson 1838 (Makushok 1973:532 [ref. 6889]). Stichaeidae.

Blennitrachus (subgenus of *Blennius*) Swainson 1839:78, 182, 274 [ref. 4303]. Masc. *Pholis quadrifasciatus* Wood 1825:282. Type by monotypy (p. 78). Spelled *Blennitrachus* by Swainson 1839:78 and 437 (index), *Blenitrachus* on pp. 182 and 274 [ref. 4303]; first reviser not researched. Synonym of *Chasmodes* Valenciennes 1836 (Williams 1983:69 [ref. 5370]). Blenniidae.

Blennius Linnaeus 1758:256 [ref. 2787]. Masc. *Blennius ocellaris* Linnaeus 1758:256. Type by subsequent designation. Type designated by Jordan & Gilbert 1883:759 [ref. 2476]. Spelled *Blennis* by Klein 1779 (not available). On Official List (Opinion 92, Direction 56). Valid (Bath 1973:519 [ref. 7212], Bath & Hutchins 1986 [ref. 5151], Zander in Whitehead et al. 1986:1097 [ref. 13677]). Blenniidae.

Blennodesmus Günther 1872:667 [ref. 1997]. Masc. *Blennodesmus scapularis* Günther 1872:667. Type by monotypy. Valid (Winterbottom 1986:5 [ref. 5727]). Pseudochromidae: Congrogadinae.

Blennodon Hardy 1987:158 [ref. 5959]. Masc. *Trypterygium dorsalis* Clarke 1879:291. Type by original designation (also monotypic). See history of name as given by Hardy on p. 157. Gender attributed to genus by Hardy was neuter, but "odon" is masculine. Correct spelling for genus of type species is *Tripterygion*. Tripterygiidae.

Blennophis Swainson 1839:75, 182, 276 [ref. 4303]. Masc. *Clinus anguillaris* Valenciennes in Cuvier & Valenciennes 1836:390. Type by original designation. "Type" given on p. 75 (also designated by Swain 1882:278 [ref. 5966]). Synonym of *Clinus* Cuvier 1816 (Bennett 1983 [ref. 5299]); valid (Smith 1986:759 [ref. 5712]). Clinidae.

Blennophis Valenciennes in Webb & Berthelot 1843:60, Pl. 20 [ref. 4502]. Masc. *Blennophis webbii* Valenciennes in Webb & Berthelot 1843:61, Pl. 20. Type by monotypy. Preoccupied by Swainson 1839 in fishes, replaced by *Ophioblennius* Gill 1860 (Smith-Vaniz & Springer 1971:35 [ref. 3722]). Objective synonym of *Ophioblennius* Gill 1860 (Smith-Vaniz & Springer 1971:35 [ref. 4145]). Blenniidae.

Blennus Klein 1779:589 [ref. 4924]. Masc. Not available, published in a work that does not conform to the principle of binominal nomenclature. Original not checked. In the synonymy of *Blennius* Linnaeus 1758. Blenniidae.

Blepharichthys Gill 1861:36 [ref. 1766]. Masc. *Zeus ciliaris* Bloch 1787:29. Type by being a replacement name. Unneeded replacement for *Blepharis* Cuvier 1816, not preoccupied. Synonym of *Alectis* Rafinesque 1815 (Daget & Smith-Vaniz 1986:308 [ref. 6207]). Carangidae.

Blepharis Cuvier 1816:322 [ref. 993]. *Zeus ciliaris* Bloch 1787:29. Type by monotypy. Synonym of *Alectis* Rafinesque 1815 (Daget & Smith-Vaniz 1986:308 [ref. 6207]). Carangidae.

Blepsias Cuvier 1829:167 [ref. 995]. Masc. *Trachinus cirrhosus* Pallas 1811:237. Type by monotypy. Valid (Bolin 1944:99 [ref. 6379], Washington et al. 1984:442 [ref. 13660], Yabe in Masuda et al. 1984:323 [ref. 6441], Yabe 1985:123 [ref. 11522] in Hemitripteridae). Cottidae.

Bleptonema Eigenmann 1914:44 [ref. 1230]. Neut. *Bleptonema paraguayensis* Eigenmann 1914:44. Type by subsequent designation. Type designated by Jordan 1920:535 [ref. 4905]. Synonym of *Prionobrama* Fowler 1913 (Géry 1977:347 [ref. 1597] based on placement of type species). Characidae.

Blicca Heckel 1843:1032 [ref. 2066]. Fem. *Cyprinus blicca* Bloch 1782:65. Type by monotypy (also by absolute tautonymy). Synonym of *Abramis* Cuvier 1816 (Howes 1981:46 [ref. 14200]); valid (Bogutskaya 1987:936 [ref. 13521]). Cyprinidae.

Bliccopsis Heckel 1843:1032 [ref. 2066]. Fem. *Cyprinus buggenhagii* Bloch 1784:137. Type by monotypy. Cyprinidae.

Blythia Talwar 1971:23 [ref. 4317]. Fem. *Umbrina dussumieri* Valenciennes in Cuvier & Valenciennes 1833:481. Type by original designation. Preoccupied by Theobald 1868 in Ophidia, replaced by *Blythsciaena* Talwar 1975. Synonym of *Johnius*, subgenus *Johnius* Bloch 1793 (Trewavas 1977:406 [ref. 4459]). Sciaenidae.

Blythsciaena Talwar 1975:17 [ref. 4318]. Fem. *Umbrina dussumieri* Valenciennes in Cuvier & Valenciennes 1833:481. Type by being a replacement name. Replacement for *Blythia* Talwar 1971, preoccupied by Theobald 1868 in Ophidia. Synonym of *Johnius*, subgenus *Johnius* Bloch 1793 (Trewavas 1977:406 [ref. 4459]). Sciaenidae.

Bodianus Bloch 1790:33 [ref. 469]. Masc. *Bodianus bodianus* Bloch 1790:33, 48. Type by absolute tautonymy. Original not checked. Type as given by Fowler (MS); see also C. L. Smith 1971:92 [ref. 14102]. Misspelled *Bodian* by Latreille 1804:83. Valid (Gomon 1979 [ref. 5480], Gomon & Randall 1978 [ref. 5481], Lobel 1981 [ref. 5536], Richards & Leis 1984:544 [ref. 13668], Yamakawa in Masuda et al. 1984:202 [ref. 6441], Randall 1986:686 [ref. 5706], Quignard & Pras in Whitehead et al. 1986:921 [ref. 13676]). Labridae.

Boehlkea Géry 1966:212 [ref. 1588]. Fem. *Boehlkea fredcochui* Géry 1966:212. Type by original designation (also monotypic). Valid (Géry 1977:375, 382 [ref. 1597]). Characidae.

Boesemania Trewavas 1977:309 [ref. 4459]. Fem. *Corvina microlepis* Bleeker 1858:11. Type by original designation (also monotypic). Valid (Kottelat 1985:273 [ref. 11441], Kottelat 1989:17 [ref. 13605]). Sciaenidae.

Boesemanichthys Abe 1952:40 [ref. 4]. Masc. *Tetraodon firmamentum* Temminck & Schlegel 1850:280. Type by original designation (also monotypic). Synonym of *Arothron* Müller 1841 (Masuda et al. 1984:364 [ref. 6441]). Tetraodontidae.

Boggiania Perugia 1897:148 [ref. 3436]. Fem. *Boggiania ocellata* Perugia 1897:148. Type by original designation (also monotypic). Synonym of *Crenicichla* Heckel 1840 (Kullander 1986:82 [ref. 12439], Kullander & Nijssen 1989:207 [ref. 14136]). Cichlidae.

Bogimba (subgenus of *Galeolamna*) Whitley 1943:125 [ref. 4702]. Neut. *Galeolamna (Bogimba) bogimba* Whitley 1943:123. Type by monotypy (also by absolute tautonymy). Synonym of *Carcharhinus* Blainville 1816 (Garrick 1982:19 [ref. 5454], Compagno 1984:449 [ref. 6846], Compagno 1988:308 [ref. 13488]). Carcharhinidae.

Bogmarus Bloch & Schneider 1801:lviii, 518 [ref. 471]. Masc. *Gymnogaster arcticus* Brünnich 1788:408. Type by monotypy. Type somewhat unclear, apparently Bloch & Schneider recognized only one species in the genus. *Bogmarus bogmarus* on p. lviii as name only; evidently intended for *islandicus*; *islandicus* used in Pl.

101; *arcticus* is only species mentioned on p. 518. Synonym of *Trachipterus* Goüan 1770 (Palmer 1973:330 [ref. 7195], Scott 1983:172 [ref. 5346]). Trachipteridae.

Bogoda Bleeker 1853:89 [ref. 341]. Fem. *Chanda nama* Hamilton 1822:109, 371. Type by monotypy, one species but with many synonyms, including the tautonym *Chanda bogoda* Hamilton 1822. (Bogodidae Bleeker apparently is an older family-group name than Ambassidae or Chandidae.) Synonym of *Chanda* Hamilton 1822 after *nama* designated type of *Chanda* by ICZN (Opinion 1121). Ambassidae.

Bogoda Blyth 1860:139 [ref. 477]. Fem. Not an original description, Blyth merely referred his new species *infuscata* to Bleeker's genus *Bogoda*; treated as an original description by Jordan but misspelled *Bogota*. In the synonymy of *Priacanthus* Oken 1817. Priacanthidae.

Bogoslovius Jordan & Evermann 1898:2563, 2574 [ref. 2445]. Masc. *Bogoslovius clarki* Jordan & Gilbert in Jordan & Evermann 1898:2575. Type by original designation. Synonym of *Coryphaenoides* Gunner 1765 (Marshall 1973:294 [ref. 7194], Marshall & Iwamoto 1973:565 [ref. 6966]). Macrouridae: Macrourinae.

Bola Günther 1868:293 [ref. 1990]. Fem. *Cyprinus bola* Hamilton 1822:274. Type by absolute tautonymy; *bola* included by Günther in synonymy of *B. goha* Hamilton 1822; second species included. Preoccupied by Hamilton 1822 in fishes, replaced by *Raiamas* Jordan 1919. Objective synonym of *Raiamas* Jordan 1919 (Lévêque & Daget 1984:332 [ref. 6186], Kuang in Chu & Chen 1989:23 [ref. 13584]). Synonym of *Barilius* Hamilton 1822 (Roberts 1989:30 [ref. 6439]). Cyprinidae.

Bola Hamilton 1822:75, 368 [ref. 2031]. Fem. *Bola coitor* Hamilton 1822:75, 368. Type by subsequent designation. Type designated by Jordan & Thompson 1911:244 [ref. 2539]. *Bola* Günther 1868, a cyprinid, is a junior homonym. Synonym of *Johnius*, subgenus *Johnius* Bloch 1793 (Trewavas 1977:406 [ref. 4459]). Sciaenidae.

Bolbometopon Smith 1956:8 [ref. 4104]. Neut. *Scarus muricatus* Valenciennes in Cuvier & Valenciennes 1839:208. Type by original designation (also monotypic). Smith wrongly treated as masculine, gender is neuter. Valid (Randall & Bruce 1983:6 [ref. 5412], Kishimoto in Masuda et al. 1984:219 [ref. 6441], Randall 1986:708 [ref. 5706], Bellwood & Choat 1989:14 [ref. 13494]). Scaridae: Scarinae.

Boleichthys Girard 1859:103 [ref. 1821]. Masc. *Boleichthys exilis* Girard 1859:103. Type by subsequent designation. Type designated by Jordan & Gilbert 1877:92 [ref. 4907]. Synonym of *Etheostoma* Rafinesque 1819, but as a valid subgenus (Page 1981:40 [ref. 3347]); as a synonym of subgenus *Oligocephalus* Girard 1859 (Bailey & Etnier 1988:25 [ref. 6873]). Percidae.

Boleophthalmus Valenciennes in Cuvier & Valenciennes 1837:198 [ref. 1006]. Masc. *Gobius boddarti* Pallas 1770:11. Type by subsequent designation. Type designated by Bleeker 1874:328 [ref. 437]. Misspelled *Bolcophthalmus* by Jordan 1923:227 (footnote 477) [ref. 2421]. Valid (Akihito in Masuda et al. 1984:286 [ref. 6441], Birdsong et al. 1988:195 [ref. 7303], Kottelat 1989:18 [ref. 13605], Murdy 1989:11 [ref. 13628]). Gobiidae.

Boleops Gill 1863:271 [ref. 1692]. Masc. *Boleophthalmus aucupatorius* Richardson 1842:148. Type by original designation (also monotypic). Type designated by Gill's style of type in parentheses in key. Synonym of *Scartelaos* Swainson 1839 (Murdy 1989:49 [ref. 13628]). Gobiidae.

Boleosoma DeKay 1842:20 [ref. 1098]. Neut. *Boleosoma tessellatum* DeKay 1842:20. Type by monotypy. Synonym of *Etheostoma* Rafinesque 1819, but as a valid subgenus (Collette & Banarescu 1977:1456 [ref. 5845], Page 1981:34 [ref. 3347], Bailey & Etnier 1988:23 [ref. 6873]). Percidae.

Bolinichthys Paxton 1972:46 [ref. 3394]. Masc. *Myctophum longipes* Brauer 1906:236. Type by original designation. Valid (Paxton 1979:6 [ref. 6440], Hulley in Whitehead et al. 1984:434 [ref. 13675], Moser et al. 1984:220 [ref. 13645], Fujii in Masuda et al. 1984:68 [ref. 6441], Hulley 1986:286 [ref. 5672], Paxton et al. 1989:254 [ref. 12442]). Myctophidae.

Bollmannia Jordan in Jordan & Bollman 1890:164 [ref. 2433]. Fem. *Bollmannia chlamydes* Jordan in Jordan & Bollman 1890:164. Type by monotypy. Valid (Birdsong et al. 1988:191 [ref. 7303]). Gobiidae.

Bombonia Herre 1927:274 [ref. 2103]. Fem. *Bombonia luzonica* Herre 1927:275. Type by monotypy. Synonym of *Hippichthys* Bleeker 1849 (Dawson 1978:133 [ref. 7026], Dawson 1985:96 [ref. 6541], Dawson 1986:282 [ref. 6201]). Syngnathidae: Syngnathinae.

Bonapartia Goode & Bean 1896:102 [ref. 1848]. Fem. *Bonapartia pedaliota* Goode & Bean 1896:102. Type by monotypy. Possibly preoccupied by Buettikofer, June 1896 in Aves; date of Goode & Bean being after July 20, 1896, and probably 24 August 1896. If preoccupied, should be replaced by *Zaphotias* Goode & Bean 1898. Valid (Witzell 1973:115 [ref. 7172], Weitzman 1974:472 [ref. 5174], Badcock in Whitehead et al. 1984:285 [ref. 13675], Ahlstrom et al. 1984:185 [ref. 13643], Schaefer et al. 1986:248 [ref. 5709], Paxton et al. 1989:183 [ref. 12442]). Gonostomatidae.

Bondia Fernández-Yépez 1948:66 [ref. 1316]. Fem. *Curimatus mivartii* Steindachner 1879:48. Type by original designation. Preoccupied by Newman 1856 in Lepidoptera, replaced by *Bondichthys* Whitley 1953. Synonym of *Curimata* Bosc 1817 (Vari 1989:6 [ref. 9189], *Bondia* not mentioned by Vari, but status based on his placement of *Bondichthys*). Curimatidae: Curimatinae.

Bondichthys Whitley 1953:134 [ref. 4718]. Masc. *Curimatus mivartii* Steindachner 1879:48. Type by being a replacement name. Replacement for *Bondia* Fernández-Yépez 1948, preoccupied by Newman 1856 in Lepidoptera. Synonym of *Curimata* Bosc 1817 (Vari 1989:6 [ref. 9189], Vari 1989:21 [ref. 13506]). Curimatidae: Curimatinae.

Boops Cuvier 1814:91 [ref. 4884]. Masc. *Sparus boops* Linnaeus 1758:208. Type by absolute tautonymy. Also in Cuvier 1815:453 [ref. 1019]. Valid (Tortonese 1973:406 [ref. 7192], Bauchot & Hureau in Whitehead et al. 1986:884 [ref. 13676]). Centracanthidae.

Boops Gronow in Gray 1854:58 [ref. 1911]. Masc. *Boops asper* Gronow in Gray 1854:58. Type by monotypy. Preoccupied by Cuvier 1814 in fishes, not replaced. Synonym of *Priacanthus* Oken 1817 (Starnes 1988:154 [ref. 6978]). Priacanthidae.

Boopsetta Alcock 1896:305 [ref. 91]. Fem. *Boopsetta umbrarum* Alcock 1896:305. Type by monotypy. Synonym of *Poecilopsetta* Günther 1880 (Norman 1934:387 [ref. 6893]). Pleuronectidae: Poecilopsettinae.

Boopsoidea Castelnau 1861:25 [ref. 767]. Fem. *Boopsoidea inornata* Castelnau 1861:26. Type by monotypy. Spelled *Boopsidea* by Castelnau (p. 26); *Boopsoidea* on p. v. and at head of genus description. Valid (Smith & Smith 1986:581 [ref. 5710]). Sparidae.

Borborodes Gistel 1848:X [ref. 1822]. Masc. *Squalus americanus* Gmelin 1789:1503. Type by being a replacement name. Replacement for *Scymnus* Cuvier, preoccupied in Coeloptera. *Barborodes* is a misspelling. Synonym of *Dalatias* Rafinesque 1810 (Compagno 1984:63 [ref. 6474], Cappetta 1987:62 [ref. 6348]). Squalidae.

Borborys Goode & Bean (ex Broussonet/Linnaeus) 1885:205 [ref. 1841]. *Cobitis heteroclitus* Linnaeus 1766:500. Type by monotypy. Not available from Goode & Bean 1885; essentially a name published in synonymy; Goode & Bean quote an annotation by Linnaeus. Subsequent availability of name not investigated. In the synonymy of *Fundulus* Lacepède 1803 (Parenti 1981:494 [ref. 7066]). Cyprinodontidae: Fundulinae.

Boreocottus Gill 1859:166 [ref. 1760]. Masc. *Boreocottus axillaris* Gill 1859:166. Type by monotypy. Synonym of *Myoxocephalus* Tilesius 1811 (Neyelov 1979:120 [ref. 3152]). Cottidae.

Boreogadus (subgenus of *Gadus*) Günther 1862:336 [ref. 1969]. Masc. *Gadus fabricii* Richardson 1836:245. Type by subsequent designation. Based on text style, described as a section of *Gadus*. Type designated by Jordan & Gilbert 1883:807 [ref. 2476]. Valid (Svetovidov 1973:305 [ref. 7169], Fahay & Markle 1984:266 [ref. 13653], Svetovidov in Whitehead et al. 1986:683 [ref. 13676]). Gadidae.

Boreogaleus Gill 1862:400, 402 [ref. 1783]. Masc. *Squalus arcticus* Faber 1829:17. Type by original designation (also monotypic). Also in Gill 1862:411 [ref. 4910]. Objective synonym of *Galeocerdo* Müller & Henle 1837 (Compagno 1973:26 [ref. 7163], Compagno 1984:503 [ref. 6846], Compagno 1988:279 [ref. 13488]). Carcharhinidae.

Boreogobius Gill 1863:269 [ref. 1691]. Masc. *Gobius stuvitzii* Duben & Koren 1844:111. Type by monotypy. Synonym of *Aphia* Risso 1826 (Miller 1973:489 [ref. 6888]). Gobiidae.

Boridia Cuvier in Cuvier & Valenciennes 1830:154 [ref. 999]. Fem. *Boridia grossidens* Cuvier in Cuvier & Valenciennes 1830:154. Type by monotypy. Valid (Johnson 1980:11 [ref. 13553]). Haemulidae.

Boroda Herre 1927:58 [ref. 2104]. Fem. *Boroda expatria* Herre 1927:59. Type by original designation. Synonym of *Bostrychus* Lacepède 1801 (Maugé 1986:390 [ref. 6218]). Eleotridae.

Borodamirus Whitley 1935:250 [ref. 4683]. Masc. *Callieleotris platycephalus* Fowler 1934:156. Type by being a replacement name. Unneeded replacement for *Callieleotris* Fowler 1934, not preoccupied by *Calleleotris* Gill 1863 in fishes. Synonym of *Bostrychus* Lacepède 1801 (Maugé 1986:390 [ref. 6218]). Eleotridae.

Borodinula Whitley 1931:334 [ref. 4672]. Fem. *Nemichthys infans* Günther 1878:251. Type by being a replacement name. An unneeded replacement for *Avocettina* Jordan & Davis 1891, not preoccupied by *Avocettinus* Mulsant & Verreaux 1866 in Aves [not investigated], nor by *Avocettinus* Bonaparte 1850 in Aves. Valid (Larsen 1973:231 [ref. 7187], Karmovskaya 1982:152 [ref. 5204]); synonym of *Avocettinops* Roule & Bertin 1924 (Smith & Nielsen 1976:4 [ref. 7084]); synonym of *Avocettina* Jordan & Davis 1891 (Smith & Nielsen 1989:447 [ref. 13290]). Nemichthyidae.

Borophryne Regan 1925:564 [ref. 3677]. Fem. *Borophryne apogon* Regan 1925:564. Type by monotypy. Linophrynidae.

Borostomias Regan 1908:217 [ref. 3634]. Masc. *Borostomias braueri* Regan 1908:217. Type by subsequent designation. Type usually given as by monotypy, but 3 included species; earliest type designated found that by Jordan 1920:529 [ref. 4905]. Valid (Gibbs 1964:332 [ref. 6960], Gibbs & Morrow 1973:127 [ref. 7174], Gibbs in Whitehead et al. 1984:331 [ref. 13675], Kawaguchi & Moser 1984:171 [ref. 13642], Fujii in Masuda et al. 1984:50 [ref. 6441], Fink 1985:11 [ref. 5171], Gibbs 1986:233 [ref. 5655], Paxton et al. 1989:195 [ref. 12442]). Astronesthidae.

Bostockia Castelnau 1873:126 [ref. 758]. Fem. *Bostockia porosa* Castelnau 1873:126. Type by monotypy. Valid (Paxton et al. 1989:510 [ref. 12442]). Percichthyidae.

Bostrichthys Duméril 1806:120, 332 [ref. 1151]. Masc. *Bostrychus sinensis* Lacepède 1801:144, 145. Type by being a replacement name. Unneeded replacement for *Bostrychus* Lacepède 1801. *Bostrychichthys* Agassiz 1846:49 [ref. 64] is an unjustified emendation. Objective synonym of *Bostrychus* Lacepède 1801 (Maugé 1986:389 [ref. 6218]). Valid (Kottelat 1989:18 [ref. 13605]). Eleotridae.

Bostrictis Rafinesque 1815:84 [ref. 3584]. Masc. Not available; name only and apparently an incorrect subsequent spelling of *Bostrichthys* Lacepède 1806. In the synonymy of *Bostrychus* (Maugé 1986:389 [ref. 6218]). Eleotridae.

Bostrychoides Lacepède 1801:144 [ref. 2710]. Masc. *Bostrychoides oculatus* Lacepède 1801:144, 145. Type by monotypy. Channidae.

Bostrychus Lacepède 1801:140 [ref. 2710]. Masc. *Bostrychus sinensis* Lacepède 1801:144, 145. Type by subsequent designation. Type apparently designated by Bleeker 1874:301 [ref. 437] through *Bostrichthys*. Not preoccupied by *Bostrichus* in insects. *Bostrichthys* Duméril 1806, *Psilus* Fischer 1813, and *Ictiopogon* Rafinesque 1815 are apparently unneeded replacements. Valid (Akihito in Masuda et al. 1984:239 [ref. 6441], Maugé 1986:389 [ref. 6218], Birdsong et al. 1988:181 [ref. 7303]). Eleotridae.

Bothragonus Gill in Jordan & Gilbert 1883:728 [ref. 2476]. Masc. *Hypsagonus swanii* Steindachner 1876:192. Type by original designation (also monotypic). Valid (Washington et al. 1984:442 [ref. 13660], Kanayama in Masuda et al. 1984:332 [ref. 6441], Yabe 1985:123 [ref. 11522], Maeda & Amaoka 1988:104 [ref. 12616], Leipertz 1988 [ref. 6233]). Agonidae.

Bothrocara Bean 1890:38 [ref. 229]. Neut. *Bothrocara mollis* Bean 1890:39. Type by monotypy. Valid (Anderson 1984:578 [ref. 13634], Toyoshima in Masuda et al. 1984:309 [ref. 6441]). Zoarcidae.

Bothrocarichthys Schmidt 1938:653 [ref. 3943]. Masc. *Bothrocarichthys microcephalus* Schmidt 1938:653. Type by monotypy. Zoarcidae.

Bothrocarina Suvorov 1935:435 (439) [ref. 4300]. Fem. *Bothrocarina nigrocaudata* Suvorov 1935:435 (439). Type by original designation (also monotypic). Valid (Anderson 1984:578 [ref. 13634], Yoyoshima in Masuda et al. 1984:308 [ref. 6441]). Zoarcidae.

Bothrocaropsis Garman 1899:127 [ref. 1540]. Fem. *Bothrocaropsis alalonga* Garman 1899:127. Type by subsequent designation. Described as "sub-gen. n." but of which genus is not clearly indicated; actually described as a new genus based on treatment on p. 390, 418 and 427. Type designated by Jordan 1920:486 [ref. 4905]. Zoarcidae.

Bothrolaemus Holbrook 1855:80 [ref. 2184]. Masc. *Trachinotus pampanus* Valenciennes in Cuvier & Valenciennes 1832:415. Type by monotypy. Synonym of *Trachinotus* Lacepède 1801 (Daget & Smith-Vaniz 1986:319 [ref. 6207]). Carangidae.

Bothus Rafinesque 1810:23 [ref. 3594]. Masc. *Bothus rumolo* Rafinesque 1810:23 (= *Pleuronectes rhombus* Linnaeus 1758:271).

Type by subsequent designation, earliest found is by Jordan 1917:79 [ref. 2407]. *Bothus rumolo* Rafinesque is an unneeded substitute for *P. rhombus*. Valid (Norman 1934:220 [ref. 6893], Amaoka 1969:161 [ref. 105], Nielsen 1973:620 [ref. 6885], Ahlstrom et al. 1984:642 [ref. 13641], Amaoka in Masuda et al. 1984:349 [ref. 6441], Nielsen in Whitehead et al. 1986:1297 [ref. 13677], Hensley 1986:855 [ref. 5669], Hensley 1986:941 [ref. 6326]). Bothidae: Bothinae.

Botia Gray 1831:8 [ref. 1879]. Fem. *Botia almorhae* Gray 1831:8. Type by monotypy. Only one valid species mentioned by name, therefore type by monotypy (not *Botia grandis* as designated by Bleeker 1863:36 [ref. 400] and 1863:3 [ref. 4859]). *Botia grandis* appeared in Gray 14 Apr. 1832:Pl. 94 [ref. 1878]. Valid (Banarescu & Nalbant 1968:341 [ref. 6554], Jayaram 1981:175 [ref. 6497], Sawada 1982:197 [ref. 14111], Kottelat 1985:267 [ref. 11441], Teugels et al. 1986 [ref. 6761], Kottelat 1989:13 [ref. 13605], Roberts 1989:101 [ref. 6439]). Cobitidae: Botiinae.

Boulengerella Eigenmann 1903:147 [ref. 1218]. Fem. *Xiphostoma lateristriga* Boulenger 1895:449. Type by original designation (also monotypic). Valid (Géry 1977:106 [ref. 1597]). Ctenoluciidae.

Boulengerina (subgenus of *Dules*) Fowler 1906:512 [ref. 1375]. Fem. *Dules mato* Lesson 1830:223. Type by original designation (also monotypic). Preoccupied by Dollo 1886 in Ophidia, replaced by *Safole* Jordan 1912. Objective synonym of *Moronopsis* Gill 1863, synonym of *Kuhlia* Gill 1861 (Maugé 1986:306 [ref. 6218]). Kuhliidae.

Boulengerochromis Pellegrin 1904:(164) 304 [ref. 3419]. Masc. *Tilapia microlepis* Boulenger 1899:94. Type by monotypy. Valid (Poll 1986:30 [ref. 6136]). Cichlidae.

Boulengeromyrus Taverne & Géry 1968:100 [ref. 4360]. Masc. *Boulengeromyrus knoepffleri* Taverne & Géry 1968:100. Type by original designation (also monotypic). Valid (Taverne 1972:171 [ref. 6367], Gosse 1984:63 [ref. 6169]). Mormyridae.

Bovichtus Valenciennes in Cuvier & Valenciennes 1831:487 [ref. 1000]. Masc. *Callionymus diacanthus* Carmichael 1818:501. Type by monotypy. Spelled *Bovichthus* by Swainson 1838:86 [ref. 4302] and *Bovichthys* by Richardson 1846:56 [ref. 3739]. The family name is correctly Bovichtidae; spelled Bovichthyidae in current literature. Valid (Stevens et al. 1984:563 [ref. 13633]). Bovichtidae.

Bovitrigla Fowler 1938:112 [ref. 1426]. Fem. *Bovitrigla acanthomoplate* Fowler 1938:113. Type by original designation. Triglidae: Triglinae.

Bowenia Haast 1873:277 [ref. 2025]. Fem. *Bowenia novaezealandiae* Haast 1873:277. Type by monotypy. Synonym of *Rhombosolea* Günther 1862 (Norman 1934:429 [ref. 6893]). Pleuronectidae: Rhombosoleinae.

Bowersia Jordan & Evermann 1903:182 [ref. 2450]. Fem. *Bowersia violescens* Jordan & Evermann 1903:183. Type by original designation. Synonym of *Pristipomoides* Bleeker 1852 (Allen 1985:141 [ref. 6843], Akazaki & Iwatsuki 1987:326 [ref. 6699]). Lutjanidae.

Box Valenciennes in Cuvier & Valenciennes 1830:346 [ref. 996]. Masc. *Sparus boops* Linnaeus 1758:280. Type by subsequent designation. Type designated by Jordan & Fesler 1893:529 [ref. 2455]. Synonym of *Boops* Cuvier 1814 (Tortonese 1973:406 [ref. 7192]). Centracanthidae.

Boxaodon Guichenot 1848:208 [ref. 1939]. Masc. *Boxaodon cyanescens* Guichenot 1848:209. Type by monotypy. Synonym of *Emmelichthys* Richardson 1845 (Heemstra & Randall 1977:378 [ref. 7057]). Emmelichthyidae.

Brachaelurus Ogilby 1907:27 [ref. 3281]. Masc. *Chiloscyllium modestum* Günther 1871:654. Type by monotypy. See *Brachaelurus* Ogilby 1908. Valid (Compagno 1984:175 [ref. 6474], Cappetta 1987:77 [ref. 6348], Paxton et al. 1989:88 [ref. 12442]). Brachyaeluridae.

Brachaelurus Ogilby 1908:2, 3 [ref. 3286]. Masc. *Brachaelurus colcloughi* Ogilby 1908:4. Type by original designation (also monotypic). Originally proposed by Ogilby 1907:27 [ref. 3281] with species as *Chiloscyllium modestum* Günther, which Ogilby in 1908 (perhaps by error) placed as the type of a new genus *Cirriscyllium*. Brachyaeluridae.

Brachaluteres Bleeker 1865:100 [ref. 416]. *Aluterius trossulus* Richardson 1846:68. Type by original designation (also monotypic). Also in Bleeker 1866:13 [ref. 417]. Correct spelling for genus of type species is *Aluterus*. Valid (Matsuura 1979:165 [ref. 7019], Tyler 1980:178 [ref. 4477], Arai 1983:199 [ref. 14249], Aboussouan & Leis 1984:452 [ref. 13661], Matsuura in Masuda et al. 1984:361 [ref. 6441], Hutchins & Swainston 1985 [ref. 5231]). Monacanthidae.

Brachionichthys Bleeker 1855:12, 21 [ref. 346]. Masc. *Cheironectes hirsutus* of Bleeker (= *Lophius hirsutus* Lacepède 1804:202, 210). Type by subsequent designation. Type designated by Bleeker 1865:5 [ref. 416]; Jordan 1919:263 [ref. 2410] wrongly lists *C. politus* Richardson as type. Correct spelling for genus of Bleeker's *hirsutus* is *Chironectes*. Valid (Paxton et al. 1989:275 [ref. 12442]). Brachionichthyidae.

Brachioptera Gracianov 1906:400 [ref. 1869]. Fem. *Brachioptera rhinoceros* Gracianov 1906:401. Type by monotypy. Based on an embryo of *Dasyatis pastinaca* Linnaeus; synonym of *Dasyatis* Rafinesque 1810. Dasyatidae.

Brachioptilon Hamilton in Newman 1849:2358 [ref. 3169]. Masc. *Brachioptilon hamiltoni* Hamilton in Newman 1849:2358. Type by monotypy. Description entirely quoted from C. B. Hamilton; name selected by Newman. Synonym of *Manta* Bancroft 1829 (Cappetta 1987:176 [ref. 6348]). Mobulidae.

Brachirus (subgenus of *Pterois*) Swainson 1839:71, 264 [ref. 4303]. Masc. *Pterois zebra* Cuvier in Cuvier & Valenciennes 1829:269. Type by subsequent designation. Type designated by Swain 1882:277 [ref. 5966] (for *Brachyrus*); *Brachyrus* Swainson 1839 regarded as a misspelling of *Brachirus* Swainson 1839 (see Eschmeyer & Randall 1975:275 [ref. 6389]); name changed to *Dendrochirus* on p. 180. See account of *Dendrochirus*. Scorpaenidae: Pteroinae.

Brachirus (subgenus of *Solea*) Swainson 1839:187, 303 [ref. 4303]. Masc. *Pleuronectes orientalis* Bloch & Schneider 1801:157. Type by subsequent designation. Type designated by Swain 1882:281 [ref. 5966]. Not *Brachirus* or *Brachyrus* Swainson 1838:71, 264 (= *Dendrochirus* Swainson). Preoccupied by *Brachirus* Swainson, replaced by *Synaptura* Cantor 1849. Objective synonym of *Synaptura* Cantor 1849 (Desoutter 1986:431 [ref. 6212]). Soleidae.

Brachyalestes Günther 1864:314 [ref. 1974]. Masc. *Myletes nurse* Rüppell 1832:12. Type by subsequent designation. Type designated by Jordan 1919:333 [ref. 2410]. Synonym of *Alestes* Müller & Troschel 1844 (Paugy 1984:140 [ref. 6183]). Alestiidae.

Brachyamblyopus Bleeker 1874:329 [ref. 437]. Masc. *Amblyopus brachysoma* Bleeker 1853:510. Type by original designation (also monotypic). Valid (Akihito in Masuda et al. 1984:287 [ref. 6441],

Birdsong et al. 1988:197 [ref. 7303], Kottelat 1989:19 [ref. 13605]). Gobiidae.

Brachybembras Fowler 1938:94 [ref. 1426]. Fem. *Brachybembras aschemeieri* Fowler 1938:94. Type by original designation (also monotypic). Bembridae.

Brachycallionymus Herre & Myers in Herre 1936:12 [ref. 2124]. Masc. *Brachycallionymus mirus* Herre 1936:12. Type by original designation (also monotypic). Synonym of *Eleutherochir* Bleeker 1879 (Nakabo 1982:109 [ref. 3139], Fricke 1982:73 [ref. 5432]). Callionymidae.

Brachycephalus Hollard 1857:326, 327 [ref. 2186]. Masc. *Tetraodon lineatus* Linnaeus 1758:333. Type by being a replacement name. Proposed without species; regarded as an unneeded replacement for the subgenus *Tetraodon* of Bibron [= *Tetraodon* Linnaeus 1758 and taking same type]; see Hollard's caption to Pl. 6. Tetraodontidae.

Brachychalcinus Boulenger 1892:11 [ref. 533]. Masc. *Brachychalcinus retrospina* Boulenger 1892:12. Type by monotypy. Valid (Géry 1977:367 [ref. 1597], Reis 1989:58 [ref. 14219]). Characidae: Stethaprioninae.

Brachycheirophis Fowler 1944:190 [ref. 1448]. Masc. *Pisoodonophis daspilotus* Gilbert in Jordan & Evermann 1898:2803. Type by original designation (also monotypic). Correct spelling for genus of type species is *Pisodonophis*. Synonym of *Pisodonophis* Kaup 1856 (McCosker 1977:83 [ref. 6836], Castle 1984:38 [ref. 6171]). Ophichthidae: Ophichthinae.

Brachyconger Bleeker 1865:116 [ref. 409]. Masc. *Muraena savanna* Bancroft 1831:135. Type by original designation (also monotypic). Synonym of *Cynoponticus* Costa 1845 (Smith 1989:436 [ref. 13285]). Muraenesocidae.

Brachyconger Norman 1922:217 [ref. 3210]. Masc. *Brachyconger platyrhynchus* Norman 1922:218. Type by monotypy. Preoccupied by *Brachyconger* Bleeker 1865, replaced by *Endeconger* Jordan 1923. Synonym of *Chilorhinus* Lütken 1852 (Smith 1989:84 [ref. 13285]). Chlopsidae.

Brachydanio (subgenus of *Danio*) Weber & de Beaufort 1916:85 [ref. 4604]. Masc. *Nuria albolineata* Blyth 1860:163. Type by monotypy. Synonym of *Danio* Hamilton 1822, but as a valid subgenus (Jayaram 1981:81 [ref. 6497]); valid genus (Kottelat 1985:261 [ref. 11441], Kottelat 1989:6 [ref. 13605]). Cyprinidae.

Brachydeuterus Gill 1862:17 [ref. 1657]. Masc. *Larimus auritus* Valenciennes in Cuvier & Valenciennes 1831:369. Type by monotypy. Valid (Roux 1973:392 [ref. 7200], Johnson 1980:11 [ref. 13553], Ben-Tuvia & McKay in Whitehead et al. 1986:859 [ref. 13676], Roux 1986:327 [ref. 6209]). Haemulidae.

Brachydicrolene (subgenus of *Dicrolene*) Norman 1939:86 [ref. 6556]. Masc. *Dicrolene nigricaudis* Alcock 1889:387. Type by monotypy, second species questionably included. Synonym of *Dicrolene* Goode & Bean 1883 (Cohen & Nielsen 1978:28 [ref. 881]). Ophidiidae: Neobythitinae.

Brachyeleotris Bleeker 1874:306 [ref. 437]. Fem. *Eleotris cyanostigma* Bleeker 1855:452. Type by original designation (also monotypic). Also appeared in Bleeker 1874:374 [ref. 436]; earliest not determined. Synonym of *Asterropteryx* Rüppell 1830 (Hoese, pers. comm.). Gobiidae.

Brachygadus Gill 1862:280 [ref. 1666]. Masc. *Gadus minutus* Linnaeus 1758:253. Type by monotypy. Also appeared in Gill 1863:230 [ref. 1687]. Synonym of *Trisopterus* Rafinesque 1814 (Svetovidov 1973:310 [ref. 7169]). Gadidae.

Brachygalaxias Eigenmann 1928:49 [ref. 1245]. Masc. *Galaxias bullocki* Regan 1908:372. Type by monotypy. Valid (McDowall 1984:153 [ref. 11850]). Galaxiidae: Galaxiinae.

Brachygenys Poey (ex Scutter) 1868:319 [ref. 3505]. Fem. *Haemulon taeniatum* Poey 1861:182. Type by monotypy. Haemulidae.

Brachyglanis Eigenmann 1912:130, 156 [ref. 1227]. Masc. *Brachyglanis frenata* Eigenmann 1912:156. Type by original designation. First published as *Breviglanis* (name only) and type species as *Breviglanis frenata* (name only, plus two more name-only species) in Eigenmann 1910:384 [ref. 1224]. *Breviglanis* is not available. Valid (Burgess 1989:276 [ref. 12860]). Pimelodidae.

Brachyglaucosoma (subgenus of *Glaucosoma*) Fowler 1934:357 [ref. 1416]. Neut. *Glaucosoma taeniatus* Fowler 1934:357. Type by original designation. Synonym of *Glaucosoma* Temminck & Schlegel 1843. Glaucosomatidae.

Brachygobius Bleeker 1874:315 [ref. 437]. Masc. *Gobius doriae* Günther 1868:265. Type by original designation (also monotypic). Valid (Kottelat 1985:274 [ref. 11441], Miller 1987:699 [ref. 6336], Birdsong et al. 1988:188 [ref. 7303], Roberts 1989:167 [ref. 6439], Miller 1989:377 [ref. 13540], Kottelat 1989:18 [ref. 13605]). Gobiidae.

Brachygramma Day 1865:304 [ref. 5295]. Neut. *Brachygramma jerdonii* Day 1865:304. Type by monotypy. Also appeared in Day 1865:216 [ref. 1074]. Cyprinidae.

Brachyistius Gill 1862:275 [ref. 1666]. Masc. *Brachyistius frenatus* Gill 1862:275. Type by monotypy. Synonym of *Micrometrus* Gibbons 1854, but as a valid subgenus (Tarp 1952:87 [ref. 12250]); valid genus (current authors). Embiotocidae.

Brachymesistius Gill 1863:233 [ref. 1687]. Masc. See *Micromesistius* Gill 1863. Gadidae.

Brachymullus Bleeker 1876:333 [ref. 448]. Masc. *Upeneus tetraspilus* Günther 1864:148. Type by original designation (also monotypic). Possibly appeared earlier as Bleeker himself in this work credits to Bleeker 1875. Synonym of *Pseudupeneus* Bleeker 1862. Mullidae.

Brachymystax Günther 1866:162 [ref. 1983]. Masc. *Salmo coregonoides* Pallas 1811:362. Type by monotypy. Valid (Kendall & Behnke 1984:144 [ref. 13638], Travers 1989:190 [ref. 13578]). Salmonidae: Salmoninae.

Brachymystus (subgenus of *Mystus*) Fowler 1937:1448 [ref. 1425]. Masc. *Bagrus nemurus* Valenciennes in Cuvier & Valenciennes 1839:423. Type by original designation, also monotypic as second species mentioned was in different subgenus. Objective synonym of *Hemibagrus* Bleeker 1862. Bagridae.

Brachynectes Scott 1957:180 [ref. 3997]. Masc. *Brachynectes fasciatus* Scott 1957:181. Type by monotypy. Valid. Tripterygiidae.

Brachyochirus Nardo 1841:1 [ref. 3150]. Masc. *Gobius aphya* of Risso (= *Gobius aphya* Linnaeus 1758:263). Original not seen. Apparently appeared without species. Spelled *Brachyochyrus* by Nardo 1844:76. Addition of species not researched. Synonym of *Aphia* Risso 1826 (Miller 1973:489 [ref. 6888]). Gobiidae.

Brachyopsis Gill 1861:167 [ref. 1775]. Fem. *Agonus rostratus* Tilesius 1810:448. Type by original designation (also monotypic). Name first appeared in Gill 1861:77 [ref. 1770] without description or species, as "*Brachyopsis* Gill = *Agonus* Swainson [not Bloch & Schneider]." Published in an available way Gill 1861:167 by reference to type species. Valid (Washington et al. 1984:442 [ref. 13660], Kanayama in Masuda et al. 1984:332 [ref. 6441], Yabe 1985:123 [ref. 11522], Maeda & Amaoka 1988:77 [ref. 12616]).

Agonidae.

Brachypetersius (subgenus of *Phenacogrammus*) Hoedeman 1956:ca. 559 [ref. 6184]. Masc. *Micralestes altus* Boulenger 1899:88. First appeared in Hoedeman 1951:8 [ref. 2178] as a new subgenus of *Alestopetersius* but not available (no fixation of type species after 1930, Art. 13b); apparently dates to Hoedeman 1956 (not seen). Valid (Poll 1967:99 [ref. 3529], Paugy 1984:164 [ref. 6183]). Alestiidae.

Brachyplatystoma Bleeker 1862:10 [ref. 393]. Neut. *Platystoma vaillanti* Valenciennes in Cuvier & Valenciennes 1840:21. Type by original designation (also monotypic). Valid (Mees 1974:120 [ref. 2969], Stewart 1986:668 [ref. 5211], Burgess 1989:282 [ref. 12860]). Pimelodidae.

Brachypleura Günther 1862:419 [ref. 1969]. Fem. *Brachypleura novaezeelandiae* Günther 1862:419. Type by monotypy. Valid (Norman 1934:400 [ref. 6893], Ahlstrom et al. 1984:640 [ref. 13641]). Citharidae: Brachypleurinae.

Brachypleurops Fowler 1934:341 [ref. 1416]. Masc. *Brachypleurops axillaris* Fowler 1934:341. Type by original designation (also monotypic). Synonym of *Citharoides* Hubbs 1915 (Amaoka 1969:80 [ref. 105]). Citharidae: Citharinae.

Brachypomacentrus (subgenus of *Eupomacentrus*) Bleeker 1877:73 [ref. 454]. Masc. *Pomacentrus albifasciatus* Schlegel & Müller 1844:21. Type by monotypy in subgenus. Also appeared in Bleeker 1877:40 [ref. 453]. Synonym of *Stegastes* Jenyns 1840 (Shen & Chan 1978:220 [ref. 6945]). Pomacentridae.

Brachyprosopon Bleeker 1862:428 [ref. 388]. Neut. *Pleuronectes microcephalus* Fleming 1828 (= *Pleuronectes microcephalus* Donovan 1803:xlii). Type by monotypy. Objective synonym of *Cynoglossa* Bonaparte 1846. Synonym of *Microstomus* Gottsche 1835 (Norman 1934:355 [ref. 6893]). Pleuronectidae: Pleuronectinae.

Brachypterois Fowler 1938:79 [ref. 1426]. Fem. *Brachypterois serrulifer* Fowler 1938:79. Type by original designation (also monotypic). Valid (Kanayama & Amaoka 1981 [ref. 5584], Amaoka in Masuda et al. 1984:316 [ref. 6441]). Scorpaenidae: Pteroinae.

Brachyrhamdia Myers 1927:123 [ref. 3096]. Fem. *Brachyrhamdia imitator* Myers 1927:123. Type by original designation (also monotypic). Valid (Lundberg & McDade 1986 [ref. 5731]). Pimelodidae.

Brachyrhamphichthys (subgenus of *Rhamphichthys*) Günther 1870:6 [ref. 1995]. Masc. *Rhamphichthys artedi* Kaup 1856:128. Type by subsequent designation. Type designated by Eigenmann & Ward 1905:169 [ref. 1267]. Synonym of *Hypopomus* Gill 1864. Gymnotidae: Hypopominae.

Brachyrhaphis Regan 1913:997 [ref. 3653]. Fem. *Gambusia rhabdophora* Regan 1908:457. Type by monotypy. Valid (Rosen & Bailey 1963:81 [ref. 7067], Parenti & Rauchenberger 1989:8 [ref. 13538]). Poeciliidae.

Brachyrhinus Gill 1862:236 [ref. 1664]. Masc. *Serranus creolus* Cuvier in Cuvier & Valenciennes 1828:265. Type by monotypy. Preoccupied by Latrielle 1802 in Crustacea, apparently not replaced. Synonym of *Paranthias* Guichenot 1868 (Smith 1971:84 [ref. 14102]). Serranidae: Epinephelinae.

Brachyrus Swainson 1839:264 [ref. 4303]. Masc. See *Dendrochirus* Swainson 1839 and *Brachirus* Swainson 1839. Scorpaenidae: Pteroinae.

Brachysomophis Kaup 1856:45 [ref. 2572]. Masc. *Brachysomophis horridus* Kaup 1856:45. Type by monotypy. Also appeared in Kaup 1856:9 [ref. 2573]. See also *Dendrophis*. Valid (McCosker 1977:74 [ref. 6836], Asano in Masuda et al. 1984:31 [ref. 6441], McCosker & Castle 1986:178 [ref. 5690], Paxton et al. 1989:116 [ref. 12442], McCosker et al. 1989:298 [ref. 13288]). Ophichthidae: Ophichthinae.

Brachystacus Van der Hoeven 1849:280 [ref. 2182]. *Platystacus chaca* Hamilton 1822:140, 374. Type by monotypy. Original not seen. Objective synonym of *Chaca* Gray 1831 (Roberts 1982:896 [ref. 6807]). Chacidae.

Brachysynodontis Bleeker 1862:6 [ref. 393]. Fem. *Synodontis batensoda* Rüppell 1832:6. Type by original designation (also monotypic). Valid (Gosse 1986:106 [ref. 6194], Burgess 1989:195 [ref. 12860]). Mochokidae.

Brama Bleeker (ex Klein) 1863:211 [ref. 397]. Fem. *Cyprinus brama* Linnaeus 1758:328. Type by monotypy, as *Abramis brama* Cuvier. On p. 25 of separate. Based on *Brama* Klein (unavailable). Preoccupied by Bloch & Schneider 1801 in fishes. Also in Bleeker 1863 [ref. 12572]. Objective synonym of *Abramis* Cuvier 1816. Cyprinidae.

Brama Bloch & Schneider 1801:98 [ref. 471]. Fem. *Sparus raii* Bloch 1791:95, 99. Type by subsequent designation. Type first designated by Bory de Saint-Vincent, v. 3, 1823:260 [ref. 3853] (see Mead 1973:386 [ref. 7199] and Whitley 1935:137 [ref. 6396]). Valid (Mead 1972:25 [ref. 6976], Mead 1973:386 [ref. 7199], Mochizuki in Masuda et al. 1984:159 [ref. 6441], Smith 1986:633 [ref. 5712], Yatsu & Nakamura 1989:190 [ref. 13449]). Bramidae.

Brama Klein 1775:61, 93 [ref. 2618]. Fem. Not available, published in a work that does not conform to the principle of binominal nomenclature. In the synonymy of *Abramis* Cuvier 1816. Cyprinidae.

Bramichthys Waite 1905:72 [ref. 4562]. Masc. *Bramichthys woodwardi* Waite 1905:72. Type by monotypy. Misspelled *Bramicthys* in Zoological Record for 1906, correctly spelled in Zoological Record for 1905. Monodactylidae.

Bramocharax Gill 1877:189 [ref. 1714]. Masc. *Bramocharax bransfordii* Gill 1877:190. Type by monotypy. Valid (Géry 1977:322 [ref. 1597]). Characidae.

Bramopsis Agassiz (L.) in A. Agassiz 1861:132 [ref. 11]. Fem. *"Bramopsis mento"* Agassiz 1861:133. Not available, manuscript name published in synonymy and apparently never made available through subsequent use. In the synonymy of *Hyperprosopon* Gibbons 1854 (Tarp 1952:31 [ref. 12250]). Embiotocidae.

Branchialepes (subgenus of *Alepes*) Fowler 1938:46 [ref. 1426]. Fem. *Selar tabulae* Barnard 1927:538. Type by original designation (also monotypic). Misspelled *Branchialepis* in Zoological Record for 1938. Synonym of *Trachurus* Rafinesque 1810. Carangidae.

Branchioica Eigenmann 1917:702 [ref. 1237]. Fem. *Branchioica bertoni* Eigenmann 1917:703. Type by original designation (also monotypic). Misspelled *Branchiogaeum* by Eigenmann in text (p. 702); misspelled *Branchoica* by Jordan 1920:563 [ref. 4905]. Synonym of *Paravandellia* Miranda-Ribeiro 1912 (Burgess 1989:324 [ref. 12860], Pinna 1989:35 [ref. 12630]). Trichomycteridae.

Branchiopsaron McKay 1971:41 [ref. 2954]. Neut. *Branchiopsaron ozawai* McKay 1972:41. Type by original designation (also monotypic). Valid (Nelson 1982:6 [ref. 5469]). Percophidae: Hemerocoetinae.

Branchiostegus Rafinesque 1815:86 [ref. 3584]. Masc. *Coryphaenoides houttuynii* Lacepède 1801:176 (= *Coryphaena japonica* Houttuyn 1782:311). Type by being a replacement name. As "*Branchiostegus* L. [sic for R.=Rafinesque] *Coryphaenoides* Lac." Available replacement name for *Coryphaenoides* Lacepède 1801 (not of Gunner). Valid (Dooley & Paxton 1975 [ref. 7419], Dooley 1978:30 [ref. 5499], Araga in Masuda et al. 1984:151 [ref. 6441], Heemstra 1986:613 [ref. 5660], Dooley & Kailola 1988 [ref. 7299], Paxton et al. 1989:565 [ref. 12442]). Malacanthidae: Latilinae.

Branchiosteus Gill 1861:52 [ref. 1673]. Masc. *Olyra laticeps* McClelland 1842:588. Type by original designation (also monotypic). Amblycipitidae.

Branderius Rafinesque 1815:93 [ref. 3584]. Masc. *Muraena branderiana* Lacepède 1800:135 (= *Muraena caeca* Linnaeus 1758:245). Type by being a replacement name. As "*Branderius* R. [Rafinesque] *Cecilia* Lac. [Lacepède]." Available replacement for *Caecilia* Lacepède 1800 (preoccupied by Linnaeus 1758 in Amphibia); earlier replaced by *Typhlotes* Fischer von Waldheim 1813. Synonym of *Apterichtus* Duméril 1806 (Blache et al. 1973:248 [ref. 7185], McCosker 1977:65 [ref. 6836], McCosker et al. 1989:318 [ref. 13288]). Ophichthidae: Ophichthinae.

Brannerella Gilbert 1900:180 [ref. 1630]. Fem. *Brannerella brasiliensis* Gilbert 1900:180. Type by original designation (also monotypic). Synonym of *Starksia* Jordan & Evermann 1896 (Rosenblatt & Taylor 1971:452 [ref. 3811]). Labrisomidae.

Bregmaceros Thompson 1840:185 [ref. 4389]. Masc. *Bregmaceros mcclellandi* Thompson 1840:185. Type by monotypy. *Bregmocerus* Agassiz 1846:53 [ref. 64] is an unjustified emendation. Species spelled originally as *mcclellandi* and *mcclellandii*. Valid (Cohen 1973:321 [ref. 6589], Houde 1984 [ref. 13654], Milliken & Houde 1984 [ref. 8132], Cohen 1984:263 [ref. 13646], Okamura in Masuda et al. 1984:92 [ref. 6441], Fahay & Markle 1984:266 [ref. 13653], Masuda et al. 1986 [ref. 5801], Smith 1986:329 [ref. 5712], Paxton et al. 1989:305 [ref. 12442]). Bregmacerotidae.

Breitensteinia Steindachner 1881:213 [ref. 4231]. Fem. *Breitensteinia insignis* Steindachner 1881:213. Type by monotypy. Valid (Burgess 1989:119 [ref. 12860], Roberts 1989:141 [ref. 6439]). Akysidae.

Breona Scott 1967:210 [ref. 3995]. Masc. *Breona greeni* Scott 1967:212. Type by original designation (also monotypic). Synonym of *Sticharium* Günther 1867 (George & Springer 1980:27 [ref. 6935]). Clinidae.

Brephamia Jordan in Jordan & Jordan 1922:43 [ref. 2487]. Fem. *Amia parvula* Smith & Radcliffe in Radcliffe 1912:432. Type by original designation (also monotypic). Synonym of *Apogon* Lacepède 1801, but as a valid subgenus (Fraser & Lachner 1985:4 [ref. 5215]). Apogonidae.

Brephostoma Alcock 1889:383 [ref. 81]. Neut. *Brephostoma carpenteri* Alcock 1889:383. Type by monotypy. Valid, family placement uncertain (Fraser 1972:42 [ref. 5195]). Acropomatidae.

Brevicephaloides (subgenus of *Clarias*) Teugels 1982:14 [ref. 6670]. Masc. *Clarias camerunensis* Lönnberg 1895. Type by original designation. Also appeared in Teugels 1982:739 [ref. 4377]. Synonym of *Clarias* Scopoli 1777 (Teugels 1986:69 [ref. 6193]). Clariidae.

Breviceps Swainson 1838:328, 343 [ref. 4302]. Neut. *Silurus bagre* Bloch 1794:Pl. 365. Type by monotypy (p. 343). Type not *S. nodosus* Bleeker as designated by Swain 1882:281 [ref. 5966]). Preoccupied by Merrem 1820 in herpetology; replaced by *Felichthys* Swainson 1839. Ariidae.

Breviglanis Eigenmann 1910:384 [ref. 1224]. Masc. Not available, appeared without description and with unavailable species; name changed and published in an available way by Eigenmann 1912 as *Brachyglanis*. Pimelodidae.

Brevigobio Tanaka 1916:102 [ref. 4327]. Masc. *Brevigobio kawabatae* Tanaka 1916:102. Type by monotypy. Cyprinidae.

Brevimyrus (subgenus of *Brienomyrus*) Taverne 1971:106, 109 [ref. 4349]. Masc. *Gnathonemus niger* Günther 1866:219. Type by monotypy in subgenus. Valid (Gosse 1984:63 [ref. 6169]). Mormyridae.

Breviperca Castelnau 1875:6 [ref. 768]. Fem. *Breviperca lineata* Castelnau 1875:6. Type by monotypy. Synonym of *Glaucosoma* Temminck & Schlegel 1843. Glaucosomatidae.

Breviraja Bigelow & Schroeder 1948:558 [ref. 301]. Fem. *Breviraja colesi* Bigelow & Schroeder 1948:559. Type by original designation. Valid (interrelationships and subgenera discussed by McEachran & Compagno 1982 [ref. 2952]; McEachran & Miyake 1987 [ref. 5973]). Rajidae.

Brevisomniosus (subgenus of *Somniosus*) Quéro 1976:463, 467 [ref. 9342]. Masc. Not available, two included species and neither designated as type after 1930 (Art. 13b); subsequent publication in an available way not researched. In the synonymy of *Somniosus* Lesueur 1818 (Compagno 1984:102 [ref. 6474]). Squalidae.

Brevoortia Gill 1861:37 [ref. 1767]. Fem. *Brevoortia menhaden* of Gill 1861 (= *Clupea menhaden* Mitchill 1814:21). Type by original designation (also monotypic). *Brevoortia menhaden* Gill is a new combination, *Clupea menhaden* Mitchill is the senior objective synonym and valid type species. Valid (Grande 1985:249 [ref. 6466], Whitehead 1985:210 [ref. 5141]). Clupeidae.

Brienomyrus Taverne 1971:106, 108 [ref. 4349]. Masc. *Marcusenius brachyistius* Gill 1862:137. Type by original designation. Misspelled *Breinomyrus* in Zoological Record for 1971. Valid (Taverne 1972:172 [ref. 6367], Gosse 1984:63 [ref. 6169], King 1989 [ref. 12831]). Mormyridae.

Brinkmannella Parr 1933:26 [ref. 3373]. Fem. *Brinkmannella elongata* Parr 1933:26. Type by original designation (also monotypic). Valid (Fraser 1972:42 [ref. 5195], Johnson 1984:469 [ref. 9681]). Epigonidae.

Brisbania Castelnau 1878:241 [ref. 761]. Fem. *Brisbania staigeri* Castelnau 1878:241. Type by monotypy. Synonym of *Megalops* Lacepède 1803 (Daget 1984:32 [ref. 6170]). Megalopidae.

Brittanichthys Géry 1965:13 [ref. 1585]. Masc. *Brittanichthys axelrodi* Géry 1965:13, 22. Type by original designation. Valid (Géry 1977:591 [ref. 1597]). Characidae.

Brochiloricaria Isbrücker & Nijssen in Isbrücker 1979:87, 90 [ref. 2302]. Fem. *Brochiloricaria chauliodon* Isbrücker 1979:102. Type by original designation. Valid (Isbrücker 1980:119 [ref. 2303], Isbrücker 1981:56 [ref. 5522], Burgess 1989:443 [ref. 12860]). Loricariidae.

Brochis Cope 1871:112 [ref. 5775]. Fem. *Brochis caeruleus* Cope 1872:277. Type by subsequent designation. Appeared first without species, more fully described in Cope 1872:77 [ref. 921] where two species were added; type designated by Cope (in describing second species he refers to first as type). Valid (Nijssen & Isbrücker 1983 [ref. 5387], Burgess 1989:364 [ref. 12860]). Callichthyidae.

Brockius (subgenus of *Labrisomus*) Clark Hubbs 1953:120 [ref. 2253]. Masc. *Labrisomus striatus* Clark Hubbs 1953:120. Type by original designation (also monotypic). Synonym of *Labrisomus* Swainson (Springer 1958:422 [ref. 10210]). Labrisomidae.

Brontes Valenciennes in Cuvier & Valenciennes 1840:341 [ref. 1008]. *Brontes prenadilla* Valenciennes in Cuvier & Valenciennes 1840:343. Type by monotypy. Preoccupied by Fabricius 1801 in Coleoptera, de Montfort 1810 in Mollusca, and Goldfuss 1839 in trilobites; replaced by *Strephon* Gistel 1848. Astroblepidae.

Brosma Schinz 1822:365 [ref. 3926]. *Gadus brosme* Müller 1776:41. Type by monotypy. Same as *Brosme* Oken, but apparently independently described by Schinz. Synonym of *Brosme* Oken 1817. Lotidae.

Brosme Oken (ex Cuvier) 1817:1182a [ref. 3303]. *Gadus brosme* Müller 1776:41. Type by monotypy (also by absolute tautonymy). Based on "Les Brosmes" Cuvier 1816:216 [ref. 993]. Unjustifiably emended or substituted as *Brosmerus* Lesueur 1819:158 [ref. 12573], *Brosma* Schinz 1822:365 [ref. 3926], *Brosmus* Stark 1828:425 [ref. 4193], *Brosmius* Cuvier 1829:334 [ref. 995] and misspelled *Brosmia* by Swainson 1839:189, 441 [ref. 4303]. See Gill 1903:966 [ref. 5768]. Valid (Svetovidov 1973:311 [ref. 7169], Fahay & Markle 1984:266 [ref. 13653]). Lotidae.

Brosme Rafinesque 1815:82 [ref. 3584]. Not available, name only; apparently same as *Brosme* of subsequent authors. Lotidae.

Brosmerus Lesueur 1819:158 [ref. 12573]. Masc. *Brosmerus flavesny* Lesueur 1819:158. Type by monotypy. Apparently independently proposed for "Le genre Brosme..." ["Les Brosmes" Cuvier 1816] in describing one new species as *Brosmerius flavesny*. Synonym of *Brosme* Oken 1817. Lotidae.

Brosmiculus Vaillant 1888:292 [ref. 4496]. Masc. *Brosmiculus imberbis* Vaillant 1888:293. Type by monotypy. Valid (Fahay & Markle 1984:266 [ref. 13653]); synonym of *Gadella* Lowe 1843 (Paulin 1989:95 [ref. 9297]). Moridae.

Brosmius Cuvier 1829:334 [ref. 995]. Masc. *Gadus brosme* Gmelin 1789 (= *Gadus brosme* Müller 1766:41). Type by monotypy. Objective synonym of *Brosme* Oken 1817. Lotidae.

Brosmodorsalis Paulin & Roberts 1989:355 [ref. 12435]. Masc. *Brosmodorsalis persicinus* Paulin & Roberts 1989:356. Type by original designation (also monotypic). Bythitidae: Brosmophycinae.

Brosmophyciops Schultz in Schultz et al. 1960:384 [ref. 3972]. Masc. *Brosmophyciops pautzkei* Schultz in Schultz et al. 1960:386. Type by original designation (also monotypic). Valid (Cohen & Nielsen 1978:53 [ref. 881], Machida & Yoshino 1984 [ref. 5362], Machida in Masuda et al. 1984:101 [ref. 6441], Paxton et al. 1989:315 [ref. 12442]). Bythitidae: Brosmophycinae.

Brosmophycis Gill 1861:168 [ref. 1775]. Fem. *Brosmius marginatus* Ayres 1854:13. Type by original designation (also monotypic). Valid (Cohen & Nielsen 1978:53 [ref. 881]). Bythitidae: Brosmophycinae.

Brosmus Fleming 1828:194 [ref. 1339]. *Brosmus vulgaris* Fleming 1828:194. Type by monotypy. May have been used first by Bosc (see Whitley 1935:136 [ref. 6396]). Lotidae.

Brosmus Stark 1828:425 [ref. 4193]. *Gadus brosme* Müller 1776:41. Type by monotypy. Objective synonym of *Brosme* Oken 1817. Lotidae.

Brotella Kaup 1858:92 [ref. 2576]. Fem. *Brotula maculata* Kaup 1846:253 (= *Brotula imberbis* Temminck & Schlegel 1846:253). Type by subsequent designation. *Brotula maculata* Kaup is an unneeded replacement for *Brotula imberbis*. Earliest subsequent designation of type not researched; usually wrongly given as by monotypy, but *B. armata* also included. Objective synonym of *Sirembo* Bleeker 1858 (Cohen & Nielsen 1978:19 [ref. 881]). Ophidiidae: Neobythitinae.

Brotula Cuvier 1829:335 [ref. 995]. Fem. *Enchelyopus barbatus* Bloch & Schneider 1801:52. Type by monotypy. Valid (Cohen & Nielsen 1978:11 [ref. 881], Machida in Masuda et al. 1984:99 [ref. 6441], Nielsen & Cohen 1986:346 [ref. 5700], Paxton et al. 1989:311 [ref. 12442]). Ophidiidae: Brotulinae.

Brotulina Fowler 1946:195 [ref. 1456]. Fem. *Brotulina fusca* Fowler 1946:195. Type by original designation (also monotypic). Valid (Cohen & Nielsen 1978:56 [ref. 881], Machida in Masuda et al. 1984:101 [ref. 6441]). Bythitidae: Brosmophycinae.

Brotuloides Robins 1961:214 [ref. 3785]. Masc. *Leptophidium emmelas* Gilbert 1890:110. Type by original designation (also monotypic). Ophidiidae: Ophidiinae.

Brotulophis Kaup 1858:93 [ref. 2576]. Masc. *Brotulophis argentistriatus* Kaup 1858:93. Type by monotypy. Ophidiidae.

Brotulotaenia Parr 1933:48 [ref. 3373]. Fem. *Brotulotaenia nigra* Parr 1933:50. Type by original designation (also monotypic). Valid (Nielsen 1973:550 [ref. 6885], Cohen 1974 [ref. 6890] as *Brotulataenia*, Nielsen in Whitehead et al. 1986:1161 [ref. 13677], Nielsen & Cohen 1986:346 [ref. 5700], Paxton et al. 1989:311 [ref. 12442]). Ophidiidae: Brotulotaeniinae.

Brunichthys Parr 1951:8 [ref. 3380]. Masc. *Alepocephalus asperifrons* Garman 1899:291. Type by original designation (also monotypic). Derivation of name not given originally [probably for Anton Bruun]; spelled *Bruunichthys* by Parr 1952:255 [ref. 3381]; name used only once in 1951 and if that is regarded as a misprint then it can be corrected; otherwise name should stand as *Brunichthys*. Alepocephalidae.

Brustiarius (subgenus of *Arius*) Herre 1935:388 [ref. 2109]. Masc. *Arius nox* Herre 1935:388. Type by original designation (also monotypic). Ariidae.

Bryanina Fowler 1932:10 [ref. 1413]. Fem. *Bryanina inana* Fowler 1932:10. Type by original designation (also monotypic). Synonym of *Sicyopterus* Gill 1860 (see Böhlke 1984:107 [ref. 13261]). Gobiidae.

Bryaninops Smith 1959:216 [ref. 4122]. Masc. *Bryaninops ridens* Smith 1959:216. Type by original designation (also monotypic). Valid (Larson 1985 [ref. 5186], Larson 1986:947 [ref. 6328], Okiyama & Tsukamoto 1989 [ref. 13564]). Gobiidae.

Brycinus Valenciennes in Cuvier & Valenciennes 1849:157 [ref. 1014]. Masc. *Brycinus macrolepidotus* Valenciennes in Cuvier & Valenciennes 1849:157. Type by monotypy. Valid (Géry 1977:19 [ref. 1597]); synonym of *Alestes* Müller & Troschel 1844 (Paugy 1984:140 [ref. 6183]). Alestiidae.

Brycochandus Eigenmann 1908:106 [ref. 1221]. Masc. *Brycochandus durbini* Eigenmann 1908:106. Type by original designation (also monotypic). Synonym of *Bryconops* Kner 1858, as a valid subgenus (Géry 1977:434 [ref. 1597]). Characidae.

Brycon Müller & Troschel 1844:90 [ref. 3070]. Masc. *Brycon falcatus* Müller & Troschel 1844:90. Type by subsequent designation. Type designated by Eigenmann 1910:430 [ref. 1224]. Valid (Géry 1977:335 [ref. 1597], Howes 1982:2 [ref. 14201], Vari 1983:5 [ref. 5419]). Characidae.

Bryconacidnus Myers in Eigenmann & Myers 1929:545 [ref. 1263]. Masc. *Hyphessobrycon ellisi* Pearson 1924:39. Type by original designation. Valid (Géry 1977:398 [ref. 1597]). Characidae.

Bryconaethiops Günther 1873:143 [ref. 2003]. Masc.

Bryconaethiops microstoma Günther 1873:143. Type by monotypy. Valid (Géry 1977:19 [ref. 1597], Paugy 1984:166 [ref. 6183]). Alestiidae.

Bryconalestes Hoedeman 1951:4 (in key) [ref. 2178]. Masc. *Brycon longipinnis* Günther 1864:315. Type by original designation (also monotypic). Type designated by use of name in parentheses (as Hoedeman used for established genera in same key), also monotypic (but with two subspecies). Synonym of *Alestes* Müller & Troschel 1844 (Paugy 1984:140 [ref. 6183]). Alestiidae.

Bryconamericus Eigenmann in Eigenmann, McAtee & Ward 1907:139 [ref. 1261]. Masc. *Bryconamericus exodon* Eigenmann in Eigenmann, McAtee & Ward 1907:139. Type by monotypy. Valid (Géry 1977:386 [ref. 1597], Malabarba 1989:131 [ref. 14217]). Characidae.

Bryconella Géry 1965:27 [ref. 1584]. Fem. *Bryconella haraldi* Géry 1965:28. Type by original designation (also monotypic). Valid (Géry 1977:511 [ref. 1597]). Characidae.

Bryconexodon Géry 1980:2 [ref. 1598]. Masc. *Bryconexodon juruenae* Géry 1980:2. Type by original designation (also monotypic). Characidae.

Bryconodon Eigenmann 1903:146 [ref. 1218]. Masc. *Brycon orthotaenia* Günther 1864:355. Type by original designation (also monotypic). Mentioned (Géry 1977:335 [ref. 1597]); synonym of *Brycon* Müller & Troschel 1844 (Howes 1982:4 [ref. 14201]). Characidae.

Bryconops Kner 1858:80 [ref. 13404]. Masc. *Bryconops alburnoides* Kner 1858:80. Type by subsequent designation. Also in Kner 1859:179 [ref. 2631]. Type designated by Eigenmann 1910:435 [ref. 1224]. Valid (Géry 1977:434 [ref. 1597]). Characidae.

Bryolophus Jordan & Snyder 1902:617 [ref. 2517]. Masc. *Bryolophus lysimus* Jordan & Snyder 1902:617. Type by monotypy. Preoccupied by Ehrenberg 1839 in Polyzoa, replaced by and objective synonym of *Bryozoichthys* Whitley 1931. Stichaeidae.

Bryostemma Jordan & Starks 1895:841 [ref. 2522]. Neut. *Blennius polyactocephalus* Pallas 1811:179. Type by original designation (also monotypic). Pholidae.

Bryozoichthys Whitley 1931:334 [ref. 4672]. Masc. *Bryolophus lysimus* Jordan & Snyder 1902:617. Type by being a replacement name. Replacement for *Bryolophus* Jordan & Snyder 1902, preoccupied by Ehrenberg 1839 in Polyzoa. Valid (Amaoka & Miki in Masuda et al. 1984:301 [ref. 6441]). Stichaeidae.

Bryssetaeres Jordan & Evermann in Jordan 1896:230 [ref. 2395]. *Gobiesox pinniger* Gilbert 1890:94. Type by original designation (also monotypic). Synonym of *Gobiesox* Lacepède 1800 (Briggs 1955:87 [ref. 637]). Gobiesocidae: Gobiesocinae.

Bryssophilus (subgenus of *Gobiesox*) Jordan & Evermann 1898: 2329, 2330 [ref. 2445]. Masc. *Gobiesox papillifer* Gilbert 1890:96. Type by original designation (also monotypic). Objective synonym of *Caulistius* Jordan & Evermann 1896. Synonym of *Gobiesox* Lacepède 1800 (Briggs 1955:87 [ref. 637]). Gobiesocidae: Gobiesocinae.

Bryttosus Jordan & Snyder 1900:354 [ref. 2502]. Masc. *Serranus kawamebari* Temminck & Schlegel 1842:5. Type by monotypy. Misspelled or unjustifiably emended to *Brittosus* by Jordan, Tanaka & Snyder 1913:150 [ref. 6448]. Serranidae.

Bryttus Valenciennes in Cuvier & Valenciennes 1831:454, 461 [ref. 4881]. Masc. *Bryttus punctatus* Valenciennes in Cuvier & Valenciennes 1831:462. Type by subsequent designation. Type designated by Jordan & Gilbert 1877:88 [ref. 4907]. Synonym of *Lepomis* Rafinesque 1819. Centrarchidae.

Bryx Herald 1940:52 [ref. 2095]. Masc. *Bryx veleronis* Herald 1940:55. Type by original designation (also monotypic). Valid (Fritzsche 1980:192 [ref. 1511], Dawson 1982:111 [ref. 6764], Dawson 1985:22 [ref. 6541]). Syngnathidae: Syngnathinae.

Bubalichthys Agassiz 1855:77 [ref. 71]. Masc. *Catostomus niger* Rafinesque 1820:355. Type by subsequent designation. Type sometimes given as *Carpiodes urus* Agassiz 1854, but *niger* was designated by Bleeker 1863:23 [ref. 4859] and Bleeker 1863:191 [ref. 397]. See Hubbs 1930:11 [ref. 5590] for comments on species. *Bubalichtys* Scudder 1882:45 [ref. 6 462] is a misspelling. Synonym of *Ictiobus* Rafinesque 1820. Catostomidae.

Bubyr Iljin 1930:53 [ref. 2297]. *Pomatoschistus caucasicus* Kawrajsky in Berg 1916. Type by original designation. Species apparently appeared first as name only in Kawrajsky in Radde 1899, made available by use of Berg 1816. Synonym of *Knipowitschia* Iljin 1927 (Miller 1973:497 [ref. 6888]). Gobiidae.

Buccochromis Eccles & Trewavas 1989:236 [ref. 13547]. Masc. *Paratilapia nototaenia* Boulenger 1902:69. Type by original designation. Cichlidae.

Buccone (subgenus of *Cynoscion*) Jordan & Evermann 1896:394 [ref. 2442]. Neut. *Cynoscion praedatorius* Jordan & Gilbert 1886:363. Type by original designation (also monotypic). Synonym of *Cynoscion* Gill 1861 (Chao 1978:34 [ref. 6983]). Sciaenidae.

Buenia Iljin 1930:51 [ref. 2297]. Fem. *Gobius affinis* Kolombatovic 1891. Type by original designation. Valid (Miller 1973:491 [ref. 6888] with type as *affinis* Iljin 1930, Miller in Whitehead et al. 1986:1026 [ref. 13677]). Gobiidae.

Bufichthys (subgenus of *Synanchia*) Swainson 1839:268 [ref. 4303]. Masc. *Scorpaena horrida* Linnaeus 1766:453. Type by subsequent designation. Not p. 181, where *Bufichthys* is a misprint for *Synanchia* = *Erosa* (see Eschmeyer & Rama Rao 1973:343 [ref. 6391]). Replaced by *Phrynichthys* Agassiz 1846. Type designated by Swain 1882:277 [ref. 5966]. Synonym of *Synanceia* Bloch & Schneider 1801 (Eschmeyer & Rama-Rao 1973:341 [ref. 6391]). Scorpaenidae: Synanceiinae.

Bufoceratias Whitley 1931:334 [ref. 4672]. Masc. *Phrynichthys wedli* Pietschmann 1926:88. Type by being a replacement name. Replacement for *Phrynichthys* Pietschmann 1926, preoccupied by *Phrynichthys* Agassiz 1846:55, 288 [ref. 64], a replacement for *Bufichthys* Swainson 1839 in fishes. *Phrynichthys* now recognized as valid (e.g. Pietsch 1986:377 [ref. 5704]) but should be replaced with *Bufoceratias*. Diceratiidae.

Buglossa Bertrand 1763:v. 1, p. 106 [ref. 6405]. Fem. Apparently based on a flatfish. Not available; on Official Index (genera), published in a rejected work. Pleuronectiformes.

Buglossidium Chabanaud 1930:14 [ref. 784]. Neut. *Solea lutea* Risso 1810:190. Type by original designation. Valid (Torchio 1973:631 [ref. 6892], Quéro et al. in Whitehead et al. 1986:1311 [ref. 13677], Desoutter 1987 [ref. 6742]). Soleidae.

Buglossus (subgenus of *Solea*) Günther 1862:462, 469-470 [ref. 1969]. Masc. *Pleuronectes variegatus* Donovan 1808:Pl. 117. Type by subsequent designation. Described in key (p. 462) as section of *Solea* with 3 species (pp. 469-470). Type designated by Jordan 1919:319 [ref. 4904]. Synonym of *Microchirus* Bonaparte 1833 (Torchio 1973:632 [ref. 6892]). Soleidae.

Bujurquina Kullander 1986:244 [ref. 12439]. Fem. *Bujurquina* *moriorum* Kullander 1986:304. Type by original designation. Valid (Kullander 1987 [ref. 6749]). Cichlidae.

Bulbonaricus (subgenus of *Ichthyocampus*) Herald in Schultz et al. 1953:241 [ref. 3975]. Masc. *Ichthyocampus davaoensis* Herald in Schultz et al. 1953:242. Type by original designation (also monotypic). Valid (Dawson 1984 [ref. 5275], Dawson 1985:24 [ref. 6541], Paxton et al. 1989:413 [ref. 12442]). Syngnathidae: Syngnathinae.

Bullisichthys Rivas 1971:718 [ref. 3762]. Masc. *Bullisichthys caribbaeus* Rivas 1971:719. Type by original designation (also monotypic). Serranidae: Serraninae.

Bullockia Arratia, Chang, Menu-Marque & Rojas 1978:162 [ref. 144]. Fem. *Hatcheria maldonadoi* Eigenmann 1927:39. Type by monotypy. Valid (Pinna 1989:31 [ref. 12630], Burgess 1989:323 [ref. 12860]). Trichomycteridae.

Bunaka Herre 1927:60 [ref. 2104]. Fem. *Bunaka pinguis* Herre 1927:61. Type by original designation (also monotypic). Valid (Birdsong et al. 1988:181 [ref. 7303]). Eleotridae.

Bungia Keyserling 1861:18 [ref. 2601]. Fem. *Bungia nigrescens* Keyserling 1861:18. Type by monotypy. Original not seen. Synonym of *Gobio* Cuvier 1816. Cyprinidae.

Bunocephalichthys Bleeker 1858:329 [ref. 365]. Masc. *Bunocephalichthys verrucosus* Bloch 1795:63. Type by subsequent designation. Not *Bunocephalichthys* Bleeker 1862. Type designated by Jordan 1919:279 [ref. 4904] (see Mees 1988:88 [ref. 6401] for discussion of problem of type species for this genus and *Bunocephalus*). Valid (if type of *Bunocephalus* Kner 1855 is *B. hypsiurus* as argued by Mees 1988 [ref. 6401]). Aspredinidae: Bunocephalinae.

Bunocephalus Kner 1855:95 [ref. 2629]. Masc. *Bunocephalus hypsiurus* Kner 1855:98. Type by subsequent designation. Type designated by Bleeker 1858:327-329 (see Mees 1988:88 [ref. 6401]), not *verrucosus* Bloch as designated by Bleeker 1862:19 and 1863:118. Valid (Mees 1988:89 [ref. 6401], Burgess 1989:303 [ref. 12860] with *verrucosus* as type, Malabarba 1989:145 [ref. 14217]). Aspredinidae: Bunocephalinae.

Bunocottus Kner 1868:28 [ref. 6074]. Masc. *Bunocottus apus* Kner 1868:28. Type by monotypy. Also appeared as new in Kner 1868:316 [ref. 2646]. Cottidae.

Buphthalmus (subgenus of *Seriola*) Smith 1959:257 [ref. 4124]. Masc. *Seriola songoro* Smith 1959:258. Type by original designation. Synonym of *Seriola* Cuvier 1816 (Smith-Vaniz, pers. comm.). Carangidae.

Burgessius (subgenus of *Heterochaetodon*) Maugé & Bauchot 1984:475 [ref. 6614]. Masc. *Chaetodon miliaris* Gmelin 1788: 1269. Type by original designation. Maugé & Bauchot included this subgenus in their new genus *Heterochaetodon*, including also *Lepidochaetodon* Bleeker 1876 as a subgenus; but *Lepidochaetodon* has priority over *Heterochaetodon* at the generic level. Type species needs research. Chaetodontidae.

Buritia Brant 1974:148 [ref. 628]. Fem. *Buritia cisalpinoi* Brant 1974:148. Type by original designation (also monotypic). Preoccupied by Young 1952 in Hemiptera (see Whitley 1976:47 [ref. 4735]); replaced by and objective synonym of *Orthospinus* Reis 1989. Characidae: Stethaprioninae.

Buro Lacepède (ex Commerson) 1803:421 [ref. 4930]. Masc. *Buro brunneus* Lacepède (ex Commerson) 1803:421, 422. Type by monotypy. Synonym of *Siganus* Forsskål 1775. Siganidae.

Burobulla Whitley 1931:321 [ref. 4672]. Fem. *Xesurus maculatus* Ogilby 1887:395. Type by original designation (also monotypic). Synonym of *Prionurus* Lacepède 1804 (Randall 1955:362 [ref. 13648]). Acanthuridae.

Buronus Rafinesque 1815:88 [ref. 3584]. Masc. *Buro brunneus* Lacepède 1803:421, 422. Type by being a replacement name. As "*Buronus* R. [Rafinesque] *Buro* Lac. [Lacepède]." An available replacement name (unneeded) for and objective synonym of *Buro* Lacepède 1803. Synonym of *Siganus* Forsskål 1775. Siganidae.

Busuanga Herre 1930:132 [ref. 2105]. Fem. *Tylosurus philippinus* Herre 1928:31. Type by original designation (also monotypic). Synonym of *Tylosurus* Cocco 1833. Belonidae.

Butigobius Whitley 1930:123 [ref. 4669]. Masc. *Lebistes scorpioides* Smitt 1899:543 (= *Gobius scorpioides* Collett 1874:447). Type by being a replacement name. Unneeded replacement for *Lebistes* [sic] Smitt 1899, not preoccupied by Fillipi 1862 in fishes. Whitley took the apparent preoccupation from Jordan 1920:487 [ref. 4905], but Jordan's entry in error for *Lebetus* Winther. Objective synonym of *Lebetus* Winther 1877 (Miller 1973:498 [ref. 6888]). Gobiidae.

Butis Bleeker 1856:412 [ref. 353]. *Cheilodipterus butis* Hamilton 1822:57, 367. Type by absolute tautonymy. Also appeared in Bleeker 1856:215 [ref. 354], and if 1856:215 was first then type is *Eleotris gymnopomus* Bleeker by monotypy. Valid (Akihito in Masuda et al. 1984:239 [ref. 6441], Kottelat 1985:274 [ref. 11441], Hoese 1986:807 [ref. 5670], Maugé 1986:390 [ref. 6218], Birdsong et al. 1988:180 [ref. 7303], Kottelat 1989:18 [ref. 13605]). Eleotridae.

Butyrinus Lacepède (ex Commerson) 1803:45 [ref. 4930]. Masc. *Butyrinus bananus* Lacepède 1803:45, 46. Type by monotypy. Spelled *Butirinus* by Cuvier 1829:329 [ref. 995] and *Buturinus* by Valenciennes in Cuvier & Valenciennes 1847:316 [ref. 4883]. Synonym of *Albula* Scopoli 1777 (Whitehead 1986:215 [ref. 5733]). Albulidae: Albulinae.

Byssochaetodon (subgenus of *Chaetodon*) Maugé & Bauchot 1984:171 [ref. 6614]. Masc. *Chaetodon robustus* Günther 1860:18. Type by original designation. Chaetodontidae.

Bythaelurus (subgenus of *Halaelurus*) Compagno 1988:146 [ref. 13448]. Masc. *Scyllium canescens* Günther 1878:18. Type by original designation. Scyliorhinidae.

Bythites Reinhardt 1835:7 [ref. 7155]. Masc. *Bythites fuscus* Reinhardt 1837:LXXIX. Type by subsequent monotypy. Genus appeared first without species; one species added by Reinhardt 1837:LXXVIII [ref. 3695]. Valid (Nielsen & Cohen 1973:72 [ref. 3200], Cohen & Nielsen 1978:46 [ref. 881], Nielsen in Whitehead et al. 1986:1154 [ref. 13677]). Bythitidae: Bythitinae.

Cabdio (subgenus of *Cyprinus*) Hamilton 1822:333, 392 [ref. 2031]. *Cyprinus (Cabdio) jaya* Hamilton 1822:333, 392. Type by subsequent designation. Type designated by Jordan 1917:115 [ref. 2407]. Presumably a senior synonym of *Aspidoparia* Heckel 1847 [?1843] of current workers; genus not treated by Jayaram 1981 [ref. 6497]. Cyprinidae.

Cabillus Smith 1959:207 [ref. 4122]. Masc. *Cabillus lacertops* Smith 1959:207. Type by original designation (also monotypic). Valid (Akihito in Masuda et al. 1984:274 [ref. 6441], Birdsong et al. 1988:192 [ref. 7303]). Gobiidae.

Caboclinus Smith 1966:73 [ref. 4140]. Masc. *Clinus robustus* Gilchrist & Thompson 1908:128. Type by original designation. Synonym of *Clinus* Cuvier 1816 (Bennett 1983 [ref. 5299], Smith 1986:761 [ref. 5712]). Clinidae.

Cabotia de Buen 1930:17 [ref. 684]. Fem. *Cabotia schmidti* de Buen 1930:17. Type by original designation (also monotypic). Apparently preoccupied by Ragonot 1888 in Lepidoptera, replaced by *Cabotichthys* Whitley 1940. Synonym of *Gobius* Linnaeus 1758 (Miller 1973:483 [ref. 6888]). Gobiidae.

Cabotichthys Whitley 1940:242 [ref. 4660]. Masc. *Cabotia schmidti* de Buen 1930:17. Type by being a replacement name. Replacement for *Cabotia* de Buen 1930, apparently preoccupied by Ragonot 1888 in Lepidoptera [not researched]. Synonym of *Gobius* Linnaeus 1758 (Miller 1973:483 [ref. 6888]). Gobiidae.

Cachius Günther 1868:339 [ref. 1990]. Masc. *Cyprinus cachius* Hamilton 1822:258, 384. Type by monotypy (also by absolute tautonymy). *C. cachius* treated by Günther as young of *C. atpar* Hamilton. Synonym of *Chela* Hamilton 1822 (Roberts 1989:31 [ref. 6439]). Cyprinidae.

Cacodoxus Cantor 1849:1145 [163] [ref. 715]. *Chaetodon argus* Linnaeus 1766:464. Type by being a replacement name. Unneeded replacement for *Scatophagus* Cuvier 1831, not preoccupied by *Scatophaga* Meigen 1802 in Diptera; *Prenes* Gistel 1848 is an earlier replacement. On page 163 of separate. Objective synonym of *Scatophagus* Cuvier 1831. Scatophagidae.

Cacumen Whitley 1931:326 [ref. 4672]. Neut. *Platycephalus speculator* Klunzinger 1872:28. Type by original designation (also monotypic). Synonym of *Platycephalus* Bloch 1795 (Paxton et al. 1989:470 [ref. 12442] based on placement of type species). Platycephalidae.

Caecilia Lacepède 1800:134 [ref. 2709]. Fem. *Caecilia branderiana* Lacepède 1800:134 (= *Muraena caeca* Linnaeus 1758:245). Type by monotypy. Preoccupied by Linnaeus 1758 in Amphibia; replaced by *Typhlotes* Fischer von Waldheim 1813 and by *Branderius* Rafinesque 1815. Synonym of *Apterichtus* Duméril 1806 (Blache et al. 1973:248 [ref. 7185], McCosker 1977:65 [ref. 6836], McCosker et al. 1989:317 [ref. 13288]). Ophichthidae: Ophichthinae.

Caecobarbus Boulenger 1921:252 [ref. 588]. Masc. *Caecobarbus geertsii* Boulenger 1921:252. Type by monotypy. Valid (Lévêque & Daget 1984:298 [ref. 6186]). Cyprinidae.

Caecocypris Banister & Bunni 1980:151 [ref. 175]. Fem. *Caecocypris basimi* Banister & Bunni 1980:151. Type by monotypy. Cyprinidae.

Caecogilbia Poll & Leleup 1965:467 [ref. 3537]. Fem. *Caecogilbia galapagosensis* Poll & Leleup 1965:467. Type by monotypy. Synonym of *Ogilbia* Jordan & Evermann 1898 (Cohen & Nielsen 1978:60 [ref. 881]). Bythitidae: Brosmophycinae.

Caecomastacembelus Poll 1958:388 [ref. 3521]. Masc. *Caecomastacembelus brichardi* Poll 1958:389. Type by original designation (also monotypic). Also appeared as new in Poll 1959:112 [ref. 3522]). Valid (Travers 1984:144 [ref. 5147], Travers et al. 1986:421 [ref. 6221], Travers 1988 [ref. 6869]). Mastacembelidae.

Caecorhamdella Borodin 1927:1 [ref. 525]. Fem. *Caecorhamdella brasiliensis* Borodin 1927:1. Type by original designation (also monotypic). Valid (Burgess 1989:278 [ref. 12860]). Pimelodidae.

Caecorhamdia Norman 1926:325 [ref. 3214]. Fem. *Caecorhamdia urichi* Norman 1926:325. Type by monotypy. Synonym of *Rhamdia* Bleeker 1858 (Mees 1974:152 [ref. 2969], Miller 1984:135 [ref. 5281]). Pimelodidae.

Caecula Vahl 1794:149 [ref. 4482]. Fem. *Caecula pterygera* Vahl 1794:153. Type by subsequent designation. Type designated by Jordan 1917:52 [ref. 2407] or Smith 1965 [ref. 4132]; for discussion of type species and a translation of Vahl's original description see Smith 1965:715-717. Valid (Böhlke & McCosker 1975:3 [ref. 607], McCosker 1977:66 [ref. 6836], McCosker et al. 1989:297 [ref. 13288]). Ophichthidae: Ophichthinae.

Caelorinchus Giorna 1809:179 [ref. 1808]. Masc. *Lepidoleprus caelorhincus* Risso 1810:200. Giorna's species "La Caelorinque-La-Ville" not latinized (unavailable). Risso 1810 placed Giorna's "Caelorinque" in *Lepidoleprus* and validly named the species. Originally included species probably date to Günther 1887:125 [ref. 2013] and type designation to Fowler 1936:459 [ref. 6546]. Original orthography was "Cæl..." and not "Cœl..."; usually as *Coelorhynchus*. Valid (Marshall & Iwamoto 1973:538 [ref. 6966], Okamura in Masuda et al. 1984:97 [ref. 6441], Iwamoto 1986:332 [ref. 5674], Paxton et al. 1989:325 [ref. 12442]. Macrouridae: Macrourinae.

Caenotropus Günther 1864:297 [ref. 1974]. Masc. *Microdus labyrinthicus* Kner 1858:77. Type by being a replacement name. Replacement for *Chilodus* Müller & Troschel 1844 and of Kner and *Chilodus* Kner 1859 (preoccupied by Nees 1812 in Hymenoptera and Emmons 1857 in fishes); on Official List, with type confirmed as *M. labyrinthicus* (through *Microdus*) by the ICZN (Opinion 1150). Spelled *Caenotropis* by Boulenger 1910:7 [not researched]. Valid (Géry 1977:211 [ref. 1597], Vari 1983:5 [ref. 5419]). Curimatidae: Chilodontinae.

Caesio Lacepède 1801:85 [ref. 2710]. Fem. *Caesio caerulaurea* Lacepède 1801:85, 86. Type by subsequent designation. Type designated by Bleeker 1876:274 [ref. 447]. *Cesio* Rafinesque 1818:85 [ref. 3584] an incorrect subsequent spelling. See Carpenter 1987:5 [ref. 6430] for discussion of why gender is feminine. Valid (Johnson 1980:10 [ref. 13553], Akazaki in Masuda et al. 1984:171 [ref. 6441], Smith 1986:579 [ref. 5712], Carpenter 1987:15 [ref. 6430], Carpenter 1988:35 [ref. 9296]). Caesionidae.

Caesioma Kaup 1864:161 From Fowler (MS), not located; apparently name only and not available. Kyphosidae: Scorpidinae.

Caesiomorus Lacepède 1801:92 [ref. 2710]. Masc. *Caesiomorus baillonii* Lacepède 1801:92, 93. Type by subsequent designation. *Cesiomorus* Rafinesque 1815:84 [ref. 3584] is an incorrect subsequent spelling. Type designated by Gill 1863:437 [ref. 1669] or by Jordan 1917:61 [ref. 2407]. Synonym of *Trachinotus* Lacepède 1801 (Daget & Smith-Vaniz 1986:319 [ref. 6207]). Carangidae.

Caesioperca Castelnau 1872:49 [ref. 757]. Fem. *Serranus rasor* Richardson 1839:95. Type by monotypy. One definitely-included species, second taxon a variety of the first. Valid (Kendall 1984:500 [ref. 13663], Paxton et al. 1989:503 [ref. 12442]). Serranidae: Anthiinae.

Caesioscorpis Whitley 1945:20 [ref. 4707]. Fem. *Caesioscorpis theagenes* Whitley 1945:21. Type by original designation (also monotypic). Valid (Johnson 1980:69 [ref. 13553], Paxton et al. 1989:490 [ref. 12442] in Serranidae). Percoidei.

Caesiosoma Bleeker (ex Kaup) 1876:299 [ref. 448]. Neut. *Caesiosoma sieboldi* Bleeker (ex Kaup) 1876:299. Type proposed as, "Spec. typ. *Caesiosoma sieboldi* Kp. (nom. manuscr.) = *Scorpis aequipinnis* Rich.?" Description perhaps validates the species name *sieboldi*, and type is by monotypy (only one species definitely included). Kyphosidae: Scorpidinae.

Caeso Gistel 1848:VIII [ref. 1822]. *Sparus aurata* Linnaeus 1758:277. Type by being a replacement name. Unexplained replacement for "*Chrysophrys* Rüppell," with no species named by Gistel (see Jordan 1919:338 [ref. 2409]). If regarded as a generic replacement, then goes back to Cuvier with type as above, else Gistel's name is unavailable. Objective synonym of *Sparus* Linnaeus 1758. Sparidae.

Caffrogobius (subgenus of *Gobius*) Smitt 1900:551 [ref. 4148]. Masc. *Gobius nudiceps* Valenciennes in Cuvier & Valenciennes 1827:65. Type by original designation (also monotypic). Valid (Hoese 1986:782 [ref. 5670], Maugé 1986:362 [ref. 6218], Birdsong et al. 1988:184, 186 [ref. 7303]). Gobiidae.

Cainosilurus Macleay 1881:211 [ref. 6222]. Masc. *Neosilurus australis* Castelnau 1845:45. Type by being a replacement name. Replacement for *Neosilurus* Castelnau 1878, preoccupied by Steindachner 1867 in fishes (actually congeneric). Synonym of *Neosilurus* Steindachner 1867 based on placement of type species (Paxton et al. 1989:224 [ref. 12442]). Plotosidae.

Cairnsichthys Allen 1980:471 [ref. 99]. Masc. *Rhadinocentrus rhombosomoides* Nichols & Raven 1928:1. Type by original designation (also monotypic). Valid (Allen & Cross 1982:104 [ref. 6251], White et al. 1984:360 [ref. 13655], Paxton et al. 1989:349 [ref. 12442]). Atherinidae: Melanotaeniinae.

Calamiana Herre 1945:79 [ref. 2140]. Fem. *Calamiana magnoris* Herre 1945:80. Type by original designation (also monotypic). Valid (Birdsong et al. 1988:188 [ref. 7303], Roberts 1989:168 [ref. 6439]). Gobiidae.

Calamoichthys Smith 1866:654 [ref. 4061]. Masc. *Erpetoichthys calabaricus* Smith 1865:278. Type by being a replacement name. Apparently an unndeeded replacement for *Erpetoichthys* Smith 1866, regarded as preoccupied by Swainson 1838 in fishes (as *Erpichthys*). Valid (Gosse 1984:8 [ref. 6169]), but probably *Erpetoichthys* should be used instead, not preoccupied by *Erpichthys* Swainson. Polypteridae.

Calamopteryx Böhlke & Cohen 1966:2 [ref. 606]. Fem. *Calamopteryx goslinei* Böhlke & Cohen 1966:4. Type by original designation (also monotypic). Valid (Cohen 1973 [ref. 7138], Cohen & Nielsen 1978:46 [ref. 881], Vergara R. 1980 [ref. 5201]). Bythitidae: Bythitinae.

Calamuraena Whitley 1944:261 [ref. 4705]. Fem. *Ophichthys calamus* Günther 1870:74. Type by original designation (also monotypic). Synonym of *Cirrhimuraena* Kaup 1856 (McCosker 1977:75 [ref. 6836]). Ophichthidae: Ophichthinae.

Calamus (subgenus of *Chrysophrys*) Swainson 1839:171, 221 [ref. 4303]. Masc. *Calamus megacephalus* Swainson 1839:222. Type by monotypy. Valid (Randall & Caldwell 1966 [ref. 9053], Matsuura in Uyeno et al. 1983:360 [ref. 14275]). Sparidae.

Calcarbrotula Fowler 1946:193 [ref. 1456]. Fem. *Calcarbrotula erythraea* Fowler 1946:193. Type by original designation (also monotypic). Synonym of *Brotulina* Fowler 1946 (Cohen & Nielsen 1978:56 [ref. 881]). Bythitidae: Brosmophycinae.

Callanthias Lowe 1839:76 [ref. 2829]. Masc. *Callanthias paradiseus* Lowe 1839:76. Type by monotypy. Ogilby 1899:175 [ref. 3279] wrongly has type as *peloritanus*. Valid (Tortonese 1973:357 [ref. 7192], Katayama in Masuda et al. 1984:138 [ref. 6441], Heemstra & Anderson 1986:538 [ref. 5664]) in Callanthiidae, Paxton et al. 1989:504 [ref. 12442]). Callanthiidae.

Callarias Klein 1777:327 [ref. 4920]. Masc. Not available, published in a work that does not conform to the principle of binominal nomenclature. In the synonymy of *Gadus* Linnaeus 1758. Gadidae.

Callaus (subgenus of *Sciaena*) Jordan & Evermann 1889:395, 401 [ref. 2439]. Fem. *Corvina deliciosa* Tschudi 1845:8. Type by original designation (also monotypic). Sciaenidae.

Callechelys Kaup 1856:51 [ref. 2572]. Fem. *Callechelys guichenoti* Kaup 1856:52. Type by monotypy. Also in Kaup 1856:28 [ref. 2573] and as name only in Kaup in Duméril 1856:199 [ref. 1154]. Valid (McCosker 1977:62 [ref. 6836], Asano in Masuda et al. 1984:30 [ref. 6441], Leiby 1984:404 [ref. 12859], McCosker & Castle 1986:178 [ref. 5690], Paxton et al. 1989:116 [ref. 12442], McCosker et al. 1989:303 [ref. 13288]). Ophichthidae: Ophichthinae.

Calleleotris Gill 1863:270 [ref. 1691]. Fem. *Gobius strigatus* Broussonet 1782:1. Type by original designation (also monotypic). Gobiidae.

Calliblennius Aoyagi 1954:213 [37] [ref. 130]. Masc. *Calliblennius rubescens* Aoyagi 1954:213 [37]. Type by original designation (also monotypic). Preoccupied by Barbour 1912 in fishes, not replaced. Synonym of *Belonepterygion* McCulloch 1915 (Hardy 1985:375 [ref. 5184]). Acanthoclinidae.

Calliblennius Barbour 1912:187 [ref. 178]. Masc. *Zacalles bryope* Jordan & Snyder 1902:448. Type by being a replacement name. Replacement for *Zacalles* Jordan & Snyder 1902, preoccupied by Foerster 1869 in Ichneumonidae (Insecta). Synonym of *Neoclinus* Girard 1858 (Clark Hubbs 1953:12 [ref. 12698]). Labrisomidae.

Callicanthus (subgenus of *Prionurus*) Swainson 1839:256 [ref. 4303]. Masc. *Aspisurus elegans* Rüppell 1818:61. Type by monotypy. Synonym of *Naso* Lacepède 1801 (Randall 1955:361 [ref. 13648]). Acanthuridae.

Callichrous (subgenus of *Silurus*) Hamilton 1822:149 [ref. 2031]. Masc. *Silurus pabda* Hamilton 1822:149. Type by subsequent designation. Type designated of Bleeker 1862:395 [ref. 391], 1862:17 [ref. 393] and 1863:115 [ref. 401]. Misspelled *Callichrus* by Swainson 1838:347, 353 [ref. 4302]; 1839:306 [ref. 4303]. Synonym of *Ompok* Lacepède 1803 (Haig 1952:103 [ref. 12607], Roberts 1989:150 [ref. 6439]). Siluridae.

Callichthys Gronow 1763:127 [ref. 1910]. Masc. Not available, published in a rejected work on Official Index (Opinion 261). Callichthyidae.

Callichthys Linck 1790:32 [ref. 4985]. Masc. *Silurus callichthys* Linnaeus 1758:307. Possibly is an available use of *Callichthys* Gronow 1763; not intended as a new genus by Linck. Callichthyidae.

Callichthys Meuschen 1778:39 Masc. *Callichthys callichthys* Linnaeus 1758:307. Original not seen; taken from Fowler (MS). Not available, published in a rejected work on Official Index (Opinion 260). In the synonymy of *Callichthys* Scopoli 1777. Callichthyidae.

Callichthys Scopoli (ex Gronow) 1777:451 [ref. 3990]. Masc. *Silurus callichthys* Linnaeus 1758:307. Appeared first without species; first addition of species not researched. Original spelling was *Calichthys*, and that spelling is regarded as a misprint for *Callichthys*. Valid (Gosline 1940:6 [ref. 6489], Burgess 1989:364 [ref. 12860], Malabarba 1989:146 [ref. 14217]). Callichthyidae.

Calliclinus Gill 1860:103 [ref. 1765]. Masc. *Clinus geniguttatus* Valenciennes in Cuvier & Valenciennes 1836:285. Type by monotypy. Valid (Stephens & Springer 1974:19 [ref. 7149]). Labrisomidae.

Callidulus (subgenus of *Eudulus*) Fowler 1907:265 [ref. 1376]. Masc. *Centropristis subligarius* Cope 1870:120. Type by original designation (also monotypic). Synonym of *Dules* Cuvier 1829. Serranidae: Serraninae.

Callieleotris Fowler 1934:155 [ref. 1417]. Fem. *Callieleotris platycephalus* Fowler 1934:156. Type by original designation (also monotypic). Synonym of *Bostrychus* Lacepède 1801 (Maugé 1986:390 [ref. 6218]). Eleotridae.

Callimucenus Whitley 1934:unpaginated [ref. 4682]. Masc. *Callionymus macdonaldi* Ogilby 1911:56. Type by original designation. Synonym of *Callionymus* Linnaeus 1758 (Fricke 1982:58 [ref. 5432]). Synonym of *Repomucenus* Whitley 1931 (Nakabo 1982:105 [ref. 3139]). Callionymidae.

Calliodon Bloch & Schneider (ex Gronow) 1801:312 [ref. 471]. Masc. *Calliodon lineatus* Bloch & Schneider 1801:312. Type by subsequent designation. Earliest type designation not researched. Scaridae: Scarinae.

Calliomorus Lacepède 1800:343 [ref. 2709]. Masc. *Callionymus indicus* Linnaeus 1758:250. Type by monotypy. Synonym of *Platycephalus* Bloch 1795. Platycephalidae.

Callionymus Linnaeus 1758:249 [ref. 2787]. Masc. *Callionymus lyra* Linnaeus 1758:249. Type by subsequent designation. Type designated by Bleeker 1879:80 [ref. 458]. On Official List (Opinion 77); *Callionimus* Goüan 1770 and *Calliongmus* Linck 1790 on Official Index as incorrect subsequent spellings (Direction 56). Valid (Wheeler 1973:516 [ref. 7190], Houde 1984:637 [ref. 13674], Fricke in Whitehead et al. 1986:1086 [ref. 13677], Fricke 1986:770 [ref. 5653]). Callionymidae.

Calliscyllium Tanaka 1912:171 [ref. 6035]. Neut. *Calliscyllium venustum* Tanaka 1912:171. Type by original designation (also monotypic). Synonym of *Proscyllium* Hilgendorf 1904 (Compagno 1984:376 [ref. 6846], Compagno 1988:189 [ref. 13488]). Proscylliidae.

Calliurichthys Jordan & Fowler 1903:941 [ref. 2462]. Masc. *Callionymus japonicus* Houttuyn 1782:311. Type by original designation. Synonym of *Callionymus* Linnaeus 1758, but as a valid subgenus (Fricke 1982:67 [ref. 5432]); valid genus (Nakabo 1982:102 [ref. 3139], Houde 1984:637 [ref. 13674], Nakabo in Masuda et al. 1984:344 [ref. 6441]). Callionymidae.

Calliurus Rafinesque 1819:420 [ref. 3590]. Masc. *Calliurus punctulatus* Rafinesque 1819:420. Type by monotypy. Synonym of *Micropterus* Lacepède 1802 (Hubbs & Bailey 1940:13 [ref. 12253]). Centrarchidae.

Callochromis Regan 1920:46 [ref. 3669]. Masc. *Pelmatochromis macrops* Boulenger 1898:13. Type by original designation. Valid (Poll 1986:107 [ref. 6136]). Cichlidae.

Callogobius Bleeker 1874:318 [ref. 437]. Masc. *Eleotris hasseltii* Bleeker 1850:253. Type by original designation (also monotypic). Valid (Lachner & McKinney 1974:878 [ref. 2547], Goren 1979 [ref. 6902], Akihito in Masuda et al. 1984:264 [ref. 6441], Hoese 1986:784 [ref. 5670], Birdsong et al. 1988:192 [ref. 7303], Kottelat 1989:18 [ref. 13605]). Gobiidae.

Callomystax Günther 1864:218 [ref. 1974]. Masc. *Pimelodus gagata* Hamilton 1822:197, 379. Type by being a replacement name. Unneeded replacement for *Gagata* Bleeker 1858; Günther replaced because Bleeker's characters were incorrect. Objective synonym of *Gagata* Bleeker 1858. Sisoridae.

Callopanchax (subgenus of *Aphyosemion*) Myers 1933:184 [ref. 3104]. Masc. *Aphyosemion occidentale* Stenholt Clausen 1966:331. Type designated by ICZN under plenary powers. On Official List (Opinion 1010). Synonym of *Fundulopanchax* Myers 1924, but as a valid subgenus (Parenti 1981:479 [ref. 7066]); synonym of *Aphyosemion* Myers 1924 (Wildekamp et al. 1986:196 [ref. 6198]). Aplocheilidae: Aplocheilinae.

Callopharynx Poll 1948:95 [ref. 3519]. Masc. *Callopharynx microdon* Poll 1948:95. Type by monotypy. Cichlidae.

Calloplesiops Fowler & Bean 1930:316 [ref. 1477]. Masc. *Calloplesiops niveus* Fowler & Bean 1930:317. Type by original designation. Valid (Hoese & Kuiter 1984:8 [ref. 5300], Hayashi in Masuda et al. 1984:141 [ref. 6441], Heemstra 1986:542 [ref. 5660], Paxton et al. 1989:524 [ref. 12442]). Plesiopidae.

Calloptilum Hutton 1873:266 [ref. 2285]. Neut. *Calloptilum punctatum* Hutton 1873:266. Type by monotypy. Described as new by Hutton, although he stated, "This genus comes next to *Bregmaceros*, Thompson, afterwards called *Calloptilum* by Sir J. Richardson, which name I have now adopted for the present genus." Preoccupied by Richardson 1845 in recent fishes; replaced by *Auchenoceros* Günther 1889. Objective synonym of *Auchenoceros* Günther 1889 (Paulin 1983:103 [ref. 5459]). Moridae.

Calloptilum Richardson 1845:94 [ref. 3739]. Neut. *Calloptilum mirum* Richardson 1845:95. Type by monotypy. Synonym of *Bregmaceros* Thompson 1840. Bregmacerotidae.

Callorhinchus Lacepède (ex Gronow) 1798:400 [ref. 2708]. Masc. *Chimaera callorynchus* Linnaeus 1758:236. Type by monotypy. Subsequently described from excellent description by Gronow as *Callorhynchus* (Cuvier 1829:382) and *Callorhincus* (Duméril 1806:104); unjustifiably emended (from Gronow 1754) by Agassiz 1846:60 [ref. 64] to *Callirhynchus*. Valid (Nakamura et al. 1986:58 [ref. 14235], Compagno 1986:147 [5648], Paxton et al. 1989:98 [ref. 12442]). Callorhynchidae.

Callorhyncus Fleming 1822:380 [ref. 5063]. Masc. *Callorhyncus antarcticus* Fleming (not of Lay & Bennett 1839) 1822:380. Type by monotypy. Original not seen. Synonym of *Callorhinchus* Lacepède 1798. Callorhynchidae.

Calloryncus Cuvier (ex Gronow) 1816:140 [ref. 993]. Masc. *Chimaera callorhynchus* Linnaeus 1758:236. Type by monotypy. The one included species given as "La Chimère antarctique (*Chimaera callorynchus* L)." Synonym of *Callorhinchus* Lacepède 1798; both being based on Gronow 1754 (pre-Linnaean). Callorhynchidae.

Calloryncus Gronow 1763:31 [ref. 1910]. Masc. Not available, published in a rejected work on Official Index (Opinion 261). Callorhynchidae.

Callosphyraena Smith 1956:38, 42 [ref. 4105]. Fem. *Sphyraena toxeuma* Fowler 1904:502. Type by original designation (also monotypic). Synonym of *Sphyraena* Rose 1793 (de Sylva 1975:76 [ref. 6302], Daget 1986:350 [ref. 6203]); as a subgenus (de Sylva 1984:534 [ref. 13666]). Sphyraenidae.

Callyodon Bloch 1788:242 [ref. 467]. Masc. Listed in Jordan 1917:45 [ref. 2407], with type presumably *Scarus croicensis* Bloch, but not seen by Jordan or by us and not treated by Fowler. Scaridae: Scarinae.

Callyodon Gronow 1763:72 [ref. 1910]. Masc. Not available, published in a rejected work on Official Index (Opinion 261). Spelled *Calliodon* by Walbaum 1792. Scaridae: Scarinae.

Callyodon Scopoli (ex Gronow) 1777:449 [ref. 3990]. Masc. Appeared first without species; first application of species not researched. Scaridae: Scarinae.

Callyodontichthys Bleeker 1861:230 [ref. 381]. Masc. *Scarus flavescens* Bleeker (not of Bloch & Schneider). Apparently appeared first as above, without species. Also appeared in Bleeker 1862:5, 15 [ref. 4858] without species. First addition of species not researched; type given by Jordan 1919:300 [ref. 4904] as above. Synonym of *Sparisoma* Swainson 1839. Scaridae: Sparisomatinae.

Calophysus Müller & Troschel in Müller 1843:318 [ref. 3063]. Masc. *Pimelodus macropterus* Lichtenstein 1819:581. Type by subsequent designation. Apparently appeared first as name only in Müller & Troschel 1842:79 [not researched]. Earliest type designation not researched. Spelled *Callophysus* by Müller & Troschel 1848:1 [ref. 3073], Eigenmann & Allen 1942:87 [ref. 1246]) and others. Valid (Stewart 1986:665 [ref. 5211], Burgess 1989:275 [ref. 12860]). Pimelodidae.

Calotomus Gilbert 1890:70 [ref. 1623]. Masc. *Calotomus xenodon* Gilbert 1890:70. Type by original designation (also monotypic). Valid (Richards & Leis 1984:544 [ref. 13668], Kishimoto in Masuda et al. 1984:218 [ref. 6441], Bruce & Randall 1985 [ref. 5234], Randall 1986:707 [ref. 5706], Bellwood & Choat 1989:12 [ref. 13494]). Scaridae: Sparisomatinae.

Calumia Smith 1958:148 [ref. 4118]. Fem. *Calumia biocellata* Smith 1958:148. Type by original designation (also monotypic). Valid (Hoese 1986:808 [ref. 5670], Birdsong et al. 1988:181 [ref. 7303]). Eleotridae.

Calycilepidotus Ayres 1855:76 [ref. 159]. Masc. *Calycilepidotus spinosus* Ayres 1855:76. Type by subsequent designation. Type designated by Jordan & Evermann 1898:1936 [ref. 2444]. Synonym of *Hemilepidotus* Cuvier 1829 (Bolin 1944:13 [ref. 6379], but as a valid subgenus (Peden 1978:16 [ref. 5530]). Cottidae.

Calymmichthys Jordan & Thompson 1914:296 [ref. 2543]. Masc. *Calymmichthys xenicus* Jordan & Thompson 1914:296. Type by monotypy. Synonym of *Diplogrammus* Gill 1865 (Nakabo 1982:97 [ref. 3139], Fricke 1982:71 [ref. 5432]). Callionymidae.

Camarina Ayres 1860:81 [ref. 158]. Fem. *Camarina nigricans* Ayres 1860:81. Type by monotypy. Synonym of *Girella* Gray 1835. Kyphosidae: Girellinae.

Campagnoia (subgenus of *Parmaturus*) Springer 1979:102 [ref. 4175]. Fem. *Parmaturus (Campagnoia) manis* Springer 1979:102. Type by original designation. No derivation of name given, perhaps for L. J. V. Compagno; *Campagnoia* regarded as the correct original spelling (that spelling used also on p. 100). Synonym of *Apristurus* Garman 1913 (Compagno 1984:257 [ref. 6846], Compagno 1988:163 [ref. 13488] as *Compagnoia*). Scyliorhinidae.

Campbellina Fowler 1958:15 [ref. 1470]. Fem. *Discus aureus* Campbell 1879:297. Type by being a replacement name. Replacement for *Discus* Campbell 1879, preoccupied by Fitzinger 1833 in Mollusca. Synonym of *Diretmus* Johnson 1863 (Woods & Sonoda 1973:291 [ref. 6899], Post & Quéro 1981:37 [ref. 3555] but as *Campellina*, Kotlyar 1987 [ref. 13522]). Diretmidae.

Campellolebias Vaz-Ferreira & Sierra 1974:14 [ref. 4517]. Masc. *Campellolebias brucei* Vaz-Ferreira & Sierra 1974:1. Type by original designation (also monotypic). Synonym of *Cynolebias* Steindachner 1876 (Parenti 1981:490 [ref. 7066]); valid (Costa et al. 1989 [ref. 9292]). Aplocheilidae: Rivulinae.

Campichthys (subgenus of *Festucalex*) Whitley 1931:313 [ref. 4672]. Masc. *Ichthyocampus tryoni* Ogilby 1890:56. Type by original designation. Valid (Dawson 1977:637 [ref. 1066], Dawson 1985:28 [ref. 6541], Paxton et al. 1989:413 [ref. 12442]). Syngnathidae: Syngnathinae.

Campilodon Cuvier 1829:205 [ref. 995]. Masc. *Notacanthus nasus* Bloch 1795:113. Type by monotypy. Appeared as "Notacanthes Bl. (*Campilodon*. oth. Fabric.)." Regarded as a name in synonymy of *Notacanthus*; possibly never made available by later use. Synonym of *Notacanthus* Bloch 1788 (Wheeler 1973:256 [ref. 7190]). Notacanthidae.

Campogramma Regan 1903:350 [ref. 3618]. Neut. *Lichia vadigo* of Risso 1810:196. Type by monotypy. Apparently based on misidentified type species (not *vadigo* Lacepède); see Smith-Vaniz & Staiger 1973:246 [ref. 7106]; Risso's *vadigo* renamed *Campogramma liro* by Dolfus 1955. Valid (Hureau & Tortonese 1973:375 [ref. 7198], Smith-Vaniz & Staiger 1973:244 [ref. 7106], Smith-Vaniz 1984:524 [ref. 13664]). Carangidae.

Camposella Fernández-Yépez 1948:60 [ref. 1316]. Fem. *Curimatus simulatus* Eigenmann & Eigenmann 1889:430. Type by original designation. Preoccupied by Cole 1919 in Diptera, replaced by *Camposichthys* Whitley 1953 (also preoccupied) and replaced by *Stupens* Whitley 1954. Synonym of *Curimata* Bosc 1817 (Vari 1989:6 [ref. 9189], not mentioned but based on placement of *Stupens*). Curimatidae: Curimatinae.

Camposichthys Travassos 1946:132 [4] [ref. 5009]. Masc. *Cynodon gibbus* Agassiz in Spix & Agassiz 1829:77. Type by original designation (also monotypic). Objective synonym of *Cynodon* Agassiz 1829 (see account of *Cynodon*). Characidae.

Camposichthys Whitley 1953:134 [ref. 4718]. Masc. *Curimatus simulatus* Eigenmann & Eigenmann 1889:430. Type by being a replacement name. Replacement for *Camposella* Fernández-Yépez 1948, preoccupied by Cole 1919 in Diptera. *Camposichthys* itself preoccupied by Travassos 1946 in fishes and replaced by *Stupens* Whitley 1954. Synonym of *Curimata* Bosc 1817 (Vari 1989:6 [ref. 9189], *Camposichthys* not mentioned but status based on placement of *Stupens*). Curimatidae: Curimatinae.

Campostoma Agassiz 1855:218 [ref. 5839]. Neut. *Rutilus anomalus* Rafinesque 1820:241. Type by original designation (p. 219). Valid (Burr 1976 [ref. 7118]). Cyprinidae.

Campylodon Fabricius 1793:22 [ref. 1288]. Masc. *Campylodon fabricii* Reinhardt 1838:120. Original not seen; apparently appeared first without species; first addition of species not researched. Synonym of *Notacanthus* Bloch 1788 (Wheeler 1973:256 [ref. 7190]). Notacanthidae.

Campylomormyrus Bleeker 1874:367 [ref. 435]. Masc. *Mormyrus tamandus* Günther 1864:22. Type by original designation (also monotypic). Valid (Taverne 1972:168 [ref. 6367], Gosse 1984:66 [ref. 6169]). Mormyridae.

Cancelloxus Smith 1961:355 [ref. 4127]. Masc. *Cancelloxus burrelli* Smith 1961:355. Type by original designation (also monotypic). Valid (Smith 1986:760 [ref. 5712], Heemstra & Wright 1986 [ref. 5997]). Clinidae.

Candidia Jordan & Richardson 1909:169 [ref. 2493]. Fem. *Opsariichthys barbatus* Regan 1908:359. Type by original designation (also monotypic). Valid, subfamily Opsariichthinae (Chen 1982:293 [ref. 824]). Cyprinidae.

Caneolepis Lahille 1908:431 [ref. 5869]. Masc. *Caneolepis acropterus* Lahille 1908:431. Type by monotypy. Synonym of *Iluocoetes* Jenyns 1842 (Gosztonyi 1977:212 [ref. 6103]). Zoarcidae.

Caninoa Nardo 1841:312 [ref. 13424]. *Caninoa chiereghini* Nardo 1841:312. Type by monotypy. Type based on *Squalus barbatus* Chierigini (manuscript) as given in Nardo 1841. Apparently based on an abnormal or mythical shark. *Caninotus* Nardo 1844 and *Thalassoklephtes* Gistel 1848 are unneeded replacements. Original not checked; taken from Fowler 1967:360 [ref. 9318]. Squaliformes.

Caninotus Nardo 1844:8 [ref. 3151]. Masc. *Caninoa chiereghini* Nardo 1841:312. Type by being a replacement name. Alternate name for *Caninoa* Nardo 1841; both *Caninoa* and *Caninotus* were used in this work as (p. 9), "Il genere porterebbe il nome di *Caninoa* o di *Caninotus*." *Caninotus* regarded by Jordan as a provisonal substitute. Objective synonym of *Caninoa* Nardo 1841. Squaliformes.

Cannorynchus Cantor 1849:1193 [211] [ref. 715]. Masc. *Fistularia tabacaria* Linnaeus 1758:312. Type by being a replacement name. Unneeded replacement for *Fistularia* Linnaeus, not preoccupied by *Fistularia* Donati 1750 (a pre-Linnaean name). On page 211 of separate. *Cannorhynchus* Bleeker 1863:236 [ref. 398] is an incorrect subsequent spelling. Objective synonym of *Fistularia* Linnaeus 1758 (Fritzsche 1976:196 [ref. 7102] but with wrong type). Fistulariidae.

Cantharus Cuvier 1816:278 [ref. 993]. Masc. *Sparus cantharus* Linnaeus 1758:280. Type by absolute tautonymy. Preoccupied by Bolton 1798 and by Montfort 1808 [not researched], replaced by *Spondyliosoma* Cantor 1849, *Cantharusa* Strand 1926, and *Caranthus* Barnard 1927. See also *Cantherus* in Whitley 1936:136 [ref. 6396]. Objective synonym of *Spondyliosoma* Cantor 1849 (Tortonese 1973:414 [ref. 7192]). Sparidae.

Cantharusa Strand 1928:54 [ref. 4285]. Fem. *Sparus cantharus* Linnaeus 1758:280. Type by being a replacement name. Replacement for *Cantharus* Cuvier 1816, preoccupied by Bolton 1798. Objective synonym of *Spondyliosoma* Cantor 1849, an earlier replacement name. Sparidae.

Cantherhines (subgenus of *Monacanthus*) Swainson 1839:194, 327 [ref. 4303]. *Monacanthus nasutus* Swainson 1839 (= *Balistes sandwichiensis* Quoy & Gaimard 1824). Type by monotypy. Spelled *Cantherhines* on pp. 194 and 437, *Cantherines* on p. 327; first reviser not located. *Cantherhinus* Agassiz 1846:64 [ref. 64] is an unjustified emendation. Swainson's *nasutus* is an unneeded substitute for *sandwichiensis*. Valid (Randall 1964:335 [ref. 3148], Matsuura 1979:165 [ref. 7019], Tyler 1980:176 [ref. 4477], Hutchins & Randall 1982 [ref. 5372], Arai 1983:199 [ref. 14249], Matsuura in Masuda et al. 1984:360 [ref. 6441], Hutchins 1986:884 [ref. 5673]). Monacanthidae.

Cantheschenia Hutchins 1977:16 [ref. 2283]. Fem. *Amanses (Cantherhines) longipinnis* Fraser-Brunner 1941:198. Type by original designation. Monacanthidae.

Canthidermis (subgenus of *Balistes*) Swainson 1839:194, 325 [ref. 4303]. Fem. *Balistes oculatus* Gray 1830:Pl. 90. Type by subsequent designation. Spelled *Canthidermes* on pp. 194, 437 (index), *Canthidermis* on p. 325. First type designation apparently by Bleeker 1866:11 [ref. 417] as *Balistes oculatus*; not *Balistes angulosus* designated by Swain 1882:282 [ref. 5966]. Valid (Matsuura 1980:66 [ref. 6943], Tyler 1980:120 [ref. 4477], Arai 1983:199 [ref. 14249], Aboussouan & Leis 1984:452 [ref. 13661], Matsuura in Masuda et al. 1984:359 [ref. 6441], Smith & Heemstra 1986:878 [ref. 5714]). Balistidae.

Canthigaster Swainson 1839:194 [ref. 4303]. Fem. *Tetraodon rostratus* Bloch 1786:8. Type by subsequent designation. Name changed to *Psilonodus* on p. 328. Type designated by Bleeker 1866:12 [ref. 417]. Misspelled or unjustifiably emended to *Canthogaster* by Bleeker 1866:19 [ref. 417]. Valid (Torchio 1973:647 [ref. 6892], Allen & Randall 1977 [ref. 6714], Tyler 1980:341 [ref. 4477], Arai 1983:207 [ref. 14249], Matsuura in Masuda et al. 1984:365 [ref. 6441], Smith & Heemstra 1986:898 [ref. 5714], Matsuura 1986 [ref. 6715], Randall & Cea Egaña 1989 [ref. 9295]). Tetraodontidae.

Canthirhynchus Swainson 1839:181, 272 [ref. 4303]. Masc. *Cottus monopterygius* Bloch 1798:156. Type by monotypy. Spelled *Canthyrhynchus* on p. 181 and 438 (index); first reviser not researched. Objective synonym of *Aspidophoroides* Lacepède 1801. Agonidae.

Canthophrys Swainson 1838:364 [ref. 4302]. Fem. *Cobitis albescens* Swainson 1839:310 (= *Cobitis cucura* Hamilton 1822:352, 394). Type by subsequent designation. Appeared first without species (1838:364); species added by Swainson 1839:190 and 310 [ref. 4303]. Type designated by Swain 1882:282 [ref. 5966]. Cobitidae: Cobitinae.

Canthopomus Eigenmann 1910:404, 407 [ref. 1224]. Fem. *Rhinelepis genibarbis* Valenciennes in Cuvier & Valenciennes 1840:484. Type by original designation. Description in key (p. 404). We regard this as the original description, not Eigenmann & Allen 1942:183 [ref. 1246](with different type, *Rhinelepis agassizii* Steindachner). Objective synonym of *Pseudorinelepis* Bleeker 1862 (Isbrücker 1980:8 [ref. 2303]). Loricariidae.

Cantor Talwar 1970:68 [ref. 5975]. *Bola cuja* Hamilton 1822:81. Type by original designation (also monotypic). Described apparently a little earlier as the new genus *Macrospinosa* by Mohan 1969. Objective synonym of *Macrospinosa* Mohan 1969 (Trewavas 1977:289 [ref. 4459]). Sciaenidae.

Cantoria Kaup 1858:106 [ref. 2579]. Fem. *Cantoria pinanganensis* Kaup 1858:106 (= *Pleuronectes potous* Cuvier 1829:344). Type by monotypy. Kaup's *pinanganensis* apparently is an unneeded replacement for *potous*. Apparently genus is not preoccupied, but *Cantorusia* Whitley 1940 is a replacement name. Synonym of *Cynoglossus* Hamilton 1822 (Menon 1977:16 [ref. 7071], Desoutter 1986:432 [ref. 6212]). Cynoglossidae: Cynoglossinae.

Cantorusia Whitley 1940:242 [ref. 4660]. Fem. *Cantoria pinanganensis* Kaup 1858:106. Type by being a replacement name. Replacement for *Cantoria* Kaup 1858, apparently not preoccupied [not researched]. Cynoglossidae: Cynoglossinae.

Capartella Chabanaud 1950:16 [ref. 801]. Fem. *Capartella polli* Chabanaud 1950:16. Type by original designation (p. 19). Soleidae.

Capellaria Gistel 1848:VIII [ref. 1822]. Fem. *Lophius commersonianus* Cuvier (ex Lacepède) 1817. Type by being a replacement name. Replacement for *Chironectes* of Cuvier and authors, preoccupied by Illiger in Mammalia. Type species uncertain, see account of *Chironectes*. Synonym of *Histrio* Fischer 1813 (Monod & Le Danois 1973:659 [ref. 7223], Pietsch 1984:37 [ref. 5380]). Antennariidae.

Capoeta Valenciennes in Cuvier & Valenciennes 1842:278 [ref. 1009]. Fem. *Capoeta capoeta* Güldenstädt 1773:507. Type by absolute tautonymy, not *amphibia* by subsequent designation of Bleeker 1863:200 [ref. 397], not *fundulus* as listed by Krupp & Schneider 1989:364 [ref. 13651]. Valid (Karaman 1969 [ref. 7823], Karaman 1971:221 [ref. 2560], Wu et al. 1977:258 [ref. 4807], Chu & Cui in Chu & Chen 1989:164 [ref. 13584], Krupp & Schneider 1989:364 [ref. 13651]); synonym of *Varicorhinus* Rüppell 1836 (Lévêque & Daget 1984:336 [ref. 6186]). Cyprinidae.

Capoetobrama Berg 1916:316 [ref. 277]. Fem. *Acanthobrama kuschakewitschi* Kessler 1872:20. Type by original designation. Valid (Bogutskaya 1987:936 [ref. 13521]). Cyprinidae.

Caprichromis Eccles & Trewavas 1989:265 [ref. 13547]. Masc. *Haplochromis orthognathus* Trewavas 1915:99. Type by original designation. Cichlidae.

Caprichthys McCulloch & Waite 1915:482 [ref. 2949]. Masc. *Caprichthys gymnura* McCulloch & Waite 1915:482. Type by monotypy. Valid (Tyler 1980:205 [ref. 4477], Winterbottom & Tyler 1983:902 [ref. 5320]). Ostraciidae: Aracaninae.

Capriscus Klein 1777:427 [ref. 4920]. Masc. Not available, published in a work that does not conform to the principle of binominal nomenclature. In the synonymy of *Balistes* Linnaeus 1758. Balistidae.

Capriscus Rafinesque 1810:41, 58 [ref. 3595]. Masc. *Capriscus porcus* Rafinesque 1810:41. Type by monotypy. Synonym of *Balistes* Linnaeus 1758. Balistidae.

Capriscus Röse 1793:114 [ref. 3833]. Masc. *Balistes capriscus* Gmelin 1788:147. Original not examined. Synonym of *Balistes* Linnaeus 1758 according to Jordan. Balistidae.

Caprodon Temminck & Schlegel 1843:64 [ref. 4371]. Masc. *Anthias schlegelii* Günther 1859:93. Proposed originally without species; one species added and type fixed by subsequent monotypy by Günther 1859:93 [ref. 1961], but Günther did not treat *Caprodon* as valid, including it in *Anthias*. Valid (Kendall 1984:500 [ref. 13663], Katayama in Masuda et al. 1984:134 [ref. 6441]). Serranidae: Anthiinae.

Capromimus Gill 1893:115, 123 [ref. 1736]. Masc. *Platystethus abbreviatus* Hector 1874:247. Type by monotypy. Zeidae.

Caprophonus Müller & Troschel 1849:28 [ref. 3073]. *Caprophonus aurora* Müller & Troschel 1849:28. Type by monotypy. Synonym of *Antigonia* Lowe 1843 (Krefft 1973:353 [ref. 7166], Parin & Borodulina 1986:143 [ref. 6005]). Caproidae.

Capropygia (subgenus of *Acerana*) Kaup 1855:220 [ref. 2571]. Fem. *Capropygia unistriata* Kaup (ex Gray) 1855:220. Type by monotypy. Valid (Tyler 1980:205 [ref. 4477], Winterbottom & Tyler 1983:902 [ref. 5320]). Ostraciidae: Aracaninae.

Capros Lacepède 1802:590 [ref. 4929]. Masc. *Zeus aper* Linnaeus 1758:267. Type by monotypy. The family Caproidae is placed in the order Perciformes by Heemstra 1986:495 [ref. 5660]; the more traditional placement is in the Zeiformes. Valid (Krefft 1973:353 [ref. 7166], Quéro in Whitehead et al. 1986:778 [ref. 13676], Heemstra 1986:506 [ref. 5660]). Caproidae.

Caprupeneus Whitley 1931:317 [ref. 4672]. Masc. *Pseudupeneus jeffi* Ogilby 1908:19. Type by original designation (also monotypic). Synonym of *Parupeneus* Bleeker 1863 or *Mullus* Linnaeus 1758. Mullidae.

Caquetaia Fowler 1945:133 [ref. 1454]. Fem. *Caquetaia amploris* Fowler 1945:133. Type by original designation (also monotypic). Synonym of *Cichlasoma* Swainson 1839 (see Kullander in Böhlke 1984:56 [ref. 13621]). Cichlidae.

Caracanthus Krøyer 1845:264, 267 [ref. 2689]. Masc. *Caracanthus typicus* Krøyer 1845:264, 267. Type by monotypy (also by use of *typicus*). Valid (Nakabo in Masuda et al. 1984:318 [ref. 6441], Eschmeyer 1986:481 [ref. 5652], Paxton et al. 1989:458 [ref. 12442]). Caracanthidae.

Caragobioides Smith 1945:568, 571 [ref. 4056]. Masc. *Caragobius geomys* Fowler 1935:161. Type by original designation (also monotypic). Valid (Kottelat 1989:19 [ref. 13605]). Gobiidae.

Caragobius Smith & Seale 1906:81 [ref. 4059]. Masc. *Caragobius typhlops* Smith & Seale 1906:81. Type by original designation (also monotypic). Valid (Birdsong et al. 1988:197 [ref. 7303]). Gobiidae.

Caragola Gray 1851:143 [ref. 4939]. Fem. *Caragola lapicida* Gray 1851:141. Type by monotypy. Also appeared in Gray 1853 [for 1851]:239 [ref. 1886]. Synonym of *Mordacia* Gray 1851 (Hubbs & Potter 1971:56 [ref. 13397]). Petromyzontidae: Mordaciinae.

Caralophia Böhlke 1955:1 [ref. 595]. Fem. *Caralophia loxochila* Böhlke 1955:2. Type by original designation (also monotypic). Valid (McCosker 1977:71 [ref. 6836], McCosker et al. 1989:338 [ref. 13288]). Ophichthidae: Ophichthinae.

Caranactis Regan & Trewavas 1932:58 [ref. 3682]. Fem. *Caranactis pumilus* Regan & Trewavas 1932:59. Type by monotypy. Synonym of *Oneirodes* Lütken 1871 (Pietsch 1974:33 [ref. 5332]). Oneirodidae.

Carangichthys Bleeker 1852:760 [ref. 335]. Masc. *Carangichthys typus* Bleeker 1852:760. Type by monotypy (also by use of *typus*). Synonym of *Caranx* Lacepède 1801 (Hureau & Tortonese 1973:373 [ref. 7198]); valid (Gushiken in Masuda et al. 1984:156 [ref. 6441], Gushiken 1988:443 [ref. 6697]); synonym of *Carangoides* Bleeker 1851 (Smith-Vaniz, pers. comm.). Carangidae.

Carangoides Bleeker 1851:343, 352, 366 [ref. 326]. Masc. *Caranx praeustus* Bennett 1830:689. Type by subsequent designation. Type designated by Jordan 1919:248 [ref. 2410]. Valid (Smith-Vaniz 1984:524 [ref. 13664], Gushiken in Masuda et al. 1984:156 [ref. 6441], Gushiken 1988:443 [ref. 6697], Paxton et al. 1989:574 [ref. 12442]). Carangidae.

Carangops Gill 1862:238 [ref. 1664]. Masc. *Caranx falcatus* Holbrook 1855:92. Type by subsequent designation. Type designated by Gill 1863:435 [ref. 1669]. Synonym of *Hemicaranx* Bleeker 1862 (Daget & Smith-Vaniz 1986:315 [ref. 6207] but with wrong type). Carangidae.

Carangulus (subgenus of *Caranx*) Jordan & Evermann 1927:505 [ref. 2453]. Masc. *Caranx latus* Agassiz in Spix & Agassiz 1831:105. Type by original designation (also monotypic). Synonym of *Caranx* Lacepède 1801 (Daget & Smith-Vaniz 1986:310 [ref. 6207]). Carangidae.

Carangus Girard 1858:168 [ref. 1813]. Masc. *Scomber carangus* Bloch 1793:69. Type by absolute tautonymy (also designated by Jordan 1919:291 [ref. 2410]). Synonym of *Caranx* Lacepède 1801 (Hureau & Tortonese 1973:373 [ref. 7198], Daget & Smith-Vaniz 1986:310 [ref. 6207]). Carangidae.

Carangus (subgenus of *Caranx*) Griffith 1834:355 [ref. 1908]. Masc. Name correctly formed [Jordan's mention as *Carangus* (1917:60 and 1919:180) wrongly withdrawn by Jordan 1923:185], but *Carangus* Griffith apparently is not available because genus and species are without distinctive characters. In the synonymy of *Caranx* Lacepède 1801. Carangidae.

Caranthus Barnard 1927:720 [ref. 194]. Masc. *Sparus cantharus* Linnaeus 1758:280. Type by being a replacement name. Replacement for *Cantharus* Cuvier 1816, preoccupied by Bolton 1798 and by Montfort 1808. Earlier replaced by *Spondyliosoma* Cantor 1849 and by *Cantharusa* Strand 1926. Objective synonym of *Spondyliosoma* Cantor 1849 (Tortonese 1973:414 [ref. 7192]). Sparidae.

Caranx Lacepède 1801:57 [ref. 2710]. Masc. *Caranx carangua* Lacepède 1801:57, 74. Type by subsequent designation. Type apparently designated by Desmarest 1874:242 [not investigated], or by Jordan & Gilbert 1883:970 [ref. 2476]. Valid (Hureau & Tortonese 1973:373 [ref. 7198], Smith-Vaniz 1984:524 [ref. 13664], Gushiken in Masuda et al. 1984:155 [ref. 6441], Smith-Vaniz

1986:646 [ref. 5718], Daget & Smith-Vaniz 1986:310 [ref. 6207], Gushiken 1988:443 [ref. 6697], Paxton et al. 1989:577 [ref. 12442]). Carangidae.

Caranxomorus Lacepède 1801:82 [ref. 2710]. Masc. *Scomber pelagicus* Linnaeus 1758:299. Type by subsequent designation. Type designated by Jordan 1917:61 [ref. 2407]. Synonym of *Coryphaena* Linnaeus 1758. Coryphaenidae.

Carapo Oken 1817:1182 [ref. 3303]. Apparently a spelling error for *Carapus* Cuvier. In synonymy of *Carapus* Cuvier 1816. Gymnotidae: Gymnotinae.

Carapus Cuvier 1816:237 [ref. 993]. Masc. *Gymnotus macrourus* Bloch & Schneider 1801:522. Earliest type designation not researched, above as given by Jordan. Preoccupied by *Carapus* Rafinesque 1810 in fishes; replaced by *Giton* Kaup. Gymnotidae: Gymnotinae.

Carapus Rafinesque 1810:37, 57 [ref. 3595]. Masc. *Gymnotus acus* Brünnich 1768:13. Type based on ICZN Opinion 42, with authorship of type credited to Linnaeus but without date. Valid (Arnold 1956:260 [ref. 5315], Wheeler 1973:557 [ref. 7190], Trott 1981:625 [ref. 14205], Williams 1984:388 [ref. 5314], Machida in Masuda et al. 1984:99 [ref. 6441], Olney & Markle 1986:351 [ref. 5701], Trott & Olney in Whitehead et al. 1986:1173 [ref. 13677], Shen & Yeh 1987:47 [ref. 6418], Paxton et al. 1989:319 [ref. 12442]). Carapidae: Carapinae.

Carasobarbus Karaman 1971:230 [ref. 2560]. Masc. *Systomus luteus* Heckel 1843:1061. Type by original designation (also monotypic). Cyprinidae.

Caraspius Nichols 1925:6 [ref. 3179]. Masc. *Caraspius agilis* Nichols 1925:6. Type by original designation (also monotypic). Cyprinidae.

Carassioides Oshima 1926:6 [ref. 3314]. Masc. *Carassioides rhombeus* Oshima 1926:7. Type by monotypy. Valid (Chen & Huang 1977:428 [ref. 13496], Wu 1987:44 [ref. 12822]). Cyprinidae.

Carassiops Ogilby 1897:732 [ref. 3274]. Masc. *Eleotris compressus* Krefft 1864:184. Type by original designation. Synonym of *Hypseleotris* Gill 1863 (Hoese, pers. comm.). Eleotridae.

Carassius (subgenus of *Cyprinus*) Nilsson 1832:32 [ref. 3204]. Masc. *Cyprinus carassius* Linnaeus 1758:321. Type by absolute tautonymy. Apparently first appeared as name only in Jarocki 1822:54, 71 [ref. 4984] (not resesarched). Valid (Chen & Huang 1977:430 [ref. 13496] credited to Jarocki, Sawada in Masuda et al. 1984:57 [ref. 6441], Paxton et al. 1989:216 [ref. 12442]). Cyprinidae.

Carcharhinus (subgenus of *Squalus*) Blainville 1816:121 [ref. 306]. Masc. *Carcharias melanopterus* Quoy & Gaimard 1824:194. Type designated by ICZN; genus placed on Official List (Opinion 723). *Carcharorhinus* Agassiz 1846:65 [ref. 64], and *Carcharinus* Cloquet 1817:7 [ref. 852] placed on the Official Index. Valid (Compagno 1973:23 [ref. 7163], Garrick 1982 [ref. 5454], Compagno 1984:449 [ref. 6846], Nakaya in Masuda et al. 1984:6 [ref. 6441], Bass et al. 1986:68 [ref. 5638], Cappetta 1987:121 [ref. 6348], Compagno 1988:307 [ref. 13488], Paxton et al. 1989:75 [ref. 12442]). Carcharhinidae.

Carcharias (subgenus of *Squalus*) Cuvier 1816:125 [ref. 993]. Masc. *Squalus carcharias* Linnaeus 1758:235. Type by monotypy (also by absolute tautonymy). Junior homonym of *Carcharias* Rafinesque 1810; not available. Placed on Official Index (Opinion 723). In the synonymy of *Carcharhinus* Blainville 1816 (Compagno 1984:449 [ref. 6846], Compagno 1988:307 [ref. 13488]). Carcharhinidae.

Carcharias Gistel 1848:VIII [ref. 1822]. Masc. *Squalus acanthias* Linnaeus 1758:233. Type by being a replacement name. Unneeded replacement for *Acanthias* [Risso] with species *vulgaris*, not preoccupied by *Acanthia* of early authors); *Carcharias* Gistel itself preoccupied by Rafinesque 1810 in fishes. Objective synonym of *Squalus* Linnaeus 1758 (Compagno 1984:109 [ref. 6474]). Squalidae.

Carcharias Rafinesque 1810:10 [ref. 3594]. Masc. *Carcharias taurus* Rafinesque 1810:10. Type by monotypy. Placed on Official Index (Opinion 723) but subsequently repealed (Opinion 1459) and put on Official List. *Carcharias* of Müller & Henle 1839, and Risso 1826 are junior homonyms on Official Index (Opinion 723). Synonym of *Eugomphodus* Gill in Compagno 1984:215 [ref. 6474], but Opinion 1459 (in 1987) makes *Carcharias* available if regarded as distinct from *Odontaspis*; valid (Paxton et al. 1989:63 [ref. 12442]). Odontaspididae: Odontaspidinae.

Carcharodon Smith in Müller & Henle 1838:37 [ref. 3066]. Masc. *Squalus carcharias* Linnaeus 1758:235. Type by subsequent monotypy. On Official List (Opinion 723). Valid (Springer 1973:13 [ref. 7162], Quéro in Whitehead et al. 1984:83 [ref. 13675], Compagno 1984:238 [ref. 6474], Bass 1986:98 [ref. 5635], Cappetta 1987:94 [ref. 6348], Paxton et al. 1989:66 [ref. 12442]). Lamnidae.

Cardiopharynx Poll 1942:346 [ref. 3516]. Fem. *Cardiopharynx schoutedeni* Poll 1942:347. Type by original designation (also monotypic). Valid (Poll 1986:100 [ref. 6136]). Cichlidae.

Careliparis (subgenus of *Liparis*) Garman 1892:62 [ref. 1537]. Masc. *Liparis agassizii* Putnam 1874:339. Type by subsequent designation. Type designated by Jordan & Evermann 1898:2114 [ref. 2444]. Synonym of *Liparis* Scopoli 1777 (Kido 1988:165 [ref. 12287]). Cyclopteridae: Liparinae.

Carelophus Krøyer 1845:227, 236 [ref. 2689]. Masc. *Gunellus stroemii* Valenciennes in Cuvier & Valenciennes 1836:444. Apparently type by monotypy, article not translated. Synonym of *Chirolophis* Swainson 1838 (Makushok 1973:532 [ref. 6889]). Stichaeidae.

Caremitra (subgenus of *Careproctus*) Jordan & Evermann 1896:452 [ref. 2442]. Fem. *Careproctus simus* Gilbert 1896:444. Type by original designation (also monotypic). Synonym of *Careproctus* Krøyer 1862 (Kido 1988:192 [ref. 12287]). Cyclopteridae: Liparinae.

Careproctus Krøyer 1862:253 [ref. 2694]. Masc. *Careproctus reinhardti* Krøyer 1862:253, 257. Type by monotypy. *Liparis palassii* also mentioned (article not translated). Valid (Lindberg 1973:610 [ref. 7220], Stein 1978:10 [ref. 4203], Kido in Masuda et al. 1984:338 [ref. 6441], Stein 1986:492 [ref. 6297], Kido 1985 [ref. 6720], Stein & Able in Whitehead et al. 1986:1275 [ref. 13677], Kido 1988:192 [ref. 12287]). Cyclopteridae: Liparinae.

Caribrhegma Breder 1927:44 [ref. 635]. Neut. *Caribrhegma gregoryi* Breder 1927:44. Type by monotypy. Serranidae: Grammistinae.

Cariburus Parr 1946:57 [ref. 3378]. Masc. *Macrurus zaniophorus* Vaillant 1888:245. Type by original designation. Synonym of *Coryphaenoides* Gunner 1765 (Marshall 1973:295 [ref. 7194], Marshall & Iwamoto 1973:565 [ref. 6966]). Macrouridae: Macrourinae.

Carinotetraodon Benl 1957:1 [ref. 258]. Masc. *Carinotetraodon chlupatyi* Benl 1957:1. Type by monotypy. Valid (Tyler 1980:341

[ref. 4477], Arai 1983:207 [ref. 14249], Leis 1984:448 [ref. 13659], Kottelat 1985:275 [ref. 11441], Kottelat 1989:21 [ref. 13605]). Tetraodontidae.

Carinotus (subgenus of *Plecostomus*) La Monte 1933:1 [ref. 2705]. Masc. *Plecostomus (Carinotus) carinotus* La Monte 1933:2. Type by original designation (also by monotypy and absolute tautonymy). Synonym of *Delturus* Eigenmann & Eigenmann 1889 (Isbrücker 1980:9 [ref. 2303]). Loricariidae.

Carinozacco Zhu, Wang & Yong 1982:267 [ref. 6473]. Masc. *Aspius spilurus* Günther 1868:311. Type by original designation. Objective synonym of *Parazacco* Chen 1982 (Kuang in Chu & Chen 1989:28 [ref. 13584]). Cyprinidae.

Caristioides Whitley 1948:87 [ref. 4710]. Masc. *Caristioides amplipinnis* Whitley 1948:88. Type by original designation (also monotypic). Synonym of *Psenes* Valenciennes 1833 (Haedrich 1967:58 [ref. 5357]). Nomeidae.

Caristius Gill & Smith 1905:249 [ref. 1748]. Masc. *Caristius japonicus* Gill & Smith 1905:249. Type by monotypy. Valid (Nielsen 1973:339 [ref. 6885], Fujii in Masuda et al. 1984:160 [ref. 6441], Post in Whitehead et al. 1986:747 [ref. 13676], Heemstra 1986:637 [ref. 5660]). Caristiidae.

Carlana Strand 1928:54 [ref. 4285]. Fem. *Cheirodon eigenmanni* Meek 1912:70. Type by being a replacement name. Replacement for *Carlia* Meek 1914, apparently preoccupied by Gray 1845 or 1854 [preoccupation not investigated]. Valid (Fink & Weitzman 1974:25 [ref. 7132], Géry 1977:543 [ref. 1597]). Characidae.

Carlastyanax Géry 1972:16 [ref. 1595]. Masc. *Astyanax aurocaudatus* Eigenmann 1913:26. Type by original designation (also monotypic). Valid (Géry 1977:379 [ref. 1597]). Characidae.

Carlhubbsia Whitley 1951:67 [ref. 4711]. Fem. *Allophallus kidderi* Hubbs 1936:236. Type by being a replacement name. Replacement for *Allophallus* Hubbs 1936, preoccupied by Dziedzicki 1923 in Diptera. Valid (Rosen & Bailey 1959:3 [ref. 12020], Rosen & Bailey 1963:114 [ref. 7067], Parenti & Rauchenberger 1989:9 [ref. 13538]). Poeciliidae.

Carlia Meek 1914:108 [ref. 2961]. Fem. *Cheirodon eigenmanni* Meek 1912:70. Type by original designation (also monotypic). Preoccupied by Gray 1845 or 1854 [not investigated], replaced by *Carlana* Strand 1928. Objective synonym of *Carlana* Strand 1928 (Fink & Weitzman 1974:25 [ref. 7132]). Characidae.

Carnegiella Eigenmann 1909:13 [ref. 1222]. Fem. *Gasteropelecus strigatus* Günther 1864:343. Type by original designation (also monotypic). Valid (Géry 1977:247 [ref. 1597], Vari 1983:5 [ref. 5419]). Gasteropelecidae.

Carpio Heckel 1843:1014 [ref. 2066]. *Cyprinus kollarii* Heckel 1836:223. Type by subsequent designation. Type designated by Bleeker 1863:24 [ref. 4859], 1863:262 [ref. 403] or 1863:191 [ref. 397]. Synonym of *Cyprinus* Linnaeus 1758. Cyprinidae.

Carpiodes (subgenus of *Catostomus*) Rafinesque 1820:302 [400] [ref. 5006]. Masc. *Catostomus cyprinus* Lesueur 1817:91. Type by subsequent designation. Type designated by Agassiz 1854:355 [ref. 69]. Also appeared in Rafinesque 1820:56 (Dec.) [ref. 3592]. Valid. Catostomidae.

Carpionichthys Bleeker 1863:262 [ref. 403]. Masc. *Cyprinus carpio* Linnaeus 1758:320. Apparently not available, no species mentioned and no description. Type above as given by Jordan 1919:322 [ref. 4904]). Synonym of *Cyprinus* Linnaeus 1758. Cyprinidae.

Cascadura Ellis 1913:387 [ref. 1270]. Fem. *Cascadura maculocephala* Ellis 1913:387. Type by monotypy. Valid (Gosline 1940:8 [ref. 6489]). Callichthyidae.

Caspialosa Berg 1915:4 [ref. 276]. Fem. *Clupea caspia* Eichwald 1838:134. Type by monotypy. Based on *Clupeonella* as treated by Berg 1913 [ref. 273], not of Kessler. Original not examined. Valid (Grande 1985:249 [ref. 6466]); synonym of *Alosa* Linck 1790 (Svetovidov 1973:105 [ref. 7169], Whitehead 1985:191 [ref. 5141]). Clupeidae.

Caspiomyzon Berg 1906:173 [ref. 264]. Masc. *Petromyzon wagneri* Kessler 1870:207, 302. Type by monotypy. Valid (Hubbs & Potter 1971:43 [ref. 13397]). Petromyzontidae: Petromyzontinae.

Caspiosoma Iljin 1927:129, 131 [ref. 5613]. Neut. *Gobiosoma caspium* Kessler 1877:38. Type by monotypy. Valid (Miller 1973:491 [ref. 6888], Miller in Whitehead et al. 1986:1027 [ref. 13677]). Gobiidae.

Cassigobius Whitley 1931:334 [ref. 4672]. Masc. *Lophiogobius ocellicauda* Günther 1873:241. Type by being a replacement name. Unneeded replacement for *Lophiogobius* Günther 1873, not preoccupied by *Lophogobius* Gill 1862 in fishes. Gobiidae.

Castelnauina (subgenus of *Solegnathus*) Fowler 1908:426 [ref. 1377]. Fem. *Solenognathus spinosissimus* Günther 1870:195. Type by original designation (also monotypic). Misspelled *Castelnauia* by Jordan 1920:523 [ref. 4905]. Synonym of *Solegnathus* Swainson 1839 (Dawson 1982:140 [ref. 5442], Dawson 1985:169 [ref. 6541]). Syngnathidae: Syngnathinae.

Catabasis Eigenmann & Norris 1900:358 [ref. 1264]. Fem. *Catabasis acuminatus* Eigenmann & Norris 1900:358. Type by original designation (also monotypic). Valid (Géry 1977:331 [ref. 1597]); synonym of *Brycon* Müller & Troschel 1844 (Howes 1982:4 [ref. 14201]). Characidae.

Catablemella Eigenmann & Eigenmann 1890:24 [ref. 1256]. Fem. *Myctophum brachychir* Eigenmann & Eigenmann 1889:126. Type by original designation (also monotypic). Synonym of *Notoscopelus* Günther 1864 (Bolin 1959:38 [ref. 503], Paxton 1979:16 [ref. 6440]). Myctophidae.

Cataetyx Günther 1887:104 [ref. 2013]. *Sirembo messieri* Günther 1878:19. Type by monotypy. Valid (Nielsen 1973:550 [ref. 6885], Hureau & Nielsen 1981:25 [ref. 5438], Machida in Masuda et al. 1984:101 [ref. 6441], Nielsen in Whitehead et al. 1986:1154 [ref. 13677], Cohen 1986:355 [ref. 5646], Sabates & Fortuño 1988 [ref. 12842], Paxton et al. 1989:316 [ref. 12442]). Bythitidae: Bythitinae.

Catalufa Snyder 1911:528 [ref. 4152]. Fem. *Catalufa umbra* Snyder 1911:528. Type by original designation. Synonym of *Pempheris* Cuvier 1829. Pempheridae.

Cataphractops Fowler 1915:231 [ref. 1392]. Masc. *Callichthys melampterus* Cope 1871:275. Type by original designation (also monotypic). Valid (Gosline 1940:8 [ref. 6489], Burgess 1989:364 [ref. 12860]). Callichthyidae.

Cataphractus Bloch 1794:80 [ref. 463]. Masc. *Silurus callichthys* Linnaeus 1758:307. Type by subsequent designation. Type designated by Jordan 1917:51 [ref. 2407]. Objective synonym of *Callichthys* Scopoli 1777 (Gosline 1940:6 [ref. 6489]). Callichthyidae.

Cataphractus Catesby 1771:9 [ref. 774]. Masc. Not available, published in a rejected work on Official Index (Opinion 89, Opinion 259), but name as appearing in the Edward's appendix is available. Doradidae.

Cataphractus Fleming 1828:216 [ref. 1339]. Masc. *Cataphractus schoneveldii* Fleming 1828:216. Type by monotypy. Agonidae.

Cataphractus Gronow 1763:115 [ref. 1910]. Masc. Not available, published in a rejected work on Official Index (Opinion 261). In the synonymy of *Pegasus* Linnaeus 1758. Pegasidae.

Cataphractus Klein 1777:828 [ref. 4920]. Masc. Not available, published in a work that does not conform to the principle of binominal nomenclature. In the synonymy of *Agonus* Bloch & Schneider 1801. Agonidae.

Catastoma Kuhl & van Hasselt in Cuvier & Valenciennes 1840:60 [ref. 1008]. Neut. *Catastoma nasutum* Kuhl & van Hasselt in Cuvier & Valenciennes 1840:60. Type by monotypy. Not available, genus and species as manuscript names mentioned in passing under *Arius nasutus*; apparently never made available by later use. In the synonymy of *Netuma* Bleeker 1858. Ariidae.

Catathyridium (subgenus of *Baeostoma*) Chabanaud 1928:28 [ref. 783]. Neut. *Baeostoma (Catathyridium) grandirivi* Chabanaud 1928:28. Type by subsequent designation. Two included species, neither designated; earliest type designation not researched. Genus of *grandirivi* is *Baiostoma*. Valid (Chapleau & Keast 1988:2799 [ref. 12625]). Achiridae.

Catesbya Böhlke & Smith 1968:35 [ref. 614]. Fem. *Catesbya pseudomuraena* Böhlke & Smith 1968:36. Type by original designation (also monotypic). Valid (Smith 1989:82 [ref. 13285]). Chlopsidae.

Cathetostoma see *Kathetostoma*. Uranoscopidae.

Cathorops (subgenus of *Arius*) Jordan & Gilbert 1882:39, 54 [ref. 2475]. Masc. *Arius hypophthalmus* Steindachner 1875:31. Type by original designation (also monotypic). Valid (Shimizu in Uyeno et al. 1983:160 [ref. 14275]). Ariidae.

Catla Valenciennes in Cuvier & Valenciennes 1844:410 [ref. 1010]. Fem. *Catla buchanani* Valenciennes in Cuvier & Valenciennes 1844:410 (= *Cyprinus catla* Hamilton 1822:187, 387). Type by monotypy. *Catla buchanani* Valenciennes is an unneeded substitute for *C. catla*. Spelled *Catlas* by Agassiz 1845:12 [ref. 4889] and 1846:68 [ref. 64]. Objective synonym of *Gibelion* Heckel 1843. Valid (Jayaram 1981:131 [ref. 6497], Kottelat 1989:6 [ref. 13605]). Cyprinidae.

Catlocarpio Boulenger 1898:450 [ref. 541]. *Catlocarpio siamensis* Boulenger 1898:451. Type by monotypy. *Catalocarpio* is a misspelling. Valid (Kottelat 1985:261 [ref. 11441], Suzuki & Taki 1988 [ref. 12747], Kottelat 1989:6 [ref. 13605]). Cyprinidae.

Catochaenum Cantor 1849:1037 [55] [ref. 715]. *Gerres vaigensis* Quoy & Gaimard 1824:292. Type by being a replacement name. Unneeded replacement for *Gerres* Cuvier 1824, apparently not preoccupied by *Gerris* (Latr.) Fabricius 1794 in Hemiptera. On p. 55 of separate. Objective synonym of *Podager* Gistel 1848. Synonym of *Gerres* Quoy & Gaimard 1824 (Roux 1986:325 [6209]). Gerreidae.

Catonotus Agassiz 1854:305 [ref. 69]. Masc. *Catonotus lineolatus* Agassiz 1854:305. Type by monotypy. Synonym of *Etheostoma* Rafinesque 1819, but as a valid subgenus (Collette & Banarescu 1977:1456 [ref. 5845], Page 1981:40 [ref. 3347], Mayden 1985 [ref. 6631, Braasch & Mayden 1985 [ref. 6874], Bailey & Etnier 1988:24 [ref. 6873]). Percidae.

Catophorhynchus Troschel (ex Bibron) 1856:88 [ref. 12559]. Masc. *Catophorhynchus lampris* Bibron in Duméril 1855:280. Appeared first as "Catophorhynque" Bibron in Duméril 1855:280 [ref. 297]. Latinized by Troschel 1856 as above, and by Hollard 1857:319 [ref. 2186]. First technical addition of species not researched. *C. lampris* as name only in Duméril 1855; perhaps never published in an available way. Type above as given by Jordan 1919:263 [ref. 2410]. Treated with question in the synonymy of *Lagocephalus* Swainson 1839 by Fraser-Brunner 1943:9 [ref. 1495]. Tetraodontidae.

Catopra Bleeker 1851:65 [ref. 327]. Fem. *Catopra fasciata* Bleeker 1851:65. Type by monotypy. Synonym of *Pristolepis* Jerdon 1849 (Roberts 1989:165 [ref. 6439]). Nandidae: Pristolepidinae.

Catoprion Müller & Troschel 1844:96 [ref. 3070]. Masc. *Serrasalmo mento* Cuvier in Cuvier & Valenciennes 1819:369. Type by monotypy. Valid (Géry 1976:54 [ref. 14199], Géry 1977:294 [ref. 1597]). Characidae: Serrasalminae.

Catostomus Lesueur 1817:89 [ref. 2734]. Masc. *Cyprinus catostomus* Forster 1773:158. Type by absolute tautonymy. Occasionally misspelled *Catastomus*. Valid (Crabtree & Buth 1987 [ref. 6770]). Catostomidae.

Catulus Garman (ex Valmont) 1913:71 [ref. 1545]. Masc. Not an original description, but included by Jordan 1920:548 [ref. 4905]. *Catulus* Valmont, published in a rejected work, is available from Smith 1838 (which Garman cites in synonymy). In the synonymy of *Scyliorhinus* Blainville 1816 (Compagno 1988:119 [ref. 13488]). Scyliorhinidae.

Catulus (subgenus of *Scyllium*) Smith (ex Willoughby) 1838:85 [ref. 4034]. Masc. *Squalus canicula* Linnaeus 1758:234. Type by subsequent designation. Earliest type designation not researched. Type apparently not *capense* Smith as given by Jordan 1919:190 [ref. 2410] (not an included available species in Smith 1838). Preoccupied by Kniphof 1759 in insects. Synonym of *Scyliorhinus* Blainville 1816 (Springer 1979:123 [ref. 4175], Compagno 1984:355 [ref. 6846], Compagno 1988:119 [ref. 13488]). Scyliorhinidae.

Catulus Valmont de Bomare 1768:114 [ref. 4507]. Masc. Not available, published in a rejected work on Official Index (Opinion 89, Direction 32). In the synonymy of *Scyliorhinus* Blainville 1816 (Springer 1973:19 [ref. 7162], Springer 1979:123 [ref. 4175], Cappetta 1987:113 [ref. 6348], Compagno 1988:119 [ref. 13488]). Scyliorhinidae.

Caucus Bory de Saint-Vincent 1823:283 [ref. 3853]. Masc. According to Whitley 1935:136 [ref. 6396], "His new genus *Caucus* (Vol. iii, 1823, 283) is a Chilean Cyprinoid." Original not seen by us. Cypriniformes.

Caudania Roule 1935:2 [ref. 3824]. Fem. *Bathytroctes mollis* Koehler 1896:517. Type by monotypy. Synonym of *Rouleina* Jordan 1923 (Krefft 1973:91 [ref. 7166]). Alepocephalidae.

Caularchus Gill 1862:330 [ref. 1668]. Masc. *Lepadogaster reticulatus* Girard 1854:155. Type by monotypy. Synonym of *Gobiesox* Lacepède 1800 (Briggs 1955:87 [ref. 637]). Gobiesocidae: Gobiesocinae.

Caulichthys (subgenus of *Carassiops*) Ogilby 1898:784, 785 [ref. 3278]. Masc. *Asterropteryx guentheri* Bleeker 1875:112. Type by original designation. Synonym of *Hypseleotris* Gill 1863. Eleotridae.

Caulistius (subgenus of *Gobiesox*) Jordan & Evermann 1896:491 [ref. 2442]. Masc. *Gobiesox papillifer* Gilbert 1890:96. Type by original designation (also monotypic). Synonym of *Gobiesox* Lacepède 1800 (Briggs 1955:87 [ref. 637]). Gobiesocidae: Gobiesocinae.

Caulolatilus Gill 1862:240 [ref. 1664]. Masc. *Latilus chrysops* Valenciennes in Cuvier & Valenciennes 1833:366. Type by monotypy. Valid (Dooley 1978:14 [ref. 5499], Dooley 1981 [ref. 5496], Marino & Dooley 1982:152 [ref. 5498]). Malacanthidae: Latilinae.

Caulolepis Gill 1883:258 [ref. 1724]. Fem. *Caulolepis longidens* Gill 1883:258. Type by monotypy. Synonym of *Anoplogaster* Günther 1859 (Nielsen 1973:348 [ref. 6885], Woods & Sonoda 1973:387 [ref. 6899]). Anoplogastridae.

Caulophryne Goode & Bean 1896:496 [ref. 1848]. Fem. *Caulophryne jordani* Goode & Bean 1896:496. Type by monotypy. Valid (Maul 1973:666 [ref. 7171], Pietsch 1979 [ref. 3474], Amaoka in Masuda et al. 1984:105 [ref. 6441], Bertelsen in Whitehead et al. 1986:1373 [ref. 13677], Paxton et al. 1989:295 [ref. 12442]). Caulophrynidae.

Caulopsetta Gill 1893:124 [ref. 1736]. Fem. *Pleuronectes scaphus* Bloch & Schneider (ex Forster) 1801:163. Type by original designation. Synonym of *Arnoglossus* Bleeker 1862 (Norman 1934:173 [ref. 6893], Amaoka 1969:186 [ref. 105]). Bothidae: Bothinae.

Caulopus (subgenus of *Alepidosaurus*) Gill 1862:128 [ref. 1660]. Masc. *Alepidosaurus altivelis* Poey 1861:302. Type by subsequent designation. Type designated by Jordan & Gilbert 1883:276 [ref. 2476]. Correct spelling for genus of type species is *Alepisaurus*. Synonym of *Alepisaurus* Lowe 1833 (Maul 1973:201 [ref. 7171]). Alepisauridae.

Cauque Eigenmann 1928:56 [ref. 1245]. Neut. *Chirostoma mauleanum* Steindachner 1896:231. Type by original designation. Synonym of *Odontesthes* Evermann & Kendall 1906 (White 1985:17 [ref. 13551]); valid (Pequeño 1989:51 [ref. 14125]). Atherinidae: Atherinopsinae.

Cavelampus (subgenus of *Collettia*) Whitley 1933:62 [ref. 4677]. Masc. *Aethoprora perspicillata* Ogilby 1898:36. Type by original designation (also monotypic). Synonym of *Diaphus* Eigenmann & Eigenmann 1890 (Nafpaktitis 1968:22 [ref. 6979], Paxton 1979:7 [ref. 6440]). Myctophidae.

Cayennia Sauvage 1880:57 [ref. 3887]. Fem. *Cayennia guichenoti* Sauvage 1880:57. Type by monotypy. Synonym of *Gobioides* Lacepède 1800 (Maugé 1986:370 [ref. 6218]). Gobiidae.

Cazon (subgenus of *Mustelus*) de Buen 1959:53 [ref. 696]. *Mustelus maculatus* Kner & Steindachner 1866. Type by monotypy. Synonym of *Triakis* Müller & Henle 1838, but as a valid subgenus (Compagno 1988:212, 216 [ref. 13488]). Triakidae: Triakinae.

Cebidichthys Ayres 1855:59 [ref. 159]. Masc. *Cebidichthys cristigalli* Ayres 1855:58. Type by monotypy. Misspelled *Cebedichthys* by Jordan & Evermann 1898:2426 [ref. 2445]. Valid (Yatsu 1986 [ref. 5150]). Stichaeidae.

Celema Goode & Bean 1896:329 [ref. 1848]. Fem. *Porogadus nudus* Vaillant 1888:262. Type by subsequent designation. Type designated by Jordan 1920:468 [ref. 4905]. Synonym of *Porogadus* Goode & Bean 1885 (Cohen & Nielsen 1978:38 [ref. 881]). Ophidiidae: Neobythitinae.

Cenisophius (subgenus of *Leucos*) Bonaparte 1846:29 [ref. 519]. Masc. *Leucos cenisophius* Bonaparte 1845:7. Type by absolute tautonymy. Bonaparte includes "Leucos cenisophius, Bp. (Rosse, Gall.)" and if that species name is available it is the type; type given as *Leucos pauperum* by Jordan and by Fowler. Synonym of *Rutilus* Rafinesque 1820 (Howes 1981:45 [ref. 14200]). Cyprinidae.

Centaurus Kaup 1855:221 [ref. 2571]. Masc. *Ostracion boops* Richardson 1845:52. Type by monotypy. Synonym of *Ranzania* Nardo 1840 (Fraser-Brunner 1943:7 [ref. 1495], Torchio 1973:650 [ref. 6892]). Molidae.

Centracantha see *Centracanthus*. Centracanthidae.

Centracanthus Rafinesque 1810:42 [ref. 3594]. Masc. *Centracanthus cirrus* Rafinesque 1810:43. Type by monotypy. Spelled *Centracantus*, emended by plenary powers of ICZN to *Centracanthus* and placed on Official List (Opinion 960); *Centracantha* Rafinesque 1810:67 (incorrect subsequent spelling) and *Centracantus* placed on Official Index. Valid (Tortonese et al. 1973:417 [ref. 7202], Johnson 1980:11 [ref. 13553], Tortonese in Whitehead et al. 1986:908 [ref. 13676]). Centracanthidae.

Centracion Gray 1831:5 [ref. 1880]. Neut. *Centracion zebra* Gray 1831:5. Type by monotypy. Perhaps intended for *Cestracion* but unclear from text. Synonym of *Heterodontus* Blainville 1816 (Compagno 1984:155 [ref. 6474]). Heterodontidae.

Centranodon Lacepède 1803:138 [ref. 4930]. Masc. *Centranodon japonicus* Lacepède 1803:138, 139. Type by monotypy. *Silurus imberbus* cited in synonymy. Regarded as unidentifiable, perhaps a synonym of *Platycephalus* Bloch 1795 (Jordan 1917:66 [ref. 2407]). Platycephalidae.

Centrarchops Fowler 1923:2 [ref. 1399]. Masc. *Centrarchops chapini* Fowler 1923:2. Type by original designation (also monotypic). Valid, in family Dinopercidae (Heemstra & Hecht 1986:14 [ref. 5971]). Dinopercidae.

Centrarchus Cuvier 1829:147 [ref. 995]. Masc. *Labrus irideus* Lacepède 1802:716. Type by subsequent designation. Type designated by Bleeker 1876:249 [ref. 447] as *irideus*; but Cuvier listed this species only as "*Labre iris*, Lac. ... que est aussi son *labre macroptére...*" Jordan 1917:126 [ref. 2407] listed the type as *Cychla aenea* Lesueur (one of two species [also *C. sparoides*] listed by Cuvier in latinized form). Valid. Centrarchidae.

Centratherina Regan 1914:283 [ref. 3660]. Fem. *Rhombatractus crassispinosus* Weber 1913:567. Type by monotypy. Synonym of *Chilatherina* Regan 1914 (Allen 1981:283 [ref. 5515], Allen & Cross 1982:85 [ref. 6251]). Atherinidae: Melanotaeniinae.

Centridermichthys Richardson 1844:73 [ref. 3739]. Masc. *Centridermichthys ansatus* Richardson 1844:74. Type by subsequent designation. Two included species; earliest type designation not established, at least can date to Jordan 1919:222 [ref. 2410]. Cottidae.

Centrina Cuvier 1816:130 [ref. 993]. Fem. *Squalus centrina* Linnaeus 1758:233. Type by absolute tautonymy (but possibly by monotypy). *Centrina* also was used by Risso 1826:135 and others, possibly independently described [not investigated]. Swainson 1838 spelled as *Centrinus*, possibly independently selected. Objective synonym of *Oxynotus* Rafinesque 1810 (Krefft & Tortonese 1973:35 [ref. 7165], Compagno 1984:124 [ref. 6474], Cappetta 1987:59 [ref. 6348]). Squalidae.

Centriscops Gill 1862:234 [ref. 1663]. Masc. *Centriscus humerosus* Richardson 1846:56. Type by monotypy. Valid (Heemstra 1986:459 [ref. 5660], Paxton et al. 1989:407 [ref. 12442]). Centriscidae: Centriscinae.

Centriscus Cuvier 1816:350 [ref. 993]. Masc. *Balistes scolopax* Linnaeus 1758:329. Type by monotypy (synonyms in footnote). Not *Centriscus* Linnaeus 1758. Cuvier did not propose this as new (citing "L." after the genus), and it could be regarded merely as a subsequent use of the name. Synonym of *Macroramphosus* Lacepède 1803 (Wheeler 1973:273 [ref. 7190]). Centriscidae: Macroramphosinae.

Centriscus Linnaeus 1758:336 [ref. 2787]. Masc. *Centriscus scutatus* Linnaeus 1758:336. Type by monotypy. Valid (Araga in Masuda et al. 1984:84 [ref. 6441], Paxton et al. 1989:410 [ref. 12442]). Centriscidae: Centriscinae.

Centristhmus Garman 1899:47 [ref. 1540]. Masc. *Centristhmus sig-*

nifer Garman 1899:48. Type by monotypy. Synonym of *Hemanthias* Steindachner 1874 (Fitch 1982:6 [ref. 5398]). Serranidae: Anthiinae.

Centroberyx Gill 1862:238 [ref. 1664]. Masc. *Beryx lineatus* Cuvier in Cuvier & Valenciennes 1829:169. Type by subsequent designation. Earliest type designation not researched; two included species. Valid (Scott 1981:115 [ref. 5533], Shimizu in Masuda et al. 1984:109 [ref. 6441], Liu & Shen 1985 [ref. 8144], Heemstra 1986:410 [ref. 5660], Paxton et al. 1989:375 [ref. 12442]). Berycidae.

Centroblennius Gill 1861:45 [ref. 1766]. Masc. *Lumpenus nubilus* Richardson 1855:359. Type by subsequent designation. Type designated by Jordan 1919:302 [ref. 4904]. Synonym of *Lumpenus* Reinhardt 1837 (Makushok 1973:536 [ref. 6889]). Stichaeidae.

Centrobranchus Fowler 1904:754 [ref. 1363]. Masc. *Centrobranchus choerocephalus* Fowler 1904:754. Type by original designation (also monotypic). Valid (Krefft & Bekker 1973:173 [ref. 7181], Paxton 1979:7 [ref. 6440], Hulley in Whitehead et al. 1984:436 [ref. 13675], Moser et al. 1984:219 [ref. 13645], Fujii in Masuda et al. 1984:67 [ref. 6441], Hulley 1986:287 [ref. 5672], Paxton et al. 1989:255 [ref. 12442]). Myctophidae.

Centrocetus Regan & Trewavas 1932:53 [ref. 3682]. Masc. *Centrocetus spinulosus* Regan & Trewavas 1932:53. Type by monotypy. Synonym of *Melanocetus* Günther 1864 (Pietsch & Van Duzer 1980:70 [ref. 5333]). Melanocetidae.

Centrochir Agassiz in Spix & Agassiz 1829:14 [ref. 13]. Fem. *Doras crocodili* Humboldt in Humboldt & Valenciennes 1821. Type by monotypy. Type species possibly dates to 1822:181 (not located). For authorship and date see Kottelat 1988:78 [ref. 13380]. Valid (Burgess 1989:224 [ref. 12860]). Doradidae.

Centrochromis Norman 1922:534 [ref. 6475]. Masc. *Glyphidodon rudis* Poey 1861:191. Type by original designation (also monotypic). Correct spelling for genus of type species is *Gliphisodon*. Pomacentridae.

Centrodoras Eigenmann 1925:304, 309 [ref. 1244]. Masc. *Doras brachiatus* Cope 1872:270. Type by original designation (also monotypic). Valid (Burgess 1989:224 [ref. 12860]). Doradidae.

Centrodraco Regan 1913:145 [ref. 3654]. Masc. *Draconetta acanthopoma* Regan 1904:130. Type by monotypy. Valid (Nakabo 1982:355 [ref. 5507], see Fricke 1982:56 [ref. 5432], Nakabo in Masuda et al. 1984:342 [ref. 6441], Fricke in Whitehead et al. 1986:1094 [ref. 13677]). Draconettidae.

Centrogaster Houttuyn 1782:333 [ref. 2220]. Fem. *Centrogaster fuscescens* Houttuyn 1782:333. Type by subsequent designation. Type designated by Jordan 1917:44 [ref. 2407]. Misspelled *Cantrogaster* by Houttuyn on p. 332; otherwise as *Centrogaster*. Synonym of *Siganus* Forsskål 1775. Siganidae.

Centrogenys Richardson 1842:(56) 120 [ref. 3734]. Fem. *Centropristis scorpaenoides* Cuvier in Cuvier & Valenciennes 1829:48 (= *Scorpaena vaigiensis* Quoy & Gaimard 1824:324). Type by monotypy. Original not examined. Valid (Mochizuki in Masuda et al. 1984:124 [ref. 6441], Paxton et al. 1989:490 [ref. 12442]). Centrogeniidae.

Centrogobius Bleeker 1874:321 [ref. 437]. Masc. *Gobius notacanthus* Bleeker 1858:210. Type by original designation (also monotypic). Apparently a synonym of *Oplopomus* Valenciennes (ex Ehrenberg) 1837. Gobiidae.

Centrolabrus Günther 1861:383 [ref. 1967]. Masc. *Labrus exoletus* Linnaeus 1758:287. Type by subsequent designation. Type designated by Jordan 1890:605 [ref. 2392]. Valid (Bauchot & Quignard 1973:430 [ref. 7204], Richards & Leis 1984:544 [ref. 13668], Quignard & Pras in Whitehead et al. 1986:922 [ref. 13676]). Labridae.

Centrolophodes Gilchrist & von Bonde 1923:2 [ref. 5931]. Masc. *Centrolophodes irvini* Gilchrist & von Bonde 1923:Pl. 17. Type by monotypy. Synonym of *Centrolophus* Lacepède 1802 (Haedrich 1967:62 [ref. 5357]). Centrolophidae.

Centrolophus Lacepède 1802:441 [ref. 4929]. Masc. *Perca nigra* Lacepède 1802:441, 442 (= *Perca nigra* Gmelin 1789:1321). Type by monotypy. *Centrolopus* is a misspelling. Valid (Haedrich 1967:62 [ref. 5357], Haedrich 1973:559 [ref. 7216], McDowall 1981:120 [ref. 5356], Horn 1984:628 [ref. 13637], Haedrich in Whitehead et al. 1986:1178 [ref. 13677], Haedrich 1986:843 [ref. 5659]). Centrolophidae.

Centromochlus Kner 1858:430 [30] [ref. 2630]. Masc. *Centromochlus megalops* Kner 1858:430. Type by subsequent designation. On p. 30 of separate. Type designated by Bleeker 1862:7 [ref. 393]. Valid (Mees 1974:44 [ref. 2969], Burgess 1989:242 [ref. 12860], Curran 1989 [ref. 12547]). Auchenipteridae.

Centronotus Bloch & Schneider 1801:165 [ref. 471]. Masc. *Blennius gunellus* Linnaeus 1758:257. Type by subsequent designation. Type designated by Bory de Saint-Vincent, v. 7, 1835:597 [ref. 3853] (see Whitley 1935:137 [ref. 6396]). Type not *C. fasciatus* Bloch & Schneider 1801 as recorded by Jordan 1917:58 [ref. 2407]. Synonym of *Pholis* Scopoli 1777 (Makushok 1973:534 [ref. 6889], Yatsu 1981:169 [ref. 4814]). Pholidae.

Centronotus Lacepède 1801:309 [ref. 2710]. Masc. *Centronotus conductor* Lacepède 1801:311 (= *Gasterosteus ductor* Linnaeus 1758:295). Type by subsequent designation. Type designated by Jordan 1917:62 [ref. 2407]. Lacepède cited *G. conductor* L. (*sic*, for *ductor*) in synonymy; and this suggests he did not intend a new species name, *conductor* could be regarded as a misspelling. Preoccupied by Bloch & Schneider 1801 in recent fishes. Synonym of *Naucrates* Rafinesque 1810 (Hureau & Tortonese 1973:377 [ref. 7198]). Carangidae.

Centropercis Ogilby 1895:320 [ref. 3268]. Fem. *Centropercis nudivittatus* Ogilby 1895:320. Type by monotypy. Synonym of *Champsodon* Günther 1867. Uranoscopidae.

Centropholis Hilgendorf 1878:1 [ref. 2171]. Fem. *Centropholis petersii* Hilgendorf 1878:2. Type by monotypy. Synonym of *Pterycombus* Fries 1837 (Mead 1972:93 [ref. 6976], Mead 1973:388 [ref. 7199]). Bramidae.

Centropholoides Smith 1949:313 [ref. 5846]. Masc. *Pterycombus falcatus* Barnard 1927:599. Type by original designation (also monotypic). Synonym of *Pterycombus* Fries 1837 (Mead 1972:93 [ref. 6976], Mead 1973:388 [ref. 7199]). Bramidae.

Centrophorus Kner 1855:167 (footnote) [ref. 2631]. Masc. *Pareiodon microps* Kner 1855:160. Type by being a replacement name. Unneeded replacement for *Pareiodon* Kner 1855, not preoccupied by *Parodon*. Preoccupied by Müller & Henle 1837 in fishes, Chevrolet 1839 in Coleoptera, and Waldheim 1846 in Orthoptera. Objective synonym of *Pareiodon* Kner 1855. Trichomycteridae.

Centrophorus Müller & Henle 1837:115 [ref. 3067]. Masc. *Squalus granulosus* Bloch & Schneider 1801:135. Type by monotypy. Dates to Müller & Henle as above. Also in Müller & Henle 1838:89 [ref. 3066]. Valid (Krefft & Tortonese 1973:38 [ref. 7165], Compagno 1984:35 [ref. 6474], Bass et al. 1986:49 [ref. 5636], Cappetta 1987:53 [ref. 6348], Paxton et al. 1989:30 [ref. 12442], Muñoz-

Chápuli & Ramos 1989 [ref. 12834]). Squalidae.

Centrophryne Regan & Trewavas 1932:84 [ref. 3682]. Fem. *Centrophryne spinulosa* Regan & Trewavas 1932:84. Not available from Regan & Trewavas 1932 (Art. 13b). Can date to Burton 1934 in Zoological Record for 1932, p. 61, where there is a reference to the description and only one available species is mentioned. Treated as valid dating to Regan & Trewavas 1932 (Bertelsen in Whitehead et al. 1986: 1401 [ref. 13677] Centrophrynidae.

Centropodus Lacepède 1801:303 [ref. 2710]. Masc. *Scomber rhombeus* Forsskål 1775:58. Type by monotypy. Synonym of *Monodactylus* Lacepède 1801 (Desoutter 1986:338 [ref. 6212]). Monodactylidae.

Centropogon Günther 1860:128 [ref. 1963]. Masc. *Cottus australis* White 1790:266. Type by subsequent designation. Type designated by Bleeker 1876:5 [ref. 12248] and 1876:297 [ref. 450] as *Apistus australis* Cuvier & Valenciennes. Valid (Washington et al. 1984:440 [ref. 13660], Paxton et al. 1989:439 [ref. 12442]). Scorpaenidae: Tetraroginae.

Centropomus Lacepède 1802:248 [ref. 4929]. Masc. *Sciaena undecimradiatus* Lacepède 1802:250, 268 (= *Sciaena undecimalis* Bloch 1792:60). Type by subsequent designation. Type is *Sciaena undecimalis* Bloch, renamed by Lacepède as *S. undecimradiatus*. Type designated by Gill 1861:48 [ref. 1768]. Spelled *Centropoma* by Duméril 1806:333 [ref. 1151]. Valid (Rivas 1986 [ref. 5210]). Centropomidae: Centropominae.

Centropristis Cuvier 1829:145 [ref. 995]. Fem. *Centropristis nigricans* Cuvier 1829:145 (= *Coryphaena nigrescens* Bloch & Schneider 1801). Type by subsequent designation. Cuvier's *nigricans* is an unneeded substitute for *nigrescens*. Type designated by Bleeker 1874:2 [ref. 5110] and 1876:254 [ref. 447]. Spelled *Centropristes* by Cuvier in Cuvier & Valenciennes (Apr.) 1829, original in Jan.-Mar. 1829. Valid (Bortone 1977 [ref. 7059], Kendall 1984:500 [ref. 13663]). Serranidae: Serraninae.

Centropus Kner 1860:531 [ref. 2633]. Masc. *Centropus staurophorus* Kner 1860:531. Type by monotypy. Synonym of *Caracanthus* Krøyer 1845. Caracanthidae.

Centropyge Kaup 1860:138 [ref. 2583]. Fem. *Holacanthus tibicen* Cuvier in Cuvier & Valenciennes 1831:173. Type by monotypy. Valid (Araga in Masuda et al. 1984:188 [ref. 6441], Smith & Heemstra 1986:624 [ref. 5714], Kosaki 1989 [ref. 13510]). Pomacanthidae.

Centroscyllium Müller & Henle 1841:191 [ref. 3069]. Neut. *Spinax fabricii* Reinhardt 1825:16. Type by monotypy. Valid (Krefft & Tortonese 1973:40 [ref. 7165], Compagno 1984:46 [ref. 6474], Nakaya & Shirai in Masuda et al. 1984:9 [ref. 6441], Bass et al. 1986:52 [ref. 5636], Paxton et al. 1989:32 [ref. 12442]). Squalidae.

Centroscymnus Bocage & Capello 1864:263 [ref. 479]. Masc. *Centroscymnus coelolepis* Bocage & Capello 1864:263. Type by monotypy. Valid (Krefft & Tortonese 1973:40 [ref. 7165], Compagno 1984:53 [ref. 6474], Bass et al. 1986:52 [ref. 5636], Taniuchi & Garrick 1986:119 [ref. 5721], Paxton et al. 1989:32 [ref. 12442]). Squalidae.

Centroselachus Garman 1913:206 [ref. 1545]. Masc. *Centrophorus crepidater* Bocage & Capello 1864:262. Type by monotypy. Synonym of *Centroscymnus* Bocage & Capello 1864 (Krefft & Tortonese 1973:40 [ref. 7165], Compagno 1984:53 [ref. 6474]). Squalidae.

Centrurophis Kaup 1856:42 [ref. 2572]. Masc. *Ophisurus spadiceus* Richardson 1846:313. Type by subsequent designation. Type designated by Jordan 1919:271 [ref. 2410]. Also appeared in Kaup 1856:2 [ref. 2573] and as name only in Kaup in Duméril 1856 [ref. 1154]. Synonym of *Ophichthus* Ahl 1789 (Blache et al. 1973:247 [ref. 7185], McCosker et al. 1989:379 [ref. 13288]); as a valid subgenus (McCosker 1977:79, 81 [ref. 6836]). Ophichthidae: Ophichthinae.

Cephacandia Rafinesque 1815:85 [ref. 3584]. Fem. *Gasterosteus spinarella* Linnaeus 1758:297. Type by being a replacement name. As "*Cephacandia* R. [Rafinesque] *Cephalacanthus* Lac. [Lacepède]." Name only but an available (unneeded) replacement for *Cephalacanthus* Lacepède 1801. Objective synonym of *Cephalacanthus* Lacepède 1801 (Monod 1973:613 [ref. 7193]). Synonym of *Dactylopterus* Lacepède 1801. Dactylopteridae.

Cephalacanthia Agassiz 1846:71 [ref. 64]. Fem. *Gasterosteus spinarella* Linnaeus 1758:297. Type by being a replacement name. Unneeded replacement for *Cephacandia* Rafinesque 1815, itself a replacement for *Cephalacanthus* Lacepède 1801. In the synonymy of *Dactylopterus* Lacepède 1801. Dactylopteridae.

Cephalacanthus Lacepède 1801:323 [ref. 2710]. Masc. *Gasterosteus spinarella* Linnaeus 1758:297. Type by monotypy. *Cephalacanthes, Cephalocanthes, Cephalocanthus* and *Chephalacanthus* are misspellings. Valid, with *Dactylopterus* as a synonym (Monod 1973:613 [ref. 7193]); synonym of *Dactylopterus* Lacepède 1801 (Eschmeyer 1986:490 [ref. 5652]). Dactylopteridae.

Cephalakompsus Herre 1924:276 [ref. 2118]. Masc. *Cephalakompsus pachycheilus* Herre 1924:276. Type by monotypy. Also in Herre 1924:1568 [ref. 2120]; date at which latter appeared not yet fully investigated. Probably valid (Kornfield & Carpenter 1984:75 [ref. 5435]). Cyprinidae.

Cephalepis Rafinesque 1810:31, 54 [ref. 3595]. Fem. *Cephalepis octomaculatus* Rafinesque 1810:31, 54. Type by monotypy. Synonym of *Regalecus* Ascanius 1772 (Palmer 1973:329 [ref. 7195]). Synonym of *Trachipterus* Goüan 1770 (Scott 1983:172 [ref. 5346]). Trachipteridae.

Cephaleutherus Rafinesque 1810:48, 61 [ref. 3595]. Masc. *Cephaleutherus maculatus* Rafinesque 1810:48, 61. Type by monotypy. Evidently based on a deformed *Raja clavata*. *Eleutherocephalus* Agassiz 1846:71, 136 [ref. 64] is an unjustified emendation. Synonym of *Raja* Linnaeus 1758. Rajidae.

Cephalinus Gronow in Gray 1854:159 [ref. 1911]. Masc. *Cephalinus glaber* Gronow in Gray 1854:159. Type by subsequent designation. Earliest type designation not researched. Synonym of *Congiopodus* Perry 1811. Congiopodidae.

Cephalocassis Bleeker 1858:62, 98, 246 [ref. 365]. Fem. *Arius melanochir* Bleeker 1852:590. Type by subsequent designation. Species also mentioned on pp. 22, 26 et seq. Type designated by Bleeker 1862:7 [ref. 393]. Synonym of *Arius* Valenciennes 1840 (Roberts 1989:110 [ref. 6439]). Ariidae.

Cephalocottus Gracianov 1907:659 [ref. 1872]. Masc. *Cottus amblystomopsis* Schmidt 1904:89. Type by original designation (also monotypic). Original not seen. Fowler (MS) has authorship as Schmidt. Synonym of *Cottus* Linnaeus 1758. Cottidae.

Cephalofarer (subgenus of *Holocentrus*) Whitley 1933:69 [ref. 4677]. *Holocentrum sicciferum* Cope 1871:465. Type by original designation (also monotypic). Correct spelling for genus of type species is *Holocentrus*. Synonym of *Sargocentron* Fowler 1904 (Randall & Heemstra 1985:5 [ref. 5144]). Holocentridae.

Cephalogobius Bleeker 1874:320 [ref. 437]. Masc. *Gobius sublitus*

Cantor 1850:1163. Type by original designation (also monotypic). Synonym of *Glossogobius* Gill 1859. Gobiidae.

Cephalopholis Bloch & Schneider 1801:311 [ref. 471]. Fem. *Cephalopholis argus* Bloch & Schneider 1801:311. Type by monotypy. Subgenus of *Epinephelus* Bloch 1793 (Smith 1971:91 [ref. 14102], Kendall 1984:501 [ref. 13663]); valid genus (Katayama in Masuda et al. 1984:127 [ref. 6441], Heemstra & Randall 1986:516 [ref. 5667], Daget & Smith 1986:299 [ref. 6204], Smith-Vaniz et al. 1988 [ref. 9299], Paxton et al. 1989:490 [ref. 12442]). Serranidae: Epinephelinae.

Cephalopsetta Dutt & Rao 1965:180 [ref. 1167]. Fem. *Cephalopsetta ventrocellatus* Dutt & Rao 1965:181. Type by monotypy. Treated by authors as masculine, but *psetta* is feminine. Valid (Ahlstrom et al. 1984:640 [ref. 13641]). Paralichthyidae.

Cephalopsis Fitzinger 1873:152, 165 [ref. 1337]. Fem. *Squalius svallize* Heckel & Kner 1858:197. Type by subsequent designation. Type designated by Jordan 1919:369 [ref. 4904]. Not preoccupied by Rafinesque 1815 (name only) in fishes. Synonym of *Leuciscus* Cuvier 1816. Cyprinidae.

Cephalopsis Rafinesque 1815:90 [ref. 3584]. Fem. As "*Cephalopsis* R. sp. do.", meaning *Cephalopsis* Rafinesque for a species in the preceding genus (*Diodon*). Not available, name only. Diodontidae.

Cephaloptera Cuvier (ex Duméril) 1816:138 [ref. 993]. Fem. *Raja cephaloptera* Bloch & Schneider 1801:365. Type by absolute tautonymy. Synonym of *Mobula* Rafinesque 1810 (Krefft & Stehmann 1973:77 [ref. 7167]). Mobulidae.

Cephalopterus Risso (ex Duméril) 1810:14 [ref. 3755]. Masc. *Raja giorna* Lacepède 1803:666. Type by subsequent designation. Type apparently first designated by Bancroft 1829:452 [ref. 5051]. Preoccupied by Geoffroy St. Hilaire 1809 in Aves; replaced by *Pterocephalus* Swainson 1838. On Official Index (Direction 44). Synonym of *Mobula* Rafinesque 1810 (Krefft & Stehmann 1973:77 [ref. 7167], Cappetta 1987:177 [ref. 6348]). Mobulidae.

Cephaloscyllium Gill 1862:407, 408 [ref. 1783]. Neut. *Scyllium laticeps* Duméril 1853:84. Type by original designation (also monotypic). Also in Gill 1862:412 [ref. 4910]. Valid (Nakaya 1975:8 [ref. 7083], Springer 1979:37 [ref. 4175], Compagno 1984:296 [ref. 6846], Nakaya in Masuda et al. 1984:4 [ref. 6441], Bass 1986:89 [ref. 5635], Compagno 1988:110 [ref. 13488], Paxton et al. 1989:72 [ref. 12442]). Scyliorhinidae.

Cephalosilurus Haseman 1911:317 [ref. 2047]. Masc. *Cephalosilurus fowleri* Haseman 1911:317. Type by monotypy. Synonym of *Pseudopimelodus* Bleeker 1858 (Mees 1974:187 [ref. 2969]). Pimelodidae.

Cephalurus Bigelow & Schroeder 1941:73 [ref. 300]. Masc. *Catulus cephalus* Gilbert 1892:541. Type by original designation (also monotypic). Valid (Springer 1979:45 [ref. 4175], Compagno 1984:305 [ref. 6846], Compagno 1988:131 [ref. 13488]). Scyliorhinidae.

Cephalus Basilewski 1855:235 [ref. 200]. Masc. *Cephalus mantschuricus* Basilewski 1855:235. Type by monotypy. Preoccupied by Shaw 1804 in fishes; apparently not replaced. Synonym of *Hypophthalmichthys* Bleeker 1859 (Howes 1981:45 [ref. 14200]). Cyprinidae.

Cephalus (subgenus of *Gardonus*) Bonaparte 1846:30 [ref. 519]. Masc. *Cyprinus cephalus* Linnaeus 1758:322. Type by absolute tautonymy. Not preoccupied by Plumier in Lacepède 1800 (unavailable), but preoccupied by Shaw 1804 in fishes. Synonym of *Leuciscus* Cuvier 1816. Cyprinidae.

Cephalus Lacepède (ex Plumier) 1800:589 (footnote) [ref. 2709]. Masc. Not available; manuscript name, as *Cephalus palustris*, mentioned in passing and not made available by subsequent use. Synonym of *Mugil* Linnaeus 1758. Mugilidae.

Cephalus Shaw 1804:437 [ref. 4015]. Masc. *Cephalus brevis* Shaw 1804:437 (= *Tetraodon mola* Linnaeus 1758:334). Type by monotypy. *Cephalus brevis* Shaw an unneeded new name for *mola* Linnaeus. Synonym of *Mola* Koelreuter 1770. Molidae.

Cephimnus Rafinesque 1815:85 [ref. 3584]. Masc. *Perca schraetzer* Linnaeus 1758:294. Type by being a replacement name. As "*Cephimnus* R. [Rafinesque] *Gymnocephalus* Bl. [Bloch]." An available (unneeded) replacement name for and objective synonym of *Gymnocephalus* Bloch 1793. Synonym of *Acerina* Güldenstädt 1774. Percidae.

Cephus Swainson 1838:319 [ref. 4302]. Masc. *Gadus macrocephalus* Tilesius 1810:360. Type by monotypy. Also in Swainson 1839:188 and 300 [ref. 4303]. Preoccupied by Latrielle 1802 in Hymenoptera, and by Oken 1817, Billberg 1828, and Fleming 1828 in Aves. Synonym of *Gadus* Linnaeus 1758. Gadidae.

Cepola Linnaeus 1766:455 [ref. 2786]. Fem. *Cepola taenia* Linnaeus 1766:455. Type by monotypy. Spelled *Cepolus* by Duméril 1806:303 [ref. 1151]. *Coepola* is a misspelling. Monod 1973 dates to Linnaeus 1764:63 with type as *rubescens* by monotypy [not seen]. Valid (Monod 1973:368 [ref. 7193], Araga in Masuda et al. 1984:201 [ref. 6441], Tortonese in Whitehead et al. 1986:810 [ref. 13676]). Cepolidae.

Cepolophis Kaup 1856:96 [ref. 2574]. Masc. *Ophidium viride* Fabricius 1780:141. Type by subsequent designation. Type designated by Jordan 1919:272 [ref. 2410]; but second species (*montagui*) perhaps only tentatively included (p. 97), if so type is by monotypy. Correct spelling for genus of type species is *Ophidion*. Objective synonym of *Gymnelus* Reinhardt 1834 (Andriashev 1973:540 [ref. 7214], McAllister et al. 1981:835 [ref. 5431], Anderson 1982:28 [ref. 5520]). Zoarcidae.

Ceracantha Rafinesque 1815:82 [ref. 3584]. Fem. Not available, name only. Unplaced genera.

Ceratacanthus Gill 1861:57 [ref. 1766]. Masc. *Balistes aurantiacus* Mitchill 1815:468. Type by monotypy. Monacanthidae.

Ceratias Krøyer 1845:638, 648 [ref. 2692]. Masc. *Ceratias holboelli* Krøyer 1845:638. Type by monotypy. Species originally as *Holbölli*, correction mandatory. Valid (Maul 1973:674 [ref. 7171], Amaoka in Masuda et al. 1984:108 [ref. 6441], Bertelsen in Whitehead et al. 1986:1403 [ref. 13677], Pietsch 1986 [ref. 5969], Pietsch 1986:374 [ref. 5704], Paxton et al. 1989:294 [ref. 12442], Abe & Iwami 1989:80 [ref. 13580]). Ceratiidae.

Ceratichthys See *Ceraticthys* Baird & Girard. Cyprinidae.

Ceraticthys Baird & Girard 1853:391 [ref. 165]. Masc. *Ceraticthys vigilax* Baird & Girard 1853:391. Type by monotypy. Spelling changed to *Ceratichthys* Baird in Girard 1856:213 [ref. 1810]. ICZN Opinion 22 regarded *Ceratichthys* Baird in Girard 1856 as a separate genus, with type as *C. biguttatus*. Hubbs & Black 1947:18 [ref. 10851] regard *Ceraticthys* as a misspelling. Synonym of *Pimephales* Rafinesque 1820 (recent authors). Cyprinidae.

Ceratobatis Boulenger 1897:227 [ref. 540]. Fem. *Ceratobatis robertsii* Boulenger 1897:227. Type by monotypy. Synonym of *Mobula* Rafinesque 1810 (Cappetta 1987:177 [ref. 6348]). Mobulidae.

Ceratobranchia Eigenmann in Eigenmann, Henn & Wilson 1914:3

[ref. 1259]. Fem. *Ceratobranchia obtusirostris* Eigenmann in Eigenmann, Henn & Wilson 1914:4. Type by monotypy. Valid (Géry 1977:398 [ref. 1597]). Characidae.

Ceratobregma Holleman 1987:174 [ref. 6747]. Neut. *Ceratobregma helenae* Holleman 1987:175. Type by original designation. Tripterygiidae.

Ceratocaulophryne Roule & Angel 1932:500 [ref. 3826]. Fem. *Ceratocaulophryne regani* Roule & Angel 1932:500. Type by monotypy. Also appeared as new in Roule & Angel 1933:55 [ref. 3827]. Synonym of *Caulophryne* Goode & Bean 1896 (Maul 1973:666 [ref. 7171], Pietsch 1979:14 [ref. 3474]). Caulophrynidae.

Ceratocheilus Miranda-Ribeiro 1918:644 [ref. 3725]. Masc. *Ceratocheilus osteomystax* Miranda-Ribeiro 1918:644. Type by monotypy. Preoccupied by Weschi 1810 in Diptera, replaced by *Osteomystax* Whitley 1940. Synonym of *Auchenipterus* Valenciennes 1840 (Mees 1974:16 [ref. 2969]). Auchenipteridae.

Ceratocottus Gill 1859:165 [ref. 1760]. Masc. *Cottus diceraus* Pallas 1783:354. Type by monotypy. Synonym of *Enophrys* Swainson 1839 (Bolin 1944:90 [ref. 6379], Neyelov 1979:145 [ref. 3152]). Cottidae.

Ceratoglanis Myers 1938:98 [ref. 3116]. Masc. *Hemisilurus scleronema* Bleeker 1862:93. Type by original designation (also monotypic). Valid (Haig 1952:65 [ref. 12607], Burgess 1989:85 [ref. 12860], Bornbusch & Lundberg 1989:441 [ref. 12543], Kottelat 1989:14 [ref. 13605], Roberts 1989:144 [ref. 6439]). Siluridae.

Ceratoptera Müller & Henle 1837:118 [ref. 3067]. Fem. *Cephaloptera giorna* Lesueur 1824:115. Type by subsequent monotypy. Genus dates to 1837:118 as above with no included species ("...und *Ceratoptera* N., deren Typus die von Lesueur beschriebene *Cephalopter* ist;.." Also in Müller & Henle 1838:91 [ref. 3066], "*Cephaloptera*, Nob. the type of which is the *Cephaloptera* described by Lesueur" [renamed *lesueurii* by Swainson 1839]. First addition of species evidently by Bonaparte 1838:6 (of separate) [ref. 4979]. Synonym of *Manta* Bancroft 1829 (Cappetta 1987:176 [ref. 6348]). Mobulidae.

Ceratorhynchus Agassiz in Spix & Agassiz 1829:10 [ref. 13]. Masc. *Silurus militaris*. Type by monotypy. As "Ceratorhynchi" in Agassiz 1829:10 for *Silurus militaris* without author; Kottelat 1988:78 [ref. 13380] regards as available (with correction to nominative singular based on Art. 11g(i)). Also appeared as Agassiz in Bleeker 1863:108 [ref. 401] as name in synonymy and not available. Synonym of *Ageneiosus* Lacepède 1803 depending on authorship of *militaris*. Ageneiosidae.

Ceratoscopelus (subgenus of *Scopelus*) Günther 1864:405, 412 [ref. 1974]. Masc. *Scopelus maderensis* Lowe 1839:87. Type by monotypy. Described in key (p. 405) as subgenus of *Scopelus* with single corresponding species on p. 412. Valid (Krefft & Bekker 1973:174 [ref. 7181], Paxton 1979:7 [ref. 6440], Hulley in Whitehead et al. 1984:437 [ref. 13675], Moser et al. 1984:220 [ref. 13645], Fujii in Masuda et al. 1984:69 [ref. 6441], Hulley 1986:287 [ref. 5672], Paxton et al. 1989:256 [ref. 12442]). Myctophidae.

Ceratostethus Myers 1937:(138) 141 [ref. 3115]. Masc. *Neostethus bicornis* Regan 1916:14. Type by original designation (also monotypic). Valid (Roberts 1971 [ref. 5528], White et al. 1984:360 [ref. 13655], Kottelat 1989:16 [ref. 13605]); synonym of *Neostethus* Regan 1916 (Parenti 1989:269 [ref. 13486]). Phallostethidae.

Cercamia Randall & Smith 1988:7 [ref. 9278]. Fem. *Cercamia cladara* Randall & Smith 1988:7. Type by original designation. Apogonidae.

Cercomitus Weber 1913:54 [ref. 4602]. Masc. *Cercomitus flagellifer* Weber 1913:55. Type by monotypy. Misspelled *Ceromitus* by Jordan 1920:551 [ref. 4905]. Synonym of *Nemichthys* Richardson 1848 (Smith & Nielsen 1989:452 [ref. 13290]). Nemichthyidae.

Cerdale Jordan & Gilbert 1882:332 [ref. 2471]. *Cerdale ionthas* Jordan & Gilbert 1882:332. Type by monotypy. Valid (Dawson 1974:414 [ref. 7122], Birdsong et al. 1988:200 [ref. 7303]). Microdesmidae: Microdesminae.

Cerdo Gistel 1848:VIII [ref. 1822]. *Gadus callarias* Linnaeus 1758:252. Type by being a replacement name. Unneeded replacement for *Asellus* Klein, an unavailable name mentioned in passing and not accepted by Klein. In the synonymy of *Gadus* Linnaeus 1758. Gadidae.

Cerictius Rafinesque 1810:12 [ref. 3594]. Masc. *Ceritius [sic] macrourus* Rafinesque 1810:12. Type by monotypy. Apparently imaginary (Jordan 1917:78 [ref. 2407]). *Cerichthys* Agassiz 1846:74 [ref. 64] is an unjustified emendation. Unplaced genera.

Cerna Bonaparte 1833:puntata 10 [ref. 516]. *Perca gigas* Brünnich 1768:65. Type by monotypy. *Cernua* Agassiz 1846:74 [ref. 64] is an unjustified emendation. Objective synonym of *Merou* Bonaparte (Cuvier) 1831. Synonym of *Epinephelus* Bloch 1793 (C. L. Smith 1971:103 [ref. 14102], Tortonese 1973:358 [ref. 7192], Daget & Smith 1986:301 [ref. 6204]). Serranidae: Epinephelinae.

Cernua Costa 1849:1 [ref. 976]. Fem. *Cernua gigas* Costa 1849:1. Type by monotypy. As *Cernua*, pp. 1-4, published Nov. 1849. Apparently an unjustified emendation of *Cerna* Bonaparte 1833; preoccupied. Original not examined. Synonym of *Epinephelus* Bloch 1793 (Tortonese 1973:358 [ref. 7192], Daget & Smith 1986:301 [ref. 6204]). Serranidae: Epinephelinae.

Cernua Fleming 1828:212 [ref. 1339]. Fem. *Perca fluviatilis* Fleming 1828:212 (= *Perca cernua* Linnaeus 1758:294). Type by monotypy; Fleming's *fluviatilis* an unneeded substitute for *cernua*. Synonym of *Gymnocephalus* Bloch 1793 (Collette & Banarescu 1977:1453 [ref. 5845]). Percidae.

Cernua Schaeffer 1761:37 [ref. 3910]. Fem. Not available, published in a rejected work on Official Index (Opinion 345). Original not examined. In the synonymy of *Gymnocephalus* Bloch 1793 (Collette & Banarescu 1977:1453 [ref. 5845]). Percidae.

Cestracion Gill (ex Klein) 1862:403 [ref. 1783]. Neut. *Squalus zygaena* Linnaeus 1758:234. Type by original designation (also monotypic). Spelled *Cestralion* by Müller & Henle 1838:85 [ref. 3068]. Objective synonym of *Sphyrna* Rafinesque 1810 (Compagno 1984:541 [ref. 6846], Compagno 1988:362 [ref. 13488]). Sphyrnidae.

Cestracion Klein 1776:523 [ref. 4919]. Neut. Not available, published in a work that does not conform to the principle of binominal nomenclature. In the synonymy of *Sphyrna* Rafinesque 1810 (Gilbert 1973:32 [ref. 7164], Cappetta 1987:127 [ref. 6348]). Sphyrnidae.

Cestracion Ogilby (ex Walbaum after Klein) 1916:81 [ref. 3295]. Neut. *Squalus zygaena* Linnaeus 1758:234. Type by original designation (name in parentheses). Validates *Cestracion* Walbaum 1792 (rejected work). Appears to have been described independently of Gill 1862. Objective synonym of *Sphyrna* Rafinesque 1810. Sphyrnidae.

Cestracion Oken (ex Cuvier) 1817:1183 [ref. 3303]. Neut. *Squalus philippi* Bloch & Schneider 1801:134. Type by subsequent monotypy. Based on "Les Cestracions" Cuvier 1816:129 [ref. 995]. Subsequent addition of species to Oken's *Cestracion* not researched. Misspelled *Cestralion* by Müller & Henle 1838:85 [ref. 3068]. Objective synonym of *Heterodontus* Blainville 1816 (Compagno 1984:155 [ref. 6474], Cappetta 1987:70 [ref. 6348]). Heterodontidae.

Cestraeus Valenciennes in Cuvier & Valenciennes 1836:157 [ref. 1005]. Masc. *Cestraeus plicatilis* Valenciennes in Cuvier & Valenciennes 1836:157. Type by subsequent designation. Type designated by Jordan 1919:185 [ref. 2410]. Mugilidae.

Cestreus Gronow in Gray 1854:49 [ref. 1911]. Masc. *Cestreus carolinensis* Gronow in Gray 1854:49. Type by monotypy. Preoccupied by McClelland 1851 in fishes; apparently not replaced. Synonym of *Cynoscion* Gill 1861 (Chao 1978:34 [ref. 6983]). Sciaenidae.

Cestreus Klein 1777:460 [ref. 4920]. Masc. Not available, published in a work that does not conform to the principle of binominal nomenclature. In the synonymy of *Mugil* Linnaeus 1758. Mugilidae.

Cestreus McClelland 1842:150 [ref. 2925]. Masc. *Cestreus minimus* McClelland 1842:151. Type by monotypy. Refers to species described by Hamilton as an *Atherina* [*Atherina danius*] but does not mention it by name, McClelland's *C. minimus* a separate species description. Eleotridae.

Cestrorhinus (subgenus of *Squalus*) Blainville 1816:121 [ref. 306]. Masc. *Squalus zygaena* Linnaeus 1758:234. Type by subsequent designation. Type apparently first designated by Fowler 1911:77 [ref. 6398]. Objective synonym of *Sphyrna* Rafinesque 1810 (Gilbert 1973:32 [ref. 7164], Compagno 1984:541 [ref. 6846], Cappetta 1987:127 [ref. 6348], Compagno 1988:362 [ref. 13488]). Sphyrnidae.

Cetengraulis Günther 1868:383 [ref. 1990]. Fem. *Engraulis edentulus* Cuvier 1829:323. Type by subsequent designation. Type designated by Jordan & Evermann 1896:450 [ref. 2443]. Valid (Grande 1985:245 [ref. 6466], Whitehead 1967:132 [ref. 6464], Whitehead et al. 1988:381 [ref. 5725]). Engraulidae.

Cetichthys Paxton 1989:152, 161 [ref. 13435]. Masc. *Cetomimus (Psapharocetus) indagator* Rofen 1959:255. Type by original designation. Cetomimidae.

Cetomimoides Koefoed 1955:3 [ref. 5621]. Masc. *Cetomimoides parri* Koefoed 1955:3. Type by monotypy. Valid (Myers & Freihofer 1966:193 [ref. 3088]). Megalomycteridae.

Cetomimus Goode & Bean 1895:452 [ref. 5767]. Masc. *Cetomimus gillii* Goode & Bean 1895:452. Type by subsequent designation. Type designated by Jordan & Evermann 1896:549 [ref. 2443]; not by monotypy as second species was provisionally described but definitely referred to genus. Valid (Paxton 1973:214 [ref. 7183], Uyeno in Masuda et al. 1984:115 [ref. 6441], Paxton in Whitehead et al. 1986:524 [ref. 13676], Paxton & Bray 1986:433 [ref. 5703]). Cetomimidae.

Cetonurichthys Sazonov & Shcherbachev 1982:714 [ref. 3908]. Masc. *Cetonurichthys subinflatus* Sazonov & Shcherbachev 1982:715. Type by original designation (also monotypic). Macrouridae: Macrourinae.

Cetonurus (subgenus of *Macrurus*) Günther 1887:124, 143 [ref. 2013]. Masc. *Coryphaenoides crassiceps* Günther 1887:25. Type by monotypy. Valid (Marshall 1973:290 [ref. 7194], Marshall 1973:613 [ref. 6965], Fahay & Markle 1984:274 [ref. 13653], Okamura in Masuda et al. 1984:95 [ref. 6441], Geistdoerfer in Whitehead et al. 1986:650 [ref. 13676], Paxton et al. 1989:324 [ref. 12442]). Macrouridae: Macrourinae.

Cetopsis Agassiz in Spix & Agassiz 1829:8, 11 [ref. 13]. Fem. *Silurus caecutiens* Lichtenstein 1829:61. Type by subsequent designation. Type designated by Bleeker 1862:16 [ref. 393] or 1862:403 [ref. 392], also 1863:111 [ref. 401]. For authorship and date see Kottelat 1988:78 [ref. 13380]. Valid (Burgess 1989:292 [ref. 12860]). Cetopsidae.

Cetopsogiton Eigenmann & Bean in Eigenmann 1910:398 [ref. 1224]. Masc. *Cetopsis occidentalis* Steindachner 1880:47. Type by original designation. Replacement for *Paracetopsis* Eigenmann & Bean 1907, perhaps preoccupied by Bleeker (ex Guichenot) 1862 but needs more investigation. Valid (Burgess 1989:292 [ref. 12860]). Cetopsidae.

Cetopsorhamdia Eigenmann & Fisher in Eigenmann 1916:83 [ref. 1233]. Fem. *Cetopsorhamdia nasus* Eigenmann & Fisher in Eigenmann 1916:83. Type by monotypy. Valid (Stewart 1985 [ref. 6788], Stewart 1986:47 [ref. 5777], Stewart 1986:667 [ref. 5211], Burgess 1989:277 [ref. 12860]). Pimelodidae.

Cetorhinus (subgenus of *Squalus*) Blainville 1816:121 [ref. 306]. Masc. *Squalus gunnerianus* Blainville 1810:256 (= *Squalus maximus* Gunnerus 1765:33). Type by subsequent designation. Gill 1862:398 [ref. 1783] lists *S. maximus* Linn. [sic] as type (not an included species); perhaps designation can date to Jordan & Evermann 1896:51 [ref. 2443] as *gunneri* = *maximus*. Spelled *Ceterhinus* and *Ceteorhinus* by Agassiz 1846:75 [ref. 64]. *Cethorhinus* is a misspelling. Valid (Springer 1973:16 [ref. 7162], Compagno 1984:233 [ref. 6474], Bass 1986:101 [ref. 5635], Cappetta 1987:107 [ref. 6348], Paxton et al. 1989:66 [ref. 12442]). Cetorhinidae.

Cetoscarus Smith 1956:16 [ref. 4104]. Masc. *Scarus pulchellus* Rüppell 1835:25. Type by original designation. Valid (Randall & Bruce 1983:6 [ref. 5412], Randall 1986:708 [ref. 5706], Bellwood & Choat 1989:13 [ref. 13494]). Scaridae: Scarinae.

Cetostoma Zugmayer 1914:4 [ref. 4848]. Neut. *Cetostoma regani* Zugmayer 1914:4. Type by monotypy. Also in Zugmayer 1940:211 [ref. 4850]. Valid (Paxton 1973:214 [ref. 7183], Amaoka in Masuda et al. 1984:115 [ref. 6441], Paxton in Whitehead et al. 1986:525 [ref. 13676], Paxton 1989:170 [ref. 13435]). Cetomimidae.

Chabanaudetta Whitley 1931:322 [ref. 4672]. Fem. *Synaptura panoides* Bleeker 1851:440. Type by being a replacement name. Apparently an unneeded replacement for *Anisochirus* Günther 1862, not preoccupied by *Anisocheirus*. Soleidae.

Chaca Gray 1831:9 [ref. 1879]. Fem. *Chaca hamiltonii* Gray 1831:9 (= *Platystacus chaca* Hamilton 1822:140, 374). Type by monotypy. Gray's *hamiltoni* is an unneeded substitute for *P. chaca* Hamilton. Valid (Jayaram 1981:274 [ref. 6497], Roberts 1982 [ref. 6807], Brown & Ferraris 1988 [ref. 6806], Burgess 1989:152 [ref. 12860], Kottelat 1989:15 [ref. 13605], Roberts 1989:143 [ref. 6439]). Chacidae.

Chaca Valenciennes 1832:386 [ref. 12986]. Fem. *Chaca lophioides* Valenciennes 1832:386 (= *Platystacus chaca* Hamilton 1822:140, 374). Type by monotypy. Valenciennes' *lophioides* apparently is an unneeded substitute for *chaca* Hamilton. Apparently described independent of *Chaca* Gray 1831. Objective synonym of *Chaca* Gray 1831 (Roberts 1982:896 [ref. 6807]). Chacidae.

Chaenichthys Richardson 1844:12 [ref. 3740]. Masc. Unjustified emendation of *Channichthys* Richardson 1844. Channichthyidae.

Chaenobryttus Gill 1864:92 [ref. 1706]. Masc. *Calliurus melanops* Girard 1856:200. Type by original designation (also monotypic). Spelled originally as *Chaenobrythus* but that spelling regarded as a misprint by contemporary workers; if the original spelling is accepted, then *Chaenobryttus* Cope 1865:84 [ref. 907] would be an unjustified emendation. Synonym of *Lepomis* Rafinesque 1819, but as a valid subgenus. Centrarchidae.

Chaenocephalus Regan 1913:287 [ref. 3651]. Masc. *Chaenichthys aceratus* Lönnberg 1906:97. Type by monotypy. Valid (DeWitt & Hureau 1979:790 [ref. 1125], Stevens et al. 1984:563 [ref. 13633], Iwami 1985:57 [ref. 13368]). Channichthyidae.

Chaenodraco Regan 1914:13 [ref. 3661]. Masc. *Chaenodraco wilsoni* Regan 1914:14. Type by subsequent designation. Type apparently first designated by Jordan 1920:554 [ref. 4905]. Valid (Stevens et al. 1984:563 [ref. 13633], Iwami 1985:57 [ref. 13368]). Channichthyidae.

Chaenogaleus Gill 1862:400, 402 [ref. 1783]. Masc. *Hemigaleus macrostoma* Bleeker 1852:46. Type by original designation (also monotypic). Also in Gill 1862:411 [ref. 4910]. Valid (Compagno 1984:437 [ref. 6846], Cappetta 1987:118 [ref. 6348], Compagno 1988:266 [ref. 13488]). Hemigaleidae.

Chaenogobius Gill 1859:12 [ref. 1751]. Masc. *Chaenogobius annularis* Gill 1859:12. Type by monotypy. Valid (Akihito in Masuda et al. 1984:276 [ref. 6441], Birdsong et al. 1988:185 [ref. 7303]). Gobiidae.

Chaenomugil Gill 1863:169 [ref. 1681]. Masc. *Mugil proboscideus* Günther 1861:459. Type by original designation (also monotypic). Mugilidae.

Chaenophryne Regan 1925:564 [ref. 3677]. Fem. *Chaenophryne longiceps* Regan 1925:564. Type by monotypy. Valid (Maul 1973:670 [ref. 7171], Pietsch 1975 [ref. 7120], Bertelsen & Pietsch 1977:186 [ref. 7063], Bertelsen & Pietsch 1983:88 [ref. 5335], Amaoka in Masuda et al. 1984:106 [ref. 6441], Bertelsen in Whitehead et al. 1986:1385 [ref. 13677], Paxton et al. 1989:290 [ref. 12442]). Oneirodidae.

Chaenopsetta Gill 1861:50 [ref. 1766]. Fem. *Pleuronectes oblongus* Mitchill 1815:391. Type by monotypy. Synonym of *Paralichthys* Girard 1858 (Norman 1934:69 [ref. 6893], Amaoka 1969:85 [ref. 105]). Paralichthyidae.

Chaenopsis Poey in Gill 1865:141 [ref. 1676]. Fem. *Chaenopsis ocellatus [a]* Poey in Gill 1865:143. Type by monotypy. Valid (Stephens 1963:98 [ref. 4270], Acero P. 1984 [ref. 5534]). Chaenopsidae.

Chaenothorax Cope 1878:679 [ref. 945]. Masc. *Chaenothorax bicarinatus* Cope 1878:679. Type by subsequent designation. Earliest type designation not researched. Synonym of *Brochis* Cope 1871 (Nijssen & Isbrücker 1983:179 [ref. 5387]). Callichthyidae.

Chaeropsodes Gilchrist & Thompson 1909:260 [ref. 1650]. Masc. *Chaeropsodes pictus* Gilchrist & Thompson 1909:260. Type by monotypy. Labridae.

Chaetichthys Gistel 1848:XI [ref. 1822]. Masc. *Trachinus trichodon* Tilesius 1813:Pl. 15. Type by being a replacement name. Unneeded replacement for *Trichodon* Cuvier, not preoccupied by *Trichoda* or *Trichodes*. Trichodontidae.

Chaetobranchopsis (subgenus of *Chaetobranchus*) Steindachner 1875:133 [ref. 4220]. Fem. *Chaetobranchus orbicularis* Steindachner 1875:133. Type by monotypy. Cichlidae.

Chaetobranchus Heckel 1840:401 [ref. 2064]. Masc. *Chaetobranchus flavescens* Heckel 1840:402. Type by subsequent designation. Type designated by Eigenmann 1910:469 [ref. 1224]. Valid (Kullander 1986:72 [ref. 12439]). Cichlidae.

Chaetoderma see *Chaetodermis*. Monacanthidae.

Chaetodermis (subgenus of *Monacanthus*) Swainson 1839:327 [ref. 4303]. Fem. *Balistes penicilligerus* Cuvier 1816:185. Type by subsequent designation. Type designated by Bleeker 1866:12, 26 [ref. 417]. On Official List (Opinion 764); treated as masculine by ICZN but classically feminine. *Choetoderma* Swainson 1839:194 [ref. 4303], and *Chaetoderma* p. 438 are misspellings and on Official Index. Valid (Matsuura 1979:164 [ref. 7019], Tyler 1980:176 [ref. 4477] and Arai 1983:199 [ref. 14249] as *Chaetoderma*, Matsuura in Masuda et al. 1984:359 [ref. 6441]). Monacanthidae.

Chaetodipterus Lacepède 1802:503 [ref. 4929]. Masc. *Chaetodipterus plumierii* Bloch 1793:104, Pl. 211. Type by monotypy. *Chetodipterus* Rafinesque 1815:83 [ref. 3584] an incorrect subsequent spelling. Valid (Matsuura in Uyeno et al. 1983:385 [ref. 14275], Johnson 1984:465 [ref. 9681], Desoutter 1986:340 [ref. 6212]). Ephippidae.

Chaetodon Linnaeus 1758:272 [ref. 2787]. Masc. *Chaetodon capistratus* Linnaeus 1758:275. Type by subsequent designation. Type designated by Jordan & Gilbert 1883:614 [ref. 2476]. *Chetodon* Rafinesque 1815:83 [ref. 3584] is an incorrect subsequent spelling. Valid (Monod 1973:422 [ref. 7193], Burgess 1978:653 [ref. 700], Ida in Masuda et al. 1984:183 [ref. 6441], Maugé & Bauchot 1984:470 [ref. 6614], Heemstra 1986:627 [ref. 5660], Nalbant 1986:169 [ref. 6135]). Chaetodontidae.

Chaetodontoplus Bleeker 1876:307 [ref. 448]. Masc. *Holacanthus septentrionalis* Temminck & Schlegel 1844:82. Type by original designation (also monotypic in ref. 448). Also in Bleeker 1876:Pl.368, 369 [ref. 6835] (earliest not determined). Valid (Yasuda & Tominaga 1976 [ref. 5505], Ida in Masuda et al. 1984:187 [ref. 6441]). Pomacanthidae.

Chaetodontops (subgenus of *Tetragonoptrus*) Bleeker 1876:305 [ref. 448]. Masc. *Chaetodon collare* Bloch 1787:116. Type by original designation (also monotypic in ref. 448). Also appeared in Bleeker 1876:313 [ref. 451] and in 1876:Pl. 374 [ref. 6835] (earliest not determined). Synonym of *Chaetodon* Linnaeus 1758, but as a valid subgenus (Burgess 1978:518 [ref. 700]); valid genus (Maugé & Bauchot 1984:467 [ref. 6614]). Chaetodontidae.

Chaetolabrus Swainson 1839:171, 216 [ref. 4303]. Masc. *Chaetodon suratensis* Bloch 1790:3, Pl. 217. Type by subsequent designation. Type designated by Swain 1882:273 [ref. 5966]. Synonym of *Etroplus* Cuvier 1830. Cichlidae.

Chaetomus McClelland 1844:405 [ref. 2927]. Masc. *Chaetomus playfairii* McClelland 1844:405. Type by subsequent designation. Type not by monotypy, second species included on p. 406 [earliest type designation not researched]. Usually spelled *Choetomus* (originally with a diphthong), but McClellan's derivation is clearly based on chaeto- a lock of hair. Synonym of *Coilia* Gray 1830 (Whitehead et al. 1988:460 [ref. 5725] as *Choetomus*). Engraulidae.

Chaetopterus Schlegel in Temminck & Schlegel 1844:78 [ref. 4372]. Masc. *Chaetopterus sieboldii* Bleeker 1857:20. Type by subsequent designation. Type designated by Jordan 1919:223 [ref. 2410]. Preoccupied by Cuvier 1829 in Annelida, replaced by *Ulaula* Jordan & Thompson 1911. Synonym of *Pristipomoides* Bleeker 1852 (Allen 1985:141 [ref. 6843], Akazaki & Iwatsuki

1987:325 [ref. 6699]). Lutjanidae.

Chaetostoma Heckel in Tschudi 1846:25 [ref. 4469]. Neut. *Chaetostoma loborhynchos* Heckel in Tschudi 1846:26. Type by monotypy. Authorship from Fowler (MS), sometimes attributed to Tschudi. Spelled *Chaetostomus* by Heckel in Kner 1854:(256) 271 [ref. 2628] and others. Valid (Isbrücker 1980:59 [ref. 2303], Burgess 1989:435 [ref. 12860]). Loricariidae.

Chaeturichthys Richardson 1844:54 [ref. 3739]. Masc. *Chaeturichthys stigmatias* Richardson 1844:55. Type by monotypy. Valid (Akihito in Masuda et al. 1984:279 [ref. 6441], Birdsong et al. 1988:183, 184 [ref. 7303]). Gobiidae.

Chagunius Smith 1938:157 [ref. 4054]. Masc. *Cyprinus chagunio* Hamilton 1822:295, 387. Type by original designation (also monotypic). Valid (Jayaram 1981:123 [ref. 6497], Rainboth 1986 [ref. 5849], Rainboth 1989:24 [ref. 13537], Kottelat 1989:6 [ref. 13605]). Cyprinidae.

Chalacoclinus (subgenus of *Auchenionchus*) de Buen 1962:57 [ref. 699]. Masc. *Auchenionchus chalaco* de Buen 1962:70. Type by original designation (also monotypic). Synonym of *Auchenionchus* Gill 1860 (Stephens & Springer 1974:11 [ref. 7149]). Labrisomidae.

Chalaroderma Norman 1943:803 [ref. 3228]. Neut. *Blennius capito* Valenciennes in Cuvier & Valenciennes 1836:260. Type by original designation (also monotypic). Valid (Springer 1986:744 [ref. 5719]). Blenniidae.

Chalcalburnus Berg 1933:709 [ref. 5569]. Masc. *Cyprinus chalcoides* Güldenstädt 1771:540. Type by original designation. Valid (Economidis 1986 [ref. 5163], Bogutskaya 1987:936 [ref. 13521]). Cyprinidae.

Chalceus (subgenus of *Myletes*) Cuvier 1817:454 [ref. 1016]. Masc. *Chalceus macrolepidotus* Cuvier 1817:454. Type by monotypy. Valid (Géry 1977:342 [ref. 1597], Vari 1983:5 [ref. 5419]). Characidae.

Chalcinopelecus Holmberg 1891:190 [ref. 2192]. Masc. *Chalcinopelecus argentinus* Holmberg 1891:190. Type by monotypy. Synonym of *Pseudocorynopoma* Perugia (30 April) 1891, *Chalcinopelecus* published June, 1891; *Bergia* Steindachner (9 July) 1891 also a synonym but preoccupied. Characidae.

Chalcinopsis Kner 1863:226 [ref. 5002]. Fem. *Chalcinopsis striatulus* Kner 1863:226. Type by subsequent designation. Earliest type designation not researched. Also appeared as new in Kner & Steindachner 1864:31 [ref. 2649]. Synonym of *Brycon* Müller & Troschel 1844 (Howes 1982:2 [ref. 14201]). Characidae.

Chalcinus Valenciennes in Cuvier & Valenciennes 1849:258 [ref. 1014]. Masc. *Chalcinus brachipomus* Valenciennes in Cuvier & Valenciennes 1849:259. Type by subsequent designation. Type designated by Eigenmann 1910:440 [ref. 1224]. Not preoccupied by *Chalcinus* Rafinesque 1815, apparently an unjustified emendation of *Chalcis* Fabricius 1787 in Hymenoptera. Synonym of *Yriportheus* Cope 1872 (Géry 1977:343 [ref. 1597]). Characidae.

Chalinochromis Poll 1974:103 [ref. 3532]. Masc. *Chalinochromis brichardi* Poll 1974:104. Type by original designation (caption to Fig. 2), also monotypic. Valid (Bailey & Stewart 1977:28 [ref. 7230], Poll 1986:72 [ref. 6136]). Cichlidae.

Chalinops Smith 1963:552 [ref. 4129]. Masc. *Callionymus floridae* Fowler 1941:92. Type by original designation (also monotypic). Valid (Fricke 1982:70 [ref. 5432]); synonym of *Diplogrammus* Gill 1865 (Nakabo 1982:97 [ref. 3139]). Callionymidae.

Chalinura Goode & Bean 1883:198 [ref. 1838]. Fem. *Chalinura simula* Goode & Bean 1883:199. Type by monotypy. Preoccupied by Dalman 1826 in Arachnida according to Fowler (MS) [not investigated]. Spelled *Chalinurus* by Günther 1887:122, 144 [ref. 2013]. Treated as valid (Marshall 1973:297 [ref. 7194], Marshall 1973:588 [ref. 6965], Fahay & Markle 1984:274 [ref. 13653], Geistdoerfer in Whitehead et al. 1986:651 [ref. 13676]). Synonym of *Coryphaenoides* Gunner 1761, but as valid subgenus (Iwamoto & Sazonov 1988:42 [ref. 6228], Merrett 1989 [ref. 12741]). Macrouridae: Macrourinae.

Chalinurus see *Chalinura*. Macrouridae: Macrourinae.

Chalisoma (subgenus of *Capriscus*) Swainson 1839:194, 325 [ref. 4303]. Neut. *Balistes pulcherrimus* Lesson. Type by subsequent designation. Spelled *Chalisomus* on p. 194 and 438, *Chalisoma* on 325. Type designated by Swain 1882:282 [ref. 5966]. Technical first reviser not researched. Details for species not located. Synonym of *Balistes* Linnaeus 1758. Balistidae.

Chalixodytes Schultz 1943:261, 262 [ref. 3957]. Masc. *Chalixodytes tauensis* Schultz 1943:263. Type by original designation (also monotypic). Valid (Nelson 1986:737 [ref. 5698]). Creediidae.

Chamaigenes Eigenmann 1910:380 [ref. 1224]. Masc. *Aspredo filamentosus* Valenciennes in Cuvier & Valenciennes 1840:437. Type by original designation (also monotypic). Description appeared in Eigenmann 1912:120 [ref. 1227], but available from 1910 by indication of included available species. Synonym of *Aspredinichthys* Bleeker 1858 (Mees 1987:188 [ref. 11510]). Aspredinidae: Aspredininae.

Chamomuraena Kaup in Duméril 1856:201 [ref. 1154]. Fem. Not available, name only without description or indication, as *Chamomuraena vitta* in list of genera and species from Kaup manuscript. Probably a misspelling for *Channomuraena vitta* Richardson. Muraenidae: Uropterygiinae.

Champsoborus Boulenger 1909:187 [ref. 576]. Masc. *Champsoborus pellegrini* Boulenger 1909:187. Type by monotypy. Citharinidae: Distichodontinae.

Champsocephalus Gill 1862:509 [ref. 1781]. Masc. *Chaenichthys esox* Günther 1861:89. Type by monotypy. Valid (Stevens et al. 1984:563 [ref. 13633], Iwami 1985:57 [ref. 13368], Nakamura in Nakamura et al. 1986:260 [ref. 14235]). Channichthyidae.

Champsochromis Boulenger 1915:433 [ref. 584]. Masc. *Paratilapia caerulea* Boulenger 1908:240. Type by subsequent designation. Type designated by Jordan 1920:558 [ref. 4905]. Valid (Eccles & Trewavas 1989:250 [ref. 13547]). Cichlidae.

Champsodon Günther 1867:102 [ref. 1986]. Masc. *Champsodon vorax* Günther 1867:102. Type by monotypy. Valid (Matsubara et al. 1964 [ref. 7061], Amaoka in Masuda et al. 1984:221 [ref. 6441], Heemstra 1986:734 [ref. 5660]). Champsodontidae.

Chanda Hamilton 1822:103, 370 [ref. 2031]. Fem. *Chanda nama* Hamilton 1822:109, Fig. 37. Type by designation of ICZN (Opinion 1121), not *Chanda lala* Hamilton 1822 of authors; on Official List. Some recent authors now use Chandidae instead of Ambassidae; according to information in Fowler (MS), the available names in date order are (1) Bogodidae Bleeker 1859, (2) Ambassidae Bleeker 1870, and (3) Chandidae Fowler 1905. Valid (Kottelat 1989:17 [ref. 13605, with other species formerly in *Chanda* now placed elsewhere). Ambassidae.

Chandramara Jayaram 1972:816 [ref. 2337]. *Pimelodus chandramara* Hamilton 1822:162, 375. Type by original designation (also by monotypy and absolute tautonymy). Valid (Jayaram

1977:18 [ref. 7005], Jayaram 1981:194 [ref. 6497], Tilak 1987 [ref. 6794], Burgess 1989:70 [ref. 12860]). Bagridae.

Channa Gronow 1763:135 [ref. 1910]. Fem. Not available, published in a rejected work on Official Index (Opinion 261). Channidae.

Channa Scopoli (Gronow) 1777:459 [ref. 3990]. Fem. *Channa orientalis* Bloch & Schneider 1801:496. Type by subsequent monotypy. Appeared without species; first addition of species apparently one treated by Bloch & Schneider 1801:496, lvi [ref. 471]. Valid (Uyeno & Arai in Masuda et al. 1984:122 [ref. 6441], Kottelat 1985:272 [ref. 11441], Kottelat 1989:20 [ref. 13605], Roberts 1989:169 [ref. 6439]). Channidae.

Channallabes (subgenus of *Gymnallabes*) Günther 1873:143 [ref. 2003]. Fem. *Gymnallabes apus* Günther 1873:142. Type by monotypy. Misspelled *Channalabes* in Zoological Record for 1873 and in Jordan 1919:369 [ref. 4904]; no evidence of a misprint in original. Valid (Poll 1977:148 [ref. 3533], Teugels 1986:66 [ref. 6193], Burgess 1989:145 [ref. 12860]). Clariidae.

Channichthys Richardson 1844:461 [ref. 3737]. Masc. *Channichthys rhinoceratus* Richardson 1844:462. Type by monotypy. Unjustifiably emended to *Chaenichthys* by Richardson 1844:12 [ref. 3740]. Valid (Stevens et al. 1984:563 [ref. 13633] as *Chaenichthys*, Iwami 1985:57 [ref. 13368]). Channichthyidae.

Channomuraena Richardson 1848:96 [ref. 3740]. Fem. *Ichthyophis vittatus* Richardson 1844:114. Type by monotypy. Proposed somewhat conditionally under *Nettastoma* but available from Richardson 1848:96. Originally as *Channo-Muraena*, correction mandatory. Valid (Böhlke et al. 1989:122 [ref. 13286]). Muraenidae: Uropterygiinae.

Chanodichthys Bleeker 1859:432 [ref. 370]. Masc. *Leptocephalus mongolicus* Basilewski 1855:234. Type by being a replacement name. Appeared in key, without included species or reference to Basilewski. Three species (two with question) included by Bleeker 1860:282, 400 [ref. 380]; indication that Basilewsky's name preoccupied and type designated on p. 400. Regarded as a replacement name. Valid (Kottelat 1989:6 [ref. 13605]). Cyprinidae.

Chanos Lacepède 1803:395 [ref. 4930]. Neut. *Chanos arabicus* Lacepède 1803:395 (= *Mugil chanos* Forsskål 1775:iv, 74). Type by monotypy. Lacepède's *arabicus* is an unneeded substitute for *M. chanos*. Valid (Arnoult 1984:128 [ref. 6179], Howes 1985 [ref. 5148], Winans 1985 [ref. 6784], Smith 1986:210 [ref. 5712], Kottelat 1989:5 [ref. 13605], Paxton et al. 1989:215 [ref. 12442]). Chanidae.

Chapalichthys Meek 1902:97 [ref. 2957]. Masc. *Characodon encaustus* Jordan & Snyder 1901:126. Type by original designation (also monotypic). Valid (Uyeno et al. 1983:503 [ref. 6818]). Goodeidae.

Chaparrudo de Buen 1931:15, 58 [ref. 686]. *Gobius flavescens* Fabricius 1779:322. Type by original designation (also monotypic). Objective synonym of *Gobiusculus* Duncker 1928 (Miller 1973:496 [ref. 6888]). Gobiidae.

Chapinus (subgenus of *Lactophrys*) Jordan & Evermann 1896:424 [ref. 2442]. Masc. *Ostracion bicaudalis* Linnaeus 1758:330. Type by original designation (also monotypic). Ostraciidae: Ostraciinae.

Characidium Reinhardt 1866:55 [ref. 3694]. Neut. *Characidium fasciatum* Reinhardt 1866:56. Type by monotypy. Valid (Géry 1977:115 [ref. 1597], Weitzman & Géry 1981:887 [ref. 14218], Malabarba 1989:131 [ref. 14217]). Characidae: Characidiinae.

Characini (subgenus of *Salmo*) Linnaeus 1758:311 [ref. 2787]. Not available, appeared in plural only as subgroup of *Salmo*. Of four subgroups proposed by Linnaeus in this way, two (Coregoni as *Coregonus* and Osmeri as *Osmerus*) have been validated by the ICZN. Characiformes.

Characinus Cuvier 1816:164 [ref. 993]. Masc. Apparently not intended by Cuvier as a new genus description, but listed by Jordan 1917:98 [ref. 2407]. Characidae.

Characinus Lacepède 1803:269 [ref. 4930]. Masc. *Salmo gibbosus* Linnaeus 1758:311. Type by subsequent designation. Type designated by Jordan 1917:66 [ref. 2407]. Objective synonym of *Charax* Scopoli 1777. Characidae.

Characodon Günther 1866:308 [ref. 1983]. Masc. *Characodon lateralis* Günther 1866:308. Type by monotypy. Valid (Fitzsimons 1972:731 [ref. 7117], Uyeno et al. 1983: 503 [ref. 6818]), Smith & Miller 1986 [ref. 5711]). Goodeidae.

Charalia (subgenus of *Eslopsarum*) de Buen 1945:505 [ref. 691]. Fem. *Chirostoma bartoni* Jordan & Evermann 1896:793. Type by original designation. Synonym of *Chirostoma* Swainson 1839. Atherinidae: Menidiinae.

Charax Gronow 1763:123 [ref. 1910]. Masc. Not available, published in a rejected work on Official Index (Opinion 261). Characidae.

Charax Risso 1826:353 [ref. 3757]. Masc. *Charax acutirostris* Delaroche 1809:348. Type by monotypy. Preoccupied by Scopoli 1777 in fishes; replaced by *Puntazzo* Bleeker 1876. Objective synonym of *Puntazzo* Bleeker 1876 (Tortonese 1973:413 [ref. 7192]). Sparidae.

Charax Scopoli (ex Gronow) 1777:455 [ref. 3990]. Masc. *Salmo gibbosus* Linnaeus 1758:311. Type by subsequent designation. Appeared without included species; first addition of species not researched; type designated by Eigenmann 1910:444 [ref. 1224] if *gibbosus* was an originally-included species. Valid (Géry 1977:307 [ref. 1597], Lucena 1989 [ref. 12852], Malabarba 1989:132 [ref. 14217]). Characidae.

Charaxodon Fernández-Yépez 1947:1 [ref. 4817]. Masc. *Charax metae* Eigenmann 1922:195. Type by original designation. Synonym of *Charax* Scopoli 1777 (Géry 1977:309 [ref. 1597] based on placement of type species). Characidae.

Charibarbitus Smith 1963:562 [ref. 4129]. *Charibarbitus celetus* Smith 1963:562. Type by original designation (also monotypic). Synonym of *Eleutherochir* Bleeker 1879 (Nakabo 1982:109 [ref. 3139]), synonym of *Draculo* Snyder 1911 (Fricke 1986:772 [ref. 5653]). Callionymidae.

Charisella Fowler 1939:90 [ref. 1429]. Fem. *Charisella fredericki* Fowler 1939:90. Type by original designation (also monotypic). Synonym of *Melanotaenia* Gill 1862 (Allen 1980:474 [ref. 99], Allen & Cross 1982:44 [ref. 6251]). Atherinidae: Melanotaeniinae.

Charybdia Facciolà 1885:265 [ref. 1295]. Fem. *Peloria ruppellii* Cocco in Krohn 1844:21. Type by subsequent designation. Type designation not researched, apparently two included species. Synonym of *Arnoglossus* Bleeker 1862 (Norman 1934:173 [ref. 6893]). Bothidae: Bothinae.

Chascanopsetta Alcock 1894:128 [ref. 90]. Fem. *Chascanopsetta lugubris* Alcock 1894:129. Type by monotypy. Valid (Norman 1934:249 [ref. 6893], Matsuura in Uyeno et al. 1983:460 [ref. 14275], Amaoka & Yamamoto 1984 [ref. 5632], Ahlstrom et al. 1984:642 [ref. 13641], Amaoka in Masuda et al. 1984:350 [ref. 6441], Hensley 1986:856 [ref. 5669]). Bothidae: Bothinae.

Chasmenchelys Fowler 1944:270 [ref. 1448]. Fem. *Muraena panamensis* Steindachner 1877:67. Type by original designation (also monotypic). Synonym of *Gymnothorax* Bloch 1795 (Böhlke et al. 1989:145 [ref. 13286]). Muraenidae: Muraeninae.

Chasmias Jordan & Snyder 1901:761 [ref. 2504]. Masc. *Chasmias misakius* Jordan & Snyder 1901:761. Type by original designation (also monotypic). Preoccupied by Ashmead 1900 in Hymenoptera, replaced by *Chasmichthys* Jordan 1901. Objective synonym of *Chasmichthys* Jordan 1901. Gobiidae.

Chasmichthys Jordan & Snyder 1901:941 [ref. 2507]. Masc. *Chasmias misakius* Jordan & Snyder 1901:761. Type by being a replacement name. Replacement for *Chasmias* Jordan & Snyder 1901 in fishes, preoccupied by Ashmead 1900 in Hymenoptera. Date for p. 941 is on or about 1 Nov. 1901; also in bound errata sheet (p. xv) for Proc. U. S. Natl. Mus. v. 23 (probably published later when volume was bound). Misspelled *Chiasmichthys* in Zoological Record for 1903. Valid (Akihito in Masuda et al. 1984:275 [ref. 6441], Birdsong et al. 1988:185, 187 [ref. 7303]). Gobiidae.

Chasmistes Jordan 1878:417 [ref. 2379]. Masc. *Catostomus fecundus* Jordan (not of Cope & Yarrow) 1878:417 (= *Chasmistes liorus* Jordan 1878:219). Type by original designation. First in Jordan 1878 with type in footnote *Catostomus fecundus*, then in Jordan 1878:219 [ref. 12254] where he recognized type was based on a misidentified type species which he renamed *C. liorus* (see Miller & Smith 1981:5 [ref. 5465]). Valid (Miller & Smith 1981 [ref. 5465]). Catostomidae.

Chasmocephalus Eigenmann 1910:384 [ref. 1224]. Masc. *Chasmocephalus longior*. Not available, appeared without description and with unavailable species; name changed and validly published by Eigenmann 1912:160 [ref. 1227] as *Chasmocranus*. Pimelodidae.

Chasmocranus Eigenmann 1912:131, 160 [ref. 1227]. Masc. *Chasmocranus longior* Eigenmann 1912:160. Type by original designation. Appeared first as *Chasmocephalus* (name only) and species *Chasmocephalus longior* (name only, along with one additional name-only species) in Eigenmann 1910:384 [ref. 1224]. *Chasmocranes* is a misspelling. Synonym of *Heptapterus* Bleeker 1858 (Mees 1974:177 [ref. 2969], but see Buckup 1988 [ref. 6635]). Pimelodidae.

Chasmodes Valenciennes in Cuvier & Valenciennes 1836:295 [ref. 1005]. Masc. *Blennius bosquianus* Lacepède 1800:493. Type by subsequent designation. Type designated by Eigenmann 1910:482 [ref. 1224]. Valid (Williams 1983 [ref. 5370]). Blenniidae.

Chatoessus Cuvier 1829:320 [ref. 995]. Masc. *Megalops cepediana* Lesueur 1818:361. Type by subsequent designation. Type designated by Valenciennes in Cuvier & Valenciennes 1848:94 [ref. 1013]; see Whitehead 1967:96 [ref. 6464]. Synonym of *Dorosoma* Rafinesque 1820 (Whitehead 1985:232 [ref. 5141]). Clupeidae.

Chatrabus Smith 1949:424 [ref. 5846]. Masc. *Batrachoides melanurus* Barnard 1927:994. Type by original designation. Valid (Hutchins 1986:359 [ref. 5673]). Batrachoididae.

Chaudhuria Annandale 1918:40 [ref. 127]. Fem. *Chaudhuria caudata* Annandale 1918:41. Type by original designation (also monotypic). Valid (Jayaram 1981:39 [ref. 6497], Travers 1984:142 [ref. 5147], Kottelat 1985:275 [ref. 11441], Kottelat 1989:20 [ref. 13605]). Chaudhuriidae.

Chauliodus Bloch & Schneider 1801:430 [ref. 471]. Masc. *Chauliodus sloani* Bloch & Schneider 1801:430. Type by monotypy. *Chauliodes* Risso 1826:441 [ref. 3757] is an incorrect subsequent spelling. *Schauliodus* Osório 1909:38 [ref. 13412] is (an intentional) unjustified emendation. Valid (Morrow 1973:130 [ref. 7175], Parin & Novikova 1974 [ref. 7528], Gibbs in Whitehead et al. 1984:336 [ref. 13675], Fujii in Masuda et al. 1984:48 [ref. 6441], Fink 1985:11 [ref. 5171], Gibbs 1986:230 [ref. 5655], Paxton et al. 1989:205 [ref. 12442]). Chauliodontidae.

Chaunax Lowe 1846:81 [ref. 2834]. Masc. *Chaunax pictus* Lowe 1846:82. Type by monotypy. Apparently appeared first as above; also in Ann. Mag. Nat. Hist. (1846) v. 18:416-418 and Trans. Zool. Soc. London (1849) v. 3:339-344 [relative dates not determined]. Valid (Monod 1973:665 [ref. 7193], Le Danois 1979 [ref. 6972], Le Danois 1984 [ref. 12846], Okamura in Masuda et al. 1984:104 [ref. 6441], Smith 1986:370 [ref. 5712], Caruso & Pietsch in Whitehead et al. 1986:1369 [ref. 13677], Caruso 1989:158 [ref. 9287], Paxton et al. 1989:282 [ref. 12442]). Chaunacidae.

Chedrus (subgenus of *Catastomus [sic]*) Swainson 1839:185, 285 [ref. 4303]. Masc. *Chedrus grayii* Swainson 1839:285. Type by monotypy. Synonym of *Barilius* Hamilton 1822 (Roberts 1989:30 [ref. 6439]). Cyprinidae.

Cheilichthys (subgenus of *Tetrodon [=Tetraodon]*) Müller 1841:252 [ref. 3061]. Masc. *Tetrodon (Cheilichthys) pachygaster* Müller & Troschel 1848. No species mentioned originally; first inclusion of species apparently by Müller & Troschel 1848:677 (Shipp 1974:34 [ref. 7147]) where genus was spelled *Chilichthys*. Synonym of *Spheroides* Duméril 1806 (Shipp 1974:34 [ref. 7147]), but see also *Sphoeroides* Ananymous. Tetraodontidae.

Cheilinoides Bleeker 1851:71 [ref. 328]. Masc. *Cheilinoides cyanopleura* Bleeker 1851:72. Type by monotypy. Synonym of *Cirrhilabrus* Temminck & Schlegel 1846 (Randall 1988:202 [ref. 14253]). Labridae.

Cheilinus Lacepède 1801:529 [ref. 2710]. Masc. *Cheilinus trilobatus* Lacepède 1801:529, 537. Type by subsequent designation. Type designated by Bonaparte 1841:puntata 156, fasc. 30 [ref. 512]. *Cheilinas* and *Chilinus* are early misspellings. Valid (Richards & Leis 1984:544 [ref. 13668], Yamakawa in Masuda et al. 1984:212 [ref. 6441], Randall 1986:688 [ref. 5706]). Labridae.

Cheilio Lacepède 1802:432 [ref. 4929]. Masc. *Cheilio auratus* Lacepède 1802:432, 433. Type by subsequent designation. Type designated by Bonaparte 1841:puntata 156, fasc. 30 [ref. 512]. Spelled *Chilio* in early literature. Valid (Araga in Masuda et al. 1984:204 [ref. 6441], Randall 1986:690 [ref. 5706]). Labridae.

Cheiliopsis Steindachner 1863:1113 [ref. 4206]. Fem. *Cheiliopsis bivittatus* Steindachner 1863:1113. Type by monotypy. Synonym of *Bodianus* Bloch 1790, subgenus *Trochocopus* Günther 1862 (Gomon & Madden 1981:122 [ref. 5482]). Labridae.

Cheilobarbus (subgenus of *Barbus*) Smith 1841:Pl. 10 [ref. 4035]. Masc. *Barbus (Cheilobarbus) capensis* Smith 1841:Pl. 10. Type by monotypy. Type designated by Jordan 1919:244 [ref. 2410]. Synonym of *Tor* Gray 1834 (Karaman 1971:224 [ref. 2560]). Synonym of *Barbus* Cuvier & Cloquet 1816 (Lévêque & Daget 1984:218 [ref. 6186]). Cyprinidae.

Cheilobranchus Richardson 1845:50 [ref. 3740]. Masc. *Cheilobranchus dorsalis* Richardson 1845:50. Type by subsequent designation. Earliest type designation not located, at least can date to Jordan 1919:223 [ref. 2410]. *Chilobranchus* Günther 1870:17 [ref. 1995] is an unjustified emendation. Synonym of *Alabes* Cloquet 1816 (Springer & Fraser 1976:1 [ref. 7086], Scott 1976:163 [ref. 7055]). Gobiesocidae: Cheilobranchinae.

Cheilochromis Eccles & Trewavas 1989:104 [ref. 13547]. Masc. *Haplochromis euchilus* Trewavas 1935:94. Type by original designation (also monotypic). Cichlidae.

Cheilodactylus Lacepède 1803:5 [ref. 4930]. Masc. *Cheilodactylus fasciatus* Lacepède 1803:5, 6. Type by monotypy. *Chilodactylus* Agassiz 1846:78, 80 [ref. 64] is an unjustified emendation. Valid (Smith 1980:2 [ref. 6907], Randall 1983 [ref. 5361], Smith 1986:667 [ref. 5712]). Cheilodactylidae.

Cheilodipterops Schultz 1940:(405) 413 [ref. 3952]. Masc. *Cheilodipterops isostigma* Schultz 1940:413. Type by original designation (also monotypic). Synonym of *Cheilodipterus* Lacepède 1801 (Fraser 1972:16 [ref. 5195]). Apogonidae.

Cheilodipterus Lacepède 1801:539 [ref. 2710]. Masc. *Cheilodipterus lineatus* Lacepède 1801:539, 54. Type by subsequent designation. Apparently earliest type designation is by Jordan 1917:63 [ref. 2407]. *Chilodipterus* Agassiz 1846:78 [ref. 64] is an unjustified emendation. Valid (Fraser 1972:16 [ref. 5195], Hayashi in Masuda et al. 1984:144 [ref. 6441], Gon 1986:555 [ref. 5657], Paxton et al. 1989:552 [ref. 12442]). Apogonidae.

Cheilolabrus Alleyne & Macleay 1877:345 [ref. 101]. Masc. *Cheilolabrus magnilabrus* Alleyne & Macleay 1877:345. Type by monotypy. Labridae.

Cheilonemus Storer (ex Baird) 1855:285 [ref. 4279]. Masc. *Leuciscus pulchellus* Storer 1839:90. Type by monotypy. Perhaps not intended as new; published as "Genus IV. *Cheilonemus*, Baird, MS." Authorship sometimes given as Baird in Storer, but description is apparently by Storer, so authorship should be Storer; but see *Chilonemus* Baird 1851. Cyprinidae.

Cheilopogon Lowe 1841:38 [ref. 2830]. Masc. *Cypselurus pulchellus* Lowe 1839:13. Type by subsequent monotypy. Name published in synonymy of *Cypselurus* Swainson; first use as an available name before 1961 and type designation not researched. Spelled *Chilopogon* by Woods & Schultz in Schultz et al. 1953:177 [ref. 3975]. Valid (Parin 1973:264 [ref. 7191], Collette et al. 1984:337 [ref. 11422], Parin in Whitehead et al. 1986:613 [ref. 13676], Heemstra & Parin 1986:392 [ref. 6293], Paxton et al. 1989:331 [ref. 12442]). Exocoetidae.

Cheiloprion Weber 1913:342 [ref. 4602]. Masc. *Pomacentrus labiatus* Day 1877:384. Type by original designation (also monotypic). Valid (Allen 1975:126 [ref. 97], Yoshino in Masuda et al. 1984:194 [ref. 6441]). Pomacentridae.

Cheilotrema Tschudi 1846:13 [ref. 4469]. Neut. *Cheilotrema fasciatum* Tschudi 1846:13. Type by monotypy. Sciaenidae.

Cheimarrichthys Haast 1874:103 [ref. 2026]. Masc. *Cheimarrichthys fosteri* Haast 1874:103. Type by monotypy. Spelled *Chimarrichthys* in literature. See also *Chimarrichthys* Sauvage. Valid (Randall 1984:41 [ref. 6067]). Pinguipedidae.

Cheimerius Smith 1938:292 [ref. 4067]. Masc. *Dentex nufar* Ehrenberg in Cuvier & Valenciennes 1830:764. Type by original designation (also monotypic). Valid (Akazaki in Masuda et al. 1984:177 [ref. 6441], Smith & Smith 1986:583 [ref. 5710]); subgenus of *Dentex* Cuvier 1814 (Bauchot & Hureau in Whitehead et al. 1986:886 [ref. 13676]). Sparidae.

Cheiragonus (subgenus of *Hypsagonus*) Herzenstein 1890:119 [ref. 2149]. Masc. *Hypsagonus gradiens* Herzenstein 1890:116. Type by monotypy. Synonym of *Hypsagonus* Gill 1861. Agonidae.

Cheiridodus Eigenmann 1922:(66) 70 [ref. 1243]. Masc. *Plecostomus hondae* Regan 1912:666. Type by original designation (also monotypic). Misspelled *Cheirododus* by Jordan 1923:153 [ref. 2421]. Synonym of *Cochliodon* Heckel 1854 (Isbrücker 1980:38 [ref. 2303]). Loricariidae.

Cheirocerus Eigenmann 1917:398 [ref. 1235]. Masc. *Cheirocerus eques* Eigenmann 1917:398. Type by original designation. Misspelled *Cheirocercus* in Zoological Record for 1917. Valid (Stewart & Pavlik 1985:357 [ref. 5240], Stewart 1986:668 [ref. 5211], Burgess 1989:277 [ref. 12860]). Pimelodidae.

Cheirodon Girard 1855:199 [ref. 1819]. Masc. *Cheirodon pisciculus* Girard 1855:199. Type by monotypy. *Chirodon* Günther 1864:332 [ref. 1974] is an unjustified emendation. Valid (Fink & Weitzman 1974:3 [ref. 7132], Géry 1977:562, 570 [ref. 1597], Arratia 1987 [ref. 6740], Malabarba 1989:133 [ref. 14217]). Characidae.

Cheirodontops Schultz 1944:319 [ref. 3960]. Masc. *Cheirodontops geayi* Schultz 1944:319. Type by original designation (also monotypic). Valid (Géry 1977:546 [ref. 1597]). Characidae.

Cheiromuroenesox Fowler 1944:60, 187 [ref. 1448]. Masc. *Muraenesox coniceps* Jordan & Gilbert 1881:348. Type by original designation (also monotypic). Apparently above is correct original spelling, not *Cheiromuraenesox*. Synonym of *Cynoponticus* Costa 1845 (Smith 1989:437 [ref. 13285]). Muraenesocidae.

Cheironebris Fowler 1944:179 [ref. 1448]. Fem. *Nebris occidentalis* Vaillant 1897:124. Type by original designation (also monotypic). Synonym of *Nebris* Cuvier 1830 (Chao 1978:31 [ref. 6983]). Haemulidae.

Cheiroxenichthys (subgenus of *Xenichthys*) Fowler 1930:634 [ref. 1405]. Masc. *Xenichthys agassizii* Steindachner 1875:34. Type by original designation (also monotypic). Haemulidae.

Chela (subgenus of *Cyprinus*) Hamilton 1822:258, 383 [ref. 2031]. Fem. *Cyprinus (Chela) cachius* Hamilton 1822:258, 384. Type by subsequent designation. Type designated by Bleeker 1863:215 [ref. 397], 1863:33 [ref. 4859] and 1863:264 [ref. 403]. Valid (Banarescu 1968 [ref. 215], Jayaram 1981:71 [ref. 6497], Kottelat 1985:261 [ref. 11441], Kottelat 1989:6 [ref. 13605], Roberts 1989:31 [ref. 6439]). Cyprinidae.

Chelaethiops Boulenger 1899:101 [ref. 589]. Masc. *Chelaethiops elongatus* Boulenger 1899:101. Type by monotypy. Valid (Lévêque & Daget 1984:298 [ref. 6186], Howes 1984:157 [ref. 5834]). Cyprinidae.

Chelidonichthys (subgenus of *Trigla*) Kaup 1873:87 [ref. 2585]. Masc. *Trigla hirundo* Linnaeus 1758:301. Type by subsequent designation. Type designated by Jordan & Evermann 1896:488 [ref. 2442]. Valid (Blanc & Hureau 1973:586 [ref. 7218], Ochiai & Yatou in Masuda et al. 1984:333 [ref. 6441], Heemstra 1986:487 [ref. 5660], Chen & Shao 1988:131 [ref. 6676], Paxton et al. 1989:454 [ref. 12442]). Triglidae: Triglinae.

Chelidoperca Boulenger 1895:304 [ref. 537]. Fem. *Centropristis hirundinaceus* Valenciennes in Cuvier & Valenciennes 1831:450. Type by subsequent designation. Type designated by Jordan 1920:466 [ref. 4905]. Valid (Akazaki 1972 [ref. 7148], Kendall 1984:500 [ref. 13663], Katayama in Masuda et al. 1984:133 [ref. 6441], Paxton et al. 1989:492 [ref. 12442]). Serranidae: Serraninae.

Chelmon Cloquet 1817:369? [ref. 852]. Masc. *Chaetodon rostratus* Linnaeus 1758:273. Type by subsequent designation. Based on "Chelmons" Cuvier 1816:334 [ref. 993]. Type designated by Bleeker 1876:303 [ref. 448]. Spelled *Chelmo* by Oken 1817:1182 [ref. 3303]; see Gill 1903:966 [ref. 5768], also *Chelmo* Schinz 1822 and *Chelmonus* Jarocki 1822 (not investigated). Valid (Burgess 1978:114 [ref. 700], Ida in Masuda et al. 1984:182 [ref. 6441], Maugé & Bauchot 1984:460 [ref. 6614], Nalbant 1986:170 [ref. 6135]). Chaetodontidae.

Chelmonops Bleeker 1876:304 [ref. 448]. Masc. *Chaetodon truncatus* Kner 1859:442. Type by original designation (also monotypic). Valid (Burgess 1978:142 [ref. 700], Maugé & Bauchot 1984:461 [ref. 6614], Kuiter 1986 [ref. 6020]). Chaetodontidae.

Chelon Röse 1793:118 [ref. 3833]. Masc. *Mugil chelo* Cuvier 1829:232. Type by subsequent designation. Type designated (though tentatively) by Jordan 1917:52 [ref. 2407]. Valid (Trewavas 1973:568 [ref. 7201], Ben-Tuvia in Whitehead et al. 1986:1198 [ref. 13677], Thomson 1986:344 [ref. 6215]). Mugilidae.

Cheloniger Plumier in Lacepède 1801:542 (footnote) [ref. 2710]. Masc. Not available; nonbinominal name mentioned in passing under *Cheilodipterus chrysopterus*. See remarks under Opinion 89 in Appendix B. Haemulidae.

Chelonodon (subgenus of *Tetrodon [=Tetraodon]*) Müller 1841:252 [ref. 3061]. Masc. *Tetraodon patoca* Hamilton 1822:7, 362. No species mentioned originally; first addition of species not established; Jordan 1919:196 [ref. 2410] lists type as above. Valid (Tyler 1980:341 [ref. 4477], Arai 1983:207 [ref. 14249], Leis 1984:448 [ref. 13659], Matsuura in Masuda et al. 1984:364 [ref. 6441], Smith & Heemstra 1986:900 [ref. 5714], Kottelat 1989:21 [ref. 13605]). Tetraodontidae.

Chelonodontops Smith 1958:156 [ref. 4121]. Masc. *Chelonodontops pulchellus* Smith 1958:157. Type by original designation (also monotypic). Tetraodontidae.

Chenia Fowler 1958:16 [ref. 1470]. Fem. *Plectropoma dentex* Cuvier in Cuvier & Valenciennes 1828:394. Type by being a replacement name. Replacement for *Colpognathus* Klunzinger 1880, preoccupied by Wesmael 1844 in Hymenoptera. *Chenia* Fowler itself preoccupied by Hsu 1954 in platyhelminths (according to Whitley 1965:25 [ref. 4733]); apparently not replaced. Synonym of *Othos* Castelnau 1875 (Paxton et al. 1989:506 [ref. 12442] based on placement of type species). Serranidae: Anthiinae.

Chenogaster Lahille 1903:375 [ref. 2711]. Fem. *Chenogaster holmbergi* Lahille 1903:375. Type by monotypy. Synonym of *Gasterochisma* Richardson 1845. Scombridae.

Cheonda Girard 1856:207 [ref. 1810]. Fem. *Cheonda cooperi* Girard 1856:207. Type by subsequent designation. Type designated by Jordan & Gilbert 1877:92 [ref. 4907]. Miller 1945:104 [ref. 3016] believes that *C. cooperi* is an intergeneric hybrid between *Mylocheilus* and *Richardsonius*. Cyprinidae.

Cheroscorpaena Mees 1964:1 [ref. 2967]. Fem. *Cheroscorpaena tridactyla* Mees 1964:1. Type by original designation (also monotypic). Valid (Washington et al. 1984:440 [ref. 13660], Paxton et al. 1989:439 [ref. 12442]). Scorpaenidae: Apistinae.

Cherublemma Trotter 1926:119 [ref. 4466]. Neut. *Cherublemma lelepris* Trotter 1926:119. Type by monotypy. Valid (Pequeño 1989:48 [ref. 14125]). Ophidiidae: Ophidiinae.

Chesnonia Iredale & Whitley 1969:45 [ref. 6763]. Fem. *Brachyopsis verrucosus* Lockington 1880:60. Type by being a replacement name. Replacement for *Occa* Jordan & Evermann 1898, preoccupied by Chesnon 1835 in Aves (see Bailey & Gruchy 1970 [ref. 6508]). Synonym of *Occella* Jordan & Hubbs 1925. Agonidae.

Chetia Trewavas 1961:53 [ref. 9385]. Fem. *Chetia flaviventris* Trewavas 1961:54. Type by original designation (also monotypic). Cichlidae.

Chiasmodon Johnson 1864:408 [ref. 5751]. Masc. *Chiasmodon niger* Johnson 1864:408. Type by monotypy. Also appeared in Johnson 1864:76 [ref. 2358]. Spelled *Chiasmodus* by Günther 1864:435 [ref. 1974]. Valid (Krefft 1973:452 [ref. 7166], Uyeno in Masuda et al. 1984:221 [ref. 6441], Johnson & Keene in Whitehead et al. 1986:957 [ref. 13676], Johnson & Keene 1986:731 [ref. 6303]). Chiasmodontidae.

Chiasmodus Günther 1864:435 [ref. 1974]. Masc. *Chiasmodon niger* Johnson 1863:408. Unjustified emendation of *Chiasmodon* Johnson 1863; name change unexplained. In the synonymy of *Chiasmodon* Johnson 1863. Chiasmodontidae.

Chilara Jordan & Evermann 1896:482 [ref. 2442]. Fem. *Ophidium taylori* Girard 1858:138. Type by original designation (also monotypic). Misspelled *Chilaria* by Jordan, Evermann & Clark 1930:485 [ref. 6476]. Correct spelling for genus of type species is *Ophidion*. Valid (Cohen & Nielsen 1978:15 [ref. 881]). Ophidiidae: Ophidiinae.

Chilatherina Regan 1914:282 [ref. 3660]. Fem. *Rhombatractus fasciatus* Weber 1913:565. Type by subsequent designation. Type designated by Jordan & Hubbs 1919:22 [ref. 2485]. Valid (Allen 1981 [ref. 5515], Allen & Cross 1982:85 [ref. 6251], White et al. 1984:360 [ref. 13655], Allen 1985:54 [ref. 6245]). Atherinidae: Melanotaeniinae.

Chilias Ogilby 1910:40 [ref. 3288]. Masc. *Perca stricticeps* De Vis 1884:545. Type by original designation (also monotypic). Synonym of *Parapercis* Bleeker 1863. Pinguipedidae.

Chilobrycon Géry & de Rham 1981:7 [ref. 1600]. Masc. *Chilobrycon deuterodon* Géry & de Rham 1981:8. Type by original designation (also monotypic). Characidae.

Chilochromis Boulenger 1902:236 [ref. 569]. Masc. *Chilochromis duponti* Boulenger 1902:236. Type by monotypy. Cichlidae.

Chiloconger Myers & Wade 1941:65 [ref. 3133]. Masc. *Chiloconger labiatus* Myers & Wade 1941:66. Type by original designation (also monotypic). Valid (Smith 1989:480 [ref. 13285]). Congridae: Bathymyrinae.

Chilodus Müller & Troschel 1844:85 [ref. 3070]. Masc. *Chilodus punctatus* Müller & Troschel 1844:85. Type by monotypy. Also published as new in Müller & Troschel 1848:634 [ref. 3072]. On Official List (Opinion 1150). Valid (Géry 1977:214 [ref. 1597], Vari 1983:5 [ref. 5419], Isbrücker & Nijssen 1988 [ref. 7319]). Curimatidae: Chilodontinae.

Chiloglanis Peters 1868:599 [ref. 3443]. Masc. *Chiloglanis deckenii* Peters 1868:599. Type by monotypy. Valid (Gosse 1986:107 [ref. 6194], Burgess 1989:197 [ref. 12860], Roberts 1989 [ref. 13302]). Mochokidae.

Chilogobio Berg 1914:488 [ref. 274]. Masc. *Chilogobio soldatovi* Berg 1914:492. Type by original designation. Synonym of *Sarcocheilichthys* Bleeker 1859 (Banarescu & Nalbant 1973:39 [ref. 173], Lu, Luo & Chen 1977:467 [ref. 13495]). Cyprinidae.

Chilomycterus Brisout de Barneville (ex Bibron) 1846:140 [ref. 296]. Masc. *Diodon reticulatus* of Brisout de Barneville 1846:142 (? = *Diodon reticulatus* Linnaeus 1758:334). Type by monotypy. Needs more study. Valid (Tortonese 1973:648 [ref. 7192], Tyler 1980:367 [ref. 4477], Arai 1983:207 [ref. 14249], Matsuura in Masuda et al. 1984:366 [ref. 6441], Tortonese in Whitehead et al. 1986:1346 [ref. 13677], Leis 1986:904 [ref. 5686]). Diodontidae.

Chilomyzon (subgenus of *Prochilodus*) Fowler 1906:309 [ref. 1373]. Masc. *Prochilodus steindachneri* Fowler 1906:309. Type by original designation. Synonym of *Prochilodus* Agassiz 1829. Curimatidae: Prochilodontinae.

Chilonemus Baird 1851:215 [ref. 5033]. Masc. *Chilonemus cataractus* Baird 1851:215. Type by monotypy. Description brief but apparently genus and species are available, with spelling as above. Later spelled *Cheilonemus*. Synonym of *Semotilus* Rafinesque 1820. Cyprinidae.

Chilopterus Philippi 1858:308 [ref. 3463]. Masc. *Ammocoetes caeruleus* Philippi 1858:306. Type by subsequent designation. Apparently two included species (*caeruleus* and *landbecki*), earliest subsequent designation not researched; type as listed by Fowler 1964:32 [ref. 7160]. Based on larval specimens. *Ammocoetus* would be the correct spelling for the genus of the type species. Petromyzontidae.

Chilorhinus Lütken 1852:16 [ref. 2852]. Masc. *Chilorhinus suensonii* Lütken 1852:16. Type by monotypy. Valid (Smith 1989:84 [ref. 13285]). Chlopsidae.

Chiloscyllium Müller & Henle 1837:112 [ref. 3067]. Neut. *Scyllium plagiosum* Bennett 1830:694. Type by subsequent monotypy (or designated by Gill 1861:407 [ref. 4910]). Appeared without species as above and in Müller & Henle 1837:395 [ref. 13421], then apparently next in Müller & Henle in Smith 1837:85. Spelled *Chyloscyllium* and *Cheiloscyllium* in early literature. Valid (Dingerkus & Defino 1983:7 [ref. 5386], Compagno 1984:189 [ref. 6474], Nakaya & Shirai in Masuda et al. 1984:8 [ref. 6441], Bass 1986:64 [ref. 5635]), Kharin 1987 [ref. 6227], Cappetta 1987:72 [ref. 6348], Paxton et al. 1989:89 [ref. 12442]). Hemiscylliidae.

Chilotilapia Boulenger 1908:243 [ref. 575]. Fem. *Chilotilapia rhoadesii* Boulenger 1908:243. Type by monotypy. Valid (Greenwood 1983:209 [ref. 5364], Ribbink et al. 1983:246 [ref. 13555], Eccles & Trewavas 1989:106 [ref. 13547]). Cichlidae.

Chimaera Linnaeus 1758:236 [ref. 2787]. Fem. *Chimaera monstrosa* Linnaeus 1758:236. Type by Linnaean tautonymy. On Official List (Opinion 77, Direction 56). *Chimaira* Duméril 1856 on Official Index as an incorrect subsequent spelling (Direction 56). Valid (Krefft 1973:78 [ref. 7166], Stehmann & Bürkel in Whitehead et al. 1984:212 [ref. 13675], Nakaya in Masuda et al. 1984:17 [ref. 6441], Compagno 1986:144 [ref. 5648]). Chimaeridae.

Chimarrhoglanis Vaillant 1897:81 [ref. 4489]. Masc. *Chimarrhoglanis leroyi* Vaillant 1897:82. Type by monotypy. Synonym of *Amphilius* Günther 1864 (Skelton & Teugels 1986:54 [ref. 6192]). Amphiliidae.

Chimarrichthys Sauvage 1874:332 [ref. 3873]. Masc. *Chimarrichthys davidi* Sauvage 1874:333. Type by monotypy. Spelled *Chimarrhichthys* by authors. *Euchiloglanis* Regan is an unneeded replacement; *Chimarrichthys* not preoccupied by *Cheimarrhichthys* Haast 1874 in fishes [any unjustified emendation of Haast's spelling probably would have been after 1874]. See *Euchiloglanis* Regan 1907. Sisoridae.

Chionobathyscus Andriashev & Neelov 1978:6 [ref. 123]. Masc. *Chionobathyscus dewitti* Andriashev & Neelov 1978:8. Type by original designation (also monotypic). Valid (Stevens et al. 1984:563 [ref. 13633], Iwami 1985:57 [ref. 13368]). Channichthyidae.

Chionodraco Lönnberg 1906:99 [ref. 12988]. Masc. *Chaenichthys rhinoceratus hamatus* Lönnberg 1905:47. Type by monotypy. For purposes of the type species, the subspecies *hamatus* is elevated to specific level; type not *rhinoceratus* which Lönnberg retained in *Chaenichthys*. Valid (DeWitt & Hureau 1979:794 [ref. 1125], Stevens et al. 1984:563 [ref. 13633], Iwami 1985:57 [ref. 13368]). Channichthyidae.

Chiramenu Rao 1971:183 [ref. 12524]. *Chiramenu fluviatilis* Rao 1971:184. Type by original designation (also monotypic). Valid (Jayaram 1981:352 [ref. 6497]). Gobiidae.

Chirocentrodon Günther 1868:463 [ref. 1990]. Masc. *Chirocentrodon taeniatus* Günther 1868:463. Type by monotypy. Valid (Shimizu in Uyeno et al. 1983:90 [ref. 14275], Grande 1985:244 [ref. 6466], Whitehead 1985:286 [ref. 5141]). Clupeidae.

Chirocentrus Cuvier 1816:178 [ref. 993]. Masc. *Clupea dorab* Forsskål 1775:XIII, 7. Type by monotypy (with synonyms mentioned in footnote). Valid (Bardack 1965:68 [ref. 6370], Uyeno in Masuda et al. 1984:20 [ref. 6441], Grande 1985:246 [ref. 6466], Whitehead 1985:23 [ref. 5141], Luther 1986 [ref. 6795], Whitehead 1986:207 [ref. 6285], Paxton et al. 1989:163 [ref. 12442]). Chirocentridae.

Chirodactylus Gill 1862:119 [ref. 1658]. Masc. *Cheilodactylus antonii* Valenciennes in Cuvier & Valenciennes 1833:494. Type by original designation (also monotypic). Valid (Smith 1986:667 [ref. 5712]). Cheilodactylidae.

Chirolophis Swainson 1838:71 [ref. 4302]. Masc. *Blennius yarellii* Valenciennes in Cuvier & Valenciennes 1836:218. Type by subsequent monotypy. Appeared first without species; one species in Swainson 1839:182 and 275 [ref. 4303]. Valid (Makushok 1973:532 [ref. 6889], Amaoka & Miki in Masuda et al. 1984:301 [ref. 6441], Makushok in Whitehead et al. 1986:1122 [ref. 13677]). Stichaeidae.

Chirolophius Regan 1903:279 [ref. 3616]. Masc. *Lophius naresi* Günther 1880:56. Type by subsequent designation. Type apparently designated first by Jordan 1920:505 [ref. 4905]. Synonym of *Lophiodes* Goode & Bean 1896 (Caruso 1981 [ref. 5169]). Lophiidae.

Chironectes Cuvier 1817:418 et seq. [ref. 1015]. Masc. *Antennarius chironectes* Lacepède (ex Commerson) 1798:325. Type by absolute tautonymy. Type as above if species is available from 1798; species mentioned by Cuvier on p. 433 (and perhaps made available); else type by subsequent designation (not researched). Also in Oken 1917 (ex Cuvier) (see Gill 1903:966 [ref. 5768]). If *Antennarius* Commerson is available, then *Chironectes* Cuvier perhaps can be considered an unneeded replacement for it. Preoccupied by Illiger 1811 in Mammalia and Rafinesque 1814 in recent fishes. Synonym of *Antennarius*. Antennariidae.

Chironectes Rafinesque 1814:19 [ref. 3582]. Masc. *Chironectes variegatus* Rafinesque 1814. Type by monotypy. Also in Rafinesque 1815:92 [ref. 3584] as name only. Preoccupied by Illiger 1811 in mammals, replaced by *Batrachopus* Goldfus 1820. *Cheironectes* and *Chironectus* are incorrect subsequent spellings. Synonym of *Histrio* Fischer 1813 (Pietsch 1984:37 [ref. 5380]). Antennariidae.

Chironemus Cuvier 1829:146 [ref. 995]. Masc. *Chironemus georgianus* Cuvier in Cuvier & Valenciennes 1829:78. Type by subsequent monotypy. Species essentially as name only in Cuvier 1829, although species was cited with a page number in Cuvier & Valenciennes [published one month later]. Cuvier & Valenciennes (April) 1829:78 [ref. 4879] described the species and serve to fix the type by subsequent monotypy. Valid. Chironemidae.

Chirophryne Regan & Trewavas 1932:81 [ref. 3682]. Fem. *Chirophryne xenolophus* Regan & Trewavas 1932:82. Type by monotypy. Valid (Pietsch 1974:32 [ref. 5332], Pietsch 1978:16 [ref. 3473]). Oneirodidae.

Chiropsis Girard 1858:201 [ref. 1811]. Fem. *Chirus constellatus* Girard 1858:42. Type by subsequent designation. Type designated by Jordan & Evermann 1898:1866 [ref. 2444]. Synonym of

Hexagrammos Steller 1809. Hexagrammidae: Hexagramminae.

Chirostoma Swainson 1839:176, 243 [ref. 4303]. Neut. *Atherina humboldtiana* Valenciennes in Cuvier & Valenciennes 1835:479, Pl. 306. Type by monotypy. Valid (Barbour 1973 [ref. 5967], Chernoff 1986:189 [ref. 5847]). Atherinidae: Menidiinae.

Chirostomias Regan & Trewavas 1930:54 [ref. 3681]. Masc. *Chirostomias pliopterus* Regan & Trewavas 1930:54. Type by monotypy. Valid (Morrow in Morrow & Gibbs 1964:367 [ref. 6962], Morrow 1973:136 [ref. 7175], Kawaguchi & Moser 1984:171 [ref. 13642], Gibbs in Whitehead et al. 1984:344 [ref. 13675], Fink 1985:11 [ref. 5171]). Melanostomiidae.

Chirus Pallas (ex Steller) 1814:279 [ref. 3351]. Masc. *Labrax superciliosus* Pallas 1810:388. Name from Steller manuscript, published in synonymy of *Labrax superciliosus*; subsequent history of use not researched. Information on type as given by Jordan 1917:84 [ref. 2407]. Synonym of *Hexagrammos* Steller 1809. Hexagrammidae: Hexagramminae.

Chitala (subgenus of *Notopterus*) Fowler 1934:244 [ref. 1416]. *Mystus chitala* Hamilton 1822:236, 282. Type by original designation (also by absolute tautonymy). Synonym of *Notopterus* Lacepède 1800 (Roberts 1989:24 [ref. 6439]). Notopteridae.

Chitonotus Lockington 1881:141 [ref. 2819]. Masc. *Chitonotus megacephalus* Lockington 1881:142. Type by original designation. Valid (Bolin 1944:19 [ref. 6379], Washington et al. 1984:442 [ref. 13660], Yabe 1985:111 [ref. 11522]). Cottidae.

Chlamydes Jenkins 1903:503 [ref. 2341]. Fem. *Chlamydes laticeps* Jenkins 1903:503. Type by original designation (also monotypic). Synonym of *Bathygobius* Bleeker 1878 (Maugé 1986:360 [ref. 6218]). Gobiidae.

Chlamydogobius Whitley 1930:122 [ref. 4669]. Masc. *Gobius eremius* Zeitz 1896:180. Type by original designation (also monotypic). Valid (Miller 1987 [ref. 6336]). Gobiidae.

Chlamydoselachus Garman 1884:8 [ref. 1531]. Masc. *Chlamydoselachus anguineus* Garman 1884:4. Type by monotypy. Also appeared in Science, v. 3, 1884 (21 Mar.), original is 17 Jan. Unjustifiably emended to *Chlamydoselache* by Günther 1887:2 [ref. 2013]. Valid (Boeseman 1973:10 [ref. 7161], Boeseman in Whitehead et al. 1984:76 [ref. 13675], Compagno 1984:14 [ref. 6474], Nakaya & Shirai in Masuda et al. 1984:3 [ref. 6441], Bass 1986:47 [ref. 5635], Paxton et al. 1989:28 [ref. 12442]). Chlamydoselachidae.

Chlevastes Jordan & Snyder 1901:867 [ref. 2508]. Masc. *Muraena colubrina* Boddaert in Pallas 1781:56. Type by original designation (also monotypic). Synonym of *Myrichthys* Girard 1859 (McCosker 1977:78 [ref. 6836], McCosker et al. 1989:372 [ref. 13288]). Ophichthidae: Ophichthinae.

Chlidichthys Smith 1953:518 [ref. 5846]. Masc. *Chlidichthys johnvoelckeri* Smith 1954:203. Type by original designation. Appeared first in 1953 edition of Smith 1949 [ref. 5846]. Also appeared in Smith 1954:200 [ref. 4091]. Valid (Lubbock 1977:12 [ref. 7039], Smith 1986:539 [ref. 5712]). Pseudochromidae: Pseudoplesiopinae.

Chloea Jordan & Snyder 1901:78 [ref. 2509]. Fem. *Gobius castaneus* O'Shaughnessy 1875:145. Type by original designation. Apparently preoccupied [not investigated], replaced by *Chloeichthys* Whitley 1940. Gobiidae.

Chloeichthys Whitley 1940:243 [ref. 4660]. Masc. *Gobius castaneus* O'Shaughnessy 1875:145. Type by being a replacement name. Replacement for *Chloea* Jordan & Snyder 1901, apparently preoccupied [not investigated]. Gobiidae.

Chlopsis Rafinesque 1810:42, 58 [ref. 3595]. Fem. *Chlopsis bicolor* Rafinesque 1810:42, 59. Type by monotypy. Recognition of the Chlopsidae, rather than the Xenocongridae, follows Smith 1989:72 [ref. 13285]. Valid (Blache et al. 1973:233 [ref. 7185], Saldanha in Whitehead et al. 1986:555 [ref. 13676], Castle 1986:186 [ref. 5644], Lavenberg 1988 [ref. 6617], Smith 1989:92 [ref. 13285]). Chlopsidae.

Chloricthys (subgenus of *Julis*) Swainson 1839:173, 232 [ref. 4303]. Masc. *Labrus bifasciatus* Bloch 1791:131, Pl. 283. Type by subsequent designation. Type designated by Swain 1882:275 [ref. 5966]. Spelled *Chlorichthys* by authors. Synonym of *Thalassoma* Swainson 1839 (Bauchot & Quignard 1973:442 [ref. 7204]). Labridae.

Chlorophthalmus Bonaparte 1840:fasc. 27 [ref. 514]. Masc. *Chlorophthalmus agassizi* Bonaparte 1840:fasc. 27. Type by monotypy. Valid (Nielsen 1973:167 [ref. 6885], Sulak 1977:53 [ref. 4299], Sulak in Whitehead et al. 1984:413 [ref. 13675], Okamura in Masuda et al. 1984:62 [ref. 6441], Sulak 1986:264 [ref. 5720], Kotlyar & Parin 1986 [ref. 5850], Paxton et al. 1989:232 [ref. 12442]). Chlorophthalmidae: Chlorophthalminae.

Chloroscombrus Girard 1858:168 [ref. 1813]. Masc. *Micropteryx cosmopolita* Agassiz in Spix & Agassiz 1829:104. Type by subsequent designation. Type designated by Jordan & Gilbert 1883:440 [ref. 2476]. Valid (Smith-Vaniz 1984:524 [ref. 13664], Smith-Vaniz 1986:649 [ref. 5718], Gushiken 1988:443 [ref. 6697], Daget & Smith-Vaniz 1986:313 [ref. 6207]). Carangidae.

Chlorurus (subgenus of *Scarus*) Swainson 1839:(173) 227 [ref. 4303]. Masc. *Scarus gibbus* Rüppell 1828:81. Type by monotypy. Spelled *Chlorogaster* by Swainson on p. 173, without species; changed to *Chlorurus* on p. 227. Technical first reviser not researched. Scaridae: Scarinae.

Choerodon Bleeker 1849:10 [ref. 317]. Masc. *Labrus macrodontus* Lacepède 1802:451, 522. Type by monotypy. Appeared first as name only and spelled *Choirodon* in Bleeker 1845:513 [ref. 312]. *Choirodon* is a misspelling. Valid (Richards & Leis 1984:544 [ref. 13668], Yamakawa in Masuda et al. 1984:202 [ref. 6441], Randall 1986:690 [ref. 5706]). Labridae.

Choerodonoides Kamohara 1958:2 [ref. 2555]. Masc. *Choerodonoides japonicus* Kamohara 1958:2. Type by original designation (also monotypic). Labridae.

Choeroichthys Kaup 1856:55 [ref. 2575]. Masc. *Choeroichthys valencienni* Kaup 1856:55. Type by original designation. Appeared first as name only in Kaup 1853:233 [ref. 2569]. Spelled *Choeoroichthys* by Weber 1913:681 [ref. 4602]. Valid (Araga in Masuda et al. 1984:88 [ref. 6441], Dawson 1985:31 [ref. 6541], Dawson 1986:447 [ref. 5650], Paxton et al. 1989:413 [ref. 12442]). Syngnathidae: Syngnathinae.

Choerojulis Gill 1862:142 [ref. 1662]. Fem. *Halichoeres bimaculatus* Rüppell 1835:17. Type by being a replacement name. Although Gill mentioned only *Julis semicinctus*, he technically proposed as a replacement for *Halichoeres*, which he stated to be preoccupied in seals. Objective synonym of *Halichoeres* Rüppell 1835. Labridae.

Choeroplotosus Kner 1866:545 [3] [ref. 2636]. Masc. *Choeroplotosus decemfilis* Kner 1867:300. Type by subsequent monotypy. On p. 3 of separate. Also described as new in Kner 1867:300 [ref. 2638]. In 1866:545 Kner listed one species as, "*Choeroplotosus limbatus* (*Plotos. limbatus* ? C. V.)", but in 1867

(p. 300) he described the species as *Choeroplotosus decemfilis* n. sp., with "Syn.? an *Plotosus limbatus* C. V." Apparently the genus can date to 1866:545 with no definitely-included named species, with species added in 1867; type *C. decemfilis* by subsequent monotypy. Plotosidae.

Choerops Rüppell 1852:20 [ref. 3846]. Masc. *Choerops meleagris* Rüppell 1852:20. Type by monotypy. Synonym of *Choerodon* Bleeker 1849. Labridae.

Choetomus see *Chaetomus*. Engraulidae.

Chologaster Agassiz 1853:135 [ref. 67]. Fem. *Chologaster cornutus* Agassiz 1853:135. Type by monotypy. Valid. Amblyopsidae.

Chondrochilus Heckel 1843:1031, 1077 [ref. 2066]. Masc. *Chondrochilus nasicus* Heckel 1843:1031, 1077. Type by subsequent designation. Type apparently first designated by Berg 1914 [not checked], also by Jordan 1919:211 [ref. 2410]. Spelled *Chondrochylus* and *Chondrochilus* by Heckel 1843:1031 and *Chondrochilus* on p. 1077. Synonym of *Chondrostoma* Agassiz 1832 or 1835 (Elvira 1987:112 [ref. 6743]). Cyprinidae.

Chondroplites Gill 1862:126 [ref. 1659]. Masc. *Stromateus atous* Valenciennes in Cuvier & Valenciennes 1833:389. Type by original designation (also monotypic). Synonym of *Pampus* Bonaparte 1837 (Haedrich 1967:109 [ref. 5357]). Stromateidae.

Chondrorhynchus Heckel 1843:1031 [ref. 2066]. Masc. *Chondrostoma soetta* Bonaparte 1840. Type by monotypy. Preoccupied by Fischer 1814 in mammals, not replaced. Synonym of *Chondrostoma* Agassiz 1832 (Elvira 1987:112 [ref. 6743]). Cyprinidae.

Chondrostoma Agassiz 1832:132 [ref. 5111]. Neut. *Cyprinus nasus* Linnaeus 1758:325. Type by monotypy. Probably can date to Agassiz 1832 as above, with type by monotypy. Spelled *Chondrostomus* by Heckel 1843:1030 [ref. 2067]. Also in Agassiz 1835:38 [ref. 22] with type designated by Bleeker 1863:197 [ref. 397] or 1863:26 [ref. 4859] if dated to 1835. Valid (Howes 1981:47 [ref. 14200], Krupp 1985 [ref. 6394], Elvira 1987 [ref. 6743], Bogutskaya 1987:936 [ref. 13521], Bogutskaya 1988:101 [ref. 12754], Nelva 1988 [ref. 12836]). Cyprinidae.

Chonerhinos Bleeker 1854:259, 260 [ref. 345]. *Tetraodon naritus* Richardson 1848. Type by subsequent designation. Type apparently designated first by Bleeker 1865:49 [ref. 416] with genus spelled *Chonerhinus*; the original correct spelling is *Chonerhinos*. Type apparently not *Tetraodon (Arothron) modestus* Bleeker 1850. Valid (Roberts 1982 [ref. 5513] with type as *modestus*, Arai 1983:208 [ref. 14249], Kottelat 1985:275 [ref. 11441], Kottelat 1989:21 [ref. 13605], Roberts 1989:186 [ref. 6439]). Tetraodontidae.

Chonophorus Poey 1860:274 [ref. 3499]. Masc. *Chonophorus bucculentus* Poey 1860:275. Type by monotypy. According to Jordan 1919:299 [ref. 4904], *Chonophorus* Poey (1860) predates *Awaous* Steindachner 1860 [ref. 4205] by a few days; but *Awaous* Steindachner is predated by *Awaous* Valenciennes in Cuvier & Valenciennes 1837. Valid (Maugé 1986:363 [ref. 6218], but with wrong author/date); apparently should be a synonym of *Awaous* Valenciennes 1837. Gobiidae.

Chopinopsetta Whitley 1931:322 [ref. 4672]. Fem. *Pleuronectes linguatula* Linnaeus 1758:270. Type by being a replacement name. Unneeded replacement for *Eucitharus* Gill, not preoccupied by *Eucithara* Fischer 1883 in Mollusca. Objective synonym of *Eucitharus* Gill 1889 (Norman 1934:168 [ref. 6893]). Citharidae: Citharinae.

Chopraia Prashad & Mukerji 1929:188 [ref. 3558]. Fem. *Chopraia rupicola* Prashad & Mukerji 1929:188. Type by original designation (also monotypic). Synonym of *Homaloptera* van Hasselt 1823 (Roberts 1989:88 [ref. 6439]). Balitoridae: Balitorinae.

Choregon Minding 1832:119 [ref. 3022]. *Salmo thymallus* Linnaeus 1758:311. Type by monotypy. Objective synonym of *Thymallus* Linck 1790. Salmonidae: Thymallinae.

Choridactylodes Gilchrist 1902:101 [ref. 1644]. Masc. *Choridactylodes natalensis* Gilchrist 1902:102. Type by monotypy. Synonym of *Choridactylus* Richardson 1848 (Eschmeyer et al. 1979:479 [ref. 6385]). Scorpaenidae: Choridactylinae.

Choridactylus Richardson 1848:8 [ref. 3744]. Masc. *Choridactylus multibarbus* Richardson 1848:8. Type by monotypy. *Chorismodactylus* Günther 1860:89, 151 [ref. 1963] is an unjustified emendation. Valid (Eschmeyer et al. 1979 [ref. 6385], Washington et al. 1984:440 [ref. 13660], Eschmeyer 1986:464 [ref. 5652]). Scorpaenidae: Choridactylinae.

Chorimycterus Cope 1894:67 [ref. 966]. Masc. *Chorimycterus tenuis* Cope 1894:67. Type by monotypy. Characidae.

Chorinemus Cuvier in Cuvier & Valenciennes 1832:367 [ref. 1000]. Masc. *Scomberoides commersonianus* Lacepède 1801:50. Type by being a replacement name. Unneeded replacement for *Scomberoides* Lacepède 1801. A replacement name, but not recognized as such by Daget & Smith-Vaniz 1986:316 [ref. 6207]). For problem with type see *Scomberoides* Lacepède. Objective synonym of *Scomberoides* Lacepède 1801 (Smith-Vaniz & Staiger 1973:190 [ref. 7106]). Carangidae.

Chorismodactylus see *Choridactylus*. Scorpaenidae: Choridactylinae.

Chorismopelor Chevey 1927:222 [ref. 829]. Neut. *Chorismopelor joubini* Chevey 1927:222. Type by monotypy. Synonym of *Inimicus* Jordan & Starks 1904 (Eschmeyer et al. 1979:483 [ref. 6385]). Scorpaenidae: Choridactylinae.

Chorisochismus Brisout de Barneville 1846:209 [ref. 641]. Masc. *Chorisochismus nudus* of Brisout de Barneville 1846:209 (not *Cyclopterus nudus* Linnaeus 1758:260). Type by monotypy. Based on a misidentified type species; type not *Cyclopterus nudus* Linnaeus; Brisout de Barneville's specimens a misidentification of *C. dentex* Pallas 1769 (Briggs 1955:39 [ref. 637]). Valid (Briggs 1955:39 [ref. 637], Briggs 1986:379 [ref. 5643]). Gobiesocidae: Gobiesocinae.

Chorististium Gill 1862:15 [ref. 1656]. Neut. *Liopropoma rubre* Poey 1861:418. Type by original designation (also monotypic). Also spelled *Chorististum* in original description; first reviser not researched. Valid (see Morgans 1982:30 [ref. 5411]); synonym of *Liopropoma* Gill 1861 (Randall & Taylor 1988:7 [ref. 6429]). Serranidae: Liopropomatinae.

Chrinorhinus Howell Rivero 1932:8 [ref. 3765]. Masc. *Chrinorhinus torrei* Howell Rivero 1932:9. Type by monotypy. Synonym of *Neoconger* Girard 1858 (Smith 1989:60 [ref. 13285]). Moringuidae.

Chriodorus Goode & Bean 1882:431 [ref. 1840]. Masc. *Chriodorus atherinoides* Goode & Bean 1882:432. Type by monotypy. Valid (Collette et al. 1984:352 [ref. 11422]). Hemiramphidae.

Chriolax (subgenus of *Prionotus*) Jordan & Gilbert 1879:374 [ref. 2465]. Fem. *Trigla evolans* Linnaeus 1766:498. Type by subsequent designation. Type designated by Jordan & Evermann 1898:2148 [ref. 2444]. Objective synonym of *Prionotus* Lacepède 1801. Triglidae: Triglinae.

Chriolepidops Smith 1958:158 [ref. 4118]. Masc. *Chriolepidops* *nebulofasciatus* Smith 1958:158. Type by original designation (also monotypic). Synonym of *Hetereleotris* Bleeker 1874 (Akihito & Meguro 1981:331 [ref. 5508], Hoese 1986:3 [ref. 5996]). Gobiidae.

Chriolepis Gilbert 1892:557 [ref. 1626]. Fem. *Chriolepis minutillus* Gilbert 1892:558. Type by original designation (also monotypic). Valid (Böhlke & Robins 1968 [ref. 609], Hastings & Bortone 1981 [ref. 5426], Birdsong et al. 1988:189 [ref. 7303]). Gobiidae.

Chriomitra Lockington 1879:133 [ref. 2816]. Fem. *Chriomitra concolor* Lockington 1879:134. Type by monotypy. Synonym of *Scomberomorus* Lacepède 1801 (Postel 1973:473 [ref. 7208], Collette & Russo 1984 [ref. 5221]). Scombridae.

Chriomystax Ginsburg 1955:628 [ref. 5606]. Masc. *Chriomystax squamentum* Ginsburg 1955:629. Type by original designation (also monotypic). Synonym of *Chrionema* Gilbert 1905 (Iwamoto & Staiger 1976:489 [ref. 7072]). Percophidae: Bembropinae.

Chrionema Gilbert 1905:645 [ref. 1631]. Neut. *Chrionema chryseres* Gilbert 1905:645. Type by original designation. Valid (Iwamoto & Staiger 1976 [ref. 7072], Okamura in Masuda et al. 1984:289 [ref. 6441]). Percophidae: Bembropinae.

Chriope Jordan 1878:787 [ref. 2377]. *Hybopsis bifrenatus* Cope 1869:384. Type by original designation (also monotypic). Synonym of *Notropis* Rafinesque 1818 (Gilbert 1978:16 [ref. 7042]). Cyprinidae.

Chriopeoides Fowler 1939:4 [ref. 1431]. Masc. *Chriopeoides pengelleyi* Fowler 1939:5. Type by original designation. Synonym of *Cubanichthys* Hubbs 1926 (Parenti 1981:520 [ref. 7066]). Cyprinodontidae: Cubanichthyinae.

Chriopeops (subgenus of *Fundulus*) Fowler 1916:425 [ref. 1394]. Masc. *Lucania goodei* Jordan 1879:240. Type by original designation (also monotypic). Synonym of *Lucania* Girard 1859 (Parenti 1981:496 [ref. 7066]). Cyprinodontidae: Fundulinae.

Christyella Trewavas 1935:(67) 77 [ref. 4451]. Fem. *Christyella nyasana* Trewavas 1935:77. Type by monotypy. Cichlidae.

Chromanthias Whitley 1935:233 [ref. 4683]. Masc. *Chromanthias exilis* Whitley 1935:233. Type by original designation (also monotypic). Synonym of *Lepidozygus* Günther 1862 (Emery 1983:1327 [ref. 5437]). Pomacentridae.

Chromaphyosemion (subgenus of *Aphyosemion*) Radda 1971:118 [ref. 9343]. Neut. *Fundulopanchax multicolor* Meinken 1930:10. Type by original designation. Synonym of *Aphyosemion* Myers 1924 (Wildekamp et al. 1986:196 [ref. 6198]); as a valid subgenus (Parenti 1981:477 [ref. 7066]). Aplocheilidae: Aplocheilinae.

Chromichthys Guichenot in Duméril 1859:257 [ref. 1149]. Masc. *Chromichthys elongatus* Guichenot in Duméril 1859:257. Type by monotypy. Original not seen. Cichlidae.

Chromidotilapia Boulenger 1898:151 [ref. 546]. Fem. *Chromidotilapia kingsleyae* Boulenger 1898:151. Type by monotypy, other species tentatively included. Valid (Greenwood 1987:164 [ref. 6166]). Cichlidae.

Chromileptes (subgenus of *Serranus*) Swainson 1839:168, 201 [ref. 4303]. Masc. *Serranus altivelis* Valenciennes in Cuvier & Valenciennes 1828:241. Type by subsequent designation. Spelled *Cromileptes* on p. 201; first technical reviser not researched. Type designated by Bleeker 1876:257 [ref. 447] (not *S. gigas* as designated by Swain 1882:272 [ref. 5966]). *Chromidoleptes* Agassiz 1846:84, 105 [ref. 64] is an unjustified emendation. Valid (Kendall 1984:500 [ref. 13663] and Katayama in Masuda et al. 1984:132 [ref. 6441] as *Cromileptes*, Heemstra & Randall 1986:519 [ref. 5667], Paxton et al. 1989:492 [ref. 12442]). Serranidae: Epinephelinae.

Chromis Cuvier 1814:88 [ref. 4884]. Fem. *Sparus chromis* Linnaeus 1758:280. Type by original designation. Type designated in subtitle (also by absolute tautonymy). Gender ruled feminine by ICZN and name placed on Official List (Opinion 1417). Not *Chromis* Plumier in Lacepède 1801. Valid (Monod 1973:424 [ref. 7193], Bailey et al. 1980 [ref. 6875], Greenfield & Woods 1980 [ref. 5581], Randall et al. 1981 [ref. 5449], Ida in Masuda et al. 1984:192 [ref. 6441], Allen 1986:673 [ref. 5631], Randall 1988 [ref. 14250], Randall 1988:202 [ref. 14252]). Pomacentridae.

Chromis Gronow in Gray 1854:149 [ref. 1911]. Fem. *Chromis epicurorum* Gronow in Gray 1854:149. Type by monotypy. Preoccupied by Cuvier 1814 in fishes and by Huebner 1819 in Lepidoptera; not replaced. Synonym of *Pomatomus* Lacepède 1802 (Monod 1973:369 [ref. 7193]). Pomatomidae.

Chromis Günther 1862:267 [ref. 1969]. Fem. Apparently a redefinition and not intended as a new genus, since "*Chromis*, pt., Cuv. Règne Anim." is given in the synonymy. Preoccupied by Cuvier 1814 in fishes. Synonym of *Tilapia* Smith 1840. Cichlidae.

Chromis Oken (ex Cuvier) 1817:1182 [ref. 3303]. Fem. *Sparus chromis* Linnaeus 1758:280. Type by absolute tautonymy. Based on "Les Chromes" of Cuvier 1816:266. Objective synonym of *Chromis* Cuvier 1814 (Monod 1973:424 [ref. 7193]). Pomacentridae.

Chromis Plumier in Lacepède 1801:546 (footnote) [ref. 2710]. Fem. Not available; mentioned in passing in footnote under *Cheilodipterus cyanopterus* Lacepède. See remarks under Opinion 89 in Appendix B. Not *Chromis* Cuvier. Sciaenidae.

Chromogobius de Buen 1930:135, 138 [ref. 685]. Masc. *Gobius quadrivittatus* Steindachner 1863:399. Type by original designation (also monotypic). *Cromogobius* is a misspelling. Valid (Miller 1973:492 [ref. 6888], Golani & Ben-Tuvia 1986:290 [ref. 6757], Miller in Whitehead et al. 1986:1028 [ref. 13677]). Gobiidae.

Chrosomus Rafinesque 1820:237 [ref. 7310]. Masc. *Luxilus erythrogaster* Rafinesque 1820:237. Type by monotypy. Also appeared in Rafinesque 1820:47 (Dec.) [ref. 3592]. Synonym of *Phoxinus* Rafinesque 1820 (Howes 1985:66 [ref. 5274]). Cyprinidae.

Chryseis Schinz 1822:438 [ref. 3926]. Masc. *Sparus aurata* Linnaeus 1758:277. Type by subsequent designation. Earliest type designation not established; see also Whitley 1935:137 [ref. 6396]. Objective synonym of *Sparus* Linnaeus 1758. Sparidae.

Chrysichthys Bleeker 1858:60, 65 [ref. 365]. Masc. *Pimelodus auratus* Geoffroy St. Hilaire 1809:Pl. 14. Type by subsequent designation. Type designated by Bleeker 1862:9 [ref. 393] and 1863:95 [ref. 401]. Valid (Bailey & Stewart 1984:5 [ref. 5232], Risch 1986:13 [ref. 6190], Risch 1987:22 [ref. 6751], Risch 1988:3 [ref. 6735], Burgess 1989:66 [ref. 12860]). Bagridae.

Chrysiptera (subgenus of *Glyphisodon*) Swainson 1839:171, 216 [ref. 4303]. Fem. *Glyphisodon azureus* Cuvier (ex Quoy & Gaimard) in Cuvier & Valenciennes 1830:479. Type by monotypy. Also designated by Swain 1883:273 [ref. 5966]. *Chrysoptera* Agassiz 1846:84 [ref. 64] is an unjustified emendation. Not preoccupied by *Chrysoptera* Latreille in Coleoptera; *Iredaleichthys* Whitley 1928 is an unneeded replacement. Valid (Yoshino in Masuda et al. 1984:198 [ref. 6441], Allen 1986:676 [ref. 5631], Allen 1987 [ref. 5995]). Pomacentridae.

Chrysobagrus Boulenger 1899:40 [ref. 548]. Masc. *Chrysobagrus* *brevibarbis* Boulenger 1899:40. Type by subsequent designation. Earliest type designation not located; Jordan 1920:485 [ref. 4905] lists type as above; two included species. Type not *Chrysobagrus longibarbis* as designated by Jayaram 1966:1072 (see Risch 1988:14 [ref. 6190]). Bagridae.

Chrysoblephus (subgenus of *Chrysophrys*) Swainson 1839:171, 221 [ref. 4303]. *Sparus gibbiceps* Valenciennes in Cuvier & Valenciennes 1830:27. Type by monotypy. Spelled *Chrysoblepus* by Swainson 1839:171 and 442 (index) [ref. 4303]; first reviser not researched. Valid (Smith & Smith 1986:583 [ref. 5710] as *Chrysoblephus*). Sparidae.

Chrysochir Trewavas & Yazdani 1966:250 [ref. 4461]. Fem. *Otolithus aureus* Richardson 1846:224. Type by original designation (also monotypic). Correct spelling for genus of type species is *Otolithes*. Valid (Trewavas 1977:344 [ref. 4459]). Sciaenidae.

Chrysomelanus Plumier in Lacepède 1802:160 [ref. 4929]. Masc. Not available; name mentioned in passing under *Sparus chrysomelanus* Lacepède; apparently never used as a valid name or homonym if considered a name published in synonymy; see remarks under Opinion 89 in Appendix B. Synonym of *Epinephelus* Bloch 1793. Serranidae: Epinephelinae.

Chrysoperca (subgenus of *Morone*) Fowler 1907:250 [ref. 1376]. Fem. *Morone interrupta* Gill 1860:118. Type by original designation. Synonym of *Morone* Mitchill 1814. Moronidae.

Chrysophekadion Bleeker 1859:424 [ref. 370]. Neut. *Rohita chrysophekadion* Bleeker 1850:20. Type by absolute tautonymy. Apparently appeared first in key without included species; one species (with synonyms) included by Bleeker 1859:145 [ref. 371] and four more on p. 259 [ref. 380]. Synonym of *Labeo* Cuvier 1816. Cyprinidae.

Chrysophris Cuvier 1829:181 [ref. 995]. *Sparus aurita* Linnaeus 1758:277. Type by subsequent designation. Type designated by Jordan 1917:128 [ref. 2407]. Objective synonym of *Sparus* Linnaeus 1758 (Tortonese 1973:405 [ref. 7192]). Sparidae.

Chrysophrys Quoy & Gaimard 1824:299 [ref. 3574]. Fem. *Chrysophrys unicolor* Quoy & Gaimard 1824:299. Type by monotypy. As "*Chrysophrys*. Cuv." but that name (as *Chrysophris*) not validated until Cuvier 1829. Apparently *Chrysophrys* is available as above. Sparidae.

Chrysostromus Lacepède 1802:697 [ref. 4929]. *Chrysostromus fiatoloides* Lacepède 1802:697. Type by monotypy. *Chrysostosus* Rafinesque 1815:84 [ref. 3585] is an incorrect subsequent spelling. Misspelled *Chrysostroma* by authors. Synonym of *Stromateus* Linnaeus 1758 (Haedrich 1967:99 [ref. 5357], Haedrich 1973:565 [ref. 7216]). Stromateidae.

Chrysotosus Lacepède 1802:586 [ref. 4929]. Masc. *Zeus luna* Gmelin 1789:1225. Type by monotypy. Synonym of *Lampris* Retzius 1799 (Palmer 1973:328 [ref. 7195]). Lampridae.

Chthamalopteryx Ogilby 1888:616 [ref. 3263]. Fem. *Gerres melbournensis* Castelnau 1872:158. Type by monotypy. Synonym of *Parequula* Steindachner 1879. Gerreidae.

Chuanchia Herzenstein 1891:223 [ref. 4917]. Fem. *Chuanchia labiosa* Herzenstein 1891:224. Type by monotypy. Valid (Tsao 1964:191 [ref. 13501], Wu 1987:47 [ref. 12822]). Cyprinidae.

Chuco Fernández-Yépez 1969:[4] [ref. 9186]. Neut. *Cichlasoma milleri* Meek 1907:142. Type by original designation. Appeared in an obscure publication, apparently available. Treated as neuter by Fernández-Yépez. Synonym of *Cichlasoma* Swainson 1839. Cichlidae.

Cibotion Kaup 1855:215 [ref. 2571]. Neut. *Ostracion cubicus* Linnaeus 1758:332. Type by subsequent designation. Earliest type designation found that by Jordan 1919:264 [ref. 2410]. Ostraciidae: Ostraciinae.

Cichla Bloch & Schneider 1801:336 [ref. 471]. Fem. *Cichla ocellaris* Bloch & Schneider 1801:310. Type by subsequent designation. Type designated by Eigenmann & Bray 1894:611 [ref. 1248]. Valid (Kullander 1986:50 [ref. 12439], Kullander & Nijssen 1989:5 [ref. 14136]). Cichlidae.

Cichlasoma (subgenus of *Plesiops*) Swainson 1839:230 [ref. 4303]. Neut. *Labrus bimaculatus* Linnaeus 1758:285. Type by subsequent designation. As *Cichlaurus* on p. 173; Swain 1882:284 [ref. 5966] acts as first reviser selecting *Cichlasoma* (see Bailey 1957:303 [ref. 6478]). *Cychlasoma* is a misspelling; *Cichlosoma* Regan 1905:61 [ref. 3622] is an unjustified emendation. For a discussion of problems involving the type species, see Kullander 1983:9 [ref. 8319). Valid (Kullander 1983 [ref. 8319], Kullander 1986:335 [ref. 12439], Malabarba 1989:163 [ref. 14217], Kullander & Nijssen 1989:131 [ref. 14136]). Cichlidae.

Cichlaurus Swainson 1839:173 [ref. 4303]. Masc. *Labrus bimaculatus* Linnaeus 1758:285. Type by being a replacement name. Without species but clear from text that this was another name for *Cichlasoma* Swainson 1839:230 [ref. 4303]; Swain 1882:284 [ref. 5966], acts as first reviser selecting *Cichlasoma* (see Bailey 1957:304 [ref. 6478]). Objective synonym of *Cichlasoma* Swainson 1839 (Kullander 1986:335 [ref. 12439], Kullander & Nijssen 1989:131 [ref. 14136]). Cichlidae.

Cichlops Müller & Troschel 1849:24 [ref. 3073]. Masc. *Cichlops cyclophthalmus* Müller & Troschel 1849:24. Type by monotypy. Preoccupied by Hodgson 1844 in Aves. Spelled *Cichlopsis* by Schlegel 1857:121 (preoccupied by Cabanis 1851 in Aves [not investigated] and named *Labracinus* by Schlegel 1858). Objective synonym of *Labracinus* Schlegel 1858; senior synonym of *Dampieria* Castelnau 1875. Pseudochromidae: Pseudochrominae.

Cichlosoma see *Cichlasoma*. Cichlidae.

Cicla Klein 1776:412 [ref. 4918]. Fem. Not available, published in a work that does not conform to the principle of binominal nomenclature. In the synonymy of *Labrus* Linnaeus 1758. Labridae.

Cicla Röse 1793:112 [ref. 3833]. Fem. *? Labrus viridis* Linnaeus 1758:286. Original not examined. Labridae.

Ciliata Couch 1832:15 [ref. 5557]. Fem. *Ciliata glauca* Couch 1832:16. Type by monotypy. Valid (Svetovidov 1973:312 [ref. 7169], Fahay & Markle 1984:266 [ref. 13653], Svetovidov in Whitehead et al. 1986:697 [ref. 13676], Stainier et al. 1986 [ref. 6754]). Lotidae.

Cilus Delfin 1900:55 [ref. 1099]. Masc. *Cilus montti* Delfin 1900:56. Type by monotypy. Family placement uncertain, in Haemulidae follows Fowler (MS). Haemulidae.

Cinetodus Ogilby 1898:32 [ref. 5861]. Masc. *Arius froggatii* Ramsay & Ogilby 1886:14. Type by original designation (also monotypic). Valid (Paxton et al. 1989:220 [ref. 12442]). Ariidae.

Cingla Fleming 1822:394 [ref. 5063]. Fem. *Perca zingel* Linnaeus 1766:482. Type by monotypy. Original not seen. Synonym of *Zingel* Cloquet 1817 (Collette & Banarescu 1977:1459 [ref. 5845]). Percidae.

Cingulogobius Herre 1927:201 [ref. 2104]. Masc. *Pleurogobius (sic) boulengeri* Seale 1909:536. Type by original designation (also monotypic). *Pleurogobius* Seale 1909 apparently a lapsus,

Seale's species referred by Herre to new genus. *Pleurogobius* as used by Herre 1927:201, 202 [ref. 2104] is name in synonymy and not available. Gobiidae.

Cirrhibarbis Valenciennes in Cuvier & Valenciennes 1836:406 [ref. 1005]. Masc. *Cirrhibarbis capensis* Valenciennes in Cuvier & Valenciennes 1836:406. Type by monotypy. Appeared first as "Les Cirribarbes" in Cuvier 1829:239 [ref. 995], without species. Synonym of *Clinus* Cuvier 1816 (Bennett 1983 [ref. 5299]); valid (Smith 1986:760 [ref. 5712]). Clinidae.

Cirrhigaleus Tanaka 1912:151 [ref. 6034]. Masc. *Cirrhigaleus barbifer* Tanaka 1912:151. Type by original designation (also monotypic). Valid (Compagno 1984:61 [ref. 6474], Paxton et al. 1989:33 [ref. 12442] as *Cirrigaleus*). Squalidae.

Cirrhilabrichthys Klausewitz 1976:12 [ref. 2615]. Masc. *Cirrhilabrichthys filamentosus* Klausewitz 1976:12. Type by original designation. Synonym of *Cirrhilabrus* Temminck & Schlegel 1846 (Randall 1988:202 [ref. 14253]). Labridae.

Cirrhilabrus Temminck & Schlegel 1845:167 [ref. 4373]. Masc. *Cirrhilabrus temminckii* Bleeker 1853:17. Type by subsequent monotypy. Original description without species; one species added by Bleeker 1853:17 [ref. 340]. Valid (Randall & Shen 1978 [ref. 7027], Richards & Leis 1984:544 [ref. 13668], Yamakawa in Masuda et al. 1984:211 [ref. 6441], Randall 1986:691 [ref. 5706], Randall 1988:202 [ref. 14253], Randall & Pyle 1989 [ref. 12854], Randall & Kuiter 1989 [ref. 13502]). Labridae.

Cirrhimuraena Kaup 1856:51 [ref. 2572]. Fem. *Cirrhimuraena chinensis* Kaup 1856:51. Type by monotypy. Also in Kaup 1856: 27 [ref. 2573] and as name only in Kaup in Duméril 1856:199 [ref. 1154]. Valid (McCosker 1977:75 [ref. 6836], McCosker & Castle 1986:178 [ref. 5690], Paxton et al. 1989:116 [ref. 12442], McCosker et al. 1989:298 [ref. 13288]). Ophichthidae: Ophichthinae.

Cirrhinichthys Bleeker 1863:202 [ref. 397]. Masc. *Cirrhina dussumieri* Valenciennes in Cuvier & Valenciennes 1842:291. Type by original designation (also monotypic). Also appeared in Bleeker 1863:263 [ref. 403] and 1863:28 [ref. 4859]. Correct spelling for genus of type species is *Cirrhinus*. Cyprinidae.

Cirrhinus Oken (ex Cuvier) 1817:1183 [ref. 3303]. Masc. *Cyprinus cirrhosus* Bloch 1795:52. Type by monotypy. Based on "Les Cirrhines" Cuvier 1816:193 [ref. 993] (see Gill 1903:966 [ref. 5768]). Misspelled or unjustifiably emended to *Cirrhina*, *Cirrhines* and *Cirrhine* by early authors. Valid (Wu et al. 1977:352 [ref. 4807], Jayaram 1981:126 [ref. 6497], Kottelat 1985:261 [ref. 11441], Kottelat 1989:6 [ref. 13605], Chu & Cui in Chu & Chen 1989:265 [ref. 13584]). Cyprinidae.

Cirrhiptera Kuhl & van Hasselt in Bleeker 1853:280 [ref. 12580]. Fem. Not available; name mentioned in passing in synonymy of *Plesiops* as *Cirrhiptera corallicola* van Hasselt. Also in Bleeker 1876:322 [ref. 448] as name in synonymy attributed to Kuhl & van Hasselt. Apparently never used as a valid name or senior homonym. In the synonymy of *Plesiops* Oken 1817. Plesiopidae.

Cirrhisomus Swainson 1839:194, 328 [ref. 4303]. Masc. *Tetraodon sprengleri* Swainson 1839:328. Type by monotypy. Species possibly dates to Bloch as *spengleri* as given by Jordan 1919:205 [ref. 2410]. Synonym of *Spheroides* Duméril 1806 [= *Sphoeroides* Anonymous 1798] (Fraser-Brunner 1943:10 [ref. 1495]). Tetraodontidae.

Cirrhitichthys Bleeker 1857:3, 39 [ref. 356]. Masc. *Cirrhites graphidopterus* Bleeker 1853:106. Type by monotypy. One available species listed with new name on p. 3, genus characterized on p. 39. Correct spelling for genus of type species is *Cirrhitus*. Valid (Araga in Masuda et al. 1984:199 [ref. 6441], Donaldson 1986:624 [ref. 6317]). Cirrhitidae.

Cirrhitoidea Jenkins 1903:489 [ref. 2341]. Fem. *Cirrhitoidea bimacula* Jenkins 1903:489. Type by original designation (also monotypic). Cirrhitidae.

Cirrhitops Smith 1951:(627) 637 [ref. 4081]. Masc. *Cirrhites fasciatus* Bennett (non Cuvier) 1829:39 (= *Cirrhites cinctus* Günther 1860:73). Type by original designation (also monotypic). Correct spelling for genus of type species is *Cirrhitus*. Valid (Araga in Masuda et al. 1984:199 [ref. 6441], Donaldson 1986:624 [ref. 6317]). Cirrhitidae.

Cirrhitopsis Gill 1862:109 [ref. 1658]. Fem. *Cirrhites aureus* Temminck & Schlegel 1842:15. Type by original designation (also monotypic). Correct spelling for genus of type species is *Cirrhitus*. Synonym of *Cirrhitichthys* Bleeker 1857. Cirrhitidae.

Cirrhitus Lacepède 1803:2 [ref. 4930]. Masc. *Cirrhitus maculatus* Lacepède 1803:2, 3. Type by monotypy. Spelled *Cirrhite* and especially *Cirrhites* in early literature. Valid (Araga in Masuda et al. 1984:199 [ref. 6441], Randall 1986:665 [ref. 5706], Donaldson 1986:624 [ref. 6317]). Cirrhitidae.

Cirrhoscyllium Smith & Radcliffe in Smith 1913:568 [ref. 4043]. Neut. *Cirrhoscyllium expolitum* Smith & Radcliffe in Smith 1913:568. Type by original designation (also monotypic). *Zev* Whitley 1927 is an unneeded replacement. Valid (Compagno 1984:167 [ref. 6474], Nakaya & Shirai in Masuda et al. 1984:8 [ref. 6441]). Parascylliidae.

Cirricaecula Schultz in Schultz et al. 1953:49 [ref. 3975]. Fem. *Cirricaecula johnsoni* Schultz in Schultz et al. 1953:50. Type by original designation (also monotypic). Valid (McCosker 1977:67 [ref. 6836], McCosker et al. 1989:297 [ref. 13288]). Ophichthidae: Ophichthinae.

Cirrimens Gill 1862:17 [ref. 1657]. Fem. *Umbrina ophicephala* Jenyns 1842:45. Type by original designation (also monotypic). Valid (Chao 1978:30 [ref. 6983]). Sciaenidae.

Cirrinasus Schultz in Schultz et al. 1960:277 [ref. 3972]. Masc. *Roxasella fusiforme* Fowler 1943:87. Type by being a replacement name. Replacement for *Roxasella* Fowler 1943, preoccupied by Merino 1936 [not investigated]. Synonym of *Matsubaraea* Taki 1953 (Iwamoto 1980 [ref. 6933]). Percophidae: Hemerocoetinae.

Cirripectes (subgenus of *Salarias*) Swainson 1839:182, 275 [ref. 4303]. Masc. *Salarias variolosus* Valenciennes in Cuvier & Valenciennes 1836:317. Type by monotypy. Spelled *Cirripectus* by Swainson 1839:79, 80 [ref. 4303], first revisers for selection of generic spelling evidently were McCulloch & McNeil 1918 (Williams 1988:7 [ref. 7000]). Valid (Smith-Vaniz & Springer 1971:19 [ref. 4145], Fukao 1984 [ref. 6726], Yoshino in Masuda et al. 1984:299 [ref. 6441], Springer 1986:745 [ref. 5719], Williams 1988 [ref. 7000], Williams 1989:17 [ref. 13549]). Blenniidae.

Cirrisalarias Springer 1976:199 [ref. 4179]. Masc. *Cirrisalarias bunares* Springer 1976:202. Type by original designation (also monotypic). Valid (Springer & Spreitzer 1978:3 [ref. 4181]). Blenniidae.

Cirriscyllium Ogilby 1908:4 [ref. 3286]. Neut. *Chiloscyllium modestum* Günther 1871:654. Type by original designation. Perhaps published through a mixup — corresponds to *Brachaelurus* Ogilby 1907, not 1908. Could be considered as an unneeded replacement for *Brachaelurus* Ogilby 1907. Objective synonym of *Brachaelurus* Ogilby 1907 (Compagno 1984:175 [ref. 6474]).

Brachyaeluridae.

Cisco (subgenus of *Leucichthys*) Jordan & Evermann 1911:3 [ref. 2452]. Masc. *Argyrosomus nigripinnis* Gill in Hoy 1874:87. Type by original designation. Synonym of *Coregonus* Lacepède 1803. Salmonidae: Coregoninae.

Citharichthys Bleeker 1862:427 [ref. 388]. Masc. *Citharichthys cayennensis* Bleeker 1862:427. Type by monotypy. Valid (Norman 1934:139 [ref. 6893], Ahlstrom et al. 1984:640 [ref. 13641], Hensley 1986:857 [ref. 5669], Desoutter 1986:428 [ref. 6212]). Paralichthyidae.

Citharidium Boulenger 1902:144 [ref. 563]. Neut. *Citharidium ansorgii* Boulenger 1902:144. Type by monotypy. Valid (Géry 1977:58 [ref. 1597], Vari 1979:339 [ref. 5490], Daget 1984:212 [ref. 6170]). Citharinidae: Citharininae.

Citharinoides (subgenus of *Citharinus*) Daget 1962:81, 102 [ref. 1024]. Masc. *Citharinus latus* Müller & Troschel 1845. Not available from Daget 1962, described with 2 included species without type fixation after 1930 (Art. 13b); perhaps made available and dates to Daget & Iltis 1965:83 (footnote) [ref. 13626, not researched] where type was designated. Treated as a synonym of *Citharinus* Cuvier 1816 (Daget 1984:213 [ref. 6170]). Citharinidae: Citharininae.

Citharinops (subgenus of *Citharinus*) Daget 1962:81, 101 [ref. 1024]. Masc. *Citharinus distichodoides* Pellegrin 1919:208. Type by monotypy. Valid (Daget 1984:212 [ref. 6170]). Citharinidae: Citharininae.

Citharinus Cuvier 1816:168 [ref. 993]. Masc. *Serrasalmus citharus* Geoffroy St. Hilaire 1809:Pl. 5. Type by monotypy. Spelled *Cytharinus* by Oken (ex Cuvier):1182 [ref. 3303]. Valid (Daget 1962 [ref. 1024], Géry 1977:55 [ref. 1597], Vari 1983:5 [ref. 5419], Daget 1984:213 [ref. 6170]). Citharinidae: Citharininae.

Citharoedus Kaup 1860:136, 141 [ref. 2583]. *Chaetodon meyeri* Bloch & Schneider 1801:223. Type by subsequent designation. Type apparently designated first by Bleeker 1876:305 [ref. 448], not *ornatissimus* as given by Jordan 1919:297 [ref. 4904]. Synonym of *Chaetodon* Linnaeus 1758, but as a valid subgenus (Burgess 1978:498 [ref. 700]); valid genus (Maugé & Bauchot 1984:466 [ref. 6614]). Chaetodontidae.

Citharoides Hubbs 1915:452 [ref. 2224]. Masc. *Citharoides macrolepidotus* Hubbs 1915:453. Type by original designation (also monotypic). Valid (Norman 1934:170 [ref. 6893], Ahlstrom et al. 1984:640 [ref. 13641], Amaoka in Masuda et al. 1984:346 [ref. 6441], Heemstra 1986:853 [ref. 5660]). Citharidae: Citharinae.

Citharus Bleeker 1862:424 [ref. 388]. Masc. *Pleuronectes macrolepidotus* Bloch 1787:34, Pl. 190. Type by monotypy. Preoccupied by Röse 1793 and Reinhardt 1838 in fishes; replaced by *Eucitharus* Gill 1889. Bleeker 1862:424 gives species as *Pleuronectes macrolepidotus* L. [Linnaeus], but that was named by Bloch. Synonym of *Citharus* Röse 1793 if available. Citharidae: Citharinae.

Citharus Reinhardt 1838:116, 130 [ref. 3691]. Masc. *Pleuronectes platessoides* Fabricius 1780:164. Type by subsequent designation. Perhaps not intended as a new genus. Type as given by Jordan 1919:193 [ref. 2410]. Preoccupied by *Citharus* Röse 1793. Synonym of *Hippoglossoides* Gottsche 1835 (Norman 1934:294 [ref. 6893]). Pleuronectidae: Pleuronectinae.

Citharus Röse 1793:116 [ref. 3833]. Masc. *Pleuronectes linguatula* Linnaeus 1758:270. Synonym of *Eucitharus* Gill 1889 (Norman 1934:168 [ref. 6893]); valid (Nielsen 1973:615 [ref. 6885], Nielsen in Whitehead et al. 1986:1286 [ref. 13677]). Citharidae: Citharinae.

Citula Cuvier 1816:315 [ref. 993]. Fem. *Citula banksii* Risso 1820:254. Type by subsequent monotypy. Appeared first without included species, one species added by Risso 1820. Treated as a possible senior synonym of *Carangoides* (e.g., by Smith-Vaniz 1986:641 [ref. 5718]) but with wrong type. With type as above, *Citula* would be a senior synonym of *Pseudocaranx*, and the ICZN should be petitioned to conserve *Pseudocaranx* (Smith-Vaniz, pers. comm., Feb. 1990). Carangidae.

Clara Gill 1862:127 [ref. 1659]. *Equula longimana* Cantor 1850:1134. Type by original designation (also monotypic). Synonym of *Pentaprion* Bleeker 1850. Gerreidae.

Clariallabes Boulenger 1900:136 [ref. 555]. Fem. *Clarias melas* Boulenger 1887:148. Type by original designation (also monotypic). Valid (Poll 1977:146 [ref. 3533], Burgess 1989:145 [ref. 12860]). Clariidae.

Clarias Gronow 1763:100 [ref. 1910]. Masc. Not available, published in a rejected work on Official Index (Opinion 261). In the synonymy of *Clarias* Scopoli 1777. Clariidae.

Clarias Scopoli (ex Gronow) 1777:455 [ref. 3990]. Masc. *Silurus anguillaris* Linnaeus 1758:305. Type by subsequent designation. Based on *Clarias* Gronow; spelled *Chlarias* by Scopoli (regarded as in error). Species added by Cuvier 1816; type designated by Teugels & Roberts 1987 [ref. 6479]. Valid, as *Clarias*, with varying type species (Teugels 1982 [ref. 4377], Teugels 1983 [ref. 12851], Sawada in Masuda et al. 1984:59 [ref. 6441], Teugels 1986:69 [ref. 6193], Teugels 1986 [ref. 12548], Teugels & Roberts 1987 [ref. 6479], Burgess 1989:145 [ref. 12860], Roberts 1989:127 [ref. 6439]). Clariidae.

Claricola (subgenus of *Etheostoma*) Jordan & Evermann 1896:1066, 1069, 1093 [ref. 2443]. Masc. *Etheostoma juliae* Meek 1891:130. Type by original designation. Synonym of *Etheostoma* Rafinesque 1819 (Collette & Banarescu 1977:1456 [ref. 5845]). Percidae.

Clariger Jordan & Snyder 1901:120 [ref. 2509]. Masc. *Clariger cosmurus* Jordan & Snyder 1901:121. Type by original designation (also monotypic). Valid (Akihito in Masuda et al. 1984:281 [ref. 6441], Shiogaki 1988 [ref. 6854], Birdsong et al. 1988:185 [ref. 7303]). Gobiidae.

Clarioides (subgenus of *Clarias*) David in David & Poll 1937:231 [ref. 1043]. Masc. *Clarias angolensis* Steindachner 1866:766. Not available, published after 1930 without type fixation (Art. 13b). Not made available in the Zoological Record (for 1960). Designation of *Clarias angolensis* Steindachner 1866 by Teugels 1982:12 may allow genus to date to that work. In the synonymy of *Clarias* Scopoli 1777 (Teugels 1986:69 [ref. 6193]). Clariidae.

Clarisilurus Fowler 1937:133 [ref. 1425]. Masc. *Clarisilurus kemratensis* Fowler 1937:133. Type by original designation (also monotypic). Misspelled *Clarasilurus* by Neave 1950:54 [ref. 6512] and in Zoological Record for 1937. Synonym of *Heteropneustes* Müller 1840 (Myers 1938:98 [ref. 3116]). Heteropneustidae.

Clarkichthys (subgenus of *Gunnellichthys*) Smith 1958:128 [ref. 4119]. Masc. *Cerdale bilineata* Clark 1936:394. Type by original designation (also monotypic). Valid (Dawson 1974:439 [ref. 7122], Birdsong et al. 1988:200 [ref. 7303]). Microdesmidae: Microdesminae.

Clarkina Jordan & Evermann 1927:502 [ref. 2453]. Fem. *Cyprinus (Leuciscus) caurinus* Richardson 1836:304. Type by original designation (also monotypic). Cyprinidae.

Clarotes Kner 1855:313 [ref. 12581]. *Clarotes heuglini* Kner 1855:313. Type by monotypy. Type not *Pimelodus laticeps* Rüppell as given by Jordan 1919:265 [ref. 2410]. Valid (Risch 1986:27 [ref. 6190] and Burgess 1989:67 [ref. 12860] but with wrong type). Bagridae.

Clathropus Smith 1966:321 [ref. 4137]. Masc. *Clathropus maugei* Smith 1966:323. Type by original designation (also monotypic). Synonym of *Eleutherochir* Bleeker 1879 (Nakabo 1982 [ref. 3139). Synonym of *Draculo* Snyder 1911 (Fricke 1982:72 [ref. 5432], Fricke 1986:772 [ref. 5653]). Callionymidae.

Clavata (subgenus of *Raja*) de Buen 1926:33 [ref. 5054]. *Raja clavata* Linnaeus 1758:232. As a "grupo" for 8 species of *Raja*. Not available on basis of Art. 1b(6) [see de Buen's definition of "grupo" on p. 11]; see Appendix A. Synonym of *Raja* Linnaeus 1758. Rajidae.

Cleidopus De Vis 1882:367 [ref. 1087]. Masc. *Cleidopus gloriamaris* De Vis 1882:368. Type by monotypy. Valid (Paxton et al. 1989:364 [ref. 12442]). Monocentridae.

Cleisthenes Jordan & Starks 1904:622 [ref. 2526]. *Cleisthenes pinetorum* Jordan & Starks 1904:622. Type by original designation (also monotypic). Valid (Norman 1934:304 [ref. 6893], Ahlstrom et al. 1984:643 [ref. 13641], Sakamoto in Masuda et al. 1984:351 [ref. 6441]). Pleuronectidae: Pleuronectinae.

Cleithracara Kullander & Nijssen 1989:173 [ref. 14136]. Fem. *Acara maronii* Steindachner 1882:141. Type by original designation (also monotypic). Cichlidae.

Clepticus Cuvier 1829:261 [ref. 995]. Masc. *Clepticus genizara* Cuvier 1829:261. Type by monotypy. Valid. Labridae.

Cleptochromis (subgenus of *Lipochromis*) Greenwood 1980:31 [ref. 1899]. Masc. *Paratilapia parvidens* Boulenger 1911:65. Type by original designation. Cichlidae.

Clevelandia Eigenmann & Eigenmann 1888:73 [ref. 1250]. Fem. *Gobiosoma longipinne* Steindachner 1880:145. Type by monotypy. Apparently based on a misidentified type species (D. Hoese, pers. comm.). Valid (Birdsong et al. 1988:185, 187 [ref. 7303]). Gobiidae.

Clidoderma Bleeker 1862:425 [ref. 388]. Neut. *Platessa asperrima* Temminck & Schlegel 1846:177. Type by monotypy. Valid (Norman 1934:314 [ref. 6893], Ahlstrom et al. 1984:643 [ref. 13641], Sakamoto 1984 [ref. 5273], Sakamoto in Masuda et al. 1984:353 [ref. 6441]). Pleuronectidae: Pleuronectinae.

Climacogrammus (subgenus of *Diplogrammus*) Smith 1963:550 [ref. 4129]. Masc. *Diplogrammus (Climacogrammus) infulatus* Smith 1963:550. Type by original designation (also monotypic). Synonym of *Diplogrammus* Gill 1865 (Nakabo 1982:97 [ref. 3139]), doubtfully as a valid subgenus (Fricke 1982:72 [ref. 5432]). Callionymidae.

Climacoporus Barnard 1935:645 [ref. 196]. Masc. *Climacoporus navalis* Barnard 1935:646. Type by monotypy. Wrongly as *Nemacoclinus* in Smith 1937:195 [ref. 6553]. Synonym of *Clinus* Cuvier 1816 (Bennett 1983 [ref. 5299]); valid (Smith 1986:761 [ref. 5712]). Clinidae.

Clinitrachus Swainson 1839:75, 192, 276 [ref. 4303]. Masc. *Blennius variabilis* Rafinesque 1810:29. Type by original designation. Description on p. 75, with type as "*Blennius variabilis* Raf." (also see footnote, p. 75), type not *superciliosus* as designated by Swain 1882:278 [ref. 5966]; based on 2 included species on Swainson p. 276. *Clinetrachus* and *Clinotrachys* are misspellings. Valid (Wheeler 1973:530 [ref. 7190], Wirtz & Zander in Whitehead et al. 1986:1117 [ref. 13677]). Clinidae.

Clinocottus Gill 1861:166 [ref. 1775]. Masc. *Oligocottus analis* Girard 1857:201. Type by monotypy. Valid (Bolin 1944:72 [ref. 6379], Washington et al. 1984:442 [ref. 13660], Yabe 1985:111 [ref. 11522], Washington 1986 [ref. 5202]). Cottidae.

Clinodon Regan 1920:45 [ref. 3669]. Masc. *Hemitilapia bayoni* Boulenger 1908:6. Type by original designation (also monotypic). Cichlidae.

Clinoides Gilchrist & Thompson 1908:98 [ref. 5840]. Masc. Proposed for non-crested species of *Clinus* in South Africa; from key (p. 111) this would include 14 species. Type apparently not yet designated. Clinidae.

Clinoporus Barnard 1927:74 [ref. 193]. Masc. *Clinus biporosus* Gilchrist & Thompson 1908:137. Type by original designation (also monotypic). Also appeared in Barnard 1927 (Oct.):864 [ref. 194]. Valid (Smith 1986:761 [ref. 5712]). Clinidae.

Clinostomus Girard 1856:211 [ref. 1810]. Masc. *Luxilus elongatus* Kirtland 1838:169, 192. Type by subsequent designation. Type designated by Jordan & Gilbert 1877:92 [ref. 4907]. Valid (Robins et al. 1980:21 [ref. 7111]). Cyprinidae.

Clinus Cuvier 1816:251 [ref. 993]. Masc. *Blennius acuminatus* Bloch & Schneider 1801:169. Type by subsequent designation. Type designated by Swainson 1839:75 [ref. 4303]. See Smith 1966:72 [ref. 4140] for discussion of type designation. Valid (Bennett 1983 [ref. 5299], Smith 1986:761 [ref. 5712]). Clinidae.

Cliola Girard 1856:192 [ref. 1810]. Fem. *Ceratichthys vigilax* Baird & Girard 1853:390. Type by subsequent designation. Type designated by Bleeker 1863:30 [ref. 4859] and 1863:207 [ref. 397]. Objective synonym of *Ceratichthys* Baird & Girard 1853. Synonym of *Pimephales* Rafinesque 1820. Cyprinidae.

Clodactylus Rafinesque 1815:87 [ref. 3584]. Masc. Not available, name only; near *Polynemus* Linnaeus 1758. Polynemidae.

Clodalus (subgenus of *Hyodon [Hiodon]*) Rafinesque 1820:175 [ref. 7309]. Masc. *Hiodon clodalus* Lesueur 1818:367. Type by absolute tautonymy. Also appeared in Rafinesque (Dec.) 1820:43 [ref. 3592]. Synonym of *Hiodon* Lesueur 1818. Hiodontidae.

Clodipterus Rafinesque 1815:86, 88 [ref. 3584]. Masc. *Cheilodipterus lineatus* Lacepède 1801:539. Type by being a replacement name. As "*Clodipterus* R. [Rafinesque] *Cheilodipterus* Lac. [Lacepède]." An available (unneeded) replacement for *Cheilodipterus* Lacepède 1801 based on style in work. Objective synonym of *Cheilodipterus* Lacepède 1801. Apogonidae.

Clupalosa Bleeker 1849:12 [ref. 320]. Fem. *Clupalosa bulan* Bleeker 1849:12. Type by monotypy. Synonym of *Sardinella* Valenciennes 1847 (Whitehead 1985:90 [ref. 5141]). Clupeidae.

Clupanodon Lacepède 1803:468 [ref. 4930]. Masc. *Clupea thrissa* Linnaeus 1758:318. Type by subsequent designation. Type apparently designated first by Bleeker 1872:112 [ref. 428], not by Jordan & Gilbert 1883:574 (see Regan 1917:308 [ref. 3665]) or by others (see Whitehead 1967:98 [ref. 6464], Whitehead 1985:238 [ref. 5141]). Valid (Grande 1985:248 [ref. 6466], Whitehead 1985:238 [ref. 5141], Kottelat 1989:4 [ref. 13605]). Clupeidae.

Clupea Linnaeus 1758:317 [ref. 2787]. Fem. *Clupea harengus* Linnaeus 1758:317. Type by subsequent designation. Type designated by Gill 1861:35 [ref. 1767]. On Official List (Opinion 77). Valid (Svetovidov 1973:99 [ref. 7169], Uyeno & Sato in Masuda et al. 1984:19 [ref. 6441], Grande 1985:249 [ref. 6466], Whitehead 1985:115 [ref. 5141]). Clupeidae.

Clupeacharax Pearson 1924:46 [ref. 3396]. Masc. *Clupeacharax* *anchoveoides* Pearson 1924:47. Type by monotypy. Not *Clupeocharax* Pellegrin 1926. Valid (Géry 1977:346 [ref. 1597]). Characidae.

Clupeichthys Bleeker 1855:274 [ref. 351]. Masc. *Clupeichthys goniognathus* Bleeker 1855:275. Type by monotypy. Valid (Grande 1985:246 [ref. 6466], Whitehead 1985:181 [ref. 5141], Kottelat 1989:4 [ref. 13605], Roberts 1989:24 [ref. 6439]). Clupeidae.

Clupeocharax Pellegrin 1926:159 [ref. 3404]. Masc. *Clupeocharax schoutedeni* Pellegrin 1926:159. Type by monotypy. Not preoccupied by *Clupeacharax* Pearson 1924 in fishes; *Clupeopetersius* Pellegrin 1928 apparently is an unneeded replacement. Valid (Géry 1977:50 [ref. 1597], Paugy 1984:167 [ref. 6183]). Alestiidae.

Clupeoides Bleeker 1851:274 [ref. 325]. Masc. *Clupeoides borneensis* Bleeker 1851:275. Type by monotypy. Valid (Grande 1985:246 [ref. 6466], Whitehead 1985:174 [ref. 5141], Kottelat 1989:4 [ref. 13605], Roberts 1989:25 [ref. 6439]). Clupeidae.

Clupeolabrus Nichols 1923:2 [ref. 3176]. Masc. *Clupeolabrus dubius* Nichols 1923:2. Type by monotypy. Synonym of *Pterocaesio* Bleeker 1876 (Carpenter 1987:29 [ref. 6430], Carpenter 1988:50 [ref. 9296]). Caesionidae.

Clupeonella Kessler 1877:187 [ref. 2597]. Fem. *Clupeonella grimmi* Kessler 1877:187. Type by monotypy. Original not seen. Valid (Svetovidov 1973:101 [ref. 7169], Grande 1985:250 [ref. 6466], Whitehead 1985:51 [ref. 5141]). Clupeidae.

Clupeonia Valenciennes in Cuvier & Valenciennes 1847:345 [ref. 1012]. Fem. *Clupanodon jussieui* Lacepède 1803:469, 474. Type by subsequent designation. Type designated by Gill 1861:35 [ref. 1767]. Synonym of *Sardinella* Valenciennes 1847 (Svetovidov 1973:102 [ref. 7169]), but sometimes as a subgenus or genus (see Whitehead 1967:58 [ref. 6464], Whitehead 1985:90 [ref. 5141]). Clupeidae.

Clupeopetersius Pellegrin 1928:82 [ref. 3409]. Masc. *Clupeocharax schoutedeni* Pellegrin 1926:159. Type by being a replacement name. Unneeded replacement for *Clupeocharax* Pellegrin 1926, not preoccupied by *Clupeacharax* Pearson 1924 in fishes. Also in Pellegrin 1928:20 [ref. 3411]. Valid (Poll 1967:71 [ref. 3529], Stewart & Roberts 1984:82 [ref. 6480]); correctly as a synonym of *Clupeocharax* (Géry 1977:50 [ref. 1597], Paugy 1984:167 [ref. 6183]). Alestiidae.

Clupisoma (subgenus of *Silurus*) Swainson 1838:347, 351, 354 [ref. 4302]. Neut. *Silurus garua* Hamilton 1822:156, 375. Type by original designation (also monotypic). Type designated on p. 347; also in Swainson 1839:189, 306 [ref. 4303]. Swainson needlessly renamed *garua* as *argentata* on p. 306. Valid (Jayaram 1977:18 [ref. 7006], Jayaram 1981:219 [ref. 6497], Burgess 1989:98 [ref. 12860]). Schilbeidae.

Clupisudis (subgenus of *Sudis*) Swainson 1839:185, 286 [ref. 4303]. Fem. *Sudis nilotica* Cuvier 1829:328. Type by monotypy. Synonym of *Heterotis* Rüppell 1828 (Daget 1984:57 [ref. 6170]). Osteoglossidae: Heterotidinae.

Clypeobarbus (subgenus of *Barbus*) Fowler 1936:272 [ref. 1424]. Masc. *Barbus kemoensis* Fowler 1936:272. Type by original designation. Synonym of *Barbus* Cuvier & Cloquet 1816 (Lévêque & Daget 1984:218 [ref. 6186]). Cyprinidae.

Clypeocottus Ayres 1854:12 [ref. 157]. Masc. *Clypeocottus robustus* Ayres 1854:11. Type by monotypy. Read at meeting of 9 Oct. 1854; appeared first in "The Pacific" newspaper, 13 Oct. 1854, 3(48):194; then in the Proceedings (pp. 11-12). On p. 11 Ayres notes that *Aspicottus bison* Girard (Aug. 1854) preceeded description of *C. robustus*. Synonym of *Enophrys* Swainson 1839 (Bolin 1944:90 [ref. 6379]; synonym of *Aspicottus* Girard 1854 (Neyelov 1979:147 [ref. 3152]). Cottidae.

Cnesterodon Garman 1895:43 [ref. 1538]. Masc. *Poecilia decemmaculata* Jenyns 1842:115. Type by original designation. Valid (Rosen & Bailey 1963:74 [ref. 7067], Parenti & Rauchenberger 1989:8 [ref. 13538], Malabarba 1989:160 [ref. 14217]). Poeciliidae.

Cnestrostoma Regan 1920:45 [ref. 3669]. Neut. *Paratilapia polyodon* Boulenger 1909:306. Type by original designation (also monotypic). Cichlidae.

Cnidoglanis Günther 1864:27 [ref. 1974]. Masc. *Plotosus megastomus* Richardson 1845:31. Type by subsequent designation. Type designated by Jordan 1919:332 [ref. 4904]. Valid (Burgess 1989:180 [ref. 12860], Paxton et al. 1989:222 [ref. 12442]). Plotosidae.

Cnidon Müller & Troschel 1849:21 [ref. 3073]. Masc. *Cnidon chinensis* Müller & Troschel 1849:21. Type by monotypy. Synonym of *Psammoperca* Richardson 1848. Centropomidae: Latinae.

Cobitichthys Bleeker 1859:304 [ref. 366]. Masc. *Cobitis barbatuloides* Bleeker 1851:435. Type by monotypy. Misspelled *Cobiitichthys* by Jordan 1919:279 [ref. 2410]. Synonym of *Misgurnus* Lacepède 1803. Cobitidae: Cobitinae.

Cobitiglanis (subgenus of *Ochmacanthus*) Fowler 1914:268 [ref. 1390]. Masc. *Ochmacanthus taxistigma* Fowler 1914:268. Type by original designation. *Cobitoglanis* is a misspelling. Synonym of *Henonemus* Eigenmann & Ward 1907. Trichomycteridae.

Cobitinula Hanko 1924:152 [ref. 2035]. Fem. *Cobitinula anatoliae* Hanko 1924:152. Type by monotypy. Synonym of *Cobitis* Linnaeus 1758. Cobitidae: Cobitinae.

Cobitis Linnaeus 1758:303 [ref. 2787]. Fem. *Cobitis taenia* Linnaeus 1758:303. Type designated by ICZN (Opinion 1500). *Cobites* Swainson 1839:190, 310 [ref. 4303] is a misspelling. Valid (Sawada 1982:199 [ref. 14111], Sawada in Masuda et al. 1984:58 [ref. 6441], Kim 1986:945 [ref. 6327], Kottelat 1989:13 [ref. 13605]). Cobitidae: Cobitinae.

Cobitophis Myers 1927:4 [ref. 3097]. Masc. *Acantophthalmus anguillaris* Vaillant 1902:151. Type by original designation. As a subgenus of *Acanthophthalmus* [or *Acantophthalmus*] van Hasselt (Nalbant 1963:368 [ref. 3140]); synonym of *Acanthophthalmus* (Roberts 1989:95 [ref.6439]); synonym of *Pangio* Blyth 1860 (Kottelat 1989:13 [ref. 13605]). Cobitidae: Cobitinae.

Coccia Günther 1864:387 [ref. 1974]. Fem. *Gonostomus ovatus* Cocco 1838:169. Type by being a replacement name. Unneeded replacement for *Ichthyococcus* Bonaparte 1840; replaced because Günther felt name was inappropriately formed. Correct spelling for genus of type species is *Gonostoma*. Objective synonym of *Ichthyococcus* Bonaparte 1840 (Witzell 1973:118 [ref. 7172]). Phosichthyidae.

Coccogenia (subgenus of *Notropis*) Cockerell & Callaway 1909:190 [ref. 876]. Fem. *Hypsilepis coccogenis* Cope 1867:160. Type by original designation. Genus of type species is correctly *Hypsolepis*. Objective synonym of *Coccotis* Jordan 1882; synonym of *Notropis* Rafinesque 1818, subgenus *Luxilus* Rafinesque 1820 (Gilbert 1978:16 [ref. 7042]). Cyprinidae.

Coccolus Bonaparte 1846:47, 97 [ref. 519]. Masc. *Coccolus annectens* Bonaparte 1846:47, 97. Type by monotypy. Based on a larva. Essentially as name only. Needs more research; Bonaparte's Note

A on p. 97 not translated; perhaps *Coccolus* is the same as *Krohnius* Cocco (a macrourid larva) and not a pleuronectiform as placed by Bonaparte. As name only in synonymy of *Caelorinchus* Giorna 1809 (Marshall & Iwamoto 1973:538 [ref. 6966]). Macrouridae: Macrourinae.

Coccorella Roule 1929:8, 11 [ref. 3822]. Fem. *Odontostomus atratus* Alcock 1893:182. Type by original designation. Type designated on p. 8, second subspecies included on p. 11. Valid (Maul 1973:200 [ref. 7171], Johnson 1982:103 [ref. 5519], Johnson in Whitehead et al. 1984:490 [ref. 13675], Fujii in Masuda et al. 1984:78 [ref. 6441], Paxton et al. 1989:249 [ref. 12442]). Evermannellidae.

Coccotis Jordan 1882:852 [ref. 2383]. Fem. *Hypsilepis coccogenis* Cope 1867:160. Type by original designation (also monotypic). Correct genus of type is *Hypsolepis*. Synonym of *Notropis* Rafinesque 1818, subgenus *Luxilus* Rafinesque 1820 (Gilbert 1978:16 [ref. 7042]). Cyprinidae.

Coccotropsis Barnard 1927:75 [ref. 193]. Fem. *Tetraroge gymnoderma* Gilchrist 1906:147. Type by original designation (also monotypic). Also appeared in Barnard 1927 (Oct.):919 [ref. 194]. Valid (Washington et al. 1984:440 [ref. 13660], Poss 1986:479 [ref. 6296]). Scorpaenidae: Tetraroginae.

Cochlefelis Whitley 1941:8 [ref. 4701]. Fem. *Arius spatula* Ramsay & Ogilby 1886:15. Type by original designation. Ariidae.

Cochleoceps Whitley 1943:141 [ref. 4702]. Neut. *Crepidogaster spatula* Günther 1861:508. Type by original designation (also monotypic). Misspelled *Cochlioceps* in Zoological Record for 1943. Valid (Briggs 1955:51 [ref. 637], Scott 1976:187 [ref. 7055], Hutchins 1983 [ref. 5374]). Gobiesocidae: Gobiesocinae.

Cochliodon Heckel in Kner 1854:255, 265 [ref. 2628]. Masc. *Hypostomus cochliodon* Kner 1854:265. Type by monotypy (also by absolute tautonymy). First published in synonymy, adopted by Günther 1864:231 [ref. 1974] as a valid subgroup in *Plecostomus* with one species. Valid (Isbrücker 1980:38 [ref. 2303], Burgess 1989:433 [ref. 12860]). Loricariidae.

Cochlognathus Baird & Girard 1854:158 [ref. 167]. Masc. *Cochlognathus ornatus* Baird & Girard 1854:158. Type by monotypy. Cyprinidae.

Cociella Whitley 1940:243 [ref. 4660]. Fem. *Platycephalus crocodilus* Tilesius 1812:59. Type by being a replacement name. Replacement for *Cocius* Jordan & Hubbs 1925, preoccupied by Navás 1921 [not researched]. Valid (Ochiai in Masuda et al. 1984:322 [ref. 6441], Knapp 1986:482 [ref. 5683]). Platycephalidae.

Cocius Jordan & Hubbs 1925:286 [ref. 2486]. Masc. *Platycephalus crocodilus* Tilesius 1812:59. Type by original designation (also monotypic). Apparently preoccupied by Navás 1921 [not researched], replaced by *Cociella* Whitley 1940. Platycephalidae.

Cocotropus Kaup 1858:333 [ref. 2580]. Masc. *Corythobatus echinatus* Cantor 1850:1027. Type by monotypy. *Coccotropus* is a misspelling; not same as *Coccotropsis*. Valid (Nakabo in Masuda et al. 1984:319 [ref. 6441], Washington et al. 1984:440 [ref. 13660], Poss 1986:480 [ref. 6296], Poss & Allen 1987 [ref. 6616]). Aploactinidae.

Codoma Girard 1856:194 [ref. 1810]. Neut. *Codoma ornata* Girard 1856:195. Type by subsequent designation. Type designated by Jordan & Gilbert 1877:91 [ref. 4907]. Synonym of *Notropis* Rafinesque 1818 (Gilbert 1978:15 [ref. 7042]); synonym of *Cyprinella* Girard 1857 (Mayden 1989:45 [ref. 12555]). Cyprinidae.

Coecilophis Kaup 1856:44 [ref. 2572]. Masc. *Ophisurus compar* Richardson 1848:103. Type by monotypy. Also appeared in Kaup 1856:6 [ref. 2573] and in Kaup in Duméril 1856:198 [ref. 1154]. Synonym of *Ophichthus* Ahl 1789 (Blache et al. 1973:247 [ref. 7185], McCosker et al. 1989:379 [ref. 13288]); as a valid subgenus (McCosker 1977:80, 81 [ref. 6836]). Ophichthidae: Ophichthinae.

Coelocephalus Gilbert & Cramer 1897:422 [ref. 1635]. Masc. *Coelocephalus acipenserinus* Gilbert & Cramer 1897:422. Type by monotypy. Preoccupied by Clark 1860 in Coleoptera (not preoccupied by Agassiz 1844, name only); replaced by *Mataeocephalus* Berg 1898. Objective synonym of *Mataeocephalus* Berg 1898 (Marshall 1973:618 [ref. 6965], Iwamoto 1979: 144 [ref. 2311]). Macrouridae: Macrourinae.

Coelonotus Peters 1855:465 [ref. 3449]. Masc. *Syngnathus argulus* Peters 1855:278. Type by monotypy. Synonym of *Microphis* Kaup 1853 (Dawson 1986:284 [ref. 6201]), as a valid subgenus (Dawson 1984 [ref. 5879], Dawson 1985:127 [ref. 6541]); valid (Araga in Masuda et al. 1984:85 [ref. 6441]). See *Hemimarsupium* Kaup 1853. Syngnathidae: Syngnathinae.

Coelophrys Brauer 1902:291 [ref. 631]. Fem. *Coelophrys brevicaudata* Brauer 1902:291. Type by monotypy. Ogcocephalidae.

Coelorinchus See Caelorinchus. The correct spelling of this genus is *Caelorinchus* (C. R. Robins, pers. comm., and based on examination of original). Macrouridae: Macrourinae.

Coelurichthys Miranda-Ribeiro 1908:[4] [ref. 3715]. Masc. *Coelurichthys iporangae* Miranda-Ribeiro 1908:[4]. Type by monotypy. On page 4, unpaginated. Valid (Géry 1977:362 [ref. 1597]); synonym of *Mimagoniates* Regan 1907 (Weitzman & Fink 1985:2 [ref. 5203]). Characidae: Glandulocaudinae.

Cogrus Rafinesque 1810:62 [ref. 3594]. Fem. *Cogrus maculatus* Rafinesque 1810:62. Type by monotypy. Synonym of *Ophichthus* Ahl 1789 (Blache et al. 1973:247 [ref. 7185], McCosker 1977:79 [ref. 6836], McCosker et al. 1989:379 [ref. 13288]). Ophichthidae: Ophichthinae.

Coilia (subgenus of *Engraulis*) Gray 1830:Pl. 85 (v. 1) [ref. 1878]. Fem. *Engraulis (Coilia) hamiltonii* Gray 1830:Pl. 85 (= *Mystus ramcarati* Hamilton 1822:233). Type by monotypy. Also appeared in Gray 1831:9 [ref. 1879] as a new genus. Valid (see Whitehead 1967:148-149 [ref. 6464], Uyeno in Masuda et al. 1984:20 [ref. 6441], Grande 1985:245 [ref. 6466], Whitehead et al. 1988:460 [ref. 5725], Kottelat 1989:4 [ref. 13605]). Engraulidae.

Coius Hamilton 1822:85, 369 [ref. 2031]. Masc. *Coius polota* Hamilton 1822:95, 370. Type by subsequent designation. Type designated by Fowler 1905:504 [ref. 1370], not *Coius cobojus* [sic] Hamilton as designated by Jordan 1917:114 [ref. 2407]. Apparently a senior objective synonym of (and should replace) *Datnioides* Bleeker 1853. Lobotidae.

Cokeridia Meek & Hildebrand 1928:905 [ref. 2964]. Fem. *Cokeridia crossota* Meek & Hildebrand 1928:906. Type by original designation (also monotypic). Synonym of *Dactyloscopus* Gill 1859 (Dawson 1975:5 [ref. 7121], Dawson 1982:19 [ref. 1072]). Dactyloscopidae.

Colefaxia (subgenus of *Neoplatycephalus*) Whitley 1935:249 [ref. 4683]. Fem. *Platycephalus macrodon* Ogilby 1886:226. Type by original designation (also monotypic). Misspelled *Colifaxia* in Zoological Record for 1935. Synonym of *Platycephalus* Bloch 1795 (Paxton et al. 1989:469 [ref. 12442] based on placement of type species). Platycephalidae.

Coleosmaris Norman 1931:359 [ref. 3220]. Fem. *Coleosmaris nigricauda* Norman 1931:359. Type by original designation (also monotypic). Centracanthidae.

Coleotropis Myers & Wade 1942:136 [ref. 3134]. Fem. *Menidia starksi* Meek & Hildebrand 1923:267. Type by original designation. Synonym of *Atherinella* Steindachner 1875 (Chernoff 1986:240 [ref. 5847]). Atherinidae: Menidiinae.

Colisa Cuvier in Cuvier & Valenciennes 1831:359 [ref. 4881]. Fem. *Colisa vulgarus* Cuvier in Cuvier & Valenciennes 1831:362 (= *Trichopodus colisa* Hamilton 1822:117, 372). Type by absolute tautonymy of senior objective synonym. Cuvier's *C. vulgarus* is an unneeded substitute for *T. colisa* Hamilton. See account of *Polyacanthus* Cuvier. Synonym of *Trichogaster* Bloch & Schneider 1801. Belontiidae.

Coliscus Cope 1871:437 [ref. 922]. Masc. *Coliscus parietalis* Cope 1871:437. Type by monotypy. Synonym of *Pimephales* Rafinesque 1820. Cyprinidae.

Colistium Norman 1926:272 [ref. 3216]. Neut. *Ammotretis nudipinnis* Waite 1910:50. Type by subsequent designation. Two included species, earliest type designation not researched; *nudipinnis* listed by Norman 1934. Valid (Norman 1934:424 [ref. 6893], Ahlstrom et al. 1984:643 [ref. 13641], Sakamoto 1984 [ref. 5273]). Pleuronectidae: Rhombosoleinae.

Collettia Goode & Bean 1896:88 [ref. 1848]. Fem. *Nyctophus rafinesquii* Cocco 1820:tab. III. Type by original designation (also monotypic). Synonym of *Diaphus* Eigenmann & Eigenmann 1890 (Nafpaktitis 1968:22 [ref. 6979], Bolin 1959:20 [ref. 503], Krefft & Bekker 1973:176 [ref. 7181], Paxton 1979:7 [ref. 6440]). Myctophidae.

Collichthys Günther 1860:312 [ref. 1963]. Masc. *Sciaena lucida* Richardson 1855:87. Type by subsequent designation. Type designated by Jordan & Evermann 1889:348 [ref. 2439] and perhaps by Günther 1867 (in Zoological Record for 1866); see discussion by Trewavas 1977:388 [ref. 4459]; see also Bleeker 1876:330 [ref. 448] for possible type designation. Valid (Trewavas 1977:400 [ref. 4459], Okamura in Masuda et al. 1984:163 [ref. 6441]). Sciaenidae.

Collybus Snyder 1904:525 [ref. 4149]. *Collybus drachme* Snyder 1904:525. Type by original designation (also monotypic). Synonym of *Brama* Bloch & Schneider 1801 (Mead 1972:25 [ref. 6976], Mead 1973:386 [ref. 7199]). Bramidae.

Coloconger Alcock 1889:456 [ref. 81]. Masc. *Coloconger raniceps* Alcock 1889:456. Type by monotypy. Misspelled *Cologonger* in Zoological Record for 1889. Valid (Blache & Bauchot 1976:428 [ref. 305], Karrer 1982:41 [ref. 5679], Asano in Masuda et al. 1984:27 [ref. 6441], Castle 1986:163 [ref. 5644], Paxton et al. 1989:144 [ref. 12442], Smith 1989:417 [ref. 13285]). Colocongridae.

Colocopus Gill 1884:279 [ref. 1726]. Masc. *Colocopus lambdurus* Gill 1884:279. Type by original designation (also monotypic). Synonym of *Paracanthurus* Bleeker 1863 (Randall 1955:363 [ref. 13648]). Acanthuridae.

Cologrammus Gill 1893:119, 124 [ref. 1736]. Masc. *Sticharium flavescens* Hutton 1872:33. Type by monotypy. Clinidae.

Cololabis Gill 1895:176 [ref. 6957]. Fem. *Scomberesox brevirostris* Peters 1866:521. Type by monotypy. Valid (Hubbs & Wisner 1980 [ref. 2267], Yoshino in Masuda et al. 1984:79 [ref. 6441], Collette et al. 1984:336 [ref. 11422]). Scomberesocidae.

Colomesus Gill 1884:422 [ref. 1727]. *Tetrodon psittacus* Bloch & Schneider 1801:505. Type by being a replacement name. Replacement for *Batrachops* Bibron, preoccupied by Heckel 1840 in fishes. Valid (Shipp 1974:108 [ref. 7147], Tyler 1980:341 [ref. 4477], Arai 1983:207 [ref. 14249], see Su et al. 1986:112 [ref. 12582]). Tetraodontidae.

Colonianus de Buen 1926:80 [ref. 5054]. As a "grupo" for 2 species of *Gobius*. Not available on basis of Art. 1b(6) [see de Buen's definition of "grupo" on p. 11]; see Appendix A. Gobiidae.

Colossoma Eigenmann & Kennedy 1903:530 [ref. 1260]. Neut. *Myletes oculus* Cope 1872:268. Type by monotypy. Also appeared in Eigenmann 1903 (Dec.):148 [ref. 1218]. *Colosoma* is a misspelling. Valid (Géry 1976:50 [ref. 14199], Géry 1977:254 [ref. 1597], Géry 1986:97 [ref. 6012], Machado-Allison 1986:1 [ref. 12757]). Characidae: Serrasalminae.

Colotrigla Gill 1905:339 [ref. 1790]. Fem. *Prionotus stearnsii* Jordan & Swain 1884:541. Type by original designation (also monotypic). Synonym of *Prionotus* Lacepède 1801. Triglidae: Triglinae.

Colpichthys Hubbs 1918:305 [ref. 2226]. Masc. *Atherinops regis* Jenkins & Evermann 1888:138. Type by original designation (also monotypic). Valid (White et al. 1984:360 [ref. 13655], White 1985:17 [ref. 13551], Crabtree 1987:861 [ref. 6771], Crabtree 1989 [ref. 12738]). Atherinidae: Atherinopsinae.

Colpognathus Klunzinger 1880:339 [ref. 2624]. Masc. *Plectropoma dentex* Cuvier in Cuvier & Valenciennes 1828:394. Type by monotypy or by original designation (not translated). Apparently preoccupied by Wesmael 1844 in Hymenoptera, replaced by *Chenia* Fowler 1958 (*Chenia* itself also apparently preoccupied). Synonym of *Othos* Castelnau 1875 (Paxton et al. 1989:506 [ref. 12442]). Serranidae: Anthiinae.

Colubrina Lacepède 1803:40 [ref. 4930]. Fem. *Colubrina chinensis* Lacepède 1803:40, 41. Type by monotypy. *Colubrinus* is a misspelling. Possibly fictitious, based on an unidentified Chinese painting. Ophichthidae.

Columatilla Whitley 1940:243 [ref. 4660]. Fem. *Columbia transmontana* Eigenmann & Eigenmann 1892:234. Type by being a replacement name. Replacement for *Columbia* Eigenmann & Eigenmann 1892, preoccupied by Rang 1834 in Mollusca [not investigated]. Synonym of *Percopsis* Agassiz 1849. Percopsidae.

Columbia Eigenmann & Eigenmann 1892:234 [ref. 1213]. Fem. *Columbia transmontana* Eigenmann & Eigenmann in Eigenmann 1892:234. Type by monotypy. Apparently preoccupied by Rang 1834 in Mollusca, replaced by *Columatilla* Whitley 1940. Synonym of *Percopsis* Agassiz 1849. Percopsidae.

Colurodontis Hutchins 1977:22 [ref. 2283]. Fem. *Colurodontis paxmani* Hutchins 1977:22. Type by original designation (also monotypic). Monacanthidae.

Comephorus Lacepède 1800:312 [ref. 2709]. Masc. *Callionymus baikalensis* Pallas 1776:290, 707. Type by monotypy. Valid (Sideleva 1982:29 [ref. 14469], Washington et al. 1984:442 [ref. 13660], Yabe 1985:123 [ref. 11522]). Comephoridae.

Commandorella Taranetz & Andriashev 1935:267, 269 [ref. 4341]. Fem. *Commandorella popovi* Taranetz & Andriashev 1935:268, 270. Type by original designation (also monotypic). Synonym of *Gymnelus* Reinhardt 1834 (Anderson 1982:28 [ref. 5520]). Zoarcidae.

Compagnoia (subgenus of *Parmaturus*) see *Campagnoia*. Scyliorhinidae.

Compsomidiama Chabanaud 1951:1 [ref. 802]. Neut. *Com-*

psomidiama medium Chabanaud 1951:1. Type by monotypy. Cynoglossidae: Cynoglossinae.

Compsura Eigenmann 1915:60 [ref. 1231]. Fem. *Compsura heterura* Eigenmann 1915:61. Type by original designation (also monotypic). Misspelled *Compsoura* by Eigenmann 1917:37 [ref. 1236]. Synonym of *Cheirodon* Girard 1855 (Fink & Weitzman 1974:3 [ref. 7132]), as a valid subgenus (Géry 1977:574 [ref. 1597]). Characidae.

Conchognathus Collett 1889:123 [ref. 889]. Masc. *Conchognathus grimaldii* Collett 1889:124. Type by monotypy. Synonym of *Simenchelys* Gill 1879 (Blache et al. 1973:223 [ref. 7185], Robins & Robins 1989:214 [ref. 13287]). Synaphobranchidae: Simenchelyinae.

Conger Bosc (ex Cuvier) 1817:450 [ref. 5126]. Masc. *Muraena conger* Linnaeus 1758:245. Type by absolute tautonymy. See discussion in Paxton et al. 1989:140-141 [ref. 12442] regarding authorship of this genus; should be credited to Bosc instead of Oken. Valid, with authorship as above (Paxton et al. 1989:140 [ref. 12442]). Congridae: Congrinae.

Conger Klein 1775:22 [ref. 2618]. Masc. Not available, published in a work that does not conform to the principle of binominal nomenclature. In the synonymy of *Conger* Oken 1817. Congridae: Congrinae.

Conger Oken (ex Cuvier) 1817:1781 [ref. 3303]. Masc. *Muraena conger* Linnaeus 1758:245. Type by absolute tautonymy. Based on "Les Congres" of Cuvier 1816:231 [ref. 993] (see Gill 1903:966 [ref. 5768]). On Official List (Opinion 93, Direction 87); unavailable names of *Conger* on Official Index. Apparently predated by and should be credited to Bosc 1817 (see Paxton et al. 1989:140-141 [ref. 12442]). Valid (Blache et al. 1973:239 [ref. 7185], Asano in Masuda et al. 1984:28 [ref. 6441], Castle 1986:164 [ref. 5644], see Paxton et al. 1989:141 [ref. 12442], Smith 1989:513 [ref. 13285]). Congridae: Congrinae.

Congermuraena Kaup 1856:71 [ref. 2572]. Fem. *Congrus habenata* Richardson 1844:109. Type by subsequent designation. Type (as *Muraena belearica* De la Roche) apparently not designated by Bleeker, contrary to Jordan (1919:272 [ref. 2410]); first designated by Ogilby 1898:284-285 [ref. 3276] as above. Also in Kaup 1856:108 [ref. 2573]. *Congromuraena* Günther 1870:40 [ref. 1995] is an unjustified emendation. Synonym of *Ariosoma* Swainson 1838 (Blache et al. 1973:240 [ref. 7185] and Smith 1989:491 [ref. 13285] with *balearica* as type). Congridae: Bathymyrinae.

Congerodon Kaup 1856:73 [ref. 2572]. Masc. *Congerodon indicus* Kaup 1856:74. Type by monotypy. Unlike other genera in this work, this genus did not appear in Kaup 1856 [ref. 2573]. Synonym of *Uroconger* Kaup 1856 (Smith 1989:545 [ref. 13285]). Congridae: Congrinae.

Congiopodus Perry 1811:unnum. p., pl. [ref. 12255]. Masc. *Congiopodus percatus* Perry 1811:unnum. p., pl. Type by monotypy. Possible derivations *Conchopodus* and *Coniopodus* listed by Günther 1872:659 [ref. 1997]; *Congiopus* is a misspelling. Valid (Paulin & Moreland 1979 [ref. 6915], Washington et al. 1984:440 [ref. 13660], Poss 1986:480 [ref. 6296], Paxton et al. 1989:475 [ref. 12442]). Congiopodidae.

Congiopus see *Congiopodus*. Congiopodidae.

Congocharax Matthes 1964:75 [ref. 2911]. Masc. *Hemigrammocharax olbrechtsi* Poll 1954:59. Type by original designation. Synonym of *Neolebias* Steindachner 1894 (Vari 1979:339 [ref. 5490]); valid (Géry 1977:66 [ref. 1597], Daget & Gosse 1984:184 [ref. 6185]). Citharinidae: Distichodontinae.

Congopanchax Poll 1971:303 [ref. 3530]. Masc. *Aplocheilichthys myersi* Poll 1952:300. Type by original designation. Valid (Wildekamp et al. 1986:187 [ref. 6198]). As a subgenus of *Aplocheilichthys* Bleeker 1863 (Parenti 1981:508 [ref. 7066]). Cyprinodontidae: Aplocheilichthyinae.

Congothrissa Poll 1964:8 [ref. 3523]. Fem. *Congothrissa gossei* Poll 1964:8. Type by original designation (also monotypic). Valid (Whitehead 1985:166 [ref. 5141]) in Clupeidae, subfamily Pellonulinae; in Congothrissidae (Grande 1985:246 [ref. 6466]). Clupeidae.

Congrammus Fowler 1906:105 [ref. 1371]. Masc. *Congrammus moorei* Fowler 1906:105. Type by original designation (also monotypic). Synonym of *Dactyloscopus* Gill 1859 (Dawson 1982:19 [ref. 1072]). Dactyloscopidae.

Congrellus Ogilby 1898:288 [ref. 3276]. Masc. *Muraena balearica* Delaroche 1809:314, 327. Type by original designation. Apparently appeared first (31 Aug.) as above; also as Ogilby in Jordan & Evermann 1898:2801 (26 Nov.). Objective synonym of *Congermuraena* Kaup 1856; synonym of *Ariosoma* Swainson 1838 (Blache et al. 1973:241 [ref. 7185], Smith 1989:492 [ref. 13285]). Congridae: Bathymyrinae.

Congresox Gill 1890:234 [ref. 1733]. Masc. *Conger talabon* Cuvier 1829:350. Type by original designation (also monotypic). Valid (Castle & Williamson 1975:2 [ref. 7115], Smith 1989:434 [ref. 13285]). Muraenesocidae.

Congrhynchus Fowler 1934:272 [ref. 1416]. Masc. *Congrhynchus talabonoides* Fowler 1934:273. Type by original designation (also monotypic). Congridae: Congrinae.

Congrina Jordan & Hubbs 1925:192, 196 [ref. 2486]. Fem. *Congermuraena aequorea* Gilbert & Cramer 1897:405. Type by original designation. Synonym of *Rhechias* Jordan 1921 (Smith & Kanazawa 1977:538 [ref. 4036], Smith 1989:532 [ref. 13285]). Congridae: Congrinae.

Congriscus Jordan & Hubbs 1925:191, 193 [ref. 2486]. Masc. *Congromuraena megastoma* Günther 1877:445. Type by original designation (also monotypic). Correct spelling for genus of type is *Congermuraena*. Valid (Karrer 1982:18 [ref. 5679], Asano in Masuda et al. 1984:28 [ref. 6441], Smith 1989:511 [ref. 13285]). Congridae: Congrinae.

Congrogadoides Borodin 1933:141 [ref. 528]. Masc. *Congrogadoides spinifer* Borodin 1933:141. Type by monotypy. Synonym of *Congrogadus* Günther 1862, but as a valid subgenus (Godkin & Winterbottom 1985 [ref. 5233], Winterbottom 1986:7 [ref. 5727]). Pseudochromidae: Congrogadinae.

Congrogadus Günther 1862:388 [ref. 1969]. Masc. *Machaerium subducens* Richardson 1843:175. Type by being a replacement name. Replacement for *Machaerium* Richardson 1843, preoccupied by Haliday 1832 in Diptera. Misspelled *Conyrodus* and *Congrodus* in literature. Valid (Winterbottom et al. 1984:1607 [ref. 5140], Amaoka in Masuda et al. 1984:293 [ref. 6441], Winterbottom 1986:7 [ref. 5727]). Pseudochromidae: Congrogadinae.

Congrosoma Garman 1899:308 [ref. 1540]. Neut. *Congrosoma evermanni* Garman 1899:309. Type by monotypy. Synonym of *Promyllantor* Alcock 1890 (Blache et al. 1973:243 [ref. 7185]); valid, but needs research (Castle, pers. comm.); valid, mentioned in passing (Smith 1989:512 [ref. 13285]). Congridae: Congrinae.

Congruogobius (subgenus of *Gobionellus*) Ginsburg 1953:26 [ref. 1806]. Masc. *Euctenogobius liolepis* Meek & Hildebrand

1928:875. Type by original designation (also monotypic). Gobiidae.

Congrus Richardson 1845:105 [ref. 3739]. Masc. Also in Richardson 1848:106 [ref. 3740]. Considered by Jordan and others as a variant spelling of *Conger* of earlier authors, with same type. If regarded as an available generic name (as by Blache et al. 1973:239 [ref. 7185]), then includes two species: *Muraenesox tricuspidatus* McClelland and *Congrus lepturus* Richardson, neither as yet apparently designated as type. Synonym of *Conger* Oken 1817 (Smith 1989:513 [ref. 13285]). Congridae: Congrinae.

Conidens Briggs 1955:15 [ref. 637]. Masc. *Crepidogaster samoensis* Steindachner 1906:1408. Type by original designation. Valid (Allen [L. G.] 1984:629 [ref. 13673], Yoshino in Masuda et al. 1984:341 [ref. 6441]). Gobiesocidae: Gobiesocinae.

Conniella Allen 1983:44 [ref. 5355]. Fem. *Conniella apterygia* Allen 1983:44. Type by original designation (also monotypic). Labridae.

Conocara Goode & Bean 1896:39 [ref. 1848]. Neut. *Conocara macdonaldi* Goode & Bean 1896:39. Type by subsequent designation. Type designated by Jordan 1920:467 [ref. 4905]. Valid (Krefft 1973:88 [ref. 7166], Markle & Quéro in Whitehead et al. 1984:238 [ref. 13675], Markle 1986:220 [ref. 5687]). Alepocephalidae.

Conodon Cuvier in Cuvier & Valenciennes 1830:156 [ref. 999]. Masc. *Conodon antillanus* Cuvier in Cuvier & Valenciennes 1830:156. Type by monotypy. Valid (Johnson 1980:11 [ref. 13553], Matsuura in Uyeno et al. 1983:350 [ref. 14275]). Haemulidae.

Conomus Rafinesque 1815:92 [ref. 3584]. As "*Conomus* R. sp. do.", meaning a new genus name by Rafinesque for a species in a preceding genus, and presumably for a species of *Lophius*. Unavailable, name only. In the synonymy of *Lophius* Linnaeus 1758. Lophiidae.

Conoporoderma (subgenus of *Poroderma*) Fowler 1934:234 [ref. 1416]. Neut. *Scyllium pantherinum* Müller & Henle 1841:13. Type by original designation. Synonym of *Poroderma* Smith 1838 (Springer 1979:112 [ref. 4175], Compagno 1984:346 [ref. 6846], Compagno 1988:115 [ref. 13488]). Scyliorhinidae.

Conorhynchos Bleeker 1858:191, 205, 209 [ref. 365]. Neut. *Pimelodus conirostris* Valenciennes in Cuvier & Valenciennes 1840:204. Type by monotypy. Spelled *Conorhynchus* by Bleeker 1862:12 [ref. 393] and 1863:102 [ref. 401]. *Conostomus* [*Conostome*] Duméril is a synonym. Valid (Burgess 1989:281 [ref. 12860] as *Conorhynchus*). Pimelodidae.

Conorynchus Nozemann 1758:381 [ref. 13433]. Masc. *Conorhynchus macrocephalus* Lacepède 1803. Type by subsequent designation. Original without included species; Gill 1861:55 [ref. 1766], as *Conorhynchus*, provided a type (see Whitehead 1986:214 [ref. 5733]). Whitehead regards *Conorynchus* Nozemann as the senior synonym of *Albula* but to be rejected as a forgotten name (nomen oblitum). Original not examined. Possibly can date to Gill 1861. Albulidae: Albulinae.

Conostome Duméril 1856:484 [ref. 1154]. *Pimelodus conirostris* Valenciennes in Cuvier & Valenciennes 1840:204. Type by original designation. Not available, vernacular name not latinized. Spelled *Conostomus* by Bleeker 1858:191, 205 [ref. 365] as name in synonymy of his *Conorhynchos*. Pimelodidae.

Conta Hora 1950:194 [ref. 2214]. Fem. *Pimelodus conta* Hamilton 1822:191. Type by original designation (also by monotypy and absolute tautonymy). Valid (Jayaram 1981:246 [ref. 6497], Tilak 1987 [ref. 6794], Burgess 1989:132 [ref. 12860]). Sisoridae.

Contusus Whitley 1947:147 [ref. 4708]. Masc. *Tetrodon richei* Fréminville 1813:250. Type by original designation. Proposed with *richei* as type; apparently not technically a replacement name for *Amblyrhynchotus* Troschel 1856, preoccupied by Tilesius 1818 in Crustacea. Valid (Arai 1983:207 [ref. 14249], Su et al. 1986:112 [ref. 12582]). Tetraodontidae.

Cookeolus (subgenus of *Priacanthus*) Fowler 1928:190 [ref. 5596]. Masc. *Anthias boops* Forster in Bloch & Schneider 1801:308. Type by original designation (also monotypic). Apparently based on a misidentified type species, and a petition is pending to have the ICZN designate *Priacanthus japonicus* Cuvier 1829 as the type to preserve current usage (see Starnes 1988:142-143 [ref. 6978]). Valid (Fitch & Crooke 1984 [ref. 4950], Yoshino in Masuda et al. 1984:143 [ref. 6441], Heemstra 1986:544 [ref. 5660], Starnes 1988:142 [ref. 6978], Paxton et al. 1989:542 [ref. 12442]). Priacanthidae.

Copadichromis Eccles & Trewavas 1989:294 [ref. 13547]. Masc. *Haplochromis quadrimaculatus* Regan 1922:703. Type by original designation. Cichlidae.

Copeina Fowler 1906:294 [ref. 1373]. Fem. *Pyrrhulina argyrops* Cope 1878:694. Type by original designation (also monotypic). Valid (Géry 1977:142 [ref. 1597], Géry et al. 1987:369 [ref. 6001]). Lebiasinidae: Pyrrhulininae.

Copelandellus Jordan & Evermann 1896:1019, 1100 [ref. 2443]. Masc. *Poecilichthys quiescens* Jordan 1884:478. Type by original designation (also monotypic). Synonym of subgenus *Hololepis* Putnam 1863 of genus *Etheostoma* Rafinesque 1819 (Collette & Banarescu 1977:1457 [ref. 5845]). Percidae.

Copelandia Jordan in Jordan & Copeland 1877:136 [ref. 5961]. Fem. *Copelandia eriarcha* Jordan 1877:136. Type by original designation (also monotypic). Also in Jordan 1877:56 [ref. 2372], where species is described in more detail. Synonym of *Enneacanthus* Gill 1864. Centrarchidae.

Copella Myers 1956:12 [ref. 3127]. Fem. *Copeina compta* Myers 1927:110. Type by original designation. Valid (Géry 1977:143 [ref. 1597], Géry et al. 1987:369 [ref. 6001]). Lebiasinidae: Pyrrhulininae.

Copidoglanis Günther 1864:25 [ref. 1974]. Masc. *Plotosus (Tandanus) tandanus* Mitchell 1838:44, 95. Type by subsequent designation. Type designated by Jordan 1919:332 [ref. 4904] with name was misprinted *Copiodoglanis*. Objective synonym of *Tandanus* Mitchell 1838. Plotosidae.

Copora Fernández-Yépez 1969:[4] [ref. 9186]. *Heros nicaraguense* Günther 1864:153. Type by original designation. Synonym of *Cichlasoma* Swainson 1839. Cichlidae.

Coptobrycon Géry 1966:226 [ref. 1588]. Masc. *Hasemania bilineata* Ellis 1911:150. Type by original designation (also monotypic). Valid (Géry 1977:402 [ref. 1597]). Characidae.

Coptodon Gervais 1853:8 [ref. 1575]. Masc. *Acerina zilli* Gervais 1848:203. Type by original designation (also monotypic). Cichlidae.

Coptostomabarbus David & Poll 1937:223 [ref. 1043]. Masc. *Coptostomabarbus wittei* David & Poll 1937:223. Type by monotypy. Valid (Lévêque & Daget 1984:300 [ref. 6186] as *Coptostomobarbus*). Cyprinidae.

Coracinus Gronow 1763:66 [ref. 1910]. Masc. Apparently not available, published in a rejected work (Opinions 89 and 261).

According to Fowler (MS), the correct genus is *Dichistus* Gill 1888, a replacement for *Dipterodon* Cuvier, preoccupied; family should be Dichistiidae. Fowler's treatment is similar to that of J.L.B. Smith 1935 [ref. 13662], but not J.L.B. Smith 1945:248 [ref. 5846] where *Coracinus* is used. Treated as valid by Johnson 1984:464 [ref. 9681] and M.M. Smith 1986:601 [ref. 5712]. Coracinidae.

Coracinus Pallas 1814:256 [ref. 3351]. Masc. *Coracinus chalcis* Pallas 1814:256. Type by subsequent designation. Type designated by Jordan 1917:84 [ref. 2407]. Not *Coracinus* Gronow. Synonym of *Sciaena* Linnaeus 1758 (Trewavas 1973:396 [ref. 7201]). Sciaenidae.

Coradion Kaup 1860:137, 146 [ref. 2583]. Neut. *Chaetodon chrysozonus* Cuvier (ex Kuhl & van Hasselt) 1831:82. Type by subsequent designation. Type designated by Bleeker 1876:304 [ref. 448]. Valid (Burgess 1978:151 [ref. 700], Ida in Masuda et al. 1984:186 [ref. 6441], Maugé & Bauchot 1984:461 [ref. 6614]). Chaetodontidae.

Coraglanis Hora & Silas 1952:12 [ref. 2218]. Masc. *Euchiloglanis kishinouyei* Kimura 1934:178. Type by original designation (also monotypic). Valid (Chu 1979:76 [ref. 831], Jayaram 1981:263 [ref. 6497], Burgess 1989:133 [ref. 12860]); synonym of *Euchiloglanis* Regan 1907 (Chu 1981:27, 30 [ref. 5249]). Sisoridae.

Corallicola (subgenus of *Auchenopterus*) Jordan & Evermann 1898:2369 [ref. 2445]. Masc. *Cremnobates marmoratus* Steindachner 1876:222. Type by original designation. Synonym of *Paraclinus* Mocquard 1888 (Clark Hubbs 1952:65 [ref. 2252]). Labrisomidae.

Coralliozetus Evermann & Marsh 1899:362 [ref. 1283]. *Coralliozetus cardonae* Evermann & Marsh 1899:362. Type by original designation (also monotypic). Valid (Stephens 1963:51 [ref. 4270], Greenfield & Johnson 1981:56 [ref. 5580], Acero P. 1984 [ref. 5534]). Chaenopsidae.

Corallochaetodon (subgenus of *Chaetodon*) Burgess 1978:474 [ref. 700]. Masc. *Chaetodon trifasciatus* Park 1794:34. Type by original designation. Wrongly treated as a synonym of *Mesochaetodon* Maugé & Bauchot 1984, but as a valid subgenus (Maugé & Bauchot 1984:477 [ref. 6614]); *Corallochaetodon* has priority over *Mesochaetodon* at the generic level). Chaetodontidae.

Coranthus Smith 1961:409 [ref. 4128]. Masc. *Cheilodipterus polyacanthus* Vaillant 1877:27. Type by original designation (also monotypic). Valid (Fraser 1972:15 [ref. 5195], Hayashi in Masuda et al. 1984:145 [ref. 6441]). Apogonidae.

Corcyrogobius Miller 1972:395 [ref. 3011]. Masc. *Gobius liechtensteini* Kolombatovic 1891:25. Type by original designation (also monotypic). Appeared first in Miller 1971:264 as name only. Valid (Miller 1973:493 [ref. 6888], Miller in Whitehead et al. 1986:1030 [ref. 13677]). Gobiidae.

Cordorinus Rafinesque 1815:89 [ref. 3584]. Masc. *Corydoras geoffroy* Lacepède 1803:148. Type by being a replacement name. As "*Cordorinus* R. [Rafinesque] *Corydoras* Lac. [Lacepède]." An available replacement name (unneeded) for and objective synonym of *Corydoras* Lacepède 1803. In the synonymy of *Corydoras* Lacepède 1803 (Nijssen & Isbrücker 1980:192 [ref. 6910]). Callichthyidae.

Cordylancistrus Isbrücker 1980:48 [ref. 2303]. Masc. *Pseudancistrus torbesensis* Schultz 1944:296. Type by original designation (also monotypic). Valid (Heitmans et al. 1983 [ref. 5278], Burgess 1989:434 [ref. 12860]). Loricariidae.

Cordylus Gronow in Gray 1854:163 [ref. 1911]. Masc. *Scomber scombrus* Linnaeus 1758:297. Type by monotypy. Apparently preoccupied by Laurenti 1768 in Reptilia and by Wagler 1828 in Amphibia (not by Gronow 1763, rejected work); apparently not replaced. Objective synonym of *Scomber* Linnaeus 1758. Scombridae.

Coregonoides Richardson 1843:426 [ref. 13395]. Masc. *Odax vittatus* Richardson 1843. Appeared as Solander manuscript name and quoted description published in synonymy of *Odax*; technically a name published in synonymy. Apparently never made available. In the synonymy of *Odax* Cuvier 1839 (Gomon & Paxton 1986:31 [ref. 5656]). Odacidae.

Coregonus Jarocki 1822:35 [ref. 4984]. Masc. Not available, on Official Index (Direction 56). Junior homonym of *Coregonus* Linnaeus 1758. Original not seen. In the synonymy of *Coregonus* Linnaeus 1758. Salmonidae: Coregoninae.

Coregonus Lacepède 1803:239 [ref. 4930]. Masc. *Coregonus lavaretus* Linnaeus 1758:310. Type by subsequent designation. Not available; on Official Index (Direction 56). Junior homonym and in synonymy of *Coregonus* Linnaeus 1758 (Svetovidov 1973:148 [ref. 7169]). Salmonidae: Coregoninae.

Coregonus (subgenus of *Salmo*) Linnaeus 1758:310 [ref. 2787]. Masc. *Salmo lavaretus* Linnaeus 1758:310. Appeared as "Coregoni", as subgroup of *Salmo*; made available by the ICZN. Type designated by Plenary Powers; on Official List (Opinion 93), *Coregonus* Lacepède 1803 and of Jarocki 1822 placed on Official Index (Direction 56). Valid (Svetovidov 1973:148 [ref. 7169], Svetovidov in Whitehead et al. 1984:374 [ref. 13675], Kendall & Behnke 1984:144 [ref. 13638]). Salmonidae: Coregoninae.

Coreius Jordan & Starks 1905:197 [ref. 2530]. Masc. *Labeo cetopsis* Kner 1866:548. Type by monotypy. Valid (Banarescu & Nalbant 1973:175 [ref. 173], Lu, Luo & Chen 1977:502 [ref. 13495], Chen & Li in Chu & Chen 1989:109 [ref. 13584]). Cyprinidae.

Corematodus Boulenger 1897:918 [ref. 538]. Masc. *Corematodus shiranus* Boulenger 1897:919. Type by monotypy. Misspelled *Corematodes* by Jordan 1920:471 [ref. 4905]. Valid (Eccles & Trewavas 1989:272 [ref. 13547]). Cichlidae.

Coreobagrus Mori 1936:672, 675 [ref. 3044]. Masc. *Coreobagrus brevicorpus* Mori 1936:672, 675. Type by monotypy. Valid (Jayaram 1968:342 [ref. 5615], Sawada in Masuda et al. 1984:59 [ref. 6441], Burgess 1989:69 [ref. 12860]). Bagridae.

Coreoleuciscus Mori 1935:161 [ref. 3043]. Masc. *Coreoleuciscus splendidus* Mori 1935:161. Type by original designation (also monotypic). Valid (Banarescu & Nalbant 1973:33 [ref. 173]). Cyprinidae.

Coreoperca Herzenstein 1896:11 [ref. 2151]. Fem. *Coreoperca herzi* Herzenstein 1896:11. Type by monotypy. Valid (Katayama in Masuda et al. 1984:124 [ref. 6441], Zhou et al. 1986:965 [ref. 6332]). Percichthyidae.

Coreosiniperca (subgenus of *Siniperca*) Fang & Chong 1932:137, 149 [ref. 1307]. Fem. *Siniperca roulei* Wu 1930:54. Type by original designation (also monotypic). Percoidei.

Corica Hamilton 1822:253, 383 [ref. 2031]. Fem. *Corica soborna* Hamilton 1822:253, 383. Type by monotypy. Valid (Jayaram 1981:37 [ref. 6497], Grande 1985:246 [ref. 6466], Whitehead 1985:179 [ref. 5141], Kottelat 1989:4 [ref. 13605]). Clupeidae.

Coridodax Günther 1862:243 [ref. 1969]. Masc. *Sparus pullus* Forster in Bloch & Schneider 1801:288. Type by monotypy. Objective synonym of *Odax* Cuvier 1839 (see Gomon & Paxton 1986:31 [ref. 5656], see also Whitley 1976:47 [ref. 4735]).

Odacidae.

Coripareius Garman 1912:120 [ref. 1544]. Masc. *Labeo cetopsis* Kner 1866:548. Type by original designation (also monotypic). Objective synonym of *Coreius* Jordan & Starks 1905 (Banarescu & Nalbant 1973:175 [ref. 173], Lu, Luo & Chen 1977:502 [ref. 13495], Chen & Li in Chu & Chen 1989:109 [ref. 13584]). Cyprinidae.

Coris Lacepède (ex Commerson) 1801:96 [ref. 2710]. Fem. *Coris aygula* Lacepède 1801:96, 97. Type by subsequent designation. Type designated by Jordan 1890:636 [ref. 2392]. Valid (Bauchot & Quignard 1973:431 [ref. 7204], Randall & Kuiter 1982 [ref. 5446], Richards & Leis 1984:544 [ref. 13668], Araga in Masuda et al. 1984:209 [ref. 6441], Randall 1986:691 [ref. 5706], Quignard & Pras in Whitehead et al. 1986:923 [ref. 13676]). Labridae.

Corniger Agassiz in Spix & Agassiz 1831:119, 121 [ref. 13]. Masc. *Corniger spinosus* Agassiz in Spix & Agassiz 1831:122. Type by monotypy. For authorship and date see Kottelat 1988:78 [ref. 13380]. Valid (Woods & Sonoda 1973:378 [ref. 6899], Uyeno & Sato in Uyeno et al. 1983:275 [ref. 14275], Lozano & Brito 1989 [ref. 12828]). Holocentridae.

Coronichthys Herre 1942:120 [ref. 2133]. Masc. *Coronichthys ornata* Herre 1942:122. Type by original designation (also monotypic). *Diademichthys* Pfaff published 9 May 1942, *Coronichthys* published 24 Aug. 1942. Synonym of *Diademichthys* Pfaff 1942 (Briggs 1955:141 [ref. 637]). Gobiesocidae: Gobiesocinae.

Coronogobius Herre 1945:80 [ref. 2140]. Masc. *Coronogobius striata* Herre 1948:81. Type by original designation (also monotypic). Synonym of *Porogobius* Bleeker 1874 (Maugé 1986:381 [ref. 6218]). Gobiidae.

Coroplopus Smith 1966:1 [ref. 4139]. Masc. *Coroplopus dicologlossops* Smith 1966:1. Type by original designation (also monotypic). Synonym of *Schedophilus* Cocco 1839 (McDowall 1981:123 [ref. 5356], but as *Coroplopos*). Centrolophidae.

Corusculus Jordan & Snyder 1901:75 [ref. 2505]. Masc. *Anthias berycoides* Hilgendorf 1879:78. Type by monotypy. Unneeded name "by accident" for *Eteliscus* Jordan & Snyder (Jordan 1920:494 [ref. 4905]). Objective synonym of *Eteliscus* Jordan & Snyder 1900. Synonym of *Doederleinia* Steindachner 1883. Acropomatidae.

Corvina Cuvier 1829:173 [ref. 995]. Fem. *Sciaena nigra* Forsskål 1775:47. Type by subsequent designation. Species cited by Cuvier as "(*Sciaena nigra* Gm.) Bl. 297." with more species listed in footnote. Type designated by Gill 1862:85 [ref. 1771] as *Corvina nigra* Cuvier, which apparently goes back to Forsskål. Preoccupied by Hahn 1822 in Aves. Synonym of *Sciaena* Linnaeus 1758 (Trewavas 1973:396 [ref. 7201]). Sciaenidae.

Corvula Jordan & Eigenmann 1889:377 [ref. 2439]. Fem. *Johnius batabanus* Poey 1861:184. Type by original designation. Tentatively a synonym of *Bairdiella* Gill 1861 (Chao 1978:38 [ref. 6983]). Sciaenidae.

Corycus Cuvier 1814:89 [ref. 4884]. Masc. *Lutjanus rostratus* Bloch 1792:Pl. 254. Type by subsequent designation. Appeared without species scientifically named; species added by Valenciennes in Cuvier & Valenciennes 1839. Type designated by Jordan 1917:93 [ref. 2407] if not earlier. As *Coricus* in Cuvier 1816:263 [ref. 993] and *Corica* by authors. Originally as a subgenus, but genus not stated. Synonym of *Symphodus* Rafinesque 1810 (Bauchot & Quignard 1973:434 [ref. 7204], see also Quignard & Pras in Whitehead et al. 1986:931 [ref. 13676]). Labridae.

Corydoras Lacepède 1803:147 [ref. 4930]. Masc. *Corydoras geoffroy* Lacepède 1803:147, 148. Type by monotypy. *Cataphractus punctatus* Bloch 1794 sometimes cited as type but not cited by Lacepède in this subgenus (see Nijssen & Isbrücker 1980:192 [ref. 6810]); Lacepède's description apparently independent of Bloch. Valid (Gosline 1940 [ref. 6489], Nijssen & Isbrücker 1980 [ref. 6910], Nijssen & Isbrücker 1986 [ref. 6010], Burgess 1989:365 [ref. 12860], Malabarba 1989:147 [ref. 14217]). Callichthyidae.

Corymbophanes Eigenmann 1909:5 [ref. 1222]. *Corymbophanes andersoni* Eigenmann 1909:5. Type by monotypy. Valid (Isbrücker 1980:14 [ref. 2303], Burgess 1989:430 [ref. 12860]). Loricariidae.

Corynolophus Gill 1878:217, 218 [ref. 5604]. Masc. *Himantolophus reinhardti* Lütken 1878:320. Type by monotypy. Synonym of *Himantolophus* Reinhardt 1837 (Bertelsen & Krefft 1988:35 [ref. 6615]). Himantolophidae.

Corynophorus Osório 1912:89 [ref. 6481]. Masc. *Corynophorus compressus* Osório 1912:90. Type by monotypy. Synonym of *Himantolophus* Reinhardt 1837 (Maul 1973:668 [ref. 7171], Bertelsen & Krefft 1988:35 [ref. 6615]). Himantolophidae.

Corynopoma Gill 1858:425 [ref. 1750]. Neut. *Corynopoma riisei* Gill 1858:426. Type by subsequent designation. Type apparently first designated by Jordan 1919:281 [ref. 2410]. Selected over *Stevardia* Gill 1858 by action of Günther (1864:287), see Weitzman & Fink 1985:2 [ref. 5203]). Valid (Géry 1977:359 [ref. 1597], Weitzman & S. Fink 1985:1 et seq. [ref. 5203]). Characidae: Glandulocaudinae.

Corynopomops Fowler 1943:6 [ref. 1442]. Masc. *Corynopomops opisthopterus* Fowler 1943:6. Type by original designation (also monotypic). Synonym of *Gephyrocharax* Eigenmann 1912 (Weitzman & S. Fink 1985:2 [ref. 5203]). Characidae: Glandulocaudinae.

Coryogalops Smith 1958:144 [ref. 4118]. Masc. *Coryogalops anomolus* Smith 1958:144. Type by original designation (also monotypic). Valid (Goren 1979 [ref. 6952]). Gobiidae.

Coryphaena Houttuyn 1782:315 [ref. 2220]. Fem. *Coryphaena japonica* Houttuyn 1782:315. Type by monotypy. Preoccupied by *Coryphaena* Linnaeus 1758, replaced by *Coryphaenoides* Lacepède 1801 (preoccupied) and *Branchiostegus* Rafinesque 1815. Objective synonym of *Branchiostegus* Rafinesque 1815 (Dooley 1978:31 [ref. 5499], Dooley & Kailola 1988:250 [ref. 7299]). Malacanthidae: Latilinae.

Coryphaena Linnaeus 1758:261 [ref. 2787]. Fem. *Coryphaena hippurus* Linnaeus 1758:261. Type by subsequent designation. Type designated by Jordan & Gilbert 1883:454 [ref. 2476]. On Official List (Opinion 77); *Coryhaena* Stiles 1922:73 placed on Official Index as an incorrect subsequent spelling. Valid (Tortonese 1973:385 [ref. 7192], Nakamura in Masuda et al. 1984:158 [ref. 6441], Collette in Whitehead et al. 1986:845 [ref. 13676], Smith 1986:661 [ref. 5712]). Coryphaenidae.

Coryphaenoides Gunner 1765:50 [ref. 1958]. Masc. *Coryphaenoides rupestris* Gunner 1765:50. Type by monotypy. Dean 1916:528 [ref. 13327] cites a Gunner 1761 article with different title but in same journal volume, pp. 43-50 [not investigated]. Current authors date to 1765. Valid (Marshall 1973:294 [ref. 7194], Marshall & Iwamoto 1973:565 [ref. 6966], Fahay & Markle 1984:274 [ref. 13653], Okamura in Masuda et al. 1984:96 [ref. 6441], Iwamoto 1986:334 [ref. 5674], Iwamoto & Sazonov 1988 [ref. 6228], Paxton et al. 1989:326 [ref. 12442]). Macrouridae: Macrourinae.

Coryphaenoides Lacepède 1801:219 [ref. 2710]. Masc. *Coryphaenoides houttuyni* Lacepède 1801:219, 220 (= *Coryphaena japonica* Houttuyn 1782:315). Type by monotypy. Preoccupied by *Coryphaenoides* Gunner 1765. Replaced by *Branchiostegus* Rafinesque 1815. Objective synonym of *Branchiostegus* Rafinesque 1815 (Dooley 1978:31 [ref. 5499], Dooley & Kailola 1988:250 [ref. 7299]). Malacanthidae: Latilinae.

Coryphaesopia Chabanaud 1930:17 [ref. 784]. Fem. *Aesopia cornuta* Kaup 1858:58. Type by original designation (also monotypic). Soleidae.

Coryphillus Chabanaud 1931:302 [ref. 785]. Masc. *Aseraggodes filiger* Weber 1913:436. Type by monotypy. Soleidae.

Coryphoblennius Norman 1943:802 [ref. 3228]. Masc. *Blennius galerita* Linnaeus 1758:256. Type by original designation (also monotypic). Valid (Bath 1973:526 [ref. 7212], Bath 1977:181 [ref. 208], Zander in Whitehead et al. 1986:1098 [ref. 13677]). Blenniidae.

Coryphopterus Gill 1863:262 [ref. 1690]. Masc. *Coryphopterus glaucofraenum* Gill 1863:263. Type by original designation (also monotypic). Misspelled *Coryphogobius* by Gill 1863:263 (footnote). Valid (Birdsong et al. 1988:192 [ref. 7303]). Gobiidae.

Coryphus Commerson in Lacepède 1801:186 (footnote) [ref. 2710]. Masc. *Coryphaena chrysurus* Linnaeus 1758:261. Type by monotypy. Probably not available; name mentioned in passing under *Coryphaena chrysurus*; Lacepède adopted Plumier's species name but not the generic name. See remarks under Opinion 89 in Appendix B. In the synonymy of *Coryphaena* Linnaeus 1758. Coryphaenidae.

Corystion Klein 1776:762 [ref. 4919]. Neut. Not available, published in a work that does not conform to the principle of binominal nomenclature. In the synonymy of *Trigla* Linnaeus 1758. Triglidae: Triglinae.

Corystion Rafinesque 1810:24 [ref. 3594]. Neut. *Corystion mustazola* Rafinesque 1810:24. Type by monotypy. Synonym of *Trachinus* Linnaeus 1758 (Wheeler 1973:449 [ref. 7190]). Trachinidae.

Corythobatus Cantor 1849:1027 [45] [ref. 715]. Masc. *Scorpaena monodactyla* Bloch & Schneider 1801:194. Type by being a replacement name. Unneeded replacement for *Minous* Cuvier 1829, not preoccupied by *Minois* Hübner 1816 in Lepidoptera. On page 45 of separate. Objective synonym of *Minous* Cuvier 1829 (Eschmeyer et al. 1979:454 [ref. 1277]). Scorpaenidae: Minoinae.

Corythoichthys Kaup 1853:231 [ref. 2569]. Masc. *Syngnathus fasciatus* Gray 1830. Type by subsequent designation. Jordan 1919:253 [ref. 2410] gives type as *C. albirostris* Heckel, but that species apparently not available; type above designated by Whitley 1948 according to Dawson 1985:36 [ref. 6541]. Misspelled *Corythroichthys* by Jordan and others. Valid (Dawson 1977 [ref. 7048], Araga in Masuda et al. 1984:87 [ref. 6441], Dawson 1985:36 [ref. 6541], Paxton et al. 1989:414 [ref. 12442]). Syngnathidae: Syngnathinae.

Coryzichthys Ogilby 1908:50, 54 [ref. 3284]. Masc. *Batrachoides diemensis* Lesueur 1824:402. Type by subsequent designation. Type designated by Jordan 1920:529 [ref. 4905]. Objective synonym of *Halophryne* Gill 1863 (Hutchins 1976:8 [ref. 6971]). Batrachoididae.

Coscinoxyron Fowler 1907:450 [ref. 1374]. Neut. *Chalcinus culter* Cope 1872:265. Type by original designation (also monotypic). Questionably a synonym of *Triportheus* Cope 1872 (Géry 1977:343 [ref. 1597]). Characidae.

Cosmocampus Dawson 1979:674 [ref. 1069]. Masc. *Corythoichthys albirostris* Heckel in Kaup 1856:25. Type by original designation. Valid (Dawson 1982:120 [ref. 6764], Dawson 1982:135 [ref. 5440], Dawson 1985:47 [ref. 6541], Dawson 1986:447 [ref. 5650], Paxton et al. 1989:415 [ref. 12442]). Syngnathidae: Syngnathinae.

Cosmochilus Sauvage 1878:240 [ref. 3879]. Masc. *Cosmochilus harmandi* Sauvage 1878:240. Type by monotypy. Also appeared in Sauvage 1882:180 [ref. 3894]. Valid (Kottelat 1985:261 [ref. 11441], Chu & Roberts 1985 [ref. 5244], Roberts 1989:31 [ref. 6439], Kottelat 1989:7 [ref. 13605], Chu & Cui in Chu & Chen 1989:162 [ref. 13584]). Cyprinidae.

Cossyphodes Bleeker 1860:37 [ref. 375]. Masc. *Labrus macrodontus* Lacepède 1802:451, 522. Type by monotypy. Objective synonym of *Choerodon* Bleeker 1849. Labridae.

Cossyphus McClelland 1844:403 [ref. 2927]. Masc. *Cossyphus ater* McClelland 1844:403. Type by monotypy. Preoccupied by Valenciennes 1839 in fishes; replaced by *Phagorus* McClelland 1844. Synonym of *Clarias* Scopoli 1777 (Teugels 1986:11 [ref. 12548]). Clariidae.

Cossyphus Valenciennes in Cuvier & Valenciennes 1839:102 [ref. 1007]. Masc. *Bodianus bodianus* Bloch 1790:33. Type by subsequent designation. Type designated by Bonaparte 1841:puntata 156, fasc. 30 [ref. 512]. Preoccupied by Olivier 1791 in Coleoptera, and by Rafinesque 1815 and Dumont 1823 in Aves. Synonym of *Bodianus* Bloch 1790 (Randall 1986:686 [ref. 5706]). Labridae.

Cottapistus Bleeker 1876:298 [ref. 450]. Masc. *Apistus cottoides* Linnaeus 1758:29. Type by monotypy. Valid (Washington et al. 1984:440 [ref. 13660], Paxton et al. 1989:440 [ref. 12442]). Scorpaenidae: Tetraroginae.

Cottinella (subgenus of *Abyssocottus*) Berg 1907:43, 45 [ref. 266]. Fem. *Abyssocottus boulengeri* Berg 1906:908. Type by monotypy. Valid (Sideleva 1982:30 [ref. 14469], Washington et al. 1984:443 [ref. 13660], Yabe 1985:123 [ref. 11522]). Cottocomephoridae.

Cottiusculus Schmidt 1904:108 [ref. 3946]. Masc. *Cottiusculus gonez* Schmidt 1904:108. Type by monotypy. Appeared as name only in Schmidt 1903:518 [ref. 3945]. *Cottiusculus schmidti* mentioned in footnote on p. 108, but that species apparently not yet available [described by Jordan & Starks in same year]. Valid (Neyelov 1979:116, 161 [ref. 3152], Washington et al. 1984:442 [ref. 13660], Yabe in Masuda et al. 1984:327 [ref. 6441], Yabe 1985:111 [ref. 11522]). Cottidae.

Cottocomephorus Pellegrin 1900:354 [ref. 3398]. Masc. *Cottocomephorus megalops* Pellegrin 1900:354. Type by monotypy. Valid (Sideleva 1982:28 [ref. 14469], Washington et al. 1984:443 [ref. 13660]). Cottocomephoridae.

Cottogaster Putnam 1863:4 [ref. 3567]. Fem. *Boleosoma tessellatum* Thompson (not of DeKay) 1853:31. Type by monotypy. Based on misidentified type species, *Boleosoma tessellatum* (not of DeKay) Thompson 1853; *Cottogaster putnami* Jordan & Gilbert 1883:498 proposed for Thompson's misidentification. Should go to ICZN on Art. 70(b). Synonym of *Percina* Haldeman 1842, but as a valid subgenus (Page 1974:84 [ref. 3346], Collette & Banarescu 1977:1455 [ref. 5845]). Percidae.

Cottogobius Koumans 1941:253 [ref. 2677]. Masc. *Cottogobius bilobatus* Koumans 1941:253. Type by original designation (also monotypic). Synonym of *Pleurosicya* Weber 1913 (Larson & Hoese 1980:33 [ref. 2725]). Gobiidae.

Cottoperca Steindachner 1875:66 [ref. 4223]. Fem. *Cottoperca rosenbergii* Steindachner 1875:67. Type by monotypy. Valid (Stevens et al. 1984:563 [ref. 13633], Nakamura in Nakamura et al. 1986:244 [ref. 14235]). Bovichtidae.

Cottopsis Girard 1850:303 [ref. 1815]. Fem. *Cottus asper* Richardson 1836:295. Type by monotypy. Synonym of *Cottus* Linnaeus 1758. Cottidae.

Cottunculoides Barnard 1927:76 [ref. 193]. Masc. *Cottunculus inermis* Vaillant 1888:365. Type by original designation. Also in Barnard (Oct.) 1927:923 [ref. 194]. Type clearly designated in 1927:76 but not in 1927:923. Most workers overlook 1927:76 as earliest. Valid (Neyelov 1973:604 [ref. 7219]). As a subgenus of *Psychrolutes* (Nelson et al. 1985 [ref. 5264]). Psychrolutidae.

Cottunculus Collett 1875:20 [ref. 884]. Masc. *Cottunculus microps* Collett 1875:20. Type by monotypy. Valid (Neyelov 1973:603 [ref. 7219], Nelson 1982:1473 [ref. 5470], Washington et al. 1984:444 [ref. 13660], Yabe 1985:122 [ref. 11522], Fedorov & Nelson in Whitehead et al. 1986:1261 [ref. 13677], Nelson 1986:491 [ref. 5698], Nelson 1989 [ref. 12546]). Psychrolutidae.

Cottus Linnaeus 1758:264 [ref. 2787]. Masc. *Cottus gobio* Linnaeus 1758:265. Type by subsequent designation. Type designated by Girard 1850:184 [ref. 1814]. On Official List (Opinion 77). Valid (Neyelov 1973:593 [ref. 7219], Sideleva 1982:27 [ref. 14469], Yabe in Masuda et al. 1984:326 [ref. 6441], Yabe 1985:111 [ref. 11522], Fedorov in Whitehead et al. 1986:1247 [ref. 13677]). Cottidae.

Cotylephorus Swainson 1838:354 [ref. 4302]. Masc. *Cotylephorus blochii* Swainson 1838:354 (= *Platystacus cotylephorus* Bloch 1794:54). Type by monotypy in 1838:354; *blochii* Swainson is an unneeded substitute for *P. cotylephorus*. Also in Swainson 1839 [ref. 4303]:189 (as *Cotilephorus*), and p. 308 (as *Cotylephorus*). *Cotilephorus* is an incorrect subsequent spelling. *Cotylophorus* Agassiz 1846:102 [ref. 64] is an unjustified emendation. Objective synonym of *Platystacus* Bloch 1794, which Mees 1987:175 [ref. 11510] treats as a synonym of *Aspredo* Scopoli 1777. Aspredinidae: Aspredininae.

Cotylichthys Jordan 1919:341 [ref. 2413]. Masc. *Cotylis fimbriata* Müller & Troschel 1849. Type by original designation (also monotypic). Synonym of *Gobiesox* Lacepède 1800 (Briggs 1955:87 [ref. 637]). Gobiesocidae: Gobiesocinae.

Cotylis Müller & Troschel in Müller 1843:297 [ref. 3063]. Fem. *Cyclopterus nudus* of Bloch & Schneider 1801. Type by monotypy. Type not *L. nudus* Linnaeus (Briggs 1955:87 [ref. 637]). Synonym of *Gobiesox* Lacepède 1800 (Briggs 1955:87 [ref. 637]). Gobiesocidae: Gobiesocinae.

Cotylopus Guichenot 1864:9 [ref. 1943]. Masc. *Cotylopus acutipinnis* Guichenot 1864:10. Type by subsequent designation. Type apparently first designated by Bleeker 1874:313 [ref. 437]. Valid (Maugé 1986:366 [ref. 6218]). Gobiidae.

Couchia Thompson 1856:190 [ref. 4390]. Fem. *Couchia minor* Thompson 1856:188. Type by monotypy. Synonym of *Ciliata* Couch 1832 (Svetovidov 1973:312 [ref. 7169]). Lotidae.

Couesius Jordan 1878:784 [ref. 2377]. Masc. *Nocomis dissimilis* Girard 1856:189. Type by original designation. Type stated as *Leucosomus dissimilis* Girard = *Nocomis milneri* Jordan; *dissimilis* regarded as type — the only species Jordan recognized as valid with the original description of the genus. Valid (Robins et al. 1980:21 [ref. 7111]). Cyprinidae.

Cranoglanis Peters 1880:1030 [ref. 3456]. Masc. *Cranoglanis sinensis* Peters 1880:1030. Type by monotypy. Valid (Burgess 1989:73 [ref. 12860]). Cranoglanididae.

Crapatalus Günther 1861:86 [ref. 1966]. Fem. *Crapatalus novaezelandiae* Günther 1861:87. Type by monotypy. Leptoscopidae.

Crassilabrus (subgenus of *Zirichthys*) Swainson 1839:172, 225 [ref. 4303]. Masc. *Cheilinus undulatus* Rüppell 1835:20. Type by monotypy. Labridae.

Crassinarke Takagi 1951:27 [ref. 4309]. Fem. *Crassinarke dormitor* Takagi 1951:30. Type by original designation (also monotypic). Valid (Nakaya in Masuda et al. 1984:12 [ref. 6441]). Torpedinidae.

Crassispinus Maul 1948:51 [ref. 2916]. Masc. *Crassispinus granulosus* Maul 1948:52. Type by monotypy. Synonym of *Neocyttus* Gilchrist 1906 (Wheeler 1973:352 [ref. 7190]). Oreosomatidae.

Craterocephalus McCulloch 1912:48 [ref. 2938]. Masc. *Craterocephalus fluviatilis* McCulloch 1912:49. Type by original designation. Valid (White et al. 1984:360 [ref. 13655], Ivantsoff et al. 1987 [ref. 6229], Crowley & Ivantsoff 1988 [ref. 12286], Paxton et al. 1989:357 [ref. 12442]). Atherinidae: Atherininae.

Cratinus Steindachner 1878:395 [ref. 4226]. Masc. *Cratinus agassizii* Steindachner 1878:395. Type by monotypy. Date may be 1879. Valid (Kendall 1984:500 [ref. 13663]). Serranidae: Serraninae.

Crayracion Bleeker (ex Klein) 1865:Pls. 205-214 [ref. 416]. Neut. Can date to many species figured on Pls. 205, 206, 208, 209, 210, 211, 212 and 214 published in part 18 (19 Apr. 1865); corresponding text (pp. 49, 65 et seq.) published in parts 19 and 20. Type as designated by Bleeker (p. 49) is *Crayracion laevissimus* Klein (unavailable). Type should be selected from among the figured specimens; type perhaps not yet validly designated. Also appeared in other Bleeker 1865 papers. In the synonymy of *Sphoeroides*. Tetraodontidae.

Crayracion Klein 1777:788 [ref. 4920]. Neut. Not available, published in a work that does not conform to the principle of binominal nomenclature. In the synonymy of *Sphoeroides* Anonymous 1798. Tetraodontidae.

Crayracion Walbaum (ex Klein) 1792:580 [ref. 4572]. Not available (see Shipp 1974:34 [ref. 7147]). Genus can date to Bleeker 1865 [ref. 416]. In the synonymy of *Sphoeroides* Anonymous 1798. Tetraodontidae.

Creagrudite Myers 1927:117 [ref. 3096]. *Creagrudite maxillaris* Myers 1927:118. Type by original designation. Synonym of *Creagrutus* Günther 1864 (Böhlke & Saul 1975 [ref. 7109]); valid (Géry 1977:383 [ref. 1597]). Characidae.

Creagrutops Schultz 1944:327 [ref. 3960]. Masc. *Creagrutops maracaiboensis* Schultz 1944:327. Type by original designation (also monotypic). Valid (Géry 1977:410 [ref. 1597]). Characidae.

Creagrutus Günther 1864:339 [ref. 1974]. Masc. *Leporinus muelleri* Günther 1859:92. Type by monotypy. Valid (Böhlke & Saul 1975 [ref. 7109], Géry 1977:403 [ref. 1597], Mahnert & Géry 1988:5 [ref. 6407], Géry & Renno 1989 [ref. 13420]). Characidae.

Creatochanes (subgenus of *Tetragonopterus*) Günther 1864:318, 329-330 [ref. 1974]. *Salmo melanurus* Bloch 1794:104. Type by subsequent designation. Described as a section or subgenus in key (p. 318) with corresponding species on pp. 329-330. Type designated by Eigenmann 1910:435 [ref. 1224]. Synonym of *Bryconops* Kner 1858, as a valid subgenus (Géry 1977:435 [ref. 1597]). Characidae.

Creedia Ogilby 1898:298 [ref. 3276]. Fem. *Creedia clathrisquamis*

Ogilby 1898:299. Type by monotypy. Valid (Nelson 1983 [ref. 5272], Nelson 1985 [ref. 5154], Shimada & Yoshino 1987 [ref. 6703]). Creediidae.

Creisson Jordan & Seale 1907:43 [ref. 2498]. Masc. *Creisson validus* Jordan & Seale 1907:43. Type by original designation (also monotypic). Synonym of *Acentrogobius* Bleeker 1874 (Hoese, pers. comm.). Valid (Kottelat 1989:18 [ref. 13605]). Gobiidae.

Cremnobates Günther 1861:374 [ref. 1968]. Masc. *Auchenopterus monophthalmus* Günther 1861:275. Type by being a replacement name. Replacement for *Auchenopterus* Günther 1861, not preoccupied by *Auchenipterus* Valenciennes but preoccupied by Agassiz' 1846 unjustified emendation of *Auchenipterus*. Synonym of *Paraclinus* Mocquard 1888 (Clark Hubbs 1952:65 [ref. 2252]). Labrisomidae.

Cremnochorites Holleman 1982:125 [ref. 2187]. Masc. *Tripterygium capense* Gilchrist & Thompson 1908:140. Type by original designation (also monotypic). Correct spelling for genus of type species is *Tripterygion*. Valid (Hardy 1984:176 [ref. 5340], Holleman 1986:756 [ref. 5671]). Tripterygiidae.

Cremnotekla Whitley 1940:242 [ref. 4660]. Fem. *Auchenopterus monophthalmus* Günther 1861:275. Type by being a replacement name. Replacement for *Auchenopterus* Günther 1861, not preoccupied by *Auchenipterus* Valenciennes but preoccupied by Agassiz' 1846 unjustified emendation *Auchenopterus*. Synonym of *Paraclinus* Mocquard 1888 (Clark Hubbs 1952:66 [ref. 2252]). Blenniidae.

Cremornea Whitley 1962:9 [ref. 4732]. Fem. *Cremornea francoisi* Whitley 1962:9. Type by original designation (also monotypic). Synonym of *Priolepis* Valenciennes 1837. Gobiidae.

Crenacara see *Crenicara*. Cichlidae.

Crenalticus Whitley 1930:21 [ref. 4671]. Masc. *Salarias crenulatus pallidus* Whitley 1926:235. Type by original designation. The subspecies *pallidus* is elevated to the species level for purposes of the type species; type not *crenulatus*. Synonym of *Salarias* Cuvier 1816 (Smith-Vaniz & Springer 1971:38 [ref. 4145]). Blenniidae.

Crenicara Steindachner 1875:99 [ref. 4220]. Neut. *Crenicara elegans* Steindachner 1875:99. Type by monotypy. Unjustifiably emended to *Crenacara* by Regan 1905:152 [ref. 12256]. Valid (Kullander 1986:140 [ref. 12439]). Cichlidae.

Crenichthys Hubbs 1932:3 [ref. 2242]. Masc. *Crenichthys nevadae* Hubbs 1932:4. Type by original designation (also monotypic). Valid (Parenti 1981:517 [ref. 7066]). Cyprinodontidae: Empetrichthyinae.

Crenicichla Heckel 1840:416 [ref. 2064]. Fem. *Crenicichla macrophthalma* Heckel 1840:427. Type by subsequent designation. Type designated by Eigenmann & Bray 1894:620 [ref. 1248]. Valid (Casciotta 1987 [ref. 6772], Kullander 1986:82 [ref. 12439], Kullander 1988 [ref. 6232], Malabarba 1989:164 [ref. 14217], Kullander & Nijssen 1989:207 [ref. 14136]). Cichlidae.

Crenidens Valenciennes in Cuvier & Valenciennes 1830:377 [ref. 996]. Masc. *Crenidens forskalii* Valenciennes in Cuvier & Valenciennes 1830:378 (= *Sparus crenidens* Forsskål 1775:xv). Type by monotypy. Valid (Tortonese 1973:416 [ref. 7192], Bauchot & Hureau in Whitehead et al. 1986:884 [ref. 13676], Smith & Smith 1986:584 [ref. 5710]). Sparidae.

Crenilabrus Oken (ex Cuvier) 1817:1182a [ref. 3303]. Masc. *Labrus lapina* Forsskål 1775:36. Type by subsequent designation. Swainson 1839:229 [ref.4303] fixed the type as *verres* Bloch; if accepted would upset current usage. Bonaparte 1841:puntata 156, fasc. 30 [ref. 512] designated *pavo* (not an included species = *lapina*) which is usually cited as the type. Based on"Les Crénilabres" of Cuvier 1816:262 [ref. 993]; also 1814:89 [ref. 4884]. See Jordan 1917:101 [ref. 2407] and Gill 1903:966 [ref. 5768]. Synonym of *Symphodus* Rafinesque 1810 (Bauchot & Quignard 1973:434 [ref. 7204]). Labridae.

Crenimugil Schultz 1946:(380) 387 [ref. 3965]. Masc. *Mugil crenilabrus* Forsskål 1775:73. Type by original designation (also monotypic). Valid (Yoshino & Senou in Masuda et al. 1984:120 [ref. 6441], Smith & Smith 1986:715 [ref. 5717]). Mugilidae.

Crenuchus Günther 1863:443 [ref. 1973]. Masc. *Crenuchus spilurus* Günther 1863:443. Type by monotypy. Valid (Géry 1977:110 [ref. 1597], Vari 1983:5 [ref. 5419]). Characidae.

Creocele Briggs 1955:12 [ref. 637]. Fem. *Gobiesox cardinalis* Ramsay 1882:148. Type by original designation (also monotypic). Valid (Scott 1976:179 [ref. 7055]). Gobiesocidae: Gobiesocinae.

Creolus Jordan & Gilbert 1883:xxxvi, 985 [ref. 2476]. Masc. *Serranus furcifer* Cuvier in Cuvier & Valenciennes 1828:264. Type by monotypy. Intended as a replacent for *Brachyrhinus* Gill 1862 (preoccupied) on p. 916; name appeared as *Creolus* in table of contents and in index, but withdrawn in Addenda (p. 973) and *Paranthias* substituted. Objective synonym of *Paranthias* Guichenot 1868 (Smith 1971:84 [ref. 14102]). Serranidae: Epinephelinae.

Creotroctes Gistel 1848:X [ref. 1822]. Masc. *Scomber sarda* Bloch 1793:44. Type by being a replacement name. Unneeded and unexplained replacement for *Sarda* Cuvier 1829. Objective synonym of *Sarda* Cuvier 1829 (Collette & Chao 1975:597 [ref. 5573]). Scombridae.

Crepidogaster Günther 1861:507 [ref. 1964]. Fem. *Crepidogaster tasmaniensis* Günther 1861:507. Type by subsequent designation. Type designated by Jordan 1919:307 [ref. 4904]. Preoccupied by Boheman 1848 in Coleoptera; replaced by *Aspasmogaster* Waite 1907. Objective synonym of *Aspasmogaster* Waite 1907 (Briggs 1955:49 [ref. 637], Scott 1976:182 [ref. 7055]). Gobiesocidae: Gobiesocinae.

Cridorsa Whitley 1938:159 [ref. 4694]. Fem. *Cridorsa moonta* Whitley 1938:159. Type by original designation (also monotypic). Kyphosidae.

Crinodus Gill 1862:112 [ref. 1658]. Masc. *Haplodactylus lophodon* Günther 1859:435. Type by original designation (also monotypic). Correct genus for type is *Aplodactylus*. Aplodactylidae.

Cristatogobius Herre 1927:170 [ref. 2104]. Masc. *Cristatogobius lophius* Herre 1927:170. Type by original designation (also monotypic). Valid (Akihito in Masuda et al. 1984:256 [ref. 6441], Birdsong et al. 1988:192 [ref. 7303]). Gobiidae.

Cristiceps Valenciennes in Cuvier & Valenciennes 1836:402 [ref. 1005]. Neut. *Cristiceps australis* Valenciennes in Cuvier & Valenciennes 1836:402. Type by monotypy. Valid (Hoese 1976:52 [ref. 7338]). Clinidae.

Cristivomer Gill & Jordan in Jordan 1878:356, 359 [ref. 2376]. Masc. *Salmo namaycush* Walbaum 1792:68. Type by subsequent designation. Type designated by Jordan & Gilbert 1883:317 [ref. 2476]. Synonym of *Salvelinus* Richardson 1836, but as a valid subgenus (Kendall & Behnke 1984:144 [ref. 13638]). Salmonidae: Salmoninae.

Cristula de Buen 1961:24, 26 [ref. 698]. Fem. *Cristula reticulata* de Buen 1961:27. Type by original designation (also monotypic). Synonym of *Maxillicosta* Whitley 1935 (Eschmeyer & Poss

1976:434 [ref. 5468]). Scorpaenidae: Neosebastinae.

Crius Valenciennes in Webb & Berthelot 1839:Pl. 9 [ref. 4502]. Masc. *Crius berthelotii* Valenciennes in Webb & Berthelot 1839:Pl. 9. Type by monotypy. In text in 1843:43, plate in 1839. Synonym of *Schedophilus* Cocco 1839 (Haedrich 1967:59 [ref. 5357], Haedrich 1973:560 [ref. 7216]). Centrolophidae.

Croaltus Smith 1959:247 [ref. 4123]. Masc. *Blennius bifilum* Günther 1861:225. Type by monotypy; author indicates one species in genus but mentions a second in text, without clear generic allocation. Synonym of *Antennablennius* Fowler 1931 (Bath 1983:48 [ref. 5393]). Blenniidae.

Crockeridius Clark 1936:391 [ref. 839]. Masc. *Crockeridius odysseus* Clark 1936:391. Type by original designation (also monotypic). Synonym of *Dialommus* Gilbert 1891 (Clark Hubbs 1952:62 [ref. 2252]). Labrisomidae.

Croilia Smith 1955:106 [ref. 4095]. Fem. *Croilia mossambica* Smith 1955:108. Type by original designation (also monotypic). Misspelled *Croila* in Zoological Record for 1955. Valid (Hoese 1986:785 [ref. 5670], Maugé 1986:366 [ref. 6218] but as *Croila*). Gobiidae.

Cromeria Boulenger 1901:445 [ref. 557]. Fem. *Cromeria nilotica* Boulenger 1901:445. Type by monotypy. Valid (Poll 1984:134 [ref. 6180] in Cromeriidae; for relationships see Howes 1985:289 [ref. 5148]). Kneriidae.

Cromis Browne 1789:449 [ref. 669]. Masc. Not available, published in a rejected work on Official Index (Opinion 89). Sciaenidae.

Crossias Jordan & Starks 1904:296 [ref. 2528]. Masc. *Crossias allisi* Jordan & Starks 1904:296. Type by original designation (also monotypic). Valid subgenus of *Porocottus Gill 1859 (Neyelov 1979:135 [ref. 3152]); valid genus (Washington et al. 1984:442 [ref. 13660]). Cottidae.*

Crossobothus (subgenus of *Bothus*) Fowler 1934:335 [ref. 1416]. Masc. *Bothus variegatus* Fowler 1934:335. Type by original designation (also monotypic). Bothidae: Bothinae.

Crossocheilichthys (subgenus of *Crossocheilos*) Bleeker 1860:122 [ref. 380]. Masc. *Crossocheilos (Crossocheilichthys) cobitis* Bleeker 1860:125. Type by subsequent designation. Type designated by Bleeker 1863:192 [ref. 397]. Correct spelling for genus of type species is *Crossocheilus*. Cyprinidae.

Crossocheilus Kuhl & van Hasselt in van Hasselt 1823:132 [ref. 5963]. Masc. *Crossocheilus oblongus* Kuhl & van Hasselt in van Hasselt 1823:132. Type by monotypy. Also spelled *Crostocheilus* in text and in 1824 [ref. 5104]. *Crossocheilus* selected by Kottelat (1987:371 [ref. 5962]). *Crossocheilos* is a misspelling; *Crossochilus* Günther 1868:73 [ref. 1990] is an unjustified emendation. Valid (Karaman 1971:236 [ref. 2560], Jayaram 1981:133 [ref. 6497], Roberts 1989:32 [ref. 6439], Chu & Cui in Chu & Chen 1989:243 [ref. 13584], Kottelat 1989:7 [ref. 13605]). Cyprinidae.

Crossochir Hubbs 1933:3 [ref. 2243]. Fem. *Crossochir koelzi* Hubbs 1933:3. Type by original designation (also monotypic). Synonym of *Amphistichus* Agassiz 1854 (Tarp 1952:39 [ref. 12250]). Embiotocidae.

Crossoderma Guichenot 1869:194 [ref. 1952]. Neut. *Crossoderma madagascariense* Guichenot 1869:195. Type by monotypy. Synonym of *Caracanthus* Krøyer 1845. Caracanthidae.

Crossogobius Koumans 1931:111 [ref. 5623]. Masc. *Gobius depressus* Ramsay & Ogilby 1887:4. Type by monotypy. Proposed as a "museum name" but treated as a genus, with a species and description, "...after which I made the genus description. I do not know who has described the genus." Regarded as an available genus name and description. Synonym of *Callogobius* Bleeker 1874. Gobiidae.

Crossolepis Norman 1927:22 [ref. 3217]. Fem. *Arnoglossus breviríctis* Alcock 1890:433. Type by original designation (also monotypic). Synonym of *Psettina* Hubbs 1915 (Norman 1934:199 [ref. 6893], Amaoka 1969:177 [ref. 105]), as a valid subgenus (Fedorov & Foroshchuk 1988 [ref. 13478]). Bothidae: Bothinae.

Crossoloricaria Isbrücker 1979:87, 90 [ref. 2302]. Fem. *Loricaria variegata* Steindachner 1879:151. Type by original designation. Valid (Isbrücker 1980:120 [ref. 2303], Isbrücker & Nijssen 1986:103 [ref. 5212], Isbrücker & Nijssen 1986:40 [ref. 7321], Burgess 1989:444 [ref. 12860]). Loricariidae.

Crossolycus Regan 1913:247 [ref. 3651]. Masc. *Lycodes fimbriatus* of Steindachner 1898:322 (= *Crossolycus chilensis* Regan 1913:247). Type by subsequent designation. Type designated by Jordan 1920:550 [ref. 4905]. Objective synonym of *Crossostomus* Lahille 1908 (Gosztonyi 1977:204 [ref. 6103]). Zoarcidae.

Crossorhinus Müller & Henle 1837:113 [ref. 3067]. Masc. *Squalus lobatus* Bloch & Schneider 1801:137. Type by monotypy. Objective synonym of *Orectolobus* Bonaparte 1834 (Compagno 1984:180 [ref. 6474]). Orectolobidae.

Crossorhombus Regan 1920:211 [ref. 3671]. Masc. *Platophrys dimorphus* Gilchrist 1905:10. Type by original designation (also monotypic). Valid (Norman 1934:217 [ref. 6893], Amaoka 1969:132 [ref. 105], Ahlstrom et al. 1984:642 [ref. 13641], Amaoka in Masuda et al. 1984:348 [ref. 6441], Hensley 1986:857 [ref. 5669], Hensley 1986:941 [ref. 6326]). Bothidae: Bothinae.

Crossosalarias Smith-Vaniz & Springer 1971:20 [ref. 4145]. Masc. *Crossosalarias macrospilus* Smith-Vaniz & Springer 1971:21. Type by original designation (also monotypic). Valid (Yoshino in Masuda et al. 1984:298 [ref. 6441]). Blenniidae.

Crossoscorpaena Fowler 1938:75 [ref. 1426]. Fem. *Sebastes hexanema* Günther 1880:40. Type by original designation (also monotypic). Synonym of *Pontinus* Poey 1860. Scorpaenidae: Scorpaeninae.

Crossostoma Sauvage 1878:88 [ref. 3878]. Neut. *Crossostoma davidi* Sauvage 1878:89. Type by monotypy. Apparently preoccupied by Morris & Lycett 1851 in Mollusca, Gosse 1855 in Polychaeta, and by Agassiz 1862 in Colenterata; apparently not replaced [preoccupation not investigated]. Treated as valid (Silas 1953:222 [ref. 4024], Chen 1980:102 [ref. 6901], Sawada 1982:205 [ref. 14111]). Balitoridae: Balitorinae.

Crossostomus Lahille 1908:408 [ref. 5869]. Masc. *Lycodes (Iluocoetes) fimbriatus* of Steindachner 1898:322 (not of Jenyns). Type by monotypy. Based on misidentified type species, species named *Crossolycus chilensis* by Regan 1913. ICZN should be requested to fix type for *Crossostomus* as *Crossolycus chilensis* Regan 1913. See also *Crossolycus*. Valid (Gosztonyi 1977:204 [ref. 6103], Anderson 1984:578 [ref. 13634], Nakamura in Nakamura et al. 1986:240 [ref. 14235], Pequeño 1989:48 [ref. 14125]). Zoarcidae.

Crotalopsis Kaup 1860:12 [ref. 2586]. Fem. *Crotalopsis punctifer* Kaup 1860:13. Type by monotypy. Misspelled *Crotalopis* by Jordan 1919:297 [ref. 4904]. Synonym of *Echiophis* Kaup 1856 (McCosker 1977:76 [ref. 6836], McCosker et al. 1989:357 [ref. 13288]). Ophichthidae: Ophichthinae.

Cruantus Smith 1959:234 [ref. 4123]. Masc. *Omobranchus dealmeida* Smith 1949:104. Type by original designation. Synonym of

Omobranchus Ehrenberg 1836 (Springer 1972:9 [ref. 4178], Springer & Gomon 1975:9 [ref. 6083]). Blenniidae.

Cruriraja Bigelow & Schroeder 1948:549 [ref. 301]. Fem. *Cruriraja atlantis* Bigelow & Schroeder 1948:550. Type by original designation. Valid (Hulley 1986:116 [ref. 5672]). Rajidae.

Cruxentina Fernández-Yépez 1948:52 [ref. 1316]. Fem. *Curimata hypostoma hastata* Allen in Eigenmann & Allen 1942:297. Type by original designation. For purposes of the type species, the subspecies *hastata* is elevated to species level; type not *hypostoma.* Synonym of *Cyphocharax* Fowler 1906 (Vari 1989:6 [ref. 9189]). Curimatidae: Curimatinae.

Cryodraco Dollo 1900:129 [ref. 1132]. Masc. *Cryodraco antarcticus* Dollo 1900:130. Type by monotypy. Valid (DeWitt & Hureau 1979:791 [ref. 1125], Stevens et al. 1984:563 [ref. 13633], Iwami 1985:57 [ref. 13368]). Channichthyidae.

Cryothenia Daniels 1981:558 [ref. 1034]. Fem. *Cryothenia peninsulae* Daniels 1981:559. Type by original designation (also monotypic). Species misspelled *peninsula* at head of species description, *peninsulae* elsewhere. Valid (Stevens et al. 1984:563 [ref. 13633], Pequeño 1989:72 [ref. 14125]). Nototheniidae.

Cryptacanthodes Storer 1839:27 (of separate) [ref. 4278]. Masc. *Cryptacanthodes maculatus* Storer 1839:28. Type by monotypy. Valid. Cryptacanthodidae.

Cryptacanthoides Lindberg in Soldatov & Lindberg 1930:482 [ref. 4164]. Masc. *Cryptacanthoides bergi* Lindberg in Soldatov & Lindberg 1930:484. Type by original designation (also monotypic). Spelled *Cryptocanthoides* by Taranetz 1937:158 [not investigated]. Valid (Amaoka in Masuda et al. 1984:303 [ref. 6441]). Cryptacanthodidae.

Cryptichthys Hardy 1987:266 [ref. 5960]. Masc. *Cryptichthys jojettae* Hardy 1987:266. Type by original designation (also monotypic). Tripterygiidae.

Cryptocentroides Popta 1922:32 [ref. 3550]. Masc. *Cryptocentroides dentatus* Popta 1922:33. Type by subsequent designation. Apparently more than one included species, earliest subsequent designation not researched; not treated by Jordan. Valid (Akihito in Masuda et al. 1984:257 [ref. 6441], Birdsong et al. 1988:192 [ref. 7303]). Gobiidae.

Cryptocentrops Smith 1958:152 [ref. 4118]. Masc. *Cryptocentrops exilis* Smith 1958:153. Type by original designation (also monotypic). Synonym of *Cryptocentrus* Valenciennes (ex Ehrenberg) 1837 (Polunin & Lubbock 1977:91 [ref. 3540]). Synonym of *Amblyeleotris* Bleeker 1974 (Yanagisawa 1978:298 [ref. 7028]). Gobiidae.

Cryptocentrus Valenciennes (ex Ehrenberg) in Cuvier & Valenciennes 1837:111 [ref. 1006]. Masc. *Gobius cryptocentrus* Valenciennes in Cuvier & Valenciennes 1837:111. First appeared as name in synonymy of *Gobius*, but made available from Valenciennes (ex Ehrenberg) 1837 by subsequent use, e.g. Bleeker 1874:322 [ref. 437], 1876:142 [ref. 449]. Type designated by Bleeker. Valid (Polunin & Lubbock 1977:76 [ref. 3540], Yanagisawa 1978:271 [ref. 7028], Akihito in Masuda et al. 1984:257 [ref. 6441], Hoese 1986:786 [ref. 5670], Birdsong et al. 1988:192 [ref. 7303], Kottelat 1989:18 [ref. 13605]). Gobiidae.

Cryptolychnus Regan & Trewavas 1932:105 [ref. 3682]. Masc. *Cryptolychnus micractis* Regan & Trewavas 1932:105. Not available from Regan & Trewavas 1932 (Art. 13b). Possible subsequent available publication not researched. Ceratioidei.

Cryptophthalmus Franz 1910:15 [ref. 1481]. Masc. *Cryptophthalmus robustus* Franz 1910:15. Type by monotypy. Preoccupied by Rafinesque 1814 in Crustacea and by Ehrenberg 1831 in Mollusca; replaced by *Unagius* Jordan 1919. Synbranchidae.

Cryptops Eigenmann 1894:626 [ref. 1214]. Masc. *Sternopygus humboldtii* Steindachner 1878:71. Type by original designation. Preoccupied by Leach 1814 in Myriapoda, Schoenherr 1823 and Solier 1851 in Coleoptera, replaced by *Eigenmannia* Jordan & Evermann 1896. Objective synonym of *Eigenmannia* Jordan & Evermann 1896 (Mago-Leccia 1978:19 [ref. 5489]). Gymnotidae: Gymnotinae.

Cryptopsaras Gill 1883:284 [ref. 1723]. *Cryptopsaras couesii* Gill 1883:284. Type by monotypy. Misspelled or unjustifiably emended to *Cryptosparas*, *Cryptosarus* and *Cryptosaras* by authors (see Pietsch 1986:488 [ref. 5969]). Valid (Maul 1973:674 [ref. 7171], Amaoka in Masuda et al. 1984:108 [ref. 6441], Bertelsen in Whitehead et al. 1986:1404 [ref. 13677], Pietsch 1986:374 [ref. 5704], Pietsch 1986 [ref. 5969], Paxton et al. 1989:294 [ref. 12442]). Ceratiidae.

Cryptopterella Fowler 1944:1 [ref. 5598]. Fem. *Cryptopterella beldti* Fowler 1944:2. Type by original designation (also monotypic). Synonym of *Kryptopterus* Bleeker 1858 (Roberts 1989:145 [ref. 6439]). Siluridae.

Cryptopterenchelys (subgenus of *Ophichthus*) Fowler 1925:1 [ref. 1401]. Fem. *Cryptopterus puncticeps* Kaup 1860:11. Type by being a replacement name. Apparently an unneeded replacement for *Cryptopterus* Kaup 1860; apparently not preoccupied by *Cryptopterus* Bleeker 1860 [relative dates in 1860 not researched], an emendation of *Kryptopterus* Bleeker 1858. Synonym of *Ophichthus* Ahl 1789 (Blache et al. 1973:247 [ref. 7185], McCosker 1977:80 [ref. 6836], McCosker et al. 1989:379 [ref. 13288]). Ophichthidae: Ophichthinae.

Cryptopterus Kaup 1860:11 [ref. 2586]. Masc. *Cryptopterus puncticeps* Kaup 1860:11. Type by monotypy. *Cryptopterus* perhaps preoccupied by *Cryptopterus* Bleeker 1860, if an unjustified emendation of *Kryptopterus* Bleeker 1858; *Cryptopterus* Günther 1864 definitely is an unjustified emendation but is later than *Cryptopterus* Kaup. Synonym of *Ophichthus* Ahl 1789 (Blache et al. 1973:247 [ref. 7185], McCosker 1977:80 [ref. 6836], McCosker et al. 1989:379 [ref. 13288]). Ophichthidae: Ophichthinae.

Cryptopterygium Ginsburg 1951:482 [ref. 1804]. Neut. *Cryptopterygium holochroma* Ginsburg 1951:482. Type by original designation (also monotypic). Synonym of *Callechelys* Kaup 1856 (McCosker 1977:62 [ref. 6836], McCosker et al. 1989:303 [ref. 13288]). Ophichthidae: Ophichthinae.

Cryptosmilia Cope 1869:401 [ref. 910]. Fem. *Cryptosmilia luna* Cope 1869:401. Type by monotypy. Synonym of *Drepane* Cuvier 1831 (Desoutter 1986:340 [ref. 6212]). Drepanidae.

Cryptostomias Gibbs & Weitzman 1965:266 [ref. 1612]. Masc. *Cryptostomias psycholutes* Gibbs & Weitzman 1965:268. Type by original designation (also monotypic). Synonym of *Astronesthes* Richardson 1845 (Fink 1985:1 [ref. 5171], Gibbs & McKinney 1988 [ref. 6628]). Astronesthidae.

Cryptotomus Cope 1870:462 [ref. 920]. Masc. *Cryptotomus roseus* Cope 1870:463. Type by monotypy. Scaridae: Sparisomatinae.

Cryptotrema Gilbert 1890:101 [ref. 1623]. Neut. *Cryptotrema corallinum* Gilbert 1890:101. Type by original designation (also monotypic). Misspelled *Crytotrema* by Gilbert 1890:index, and *Chryptotrema* by Jordan, Evermann & Clark 1930:456 [ref. 6476]. Valid (Clark Hubbs 1952:100 [ref. 2252]). Labrisomidae.

Crystallaria Jordan & Gilbert in Jordan 1885:866 [78] [ref. 2385]. Fem. *Pleurolepis asprellus* Jordan 1878:38. Type by original designation (also monotypic). On p. 78 of separate. Synonym of *Ammocrypta* Jordan 1877, but as a valid subgenus (Collette & Banarescu 1977:1455 [ref. 5845], Page 1981:28 [ref. 3347]); valid genus (some authors). Percidae.

Crystallias Jordan & Snyder 1902:349 [ref. 2512]. Masc. *Crystallias matsushimae* Jordan & Snyder 1902:350. Type by original designation (also monotypic). Synonym of *Crystallichthys* Jordan & Gilbert 1898 (Kido 1988:248 [ref. 12287]). Cyclopteridae: Liparinae.

Crystallichthys Jordan & Gilbert in Jordan & Evermann 1898:2864 [ref. 2445]. Masc. *Crystallichthys mirabilis* Jordan & Gilbert in Jordan & Evermann 1898:2865. Type by original designation (also monotypic). Also in Jordan & Gilbert 1898:476 [ref. 1793]. Valid (Kido 1988:248 [ref. 12287]). Cyclopteridae: Liparinae.

Crystallodytes Fowler 1923:390 [ref. 1398]. Masc. *Crystallodytes cookei* Fowler 1923:391. Type by original designation (also monotypic). Valid (Nelson & Randall 1985 [ref. 5271]). Creediidae.

Crystallogobius Gill 1863:269 [ref. 1691]. Masc. *Gobius nilssonii* van Düben & Koren 1846:53. Type by monotypy. *Cristallogobius* Bleeker 1874:310 [ref. 437] is an incorrect subsequent spelling. Valid (Miller 1973:493 [ref. 6888], Miller in Whitehead et al. 1986:1031 [ref. 13677]). Gobiidae.

Ctenacis Compagno 1973:258 [ref. 897]. *Triakis fehlmanni* Springer 1968:614. Type by original designation (also monotypic). Valid (Compagno 1984:370 [ref. 6846], Bass & Compagno 1986:87 [ref. 5637], Compagno 1988:183 [ref. 13488]). Proscylliidae.

Ctenichthys Howell Rivero 1936:69 [ref. 12257]. Masc. *Ctenichthys interrupta* Howell Rivero 1936:69. Type by original designation (also monotypic). Synonym of *Labrisomus* Swainson (Springer 1958:422 [ref. 10210]). Labrisomidae.

Ctenilorícaria Isbrücker & Nijssen in Isbrücker 1979:88, 91 [ref. 2302]. Fem. *Loricaria platystoma* Günther 1868:478. Type by original designation. Valid (Isbrücker 1980:90 [ref. 2303], Burgess 1989:439 [ref. 12860]). Loricariidae.

Ctenobrycon Eigenmann 1908:94 [ref. 1221]. Masc. *Tetragonopterus hauxwellianus* Cope 1970:560. Type by original designation (also monotypic). Valid (Géry 1977:431 [ref. 1597]). Characidae.

Ctenochaetus Gill 1884:279 [ref. 1726]. Masc. *Acanthurus strigosus* Bennett 1828:41. Type by original designation (also monotypic). Not expressly proposed as a replacement name. Valid (Leis & Richards 1984:548 [ref. 13669], Kishimoto in Masuda et al. 1984:232 [ref. 6441], Randall 1986:816 [ref. 5706], Tyler et al. 1989:38 [ref. 13460]). Acanthuridae.

Ctenocharax Regan 1907:403 [ref. 3631]. Masc. *Ctenocharax bogotensis* Regan 1907:403. Type by monotypy. Characidae.

Ctenochirichthys Regan & Trewavas 1932:82 [ref. 3682]. Masc. *Ctenochirichthys longimanus* Regan & Trewavas 1932:82. Type by monotypy. Valid (Maul 1973:671 [ref. 7171], Pietsch 1974:32 [ref. 5332], Pietsch 1978:12 [ref. 3473], Bertelsen in Whitehead et al. 1986:1387 [ref. 13677]). Oneirodidae.

Ctenochromis Pfeffer 1893:153 [25] [ref. 3461]. Masc. *Ctenochromis pectoralis* Pfeffer 1893:153 [25]. Type by subsequent designation. On p. 25 of separate. Two included species; first subsequent designation of type not researched. Valid (Poll 1986:38 [ref. 6136]). Cichlidae.

Ctenocorissa Whitley 1931:323 [ref. 4672]. Fem. *Labrus pictus* Bloch & Schneider 1801:251. Type by original designation (also monotypic). Labridae.

Ctenodax Macleay 1886:718 [ref. 2874]. Masc. *Ctenodax wilkinsoni* Macleay 1886:719. Type by monotypy. Synonym of *Tetragonurus* Risso 1810 (Haedrich 1967:96 [ref. 5357], Haedrich in Whitehead et al. 1986:1189 [ref. 13677]). Tetragonuridae.

Ctenodon (subgenus of *Teuthis*) Bonaparte 1831:175 [ref. 4978]. Masc. Appeared as a section under *Teuthis* as, "4. Ctenodon, Nob." Not available, no description or indication; see *Ctenodon* Klunzinger 1884. In the synonymy of *Acanthurus* Forsskål 1775 (Randall 1955:364 [ref. 13648]). Acanthuridae.

Ctenodon (subgenus of *Acanthurus*) Klunzinger 1871:509 [ref. 2622]. Masc. *Acanthurus strigosus* Bennett 1828:41. Type by monotypy. Not described as new but validates this use of *Ctenodon* by Bonaparte. Apparently preoccupied by Wagler 1830 in Insecta, preoccupied by Swainson 1839 in fishes. *Ctenochaetus* Gill 1884 is an available objective synonym. In the synonymy of *Ctenochaetus* Gill 1884 (Randall 1955:365 [ref. 13648]). Acanthuridae.

Ctenodon (subgenus of *Lumpenus*) Nilsson 1855:190 [ref. 3205]. Masc. *Clinus maculatus* Fries 1838:49. Type by monotypy. Preoccupied by Wagler 1830, Ehrenberg 1838 in rotifers and Swainson 1839 in fishes. Synonym of *Leptoclinus* Gill 1861 (Makushok 1973:538 [ref. 6889]). Stichaeidae.

Ctenodon (subgenus of *Acanthurus*) Swainson 1839:178, 255, 256 [ref. 4303]. Masc. *Ctenodon ruppellii* Swainson 1839:256. Type by subsequent designation. Type designated by Swain 1882:276 [ref. 5966]. Apparently preoccupied by Wagler 1830, not replaced. Not *Ctenodon* Bonaparte 1831 or Klunzinger 1884. Synonym of *Acanthurus* Forsskål 1775. Acanthuridae.

Ctenoglyphidodon (subgenus of *Abudefduf*) Fowler 1918:58 [ref. 1396]. Masc. *Abudefduf melanopselion* Fowler 1918:59. Type by original designation (also monotypic). Synonym of *Hemiglyphidodon* Bleeker 1877 (see Böhlke 1984:146 [ref. 13621]). Pomacentridae.

Ctenogobiops Smith 1959:191 [ref. 4122]. Masc. *Ctenogobiops crocineus* Smith 1959:191. Type by original designation; also monotypic as second species was tentatively referred to genus. Valid (Polunin & Lubbock 1977:70 [ref. 3540], Yanagisawa 1978:293 [ref. 7028], Yoshino & Senou 1983:2 [ref. 5395], Yoshino in Masuda et al. 1984:261 [ref. 6441], Birdsong et al. 1988:192 [ref. 7303]). Gobiidae.

Ctenogobius Gill 1858:374 [ref. 1750]. Masc. *Ctenogobius fasciatus* Gill 1858:376. Type by original designation. Type designated on p. 376. Synonym of *Gobionellus* Girard 1859 (Maugé 1986:371 [ref. 6218]), but *Ctenogobius* may have been published earlier (in 1858 in the actual journal or as a separate; *Gobionellus* is 1859); valid (Birdsong et al. 1988:188 [ref. 7303]). Gobiidae.

Ctenolabrus Valenciennes in Cuvier & Valenciennes 1839:223 [ref. 1007]. Masc. *Labrus rupestris* Linnaeus 1758:286. Type by subsequent designation. Type apparently designated first by Jordan 1890:622 [ref. 2392]. Valid (Bauchot & Quignard 1973:432 [ref. 7204], Richards & Leis 1984:544 [ref. 13668], Quignard & Pras in Whitehead et al. 1986:925 [ref. 13676]). Labridae.

Ctenolates Günther 1871:320 [ref. 1996]. Masc. *Ctenolates macquariensis* Günther 1871:320. Type by original designation (also monotypic). Synonym of *Macquaria* Cuvier 1830 (Paxton et al. 1989:512 [ref. 12442]). Percichthyidae.

Ctenolucius Gill 1861:8 [ref. 5014]. Masc. *Xiphostoma hujeta*

Valenciennes in Cuvier & Valenciennes 1848:358. Type by subsequent monotypy. Appeared first without a definite species for specimens similar to *Xiphostoma hujeta*; type established by Bean 1908:701 [ref. 5014], who identified the specimens as *X. hujeta*. Valid (Géry 1977:103 [ref. 1597]). Ctenoluciidae.

Ctenophallus Herre 1939:144 [ref. 2129]. Masc. *Solenophallus ctenophorus* Aurich 1937:272. Type by original designation (also monotypic). Synonym of *Neostethus* Regan 1916 (Parenti 1989:269 [ref. 13486]). Phallostethidae.

Ctenopharyngodon Steindachner 1866:782 [ref. 5030]. Masc. *Ctenopharyngodon laticeps* Steindachner 1866:782. Type by monotypy. Valid (Yang & Hwang 1964:13 [ref. 13497], Howes 1981:40 [ref. 14200], Jayaram 1981:131 [ref. 6497], Sawada in Masuda et al. 1984:58 [ref. 6441], Bogutskaya 1987:936 [ref. 13521], Chen & Li in Chu & Chen 1989:40 [ref. 13584], Kottelat 1989:7 [ref. 13605]). Cyprinidae.

Ctenopharynx Eccles & Trewavas 1989:180 [ref. 13547]. Masc. *Hemichromis intermedius* Günther 1893:312. Type by original designation. Cichlidae.

Ctenopoma Peters 1844:34 [ref. 13442]. Neut. *Ctenopoma multispinis* Peters 1844:34. Type by monotypy. Also appeared in Peters 1846 [translation, ref. 3448] and 1847 [ref. 6176]. Valid (Gosse 1986:402 [ref. 6194], Norris et al. 1988 [ref. 6415], Skelton 1988 [ref. 6737]). Anabantidae.

Ctenops McClelland 1845:281 [ref. 2929]. Masc. *Ctenops nobilis* McClelland 1845:281. Type by monotypy. Valid (Jayaram 1981:381 [ref. 6497]). Belontiidae.

Ctenosciaena (subgenus of *Sciaena*) Fowler & Bean 1923:15 [ref. 1474]. Fem. *Sciaena (Ctenosciaena) dubia* Fowler & Bean 1923:15. Type by original designation (also monotypic). Valid (Chao 1978:29 [ref. 6983], Uyeno & Sato in Uyeno et al. 1983:365 [ref. 14275], de Lucena 1988 [ref. 12613]). Sciaenidae.

Ctenoscolopsis (subgenus of *Scolopsis*) Fowler 1931:273, 300 [ref. 1407]. Fem. *Holocentrus ciliatus* Lacepède 1802:333, 367. Type by original designation (also monotypic). Nemipteridae.

Ctenoscopelus (subgenus of *Myctophum*) Fraser-Brunner 1949:1059 [ref. 1496]. Masc. *Scopelus phengodes* Lütken 1892:253. Type by original designation (also monotypic). Synonym of *Myctophum* Rafinesque 1810 (Krefft & Bekker 1973:176 [ref. 7181], Paxton 1979:15 [ref. 6440]). Myctophidae.

Ctenotrypauchen Steindachner 1867:530 [ref. 4215]. *Ctenotrypauchen chinensis* Steindachner 1867:530. Type by monotypy. Valid (Akihito in Masuda et al. 1984:288 [ref. 6441], Maugé 1986:366 [ref. 6218], Kottelat 1989:19 [ref. 13605]). Gobiidae.

Cualac Miller 1956:1 [ref. 3018]. Masc. *Cualac tessellatus* Miller 1956:9. Type by original designation (also monotypic). Valid (Parenti 1981:529 [ref. 7066]). Cyprinodontidae: Cyprinodontinae.

Cubanichthys Hubbs 1926:4 [ref. 2233]. Masc. *Fundulus cubensis* Eigenmann 1903:222. Type by original designation (also monotypic). Valid (Parenti 1981:520 [ref. 7066]). Cyprinodontidae: Cubanichthyinae.

Cubiceps Lowe 1843:82 [ref. 2832]. Masc. *Seriola gracilis* Lowe 1843:82. Type by subsequent designation. Type designated by Jordan 1919:215 [ref. 2410]. On Official List (Opinion 461). Valid (Haedrich 1967:78 [ref. 5357], Haedrich 1973:562 [ref. 7216], Scott 1982:185 [ref. 5472], Aboussouan 1983:8 [ref. 12850], Horn 1984:628 [ref. 13637], Nakabo in Masuda et al. 1984:235 [ref. 6441], Haedrich in Whitehead et al. 1986:1184 [ref. 13677], Haedrich 1986:847 [ref. 5659], Agafonova 1988 [ref. 13479]). Nomeidae.

Cuchia Hamilton in Taylor 1831:42 [ref. 6560]. Fem. *Unibranchapertura cuchia* Hamilton 1822:16, 363. Type by monotypy (also by absolute tautonymy). Probably unavailable and a vernacular name not distinct from *Unibranchapertura* as used by Taylor (see discussion in Rosen & Greenwood 1976:56 [ref. 7094]); possibly as *Cuchia* for the species *cuchia*. Synonym of *Monopterus* Lacepède 1800. Synbranchidae.

Cugupuguacu Catesby 1771:14 [ref. 774]. Not available, published in a rejected work on Official Index (Opinion 89, Opinion 259). In the synonymy of *Epinephelus* Bloch 1793. Serranidae: Epinephelinae.

Culaea Whitley 1950:44 [ref. 4713]. Fem. *Gasterosteus inconstans* Kirtland 1841:273. Type by being a replacement name. Replacement for *Eucalia* Jordan 1876, preoccupied by Felder 1861 in Lepidoptera. Valid (Nelson 1969 [ref. 7145]). Gasterosteidae: Gasterosteinae.

Culius Bleeker 1856:385, 411 [ref. 353]. Masc. *Cheilodipterus culius* Hamilton 1822:55, 367. Type by absolute tautonymy, not *fuscus* = *nigra* as designated by Bleeker 1874:303 [ref. 437]. Synonym of *Eleotris* Bloch & Schneider 1801 (Maugé 1986:391 [ref. 6218] but with wrong type). Eleotridae.

Culter Basilewski 1855:236 [ref. 200]. Masc. *Culter alburnus* Basilewski 1855:236. Type by subsequent designation. Type designated by Bleeker 1863:33 [ref. 4859] or 1863:214 [ref. 397]. On Official List (Opinion 513). Valid (Yih & Wu 1964:112 [ref. 13499]). Cyprinidae.

Culticula Abbott 1901:485 [ref. 2]. Fem. *Culticula emmelas* Abbott 1901:485. Type by monotypy. Misspelled *Culticola* in Zoological Record for 1901. Cyprinidae.

Cultrichthys Smith 1938:410 [ref. 4053]. Masc. *Culter brevicauda* Günther 1868:329. Type by original designation (also monotypic). Cyprinidae.

Cultriculus Oshima 1919:252 [ref. 3312]. Masc. *Culter leucisculus* Kner (not of Basilewski) 1867:362 (= *Hemiculter kneri* Kreyenberg 1908). Type by original designation (also monotypic). Synonym of *Hemiculter* Bleeker 1859 (Chen in Chu & Chen 1989:80 [ref. 13584]). Cyprinidae.

Cultrops Smith 1938:410 [ref. 4053]. Masc. *Culter siamensis* Hora 1923:149. Type by original designation (also monotypic). Synonym of *Paralaubucca* Bleeker 1865 (Banarescu & Bailey in Böhlke 1984:95 [ref. 13621]). Cyprinidae.

Cumbel Whitley 1952:32 [ref. 4714]. *Platycephalus haackei* Steindachner 1883:1081. Type by original designation (also monotypic). Synonym of *Leviprora* Whitley 1931 (Paxton et al. 1989:467 [ref. 12442] based on placement of the type species). Platycephalidae.

Cunningtonia Boulenger 1906:573 [ref. 573]. Fem. *Cunningtonia longiventralis* Boulenger 1906:574. Type by monotypy. Valid (Liem 1981:192 [ref. 6897], Poll 1986:97 [ref. 6136]). Cichlidae.

Curimata Bosc 1817:9 [ref. 5126]. Fem. *Salmo edentulus* Bloch 1794:Pl. 380. Type designated by ICZN and placed on Official List (Opinion 772). Same as *Curimata* Cloquet 1818:240 [v. 12, ref. 852]. See important discussion by Taylor 1964:260 [ref. 12563]. Valid (Géry 1977:227 [ref. 1597], Vari 1983:4 [ref. 5419], Géry et al. 1987:415 [ref. 6001], Vari 1987 [ref. 6059], Vari 1989:6 [ref. 9189], Vari 1989:21 [ref. 13506]). Curimatidae: Curimatinae.

Curimata Walbaum 1792:80 [ref. 4572]. Fem. *Salmo (Curimata)* *marggravii* Walbaum 1792:80. Type by monotypy. Not described as a genus or subgenus (see Opinion 772), placed on Official Index; *Curimates* Goldfuss 1820 and *Curimate* Quoy & Gaimard 1825 based on Walbaum are not original descriptions. In the synonymy of *Curimata* Bosc 1817. Curimatidae: Curimatinae.

Curimatella (subgenus of *Curimatus*) Eigenmann & Eigenmann 1889:415 [ref. 1254]. Fem. *Curimatus lepidurus* Eigenmann & Eigenmann 1889:417. Type by subsequent designation. Type designated by Eigenmann 1910:420 [ref. 1224]. *Curimatella* Pellegrin as given by Jordan 1920:533 [ref. 4905] introduced by error. Valid (Géry 1977:238 [ref. 1597], Géry et al. 1987:431 [ref. 6001], Vari 1989:6 [ref. 9189]). Curimatidae: Curimatinae.

Curimatichthys Fernández-Yépez 1948:71 [ref. 1316]. Masc. *Curimatopsis microlepis* Eigenmann & Eigenmann 1889:414. Type by original designation (also monotypic). Misspelled once as *Curimatichtys* on p. 71, correctly once as *Curimatichthys* on p. 71 and in index. Synonym of *Curimatopsis* Steindachner 1876 (Vari 1982: 12 [ref. 5485], Vari 1989:6 [ref. 9189]). Curimatidae: Curimatinae.

Curimatoides Fowler 1940:255 [ref. 1432]. Masc. *Curimatoides ucayalensis* Fowler 1940:256. Type by original designation (also monotypic). Synonym of *Cyphocharax* Fowler 1906 (Vari 1989:6 [ref. 9189]). Curimatidae: Curimatinae.

Curimatopsis (subgenus of *Curimatus*) Steindachner 1876:81 [ref. 4225]. Fem. *Curimatus (Curimatopsis) macrolepis* Steindachner 1876:81. Type by monotypy. Valid (Vari 1982 [ref. 5485], Vari 1983:4 [ref. 5419], see also Géry et al. 1987:435 [ref. 6001], Vari 1989:6 [ref. 9189]). Curimatidae: Curimatinae.

Curimatorbis Fernández-Yépez 1948:42 [ref. 1316]. Masc. *Curimata atratoensis* Eigenmann 1912:19. Type by original designation. Synonym of *Steindachnerina* Fowler 1906 (Vari 1989:6 [ref. 9189]). Curimatidae: Curimatinae.

Curimatus Oken (ex Cuvier) 1817:1183 [ref. 3303]. Masc. *Salmo edentulus* Bloch 1794:Pl. 380. Type by subsequent designation. See Gill 1903:966 [ref. 5768]. Type designated by Eigenmann 1910:421 [ref. 1224]. Not mentioned in Opinion 772. Objective synonym of *Curimata* Bosc 1817. Curimatidae: Curimatinae.

Curioptera Whitley 1951:68 [ref. 4711]. Fem. *Oncopterus darwinii* Steindachner 1875:363. Type by being a replacement name. Apparently an unneeded replacement for *Oncopterus* Steindachner 1875, not preoccupied by *Oncoptera*. Pleuronectidae: Rhombosoleinae.

Curraichthys Fernández-Yépez 1969:[3] [ref. 9186]. Masc. *Heros lobochilus* Günther 1868:457. Type by original designation. Synonym of *Cichlasoma* Swainson 1839. Cichlidae.

Currupiscis Whitley 1931:327 [ref. 4672]. Masc. *Currupiscis volucer* Whitley 1931:327. Type by original designation (also monotypic). Triglidae: Triglinae.

Curtipenis Rivas & Myers 1950:289 [ref. 3764]. Masc. *Mollienesia elegans* Trewavas 1948:409. Type by original designation (also monotypic). Synonym of *Poecilia* Bloch & Schneider 1801 (Rosen & Bailey 1963:45 [ref. 7067]). Poeciliidae.

Cyanichthys Kaup 1855:231 [ref. 2571]. Masc. *Cyanichthys coeruleus* of Kaup (not of Quoy & Gaimard) 1855:231. Type by monotypy. Evidently based on a misidentified type species, not *Diodon coeruleus* Quoy & Gaimard according to Jordan 1919:265 [ref. 2410]. Diodontidae.

Cyathochromis Trewavas 1935:(67) 77 [ref. 4451]. Masc. *Cyathochromis obliquidens* Trewavas 1935:77. Type by monotypy. Valid (Ribbink et al. 1983:242 [ref. 13555]). Cichlidae.

Cyathopharynx Regan 1920:42 [ref. 3669]. Masc. *Tilapia grandoculis* Boulenger 1899:94. Type by original designation. Valid (Poll 1986:98 [ref. 6136]). Cichlidae.

Cybiosarda (subgenus of *Scomberomorus*) Whitley 1935:236 [ref. 4683]. Fem. *Scomberomorus (Cybiosarda) elegans* Whitley 1935:236. Type by monotypy. Valid (Collette & Nauen 1983:31 [ref. 5375], Collette et al. 1984:600 [ref. 11421]). Scombridae.

Cybium Cuvier 1829:199 [ref. 995]. Neut. *Scomber commerson* Lacepède 1800:598, 600. Type by subsequent designation. Type designated by Gill 1862:126 [ref. 1649]. Synonym of *Scomberomorus* Lacepède 1801 (Postel 1973:473 [ref. 7208], Collette & Russo 1984:611 [ref. 5221]). Scombridae.

Cycleptus Rafinesque 1819:421 [ref. 3590]. Masc. *Cycleptus nigrescens* Rafinesque 1819:421. Type by monotypy. Also treated in Rafinesque 1820:355 (July) [ref. 7311] and 1820:61 (Dec.) [ref. 3592]. Valid. Catostomidae.

Cyclichthys Kaup 1855:231 [ref. 2571]. Masc. *Diodon orbicularis* Bloch 1785:73. Type by subsequent designation. Type apparently designated first by Bleeker 1865:48 [ref. 416]. Valid (Leis 1986:904 [ref. 5686]). Diodontidae.

Cyclocheilichthys Bleeker 1859:431 [ref. 370]. Masc. *Barbus enoplus* Bleeker 1850:16. Type by subsequent designation. Apparently appeared first in key, without included species. Species added by Bleeker 1859:148 [ref. 371] and perhaps in other 1859-60 articles. Type apparently designated first by Bleeker 1863:27 [ref. 4859] and 1863:199 [ref. 397]; type not *armatus* Bleeker. Valid (Wu et al. 1977:321 [ref. 4807], Kottelat 1985:262 [ref. 11441], Chen & Chu 1985:82 [ref. 5250], Kottelat 1989:7 [ref. 13605], Roberts 1989:33 [ref. 6439]). Cyprinidae.

Cyclocottus Popov in Soldatov & Lindberg 1930:325 [ref. 4164]. Masc. Not available; name only, same as *Cyclopterocottus* Popov 1930 (see Lindberg & Legeza 1955 [ref. 2785]). Cyclopteridae: Cyclopterinae.

Cyclogaster Gronow 1763:55 [ref. 1910]. Fem. Also in Gronow 1760 [not investigated] which is regarded as non-binominal and unavailable (see Cohen & Russo 1979:101 [ref. 6975]). Gronow 1763 is a rejected work on Official Index (Opinion 261). Subsequent availability not researched. In the synonymy of *Liparis* Scopoli 1777 (Lindberg 1973:609 [ref. 7220]). Cyclopteridae: Liparinae.

Cyclogobius Steindachner 1860:285 [ref. 4205]. Masc. *Gobius lepidus* Girard 1858:127. Type by monotypy. Objective synonym of *Lepidogobius* Gill 1859. Gobiidae.

Cyclolumpus Tanaka 1912:86 [ref. 4323]. Masc. *Cyclolumpus asperrimus* Tanaka 1912:86. Type by monotypy. Synonym of *Eumicrotremus* Gill 1862 (Lindberg & Legeza 1955 [ref. 2785]). Cyclopteridae: Cyclopterinae.

Cyclonarce Gill 1862:387 [ref. 1783]. Fem. *Raja timlei* Bloch & Schneider 1801:359. Type by original designation (also monotypic). Type stated (name in parentheses in key) as "*Narcine Timlei* Henle" which is *R. timlei* Bloch & Schneider. Synonym of *Narcine* Henle 1834 (Cappetta 1987:162 [ref. 6348]). Narkidae.

Cyclopharynx Poll 1948:94 [ref. 3519]. Masc. *Cyclopharynx fwae* Poll 1948:94. Type by monotypy. Cichlidae.

Cyclophichthys (subgenus of *Malvoliophis*) Whitley 1951:392 [ref. 4715]. Masc. *Ophichthus cyclorhinus* Fraser-Brunner 1934:466. Type by original designation (also monotypic). Synonym of *Elapsopis* Kaup 1856 (McCosker 1977:77 [ref. 6836]). Ophichthidae: Ophichthinae.

Cyclopium Swainson 1838:356 [ref. 4302]. Neut. *Cyclopium humboldtii* Swainson 1839:305 (= *Pimelodus cyclopium* Humboldt 1805). Type by monotypy. Genus dates to 1838:356, without species. Also in Swainson 1839:189 and 305 [ref. 4303] (species added). *C. humboldtii* Swainson is unneeded substitute for *cyclopius*). Synonym of *Astroblepus* Humboldt 1805. Astroblepidae.

Cyclopsetta Gill 1889:601 [ref. 1730]. Fem. *Hemirhombus fimbriatus* Goode & Bean 1886:591. Type by original designation (also monotypic). Valid (Norman 1934:134 [ref. 6893], Matsuura in Uyeno et al. 1983:458 [ref. 14275], Ahlstrom et al. 1984:640 [ref. 13641]). Paralichthyidae.

Cyclopsis Popov 1930:74 [ref. 3545]. Fem. *Cyclopsis tentacularis* Popov 1930:76. Type by monotypy. Appeared as name only in Soldatov & Popov 1929:239 [ref. 4163]. Also appeared as new in Popov 1931:86 [ref. 3543]. Valid (Lindberg & Legeza 1955 [ref. 2785]). Cyclopteridae: Cyclopterinae.

Cyclopterichthys Steindachner 1881:192 [ref. 4231]. Masc. *Cyclopterichthys glaber* Steindachner 1881:192. Type by monotypy. Valid (Lindberg & Legeza 1955 [ref. 2785]). Cyclopteridae: Cyclopterinae.

Cyclopterocottus Popov 1930:74 [ref. 3545]. Masc. *Eumicrotremus brashnikowi* Schmidt 1904:3129. Type by subsequent designation. Type designated by Lindberg & Legeza 1955 [ref. 2785]. Cyclopteridae: Cyclopterinae.

Cyclopteroides Garman 1892:37 [ref. 1537]. Masc. *Cyclopteroides gyrinops* Garman 1892:37. Type by monotypy. Synonym of *Eumicrotremus* Gill 1862 (Lindberg & Legeza 1955 [ref. 2785]). Cyclopteridae: Cyclopterinae.

Cyclopteropsis Soldatov & Popov 1929:240 [ref. 4163]. Fem. *Cyclopteropsis bergi* Popov 1929. Type by original designation. Type designated on p. 241. Valid (Lindberg & Legeza 1955 [ref. 2785], Lindberg 1973:607 [ref. 7220], Kido in Masuda et al. 1984:336 [ref. 6441], Stein in Whitehead et al. 1986:1270 [ref. 13677]). Cyclopteridae: Cyclopterinae.

Cyclopterus Linnaeus 1758:260 [ref. 2787]. Masc. *Cyclopterus lumpus* Linnaeus 1758:260. Type by Linnaean tautonymy. On Official List (Opinion 77). Valid (Lindberg 1973:607 [ref. 7220], Stein in Whitehead et al. 1986:1271 [ref. 13677]). Cyclopteridae: Cyclopterinae.

Cyclothone Goode & Bean 1883:221 [ref. 1838]. Fem. *Cyclothone lusca* Goode & Bean 1883:221. Type by monotypy. Valid (Witzell 1973:116 [ref. 7172], Weitzman 1974:472 [ref. 5174], Badcock in Whitehead et al. 1984:286 [ref. 13675], Ahlstrom et al. 1984:185 [ref. 13643], Fujii in Masuda et al. 1984:46 [ref. 6441], Schaefer et al. 1986:248 [ref. 5709], Paxton et al. 1989:183 [ref. 12442]). Gonostomatidae.

Cyema Günther 1878:251 [ref. 2010]. Neut. *Cyema atrum* Günther 1878:251. Type by monotypy. Valid (Bauchot & Saldanha 1973:234 [ref. 7186], Saldanha & Bauchot in Whitehead et al. 1986:557 [ref. 13676], Castle 1986:193 [ref. 5644], Paxton et al. 1989:136 [ref. 12442], Smith 1989:633 [ref. 13285]). Cyematidae.

Cygnodraco Waite 1916:32 [ref. 4568]. Masc. *Cygnodraco mawsoni* Waite 1916:33. Type by monotypy. Valid (DeWitt & Hureau 1979:789 [ref. 1125], Stevens et al. 1984:563 [ref. 13633], Voskoboinikova 1988:45 [ref. 12756]). Bathydraconidae.

Cylindrosteus (subgenus of *Lepisosteus*) Rafinesque 1820:168 [ref. 7306]. Masc. *Lepisosteus (Cylindrosteus) platostomus* Rafinesque 1820:168. Type by subsequent designation. Type designated by Jordan & Copeland 1877:160 [ref. 5961]. Also in Rafinesque 1820:72 (Dec.) [ref. 3592]. Synonym of *Lepisosteus* Lacepède 1803 (Suttkus 1963:69 [ref. 7110], Wiley 1976:41 [ref. 7091]). Lepisosteidae.

Cymatoceps Smith 1938:259 [ref. 4067]. Neut. *Chrysophrys nasutus* Castelnau 1861:24. Type by original designation (also monotypic). Valid (Smith & Smith 1986:585 [ref. 5710]). Sparidae.

Cymatogaster Gibbons 1854:2, col. 3 [ref. 5207]. Fem. *Cymatogaster aggregata* Gibbons 1854:2, col. 3. Type by subsequent designation. Type designated by Gill 1862:275 [ref. 1666]. Not of Gibbons 1854 (June 21) in "Placer Times" or 1854:123 [ref. 1610]; when name first appeared it did not mention the species for which Gibbons intended the genus, see *Micrometrus*. Valid (Tarp 1952:72 [ref. 12250]). Embiotocidae.

Cymbacephalus Fowler 1938:90 [ref. 1426]. Masc. *Platycephalus nematophthalmus* Günther 1860:184. Type by original designation. Valid (Paxton et al. 1989:466 [ref. 12442]). Platycephalidae.

Cymolutes Günther 1861:387 [ref. 1967]. Masc. *Julis praetextata* Quoy & Gaimard 1834:712. Type by subsequent designation. Also appeared in Günther 1862:207 [ref. 1969]. Type designated by Jordan 1919:318 [ref. 4904]. Valid (Yamakawa in Masuda et al. 1984:211 [ref. 6441], Randall 1986:692 [ref. 5706]). Labridae.

Cynaedus Gronow 1763:60 [ref. 1910]. Not available, published in a rejected work on Official Index (Opinion 261). Sparidae.

Cynaedus (subgenus of *Crenilabrus*) Swainson 1839:229 [ref. 4303]. *Labrus rupestris* of Bloch (= *Labrus rupestris* Linnaeus 1758:286). Type by subsequent designation. Type apparently designated first by Bonaparte 1841:fasc. 30 [ref. 512], not *Labrus tinca* as designated by Swain 1882:274 [ref. 5966]. Objective synonym of *Ctenolabrus* Valenciennes 1839 (Bauchot & Quignard 1973:432 [ref. 7204]). Labridae.

Cynedus Scopoli (ex Gronow) 1777:455 [ref. 3990]. Appeared first without species and with spelling as *Cynedus* (the correct original spelling), *Cynaedus* used by Jordan and authors. First addition of species not researched. See also Whitley 1936:199 [ref. 6397]. Sparidae.

Cyneichthys (subgenus of *Petroscirtes*) Ogilby 1910:55 [ref. 3288]. Masc. *Blennechis anolius* Valenciennes in Cuvier & Valenciennes 1836:288. Type by original designation (also monotypic). Type by use of species in parentheses in footnote. Synonym of *Omobranchus* Ehrenberg 1836 (Springer 1972:9 [ref. 4178], Springer & Gomon 1975:9 [ref. 6083]). Blenniidae.

Cynias Gill 1903:960 [ref. 4983]. Masc. *Mustelus canis* of Jordan & Evermann 1896 (= *Squalus canis* Mitchill 1815:486). Type by monotypy. Synonym of *Mustelus* Linck 1790 (Compagno 1984:397 [ref. 6846], Cappetta 1987:116 [ref. 6348], Compagno 1988:219 [ref. 13488]). Triakidae: Triakinae.

Cynichthys (subgenus of *Serranus*) Swainson 1839:168, 201 [ref. 4303]. Masc. *Perca flavopurpurea* Bennett 1830:Pl. 19. Type by monotypy. Synonym of *Epinephelus* Bloch 1793 (C. L. Smith 1971:103 [ref. 14102], Daget & Smith 1986:301 [ref. 6204]). Serranidae: Epinephelinae.

Cynicoglossus Bonaparte 1837:puntata 97 [ref. 4893]. Masc. *Pleuronectes cynoglossus* Linnaeus 1758:269. Type by monotypy. Apparently appeared first in puntata 97, fasc. 19 under *Platessa passer*. Bonaparte stated that the species was *P. cynoglossus* Linnaeus; possibly based on a misidentified type species (see Norman 1934:355). Synonym of *Microstomus* Gottsche 1835 (Norman

1934:355 [ref. 6893]). Pleuronectidae: Pleuronectinae.

Cynocephalus Gill (ex Klein) 1862:400, 401 [ref. 1783]. Masc. *Squalus glaucus* Linnaeus 1758:235. Type by original designation (also monotypic). Preoccupied by Boddaert 1768 and Geoffroy & Cuvier 1795 in Mammalia. Objective synonym of *Prionace* Cantor 1849 (Compagno 1984:521 [ref. 6846], Compagno 1988:346 [ref. 13488]). Carcharhinidae.

Cynocephalus Klein 1777:161 [ref. 2618]. Masc. Not available, published in a work that does not conform to the principle of binominal nomenclature. Also preoccupied by Boddaert 1768 in bats. In the synonymy of *Prionace* Cantor 1849. Carcharhinidae.

Cynocharax (subgenus of *Roeboides*) Fowler 1907:457 [ref. 1374]. Masc. *Anacyrtus affinis* Günther 1868:481. Type by original designation. Synonym of *Roeboides* Günther 1864. Characidae.

Cynodon Agassiz in Spix & Agassiz 1829:76 [ref. 13]. Masc. *Rhaphiodon gibbus* Agassiz in Spix & Agassiz 1829:77. Type by subsequent designation. Name first published in synonymy of *Rhaphiodon* Agassiz 1829, but later made available back to Agassiz; this interpretion differs from that of Kottelat 1988:82 [ref. 13380]. Type designated by Eigenmann 1910:444 [ref. 1224] (not first by Campos 1945 as indicated by Kottelat). *Rhaphiodon* cannot be regarded as a replacement name for *Cynodon*. Valid (Géry 1986:63 [ref. 6019]). Cynodontidae.

Cynodonichthys Meek 1904:101 [ref. 2958]. Masc. *Cynodonichthys tenuis* Meek 1904:401. Type by original designation (also monotypic). Synonym of *Rivulus* Poey 1860 (Parenti 1981:481 [ref. 7066]). Aplocheilidae: Rivulinae.

Cynoglossa Bonaparte 1846:48 [ref. 519]. Fem. *Pleuronectes microcephalus* Donovan 1803:xlii. Type by monotypy. Synonym of *Microstomus* Gottsche 1835 (Norman 1934:355 [ref. 6893], Nielsen 1973:625 [ref. 6885]). Pleuronectidae: Pleuronectinae.

Cynoglossoides Smith 1949:165 [ref. 5846]. Masc. *Cynoglossus acaudatus* Gilchrist 1906:162. Type by original designation. Preoccupied by von Bonde 1922 in same family, replaced by *Notrullus* Whitley 1951. Species misspelled *ecaudatus* by authors. Synonym of *Cynoglossus* Hamilton 1822 (Menon 1977:16 [ref. 7071], Desoutter 1986:432 [ref. 6212]). Cynoglossidae: Cynoglossinae.

Cynoglossoides von Bonde 1922:23 [ref. 520]. Masc. *Cynoglossus attenuatus* Gilchrist 1905:11. Type by monotypy. Not same as *Cynoglossoides* Smith 1949. Synonym of *Cynoglossus* Hamilton 1822 (Menon 1977:16 [ref. 7071], Desoutter 1986:432 [ref. 6212]). Cynoglossidae: Cynoglossinae.

Cynoglossus Hamilton 1822:32, 365 [ref. 2031]. Masc. *Cynoglossus lingua* Hamilton 1822:32, 365. Type by monotypy. Valid (Torchio 1973:635 [ref. 6892], Menon 1977 [ref. 7071], Ahlstrom et al. 1984:643 [ref. 13641], Ochiai in Masuda et al. 1984:356 [ref. 6441], Kottelat 1985:274 [ref. 11441], Heemstra 1986:865 [ref. 5660], Quéro et al. in Whitehead et al. 1986:1325 [ref. 13677], Desoutter 1986:432 [ref. 6212], Chapleau 1988:1231 [ref. 13819], Kottelat 1989:20 [ref. 13605], Roberts 1989:184 [ref. 6439]). Cynoglossidae: Cynoglossinae.

Cynolebias Steindachner 1876:172 [ref. 4225]. Masc. *Cynolebias porosus* Steindachner 1876:173. Type by monotypy. Misspelled *Cynelebias* in Zoological Record for 1876. Valid (Parenti 1981:490 [ref. 7066], Costa et al. 1988 [ref. 6372], Malabarba 1989:158 [ref. 14217], Costa 1989 [ref. 14323]). Aplocheilidae: Rivulinae.

Cynomacrurus Dollo 1909:318, 319 [ref. 1137]. Masc. *Cynomacrurus piriei* Dollo 1909:320. Type by monotypy. Valid (Marshall & Iwamoto 1973:534 [ref. 6963], Fahay & Markle 1984:274 [ref. 13653], Iwamoto & Sazonov 1988:39 [ref. 6228], Paxton et al. 1989:327 [ref. 12442]). Macrouridae: Macrourinae.

Cynopanchax Ahl 1928:115 [ref. 78]. Masc. *Haplochilichthys bukobanus* Ahl 1924:137. Type by original designation (also monotypic). Correct spelling for genus of type species is *Aplocheilichthys*. Valid (Parenti 1981:513 [ref. 7066], Wildekamp et al. 1986:187 [ref. 6198]). Cyprinodontidae: Aplocheilichthyinae.

Cynoperca (subgenus of *Stizostethium (sic)*) Gill & Jordan in Jordan 1877:44, 45 [ref. 2374]. Fem. *Lucioperca canadense* Smith 1834:275. Type by monotypy; "typified by" not specific enough for original designation. Synonym of *Stizostedion* Rafinesque 1820 (Collette & Banarescu 1977:1457 [ref. 5845]). Percidae.

Cynophidium Regan 1914:16 [ref. 3661]. Neut. *Cynophidium punctatum* Regan 1914:16. Type by monotypy. Synonym of *Pyramodon* Smith & Radcliffe 1913 (Cohen & Nielsen 1978:6 [ref. 881], Williams 1983:848 [ref. 5367]). Carapidae: Pyramodontinae.

Cynopoecilus Regan 1912:642 [ref. 3649]. Masc. *Cynolebias melanotaenia* Regan 1912:506. Type by original designation (also monotypic). Synonym of *Cynolebias* Steindachner 1876 (Parenti 1981:490 [ref. 7066]). Aplocheilidae: Rivulinae.

Cynoponticus Costa 1845:1 [ref. 976]. Masc. *Cynoponticus ferox* Costa 1846:10. Type by subsequent monotypy. On p. 1 of "Genre Cinopontico," with species named on p. 10 of same section; pp. 1-8 published 6 Nov. 1845, pp. 9-12 in 1846. Valid (Blache et al. 1973:235 [ref. 7185], Castle & Williamson 1975:2 [ref. 7115], Bauchot & Saldanha in Whitehead et al. 1986:559 [ref. 13676], Smith 1989:436 [ref. 13285]). Muraenesocidae.

Cynopotamus Valenciennes in Cuvier & Valenciennes 1849:317 [ref. 1014]. Masc. *Hydrocyon argenteus* Valenciennes 1847:9. Type by subsequent designation. Type designated by Eigenmann 1912:403 [ref. 1227]. Valid (Menezes 1976:22 [ref. 7073] in subfamily Cynopotaminae, Géry 1977:306 [ref. 1597]). Characidae.

Cynopsetta Jordan & Starks (ex Schmidt) 1906:188 [ref. 2531]. Fem. *Hippoglossoides dubius* Schmidt 1904:227. Genus and species apparently appeared first as name only (*Cynopsetta dubia* n. g. n. sp.) in Schmidt 1903:521 [ref. 3945], genus made available by Jordan & Starks 1906; species made available by Schmidt 1904. Synonym of *Hippoglossoides* Gottsche 1835 (Norman 1934:294 [ref. 6893]). Pleuronectidae: Pleuronectinae.

Cynoscartes Norman 1943:810 [ref. 3228]. Masc. *Salarias atlanticus* Valenciennes in Cuvier & Valenciennes 1836:321. Type by original designation (also monotypic). Synonym of *Ophioblennius* Gill 1860 (Smith-Vaniz & Springer 1971:35 [ref. 4145]). Blenniidae.

Cynoscion Gill 1861:81 [ref. 1771]. Masc. *Johnius regalis* Bloch & Schneider 1801:75. Type by original designation (also monotypic). Valid (Chao 1978:34 [ref. 6983], Uyeno & Sato in Uyeno et al. 1983:370 [ref. 14275]). Sciaenidae.

Cynothrissa Regan 1917:203 [ref. 3668]. Fem. *Cynothrissa mento* Regan 1917:204. Type by subsequent designation. Type designated by Jordan 1920:563 [ref. 4905]. Valid (Poll et al. 1984:41 [ref. 6172], Grande 1985:246 [ref. 6466], Whitehead 1985:136 [ref. 5141]). Clupeidae.

Cynotilapia Regan 1922:684 [ref. 3673]. Fem. *Hemichromis afra* Günther 1893:626. Type by monotypy. Valid (Ribbink et al. 1983:233 [ref. 13555]). Cichlidae.

Cypho Myers 1940:35 [ref. 3118]. *Nesiotes purpurascens* De Vis 1884:453. Type by being a replacement name. Replacement for

Nesiotes De Vis 1884, preoccupied by Martens 1860 in Mollusca, Wollaston 1861 in Coleoptera and Stål 1873 in insects. Valid (Gill, pers. comm.). Pseudochromidae: Pseudochrominae.

Cyphocharax (subgenus of *Curimata*) Fowler 1906:297 [ref. 1373]. Masc. *Curimatus spilurus* Günther 1864:288. Type by original designation. Valid (Vari 1989:6 [ref. 9189], Vari 1989:10 [ref. 13475], Malabarba 1989:124 [ref. 14217]). Curimatidae: Curimatinae.

Cyphomycter (subgenus of *Naso*) Fowler & Bean 1929:264, 273 [ref. 1476]. Masc. *Naso tuberosus* Lacepède 1801:105. Type by original designation. Synonym of *Naso* Lacepède 1801 (Randall 1955:362 [ref. 13648]). Acanthuridae.

Cyphomyrus Myers 1960:124 [ref. 3128]. Masc. *Marcusenius psittacus* Boulenger 1898:798. Type by original designation. Synonym of *Hippopotamyrus* Pappenheim 1906 (Taverne 1972:170 [ref. 6367], Gosse 1984:73 [ref. 6169]). Mormyridae.

Cyphoscopelus Fowler 1925:2 [ref. 1401]. Masc. *Scopelus langerhansi* Johnson 1890:454. Type by original designation (also monotypic). Type species unplaceable to genus (Paxton 1979:18 [ref. 6440]). Myctophidae.

Cyphotilapia Regan 1920:43 [ref. 3669]. Fem. *Pelmatochromis frontosus* Boulenger 1906:561. Type by original designation. Valid (Poll 1986:84 [ref. 6136]). Cichlidae.

Cyprichromis Scheuermann 1977:71 [ref. 3924]. Masc. *Paratilapia leptosoma* Boulenger 1898:14. Type by original designation. Valid (Poll 1981:171 [ref. 3534], Poll 1986:146 [ref. 6136]). Cichlidae.

Cyprichthys Whitley 1936:51 [ref. 4687]. Masc. *Tetraodon mappa* Lesson 1831:102. Type by original designation (also monotypic). Tetraodontidae.

Cyprinella Girard 1856:196 [ref. 1810]. Fem. *Leuciscus bubalinus* Baird & Girard 1853:249. Type by subsequent designation. Type designated by Jordan & Gilbert 1877:91 [ref. 4907]. Synonym of *Notropis* Rafinesque 1818 (Gilbert 1978:15 [ref. 7042]); valid (Matthews 1987 [ref. 6774], Mayden 1989 [ref. 12555]. Cyprinidae.

Cyprinion Heckel 1843:1015 [ref. 2066]. Neut. *Cyprinion macrostomus* Heckel 1843:1065. Type by subsequent designation. Type designated by Jordan 1919:211 [ref. 2410]. *Cyprinium* Agassiz 1846:114 [ref. 64] is an unjustified emendation. Valid (Karaman 1971:221 [ref. 2560], Howes 1982:331 [ref. 14202], Jayaram 1981:130 [ref. 6497], Kottelat 1989:7 [ref. 13605], Chen 1989:118 [ref. 14144]). Cyprinidae.

Cyprinocirrhites Tanaka 1917:269 [ref. 4332]. Masc. *Cyprinocirrhites ui* Tanaka 1917:269. Type by monotypy. Appeared first in Japanese (15 July) 1917, in English in 1918 (28 Nov.):507 [ref. 6037]. Valid (Araga in Masuda et al. 1984:200 [ref. 6441], Randall 1986:666 [ref. 5706], Donaldson 1986:624 [ref. 6317]). Cirrhitidae.

Cyprinodon Lacepède (ex Bosc) 1803:486 [ref. 4930]. Masc. *Cyprinodon variegatus* Lacepède 1803:486, 487. Type by monotypy. Valid (Miller 1976 [ref. 7032], Parenti 1981:526 [ref. 7066]). Cyprinodontidae: Cyprinodontinae.

Cyprinogobius Koumans 1937:11 [ref. 2675]. Masc. *Lophogobius chrysosoma* Bleeker 1875:114. Type by original designation. Synonym of *Redigobius* Herre 1927 (Miller 1987:698 [ref. 6336]). Gobiidae.

Cyprinopsis Blanchard 1866:335 [ref. 310]. Fem. Blanchard (p. 335) clearly refers to Fitzinger as author of genus, so Blanchard's treatment not regarded as an original description; see Fitzinger 1832. Cyprinidae.

Cyprinopsis Fitzinger 1832:334 [ref. 5019]. Fem. *Cyprinus auratus* Linnaeus 1758:322. Type by monotypy. Original not seen. Synonym of *Carassius* Nilsson 1832. Cyprinidae.

Cyprinus Linnaeus 1758:320 [ref. 2787]. Masc. *Cyprinus carpio* Linnaeus 1758:320. Type by subsequent designation. Type designated by Jordan & Gilbert 1883:254 [ref. 2476]. On Official List (Opinion 77). Valid (Chen & Huang 1977:401 [ref. 13496], Sawada in Masuda et al. 1984:58 [ref. 6441], Zhou in Chu & Chen 1989:329 [ref. 13584]). Cyprinidae.

Cypselichthys Steindachner & Döderlein 1883:14 [ref. 4247]. Masc. *Cypselichthys japonicus* Steindachner & Döderlein 1883:15. Type by monotypy. Kyphosidae: Scorpidinae.

Cypselurus Swainson 1838:299 [ref. 4302]. Masc. *Exocoetus appendiculatus* Wood 1825:283. Type by monotypy. In 1838:299 as genus *Cypsilurus* and type by monotypy; then 1839:187 and 296 [ref. 4303] as *Cypsilurus* subgenus of *Exocoetus*. Spelled *Cypsilurus* 5 times (including index) by Swainson, but ICZN (Opinion 26) ruled that this was in error for *Cypselurus*. Valid (Collette et al. 1984:338 [ref. 11422], Yoshino in Masuda et al. 1984:80 [ref. 6441], Heemstra & Parin 1986:393 [ref. 6293], Paxton et al. 1989:333 [ref. 12442]). Exocoetidae.

Cypsilurus see *Cypselurus*. Exocoetidae.

Cyrene Heckel 1843:1024 [ref. 2066]. Fem. *Cyrene ocellata* Heckel 1843:1025. Type by subsequent designation. Type apparently designated first by Jordan 1919:215 [ref. 2410]. Possibly preoccupied by *Cyrene* Schleuter 1838:34, if a justified emendation for *Cyrena* Lamarck 1818 in Mollusca. Synonym of *Dangila* Valenciennes 1842 (Roberts 1989:37 [ref. 6439]); synonym of *Labiobarbus* van Hasselt 1823 (if recognized). Cyprinidae.

Cyrtocara Boulenger 1902:69 [ref. 567]. Neut. *Cyrtocara moorii* Boulenger 1902:70. Type by monotypy. Valid (Ribbink et al. 1983:246 [ref. 13555], Stauffer & McKaye 1985 [ref. 6786], Eccles & Trewavas 1989:199 [ref. 13547]). Cichlidae.

Cyrtocharax Fowler 1907:454 [ref. 1374]. Masc. *Anacyrtus limaesquamis* Cope 1878:686. Type by original designation (also monotypic). Synonym of *Cynopotamus* Valenciennes 1849 (Menezes 1976:22 [ref. 7073] in subfamily Cynopotaminae). Characidae.

Cyrtorhynchus Costa 1855:suppl. [ref. 976]. Masc. *Cyrtorhynchus leopoldi* Costa 1855:suppl. Type by monotypy. Myctophiformes.

Cyrtus Minding 1832:113 [ref. 3022]. Masc. *Cyrtus indicus*. Name not in current literature. Unplaced genera.

Cyttoides Smith 1947:795 [ref. 4073]. Masc. *Cyttoides jacksoni* Smith 1907:795. Type by original designation (also monotypic). Preoccupied by Wettstein 1886 in fossil fishes, replaced by *Cyttoidops* Smith 1949. Synonym of *Cyttus* Günther 1860 (James 1976:495 [ref. 7081], Heemstra 1980:7 [ref. 14195]). Zeidae.

Cyttoidops Smith 1949:143 [ref. 5846]. Masc. *Cyttoides jacksoni* Smith 1947:795. Type by original designation. Apparently a replacement for *Cyttoides* Smith 1947, preoccupied by Wettstein 1886 in fossil fishes, but not so stated by Smith. Synonym of *Cyttus* Günther 1860 (James 1976:495 [ref. 7081], Heemstra 1980:7 [ref. 14195]). Zeidae.

Cyttomimus Gilbert 1905:623 [ref. 1631]. Masc. *Cyttomimus stelgis* Gilbert 1905:624. Type by original designation (type in parentheses), also monotypic—additional species listed are regarded as not definitely referred to genus. Valid (Machida in Masuda et al. 1984:118 [ref. 6441], Paxton et al. 1989:388 [ref. 12442], Pequeño 1989:54 [ref. 14125]). Zeidae.

Cyttopsis Gill 1862:126 [ref. 1659]. Fem. *Zeus roseus* Lowe 1843:85. Type by original designation (also monotypic). Valid (Wheeler 1973:350 [ref. 7190], Heemstra 1980:3 [ref. 14195], Machida in Masuda et al. 1984:118 [ref. 6441], Quéro in Whitehead et al. 1986:769 [ref. 13676], Heemstra 1986:436 [ref. 5660], Paxton et al. 1989:388 [ref. 12442]). Zeidae.

Cyttosoma Gilchrist 1904:6 [ref. 1645]. Neut. *Cyttosoma boops* Gilchrist 1904:6. Type by monotypy. Synonym of *Oreosoma* Cuvier 1829 (Karrer 1986:439 [ref. 5680], James et al. 1988:302 [ref. 6639]). Oreosomatidae.

Cyttula Weber 1913:411 [ref. 4602]. Fem. *Cyttula macrops* Weber 1913:411. Type by monotypy. Macrurocyttidae.

Cyttus Günther 1860:396 [ref. 1963]. Masc. *Capros australis* Richardson 1843:170. Type by subsequent designation. Type designated by Gill 1862:126 [ref. 1659]. Valid (Wheeler 1973:349 [ref. 7190], James 1976:495 [ref. 7081], Heemstra 1980:7 [ref. 14195], Heemstra 1986:437 [ref. 5660], Paxton et al. 1989:389 [ref. 12442]). Zeidae.

Czekanowskiella (subgenus of *Phoxinus*) Dybowski 1916:ca. 100 [ref. 6519]. Fem. *Phoxinus czekanowskii* Dybowski 1869:953. Original not seen. Questionably a synonym of *Lagowskiella* Dybowski 1916 (Howes 1985:63 [ref. 5274]). Cyprinidae.

Daba (subgenus of *Perca*) Forsskål 1775:44 [ref. 1351]. Fem. *Perca summana areolata* Forsskål 1775:42. Not available, regarded as non-latinized Arabic name (see Jordan 1917:33-34 [ref. 2407]). In the synonymy of *Epinephelus* Bloch 1793. Serranidae: Epinephelinae.

Dacentrus Jordan 1878:667 [ref. 5860]. Masc. *Dacentrus lucens* Jordan 1878:667. Type by monotypy. Synonym of *Hysterocarpus* Gibbons 1854 (Tarp 1952:77 [ref. 12250]). Embiotocidae.

Dacodraco Waite 1916:35 [ref. 4568]. Masc. *Dacodraco hunteri* Waite 1916:36. Type by monotypy. Valid (DeWitt & Hureau 1979:790 [ref. 1125], Stevens et al. 1984:563 [ref. 13633], Iwami 1985:57 [ref. 13368]). Channichthyidae.

Dactylagnus Gill 1863:505 [ref. 1672]. Masc. *Dactylagnus mundus* Gill 1863:505. Type by monotypy. Valid (Dawson 1982:75 [ref. 1072]). Dactyloscopidae.

Dactylanthias Bleeker 1871:Pl. 282 [ref. 4861]. Masc. *Anthias aplodactylus* Bleeker 1858:3. Type by monotypy. Apparently correctly dates to Pl. 282 (probably published in 1871) as above; corresponding legend (p. 123) not published until 1876, corresponding text (p. 15) published in 1875. Also published in Bleeker 1873:156, 168 [ref. 432]. Valid (Kendall 1984:500 [ref. 13663]). Serranidae: Anthiinae.

Dactyleleotris Smith 1958:161 [ref. 4118]. Fem. *Dactyleleotris tentaculatus* Smith 1958:161. Type by original designation (also monotypic). Synonym of *Hetereleotris* Bleeker 1874 (Akihito & Meguro 1981:331 [ref. 5508], Hoese 1986:3 [ref. 5996]). Gobiidae.

Dactyleptus Rafinesque 1815:82 [ref. 3584]. Masc. *Blennius muraenoides* Sujef 1779:195. Type by being a replacement name. As "*Dactyleptus* R. [Rafinesque] *Muraenoide* Lac. [Lacepède]." Apparently an available (unneeded) replacement name for *Muraenoides* Lacepède 1800. Synonym of *Pholis* Scopoli 1777 (Makushok 1973:534 [ref. 6889], Yatsu 1981:169 [ref. 4814]). Pholidae.

Dactylobatus Bean & Weed 1909:459 [ref. 220]. Masc. *Dactylobatus armatus* Bean & Weed 1909:459. Type by original designation (also monotypic). Rajidae.

Dactylopagrus Gill 1862:114 [ref. 1658]. Masc. *Cheilodactylus carponemus* Cuvier in Cuvier & Valenciennes 1830:362. Type by original designation (also monotypic). Spelled *Dactylosparus* on p. 117; Jordan 1919:314 [ref. 4904] serves as first reviser selecting *Dactylopagrus* [earlier first reviser not researched]. Cheilodactylidae.

Dactylophallus Howell Rivero & Rivas 1944:8, 15 [ref. 7312]. Masc. *Girardinus denticulatus* Garman 1895:47. Type by original designation (also monotypic). Synonym of *Girardinus* Poey 1854 (Rosen & Bailey 1963:109 [ref. 7067]). Poeciliidae.

Dactylophora De Vis 1883:284 [ref. 1088]. Fem. *Dactylophora semimaculata* De Vis 1883:284. Type by monotypy. Cirrhitidae.

Dactylophorus Swainson 1839:55, 179, 262 [ref. 4303]. Masc. *Dactylophorus volitans* Swainson 1839:262 (= *Gasterosteus volitans* Linnaeus 1758:296). Type by subsequent designation. Type designated by Whitley 1929:127 [ref. 4665]. Perhaps described independently of *Dactylopterus* Lacepède 1801, else an incorrect subsequent spelling. Objective synonym of *Dactylopterus* Lacepède 1801. Dactylopteridae.

Dactyloptena Jordan & Richardson 1908:665 [ref. 2491]. Fem. *Dactylopterus orientalis* Cuvier in Cuvier & Valenciennes 1829:134. Type by original designation (also monotypic). Valid (Washington et al. 1984:441 [ref. 13660], Okamura in Masuda et al. 1984:336 [ref. 6441], Eschmeyer 1986:490 [ref. 5652], Paxton et al. 1989:480 [ref. 12442]). Dactylopteridae.

Dactylopterus Lacepède 1801:325 [ref. 2710]. Masc. *Gasterosteus pirapeda* Lacepède 1801:325, 326 (= *Gasterosteus volitans* Linnaeus 1758:296). Type by subsequent designation. Type apparently designated first by Jordan 1917:62 [ref. 2407]. Synonym of *Cephalacanthus* Lacepède 1801 (Monod 1973:613 [ref. 7193]); valid (Washington et al. 1984:441 [ref. 13660], Roux in Whitehead et al. 1986:1284 [ref. 13677], Eschmeyer 1986:490 [ref. 5652]). Dactylopteridae.

Dactylopus Gill 1859:130 [ref. 1761]. Masc. *Callionymus dactylopus* Bennett in Valenciennes in Cuvier & Valenciennes 1837:310. Type by monotypy. Valid (Nakabo 1982:101 [ref. 3139], Fricke 1982:71 [ref. 5432], Houde 1984:637 [ref. 13674], Nakabo in Masuda et al. 1984:344 [ref. 6441]). Callionymidae.

Dactylosargus Gill 1862:112 [ref. 1658]. Masc. *Aplodactylus arcidens [arctidens]* Richardson 1839:96. Type by monotypy, second species included with doubt. Aplodactylidae.

Dactyloscopus Gill 1859:132 [ref. 1792]. Masc. *Dactyloscopus tridigitatus* Gill 1859:132. Type by monotypy. Valid (Dawson 1975 [ref. 7121], Dawson 1982:19 [ref. 1072]). Dactyloscopidae.

Dactylosparus Gill 1862:117 [ref. 1658]. Masc. *Cheilodactylus carponemus* Cuvier in Cuvier & Valenciennes 1830:362. Type by original designation (also monotypic). *Dactylopagrus* used for this genus on p. 114; Jordan, 1919:314 [ref. 4904] serves as first reviser, selecting *Dactylopagrus*. Objective synonym of *Dactylopagrus* Gill 1862. Cheilodactylidae.

Dactylostomias Garman 1899:279 [ref. 1540]. Masc. *Dactylostomias filifer* Garman 1899:279. Type by monotypy. Synonym of *Bathophilus* Giglioli 1882 (Morrow in Morrow & Gibbs 1964:456 [ref. 6962], Morrow 1973:135 [ref. 7175]). Melanostomiidae.

Dacymba Jordan & Hubbs 1917:464 [ref. 2484]. Fem. *Pristipoma bennettii* Lowe 1841:176. Type by original designation (also monotypic). Synonym of *Pomadasys* Lacepède 1802 (Roux 1973:391 [ref. 7200], Roux 1986:328 [ref. 6209]). Haemulidae.

Dadyanos Whitley 1951:68 [ref. 4711]. *Platea insignis* Steindachner

1898:323. Type by being a replacement name. Replacement for *Platea* Steindachner 1898, preoccupied [not investigated]. Valid (Gosztonyi 1977:210 [ref. 6103], Anderson 1984:578 [ref. 13634]). Zoarcidae.

Daector Jordan & Evermann 1898:2313, 2325 [ref. 2445]. Masc. *Thalassophryne dowi* Jordan & Gilbert 1887:388. Type by original designation (also monotypic). Valid (Collette 1966:859 [ref. 14192]). Batrachoididae.

Daemomanta Whitley 1932:327 [ref. 4674]. Fem. *Manta alfredi* Krefft 1868:3, 9. Type by original designation (also monotypic). Date for type species still under investigation, see Whitley 1932:328 [ref. 4674]. Synonym of *Manta* Bancroft 1829 (Cappetta 1987:176 [ref. 6348]). Mobulidae.

Dagetia (subgenus of *Coptodon*) Thys van den Audenaerde 1970:290 [ref. 12518]. Fem. Not available, name only; possible subsequent use not researched. Cichlidae.

Dagetichthys Stauch & Blanc 1964:172 [ref. 4200]. Masc. *Dagetichthys lakdoensis* Stauch & Blanc 1964:173. Type by monotypy. Valid (Desoutter 1986:430 [ref. 6212]). Soleidae.

Daia Ogilby 1903:9 [ref. 3280]. Fem. *Centropogon indicus* Day 1875:155. Type by monotypy. Second species doubtfully referred to genus in footnote. Synonym of *Paracentropogon* Bleeker 1876. Scorpaenidae: Tetraroginae.

Daicocus Jordan & Richardson 1908:667 [ref. 2491]. *Dactylopterus peterseni* Nyström 1887:24. Type by original designation (also monotypic). Synonym of *Dactyloptena* Jordan & Richardson 1908 (Eschmeyer, pers. comm.); valid (Okamura in Masuda et al. 1984:336 [ref. 6441]). Dactylopteridae.

Dajaus Valenciennes in Cuvier & Valenciennes 1836:164 [ref. 1005]. *Mugil monticola* Bancroft in Griffith 1834:367. Type by monotypy. Synonym of *Agonostomus* Bennett 1832 (Thomson 1986:344 [ref. 6215]). Mugilidae.

Dalatias Rafinesque 1810:10 [ref. 3594]. Masc. *Dalatias sparophagus* Rafinesque 1810:10. Type by subsequent designation. Type designated by Jordan, Tanaka & Snyder 1913:22 [ref. 6448]. *Dalatius* an incorrect subsequent spelling. Valid (Compagno 1984:63 [ref. 6474], Nakaya & Shirai in Masuda et al. 1984:11 [ref. 6441]). Doubtfully a senior synonym of *Scymnorhinus* Bonaparte 1846 (Krefft & Tortonese 1973:46 [ref. 7165], Cappetta 1987:62 [ref. 6348], Paxton et al. 1989:33 [ref. 12442]). Squalidae.

Dallia Bean 1880:358 [ref. 222]. Fem. *Dallia pectoralis* Bean 1880:358. Type by monotypy. Valid (Wilson & Veilleux 1982 [ref. 14203], Balushkin & Chereshnev 1982 [ref. 5251], Martin 1984:140 [ref. 13639]). Umbridae.

Dalophis Rafinesque 1810:68 [ref. 3594]. Masc. *Dalophis serpa* Rafinesque 1810:69. Type by subsequent designation. Spelled *Dalaphis* on legend page (p. 100) and on Pl. VII. Two species; earliest first reviser not researched; perhaps type first designated by Jordan 1917:81 [ref. 2407], but Fowler (MS) says type is *bimaculata*. Valid (Blache et al. 1973:249 [ref. 7185], McCosker 1977:71 [ref. 6836], Castle 1984:38 [ref. 6171], Bauchot in Whitehead et al. 1986:579 [ref. 13676], McCosker et al. 1989:298 [ref. 13288]). Ophichthidae: Ophichthinae.

Damalichthys Girard 1855:321 [ref. 1820]. Masc. *Damalichthys vacca* Girard 1855:321. Type by monotypy. Synonym of *Rhacochilus* Agassiz 1854 (Tarp 1952:53 [ref. 12250]). Embiotocidae.

Damania Smith 1959:239 [ref. 4123]. Fem. *Andamia anjouanae* Fourmanoir 1954:207. Type by original designation. Synonym of *Alticus* Commerson 1800 (Smith-Vaniz & Springer 1971:14 [ref. 4145], Bath 1986:355 [ref. 6217]). Blenniidae.

Dameus Rafinesque 1815:91 [ref. 3584]. Not available, name only. Presumably for a species of gymnotid. Gymnotidae.

Dampieria Castelnau 1875:30 [ref. 768]. Fem. *Dampieria lineata* Castelnau 1875:30. Type by monotypy. Synonym of *Labracinus* Schlegel 1858 (Hayashi in Masuda et al. 1984:140 [ref. 6441], Paxton et al. 1989:518 [ref. 12442]). Pseudochromidae: Pseudochrominae.

Dampierosa Whitley 1932:346 [ref. 4674]. Fem. *Dampierosa daruma* Whitley 1932:346. Type by original designation (also monotypic). Valid (Eschmeyer & Rama-Rao 1973:367 [ref. 6391], Washington et al. 1984:440 [ref. 13660], Paxton et al. 1989:440 [ref. 12442]). Scorpaenidae: Synanceiinae.

Danacetichthys Paxton 1989:151, 168 [ref. 13435]. Masc. *Danacetichthys galathenus* Paxton 1989:169. Type by original designation (also monotypic). Cetomimidae.

Danakilia Thys van den Audenaerde 1970:290, 291 [ref. 12518]. Fem. Not available, name only; as a subgroup of *Sarotherodon (Oreochromis)*. Cichlidae.

Danaphos Bruun 1931:286 [ref. 672]. Masc. *Danaphos asteroscopus* Bruun 1931:287. Type by original designation (also monotypic). Second species questionably referred to genus. Valid (Weitzman 1974:472 [ref. 5174], Ahlstrom et al. 1984:185 [ref. 13643], Weitzman 1986:254 [ref. 6287]). Sternoptychidae: Maurolicinae.

Danaphryne Bertelsen 1951:101 [ref. 287]. Fem. *Dolopichthys (Dermatias) nigrifilis* Regan & Trewavas 1932:67. Type by monotypy. Valid (Pietsch 1974:32 [ref. 5332], Bertelsen & Pietsch 1977:183 [ref. 7063]). Oneirodidae.

Dangila Valenciennes in Cuvier & Valenciennes 1842:229 [ref. 1009]. Fem. *Dangila cuvieri* Valenciennes in Cuvier & Valenciennes 1842:230. Type by subsequent designation. Type designated by Bleeker 1863:24 [ref. 4859] or 1863:193 [ref. 397], as "*Dangila leptocheilus* Val. = *Dangila Cuvieri* Val." Synonym of *Labiobarbus* van Hasselt 1823 (Jayaram 1981:121 [ref. 6497]); valid (Roberts 1989:37 [ref. 6439] with *Labiobarbus* as unidentifiable). Cyprinidae.

Danichthys Bruun 1934:134 [ref. 5129]. Masc. *Exocoetus rondeletii* Valenciennes in Cuvier & Valenciennes 1847:115. Type by original designation (also monotypic). Synonym of *Hirundichthys* Bleeker 1928 (Parin 1973:265 [ref. 7191]), but as a valid subgenus (Heemstra & Parin 1986:394 [ref. 6293]); valid genus (Yoshino in Masuda et al. 1984:82 [ref. 6441]). Exocoetidae.

Danio (subgenus of *Cyprinus*) Hamilton 1822:321, 390 [ref. 2031]. Masc. *Cyprinus (Danio) dangila* Hamilton 1822:321, 390. Type by subsequent designation. Type designated by Bleeker 1863:203 [ref. 397], 1863:264 [ref. 403] and 1863:29 [ref. 4859]. Valid (Yang & Hwang 1964:54 [ref. 13497], Jayaram 1981:78 [ref. 6497], Chu 1981 [ref. 5248], Kuang in Chu & Chen 1989:11 [ref. 13584], Kottelat 1989:7 [ref. 13605]). Cyprinidae.

Danioides Chu 1935:10 [ref. 832]. Masc. *Danio kakhienensis* Anderson 1878:868. Type by original designation. Synonym of *Danio* Hamilton 1822 (Chu 1981:145 [ref. 5248], Kuang in Chu & Chen 1989:11 [ref. 13584]). Cyprinidae.

Danionella Roberts 1986:232 [ref. 5942]. Fem. *Danionella translucida* Roberts 1986:233. Type by original designation (also monotypic). Cyprinidae.

Daniops Smith 1945:91 [ref. 4056]. Masc. *Daniops myersi* Smith

1945:92. Type by original designation (also monotypic). Synonym of *Danio* Hamilton 1822 (Chu 1981:145 [ref. 5248], Kottelat 1982:524 [ref. 5400], Kuang in Chu & Chen 1989:12 [ref. 13584]). Cyprinidae.

Dannevigia Whitley 1941:42 [ref. 4701]. Fem. *Dannevigia tusca* Whitley 1941:42. Type by original designation (also monotypic). Valid (Cohen & Nielsen 1978:19 [ref. 881], Paxton et al. 1989:311 [ref. 12442]). Ophidiidae: Neobythitinae.

Daramattus Smith 1960:231 [ref. 4125]. Masc. *Daramattus armatus* Smith 1960:231. Type by original designation. Synonym of *Grammicolepis* Poey 1873 (Karrer & Heemstra 1986:440 [ref. 5681]); valid (Shimizu in Uyeno et al. 1983:290 [ref. 14275], Paxton et al. 1989:391 [ref. 12442]). Grammicolepididae.

Darienichthys Hubbs 1924:8 [ref. 2231]. Masc. *Gambusia darienensis* Meek & Hildebrand 1913:88. Type by original designation (also monotypic). Synonym of *Priapichthys* Regan 1913 (Rosen & Bailey 1963:120 [ref. 7067]). Poeciliidae.

Daruma Jordan & Starks 1904:241 [ref. 2528]. Fem. *Daruma sagamia* Jordan & Starks 1904:241. Type by original designation (also monotypic). Valid (Washington et al. 1984:442 [ref. 13660], Yabe in Masuda et al. 1984:325 [ref. 6441]). Cottidae.

Dascillus Gronow in Gray 1854:171 [ref. 1911]. Masc. No included species. Subsequent use not researched; Jordan 1919:259 [ref. 2410] regards as a clupeid. Gray (Preface p. vi) indicates that Gronow's description was incomplete. Not *Dascyllus* Cuvier 1829. Clupeidae.

Dascyllus Cuvier 1829:179 [ref. 995]. Masc. *Chaetodon aruanus* Linnaeus 1758:275. Type by monotypy. Spelled *Dascylus*, *Dascilus* and *Dascillus* in early literature. Valid (Randall & Allen 1977 [ref. 6482], Ida in Masuda et al. 1984:191 [ref. 6441], Allen 1986:677 [ref. 5631]). Pomacentridae.

Dasson Jordan & Hubbs 1925:318 [ref. 2486]. Masc. *Aspidontus trossulus* Jordan & Snyder 1902:455. Type by original designation. Synonym of *Petroscirtes* Rüppell 1830, but as a valid subgenus (Smith-Vaniz 1976:19, 23 [ref. 4144]). Blenniidae.

Dasyacanthurus (subgenus of *Xesurus*) Fowler 1944:333 [ref. 1448]. Masc. *Xesurus hopkinsi* Gilbert & Starks 1904:155. Type by original designation (also monotypic). Synonym of *Xesurus* Jordan & Evermann 1896. Acanthuridae.

Dasyatis Gray 1851:121 [ref. 4939]. Fem. *Raja altavela* Linnaeus 1758:232. Type by subsequent designation. Type designated by Bigelow & Schroeder 1953:397 [ref. 6568]. Not *Dasyatis* Rafinesque. Probably should not be regarded as an original description as Gray cites *Dasyatis* Rafinesque in synonymy. In the synonymy of *Gymnura* van Hasselt 1823 (Krefft & Stehmann 1973:72 [ref. 7167]). Gymnuridae.

Dasyatis Rafinesque 1810:16 [ref. 3594]. Fem. *Dasyatis ujo* Rafinesque 1810:16. Type by monotypy. *Dasibatis* Agassiz 1846:117 [ref. 64] is an unjustified emendation. Valid (Krefft & Stehmann 1973:70 [ref. 7167], Nakaya in Masuda et al. 1984:15 [ref. 6441], Compagno 1986:136 [ref. 5648], Cappetta 1987:163 [ref. 6348], Nishida & Nakaya 1988 [ref. 12554], Paxton et al. 1989:42 [ref. 12442]). Dasyatidae.

Dasybatis Blainville 1825:12 [ref. 4991]. Fem. *Raja batis* Linnaeus 1758:231. Type by subsequent designation. Jordan 1917:134 [ref. 2407] lists as above with author as Serville, but name can be considered an incorrect subsequent spelling of *Dasybatus* Blainville and author is Blainville; see remarks under Blainville 1825 [ref. 4991]. Synonym of *Raja* Linnaeus 1758. Rajidae.

Dasybatus (subgenus of *Raia [Raja]*) Blainville 1816:112 [= 120] [ref. 306]. Masc. *Raja clavata* Linnaeus 1758:232. Type by subsequent designation. Type apparently first designated by Bonaparte 1838:203 [ref. 4979]. Not *Dasybatus* Klein 1775. Synonym of *Raja* Linnaeus 1758 (Stehmann 1973:58 [ref. 7168]). Rajidae.

Dasybatus Bonaparte 1834:puntata 32 [ref. 517]. Masc. *Raia radula* Delaroche 1809:321. Apparently appeared first in puntata 32, fasc. 6 under *Raja marginata* and spelled *Leiobatus* and *Leiobatis*; also appeared in puntata 68 under *Raja radula*. Bonaparte attributes the name to Blainville, so Bonapart's treatment is not regarded as an original description. Synonym of *Raja* Linnaeus 1758. Rajidae.

Dasybatus Garman (ex Klein) 1885:221 [ref. 1532]. Masc. *Raja pastinaca* Linnaeus 1758:232. Type by monotypy. Based on *Dasybatus* Klein 1775. Walbaum 1792 did not make available; names reproduced by Walbaum from Klein have been rejected by the ICZN. Synonym of *Dasyatis* Rafinesque 1810. Dasyatidae.

Dasybatus Klein 1775:991 [ref. 2618]. Masc. Not available, published in a work that does not conform to the principle of binominal nomenclature. Not *Dasybatus* Blainville 1816. In the synonymy of *Dasyatis* Rafinesque 1810. Dasyatidae.

Dasycottus Bean 1890:42 [ref. 229]. Masc. *Dasycottus setiger* Bean 1890:42. Type by monotypy. Valid (Nelson 1982:1473 [ref. 5470], Washington et al. 1984:444 [ref. 13660], Yabe in Masuda et al. 1984:330 [ref. 6441], Yabe 1985:122 [ref. 11522]). Psychrolutidae.

Dasyloricaria Isbrücker & Nijssen in Isbrücker 1979:87, 90 [ref. 2302]. Fem. *Loricaria filamentosa* Steindachner 1878:90. Type by original designation. Valid (Isbrücker 1980:111 [ref. 2303], Burgess 1989:443 [ref. 12860]). Loricariidae.

Dasyscopelus (subgenus of *Scopelus*) Günther 1864:405, 411 [ref. 1974]. Masc. *Myctophum asperum* Richardson 1845:41. Type by subsequent designation. Described in key (p. 405) as subgenus of *Scopelus* with two corresponding species on p. 411. Type designated by Goode & Bean 1896:91 [ref. 1848]. Synonym of *Myctophum* Rafinesque 1810 (Bolin 1959:13 [ref. 503], Krefft & Bekker 1973:171 [ref. 7181], Paxton 1979:15 [ref. 6440]). Myctophidae.

Datnia Cuvier 1829:148 [ref. 995]. Fem. *Coius datnia* Hamilton 1822:88, 369. Type by absolute tautonymy. Appeared first in Cuvier (Mar.) 1829:147 (footnote) as above; then in Cuvier in Cuvier & Valenciennes (Apr.) 1829 [ref. 4879]. Labridae.

Datnioides Bleeker 1853:440 [ref. 338]. Masc. *Datnioides polota* Bleeker 1853:440 (= *Coius polota* Hamilton 1822:95, 370). Type by subsequent designation. Type designated by Bleeker 1876:272 [as "*Datnioides quadrifasciatus* Blkr = *Datnioides polota* Blkr = *Chaetodon quadrifasciatus* Seuvast."; *polota* and *microlepis* are the two original included species; *polota* Hamilton the type.] See *Coius* Hamilton 1822. Treated as valid (Kottelat 1989:17 [ref. 13605]). Placed in Percoidei incerte sedis by Johnson 1984:465 [ref. 9681]. Lobotidae.

Datnioides Canestrini 1860:305 [ref. 712]. Masc. Not proposed as a new name (see Mees & Kailola 1977:8 [ref. 5183]) but a subsequent use of *Datnioides* of authors. Lobotidae.

Daurada Stark 1828:452 [ref. 4193]. Masc. *Sparus aurata* Linnaeus 1758:277. Type by subsequent designation. Type apparently first designated by Jordan 1917:123 [ref. 2407]. Treated by Stark as masculine. Objective synonym of *Sparus* Linnaeus 1758. Sparidae.

Davalla Bleeker 1858:58, 64 [ref. 365]. Fem. *Davalla schomburgkii* Bleeker 1858:64 (= *Hypophthalmus davalla* Schomburgk

1849:191). Type by monotypy. Bleeker's *schomburgkii* is an unneeded substitute for *davalla*. Synonym of *Ageneiosus* Lacepède 1803. Ageneiosidae.

Davidia Miranda-Ribeiro 1915:9 [ref. 3711]. Fem. *Alutera punctata* Agassiz in Spix & Agassiz 1829:137. Type by monotypy. Appears on p. 9 in section titled Monacanthidae. Monacanthidae.

Davidijordania Popov 1931:212 [ref. 3544]. Fem. *Lycenchelys lacertinus* Pavlenko 1910:53. Type by original designation. Spelled *Davidojordania* by Schmidt 1936:97 [ref. 3942]. Valid (Anderson 1984:578 [ref. 13634], Toyoshima in Masuda et al. 1984:305 [ref. 6441]). Zoarcidae.

Daya Bleeker 1877:71 [ref. 454]. Fem. *Pomacentrus jerdoni* Day 1873:237. Type by monotypy. Synonym of *Pristotis* Rüppell 1838 (Allen 1975:227 [ref. 97], Shen & Chan 1978:211 [ref. 6945]). Pomacentridae.

Dayella Talwar & Whitehead 1971:63 [ref. 4320]. Fem. *Spratelloides malabaricus* Day 1873:240. Type by original designation (also monotypic). Valid (Jayaram 1981:37 [ref. 6497], Whitehead 1985:173 [ref. 5141]). Clupeidae.

Daysciaena Talwar 1970:192 [ref. 12258]. Fem. *Corvina albida* Cuvier 1830:93. Type by original designation (also monotypic). Valid (Jayaram 1981:331 [ref. 6497]). Sciaenidae.

Deania Jordan & Snyder 1902:80 [ref. 2515]. Fem. *Deania eglantina* Jordan & Snyder 1902:80. Type by monotypy. Valid (Krefft & Tortonese 1973:41 [ref. 7165], Compagno 1984:65 [ref. 6474], Bass et al. 1986:53 [ref. 5636], Cappetta 1987:55 [ref. 6348], Paxton et al. 1989:34 [ref. 12442]). Squalidae.

Deaniops Whitley 1932:326 [ref. 4674]. Masc. *Acanthidium quadrispinosum* McCulloch 1915:100. Type by original designation (also monotypic). Synonym of *Deania* Jordan & Snyder 1902 (Compagno 1984:65 [ref. 6474]). Squalidae.

Decactylus (subgenus of *Catostomus*) Rafinesque 1820:306 [ref. 5006]. Masc. *Catostomus bostoniensis* Lesueur 1817:95. Type by subsequent designation. Type designated by Jordan & Gilbert 1877:87 [ref. 4907]. Also appeared in Rafinesque 1820:60 (Dec.) [ref. 3592] as *Decadactylus*. Synonym of *Catostomus* Lesueur 1817. Catostomidae.

Decagrammus Hubbs 1928:13 [ref. 2237]. Masc. *Chiropsis constellatus* Girard 1858:42. Type by original designation (also monotypic). Objective synonym of *Chiropsis* Girard 1858; synonym of *Hexagrammos* Steller 1809. Hexagrammidae: Hexagramminae.

Decapogon Eigenmann & Eigenmann 1888:165 [ref. 1249]. Masc. *Callichthys adspersus* Steindachner 1876:135. Type by monotypy. Callichthyidae.

Decapterus Bleeker 1851:342, 352, 358 [ref. 326]. Masc. *Caranx kurra* Cuvier in Cuvier & Valenciennes 1833:44. Type by subsequent designation. Type designated by Jordan & Gilbert 1883:432 [ref. 2476]. Valid (Hureau & Tortonese 1973:375 [ref. 7198], Smith-Vaniz 1984:524 [ref. 13664], Gushiken in Masuda et al. 1984:154 [ref. 6441], Smith-Vaniz 1986:649 [ref. 5718], Daget & Smith-Vaniz 1986:314 [ref. 6207], Gushiken 1988:443 [ref. 6697], Paxton et al. 1989:578 [ref. 12442]). Carangidae.

Decaptus Poey 1861:374, 391 [ref. 3499]. Masc. *Seriola pinnulata* Poey 1860:233. Type by monotypy. Synonym of *Elagatis* Bennett 1840 (Smith-Vaniz, pers. comm., Nov. 1989). Carangidae.

Decodon Günther 1861:384 [ref. 1967]. Masc. *Cossyphus puellaris* Poey 1860:210. Type by monotypy. Valid (Gomon 1974 [ref. 7103], Randall 1986:693 [ref. 5706]). Labridae.

Decterias Jordan & Starks 1904:154 [ref. 2527]. Masc. *Minous pusillus* Temminck & Schlegel 1843:50. Type by original designation (also monotypic). Synonym of *Minous* Cuvier 1829 (Eschmeyer et al. 1979:454 [ref. 1277]). Scorpaenidae: Minoinae.

Dekaya Cooper 1863:70 [ref. 905]. Fem. *Dekaya anomala* Cooper 1863:70. Type by monotypy. Synonym of *Caulolatilus* Gill 1862 (Dooley 1978:14 [ref. 5499]). Malacanthidae: Latilinae.

Dekeyseria Rapp Py-Daniel 1985:178 [ref. 6101]. Fem. *Dekeyseria amazonica* Rapp Py-Daniel 1985:180. Type by original designation. Loricariidae.

Deleastes Seale 1906:80 [ref. 3999]. Masc. *Deleastes daector* Seale 1906:81. Type by monotypy. Synonym of *Synanceia* Bloch & Schneider 1801 (Eschmeyer & Rama-Rao 1973:342 [ref. 6391]). Scorpaenidae: Synanceiinae.

Dellichthys Briggs 1955:14 [ref. 637]. Masc. *Dellichthys morelandi* Briggs 1955:14. Type by original designation (also monotypic). Gobiesocidae: Gobiesocinae.

Delolepis Bean 1882:465 [ref. 224]. Fem. *Delolepis virgatus* Bean 1882:466. Type by original designation (also monotypic). Valid. Cryptacanthodidae.

Delothyris Goode 1883:109 [ref. 1835]. Fem. *Thyris pellucidus* Goode 1880:344. Type by being a replacement name. Replacement for *Thyris* Goode 1880, preoccupied by Laspeyres 1803 and Ochsenheimer 1808 in Lepidoptera. Objective synonym of *Thyris* Goode 1880. Synonym of *Monolene* Goode 1880 (Norman 1934:164 [ref. 6893]). Bothidae: Bothinae.

Delsmania (subgenus of *Scleropages*) Fowler 1934:243 [ref. 1416]. Fem. *Osteoglossum formosum* Mu("ller & Schlegel 1844:1. Type by original designation (also monotypic). Synonym of *Scleropages* Günther 1864 (Roberts 1989:23 [ref. 6439]). Osteoglossidae: Osteoglossinae.

Deltadoras Fernández-Yépez 1968:36 [ref. 1325]. Masc. *Deltadoras guayoensis* Fernández-Yépez 1968:37. Type by original designation (also monotypic). Valid (Burgess 1989:224 [ref. 12860]). Doradidae.

Deltaraia (subgenus of *Raja*) Leigh-Sharpe 1924:567, 573 [ref. 5748]. Fem. *Raja radiata* Donovan 1808:114. Type by original designation. As a "pseudogenus" of *Raia* [=*Raja*]. Not available [Art. 1b (6)], used as an artificial category (see Leigh-Sharpe 1928 [ref. 6152]). In the synonymy of *Raja* Linnaeus 1758, subgenus *Amblyraja* Malm 1877 (Stehmann 1973:61 [ref. 7168]). Rajidae.

Deltascyllium (subgenus of *Scyllium*) Leigh-Sharpe 1926:330 [ref. 5627]. Neut. *Scyllium marmoratum* Bennett 1830:693. Type by original designation. As a "pseudogenus" of *Scyllium*. Not available [Art. 1b (6)], used as an artificial category (see Leigh-Sharpe 1928 [ref. 6152]). In the synonymy of *Atelomycterus* Garman 1913 (Compagno 1984:292 [ref. 6846], Compagno 1988:100 [ref. 13488]). Scyliorhinidae.

Deltatylosurus Martin 1954:4 [ref. 2897]. Masc. *Deltatylosurus guayoensis* Martin 1954:5. Type by monotypy. Synonym of *Pseudotylosurus* Fernández-Yépez 1948 (Collette 1974:171 [ref. 7131]). Belonidae.

Deltentosteus Gill 1863:263 [ref. 1690]. Masc. *Gobius quadrimaculatus* Valenciennes in Cuvier & Valenciennes 1837:44. Type by original designation (also monotypic). Valid (Miller 1973:494 [ref. 6888], Miller in Whitehead et al. 1986:1031 [ref. 13677], Birdsong et al. 1988:202 [ref. 7303]). Gobiidae.

Deltistes Seale 1896:269 [ref. 3998]. Masc. *Chasmistes luxatus* Cope 1879:784. Type by subsequent designation. Type designated by Jordan & Evermann 1898:2794 [ref. 2445]; Seale's use of "typified by" not precise enough for original designation. Catostomidae.

Delturus Eigenmann & Eigenmann 1889:45 [ref. 1253]. Masc. *Delturus parahybae* Eigenmann & Eigenmann 1889:45. Type by original designation. Valid (Isbrücker 1980:9 [ref. 2303], Burgess 1989:429 [ref. 12860]). Loricariidae.

Demicoilia Jordan & Seale 1925:28 [ref. 2499]. Fem. *Coilia quadragesimalis* Valenciennes in Cuvier & Valenciennes 1848:79. Type by original designation (also monotypic). Synonym of *Coilia* Gray 1830 (Whitehead 1967:149 [ref. 6464], Whitehead et al. 1988:460 [ref. 5725]). Engraulidae.

Demiurga Gistel 1848:X [ref. 1822]. Fem. *Rhina ancylostoma* Bloch & Schneider 1801:352. Type by being a replacement name. Unneeded replacement for *Rhina* Bonaparte and Müller (with species *ancylostoma*), preoccupied in beetles [Oliver 1807], but *Rhina* dates to Bloch & Schneider 1801 (see Jordan 1919:339 [ref. 2409]) and predates Oliver 1807. Synonym of *Rhina* Bloch & Schneider 1801. Rhinobatidae: Rhininae.

Demoisellea Whitley 1928:295 [ref. 4663]. Fem. *Furcaria puncta* Poey 1860:195. Type by being a replacement name. Replacement for *Furcaria* Poey 1860, preoccupied by Lesson 1838 in Aves. Pomacentridae.

Denariusa Whitley 1948:92 [ref. 4710]. Fem. *Denariusa bandata* Whitley 1948:92. Type by original designation (also monotypic). Valid (Paxton et al. 1989:486 [ref. 12442]). Ambassidae.

Dendrochirus Swainson 1839:180 [ref. 4303]. Masc. *Pterois zebra* Cuvier in Cuvier & Valenciennes 1829:269. Type by subsequent designation. As *Dendrochirus* on p. 180; *Brachirus* (p. 71) and *Brachyrus* (p. 264). Bleeker 1876:42 serves as first reviser selecting *Dendrochirus* (see Eschmeyer & Randall 1975:275 [ref. 6389]). Type designated by Swain 1882 for *Brachyrus*. Valid (Amaoka in Masuda et al. 1984:316 [ref. 6441], Eschmeyer 1986:465 [ref. 5652], Paxton et al. 1989:440 [ref. 12442]). Scorpaenidae: Pteroinae.

Dendrophis Kaup in Duméril 1856:199 [ref. 1154]. Not available; name only, as *Dendrophis horridus*, apparently for *Brachysomophis horridus*. In the synonymy of *Brachysomophis* Kaup 1856. Ophichthidae: Ophichthinae.

Dendrophysa Trewavas 1964:110 [ref. 4457]. Fem. *Umbrina russelii [russelli]* Cuvier 1830:178. Type by original designation (also monotypic). Species emended from *russelii* to *russelli* by Trewavas 1964:111 as an inadvertent error originally. Valid (Trewavas 1977:367 [ref. 4459], Jayaram 1981:330 [ref. 6497], Kottelat 1989:17 [ref. 13605]). Sciaenidae.

Dendroscorpaena Smith 1957:60 [ref. 4112]. Fem. *Perca cirrhosa* Thunberg 1793:199. Type by being a replacement name. Replacement for *Scorpaenichthys* Bleeker 1862, preoccupied by Girard 1854 in fishes. As a group within *Scorpaenopsis* Heckel 1837 (Eschmeyer & Randall 1975:297 [ref. 6389]). Scorpaenidae: Scorpaeninae.

Denius Gistel 1848:X [ref. 1822]. Masc. *Sparus sargus* Linnaeus 1758:278. Type by being a replacement name. Replacement for *Sargus* Cuvier 1817, preoccupied by Fabricius 1798 in Diptera. Misspelled *Demius* by Neave 1940:33 [ref. 12569]. Synonym of *Diplodus* Rafinesque 1810. Sparidae.

Dentatherina Patten & Ivantsoff 1983:331 [ref. 5424]. Fem. *Dentatherina merceri* Patten & Ivantsoff 1983:331. Type by original designation (also monotypic). Valid (Ivantsoff et al. 1987 [ref. 6230] as family Dentatherinidae). Valid, in Atherinidae (Paxton et al. 1989:359 [ref. 12442]). Atherinidae: Dentatherininae.

Dentectus Martín Salazar, Isbrücker & Nijssen 1982:127 [ref. 2900]. *Dentectus barbarmatus* Martín Salazar, Isbrücker & Nijssen 1982:130. Type by original designation (also monotypic). Valid (Isbrücker & Nijssen 1986:103 [ref. 5212], Isbrücker & Nijssen 1986:40 [ref. 7321], Burgess 1989:444 [ref. 12860]). Loricariidae.

Dentex Cuvier 1814:92 [ref. 4884]. Masc. *Sparus dentex* Linnaeus 1758:281. Type by absolute tautonymy. Valid (Tortonese 1973:407 [ref. 7192], Akazaki in Masuda et al. 1984:177 [ref. 6441], Bauchot & Hureau in Whitehead et al. 1986:885 [ref. 13676]). Sparidae.

Denticeps Clausen 1959:147 [ref. 842]. Neut. *Denticeps clupeoides* Clausen 1959:147. Type by original designation (also monotypic). Valid (Daget 1984:40 [ref. 6170], Grande 1985:244 [ref. 6466]). Denticipitidae.

Dentiraja (subgenus of *Raja*) Whitley 1940:186 [ref. 4700]. Fem. *Raja dentata* Klunzinger 1872:46. Type by original designation (also monotypic). Synonym of *Raja* Linnaeus 1758. Rajidae.

Dentirostrum Herald & Randall 1972:123 [ref. 2097]. Neut. *Dentirostrum janssi* Herald & Randall 1972:124. Type by original designation (also monotypic). Synonym of *Doryrhamphus* Kaup 1856 (Dawson 1981:2 [ref. 5511], Dawson 1985:58 [ref. 6541]). Syngnathidae: Syngnathinae.

Deportator Gistel 1848:X [ref. 1822]. Masc. *Platystacus anguillaris* Bloch 1794:61. Type by being a replacement name. Unneeded replacement for *Plotosus* Lacepède 1803, not preoccupied by *Plotus* Linnaeus 1766 in Aves. Objective synonym of *Plotosus* Lacepède 1803 (Taylor & Gomon 1986:160 [ref. 6196]). Plotosidae.

Deratoptera Krefft 1868:3, 9 [ref. 5074]. Fem. *Deratoptera alfredi* Krefft 1868:3, 9. Type by monotypy. Appeared in newspaper article (original not seen); later described as *Daemomanta* by Whitley 1932. Synonym of *Manta* Bancroft 1829. Mobulidae.

Derepodichthys Gilbert 1896:456 [ref. 1628]. Masc. *Derepodichthys alepidotus* Gilbert 1895:456. Type by original designation (also monotypic). Valid (Anderson & Hubbs 1981:341 [ref. 5476], Anderson 1984:578 [ref. 13634], Toyoshima 1985:144 [ref. 5722]). Zoarcidae.

Derichthys Gill 1884:433 [ref. 1728]. Masc. *Derichthys serpentinus* Gill 1884:433. Type by monotypy. *Derichtys* is a misspelling. Valid (Blache et al. 1973:244 [ref. 7185], Bauchot & Saldanha in Whitehead et al. 1986:575 with author as Schmidt 1930, Castle 1986:192 [ref. 5644], Robins 1989:424 [ref. 13289]). Derichthyidae.

Derilissus Briggs 1969:333 [ref. 639]. Masc. *Derilissus nanus* Briggs 1969:333. Type by original designation (also monotypic). Valid. Gobiesocidae: Gobiesocinae.

Derjuginia Popov 1931:137 [ref. 12552]. Fem. *Derjuginia ochotensis* Popov 1931:137. Type by monotypy. Synonym of *Gymnelopsis* Soldatov 1922 (Anderson 1982:49 [ref. 5520]); valid (Toyoshima in Masuda et al. 1984:306 [ref. 6441]). Zoarcidae.

Dermatias Smith & Radcliffe in Radcliffe 1912:206 [ref. 3577]. Masc. *Dermatias platynogaster* Smith & Radcliffe in Radcliffe 1912:206. Type by original designation (also monotypic). Synonym of *Oneirodes* Lütken 1871 (Pietsch 1974:33 [ref. 532]). Oneirodidae.

Dermatocheir Durbin 1909:55 [ref. 1166]. Fem. *Dermatocheir catablepta* Durbin 1909:55. Type by original designation (also monotypic). Synonym of *Hyphessobrycon* Durbin in Eigenmann 1980 (Géry 1977:462 [ref. 1597] based on placement of type species). Characidae.

Dermatolepis Gill 1861:54 [ref. 1769]. Fem. *Dermatolepis punctatus* Gill 1861:54. Type by monotypy. Subgenus of *Epinephelus* Bloch 1793 (C. L. Smith 1971:157 [ref. 14102], Kendall 1984:500, 507 [ref. 13663]); valid (Heemstra & Randall 1986:520 [ref. 5667]). Serranidae: Epinephelinae.

Dermatopsis Ogilby 1896:138 [ref. 3270]. Fem. *Dermatopsis macrodon* Ogilby 1896:140. Type by monotypy. Valid (Cohen & Nielsen 1978:56 [ref. 881], Paxton et al. 1989:316 [ref. 12442]). Bythitidae: Brosmophycinae.

Dermatopsoides Smith 1948:344 [ref. 4074]. Masc. *Dermatopsis kasougae* Smith 1943:72. Type by original designation (also monotypic). Valid (Cohen & Nielsen 1978:57 [ref. 881], Cohen 1986:355 [ref. 5646]). Bythitidae: Brosmophycinae.

Dermatorus Alcock 1890:298 [ref. 83]. Masc. *Dermatorus trichiurus* Alcock 1890:298. Type by monotypy. Synonym of *Porogadus* Goode & Bean 1885 (Cohen & Nielsen 1978:38 [ref. 881]). Ophidiidae: Neobythitinae.

Dermatostethus Gill 1862:283 [ref. 1667]. Masc. *Dermatostethus punctipinnis* Gill 1862:283. Type by monotypy. Synonym of *Syngnathus* Linnaeus 1758 (Fritzsche 1980:198 [ref. 1511], Dawson 1982:55 [ref. 6764], Dawson 1985:181 [ref. 6541]). Syngnathidae: Syngnathinae.

Dermocassis (subgenus of *Leiocassis*) Nichols 1925:1 [ref. 3180]. Fem. *Bagrus ussuriensis* Dybowski 1872:210. Type by original designation (also monotypic). Bagridae.

Dermogenys Kuhl & van Hasselt in van Hasselt 1823:131 [ref. 5963]. Fem. *Dermogenys pusillus [a]* van Hasselt 1823:131. Type by monotypy. Spelled *Dermatogenys* by Peters 1865:163 [not researched]. Species apparently should be emended to *pusilla*. Valid (Collette et al. 1984:336 [ref. 11422], Kottelat 1985:271 [ref. 11441], Kottelat 1987:370 [ref. 5962], Kottelat 1989:16 [ref. 13605], Roberts 1989:154 [ref. 6439]). Hemiramphidae.

Dermosteira Schultz 1943:267 [ref. 3957]. Fem. *Dermosteira dorotheae* Schultz 1943:267. Type by original designation (also monotypic). Synonym of *Diplogrammus* Gill 1865 (Nakabo 1982:97 [ref. 3139], Fricke 1982:71 [ref. 5432]). Callionymidae.

Deschauenseeia Fowler 1934:147 [ref. 1417]. Fem. *Deschauenseeia chryseus* Fowler 1934:147. Type by original designation (also monotypic). Misspelled *Deschauensella* in Zoological Record for 1934. Synonym of *Trichogaster* Bloch & Schneider 1801 (Kottelat, pers. comm.). Belontiidae.

Desmoamia (subgenus of *Cheilopterus*) Fowler & Bean 1930:123 [ref. 1477]. Fem. *Cheilodipterus zonatus* Smith & Radcliffe 1912:443. Type by original designation (also monotypic). Synonym of *Cheilodipterus* Lacepède 1801 (Fraser 1972:16 [ref. 5195]). Apogonidae.

Desmodema Walters & Fitch 1960:446 [ref. 4580]. Neut. *Trachypterus jacksoniensis polystictus* Ogilby 1897:649. Type by original designation (also monotypic). For purposes of the type species, the subspecies *polystictus* is elevated to specific rank; type not *jacksoniensis*. Valid (Olney 1984:369 [ref. 13656], Heemstra & Kannemeyer 1984:15 [ref. 5349], Fujii in Masuda et al. 1984:117 [ref. 6441], Heemstra & Kannemeyer 1986:400 [ref. 5666], Paxton et al. 1989:399 [ref. 12442]). Trachipteridae.

Desmoholacanthus Fowler 1941:256 [ref. 1438]. Masc. *Holacanthus arcuatus* Gray 1831:33. Type by original designation (also monotypic). Pomacanthidae.

Desmoprenes (subgenus of *Scatophagus*) Fowler & Bean 1929:35, 40 [ref. 1476]. *Chaetodon tetracanthus* Lacepède 1802:726. Type by original designation (also monotypic). Synonym of *Scatophagus* Cuvier 1831. Scatophagidae.

Deuteracanthus Fowler 1944:398 [ref. 1448]. Masc. *Deuteracanthus lonchophorus* Fowler 1944:398. Type by original designation (also monotypic). Based on a postlarval specimen. Synonym of *Lutjanus* Bloch 1790 (Heemstra 1974:22 [ref. 7125]). Lutjanidae.

Deuterodon Eigenmann in Eigenmann, McAtee & Ward 1907:140 [ref. 1261]. Masc. *Deuterodon iguape* Eigenmann in Eigenmann, McAtee & Ward 1907:140. Type by monotypy. Valid (Géry 1977:519 [ref. 1597], Géry et al. 1988:10 [ref. 6408]). Characidae.

Deuterophysa (subgenus of *Nemacheilus*) Rendahl 1933:23 [ref. 3704]. Fem. *Diplophysa strauchii* Kessler 1874:58. Type by original designation. Preoccupied by Warren 1889 in Lepidoptera; also an objective synonym of earlier *Diplophysa* Kessler 1874 (also preoccupied). *Didymophysa* Whitley 1950 a replacement for both as is *Diplophysoides* Fowler 1958. Objective synonym of *Triplophysa* Rendahl 1933 (Kottelat 1990:21 [ref. 14137]). Balitoridae: Nemacheilinae.

Deuteropterus Gill 1861:51 [ref. 1768]. Masc. *Perca marginata* Cuvier in Cuvier & Valenciennes 1802:53. Type by original designation (also monotypic). Percichthyidae.

Devario Heckel 1843:1015 [ref. 2066]. *Cyprinus devario* Hamilton 1822:341, 393. Type by absolute tautonymy. Synonym of *Danio* Hamilton 1822. Cyprinidae.

Deveximentum Fowler 1904:517 [ref. 1367]. Neut. *Zeus insidiator* Bloch 1787:41. Type by original designation (also monotypic). Synonym of *Secutor* Gistel 1848 (James 1978:165 [ref. 5317]). Leiognathidae.

Devisina (subgenus of *Pseudochromis*) Fowler 1931:20, 26 [ref. 1407]. Fem. *Pseudochromis quinquedentatus* McCulloch 1926:190. Type by original designation. Synonym of *Pseudochromis* Rüppell 1835. Pseudochromidae: Pseudochrominae.

Dexillichthys Whitley 1931:322 [ref. 4672]. Masc. *Synaptura macrolepis* Bleeker 1858:7. Type by being a replacement name. Unneeded replacement for *Dexillus* Chabanaud 1930, not preoccupied by *Dexilla* Westwood 1840 in Diptera. Soleidae.

Dexillus Chabanaud 1930:16 [ref. 784]. Masc. *Synaptura macrolepis* Bleeker 1858:7. Type by original designation (also monotypic). *Dexillichthys* Whitley 1931 is an unneeded replacement, not preoccupied by *Dexilla* Westwood 1840 in Diptera. Valid (Chapleau & Keast 1988:2799 [ref. 12625]). Soleidae.

Dexiourius Chabanaud 1947:443 [ref. 800]. Masc. *Cynoglossus semilaevis* Günther 1873:379. Type by original designation (also monotypic). Synonym of *Cynoglossus* Hamilton 1822 (Menon 1977:16 [ref. 7071], Desoutter 1986:432 [ref. 6212]). Cynoglossidae: Cynoglossinae.

Dexistes Jordan & Starks 1904:624 [ref. 2526]. Masc. *Dexistes rikuzenius* Jordan & Starks 1904:624. Type by original designation (also monotypic). Valid (Norman 1934:347 [ref. 6893], Sakamoto 1984 [ref. 5273], Ahlstrom et al. 1984:643 [ref. 13641], Sakamoto in Masuda et al. 1984:352 [ref. 6441]). Pleuronectidae: Pleuronectinae.

Dhoma Talwar & Joglekar 1970:361 [ref. 4319]. *Corvina axillaris* Cuvier in Cuvier & Valenciennes 1830:113. Type by original designation (also monotypic). Objective synonym of *Kathala* Mohan 1969 (Trewavas 1977:292 [ref. 4459]). Sciaenidae.

Diabasis Desmarest 1823:30, 34 [ref. 1120]. Fem. *Diabasis parra* Desmarest 1823:30. Type by subsequent designation. Fowler

(MS) lists a *Diabasis* Desmarest 1818 (not researched). Earliest type designation not researched. Apparently preoccupied in Coleoptera. Synonym of *Haemulon* Cuvier 1829. Haemulidae.

Diabolicthys Holmes 1856:45 [ref. 2194]. Masc. *Diabolicthys elliotti* Holmes 1856:45. Type by monotypy. Spelled *Diabolichthys* by authors. Synonym of *Manta* Bancroft 1829 (Cappetta 1987:176 [ref. 6348] as *Diabolichthys*). Mobulidae.

Diabolidium Beebe 1926:80 [ref. 244]. Neut. *Diabolidium arcturi* Beebe 1926:80. Type by monotypy. Ceratioidei.

Diacantha (subgenus of *Canthophrys*) Swainson 1839:190, 310 [ref. 4303]. Fem. *Diacantha zebra* Swainson 1839:310 (= *Cobitis geto* Hamilton 1822:355, 394). Type by monotypy. As *Diacanthus* on p. 190. Swainson's *D. zebra* is an unneeded name change for *C. geto* Hamilton. Apparently not preoccupied by Chevrolat in Dejean 1835 (nomen nudum) in Coleoptera. Synonym of *Botia* Gray 1831. Cobitidae: Botiinae.

Diacope Cuvier 1815:360 [ref. 1019]. Fem. *Holocentrus bengalensis* Bloch 1790:102. Type by subsequent designation. Possibly dates to Cuvier 1814:89. Type designated by Jordan 1917:94 [ref. 2407]. Also in Cuvier 1816:280 [ref. 993]. *Genyoroge* Cantor 1850 is an unneeded replacement; *Diacope* not preoccupied by Hübner 1816 in Lepidoptera. Synonym of *Lutjanus* Bloch 1790 (Allen 1985:33 [ref. 6843], Allen & Talbot 1985:8 [ref. 6491], Allen 1986:323 [6208]). Lutjanidae.

Diademichthys Pfaff 1942:413 [ref. 3459]. Masc. *Diademichthys deversor* Pfaff 1942:414. Type by original designation (also monotypic). According to Briggs (1955:141 [ref. 637]), *Diademichthys* and *Coronichthys* Herre Aug. 1942 are synonyms, *Diademichthys* appeared in May 1942 and is therefore the older name. Valid (Briggs 1955:141 [ref. 637], Yoshino in Masuda et al. 1984:342 [ref. 6441]). Gobiesocidae: Gobiesocinae.

Diagramma Oken (ex Cuvier) 1817:1182 [ref. 3303]. Neut. *Anthias diagramma* Bloch 1792:320. Based on "Les Diagrammes" Cuvier 1816 (see Gill 1903:966 [ref. 5768]). Subsequent addition of species after latinization not researched. Valid (Johnson 1980:12 [ref. 13553], Smith & McKay 1986:565 [ref. 5716]); synonym of *Plectorhinchus* Lacepède 1801 (Roux 1973:394 [ref. 7200], Roux 1986:327 [ref. 6209]). Haemulidae.

Diagrammella (subgenus of *Diagramma*) Pellegrin 1912:295 [ref. 3426]. Fem. *Diagramma macrops* Pellegrin 1912:295. Type by original designation. Type designated on p. 294. Misspelled *Diagramella* in Zoological Record for 1913 and by others. Synonym of *Parapristipoma* Bleeker 1873 (Roux 1973:393 [ref. 7200]). Haemulidae.

Dialarchus Greeley 1901:14 [ref. 1889]. Masc. *Oligocottus snyderi* Greeley in Jordan & Evermann 1898:2871. Type by monotypy. Synonym of *Oligocottus* Girard 1856 (Bolin 1944:65 [ref. 6379]). Cottidae.

Dialommus Gilbert 1891:452 [ref. 1624]. Masc. *Dialommus fuscus* Gilbert 1891:452. Type by original designation (also monotypic). Valid (Clark Hubbs 1952:62 [ref. 2252]). Labrisomidae.

Diana Risso 1826:267 [ref. 3757]. Fem. *Diana semilunata* Risso 1826:267. Type by monotypy. Synonym of *Luvarus* Rafinesque 1810 (Topp 1973:476 [ref. 7209]). Luvaridae.

Diancistrus Ogilby 1899:743 [ref. 3277]. Masc. *Diancistrus longifilis* Ogilby 1899:744. Type by monotypy. Valid (Paxton et al. 1989:316 [ref. 12442]). Bythitidae: Brosmophycinae.

Dianema Cope 1871:112 [ref. 5775]. Neut. *Dianema longibarbis* Cope 1872:276. Type by subsequent monotypy. Appeared first as above, with brief description and no species; species added by Cope 1872:276 [ref. 921]. Valid (Gosline 1940:9 [ref. 6489], Burgess 1989:364 [ref. 12860]). Callichthyidae.

Diapeltoplites (subgenus of *Hypoptopoma*) Fowler 1915:237 [ref. 1392]. Masc. *Hypoptopoma gulare* Cope 1878:678. Type by original designation. Misspelled *Diapaletoplites* in Zoological Record for 1915 and in Jordan 1920:556 [ref. 4905]. Synonym of *Hypoptopoma* Günther 1868 (Isbrücker 1980:87 [ref. 2303]). Loricariidae.

Diaphanichthys (subgenus of *Leptocephalus*) Peters 1864:399 [ref. 3437]. Masc. *Leptocephalus (Diaphanichthys) brevicaudus* Peters 1864:299. Type by monotypy. Based on a leptocephalus. Questionably a synonym of *Ariosoma* Swainson 1838 (Smith 1989:491 [ref. 13285]). Congridae: Bathymyrinae.

Diaphasia Lowe 1843:92 [ref. 2832]. Fem. *Gymnotus acus* Brünnich 1768:13. Type by monotypy. Lowe gives synonymy as: *Diaphus acus* no author, *Ophidium fierasfer* of Risso and "Les Fierasfers" (*Ophidium imberbe*, L.); proposes *Diaphasia* for "barbarous" vernacular "Fierasfer." Synonym of *Carapus* Rafinesque 1810 (Arnold 1956:260 [ref. 5315], Wheeler 1973:557 [ref. 7190]). Carapidae: Carapinae.

Diaphoroculius Fowler 1938:134 [ref. 1428]. Masc. *Diaphoroculius rangiroae* Fowler 1938:134. Type by original designation (also monotypic). Eleotridae.

Diaphus Eigenmann & Eigenmann 1890:3 [ref. 1256]. Masc. *Diaphus theta* Eigenmann & Eigenmann 1890:4. Type by original designation. Valid (Nafpaktitis 1968:22 [ref. 6979], Krefft & Bekker 1973:176 [ref. 7181], Paxton 1979:7 [ref. 6440], Hulley in Whitehead et al. 1984:439 [ref. 13675], Okiyama 1984:207 [ref. 13644], Moser et al. 1984:219 [ref. 13645], Fujii in Masuda et al. 1984:71 [ref. 6441], Hulley 1986:287 [ref. 5672], Paxton et al. 1989:256 [ref. 12442]). Myctophidae.

Diapoma Cope 1894:67 [ref. 966]. Neut. *Diapoma speculiferum* Cope 1894:67. Type by monotypy. Valid (Géry 1977:359 [ref. 1597], Weitzman & S. Fink 1985:1 et seq. [ref. 5203], Weitzman et al. 1988:383 [ref. 13557], Malabarba 1989:134 [ref. 14217]). Characidae: Glandulocaudinae.

Diapteron (subgenus of *Aphyosemion*) Huber & Seegers 1977:146 [ref. 2273]. *Aphyosemion georgiae* Lambert & Géry 1967:306. Type by original designation. Also published as new in Huber & Seegers 1978:115 [ref. 2272]. Subgenus of *Aphyosemion* Myers 1824 (Parenti 1981:477 [ref. 7066]). Valid (Wildekamp et al. 1986:242 [ref. 6198]). Aplocheilidae: Aplocheilinae.

Diapterus Ranzani 1842:340 [ref. 9017]. Masc. *Diapterus auratus* Ranzani 1842:340. Type by monotypy. Synonym of *Gerres* Quoy & Gaimard 1824 (Roux 1986:325 [ref. 6209]); valid (Deckert & Greenfield 1987:184 [ref. 6778]). Gerreidae.

Diastatomycter Vaillant 1891:182 [ref. 4497]. Masc. *Diastatomycter chaperi* Vaillant 1891:182. Type by monotypy. Also appeared in Vaillant 1893:61 [ref. 4485]. Synonym of *Hemisilurus* Bleeker 1858 (Haig 1952:94 [ref. 12607], Bornbusch & Lundberg 1989:442 [ref. 12543, Roberts 1989:145 [ref. 6439]). Siluridae.

Diastobranchus Barnard 1923:441 [ref. 191]. Masc. *Diastobranchus capensis* Barnard 1923:441. Type by monotypy. *Diactobranchus* is a misspelling. Valid (Castle 1986:188 [ref. 5644], Paxton et al. 1989:107 [ref. 12442]); synonym of *Synaphobranchus* Johnson 1862 (Robins & Robins 1989:219 [ref. 13287]). Synaphobranchidae: Synaphobranchinae.

Diastodon Bowdich 1825:xii, 238 [ref. 590]. Masc. *Diastodon* *speciosus* Bowdich 1825:238. Type by monotypy. Also involves fig. 41 opposite p. 234 in conjunction with p. xii. Valid (Bauchot & Quignard 1973:433 [ref. 7204]). Labridae.

Dibranchichthys Garman 1899:99 [ref. 1540]. Masc. *Dibranchichthys nudivomer* Garman 1899:99. Type by monotypy. Synonym of *Dibranchus* Peters 1876. Ogcocephalidae.

Dibranchopsis Garman 1899:96 [ref. 1540]. Fem. *Halieutaea spongiosa* Gilbert 1890:124. Type by original designation (also monotypic). Synonym of *Dibranchus* Peters 1876. Ogcocephalidae.

Dibranchus Peters 1876:737 [ref. 3453]. Masc. *Dibranchus atlanticus* Peters 1876:738. Type by monotypy. Valid (Mochizuki in Masuda et al. 1984:105 [ref. 6441], Bradbury 1986:371 [ref. 6291], Paxton et al. 1989:284 [ref. 12442]). Ogcocephalidae.

Dicallionymus Fowler 1941:29 [ref. 1439]. Masc. *Callionymus goramensis* Bleeker 1858:214. Type by original designation (also monotypic). Objective synonym of *Diplogrammus* Gill 1865 (Nakabo 1982:97 [ref. 3139], Fricke 1982:71 [ref. 5432]). Callionymidae.

Dicentrarchus Gill 1860:109, 111 [ref. 1793]. Masc. *Perca elongata* Geoffroy St. Hilaire 1809:Pl. 19. Type by original designation (also monotypic). Valid (some authors, e.g. Tortonese 1973:357 [ref. 7192], Tortonese in Whitehead et al. 1986:793 [ref. 13676], Daget & Smith 1986:299 [ref. 6204]); synonym of *Morone* Mitchill 1814 (some authors). Moronidae.

Diceratias (subgenus of *Ceratias*) Günther 1887:52 [ref. 2013]. Masc. *Ceratias bispinosus* Günther 1887:53. Type by monotypy. Valid (Uwate 1979 [ref. 7015], Fujii in Uyeno et al. 1983:259 [ref. 14275]). Diceratiidae.

Dicerobatis Blainville 1825:40 [ref. 4991]. Fem. Regarded as an unjustified emendation of, or new spelling for, *Dicerobatus* Blainville, and not a replacement for it (contrary to current literature). See also remarks in Literature Cited under this reference. In the synonymy of *Mobula* Rafinesque 1810. Mobulidae.

Dicerobatus (subgenus of *Raia [Raja]*) Blainville 1816:112 [= 120] [ref. 306]. Masc. *Raja mobular* Bonnaterre 1788:5. Type by subsequent designation. The species *fimbriata* Lacepède was designated type by Bancroft 1829:452 [ref. 5051]. Type *mobular* listed as type by Jordan 1917:95 [ref. 2407]. Spelled *Dicerobatis* by Agassiz 1845:22 [ref. 4889] and 1846:122 [ref. 64]. Synonym of *Mobula* Rafinesque 1810 (Krefft & Stehmann 1973:77 [ref. 7167], Cappetta 1987:177 [ref. 6348]). Mobulidae.

Dicerophallus Alvarez 1952:95 [ref. 102]. Masc. *Dicerophallus echeagarayi* Alvarez 1952:95. Type by original designation (also monotypic). Synonym of *Gambusia* Poey 1854 (Rosen & Bailey 1963:90 [ref. 7067]). Poeciliidae.

Dichichthys Chan 1966:223 [ref. 806]. Masc. *Dichichthys melanobranchus* Chan 1966:226. Type by original designation (also monotypic). Synonym of *Parmaturus* Garman 1906 (Compagno 1984:339 [ref. 6846], Compagno 1988:157 [ref. 13488]). Scyliorhinidae.

Dichistius Gill 1888:68 [ref. 1732]. Masc. *Dipterodon capensis* Cuvier in Cuvier & Valenciennes 1831:276. Type by being a replacement name. Replacement for *Dipterodon* Cuvier 1829, preoccupied by Lacepède 1802 in fishes. See remarks under *Coracinus* Gronow. Coracinidae.

Dichotomycter Troschel (ex Bibron) 1856:88 [ref. 12559]. Masc. *Tetraodon fluviatilis* Hamilton 1822:6, 362. Appeared first as "Dichotomyctère" Bibron in Duméril 1855:279 [ref. 297]; latinized by Troschel as above, also by Hollard 1857:319 [ref. 2186]. First technical addition of species not researched; type above as given by Jordan 1919: 263 [ref. 2410]. Synonym of *Tetraodon* Linnaeus 1758 Tetraodontidae.

Dicologlossa Chabanaud 1927:14 [ref. 782]. Fem. *Solea cuneata* Moreau (ex de la Pylaie) 1881:312. Type by original designation. Spelling unnecessarily (intentionally) changed to *Dicologoglossa* by Chabanaud 1930:7, 12 [ref. 784]. Valid (Torchio 1973:631 [ref. 6892], Matallanas 1984 [ref. 12848] and Quéro et al. in Whitehead et al. 1986:1312 [ref. 13677] as *Dicologoglossa*, Heemstra & Gon 1986:870 [ref. 5665]). Soleidae.

Dicotylichthys Kaup 1855:230 [ref. 2571]. Masc. *Dicotylichthys punctulatus* Kaup 1855:230. Type by monotypy. Valid (Fraser-Brunner 1943:17 [ref. 1495]); synonym of *Diodon* Linnaeus 1758 (Tyler 1980:367 [ref. 4477]). Diodontidae.

Dicrolene Goode & Bean 1883:202 [ref. 1838]. Masc. *Dicrolene intronigra* Goode & Bean 1883:202. Type by original designation (also monotypic). Valid (Cohen & Nielsen 1978:28 [ref. 881], Hureau & Nielsen 1981 [ref. 5438], Machida in Masuda et al. 1984:100 [ref. 6441], Nielsen & Cohen 1986:346 [ref. 5700]). Ophidiidae: Neobythitinae.

Dicromita Goode & Bean 1896:319 [ref. 1848]. Fem. *Dicromita agassizii* Goode & Bean 1896:319. Type by subsequent designation. Type designated by Radcliffe 1913:148 [ref. 3579]. Synonym of *Monomitopus* Alcock 1890 (Nielsen 1973:551 [ref. 6885], Cohen & Nielsen 1978:35 [ref. 881]). Ophidiidae: Neobythitinae.

Dicrossus Steindachner (ex Agassiz) 1875:102 [ref. 4220]. Masc. *Dicrossus maculatus* Steindachner 1875:102. Type by monotypy. Synonym of *Crenicara* Steindachner 1875 (Kullander 1986:140 [ref. 12439]). Cichlidae.

Dicrotus Günther 1860:349 [ref. 1963]. Masc. *Dicrotus armatus* Günther 1860:349. Type by monotypy. Questionably a synonym of *Promethichthys* Gill 1893 (Parin & Bekker 1973:459 [ref. 7206]). Gempylidae.

Dictyosoma Temminck & Schlegel 1845:139 [ref. 4373]. Neut. *Dictyosoma burgeri* Van der Hoeven 1850:347. Type by subsequent monotypy. Original description without species; one species added [not checked] by Van der Hoeven 1850:347 [ref. 2182]. Valid (Amaoka & Miki in Masuda et al. 1984:303 [ref. 6441], Yatsu 1986 [ref. 5150]). Stichaeidae.

Didogobius Miller 1966:161 [ref. 3009]. Masc. *Didogobius bentuvii* Miller 1966:162. Type by original designation (also monotypic). Valid (Miller 1973:495 [ref. 6888], Miller in Whitehead et al. 1986:1033 [ref. 13677]). Gobiidae.

Didymophysa Whitley 1950:44 [ref. 4713]. Fem. *Diplophysa strauchii* Kessler 1874:58. Type by being a replacement name. Replacement for *Deuterophysa* Rendahl 1933 and *Diplophysa* Kessler 1874, both preoccupied. See also *Diplophysoides* Fowler 1958, also a replacement for both genera. Synonym of *Triplophysa* Rendahl 1933 (Kottelat 1990:21 [ref. 14137]). Balitoridae: Nemacheilinae.

Dieidolycus Anderson 1988:72 [ref. 7304]. Masc. *Dieidolycus leptodermatus* Anderson 1988:72. Type by original designation (also monotypic). Zoarcidae.

Diepinotus Rafinesque 1815:91 [ref. 3584]. *Trichiurus lepturus* Linnaeus 1758:246. Type by subsequent designation. Species added by Fowler 1936:641 [ref. 6546], but with genus in synonymy; not available from Rafinesque and not made available by Fowler. Used as name only; perhaps intended to be *Dispinotus* as used by Jordan

1917:92 [ref. 2407]. In the synonymy of *Trichiurus* Linnaeus 1758. Trichiuridae: Trichiurinae.

Dietrichthys (subgenus of *Chlopsis*) Whitley 1935:219 [ref. 4683]. Masc. *Chlopsis (Dietrichthys) finitimus* Whitley 1935:219. Type by original designation (also monotypic). Synonym of *Saurenchelys* Peters 1864 (Smith 1989:590 [ref. 13285]). Nettastomatidae.

Dikellorhynchus Smith 1956:54 [ref. 4102]. Masc. *Dikellorhynchus incredibilis* Smith 1956:54. Type by original designation (also monotypic). Synonym of *Malacanthus* Cuvier 1829 (Dooley 1978:54 [ref. 5499]). Malacanthidae: Malacanthinae.

Dilepidion (subgenus of *Gobiosoma*) Ginsburg 1933:17 [ref. 1800]. Neut. *Gobiosoma ginsburgi* Hildebrand & Schroeder 1928:324. Type by original designation. Gobiidae.

Dillonia Heckel 1847:285 [ref. 2068]. Fem. *Chondrostoma dillonii* Valenciennes in Cuvier & Valenciennes 1844:404. Type by monotypy. Lévêque and Daget 1984, Fowler (MS), and authors cite Heckel 1842:1020 [ref. 2067], but *Dillonia* not found there; apparently dates to 1847 as above. Synonym of *Varicorhinus* Rüppell 1836 (Lévêque & Daget 1984:336 [ref. 6186]). Cyprinidae.

Dilobomycter Troschel (ex Bibron) 1856:88 [ref. 12559]. Masc. *Tetraodon reticularis* Bloch & Schneider 1801:506. Appeared first as "Dilobomyctére" Bibron in Duméril 1855:279 [ref. 297]; latinized by Troschel 1856 as above, also by Hollard 1857:319 [ref. 2186]. First technical addition of species not researched (one species included by Bibron); type above as given by Jordan 1919:263 [ref. 2410]. Tetraodontidae.

Dimalacocentrus Gill 1863:223 [ref. 1685]. Masc. *Novacula kallosoma* Bleeker 1860:5. Type by monotypy. Synonym of *Novaculichthys* Bleeker 1862. Labridae.

Dimidiochromis Eccles & Trewavas 1989:88 [ref. 13547]. Masc. *Haplochromis strigatus* Regan 1922:697. Type by original designation. Cichlidae.

Dinematichthys Bleeker 1855:318 [ref. 348]. Masc. *Dinematichthys iluocoeteoides* Bleeker 1855:319. Type by monotypy. Spelled *Dinematichthijs* (p. 318) and *Dinematichthys* (p. 306, 308, 319) when first proposed; the latter spelling correctly latinized (first a typographical error); first technical reviser not researched. Valid (Cohen & Nielsen 1978:57 [ref. 881], but see Cohen 1986:356 [ref. 5646], Sedor & Cohen 1987 [ref. 6041], Paxton et al. 1989:316 [ref. 12442]). Bythitidae: Brosmophycinae.

Dinematochirus Regan & Trewavas 1930:73, 97 [ref. 3681]. Masc. *Neostomias fissibarbis* Pappenheim 1914:175. Type by original designation. Synonym of *Eustomias* Vaillant 1888 (Gibbs in Morrow & Gibbs 1964:377 [ref. 6962], Morrow 1973:138 [ref. 7175]). Melanostomiidae.

Dinemus Poey 1860:161 [ref. 3499]. Masc. *Dinemus venustus* Poey 1860:161. Type by monotypy. Synonym of *Polymixia* Lowe 1836 (Nielsen 1973:336 [ref. 6885], Woods & Sonoda 1973:269 [ref. 6899]). Polymixiidae.

Dinichthys Kaup 1873:83 [ref. 2585]. Masc. *Prionotus horrens* Richardson 1843:79. Type by subsequent designation. Type apparently first designated by Whitley 1950:44 [ref. 4713]. Preoccupied by Newberry 1868 in fossil fishes, replaced by *Marubecula* Whitley 1950. Triglidae: Triglinae.

Dinoctus Rafinesque 1818:445 [ref. 3587]. Masc. *Dinoctus truncatus* Rafinesque 1818:445. Type by monotypy. Spelled *Dinectus* by Rafinesque 1820:249 [ref. 5088]. Based on an Audubon drawing, apparently of a mythical sturgeon. In the synonymy of *Acipenser* Linnaeus 1758. Acipenseridae: Acipenserinae.

Dinogunellus (subgenus of *Stichaeus*) Herzenstein 1890:121 [ref. 2149]. Masc. *Stichaeus grigorjewi* Herzenstein 1890:119. Type by monotypy. Valid. Stichaeidae.

Dinolestes Klunzinger 1872:29 [ref. 2623]. Masc. *Dinolestes muelleri* Klunzinger 1872:30. Type by monotypy. Original spelling of species is *mülleri*; correction to *muelleri* is mandatory. Valid (Scott 1981:130 [ref. 5533], Paxton et al. 1989:560 [ref. 12442]). Dinolestidae.

Dinoperca Boulenger 1895:153 [ref. 537]. Fem. *Hapalogenys petersii* Day 1875:77. Type by monotypy. Valid (Heemstra 1986:571 [ref. 5660], Heemstra & Hecht 1986 [ref. 5971]). Dinopercidae.

Dinotopteroides Fowler 1930:41 [ref. 1406]. Masc. *Dinotopteroides prentissgrayi* Fowler 1930:41. Type by original designation (also monotypic). Synonym of *Clarias* Scopoli 1777 (Teugels 1986:69 [ref. 6193], Teugels 1986:11 [ref. 12548]); as a valid subgenus (Teugels 1983 [ref. 12851]). Clariidae.

Dinotopterus Boulenger 1906:550 [ref. 573]. Masc. *Dinotopterus cunningtoni* Boulenger 1906:550. Type by monotypy. Valid (Poll 1977:145 [ref. 3533], Teugels 1986:95 [ref. 6193], Burgess 1989:146 [ref. 12860]). Clariidae.

Diodon Linnaeus 1758:334 [ref. 2787]. Masc. *Diodon hystrix* Linnaeus 1758:335. Type designated by ICZN. Name put on Official List (Opinion 77) but later withdrawn. *Diodon* Lesson 1828 and 1830, and Storr 1780 of other animal groups placed on Official Index as junior homonyms of *Diodon* Linnaeus. Valid (Fraser-Brunner 1943:17 [ref. 1495], Tortonese 1973:648 [ref. 7192], Leis 1978 [ref. 5529], Tyler 1980:367 [ref. 4477], Arai 1983:207 [ref. 14249], Matsuura in Masuda et al. 1984:365 [ref. 6441], Leis 1986:905 [ref. 5686], Tortonese in Whitehead et al. 1986:1347 [ref. 13677]). Diodontidae.

Diogenichthys Bolin 1939:119 [ref. 508]. Masc. *Myctophum laternatum* Garman 1899:267. Type by original designation. Valid (Krefft & Bekker 1973:181 [ref. 7181], Paxton 1979:10 [ref. 6440], Hulley in Whitehead et al. 1984:450 [ref. 13675], Moser et al. 1984:219 [ref. 13645], Fujii in Masuda et al. 1984:66 [ref. 6441], Hulley 1986:296 [ref. 5672], Paxton et al. 1989:260 [ref. 12442]). Myctophidae.

Diogenides Koumans 1931:73 [ref. 5623]. Not available, no description. Gobiidae.

Dionda Girard 1856:176 [ref. 1810]. Fem. *Dionda episcopa* Girard 1856:177. Type by subsequent designation. Type designated by Bleeker 1863:29 [ref. 4859] and 1863:206 [ref. 397]. Valid (Contreras-Balderas & Verduzco-Martínez 1977 [ref. 7058], Hubbs & Miller 1977 [ref. 7060]). Cyprinidae.

Dionisia Lahille 1915:374, 380 [ref. 5625]. Fem. *Dionisia patagonica* Lahille 1915:374. Type by monotypy. Proposed on p. 374 as distinguished provisionally from *Geotria chilensis* and in the synonymy of *G. chilensis* on p. 380. Evidently missed by authors until Hubbs & Potter 1971, but perhaps not available since *Dionisia* can be considered as a name published in synonymy and species not separately distinguished from *G. chilensis* and not treated as valid. Synonym of *Geotria* Gray 1851 (Hubbs & Potter 1971:55 [ref. 13397]). Petromyzontidae: Geotriinae.

Dioplites (subgenus of *Lepomis*) Rafinesque 1820:52 [ref. 7305]. Masc. *Lepomis (Dioplites) salmonea* Rafinesque 1820:52. Type by subsequent designation. Also appeared in Rafinesque 1820:32 (Dec.) [ref. 3592]. Type designated by Jordan & Gilbert 1877:86 [ref. 4907]. Synonym of *Micropterus* Lacepède 1802 (Hubbs &

Bailey 1940:13 [ref. 12253]). Centrarchidae.

Diphreutes Cantor 1849:1141 [159] [ref. 715]. Masc. *Chaetodon macrolepidotus* Linnaeus 1758:274. Type by being a replacement name. Unneeded replacement for *Heniochus* Cuvier 1816, not preoccupied by *Henioche* Hübner 1816 in Lepidoptera. On page 159 of separate. Objective synonym of *Heniochus* Cuvier 1816 (Burgess 1978:218 [ref. 700]). Chaetodontidae.

Diphyacantha Henn 1916:113 [ref. 2093]. Fem. *Diphyacantha chocoensis* Henn 1916:114. Type by monotypy. Synonym of *Priapichthys* Regan 1913 (Rosen & Bailey 1963:120 [ref. 7067]). Poeciliidae.

Diplacanthopoma Günther 1887:115 [ref. 2013]. Neut. *Diplacanthopoma brachysoma* Günther 1887:115. Type by monotypy. Valid (Cohen & Nielsen 1978:47 [ref. 881], Machida in Masuda et al. 1984:101 [ref. 6441], Cohen 1986:356 [ref. 5646], Machida 1988 [ref. 13418]). Bythitidae: Bythitinae.

Diplanchias Rafinesque 1810:17 [ref. 3594]. Masc. *Diplanchias nasus* Rafinesque 1810:17. Type by monotypy. Synonym of *Mola* Koelreuter 1770 (Fraser-Brunner 1943:8 [ref. 1495]). Molidae.

Diplecogaster Fraser-Brunner 1938:415 [ref. 1492]. Fem. *Cyclopterus bimaculatus* Bonnaterre 1788:29. Type by original designation. Valid (Briggs 1955:28 [ref. 637], Briggs 1973:652 [ref. 7222], Allen [L. G.] 1984:629 [ref. 13673], Briggs in Whitehead et al. 1986:1353 [ref. 13677], Briggs 1986:379 [ref. 5643]). Gobiesocidae: Gobiesocinae.

Diplectrum Holbrook 1855:32, 42 [ref. 2184]. Neut. *Serranus fasicularis* Valenciennes in Cuvier & Valenciennes 1828:245. Type by monotypy. Also appeared in Holbrook 1860:35 [ref. 2185]. Not preoccupied by Agassiz 1846:125 [ref. 64], an unjustified emendation for *Diplectron* Vieillot 1816 in Aves. *Diplectron* Troschel 1858 is a misspelling. Valid (Bortone 1977 [ref. 7064], Kendall 1984:500 [ref. 13663]). Serranidae: Serraninae.

Diplesion (subgenus of *Etheostoma*) Rafinesque 1820:169 [ref. 7309]. Neut. *Etheostoma blennioides* Rafinesque 1819:419. Type by monotypy. Also appeared in Rafinesque 1820:37 [ref. 3592]. *Diplesium* Agassiz 1846:125 [ref. 64] is an unjustified emendation. Objective synonym of *Etheostoma* Rafinesque 1819 (Collette & Banarescu 1977:1455 [ref. 5845]). Percidae.

Diplobatis Bigelow & Schroeder 1948:562 [ref. 301]. Fem. *Discopyge ommata* Jordan & Gilbert in Jordan & Bollman 1889:151. Type by original designation (also monotypic). Valid (Fechhelm & McEachran 1984 [ref. 5227]). Narkidae.

Diplocheilichthys Bleeker 1859:423 [ref. 370]. Masc. *Lobocheilos pleurotaenia* Bleeker 1855:267. Type by subsequent monotypy. Apparently appeared first in key without species; one species included by Bleeker 1859:144 [ref. 371] and 1860:143 [ref. 380]. Regarded as a nomen oblitum by Roberts 1989:45 [ref. 6439] and in synonymy of *Osteochilus* Günther 1868. Predates *Osteochilus* Günther 1868 (see remarks by Kottelat 1989:10 [ref. 13605]). Cyprinidae.

Diplocheilos (subgenus of *Labeo*) Bleeker 1860:133, 135 [ref. 380]. Masc. *Labeo erythropterus* Valenciennes in Cuvier & Valenciennes 1842:354. Type by subsequent designation. Type designated as *Diplocheilus erythropterus* van Hasselt by Bleeker 1863:194 [ref. 397]. Genus *Diplocheilus* and species *erythropterus* van Hasselt 1823 regarded as without diagnostic features (see Kottelat 1987:371 [ref. 5962]). Treated by Roberts 1989:45 [ref. 6439] as a nomen oblitum in the synonymy of *Osteochilus* Günther 1868, but with type as *Labeo rohitoides* Bleeker 1857 by monotypy. Cyprinidae.

Diplocheilus van Hasselt 1823:132 [ref. 5963]. Masc. *Diplocheilus erythopterus* van Hasselt 1823:132. Type by monotypy. Brief description of genus and species regarded as without distinguishing features and therefore nomina nuda (Kottelat 1987:371 [ref. 5962]); validly described by Bleeker 1860 as *Diplocheilos* to which genus can date. Cyprinidae.

Diploconger Kotthaus 1968:34 [ref. 2669]. Masc. *Diploconger polystigmatus* Kotthaus 1968:34. Type by original designation (also monotypic). Valid (Paxton et al. 1989:141 [ref. 12442], Smith 1989:511 [ref. 13285]). Congridae: Congrinae.

Diplocrepis Günther 1861:506 [ref. 1964]. *Lepadogaster puniceus* Richardson 1846:71. Type by monotypy. Valid (Briggs 1955:41 [ref. 637], Allen [L. G.] 1984:629 [ref. 13673]). Gobiesocidae: Gobiesocinae.

Diplodus Rafinesque 1810:26, 54 [ref. 3595]. Masc. *Sparus annularis* Linnaeus 1758:278. Type by monotypy. *Diploctus* is a misspelling. Valid (Tortonese 1973:408 [ref. 7192], Bauchot & Hureau in Whitehead et al. 1986:890 [ref. 13676], Smith & Smith 1986:585 [ref. 5710]). Sparidae.

Diplogonurus Noronha 1926:381 [ref. 3229]. Masc. *Diplogonurus maderensis* Noronha 1926:381. Type by monotypy. Synonym of *Lepidocybium* Gill 1862 (Parin & Bekker 1973:458 [ref. 7206]). Gempylidae.

Diplogrammoides (subgenus of *Diplogrammus*) Smith 1963:551 [ref. 4129]. Masc. *Diplogrammus (Diplogrammoides) gruveli* Smith 1963:551. Type by original designation (also monotypic). Synonym of *Diplogrammus* Gill 1865 (Nakabo 1982:97 [ref. 3139]); as a valid subgenus (Fricke 1982:72 [ref. 5432]). Callionymidae.

Diplogrammus Gill 1865:143 [ref. 1676]. Masc. *Callionymus goramensis* Bleeker 1858:214. Technically type is by monotypy, use of "may be regarded as a distinct type" not sufficient for original designation. Valid (Nakabo 1982:97 [ref. 3139], Fricke 1982:71 [ref. 5432], Fricke & Zaiser 1982 [ref. 5452], Houde 1984:637 [ref. 13674], Nakabo in Masuda et al. 1984:344 [ref. 6441], Fricke 1986:772 [ref. 5653]). Callionymidae.

Diplolepis Steindachner 1863:164 [ref. 4208]. Fem. *Sciaena squamosissima* Heckel 1840:438. Type by monotypy. Preoccupied by Geoffroy 1762 and by Fabricius 1805 in Hymenoptera. Objective synonym of *Plagioscion* Gill 1861 (Chao 1978:43 [ref. 6983]). Sciaenidae.

Diplolychnus Regan & Trewavas 1929:27 [ref. 3680]. Masc. *Diplolychnus lucifer* Regan & Trewavas 1929:28. Type by subsequent designation. Type apparently designated first by Fowler 1936:1196 [ref. 6546]. Valid (Gibbs 1964:339 [ref. 6960]); synonym of *Borostomias* Regan 1908 (Gibbs & Morrow 1973:127 [ref. 7174], Fink 1985:1 [ref. 5171]). Astronesthidae.

Diplomystax Günther (ex Duméril) 1864:180 [ref. 1974]. Masc. Latinization of "Diplomyste" Duméril 1856, but predated by Bleeker (1858:63 [ref. 365] as *Diplomystes*; since Bleeker's *Diplomystes* is listed in synonymy by Günther, *Diplomystax* could be regarded as an unjustified emendation. In the synonymy of *Diplomystes* Bleeker 1858. Diplomystidae.

Diplomyste Duméril 1856:487 [ref. 1154]. Not available, French vernacular not latinized. Published in an available way as *Diplomystes* by Bleeker 1858:63, and as *Diplomystax* by Günther 1864:180. Diplomystidae.

Diplomystes Bleeker (ex Duméril) 1858:63, 68 [ref. 365]. Masc.

Arius papillosus Valenciennes in Cuvier & Valenciennes 1840:118. Type by monotypy. Also in Bleeker 1862:8 [ref. 393]. Valid (Arratia 1987 [ref. 5957] as *Diplomystes* and type wrongly *Silurus chilensis* Molina 1782, Burgess 1989:25 [ref. 12860]). Diplomystidae.

Diplophos Günther 1873:101 [ref. 6423]. Masc. *Diplophos taenia* Günther 1873:102. Type by monotypy. Valid (Witzell 1973:118 [ref. 7172], Weitzman 1974:472 [ref. 5174], Fink & Weitzman 1982 [ref. 5177], Badcock in Whitehead et al. 1984:295 [ref. 13675], Ahlstrom et al. 1984:185 [ref. 13643], Fujii in Masuda et al. 1984:44 [ref. 6441], Schaefer et al. 1986:250 [ref. 5709], Paxton et al. 1989:185 [ref. 12442]). Gonostomatidae.

Diplophysa Kessler 1874:57 [ref. 2596]. Fem. *Diplophysa strauchii* Kessler 1874:58. Type by subsequent designation. Type designation by Berg 1916 (not investigated). Preoccupied by Gegenbaur 1853 in Coelenterata. *Deuterophysa* Rendahl 1933 based on same type is also preoccupied; both replaced by *Didymophysa* Whitley 1950 and by *Diplophysoides* Fowler 1958. Synonym of *Triplophysa* Rendahl 1933 (Kottelat 1990:21 [ref. 14137]). Balitoridae: Nemacheilinae.

Diplophysoides Fowler 1958:13 [ref. 1470]. Masc. *Diplophysa strauchii* Kessler 1874:58. Type by being a replacement name. Unneeded replacement for *Diplophysa* Kessler 1874, preoccupied by Gegenbaur 1853 in Coelenterata; also replacement for *Deuterophysa* Rendahl 1933, preoccupied by Warren 1889 in Lepidoptera; both earlier replaced by *Didymophysa* Whitley. Objective synonym of *Didymophysa* Whitley 1950. Synonym of *Triplophysa* Rendahl 1933 (Kottelat 1990:21 [ref. 14137]). Balitoridae: Nemacheilinae.

Diploprion Cuvier (ex Kuhl & van Hasselt) in Cuvier & Valenciennes 1828:137 [ref. 997]. Masc. *Diploprion bifasciatum* Cuvier (ex Kuhl & van Hasselt) in Cuvier & Valenciennes 1828:137. Type by monotypy. Species should be *Diploprion bifasciatus*. Valid (Katayama in Masuda et al. 1984:139 [ref. 6441], Paxton et al. 1989:517 [ref. 12442] in Grammistidae). Serranidae: Grammistinae.

Diplopterus Gray 1830:Pl. 87 (v. 1) [ref. 1878]. Masc. *Diplopterus pulcher* Gray 1830:Pl. 87. Type by monotypy. Also appeared with description in Gray 1831:8 [ref. 1879]. Preoccupied by Boie 1826 in Aves and by Agassiz 1835 in fossil fishes. Replaced by *Luciocephalus* Bleeker 1851. Objective synonym of *Luciocephalus* Bleeker 1851 (Roberts 1989:178 [ref. 6439]). Luciocephalidae.

Diplospinus Maul 1948:42 [ref. 2916]. Masc. *Diplospinus multistriatus* Maul 1948:42. Type by monotypy. Valid (Parin & Bekker 1973:457 [ref. 7206], Collette et al. 1984:600 [ref. 11421], Nakamura in Masuda et al. 1984:227 [ref. 6441], Parin in Whitehead et al. 1986:968 [ref. 13676], Nakamura 1986:826 [ref. 5696]). Gempylidae.

Diplostomias Kotthaus 1967:32 [ref. 2668]. Masc. *Diplostomias indicus* Kotthaus 1967:33. Type by original designation (also monotypic). Melanostomiidae.

Diplotaxodon Trewavas 1935:(68) 116 [ref. 4451]. Masc. *Diplotaxodon argenteus* Trewavas 1935:116. Type by monotypy. Valid (Eccles & Trewavas 1989:268 [ref. 13547]). Cichlidae.

Diproctacanthus Bleeker 1862:415 [ref. 382]. Masc. *Labroides xanthurus* Bleeker 1856:52. Type by original designation (also monotypic). Also appeared in Bleeker 1862:104 [ref. 386]. Valid (Randall & Springer 1973:293 [ref. 3603]). Labridae.

Dipterodon Cuvier 1829:194 [ref. 995]. Masc. *Dipterodon capensis* Cuvier in Cuvier & Valenciennes 1831:276. Type by monotypy. Preoccupied by Lacepède 1802 in fishes; replaced by *Dichistius* Gill 1888. Coracinidae.

Dipterodon Lacepède 1802:165, 167 [ref. 4929]. Masc. *Dipterodon hexacanthus* Lacepède 1802:166-168. Type by subsequent designation. Type designated by Jordan & Evermann 1896:1106 [ref. 2443] by use of their style of name in parentheses. Questionably a synonym of *Apogon* Lacepède 1801 (Fraser 1972:17 [ref. 5195], see also Gon 1987:144 [ref. 6706]). Apogonidae.

Dipterygonotus Bleeker 1849:70 [ref. 316]. Masc. *Dipterygonotus leucogrammicus* Bleeker 1849:71. Type by monotypy. Valid (Johnson 1980:10 [ref. 13553], Carpenter 1987:52 [ref. 6430], Carpenter 1988:47 [ref. 9296]). Caesionidae.

Dipturus Rafinesque 1810:16 [ref. 3594]. Masc. *Raja batis* Linnaeus 1758:231. Type by monotypy. Synonym of *Raja* Linnaeus 1758, usually recognized as a valid subgenus (Stehmann 1973:62 [ref. 7168], Ishihara & Ishiyama 1986:274 [ref. 5142], Ishihara 1987:242 [ref. 6264], Séret 1989 [ref. 12827]). Rajidae.

Diptychus Steindachner 1866:787 [ref. 5030]. Masc. *Diptychus maculatus* Steindachner 1866:788. Type by monotypy. Valid (Tsao 1964:169 [ref. 13501], Jayaram 1981:69 [ref. 6497], Wu 1987:47 [ref. 12822]). Cyprinidae.

Dipulus Waite 1905:77 [ref. 4562]. Masc. *Dipulus caecus* Waite 1905:78. Type by monotypy. Valid (Cohen & Nielsen 1978:59 [ref. 881], Paxton et al. 1989:316 [ref. 12442]). Bythitidae: Brosmophycinae.

Dipurus Rafinesque 1815:222 [ref. 3584]. Not available, name only. In corrigenda for this work. Unplaced genera.

Diretmoides Post & Quero 1981:41 [ref. 3555]. Masc. *Diretmus pauciradiatus* Woods 1973:296. Type by original designation. Valid (Shimizu in Masuda et al. 1984:109 [ref. 6441], Post in Whitehead et al. 1986:743 [ref. 13676], Post 1986:414 [ref. 5705], Kotlyar 1987 [ref. 13522], Paxton et al. 1989:370 [ref. 12442]). Diretmidae.

Diretmus Johnson 1864:403 [ref. 5751]. Masc. *Diretmus argenteus* Johnson 1864:403. Type by monotypy. Also appeared in Johnson 1864 (July):70-71 [ref. 2358]. Valid (Maul 1973:338 [ref. 7171], Woods & Sonoda 1973:291 [ref. 6899], Post 1976 [ref. 5541], Post & Quéro 1981:35 [ref. 3555], Post in Whitehead et al. 1986:745 [ref. 13676], Post 1986:414 [ref. 5705], Kotlyar 1987 [ref. 13522], Paxton et al. 1989:370 [ref. 12442]). Diretmidae.

Dirrhizodon Klunzinger 1871:664 [ref. 2622]. Masc. *Dirrhizodon elongatus* Klunzinger 1871:665. Type by monotypy. Synonym of *Hemipristis* Agassiz 1843 (Compagno 1984:440 [ref. 6846], Cappetta 1987:119 [ref. 6348], Compagno 1988:269 [ref. 13488]). Hemigaleidae.

Disceus Garman 1877:208 [ref. 1528]. Masc. *Trygon strongylopterus* Schomburgk 1843:184. Type by monotypy. Based on a misidentified type species according to Fowler 1970:571 [ref. 7313], Garman's specimens are *Disceus thayeri* Garman 1913. Synonym of *Elipesurus* Schomburgk 1843 (Fowler 1970:571 [ref. 7313]). Potamotrygonidae.

Discherodontus Rainboth 1989:4 [ref. 13537]. Masc. *Barbus ashmeadi* Fowler 1937:193. Type by original designation. Cyprinidae.

Dischistodus Gill 1863:214 [ref. 1684]. Masc. *Pomacentrus fasciatus* Cuvier in Cuvier & Valenciennes 1830:426. Type by original designation (also monotypic). Valid (Allen 1975:127 [ref. 97], Shen & Chan 1978:235 [ref. 6945], Yoshino 1982 [ref. 5402],

Yoshino in Masuda et al. 1984:195 [ref. 6441]). Pomacentridae.

Discobatis Miklukho-Maclay & Macleay 1886:676 [ref. 2996]. Fem. *Discobatis marginipinnis* Miklukho-Maclay & Macleay 1886:676. Type by monotypy. Not preoccupied by *Discobatus* Garman 1881 in fishes; *Discotrygon* Fowler 1910 is an unneeded replacement. Synonym of *Taeniura* Müller & Henle 1837. Dasyatidae.

Discobatus Garman 1881:523 [ref. 1529]. Masc. *Raja sinensis* Bloch & Schneider 1801:352. Type by being a replacement name. Unneeded replacement for *Platyrhina* Müller & Henle 1831, not preoccupied by *Platyrhinus* Clairville-Shellenberg 1798 (not researched). Placed on Official Index along with *Analithis* Gistel 1848 (Opinion 345). Objective synonym of *Platyrhina* Müller & Henle 1838. Platyrhinidae.

Discochaetodon (subgenus of *Chaetodon*) Nalbant 1971:222 [ref. 6642]. Masc. *Chaetodon octofasciatus* Bloch 1787:113. Type by original designation. Synonym of *Chaetodon* Linnaeus 1758, but as a valid subgenus (Burgess 1978:641 [ref. 700]); valid (Maugé & Bauchot 1984:466 [ref. 6614]). Chaetodontidae.

Discognathichthys Bleeker 1859:423 [ref. 370]. Masc. *Discognathus variabilis* Heckel 1843:1069. Type by subsequent designation. Apparently appeared first in key, without species. Species added by Bleeker 1860:111, 128 [ref. 380] and type designated (p. 128). Synonym of *Garra* Hamilton 1822 (Karaman 1971:232 [ref. 2560], Roberts 1989:40 [ref. 6439], Krupp & Schneider 1989:367 [ref. 13651]). Cyprinidae.

Discognathus Heckel 1843:1027 [ref. 2066]. Masc. *Discognathus variabilis* Heckel 1843:1069. Type by subsequent designation. Type designated by Bleeker 1863:24 [ref. 4859], 1863:262 [ref. 403], and 1863:192 [ref. 397]. Synonym of *Garra* Hamilton 1822 (Karaman 1971:232 [ref. 2560], Wu et al. 1977:372 [ref. 4807], Lévêque & Daget 1984:301 [ref. 6186], Roberts 1989:40 [ref. 6439], Krupp & Schneider 1989:367 [ref. 13651]). Cyprinidae.

Discogobio Lin 1931:72 [ref. 4019]. Masc. *Discogobio tetrabarbatus* Lin 1931:72. Type by monotypy. Valid (Wu et al. 1977:384 [ref. 4807], Chu & Cui in Chu & Chen 1989:281 [ref. 13584]). Cyprinidae.

Discolabeo Fowler 1937:210 [ref. 1425]. Masc. *Discolabeo fisheri* Fowler 1937:211. Type by original designation (also monotypic). Synonym of *Garra* Hamilton 1822 (Roberts 1989:40 [ref. 6439]). Cyprinidae.

Discolophius Fowler 1943:333 [ref. 1444]. Masc. *Lophius gastrophysus* Miranda-Ribeiro 1915:2, 4. Type by original designation (also monotypic). Synonym of *Lophius* Linnaeus 1758 (Caruso 1983 [ref. 5168]). Lophiidae.

Discopyge Heckel in Tschudi 1846:32 [ref. 4469]. Fem. *Discopyge tschudii* Heckel in Tschudi 1846:32. Type by monotypy. Valid (Fechhelm & McEachran 1984 [ref. 5227], Pequeño et al. 1988 [ref. 12550]). Narkidae.

Discordipinna Hoese & Fourmanoir 1978:19 [ref. 2181]. Fem. *Discordipinna griessingeri* Hoese & Fourmanoir 1978:21. Type by original designation (also monotypic). Valid (Birdsong et al. 1988:202 [ref. 7303]). Gobiidae.

Discotrema Briggs 1976:339 [ref. 640]. Neut. *Discotrema crinophila* Briggs 1976:340. Type by original designation (also monotypic). Valid (Yoshino in Masuda et al. 1984:342 [ref. 6441]). Gobiesocidae: Gobiesocinae.

Discotrygon Fowler 1910:468 [ref. 1379]. Fem. *Discobatis marginipinnis* Miklukho-Maclay & Macleay 1886:676. Type by being a replacement name. Unneeded replacement for *Discobatis* Miklukho-Maclay & Macleay 1886, not preoccupied by *Discobatus* Garman 1881 in fishes. Synonym of *Taeniura* Müller & Henle 1837. Dasyatidae.

Discoverichthys Merrett & Nielsen 1987:452 [ref. 6058]. Masc. *Discoverichthys praecox* Merrett & Nielsen 1987:455. Type by original designation (also monotypic). Chlorophthalmidae: Ipnopinae.

Discus Campbell 1879:297 [ref. 711]. Masc. *Discus aureus* Campbell 1879:298. Type by monotypy. Preoccupied by Fitzinger 1833 in Mollusca, replaced by *Campbellina* Fowler 1958. Synonym of *Diretmus* Johnson 1863 (Woods & Sonoda 1973:291 [ref. 6899], Post & Quéro 1981:35 [ref. 3555], Kotlyar 1987 [ref. 13522]). Diretmidae.

Disparichthys Herre 1935:383 [ref. 2109]. Masc. *Disparichthys fluviatilis* Herre 1935:384. Type by original designation (also monotypic). Synonym of *Carapus* Rafinesque 1810 (Arnold 1956:260 [ref. 5315]). Carapidae: Carapinae.

Dispinus Li in Li, Wang & Wu 1981:78 [ref. 6437]. Masc. *Sciaena ruber* Forsskål 1775:48. Type by original designation (also monotypic). Holocentridae.

Dissomma Brauer 1902:278 [ref. 631]. Neut. *Dissomma anale* Brauer 1902:278. Type by monotypy. Synonym of *Scopelarchus* Alcock 1896 (Johnson 1974:153 [ref. 7050]). Scopelarchidae.

Dissostichus Smitt 1898:3 [ref. 4147]. Masc. *Dissostichus eleginoides* Smitt 1898:4. Type by monotypy. Valid (Stevens et al. 1984:563 [ref. 13633], Andersen 1984:23 [ref. 13369], Nakamura in Nakamura et al. 1986:258 [ref. 14235], Oyarzún & Campos 1987 [ref. 12877], Abe & Iwami 1989:79 [ref. 13580]). Nototheniidae.

Distichodina (subgenus of *Distichodus*) Fowler 1935:260 [ref. 1423]. Fem. *Distichodus stigmaturus* Fowler 1935:260. Type by original designation (also monotypic). Synonym of *Hemigrammocharax* Pellegrin 1923 (Daget & Gosse 1984:194 [ref. 6185]). Citharinidae: Distichodontinae.

Distichodomicrura (subgenus of *Distichodus*) Fowler 1936:266 [ref. 1424]. Fem. *Distichodus maculatus* Boulenger 1898:27. Type by original designation (also monotypic). Synonym of *Distichodus* Müller & Troschel 1844 (Daget & Gosse 1984:185 [ref. 6185]). Citharinidae: Distichodontinae.

Distichodura (subgenus of *Distichodus*) Fowler 1936:266 [ref. 1424]. Fem. *Distichodus affinis* Günther 1873:144. Type by original designation (also monotypic). Synonym of *Distichodus* Müller & Troschel 1844 (Daget & Gosse 1984:185 [ref. 6185]). Citharinidae: Distichodontinae.

Distichodus Müller & Troschel 1844:87 [ref. 3070]. Masc. *Characinus nefasch* Lacepède 1803:270, 274. Type by monotypy. Valid (Géry 1977:67 [ref. 1597], Vari 1979:340 [ref. 5490], Daget & Gosse 1984:185 [ref. 6185] but with wrong date and apparently the wrong type). Citharinidae: Distichodontinae.

Distocyclus Mago-Leccia 1978:17, 25 [ref. 5489]. Masc. *Eigenmannia conirostris* Eigenmann & Allen 1942:316. Type by original designation. Gymnotidae: Sternopyginae.

Distoechodon Peters 1880:924 [ref. 3455]. Masc. *Distoechodon tumirostris* Peters 1880:925. Type by monotypy. Valid (Yang 1964:129 [ref. 13500], Howes 1981:45 [ref. 14200], Li 1986:480 [ref. 6154], Chen & Li in Chu & Chen 1989:96 [ref. 13584]). Cyprinidae.

Distoechus Gomes 1947:12 [ref. 1830]. Masc. *Distoechus stigmaturus* Gomes 1947:13. Type by original designation (also monotypic). Synonym of *Deuterodon* Eigenmann 1907 (Böhlke

1952:793 [ref. 13618]). Characidae.

Ditrema Temminck & Schlegel 1844:77 [ref. 4372]. Neut. *Ditrema temminckii* Bleeker 1853:33. Type by subsequent monotypy. Original description without species; one species added by Bleeker 1853:33 [ref. 340]. Valid (Tarp 1952:64 [ref. 12250], Nakabo in Masuda et al. 1984:190 [ref. 6441]). Embiotocidae.

Ditropichthys Parr 1934:21 [ref. 3375]. Masc. *Cetomimus storeri* Goode & Bean 1895:453. Type by original designation (also monotypic). Valid (Paxton 1989:156 [ref. 13435]). Cetomimidae.

Dixiphichthys Fowler 1938:119 [ref. 1426]. Masc. *Dixiphichthys hoplites* Fowler 1938:120. Type by original designation (also monotypic). Triglidae: Triglinae.

Dixiphistes Fowler 1938:117 [ref. 1426]. Masc. *Dixiphistes macrorhynchus* Fowler 1938:118. Type by original designation (also monotypic). Triglidae: Triglinae.

Dixiphistops Fowler 1938:115 [ref. 1426]. Masc. *Dixiphistops megalops* Fowler 1938:116. Type by original designation (also monotypic). Triglidae: Triglinae.

Dixonina Fowler 1911:651 [ref. 1381]. Fem. *Dixonina nemoptera* Fowler 1911:651. Type by original designation (also monotypic). Synonym of *Albula* Scopoli 1777 (Whitehead 1986:216 [ref. 5733]). Albulidae: Albulinae.

Djabub (subgenus of *Sciaena*) Forsskål 1775:44 [ref. 1351]. *Sciaena jarbua* Forsskål 1775:50. Not available, regarded as non-latinized Arabic name (see Jordan 1917:33-34 [ref. 2407]). In the synonymy of *Terapon* Cuvier 1816. Terapontidae.

Djulongius Whitley 1935:223 [ref. 4683]. Masc. *Belone melanotus* Bleeker 1850:94. Type by original designation (also monotypic). Belonidae.

Dobula Rafinesque 1820:236 [ref. 7310]. Fem. *Cyprinus dobula* Linnaeus 1758:323. Type usually stated as understood by tautonymy, genus proposed for European species but species name not given; technical addition of species not researched. Also appeared in Rafinesque 1820:46 (Dec.) [ref. 3592]. Synonym of *Leuciscus* Cuvier 1816. Cyprinidae.

Docimodus Boulenger 1897:917 [ref. 538]. Masc. *Docimodus johnstonii* Boulenger 1897:917. Type by monotypy. Valid (Ribbink et al. 1983:249 [ref. 13555], Eccles & Trewavas 1989:270 [ref. 13547]). Cichlidae.

Dodecatrema Fowler 1947:3 [ref. 1458]. Neut. *Bdellostoma polytrema* Girard 1854:199. Type by original designation (also monotypic). Myxinidae: Eptatretinae.

Dodekablennos Springer & Spreitzer 1978:10 [ref. 4181]. *Dodekablennos fraseri* Springer & Spreitzer 1978:11. Type by original designation (also monotypic). Blenniidae.

Doederleinia Steindachner in Steindachner & Döderlein 1883:237 [ref. 4246]. Fem. *Doederleinia orientalis* Steindachner & Döderlein 1883:237. Type by monotypy. Originally as *Döderleinia*, correction to *Doederleinia* mandatory; as emended is apparently preoccupied by Mayer 1872 in Mollusca (not researched). Valid in Percichthyidae (Katayama in Masuda et al. 1984:124 [ref. 6441], Paxton et al. 1989:511 [ref. 12442]); valid in Acropomatidae (Johnson 1984:464 [ref. 9681]). Acropomatidae.

Doidyxodon Valenciennes 1846:Pl. 5 [ref. 6165]. Masc. *Doidyxodon freminvillii* Valenciennes 1846:Pl. 5. Type by monotypy. Originally named *Doidyxodon* on Pl. 5 (Atlas, 1846) to which genus and species date; name spelled *Doydixodon* in accompanying text which was not published until 1855:323 [ref. 4504]. *Doydixodon* used by authors (e.g., Kner & Steindachner 1867:358 [ref. 2640]). Kyphosidae: Girellinae.

Doiichthys Weber 1913:532 [ref. 4603]. Masc. *Doiichthys novaeguineae* Weber 1913:534. Type by monotypy. Species originally given as *novae-guineae*; emendation mandatory. Valid (Burgess 1989:167 [ref. 12860]). Ariidae.

Dolichallabes Poll 1942:95 [ref. 3515]. *Dolichallabes microphthalmus* Poll 1942:97. Type by monotypy. Valid (Poll 1977:148 [ref. 3533], Teugels 1986:97 [ref. 6193], Burgess 1989:146 [ref. 12860]). Clariidae.

Dolichancistrus Isbrücker 1980:47 [ref. 2303]. Masc. *Pseudancistrus pediculatus* Eigenmann 1917:679. Type by original designation. Valid (Heitmans et al. 1983 [ref. 5278], Burgess 1989:434 [ref. 12860]). Loricariidae.

Dolichodon Parr 1931:45 [ref. 3371]. Masc. *Dolichodon normani* Parr 1931:46. Type by original designation. *Hemicyclodon* Parr 1931 is an unneeded replacement, apparently not preoccupied by *Dolicodon* Fanzango 1874 as unjustifiably emended to *Dolichodon* by Cambridge in Zoological Record for 1875:262. Possibly preoccupied by Gray 1866 in Mammalia. Synonym of *Kali* Lloyd 1909 (Krefft 1973:453 [ref. 7166], Johnson & Cohen 1974:34 [ref. 7133]). Chiasmodontidae.

Dolicholagus Kobyliansky 1986:46 [ref. 6002]. Masc. *Bathylagus longirostris* Maul 1948:35. Type by original designation (also monotypic). Bathylagidae.

Dolichopteryx Brauer 1901:127 [ref. 630]. Fem. *Dolichopteryx anascopa* Brauer 1901:127. Type by monotypy. Valid (Cohen 1973:157 [ref. 6589], Cohen in Whitehead et al. 1984:396 [ref. 13675], Ahlstrom et al. 1984:156 [ref. 13627], Fujii in Masuda et al. 1984:42 [ref. 6441]). Opisthoproctidae.

Dolichostomias (subgenus of *Photonectes*) Parr 1927:106, 111 [ref. 3367]. Masc. *Photonectes gracilis* Goode & Bean 1896:112. Type by subsequent designation. *P. gracilis* regarded as "typical" for subgenus, but type technically not designated by Parr; subsequent designator not investigated. Synonym of *Photonectes* Günther 1887, but as a valid subgenus (Morrow in Morrow & Gibbs 1964:489 [ref. 6962]). Stomiidae.

Dolichosudis Post 1969:15 [ref. 3554]. Fem. *Dolichosudis fuliginosa* Post 1969:17. Type by original designation (also monotypic). Valid (Post 1980 [ref. 5577], Okiyama 1984:207 [ref. 13644], Fujii in Masuda et al. 1984:77 [ref. 6441]). Paralepididae.

Doliichthys Sauvage 1874:336 [ref. 3873]. Masc. *Doliichthys stellatus* Sauvage 1874:336. Type by monotypy. Synonym of *Benthophilus* Eichwald 1831 (Miller 1973:490 [ref. 6888]). Gobiidae.

Doliodon Girard 1858:168 [ref. 1813]. Masc. *Gasterosteus carolinus* Linnaeus 1766:490 (= *Lichia carolina* of DeKay 1842:114). Type by original designation. Synonym of *Trachinotus* Lacepède 1801 (Daget & Smith-Vaniz 1986:319 [ref. 6207]). Carangidae.

Dollfusetta Whitley 1950:44 [ref. 4713]. Fem. *Peloria rueppellii* Cocco 1844:21. Type by being a replacement name. Replacement for *Dollfusina* Chabanaud 1933; *Dollfusina* preoccupied according to Whitley, but details of preoccupation not given by Whitley. Synonym of *Arnoglossus* Bleeker 1862 (Nielsen 1973:621 [ref. 6885] based on placement of *Dollfusina*). Bothidae: Bothinae.

Dollfusichthys Chabanaud 1931:304 [ref. 785]. Masc. *Dollfusichthys sinusarabici* Chabanaud 1931:304. Type by monotypy. Synonym of *Cynoglossus* Hamilton 1822 (Torchio 1973:635 [ref. 6892], Menon 1977:16 [ref. 7071], Desoutter 1986:432 [ref. 6212]). Cynoglossidae: Cynoglossinae.

Dollfusina (subgenus of *Arnoglossus*) Chabanaud 1933:31, 44 [ref. 787]. Fem. *Peloria rueppellii* Cocco 1844:21. Type by monotypy. Apparently preoccupied [not researched], replaced by *Dollfusetta* Whitley 1950. Synonym of *Arnoglossus* Bleeker 1862 (Norman 1934:173 [ref. 6893], Nielsen 1973:621 [ref. 6885]). Bothidae: Bothinae.

Dolloa Jordan 1900:897 [ref. 2397]. Fem. *Coryphaenoides longifilis* Günther 1877:439. Type by being a replacement name. Replacement for *Moseleya* Goode & Bean 1896, preoccupied by Quelch 1884 in Coelenterata. Synonym of *Coryphaenoides* Gunner 1765 (Marshall 1973:295 [ref. 7194], Marshall & Iwamoto 1973:565 [ref. 6966]). Macrouridae: Macrourinae.

Dolloidraco Roule 1913:15 [ref. 3815]. Masc. *Dolloidraco longidorsalis* Roule 1913:15. Original not examined. Valid (Eakin 1981:138 [ref. 14216], Stevens et al. 1984:563 [ref. 13633] as *Dolliodraco*). Harpagiferidae.

Dolopichthys Garman 1899:81 [ref. 1540]. Masc. *Dolopichthys allector* Garman 1899:81. Type by monotypy. Valid (Maul 1973:671 [ref. 7171], Pietsch 1974:33 [ref. 5332], Bertelsen & Pietsch 1977:185 [ref. 7063], Bertelsen in Whitehead et al. 1986:1387 [ref. 13677], Leipertz & Pietsch 1987 [ref. 5972], Paxton et al. 1989:290 [ref. 12442]). Oneirodidae.

Dorada Jarocki 1822:200 [ref. 4984]. *Sparus aurata* Linnaeus 1758:277. Original not seen. Objective synonym of *Sparus* Linnaeus 1758. Sparidae.

Doraops Schultz 1944:(269) 270 [ref. 3959]. Masc. *Doraops zuloagai* Schultz 1944:(269) 271. Type by original designation (also monotypic). Valid (Burgess 1989:224 [ref. 12860]). Doradidae.

Doras Lacepède 1803:116 [ref. 4930]. Masc. *Silurus carinatus* Linnaeus 1766:504. Type by subsequent designation. Type designated by Bleeker 1862:5 [ref. 393], not *Silurus costatus* Linnaeus. Valid (Burgess 1989:223 [ref. 12860]). Doradidae.

Doration Jordan 1929:156 [ref. 6443]. Neut. *Boleosoma stigmaeum* Jordan 1887:1877. Type by original designation (also monotypic). Synonym of *Etheostoma* Rafinesque 1819, but as a valid subgenus (Collette & Banarescu 1977:1456 [ref. 5845], Page 1981:33 [ref. 3347], Bailey & Etnier 1988:23 [ref. 6873]). Percidae.

Doratonotus Günther 1861:385 [ref. 1967]. Masc. *Doratonotus megalepis* Günther 1862:125. Type by subsequent monotypy. Genus appeared first in Günther 1861:385 [ref. 1967], with species as name only; genus more fully described and species described in Günther 1862:124 [ref. 1969]. Labridae.

Dormitator Gill 1861:44 [ref. 1766]. Masc. *Eleotris somnulentus* Girard 1858:169. Type by monotypy. Valid (Maugé 1986:391 [ref. 6218], Birdsong et al. 1988:181 [ref. 7303]). Eleotridae.

Dorosoma Rafinesque 1820:171 [ref. 7309]. Neut. *Dorosoma notatum* Rafinesque 1820:172. Type by monotypy. Also appeared in Rafinesque 1820:39 (Dec.) [ref. 3592]. Valid (Grande 1985:248 [ref. 6466], Whitehead 1985:232 [ref. 5141]). Clupeidae.

Dorsadena Coleman & Nafpaktitis 1972:1 [ref. 883]. Fem. *Dorsadena yaquinae* Coleman & Nafpaktitis 1972:2. Type by original designation (also monotypic). Synonym of *Lampadena* Goode & Bean in Gill 1893, but as a valid subgenus (Paxton 1979:12 [ref. 6440], Moser et al. 1984:220 [ref. 13645]). Myctophidae.

Dorsopsetta Nielsen 1963:379 [ref. 3194]. Fem. *Dorsopsetta norma* Nielsen 1963:379. Type by original designation (also monotypic). Bothidae: Bothinae.

Dorsuarius Lacepède (ex Commerson) 1803:482 [ref. 4930]. Masc. *Dorsuarius nigrescens* Lacepède 1803:482, 483. Type by monotypy. Synonym of *Kyphosus* Lacepède 1801 (Desoutter 1973:420 [ref. 7203]). Kyphosidae: Kyphosinae.

Dorybelone Fowler 1944:215 [ref. 1448]. Fem. *Belone stolzmanni* Steindachner 1878:397. Type by original designation (also monotypic). Belonidae.

Dorychromis (subgenus of *Heliases*) Fowler & Bean 1928:31, 60 [ref. 1475]. Masc. *Heliases analis* Cuvier in Cuvier & Valenciennes 1830:496. Type by original designation (also monotypic). Pomacentridae.

Doryichthys Kaup 1853:233 [ref. 2569]. Masc. Type by subsequent designation. Dawson 1981:2 [ref. 5526] and 1985:55 [ref. 6541] dates to 1856:56, but several species mentioned in 1853 were available (but not *bilineatus* which Dawson regarded as type). Dawson 1981:3 mentions a designation of *Syngnathus cuncalus* Hamilton 1822 by Duncker (1912) and that should be examined as the first valid type designation. Spelled *Dorichthys* by Duncker 1909. Valid (Dawson 1981:2 [ref. 5527], Dawson 1985:55 [ref. 6541], Roberts 1989:158 [ref. 6439]). Syngnathidae: Syngnathinae.

Doryptena Snyder 1908:102 [ref. 4150]. Fem. *Doryptena okinawae* Snyder 1908:103. Type by original designation. Synonym of *Callogobius* Bleeker 1874. Gobiidae.

Doryrhamphinarum Kaup 1856:62 [ref. 2575]. *Syngnathus heterosoma* Bleeker 1851:441. Type by original designation (also monotypic). Fowler (MS), treats as a lapsus for *Doryichthys* Kaup 1856 [= 1853]; Dawson 1981 treats as a nomen nudum. Kaup provides a description from Bleeker, and states (p. 63), "...leaves me in no doubt of this species being the type of a genus hitherto undescribed..." Kaup's heading "Genus novem, 5. *Doryrhamphinarum*" is regarded here as meaning of the family Doryrhamphidae, without proposal of a new genus. Synonym of *Doryichthys* Kaup 1853 (Dawson 1981:2 [ref. 5511]). Syngnathidae: Syngnathinae.

Doryrhamphus Kaup 1856:54 [ref. 2575]. Masc. *Doryrhamphus excisus* Kaup 1856:54. Type by monotypy. Apparently no available species included with genus in Kaup 1853:233 [ref. 2569]; genus as name only; apparently dates to 1856 as above. *Doryramphus* Bleeker 1860 is an incorrect subsequent spelling. Valid (Fritzsche 1980:187 [ref. 1511], Dawson 1981 [ref. 5511], Araga in Masuda et al. 1984:85 [ref. 6441], Dawson 1985:58 [ref. 6541], Dawson 1986:448 [ref. 5650], Paxton et al. 1989:416 [ref. 12442]). Syngnathidae: Syngnathinae.

Dotalabrus Whitley 1930:251 [ref. 4670]. Masc. *Cheilinus aurantiacus* Castelnau 1872:245. Type by original designation (also monotypic). Valid (Russell 1988:8 [ref. 12549]). Labridae.

Doumea Sauvage 1879:96 [ref. 3881]. Fem. *Doumea typica* Sauvage 1879:97. Type by monotypy (also by use of *typica*). Valid (Skelton & Teugels 1986:60 [ref. 6192], Burgess 1989:114 [ref. 12860], Skelton 1989:6 [ref. 14123]). Amphiliidae.

Doydixodon see *Doidixodon*. Kyphosidae: Girellinae.

Draciscus Jordan & Snyder 1901:379 [ref. 2503]. Masc. *Draciscus sachi* Jordan & Snyder 1901:379. Type by original designation (also monotypic). Agonidae.

Draco Goüan 1770:117 [ref. 1863]. Placed on Official Index as nomen nudum (Direction 56). Unplaced genera.

Draconetta Jordan & Fowler 1903:939 [ref. 2462]. Fem. *Draconetta xenica* Jordan & Fowler 1903:939. Type by original designation (also monotypic). Valid (Nakabo 1982 [ref. 5507], see Fricke

1982:57 [ref. 5432], Parin 1982 [ref. 5305], Nakabo in Masuda et al. 1984:342 [ref. 6441]). Draconettidae.

Draculo Snyder 1911:545 [ref. 4152]. *Draculo mirabilis* Snyder 1911:545. Type by original designation (also monotypic). Misspelled *Draculus* by Jordan, Tanaka & Snyder 1913:377 [ref. 6448]. Valid (Fricke 1982:72 [ref. 5432], Fricke 1986:772 [ref. 5653]); synonym of *Eleutherochir* Bleeker 1879 (Nakabo 1982:109 [ref. 3139]). Callionymidae.

Drepane Cuvier in Cuvier & Valenciennes 1831:132 [ref. 4881]. Fem. *Chaetodon punctatus* Linnaeus 1758:273. Type by subsequent designation. Type designated by Jordan 1917:136 [ref. 2407]. *Enixe* Gistel 1848, *Harpochris* Cantor 1849, and *Drepanichthys* Bonaparte 1831 are unneeded replacement names on Official Index (Opinion 1046); *Drepane* not preoccupied by *Drepana*. *Drepane* Cuvier on Official List. Valid (Johnson 1984:465 [ref. 9681], Hayashi in Masuda et al. 1984:181 [ref. 6441], Desoutter 1986:340 [ref. 6212], Smith 1986:609 [ref. 5712]). Drepanidae.

Drepanichthys (subgenus of *Ephippus*) Bonaparte 1831:172 [ref. 4978]. Masc. *Chaetodon punctatus* Linnaeus 1758:273. Type by being a replacement name. Appeared as a section under *Ephippus* as "*Drepanichthys*, N. (*Drepanis*, C. nec Orn.)". Unneeded replacement for *Drepane* Cuvier 1831. On Official Index (Opinion 1046). Objective synonym of *Drepane* Cuvier 1831. Drepanidae.

Drepanopsetta Gill 1861:50 [ref. 1766]. Fem. *Pleuronectes platessoides* Fabricius 1780:164. Type by monotypy. Synonym of *Hippoglossoides* Gottsche 1835 (Norman 1934:294 [ref. 6893], Nielsen 1973:624 [ref. 6885]). Pleuronectidae: Pleuronectinae.

Drepanoscorpis Fowler 1934:476 [ref. 1419]. Fem. *Drepanoscorpis gilchristi* Fowler 1934:476. Type by original designation (also monotypic). Synonym of *Dichistius* Gill 1888. Coracinidae.

Drombus Jordan & Seale 1905:797 [ref. 2495]. *Drombus palackyi* Jordan & Seale 1905:797. Type by monotypy. Valid (Akihito in Masuda et al. 1984:250 [ref. 6441], Hoese 1986:786 [ref. 5670], Maugé 1986:367 [ref. 6218], Birdsong et al. 1988:192 [ref. 7303]). Gobiidae.

Dropsarus Rafinesque 1815:82 [ref. 3584]. Masc. Not available; name only and evidently an incorrect subsequent spelling (shortened version) of *Gaidropsarus* Rafinesque 1810. In the synonymy of *Gaidropsarus* Rafinesque 1810 (Svetovidov 1973:318 [ref. 7169], Svetovidov 1986 [ref. 8033]). Lotidae.

Dubiblennius Whitley 1930:20 [ref. 4671]. Masc. *Blennius tonganus* Jordan & Seale 1906:420. Type by original designation (also monotypic). Synonym of *Blennius* Linnaeus 1758 (Bath 1973:519 [ref. 7212]). Blenniidae.

Duboisialestes Poll 1967:133 [ref. 3529]. Masc. *Alestopetersius xenurus tumbensis* Hoedeman 1951:8. Type by original designation. For purposes of the type species, the subspecies *tumbensis* is raised to species rank; type not *A. xenurus*. Synonym of *Hemigrammopetersius* Pellegrin 1926 (Géry 1977:46 [ref. 1597]); valid (Paugy 1984:167 [ref. 6183]). Alestiidae.

Dules Cuvier in Cuvier & Valenciennes 1829:111 [ref. 4879]. *Dules auriga* Cuvier in Cuvier & Valenciennes 1829:117. Type by subsequent designation. Type apparently first designated by Bleeker 1874:2 [ref. 5110]. Valid (Ringuelet & Aramburu 1960:62 [ref. 14229], Indada in Nakamura et al. 1986:198 [ref. 14235], Kendall 1986:501 [ref. 13663]). Serranidae: Serraninae.

Dulichthys Bonaparte 1831:167 [ref. 4978]. Masc. *Dules auriga* Cuvier in Cuvier & Valenciennes 1829:112. Type by being a replacement name. Appeared as "*Dulichthys*. Nob. (*Dules*, Cuv.)". Unneeded replacement for *Dules* Cuvier 1829, not preoccupied by *Dulus* Viellot 1816 in Aves. Misspelled *Dulichethys* by Swainson 1838:85 [ref. 4302]. Objective synonym of *Dules* Cuvier 1829. Serranidae: Serraninae.

Dulosparus (subgenus of *Sparus*) Fowler 1933:148, 168 [ref. 1414]. Masc. *Pagrus filamentosus* Valenciennes in Cuvier & Valenciennes 1830:158. Type by original designation (also monotypic). Synonym of *Sparus* Linnaeus 1758. Sparidae.

Dunckerocampus Whitley 1933:67 [ref. 4677]. Masc. *Syngnathus dactyliophorus* Bleeker 1853:506. Type by being a replacement name. Replacement for *Acanthognathus* Duncker 1912, preoccupied by Mayr 1887 in Hymenoptera. Synonym of *Doryrhamphus* Kaup 1856, but as a valid subgenus (Dawson 1985:58 [ref. 6541], Winterbottom 1987 [ref. 6776] but spelled *Dunkerocampus*); valid (Araga in Masuda et al. 1984:86 [ref. 6441]). Syngnathidae: Syngnathinae.

Dundocharax Poll 1967:129 [ref. 3528]. Masc. *Dundocharax bidentatus* Poll 1967:129. Type by original designation (also monotypic). Synonym of *Neolebias* Steindachner 1894 (see Vari 1979:339 [ref. 5490]); valid (Géry 1977:66 [ref. 1597], Daget & Gosse 1984:193 [ref. 6185]). Citharinidae: Distichodontinae.

Duohemipteronotus (subgenus of *Hemipteronotus*) Fowler 1956:281 [ref. 1469]. Masc. *Hemipteronotus evides* Jordan & Richardson 1909:196. Type by original designation (also monotypic). Labridae.

Duopalatinus Eigenmann & Eigenmann 1888:136 [ref. 1249]. Masc. *Platystoma emarginatum* Valenciennes in Cuvier & Valenciennes 1840:25. Type by monotypy. *Duoplatinus* is a misspelling. Valid (Burgess 1989:282 [ref. 12860]). Pimelodidae.

Dupouyichthys Schultz 1944:244 [ref. 3959]. Masc. *Dupouyichthys sapito* Schultz 1944:245. Type by original designation (also monotypic). Valid (Stewart 1985:10 [ref. 5239], Mees 1988:90 [ref. 6401], Burgess 1989:304 [ref. 12860] as *Dupuoyichthys*). Aspredinidae: Bunocephalinae.

Dussumieria Valenciennes in Cuvier & Valenciennes 1847:467 [ref. 1012]. Fem. *Dussumieria acuta* Valenciennes in Cuvier & Valenciennes 1847:467. Type by monotypy. Valid (Whitehead & Ben-Tuvia 1973:110 [ref. 7170], Uyeno & Sato in Masuda et al. 1984:18 [ref. 6441], Grande 1985:248 [ref. 6466], Whitehead 1985:28 [ref. 5141], Paxton et al. 1989:152 [ref. 12442]). Clupeidae.

Duxordia Tickell in Day 1888:805 [ref. 1082]. Fem. *Leiocassis fluviatilis* Day 1888:805. Type by subsequent monotypy. Appeared as a manuscript name in synonymy of *Leiocassis fluviatilis*. See Myers 1951:26 [ref. 13464]; Myers apparently did not make the name available back to Tickell in Day (see Appendix A). In the synonymy of *Leiocassis* Bleeker 1858. Bagridae.

Duymaeria Bleeker 1856:52 [ref. 311]. Fem. *Duymaeria amboinensis* Bleeker 1856:54. Type by subsequent designation. Type apparently designated first by Jordan, Tanaka & Snyder 1913:199 [ref. 6448]. Synonym of *Pteragogus* Peters 1855 (Randall 1986:701 [ref. 5706]). Labridae.

Dysalotus MacGilchrist 1905:268 [ref. 2953]. Masc. *Dysalotus alcocki* MacGilchrist 1905:268. Type by monotypy. Valid (Johnson & Cohen 1974:29 [ref. 7133], Johnson & Keene 1986:732 [ref. 6303]). Chiasmodontidae.

Dysichthys Cope 1874:133 [ref. 931]. Masc. *Dysichthys coracoideus* Cope 1874:133. Type by monotypy. Valid (Mees 1988:89 [ref. 6401], Mees 1989 [ref. 13383]). Aspredinidae: Bunocephalinae.

Dysomma Alcock 1889:459 [ref. 81]. Neut. *Dysomma bucephalus* Alcock 1889:459. Type by monotypy. Valid (Robins & Robins 1976:256 [ref. 3784], Karrer 1982:89 [ref. 5679], Asano in Masuda et al. 1984:27 [ref. 6441], Saldanha & Bauchot in Whitehead et al. 1986:587 [ref. 13676], Castle 1986:189 [ref. 5644], Robins & Robins 1989:244 [ref. 13287]). Synaphobranchidae: Ilyophinae.

Dysommina Ginsburg 1951:450 [ref. 1804]. Fem. *Dysommina rugosa* Ginsburg 1951:450. Type by original designation (also monotypic). Valid (Karrer 1982:96 [ref. 5679], Robins & Robins 1989:242 [ref. 13287]). Synaphobranchidae: Ilyophinae.

Dysommopsis Alcock 1891:137 [ref. 87]. Fem. *Dysommopsis muciparus* Alcock 1891:137. Type by monotypy. Misspelled *Dsyommopsis* in Zoological Record for 1891. Synonym of *Dysomma* Alcock 1889 (Robins & Robins 1976:256 [ref. 3784], Robins & Robins 1989:244 [ref. 13287]). Synaphobranchidae: Ilyophinae.

Ebinania Sakamoto 1932:1 [ref. 3860]. Fem. *Ebinania vermiculata* Sakamoto 1932:2. Type by monotypy. Valid (Nelson 1982:1482 [ref. 5470], Washington et al. 1984:444 [ref. 13660], Yabe in Masuda et al. 1984:330 [ref. 6441], Yabe 1985:122 [ref. 11522], Nelson 1986:491 [ref. 5698]). Psychrolutidae.

Ebisinus Jordan & Richardson 1908:665 [ref. 2491]. Masc. *Dactylopterus chirophthalmus* Bleeker 1854:494. Type by original designation (also monotypic). Synonym of *Dactyloptena* Jordan & Richardson 1908. Dactylopteridae.

Ebisus Jordan & Snyder 1901:308 [ref. 2506]. Masc. *Ebisus sagamius* Jordan & Snyder 1901:308. Type by monotypy. Synonym of *Erilepis* Gill 1894. Anoplopomatidae.

Ebomegobius Herre 1946:124 [ref. 2142]. Masc. *Ebomegobius goodi* Herre 1946:124. Type by original designation (also monotypic). Valid (Maugé 1986:388 [ref. 6218]). Gobiidae.

Ebosia Jordan & Starks 1904:145 [ref. 2527]. Fem. *Pterois bleekeri* Döderlein in Steindachner & Döderlein 1884:200. Type by original designation (also monotypic). Valid (Eschmeyer & Rama-Rao 1978 [ref. 6386], Shimizu in Masuda et al. 1984:316 [ref. 6441]). Scorpaenidae: Pteroinae.

Echelus Rafinesque 1810:63 [ref. 3594]. Masc. *Echelus punctatus* Rafinesque 1810:65. Type by subsequent designation. Type designated by Bleeker 1864:20 [ref. 4860] and 1865:117 [ref. 409]. Valid (Blache et al. 1973:245 [ref. 7185], McCosker 1977:75 [ref. 6836], Karrer 1982:76 [ref. 5679], Asano in Masuda et al. 1984:30 [ref. 6441], Bauchot in Whitehead et al. 1986:580 [ref. 13676], McCosker et al. 1989:298 [ref. 13288]). Ophichthidae: Ophichthinae.

Echemythes Gistel 1848:VIII [ref. 1822]. *Zeus luna* Gmelin 1789:1225. Type by being a replacement name. Unneeded replacement for and objective synonym of *Chrysotosus* Lacepède 1802; no reason given by Gistel for the new name. Synonym of *Lampris* Retzius 1799 (Palmer 1973:328 [ref. 7195]). Lampridae.

Echeneis Linnaeus 1758:260 [ref. 2787]. Fem. *Echeneis naucrates* Linnaeus 1758:261. Type designated by ICZN under plenary powers (emendation of *neucrates*). On Official List (Opinions 92 and 242). Valid (Lachner 1973:637 [ref. 7221], Okamura in Masuda et al. 1984:222 [ref. 6441], Heemstra 1986:662 [ref. 5660], Lachner in Whitehead et al. 1986:1330 [ref. 13677], Paxton et al. 1989:571 [ref. 12442]). Echeneidae.

Echidna Forster 1777:81 [ref. 1353]. Fem. *Echidna variegata* Forster in Lichtenstein 1844. Original not seen, needs further study. Valid (Hatooka in Masuda et al. 1984:25 [ref. 6441], Castle & McCosker 1986:166 [ref. 5645], Paxton et al. 1989:127 [ref. 12442], Böhlke et al. 1989:130 [ref. 13286]). Muraenidae: Muraeninae.

Echiichthys Bleeker 1861:378 [ref. 384]. Masc. *Echiichthys vipera* Cuvier 1829:152. Type by monotypy. Also as Bleeker 1862:117 [ref. 385], with type designated on p. 115. Synonym of *Trachinus* Linnaeus 1758 (Wheeler 1973:449 [ref. 7190]); valid (Bentivegna & Fiorito 1983:51 [ref. 12849], Tortonese in Whitehead et al. 1986:951 [ref. 13676]). Trachinidae.

Echinomacrurus Roule 1916:22 [ref. 3818]. Masc. *Echinomacrurus mollis* Roule 1916:22. Type by monotypy. Valid (Marshall 1973:289 [ref. 7194], Iwamoto 1979:142 [ref. 2311], Fahay & Markle 1984:274 [ref. 13653], Geistdoerfer in Whitehead et al. 1986:661 [ref. 13676]). Macrouridae: Macrourinae.

Echinophryne McCulloch & Waite 1918:66 [ref. 2950]. Fem. *Echinophryne crassispina* McCulloch & Waite 1918:67. Type by original designation (also monotypic). Valid (Pietsch & Kuiter 1984 [ref. 5194], Pietsch 1984:39 [ref. 5380], Paxton et al. 1989:279 [ref. 12442]). Antennariidae.

Echinorhinus (subgenus of *Squalus*) Blainville 1816:121 [ref. 306]. Masc. *Squalus spinosus* Gmelin 1789:1500. Type by monotypy. Also spelled *Echinorrhinus* in early literature (e.g., Müller & Henle 1837:116 [ref. 3067]). Valid (Krefft & Tortonese 1973:45 [ref. 7165], Compagno 1984:25 [ref. 6474], Nakaya & Shirai in Masuda et al. 1984:11 [ref. 6441], Bass & Compagno 1986:63 [ref. 5637], Cappetta 1987:51 [ref. 6348], Paxton et al. 1989:34 [ref. 12442]). Echinorhinidae.

Echinosolea Chabanaud 1927:5, 10 [ref. 782]. Fem. *Solea oculata* Rondelet (= *Pleuronectes ocellatus* Linnaeus 1758:269). Type by original designation. Synonym of *Microchirus* Bonaparte 1833 (Torchio 1973:632 [ref. 6892]). Soleidae.

Echiodon Thompson 1837:55 [ref. 4388]. Masc. *Echiodon drummondii* Thompson 1837:55. Type by monotypy. Valid (Arnold 1956:288 [ref. 5315], Wheeler 1973:558 [ref. 7190], Williams 1984 [ref. 6813], Williams 1984:391 [ref. 5314], Trott & Olney in Whitehead et al. 1986:1175 [ref. 13677], Shen & Yeh 1987:51 [ref. 6418], Paxton et al. 1989:320 [ref. 12442]). Carapidae: Carapinae.

Echiophis Kaup 1856:46 [ref. 2572]. Masc. *Ophisurus intertinctus* Richardson 1848:102. Type by monotypy. Also in Kaup 1856:13 [ref. 2573] and as Kaup in Dumeril 1856:198 [ref. 1154] but as *Echiopsis* [which technically must be treated as a misspelling on p. 13 [ref. 2573]]; *Echiopsis* also preoccupied by Fitzinger 1843 in Reptilia. Valid (McCosker 1977:76 [ref. 6836], McCosker et al. 1989:357 [ref. 13288]). Ophichthidae: Ophichthinae.

Echiostoma Lowe 1843:87 [ref. 2832]. Neut. *Echiostoma barbatum* Lowe 1843:88. Type by monotypy. *Echiostomias* is a misspelling. Valid (Morrow in Morrow & Gibbs 1964:480 [ref. 6962], Morrow 1973:137 [ref. 7175], Gibbs in Whitehead et al. 1984:345 [ref. 13675], Kawaguchi & Moser 1984:171 [ref. 13642], Fujii in Masuda et al. 1984:52 [ref. 6441], Fink 1985:11 [ref. 5171], Gibbs 1986:238 [ref. 5655], Paxton et al. 1989:198 [ref. 12442]). Melanostomiidae.

Eckloniaichthys Smith 1943:67 [ref. 4071]. Masc. *Eckloniaichthys scylliorhiniceps* Smith 1943:67. Type by monotypy. Valid (Briggs 1955:71 [ref. 637], Briggs 1986:379 [ref. 5643]). Gobiesocidae: Gobiesocinae.

Eclectochromis Eccles & Trewavas 1989:277 [ref. 13547]. Masc. *Haplochromis ornatus* Regan 1922:691. Type by original designation. Cichlidae.

Economidichthys Bianco, Bullock, Miller & Roubal 1987:797 [ref.

6337]. Masc. *Gobius pygmaeus* Holly 1929:487. Type by original designation (also monotypic). Gobiidae.

Ecsenius McCulloch 1923:121 [ref. 2946]. Masc. *Ecsenius mandibularis* McCulloch 1923:122. Type by original designation (also monotypic). Valid (Smith-Vaniz & Springer 1971:22 [ref. 4145], McKinney & Springer 1976 [ref. 7087], Yoshino in Masuda et al. 1984:300 [ref. 6441], Springer 1986:745 [ref. 5719], Springer 1988 [ref. 6804]). Blenniidae.

Ectenias Jordan & Thompson 1914:241 [ref. 2543]. Masc. *Ectenias brunneus* Jordan & Thompson 1914:241. Type by monotypy. Synonym of *Coryphaena* Linnaeus 1758. Coryphaenidae.

Ectodus Boulenger 1898:21 [ref. 547]. Masc. *Ectodus descampsi* Boulenger 1898:21. Type by subsequent designation. Type designated by Jordan 1920:576 [ref. 4905]. Valid (Liem 1981:192 [ref. 6897], Poll 1986:93 [ref. 6136]). Cichlidae.

Ectrepopterus (subgenus of *Megalamphodus*) Fowler 1943:313 [ref. 1444]. Masc. *Megalamphodus uruguayensis* Fowler 1943:313. Type by original designation (also monotypic). Characidae.

Ectreposebastes Garman 1899:53 [ref. 1540]. Masc. *Ectreposebastes imus* Garman 1899:53. Type by monotypy. Valid (Eschmeyer & Collette 1966:366 [ref. 6485], Eschmeyer & Randall 1975:291 [ref. 6389], Amaoka in Masuda et al. 1984:317 [ref. 6441], Paxton et al. 1989:441 [ref. 12442]). Scorpaenidae: Setarchinae.

Edelia Castelnau 1873:123 [ref. 758]. Fem. *Edelia vittata* Castelnau 1873:124. Type by subsequent designation. Type designated by Bleeker 1876:334 [ref. 448]. Treated as valid but possibly a synonym of *Nannoperca* Günther 1861 (Kuiter & Allen 1986:109 [ref. 5213]). Valid (Paxton et al. 1989:539 [ref. 12442]). Percichthyidae.

Edomus Rafinesque 1815:88 [ref. 3584]. Not available, name only. Unplaced genera.

Edriolychnus Regan 1925:398 [ref. 3678]. Masc. *Edriolychnus schmidti* Regan 1925:398. Type by monotypy. Valid (Maul 1973:677 [ref. 7171]); synonym of *Haplophryne* Regan 1912 (Bertelsen in Whitehead et al. 1986:1408 [ref. 13677]). Linophrynidae.

Eeyorius Paulin 1986:201 [ref. 5327]. Masc. *Eeyorius hutchinsi* Paulin 1986:204. Type by original designation (also monotypic). Moridae.

Egglestonichthys Miller & Wongrat 1979:240 [ref. 3014]. Masc. *Egglestonichthys patriciae* Miller & Wongrat 1979:242. Type by original designation (also monotypic). Valid. Gobiidae.

Ehirava Deraniyagala 1929:34 [ref. 1115]. *Ehirava fluviatilis* Deraniyagala 1929:35. Type by monotypy. Valid (Jayaram 1981:38 [ref. 6497], Grande 1985:246 [ref. 6466], Whitehead 1985:171 [ref. 5141]). Clupeidae.

Eichwaldia (subgenus of *Gobius*) Smitt 1900:545 [ref. 4148]. Fem. *Gobius caspius* Eichwald 1831:76. Type by monotypy. Preoccupied by Billings 1858 in fossil brachiopods, replaced by and objective synonym of *Eichwaldiella* Whitley 1930. Synonym of *Neogobius* Iljin 1927 (Miller 1973:501 [ref. 6888]). Gobiidae.

Eichwaldiella Whitley 1930:123 [ref. 4669]. Fem. *Gobius caspius* Eichwald 1831:76. Type by being a replacement name. Replacement for *Eichwaldia* Smitt 1899, preoccupied by Billings 1858 in fossil brachiopods. Synonym of *Neogobius* Iljin 1927 (Miller 1973:502 [ref. 6888]). Gobiidae.

Eigenmannia Jordan & Evermann 1896:340, 341 [ref. 2443]. Fem. *Sternopygus humboldtii* Steindachner 1878:71. Type by being a replacement name. Replacement for *Cryptops* Eigenmann 1894, preoccupied by Leach 1814 in Myriopoda, Schoenherr 1823 and Solier 1851 in Coleoptera. Valid (Mago-Leccia 1978:19 [ref. 5489], Malabarba 1989:156 [ref. 14217]). Gymnotidae: Sternopyginae.

Eigenmannina Fowler 1906:307 [ref. 1373]. Fem. *Anodus melanopogon* Cope 1878:692. Type by original designation. Hemiodontidae: Hemiodontinae.

Eilatia Klausewitz 1974:206 [ref. 2614]. Fem. *Eilatia latruncularia* Klausewitz 1974:206. Type by original designation (also monotypic). Synonym of *Flabelligobius* Smith 1956 (Hoese, pers. comm.). Gobiidae.

Eilichthys Pellegrin 1929:204 [ref. 3412]. Masc. *Eilichthys microphthalmus* Pellegrin 1929:204. Type by monotypy. Misspelled *Eileichthys* in Zoological Record for 1929. Synonym of *Barbopsis* Caporiacco 1926 (Lévêque & Daget 1984:218 [ref. 6186]). Cyprinidae.

Einara Parr 1951:10 [ref. 3380]. Fem. *Alepocephalus macrolepis* Koefoed 1927:43. Type by original designation (also monotypic). Valid (Krefft 1973:89 [ref. 7166], Markle & Quéro in Whitehead et al. 1984:242 [ref. 13675], Markle 1986:220 [ref. 5687]). Alepocephalidae.

Eirmotus Schultz 1959:10 [ref. 3971]. Masc. *Eirmotus octozona* Schultz 1959:11. Type by original designation (also monotypic). Valid (Kottelat 1982:431 [ref. 2667], Kottelat 1989:7 [ref. 13605], Roberts 1989:38 [ref. 6439]). Cyprinidae.

Ekemblemaria Stephens 1963:21 [ref. 4270]. Fem. *Ekemblemaria myersi* Stephens 1963:23. Type by original designation. Valid (Acero P. 1984 [ref. 5534]). Chaenopsidae.

Elacate Cuvier in Cuvier & Valenciennes 1832:328 [ref. 1000]. Fem. *Elacate malabarica* Cuvier in Cuvier & Valenciennes 1832:332. Type by subsequent designation. Type designated by Jordan & Gilbert 1883:418 [ref. 2476]. *Elecate* is a misspelling. Synonym of *Rachycentron* Kaup 1826 (Monod 1973:371 [ref. 7193]). Rachycentridae.

Elacatinus Jordan 1904:542 [ref. 2400]. Masc. *Elacatinus oceanops* Jordan 1904:542. Type by original designation (also monotypic). Valid. Gobiidae.

Elachocharax Myers 1927:114 [ref. 3096]. Masc. *Elachocharax pulcher* Myers 1927:115. Type by original designation (also monotypic). Valid (Géry 1977:119 [ref. 1597], Weitzman & Géry 1981 [ref. 14218], Weitzman 1986 [ref. 5983]). Characidae: Characidiinae.

Elaeorhous Pallas 1814:122 [ref. 3351]. *Callionymus baicalensis* Pallas 1776:290, 707. Type by monotypy. Junior objective synonym of *Comephorus* Lacepède 1800. Comephoridae.

Elagatis Bennett 1840:283 [ref. 260]. Fem. *Elagatis bipinnulatus* Bennett 1840:283. Type by monotypy. Type usually given as *Seriola bipinnulata* Quoy & Gaimard 1825, but Bennett treats only "*Elagatis Bipinnulatus*, n. sp."; names were selected independently, but are treated as synonyms. Genus is feminine so correct spelling is *bipinnulata*. Valid (Hureau & Tortonese 1973:376 [ref. 7198], Smith-Vaniz 1984:524 [ref. 13664], Gushiken in Masuda et al. 1984:153 [ref. 6441], Smith-Vaniz 1986:652 [ref. 5718], Paxton et al. 1989:580 [ref. 12442]). Carangidae.

Elampa (subgenus of *Electrona*) Fraser-Brunner 1949:1048 [ref. 1496]. Fem. *Scopelus subasper* Günther 1864:411. Type by original designation. *Elampadena* Whitley 1953 is an unneeded replacement, *Elampa* apparently not preoccupied. Synonym of *Electrona* Goode & Bean 1896 (Paxton 1979:10 [ref. 6440]). Myctophidae.

Elampadena Whitley 1953:135 [ref. 4718]. Fem. *Scopelus subasper* Günther 1864:411. Type by being a replacement name. Unneeded replacement for and objective synonym of *Elampa* Fraser-Brunner 1949, not preoccupied by *Elampus* Spinola 1806 in Hymenoptera. Synonym of *Electrona* Goode & Bean 1896 (Paxton 1979:10 [ref. 6440]). Myctophidae.

Elanura Gilbert 1896:429 [ref. 1628]. Fem. *Elanura forficata* Gilbert 1896:430. Type by monotypy. Synonym of *Triglops* Reinhardt 1831. Cottidae.

Elaphichthys Jordan & Starks 1904:301 [ref. 2528]. Masc. *Centridermichthys elongatus* Steindachner 1881:186. Type by original designation (also monotypic). Cottidae.

Elaphocottus (subgenus of *Cottus*) Sauvage 1878:137, 139 [ref. 3880]. Masc. *Cottus pistilliger* Pallas 1811:143. Type by subsequent designation. Two included species; earliest type designation located that of Jordan 1919:397 [ref. 4904]. Synonym of *Gymnocanthus* Swainson 1839. Cottidae.

Elaphrotoxon (subgenus of *Caranx*) Fowler 1905:76 [ref. 1369]. Neut. *Scomber ruber* Bloch 1793:75. Type by original designation (also monotypic). Spelled *Elaphotoxon* by Jordan, Evermann & Clark 1930:271 [ref. 6476], and by Jordan 1920:512 [ref. 4905]. Synonym of *Carangoides* Bleeker 1851 (Smith-Vaniz, pers. comm.). Carangidae.

Elapsopis Kaup 1856:45 [ref. 2572]. Fem. *Ophisurus versicolor* Richardson 1846:103. Type by monotypy. Also appeared as *Elapsopsis* in Kaup 1856:10 [ref. 2573] and in Kaup in Duméril 1856:199 [ref. 1154]. Valid (Blache et al. 1973:247 [ref. 7185], McCosker 1977:77 [ref. 6836], Paxton et al. 1989:116 [ref. 12442]. Synonym of *Leiuranus* Bleeker 1853 (McCosker et al. 1989:354 [ref. 13288]). Ophichthidae: Ophichthinae.

Elapterostomias Fowler 1934:258 [ref. 1416]. Masc. *Elapterostomias philippinus* Fowler 1934:259. Type by original designation (also monotypic). Synonym of *Borostomias* Regan 1908 (Gibbs 1964:332 [ref. 6960]). Astronesthidae.

Elassichthys Hubbs & Wisner 1980:534 [ref. 2267]. Masc. *Cololabis adocetus* Böhlke 1951:83. Type by original designation (also monotypic). Valid (Collette et al. 1984:352 [ref. 11422]). Scomberesocidae.

Elassodiscus Gilbert & Burke 1912:81 [ref. 1634]. Masc. *Elassodiscus tremebundus* Gilbert & Burke 1912:81. Type by original designation (also monotypic). Valid (Stein 1978:26 [ref. 4203]); synonym of *Paraliparis* Collett 1878 (Kido 1988:230 [ref. 12287]). Cyclopteridae: Liparinae.

Elassoma Jordan 1877:50 [ref. 2374]. Neut. *Elassoma zonata* Jordan 1877:50. Type by original designation (also monotypic). Misspelled *Elassosoma* in Zoological Record for 1877. In this case, "Typical species *Elassoma zonata*, Jordan" is regarded as type by original designation; the expression typical used in the sense of the type species. Valid (Johnson 1984:465 [ref. 9681], Rohde & Arndt 1987 [ref. 13524]). Elassomatidae.

Elastoma (subgenus of *Eteles*) Swainson 1839:168, 202 [ref. 4303]. Neut. *Etelis oculatus* Cuvier in Cuvier & Valenciennes 1828:266. Type by monotypy. Synonym of *Etelis* Cuvier 1828 (Allen 1985:24 [ref. 6843]). Lutjanidae.

Elates Jordan & Seale 1907:39 [ref. 2498]. Masc. *Elates thompsoni* Jordan & Seale 1907:39. Type by original designation (also monotypic). Valid (Paxton et al. 1989:466 [ref. 12442]). Platycephalidae.

Elattarchus Jordan & Evermann 1896:397 [ref. 2442]. Masc. *Odontoscion archidium* Jordan & Gilbert 1882:317. Type by original designation (also monotypic). Sciaenidae.

Elattonistius (subgenus of *Hyodon*) Gill & Jordan in Jordan 1877:67 [ref. 2374]. Masc. *Hyodon chrysopsis* Richardson 1836:232. Type by monotypy. Correct spelling for genus of the type species is *Hiodon*. Synonym of *Hiodon* Lesueur 1818. Hiodontidae.

Electrona Goode & Bean 1896:91 [ref. 1848]. Fem. *Scopelus risso* Cocco 1829:144. Type by original designation (also monotypic). Valid (Krefft & Bekker 1973:181 [ref. 7181], Paxton 1979:10 [ref. 6440], Hulley in Whitehead et al. 1984:450 [ref. 13675], Moser et al. 1984:219 [ref. 13645], Fujii in Masuda et al. 1984:65 [ref. 6441], Hulley 1986:297 [ref. 5672], Paxton et al. 1989:260 [ref. 12442]). Myctophidae.

Electrophorus Gill 1864:151 [ref. 1698]. Masc. *Gymnotus electricus* Linnaeus 1766:427. Type by monotypy. Valid. Gymnotidae: Electrophorinae.

Eleginops Gill 1862:522 [ref. 1782]. Masc. *Aphritis undulatus* Jenyns 1842:160. Type by subsequent designation. Earliest type designation not researched. Valid (Stevens et al. 1984:563 [ref. 13633], Andersen 1984:23 [ref. 13369] with type as *maclovinus* [type of *Eleginus* not *Eleginops*], Nakamura in Nakamura et al. 1986:256 [ref. 14235]). Nototheniidae.

Eleginus Cuvier in Cuvier & Valenciennes 1830:158 [ref. 999]. Masc. *Eleginus maclovinus* Cuvier in Cuvier & Valenciennes 1830:158. Type by monotypy. Preoccupied by Fischer von Waldheim 1813 in fishes, not replaced. Synonym of *Eleginops* Gill 1862. Nototheniidae.

Eleginus Fischer von Waldheim 1813:252 [ref. 1332]. Masc. *Gadus navaga* Pallas (ex Koelreuter) 1811:196. Type by monotypy. Original not seen; see Gill 1891:302 [ref. 1734]. Not *Eleginus* Cuvier 1830. Valid (Svetovidov 1973:305 [ref. 7169], Fahay & Markle 1984:266 [ref. 13653], Okamura in Masuda et al. 1984:92 [ref. 6441], Svetovidov in Whitehead et al. 1986:684 [ref. 13676]). Gadidae.

Eleotrica Ginsburg 1933:10 [ref. 1800]. Fem. *Eleotrica cableae* Ginsburg 1933:11. Type by original designation (also monotypic). Valid (Birdsong et al. 1988:189 [ref. 7303]). Gobiidae.

Eleotriculus (subgenus of *Chriolepis*) Ginsburg 1938:111 [ref. 1802]. Masc. *Chriolepis zebra* Ginsburg 1938:109. Type by original designation (also monotypic). Synonym of *Chriolepis* Gilbert 1892 (Hoese, pers. comm.). Gobiidae.

Eleotriodes Bleeker 1857:372 [ref. 358]. Masc. *Eleotris sexguttata* Valenciennes in Cuvier & Valenciennes 1837:254. Type by monotypy. Appeared as above as name with existing species and therefore available. Also appeared in Bleeker 1858:212 [ref. 362] as a new genus based on Bleeker's style, but in conjunction with *E. helsdingenii* which Bleeker subsequently regarded as type. Gobiidae.

Eleotris Bloch & Schneider 1801:65 [ref. 471]. Fem. *Gobius pisonis* Gmelin in Linnaeus 1789:1206. Type designated by ICZN by use of plenary powers; on Official List (Opinion 93, Direction 56). *Eleotris* Gronow 1763 placed on Official Index (Direction 56) as a name published in a rejected work. Valid (Akihito in Masuda et al. 1984:239 [ref. 6441], Hoese 1986:809 [ref. 5670], Maugé 1986:391 [ref. 6218] but with wrong type, Birdsong et al. 1988:181 [ref. 7303], Kottelat 1989:18 [ref. 13605], Roberts 1989:166 [ref. 6439]). Eleotridae.

Elephantichthys Hubbs & Schultz 1934:21 [ref. 5610]. Masc. *Elephantichthys copeianus* Hubbs & Schultz 1934:22. Type by monotypy. Synonym of *Cyclopterichthys* Steindachner 1881 (Lindberg & Legeza 1955 [ref. 2785]). Cyclopteridae: Cyclopterinae.

Elephenor Jordan 1919:330, 332 [ref. 2411]. *Pteraclis macropus* Bellotti 1903:137. Type by original designation (also monotypic). Synonym of *Caristius* Gill & Smith 1905 (Nielsen 1973:339 [ref. 6885]). Caristiidae.

Eleria Jordan & Seale 1905:774 [ref. 2495]. Fem. *Eleria philippina* Jordan & Seale 1905:774. Type by monotypy. Synonym of *Scomberoides* Lacepède 1801 (Smith-Vaniz & Staiger 1973:190 [ref. 7106], Daget & Smith-Vaniz 1986:316 [ref. 6207]). Carangidae.

Eleutheractis Cope 1870:467 [ref. 920]. Fem. *Eleutheractis coriaceus* Cope 1870:467. Type by original designation. Synonym of *Rypticus* Cuvier 1829. Serranidae: Grammistinae.

Eleutherocephalus Agassiz 1846 [ref. 64]. See *Cephaleutherus* Rafinesque 1810. Rajidae.

Eleutherochir Bleeker 1879:102 [ref. 458]. Fem. *Callionymus opercularioides* Bleeker 1851:32. Type by original designation (also monotypic). Valid (Fricke 1982:73 [ref. 5432], Nakabo 1982:109 [ref. 3139], Houde 1984:637 [ref. 13674], Nakabo in Masuda et al. 1984:345 [ref. 6441]). Callionymidae.

Eleutheronema Bleeker 1862:110 [ref. 387]. Neut. *Polynemus tetradactylus* Shaw 1804:155. Type by monotypy. Also appeared in Bleeker 1862:124 [ref. 389]. Valid (Jayaram 1981:348 [ref. 6497], de Sylva 1984:540 [ref. 13667], Kottelat 1989:18 [ref. 13605]). Polynemidae.

Eleuthurus Rafinesque 1815:91 [ref. 3584]. Not available, name only. Unplaced genera.

Elipesurus Schomburgk 1843:184 [ref. 3948]. Masc. *Elipesurus spinicauda* Schomburgk 1843:184. Type by monotypy. Original is *Elipesurus*; *Ellipesurus* is a misspelling or unjustified emendation. Valid (Bailey 1969:133 [ref. 14234], Fowler 1970:571 [ref. 7313]; see Rosa et al. 1987:447 [ref. 5974]). Potamotrygonidae.

Ellerkeldia Whitley 1927:298 [ref. 4662]. Fem. *Plectropoma annulatum* Günther 1859:158. Type by original designation. Not regarded as a replacement for *Gilbertia* Jordan 1891; see Appendix A; type therefore not *Plectropoma semicinctum* Valenciennes 1833:442. Valid (Allen & Moyer 1980 [ref. 6925], Kendall 1984:500 [ref. 13663], Paxton et al. 1989:504 [ref. 12442]); synonym of *Hypoplectrodes* Gill 1862 (Anderson & Heemstra 1989:1002 [ref. 13526] with type as *semicinctum*). Serranidae: Anthiinae.

Ellerya Castelnau 1873:95 [ref. 758]. Fem. *Ellerya unicolor* Castelnau 1873:95. Type by monotypy. *Ellyria* Castelnau 1875:21 [ref. 768] is an incorrect subsequent spelling. Synonym of *Gobiodon* Bleeker 1856 (Maugé 1986:369 [ref. 6218]). Gobiidae.

Elliops (subgenus of *Ictalurus*) Rafinesque 1820:356 [ref. 7311]. Masc. *Silurus maculatus* Rafinesque 1819:48. Type by subsequent designation. Described as a section of the subgenus *Ictalurus*. Type designated by Jordan & Gilbert 1877:87 [ref. 4907]. Also appeared in Rafinesque 1820:62 (Dec.) [ref. 3592]. Synonym of *Ictalurus* Rafinesque 1820. Ictaluridae.

Ellisichthys Miranda-Ribeiro 1920:11 [ref. 3727]. Masc. *Cascadura maculocephala* Ellis 1913:387. Type by being a replacement name. Unneeded replacement for *Cascadura* Ellis 1913, apparently not preoccupied. In the synonymy of *Cascadura* Ellis 1913 (Gosline 1940:8 [ref. 6489]). Callichthyidae.

Ello Gistel 1848:109 [ref. 1822]. *Mugil cephalus* Linnaeus 1758: 316. Type by being a replacement name. Unneeded replacement for *Mugil* Linnaeus 1758. Objective synonym of *Mugil* Linnaeus 1758. Mugilidae.

Ellochelon Whitley 1930:251 [ref. 4670]. Masc. *Mugil vaigiensis* Quoy & Gaimard 1825:337. Type by original designation (also monotypic). Synonym of *Liza* Jordan & Swain 1884 (Smith & Smith 1986:715 [ref. 5717]). Mugilidae.

Ellogobius Whitley 1933:92 [ref. 4677]. Masc. *Gobius stigmaticus* De Vis 1884:686. Type by original designation. Synonym of *Mugilogobius* Smitt 1900 (Hoese, pers. comm.). Gobiidae.

Ellopostoma Vaillant 1902:145 [ref. 4490]. Neut. *Aperioptus megalomycter* Vaillant 1902:145. Type by monotypy. Placement uncertain, possibly near Cobitidae (Roberts 1972:13 [ref. 12567]). Valid (Roberts 1972 [ref. 12567], Kottelat 1989:12 [ref. 13605], Roberts 1989:103 [ref. 6439]). Balitoridae: Nemacheilinae.

Ellops Gistel 1848:IX [ref. 1822]. Masc. *Acipenser helops* Pallas 1811:97. Type by being a replacement name. Unneeded replacement for *Helops* [Browne 1789 in fishes, not available]. *Ellops* itself possibly preoccupied by Minding 1832 in fishes. Synonym of *Acipenser* Linnaeus 1758. Acipenseridae: Acipenserinae.

Ellops Minding 1832:124 [ref. 3022]. Masc. *Ellops saurus* Minding 1832:125 (= *Elops saurus* Linnaeus 1766:518). Type by monotypy. Perhaps not intended as a new name, unclear from text. Objective synonym of *Elops* Linnaeus 1766. Elopidae.

Elopichthys Bleeker 1859:436 [ref. 370]. Masc. *Leuciscus bambusa* Richardson 1845:141. Type by subsequent designation. Apparently appeared first in key without included species. Two species included by Bleeker 1860:286, 428 [ref. 380]. Type designated by Bleeker 1863:32 [ref. 4859] and 1863:212 [ref. 397]. Valid (Yang & Hwang 1964:38 [ref. 13497], Bogutskaya 1987:936 [ref. 13521], Bogutskaya 1988:107 [ref. 12754], Chen & Li in Chu & Chen 1989:45 [ref. 13584]). Cyprinidae.

Elopomorphus Gill 1878:167 [ref. 5755]. Masc. *Elopomorphus jordanii* Gill 1878:168. Type by monotypy. One species definitely included, "The *Anodus elongatus* of Spix seems to be a congeneric ..." Also published in Gill (July) 1878:212 [ref. 1716]. Synonym of *Anodus* Cuvier 1829 (but see account of *Anodus*). Hemiodontidae: Hemiodontinae.

Elops Bonaparte (ex Commerson) 1831:178 [ref. 4978]. Masc. *Gomphosus tricolor* Quoy & Gaimard 1824:280. Appeared as "*Elops*, Commers. (*Gomphosus*, Lacep.)" but not recorded by Bonaparte as "Nob." which was his style for replacement names. Not available. Jordan regarded as of doubtful elegibility and as a substitute for *Gomphosus*. Labridae.

Elops Commerson in Lacepède 1801:100 (footnote) [ref. 2710]. Masc. Not available; preoccupied; name mentioned in passing under *Gomphosus*. See remarks under Opinion 89 in Appendix B. Not *Elops* Linnaeus 1766. In the synonymy of *Gomphosus* Lacepède 1801. Labridae.

Elops Linnaeus 1766:518 [ref. 2786]. Masc. *Elops saurus* Linnaeus 1766:518. Type by monotypy. *Helops* Agassiz 1846 is an unjustified emendation. Valid (Daget 1984:30 [ref. 6170], Uyeno in Masuda et al. 1984:21 [ref. 6441], Smith 1986:155 [ref. 5712], Paxton et al. 1989:104 [ref. 12442], Smith 1989:962 [ref. 13285]). Elopidae.

Elxis Jordan & Fowler 1903:768 [ref. 2461]. *Elxis nikkonis* Jordan & Fowler 1903:768. Type by original designation (also monotypic). Synonym of *Oreonectes* Günther 1868 (Banarescu & Nalbant 1968:339 [ref. 6554]); synonym of *Lefua* Herzenstein 1888 (Kottelat 1990:19 [ref. 14137]). Balitoridae: Nemacheilinae.

Embassichthys Jordan & Evermann 1896:506 [ref. 2442]. Masc. *Cynicoglossus bathybius* Gilbert 1890:123. Type by original designation (also monotypic). Valid (Norman 1934:361 [ref. 6893], Amaoka, Sakamoto & Abe 1981 [ref. 5578], Ahlstrom et al. 1984:643 [ref. 13641], Sakamoto 1984 [ref. 5273], Sakamoto in Masuda et al. 1984:353 [ref. 6441]). Pleuronectidae: Pleuronectinae.

Embiotoca Agassiz 1853:386 [ref. 68]. Fem. *Embiotoca jacksoni* Agassiz 1853:387. Type by subsequent designation. Earliest type designation found is by Bleeker 1876:290 [ref. 448]). Valid (Tarp 1952:58 [ref. 12250]). Embiotocidae.

Emblemaria Jordan & Gilbert 1883:627 [ref. 2474]. Fem. *Emblemaria nivipes* Jordan & Gilbert 1883:627. Type by monotypy. Valid (Stephens 1963:68 [ref. 4270], Greenfield & Johnson 1981:57 [ref. 5580], Acero P. 1984 [ref. 5534], Acero P. 1984 [ref. 8191]). Chaenopsidae.

Emblemariopsis Longley 1927:222 [ref. 5630]. Fem. *Emblemariopsis diaphana* Longley 1927:223. Type by original designation (also monotypic). Synonym of *Coralliozetus* Evermann & Marsh 1899 (Acero P. 1984 [ref. 5534]); valid (Stephens 1963:91 [ref. 4270], Stephens 1970:283 [ref. 6994], Greenfield & Johnson 1981:61 [ref. 5580]). Chaenopsidae.

Embolichthys Jordan & Evermann in Jordan 1903:693 [ref. 2398]. Masc. *Bleekeria mitsukurii* Jordan & Evermann 1902:333. Type by original designation (also monotypic). Valid (Stevens et al. 1984:574 [ref. 13671], Ida in Masuda et al. 1984:222 [ref. 6441]). Ammodytidae.

Embryx Jordan & Evermann 1898:2456, 2458 [ref. 2445]. Masc. *Lycodopsis crotalinus* Gilbert 1890:105. Type by original designation. Valid (Toyoshima 1985:176 [ref. 5722]); synonym of *Lycenchelys* Gill 1884 (Anderson 1988:87 [ref. 7304]). Zoarcidae.

Emissola Jarocki 1822:448 [ref. 4984]. Fem. *Squalus mustelus* Linnaeus 1758:235. Type by subsequent designation. Type apparently first designated by Hubbs 1938:12 [ref. 5958]. Original not seen. Objective synonym of *Mustelus* Linck 1790 (Compagno 1973:28 [ref. 7163], Compagno 1984:397 [ref. 6846], Compagno 1988:219 [ref. 13488]). Triakidae: Triakinae.

Emmeekia Jordan & Evermann 1896:413 [ref. 2442]. Fem. *Pseudojulis venustus* Jenkins & Evermann 1888:145. Type by original designation (also monotypic). Labridae.

Emmelanthias Smith 1955:(337) 342 [ref. 4097]. Masc. *Emmelanthias stigmapteron* Smith 1955:342. Type by original designation (also monotypic). Synonym of *Nemanthias* Smith 1954. Serranidae: Anthiinae.

Emmelas (subgenus of *Sebastodes*) Jordan & Evermann 1898:1765 et seq. [ref. 2444]. *Sebastodes glaucus* Hilgendorf 1880:170. Type by original designation (also monotypic). Synonym of *Sebastes* Cuvier 1829. Scorpaenidae: Sebastinae.

Emmelichthyops Schultz 1945:133 [ref. 3963]. Masc. *Emmelichthyops atlanticus* Schultz 1945:133. Type by original designation (also monotypic). *Emmelichthops* is a misspelling. Valid (Johnson 1980:12 [ref. 13553]). Inermiidae.

Emmelichthys Richardson 1845:47 [ref. 3740]. Masc. *Emmelichthys nitidus* Richardson 1845:47. Type by monotypy. Valid (Heemstra & Randall 1977:378 [ref. 7057], Scott 1983:194 [ref. 5346], Mochizuki in Masuda et al. 1984:161 [ref. 6441], Nakamura in Nakamura et al. 1986:216 [ref. 14235], Heemstra 1986:637 [ref. 5660]). Emmelichthyidae.

Emmnion Jordan in Gilbert 1897:454 [ref. 1629]. Neut. *Emmnion bristolae* Jordan in Gilbert 1897:454. Type by original designation (also monotypic). Type designated on p. 455. Synonym of *Dialommus* Gilbert 1891 (Clark Hubbs 1952:62 [ref. 2252]). Labrisomidae.

Emmydrichthys Jordan & Rutter in Jordan 1896:221 [ref. 2395]. Masc. *Emmydrichthys vulcanus* Jordan & Rutter in Jordan 1896:221, 562. Type by monotypy. Synonym of *Synanceia* Bloch & Schneider 1801 (Eschmeyer & Rama-Rao 1973:341 [ref. 6391]). Scorpaenidae: Synanceiinae.

Empetrichthys Gilbert 1893:233 [ref. 1627]. Masc. *Empetrichthys merriami* Gilbert 1893:234. Type by monotypy. Valid (Parenti 1981:516 [ref. 7066]). Cyprinodontidae: Empetrichthyinae.

Emphycus (subgenus of *Urophycis*) Jordan & Evermann 1898:2552, 2555 [ref. 2445]. Masc. *Phycis tenuis* Mitchill 1814:5. Type by original designation. Phycidae.

Enantioliparis Vaillant 1888:22 [ref. 4495]. Masc. *Enantioliparis pallidus* Vaillant 1888:22. Type by monotypy. Synonym of *Careproctus* Krøyer 1862 (Stein 1978:10 [ref. 4203], Kido 1988:192 [ref. 12287]). Cyclopteridae: Liparinae.

Enantiopus Boulenger 1906:569 [ref. 573]. Masc. *Ectodus melanogenys* Boulenger 1898:21. Type by subsequent designation. Type apparently first designated by Regan 1920:48 [ref. 3669]. Valid (Poll 1986:115 [ref. 6136]). Cichlidae.

Encaeura Jordan & Hubbs 1925:303 [ref. 2486]. Fem. *Encaeura evides* Jordan & Hubbs 1925:303. Type by original designation (also monotypic). Synonym of *Ptereleotris* Gill 1863 (Randall & Hoese 1985 [ref. 5197]). Microdesmidae: Ptereleotrinae.

Encheiridiodon Smith 1967:128 [ref. 4141]. Masc. *Encheiridiodon hendersoni* Smith 1967:129. Type by original designation, "holotype" in first line apparently a slip for "type" based on style for other accounts, also monotypic. Synonym of *Centrophorus* Müller & Henle 1837 (Compagno 1984:35 [ref. 6474] as *Enchiridiodon*, Bass et al. 1986:49 [ref. 5636]). Squalidae.

Encheliophiops Reid 1940:47 [ref. 3685]. Masc. *Encheliophiops hancocki* Reid 1940:47. Type by original designation (also monotypic). Synonym of *Encheliophis* Müller 1842 (Williams 1984:389 [ref. 5314]). Carapidae: Carapinae.

Encheliophis Müller 1842:205 [ref. 3062]. Masc. *Encheliophis vermicularis* Müller 1842:205. Type by monotypy. Possibly appeared in other Müller papers, 1842-43. Valid (Trott 1981:625 [ref. 14205], Williams 1984:389 [ref. 5314], Machida in Masuda et al. 1984:99 [ref. 6441], Olney & Markle 1986:353 [ref. 5701]). Carapidae: Carapinae.

Encheloclarias Herre & Myers 1937:66 [ref. 2123]. Masc. *Heterobranchus tapeinopterus* Bleeker 1852:732. Type by original designation (also monotypic). Valid (Kottelat 1989:15 [ref. 13605], Roberts 1989:128 [ref. 6439]). Clariidae.

Enchelybrotula Smith & Radcliffe in Radcliffe 1913:154 [ref. 3579]. Fem. *Enchelybrotula paucidens* Smith & Radcliffe in Radcliffe 1913:154. Type by original designation (also monotypic). Valid (Cohen & Nielsen 1978:29 [ref. 881], Cohen 1982 [ref. 5521]). Ophidiidae: Neobythitinae.

Enchelycore Kaup 1856:60 [ref. 2572]. Fem. *Muraena nigricans* Bonnaterre 1788:34. Type by subsequent designation. *E. euryrhina* appeared as name only (not available) in Kaup 1856 [ref. 2572]. Genus also in Kaup 1856:72 [ref. 2573] to which type fixation dates. Appeared as *Enchelycotte* in Kaup in Duméril 1856:200 (as name only and not available). Valid (Hatooka in Masuda et al. 1984:23 [ref. 6441], Bauchot in Whitehead et al.

1986:539 [ref. 13676], Paxton et al. 1989:127 [ref. 12442], Böhlke et al. 1989:134 [ref. 13286]). Muraenidae: Muraeninae.

Enchelycotte Kaup in Duméril 1856:200 [ref. 1154]. Not available, as name only with no description or indication in list of genera and species taken from Kaup manuscript, published as *Enchelycore* by Kaup. In the synonymy of *Enchelycore* Kaup 1856 (Böhlke et al. 1989:134 [ref. 13286]). Muraenidae: Muraeninae.

Enchelynassa Kaup 1855:213 [ref. 2570]. Fem. *Enchelynassa bleekeri* Kaup 1855:214. Type by monotypy. Valid (Böhlke et al. 1989:130 [ref. 13286]). Muraenidae: Muraeninae.

Enchelyocampus Dawson & Allen 1978:405 [ref. 1073]. Masc. *Enchelyocampus brauni* Dawson & Allen 1978:407. Type by original designation (also monotypic). Synonym of *Bulbonaricus* Herald 1953 (Dawson 1984 [ref. 5275], Dawson 1985:24 [ref. 6541]). Syngnathidae: Syngnathinae.

Enchelyopus Bleeker 1862:109 [ref. 387]. Masc. *Trichiurus haumela* Valenciennes in Cuvier & Valenciennes 1832:248 (= *Clupea haumela* Forsskål 1775:xiii, 72). Type by monotypy. As used by Bleeker 1862 et seq., genus is same as *Enchelyopus* Klein 1775 (not available). Preoccupied by Bloch & Schneider 1801. Synonym of *Trichiurus* Linnaeus 1758. Trichiuridae: Trichiurinae.

Enchelyopus Bloch & Schneider 1801:50 (xxvi) [ref. 471]. Masc. *Gadus cimbricus* Linnaeus 1766:440. Type by subsequent designation. Type designated by Jordan & Evermann 1898:2560 [ref. 2445]. Apparently not preoccupied by Gronow 1760 and 1763 (non-binominal works) or by Klein 1775 in Trichiuridae. Synonym of *Rhinonemus* Gill 1863 (authors); valid (Cohen & Russo 1979 [ref. 6975], Fahay & Markle 1984:266 [ref. 13653]). Lotidae.

Enchelyopus Gronow 1760:259 [ref. 13466]. Masc. *Blennius viviparus* Linnaeus 1758:258. Type by subsequent designation. Regarded as unavailable (see Cohen & Russo 1979:100 [ref. 6975]). Also in Gronow 1763 but not available, rejected work on Official Index (Opinion 261). But see also *Enchelyope* Bosc as discussed by Whitley 1936:190 [ref. 6397]. In the synonymy of *Zoarces* Cuvier 1829 (Andriashev 1973:540 [ref. 7214]). Zoarcidae.

Enchelyopus Klein 1775:32 [ref. 2618]. Masc. Not available, published in a work that does not conform to the principle of binominal nomenclature. In the synonymy of *Trichiurus* Linnaeus 1758. Trichiuridae: Trichiurinae.

Enchelyurus Peters 1868:268 [ref. 3442]. Masc. *Enchelyurus flavipes* Peters 1868:268. Type by monotypy. Valid (Springer 1972:4 [ref. 4178], Yoshino in Masuda et al. 1984:296 [ref. 6441], Springer 1985:91 [ref. 6107]). Blenniidae.

Enchura Minding 1832:84 [ref. 3022]. Fem. *Enchura brasma* Minding 1832:84 (= *Gadus brosme* Müller 1776:41). Type by monotypy. Name not found in current literature; apparently a synonym of *Brosme* Oken 1817. Lotidae.

Encrasicholina Fowler 1938:156 [ref. 1428]. Fem. *Encrasicholina punctifer* Fowler 1938:157. Type by original designation (also monotypic). Valid (G. Nelson 1983 [ref. 5189], Grande 1985:245 [ref. 6466], Whitehead et al. 1988:394 [ref. 5725]). Engraulidae.

Encrasicholus Commerson in Lacepède 1803:458 (footnote) [ref. 4930]. Masc. Not available, name from Commerson manuscript mentioned in passing under *Clupea vittargentea* (see Whitehead 1967:136 [ref. 6464]). Commerson names in footnotes in this volume placed on Official Index of Rejected Works (see remarks under Opinion 89 in Appendix B). Engraulidae.

Encrasicholus Fleming 1828:183 [ref. 1339]. Masc. *Clupea encrasicolus* Linnaeus 1758:318. Type by monotypy. Fleming withdrew name in corrigenda ("for *Encrasicholus* read *Engraulis*"); see Whitehead 1967:124 [ref. 6464]; not the same as (nor preoccupied by) *Encrasicholus* Commerson in Lacepède 1803. Probably best treated as a name first published in synonymy; subsequent availability not researched. Objective synonym of *Engraulis* Cuvier 1816 (Svetovidov 1973:111 [ref. 7169], Whitehead et al. 1988:311 [ref. 5725]). Engraulidae.

Encrates Gistel 1848:IX [ref. 1822]. Fem. *Cyprinodon variegatus* Lacepède 1803:486, 487. Type by being a replacement name. Replacement for *Lebia* of "Bon., Räf." [Cuvier], preoccupied by *Lebias* Cuvier according to Gistel; *Lebia* is preoccupied by Latreille 1802 in Coleoptera. Objective synonym of *Cyprinodon* Lacepède 1803 (Parenti 1981:526 [ref. 7066]). Cyprinodontidae: Cyprinodontinae.

Endeconger Jordan 1923:131 [ref. 2421]. Masc. *Brachyconger platyrhynchus* Norman 1922:218. Type by being a replacement name. Replacement for *Brachyconger* Norman 1922, preoccupied by Bleeker 1865 in fishes. Synonym of *Chilorhinus* Lütken 1852 (Smith 1989:84 [ref. 13285]). Chlopsidae.

Endemichthys Hopkirk 1974:56 [ref. 2199]. Masc. *Endemichthys grandipinnis* Hopkirk 1974:57. Type by original designation (also monotypic). Appeared first as nomen nudum in Hopkirk 1968:414 [ref. 2198]. Preoccupied by Forey & Gardiner 1973 in fossil fishes. A hybrid of *Lavinia exilicauda x Orthodon microlepidotus* (some authors); possibly an extinct lake-adapted species of *Hesperoleucus* Snyder 1913 (Hopkirk 1988:185 [ref. 13463]). Cyprinidae.

Endorrhis Ogilby 1898:283 [ref. 3276]. Fem. *Copidoglanis longifilis* Macleay 1881:207. Type by original designation (also monotypic). Synonym of *Paraplotosus* Bleeker 1862 (Paxton et al. 1989:225 [ref. 12442] based on placement of type species). Plotosidae.

Enedrias Jordan & Gilbert in Jordan & Evermann 1898:2414 [ref. 2445]. Masc. *Gunnellus nebulosus* Temminck & Schlegel 1845:138. Type by original designation (also monotypic). Valid (Amaoka in Masuda et al. 1984:303 [ref. 6441]); synonym of *Pholis* Scopoli 1777 (Yatsu 1985:273 [ref. 5149], Makushok in Whitehead et al. 1986:1124 [ref. 13677], Yatsu 1986:674 [ref. 5150]). Pholidae.

Englottogaster Gistel 1848:X [ref. 1822]. Fem. *Oreinus guttatus* McClelland 1839:273, 344. Type by being a replacement name. Unneeded replacement for "*Oreina* [sic] Valenc. XVI, 1842, p. 224" [=*Oreinus* McClelland 1839], not preoccupied by *Oreina* of earlier authors. Synonym of *Schizothorax* Heckel 1838 (Mo in Chu & Chen 1989:287 [ref. 13584]). Cyprinidae.

Engraulicypris Günther 1894:626 [ref. 2018]. Fem. *Engraulicypris pinguis* Günther 1894:626. Type by monotypy. Valid (Lévêque & Daget 1984:301 [ref. 6186]). Cyprinidae.

Engrauligobius Iljin 1930:53 [ref. 2297]. Masc. *Gobius quagga* Heckel 1840:150. Type by original designation (also monotypic). Synonym of *Pomatoschistus* Gill 1863 (Miller 1973:506 [ref. 6888], Maugé 1986:380 [ref. 6218]). Gobiidae.

Engraulis Cuvier 1816:174 [ref. 993]. Fem. *Clupea encrasicolus* Linnaeus 1758:318. Type by subsequent designation. Type designated by Fleming 1822:385 according to Whitehead 1967:124 [ref. 6464]. See Whitley 1935:136 [ref. 6396] for possible earlier publication. Valid (Svetovidov 1973:111 [ref. 7169], Uyeno & Sato in Masuda et al. 1984:20 [ref. 6441], Grande 1985:245 [ref. 6466], Whitehead & Wongratana 1986:205 [ref. 6284], Whitehead et al.

1988:311 [ref. 5725], Paxton et al. 1989:159 [ref. 12442]). Engraulidae.

Engraulisoma Castro 1981:135 [ref. 773]. Neut. *Engraulisoma taeniatum* Castro 1981:137. Type by original designation (also monotypic). Characidae.

Engyophrys Jordan & Bollman 1890:176 [ref. 2433]. Fem. *Engyophrys sanctilaurentii* Jordan & Bollman 1890:176. Type by original designation (also monotypic). Valid (Norman 1934:161 [ref. 6893], Ahlstrom et al. 1984:642 [ref. 13641], Hensley 1986:941 [ref. 6326]). Bothidae: Taeniopsettinae.

Engyprosopon (subgenus of *Rhomboidichthys*) Günther 1862:431, 438 [ref. 1969]. Neut. *Rhombus mogkii* Bleeker 1854:256. Type by monotypy. Described as a section of *Rhomboidichthys*. Valid (Norman 1934:203 [ref. 6893], Amaoka 1969:142 [ref. 105], Ahlstrom et al. 1984:642 [ref. 13641], Amaoka in Masuda et al. 1984:348 [ref. 6441], Hensley 1986:858 [ref. 5669], Hensley 1986:941 [ref. 6326]). Bothidae: Bothinae.

Enigmapercis Whitley 1936:19 [ref. 7315]. Fem. *Enigmapercis reducta* Whitley 1936:19. Type by monotypy. Valid (see Nelson 1982:9 [ref. 5469]). Percophidae: Hemerocoetinae.

Enixe Gistel 1848:IX [ref. 1822]. *Chaetodon punctatus* Linnaeus 1758:273. Type by being a replacement name. Unneeded replacement for *Drepane* Cuvier 1831. On Official Index (Opinion 1046). Objective synonym of *Drepane* Cuvier 1831. Drepanidae.

Enneacampus Dawson 1981:466 [ref. 1071]. Masc. *Syngnathus ansorgii* Boulenger 1910:559. Type by original designation. Valid (Dawson 1986:281 [ref. 6201]). Syngnathidae: Syngnathinae.

Enneacanthus Gill 1864:92 [ref. 1706]. Masc. *Pomotis obesus* Girard 1856:40. Type by original designation (also monotypic). Valid (Peterson & Ross 1987 [ref. 6231]). Centrarchidae.

Enneacentrus Gill 1865:105 [ref. 1710]. Masc. *Serranus outalibi* Cuvier in Cuvier & Valenciennes 1828:381. Type by original designation (also monotypic). Synonym of *Epinephelus* Bloch 1793, subgenus *Cephalopholis* Bloch & Schneider 1801 (C. L. Smith 1971:92 [ref. 14102]); synonym of *Cephalopholis* (Daget & Smith 1986:299 [ref. 6204]). Serranidae: Epinephelinae.

Enneanectes Jordan & Evermann in Jordan 1895:501 [ref. 2394]. Masc. *Tripterygium carminale* Jordan & Gilbert in Jordan 1895:501. Type by monotypy. Correct spelling for genus of type species is *Tripterygion*. Valid (Greenfield & Johnson 1981:46 [ref. 5580]). Tripterygiidae.

Enneapterygius Rüppell 1835:2 [ref. 3844]. Masc. *Enneapterygius pusillus* Rüppell 1835:2. Type by monotypy. Valid (Holleman 1982:120 [ref. 2187], Yoshino in Masuda et al. 1984:294 [ref. 6441], Holleman 1986:756 [ref. 5671]). Tripterygiidae.

Enneistus (subgenus of *Bodianus*) Jordan & Evermann 1896:1143, 1147 [ref. 2443]. Masc. *Bodianus acanthistius* Gilbert 1891:552. Type by original designation (also monotypic). Synonym of subgenus *Cephalopholis* Bloch & Schneider 1801 of genus *Epinephelus* Bloch 1793 (Smith 1971:92 [ref. 14102]). Serranidae: Epinephelinae.

Ennichthys Girard 1855:322 [ref. 1820]. Masc. *Holconotus megalops* Girard 1854:152. Type by subsequent designation. Type designated by Jordan & Evermann 1898:1501 [ref. 2444]. Misspelled *Eunichthys* by Jordan, Evermann & Clark 1930:410 [ref. 6476]. Synonym of *Hyperprosopon* Gibbons 1854 (Tarp 1952:31 [ref. 12250]). Embiotocidae.

Enobarbichthys Whitley 1931:107 [ref. 4673]. Masc. *Platacanthus maculatus* Day 1867:941. Type by being a replacement name. Apparently an unneeded replacement for *Enobarbus* Whitley 1928, not preoccupied by *Aenobarbus* Temminck 1838 in Aves. Treated as valid (Jayaram 1981:178 [ref. 6497], Sawada 1982:200 [ref. 14111] as *Enobarichthys*). Cobitidae: Cobitinae.

Enobarbus Whitley 1928:296 [ref. 4663]. Masc. *Platacanthus maculatus* Day 1867:941. Type by being a replacement name. Replacement for *Jerdonia* Day 1870, apparently preoccupied by Blanford 1832 in Mollusca. *Enobarbichthys* Whitley 1931 apparently is an unneeded replacement of *Enobarbus*, not preoccupied by *Aenobarbus* Temminck 1838 in Aves. Cobitidae: Cobitinae.

Enophrys Swainson 1839:181, 271 [ref. 4303]. Fem. *Cottus claviger* Cuvier in Cuvier & Valenciennes 1829:195. Type by monotypy. Valid (Bolin 1944:90 [ref. 6379], Neyelov 1979:115, 145 [ref. 3152], Washington et al. 1984:442 [ref. 13660], Yabe in Masuda et al. 1984:328 [ref. 6441], Yabe 1985:111 [ref. 11522]). Cottidae.

Enoplosus Lacepède 1802:540 [ref. 4929]. Masc. *Enoplosus white* Lacepède 1802:540, 541 (= *Chaetodon armatus* White 1790:254). Type by monotypy. *Enoplosus white* Lacepède is an unneeded substitute for *Chaetodon armatus* White. Valid. Enoplosidae.

Entelurus Duméril 1870:605 [ref. 1147]. Masc. *Syngnathus aequoreus* Linnaeus 1758:337. Type by subsequent designation. Earliest type designation not researched. See *Acus* Swainson (ex Willoughby) 1839. Valid (Wheeler 1973:278 [ref. 7190], Dawson in Whitehead et al. 1986:629 [ref. 13676]). Syngnathidae: Syngnathinae.

Enterochromis Greenwood 1980:43 [ref. 1899]. Masc. *Haplochromis erythrocephalus* Greenwood & Gee 1969:19. Type by original designation. Cichlidae.

Enteromius Cope 1869:405 [ref. 910]. Masc. *Enteromius potamogalis* Cope 1867:405. Type by monotypy. Valid (Karaman 1971: 189 [ref. 2560]); synonym of *Barbus* Cuvier & Cloquet 1816 (Lévêque & Daget 1984:218 [ref. 6186]). Cyprinidae.

Entomacrodops Fowler 1944:401 [ref. 1448]. Masc. *Entomacrodops macropus* Fowler 1944:402. Type by original designation (also monotypic). Blenniidae.

Entomacrodus Gill 1859:168 [ref. 1755]. Masc. *Entomacrodus nigricans* Gill 1859:168. Type by monotypy. Valid (Smith-Vaniz & Springer 1971:23 [ref. 4145], Greenfield & Johnson 1981:67 [ref. 5580], Yoshino in Masuda et al. 1984:299 [ref. 6441], Springer 1986:746 [ref. 5719], Williams 1989:12 [ref. 13549]). Blenniidae.

Entomocorus Eigenmann 1917:403 [ref. 1235]. Masc. *Entomocorus benjamini* Eigenmann 1917:403. Type by monotypy. Valid (Burgess 1989:241 [ref. 12860], Curran 1989 [ref. 12547]). Auchenipteridae.

Entomolepis Eigenmann 1917:63 [ref. 1236]. Fem. *Tetragonopterus steindachneri* Eigenmann 1893:53. Type by original designation (also monotypic). Preoccupied by Brady 1889 in Crustacea; replaced by *Bario* Myers 1940. Objective synonym of *Bario* Myers 1940. Characidae.

Entonanthias Jordan & Tanaka 1927:385 [ref. 2537]. Masc. *Entonanthias pascalus* Jordan & Tanaka 1927:385. Type by original designation (also monotypic). Synonym of subgenus *Mirolabrichthys* Herre & Montalban 1927 of genus *Anthias* Bloch 1792 (Randall & Lubbock 1981:2 [ref. 6912]). Serranidae: Anthiinae.

Entosphenus Gill 1862:331 [ref. 1668]. Masc. *Petromyzon tridentatus* Richardson 1836:293. Type by subsequent designation. Type designated by Jordan & Gilbert 1877:93 [ref. 4907]. Valid (some authors, e.g., Hubbs & Potter 1971:49 [ref. 13397], Sato in Masuda et al. 1984:2 [ref. 6441]); synonym of *Lampetra* Gray 1851 (authors), as a valid subgenus of *Lampetra* (Hubbs 1971:126 [ref. 7683], Bailey 1980:1627 [ref. 5243]). Petromyzontidae: Petromyzontinae.

Entoxychirus Gill 1863:496, 498 [ref. 1671]. Masc. *Squalus uyato* Rafinesque 1810:13. Type by original designation (also monotypic). Spelled *Entoxychyrus* by Duméril 1865:699 [ref. 1150]. Synonym of *Centrophorus* Müller & Henle 1837 (Krefft & Tortonese 1973:38 [ref. 7165], Compagno 1984:35 [ref. 6474], Cappetta 1987:53 [ref. 6348]). Squalidae.

Enypnias (subgenus of *Garmannia*) Jordan & Evermann 1898:2231, 2233 [ref. 2445]. Masc. *Gobius seminudus* Günther 1861:554. Type by original designation (also monotypic). Valid (Birdsong et al. 1988:189 [ref. 7303]). Gobiidae.

Eocallionymus Nakabo 1982:89 [ref. 3139]. Masc. *Callionymus papilio* Günther 1864:197. Type by original designation (also monotypic). Synonym of *Synchiropus* Gill 1859 (Fricke 1982:74 [ref. 5432]); valid (Houde 1984:637 [ref. 13674]). Callionymidae.

Eonemachilus Berg 1938:314, 316 [ref. 281]. Masc. *Nemachilus nigromaculatus* Regan 1904:192. Type by original designation (also monotypic). Synonym of *Yunnanilus* Nichols 1925 (Kottelat & Chu 1988:66 [ref. 13392], Kottelat 1990:21 [ref. 14137]). Balitoridae: Nemacheilinae.

Eopeyeria Whitley 1947:150 [ref. 4708]. Fem. *Ariopsis aegyptiacus* Peyer 1928:43. Type by being a replacement name. Replacement for *Peyeria* Whitley 1940, preoccupied by Weiler 1935 in fossil fishes. Ariidae.

Eopsetta (subgenus of *Hippoglossoides*) Jordan & Goss in Jordan 1885:923 [135] [ref. 2385]. Fem. *Hippoglossoides jordani* Lockington 1879:73. Type by original designation (also monotypic). On p. 135 of separate. Valid (Norman 1934:307 [ref. 6893], Ahlstrom et al. 1984:643 [ref. 13641], Sakamoto 1984 [ref. 5273], Sakamoto in Masuda et al. 1984:351 [ref. 6441]). Pleuronectidae: Pleuronectinae.

Eosebastes (subgenus of *Sebastodes*) Jordan & Evermann 1896:430 [ref. 2442]. Masc. *Sebastichthys aurora* Gilbert 1890:80. Type by original designation. Synonym of *Sebastes* Cuvier 1829. Scorpaenidae: Sebastinae.

Epalzeorhynchos Bleeker 1855:258, 270 [ref. 351]. Neut. *Barbus kalopterus* Bleeker 1850:13. Type by monotypy. Spelled two ways when originally proposed: *Epalzeorhijnchos* (p. 258, 270) and *Epalzeorhynchos* (p. 260, 270), the later correctly formed. Spelled *Epalzeorhynchus* by Bleeker 1863:192 [ref. 397] and authors. Valid (Wu et al. 1977:357 [ref. 4807], Bailey in Böhlke 1984:76 [ref. 13621], Kottelat 1985:262 [ref. 11441], Roberts 1989:38 [ref. 6439], Chu & Cui in Chu & Chen 1989:232 [ref. 13584], Kottelat 1989:7 [ref. 13605]). Cyprinidae.

Epapterus Cope 1878:677 [ref. 945]. Masc. *Epapterus dispilurus* Cope 1878:677. Type by monotypy. Valid (Vari et al. 1984 [ref. 5261], Burgess 1989:241 [ref. 12860], Curran 1989 [ref. 12547]). Auchenipteridae.

Epelytes Evermann & Radcliffe 1917:71 [ref. 1284]. Masc. *Epelytes punctatus* Eigenmann & Radcliffe 1917:71. Type by original designation (also monotypic). Preoccupied [details not investigated], replaced by ***Pinguilabrum*** Hildebrand 1946. Synonym of *Graus* Philippi 1887 (Johnson & Fritzsche 1989:2 [ref. 13513]). Kyphosidae: Girellinae.

Eperlanio Jordan 1919:341 [ref. 2413]. *Osmerus albatrossis* Jordan & Gilbert in Jordan & Evermann 1898:2823. Type by original designation (also monotypic). Described as a "genus or subgenus" [of *Osmerus*]. Osmeridae.

Eperlanus Basilewski 1855:242 [ref. 200]. Masc. *Eperlanus chinensis* Basilewski 1855:242. Type by monotypy. Synonym of *Protosalanx* Regan 1908 (Roberts 1984:204 [ref. 5318]). Osmeridae.

Eperlanus Gaimard 1851 [ref. 1523]. Masc. *Salmo eperlanus* Linnaeus 1758:310. Type by monotypy. Not seen, quoted from Jordan 1919:249 [ref. 2410]. Objective synonym of *Osmerus* Linnaeus 1758. Osmeridae.

Eperlanus Rutty 1772:358 [ref. 7179]. Masc. *Eperlanus schonfoldii* Rutty 1772:358. Type by monotypy. Not available, no distinguishing features for either genus or species. In the synonymy of *Osmerus* Linnaeus 1758 (Kljukanov & McAllister 1973:158 [ref. 7178]). Osmeridae.

Epetriodus Cohen & Nielsen 1978:29 [ref. 881]. Masc. *Epetriodus freddyi* Cohen & Nielsen 1978:30. Type by original designation (also monotypic). Valid (Nielsen & Cohen 1986:347 [ref. 5700]). Ophidiidae: Neobythitinae.

Ephippicharax Fowler 1913:51 [ref. 1387]. Masc. *Tetragonopterus compressus* Günther 1864:319. Type by being a replacement name. Replacement for *Fowlerina* Eigenmann 1907, preoccupied by Pelseneer 1906 in Mollusca. Synonym of *Poptella* Eigenmann 1907 (Géry 1977:367 [ref. 1597], Reis 1989:18 [ref. 14219]). Characidae: Stethaprioninae.

Ephippion Bibron in Duméril 1855:280 [ref. 297]. Neut. *Ephippion maculatum* Bibron in Duméril 1855:280 (= *Tetraodon guttifer* Bennett 1831:148). Treated as latinized when appeared as above. *E. maculatum* Bibron apparently never published in an available way; technical addition of *T. guttifer* not researched. *Hemiconiatus* Günther 1870 is an unneeded replacement. Valid (Tortonese 1973:645 [ref. 7192], Shipp 1974:116 [ref. 7147], Tyler 1980:341 [ref. 4477], Arai 1983:207 [ref. 14249], Tortonese in Whitehead et al. 1986:1342 [ref. 13677]). Tetraodontidae.

Ephippus Cuvier 1816:335 [ref. 993]. Masc. *Chaetodon orbis* Bloch 1787:81. Type by subsequent designation. Type as given by Jordan 1917:105 [ref. 2407]. Type possibly *E. argus* of Bloch as designated by Bleeker 1876:302 [ref. 448] for Cuvier 1817 [=1816] but not Cuvier 1829 which would upset current usage of *Scatophagus*. Jordan indicated that type was restricted by Cuvier & Valenciennes 1831 [ref. 4881], but they apparently did not fix the type. Valid (Hayashi in Masuda et al. 1984:181 [ref. 6441]); synonym of *Chaetodipterus* Lacepède 1801 (Smith 1986:605 [ref. 5712]). Ephippidae.

Epibulus Cuvier 1815:111 [ref. 5017]. Masc. *Sparus insidiator* Pallas 1770:41. Type by monotypy. Apparently can date to Cuvier 1815 as "...le *sparus insidiator* que je détache du genre *sparus* pour le reporter sous le nom d'*epibulus*, vers la famille naturelle des labres..." Valid (Yamakawa in Masuda et al. 1984:212 [ref. 6441], Randall 1986:693 [ref. 5706]). Labridae.

Epiceratodus Teller 1891:37 [ref. 4369]. Masc. *Ceratodus forsteri* Krefft 1870:221. Type by monotypy. The genus *Ceratodus* is not included since its type species is based on a fossil. Synonym of *Neoceratodus* Castelnau 1876 (Paxton et al. 1989:102 [ref. 12442]. Ceratodontidae.

Epicopus Günther 1860:248 [ref. 1963]. Masc. *Merlus gayi* Guichenot 1847:329. Type by being a replacement name. New name for *Merlus* Guichenot 1847, regarded by Günther as in the

French form, but serves as a replacement name, *Merlus* preoccupied by de la Fresnaye 1838 in Aves. Synonym of *Merluccius* Rafinesque 1810. Merlucciidae: Merlucciinae.

Epicyrtus Müller & Troschel 1844:92 [ref. 3070]. Masc. *Salmo gibbosus* Linnaeus 1758:311. Type by monotypy. Preoccupied by Dejean 1833 in Coleoptera, replaced by *Anacyrtus* Günther 1864. Objective synonym of *Charax* Scopoli 1777. Characidae.

Epidesmus Ranzani 1818:137 [ref. 3604]. Masc. *Epidesmus maculatus* Ranzani 1818:137. Type by monotypy. Synonym of *Trachipterus* Goüan 1770 (Palmer 1973:330 [ref. 7195], Scott 1983:172 [ref. 5346]). Trachipteridae.

Epigeichthys Hubbs 1927:385 [ref. 2236]. Masc. *Xiphister rupestris* Jordan & Gilbert 1880:137. Type by original designation of *Xiphister rupestris* which Hubbs placed in the synonymy of *Ophidium atropurpureum* Kittlitz 1858. Stichaeidae.

Epigonus Rafinesque 1810:64 [ref. 3595]. Masc. *Epigonus macrophthalmus* Rafinesque 1810:64. Type by monotypy. Definition of the family Epigonidae follows Johnson 1984:469 [ref. 9681]. Valid (Tortonese 1973:366 [ref. 7192], Mayer 1974 [ref. 6007], Mochizuki & Shirakihara 1983 [ref. 8302], Hayashi in Masuda et al. 1984:151 [ref. 6441], Parin & Abramov 1986 [ref. 6006], Gon 1986:558 [ref. 5657], Abramov 1987 [ref. 13520], Paxton et al. 1989:553 [ref. 12442]). Epigonidae.

Epimonus Rafinesque 1815:92 [ref. 3584]. As "*Epimonus* R. sp. do." meaning *Epimonus* Rafinesque for a species in a preceding genus (*Balistes*). Not available, name only. Balistidae.

Epinephelides Ogilby 1899:169 [ref. 3279]. Masc. *Epinephelides leai* Ogilby 1899:170. Type by original designation (also monotypic). Valid (Paxton et al. 1989:505 [ref. 12442] in Anthiinae). Serranidae: Anthiinae.

Epinephelus Bloch 1793:11 [ref. 4868]. Masc. *Epinephelus marginalis* Bloch 1793:14. Type designated by ICZN under plenary powers; on Official List (Opinion 93). *Epinelephus* Rafinesque 1815:85 [ref. 3584] is an incorrect subsequent spelling. Valid (C. L. Smith 1971:90 [ref. 14102], Tortonese 1973:358 [ref. 7192], Kendall 1984:500 [ref. 13663], Katayama in Masuda et al. 1984:128 [ref. 6441], Heemstra & Randall 1986:520 [ref. 5667], Daget & Smith 1986:301 [ref. 6204], Randall & Allen 1987 [ref. 6249], Paxton et al. 1989:493 [ref. 12442]). Serranidae: Epinephelinae.

Epinnula Poey 1854:369 [ref. 3497]. Fem. *Epinnula magistralis* Poey 1854:371. Type by monotypy. Valid (Collette et al. 1984:600 [ref. 11421], Nakamura in Masuda et al. 1984:226 [ref. 6441]). Gempylidae.

Epinotus Rafinesque 1815:93 [ref. 3584]. Not available, name only; for a shark. Elasmobranchii.

Epipedorhynchus Troschel (ex Bibron) 1856:88 [ref. 12559]. Masc. Appeared first as "Epipédorhynque" Bibron in Duméril 1855:278 [ref. 297]; latinized by Troschel as above, also by Hollard 1857:319 [ref. 2186]. First technical additional of species not researched. Type as given by Jordan 1919:263 [ref. 2410] is *Tetraodon preycineti* Bibron [name only]. Perhaps not available for lack of description or diagnosis; see also Su et al. 1986:109 [ref. 12582]. Tetraodontidae.

Epiphthalmus Rafinesque 1815:86 [ref. 3584]. Masc. *Gobiomoroides piso* Lacepède 1800:592 (= *Gobius pisonis* Gmelin 1789:1206). Type by being a replacement name. As "*Epiphthalmus* R. [Rafinesque] *Gobiomoroides* Lac. [Lacepède]." Unneeded replacement for and objective synonym of *Gobiomoroides* Lacepède 1800. Synonym of *Eleotris* Bloch & Schneider 1801 (Maugé 1986:391 [ref. 6218]). Eleotridae.

Epiplatys Gill 1862:136 [ref. 1661]. Masc. *Epiplatys sexfasciatus* Gill 1862:136. Type by subsequent designation. Earliest type designation found that of Jordan 1919:314 [ref. 4904]. Valid (Parenti 1981:474 [ref. 7066], Wildekamp et al. 1986:244 [ref. 6198]). Aplocheilidae: Aplocheilinae.

Episema Cope & Jordan in Jordan 1877:77 [ref. 2372]. Neut. *Photogenis scabriceps* Cope 1868:166. Type by original designation. Preoccupied by Ochsenheimer 1816 in Lepidoptera, replaced by *Paranotropis* Fowler 1904. On Official Index (Opinion 494). Synonym of *Notropis* Rafinesque 1818 (Gilbert 1978:15 [ref. 7042]). Cyprinidae.

Episemion (subgenus of *Epiplatys*) Radda & Pürzl 1987:18 [ref. 12592]. Neut. *Episemion callipteron* Radda & Pürzl 1987:18. Type by monotypy. The authors also treated the name as a valid genus. Aplocheilidae: Aplocheilinae.

Epitomynis (subgenus of *Salmo*) Schulze 1890:174 [25] [ref. 3984]. *Salmo hucho* Linnaeus 1758:309. Type by subsequent designation. On p. 25 of 1892 edition [original not seen]. Type apparently first designated by Jordan 1920:448 [ref. 4905]. Objective synonym of *Hucho* Günther 1866. Salmonidae: Salmoninae.

Epitrachys (subgenus of *Perca*) Schulze 1890:209 [89] [ref. 3984]. Fem. *Perca fluviatilis* Linnaeus 1758:289. Type by monotypy. On p. 89 of 1892 edition [original not seen]. Preoccupied by Ehlers 1869 in Vermes. Objective synonym of *Perca* Linnaeus 1758 (Collette & Banarescu 1977:1452 [ref. 5845]). Percidae.

Epsilonraia (subgenus of *Raja*) Leigh-Sharpe 1925:568, 574 [ref. 5748]. Fem. *Raja platana* Günther 1880:11. Type by original designation. As a "Psudogenus" of *Raia* [= *Raja*]. Not available [Art. 1b (6)], used as an artificial category (see Leigh-Sharpe 1928 [ref. 6152]). In the synonymy of *Raja* Linnaeus 1758. Rajidae.

Eptatretus Cloquet (ex Duméril) 1819:134 [ref. 852]. Masc. *Gastrobranche dombey* Lacepède 1798:414. Type by monotypy. Spelled *Heptatremus* by Swainson 1838:197, 338 [ref. 4302] on Duméril's *Heptatrema* and as *Heptatretus* by authors. According to Wisner & McMillan 1986:240, the type is "apparently a myxinid, but genus and species indeterminate." Valid (Shimizu in Uyeno et al. 1983:43 [ref. 14275], Hensley 1985 [ref. 6783], Fernholm 1986:35 [ref. 6283], Wisner & McMillan 1988 [ref. 6335], Paxton et al. 1989:25 [ref. 12442]). Myxinidae: Eptatretinae.

Eques Bloch 1793:90 [ref. 4868]. Masc. *Eques americanus* Bloch 1793:91. Type by monotypy. Preoccupied by Linnaeus 1758 in Lepidoptera, replaced by *Equetus* Rafinesque 1815. Objective synonym of *Equetus* Rafinesque 1815 (Chao 1978:27 [ref. 6983]). Sciaenidae.

Equetus Rafinesque 1815:86 [ref. 3584]. *Eques americanus* Bloch 1793:91. Type by being a replacement name. As "*Equetus* R. [Rafinesque] *Eques* Bl. [Bloch]." Available replacement name for *Eques* Bloch 1793 (preoccupied by Linnaeus 1758 in Lepidoptera). *Equietus* is a misspelling. Valid (Chao 1978:27 [ref. 6983], Uyeno & Sato in Uyeno et al. 1983:362 [ref. 14275]). Sciaenidae.

Equula Cuvier 1815:462 [ref. 1019]. Fem. *Centrogaster equula* of Gmelin 1788 (= *Scomber equula* Forsskål 1775:58). Type by absolute tautonymy. Cuvier stated (p. 463), "...je nommerai *equula*"; it was Cuvier's style in this article to begin generic names with a lower case letter. Synonym of *Leiognathus* Lacepède 1802 (Tortonese 1973:390 [ref. 7192], James 1978:141 [ref. 5317]). Leiognathidae.

Equulites (subgenus of *Leiognathus*) Fowler 1904:513 [ref. 1367]. Masc. *Leiognathus vermiculatus* Fowler 1904:513. Type by original designation. Synonym of *Leiognathus* Lacepède 1802 (Böhlke 1984:119 [ref. 13621]). Leiognathidae.

Eremichthys Hubbs & Miller 1948:14 [ref. 2258]. Masc. *Eremichthys acros* Hubbs & Miller 1948:20. Type by original designation (also monotypic). Valid (Robins et al. 1980:21 [ref. 7111]). Cyprinidae.

Eremophilus Humboldt 1805:35 [ref. 2278]. Masc. *Eremophilus mutisii* Humboldt 1805:35. Type by monotypy. Original not examined; two publications may be involved. Variously given as 1805:35, 1806:17 and 1811 (not investigated). Valid (Pinna 1989:31 [ref. 12630], Burgess 1989:323 [ref. 12860]). Trichomycteridae.

Erethistes (subgenus of *Bagrus*) Müller & Troschel 1849:12 [ref. 3073]. Masc. *Erethistes pusillus* Müller & Troschel 1849:12. Type by monotypy. Date may be 1845 as given by Kottelat. Valid (Jayaram 1981:243 [ref. 6497], Kottelat 1983 [ref. 5289], Burgess 1989:132 [ref. 12860], Kottelat 1989:15 [ref. 13605]). Sisoridae.

Erethistoides Hora 1950:190 [ref. 2214]. Masc. *Erethistoides montana* Hora 1950:191. Type by original designation (also monotypic). Valid (Jayaram 1981:243 [ref. 6497], Burgess 1989:132 [ref. 12860]). Possibly a synonym of *Erethistes* Müller & Troschel 1849 [?1845] (Kottelat 1983:73 [ref. 5289]). Sisoridae.

Eretmichthys Garman 1899:164 [ref. 1540]. Masc. *Eretmichthys pinnatus* Garman 1899:165. Type by subsequent designation. Earliest type designation found that by Jordan 1920:486 [ref. 4905]. Valid (Cohen & Nielsen 1978:31 [ref. 881], Machida 1989:189 [ref. 13417]). Ophidiidae.

Eretmobrycon Fink 1976:332 [ref. 1330]. Masc. *Eretmobrycon bayano* Fink 1976:334. Type by original designation (also monotypic). Characidae.

Eretmodus Boulenger 1898:16 [ref. 547]. Masc. *Eretmodus cyanostictus* Boulenger 1898:16. Type by monotypy. Valid (Poll 1986:88 [ref. 6136]). Cichlidae.

Eretmophorus Giglioli 1889:328 [ref. 1621]. Masc. *Eretmophorus kleinenbergi* Giglioli 1889:328. Type by monotypy. Valid (Cohen 1973:322 [ref. 6589], Fahay & Markle 1984:266 [ref. 13653], Cohen in Whitehead et al. 1986:714 [ref. 13676]). Moridae.

Ereunias Jordan & Snyder 1901:377 [ref. 2503]. Masc. *Ereunias grallator* Jordan & Snyder 1901:378. Type by monotypy. Valid (Yabe 1981 [ref. 5547], Washington et al. 1984:443 [ref. 13660], Yabe in Masuda et al. 1984:323 [ref. 6441], Yabe 1985:122 [ref. 11522]). Ereuniidae.

Ericara Gill & Townsend 1897:232 [ref. 1749]. Neut. *Ericara salmonea* Gill & Townsend 1897:232. Type by monotypy. Valid (Paxton et al. 1989:210 [ref. 12442]). Alepocephalidae.

Ericentrus Gill 1893:119, 123 [ref. 1736]. Masc. *Sticharium rubrum* Hutton 1872:33. Type by monotypy. Clinidae.

Erichaeta Jordan in Klippart 1877:48 [ref. 2375]. Fem. *Pomotis incisor* Valenciennes in Cuvier & Valenciennes 1831:350. Type by monotypy. Appeared in brief letter to Klippart in footnote on p. 48; Jordan 1877 used the name *Helioperca* instead; Jordan 1919:391 [ref. 4904] says "A slip for *Helioperca* due to uncorrected proof." In the synonymy of *Lepomis* Rafinesque 1819. Centrarchidae.

Ericius Tilesius 1809:243 [ref. 4406]. Masc. *Monocentris carinata* Bloch & Schneider 1801:100. Appeared without species, but *Ericius* was proposed for the same species that Bloch & Schneider, p. 100, called *Monocentris*; possibly can be regarded as a replacement for or alternate name for *Monocentris* Bloch & Schneider 1801. In the synonymy of *Monocentris* Bloch & Schneider 1801. Monocentridae.

Ericosma Jordan & Copeland in Jordan 1877:8 [ref. 2374]. *Alvordius evides* Jordan & Copeland 1877:51. Type by original designation (also monotypic). Synonym of *Percina* Haldeman 1842, but as a valid subgenus (Page 1974:83 [ref. 3346], Collette & Banarescu 1977:1454 [ref. 5845]). Percidae.

Ericteis Jordan 1904:543 [ref. 2400]. Masc. *Ericteis kalisherae* Jordan 1904:543. Type by original designation (also monotypic). Synonym of *Labrisomus* Swainson 1839 (Hubbs 1953:117 [ref. 2253], Springer 1958:422 [ref. 10210]). Labrisomidae.

Ericymba Cope 1865:88 [ref. 907]. Fem. *Ericymba buccata* Cope 1865:88. Type by monotypy. Valid (authors); synonym of *Notropus* Rafinesque 1818 (Coburn & Cavender, pers. comm.). Cyprinidae.

Eridacnis Smith 1913:599 [ref. 4044]. *Eridacnis radcliffei* Smith 1913:599. Type by original designation (also monotypic). Valid (Compagno 1984:372 [ref. 6846], Bass & Compagno 1986:87 [ref. 5637], Compagno 1988:185 [ref. 13488]). Proscylliidae.

Erilepis Gill 1894:52 [ref. 1737]. Fem. *Myriolepis zonifer* Lockington 1880:248. Type by being a replacement name. Replacement for *Myriolepis* Lockington 1880, preoccupied by Egerton 1864 in fossil fishes. Valid (Washington et al. 1984:442 [ref. 13660], Amaoka in Masuda et al. 1984:320 [ref. 6441]). Anoplopomatidae.

Erimonax Jordan 1924:52 [ref. 2423]. Masc. *Ceratichthys monacus* Cope 1868:227. Type by original designation (also monotypic). Synonym of *Cyprinella* Girard 1856 (Coburn & Cavender, pers. comm.). Cyprinidae.

Erimystax Jordan 1882:858 [ref. 2383]. Masc. *Luxilus dissimilis* Kirtland 1840:341. Type by original designation. Valid. Cyprinidae.

Erimyzon Jordan 1876:95 [ref. 2370]. Masc. *Cyprinus oblongus* Mitchill 1814:23. Type by original designation. Valid. Catostomidae.

Erinemus Jordan 1876:279 [ref. 2371]. Masc. *Ceratichthys hyalinus* Cope 1868:180. Type by subsequent designation. Original not examined. Type designated by Jordan & Gilbert 1877:95 [ref. 4907]. Synonym of *Hybopsis* Agassiz 1854 (Gilbert 1978:17 [ref. 7042]); as a valid subgenus of *Notropis* Rafinesque 1818 (Coburn & Cavender, pers. comm.). Cyprinidae.

Eriscion (subgenus of *Cynoscion*) Jordan & Evermann 1927:506 [ref. 2453]. Masc. *Cynoscion nebulosus* Cuvier in Cuvier & Valenciennes 1830:79. Type by original designation (also monotypic). Synonym of *Cynoscion* Gill 1861 (Chao 1978:34 [ref. 6983]). Sciaenidae.

Erisphex Jordan & Starks 1904:169 [ref. 2527]. Masc. *Cocotropus pottii* Steindachner 1896:203. Type by original designation. Valid (Poss & Eschmeyer 1978:404 [ref. 6387], Washington et al. 1984:441 [ref. 13660], Nakabo in Masuda et al. 1984:319 [ref. 6441]). Aploactinidae.

Eritrema (subgenus of *Apocope*) Cope & Yarrow 1875:645 [ref. 968]. Neut. *Apocope henshavii* Cope 1874:133. Type by subsequent designation. Type designated by Jordan & Gilbert 1877:95 [ref. 4907]. Synonym of *Rhinichthys* Agassiz 1849. Cyprinidae.

Ernogrammoides Chen & Liang 1948:32 [ref. 823]. Masc. *Ernogrammoides fasciatus* Chen & Liang 1948:32. Type by original designation (also monotypic). Valid (Yoshino & Kishimoto in

Masuda et al. 1984:141 [ref. 6441]); synonym of *Belonepterygion* McCulloch 1915 (Hardy 1985:375 [ref. 5184]). Acanthoclinidae.

Ernogrammus Jordan & Evermann 1898:2441 [ref. 2445]. Masc. *Stichaeus enneagrammus* Kner 1868:30. Type by monotypy. Valid (Amaoka & Miki in Masuda et al. 1984:302 [ref. 6441], Yatsu 1986:664 [ref. 5150], Follett & Powell 1988 [ref. 6234]). Stichaeidae.

Ernstichthys Fernández-Yépez 1953:3, 4 [ref. 1322]. Masc. *Ernstichthys anduzei* Fernández-Yépez 1953:5. Type by original designation (also monotypic). Valid (Stewart 1985:12 [ref. 5239], Mees 1988:91 [ref. 6401], Burgess 1989:304 [ref. 12860]). Aspredinidae: Bunocephalinae.

Erogala (subgenus of *Codoma*) Jordan in Jordan & Brayton 1878:20 [ref. 2436]. Neut. *Photogenis stigmaturus* Jordan 1876:377. Type by original designation. Synonym of *Notropis* Rafinesque 1818; synonym of subgenus *Cyprinella* Girard 1856 (Gilbert 1978:16 [ref. 7042]); synonym of *Cyprinella* Girard 1857 (Mayden 1989:45 [ref. 12555]). Cyprinidae.

Erosa Swainson 1839:61 [ref. 4303]. Fem. *Synanceia erosa* Langsdorf in Cuvier in Cuvier & Valenciennes 1829:459. Type by monotypy. As *Bufichthys* on p. 181 and as subgenus *Synanchia* on p. 268; see Eschmeyer & Rama-Rao 1973:363 [ref. 6391] for discussion. Type established based on equivalence of names, but technically may need a subsequent application of species and a type designation. Valid (Eschmeyer & Rama-Rao 1973:363 [ref. 6391], Washington et al. 1984:440 [ref. 13660], Shimizu in Masuda et al. 1984:318 [ref. 6441], Paxton et al. 1989:441 [ref. 12442]). Scorpaenidae: Synanceiinae.

Erotelis Poey 1860:272 [ref. 3499]. Fem. *Erotelis valenciennesi* Poey 1860:273. Type apparently by monotypy [not translated]; type usually given as designated by Jordan & Eigenmann 1886:484 [ref. 8016]. Valid (Birdsong et al. 1988:181 [ref. 7303]). Eleotridae.

Erpetoichthys Smith 1865:273 [ref. 4061]. Masc. *Erpetoichthys calabaricus* Smith 1865:278. Type by monotypy. Unjustifiably emended or misspelled *Herpetoichthys* by authors. Apparently not preoccupied by *Erpichthys* Swainson 1838 in fishes; replacement *Calamoichthys* Smith 1866 not needed. Should be treated as valid; see *Calamoichthys*. Polypteridae.

Erpicthys (subgenus of *Salarias*) Swainson 1839:79, 182, 275 [ref. 4303]. Masc. *Salarias quadripennis* Cuvier 1817:251. Type by subsequent designation. Type designated by Swain 1882:279 [ref. 5966]. Misspelled *Erpichthys* by Swainson 1839:439 (index). Synonym of *Salarias* Cuvier 1816 (Smith-Vaniz & Springer 1971:38 [ref. 4145]). Blenniidae.

Errex Jordan 1919:343 [ref. 2413]. Masc. *Glyptocephalus zachirus* Lockington 1879:42. Type by original designation (also monotypic). Synonym of *Glyptocephalus* Gottsche 1835 (Norman 1934:363 [ref. 6893]); valid (Sakamoto 1984 [ref. 5273]). Pleuronectidae: Pleuronectinae.

Erychthys (subgenus of *Petronason*) Swainson 1839:172, 226 [ref. 4303]. Masc. *Scarus croicensis* Bloch 1790:27. Type by subsequent designation. Spelled *Erycthys* on p. 172; *Erychthys* on 226 and 439 (index). Type designated by Swain 1883:274 [ref. 5966]. Synonym of *Scarus* Forsskål 1775. Scaridae: Scarinae.

Erythrichthus (subgenus of *Cichlasoma*) Meek 1907:118, 121 [ref. 2959]. Masc. *Heros citrinellus* Günther 1864:153. Type by original designation. Cichlidae.

Erythrichthys Bonaparte 1831:182 [ref. 4978]. Masc. *Synodus erythrinus* Bloch & Schneider 1801:397. Appeared as "*Erythrichthys*, Nob. (*Erythrinus*, Gr.)." Unneeded replacement for *Erythrinus* Scopoli (ex Gronow) 1777. Objective synonym of *Erythrinus* Scopoli 1777. Erythrinidae.

Erythrichthys Temminck & Schlegel 1845:117 [ref. 4373]. Masc. *Emmelichthys schlegelii* Richardson 1846:272. Type by subsequent monotypy. Original description without species; one species added by Richardson 1846:372 [ref. 3742] and *Erythrichthys* synonymized with *Emmelichthys*. Preoccupied by Bonaparte 1831 in fishes, replaced by *Erythrocles* Jordan 1919. Objective synonym of *Erythrocles* Jordan 1919 (Heemstra & Randall 1977:371 [ref. 7057]). Emmelichthyidae.

Erythrinus Gronow 1763:114 [ref. 1910]. Masc. Not available, published in a rejected work on Official Index (Opinion 261). Erythrinidae.

Erythrinus Plumier in Lacepède 1802:347 (footnote) [ref. 4929]. Masc. Not available. Name without description (as *Erythrinus polygrammos*) mentioned in passing under *Holocentrus sogo*. See remarks under Opinion 89 in Appendix B. In the synonymy of *Holocentrus* Scopoli 1777 (Woods & Sonoda 1973:333 [ref. 6899]). Holocentridae.

Erythrinus Scopoli (ex Gronow) 1777:449 [ref. 3990]. Masc. *Synodus erythrinus* Bloch & Schneider 1801:397. Type by subsequent designation. Appeared without species, earliest addition of species not researched; type possibly designated first by Eigenmann & Eigenmann 1889:105 [ref. 12497], but the type of *Erythrinus* of authors was first designated by Bory de Saint-Vincent, v. 6, 1824:293 [ref. 3853] and may suffice (see Whitley 1935:137 [ref. 6396]). Misspelled *Eritrinus* by Jordan 1917:72 [ref. 2407]. Valid (Géry 1977:103 [ref. 1597]). Erythrinidae.

Erythrobussothen Parr 1933:31 [ref. 3373]. *Erythrobussothen gracilis* Parr 1933:32. Type by original designation (also monotypic). Synonym of *Etelis* Cuvier 1828 (Anderson & Fourmanoir 1975 [ref. 6028]). Not treated by Allen 1985 [ref. 6843] in world review of Lutjanidae. Lutjanidae.

Erythrocles Jordan 1919:342 [ref. 2413]. Masc. *Erythrichthys schlegelii* Richardson 1846:372. Type by being a replacement name. Replacement for *Erythrichthys* Temminck & Schlegel 1845, preoccupied by Bonaparte 1831 in fishes. Valid (Heemstra & Randall 1977:371 [ref. 7057], Mochizuki in Masuda et al. 1984:160 [ref. 6441], Heemstra 1986:638 [ref. 5660]). Emmelichthyidae.

Erythroculter (subgenus of *Culter*) Berg 1909:138 [ref. 5116]. Masc. *Culter erythropterus* Basilewski 1855:236. Type by subsequent designation. Type apparently first designated by Nichols and Pope 1927:371 [ref. 5747]. Valid (Yih & Wu 1964:97 [ref. 13499], Chen in Chu & Chen 1989:89 [ref. 13584]). Cyprinidae.

Erythrodon Rüppell 1852:34 [ref. 3846]. Masc. *Xenodon niger* Rüppell 1837:53. Type by being a replacement name. Replacement for *Xenodon* Rüppell 1836, preoccupied in Amphibia; replaced earlier by *Odonus* Gistel 1848. Objective synonym of *Odonus* Gistel 1848 (Matsuura 1980:33 [ref. 6943]). Balistidae.

Escadotus (subgenus of *Aspidontus*) Smith 1959:235 [ref. 4123]. Masc. *Petroscirtes fluctuans* Weber 1909:149. Type by original designation. Objective synonym of *Oncesthes* Jordan & Hubbs 1925; synonym of *Aspidontus* Cuvier 1834 (Smith-Vaniz 1976:53 [ref. 4144]). Blenniidae.

Eschmeyer Poss & Springer 1983:309 [ref. 5394]. Masc. *Eschmeyer nexus* Poss & Springer 1983:310. Type by original designation (also monotypic). Valid (Washington et al. 1984:441 [ref. 13660],

Poss 1986:955 [ref. 6331]). Aploactinidae.

Escolar Jordan & Evermann in Goode & Bean 1896:519 [ref. 1848]. *Thyrsitops violaceus* Bean 1887:513. Type by monotypy. Called *Bipinnula* in Jordan & Evermann 1896:877 (3 Oct., ref. 2443) through slip in proof-reading. Synonym of *Nesiarchus* Johnson 1862 (Parin & Bekker 1973:459 [ref. 7206], Nakamura et al. 1981:340 [ref. 5477]). Gempylidae.

Escualosa Whitley 1940:402 [ref. 4699]. Fem. *Clupea macrolepis* Steindachner 1879:13. Type by original designation (also monotypic). Valid (Grande 1985:250 [ref. 6466], Whitehead 1985:118 [ref. 5141], Kottelat 1989:4 [ref. 13605], Paxton et al. 1989:152 [ref. 12442]). Clupeidae.

Eslopsarum Jordan & Evermann 1896:330 [ref. 2442]. Neut. *Chirostoma jordani* Woolman 1894:62. Type by original designation. Misspelled *Elopsarum* by Schultz 1948:30 [ref. 3966]. Synonym of *Chirostoma* Swainson 1839. Atherinidae: Menidiinae.

Esloscopus (subgenus of *Dactyloscopus*) Jordan & Evermann 1896:465 [ref. 2442]. Masc. *Dactyloscopus zelotes* Jordan & Gilbert in Jordan & Evermann 1896:465. Type by original designation (also monotypic). Synonym of *Dactyloscopus* Gill 1859 (Dawson 1975:5 [ref. 7121], Dawson 1982:19 [ref. 1072]). Dactyloscopidae.

Esomus (subgenus of *Leuciscus*) Swainson 1839:185, 285 [ref. 4303]. Masc. *Esomus vittatus* Swainson 1839:285 (= *Cyprinus danrica* Hamilton 1822:325, 390). Type by monotypy. Swainson's *E. vittatus* is an unneeded new name for *C. danrica* Hamilton (Swainson's reference to "Ham. f. 88" is Hamilton, Pl. 16, fig. 88). Valid (Jayaram 1981:77 [ref. 6497], Kottelat 1985:262 [ref. 11441], Kottelat 1989:7 [ref. 13605]). Cyprinidae.

Esosynodus (subgenus of *Synodus*) Whitley 1937:219 [ref. 4690]. Masc. *Saurus lucioceps* Ayres 1855:69. Type by original designation (also monotypic). Synonym of *Synodus* Scopoli 1777 (Anderson et al. 1966:46 [ref. 6977]). Synodontidae: Synodontinae.

Esox Linnaeus 1758:313 [ref. 2787]. Masc. *Esox lucius* Linnaeus 1758:314. Type by subsequent designation. Type designated by Jordan & Gilbert 1883:352 [ref. 2476]. On Official List (Opinion 92, Direction 56). Valid (Crossman 1978:15 [ref. 6974], Martin 1984:140 [ref. 13639]). Esocidae.

Estevea Whitley 1953:133 [ref. 4718]. Fem. *Barbus (Hemigrammocapoeta) mirei* Estève 1952:177. Type by being a replacement name. Replacement for *Hemigrammocapoeta* Estève 1952, preoccupied by Pellegrin 1927 in same family. Synonym of *Barbus* Cuvier & Cloquet 1816 (Lévêque & Daget 1984:219 [ref. 6186]). Cyprinidae.

Estrella Girard 1859:65 [ref. 1821]. Fem. *Estrella atromaculata* Girard 1859:66. Type by monotypy. Synonym of subgenus *Boleosoma* DeKay 1842 of genus *Etheostoma* Rafinesque 1819 (Collette & Banarescu 1977:1456 [ref. 5845]). Percidae.

Esunculus Kaup 1856:143 [ref. 2573]. Masc. *Esunculus costai* Kaup 1856:143. Type by monotypy. Synonym (leptocephalus) of *Albula* Scopoli 1771 (Whitehead 1986:216 [ref. 5733], but genus credited to Cope). Albulidae: Albulinae.

Etaraia (subgenus of *Raja*) Leigh-Sharpe 1924:568, 576 [ref. 5748]. Fem. *Raja murrayi* Günther 1880:15. Type by original designation (also monotypic). As a "pseudogenus" of *Raia* [=*Raja*]. Not available [Art 1b (6)], used as an artificial category (see Leigh-Sharpe 1928 [ref. 6152]). In the synonymy of *Bathyraja* Ishiyama 1958. Rajidae.

Eteira Kaup 1860:137, 147 [ref. 2583]. Fem. *Chaetodon triangularis* Rüppell 1828:42. Type by subsequent designation. Type designated by Jordan 1919:297 [ref. 2410]. Synonym of *Chaetodon* Linnaeus 1758, subgenus *Megaprotodon* Guichenot 1848 (Burgess 1978:415 [ref. 700]). Synonym of *Megaprotodon* Guichenot 1848 (Maugé & Bauchot 1984:464 [ref. 6614]). Chaetodontidae.

Etelides Jordan & Thompson 1905:241 [ref. 2538]. Masc. *Etelis aquilionaris* Goode & Bean 1896:238. Type by monotypy. Synonym of *Etelis* Cuvier 1828 (Allen 1985:24 [ref. 6843]); synonym of *Pristipomoides* Bleeker 1852 (Akazaki & Iwatsuki 1987:326 [ref. 6699]). Lutjanidae.

Etelinus Jordan in Jordan & Thompson 1911:465 [ref. 2540]. Masc. *Etelis marshi* Jenkins 1903:452. Type by original designation (also monotypic). Synonym of *Etelis* Cuvier 1828 (Allen 1985:24 [ref. 6843]). Lutjanidae.

Etelis Cuvier in Cuvier & Valenciennes 1828:127 [ref. 997]. Masc. *Etelis carbunculus* Cuvier in Cuvier & Valenciennes 1828:127. Type by monotypy. Spelled *Eteles* by Swainson 1839:127, 202 [ref. 4303]. Valid (Johnson 1980:9 [ref. 13553], Yoshino in Masuda et al. 1984:167 [ref. 6441], Allen 1985:24 [ref. 6843], Anderson 1981 [ref. 5433], Anderson 1986:573 [ref. 5634], Akazaki & Iwatsuki 1986:601 [ref. 6316]). Lutjanidae.

Eteliscus Jordan & Snyder 1900:355 [ref. 2502]. Masc. *Etelis berycoides* Hilgendorf 1879:78. Type by monotypy. By mistake spelled *Corusculus* in Jordan & Snyder 1901:75 [ref. 2505]. Acropomatidae.

Ethadophis Rosenblatt & McCosker 1970:498 [ref. 3809]. Masc. *Ethadophis byrnei* Rosenblatt & McCosker 1970:499. Type by original designation. Valid (McCosker 1977:72 [ref. 6836], McCosker & Böhlke 1984:40 [ref. 5316], McCosker et al. 1989:341 [ref. 13288]). Ophichthidae: Ophichthinae.

Etheostoma Rafinesque 1819:419 [ref. 3590]. Neut. *Etheostoma blennioides* Rafinesque 1819:419. Type by subsequent designation. Type designated by Agassiz 1854:304 [ref. 69], and confirmed as type species by ICZN (Opinion 14). Valid (Collette & Banarescu 1977:1455 [ref. 5845], Page 1981:28 [ref. 3347], Bailey & Etnier 1988:12 [ref. 6873]). Percidae.

Ethmalosa Regan 1917:302 [ref. 3665]. Fem. *Alausa dorsalis* Valenciennes in Cuvier & Valenciennes 1847:418. Type by monotypy. Valid (Poll et al. 1984:42 [ref. 6172], Grande 1985:249 [ref. 6466], Whitehead 1985:218 [ref. 5141]). Clupeidae.

Ethmidium Thompson 1916:458 [ref. 4391]. Neut. *Clupea (Alosa) notacanthoides* Steindachner 1869:309. Type by original designation (also monotypic). Valid (Grande 1985:249 [ref. 6466], Whitehead 1985:217 [ref. 5141]). Clupeidae.

Etmopterus Rafinesque 1810:14 [ref. 3594]. Masc. *Etmopterus aculeatus* Rafinesque 1810:14. Type by monotypy. Valid (Krefft & Tortonese 1973:42 [ref. 7165], Compagno 1984:69 [ref. 6474], Nakaya & Shirai in Masuda et al. 1984:9 [ref. 6441], Springer & Burgess 1985 [ref. 6785], Bass et al. 1986:55 [ref. 5636], Yamakawa et al. 1986 [ref. 5729], Cappetta 1987:58 [ref. 6348], Yano 1988 [ref. 6695], Paxton et al. 1989:34 [ref. 12442]). Squalidae.

Etroplus Cuvier in Cuvier & Valenciennes 1830:486 [ref. 999]. Masc. *Etroplus meleagris* Cuvier in Cuvier & Valenciennes 1830:486 (= *Chaetodon suratensis* Bloch 1790:Pl. 217). Type by subsequent designation. Type apparently designated first by Bleeker [not researched]. Bloch's species *suratensis* needlessly renamed *meleagris* by Cuvier. Valid (Jayaram 1981:337 [ref.

6497]). Cichlidae.

Etropus Jordan & Gilbert 1882:364 [ref. 2470]. Masc. *Etropus crossotus* Jordan & Gilbert 1882:364. Type by monotypy. Valid (Norman 1934:154 [ref. 6893], Matsuura in Uyeno et al. 1983:455 [ref. 14275], Ahlstrom et al. 1984:642 [ref. 13641], Leslie & Stewart 1986:140 [ref. 5948]). Paralichthyidae.

Etrumeus Bleeker 1853:48 [ref. 340]. Masc. *Clupea micropus* Schlegel in Temminck & Schlegel 1846:236. Type by monotypy. Valid (Whitehead & Ben-Tuvia 1973:110 [ref. 7170], Uyeno & Sato in Masuda et al. 1984:18 [ref. 6441], Grande 1985:248 [ref. 6466], Whitehead 1985:30 [ref. 5141], Whitehead & Wongratana 1986:200 [ref. 6284], Paxton et al. 1989:153 [ref. 12442]). Clupeidae.

Euacanthagenys Fowler 1945:123 [ref. 1454]. Fem. *Loricaria caquetae* Fowler 1943:261. Type by original designation (also monotypic). Synonym of *Spatuloricaria* Schultz 1944 (Isbrücker 1980:112 [ref. 2303]). Loricariidae.

Euanemus Müller & Troschel in Müller 1842:203 [ref. 3062]. Masc. *Euanemus columbetes* Müller & Troschel in Müller 1842:203. Type by monotypy. Also appeared in Müller 1843:318 [ref. 3063]. Synonym of *Auchenipterus* Valenciennes 1840 (Mees 1974:16 [ref. 2969]). Auchenipteridae.

Eubalichthys Whitley 1930:179 [ref. 5811]. Masc. *Monacanthus mosaicus* Ramsay & Ogilby 1886:5. Type by original designation (also monotypic). Valid (Hutchins 1977:28 [ref. 2283], Matsuura 1979:165 [ref. 7019], Tyler 1980:183 [ref. 4477], Arai 1983:199 [ref. 14249]). Monacanthidae.

Eubleekeria (subgenus of *Leiognathus*) Fowler 1904:516 [ref. 1367]. Fem. *Equula splendens* Cuvier 1829:212. Type by original designation. Synonym of *Leiognathus* Lacepède 1802 (James 1978:141 [ref. 5317]). Leiognathidae.

Eucalia Jordan 1876:248 [ref. 2371]. Fem. *Gasterosteus inconstans* Kirtland 1841:273. Type by monotypy. Described with one included species plus two additional varieties. More complete treatment in Jordan 1877:65 [ref. 2372]. Preoccupied by Felder 1861 in Lepidoptera; replaced by *Culaea* Whitley 1950. Objective synonym of *Culaea* Whitley 1950. Gasterosteidae: Gasterosteinae.

Eucentrarchus Gill 1864:93 [ref. 1706]. Masc. *Labrus irideus* Lacepède 1802:716. Type by monotypy. Objective synonym of *Centrarchus* Cuvier 1829. Centrarchidae.

Eucentronotus Ogilby 1898:294 [ref. 3276]. Masc. *Eucentronotus zietzi* Ogilby 1898:294. Type by monotypy. Synonym of *Peronedys* Steindachner 1884 (George & Springer 1980:24 [ref. 6935]). Clinidae.

Euchalarodus Gill 1864:216 [ref. 1704]. Masc. *Euchalarodus putnami* Gill 1864:216. Type by monotypy. Described in more detail in Gill 1864:221-223 [ref. 5773]. Synonym of *Liopsetta* Gill 1864 (Norman 1934:368 [ref. 6893]). Pleuronectidae: Pleuronectinae.

Euchilichthys Boulenger 1900:522 [ref. 554]. Masc. *Atopochilus guentheri* Schilthuis 1891:86. Type by subsequent designation. Type designated by Jordan 1920:488 [ref. 4905]). Valid (Gosse 1986:113 [ref. 6194], Burgess 1989:198 [ref. 12860], Roberts 1989:164 [ref. 13302]). Mochokidae.

Euchiloglanis Regan 1907:158 [ref. 12987]. Masc. *Chimarrichthys davidi* Sauvage 1874:333. Type by being a replacement name. Probably an unneeded replacement for *Chimarrichthys* Sauvage 1874, not preoccupied by *Cheimarrichthys* Haast 1874 [treatment in Zoological Record for 1874:95 perhaps can be regarded as an unjustified emendation, but that emendation is after 1874]. Treated as valid by Chu 1979 [ref. 831], Burgess 1989:133 [ref. 12860], and Kottelat 1989:15 [ref. 13605]. Sisoridae.

Euchilomycterus Waite 1900:208 [ref. 4558]. Masc. *Euchilomycterus quadradicatus* Waite 1900:208. Type by original designation (also monotypic). Synonym of *Diodon* Linnaeus 1758 (Fraser-Brunner 1943:17 [ref. 1495]). Diodontidae.

Euchoristopus Gill 1863:271 [ref. 1692]. Masc. *Gobius kolreuteri* Pallas 1770:8. Type by monotypy. Synonym of *Periophthalmus* Bloch & Schneider 1801 (Maugé 1986:399 [ref. 6218], Murdy 1989:30 [ref. 13628]). Gobiidae.

Eucinostomus Baird & Girard in Baird 1855:334 [20] [ref. 164]. Masc. *Eucinostomus argenteus* Baird & Girard in Baird 1855:335 [21]. Type by monotypy. On page 20 of separate. Authorship is as above, with "B. and G." given with the original description (interpretation by Hubbs & Miller 1965:7 [ref. 9217] is in error). Valid (Matheson & McEachran 1984 [ref. 5228], Roux 1986:325 [ref. 6209], Deckert & Greenfield 1987:184 [ref. 6778]). Gerreidae.

Eucirrhichthys Perugia 1892:1009 [ref. 3432]. Masc. *Eucirrhichthys doriae* Perugia 1892:1009. Type by monotypy. Originally described as a cyprinid. Misspelled *Eucirrichthys* in Zoological Record for 1892. Valid (Nalbant 1963:367 ref. 3140], Sawada 1982:202 [ref. 14111]); questionably a synonym of *Acanthophthalmus* [or *Acantophthalmus*] van Hasselt 1823 (Roberts 1989:95 [ref. 6439]); synonym of *Pangio* Blyth 1860 (Kottelat 1989:13 [ref. 13605]). Cobitidae: Cobitinae.

Eucitharus Gill 1889:599 [ref. 1730]. Masc. *Pleuronectes macrolepidotus* Bloch 1787:34, Pl. 190. Type by being a replacement name. Replacement for *Citharus* Bleeker 1862, preoccupied by Reinhardt 1838 in fishes but also predated by *Citharus* Rose 1793 in fishes. Norman 1934:168 [ref. 6893] does not accept *Citharus* Röse 1793 as available. Synonym of *Citharus* Röse 1793 (Nielsen 1973:615 [ref. 6885]); valid (Norman 1934:168 [ref. 6893], Ahlstrom et al. 1984:640 [ref. 13641], Aboussouan 1988 [ref. 12841]). Citharidae: Citharinae.

Euclichthys McCulloch 1926:174 [ref. 2947]. Masc. *Euclichthys polynemus* McCulloch 1926:174. Type by original designation (also monotypic). Family placement follows articles in Cohen 1989 [ref. 13632]. Valid (Paulin 1983:88 [ref. 5459], Cohen 1984:263 [ref. 13646], Fahay & Markle 1984:266 [ref. 13653], Paxton et al. 1989:299 [ref. 12442]). Euclichthyidae.

Euclyptosternum Günther 1864:182 [ref. 1974]. Neut. Apparently an unjustified emendation of *Aglyptosternon* Bleeker 1863. Synonym of *Glyptothorax* Blyth 1860 (Li 1986:522 [ref. 6132]). Sisoridae.

Eucrossorhinus Regan 1908:357 [ref. 3635]. Masc. *Crossorhinus dasypogon* Bleeker 1867:400. Type by monotypy. Valid (Compagno 1984:178 [ref. 6474], Paxton et al. 1989:89 [ref. 12442]). Orectolobidae.

Eucrotus Bean 1912:123 [ref. 232]. Masc. *Eucrotus ventralis* Bean 1912:123. Type by monotypy. Synonym of *Schedophilus* Cocco 1839 (Haedrich 1967:59 [ref. 5357]). Centrolophidae.

Eucryphycus Anderson 1988:93 [ref. 6021]. Masc. *Maynea californica* Starks & Mann 1911:16. Type by original designation (also monotypic). Zoarcidae.

Euctenogobius Gill 1859:45 [ref. 1754]. Masc. *Euctenogobius badius* Gill 1859:45. Type by monotypy. Synonym of *Chonophorus* Poey 1860 (Maugé 1986:363 [ref. 6218]). Synonym of *Awaous* Valenciennes 1837 (Hoese, pers. comm.). Gobiidae.

Eucyclogobius Gill 1862:279 [ref. 1666]. Masc. *Gobius newberryi*

Girard 1856:136. Type by original designation (also monotypic). Valid. Gobiidae.

Eucynopotamus Fowler 1904:119 [ref. 1364]. Masc. *Cynopotamus biserialis* Garman 1890:14. Type by being a replacement name. Replacement for *Evermannella* Eigenmann 1903, preoccupied by Fowler 1901 in fishes. Valid (Géry 1977:315 [ref. 1597]). Characidae.

Eucypsilurus (subgenus of *Cypsilurus [Cypselurus]*) Bruun 1935:84 [ref. 5130]. Masc. *Exocoetus heterurus* Rafinesque 1810:58. Type by original designation. Exocoetidae.

Eudontomyzon Regan 1911:200 [ref. 3640]. Masc. *Eudontomyzon danfordi* Regan 1911:200. Type by monotypy. Valid (Hubbs & Potter 1971:44 [ref. 13397]); as a subgenus of *Lampetra* (Bailey 1980:1627 [ref. 5253]). Petromyzontidae: Petromyzontinae.

Eudulus Fowler 1907:264 [ref. 1376]. Masc. *Dules auriga* Cuvier in Cuvier & Valenciennes 1829:112. Type by being a replacement name. Unneeded replacement for *Dules* Cuvier 1828, not preoccupied by *Dulus* Viellot 1816 in Aves. Replaced earlier by *Dulichthys* Bonaparte 1832. Objective synonym of *Dules* Cuvier 1829. Serranidae: Serraninae.

Eudynama Gistel 1848:XIII [ref. 1822]. Neut. *Sparus aurata* Linnaeus 1758:277. Type by being a replacement name. Unneeded replacement for *Chrysophris* Cuvier 1829, apparently not preoccupied. Objective synonym of *Sparus* Linnaeus 1758. Sparidae.

Euelatichthys (subgenus of *Plectorhinchus*) Fowler 1904:527 [ref. 1367]. Masc. *Diagramma affine* Günther 1859:319. Type by original designation (also monotypic). Synonym of *Plectorhinchus* Lacepède 1801. Haemulidae.

Eugaleus Gill 1864:148 [ref. 1697]. Masc. *Squalus galeus* Linnaeus 1758:234. Type by being a replacement name. Replacement for *Galeus* Cuvier 1816, preoccupied by Rafinesque 1810 in fishes. Objective synonym of *Galeorhinus* Blainville 1816 after type restrictions (Compagno 1973:27 [ref. 7163], Compagno 1984:386 [ref. 6846], Compagno 1988:247 [ref. 13488]). Triakidae: Galeorhininae.

Eugerres Jordan & Evermann 1927:506 [ref. 2453]. Masc. *Gerres plumieri* Cuvier in Cuvier & Valenciennes 1830:452. Type by original designation. Synonym of *Gerres* Quoy & Gaimard 1824 (Roux 1986:325 [ref. 6209]); valid (Deckert & Greenfield 1987:188 [ref. 6778]). Gerreidae.

Euglyptosternum Day (ex Bleeker) 1877:499 [ref. 4886]. Neut. Not an original description. "Aclyptostenon [sic.], Bleeker" listed in synonymy by Day; Bleeker spelled genus *Anglypsternon*. Misspelling of *Euclyptosternum* Günther 1864, an unjustified emendation of *Anglyptosternon*. Sisoridae.

Eugnathichthys Boulenger 1898:25 [ref. 4864]. Masc. *Eugnathichthys eetveldii* Boulenger 1898:26. Type by original designation (also monotypic). Valid (Géry 1977:90 [ref. 1597], Vari 1979:340 [ref. 5490] as *Eugnatichthys*, Daget & Gosse 1984:193 [ref. 6185]). Citharinidae: Distichodontinae.

Eugnathogobius Smith 1931:37 [ref. 4047]. Masc. *Eugnathogobius microps* Smith 1931:37. Type by monotypy. Valid (Kottelat 1989:19 [ref. 13605]). Gobiidae.

Eugnathosaurus Regan 1913:234 [ref. 3651]. Masc. *Eugnathosaurus vorax* Regan 1913:234. Type by original designation (also monotypic). Based on head only. Synonym of *Anotopterus* Zugmayer 1911. Alepisauridae.

Eugomphodus Gill 1861:60 [ref. 1766]. Masc. *Squalus griseus* Ayres 1842:58. Type by monotypy. Appeared first as above, with mention of *Eugomphodus griseus*. Opinion 1459 (reversing Opinion 723) makes *Carcharias* Rafinesque 1809 available over *Eugomphodus* when recognized as congeneric. Valid (Bass & Compagno 1986:104 [ref. 5637], but should be regarded as a synonym of *Carcharias*); synonym of fossil genus *Synodontaspis* (Cappetta 1987:90 [ref. 6348]); valid (Compagno 1984:215 [ref. 6474], Grande & Eastman 1986:122 [ref. 6054]). Odontaspididae: Odontaspidinae.

Euhypsocara Gill 1863:222 [ref. 1685]. Neut. *Cossyphus anthioides* of Günther (= *Crenilabrus anthioides* Bennett 1831:167). Type by original designation (also monotypic). Misspelled *Euphysocara* by Jordan 1919:325 [ref. 4904]. Labridae.

Eulamia Gill 1862:399, 401 [ref. 1783]. Fem. *Carcharias (Prionodon) milberti* Valenciennes in Müller & Henle 1841:38. Type by monotypy. Type (p. 401) as "*Eulamia lamia* Gill" which might refer to *C. lamia* Blainville but as given is a nomen nudum; Gill 1962:409 [ref. 4910] includes only *milberti*. Synonym of *Carcharhinus* Blainville 1816 (Compagno 1973:23 [ref. 7163], Garrick 1982:19 [ref. 5454], Cappetta 1987:121 [ref. 6348], Compagno 1988:307 [ref. 13488]). Carcharhinidae.

Eulepidorhamphus (subgenus of *Hyporhamphus*) Fowler 1919:7 [ref. 1397]. Masc. *Hemirhamphus sajori* Schlegel in Temminck & Schlegel 1846:246. Type by original designation (also monotypic). Correct spelling for genus of the type species is Hemiramphus. Synonym of *Hyporhamphus* Gill 1859 (Collette et al. 1984:337 [ref. 11422] based on placement of the type species). Hemiramphidae.

Euleptocephalus (subgenus of *Leptocephalus*) Strömman 1896:5 [ref. 4294]. Masc. *Leptocephalus sicanus* Facciolà 1883:5. Type by subsequent designation. Included species unclear, at least two. On p. 5 of separate [original not examined]. Type designated by Jordan 1920:470 [ref. 4905]. Synonym of *Gnathophis* Kaup 1860 (Castle 1969:11 [ref. 12436]). Congridae: Congrinae.

Euleptoeleotris Hildebrand 1938:351 [ref. 11966]. Fem. *Euleptoeleotris clarki* Hildebrand 1838:352. Type by original designation. Eleotridae.

Euleptorhamphus Gill 1859:156 [ref. 1757]. Masc. *Euleptorhamphus brevoortii* Gill 1859:156. Type by original designation. Valid (Parin et al. 1980:139 [ref. 6895], Yoshino in Masuda et al. 1984:80 [ref. 6441], Collette et al. 1984:336 [ref. 11422], Collette 1986:389 [ref. 5647], Collette & Su 1986:253 [ref. 5998], Paxton et al. 1989:336 [ref. 12442]). Hemiramphidae.

Eulinneela (subgenus of *Phoxinus*) Dybowski 1916:101 [ref. 6519]. Fem. *Cyprinus phoxinus* Linnaeus 1758:322. Original not seen. Synonym of *Phoxinus* Rafinesque 1820 (Howes 1985:66 [ref. 5274]). Cyprinidae.

Eulophias Smith 1902:93 [ref. 4039]. Masc. *Eulophias tanneri* Smith 1902:94. Type by original designation (also monotypic). Valid (Amaoka & Miki in Masuda et al. 1984:303 [ref. 6441]). Stichaeidae.

Eumakaira Hirasaka & Nakamura 1947:16 [ref. 2174]. Fem. *Eumakaira nigra* Hirasaka & Nakamura 1947:16. Type by monotypy. Synonym of *Makaira* Lacepède 1802 (de Sylva 1973:479 [ref. 7210], Nakamura 1983:321 [ref. 5371]). Istiophoridae.

Eumecichthys Regan 1907:638 [ref. 7317]. Masc. *Lophotes fiskii* Günther 1890:244. Type by monotypy. Valid (Olney 1984:369 [ref. 13656], Fujii in Masuda et al. 1984:116 [ref. 6441] as *Eumethichthys*, Heemstra 1986:402 [ref. 5660]). Lophotidae.

Eumeda Castelnau 1878:143 [ref. 763]. Fem. *Eumeda elongata*

Castelnau 1878:144. Type by monotypy. Fowler (MS) indicates the *Eumeda elongata* Castelnau is the same as *Plotosus elongatus* Castelnau, which makes *Eumeda* the senior objective synonym of *Euristhmus* Ogilby 1899. Plotosidae.

Eumegistus Jordan & Jordan 1922:35 [ref. 2487]. Masc. *Eumegistus illustris* Jordan & Jordan 1922:36. Type by original designation (also monotypic). Valid (Mead 1972:8 [ref. 6976], Mochizuki in Masuda et al. 1984:160 [ref. 6441], Yatsu & Nakamura 1989:190 [ref. 13449]). Bramidae.

Eumesogrammus Gill 1864:210 [ref. 1703]. Masc. *Clinus praecisus* Krøyer 1837:25. Type by monotypy. Valid. Stichaeidae.

Eumicrotremus Gill 1862:330 [ref. 1668]. Masc. *Cyclopterus spinosus* Müller 1777. Type by original designation. Valid (Lindberg 1973:608 [ref. 7220], Kido in Masuda et al. 1984:336 [ref. 6441], Kido 1984 [ref. 6731], Stein in Whitehead et al. 1986:1272 [ref. 13677]). Cyclopteridae: Cyclopterinae.

Eumycterias Jenkins 1901:399 [ref. 2340]. Masc. *Eumycterias bitaeniatus* Jenkins 1901:400. Type by monotypy. Synonym of *Canthigaster* Swainson 1839 (Allen & Randall 1977:478 [ref. 6714]). Tetraodontidae.

Eunarce (subgenus of *Narcobatus*) Fowler 1910:472 [ref. 1379]. Fem. *Torpedo narke* Risso 1810:10. Type by original designation. Synonym of *Torpedo* Houttuyn 1764 (Krefft & Stehmann 1973:55 [ref. 7167], Cappetta 1987:161 [ref. 6348]). Torpedinidae.

Eupallasella Dybowski 1916:100 [ref. 6519]. Fem. *Cyprinus percnurus* Pallas 1811:299. Type by monotypy. Original not seen. Valid (Howes 1985:61 [ref. 5274]). Cyprinidae.

Eupemis (subgenus of *Julis/Gomphosis*) Swainson 1839:173, 232 [ref. 4303]. *Labrus fusiformis* Rüppell 1835:7. Type by monotypy. As a subgenus of *Julis* on p. 173, as subgenus of *Gomphosis* on p. 232. Labridae.

Eupetrichthys Ramsay & Ogilby 1888:631 [ref. 3597]. Masc. *Eupetrichthys angustipes* Ramsay & Ogilby 1888:632. Type by monotypy. Valid (Russell 1988:41 [ref. 12549]). Labridae.

Euplatygaster (subgenus of *Ilisha*) Fowler 1934:246 [ref. 1416]. Fem. *Pellona brachysoma* Bleeker 1852:22. Type by original designation. Synonym of *Ilisha* Richardson 1846 (Poll et al. 1984:44 [ref. 6172], Whitehead 1985:261 [ref. 5141]). Clupeidae.

Eupleurogrammus Gill 1862:126 [ref. 1659]. Masc. *Trichiurus muticus* Gray 1831:10. Type by original designation (also monotypic). Valid (Collette et al. 1984:600 [ref. 11421], Nakamura in Masuda et al. 1984:228 [ref. 6441]). Trichiuridae: Lepidopinae.

Eupnoea Gistel 1848:105 [ref. 1822]. Fem. *Plagusia lactea* Bonaparte 1833:5. Type by monotypy. Synonym of *Symphurus* Rafinesque 1810. Cynoglossidae: Symphurinae.

Eupomacentrus Bleeker 1877:73 [ref. 454]. Masc. *Pomacentrus lividus* Bloch & Schneider 1801:235. Type by monotypy in subgenus. Also appeared in Bleeker 1877:40 [ref. 453]. Synonym of *Pomacentrus* Lacepède 1802 (Robins et al. 1980:48, 87 [ref. 7111]; synonym of *Stegastes* Jenyns 1840 (Shen & Chan 1978:220 [ref. 6945], Emery & Allen 1980 [ref. 6917], Allen & Emery 1985:8 [ref. 5236]). Pomacentridae.

Eupomotis Gill & Jordan in Gill 1877:190 [ref. 1745]. Fem. *Sparus aureus* Walbaum 1792:290. Type by monotypy. Synonym of *Lepomis* Rafinesque 1819. Centrarchidae.

Euporista Gistel 1848:X [ref. 1822]. *Pleuronectes plagiusa* Linnaeus 1766:455. Type by being a replacement name. Replacement for *Plagusia* Bonaparte, preoccupied. Synonym of *Symphurus* Rafinesque 1810. Cynoglossidae: Symphurinae.

Euproserpa (subgenus of *Microstoma*) Fowler 1934:256 [ref. 1416]. Fem. *Microstoma schmitti* Fowler 1934:256. Type by original designation (also monotypic). Synonym of *Nansenia* Jordan & Evermann 1896. Microstomatidae.

Euprotomicroides Hulley & Penrith 1966:222 [ref. 2277]. Masc. *Euprotomicroides zantedeschia* Hulley & Penrith 1966:222. Type by monotypy. Valid (Compagno 1984:89 [ref. 6474], Bass et al. 1986:57 [ref. 5636], Stehmann & Krefft 1988 [ref. 13264]). Squalidae.

Euprotomicrus Gill 1865:264 [ref. 1705]. *Scymnus (Laemargus) labordii* Müller & Henle 1841:94. Type by monotypy. Valid (Compagno 1984:90 [ref. 6474], Bass et al. 1986:58 [ref. 5636], Paxton et al. 1989:35 [ref. 12442]). Squalidae.

Euristhmus Ogilby 1899:154 [ref. 3279]. Masc. *Plotosus elongatus* Castelnau 1878:144. Type by original designation. Objective synonym of *Eumeda* Castelnau 1878 according to Fowler (MS) [not researched], but now treated as valid (Burgess 1989:180 [ref. 12860], Paxton et al. 1989:223 [ref. 12442]). Plotosidae.

Europus Klein 1775:922 [ref. 2618]. Masc. Not available, published in a work that does not conform to the principle of binominal nomenclature. In the synonymy of *Acanthurus* Forsskål 1775. Acanthuridae.

Eurumetopos Morton 1888:77 [ref. 3046]. *Eurumetopos johnstonii* Morton 1888:77. Type by monotypy. Synonym of *Hyperoglyphe* Günther 1859 (Haedrich 1967:55 [ref. 5357], McDowall 1981:105 [ref. 5356]). Centrolophidae.

Euryarges (subgenus of *Nectarges*) Myers & Wade 1942:128 [ref. 3134]. Masc. *Nectarges nesiotes* Myers & Wade 1942:128. Type by original designation (also monotypic in subgenus *Nectarges*). Synonym of *Atherinella* Steindachner 1875. Atherinidae: Menidiinae.

Eurycaulus (subgenus of *Tylosurus*) Ogilby 1908:91 [ref. 3287]. Masc. *Belone platyura* Bennett 1831:168. Type by original designation (also monotypic). Apparently intended as a subgenus but text unclear. Preoccupied by Fairmaire 1868 [details not investigated], replaced by *Tropidocaulus* Ogilby 1921. Synonym of *Belone* Cuvier 1816. Belonidae.

Euryglossa Kaup 1858:99 [ref. 2578]. Fem. *Pleuronectes orientalis* Bloch & Schneider 1801:157. Type by monotypy. Valid (Kottelat 1985:274 [ref. 11441], Kottelat 1989:20 [ref. 13605]). Soleidae.

Eurymen Gilbert & Burke 1912:64 [ref. 1634]. Masc. *Eurymen gyrinus* Gilbert & Burke 1912:64. Type by original designation (also monotypic). Valid (Nelson 1982:1478 [ref. 5470], Washington et al. 1984:444 [ref. 13660], Yabe in Masuda et al. 1984:330 [ref. 6441], Yabe 1985:122 [ref. 11522]). Psychrolutidae.

Eurymyctera Kaup 1856:59 [ref. 2572]. Fem. *Eurymyctera crudelis* Kaup 1856:59. Type by monotypy. Also in Kaup 1856:72 [ref. 2573] and as name only in Kaup in Duméril 1856:200 [ref. 1154]. Synonym of *Lycodontis* McClelland (Blache et al. 1973:225 [ref. 7185]). Synonym of *Enchelycore* Kaup 1856 (Böhlke et al. 1989:134 [ref. 13286]). Muraenidae: Muraeninae.

Eurypegasus Bleeker 1863:250 [ref. 402]. Masc. *Pegasus draconis* Linnaeus 1766:418. Type by monotypy. Valid (Smith 1986:443 [ref. 5712], Paxton et al. 1989:434 [ref. 12442], Palsson & Pietsch 1989:7 [ref. 13536]). Pegasidae.

Eurypharynx Vaillant 1882:1226 [ref. 4493]. Masc. *Eurypharynx pelecanoides* Vaillant 1882:1226. Type by monotypy. Valid (Böhlke 1966:610 [ref. 5356], Bauchot 1973:218 [ref. 7184], Fujii in Masuda et al. 1984:32 [ref. 6441], Bertelsen & Nielsen in

Whitehead et al. 1986:534 [ref. 13676], Paxton et al. 1989:109 [ref. 12442], Bertelsen et al. 1989:649 [ref. 13293], Nielsen et al. 1989 [ref. 14467]). Eurypharyngidae.

Eurypleura Kaup 1858:100 [ref. 2578]. Fem. *Plagusia melanorhynchus* Bleeker 1851:15. Type by being a replacement name. Unneeded substitute for *Achiroides* Bleeker 1851. Objective synonym of *Achiroides* Bleeker 1851. Soleidae.

Eurystole Jordan & Evermann in Jordan 1895:418 [ref. 2394]. *Atherinella eriarcha* Jordan & Gilbert 1881:348. Type by original designation (also monotypic). Appeared first in Jordan 1895 as above, with reference to Jordan & Evermann's genus name and characters; also appeared as new in Jordan & Evermann 1896:802 [ref. 2443]. Synonym of *Atherinella* Steindachner 1875, but as a valid subgenus (Chernoff 1986:243 [ref. 5847]). Atherinidae: Menidiinae.

Eurystomus Rafinesque 1820:306 [ref. 5006]. Masc. *Catostomus megastomus* Rafinesque 1820:306. Type by monotypy. Also appeared in Rafinesque 1820:59 (Dec.) [ref. 3592]. Name proposed conditionally for uncertain species "seen by Mr. Audubon." Apparently mythical. Catostomidae.

Eusalpa Fowler 1925:4 [ref. 1401]. Fem. *Sparus salpa* Linnaeus 1758:280. Type by original designation (also monotypic). Objective synonym of *Sarpa* Bonaparte 1831 (Tortonese 1973:413 [ref. 7192]). Sparidae.

Euscarus (subgenus of *Sparisoma*) Jordan & Evermann 1896:416 [ref. 2442]. Masc. *Labrus cretensis* Linnaeus 1758:474. Type by original designation. *Euscaris* is a misspelling. Synonym of *Sparisoma* Swainson 1839 (Monod 1973:444 [ref. 7193]); as a valid subgenus (Quignard & Pras in Whitehead et al. 1986:943 [ref. 13676]). Scaridae: Sparisomatinae.

Euschistodus Gill 1862:145 [ref. 1662]. Masc. *Euschistodus declivifrons* Gill 1862:146. Type by subsequent designation. Type designated by Jordan 1919:315 [ref. 4904]. Synonym of *Abudefduf* Forsskål 1775. Pomacentridae.

Eusebastes (subgenus of *Sebastes*) Sauvage 1878:115 [ref. 3880]. Masc. *Sebastes septentrionalis* Gaimard 1842:Pl. 9. Type by monotypy. Synonym of *Sebastes* Cuvier 1829 (Blanc & Hureau 1973:583 [ref. 7218]). Scorpaenidae: Sebastinae.

Eusolea Roule 1919 Fem. *Solea capellonis* Steindachner 1868:722. Type by monotypy. Original not traced, reported by Jordan 1923:171 [ref. 2421] as a new name perhaps not intended as a generic name distinct from *Solea*. Soleidae.

Eusphyra Gill 1862:403 [ref. 1783]. Fem. *Zygaena blochii* Cuvier 1816:127. Type by original designation (also monotypic). Also in Gill 1862:412 [ref. 4910] where author of species is clear. Valid (Compagno 1984:540 [ref. 6846], Compagno 1988:370 [ref. 13488]). Sphyrnidae.

Eustira Günther 1868:331 [ref. 1990]. Fem. *Eustira ceylonensis* Günther 1868:331. Type by monotypy. Synonym of *Danio* Hamilton 1822 (Silas 1957:61 [ref. 11967]). Cyprinidae.

Eustomatodus (subgenus of *Decapterus*) Gill 1862:261 [ref. 4909]. Masc. *Decapterus kurroides* Bleeker 1855:(393) 420. Type by subsequent designation. Type designated by Jordan & Gilbert 1883:189 [ref. 2476]. Synonym of *Decapterus* Bleeker 1851 (Daget & Smith-Vaniz 1986:314 [ref. 6207]). Carangidae.

Eustomias Filhol 1884:185 [ref. 1326]. Masc. *Eustomias obscurus* Filhol 1884:185. Name only, published in an available way in Vaillant 1888. In the synonymy of *Eustomias* Vaillant 1888 (Gibbs in Morrow & Gibbs 1964:377 [ref. 6962]). Melanostomiidae.

Eustomias Vaillant 1888:112 [ref. 4496]. Masc. *Eustomias obscurus* Vaillant 1888:113. Type by monotypy. Valid (Gibbs in Morrow & Gibbs 1964:377 [ref. 6962], Morrow 1973:137 [ref. 7175], Gibbs et al. 1983 [ref. 5269], Gibbs in Whitehead et al. 1984:346 [ref. 13675], Fujii in Masuda et al. 1984:52 [ref. 6441], Fink 1985:11 [ref. 5171], Gomon & Gibbs 1985 [ref. 5268], Gibbs 1986:238 [ref. 5655], Paxton et al. 1989:199 [ref. 12442]). Melanostomiidae.

Eutaeniichthys Jordan & Snyder 1901:122 [ref. 2509]. Masc. *Eutaeniichthys gilli* Jordan & Snyder 1901:122. Type by original designation (also monotypic). Valid (Akihito in Masuda et al. 1984:280 [ref. 6441], Birdsong et al. 1988:185 [ref. 7303]). Gobiidae.

Eutaeniophorus Bertelsen & Marshall 1958:9 [ref. 291]. Masc. *Taeniophorus festivus* Bertelsen & Marshall 1956:6. Type by being a replacement name. Replacement for *Taeniophorus* Bertelsen & Marshall 1956, preoccupied by Linnavuori 1952 in Hemiptera. Combining the Mirapinnidae and Eutaeniophoridae follows Bertelsen & Marshall 1984:380 [ref. 13657]. Valid (Paxton 1973:213 [ref. 7183], Bertelsen & Marshall 1984:380 [ref. 13657], Bertelsen in Whitehead et al. 1986:522 [ref. 13676], Bertelsen 1986:406 [ref. 5642]). Mirapinnidae.

Eutelichthys Tortonese 1959:226 [ref. 4417]. Masc. *Eutelichthys leptochirus* Tortonese 1959:227. Type by original designation (also monotypic). Synonym of *Paraliparis* Collett 1878 (Lindberg 1973:611 [ref. 7220], Stein 1978:38 [ref. 4203], Andriashev 1986:14 [ref. 12760], Kido 1988:230 [ref. 12287]). Cyclopteridae: Liparinae.

Eutherapon (subgenus of *Therapon*) Fowler 1904:527 [ref. 1367]. Masc. *Therapon theraps* Cuvier in Cuvier & Valenciennes 1829:129. Type by original designation (also monotypic). Synonym of *Terapon* Cuvier 1816 (Vari 1978:254 [ref. 4514], Vari 1986:304 [ref. 6205]). Terapontidae.

Euthynnus Lütken in Jordan & Gilbert 1883:429 [ref. 2476]. Masc. *Thynnus thunnina* Cuvier 1829. Type by original designation. Apparently not technically a replacement name. Valid (Collette & Nauen 1983:32 [ref. 5375], Collette et al. 1984:600 [ref. 11421], Nakamura in Masuda et al. 1984:226 [ref. 6441], Collette 1986:833 [ref. 5647]). Scombridae.

Euthyopteroma Fowler 1904:527 [ref. 1367]. *Dentex blochii* Bleeker 1851:176. Type by original designation. Synonym of *Nemipterus* Swainson 1839. Nemipteridae.

Eutrigla Fraser-Brunner 1938:413 [ref. 1492]. Fem. *Trigla gurnardus* Linnaeus 1758:301. Type by original designation (also monotypic). Valid (Blanc & Hureau 1973:588 [ref. 7218], Hureau in Whitehead et al. 1986:1233 [ref. 13677]). Triglidae: Triglinae.

Eutropiellus Nichols & La Monte 1933:5 [ref. 3187]. Masc. *Eutropiellus kasai* Nichols & La Monte 1933:5. Type by original designation. Valid (De Vos 1986:36 [ref. 6191], Burgess 1989:99 [ref. 12860]). Schilbeidae.

Eutropiichthys Bleeker 1862:398 [ref. 391]. Masc. *Pimelodus vacha* Hamilton 1822:196, 378. Type by original designation (also monotypic). Also in Bleeker 1862:14 [ref. 393] and 1863:107 [ref. 401]. Valid (Jayaram 1977:21 [ref. 7006], Jayaram 1981:222 [ref. 6497], Burgess 1989:98 [ref. 12860], Kottelat 1989:14 [ref. 13605]). Schilbeidae.

Eutropius (subgenus of *Bagrus*) Müller & Troschel 1849:6 [ref. 3073]. Masc. *Bagrus schilbeides* Valenciennes 1840:289. Type by monotypy. Type given as "*Bagrus schilboides* Val. (*Hypophthalmus niloticus* Rüppell)..." Valid (De Vos 1984:3 [ref. 5157];

synonym of *Schilbe* Oken 1817, but as a valid subgenus (De Vos 1986:41 [ref. 6191], Burgess 1989:99 [ref. 12860]). Schilbeidae.

Eutychelithus Jordan 1876:242 [ref. 2371]. Masc. *Corvina richardsonii* Cuvier in Cuvier & Valenciennes 1830:100. Type by monotypy. Synonym of *Aplodinotus* Rafinesque 1819 (Chao 1978:41 [ref. 6983]). Sciaenidae.

Eutyx Heller & Snodgrass 1903:224 [ref. 2089]. *Eutyx diagrammus* Heller & Snodgrass 1903:224. Type by monotypy. Synonym of *Oligopus* Risso 1810 (Cohen 1964:2 [ref. 6891], Cohen & Nielsen 1978:49 [ref. 881]), but see account of *Oligopus*. Bythitidae: Bythitinae.

Euxiphipops Fraser-Brunner 1934:192 [ref. 1488]. Masc. *Holacanthus xanthometopon* Bleeker 1853:258. Type by being a replacement name. Replacement for *Heteropyge* Fraser-Brunner 1933, preoccupied by Silvestri 1897 in Myriopoda. Pomacanthidae.

Evapristis Jordan & Evermann 1896:388 [ref. 2442]. Fem. *Orthopristis lethopristis* Jordan & Fesler 1889:36. Type by original designation (also monotypic). Synonym of *Orthopristis* Girard 1858. Haemulidae.

Evarra Woolman 1894:64 [ref. 4804]. Fem. *Evarra eigenmanni* Woolman 1894:64. Type by original designation (also monotypic). Mexican genus, now extinct. Cyprinidae.

Evenchelys Jordan & Evermann 1902:327 [ref. 2447]. Fem. *Gymnothorax macrurus* Bleeker 1854:(314) 324. Type by original designation (also monotypic). Valid (Hatooka in Masuda et al. 1984:22 [ref. 6441]). Muraenidae: Muraeninae.

Evenichthys Whitley 1935:250 [ref. 4683]. Masc. *Tetragonopterus fasslii* Steindachner 1915:34. Type by being a replacement name. Replacement for *Aequidens* Steindachner 1915, preoccupied by Eigenmann & Bray 1894. Misspelled *Evemichthys* in Zoological Record for 1935. Written in Stanford reprint, "*Aequidens* Stdr. 1915 was a lapsus calami for *Astyanax*." Synonym of *Astyanax* Baird & Girard 1854. Characidae.

Evepigymnus (subgenus of *Decapterus*) Gill 1862:261 [ref. 4909]. Masc. *Decapterus hypodus* Gill 1862:262. Type by monotypy. Synonym of *Decapterus* Bleeker 1851 (Daget & Smith-Vaniz 1986:314 [ref. 6207]). Carangidae.

Evermannella Eigenmann 1903:146 [ref. 1218]. Fem. *Cynopotamus biserialis* Garman 1890:14. Type by original designation (also monotypic). Preoccupied by Fowler 1901 in fishes; replaced by *Eucynopotamus* Fowler 1904 and by *Evermannolus* Eigenmann in Eigenmann & Ogle 1907. Characidae.

Evermannella Fowler 1901:211 [ref. 1359]. Fem. *Odontostomus hyalinus* Cocco 1838:192. Type by being a replacement name. Misspelled once as *Evermanella* on p. 211. Replacement for *Odontostomus* Cocco 1838, preoccupied by Beck 1837 in Mollusca. Type usually given as *O. balbo* Risso, but *Evermannella* is a replacement name. Valid (Maul 1973:200 [ref. 7171], Johnson 1982:123 [ref. 5519], Johnson in Whitehead et al. 1984:491 [ref. 13675], Okiyama 1984:207 [ref. 13644], Fujii in Masuda et al. 1984:78 [ref. 6441], Johnson 1986:279 [ref. 5677], Paxton et al. 1989:249 [ref. 12442]). Evermannellidae.

Evermannia Jordan 1895:592 [ref. 2393]. Fem. *Gobiosoma zosterurum* Jordan & Gilbert 1881:361. Type by original designation (also monotypic). Valid. Gobiidae.

Evermanniana Taranetz 1935:91 [ref. 4339]. Fem. *Blennicottus clarki* Evermann & Gill 1907:323. Type by original designation (also monotypic). Synonym of *Artediellus* Jordan 1885 (Neyelov 1979:153 [ref. 3152], D. Nelson 1986:34 [ref. 5808]). Cottidae.

Evermannichthys Metzelaar 1920:139 [ref. 2982]. Masc. *Evermannichthys spongicola* Metzelaar 1920:189. Type by monotypy. Also appeared as new in Metzelaar 1922:141 [ref. 5741]. Valid (Gilbert & Burgess 1986 [ref. 5949], Birdsong et al. 1988:189 [ref. 7303]). Gobiidae.

Evermannolus Eigenmann in Eigenmann & Ogle 1907:2, 3 [ref. 1266]. Masc. *Cynopotamus biserialis* Garman 1890:14. Type by being a replacement name. Replacement for *Evermannella* Eigenmann 1903, preoccupied by Fowler 1901 in fishes; objective synonym of earlier replacement *Eucynopotamus* Fowler 1904. Characidae.

Eviota Jenkins 1903:501 [ref. 2341]. *Eviota epiphanes* Jenkins 1903:501. Type by original designation (also monotypic). Valid (Lachner & Karnella 1980 [ref. 6916], Jewett & Lachner 1983 [ref. 5368], Yoshino & Shimada in Masuda et al. 1984:243 [ref. 6441], Hoese 1986:787 [ref. 5670], Birdsong et al. 1988:192 [ref. 7303], Sunobe 1988 [ref. 12744]). Gobiidae.

Eviotops Smith 1957:825 [ref. 4110]. Masc. *Eviotops infulatus* Smith 1957:825. Type by original designation (also monotypic). Synonym of *Eviota* Jenkins 1903 (Lachner & Karnella 1980:12 [ref. 6916]). Gobiidae.

Evips McCosker 1972:113 [ref. 2932]. Masc. *Evips percinctus* McCosker 1972:114. Type by original designation (also monotypic). Valid (McCosker 1977:77 [ref. 6836], McCosker et al. 1989:298 [ref. 13288]). Ophichthidae: Ophichthinae.

Evistias Jordan 1907:236, 237 [ref. 2401]. Masc. *Histiopterus acutirostris* Temminck & Schlegel 1844:88. Type by original designation (also monotypic). Not preoccupied by *Evistius* Gill 1893 in fishes, *Evistiopterus* Whitley 1932 is an unneeded replacement. Valid (Hardy 1983:185 [ref. 5385], Hardy 1983:374 [ref. 5392], Mochizuki in Masuda et al. 1984:189 [ref. 6441]). Pentacerotidae.

Evistiopterus Whitley 1932:334 [ref. 4674]. Masc. *Histiopterus acutirostris* Temminck & Schlegel 1844:88. Type by being a replacement name. Unneeded replacement for *Evistias* Jordan 1907, not preoccupied by *Evistius* Gill 1893 in fishes. Objective synonym of *Evistias* Jordan 1907 (Hardy 1983:185 [ref. 5385]). Pentacerotidae.

Evistius Gill 1893:114, 123 [ref. 1736]. Masc. *Platystethus huttonii* Günther 1876:395. Type by monotypy. Apparently based on a juvenile of *Latridopsis* Gill 1862, family Latridae (see Paxton et al. 1989:567 [ref. 12442]). Latridae.

Evolantia Heller & Snodgrass 1903:189 [ref. 2089]. Fem. *Exocoetus micropterus* Valenciennes in Cuvier & Valenciennes 1847:127. Type by monotypy. Synonym of *Oxyporhamphus* Gill 1864 (Parin et al. 1980:145 [ref. 6895]). Exocoetidae.

Evoplites Gill 1862:236 [ref. 1664]. Masc. *Mesoprion pomacanthus* Bleeker 1855:407. Type by monotypy. Synonym of *Lutjanus* Bloch 1790 (Allen 1985:33 [ref. 6843], Allen & Talbot 1985:8 [ref. 6491]). Lutjanidae.

Evorthodus Gill 1859:195 [ref. 1758]. Masc. *Evorthodus breviceps* Gill 1859:195. Type by monotypy. Valid (Birdsong et al. 1988:198 [ref. 7303]). Gobiidae.

Evoxymetopon Gill 1863:227 [ref. 1686]. Neut. *Evoxymetopon taeniatus* Gill 1863:228. Type by monotypy. Misspelled *Euoxymetopon* by Günther 1887:39 [ref. 2013]. Authorship is Gill, not Poey. Valid (Collette et al. 1984:600 [ref. 11421], Nakamura in Masuda et al. 1984:228 [ref. 6441]). Trichiuridae: Lepidopinae.

Evynnis Jordan & Thompson 1912:573 [ref. 2541]. *Sparus car-*

dinalis Lacepède 1803:46, 141. Type by original designation (also monotypic). Valid (Akazaki in Masuda et al. 1984:177 [ref. 6441]). Sparidae.

Exallias Jordan & Evermann 1905:503 [ref. 2451]. Masc. *Salarias brevis* Kner 1868:334. Type by original designation (also monotypic). Valid (Yoshino in Masuda et al. 1984:299 [ref. 6441], Springer 1986:746 [ref. 5719], Williams 1989:17 [ref. 13549]). Blenniidae.

Exastilithoxus Isbrücker & Nijssen in Isbrücker 1979:88, 91 [ref. 2302]. Masc. *Pseudacanthicus fimbriatus* Steindachner 1915:201. Type by original designation (also monotypic). Valid (Isbrücker 1980:78 [ref. 2303], Burgess 1989:438 [ref. 12860]). Loricariidae.

Excursor Gistel 1848:XIII [ref. 1822]. *Corvina nigra* of Cuvier 1829 (= *Sciaena umbra* Linnaeus 1758:289). Type by being a replacement name. Unneeded replacement for *Melantha* Gistel 1848 (p. 109), not preoccupied by *Melanthia* Duponchee 1829. In the synonymy of *Sciaena* Linnaeus 1758 (Trewavas 1973:396 [ref. 7201]). Sciaenidae.

Execestides Jordan & Thompson 1905:253 [ref. 2538]. Masc. *Execestides egregius* Jordan & Thompson 1905:253. Type by monotypy. Valid (Mees 1960:47 [ref. 11931]); synonym of *Gnathagnus* Gill 1861 (Pietsch 1989:294 [ref. 12541], Kishimoto 1989:303 [ref. 13562]). Uranoscopidae.

Exechodontes DeWitt 1977:789 [ref. 1124]. Masc. *Exechodontes daidaleus* DeWitt 1977:790. Type by original designation (also monotypic). Valid (Anderson 1984:578 [ref. 13634]). Zoarcidae.

Exerpes Jordan & Evermann in Jordan 1896:232 [ref. 2395]. *Auchenopterus asper* Jenkins & Evermann 1888:154. Type by monotypy. Valid (Clark Hubbs 1952:90 [ref. 2252]). Labrisomidae.

Exilichthys Whitley 1933:65 [ref. 4677]. Masc. *Cnidoglanis nudiceps* Günther 1880:49. Type by original designation (also monotypic). Plotosidae.

Eximia Greeley 1901:18 [ref. 1889]. Fem. *Eximia rubellio* Greeley 1901:18. Type by monotypy. Preoccupied by [K.] Jordan 1894 [not investigated], replaced by *Greeleya* Jordan 1920. Synonym of *Oligocottus* Girard 1856. Cottidae.

Exocallus De la Pylaie 1835:532 [ref. 1086]. Masc. *Exocallus insignis* De la Pylaie 1835. Type by being a replacement name. Original not seen. Perhaps an unneeded substitute for *Boops* Cuvier 1814. If a substitute, then type species is *Sparus boops* Linnaeus 1758: 208. Objective synonym of *Boops* Cuvier 1814. Kyphosidae: Girellinae.

Exochochromis Eccles & Trewavas 1989:186 [ref. 13547]. Masc. *Cyrtocara anagenys* Oliver 1984:218. Type by original designation (also monotypic). Cichlidae.

Exocoetus Linnaeus 1758:316 [ref. 2787]. Masc. *Exocoetus volitans* Linnaeus 1758:316. Type by monotypy. Spelled *Exoceothus*, *Exocetus*, *Exocaetus*, and *Exococtus* in early literature. Valid (Parin 1973:263 [ref. 7191], Collette et al. 1984:338 [ref. 11422], Yoshino in Masuda et al. 1984:80 [ref. 6441], Parin in Whitehead et al. 1986:615 [ref. 13676], Heemstra & Parin 1986:394 [ref. 6293], Paxton et al. 1989:333 [ref. 12442]). Exocoetidae.

Exodomegas Gill 1883:524 [ref. 4941]. Masc. Not available; manuscript name published in synonymy of *Exomegas* Gill 1883 and apparently never made available by later use. Petromyzontidae: Geotriinae.

Exodon Müller & Troschel 1844:91 [ref. 3070]. Masc. *Exodon paradoxus* Müller & Troschel 1844:91. Type by monotypy. Perhaps appeared in several publications, Jordan lists as 1844:69, Fowler as 1845:31 [not researched]. Also as new in Müller & Troschel 1848:634 [ref. 3972]. Apparently not preoccupied, *Hystricodon* Günther 1864 is an unneeded replacement. Valid (Géry 1977:318 [ref. 1597]). Characidae.

Exoglossops Fowler & Bean 1920:311 [ref. 1472]. Masc. *Exoglossops geei* Fowler & Bean 1920:311. Type by original designation (also monotypic). Synonym of *Sarcocheilichthys* Bleeker 1859 (Banarescu & Nalbant 1973:39 [ref. 173], Lu, Luo & Chen 1977:467 [ref. 13495]). Cyprinidae.

Exoglossops Hubbs in Osburn et al. 1930:173 [ref. 5943]. Masc. *Exoglossops laurae* Hubbs MS. Not available; name (from Hubbs MS) used in list without description or available species; called *Parexoglossum* when published by Hubbs in 1931. *Exoglossops* is preoccupied by Fowler & Bean 1920 in fishes. In the synonymy of *Exoglossum* Rafinesque 1818. Cyprinidae.

Exoglossum Rafinesque 1818:419 [ref. 3588]. Neut. *Cyprinus maxillingua* Lesueur 1817:85. Type by subsequent designation. Type designated by Bleeker 1863:29 [ref. 4859] and 1863:205 [ref. 397]. Also appeared in Rafinesque 1819:155 [ref. 4938]. *Exoglossum lesurianum* Rafinesque 1818:420 is an unneeded substitute for *C. maxillingua* Lesueur 1817. Valid. Cyprinidae.

Exoles Gistel 1848:IX [ref. 1822]. Masc. *Squalus nasus* Bonnaterre 1788:10. Type by being a replacement name. Proposed as replacement for *Lamia* Bonaparte, apparently not an original description, but in the synonymy of *Lamna* Cuvier. Gistel's name is unvailable if Bonaparte's *Lamia* is not regarded as an original description. Synonym of *Lamna* Cuvier 1816 (Compagno 1984:246 [ref. 6474]). Lamnidae.

Exolissus Jordan 1923:217 [ref. 2421]. Masc. *Prionotus alepis* Alcock 1889:303. Type by original designation (also monotypic). Triglidae: Triglinae.

Exomegas Gill 1883:524 [ref. 4941]. Masc. *Petromyzon macrostomus* Burmeister 1868:xxxvi. Type by original designation (also monotypic). *Exodomegas* Gill MS mentioned in passing on p. 524 in synonymy of *Exomegas*. Synonym of *Geotria* Gray 1851. Petromyzontidae: Geotriinae.

Exonautes Jordan & Evermann 1896:322 [ref. 2442]. Masc. *Exocoetus exsiliens* Linnaeus 1771:529. Type by original designation (name in parentheses). Synonym of *Hirundichthys* Breder 1928 (Parin 1973:265 [ref. 7191]). Exocoetidae.

Exornator (subgenus of *Chaetodon*) Nalbant 1971:215 [ref. 6642]. *Chaetodon punctatofasciatus* Cuvier 1831:28. Type by original designation. Synonym of *Chaetodon* Linnaeus 1758 (Burgess 1978:653 [ref. 700]); valid (Maugé & Bauchot 1984:473 [ref. 6614]). Chaetodontidae.

Exostoma Blyth 1860:155 [ref. 477]. Neut. *Exostoma berdmorei* Blyth 1860:155. Type by subsequent designation. Type designated by Bleeker 1863:105 [ref. 401]. Valid (Chu 1979:76 [ref. 831], Jayaram 1981:265 [ref. 6497], Burgess 1989:133 [ref. 12860], Kottelat 1989:15 [ref. 13605]). Sisoridae.

Exotirichthys (subgenus of *Synodus*) Whitley 1937:219 [ref. 4690]. Masc. *Saurus altipinnis* Günther 1864:397. Type by original designation (also monotypic). Two additional species referred with question. Synonym of *Synodus* Scopoli 1777 (Anderson et al. 1966:47 [ref. 6977]). Synodontidae: Synodontinae.

Expedio Snyder 1909:606 [ref. 4151]. Masc. *Expedio parvulus* Snyder 1909:606. Type by original designation (also monotypic).

Valid (Hoese, pers. comm.). Gobiidae.

Extrarius Jordan 1919:342 [ref. 2413]. Masc. *Hybopsis tetranemus* Gilbert 1886:208. Type by original designation (also monotypic). Synonym of *Macrhybopsis* Cockerell & Allison 1909 (Coburn & Cavender, pers. comm.). Cyprinidae.

Exyrias Jordan & Seale 1906:405 [ref. 2497]. Masc. *Gobius puntangoides* Bleeker 1853:242. Type by original designation (also monotypic). Valid (Yoshino in Masuda et al. 1984:250 [ref. 6441], Birdsong et al. 1988:192 [ref. 7303]). Gobiidae.

Facciolella Whitley 1938:197 [ref. 4692]. Fem. *Nettastomella physonema* Facciolà 1914:47. Type by being a replacement name. Replacement for *Nettastomella* Facciolà 1911, preoccupied by Carpenter 1865 in Mollusca. Valid (Blache et al. 1973:237 [ref. 7185], Smith & Castle 1982:34 [ref. 5453], Saldanha in Whitehead et al. 1986:562 [ref. 13676], Smith 1989:596 [ref. 13285]). Nettastomatidae.

Fagasa Schultz 1943:252 [ref. 3957]. Fem. *Fagasa tutuilae* Schultz 1943:253. Type by original designation (also monotypic). Valid (Birdsong et al. 1988:202 [ref. 7303] as *Fagasia*). Status uncertain (Hoese, pers. comm). Eleotridae.

Fagea de Buen 1940:9 [ref. 689]. Fem. *Cabotia schmidti* de Buen 1930:17. Type by being a replacement name. Unneeded replacement for *Cabotia* de Buen 1930, preoccupied by Ragonot 1888 in Lepidoptera but apparently replaced earlier in same year by *Cabotichthys* Whitley 1940. Synonym of *Gobius* Linnaeus 1758 (Miller 1973:483 [ref. 6888]). Gobiidae.

Falcula Jordan & Snyder 1899:124 [ref. 2501]. Fem. *Falcula chapalae* Jordan & Snyder 1899:124. Type by original designation (also monotypic). Preoccupied by Hodgson 1837 in Aves and by Conrad 1870 in Mollusca, replaced by *Falcularius* Jordan & Snyder 1903. Cyprinidae.

Falcularius Jordan & Snyder 1903:360 [ref. 2399]. Masc. *Falcula chapalae* Jordan & Snyder 1899:124. Type by being a replacement name. Replacement for *Falcula* Jordan & Snyder 1899, preoccupied by Hodgson 1837 in Aves and Conrad 1870 in Mollusca. Synonym of *Yuriria* Jordan & Evermann 1896. Cyprinidae.

Fallacirripectes Schultz & Chapman in Schultz et al. 1960:362 [ref. 3972]. Masc. *Fallacirripectes minutus* Schultz & Chapman in Schultz et al. 1960:363. Type by original designation. Synonym of *Stanulus* Smith 1959 (Smith-Vaniz & Springer 1971:40 [ref. 4145]). Blenniidae.

Faremusca (subgenus of *Holocentrus*) Whitley 1933:68 [ref. 4677]. Fem. *Holocentrum punctatissimum* Cuvier in Cuvier & Valenciennes 1829:215. Type by original designation (also monotypic). Correct spelling for genus of type species is *Holocentrus*. Synonym of *Sargocentron* Fowler 1904 (Randall & Heemstra 1985:5 [ref. 5144]). Holocentridae.

Farer (subgenus of *Sciaena*) Forsskål 1775:44 [ref. 1351]. Not available, regarded as non-latinized Arabic name (see Jordan 1917:33 [ref. 2407]). Intended included species assumed to be *Holocentrus samara* Forsskål 1775, with common name Farer. In the synonymy of *Holocentrus* Scopoli 1777. Holocentridae.

Fares (subgenus of *Aphareus*) Jordan, Evermann & Tanaka 1927:673 [ref. 2454]. *Aphareus thompsoni* Fowler 1923:382. Type by original designation (also monotypic). Apparently preoccupied [details not investigated], replaced by *Humefordia* Whitley 1931. Synonym of *Aphareus* Cuvier 1830 (Allen 1985:18 [ref. 6843]). Lutjanidae.

Farhians Whitley 1930:250 [ref. 4670]. *Hemiramphus commersonii* Cuvier 1829:286 (= *Esox far* Forsskål 1775:67). Type by original designation. Synonym of *Hemiramphus* Cuvier 1816 (Parin 1973:268 [ref. 7191], Parin et al. 1980:111 [ref. 6895]). Hemiramphidae.

Fario Valenciennes in Cuvier & Valenciennes 1848:277 [ref. 1013]. Masc. *Fario argenteus* Valenciennes in Cuvier & Valenciennes 1848:294. Type by subsequent designation. Type designated by Berg 1916 according to Behnke 1984. Text should be examined closely, as *Salmo fario* Linnaeus is mentioned, and if was included in the genus *Fario*, then it would be the type species by absolute tautonymy. Synonym of *Salmo* Linnaeus 1758 (Svetovidov 1973:145 [ref. 7169], Behnke 1984:125 [ref. 6177]). Salmonidae: Salmoninae.

Farionella Valenciennes in Cuvier & Valenciennes 1849:507 [ref. 1014]. Fem. *Farionella gayi* Valenciennes in Cuvier & Valenciennes 1849:508. Type by monotypy. Synonym of *Aplochiton* Jenyns 1842. Galaxiidae: Aplochitoninae.

Farlapiscis Whitley 1931:313 [ref. 4672]. Masc. *Hippocampus breviceps* Peters 1870:710. Type by original designation. Synonym of *Hippocampus* Rafinesque 1810 (Fritzsche 1980:185 [ref. 1511] and Vari 1982:175 [ref. 6765], as *Farlapiscus*). Syngnathidae: Hippocampinae.

Farlowella Eigenmann & Eigenmann 1889:32 [ref. 1253]. Fem. *Acestra acus* Kner 1853:93. Type by being a replacement name. Replacement for *Acestra* Kner 1853, preoccupied by Jardine in Bonaparte 1846 in fishes and in 1852 in Hemiptera [not researched]. Valid (Isbrücker 1980:96 [ref. 2303], Burgess 1989:440 [ref. 12860]). Loricariidae.

Favonigobius Whitley 1930:122 [ref. 4669]. Masc. *Gobius lateralis* Macleay 1881:602. Type by original designation. Valid (Akihito in Masuda et al. 1984:250 [ref. 6441], Hoese 1986:788 [ref. 5670], Maugé 1986:367 [ref. 6218], Birdsong et al. 1988:192 [ref. 7303]). Gobiidae.

Feia Smith 1959:205 [ref. 4122]. Fem. *Feia nympha* Smith 1959:206. Type by original designation (also monotypic). Valid (Lachner & McKinney 1979:11 [ref. 7018], Birdsong et al. 1988:192 [ref. 7303]). Gobiidae.

Felichthys Swainson 1839:305 [ref. 4303]. Masc. *Silurus bagre* Bloch 1794:Pl. 365. Type by being a replacement name. Replacement for *Breviceps* Swainson 1838, preoccupied by Merrem 1820 in herpetology. Synonym of *Bagre* Cloquet 1816. Ariidae.

Fenestraja (subgenus of *Neoraja*) McEachran & Compagno 1982:423 [ref. 2952]. Fem. *Raja plutonia* Garman 1881:236. Type by original designation. Synonym of *Gurgesiella* de Buen 1959, but as a valid subgenus (McEachran 1984:57 [ref. 5225], Séret 1989 [ref. 12833]). Rajidae.

Ferdauia Jordan, Evermann & Wakiya in Jordan, Evermann & Tanaka 1927:662 [ref. 2454]. Fem. *Caranx jordani* Nichols 1922:24. Type by original designation. Synonym of *Carangoides* Bleeker 1851 (Smith-Vaniz, pers. comm., Nov. 1989). Carangidae.

Fereleotris (subgenus of *Amblyeleotris*) Smith 1958:152 [ref. 4118]. Fem. *Amblyeleotris delicatulus* Smith 1958:152. Type by original designation (also monotypic). Genus wrongly treated as masculine by author, species should be *delicatula*. Synonym of *Amblyeleotris* Bleeker 1874 (Hoese, pers. comm.). Gobiidae.

Feroxodon Su, Hardy & Tyler 1986:102 [ref. 12582]. Masc. *Anchisomus multistriatus* Richardson 1854:160. Type by original designation (also monotypic). Tetraodontidae.

Festucalex Whitley 1931:312 [ref. 4672]. Masc. *Syngnathus cinctus*

Ramsay 1882:111. Type by original designation. Valid (Dawson 1977:622 [ref. 1066], Dawson 1984 [ref. 5290], Araga in Masuda et al. 1984:88 [ref. 6441], Dawson 1985:68 [ref. 6541], Dawson 1986:448 [ref. 5650], Paxton et al. 1989:417 [ref. 12442]). Syngnathidae: Syngnathinae.

Fiatola Cuvier 1816:342 [ref. 993]. Fem. *Stromateus fiatola* Linnaeus 1758:248. Type by monotypy. Objective synonym of *Stromateus* Linnaeus 1758 (Haedrich 1967:99 [ref. 5357], Haedrich 1973:565 [ref. 7216]). Stromateidae.

Fiatola Risso 1826:289 [ref. 3757]. Fem. *Fiatola fasciata* Risso 1826:289. Type by monotypy. Apparently described independent of and preoccupied by *Fiatola* Cuvier 1816 in same family. Stromateidae.

Fierasfer Oken (ex Cuvier) 1817:1182 [ref. 3303]. *Ophidium [sic] imberbe* Cuvier 1815:119. Type designated by ICZN (Opinion 42), not *Ophidion imberbe* Linnaeus 1758. Based on "Les Fierasfers" of Cuvier 1816:239 [ref. 993] (see Gill 1903:966 [ref. 5768]). Synonym of *Carapus* Rafinesque 1810 (Arnold 1956:260 [ref. 5315], Wheeler 1973:557 [ref. 7190]). Carapidae: Carapinae.

Figaro (subgenus of *Pristiurus*) Whitley 1928:238 [ref. 4661]. *Pristiurus (Figaro) boardmani* Whitley 1928:238. Type by original designation (also monotypic). Synonym of *Galeus* Rafinesque 1810 (Nakaya 1975:40 [ref. 7083], Springer 1979:48 [ref. 4175], Compagno 1984:306 [ref. 6846], Cappetta 1987:111 [ref. 6348], Compagno 1988:134 [ref. 13488]). Scyliorhinidae.

Filialosa Fowler 1944:207 [ref. 1448]. Fem. *Meletta libertate* Günther 1866:603. Type by original designation (also monotypic). Synonym of *Opisthonema* Gill 1861 (Whitehead 1985:67 [ref. 5141]). Clupeidae.

Filicampus Whitley 1948:75 [ref. 4710]. Masc. *Syngnathus superciliaris* Günther 1880:30. Type by original designation (also monotypic). Valid (Dawson 1985:73 [ref. 6541], Paxton et al. 1989:417 [ref. 12442]). Syngnathidae: Syngnathinae.

Filimanus Myers 1936:380 [ref. 3112]. Fem. *Polynemus melanochir* Valenciennes in Cuvier & Valenciennes 1831:513. Type by original designation (also monotypic). Apparently based on a misidentified type species (Feltes, pers. comm.). Valid (de Sylva 1984: 540 [ref. 13667]). Polynemidae.

Filirasbora Fowler 1937:172 [ref. 1425]. Fem. *Filirasbora rubripinna* Fowler 1937:172. Type by original designation (also monotypic). Synonym of *Leptobarbus* Bleeker 1859 (Bailey in Böhlke 1984:90 [ref. 13621], Roberts 1989:41 [ref. 6439]). Cyprinidae.

Fimbriceps Whitley 1946:62 [ref. 9300]. Neut. *Fimbriceps umbrellabia* Whitley 1946:62. Type by monotypy. Synonym of *Gnathophis* Kaup 1860 (Castle 1977 [ref. 9301], Smith 1989:521 [ref. 13285]). Congridae: Congrinae.

Fimbriclupea Whitley 1940:399 [ref. 4699]. Fem. *Fimbriclupea dactylolepis* Whitley 1940:399. Type by original designation. Synonym of *Sardinella* Valenciennes 1847 (Whitehead 1985:90 [ref. 5141]). Clupeidae.

Fimbrinares Whitley 1948:72 [ref. 4710]. *Fimbrinares mosaica* Whitley 1948:72. Type by original designation (also monotypic). Synonym of *Enchelycore* Kaup 1856 (Böhlke et al. 1989:134 [ref. 13286]). Muraenidae: Muraeninae.

Fimbriotorpedo (subgenus of *Torpedo*) Fritsch 1884:451 [ref. 1510]. Fem. *Torpedo marmorata* Risso 1810:20. Type by subsequent designation. Three included species; type apparently first designated by Jordan 1920:435 [ref. 4905]. Also published by Fritsch 1886:365 [see under ref. 1510]. Synonym of *Torpedo* Houttuyn 1764 (Krefft & Stehmann 1973:55 [ref. 7167], Cappetta 1987:161 [ref. 6348]). Torpedinidae.

Fiscina Whitley 1940:400 [ref. 4699]. Fem. *Amblygaster posterus* Whitley 1931:144. Type by original designation (also monotypic). Synonym of *Sardinella* Valenciennes 1847 (Whitehead 1985:90 [ref. 5141]). Clupeidae.

Fissala (subgenus of *Prionotus*) Gill 1905:342 [ref. 1790]. *Prionotus alatus* Goode & Bean 1883:210. Type by monotypy. Synonym of *Prionotus* Lacepède 1801. Triglidae: Triglinae.

Fistularia Linnaeus 1758:312 [ref. 2787]. Fem. *Fistularia tabacaria* Linnaeus 1758:312. Type by monotypy. On Official List (Opinion 75). Valid (Fritzsche 1976 [ref. 7102], Fritzsche 1984 [ref. 13658], Araga in Masuda et al. 1984:84 [ref. 6441], Heemstra 1986:444 [ref. 5660], Paxton et al. 1989:405 [ref. 12442]). Fistulariidae.

Fitzroyia Günther 1866:307 [ref. 1983]. Fem. *Lebias multidentata* Jenyns 1842:117. Type by monotypy. Spelled *Fitzroya* by Eigenmann 1907:429 [ref. 1219] and 1910:457 [ref. 1224]. Regarded as same as *Jenynsia* Günther in same work; earliest first reviser selecting *Jenynsia* over *Fitzroyia* not researched in detail; earliest found is Garman 1895:69 [ref. 1538]. Synonym of *Jenynsia* Günther 1866 (Parenti 1981:503 [ref. 7066]). Anablepidae: Jenynsiinae.

Flabelliclinus (subgenus of *Auchenionchus*) de Buen 1962:57 [ref. 699]. Masc. *Auchenionchus verrucosus* de Buen 1962:68. Type by original designation. Synonym of *Auchenionchus* Gill 1860 (Stephens & Springer 1974:11 [ref. 7149]). Labrisomidae.

Flabelligobius Smith 1956:553 [ref. 4103]. Masc. *Flabelligobius fourmanoiri* Smith 1956:553. Type by original designation (also monotypic). Valid (Akihito in Masuda et al. 1984:259 [ref. 6441], Birdsong et al. 1988:192 [ref. 7303]). Gobiidae.

Flagellaria Gronow in Gray 1854:146 [ref. 1911]. Fem. *Fistularia fistularis* Gronow in Gray 1854:146 (= *Fistularia tabacaria* Linnaeus 1758:312). Type by monotypy. Synonym of *Fistularia* Linnaeus 1758 (Fritzsche 1976:196 [ref. 7102]). Fistulariidae.

Flagelloserranus Kotthaus 1970:5 [ref. 2670]. Masc. *Flagelloserranus meteori* Kotthaus 1970:11. Type by original designation (also monotypic). Synonym of *Liopropoma* Gill 1861 (Randall & Taylor 1988:7 [ref. 6429]). Serranidae: Liopropomatinae.

Flagellostomias Parr 1927:49 [ref. 3367]. Masc. *Flagellostomias tyrannus* Parr 1927:50. Type by monotypy. Valid (Morrow in Morrow & Gibbs 1964:429 [ref. 6962], Morrow 1973:139 [ref. 7175], Gibbs in Whitehead et al. 1984:352 [ref. 13675], Kawaguchi & Moser 1984:171 [ref. 13642], Fujii in Masuda et al. 1984:50 [ref. 6441], Fink 1985:11 [ref. 5171], Gibbs 1986:240 [ref. 5655], Paxton et al. 1989:200 [ref. 12442]). Melanostomiidae.

Flakeus (subgenus of *Squalus*) Whitley 1939:242 [ref. 4695]. Masc. *Squalus meglops* Macleay 1881:367. Type by original designation. Synonym of *Squalus* Linnaeus 1758 (Compagno 1984:109 [ref. 6474]). Squalidae.

Flammeo Jordan & Evermann 1898:2871 [ref. 2445]. *Holocentrum marianum* Cuvier in Cuvier & Valenciennes 1829:219. Type by original designation (also monotypic). Correct spelling for genus of type species is *Holocentrus*. Valid [over older *Neoniphon* Castelnau 1875] (Woods & Sonoda 1973:345 [ref. 6899], Shimizu in Masuda et al. 1984:112 [ref. 6441]); correctly as a synonym of *Neoniphon* Castelnau 1875 (Randall & Heemstra 1985:2 [ref. 5144], Randall & Heemstra 1986:416 [ref. 5707]). Holocentridae.

Flavicaesio (subgenus of *Caesio*) Carpenter 1987:19 [ref. 6430].

Fem. *Caesio suevica* Klunzinger 1884:46. Type by original designation. Synonym of *Caesio* Lacepède 1801, but as a valid subgenus (Carpenter 1988:4 [ref. 9296]). Caesionidae.

Flesus Moreau 1881:298 (v. 3) [ref. 3040]. Masc. *Pleuronectes flesus* Linnaeus 1758:270. Type by absolute tautonymy of name in synonymy of one of two included species. Synonym of *Platichthys* Girard 1854 (Norman 1934:376 [ref. 6893], Nielsen 1973:626 [ref. 6885]). Pleuronectidae: Pleuronectinae.

Flexipenis Hubbs in Rivas 1963:334 [ref. 3761]. Masc. *Gambusia vittata* Hubbs 1926:26. Type by original designation (also monotypic). Appeared first in Turner 1940 without distinguishing features. Synonym of *Gambusia* Poey 1854 (Rosen & Bailey 1963:90 [ref. 7067]). Poeciliidae.

Florenciella Mead & De Falla 1965:268 [ref. 2955]. Fem. *Florenciella lugubris* Mead & De Falla 1965:268. Type by original designation (also monotypic). Valid (Johnson 1984:464 [ref. 9681], Gon 1986:559 [ref. 5657]). Epigonidae.

Floridichthys Hubbs 1926:16 [ref. 2233]. Masc. *Cyprinodon carpio* Günther 1866:306. Type by original designation (also monotypic). Type designated as "*Cyprinodon mydrus* Goode & Bean = *Cyprinodon carpio* Günther" 1866. Valid (Parenti 1981:530 [ref. 7066]). Cyprinodontidae: Cyprinodontinae.

Fluta Bloch & Schneider 1801:565 [ref. 471]. Fem. *Monopterus javanensis* Lacepède 1800:138, 139. Type by being a replacement name. Regarded as an unneeded substitute for *Monopterus* Lacepède 1800. *Monopterus* not preoccupied by *Monopteros* Volta 1796. Objective synonym of *Monopterus* Lacepède 1800 (Rosen & Greenwood 1976:56 [ref. 7094] but with wrong type for *Monopterus*, Daget 1986:291 [ref. 6203], Roberts 1989:183 [ref. 6439]). Synbranchidae.

Fluvialosa Whitley 1943:170 [ref. 4703]. Fem. *Chatoessus elongatus* Macleay 1883:209. Type by original designation. Synonym of *Nematalosa* Regan 1917 (Whitehead 1985:241 [ref. 5141]). Clupeidae.

Fluviatilis de Buen 1926:46 [ref. 5054]. As a "grupo" for 2 species of Clupeidae. Not available on basis of Art. 1b(6) [see de Buen's definition of "grupo" on p. 11]; see Appendix A. Clupeidae.

Fluvicola Iljin 1930:56 [ref. 2297]. Masc. *Gobius martensi* Günther 1861:15. Type by original designation (also monotypic). Type given as *G. martensi* Günther 1861 = *G. fluviatilis* Cuvier & Valenciennes 1828. Gobiidae.

Fluvidraco Jordan & Fowler 1903:904 [ref. 2464]. Masc. *Pseudobagrus ransonnetii* Steindachner 1887:287. Type by original designation. Synonym of *Pelteobagrus* Bleeker 1865 (Jayaram 1968:295 [ref. 5615]). Bagridae.

Fluviphylax Whitley 1965:25 [ref. 4733]. Masc. *Potamophylax pygmaeus* Myers 1955:7. Type by being a replacement name. Replacement for *Potamophylax* Myers & Carvalho 1955, preoccupied by Wallengren 1891 in Trichoptera. Valid (Parenti 1981:515 [ref. 7066]). Cyprinodontidae: Fluviphylacinae.

Foa Jordan & Evermann in Jordan & Seale 1905:779 [ref. 2495]. *Fowleria brachygramma* Jenkins 1903:447. Type by subsequent designation; technically two included species. Appeared first in Jordan & Seale (3 July 1905) with description of *Foa fo*, but figure labelled *Foa brachygramma* (Jenkins). Then in Jordan & Evermann (29 July 1905:210 [ref. 2451]) with *F. brachygramma* as type [*Foa fo* not mentioned]. Type designated by Jordan & Evermann 29 July (style of type in parentheses). Valid (Fraser 1972:10 [ref. 5195], Hayashi in Masuda et al. 1984:144 [ref. 6441], Gon 1986: 556 [ref. 5657], Paxton et al. 1989:553 [ref. 12442]). Apogonidae.

Fodiator Jordan & Meek 1885:45 [ref. 2489]. Masc. *Exocoetus acutus* Valenciennes in Cuvier & Valenciennes 1847:125. Type by monotypy. Valid (Collette et al. 1984:338 [ref. 11422]). Exocoetidae.

Fodifoa Whitley 1936:26 [ref. 4687]. Fem. *Foa fistulosa* Weber 1909:162. Type by original designation (also monotypic). Synonym of *Siphamia* Weber 1909 (Fraser 1972:14 [ref. 5195]). Apogonidae.

Foerschichthys Scheel & Romand 1981:22, 30 [ref. 3923]. Masc. *Aplocheilichthys flavipinnis* Meinken 1932:54. Type by original designation (also monotypic). Valid (Parenti 1982 [ref. 5427], Wildekamp et al. 1986:262 [ref. 6198]). Aplocheilidae: Aplocheilinae.

Foetorepus Whitley 1931:323 [ref. 4672]. *Callionymus calauropomus* Richardson 1844:10. Type by original designation. Synonym of *Synchiropus* Gill 1860 (Fricke 1981:18 [ref. 1499], Fricke 1982:74 [ref. 5432]); valid (Houde 1984:637 [ref. 13674], Nakabo in Masuda et al. 1984:343 [ref. 6441], Nakabo 1987 [ref. 6375]). Callionymidae.

Folifer (subgenus of *Tor*) Wu in Wu, Lin, Chen, Chen & He 1977:327 [ref. 4807]. Masc. *Barbus (Labeobarbus) brevifilis* Peters 1880: 1033. Type by original designation (one species, two subspecies). Synonym of *Tor* Gray 1833, but as a valid subgenus (Chen & Chu 1985 [ref. 5250], Chu & Cui in Chu & Chen 1989:137 [ref. 13584]). Cyprinidae.

Fonticulus (subgenus of *Pseudotolithus*) Trewavas 1962:169 [ref. 4455]. Masc. *Corvina nigrita* Cuvier in Cuvier & Valenciennes 1830:103. Type by original designation (also monotypic). Synonym of *Pseudotolithus* Bleeker 1863 (Daget & Trewavas 1986:335 [ref. 6211]). Sciaenidae.

Fontinus (subgenus of *Fundulus*) Jordan & Evermann 1896:633, 634, 645 [ref. 2443]. Masc. *Fundulus seminolis* Girard 1859:59. Type by original designation. As *Fonticola* in Jordan, Evermann & Clark 1930, appendix:178 [ref. 6476]. Type by use of name in parentheses on p. 633 as was Jordan's style. Synonym of *Plancterus* Garman 1895 (Parenti 1981:493 [ref. 7066] but with type as *F. zebrinus*). Cyprinodontidae: Fundulinae.

Forbesella Jordan & Evermann 1927:503 [ref. 2453]. Fem. *Chologaster papilliferus* Forbes 1882:1. Type by original designation (also monotypic). *Forbesichthys* Jordan 1929 is an unneeded replacement, not preoccupied. Synonym of *Chologaster* Agassiz 1853. Amblyopsidae.

Forbesichthys Jordan 1929:68 [ref. 2431]. Masc. *Chologaster papilliferus* Forbes 1882:1. Type by being a replacement name. Unneeded replacement for and objective synonym of *Forbesella* Jordan & Evermann 1927, apparently not preoccupied. Synonym of *Chologaster* Agassiz 1853. Amblyopsidae.

Forcipiger Jordan & McGregor in Jordan & Evermann 1898:1670, 1671 [ref. 2444]. Masc. *Chelmon longirostris* Broussonet 1782:not paginated. Type by original designation. Also appeared in Jordan & McGregor 1899:279 [ref. 2488]. Valid (Burgess 1978:174 [ref. 700], Ida in Masuda et al. 1984:182 [ref. 6441], Maugé & Bauchot 1984:462 [ref. 6614], Heemstra 1986:630 [ref. 5660]). Chaetodontidae.

Formio Whitley in McCulloch 1929:193 [ref. 2948]. *Apolectus stromateus* Cuvier & Valenciennes 1832:439. Type by being a replacement name. Replacement for *Apolectus* Cuvier 1832, preoccupied by Bennett 1831 in fishes. Misspelled *Fonnio* in Zoological Record for 1929. Authorship attributed to Whitley who provided name and recognized preoccupation. Synonym of *Parastromateus* Bleeker 1865 (Smith-Vaniz 1986:653 [ref. 5718]). Carangidae.

Formosania Oshima 1919:194 [ref. 3312]. Fem. *Formosania gilberti* Oshima 1919:194. Type by original designation (also monotypic). Misspelled *Formosiana* in Zoological Record for 1919. Valid (Silas 1953:229 [ref. 4024] but with type as *lacustre* Steindachner); synonym of *Crossostoma* Sauvage 1878 (Chen 1980:102 [ref. 6901]). Balitoridae: Balitorinae.

Forskalichthys Whitley 1935:219 [ref. 4683]. Masc. *Conger cinereus* Rüppell 1828:115. Type by original designation. Synonym of *Conger* Oken 1817 (Blache et al. 1973:239 [ref. 7185], Smith 1989:513 [ref. 13285]). Congridae: Congrinae.

Forsterygion Whitley & Phillipps 1939:236 [ref. 4737]. Neut. *Blennius varius* Bloch & Schneider 1801:178. Type by original designation (also monotypic). Valid (Hardy 1989 [ref. 12485]). Tripterygiidae.

Fossorochromis Eccles & Trewavas 1989:275 [ref. 13547]. Masc. *Tilapia rostrata* Boulenger 1899:131. Type by original designation (also monotypic). Cichlidae.

Fowlerella Smith 1957:100, 104 [ref. 4113]. Fem. *Labroides bicolor* Fowler & Bean 1928:224. Type by original designation (also monotypic). Labridae.

Fowleria Jordan & Evermann 1903:180 [ref. 2450]. Fem. *Apogon auritus* Valenciennes in Cuvier & Valenciennes 1831:443. Type by original designation. Valid (Fraser 1972:11 [ref. 5195], Goren & Karplus 1980 [ref. 6903], Hayashi in Masuda et al. 1984:143 [ref. 6441], Gon 1986:556 [ref. 5657], Paxton et al. 1989:554 [ref. 12442]). Apogonidae.

Fowlerichthys Barbour 1941:12 [ref. 179]. Masc. *Fowlerichthys floridanus* Barbour 1941:12. Type by original designation (also monotypic). Synonym of *Antennarius* Daudin 1816 (Monod & Le Danois 1973:659 [ref. 7223], Pietsch in Whitehead et al. 1986:1364 [ref. 13677]); as a valid subgenus (Pietsch 1984:34 [ref. 5380]). Antennariidae.

Fowlerina Eigenmann 1907:771 [ref. 1220]. Fem. *Tetragonopterus compressus* Günther 1864:319. Type by monotypy. Preoccupied by Pelseneer 1906 in Mollusca, replaced by and objective synonym of *Ephippicharax* Fowler 1913. Synonym of *Poptella* Eigenmann 1907 (Reis 1989:18 [ref. 14219]). Characidae: Stethaprioninae.

Franciscodoras Eigenmann 1925:317 [ref. 1244]. Masc. *Doras marmoratus* Reinhardt in Lütken 1874:30. Type by original designation (also monotypic). Valid (Burgess 1989:224 [ref. 12860]). Doradidae.

Franzia Jordan & Thompson 1914:251 [ref. 2543]. Fem. *Anthias nobilis* Franz 1910:38. Type by original designation. Synonym of *Anthias* Bloch 1792 (Heemstra & Randall 1986:511 [ref. 5667]); valid genus (Kendall 1984:501, 503 [ref. 13663], Kanayama in Masuda et al. 1984:136 [ref. 6441]); valid, but close to *Pseudanthias* Bleeker 1873 (Katayama & Amaoka 1986:221 [ref. 6680]); as a subgenus of *Pseudanthias* (Randall & Hutomo 1988:672 [ref. 6679]). Serranidae: Anthiinae.

Fraudella Whitley 1935:229 [ref. 4683]. Fem. *Fraudella carassiops* Whitley 1935:229. Type by original designation (also monotypic). Placement in the Plesiopidae follows Hoese & Kuiter 1984; probably valid (Hoese & Kuiter 1984:8 [ref. 5300]); valid (Paxton et al. 1989:525 [ref. 12442]). Plesiopidae.

Frontilabrus Randall & Condé 1989:90 [ref. 9294]. Masc. *Frontilabrus caeruleus* Randall & Condé 1989:91. Type by monotypy. Labridae.

Fucomimus Smith 1946:544 [ref. 4072]. Masc. *Clinus mus* Gilchrist & Thompson 1908:119. Type by original designation (also monotypic). Valid (Smith 1986:765 [ref. 5712]). Clinidae.

Fugu Abe 1952:36 [ref. 4]. Masc. *Tetraodon rubripes* Temminck & Schlegel 1850:123. Type by original designation. See also Abe 1954:122 [ref. 5] and *Torafugu* Abe 1949. Valid (Tyler 1980:341 [ref. 4477], Arai 1983:207 [ref. 14249]); synonym of *Takifugu* Abe 1949 (Matsuura in Masuda et al. 1984:363 [ref. 2902] based on placement of type species). Tetraodontidae.

Fundulichthys Bleeker 1859:439 [ref. 370]. Masc. *Fundulus virescens* Temminck & Schlegel 1846:225. Type by subsequent designation (also monotypic). Apparently appeared first in key, without included species. Type designated by Bleeker 1864:139 [ref. 4859], which also may be the first inclusion of a species. Synonym of *Pseudorasbora* Bleeker 1859 (Banarescu & Nalbant 1973:20 [ref. 173]). Cyprinidae.

Fundulopanchax (subgenus of *Fundulus*) Myers 1924:4 [ref. 3091]. Masc. *Fundulus gularis var. caerulea* Boulenger 1915:30. Type by original designation. For purposes of the type species, the variety *caerulea* is raised to species level; type not *gularis*. On Official List (Opinion 1010). As a valid subgenus of *Aphyosemion* Myers 1924 (Radda 1977:209 [ref. 3580]); valid genus (Parenti 1981:477 [ref. 7066]); synonym of *Aphyosemion* Myers 1924 (Wildekamp et al. 1986:196 [ref. 6198]). Aplocheilidae: Aplocheilinae.

Fundulosoma Ahl 1924:50, 52 [ref. 76]. Neut. *Fundulosoma thierryi* Ahl 1924:54. Type by original designation (also monotypic). Synonym of *Nothobranchius* Peters 1868 (Parenti 1981:479 [ref. 7066]); valid (Wildekamp et al. 1986:262 [ref. 6198]). Aplocheilidae: Aplocheilinae.

Fundulus Lacepède 1803:37 [ref. 4930]. Masc. *Fundulus mudfish* Lacepède 1803:37, 38 (= *Cobitis heteroclita* Linnaeus 1766:500). Type by monotypy. See also Bailey & Wiley 1976 [ref. 7090]. Valid (Parenti 1981:494 [ref. 7066]). Cyprinodontidae: Fundulinae.

Fur Whitley 1943:167 [ref. 4703]. Masc. *Fur macki* Whitley 1943:168. Type by original designation (also monotypic). Preoccupied by Jones 1935 or 1940 in Diptera, replaced by *Furgaleus* Whitley 1951. Objective synonym of *Furgaleus* Whitley 1951 (Compagno 1984:384 [ref. 6846], Compagno 1988:233 [ref. 13488], Paxton et al. 1989:80 [ref. 12442]). Triakidae: Galeorhininae.

Furcaria Poey 1860:194 [ref. 3499]. Fem. *Furcaria puncta* Poey 1860:195. Type by subsequent designation. Earliest type designation located that of Jordan & Evermann 1898:1545 [ref. 2444]. Preoccupied by Lesson 1838 in Aves, replaced by *Demoisellea* Whitley 1928. Pomacentridae.

Furcella (subgenus of *Lycenchelys*) Jordan & Evermann 1896:480 [ref. 2442]. Fem. *Lycodes diapterus* Gilbert 1891:564. Type by original designation (also monotypic). Preoccupied by Lamarck 1801 in Mollusca, replaced by *Furcimanus* Jordan & Evermann 1898. Synonym of *Lycodes* Reinhardt 1831 (McAllister et al. 1981:824 [ref. 5431]). Zoarcidae.

Furcimanus Jordan & Evermann 1898:2456, 2472 [ref. 2445]. Fem. *Lycodes diapterus* Gilbert 1891:564. Type by being a replacement name. Replacement for *Furcella* Jordan & Evermann 1896, preoccupied by Lamarck 1801 in Mollusca. Synonym of *Lycodes* Reinhardt 1831 (McAllister et al. 1981:824 [ref. 5431], Toyoshima 1985:180 [ref. 5722]). Zoarcidae.

Furcina Jordan & Starks 1904:303 [ref. 2528]. Fem. *Furcina* *ishikawae* Jordan & Starks 1904:303. Type by original designation. Valid (Washington et al. 1984:442 [ref. 13660], Yabe in Masuda et al. 1984:329 [ref. 6441], Yabe 1985:111 [ref. 11522]). Cottidae.

Furcipenis Hubbs 1931:1 [ref. 2240]. Masc. *Priapichthys huberi* Fowler 1923:27. Type by original designation (also monotypic). Synonym of *Alfaro* Meek 1912 (Rosen & Bailey 1963:42 [ref. 7067]). Poeciliidae.

Furcodontichthys Rapp Py-Daniel 1981:2 [ref. 3568]. Masc. *Furcodontichthys novaesi* Rapp Py-Daniel 1981:4. Type by original designation (also monotypic). Valid (Burgess 1989:441 [ref. 12860]). Loricariidae.

Furgaleus Whitley 1951:67 [ref. 4711]. Masc. *Fur macki* Whitley 1943:168. Type by being a replacement name. Replacement for *Fur* Whitley 1943, preoccupied by Jones 1935 or 1940 in Diptera. Valid (Compagno 1984:384 [ref. 6846], Paxton et al. 1989:80 [ref. 12442], Herman et al. 1988:103 [ref. 13267] with *ventrosa* as type, Compagno 1988:233 [ref. 13488]). Triakidae: Galeorhininae.

Furmastix Whitley 1951:67 [ref. 4711]. Fem. *Pluto infernalis* Hubbs 1938:291. Type by being a replacement name. Replacement for *Pluto* Hubbs 1938, preoccupied in Hymenoptera [details not researched]. Synonym of *Ophisternon* McClelland 1844 (Rosen & Greenwood 1976:50 [ref. 7094], Daget 1986:291 [ref. 6203]). Synbranchidae.

Fusania Jordan & Starks 1905:198 [ref. 2530]. Fem. *Fusania ensarca* Jordan & Starks 1905:198. Type by monotypy. Cyprinidae.

Fuscatelum (subgenus of *Etheostoma*) Page 1981:36 [ref. 3347]. Neut. *Etheostoma parvipinne* Gilbert & Swain 1887:59. Type by original designation (also monotypic). Synonym of *Etheostoma* Rafinesque 1819, but as a valid subgenus (Bailey & Etnier 1988:26 [ref. 6873]). Percidae.

Fusiclupea (subgenus of *Sardinops*) Whitley 1940:401 [ref. 4699]. Fem. *Sardinops dakini* Whitley 1937:114. Type by original designation (also monotypic). Synonym of *Amblygaster* Bleeker 1849 (Whitehead 1985:86 [ref. 5141]). Clupeidae.

Fusigobius Whitley 1930:122 [ref. 4669]. Masc. *Gobius neophytus* Günther 1877:174. Type by original designation (also monotypic). Valid (Yoshino in Masuda et al. 1984:251 [ref. 6441], Hoese 1986:789 [ref. 5670], Birdsong et al. 1988:192 [ref. 7303], Hoese & Obika 1988 [ref. 12745]). Gobiidae.

Fusiloricaria (subgenus of *Loricaria*) Fowler 1940:247 [ref. 1432]. Fem. *Loricaria (Fusiloricaria) clavipinna* Fowler 1940:247. Type by original designation (also monotypic). Synonym of *Loricaria* Linnaeus 1758 (Isbrücker 1980:115 [ref. 2303], Isbrücker 1981:57 [ref. 5522]). Loricariidae.

Fustis Lin 1932:517 [ref. 2781]. Masc. *Fustis vivus* Lin 1932:517. Type by monotypy. Valid (Wu et al. 1977:268 [ref. 4807]); synonym of *Luciocyprinus* Vaillant 1904 (Kottelat 1983 [ref. 6013], Chu & Cui in Chu & Chen 1989:159 [ref. 13584]). Cyprinidae.

Fuyangia Whitley 1931:334 [ref. 4672]. Fem. *Chalinura simula* Goode & Bean 1883:199. Type by being a replacement name. Replacement for *Chalinura* Goode & Bean 1883, preoccupied by Dalman 1826 in Arachnida [not researched]. Macrouridae: Macrourinae.

Gaboa (subgenus of *Centrophorus*) Whitley 1940:146 [ref. 4700]. *Centrophorus harrissoni* McCulloch 1915:99. Type by original designation (also monotypic). Synonym of *Centrophorus* Müller & Henle 1837 (Compagno 1984:35 [ref. 6474]). Squalidae.

Gadapistus de Beaufort 1949:68 [ref. 241]. Masc. *Paracentropogon aeglefinus* Weber 1913:500. Type by monotypy. Objective synonym of *Neocentropogon* Matsubara 1943. Scorpaenidae: Tetraroginae.

Gadella Lowe 1843:91 [ref. 2832]. Fem. *Gadella gracilis* Lowe 1843:91. Type by monotypy. Valid (Cohen 1973:323 [ref. 6589], Fahay & Markle 1984:266 [ref. 13653], Cohen in Whitehead et al. 1986:715 [ref. 13676], Paulin 1989:95 [ref. 9297]). Moridae.

Gadiculus Guichenot 1850:101 [ref. 1940]. Masc. *Gadiculus argenteus* Guichenot 1850:102. Type by monotypy. Valid (Svetovidov 1973:305 [ref. 7169], Fahay & Markle 1984:266 [ref. 13653], Svetovidov in Whitehead et al. 1986:685 [ref. 13676]). Gadidae.

Gadomus Regan 1903:459 [ref. 3617]. Masc. *Bathygadus longifilis* Goode & Bean 1886:599. Type by original designation (also monotypic). Valid (Marshall 1973:288 [ref. 7194], Marshall & Iwamoto 1973:519 [ref. 6963], Fahay & Markle 1984:274 [ref. 13653], Okamura in Masuda et al. 1984:93 [ref. 6441], Geistdoerfer in Whitehead et al. 1986:647 [ref. 13676]). Macrouridae: Bathygadinae.

Gadopsis Filippi 1855:170 [ref. 1327]. Fem. *Oligopus ater* Risso 1810:142. Type by monotypy. Preoccupied by Richardson 1848 in fishes, replaced by *Verater* Jordan 1919 [second *Verater*], but earlier replaced by *Pteridium* Filippi & Verany 1859. Synonym of *Oligopus* Risso 1810 (Cohen 1964:2 [ref. 6891]), but see account of *Oligopus* Risso. Bythitidae: Bythitinae.

Gadopsis Richardson 1848:122 [ref. 3740]. Fem. *Gadopsis marmoratus* Richardson 1848:122. Type by monotypy. Valid. Percichthyidae.

Gadulus Malm 1877:106, 482 [ref. 2881]. Masc. *Gadus luscus* Linnaeus 1758:252. Type by original designation. Probably not preoccupied by *Gadulus* [apparently in error for *Cadulus* Philippi 1844] Issel 1876 in Mollusca. Synonym of *Trisopterus* Rafinesque 1814 (Svetovidov 1973:310 [ref. 7169]). Gadidae.

Gadus Linnaeus 1758:251 [ref. 2787]. Masc. *Gadus morhua* Linnaeus 1758:252. Type by subsequent designation. Type designated by Jordan & Gilbert 1883:802 [ref. 2476]; on Official List (Opinion 77, Direction 56). Valid (Svetovidov 1973:303 [ref. 7169], Fahay & Markle 1984:266 [ref. 13653], Okamura in Masuda et al. 1984:92 [ref. 6441], Svetovidov in Whitehead et al. 1986:686 [ref. 13676]). Gadidae.

Gagata Bleeker 1858:204, 206 [ref. 365]. *Pimelodus gagata* Hamilton 1822:197, 379. Type by absolute tautonymy. Valid (Jayaram 1981:238 [ref. 6497], Burgess 1989:133 [ref. 12860], Kottelat 1989:15 [ref. 13605]). Sisoridae.

Gaidropsarus Rafinesque 1810:11, 51 [ref. 3595]. Masc. *Gaidropsarus mustellaris* Rafinesque 1810:51. Type by monotypy. Valid (Svetovidov 1973:317 [ref. 7169], Markle 1982:3423 [ref. 5439], Fahay & Markle 1984:266 [ref. 13653], Svetovidov in Whitehead et al. 1986:699 [ref. 13676], Cohen 1986:324 [ref. 5646], Svetovidov 1986 [ref. 8033], Paxton et al. 1989:307 [ref. 12442]). Lotidae.

Galasaccus (subgenus of *Fundulus*) Fowler 1916:416 [ref. 1394]. Masc. *Hydrargira similis* Baird & Girard 1853:389. Type by original designation. Misspelled *Gelasaceus* by Jordan, Evermann & Clark 1930:177 [ref. 6476]. Synonym of *Fundulus* Lacepède 1803 (Parenti 1981:495 [ref. 7066] as *Galasaceus*). Cyprinodontidae: Fundulinae.

Galatheathauma (subgenus of *Thaumatichthys*) Bruun 1953:174 [ref. 6265]. Fem. *Galatheathauma axeli* Bruun 1953:174. Original not seen; information above from Bertelsen & Struhsaker 1977. Synonym of *Thaumatichthys* Smith & Radcliffe 1912 (Bertelsen & Struhsaker 1977:35 [ref. 5331]). Thaumatichthyidae.

Galaxias Cuvier 1816:183 [ref. 993]. Masc. *Esox truttaceus* Cuvier 1816:184 (footnote). Type by monotypy. Cuvier's species *truttaceus* essentially as name only in footnote, but tied to description in text and perhaps available; else type is *G. fasciatus* Gray 1842 by subsequent monotypy. Valid (McDowall & Frankenberg 1981:455 [ref. 5500], McDowall 1984:151 [ref. 11850], McDowall 1984:126 [ref. 6178], Paxton et al. 1989:175 [ref. 12442]). Galaxiidae: Galaxiinae.

Galaxiella McDowall 1978:116 [ref. 2951]. Fem. *Galaxias pusillus* Mack 1936:101. Type by original designation. Valid (McDowall & Frankenberg 1981:552 [ref. 5500], McDowall 1984:150 [ref. 11850], Paxton et al. 1989:179 [ref. 12442], Berra & Allen 1989 [ref. 13529]). Galaxiidae: Galaxiinae.

Galeagra Heller & Snodgrass 1903:193 [ref. 2089]. Fem. *Galeagra pammelas* Heller & Snodgrass 1903:193. Percoidei.

Galeichthys Valenciennes in Cuvier & Valenciennes 1840:28 [ref. 1008]. Masc. *Galeichthys feliceps* Valenciennes in Cuvier & Valenciennes 1840:29. Type by subsequent designation. Type designated by Bleeker 1862:7 [ref. 393] and 1863:90 [ref. 401]. Valid (Taylor 1986:212 [ref. 6282]). Ariidae.

Galeocerdo Müller & Henle 1837:115 [ref. 3067]. Fem. *Squalus arcticus* Faber 1829:17. Type by subsequent designation. Also in Müller & Henle 1837:397 [ref. 13421]; and in Bonaparte 1838:211 [p. 10 of separate, ref. 4979] where type is designated (see Bonaparte p. 2 of separate). Valid (Compagno 1973:26 [ref. 7163], Compagno 1984:503 [ref. 6846], Nakaya in Masuda et al. 1984:5 [ref. 6441], Bass et al. 1986:78 [ref. 5638], Cappetta 1987:123 [ref. 6348], Compagno 1988:279 [ref. 13488], Paxton et al. 1989:80 [ref. 12442]). Carcharhinidae.

Galeocharax Fowler 1910:790 [ref. 4994]. Masc. *Cynopotamus gulo* Cope 1870:565. Type by original designation. Valid (Menezes 1976:40 [ref. 7073] in subfamily Cynopotaminae). Characidae.

Galeoides Günther 1860:319, 332 [ref. 1963]. Masc. *Polynemus polydactylus* Vahl 1798:164. Type by monotypy. Valid (Monod 1973:575 [ref. 7193], de Sylva 1984:540 [ref. 13667], Hureau in Whitehead et al. 1986:1205 [ref. 13677], Daget & Njock 1986:352 [ref. 6216]). Polynemidae.

Galeolamna Owen 1853:96 [ref. 4988]. Fem. *Galeolamna greyi* Owen 1853:96. Type by original designation. Original not seen. Synonym of *Carcharhinus* Blainville 1816 (Garrick 1982:19 [ref. 5454], Compagno 1984:449 [ref. 6846], Cappetta 1987:121 [ref. 6348], Compagno 1988:307 [ref. 13488]). Carcharhinidae.

Galeolamnoides Whitley 1934:191 [ref. 4949]. Masc. *Carcharias macrurus* Ramsay & Ogilby 1887:163. Type by original designation. Synonym of *Carcharhinus* Blainville 1816 (Garrick 1982:19 [ref. 5454], Compagno 1984:449 [ref. 6846], Cappetta 1987:121 [ref. 6348], Compagno 1988:308 [ref. 13488]). Carcharhinidae.

Galeorhinus (subgenus of *Squalus*) Blainville 1816:121 [ref. 306]. Masc. *Squalus galeus* Linnaeus 1758:234. Type by subsequent designation. Type apparently first designated by Gill 1862:402 [ref. 1783] as *Galeorhinus galeus* Blainville; *Squalus canis* and *S. mustelus* also listed as type by authors. Valid (Compagno 1973:27 [ref. 7163], Compagno 1984:386 [ref. 6846], Bass et al. 1986:78 [ref. 5638], Cappetta 1987:115 [ref. 6348], Paxton et al. 1989:80 [ref. 12442], Herman et al. 1988:106 [ref. 13267], Compagno 1988:246 [ref. 13488]). Triakidae: Galeorhininae.

Galera Herre 1927:103 [ref. 2104]. Fem. *Galera producta* Herre 1927:104. Type by original designation (also monotypic). Preoccupied by Gray 1842 in Mammalia, replaced by *Herrea* Whitley 1930. Synonym of *Callogobius* Bleeker 1874 (Hoese, pers. comm.). Gobiidae.

Galeus (subgenus of *Squalus*) Cuvier 1816:127 [ref. 993]. Masc. *Squalus galeus* Linnaeus 1758:234. Type by monotypy. Preoccupied by *Galeus* Rafinesque 1810 in Scyliorhinidae. Objective synonym of *Galeorhinus* Blainville 1816 (Compagno 1984:386 [ref. 6846], Compagno 1988:246 [ref. 13488]). Triakidae: Galeorhininae.

Galeus Garman 1913:145 [ref. 1545]. Masc. *Squalus glaucus* Linnaeus 1758:235. Type by monotypy. Garman's use of *Galeus* Valmont de Bomare 1768 (not available, rejected work) creates the genus *Galeus* Garman 1913. Preoccupied by Rafinesque 1810 in fishes. In the synonymy of *Prionace* Cantor 1849 (Compagno 1984:521 [ref. 6846], Compagno 1988:346 [ref. 13488]). Triakidae: Triakinae.

Galeus Leach 1818:62 [ref. 12565]. Masc. *Squalus mustelus* Linnaeus 1758:235. Type by monotypy. Independently described. Preoccupied by *Galeus* Rafinesque 1810 and *Galeus* Cuvier 1816. Objective synonym of *Mustelus* Linck 1790 (Compagno 1984:397 [ref. 6846], Compagno 1988:219 [ref. 13488]). Triakidae: Triakinae.

Galeus Rafinesque 1810:13 [ref. 3594]. Masc. *Galeus melastomus* Rafinesque 1810:13. Type by subsequent designation. Type designated by Fowler 1908:53 [ref. 6847]; *Squalus mustelus* as used by Jordan & Evermann 1896:29 [ref. 2443] not precise enough for type designation. Valid (Springer 1973:20 [ref. 7162], Nakaya 1975:40 [ref. 7083], Springer 1979:47 [ref. 4175], Compagno 1984:306 [ref. 6846], Bass 1986:90 [ref. 5635], Séret 1987:18 [6267], Cappetta 1987:111 [ref. 6348], Tachikawa & Taniuchi 1987 [ref. 6712], Compagno 1988:134 [ref. 13488], Paxton et al. 1989:73 [ref. 12442]). Scyliorhinidae.

Galeus Schaeffer 1760:20 [ref. 4989]. Masc. Not available, published in a rejected work on Official Index (Opinion 345). Author's name spelled Schaefer by Jordan, Schaeffer by ICZN. Original not examined. In the synonymy of *Galeorhinus* Blainville 1816. Triakidae: Galeorhininae.

Galeus Valmont de Bomare 1768:371 [ref. 4507]. Masc. Not available, published in a rejected work on Official Index (Opinion 89, Direction 32). In the synonymy of *Prionace* Cantor 1849. Carcharhinidae.

Gallichtys Cuvier in Cuvier & Valenciennes 1833:168 [ref. 1002]. Masc. *Gallichtys major* Cuvier in Cuvier & Valenciennes 1833:168. Type by subsequent designation. Type designated by Jordan 1919:178 [ref. 2410]. Spelled *Gallichtys* in 3 places and in index; *Gallichthys* of Agassiz 1845:26 [ref. 4889] and others is an unjustified emendation or incorrect subsequent spelling. Synonym of *Alectis* Rafinesque 1815 (Daget & Smith-Vaniz 1986:308 [ref. 6207], as *Gallichthys*). Carangidae.

Gallus Lacepède 1802:583 [ref. 4929]. Masc. *Gallus virescens* Lacepède 1802:583. Type by monotypy. *Gallus* preoccupied by Linnaeus 1758 in Aves, replaced by *Alectis* Rafinesque 1815 (see Daget & Smith-Vaniz 1986:308 [ref. 6207]). Objective synonym of *Alectis* Rafinesque 1815 (Paxton et al. 1989:573 [ref. 12442]). Carangidae.

Gambusia Poey 1854:382, 390 [ref. 3497]. Fem. *Gambusia punctata* Poey 1854:384. Type by subsequent designation. Type apparently designated first by Bleeker 1864:140 [ref. 4859], also by Jordan & Copeland 1877:142 [ref. 5961]. On Official List

(Opinion 375). Valid (Rivas 1963 [ref. 3761], Rosen & Bailey 1963:90 [ref. 7067], Paxton et al. 1989:346 [ref. 12442], Parenti & Rauchenberger 1989:8 [ref. 13538]). Poeciliidae.

Gambusinus (subgenus of *Fundulus*) Jordan & Evermann 1896:633, 635, 649 [ref. 2443]. Masc. *Fundulus rathbuni* Jordan & Meek 1888:356. Type by original designation. Synonym of *Fundulus* Lacepède 1803 (Parenti 1981:495 [ref. 7066]). Cyprinodontidae: Fundulinae.

Gammaraia (subgenus of *Raja*) Leigh-Sharpe 1924:567, 571 [ref. 5748]. Fem. *Raja batis* Linnaeus 1758:231. Type by original designation. As a "pseudogenus" of *Raia* [=*Raja*]. Not available [Art. 1b (6)], used as an artificial category (see Leigh-Sharpe 1928 [ref. 6152]). In the synonymy of *Raja* Linnaeus 1758, subgenus *Dipturus* Rafinesque 1810 (Stehmann 1973:62 [ref. 7168]). Rajidae.

Gammascyllium Leigh-Sharpe 1926:326 [ref. 5627]. Neut. *Scyllium burgerii* Müller & Henle 1838. Type by original designation. As a "pseudogenus" of *Scyllium*. Not available [Art. 1b(6)], used as an artificial category (see Leigh-Sharpe 1928 [ref. 6152]). In the synonymy of *Halaelurus* Gill 1862 (Compagno 1984:319 [ref. 6846], Compagno 1988:143 [ref. 13488]). Scyliorhinidae.

Gammogobius Bath 1971:201 [ref. 206]. Masc. *Gammogobius steinitzi* Bath 1971:202. Type by original designation (also monotypic). Valid (Miller 1973:495 [ref. 6888], Miller in Whitehead et al. 1986:1034 [ref. 13677]). Gobiidae.

Ganoideus Whitley 1950:44 [ref. 4713]. Masc. *Agonus vulsus* Jordan & Gilbert 1880:330. Type by being a replacement name. Replacement for *Stelgis* Cramer in Jordan & Starks 1895, preoccupied by Pomel 1872 in sponges; also replaced by *Acanthostelgis* Fowler 1958. Objective synonym of *Stelgis* Cramer 1895; synonym of *Agonopsis* Gill 1861 (Lea & Dempster 1982:250 [ref. 14236]). Agonidae.

Garariscus Smith 1917:145 [ref. 4045]. Masc. *Gargariscus semidentatus* Smith 1917:145. Triglidae: Peristediinae.

Gardonus Bonaparte 1846:29 [ref. 519]. *Leuciscus decipiens* Agassiz 1834:38. Type by subsequent designation. Earliest subsequent designation not researched. Synonym of *Rutilus* Rafinesque 1820 (Howes 1981:45 [ref. 14200] as *Gardanus*). Cyprinidae.

Gareus (subgenus of *Liopsetta*) Hubbs 1915:486 [ref. 2224]. Masc. *Pleuronectes obscurus* Herzenstein 1891:49. Type by original designation (also monotypic). Synonym of *Liopsetta* Gill 1864 (Norman 1934:368 [ref. 6893]). Pleuronectidae: Pleuronectinae.

Gargariscus Smith 1917:145 [ref. 4045]. Masc. *Gargariscus semidentatus* Smith 1917:145. Type by original designation (also monotypic). Valid (Ochiai & Yatou in Masuda et al. 1984:334 [ref. 6441], Chen & Shao 1988:129 [ref. 6676], Paxton et al. 1989:454 [ref. 12442]). Triglidae: Peristediinae.

Gargaropteron Smith 1965:569 [ref. 4134]. *Gargaropteron pterodactylops* Smith 1965:569. Type by original designation (also monotypic). Synonym of *Kali* Lloyd 1909 (Johnson & Cohen 1974:34 [ref. 7133]). Chiasmodontidae.

Gargilius Jensen in Koefoed 1953:11 [ref. 6486]. Masc. *Gargilius lucullus* Jensen in Koefoed 1953:11. Type by subsequent designation. Type designated by Cohen 1973:326 [ref. 6589], but that designation invalid as genus established after 1930 without type fixation. Appeared first without description in Jensen in Schmidt 1906:177 and Holt & Byrne 1908:58 [ref. 6487]. Preoccupied by Faimaire 1891 in Insecta, replaced by *Svetovidovia* Cohen 1973, but since *Gargilius* was not available it cannot be replaced; *Svetovidovia* stands on its own with type by original designation (also monotypic). Moridae.

Garichthys Whitley 1934:unpaginated [ref. 4682]. Masc. *Coelorhynchus (Paramacrurus) mirus* McCulloch 1926:178. Type by original designation (also monotypic). Synonym of *Caelorinchus* Giorna 1809 (Marshall 1973:293 [ref. 7194], Marshall & Iwamoto 1973:538 [ref. 6966]). Macrouridae: Macrourinae.

Garmanella Hubbs 1936:218 [ref. 2247]. Fem. *Garmanella pulchra* Hubbs 1936:219. Type by original designation (also monotypic). Valid (some authors); synonym of *Jordanella* Goode & Bean 1879 (Parenti 1981:528 [ref. 7066]). Cyprinodontidae: Cyprinodontinae.

Garmanichthys Seale 1917:80 [ref. 4001]. Masc. *Garmanichthys dentatus* Seale 1917:80. Type by monotypy. Synonym of *Chlopsis* Rafinesque 1810 (Smith 1989:92 [ref. 13285]). Chlopsidae.

Garmanina (subgenus of *Rhytiodus*) Fowler 1906:326 [ref. 1373]. Fem. *Rhytiodus argenteofuscus* Kner 1859:166. Type by original designation (also monotypic). Synonym of *Rhytiodus* Kner 1858. Curimatidae: Anostominae.

Garmannia Jordan & Evermann in Jordan 1895:495 [ref. 2394]. Fem. *Gobius paradoxus* Günther 1861:549. Type by original designation (also monotypic). Valid. Gobiidae.

Garo Yazdani & Talwar 1981:287 [ref. 4816]. *Pillaia khajuriai* Talwar, Yazdani & Kundu 1977:53. Type by original designation (also monotypic). Synonym of *Chaudhuria* Annandale 1918 (Travers 1984:142 [ref. 5147]). Chaudhuriidae.

Garra (subgenus of *Cyprinus*) Hamilton 1822:343, 393 [ref. 2031]. Fem. *Cyprinus (Garra) lamta* Hamilton 1822:343, 393. Type by subsequent designation. Type designated by Bleeker 1863:192 [ref. 397], 1863:262 [ref. 403] or 1863:24 [ref. 4859]. Valid (Karaman 1971:232 [ref. 2560], Wu et al. 1977:372 [ref. 4807], Jayaram 1981:134 [ref. 6497], Lévêque & Daget 1984:301 [ref. 6186], Kottelat 1985:262 [ref. 11441], Roberts 1989:40 [ref. 6439], Chu & Cui in Chu & Chen 1989:269 [ref. 13584], Kottelat 1989:8 [ref. 13605], Krupp & Schneider 1989:366 [ref. 13651]). Cyprinidae.

Garrupa (subgenus of *Epinephelus*) Jordan in Jordan & Eigenmann 1890:350, 362 [ref. 2440]. *Serranus nigritus* Holbrook 1856:173. Type by original designation. Jordan is listed as author on p. 350, on p. 361-362 "We [Jordan & Eigenmann] have suggested...name...*Garrupa*..."; Jordan probably responsible for description. Synonym of *Epinephalus* Bloch 1793 (Smith 1971:103 [ref. 14102]). Serranidae: Epinephelinae.

Gasteracanthus Pallas 1814:228 [ref. 3351]. Masc. *Gasteracanthus cataphractus* Pallas 1814. Type by subsequent designation. Earliest type designation not researched. Synonym of *Gasterosteus* Linnaeus 1758 (Monod 1973:280 [ref. 7193] as *Gasteracenthus*). Gasterosteidae: Gasterosteinae.

Gasterochisma Richardson 1845:346 [ref. 3741]. *Gasterochisma melampus* Richardson 1845:346. Type by monotypy. Misspelled *Gasteroschisma* by Jordan 1919:227 [ref. 2410] and 1923:179 [ref. 2421]. Valid (Scott 1981:134 [ref. 5533], Collette & Nauen 1983: 37 [ref. 5375], Kohno 1984 [ref. 5796], Collette et al. 1984:600 [ref. 11421], Collette 1986:833 [ref. 5647], Johnson 1986:37 [ref. 5676]). Scombridae.

Gasterodon Rafinesque 1815:88 [ref. 3584]. Masc. Not available, name only. Unplaced genera.

Gasteropelecus Scopoli (ex Gronow) 1777:458 [ref. 3990]. Masc. *Clupea sternicla* Linnaeus 1758:319. Appeared without species;

first addition of species and subsequent designation of type not researched. Frequently misspelled. *Gastropelecys* Agassiz 1846:160 is an unjustified emendation or replacement for *Gasteropelecus* Gronow 1763 (not available). Valid (Géry 1977:2463, Vari 1983:5 [ref. 5419] in Characidae). Gasteropelecidae.

Gasterostea (subgenus of *Gasterosteus*) Sauvage 1874:7, 29 [ref. 3904]. Fem. *Gasterosteus pungitius* Linnaeus 1758:296. Type by subsequent designation. Type designated by Jordan 1919:377 [ref. 4904]. Objective synonym of *Pungitius* Coste 1848 (Monod 1973:283 [ref. 7193]). Gasterosteidae: Gasterosteinae.

Gasterosteus Linnaeus 1758:295 [ref. 2787]. Masc. *Gasterosteus aculeatus* Linnaeus 1758:295. Type by subsequent designation. Type designated by Jordan & Gilbert 1883:393 [ref. 2476]. On Official List (Opinion 77, Direction 56). Misspellings include *Gasterosterus* and *Gastrosteus*. Valid (Monod 1973:280 [ref. 7193], Ida in Masuda et al. 1984:83 [ref. 6441], Banister in Whitehead et al. 1986:640 [ref. 13676]). Gasterosteidae: Gasterosteinae.

Gasterotokeus Heckel in Kaup 1853:230 [ref. 2569]. Masc. *Syngnathus biaculeatus* Bloch 1785:10. Type by monotypy. Misspelled *Gastrotokeus* by authors. Synonym of *Syngnathoides* Bleeker 1851 (Dawson 1985:179 [ref. 6541]). Syngnathidae: Syngnathinae.

Gasterotomus Eigenmann 1910:422 [ref. 1224]. Masc. *Anodus latior* Agassiz in Spix & Agassiz 1829:61. Type by original designation (also monotypic). Misspelled *Gasterostomus* by authors. Synonym of *Potamorhina* Cope 1878 (Vari 1984:11 [ref. 5307], Vari 1989:6 [ref. 9189]). Curimatidae: Curimatinae.

Gastraea (subgenus of *Gasterosteus*) Sauvage 1874:7 [ref. 3904]. Fem. *Gasterosteus spinachia* Linnaeus 1758:296. Type by monotypy. Objective synonym of *Spinachia* Cuvier 1816 (Monod 1973:286 [ref. 7193]). Gasterosteidae: Gasterosteinae.

Gastrobranchus Bloch 1791:26 [ref. 6882]. Masc. *Gastrobranchus coecus* Bloch 1791:26. Type by monotypy. Also appeared in Cuvier & Valenciennes 1791:26 as abstract [see note under Bloch 1791, ref. 6882]. Species also appeared in Bloch 1795:67. Synonym of *Myxine* Linnaeus 1758 (Vladykov 1973:6 [ref. 7159]). Myxinidae: Myxininae.

Gastrocyathus Briggs 1955:46 [ref. 637]. Masc. *Gastrocyathus gracilis* Briggs 1955:47. Type by original designation (also monotypic). Valid (Allen [L. G.] 1984:629 [ref. 13673]). Gobiesocidae: Gobiesocinae.

Gastrocymba Briggs 1955:11 [ref. 637]. Fem. *Diplocrepis quadriradiatus* Rendahl 1925:8. Type by original designation (also monotypic). Species originally as "4-*radiatus*", emendation mandatory. Valid. Gobiesocidae: Gobiesocinae.

Gastrodermus Cope 1878:681 [ref. 945]. Masc. *Corydorus elegans* Steindachner 1876:141. Type by subsequent designation. Type apparently first designated by Gosline 1940:10 [ref. 6489]. Correct spelling for genus of type is *Corydoras*. Synonym of *Corydoras* Lacepède 1803 (Nijssen & Isbrücker 1980:192 [ref. 6910]). Callichthyidae.

Gastrogonus Rafinesque 1815:85 [ref. 3584]. Masc. Not available, name only. Unplaced genera.

Gastromyzon Günther 1874:454 [ref. 5753]. Masc. *Gastromyzon borneensis* Günther 1874:454. Type by monotypy. Valid (Silas 1953:240 [ref. 4024], Sawada 1982:206 [ref. 14111], Roberts 1982 [ref. 6689], Roberts 1989:85 [ref. 6439]). Balitoridae: Balitorinae.

Gastronemus Bonaparte (ex Cocco) 1846:68 [ref. 519]. Masc. *Pharopteryx benoiti* Rüppell 1852:16. Not available, name in synonymy of *Pharopteryx*. Perhaps first appeared in Cocco 1846:749 [not researched]. Synonym of *Mora* Risso 1826. Moridae.

Gastropelecys Agassiz 1846:160 [ref. 64]. *Clupea sternicla* Linnaeus 1758:319. Type by being a replacement name. An intended unjustified emendation for *Gasteropelecus* Gronow 1763:135, not available; but *Gasteropelecus* was published in an available way first by Scopoli 1777. Objective synonym of *Gasteropelecus* Scopoli 1777. Gasteropelecidae.

Gastrophysus Müller 1843:330 [ref. 3063]. Masc. *Tetraodon oblongus* Bloch 1786:6. Type by being a replacement name. Replacement for *Physogaster* Müller 1841, apparently preoccupied in insects. Synonym of *Lagocephalus* Swainson 1839 (Shipp 1974:17 [ref. 7147]); as a valid genus (Li 1986 [ref. 6329]). Tetraodontidae.

Gastropristis Eigenmann 1915:238 [ref. 1232]. Fem. *Serrasalmo (Pygocentrus) ternetzi* Steindachner 1908:359. Type by original designation (also monotypic). Synonym of *Serrasalmus* Lacepède 1803, but as a synonym of the later subgenus *Taddyella* von Ihering 1928 (Géry 1976:52 [ref. 14199]). Characidae: Serrasalminae.

Gastropsetta Bean 1895:633 [ref. 231]. Fem. *Gastropsetta frontalis* Bean 1895:633. Type by monotypy. Valid (Norman 1934:128 [ref. 6893], Ahlstrom et al. 1984:642 [ref. 13641]). Paralichthyidae.

Gastropterus Cope 1878:700 [ref. 945]. Masc. *Gastropterus archaeus* Cope 1878:700. Type by monotypy. Synonym of *Basilichthys* Girard 1855 (White 1985:17 [ref. 13551]). Atherinidae: Atherinopsinae.

Gastroscyphus Briggs 1955:45 [ref. 637]. Masc. *Crepidogaster hectoris* Günther 1876:396. Type by original designation (also monotypic). Valid (Allen [L. G.] 1984:629 [ref. 13673]). Gobiesocidae: Gobiesocinae.

Gastrostomus Gill & Ryder 1883:271 [ref. 1747]. Masc. *Gastro stomus bairdii* Gill & Ryder 1883:271. Type by monotypy. Synonym of *Eurypharynx* Vaillant 1882 (Böhlke 1966:610 [ref. 5256], Bauchot 1973:218 [ref. 7184], Bertelsen et al. 1989:649 [ref. 13293]). Eurypharyngidae.

Gaterin (subgenus of *Sciaena*) Forsskål 1775:45 [ref. 1351]. *Sciaena gaterina* Forsskål 1775:50. Not available, regarded as non-latinized Arabic name (see Jordan 1917:33-34 [ref. 2407]). Subsequent use in an available way not researched. In the synonymy of *Plectorhinchus* Lacepède 1801. Haemulidae.

Gaurochromis Greenwood 1980:32 [ref. 1899]. Masc. *Haplochromis empodisma* Greenwood 1960:262. Type by original designation. Described as a new genus on p. 32, as a new subgenus on p. 36. Cichlidae.

Gavialiceps Alcock (ex Wood-Mason) 1889:460 [ref. 81]. Neut. *Gavialiceps taeniola* Alcock (ex Wood-Mason) 1889:460. Type by subsequent designation. Described first with 2 included species. Alcock (1891:137 [ref. 87]) says *taeniola* is not a *Gavialiceps*, but does not technically fix the type of *Gavialiceps* as *microps*. Type selected by Gilbert 1905:586 [ref. 1631]. See Tighe 1989:617 [ref. 13291]. Valid (Karrer 1982:52 [ref. 5679], Machida in Masuda et al. 1984:29 [ref. 6441]). Muraenesocidae.

Gavialocharax Pellegrin 1927:390 [ref. 3405]. Masc. *Gavialocharax monodi* Pellegrin 1927:391. Type by monotypy. Valid (Géry 1977:86 [ref. 1597]); synonym of *Ichthyborus* Günther 1864 (Vari 1979:339 [ref. 5490], Daget & Gosse 1984:197 [ref. 6185]). Citharinidae: Distichodontinae.

Gazza Rüppell 1835:3 [ref. 3844]. Fem. *Gazza equulaeformis* Rüppell 1835:4. Type by monotypy. Valid (James 1978:168 [ref. 5317], Yabumoto et al. 1984 [ref. 6728], Uyeno & Yabumoto in Masuda et al. 1984:159 [ref. 6441], James 1985:397 [ref. 12861], Smith 1986:620 [ref. 5712]). Leiognathidae.

Geisleria Géry 1971:154 [ref. 1593]. Fem. *Geisleria junki* Géry 1971:154. Type by original designation (also monotypic). Valid (Géry 1977:122 [ref. 1597]); synonym of *Elachocharax* Myers 1927 (Weitzman & Géry 1981:888 [ref. 14218]). Characidae: Characidiinae.

Gelanoglanis Böhlke 1980:150 [ref. 605]. Masc. *Gelanoglanis stroudi* Böhlke 1980:152. Type by original designation (also monotypic). Valid (Burgess 1989:241 [ref. 12860], Curran 1989 [ref. 12547]). Auchenipteridae.

Gelidus Whitley 1937:19 [ref. 4691]. Masc. *Pleuragramma antarcticum* Boulenger 1902:187. Type by being a replacement name. Unneeded replacement for *Pleuragramma* Boulenger 1902, not preoccupied by *Pleurogrammus* Gill 1861 in fishes. Objective synonym of *Pleuragramma* Boulenger 1902. Nototheniidae.

Gempylus Cuvier 1829:200 [ref. 995]. Masc. *Gempylus serpens* Cuvier 1829:200. Type by monotypy. As "Les Gempyles," but with genus latinized in footnote. On Official List (Opinion 487). *Lucoscombrus* Van der Hoeven 1855:267 placed on Official Index as a junior objective synonym (Opinion 487). Valid (Parin & Bekker 1973:457 [ref. 7206], Collette et al. 1984:600 [ref. 11421], Nakamura in Masuda et al. 1984:227 [ref. 6441], Parin in Whitehead et al. 1986:968 [ref. 13676], Nakamura 1986:826 [ref. 5696]). Gempylidae.

Geneiates Tickell in Day 1888:804 [ref. 1082]. Masc. *Geneiates ferruginosus* Tickell in Day 1888:804. Type by subsequent designation (also monotypic). Appeared as a Tickell manuscript name mentioned by Day in the synonymy of *Brotula multibarbata*. See Myers 1951:26 [ref. 13464]; Myers did not make available by his statement, "Probably a synonym of *Brotula* but perhaps a good genus." Type designated by Myers 1951 [ref. 13464]. In the synonymy of *Brotula* Cuvier 1829 (Cohen & Nielsen 1978:11 [ref. 881]). Ophidiidae: Brotulinae.

Geneion Bibron in Duméril 1855:280 [ref. 297]. Neut. *Geneion maculatus* Bibron in Duméril 1855:280. Unlike most other genera in this work, *Geneion* has been regarded as latinized when originally proposed (e.g., by Troschel 1856:88 [ref. 12559] and by Hollard 1857:319 [ref. 2186]). But species appeared as name only unless it can take the monotypic genus description; addition of available species not researched; perhaps unavailable. Treated as a synonym of *Lagocephalus* Swainson 1839 by Fraser-Brunner 1943:9 [ref. 1495]. Tetraodontidae.

Gengea Katayama 1943:101 [ref. 2567]. Fem. *Gengea japonica* Katayama 1943:101. Type by original designation (also monotypic). Synonym of *Gymnelopsis* Soldatov 1922 (Anderson 1982:49 [ref. 5520]). Zoarcidae.

Genghis Howes 1984:289 [ref. 5312]. Masc. *Squalius mongolicus* Kessler in Prejevalsky 1876:21. Type by original designation (also monotypic). Cyprinidae.

Genicanthus (subgenus of *Holacanthus*) Swainson 1839:170, 212 [ref. 4303]. Masc. *Holacanthus lamarck* Lacepède 1802:526, 530. Type by subsequent designation. Type designated by Swain 1882:273 [ref. 5966]. Valid (Randall 1975 [ref. 6490], Araga in Masuda et al. 1984:188 [ref. 6441], Smith & Heemstra 1986:624 [ref. 5714]). Pomacanthidae.

Genidens Castelnau 1855:33 [ref. 766]. Masc. *Bagrus genidens* Valenciennes in Cuvier & Valenciennes 1840:453. Type by original designation (or by absolute tautonymy). *Bagrus genidens* renamed *G. cuvieri* by Castelnau. Valid (Burgess 1989:167 [ref. 12860]). Ariidae.

Genioliparis Andriashev & Neelov 1976:70 [ref. 124]. Masc. *Genioliparis lindbergi* Andriashev & Neelov 1976:73. Type by original designation (also monotypic). Cyclopteridae: Liparinae.

Gennadius Jordan & Seale 1907:37 [ref. 2498]. Masc. *Sebastes stoliczkae* Day 1877:149. Type by original designation (also monotypic). Synonym of *Centrogenys* Richardson 1842. Centrogeniidae.

Genyagnus Gill 1861:115 [ref. 1774]. Masc. *Uranoscopus monopterygius* Bloch & Schneider 1801:49. Type by monotypy. *Geniagnus* Waite 1907:30 [ref. 11968] is an incorrect subsequent spelling. Valid (Mees 1960:47 [ref. 11931], Pietsch 1989:296 [ref. 12541]). Uranoscopidae.

Genyatremus Gill 1862:256 [ref. 4909]. Masc. *Pristipoma bilineatum* Cuvier in Cuvier & Valenciennes 1830:271. Type by original designation. Spelled *Genytremus* four times and once as *Genyatremus* in original description. First reviser not researched; *Genyatremus* in recent literature. Valid (Johnson 1980:11 [ref. 13553] as *Genyatremus*, Matsuura in Uyeno et al. 1983:354 [ref. 14275]). Haemulidae.

Genycharax Eigenmann 1912:22 [ref. 1228]. Masc. *Genycharax tarpon* Eigenmann 1912:22. Type by original designation (also monotypic). Valid (Géry 1977:531 [ref. 1597]). Characidae.

Genyochromis Trewavas 1935:(68) 79 [ref. 4451]. Masc. *Genyochromis mento* Trewavas 1935:79. Type by monotypy. Valid (Ribbink et al. 1983:241 [ref. 13555]). Cichlidae.

Genyomyrus Boulenger 1898:17 [ref. 542]. Masc. *Genyomyrus donnyi* Boulenger 1898:17. Type by original designation (also monotypic). Valid (Taverne 1972:170 [ref. 6367], Gosse 1984:70 [ref. 6169]). Mormyridae.

Genyonemus Gill 1861:87 [ref. 1771]. Neut. *Leiostomus lineatus* Ayres 1855:24. Type by original designation (also monotypic). Valid. Sciaenidae.

Genyoroge Cantor 1849:994 [12] [ref. 715]. *Holocentrus bengalensis* Bloch 1790:264. Type by being a replacement name. Unneeded replacement for *Diacope* Cuvier 1815, not preoccupied by Hübner 1816. On page 12 of separate. Synonym of *Lutjanus* Bloch 1790 (Allen 1985:33 [ref. 6843], Allen & Talbot 1985:8 [ref. 6491], Allen 1986:323 [ref. 6208]). Lutjanidae.

Genypterus Philippi 1857:268 [ref. 3462]. Masc. *Genypterus nigricans* Philippi 1857:269. Type by monotypy. On Official List (Opinion 1200). Valid (Inada in Nakamura et al. 1986:142 [ref. 14235], Nielsen & Cohen 1986:347 [ref. 5700], Paxton et al. 1989:311 [ref. 12442], Pequeño 1989:48 [ref. 14125]). Ophidiidae: Ophidiinae.

Geophagus Heckel 1840:383 [ref. 2064]. Masc. *Geophagus altifrons* Heckel 1840:385. Type by subsequent designation. Type designated by Eigenmann & Bray 1894:621 [ref. 1248], not *Sparus surinamensis* Bloch as designated by Eigenmann 1910:478 [ref. 1224]. Valid (Gosse 1975 [ref. 7029], Kullander 1980:23 [ref. 5526], Kullander 1986:120 [ref. 12439], Kullander & Nijssen 1989:30 [ref. 14136], Malabarba 1989:166 [ref. 14217]). Cichlidae.

Georgichthys Nichols 1918:17 [ref. 3171]. Masc. *Georgichthys scaphignathus* Nichols 1918:17. Type by original designation (also monotypic). Synonym of *Sarcocheilichthys* Bleeker 1859 (Banarescu & Nalbant 1973:39 [ref. 173], Lu, Luo & Chen 1977:467 [ref. 13495]). Cyprinidae.

Geotria Gray 1851:142 [ref. 4939]. Fem. *Geotria australis* Gray 1851:142. Type by monotypy. Also appeared in Gray 1853 [for 1851]:239 [ref. 1886]. Valid (Hubbs & Potter 1971:55 [ref. 13397], Pequeño 1989:6 [ref. 14125]). Petromyzontidae: Geotriinae.

Gephyroberyx Boulenger 1902:203 [ref. 565]. Masc. *Trachichthys darwinii* Johnson 1866:311. Type by monotypy. Misspelled *Geophroberyx* by Jordan 1920:497 [ref. 4905]. Valid (Nielsen 1973:340 [ref. 6885], Woods & Sonoda 1973:300 [ref. 6899], Yamakawa in Masuda et al. 1984:109 [ref. 6441], Maul in Whitehead et al. 1986:749 [ref. 13676], Heemstra 1986:410 [ref. 5660], Paxton et al. 1989:366 [ref. 12442]). Trachichthyidae.

Gephyrocharax Eigenmann 1912:23 [ref. 1228]. Fem. *Gephyrocharax chocoensis* Eigenmann 1912:23. Type by original designation. Valid (Géry 1977:358 [ref. 1597], Weitzman & S. Fink 1985:1 et seq. [ref. 5203]). Characidae: Glandulocaudinae.

Gephyrochromis Boulenger 1901:4 [ref. 5758]. Masc. *Gephyrochromis moorii* Boulenger 1901:4. Type by monotypy. Appeared first in Boulenger (Jan.) 1901:4 as above; also in Boulenger (Oct.) 1901:156 [ref. 556]. Valid (Ribbink et al. 1983:240 [ref. 13555]). Cichlidae.

Gephyroglanis Boulenger 1899:42 [ref. 548]. Masc. *Gephyroglanis congicus* Boulenger 1899:42. Type by monotypy. Valid (Skelton et al. 1984 [ref. 5835], Risch 1986:29 [ref. 6190], Burgess 1989:68 [ref. 12860]). Bagridae.

Gephyromochlus (subgenus of *Centromochlus*) Hoedeman 1961:135 [ref. 11969]. *Centromochlus (Gephyromochlus) leopardus* Hoedeman 1961:135. Type by monotypy. Synonym of *Glanidium* Lütken 1874 (Mees 1974:93 [ref. 2969]). Auchenipteridae.

Gergobius (subgenus of *Calleleotris*) Whitley 1930:22 [ref. 4671]. Masc. *Eleotris taeniura* Macleay 1881:624. Type by original designation (also monotypic). Synonym of *Valenciennea* Bleeker 1868 (Hoese, pers. comm.). Gobiidae.

Gerhardinus Meek & Hildebrand 1928:889 [ref. 2964]. Masc. *Gerhardinus nudus* Meek & Hildebrand 1928:889. Type by original designation (also monotypic). Synonym of *Gobiosoma* Girard 1858 (Hoese, pers. comm.). Gobiidae.

Gerlachea Dollo 1900:195 [ref. 1133]. Fem. *Gerlachea australis* Dollo 1900:196. Type by monotypy. Spelled *Gerlachia* by Boulenger 1904:706 [in Harmer & Shipley, Cambridge Nat. Hist. v. 7; not seen]. Valid (DeWitt & Hureau 1979:789 [ref. 1125], Stevens et al. 1984:563 [ref. 13633], Voskoboinikova 1988:45 [ref. 12756]). Bathydraconidae.

Germo Jordan 1888:180 [ref. 2389]. *Scomber germo* Lacepède 1801:1. Type by being a replacement name. See *Orcynus* Cuvier 1831. Replacement for *Orcynus* Cuvier 1816, preoccupied by Rafinesque 1815 in fishes. Synonym of *Thunnus* South 1845 (Gibbs & Collette 1967:97 [ref. 13640]); as a valid subgenus (Postel 1973:468 [ref. 7208]). Scombridae.

Gerreomorpha Alleyne & Macleay 1877:274 [ref. 101]. Fem. *Gerreomorpha rostrata* Alleyne & Macleay 1877:274. Type by monotypy. Synonym of *Gerres* Quoy & Gaimard 1824 (Roux 1986:325 [ref. 6209]). Gerreidae.

Gerres Quoy & Gaimard (ex Cuvier) 1824:292 [ref. 3574]. Masc. *Gerres vaigiensis* Quoy & Gaimard 1824:292. Type by subsequent designation. Type designated by Jordan 1917:117 [ref. 2407]. On Official List (Opinion 962). Misspelled *Gerris* by Swainson 1839: 28 [ref. 4303]. Valid (Akazaki & Juso in Masuda et al. 1984:161 [ref. 6441], Roux 1986:325 [ref. 6209], Woodland 1986: 608 [ref. 6299], Deckert & Greenfield 1987 [ref. 6778]). Gerreidae.

Ghanan (subgenus of *Sciaena*) Forsskål 1775:44 [ref. 1351]. *Sciaena ghanan* Forsskål 1775:50. Not available, regarded as non-latinized Arabic name (see Jordan 1917:33-34 [ref. 2407]). In the synonymy of *Scolopsis* Cuvier 1814. Nemipteridae.

Gibberichthys Parr 1933:5 [ref. 3373]. Masc. *Gibberichthys pumilus* Parr 1933:5. Type by monotypy. Valid (de Sylva & Eschmeyer 1977 [ref. 5936], Uyeno & Sato in Uyeno et al. 1983: 279 [ref. 14275]). Gibberichthyidae.

Gibbonsia Cooper 1864:109 [ref. 4877]. Fem. *Myxodes elegans* Cooper 1864:109. Type by monotypy. Valid (Clark Hubbs 1952:116 [ref. 2252], Stepien et al. 1988 [ref. 6384]). Clinidae.

Gibelion Heckel 1843:1014 [ref. 2066]. Neut. *Cyprinus catla* Hamilton 1822:187, 387. Type by subsequent designation. Species misspelled *Cyprinus catta* by Heckel. Type designated by Jordan 1919:211 [ref. 2410]. Apparently predates *Catla* Valenciennes 1844. Valid. Cyprinidae.

Giffordella Fowler 1932:14 [ref. 1412]. Fem. *Giffordella corneliae* Fowler 1932:14. Type by original designation (also monotypic). Synonym of *Entomacrodus* Gill 1859 (Smith-Vaniz & Springer 1971:23 [ref. 4145]). Blenniidae.

Gigantactis Brauer 1902:295 [ref. 631]. Fem. *Gigantactis vanhoeffeni* Brauer 1902:296. Type by monotypy. Valid (Maul 1973:675 [ref. 7171], Bertelsen et al. 1981 [ref. 5330], Bertelsen & Pietsch 1983:91 [ref. 5335], Amaoka in Masuda et al. 1984:106 [ref. 6441], Bertelsen in Whitehead et al. 1986:1406 [ref. 13677], Paxton et al. 1989:292 [ref. 12442]). Gigantactinidae.

Giganthias Katayama 1954:56 [ref. 5619]. Masc. *Giganthias immaculatus* Katayama 1954:57. Type by original designation (also monotypic). Valid (Kendall 1984:500 [ref. 13663], Katayama in Masuda et al. 1984:132 [ref. 6441]). Serranidae: Anthiinae.

Gigantogobius Fowler 1905:511 [ref. 1370]. Masc. *Gigantogobius jordani* Fowler 1905:511. Type by original designation (also monotypic). Synonym of *Bostrychus* Lacepède 1801 (Maugé 1986:390 [ref. 6218]); questionably a synonym of *Oxyeleotris* Bleeker 1874 (Roberts 1989:166 [ref. 6439]). Eleotridae.

Gigantura Brauer 1901:128 [ref. 630]. Fem. *Gigantura chuni* Brauer 1901:128. Type by monotypy. Valid (Johnson 1984:199 [ref. 13623], Johnson 1986:273 [ref. 5677], Paxton et al. 1989:245 [ref. 12442]). Giganturidae.

Gigliolia Goode & Bean 1895:464 [ref. 1847]. Fem. *Gigliolia moseleyi* Goode & Bean 1895:465. Type by monotypy. Also appeared as new in Goode & Bean 1896:169 [ref. 1848]. Synonym of *Notacanthus* Bloch 1788. Notacanthidae.

Gignimentum Whitley 1933:88 [ref. 4677]. Neut. *Gignimentum penicillum* Whitley 1933:89. Type by original designation (also monotypic). Valid, in Xenisthmidae (Hoese, pers. comm.). Xenisthmidae.

Gila Baird & Girard 1853:368 [ref. 166]. Fem. *Gila robusta* Girard 1853:369. Type by subsequent designation. Type designated by Jordan & Gilbert 1877:89 [ref. 4907]. Valid (Kaeding et al. 1986 [ref. 6781], Douglas et al. 1989 [ref. 12740]). Cyprinidae.

Gilbertella Eigenmann 1903:147 [ref. 1218]. Fem. *Anacyrtus alatus* Steindachner 1879:65. Type by original designation (also monotypic). Preoccupied by Waite 1902 in fishes, replaced by *Gilbertolus* Eigenmann in Eigenmann & Ogle 1907. Synonym of *Roestes* Günther 1864 (Menezes 1974:220 [ref. 7129]).

Characidae.

Gilbertella (subgenus of *Hypoplectrodes*) Waite 1902:182 [ref. 4559]. Fem. *Serranus armatus* Castelnau 1875:7. Type by monotypy. Synonym of *Epinephelides* Ogilby 1899. Serranidae: Anthiinae.

Gilbertia Jordan in Jordan & Eigenmann 1890:333, 346 [ref. 2440]. Fem. *Plectropoma semicinctum* Valenciennes in Cuvier & Valenciennes 1833:442. Type by original designation. Preoccupied by Cossman 1889 in Mollusca; replaced by *Ellerkeldia* Whitley 1927 (see our Appendix A). Synonym of *Hypoplectrodes* Gill 1862 (Anderson & Heemstra 1989:1002 [ref. 13526]). Serranidae: Anthiinae.

Gilbertidia Berg 1898:42 [ref. 262]. Fem. *Gilbertidia sigalutes* Jordan & Starks 1895:811. Type by being a replacement name. Replacement for *Gilbertina* Jordan & Starks 1895, preoccupied by Morlet 1888 in Mollusca. Valid (see Nelson 1982:1499 [ref. 5470], Yabe 1985:123 [ref. 11522]). Psychrolutidae.

Gilbertina Jordan & Starks 1895:811 [ref. 2522]. Fem. *Gilbertina sigalutes* Jordan & Starks 1895:811. Type by original designation (also monotypic). Preoccupied by Morlet 1888 in Mollusca, replaced by *Gilbertidia* Berg 1898. Objective synonym of *Gilbertidia* Berg 1898. Psychrolutidae.

Gilbertolus Eigenmann in Eigenmann & Ogle 1907:2, 3 [ref. 1266]. Masc. *Anacyrtus alatus* Steindachner 1879:65. Type by being a replacement name. Replacement for *Gilbertella* Eigenmann 1903, preoccupied by Waite 1902 in fishes. Misspelled *Gilbertollus* by Eigenmann 1910:445 [ref. 1224]. Valid (Géry 1977:311 [ref. 1597]); synonym of *Roestes* Günther 1864 (Menezes 1974:221 [ref. 7129]). Characidae.

Gilchristella Fowler 1935:365 [ref. 1421]. Fem. *Spratelloides aestuarius* Gilchrist 1914:55. Type by original designation (also monotypic). Valid (Poll et al. 1984:44 [ref. 6172], Grande 1985:246 [ref. 6466], Whitehead 1985:167 [ref. 5141], Whitehead & Wongratana 1986:201 [ref. 6284]). Clupeidae.

Gilchristia Jordan 1907:236 [ref. 2401]. Fem. *Histiopterus richardsoni* Smith 1844:Pl. 21. Type by original designation (also monotypic). Objective synonym of *Pseudopentaceros* Bleeker 1876 (Hardy 1983:206 [ref. 5385]). Pentacerotidae.

Gillellus Gilbert 1890:98 [ref. 1623]. Masc. *Gillellus semicinctus* Gilbert 1890:98. Type by original designation. Valid (Dawson 1977:127 [ref. 1067], Dawson 1982:50 [ref. 1072]). Dactyloscopidae.

Gillia Günther 1865:157 [ref. 1980]. Fem. *Gillichthys mirabilis* Cooper 1863:109. Type by being a replacement name. Unneeded replacement for *Gillichthys* Cooper 1863, deemed barbarous by Günther. Objective synonym of *Gillichthys* Cooper 1863. Gobiidae.

Gillias Evermann & Marsh 1900:357 [ref. 1283]. Masc. *Gillias jordani* Evermann & Marsh 1900:357. Type by original designation (also monotypic). Stichaeidae.

Gillichthys Cooper 1863:109 [ref. 4877]. Masc. *Gillichthys mirabilis* Cooper 1863:111. Type by monotypy. Valid (Birdsong et al. 1988:185, 187 [ref. 7303]). Gobiidae.

Gillisqualus Whitley 1934:189 [ref. 4949]. Masc. *Carcharinus amblyrhynchoides* Whitley 1934:189. Type by original designation (also monotypic). Correct spelling for genus of type species is *Carcharhinus*. Synonym of *Carcharhinus* Blainville 1816 (Garrick 1982:19 [ref. 5454] but with wrong type species, Compagno 1984:449 [ref. 6846], Cappetta 1987:121 [ref. 6348], Compagno 1988:307 [ref. 13488]). Carcharhinidae.

Gilloblennius Whitley & Phillipps 1939:235 [ref. 4737]. Masc. *Blennius tripennis* Bloch & Schneider 1801:174. Type by original designation (also monotypic). Valid (Hardy 1986:940 [ref. 6325], Hardy 1986 [ref. 6139]). Tripterygiidae.

Ginesia Fernández-Yépez 1951:1 [unnumbered] [ref. 14283]. Fem. *Ginesia cunaguaro* Fernández-Yépez 1951:2 [unnumbered]. Type by original designation (also monotypic). Pimelodidae.

Ginglymostoma Müller & Henle 1837:113 [ref. 3067]. Neut. *Squalus cirratus* Bonnaterre 1788:7. Type by subsequent designation. Dates to 1837:113 without species; species added by Müller & Henle 1838:22 [ref. 3069]. Type designated by Jordan & Gilbert 1883:18 [ref. 2476] (and possibly by Bonaparte 1839:11 of separate [ref. 4979]). *Ginglimostoma*, *Gynglimostoma* and *Gingylostoma* are misspellings. Valid (Springer 1973:18 [ref. 7162], Quéro in Whitehead et al. 1984:93 [ref. 13675], Compagno 1984:204 [ref. 6474], Bass 1986:64 [ref. 5635], Cappetta 1987:79 [ref. 6348]). Ginglymostomatidae.

Ginsburgellus Böhlke & Robins 1968:140 [ref. 609]. Masc. *Gobiosoma novemlineatum* Fowler 1950:89. Type by original designation (also monotypic). Valid (Birdsong et al. 1988:189 [ref. 7303]). Gobiidae.

Girardinichthys Bleeker 1860:481 [ref. 380]. Masc. *Girardinichthys innominatus* Bleeker 1860:484. Type by monotypy. *Limnurgus* Günther 1866 is an unneeded replacement. Valid (Miller & Fitzsimons 1971:10 [ref. 3019], Uyeno et al. 1983:503 [ref. 6818]). Goodeidae.

Girardinus Poey 1854:383, 390 [ref. 3497]. Masc. *Girardinus metallicus* Poey 1854:387, 391. Type by monotypy. Valid (Rosen & Bailey 1963:109 [ref. 7067], Parenti & Rauchenberger 1989:9 [ref. 13538]). Poeciliidae.

Girella Gray 1835:Pl. 98 (v. 2) [ref. 1878]. Fem. *Girella punctata* Gray 1835:Pl. 98. Type by monotypy. Valid (Araga in Masuda et al. 1984:165 [ref. 6441]). Kyphosidae: Girellinae.

Girellichthys (subgenus of *Girella*) Klunzinger 1872:22 [ref. 2623]. Masc. *Crenidens zebra* of Steindachner (? = *Crenidens zebra* Richardson 1846:70). Type by monotypy. Single included species as "*Girella (Girellichthys) zebra* (Rich.?) Steindachner." *Neotephraeops* Castelnau 1872 is an objective synonym; apparently *Girellichthys* appeared slightly earlier in 1872. Kyphosidae: Girellinae.

Girellipiscis Whitley 1931:320 [ref. 4672]. Masc. *Girella elevata* Macleay 1881:408. Type by original designation (also monotypic). Synonym of *Girella* Gray 1835. Kyphosidae: Girellinae.

Girellops Regan 1913:369 [ref. 3652]. Masc. *Girella nebulosa* Kendall & Radcliffe 1912:120. Type by monotypy. Kyphosidae: Girellinae.

Giscenchelys (subgenus of *Ophichthus*) Fowler 1944:188 [ref. 1448]. Fem. *Ophichthys zophochir* Jordan & Gilbert 1881:347. Type by original designation (also monotypic). Synonym of *Ophichthus* Ahl 1789 (McCosker 1977:80 [ref. 6836] and McCosker et al. 1989:379 [ref. 13288] but as *Gisenchelys*). Ophichthidae: Ophichthinae.

Giton Kaup in Duméril 1856:201 [ref. 1154]. Masc. *Gymnotus fasciatus* Pallas 1767:35. Not available, name only as "*Giton arhea, fasciata*" in list of genera. Apparently for *Gymnotus fasciatus* Pallas. In the synonymy of *Gymnotus* Linnaeus 1758. Gymnotidae: Gymnotinae.

Giuris (subgenus of *Eleotris*) Sauvage 1880:54 [ref. 3887]. *Giuris vanicolensis* Sauvage 1880:54. Type by subsequent designation.

Type designated by Jordan 1919:401 [ref. 4904]. Appeared without description with four species of *Eleotris*. Eleotridae.

Glabrilutjanus (subgenus of *Lutjanus*) Fowler 1931:88, 95 [ref. 1407]. Masc. *Mesoprion nematophorus* Bleeker 1860:56. Type by original designation (also monotypic). Synonym of *Symphorus* Günther 1872 (Allen & Talbot 1985:9 [ref. 6491]). Lutjanidae.

Glabrobarbus (subgenus of *Barbus*) Fowler 1930:594 [ref. 1404]. Masc. *Barbus nigriparipinnis* Fowler 1930:594. Type by original designation (also monotypic). Status uncertain (see Böhlke 1984:85 [ref. 13621]). Cyprinidae.

Gladioglanis Ferraris & Mago-Leccia 1989:166 [ref. 9288]. Masc. *Gladioglanis machadoi* Ferraris & Mago-Leccia 1989:167. Type by original designation (also monotypic). Pimelodidae.

Gladiogobius Herre 1933:23 [ref. 2106]. Masc. *Gladiogobius ensifer* Herre 1933:23. Type by monotypy. Misspelled *Gladigobius* in Zoological Record for 1933. Valid (Akihito in Masuda et al. 1984:242 [ref. 6441], Birdsong et al. 1988:193 [ref. 7303]). Gobiidae.

Gladiunculus (subgenus of *Gasterosteus*) Jordan & Evermann 1927:504 [ref. 2453]. Masc. *Gasterosteus gladiunculus* Kendall 1896:623. Type by monotypy (also by absolute tautonymy). Described as a new subgenus but no genus specifically mentioned. Synonym of *Gasterosteus* Linnaeus 1758 (Monod 1973:280 [ref. 7193]). Gasterosteidae: Gasterosteinae.

Gladostomus (subgenus of *Acipenser*) Holly 1936:31 [ref. 6492]. Masc. *Acipenser stellatus* Pallas 1771:131. Type by monotypy. Synonym of *Acipenser* Linnaeus 1758 (Svetovidov 1973:82 [ref. 7169]). Acipenseridae: Acipenserinae.

Glanapteryx Myers 1927:128 [ref. 3096]. Fem. *Glanapteryx anguilla* Myers 1927:127. Type by original designation (also monotypic). Valid (Burgess 1989:325 [ref. 12860], Pinna 1989 [ref. 13515]). Trichomycteridae.

Glandulocauda Eigenmann 1911:168 [ref. 1226]. Fem. *Glandulocauda melanogenys* Eigenmann 1911:168. Type by original designation. See Weitzman and S. Fink 1985 [ref. 5203] for a review of the Glandulocaudinae; they suggest that the monophyly of this group remains uncertain. See their pp. 2-3 for family names — Glandulocaudinae would not be the oldest available one. Valid (Géry 1977:362 [ref. 1597], Weitzman & S. Fink 1985:1 et seq. [ref. 5203], Weitzman et al. 1988:384 [ref. 13557]). Characidae: Glandulocaudinae.

Glanide Agassiz in Spix & Agassiz 1829:10 [ref. 13]. Not available, not latinized. Ariidae.

Glanidium Lütken 1874:31 [3] [ref. 2855]. Neut. *Glanidium albescens* Reinhardt in Lütken 1874:31. Type by monotypy. On p. 3 of separate. Valid (Mees 1974:93 [ref. 2969], Burgess 1989:241 [ref. 12860], Curran 1989 [ref. 12547], Malabarba 1989:139 [ref. 14217]). Auchenipteridae.

Glaniopsis Boulenger 1899:228 [ref. 553]. Fem. *Glaniopsis hanitschi* Boulenger 1899:228. Type by monotypy. Valid (Silas 1953:220 [ref. 4024], Sawada 1982:204 [ref. 14111], Roberts 1982 [ref. 6689]). Balitoridae: Balitorinae.

Glanis Agassiz 1857:333 [ref. 72]. Masc. *Glanis aristotelis* Agassiz 1857:333. Type by monotypy. Preoccupied several times. Synonym of *Silurus* Linnaeus 1758 (Haig 1952:97 [ref. 12607], Kobayakawa 1989:157 [ref. 13476]). Siluridae.

Glanis Agassiz in Spix & Agassiz 1829:46 [ref. 13]. *Silurus bagre* Linnaeus 1766:505. Type by subsequent designation. Type designated by Kottelat 1988; see Kottelat 1988:78 [ref. 13380] for authorship and date. Objective synonym of *Bagre* Cloquet 1816. Ariidae.

Glanis Gronow in Gray 1854:135 [ref. 1911]. Masc. *Glanis imberbis* Gronow in Gray 1854:135. Type by monotypy. Notopteridae.

Glaridichthys Garman 1896:232 [ref. 1539]. Masc. *Girardinus uninotatus* Poey 1861:309, 383. Type by being a replacement name. Replacement for *Glaridodon* Garman 1895, preoccupied by Seeley 1888 in Reptilia. Synonym of *Girardinus* Poey 1854 (Rosen & Bailey 1963:109 [ref. 7067]). Poeciliidae.

Glaridodon Garman 1895:40 [ref. 1538]. Masc. *Glaridodon uninotatus* Poey 1861:309, 383. Type by original designation. Type not *latidens* as sometimes given; type clearly designated. Preoccupied by Seeley 1888 in Reptilia, replaced by *Glaridichthys* Garman 1896. Synonym of *Girardinus* Poey 1854 (Rosen & Bailey 1963:109 [ref. 7067]). Poeciliidae.

Glaridoglanis Norman 1925:574 [ref. 6493]. Masc. *Exostoma andersonii* Day 1869:524. Type by monotypy. Valid (Chu 1979:76 [ref. 831], Burgess 1989:133 [ref. 12860]). Sisoridae.

Glaucosoma Temminck & Schlegel 1843:62 [ref. 4371]. Neut. *Glaucosoma buergeri* Richardson 1844:27. Original description without species; two species (*bürgeri* and *hebraicum*) added by Richardson 1844:27 [ref. 3740]; *hebraicum* included with some doubt but regarded as an included species; first subsequent designation not researched. Valid (Katayama in Masuda et al. 1984:142 [ref. 6441], Paxton et al. 1989:529 [ref. 12442]). Glaucosomatidae.

Glaucostegus Bonaparte 1846:14 [ref. 519]. Masc. *Raja rhinobatos* Linnaeus 1758:232. Type by subsequent designation. Earliest type designation apparently Jordan & Evermann 1896:61 [ref. 2443]. Objective synonym of *Rhinobatos* Linck 1790 (Krefft & Stehmann 1973:53 [ref. 7167]). Rhinobatidae: Rhinobatinae.

Glaucus Bleeker (ex Klein) 1863:14, 75 [ref. 395]. Masc. *Scomber rondeletii* Bleeker 1863:298 (= *Scomber glaucus* Linnaeus 1758:298). Type by monotypy. Genus based on *Glaucus* of earlier authors (not available) and species on non-binominal *Glaucus primus Rondeletii* Willughby, with *S. glaucus* Linnaeus in synonymy; Bleeker's action creates a genus and species dating to Bleeker. Synonym of *Trachinotus* Lacepède 1801 (as treated by Hureau & Tortonese 1973:383 [ref. 7198]). Carangidae.

Glaucus Fowler (ex Klein in Walbaum) 1906:116 [ref. 1372]. Masc. *Scomber amia* Linnaeus 1758:299. Type by original designation (also monotypic). *Glaucus* Klein is unavailable, as are Klein's genera reprinted in condensed form in Walbaum 1792 (Opinion 21); Fowler's action creates a genus *Glaucus* credited to Fowler 1906. With type as above would be a synonym of *Lichia* Cuvier 1816 (as treated by Hureau & Tortonese 1973:377 [ref. 7198]). Carangidae.

Glaucus Jordan & Hubbs (ex Klein) 1917:463 [ref. 2484]. Masc. *Scomber glaucus* Linnaeus 1758:298. Type by original designation (also monotypic). Based on *Glaucus* Klein (unavailable); creates a *Glaucus* Jordan & Hubbs 1917. With type as above would be a synonym of *Trachinotus* Lacepède 1801 (as teated by Hureau & Tortonese 1973:383 [ref. 7198]). Carangidae.

Glaucus Klein 1775:829 [ref. 2618]. Masc. Not available, published in a work that does not conform to the principle of binominal nomenclature. Carangidae.

Glaucus Klein in Walbaum 1792:585 [ref. 4572]. Masc. Not available (Opinion 21). Carangidae.

Glauertichthys (subgenus of *Paristiopterus*) Whitley 1945:28 [ref. 4707]. Masc. *Paristiopterus gallipavo* Whitley 1945:28. Type by original designation. Synonym of *Paristiopterus* Bleeker 1876

(Hardy 1983:189 [ref. 5385]). Pentacerotidae.

Glenoglossa McCosker 1982:60 [ref. 2934]. Fem. *Glenoglossa wassi* McCosker 1982:61. Type by original designation (also monotypic). Valid (McCosker et al. 1989:271 [ref. 13288]). Ophichthidae: Myrophinae.

Gloriella Schultz 1941:17 [ref. 3953]. Fem. *Cirripectes caninus* Herre 1936:284. Type by original designation (also monotypic). Synonym of *Exallias* Jordan & Evermann 1905 (Smith-Vaniz & Springer 1971:23 [ref. 4145]). Blenniidae.

Glossamia Gill 1863:82 [ref. 1679]. Fem. *Apogon aprion* Richardson 1842:16. Type by original designation, Gill's style of placing type in parentheses in key (also monotypic). Valid (Fraser 1972:8 [ref. 5195], Paxton et al. 1989:555 [ref. 12442]). Apogonidae.

Glossanodon Guichenot 1867:[9] [ref. 1946]. Masc. *Argentina leioglossa* Valenciennes in Cuvier & Valenciennes 1848:417. Type by original designation (also monotypic). Valid (Cohen 1973:153 [ref. 6589], Parin & Shcherbachev 1982 [ref. 5344], Cohen in Whitehead et al. 1984:388 [ref. 13675], Ahlstrom et al. 1984:156 [ref. 13627], Uyeno in Masuda et al. 1984:40 [ref. 6441], Cohen 1986:215 [ref. 5646], Paxton et al. 1989:167 [ref. 12442]). Argentinidae.

Glossichthys Gill 1861:51 [ref. 1766]. Masc. *Glossichthys plagiusa* Gill 1861 (= *Pleuronectes plagiusa* Linnaeus 1766:455). Type by monotypy. Single included species given as "*Glossichthys plagiusa* Gill" with *Plagusia fasciata* Storer in synonymy; species apparently is *Pleuronectes plagiusa* Linnaeus. Synonym of *Symphurus* Rafinesque 1810. Cynoglossidae: Symphurinae.

Glossodon Heckel 1843:1033 [ref. 2066]. Masc. *Cyprinus (Abramis?) smithii* Richardson 1836:110. Type by monotypy. Preoccupied by Rafinesque 1818 in fishes; not replaced. Cyprinidae.

Glossodon Rafinesque 1818:354 [ref. 3586]. Masc. *Glossodon harengoides* Rafinesque 1818:354. Type by subsequent designation. Type designated by Jordan & Gilbert 1877:84 [ref. 4907]. Treated as subgenus of *Hyodon [Hiodon]* in Rafinesque 1820:174 (Apr.) [ref. 7309] and 1820:42 (Dec.) [ref. 3592]. Synonym of *Hiodon* Lesueur 1818. Hiodontidae.

Glossodonta Cuvier 1815:232, 233 [ref. 1019]. Masc. *Argentina glossodonta* Forsskål 1775:68. Type by monotypy (also by absolute tautonymy). Synonym of *Albula* Scopoli 1777 (see Whitehead 1986:215 [ref. 5733]). Albulidae: Albulinae.

Glossodus Agassiz in Spix & Agassiz 1829:48 [ref. 13]. Masc. *Glossodus forskalii* Agassiz in Spix & Agassiz 1829:68 (= *Argentina glossodonta* Forsskål 1775:68). Type by monotypy. Based on *Glossodonta* Cuvier 1815, not available. Agassiz's species *Glossodus forskalii* is an unneeded substitute for *A. glossodonta*. See also Kottelat 1988:78 [ref. 13380]. Synonym of *Albula* Scopoli 1777 (Whitehead 1986:215 [ref. 5733]). Albulidae: Albulinae.

Glossognathus Rafinesque 1818:420 [ref. 3588]. Masc. *Cyprinus maxillingua* Lesueur 1817:85. Mentioned by Rafinesque as an equivalent of *Exoglossum* Rafinesque but a name he did not wish to use. Can be regarded as a name published in synonymy of *Exoglossum* or as a name mentioned in passing. Subsequent use as a valid name or senior homonym not researched. Cyprinidae.

Glossogobius Gill 1859:46 [ref. 1754]. Masc. *Gobius platycephalus* Richardson 1846:204, 318. Type by monotypy. Date may be 1860. Valid (Akihito in Masuda et al. 1984:274 [ref. 6441], Kottelat 1985:274 [ref. 11441], Hoese 1986:789 [ref. 5670], Birdsong et al. 1988:186 [ref. 7303], Kottelat 1989:19 [ref. 13605]). Gobiidae.

Glossolepis Weber 1907:241 [ref. 4599]. Fem. *Glossolepis incisus* Weber 1907:241. Type by monotypy. Valid (Allen 1981:301 [ref. 5514], Allen & Cross 1982:96 [ref. 6251], White et al. 1984:360 [ref. 13655], Allen 1985:56 [ref. 6245]). Atherinidae: Melanotaeniinae.

Glossoplites Jordan 1876:233 [ref. 2371]. Masc. *Calliurus melanops* Girard 1857:200. Type by original designation. Objective synonym of *Chaenobryttus* Gill 1864. Centrarchidae.

Glyphidodontops Bleeker 1877:128 [ref. 454]. Masc. *Glyphidodon azureus* Cuvier (ex Quoy & Gaimard) in Cuvier & Valenciennes 1830:479 (= *Glyphidodon cyaneus* Quoy & Gaimard 1825:392). Type by being a replacement name (see text). Not usually regarded as a replacement name, but from text it is clearly an unneeded replacement for *Chrysiptera* Swainson (with same type), *Chrysiptera* not preoccupied as thought by Bleeker. Also appeared in Bleeker 1877:41 [ref. 453]. Correct spelling for genus of type species is *Glyphisodon*. Objective synonym of *Chrysiptera* Swainson; incorrectly regarded as valid (Shen & Chan 1979:72 [ref. 6944]). Pomacentridae.

Glyphis Agassiz 1843:243 [Tome 3] [ref. 13390]. Fem. *Carcharias (Prionodon) glyphis* Müller & Henle 1839:40. Type by absolute tautonymy, *C. glyphis* mentioned in text. Type is not the fossil species *Glyphis hastalis* Agassiz 1843 (see discussion in Compagno 1984:506 [ref. 6846]). Valid (Compagno 1984:506 [ref. 6846], Compagno 1988:328 [ref. 13488]). Carcharhinidae.

Glyphisodon Lacepède 1802:542 [ref. 4929]. Masc. *Glyphisodon moucharra* Lacepède 1802:542. Type by subsequent designation. Earliest designation possibly by Jordan 1917:64 [ref. 2407]; not by Bleeker 1877:91 [ref. 454] as *saxatilis*. *Glyphidodon* Agassiz 1846:164 [ref. 64] is an unjustified emendation; also as *Gliphysodon* and *Glyphidon* in literature. Synonym of *Abudefduf* Forsskål 1775 (Shen & Chan 1979:37 [ref. 6944], Hensley 1986:857 [ref. 5734]). Pomacentridae.

Glyphodes Guichenot 1864:3 [ref. 1943]. Masc. *Glyphodes aprionoides* Guichenot 1864:3. Type by original designation (also monotypic). Preoccupied in Lepidoptera [details not investigated], replaced by *Guichenotia* Whitley 1950. Kyphosidae: Girellinae.

Glyptauchen Günther 1860:121 [ref. 1963]. Masc. *Apistes panduratus* Richardson 1850:58. Type by monotypy. Valid (Washington et al. 1984:440 [ref. 13660], Paxton et al. 1989:441 [ref. 12442]). Scorpaenidae: Tetraroginae.

Glyptocephalus Gottsche 1835:136, 156 [ref. 1862]. Masc. *Pleuronectes saxicola* Faber 1828:244. Type by monotypy. Valid (Norman 1934:363 [ref. 6893], Nielsen 1973:623 [ref. 6885], Ahlstrom et al. 1984:643 [ref. 13641], Sakamoto 1984 [ref. 5273], Sakamoto in Masuda et al. 1984:353 [ref. 6441], Nielsen in Whitehead et al. 1986:1299 [ref. 13677]). Pleuronectidae: Pleuronectinae.

Glyptoparus Smith 1959:249 [ref. 4123]. Masc. *Glyptoparus delicatulus* Smith 1959:249. Type by original designation. Valid (Smith-Vaniz & Springer 1971:24 [ref. 4145], Yoshino in Masuda et al. 1984:298 [ref. 6441]). Blenniidae.

Glyptophidium Alcock 1889:390 [ref. 81]. Neut. *Glyptophidium argenteum* Alcock 1889:390. Type by monotypy. Valid (Cohen & Nielsen 1978:32 [ref. 881], Machida in Masuda et al. 1984:100 [ref. 6441], Nielsen & Machida 1988 [ref. 12746], Paxton et al. 1989: 312 [ref. 12442]). Ophidiidae: Neobythitinae.

Glyptosternon McClelland 1842:584 [ref. 2926]. Neut. *Glyptosternon reticulatus* McClelland 1842:584. Type by subsequent designation. One species listed with main account, others listed on p. 574, 587-588. Type designated by Bleeker 1862:12 [ref. 393] and 1863:104 [ref. 401]. *Glyptosternum* Agassiz 1846:164 [ref. 64] and others is an unjustified emendation. Valid (Jayaram 1981:248 [ref. 6497], Chu 1979 [ref. 831] and Wu 1987:109 [ref. 12824] but as *Glyptosternum*, Burgess 1989:133 [ref. 12860]). Sisoridae.

Glyptothorax Blyth 1860:154 [ref. 477]. Masc. *Glyptosternon striatus* McClelland 1842:290, 397. Type by subsequent designation. Text somewhat unclear, but apparently three species included. Type designated by Bleeker 1863:105 [ref. 401]. Valid (Jayaram 1981:252 [ref. 6497], Kottelat 1985:271 [ref. 11441], Coad & Delmastro 1985 [ref. 6495], Li 1986 [ref. 6132], Burgess 1989:132 [ref. 12860], Kottelat 1989:15 [ref. 13605], Roberts 1989:134 [ref. 6439]). Sisoridae.

Gnathagnoides Whitley & Phillipps 1939:235 [ref. 4737]. Masc. *Gnathagnus innotabilis* Waite 1904:238. Type by original designation (also monotypic). Synonym of *Gnathagnus* Gill 1861 (Mees 1960:47 [ref. 11931], Pietsch 1989:294 [ref. 12541]). Uranoscopidae.

Gnathagnus Gill 1861:115 [ref. 1774]. Masc. *Uranoscopus elongatus* Temminck & Schlegel 1842:27. Type by monotypy. Valid (Mees 1960:47 [ref. 11931], Kishimoto in Masuda et al. 1984:293 [ref. 6441], Pietsch 1989:294 [ref. 12541], Kishimoto 1989 [ref. 13562]). Uranoscopidae.

Gnathanacanthus Bleeker 1855:2, 21 [ref. 346]. Masc. *Gnathanacanthus goetzeei* Bleeker 1855:21. Type by monotypy. Misspelled *Gnathacanthus* and *goetzei* by Bleeker on p. 31 (plate legend). Bleeker says named for J. W. Goetzee, so *goetzeei* is correct. Valid (Washington et al. 1984:440 [ref. 13660], Scott 1986 [ref. 5807], Paxton et al. 1989:464 [ref. 12442]). Gnathanacanthidae.

Gnathanodon Bleeker 1851:160 [ref. 324]. Masc. *Scomber speciosus* Forsskål 1775:54. Type by monotypy. Appeared without description as "*Gnathanodon speciosus* Blkr. = *Caranx speciosus* CV.", but new name plus existing species is sufficient for availability. Diagnosis followed in Bleeker 1862:72 [ref. 332] and 1862:352 [ref. 326]. Valid (Smith-Vaniz 1984:524 [ref. 13664], Gushiken in Masuda et al. 1984:157 [ref. 6441], Smith-Vaniz 1986:652 [ref. 5718], Gushiken 1988:443 [ref. 6697]). Carangidae.

Gnathendalia Castelnau 1861:57 [ref. 767]. Fem. *Gnathendalia vulnerata* Castelnau 1861:57. Type by monotypy. Synonym of *Barbus* Cuvier & Cloquet 1816 (Lévêque & Daget 1984:218 [ref. 6186]). Cyprinidae.

Gnathobagrus Nichols & Griscom 1917:711 [ref. 3185]. Masc. *Gnathobagrus depressus* Nichols & Griscom 1917:712. Type by monotypy. Valid (Risch 1986:30 [ref. 6190], Burgess 1989:67 [ref. 12860]). Bagridae.

Gnathobolus Bloch & Schneider 1801:556 [ref. 471]. Masc. *Odontognathus mucronatus* Lacepède 1800:221. Type by being a replacement name. Apparently an unneeded substitute for *Odontognathus* Lacepède 1800. Objective synonym of *Odontognathus* Lacepède 1800 (Whitehead 1967:103 [ref. 6464], Whitehead 1985:297 [ref. 5141]). Clupeidae.

Gnathocentrum Guichenot 1866:[5] [ref. 1945]. Neut. *Zanclus centrognathus* Cuvier in Cuvier & Valenciennes 1831:528. Type by original designation (also monotypic). Described as "le type d'un petit genre ou sous-genre [of *Zanclus*] particulier..." Synonym of *Zanclus* Cuvier 1831. Zanclidae.

Gnathocharax Fowler 1913:560 [ref. 1389]. Masc. *Gnathocharax steindachneri* Fowler 1913:561. Type by original designation (also monotypic). Valid (Géry 1977:311 [ref. 1597]). Characidae.

Gnathochromis Poll 1981:168 [ref. 3534]. Masc. *Limnochromis permaxillaris* David 1936. Type by original designation. Valid (Poll 1986:136 [ref. 6136]). Cichlidae.

Gnathodentex Bleeker 1873:41 [ref. 433]. Masc. *Sparus aureolineatus* Lacepède 1802:42, 132. Type by monotypy. Valid (Johnson 1980:11 [ref. 13553], Sato in Masuda et al. 1984:179 [ref. 6441], Smith 1986:595 [ref. 5712], Sato 1986:604 [ref. 5152], Carpenter & Allen 1989:17 [ref. 13577]). Lethrinidae.

Gnathodolus Myers 1927:108 [ref. 3096]. Masc. *Gnathodolus bidens* Myers 1927:108. Type by original designation (also monotypic). Valid (Géry 1977:187 [ref. 1597], Winterbottom 1980:21 [ref. 4755], Vari 1983:5 [ref. 5419]). Curimatidae: Anostominae.

Gnathogobius Smith 1945:522 [ref. 4056]. Masc. *Gnathogobius aliceae* Smith 1945:523. Type by original designation (also monotypic). Synonym of *Calamiana* Herre 1945 (Hoese, pers. comm.). Valid (Kottelat 1989:19 [ref. 13605]). Gobiidae.

Gnatholepis (subgenus of *Stenogobius*) Bleeker 1874:318 [ref. 437]. Fem. *Gobius anjerensis* Bleeker 1850:251. Type by original designation (also monotypic). Valid (Yoshino in Masuda et al. 1984:251 [ref. 6441], Hoese 1986:790 [ref. 5670], Maugé 1986:369 [ref. 6218], Birdsong et al. 1988:188 [ref. 7303], Kottelat 1989:19 [ref. 13605]). Gobiidae.

Gnathonemus Gill 1863:444 [ref. 1670]. Masc. *Mormyrus petersii* Günther 1862:54. Type by monotypy. Valid (Taverne 1972:168 [ref. 6367], Gosse 1984:71 [ref. 6169]). Mormyridae.

Gnathonotacanthus Fowler 1934:266 [ref. 1416]. Masc. *Polyacanthonotus vaillanti* Fowler 1934:266. Type by original designation. Synonym of *Polyacanthonotus* Bleeker 1874 (Wheeler 1973:257 [ref. 7190]). Notacanthidae.

Gnathophis Kaup 1860:7 [ref. 2586]. Masc. *Myrophis heterognathus* Bleeker 1858:9. Type by monotypy. Valid (Blache et al. 1973:241 [ref. 7185], Blache & Bauchot 1976:410 [ref. 305], Smith & Kanazawa 1977:534 [ref. 4036], Karrer 1982:21 [ref. 5679], Asano in Masuda et al. 1984:28 [ref. 6441], Bauchot & Saldanha in Whitehead et al. 1986:569 [ref. 13676], Castle 1986:164 [ref. 5644], Paxton et al. 1989:142 [ref. 12442], Smith 1989:521 [ref. 13285]). Congridae: Congrinae.

Gnathoplax Myers 1960:209 [ref. 3129]. Fem. *Exodon guyanensis* Puyo 1960:209. Type by original designation (also monotypic). Synonym of *Roeboexodon* Géry 1959 (Géry 1977:322 [ref. 1597] based on placement of type species). Characidae.

Gnathopogon Bleeker 1859:435 [ref. 370]. Masc. *Capoeta elongata* Temminck & Schlegel 1846:200. Type by subsequent designation. Apparently appeared first in key, without included species. Two species included by Bleeker 1860:285, 434 [ref. 380]. Type designated by Bleeker 1863:28 [ref. 4859] or 1863:202 [ref. 397]. Valid (Banarescu & Nalbant 1973:61 [ref. 173], Lu, Luo & Chen 1977:478 [ref. 13495], Sawada in Masuda et al. 1984:56 [ref. 6441]). Cyprinidae.

Gnathostomias Pappenheim 1914:171 [ref. 3361]. Masc. *Gnathostomias longifilis* Pappenheim 1914:172. Type by monotypy. Synonym of *Bathophilus* Giglioli 1882 (Morrow in Morrow & Gibbs 1964:456 [ref. 6962], Morrow 1973:135 [ref. 7175]). Melanostomiidae.

Gnathypops Gill 1862:241 [ref. 1664]. Masc. *Opisthognathus maxillosus* Poey 1861:286. Type by subsequent designation. Earliest type designation found that of Jordan & Evermann 1898:2283 [ref. 2445]. Correct spelling for genus of type species is *Opistognathus*. Synonym of *Opistognathus* Cuvier 1816 (Smith-Vaniz & Yoshino 1985:18 [ref. 6721]). Opistognathidae.

Gobatinus (subgenus of *Gobionellus*) Ginsburg 1953:25 [ref. 1806]. Masc. *Euctenogobius panamensis* Meek & Hildebrand 1928:874. Type by original designation (also monotypic). Synonym of *Gobionellus* Girard 1858 (Hoese, pers. comm.). Gobiidae.

Gobatus (subgenus of *Gobionellus*) Ginsburg 1932:45 [ref. 1798]. Masc. *Gobius microdon* Gilbert 1891:554. Type by original designation. Synonym of *Gobionellus* Girard 1858 (Hoese, pers. comm.). Gobiidae.

Gobica (subgenus of *Gobionellus*) Ginsburg 1932:45 [ref. 1798]. Fem. *Gobius boleosoma* Jordan & Gilbert 1882:295. Type by original designation. Synonym of *Gobionellus* Girard 1858 (Maugé 1986:371 [ref. 6218], but see *Ctenogobius*). Gobiidae.

Gobicula (subgenus of *Garmannia*) Ginsburg 1944:379 [ref. 1803]. Fem. *Garmannia gemmata* Ginsburg 1939:3. Type by original designation (also monotypic). Synonym of *Elacatinus* Jordan 1904 (Hoese, pers. comm.). Gobiidae.

Gobiculina (subgenus of *Garmannia*) Ginsburg 1944:380 [ref. 1803]. Fem. *Garmannia homochroma* Ginsburg 1939:62. Type by original designation (also monotypic). Synonym of *Gobiosoma* Girard 1858 (Hoese, pers. comm.). Gobiidae.

Gobidus (subgenus of *Gobionellus*) Ginsburg 1953:25 [ref. 1806]. Masc. *Gobius longicaudus* Jenkins & Evermann 1889:146. Type by original designation. Gobiidae.

Gobiella Smith 1931:33 [ref. 4047]. Fem. *Gobiella pellucida* Smith 1931:33. Type by monotypy. Synonym of *Gobiopterus* Bleeker 1874 (Hoese, pers. comm.). Gobiidae.

Gobiesox Lacepède 1800:595 [ref. 2709]. Masc. *Gobiesox cephalus* Lacepède 1800:595. Type by monotypy. *Gobiesox* of Müller & Troschel 1849 (not of Lacepède) is a synonym of *Chorisochismus* Brisout de Barneville (Briggs 1955:39 [ref. 637]). Valid (Briggs 1955:87 [ref. 637], Allen [L. G.] 1984:629 [ref. 13673], Pequeño 1989:41 [ref. 14125]). Gobiesocidae: Gobiesocinae.

Gobiex (subgenus of *Gobionellus*) Ginsburg 1932:44 [ref. 1798]. *Gobius stigmaturus* Goode & Bean 1882:418. Type by original designation (also monotypic). Synonym of *Gobionellus* Girard 1858 (Hoese, pers. comm.). Gobiidae.

Gobiichthys (subgenus of *Apocryptes*) Klunzinger 1871:479 [ref. 2622]. Masc. *Gobiichthys petersii* Klunzinger 1871:480. Type by monotypy. Synonym of *Oxyurichthys* Bleeker 1857 (Maugé 1986:378 [ref. 6218]). Gobiidae.

Gobileptes Bleeker (ex Swainson) 1874:327 [ref. 437]. Masc. Not available, appeared as name in synonymy of *Apocryptes* Valenciennes. Apparently not later made available. See *Gobileptes* Swainson. Gobiidae.

Gobileptes (subgenus of *Gobius*) Swainson 1839:183 [ref. 4303]. Masc. As a subgenus of *Gobius*, without included species. Bleeker 1874:327 [ref. 437] designated a type for *Apocryptes* Valenciennes and included *Gobileptes* in synonymy; this has been regarded wrongly as type designation for *Gobileptes*. First addition of species not researched; type designation may date to Jordan 1919:198 [ref. 2410] as *Gobius acutipinnis*. See Murdy 1989:7 [ref. 13628]). Gobiidae.

Gobio Bertrand 1763:v. 1, p. 250 [ref. 6405]. Masc. Not available; on Official Index, published in a rejected work (Opinion 592). Unplaced genera.

Gobio Cuvier 1816:193 [ref. 993]. Masc. *Cyprinus gobio* Linnaeus 1758:320. Type by monotypy (also by absolute tautonymy). *Gobio* Walbaum (ex Klein) 1792 would preoccupy but is not admissible. Valid (Banarescu & Nalbant 1973:106 [ref. 173], Lu, Luo & Chen 1977:493 [ref. 13495], Hosoya 1986:488 [ref. 6155], Travers 1989:199 [ref. 13578]). Cyprinidae.

Gobio Klein 1779:178 [ref. 4923]. Masc. Not available, published in a work that does not conform to the principle of binominal nomenclature. Not *Gobio* Cuvier 1816. Original not checked. In the synonymy of *Gobius* Linnaeus 1758. Gobiidae.

Gobiobarbus Dybowski 1869:951 [ref. 1169]. Masc. *Cyprinus labeo* Pallas 1776:207, 730. Type by monotypy. Synonym of *Hemibarbus* Bleeker 1859 (Lu, Luo & Chen 1977:443 [ref. 13495], Chen & Li in Chu & Chen 1989:102 [ref. 13584]). Cyprinidae.

Gobiobotia Kreyenberg 1911:417 [ref. 2688]. Fem. *Gobiobotia pappenheimi* Kreyenberg 1911:417. Type by monotypy. Under specimens is given "4 Exemplare...die Type der Gattung und Art..." does not constitute designation of a type species. Valid (Banarescu & Nalbant 1973:201 [ref. 173], Chen & Tsao 1977:551 [ref. 825], Zheng & Yan 1986:58 [ref. 5852], Hosoya 1986:488 [ref. 6155], Chen & Li in Chu & Chen 1989:119 [ref. 13584]). Cyprinidae.

Gobiochromis Poll 1939:48 [ref. 3513]. Masc. *Gobiochromis tinanti* Poll 1939:49. Type by monotypy. Cichlidae.

Gobiocichla Kanazawa 1951:378 [ref. 2558]. Fem. *Gobiocichla wonderi* Kanazawa 1951:378. Type by original designation (also monotypic). Valid (Roberts 1982:576 [ref. 5460]). Cichlidae.

Gobioclinus Gill 1860:103 [ref. 1765]. Masc. *Clinus gobio* Valenciennes in Cuvier & Valenciennes 1836:395. Type by original designation (also monotypic). Synonym of *Labrisomus* Swainson (Springer 1958:422 [ref. 10210]). Labrisomidae.

Gobiocypris Ye & Fu 1983:434 [436] [ref. 6669]. *Gobiocypris rarus* Ye & Fu 1983:434 [436]. Type by original designation (also monotypic). In English on pp. 436-437. Cyprinidae.

Gobiodon Bleeker (ex Kuhl & van Hasselt) 1856:385, 407 [ref. 353]. Masc. *Gobius heterospilus* Bleeker 1856:409. Type by subsequent designation. Earliest type designation found is Jordan 1919:267 [ref. 2410]; type not *Gobius histrio* as listed by Maugé 1986, apparently not designated by Bleeker 1874:309 [ref. 437] where two types are listed. Valid (Yoshino & Yamamoto in Masuda et al. 1984:265 [ref. 6441], Hoese 1986:791 [ref. 5670], Maugé 1986:369 [ref. 6218], Birdsong et al. 1988:193 [ref. 7303]). Gobiidae.

Gobiodonella Lindberg 1934:336, 440 [ref. 6496]. Fem. *Gobiodonella macrops* Lindberg 1934:440. Type by original designation (also monotypic). Synonym of *Lubricogobius* Tanaka 1915 (Hoese, pers. comm.). Gobiidae.

Gobiohelpis (subgenus of *Gramannia*) Ginsburg 1944:380 [ref. 1803]. *Garmannia spes* Ginsburg 1939:62. Type by original designation. Synonym of *Gobiosoma* Girard 1858 (Hoese, pers. comm.). Gobiidae.

Gobioides Lacepède 1800:576 [ref. 2709]. Masc. *Gobius broussonnetii* Lacepède 1800:280. Type by subsequent designation. Type designated by Bleeker 1874:329 [ref. 437]. Valid (Maugé 1986:370 [ref. 6218], Birdsong et al. 1988:196 [ref. 7303]). Gobiidae.

Gobiolepis (subgenus of *Garmannia*) Ginsburg 1944:379 [ref. 1803]. Fem. *Garmannia hildebrandi* Ginsburg 1939:62. Type by original designation. Synonym of *Gobiosoma* Girard 1858 (Hoese, pers. comm.). Gobiidae.

Gobiomoroides Lacepède 1800:592 [ref. 2709]. Masc. *Gobiomoroides piso* Lacepède 1800:593 (= *Gobius pisonis* Gmelin

1789:1206). Type by monotypy. Synonym of *Eleotris* Bloch & Schneider 1801 (Maugé 1986:391 [ref. 6218]). Eleotridae.

Gobiomorphus Gill 1863:270 [ref. 1691]. Masc. *Eleotris gobiodes* Valenciennes in Cuvier & Valenciennes 1837:247. Type by original designation (also monotypic). Valid (McDowall 1975 [ref. 7113], Hoese & Larson 1987:43 [ref. 6609], Birdsong et al. 1988:182 [ref. 7303]). Eleotridae.

Gobiomorus Lacepède 1800:583 [ref. 2709]. Masc. *Gobiomorus dormitor* Lacepède 1800:583, 589. Type by subsequent designation. Type designated by Jordan 1917:57 [ref. 2407]. Valid (Birdsong et al. 1988:180 [ref. 7303]). Eleotridae.

Gobionellus Girard 1858:168 [ref. 1813]. Masc. *Gobius lanceolatus* Bloch 1783:8. Type by subsequent designation. Type apparently designated by Bleeker 1874:325 [ref. 437] as "Sp. typ. *Gobius lanceolatus* Bl. (Sp. typ. Girardiana *Gobionellus hastatus* non satis cognita)." Valid (Gilbert & Randall 1979 [ref. 6929], Maugé 1986:371 [ref. 6218], Pezold & Gilbert 1987 [ref. 6777], Pezold & Grady 1989 [ref. 13579]). But see *Ctenogobius*. Gobiidae.

Gobionichthys (subgenus of *Lobocheilos*) Bleeker 1859:145 [ref. 371]. Masc. *Gobio microcephalus* Bleeker 1857:357. Type by subsequent designation. Also appeared in Bleeker 1860:145 [ref. 380]. Earliest type designation not established; Bleeker's 1863:194 [ref. 397] and 1863:25 [ref. 4859] designation of *lipocheilus* is invalid (not an included species in 1859:145). Synonym of *Lobocheilos* Bleeker 1853 (Roberts 1989:41 [ref. 6439]). Cyprinidae.

Gobionotothen Balushkin 1976:122, 128 [ref. 170]. *Notothenia gibbifrons* Lönnberg 1905:33. Type by original designation. Synonym of *Notothenia* Richardson 1844, but as a valid subgenus (Andersen 1984:24 [ref. 13369]); valid genus (Voskoboinikova & Balushkin 1987 [ref. 6342]). Nototheniidae.

Gobiopsis Steindachner 1860:291 [ref. 4205]. Fem. *Gobius macrostomus* Heckel in Steindachner 1860:291. Type by monotypy. Valid (Lachner & McKinney 1978 [ref. 6603], Lachner & McKinney 1979 [ref. 7018], Akihito in Masuda et al. 1984:267 [ref. 6441], Hoese 1986:791 [ref. 5670], Birdsong et al. 1988:193 [ref. 7303], Kottelat 1989:19 [ref. 13605]). Gobiidae.

Gobiopterus Bleeker 1874:311 [ref. 437]. Masc. *Apocryptes brachypterus* Bleeker 1855:401. Type by original designation (also monotypic). Valid (Birdsong et al. 1988:188 [ref. 7303], Kottelat 1989:19 [ref. 13605]). Gobiidae.

Gobiopus Gill 1874:160 [ref. 1713]. Masc. Not available, no description; Gill states, "The question then arose whether that fin [first dorsal fin] had been atrophied (as in *Aspidophoroides, Gobiopus*, &c.)..." Gobiidae.

Gobiosoma Dybowski 1872:211 [ref. 1170]. Neut. *Gobiosoma amurensis* Dybowski 1872:211. Type by monotypy. Preoccupied by Girard 1858 in fishes. Synonym of *Saurogobio* Bleeker 1870 (Banarescu & Nalbant 1973:282 [ref. 173], Lu, Luo & Chen 1977:537 [ref. 13495], Chen & Li in Chu & Chen 1989:116 [ref. 13584]). Cyprinidae.

Gobiosoma Girard 1858:169 [ref. 1813]. Neut. *Gobiosoma molestum* Girard 1858:169. Type by subsequent designation. Type apparently designated first by Bleeker 1874:310 [ref. 437]. Valid (Birdsong et al. 1988:186, 189 [ref. 7303]). Gobiidae.

Gobitrichinotus Fowler 1943:85 [ref. 1441]. Masc. *Gobitrichinotus radiocularis* Fowler 1943:86. Type by original designation (also monotypic). Misspelled *Gobitrichonotus* in Zoological Record for 1943. Valid (Hayashi in Masuda et al. 1984:287 [ref. 6441], Birdsong et al. 1988:201 [ref. 7303]). Kraemeriidae.

Gobius Linnaeus 1758:262 [ref. 2787]. Masc. *Gobius niger* Linnaeus 1758:262. Type by subsequent designation. Type apparently first designated by Gill 1863:268 [ref. 1690]. On Official List (Opinion 77, Direction 56). Valid (Miller 1973:483 [ref. 6888], Miller in Whitehead et al. 1986:1035 [ref. 13677], Birdsong et al. 1988:190 [ref. 7303]). Gobiidae.

Gobiusculus Duncker 1928:123 [ref. 6525]. Masc. *Gobius flavescens* Fabricius 1779:322. Type by subsequent designation. Type apparently first designated by Miller 1973:496 [ref. 6888]. Valid (Miller 1973:496 [ref. 6888], Miller in Whitehead et al. 1986:1046 [ref. 13677]). Gobiidae.

Gobulus Ginsburg 1933:12 [ref. 1800]. Masc. *Gobiosoma crescentalis* Gilbert 1891:557. Type by original designation (also monotypic). Valid (Birdsong et al. 1988:189 [ref. 7303]). Gobiidae.

Goeldiella Eigenmann & Norris 1900:353 [ref. 1264]. Fem. *Pimelodus eques* Müller & Troschel 1848:628. Type by monotypy. Valid (Burgess 1989:281 [ref. 12860]). Pimelodidae.

Gogolia Compagno 1973:383 [ref. 898]. Fem. *Gogolia filewoodi* Compagno 1973:394. Type by original designation (also monotypic). Valid (Compagno 1984:389 [ref. 6846], Herman et al. 1988:106 [ref. 13267], Compagno 1988:241 [ref. 13488]). Triakidae: Galeorhininae.

Gogrius Day 1867:563 [ref. 1075]. Masc. *Gogrius sykesi* Day 1867:563 (= *Pimelodus gogra* Sykes 1834:164). Type by monotypy. Species *gogra* needlessly renamed *sykesi* by Day. Synonym of *Rita* Bleeker 1853 (Jayaram 1977:12 [ref. 7005] and Jayaram 1981:109 [ref. 6497] but as *Gogra*). Bagridae.

Golem Whitley 1957:70 [ref. 4727]. Masc. *Antennarius cryptacanthus* Weber 1913:564. Type by original designation (also monotypic). Treated as masculine by author. Synonym of *Histiophryne* Gill 1863 (Pietsch 1984:40 [ref. 5380]). Antennariidae.

Gollum Compagno 1973:264 [ref. 897]. Masc. *Triakis attenuata* Garrick 1954:698. Type by original designation (also monotypic). Valid (Compagno 1984:375 [ref. 6846], Compagno 1988:193 [ref. 13488] in new subfamily Golluminae of Proscylliidae). Proscylliidae.

Gomphosus Lacepède 1801:100 [ref. 2710]. Masc. *Gomphosus caeruleus* Lacepède 1801:100, 101. Type by subsequent designation. Type designated by Jordan 1917:61 [ref. 2407]. Valid (Araga in Masuda et al. 1984:205 [ref. 6441], Randall 1986:693 [ref. 5706]). Labridae.

Gonenion Rafinesque 1810:53 [ref. 3594]. Neut. *Gonenion serra* Rafinesque 1810:53. Type by monotypy. *Gonenium* Agassiz 1846:165 [ref. 64] is an unjustified emendation. Synonym of *Pomatomus* Lacepède 1802 (Monod 1973:369 [ref. 7193]). Pomatomidae.

Gonialosa Regan 1917:315 [ref. 3665]. Fem. *Chatoessus modestus* Day 1869:622. Type by subsequent designation. Type designated by Jordan 1920:560 [ref. 4905]. Valid (Jayaram 1981:42 [ref. 6497] but as *Goniolosa*, Grande 1985:248 [ref. 6466], Whitehead 1985:256 [ref. 5141], Kottelat 1989:4 [ref. 13605]). Clupeidae.

Gonichthys Gistel 1850:71 [ref. 5020]. Masc. *Alysia loricata* Lowe 1839:87. Type by being a replacement name. Replacement for *Alysia* Lowe 1839, preoccupied by Latreille 1804 in Hymenoptera. Original not seen. Valid (Krefft & Bekker 1973:182 [ref. 7181], Paxton 1979:11 [ref. 6440], Hulley in Whitehead et al. 1984:452 [ref. 13675], Moser et al. 1984:219 [ref. 13645], Paxton et al.

1984:241 [ref. 13625], Hulley 1986:298 [ref. 5672], Paxton et al. 1989:261 [ref. 12442]). Myctophidae.

Goniistius Gill 1862:120 [ref. 1658]. Masc. *Cheilodactylus zonatus* Cuvier in Cuvier & Valenciennes 1830:365. Type by original designation. Synonym of *Cheilodactylus* Lacepède 1803, but as a valid subgenus (Randall 1983 [ref. 5361]); valid genus (Araga in Masuda et al. 1984:200 [ref. 6441]). Cheilodactylidae.

Goniobatus Agassiz 1858:385 [ref. 73]. Masc. *Raja flagellum* Bloch & Schneider 1801:361. Type by monotypy. Synonym of *Aetobatus* Blainville 1816 (Cappetta 1987:170 [ref. 6348]). Myliobatidae.

Gonionarce Gill 1862:387 [ref. 1783]. Fem. *Narcine indica* Henle 1834:35. Type by original designation (also monotypic). Synonym of *Narcine* Henle 1834 (Cappetta 1987:162 [ref. 6348]). Narkidae.

Gonioperca Gill 1862:236 [ref. 1664]. Fem. *Serranus albomaculatus* Jenyns 1840:3. Type by monotypy. Synonym of *Paralabrax* Girard 1856. Serranidae: Serraninae.

Gonioplectrus Gill 1862:236, 237 [ref. 1664]. Masc. *Plectropoma hispanum* Cuvier in Cuvier & Valenciennes 1828:396. Type by monotypy. Valid (Kendall 1984:500, 508 [ref. 13663]). Serranidae: Epinephelinae.

Goniosoma Costa 1844:1 [ref. 976]. Neut. *Argentina sphyraena* Linnaeus 1758:315. Type by monotypy. Objective synonym of *Argentina* Linnaeus 1758 (Cohen 1973:152 [ref. 6589]). Argentinidae.

Gonipus Rafinesque 1815:88 [ref. 3584]. Not available, name only. Unplaced genera.

Gonocephalus Gronow in Gray 1854:105 [ref. 1911]. Masc. *Gonocephalus macrocephalus* Gronow in Gray 1854 (= *Trigla volitans* Linnaeus 1758:302). Type by subsequent designation. Two included species, earliest type designation not researched. Synonym of *Dactylopterus* Lacepède 1801. Dactylopteridae.

Gonocephalus Kner 1855:313 [ref. 12581]. Masc. *Clarotes heuglini* Kner 1855:313. Type by monotypy. Proposed as "...Gattungsname *Clarotes* oder *Gonocephalus*..." Can be regarded as a name published in synonymy of *Clarotes*. Not *Gonocephalus* Gronow in Gray 1854. Synonym of *Clarotes* Kner 1855 (Risch 1986:27 [ref. 6190]). Bagridae.

Gonochaetodon (subgenus of *Tetragonoptrus* (sic)) Bleeker 1876:306 [ref. 448]. Masc. *Chaetodon triangulum* Cuvier (ex Kuhl & van Hasselt) in Cuvier & Valenciennes 1831:44. Type by original designation (also monotypic [in ref. 448]). Also appeared in Bleeker 1876:314 [ref. 451] and 1876:Pl. 374 [ref. 6835] (earliest not established). Misspelled *Gonoehaetodon* in Zoological Record for 1876. Synonym of *Chaetodon* Linnaeus 1758, but as a valid subgenus (Burgess 1978:426 [ref. 700]). Synonym of *Citharoedus* Kaup 1860, but as a valid subgenus (Maugé & Bauchot 1984:466 [ref. 6614]). Chaetodontidae.

Gonodermus Rafinesque 1815:90 [ref. 3584]. Masc. As "*Gonodermus* R. sp. do.", meaning *Gonodermus* Rafinesque for a species previously in preceding genus (*Ostracion*). Not available, name only. Ostraciidae: Ostraciinae.

Gonoproktopterus (subgenus of *Hypselobarbus*) Bleeker 1860:275, 311, 312 [ref. 380]. Masc. *Barbus kolus* Sykes 1841:357. Type by monotypy. Appeared first in Bleeker 1859:430 [ref. 370] as name only in key. Description in Bleeker 1860, with one included species. Spelled *Gonoproktopterys* by Jordan 1923:141 [ref 2421] and *Gonoproctopterus* by Bleeker 1863:199 [ref. 397] and 1863:27 [ref. 4859]. Valid (see Rainboth 1986:11 [ref. 5849]); synonym of *Hypselobarbus* Bleeker, but as a valid subgenus (Rainboth 1989:24 [ref. 13537]). Cyprinidae.

Gonopterus Gronow in Gray 1854:77 [ref. 1911]. Masc. *Gonopterus moerens* Gronow in Gray 1854:77. Type by monotypy. Synonym of *Zanclus* Cuvier 1831. Zanclidae.

Gonorhynchus McClelland 1839:366 [ref. 2923]. Masc. *Gonorhynchus brevis* McClelland 1839:373 (= *Cyprinus gohama* Hamilton 1822:346, 393). Type by subsequent designation. McClelland needlessly renamed Hamilton's species as *G. brevis*. Earliest type designation not researched. Not *Gonorynchus* Scopoli 1777. Cyprinidae.

Gonorynchus Gronow 1763:56 [ref. 1910]. Masc. Not available, published in a rejected work on Official Index (Opinion 261). Gonorynchidae.

Gonorynchus Scopoli (ex Gronow) 1777:450 [ref. 3990]. Masc. *Cyprinus gonorhynchus* Linnaeus 1766:528. Described without species; first addition of species not researched. See also *Gonorynche* Bosc as discussed by Whitley 1936:190 [ref. 6397]. Original spelling is *Gonorynchus*. Valid (see Howes 1985 [ref. 5148], Smith 1986:209 [ref. 5712], Paxton et al. 1989:214 [ref. 12442]). Gonorynchidae.

Gonostoma Rafinesque 1810:64 [ref. 3595]. Neut. *Gonostoma denudatum* Rafinesque 1810:64. Type by monotypy. Species originally spelled *denudata*, termination changed to agree with gender of genus. Valid (Witzell 1973:114 [ref. 7172], Weitzman 1974:472 [ref. 5174], Badcock in Whitehead et al. 1984:297 [ref. 13675], Ahlstrom et al. 1984:185 [ref. 13643], Fujii in Masuda et al. 1984:45 [ref. 6441], Schaefer et al. 1986:251 [ref. 5709], Paxton et al. 1989:185 [ref. 12442]). Gonostomatidae.

Gonostoma van Hasselt 1823:329 [ref. 5105]. Neut. *Gonostoma javanicum* Hyrtl 1855:49. Type by monotypy. Proposed in brief description, no included species. Preoccupied by Rafinesque 1810 in fishes; Bleeker 1849 described as *Anodontostoma*, with his species hasseltii (with "*Gonostoma javanicum* K. v. H." in synonymy but never described by them). Apparently Hyrtl 1855 was first to technically add a species to *Gonostoma* Van Hasselt. Questionably in synonymy of *Anodontostoma* Bleeker 1849 (Whitehead 1985:252 [ref. 5141]), but in any event preoccupied. Clupeidae.

Gonostomyxus Macdonald 1869:38 [ref. 2866]. Masc. *Gonostomyxus loaloa* Macdonald 1869:38. Type by original designation (also monotypic). Type designated in title to article. Mugilidae.

Gonurus Rafinesque 1815:85 [ref. 3584]. Masc. Not available, name only. As "*Gonurus* Lac.". Unplaced genera.

Goodea Jordan 1880:299 [ref. 2382]. Fem. *Goodea atripinnis* Jordan 1880:299. Type by monotypy. Valid (Parenti 1981:519 [ref. 7066], Uyeno et al. 1983:503 [ref. 6818]). Goodeidae.

Goodella Ogilby 1897:249 [ref. 3273]. Fem. *Goodella hypozona* Ogilby 1897:250. Type by monotypy. Synonym of *Trachinocephalus* Gill 1861 (Anderson et al. 1966:46 [ref. 6977]). Synodontidae: Synodontinae.

Gordiichthys Jordan & Davis 1891:644 [ref. 2437]. Masc. *Gordiichthys irretitus* Jordan & Davis 1891:644. Type by original designation (also monotypic). Valid (McCosker 1977:72 [ref. 6836], McCosker & Böhlke 1984:34 [ref. 5316], McCosker et al. 1989:343 [ref. 13288]). Ophichthidae: Ophichthinae.

Gorgasia Meek & Hildebrand 1923:133 [ref. 2963]. Fem. *Gorgasia punctata* Meek & Hildebrand 1923:133. Type by original designation (also monotypic). Valid (Randall & Chess 1979 [ref. 6924], Robison & Lancraft 1984 [ref. 6812], Asano in Masuda et al. 1984:29 [ref. 6441], Smith 1989:484 [ref. 13285]). Congridae:

Heterocongrinae.

Gorogobius Miller 1978:28 [ref. 3012]. Masc. *Gobius nigricinctus* Delais 1951:356. Type by original designation (also monotypic). Valid (Birdsong et al. 1988:186 [ref. 7303]). Gobiidae.

Goslinia Myers 1941:88 [ref. 3120]. Fem. *Taenionema steerei* Eigenmann & Bean 1907:662. Type by being a replacement name. Replacement for *Taenionema* Eigenmann & Bean 1907, preoccupied by Banks 1905 in Plecoptera and by Bolivar 1906 in Orthoptera. Valid (Stewart 1986:668 [ref. 5211], Burgess 1989:282 [ref. 12860]). Pimelodidae.

Gouania Nardo 1833:548 [ref. 5746]. Fem. *Gouania prototypus* Nardo 1833:548. Type by original designation. Type as given by Briggs 1973:653 [original not seen]. Valid (Briggs 1955:22 [ref. 637], Briggs 1973:653 [ref. 7222], Briggs in Whitehead et al. 1986:1355 [ref. 13677]). Gobiesocidae: Gobiesocinae.

Gracila Randall 1964:281 [ref. 3600]. Fem. *Cephalopholis albomarginatus* Fowler & Bean 1930:235. Type by original designation (also monotypic). Valid (Kendall 1984:500 [ref. 13663], Katayama in Masuda et al. 1984:127 [ref. 6441], Heemstra & Randall 1986:533 [ref. 5667], Smith-Vaniz et al. 1988 [ref. 9299], Paxton et al. 1989:499 [ref. 12442]). Serranidae: Epinephelinae.

Graciieotris Herre 1953:189 [ref. 2144]. Fem. *Gracileotris bockensis* Herre 1953:190. Type by original designation (also monotypic). Synonym of *Ptereleotris* Gill 1863 (Randall & Hoese 1985 [ref. 5197]). Microdesmidae: Ptereleotrinae.

Gracilimugil Whitley 1941:18 [ref. 4701]. Masc. *Mugil ramsayi* Macleay 1883:208. Type by original designation (also monotypic). Mugilidae.

Grahamichthys Whitley 1956:34 [ref. 4726]. Masc. *Eleotris radiata* Valenciennes in Cuvier & Valenciennes 1837:250. Type by original designation (also monotypic). Valid (Hoese, pers. comm.). Eleotridae.

Gramma Poey 1868:296 [ref. 3505]. Neut. *Gramma loreto* Poey 1868:296. Type by monotypy. Valid (Johnson 1984:465 [ref. 9681]). Grammatidae.

Grammabrycon Fowler 1941:190 [ref. 1437]. Masc. *Grammabrycon calverti* Fowler 1941:190. Type by original designation (also monotypic). Synonym of *Phenacogaster* Eigenmann 1907 (see Böhlke 1984:44 [ref. 13621]). Characidae.

Grammateus Poey 1872:182 [ref. 3508]. Masc. *Pagellus microps* Guichenot 1843:188. Type by subsequent designation. Type designated by Jordan & Fesler 1893:508 [ref. 2455] as *microps*; two included species are *humilis* (*microps* in synonymy) and *medius*. Synonym of *Calamus* Swainson 1839 (Randall & Caldwell 1966:5 [ref. 9053]). Sparidae.

Grammatobothus Norman 1926:253 [ref. 3216]. Masc. *Platophrys polyophthalmus* Bleeker 1866:46. Type by original designation. Valid (Norman 1934:244 [ref. 6893], Ahlstrom et al. 1984:642 [ref. 13641], Hensley 1986:941 [ref. 6326]). Bothidae: Bothinae.

Grammatocephalus Norman 1930:338 [ref. 3219]. Masc. *Grammatocephalus kempi* Norman 1930:339. Type by original designation (also monotypic). Synonym of *Derichthys* Gill 1884 (Blache et al. 1973:244 [ref. 7185], Robins 1989:424 [ref. 13289]). Derichthyidae.

Grammatonotus Gilbert 1905:618 [ref. 1631]. Masc. *Grammatonotus laysanus* Gilbert 1905:619. Type by original designation (also monotypic). Valid (Katayama et al. 1980 [ref. 5548], Katayama et al. 1982 [ref. 5397], Katayama in Masuda et al. 1984:138 [ref. 6441] in Serranidae, Johnson 1984:465 [ref. 9681] in Callanthiidae). Callanthiidae.

Grammatopleurus Gill 1861:166 [ref. 1775]. Masc. *Labrax lagocephalus* Pallas 1810:384. Type by original designation (also monotypic). Synonym of *Hexagrammos* Steller 1809. Hexagrammidae: Hexagramminae.

Grammatorycnus Gill 1862:125 [ref. 1659]. Masc. *Thynnus bilineatus* Rüppell 1835:39. Type by monotypy. Originally spelled *Grammatorycnus*, regarded as a misspelling and corrected to *Grammatorcynus* [but probably incorrectly so based on Art. 32(c)(ii)]; suffix apparently based on *Orcynus* of Cuvier, wrongly cited by Gill as *Orycnus*). Valid (Collette 1983 [ref. 5220], Collette & Nauen 1983:38 [ref. 5375], Collette et al. 1984:600 [ref. 11421], Collette & Russo 1984 [ref. 5221], Nakamura in Masuda et al. 1984:224 [ref. 6441]). Scombridae.

Grammatostomias Goode & Bean 1896:110 [ref. 1848]. Masc. *Grammatostomias dentatus* Goode & Bean 1896:110. Type by monotypy. Misspelled *Grammastomias* in Zoological Record for 1896 and *Grammatististomias* in Jordan 1920:536 [ref. 4905]. *Grammatostomias* Holt & Byrne 1910 [ref. 2196] not an original description but a misidentification (= *Lamprotoxus*). Valid (Morrow in Morrow & Gibbs 1964:448 [ref. 6962], Morrow 1973:139 [ref. 7175], Kawaguchi & Moser 1984:171 [ref. 13642], Gibbs in Whitehead et al. 1984:353 [ref. 13675], Fink 1985:11 [ref. 5171]). Melanostomiidae.

Grammatotria Boulenger 1899:90 [ref. 550]. Fem. *Grammatotria lemairii* Boulenger 1899:90. Type by monotypy. Valid (Poll 1986:113 [ref. 6136]). Cichlidae.

Grammichthys Kaup 1858:101 [ref. 2578]. Masc. *Pleuronectes lineatus* Linnaeus 1758:268. Type by monotypy. Synonym of *Achirus* Lacepède 1802. Achiridae.

Grammicolepis Poey 1873:403 et seq. [ref. 3507]. Fem. *Grammicolepis brachiusculus* Poey 1873:403 et seq. Type by monotypy. Valid (Quéro 1973:351 [ref. 7196], Machida in Masuda et al. 1984:118 [ref. 6441], Quéro in Whitehead et al. 1986:773 [ref. 13676], Karrer & Heemstra 1986:440 [ref. 5681]). Grammicolepididae.

Grammiconotus Costa 1862:55 [ref. 4852]. Masc. *Grammiconotus bicolor* Costa 1862:55. Type by monotypy. Synonym of *Scomberesox* Lacepède 1803 (Parin 1973:261 [ref. 7191]). Scomberesocidae.

Grammistes Bloch & Schneider 1801:182 [ref. 471]. Masc. *Grammistes orientalis* Bloch & Schneider 1801:188 (= *Perca sexlineata* Thunberg 1792:142). Type by subsequent designation. Type designated by Jordan 1917:58 [ref. 2407]. Valid (Kendall 1984:501 [ref. 13663], Katayama in Masuda et al. 1984:139 [ref. 6441], Randall 1986:538 [ref. 5706], Paxton et al. 1989:517 [ref. 12442]). Serranidae: Grammistinae.

Grammistops Schultz in Schultz et al. 1953:386 [ref. 3975]. Masc. *Grammistops ocellatus* Schultz in Schultz et al. 1953:386. Type by original designation (also monotypic). Valid (Kendall 1984:501 [ref. 13663], Katayama in Masuda et al. 1984:139 [ref. 6441], Randall 1986:538 [ref. 5706], Paxton et al. 1989:517 [ref. 12442]). Serranidae: Grammistinae.

Grammonoides Smith 1948:343 [ref. 4074]. Masc. *Grammonus opisthodon* Smith 1934:90. Type by original designation (also monotypic). Valid (Cohen & Nielsen 1978:47 [ref. 881], Cohen 1986:356 [ref. 5646]). Bythitidae: Bythitinae.

Grammonus Gill in Goode & Bean 1896:317 [ref. 1848]. *Oligopus ater* Risso 1810:142. Type by monotypy. Authorship is given as

Gill by Goode and Bean, but Gill evidently only responsible for name and workers may wish to credit authorship to Goode & Bean. Synonym of *Oligopus* Risso 1810 (Cohen 1964:2 [ref. 6891], Nielsen 1973:551 [ref. 6885], Cohen & Nielsen 1978:49 [ref. 881]), but see *Oligopus* Risso. Apparently *Grammonus* should be the valid genus for *O. ater* Risso 1810. Bythitidae: Bythitinae.

Grammoplites Fowler 1904:550 [ref. 1367]. Masc. *Cottus scaber* Linnaeus 1758:265. Type by original designation (also monotypic). Valid (Knapp 1979:51 [ref. 14196], Knapp 1986:483 [ref. 5683]). Platycephalidae.

Grandisquamachela (subgenus of *Parachela*) Fowler 1934:111 [ref. 1417]. Fem. *Parachela williaminae* Fowler 1934:111. Synonym of *Oxygaster* van Hasselt 1823 (see Böhlke 1984:95 [ref. 13262]). Cyprinidae.

Graodus Günther 1868:485 [ref. 1990]. Masc. *Graodus nigrotaeniatus* Günther 1868:485. Type by monotypy. Synonym of *Notropis* Rafinesque 1818 (Gilbert 1978:15 [ref. 7042]). Cyprinidae.

Grasseichthys Géry 1964:4805 [ref. 1581]. Masc. *Grasseichthys gabonensis* Géry 1964:4806. Type by original designation (also monotypic). Valid (Poll 1984:135 [ref. 6180] in Grasseichthyidae, Howes 1985:301 [ref. 5148] with family placement uncertain). Kneriidae.

Graus Philippi 1887:572 [40] [ref. 3464]. Fem. *Graus nigra* Philippi 1887:572 [40]. Type by monotypy. On p. 40 of separate. Valid (Johnson & Fritzsche 1989 [ref. 13513]). Kyphosidae: Girellinae.

Graviceps Fowler 1903:170 [ref. 1360]. Neut. *Petroscirtes elegans* Steindachner 1877:169. Type by original designation (also monotypic). Synonym of *Omobranchus* Ehrenberg 1836 (Springer 1972:9 [ref. 4178], Springer & Gomon 1975:9 [ref. 6083]). Blenniidae.

Grecarchopterus Mohsen 1962:119 [ref. 3035]. Masc. *Zenarchopterus novaeguineae* Weber 1913. Type by original designation (also monotypic). Synonym of *Zenarchopterus* Gill 1864 (Collette 1986:163 [ref. 6197] but as *Grecarhopterus*). Hemiramphidae.

Greeleya Jordan 1920:493, 571 [ref. 4905]. Fem. *Eximia rubellio* Greeley 1901:18. Type by being a replacement name. Replacement for *Eximia* Greeley 1901, preoccupied by [K.] Jordan 1894 [details not researched]. Synonym of *Oligocottus* Girard 1856 (Bolin 1944:65 [ref. 6379]). Cottidae.

Greenwoodochromis Poll 1983:46 [ref. 6498]. Masc. *Limnochromis christyi* Trewavas 1953:1. Type by original designation. Replacement for *Lepidochromis* Poll 1981, preoccupied by Fowler & Bean 1928. Valid (Poll 1986:139 [ref. 6136]). Cichlidae.

Gregoryina Fowler & Ball 1924:269 [ref. 1471]. Fem. *Gregoryina gygis* Fowler & Ball 1924:270. Type by original designation (also monotypic). Synonym of subgenus *Goniistius* Gill 1862 of genus *Cheilodactylus* Lacepède 1803 (Randall 1983:2 [ref. 5361]). Cheilodactylidae.

Gremilla Gistel 1848:VIII [ref. 1822]. Fem. *Perca cernua* Linnaeus 1758:294. Type by being a replacement name. Replacement for *Acerina* Cuvier 1816, preoccupied; unneeded, as earlier names are available (e.g., *Gymnocephalus* Bloch 1793. Objective synonym of *Acerina* Güldenstädt 1774. Percidae.

Grenurus Parr 1946:46 [ref. 3378]. Masc. *Grenurus grenadae* Parr 1946:47. Type by original designation (also monotypic). Synonym of *Sphagemacrurus* Fowler 1925 (Marshall 1973:291 [ref. 7194], Marshall 1973:621 [ref. 6965]). Macrouridae: Macrourinae.

Griffinetta Whitley & Phillipps 1939:233 [ref. 4737]. Fem. *Griffinetta nelsonensis* Whitley & Phillipps 1939:233. Type by original designation (also monotypic). Synonym of *Pseudopentaceros* Bleeker 1876 (Hardy 1983:206 [ref. 5385]). Pentacerotidae.

Grimaldia Chapman 1942:(272) 299 [ref. 818]. Fem. *Opisthoproctus grimaldii* Zugmayer 1911:2. Type by original designation (also monotypic). Preoccupied by Chevreux 1889 in Crustacea, replaced by *Monacoa* Whitley 1943. Objective synonym of *Monacoa* Whitley 1943; synonym of *Opisthoproctus* Vaillant 1888 (Cohen 1973:156 [ref. 6589]). Opisthoproctidae.

Grimaldichthys Roule 1913:2 [ref. 3816]. Masc. *Grimaldichthys profundissimus* Roule 1913:3. Type by monotypy. Also in Roule (Apr.) 1914:498 [ref. 3814]. Synonym of *Bassogigas* Goode & Bean 1896 (Nielsen 1973:549 [ref. 6885]); synonym of *Holcomycteronus* Garman 1899 (Cohen & Nielsen 1978:32 [ref. 881]). Ophidiidae: Neobythitinae.

Grimatroctes Parr 1952:265 [ref. 3381]. Masc. *Bathytroctes grimaldii* Zugmayer 1911:1. Type by original designation. Valid (Krefft 1973:90 [ref. 7166]). Alepocephalidae.

Gristes Cuvier 1829:145 [ref. 995]. Masc. *Labrus salmoides* Lacepède 1802:716. Type by subsequent designation. Also appeared in Cuvier in Cuvier & Valenciennes (Apr.) 1829:54 [ref. 4879] as *Grystes*. Spelled *Gryptes* and *Gristes* in early literature. Type designated by Jordan & Gilbert 1877:88 [ref. 4907]. Type apparently misidentified (see Hubbs & Bailey). Synonym of *Micropterus* Lacepède 1802 (Hubbs & Bailey 1940:13 [ref. 12253] as *Grystes*). Centrarchidae.

Gronias Cope 1864:231 [ref. 906]. Masc. *Gronias nigrilabris* Cope 1864:231. Type by monotypy. Synonym of *Ameiurus* Rafinesque 1820 (Hubbs & Bailey 1947:12 [ref. 2254]). Ictaluridae.

Gronovichthys Whitley 1930:302 [ref. 13468]. Masc. *Amia percaeformis* Gronow in Gray 1854:173. Type by being a replacement name. Replacement for *Amia* of Meuschen 1781 (on unavailable *Amia* Gronow 1763 and on Gronow in Gray 1854), preoccupied by *Amia* Linnaeus 1766 in fishes. Synonym of *Apogon* Lacepède 1801 (Fraser 1972:17 [ref. 5195]). Apogonidae.

Grundulus Valenciennes in Cuvier & Valenciennes 1846:216 [ref. 1011]. Masc. *Poecilia bogotensis* Humboldt 1821:154, 159. Type by monotypy. Valid (Géry 1977:607 [ref. 1597]). Characidae.

Grystes see *Gristes* Cuvier 1829. Centrarchidae.

Guaperva Plumier in Lacepède 1802:562 (footnote) [ref. 4929]. Fem. Not available, name mentioned in passing under *Selene argentea*. See remarks under Opinion 89 in Appendix B. Carangidae.

Guaris Rafinesque 1815:90 [ref. 3584]. Not available, name only. Unplaced genera.

Guavina Bleeker 1874:302 [ref. 437]. Fem. *Eleotris guavina* Valenciennes in Cuvier & Valenciennes 1837:223. Type by original designation (also monotypic and by absolute tautonymy). Valid (Birdsong et al. 1988:181 [ref. 7303]). Eleotridae.

Gudusia (subgenus of *Sardinella*) Fowler 1911:207 [ref. 1382]. Fem. *Clupanodon chapra* Hamilton 1822:248, 383. Type by original designation (also monotypic). Misspelled *Gadusia* by authors. Valid (Jayaram 1981:40 [ref. 6497], Grande 1985:249 [ref. 6466], Whitehead 1985:228 [ref. 5141]). Clupeidae.

Guebucus Rafinesque 1815:86 [ref. 3584]. Not available, name only; listed as a genus of istiophorid. Istiophoridae.

Guentheria Bleeker 1862:413 [ref. 382]. Fem. *Guentheria caeruleovittatus* Rüppell 1835:Pl. 14. Type by original designation (also monotypic). Also appeared in Bleeker 1862:101 [ref. 386].

Synonym of *Halichoeres* Rüppell 1835. Labridae.

Guentheridia Gilbert & Starks 1904:158 [ref. 1639]. Fem. *Tetraodon formosus* Günther 1870:283. Type by original designation (also monotypic). Valid (Tyler 1980:341 [ref. 4477], Arai 1983:207 [ref. 14249]). Tetraodontidae.

Guentherus Osório 1917:117 [ref. 3318]. Masc. *Guentherus altivela* Osório 1917:117. Type by monotypy. Spelled *Güntherus* two of four times and *Guntherus* two of four times (pp. 105, 117); correct spelling will be *Guentherus* or *Guntherus* depending on first reviser [not researched]. Although genus is masculine, species spelling should not be emended according to Bussing & López 1977:181 [ref. 7001]). Valid (Bussing & López 1977 [ref. 7001], Paxton in Whitehead et al. 1986:528 [ref. 13676], Smith 1986:405 [ref. 5712]). Ateleopodidae.

Guianacara Kullander & Nijssen 1989:90, 92 [ref. 14136]. Fem. *Guianacara owroewefi* Kullander & Nijssen 1989:97. Type by original designation. Cichlidae.

Guichenotia Whitley 1950:44 [ref. 4713]. Fem. *Glyphodes aprionoides* Guichenot 1862:3. Type by being a replacement name. Replacement for *Glyphodes* Guichenot 1862, preoccupied in Lepidoptera [details not investigated]. Kyphosidae: Girellinae.

Guichthys Fernández-Yépez 1968:[5] [ref. 7318]. Masc. *Guichthys caviceps* Fernández-Yépez 1968:[5]. Type by original designation (also monotypic). Synonym of *Rhabdolichops* Eigenmann & Allen 1942 (Mago-Leccia 1978:14 [ref. 5489]). Gymnotidae: Sternopyginae.

Guiritinga Bleeker 1858:62, 67 [ref. 365]. Fem. *Pimelodus commersonii* Lacepède 1803:95, 103, 108. Type by monotypy. Synonym of *Netuma* Bleeker 1858, but may be valid for South American species (Higuchi et al. 1982:3 [ref. 11467]). Ariidae.

Gulaphallus Herre 1925:508 [ref. 2121]. Masc. *Gulaphallus eximius* Herre 1925:509. Type by subsequent designation. Type designated by Myers 1928:9 [ref. 3101]. Valid (White et al. 1984:360 [ref. 13655], Parenti 1989:273 [ref. 13486]). Phallostethidae.

Gulapinnus Langer 1913:207 [ref. 2717]. Masc. *Poecilia decemmaculata* Jenyns 1842:115. Type by monotypy. Synonym of *Cnesterodon* Garman 1895 (Rosen & Bailey 1963:74 [ref. 7067]). Poeciliidae.

Gularopanchax (subgenus of *Aphyosemion*) Radda 1977:210 [ref. 3580]. Masc. *Fundulus gularis* Boulenger 1901:623. Type by original designation. Synonym of *Fundulopanchax* Myers 1924, but as a valid subgenus (Parenti 1981:477 [ref. 7066]); synonym of *Aphyosemion* Myers 1924 (Wildekamp et al. 1986:197 [ref. 6198]). Aplocheilidae: Aplocheilinae.

Gularus (subgenus of *Elops*) Whitley 1940:397 [ref. 4699]. Masc. *Elops australis* Regan 1909:39. Type by original designation. Elopidae.

Gulliveria Castelnau 1878:45 [ref. 762]. Fem. *Gulliveria fusca* Castelnau 1878:45. Type by subsequent designation. Type designated by Jordan 1919:393 [ref. 4904]. Synonym of *Glossamia* Gill 1863 (Fraser 1972:8 [ref. 5195], Paxton et al. 1989:555 [ref. 12442]). Apogonidae.

Gunnamatta Whitley 1928:225 [ref. 4661]. Fem. *Gunnamatta insolita* Whitley 1928:225. Type by original designation (also monotypic). Synonym of *Callogobius* Bleeker 1874. Gobiidae.

Gunnellichthys Bleeker 1858:3, 9 [ref. 361]. Masc. *Gunnellichthys pleurotaenia* Bleeker 1858:3, 10. Type by monotypy. Valid (Hayashi in Masuda et al. 1984:288 [ref. 6441], Birdsong et al. 1988:200 [ref. 7303]). Microdesmidae: Microdesminae.

Gunnellops Bleeker 1874:368 [ref. 435]. Masc. *Gunnellus roseus* Pallas 1811:197. Type by original designation (also monotypic). Pholidae.

Gunnellus Fleming 1828:207 [ref. 1339]. Masc. *Gunnellus vulgaris* Fleming 1818:207 (= *Blennius gunnellus* Linnaeus 1758:257). Type by monotypy. Synonym of *Pholis* Scopoli 1777 (Makushok 1973:534 [ref. 6889], Yatsu 1981:169 [ref. 4814]). Pholidae.

Gunterichthys Dawson 1966:205 [ref. 1063]. Masc. *Gunterichthys longipenis* Dawson 1966:206. Type by original designation (also monotypic). Valid (Cohen & Nielsen 1978:59 [ref. 881]). Bythitidae: Brosmophycinae.

Gurgesiella de Buen 1959:184 [ref. 697]. Fem. *Gurgesiella furvescens* de Buen 1959:185. Type by original designation (also monotypic). Valid (McEachran & Compagno 1979 [ref. 5226], McEachran & Compagno 1980 [ref. 6896], McEachran 1984:56 [ref. 5225]). Rajidae.

Gurnardus (subgenus of *Prionotus*) Jordan & Evermann 1898:2148, 2152 [ref. 2444]. Masc. *Prionotus gymnostethus* Gilbert 1891:559. Type by original designation. Synonym of *Prionotus* Lacepède 1801. Triglidae: Triglinae.

Guttigadus (subgenus of *Laemonema*) Taki 1953:205, 209 [ref. 4314]. Masc. *Laemonema (Guttigadus) nana* Taki 1953:205. Type by original designation (also monotypic). Synonym of *Laemonema* Günther 1862. Moridae.

Gvozdarus Balushkin 1989:83 [ref. 13490]. Masc. *Gvozdarus svetovidovi* Balushkin 1989:85. Type by original designation (also monotypic). Nototheniidae.

Gymnacanthus see *Gymnocanthus*. Cottidae.

Gymnachirus Kaup 1858:101 [ref. 2578]. Masc. *Gymnachirus nudus* Kaup 1858. Type by monotypy. Valid (Matsuura in Uyeno et al. 1983:462 [ref. 14275], Chapleau & Keast 1988:2799 [ref. 12625]). Achiridae.

Gymnallabes Günther 1867:111 [ref. 1989]. Fem. *Gymnallabes typus* Günther 1867:111. Type by monotypy (also by use of *typus*). Valid (Poll 1977:124 [ref. 3533], Teugels 1986:97 [ref. 6193], Burgess 1989:147 [ref. 12860]). Clariidae.

Gymnammodytes Duncker & Mohr 1935:216 [ref. 5561]. Masc. *Ammodytes cicerelus* Rafinesque 1810:21. Type apparently by monotypy. Text somewhat unclear, apparently additional species all referred to (or questionably referred to) *circerelus*; if more than one species is included then this name is not available from Duncker & Möhr (no designation of type after 1930). Valid (Wheeler 1973:447 [ref. 7190], Stevens et al. 1984:574 [ref. 13671], Heemstra 1986:770 [ref. 5660], Reay in Whitehead et al. 1986:947 [ref. 13676] dating to Duncker & Mohr 1939). Ammodytidae.

Gymnapistes (subgenus of *Apistes*) Swainson 1839:65, 180, 265 [ref. 4303]. Masc. *Apistus marmoratus* Cuvier in Cuvier & Valenciennes 1829:416. Type by subsequent designation. Type designated by Bleeker 1876:7 [ref. 12248] and 1876:299 [ref. 450], also by Swain 1882:277 [ref. 5966]. Spelled *Gymnapistus* by Bleeker 1876:7 and 1876:299. Valid (Scott 1976:200 [ref. 7055], Washington et al. 1984:440 [ref. 13660], Paxton et al. 1989:441 [ref. 12442]). Scorpaenidae: Tetraroginae.

Gymnapogon Regan 1905:19 [ref. 3624]. Masc. *Gymnapogon japonicus* Regan 1905:20. Type by monotypy. Valid (Fraser 1972:31 [ref. 5195], Hayashi in Masuda et al. 1984:150 [ref. 6441], Gon 1986:560 [ref. 5657], Paxton et al. 1989:555 [ref. 12442]).

Apogonidae.

Gymnarchus Cuvier 1829:357 [ref. 995]. Masc. *Gymnarchus niloticus* Cuvier 1829:358. Type by monotypy. Valid (Taverne 1972:125, 174 [ref. 6367], Gosse 1984:123 [ref. 6169]). Gymnarchidae.

Gymneleotris Bleeker 1874:304 [ref. 437]. Fem. *Eleotris seminudus* Günther 1864:24. Type by original designation. Valid (Birdsong et al. 1988:189 [ref. 7303]). Gobiidae.

Gymnelichthys Fischer 1885:60 [ref. 1333]. Masc. *Gymnelichthys antarcticus* Fischer 1885:61. Type by monotypy. Synonym of *Maynea* Cunningham 1871 (Gosztonyi 1977:220 [ref. 6103]). Synonym of *Gymnelus* Reinhardt 1834 (Andriashev 1973:540 [ref. 7214], McAllister et al. 1981:835 [ref. 5431], Anderson 1982:28 [ref. 5520]). Zoarcidae.

Gymnelopsis Soldatov 1922:160 [ref. 4159]. Fem. *Gymnelopsis ocellatus* Soldatov 1922:161. Type by original designation. Valid (Anderson 1982 [ref. 5520], Anderson 1984:578 [ref. 13634], Toyoshima in Masuda et al. 1984:306 [ref. 6441]). Zoarcidae.

Gymnelus Reinhardt 1834:4 [ref. 13469]. Masc. *Ophidium viride* Fabricius 1780:141. Type by monotypy. Later spelled *Gymnelis* by Reinhardt and authors (Andriashev 1973:540 [ref. 7214]); see also Krøyer 1862:258 [ref. 2694]. Correct spelling for genus of type species is *Ophidion*. Valid (Andriashev 1973:540 [ref. 7214], McAllister et al. 1981:835 [ref. 5431], Anderson 1982 [ref. 5520], Anderson 1984:578 [ref. 13634], Toyoshima in Masuda et al. 1984:306 [ref. 6441], Andriashev in Whitehead et al. 1986:1131 [ref. 13677]). Zoarcidae.

Gymnepignathus (subgenus of *Decapterus*) Gill 1862:261 [ref. 4909]. Masc. *Decapterus macrosoma* Bleeker 1851:358. Type by monotypy. Misspelled *Gymneipignathus* by Jordan 1919:316 [ref. 4904]. Synonym of *Decapterus* Bleeker 1851 (Daget & Smith-Vaniz 1986:314 [ref. 6207]). Carangidae.

Gymnetrus Bloch 1795:94 [ref. 464]. *Gymnetrus hawkenii* Bloch 1795:95. Type by monotypy. Synonym of *Regalecus* Ascanius 1772 (Palmer 1973:329 [ref. 7195]). Regalecidae.

Gymnobatrachus Smith 1949:423 [ref. 5846]. Masc. *Amphichthys ophiocephalus* Smith 1947:819. Type by original designation. Synonym of *Batrichthys* Smith 1934 (based on placement of type species by Hutchins 1986:359 [ref. 5673]). Batrachoididae.

Gymnobutis Bleeker 1874:304 [ref. 437]. *Eleotris gymnocephalus* Steindachner 1866:453. Type by original designation (also monotypic). Eleotridae.

Gymnocaesio Bleeker 1876:152 [ref. 445]. Fem. *Caesio gymnopterus* Bleeker 1856:372. Type by original designation (also monotypic). Possibly appeared first in Atlas in 1876 on legend page 125 (for Pl. 310 published in 1872 but with *Caesio* on plate) [ref. 4861]. Also in Bleeker 1876:8 [ref. 4862] and as above (earliest not determined). Valid (Johnson 1980:10 [ref. 13553], Carpenter 1987:50 [ref. 6430], Carpenter 1988:48 [ref. 9296]). Caesionidae.

Gymnocanthus Swainson 1839:181, 271 [ref. 4303]. Masc. *Cottus ventralis* Cuvier in Cuvier & Valenciennes 1829:194. Type by monotypy. Spelled *Gymnacanthus* by authors; spelled *Gymnocanthus* three times by Swainson and therefore there is no evidence for an inadvertent error. Valid (Neyelov 1973:595 [ref. 7219] as *Gymnacanthus*, Washington et al. 1984:442 [ref. 13660], Yabe in Masuda et al. 1984:328 [ref. 6441], Yabe 1985:111 [ref. 11522], Fedorov in Whitehead et al. 1986:1249 [ref. 13677] as *Gymnacanthus*). Cottidae.

Gymnocephalus Bloch 1793:24 [ref. 4868]. Masc. *Perca schraetser* Linnaeus 1758:294. Type by subsequent designation. Type designated by Bleeker 1876:266 [ref. 447]. See *Acerina* Güldenstädt 1774. Valid (Collette & Banarescu 1977:1453 [ref. 5845]). Percidae.

Gymnocephalus Cocco 1838:26 [ref. 6499]. Masc. *Gymnocephalus messinensis* Cocco 1838:26. Type by monotypy. Preoccupied by Bloch 1793 in fishes, apparently not replaced. Synonym of *Centrolophus* Lacepède 1802 (Haedrich 1967:62 [ref. 5357], Haedrich 1973:559 [ref. 7216]). Centrolophidae.

Gymnochanda Boeseman 1957:75 [ref. 487]. Fem. *Gymnochanda filamentosa* Boeseman 1957:75. Type by original designation (also monotypic). Homonym and subjective synonym of *Gymnochanda* Fraser-Brunner 1955 (Boeseman independently chose the same genus and species names for this species [as stated in correction notice circulated by Boeseman]). Synonym of *Gymnochanda* Fraser-Brunner 1955 (Roberts 1989:159 [ref. 6439]). Ambassidae.

Gymnochanda Fraser-Brunner 1955:209 [ref. 1498]. Fem. *Gymnochanda filamentosa* Fraser-Brunner 1955:210. Type by original designation (also monotypic). Boeseman 1957:75 [ref. 487] independently chose the same genus and species name for this species; *Gymnochanda* Boeseman is a homonym and synonym of *Gymnochanda* Fraser-Brunner. Valid (Kottelat 1989:17 [ref. 13605], Roberts 1989:159 [ref. 6439]). Ambassidae.

Gymnocharacinus Steindachner 1903:20 [ref. 4240]. Masc. *Gymnocharacinus bergii* Steindachner 1903:20. Type by monotypy. Valid (Géry 1977:535 [ref. 1597]). Characidae.

Gymnocirrhites Smith 1951:638 [ref. 4081]. Masc. *Cirrhites arcatus* Cuvier in Cuvier & Valenciennes 1829:74. Type by original designation. Correct spelling for genus of type species is *Cirrhitus*. Cirrhitidae.

Gymnoclinus Gilbert & Burke 1912:86 [ref. 1634]. Masc. *Gymnoclinus cristulatus* Gilbert & Burke 1912:86. Type by original designation (also monotypic). Valid. Stichaeidae.

Gymnocorymbus Eigenmann 1908:93 [ref. 1221]. Masc. *Gymnocorymbus thayeri* Eigenmann 1908:93. Type by original designation (also monotypic). Valid (Géry 1977:451 [ref. 1597]). Characidae.

Gymnocranius (subgenus of *Dentex*) Klunzinger 1870:764 [ref. 2621]. Masc. *Dentex rivulatus* Rüppell 1838:116 (= *Canthatus grandoculis* Valenciennes 1830:255). Type by monotypy. *Dentex rivulatus* of Rüppell 1838 is not the same as *Dentex rivulatus* Bennett 1835 (see Carpenter & Allen 1989:19 [ref. 13577]). Valid (Johnson 1980:11 [ref. 13553], Sato in Masuda et al. 1984:179 [ref. 6441], Smith 1986:595 [ref. 5712], Sato 1986:604 [ref. 5152], Carpenter & Allen 1989:18 [ref. 13577]). Lethrinidae.

Gymnocrotaphus Günther 1859:413, 432 [ref. 1961]. Masc. *Gymnocrotaphus curvidens* Günther 1859:432. Type by monotypy. Valid (Smith & Smith 1986:586 [ref. 5710]). Sparidae.

Gymnocypris Günther 1868:169 [ref. 1990]. Fem. *Gymnocypris dobula* Günther 1868:170. Type by monotypy. Valid (Tsao 1964:178 [ref. 13501], Tchang et al. 1964 [ref. 3501], Jayaram 1981:69 [ref. 6497], Wu 1987:43 [ref. 12822], Wu 1987:111 [ref. 12824]). Cyprinidae.

Gymnodiptychus Herzenstein 1892:225 [ref. 5037]. Masc. *Diptychus dybowskii* Kessler 1874:55. Type by original designation. Type designated by Jordan 1920:458 [ref. 4905]. Synonym of *Diptychus* Steindachner 1866, but as a valid subgenus (Tsao 1964:175 [ref. 13501]); valid genus (Wu 1987:47 [ref. 12822], Mo in Chu & Chen 1989:319 [ref. 13584]). Cyprinidae.

Gymnodraco Boulenger 1902:186 [ref. 561]. Masc. *Gymnodraco acuticeps* Boulenger 1902:186. Type by monotypy. Valid (Stevens et al. 1984:563 [ref. 13633], Voskoboinikova 1988:44 [ref. 12756]). Bathydraconidae.

Gymnogaster Brünnich 1788:408 [ref. 5131]. Fem. *Gymnogaster arcticus* Brünnich 1788:408. Type by monotypy. Possibly published in 1771 [ref. 675, not seen] (see Palmer 1973:330 [ref. 7195]). Synonym of *Trachipterus* Goüan 1770 (Palmer 1973:330 [ref. 7195], Scott 1983:172 [ref. 5346]). Trachipteridae.

Gymnogaster Gronow 1763:136 [ref. 1910]. Fem. Not available, published in a rejected work on Official Index (Opinion 261). In the synonymy of *Trichiurus* Linnaeus 1758. Trichiuridae: Trichiurinae.

Gymnogeophagus Miranda-Ribeiro 1918:790 [ref. 3724]. Masc. *Gymnogeophagus cyanopterus* Miranda-Ribeiro 1918:790. Type by monotypy. Valid (Gosse 1975:109 [ref. 7029], Kullander 1980:23 [ref. 5526], Reis & Malabarba 1988 [ref. 6638], Malabarba 1989:167 [ref. 14217]). Cichlidae.

Gymnognathus Sauvage 1884:214 [ref. 3886]. Masc. *Gymnognathus harmandi* Sauvage 1884:214. Type by monotypy. Preoccupied by Schoenherr 1823 and by Solier 1851 in Coleoptera; not replaced. Cyprinidae.

Gymnogobius Gill 1863:269 [ref. 1691]. Masc. *Gobius macrognathos* Bleeker 1860:53. Type by monotypy. Gobiidae.

Gymnolycodes Vaillant 1888:312 [ref. 4496]. Masc. *Gymnolycodes edwardsi* Vaillant 1888:313. Type by monotypy. Synonym of *Paraliparis* Collett 1878 (Lindberg 1973:611 [ref. 7220], Stein 1978:37 [ref. 4203], Andriashev 1986:14 [ref. 12760], Kido 1988:230 [ref. 12287]). Cyclopteridae: Liparinae.

Gymnomuraena Lacepède 1803:648 [ref. 4930]. Fem. *Gymnomuraena doliata* Lacepède 1803:648, 649. Type by subsequent designation. Earliest valid type designation not researched; not *G. pantherina* as designated by Bleeker 1865:74 [ref. 4860]. Valid (Hatooka in Masuda et al. 1984:25 [ref. 6441], Böhlke et al. 1989:130 [ref. 13286]). Muraenidae: Muraeninae.

Gymnopropoma Gill 1863:222 [ref. 1685]. Neut. *Labrus bilunulatus* Lacepède 1801:454. Type by original designation (also monotypic). Synonym of *Lepidaplois* Gill 1862. Labridae.

Gymnopsis Rafinesque 1815:93 [ref. 3584]. Fem. *Gymnomuraena doliata* Lacepède 1803:648. Type by being a replacement name. As "*Gymnopsis* R. [Rafinesque] *Gymnomuraena* Lac. [Lacepède]". An available replacement name (unneeded) for *Gymnomuraena* Lacepède 1803. Synonym of *Echidna* Forster 1777. Muraenidae: Muraeninae.

Gymnorhamphichthys Ellis in Eigenmann 1912:423, 436 [ref. 1227]. Masc. *Gymnorhamphichthys hypostomus* Ellis in Eigenmann 1912:436. Type by monotypy. Also appeared in Ellis 1913:139 [ref. 1271]. Valid (Nijssen et al. 1976 [ref. 7078], Mago-Leccia 1978:14 [ref. 5489], Schwassmann 1989 [ref. 13745]). Gymnotidae: Rhamphichthyinae.

Gymnorhinus Hilgendorf in Hemprich & Ehrenberg 1899:8 [ref. 4977]. Masc. *Gymnorhinus pharaonis* Hemprich & Ehrenberg 1899. Preoccupied by Maxillian 1840 or 1841 in Aves. Also apparently as *Gymnorrhinus* on Pl. 7. Original not examined; see Compagno 1988:307 [ref. 13488] and Fowler 1968:425 [ref. 9319]. Synonym of *Carcharhinus* Blainville 1816 (Garrick 1982:19 [ref. 5454], Compagno 1984:449 [ref. 6846], Compagno 1988:307 [ref. 13488]). Carcharhinidae.

Gymnosarda Gill 1862:125 [ref. 1659]. Fem. *Thynnus unicolor* Rüppell 1836:40. Type by original designation (also monotypic). Valid (Collette & Nauen 1983:40 [ref. 5375], Collette et al. 1984:600 [ref. 11421], Nakamura in Masuda et al. 1984:225 [ref. 6441], Collette 1986:833 [ref. 5647]). Scombridae.

Gymnoscopelus Günther 1873:91 [ref. 6424]. Masc. *Gymnoscopelus aphya* Günther 1873:91. Type by monotypy. Valid (Paxton 1979:11 [ref. 6440], Moser et al. 1984:220 [ref. 13645], Hulley 1986:299 [ref. 5672], Hulley 1989 [ref. 12284], Paxton et al. 1989:261 [ref. 12442]). Myctophidae.

Gymnoscyphus Böhlke & Robins 1970:3 [ref. 610]. Masc. *Gymnoscyphus ascitus* Böhlke & Robins 1970:3. Type by original designation (also monotypic). Valid. Gobiesocidae: Gobiesocinae.

Gymnosimenchelys Tanaka 1908:2 [ref. 4321]. Fem. *Gymnosimenchelys leptosomus* Tanaka 1908:2. Type by monotypy. Synonym of *Simenchelys* Gill 1879 (Robins & Robins 1989:214 [ref. 13287]). Synaphobranchidae: Simenchelyinae.

Gymnostomus Heckel 1843:1030 [ref. 2066]. Masc. *Cyprinus ariza* Hamilton 1822:344. Type by subsequent designation. Type apparently designated first by Bleeker 1863:197 [ref. 397]; not Bleeker 1860 and not *Capoeta syriaca* (not an included species). Synonym of *Varicorhinus* Rüppell 1836 (Lévêque & Daget 1984 [ref. 6186]). Cyprinidae.

Gymnotes Gill 1864:152 [ref. 1698]. *Gymnotus aequilabiatus* Humboldt 1811:46. Type by monotypy. Synonym of *Gymnotus* Linnaeus 1758. Gymnotidae: Gymnotinae.

Gymnothorax Bloch 1795:83 [ref. 464]. Masc. *Gymnothorax reticularis* Bloch 1795:85. Type designated by ICZN by use of plenary powers; on Official List (Opinion 93); *Gymnothorax* Cuvier 1800 (nomen nudum) placed on Official Index (Direction 56). Valid (Blache et al. 1983:226 [ref. 7185], Hatooka in Masuda et al. 1984:23 [ref. 6441], Bauchot in Whitehead et al. 1986:540 [ref. 13676], Castle & McCosker 1986:167 [ref. 5645], Paxton et al. 1989:128 [ref. 12442], Böhlke et al. 1989:145 [ref. 13286]). Muraenidae: Muraeninae.

Gymnotichthys Fernández-Yépez 1950:9 [ref. 1323]. Masc. *Gymnotichthys hildae* Fernández-Yépez 1950:10. Type by original designation (also monotypic). Mentioned (Géry 1977:451 [ref. 1597]). Characidae.

Gymnotorpedo (subgenus of *Torpedo*) Fritsch 1884:451 [ref. 1510]. Fem. *Torpedo occidentalis* Storer 1843:166. Type by subsequent designation. Three included species; first subsequent type designation not researched. Also published in Fritsch 1886:365 [see under ref. 1510]. Objective synonym of *Tetronarce* Gill 1862; synonym of *Torpedo* Houttuyn 1764 (Cappetta 1987:161 [ref. 6348]). Torpedinidae.

Gymnotus Linnaeus 1758:246 [ref. 2787]. Masc. *Gymnotus carapo* Linnaeus 1758:246. Type by Linnaean tautonymy (also designated by Eigenmann 1910:450 [ref. 1224]). Unjustifiably emended to *Gymnonotus* by Bloch & Schneider 1801:521 [ref. 471]. Valid (Malabarba 1989:158 [ref. 14217]). Gymnotidae: Gymnotinae.

Gymnura Müller & Henle 1837:117 [ref. 3067]. Fem. *Raja asperrima* Bloch & Schneider 1801:367. Type by monotypy. Preoccupied by van Hasselt 1823 in fishes, replaced by *Urogymnus* Müller & Henle 1837. Objective synonym of *Urogymnus* Müller & Henle 1837 (Paxton et al. 1989:43 [ref. 12442]). Dasyatidae.

Gymnura van Hasselt 1823:316 [ref. 4513]. Fem. *Raja micrura* Bloch & Schneider 1801:360. Type by monotypy. Valid (Krefft & Stehmann 1973:72 [ref. 7167], Nakaya in Masuda et al. 1984:16 [ref. 6441], Compagno 1986:138 [ref. 5648], Cappetta 1987:165

[ref. 6348], Paxton et al. 1989:45 [ref. 12442]). Gymnuridae.

Gymnurus Rafinesque 1815:84 [ref. 3584]. Masc. *Taenioides hermanni* Lacepède 1800:532. Type by being a replacement name. As "*Gymnurus* L. *Taenioides* Lac. [Lacepède]." An available (unneeded) replacement name for and objective synonym of *Taenioides* Lacepède 1800; the "L" after *Gymnurus* should have been an "R" for Rafinesque. Gobiidae.

Gynutoclinus Smith 1946:545 [ref. 4072]. Masc. *Clinus rotundifrons* Barnard 1937:63. Type by original designation (also monotypic). Synonym of *Clinus* Cuvier 1816 (Bennett 1983 [ref. 5299], Smith 1986:761 [ref. 5712]). Clinidae.

Gyrinichthys Gilbert 1896:444 [ref. 1628]. Masc. *Gyrinichthys minytremus* Gilbert 1896:444. Type by original designation (also monotypic). Cyclopteridae: Liparinae.

Gyrinocheilops Fowler 1937:160 [ref. 1425]. Masc. *Gyrinocheilops pennocki* Fowler 1937:160. Type by original designation. Synonym of *Gyrinocheilus* Vaillant 1902. Gyrinocheilidae.

Gyrinocheilus Vaillant 1902:107 [ref. 4490]. Masc. *Gyrinocheilus pustulosus* Vaillant 1902:111. Type by monotypy. Misspelled *Gyrinochilus* by Jordan 1920:500 [ref. 4905]. Valid (Kottelat 1985:267 [ref. 11441], Krasyukova & Gusev 1987:67 [ref. 6340], Kottelat 1989:13 [ref. 13605], Roberts 1989:81 [ref. 6439]). Gyrinocheilidae.

Gyrinomene Vaillant 1888:18, 45, 355 [ref. 4496]. Fem. *Gyrinomene nummularis* Vaillant 1888:18, 45, 355. Genus and species as name only (pp. 18, 45), identified as *Diretmus argentius* on p. 355; technically probably a name published in synonymy [subsequent availability not researched]. Misspelled *Gyrinonemus* by Jordan 1920:443 [ref. 4905]. In the synonymy of *Diretmus* Johnson 1863 (Maul 1973:338 [ref. 7171], Woods & Sonoda 1973:291 [ref. 6899], Post & Quéro 1981:37 [ref. 3555], Kotlyar 1987 [ref. 13522] as *Gyriomene*). Diretmidae.

Gyrinomimus Parr 1934:21, 29 [ref. 3375]. Masc. *Gyrinomimus myersi* Parr 1934:29. Type by original designation (also monotypic). Valid (Paxton et al. 1989:384 [ref. 12442], Paxton 1989:175 [ref. 13435]). Cetomimidae.

Gyrinostomus Rochebrune 1885:96 [ref. 3791]. Masc. *Gyrinostomus marchei* Rochebrune 1885:96. Type by monotypy. Mastacembelidae.

Gyrinurus Miranda-Ribeiro 1912:27 [ref. 3718]. Masc. *Gyrinurus batrachostoma* Miranda-Ribeiro 1912:28. Type by monotypy. Trichomycteridae.

Gyropleurodus Gill 1862:331 [ref. 1668]. Masc. *Cestracion francisci* Girard 1854:196. Type by monotypy. Synonym of *Heterodontus* Blainville 1816 (Compagno 1984:155 [ref. 6474]). Heterodontidae.

Habrolepis Fitzinger 1873:152, 167 [ref. 1337]. Fem. *Squalius ukliva* Heckel 1873:1042. Type by subsequent designation. Type apparently first designated by Jordan 1919:369 [ref. 4904]. Fitzinger spelled as *Habrolopis* on p. 152. Synonym of *Leuciscus* Cuvier 1816. Cyprinidae.

Hadropareia Schmidt 1904:204 [ref. 3946]. Fem. *Hadropareia middendorffii* Schmidt 1904:204. Type by monotypy. Valid (Anderson 1984:578 [ref. 13634]). Zoarcidae.

Hadropogonichthys Fedorov 1982:722 [ref. 1311]. Masc. *Hadropogonichthys lindbergi* Fedorov 1982:724. Type by original designation (also monotypic). Valid (Anderson 1984:578 [ref. 13634], Toyoshima 1985:142 [ref. 5722]). Zoarcidae.

Hadropterus Agassiz 1854:305 [ref. 69]. Masc. *Hadropterus nigrofasciatus* Agassiz 1854:305. Type by monotypy. Synonym of *Percina* Haldeman 1842, but as a valid subgenus (Page 1974:82 [ref. 3346], Collette & Banarescu 1977:1454 [ref. 5845]). Percidae.

Haemomaster Myers 1927:131 [ref. 3096]. Masc. *Haemomaster venezuelae* Myers 1927:131. Type by original designation (also monotypic). Valid (Burgess 1989:324 [ref. 12860], Pinna 1989 [ref. 12630]). Trichomycteridae.

Haemulon Cuvier 1829:175 [ref. 995]. Neut. *Haemulon elegans* Cuvier 1829:175 (on *Anthias formosus* Bloch). Type by subsequent designation. Type apparently designated first by Jordan 1917:128 [ref. 2407]. Spelled *Haemulion* by Swainson 1839:17 [ref. 4303]. *Haemylum* Agassiz 1846:170 [ref. 64] is an unjustified emendation. Valid (Johnson 1980:11 [ref. 13553], Matsuura in Uyeno et al. 1983:355 [ref. 14275]). Haemulidae.

Haemulopsis (subgenus of *Pristipoma*) Steindachner 1869:128 [ref. 4216]. Fem. *Haemulon corvinaeforme* Steindachner 1868:980. Type by subsequent designation. Type designated by Jordan 1919:355 [ref. 4904]. Synonym of *Pomadasys* Lacepède 1802 (Roux 1973:391 [ref. 7200] with type as *H. nitidum*); synonym of *Brachydeuterus* Gill 1862 (Roux 1986:327 [ref. 6209]); as a subgenus of *Pomadasys* Lacepède 1802 (López 1981 [ref. 5187]); valid genus (Johnson 1980:11 [ref. 13553]). Haemulidae.

Hainania Koller 1927:45 [ref. 5622]. Fem. *Hainania serrata* Koller 1927:45. Type by monotypy. Valid (Yih & Wu 1964:78 [ref. 13499]); synonym of *Hemiculter* Bleeker 1859 (authors). Cyprinidae.

Halaelurus Gill 1862:407 [ref. 1783]. Masc. *Scyllium burgeri* Müller & Henle 1841:8. Type by original designation (also monotypic). Also in Gill 1862:412 [ref. 4910] where author of species is clear. Valid (Nakaya 1975:60 [ref. 7083], Springer 1979:68 [ref. 4175], Compagno 1984:319 [ref. 6846], Nakaya in Masuda et al. 1984:4 [ref. 6441], Bass 1986:90 [ref. 5635], Séret 1987 [ref. 6267], Compagno 1988:143 [ref. 13488]). Scyliorhinidae.

Halaphya Günther 1889:38 [ref. 2017]. Fem. *Halaphya elongata* Günther 1889:39. Type by monotypy. Misspelled *Halophya* in Zoological Record for 1889. Based on very small specimens; family placement uncertain (see Cohen 1958:134 [ref. 13649]); specimens not located at the British Museum by Cohen (pers. comm., May 1990). Argentinoidei.

Halargyreus Günther 1862:342 [ref. 1969]. Masc. *Halargyreus johnsonii* Günther 1862:342. Type by monotypy. Valid (Cohen 1973:323 [ref. 6589], Cohen 1973 [ref. 7137], Paulin 1983:108 [ref. 5459], Fahay & Markle 1984:266 [ref. 13653], Okamura in Masuda et al. 1984:90 [ref. 6441], Cohen in Whitehead et al. 1986:716 [ref. 13676], Paxton et al. 1989:299 [ref. 12442]). Moridae.

Halatractus Gill 1863:442 [ref. 1669]. Masc. *Scomber zonatus* Mitchill 1815:440. Type by original designation. Jordan (1919:317 [ref. 4904]) states that this is a replacement for *Seriola* Cuvier 1816 (type *Seriola dumerili*), but there is no evidence in the original description that this is the case, and *zonatus* is clearly designated type. Synonym of *Seriola* Cuvier 1816 (Smith-Vaniz, pers. comm.). Carangidae.

Halecula Jordan 1925:41 [ref. 2428]. Fem. *Etrumeus acuminatus* Gilbert 1890:56. Type by monotypy. Preoccupied by Facciolà 1891 [not researched], replaced by *Parahalecula* Fowler 1958. Synonym of *Etrumeus* Bleeker 1853 (Whitehead 1985:30 [ref. 5141]). Clupeidae.

Haletta Whitley 1947:146 [ref. 4708]. Fem. *Odax semifasciatus* Valenciennes in Cuvier & Valenciennes 1840:299. Type by original designation (also monotypic). Synonym of *Neoodax* Castelnau 1875 (Scott 1976:352 [ref. 3996]); valid (Gomon & Paxton 1986:29 [ref. 5656]). Odacidae.

Halex Commerson in Lacepède 1803:460 (footnote) [ref. 4930]. Masc. *Clupea fasciata* Lacepède 1803:460. Not available. Names from Commerson footnotes in this volume of Lacepède placed on Official Index of Rejected Works (see remarks under Opinion 89 in Appendix B). Leiognathidae.

Halias Ayres 1860:52 [ref. 156]. Masc. *Brosmius marginatus* Ayres 1854:13. Type by monotypy. Apparently preoccupied by Treitschke 1829 in Lepidoptera [not researched]; *Brosmophycis* Gill 1861 apparently described independently and may be used as the available name. Objective synonym of *Brosmophycis* Gill 1861 (Cohen & Nielsen 1978:53 [ref. 881] with date as 1863). Bythitidae: Brosmophycinae.

Halicampoides Fowler 1956:204 [ref. 1468]. Masc. *Halicampus macrorhynchus* Bamber 1915:480. Type by original designation (also monotypic). Synonym of *Halicampus* Kaup 1856 (Dawson 1985:75 [ref. 6541]). Syngnathidae: Syngnathinae.

Halicampus Kaup 1856:22 [ref. 2575]. Masc. *Halicampus grayi* Kaup 1856:22. Type by monotypy. Appeared first as name only in Kaup 1853:231 [ref. 2569] with unavailable species *H. grayi* Kaup. See Opinion 53 for action involving *grayi* Kaup. Valid (Araga in Masuda et al. 1984:87 [ref. 6441], Dawson 1985:75 [ref. 6541], Dawson 1986:451 [ref. 5650], Paxton et al. 1989:418 [ref. 12442]). Syngnathidae: Syngnathinae.

Halichoeres Rüppell 1835:(10) 14 [ref. 3844]. Masc. *Halichoeres bimaculatus* Rüppell 1835:17. Type by subsequent designation. Type designated by Jordan 1919:184 [ref. 2410]. Spelled *Halychoeres* by Bonaparte 1841:puntata 156, fasc. 30 [ref. 512]. Unneeded replacement names are *Hemiulis* Swainson 1839 and *Choerojulis* Gill 1862. Valid (Randall 1981 [ref. 5542], Richards & Leis 1984:544 [ref. 13668], Araga in Masuda et al. 1984:208 [ref. 6441], Randall 1986:694 [ref. 5706]). Labridae.

Halicmetus Alcock 1891:27 [ref. 87]. Masc. *Halicmetus ruber* Alcock 1891:27. Type by monotypy. Valid (Mochizuki in Masuda et al. 1984:104 [ref. 6441] but as *Halicmetes*). Ogcocephalidae.

Halidesmus Günther 1872:668 [ref. 1997]. Masc. *Halidesmus scapularis* Günther 1872:668. Type by monotypy. Valid (Winterbottom 1982 [ref. 5436], Winterbottom 1986:17 [ref. 5727], Winterbottom 1986:729 [ref. 5728]). Pseudochromidae: Congrogadinae.

Halieutaea Valenciennes in Cuvier & Valenciennes 1837:455 [ref. 1006]. Fem. *Halieutaea stellata* Valenciennes in Cuvier & Valenciennes 1837:456 (= *Lophius stellatus* Vahl 1797:214). Type by monotypy. Spelled *Halieutea* in early literature. Valid (Mochizuki in Masuda et al. 1984:105 [ref. 6441], Bradbury 1986:371 [ref. 6291], Paxton et al. 1989:285 [ref. 12442]). Ogcocephalidae.

Halieutella Goode & Bean 1885:88 [ref. 1843]. Fem. *Halieutella lappa* Goode & Bean 1885:88. Type by monotypy. Ogcocephalidae.

Halieutichthys Poey in Gill 1863:90 [ref. 1680]. Masc. *Halieutichthys reticulatus* Poey in Gill 1863:91. Ogcocephalidae.

Halieutopsis Garman 1899:89 [ref. 1540]. Fem. *Halieutopsis tumifrons* Garman 1899:90. Type by original designation (also monotypic). Valid (Mochizuki in Masuda et al. 1984:104 [ref. 6441], Bradbury 1986:372 [ref. 6291], Okamura et al. 1987 [ref. 6850], Bradbury 1988 [ref. 6428]). Ogcocephalidae.

Haligenes Günther 1859:471 [ref. 1962]. *Haligenes tristrami* Günther 1859:471. Type by monotypy. Synonym of *Tilapia* Smith 1840. Cichlidae.

Haliichthys Gray 1859:38 [ref. 1887]. Masc. *Haliichthys taeniophora* Gray 1859:39. Type by monotypy. Valid (Paxton et al. 1989:419 [ref. 12442]). Syngnathidae.

Halimochirurgus Alcock 1899:78 [ref. 93]. Masc. *Halimochirurgus centriscoides* Alcock 1899:78. Type by original designation (also monotypic). Misspelled *Halimochirus* by Jordan 1920:484 [ref. 4905]. Valid (Tyler 1968:217 [ref. 6438], Tyler 1980:56 [ref. 4477], Matsuura in Masuda et al. 1984:357 [ref. 6441], Tyler 1986:888 [ref. 5723]). Triacanthodidae.

Halimuraena Smith 1952:92 [ref. 4082]. Fem. *Halimuraena hexagonata* Smith 1952:92. Type by original designation (also monotypic). Valid (Maugé & Bardach 1985:378 [ref. 5162], Winterbottom 1986:19 [ref. 5727], Winterbottom 1986:729 [ref. 5728]). Pseudochromidae: Congrogadinae.

Halimuraenoides Maugé & Bardach 1985:381 [ref. 5162]. Masc. *Halimuraenoides isostigma* Maugé & Bardach 1985:382. Type by original designation (also monotypic). Valid (Winterbottom 1986:22 [ref. 5727]). Pseudochromidae: Congrogadinae.

Halinanodes Whitley 1931:113 [ref. 4673]. Masc. *Halichoeres leucostigma* Fowler & Bean 1928:299. Type by original designation (also monotypic). Labridae.

Haliophis Rüppell 1829:49 [ref. 3843]. Masc. *Muraena guttata* Forsskål 1775:22. Type by monotypy. Valid (Winterbottom 1985:209 [ref. 5241], Maugé & Bardach 1985:377 [ref. 5162], Winterbottom 1986:23 [ref. 5727]). Pseudochromidae: Congrogadinae.

Haliperca Gill 1862:236 [ref. 1664]. Fem. *Serranus bivittatus* Cuvier in Cuvier & Valenciennes 1828:241. Type by subsequent designation. Type designated by Jordan & Gilbert 1883:535 [ref. 2476]. Synonym of *Diplectrum* Holbrook 1855 (Bortone 1977:3 [ref. 7064]). Serranidae: Serraninae.

Halisauriceps Fowler 1934:247 [ref. 1416]. Neut. *Alepocephalus longiceps* Lloyd 1909:147. Type by original designation (also monotypic). Synonym of *Alepocephalus* Risso 1820 (Parr 1951:4 [ref. 3380]). Alepocephalidae.

Halmablennius Smith 1948:340 [ref. 4074]. Masc. *Salarias unicolor* Rüppell 1835:136. Type by original designation. Synonym of *Istiblennius* Whitley 1943 (Smith-Vaniz & Springer 1971:25 [ref. 4145], Bath 1986:356 [ref. 6217]). Blenniidae.

Halobatrachus Ogilby 1908:46, 53 [ref. 3284]. Masc. *Batrachus didactylus* Bloch & Schneider 1801:42. Type by original designation. Valid (Monod 1973:657 [ref. 7193], Roux in Whitehead et al. 1986:1360 [ref. 13677]). Batrachoididae.

Halocypselus Weinland 1858:385 [ref. 4615]. Masc. *Halocypselus mesogaster* Weinland 1858 (= *Exocoetus evolans* Linnaeus 1766:521). Type by monotypy. Synonym of *Exocoetus* Linnaeus 1758 (Parin 1973:263 [ref. 7191]). Exocoetidae.

Halophryne Gill 1863:170 [ref. 1681]. Fem. *Batrachoides diemensis* Lesueur 1824:402. Type by original designation (also monotypic). Valid (Hutchins 1974 [ref. 6970], Hutchins 1976:8 [ref. 6971], Paxton et al. 1989:272 [ref. 12442]). Batrachoididae.

Haloporphyrus Günther in Johnson 1862:166 [ref. 5804]. Masc. *Gadus lepidion* Risso 1810:118. Type by being a replacement name. Appeared first in Johnson (Sept. 1862) attributed to Günther (publ. Dec. 1862:358). Unneeded replacement for *Lepidion* Swainson 1838, not preoccupied by *Lepidia* Savigny 1817 (see Paulin 1983:106 [ref. 5459]). Objective synonym of *Lepidion* Swainson 1838 (Cohen 1973:324 [ref. 6589], Paulin 1983:106 [ref. 5459]). Moridae.

Halosaurichthys Alcock 1889:454 [ref. 81]. Masc. *Halosaurichthys carinicauda* Alcock 1889:454. Type by monotypy. Synonym of *Halosaurus* Johnson 1863. Halosauridae.

Halosauropsis Collett 1896:143 [ref. 890]. Fem. *Halosaurus macrochir* Günther 1878:250. Type by original designation. Valid (Harrisson 1973:254 [ref. 7189], Sulak 1986:196 [ref. 5720], Sulak in Whitehead et al. 1986:595 [ref. 13676], Machida et al. 1988 [ref. 6623], Paxton et al. 1989:147 [ref. 12442]). Halosauridae.

Halosaurus Johnson 1864:406 [ref. 5751]. Masc. *Halosaurus ovenii* Johnson 1864:406. Type by monotypy. Also appeared in Johnson 1864:74 [ref. 2358]. Valid (Harrisson 1973:254 [ref. 7189], Sulak 1986:197 [ref. 5720], Sulak in Whitehead et al. 1986:596 [ref. 13676], Paxton et al. 1989:147 [ref. 12442]). Halosauridae.

Halsydrus Fleming (ex Neil) in Brewster 1817:17 *Halsydrus pontoppidiani* Fleming or Neil 1809:17. Apparently appeared first in Neil 1809 [Scottish Mag., v. 7] as name only, apparently published in an available way by Fleming 1817 in Brewster's Edinburgh Encylopedia [not investigated]. Synonym of *Cetorhinus* Blainville 1816 (Compagno 1984:234 [ref. 6474], Cappetta 1987:107 [ref. 6348]). Cetorhinidae.

Hamatichthys Fernández-Yépez 1948:33 [ref. 1316]. Masc. *Anodus ciliatus* Müller & Troschel 1845:25. Type by original designation (also monotypic). Synonym of *Psectrogaster* Eigenmann & Eigenmann 1889 (Vari 1989:6 [ref. 9189], Vari 1989:12 [ref. 13548]). Curimatidae: Curimatinae.

Hamiltonia (subgenus of *Equula*) Swainson 1839:176, 250 [ref. 4303]. Fem. *Chanda nama* Hamilton 1822:109, 371. Type by being a replacement name. Technically a replacement for *Chanda* Hamilton; type is *C. nama* as designated by ICZN for *Chanda* (not *H. ovata* as designated by Swain 1882). *Hamiltonia* placed on Official Index (Opinion 1121). Objective synonym of *Chanda* Hamilton 1822. Ambassidae.

Hampala Bleeker 1860:275 [ref. 380]. Fem. *Capoeta macrolepidota* Valenciennes in Cuvier & Valenciennes 1842:280. Type by subsequent designation. Type designated by Bleeker 1863:200 [ref. 397] or 1863:27 [ref. 4859] through *Hampla macrolepidota* van Hasselt 1823. See *Hampala* Kuhl & van Hasselt 1823. Valid (Kottelat 1985:262 [ref. 11441], Kottelat 1989:8 [ref. 13605], Roberts 1989:40 [ref. 6439]). Cyprinidae.

Hampala Kuhl & van Hasselt in van Hasselt 1823:132 [ref. 5963]. Fem. *Hampala macrolepidota* Kuhl & van Hasselt in van Hasselt 1823:132. Type by monotypy. Also appeared in French version 1823:376 [ref. 5104]; regarded by Kottelat (1987:370 [ref. 5962]) as available; genus usually credited to Bleeker 1860 and species to Valenciennes 1842; both authors providing complete descriptions. As a nomen nudum in synonymy of *Hampala* Bleeker 1860 (Roberts 1989:40 [ref. 6439]). Valid (Chu & Cui in Chu & Chen 1989:157 [ref. 13584]). Cyprinidae.

Hannia Vari 1978:244 [ref. 4514]. Fem. *Hannia greenwayi* Vari 1978:244. Type by original designation (also monotypic). Valid (Paxton et al. 1989:532 [ref. 12442]). Terapontidae.

Hanno Herre 1946:123 [ref. 2142]. Masc. *Eleotris africanus* Steindachner 1880:153. Type by original designation (also monotypic). Preoccupied by Gray 1821 in Mammalia, replaced by *Hannoichthys* Herre 1950. Synonym of *Bostrychus* Lacepède 1801 (Maugé 1986:390 [ref. 6218]). Eleotridae.

Hannoichthys Herre 1950:198 [ref. 2113]. Masc. *Eleotris africanus* Steindachner 1880:153. Type by being a replacement name. Replacement for *Hanno* Herre 1946, preoccupied by Gray 1821 in Mammalia. Synonym of *Bostrychus* Lacepède 1801 (Maugé 1986:390 [ref. 6218]); valid (Birdsong et al. 1988:180 [ref. 7303]). Eleotridae.

Hanomanctus Smith 1949:403 [ref. 5846]. Masc. *Hanomanctus bovinus* Smith 1949:403. Type by original designation (also monotypic). Synonym of *Cantherhines* Swainson 1839 (Randall 1964:335 [ref. 3148]). Balistidae.

Hapalogenys Richardson 1844:462 [ref. 3736]. Fem. *Hapalogenys nitens* Richardson 1844:463. Type by subsequent designation. Type designated by Bleeker 1876:271 [ref. 447]. Placement in Percoidei incertae sedis follows Johnson 1984:465 [ref. 9681]. Valid (Akazaki in Masuda et al. 1984:173 [ref. 6441]). Percoidei.

Haploactis see *Aploactis*. Aploactinidae.

Haploactisoma see *Aploactisoma*. Aploactinidae.

Haploblepharus Garman 1913:101 [ref. 1545]. Masc. *Scyllium edwardsii* Cuvier in Müller & Henle 1841. Type by monotypy. Type species needs work. Valid (Springer 1979:88 [ref. 4175], Compagno 1984:332 [ref. 6846], Bass 1986:91 [ref. 5635], Compagno 1988:148 [ref. 13488]). Scyliorhinidae.

Haplochilus see *Aplocheilus*. Aplocheilidae: Aplocheilinae.

Haplochiton Agassiz 1846 [ref. 64]. see *Aplochiton* Jenyns 1842. Galaxiidae: Aplochitoninae.

Haplochromis (subgenus of *Chromis*) Hilgendorf 1888:76 [ref. 2168]. Masc. *Haplochromis obliquidens* Hilgendorf 1888:76. Type by monotypy. Valid (Greenwood 1980 [ref. 1899], Snoeks 1988 [ref. 6867]). Cichlidae.

Haploclonus Regan & Trewavas 1930:72, 78 [ref. 3681]. Masc. *Eustomias enbarbatus* Welsh 1923:7. Type by original designation. Synonym of *Eustomias* Vaillant 1888 (Gibbs in Morrow & Gibbs 1964:377 [ref. 6962], Morrow 1973:137 [ref. 7175]). Melanostomiidae.

Haplocylix Briggs 1955:21 [ref. 637]. Fem. *Cyclopterus littoreus* Forster in Bloch & Schneider 1801:199. Type by original designation (also monotypic). Valid. Gobiesocidae: Gobiesocinae.

Haploglossa (subgenus of *Agnathomyzon*) Gracianov 1906:18 [ref. 1870]. Fem. *Agnathomyzon (Haploglossa) caspicus* Gracianov 1906:18. Original not seen. Fowler 1964:39 [ref. 7160] says published in 1907. Preoccupied by Kraatz 1858 in Coleoptera. Synonym of *Caspiomyzon* Berg 1906 (Sept.), date for Gracianov is Dec. 1906 (Hubbs & Potter 1971:43 [ref. 13397]). Petromyzontidae: Petromyzontinae.

Haploidonotus [ref. 1773]. see *Aplodinotus*. Sciaenidae.

Haplomacrourus Trunov 1980:3 [ref. 4467]. Masc. *Haplomacrourus nudirostris* Trunov 1980:5. Type by original designation (also monotypic). Valid (Paxton et al. 1989:327 [ref. 12442]). Macrouridae: Macrourinae.

Haplophryne Regan 1912:289 [ref. 3644]. Fem. *Aceratias mollis* Brauer 1906:323. Type by monotypy. Based on larval males. Valid (Bertelsen in Whitehead et al. 1986:108 [ref. 13677]); synonym of *Linophryne* Collett 1886 (Paxton et al. 1989:296 [ref. 12442]). Linophrynidae.

Haplostomias Regan & Trewavas 1930:109 [ref. 3681]. Masc. *Haplostomias tenaculatus* Regan & Trewavas 1930:109. Two included species, neither designated. Earliest type designation not researched; possibly first by Fowler 1974:279 [ref. 7156]. Synonym of *Melanostomias* Brauer 1902 (Gibbs in Morrow & Gibbs 1964:354 [ref. 6962], Morrow 1973:134 [ref. 7175]). Melanostomiidae.

Haplotaxodon Boulenger 1906:565 [ref. 573]. Masc. *Haplotaxodon microlepis* Boulenger 1906:566. Type by monotypy. Valid (Poll 1986:155 [ref. 6136]). Cichlidae.

Haplozebrias Chabanaud 1943:292 [ref. 799]. Masc. *Synaptura fasciata* Macleay 1883:14. Type by original designation (also monotypic). Misspelled *Haplozelrias* in Zoological Record for 1944. Soleidae.

Haptenchelys Robins & Martin in Robins & Robins 1976:267 [ref. 3784]. Fem. *Haptenchelys texis* Robins & Martin in Robins & Robins 1976:267. Type by original designation (also monotypic). Valid (Anderson et al. 1985 [ref. 5164], Robins & Robins 1989:232 [ref. 13287]). Synaphobranchidae: Synaphobranchinae.

Haptoclinus Böhlke & Robins 1974:1 [ref. 611]. Masc. *Haptoclinus apectolophus* Böhlke & Robins 1974:1. Type by original designation (also monotypic). Labrisomidae.

Haptogenys Springer 1972:8 [ref. 4178]. Fem. *Haptogenys quadripora* Springer 1972:8. Type by original designation (also monotypic). Valid (Springer 1985:91 [ref. 6107]). Blenniidae.

Hara Blyth 1860:152 [ref. 477]. *Hara buchanani* Blyth 1860:152 (= *Pimelodus hara* Hamilton 1822:190, 378). Type by original designation. Type designated as *H. buchanani*, nobis; *Pimelodus hara*, B.H."; Blyth's new name *buchanani* is an unneeded substitute for *P. hara*. Valid (Jayaram 1981:245 [ref. 6497], Burgess 1989:132 [ref. 12860]). Possibly a synonym of *Erethistes* Müller & Troschel 1849 [?1845] (Kottelat 1983:74 [ref. 5289]). Sisoridae.

Harengula Valenciennes in Cuvier & Valenciennes 1847:277 [ref. 1012]. Fem. *Harengula latulus* Valenciennes 1847:280 (= *Clupea clupeola* Cuvier 1829:318). Type by subsequent designation. Type designated by Gill 1861:36 [ref. 1767]. Valid (Grande 1985:250 [ref. 6466], Whitehead 1985:63 [ref. 5141]). Clupeidae.

Harengus Catesby 1771:24 [ref. 774]. Masc. Not available, published in a rejected work on Official Index (Opinion 89, Opinion 259). Clupeidae.

Harengus Geoffroy St. Hilaire 1767:405 [ref. 1570]. Masc. Original not seen. Apparently not available, no included species; type assumed to be *Clupea harengus* Linnaeus 1758. In the synonymy of *Clupea* Linnaeus 1758. Clupeidae.

Harengus Klein 1775:209 [ref. 2618]. Masc. Not available, published in a work that does not conform to the principle of binominal nomenclature. Clupeidae.

Harpadon (subgenus of *Saurus*) Lesueur 1825:50 [ref. 5024]. Masc. *Salmo microps* Lesueur 1825:48. Type by original designation (also monotypic). Spelled *Harpodon* by Cuvier 1829:314 [ref. 995]. Lesueur states, "type of a new subgenus near to *Saurus*"; it is somewhat unclear if he was describing *Harpadon* as a subgenus of *Salmo* or *Saurus*. Spelling of subfamily correctly is Harpadontinae. Valid (Klausewitz 1983 [ref. 6011], Okiyama 1984:207 [ref. 13644], Fujii in Masuda et al. 1984:62 [ref. 6441], Paxton et al. 1989:242 [ref. 12442]). Synodontidae: Harpadontinae.

Harpage De Vis 1884:447 [ref. 1089]. *Harpage rosea* De Vis 1884:448. Type by monotypy. Synonym of *Plectrypops* Gill 1862 (Woods & Sonoda 1973:382 [ref. 6899]). Holocentridae.

Harpagifer Richardson 1844:11 [ref. 3740]. Masc. *Callionymus bispinis* Forster in Bloch & Schneider 1801:45. Type by monotypy. Valid (Hureau et al. 1980 [ref. 6932], Eakin 1981:138 [ref. 14216], Stevens et al. 1984:563 [ref. 13633]). Harpagiferidae.

Harpagochromis Greenwood 1980:10 [ref. 1899]. Masc. *Hemichromis serranus* Pfeffer 1896:23. Type by original designation. Cichlidae.

Harpe Lacepède 1802:426 [ref. 4929]. Masc. *Harpe caeruleoaureus* Lacepède 1802:426, 427. Type by monotypy. Synonym of *Bodianus* Bloch 1790. Labridae.

Harpochris Cantor 1849:1144 [162] [ref. 715]. Masc. *Chaetodon punctatus* Linnaeus 1758:273. Type by being a replacement name. Unneeded replacement for *Drepane* Cuvier 1831, not preoccupied by *Drepana*. On Official Index (Opinion 1046). Earlier replaced by *Enixe* Gistel 1848. On page 162 of separate. Spelled *Harpochirus* by Bleeker 1876:301 [ref. 448] and 1877:19 [ref. 6835]. Objective synonym of *Drepane* Cuvier 1831. Drepanidae.

Harpodon Cuvier 1829:footnote on 314 [ref. 995]. Masc. *Salmo microps* Lesueur 1825:48. Apparently an incorrect subsequent spelling of *Harpadon* Lesueur 1825, misquoted by Cuvier as *Harpodon*. In the synonymy of *Harpadon* Lesueur 1825. Synodontidae: Harpadontinae.

Harpurina (subgenus of *Hepatus*) Fowler & Bean 1929:210, 253 [ref. 1476]. Fem. *Hepatus nubilus* Fowler & Bean 1929:253. Type by original designation (also monotypic). Synonym of *Acanthurus* Forsskål 1775 (Randall 1955:364 [ref. 13648]). Acanthuridae.

Harpurus Forster 1778:84 [ref. 1354]. Masc. *Chaetodon sohal* Forsskål 1775:63. Type by subsequent designation. Type designated by Fowler 1904:544 [ref. 1367]; Jordan lists *Hapurus fasciatus* Forster 1778 as type. Original not seen, but without species according to Fowler 1904; first addition of species and type designation needs research. Synonym of *Acanthurus* Forsskål 1775 (Randall 1955:363 [ref. 13648]). Acanthuridae.

Harriotta Goode & Bean 1895:471 [ref. 1846]. Fem. *Harriotta raleighana* Goode & Bean 1895:472. Type by monotypy. Appeared first in Goode 1886:104 [ref. 12455] in footnote as "...a long-rostrated chimaeroid fish from deep water off the Atlantic coast of North America." [regarded as insufficient diagnosis]. Above is Jan. 1895. Also in Goode & Bean 1896:32 [ref. 1848]. As *Hariotta* in Mitsukuri (June) 1895 [ref. 5935] on Goode & Bean. Valid (Krefft 1973:80 [ref. 7166], Nakaya in Masuda et al. 1984:17 [ref. 6441], Compagno 1986:146 [ref. 5648], Paxton et al. 1989:100 [ref. 12442]). Rhinochimaeridae.

Harttia Steindachner 1876:668 [110] [ref. 4224]. Fem. *Harttia loricariformis* Steindachner 1876:669. Type by monotypy. Apparently appeared first as name only 1876:191 [ref. 12584]; dates to p. 668 as above; on p. 110 of separate. Valid (Isbrücker 1980:89 [ref. 2303], Burgess 1989:439 [ref. 12860]). Loricariidae.

Harttiella Boeseman 1971:25 [ref. 490]. Fem. *Harttia crassicauda* Boeseman 1953:10. Type by original designation. Misspelled *Hartiella* in Zoological Record for 1971, corrected in 1972. Valid (Isbrücker 1980:89 [ref. 2303], Burgess 1989:439 [ref. 12860]). Loricariidae.

Hasemania Ellis 1911:148 [ref. 1269]. Fem. *Hasemania melanura* Ellis 1911:149. Type by original designation. Valid (Géry 1977:518 [ref. 1597]). Characidae.

Hassar (subgenus of *Hemidoras*) Eigenmann & Eigenmann 1888:158 [ref. 1249]. *Doras orestes* Agassiz in Steindachner 1875:138. Type by subsequent designation. Type designated by Eigenmann 1910:394 [ref. 1224]. Valid (Burgess 1989:222 [ref. 12860]). Doradidae.

Hatcheria Eigenmann 1909:250 [ref. 1223]. Fem. *Hatcheria* *patagoniensis* Eigenmann 1909:250. Type by original designation. Valid (Arratia et al. 1978 [ref. 144], Arratia & Menu-Marque 1981 [ref. 6024] with type as *macraei*, Pinna 1989:31 [ref. 12630]). Trichomycteridae.

Hatha Whitley 1959:25 [ref. 4730]. Fem. *Lepidotrigla mulhalli* Macleay 1884:460. Type by original designation (also monotypic). Synonym of *Lepidotrigla* Günther 1860 (Richards & Saksena 1977:209 [ref. 5285]). Triglidae: Triglinae.

Hatumeus (subgenus of *Sebastes*) Matsubara 1943:192 [ref. 2905]. Masc. *Sebastodes owstoni* Jordan & Thompson 1914:270. Type by original designation (also monotypic). Synonym of *Sebastes* Cuvier 1829. Scorpaenidae: Sebastinae.

Haustor (subgenus of *Ameiurus*) Jordan & Evermann 1896:135, 136, 137 [ref. 2443]. Masc. *Gadus lacustris* Walbaum 1792:144. Type by original designation. Based on a misidentified type species (see Speirs 1952 [ref. 14251]). The description given by Jordan & Evermann is of an *Ictalurus*, the type species is a *Lota* (Lotidae). Synonym of *Ictalurus* Rafinesque 1820 (some authors); synonym of *Lota* (Spiers 1952:102 [ref. 14251]). Lotidae.

Hazeus Jordan & Snyder 1901:51 [ref. 2509]. Masc. *Hazeus otakii* Jordan & Snyder 1901:51. Type by original designation. Synonym of *Gnatholepis* Bleeker 1874 (Maugé 1986:369 [ref. 6218]); valid (Akihito in Masuda et al. 1984:253 [ref. 6441], Birdsong et al. 1988:193 [ref. 7303]). Gobiidae.

Hectoria Castelnau 1873:151 [ref. 758]. Fem. *Oligorus gigas* Günther 1859 (= *Centropristis gigas* Owen 1853:51). Type by monotypy. Synonym of *Polyprion* Oken 1817. Polyprionidae.

Hedinichthys (subgenus of *Nemacheilus*) Rendahl 1933:26 [ref. 3704]. Masc. *Nemocheilus yarkandensis* Day 1876:796. Type by original designation (also monotypic). Valid (Kottelat 1990:19 [ref. 14137]). Balitoridae: Nemacheilinae.

Heegerius (subgenus of *Scardinius*) Bonaparte 1846:31 Masc. *Leuciscus hegeri* Bonaparte 1839:fasc. 24 (= *Heegerius typus* Bonaparte 1845:10). Type by monotypy. Apparently appeared first as *Heegerius* Bonaparte 1845:10 [ref. 13472], perhaps as a name in synonymy (not seen). Then (according to Fowler MS) it appeared in Atti. Riun. Sci. Ital., v. 6 (1845):398. Later (1846, ref. 519) spelled *Hegerius* by Bonaparte. Original not examined. Synonym of *Rutilus* Rafinesque 1820 (Howes 1981:45 [ref. 14200]) as *Hegerius*); synonym of *Scardinius* Bonaparte 1837. Cyprinidae.

Helcogramma McCulloch & Waite 1918:51 [ref. 2950]. Neut. *Helcogramma decurrens* McCulloch & Waite 1918:52. Type by original designation. Valid (Yoshino in Masuda et al. 1984:293 [ref. 6441], Hadley Hansen 1986 [ref. 5810], Holleman 1986:757 [ref. 5671], Hardy 1987 [ref. 5960]). Tripterygiidae.

Helgia Vinciguerra 1890:328 [ref. 4520]. Fem. *Homaloptera bilineata* Blyth 1860:172. Type by subsequent designation. Earliest type designation found that of Jordan 1920:448 [ref. 4905] as above. Synonym of *Homaloptera* van Hasselt 1823 (Roberts 1989:88 [ref. 6439]). Balitoridae: Balitorinae.

Heliases Cuvier in Cuvier & Valenciennes 1830:493 et seq. [ref. 999]. *Heliases insolatus* Cuvier in Cuvier & Valenciennes 1830:494. Type by subsequent designation. Based on "Les Héliases" Cuvier 1829:160; latinized first as above, with six included species. Type apparently designated first by Valenciennes 1845:503 in Dict. Univ. Hist. Nat. v. 6 according to Fowler, MS. Variously misspelled or emended to *Haliastes*, *Heliasus*, and *Heliazes* in early literature (see Monod 1973:424 [ref. 7193]). Synonym of *Chromis* Cuvier 1814. Pomacentridae.

Heliastes Lowe 1838:177 [ref. 2831]. Masc. Unjustified emendation of *Heliases* Cuvier 1815. Synonym of *Chromis* Cuvier 1814 (Monod 1973:424 [ref. 7193]). Pomacentridae.

Helicobranchus Hyrtl 1854:86 [ref. 2290]. Masc. *Sudis niloticus* Cuvier (ex Ehrenberg) 1829:469. Type by being a replacement name. Apparently an unneeded replacement for *Heterotis* Rüppell. Objective synonym of *Heterotis* Rüppell 1828 (Daget 1984:57 [ref. 6170]). Osteoglossidae: Heterotidinae.

Helicolenus Goode & Bean 1896:248 [ref. 1848]. Masc. *Scorpaena dactyloptera* Delaroche 1809:337. Type by original designation. Valid (Barsukov 1973 [ref. 7154], Blanc & Hureau 1973:582 [ref. 7218], Barsukov 1981 [ref. 5306], Washington et al. 1984:440 [ref. 13660], Shimizu & Amaoka in Masuda et al. 1984:313 [ref. 6441], Hureau & Litvinenko in Whitehead et al. 1986:1212 [ref. 13677], Eschmeyer 1986:477 [ref. 5652], Paxton et al. 1989:442 [ref. 12442]) Scorpaenidae: Sebastinae.

Helicophagus Bleeker 1858:45 [ref. 359]. Masc. *Helicophagus typus* Bleeker 1858:46. Species listed on p. 28 et seq.; type by use of *typus*. Valid (Kottelat 1985:269 [ref. 11441], Burgess 1989:105 [ref. 12860], Kottelat 1989:14 [ref. 13605]). Pangasiidae.

Helioperca Jordan 1877:355 [ref. 2373]. Fem. *Labrus palladus* Mitchill 1815:407. Type by original designation. Type species unjustifiably emended by Jordan to *Labrus pallidus* Mitchill [not *Lepomis pallida* Rafinesque 1820]. Type species misidentified according to Hubbs 1935 [ref. 5593]); probably should be submitted to the ICZN. Originally type given as "*Labrus pallidus* Mitch. (=*Pomotis incisor* C. and V.);" *incisor* agrees with the original description according to Hubbs. Synonym of *Lepomis* Rafinesque 1819. Centrarchidae.

Helmichthys Costa 1844:Pl. 31 [ref. 980]. Masc. *Helmichthys diaphanus* Costa 1844:Pl. 31. Type by monotypy. Based on a leptocephalus. Not seen. Synonym of *Conger* Oken 1817 (see Castle 1969:10 [ref. 12436]). Synonym of *Ariosoma* Swainson 1838 (Smith 1989:491 [ref. 13285]). Congridae: Bathymyrinae.

Helmictis Rafinesque 1810:49, 62 [ref. 3595]. Masc. *Helmictis punctatus* Rafinesque 1810:62. Type by monotypy. Spelled *Helminctis* by Bonaparte 1841 and *Helminthichthys* by Agassiz 1846 (see Smith 1989:514 [ref. 13285] for nomenclatural comments). Possibly a synonym of *Conger* Oken 1817. Congridae: Congrinae.

Helminthodes Gill 1864:203 [ref. 1702]. Masc. *Oxybeles lumbricoides* Bleeker 1854:163. Type by monotypy. Apparently preoccupied by Marsh 1864 [not researched; Gill 1864 published in Dec.], replaced by *Pirellinus* Whitley 1928. *Helminthoides* is a misspelling. Synonym of *Carapus* Rafinesque 1810 (Arnold 1956:260 [ref. 5315]). Carapidae: Carapinae.

Helminthostoma Günther (ex Cocco) 1870:145 [ref. 1995]. Neut. Not available, passing reference to manuscript name placed by Günther in synonymy of *Porobranchus*. In the synonymy of *Carapus* Rafinesque 1810 (Arnold 1956:260 [ref. 5315]). Carapidae: Carapinae.

Helogenes Günther 1863:443 [ref. 1973]. Masc. *Helogenes marmoratus* Günther 1863:443. Type by monotypy. Valid (Glodek & Carter 1978 [ref. 6159], Vari & Ortega 1986 [ref. 5837], Burgess 1989:288 [ref. 12860]). Helogeneidae.

Helops Agassiz 1846:136 [ref. 64]. Masc. Unjustified emendation of *Elops* Linnaeus 1766; also perhaps preoccupied by Brandt & Ratzeburg 1833 in fishes. Whitley 1935:136 [ref. 6396] states that Bory de Saint-Vincent earlier made this emendation [not investigated]. Objective synonym of *Elops* Linnaeus 1766 (Daget

1984:30 [ref. 6170]). Elopidae.

Helops Brandt & Ratzeburg 1833:3 [ref. 619]. Masc. *Acipenser stellatus* Pallas 1771:131. Type by subsequent designation. As *Helopes* [apparently a vernacular and not available], a group within *Acipenser* later used by Heckel & Kner 1858:342 [ref. 2078]. Norman 1966 [ref. 13535] lists a *Helops* Brandt 1835 in Müller (not investigated). In the synonymy of *Acipenser* Linnaeus 1758. Acipenseridae: Acipenserinae.

Helops Browne 1789:445 [ref. 669]. Masc. Not available, published in a rejected work on Official Index (Opinion 89). Labridae.

Helostoma Cuvier (ex Kuhl) 1829:228 [ref. 995]. Neut. *Helostoma temminckii* Cuvier 1829:228. Type by monotypy. Valid (Kottelat 1989:20 [ref. 13605], Roberts 1989:177 [ref. 6439]). Helostomatidae.

Helotes Cuvier 1829:148 [ref. 995]. Fem. *Terapon sexlineatus* Quoy & Gaimard 1824:340. Type by monotypy. Appeared first in Cuvier (Mar.) 1829:148 as above, then in Cuvier in Cuvier & Valenciennes (Nov.) 1829:149 [4879]. Synonym of *Pelates* Cuvier 1829 (Vari 1978:249 [ref. 4514]); valid (Mees & Kailola 1977:31 [ref. 5183]). Terapontidae.

Helotosoma Kaup 1863:162 [ref. 2584]. Neut. *Helotosoma servus* Kaup 1863:162. Type by monotypy. Original not seen. Synonym of *Atypichthys* Günther 1862 (Fowler). Kyphosidae: Microcanthinae.

Hemanthias (subgenus of *Anthias*) Steindachner 1874:378 [ref. 4219]. Masc. *Anthias (Hemanthias) peruanus* Steindachner 1874:378. Type by monotypy. Misspelled *Hemianthias* by Jordan 1919:377 [ref. 4904]. Valid (Fitch 1982:6 [ref. 5398], Matsuura in Uyeno et al. 1983:314 [ref. 14275], Kendall 1984:500 [ref. 13663]). Serranidae: Anthiinae.

Hemerocoetes Valenciennes in Cuvier & Valenciennes 1837:311 [ref. 1006]. Masc. *Callionymus acanthorhynchus* Forster in Bloch & Schneider 1801:41 (= *C. monopterygius* Bloch & Schneider 1801:42). Type by monotypy. Valid (Nelson 1979 [ref. 6951]). Percophidae: Hemerocoetinae.

Hemerorhinus Weber & de Beaufort 1916:281 [ref. 4604]. Masc. *Sphagebranchus heyningi* Weber 1913:46. Type by monotypy. Valid (McCosker 1977:67 [ref. 6836], McCosker et al. 1989:297 [ref. 13288]). Ophichthidae: Ophichthinae.

Hemiancistrus Bleeker 1862:2 [ref. 393]. Masc. *Ancistrus medians* Kner 1854:256, 281. Type by original designation (also monotypic). Valid (Isbrücker 1980:49 [ref. 2303], Heitmans et al. 1983 [ref. 5278], Burgess 1989:434 [ref. 12860], Malabarba 1989:148 [ref. 14217]). Loricariidae.

Hemiarius Bleeker 1862:7, 29 [ref. 393]. Masc. *Cephalocassis stormii* Bleeker 1858:246. Type by original designation. Dates to part 6 (26 Nov. 1862); Pl. 100 dates to part 9 (before 8 Oct. 1863). Also appeared in Bleeker 1862:392 [ref. 391] as name only and in Bleeker 1863:90 [ref. 401]. Synonym of *Arius* Valenciennes 1840 (Roberts 1989:110 [ref. 6439]). Ariidae.

Hemibagrus Bleeker 1862:9, Pls. 69-72 [ref. 393]. Masc. *Bagrus nemurus* Valenciennes in Cuvier & Valenciennes 1839:423. Type by original designation. Dates to text p. 9 published in part 6 (26 Nov. 1862) and Pls. 69-72 published in part 6; text p. 54 published in part 7 (27 Jan. 1863). Appeared as name only in Bleeker 1862:393 [ref. 391]. Synonym of *Mystus* Scopoli 1777 (Roberts 1989:120 [ref. 6439]). Bagridae.

Hemibalistes (subgenus of *Sufflamen*) Fraser-Brunner 1935:662 [ref. 1489]. Masc. *Balistes bursa* Bloch & Schneider 1801:476. Not available from Fraser-Brunner 1935; two included species and no type designated after 1930 (Art. 13b). Can date to Burton 1936 in Zoological Record for 1935 (see remarks on Art. 13b in Appendix A). In the synonymy of *Sufflamen* Jordan 1916 (Matsuura 1980:48 [ref. 6943]). Balistidae.

Hemibarboides Wang 1935:59 [ref. 4582]. Masc. *Hemibarboides tientaiensis* Wang 1935:60. Type by original designation (also monotypic). Synonym of *Hemibrabus* Bleeker 1859, subgenus *Belligobio* Jordan & Hubbs 1925 (Banarescu & Nalbant 1973:183 [ref. 173]); synonym of *Belligobio* (Lu, Luo & Chen 1977:459 [ref. 13495]). Cyprinidae.

Hemibarbus Bleeker 1859:431 [ref. 370]. Masc. *Gobio barbus* Schlegel in Temminck & Schlegel 1846:198. Type by subsequent monotypy. Apparently appeared first in key, without included species. One species included by Bleeker 1860:281, 394 [ref. 380]. Valid (Banarescu & Nalbant 1973:181 [ref. 173], Lu, Luo & Chen 1977:443 [ref. 13495], Sawada in Masuda et al. 1984:56 [ref. 6441], Hosoya 1986:488 [ref. 6155], Chen & Li in Chu & Chen 1989:101 [ref. 13584]). Cyprinidae.

Hemibates Regan 1920:49 [ref. 3669]. Masc. *Paratilapia stenosoma* Boulenger 1901:2. Type by original designation (also monotypic). Valid (Bailey & Stewart 1977:6 [ref. 7230], Poll 1986:128 [ref. 6136]). Cichlidae.

Hemibrycon (subgenus of *Tetragonopterus*) Günther 1864:318, 330 [ref. 1974]. Masc. *Tetragonopterus polyodon* Günther 1864:330. Type by monotypy. Described in key (p. 318) as section or subgenus of *Tetragonopterus* with corresponding species on p. 330. Valid (Géry 1977:378 [ref. 1597]). Characidae.

Hemicaranx Bleeker 1862:135 [ref. 389]. Masc. *Hemicaranx marginatus* Bleeker 1862:135, 139. Type by original designation. Valid (Smith-Vaniz 1984:524 [ref. 13664], Daget & Smith-Vaniz 1986:315 [ref. 6207], Gushiken 1988:443 [ref. 6697]). Carangidae.

Hemicetopsis Bleeker 1862:403 [ref. 392]. Fem. *Cetopsis candiru* Agassiz in Spix & Agassiz 1829:13. Type by original designation (also monotypic). Also appeared [perhaps earlier] in Bleeker 1862:16 [ref. 393]. Valid (Burgess 1989:291 [ref. 12860]). Cetopsidae.

Hemichaetodon (subgenus of *Tetragonopterus*) Bleeker 1876:305 [ref. 448]. Masc. *Chaetodon capistratus* of Bloch (= *Chaetodon capistratus* Linnaeus 1758:275). Type by original designation (also monotypic). Also appeared in Bleeker 1876:313 [ref. 451]. Objective synonym of *Chaetodon* Linnaeus 1758 (Burgess 1978:653 [ref. 700]). Chaetodontidae.

Hemichromis Peters 1858:403 [ref. 3450]. Masc. *Hemichromis fasciatus* Peters 1858:403. Type by monotypy. Valid. Cichlidae.

Hemiconiatus (subgenus of *Tetraodon*) Günther 1870:272 [ref. 1995]. *Tetraodon guttifer* Bennett 1830:148. Type by monotypy. Unneeded replacement for *Ephippion* Bibron (ex Duméril) 1855, not preoccupied by near-spellings. Objective synonym of *Ephippion* Bibron 1855 (Shipp 1974:116 [ref. 7147]). Tetraodontidae.

Hemicoris Bleeker 1862:411 [ref. 382]. Fem. *Halichoeres variegatus* Rüppell 1835:14. Type by original designation (also monotypic). Also appeared in Bleeker 1862:99 [ref. 386]. Labridae.

Hemiculter Bleeker 1859:432 [ref. 370]. Masc. *Culter leucisculus* Basilewski 1860:401. Type by subsequent monotypy. Apparently appeared first in key, without included species. One species included by Bleeker 1860:282, 401 [ref. 380]. Valid (Yih & Wu 1964:86 [ref. 13499], Vasil'yeva & Kozlova 1988 [ref. 13523],

Chen in Chu & Chen 1989:80 [ref. 13584], Kottelat 1989:8 [ref. 13605]). Cyprinidae.

Hemiculterella Warpachowski 1887:23 [ref. 4516]. Fem. *Hemiculterella sauvagei* Warpachowski 1887:23. Type by monotypy. Valid (Yih & Wu 1964:77 [ref. 13499], Chen in Chu & Chen 1989:75 [ref. 13584]). Cyprinidae.

Hemicurimata (subgenus of *Curimata*) Myers 1929:620 [ref. 3102]. Fem. *Curimata esperanzae* Myers 1929:620. Type by original designation. Valid (see Vari 1982:11 [ref. 5485]); synonym of *Cyphocharax* Fowler 1906 (Vari 1989:6 [ref. 9189]). Curimatidae: Curimatinae.

Hemicyclodon Parr 1931:162 [ref. 3372]. Masc. *Dolichodon normani* Parr 1931. Type by being a replacement name. Unneeded replacement for *Dolichodon* Parr 1931, not preoccupied by *Dolicodon* Fanzango 1874, unjustifiably emended or misspelled *Dolichodon* by Cambridge in Zoological Record for 1875:262. Possibly preoccupied by Gray 1866 in Mammalia [not researched]. Synonym of *Kali* Lloyd 1909 (Krefft 1973:453 [ref. 7166], Johnson & Cohen 1974:34 [ref. 7133]). Chiasmodontidae.

Hemidoras Bleeker 1858:35, 53, 54 [ref. 365]. Masc. *Doras (Oxydoras) stenopeltis* Kner 1855:142. Type by monotypy. Valid (Burgess 1989:222 [ref. 12860]). Doradidae.

Hemieleotris Meek & Hildebrand 1916:364 [ref. 2962]. Fem. *Eleotris latifasciatus* Meek & Hildebrand 1912:68. Type by original designation (also monotypic). Valid (Birdsong et al. 1988:182 [ref. 7303]). Eleotridae.

Hemiemblemaria Longley & Hildebrand 1940:273 [ref. 2822]. Fem. *Hemiemblemaria simulus* Longley & Hildebrand 1940:273. Type by monotypy. Valid (Stephens 1963:96 [ref. 4270], Greenfield & Johnson 1981:65 [ref. 5580], Acero P. 1984 [ref. 5534]). Chaenopsidae.

Hemiexocoetus Fowler 1901:293 [ref. 1358]. Masc. *Hemiexocoetus caudimaculatus* Fowler 1901:294. Type by monotypy. Synonym of *Fodiator* Jordan & Meek 1885 (Fowler MS). Exocoetidae.

Hemigaleops Schultz & Welander in Schultz et al. 1953:8 [ref. 3975]. Masc. *Hemigaleops forsteri* Schultz & Welander in Schultz et al. 1953:9. Type by original designation (also monotypic). Authorship of species is Schultz and Welander; genus regarded as authored by both ("Our new genus..."). Synonym of *Negaprion* Whitley 1940 (Compagno 1984:516 [ref. 6846], Compagno 1988:341 [ref. 13488]). Carcharhinidae.

Hemigaleus Bleeker 1852:45 [ref. 333]. Masc. *Hemigaleus microstoma* Bleeker 1852:46. Type by subsequent designation. Type designated by Gill 1862:402 [ref. 1783]. *Negogaleus* Whitley 1931 is an unneeded replacement. Valid (Compagno 1984:438 [ref. 6846], Compagno 1988:262 [ref. 13488], Paxton et al. 1989:81 [ref. 12442]). Hemigaleidae.

Hemigarra Karaman 1971:241 [ref. 2560]. Fem. *Tylognathus elegans* Günther 1868:64. Type by original designation (also monotypic). Probably a synonym of *Hemigrammocapoeta* Pelegrin 1927 (Krupp & Schneider 1989:372 [ref. 13651]). Cyprinidae.

Hemiglyphidodon (subgenus of *Glyphidodon*) Bleeker 1877:91, 93 [ref. 454]. Masc. *Glyphisodon plagiometopon* Bleeker 1852:67. Type by original designation (also monotypic). Valid (Allen 1975:163 [ref. 97], Yoshino in Masuda et al. 1984:199 [ref. 6441]). Pomacentridae.

Hemigobius Bleeker 1874:319 [ref. 437]. Masc. *Gobius melanurus* Bleeker 1849:31 (= *Hemigobius bleekeri* Koumans 1953:191). Type by original designation (also monotypic). Type species apparently preoccupied, renamed *Hemigobius bleekeri* by Koumans 1953:191 [ref. 2678]. Valid (Miller 1987:695 [ref. 6336]). Gobiidae.

Hemigrammalestes Pellegrin 1926:158 [ref. 3404]. Masc. *Micralestes urotaenia* Pellegrin 1909:228. Type by subsequent designation. Type apparently designated first by Burton in Zoological record for 1926, not *M. interruptus* as designated by Myers 1929. Alestiidae.

Hemigrammocapoeta (subgenus of *Barbus*) Estève 1952:177 [ref. 5564]. Fem. *Barbus mirei* Estève 1952:177. Type by monotypy. Preoccupied by Pellegrin 1927 in same family, replaced by *Estevea* Whitley 1953. Valid (Karaman 1971:236 [ref. 2560]); synonym of *Barbus* Cuvier & Cloquet 1816 (Lévêque & Daget 1984:219 [ref. 6186]). Cyprinidae.

Hemigrammocapoeta Pellegrin 1927:34 [ref. 5042]. Fem. *Hemigrammocapoeta culiciphaga* Pellegrin 1927:34. Type by monotypy. Valid (Krupp & Schneider 1989:371 [ref. 13651]). Cyprinidae.

Hemigrammocharax (subgenus of *Nannocharax*) Pellegrin 1923:115 [ref. 3403]. Masc. *Nannocharax ocellicauda* Boulenger 1907:485. Type by monotypy. Valid (Géry 1977:74 [ref. 1597], Vari 1979:340 [ref. 5490], Daget & Gosse 1984:194 [ref. 6185]). Citharinidae: Distichodontinae.

Hemigrammocypris Fowler 1910:483 [ref. 1380]. Fem. *Hemigrammocypris rasborella* Fowler 1910:484. Type by original designation (also monotypic). Valid (Sawada in Masuda et al. 1984:57 [ref. 6441]). Cyprinidae.

Hemigrammonannocharax Holly 1930:198, 233 [ref. 2190]. Masc. *Nannocharax ocellicauda* Boulenger 1907:495. Type by original designation (also monotypic). Objective synonym of *Hemigrammocharax* Pellegrin 1923 (Daget & Gosse 1984:194 [ref. 6185]). Citharinidae: Distichodontinae.

Hemigrammopetersius Pellegrin 1926:158 [ref. 3404]. Masc. *Petersius pulcher* Boulenger 1909:237. Type by subsequent designation. Type designated by Burton in Zoological Record for 1926. Valid (Géry 1977:38 [ref. 1597], Paugy 1984:168 [ref. 6183]). Alestiidae.

Hemigrammopuntius (subgenus of *Barbus*) Pellegrin 1923:128 [ref. 3403]. Masc. *Barbus salessei* Pellegrin 1908:207. Type by monotypy. Type designated by Myers 1927:4 [ref. 3097]. Synonym of *Barbus* Cuvier & Cloquet 1816 (Lévêque & Daget 1984:218 [ref. 6186]). Cyprinidae.

Hemigrammus (subgenus of *Poecilurichthys*) Gill 1858:416, 420 [ref. 1750]. Masc. *Poecilurichthys (Hemigrammus) unilineatus* Gill 1858:420. Type by monotypy in subgenus. Valid (Géry 1977:490 [ref. 1597]). Characidae.

Hemigymnus Günther 1861:386 [ref. 1967]. Masc. *Mullus fasciatus* Thunberg 1776:351. Type by subsequent designation. Earliest type designation found that of Jordan 1919:308 [ref. 4904]. Type not *Mullus fasciatus* White 1790 (an apogonid). Valid (Araga in Masuda et al. 1984:205 [ref. 6441], Randall 1986:696 [ref. 5706]). Labridae.

Hemihaplochromis Wickler 1963:90 [ref. 4738]. Masc. *Haplochromis multicolor* Hilgendorf 1903. Type by original designation (also monotypic). Synonym of *Pseudocrenilabrus* Fowler 1934 (Greenwood 1984:213 [ref. 5311], Greenwood 1989:2 [ref. 14120]). Cichlidae.

Hemilepidotus Cuvier 1829:165 [ref. 995]. Masc. *Cottus hemilepidotus* Tilesius 1810:262. Type by absolute tautonymy (two species mentioned, one possibly the same as the other). Valid (Bolin 1944:13 [ref. 6379], Peden 1978 [ref. 5530], Washington et al. 1984:442 [ref. 13660], Yabe in Masuda et al. 1984:323 [ref. 6441], Yabe 1985:111 [ref. 11522]). Cottidae.

Hemiloricaria Bleeker 1862:3 [ref. 393]. Fem. *Hemiloricaria caracasensis* Bleeker 1862:3. Type by original designation (also monotypic). Species as name only in 1862:3, apparently dates to 1863:81. Doubtfully a synonym of *Rineloricaria* Bleeker 1862 (Isbrücker 1980:103 [ref. 2303]). Loricariidae.

Hemilutjanus Bleeker 1876:277 [ref. 447]. Masc. *Plectropoma macrophthalmus* Tschudi 1844:6. Type by original designation (also monotypic). Placement uncertain, not a lutjanid. Treated by Johnson 1984:465 [ref. 9681] as *incertae sedis* in suborder Percoidei. Percoidei.

Hemimacrurus Fraser-Brunner 1935:322 [ref. 1491]. Masc. *Macrurus acrolepis* Bean 1883:362. Type by original designation (also monotypic). Synonym of *Coryphaenoides* Gunner 1765 (Marshall 1973:295 [ref. 7194], Marshall & Iwamoto 1973:565 [ref. 6966]), but see Iwamoto & Sazonov 1988:39 [ref. 6228]. Macrouridae: Macrourinae.

Hemimarsupium Kaup 1853:234 [ref. 2569]. Neut. Treated as a nomen nudum by Dawson 1984:124 [ref. 5879], in synonymy of *Microphis (Coelonotus)*. Type listed by Jordan 1919:272 [ref. 2410] as *Typhlus gondotii* [sic *goudoti*] but that name apparently never published in an available way and renamed *Syngnathus leiaspis* by Bleeker. *Hemithylacus* Kaup 1856 is the same as *Hemimarsupium*. Syngnathidae: Syngnathinae.

Hemimyzon Regan 1911:32 [ref. 3642]. Masc. *Homaloptera formosanum* Boulenger 1894:463. Type by original designation (also monotypic). Valid (Silas 1953:212 [ref. 4024], Chen 1978:338 [ref. 6900], Sawada 1982:204 [ref. 14111], Kottelat & Chu 1988:192 [ref. 13491], Kottelat 1989:12 [ref. 13605]). Balitoridae: Balitorinae.

Heminigellus Nalbant 1984:239 [ref. 5855]. Masc. *Chaetodon tinkeri* Schultz 1951:485. Type by original designation. Synonym of *Roaops* Maugé & Bauchot 1984 (Nalbant 1986:163 [ref. 6135]). Chaetodontidae.

Heminodus Smith 1917:146 [ref. 4045]. Masc. *Heminodus philippinus* Smith 1917:146. Type by original designation (also monotypic). Valid (Ochiai & Yatou in Masuda et al. 1984:335 [ref. 6441]). Triglidae: Peristediinae.

Heminoemacheilus Zhu & Cao 1987:324, 330 [ref. 14139]. Masc. *Heminoemacheilus zhengbaoshani* Zhu & Cao 1987. Appeared first as name only in Banarescu 1977:44 [ref. 14138] in different context. English summary on p. 330. Valid (Kottelat 1990:19 [ref. 14137]). Balitoridae: Nemacheilinae.

Hemiodon Kner 1853:119 [ref. 2627]. Masc. *Hemiodon depressus* Kner 1854:91. Type by subsequent designation. Appeared first without species. Species added and type designated by Bleeker 1862:4 [ref. 393] and 1863:82 [ref. 401]. Preoccupied by Swainson 1840 in Mollusca; replaced by *Reganella* Eigenmann 1905. Objective synonym of *Reganella* Eigenmann 1905 (Isbrücker 1980:123 [ref. 2303]). Loricariidae.

Hemiodontichthys Bleeker 1862:4 [ref. 393]. Masc. *Hemiodon acipenserinus* Kner 1854:92. Type by original designation (also monotypic). *Homiodontichthys* is a misspelling. Valid (Isbrücker & Nijssen 1974:201 [ref. 7126], Isbrücker 1980:130 [ref. 2303], Burgess 1989:445 [ref. 12860]). Loricariidae.

Hemiodopsis (subgenus of *Hemiodus*) Fowler 1906:318 [ref. 1373]. Fem. *Hemiodus microlepis* Kner 1859:155. Type by original designation (also monotypic). Synonym of *Hemiodus* Müller 1843 (Roberts 1974:432 [ref. 6872]); valid (Géry 1977:194 [ref. 1597], Vari 1983:5 [ref. 5419], Géry et al. 1987:403 [ref. 6001]). Hemiodontidae: Hemiodontinae.

Hemiodus Müller 1842:206 [ref. 3062]. Masc. *Hemiodus crenidens* Müller 1842:206. Type by monotypy. Also in Müller 1843:316 [ref. 3063]. Valid (Roberts 1974:432 [ref. 6872], Géry 1977:198 [ref. 1597], Vari 1983:5 [ref. 5419], Géry et al. 1987:403 [ref. 6001]). Hemiodontidae: Hemiodontinae.

Hemioplites Cope 1868:217 [ref. 909]. Masc. *Hemioplites simulans* Cope 1868:217. Type by monotypy. Synonym of *Enneacanthus* Gill 1864. Centrarchidae.

Hemipimelodus Bleeker 1858:205, 236 [ref. 365]. Masc. *Pimelodus borneensis* Bleeker 1851:430. Type by subsequent designation. Type designated by Bleeker 1862:8 [ref. 393] and 1863:92 [ref. 401]. Valid (Jayaram & Dhanze 1979:48 [ref. 6800]), Jayaram 1981:283 [ref. 6497], Kottelat 1985:271 [ref. 11441], Burgess 1989:167 [ref. 12860], Kottelat 1989:15 [ref. 13605], Roberts 1989:110 [ref. 6439]). Ariidae.

Hemiplatystoma Bleeker 1862:10 [ref. 393]. Neut. *Platystoma tigrinum* Valenciennes in Cuvier & Valenciennes 1840:10. Type by original designation (also monotypic). Synonym of *Pseudoplatystoma* Bleeker 1862 (Mees 1974:127 [ref. 2969]). Pimelodidae.

Hemiplus Rafinesque 1820:6 [ref. 3591]. Masc. *Hemiplus lacustris* Rafinesque 1820:6. Type by monotypy. Synonym of *Notemigonus* Rafinesque 1819. Cyprinidae.

Hemipristis Agassiz 1843:237, 302 [Tome 3] [ref. 13390]. Fem. *Hemipristis serra* Agassiz 1843. Type by subsequent designation. Based on a fossil type species but a Recent species has been referred to this genus (see Paxton et al. 1989:81 [ref. 12442]). Valid (Compagno 1988:269 [ref. 13488] in Hemipristinae of family Hemigaleidae). Hemigaleidae.

Hemipsilichthys Eigenmann & Eigenmann 1889:46 [ref. 1253]. Masc. *Xenomystus gobio* Lütken 1874:217. Type by being a replacement name. Replacement for *Xenomystus* Lütken 1874, preoccupied by Günther 1868 in fishes. Valid (Isbrücker 1980:11 [ref. 2303], Burgess 1989:429 [ref. 12860], Malabarba 1989:151 [ref. 14217]). Loricariidae.

Hemipterois Regan 1911:126 [ref. 3639]. *Bathypterois guentheri* Alcock 1889:450. Type by original designation (also monotypic). Type designated on p. 127. Synonym of subgenus *Benthosaurus* Goode & Bean 1886, genus *Bathypterois* Günther 1878 (Sulak 1977:76 [ref. 4299]). Chlorophthalmidae: Ipnopinae.

Hemipteronotus Lacepède 1801:214 [ref. 2710]. Masc. *Hemipteronotus quinquemaculatus* Lacepède 1801:214, 215. Type by subsequent designation. Type designated by Bleeker 1862:414 [ref. 382]. Lacepède's account based on several sources; *C. pentadactyla* Linnaeus cited in synonymy; Bauchot & Quignard (1973:442 [ref. 7204]) treat as unavailable but it apparently is available. In the synonymy of *Xyrichtys* Cuvier 1814. Labridae.

Hemiramphus Cuvier 1816:186 [ref. 993]. Masc. *Esox brasiliensis* Linnaeus 1758:186. Type by subsequent designation. Type designated by Gill 1863:273 [ref. 1693]. Originally *Hemi-Ramphus* (correction mandatory); sometimes spelled *Hemirhamphus*. Valid (Parin 1973:268 [ref. 7191], Parin et al. 1980:111 [ref. 6895], Yoshino in Masuda et al. 1984:79 [ref. 6441], Collette et al. 1984:336 [ref. 11422], Collette & Parin in Whitehead et al. 1986:621 [ref. 13676], Collette 1986:389 [ref. 5647], Paxton et al.

1989:337 [ref. 12442]). Hemiramphidae.

Hemirhamphodon Bleeker 1866:140 [ref. 419]. Masc. *Hemirhamphus phaiosoma* Bleeker 1852:88, 99. Type by original designation. Correct spelling for genus of type species is *Hemiramphus*. Valid (Collette et al. 1984:337 [ref. 11422], Kottelat 1989:16 [ref. 13605], Roberts 1989:154 [ref. 6439]). Hemiramphidae.

Hemirhombus Bleeker 1862:425 [ref. 388]. Masc. *Hemirhombus guineensis* Günther (ex Bleeker) 1862:423. Type by subsequent designation. Species as name only at end of generic account and apparently unavailable at that time; species was described by Günther from Bleeker in same year. Günther referred three species (one with question) to the genus; earliest technical type designation not researched. Synonym of *Syacium* Ranzani 1842 (Norman 1934:129 [ref. 6893]). Paralichthyidae.

Hemisalanx Regan 1908:444 [ref. 3632]. Masc. *Hemisalanx prognathus* Regan 1908:445. Type by monotypy. Synonym of *Salanx* Oken 1817, but as a valid subgenus (Roberts 1984:206 [ref. 5318]). Salangidae.

Hemiscaphirhynchus (subgenus of *Pseudoscaphirhynchus*) Berg 1911:309, 310 [ref. 272]. Masc. *Scaphirhynchus kaufmanni* Bogdanov 1874:48. Type by original designation. Synonym of *Pseudoscaphirhynchus* Nikolskii 1900. Acipenseridae: Scaphirhynchinae.

Hemisciaena Bleeker 1863:140 [ref. 396]. Fem. *Sciaena lucida* Richardson 1844:87. Type by monotypy. Objective synonym of *Collichthys* Günther 1860 (Trewavas 1977:400, and see also p. 387 [ref. 4459]). Sciaenidae.

Hemiscyllium Müller & Henle 1838:34 [ref. 3066]. Neut. *Squalus ocellatus* Bonnaterre 1788:8. Type by monotypy. Predates *Hemiscyllium* Müller & Henle in Smith (13 Feb. 1838), Müller & Henle apparently published 2 Jan. 1838. Also in Müller & Henle 1838:83 [ref. 3068]. Valid (Compagno 1984:195 [ref. 6474], Cappetta 1987:73 [ref. 6348], Paxton et al. 1989:89 [ref. 12442]). Hemiscylliidae.

Hemisilurus Bleeker 1858:255, 257, 295 [ref. 365]. Masc. *Wallago heterorhynchus* Bleeker 1853:514. Type by subsequent designation. Also on p. 33 et seq. Type designated by Bleeker 1862:395 [ref. 391], 1862:18 [ref. 393] and 1863:116 [ref. 401]. Type species spelled *heterorrhynchus* by Bleeker 1862:18, 94 [ref. 393]. Valid (Haig 1952:63 [ref. 12607], Kottelat 1985:268 [ref. 11441], Burgess 1989:85 [ref. 12860], Bornbusch & Lundburg 1989 [ref. 12543], Kottelat 1989:14 [ref. 13605], Roberts 1989:145 [ref. 6439]). Siluridae.

Hemisorubim Bleeker 1862:10 [ref. 393]. *Platystoma platyrhynchos* Valenciennes in Cuvier & Valenciennes 1840:27. Type by original designation (also monotypic). Valid (Mees 1974:117 [ref. 2969], Stewart 1986:668 [ref. 5211], Burgess 1989:282 [ref. 12860]). Pimelodidae.

Hemistichodus Pellegrin 1900:352 [ref. 6253]. Masc. *Hemistichodus vaillanti* Pellegrin 1900:352. Type by monotypy. Valid (Géry 1977:82 [ref. 1597], Vari 1979:340 [ref. 5490], Daget & Gosse 1984:196 [ref. 6185]). Citharinidae: Distichodontinae.

Hemistoma (subgenus of *Scarus*) Swainson 1839:172, 226 [ref. 4303]. Neut. *Hemistoma reticulata* Swainson 1839:226 (= *Scarus pepo* Bennett 1834:28). Type by monotypy. *H. reticulata* Swainson is an unneeded substitute for *S. pepo* Bennett. Synonym of *Scarus* Forsskål 1775. Scaridae: Scarinae.

Hemisynodontis Bleeker 1862:6 [ref. 393]. Fem. *Pimelodus membranaceus* Geoffroy St. Hilaire 1809:Pl. 13. Type by original designation (also monotypic). Valid (Gosse 1986:114 [ref. 6194], Burgess 1989:195 [ref. 12860]). Mochokidae.

Hemitaeniochromis Eccles & Trewavas 1989:71 [ref. 13547]. Masc. *Haplochromis urotaenia* Regan 1922:695. Type by original designation (also monotypic). Cichlidae.

Hemitaurichthys Bleeker 1876:304 [ref. 448]. Masc. *Chaetodon polylepis* Bleeker 1857:(4) 54. Type by original designation (also monotypic [in ref. 448]). Also in Bleeker 1876:Pl. 378 [ref. 6835]. Valid (Burgess 1978:194 [ref. 700], Ida in Masuda et al. 1984:186 [ref. 6441], Maugé & Bauchot 1984:462 [ref. 6614], Heemstra 1986:631 [ref. 5660], Nalbant 1986:169 [ref. 6135]). Chaetodontidae.

Hemitautoga Bleeker 1862:413 [ref. 382]. Fem. *Labrus centiquadrus* Lacepède 1801:437, 493. Type by original designation (also monotypic). Also appeared in Bleeker 1862:101 [ref. 386]. Synonym of *Halichoeres* Rüppell 1835 (Fowler). Labridae.

Hemithylacus Kaup 1856:61 [ref. 2575]. *Syngnathus leiaspis* Bleeker 1853:20. Type by monotypy. A substitute for *Hemimarsupium* according to Jordan 1919:272 [ref. 2410]; Dawson 1984:124 [ref. 5879] treats *Hemimarsupium* as a nomen nudum and in synonymy of *Microphis (Coelonotus)*. See *Hemimarsupium* Kaup 1853. Synonym of *Microphis* Kaup 1853 (Dawson 1985:126 [ref. 6541]). Syngnathidae: Syngnathinae.

Hemitilapia Boulenger 1902:70 [ref. 567]. Fem. *Hemitilapia oxyrhynchus* Boulenger 1902:71. Type by monotypy. Valid (Eccles & Trewavas 1989:195 [ref. 13547]). Cichlidae.

Hemitremia Cope 1870:462 [ref. 913]. Fem. *Hemitremia vittata* Cope 1870:462. Type by monotypy. Species *vittata* preoccupied when placed in *Leuciscus*, renamed *flammeus* by Jordan. Cyprinidae.

Hemitriakis Herre 1923:70 [ref. 2116]. Fem. *Hemitriakis leucoperiptera* Herre 1923:71. Type by monotypy. Valid (Compagno 1984:390 [ref. 6846], Nakaya in Masuda et al. 1984:5 [ref. 6441], Herman et al. 1988:102 [ref. 13267], Compagno 1988:230 [ref. 13488]). Triakidae: Galeorhininae.

Hemitripterus Cuvier 1829:164 [ref. 995]. Masc. *Cottus tripterygius* Bloch & Schneider 1801:63. Type by monotypy (synonyms included in footnote). Also appeared in Cuvier & Valenciennes (Nov.) 1829:268 [ref. 998]. Valid (Washington et al. 1984:442 [ref. 13660], Yabe in Masuda et al. 1984:323 [ref. 6441], Yabe 1985:123 [ref. 11522] in a family Hemitripteridae). Cottidae.

Hemitrygon (subgenus of *Trygon*) Müller & Henle 1838:90 [ref. 3066]. Fem. *Trygon bennettii* Müller & Henle 1841:160. Type by subsequent monotypy. Appeared first without species, one species added by Müller & Henle 1841:160 [ref. 3069]. Synonym of *Dasyatis* Rafinesque 1810. Dasyatidae.

Hemiulis (subgenus of *Labrus*) Swainson 1839:173, 228 [ref. 4303]. Fem. *Labrus guttatus* Bloch 1791:149. Type by subsequent designation. Type designated by Bonaparte 1841:puntata 156, fasc. 30 [ref. 512]; Bonaparte spelled the name *Hemijulis*, and that spelling is regarded as an incorrect subsequent spelling. Labridae.

Hemixiphophorus Bleeker 1859:440 [ref. 370]. Masc. *Xiphophorus gracilis* Heckel 1848:300. Type by subsequent monotypy. Appeared first in key, without included species. One species added by Bleeker 1860:485. See discussion in Rosen & Bailey 1963:131 [ref. 7067]. Would be a senior objective synonym of *Poeciliopsis* Regan 1913 but not recognized as valid (see Rosen & Bailey 1963:131 [ref. 7067]). Poeciliidae.

Henicichthys Tanaka 1915:568 [ref. 4324]. Masc. *Henicichthys* *foraminosus* Tanaka 1915:568. Type by monotypy. Translation of original description appeared in Jordan 1923:203 [ref. 2421]. Synonym of *Gymnapogon* Regan 1905 (Fraser 1972:31 [ref. 5195]). Apogonidae.

Henicorhynchus Smith 1945:256 [ref. 4056]. Masc. *Henicorhynchus lobatus* Smith 1945:257. Type by original designation (also monotypic). Valid (Kottelat 1985:263 [ref. 11441], Chu & Cui in Chu & Chen 1989:250 [ref. 13584], Kottelat 1989:8 [ref. 13605]). Cyprinidae.

Heniochus Cuvier 1816:335 [ref. 993]. Masc. *Chaetodon macrolepidotus* Linnaeus 1758:274. Type confirmed by ICZN (Opinion 40). Valid (Burgess 1978:218 [ref. 700], Ida in Masuda et al. 1984:186 [ref. 6441], Maugé & Bauchot 1984:463 [ref. 6614], Heemstra 1986:631 [ref. 5660], Nalbant 1986:171 [ref. 6135]). Chaetodontidae.

Henochilus Garman 1890:49 [ref. 1536]. Masc. *Henochilus wheatlandii* Garman 1890:49. Type by monotypy. Valid (Géry 1977:578 [ref. 1597]). Characidae.

Henonemus Eigenmann & Ward in Eigenmann, McAtee & Ward 1907:118 [ref. 1261]. Masc. *Stegophilus intermedius* Eigenmann & Eigenmann 1889:54. Type by original designation (also monotypic). Valid (Pinna 1989 [ref. 12630]). Trichomycteridae.

Hepatoscartes Fowler 1944:230 [ref. 1448]. Masc. *Hepatoscartes umbrifasciatus* Fowler 1944:230. Type by original designation (also monotypic). Synonym of *Ophioblennius* Gill 1860 (Smith-Vaniz & Springer 1971:35 [ref. 4145]). Blenniidae.

Hepatus Gronow 1763:113 [ref. 1910]. Masc. Not available, published in a rejected work on Official Index (Opinion 261). Perhaps made available by Jordan & Seale 1906. In the synonymy of *Acanthurus* Forsskål 1775 (Randall 1955:363 [ref. 13648]). Acanthuridae.

Hepatus Röse 1793:113 [ref. 3833]. Masc. Original not examined. Not available, no included species; based on *Hepatos* Aristotle which probably is *Labrus hepatus* Linnaeus 1758. In the synonymy of *Paracentropristis* Klunzinger 1884. Serranidae: Serraninae.

Hephaestus De Vis 1884:399 [ref. 1090]. Masc. *Hephaestus tulliensis* De Vis 1884:399. Type by monotypy. Synonym of *Terapon* Cuvier 1816 (Mees & Kailola 1977:32 [ref. 5183]); valid (Vari 1978:279 [ref. 4514], Allen 1984 [ref. 6243], Paxton et al. 1989:533 [ref. 12442]). Terapontidae.

Hephthocara Alcock 1892:349 [ref. 88]. Neut. *Hephthocara simum* Alcock 1892:349. Type by monotypy. Valid (Cohen & Nielsen 1978:48 [ref. 881]). Bythitidae: Bythitinae.

Hepsetia (subgenus of *Atherina*) Bonaparte 1836:puntata 91 [ref. 4892]. Fem. *Atherina boyeri* Risso 1810:338. Type by monotypy. Apparently appeared first in puntata 91 under *Atherina hepsetus*. Synonym of *Atherina* Linnaeus 1758 (Kiener & Spillmann 1973:576 [ref. 7217], Maugé 1986:277 [ref. 6218]); as a valid subgenus (Quignard & Pras in Whitehead et al. 1986:1208 [ref. 13677]). Atherinidae: Atherininae.

Hepsetus (subgenus of *Xiphosoma*) Swainson 1838:259 [ref. 4302]. *Salmo odoe* Bloch 1794:122. Appeared without species; first addition of species not researched; type by subsequent monotypy or by subsequent designation of Hubbs 1939:168 [ref. 5012]. Valid (Géry 1977:17 [ref. 1597], Vari 1983:5 [ref. 5419], Roberts 1984:138 [ref. 6182]). Hepsetidae.

Heptadecanthus Alleyne & Macleay 1877:343 [ref. 101]. Masc. *Heptadecanthus longicaudus* Alleyne & Macleay 1877:343. Type by monotypy. Misspelled *Heptadecacanthus* by Jordan 1919:387 [ref. 4904]. Synonym of *Acanthochromis* Gill 1863. Pomacentridae.

Heptanchus Müller & Henle 1841:81 [ref. 3069]. Masc. Unjustified emendation of *Heptranchias* Rafinesque 1810. Hexanchidae.

Heptapterus Bleeker 1858:197, 204, 208 [ref. 365]. Masc. *Pimelodus mustelinus* Valenciennes in Cuvier & Valenciennes 1840:165. Type by monotypy. Valid (Mees 1974:177 [ref. 2969], Stewart 1986:668 [ref. 5211], Mees 1986:320 [ref. 5693], Mees 1987 [ref. 6619], Buckup 1988 [ref. 6635], Burgess 1989:276 [ref. 12860], Malabarba 1989:139 [ref. 14217]). Pimelodidae.

Heptatrema Duméril in Voigt 1832:529 [ref. 4948]. Neut. *Eptatretus dombey* Latreille 1804. Type by monotypy. Original not seen; taken from Fowler 1964:45 [ref. 7160]. Synonym of *Eptatretus* Cloquet 1819. Myxinidae: Eptatretinae.

Heptatremus (subgenus of *Petromyzon*) Swainson 1839:197, 338 [ref. 4303]. Masc. Not available; unjustified emendation or misspelling of *Heptatrema* Duméril 1832. In the synonymy of *Eptatretus* Cloquet 1819. Myxinidae: Eptatretinae.

Heptatretus Regan 1912:534 [ref. 12438]. Masc. Unjustified emendation of *Eptatretus* Cloquet 1819. Myxinidae: Eptatretinae.

Heptranchias Rafinesque 1810:13 [ref. 3594]. Masc. *Squalus cinereus* Gmelin 1789:1497. Type by monotypy. *Heptanchus* Müller & Henle is an unjustified emendation. Spelled *Heptranchus* and *Heptancus* by authors. Valid (Boeseman 1973:8 [ref. 7161], Boeseman in Whitehead et al. 1984:72 [ref. 13675], Compagno 1984:17 [ref. 6474], Nakaya & Shirai in Masuda et al. 1984:3 [ref. 6441], Bass et al. 1986:45 [ref. 5638], Cappetta 1987:49 [ref. 6348], Paxton et al. 1989:26 [ref. 12442]. Hexanchidae.

Heraldia Paxton 1975:441 [ref. 3395]. Fem. *Heraldia nocturna* Paxton 1975:441. Type by original designation (also monotypic). Valid (Dawson 1985:95 [ref. 6541], Paxton et al. 1989:419 [ref. 12442]). Syngnathidae: Syngnathinae.

Herichthys Baird & Girard 1854:25 [ref. 168]. Masc. *Herichthys cyanoguttatus* Baird & Girard 1854:25. Type by monotypy. Synonyn of *Cichlasoma* Swainson 1839 (authors). Cichlidae.

Heringia Fowler 1911:207 [ref. 1382]. Fem. *Clupea amazonica* Steindachner 1879:183. Type by original designation (also monotypic). Preoccupied by Rondani 1856 in Diptera; not replaced. Synonym of *Rhinosardinia* Eigenmann 1912 (Whitehead 1985:125 [ref. 5141]). Clupeidae.

Herklotsella (subgenus of *Harengula*) Fowler 1934:246 [ref. 1416]. Fem. *Harengula dispilonotus* Bleeker 1852:456 (445). Type by original designation (also monotypic). Preoccupied by Herre 1933 in fishes, replaced by *Herklotsichthys* Whitley 1951. Objective synonym of *Herklotsichthys* Whitley 1951 (Whitehead 1985:73 [ref. 5141], Paxton et al. 1989:153 [ref. 12442]). Clupeidae.

Herklotsella Herre 1933:179 [ref. 2107]. Fem. *Herklotsella anomala* Herre 1933:179. Type by original designation (also monotypic). Published as Dec. 1933, but perhaps appeared later; regarded as predating *Herklotsella* Fowler (Jan.) 1934. Synonym of *Silurus* Linnaeus 1758 (Haig 1952:97 [ref. 12607], Kobayakawa 1989:157 [ref. 13476] but spelled *Herklostella*). Siluridae.

Herklotsichthys Whitley 1951:67 [ref. 4711]. Masc. *Harengula dispilonotus* Bleeker 1852:456. Type by being a replacement name. Replacement for *Herklotsella* Fowler 1934 (Jan.), preoccupied by Herre 1933 in fishes. Valid (Uyeno & Sato in Masuda et al. 1984:10 [ref. 6441], Grande 1985:250 [ref. 6466], Whitehead 1985:73 [ref. 5141], Whitehead & Wongratana 1986:201 [ref. 6284], Kottelat

1989:4 [ref. 13605], Paxton et al. 1989:153 [ref. 12442]). Clupeidae.

Herklotsina Fowler 1931:311 [ref. 1408]. Fem. *Herklotsina viridianguilla* Fowler 1931:311. Type by original designation (also monotypic). Synonym of *Bleekeria* Günther 1862. Ammodytidae.

Hermosilla Jenkins & Evermann 1889:144 [ref. 2342]. Fem. *Hermosilla azurea* Jenkins & Evermann 1889:144. Type by monotypy. Valid. Kyphosidae: Kyphosinae.

Herops De Vis 1884:392 [ref. 1090]. Masc. *Herops munda* De Vis 1884:392. Type by monotypy. Synonym of *Kuhlia* Gill 1861 (Maugé 1986:306 [ref. 6218]). Kuhliidae.

Heros Heckel 1840:362 [ref. 2064]. Masc. *Heros severus* Heckel 1840:362. Type by subsequent designation. Type designated by Jordan & Gilbert 1883:608 [ref. 2476]. Valid (Kullander 1986:219 [ref. 12439]). Cichlidae.

Herotilapia Pellegrin 1904:(165) 247 [ref. 3419]. Fem. *Heros multispinosus* Günther 1869:453. Type by monotypy. Misspelled *Heterotilapia* in Zoological Record for 1904. Cichlidae.

Herpetoichthys Kaup 1856:44 [ref. 2572]. Masc. *Herpetoichthys ornatissimus* Kaup 1856:44. Type by subsequent designation. Type designated by Jordan 1919:271 [ref. 2410]. Also appeared in Kaup 1856:7 [ref. 2573] and as name only in Kaup in Duméril 1856:199 [ref. 1154]. Synonym of *Ophichthus* Ahl 1789 (Blache et al. 1973:247 [ref. 7185], McCosker 1977:80 [ref. 6836]); valid (McCosker et al. 1989:364 [ref. 13288]). Ophichthidae: Ophichthinae.

Herrea Smith 1931:40 [ref. 4047]. Fem. *Herrea formosa* Smith 1931:40. Type by monotypy. Preoccupied by Gray 1842 in Mammalia and by Whitley 1930 in fishes, replaced by *Herreolus* Smith 1931. Synonym of *Parioglossus* Regan 1912 (Rennis & Hoese 1985:172 [ref. 5859]). Microdesmidae: Ptereleotrinae.

Herrea Whitley 1930:123 [ref. 4669]. Fem. *Galera producta* Herre 1927:104. Type by being a replacement name. Replacement for *Galera* Herre 1927, preoccupied by Gray 1842 in mammals. Gobiidae.

Herreichthys Koumans 1931:163 [ref. 5623]. Masc. *Herrea formosa* Smith 1931:40. Type by being a replacement name. Unneeded replacement for *Herrea* Smith 1931, earlier replaced by *Herreolus* Smith 1931. Synonym of *Parioglossus* Regan 1912 (Rennis & Hoese 1985:172 [ref. 5859]). Microdesmidae: Ptereleotrinae.

Herreogobius Koumans 1940:139 [ref. 2676]. Masc. *Ctenogobius malekulae* Herre 1931:14. Type by original designation (also monotypic). Synonym of *Gobiopsis* Steindachner 1860 (Lachner & McKinney 1978:10 [ref. 6603]). Gobiidae.

Herreolus Smith 1931:190 [ref. 4048]. Masc. *Herrea formosa* Smith 1931:40. Type by being a replacement name. Replacement for *Herrea* Smith 1931, preoccupied by Whitley 1930 in fishes. Synonym of *Parioglossus* Regan 1912 (Rennis & Hoese 1985:172 [ref. 5859]). Microdesmidae: Ptereleotrinae.

Herwigia Nielsen 1972:30 [ref. 3197]. Fem. *Bathylaco kreffti* Nielsen & Larsen 1970:35. Type by original designation (also monotypic). Valid (Iwamoto et al. 1976 [ref. 7089], Markle & Quéro in Whitehead et al. 1984:243 [ref. 13675], Markle 1986:220 [ref. 5687], Paxton et al. 1989:210 [ref. 12442]). Alepocephalidae.

Herzensteinia Chu 1935:13 [ref. 832]. Fem. *Schizopygopsis microcephalus* Herzenstein 1891:219. Type by original designation (also monotypic). Valid (Tsao 1964:193 [ref. 13501]). Cyprinidae.

Hesperanthias Lowe 1843:14 [ref. 2832]. Masc. *Serranus oculatus* Cuvier in Cuvier & Valenciennes 1828:266. Type by monotypy. Objective synonym of *Elastoma* Swainson 1839, synonym of *Etelis* Cuvier 1828 (Allen 1985:24 [ref. 6843]). Lutjanidae.

Hesperoleucus Snyder 1913:63 [ref. 4153]. Masc. *Pogonichthys symmetricus* Baird & Girard 1854:136. Type by original designation. Valid. Cyprinidae.

Hesperomyrus Myers & Storey 1939:157 [ref. 3132]. Masc. *Hesperomyrus fryi* Myers & Storey 1939:157. Type by monotypy. Synonym of *Myrophis* Lütken 1852 (McCosker 1977:59 [ref. 6836], McCosker et al. 1989:279 [ref. 13288]). Ophichthidae: Myrophinae.

Heterandria Agassiz 1853:135 [ref. 67]. Fem. *Heterandria formosa* Agassiz 1855:136. Appeared in 1853 without mention of species. Type designated under plenary powers by ICZN; on Official List (Opinion 375). Valid (Rosen & Bailey 1963:128 [ref. 7067], Rosen 1979:278 [ref. 7020], Parenti & Rauchenberger 1989:9 [ref. 13538]). Poeciliidae.

Hetereleotris Bleeker 1874:306 [ref. 437]. Fem. *Gobius diadematus* Rüppell 1830:137. Type by original designation (also monotypic). Valid (Akihito & Meguro 1981 [ref. 5508], Akihito in Masuda et al. 1984:241 [ref. 6441], Hoese 1986 [ref. 5996], Hoese 1986:791 [ref. 5670], Birdsong et al. 1988:184, 186 [ref. 7303]). Gobiidae.

Heterenchelys Regan 1912:323 [ref. 3647]. Fem. *Heterenchelys microphthalmus* Regan 1912:323. Type by subsequent designation. Type designated by Jordan 1920:545 [ref. 4905]. Valid (Smith 1989:52 [ref. 13285]). Heterenchelyidae.

Hetererythrinus (subgenus of *Erythrinus*) Günther 1864:283, 284 [ref. 1974]. Masc. *Erythrinus salmoneus* Gronow in Gray 1854:170. Type by subsequent designation. Described in key (p. 283) with 3 corresponding species on pp. 284-285. Type by subsequent designation of Jordan 1919:332 [ref. 4904]. Erythrinidae.

Heteristius Myers & Wade 1946:160 [ref. 3135]. Masc. *Heteristius jalisconis* Myers & Wade 1946:161. Type by original designation (also monotypic). Valid (Dawson 1977:155 [ref. 1067], Dawson 1982:83 [ref. 1072]). Dactyloscopidae.

Heterobagrus Bleeker 1864:355 [ref. 404]. Masc. *Heterobagrus bocourti* Bleeker 1864:355. Type by original designation (also monotypic). Valid (Jayaram 1968:369 [ref. 5615], Kottelat 1985:270 [ref. 11441], Burgess 1989:71 [ref. 12860], Kottelat 1989:13 [ref. 13605]); synonym of *Mystus* Scopoli 1777 (Roberts 1989:120 [ref. 6439]). Bagridae.

Heterobranchoides (subgenus of *Clarias*) David 1935:82, 99 [ref. 5559]. Masc. Apparently unavailable, after 1930 without type fixation (article not fully translated); not validated by David in David & Poll 1937:230 [ref. 1043]. In the synonymy of *Clarias* Scopoli 1777 (Teugels 1986:69 [ref. 6193]). Clariidae.

Heterobranchus Geoffroy St. Hilaire 1808:Pls. 16-17 [ref. 4182]. Masc. *Heterobranchus bidorsalis* Geoffroy St. Hilaire 1808:Pls. 16-17. Type by monotypy. Original not seen; above from Fowler (MS). Plates apparently appeared in 1808 (see Taylor 1985:14 [ref. 6640]). Valid (Poll 1977:144 [ref. 3533], Teugels 1986:98 [ref. 6193], Burgess 1989:147 [ref. 12860], Teugels et al. 1990 [ref. 14142]). Clariidae.

Heterobuglossus Chabanaud 1931:293 [ref. 785]. Masc. *Synaptura aspilos* Bleeker 1852:74. Type by original designation (also monotypic). Soleidae.

Heterochaetodon Maugé & Bauchot 1984:474 [ref. 6614]. Masc. *Chaetodon assarius* Waite 1905:66. Type by original designation. Also described as a new subgenus. Maugé & Bauchot included

Lepidochaetodon Bleeker 1876 as a valid subgenus in their genus *Heterochaetodon*, but at the generic level, *Lepidochaetodon* has priority. Chaetodontidae.

Heterocharax Eigenmann 1912:258, 405 [ref. 1227]. Masc. *Heterocharax macrolepis* Eigenmann 1912:406. Type by original designation (also monotypic). Valid (Géry 1977:314 [ref. 1597]). Characidae.

Heterochoerops Steindachner 1866:461 [ref. 4210]. Masc. *Heterochoerops viridis* Steindachner 1866:461. Type by monotypy. Labridae.

Heterochromis Regan 1922:252 [ref. 3674]. Masc. *Paratilapia multidens* Pellegrin 1900:98. Type by original designation (also monotypic). Cichlidae.

Heteroclinus Castelnau 1872:247 [ref. 757]. Masc. *Heteroclinus adelaidae* Castelnau 1872:247. Type by monotypy. Valid (Hoese 1976 [ref. 7338]). Clinidae.

Heteroconger Bleeker 1868:331 [ref. 425]. Masc. *Heteroconger polyzona* Bleeker 1868:332. Type by original designation (also monotypic). Valid (Asano in Masuda et al. 1984:29 [ref. 6441], Paxton et al. 1989:142 [ref. 12442], Smith 1989:484 [ref. 13285]). Congridae: Heterocongrinae.

Heterodon Bleeker 1845:523 [ref. 312]. Masc. *Heterodon zonatus* Bleeker 1845:523. Type by monotypy. Treated by Jordan 1919:225 [ref. 2410] as an original description, but account perhaps without sufficient distinguishing features. Apparently preoccupied in Ophidia, replaced by *Heterognathodon* Bleeker 1848. Synonym of *Pentapodus* Quoy & Gaimard 1824. Nemipteridae.

Heterodontus (subgenus of *Squalus*) Blainville 1816:121 [ref. 306]. Masc. *Squalus philippi* Bloch & Schneider 1801:134. Type by monotypy. Valid (Taylor & Castro-Aguirre 1972 [ref. 7158], Compagno 1984:155 [ref. 6474], Nakaya & Shirai in Masuda et al. 1984:3 [ref. 6441], Bass 1986:48 [ref. 5635], Cappetta 1987:70 [ref. 6348], Paxton et al. 1989:95 [ref. 12442]). Heterodontidae.

Heterogaleus Gohar & Mazhar 1964:28 [ref. 1827]. Masc. *Heterogaleus ghardaqensis* Gohar & Mazhar 1964:29. Type by monotypy. Synonym of fossil genus *Hemipristis* Agassiz 1843 (Compagno 1984:440 [ref. 6846], Compagno 1988:269 [ref. 13488]). Hemigaleidae.

Heterognathodon Bleeker 1848:634, 636 [ref. 315]. Masc. *Heteoodon zonatus* Bleeker 1845:513. Type by being a replacement name. Replacement for *Heterodon* Bleeker 1845, preoccupied several times (see Agassiz 1846:180 [ref. 64]). Synonym of *Pentapodus* Quoy & Gaimard 1824. Nemipteridae.

Heterognathus Girard 1855:198 [ref. 1819]. Masc. *Atherina humboldtiana* Valenciennes in Cuvier & Valenciennes 1835:479. Type by subsequent designation. Earliest type designation found that of Jordan & Evermann 1896:792 [ref. 2443]. Synonym of *Chirostoma* Swainson 1839. Atherinidae: Menidiinae.

Heterogobius Bleeker 1874:320 [ref. 437]. Masc. *Gobius chiloensis* Guichenot in Gay 1848:293. Type by original designation. Gobiidae.

Heterogramma Regan 1906:60 [ref. 3626]. Neut. *Mesops taeniatus* Günther 1862:312. Type by subsequent designation. Type designated by Eigenmann 1910:473 [ref. 1224] (not *H. borelli* listed by Jordan 1920:530 [ref. 4905]; see Myers & Harry 1948:7 [ref. 5458]). Preoccupied by Guenée 1854 [not researched], replaced by *Apistogramma* Regan 1913. Objective synonym of *Apistogramma* Regan 1913 (Kullander 1980:21 [ref. 5526], Kullander 1986:155 [ref. 12439], Kullander & Nijssen 1989:74 [ref. 14136]). Cichlidae.

Heterolenciscus Sauvage 1874:339 [ref. 3873]. Masc. *Heterolenciscus jullieni* Sauvage 1874:339. Type by monotypy. Spelled *Heterolenciscus* twice; described as in "Du groupe des Leuciscus." Apparently intended as *Heteroleuciscus*. Cyprinidae.

Heteromormyrus (subgenus of *Mormyrus*) Steindachner 1866:765 [ref. 5030]. Masc. *Mormyrus pauciradiatus* Steindachner 1866:765. Type by monotypy. Valid (Taverne 1972:168 [ref. 6367], Gosse 1984:73 [ref. 6169]). Mormyridae.

Heteromugil Schultz 1946:(381) 394 [ref. 3965]. Masc. *Mugil tricuspidens* Smith 1935:618. Type by original designation (also monotypic). Synonym of *Liza* Jordan & Swain 1884 (Smith & Smith 1986:715 [ref. 5717]). Mugilidae.

Heteromycteris Kaup 1858:103 [ref. 2578]. *Heteromycteris capensis* Kaup 1858:103. Type by monotypy. Valid (Ochiai in Masuda et al. 1984:354 [ref. 6441], Heemstra & Gon 1986:870 [ref. 5665], Desoutter 1986:430 [ref. 6212]). Soleidae.

Heteromyrus Pietschmann 1935:93 [ref. 3477]. Masc. *Heteromyrus atolli* Pietschmann 1935:93. Type by monotypy. Muraenidae.

Heteronarce Regan 1921:414 [ref. 3672]. Fem. *Heteronarce garmani* Regan 1921:414. Type by subsequent designation. Current authors say type by monotypy, but clearly two included species; earliest type designation not researched. Valid (Compagno 1986:113 [ref. 5648]). Narkidae.

Heterophallina (subgenus of *Gambusia*) Hubbs 1926:21, 26 [ref. 2233]. Fem. *Gambusia regani* Hubbs 1926:28. Type by original designation. Synonym of *Gambusia* Poey 1854 (Rosen & Bailey 1963:90 [ref. 7067]), as a valid subgenus (Rivas 1963:333 [ref. 3761], Parenti & Rauchenberger 1989:9 [ref. 13538]). Poeciliidae.

Heterophallus Regan 1914:65 [ref. 3664]. Masc. *Heterophallus rachovii* Regan 1914:66. Type by monotypy. Synonym of *Gambusia* Poey 1854 (Rosen & Bailey 1963:90 [ref. 7067]). Poeciliidae.

Heterophotus Regan & Trewavas 1929:28 [ref. 3680]. Masc. *Heterophotus ophistoma* Regan & Trewavas 1929:29. Type by monotypy. Valid (Gibbs 1964:340 [ref. 6960], Kawaguchi & Moser 1984:171 [ref. 13642], Fujii in Masuda et al. 1984:50 [ref. 6441], Fink 1985:11 [ref. 5171], Paxton et al. 1989:196 [ref. 12442]). Astronesthidae.

Heterophthalmus Bleeker 1856:42 [ref. 352]. Masc. *Heterophthalmus katopron* Bleeker 1856:43. Type by monotypy. Preoccupied by Blanchard 1851 in Coleoptera, apparently not replaced. Synonym of *Anomalops* Kner 1868 (McCosker & Rosenblatt 1987 [ref. 6707]). Anomalopidae.

Heteroplopomus Tomiyama 1936:39, 58 [ref. 4413]. Fem. *Rhinogobius barbatus* Tomiyama 1934:325. Type by original designation (also monotypic). Valid (Akihito in Masuda et al. 1984:267 [ref. 6441], Birdsong et al. 1988:193 [ref. 7303]). Gobiidae.

Heteropneustes Müller 1840:115 [ref. 12523]. Masc. *Silurus fossilis* Bloch 1797:36. Type by monotypy. Apparently appeared first as above [not seen]; then in Müller 1841:243 [ref. 3061]. Valid (Jayaram 1981:273 [ref. 6497], Burgess 1989:150 [ref. 12860], Kottelat 1989:15 [ref. 13605]). Heteropneustidae.

Heteropriacanthus Fitch & Crooke 1984:310 [ref. 4950]. Masc. *Labrus cruentatus* Lacepède 1801:452. Type by original designation (also monotypic). Technically a synonym of *Cookeolus* Fowler 1928, but petition pending to ICZN (see Starnes 1988:149). Valid (Starnes 1988:149 [ref. 6978], Paxton et al. 1989:542 [ref. 12442]). Priacanthidae.

Heteroprosopon Bleeker 1862:429 [ref. 388]. Neut. *Platessa cornuta* Temminck & Schlegel 1846:179. Type by monotypy. Synonym of *Pleuronichthys* Girard 1854 (Norman 1934:317 [ref. 6893]). Pleuronectidae: Pleuronectinae.

Heteropyge Fraser-Brunner 1933:569 [ref. 671]. Fem. *Holacanthus xanthometopon* Bleeker 1853:258. Type by original designation. Preoccupied by Silvestri 1897 in Myriapoda, replaced by *Euxiphipops* Fraser-Brunner 1934. Pomacanthidae.

Heteroscarus Castelnau 1872:245 [ref. 757]. Masc. *Heteroscarus filamentosus* Castelnau 1872:246. Type by subsequent designation. Type designated by Jordan 1919:363 [ref. 4904]. Synonym of *Odax* Cuvier 1839 (Gomon & Paxton 1986 [ref. 5656]). Odacidae.

Heteroscyllium Regan 1908:455 [ref. 3633]. Neut. *Brachaelurus colcloughi* Ogilby 1908:4. Type by monotypy. Perhaps intended as a replacement name for *Barchaelurus* Ogilby 1908 but text unclear, not Ogilby 1907. Valid (Compagno 1984:176 [ref. 6474]). Brachyaeluridae.

Heteroscymnoides Fowler 1934:239 [ref. 1416]. Masc. *Hetero scymnoides marleyi* Fowler 1934:240. Type by original designation (also monotypic). *Heteroscymnodes* is a misspelling. Valid (Compagno 1984:91 [ref. 6474], Bass et al. 1986:58 [ref. 5636]). Squalidae.

Heteroscymnus Tanaka 1912:102 [ref. 6033]. Masc. *Heteroscymnus longus* Tanaka 1912:102. Type by original designation (also monotypic). Synonym of *Somniosus* Lesueur 1818 (Compagno 1984:102 [ref. 6474]). Squalidae.

Heterostichus Girard 1854:143 [ref. 5769]. Masc. *Heterostichus rostratus* Girard 1854:143. Type by monotypy. Valid (Clark Hubbs 1952:111 [ref. 2252]). Clinidae.

Heterothrissa (subgenus of *Engraulis*) Günther 1868:385, 401 [ref. 1990]. Fem. *Engraulis breviceps* Cantor 1850:1288. Type by monotypy. Described in key (p. 385) for one species treated on p. 401. Synonym of *Setipinna* Swainson 1839 (Whitehead et al. 1988:451 [ref. 5725], Roberts 1989:26 [ref. 6439]). Engraulidae.

Heterotilapia (subgenus of *Tilapia*) Regan 1920:38 [ref. 3669]. Fem. *Tilapia buettikoferi* Hubrecht 1881:66. Type by original designation (also monotypic). Preoccupied [details not researched], replaced by *Reganotilapia* Whitley 1950. Cichlidae.

Heterotis Rüppell (ex Ehrenberg) 1828:10 [ref. 3843]. Masc. *Sudis niloticus* Cuvier (ex Ehrenberg) 1828:328. Type by monotypy. On Official List (Opinion 1132); gender given as masculine by ICZN but is classically feminine. Ruled by ICZN to be available from publication in synonymy by Rüppell. Previously credited to Ehrenberg 1834:432 [ref. 5036]. Valid (Daget 1984:57 [ref. 6170]). Osteoglossidae: Heterotidinae.

Heterotrema Girard 1855:251 [ref. 4912]. Neut. *Bdellostoma heterotrema* Müller 1834:79. Type by monotypy. Type inferred from text on p. 251. Myxinidae: Eptatretinae.

Hexabranchus Schultze 1836:757 [ref. 3978]. Masc. *Hexabranchus lichtensteinii* Schultze 1836. Preoccupied by Ehrenberg 1828 in Mollusca. Synonym of *Eptatretus* Cloquet 1819. Myxinidae: Eptatretinae.

Hexacanthus Nordmann 1838:332 [ref. 3208]. Masc. *Gobius macrocephalus* Pallas 1787:52. Type by monotypy. Objective synonym of *Benthophilus* Eichwald 1831 (Miller 1973:490 [ref. 6888]). Gobiidae.

Hexagrammoides Gracianov 1907:289 [ref. 1871]. Masc. *Hexagrammoides nudigenis* Gracianov 1907. Original not seen. Synonym of *Hexagrammos* Steller 1809. Hexagrammidae: Hexagramminae.

Hexagrammos Steller in Tilesius 1809:335 [ref. 12816]. Masc. *Hexagrammos stelleri* Tilesius 1809:335. Type by monotypy. Unjustifiably emended to *Hexagramus* by Jordan & Gilbert 1883:641 [ref. 2476]. Valid (Washington et al. 1984:443 [ref. 13660], Amaoka in Masuda et al. 1984:320 [ref. 6441]). Hexagrammidae: Hexagramminae.

Hexanchus Rafinesque 1810:14 [ref. 3594]. Masc. *Squalus griseus* Bonnaterre 1788:9. Type by monotypy. *Hexancus* Agassiz 1846:181 [ref. 64] is an unjustified emendation; spelled *Hexanchias* by Swainson 1838:148 [ref. 4302]). Valid (Boeseman 1973:8 [ref. 7161], Boeseman in Whitehead et al. 1984:73 [ref. 13675], Compagno 1984:19 [ref. 6474], Nakaya & Shirai in Masuda et al. 1984:3 [ref. 6441], Bass et al. 1986:46 [ref. 5638], Cappetta 1987:46 [ref. 6348], Paxton et al. 1989:27 [ref. 12442]). Hexanchidae.

Hexanematichthys Bleeker 1858:2 [ref. 364]. Masc. *Bagrus sondaicus* Valenciennes in Cuvier & Valenciennes 1840:444. Type by monotypy. Also in Bleeker 1858:24 et seq., 61, 126 [ref. 365]; earliest publication in 1858 not established. Synonym of *Arius* Valenciennes 1840 (Roberts 1989:110 [ref. 6439]). Ariidae.

Hexatrema Girard 1855:251 [ref. 4912]. Neut. *Bdellostoma hexatrema* Müller 1834:79. Type by monotypy (also by absolute tautonymy). Proposed conditionally; type by inference from text on p. 251, but technically no originally included species. Myxinidae: Eptatretinae.

Hexatrematobatis Chu & Meng in Zhu et al. 1981:111 [ref. 4841]. Fem. *Hexatrematobatis longirostrum* Chu & Meng 1981:111. Type by original designation (also monotypic). Misspelled once as *Hexatrematibatis* (p. 116). Synonym of *Hexatrygon* Heemstra & Smith 1980 (Smith & Heemstra 1986:142 [ref. 5714]). Hexatrygonidae.

Hexatrygon Heemstra & Smith 1980:1 [ref. 2081]. Fem. *Hexatrygon bickelli* Heemstra & Smith 1980:6. Type by original designation (also monotypic). Valid (Nakaya in Masuda et al. 1984:15 [ref. 6441], Smith & Heemstra 1986:142 [ref. 5714], Shen 1986 [ref. 6381], Shen 1986 [ref. 8041]). Hexatrygonidae.

Hiatula Lacepède 1800:522 [ref. 2709]. Fem. *Hiatula gardeniana* Lacepède 1800:522. Type by monotypy. Preoccupied by Modeer 1792 in Mollusca, not replaced. Synonym of *Tautoga* Mitchill 1814. Labridae.

Hierichthys Jordan & Fowler 1902:744 [ref. 2459]. Masc. *Hierichthys encryptes* Jordan & Fowler 1902:744. Type by original designation (also monotypic). Synonym of *Congrogadus* Günther 1862 (Winterbottom et al. 1984:1607 [ref. 5140]). Pseudochromidae: Congrogadinae.

Hierops (subgenus of *Electrona*) Fraser-Brunner 1949:1046 [ref. 1496]. Masc. *Scopelus arcticus* Lütken 1892:249. Type by original designation. Synonym of *Protomyctophum* Fraser-Brunner 1949 (Krefft & Bekker 1973:196 [ref. 7181]); as a valid subgenus (Paxton 1979:17 [ref. 6440], Moser et al. 1984:219 [ref. 13645], Hulley 1986:316 [ref. 5672]). Myctophidae.

Hieroptera Fleming 1841:238 [ref. 1340]. Fem. *Hieroptera abredonensis* Fleming 1841:236. Type by original designation (also monotypic). Based on a deformed specimen of *Raja clavata*. Synonym of *Raja* Linnaeus 1758. Rajidae.

Higanfugu (subgenus of *Sphaeroides*) Abe 1949:93 (in key) [ref. 3]. Masc. *Tetraodon pardalis* Temminck & Schlegel 1850:282. Type by monotypy. Synonym of *Takifugu* Abe 1949 (Masuda et al.

1984:363 [ref. 6441] based on placement of type species). Tetraodontidae.

Hildadoras Fernández-Yépez 1968:41 [ref. 1325]. Masc. *Hildadoras orinocensis* Fernández-Yépez 1968:41. Type by original designation. Valid (Burgess 1989:223 [ref. 12860]). Doradidae.

Hildatia Fernández-Yépez 1968:[3] [ref. 7318]. Fem. *Hildatia brasiliensis* Fernández-Yépez 1968:[3]. Type by original designation (also monotypic). Synonym of *Sternopygus* Müller & Troschel 1848 (Mago-Leccia 1978:14, footnote [ref. 5489], Fink 1979 [ref. 6949]). Gymnotidae: Sternopyginae.

Hildebrandella Nichols 1950:20 [ref. 3183]. Fem. *Citula halli* Evermann & Seale 1907:65. Type by original designation (also monotypic). Synonym of *Apolectus* Cuvier 1832 (Witzell 1978:74 [ref. 6802]), which is a synonym of *Parastromateus* Bleeker 1865. Carangidae.

Hildebrandia Jordan & Evermann 1927:502 [ref. 2453]. Fem. *Congermuraena flava* Goode & Bean 1896:138. Type by original designation (also monotypic). Valid (Smith & Kanazawa 1977:536 [ref. 4036]); synonym of *Rhynchoconger* Jordan & Hubbs 1925 (Smith 1989:525 [ref. 13285]). Congridae: Congrinae.

Hildebrandichthys Schultz 1949:49 [ref. 3967]. Masc. *Hildebrandichthys setiger* Schultz 1949:49. Type by original designation (also monotypic). Synonym of *Engraulis*, subgenus *Cetengraulis* Günther 1868 (G. Nelson 1984 [ref. 5190]). Engraulidae.

Hilgendorfia Goode & Bean 1896:280 [ref. 1848]. Fem. *Paraliparis membranaceus* Günther 1887:69. Type by monotypy. Synonym of *Paraliparis* Collett 1878 (Stein 1978:38 [ref. 4203], Andriashev 1986:14 [ref. 12760] as *Hilgendorphia*, Kido 1988:230 [ref. 12287]). Cyclopteridae: Liparinae.

Hilsa Regan 1917:303 [ref. 3665]. Fem. *Clupea durbanensis* Regan 1906:4. Type by being a replacement name. Replacement for *Paralosa* Regan 1916, preoccupied by Bleeker 1868 in fishes. Treated by some authors as a junior synonym of *Macrura* van Hasselt [see account of *Macrura* van Hasselt]. Valid (Jayaram 1981:39 [ref. 6497], Grande 1985:249 [ref. 6466], Whitehead 1985:220 [ref. 5141], Whitehead & Wongratana 1986:201 [ref. 6284]). Clupeidae.

Himantolophus Reinhardt 1837:116 [ref. 13398]. Masc. *Himantolophus groenlandicus* Reinhardt 1837:116. Type by monotypy. Original not seen. Valid (Maul 1973:668 [ref. 7171], Amaoka in Masuda et al. 1984:105 [ref. 6441], Pietsch 1986:376 [ref. 5704], Bertelsen in Whitehead et al. 1986:1378 [ref. 13677], Bertelsen & Krefft 1988 [ref. 6615], Paxton et al. 1989:289 [ref. 12442]). Himantolophidae.

Himantura Müller & Henle 1837:400 [ref. 13421]. Fem. *Raja uarnak* Forsskål 1775:18. Type by subsequent designation. Also appeared in (and may date to) Müller & Henle 1837:117. Type designated by Garman 1913:375 [ref. 1545], who unjustifiably emended spelling to *Himanturus*, as a subgenus of *Dasybatus*. Valid (Krefft & Stehmann 1973:72 [ref. 7167], Nakaya in Masuda et al. 1984:16 [ref. 6441], Compagno 1986:138 [ref. 5648], Paxton et al. 1989:42 [ref. 12442], Roberts 1989:22 [ref. 6439]). Dasyatidae.

Hime Starks 1924:30 [ref. 4198]. Fem. *Aulopus japonicus* Günther 1880:72. Type by original designation (also monotypic). Synonym of *Aulopus* Cloquet 1816 (Sulak 1977:53 [ref. 4299]); valid (Parin & Kotlyar 1989 [ref. 12748]). Aulopidae.

Hinalea Jordan & Jordan 1922:69 [ref. 2487]. Fem. *Julis axillaris* Quoy & Gaimard 1824:72. Type by original designation. Labridae.

Hintonia Fraser-Brunner 1949:1098 [ref. 1496]. Fem. *Hintonia candens* Fraser-Brunner 1949:1098. Type by original designation (also monotypic). Valid (Paxton 1979:11 [ref. 6440], Moser et al. 1984:220 [ref. 13645], Paxton et al. 1984:241 [ref. 13625], Hulley 1986:301 [ref. 5672]). Myctophidae.

Hiodon Lesueur 1818:364 [ref. 2735]. Masc. *Hiodon tergisus* Lesueur 1818:366. Type by subsequent designation. Type designated by Jordan & Gilbert 1877:84 [ref. 4907]. Spelled *Hyodon* in early literature. Valid. Hiodontidae.

Hippichthys (subgenus of *Syngnathus*) Bleeker 1849:15 [ref. 320]. Masc. *Hippichthys heptagonus* Bleeker 1849:15. Type by monotypy. Proposed as a section of *Syngnathus*. Valid (Dawson 1978 [ref. 7026], Araga in Masuda et al. 1984:86 [ref. 6441], Dawson 1985:97 [ref. 6541], Dawson 1986:282 [ref. 6201], Dawson 1986: 451 [ref. 5650], Paxton et al. 1989:419 [ref. 12442], Kottelat 1989: 16 [ref. 13605]). Syngnathidae: Syngnathinae.

Hippocampus Cuvier 1816:157 [ref. 993]. Masc. *Syngnathus hippocampus* Linnaeus 1758:338. Type by absolute tautonymy. Same as *Hippocampus* Rafinesque 1810, but Cuvier does not cite Rafinesque. In the synonymy of *Hippocampus* Rafinesque 1810. Syngnathidae: Hippocampinae.

Hippocampus Leach 1814:103 [ref. 2738]. Masc. *Hippocampus antiquorum* Leach 1814 (= *Syngnathus hippocampus* Linnaeus 1758:338). Apparently not intended as a new genus (original not seen). In the synonymy of *Hippocampus* Rafinesque 1810. Syngnathidae: Hippocampinae.

Hippocampus Perry 1810:Pl. 45 Masc. *Syngnathus hippocampus* Linnaeus 1758:338. Type by monotypy. Above from Fowler (MS); listed by him under *Hippocampus*, but stated to be not of Rafinesque. Published in "Arcana 1810" according to Fowler. Not examined. Syngnathidae: Hippocampinae.

Hippocampus Rafinesque 1810:18 [ref. 3594]. Masc. *Syngnathus heptagonus* Rafinesque 1810 (= *Syngnathus hippocampus* Linnaeus 1758:338). Type by monotypy. Valid (Wheeler 1973:278 [ref. 7190], Fritzsche 1980:185 [ref. 1511], Vari 1982:175 [ref. 6765], Fritzsche 1984 [ref. 13658], Araga in Masuda et al. 1984:89 [ref. 6441], Dawson in Whitehead et al. 1986:630 [ref. 13676], Dawson 1986:452 [ref. 5650], Paxton et al. 1989:420 [ref. 12442]). Syngnathidae: Hippocampinae.

Hippocephalus Swainson 1839:181, 272 [ref. 4303]. Masc. *Cottus japonicus* Pallas 1772:30. Type by subsequent designation. Type designated by Gill 1861:167 [ref. 1775]. Synonym of *Percis* Scopoli 1777. Agonidae.

Hippoglossina Steindachner 1876:61 [ref. 4225]. Fem. *Hippoglossina macrops* Steindachner 1876:61. Type by monotypy. Valid (Norman 1934:65 [ref. 6893], Ahlstrom et al. 1984:642 [ref. 13641]). Paralichthyidae.

Hippoglossoides Gottsche 1835:164, 168 [ref. 1862]. Masc. *Hippoglossoides limanda* Gottsche 1835:168 (= *Pleuronectes limandoides* Bloch 1787:27). Type by monotypy. Valid (Norman 1934:294 [ref. 6893], Nielsen 1973:623 [ref. 6885], Ahlstrom et al. 1984:643 [ref. 13641], Sakamoto 1984 [ref. 5273], Sakamoto in Masuda et al. 1984:351 [ref. 6441], Nielsen in Whitehead et al. 1986:1300 [ref. 13677]). Pleuronectidae: Pleuronectinae.

Hippoglossus Cuvier 1816:221 [ref. 993]. Masc. *Pleuronectes hippoglossus* Linnaeus 1758:269. Type by absolute tautonymy. Valid (Norman 1934:291 [ref. 6893], Nielsen 1973:624 [ref. 6885], Ahlstrom et al. 1984:643 [ref. 13641], Sakamoto 1984 [ref. 5273],

Sakamoto in Masuda et al. 1984:351 [ref. 6441], Nielsen in Whitehead et al. 1986:1301 [ref. 13677]). Pleuronectidae: Pleuronectinae.

Hippohystrix Whitley 1940:414 [ref. 4699]. Fem. *Hippocampus spinosissimus* Weber 1913:120. Type by original designation (also monotypic). Synonym of *Hippocampus* Rafinesque 1810 (Fritzsche 1980:185 [ref. 1511], Vari 1982:175 [ref. 6765]). Syngnathidae: Hippocampinae.

Hippopotamyrus Pappenheim 1906:260 [ref. 3360]. Masc. *Hippopotamyrus castor* Pappenheim 1906:260. Type by monotypy. Valid (Taverne 1972:170 [ref. 6367], Gosse 1984:73 [ref. 6169], Lévêque & Bigorne 1985 [ref. 5160]). Mormyridae.

Hipposcarus Smith 1956:17 [ref. 4104]. Masc. *Scarus harid* Forsskål 1775:30. Type by original designation (also monotypic). Valid (Randall & Bruce 1983:7 [ref. 5412], Randall 1986:709 [ref. 5706], Bellwood & Choat 1989:15 [ref. 13494]). Scaridae: Scarinae.

Hipposcorpaena Fowler 1938:71 [ref. 1426]. Fem. *Hipposcorpaena filamentosa* Fowler 1938:72. Type by original designation (also monotypic). Valid (Eschmeyer et al. 1973:304 [ref. 6390]). Scorpaenidae: Scorpaeninae.

Hippurus Klein 1779:788 [ref. 4923]. Masc. Not available; published in a work that does not conform to the principle of binominal nomenclature. Also as *Hippuris* by Klein in Walbaum 1792 (not available). Original not checked. In the synonymy of *Coryphaena* Linnaeus 1758. Coryphaenidae.

Hirculops Smith 1959:247 [ref. 4123]. Masc. *Blennius cornifer* Rüppell 1828:112. Type by original designation (also monotypic). Valid (Springer 1986:747 [ref. 5719]). Blenniidae.

Hirundichthys Breder 1928:14, 20 [ref. 636]. Masc. *Exocoetus rubescens* Rafinesque 1818:205. Type by original designation (also monotypic). Valid (Parin 1973:265 [ref. 7191], Collette et al. 1984:338 [ref. 11422], Yoshino in Masuda et al. 1984:82 [ref. 6441], Parin in Whitehead et al. 1986:617 [ref. 13676], Heemstra & Parin 1986:394 [ref. 6293], Paxton et al. 1989:333 [ref. 12442]). Exocoetidae.

Hirundo Catesby 1771:8 [ref. 774]. Fem. Not available, published in a rejected work on Official Index (Opinion 89, Opinion 259). Exocoetidae.

Hisonotus Eigenmann & Eigenmann 1889:40 [ref. 1253]. Masc. *Hisonotus notatus* Eigenmann & Eigenmann 1889:42. Type by original designation (also monotypic). Synonym of *Otocinclus* Cope 1871 (Isbrücker 1980:81 [ref. 2303]). Loricariidae.

Hispaniscus (subgenus of *Sebastodes*) Jordan & Evermann 1896:431 [ref. 2442]. Masc. *Sebastichthys rubrivinctus* Jordan & Gilbert 1880:291. Type by original designation. Synonym of *Sebastes* Cuvier 1829. Scorpaenidae: Sebastinae.

Hispidoberyx Kotlyar 1981:411 [ref. 2666]. Masc. *Hispidoberyx ambagiosus* Kotlyar 1981:412. Type by original designation (also monotypic). Valid (Yang et al. 1988 [ref. 7301]). Hispidoberycidae.

Histiobranchus Gill 1883:255 [ref. 1724]. Masc. *Histiobranchus infernalis* Gill 1883:255. Type by monotypy. Valid (Blache et al. 1973:252 [ref. 7185], Asano in Masuda et al. 1984:26 [ref. 6441], Saldanha & Bauchot in Whitehead et al. 1986:588 [ref. 13676], Castle 1986:189 [ref. 5644], Paxton et al. 1989:107 [ref. 12442], Robins & Robins 1989:219 [ref. 13287]). Synaphobranchidae: Synaphobranchinae.

Histioclinus Metzelaar 1919:157 [ref. 2982]. Masc. *Histioclinus veliger* Metzelaar 1919:157. Type by monotypy. Also appeared as new in Metzelaar 1922:141 [ref. 5741]. Synonym of *Auchenistius* Evermann & Marsh 1899 (Clark Hubbs 1952:65 [ref. 2252]). Synonym of *Stathmonotus* Bean 1885 (Springer 1955:74 [ref. 10208]). Labrisomidae.

Histiocottus Gill 1889:573 [ref. 1729]. Masc. *Peropus bilobus* of Lay & Bennett 1839 (= *Blepsias bilobus* Cuvier 1829:279). Type by being a replacement name. Replacement for *Peropus* Lay & Bennett 1839, apparently preoccupied in herpetology [not investigated]. *P. bilobus* of Lay & Bennett apparently same as *Blepsias bilobus* Cuvier 1829:279 (not investigated). Synonym of *Blepsias* Cuvier 1829 (Bolin 1944:99 [ref. 6379]). Cottidae.

Histiodraco Regan 1914:9 [ref. 3659]. Masc. *Dolloidraco velifer* Regan 1914:12. Type by monotypy. Valid (Eakin 1981:138 [ref. 14216], Stevens et al. 1984:563 [ref. 13633]). Harpagiferidae.

Histiodromus Gistel 1848:VIII [ref. 1822]. Masc. *Salmo anostomus* Linnaeus 1758:312. Type by being a replacement name. Unneeded replacement for *Anostomus* Gronow 1763 and others, not preoccupied by *Anastomus* Illiger 1835; published earlier in an available way by Scopoli 1777. Objective synonym of *Anostomus* Scopoli 1777 (Winterbottom 1980:9 [ref. 4755]). Curimatidae: Anostominae.

Histiogamphelus McCulloch 1914:30 [ref. 2939]. Masc. *Histiogamphelus briggsii* McCulloch 1914:30. Type by original designation. Valid (Dawson 1985:101 [ref. 6541], Paxton et al. 1989:422 [ref. 12442]). Syngnathidae: Syngnathinae.

Histiophorus Cuvier in Cuvier & Valenciennes 1832:291, 293 [ref. 1000]. Masc. Apparently an unjustifiable emendation of or new spelling of *Istiophorus* Lacepède 1801; *Histiophorus* regarded by some as separate genus, with type as *Histiophorus americanus* Cuvier. In the synonymy of *Istiophorus* Lacepède 1801 (de Sylva 1973:477 [ref. 7210], Nakamura 1983:276 [ref. 5371]). Istiophoridae.

Histiophryne Gill 1863:90 [ref. 1680]. Fem. *Chironectes bougainvilli* Valenciennes in Cuvier & Valenciennes 1837:431. Type by original designation (also monotypic). Valid (Pietsch 1984:40 [ref. 5380] and Paxton et al. 1989:279 [ref. 12442]) but with 1879 as date). Antennariidae.

Histiopterus Temminck & Schlegel 1844:86 [ref. 4372]. Masc. *Histiopterus typus* Temminck & Schlegel 1844:88. Type by use of *typus*. Valid (Hardy 1983:179 [ref. 5385], Hardy 1983:374 [ref. 5392], Mochizuki in Masuda et al. 1984:189 [ref. 6441], Heemstra 1986:622 [ref. 5660]). Pentacerotidae.

Histrio Fischer von Waldheim 1813:70, 78 [ref. 1331]. *Lophius histrio* Linnaeus 1758:237. No species included originally; first addition of species not researched. Type generally regarded as by tautonymy. Original not seen. Valid (Monod & Le Danois 1973:659 [ref. 7223], Pietsch 1984:37 [ref. 5380], Araga in Masuda et al. 1984:103 [ref. 6441], Pietsch in Whitehead et al. 1986:1367 [ref. 13677], Pietsch 1986:369 [ref. 5704], Paxton et al. 1989:279 [ref. 12442]). Antennariidae.

Hito Herre 1924:702 [ref. 2119]. *Hito taytayensis* Herre 1924:703. Type by original designation (also monotypic). Also described as *Hitoichthys* by Herre 1924:1570 [ref. 2120]; but dates of publication not fully investigated. Haig 1952:82 [ref. 12607] selected *Hito* over *Hitoichthys* and indicated earliest could not be determined. Valid (Haig 1952:81 [ref. 12607], Burgess 1989:86 [ref. 12860]). Siluridae.

Hitoichthys Herre 1924:1570 [ref. 2120]. Masc. *Hitoichthys* *taytayensis* Herre 1924:1570. Type by original designation (also monotypic). See *Hito* Herre 1924. Possibly *Hitoichthys* was published first, but dates not fully investigated. Objective synonym of *Hito* Herre 1924. Siluridae.

Hobar (subgenus of *Sciaena*) Forsskål 1775:44 [ref. 1351]. *Sciaena bohar* Forsskål 1775:xi, 46. Not available, regarded as non-latinized Arabic name (see Jordan 1917:33-34 [ref. 2407]). In the synonymy of *Lutjanus* Bloch 1790. Lutjanidae.

Hogbinia (subgenus of *Pseudupeneus*) Whitley 1929:92 [ref. 4667]. Fem. *Pseudupeneus filamentosus* Macleay 1883:264. Type by original designation (also monotypic). Possibly additional species included (see p. 95) but unclear. Mullidae.

Holacanthus Gronow in Gray 1854:23 [ref. 1911]. Masc. *Holacanthus leionothos* Gronow in Gray 1854:23. Type by subsequent designation. Type designated by Jordan 1919:258 [ref. 2410]. Synonym of *Spheroides* Duméril 1806. Tetraodontidae.

Holacanthus Lacepède 1802:525 [ref. 4929]. Masc. *Chaetodon tricolor* Bloch 1795:103. Type by subsequent designation. Type designated by Bleeker 1876:307-308 [ref. 448]. *Holacantha* Rafinesque 1815:83 [ref. 3584] and *Holocanthus* Gray 1831:35 (not investigated) are apparently incorrect subsequent spellings. Valid (Matsuura in Uyeno et al. 1983:392 [ref. 14275], Araga in Masuda et al. 1984:188 [ref. 6441]). Pomacanthidae.

Holanthias Günther 1868:226 [ref. 1991]. Masc. *Anthias fronticinctus* Günther 1868:226. Type by original designation (also monotypic). Valid (Kendall 1984:500 [ref. 13663], Katayama in Masuda et al. 1984:135 [ref. 6441], Heemstra & Randall 1986:512 [ref. 5667]). Serranidae: Anthiinae.

Holapogon Fraser 1973:2 [ref. 1483]. Masc. *Apogon maximus* Boulenger 1887:655. Type by original designation (also monotypic). Apogonidae.

Holcomycteronus Garman 1899:162 [ref. 1540]. Masc. *Holcomycteronus digittatus* Garman 1899:163. Type by monotypy. Synonym of *Bassogigas* Goode & Bean 1896 (Nielsen 1973:549 [ref. 6885]); valid (Cohen & Nielsen 1978:32 [ref. 881], Nielsen 1980 [ref. 6926], Anderson et al. 1985 [ref. 5164], Nielsen in Whitehead et al. 1986:1162 [ref. 13677], Nielsen & Cohen 1986:347 [ref. 5700]). Ophidiidae: Neobythitinae.

Holconotus Agassiz 1854:367 [ref. 70]. Masc. *Holconotus rhodoterus* Agassiz 1854:368. Type by monotypy. Preoccupied by Schmidt-Goebel 1846 in Coleoptera, not replaced. Synonym of *Amphistichus* Agassiz 1854 (Tarp 1952:39 [ref. 12250]). Embiotocidae.

Hollandichthys Eigenmann 1910:432 [ref. 1224]. Masc. *Tetragonopterus multifasciatus* Eigenmann & Norris 1900:358. Type by monotypy. Characidae.

Hollardia Poey 1861:348 [ref. 3499]. Fem. *Hollardia hollardi* Poey 1861:348. Type by monotypy. Valid (Tyler 1968:92 [ref. 6438], Tyler 1980:56 [ref. 4477], Matsuura in Uyeno et al. 1983:464 [ref. 14275]). Triacanthodidae.

Holobrycon Eigenmann 1909:33 [ref. 1222]. Masc. *Brycon pesu* Müller & Troschel 1845:16. Type by original designation (also monotypic). Tentatively distinct from *Brycon* (Géry 1977:335 [ref. 1597]); synonym of *Brycon* Müller & Troschel 1844 (Howes 1982:4 [ref. 14201]). Characidae.

Holocentrus Bloch 1790:59 [ref. 469]. Masc. *Holocentrus sogo* Bloch 1790:61. Type by subsequent designation. Fowler (MS) lists a first occurrence of this name as Bloch 1767, "Ichthyologie 7":46 (not investigated). *Holocentrum* of Cuvier 1829:95 [ref. 995] and authors are misspellings or unjustified emendations. Type designated by Jordan & Gilbert 1883:459 [ref. 2476]. Synonym of *Holocentrus* Scopoli 1777 (Woods & Sonoda 1973:333 [ref. 6899]). Holocentridae.

Holocentrus Gronow 1763:65 [ref. 1910]. Masc. Not available, published in a rejected work on Official Index (Opinion 261). Holocentridae.

Holocentrus Scopoli (ex Gronow) 1777:449 [ref. 3990]. Masc. *Perca adscenisionis* Osbeck 1765:388. Type by subsequent designation. Appeared originally as *Holocenthrus* (regarded as a typographical error by authors), after *Holocentrus maxilla* Gronow (rejected work). Type perhaps first designated by Jordan & Gilbert 1883:459 [ref. 2476], but Whitley 1933:68 [ref. 4677] regards *sogo* Bloch as type [needs investigation]. Valid (Woods & Sonoda 1973:333 [ref. 6899]). Holocentridae.

Hologymnosus Lacepède 1801:556 [ref. 2710]. Masc. *Hologymnosus fasciatus* Lacepède 1801:556, 557. Type by monotypy. Spelled *Hologymnos* by Duméril 1806 (not investigated). Valid (Randall 1982 [ref. 5448], Araga in Masuda et al. 1984:210 [ref. 6441], Randall 1986:697 [ref. 5706], Randall & Yamakawa 1988 [ref. 6410]). Labridae.

Holohalaelurus (subgenus of *Halaelurus*) Fowler 1934:235 [ref. 1416]. Masc. *Scyliorhinus regani* Gilchrist 1922:45. Type by original designation (also monotypic). Valid (Springer 1979:92 [ref. 4175], Compagno 1984:336 [ref. 6846], Bass 1986:92 [ref. 5635], Compagno 1988:152 [ref. 13488]). Scyliorhinidae.

Hololepis Putnam (ex Agassiz) 1863:4 [ref. 3567]. Fem. *Boleosoma barratti* Holbrook 1855:56. Type by subsequent designation. Type designated by Jordan & Gilbert 1877:93 [ref. 4907]. Synonym of *Etheostoma* Rafinesque 1819, but as a valid subgenus (Collette & Banarescu 1977:1457 [ref. 5845], Bailey & Etnier 1988:27 [ref. 6873]). Percidae.

Holomeiacanthus (subgenus of *Meiacanthus*) Smith-Vaniz 1976:82 [ref. 4144]. Masc. *Petroscirtes anema* Bleeker 1852:273. Type by original designation (also monotypic). Blenniidae.

Holonodus (subgenus of *Zebrias*) Chabanaud 1936:383 [ref. 792]. Masc. *Synaptura synapturoides* Jenkins 1910:28. Type by original designation (also monotypic). Soleidae.

Holoprion Eigenmann 1903:145 [ref. 1218]. Masc. *Chirodon agassizii* Steindachner 1882:180. Type by original designation (also monotypic). Correct spelling for genus of type is *Cheirodon*. Synonym of *Aphyocharax* Günther 1868 (Géry 1977:351 [ref. 1597]). Characidae.

Holopristis Eigenmann 1903:145 [ref. 1218]. Fem. *Tetragonopterus ocellifer* Steindachner 1883:32. Type by original designation (also monotypic). Unjustifiably emended or misspelled *Holopristes* by Eigenmann & Ogle 1907:11 [ref. 1266]. Characidae.

Holopterura Cope 1871:482 [ref. 920]. Fem. *Holopterura plumbea* Cope 1871:482. Type by monotypy. Synonym of *Myrophis* Lütken 1852 (McCosker et al. 1989:279 [ref. 13288]). Ophichthidae: Myrophinae.

Holorhinus Gill 1862:331 [ref. 1668]. Masc. *Rhinoptera vespertilio* Girard 1856:137. Type by monotypy. Synonym of *Myliobatis* Cuvier 1816 (Krefft & Stehmann 1973:74 [ref. 7167], Cappetta 1987:172 [ref. 6348]). Myliobatidae.

Holoscorpaena Fowler 1944:277 [ref. 1448]. Fem. *Holoscorpaena didymogramma* Fowler 1944:277. Type by original designation (also monotypic). Synonym of *Scorpaena* Linnaeus 1758 (see Böhlke 1984:153 [ref. 13621]). Scorpaenidae: Scorpaeninae.

Holoshesthes Eigenmann 1903:144 [ref. 1218]. Fem. *Chirodon pequira* Steindachner 1882:179. Type by original designation (also monotypic). Spelled *Holesthes* by Eigenmann 1915:83 [ref. 1231] and *Holoesthes* by Eigenmann 1917:35 [ref. 1236]. Correct spelling for genus of type is *Cheirodon*. Valid (Géry 1977:551 [ref. 1597]). Characidae.

Holotaxis Cope 1870:563 [ref. 914]. Fem. *Holotaxis melanostomus* Cope 1870:563. Type by monotypy. Synonym of *Pyrrhulina* Valenciennes 1846. Lebiasinidae: Pyrrhulininae.

Holotrachys (subgenus of *Myripristis*) Günther 1874:93 [ref. 2005]. Fem. *Myripristis lima* Valenciennes in Cuvier & Valenciennes 1831:493. Type by monotypy. Synonym of *Plectrypops* Gill 1862 (Woods & Sonoda 1973:382 [ref. 6899], Randall & Heemstra 1986:426 [ref. 5707]). Holocentridae.

Holotylognathus Fowler 1934:135 [ref. 1417]. Masc. *Holotylognathus reticulatus* Fowler 1934:135. Type by original designation (also monotypic). Synonym of *Crossocheilus* Kuhl & van Hasselt 1823 (see Böhlke 1984:89 [ref. 13261]). Cyprinidae.

Holoxenus Günther 1876:393 [ref. 2007]. Masc. *Holoxenus cutaneus* Günther 1876:393. Type by monotypy. Synonym of *Gnathanacanthus* Bleeker 1855 (Scott 1986:53 [ref. 5807], Paxton et al. 1989:464 [ref. 12442]). Gnathanacanthidae.

Holtbyrnia Parr 1937:6 [ref. 3376]. Fem. *Bathytroctes innesi* Fowler 1934:252. Type by original designation (also monotypic). Valid (Krefft 1973:96 [ref. 7166], Quéro et al. in Whitehead et al. 1984:259 [ref. 13675], Matsui & Rosenblatt 1986:222 [ref. 5688], Sazonov 1986 [ref. 6003], Paxton et al. 1989:212 [ref. 12442]). Platytroctidae.

Homalogrystes Alleyne & Macleay 1877:268 [ref. 101]. Masc. *Homalogrystes guentheri* Alleyne & Macleay 1877:269. Type by monotypy. Synonym of *Epinephelus* Bloch 1793 (Smith 1971:103 [ref. 14102], Daget & Smith 1986:301 [ref. 6204]). Serranidae: Epinephelinae.

Homalopomus Girard 1856:132 [ref. 1809]. Fem. *Homalopomus trowbridgii* Girard 1856:132. Type by monotypy. Synonym of *Merluccius* Rafinesque 1810. Merlucciidae: Merlucciinae.

Homaloptera van Hasselt 1823:133 [ref. 5963]. Fem. *Homaloptera ocellata* Van der Hoeven 1833. Type by subsequent monotypy. The two originally included species (*fasciata* and *javanica*) are nomina nuda (see Kottelat 1987:373 [ref. 5962]); first addition of species is in van der Hoeven 1833. Also spelled *Homalophra* by van Hasselt (p. 132), with Kottelat serving as first reviser, selecting *Homaloptera*. Valid (Kottelat 1985:267 [ref. 11441], Menon 1987:221 [ref. 14149], Kottelat & Chu 1988 [ref. 12840], Roberts 1989:88 [ref. 6439] dating to Hoeven 1833, Kottelat 1989:12 [ref. 13605]). Balitoridae: Balitorinae.

Homalopteroides Fowler 1905:476 [ref. 1370]. Masc. *Homaloptera wassinkii* Bleeker 1853:163. Type by original designation (also monotypic). Synonym of *Homaloptera* van Hasselt 1823 (Menon 1987:221 [ref. 14149], Roberts 1989:88 [ref. 6439]). Balitoridae: Balitorinae.

Homalopterula Fowler 1940:379 [ref. 1433]. Fem. *Homalopterula ripleyi* Fowler 1940:379. Type by original designation (also monotypic). Synonym of *Homaloptera* van Hasselt 1823 (Roberts 1989:88 [ref. 6439]). Balitoridae: Balitorinae.

Homalosoma Boulenger 1901:270 [ref. 5127]. Neut. *Homalosoma stenosoma* Boulenger 1901:270. Type by monotypy. Apparently in error for *Homaloptera*; not labeled a new genus in the original description or in list of new genera in volume; spelled consistently as *Homalosoma* in original description, on plate, etc.; see Hora 1932:309 [ref. 2208]. In the synonymy of *Vanmanenia* Hora 1932 (Chen 1980:97 [ref. 6901]). Balitoridae: Balitorinae.

Homatula (subgenus of *Barbatula*) Nichols 1925:2 [ref. 3178]. Fem. *Nemacheilus potanini* Günther 1896:218. Type by original designation (also monotypic). Valid (Kottelat 1990:19 [ref. 14137]). Balitoridae: Nemacheilinae.

Homea Fleming 1822:374 [ref. 5063]. Fem. *Homea banksii* Fleming 1822:375. Type by monotypy. Original not seen. Synonym of *Eptatretus* Cloquet 1819. Myxinidae: Eptatretinae.

Homesthes Gilbert in Jordan & Evermann 1898:2346, 2394 [ref. 2445]. Fem. *Homesthes caulopus* Gilbert in Jordan & Evermann 1898:2394. Type by original designation (also monotypic). Synonym of *Hypsoblennius* Gill 1861 (Bath 1977:186 [ref. 208]). Blenniidae.

Homodemus De Vis 1884:395 [ref. 1090]. Masc. *Homodemus cavifrons* De Vis 1884:396. Type by monotypy. Preoccupied by Fischer 1858 in Hymenoptera. In the synonymy of *Maccullochella* Whitley 1929. Percichthyidae.

Homodiaetus Eigenmann & Ward in Eigenmann, McAtee & Ward 1907:117 [ref. 1261]. Masc. *Homodiaetus anisitsi* Eigenmann & Ward in Eigenmann, McAtee & Ward 1907:119. Type by original designation (also monotypic). Valid (Burgess 1989:324 [ref. 12860], Pinna 1989 [ref. 12630], Malabarba 1989:145 [ref. 14217]). Trichomycteridae.

Homodon Brisout de Barneville 1847:133 [ref. 643]. Masc. *Centropristis georgianus* Valenciennes in Cuvier & Valenciennes 1831: 451. Type by subsequent designation. Two included species; earliest subsequent designation not researched. Objective synonym of *Arripis* Jenyns 1840. Arripidae.

Homolenus Rafinesque 1815:90 [ref. 3584]. Not available, name only. Unplaced genera.

Homoprion Holbrook 1855:168 [ref. 2184]. Masc. *Homoprion lanceolatus* Holbrook 1855. Type by monotypy. Synonym of *Stellifer* Oken 1817 (Chao 1978:40 [ref. 6983]). Sciaenidae.

Homostolus Smith & Radcliffe in Radcliffe 1913:146 [ref. 3579]. Masc. *Homostolus acer* Smith & Radcliffe in Radcliffe 1913:147. Type by original designation (also monotypic). Valid (Cohen & Nielsen 1978:32 [ref. 881], Machida in Masuda et al. 1984:100 [ref. 6441]). Ophidiidae: Neobythitinae.

Hopladelus see *Opladelus*. Ictaluridae.

Hoplarchus Kaup 1860:128 [ref. 2581]. Masc. *Hoplarchus pentacanthus* Kaup 1860:129. Type by subsequent designation. Two included species, apparently neither designated as type [article not fully translated]; earliest subsequent designation probably Eigenmann 1910:475 [ref. 1224]. Synonym of *Cichlasoma* Swainson 1839. Cichlidae.

Hoplerythrinus Gill 1896:208 [ref. 1739]. Masc. *Erythrinus unitaeniatus* Agassiz in Spix & Agassiz 1829:42. Type by monotypy. Valid (Géry 1977:103 [ref. 1597], Géry et al. 1987 [ref. 6001]). Erythrinidae.

Hopliancistrus Isbrücker & Nijssen 1989:543 [ref. 13622]. Masc. *Hopliancistrus tricomis* Isbrücker & Nijssen 1989:543. Type by original designation (also monotypic). Loricariidae.

Hoplias Gill 1903:1016 [ref. 1786]. Masc. *Esox malabaricus* Bloch 1794:149. Type by being a replacement name. Replacement for *Macrodon* Müller 1842, preoccupied by Schinz 1822 in fishes. Valid (Géry 1977:102 [ref. 1597], Malabarba 1989:127 [ref. 14217]). Erythrinidae.

Hoplichthys Cuvier in Cuvier & Valenciennes 1829:264 [ref. 998]. Masc. *Hoplichthys langsdorfii* Cuvier in Cuvier & Valenciennes 1829:194. Type by monotypy. Spelled *Oplichthys* several times on p. 264, *Hoplichthys* in table of contents; technical first reviser not located. Valid (Ochiai in Masuda et al. 1984:322 [ref. 6441], Smith 1986:486 [ref. 5712], Paxton et al. 1989:473 [ref. 12442]). Hoplichthyidae.

Hoplisoma Swainson 1838:336 [ref. 4302]. Neut. *Cataphractus punctatus* Bloch 1794:377. Type by original designation (also monotypic). Also in Swainson 1839:188, 189, 304 [ref. 4303]. *Hoplosoma* Agassiz 1846:185, 186 [ref. 64] is an unjustified emendation. Synonym of *Corydoras* Lacepède 1803 (Nijssen & Isbrücker 1980:192 [ref. 6910]). Callichthyidae.

Hoplites see *Aplites*. Centrarchidae.

Hoplobrotula Gill 1863:253 [ref. 1688]. Fem. *Brotula armata* Temminck & Schlegel 1846:255. Type by original designation (also monotypic). Misspelled *Haplobrotula* in Zoological Record for 1921 and in Gilchrist 1922:76 [ref. 1648]. Valid (Cohen & Nielsen 1978:19 [ref. 881], Machida in Masuda et al. 1984:100 [ref. 6441], Nielsen & Cohen 1986:348 [ref. 5700], Paxton et al. 1989:312 [ref. 12442]). Ophidiidae: Neobythitinae.

Hoplocharax Géry 1966:286 [ref. 1589]. Masc. *Hoplocharax goethei* Géry 1966:291. Type by original designation (also monotypic). Valid (Géry 1977:314 [ref. 1597]). Characidae.

Hoplochromis (subgenus of *Chromis*) Fowler 1918:66 [ref. 1396]. Masc. *Heliastes caeruleus* Cuvier in Cuvier & Valenciennes 1830:496. Type by original designation (also monotypic). Pomacentridae.

Hoplocoryphis Gill 1862:127 [ref. 1659]. *Schedophilus maculatus* Günther 1860:412. Type by original designation (also monotypic). Synonym of *Schedophilus* Cocco 1839 (Haedrich 1967:59 [ref. 5357]). Centrolophidae.

Hoplocottus Kaup 1858:339 [ref. 2580]. Masc. *Podabrus cottoides* Richardson 1850:13. Type by subsequent designation. Type apparently first designated by Jordan 1919:282 [ref. 2410]. Synonym of *Pseudoblennius* Temminck & Schlegel 1850. Cottidae.

Hoplodoras Eigenmann 1925:304, 310 [ref. 1244]. Masc. *Doras uranoscopus* Eigenmann & Eigenmann 1888:159. Type by original designation (also monotypic). Misspelled by Eigenmann once as *Haplodoras* on p. 311 and *Hoplodoros* on fig. 12c; correctly *Hoplodoras* in key and main account. First reviser not investigated. Valid (Burgess 1989:224 [ref. 12860]). Doradidae.

Hoplolatilus Günther 1887:550 [ref. 2014]. Masc. *Latilus fronticinctus* Günther 1887:550. Type by monotypy. Valid (Randall & Dooley 1974 [ref. 5336], Dooley 1978:62 [ref. 5499], Klausewitz et al. 1978 [ref. 5337], Randall 1981 [ref. 5495], Araga in Masuda et al. 1984:152 [ref. 6441], Heemstra 1986:614 [ref. 5660], Paxton et al. 1989:566 [ref. 12442], Allen & Kuiter 1989 [ref. 13504]). Malacanthidae: Latilinae.

Hoplomyzon Myers 1942:94 [ref. 3121]. Masc. *Hoplomyzon atrizona* Myers 1942:95. Type by original designation (also monotypic). Misspelled *Haplomyzon* in Zoological Record for 1943. Valid (Stewart 1985:5 [ref. 5239], Mees 1988:90 [ref. 6401], Burgess 1989:304 [ref. 12860]). Aspredinidae: Bunocephalinae.

Hoplonotus Guichenot 1866:[3] [ref. 1944]. Masc. *Trigla polyommata* Richardson 1839:96. Type by monotypy. Preoccupied by Schmidt 1846 in Coleoptera, replaced by *Pterygotrigla* Waite 1899. Objective synonym of *Pterygotrigla* Waite 1899 (Paxton et al. 1989:456 [ref. 12442]). Triglidae: Triglinae.

Hoplopagrus Gill 1861:78 [ref. 1770]. Masc. *Hoplopagrus guntherii* Gill 1862:253. Type by subsequent monotypy. Genus described without species, except "... in testimony of his appreciation... rendered by Dr. Günther... [Gill] would dedicate it [species] to that gentleman." Species named in 1862. Valid (Johnson 1980:10 [ref. 13553], Allen 1985:30 [ref. 6843], Akazaki & Iwatsuki 1986 [ref. 6316]). Lutjanidae.

Hoplophycis Kaup 1858:92 [ref. 2576]. Fem. *Hoplophycis lalandi* Kaup 1858:93. Type by monotypy. Ophidiidae: Ophidiinae.

Hoplopomus see *Oplopomus*. Gobiidae.

Hoplosebastes Schmidt 1929:194 [ref. 3936]. Masc. *Hoplosebastes armatus* Schmidt 1929:194. Type by monotypy. Valid (Shimizu in Masuda et al. 1984:314 [ref. 6441]). Scorpaenidae: Scorpaeninae.

Hoplosternum Gill 1858:395 [ref. 1750]. Neut. *Callichthys laevigatus* Valenciennes in Cuvier & Valenciennes 1840:314. Type by original designation. Spelled *Hoplosternon* by Bleeker 1862:391 [ref. 391]. Valid (Gosline 1940:6 [ref. 6489], Burgess 1989:364 [ref. 12860], Malabarba 1989:148 [ref. 14217]). Callichthyidae.

Hoplostethus Cuvier in Cuvier & Valenciennes 1829:469 [ref. 998]. Masc. *Hoplostethus mediterraneus* Cuvier in Cuvier & Valenciennes 1829:469. Type by monotypy. Valid (Nielsen 1973:340 [ref. 6885], Woods & Sonoda 1973:305 [ref. 6899], Paulin 1979:73 [ref. 6918], Yamakawa in Masuda et al. 1984:109 [ref. 6441], Maul in Whitehead et al. 1986:750 [ref. 13676], Heemstra 1986:411 [ref. 5660], Kotlyar 1986:100 [ref. 6004], Paxton et al. 1989:366 [ref. 12442]). Trachichthyidae.

Hoplotilapia Hilgendorf 1888:77 [ref. 2168]. Fem. *Paratilapia retrodens* Hilgendorf 1888:76. Type by monotypy. Valid (Greenwood 1980:72 [ref. 1899]). Cichlidae.

Hoplunnis Kaup 1860:19 [ref. 2586]. Masc. *Hoplunnis schmidti* Kaup 1860:19. Type by monotypy. Valid (Smith & Castle 1982:19 [ref. 5453], Smith 1989:576 [ref. 13285]). Nettastomatidae.

Horabagrus Jayaram 1955:261 [ref. 5614]. Masc. *Pseudobagrus brachysoma* Günther 1864:86. Type by original designation (also monotypic). Valid (Jayaram 1977:19 [ref. 7005], Jayaram 1981:195 [ref. 6497], Burgess 1989:69 [ref. 12860]). Bagridae.

Horadandia Deraniyagala 1943:158 [1] [ref. 1118]. Fem. *Horadandia atukorali* Deraniyagala 1943:158 [1]. Type by original designation (also monotypic). On page one of separate [original pagination not checked]. Valid (Jayaram 1981:82 [ref. 6497]). Cyprinidae.

Horaglanis Menon 1950:60 [ref. 2980]. Masc. *Horaglanis krishnai* Menon 1950:64. Type by original designation (also monotypic). Valid (Jayaram 1981:272 [ref. 6497], Burgess 1989:147 [ref. 12860]). Clariidae.

Horaichthys Kulkarni 1940:385 [ref. 2697]. Masc. *Horaichthys setnai* Kulkarni 1940:385. Type by original designation (also monotypic). Valid (Jayaram 1981:292 [ref. 6497], Rosen & Parenti 1981:2 [ref. 5538], Collette et al. 1984:335 [ref. 11422]). Adrianichthyidae: Horaichthyinae.

Horalabiosa Silas 1954:28 [ref. 4025]. Fem. *Horalabiosa joshuai* Silas 1954:30. Type by original designation (also monotypic). Cyprinidae.

Horiomyzon Stewart 1986:47 [ref. 5777]. Masc. *Horiomyzon retropinnatus* Stewart 1986:48. Type by original designation (also monotypic). Pimelodidae.

Hospilabrus Whitley 1931:334 [ref. 4672]. Masc. *Malapterus reticulatus* Valenciennes in Cuvier & Valenciennes 1839:355. Type by being a replacement name. Unneeded replacement for *Malap-*

terus Valenciennes 1839, apparently not preoccupied by *Malapterus* Jarocki 1822 an incorrect subsequent spelling of *Malapterurus* Lacepède in fishes. Labridae.

Hostia (subgenus of *Pseudotolithus*) Trewavas 1962:170 [ref. 4455]. Fem. *Corvina moorii* Günther 1865:48. Type by original designation (also monotypic). Synonym of *Pseudotolithus* Bleeker 1863 (Daget & Trewavas 1986:335 [ref. 6211]). Sciaenidae.

Howella Ogilby 1899:734 [ref. 3277]. Fem. *Howella brodiei* Ogilby 1899:734. Type by monotypy. Family placement uncertain; sometimes placed in the Percichthyidae; placement here follows Johnson 1984:465 [ref. 9681]. Valid (Tortonese 1973:366 [ref. 7192], Mouchizuki in Masuda et al. 1984:125 [ref. 6441], Tortonese in Whitehead et al. 1986:795 [ref. 13676], Heemstra 1986:562 [ref. 5660], Fraser 1972:41 [ref. 5195], Paxton et al. 1989:511 [ref. 12442]). Percoidei.

Hozukius Matsubara 1934:199 [ref. 2903]. Masc. *Helicolenus emblemarius* Jordan & Starks 1904:127. Type by original designation (also monotypic). Valid (Barsukov & Fedorov 1975 [ref. 7011], Washington et al. 1984:440 [ref. 13660], Amaoka in Masuda et al. 1984:313 [ref. 6441], Ishida & Amaoka 1986 [ref. 11443]). Scorpaenidae: Sebastinae.

Hubbesia Jordan 1919:310 [ref. 2415]. Fem. *Menidia gilberti* Jordan & Bollman 1889:155. Type by monotypy. Synonym of *Membras* Bonaparte 1836 (Chernoff 1986:239 [ref. 5847]). Atherinidae: Menidiinae.

Hubbsichthys Schultz 1949:95 [ref. 3967]. Masc. *Hubbsichthys laurae* Schultz 1949:96. Type by original designation (also monotypic). Synonym of *Poecilia* Bloch & Schneider 1801 (Parenti 1981:546 [ref. 7066]); placement uncertain (R. M. Bailey). Poeciliidae.

Hubbsiella Breder 1936:6 [ref. 634]. Fem. *Menidia clara* Evermann & Jenkins 1891:136. Type by original designation (also monotypic). Synonym of *Leuresthes* Jordan & Gilbert 1880 (White 1985:17 [ref. 13551]). Atherinidae: Atherinopsinae.

Hubbsina de Buen 1940:135 [ref. 688]. Fem. *Hubbsina turneri* de Buen 1940:135. Type by monotypy. Valid (Uyeno et al. 1983:505 [ref. 6818]). Goodeidae.

Hucho (subgenus of *Salmo*) Günther 1866:125 [ref. 1983]. Masc. *Salmo hucho* Linnaeus 1758:309. Type by monotypy, only one species mentioned (also by absolute tautonymy). Proposed somewhat conditionally (but available), and probably can be interpreted as proposed as a subgenus of *Salmo*. Valid (Araga in Masuda et al. 1984:36 [ref. 6441], Kendall & Behnke 1984:144 [ref. 13638]). Salmonidae: Salmoninae.

Hudsonius Girard 1856:210 [ref. 1810]. Masc. *Hudsonius fluviatilis* Girard 1856:210 (= *Clupea hudsonia* Clinton 1824:49). Type by subsequent designation. Type designated by Bleeker 1863:211 [ref. 397] and 1863:32 [ref. 4859]. *H. fluviatilis* Girard is an unneeded substitute for *C. hudsonia* Clinton. Synonym of *Notropis* Rafinesque 1818 (Gilbert 1978:15 [ref. 7042]). Cyprinidae.

Hughichthys Schultz 1943:131, 136 [ref. 3957]. Masc. *Cirrhites melanotus* Günther 1874:72. Type by original designation (also monotypic). Correct spelling for genus of type species is *Cirrhitus*. Cirrhitidae.

Huigobio Fang 1938:239 [ref. 1305]. Masc. *Huigobio chenshienensis* Fang 1938:239. Type by monotypy. Misspelled *Hingobio* in Zoological Record for 1938. Synonym of *Microphysogobio* Mori 1934 (Banarescu & Nalbant 1973:244 [ref. 173]); valid (Lu, Luo & Chen 1977:530 [ref. 13495]). Cyprinidae.

Humefordia Whitley 1931:334 [ref. 4672]. Fem. *Aphareus thompsoni* Fowler 1923:382. Type by being a replacement name. Replacement for *Fares* Jordan, Evermann & Tanaka 1927, preoccupied according to Whitley [not investigated]. Synonym of *Aphareus* Cuvier 1830 (Allen 1985:18 [ref. 6843]). Lutjanidae.

Huro Cuvier in Cuvier & Valenciennes 1828:124 [ref. 997]. Masc. *Huro nigricans* Cuvier in Cuvier & Valenciennes 1828:124. Type by monotypy. Synonym of *Micropterus* Lacepède 1802 (Bailey & Hubbs 1949:17 [ref. 11647]). Centrarchidae.

Huso Brandt & Ratzeburg 1833:3, 349 [ref. 619]. Masc. *Acipenser huso* Linnaeus 1758:238. Type by absolute tautonymy. As *Husones*, a group within *Acipenser*. According to Fowler 1972:205 [ref. 9327], *Huso* is predated by *Ichthyocolla* Geoffroy St. hilaire 1767. Valid (Svetovidov 1973:82 [ref. 7169], Svetovidov in Whitehead et al. 1984:225 [ref. 13675], Nakaya in Masuda et al. 1984:18 [ref. 6441]). Acipenseridae: Acipenserinae.

Huttonichthys (subgenus of *Merluccius*) Whitley 1937:122 [ref. 4689]. Masc. *Gadus australis* Hutton 1872:45, 115. Type by original designation (also monotypic). Synonym of *Merluccius* Rafinesque 1810. Merlucciidae: Merlucciinae.

Hyaloceratias Koefoed 1944:16 [ref. 2651]. Masc. *Hyaloceratias parri* Koefoed 1944:16. Type by monotypy. Based on larval males or more than one species. Synonym of *Linophryne* Collett 1886. Linophrynidae.

Hyalorhynchus Gilchrist & von Bonde 1924:4 [ref. 1649]. Masc. *Hyalorhynchus natalensis* Gilchrist & von Bonde 1924:4. Type by monotypy. Preoccupied by Ogilby 1910 in fishes, replaced by *Rhynchohyalus* Barnard 1925. Objective synonym of *Rhynchohyalus* Barnard 1925 (Cohen 1973:157 [ref. 6589], Paxton et al. 1989:170 [ref. 12442]). Opisthoproctidae.

Hyalorhynchus Ogilby 1910:118 [ref. 3289]. Masc. *Hyalorhynchus pellucidus* Ogilby 1910:118. Type by monotypy. Synonym of *Elates* Jordan & Seale 1907 (Paxton et al. 1989:466 [ref. 12242] based on placement of the type species). Platycephalidae.

Hyalosprattus (subgenus of *Hyperlophus*) Whitley 1936:25 [ref. 4687]. Masc. *Hyperlophus translucidus* McCulloch 1917:165. Type by original designation (also monotypic). Synonym of *Hyperlophus* Ogilby 1892 (Whitehead 1985:187 [ref. 5141]). Clupeidae.

Hybocharax (subgenus of *Cynopotamus*) Géry & Vu-Tân-Tuê 1963:240 [ref. 1602]. Masc. *Cynopotamus bipunctatus* Pellegrin 1909. Type by original designation. Synonym of *Cynopotamus* Valenciennes 1849 (Menezes 1976:22 [ref. 7073] in subfamily Cynopotaminae); as a valid subgenus of *Cynopotamus* (Géry 1977:306 [ref. 1597]). Characidae.

Hybognathus Agassiz 1855:223 [ref. 5839]. Masc. *Hybognathus nuchalis* Agassiz 1855:224. Type by original designation (also monotypic). Valid. Cyprinidae.

Hybopsis Agassiz 1854:358 [ref. 69]. Fem. *Hybopsis gracilis* Agassiz 1854:358. Type by subsequent designation. Type designated by Bleeker 1863:211 [ref. 397] and 1863:32 [ref. 4859], the use of "This genus is founded upon a small species from Huntsville." is not explicit enough for original designation. Valid (Mayden 1989: 25 [ref. 12555]); subgenus of *Notropis* Rafinesque 1818 (Coburn & Cavender, in prep.). Cyprinidae.

Hyborhynchus Agassiz 1855:222 [ref. 5839]. Masc. *Minnilus notatus* Rafinesque 1820:236. Type by original designation (also monotypic). Misspelled *Hyborrhynchus* in Zoological Record for 1876. Synonym of *Pimephales* Rafinesque 1820. Cyprinidae.

Hydrargira Lacepède 1803:378 [ref. 4930]. Fem. *Hydrargira* *swampina* Lacepède 1803:378, 379. Type by monotypy. *Hydrargyra* Rafinesque 1815:88 [ref. 3584] and authors is an incorrect subsequent spelling or unjustified emendation. Synonym of *Fundulus* Lacepède 1803 (Bailey & Wiley 1976 [ref. 7090], Parenti 1981:494 [ref. 7066]). Cyprinodontidae: Fundulinae.

Hydrocionichthys Travassos 1952:142 [ref. 4450]. Masc. *Hydrocynus lucius* Cuvier 1816:168. Type by being a replacement name. Apparently an unneeded replacement for *Hydrocynus* Cuvier 1816, not preoccupied. See account of *Hydrocynus*. Objective synonym of *Hydrocynus* Cuvier 1816 (Paugy 1984:169 [ref. 6183]). Alestiidae.

Hydrocynus (subgenus of *Salmo*) Cuvier 1816:167 [ref. 993]. *Hydrocynus lucius* Cuvier 1816:168. Type by subsequent designation. Type apparently designated first by Eigenmann 1910:446 [ref. 1224] (see Travassos 1951 [ref. 4450]), and not by Agassiz in Spix & Agassiz 1829:67 [ref. 13]. *Hydrocion* Duméril 1856 and *Hydrocinus* Boulenger (ex Cuvier) 1909 are unjustified emendations or incorrect subsequent spellings. Type apparently not *H. forskalii* Cuvier. *Hydrocionichthys* Travassos 1952 is an unneeded replacement. Valid (Géry 1977:54 [ref. 1597], Paugy 1984:169 [ref. 6183]). Alestiidae.

Hydrocyon Cuvier 1819:353 [ref. 1017]. Masc. Not intended as new; same as *Hydrocynus*, and can be regarded as an incorrect subsequent spelling; see account of *Hydocynus* Cuvier 1816. In the synonymy of *Hydrocynus* Cuvier 1816. Alestiidae.

Hydrocyonoides Castelnau 1861:66 [ref. 767]. Masc. *Hydrocyonoides cuvieri* Castelnau 1861:66. Type by monotypy. Synonym of *Hepsetus* Swainson 1838 (Roberts 1984:138 [ref. 6182]). Hepsetidae.

Hydrolagus Gill 1862:331 [ref. 1668]. Masc. *Chimaera colliei* Lay & Bennett 1839:71. Type by monotypy. Valid (Krefft 1973:78 [ref. 7166], Stehmann & Bürkel in Whitehead et al. 1984:214 [ref. 13675], Nakaya in Masuda et al. 1984:17 [ref. 6441], Compagno 1986:145 [ref. 5648], Paxton et al. 1989:97 [ref. 12442]). Chimaeridae.

Hydrolycus Müller & Troschel 1844:93 [ref. 3070]. Masc. *Hydrocyon scomberoides* Cuvier 1819:357. Type by monotypy. Type species confirmed and genus name placed on Official List (Opinion 1581). Valid (Géry 1977:299 [ref. 1597], Vari 1983:5 [ref. 5419] in Characidae, Géry 1986 [ref. 6019], see Gé'ry & Mahnert 1988 [ref. 6881]). Cynodontidae.

Hydronus Minding 1832:83 [ref. 3022]. *Hydronus marlucius* Minding 1832:84 (= *Gadus merluccius* Linnaeus 1758:254). Type by monotypy. Synonym of *Merluccius* Rafinesque 1810 (Svetovidov 1973:300 [ref. 7169]). Merlucciidae: Merlucciinae.

Hydropardus Reinhardt 1849:46 [ref. 3692]. Masc. *Hydropardus rapax* Reinhardt 1849:46. Type by monotypy. Synonym of *Rhaphiodon* Agassiz 1829. Characidae.

Hydrophlox Jordan in Jordan & Brayton 1878:18 [ref. 2436]. Fem. *Hybopsis rubricroceus* Cope 1868:231. Type by original designation. Synonym of *Notropis* Rafinesque 1818, but as a valid subgenus (Gilbert 1978:16 [ref. 7042], Mayden 1989:41 [ref. 12555]). Cyprinidae.

Hygophum (subgenus of *Myctophum*) Bolin (ex Tåning) 1939:113 [ref. 508]. Neut. *Scopelus hygomi* Lütken 1892:237, 256. Type by original designation. Appeared first in Tåning 1932:133 [ref. 5031], but not available, after 1930 without designation of type species (Art. 13b) or distinguishing characters. Can date to Bolin 1939 as above. Valid (Krefft & Bekker 1973:183 [ref. 7181], Paxton 1979:11 [ref. 6440], Hulley in Whitehead et al. 1984:433 [ref. 13675], Moser et al. 1984:219 [ref. 13645], Fujii in Masuda et al. 1984:65 [ref. 6441], Hulley 1986:301 [ref. 5672], Paxton et al. 1989:261 [ref. 12442]). Myctophidae.

Hygrogonus Günther 1862:303 [ref. 1969]. Masc. *Lobotes ocellatus* Agassiz in Spix & Agassiz 1829:129. Type by monotypy. Objective synonym of *Astronotus* Swainson 1839 (Kullander 1986:60 [ref. 12439]). Cichlidae.

Hylomyzon Agassiz 1855:90 [ref. 71]. Masc. *Catostomus nigricans* Lesueur 1817:102. Type by original designation (also monotypic). Synonym of *Hypentelium* Rafinesque 1818. Catostomidae.

Hylopanchax Poll & Lambert 1965:623 [ref. 3535]. Masc. *Hypsopanchax silvestris* Poll & Lambert 1958:328. Type by original designation. Synonym of *Procatopus* Boulenger 1904 (Parenti 1981:511 [ref. 7066]); valid (Wildekamp et al. 1986:188 [ref. 6198]). Cyprinodontidae: Aplocheilichthyinae.

Hymenocephalus Giglioli in Giglioli & Issel 1884:228 [ref. 5325]. Masc. *Hymenocephalus italicus* Giglioli in Giglioli & Issel 1884:228. Type by original designation (also monotypic). Species appeared first as *Malacocephalus laevis* [Lowe] in Giglioli 1882:535 [ref. 1618] without description, to which name *Hymenocephalus italicus* was applied by Giglioli (1883:199 [ref. 1620]) without description. Available as above. Valid (Marshall 1973:289 [ref. 7194], Marshall & Iwamoto 1973:601 [ref. 6966], Iwamoto 1979:140 [ref. 2311], Fahay & Markle 1984:274 [ref. 13653], Okamura in Masuda et al. 1984:93 [ref. 6441], Paxton et al. 1989:327 [ref. 12442]). Macrouridae: Macrourinae.

Hymenogadus (subgenus of *Hymenocephalus*) Gilbert & Hubbs 1920:521 [ref. 1638]. Masc. *Hymenocephalus gracilis* Gilbert & Hubbs 1920:522. Type by original designation. Synonym of *Hymenocephalus* Giglioli 1884 (Iwamoto 1979:140 [ref. 2311]); valid (Okamura in Masuda et al. 1984:93 [ref. 6441]). Macrouridae: Macrourinae.

Hymenolomus Duméril 1870:607 [ref. 1147]. Masc. *Hymenolomus richardsonii* Duméril 1870:52 (= *Syngnathus hymenolomus* Richardson 1845:52). Type by monotypy. Duméril's *S. richardsonii* is an unneeded substitute for *S. hymenolomus* Richardson. Apparently predates *Protocampus* Günther 1870 [but months of publication not researched]. Synonym of *Entelurus* Duméril 1870 (Wheeler 1973:278 [ref. 7190]). Syngnathidae: Syngnathinae.

Hymenphysa McClelland 1839:443 [ref. 2923]. Fem. *Cobitis dario* Hamilton 1822:354, 394. Type by subsequent designation. Earliest subsequent designation not researched. Spelled *Hymenophysa* by Bleeker 1858-59:303 [ref. 366] and by Günther 1868:366 [ref. 1990] and authors; original spelling probably should be used; Bleeker's spelling is an incorrect subsequent spelling. Synonym of *Botia* Gray 1831, but as a valid subgenus (see Mirza et al. 1981:106 [ref. 5390]); synonym of *Botia* Gray 1831 (Roberts 1989:101 [ref. 6439]). Cobitidae: Botiinae.

Hynnis Cuvier in Cuvier & Valenciennes 1833:195 [ref. 1002]. Fem. *Hynnis goreensis* Cuvier in Cuvier & Valenciennes 1833:195. Type by monotypy. Synonym of *Alectis* Rafinesque 1815 (Daget & Smith-Vaniz 1986:308 [ref. 6207]). Carangidae.

Hynnodus Gilbert 1905:617 [ref. 1631]. Masc. *Hynnodus atherinoides* Gilbert 1905:618. Type by original designation, also monotypic; type included in parentheses after genus, second species doubtfully referred to genus. Synonym of *Epigonus* Rafinesque 1810 (Mayer 1974:151 [ref. 6007]). Epigonidae.

Hyomacrurus (subgenus of *Coryphaenoides*) Gilbert & Hubbs 1920:422 [ref. 1638]. Masc. *Macrourus hyostomus* Smith & Radcliffe 1912:121. Type by original designation (also monotypic). Appeared as *Hyostomus* Gilbert & Hubbs MS in Jordan (Aug.) 1920:570 [ref. 4905] by error; name changed in proof sheets to *Hyomacrurus* and published in Gilbert & Hubbs 1920 as above. Valid (Marshall 1973:564 [ref. 6965], Fahay & Markle 1984:274 [ref. 13653]). Probably valid (see Iwamoto & Sazonov 1988:39 [ref. 6228]). Macrouridae: Macrourinae.

Hyoprorus Kölliker 1853:101 [ref. 2680]. Masc. *Hyoprorus messanensis* Kölliker 1853:102. Type by monotypy. Species originally spelled *messanensis*, perhaps in error for *messinaensis*. Synonym of *Nettastoma* Rafinesque 1810 (Smith et al. 1981:538 [ref. 6158], Smith 1989:604 [ref. 13285]). Nettastomatidae.

Hyostoma Agassiz 1854:305 [ref. 69]. Neut. *Hyostoma newmanii* Agassiz 1854:305. Type by monotypy. Synonym of subgenus *Etheostoma* of genus *Etheostoma* Rafinesque 1819 (Collette & Banarescu 1977:1456 [ref. 5845]). Percidae.

Hyostomus Jordan (ex Gilbert & Hubbs) 1920:570 [ref. 4905]. Masc. *Macrourus hyostomus* Smith & Radcliffe 1912:121. Type by original designation (also monotypic). Name taken from Gilbert & Hubbs manuscript but published as *Hyomacrurus* by Gilbert & Hubbs 1920 [ref. 1638], *Hyostomus* published Aug. 1920. In the synonymy of *Hyomacrurus* Gilbert & Hubbs 1920. Macrouridae: Macrourinae.

Hypacantha Lacepède 1810:67 [ref. 3595]. Fem. See *Hypacantus* Rafinesque. Also appears with this spelling as name only in Rafinesque 1815:84 [ref. 3584]. On Official Index (Opinion 1124). Carangidae.

Hypacantus Rafinesque 1810:43 [ref. 3594]. Masc. *Centronotus vadigo* Lacepède 1802:310. Type by subsequent designation. On Official Index for purposes of priority (Opinion 1124); the incorrect subsequent spellings *Hypacantha* Rafinesque and *Hypacanthus* Rafinesque also placed on Official Index (Opinion 1124). Type perhaps validly designated by Smith-Vaniz & Staiger 1973:228 [ref. 7106] with genus spelling *Hypacanthus*. In the synonymy of *Lichia* Cuvier 1816 (Smith-Vaniz & Staiger 1973:228 [ref. 7106] as *Hypacanthus*). Carangidae.

Hypanus Rafinesque 1818:274 [ref. 5087]. Masc. *Raja say* Lesueur 1817:42. Original not seen. Apparently a synonym *Dasyatis* Rafinesque 1810. Dasyatidae.

Hypargyrus Forbes in Gilbert 1884:200 [ref. 1622]. Masc. *Hybopsis tuditanus* Cope 1866:381. Type by original designation (also monotypic). Authorship unclear, perhaps most of description is by Gilbert; footnote indicates genus name is from Forbes' manuscript; Jordan & Evermann 1896:252 [ref. 2443] credit to Forbes. Synonym of *Pimephales* Rafinesque 1820, of subgenus *Hyborhynchus* Agassiz 1855. Cyprinidae.

Hypeneus Agassiz 1846:190 [ref. 64]. Masc. *Mullus vittatus* Forsskål 1775:31. Unjustified emendation of *Upeneus* Cuvier 1829. In the synonymy of *Upeneus* Cuvier 1829 (Hureau 1973:403 [ref. 7197]). Mullidae.

Hypentelium (subgenus of *Exoglossum*) Rafinesque 1818:421 [ref. 3588]. Neut. *Exoglossum macropterum* Rafinesque 1818:420. Type by monotypy. Valid (Buth 1980 [ref. 6942]). Catostomidae.

Hyperchoristus Gill 1883:256 [ref. 1724]. Masc. *Hyperchoristus tanneri* Gill 1883:256. Type by monotypy. Synonym of *Echiostoma* Lowe 1843 (Morrow in Morrow & Gibbs 1964:480 [ref. 6962], Morrow 1973:137 [ref. 7175]). Melanostomiidae.

Hypergastromyzon Roberts 1989:91 [ref. 6439]. Masc. *Hypergastromyzon humilis* Roberts 1989:92. Type by original designation (also monotypic). Misspelled once as *Hypogastromyzon* in key on p. 71, elsewhere as above. Balitoridae: Balitorinae.

Hyperistius Gill 1864:92 [ref. 1706]. Masc. *Centrarchus hexacanthus* Valenciennes in Cuvier & Valenciennes 1831:459. Type by original designation (also monotypic). Synonym of *Pomoxis* Rafinesque 1818. Centrarchidae.

Hyperlophus Ogilby 1892:26 [ref. 3266]. Masc. *Clupea sprattellides* Ogilby 1892:24. Text somewhat unclear, but type apparently by monotypy; also designated by Ogilby 1897:71 [ref. 3272]. Valid (Grande 1985:246 [ref. 6466], Whitehead 1985:187 [ref. 5141], Paxton et al. 1989:154 [ref. 12442]). Clupeidae.

Hyperoglyphe Günther 1859:337 [ref. 1961]. Fem. *Diagramma porosa* Richardson 1845:26. Type by monotypy. Valid (Haedrich 1967:54 [ref. 5357], Haedrich 1973:560 [ref. 7216], McDowall 1981:105 [ref. 5356], Horn 1984:628 [ref. 13637], Nakabo in Masuda et al. 1984:234 [ref. 6441], Haedrich in Whitehead et al. 1986:1179 [ref. 13677], Haedrich 1986:843 [ref. 5659], Karrer 1986 [ref. 6762]). Centrolophidae.

Hyperopisus Gill 1862:139 [ref. 1661]. Masc. *Mormyrus dorsalis* Geoffroy St. Hilaire 1809:276, Pl. 8. Type by monotypy. Valid (Taverne 1972:55 [ref. 6367] but with wrong type species, Gosse 1984:77 [ref. 6169]). Mormyridae.

Hyperoplus (subgenus of *Ammodytes*) Günther 1862:384 [ref. 1969]. Masc. *Ammodytes lanceolatus* Sauvage 1825:262. Type by monotypy. Described as a section of *Ammodytes*. Synonym of *Ammodytes* Linnaeus 1758 (authors); valid (Wheeler 1973:447 [ref. 7190], Stevens et al. 1984:574 [ref. 13671], Reay in Whitehead et al. 1986:949 [ref. 13676]). Ammodytidae.

Hyperphotops (subgenus of *Diaphus*) Fraser-Brunner 1949:1066 [ref. 1496]. Masc. *Nyctophus gemellari* Cocco 1838:186. Type by original designation. Synonym of *Lobianchia* Gatti 1904 (Bolin 1959:18 [ref. 503], Nafpaktitis 1968:11 [ref. 6979], Krefft & Bekker 1973:191 [ref. 7181], Paxton 1979:15 [ref. 6440]). Myctophidae.

Hyperprosopon Gibbons 1854:2, col. 3 [ref. 5207]. Neut. *Hyperprosopon argenteus* [sic] Gibbons 1854:2, col. 3. Type by monotypy. Also appeared in Gibbons 1854:124 [ref. 1610]. Species should be spelled *argenteum*. *Hyperprosodon* is a misspelling. Valid (Tarp 1952:30 [ref. 12250]). Embiotocidae.

Hyphalonedrus Goode 1881:483 [ref. 1833]. *Hyphalonedrus chalybeius* Goode 1881:483, 484. Type by original designation (also monotypic). Synonym of *Chlorophthalmus* Bonaparte 1840. Chlorophthalmidae: Chlorophthalminae.

Hyphalophis McCosker & Böhlke 1982:116 [ref. 2935]. Masc. *Hyphalophis devius* McCosker & Böhlke 1982:117. Type by original designation (also monotypic). Valid (McCosker et al. 1989:367 [ref. 13288]). Ophichthidae: Ophichthinae.

Hyphessobrycon (subgenus of *Hemigrammus*) Durbin in Eigenmann 1908:100 [ref. 1221]. Masc. *Hemigrammus compressus* Meek in Eigenmann & Ogle 1908:14. Type by original designation (also monotypic). Genus credited to Durbin based on footnote on p. 99. Valid (Géry 1977:458 [ref. 1597], Malabarba 1989:134 [ref. 14217]). Characidae.

Hypleurochilus Gill 1861:44 [ref. 1766]. Masc. *Blennius multifilis* Girard 1858:168. Type by subsequent designation. Type designated by Gill 1861:168 [ref. 1775] and by Jordan & Gilbert 1883:758 [ref. 2476]. Valid (Bath 1973:527 [ref. 7212], Bath

1977:183 [ref. 208], Greenfield & Johnson 1981:69 [ref. 5580], Zander in Whitehead et al. 1986:1099 [ref. 13677], Bath 1986:355 [ref. 6217]). Blenniidae.

Hypnarce Waite 1902:180 [ref. 4559]. Fem. *Hypnos subnigerum* Duméril 1852:279. Type by being a replacement name. Apparently an unneeded replacement for *Hypnos* Duméril 1852, not preoccupied by *Hypna* Hübner 1816 in Lepidoptera. Spelled *Hypnarea* in index p. 9 to Zoological Record for 1902. Torpedinidae.

Hypnos Duméril 1852:277 [ref. 1148]. Masc. *Hypnos subnigrum* Duméril 1852:279. Type by monotypy. Apparently not preoccupied, *Hypnarce* Waite 1902 is an unneeded replacement. Valid (Paxton et al. 1989:60 [ref. 12442]). Torpedinidae.

Hypoatherina Schultz 1948:(8) 23 [ref. 3966]. Fem. *Atherina uisila* Jordan & Seale 1905:216. Type by original designation. Valid (Whitehead & Ivantsoff 1983:361 [ref. 5418], Yoshino in Masuda et al. 1984:119 [ref. 6441], Ivantsoff 1986:383 [ref. 6292], Ivantsoff & Kottelat 1988 [ref. 6856], Paxton et al. 1989:359 [ref. 12442], Kottelat 1989:16 [ref. 13605]). Atherinidae: Atherininae.

Hypocaranx (subgenus of *Caranx*) Klunzinger 1884:92 [ref. 2625]. Masc. *Scomber speciosus* Forsskål 1775:54. Type by subsequent designation. Type designated by Jordan 1920:429 [ref. 4905]. Objective synonym of *Gnathanodon* Bleeker 1851. Carangidae.

Hypoclinemus Chabanaud 1928:32 [ref. 783]. *Hypoclinemus paraguayensis* Chabanaud 1928:35. Type by subsequent designation. Two included species; earliest type designation not researched. Valid (Chapleau & Keast 1988:2799 [ref. 12625]). Achiridae.

Hypoclydonia Goode & Bean 1896:236 [ref. 1848]. Fem. *Hypoclydonia bella* Goode & Bean 1896:236. Type by monotypy. Synonym of *Synagrops* Günther 1887. Acropomatidae.

Hypocolpterus Fowler 1943:259 [ref. 1443]. Masc. *Hypocolpterus analis* Fowler 1943:261. Type by original designation (also monotypic). Valid (Isbrücker 1980:59 [ref. 2303], Heitmans et al. 1983 [ref. 5278], Burgess 1989:435 [ref. 12860]). Loricariidae.

Hypocritichthys Gill 1862:275 [ref. 1666]. Masc. *Hyperprosopon analis* Agassiz 1861:133. Type by monotypy. Synonym of *Hyperprosopon* Gibbons 1854, but as a valid subgenus (Tarp 1952:36 [ref. 12250]). Embiotocidae.

Hypodis Rafinesque 1810:41 [ref. 3594]. *Scomber glaucus* Linnaeus 1758:298. Type by subsequent designation (also subsequent monotypy). Originally without species, one species included and type designated by Jordan 1917:79 [ref. 2407]. Synonym of *Trachinotus* Lacepède 1801. Carangidae.

Hypodoras Eigenmann 1925:329 [ref. 1244]. Masc. *Hypodoras forficulatus* Eigenmann 1925:330. Type by original designation (also monotypic). Valid (Burgess 1989:223 [ref. 12860]). Doradidae.

Hypodytes Gistel 1848:VIII [ref. 1822]. Masc. *Apistus alatus* Cuvier in Cuvier & Valenciennes 1829:392. Type by being a replacement name. Apparently technically is a replacement for *Apistes* Cuvier. *Hypodytes* was proposed by Gistel as a replacement for "*Aspistes* Quoy, Astrol., Fisch.", but *Apistus* Cuvier was used by Quoy & Gaimard, not the earlier non-latinized "Apistes" Cuvier 1829. Should be treated as an objective synonym of *Apistus* Cuvier 1829. Valid (Nakabo in Masuda et al. 1984:319 [ref. 6441], Paxton et al. 1989:442 [ref. 12442] with wrong authorship). Scorpaenidae: Apistinae.

Hypogaleus (subgenus of *Galeorhinus*) Smith 1957:(585) 589 [ref. 4115]. Masc. *Galeorhinus (Hypogaleus) zanzibarensis* Smith 1957:589. Type by original designation (also monotypic). Only one species definitely referred to subgenus. Valid (Compagno 1984:393 [ref. 6846], Nakaya in Masuda et al. 1984:5 [ref. 6441], Bass et al. 1986:79 [ref. 5638], Paxton et al. 1989:81 [ref. 12442], Herman et al. 1988:106 [ref. 13267]). Triakidae: Galeorhininae.

Hypogymnogobius Bleeker 1874:318 [ref. 437]. Masc. *Gobius xanthozona* Bleeker 1849:5. Type by original designation (also monotypic). Synonym of *Brachygobius* Bleeker 1874 (Miller 1987:699 [ref. 6336]); valid (Miller 1989:376 [ref. 13540]). Gobiidae.

Hypohomus Cope 1870:449 [ref. 913]. Masc. *Cottogaster aurantiacus* Cope 1869:211. Type by monotypy. Misspelled *Hypochromus* in Zoological Record for 1871. Synonym of *Percina* Haldeman 1842, but as a valid subgenus (Page 1974:84 [ref. 3346], Collette & Banarescu 1977:1455 [ref. 5845]). Percidae.

Hypolophus Müller & Henle 1837:117 [ref. 3067]. Masc. *Raja sephen* Forsskål 1775:17. Also in Müller & Henle 1837:400 [ref. 13421] without species. Species added by Müller & Henle 1841:170 [ref. 3069] but earlier Bonaparte 1838:202 (p. 6 of separate) included one species and designated type (see p. 2 of separate). Spelled *Hyplophus* by Jordan 1923:104 [ref. 2421]. Valid (Compagno 1986:140 [ref. 5648]). Valid, but *Pastinachus* Rüppell 1828 may be a senior synonym (Paxton et al. 1989:43 [ref. 12442]). Dasyatidae.

Hypolycodes Hector 1881:194 [ref. 2080]. Masc. *Hypolycodes haastii* Hector 1881:194. Type by monotypy. Zoarcidae.

Hypomacrus Evermann & Seale 1907:101 [ref. 1285]. Masc. *Hypomacrus albaiensis* Evermann & Seale 1907:102. Type by original designation (also monotypic). Synonym of *Scorpaenodes* Bleeker 1857. Scorpaenidae: Scorpaeninae.

Hypomasticus (subgenus of *Leporinus*) Borodin 1929:272 [ref. 527]. Masc. *Leporinus mormyrops* Steindachner 1876:240. Type by original designation. Synonym of *Leporinus* Agassiz 1829, but as a valid subgenus (Géry 1977:158 [ref. 1597]). Curimatidae: Anostominae.

Hypomesus Gill 1862:15 [ref. 1655]. Masc. *Argentina pretiosa* Girard 1854:155. Type by monotypy. See *Mesopus* Gill 1862. Technical first reviser (if needed) selecting *Hypomesus* over *Mesopus* apparently Gill, but reference not researched. Valid (Uyeno in Masuda et al. 1984:33 [ref. 6441]). Osmeridae.

Hypophthalmichthys Bleeker 1859:433 [ref. 370]. Masc. *Leuciscus molitrix* Valenciennes in Cuvier & Valenciennes 1842:360. Type by subsequent designation. Apparently appeared first in key, without included species. Six species (3 with question) included by Bleeker 1860:283, 405 [ref. 380]. Type designated by Bleeker 1863:28 [ref. 4859] and 1863:201 [ref. 397]. Valid (Yang 1964:225 [ref. 13500], Howes 1981:45 [ref. 14200], Jayaram 1981:76 [ref. 6497], Sawada in Masuda et al. 1984:58 [ref. 6441], Bogutskaya 1987:936 [ref. 13521], Bogutskaya 1988:107 [ref. 12754], Chen & Li in Chu & Chen 1989:99 [ref. 13584]). Cyprinidae.

Hypophthalmus Agassiz in Spix & Agassiz 1829:16 [ref. 13]. Masc. *Hypophthalmus edentatus* Agassiz in Spix & Agassiz 1829:14. Type by subsequent designation. Type designated by Bleeker 1862:15 [ref. 393] and 1863:109 [ref. 401] as *edentatus*. Treated as valid (Stewart 1986:667 et seq. [ref. 5211], Burgess 1989:294 [ref. 12860]), but genus dates to Cuvier 1829 (see Kottelat 1988:78 [ref. 13380]). Hypophthalmidae.

Hypophthalmus Cuvier 1829:293 [ref. 995]. Masc. *Hypophthalmus edentatus* Agassiz in Spix & Agassiz 1829:14. Type by subsequent designation. Type designated by Bleeker 1862:15 [ref. 393].

Cuvier's *Hypophthalmus* predates Agassiz's treatment (see Kottelat 1988:78 [ref. 13380]). Valid, with Cuvier as author (Kottelat 1988:78 [ref. 13380]). Hypophthalmidae.

Hypoplectrodes Gill 1862:236 [ref. 1664]. Masc. *Plectropoma nigrorubrum* Cuvier in Cuvier & Valenciennes 1828:402. Type by monotypy. Valid (Fischer 1980 [ref. 6905], Paxton et al. 1989:505 [ref. 12442], Anderson & Heemstra 1989:1002 [ref. 13526]). Serranidae: Anthiinae.

Hypoplectrus Gill 1861:98 [ref. 1772]. Masc. *Plectropoma puella* Cuvier in Cuvier & Valenciennes 1829:405. Type by monotypy. Valid (Kendall 1984:500 [ref. 13663]). Serranidae: Serraninae.

Hypopleuron Smith & Radcliffe in Radcliffe 1913:164 [ref. 3579]. Neut. *Hypopleuron caninum* Smith & Radcliffe in Radcliffe 1913:165. Type by original designation (also monotypic). Valid (Cohen & Nielsen 1978:33 [ref. 881], Paxton et al. 1989:312 [ref. 12442]). Ophidiidae: Neobythitinae.

Hypoplites Gill 1862:236 [ref. 1664]. Masc. *Mesoprion retrospinis* Valenciennes in Cuvier & Valenciennes 1830:407. Type by monotypy. Status uncertain based on questionable species placement (see Allen 1985:165 [ref. 6843]). Lutjanidae.

Hypopomus Gill 1864:152 [ref. 1698]. Fem. *Rhamphichthys mulleri* Kaup 1856:129. Type by monotypy. Valid (Mago-Leccia 1978:14 [ref. 5489], Malabarba 1989:157 [ref. 14217]). Gymnotidae: Hypopominae.

Hypopostomatinum Günther 1868:234 [ref. 5756]. *Hypoptopoma thoracatum* Günther 1868:477. Type by monotypy. As *Hypoptopoma* in Günther (June) 1868 [ref. 1992]. Appeared above (Sept.) as "*Hypoptopoma* (g. n. *Hypostomatinum*)"; reason for name change not stated; can be considered as name published in synonymy and perhaps never made available Objective synonym of *Hypoptopoma* Günther 1868. Loricariidae.

Hypoprion (subgenus of *Carcharias*) Müller & Henle 1838:34 [ref. 3069]. Masc. *Carcharias (Hypoprion) macloti* Müller & Henle 1838:34. Type by subsequent designation. Type designated by Gill 1862:401 [ref. 1783]. Synonym of *Carcharhinus* Blainville 1816 (Raschi et al. 1982 [ref. 6823], Garrick 1985:1 [ref. 5654], Compagno 1988:307 [ref. 13488]); valid (Nakaya in Masuda et al. 1984:6 [ref. 6441]). Carcharhinidae.

Hypoprionodon Gill 1862:400, 401 [ref. 1783]. Masc. *Carcharias (Hypoprion) hemiodon* Valenciennes in Müller & Henle 1841:35. Type by original designation (also monotypic). Also in Gill 1862:409 [ref. 4910]. Synonym of *Carcharhinus* Blainville 1816 (Compagno 1984:449 [ref. 6846], Compagno 1988:307 [ref. 13488]). Carcharhinidae.

Hypopterus Gill 1861:50 [ref. 1768]. Masc. *Psammoperca macroptera* Günther 1859:69. Type by original designation (also monotypic). Valid (Paxton et al. 1989:482 [ref. 12442]). Centropomidae: Latinae.

Hypoptopoma Günther 1868:477 [ref. 1992]. Neut. *Hypoptopoma thoracatum* Günther 1868:477. Type by monotypy. Also in Günther 1868:234 [ref. 5756]. Valid (Isbrücker 1980:86 [ref. 2303], Burgess 1989:439 [ref. 12860]). Loricariidae.

Hypoptychus Steindachner 1881:257 [ref. 4230]. Masc. *Hypoptychus dybowskii* Steindachner 1881:257. Type by monotypy. Valid (Fritzsche 1984 [ref. 13658], Ida in Masuda et al. 1984:83 [ref. 6441]). Hypoptychidae.

Hypopygus Hoedeman 1962:99 [ref. 12585]. Masc. *Hypopygus lepturus* Hoedeman 1962:99. Type by monotypy. Valid (see Mago-Leccia 1978:14 [ref. 5489]). Gymnotidae: Hypopominae.

Hyporhamphus Gill 1859:131 [ref. 1759]. Masc. *Hyporhamphus tricuspidatus* Gill 1859:131. Type by monotypy. Valid (Parin 1973:269 [ref. 7191], Parin et al. 1980:13 [ref. 6895], Collette et al. 1984:337 [ref. 11422], Yoshino in Masuda et al. 1984:79 [ref. 6441], Kottelat 1985:271 [ref. 11441], Collette 1986:163 [ref. 6197], Collette & Parin in Whitehead et al. 1986:622 [ref. 13676], Collette 1986:390 [ref. 5647], Collette & Su 1986:256 [ref. 5998], Paxton et al. 1989:337 [ref. 12442], Kottelat 1989:16 [ref. 13605]). Hemiramphidae.

Hyporthodus Gill 1861:98 [ref. 1772]. Masc. *Hyporthodus flavicaudus* Gill 1861:98. Type by monotypy. Synonym of *Epinephelus* Bloch 1793 (C. L. Smith 1971:103 [ref. 14102], Daget & Smith 1986:301 [ref. 6204]). Serranidae: Epinephelinae.

Hyposerranus (subgenus of *Serranus*) Klunzinger 1884:3 [ref. 2625]. Masc. *Serranus morrhua* Valenciennes in Cuvier & Valenciennes 1833:434. Type by subsequent designation. Type designated by Jordan 1920:429 [ref. 4905]. Synonym of *Epinephelus* Bloch 1793 (Smith 1971:103 [ref. 14102], Daget & Smith 1986:301 [ref. 6204]). Serranidae: Epinephelinae.

Hypostomus Lacepède 1803:144 [ref. 4930]. Masc. *Hypostomus guacari* Lacepède 1803:144 (= *Acipenser plecostomus* Linnaeus 1758:238). Type by monotypy. *H. guacari* Lacepède is an unneeded substitute for *A. plecostomus*. Valid (Isbrücker 1980:17 [ref. 2303], Weber 1987 [ref. 6241], Burgess 1989:430 [ref. 12860]). Loricariidae.

Hypsagonus Gill 1861:167 [ref. 1775]. Masc. *Aspidophorus quadricornis* Cuvier in Cuvier & Valenciennes 1829:221. Type by original designation (also monotypic). Valid (Washington et al. 1984:442 [ref. 13660], Kanayama in Masuda et al. 1984:331 [ref. 6441], Yabe 1985:123 [ref. 11522], Maeda & Amaoka 1988:60 [ref. 12616]). Agonidae.

Hypselecara Kullander 1986:232 [ref. 12439]. Fem. *Heros temporalis* Günther 1862:286. Type by original designation. Cichlidae.

Hypseleotris Gill 1863:270 [ref. 1691]. Fem. *Eleotris cyprinoides* Valenciennes in Cuvier & Valenciennes 1837:248. Type by original designation (also monotypic). Valid (Akihito in Masuda et al. 1984:241 [ref. 6441], Hoese 1986:809 [ref. 5670], Maugé 1986:394 [ref. 6218], Birdsong et al. 1988:182 [ref. 7303]). Eleotridae.

Hypselobagrus Bleeker 1862:10 [ref. 393]. Masc. *Bagrus macronema* Bleeker 1846:150. Type by original designation (also monotypic). Dates to p. 10 published in part 6 (26 Nov. 1862); p. 57 and Pls. 73-74 published in part 7 (27 Jan. 1863). Synonym of *Mystus* Scopoli 1777 (Roberts 1989:120 [ref. 6439]). Bagridae.

Hypselobarbus Bleeker 1859:430 [ref. 370]. Masc. *Barbus mussullah* Sykes 1838:159. Type by subsequent designation. Appeared in key, without included species. Two species (*mussullah* and *nancar*) apparently first added in *Hypselobarbus* (subgenus *Hypselobarbus*) by Bleeker 1860:275 [ref.380]. Type first designated by Bleeker 1863:199 [ref. 397] or 1863:27 [ref. 4859]. Synonym of *Tor* Gray (see Rainboth 1986:12 [ref. 5849]); valid (see Rainboth 1989:24 [ref. 13537]). Cyprinidae.

Hypselognathus Whitley 1948:76 [ref. 4710]. Masc. *Histiogamphelus rostratus* Waite & Hale 1921:303. Type by original designation (also monotypic). Valid (Dawson & Glover 1982 [ref. 5444], Dawson 1985:104 [ref. 6541], Paxton et al. 1989:423 [ref. 12442]). Syngnathidae: Syngnathinae.

Hypsicometes Goode 1880:337, 347 [ref. 1834]. Masc. *Hypsicometes gobioides* Goode 1880:337, 348. Type by monotypy.

Percophidae: Bembropinae.

Hypsifario Gill 1862:330 [ref. 1668]. Masc. *Salmo kennerlyi* Suckley 1861:307. Type by monotypy. Synonym of *Oncorhynchus* Suckley 1861 (Svetovidov 1973:146 [ref. 7169]). Salmonidae: Salmoninae.

Hypsigenys Günther 1861:383 [ref. 1967]. Fem. *Labrus macrodontus* Lacepède 1801:451, 522. Type by subsequent designation. Three included species, none designated type; first subsequent designation of type not researched. If type is as above, then name is an objective synonym of *Choerodon* Bleeker 1849 and of *Cossyphodes* Bleeker 1860. Labridae.

Hypsinotus Temminck & Schlegel 1844:84 [ref. 4372]. Masc. *Hypsinotus rubescens* Günther 1860:63. Type by subsequent designation. Original description without species; one species added and type fixed by subsequent monotypy by Günther 1860:63 [ref. 1963]; Bleeker's (1876:310 [ref. 448]) designation of *H. benhatatate* Bleeker invalid. Synonym of *Antigonia* Lowe 1843 (Parin & Borodulina 1986:143 [ref. 6005]). Caproidae.

Hypsiptera Günther 1860:386 [ref. 1963]. Fem. *Hypsiptera argentea* Günther 1860:386. Type by monotypy. Lotidae.

Hypsirhynchus Facciolà 1884:112 [ref. 1292]. Masc. *Hypsirhynchus hepaticus* Facciolà 1884:113. Type by monotypy. Preoccupied by Günther 1858 in Reptilia, replaced by *Rhynchogadus* Tortonese 1948 and *Olssonichthys* Fowler 1958. Objective synonym of *Rhynchogadus* Tortonese 1948 (Cohen 1973:326 [ref. 6589]). Moridae.

Hypsoblenniops Schultz 1941:153 [ref. 3955]. Masc. *Hypsoblenniops rickettsi* Schultz 1941:154. Type by original designation (also monotypic). Synonym of *Hypsoblennius* Gill 1861 (Bath 1977:186 [ref. 208]). Blenniidae.

Hypsoblennius Gill 1861:44 [ref. 1766]. Masc. *Blennius hentzi* Lesueur 1825:363. Type by monotypy. Valid (Smith-Vaniz 1980 [ref. 5525]). Blenniidae.

Hypsolepis Agassiz (ex Baird) 1854:359 [ref. 69]. Fem. *Cyprinus cornutus* Mitchill 1818:324. Type by original designation. *Hypsilepis* is a misspelling. Synonym of *Notropis* Rafinesque 1818, subgenus *Luxilus* Rafinesque 1820 (Gilbert 1978:15 [ref. 7042]); synonym of genus *Luxilus* Rafinesque 1820 (Mayden 1989 [ref. 12555]). Cyprinidae.

Hypsopanchax Myers 1924:41 [ref. 3092]. Masc. *Haplochilus platysternus* Nichols & Griscom 1917:724. Type by original designation (also monotypic). Valid (Parenti 1981:513 [ref. 7066], Wildekamp et al. 1986:188 [ref. 6198]). Cyprinodontidae: Aplocheilichthyinae.

Hypsophrys Agassiz 1859:408 [ref. 74]. Fem. *Hypsophrys unimaculatus* Agassiz 1859:408. Type by monotypy. Cichlidae.

Hypsopsetta Gill 1862:330 [ref. 1668]. Fem. *Pleuronichthys guttulatus* Girard 1856:137. Type by monotypy. Valid (Norman 1934:315 [ref. 6893], Ahlstrom et al. 1984:643 [ref. 13641], Sakamoto 1984 [ref. 5273]). Pleuronectidae: Pleuronectinae.

Hypsurus Agassiz 1861:133 [ref. 11]. Masc. *Embiotoca caryi* Agassiz 1853:389. Type by monotypy. Valid (Tarp 1952:46 [ref. 12250]). Embiotocidae.

Hypsypops Gill 1861:165 [ref. 1775]. Masc. *Glyphisodon rubicundus* Girard 1854:148. Type by monotypy. Valid (see Hensley 1986:857 [ref. 5734]). Pomacentridae.

Hyrcanogobius Iljin 1928:44 [ref. 2296]. Masc. *Hyrcanogobius bergi* Iljin 1928:44. Type by monotypy. Valid (Hoese, pers. comm.). Gobiidae.

Hyrtlinus Fowler 1958:5 [ref. 1470]. Masc. *Hyrtlinus altiformus* Fowler 1958:6. Type by original designation (also monotypic). Synonym of *Harengula* Valenciennes 1847 (Whitehead 1985:63 [ref. 5141]). Clupeidae.

Hysterocarpus Gibbons 1854:2, col. 3 [ref. 5207]. Masc. *Hysterocarpus traskii* Gibbons 1854:2, col. 3. Type by monotypy. Also appeared in Gibbons 1854:124 [ref. 1610]. Valid (Tarp 1952:77 [ref. 12250], Baltz & Moyle 1981 [ref. 6827]). Embiotocidae.

Hysteronotus Eigenmann 1911:171 [ref. 1226]. Masc. *Hysteronotus megalostomus* Eigenmann 1911:171. Type by original designation (also monotypic). Valid (Géry 1977:358 [ref. 1597], Weitzman & S. Fink 1985:1 et seq. [ref. 5203]). Characidae: Glandulocaudinae.

Hystricodon Günther 1864:349 [ref. 1974]. Masc. *Exodon paradoxus* Müller & Troschel 1845:31. Type by being a replacement name. Unneeded replacement for *Exodon*, wrongly thought preoccupied. Objective synonym of *Exodon* Müller & Troschel 1844. Characidae.

Iago Compagno & Springer 1971:616 [ref. 899]. *Eugaleus omanensis* Norman 1939:11. Type by original designation (also monotypic). Valid (Compagno 1984:395 [ref. 6846], Bass et al. 1986:80 [ref. 5638], Herman et al. 1988:107 [ref. 13267], Compagno 1988:236 [ref. 13488]). Triakidae: Galeorhininae.

Iberocobitis (subgenus of *Cobitis*) Bacescu 1962:438 [ref. 6454]. Fem. *Cobitis paludicola* de Buen 1930. Type by original designation. Cobitidae: Cobitinae.

Iberocypris Doadrio 1980:6 [ref. 1129]. Fem. *Iberocypris palaciosi* Doadrio 1980:7. Type by original designation (also monotypic). Cyprinidae.

Iburiella Jordan & Hubbs 1925:290, 291 [ref. 2486]. Fem. *Iburiella kasawae [kazawai]* Jordan & Hubbs 1925:271. Type by original designation (also monotypic). Type species named after Mr. Kazawa, emended to *kazawai* by Bailey & Gruchy 1970 [ref. 6508]). Synonym of *Occella* Jordan & Hubbs 1925 (see Bailey & Gruchy 1970 [ref. 6508]). Agonidae.

Iburina Jordan & Hubbs 1925:290, 291 [ref. 2486]. Fem. *Occa iburia* Jordan & Starks 1904:585. Type by original designation (also monotypic). Synonym of *Occella* Jordan & Hubbs 1925 (Bailey & Gruchy 1970:982 [ref. 6508]). Agonidae.

Icania Kaup 1858:109 [ref. 2579]. Fem. *Achirus cynoglossus* Hamilton 1822:132, 373. Type by monotypy. Synonym of *Cynoglossus* Hamilton 1822 (Menon 1977:16 [ref. 7071], Desoutter 1986:432 [ref. 6212]). Cynoglossidae: Cynoglossinae.

Icelichthys (subgenus of *Icelus*) Schmidt 1935:416 [ref. 3939]. Masc. *Icelus gilberti* Taranetz in Schmidt 1935:416. Type by monotypy. Synonym of *Icelus* Krøyer 1845 (Nelson 1984:19 [ref. 5391]). Cottidae.

Icelinus Jordan 1885:898 [110] [ref. 2385]. Masc. *Artedius quadriseriatus* Lockington 1880:330. Type by original designation (also monotypic). Proposed as a genus or subgenus, but treated as a genus. Valid (Bolin 1944:22 [ref. 6379], Washington et al. 1984:442 [ref. 13660], Yabe in Masuda et al. 1984:325 [ref. 6441], Peden 1984 [ref. 5193], Yabe 1985:111 [ref. 11522]). Cottidae.

Icelopsis (subgenus of *Icelus*) Taranetz 1936:149 [ref. 6509]. Fem. *Icelus gilberti* Taranetz in Schmidt 1935:416. Apparently not intended as a new genus; a lapsus for *Icelichthys* Taranetz 1935 and considered an incorrect subsequent spelling; appeared in footnote as "P. J. Schmidt [1935] determined this genus as a separate subgenus *Icelopsis*." In the synonymy of *Icelus* Krøyer 1845 (Nelson 1984:19 [ref. 5391]). Cottidae.

Icelus Krøyer 1845:253, 261 [ref. 2689]. Masc. *Icelus hamatus* Krøyer 1845:253. Type by monotypy. Valid (Neyelov 1973:596 [ref. 7219], Yabe 1981 [ref. 5547], Washington et al. 1984:442 [ref. 13660], Yabe in Masuda et al. 1984:324 [ref. 6441], Nelson 1984:19 [ref. 5391], Yabe 1985:111 [ref. 11522], Fedorov in Whitehead et al. 1986:1250 [ref. 13677]). Cottidae.

Ichthyacus Fernández-Yépez 1948:[1] [ref. 1318]. Masc. *Ichthyacus breederi* Fernández-Yépez 1948:[1]. Type by original designation (also monotypic). Hemiramphidae.

Ichthyapus Brisout de Barneville 1847:219 [ref. 644]. Masc. *Ichthyapus acutirostris* Brisout de Barneville 1847:219. Type by monotypy. Valid (McCosker 1977:67 [ref. 6836], McCosker & Castle 1986:179 [ref. 5690], Paxton et al. 1989:116 [ref. 12442], McCosker et al. 1989:322 [ref. 13288]). Ophichthidae: Ophichthinae.

Ichthyborus Günther 1864:362 [ref. 1974]. Masc. *Ichthyborus microlepis* Günther 1864:363. Type by subsequent designation. Type designated by Jordan 1919:333 [ref. 4904]. *Ichthyoborus* Boulenger 1907:134 [ref. 6510] is an unjustified emendation (*Ichthyoborus* in preoccupied by Kaup 1845 in birds); *Ra* Whitley 1931 is an unneeded replacement. Valid (Géry 1977:87 [ref. 1597], Vari 1979:340 [ref. 5490], Daget & Gosse 1984:196 [ref. 6185]). Citharinidae: Distichodontinae.

Ichthycallus (subgenus of *Julis*) Swainson 1839:173, 232 [ref. 4303]. Masc. *Julis semipunctatus* Rüppell 1835:12. Type by subsequent designation. Swain 1883:275 [ref. 5966] selected *Julis semipunctatus* Rüppell as type. Spelled *Ichtycollus* once by Bonaparte 1841:puntata 156, fasc. 30 [ref. 512]. Synonym of *Halichoeres* Rüppell 1835. Labridae.

Ichthyocampus Kaup 1853:231 [ref. 2569]. Masc. *Syngnathus carce* Hamilton 1822:13. Type by monotypy [not fully investigated] or designated by Duncker 1912 [ref. 1156]; not *I. belcheri* Kaup as cited by Jordan which was unavailable (name only) with original generic description. Valid (Dawson 1977:600 [ref. 1066], Dawson 1985:105 [ref. 6541], Kottelat 1989:16 [ref. 13605]). Syngnathidae: Syngnathinae.

Ichthyococcus Bonaparte 1840:puntata 138 [ref. 514]. Masc. *Gonostomus ovatus* Cocco 1838:169. Type by subsequent designation. Appeared first in puntata 138, fasc. 27 on unnumbered p. 3 under *Gonostoma denudata* as *Ichtyococcus*; on pp. 5 and 6 Bonaparte treated *Ichthyococcus ovatus* and *I. poweriae*. First subsequent designation of type not researched. *Coccia* Günther 1864 is an unneeded replacement. Valid (Witzell 1973:118 [ref. 7172], Weitzman 1974:472 [ref. 5174], Ahlstrom et al. 1984:185 [ref. 13643], Schaefer et al. 1986:244 [ref. 5709], Paxton et al. 1989:187 [ref. 12442]). Phosichthyidae.

Ichthyocolla Geoffroy St. Hilaire 1767:399 [ref. 1570]. Fem. *Acipenser huso* Linnaeus 1758:238. Type by monotypy. Original not examined; taken from Fowler 1972:205 [ref. 9327]. Predates *Huso* Brandt & Ratzeburg 1833. Synonym of *Acipenser* Linnaeus 1758 (when *Huso*/*Ichthyocolla* is not recognized). Acipenseridae: Acipenserinae.

Ichthyocoris Bonaparte 1840:fasc. 28 [ref. 514]. Fem. *Salarias varus* Risso 1826:237. Type by subsequent designation. Type designated by Jordan 1919:206 [ref. 2410]. Synonym of *Blennius* Linnaeus 1758 (Bath 1973:519 [ref. 7212]). Synonym of *Salaria* Forsskål 1775 (Bath 1977:208 [ref. 208], Bath 1986:356 [ref. 6217]). Blenniidae.

Ichthyoelephas Posada 1909:300 [ref. 5005]. *Ichthyoelephas patalo* Posada 1909:302. Type by monotypy. Valid (Géry 1977:226 [ref. 1597], Vari 1983:4 [ref. 5419], Roberts 1973:213 [ref. 7051]). Curimatidae: Prochilodontinae.

Ichthyomyzon Girard 1858:381 [ref. 4911]. Masc. *Petromyzon argenteus* Kirtland 1838:170, 197. Type by subsequent designation. Type designated by Jordan & Gilbert 1883:9 [ref. 2476]. Valid (Hubbs & Potter 1971:40 [ref. 13397]). Petromyzontidae: Petromyzontinae.

Ichthyophis Lesson 1828:397 [ref. 2775]. Masc. *Ichthyophis tigrinus* Lesson 1828:399. Type by monotypy. Apparently preoccupied by Fitzinger 1826 in Reptilia [details not investigated]. Muraenidae: Uropterygiinae.

Ichthyorhamphos Castelnau 1861:35 [ref. 767]. Neut. *Ichthyo rhamphos pappei* Castelnau 1861:35. Type by monotypy. Synonym of *Oplegnathus* Richardson 1840. Oplegnathidae.

Ichthyscopus (subgenus of *Uranoscopus*) Swainson 1839:181, 269 [ref. 4303]. Masc. *Uranoscopus inermis* Cuvier in Cuvier & Valenciennes 1829:310. Type by subsequent designation. Genus restricted by Gill 1861:114 [ref. 1774] but type not designated; type designated by Swain 1882:278 [ref. 5966]. *Ichthyoscopus* Agassiz 1846:193 [ref. 64] is an unjustified emendation. Valid (Mees 1960:46 [ref. 11931], Kishimoto in Masuda et al. 1984:293 [ref. 6441], Pietsch 1989:297 [ref. 12541]). Uranoscopidae.

Icichthys Jordan & Gilbert 1880:305 [ref. 2469]. Masc. *Icichthys lockingtoni* Jordan & Gilbert 1880:305. Type by monotypy. Valid (Haedrich 1967:65 [ref. 5357], McDowall 1981:130 [ref. 5356], Horn 1984:628 [ref. 13637], Nakabo in Masuda et al. 1984:234 [ref. 6441], Nakamura in Nakamura et al. 1986:288 [ref. 14235]). Centrolophidae.

Icosteus Lockington 1880:63 [ref. 2817]. Masc. *Icosteus aenigmaticus* Lockington 1880:63. Type by monotypy. Valid (Matarese et al. 1984 [ref. 13672], Mochizuki in Masuda et al. 1984:309 [ref. 6441]). Icosteidae.

Ictaetus Rafinesque 1815:93 [ref. 3584]. Not available, name only; for a ray. Myliobatidae.

Ictalurus (subgenus of *Pimelodus*) Rafinesque 1820:355 [ref. 7311]. Masc. *Silurus cerulescens* Rafinesque 1820:49. Type by subsequent designation. Type designated by Gill 1861:49 [ref. 12585] as *P. coerulescens* — not *punctatus* (not an included species) or *maculatus*. Also in Rafinesque 1820:61 (Dec.) [ref. 3592]. Spelled *Ichthaelurus* by Cope 1868:237 [ref. 909] and *Ichthyaelurus* by Meek 1904:10 [ref. 2958]. Valid (Burgess 1989:35 [ref. 12860]). Ictaluridae.

Icthelis Rafinesque 1820:375 [ref. 7308]. Fem. *Icthelis megalotis* Rafinesque 1820:377. Type by subsequent designation. Type designated by Jordan & Copeland 1877:134, 138 [ref. 5961] (not *auritus* as listed by Jordan & Gilbert 1877:86 [ref. 4907]). On *Lepomis* of Rafinesque 1819. *Ichthelis* is an unjustified emendation. Synonym of *Lepomis* Rafinesque 1819. Centrarchidae.

Ictias Rafinesque 1815:82 [ref. 3584]. Masc. Not available, name only; for a species of *Pacamus* (name only). Unplaced genera.

Icticus Jordan & Thompson 1914:242 [ref. 2543]. Masc. *Icticus ischanus* Jordan & Thompson 1914:242. Type by monotypy. Synonym of *Psenes* Valenciennes 1833. Nomeidae.

Ictiobus (subgenus of *Catostomus*) Rafinesque 1820:301 [299] [ref. 5006]. Masc. *Amblodon bubalus* Rafinesque 1818:421. Type by subsequent designation. Type designated by Agassiz 1854:354 [ref. 69]. Also in Rafinesque 1820:55, 89 (Dec.) [ref. 3592] as *Ictiorus*. Name placed on Official List (Opinion 1582), conserving over *Amblodon* Rafinesque 1819 which was placed on Official Index. Valid (see Bailey & Eschmeyer 1988 [ref. 6624]). Catostomidae.

Ictiopogon Rafinesque 1815:91 [ref. 3584]. Masc. *Bostrychus sinensis* Lacepède 1801:141. Type by being a replacement name. As "*Ictiopogon* R. *Botrychus* [sic] Lac.," meaning *Ictiopogon* Rafinesque *Bostrychus* Lacepède." Unneeded replacement for and objective synonym of *Bostrychus* Lacepède 1801. *Ichthyopogon* Agassiz 1846:193 [ref 64] is an unjustified emendation. Eleotridae.

Ictiorus see *Ictiobus*. Catostomidae.

Idiacanthus Peters 1877:846 [ref. 3454]. Masc. *Idiacanthus fasciola* Peters 1877:847. Type by monotypy. Valid (Gibbs 1964:513 [ref. 6961], Krueger 1973:144 [ref. 7177], Kawaguchi & Moser 1984:171 [ref. 13642], Gibbs in Whitehead et al. 1984:371 [ref. 13675], Fujii in Masuda et al. 1984:53 [ref. 6441], Fink 1985:11 [ref. 5171], Hulley 1986:234 [ref. 5672], Paxton et al. 1989:208 [ref. 12442]). Idiacanthidae.

Idiastion Eschmeyer 1965:530 [ref. 1273]. Neut. *Idiastion kyphos* Eschmeyer 1965:530. Type by original designation (also monotypic). Valid (Anderson et al. 1975 [ref. 7056]). Scorpaenidae: Scorpaeninae.

Idiolophorhynchus Sazonov 1981:1358 [ref. 3906]. Masc. *Idiolophorhynchus andriashevi* Sazonov 1981:1360. Type by original designation (also monotypic). Valid (Paxton et al. 1989:327 [ref. 12442]). Macrouridae: Trachyrincinae.

Idiolychnus Nafpaktitis & Paxton 1978:495 [ref. 3138]. Masc. *Diaphus urolampus* Gilbert & Cramer 1897:408. Type by original designation (also monotypic). Misspelled *Idiolychus* in Zoological Record for 1978. Valid (Paxton 1979:12 [ref. 6440], Fujii in Masuda et al. 1984:71 [ref. 6441], Moser et al. 1984:219 [ref. 13645], Paxton et al. 1984:241 [ref. 13625]). Myctophidae.

Idiotropiscis Whitley 1947:150 [ref. 4708]. Masc. *Acentronura australe* Waite & Hale 1921:317. Type by original designation (also monotypic). Synonym of *Acentronura* Kaup 1853, but as a valid subgenus (Dawson 1985:15 [ref. 6541], Dawson 1984 [ref. 5276], Dawson 1986:446 [ref. 5650]). Syngnathidae: Syngnathinae.

Idus Heckel 1843:1037 [ref. 2066]. Masc. *Cyprinus idus* Linnaeus 1758:324. Type by absolute tautonymy. Cyprinidae.

Igborichthys Clausen 1959:141 [ref. 842]. Masc. *Denticeps clupeoides* Clausen 1959:141. Type by original designation. Objective synonym of *Denticeps*; proposed as alternative name for (and at same time as) *Denticeps* Clausen, "In the event of *Denticeps* being found a homonym..." Perhaps best considered a name published in synonymy. Denticipitidae.

Iguanobrycon (subgenus of *Iguanodectes*) Géry 1970:424 [ref. 1592]. Masc. *Iguanodectes geisleri* Géry 1970:422. Type by original designation (also monotypic). Synonym of *Iguanodectes* Cope 1872 (Géry 1977:369 [ref. 1597] based on placement of type species). Characidae.

Iguanodectes Cope 1872:260 [ref. 921]. Masc. *Iguanodectes tenuis* Cope 1872:260. Type by monotypy. Valid (Géry 1977:374 [ref. 1597], Vari 1977:1 [ref. 7037]). Characidae.

Iheringichthys Eigenmann & Norris 1900:354 [ref. 1264]. Masc. *Pimelodus labrosus* Krøyer 1874:200. Type by original designation (also monotypic). Valid (Burgess 1989:280 [ref. 12860]). Pimelodidae.

Ijimaia Sauter 1905:235 [ref. 3867]. Fem. *Ijimaia dofleini* Sauter 1905:235. Type by original designation (also monotypic). Possibly the large adult of *Ateleopus* Schlegel 1846 (Stauch & Blache 1964 [ref. 6081]); valid (Paxton 1973:215 [ref. 7183], Mochizuki in Masuda et al. 1984:115 [ref. 6441], Paxton in Whitehead et al. 1986:529 [ref. 13676], Smith 1986:405 [ref. 5712]). Ateleopodidae.

Ilarches Cantor 1849:1142 [160] [ref. 715]. *Chaetodon orbis* Bloch 1787:81. Type by being a replacement name. Unneeded replacement for *Ephippus* Cuvier 1816, not preoccupied by *Ephippium* Latreille 1802 in Diptera. On page 160 of separate. Objective synonym of *Ephippus* Cuvier 1816. Ephippidae.

Ilictis (subgenus of *Ictalurus*) Rafinesque 1820:360 [ref. 7311]. Masc. *Silurus limosus* Rafinesque 1820:51. Type by monotypy. Described as a section of the subgenus *Ictalurus*. Also in Rafinesque 1820:66 (Dec.) [ref. 3592]. Synonym of *Pylodictis* Rafinesque 1819. Ictaluridae.

Ilisha Richardson (ex Gray) 1846:306 [ref. 3742]. Fem. *Ilisha abnormis* Richardson (ex Gray) 1846:306. Type usually regarded as by monotypy, but second species cited by scientific name in footnote and apparently included in *Ilisha*; earliest type designation not researched. Valid (Poll et al. 1984:44 [ref. 6172], Uyeno & Sato in Masuda et al. 1984:20 [ref. 6441], Grande 1985:244 [ref. 6466], Whitehead 1985:261 [ref. 5141], Kottelat 1989:4 [ref. 13605], Paxton et al. 1989:155 [ref. 12442]). Clupeidae.

Iljinia de Buen 1930:130, 132 [ref. 685]. Fem. *Gobius microps* Krøyer 1838:416. Type by original designation. Synonym of *Pomatoschistus* Gill 1863 (Miller 1973:506 [ref. 6888], Maugé 1986:380 [ref. 6218]). Gobiidae.

Illana Smith & Seale 1906:79 [ref. 4059]. *Illana cacabet* Smith & Seale 1906:80. Type by original designation (also monotypic). Second species questionably referred to genus. Synonym of *Glossogobius* Gill 1859 (Hoese, pers. comm.). Gobiidae.

Iluocoetes Jenyns 1842:165 [ref. 2344]. Masc. *Iluocoetes fimbriatus* Jenyns 1842:166. Type by monotypy. *Ilyocoetes* Agassiz 1846:194 [ref. 64] is an unjustified emendation. Treated as masculine by Jenyns. Valid (Gosztonyi 1977:212 [ref. 6103], Anderson 1984:578 [ref. 13634], Nakamura in Nakamura et al. 1986:232 [ref. 14235]). Zoarcidae.

Ilyodon Eigenmann 1907:425, 427 [ref. 1219]. Masc. *Ilyodon paraguayense* Eigenmann 1907:428. Type by original designation (also monotypic). Valid (Miller & Fitzsimons 1971:10 [ref. 3019], Uyeno et al. 1983:505 [ref. 6818]). Goodeidae.

Ilyophis Gilbert 1891:351 [ref. 1625]. Masc. *Ilyophis brunneus* Gilbert 1891:352. Type by original designation (also monotypic). Valid (Blache et al. 1973:253 [ref. 7185] as *Iliophis*, Robins & Robins 1976:264 [ref. 3784], Karrer 1982:99 [ref. 5679], Machida in Masuda et al. 1984:26 [ref. 6441], Saldanha & Bauchot in Whitehead et al. 1986:589 [ref. 13676], Castle 1986:189 [ref. 5644], Robins & Robins 1989:235 [ref. 13287]). Synaphobranchidae: Ilyophinae.

Ilypnus Jordan & Evermann 1896:460 [ref. 2442]. Masc. *Lepidogobius gilberti* Eigenmann & Eigenmann 1888:464. Type by original designation (also monotypic). Valid (Birdsong et al. 1988:187 [ref. 7303]). Gobiidae.

Imostoma Jordan 1877:49 [ref. 2372]. Neut. *Hadropterus shumardi* Girard 1860:100. Type by original designation (also monotypic). Synonym of *Percina* Haldeman 1842, but as a valid subgenus (Page 1974:85 [ref. 3346], Collette & Banarescu 1977:1455 [ref. 5845]). Percidae.

Imparales Schultz 1944:93 [ref. 3958]. Masc. *Imparales mariai*

Schultz 1944:94. Type by original designation (also monotypic). Synonym of *Heptapterus* Bleeker 1858 (Mees 1974:177 [ref. 2969], but see Buckup 1988 [ref. 6635]). Pimelodidae.

Imparfinis Eigenmann & Norris 1900:351 [ref. 1264]. Masc. *Imparfinis piperatus* Eigenmann & Norris 1900:352. Type by monotypy. Valid (Mees 1974:167 [ref. 2969], Stewart 1986:46 [ref. 5777], Stewart 1986:667 [ref. 5211], Burgess 1989:277 [ref. 12860], Mees & Cala 1989 [ref. 14277]). Pimelodidae.

Incara Rao 1971:329 [ref. 12496]. Masc. *Incara multisquamatus* Rao 1971:329. Type by original designation (also monotypic). Name an arbitrary combination of letters; treated by author as masculine. Valid (Jayaram 1981:374 [ref. 6497]). Eleotridae.

Incisidens Gill 1862:244 [ref. 1665]. Masc. *Crenidens simplex* Richardson 1848:120. Type by monotypy. Synonym of *Girella* Gray 1835. Kyphosidae: Girellinae.

Incisilabeo (subgenus of *Labeo*) Fowler 1937:206 [ref. 1425]. Masc. *Labeo behri* Fowler 1937:206. Type by original designation (also monotypic). Spelled *Incislabeo* by Neave 1950:123 [ref. 6512]. Synonym of *Labeo* Cuvier 1816 (Böhlke 1984:70 [ref. 13621] based on placement of type species). Cyprinidae.

Indialosa (subgenus of *Gonialosa*) Herre & Myers 1931:238 [ref. 2115]. Fem. *Clupanodon manmina* Hamilton 1822:247, 249, 383. Type by original designation (also monotypic). Synonym of *Gonialosa* Regan 1917 (Whitehead 1985:256 [ref. 5141]). Clupeidae.

Indocybium (subgenus of *Scomberomorus*) Munro 1943:68 [ref. 3056]. Neut. *Cybium semifasciatum* Macleay 1884:205. Type by original designation. Synonym of *Scomberomorus* Lacepède 1801 (Collette & Russo 1984:611 [ref. 5221]). Scombridae.

Indoglyphidodon Fowler 1944:25 [ref. 6513]. Masc. *Indoglyphidodon abbotti* Fowler 1944:26. Type by original designation (also monotypic). Pomacentridae.

Indomanta Whitley 1936:11 [ref. 4688]. Fem. *Indomanta tombazii* Whitley 1936:11. Type by monotypy. Myliobatidae.

Indonotothenia Balushkin 1984:14 [ref. 6138]. Fem. *Notothenia cyanobrancha* Richardson 1848:7. Type by original designation. Synonym of *Notothenia* Richardson 1844. Nototheniidae.

Indoreonectes (subgenus of *Oreonectes*) Rita & Banarescu in Rita, Banarescu & Nalbant 1978:185 [ref. 3758]. Masc. *Oreonectes (Indoreonectes) keralensis* Rita & Nalbant in Rita, Banarescu & Nalbant 1978:186. Type by original designation (also monotypic). Synonym of *Noemacheilus* Kuhl & van Hasselt 1823, but as a valid subgenus (Menon 1987:190 [ref. 14149]); valid genus (Kottelat 1990:19 [ref. 14137]). Balitoridae: Nemacheilinae.

Indosphyraena Smith 1956:38, 39 [ref. 4105]. Fem. *Sphyraena africana* Gilchrist & Thompson 1909:213. Type by original designation (also monotypic). Synonym of *Sphyraena* Röse 1793 (de Sylva 1975:76 [ref. 6302], Daget 1986:350 [ref. 6203]). Sphyraenidae.

Indostomus Prashad & Mukerji 1929:220 [ref. 3558]. Masc. *Indostomus paradoxus* Prashad & Mukerji 1929:220. Type by original designation (also monotypic). Valid (Jayaram 1981:299 [ref. 6497], Kottelat 1985:272 [ref. 11441], Kottelat 1989:16 [ref. 13605]). Indostomidae.

Inegocia Jordan & Thompson 1913:70 [ref. 2542]. Fem. *Platycephalus japonicus* Tilesius 1812:Pl. 59. Type by original designation. Valid (Ochiai in Masuda et al. 1984:321 [ref. 6441], Paxton et al. 1989:466 [ref. 12442]). Platycephalidae.

Inermia Poey 1860:193 [ref. 3499]. Fem. *Inermia vittata* Poey 1860:193. Type by monotypy. Valid (Johnson 1980:12 [ref. 13553]). Inermiidae.

Infratridens Schultz 1944:57 [ref. 3961]. Masc. *Gobiesox rhessodon* Smith in Jordan & Gilbert 1881:63. Type by original designation (also monotypic). Synonym of *Gobiesox* Lacepède 1800 (Briggs 1955:87 [ref. 637]). Gobiesocidae: Gobiesocinae.

Infundibulatus (subgenus of *Noemacheilus*) Menon 1987:177 [ref. 14149]. Masc. *Nemacheilus peguensis* Hora 1929:320. Type by original designation. Balitoridae: Nemacheilinae.

Iniistius Gill 1862:143 [ref. 1662]. Masc. *Xyrichthys pavo* Valenciennes in Cuvier & Valenciennes 1839:61. Type by original designation (also monotypic). Type designated by Gill's style of one species in parentheses in key. Valid (Richards & Leis 1984:544 [ref. 13668]); synonym of *Xyrichtys* Cuvier 1814 (Randall 1986:705 [ref. 5706]). Labridae.

Inimicus Jordan & Starks 1904:158 [ref. 2527]. Masc. *Pelor japonicum* Cuvier in Cuvier & Valenciennes 1829:437. Type by original designation. Valid (Eschmeyer et al. 1979:483 [ref. 6385], Washington et al. 1984:440 [ref. 13660], Shimizu in Masuda et al. 1984:318 [ref. 6441], Eschmeyer 1986:464 [ref. 5652], Paxton et al. 1989:442 [ref. 12442]). Scorpaenidae: Choridactylinae.

Inlecypris Howes 1980:171 [ref. 2222]. Fem. *Barilius auropurpureus* Annandale 1918. Type by original designation (also monotypic). Valid (Kottelat 1989:8 [ref. 13605]). Cyprinidae.

Innoculus Whitley 1952:25 [ref. 4717]. Masc. *Gobius nigroocellatus* Günther 1873:101. Type by original designation (also monotypic). Murdy & Hoese (1985:9 [ref. 5237]) refer Whitley's specimens of *nigroocellatus* Günther to *Istigobius ornatus* (Rüppell), so *Innoculus* is based on a misidentified type species and case should go to ICZN. Synonym of *Istigobius* Whitley 1932 (Murdy & Hoese 1985:5 [ref. 5237]). Gobiidae.

Innominado Parra 1787:96, Pl. 37 [ref. 6840]. Not available; a vernacular name for a species; work also probably can be considered as not following the principle of binominal nomenclature. In the synonymy of *Ophichthus* Ahl 1789 (McCosker 1977:79 [ref. 6836], McCosker et al. 1989:379 [ref. 13288]). Ophichthidae: Ophichthinae.

Inopsetta Jordan & Goss in Jordan 1885:924 [136] [ref. 2385]. Fem. *Parophrys ischyrus* Jordan & Gilbert 1881:276. Type by original designation (also monotypic). On p. 136 of separate. Valid (Norman 1934:375 [ref. 6893]). Pleuronectidae: Pleuronectinae.

Inpaichthys Géry & Junk 1977:417 [ref. 1601]. Masc. *Inpaichthys kerri* Géry & Junk 1977:418. Type by original designation (also monotypic). Characidae.

Insidiator Jordan & Snyder 1900:368 [ref. 2502]. Masc. *Platycephalus rudis* Günther 1880:66. Type by original designation (also monotypic). Apparently preoccupied by Oken 1842 [not investigated], not preoccupied by Amoyt 1846 (non-binominal) in insects; replaced by *Suggrundus* Whitley 1930. Objective synonym of *Suggrundus* Whitley 1930. Platycephalidae.

Insopiscis Whitley 1933:102 [ref. 4677]. Masc. *Cocotropus altipinnis* Waite 1903:41. Type by original designation (also monotypic). Probably a synonym of *Cocotropus* Kaup 1858 (Poss & Eschmeyer 1978:404 [ref. 6387]). Aploactinidae.

Intonsagobius Herre 1943:91 [ref. 2136]. Masc. *Intonsagobius kuderi* Herre 1943:93. Type by original designation (also monotypic). Synonym of *Callogobius* Bleeker 1874. Gobiidae.

Inu Snyder 1909:607 [ref. 4151]. Fem. *Inu koma* Snyder 1909:607. Type by original designation. Synonym of *Luciogobius* Gill 1859

(Akihito in Masuda et al. 1984:281 [ref. 6441] based on placement of type species). Gobiidae.

Investigator Goode in Goode & Bean 1896:518 [ref. 1848]. Masc. *Nemichthys acanthonotus* Alcock 1894:22. Type by original designation (also monotypic). Synonym of *Nemichthys* Richardson 1848 (Smith & Nielsen 1989:452 [ref. 13290]). Nemichthyidae.

Ioa Jordan & Brayton 1878:88 [ref. 2436]. Fem. *Poecilichthys vitreus* Cope 1870:263. Type by original designation (also monotypic). Synonym of *Etheostoma* Rafinesque 1819, but as a valid subgenus (Collette & Banarescu 1977:1455 [ref. 5845], Page 1981:34 [ref. 3347], Bailey & Etnier 1988:23 [ref. 6873]). Percidae.

Ioamia (subgenus of *Archamia*) Fowler & Bean 1930:110, 120 [ref. 1477]. Fem. *Apogonichthys gracilis* Bleeker 1856:371. Type by original designation (also monotypic). Synonym of *Rhabdamia* Weber 1909, but as a valid subgenus (Fraser 1972:27 [ref. 5195]). Apogonidae.

Iodotropheus Oliver & Loiselle 1972:310 [ref. 3305]. Masc. *Iodotropheus sprengerae* Oliver & Loiselle 1972:310. Type by original designation (also monotypic). Valid (Ribbink et al. 1983:241 [ref. 13555]). Cichlidae.

Ioglossus Bean in Jordan & Gilbert 1882:297 [ref. 2472]. Masc. *Ioglossus calliurus* Bean in Jordan & Gilbert 1882:297. Type by monotypy. Also appeared in Goode & Bean 1882 (about 18 Sept.):419 [ref. 1840], Bean in Jordan & Gilbert is 15 Aug. 1882. Synonym of *Ptereleotris* Gill 1863 (Randall & Hoese 1985 [ref. 5197], Birdsong et al. 1988:198 [ref. 7303]). Microdesmidae: Ptereleotrinae.

Iotabrycon Roberts 1973:491 [ref. 3776]. Masc. *Iotabrycon praecox* Roberts 1973:492. Type by original designation (also monotypic). Valid (Géry 1977:359 [ref. 1597], Weitzman & Fink 1985:1 et seq. [ref. 5203]). Characidae: Glandulocaudinae.

Iotaraia (subgenus of *Raja*) Leigh-Sharpe 1924:568, 577 [ref. 5748]. Fem. *Raja marginata* Lacepède 1803:662, 663. Type by original designation (also monotypic). As a "pseudogenus" of *Raia* [=*Raja*]. Not available [Art. 1b (6)], used as an artificial category (see Leigh-Sharpe 1928 [ref. 6152]). In the synonymy of *Raja* Linnaeus 1758 (Stehmann 1973:58 [ref. 7168]). Rajidae.

Iotichthys (subgenus of *Leuciscus*) Jordan & Evermann 1896:228, 231, 243 [ref. 2443]. Masc. *Clinostomus phlegethontis* Cope 1874:134. Type by original designation (also monotypic). Valid (Robins et al. 1980:22 [ref. 7111]). Cyprinidae.

Iotogobius Smith 1959:195 [ref. 4122]. Masc. *Iotogobius malindiensis* Smith 1959:195. Type by original designation (also monotypic). Synonym of *Cryptocentrus* Valenciennes (ex Ehrenberg) 1837 (Polunin & Lubbock 1977:91 [ref. 3540]). Gobiidae.

Ipnoceps Fowler 1943:56 [ref. 1441]. Neut. *Ipnoceps pristibrachium* Fowler 1943:56. Type by original designation (also monotypic). Synonym of *Ipnops* Günther 1878 (Sulak 1977:53 [ref. 4299]). Chlorophthalmidae: Ipnopinae.

Ipnops Günther 1878:187 [ref. 2010]. Masc. *Ipnops murrayi* Günther 1878:187. Type by monotypy. On Official List (Opinion 1333), with *Lychnoculus* Murray 1877 suppressed. Valid (Sulak 1977:53 [ref. 4299], Okiyama 1984:207 [ref. 13644], Sulak 1986:264 [ref. 5720], Merrett & Nielsen 1987 [ref. 6058], Paxton et al. 1989:236 [ref. 12442]). Chlorophthalmidae: Ipnopinae.

Iracundus Jordan & Evermann 1903:209 [ref. 2449]. Masc. *Iracundus signifer* Jordan & Evermann 1903:210. Type by original designation (also monotypic). Valid (Eschmeyer & Randall 1975:287 [ref. 6389], Kishimoto in Masuda et al. 1984:317 [ref. 6441], Eschmeyer 1986:468 [ref. 5652]). Scorpaenidae: Scorpaeninae.

Iranocichla Coad 1982:28 [ref. 854]. Fem. *Iranocichla hormuzensis* Coad 1982:29. Type by original designation (also monotypic). Cichlidae.

Iranocypris Bruun & Kaiser 1944:4 [ref. 674]. Fem. *Iranocypris typhlops* Bruun & Kaiser 1944:5. Type by original designation (also monotypic). Valid (Banister & Bunni 1980:151 [ref. 175]). Cyprinidae.

Iredaleichthys Whitley 1928:296 [ref. 4663]. Masc. *Glyphisodon azureus* Cuvier in Cuvier & Valenciennes 1830:479. Type by being a replacement name. Unneeded replacement for *Chrysiptera* Swainson 1839, not preoccupied by *Chrysoptera* Lincken 1817 in Lepidoptera. Objective synonym of *Chrysiptera* Swainson 1839. Pomacentridae.

Iredalella Whitley 1931:320 [ref. 4672]. Fem. *Girella cyanea* Macleay 1881:409. Type by original designation (also monotypic). Synonym of *Girella* Gray 1835. Kyphosidae: Girellinae.

Irex Valenciennes 1862:1204 [ref. 4506]. Masc. *Irex indicus* Valenciennes 1862:1205. Type by subsequent designation. Type apparently first designated by Jordan 1919:321 [ref. 4904]; two originally-included species. Synonym of *Elagatis* Bennett 1840 (Smith-Vaniz et al. 1979:23 [ref. 12247]). Carangidae.

Iriatherina Meinken 1974:9 [ref. 2973]. Fem. *Iriatherina werneri* Meinken 1974:9. Type by original designation (also monotypic). Also appeared in Meinken 1975:60 [ref. 2974]. Valid (Allen 1980:472 [ref. 99], Allen & Hoese 1980:55 [ref. 5517], Allen & Cross 1982:112 [ref. 6251], White et al. 1984:360 [ref. 13655], Paxton et al. 1989:349 [ref. 12442]). Atherinidae: Melanotaeniinae.

Iridio Jordan & Evermann 1896:412 [ref. 2442]. Fem. *Labrus radiatus* Linnaeus 1758:288. Type by original designation. Labridae.

Irillion Jordan 1919:342 [ref. 2413]. Neut. *Coregonus oregonius* Jordan & Snyder 1911:425. Type by original designation (also monotypic). Synonym of *Prosopium* Jordan 1878. Salmonidae: Coregoninae.

Irolita Whitley 1931:97 [ref. 4673]. Fem. *Raja waitii* McCulloch 1911:12. Type by original designation (also monotypic). Valid (Paxton et al. 1989:55 [ref. 12442]). Rajidae.

Irvineia Trewavas 1943:165 [ref. 4453]. Fem. *Irvineia voltae* Trewavas 1943:165. Type by monotypy. Valid (De Vos 1986:38 [ref. 6191], Burgess 1989:99 [ref. 12860]). Schilbeidae.

Isacia Jordan & Fesler 1893:501 [ref. 2455]. Fem. *Pristipoma conceptione* Cuvier in Cuvier & Valenciennes 1830:268. Type by original designation (also monotypic). Valid (Johnson 1980:11 [ref. 13553]). Haemulidae.

Isaciella (subgenus of *Orthopristis*) Jordan & Fesler 1893:495, 497, 500 [ref. 2455]. Fem. *Pristipoma brevipinne* Steindachner 1869: 10. Type by original designation (also monotypic). Haemulidae.

Isaciops Miles 1953:273 [ref. 2999]. Masc. *Isaciops facis* Miles 1953:274. Type by monotypy. Haemulidae.

Ischikauia Jordan & Snyder 1900:346 [ref. 2502]. Fem. *Opsariichthys steenackeri* Sauvage 1883:48. Type by monotypy. Misspelled *Ischikavia* in Zoological Record for 1901. Valid (Sawada in Masuda et al. 1984:57 [ref. 6441]). Cyprinidae.

Ischnomembras Fowler 1903:730 [ref. 1362]. Fem. *Ischnomembras gabunensis* Fowler 1903:731. Type by original designation (also monotypic). Type species with wrong type locality, not Africa.

Synonym of *Menidia* Bonaparte 1836 (see Maugé 1986:279 [ref. 6218]). Atherinidae: Menidiinae.

Ischnosoma Agassiz in Spix & Agassiz 1829:46, 47 [ref. 13]. Neut. *Osteoglossum bicirrhosum* Vandelli in Spix & Agassiz 1829:47. Not available, name published in synonymy of *Osteoglossum* Cuvier 1829, and apparently never made available. Type as given by Jordan 1917:132 [ref. 2407]; if not technically available then it would have no type species. Kottelat differs in that he feels Agassiz's use validates the name *Ischnosoma* back to Cuvier, but Agassiz used the name only in synonymy. See account of *Osteoglossum*. In the synonymy of *Osteoglossum* Cuvier 1829 (see Kottelat 1988:81 [ref. 13380]). Osteoglossidae: Osteoglossinae.

Isesthes Jordan & Gilbert 1883:757 [ref. 2476]. Fem. *Blennius gentilis* Girard 1854:149. Type by original designation (also monotypic). Identification of species corrected in Addenda, p. 959. *Isethes* is a misspelling. Synonym of *Hypsoblennius* Gill 1861 (Bath 1977:186 [ref. 208]). Blenniidae.

Isichthys Gill 1863:444 [ref. 1670]. Masc. *Isichthys henryi* Gill 1863:444. Type by monotypy. In error as *Isistius* in Sauvage 1884:207; there is no evidence that this was an emendation, and it should be regarded as an incorrect subsequent spelling of *Isichthys*. Valid (Taverne 1972:71 [ref. 6367], Gosse 1984:79 [ref. 6169]). Mormyridae.

Isistius Gill 1865:264 [ref. 1705]. Masc. *Scymnus brasiliensis* Cuvier in Quoy & Gaimard 1824:198. Type by monotypy. Valid (Compagno 1984:93 [ref. 6474], Nakaya & Shirai in Masuda et al. 1984:11 [ref. 6441], Bass et al. 1986:59 [ref. 5636], Cappetta 1987:62 [ref. 6348], Paxton et al. 1989:36 [ref. 12442]). Squalidae.

Iso Jordan & Starks 1901:204 [ref. 2524]. *Iso flosmaris* Jordan & Starks 1901:205. Type by monotypy. Misspelled *Ios* in Zoological Record for 1901. Valid (White et al. 1984:360 [ref. 13655], Yoshino in Masuda et al. 1984:119 [ref. 6441], Ivantsoff 1986:384 [ref. 6292] in family Notocheiridae which predates Isonidae); valid (Paxton et al. 1989:361 [ref. 12442] in Isonidae). Atherinidae: Notocheirinae.

Isobuna Jordan in Jordan & Herre 1907:158 [ref. 2483]. Fem. *Paracirrhites japonicus* Steindachner 1884:25. Type by being a replacement name. Replacement for *Paracirrhites* Steindachner 1884, preoccupied by Bleeker 1875 in fishes (same family). Synonym of *Plectranthias* Bleeker 1873 (Randall & Heemstra 1978 [ref. 6993], Randall 1980:105 [ref. 6717]). Serranidae: Anthiinae.

Isocephalus Heckel 1843:1029 [ref. 2067]. Masc. Type by subsequent designation. Possibly type never designated; Jordan lists type as *Cyprinus bandon* Hamilton (not an included species) and wrongly credits genus to Bleeker 1863. Cyprinidae.

Isocirrhitus Randall 1963:422 [ref. 3599]. Masc. *Cirrhitoidea sexfasciata* Schultz 1960:255. Type by original designation (also monotypic). Valid (Donaldson 1986:624 [ref. 6317]). Cirrhitidae.

Isognatha Gill (ex DeKay) 1861:56 [ref. 1766]. Fem. *Anguilla oceanica* Mitchill 1818:407. Type by monotypy. Synonym of *Conger* Oken 1817 (Blache et al. 1973:239 [ref. 7185], Smith 1989:513 [ref. 13285]). Congridae: Congrinae.

Isogomphodon Gill 1862:400, 401 [ref. 1783]. Masc. *Carcharias (Prionodon) oxyrhynchus* Müller & Henle 1839:41. Type by original designation (also monotypic). Also in Gill 1862:410 [ref. 4910]. Valid (Compagno 1984:510 [ref. 6846], Cappetta 1987:120 [ref. 6348], Compagno 1988:301 [ref. 13488]). Carcharhinidae.

Isopisthus Gill 1862:18 [ref. 1657]. Masc. *Ancylodon parvipinnis* Cuvier in Cuvier & Valenciennes 1830:84. Type by original designation (also monotypic). Type designated on p. 16. Valid (Chao 1978:37 [ref. 6983], Uyeno & Sato in Uyeno et al. 1983:374 [ref. 14275]). Sciaenidae.

Isoplagiodon Gill 1862:400, 401 [ref. 1783]. Masc. *Carcharias (Prionodon) sorrah* Valenciennes in Müller & Henle 1841:45. Type by original designation (also monotypic). Also in Gill 1862:410 [ref. 4910]. Synonym of *Carcharhinus* Blainville 1816 (Garrick 1982:19 [ref. 5454], Compagno 1984:449 [ref. 6846], Cappetta 1987:121 [ref. 6348], Compagno 1988:307 [ref. 13488]). Carcharhinidae.

Isopsetta Lockington in Jordan & Gilbert 1883:832 [ref. 2476]. Fem. *Lepidopsetta isolepis* Lockington 1880:325. Type by original designation (also monotypic). Valid (Norman 1934:326 [ref. 6893], Ahlstrom et al. 1984:643 [ref. 13641]). Pleuronectidae: Pleuronectinae.

Isorineloricaria Isbrücker 1980:15, 181 [ref. 2303]. Fem. *Plecostomus spinosissimus* Steindachner 1880:98. Type by original designation (also monotypic). Valid (Burgess 1989:430 [ref. 12860]). Loricariidae.

Isosillago Macleay 1878:34 [ref. 2868]. Fem. *Isosillago maculata* Macleay 1878:34. Type by monotypy. Synonym of *Sillaginodes* Gill 1862. Sillaginidae.

Isthmogobius Koumans (ex Bleeker) 1931:86 [ref. 5623]. Masc. *Gobius baliurus* Kuhl & van Hasselt in Cuvier & Valenciennes 1837:61. Type by original designation. Appeared in synonymy of *Gnatholepis* Bleeker as "?*Isthmogobius* Bleeker (Museum name) (*Gobius baliurus* C. & V.)." Regarded as a name in synonymy; apparently never made available; type as given by authors. In the synonymy of *Gnatholepis* Bleeker 1874. Gobiidae.

Istiblennius Whitley 1943:185 [ref. 4703]. Masc. *Salarias mulleri* Klunzinger 1879:388. Type by original designation (also monotypic). Valid (Smith-Vaniz & Springer 1971:24 [ref. 4145], Yoshino in Masuda et al. 1984:299 [ref. 6441], Springer 1986:747 [ref. 5719], Bath 1986:356 [ref. 6217], Williams 1989:11 [ref. 13549]). Blenniidae.

Istigobius (subgenus of *Gobius*) Whitley 1932:301 [ref. 4676]. Masc. *Gobius (Istigobius) stephensoni* Whitley 1932:301. Type by original designation (also monotypic). Valid (Akihito in Masuda et al. 1984:252 [ref. 6441], Murdy & Hoese 1985 [ref. 5237], Hoese 1986:793 [ref. 5670], Maugé 1986:374 [ref. 6218], Birdsong et al. 1988:193 [ref. 7303], Kottelat 1989:19 [ref. 13605]). Gobiidae.

Istiompax Whitley 1931:321 [ref. 4672]. Fem. *Istiompax australis* Whitley 1931:321. Type by original designation (also monotypic). Misspelled *Istiopomax* in Zoological Record for 1931. Synonym of *Makaira* Lacepède 1802 (de Sylva 1973:479 [ref. 7210], Nakamura 1983:321 [ref. 5371]). Istiophoridae.

Istiophorus Lacepède 1801:374 [ref. 2710]. Masc. *Xiphias platypterus* Shaw & Nodder 1792:Pl. 88. Type designated by ICZN; on Official List (Opinion 903). Unjustifiably emended to *Histiophorus* by Cuvier in Cuvier & Valenciennes 1831:293 [ref. 4881]. Valid (de Sylva 1973:477 [ref. 7210], Nakamura 1983:276 [ref. 5371], Collette et al. 1984:600 [ref. 11421], Nakamura in Masuda et al. 1984:223 [ref. 6441], Heemstra 1986:840 [ref. 5660]). Istiophoridae.

Istiorhombus Whitley 1931:322 [ref. 4672]. Masc. *Pseudorhombus spinosus* McCulloch 1914:129. Type by original designation (also monotypic). Synonym of *Pseudorhombus* Bleeker 1862 (Norman 1934:89 [ref. 6893], Amaoka 1969:88 [ref. 105], Desoutter

1986:428 [ref. 6212]). Paralichthyidae.

Istlarius Jordan & Snyder 1899:118 [ref. 2501]. Masc. *Istlarius balsanus* Jordan & Snyder 1899:118. Type by original designation (also monotypic). Synonym of *Ictalurus* Rafinesque 1820. Ictaluridae.

Isuropsis Gill 1862:397, 398 [ref. 1783]. Fem. *Oxyrhina glauca* Müller & Henle 1841:69. Type by original designation (also monotypic). Also in Gill 1862:409 [ref. 4910]. Synonym of *Isurus* Rafinesque 1810 (Springer 1973:14 [ref. 7162], Compagno 1984:242 [ref. 6474], Cappetta 1987:96 [ref. 6348]). Lamnidae.

Isurus Rafinesque 1810:11 [ref. 3594]. Masc. *Isurus oxyrinchus* Rafinesque 1810:12. Type by monotypy. Valid (Springer 1973:14 [ref. 7162], Quéro in Whitehead et al. 1984:85 [ref. 13675], Compagno 1984:242 [ref. 6474], Nakaya in Masuda et al. 1984:9 [ref. 6441], Bass 1986:99 [ref. 5635], Cappetta 1987:96 [ref. 6348], Paxton et al. 1989:67 [ref. 12442]). Lamnidae.

Itaiara (subgenus of *Serranus*) Vaillant & Bocourt 1878:70, 90 [ref. 4498]. Fem. *Serranus itaiara* Lichtenstein 1822:278. Type by monotypy (also absolute tautonymy). Synonym of *Epinephelus* Bloch 1793 (Smith 1971:103 [ref. 14102]). Serranidae: Epinephelinae.

Itatius Matsubara 1943:40 [ref. 6514]. Masc. *Itatius microlepis* Matsubara 1943:41. Type by original designation (also monotypic). Synonym of *Pycnocraspedum* Alcock 1889 (Cohen & Nielsen 1978:38 [ref. 881]). Ophidiidae: Neobythitinae.

Itbaya Herre 1927:288 [ref. 2104]. Fem. *Itbaya nuda* Herre 1927:288. Type by original designation (also monotypic). Synonym of *Kelloggella* Jordan & Seale 1905 (Hoese 1975:474 [ref. 5294]). Gobiidae.

Ivindomyrus Taverne & Géry 1975:555 [ref. 4348]. Masc. *Ivindomyrus opdenboschi* Taverne & Géry 1975:556. Type by original designation (also monotypic). Valid (Gosse 1984:79 [ref. 6169]). Mormyridae.

Ixinandria Isbrücker & Nijssen in Isbrücker 1979:87, 91 [ref. 2302]. Fem. *Loricaria steinbachi* Regan 1906:97. Type by original designation. Valid (Isbrücker 1980:103 [ref. 2303], Burgess 1989:441 [ref. 12860]). Loricariidae.

Jadamga Schultz 1940:(406) 416 [ref. 3952]. Fem. *Cheilodipterus quinquelineatus* Cuvier in Cuvier & Valenciennes 1828:167. Type by original designation (also monotypic). Objective synonym of *Paramia* Bleeker 1863. Synonym of *Cheilodipterus* Lacepède 1801 (Fraser 1972:16 [ref. 5195]). Apogonidae.

Jamsus (subgenus of *Hippocampus*) Ginsburg 1937:584 [ref. 1801]. Masc. *Hippocampus regulus* Ginsburg 1937:584. Type by original designation. Synonym of *Hippocampus* Rafinesque 1810 (Vari 1982:175 [ref. 6765]). Syngnathidae: Hippocampinae.

Japanopsychrolutes Nojima 1936:246 [ref. 3207]. Masc. *Japanopsychrolutes dentatus* Nojima 1936:246. Type by original designation (also monotypic). Synonym of *Eurymen* Gilbert & Burke 1912. Psychrolutidae.

Japonoconger Asano 1958:316 [ref. 146]. Masc. *Arisoma [sic] sivicola* Matsubara & Ochiai 1951:11. Type by original designation (also monotypic). Correct genus for type species is *Ariosoma*. Valid (Blache & Bauchot 1976:397 [ref. 305], Smith & Kanazawa 1977:540 [ref. 4036], Asano in Masuda et al. 1984:28 [ref. 6441], Smith 1989:549 [ref. 13285]). Congridae: Congrinae.

Japonolaeops Amaoka 1969:200 [136] [ref. 105]. Masc. *Japonolaeops dentatus* Amaoka 1969:200 [138]. Type by original designation (also monotypic). Valid (Ahlstrom et al. 1984:642 [ref. 13641], Amaoka in Masuda et al. 1984:350 [ref. 6441], Hensley 1986:941 [ref. 6326]). Bothidae: Bothinae.

Javichthys Hardy 1985:145 [ref. 5185]. Masc. *Javichthys kailolae* Hardy 1985:147. Type by original designation (also monotypic). Valid (see Su et al. 1986:112 [ref. 12582]). Tetraodontidae.

Jaydia Smith 1961:375, 392 [ref. 4128]. Fem. *Apogon ellioti* Day 1875:63. Type by original designation. Apogonidae.

Jeboehlkia Robins 1967:593 [ref. 3786]. Fem. *Jeboehlkia gladifer* Robins 1967:593. Type by original designation (also monotypic). Author wrongly regarded gender as masculine. Valid (Kendall 1984:500, 508 [ref. 13663]). Serranidae: Liopropomatinae.

Jenkinsia Jordan & Evermann 1896:417, 418 [ref. 2443]. Fem. *Dussumieria stolifera* Jordan & Gilbert 1884:25. Type by original designation. Valid (Grande 1985:248 [ref. 6466], Whitehead 1985:37 [ref. 5141]). Clupeidae.

Jenkinsiella Jordan & Evermann 1905:82 [ref. 2451]. Fem. *Microdonophis macgregori* Jenkins 1903:422. Type by original designation (also monotypic). Synonym of *Cirrhimuraena* Kaup 1856, but as a valid subgenus (McCosker 1977:75 [ref. 6836]). Ophichthidae: Ophichthinae.

Jenynsella Ogilby 1908:3, 15 [ref. 3285]. Fem. *Jenynsella weatherilli* Ogilby 1908:15. Type by original designation (also monotypic). Synonym of *Retropinna* Gill 1862 (McDowall 1979:90 [ref. 7021]). Retropinnidae: Retropinninae.

Jenynsia Günther 1866:331 [ref. 1983]. Fem. *Lebias lineata* Jenyns 1842:116. Type by monotypy. *Fitzroyia* and *Jenynsia* both described by Günther in the same work and long regarded as synonyms; earliest technical "first reviser" not fully researched [see *Fitzroyia*]. Valid (Parenti 1981:502 [ref. 7066], Malabarba 1989:160 [ref. 14217]). Anablepidae: Jenynsiinae.

Jerdonia Day 1871:700 [ref. 1078]. Fem. *Platacanthus maculatus* Day 1867:941. Type by monotypy. Apparently preoccupied by Blanford 1862 in Mollusca; *Enobarbus* Whitley 1928 (and its replacement *Enobarbichthys* Whitley 1931) and *Madrasia* Nalbant 1963 are replacement names. In the synonymy of *Enobarbus* Whitley 1928. Cobitidae: Cobitinae.

Jinshaia Kottelat & Chu 1988:191 [ref. 13491]. Fem. *Psilorhynchus sinensis* Sauvage & Dabry de Thiersant 1874:14. Type by original designation. Balitoridae: Balitorinae.

Jobertina (subgenus of *Characidium*) Pellegrin 1909:151 [ref. 3424]. Fem. *Characidium (Jobertina) interruptum* Pellegrin 1909:151. Type by monotypy. Valid (Géry 1977:114 [ref. 1597], Malabarba 1989:136 [ref. 14217]). Characidae: Characidiinae..

Johnieops Mohan 1972:85 [ref. 5743]. Masc. *Sciaena osseus* Day 1876:193. Type by original designation. Synonym of *Johnius* Bloch 1793, but as a valid subgenus (Trewavas 1977:428 [ref. 4459], Sasaki & Amaoka 1989:466 [ref. 12749]); valid genus (Daget & Trewavas 1986:334 [ref. 6211]). Sciaenidae.

Johnius Bloch 1793:132 [ref. 4868]. Masc. *Johnius carutta* Bloch 1793:133. Type by subsequent designation. Type designated by Gill 1861:85 [ref. 1771], also by Bleeker 1876:327 [ref. 448]. Valid (Trewavas 1977:405 [ref. 4459], Okamura in Masuda et al. 1984:162 [ref. 6441], Heemstra 1986:618 [ref. 5660], Sasaki & Amaoka 1989 [ref. 12749], Kottelat 1989:17 [ref. 13605]). Sciaenidae.

Johnrandallia Nalbant 1974:308 [ref. 6641]. Fem. *Sarothrodus nigrirostris* Gill 1862:243. Type by original designation (also monotypic). Chaetodontidae.

Johnsonina Myers 1934:5 [ref. 3107]. Fem. *Johnsonina eriomma*

Myers 1934:5. Type by original designation (also monotypic). Valid (Tyler 1968:149 [ref. 6438], Tyler 1980:56 [ref. 4477]). Triacanthodidae.

Joinvillea Steindachner 1908:30 [ref. 4243]. Fem. *Joinvillea rosae* Steindachner 1908:30. Type by monotypy. Synonym of *Deuterodon* Eigenmann 1907. Characidae.

Jopaica Pinto 1970:47 [ref. 3481]. Fem. *Springeria santosi* Carvalho & Pinto 1965:113. Type by being a replacement name. Replacement for *Springeria* Carvalho & Pinto 1965, preoccupied by Bigelow & Schroeder 1951 in fishes. Synonym of *Dactyloscopus* Gill 1859 (Dawson 1982:20 [ref. 1072]). Dactyloscopidae.

Jordanella Goode & Bean in Goode 1879:117 [ref. 1836]. Fem. *Jordanella floridae* Goode & Bean in Goode 1879:117. Type by monotypy. Valid (Parenti 1981:528 [ref. 7066]). Cyprinodontidae: Cyprinodontinae.

Jordania Starks 1895:410 [ref. 4194]. Fem. *Jordania zonope* Starks 1895:410. Type by monotypy. Valid (Bolin 1944:8 [ref. 6379], Washington et al. 1984:442 [ref. 13660], Yabe 1985:111 [ref. 11522]). Cottidae.

Jordanichthys Evermann & Clark 1928:687 [ref. 5565]. Masc. *Jordanichthys holei* Evermann & Clark 1928:687. Type by original designation (also monotypic). Based on a skin; family placement uncertain, not treated by Allen 1985 [ref. 6843] in Lutjanidae. Lutjanidae.

Jordanicus Gilbert 1905:656 [ref. 1631]. Masc. *Fierasfer umbratilis* Jordan & Evermann 1904:206. Type by original designation (also monotypic). Synonym of *Encheliophis* Müller 1842 (Williams 1984:389 [ref. 5314]); as a valid subgenus (Arnold 1956:299 [ref. 5315]); as a valid genus (Trott 1981:625 [ref. 14205], Shen & Yeh 1987:47 [ref. 6418]). Carapidae: Carapinae.

Jordanidia Snyder 1911:527 [ref. 4152]. Fem. *Jordanidia raptoria* Snyder 1911:527. Type by original designation (also monotypic). Synonym of *Rexea* Waite (18 Jan.) 1911, *Jordanidia* published on 26 May. Gempylidae.

Jordanites Fowler 1925:75 [ref. 1400]. Masc. *Eurypharynx richardi* Roule 1914:1821. Type by being a replacement name. Replacement for *Rouleina* Fowler (Mar.) 1925, preoccupied by Jordan 1923 in fishes; Fowler 1925:75 misspells as *Rouelina*. Synonym of *Eurypharynx* Vaillant 1882 (Böhlke 1966:610 [ref. 5256], Bauchot 1973:218 [ref. 7184], Bertelsen et al. 1989:649 [ref. 13293]). Eurypharyngidae.

Joturus Poey 1860:263 [ref. 3499]. Masc. *Joturus pichardi* Poey 1860:263. Type by monotypy. Mugilidae.

Julichthys De Vis 1885:884 [ref. 1091]. Masc. *Julichthys inornata* De Vis 1885:884. Type by monotypy. Labridae.

Julidio Jordan & Evermann 1896:413 [ref. 2442]. Fem. *Pseudojulis adustus* Gilbert 1890:66. Type by original designation (also monotypic). Labridae.

Julidochromis Boulenger 1898:11 [ref. 547]. Masc. *Julidochromis ornatus* Boulenger 1898:12. Type by monotypy. Valid (Poll 1986:70 [ref. 6136]). Cichlidae.

Julis Cuvier 1814:90 [ref. 4884]. Fem. *Labrus julis* Linnaeus 1758:284. Type by absolute tautonymy. Apparently appeared first in Goüan 1770:41 [ref. 1863] without species and essentially as name only, then as above, and in Cuvier 1816:261 [ref. 993]. Spelled *Julus* and *Julius* in early literature. Synonym of *Coris* Lacepède 1801 (Bauchot & Quignard 1973:431 [ref. 7204]). Labridae.

Juncrus (subgenus of *Scyliorhinus*) Whitley 1939:229 [ref. 4695]. *Scyllium vincenti* Zeitz 1908:287. Type by original designation. Compagno 1984:289 serves as first reviser, selecting *Asymbolus* Whitley 1939 over *Juncrus* Whitley 1939, both genera appearing in the same work and treated by Compagno as synonyms. Valid (Springer 1979:95 [ref. 4175]); synonym of *Asymbolus* Whitley 1939 (Compagno 1984:289 [ref. 6846], Compagno 1988:127 [ref. 13488]). Scyliorhinidae.

Jurengraulis Whitehead, Nelson & Wongratana 1988:384 [ref. 5725]. Fem. *Cetengraulis juruensis* Boulenger 1898:421. Type by original designation (also monotypic). Engraulidae.

Juvenella Whitley 1948:90 [ref. 4710]. Fem. *Juvenella carangoides* Whitley 1948:90. Type by original designation (also monotypic). Described as a carangid. Appears to be a juvenile *Scorpis lineolatus* (Paxton, pers. comm., based on examination of holotype), and therefore a junior synonym of *Scorpis* Valenciennes 1832. Kyphosidae: Scorpidinae.

Kaiwarinus Suzuki 1962:204 [ref. 4301]. Masc. *Caranx equula* Temminck & Schlegel 1844:111. Type by original designation (also monotypic). Valid (Gushiken in Masuda et al. 1984:155 [ref. 6441], Kijima et al. 1986:841 [ref. 6320], Gushiken 1988:443 [ref. 6697]); synonym of *Carangoides* Bleeker 1851 (Smith-Vaniz, pers. comm.). Carangidae.

Kajikia Hirasaka & Nakamura 1947:12 [ref. 2174]. Fem. *Kajikia formosana* Hirasaka & Nakamura 1947:13. Type by subsequent designation. Apparently not available as above, described after 1930 without designation of a type species. Can date to treatment in Zoological Record for 1947, Pisces, p. 61 (see remarks on Art. 13b in Appendix A). In the synonymy of *Tetrapturus* Rafinesque 1810 (de Sylva 1973:480 [ref. 7210], Nakamura 1983:294 [ref. 5371]). Istiophoridae.

Kali Lloyd 1909:154 [ref. 2814]. Fem. *Kali indica* Lloyd 1909:154. Type by monotypy. Valid (Krefft 1973:453 [ref. 7166], Johnson & Cohen 1974:34 [ref. 7133], Johnson & Keene in Whitehead et al. 1986:959 [ref. 13676], Johnson & Keene 1986:732 [ref. 6303]). Chiasmodontidae.

Kalimantania Banarescu 1980:471 [ref. 216]. Fem. *Systomus lawak* Bleeker 1855:411. Type by original designation (also monotypic). Type given as *Systomus lawak* Bleeker = *Amblyrhynchichthys altus* Vaillant. Valid (Roberts 1989:40 [ref. 6439]). Cyprinidae.

Kalthala Mohan 1969:295 [ref. 3034]. *Corvina axillaris* Cuvier 1830:113. Type by original designation (also monotypic). Objective synonym of *Dhoma* Talwar & Joglekar 1970. Sciaenidae.

Kamoharaia Kuronuma 1940:35 [ref. 2701]. Fem. *Chascanopsetta megastoma* Kamohara 1936:308. Type by monotypy. Valid (Amaoka 1969:216 [ref. 105], Ahlstrom et al. 1984:642 [ref. 13641], Amaoka in Masuda et al. 1984:350 [ref. 6441], Hensley 1986:941 [ref. 6326]). Bothidae: Bothinae.

Kanazawaichthys Schultz 1957:(55) 62 [ref. 3969]. Masc. *Kanazawaichthys scutatus* Schultz 1957:63. Type by original designation (also monotypic). Synonym of *Antennarius* Daudin 1816 (Pietsch 1984:34 [ref. 5380], Pietsch in Whitehead et al. 1986:1364 [ref. 13677]). Antennariidae.

Kanduka Hora 1925:579 [ref. 2206]. Fem. *Kanduka michiei* Hora 1925:581. Type by monotypy. Synonym of *Arothron* Müller 1841 (Fraser-Brunner 1943:15 [ref. 1495]). Tetraodontidae.

Kanekonia Tanaka 1915:566 [ref. 4324]. Fem. *Kanekonia florida* Tanaka 1915:566. Type by monotypy. Appeared first in Japanese (15 Nov.), English version 28 Nov. 1918:510 [ref.6037]. Valid (Poss & Eschmeyer 1978:404 [ref. 6387], Poss 1982 [ref. 5474],

Washington et al. 1984:441 [ref. 13660], Nakabo in Masuda et al. 1984:319 [ref. 6441], Paxton et al. 1989:460 [ref. 12442]). Aploactinidae.

Kantaka (subgenus of *Osteochilus*) Hora 1942:9 [ref. 2213]. *Semiplotus brevidorsalis* Day 1873:239. Type by original designation (also monotypic). Synonym of *Osteochilus* Günther 1868, but as a valid subgenus (Jayaram 1981:128 [ref. 6497]). Cyprinidae.

Kantapus Smith 1947:817 [ref. 4073]. Masc. *Kantapus oglinus* Smith 1947:817. Type by original designation (also monotypic). Scorpaenidae: Scorpaeninae.

Kapparaia (subgenus of *Raja*) Leigh-Sharpe 1926:353 [ref. 5628]. Fem. *Raja ocellata* Mitchill 1815:477. Type by original designation (also monotypic). As a "pseudogenus" of *Raia* [=*Raja*]. Not available [Art. 1b (6)], used as an artificial category (see Leigh-Sharpe 1928 [ref. 6152]). In the synonymy of *Raja* Linnaeus 1758. Rajidae.

Karalepis Hardy 1984:176 [ref. 5340]. Fem. *Karalepis stewarti* Hardy 1984:177. Type by original designation (also monotypic). Tripterygiidae.

Kareius Jordan & Snyder 1900:379 [ref. 2502]. Masc. *Pleuronectes scutifer* Steindachner 1870:628. Type by original designation (also monotypic). Valid (Norman 1934:376 [ref. 6893], Sakamoto 1984 [ref. 5273], Sakamoto in Masuda et al. 1984:353 [ref. 6441]). Pleuronectidae: Pleuronectinae.

Karumba Whitley 1966:242 [ref. 4734]. Fem. *Bathyaploactis curtisensis ornatissimus* Whitley 1933:103. Type by original designation (also monotypic). Type is Whitley's subspecies *ornatissimus* (elevated to species as *B. ornatissimus* for technical designation of the type) and not the species *curtisensis*. Valid (Poss & Eschmeyer 1978:404 [ref. 6387], Paxton et al. 1989:460 [ref. 12442]). Aploactinidae.

Kasatkia Soldatov & Pavlenko 1916:638 [ref. 4162]. Fem. *Kasatkia memorabilis* Soldatov & Pavlenko 1916:639. Type by original designation (also monotypic). Stichaeidae.

Kasidoron Robins & De Sylva 1965:190 [ref. 3788]. *Kasidoron edom* Robins & De Sylva 1965:190. Type by original designation (also monotypic). Synonym of *Gibberichthys* Parr 1933 (de Sylva & Eschmeyer 1977:228 [ref. 5936]). Gibberichthyidae.

Kathala Mohan 1969:295 [ref. 3034]. *Corvina axillaris* Cuvier in Cuvier & Valenciennes 1830:113. Type by original designation (also monotypic). Valid (Trewavas 1977:292 [ref. 4459]). Sciaenidae.

Kathetostoma Günther 1860:231 [ref. 1963]. Neut. *Uranoscopus laevis* Bloch & Schneider 1801:47. Type by monotypy. Spelled *Cathetostoma* by Boulenger 1901:266 [ref. 558]; technically an incorrect subsequent spelling. Valid (Mees 1960:47 [ref. 11931], Pietsch 1989:296 [ref. 12541]). Uranoscopidae.

Kathetys (subgenus of *Aphyosemion*) Huber 1977:unnum. p. 10 [ref. 2268]. *Haplochilus exiguum* Boulenger 1911:265. Type by original designation. Synonym of *Aphyosemion* Myers 1924 (Wildekamp et al. 1986:196 [ref. 6198]); as a valid subgenus (Parenti 1981:477 [ref. 7066]). Aplocheilidae: Aplocheilinae.

Katsuwonus Kishinouye 1915:21 [ref. 2609]. Masc. *Thynnus pelamis* Linnaeus 1758:297. Type by original designation (also monotypic). Appeared first in Japanese as cited by Kishinouye 1923 [1915 reference not examined]; in English in 1923 [ref. 2609]. Valid (Postel 1973:471 [ref. 7208], Collette & Nauen 1983:42 [ref. 5375], Collette et al. 1984:600 [ref. 11421], Nakamura in Masuda et al. 1984:226 [ref. 6441], Collette 1986:834 [ref. 5647]). Scombridae.

Kaupia Smith 1963:533 [ref. 6516]. Fem. *Syngnathus boaja* Bleeker 1851:3 et seq. Type by original designation. Synonym of *Doryichthys* Kaup 1853 (Dawson 1981:2 [ref. 5527], Dawson 1985:55 [ref. 6541], Roberts 1989:158 [ref. 6439]). Syngnathidae: Syngnathinae.

Kaupichthys Schultz 1943:50 [ref. 3957]. Masc. *Kaupichthys diodontus* Schultz 1943:50. Type by original designation (also monotypic). Valid (Asano in Masuda et al. 1984:22 [ref. 6441], Castle 1986:187 [ref. 5644], Paxton et al. 1989:137 [ref. 12442], Smith 1989:86 [ref. 13285]). Chlopsidae.

Kaupus (subgenus of *Leptonotus*) Whitley 1951:392 [ref. 4715]. Masc. *Leptonotus costatus* Waite & Hale 1921:301. Type by original designation (also monotypic). Valid (Dawson 1985:107 [ref. 6541], Paxton et al. 1989:423 [ref. 12442]). Syngnathidae: Syngnathinae.

Kelloggella Jordan & Seale in Jordan & Evermann 1905:488 [ref. 2451]. Fem. *Enypnias oligolepis* Jenkins 1903:504. Type by monotypy. First as above (29 July 1905), then in Jordan & Seale 1906:409 [ref. 2497], with "type" *K. cardinalis* Jordan & Seale. Intended type was *cardinalis* (in parentheses after genus in 29 July), but that species not then available. Valid (Hoese 1975 [ref. 5294], Sawada 1977 [ref. 6984], Yoshino in Masuda et al. 1984:268 [ref. 6441], Birdsong et al. 1988:190 [ref. 7303]). Gobiidae.

Kendallia Evermann & Shaw 1927:108 [ref. 1286]. Fem. *Kendallia goldsboroughi* Evermann & Shaw 1927:108. Type by original designation (also monotypic). Synonym of *Cultriculus* Oshima 1919 (Chu 1935:39 [ref. 832]). Synonym of *Hemiculter* Bleeker 1859 (Chen in Chu & Chen 1989:80 [ref. 13584]). Cyprinidae.

Kenoza (subgenus of *Lucius*) Jordan & Evermann 1896:625, 626 [ref. 2443]. Fem. *Esox lucius var. americanus* Gmelin 1789:1319. Type by original designation (also monotypic). Type by use of name in parentheses. For purposes of the type species, the variety *americanus* is raised to species level; type not *lucius*. Synonym of *Esox* Linnaeus 1758, but as a valid subgenus (Crossman 1978:20 [ref. 6974]). Esocidae.

Kentrocapros (subgenus of *Acerana*) Kaup 1855:220 [ref. 2571]. Masc. *Ostracion hexagonus* Thunberg 1787:30. Type by monotypy. Valid (Tyler 1980:205 [ref. 4477], Matsuura & Yamakawa 1982 [ref. 5504], Winterbottom & Tyler 1983:902 [ref. 5320], Arai 1983:202 [ref. 14249], Matsuura in Masuda et al. 1984:361 [ref. 6441], Smith 1986:891 [ref. 5712]). Ostraciidae: Aracaninae.

Keris Valenciennes in Cuvier & Valenciennes 1835:304 [ref. 1004]. Masc. *Keris anguinosus* Valenciennes in Cuvier & Valenciennes 1835:304. Type by monotypy. Spelled *Ceris* by Günther in Zoological Record for 1865:87. Synonym of *Naso* Lacepède 1801 (Randall 1955:361 [ref. 13648]). Acanthuridae.

Kertomichthys McCosker & Böhlke 1982:119 [ref. 2935]. Masc. *Mystriophis blastorhinos* Kanazawa 1963:282. Type by original designation (also monotypic). Valid (McCosker et al. 1989:368 [ref. 13288]). Ophichthidae: Ophichthinae.

Kessleria Boghdanov 1882:3 [ref. 499]. Fem. *Scaphirhynchus fedtschenkoi* Kessler 1872:70. Type by monotypy. Preoccupied by Nowicki 1864 in Lepidoptera. Not replaced; see Myers 1940:35 [ref. 3118]. Synonym of *Pseudoscaphirhynchus* Nikolski 1900. Acipenseridae: Scaphirhynchinae.

Kestratherina Pavlov, Ivantsoff, Last & Crowley 1988:387 [ref. 12285]. *Atherinichthys esox* Klunzinger 1872:34. Type by original designation. Atherinidae: Atherininae.

Ketengus Bleeker 1847:167 [ref. 314]. Masc. *Ketengus typus* Bleeker 1847:167. Type by monotypy (also by use of *typus*). Valid (Jayaram & Dhanze 1979:48 [ref. 6800], Jayaram 1981:282 [ref. 6497], Burgess 1989:167 [ref. 12860], Kottelat 1989:15 [ref. 13605]). Ariidae.

Kieneria (subgenus of *Eleotris*) Maugé 1984:98 [ref. 5945]. Fem. *Eleotris (Kieneria) vomerodentata* Maugé 1984:98. Type by original designation (also monotypic). Synonym of *Eleotris* Bloch & Schneider 1801 (Maugé 1986:391 [ref. 6218]). Eleotridae.

Kimberleyeleotris Hoese & Allen 1987:36 [ref. 6604]. Fem. *Kimberleyeleotris hutchinsi* Hoese & Allen 1987:36. Type by original designation. Eleotridae.

Kimblaeus Dawson 1980:518 [ref. 1070]. Masc. *Kimblaeus bassensis* Dawson 1980:518. Type by original designation (also monotypic). Valid (Dawson 1985:108 [ref. 6541], Paxton et al. 1989:423 [ref. 12442]). Syngnathidae: Syngnathinae.

Kirtlandia Jordan & Evermann 1896:789, 794 [ref. 2443]. Fem. *Chirostoma vagrans* Goode & Bean 1879:148. Type by original designation. Synonym of *Membras* Bonaparte 1836 (Chernoff 1986:239 [ref. 5847]). Atherinidae: Menidiinae.

Kishinoella Jordan & Hubbs 1925:219 [ref. 2486]. Fem. *Thunnus rarus* Kishinouye 1915:28. Type by original designation (also monotypic). Synonym of *Thunnus* South 1845 (Gibbs & Collette 1967:97 [ref. 13640]). Scombridae.

Kiunga Allen 1983:72 [ref. 5350]. *Kiunga ballochi* Allen 1983:73. Type by original designation (also monotypic). Valid (Saeed et al. 1989:721, 779 [ref. 13533] in Pseudomugilidae as subfamily Kiunginae). Atherinidae: Pseudomugilinae.

Klamathella (subgenus of *Gila*) Miller 1945:105 [ref. 3016]. Fem. *Tigoma bicolor* Girard 1856:206. Type by original designation (also monotypic). Cyprinidae.

Klausewitzia Géry 1965:198 [ref. 1586]. Fem. *Klausewitzia ritae* Géry 1965:199. Type by original designation (also monotypic). Valid (Géry 1977:119 [ref. 1597]). Characidae: Characidiinae.

Kleiwegia de Beaufort 1952:45 [ref. 234]. Fem. *Cocotropus dezwaani* Weber & de Beaufort 1952:45. Type by monotypy. Synonym of *Acanthosphex* Fowler 1938 (Poss & Eschmeyer 1978:404 [ref. 6387]). Aploactinidae.

Klunzingerina (subgenus of *Pseudochromis*) Fowler 1931:21, 33 [ref. 1407]. Fem. *Pseudochromis novaehollandiae* Steindachner 1879:160. Type by original designation. Synonym of *Ogilbyina* Fowler 1931 (Gill, pers. comm.). Pseudochromidae: Pseudochrominae.

Kneria Steindachner 1866:769 [ref. 5030]. Fem. *Kneria angolensis* Steindachner 1866:770. Type by monotypy. Valid (Poll 1984:129 [ref. 6180], for relationships see Howes 1985 [ref. 5148]). Kneriidae.

Knipowitschia Iljin 1927:129, 131 [ref. 5613]. Fem. *Gobius longicaudatus* Kessler 1877:35. Type by monotypy. Also appeared in Iljin 1928:43 [ref. 2296], and spelled once as *Knipovitschia*. Valid (Miller 1973:496 [ref. 6888], Miller in Whitehead et al. 1986:1047 [ref. 13677]). Gobiidae.

Knodus Eigenmann 1911:216 [ref. 1225]. Masc. *Knodus meridae* Eigenmann 1911:216. Type by monotypy. Also appeared as new genus in Eigenmann 1918:114 [ref. 1240] with type given as *Bryconamericus breviceps* Eigenmann. Valid (Géry 1977:391 [ref. 1597]). Characidae.

Kochia Kamohara 1960:11 [ref. 2556]. Fem. *Neopercis flavofasciata* Kamohara 1936:309. Type by original designation (also monotypic). Preoccupied [details not investigated], replaced by *Kochichthys* Kamohara 1961. Pinguipedidae.

Kochichthys Kamohara 1961:8 [ref. 2557]. Masc. *Neopercis flavofasciata* Kamohara 1936:309. Type by being a replacement name. Replacement for *Kochia* Kamohara 1960, preoccupied [details not investigated]. Valid (Randall 1984:41 [ref. 6067], Okamura in Masuda et al. 1984:292 [ref. 6441]). Pinguipedidae.

Koinga (subgenus of *Squalus*) Whitley 1939:242 [ref. 4695]. Fem. *Squalus whitleyi* Phillipps 1931:361. Type by original designation. Synonym of *Squalus* Linnaeus 1758 (Compagno 1984:109 [ref. 6474]). Squalidae.

Konia Trewavas, Green & Corbet 1972:61 [ref. 4460]. Fem. *Tilapia eisentrauti* Trewavas 1962:168. Type by original designation. Cichlidae.

Konopickia Whitley 1937:133 [ref. 4689]. Fem. *Ambassis mulleri* Klunzinger 1879:346. Type by original designation (also monotypic). Ambassidae.

Konosirus Jordan & Snyder 1900:349 [ref. 2502]. Masc. *Chatoessus punctatus* Schlegel in Temminck & Schlegel 1846:240. Type by original designation (also monotypic). Type not *Chatoessus nasus* as given by Jordan 1920:490 [ref. 4905], but clearly *C. punctatus* by original designation. Misspelled *Konoshirus* by Jordan & Snyder 1901:53 [ref. 2505]. Valid (Uyeno & Sato in Masuda et al. 1984:19 [ref. 6441], Grande 1985:248 [ref. 6466], Whitehead 1985:240 [ref. 5141]). Clupeidae.

Kopua Hardy 1984:244 [ref. 5338]. *Kopua nuimata* Hardy 1984: 246. Type by original designation (also monotypic). Gobiesocidae: Gobiesocinae.

Korsogaster Parr 1933:9 [ref. 3373]. Fem. *Korsogaster nanus* Parr 1933:9. Type by original designation (also monotypic). Synonym of *Hoplostethus* Cuvier 1829 (Woods & Sonoda 1973:306 [ref. 6899]). Trachichthyidae.

Kosswigichthys Sözer 1942:308 [ref. 4171]. Masc. *Kosswigichthys asquamatus* Sözer 1942:308. Type by monotypy. Valid (Parenti 1981:524 [ref. 7066]). Cyprinodontidae: Cyprinodontinae.

Kosswigobarbus Karaman 1971:239 [ref. 2560]. Masc. *Cyclocheilichthys kosswigi* Ladiges 1960:135. Type by original designation (also monotypic). Synonym of *Barbus* Cuvier 1816 in broad sense (Coad 1982 [ref. 5430]). Cyprinidae.

Koumansetta Whitley 1940:425 [ref. 4699]. Fem. *Koumansetta rainfordi* Whitley 1940:426. Type by original designation (also monotypic). Synonym of *Amblygobius* Bleeker 1874 (Hoese, pers. comm.). Gobiidae.

Koumansiasis Visweswara Rao 1968:17 [ref. 4524]. Fem. *Koumansiasis macrocephalus* Visweswara Rao 1968:17. Type by original designation (also monotypic). Synonym of *Bathygobius* Bleeker 1878 (Hoese, pers. comm.). Gobiidae.

Kowala Valenciennes in Cuvier & Valenciennes 1847:362 [ref. 1012]. *Kowala albella* Valenciennes in Cuvier & Valenciennes 1847:362. Type by subsequent designation. Type designated by Gill 1861:36 [ref. 1767]; type not *kowal* Rüppell [not absolute tautonymy] (see Whitehead 1967:52, 72 [ref. 6464]). Synonym of *Sardinella* Valenciennes 1847 (Whitehead 1985:90 [ref. 5141]). Clupeidae.

Kraemeria Steindachner 1906:1409 [ref. 4242]. Fem. *Kraemeria samoensis* Steindachner 1906:1409. Type by monotypy. Maugé 1986:375 cites original as Steindachner 1906:338 (Anz. Akad. Wiss. Wien, v. 43:338-339) which is an abstract of Steindachner (July) 1906 [relative dates not investigated]. Valid (Hayashi in

Masuda et al. 1984:287 [ref. 6441], Hoese 1986:811 [ref. 5670], Maugé 1986:375 [ref. 6218], Goren 1987 [ref. 6611], Birdsong et al. 1988:200 [ref. 7303]). Kraemeriidae.

Kraemericus Schultz in Schultz et al. 1966:8 [ref. 5366]. Masc. *Kraemericus chapmani* Schultz in Schultz et al. 1966:8. Type by original designation (also monotypic). Valid (Birdsong et al. 1988:183 [ref. 7303]). Xenisthmidae.

Krefftia (subgenus of *Holtbyrnia*) Parr 1960:63, 71 [ref. 3384]. Fem. *Searsia schnakenbecki* Krefft 1960:71. Type by original designation. Synonym of *Sagamichthys* Parr 1953 (Krefft 1973:97 [ref. 7166]). Platytroctidae.

Krefftichthys Hulley 1981:9 [ref. 2276]. Masc. *Myctophum anderssoni* Lönnberg 1905:763. Type by original designation (also monotypic). Valid (Moser et al. 1984:219 [ref. 13645], Paxton et al. 1984:241 [ref. 13625], Hulley 1986:303 [ref. 5672]). Myctophidae.

Krefftius Ogilby 1897:736 [ref. 3274]. Masc. *Eleotris australis* Krefft 1864:183. Type by original designation (also monotypic). Synonym of *Gobiomorphus* Gill 1863. Eleotridae.

Kribia Herre 1946:123 [ref. 2142]. Fem. *Eleotris kribensis* Boulenger 1907:52. Type by original designation (also monotypic). Valid (Miller 1981:282 [ref. 3013], Maugé 1986:395 [ref. 6218], Birdsong et al. 1988:181 [ref. 7303]). Eleotridae.

Krobia Kullander & Nijssen 1989:148 [ref. 14136]. Fem. *Acara guianensis* Regan 1905:340. Type by original designation. Cichlidae.

Krohnius Cocco 1844:22 [ref. 866]. Masc. *Krohnius filamentosus* Cocco 1844:23. Type by monotypy. Based on a larva. Apparently a synonym of *Caelorinchus* Giorna 1809. Macrouridae: Macrourinae.

Kronia Miranda-Ribeiro 1915:9 [ref. 3711]. Fem. *Kronia iguapensis* Miranda-Ribeiro 1915:10. Type by monotypy. Appears on p. 9 in section titled Trematolepides. Synonym of *Odontesthes* Evermann & Kendall 1906 (White 1985:17 [ref. 13551]). Atherinidae: Atherinopsinae.

Kronichthys Miranda-Ribeiro 1908:[1] [ref. 3715]. Masc. *Kronichthys subteres* Miranda-Ribeiro 1908:[2]. Type by monotypy. Unpaginated. Valid (Isbrücker 1980:13 [ref. 2303], Burgess 1989:430 [ref. 12860]). Loricariidae.

Kroseriphus Whitley 1950:44 [ref. 4713]. Masc. *Seriphus politus* Ayres 1860:80. Type by being a replacement name. Replacement for *Seriphus* Ayres 1860 [preoccupation not researched]; *Seriphus* is used in current literature as valid. Sciaenidae.

Krusensterniella Schmidt 1904:197 [ref. 3946]. Fem. *Krusensterniella notabilis* Schmidt 1904:198. Type by monotypy. *Krusensteiniella* Popov 1931 evidently is a misspelling [not researched]. Valid (Anderson 1984:578 [ref. 13634], Toyoshima in Masuda et al. 1984:305 [ref. 6441]). Zoarcidae.

Kryptophanaron Silvester & Fowler 1926:246 [ref. 4028]. Neut. *Kryptophanaron alfredi* Silvester & Fowler 1926:246. Type by original designation (also monotypic). Valid (Woods & Sonoda 1973:328 [ref. 6899] as *Kryptophaneron*, McCosker & Rosenblatt 1987:158 [ref. 6707], Johnson & Rosenblatt 1988 [ref. 6682]). Anomalopidae.

Kryptopterichthys Bleeker 1858:255, 257, 288 [ref. 365]. Masc. *Silurus palembangensis* Bleeker 1852:584. Type by subsequent designation. Also on pp. 24, 26, 27 et seq.; misspelled once on p. 288 as *Kryptopterichthijs*. Type designated by Bleeker 1862:395 [ref. 391], 1862:18 [ref. 393] and 1863:116 [ref. 401]. Synonym of *Kryptopterus* Bleeker 1858 (Haig 1952:106 [ref. 12607], Roberts 1989:145 [ref. 6439]). Siluridae.

Kryptopterus Bleeker 1858:255, 257, 283 [ref. 365]. Masc. *Kryptopterus micropus* Bleeker 1858:284. Type by subsequent designation. Type designated by Bleeker 1862:395 [ref. 391] or 1862:18 [ref. 393], also 1863:116 [ref. 401]. *Cryptopterus* Günther 1864:6, 38 [ref. 1974] is an unjustified emendation (as emended is preoccupied by Kaup 1860 in fishes). Valid (Haig 1952:92, 106 [ref. 12607], Kottelat 1985:268 [ref. 11441], Burgess 1989:86 [ref. 12860], Kottelat 1989:14 [ref. 13605], Roberts 1989:145 [ref. 6439]). Siluridae.

Kuhlia Gill 1861:48 [ref. 1768]. Fem. *Perca ciliata* Cuvier (ex Kuhl & van Hasselt) in Cuvier & Valenciennes 1828:52. Type by original designation (also monotypic). Valid (Mochizuki in Masuda et al. 1984:142 [ref. 6441], Maugé 1986 [ref. 6218], Smith 1986:508 [ref. 5712], Paxton et al. 1989:539 [ref. 12442]). Kuhliidae.

Kuiterichthys Pietsch 1984:37 [ref. 5380]. Masc. *Chironectes furcipilis* Cuvier 1817:429. Type by original designation (also monotypic). Valid (Paxton et al. 1989:280 [ref. 12442]). Antennariidae.

Kumba Marshall 1973:616 [ref. 6965]. Fem. *Kumba dentoni* Marshall 1973:617. Type by original designation (also monotypic). Valid (Fahay & Markle 1984:274 [ref. 13653]). Macrouridae: Macrourinae.

Kumococius Matsubara & Ochiai 1955:89 [ref. 2907]. Masc. *Insidiator detrusus* Jordan & Seale 1905:10. Type by original designation (also monotypic). Valid (Ochiai in Masuda et al. 1984:322 [ref. 6441] but spelled *Kumococcius*). Platycephalidae.

Kurandapogon Whitley 1939:1 [ref. 4696]. Masc. *Kurandapogon blanchardi* Whitley 1939:1. Type by original designation (also monotypic). Synonym of *Glossamia* Gill 1863 (Fraser 1972:8 [ref. 5195], Paxton et al. 1989:555 [ref. 12442]). Apogonidae.

Kuronezumia (subgenus of *Nezumia*) Iwamoto 1974:509 [ref. 2310]. Fem. *Nezumia bubonis* Iwamoto 1974:509. Type by monotypy. Second unnamed species mentioned on p. 513. Macrouridae: Macrourinae.

Kurtus Bloch 1786:121 [ref. 465]. Masc. *Kurtus indicus* Bloch 1786:122. Type by monotypy. Spelled *Kyrtus* in Bloch & Schneider 1801:xxxv [ref. 471]; unjustifiably emended to *Cyrtus* by Agassiz 1846:198 [ref. 64]; misspelled *Curtus* by authors. Valid. Kurtidae.

Kutaflammeo (subgenus of *Holocentrus*) Whitley 1933:69 [ref. 4677]. *Holocentrus tahiticum* Kner 1864:482. Type by original designation (also monotypic). Synonym of *Neoniphon* Castelnau 1875 (Randall & Heemstra 1985:2 [ref. 5144]). Holocentridae.

Kyleia Chabanaud 1931:393 [ref. 6057]. Fem. *Arnoglossus thori* Kyle 1913:55. Type by original designation (also monotypic). Also described as new in Chabanaud 1933:49 [ref. 787]). Synonym of *Arnoglossus* Bleeker 1862 (Norman 1934:173 [ref. 6893], Nielsen 1973:621 [ref. 6885]). Bothidae: Bothinae.

Kyphosus Lacepède 1801:114 [ref. 2710]. Masc. *Kyphosus bigibbus* Lacepède 1801:114, 115. Type by monotypy. Unjustifiably emended to *Cyphosus* by Jordan & Gilbert 1883:792 [ref. 2476] (see Briggs 1961:162 [ref. 13439]). Valid (Desoutter 1973:420 [ref. 7203], Araga in Masuda et al. 1984:166 [ref. 6441], Tortonese in Whitehead et al. 1986:912 [ref. 13676], Smith 1986:603 [ref. 5712]). Kyphosidae: Kyphosinae.

Labeo Bowdich 1825:xii, 122 [ref. 590]. Masc. *Labeo sparoides*

Bowdich 1825:122. Type by monotypy. Also involves fig. 29 opposite p. 140 in conjunction with p. xii. Preoccupied by Cuvier 1816 in fishes, replaced by *Labeova* Whitley 1950. Sparidae.

Labeo Cuvier 1816:194 [ref. 993]. Masc. *Cyprinus niloticus* Forsskål 1775. Type by subsequent designation. Type designated by Bleeker 1863:194 [ref. 397] or 1863:25 [ref. 4859]. Misspelled *Labes* by Goldfuss 1820. Type apparently not *Cyprinus niloticus* Linnaeus. Valid (Wu et al. 1977:351 [ref. 4807], Jayaram 1981:116 [ref. 6497], Lévêque & Daget 1984:305 [ref. 6186], Kottelat 1985:263 [ref. 11441], Chu & Cui in Chu & Chen 1989:248 [ref. 13584], Kottelat 1989:8 [ref. 13605]). Cyprinidae.

Labeobarbus Rüppell 1836:14 [ref. 3845]. Masc. *Labeobarbus nedgia* Rüppell 1836:14. Type by monotypy. Synonym of *Tor* Gray 1834 (Karaman 1971:224 [ref. 2560], Chu & Cui in Chu & Chen 1989:136 [ref. 13584]). Cyprinidae.

Labeotropheus Ahl 1926:52 [ref. 77]. Masc. *Labeotropheus fuelleborni* Ahl 1926:52. Type by original designation. Valid (Ribbink et al. 1983:237 [ref. 13555]). Cichlidae.

Labeova Whitley 1950:44 [ref. 4713]. Fem. *Labeo sparoides* Bowdich 1825:122. Type by being a replacement name. Replacement for *Labeo* Bowdich 1825, preoccupied by Cuvier 1816 in fishes. Sparidae.

Labichthys Gill & Ryder 1883:261 [ref. 1746]. Masc. *Labichthys carinatus* Gill & Ryder 1883:261. Type by subsequent designation. Appeared first as name only in Gill 1883:253 [ref. 1724]. Type designated by Jordan & Davis 1891:655 [ref. 2437]. Valid (Karmovskaya 1982:154 [ref. 5204], Smith & Nielsen 1989:450 [ref. 13290]). Nemichthyidae.

Labidesthes Cope 1870:455 [ref. 913]. Fem. *Chirostoma sicculum* Cope 1865:81. Type by monotypy. Valid (Chernoff 1986:189 [ref. 5847]). Atherinidae: Menidiinae.

Labidochromis Trewavas 1935:(68) 80 [ref. 4451]. Masc. *Labidochromis vellicans* Trewavas 1935:80. Type by monotypy. Valid (Ribbink et al. 1983:228 [ref. 13555]). Cichlidae.

Labidorhamphus Fowler 1905:493 [ref. 1370]. Masc. *Hemirhamphus amblyurus* Bleeker 1849:11. Type by original designation (also monotypic). Correct spelling for genus of type species is *Hemiramphus*. Synonym of *Zenarchopterus* Gill 1864 (Collette 1986:163 [ref. 6197]). Hemiramphidae.

Labiobarbus van Hasselt 1823:132 [ref. 5963]. Masc. *Labiobarbus leptocheilus* Valenciennes in Cuvier & Valenciennes 1842:234. Type by subsequent designation. Originally two species (*leptocheilus* and *lipocheilus*), both nomina nuda (see Kottelat 1987: 370 [ref. 5962]). Type designated by Smith 1945:221 [ref. 4056] as *Labiobarbus leptocheilus* van Hasselt (validly published by Valenciennes 1842). Valid (Wu et al. 1977:354 [ref. 4807], Jayaram 1981:121 [ref. 6497], Kottelat 1985:263 [ref. 11441], Chu & Cui in Chu & Chen 1989:230 [ref. 13584],Kottelat 1989:8 [ref. 13605]). Unidentifiable (Roberts 1989:37 [ref. 6439]). Cyprinidae.

Labracinus Schlegel 1858:121 [ref. 6605]. Masc. *Cichlops cyclophthalmus* Müller & Troschel 1849:24. Type by monotypy. First published in synonymy of *Cichlopsis* [error for *Cichlops*] Müller & Troschel, but treated as valid before 1961 (Gill 1904:119 [ref. 6606] and by Bleeker 1875:2 [ref. 444]) and therefore available from Schlegel 1858. Type first technically fixed by Jordan 1919:383 [ref. 4904], else by Schultz 1967:20 [ref. 9645]. Predates *Dampieria* Castelnau 1875. Valid (Paxton et al. 1989:518 [ref. 12442] with Bleeker 1875 as author). Pseudochromidae: Pseudochrominae.

Labracoglossa Peters 1866:513 [ref. 3439]. Fem. *Labracoglossa argenteiventris* Peters 1866:513. Type by monotypy. Valid (Gosline 1985:353 [ref. 5283] in Scorpididae, Araga in Masuda et al. 1984:152 [ref. 6441] and Paxton et al. 1989:567 [ref. 12442] in Labracoglossidae). Kyphosidae: Scorpidinae.

Labracopsis (subgenus of *Pikea*) Steindachner & Döderlein 1883:235 [ref. 4246]. Fem. *Labracopsis japonicus* Döderlein in Steindachner & Döderlein 1883:235. Type by monotypy. Appeared first as name only in Steindachner & Döderlein 1883:49 [not investigated]. Authorship attributed here to Steindachner & Döderlein as both participated in the description. Synonym of *Liopropoma* Gill 1861 (Randall & Taylor 1988:7 [ref. 6429]). Serranidae: Liopropomatinae.

Labrastrum Guichenot 1860:153 [ref. 1942]. Neut. *Ctenolabrus flagellifer* Valenciennes in Cuvier & Valenciennes 1839:240. Type by original designation (also monotypic). As *Lebrastres* and *Labrastre*, but latinized on p. 153 as *Labrastrum*. Synonym of *Duymaeria* Bleeker 1856. Labridae.

Labrax Cuvier in Cuvier & Valenciennes 1828:55 [ref. 997]. Masc. *Perca labrax* Linnaeus 1758:290. Type by absolute tautonymy. Preoccupied by *Labrax* Pallas 1810; not replaced. Synonym of *Morone* Mitchill 1814 (some authors), synonym of *Dicentrarchus* Gill 1860 (others, e.g. Daget & Smith 1986:299 [ref. 6204]). Moronidae.

Labrax Klein 1776:32 [ref. 4918]. Masc. Also in Klein 1779:164 [ref. 4924]. Not available, published in a work that does not conform to the principle of binominal nomenclature. Not *Labrax* Pallas. In the synonymy of *Labrax* Cuvier 1828. Moronidae.

Labrax Klein in Walbaum 1792:584 [ref. 4572]. Masc. Not available (Opinion 21). In the synonymy of *Dicentrarchus* Gill 1860 (Tortonese 1973:357 [ref. 7192]). Moronidae.

Labrax Pallas 1810:384 [ref. 3350]. Masc. *Labrax lagocephalus* Pallas 1810:384. Type by subsequent designation [not researched]. Not *Labrax* of Klein or Cuvier. Synonym of *Hexagrammos* Steller 1809. Hexagrammidae: Hexagramminae.

Labrichthys Bleeker 1854:331 [ref. 343]. Masc. *Labrichthys cyanotaenia* Bleeker 1854:331. Type by monotypy. Valid (Randall & Springer 1973:283 [ref. 3603], Araga in Masuda et al. 1984:207 [ref. 6441], Randall 1986:697 [ref. 5706]). Labridae.

Labrisomus Swainson 1839:75, 76, 182, 277 [ref. 4303]. Masc. *Clinus pectinifer* Valenciennes in Cuvier & Valenciennes 1836:374. Type by original designation (p. 75). *Labrosomus* Agassiz 1846:199 [ref. 64] and others is an unjustified emendation. Valid (Hubbs 1953:117 [ref. 2253], Springer 1958:422 [ref. 10210], Greenfield & Johnson 1981:15 [ref. 5580]). Labrisomidae.

Labristoma (subgenus of *Plesiops*) Swainson 1839:230 [ref. 4303]. Neut. *Pseudochromis olivaceus* Rüppell 1835:9. Type by being a replacement name. Unneeded replacement for *Pseudochromis* Rüppell 1835. Objective synonym of *Pseudochromis* Rüppell 1835. Pseudochromidae: Pseudochrominae.

Labroblennius Borodin 1928:31 [ref. 526]. Masc. *Labroblennius nicholsi* Borodin 1928:31. Type by monotypy. Synonym of *Ophioblennius* Gill 1860 (Smith-Vaniz & Springer 1971:35 [ref. 4145]). Blenniidae.

Labrochromis Daget 1952:226 [ref. 1023]. Masc. *Labrochromis polli* Daget 1952:227. Type by monotypy. Described as a new genus, not *Labrochromis* Regan 1920. Synonym of *Gobiocichla* Kanazawa 1951. Cichlidae.

Labrochromis Regan 1920:45 [ref. 3669]. Masc. *Tilapia pallida* not of Boulenger 1911:72. Type by original designation. Based on a misidentified type species (see Greenwood 1980:37 [ref. 1899]), specimens misidentified by Regan as *T. pallida* were *Haplochromis ishmaeli* Boulenger 1906, as recognized by Regan (1922). Probably should go to ICZN. *Labrochromis* treated as valid by Greenwood 1980:37 [ref. 1899]. Cichlidae.

Labroclinus Smith 1946:544 [ref. 4072]. Masc. *Cristiceps mentalis* Gilchrist & Thompson 1908:139. Type by original designation. Synonym of *Pavoclinus* Smith 1946, but as a valid subgenus (Smith 1986:766 [ref. 5712]). Clinidae.

Labrodascyllus Caporiacco 1947:198 [ref. 721]. Masc. *Labrodascyllus cimballii* Caporiacco 1947:198. Type by monotypy. Pomacentridae.

Labroides Bleeker 1851:227, 249 [ref. 331]. Masc. *Labroides paradiseus* Bleeker 1851:249 (= *Cossyphus dimidiatus* Valenciennes 1839:136). Type by monotypy. Bleeker's *L. paradiseus* apparently is an unneeded substitute for *Cossyphus dimidiatus* Valenciennes. Valid (Richards & Leis 1984:544 [ref. 13668], Araga in Masuda et al. 1984:206 [ref. 6441], Randall 1986:697 [ref. 5706]). Labridae.

Labroperca Gill 1862:236 [ref. 1664]. Fem. *Serranus labriformis* Jenyns 1842:8. Type by monotypy. Synonym of *Epinephelus* Bloch 1793 (C. L. Smith 1971:103 [ref. 14102], Daget & Smith 1986:301 [ref. 6204]). Serranidae: Epinephelinae.

Labropsis Schmidt 1930:75 [ref. 3937]. Fem. *Labropsis manabei* Schmidt 1930:76. Type by original designation (also monotypic). Apparently appeared first as name only in Schmidt 1929:515 [Fourth Pac. Sci. Congress v. 3, not investigated]. Valid (Randall 1981 [ref. 5493], Araga in Masuda et al. 1984:206 [ref. 6441]). Labridae.

Labrus Linnaeus 1758:282 [ref. 2787]. Masc. *Labrus bimaculatus* Linnaeus 1758:285. Type by subsequent designation. Type usually given as first designated by Bonaparte 1841:puntata 156, fasc. 30 [ref. 512] but Bonaparte listed the type only as *L. vetula* Bloch (not an included species). Earliest technical designation not researched. Valid (Bauchot & Quignard 1973:426 [ref. 7204], Richards & Leis 1984:544 [ref. 13668], Quignard & Pras in Whitehead et al. 1986:925 [ref. 13676]). Labridae.

Laccoeleotris Fowler 1935:403 [ref. 1421]. Fem. *Laccoeleotris lineopinnis* Fowler 1935:403. Type by original designation (also monotypic). Synonym of *Ptereleotris* Gill 1863 (Randall & Hoese 1985 [ref. 5197]). Microdesmidae: Ptereleotrinae.

Lacepedia Castelnau 1873:42 [ref. 758]. Fem. *Lacepedia cataphracta* Castelnau 1873:43. Type by monotypy. Status uncertain; placement in the subfamily Anthiinae follows Hoese & Kuiter 1984:10 [ref. 5300]. Serranidae: Anthiinae.

Lachneria Smith 1954:794 [ref. 4093]. Fem. *Gymnapogon gracilicauda* Lachner 1953:497. Type by original designation (also monotypic). Synonym of *Pseudamiops* Smith 1954 (Fraser 1972:31 [ref. 5195], Randall et al. 1985:4 [ref. 9188]). Apogonidae.

Lachnolaimus Cuvier 1829:257 [ref. 995]. Masc. *Lachnolaimus suillus* Cuvier 1829:257. Type by subsequent designation. Two species listed in footnote; type designated by Jordan 1890:626 [ref. 2392]. Based on *Suillus* Catesby 1750. *Lachnolaemus* Agassiz 1846:199 [ref. 64] is an unjustified emendation. Valid (Richards & Leis 1984:544 [ref. 13668]). Labridae.

Laciris Huber 1981:33 [ref. 2271]. Fem. *Haplochilichthys pelagicus* Worthington 1932:33. Type by monotypy. Correct spelling of genus of type species is *Aplocheilichthys*. Valid (Wildekamp et al. 1986:190 [ref. 6198]). Cyprinodontidae: Aplocheilichthyinae.

Lacrimolycus (subgenus of *Ophthalmolycus*) Andriashev & Fedorov 1986:28 [ref. 6133]. Masc. *Ophthalmolycus (Lacrimolycus) campbellensis* Andriashev & Fedorov 1986:28. Type by original designation (also monotypic). Zoarcidae.

Lactarius Valenciennes in Cuvier & Valenciennes 1833:237 [ref. 1002]. Masc. *Lactarius delicatulus* Valenciennes 1833:258 (= *Scomber lactarius* Bloch & Schneider 1801:31). Type by monotypy (also by absolute tautonymy of cited synonym); *Lactarius delicatulus* Valenciennes is an unneeded replacement for *S. lactarius*. Valid (Paxton et al. 1989:569 [ref. 12442]). Lactariidae.

Lactophrys (subgenus of *Tetrosomus*) Swainson 1839:194, 324 [ref. 4303]. Fem. *Ostracion trigonus* Linnaeus 1758:330. Type by subsequent designation. Type designated by Bleeker 1865:27 [ref. 416] (but genus misspelled *Laetophrys*); also designated by Swain 1882:282 [ref. 5966]. Valid (Tyler 1980:239 [ref. 4477], Arai 1983:203 [ref. 14249]). Ostraciidae: Ostraciinae.

Lactoria (subgenus of *Ostracion*) Jordan & Fowler 1902:278, 279 [ref. 2457]. Fem. *Ostracion cornutus* Linnaeus 1758:331. Type by original designation. Description in key as a subgenus. Valid (Tyler 1980:239 [ref. 4477], Arai 1983:203 [ref. 14249], Matsuura in Masuda et al. 1984:362 [ref. 6441], Smith 1986:891 [ref. 5712]). Ostraciidae: Ostraciinae.

Lacustricola (subgenus of *Micropanchax*) Myers 1924:43 [ref. 3092]. Masc. *Haplochilus pumilus* Boulenger 1906:554. Type by monotypy. Synonym of *Aplocheilichthys* Bleeker 1863 (Wildekamp et al. 1986:170 [ref. 6198]); as a valid subgenus (Parenti 1981:508 [ref. 7066]). Cyprinodontidae: Aplocheilichthyinae.

Ladigesia Géry 1968:78 [ref. 1591]. Fem. *Ladigesia roloffi* Géry 1968:83. Type by original designation (also monotypic). Valid (Géry 1977:50 [ref. 1597], Paugy 1984:173 [ref. 6183]). Alestiidae.

Ladigesocypris Karaman 1972:143 [ref. 2561]. Fem. *Leucaspius ghigii* Gianferrari 1927:123. Type by original designation (also monotypic). Cyprinidae.

Ladislavia Dybowski 1869:954 [ref. 1169]. Fem. *Ladislavia taczanowskii* Dybowski 1869:954. Type by monotypy. Valid (Banarescu & Nalbant 1973:37 [ref. 173], Lu, Luo & Chen 1977:466 [ref. 13495]). Cyprinidae.

Laemargus Müller & Henle 1837:116 [ref. 3067]. Masc. *Squalus borealis* Scoresby 1820:538. Type by subsequent designation. Dates to Müller & Henle 1837:116 without species. Three species in Müller & Henle 1839:93 [ref. 3069]. Type apparently designated first by Jordan 1919:192 [ref. 2410]. Synonym of *Somniosus* Lesueur 1818 (Krefft & Tortonese 1973:46 [ref. 7165], Compagno 1984:102 [ref. 6474], Cappetta 1987:62 [ref. 6348]). Squalidae.

Laemolyta Cope 1872:258 [ref. 921]. *Schizodon taeniatus* Kner 1859:159. Type by monotypy. Synonym of *Anostomus* Scopoli 1777, but as a valid subgenus (Géry 1977:178 [ref. 1597]); valid (Winterbottom 1980:2 [ref. 4755], Vari 1983:5 [ref. 5419]). Curimatidae: Anostominae.

Laemonema Günther in Johnson 1862:171 [ref. 2357]. Neut. *Laemonema robustum* Johnson 1862:171. Apparently first in Johnson (Sept.) 1862:171, attributed to Günther MS (published Nov. 1862:356 [ref. 1969]), with *L. robustum* the only included species, so type by monotypy even though that species not intended by Günther as type. Valid (Paulin 1983:113 [ref. 5459], Fahay & Markle 1984:266 [ref. 13653], Okamura in Masuda et al. 1984:91 [ref. 6441], Cohen 1986:326 [ref. 5646], Markle & Melendez C.

1988 [ref. 9283], Paxton et al. 1989:299 [ref. 12442]). Moridae.

Laemonemodes Gilchrist 1903:208 [ref. 1645]. Masc. *Laemonemodes compressicauda* Gilchrist 1903:208. Type by monotypy. Misspelled *Laemonemodus* by Jordan 1920:503 [ref. 4905] and 1923:164 [ref. 2421]. Moridae.

Laeops Günther 1880:28 [ref. 2011]. Masc. *Laeops parviceps* Günther 1880:29. Type by monotypy. Valid (Norman 1934:252 [ref. 6893], Amaoka 1969:204 [ref. 105], Ahlstrom et al. 1984:642 [ref. 13641], Amaoka in Masuda et al. 1984:350 [ref. 6441], Hensley 1986:859 [ref. 5669], Hensley 1986:941 [ref. 6326]). Bothidae: Bothinae.

Laeoptichthys Hubbs 1915:460 [ref. 2224]. Masc. *Laeoptichthys fragilis* Hubbs 1915:460. Type by original designation (also monotypic). Synonym of *Laeops* Günther 1880 (Norman 1934:252 [ref. 6893], Amaoka 1969:204 [ref. 105]). Bothidae: Bothinae.

Laephichthys Ogilby 1916:173 [ref. 3297]. Masc. *Acanthurus rostratus* Günther 1875:117. Type by original designation (also monotypic). Spelling somewhat unclear with regard to dipthong "ae" or "oe" in original description, apparently "ae". Synonym of *Zebrasoma* Swainson 1839 (Randall 1955:363 [ref. 13648]). Acanthuridae.

Laetacara Kullander 1986:321 [ref. 12439]. Fem. *Acara flavilabris* Cope 1870:570. Type by original designation. Cichlidae.

Laeviraja Bonaparte 1834:puntata 32 [ref. 517]. Fem. *Raja oxyrinchus* Linnaeus 1758:231. Type by subsequent designation. Described in puntata 32, fasc. 6, under *Raja marginata* with other species mentioned; also in puntata 130, fasc. 25. Earliest subsequent type designation not researched, possibly by Bonaparte 1838:7 (of separate) [ref. 4979]. Synonym of *Raja* Linnaeus 1758, subgenus *Dipturus* Rafinesque 1810 (Stehmann 1973:62 [ref. 7168]). Rajidae.

Laevirajae Nardo 1827:11 [ref. 3146]. Not available, name given in pleural form; listed in Jordan 1919:121 [ref. 2410]. Original not examined; also in Isis, v. 20:476 [seen]. Rajidae.

Laeviscutella Poll, Whitehead & Hopson 1965:279 [ref. 3524]. Fem. *Laeviscutella dekimpei* Poll, Whitehead & Hopson 1965:280. Type by monotypy. Valid (Poll et al. 1984:45 [ref. 6172], Grande 1985:247 [ref. 6466], Whitehead 1985:164 [ref. 5141]). Clupeidae.

Laevoceratias Parr 1927:33 [ref. 3366]. Masc. *Laevoceratias liparis* Parr 1927:33. Type by monotypy. Synonym of *Gigantactis* Brauer 1902 (Bertelsen et al. 1981:24 [ref. 5330]). Gigantactinidae.

Lagocephalus Swainson 1839:194, 328 [ref. 4303]. Masc. *Tetraodon stellatus* Donovan 1802:66. Type by subsequent designation. Type as designated by Swain 1882:283 [ref. 5966]. Valid (Tortonese 1973:645 [ref. 7192], Shipp 1974 [ref. 7147], Tyler 1980:341 [ref. 4477], Arai 1983:206 [ref. 14249], Matsuura in Masuda et al. 1984:364 [ref. 6441], Tortonese in Whitehead et al. 1986:1343 [ref. 13677], Smith & Heemstra 1986:900 [ref. 5714], see Su et al. 1986:112 [ref. 12582]). Tetraodontidae.

Lagochila Jordan & Brayton 1877:280 [ref. 2435]. Fem. *Lagochila lacera* Jordan & Brayton 1877:280. Type by monotypy. Apparently not preoccupied by several near-identical spellings (see Fowler 1976:11 [ref. 7323]); *Quassilabia* Jordan & Brayton 1878 is an unneeded replacement. Valid (authors); synonym of *Moxostoma* Rafinsque 1820 (G. R. Smith, pers. comm.). Catostomidae.

Lagodon Holbrook 1855:56 [ref. 2184]. Masc. *Sparus rhomboides* Linnaeus 1766:470. Type by monotypy. Valid. Sparidae.

Lagowskiella (subgenus of *Phoxinus*) Dybowski 1916:ca. 100 [ref. 6519]. Fem. *Phoxinus lagowskii* Dybowski 1869:952. Original not seen. Valid (Howes 1985:63 [ref. 5274], Travers 1989:197 [ref. 13578]). Cyprinidae.

Lagusia Vari 1978:247 [ref. 4514]. Fem. *Datnia micracanthus* Bleeker 1860:55. Type by original designation (also monotypic). Terapontidae.

Laguvia Hora 1921:739 [ref. 2203]. Fem. *Laguvia shawi* Hora 1921:740. Type by subsequent designation. Three included species, type perhaps first designated by Jordan 1921:148 [ref. 2421] as *Pimelodus asperus* McClelland, but authors apparently regard *shawi* as type [not investigated]. Synonym of *Glyptothorax* Blyth 1860 (Jayaram 1981:249 [ref. 6497], Li 1986:522 [ref. 6132]). Sisoridae.

Lahilliella (subgenus of *Anostomus*) Eigenmann & Kennedy in Eigenmann 1903:144 [ref. 1218]. Fem. *Schizodon nasutus* Kner 1859:164. Type by original designation (also monotypic). Misspelled *Lahiliella* by Jordan 1920:502 [ref. 4905]. Curimatidae: Anostominae.

Laichowcypris Yen 1978:28 [ref. 13511]. *Laichowxypris day* Yen 1978:28. Type apparently by monotypy. Apparently available; see Kottelat 1989:1103 [ref. 14361]. Cyprinidae.

Laides Jordan 1919:293 [ref. 4904]. Masc. *Pangasius hexanema* Bleeker 1852:588. Type by being a replacement name. Replacement for *Lais* Bleeker 1858, preoccupied by Gistel 1848 in Tunicata. Valid (Burgess 1989:105 [ref. 12860], Kottelat 1989:14 [ref. 13605], Roberts 1989:131 [ref. 6439]). In family Schilbeidae (T. Roberts, pers. comm., Feb. 1990). Schilbeidae.

Laimumena Sauvage 1884:147 [ref. 3898]. Fem. *Laimumena barbonica* Sauvage 1884:147. Type by monotypy. Doradidae.

Laiopteryx Weber 1913:423 [ref. 4602]. Fem. *Brachypleura xanthosticta* Alcock 1889:281. Type by monotypy. Misspelled *Liopteryx* by Jordan 1920:551 [ref. 4905]. Synonym of *Brachypleura* Günther 1862 (Norman 1934:400 [ref. 6893]). Citharidae: Brachypleurinae.

Laiphognathus Smith 1955:23 [ref. 4101]. Masc. *Laiphognathus multimaculatus* Smith 1955:24. Type by original designation (also monotypic). Valid (Springer 1972:8 [ref. 4178], Springer 1985:91 [ref. 6107], Springer 1986:749 [ref. 5719]). Blenniidae.

Lairdina Fowler 1953:385 [ref. 1464]. Fem. *Lairdina hopletupus* Fowler 1953:386. Type by original designation (also monotypic). Eleotridae.

Lais Bleeker 1858:170 [ref. 365]. *Pangasius hexanema* Bleeker 1852:589. Type by monotypy. Apparently preoccupied by Gistel 1848 in Tunicata [not investigated], replaced by *Laides* Jordan 1919. Objective synonym of *Laides* Jordan 1919 (Roberts 1989:131 [ref. 6439]). In family Schilbeidae (T. Roberts, pers. comm., Feb. 1990). Schilbeidae.

Lambdopsetta Smith & Pope 1906:496 [ref. 4058]. Fem. *Lambdopsetta kitaharae* Smith & Pope 1906:496. Type by original designation (also monotypic). Synonym of *Laeops* Günther 1880 (Norman 1934:252 [ref. 6893], Amaoka 1969:204 [ref. 105]). Bothidae: Bothinae.

Lambepiedra Fernández-Yépez 1948:62 [ref. 1316]. *Lambepiedra alleni* Fernández-Yépez 1948:62. Type by original designation. Synonym of *Curimata* Bosc 1817 (Vari 1989:6 [ref. 9189], Vari 1989:21 [ref. 13506]). Curimatidae: Curimatinae.

Lambertia Perugia 1894:550 [ref. 3435]. Fem. *Lambertia atra* Perugia 1894:551. Type by monotypy. Preoccupied by Robineau-Desvoidy 1863 in Diptera and by Souverbie 1869 in Mollusca; replaced by *Lambertichthys* Whitley 1938. Plotosidae.

Lambertichthys Whitley 1938:223 [ref. 4693]. Masc. *Lambertia atra* Perugia 1894:550. Type by being a replacement name. Replacement for *Lambertia* Perugia 1894, preoccupied by Robineau-Desvoidy 1863 in Diptera and by Souverbie 1869 in Mollusca. Plotosidae.

Lamia Risso 1826:123 [ref. 3757]. Fem. *Squalus cornubicus* Gmelin in Linnaeus 1789:1497. Type by monotypy. Preoccupied by Edwards 1771 [not researched] and by Fabricus 1775 in Coleoptera; not replaced. Objective synonym of *Lamna* Cuvier 1816 (Compagno 1984:246 [ref. 6474]). Lamnidae.

Lamiopsis Gill 1862:399, 401 [ref. 1783]. Fem. *Carcharias (Prionodon) temminckii* Müller & Henle 1839:48. Type by original designation (also monotypic). Also in Gill 1862:410 [ref. 4910]. Valid (Compagno 1984:511 [ref. 6846], Compagno 1988:334 [ref. 13488]). Carcharhinidae.

Lamiostoma Glückman 1964:105 [ref. 1824]. Neut. *Lamiostoma belyaevi* Glückman 1964:105. Type by original designation. The type is a Recent species; fossil species also included. Synonym of *Isurus* Rafinesque 1810 (Compagno 1984:242 [ref. 6474]). Lamnidae.

Lamna (subgenus of *Squalus*) Cuvier 1816:126 [ref. 993]. Fem. *Squalus cornubicus* Gmelin in Linnaeus 1789:1497. Type by subsequent designation. Type apparently designated first by Bonaparte 1839: 9 (of separate; also see p. 2 of separate) [ref. 4979]; also designated by Gill 1862:398 [ref. 1783]. Valid (Springer 1973:13 [ref. 7162], Quéro in Whitehead et al. 1984:87 [ref. 13675], Compagno 1984:246 [ref. 6474], Nakaya in Masuda et al. 1984:9 [ref. 6441], Bass 1986:100 [ref. 5635], Cappetta 1987:97 [ref. 6348], Paxton et al. 1989:68 [ref. 12442]). Lamnidae.

Lamnarius (subgenus of *Galeolamna*) Whitley 1943:119 [ref. 4702]. Masc. *Carcharias spenceri* Ogilby 1910:3. Type by original designation (also monotypic). Synonym of *Carcharhinus* Blainville 1816 (Garrick 1982:19 [ref. 5454], Compagno 1984:449 [ref. 6846], Compagno 1988:308 [ref. 13488]). Carcharhinidae.

Lamnostoma Kaup 1856:49 [ref. 2572]. Neut. *Lamnostoma pictum* Kaup 1856:50. Type by monotypy. Also appeared in Kaup 1856:24 [ref. 2573]. Valid (McCosker 1977:68 [ref. 6836], McCosker & Castle 1986:179 [ref. 5690], McCosker et al. 1989:297 [ref. 13288]). Ophichthidae: Ophichthinae.

Lamontella Smith 1956:32 [ref. 4107]. Fem. *Tetrapturus albida [albidus]* Poey 1860:237. Type by original designation (also monotypic). Synonym of *Tetrapturus* Rafinesque 1810 (de Sylva 1973:480 [ref. 7210], Nakamura 1983:294 [ref. 5371]). Istiophoridae.

Lamontichthys Miranda-Ribeiro 1939:12 [ref. 3024]. Masc. *Harttia filamentosa* La Monte 1935:5. Type by original designation (also monotypic). Valid (Isbrücker & Nijssen 1978 [ref. 2305], Isbrücker 1980:91 [ref. 2303], Burgess 1989:440 [ref. 12860]). Loricariidae.

Lampadena Goode & Bean in Gill 1893:113 [ref. 1736]. Fem. *Lampadena speculigera* Goode & Bean 1896:85. Type by subsequent monotypy. *Lampeda* is a misspelling. Valid (Krefft & Bekker 1973:184 [ref. 7181], Paxton 1979:12 [ref. 6440], Hulley in Whitehead et al. 1984:456 [ref. 13675], Moser et al. 1984:220 [ref. 13645], Fujii in Masuda et al. 1984:68 [ref. 6441], Hulley 1986:303 [ref. 5672], Paxton et al. 1989:263 [ref. 12442]). Myctophidae.

Lampanyctodes Fraser-Brunner 1949:1080 [ref. 1496]. Masc. *Scopelus hectoris* Günther 1876:399. Type by original designation (also monotypic). Valid (Paxton 1979:12 [ref. 6440], Moser et al. 1984:220 [ref. 13645], Paxton et al. 1984:241 [ref. 13625], Hulley 1986:305 [ref. 5672]). Myctophidae.

Lampanyctus Bonaparte 1840:fasc. 27 [ref. 514]. Masc. *Nyctophus (sic) bonapartii* Cocco 1838:189. Type by monotypy. Valid (Krefft & Bekker 1973:186 [ref. 7181], Hulley in Whitehead et al. 1984:459 [ref. 13675], Moser et al. 1984:220 [ref. 13645], Fujii in Masuda et al. 1984:69 [ref. 6441], Hulley 1986:305 [ref. 5672], Paxton et al. 1989:263 [ref. 12442]). Myctophidae.

Lampetra Bonnaterre 1788:li, 1 [ref. 4940]. Fem. *Petromyzon planeri* Bloch 1784:47. Type by subsequent designation. Type designated by Fowler 1958:1 [ref. 1470]. Fowler 1964:37 [ref. 7160] regards *Lampetra* Bonnaterre as the first available use of this pre-Linnaean name, predating Gray 1851 (the author and date usually given for this genus). Apparently should replace *Lampetra* Gray 1851. Petromyzontidae: Petromyzontinae.

Lampetra Gray 1851:140 [ref. 4939]. Fem. *Petromyzon fluviatilis* Linnaeus 1758:230. Type by subsequent designation. Type designated by Gray 1853:237 [ref. 1886]. Also in Gray 1853 [for 1851]:237 [ref. 1886]. Current authors credit genus to Gray, but according to Fowler 1964:37 [ref. 7160] available use of this pre-Linnaean name was first done by Bonnaterre 1788 and the type is *Petromyzon planeri* Bloch 1784. Valid (Hubbs & Potter 1971:49 [ref. 13397], Vladykov 1973:3 [ref. 7159] with Gray as author and type as *fluviatilis*, Sato in Masuda et al. 1984:2 [ref. 6441]). Petromyzontidae: Petromyzontinae.

Lampichthys Fraser-Brunner 1949:1095 [ref. 1496]. Masc. *Myctophum (Lampanyctus) procerum* Brauer 1904:402. Type by original designation. Valid (Paxton 1979:14 [ref. 6440], Moser et al. 1984:220 [ref. 13645], Hulley 1986:310 [ref. 5672], Paxton et al. 1989:265 [ref. 12442]). Myctophidae.

Lampreda Rafinesque 1815:94 [ref. 3584]. Fem. As "*Lampreda* R. sp. do.," meaning *Lampreda* Rafinesque based on a species in the preceding listed genus [*Petromyzon*]. Not available, name only; probably intended for *Lampetra* of pre-Linnaean authors. Petromyzontidae: Petromyzontinae.

Lamprichthys Regan 1911:325 [ref. 5761]. Masc. *Haplochilus tanganicanus* Boulenger 1898:25. Type by monotypy. Valid (Parenti 1981:508 [ref. 7066], Wildekamp et al. 1986:191 [ref. 6198]). Cyprinodontidae: Aplocheilichthyinae.

Lampris Retzius 1799:97 [ref. 3706]. Masc. *Zeus guttatus* Brünnich 1788:398. Type by monotypy. Valid (Palmer 1973:328 [ref. 7195], Olney 1984:369 [ref. 13656], Fujii in Masuda et al. 1984:116 [ref. 6441], Palmer in Whitehead et al. 1986:725 [ref. 13676], Heemstra 1986:398 [ref. 5660], Paxton et al. 1989:396 [ref. 12442]). Lampridae.

Lamprocheirodon (subgenus of *Cheirodon*) Géry 1960:13 [ref. 1603]. Masc. *Cheirodon axelrodi* Schultz 1956:42. Type by original designation (also monotypic). Synonym of *Cheirodon* Girard 1854, as a valid subgenus (Géry 1977:563 [ref. 1597]); synonym of *Paracheirodon* Géry 1960 (Weitzman & Fink 1983:353 [ref. 5383]). Characidae.

Lamprogrammus Alcock 1891:32 [ref. 87]. Masc. *Lamprogrammus niger* Alcock 1891:33. Type by monotypy. Valid (Cohen & Nielsen 1978:33 [ref. 881], Nielsen & Cohen 1986:348 [ref. 5700]). Ophidiidae: Neobythitinae.

Lamprologus Schilthuis 1891:85 [ref. 3925]. Masc. *Lamprologus congoensis* Schilthuis 1891:85. Type by monotypy. Valid (Bailey & Stewart 1977:18 [ref. 7230], Poll 1986:48 [ref. 6136]). Cichlidae.

Lamprossa Jordan & Hubbs 1925:156 [ref. 2486]. Fem. *Diaphus* *anteorbitalis* Gilbert 1913:92. Type by original designation. Synonym of *Diaphus* Eigenmann & Eigenmann 1890 (Nafpaktitis 1968:22 [ref. 6979], Krefft & Bekker 1973:176 [ref. 7181], Paxton 1979:7 [ref. 6440]). Myctophidae.

Lamprotoxus Holt & Bryne 1913:7 [ref. 2197]. Masc. *Grammatostomias flagellibarba* Holt & Byrne 1910:294. Type by monotypy. Synonym of *Grammatostomias* Goode & Bean 1896 (Morrow in Morrow & Gibbs 1964:448 [ref. 6962], Morrow 1973:139 [ref. 7175]). Melanostomiidae.

Lampugus Valenciennes in Cuvier & Valenciennes 1833:317 [ref. 1002]. *Scomber pelagicus* Linnaeus 1758:299. Type by subsequent designation. Type designated by Jordan 1917:143 [ref. 2407]. Objective synonym of *Caranxomorus* Lacepède 1801; synonym of *Coryphaena* Linnaeus 1758 (Tortonese 1973:385 [ref. 7192]). Coryphaenidae.

Lanceabarbus (subgenus of *Barbus*) Fowler 1936:287 [ref. 1424]. Masc. *Barbus tanensis* Günther 1894:90. Type by original designation. Synonym of *Barbus* Cuvier & Cloquet 1816 (Lévêque & Daget 1984:219 [ref. 6186]). Cyprinidae.

Landonia Eigenmann & Henn in Eigenmann, Henn & Wilson 1914:1 [ref. 1259]. Fem. *Landonia latidens* Eigenmann & Henn in Eigenmann, Henn & Wilson 1914:2. Type by monotypy. Valid (Roberts 1973:491 [ref. 3776], Géry 1977:359 [ref. 1597], Weitzman & S. Fink 1985:1 et seq. [ref. 5203]). Characidae: Glandulocaudinae.

Lanioperca Günther 1872:183 [ref. 2001]. Fem. *Lanioperca mordax* Günther 1872:183. Type by monotypy. Synonym of *Dinolestes* Klunzinger (early) 1872 (Scott 1981:130 [ref. 5533], Paxton et al. 1989:560 [ref. 12442]); also a synonym of *Neosphyraena* Castelnau (July 15, 1872), *Lanioperca* dating to Sept. 1, 1872 (Fowler MS). Dinolestidae.

Laomeda Rafinesque 1815:220 [ref. 3584]. Fem. Appeared in "Additions et Corrections" to this work. Not available, name only; for a species formerly in *Clupea* but not specified. Clupeidae.

Lappanella (subgenus of *Ctenolabrus*) Jordan 1890:622, 689 [ref. 2392]. Fem. *Ctenolabrus iris* Valenciennes in Cuvier & Valenciennes 1839:236. Type by monotypy. Valid (Bauchot & Quignard 1973:433 [ref. 7204], Quignard & Pras in Whitehead et al. 1986:929 [ref. 13676]). Labridae.

Laputa Whitley 1930:179 [ref. 5811]. *Monacanthus knerii* Steindachner 1867:591. Type by being a replacement name. Replacement for *Paramonacanthus* Steindachner 1867, preoccupied by Bleeker 1866 in same family. Valid (Tyler 1980:176 [ref. 4477]). Monacanthidae.

Larabicus Randall & Springer 1973:289 [ref. 3603]. Masc. *Labrus quadrilineatus* Rüppell 1835:6. Type by original designation (also monotypic). Labridae.

Larimichthys Jordan & Starks 1905:204 [ref. 2530]. Masc. *Larimichthys rathbunae* Jordan & Starks 1905:204. Type by monotypy. Valid (Trewavas 1977:392 [ref. 4459]). Sciaenidae.

Larimodon Bleeker (ex Kaup) 1876:329 [ref. 448]. Masc. First appeared as name in synonymy of *Odontoscion* Gill 1862 and then in Bleeker 1876 as above; apparently never used as an available name, and therefore not available and with no type validly established. In the synonymy of *Odontoscion* Gill 1862. Sciaenidae.

Larimus Cuvier in Cuvier & Valenciennes 1830:145 [ref. 999]. Masc. *Larimus breviceps* Cuvier in Cuvier & Valenciennes 1830:146. Type by monotypy. Valid (Chao 1978:31 [ref. 6983], Uyeno & Sato in Uyeno et al. 1983:367 [ref. 14275]). Sciaenidae.

Larvicampus Whitley 1948:75 [ref. 4710]. Masc. *Festucalex (Campichthys) runa* Whitley 1931:313. Type by original designation (also monotypic). Synonym of *Lissocampus* Waite & Hale 1921 (Dawson 1977:600 [ref. 7047], Dawson 1985:114 [ref. 6541]). Syngnathidae: Syngnathinae.

Lasiancistrus (subgenus of *Ancistrus*) Regan 1904:224 [ref. 3621]. Masc. *Chaetostomus heteracanthus* Günther 1869:425. Type by subsequent designation. Type designated by Eigenmann 1910:409 [ref. 1224]. Correct spelling for genus of type species is *Chaetostoma*. Valid (Isbrücker 1980:43 [ref. 2303], Heitmans et al. 1983 [ref. 5278], Nijssen & Isbrücker 1985 [ref. 9706], Burgess 1989:433 [ref. 12860]). Loricariidae.

Lasiognathus Regan 1925:563 [ref. 3677]. Masc. *Lasiognathus saccostoma* Regan 1925:563. Type by monotypy. Valid (Maul 1973:672 [ref. 7171], Nolan & Rosenblatt 1975 [ref. 6266], Bertelsen & Struhsaker 1977:35 [ref. 5331], Bertelsen in Whitehead et al. 1986:1400 [ref. 13677]). Thaumatichthyidae.

Latargus Klein 1775:298 [ref. 2618]. Masc. Not available; published in a work that does not conform to the principle of binominal nomenclature. In the synonymy of *Anarhichas* Linnaeus 1758. Anarhichadidae.

Latebrus Poey 1860:168 [ref. 3499]. Masc. *Latebrus oculatus* Poey 1860:168. Type by monotypy. Scombropidae.

Lateolabrax Bleeker 1857:53 [ref. 357]. Masc. *Labrax japonicus* Cuvier in Cuvier & Valenciennes 1828:85. Type by monotypy. Placement as an incertae sedis genus in the Percoidei follows Johnson 1984:465 [ref. 9681]. Valid (Katayama in Masuda et al. 1984:123 [ref. 6441], Kinoshita & Fujita 1988 [ref. 6698], Paxton et al. 1989:511 [ref. 12442]). Percoidei.

Laterosculatus de Buen 1926:103 [ref. 5054]. As a "grupo" of Carangidae. Not available on basis of Art. 1b(6) [see de Buen's definition of "grupo" on p. 11]; see Appendix A. Carangidae.

Laterosquamatus de Buen 1926:102 [ref. 5054]. As a "grupo" of Carangidae including *Lichia* and *Seriola*. Not available on basis of Art. 1b(6) [see de Buen's definition of "grupo" on p. 11]; see Appendix A. Carangidae.

Lates Cuvier in Cuvier & Valenciennes 1828:88 [ref. 997]. Masc. *Perca nilotica* Linnaeus 1758:290. Type by subsequent designation. Type designated by Gill 1861:52 [ref. 1769] as *Lates niloticus* Cuvier. Valid (Greenwood 1976:77 [ref. 14198], Katayama et al. 1977:46 [ref. 7052], Katayama in Masuda et al. 1984:122 [ref. 6441], Jayaram 1981:315 [ref. 6497], Daget 1986:293 [ref. 6203], Van Neer 1987 [ref. 12843], Paxton et al. 1989:482 [ref. 12442]). Centropomidae: Latinae.

Latilus Cuvier in Cuvier & Valenciennes 1830:368 [ref. 999]. Masc. *Latilus argentatus* Cuvier in Cuvier & Valenciennes 1830:369. Type by subsequent designation. Type designated by Bleeker 1876:280 [ref. 447]. Synonym of *Branchiostegus* Rafinesque 1815 (Dooley 1978:31 [ref. 5499], Dooley & Kailola 1988:250 [ref. 7299]). Malacanthidae: Latilinae.

Latimeria Smith 1939:455 [ref. 4068]. Fem. *Latimeria chalumnae* Smith 1939:455. Type by monotypy. Valid (see McCosker & Lagios (eds.) 1979 [ref. 6998], Smith 1986:152 [ref. 5712]). Latimeriidae.

Latridopsis Gill 1862:115 [ref. 1658]. Fem. *Anthias ciliaris* Bloch & Schneider 1801:310. Type by original designation (also monotypic). Latridae.

Latris Richardson 1839:98 [ref. 3732]. Fem. *Latris hecateia* Richardson 1839:97. Type by monotypy. Valid. Latridae.

Latropiscis Whitley 1931:312 [ref. 4672]. Masc. *Aulopus milesii*

Valenciennes in Cuvier & Valenciennes 1849:519. Type by original designation. Synonym of *Aulopus* Cloquet 1816 (Sulak 1977:53 [ref. 4299] as *Latropiscus*). Aulopidae.

Latrunculodes Collett 1874:151 [ref. 6521]. Masc. *Gobius nilssonii* van Düben & Koren 1846:53. Type by original designation (also monotypic). Also appeared in Collette 1875:60 [ref. 884]. Objective synonym of *Crystallogobius* Gill 1863 (Miller 1973:493 [ref. 6888]). Gobiidae.

Latrunculus Günther 1861:80 [ref. 1964]. Masc. *Gobius albus* Parnell 1838:248. Type by monotypy. Preoccupied by Gray 1847 in Mollusca, replaced by *Aphyogobius* Whitley 1931. Synonym of *Aphia* Risso 1826 (Miller 1973:489 [ref. 6888]). Gobiidae.

Laubuca Bleeker 1859:438 [ref. 370]. Fem. *Cyprinus (Chela) laubuca* Hamilton 1822:260, 342. Type by subsequent monotypy. Apparently appeared first in key, without species. One species (with synonyms) included in *Laubuka* by Bleeker 1859:261 [ref. 371] (two species in Bleeker 1860:297, 468-469 [ref. 380]). Misspelled once as *Lauuca* by Bleeker 1863:215 [ref. 397]. If 1859:261 was published first, then the spelling *Laubuka* apparently takes precedence and type would be by subsequent designation. Synonym of *Chela* Hamilton 1822 (Jayaram 1981:71 [ref. 6497], Roberts 1989:31 [ref. 6439]). Cyprinidae.

Laurida Swainson 1838:242, 246 [ref. 4302]. Fem. *Salmo foetans* of Swainson (= *Salmo foetens* Linnaeus 1766:50). Type by subsequent designation. Also in Swainson 1839:185, 287-288 [ref. 4303]. Dates to 1838:242, 246 (with 3 included species in 1838); also mentioned on pp. 43, 221, 245, 250-252, 258. Type designated by Swain 1882:279 [ref. 5966]. Synonym of *Synodus* Scopoli 1777 (Nielsen 1973:161 [ref. 6885], see Anderson et al. 1966:47 [ref. 6977]). Synodontidae: Synodontinae.

Lavinia Girard 1854:137 [ref. 1817]. Fem. *Lavinia exilicauda* Baird & Girard in Girard 1854:137. Type by subsequent designation. Type designated by Bleeker 1863:29 [ref. 4859] and 1863:206 [ref. 397]. Valid. Cyprinidae.

Lebetus Winther 1877:49 [ref. 4758]. Masc. *Gobius scorpioides* Collett 1874:447. Type by monotypy. See *Lebistes* Smitt 1900. Valid (Miller 1973:498 [ref. 6888], Miller in Whitehead et al. 1986:1049 [ref. 13677]). Gobiidae.

Lebia Oken (ex Cuvier) 1817:1183 [ref. 3303]. Fem. *Cyprinodon variegatus* Lacepède (ex Bosc) 1803:486, 487. Type by subsequent monotypy. See Gill 1903:966 [ref. 5768]. Preoccupied by Latreille 1802 in Coleoptera; replaced by *Encrotes* Gistel 1848. Later spelled *Lebias*. Objective synonym of *Cyprinodon* Lacepède 1803. Cyprinodontidae: Cyprinodontinae.

Lebias of authors Masc. Not *Lebia* Oken (ex Cuvier). Fowler credits this spelling first to Goldfuss 1826. Synonym of *Aphanius* Nardo 1827 (Parenti 1981:521 [ref. 7066]). Cyprinodontidae: Cyprinodontinae.

Lebiasina Valenciennes in Cuvier & Valenciennes 1846:531 [ref. 1011]. Fem. *Lebiasina bimaculata* Valenciennes in Cuvier & Valenciennes 1846:531. Type by monotypy. Valid (Weitzman & Cobb 1975:2 [ref. 7134], Géry 1977:123 [ref. 1597]). Lebiasinidae: Lebiasininae.

Lebistes Filippi 1861:69 [ref. 1328]. Masc. *Lebistes poecilioides* Filippi 1861:69. Type by monotypy. Synonym of *Poecilia* Bloch & Schneider 1801, but as a valid subgenus (Rosen & Bailey 1963:44, 55 [ref. 7067], Parenti & Rauchenberger 1989:8 [ref. 13538]). Poeciliidae.

Lebistes (subgenus of *Gobius*) Smitt 1900:487 [ref. 4148]. Masc. Not available; appeared by mistake as a genus authored by Smitt, but Smitt attributed the name correctly to Winther and spelled the name correctly as *Lebetus*. *Butigobius* Whitley 1930 is an unneeded replacement. In the synonymy of *Lebetus* Winther 1877 (Miller 1973:498 [ref. 6888]). Gobiidae.

Lebius Pallas (ex Steller) 1814:279 [ref. 3351]. Masc. *Labrax superciliosus* Pallas 1810:388. Type by subsequent designation. Name from Steller manuscript, published in the synonymy of *Labrax superciliosus* (along with *Chirus* also); subsequent history of available use not researched. Type as given by Jordan 1917:84 [ref. 2407]. Synonym of *Hexagrammos* Steller 1809. Hexagrammidae: Hexagramminae.

Lecanogaster Briggs 1957:204 [ref. 638]. Fem. *Lecanogaster chrysea* Briggs 1957:205. Type by original designation (also monotypic). Gobiesocidae: Gobiesocinae.

Lefroyia Jones 1874:3838 [ref. 2362]. Fem. *Lefroyia bermudensis* Jones 1874:3838. Type by monotypy. Synonym of *Carapus* Rafinesque 1810 (Arnold 1956:260 [ref. 5315]). Carapidae: Carapinae.

Lefua Herzenstein 1888:3 [ref. 2147]. Fem. *Octonema pleskei* Herzenstein in Herzenstein & Warpachowski 1887:48. Type by being a replacement name. Replacement for *Octonema* Herzenstein 1887, preoccupied by Martens 1868 in fishes and by Haecker 1879 in Coelenterata. Also appeared in Herzenstein 1888:91 [ref. 2148]. Synonym of *Oreonectes* Günther 1868 (Banarescu & Nalbant 1968:339 [ref. 6554]); valid (Sawada 1982:202 [ref. 14111], Sawada in Masuda et al. 1984:59 [ref. 6441], Kottelat 1990:19 [ref. 14137]). Balitoridae: Nemacheilinae.

Leiarius Bleeker 1862:10 [ref. 393]. Masc. *Arius? longibarbis* Castelnau 1855:36. Type by original designation (also monotypic). Valid (Stewart 1986:667 [ref. 5211], Burgess 1989:282 [ref. 12860] but as Müller & Troschel 1849 and with type as *pictus*). [*A. pictus* apparently is the same as *longibarbis*, however.] Pimelodidae.

Leihala Jordan 1925:5 [ref. 2544]. Fem. *Poecilophis tritor* Vaillant & Sauvage 1875:287. Type by original designation. Type given as "*Poecilophis tritor* = *Echidna leihala* Jenkins." Synonym of *Echidna* Forster 1777 (Böhlke et al. 1989:130 [ref. 13286]). Muraenidae: Muraeninae.

Leiobatis von Bonde & Swart 1923:18 [ref. 522]. Fem. *Leiobatis marmoratus* von Bonde & Swart 1923:18. Type by subsequent designation [not researched]. Preoccupied by use of Blainville 1825 in fishes (see under *Leiobatus* Rafinesque 1810); replaced by *Anacanthobatis* in a bound printed errata sheet appearing with article. Objective synonym of *Anacanthobatis* von Bonde & Swart 1923. Anacanthobatidae.

Leiobatus (subgenus of *Raia [Raja]*) Blainville 1816:121 [ref. 306]. Masc. *Leiobatus sloani* Blainville 1816:121. Type given as above by Jordan 1917:95 [ref. 2407], but Blainville listed 3 species, all of which are apparently name only and unavailable. Subsequent addition of species not researched. Not *Leiobatus* as treated by Rafinesque. Synonym of *Urolophus* Müller & Henle 1837 (Cappetta 1987:165 [ref. 6348]). Urolophidae.

Leiobatus Klein 1775:316 [ref. 2618]. Masc. Not available, published in a work that does not conform to the principle of binominal nomenclature. Not *Leiobatis* von Bonde & Swart 1923. In the synonymy of *Raja* Linnaeus 1758. Rajidae.

Leiobatus Rafinesque 1810:16 [ref. 3594]. Masc. *Leiobatus panduratus* Rafinesque 1810:16. Type by monotypy. Apparently *Leiobatis* Blainville 1825:43 [ref. 4991] is an unjustified emendation or incorrect subsequent spelling. Synonym of *Rhinobatos* Linck 1790 (Krefft & Stehmann 1973:53 [ref. 7167]). Rhinobatidae: Rhinobatinae.

Leiocassis Bleeker 1858:59, 139 [ref. 365]. Fem. *Bagrus poecilopterus* Kuhl & van Hasselt in Cuvier & Valenciennes 1839:421. Type by subsequent designation. Also on p. 24 et seq. Type designated by Bleeker 1862:9 [ref. 393] and 1863:95 [ref. 401]. Also appeared in Bleeker 1858:225 [ref. 363], and if earlier then the type is *Bagrus micropogon* Bleeker by monotypy. Unjustifiably emended to *Liocassis* by Günther 1864. Valid (Jayaram 1968:347 [5615], Kottelat 1985:270 [ref. 11441], Burgess 1989:70 [ref. 12860], Kottelat 1989:13 [ref. 13605], Roberts 1989:116 [ref. 6439]). Bagridae.

Leiocottus Girard 1856:133 [ref. 1809]. Masc. *Leiocottus hirundo* Girard 1856:133. Type by monotypy. Valid (Bolin 1944:86 [ref. 6379], Washington et al. 1984:443 [ref. 13660], Yabe 1985:111 [ref. 11522]). Cottidae.

Leiodon Swainson 1839:194 [ref. 4303]. Masc. *Tetraodon laevissimus* Swainson 1839. Type by subsequent designation. Appeared without species on p. 194; Swainson changed name to *Leisomus* on p. 328. Type designated by Bleeker 1865:45 [416], not by Bleeker 1865:49 [ref. 416] as *T. patoca* Hamilton (not an included species if one accepts the equivalence of *Leiodon* and *Leisomus*). Species *laevissimus* perhaps not available. Bleeker 1865:45 apparently serves as first reviser, selecting *Leiodon* over *Leisomus*. Tetraodontidae.

Leiodon Wood 1846:174 [ref. 4760]. Masc. *Leiodon echinatum* Wood 1846:174. Type by monotypy. Preoccupied by Swainson 1839 in fishes and by Owen 1841 in Reptilia, apparently not replaced. Synonym of *Somniosus* Lesueur 1818 (Compagno 1984:102 [ref. 6474], Cappetta 1987:62 [ref. 6348]). Squalidae.

Leioeleotris Fowler 1934:494 [ref. 1419]. Fem. *Leioeleotris zonatus* Fowler 1934:494. Type by original designation (also monotypic). Synonym of *Heterelotris* Bleeker 1874 (Akihito & Meguro 1981:331 [ref. 5508], Hoese 1986:3 [ref. 5996]). Gobiidae.

Leiogaster Weber 1913:179 [ref. 4602]. Fem. *Leiogaster melanopus* Weber 1913:180. Type by monotypy. Synonym of *Hoplostethus* Cuvier 1829 (Woods & Sonoda 1973:305 [ref. 6899]); as a valid subgenus (Kotlyar 1986:132 [ref. 6004]). Trachichthyidae.

Leioglossus Bleeker 1851:343, 352, 367 [ref. 326]. Masc. *Leioglossus carangoides* Bleeker 1851:367. Type by monotypy. Also appeared in Bleeker 1852:70 [ref. 332] with type by monotypy. Carangidae.

Leiognathus Lacepède 1802:448 [ref. 4929]. Masc. *Leiognathus argenteus* Lacepède 1802:448, 449 (= *Scomber edentulus* Bloch 1785:109). Type by monotypy. *L. argenteus* Lacepède is an unneeded substitute for *S. edentulus* Bloch. *Liognathus* Agassiz 1846:203, 212 [ref. 64] is an unjustified emendation (see Briggs 1961:162 [ref. 13439]). Valid (Tortonese 1973:390 [ref. 7192], Uyeno & Yabumoto in Masuda et al. 1984:158 [ref. 6441], James 1985:397 [ref. 12861], Smith 1986:620 [ref. 5712], Kottelat 1989:17 [ref. 13605]). Leiognathidae.

Leionura Bleeker 1860:68 [ref. 373]. Fem. Not available, name only in synonymy of *Thyrisites*. Gempylidae.

Leiopotherapon (subgenus of *Terapon*) Fowler 1931:328, 353 [ref. 1407]. Masc. *Datnia plumbea* Kner 1864:484. Type by original designation. Misspelled *Leispotherapon* in Zoological Record for 1931. Synonym of *Terapon* Cuvier 1816 (Mees & Kailola 1977:32 [ref. 5183]); valid (Vari 1978:227 [ref. 4514], Paxton et al. 1989:533 [ref. 12442]). Terapontidae.

Leiopsis Bennett 1830:688 [ref. 259]. Fem. *Pentapodus rafflesii* Bennett 1830:688. Type by monotypy. Synonym of *Pentapodus* Quoy & Gaimard 1824. Nemipteridae.

Leiostomus Lacepède 1802:438 [ref. 4929]. Masc. *Leiostomus xanthurus* Lacepède 1802:438, 439. Type by monotypy. *Liostomus* Agassiz 1846:204, 212 [ref. 64] is an unjustified emendation. Valid (Chao 1978:29 [ref. 6983]). Sciaenidae.

Leiosynodontis Bleeker 1862:6 [ref. 393]. Fem. *Synodontis maculosus* Rüppell 1829:10. Type by original designation (also monotypic). Synonym of *Synodontis* Cuvier 1816 (Gosse 1986:117 [ref. 6194]). Mochokidae.

Leirus Lowe 1833:143 [ref. 2826]. Masc. *Leirus bennettii* Lowe 1833:143. Type by monotypy. Apparently preoccupied by Meigen 1823 in Coleoptera or Zimmermann in Gistel 1832 in Coleoptera, not preoccupied by Dahl 1823 in Lepidoptera (nomen nudum). *Liurus* Agassiz 1846:204, 214 [ref. 64] is an unjustified emendation. Synonym of *Schedophilus* Cocco 1839 (Haedrich 1967:59 [ref. 5357], Haedrich 1973:560 [ref. 7216]). Centrolophidae.

Leisomus Swainson 1839:328 [ref. 4303]. Masc. *Tetraodon laevissimus* Swainson 1839. Type by subsequent designation. As *Leiodon* on p. 194. Type designated by Swain 1883:283 [ref. 5966]. Spelled *Leiosomus* by authors. See account of *Leiodon* Swainson. Species name perhaps not available. Tetraodontidae.

Leitectus (subgenus of *Gaterin*) Smith 1952:711, 712 [ref. 4085]. *Gaterin (Leitectus) harrawayi* Smith 1952:712. Type by original designation (also monotypic). Haemulidae.

Leiuranus (subgenus of *Ophisurus*) Bleeker 1853:11, 24, 36 [ref. 339]. Masc. *Leiuranus lacepedii* Bleeker 1853:(11) 36. Type by monotypy. Based on style, Bleeker treated as a subgenus of *Ophisurus* (p. 24) and as a genus (p. 11, 36), with one species. Type not *L. colubrinus* as stated by Bleeker 1864:36 [ref. 4860] and 1865:119 [ref. 409]. *Liuranus* Günther 1870:54 [ref. 1995] is an unjustified emendation. Valid (McCosker 1977:77 [ref. 6836], Asano in Masuda et al. 1984:30 [ref. 6441], McCosker & Castle 1986:180 [ref. 5690], Paxton et al. 1989:117 [ref. 12442], McCosker et al. 1989:299 [ref. 13288]). Ophichthidae: Ophichthinae.

Leiurus Kaup in Duméril 1856:198 [ref. 1154]. Masc. Apparently not available, name only as "*Leiurus colubrinus*" in list of genera taken from Kaup manuscript; probably for *Leiuranus colubrinus*. Preoccupied by Swainson 1839 in fishes, replaced by *Chlevastes* Jordan & Snyder 1901. In the synonymy of *Leiuranus* Bleeker 1853. Ophichthidae: Ophichthinae.

Leiurus (subgenus of *Gasterosteus*) Swainson 1839:175, 242 [ref. 4303]. Masc. *Gasterosteus aculeatus* Linnaeus 1758:295. Type by subsequent designation. Type designated by Swain 1882:276 [ref. 5966]. *Leiurus* on Swainson page 326 not same genus. Synonym of *Gasterosteus* Linnaeus 1758 (Monod 1973:280 [ref. 7193]). Gasterosteidae: Gasterosteinae.

Leiurus (subgenus of *Capriscus*) Swainson 1839:326 [ref. 4303]. Masc. *Leiurus macrophthalmus* Swainson 1839:326. Type by subsequent designation. Type designated by Swain 1883:282 [ref. 5966]. Preoccupied by Swainson on p. 242 of same work, replaced by *Abalistes* Jordan & Seale 1906. Balistidae.

Leius Kner 1864:186 [ref. 2637]. Masc. *Leius ferox* Kner 1864:186. Type by monotypy. Also as Kner 1865:9 [ref. 6174], and in Anonymous 1865:78 [ref. 6173]; assume 1864:186 was published first. Synonym of *Isistius* Gill 1865 (Compagno 1984:93 [ref. 6474], Cappetta 1987:62 [ref. 6348]). Squalidae.

Lembeichthys Herre 1936:283 [ref. 2125]. Masc. *Lembeichthys celebesensis* Herre 1936:283. Type by original designation (also monotypic). Synonym of *Plagiotremus* Gill 1865 (Smith-Vaniz 1976:108 [ref. 4144], Smith-Vaniz 1987:47 [ref. 6404]). Blenniidae.

Lembesseia Fowler 1949:267 [ref. 1461]. Fem. *Lembesseia parvianalis* Fowler 1949:267. Type by original designation (also monotypic). Synonym of *Poecilia* Bloch & Schneider 1801 (Rosen & Bailey 1963:45 [ref. 7067]). Poeciliidae.

Lembus Günther 1859:505 [ref. 1961]. Masc. *Lembus maculatus* Günther 1859:505. Type by monotypy. Synonym of *Gobiomorus* Lacepède 1800. Eleotridae.

Leme De Vis 1883:286 [ref. 1088]. Fem. *Leme mordax* De Vis 1883:286. Type by monotypy. Gobiidae.

Lemkea Kotthaus 1968:33 [ref. 2669]. Fem. *Lemkea heterolinea* Kotthaus 1968:33. Type by original designation (also monotypic). Synonym of *Gnathophis* Kaup 1860 (Blache & Bauchot 1976:411 [ref. 305], Smith 1989:521 [ref. 13285]). Congridae: Congrinae.

Lemnisoma Lesson 1831:160 [ref. 2776]. Neut. *Lemnisoma thyrsitoides* Lesson 1831:160. Type by monotypy. *Lemniscosoma* Agassiz 1846:204 [ref. 64] is an unjustified emendation. Synonym of *Gempylus* Cuvier 1829. Gempylidae.

Lentipes Günther 1861:96 [ref. 1964]. Masc. *Sicyogaster concolor* Gill 1860:102. Type by monotypy. Replacement for *Sicyogaster* Gill 1860, preoccupied by Brissout in fishes. Valid (Akihito in Masuda et al. 1984:285 [ref. 6441], Nishimoto & Fitzsimons 1986 [ref. 6319], Birdsong et al. 1988:198 [ref. 7303]). Gobiidae.

Leoblennius Reid 1943:382 [ref. 3686]. Masc. *Leoblennius schultzi* Reid 1943:382. Type by original designation (also monotypic). Synonym of *Exallias* Jordan & Evermann 1905 (Smith-Vaniz & Springer 1971:23 [ref. 4145]). Blenniidae.

Leocottus (subgenus of *Paracottus*) Taliev 1955:235, 243 [ref. 4316]. Masc. *Paracottus (Leocottus) pelagicus* Taliev 1955:235. Two included species, one with subspecies; article not fully translated, but if no type was designated, then this genus is unavailable from Taliev 1955 (Art. 13b). Zoological Record for 1958 lists the type as *pelagicus* and Fowler (MS) lists the type as *kessleri*. Cottocomephoridae.

Lepadichthys Waite 1904:(139) 180 [ref. 4561]. Masc. *Lepadichthys frenatus* Waite 1904:180. Type by original designation (also monotypic). Type designated on p. 139. Valid (Briggs 1955:136 [ref. 637], Allen [L. G.] 1984:629 [ref. 13673], Yoshino in Masuda et al. 1984:342 [ref. 6441], Briggs 1986:379 [ref. 5643]). Gobiesocidae: Gobiesocinae.

Lepadogaster Goüan 1770:106, 177 [ref. 1863]. Fem. *Cyclopterus lepadogaster* Bonnaterre 1778:29. Appeared without species, first species apparently added by Bonnaterre; type by subsequent monotypy (also by absolute tautonymy). *Lepidogaster* Kent 1883:55 placed on Official Index as incorrect subsequent spelling (Opinion 638). Valid (Briggs 1955:33 [ref. 637], Briggs 1973:653 [ref. 7222], Briggs in Whitehead et al. 1986:1356 [ref. 13677], Allen [L. G.] 1984:629 [ref. 13673]). Gobiesocidae: Gobiesocinae.

Lepadogasterus Duméril 1806:108, 337 [ref. 1151]. Masc. *Cyclopterus lepadogaster* Bonnaterre 1788:29. Type by subsequent designation. Type designated by Fowler 1936:1078 [ref. 6546]. "*Lepadogasterus* Gouan" given in parentheses; probably can be considered an incorrect subsequent spelling of *Lepadogaster* Goüan 1770. Objective synonym of *Lepadogaster* Goüan 1770 (Briggs 1955:33 [ref. 637], Briggs 1973:653 [ref. 7222]). Gobiesocidae: Gobiesocinae.

Lepibema (subgenus of *Perca*) Rafinesque 1820:371 [ref. 7308]. Neut. *Perca chrysops* Rafinesque 1820:370. Type by monotypy. Also appeared in Rafinesque 1820:23 (Dec.) [ref. 3592]. Synonym of *Morone* Mitchill 1814. Moronidae.

Lepicantha Rafinesque 1815:85 [ref. 3584]. Fem. Not available; name only and apparently an incorrect subsequent spelling of *Lepisacanthus* Lacepède 1801. Monocentridae.

Lepicephalochromis Fowler 1943:78 [ref. 1441]. Masc. *Chromis cupreus* Fowler & Bean 1923:22. Type by original designation (also monotypic). Pomacentridae.

Lepidamia Gill 1863:81 [ref. 1679]. Fem. *Apogon kalosoma* Bleeker 1852:448. Type by original designation (also monotypic). Type by original designation, Gill's style of type in parentheses in key. Synonym of *Apogon* Lacepède 1801, but as a valid subgenus (Fraser & Lachner 1985:4 [ref. 5215]). Apogonidae.

Lepidaplois Gill 1862:140 [ref. 1662]. *Cossyphus axillaris* Valenciennes in Cuvier & Valenciennes 1839:95. Type by monotypy. Synonym of *Bodianus* Bloch 1790 (see Gomon & Randall 1978:32 [ref. 5481], Randall 1986:686 [ref. 5706]). Labridae.

Lepidarchus Roberts 1966:209 [ref. 3769]. Masc. *Lepidarchus adonis* Roberts 1966:210. Type by original designation (also monotypic). Valid (Géry 1977:51 [ref. 1597], Paugy 1984:173 [ref. 6183]). Alestiidae.

Lepidiolamprologus Pellegrin 1904:(163) 295 [ref. 3419]. Masc. *Lamprologus elongatus* Boulenger 1898:9. Type by monotypy. Misspelled *Lepidolamprologus* by Jordan 1920:510 [ref. 4905]. Valid (Poll 1986:52 [ref. 6136]). Cichlidae.

Lepidion Swainson 1838:318 [ref. 4302]. Neut. *Gadus lepidion* Risso 1810:118. Type by monotypy. Also in Swainson 1839:188, 300 [ref. 4303]. Risso's *lepidion* renamed *rissoii* (p. 319) and *rubescens* (1839:300) by Swainson. *Haloporphyrus* Günther 1862 is an unneeded replacement. Valid (Cohen 1973:324 [ref. 6589], Paulin 1983:106 [ref. 5459], Fahay & Markle 1984:266 [ref. 13653], Okamura in Masuda et al. 1984:90 [ref. 6441], Cohen in Whitehead et al. 1986:719 [ref. 13676], Cohen 1986:327 [ref. 5646], Paxton et al. 1989:300 [ref. 12442]). Moridae.

Lepidoblennius Sauvage 1874:337 [ref. 3873]. Masc. *Lepidoblennius caledonicus* Sauvage 1874:338. Type by monotypy. Preoccupied by Steindachner 1867 in fishes, replaced by *Sauvagea* Jordan & Seale 1906. Tripterygiidae.

Lepidoblennius Steindachner 1867:11 [ref. 4214]. Masc. *Lepidoblennius haplodactylus* Steindachner 1867:12. Type by monotypy. Valid (Hardy 1987:254 [ref. 5960]). Tripterygiidae.

Lepidoblepharon Weber 1913:421 [ref. 4602]. Neut. *Lepidoblepharon ophthalmolepis* Weber 1913:422. Type by monotypy. Valid (Norman 1934:401 [ref. 6893], Ahlstrom et al. 1984:640 [ref. 13641], Amaoko in Masuda et al. 1984:346 [ref. 6441]). Citharidae: Brachypleurinae.

Lepidocephalichthys Bleeker 1863:38, 42 [ref. 400]. Masc. *Cobitis hasseltii* Valenciennes in Cuvier & Valenciennes 1846:74. Type by original designation. Also may date to Bleeker 1863: Pl. 103 in part 9 [ref. 4859]. Type given as *Lepidocephalichthys hasseltii* Bleeker (p. 42) = *Cobitis hasseltii* Valenciennes. Synonym of *Lepidocephalus* Bleeker 1859 (Banarescu & Nalbant 1968:343 [ref. 6554]); valid subgenus of *Lepidocephalus* (Jayaram 1981:181 [ref. 6497]); valid genus (Nalbant 1963:366 [ref. 3140], Kottelat 1989:13 [ref. 13605], Roberts 1989:103 [ref. 6439]). Cobitidae: Cobitinae.

Lepidocephalus Bleeker 1859:303 [ref. 366]. Masc. *Cobitis macrochir* Bleeker 1854:97. Type by subsequent designation. Type designated by Bleeker 1863:35 [ref. 400] and 1863:4 [ref. 4859]. Valid (Nalbant 1963:366 [ref. 3140], Banarescu & Nalbant 1968:343 [ref. 6554], Jayaram 1981:180 [ref. 6497], Sawada 1982:201 [ref. 14111], Kottelat 1985:268 [ref. 11441], Roberts 1989:106 [ref. 6439]). Cobitidae: Cobitinae.

Lepidochaetodon (subgenus of *Tetragonoptrus*) Bleeker 1876:306 [ref. 448]. Masc. *Chaetodon unimaculatus* Bloch 1787:75. Type by original designation, also monotypic [in ref. 448]. Also in Bleeker 1876:Pls. 373, 375 [ref. 6835] (earliest not established). Synonym of *Chaetodon* Linnaeus 1758, but as a valid subgenus (Burgess 1978:636 [ref. 700]). Apparently incorrectly as a synonym of *Heterochaetodon* Maugé & Bauchot 1984:475 (Maugé & Bauchot 1984:475 [ref. 6614] since *Lepidochaetodon* has priority). Chaetodontidae.

Lepidochromis (subgenus of *Chromis*) Fowler & Bean 1928:31, 58 [ref. 1475]. Masc. *Chromis lepidolepis* Bleeker 1876:389. Type by original designation. Pomacentridae.

Lepidochromis Poll 1981:169 [ref. 3534]. Masc. *Limnochromis christyi* Trewavas 1953:1. Type by original designation. Preoccupied by Fowler & Bean 1928 in fishes, apparently not replaced. Cichlidae.

Lepidocybium Gill 1862:125 [ref. 1659]. Neut. *Cybium flavobrunneum* Smith 1849:Pl. 20. Type by original designation (also monotypic). Valid (Parin & Bekker 1973:458 [ref. 7206], Collette et al. 1984:600 [ref. 11421], Nakamura in Masuda et al. 1984:227 [ref. 6441], Parin in Whitehead et al. 1986:969 [ref. 13676], Nakamura 1986:826 [ref. 5696]). Gempylidae.

Lepidogalaxias Mees 1961:33 [ref. 2965]. Masc. *Lepidogalaxias salamandroides* Mees 1961:33. Type by original designation (also monotypic). Valid (McDowall & Pusey 1983 [ref. 6522], Paxton et al. 1989:182 [ref. 12442], Berra & Allen 1989 [ref. 13531]). Lepidogalaxiidae.

Lepidoglanis Vaillant 1889:82 [ref. 4483]. Masc. *Lepidoglanis monticola* Vaillant 1889:82. Type by monotypy. Synonym of *Gastromyzon* Günther 1874 (Roberts 1982:500 [ref. 6689], Roberts 1989:85 [ref. 6439]). Balitoridae: Balitorinae.

Lepidogobius Gill 1859:14 [ref. 1751]. Masc. *Gobius lepidus* Girard 1858:127 (= *Gobius gracilis* Girard 1854:134). Type by subsequent designation. Type designated by Gill 1862:279 [not researched] and by Bleeker 1874:319 [ref. 437] as *gracilis*. *Gobius gracilis* Girard 1854 preoccupied, replaced by *G. lepidus* Girard 1858. Valid (Birdsong et al. 1988:185, 187 [ref. 7303]). Gobiidae.

Lepidoleprus Risso 1810:197 [ref. 3755]. Masc. *Lepidoleprus trachyrincus* Risso 1810:197. Type by subsequent designation. Earliest type designation not researched. Name unneeded; *Trachyrincus* Giorna 1809 is available. *Lepidosoma* Swainson 1839 apparently in error for *Lepidoleprus*. Objective synonym of *Trachyrincus* Giorna 1809 (Marshall 1973:287 [ref. 7194], Marshall & Iwamoto 1973:516 [ref. 6963]). Macrouridae: Trachyrincinae.

Lepidomeda Cope 1874:131 [ref. 932]. Fem. *Lepidomeda vittata* Cope 1874:131. Type by subsequent designation. Type designated by Jordan & Gilbert 1877:95 [ref. 4907]. Valid (Miller & Hubbs 1960:18 [ref. 11934]). Cyprinidae.

Lepidomegas Thominot 1880:173 [ref. 4383]. Masc. *Lepidomegas muelleri* Thominot 1880:173. Type by monotypy. Synonym of *Seriola* Cuvier 1816 in family Carangidae (authors); synonym of *Arripis* Jenyns 1840 in family Arripidae (Smith-Vaniz et al. 1979:52 [ref. 12247]). Arripidae.

Lepidonotothen Balushkin 1976:130 [ref. 170]. *Notothenia kempi* Norman 1938. Type by original designation. Synonym of *Notothenia* Richardson 1844, but as a valid subgenus (Andersen 1984:24 [ref. 13369]). Nototheniidae.

Lepidoperca Regan 1914:15 [ref. 3661]. Fem. *Lepidoperca inornata* Regan 1914:15. Type by monotypy. Valid (Paxton et al. 1989:505 [ref. 12442], Roberts 1989 [ref. 12486]). Serranidae: Anthiinae.

Lepidophanes (subgenus of *Lampanyctus*) Fraser-Brunner 1949: 1090 [ref. 1496]. *Lampanyctus guentheri* Goode & Bean 1896:79. Type by original designation. Valid (Krefft & Bekker 1973:190 [ref. 7181], Paxton 1979:14 [ref. 6440], Hulley in Whitehead et al. 1984:466 [ref. 13675], Moser et al. 1984:220 [ref. 13645], Paxton et al. 1984:241 [ref. 13625], Hulley 1986:310 [ref. 5672]). Myctophidae.

Lepidopomacentrus (subgenus of *Pomacentrus*) Allen 1975:39, 43 [ref. 97]. Masc. *Pomacentrus lepidogenys* Fowler & Bean 1928:98. Type by original designation (also monotypic). Pomacentridae.

Lepidopristis (subgenus of *Orthopristis*) Fowler 1944:328 [ref. 1448]. Fem. *Orthopristis forbesi* Jordan & Starks in Gilbert 1897:443. Type by original designation (also monotypic). Haemulidae.

Lepidopsetta Gill 1862:330 [ref. 1668]. Fem. *Platichthys umbrosus* Girard 1857:136. Type by monotypy. Valid (Norman 1934:329 [ref. 6893], Ahlstrom et al. 1984:643 [ref. 13641], Sakamoto in Masuda et al. 1984:352 [ref. 6441]). Pleuronectidae: Pleuronectinae.

Lepidopsetta Günther 1880:18 [ref. 2011]. Fem. *Lepidopsetta maculata* Günther 1880:18. Type by monotypy. Preoccupied by Gill 1862 in fishes, replaced by *Mancopsetta* Gill 1881. Objective synonym of *Mancopsetta* Gill 1881 (Norman 1934:247 [ref. 6893]). Achiropsettidae.

Lepidopus Goüan 1770:107, 185 [ref. 1863]. Masc. *Lepidopus gouanianus* Lacepède 1800:519 (= *Trichiurus caudatus* Euphrasen 1788:49). Type by subsequent monotypy or subsequent designation. No included species; first addition possibly by Cuvier 1798:344 [ref. 5558], and if first then type is *argenteus*. If Cuvier 1798 was not first, then probably type was designated by Bory de Saint-Vincent, v. 9, 1826:291 [ref. 3853] on Lacepède (see Whitley 1935:137 [ref. 6396]). Jordan 1917:28 [ref. 2407] says type is *L. gouani* = *Trichiurus caudatus*. Valid (Parin & Bekker 1973:464 [ref. 7206], Nakamura 1986:830 [ref. 5696], Rosenblatt & Wilson 1987 [ref. 6711]). Trichiuridae: Lepidopinae.

Lepidopygopsis Raj 1941:210 [ref. 3596]. Fem. *Lepidopygopsis typus* Raj 1941:210. Type by original designation (also monotypic and by use of *typus*). Valid (Jayaram 1981:66 [ref. 6497]). Cyprinidae.

Lepidorbidus (subgenus of *Sphoeroides*) Fowler 1929:263 [ref. 1403]. Masc. *Sphoeroides marleyi* Fowler 1929:263. Type by original designation (also monotypic). Synonym of *Spheroides* Duméril 1806 [or *Sphoeroides* Anonymous 1798] (Fraser-Brunner 1943:11 [ref. 1495]). Tetraodontidae.

Lepidorhinus Bonaparte 1838:207 [9] [ref. 4979]. Masc. *Squalus squamosus* Bonnaterre 1788:12. Type by original designation (see p. 2 of separate; also monotypic). On p. 9 of separate. Valid (Krefft & Tortonese 1973:40 [ref. 7165]); synonym of *Centrophorus*

Müller & Henle 1837 (Compagno 1984:35 [ref. 6474], Bass et al. 1986:49 [ref. 5636]). Squalidae.

Lepidorhombus (subgenus of *Rhombus*) Günther 1862:407, 411 [ref. 1969]. Masc. *Pleuronectes megastoma* Donovan 1804:407. Type by subsequent designation. Type apparently first designated by Jordan 1919:319 [ref. 4904]. Valid (Norman 1934:272 [ref. 6893], Nielsen 1973:616 [ref. 6885], Ahlstrom et al. 1984:640 [ref. 13641], Nielsen in Whitehead et al. 1986:1287 [ref. 13677]). Scophthalmidae.

Lepidorhynchus Richardson 1846:53 [ref. 3740]. Masc. *Macrourus "vel" Lepidorhynchus denticulatus* Richardson 1846:53. Type by monotypy. First published in synonymy, but apparently made available [Art. 11e] by Bleeker 1879:21 [ref. 460], but spelled *Lepidorynchus*; dates to Richardson 1846 with type *denticulatus* Richardson. Valid (Scott 1979:107 [ref. 6995], Fahay & Markle 1984:274 [ref. 13653], Iwamoto & Sazonov 1988:39 [ref. 6228], Paxton et al. 1989:328 [ref. 12442]). Macrouridae: Macrourinae.

Lepidosarda Kishinouye 1926:377 [ref. 2610]. Fem. *Lepidosarda retigramma* Kishinouye 1926:378. Type by monotypy. Synonym of *Lebidocybium* Gill 1862. Scombroidei.

Lepidosiren Fitzinger 1837:379 [ref. 1338]. Fem. *Lepidosiren paradoxa* Fitzinger 1837:379. Earliest description not determined; variously given as: Frorieps Notizen, vol. 1:90 (or p. 50 and 90); Wiegmann's Archiv. 1837:232; and perhaps the earliest: Natterer, Ann. Wierner Museums Natur. 1837, v. 2:165; or as given above. Valid. Lepidosirenidae: Lepidosireninae.

Lepidosoma Swainson 1839:261 [ref. 4303]. Neut. *Lepidoleprus trachyrincus* Risso 1810:197. Type by being a replacement name. Unneeded substitute for (or error for) *Lepidoleprus* Risso 1810. Preoccupied by Wagler 1830 in Reptilia. Objective synonym of *Trachyrincus* Giorna 1809 (Marshall 1973:287 [ref. 7194], Marshall & Iwamoto 1973:516 [ref. 6963]). Macrouridae: Trachyrincinae.

Lepidothynnus Günther 1889:15 [ref. 2017]. Masc. *Lepidothynnus huttonii* Günther 1889:15. Type by monotypy. Synonym of *Gasterochisma* Richardson 1845 (Scott 1981:134 [ref. 5533]). Scombridae.

Lepidotrigla Günther 1860:196 [ref. 1963]. Fem. *Trigla aspera* Cuvier in Cuvier & Valenciennes 1829:77 (= *Trigla cavillone* Lacepède 1801:341, 367). Type by subsequent designation. Type designated by Jordan 1919:286 [ref. 4904]. Valid (Blanc & Hureau 1973:589 [ref. 7218], Richards & Saksena 1977 [ref. 5285], Ochiai & Yatou in Masuda et al. 1984:333 [ref. 6441], Heemstra 1986:487 [ref. 5660], Hureau in Whitehead et al. 1986:1234 [ref. 13677], Chen & Shao 1988:132 [ref. 6676], Paxton et al. 1989:454 [ref. 12442]). Triglidae: Triglinae.

Lepidotus Asso 1801:38 [ref. 6523]. Masc. *Lepidotus catalonicus* Asso 1801:38. Type by monotypy. Synonym of *Brama* Bloch & Schneider 1801 (Mead 1972:25 [ref. 6976], Mead 1973:386 [ref. 7199]). Bramidae.

Lepidozygus Günther 1862:15 [ref. 1969]. Masc. *Pomacentrus tapeinosoma* Bleeker 1856:376. Type by monotypy. Valid (Emery 1980 [ref. 6928], Emery 1983 [ref. 5437], Kishimoto in Masuda et al. 1984:194 [ref. 6441], Allen 1986:678 [ref. 5631]). Pomacentridae.

Lepimphis Rafinesque 1810:34 [ref. 3594]. *Lepimphis hippuroides* Rafinesque 1810:34. Type by subsequent designation. Type designated by Jordan 1917:79 [ref. 2407]. Synonym of *Coryphaena* Linnaeus 1758 (Tortonese 1973:385 [ref. 7192]). Coryphaenidae.

Lepinannocharax (subgenus of *Nannocharax*) Fowler 1936:271 [ref. 1424]. Masc. *Nannocharax pteron* Fowler 1936:272. Type by original designation. Synonym of *Nannocharax* Günther 1867 (Daget & Gosse 1984:200 [ref. 6185]). Citharinidae: Distichodontinae.

Lepipinna Fernández-Yépez 1948:26 [ref. 1316]. Fem. *Anodus alburnus* Müller & Troschel 1844:83. Type by original designation. Synonym of *Curimatella* Eigenmann & Eigenmann 1889 (Vari 1989:6 [ref. 9189]). Curimatidae: Curimatinae.

Lepipterus Cuvier in Cuvier & Valenciennes 1830:151 [ref. 999]. Masc. *Lepipterus francisci* Cuvier in Cuvier & Valenciennes 1830:152. Type by monotypy. Not preoccupied by Rafinesque 1815 in fishes (name only). Wrongly as a synonym of *Pachyurus* Agassiz [1831] (Chao 1978:42 [ref. 6983]). Valid. Sciaenidae.

Lepipterus Rafinesque 1815:85 [ref. 3584]. Masc. Not available, name only. Type designation (*Stromateus fiatola* Linnaeus 1758:248) by Fowler 1936:671 [ref. 6546] invalid; not recognized by Fowler as a valid genus. Stromateidae.

Lepisacanthus Lacepède 1801:320 [ref. 2710]. Masc. *Lepisacanthus japonicus* Lacepède 1801:320, 321 (= *Gasterosteus japonicus* Houttuyn 1782:329). Type by monotypy. *Lepicantha* Rafinesque 1815 evidently is an unjustified emendation or incorrect subsequent spelling. Objective synonym of *Monocentris* Bloch & Schneider 1801. Monocentridae.

Lepisoma DeKay 1842:41 [ref. 1098]. Neut. *Lepisoma cirrhosum* DeKay 1842:41. Type by monotypy. Apparently not preoccupied by *Lepisomus* Kirby 1837. Synonym of *Labrisomus* Swainson 1839 (Hubbs 1953:117 [ref. 2253], Springer 1958:422 [ref. 10210]). Labrisomidae.

Lepisosteus Lacepède 1803:331 [ref. 4930]. Masc. *Lepisosteus gavial* Lacepède 1803:331, 333. Type by subsequent designation. Type designated by Jordan & Gilbert 1877:84 [ref. 4907]. *Lepidosteus* of authors is an incorrect subsequent spelling or unjustified emendation (see Briggs 1961:162 [ref. 13439]). Original spelling of species is *gravial*; often cited as *gravialis*. Valid (Suttkus 1963 [ref. 7110], Wiley 1976:41 [ref. 7091]). Lepisosteidae.

Lepodus Rafinesque 1810:53 [ref. 3594]. Masc. *Lepodus saragus* Rafinesque 1810:54. Type by monotypy. Synonym of *Brama* Bloch & Schneider 1801 (Mead 1972:25 [ref. 6976], Mead 1973:386 [ref. 7199]). Bramidae.

Lepogenys Parr 1951:5 [ref. 3380]. Fem. *Bathytroctes squamosus* Alcock 1890:300. Type by original designation (also monotypic). Alepocephalidae.

Lepomis Rafinesque 1819:420 [ref. 3590]. Fem. *Labrus auritus* Linnaeus 1758:283. Type by original designation. *Lepomotis*, *Lepiopomus*, *Lepidopomus*, *Lepidopoma*, and *Lepipomus* in early literature are incorrect subsequent spellings or unjustified emendations. Valid. Centrarchidae.

Lepomus Rafinesque 1815:86 [ref. 3584]. Masc. Not available, name only. Unplaced genera.

Lepophidium Gill 1895:167 [ref. 1742]. Neut. *Leptophidium profundorum* Gill 1863:211. Type by being a replacement name. Replacement for *Leptophidium* Gill 1863, preoccupied by Hallowell 1860 in Ophidia. Valid (Nielsen 1973:553 [ref. 6885], Cohen & Nielsen 1978:14 [ref. 881]). Ophidiidae: Ophidiinae.

Leporacanthicus Isbrücker & Nijssen 1989:544 [ref. 13622]. Masc. *Leporacanthicus galaxias* Isbrücker & Nijssen 1989:546. Type by original designation. Loricariidae.

Leporellus Lütken 1875:129 [ref. 2856]. Masc. *Leporinus pictus*

Kner 1859:172. Type by monotypy. Valid (Géry 1977:151 [ref. 1597], Winterbottom 1980:2 [ref. 4755], Géry et al. 1987:371 [ref. 6001]). Curimatidae: Anostominae.

Leporinodus Eigenmann 1922:116 [ref. 1243]. Masc. *Leporinodus retropinnis* Eigenmann 1922:116. Type by original designation. Curimatidae: Anostominae.

Leporinops (subgenus of *Leporinus*) Géry 1960:308 [ref. 1604]. Masc. *Leporinus moralesi* Fowler 1942:18. Type by original designation (also monotypic). Synonym of *Leporinus* Agassiz 1829,. but as a valid subgenus (Géry 1977:155 [ref. 1597]). Curimatidae: Anostominae.

Leporinus Agassiz in Spix & Agassiz 1829:58, 65 [ref. 13]. Masc. *Leporinus novemfasciatus* Agassiz in Spix & Agassiz 1829:65 (= *Salmo fasciatus* Bloch 1794:96). Type by monotypy. *L. novemfasciatus* is an unneeded substitute for and objective synonym of *S. fasciatus* Bloch. For authorship and date see Kottelat 1988:78 [ref. 13380]. Valid (Géry 1977:155 [ref. 1597], Vari 1983:5 [ref. 5419], Géry et al. 1987:383 [ref. 6001], Garavello & Britski 1987 [ref. 6851], Garavello 1988 [ref. 14272], Garavello 1989 [ref. 14273], Malabarba 1989:126 [ref. 14217]). Curimatidae: Anostominae.

Leprogaster (subgenus of *Monacanthus*) Fraser-Brunner 1941:184 [ref. 1494]. Fem. *Balistes ciliatus* Mitchill 1818:326. Type by original designation. Monacanthidae.

Leptacanthichthys (subgenus of *Dolopichthys*) Regan & Trewavas 1932:66, 80 [ref. 3682]. Masc. *Dolopichthys gracilispinis* Regan 1925:563. Type by monotypy. Valid (Pietsch 1974:32 [ref. 5332], Pietsch 1978:19 [ref. 3473], Bertelsen in Whitehead et al. 1986:1390 [ref. 13677]). Oneirodidae.

Leptagoniates Boulenger 1887:281 [ref. 532]. Masc. *Leptagoniates steindachneri* Boulenger 1887:282. Type by monotypy. Misspelled *Leptogoniates* by Jordan 1920:437 [ref. 4905]. Valid (Géry 1977:347 [ref. 1597], Vari 1978 [ref. 7036]). Characidae.

Leptagonus Gill 1861:167 [ref. 1775]. Masc. *Agonus spinosissimus* Krøyer 1844:250. Type by original designation (also monotypic). Valid (Lindberg 1973:605 [ref. 7220], Yabe 1985:123 [ref. 11522], Andriashev in Whitehead et al. 1986:1266 [ref. 13677]). Agonidae.

Leptanthias Tanaka 1918:525 [ref. 4331]. Masc. *Leptanthias kashiwae* Tanaka 1918:525. Type by original designation (also monotypic). Synonym of *Pseudanthias* Bleeker 1871 (Katayama in Masuda et al. 1984:137 [ref. 6441] based on placement of type species). Serranidae: Anthiinae.

Leptarius Gill 1863:170 [ref. 1681]. Masc. *Leptarius dowii* Gill 1863:170. Type by monotypy. Synonym of *Selenaspis* Bleeker 1858. Ariidae.

Leptaspis Bleeker 1852:71 [ref. 332]. Fem. *Caranx leptolepis* Cuvier (ex Kuhl & van Hasselt) in Cuvier & Valenciennes 1833:48. Type by monotypy. Earlier as *Selaroides* by Bleeker 1851; reason for change unstated. Objective synonym of *Selaroides* Bleeker 1851. Carangidae.

Leptatherina Pavlov, Ivantsoff, Last & Crowley 1988:393 [ref. 12285]. Fem. *Atherina presbyteroides* Richardson 1843:179. Type by original designation. Atherinidae: Atherininae.

Leptecheneis Gill 1864:60 [ref. 1695]. Fem. *Echeneis naucrates* Linnaeus 1758:261. Type by original designation (also monotypic). Objective synonym of *Echeneis* Linnaeus 1758 (Lachner 1973:637 [ref. 7221]). Echeneidae.

Leptenchelys Myers & Wade 1941:72 [ref. 3133]. Fem. *Leptenchelys vermiformis* Myers & Wade 1941:73. Type by original designation (also monotypic). Valid (McCosker 1977:72 [ref. 6836], McCosker et al. 1989:298 [ref. 13288]). Ophichthidae: Ophichthinae.

Lepterus Rafinesque 1810:52 [ref. 3594]. Masc. *Lepterus fetula* Rafinesque 1810:52. Type by monotypy. Synonym of *Stromateus* Linnaeus 1758. Stromateidae.

Lepthaemulon (subgenus of *Orthopristis*) Fowler & Bean 1923:14 [ref. 1474]. Neut. *Orthopristis rhabdotus* Fowler & Bean 1923:14. Type by original designation (also monotypic). Synonym of *Orthopristis* Girard 1858. Haemulidae.

Leptoancistrus Meek & Hildebrand 1916:254 [ref. 2962]. Masc. *Acanthicus canensis* Meek & Hildebrand 1913:80. Type by original designation (also monotypic). Valid (Isbrücker 1980:65 [ref. 2303], Heitmans et al. 1983 [ref. 5278], Burgess 1989:436 [ref. 12860]). Loricariidae.

Leptobarbus Bleeker 1859:435 [ref. 370]. Masc. *Barbus hoevenii* Bleeker 1851:207. Type by subsequent monotypy. Apparently appeared first in key, without included species. One species included by Bleeker 1859:153 [ref. 371] and 1860:285, 432 [ref. 380]. Valid (Kottelat 1985:263 [ref. 11441], Roberts 1989:41 [ref. 6439]). Cyprinidae.

Leptoblennius Bath 1978:184 [ref. 209]. Masc. *Hypsoblennius piersoni* Gilbert & Starks 1904:191. Type by original designation (also monotypic). Preoccupied by Gill 1860 in fishes, replaced by *Parahypsos* Bath 1982. Blenniidae.

Leptoblennius Gill 1860:21 [ref. 1763]. Masc. *Blennius serpentinus* Storer 1848:30. Type by monotypy. Synonym of *Lumpenus* Reinhardt 1837 (Makushok 1973:536 [ref. 6889]). Stichaeidae.

Leptobotia Bleeker 1870:256 [ref. 5871]. Fem. *Botia (Leptobotia) elongata* Bleeker 1870:254. Type by monotypy. Species described in *Botia* but put in *Leptobotia* at end of description. Valid (Nalbant 1963:357 [ref. 3140], Sawada 1982:197 [ref. 14111], Sawada in Masuda et al. 1984:58 [ref. 6441]). Cobitidae: Botiinae.

Leptobrama Steindachner 1878:388 [ref. 4226]. Fem. *Leptobrama muelleri* Steindachner 1878:388. Type by monotypy. Date may be 1879. Valid. Leptobramidae.

Leptobrotula Nielsen 1986:166 [ref. 3199]. Fem. *Leptobrotula breviventralis* Nielsen 1986:166. Type by original designation (also monotypic). Ophidiidae.

Leptobrycon Eigenmann 1915:46 [ref. 1231]. Masc. *Leptobrycon jutuaranae* Eigenmann 1915:46. Type by original designation (also monotypic). Characidae.

Leptocarcharias Günther 1870:384 [ref. 1995]. Masc. *Triaenodon smithii* Müller & Henle 1841:56. Type by monotypy. *Leptocarias* listed in synonymy and attributed to Smith (manuscript), but description of genus and species appears to be by Günther, therefore authorship solely to Günther; not technically an emendation of *Leptocharias*. Objective synonym of *Leptocharias* Smith 1838 (Compagno 1973:27 [ref. 7163], Compagno 1988:202 [ref. 13488]). Leptochariidae.

Leptocarias Müller & Henle (ex Smith) 1839:56 [ref. 3069]. Masc. *Leptocarias smithii* Müller & Henle 1839:56. Type by monotypy. As appeared in footnote in Müller & Henle can probably be regarded as a name in synonymy of *Triaenodon*. Appeared first as *Leptocharias* Smith 1838; perhaps Müller and Henle's treatment can be regarded as an incorrect subsequent spelling. Synonym of *Leptocharias* Smith 1838 (Compagno 1973:27 [ref. 7163], Compagno 1988:202 [ref. 13488]). Leptochariidae.

Leptocephalichthys Bleeker 1856:69 [ref. 352]. Masc. *Leptocephalichthys hypselosoma* Bleeker 1856:69. Type by monotypy. Congridae: Congrinae.

Leptocephalus Basilewski (ex Pallas) 1855:234 [ref. 200]. Masc. *Leptocephalus mongolicus* Basilewski 1855:234. Type by monotypy. Preoccupied by Scopoli 1777 in fishes, replaced by *Chanodichthys* Bleeker 1859. On Official Index as a junior homonym of Scopoli 1777 (Direction 87). Cyprinidae.

Leptocephalus Gronow 1763:135 [ref. 1910]. Masc. Not available, published in a rejected work on Official Index (Opinion 261). Congridae: Congrinae.

Leptocephalus Scopoli (ex Gronow) 1777:453 [ref. 3990]. Masc. Type by monotypy. *Leptocephalus* Scopoli placed on Official Index (Direction 87), suppressed for purposes of priority but not homonymy (Opinion 93). *Leptocephalus* Cuvier 1797 placed on Official Index (Opinion 87) as a junior homonym; *Leptocephalus* of Gmelin in Linnaeus 1789:1130 and Gronovius 1763:135 also placed on Official Index (Direction 87). In the synonymy of *Conger* Oken 1817. Congridae: Congrinae.

Leptocerdale Weymouth 1910:142 [ref. 4632]. *Leptocerdale longipinnis* Weymouth 1910:142. Type by original designation (also monotypic). Synonym of *Microdesmus* Günther 1864. Microdesmidae: Microdesminae.

Leptocharias Smith in Müller & Henle 1838:36 [ref. 3066]. Masc. *Triaenodon smithii* Müller & Henle 1839:56. Type by subsequent monotypy. Appeared first without species, one species added by Müller & Henle 1839:56 [ref. 3069] where genus was spelled *Leptocarias*. See *Leptocarcharias* Günther 1870 [ref. 1995]. Valid (Compagno 1973:27 [ref. 7163], Compagno 1984:380 [ref. 6846], Bass et al. 1986:80 [ref. 5638], Compagno 1988:202 [ref. 13488]). Leptochariidae.

Leptochilichthys Garman 1899:284 [ref. 1540]. Masc. *Leptochilichthys agassizii* Garman 1899:285. Type by monotypy. Valid (Krefft 1973:90 [ref. 7166], Markle & Quéro in Whitehead et al. 1984:254 [ref. 13675], Markle 1986:225 [ref. 5687], Machida & Shiogaki 1988 [ref. 6622]). Leptochilichthyidae.

Leptochromis (subgenus of *Pseudochromis*) Bleeker 1875:14 [ref. 444]. Masc. *Pseudochromis melanotaenia* Bleeker 1863:273. Type by subsequent designation. Type designated by Bleeker 1876:321 [ref. 448], not *cyanotaenia* designated by Jordan 1919:382 [ref. 4904]. Synonym of *Pseudochromis* Rüppell 1835. Pseudochromidae: Pseudochrominae.

Leptochromis Regan 1920:46 [ref. 3669]. Masc. *Paratilapia calliura* Boulenger 1901:2. Type by original designation (also monotypic). Preoccupied by Bleeker 1875 in fishes, replaced by *Reganochromis* Whitley 1929. Cichlidae.

Leptoclinus Gill 1861:45 [ref. 1766]. Masc. *Lumpenus aculeatus* Reinhardt 1837:cx. Type by monotypy. Valid (Makushok 1973:538 [ref. 6889], Makushok in Whitehead et al. 1986:1127 [ref. 13677], Miki et al. 1987:131 [ref. 6704]). Stichaeidae.

Leptoclupea Whitehead, Boeseman & Wheeler (ex Bleeker) 1966:12 [ref. 6860]. Fem. Cited as a name mentioned in a letter from Bleeker to Günther; not available, not used as a valid name by Whitehead, Boeseman & Wheeler. Clupeidae.

Leptoconger Poey 1880:250 [ref. 6524]. Masc. *Neoconger perlongus* Poey 1874:67. Type by monotypy. Synonym of *Myrophis* Lütken 1852 (McCosker et al. 1989:279 [ref. 13288]). Ophichthidae: Myrophinae.

Leptocottus Girard 1854:130 [ref. 1817]. Masc. *Leptocottus armatus* Girard 1854:131. Type by monotypy. Valid (Bolin 1944:96 [ref. 6379], Washington et al. 1984:443 [ref. 13660], Yabe 1985:111 [ref. 11522]). Cottidae.

Leptocypris Boulenger 1900:133 [ref. 555]. Fem. *Leptocypris modestus* Boulenger 1900:134. Type by monotypy. Valid (Lévêque & Daget 1984:324 [ref. 6186], Howes & Teugels 1989 [ref. 13624]). Cyprinidae.

Leptoderma Vaillant 1886:1239 [ref. 4494]. Neut. *Leptoderma macrops* Vaillant 1886:1239. Type by monotypy. Valid (Krefft 1973:91 [ref. 7166], Markle & Quéro in Whitehead et al. 1984:244 [ref. 13675], Machida in Masuda et al. 1984:43 [ref. 6441], Markle 1986:221 [ref. 5687]). Alepocephalidae.

Leptodes Swainson 1838:303 [ref. 4302]. Masc. *Chauliodus sloani* Bloch & Schneider 1801:430. Type by being a replacement name. Also in Swainson 1839:187, 298, 388 [ref. 4303]. Unneeded replacement for *Chauliodus* Bloch & Schneider 1801. Objective synonym of *Chauliodus* Bloch & Schneider 1801 (Morrow 1973:130 [ref. 7175]). Chauliodontidae.

Leptodoras Boulenger 1898:477 [ref. 545]. Masc. *Oxydoras acipenserinus* Günther 1868:230. Type by subsequent designation. Type apparently first designated by Eigenmann 1910:395 [ref. 1224]. Valid (Böhlke 1970 [ref. 7150], Burgess 1989:222 [ref. 12860]). Doradidae.

Leptofierasfer Meek & Hildebrand 1928:964 [ref. 2964]. *Leptofierasfer macrurus* Meek & Hildebrand 1928:964. Type by original designation (also monotypic). Synonym of *Carapus* Rafinesque 1810 (Arnold 1956:260 [ref. 5315]). Carapidae: Carapinae.

Leptogadus Gill 1863:248 [ref. 1688]. Masc. *Gadus blennioides* Pallas 1770:47. Type by original designation, Gill's style of type in parentheses in key (also monotypic). Species may date to Brünnich 1768:24 (not researched). Gadiformes.

Leptogaster Bleeker 1870:Pl. 264 [ref. 428]. Fem. *Spratelloides argyrotaenia* Bleeker 1849:72. Type by monotypy. Jordan 1919:362 [ref. 4904] regarded as introduced in error, probably overlooked in proofreading. Whitehead et al. 1966:70 [ref. 6860] treat as a forgotten name and place in synonymy of *Escualosa* Whitley 1940. Correctly dates to 1870, Pl. 264 in part 22 [ref. 428], with corresponding legend page published in 1875; in corresponding text page 101 published in 1872 Bleeker used the name *Clupeoides*. In synonymy of *Escualosa* Whitley 1940 (Whitehead 1985:118 [ref. 5141]). Clupeidae.

Leptoglanis Boulenger 1902:42 [ref. 562]. Masc. *Leptoglanis xenognathus* Boulenger 1902:43. Type by monotypy. Also placed in the Bagridae by authors. Valid (Bailey & Stewart 1984:9 [ref. 5232] in Amphiliidae, Risch 1986:30 [ref. 6190], Burgess 1989:68 [ref. 12860]). Amphiliidae.

Leptoglanis Eigenmann 1912:130, 158 [ref. 1227]. Masc. *Leptoglanis essequibensis* Eigenmann 1912:158. Type by original designation (also monotypic). Genus and species appeared first without description or available species name in Eigenmann 1910:384 [ref. 1224]. Preoccupied by Boulenger 1902 in fishes, replaced by and objective synonym of *Leptorhamdia* Eigenmann 1918. Pimelodidae.

Leptognathus Swainson 1838:221 [ref. 4302]. Masc. *Leptognathus oxyrhynchus* Swainson 1838:221. Type by monotypy. Also in Swainson 1839:196, 334 [ref. 4303] as a subgenus of *Anguilla*. Synonym of *Ophisurus* Lacepède 1800 (Blache et al. 1973:249 [ref. 7185], McCosker 1977:82 [ref. 6836]). Ophichthidae: Ophichthinae.

Leptogobius Bleeker 1874:311 [ref. 437]. Masc. *Gobius oxypterus*

Bleeker 1855:400. Type by original designation (also monotypic). Also appeared in Bleeker 1876:292 [ref. 442]. Synonym of *Gobiopterus* Bleeker 1874 (Hoese, pers. comm.). Gobiidae.

Leptogunnellus Ayres 1855:26 [ref. 159]. Masc. *Leptogunnellus gracilis* Ayres 1855:26. Type by monotypy. Read at the meeting of 22 Jan. 1855; appeared first in "The Pacific" newspaper, v. 4(8), 26 Jan. 1855, then in the Proceedings, p. 26. Synonym of *Lumpenus* Reinhardt 1837. Stichaeidae.

Leptoichthys Kaup 1853:233 [ref. 2569]. Masc. *Typhlus fistularius* Kaup 1853:233. Type by monotypy. Valid (Dawson 1985:110 [ref. 6541], Paxton et al. 1989:423 [ref. 12442]). Syngnathidae: Syngnathinae.

Leptojulis Bleeker 1862:412 [ref. 382]. Fem. *Julis (Halichoeres) cyanopleura* Bleeker 1853:489. Type by original designation (also monotypic). Also appeared in Bleeker 1862:100 [ref. 386]. Valid (Randall & Ferraris 1981 [ref. 5492]). Labridae.

Leptokyphosus (subgenus of *Segutilum*) Whitley 1931:320 [ref. 4672]. Masc. *Kyphosus gibsoni* Ogilby 1912:50. Type by original designation (also monotypic). Synonym of *Kyphosus* Lacepède 1801. Kyphosidae: Kyphosinae.

Leptolaeops (subgenus of *Laeops*) Fowler 1934:335 [ref. 1416]. Masc. *Laeops clarus* Fowler 1934:337. Type by original designation (also monotypic). Bothidae: Bothinae.

Leptolamprologus Pellegrin 1927:55 [ref. 3408]. Masc. *Leptolamprologus monogramma* Pellegrin 1927:55. Type by monotypy. Also appeared in Pellegrin 1928:34 [ref. 3411]. Cichlidae.

Leptolebias (subgenus of *Cynolebias*) Myers 1952:140 [ref. 3125]. Masc. *Cynolebias marmoratus* Ladiges 1934. Type by original designation. Synonym of *Cynolebias* Steindachner 1876 (Parenti 1981:490 [ref. 7066]). Aplocheilidae: Rivulinae.

Leptolepis Guichenot (ex van Hasselt MS) 1867:68 [ref. 1950]. Fem. Genus and species (*argentea*) appeared as name only, from van Hasselt manuscript; apparently never made available; possibly intended for *Pampus argenteus*. Preoccupied by Agassiz 1832 in fossil fishes. In the synonymy of *Pampus* Bonaparte 1837. Stromateidae.

Leptoligoplites (subgenus of *Oligoplites*) Fowler 1944:223 [ref. 1448]. Masc. *Oligoplites refulgens* Gilbert & Starks 1904:73. Type by original designation (also monotypic). Synonym of *Oligoplites* Gill 1863 (Smith-Vaniz & Staiger 1973:213 [ref. 7106]). Carangidae.

Leptolucania (subgenus of *Lucania*) Myers 1924:8 [ref. 3091]. Fem. *Heterandria ommata* Jordan 1884:323. Type by original designation (also monotypic). Valid (Parenti 1981:497 [ref. 7066]). Cyprinodontidae: Fundulinae.

Leptometopon (subgenus of *Polyamblyodon*) Smith 1940:178 [ref. 4069]. Neut. *Polyamblyodon (Leptometopon) cristiceps* Smith 1940:178. Apparently not available from Smith 1940, two included species in subgenus, neither designated as type (Art. 13b). Genus apparently can date to treatment in Zoological Record for 1940 where only one species was mentioned with the name; *Leptometopon* also was spelled two ways. See remarks on Art. 13b in Appendix A. Sparidae.

Leptonotus Kaup 1853:232 [ref. 2569]. Masc. *Syngnathus blainvillianus* Eydoux & Gervais 1837:3. Type by monotypy, second included species as name only and not available; *blainvillianus* spelled *blainvillei* by Kaup. Also appeared in Kaup 1856:46 [ref. 2573]. Valid (Fritzsche 1980:190 [ref. 1511], Dawson 1982:40 [ref. 6764], Dawson 1985:111 [ref. 6541]). Syngnathidae: Syngnathinae.

Leptonurus Bleeker 1849:14 [ref. 320]. Masc. *Leptonurus chrysostigma* Bleeker 1849:14. Type by monotypy. Synonym of *Coilia* Gray 1830 (Whitehead et al. 1988:460 [ref. 5725]). Engraulidae.

Leptopegasus Bleeker 1873:125 [ref. 431]. Masc. *Pegasus natans* Linnaeus 1766:418. Type by monotypy. Objective synonym of *Parapegasus* Duméril (ex Bleeker) 1870; synonym of *Pegasus* Linnaeus 1758 (Palsson & Pietsch 1989:18 [ref. 13536]). Pegasidae.

Leptoperca Gill 1862:502, footnote [ref. 1780]. Fem. *Perca schraetzer* Linnaeus 1758:294. Type by original designation (also monotypic). Synonym of *Gymnocephalus* Bloch 1793 (Collette & Banarescu 1977:1453 [ref. 5845]). Percidae.

Leptophidium Gill 1863:210 [ref. 1683]. Neut. *Leptophidium profundorum* Gill 1863:211. Type by monotypy, second species included conditionally. Preoccupied by Hallowell 1860 in Ophidia (snakes), replaced by *Lepophidium* Gill 1895. Objective synonym of *Lepophidium* Gill 1895 (Cohen & Nielsen 1978:14 [ref. 881]). Ophidiidae: Ophidiinae.

Leptophilypnus Meek & Hildebrand 1916:361 [ref. 2962]. Masc. *Leptophilypnus fluviatilis* Meek & Hildebrand 1916:361. Type by original designation (also monotypic). Valid (Birdsong et al. 1988:202 [ref. 7303]). Eleotridae.

Leptophycis Garman 1899:182 [ref. 1540]. Fem. *Leptophycis filifer* Garman 1899:182. Type by monotypy. Synonym of *Gadella* Lowe 1843 (Paulin 1989:95 [ref. 9297]). Moridae.

Leptops (subgenus of *Ictalurus*) Rafinesque 1820:358 [ref. 7311]. Masc. *Pimelodus viscosus* Rafinesque 1820:50. Type by subsequent designation. As a section of the subgenus *Ictalurus*. Type designated by Jordan & Gilbert 1877:87 [ref. 4907]. Also appeared in Rafinesque 1820:64 (Dec.) [ref. 3592]. Synonym of *Pylodictis* Rafinesque 1819. Ictaluridae.

Leptopterygius Troschel 1860:206 [ref. 4464]. Masc. *Leptopterygius coccoi* Troschel 1860:207. Type by subsequent designation. Apparently two included species; earliest subsequent designation not researched. Synonym of *Gouania* Nardo 1833 (Briggs 1955:23 [ref. 637], Briggs 1973:653 [ref. 7222]). Gobiesocidae: Gobiesocinae.

Leptopus Rafinesque 1814:16 [ref. 3581]. Masc. *Leptopus peregrinus* Rafinesque 1814:16. Type by monotypy. Synonym of *Lophotus* Giorna 1809 (Palmer 1973:334 [ref. 7195]). Lophotidae.

Leptorhamdia Eigenmann 1918:260 [ref. 1239]. Fem. *Leptoglanis essequibensis* Eigenmann 1912:158. Type by being a replacement name. Replacement for *Leptoglanis* Eigenmann 1912, preoccupied by Boulenger 1902 in fishes. Pimelodidae.

Leptorhaphis Regan 1913:998 [ref. 3653]. Fem. *Gambusia infans* Woolman 1894:62. Type by monotypy. Synonym of *Poeciliopsis* Regan 1913 (Rosen & Bailey 1963:131 [ref. 7067]). Poeciliidae.

Leptorhinophis Kaup 1856:46 [ref. 2572]. Masc. *Ophisurus gomesii* Castelnau 1855:pl. 44. Type by subsequent designation. Type designated by Jordan 1919:271 [ref. 2410]. Also appeared in Kaup 1856:14 [ref. 2573]. Synonym of *Ophichthus* Ahl 1789 (Blache et al. 1973:247 [ref. 7185], McCosker 1977:80 [ref. 6836], McCosker et al. 1989:379 [ref. 13288]). Ophichthidae: Ophichthinae.

Leptorhynchus Lowe 1852:252 [ref. 2835]. Masc. *Leptorhynchus leuchtenbergi* Lowe 1852:252. Type by monotypy. Also in Lowe 1852:54 [ref. 2836] and in Lowe 1854:172 [ref. 9184]. Preoccupied by Clift 1828 in Reptilia, Du Bus 1835 and Ménétries 1835 in Aves, and Smith 1840 in fishes; replaced by *Belonopsis* Brandt 1854. Synonym of *Nemichthys* Richardson 1848 (Larsen 1973:231 [ref. 7187], Smith & Nielsen 1989:452 [ref. 13290]). Nemichthyidae.

Leptorhynchus Smith 1840:Pl. 6 [ref. 4035]. Masc. *Leptorhynchus capensis* Smith 1840:Pl. 6. Type by monotypy. Preoccupied by Clift 1828 in Reptilia, Du Bus 1835 and Ménetriés 1835 in Aves; replaced by *Anepistomon* Gistel 1848. Synonym of *Ophisurus* Lacepède 1800 (Blache et al. 1973:249 [ref. 7185], McCosker 1977:82 [ref. 6836]). Ophichthidae: Ophichthinae.

Leptoscarus (subgenus of *Scarus*) Swainson 1839:172, 226 [ref. 4303]. Masc. *Scarus vaigiensis* Quoy & Gaimard 1824:288. Type by monotypy. Valid (Kishimoto in Masuda et al. 1984:218 [ref. 6441], Bruce & Randall 1985 [ref. 5234], Randall 1986:708 [ref. 5706], Bellwood & Choat 1989:12 [ref. 13494]). Scaridae: Sparisomatinae.

Leptoscolopsis Tanaka 1915:365 [ref. 6036]. Fem. *Leptoscolopsis nagasakiensis* Tanaka 1915:365. Type by original designation (also monotypic). Nemipteridae.

Leptoscopus Gill 1859:132 [ref. 1792]. Masc. *Uranoscopus macropygos* Richardson 1846:55. Type by monotypy. Valid. Leptoscopidae.

Leptosoma Nardo 1827:15, 22 [ref. 3146]. Neut. *Leptosoma atrum* Nardo 1827. Original not examined. Also in Isis, v. 20:482 (seen). Preoccupied by Leach 1819 in Crustacea; replaced by *Spanius* Gistel 1848. Soleidae.

Leptostichaeus Miki 1985:137 [ref. 5798]. Masc. *Leptostichaeus pumilus* Miki 1985:139. Type by original designation (also monotypic). Stichaeidae.

Leptostomias Gilbert 1905:606 [ref. 1631]. Masc. *Leptostomias macronema* Gilbert 1905:607. Type by original designation (also monotypic). Type in parentheses. Valid (Morrow in Morrow & Gibbs 1964:433 [ref. 6962], Morrow 1973:140 [ref. 7175], Kawaguchi & Moser 1984:171 [ref. 13642], Gibbs in Whitehead et al. 1984:354 [ref. 13675], Fujii in Masuda et al. 1984:51 [ref. 6441], Fink 1985:11 [ref. 5171], Gibbs 1986:240 [ref. 5655]). Melanostomiidae.

Leptosynanceia Bleeker 1874:17 [ref. 439]. Fem. *Synanceia astroblepa* Richardson 1848:69. Type by monotypy. Valid (Eschmeyer & Rama-Rao 1973:375 [ref. 6391], Washington et al. 1984:440 [ref. 13660]). Scorpaenidae: Synanceiinae.

Leptotilapia Pellegrin 1928:112 [ref. 3410]. Fem. *Leptotilapia rouxi* Pellegrin 1928:112. Type by monotypy. Cichlidae.

Lepturacanthus (subgenus of *Trichiurus*) Fowler 1905:770 [ref. 1368]. Masc. *Trichiurus savala* Cuvier 1829:219. Type by original designation (also monotypic). Valid (Collette et al. 1984:600 [ref. 11421]). Trichiuridae: Trichiurinae.

Lepturichthys Regan 1911:31 [ref. 3642]. Masc. *Homaloptera fimbriatum* Günther 1888:433. Type by original designation (also monotypic). Valid (Silas 1953:210 [ref. 4024], Chen 1978:337 [ref. 6900], Sawada 1982:204 [ref. 14111]). Balitoridae: Balitorinae.

Lepturus Gill 1861:35 [ref. 1766]. Masc. *Trichiurus lepturus* Linnaeus 1758:246. Type by monotypy. Revival of pre-Linnaean name; apparently preoccupied by Molhring 1758 in Aves [not researched]. Objective synonym of *Trichiurus* Linnaeus 1758. Trichiuridae: Trichiurinae.

Lepturus Gronow in Gray 1854:165 [ref. 1911]. Masc. *Lepturus brevirostris* Gronow in Gray 1854:166. Type by monotypy. Preoccupied by Moehring 1758 and by Bibron 1760 and Swainson 1837 in Aves. Synonym of *Coryphaenoides* Gunner 1765. Macrouridae: Macrourinae.

Lermichthys Hubbs 1926:18 [ref. 2233]. Masc. *Characodon multiradiatus* Meek 1904:119. Type by original designation (also monotypic). Synonym of *Girardinichthys* Bleeker 1860 (Miller & Fitzsimons 1971:10 [ref. 3019]). Goodeidae.

Lestidiops Hubbs 1916:154 [ref. 2225]. Masc. *Lestidiops sphyraenopsis* Hubbs 1916:155. Type by original designation (also monotypic). Valid (Post 1973:205 [ref. 7182], Post in Whitehead et al. 1984:498 [ref. 13675], Okiyama 1984:207 [ref. 13644], Fujii in Masuda et al. 1984:76 [ref. 6441], Post 1986:275 [ref. 5705], Paxton et al. 1989:246 [ref. 12442]). Paralepididae.

Lestidium Gilbert 1905:607 [ref. 1631]. Neut. *Lestidium nudum* Gilbert 1905:607. Type by original designation (also monotypic). Type given in parentheses as was Gilbert's style. Valid (Okiyama 1984:207 [ref. 13644], Fujii in Masuda et al. 1984:76 [ref. 6441], Post 1986:275 [ref. 5705], Paxton et al. 1989:246 [ref. 12442]). Paralepididae.

Lestradea Poll 1943:307 [ref. 3518]. Fem. *Lestradea perspicax* Poll 1943:308. Type by original designation (also monotypic). Valid (Liem 1981:192 [ref. 6897], Poll 1986:103 [ref. 6136]). Cichlidae.

Lestrolepis (subgenus of *Lestidium*) Harry 1953:240 [ref. 2045]. Fem. *Paralepis philippinus* Fowler 1934:281. Type by original designation. Valid (Okiyama 1984:207 [ref. 13644], Fujii in Masuda et al. 1984:77 [ref. 6441], Post 1986:275 [ref. 5705], Paxton et al. 1989:247 [ref. 12442]). Paralepididae.

Lesueuri de Buen 1926:80 [ref. 5054]. As a "grupo" for 2 species of *Gobius*. Not available on basis of Art. 1b(6) [see de Buen's definition of "grupo" on p. 11]; see Appendix A. Gobiidae.

Lesueuria (subgenus of *Gobius*) Duncker 1928:124 [ref. 6525]. Fem. *Gobius suerii* Risso 1810:387. Type by subsequent designation. Type designated by Iljin 1930:50 [ref. 2297]. Preoccupied by Milne-Edwards 1841 in Coelenterata, replaced by *Lesueurigobius* Whitley 1950. Objective synonym of *Lesueurigobius* Whitley 1950 (Miller 1973:499 [ref. 6888]). Gobiidae.

Lesueurigobius Whitley 1950:44 [ref. 4713]. Masc. *Gobius suerii* Risso 1810:387. Type by being a replacement name. Replacement for *Lesueuria* Duncker 1928, preoccupied by Milne-Edwards 1841 in Coelenterata. Valid (Miller 1973:499 [ref. 6888], Miller 1984:380 [ref. 6338], Miller in Whitehead et al. 1986:1051 [ref. 13677], Birdsong et al. 1988:186 [ref. 7303] as *Lesuerigobius*). Gobiidae.

Lesueurina Fowler 1908:440 [ref. 1377]. Fem. *Lesueurina platycephala* Fowler 1908:440. Type by original designation (also monotypic). Misspelled once as *Lesueurella* by Fowler on p. 440 and *Lesueuriella* by Jordan 1920:523 [ref. 4905]. Trichonotidae.

Letharchus Goode & Bean 1882:436 [ref. 1840]. Masc. *Letharchus velifer* Goode & Bean 1882:437. Type by monotypy. Misspelled *Letharcus* by Goode & Bean on p. 437 (corrected in "List of Corrections" on p. xi). Valid (McCosker 1974 [ref. 2933], McCosker 1977:63 [ref. 6836], Leiby 1984:414 [ref. 12859], McCosker et al. 1989:313 [ref. 13288]). Ophichthidae: Ophichthinae.

Lethenteron (subgenus of *Lampetra*) Creaser & Hubbs 1922:6 [ref. 990]. Neut. *Lampetra wilderi* Gage in Jordan & Evermann 1896:13. Type by original designation. Valid (Vladykov 1973:4 [ref. 7159], Vladykov & Kott 1978 [ref. 7038], Vladykov in Whitehead et al. 1984:65 [ref. 13675]); as a subgenus of *Lampetra* Gray 1851 (Hubbs & Potter 1971:49[ref. 13397], Bailey 1980:1627 [ref. 5253] and most current workers). Petromyzontidae:

Petromyzontinae.

Lethogoleos McCosker & Böhlke 1982:114 [ref. 2935]. Masc. *Lethogoleos andersoni* McCosker & Böhlke 1982:114. Type by original designation (also monotypic). Valid (McCosker et al. 1989:370 [ref. 13288]). Ophichthidae: Ophichthinae.

Letholycus Anderson 1988:272 [ref. 6334]. Masc. *Melanostigma microphthalmus* Norman 1937:110. Type by original designation. Zoarcidae.

Lethops Hubbs 1926:4 [ref. 2234]. Masc. *Lethops connectens* Hubbs 1926:5. Type by original designation (also monotypic). Valid (Birdsong et al. 1988:202 [ref. 7303] as *Lethrops). Gobiidae.*

Lethostole Jordan & Evermann 1896:789, 792 [ref. 2443]. *Chirostoma estor* Jordan 1879:298. Type by original designation (also monotypic). Misspelled *Lethestole* by Eigenmann 1910:465 [ref. 1224]. Synonym of *Chirostoma* Swainson 1839. Atherinidae: Menidiinae.

Lethotremus Gilbert 1896:469 [ref. 1628]. Masc. *Lethotremus multicus* Gilbert 1896:469. Type by monotypy. Valid (Lindberg & Legeza 1955 [ref. 2785], Kido in Masuda et al. 1984:337 [ref. 6441]). Cyclopteridae: Cyclopterinae.

Lethrinella (subgenus of *Lethrinus*) Fowler 1904:529 [ref. 1367]. Fem. *Sparus miniatus* Bloch & Schneider 1801:281. Type by original designation (also monotypic). Synonym of *Lethrinus* Cuvier 1829 (Carpenter & Allen 1989:33 [ref. 13577]). Lethrinidae.

Lethrinichthys Jordan & Thompson 1912:558 [ref. 2541]. Masc. *Lethrinus nematacanthus* Bleeker 1854:403. Type by original designation. Synonym of *Lethrinus* Cuvier 1829 (Carpenter & Allen 1989:33 [ref. 13577]). Lethrinidae.

Lethrinops Regan 1922:719 [ref. 3673]. Masc. *Chromis lethrinus* Günther 1893:622. Type by original designation. Valid (Eccles & Lewis 1977 [ref. 7049], Eccles & Lewis 1978 [ref. 7012], Eccles & Lewis 1979 [ref. 6939], Eccles & Trewavas 1989:120 [ref. 13547]). Cichlidae.

Lethrinus Cuvier 1829:184 [ref. 995]. Masc. *Sparus choerorynchus* Bloch & Schneider 1801:278. Type by subsequent designation. Type designated by Jordan & Thompson 1912:558 [ref. 2541] (not by Bleeker 1876:281 of a non-included species). Spelled *Lethrynus* by Temminck & Schlegel 1844:74 [ref. 4372]. Valid (Sato 1978 [ref. 8884], Johnson 1980:11 [ref. 13553], Sato in Masuda et al. 1984:179 [ref. 6441], Smith 1986:596 [ref. 5712], Carpenter & Allen 1989:33 [ref. 13577]). Lethrinidae.

Leucabramis Smitt 1895:798 [ref. 4146]. Fem. *Cyprinus vimba* Linnaeus 1758:325. Type by monotypy. Objective synonym of *Vimba* Fitzinger 1873. Synonym of *Abramis* Cuvier 1816 (Howes 1981:46 [ref. 14200]). Cyprinidae.

Leucalburnus Berg 1916:292 [ref. 277]. Masc. *Phoxinus satunini* Berg 1910:127. Type by monotypy. Valid (Bogutskaya 1987:936 [ref. 13521]). Cyprinidae.

Leucaspius Heckel & Kner 1858:145 [ref. 2078]. Masc. *Leucaspius abruptus* Heckel & Kner 1858:145. Type by monotypy. Misspelled *Leucaspis* by Jordan 1923:141 [ref. 2421]. Valid (Bogutskaya 1987:936 [ref. 13521], but see Coad 1981:2062 [ref. 5572]). Cyprinidae.

Leucichthys (subgenus of *Coregonus*) Dybowski 1874:390 [ref. 1172]. Masc. *Salmo omul* Pallas 1811:406. Type by subsequent designation. Type apparently first designated by Jordan & Evermann 1911:3 [ref. 2452]. Synonym of *Coregonus* Linnaeus 1758 (Svetovidov 1973:148 [ref. 7169]), as a valid subgenus (Kendall & Behnke 1984:144 [ref. 13638]). Salmonidae: Coregoninae.

Leucicorus Garman 1899:146 [ref. 1540]. Masc. *Leucicorus lusciosus* Garman 1899:146. Type by monotypy. Valid (Cohen & Nielsen 1978:34 [ref. 881], Anderson et al. 1985 [ref. 5164]). Ophidiidae: Neobythitinae.

Leucidius Snyder 1917:64 [ref. 4156]. Masc. *Leucidius pectinifer* Snyder 1917:64. Type by original designation (also monotypic). Synonym of *Gila* Baird & Girard 1853. Cyprinidae.

Leucisculus Oshima 1920:128 [ref. 3313]. Masc. *Leucisculus fuscus* Oshima 1920:129. Type by original designation (also monotypic). Synonym of *Mylopharyngodon* Peters 1873 (Howes 1981:41 [ref. 14200]). Cyprinidae.

Leuciscus Cuvier (ex Klein) 1816:194 [ref. 993]. Masc. *Cyprinus leuciscus* Linnaeus 1758:323. Type by absolute tautonymy. Appeared first in Klein 1775, unavailable. Valid (Yang & Hwang 1964:28 [ref. 13497]; see discussion in Howes 1984:284 [ref. 5312], Bogutskaya 1987 [ref. 13521]). Cyprinidae.

Leuciscus Klein 1775:172 [ref. 2618]. Masc. Not available, published in a work that does not conform to the principle of binominal nomenclature. In the synonymy of *Leuciscus* Cuvier 1816. Cyprinidae.

Leucobrotula Koefoed 1952:20 [ref. 2652]. Fem. *Leucobrotula adipatus* Koefoed 1952:20. Type by monotypy. Valid (Nielsen 1973:548 [ref. 6885], Nielsen in Whitehead et al. 1986:1151 [ref. 13677], Anderson 1986:343 [ref. 5633]). Ophidiidae.

Leucochlamys Zugmayer 1911:11 [ref. 6161]. Fem. *Leucochlamys cryptophthalmus* Zugmayer 1911:11. Type by monotypy. Also appeared in Zugmayer 1911 (Dec.):131 [ref. 4846]. Valid (Nielsen 1969:69 [ref. 3195], Nielsen 1973:555 [ref. 6885], Cohen & Nielsen 1978:62 [ref. 881]); synonym of *Sciadonus* Garman 1899 (Nielsen in Whitehead et al. 1986:1171 [ref. 13677] based on placement of type species). Aphyonidae.

Leucoglossa Jordan & Evermann in Jordan, Evermann & Tanaka 1927:660 [ref. 2454]. Fem. *Leucoglossa candens* Jordan, Evermann & Wakiya in Jordan, Evermann & Tanaka 1927:660. Type by original designation. Synonym of *Uraspis* Bleeker 1855 (Smith-Vaniz, pres. comm.). Carangidae.

Leucogobio Günther 1896:212 [ref. 2019]. Masc. *Leucogobio herzensteini* Günther 1896:213. Type by monotypy. Species spelled *herzensteini* on p. 212 and *herzensteinii* on Pl. 2. Synonym of *Gnathopogon* Bleeker 1859 (Banarescu & Nalbant 1973:61 [ref. 173], Lu, Luo & Chen 1977:478 [ref. 13495]). Cyprinidae.

Leucops Rafinesque 1819:419 [ref. 3590]. Masc. *Pogostoma leucops* Rafinesque 1818:447. Type by being a replacement name. Unneeded replacement for *Pogostoma* Rafinesque 1818, not preoccupied. Apparently a mythical fish, based on Audubon drawing. Percidae.

Leucopsarion Hilgendorf 1880:340 [ref. 2167]. Neut. *Leucopsarion petersi* Hilgendorf 1880:340. Type by monotypy. Valid (Akihito in Masuda et al. 1984:283 [ref. 6441], Birdsong et al. 1988:185 [ref. 7303]). Gobiidae.

Leucoraja Malm 1877:121, 609 [ref. 2881]. Fem. *Raja fullonica* Linnaeus 1758:231. Type by subsequent designation. Type designated by Jordan 1919:391 [ref. 4904]. Synonym of *Raja* Linnaeus 1758, but as a valid subgenus (Stehmann 1973:64 [ref. 7168]). Rajidae.

Leucos Heckel 1843:1038 [ref. 2066]. Masc. *Leucos cisalpinus* Heckel 1843:1038. Type by subsequent designation. Earliest subsequent type designation found is by Jordan & Gilbert 1883:244

[ref. 2476]. Not preoccupied by *Leucus* Kaup 1829 in Aves. Synonym of *Rutilus* Rafinesque 1820 (Howes 1981:45 [ref. 14200]). Cyprinidae.

Leucosoma Gray 1831:4 [ref. 1880]. Neut. *Leucosoma reevesii* Gray 1831:4. Type by monotypy. Synonym of *Salanx* Oken 1817, but as a valid subgenus (Roberts 1984:206 [ref. 5318]). Salangidae.

Leucosomus Heckel 1843:1042 [ref. 2066]. Masc. *Cyprinus crysoleucus* Mitchill 1814. Type by subsequent designation. Earliest type designation not researched. Jordan 1919:211 [ref. 2410] says type is *chrysoleucus* Heckel (not of Mitchill) = *Cyprinus corporalis* Mitchill. The description is of *Notemigonus crysoleucas* of current authors. Synonym of *Notemigonus* Rafinesque 1819. Cyprinidae.

Leuresthes Jordan & Gilbert 1880:29 [ref. 2466]. Fem. *Atherinopsis tenuis* Ayres 1860:75. Type by monotypy. Valid (White et al. 1984:360 [ref. 13655], White 1985:17 [ref. 13551], Crabtree 1987:861 [ref. 6771]). Atherinidae: Atherinopsinae.

Leurochilus Böhlke 1968:2 [ref. 604]. Masc. *Leurochilus acon* Böhlke 1968:4. Type by original designation (also monotypic). Valid (Dawson 1982:46 [ref. 1072]). Dactyloscopidae.

Leuroglossus Gilbert 1890:57 [ref. 1623]. Masc. *Leuroglossus stilbius* Gilbert 1890:57. Type by original designation (also monotypic). Valid (Peden 1981 [ref. 5512], Uyeno in Masuda et al. 1984:41 [ref. 6441], Kobyliansky 1986:44 [ref. 6002], Matallanas 1986 [ref. 6755]). Synonym of *Bathylagus* Günther 1878 (Ahlstrom et al. 1984:156 [ref. 13627]). Bathylagidae.

Leuropharus Rosenblatt & McCosker 1970:502 [ref. 3809]. *Leuropharus lasiops* Rosenblatt & McCosker 1970:502. Type by original designation (also monotypic). Valid (McCosker 1977:64 [ref. 6836], McCosker et al. 1989:296 [ref. 13288]). Ophichthidae: Ophichthinae.

Leurynnis Lockington 1880:326 [ref. 2815]. *Leurynnis paucidens* Lockington 1880:326. Type by monotypy. Synonym of *Lycodopsis* Collett (1 Aug.) 1879, Lockington is 25 Mar. 1880 (Toyoshima 1985:238 [ref. 5722]). Zoarcidae.

Levanaora Whitley 1933:95 [ref. 4677]. Fem. *Platycephalus isacanthus* Cuvier in Cuvier & Valenciennes 1829:246. Type by original designation (also monotypic). Synonym of *Inegocia* Jordan & Thompson 1913 (Paxton et al. 1989:467 [ref. 12442] based on placement of the type species). Platycephalidae.

Leviprora Whitley 1931:327 [ref. 4672]. Fem. *Platycephalus inops* Jenyns 1840:33. Type by original designation (also monotypic). Valid (Paxton et al. 1989:467 [ref. 12442]). Platycephalidae.

Lewinichthys Whitley 1933:67 [ref. 4677]. Masc. *Belone ferox* Günther 1866:242. Type by original designation (also monotypic). Belonidae.

Leyvaichthys Dahl 1960:302 [ref. 5836]. Masc. *Leyvaichthys castaneus* Dahl 1960:302. Type by original designation (also monotypic). Spelled *Leyvaichthys* in at least 3 places (pp. 302, 303, 305), *Leyvaichths* in one place (p. 303, an obvious typographical error); as *Lavichthys* in Glodek & Carter 1978:76 [ref. 6159] and others. Named for Jose P. Leyva. Synonym of *Helogenes* Günther 1863 (Glodek & Carter 1978:81 [ref. 6159], Vari & Ortega 1986:6 [ref. 5837]). Helogeneidae.

Lhotskia Whitley 1933:67 [ref. 4677]. Fem. *Belone macleayana* Ogilby 1886:53. Type by original designation (also monotypic). Valid (Parin 1967:41 [ref. 10272]); synonym of *Tylosurus* Cocco 1833 (Paxton et al. 1989:343 [ref. 12442] based on placement of type species). Exocoetidae.

Liachirus Günther 1862:479 [ref. 1969]. Masc. *Liachirus nitidus* Günther 1862:479. Type by monotypy. Valid (Ochiai in Masuda et al. 1984:354 [ref. 6441]). Soleidae.

Liauchenoglanis Boulenger 1916:314 [ref. 585]. Masc. *Liauchenoglanis maculatus* Boulenger 1916:314. Type by monotypy. Valid (Risch 1986:32 [ref. 6190], Burgess 1989:71 [ref. 12860]). Bagridae.

Lichia Cuvier 1816:321 [ref. 993]. Fem. *Scomber amia* Linnaeus 1758:299. Type by subsequent designation. Type designated by Regan 1903:348 [ref. 3618]. On Official List (Opinion 1124). Valid (Hureau & Tortonese 1973:377 [ref. 7198], Smith-Vaniz 1986:652 [ref. 5718], Daget & Smith-Vaniz 1986:315 [ref. 6207]). Carangidae.

Lichnochromis Trewavas 1935:(69) 117 [ref. 4451]. Masc. *Lichnochromis acuticeps* Trewavas 1935:117. Type by monotypy. Valid (Eccles & Trewavas 1989:255 [ref. 13547]). Cichlidae.

Lienardella (subgenus of *Lepidaplois*) Fowler & Bean 1928:202 [ref. 1475]. Fem. *Lepidaplois mirabilis* Snyder 1909:96. Type by original designation (also monotypic). Valid (Yamakawa in Masuda et al. 1984:202 [ref. 6441]). Labridae.

Lile (subgenus of *Sardinella*) Jordan & Evermann 1896:428, 431 [ref. 2443]. *Clupea stolifera* Jordan & Gilbert 1881:339. Type by original designation. Valid (Grande 1985:250 [ref. 6466], Whitehead 1985:128 [ref. 5141]). Clupeidae.

Limanda Gottsche 1835:136, 160 [ref. 1862]. Fem. *Limanda vulgaris* Gottsche 1835 (= *Pleuronectes limanda* Nilsson [= Linnaeus]). Type by monotypy. *Limanda vulgaris* Gottsche an unneeded replacement for *P. limanda* Nilsson; apparently the species goes back to *Pleuronectes limanda* Linnaeus 1758. Valid (Norman 1934:333 [ref. 6893], Nielsen 1973:624 [ref. 6885], Ahlstrom et al. 1984:643 [ref. 13641], Sakamoto in Masuda et al. 1984:352 [ref. 6441], Nielsen in Whitehead et al. 1986:1302 [ref. 13677]). Pleuronectidae: Pleuronectinae.

Limandella (subgenus of *Limanda*) Jordan & Starks 1906:204 [ref. 2532]. Fem. *Pleuronectes yokohamae* Günther 1877:442. Type by original designation. Synonym of *Pseudopleuronectes* Bleeker 1862 (Norman 1934:342 [ref. 6893]). Pleuronectidae: Pleuronectinae.

Limatulichthys Isbrücker & Nijssen in Isbrücker 1979:88, 91 [ref. 2302]. Masc. *Loricaria (Pseudoloricaria) punctata* Regan 1904:285. Type by original designation (also monotypic). Valid (Isbrücker 1980:123 [ref. 2303], Burgess 1989:444 [ref. 12860]). Loricariidae.

Limbochromis Greenwood 1987:188 [ref. 6166]. Masc. *Nanochromis robertsi* Thys van den Audenaerde & Loiselle 1971:194. Type by original designation. Cichlidae.

Limia Poey 1854:382, 390 [ref. 3497]. Fem. *Limia cubensis* Poey 1854:388, 391. Type by subsequent designation. Type apparently first designated by Henn 1916:137 [ref. 2093]. Synonym of *Poecilia* Bloch & Schneider 1801, but as a valid subgenus (Rosen & Bailey 1963:44, 58 [ref. 7067], Parenti & Rauchenberger 1989:8 [ref. 13538]); valid genus (Rivas 1980 [ref. 3763]). Poeciliidae.

Limiculina (subgenus of *Macrorhamphosus*) Fowler 1907:425 [ref. 1377]. Fem. *Centriscus humerosus* Richardson 1846:56. Type by original designation (also monotypic). Objective synonym of *Centriscops* Gill 1862. Centriscidae: Macroramphosinae.

Limmamuraena Kaup in Duméril 1856:200 [ref. 1154]. Fem. Not available; appeared as *Limmamuraena guttata*, without description or indication in list of genera and species taken from Kaup manuscript. Named *Limomuraena* by Kaup 1856:65 [ref. 2572], and misspelled *Limamuraena* by authors. In the synonymy of *Muraena* Linnaeus 1758. Muraenidae: Muraeninae.

Limnichthys Waite 1904:178 [ref. 4561]. Masc. *Limnichthys fasciatus* Waite 1904:178. Type by original designation (also monotypic). Type designated on p. 139. Valid (Nelson 1983:34 [ref. 5272], Yoshino & Shimada in Masuda et al. 1984:292 [ref. 6441], Nelson 1985 [ref. 5154], Nelson 1986:737 [ref. 5698]). Creediidae.

Limnochromis Regan 1920:43 [ref. 3669]. Masc. *Paratilapia aurita* Boulenger 1901:2. Type by original designation. Valid (Poll 1981 [ref. 3534], Poll 1986:131 [ref. 6136]). Cichlidae.

Limnocottus Berg 1906:908 [ref. 265]. Masc. *Cottus godlewskii* Dybowski 1874:385. Type by subsequent designation. Two included species; earliest subsequent designation not researched. Valid (Sideleva 1982:30 [ref. 14469], Yabe 1985:123 [ref. 11522]). Cottocomephoridae.

Limnothrissa Regan 1917:207 [ref. 3668]. Fem. *Pellonula miodon* Boulenger 1906:546. Type by monotypy. Type not *L. miodon* Regan 1917 as cited by some authors; Regan (1917: 206-207) split Boulenger's (1909) material among two species (one new) in two new genera; type specimen of *miodon* went with *Limnothrissa*. Valid (Poll et al. 1984 [ref. 6172], Grande 1985:247 [ref. 6466], Whitehead 1985:159 [ref. 5141]). Clupeidae.

Limnotilapia Regan 1920:39 [ref. 3669]. Fem. *Tilapia dardennii* Boulenger 1899:91. Type by original designation. Valid (Poll 1986:82 [ref. 6136]). Cichlidae.

Limnurgus Günther 1866:309 [ref. 1983]. *Girardinichthys innominatus* Bleeker 1860:481. Type by being a replacement name. Unneeded replacement for and objective synonym of *Girardinichthys* Bleeker, both genus and species thought by Günther to be barbarous names; *L. variegatus* an unneeded new name for *G. innominatus*. Goodeidae.

Limomuraena Kaup 1856:65 [ref. 2572]. Fem. *Limomuraena guttata* Kaup 1856:65. Type by monotypy. Also in Kaup 1856:95 [ref. 2573] and as *Limamuraena* Kaup in Dumeril 1856 as name only and unavailable [ref. 1154]. Misspelled *Limamuraena* by authors, including Jordan 1919:271 [ref. 2410]. Synonym of *Muraena* Linnaeus 1758 (Blache et al. 1973:224 [ref. 7185], Böhlke et al. 1989:194 [ref. 13286]). Muraenidae: Muraeninae.

Lindbergia Balushkin 1976:122, 129 [ref. 170]. Fem. *Notothenia mizops* Günther 1880:16. Type by original designation. Preoccupied by Riedel 1959 in Gastropoda, replaced by *Lindbergichthys* Balushkin 1979. Synonym of *Nototheniops* Balushkin 1976 (Andersen 1984:24 [ref. 13369]). Nototheniidae.

Lindbergichthys Balushkin 1979:930 [ref. 171]. Masc. *Notothenia mizops* Günther 1880:16. Type by being a replacement name. Replacement for *Lindbergia* Balushkin 1976, preoccupied by Riedel 1959 in Gastropoda. Synonym of *Nototheniops* Balushkin 1976 (Andersen 1984:24 [ref. 13369]). Nototheniidae.

Lindemanella Whitley 1935:241 [ref. 4683]. Fem. *Lindemanella iota* Whitley 1935:242. Type by original designation (also monotypic). Synonym of *Ophiocara* Gill 1863 (Hoese, pers. comm.). Eleotridae.

Liniparhomaloptera Fang 1935:93 [ref. 1300]. Fem. *Parhomaloptera disparis* Lin 1934:225. Type by original designation (also monotypic). Misspelled *Limparhomaloptera* in Zoological Record for 1935. Valid (Silas 1953:224 [ref. 4024], Chen 1980:96 [ref. 6901], Sawada 1982:205 [ref. 14111]). Balitoridae: Balitorinae.

Linkenchelys Smith 1989:78 [ref. 13285]. Fem. *Linkenchelys multipora* Smith 1989:78. Type by original designation (also monotypic). Family placement follows K. Tighe (pers. comm., June 1990). Synaphobranchidae: Ilyophinae.

Linophora Kaup 1860:137, 155 [ref. 2583]. Fem. *Chaetodon auriga* Forsskål 1775:xii, 60. Type by subsequent designation. Type designated by Bleeker 1876:306 [ref. 448]. Synonym of *Chaetodon* Linnaeus 1758, subgenus *Rabdophorus* Swainson 1839 (Burgess 1978:578 [ref. 700]). Synonym of *Rabdophorus* Swainson 1839, but as a valid subgenus (Maugé & Bauchot 1984:468 [ref. 6614]). Chaetodontidae.

Linophryne Collett 1886:138 [ref. 888]. Fem. *Linophryne lucifer* Collett 1886:138. Type by monotypy. Valid (Maul 1973:676 [ref. 7171], Bertelsen 1980 [ref. 6927], Bertelsen 1982 [ref. 288], Bertelsen & Pietsch 1983:94 [ref. 5335], Amaoka in Masuda et al. 1984:108 [ref. 6441], Bertelsen in Whitehead et al. 1986:1409 [ref. 13677], Paxton et al. 1989:296 [ref. 12442]). Linophrynidae.

Liobagrus Hilgendorf 1878:155 [ref. 2166]. Masc. *Liobagrus reinii* Hilgendorf 1878:155. Type by monotypy. Valid (Sawada in Masuda et al. 1984:59 [ref. 6441], Burgess 1989:108 [ref. 12860]). Amblycipitidae.

Lioblennius Svetovidov 1958:591 [ref. 6528]. Masc. *Blennius galerita* Linnaeus 1758:256. Type by monotypy. Apparently not intended as a new name; "... and based on this it has been classified as a separate genus *Lioblennius* (J. R. Norman, 1943)." But Norman used the name *Coryphoblennius*; *Lioblennius* first used by Svetovidov as above. Objective synonym of *Coryphoblennius* Norman 1943. Blenniidae.

Liobranchia Briggs 1955:132 [ref. 637]. Fem. *Liobranchia stria* Briggs 1955:133. Type by original designation (also monotypic). Valid. Gobiesocidae: Gobiesocinae.

Liocaesio Bleeker 1876:153 [ref. 445]. Fem. *Caesio cylindricus* Günther 1859:393. Type by original designation (also monotypic). Synonym of *Pterocaesio* Bleeker 1876 (Carpenter 1987:29 [ref. 6430], Carpenter 1988:50 [ref. 9296]). Caesionidae.

Liocetus (subgenus of *Melanocetus*) Günther 1887:56 [ref. 2013]. Masc. *Melanocetus murrayi* Günther 1887:57. Type by monotypy. Misspelled *Linocetus* by authors. Synonym of *Melanocetus* Günther 1864 (Maul 1973:667 [ref. 7171] as *Linocetus*, Pietsch & Van Duzer 1980:70 [ref. 5333]). Melanocetidae.

Liocornus (subgenus of *Cantherines*) Tortonese 1939:389 [ref. 4414]. Fem. *Balistes unicornus* Basilewski 1855:263. Type by original designation (also monotypic). Balistidae.

Liocranium Ogilby 1903:23 [ref. 3280]. Neut. *Liocranium praepositum* Ogilby 1903:25. Type by monotypy. *Abcichthys* Whitley 1927 is an unneeded replacement. Valid (Washington et al. 1984:440 [ref. 13660]). Scorpaenidae: Tetraroginae.

Lioglossina Gilbert 1890:122 [ref. 1623]. Fem. *Lioglossina tetrophthalmus [a]* Gilbert 1891:122. Type by original designation (also monotypic). Valid (Norman 1934:68 [ref. 6893], Ahlstrom et al. 1984:642 [ref. 13641]). Paralichthyidae.

Liomonacanthus Bleeker 1865:Pl. 230 [ref. 416]. Masc. *Monacanthus pardalis* Rüppell 1835:57. Apparently dates to Pl. 230 published in part 20 (1865), with type by monotypy; corresponding text (p. 99) published in part 21 (in 1869). Also in Bleeker 1866:13 [ref. 417]. Synonym of *Cantherhines* Swainson 1839 (Randall 1964:335 [ref. 3148]). Monacanthidae.

Lioniscus (subgenus of *Acipenser*) Bonaparte (ex Heckel & Fitzinger) 1846:20 [ref. 519]. Masc. *Acipenser glaber* Heckel &

Fitzinger 1836:270. Type by monotypy. Latinization of "Lionisci" Heckel & Fitzinger 1836. Synonym of *Acipenser* Linnaeus 1758. Acipenseridae: Acipenserinae.

Lioniscus Heckel & Fitzinger 1836:370 [ref. 2077]. Masc. *Acipenser glaber* Heckel & Fitzinger 1836:270. Type by monotypy. Original not seen, apparently only in vernacular "Lionisci"; latinized by Bonaparte 1846. Later "Lionisci" used as a group within *Acipenser* by Heckel & Kner 1858:332 [ref. 2078]. Synonym of *Acipenser* Linnaeus 1758 (Svetovidov 1973:82 [ref. 7169]). Acipenseridae: Acipenserinae.

Lionurus (subgenus of *Macrurus*) Günther 1887:124, 141 [ref. 2013]. Masc. *Coryphaenoides filicauda* Günther 1878:27. Type by subsequent designation. Earliest type designation not researched; not designated by Goode & Bean 1896:409 [ref. 1848]. Valid (Marshall 1973:298 [ref. 7194], Marshall 1973:595 [ref. 6965], Fahay & Markle 1984:274 [ref. 13653], Geistdoerfer in Whitehead et al. 1986:665 [ref. 13676]); synonym of *Coryphaenoides* Gunner 1761, but as a valid subgenus (Iwamoto & Sazonov 1988:42 [ref. 6228]). Macrouridae: Macrourinae.

Liopempheris Ogilby 1913:61, 62, 66 [ref. 3291]. Fem. *Pempheris multiradiata* Klunzinger 1879:381. Type by original designation. Synonym of *Pempheris* Cuvier 1829 (Fowler). Pempheridae.

Lioperca Gill 1862:236, 237 [ref. 1664]. Fem. *Serranus inermis* Valenciennes in Cuvier & Valenciennes 1833:436. Type by monotypy. Synonym of subgenus *Dermatolepis* Gill 1861 of genus *Epinephelus* Bloch 1793 (Smith 1971:157 [ref. 14102]). Serranidae: Epinephelinae.

Liopropoma Gill 1861:52 [ref. 1768]. Neut. *Perca aberrans* Poey 1861:125. Type by original designation (also monotypic). Valid (Bussing 1980 [ref. 6904], Kendall 1984:500 [ref. 13663], Katayama in Masuda et al. 1984:133 [ref. 6441], Randall & Taylor 1988 [ref. 6429], Paxton et al. 1989:499 [ref. 12442]). Serranidae: Liopropomatinae.

Liopsaron McKay 1972:45 [ref. 2954]. Neut. *Liopsaron insolitum* McKay 1972:45. Type by original designation (also monotypic). Synonym of *Centrodraco* Regan 1913 (Fricke 1982:56 [ref. 5432]). Draconettidae.

Liopsetta Gill 1864:217 [ref. 1704]. Fem. *Platessa glabra* Storer 1844:130. Type by original designation. Valid (Norman 1934:368 [ref. 6893], Nielsen 1973:625 [ref. 6885], Ahlstrom et al. 1984:643 [ref. 13641], Sakamoto in Masuda et al. 1984:353 [ref. 6441], Nielsen in Whitehead et al. 1986:1303 [ref. 13677]). Pleuronectidae: Pleuronectinae.

Liosaccus (subgenus of *Tetrodon*) Günther 1870:272, 287 [ref. 1995]. Masc. *Liosaccus cutaneus* Günther 1870:287. Type by subsequent designation. Described in key (p. 272) for 4 species treated on pp. 287-288. Type designated by Jordan 1919:357 [ref. 4904]. Spelled *Liosarcus* and wrongly credited to Hilgendorf by Abe 1949:93 [ref. 3], see Abe 1954:122 [ref. 5]. Synonym of *Spheroides* Duméril 1806 or *Sphoeroides* Anonymous 1798 (Fraser-Brunner 1943:11 [ref. 1495]); valid (Arai 1983:206 [ref. 14249]). Tetraodontidae.

Lioscorpius Günther 1880:40 [ref. 2011]. Masc. *Lioscorpius longiceps* Günther 1880:40. Type by monotypy. Valid (Eschmeyer & Collette 1966:365 [ref. 6485], Amaoka in Masuda et al. 1984:316 [ref. 6441], Paxton et al. 1989:443 [ref. 12442]). Scorpaenidae: Setarchinae.

Liosomadoras Fowler 1940:226 [ref. 1432]. Masc. *Liosomadoras morrowi* Fowler 1940:226. Type by original designation (also monotypic). Valid (Burgess 1989:241 [ref. 12860]). Auchenipteridae.

Lioteres Smith 1958:156 [ref. 4118]. Masc. *Lioteres caminatus* Smith 1958:156. Type by original designation. Described as a new genus and new subgenus. Valid (Hoese & Winterbottom 1979 [ref. 7022]); synonym of *Hetereleotris* Bleeker 1874 (Akihito & Meguro 1981:331 [ref. 5508], Hoese 1986:3 [ref. 5996]). Gobiidae.

Lipactis Regan 1925:566 [ref. 3677]. Fem. *Lipactis tumidus* Regan 1925:566. Type by monotypy. Synonym of *Himantolophus* Reinhardt 1837 (Bertelsen & Krefft 1988:35 [ref. 6615]). Himantolophidae.

Liparis Röse 1793:117 [ref. 3833]. Masc. *Liparis nostras* Johnson (? = *Cyclopterus liparis* Linnaeus 1766:414). Original not seen. Cyclopteridae: Liparinae.

Liparis Scopoli (ex Artedi) 1777:453 [ref. 3990]. Masc. *Cyclopterus liparis* Linnaeus 1766:414. Appeared without species; first addition of species not researched; type designated at least by Jordan 1917:41 [ref. 2407]). Petition to ICZN is pending (see Vogt 1988 [ref. 6625]). Valid (Lindberg 1973:609 [ref. 7220], Able & McAllister 1980 [ref. 6908], Kido in Masuda et al. 1984:337 [ref. 6441], Stein & Able in Whitehead et al. 1986:1277 [ref. 13677], Chernova 1987 [ref. 6341], Chernova 1988 [ref. 13480], Kido 1988:165 [ref. 12287]). Cyclopteridae: Liparinae.

Lipariscus Gilbert 1915:358 [ref. 1632]. Masc. *Lipariscus nanus* Gilbert 1915:358. Type by original designation (also monotypic). Valid (Stein 1978:28 [ref. 4203], Kido in Masuda et al. 1984:341 [ref. 6441]); synonym of *Paraliparis* Collett 1878 (Kido 1988:230 [ref. 12287]). Cyclopteridae: Liparinae.

Liparius Rafinesque 1815:87 [ref. 3584]. Masc. As "*Liparius* R. sp. do." meaning *Liparius* Rafinesque, a new genus for a species of a previous genus. Not available, name only. Apparently for a species of *Cyclopterus* Linnaeus but not so specified. Cyclopteridae: Cyclopterinae.

Liparoides Lloyd 1909:163 [ref. 2814]. Masc. *Liparoides beauchampi* Lloyd 1909:163. Type by monotypy. Cyclopteridae: Cyclopterinae.

Liparops Garman 1892:42 [ref. 1537]. Masc. *Cyclopterus stelleri* Pallas 1831:73. Type by monotypy. Cyclopteridae: Liparinae.

Liparus (subgenus of *Leuciscus*) Schulze 1890:161 [61] [ref. 3984]. Masc. *Cyprinus rutilus* Linnaeus 1758:324. Type by monotypy. On p. 61 of 1892 edition. Preoccupied by Olivier 1807 in Coleoptera, Harris 1841 in Lepidoptera, and Albers 1850 in Mollusca; not replaced. Objective synonym of *Rutilus* Rafinesque 1820. Cyprinidae.

Lipocheilus Anderson, Talwar & Johnson 1977:510 [ref. 116]. Masc. *Tangia carnolabrum* Chan 1970:20. Type by being a replacement name. Replacement for *Tangia* Chan 1970, preoccupied by Stål 1859 in Hemiptera. Valid (Johnson 1980:10 [ref. 13553], Yoshino & Sata 1981 [ref. 5506], Yoshino in Masuda et al. 1984:168 [ref. 6441], Allen 1985:32 [ref. 6843], Akazaki & Iwatsuki 1986 [ref. 6316]). Lutjanidae.

Lipochromis Regan 1920:45 [ref. 3669]. Masc. *Pelmatochromis obesus* Boulenger 1906:442. Type by original designation (also monotypic). Valid (Greenwood 1980:26 [ref. 1899]). Cichlidae.

Lipogenys Goode & Bean 1895:469 [ref. 1847]. Fem. *Lipogenys gillii* Goode & Bean 1895:469. Type by monotypy. Also appeared as new in Goode & Bean 1896:173 [ref. 1848]. Misspelled *Lypogenys* in Zoological Record for 1894. Valid (Sheiko 1988 [ref. 13519], Paxton et al. 1989:149 [ref. 12442]). Lipogenyidae.

Lipogramma Böhlke 1960:6 [ref. 5941]. Neut. *Lipogramma* *anabantoides* Böhlke 1960:8. Type by original designation (also monotypic). Valid (Robins & Colin 1979 [ref. 6986], Gilmore & Jones 1988 [ref. 12879]). Grammatidae.

Lipolagus Kobyliansky 1986:47 [ref. 6002]. Masc. *Bathylagus ochotensis* Schmidt 1938:654. Type by original designation (also monotypic). Bathylagidae.

Lipomyzon Cope 1881:59 [ref. 949]. Masc. *Chasmistes brevirostris* Cope 1879:785. Type by subsequent designation. Type designated by Jordan & Gilbert 1883:132 [ref. 2476]. Synonym of *Chasmistes* Jordan 1878. Catostomidae.

Lipophrys Gill 1896:498 [ref. 1744]. Fem. *Blennius pholis* Linnaeus 1758:257. Type by being a replacement name. Replacement for *Pholis* Cuvier 1816, preoccupied by Scopoli 1777 in fishes. Synonym of *Blennius* Linnaeus 1758 (Bath 1973:519 [ref. 7212]); valid (Wirtz & Bath 1982 [ref. 5475], Bath 1983:153 [ref. 5420], Zander in Whitehead et al. 1986:1100 [ref. 13677], Springer 1986:742 [ref. 5719], Wertz & Bath 1989 [ref. 9298]). Blenniidae.

Lipopterichthys Norman 1935:627 [ref. 3223]. Masc. *Lipopterichthys carrioni* Norman 1935:628. Type by original designation (also monotypic). Valid (Isbrücker 1980:65 [ref. 2303], Heitmans et al. 1983 [ref. 5278], Burgess 1989:436 [ref. 12860]). Loricariidae.

Liposarcus Günther 1864:238 [ref. 1974]. Masc. *Hypostomus multiradiatus* Hancock 1828:246. Type by subsequent designation. Type designated by Jordan 1919:332 [ref. 4904]. Synonym of *Pterygoplichthys* Gill 1858 (Isbrücker 1980:40 [ref. 2303]). Loricariidae.

Lissocampus Waite & Hale 1921:306 [ref. 4569]. Masc. *Lissocampus caudalis* Waite & Hale 1921:306. Type by monotypy. Valid (Dawson 1977 [ref. 7047], Dawson 1985:114 [ref. 6541], Paxton et al. 1989:424 [ref. 12442]). Syngnathidae: Syngnathinae.

Lissochilichthys Oshima 1920:124 [ref. 3313]. Masc. *Lissochilichthys matsudai* Oshima 1920:124. Type by original designation (also monotypic). Misspelled *Lissocheilichthys* by Jordan 1920:572 [ref. 4905]. Synonym of *Acrossocheilus* Oshima 1919, but as a valid subgenus (Wu et al. 1977:274 [ref. 4807]). Cyprinidae.

Lissochilus Weber & de Beaufort 1916:167 [ref. 4604]. Masc. *Lissochilus sumatranus* Weber & de Beaufort 1916:169. Type by subsequent designation. Type designated by Jordan 1920:561 [ref. 4905]. Apparently preoccupied by Pethoe in Zittel 1882 [not researched], not replaced. Synonym of *Acrossocheilus* Oshima 1919 (Wu et al. 1977:273 [ref. 4807]). Cyprinidae.

Lissonanchus Smith 1966:642 [ref. 4138]. Masc. *Lissonanchus lusheri* Smith 1966:642. Type by original designation (also monotypic). Valid (Briggs 1986:380 [ref. 5643]). Gobiesocidae: Gobiesocinae.

Lissorhynchus Bleeker 1859:422 [ref. 370]. Masc. *Gobio lissorhynchus* McClelland 1839:277. Apparently appeared first in key, without species, as *Lissorhynchus*. One species included in Bleeker 1860:85-86 [ref. 380]. Type by subsequent monotypy. Misspelled *Lissorhynchos* by Bleeker 1860:86, *Lissorhynchus* on p. 85. Synonym of *Garra* Hamilton 1822 (Karaman 1971:232 [ref. 2560], Roberts 1989:40 [ref. 6439]). Cyprinidae.

Listrura de Pinna 1988:3 [ref. 5999]. Fem. *Listrura nematopteryx* de Pinna 1988:4. Type by original designation. Valid (Pinna 1989:31 [ref. 12630], Pinna 1989:372 [ref. 13515]). Trichomycteridae.

Litanchus (subgenus of *Antennablennius*) Smith 1959:247, 248 [ref. 4123]. Masc. *Antennablennius (Litanchus) velifer* Smith 1959:249. Type by original designation. Synonym of *Antennablennius* Fowler 1931 (Bath 1983:48 [ref. 5393]). Blenniidae.

Lithodoras Bleeker 1862:5 [ref. 393]. Masc. *Doras lithogaster* Heckel in Kner 1855:132. Type by original designation (also monotypic). Valid (Burgess 1989:224 [ref. 12860]). Doradidae.

Lithogenes Eigenmann 1909:6 [ref. 1222]. Masc. *Lithogenes villosus* Eigenmann 1909:6. Type by monotypy. Valid (Isbrücker 1980:6 [ref. 2303]; transferred from Loricariidae to Astroblepidae by Nijssen & Isbrücker 1987 [ref. 5993], Burgess 1989:429 [ref. 12860]). Astroblepidae.

Lithognathus (subgenus of *Pagellus*) Swainson 1839:172, 222 [ref. 4303]. Masc. *Lithognathus capensis* Swainson 1839:222 (= *Pagellus lithognathus* Cuvier 1830:151). Type by monotypy. *L. capensis* Swainson is an unneeded substitute for *P. lithognathus*. Valid (Tortonese 1973:410 [ref. 7192], Bauchot & Hureau in Whitehead et al. 1986:896 [ref. 13676], Smith & Smith 1986:587 [ref. 5710]). Sparidae.

Litholepis Rafinesque 1818:445 [ref. 3587]. Fem. *Litholepis adamantinus* Rafinesque 1818:445. Type by monotypy. Regarded (e.g., by Jordan 1917:109 [ref. 2407]) as based on a mythical gar, but original description is reasonably correct for *Lepisosteus spatula*. Synonym of *Lepisosteus* Lacepède 1803 (Suttkus 1963:69 [ref. 7110]). Lepisosteidae.

Lithoxancistrus Isbrücker, Nijssen & Cala 1988:14 [ref. 6409]. Masc. *Lithoxancistrus orinoco* Isbrücker, Nijssen & Cala 1988:14. Type by original designation (also monotypic). Valid (Burgess 1989:436 [ref. 12860]). Loricariidae.

Lithoxus Eigenmann 1910:405, 412 [ref. 1224]. Masc. *Lithoxus lithoides* Eigenmann 1910:412. Appeared in key in footnote (p. 405); we agree with Boeseman (1982:43 [ref. 492]) that this constitutes original description; described fully in Eigenmann 1912:242 [ref. 1227]. Type as name only in 1910; type by subsequent monotypy. Valid (Isbrücker 1980:77 [ref. 2303], Boeseman 1982 [ref. 492], Burgess 1989:438 [ref. 12860]). Loricariidae.

Lithulcus Gistel 1848:XI [ref. 1822]. Neut. *Labrus trichopterus* Pallas 1770:45. Type by being a replacement name. Unneeded replacement for *Trichopodus* Valenciennes [= Lacepède 1801]; thought preoccupied in botany and by *Trichopoda* in Diptera. See accounts of *Trichopodus* and *Trichogaster* for problems with type. Synonym of *Trichopodus* Bloch & Schneider 1801 or of *Osphronemus* Lacepède 1801. Belontiidae.

Litobranchus Smith-Vaniz & Springer 1971:26 [ref. 4145]. Masc. *Salarias fowleri* Herre 1926:364. Type by original designation (also monotypic). Valid (Springer & Spreitzer 1978:3 [ref. 4181]). Blenniidae.

Litocara (subgenus of *Poecilichthys*) Bailey 1948:79 [ref. 160]. Neut. *Poecilichthys sagitta* Jordan & Swain 1883:250. Type by original designation. Synonym of *Etheostoma* Rafinesque 1819, but as a valid subgenus (Collette & Banarescu 1977:1456 [ref. 5845], Page 1981:30 [ref. 3347], Bailey & Etnier 1988:12 [ref. 6873]). Percidae.

Littocottus (subgenus of *Myoxocephalus*) Neelov 1979:123 [ref. 3152]. Masc. *Cottus niger* Bean 1882:151. Type by monotypy. Cottidae.

Lixagasa (subgenus of *Saxilaga*) Scott 1936:110 [ref. 3994]. Masc. *Galaxias burrowsius* Phillips 1926:531. Type by original designation (also monotypic). Name an anagram of *Galaxias* and apparently treated as masculine by Scott. Galaxiidae: Galaxiinae.

Liza (subgenus of *Mugil*) Jordan & Swain 1884:261 [ref. 2535]. Fem. *Mugil capito* Cuvier 1829:232. Type by original designation (also monotypic). Valid (Trewavas 1973:570 [ref. 7201], Yoshino & Senou in Masuda et al. 1984:119 [ref. 6441], Smith & Smith 1986:715 [ref. 5717], Ben-Tuvia in Whitehead et al. 1986:1199 [ref. 13677], Thomson 1986:345 [ref. 6215], Kottelat 1989:18 [ref. 13605]). Mugilidae.

Lizagobius (subgenus of *Ellogobius*) Whitley 1933:93 [ref. 4677]. Masc. *Mugilogobius galwayi* McCulloch & Waite 1918:50. Type by original designation (also monotypic). Gobiidae.

Lizettea Herre 1936:275 [ref. 2125]. Fem. *Lizettea pelewensis* Herre 1936:276. Type by original designation (also monotypic). Synonym of *Bunaka* Herre 1927 (Hoese, pers. comm.). Eleotridae.

Lloydiella (subgenus of *Alepocephalus*) Parr 1952:256, 259 [ref. 3381]. Fem. *Alepocephalus bicolor* Alcock 1891:133. Type by original designation (also monotypic). Type designated in key. Alepocephalidae.

Lo Seale 1906:71 [ref. 3999]. Masc. *Amphacanthus vulpinus* Schlegel & Müller 1844:142. Type by monotypy. Also appeared apparently later as Seale in Jordan & Seale 1906:360 [ref. 2497]. Treated by author as masculine. Valid. Siganidae.

Loa Jordan 1921:652 [ref. 2419]. Fem. *Loa excelsa* Jordan 1921:652. Type by original designation (also monotypic). Preoccupied by Stiles 1902 in Nematoda, replaced by *Roa* Jordan 1923. Synonym of *Chaetodon* Linnaeus 1758, subgenus *Roa* (Burgess 1978:347 [ref. 700]). Chaetodontidae.

Lobianchia Gatti 1904:28 [ref. 6529]. Fem. *Nyctophus gemellarii* Cocco 1838:18. Type by monotypy. May date to 1903. Valid (Nafpaktitis 1968:11 [ref. 6979], Krefft & Bekker 1973:191 [ref. 7181], Paxton 1979:15 [ref. 6440], Hulley in Whitehead et al. 1984:468 [ref. 13675], Moser et al. 1984:219 [ref. 13645], Fujii in Masuda et al. 1984:71 [ref. 6441], Hulley 1986:310 [ref. 5672]). Myctophidae.

Lobocheilos Bleeker 1853:520 [ref. 5965]. Masc. *Labeo falcifer* Valenciennes in Cuvier & Valenciennes 1842:358. Type by subsequent designation. Genus and species appeared first as *Lobocheilus falcifer*, name only, in van Hasselt 1823:132 [ref. 5963]. Validly described as above. Type designated by Bleeker 1863:194 [ref. 397] or 1863:25 [ref. 4859] with genus spelled *Lobocheilus*. Valid (Kottelat 1985:263 [ref. 11441] and Chu & Cui in Chu & Chen 1989:236 [ref. 13584] as *Lobocheilus*, Kottelat 1989:8 [ref. 13605], Roberts 1989:41 [ref. 6439]). Cyprinidae.

Lobocheilus Kuhl & van Hasselt in van Hasselt 1823:132 [ref. 5963]. Masc. *Lobocheilus falcifer* Kuhl & van Hasselt in van Hasselt 1823:133. Type by monotypy. Not available, both genus and species are nomina nuda (see Kottelat 1987:371 [ref. 5962]). Validly described by Bleeker 1853:520 [ref. 5965] as *Lobocheilos*. Valid (Wu et al. 1977:346 [ref. 4807] credited to van Hasselt). Cyprinidae.

Lobochilotes Boulenger 1915:280 [ref. 584]. Fem. *Tilapia labiata* Boulenger 1898:17. Type by monotypy. Valid (Poll 1986:81 [ref. 6136]). Cichlidae.

Lobodeuterodon (subgenus of *Deuterodon*) Fowler 1945:100 [ref. 1454]. Masc. *Deuterodon euspilurus* Fowler 1945:102. Type by original designation (also monotypic). Possibly a synonym of *Odontostilbe* Cope 1870 (see Böhlke 1984:46 [ref. 13621]). Characidae.

Lobotes Cuvier in Cuvier & Valenciennes 1830:319 [ref. 999]. Fem. *Holocentrus surinamensis* Bloch 1790:98. Type by subsequent designation. Appeared first as "Les Lobotes" in Cuvier 1829:177 [ref. 995]; apparently first latinized as above in 1830. Subsequent designation of type not researched. Valid (Tortonese 1973:389 [ref. 7192], Mochizuki in Masuda et al. 1984:161 [ref. 6441], Heemstra 1986:622 [ref. 5660]). Lobotidae.

Lobulogobius Koumans in Blegvad & Løppenthin 1944:168 [ref. 462]. Masc. *Lobulogobius omanensis* Koumans in Blegvad & Løppenthin 1944:168. Type by original designation (also monotypic). Valid (Larson & Hoese 1980:38 [ref. 2725], Larson 1986:947 [ref. 6328]). Gobiidae.

Loligorhamphus Whitley 1931:105 [ref. 4673]. Masc. *Loligorhamphus normani* Whitley 1931:105. Type by original designation (also monotypic). Synonym of *Rhynchorhamphus* Fowler 1928 (Collette 1976:73 [ref. 7107], Parin et al. 1980:99 [ref. 6895]). Hemiramphidae.

Lomanetia Whitley 1936:25 [ref. 4687]. Fem. *Melanotaenia multisquamata* Weber & de Beaufort 1922:290. Type by original designation (also monotypic). Synonym of *Glossolepis* Weber 1908 (Allen 1980:488 and 476 [ref. 99] based on placement of the type species). Atherinidae: Melanotaeniinae.

Lonchistium Myers 1935:3 [ref. 3111]. Neut. *Lonchistium lemur* Myers 1935:3. Type by original designation (also monotypic). Synonym of *Lonchopisthus* Gill 1862 (Smith-Vaniz, pers. comm., Dec. 1989). Opistognathidae.

Lonchogenys Myers 1927:121 [ref. 3096]. Fem. *Lonchogenys ilisha* Myers 1927:122. Type by original designation (also monotypic). Valid (Géry 1977:314 [ref. 1597]). Characidae.

Lonchopisthus Gill 1862:241 [ref. 1664]. Masc. *Opisthognathus micrognathus* Poey 1861:287. Type by monotypy. Correct spelling for genus of type species is *Opistognathus*. Valid (Shimizu in Uyeno et al. 1983:401 [ref. 14275]). Opistognathidae.

Lonchurus Bloch 1793:143 [ref. 4868]. Masc. *Lonchurus barbatus* Bloch 1793:Pl. 360. Type by monotypy. *Longurus* and *Lonchiurus* are misspellings. Valid (Chao 1978:37 [ref. 6983]). Sciaenidae.

Longiculter Fowler 1937:162 [ref. 1425]. Masc. *Longiculter siahi* Fowler 1937:162. Type by original designation (also monotypic, other species to a different subgenus). Misspelled *Longicultur* in Zoological Record for 1937. Valid (Kottelat 1985:263 [ref. 11441], Kottelat 1989:8 [ref. 13605]). Cyprinidae.

Longirostrum Wakiya 1924:202 [ref. 4570]. Neut. *Caranx luna* Geoffroy St. Hilaire 1809:182; Pl. 23. Type by being a replacement name. Replacement for *Selenia* Bonaparte 1846, preoccupied by Hubner 1816 in Coleoptera. *Usa* Whitley 1927 apparently is an unneeded replacement for *Longirostrum*. Synonym of *Pseudocaranx* Bleeker 1863 (Smith-Vaniz, pers. comm., Nov. 1989). Carangidae.

Longisudis Maul 1965:55 [ref. 2918]. Fem. *Longisudis nigra* Maul 1965:56. Type by original designation (also monotypic). Synonym of *Macroparalepis* Ege 1933 (Post 1973:207 [ref. 7182]) [but *Macroparalepis* is not available from Ege 1933]. Paralepididae.

Longitrudis Whitley 1931:327 [ref. 4672]. Fem. *Platycephalus longispinis* Macleay 1884:170. Type by original designation (also monotypic). Synonym of *Platycephalus* Bloch 1795 (Paxton et al. 1989:469 based on placement of type species). Platycephalidae.

Longmania Whitley 1939:231 [ref. 4695]. Fem. *Carcharias (Aprion) brevipinna* Müller & Henle 1841:31. Type by original designation (also monotypic). Synonym of *Carcharhinus* Blainville 1816 (Compagno 1973:23 [ref. 7163], Garrick 1982:19 [ref. 5454], Compagno 1984:449 [ref. 6846], Cappetta 1987:121 [ref. 6348],

Compagno 1988:308 [ref. 13488]). Carcharhinidae.

Longurio Jordan & Starks 1905:196 [ref. 2530]. Masc. *Longurio athymius* Jordan & Starks 1905:197. Type by monotypy. Apparently preoccupied in Diptera, not replaced. Synonym of *Saurogobio* Bleeker 1870 (Banarescu & Nalbant 1973:283 [ref. 173]). Cyprinidae.

Lophalticus Smith 1957:889 [ref. 4111]. Masc. *Salarias kirkii* Günther 1868:458. Type by original designation (also monotypic). Synonym of *Alticus* Commerson 1800 (Smith-Vaniz & Springer 1971:14 [ref. 4145], Bath 1986:355 [ref. 6217]). Blenniidae.

Lopharis Rafinesque 1810:52 [ref. 3594]. *Perca lophar* Forsskål 1775:38. Type by monotypy. Synonym of *Pomatomus* Lacepède 1802 (Monod 1973:369 [ref. 7193]). Pomatomidae.

Lophenchelys Ben-Tuvia 1953:9 [ref. 257]. Fem. *Lophenchelys fowleri* Ben-Tuvia 1953:9. Type by monotypy. Synonym of *Panturichthys* Pellegrin 1913 (Blache et al. 1973:228 [ref. 7185]). Heterenchelyidae.

Lophichthys Boeseman 1964:12 [ref. 488]. Masc. *Lophichthys boschmai* Boeseman 1964:13. Type by original designation (also monotypic). Valid. Lophichthyidae.

Lophidius Rafinesque 1815:92 [ref. 3584]. Masc. *Lophius piscatorius* Linnaeus 1758:236. As "*Lophidius* R. *Lophius* L." Style of Rafinesque in this work indicates that this is his substitute name for *Lophius* Linnaeus 1758. In that context it is an available (unneeded) replacement name. Objective synonym of *Lophius* Linnaeus 1758. Lophiidae.

Lophiobagrus Poll 1942:318 [ref. 3514]. Masc. *Lophiobagrus lestradei* Poll 1942:320. Type by monotypy. Valid (Bailey & Stewart 1984:17 [ref. 5232], Risch 1986:32 [ref. 6190], Burgess 1989:67 [ref. 12860]). Bagridae.

Lophiocharon Whitley 1933:104 [ref. 4677]. Masc. *Lophiocharon broomensis* Whitley 1933:104. Type by original designation (also monotypic). Valid (Pietsch 1984:38 [ref. 5380], Araga in Masuda et al. 1984:103 [ref. 6441], Paxton et al. 1989:280 [ref. 12442]). Antennariidae.

Lophiodes Goode & Bean 1896:537 [ref. 1848]. Masc. *Lophius mutilus* Alcock 1883:11. Type by monotypy. Valid (Caruso 1981 [ref. 5169], Nakabo in Masuda et al. 1984:102 [ref. 6441], Saruwatari & Mochizuki 1985 [ref. 5800], Caruso 1986:364 [ref. 6290], Paxton et al. 1989:273 [ref. 12442]). Lophiidae.

Lophiogobius Günther 1873:241 [ref. 2004]. Masc. *Lophiogobius ocellicauda* Günther 1873:241. Type by monotypy. Not preoccupied by *Lophogobius* Gill 1862; *Cassigobius* Whitley 1931 is an unneeded replacement. Valid (Birdsong et al. 1988:184 [ref. 7303]). Gobiidae.

Lophioides Minding 1832:57 [ref. 3022]. Italicized, but a vernacular used at the family level based on style; also applies to several other names in this work. Lophiidae.

Lophiomus Gill 1883:552 [ref. 1722]. Masc. *Lophius setigerus* Vahl 1797:215. Type by original designation (also monotypic). Valid (Caruso 1983 [ref. 5168], Nakabo in Masuda et al. 1984:102 [ref. 6441], Caruso 1986:365 [ref. 6290], Paxton et al. 1989:274 [ref. 12442]). Lophiidae.

Lophiopside(s) see *Lophiopsis*. Lophiidae.

Lophiopsis Guichenot 1867:105 [23] [ref. 1948]. Fem. *Lophius vomerinus* Valenciennes in Cuvier & Valenciennes 1837:381. Type by original designation (also monotypic). Guichenot also used the vernacular Lophiopside, but latinized on p. 105 [separate p. 23] as *Lophiopsis*; Jordan's 1919:345 [ref. 4904] *Lophiopsides* is an incorrect subsequent spelling. Synonym of *Lophius* Linnaeus 1758 (Caruso 1983 [ref. 5168]). Lophiidae.

Lophiosilurus Steindachner 1876:154 [ref. 4225]. Masc. *Lophiosilurus alexandri* Steindachner 1876:154. Type by monotypy. Valid (Burgess 1989:275 [ref. 12860]). Pimelodidae.

Lophius Linnaeus 1758:236 [ref. 2787]. Masc. *Lophius piscatorius* Linnaeus 1758:236. Type by subsequent designation. Type designated by Jordan & Gilbert 1883:844 [ref. 2476]. On Official List (Opinion 77, Direction 56). Valid (Monod & Le Danois 1973:659 [ref. 7223], Caruso 1983 [ref. 5168], Nakabo in Masuda et al. 1984:102 [ref. 6441], Caruso in Whitehead et al. 1986:1362 [ref. 13677], Caruso 1986:365 [ref. 6290]). Lophiidae.

Lophocampus (subgenus of *Microphis*) Dawson 1984:166 [ref. 5879]. Masc. *Syngnathus retzii* Bleeker 1856:6, 29, 76. Type by original designation. Synonym of *Microphis* Kaup 1853 (Dawson 1986:284 [ref. 6201]), but as a valid subgenus (Dawson 1985:126, 127 [ref. 6541]). Syngnathidae: Syngnathinae.

Lophocephalus Osório 1906:173 [ref. 3316]. Masc. *Lophocephalus anthrax* Osório 1906:172. Type by monotypy. Also described as new in Osório 1909:8 [ref. 3317]. Synonym of *Poromitra* Goode & Bean 1883 (Maul 1973:344 [ref. 7171]). Melamphaidae.

Lophodiodon (subgenus of *Diodon*) Fraser-Brunner 1943:17 [ref. 1495]. Masc. *Diodon calori* Bianconi 1855:223. Type by original designation (also monotypic). Valid (Leis 1986:906 [ref. 5686]). Diodontidae.

Lophodolos Lloyd 1909:167 [ref. 2814]. Masc. *Lophodolos indicus* Lloyd 1909:167. Type by monotypy. Valid (Maul 1973:672 [ref. 7171] as *Lophodolus*, Pietsch 1974:33 [ref. 5332], Pietsch 1974 [ref. 7116], Bertelsen & Pietsch 1977:188 [ref. 7063], Bertelsen in Whitehead et al. 1986:1391 [ref. 13677]). Oneirodidae.

Lophogobius Gill 1862:240 [ref. 1664]. Masc. *Gobius cristagalli* Valenciennes in Cuvier & Valenciennes 1837:130. Type by monotypy. Valid (Birdsong et al. 1988:193 [ref. 7303]). Gobiidae.

Lopholatilus Goode & Bean 1879:205 [ref. 1837]. Masc. *Lopholatilus chamaeleonticeps* Goode & Bean 1879:205. Type by original designation (also monotypic). Valid (Dooley 1978:47 [ref. 5499], Marino & Dooley 1982:152 [ref. 5498],). Malacanthidae: Latilinae.

Lophonectes Günther 1880:28 [ref. 2011]. Masc. *Lophonectes gallus* Günther 1880:29. Type by monotypy. Valid (Norman 1934:202 [ref. 6893], Ahlstrom et al. 1984:642 [ref. 13641]). Bothidae: Bothinae.

Lophopsetta Gill 1861:51 [ref. 1766]. Fem. *Pleuronectes maculatus* Mitchill 1814:9. Type by monotypy. Synonym of *Scophthalmus* Rafinesque 1810 (Norman 1934:262 [ref. 6893], Nielsen 1973:616 [ref. 6885]). Scophthalmidae.

Lophorhombus Macleay 1882:14 [ref. 2870]. Masc. *Lophorhombus cristatus* Macleay 1882:14. Type by monotypy. Synonym of *Lophonectes* Günther 1880 (Norman 1934:202 [ref. 6893]). Bothidae: Bothinae.

Lophotes Bosc 1817:185 [ref. 5126]. Fem. *Lophotus lacepede* Bosc (ex Giorna) 1817:185. Type by monotypy. See account of *Lophotus*. Original not examined. Synonym of *Lophotus* Giorna 1809 (Palmer 1973:334 [ref. 7195]). Lophotidae.

Lophotopsis Barnard 1925:357 [ref. 192]. Fem. *Lophotes fiskii* Günther 1890:244. Type by monotypy. Objective synonym of *Eumecichthys* Regan 1907. Lophotidae.

Lophotus Giorna 1809:179 [ref. 1808]. Masc. *Lophotus lacepede* Bosc 1817:185. Type by subsequent monotypy. Giorna's species,

"Le Lophote-Lacepede" considered as non-latinized (see Appendix A). Type by subsequent monotypy [if by Bosc then type is *lacepede*]; Gioma's description without available species. Valid (Olney 1984:369 [ref. 13656], Fujii in Masuda et al. 1984:116 [ref. 6441], Palmer in Whitehead et al. 1986:734 [ref. 13676], Heemstra 1986:402 [ref. 5660], Paxton et al. 1989:398 [ref. 12442]). Lophotidae.

Loricaria Linnaeus 1758:307 [ref. 2787]. Fem. *Loricaria cataphracta* Linnaeus 1758:307. Type by monotypy. Valid (Isbrücker 1981 [ref. 5522], Burgess 1989:443 [ref. 12860]). Loricariidae.

Loricariichthys Bleeker 1862:3 [ref. 393]. Masc. *Loricaria maculata* Bloch 1794:73. Type by original designation (also monotypic). Valid (Isbrücker 1980:125 [ref. 2303] and see Isbrücker remarks on *Plecostomus*, Burgess 1989:444 [ref. 12860], Malabarba 1989:154 [ref. 14217]). Loricariidae.

Loro Jordan & Evermann 1896:418 [ref. 2442]. Masc. *Scarus guacamaia* Cuvier 1829:265. Type by original designation. Synonym of *Scarus* Forsskål 1775. Scaridae: Scarinae.

Loruwiala Thys van den Audenaerde 1970:290, 291 [ref. 12518]. Fem. Not available, name only; as a subgroup of *Sarotherodon (Oreochromis)*. Cichlidae.

Lota Oken (ex Cuvier) 1817:1182a [ref. 3303]. Fem. *Gadus lota* Linnaeus 1758:255. Type by subsequent absolute tautonymy. Technical addition of species not researched; type usually given as by tautonymy. Based on "Les Lottes" of Cuvier 1816:215 [ref. 993](see Gill 1903:966 [ref. 5768]). Valid (Fahay & Markle 1984:266 [ref. 13653]). Lotidae.

Lotella Kaup 1858:88 [ref. 2576]. Fem. *Lota schlegeli* Kaup 1858:88 (= *Lota phycis* Temminck & Schlegel 1846:248). Type by monotypy. *L. schlegeli* Kaup is an unneeded substitute for *Lota phycis*. Valid (Cohen 1979 [ref. 6950], Paulin 1983:98 [ref. 5459], Fahay & Markle 1984:266 [ref. 13653], Okamura in Masuda et al. 1984:91 [ref. 6441], Paxton et al. 1989:300 [ref. 12442]). Moridae.

Lotilia Klausewitz 1960:158 [ref. 2613]. Fem. *Lotilia graciliosa* Klausewitz 1960:158. Type by original designation (also monotypic). Valid (Hayashi in Masuda et al. 1984:262 [ref. 6441], Birdsong et al. 1988:193 [ref. 7303]). Gobiidae.

Lotta Risso 1826:217 [ref. 3757]. Fem. *Gadus elongatus* of Risso 1826 (= *Gadus elongatus* Otto 1821). Type by subsequent designation. Earliest subsequent designation not researched. Synonym of *Molva* Lesueur 1819 (Svetovidov 1973:313 [ref. 7169]). Lotidae.

Louti (subgenus of *Perca*) Forsskål 1775:44 [ref. 1351]. *Perca louti* Forsskål 1775:40. Not available, regarded as non-latinized Arabic name (see Jordan 1917:33-34 [ref. 2407]). In the synonymy of *Variola* Swainson 1839. Serranidae: Epinephelinae.

Lovamia Whitley 1930:10 [ref. 4671]. Fem. *Mullus fasciatus* White 1790:268. Type by original designation. Synonym of *Apogon* Lacepède 1801 (Fraser 1972:17 [ref. 5195]). Apogonidae.

Lovettia McCulloch 1915:259 [ref. 2942]. Fem. *Haplochiton sealii* Johnson 1883:128. Type by monotypy. Valid (McDowall 1984:151 [ref. 11850], McDowall & Nakaya 1987:377 [ref. 6701], Paxton et al. 1989:181 [ref. 12442]). Galaxiidae: Aplochitoninae.

Loweina (subgenus of *Rhinoscopelus*) Fowler 1925:2 [ref. 1401]. Fem. *Scopelus (Rhinoscopelus) rarus* Lütken 1892:246. Type by original designation (also monotypic). Valid (Krefft & Bekker 1973:192 [ref. 7181], Paxton 1979:15 [ref. 6440], Hulley in Whitehead et al. 1984:470 [ref. 13675], Moser et al. 1984:219 [ref. 13645], Paxton et al. 1984:241 [ref. 13625], Hulley 1986:311 [ref. 5672], Paxton et al. 1989:265 [ref. 12442]). Myctophidae.

Loxodon Müller & Henle 1838:36 [ref. 3066]. Masc. *Loxodon macrorhinus* Müller & Henle 1839:61. Type by subsequent monotypy. Appeared first with no included species; species added in Müller & Henle 1839:61 [ref. 3069]. As name only in Müller & Henle 1838:84 [ref. 3068]. Valid (Compagno 1984:513 [ref. 6846], Nakaya in Masuda et al. 1984:5 [ref. 6441], Bass et al. 1986:80 [ref. 5638], Compagno 1988:291 [ref. 13488], Paxton et al. 1989:82 [ref. 12442]). Carcharhinidae.

Loxolutjanus (subgenus of *Lutjanus*) Fowler 1931:90, 165 [ref. 1407]. Masc. *Lutjanus erythropterus* Bloch 1790:115. Type by original designation. Synonym of *Lutjanus* Bloch 1790 (Allen 1985:33 [ref. 6843], Allen & Talbot 1985:8 [ref. 6491]). Lutjanidae.

Loxopseudochromis Fowler 1934:354 [ref. 1416]. Masc. *Loxopseudochromis dorypterus* Fowler 1934:355. Type by original designation (also monotypic). Family uncertain; placed in Owstoniidae by Fowler (MS). Cepolidae.

Lubricogobius Tanaka 1915:567 [ref. 4324]. Masc. *Lubricogobius exiguus* Tanaka 1915:567. Type by monotypy. Valid (Larson & Hoese 1980:41 [ref. 2725], Akihito in Masuda et al. 1984:267 [ref. 6441]). Gobiidae.

Lucania Girard 1859:118 [ref. 1821]. Fem. *Limia venusta* Girard 1859:71. Type by subsequent designation. Use of "typical" species not precise enough for original designation; type designated by Bleeker 1864:139 [ref. 4859], also by Jordan & Gilbert 1877:92 [ref. 4907]. Valid (Parenti 1981:496 [ref. 7066] with type as *parvus*; Duggins et al. 1983 [ref. 6819]). Cyprinodontidae: Fundulinae.

Lucaya Böhlke 1957:83 [ref. 599]. Fem. *Lucaya zingaro* Böhlke 1957:84. Type by original designation (also monotypic). Preoccupied by Chase 1939 in Crustacea, replaced by *Lucayablennius* Böhlke 1958. Objective synonym of *Lucayablennius* Böhlke 1958 (Stephens 1963:98 [ref. 4270]). Chaenopsidae.

Lucayablennius Böhlke 1958:59 [ref. 600]. Masc. *Lucaya zingaro* Böhlke 1957:84. Type by being a replacement name. Replacement for *Lucaya* Böhlke 1957, preoccupied by Chase 1939 in Crustacea. Valid (Stephens 1963:98 [ref. 4270], Greenfield & Johnson 1981:66 [ref. 5580], Acero P. 1984 [ref. 5534]). Chaenopsidae.

Lucifer Döderlein 1882:26 [ref. 1139]. Masc. *Lucifer albipennis* Döderlein 1882:26. Type by monotypy. Also appeared in Steindachner & Döderlein 1883:35 [ref. 4249]. Preoccupied by Thompson 1830 in Crustacea and by Reichenbach 1849 in Aves; replaced by *Photonectes* Günther 1887. Objective synonym of *Photonectes* Günther 1887 (Morrow in Morrow & Gibbs 1964:487 [ref. 6962], Morrow 1973:140 [ref. 7175]). Melanostomiidae.

Lucifuga Poey 1858:95 [ref. 3499]. Fem. *Lucifuga subterraneus* Poey 1858:96. Type by monotypy. Genus specifically regarded ("sustantivo masculino") as masculine by Poey (p. 95), but gender is feminine. Valid (Cohen & Nielsen 1978:54 [ref. 881], Vergara R. 1980 [ref. 5201]). Bythitidae: Brosmophycinae.

Lucigadella (subgenus of *Ventrifossa*) Gilbert & Hubbs 1920:544, 545, 552 [ref. 1638]. Fem. *Macrourus nigromarginatus* Smith & Radcliffe 1912:114. Type by original designation (also monotypic). Macrouridae: Macrourinae.

Lucigadus (subgenus of *Ventrifossa*) Gilbert & Hubbs 1920:545, 553 [ref. 1638]. Masc. *Macrourus lucifer* Smith & Radcliffe 1912:113. Type by original designation (also monotypic). Synonym of *Ventrifossa* Gilbert & Hubbs 1920, but as a valid subgenus (Iwamoto 1979:151 [ref. 2311]). Macrouridae: Macrourinae.

Luciobarbus Heckel 1843:1019, 1054 [ref. 2066]. Masc. *Luciobarbus esocinus* Heckel 1843:1054. Type by subsequent designation. Earliest designation located is Jordan 1919:211 [ref. 2410]. Synonym of *Barbus* Cuvier & Cloquet 1816 (Karaman 1971:192 [ref. 2560], Krupp & Schneider 1989:359 [ref. 13651]). Cyprinidae.

Lucioblennius Gilbert 1890:103 [ref. 1623]. Masc. *Lucioblennius alepidotus* Gilbert 1890:103. Type by original designation (also monotypic). Synonym of *Chaenopsis* Poey 1865 (Stephens 1963:98 [ref. 4270]). Chaenopsidae.

Luciobrama Bleeker 1870:252, 253 [ref. 429]. Fem. *Luciobrama typus* Bleeker 1871:51. Type by subsequent monotypy (also by use of *typus*). Species appeared as name only in Bleeker 1870:252, described in Bleeker 1871:51 [ref. 6421]. If Bleeker's remarks on p. 253 are insufficient to validate the genus, then genus dates to Bleeker 1871:51. Valid (Yang & Hwang 1964:21 [ref. 13497], Chen & Li in Chu & Chen 1989:38 [ref. 13584]). Cyprinidae.

Luciobrotula Smith & Radcliffe in Radcliffe 1913:170 [ref. 3579]. Fem. *Luciobrotula bartschi* Smith & Radcliffe in Radcliffe 1913:171. Type by original designation (also monotypic). Valid (Cohen 1974 [ref. 7139], Cohen & Nielsen 1978:35 [ref. 881], Machida 1982 [ref. 5473], Machida in Masuda et al. 1984:100 [ref. 6441], Nielsen & Cohen 1986:349 [ref. 5700]). Ophidiidae: Neobythitinae.

Luciocephalus Bleeker 1851:273 [ref. 325]. Masc. *Diplopterus pulcher* Gray 1831:8. Type by being a replacement name. Evidently proposed as a replacement name for *Diplopterus* Gray 1831, preoccupied by Boie 1826 in Aves. Valid (Kottelat 1989:20 [ref. 13605], Roberts 1989:178 [ref. 6439]). Luciocephalidae.

Luciocharax Steindachner 1878:67 [ref. 4227]. Masc. *Luciocharax insculptus* Steindachner 1878:67. Type by monotypy. *Ctenolucius* Gill 1861 is regarded as available and predates *Luciocharax* when treated as congeneric. Ctenoluciidae.

Luciocyprinus Vaillant 1904:298 [ref. 4491]. Masc. *Luciocyprinus langsoni* Vaillant 1904:299. Type by monotypy. Valid (Kottelat 1983 [ref. 6013], Cui & Chu 1986 [ref. 8097], Chu & Cui in Chu & Chen 1989:159 [ref. 13584]). Cyprinidae.

Luciogobius Gill 1859:146 [ref. 1762]. Masc. *Luciogobius guttatus* Gill 1859:146. Type by monotypy. Valid (Akihito in Masuda et al. 1984:281 [ref. 6441], Birdsong et al. 1988:185 [ref. 7303]). Gobiidae.

Luciolates Boulenger 1914:443 [ref. 583]. Masc. *Luciolates stappersii* Boulenger 1914:443. Type by subsequent designation. Type designated by Jordan 1920:552 [ref. 4905]. Synonym of *Lates* Cuvier 1828, but as a valid subgenus (Greenwood 1976:78 [ref. 14198], Daget 1986:293 [ref. 6203]). Centropomidae: Latinae.

Lucioperca Cuvier in Cuvier & Valenciennes 1828:110 [ref. 997]. Fem. *Perca lucioperca* Linnaeus 1758:289. Type by monotypy (also by absolute tautonymy). Appeared first as a vernacular species "lucio perca" in Cuvier 1816:295 [ref. 993] (see Collette 1963:617 [ref. 6459]). Preoccupied by Fleming 1822 and Schinz 1822 in fishes. Synonym of *Stizostedion* Rafinesque 1820 (Collette & Banarescu 1977:1457 [ref. 5845]). Percidae.

Lucioperca Fleming 1822:394 [ref. 5063]. Fem. *Lucioperca vulgaris* Fleming 1822:394 (= *Perca lucioperca* Linnaeus 1758:289). Type by monotypy. Original not seen. Synonym of *Stizostedion* Rafinesque 1820 (Collette & Banarescu 1977:1457 [ref. 5845]). Percidae.

Lucioperca Schinz 1822:475 [ref. 3926]. Fem. *Perca lucioperca* Linnaeus 1758:289. Type by monotypy (also by absolute tautonymy). Predates *Lucioperca* Cuvier 1828. Synonym of *Stizostedion* Rafinesque 1820 (Collette & Banarescu 1977:1457 [ref. 5845). Percidae.

Luciopimelodus Eigenmann & Eigenmann 1888:122 [ref. 1249]. Masc. *Pimelodus pati* Valenciennes in Cuvier & Valenciennes 1840:176. Type by original designation. Valid (Stewart 1986:665 [ref. 5211], Burgess 1989:275 [ref. 12860]). Pimelodidae.

Luciosoma Bleeker 1855:263 [ref. 351]. Neut. *Barbus setigerus* Valenciennes in Cuvier & Valenciennes 1842:203. Type by subsequent designation. Type designated by Bleeker 1863:29 [ref. 4859] and 1863:204 [ref. 397]. Valid (Yang & Hwang 1964:53 [ref. 13497], Kottelat 1985:263 [ref. 11441], Roberts 1989:42 [ref. 6439], Kottelat 1989:8 [ref. 13605]). Cyprinidae.

Luciosudis Fraser-Brunner 1931:220 [ref. 1486]. Fem. *Luciosudis normani* Fraser-Brunner 1931:220. Type by monotypy. Valid (Bertelsen et al. 1976:92 [ref. 289], Okiyama 1984:207 [ref. 13644], Krefft 1986:268 [ref. 5684], Paxton et al. 1989:229 [ref. 12442]). Notosudidae.

Luciotrutta Günther 1866:164 [ref. 1983]. Fem. *Salmo mackenzii* Richardson 1823:707. Type by monotypy; two included species but second questionably referred to genus (type also designated by Jordan & Gilbert 1877:94 [ref. 4907]). Objective synonym of *Stenodus* Richardson 1836 (Svetovidov 1973:151 [ref. 7169]). Salmonidae: Coregoninae.

Lucius Geoffroy St. Hilaire 1767:407 [ref. 1570]. Masc. *Esox lucius* Linnaeus 1758:314. Type by subsequent designation. Type designated by Jordan 1917:24 [ref. 2407]. Original not seen. Esocidae.

Lucius Klein 1776:506 [ref. 4919]. Masc. Not available, published in a work that does not conform to the principle of binominal nomenclature. In the synonymy of *Esox* Linnaeus 1758. Esocidae.

Lucius Rafinesque 1810:59 [ref. 3594]. Masc. *Esox lucius* Linnaeus 1758:314. Type by subsequent designation. Appeared without included species but clearly established for *E. lucius*. Earliest to technically add species or fix type species is unclear, dates at least to Jordan & Evermann 1896:625 [ref. 2443]. Esocidae.

Lucoscombrus Van der Hoeven 1855:367 [ref. 6527]. *Gempylus serpens* Cuvier 1829:200. Type by subsequent designation. Type apparently designated by Whitley 1929:119. Appeared on p. 161 of English translation by W. Clark. Not available; on Official Index as junior objective synonym of *Gempylus* Cuvier 1829 (Opinion 487). *Leucoscombrus* is a misspelling. In the synonymy of *Gempylus* Cuvier 1829 (Parin & Bekker 1973:457 [ref. 7206]). Gempylidae.

Lucubrapiscis Whitley 1931:334 [ref. 4672]. Masc. *Eumycterias bitaeniatus* Jenkins 1901:400. Type by being a replacement name. Apparently an unneeded replacement for *Eumycterias* Jenkins 1901, not preoccupied by *Eumycterus* Schoenherr 1838 in Coleoptera. Objective synonym of *Eumycterias* Jenkins 1901. Synonym of *Canthigaster* Swainson 1839 (Allen & Randall 1977:478 [ref. 6714]). Tetraodontidae.

Luetkenia Steindachner 1876:85 [ref. 4225]. Fem. *Luetkenia insignis* Steindachner 1876:86. Type by monotypy. Originally as *Lütkenia*; correction mandatory. Apparently preoccupied by *Lütkenia* Claus 1864 in Crustacea [not investigated], replaced by *Stichonodon* Eigenmann 1903. Objective synonym of *Stichonodon* Eigenmann 1903. Characidae.

Lumiconger Castle & Paxton 1984:73 [ref. 5259]. Masc. *Lumiconger arafura* Castle & Paxton 1984:73. Type by original designation (also monotypic). Valid (Paxton et al. 1989:142 [ref. 12442], Smith 1989:512 [ref. 13285]). Congridae: Congrinae.

Lumpenella Hubbs 1927:378 [ref. 2236]. Fem. *Lumpenus longirostris* Evermann & Goldsborough 1907:340. Type by original designation (also monotypic). Valid (Amaoka & Miki in Masuda et al. 1984:301 [ref. 6441], Miki et al. 1987:131 [ref. 6704]). Stichaeidae.

Lumpenopsis Soldatov 1916:635 [ref. 4158]. Fem. *Lumpenopsis pavlenkoi* Soldatov 1916:636. Type by original designation (also monotypic). Valid (Amaoka & Miki in Masuda et al. 1984:302 [ref. 6441]). Stichaeidae.

Lumpenus Reinhardt 1837:CX [ref. 3695]. Masc. *Blennius lumpenus* Fabricius 1793. Type by absolute tautonymy. Valid (Makushok 1973:536 [ref. 6889], Amaoka & Miki in Masuda et al. 1984:301 [ref. 6441], Makushok in Whitehead et al. 1986:1128 [ref. 13677], Miki et al. 1987:131 [ref. 6704]). Stichaeidae.

Lumpus Oken (ex Cuvier) 1817:1182a [ref. 3303]. *Cyclopterus lumpus* Linnaeus 1758:260. Type apparently by subsequent monotypy (also by absolute tautonymy). Based on "Les Lumps" of Cuvier 1816:226 [ref. 993] (see Gill 1903:966 [ref. 5768]). Technical addition of species after latinization not researched. Objective synonym of *Cyclopterus* Linnaeus 1758 (Lindberg 1973:607 [ref. 7220]). Cyclopteridae: Cyclopterinae.

Lumpus Rafinesque 1815:87 [ref. 3584]. As "*Lumpus* R. sp. do." meaning *Lumpus* Rafinesque, a new genus for a species previously in another genus. Not available, name only; apparently for a species of *Cyclopterus* but not so specified. Cyclopteridae: Cyclopterinae.

Lunicauda Whitley 1947:144 [ref. 4708]. Fem. *Mesoprion?? emeryii* Richardson 1843:7. Type by original designation (also monotypic). Nemipteridae.

Lunolabrus (subgenus of *Pseudolabrus*) Whitley 1933:86 [ref. 4677]. Masc. *Labrus miles* Bloch & Schneider 1801:264. Type by original designation. Synonym of *Pseudolabrus* Bleeker 1862, but as a valid subgenus (Russell 1988:23, 33 [ref. 12549]). Labridae.

Lupinoblennius Herre 1942:302 [ref. 2135]. Masc. *Lupinoblennius dispar* Herre 1942:303. Type by original designation (also monotypic). Valid (Greenfield & Johnson 1981:70 [ref. 5580]). Blenniidae.

Luposicya Smith 1959:217 [ref. 4122]. Fem. *Luposicya lupus* Smith 1959:217. Type by original designation (also monotypic). Valid (Yoshino in Masuda et al. 1984:284 [ref. 6441], Larson 1986:947 [ref. 6328], Birdsong et al. 1988:193 [ref. 7303]). Gobiidae.

Lutianus see *Lutjanus*. Lutjanidae.

Lutjanus Bloch 1790:105 [ref. 469]. Masc. *Lutjanus lutjanus* Bloch 1790:107. Type by absolute tautonymy. Also spelled *Lutianus* by Bloch 1790:Pl. 245, and subsequent authors, but as *Lutjanus* throughout text (pp. 107-127). Valid (Johnson 1980:10 [ref. 13553], Akazaki in Masuda et al. 1984:169 [ref. 6441], Allen & Talbot 1985 [ref. 6491], Allen 1986:323 [ref. 6208], Iwatsuki et al. 1989 [ref. 12750]). Lutjanidae.

Lutodeira van Hasselt 1823:330 [ref. 5105]. Fem. *Lutodeira indica* van Hasselt 1823:330. Type by monotypy. *Lutodira* Agassiz 1846:217 [ref. 64] is an unjustified emendation. Synonym of *Chanos* Lacepède 1803 (Arnoult 1984:128 [ref. 6179] but attributed to Rüppell 1828; see Kottelat 1987:370 [ref. 5962]). Chanidae.

Luvarus Rafinesque 1810:22 [ref. 3594]. Masc. *Luvarus imperialis* Rafinesque 1810:22. Type by monotypy. Misspelled *Luvaris* in literature. Valid (Topp 1973:476 [erf. 7209], Leis & Richards 1984:548 [ref. 13669], Nakamura in Masuda et al. 1984:223 [ref. 6441], Decamps in Whitehead et al. 1986:998 [ref. 13676], Heemstra 1986:838 [ref. 5660], Tyler et al. 1989 [ref. 13460]). Luvaridae.

Luxilinus Jordan 1885:126 [ref. 2384]. Masc. *Leucosomus occidentalis* Baird & Girard in Girard 1856:186. Type by original designation (also monotypic). Synonym of *Lavinia* Girard 1854. Cyprinidae.

Luxilus Rafinesque 1820:237 [ref. 7310]. Masc. *Luxilus chrysocephalus* Rafinesque 1820:238. Type by subsequent designation. Also appeared in Rafinesque 1820:47 (Dec.) [ref. 3592]. Type designated by Jordan & Gilbert 1877:86 [ref. 4907]. *Luxulus* is a misspelling. Synonym of *Notropis* Rafinesque 1818, but as a valid subgenus (Gilbert 1978:15 [ref. 7042], Mayden 1988 [ref. 6235]); valid genus (Mayden 1989:38 [ref. 12555]). Cyprinidae.

Luzoneleotris Herre 1938:59 [ref. 2126]. Fem. *Luzoneleotris nasugbua* Herre 1938:60. Type by original designation (also monotypic). In Xenisthmidae (Hoese, pers. comm.). Xenisthmidae.

Luzonichthys Herre 1936:366 [ref. 5609]. Masc. *Mirolabrichthys waitei* Fowler 1931:228. Type by original designation (also monotypic). Valid (Randall 1981:13 [ref. 5549], Kendall 1984:500 [ref. 136663], Heemstra & Randall 1986:513 [ref. 5667], Paxton et al. 1989:506 [ref. 12442]). Serranidae: Anthiinae.

Lycenchelys Gill 1884:180 [ref. 1725]. Fem. *Lycodes muraena* Collett 1878:14, 15. Type by subsequent designation. Proposed for "...Collett's second group which have the body elongate..." but with no species mentioned. First addition of species not investigated. Type designated by Jordan 1920:428 [ref. 4905]. Misspelled *Lycenchelis* in Zoological Record for 1923. Valid (Andriashev 1973:541 [ref. 7214], Gosztonyi 1977:217 [ref. 6103], Anderson 1984:578 [ref. 13634], Toyoshima in Masuda et al. 1984:306 [ref. 6441], Toyoshima 1985:145 [ref. 5722], Anderson 1988:86 [ref. 7304]). Zoarcidae.

Lycengraulis (subgenus of *Engraulis*) Günther 1868:385, 399 [ref. 1990]. Fem. *Engraulis grossidens* Agassiz (ex Cuvier) 1828:50. Type by subsequent designation. Described in key (p. 385) as a subgenus of *Engraulis* for two species on p. 399. Type designated by Jordan & Evermann 1896:451 [ref. 2443] (see Whitehead 1967:134 [ref. 6464]). Valid (Grande 1985:245 [ref. 6466]). Engraulidae.

Lychnoculus Murray 1877:132 [ref. 6531]. Masc. *Lychnoculus mirabilis* Murray 1877:132. Type by monotypy. Suppressed for priority but not homonymy and placed on Official Index (Opinion 1333). Original not seen. In the synonymy of *Ipnops* Günther 1878. Chlorophthalmidae: Ipnopinae.

Lychnophora (subgenus of *Lampadena*) Fraser-Brunner 1949:1080 [ref. 1496]. Fem. *Lampadena nitida* Tåning 1928:62. Type by original designation. Synonym of *Lampadena* Goode & Bean in Gill 1893, but as a valid subgenus (Paxton 1979:12 [ref. 6440]). Myctophidae.

Lychnopoles Garman 1899:244 [ref. 1540]. *Lychnopoles argenteolus* Garman 1899:244. Type by monotypy. Sternoptychidae: Maurolicinae.

Lycias (subgenus of *Lycodes*) Jordan & Evermann 1898:2461, 2468 [ref. 2445]. Masc. *Lycodes seminudus* Reinhardt 1837:117. Type by original designation. Synonym of *Lycodes* Reinhardt 1831 (Andriashev 1973:542 [ref. 7214], McAllister et al. 1981:824 [ref. 5431], Toyoshima 1985:180 [ref. 5722] with wrong type). Zoarcidae.

Lycichthys Gill 1877:clxvii [ref. 1715]. Masc. *Anarrhichas latifrons* Steenstrup & Hallgrimmson 1842:647. Type by subsequent designation. Two included species; earliest type designation not researched. Gill cites as from a monograph by Steenstrup [not investigated]. Synonym of *Anarhichas* Linnaeus 1758 (Barsukov 1973:528 [ref. 7213]). Anarhichadidae.

Lyciscus Evermann & Goldsborough 1907:342 [ref. 6532]. Masc. *Lycodopsis crotalinus* Gilbert 1890:105. Type by monotypy. Apparently preoccupied by Smith 1839 [not investigated]. No description, but name with available species. Objective synonym of *Embryx* Jordan & Evermann 1898. Synonym of *Lycenchelys* Gill 1884 (Anderson 1988:87 [ref. 7304]). Zoarcidae.

Lycocara Gill 1884:180 [ref. 1725]. Neut. *Ophidium parrii* Ross 1826:109. Type by being a replacement name. Replacement for *Uronectes* Günther 1862, preoccupied by Brown 1850 in Crustacea. Correct spelling for genus of type species is *Ophidion*. Synonym of *Liparis* Scopoli 1777 (Andriashev & McAllister 1978 [ref. 6988] and not a zoarcid). Cyclopteridae: Liparinae.

Lycocyprinus Peters 1868:146 [ref. 7935]. Masc. *Poecilia sexfasciata* Peters 1864:396. Type by monotypy. *Poecilia sexfasciata* Peters 1864 preoccupied by *Epiplatys sexfasciatus* Gill 1863 when both are placed in *Epiplatys*; Peter's species equals *Epiplatys dageti* Poll 1953 according to Wildekamp et al. 1986:244 [ref. 6198]. Synonym of *Epiplatys* Gill 1862, but as a valid subgenus (Parenti 1981:475 [ref. 7066]). Aplocheilidae: Aplocheilinae.

Lycodalepis Bleeker 1874:369 [ref. 435]. Fem. *Lycodes mucosus* Richardson 1855:362. Type by original designation (also monotypic). Synonym of *Lycodes* Reinhardt 1831 (Andriashev 1973:542 [ref. 7214], McAllister et al. 1981:824 [ref. 5431], Toyoshima 1985:180 [ref. 5722]). Zoarcidae.

Lycodapus Gilbert 1890:107 [ref. 1623]. Masc. *Lycodapus fierasfer* Gilbert 1890:107. Type by original designation (also monotypic). Valid (Peden & Anderson 1981 [ref. 5531], Anderson 1984:578 [ref. 13634], Toyoshima in Masuda et al. 1984:309 [ref. 6441], Anderson 1988:104 [ref. 7304], Anderson 1989 [ref. 13419]). Zoarcidae.

Lycodes Reinhardt 1831:18 [ref. 6533]. Masc. *Lycodes vahlii* Reinhardt 1831:18. Type by monotypy. Valid (Andriashev 1973:542 [ref. 7214], McAllister et al. 1981:824 [ref. 5431], Anderson 1984:578 [ref. 13634], Toyoshima in Masuda et al. 1984:307 [ref. 6441], Toyoshima 1985:180 [ref. 5722], Andriashev in Whitehead et al. 1986:1135 [ref. 13677], Anderson 1986:342 [ref. 5633]). Zoarcidae.

Lycodichthys Pappenheim 1911:382 [ref. 6534]. Masc. *Lycodichthys antarcticus* Pappenheim 1911:382. Type by monotypy. Valid (Anderson 1984:578 [ref. 13634], Anderson 1988:78 [ref. 7304]). Zoarcidae.

Lycodon Kner 1860:52 [ref. 7130]. *Cynopotamus molossus* Kner 1860:51. Type by monotypy. Kner placed his new species *molossus* in the established genus *Cynopotamus* but suggested it might represent a distinct genus for which he proposed *Lycodon*. Preoccupied by *Lycodon* Fitzinger 1826 in Reptilia. In the synonymy of *Roestes* Günther 1864 (Menezes 1974:219 [ref. 7129]). Characidae.

Lycodontis McClelland 1844:173, 185 [ref. 2928]. Fem. *Lycodontis literata* McClelland 1844:186. Type by subsequent designation. Not available from McClelland; an incorrect original spelling (see *Strophidon* McClelland). Probably can date to Jordan & Evermann who provide a description. Type designated by Jordan & Evermann 1896:392 [ref. 2443]. Valid (Blache et al. 1973:225 [ref. 7185], Ajiad & El-Absy 1986 [ref. 6758]); synonym of *Gymnothorax* Bloch 1795 (Böhlke et al. 1989:145 [ref. 13286] but as a valid subgenus on p. 155). Muraenidae: Muraeninae.

Lycodonus Goode & Bean 1883:208 [ref. 1838]. Fem. *Lycodonus mirabilis* Goode & Bean 1883:208. Type by monotypy. Valid (Andriashev 1973:546 [ref. 7214], Anderson 1984:578 [ref. 13634], Toyoshima 1985:143 [ref. 5722], Andriashev in Whitehead et al. 1986:1146 [ref. 13677], Anderson 1986:343 [ref. 5633]). Zoarcidae.

Lycodophis Vaillant 1888:311 [ref. 4496]. Masc. *Lycodophis albus* Vaillant 1888:309. Type by monotypy. Proposed somewhat conditionally (but available). Synonym of *Lycenchelys* Gill 1884 (Andriashev 1973:541 [ref. 7214], Anderson 1988:86 [ref. 7304]). Zoarcidae.

Lycodopsis Collett 1879:382 [ref. 886]. Fem. *Lycodes pacificus* Collett 1879:381. Type by monotypy. Predates *Leurynnis* Lockington 1880 (25 Mar.), *Lycodopsis* published 1 Aug. 1879 (see Gill 1880:247-248 [ref. 5766]). Valid (Toyoshima 1985:238 [ref. 5722]). Zoarcidae.

Lycogenis Cuvier (ex Kuhl & van Hasselt) in Cuvier & Valenciennes 1830:346 [ref. 999]. Fem. *Lycogenis argyrosoma* Cuvier (ex Kuhl & van Hasselt) in Cuvier & Valenciennes 1830:346. Not available, both genus and species names published in passing in synonymy; apparently never made available. In the synonymy of *Scolopsis* Cuvier 1814. Nemipteridae.

Lycogramma Gilbert 1915:364 [ref. 1632]. Neut. *Maynea brunnea* Bean 1890:39. Type by original designation (also monotypic). Zoarcidae.

Lycogrammoides Soldatov & Lindberg 1929:40 [ref. 4161]. Masc. *Lycogrammoides schmidti* Soldatov & Lindberg 1929:41. Type by original designation (also monotypic). Valid (Anderson 1984:578 [ref. 13634]). Zoarcidae.

Lyconectes Gilbert 1896:452 [ref. 1628]. Masc. *Lyconectes aleuticus* Gilbert 1896:452. Type by original designation (also monotypic). Valid. Cryptacanthodidae.

Lyconema Gilbert 1896:471 [ref. 1628]. Neut. *Lyconema barbatum* Gilbert 1896:471. Type by original designation (also monotypic). Valid (Anderson 1984:578 [ref. 13634], Toyoshima 1985:142 [ref. 5722]). Zoarcidae.

Lyconodes Gilchrist 1922:59 [ref. 1648]. Masc. *Lyconodes argentrus* Gilchrist 1922:59. Type by monotypy. Valid (Cohen 1986:325 [ref. 5646]). Merlucciidae: Merlucciinae.

Lyconus Günther 1887:158 [ref. 2013]. Masc. *Lyconus pinnatus* Günther 1887:158. Type by monotypy. Valid (Svetovidov 1973:301 [ref. 7169], Marshall 1973:298 [ref. 7194], Fahay & Markle 1984:267 [ref. 13653], Svetovidov in Whitehead et al. 1986:679 [ref. 13676]. Cohen 1986:325 [ref. 5646], Cohen 1984:264 [ref. 13646]). Merlucciidae: Merlucciinae.

Lycothrissa (subgenus of *Engraulis*) Günther 1868:385, 399 [ref. 1990]. Fem. *Engraulis crocodilus* Bleeker 1851:15. Type by monotypy. Described in key (p. 385) as subgenus of *Engraulis* for a species on p. 399. Valid (Grande 1985:245 [ref. 6466], Whitehead et al. 1988:448 [ref. 5725], Kottelat 1989:6 [ref. 13605], Roberts 1989:26 [ref. 6439]). Engraulidae.

Lycozoarces Popov 1935:303 [ref. 3546]. Masc. *Lycozoarces hubbsi* Popov 1935:303. Type by monotypy. Appeared first in Popov 1933:151 as name only and species *regani* as name only, then in

1935 as above. In 1935 *hubbsi* and *regani* were both mentioned, and name *Lycozoarces* would not be available (after 1930 without type designated), but apparently *regani* still not available, so genus is available from 1935 with type by monotypy. Valid (Anderson 1984:578 [ref. 13634], Toyoshima in Masuda et al. 1984:305 [ref. 6441]). Zoarcidae.

Lymnea Rafinesque 1815:93 [ref. 3584]. Not available, name only; perhaps an incorrect subsequent spelling of *Lamna*. Rafinesque changed name from *Lymnea* to *Noelius* in "Additions et Corrections" on p. 220 without explanation. Lamnidae.

Lyocetus (subgenus of *Melanocetus*) Günther 1887:57 [ref. 2013]. Masc. *Lyocetus murrayi* Günther 1887:57. Type by monotypy. Melanocetidae.

Lyoliparis (subgenus of *Liparis*) Jordan & Evermann 1896:451 [ref. 2442]. Masc. *Liparis pulchellus* Ayres 1855:22. Type by original designation (also monotypic). Synonym of *Liparis* Scopoli 1777 (Kido 1988:165 [ref. 12287]). Cyclopteridae: Liparinae.

Lyopsetta (subgenus of *Hippoglossoides*) Jordan & Goss in Jordan 1885:923 [135] [ref. 2385]. Fem. *Hippoglossoides exilis* Jordan & Gilbert 1881:154, 454. Type by original designation (also monotypic). On p. 135 of separate. Valid (Norman 1934:306 [ref. 6893], Ahlstrom et al. 1984:643 [ref. 13641]). Pleuronectidae: Pleuronectinae.

Lyosphaera Evermann & Kendall 1898:131 [ref. 1281]. Fem. *Lyosphaera globosa* Evermann & Kendall 1898:131. Type by original designation (also monotypic). Diodontidae.

Lyragalaxias Whitley 1935:Pl. 3 legend [ref. 4686]. Masc. *Galaxias oconnori* Ogilby 1912:33. Not available from this reference, no description after 1930 [Art. 13a(i)]; subsequent use in an available way not investigated. In the synonymy of *Galaxias* Cuvier 1816. Galaxiidae: Galaxiinae.

Lyrichthys (subgenus of *Trigla*) Kaup 1873:88 [ref. 2585]. Masc. *Trigla lyra* Linnaeus 1758:300. Type by subsequent designation. Type designated by Jordan 1919:370 [ref. 4904]. Synonym of *Trigla* Linnaeus 1758 (Blanc & Hureau 1973:586 [ref. 7218]). Triglidae: Triglinae.

Lysodermus Smith & Pope 1906:483 [ref. 4058]. Masc. *Lysodermus satsumae* Smith & Pope 1906:484. Type by original designation (also monotypic). Synonym of *Minous* Cuvier 1829 (Eschmeyer et al. 1979:454 [ref. 1277]). Scorpaenidae: Minoinae.

Lythrichthys Jordan & Starks 1904:140 [ref. 2527]. Masc. *Lythrichthys eulabes* Jordan & Starks 1904:140. Type by original designation (also monotypic). Synonym of *Setarches* Johnson 1862:355 (Eschmeyer & Collette 1966:355 [ref. 6485]). Scorpaenidae: Setarchinae.

Lythrulon (subgenus of *Haemulon*) Jordan & Swain 1884:284, 287, 315 [ref. 2536]. Neut. *Haemulon flaviguttatus* Gill 1862:254. Type by original designation (also monotypic). Type designated on p. 315. Haemulidae.

Lythrurus Jordan 1876:272 [ref. 2371]. Masc. *Semotilus diplemia* Rafinesque 1820:50. Type by subsequent designation. Type designated by Jordan & Gilbert 1877:95 [ref. 4907]. Synonym of *Notropis* Rafinesque 1818, but as a valid subgenus (Gilbert 1978:15 [ref. 7042]); valid genus (Mayden 1989:34 [ref. 12555]). Cyprinidae.

Lythrypnus (subgenus of *Gobius*) Jordan & Evermann 1896:458 [ref. 2442]. Masc. *Gobius dalli* Gilbert 1890:73. Type by original designation (also monotypic). Valid (Greenfield 1988 [ref. 6413], Birdsong et al. 1988:193 [ref. 7303]). Gobiidae.

Maccullochella Whitley 1929:109 [ref. 4665]. Fem. *Grystes macquariensis* Cuvier in Cuvier & Valenciennes 1829:58. Type by being a replacement name. Replacement for *Oligorus* Günther 1859, preoccupied by Dejean 1834 in Coleoptera. Correct spelling of genus of type species is *Gristes*. Valid (Berra & Weatherley 1972 [ref. 7104], Paxton et al. 1989:511 [ref. 12442]). Percichthyidae.

Maccullochina Jordan in Jordan & Jordan 1922:44 [ref. 2487]. Fem. *Synagrops serratospinosa* Smith & Radcliffe 1912:444. Type by original designation (also monotypic). Near *Synagrops*. Acropomatidae.

Macdonaldia Goode & Bean 1895:467 [ref. 1847]. Fem. *Notacanthus rostratus* Collett 1889:307. Type by original designation (also monotypic). Also appeared as new in Goode & Bean 1896:171 [ref. 1848]. Valid (Wheeler 1973:257 [ref. 7190]). Notacanthidae.

Macgregorella Seale 1910:533 [ref. 4000]. Fem. *Macgregorella moroana* Seale 1910:533. Type by original designation (also monotypic). Synonym of *Callogobius* Bleeker 1874 (Lachner & McKinney 1974:878 [ref. 2547]). Gobiidae.

Machaerenchelys Fowler 1938:85 [ref. 1428]. Fem. *Machaerenchelys vanderbilti* Fowler 1938:85. Type by original designation (also monotypic). Synonym of *Leiuranus* Bleeker 1853 (McCosker 1977:77 [ref. 6836]). Ophichthidae: Ophichthinae.

Machaerium Richardson 1843:176 [ref. 3735]. Neut. *Machaerium subducens* Richardson 1843:176. Type by monotypy. Richardson 1843:176 published Sept. 1843; also in Günther, Rept. British Assoc. Adv. Sci. 1843:69 (not checked), apparently published later. Preoccupied by Holliday 1832 in Diptera, replaced by *Congrogadus* Günther 1862. Objective synonym of *Congrogadus* Günther 1862 (Winterbottom et al. 1984:1607 [ref. 5140]). Pseudochromidae: Congrogadinae.

Machaerochilus Fitzinger 1873:152, 170 [ref. 1337]. Masc. *Chondrostoma phoxinus* Heckel 1843:1031. Type by subsequent designation. Type apparently first designated by Jordan 1919:369 [ref. 4904]). Synonym of *Chondrostoma* Agassiz 1832 or 1835 (Elvira 1987:112 [ref. 6743]). Cyprinidae.

Machaerope Ogilby 1899:736 [ref. 3277]. Fem. *Machaerope latispinis* Ogilby 1899:737. Type by monotypy. Gempylidae.

Machephilus Johnson 1868:713 [ref. 2360]. Masc. *Machephilus dumerilli* Johnson 1868:713. Type by monotypy. Synonym of *Lepidorhinus* Bonaparte 1838 (Krefft & Tortonese 1973:40 [ref. 7165]); synonym of *Centrophorus* Müller & Henle 1837 (Compagno 1984:35 [ref. 6474]). Squalidae.

Macilentichthys Whitley 1932:114 [ref. 4675]. Masc. *Macilentichthys popei* Whitley 1932:115. Type by original designation. Leiognathidae.

Macleayina Fowler 1907:426 [ref. 1377]. Fem. *Hippocampus bleekeri* Fowler 1907:426. Type by original designation. Synonym of *Hippocampus* Rafinesque 1810 (Vari 1982:175 [ref. 6765]). Syngnathidae: Hippocampinae.

Macolor Bleeker 1860:25 [ref. 379]. Masc. *Macolor typus* Bleeker 1867:277 (= *Diacope macolor* Lesson 1827:138). Type by monotypy (also by use of *typus*). Lesson's species *macolor* needlessly renamed *typus* by Bleeker. Valid (Johnson 1980:10 [ref. 13553], Akazaki in Masuda et al. 1984:168 [ref. 6441], Allen 1985:125 [ref. 6843], Anderson 1986:577 [ref. 5634], Kishimoto et al. 1987 [ref. 6061]). Lutjanidae.

Macquaria Cuvier in Cuvier & Valenciennes 1830:377 [ref. 999]. Fem. *Macquaria australasica* Cuvier in Cuvier & Valenciennes 1830:377. Type by monotypy. *Paschalestes* Gistel 1848 apparently is an unneeded replacement. Valid (Paxton et al. 1989:512 [ref. 12442]) Percichthyidae.

Macrhybopsis (subgenus of *Hybopsis*) Cockerell & Allison 1909:162 [ref. 875]. Fem. *Gobio gelidus* Girard 1856:188. Type by original designation (also monotypic). Synonym of *Hybopsis* Agassiz 1854 (authors); valid (Coburn & Cavender, in prep.). Cyprinidae.

Macrias Gill & Townsend 1901:937 [ref. 1791]. Masc. *Macrias amissus* Gill & Townsend 1901:837. Type by monotypy. Type specimen not available, only known specimen was thrown overboard. Chlorophthalmidae: Ipnopinae.

Macristiella Berry & Robins 1967:46 [ref. 286]. Fem. *Macristiella perlucens* Berry & Robins 1967:46. Type by original designation (also monotypic). Synonym of *Bathytyphlops* Nybelin 1957 (Sulak 1977:53 [ref. 4299]). Chlorophthalmidae: Ipnopinae.

Macristium Regan 1903:345 [ref. 3619]. Neut. *Macristium chavesi* Regan 1903:345. Type by monotypy. Valid (Maul 1973:113 [ref. 7171]); synonym of *Bathysaurus* Günther 1878 (Johnson 1974 [ref. 7135], Sulak 1977:53 [ref. 4299]). Synodontidae: Bathysaurinae.

Macrocephalus Bleeker (ex Browne) 1876:336 [ref. 448]. Masc. *Sciaena undecimalis* Bloch 1792:60. Not available, name published in synonymy of *Oxylabrax* Bleeker; apparently never made available. In the synonymy of *Centropomus* Lacepède 1802. Centropomidae: Centropominae.

Macrocephalus Browne 1789:450 [ref. 669]. Masc. Not available, published in a rejected work on Official Index (Opinion 89). Also preoccupied by Swederus 1787 in Hemiptera. Appeared as name in synonymy (not available) in Bleeker 1876:336 [ref. 448]. Centropomidae: Centropominae.

Macrocephenchelys Fowler 1934:275 [ref. 1416]. Fem. *Macrocephenchelys brachialis* Fowler 1934:277. Type by original designation (also monotypic). Has been placed in its own family Macrocephenchelyidae; now placed in the Congridae (see McCosker et al. 1989:256 [ref. 13288], also Smith 1989:512 [ref. 13285]). Valid (Robins & Robins 1971 [ref. 7127], Karrer 1982:48 [ref. 5679]). Congridae: Congrinae.

Macrochirichthys Bleeker 1859:439 [ref. 370]. Masc. *Macrochirichthys uranoscopus* Bleeker 1851:14. Apparently appeared first in key, without included species. Two species (one with question) included by Bleeker 1859:155 [ref. 371] and 1860:298 [ref. 380]; therefore type by subsequent monotypy. Valid (Yih & Wu 1964:92 [ref. 13499], Kottelat 1985:263 [ref. 11441], Roberts 1989:44 [ref. 6439], Chen in Chu & Chen 1989:82 [ref. 13584], Kottelat 1989:8 [ref. 13605]). Cyprinidae.

Macrochirus Swainson 1839:70, 71, 180 [ref. 4303]. Masc. *Scorpaena miles* Bennett 1828:9. Type by monotypy. Spelled *Machrochirus* on p. 65, *Macrochirus* 3 times on pp. 70-71, and once each on p. 180 and 441 (index) and *Macrochyrus* on 264. *Macrochirus* here regarded as the correct original spelling unless first reviser can be located for all three names. Synonym of *Pterois* Oken 1817. Scorpaenidae: Pteroinae.

Macrochoerodon Fowler & Bean 1928:200 [ref. 1475]. Masc. *Crenilabrus oligacanthus* Bleeker 1851:489. Type by original designation (also monotypic). Labridae.

Macrodon Müller 1843:316 [ref. 3063]. Masc. *Esox malabaricus* Bloch 1794:149. Type by subsequent designation. Type designated by Eigenmann & Eigenmann 1889:102 [ref. 12497] as *trahira* Spix (not an included species but placed in synonymy of *malabaricus*). Apparently preoccupied by Schinz 1822 in fishes, replaced by *Hoplias* Gill 1903. Objective synonym of *Hoplias* Gill 1903. Erythrinidae.

Macrodon Schinz 1822:482 [ref. 3926]. Masc. *Lonchurus ancylodon* Bloch & Schneider 1801:102. Type by being a replacement name. Replacement for *Ancylodon* Cuvier 1816 [Oken], preoccupied by Illiger 1811 in Mammalia. Valid (Chao 1978:36 [ref. 6983], Uyeno & Sato in Uyeno et al. 1983:373 [ref. 14275]). Sciaenidae.

Macrodonophis Poey 1868:251 [ref. 3503]. Masc. *Conger mordax* Poey 1860:319. Type by monotypy. Synonym of *Echiophis* Kaup 1856 (McCosker 1977:76 [ref. 6836], McCosker et al. 1989:357 [ref. 13288]). Ophichthidae: Ophichthinae.

Macrodontogobius Herre 1936:278 [ref. 2125]. Masc. *Macrodontogobius wilburi* Herre 1936:279. Type by monotypy. Valid (Murdy & Hoese 1984 [ref. 5377], Akihito in Masuda et al. 1984:253 [ref. 6441], Birdsong et al. 1988:193 [ref. 7303] as *Macrodontigobius*). Gobiidae.

Macrognathus Gronow in Gray 1854:147 [ref. 1911]. Masc. *Balistes scolopax* Linnaeus 1758:329. Type by monotypy. Preoccupied by Lacepède 1800 in fishes and by Burmeister in Hope 1845 in Coleoptera. Synonym of *Macroramphosus* Lacepède 1803. Centriscidae: Macroramphosinae.

Macrognathus Lacepède 1800:283 [ref. 2709]. Masc. *Ophidium aculeatum* Bloch 1786:478. Type by subsequent designation. Earliest type designation located is Jordan 1917:56 [ref. 2407]. Correct spelling for genus of type species is *Ophidion*. Valid (Sufi 1956:99 [ref. 12498], Jayaram 1981:387 [ref. 6497], Travers 1984:143 [ref. 5147], Kottelat 1985:274 [ref. 11441], Roberts 1986:98 [ref. 5802], Kottelat 1989:20 [ref. 13605], Roberts 1989:178 [ref. 6439]). Mastacembelidae.

Macrogobius de Buen 1930:135, 138 [ref. 685]. Masc. *Gobius cobitis* Pallas 1814:160. Type by original designation. Synonym of *Gobius* Linnaeus 1758 (Miller 1973:483 [ref. 6888]). Gobiidae.

Macrohoplostethus (subgenus of *Hoplostethus*) Kotlyar 1986:99, 130 [ref. 6004]. Masc. *Hoplostethus atlanticus* Collett 1889:306. Type by original designation. Trachichthyidae.

Macrolepis Rafinesque 1815:86 [ref. 3584]. Fem. Not available; name only. Regarded as a synonym of *Apogon* Lacepède 1801 (Fraser 1972:17 [ref. 5195]), but based on style in Rafinesque 1815, was proposed as a new name based on "sp. do.," meaning on a species included in a preceding genus. Apogonidae.

Macromastax Beebe 1933:161 [ref. 5873]. Fem. *Macromastax gymnos* Beebe 1933:162. Type by monotypy. Also as Beebe 1933 (Aug.):80 [ref. 245]. Synonym of *Bathylaco* Goode & Bean 1896 (Nielsen 1973:85 [ref. 6885]). Alepocephalidae.

Macrones Duméril 1856:484 [ref. 1154]. Masc. *Bagrus lamarrii* Valenciennes in Cuvier & Valenciennes 1840:407. Type by monotypy. Possibly can be considered a French vernacular and not available. Preoccupied by Newman 1841 in Coleoptera, replaced by *Aoria* Jordan 1917 (preoccupied by Baly 1863 and replaced by *Aorichthys* Wu 1939 and *Macronichthys* White & Moy-Thomas 1940); *Macrones* also replaced by *Sperta* Holly 1939. Synonym of *Mystus* Scopoli 1777 (Roberts 1989:120 [ref. 6439]). Bagridae.

Macronichthys White & Moy-Thomas 1940:505 [ref. 4650]. Masc. *Bagrus lamarrii* Valenciennes in Cuvier & Valenciennes 1840:407. Type by being a replacement name. Replacement for *Aoria* Jordan 1917. *Aoria* itself is a replacement for *Macrones* Duméril 1856 (preoccupied, replaced earlier by *Sperata* Holly 1939); *Aoria* replaced earlier by *Aorichthys* Wu 1939. Objective synonym of *Sperata* and *Aorichthys*. Synonym of *Mystus* Scopoli 1777

(Roberts 1989:120 [ref. 6439]). Bagridae.

Macronoides (subgenus of *Macrones*) Hora 1921:179 [ref. 2202]. Masc. *Batasio affinis* Blyth 1861:150. Type by subsequent designation. Three included species, earliest type designation not located. Synonym of *Batasio* Blyth 1860 (Jayaram 1977:16 [ref. 7005], Jayaram 1981:191 [ref. 6497]). Bagridae.

Macronotothen Gill 1862:520 [ref. 1782]. *Notothenia rossii* Richardson 1845:9. Type by original designation (also monotypic). Synonym of *Notothenia* Richardson 1844 (Andersen 1984:24 [ref. 13369]). Nototheniidae.

Macroparalepis Ege 1933:229 [ref. 1186]. Fem. *Macroparalepis danae* Ege 1933. Not available, after 1930 with 9 species and no type fixed. Genus dates to Zoological Record for 1933 (1934) where *M. danae* Ege is listed as type; authorship probably Burton (see Art. 13b in Appendix A). Harry 1953:240 [ref. 2045] lists *affinis* as type. Valid as Ege 1933 (Post 1973:207 [ref. 7182], Post 1980 [ref. 5577], Post in Whitehead et al. 1984:501 [ref. 13675], Okiyama 1984:207 [ref. 13644], Post 1986:276 [ref. 5705], Paxton et al. 1989:247 [ref. 12442]). Paralepididae.

Macropharyngodon Bleeker 1862:412 [ref. 382]. Masc. *Julis geoffroy* Quoy & Gaimard 1824:270. Type by original designation (also monotypic). Also appeared in Bleeker 1862:100 [ref. 386]. Valid (Randall 1978 [ref. 7004], Araga in Masuda et al. 1984:207 [ref. 6441], Randall 1986:698 [ref. 5706]). Labridae.

Macropharynx Brauer 1902:290 [ref. 631]. Masc. *Macropharynx longicaudatus* Brauer 1902:290. Type by monotypy. Mentioned earlier by Brauer in Chun (1900:290 [ref. 629]) as *Megalopharynx*. Synonym of *Eurypharynx* Vaillant 1882 (Böhlke 1966:610 [ref. 5256], Bauchot 1973:218 [ref. 7184], Bertelsen et al. 1989:649 [ref. 13293]). Eurypharyngidae.

Macrophthalmia Plate 1897:137, 140 [ref. 3489]. Fem. *Macrophthalmia chilensis* Plate 1897:137, 140. Type by monotypy. Synonym of *Geotria* Gray 1851. Petromyzontidae: Geotriinae.

Macropinna Chapman 1939:509 [ref. 817]. Fem. *Macropinna microstoma* Chapman 1939:509. Type by original designation (also monotypic). Valid (Fujii in Masuda et al. 1984:41 [ref. 6441], Ahlstrom et al. 1984:156 [ref. 13627]). Opisthoproctidae.

Macropleurodus Regan 1922:189 [ref. 3675]. Masc. *Haplochromis bicolor* Boulenger 1906:444. Type by monotypy. See Greenwood 1956:299-300 [ref. 1894]. Valid (Greenwood 1980:80 [ref. 1899], Greenwood 1983:209 [ref. 5364]). Cichlidae.

Macropodus Lacepède 1801:416 [ref. 2710]. Masc. *Macropodus viridiauratus* Lacepède 1801:416, 417. Type by monotypy. Unjustifiably emended to *Macropus* (not of Shaw 1790, Latrielle 1802 or Thunberg 1805) by Günther 1861:(372) 381 [ref. 1964]. Valid (Jayaram 1981:381 [ref. 6497], Uyeno & Arai in Masuda et al. 1984:122 [ref. 6441]). Belontiidae.

Macrops Duméril 1856:279 [ref. 1154]. Masc. *Serranus aculeatus [oculatus]* Cuvier in Cuvier & Valenciennes 1828:266. Type by monotypy. Preoccupied by Wagler 1830 in Reptilia, Burmeister 1835 in Hemiptera and Kirby 1837 in Coleoptera. Species given by Duméril as *aculeatus* by error for *oculatus* (with clear citation to page and plate in Cuvier & Valenciennes). Objective synonym of *Elastoma* Swainson 1839 and *Hesperanthias* Lowe 1843. Synonym of *Etelis* Cuvier 1828 (Allen 1985:24 [ref. 6843]). Lutjanidae.

Macropsobrycon Eigenmann 1915:48 [ref. 1231]. Masc. *Macropsobrycon uruguayanae* Eigenmann 1915:48. Type by original designation (also monotypic). Valid (Malabarba 1989:136 [ref. 14217]). Characidae.

Macropterobagrus (subgenus of *Hemibagrus*) Nichols 1925:1 [ref. 3180]. Masc. *Hemibagrus macropterus* Bleeker 1870:257. Type by monotypy. Bagridae.

Macropteronotus Lacepède 1803:84 [ref. 4930]. Masc. *Macropteronotus charmuth* Lacepède 1803:84, 85. Type by monotypy. Synonym of *Clarias* Scopoli 1777 (Teugels 1986:69 [ref. 6193], Teugels 1986:11 [ref. 12548]). Clariidae.

Macroramphosus Lacepède 1803:136 [ref. 4930]. Masc. *Silurus cornutus* Forsskål 1775:xiii, 66. Type by monotypy. Also spelled *Macrorhamphosus*, *Macramphosus* and *Macrorhamphus* by authors. See Paxton et al. 1989:406 [ref. 12442] for discussion of nomenclatural problems. Valid (Wheeler 1973:273 [ref. 7190], Fritzsche 1984 [ref. 13658], Clarke 1984 [ref. 6811], Araga in Masuda et al. 1984:84 [ref. 6441], Ehrich in Whitehead et al. 1986:627 [ref. 13676], Heemstra 1986:460 [ref. 5660], Paxton et al. 1989:408 [ref. 12442]). Centriscidae: Macroramphosinae.

Macrorhamphosodes Fowler 1934:364 [ref. 1416]. Masc. *Macrorhamphosodes platycheilus* Fowler 1934:365. Type by original designation (also monotypic). Valid (Tyler 1968:192 [ref. 6438], Tyler 1980:56 [ref. 4477]), Aboussouan & Leis 1984:452 [ref. 13661], Matsuura in Masuda et al. 1984:357 [ref. 6441], Tyler 1986:888 [ref. 5723], Matsuura 1987 [ref. 6710]). Triacanthodidae.

Macrorhyncus Lacepède in Duméril 1806:342 [ref. 1152]. Masc. *"Macrorhinque argentee"* Lacepède (= *Syngnathus argenteus* Osbeck 1765:396). *Macrorinchus* and *Macrorhynchus* of authors are misspellings or incorrect subsequent spellings. Scombridae.

Macroscorpius Fowler 1938:75 [ref. 1426]. Masc. *Macroscorpius pallidus* Fowler 1938:76. Type by original designation (also monotypic). Synonym of *Lioscorpius* Günther 1880 (Eschmeyer & Collette 1966:365 [ref. 6485]). Scorpaenidae: Setarchinae.

Macrosmia Merritt, Sazonov & Shcherbachev 1983:550 [ref. 6672]. Fem. *Macrosmia phalacra* Merritt, Sazonov & Shcherbachev 1983:554. Type by original designation (also monotypic). Valid (Fahay & Markle 1984:274 [ref. 13653]). Macrouridae: Macrourinae.

Macrospinosa Mohan 1969:295 [ref. 3034]. Fem. *Bola cuja* Hamilton 1822:81. Type by original designation (also monotypic). Spelled *Macropinos* in main heading on p. 295; spelled *Macrospinosa* in abstract, figure caption and p. 296; former regarded as a typesetting error [but the possibility that both names are preoccupied should be investigated]. Date on cover is 20 June 1969; *B. cuja* placed in a new genus *Cantor* by Talwar, with date of 1970. Valid (Trewavas 1977:289 [ref. 4459], Jayaram 1981:328 [ref. 6497]). Sciaenidae.

Macrostoma Risso 1826:447 [ref. 3757]. Neut. *Scopelus angustidens* Risso 1820:267. Type by monotypy. *Notoscopelus* Günther 1864 is an unneeded replacement name, *Macrostoma* not preoccupied by *Macrostomus* Weidmann 1817 in Diptera. Myctophidae.

Macrostomias Brauer 1902:283 [ref. 631]. Masc. *Macrostomias longibarbatus* Brauer 1902:283. Type by monotypy. Synonym of *Stomias* Cuvier 1816 (Morrow 1973:133 [ref. 7175], Fink 1985:1 [ref. 5171], Fink & Fink 1986:500 [ref. 5176]); valid (Gibbs in Whitehead et al. 1984:338 [ref. 13675], Fujii in Masuda et al. 1984:49 [ref. 6441], Gibbs 1986:229 [ref. 5655], Paxton et al. 1989:206 [ref. 12442]). Stomiidae.

Macrotrema Regan 1912:390 [ref. 3645]. Neut. *Symbranchus caligans* Cantor 1850:1316. Type by monotypy. Correct spelling for genus of type species is *Synbranchus*. Valid (Rosen & Greenwood 1976:50 [ref. 7094], Kottelat 1989:16 [ref. 13605]). Synbranchidae.

Macrouroides Smith & Radcliffe in Radcliffe 1912:139 [ref. 3578]. Masc. *Macrouroides inflaticeps* Smith & Radcliffe in Radcliffe 1912:139. Type by original designation (also monotypic). Misspelled *Macruroides* in Zoological Record for 1912. Valid (Fahay & Markle 1984:274 [ref. 13653]). Macrouridae: Macrouroidinae.

Macrourus Bloch 1786:150 [ref. 465]. Masc. *Coryphaena rupestris* of Fabricius, Bloch, and of others. Type by monotypy. Misidentified type species, not *rupestris* Gunner; case should be referred to the ICZN. Jordan 1917:44 [ref. 2407] regards *Coryphaenodes berglax* Lacepède as type, to which Fabricius' and Bloch's misidentifications are assigned. Spelled *Macrurus* in early literature. Valid (Marshall 1973:296 [ref. 7194], Marshall 1973:581 [ref. 6965], Fahay & Markle 1984:274 [ref. 13653], Geistdoerfer in Whitehead et al. 1986:666 [ref. 13676]). Macrouridae: Macrourinae.

Macrozoarces Gill 1863:258 [ref. 1689]. Masc. *Blennius labrosus* Mitchill 1815:375. Type by monotypy. Valid (Anderson 1984:578 [ref. 13634]). Zoarcidae.

Macrura Fowler 1941:626 [ref. 6536]. Fem. *Clupea kelee* Cuvier 1829:320. Type by original designation. Available from this date if not from van Hasselt 1823; *Macrura* van Hasselt a species name according to Kottelat 1987:369-370 [ref. 5962], but not of other authors (see *Macrura* van Hasselt). Synonym of *Hilsa* Regan 1917 (Whitehead 1985:202 [ref. 5141]); would replace *Hilsa* if it dates to van Hasselt. Clupeidae.

Macrura van Hasselt 1823:329 [ref. 5105]. Fem. Van Hasselt text unclear if intended as a species or genus. Regarded by Kottelat (1987:370 [ref. 5962]) as a species name; but Fowler, Whitley [refs. 4709 and 4718] and others regard as a genus, taking precedence over *Hilsa* Regan 1917. Whitehead 1985:220, 222 [ref. 5141] credits the genus to Fowler 1941:626 and places in synonymy of *Hilsa* Regan 1917 and (in part) *Tenualosa* Fowler 1934. Case probably should be submitted to ICZN to conserve *Hilsa*. Clupeidae.

Macrurocyttus Fowler 1934:350 [ref. 1416]. Masc. *Macrurocyttus acanthopodus* Fowler 1934:351. Type by original designation (also monotypic). Macrurocyttidae.

Macruronus Günther 1873:103 [ref. 1999]. Masc. *Coryphaenoides novaezelandiae* Hector 1871:136. Type by original designation (also monotypic). Valid (Svetovidov 1973:301 [ref. 7169], Marshall 1973:299 [ref. 7194], Fahay & Markle 1984:267 [ref. 13653], Cohen 1986:325 [ref. 5646], Cohen 1984:263 [ref. 13646], Paxton et al. 1989:308 [ref. 12442]). Merlucciidae: Merlucciinae.

Macruroplus Bleeker 1874:369 [ref. 435]. Masc. *Macrurus serratus* Lowe 1843:91. Type by original designation (also monotypic). Misspelled *Macuroplus* by Jordan 1919:372 [ref. 4904]. Regarded by Iwamoto (1986:337 [ref. 5674]) as unidentifiable, type species a nomen nudum. Macrouridae.

Macrurrhynchus Ogilby 1896:136 [ref. 3270]. Masc. *Macrurrhynchus maroubrae* Ogilby 1896:137. Type by subsequent designation. Type designated by Ogilby 1910:55 [ref. 3288]. Synonym of *Plagiotremus* Gill 1865 (Smith-Vaniz 1976:108 [ref. 4144]). Blenniidae.

Macrurus see *Macrourus*. Macrouridae: Macrourinae.

Maculisudis Kotthaus 1967:81 [ref. 2668]. Fem. *Maculisudis longipinnis* Kotthaus 1967:82. Type by original designation (also monotypic). Paralepididae.

Macullochia Waite 1910:25 [ref. 4565]. Fem. *Richardsonia insignis* Castelnau 1872:112. Type by being a replacement name. Text somewhat unclear, but must be regarded as an unneeded replacement for *Richardsonia* Castelnau 1872, preoccupied by Steindachner 1866, but earlier replaced by *Paristiopterus* Bleeker 1876. Spelled *Maccullochia* by Waite 1911:217 and Jordan 1920:537 [ref. 4905]. Objective synonym of *Paristiopterus* Bleeker 1876. Synonym of *Paristiopterus* but with type as *Histiopterus labiosus* Günther (Hardy 1983:188 [ref. 5385]). Pentacerotidae.

Maculocoetus Whitley & Colefax 1938:287 [ref. 4736]. Masc. *Maculocoetus suttoni* Whitley & Colefax 1938:288. Type by original designation. Exocoetidae.

Madigania Whitley 1945:10 [ref. 4706]. Fem. *Therapon unicolor* Günther 1859:277. Type by original designation (also monotypic). Synonym of *Leiopotherapon* Fowler 1931 (Vari 1978:227 [ref. 4514]). Synonym of *Terapon* Cuvier 1816 (Mees & Kailola 1977:32 [ref. 5183]). Terapontidae.

Madrasia Nalbant 1963:364 [ref. 3140]. Fem. *Platacanthus maculatus* Day 1867:941. Type by being a replacement name. Replacement for *Jerdonia* Day 1871, preoccupied by Blanford 1861 in Mollusca. *Madrassia* is a misspelling. Objective synonym of *Enobarbichthys* Whitley 1931 [but see *Enobarbus*] (Jayaram 1981:178 [ref. 6497]). Cobitidae: Cobitinae.

Maena Cuvier 1829:186 [ref. 995]. *Sparus maena* Linnaeus 1758:278. Type by absolute tautonymy. Spelled *Mena* by Swainson 1839:170, 215 [ref. 4303]. Synonym of *Spicara* Rafinesque 1810 (Tortonese et al. 1973:417 [ref. 7202]). Centracanthidae.

Maenas Bleeker (ex Klein) 1876:273 [ref. 447]. *Sparus maena* Linnaeus 1758:278. Type by original designation (also monotypic). Objective synonym of *Maena* Cuvier 1829. Centracanthidae.

Maenas Klein 1776:360 [ref. 4918]. Not available, published in a work that does not conform to the principle of binominal nomenclature. In the synonymy of *Maena* Cuvier 1829. Centracanthidae.

Maenichthys Bleeker (ex Kaup) 1876:291 [ref. 447]. Masc. *Ditrema temmincki* Bleeker. Not available, manuscript name published as synonym of *Ditrema*, apparently never used as valid name before 1931. Embiotocidae.

Maenoides Richardson 1843:8 [ref. 6537]. Masc. *Maenioides? aurofrenatus* Richardson 1843:8, Pl. 5. Type by subsequent designation. Apparently not intended as a new genus and perhaps used as a vernacular (though latinized); Bleeker states, "I am unable...to assign this fish to a genus ... , and have not therefore attempted it." Type designated by Jordan 1923:197 [ref. 2421] but genus spelled *Maenioides*. Synonym of *Pentapodus* Quoy & Gaimard 1824. Nemipteridae.

Magnisudis Harry 1953:234 [ref. 2045]. Fem. *Magnisudis barysoma* Harry 1953:234. Type by original designation (also monotypic). Synonym of *Paralepis* Cuvier 1816 (some authors, including Post 1973:203 [ref. 7182]); valid (Post 1986:276 [ref. 5705], Post 1987:88 [ref. 6225]). Paralepididae.

Mahia McCann & McKnight 1980:53 [ref. 2922]. Fem. *Mahia matamua* McCann & McKnight 1980:53. Type by original designation (also monotypic). Valid (Fahay & Markle 1984:274 [ref. 13653], Nakamura in Nakamura et al. 1986:132 [ref. 14235], Iwamoto 1986:336 [ref. 5674]). Macrouridae: Macrourinae.

Mahidolia Smith 1932:255 [ref. 4050]. Fem. *Mahidolia normani* Smith & Koumans in Smith 1932:256. Type by monotypy. The name *Rictugobius* is mentioned in passing (p. 258), not available.

Valid (Yanagisawa 1978:309 [ref. 7028], Hayashi in Masuda et al. 1984:262 [ref. 6441] as *Mahidoria*, Hoese 1986:794 [ref. 5670], Birdsong et al. 1988:193 [ref. 7303], Kottelat 1989:19 [ref. 13605]); synonym of *Waitea* Jordan & Seale 1906 (Maugé 1986:386 [ref. 6218]). Gobiidae.

Maina Gistel 1848:IX [ref. 1822]. *Sparus choerorhynchus* Bloch & Schneider 1801:xii, 52. Type by being a replacement name. Unneeded replacement for *Lethrinus* Cuvier 1829, not preoccupied by *Lethrus* in Coleoptera; *Maina* itself preoccupied by Hodgson 1837 in Aves. Objective synonym of *Lethrinus* Cuvier 1829. Lethrinidae.

Makaira Lacepède 1802:688 [ref. 4929]. Fem. *Makaira nigricans* Lacepède 1802:688, 689. Type by monotypy. *Machaera*, *Macaira* and *Macaria* are misspellings or unjustified emendations. Valid (de Sylva 1973:478 [ref. 7210], Nakamura 1983:321 [ref. 5371], Collette et al. 1984:600 [ref. 11421], Nakamura in Masuda et al. 1984:223 [ref. 6441], Heemstra 1986:840 [ref. 5660]). Istiophoridae.

Malacanthus Cuvier 1829:264 [ref. 995]. Masc. *Malacanthus trachinus* Cuvier 1829:119 (= *Coryphaena plumieri* Bloch 1786:119). Type by monotypy; other mentioned species in synonymy. Valid (Dooley 1978:54 [ref. 5499], Araga in Masuda et al. 1984:152 [ref. 6441], Heemstra 1986:614 [ref. 5660], Paxton et al. 1989:566 [ref. 12442]). Malacanthidae: Malacanthinae.

Malacobagrus Bleeker 1862:11 [ref. 393]. Masc. *Pimelodus filamentosus* Lichtenstein 1819:60. Type by original designation (also monotypic). Synonym of *Brachyplatystoma* Bleeker 1862 (Mees 1974:120 [ref. 2969]). Pimelodidae.

Malacobatis Gracianov 1907:39 [ref. 1871]. Fem. *Raja mucosa* Pallas 1811:61. Type by monotypy. Original not seen. Rajidae.

Malacocanthus Tickell in Day 1888:791 [ref. 1082]. Masc. *Malacocanthus cocinicauda* Tickell in Day 1888:791. Myers 1951:26 [ref. 13464] mentioned this name as a forgotten one appearing in synonymy of *Pseudochromis* as quoted by Day from a Tickell manuscript; two species were mentioned, and Myers included both and designated *cocinicauda* as type. Myers' use apparently does not make names available from Tickell in Day 1888; Myers' stated, "Apparently a synonym of *Pseudochromis*, but perhaps available for a subgenus." Pseudochromidae: Pseudochrominae.

Malacocentrus Gill 1862:143 [ref. 1662]. Masc. *Xyrichthys taeniurus* Valenciennes in Cuvier & Valenciennes 1840:41. Type by original designation (also monotypic). Type designated by Gill's style of one species in parentheses in key. Correct spelling for genus of type species is *Xyrichtys*. Labridae.

Malacocephalus Günther 1862:396 [ref. 1969]. Masc. *Macrourus laevis* Lowe 1843:92. Type by monotypy. Valid (Marshall 1973:292 [ref. 7194], Marshall 1973:650 [ref. 6965], Iwamoto 1979:149 [ref. 2311], Fahay & Markle 1984:274 [ref. 13653], Geistdoerfer in Whitehead et al. 1986:667 [ref. 13676], Iwamoto 1986:337 [ref. 5674], Iwamoto & Arai 1987 [ref. 6779], Paxton et al. 1989:328 [ref. 12442]). Macrouridae: Macrourinae.

Malacocottus Bean 1890:42 [ref. 229]. Masc. *Malacocottus zonurus* Bean 1890:43. Type by monotypy. Misspelled *Malacottus* in Zoological Record for 1890. Valid (Nelson 1982:1473 [ref. 5470], Washington et al. 1984:444 [ref. 13660], Yabe in Masuda et al. 1984:330 [ref. 6441], Yabe 1985:122 [ref. 11522]). Psychrolutidae.

Malacoctenus Gill 1860:103 [ref. 1765]. Masc. *Clinus delalandii* Valenciennes in Cuvier & Valenciennes 1836:279. Type by monotypy. Valid (Springer 1958:438 [ref. 10210], Greenfield & Johnson 1981:24 [ref. 5580]). Labrisomidae.

Malacoglanis Myers & Weitzman 1966:281 [ref. 3136]. Masc. *Malacoglanis gelatinosus* Myers & Weitzman 1966:282. Type by original designation (also monotypic). Valid (Burgess 1989:325 [ref. 12860], Pinna 1989:25 [ref. 12630]). Trichomycteridae.

Malacoraja (subgenus of *Raja*) Stehmann 1970:151 [ref. 4202]. Fem. *Raja mollis* Bigelow & Schroeder 1950:388. Type by original designation. Type clearly designated originally as above on both pages 151 and 159, but in subsequent articles workers wrongly list *Raja spinacidermis* Barnard 1923 as type. As a subgenus of *Raja* Linnaeus 1758 (Stehmann 1973:65 [ref. 7168]). Valid (Stehmann 1977:89 [ref. 6982] and McEachran 1984:55 [ref. 5225] but with *spinacidermis* as type). Rajidae.

Malacorhina (subgenus of *Raja*) Garman 1877:203, 207 [ref. 1528]. Fem. *Raja (Malacorhina) mira* Garman 1877:207. Type by monotypy. Synonym of *Psammobatis* Günther 1870. Rajidae.

Malacosarcus Günther 1887:30 [ref. 2013]. Masc. *Scopelus macrostomus* Günther 1878:186. Type by original designation (also monotypic). Valid (Ebeling & Weed 1973:415 [ref. 6898]). Stephanoberycidae.

Malacosteus Ayres 1848:69 [ref. 154]. Masc. *Malacosteus niger* Ayres 1848:69. Type by monotypy. Appeared first in Ayres (Nov.) 1848 as above, than in Ayres (Sept.) 1849:53 [ref. 5864] (not investigated). Valid (Morrow 1964:543 [ref. 6958], Goodyear 1973:142 [ref. 7176], Kawaguchi & Moser 1984:171 [ref. 13642], Gibbs in Whitehead et al. 1984:369 [ref. 13675], Fujii in Masuda et al. 1984:53 [ref. 6441], Fink 1985:11 [ref. 5171], Goodyear & Gibbs 1986:235 [ref. 5658], Paxton et al. 1989:204 [ref. 12442]). Malacosteidae.

Malakichthys Döderlein in Steindachner & Döderlein 1883:240 [ref. 4246]. Masc. *Malakichthys griseus* Döderlein in Steindachner & Döderlein 1883:240. Type by monotypy. Spelled *Malacichthys* by Boulenger & Ogilvie-Grant in Zoological Record for 1883. Valid (Johnson 1984:464 [ref. 9681], Mochizuki in Masuda et al. 1984:125 [ref. 6441], Paxton et al. 1989:514 [ref. 12442]). Acropomatidae.

Malania Smith 1953:99 [ref. 4088]. Fem. *Malania anjouanae* Smith 1953:100. Type by original designation (also monotypic). Based on an abnormal specimen of *Latimeria*. In describing the genus Smith proposed an alternate name *Melanius* (p. 99) which technically was a name in synonymy and never made available. Synonym of *Latimeria* Smith 1939. Latimeriidae.

Malapterurus Lacepède 1803:90 [ref. 4930]. Masc. *Silurus electricus* Gmelin 1789:1354. Type designated by ICZN; on Official List (Opinion 93, Direction 56). *Malapterus* Jarocki 1822 and *Malapturus* Swainson 1839 both on Official Index as incorrect subsequent spellings (Direction 56). Unjustifiably emended to *Malopterurus* by Agassiz 1846; as *Malacopterurus* by Gill 1890:3591 [Century Dictionary, v. 4 - not investigated]. Valid (Gosse 1986:102 [ref. 6194], Burgess 1989:157 [ref. 12860]). Malapteruridae.

Malapterus Valenciennes in Cuvier & Valenciennes 1839:355 [ref. 1007]. Masc. *Malapterus reticulatus* Valenciennes in Cuvier & Valenciennes 1839:355. Type by monotypy. Not preoccupied by Jarocki 1822 (an incorrect subsequent spelling of *Malapterurus* Lacepède 1803 and on Official Index). *Hospilabrus* Whitley is an unneeded replacement. Unjustifiably emended to *Malacopterus* by

Günther 1862 [itself preoccupied by Audinet-Serville 1834 in Coleoptera]. Labridae.

Malayochela (subgenus of *Chela*) Banarescu 1968:59 [ref. 215]. Fem. *Eustira maassi* Weber & de Beaufort 1912:531. Type by original designation (also monotypic). Synonym of *Chela* Hamilton 1822 (Roberts 1989:31 [ref. 6439]). Cyprinidae.

Mallotus Cuvier 1829:305 [ref. 995]. Masc. *Clupea groenlandicus* Bloch 1794:Pl. 381 (= *Clupea villosa* Müller 1776:50, 245). Type by subsequent designation. Earliest subsequent designation not researched. Fowler 1974:110 [ref. 7180] and Jordan & Evermann 1896:520 [ref. 2443] list *villosa* as type; Cuvier includes *villosa* Gmelin (which apparently is *villosa* Müller) and *groenlandicus* Bloch. Jordan 1917:130 [ref. 2407] lists *groenlandicus* (*villosa* Gmelin) as type. Valid (Kljukanov & McAllister 1973:159 [ref. 7178], McAllister in Whitehead et al. 1984:399 [ref. 13675], Uyeno in Masuda et al. 1984:33 [ref. 6441]). Osmeridae.

Malpulutta Deraniyagala 1937:351 [ref. 1117]. *Malpulutta kretseri* Deraniyagala 1937:352. Type by monotypy. Belontiidae.

Malthe Cuvier 1816:311 [ref. 993]. *Lophius vespertilio* Linnaeus 1758:236. Type by subsequent designation. Type designated by Bleeker 1865:3 [ref. 416], also by Gill 1878:232 [ref. 12021]. Spelled *Malthea* and *Malthaea* by Valenciennes in Cuvier & Valenciennes 1837:440 [ref. 1006]. Synonym of *Ogcocephalus* Fischer 1813 (Bradbury 1980:234 [ref. 6538]). Ogcocephalidae.

Malthopsis Alcock 1891:26 [ref. 87]. Fem. *Malthopsis luteus* Alcock 1891:26. Type by monotypy. Valid (Okamura in Masuda et al. 1984:104 [ref. 6441], Bradbury 1986:372 [ref. 6291], Paxton et al. 1989:285 [ref. 12442]). Ogcocephalidae.

Malvoliophis Whitley 1934:154 [ref. 4681]. Masc. *Bascanichthys hemizona* Ogilby 1897:248. Type by original designation. Type (*hemizona*) regarded by Whitley as a possible synonym of *Ophichthys pinguis* Günther 1872. Valid (McCosker 1977:78 [ref. 6836], Paxton et al. 1989:117 [ref. 12442], McCosker et al. 1989:300 [ref. 13288]). Ophichthidae: Ophichthinae.

Manacopus Herre 1940:141 [ref. 5781]. Masc. *Gulaphallus falcifer* Manacop 1936:375. Type by being a replacement name. Replacement for *Acanthostethus* Herre 1939, preoccupied by Smith 1869 in Hymenoptera. Valid (White et al. 1984:360 [ref. 13655]); synonym of *Gulaphallus* Herre 1925 (Parenti 1989:274 [ref. 13486]). Phallostethidae.

Mancalias Gill 1878:227, 228 [ref. 1718]. Masc. *Ceratias uranoscopus* Murray in Thompson 1877:70. Type by original designation (also monotypic). Misspelled *Mancalius* by Beebe & Crane 1947:169 [ref. 6539]. Synonym of *Ceratias* Krøyer 1845 (Pietsch 1986:481 [ref. 5969]). Ceratiidae.

Mancopsetta Gill 1881:372 [ref. 5954]. Fem. *Lepidopsetta maculata* Günther 1880:18. Type by being a replacement name. Replacement for *Lepidopsetta* Günther 1880, preoccupied by Gill 1862 in fishes. Valid (Norman 1934:247 [ref. 6893], Ahlstrom et al. 1984:642 [ref. 13641]. Hensley 1986:860 [ref. 5669], Hensley 1986:941 [ref. 6326]). Achiropsettidae.

Mandelichthys (subgenus of *Cubiceps*) Nichols & Murphy 1944:247 [ref. 3189]. Masc. *Cubiceps carinatus* Nichols & Murphy 1944:245. Type by monotypy. Synonym of *Cubiceps* Lowe 1843 (Haedrich 1967:78 [ref. 5357]). Nomeidae.

Mandibularca Herre 1924:272 [ref. 2118]. Fem. *Mandibularca resinus* Herre 1924:273. Type by monotypy. Probably valid (Kornfield & Carpenter 1984:75 [ref. 5435]). Cyprinidae.

Manducus Goode & Bean 1896:514 [ref. 1848]. Masc. *Gonostoma maderense* Johnson 1890:458. Type by monotypy. *Paraphotichthys* Whitley 1931 is an unneeded replacement, not preoccupied by *Manduca* Huebner ca. 1806 in Lepidoptera. Synonym of *Diplophos* Günther 1873 (Witzell 1973:118 [ref. 7172]). Valid (Ahlstrom et al. 1984:185 [ref. 13643]). Gonostomatidae.

Mangarinus Herre 1943:94 [ref. 2136]. Masc. *Mangarinus waterousi* Herre 1943:94. Type by original designation (also monotypic). Valid (Akihito & Meguro 1977 [ref. 7043], Akihito in Masuda et al. 1984:262 [ref. 6441], Birdsong et al. 1988:193 [ref. 7303]). Gobiidae.

Mannarichthys Dawson 1977:606 [ref. 1066]. Masc. *Ichthyocampus pictus* Duncker 1915:95. Type by original designation (also monotypic). Second species questionably included in genus. Synonym of *Nannocampus* Günther 1870, but as a valid subgenus (Dawson 1986:456 [ref. 5650], Dawson 1985:148, 149 [ref. 6541]). Syngnathidae: Syngnathinae.

Mannichthys Schultz 1942:320 [ref. 3956]. Masc. *Mannichthys lucileae* Schultz 1942:321. Type by original designation (also monotypic). Synonym of *Enteromius* Cope 1867 (Karaman 1971:189 [ref. 2560]). Synonym of *Barbus* Cuvier & Cloquet 1816 (Lévêque & Daget 1984:219 [ref. 6186]). Cyprinidae.

Manta Bancroft 1829:454 [ref. 5051]. Fem. *Cephalopterus manta* Bancroft 1829:453. Type by monotypy (also by absolute tautonymy). *Manta americana* given on p. 454 if *Cephalopterus manta* proved not to be a *Cephalopterus*. Valid (Nakaya in Masuda et al. 1984:16 [ref. 6441], Compagno 1986:134 [ref. 5648], Cappetta 1987:176 [ref. 6348], Paxton et al. 1989:51 [ref. 12442]). Mobulidae.

Mapo (subgenus of *Gobius*) Smitt 1900:551 [ref. 4148]. *Gobius soporator* Valenciennes in Cuvier & Valenciennes 1837:56. Type by monotypy. Synonym of *Bathygobius* Bleeker 1878 (Miller 1973:515 [ref. 6888], Maugé 1986:360 [ref. 6218]). Gobiidae.

Mapolamia Whitley 1934:188 [ref. 4949]. Fem. *Carcharias melanopterus* Quoy & Gaimard 1824:194. Type by original designation. Objective synonym of *Carcharhinus* Blainville (Compagno 1973:23 [ref. 7163], Garrick 1982:19 [ref. 5454], Compagno 1984:449 [ref. 6846], Cappetta 1987:121 [ref. 6348], Compagno 1988:307 [ref. 13488]). Carcharhinidae.

Maravichromis Eccles & Trewavas 1989:203 [ref. 13547]. Masc. *Haplochromis ericotaenia* Regan 1922:704. Type by original designation. Cichlidae.

Marcgravia Jordan 1887:546 [ref. 2387]. Fem. *Batrachus cryptocentrus* Valenciennes in Cuvier & Valenciennes 1837:485. Type by original designation. *Marcgravichthys* Miranda-Ribeiro 1915 is an unneeded replacement. Synonym of *Amphichthys* Swainson 1839 (Greenfield & Greenfield 1973:562 [ref. 7128]). Batrachoididae.

Marcgravichthys Miranda-Ribeiro 1915:3 [ref. 3711]. Masc. *Batrachus cryptocentrus* Valenciennes in Cuvier & Valenciennes 1837:485. Type by being a replacement name. Appears on p. 3 of section titled Batrachoididae. Unneeded replacement for *Marcgravia* Jordan 1887; name used in botany but does not cause preoccupation in zoology. Synonym of *Amphichthys* Swainson 1839 (Greenfield & Greenfield 1973:562 [ref. 7128]). Batrachoididae.

Marcusenius Gill 1862:139 [ref. 1661]. Masc. *Mormyrus anguilloides* Linnaeus 1758:327. Type by subsequent designation. Gill (1862:139) described *M. brachistius* and included with it *anguilloides*, *tuckeri* and *zambanenje*, but in key on same page (in error) associated *cyprinoides* with *Marcusenius* as the implied type, with *anguilloides* in *Mormyrops*. Gill 1863:44 designated *anguilloides* as type. Treated as valid (Taverne 1972:165 [ref. 6367], but apparently with wrong type). Mormyridae.

Margariscus (subgenus of *Richardsonius*) Cockerell 1909:217 [ref. 868]. Masc. *Clinostomus margarita* Cope 1869:377. Type by original designation. Synonym of *Semotilus* Rafinesque 1820 (authors); valid (most current authors). Cyprinidae.

Margaritodon Smith 1956:15 [ref. 4104]. Masc. *Callyodon verweyi* Weber & de Beaufort 1940:15. Type by original designation. Misspelled *Margaritdon* on p. 4 (corrected in 1969 edition). Scaridae: Scarinae.

Margrethia Jespersen & Tåning 1919:222 [ref. 2350]. Fem. *Margrethia obtusirostra* Jespersen & Tåning 1919:222. Type by original designation (also monotypic). Valid (Witzell 1973:119 [ref. 7172], Weitzman 1974:472 [ref. 5174], Badcock in Whitehead et al. 1984:301 [ref. 13675], Ahlstrom et al. 1984:185 [ref. 13643], Fujii in Masuda et al. 1984:46 [ref. 6441], Schaefer et al. 1986:252 [ref. 5709], Paxton et al. 1989:186 [ref. 12442]). Gonostomatidae.

Marilyna Hardy 1982:2 [ref. 2038]. Fem. *Tetrodon pleurostictus* Günther 1872:653, 674. Type by original designation. Correct spelling for genus of type species is *Tetraodon*. Valid (see Su et al. 1986:112 [ref. 12582]). Tetraodontidae.

Marinus de Buen 1926:47 [ref. 5054]. As a "grupo" for 3 species of Clupeidae. Not available on basis of Art. 1b(6) [see de Buen's definition of "grupo" on p. 11]; see Appendix A. Clupeidae.

Markiana Eigenmann 1903:145 [ref. 1218]. Fem. *Tetragonopterus nigripinnis* Perugia 1891:643. Type by original designation (also monotypic). Valid (Géry 1977:455 [ref. 1597]). Characidae.

Marleyella (subgenus of *Poecilopsetta*) Fowler 1925:203 [ref. 5570]. Fem. *Poecilopsetta bicolorata* von Bonde 1922:14. Type by original designation (also monotypic). Valid (Norman 1934:396 [ref. 6893], Ahlstrom et al. 1984:643 [ref. 13641], Sakamoto 1984 [ref. 5273], Heemstra 1986:863 [ref. 5660]). Pleuronectidae: Poecilopsettinae.

Marlina Grey 1928:47 [ref. 6540]. Fem. *Tetrapturus mitsukurii* Jordan & Snyder 1901:303. Type by monotypy. There is no indication that this name was being proposed as a new genus, but it is an available generic name. Synonym of *Tetrapturus* Rafinesque 1810 (de Sylva 1973:480 [ref. 7210], Nakamura 1983:294 [ref. 5371]). Istiophoridae.

Marlina Hirasaka & Nakamura 1947:15 [ref. 2174]. Fem. *Marlina marlina* Jordan & Hill in Jordan & Evermann 1926:59. Type by monotypy (also by absolute tautonymy). Preoccupied by *Marlina* Grey 1928 in same family; not replaced. Synonym of *Makaira* Lacepède 1802 (de Sylva 1973:480 [ref. 7210], Nakamura 1983:321 [ref. 5371]). Istiophoridae.

Maroubra Whitley 1948:74 [ref. 4710]. Fem. *Maroubra perserrata* Whitley 1948:74. Type by original designation (also monotypic). Valid (Araga in Masuda et al. 1984:86 [ref. 6441], Dawson 1985:119 [ref. 6541], Paxton et al. 1989:424 [ref. 12442]). Syngnathidae: Syngnathinae.

Mars Jordan & Seale 1906:408 [ref. 2497]. Masc. *Mars strigilliceps* Jordan & Seale 1906:408. Type by original designation (also monotypic). Valid (Yanagisawa 1978:278 [ref. 7028]); synonym of *Cryptocentrus* Ehrenberg 1837 (Hoese, pers. comm.). Gobiidae.

Marsis Barnard 1927:682 [ref. 194]. Masc. *Sparus smaris* Linnaeus 1758:278. Type by being a replacement name. Replacement for *Smaris* Cuvier 1814, preoccupied by Latreille 1796 in Arachnida. Synonym of *Spicara* Rafinesque 1810 (Tortonese et al. 1973:417 [ref. 7202]). Centracanthidae.

Marubecula Whitley 1950:44 [ref. 4713]. Fem. *Prionotus horrens* Richardson 1843:79. Type by being a replacement name. Replacement for *Dinichthys* Kaup 1873, preoccupied by Newberry 1868 in fossil fishes. Triglidae: Triglinae.

Marukawichthys Sakamoto 1931:54 [ref. 3859]. Masc. *Marukawichthys ambulator* Sakamoto 1931:54. Type by original designation (also monotypic). Valid (Yabe 1981 [ref. 5547], Washington et al. 1984:443 [ref. 13660], Yabe in Masuda et al. 1984:323 [ref. 6441], Yabe 1985:122 [ref. 11522]). Ereuniidae.

Marzapanus Facciolà 1916:148 [ref. 5566]. Masc. *Coricus fasciatus* Cocco 1833. Type by monotypy. Correct spelling of genus of type species is *Corycus*. Synonym of *Lappanella* Jordan 1890 (Bauchot & Quignard 1973:433 [ref. 7204]). Labridae.

Mascalongus Jordan 1878:92 [ref. 2380]. Masc. *Esox nobilior* Thompson 1850:163, 173. Type by monotypy. Original not seen. Synonym of *Esox* Linnaeus 1758. Esocidae.

Massaria Gistel 1848:IX [ref. 1822]. Fem. *Cyclopterus liparis* Linnaeus 1766:414. Type by being a replacement name. Unneeded replacement for *Liparis* "Artedi", not preoccupied by use of same name in botany. Objective synonym of *Liparis* Scopoli 1777. Cyclopteridae: Liparinae.

Mastaccembelus Klein 1776:271 [ref. 4919]. Masc. Not available, published in a work that does not conform to the principle of binominal nomenclature. Not *Mastacembelus* of Gronow or Scopoli. In the synonymy of *Belone* Cuvier 1816. Belonidae.

Mastacembelus Gronow 1763:132 [ref. 1910]. Masc. Not available, published in a rejected work on Official Index (Opinion 261). Mastacembelidae.

Mastacembelus Scopoli (ex Gronow) 1777:458 [ref. 3990]. Masc. *Ophidium [sic] mastacembelus* Banks & Solander in Russell 1794:209. Type apparently by subsequent monotypy. Appeared first without species; addition of species not researched. Scopoli's spelling is *Mastocembelus* on Gronow's 1763 unavailable [*Mastacembelus*]; Scopoli's spelling regarded as in error (see Sufi 1956:106 [ref. 12498]; see also Wheeler 1956:91 [ref. 12499] for type species). Valid (Sufi 1956:105 [ref. 12498], Jayaram 1981:388 [ref. 6497], Travers 1984:143 [ref. 5147], Roberts 1986 [ref. 5802], Kottelat 1989:20 [ref. 13605], Roberts 1989:180 [ref. 6439]. Mastacembelidae.

Masticbarbus Tang 1942:158 [ref. 4335]. Masc. *Masticbarbus pentafasciatus* Tang 1942:158. Type by original designation (also monotypic). Spelled *Mastibarbus* by Fowler 1976:378 [ref. 9335]; spelle as above several times in original description. Cyprinidae.

Mastigophorus Kaup 1873:82 [ref. 2585]. Masc. A forgotten name needing more study. Three included species, *orientalis*, *macracanthus* and *chirophthalmus*. It predates *Dactyloptera* Jordan & Richardson 1908 but apparently is preoccupied by *Mastigophorus* Poey 1832 in Lepidoptera. Dactylopteridae.

Mastigopterus Smith & Radcliffe in Radcliffe 1913:158 [ref. 3579]. Masc. *Mastigopterus imperator* Smith & Radcliffe in Radcliffe 1913:159. Type by original designation (also monotypic). Valid (Cohen & Nielsen 1978:35 [ref. 881]). Ophidiidae: Neobythitinae.

Masturus Gill 1884:425 [ref. 1727]. Masc. *Orthagoriscus oxyuropterus* Bleeker 1873:151. Type by original designation (also monotypic). Synonym of *Mola* Koelreuter 1770 (Fraser-Brunner 1943:8 [ref. 1495]); valid (Tortonese 1973:649 [ref. 7192], Tyler 1980:391 [ref. 4477], Matsuura in Masuda et al. 1984:366 [ref.

6441], Tortonese in Whitehead et al. 1986:1348 [ref. 13677], Kan 1986 [ref. 6313], Heemstra 1986:907 [ref. 5660]). Molidae.

Mataeocephalus Berg 1898:43 [ref. 262]. Masc. *Coelocephalus acipenserinus* Gilbert & Cramer 1897:422. Type by being a replacement name. Replacement for *Coelocephalus* Gilbert & Cramer 1897, preoccupied by Clark 1860 in Coleoptera (not preoccupied by Agassiz 1844, name only). Misspelled *Metaeocephalus* in Zoological Record for 1899. Valid (Marshall 1973:618 [ref. 6965], Iwamoto 1979:144 [ref. 2311], Fahay & Markle 1984:274 [ref. 13653]). Macrouridae: Macrourinae.

Matsubaraea Taki 1953:201 [ref. 4314]. Fem. *Matsubaraea setouchiensis* Taki 1953:202. Type by monotypy. Valid (Iwamoto 1980 [ref. 6933], Nelson 1982:9 [ref. 5469], Okamura in Masuda et al. 1984:290 [ref. 6441]). Percophidae: Hemerocoetinae.

Matsya Day 1889:292 [ref. 1083]. Fem. *Acanthonotus argenteus* Tickell in Day 1888:807. Type by being a replacement name. Apparently a replacement for *Acanthonotus* Tickell (in Day) 1888, apparently preoccupied by Bloch 1797, Goldfus 1809 in Mammalia, and Gray 1831 in fishes [preoccupations not researched]. Synonym of *Mystacoleucus* Günther 1868 (Chu & Kottelat 1989:1 [ref. 12575], Roberts 1989:45 [ref. 6439]). Cyprinidae.

Maturacus Rafinesque 1815:88 [ref. 3584]. Not available, name only. Unplaced genera.

Maugeclupea Whitley 1932:332 [ref. 4674]. Fem. *Clupea (Pomolobus) bassensis* McCulloch 1911:16. Type by original designation (also monotypic). Misspelled *Mangeclupea* in Zoological Record for 1932. Synonym of *Sprattus* Girgensohn 1846 (Whitehead 1985:45 [ref. 5141], Whitehead et al. 1985:263 [ref. 6542]; see also Whitehead 1967:20 [ref. 6464]). Clupeidae.

Maulichthys Rofen 1963:2 [ref. 3794]. Masc. *Paralepis harryi* Maul 1954:54. Type by monotypy. Synonym of *Paralepis* Cuvier 1816 (Post 1973:203 [ref. 7182]). Valid (Okiyama 1984:207 [ref. 13644]). Paralepididae.

Mauligobius Miller 1984:384 [ref. 6338]. Masc. *Gobius maderensis* Valenciennes 1837:41. Type by original designation. Not available from Miller 1981:6, 8 [ref. 6219] (after 1930 without type designation, Art. 13b). Can date to Miller 1984 as given above. Valid (Maugé 1986:375 [ref. 6218], Miller in Whitehead et al. 1986:1054 [ref. 13677], Birdsong et al. 1988:190 [ref. 7303]). Gobiidae.

Maulisia Parr 1960:81 [ref. 3384]. Fem. *Maulisia mauli* Parr 1960:82. Type by original designation (also monotypic). Valid (Krefft 1973:96 [ref. 7166], Matsui & Rosenblatt 1979 [ref. 7024], Quéro et al. in Whitehead et al. 1984:260 [ref. 13675], Matsui & Rosenblatt 1986:224 [ref. 5688], Sazonov 1986 [ref. 6003], Paxton et al. 1989:212 [ref. 12442]). Platytroctidae.

Maurolicus Cocco 1838:192, 193 [32] [ref. 865]. Masc. *Maurolicus amethystinopunctatus* Cocco 1838:193 [33]. Type by monotypy. On pages 32-33 of separate. Valid (Witzell 1973:119 [ref. 7172], 1974:472 [ref. 5174], Badcock in Whitehead et al. 1984:311 [ref. 13675], Ahlstrom et al. 1984:185 [ref. 13643], Fujii in Masuda et al. 1984:47 [ref. 6441], Weitzman 1986:254 [ref. 6287], Paxton et al. 1989:192 [ref. 12442]). Sternoptychidae: Maurolicinae.

Maxillicosta Whitley 1935:246 [ref. 4683]. Fem. *Maxillicosta scabriceps* Whitley 1935:246. Type by original designation (also monotypic). Valid (Eschmeyer & Poss 1976 [ref. 5468], Paxton et al. 1989:443 [ref. 12442]). Scorpaenidae: Neosebastinae.

Maxillingua (subgenus of *Exoglossum*) Rafinesque 1818:420, 421 [ref. 3588]. Fem. *Cyprinus maxillingua* Lesueur 1817:85. Type by absolute tautonymy. Proposed as a possible section [subgenus] of *Exoglossum*, and from text taxon included more than one species. Objective junior synonym of *Exoglossum* Rafinesque 1818. Cyprinidae.

Mayerina Silvester 1915:214 [ref. 4027]. Fem. *Mayerina mayeri* Silvester 1915:214. Type by original designation (also monotypic). Synonym of *Moringua* Gray 1831 (Smith 1989:65 [ref. 13285]). Moringuidae.

Maylandia (subgenus of *Pseudotropheus*) Meyer & Foerster 1984:112 [ref. 6645]. Fem. *Pseudotropheus (Maylandia) greshakei* Meyer & Foerster 1984:108. Type by original designation. Cichlidae.

Maynea Cunningham 1871:471 [ref. 992]. Fem. *Maynea patagonica* Cunningham 1871:472. Type by original designation (also monotypic). Valid (Gosztonyi 1977:220 [ref. 6103], Anderson 1984:578 [ref. 13634], Toyoshima 1985:143 [ref. 5722]). Zoarcidae.

Mayoa Day 1870:553 [ref. 1077]. Fem. *Mayoa modesta* Day 1870:553. Type by monotypy. Synonym of *Garra* Hamilton 1822 (Karaman 1971:232 [ref. 2560], Lévêque & Daget 1984:301 [ref. 6186]). Cyprinidae.

Mccoskerichthys Rosenblatt & Stephens 1978:2 [ref. 3810]. Masc. *Mccoskerichthys sandae* Rosenblatt & Stephens 1978:5. Type by original designation (also monotypic). Valid (Acero P. 1984 [ref. 5534]). Chaenopsidae.

Meadia Böhlke 1951:6 [ref. 591]. Fem. *Dysomma abyssale* Kamohara 1938:12. Type by original designation (also monotypic). Valid (Robins & Robins 1976:251 [ref. 3784], Asano in Masuda et al. 1984:27 [ref. 6441], Robins & Robins 1989:239 [ref. 13287]). Synaphobranchidae: Ilyophinae.

Mearnsella Seale & Bean 1907:231 [ref. 4002]. Fem. *Mearnsella alestes* Seale & Bean 1907:231. Type by original designation (also monotypic). Cyprinidae.

Mebarus (subgenus of *Sebastes*) Matsubara 1943:194 [ref. 2905]. Masc. *Sebastes inermis* Cuvier in Cuvier & Valenciennes 1829:346. Type by original designation. Synonym of *Sebastes* Cuvier 1829, but as a valid subgenus (Chen 1985 [ref. 6543]). Scorpaenidae: Sebastinae.

Mecaenichthys Whitley 1929:218 [ref. 4666]. Masc. *Heliastes immaculatus* Ogilby 1885:446. Type by original designation (also monotypic). Pomacentridae.

Meda Girard 1856:191 [ref. 1810]. Fem. *Meda fulgida* Girard 1856:191. Type by monotypy. Valid (Miller & Hubbs 1960:31 [ref. 11934]). Cyprinidae.

Medemichthys Dahl 1961:490 [ref. 1027]. Masc. *Medemichthys guayaberensis* Dahl 1961:491. Type by monotypy. Synonym of *Heptapterus* Bleeker 1858 (Mees 1974:177 [ref. 2969], but see Buckup 1988 [ref. 6635]). Pimelodidae.

Medialuna Jordan & Fesler 1893:536 [ref. 2455]. Fem. *Scorpis californiensis* Steindachner 1875:47. Type by original designation (also monotypic). Valid (Chirichigno-F. 1987 [ref. 12856]). Kyphosidae: Scorpidinae.

Medicelinus (subgenus of *Icelinus*) Bolin 1936:156 [ref. 506]. Masc. *Icelinus burchami* Evermann & Goldsborough 1907:221, 223, 297. Type by original designation (also monotypic). Synonym of *Icelinus* Jordan 1885 (Bolin 1944:29 [ref. 6379]). Cottidae.

Medipellona Jordan & Seale 1926:417 [ref. 2500]. Fem. *Pellona bleekeriana* Poey 1867:242. Type by original designation (also monotypic). Synonym of *Chirocentrodon* Günther 1868

(Whitehead 1985:286 [ref. 5141]). Clupeidae.

Medusablennius Springer 1966:56 [ref. 4177]. Masc. *Medusablennius chani* Springer 1966:56. Type by original designation (also monotypic). Valid (Smith-Vaniz & Springer 1971:28 [ref. 4145]). Blenniidae.

Megabatus Rafinesque 1815:93 [ref. 3584]. Masc. Not available, name only; for a ray. Torpediniformes.

Megachasma Taylor, Compagno & Struhsaker 1983:96 [ref. 5428]. Fem. *Megachasma pelagios* Taylor, Compagno & Struhsaker 1983:96. Type by original designation (also monotypic). Valid (Compagno 1984:227 [ref. 6474], Maisey 1985 [ref. 6793] in Cetorhinidae). Megachasmidae.

Megaderus Rafinesque 1815:220 [ref. 3584]. Appears in "Additions et Corrections" on p. 220, referring back to p. 93. An available but unneeded replacement name for *Echidna* Forster 1777. Objective synonym of *Echidna* Forster 1777 (Böhlke et al. 1989:130 [ref. 13286]). Muraenidae: Muraeninae.

Megagobio Kessler 1876:16 [ref. 2595]. Masc. *Megagobio nasutus* Kessler 1876:16. Type by monotypy. Original not seen. Synonym of *Rhinogobio* Bleeker 1870 (Banarescu & Nalbant 1973:166 [ref. 173], Lu, Luo & Chen 1977:507 [ref. 13495], Chen & Li in Chu & Chen 1989:107 [ref. 13584]). Cyprinidae.

Megalamphodus Eigenmann 1915:49 [ref. 1231]. Masc. *Megalamphodus megalopterus* Eigenmann 1915:50. Type by original designation. Valid (Géry 1977:583 [ref. 1597]). Characidae.

Megalancistrus Isbrücker 1980:52 [ref. 2303]. Masc. *Chaetostomus gigas* Boulenger 1895:526. Type by original designation. Valid (Heitmans et al. 1983 [ref. 5278], Burgess 1989:434 [ref. 12860]). Loricariidae.

Megalaspis Bleeker 1851:342, 352 [ref. 326]. Fem. *Scomber rottleri* Bloch 1793:88. Type by monotypy. Valid (Smith-Vaniz 1984:524 [ref. 13664], Gushiken in Masuda et al. 1984:155 [ref. 6441], Smith-Vaniz 1986:653 [ref. 5718, Gushiken 1988:443 [ref. 6697], Paxton et al. 1989:581 [ref. 12442]). Carangidae.

Megalepis Bianconi 1857:270 [ref. 295]. Fem. *Megalepis alessandrini* Bianconi 1857:ca 270. Type by monotypy. Original not seen. Apparently as Rec. Acad. Sci. Bologna, 1857:100 [see ref. 295]. Synonym of *Upeneus* Cuvier 1829. Mullidae.

Megalepocephalus (subgenus of *Asquamiceps*) Fowler 1934:248 [ref. 1416]. Masc. *Asquamiceps longmani* Fowler 1934:248. Type by original designation (also monotypic). Synonym of *Asquamiceps* Zugmayer 1911 (Markle 1980:45 [ref. 6077]). Alepocephalidae.

Megalobrama Dybowski 1872:212 [ref. 1170]. Fem. *Megalobrama skolkovii* Dybowski 1872:213. Type by subsequent designation. Also included was a variety *M. carinatus* Dybowski, which is regarded as a second included species. Type perhaps first designated by Jordan 1919:364 [ref. 4904], but misspelled *akolkovii*. Valid (Yih & Wu 1964:93 [ref. 13499], Chen in Chu & Chen 1989:87 [ref. 13584]). Cyprinidae.

Megalobrycon Günther 1870:423 [ref. 5780]. Masc. *Megalobrycon cephalus* Günther 1870:423. Type by monotypy. Mention (Géry 1977:335 [ref. 1597]); synonym of *Brycon* Müller & Troschel 1844 (Howes 1982:2 [ref. 14201]). Characidae.

Megalocottus Gill 1861:166 [ref. 1775]. Masc. *Cottus platycephalus* Pallas 1811:135. Type by monotypy. Valid (Neyelov 1979:115, 129 [ref. 3152], Washington et al. 1984:443 [ref. 13660]). Cottidae.

Megalodoras Eigenmann 1925:304, 306 [ref. 1244]. Masc. *Megalodoras irwini* Eigenmann 1925:307. Type by original designation. Valid (Burgess 1989:223 [ref. 12860]). Doradidae.

Megalomycter Myers & Freihofer 1966:195 [ref. 3088]. Masc. *Megalomycter teevani* Myers & Freihofer 1966:195. Type by original designation (also monotypic). Megalomycteridae.

Megalonema Eigenmann 1912:130, 150 [ref. 1227]. Neut. *Megalonema platycephalum* Eigenmann 1912:150. Type by original designation (also monotypic). Genus and species first appeared as name only in Eigenmann 1910:383 [ref. 1224], not available. Valid (Stewart 1986:669 [ref. 5211], Burgess 1989:275 [ref. 12860]). Pimelodidae.

Megalonibea Chu, Lo & Wu 1963:34, 89 [ref. 833]. Fem. *Megalonibea fusca* Chu, Lo & Wu 1963:35, 90. Type by original designation (also monotypic). Valid (Trewavas 1977:359 [ref. 4459], Okamura in Masuda et al. 1984:162 [ref. 6441]). Sciaenidae.

Megalopharynx Brauer in Chun 1900:521 [ref. 629]. Masc. *Macropharynx longicaudatus* Brauer 1902:291. Type apparently by subsequent monotypy [but not researched]. Original not seen; apparently appeared first as above, without species; name changed to *Macropharynx* by Brauer 1902:290 [ref. 631] and 1906:134 [ref. 632]. Synonym of *Eurypharynx* Vaillant 1882 (Böhlke 1966:610 [ref. 5256], Bauchot 1973:218 [ref. 7184], Bertelsen et al. 1989:649 [ref. 13293]). Eurypharyngidae.

Megalops Lacepède 1803:289 [ref. 4930]. Masc. *Megalops filamentosus* Lacepède 1803:289, 290. Type by monotypy. Spelled *Megalopus* by Minding 1832:124 [ref. 3022]. Valid (Daget 1984:32 [ref. 6170], Uyeno in Masuda et al. 1984:21 [ref. 6441], Smith 1986:156 [ref. 5712], Kottelat 1989:4 [ref. 13605], Paxton et al. 1989:104 [ref. 12442], Smith 1989:968 [ref. 13285]). Megalopidae.

Megaperca Hilgendorf 1878:155 [ref. 2166]. Fem. *Megaperca ischinagi* Hilgendorf 1878:156. Type by monotypy. Synonym of *Stereolepis* Ayres 1859. Polyprionidae.

Megaphalus Rafinesque 1815:86 [ref. 3584]. Masc. *Gobiesox cephalus* Lacepède 1800:595. Type by being a replacement name. As "*Megaphalus* R. [Rafinesque] *Gobiesox* Lac. [Lacepède]." An available replacement name (unneeded) for *Gobiesox* Lacepède 1800. Objective synonym of *Gobiesox* Lacepède 1800 (Briggs 1955:87 [ref. 637]). Gobiesocidae: Gobiesocinae.

Megapharynx Legendre 1942:228 [ref. 2740]. Fem. *Moxostoma valenciennesi* not of Jordan 1885:73 (= *Megapharynx hubbsi* Legendre 1952). Type by original designation (also monotypic). Evidently based on a misidentified type species (see Robins & Raney 1956:5 [ref. 12222]); specimens renamed *M. hubbsi*. Synonym of *Moxostoma* Rafinesque 1820 (Robins & Raney 1956:5 [ref. 12222]).

Megaprotodon Guichenot 1848:12 [ref. 1938]. Masc. *Chaetodon bifascialis* Cuvier 1829:190 (= *Chaetodon trifascialis* Quoy & Gaimard 1825:379). Type by subsequent designation. Two included species; earliest subsequent designation not researched. Synonym of *Chaetodon* Linnaeus 1758, but as a valid subgenus (Burgess 1978:415 [ref. 700]); valid (Maugé & Bauchot 1984:464 [ref. 6614]). Chaetodontidae.

Megarasbora (subgenus of *Rasbora*) Günther 1868:193, 198 [ref. 1990]. Fem. *Cyprinus elanga* Hamilton 1822:281, 386. Type by monotypy. Described in key (p. 193) as section or subgenus of *Rasbora* for one species on p. 198. Synonym of *Rasbora* Bleeker 1859, but as a valid subgenus (Jayaram 1981:83 [ref. 6497]). Cyprinidae.

Megarhinus Rafinesque 1820:251 [ref. 5088]. Masc. *Megarhinus paradoxus* Rafinesque 1820:251. Type by monotypy. Also in Rafinesque 1820:83 (Dec.) [ref. 3592]. *Megarhinus paradoxus* mentioned in passing as "his" name for *Platirostra edentula* Lesueur 1818:227. Synonym of *Polyodon* Lacepède 1797. Polyodontidae.

Megastomatobus (subgenus of *Amblodon*) Fowler 1913:45 [ref. 1388]. Masc. *Sclerognathus cyprinella* Valenciennes in Cuvier & Valenciennes 1844:477. Type by original designation (also monotypic). Misspelled *Macrostomatobus* by Hubbs 1926:19 [ref. 12022]. Synonym of *Ictiobus* Rafinesque 1820. Catostomidae.

Megupsilon Miller & Walters 1972:2 [ref. 3020]. Neut. *Megupsilon aporus* Miller & Walters 1972:5. Type by original designation (also monotypic). Valid (Parenti 1981:531 [ref. 7066]). Cyprinodontidae: Cyprinodontinae.

Meiacanthus Norman 1943:805 [ref. 3228]. Masc. *Petroscirtes oualensis* Günther 1880:35. Type by original designation. Species originally misspelled *oualanensis*, corrected by Smith-Vaniz to *Ovalanensis*. Valid (Smith-Vaniz 1976:73 [ref. 4144], Yoshino in Masuda et al. 1984:296 [ref. 6441], Smith-Vaniz 1987:5 [ref. 6404]). Blenniidae.

Mekongina Fowler 1937:200 [ref. 1425]. Fem. *Mekongina erythrospila* Fowler 1937:200. Type by original designation (also monotypic). Valid (Kottelat 1985:264 [ref. 11441], Kottelat 1989:8 [ref. 13605]). Cyprinidae.

Meladerma (subgenus of *Elacate*) Swainson 1839:176, 243 [ref. 4303]. Neut. *Meladerma nigerrima* Swainson 1839:243. Type by monotypy. Synonym of *Rachycentron* Kaup 1826 (Monod 1973:371 [ref. 7193]). Rachycentridae.

Melambaphes Günther 1863:115 [ref. 1972]. Masc. *Glyphidodon nigroris* of Günther (not of Cuvier) 1883. Type by monotypy. Apparently based on a misidentified type species, not *Glyphidodon nigroris* Cuvier in Cuvier & Valenciennes, but is the species later named *Melambaphes guentheri* Gill 1863. Correct spelling for genus of type species is *Glyphisodon*. In the synonymy of *Girellichthys* Klunzinger 1872. Kyphosidae: Girellinae.

Melamphaes Günther 1864:433 [ref. 1974]. *Metopias typhlops* Lowe 1843:90. Type by being a replacement name. Replacement for *Metopias* Lowe 1843, preoccupied by Gory 1832 [not researched]. Valid (Maul 1973:343 [ref. 7171], Ebeling & Weed 1973:451 [ref. 6898], Fujii in Masuda et al. 1984:111 [ref. 6441], Maul in Whitehead et al. 1986:757 [ref. 13676], Ebeling 1986:427 [ref. 5651], Paxton et al. 1989:371 [ref. 12442]). Melamphaidae.

Melanictis Rafinesque 1815:92 [ref. 3584]. Masc. Not available, name only; near *Sternoptyx*. Sternoptychidae: Sternoptychinae.

Melaniris Meek 1902:117 [ref. 2957]. Fem. *Melaniris balsanus* Meek 1902:117. Type by original designation (also monotypic). Valid (Bussing 1978 [ref. 6973]); synonym of *Atherinella* Steindachner 1875 (Chernoff 1986:240 [ref. 5847]). Atherinidae: Menidiinae.

Melanobranchus Regan 1903:459 (footnote) [ref. 3617]. Masc. *Bathygadus melanobranchus* Vaillant 1888:206. Type by monotypy. Synonym of *Bathygadus* Günther 1878 (Marshall 1973:288 [ref. 7194], Marshall & Iwamoto 1973:525 [ref. 6963]). Macrouridae: Bathygadinae.

Melanocetus Günther 1864:302 [ref. 5750]. Masc. *Melanocetus johnsonii* Günther 1864:302. Type by monotypy. Also as Günther 1865:333 [ref. 1977]. Valid (Maul 1973:667 [ref. 7171], Pietsch & Van Duzer 1980:70 [ref. 5333], Bertelsen & Pietsch 1983:81 [ref. 5335], Amaoka in Masuda et al. 1984:108 [ref. 6441], Bertelsen in Whitehead et al. 1986:1376 [ref. 13677], Pietsch 1986:375 [ref. 5704], Paxton et al. 1989:287 [ref. 12442]). Melanocetidae.

Melanochromis Trewavas 1935:(67) 77 [ref. 4451]. Masc. *Melanochromis melanopterus* Trewavas 1935:79. Type by original designation. Valid (Ribbink et al. 1983:200 [ref. 13555]); status somewhat uncertain, similar to *Pseudotropheus* Regan 1922 (see Trewavas 1984:97 [ref. 5303]). Cichlidae.

Melanodactylus Bleeker 1858:60, 65 [ref. 365]. Masc. *Arius acutivelis* Valenciennes in Cuvier & Valenciennes 1840:85. Type by subsequent designation. Type designated by Bleeker 1862:9 [ref. 393] and Bleeker 1863:95 [ref. 401]. Type not *Pimelodus nigrodigitatus* Lacepède since original description mentioned only *acutivelis* and *cous* by name. Bagridae.

Melanogenes Bleeker 1863:35 [ref. 395]. Masc. *Melanogenes macrocephalus* Bleeker 1863:36. Type by subsequent designation. Two included species, first subsequent designation not researched. Cichlidae.

Melanogloea Barnard 1941:10 [ref. 198]. Fem. *Melanogloea ventralis* Branard 1941:10. Type by monotypy. Originally typset *Mesogloea* on p. 10, *Melanogloea* on plate and as pasted-over correction on p. 10. Synonym of *Guentherus* Osório 1917 (Bussing & López S. 1977:181 [ref. 7001]). Ateleopodidae.

Melanogrammus Gill 1862:280 [ref. 1666]. Masc. *Gadus aeglefinus* Linnaeus 1758:251. Type by original designation (also monotypic). Valid (Svetovidov 1973:306 [ref. 7169], Fahay & Markle 1984:267 [ref. 13653], Svetovidov in Whitehead et al. 1986:687 [ref. 13676]). Gadidae.

Melanolagus Kobyliansky 1986:45 [ref. 6002]. Masc. *Bathylagus bericoides* Borodin 1929:110. Type by original designation (also monotypic). Bathylagidae.

Melanonectes (subgenus of *Photonectes*) Regan & Trewavas 1930:119, 120 [ref. 3681]. Masc. *Photonectes dinema* Regan & Trewavas 1930:120. Type by subsequent designation. Type designated in Zoological Record for 1930 (Pisces):48; also designated by Fowler 1936:1186 [ref. 6546]. Synonym of *Photonectes* Günther 1887, but as a valid subgenus (Morrow in Morrow & Gibbs 1964:489 [ref. 6962]). Melanostomiidae.

Melanonosoma Gilchrist 1902:106 [ref. 1644]. Neut. *Melanonosoma acutecaudatum* Gilchrist 1902:106. Type by monotypy. Synonym of *Melanonus* Günther 1878 (Cohen 1986:328 [ref. 5646] but misspelled *Melanosoma*). Melanonidae.

Melanonus Günther 1878:19 [ref. 2010]. Masc. *Melanonus gracilis* Günther 1878:19. Type by monotypy. Valid (Cohen 1973:327 [ref. 6589], Cohen 1986:328 [ref. 5646], Cohen 1984:263 [ref. 13646], Fahay & Markle 1984:266 [ref. 13653], Cohen in Whitehead et al. 1986:724 [ref. 13676], Paxton et al. 1989:304 [ref. 12442]). Melanonidae.

Melanorhinus Metzelaar 1919:38 [ref. 2982]. Masc. *Melanorhinus boekei* Metzelaar 1919:38. Type by monotypy. Also appeared as new in Metzelaar 1922:141 [ref. 5741]. Valid (Chernoff 1986:245 [ref. 5847]). Atherinidae: Menidiinae.

Melanostigma Günther 1881:20 [ref. 2012]. Neut. *Melanostigma gelatinosum* Günther 1881:21. Type by monotypy. Valid (Andriashev 1973:547 [ref. 7214], Anderson 1984:578 [ref. 13634], Toyoshima in Masuda et al. 1984:309 [ref. 6441], Andriashev in Whitehead et al. 1986:1148 [ref. 13677], Anderson 1986:343 [ref. 5633], Anderson 1988:61 [ref. 7304], Paxton et al. 1989:322 [ref. 12442]). Zoarcidae.

Melanostoma Döderlein in Steindachner & Döderlein 1883:5 [ref. 4247]. Neut. *Melanostoma japonicum* Döderlein in Steindachner & Döderlein 1883:5. Type by monotypy. Preoccupied by Schiner 1860 in Diptera and Stål 1872 in Hemiptera, replaced by *Synagrops* Günther 1887. Objective synonym of *Synagrops* Günther 1887. Acropomatidae.

Melanostomias Brauer 1902:284 [ref. 631]. Masc. *Melanostomias valdiviae* Brauer 1902:225. Type by subsequent designation. Type apparently designated first by Jordan 1920:497 [ref. 4905]; not *M. melanops*. Valid (Gibbs in Morrow & Gibbs 1964:354 [ref. 6962], Morrow 1973:134 [ref. 7175], Kawaguchi & Moser 1984:171 [ref. 13642], Gibbs in Whitehead et al. 1984:357 [ref. 13675], Fujii in Masuda et al. 1984:51 [ref. 6441], Fink 1985:11 [ref. 5171], Gibbs 1986:241 [ref. 5655], Paxton et al. 1989:200 [ref. 12442]). Melanostomiidae.

Melanotaenia Gill 1862:280 [ref. 1666]. Fem. *Atherina nigrans* Richardson 1843:180. Type by original designation (also monotypic). Valid (Allen & Cross 1982:44 [ref. 6251], White et al. 1984:360 [ref. 13655], Allen 1985:58 [ref. 6245], Paxton et al. 1989:349 [ref. 12442]). Atherinidae: Melanotaeniinae.

Melantha Gistel 1848:109 [ref. 1822]. Fem. *Sciaena nigra* Forsskål 1775:47 (= *Sciaena umbra* Linnaeus 1758:289). Type by being a replacement name. Apparently an unneeded replacement for *Corvina* Cuvier 1829. Synonym of *Sciaena* Linnaeus 1758 (Trewavas 1973:396 [ref. 7201]). Sciaenidae.

Melanura Agassiz 1853:135 [ref. 67]. Fem. Appeared in 1853 without species and with brief characterization. Jordan & Evermann 1896:624 [ref. 2443] list *Melanura annulata* Agassiz 1854 (sic 1853):135 in synonymy of *pygmaea* but *annulata* not mentioned on p. 135; Jordan 1919:252 [ref. 2410] wrongly says type is *Exoglossum annulatum* Rafinesque and that it was designated on p. 217 of same journal [as 1853 paper]. Included species (as *limi* and *pygmaea*) may date to ref. 2443. Synonym of *Umbra* Kramer 1777. Umbridae.

Melanychthys Temminck & Schlegel 1844:75 [ref. 4372]. Masc. *Crenidens melanichthys* Richardson 1846:243. Original description without species. Richardson 1846:243 [ref. 3742] described *Crenidens melanichthys* but did not recognize *Melanychthys*. In a footnore under *Melanichthes*, Temminck & Schlegel 1850:317 [ref. 4375] list Richardson's species, and this can constitute type by subsequent monotypy. Often spelled *Melanichthys*, but original was *Melanychthys*. Synonym of *Girella* Gray 1835. Kyphosidae: Girellinae.

Melapedalion Fowler 1934:326 [ref. 1416]. Neut. *Oxyporhamphus brevis* Seale 1910:495. Type by original designation (also monotypic). Valid (Parin et al. 1980:97 [ref. 6895], Collette et al. 1984:337 [ref. 11422], Kottelat 1989:16 [ref. 13605]). Hemiramphidae.

Melbanella Whitley 1937:132 [ref. 4689]. Fem. *Micropus mulleri* Steindachner 1879:7. Type by original designation (also monotypic). Sometimes placed in the Carangidae; placement in Latrididae follows Smith-Vaniz (pers. comm., Nov. 1989). Latridae.

Meletta Valenciennes in Cuvier & Valenciennes 1847:366 [ref. 1012]. Fem. *Meletta vulgaris* Valenciennes in Cuvier & Valenciennes 1847:366. Type by subsequent designation. Type designated by Gill 1861:36 [ref. 1767]. Synonym of *Sprattus* Girgensohn 1846 (Svetovidov 1973:104 [ref. 7169], Whitehead 1985:45 [ref. 5141], Whitehead et al. 1985:263 [ref. 6542]; see also Whitehead 1967:20 [ref. 6464]). Clupeidae.

Melichthys (subgenus of *Balistes*) Swainson 1839:194, 325 [ref. 4303]. Masc. *Balistes ringens* Osbeck (not of Linnaeus) 1765 (= *Balistes niger* Bloch 1786:27). Type by subsequent designation. Type designated by Bleeker 1866:10 [ref. 417] as "*Balistes ringens* Osb." Possibly based on a misidentified type species. *Melanichthys* Günther 1870:212, 227 [ref. 1995] (not of Temminck & Schlegel) apparently is an unjustified emendation. Valid (Matsuura 1980:40 [ref. 6943], Tyler 1980:120 [ref. 4477], Arai 1983:199 [ref. 14249], Matsuura in Masuda et al. 1984:358 [ref. 6441], Smith & Heemstra 1986:879 [ref. 5714]). Balistidae.

Melletes Bean 1880:354 [ref. 222]. Masc. *Melletes papilio* Bean 1880:354. Type by original designation (also monotypic). Synonym of *Hemilepidotus* Cuvier 1829, but as a valid subgenus (Peden 1978:39 [ref. 5530]). Cottidae.

Melloina Amaral Campos 1946:219 [ref. 107]. Fem. *Melloina tambaqui* Amaral Campos 1946:220. Type by original designation (also monotypic). Synonym of *Colossoma* Eigenmann & Kennedy 1903 (Géry 1976:50 [ref. 14199]). Characidae: Serrasalminae.

Melodichthys Nielsen & Cohen 1986:381 [ref. 6039]. Masc. *Melodichthys hadrocephalus* Nielsen & Cohen 1986:383. Type by original designation. Bythitidae: Brosmophycinae.

Memarchus Kaup in Duméril 1856:201 [ref. 1154]. Masc. *Gymnotus albifrons* Linnaeus 1766:428. Not available, name only without description or indication; authorship of type inferred. Objective synonym of *Sternarchus* Bloch & Schneider 1801, synonym of *Apteronotus* Lacepède 1800. Gymnotidae: Apteronotinae.

Membracidichthys Whitley 1933:102 [ref. 4677]. Masc. *Coccotropus [sic] obbesi* Weber 1913:503. Type by original designation (also monotypic). Synonym of *Paraploactis* Bleeker 1865 (Poss & Eschmeyer 1978:405 [ref. 6387]). Aploactinidae.

Membras Bonaparte 1836:puntata 91 [ref. 4892]. Fem. *Atherina martinica* Valenciennes in Cuvier & Valenciennes 1835:459. Type by subsequent designation. Appeared in puntata 91 under *Atherina hepsetus*. Originally without included species; first addition of species not researched. Type above as listed by Jordan 1917:142 [ref. 2407]. Valid (Chernoff 1986:239 [ref. 5847]). Atherinidae: Menidiinae.

Mendosoma Guichenot 1848:212 [ref. 1939]. Neut. *Mendosoma lineata [lineatum]* Guichenot (ex Gay) 1848:213. Type by subsequent designation. Type designated by Bleeker 1876:316 [ref. 448]. Valid (see Pequeño 1980 [ref. 5422], Gon & Heemstra 1987 [ref. 6748). Latridae.

Mene Lacepède 1803:479 [ref. 4930]. Fem. *Mene annacarolina* Lacepède 1803:479, 480. Type by monotypy. Valid (Nakamura in Masuda et al. 1984:158 [ref. 6441], Smith 1986:619 [ref. 5712]). Menidae.

Menephorus Poey 1871:50 [ref. 3506]. Masc. *Serranus dubius* Poey 1861:142. Type by original designation (also monotypic). Serranidae: Epinephelinae.

Meneus Rafinesque 1815:88 [ref. 3584]. Masc. Not available, name only. Apparently an incorrect subsequent spelling of *Mene* Lacepède 1803 based on style of Rafinesque in this work. Menidae.

Menidia Bonaparte 1836:puntata 91 [ref. 4892]. Fem. *Atherina menidia* Linnaeus 1766:519. Apparently appeared first in puntata 91 under *Atherina hepsetus* without mention of included species. Technical first addition of species not researched; type usually given as *A. menidia*. Valid (Chernoff et al. 1981 [ref. 5466], Echelle

& Mosier 1982 [ref. 6821], Chernoff 1986:189 [ref. 5847]). Atherinidae: Menidiinae.

Menidia Browne 1789:441 [ref. 669]. Fem. Not available; published in a rejected work on Official Index (Opinion 89). Engraulidae.

Menidiella Schultz 1948:(13) 33 [ref. 3966]. Fem. *Menidia colei* Hubbs 1936:248. Type by original designation. Synonym of *Menidia* Bonaparte 1836. Atherinidae: Menidiinae.

Menticirrhus Gill 1861:86 [ref. 1771]. Masc. *Perca alburnus* Linnaeus 1766:482. Type by original designation (also monotypic). Type as proposed was *Umbrina alburnus* Holbrook. *Menticirrus* is a misspelling. Valid (Chao 1978:30 [ref. 6983], Uyeno & Sato in Uyeno et al. 1983:366 [ref. 14275]). Sciaenidae.

Mentiperca Gill 1862:236 [ref. 1664]. Fem. *Serranus luciopercanus* Poey 1852:56. Type by monotypy. Synonym of *Serranus* Cuvier 1814 (Johnson & Smith-Vaniz 1987:53 [ref. 9235]). Serranidae: Serraninae.

Mentodus (subgenus of *Holtbyrnia*) Parr 1951:16, 18 [ref. 3380]. Masc. *Bathytroctes rostratus* Günther 1878:227. Type by original designation (also monotypic). Valid (Krefft 1973:97 [ref. 7166], Sazonov 1986 [ref. 6003]). Platytroctidae.

Mephisto Tyler 1966:1 [ref. 4474]. *Mephisto fraserbrunneri* Tyler 1966:3. Type by original designation (also monotypic). Valid (Tyler 1968:133 [ref. 6438], Tyler 1980:56 [ref. 4477], Tyler 1986:889 [ref. 5723]). Triacanthodidae.

Merinthe Snyder 1904:535 [ref. 4149]. Fem. *Sebastes macrocephalus* Sauvage 1882:169. Type by monotypy. Treated as feminine by author. Synonym of *Pontinus* Poey 1860. Scorpaenidae: Scorpaeninae.

Merinthichthys Howell Rivero 1934:343 [ref. 3767]. Masc. *Merinthichthys sanchezi* Howell Rivero 1934:343. Type by original designation (also monotypic). Synonym of *Moringua* Gray 1831 (Smith 1989:65 [ref. 13285]). Moringuidae.

Merlangius Geoffroy St. Hilaire 1767:401 [ref. 1570]. Masc. *Gadus merlangus* Linnaeus 1758:253. Original not seen. Valid (Svetovidov 1973:307 [ref. 7169], Fahay & Markle 1984:267 [ref. 13653], Svetovidov in Whitehead et al. 1986:688 [ref. 13676]). Gadidae.

Merlangus Oken (ex Cuvier) 1817:1182a [ref. 3303]. *Gadus merlangus* Linnaeus 1758:253. Type apparently by subsequent absolute tautonymy. Based on "Les Merlans" of Cuvier 1816:213 [ref. 993] (see Gill 1903:966 [ref. 5768], but as *Merlongus*). First technical addition of species not researched. Also described apparently independently by Nilsson 1832:41 [ref. 3204]. Synonym of *Merlangius* Geoffroy St. Hilaire 1767 (Svetovidov 1973:307 [ref. 7169]). Gadidae.

Merlangus Rafinesque 1810:67 [ref. 3595]. *Gadus merluccius* Linnaeus 1758:254. Type by being a replacement name. Appeared in Additions and Corrections as, "In vece di *Onus*, sp. 30. leggete *Merlangus*" Species 30 was *Onus riali*; *Onus* apparently a replacement for *Merluccius*; *Merlangus* also an unneeded substitute for *Merluccius* Rafinesque 1810. Synonym of *Merluccius* Rafinesque 1810 (Svetovidov 1973:300 [ref. 7169]). Merlucciidae: Merlucciinae.

Merluccius Rafinesque 1810:25 [ref. 3594]. Masc. *Merluccius smiridus* Rafinesque 1810 (= *Gadus merluccius* Linnaeus 1758: 254). Type by monotypy. Linnaeus' species spelled *merlucius* by Rafinesque. Spelled *Merlucius* by Schinz 1822:362 [ref. 3926] and some subsequent authors. Perhaps *Onus* Rafinesque 1810:12 [ref. 3595] predates *Merluccius* Rafinesque. Valid (Svetovidov 1973:300 [ref. 7169], Cohen 1986:325 [ref. 5646], Cohen 1984:264 [ref. 13646], Paxton et al. 1989:309 [ref. 12442]). Merlucciidae: Merlucciinae.

Merlucius Gronow in Gray 1854:129 [ref. 1911]. Masc. *Merlucius lanatus* Gronow in Gray 1854:130. Type by monotypy. In the synonymy of *Merluccius* Rafinesque 1810 (Svetovidov 1973:300 [ref. 7169]). Merlucciidae: Merlucciinae.

Merlus Guichenot 1848:328 [ref. 1939]. *Merlus gayi* Guichenot 1848:329. Type by monotypy. Preoccupied by de la Fresnaye 1838 in Aves, replaced by *Epicopus* Günther 1860. Synonym of *Merluccius* Rafinesque 1810. Merlucciidae: Merlucciinae.

Merodontotus Britski 1981:109 [ref. 645]. Masc. *Merodontotus tigrinus* Britski 1981:110. Type by original designation (also monotypic). Valid (Castro 1984 [ref. 5296], Stewart 1986:668 [ref. 5211], Burgess 1989:282 [ref. 12860]). Pimelodidae.

Merogymnoides Whitley 1966:239 [ref. 4734]. Masc. *Merogymnoides carpentariae* Whitley 1966:240. Type by original designation. Opistognathidae.

Merogymnus Ogilby 1908:18 [ref. 3286]. Masc. *Merogymnus eximius* Ogilby 1908:18. Type by original designation (also monotypic). Type designated on p. 2. Synonym of *Opistognathus* Cuvier 1816 (Smith-Vaniz & Yoshino 1985:18 [ref. 6721]). Opistognathidae.

Merolepis Rafinesque 1810:25 [ref. 3595]. Fem. *Sparus massiliensis* Lacepède in Buffon 1802:33, 108. Type by monotypy. On Official List (Opinion 960). Synonym of *Spicara* Rafinesque 1810 (Tortonese et al. 1973:417 [ref. 7202]). Centracanthidae.

Merou (subgenus of *Serranus*) Bonaparte (ex Cuvier) 1831:167 [ref. 4978]. *Perca gigas* Brünnich 1768:65. Type by subsequent designation. Appeared as a section under *Serranus* as "2. *Merou*, Cuv. (*Holocentrum, Bodianus, Lutjanus, ...Gymnocephalus*, Bl.) Tutt'i mari. 98 [= species]". Probably not available from Bonaparte. Type as given by Jordan 1919:175 [ref. 2410]. Synonym of *Epinephelus* Bloch 1793. Serranidae: Epinephelinae.

Merulinus (subgenus of *Prionotus*) Jordan & Evermann 1898:2148, 2149, 2156 [ref. 2444]. Masc. *Trigla carolina* Linnaeus 1771:528. Type by original designation. Not preoccupied by *Merulina* Ehrenberg 1834, *Triscurrichthys* Whitley 1931 is an unneeded replacement. Synonym of *Prionotus* Lacepède 1801. Triglidae: Triglinae.

Merus Poey (ex Cuvier) 1871:39 [ref. 3506]. *Perca gigas* Brünnich 1768:65. Type by original designation. Preoccupied by Gistel 1857 in Coleoptera, not replaced. Objective synonym of *Merou* Bonaparte (ex Cuvier) 1831 and of *Cerna* Bonaparte 1833. Synonym of *Epinephelus* Bloch 1793 (Smith 1971:103 [ref. 14102], Daget & Smith 1986:301 [ref. 6204]). Serranidae: Epinephelinae.

Mesites Jenyns 1842:118 [ref. 2344]. Masc. *Mesites attenuatus* Jenyns 1842:121. Type by subsequent designation. Type designated by Jordan 1919:212 [ref. 2410]. Preoccupied by Schoenherr 1838 in Coleoptera, replaced by *Austrocobitis* Ogilby 1899. Synonym of *Galaxias* Cuvier 1816 (McDowall & Frankenberg 1981:455 [ref. 5500], McDowall 1984:126 [ref. 6178]). Galaxiidae: Galaxiinae.

Mesoaphyosemion (subgenus of *Aphyosemion*) Radda 1977:213 [ref. 3580]. Neut. *Haplochilus cameronense* Boulenger 1903:435. Type by original designation. Synonym of *Aphyosemion* Myers 1924 (Wildekamp et al. 1986:197 [ref. 6198]); as a valid subgenus (Parenti 1981:477 [ref. 7066]). Aplocheilidae: Aplocheilinae.

Mesobius Hubbs & Iwamoto 1977:235 [ref. 2257]. Masc. *Mesobius berryi* Hubbs & Iwamoto 1977:236. Type by original designation.

Valid (Iwamoto 1979:141 [ref. 2311], Fahay & Markle 1984:274 [ref. 13653], Iwamoto 1986:337 [ref. 5674], Paxton et al. 1989:328 [ref. 12442]). Macrouridae: Macrourinae.

Mesobola Howes 1984:168 [ref. 5834]. Fem. *Engraulicypris brevianalis* Boulenger 1908:231. Type by original designation. Cyprinidae.

Mesoborus Pellegrin 1900:178 [ref. 3397]. Masc. *Mesoborus crocodilus* Pellegrin 1900:179. Type by monotypy. Valid (Géry 1977:87 [ref. 1597], Vari 1979:340 [ref. 5490], Daget & Gosse 1984:198 [ref. 6185]). Citharinidae: Distichodontinae.

Mesochaetodon Maugé & Bauchot 1984:476 [ref. 6614]. Masc. *Chaetodon nippon* Döderlein 1884:23. Type by original designation. Also described as a new monotypic subgenus. Maugé & Bauchot included in their new genus *Mesochaetodon* the genus *Corallochaetodon* Burgess 1978; but *Corallochaetodon* Burgess has priority over *Mesochaetodon* at the generic level. Chaetodontidae.

Mesocottus Gracianov 1907:655, 660 [ref. 1872]. Masc. *Cottus haitei* Dybowski 1869:949. Type by original designation (also monotypic). Original not seen; from Berg 1949:1138. Valid (Washington et al. 1984:443 [ref. 13660]). Cottidae.

Mesocyprinus Cheng 1950:568 [ref. 828]. Masc. *Cyprinus micristius* Regan 1906:332. Type by monotypy. Described as a new genus, but described earlier by Fang 1936 with same name and type species. Cyprinidae.

Mesocyprinus Fang 1936:690, 699 [ref. 1304]. Masc. *Cyprinus micristius* Regan 1906:332. Type by original designation (also monotypic). See also *Mesocyprinus* Cheng 1950. Synonym of *Cyprinus* Linnaeus 1758, but as a valid subgenus (Chen & Huang 1977:403 [ref. 13496], Zhou in Chu & Chen 1989:330 [ref. 13584]). Cyprinidae.

Mesogobio Banarescu & Nalbant 1973:198 [ref. 173]. Masc. *Mesogobio lachneri* Banarescu & Nalbant 1973:199. Type by original designation (also monotypic). Valid (Hosoya 1986:488 [ref. 6155]). Cyprinidae.

Mesogobius (subgenus of *Gobius*) Bleeker 1874:317 [ref. 437]. Masc. *Gobius batrachocephalus* Pallas 1811:149. Type by original designation (also monotypic). Valid (Miller 1973:501 [ref. 6888], Miller in Whitehead et al. 1986:1054 [ref. 13677]). Gobiidae.

Mesogonistius Gill 1864:92 [ref. 1706]. Masc. *Pomotis chaetodon* Baird 1855:324. Type by original designation (also monotypic). Synonym of *Enneacanthus* Gill 1864. Centrarchidae.

Mesomisgurnus Fang 1935:129 [ref. 1301]. Masc. *Nemacheilus bipartitus* Sauvage & Dabry de Thiersant 1874:16. Type by original designation. Cobitidae: Cobitinae.

Mesonauta Günther 1862:300 [ref. 1969]. Masc. *Heros insignis* Heckel 1840:378. Type by monotypy. Valid (Kullander 1986:200 [ref. 12439]). Cichlidae.

Mesonoemacheilus (subgenus of *Noemacheilus*) Banarescu & Nalbant in Singh et al. 1982:202 [ref. 4030]. Masc. *Noemacheilus triangularis* Day 1865. Type by original designation. Synonym of *Noemacheilus* Kuhl & van Hasselt 1823, but as a valid subgenus (Menon 1984 [ref. 12845], Menon 1987:160 [ref. 14149]); valid (Kottelat 1990:19 [ref. 14137]). Balitoridae: Nemacheilinae.

Mesopodus Rafinesque 1815:86 [ref. 3584]. Masc. Not available, name only. Unplaced genera.

Mesopotamichthys Karaman 1971:227 [ref. 2560]. Masc. *Barbus sharpeyi* Günther 1874:38. Type by original designation (one species, two subspecies). Cyprinidae.

Mesoprion Cuvier in Cuvier & Valenciennes 1828:439-440 [ref. 997]. Masc. *Lutjanus lutjanus* Bloch 1790:107. Type by being a replacement name. Regarded as a replacement name for *Lutjanus* Bloch; if not then type designation is by Jordan 1917:124 [ref. 2407]. Type spelled *Lutianus lutianus* by Bloch 1790: Pl. 245 [ref. 469]. Objective synonym of *Lutjanus* Bloch 1790 (Allen 1985:32 [ref. 6843], Allen & Talbot 1985:8 [ref. 6491], Allen 1986:323 [ref. 6208]). Lutjanidae.

Mesopristes Bleeker 1873:372, 383 [ref. 12588]. Masc. *Mesopristes macracanthus* Bleeker 1873 (= *Datnia argentea* Cuvier 1829:139). Type by subsequent designation. As name only in Bleeker 1845:523 [ref. 312], then as name in synonymy in Bleeker 1873:372, 383 [ref. 12588] (see Mees & Kailola 1977:33-34 [ref. 5183]). Validly used by Fowler 1918:36 [ref. 1396] so dates to Bleeker 1873, with included species by Fowler as above. Valid (Vari 1978:270 [ref. 4514], Yoshino in Masuda et al. 1984:174 [ref. 6441], Vari 1986:304 [ref. 6205] and Paxton et al. 1989:534 [ref. 12442] but with date as Bleeker 1845 and type as *macracanthus*). Terapontidae.

Mesopristes Fowler (ex Bleeker) 1918:36 [ref. 1396]. Masc. *Datnia argentea* Cuvier 1829:139. Type by original designation. Validates *Mesopristes* Bleeker 1873, unavailable from Bleeker 1845 (see previous entry). Type as "*M. macracanthus* Bleeker (= *Datnia argentea* Cuvier)." *M. macracanthus* is a nomen nudum and type is therefore *argentea*. *Mesopristes* Fowler 1918 would be recognized only if one disagrees with analysis of name in synonymy as applied to *Mesopristes* Bleeker 1873. Terapontidae.

Mesops Günther 1862:311 [ref. 1969]. Masc. *Geophagus cupido* Heckel 1840:399. Type by subsequent designation. Type designated by Eigenmann & Bray 1894:621 [ref. 1248]. Preoccupied by Billberg 1820 in Coleoptera and by Audinet-Serville 1831 in Orthoptera; replaced by *Biotodoma* Eigenmann & Kennedy 1903. Objective synonym of *Biotodoma* Eigenmann & Kennedy 1903 (Kullander 1986:128 [ref. 12439]). Cichlidae.

Mesopus Gill 1862:14 [ref. 1655]. Masc. *Argentina pretiosa* Girard 1854:155. Type by original designation (also monotypic). Introduced as a proofing error (see Jordan 1919:313 [ref. 4904]) for *Hypomesus* Gill on p. 15. Objective synonym of *Hypomesus* Gill 1862. Osmeridae.

Mesoscorpia (subgenus of *Trachyscorpia*) Eschmeyer 1969:50 [ref. 1274]. Fem. *Scorpaena capensis* Gilchrist & von Bonde 1924:18. Type by original designation (also monotypic). Scorpaenidae: Sebastolobinae.

Mesozygaena (subgenus of *Sphyrna*) Compagno 1988:362, 366 [ref. 13488]. Fem. *Sphyrna corona* Springer 1940:163. Type by original designation. Sphyrnidae.

Metacottus Taliev 1946:90 [ref. 4315]. Masc. *Metacottus gurwicii* Taliev 1946:90. Type by monotypy. Valid (Washington et al. 1984:443 [ref. 13660]). Cottocomephoridae.

Metagobius Whitley 1930:122 [ref. 4669]. Masc. *Eleotris sclateri* Steindachner 1880:157. Type by original designation (also monotypic). Synonym of *Callogobius* Bleeker 1874 (Hoese, pers. comm.). Gobiidae.

Metahomaloptera Chang 1944:54 [ref. 5136]. Fem. *Metahomaloptera omeiensis* Chang 1944:54. Type by monotypy. Valid (Silas 1953:217 [ref. 4024], Chen 1978:345 [ref. 6900], Sawada 1982:204 [ref. 14111], Kottelat & Chu 1988:194 [ref. 13491]). Balitoridae: Balitorinae.

Metallites Schulze 1890:184 Masc. *Cyprinus rutilus* Linnaeus 1758:324. Type by monotypy. Original not examined; could not locate in ref. 3984. Preoccupied by Schoenherr 1824 in Coleoptera; apparently not replaced. Objective synonym of *Rutilus* Rafinesque 1820. Cyprinidae.

Metaloricaria Isbrücker 1975:2 [ref. 2301]. Fem. *Metaloricaria paucidens* Isbrücker 1975:2. Type by original designation (also monotypic). Valid (Isbrücker 1980:96 [ref. 2303]), Isbrücker & Nijssen 1982 [ref. 5277], Burgess 1989:440 [ref. 12860]). Loricariidae.

Metasalanx Wakiya & Takahasi 1937:293 [ref. 4571]. Masc. *Metasalanx coreanus* Wakiya & Takahasi 1937:293. Type by monotypy. Not available; manuscript name in synonymy of *Hemisalanx* Regan 1908, and apparently never made available by subsequent use. In the synonymy of *Salanx* Cuvier 1816 (Roberts 1984:206 [ref. 5318]). Salangidae.

Metavelifer Walters 1960:246 [ref. 4577]. Masc. *Velifer multiradiatus* Regan 1907:633. Type by original designation (also monotypic). Valid (Olney 1984:369 [ref. 13656], Fujii in Masuda et al. 1984:116 [ref. 6441], Heemstra 1986:399 [ref. 5660]). Veliferidae.

Metelectrona Wisner 1963:24 [ref. 4759]. Fem. *Metelectrona ahlstromi* Wisner 1963:25. Type by original designation (also monotypic). Synonym of *Electrona* Goode & Bean 1896, but as a valid subgenus (Paxton 1979:11 [ref. 6440]; valid genus (Moser et al. 1984:219 [ref. 13645], Paxton et al. 1984:241 [ref. 13625], Hulley 1986:312 [ref. 5672], Paxton et al. 1989:266 [ref. 12442]). Myctophidae.

Meteoria Nielsen 1969:57 [ref. 3195]. Fem. *Meteoria erythrops* Nielsen 1969:58. Type by original designation (also monotypic). Valid (Nielsen 1973:555 [ref. 6885], Cohen & Nielsen 1978:62 [ref. 881], Nielsen in Whitehead et al. 1986:1169 [ref. 13677]). Aphyonidae.

Metopias Lowe 1843:89 [ref. 2832]. Masc. *Metopias typhlops* Lowe 1843:90. Type by monotypy. Preoccupied by Gory 1821 [or 1832] [not researched], replaced by *Melamphaes* Günther 1864. Objective synonym of *Melamphaes* Günther 1864 (Maul 1973:343 [ref. 7171], Ebeling & Weed 1973:451 [ref. 6898], Paxton et al. 1989:371 [ref. 12442]). Melamphaidae.

Metopomycter Gilbert 1905:585 [ref. 1631]. Masc. *Metopomycter denticulatus* Gilbert 1905:585. Type by original designation (also monotypic). Synonym of *Nettastoma* Rafinesque 1810 (Smith et al. 1981:538 [ref. 6158], Smith 1989:604 [ref. 13285]). Nettastomatidae.

Metoponops Gill 1864:198 [ref. 5770]. Masc. *Metoponops copperi* Gill 1864:199. Type by monotypy. Appeared first in Gill 1864:198 [ref. 1702] without description and name-only species in article immediately preceding the original description (but on same page 198). Synonym of *Citharichthys* Bleeker 1862 (Norman 1934:139 [ref. 6893], Desoutter 1986:428 [ref. 6212]). Paralichthyidae.

Metrogaster Agassiz 1861:128, 129, 133 [ref. 11]. Fem. *Cymatogaster aggregata* Gibbons 1854:2, col. 3. Type by monotypy. Name published in synonymy (pp. 128, 129) but as an available name on p. 133 (Note). Synonym of *Cymatogaster* Gibbons 1854 (Tarp 1952:72 [ref. 12250]). Embiotocidae.

Metynnis Cope 1878:692 [ref. 945]. *Metynnis luna* Cope 1878:692. Type by monotypy. Valid (Géry 1976:50 [ref. 14199], Géry 1977:270 [ref. 1597], Géry et al. 1987:447 [ref. 6001]). Characidae: Serrasalminae.

Metzelaaria Jordan 1923:209 [ref. 2421]. Fem. *Scorpaena tridecimspinosa* Metzelaar 1919:146. Type by original designation (also monotypic). Synonym of *Scorpaenodes* Bleeker 1857. Scorpaenidae: Scorpaeninae.

Metzia Jordan & Thompson 1914:227 [ref. 2543]. Fem. *Acheilognathus mesembrinus* Jordan & Evermann 1902:323. Type by original designation (also monotypic). Cyprinidae.

Meuschenia Whitley 1929:138 [ref. 4665]. Fem. *Monacanthus trachylepis* Günther 1870:248. Type by original designation (also monotypic). Valid (Hutchins 1977:40 [ref. 2283], Matsuura 1979:165 [ref. 7019], Tyler 1980:178 [ref. 4477], Arai 1983:199 [ref. 14249]). Monacanthidae.

Meuschenula Whitley 1931:325 [ref. 4672]. Fem. *Agonostoma darwiniense* Macleay 1878:360. Type by original designation (also monotypic). Correct spelling for genus of type is *Agonostomus*. Synonym of *Ophiocara* Gill 1863 (Hoese, pers. comm.). Eleotridae.

Micracanthus Sauvage 1879:95 [ref. 3881]. Masc. *Micracanthus marchei* Sauvage 1879:96. Type by monotypy. Not preoccupied by *Microcanthus* Swainson 1839, *Oshimia* Jordan 1919 is an unneeded replacement. Synonym of *Betta* Bleeker 1850 Roberts 1989:171 [ref. 6439]). Belontiidae.

Micraethiops (subgenus of *Neolebias*) Daget 1965:20 [ref. 1025]. Masc. *Neolebias ansorgii* Boulenger 1912:8. Type by original designation. Valid (Daget & Gosse 1984:205 [ref. 6185]). Citharinidae: Distichodontinae.

Micralestes Boulenger 1899:86 [ref. 549]. Masc. *Micralestes humilis* Boulenger 1899:87. Type by subsequent designation. Type designated by Jordan 1920:485 [ref. 4905]. Valid (Poll 1967:28 [ref. 3529], Géry 1977:28 [ref. 1597], Paugy 1984:173 [ref. 6183]). Alestiidae.

Micrapocryptes Hora 1923:751 [ref. 2204]. Masc. *Micrapocryptes fragilis* Hora 1923:751. Type by original designation. Misspelled *Micropocryptes* in Zoological Record for 1923. Synonym of *Gobiopterus* Bleeker 1874 (Hoese, pers. comm.). Gobiidae.

Micraspius Dybowski 1869:953 [ref. 1169]. Masc. *Micraspius mianowskii* Dybowski 1869:954. Type by monotypy. Synonym of *Pseudorasbora* Bleeker 1859 (Banarescu & Nalbant 1973:20 [ref. 173]). Cyprinidae.

Micrenophrys (subgenus of *Taurulus*) Andriashev 1954:400 [ref. 6547]. Fem. *Cottus lilljeborgi* Collett 1875. Type by monotypy. Synonym of *Taurulus* Gracianov 1907 (Neyelov 1973:600 [ref. 7219]); valid (Neyelov 1979:116, 149 [ref. 3152], Fedorov in Whitehead et al. 1986:1252 [ref. 13677]). Cottidae.

Micristius Gill 1865:266 [24] [ref. 1707]. Masc. *Fundulus zonatus* Valenciennes in Cuvier & Valenciennes 1846:196. Type by subsequent designation. Type designated by Jordan & Gilbert 1877:94 [ref. 4907]. On p. 24 of separate. Synonym of *Fundulus* Lacepède 1803 (Parenti 1981:494 [ref. 7066]). Cyprinodontidae: Fundulinae.

Micristodus Gill 1865:177 [ref. 1711]. Masc. *Micristodus punctatus* Gill 1865:177. Type by monotypy. Synonym of *Rhincodon* Smith 1829 (Compagno 1984:210 [ref. 6474], Cappetta 1987:81 [ref. 6348]). Rhincodontidae.

Microbarbus Géry 1957:6 et seq. [ref. 2024]. Masc. Apparently not available from this reference; published after 1930 without fixation of a type species (Art. 13b); many included species. Later publication in an available way not researched. Cyprinidae.

Microbrotula Gosline 1953:218 [ref. 1859]. Fem. *Microbrotula* *rubra* Gosline 1953:218. Type by original designation. Valid (Cohen & Nielsen 1978:49 [ref. 881], Cohen & Wourms 1976 [ref. 7046]). Bythitidae: Bythitinae.

Microbrycon Eigenmann & Wilson in Eigenmann, Henn & Wilson 1914:3 [ref. 1259]. Masc. *Microbrycon minutus* Eigenmann & Wilson in Eigenmann, Henn & Wilson 1914:3. Type by monotypy. Synonym of *Pterobrycon* Eigenmann 1913 (Géry 1977:359 [ref. 1597]); status uncertain (see Weitzman & S. Fink 1985:2 [ref. 5203]). Characidae: Glandulocaudinae.

Microbuglossus (subgenus of *Solea*) Günther 1862:462, 471-472 [ref. 1969]. Masc. *Solea humilis* Cantor 1850:219. Type by subsequent designation. Described in key (p. 462) as section of *Solea* with 2 species (pp. 471-472). Type designated by Jordan 1919:319 [ref. 4904]. Soleidae.

Microcaelurus Miranda-Ribeiro 1939:362 [ref. 3023]. Masc. *Microcaelurus odontocheilus* Miranda-Ribeiro 1939:362. Type by monotypy. A translation of the original description may be found in Myers & Böhlke 1956:11-12 [ref. 5937]. Synonym of *Tyttocharax* Fowler 1913 (Weitzman & S. Fink 1985:2 [ref. 5203]). Characidae: Glandulocaudinae.

Microcanthus (subgenus of *Chaetodon*) Swainson 1839:170, 215 [ref. 4303]. Masc. *Chaetodon strigatus* Cuvier in Cuvier & Valenciennes 1831:25. Type by monotypy. Valid (Hayashi in Masuda et al. 1984:181 [ref. 6441], Gosline 1985:353 [ref. 5283]). Kyphosidae: Microcanthinae.

Microcephalocongrus (subgenus of *Bathycongrus*) Fowler 1934:270 [ref. 1416]. Masc. *Bathycongrus megalops* Fowler 1934:270. Type by original designation. Valid (Smith 1989:512 [ref. 13285]). Congridae: Congrinae.

Microcharax Eigenmann 1909:35 [ref. 1222]. Masc. *Nannostomus lateralis* Boulenger 1895:2. Type by original designation (also monotypic). In Characidiinae, status uncertain (P. Buckup, pers. comm., July 1990). Characidae: Characidiinae.

Microchirichthys (subgenus of *Photonectes*) Regan & Trewavas 1930:120, 124 [ref. 3681]. Masc. *Photonectes parvimanus* Regan & Trewavas 1930:124. Type by subsequent designation. Type designated in Zoological Record for 1930 (Pisces):48; also by Fowler 1936:1186 [ref. 6546]. Stomiidae.

Microchiropsis Chabanaud 1956:447 [ref. 803]. Fem. *Solea (Microchirus) boscanion* Chabanaud 1926:127. Type by monotypy. Misspelled *Michrochiropsis* in Zoological Record for 1956. Synonym of *Buglossidium* Chabanaud 1930 (Torchio 1973:631 [ref. 6892]). Soleidae.

Microchirus (subgenus of *Solea*) Bonaparte 1833:puntata 27 [ref. 516]. Masc. *Pleuronectes microchirus* Delaroche 1809:356. Type by absolute tautonymy. Type possibly *Pleuronectes mangili* Risso, by monotypy in puntata 27— the name adopted by Bonaparte; *microchirus* in synonymy of *mangili*. Also published in puntata 28. Valid (Torchio 1973:632 [ref. 6892], Quéro et al. in Whitehead et al. 1986:1313 [ref. 13677], Desoutter 1987 [ref. 6742], Chapleau & Keast 1988:2799 [ref. 12625]). Soleidae.

Microchromis Johnson 1975:16 [ref. 2356]. Masc. *Microchromis zebroides* Johnson 1975:16. Type by monotypy. Apparently a synonym of *Cynotilapia* Regan 1922. See also Ribbink et al. 1983:243 [ref. 13555]). Cichlidae.

Microconger (subgenus of *Leptocephalus*) Fowler 1912:9 [ref. 1385]. Masc. *Leptocephalus caudalis* Fowler 1912:9. Type by original designation (also monotypic). Synonym of *Conger* Oken 1817 (Blache et al. 1973:239 [ref. 7185], Smith 1989:513 [ref. 13285]). Congridae: Congrinae.

Microcorydoras (subgenus of *Corydoras*) Myers 1953:270 [ref. 5745]. Masc. *Corydoras hastatus* Eigenmann & Eigenmann 1888:166. Type by original designation (also monotypic). Synonym of *Corydoras* Lacepède 1803 (Nijssen & Isbrücker 1980:192 [ref. 6910]). Callichthyidae.

Microcottus Schmidt 1940:378 [ref. 3944]. Masc. *Porocottus sellaris* Gilbert 1895:419. Type by monotypy. Valid (Neyelov 1979:115, 134 [ref. 3152], Yabe et al. 1983:460-461 [ref. 5423], Washington et al. 1984:443 [ref. 13660], Yabe in Masuda et al. 1984:327 [ref. 6441], Yabe 1985:111 [ref. 11522]). Cottidae.

Microdesmus Günther 1864:26 [ref. 5752]. Masc. *Microdesmus dipus* Günther 1864:26. Type by monotypy. Also as Günther 1864 (Sept.):231 [ref. 1976]. Valid (Dawson 1979 [ref. 6947], Birdsong et al. 1988:200 [ref. 7303]). Microdesmidae: Microdesminae.

Microdistichodus Pellegrin 1926:161 [ref. 3404]. Masc. *Microdistichodus uriocellatus* Pellegrin 1926:162. Type by monotypy. Also appeared in Pellegrin 1928:23 [ref. 3411]. Synonym of *Hemigrammocharax* Pellegrin 1923 (Daget & Gosse 1984:194 [ref. 6185]). Citharinidae: Distichodontinae.

Microdonophis Kaup 1856:43 [ref. 2572]. Masc. *Microdonophis altipennis* Kaup 1856:43. Type by monotypy. Also appeared in Kaup 1856:6 [ref. 2573] and as name only in Kaup in Duméril 1856:198 [ref. 1154]. Synonym of *Ophichthus* Ahl 1789 (Blache et al. 1973:247 [ref. 7185], McCosker et al. 1989:379 [ref. 13288]); as a valid subgenus (McCosker 1977:80, 81 [ref. 6836]). Ophichthidae: Ophichthinae.

Microdontochromis Poll 1986:117 [ref. 6136]. Masc. *Xenotilapia tenuidentata* Poll 1951:6. Type by original designation (also monotypic). Cichlidae.

Microdontostomias Fowler 1934:259 [ref. 1416]. Masc. *Microdontostomias orientalis* Fowler 1934:261. Type by original designation (also monotypic). Synonym of *Stomias* Cuvier 1816 (Morrow 1964:292 [ref. 6967], Morrow 1973:132 [ref. 7175]). Stomiidae.

Microdus Kner 1858:77 [ref. 13404]. Masc. *Microdus labyrinthicus* Kner 1858:77. Type by monotypy. Also appeared in Kner 1859:149 [ref. 2631]. Preoccupied by Nees 1812 in Hymenoptera and by Emmons 1857 in fossil fishes. Placed on Official Index, and *Caenotropus* Günther 1864 established as a replacement name by ICZN (Opinion 1150). Curimatidae: Chilodontinae.

Microeleotris Meek & Hildebrand 1916:362 [ref. 2962]. Fem. *Microeleotris panamensis* Meek & Hildebrand 1916:363. Type by original designation. Synonym of *Leptophilypnus* Meek & Hildebrand 1916. Eleotridae.

Microgadus Gill 1865:69 [ref. 1709]. Masc. *Gadus proximus* Girard 1854:141, 154. Type regarded as by monotypy, a second species, *Gadus tomcodus* Mitchill "exhibits similar modifications of the cranium, and should be approximated to *G. proximus*." Valid (Fahay & Markle 1984:267 [ref. 13653]). Gadidae.

Microgaster (subgenus of *Glyphisodon*) Swainson 1839:171, 216 [ref. 4303]. Fem. *Microgaster maculatus* Swainson 1839:216 (= *Etroplus coruchii* Cuvier 1830:491). Type by monotypy. One included species as, "*maculata*. Cuv. pl. 136." Swainson's *maculata* is an unneeded substitute for *coruchii* Cuvier in Cuvier & Valenciennes. Cichlidae.

Microgenys Eigenmann 1913:22 [ref. 1229]. Fem. *Microgenys minutus* Eigenmann 1913:22. Type by original designation (also monotypic). Valid (Géry 1977:398 [ref. 1597]). Characidae.

Microgeophagus Axelrod 1971:344 [ref. 5456]. Masc. *Apistogram-*

ma ramirezi Myers & Harry 1948:77. Type by monotypy. Needs more research. Robins & Bailey 1982:208 [ref. 6548] regard the genus as unavailable from Frey 1957:56, 375 [ref. 5455] and attribute it to Axelrod 1971 as above. Frey's mention of the name with an existing species is probably sufficient to validate. See also Kullander 1985 [ref. 14221, not seen] and *Papiliochromis* Kullander 1977 with same type. Cichlidae.

Microglanis Eigenmann 1912:130, 155 [ref. 1227]. Masc. *Microglanis poecilus* Eigenmann 1912:155. Type by original designation (also monotypic). Valid (Mees 1974:221 [ref. 2969], Mees 1978:259 [ref. 5691], Burgess 1989:276 [ref. 12860], Malabarba 1989:140 [ref. 14217]). Pimelodidae.

Micrognathus Duncker 1912:235 [ref. 1156]. Masc. *Syngnathus brevirostris* Rüppell 1838:144. Type by original designation (also monotypic). Valid (Dawson 1982:25 [ref. 6764], Dawson 1982 [ref. 5441], Araga in Masuda et al. 1984:87 [ref. 6441], Dawson 1985:121 [ref. 6541], Dawson 1986:454 [ref. 5650], Paxton et al. 1989:425 [ref. 12442]). Syngnathidae: Syngnathinae.

Microgobius Koumans (ex Bleeker) 1931:101 [ref. 5623]. Masc. Not available, museum name from Bleeker cited in passing in synonymy of *Stigmatogobius*; much later than *Microgobius* Poey 1876. Gobiidae.

Microgobius Poey 1876:168 [ref. 3510]. Masc. *Microgobius signatus* Poey 1876:169. Type by monotypy. On pp. 126-127 of separate. Valid (Birdsong 1981 [ref. 5425], Birdsong et al. 1988:191 [ref. 7303]). Gobiidae.

Microichthys Rüppell 1852:1 [ref. 3846]. Masc. *Microichthys coccoi* Rüppell 1852:1. Type by monotypy. Status uncertain, possibly a synonym of *Epigonus* (see Fraser 1972:5 [ref. 5195], Mayer 1974:199 [ref. 6007]). Valid (Tortonese 1973:367 [ref. 7192], Tortonese in Whitehead et al. 1986:808 [ref. 13676]). Epigonidae.

Microlepidalestes (subgenus of *Alestopetersius*) Hoedeman 1951:8 (in key) [ref. 2178]. Masc. *Micralestes caudomaculatus* Pellegrin 1925:101. Type by monotypy. Synonym of *Bathyaethiops* Fowler 1949 (Paugy 1984:163 [ref. 6183]). Alestiidae.

Microlepidium Garman 1899:180 [ref. 1540]. Neut. *Lepidion verecundum* Jordan & Cramer in Gilbert 1897:456. Type by subsequent designation. Earliest type designation not researched, above as given by Jordan; second included species is *M. grandiceps* Garman 1899. Valid (Fahay & Markle 1984:266 [ref. 13653]). Moridae.

Microlepidogaster Eigenmann & Eigenmann 1889:8 [ref. 1258]. Fem. *Microlepidogaster perforatus [a]* Eigenmann & Eigenmann 1889:9. Type by original designation (also monotypic). Also appeared in Eigenmann & Eigenmann 1889:42 (18 Aug.) [ref. 1253], original in Apr. 1889. Species originally given as *perforatus*, emended to *perforata*. Synonym of *Otocinclus* Cope 1871 (Isbrücker 1980:81 [ref. 2303]); valid (Burgess 1989:439 [ref. 12860], Malabarba 1989:149 [ref. 14217]). Loricariidae.

Microlepidotus Gill 1862:255 [ref. 4909]. Masc. *Microlepidotus inornatus* Gill 1862:256. Type by monotypy. Haemulidae.

Microlepis (subgenus of *Leuciscus*) Bonaparte 1846:30 [ref. 519]. Fem. *Squalius microlepis* Heckel 1843:1041. Type by absolute tautonymy. Synonym of *Leuciscus* Cuvier 1816. Cyprinidae.

Microlophichthys (subgenus of *Dolopichthys*) Regan & Trewavas 1932:77 [ref. 3682]. Masc. *Dolopichthys microlophus* Regan 1925:29. Not available from Regan & Trewavas 1932 (Art. 13b), no designation of type species after 1930 (Art. 13b). Can date to Burton 1933 (Zoological Record for 1932) where citation occurred and type was designated; authorship is Burton (ex Regan & Trewavas); see Appendix A. Treated as valid by Pietsch 1974:32 [ref. 5332], Bertelsen & Pietsch 1977:185 [ref. 7063], Bertelsen in Whitehead et al. 1986:1392 [ref. 13677]). Oneirodidae.

Micromesistius Gill 1863:231 [ref. 1687]. Masc. *Gadus poutassou* Risso 1826:227. Type by original designation (also monotypic). Spelled *Brachymesistius* on page 233 (regarded as a lapsus for *Micromesistius*). Valid (Svetovidov 1973:308 [ref. 7169], Inada & Nakamura 1975 [ref. 7099], Fahay & Markle 1984:267 [ref. 13653], Svetovidov in Whitehead et al. 1986:689 [ref. 13676]). Gadidae.

Micromesus Gill 1865:136 [ref. 1712]. Masc. *Rhinoptera adspersa* Valenciennes in Müller & Henle 1841:183. Type by original designation (also monotypic). Synonym of *Rhinoptera* Cuvier 1829 (Cappetta 1987:173 [ref. 6348]). Myliobatidae.

Micrometrus Gibbons 1854:1, col. 1 [ref. 6064]. Masc. *Cymatogaster minimus* Gibbons 1854:2, col. 3. Type by subsequent designation. Type designated by Agassiz 1861:129 [ref. 11]. Also in Gibbons 1854:125 [Oct., ref. 1610]. Same two species included in this genus also put in *Cymatogaster* Gibbons of 18 May 1854, although he apparently originally intended *Cymatogaster* for a different species. Valid (Tarp 1952:81 [ref. 12250]). Embiotocidae.

Micromischodus Roberts 1971:4 [ref. 3773]. Masc. *Micromischodus sugillatus* Roberts 1971:5. Type by original designation (also monotypic). Valid (Roberts 1974:413 [ref. 6872], Géry 1977:190 [ref. 1597], Vari 1983:5 [ref. 5419]). Hemiodontidae: Hemiodontinae.

Micromugil Gulia 1861:11 [ref. 1956]. Masc. *Micromugil tumidus* Gulia 1861:11. Type by subsequent designation. Type usually given as by monotypy, but 2 included species (*timidus* and *macrogaster*); first subsequent designation perhaps by Jordan 1919:307 [ref. 4904]. Synonym of *Aphanius* Nardo 1827 (Tortonese 1973:270 [ref. 7192], Parenti 1981:521 [ref. 7066], Wildekamp et al. 1986:165 [ref. 6198]). Cyprinodontidae: Cyprinodontinae.

Micronema Bleeker 1858:255, 257, 298 [ref. 365]. Neut. *Micronema typus* Bleeker 1858:429 (= *Silurus micronemus* Bleeker 1846:18). Also on p. 26 et seq.; misspelled once on p. 32 as *Mircronema*. Type possibly by original designation (text not translated), else by use of *typus*. Bleeker's *typus* is an unneeded substitute for *Silurus micronemus*. Synonym of *Kryptopterus* Bleeker 1858 (Haig 1952:106 [ref. 12607], Roberts 1989:145 [ref. 6439]). Siluridae.

Micronemacheilus (subgenus of *Nemacheilus*) Rendahl 1944:45 [ref. 3705]. Masc. *Nemacheilus (Micronemacheilus) cruciatus* Rendahl 1944:37. Type by original designation. Valid (Zhu & Cao 1987: [ref. 14139] as *Micronoemacheilus*, Kottelat 1989:12 [ref. 13605], Kottelat 1990:19 [ref. 14137]). Balitoridae: Nemacheilinae.

Micropanchax Myers 1924:42 [ref. 3092]. Masc. *Haplochilus schoelleri* Boulenger 1904:136. Type by original designation. Misspelled *Microphanchax* in Zoological Record for 1924. Synonym of *Aplocheilichthys* Bleeker 1863 (Wildekamp et al. 1986:170 [ref. 6198]); as a valid subgenus (Parenti 1981:506 [ref. 7066]). Cyprinodontidae: Aplocheilichthyinae.

Microperca Castelnau 1872:48 [ref. 757]. Fem. *Microperca yarrae* Castelnau 1872:48. Type by monotypy. Preoccupied by Putnam 1863 in fishes, replaced by *Percamia* Bleeker 1876. Synonym of *Nannoperca* Günther 1861. Kuhliidae.

Microperca Putnam 1863:4 [ref. 3567]. Fem. *Microperca punctulata* Putnam 1863:4. Type by monotypy. Type species preoccupied when in *Etheostoma*, species replaced by *Etheostoma microperca* Jordan & Gilbert. Synonym of *Etheostoma* Rafinesque 1819, but as a valid subgenus (Collette & Banarescu 1977:1457 [ref. 5845], Burr 1978 [ref. 7035], Bailey & Etnier 1988:28 [ref. 6873]). Percidae.

Micropercops Fowler & Bean 1920:318 [ref. 1472]. Masc. *Micropercops dabryi* Fowler & Bean 1920:319. Type by original designation (also monotypic). Valid (Birdsong et al. 1988:183 [ref. 7303]). Eleotridae.

Microphilypnus Myers 1927:133 [ref. 3096]. Masc. *Microphilypnus ternetzi* Myers 1927:134. Type by original designation. Valid (Birdsong et al. 1988:202 [ref. 7303]). Eleotridae.

Microphis Kaup 1853:234 [ref. 2569]. Masc. *Syngnathus deocata* Hamilton 1822:14, 363. Type by subsequent designation. Type designated by Jordan 1919:254 [ref. 2410]. Duncker 1912 wrongly says type is *Microphis brachyurus* Bleeker 1853, but it was not an originally-included species. Valid (Dawson 1984 [ref. 5879], Dawson 1985:126 [ref. 6541], Dawson 1986:454 [ref. 5650], Paxton et al. 1989:425 [ref. 12442], Kottelat 1989:16 [ref. 13605]). Syngnathidae: Syngnathinae.

Microphotolepis Sazonov & Parin 1977:49 [ref. 3907]. Fem. *Microphotolepis multipunctata* Sazonov & Parin 1977:50. Type by original designation (also monotypic). Alepocephalidae.

Microphysogobio Mori 1934:39 [ref. 3042]. Masc. *Microphysogobio hsinglungshanensis* Mori 1934:40. Type by monotypy. Appeared first in Mori 1933:114 [ref. 7968] without species and unavailable (no fixation of type species after 1930). Apparently can date to 1934 as above with type as *hsinglungshanensis* by monotypy. Else genus dates to Mori 1935:171 [ref. 3043] with type as *koreensis* Mori 1935 by original designation in synonymy on p. 171. Valid (Banarescu & Nalbant 1973:244 [ref. 173], Hosoya 1986:488 [ref. 6155]). Cyprinidae.

Micropodus Rafinesque 1815:86 [ref. 3584]. Masc. *Cheilio auratus* Lacepède 1802:432. Type by being a replacement name. As "*Micropodus* R. [Rafinesque] *Cheilio* Lac. [Lacepède]." Available replacement name (unneeded) for and objective synonym of *Cheilio* Lacepède 1802. Labridae.

Micropoecilia Hubbs 1926:73 [ref. 2233]. Fem. *Poecilia vivipara parae* Eigenmann 1894:629. Type by original designation. For purposes of the type species, the subspecies *parae* is elevated to species level; type not *vivipara*. *Recepoecilia* Whitley 1951 is an unneeded replacement. Synonym of *Poecilia* Bloch & Schneider 1801 (Rosen & Bailey 1963:45 [ref. 7067]). Poeciliidae.

Micropogon Cuvier in Cuvier & Valenciennes 1830:213 [ref. 999]. Masc. *Micropogon lineatus* Cuvier in Cuvier & Valenciennes 1830:215. Type by subsequent designation. Type designated by Bleeker 1876:326 [ref. 448] as *M. costatus* DeKay [not an included species] = *M. lineatus*. Preoccupied by Boie 1826 in Aves, replaced by *Micropogonias* Bonaparte 1831. Objective synonym of *Micropogonias* Bonaparte 1831 (Chao 1978:32 [ref. 6983]). Sciaenidae.

Micropogonias Bonaparte 1831:170 [ref. 4978]. Masc. *Perca lineatus* Cuvier in Cuvier & Valenciennes 1830:215. Type by being a replacement name. Replacement for *Micropogon* Cuvier 1830, preoccupied by Boie 1826 in Aves. After lectotype designation (Chao 1978:32 [ref. 6983]), Cuvier's *P. lineatus* is a synonym of *Umbrina furnieri* Desmarest 1823. *Micropogonoides* is a misspelling. Valid (Chao 1978:32 [ref. 6983], Uyeno & Sato in Uyeno et al. 1983:369 [ref. 14275]). Sciaenidae.

Micropterus Lacepède 1802:324 [ref. 4929]. Masc. *Micropterus dolomieu* Lacepède 1802:324, 325. Type by monotypy. Valid (Hubbs & Bailey 1940:13 [ref. 12253]). Centrarchidae.

Micropteryx Agassiz in Spix & Agassiz 1831:102, 104 [ref. 13]. Fem. *Seriola dumerili* Risso 1810:175. Type by being a replacement name. For authorship and date see Kottelat 1988:78 [ref. 13380]. Unneeded replacement for *Seriola*, regarded as preoccupied in botany but names in botany do not compete with names in zoology. Objective synonym of *Seriola* Cuvier 1816 (Hureau & Tortonese 1973:379 [ref. 7198]). Carangidae.

Micropus Gray 1831:20 [ref. 1881]. Masc. *Micropus maculatus* Gray 1831:20. Type by monotypy. Preoccupied by Wolf 1810 in Aves, not replaced. On Official Index (Opinion 502) because of homonymy with *Micropus* Wolf. In the synonymy of *Caracanthus* Krøyer 1845. Caracanthidae.

Micropus Kner 1868:29 [ref. 6074]. Masc. *Micropteryx polycentrus* Kner 1868:323. Type by monotypy. As "*Micropteryx polycentrus* nov. sp. vel potius nov. gen. *Micropus polycentrus*." Also appeared as new in Kner 1868:322 [ref. 2646]. Preoccupied four times, replaced by *Orqueta* Jordan 1919. On Official Index (Opinion 502). Not a carangid, belongs in Latridae (Smith-Vaniz, pers. comm., Nov. 1989). Latridae.

Microrasbora Annandale 1918:50 [ref. 127]. Fem. *Microrasbora rubescens* Annandale 1918:50. Type by original designation. Valid (Jayaram 1981:82 [ref. 6497], Kottelat 1989:8 [ref. 13605]). Cyprinidae.

Microrhynchus Blache & Bauchot 1972:728 [ref. 304]. Masc. *Sphagebranchus foresti* Cadenat & Roux 1964:3. Type by original designation. Preoccupied by Megerle in Dahl 1823 in Lepidoptera, Jourdan 1834 in Mammalia, and four more times (McCosker & Böhlke 1984:40 [ref. 5316]); not replaced. Synonym of *Ethadophis* Rosenblatt & McCosker 1970 (McCosker & Böhlke 1984:40 [ref. 5316], McCosker et al. 1989:341 [ref. 13288]). Ophichthidae: Ophichthinae.

Microschemobrycon Eigenmann 1915:56 [ref. 1231]. Masc. *Microschemobrycon guaporensis* Eigenmann 1915:56. Type by original designation (also monotypic). Valid (Géry 1977:598 [ref. 1597]). Characidae.

Microsicydium Bleeker 1874:314 [ref. 437]. Neut. *Sicydium gymnauchen* Bleeker 1874:314. Type by original designation (also monotypic). Gobiidae.

Microspathodon Günther 1862:35, 57 [ref. 1969]. Masc. *Glyphidodon chrysurus* Cuvier in Cuvier & Valenciennes 1830:476. Type by monotypy. Described in key (p. 35) as "II. Teeth in the upper jaw moveable: *Microspathodon*, p. 57." On p. 57 *Glyphidodon chrysurus* is treated but without mention of *Microspathodon*, but is only species in Section II (with moveable teeth). Correct spelling for genus of type species is *Glyphisodon*. Valid (Richards & Leis 1984:544 [ref. 13668]). Pomacentridae.

Microsternarchus Fernández-Yépez 1968:[4] [ref. 7318]. Masc. *Microsternarchus bilineatus* Fernández-Yépez 1968:[4]. Type by original designation (also monotypic). Synonym of *Hypopomus* Gill 1864 (Mago-Leccia 1978:14, footnote [ref. 5489]). Gymnotidae: Hypopominae.

Microstoma Cuvier 1816:184 [ref. 993]. Neut. *Gasteropelecus microstoma* Risso 1810:356. Type by monotypy (also by absolute tautonymy). Recognition of the Microstomatidae as a family follows Ahlstrom et al. 1984:156 [ref. 13627]. Valid (Cohen 1973:153 [ref. 6589], Cohen in Whitehead et al. 1984:390 [ref. 13675], Ahlstrom et al. 1984:156 [ref. 13627], Cohen 1986:215 [ref. 5646], Paxton et al. 1989:166 [ref. 12442]). Microstomatidae.

Microstomatichthyoborus Nichols & Griscom 1917:685 [ref. 3185]. Masc. *Microstomatichthyoborus bashforddeani* Nichols & Griscom 1917:685. Type by monotypy. [The longest generic-group name in fishes.] Valid (Géry 1977:67 [ref. 1597], Vari 1979:340 [ref. 5490], Daget & Gosse 1984:199 [ref. 6185]). Citharinidae: Distichodontinae.

Microstomus Gottsche 1835:136, 150 [ref. 1862]. Masc. *Microstomus latidens* Gottsche 1835:150. Type by monotypy. Valid (Norman 1934:355 [ref. 6893], Nielsen 1973:625 [ref. 6885], Ahlstrom et al. 1984:643 [ref. 13641], Sakamoto 1984 [ref. 5273], Sakamoto in Masuda et al. 1984:353 [ref. 6441], Nielsen in Whitehead et al. 1986:1303 [ref. 13677]). Pleuronectidae: Pleuronectinae.

Microsyngnathus (subgenus of *Syngnathus*) Herald 1959:468 [ref. 2096]. Masc. *Syngnathus dunckeri* Metzelaar 1919. Type by original designation. Synonym of *Bryx* Herald 1940 (Fritzsche 1980:192 [ref. 1511], Dawson 1982:111 [ref. 6764], Dawson 1985:22 [ref. 6541]). Syngnathidae: Syngnathinae.

Microsynodontis Boulenger 1903:26 [ref. 570]. Fem. *Microsynodontis batesii* Boulenger 1903:26. Type by monotypy. Valid (Gosse 1986:116 [ref. 6194], Burgess 1989:197 [ref. 12860]). Mochokidae.

Microthrissa Boulenger 1902:26 [ref. 562]. Fem. *Microthrissa royauxi* Boulenger 1902:26. Type by monotypy. Valid (Poll et al. 1984:46 [ref. 6172], Grande 1985:247 [ref. 6466], Whitehead 1985:151 [ref. 5141], Whitehead 1986 [ref. 6756], Gourène & Teugels 1988 [ref. 12839]). Clupeidae.

Microtrigla (subgenus of *Trigla*) Kaup 1873:86 [ref. 2585]. Fem. *Trigla papilio* Cuvier in Cuvier & Valenciennes 1829:80. Type by subsequent designation. Based on style, described as a subgenus. Type designated by Jordan 1919:369 [ref. 4904]. Synonym of *Lepidotrigla* Günther 1860 (Richards & Saksena 1977:209 [ref. 5285]). Triglidae: Triglinae.

Microzeus Blyth 1860:142 [ref. 477]. Masc. *Microzeus armatus* Blyth 1860:143. Type by monotypy. Zeidae.

Miichthys Lin 1938:165 [ref. 12501]. Masc. *Sciaena miiuy* Basilewski 1855:22. Type by original designation (also monotypic). Synonym of *Argyrosomus* De la Pylaie 1835 (Trewavas 1977:322 [ref. 4459]); valid (Okamura in Masuda et al. 1984:162 [ref. 6441]). Sciaenidae.

Millerigobius Bath 1973:304 [ref. 207]. Masc. *Gobius macrocephalus* Kolombatovic 1891:22. Type by original designation (also monotypic). Valid (Miller in Whitehead et al. 1986:1055 [ref. 13677]). Gobiidae.

Milyeringa Whitley 1945:36 [ref. 4707]. Fem. *Milyeringa veritas* Whitley 1945:36. Type by original designation (also monotypic). Valid (Springer 1983:33 [ref. 5365]). Eleotridae.

Mimagoniates Regan 1907:402 [ref. 3631]. Masc. *Mimagoniates barberi* Regan 1907:402. Type by monotypy. Valid (Géry 1977:362 [ref. 1597], Weitzman & S. Fink 1985:1 et seq. [ref. 5203], Weitzman et al. 1988:384 [ref. 13557], Malabarba 1989:136 [ref. 14217]). Characidae: Glandulocaudinae.

Mimasea Kamohara 1936:929 [ref. 2550]. Fem. *Mimasea taeniosoma* Kamohara 1936:929. Type by original designation (also monotypic). Synonym of *Thyrsitoides* Fowler 1929 (Nakamura 1980:357 [ref. 5478], Nakamura 1986:828 [ref. 5696]). Gempylidae.

Mimoblennius Smith-Vaniz & Springer 1971:29 [ref. 4145]. Masc. *Blennius atrocinctus* Regan 1909:404. Type by original designation. Valid (Springer & Spreitzer 1978:12 [ref. 4181], Yoshino in Masuda et al. 1984:298 [ref. 6441], Springer 1986:749 [ref. 5719]). Blenniidae.

Mimocubiceps Fowler 1944:1 [ref. 1446]. Neut. *Mimocubiceps virginiae* Fowler 1944:2. Type by original designation (also monotypic). Synonym of *Stenotomus* Gill 1865 (Robins & de Sylva 1964:589 [ref. 6550]). Sparidae.

Mimoperca (subgenus of *Stizostethium (sic)*) Gill & Jordan in Jordan 1877:44 [ref. 2374]. Fem. *Perca volgensis* Pallas 1776:461. Type by original designation (based on context of "typified by"), also monotypic. Objective synonym of *Schilius* Krynicki 1832. Synonym of *Stizostedion* Rafinesque 1820 (Collette & Banarescu 1977:1457 [ref. 5845]). Percidae.

Mindorogobius Herre 1945:11 [ref. 2139]. Masc. *Mindorogobius lopezi* Herre 1945:13. Type by original designation (also monotypic). Synonym of *Amoya* Herre 1927 (Hoese, pers. comm.). Gobiidae.

Minictenogobiops Goren 1978:192 [ref. 1851]. Masc. *Minictenogobiops sinaii* Goren 1978:192. Type by original designation (also monotypic). Synonym of *Silhouettea* Smith 1959 (Miller & Fouda 1986:395 [ref. 12844]). Gobiidae.

Miniellus (subgenus of *Notropis*) Jordan 1888:56 [ref. 2390]. Masc. *Hybopsis procne* Cope 1864:283. Type by subsequent designation. Type designated by Jordan and Evermann 1896:254 [ref. 2443]. Synonym of *Notropis* Rafinesque 1818 (Gilbert 1978:16 [ref. 7042]). Cyprinidae.

Minilabrus Randall & Dor 1980:155 [ref. 3601]. Masc. *Minilabrus striatus* Randall & Dor 1980:155. Type by original designation (also monotypic). Labridae.

Minnilus Rafinesque 1820:235 [ref. 7310]. Masc. *Minnilus dinemus* Rafinesque 1820:236. Type by subsequent designation. Type designated by Jordan & Gilbert 1877:86 [ref. 4907]. Also appeared in Rafinesque 1820 (Dec.):45 [ref. 3592]. Misspelled on p. 236 as *Minulus* and on p.237 as *Minnulus*. Synonym of *Notropis* Rafinesque 1818 (Gilbert 1978:15 [ref. 7042]). Cyprinidae.

Minomus Girard 1856:173 [ref. 1810]. Masc. *Catostomus insignis* Baird & Girard 1854:28. Type by subsequent designation. Type designated by Bleeker 1863:23 [ref. 4859] or 1863:189 [ref. 397]. Synonym of *Catostomus* Lesueur 1817. Catostomidae.

Minous Cuvier in Cuvier & Valenciennes 1829:420 [ref. 998]. Masc. *Scorpaena monodactyla* Bloch & Schneider 1801:194. Type by subsequent designation. Type designated by Bleeker 1876:6 [ref. 12248] and 1876:298 [ref. 450] as *Minous monodactylus* Cuvier & Valenciennes. Valid (Eschmeyer et al. 1979 [ref. 1277], Amaoka & Kanayama 1981 [ref. 5579], Shimizu in Masuda et al. 1984:318 [ref. 6441], Eschmeyer 1986:464 [ref. 5652], Paxton et al. 1989:443 [ref. 12442]). Scorpaenidae: Minoinae.

Minutus de Buen 1926:61 [ref. 5054]. As a "grupo" for 3 species of *Gadus*. Not available on basis of Art. 1b(6) [see de Buen's definition of "grupo" on p. 11]; see Appendix A. Gadidae.

Minutus de Buen 1926:80 [ref. 5054]. As a "grupo" for 4 species of *Gobius*. Not available on basis of Art. 1b(6) [see de Buen's definition of "grupo" on p. 11]; see Appendix A. Gobiidae.

Minyichthys (subgenus of *Micrognathus*) Herald & Randall 1972:137 [ref. 2097]. Masc. *Micrognathus brachyrhinus* Herald 1953:262. Type by original designation (also monotypic). Valid

(Dawson 1982:137 [ref. 5440], Dawson 1985:142 [ref. 6541], Dawson in Whitehead et al. 1986:631 [ref. 13676]). Syngnathidae: Syngnathinae.

Minysynchiropus Nakabo 1982:94 [ref. 3139]. Masc. *Synchiropus laddi* Schultz 1960:406. Type by original designation (also monotypic). Synonym of *Synchiropus* Gill 1859 (Fricke 1982:74 [ref. 5432]); valid (Houde 1984:637 [ref. 13674], Nakabo in Masuda et al. 1984:344 [ref. 6441]). Callionymidae.

Minytrema Jordan 1878:318 [ref. 2376]. Neut. *Catostomus melanops* Rafinesque 1820:302. Type by monotypy. Valid. Catostomidae.

Mionorus Krefft 1867:942 [ref. 2686]. Masc. *Mionorus lunatus* Krefft 1867:943. Type by monotypy. Apparently misspelled *Mionurus* by Jordan 1917:46 [ref. 2406] and by Fraser 1972:8 [ref. 5195]. Synonym of *Glossamia* Gill 1863 (Fraser 1972:8 [ref. 5195], Paxton et al. 1989:555 [ref. 12442]). Apogonidae.

Miopsaras Gilbert 1905:694 [ref. 1631]. *Miopsaras myops* Gilbert 1905:694. Type by original designation (also monotypic). Misspelled or unjustifiably emended to *Myosparas* by Regan 1926:37 [ref. 3679] and to *Myopsaras* by Roule & Angel 1933:58 [ref. 3827]. Synonym of *Ceratias* Krøyer 1845 (Pietsch 1986:481 [ref. 5969]). Ceratiidae.

Miracorvina Trewavas 1962:170 [ref. 4455]. Fem. *Sciaena angolensis* Norman 1935:14. Type by original designation (also monotypic). Sciaenidae.

Mirapinna Bertelsen & Marshall 1956:4 [ref. 290]. Fem. *Mirapinna esau* Bertelsen & Marshall 1956:4. Type by monotypy. Valid (Paxton 1973:212 [ref. 7183], Bertelsen & Marshall 1984:380 [ref. 13657], Bertelsen in Whitehead et al. 1986:521 [ref. 13676]). Mirapinnidae.

Mirbelia Canestrini 1864:189 [ref. 714]. Fem. *Lepadogaster decandollii* Risso 1826:273. Type by subsequent designation. Type apparently first designated by Jordan 1919:329 [ref. 4904]. Synonym of *Lepadogaster* Goüan 1770 (Briggs 1955:33 [ref. 637], Briggs 1973:655 [ref. 7222]). Gobiesocidae: Gobiesocinae.

Mirognathus Parr 1951:4, 10 [ref. 3380]. Masc. *Mirognathus normani* Parr 1951:10. Type by original designation (also monotypic). Species spelled *normanii* on p. 4, *normani* on p. 10. Valid (Markle & Quéro in Whitehead et al. 1984:245 [ref. 13675], Markle 1986:221 [ref. 5687]). Alepocephalidae.

Mirogobius Herre 1927:91 [ref. 2104]. Masc. *Mirogobius stellatus* Herre 1927:92. Type by original designation. Synonym of *Gobiopterus* Bleeker 1874 (Hoese, pers. comm.). Gobiidae.

Mirogrex Goren, Fishelson & Trewavas 1973:306 [ref. 1853]. Masc. *Acanthobrama terraesanctae* Steinitz 1952:295. Type by original designation (also monotypic). Synonym of *Rutilus* Rafinesque 1820 (Howes 1981:46 [ref. 14200]); synonym of *Acanthobrama* Heckel 1843 (Coad 1984 [ref. 5347], Krupp & Schneider 1989:354 [ref. 13651]). Cyprinidae.

Mirolabrichthys Herre 1927:413 [ref. 2102]. Masc. *Mirolabrichthys tuka* Herre & Montalban in Herre 1927:413. Type by monotypy. Misspelled *Microlabrichthys* in Zoological Record for 1931. Synonym of *Anthias* Bloch 1792 (Heemstra & Randall 1986:511 [ref. 5667]). Valid subgenus of *Anthias* Bloch 1792 (Randall & Lubbock 1981 [ref. 6912]). Valid (Katayama in Masuda et al. 1984:137 [ref. 6441], Katayama & Amaoka 1986 [ref. 6680]). Valid subgenus of *Pseudanthias* Bleeker 1873 (Randall & Hutomo 1988:671 [ref. 6679]). Serranidae: Anthiinae.

Mirophallus Herre 1926:539 [ref. 2122]. Masc. *Mirophallus bikolanus* Herre 1926:540. Type by monotypy. Misspelled *Microphallus* in Zoological Record for 1926. Valid (White et al. 1984:360 [ref. 13655]); synonym of *Gulaphallus* Herre 1925 (Parenti 1989:274 [ref. 13486]). Phallostethidae.

Mirorictus Parr 1947:59 [ref. 3379]. Masc. *Mirorictus taningi* Parr 1947:60. Type by monotypy. Alepocephalidae.

Mischommatus (subgenus of *Euryglossa*) Chabanaud 1938:110 [ref. 795]. Masc. *Synaptura muelleri* Steindachner 1879:4. Type by monotypy (one species with two subspecies). Objective synonym of *Strandichthys* Whitley 1937; synonym of *Dexillus* Chabanaud 1930 (Chabanaud 1943:291 [ref. 799]). Soleidae.

Misgurnus Lacepède 1803:16 [ref. 4930]. Masc. *Cobitis fossilis* Linnaeus 1758:303. Type by monotypy. Valid (Jayaram 1981:182 [ref. 6497], Sawada 1982:198 [ref. 14111], Sawada in Masuda et al. 1984:58 [ref. 6441], Kottelat 1989:13 [ref. 13605], Travers 1989:203 [ref. 13578]). Cobitidae: Cobitinae.

Mistichthys Smith 1902:30 [ref. 4038]. Masc. *Mistichthys luzonensis* Smith 1902:30. Type by monotypy. Valid (Birdsong et al. 1988:188 [ref. 7303]). Gobiidae.

Mitchillina Jordan & Evermann 1896:452, 453 [ref. 2443]. Fem. *Alepocephalus bairdii* Goode & Bean 1879:55. Type by original designation. Alepocephalidae.

Mitotichthys Whitley 1948:75 [ref. 4710]. Masc. *Syngnathus tuckeri* Scott 1942:17. Type by original designation (also monotypic). Valid (Dawson 1985:145 [ref. 6541], Paxton et al. 1989:426 [ref. 12442]). Syngnathidae: Syngnathinae.

Mitsukurina Jordan 1898:199 [ref. 2396]. Fem. *Mitsukurina owstoni* Jordan 1898:200. Type by monotypy. Valid (Springer 1973:12 [ref. 7162], Quéro in Whitehead et al. 1984:82 [ref. 13675], Compagno 1984:222 [ref. 6474], Nakaya & Shirai in Masuda et al. 1984:7 [ref. 6441], Bass & Compagno 1986:103 [ref. 5637], Cappetta 1987:92 [ref. 6348], Paxton et al. 1989:65 [ref. 12442]). Odontaspididae: Mitsukurininae.

Miuroglanis Eigenmann & Eigenmann 1889:55 [ref. 1253]. Masc. *Miuroglanis platycephalus* Eigenmann & Eigenmann 1889:56. Type by original designation (also monotypic). Valid (Burgess 1989:325 [ref. 12860]). Trichomycteridae.

Mixobrycon Eigenmann 1915:62 [ref. 1231]. Masc. *Cheirodon ribeiroi* Eigenmann 1907:9. Type by original designation (also monotypic). Valid (Géry 1977:550 [ref. 1597]). Characidae.

Mixomyrophis McCosker 1985:10 [ref. 5238]. Masc. *Mixomyrophis pusillipinna* McCosker 1985:10. Type by original designation (also monotypic). Valid (McCosker et al. 1989:277 [ref. 13288]). Ophichthidae: Myrophinae.

Mixonus Günther 1887:108 [ref. 2013]. Masc. *Bathynectes laticeps* Günther 1878:20. Type by monotypy. Valid (Nielsen 1973:551 [ref. 6885] but with *Bathynectes* as a synonym [*Bathyonus*, a replacement for *Bathynectes*, has priority over *Mixonus*]); synonym of *Bathyonus* Goode & Bean 1886 (Cohen & Nielsen 1978:27 [ref. 881]). Ophidiidae: Neobythitinae.

Mnierpes Jordan & Evermann 1896:468 [ref. 2442]. *Clinus macrocephalus* Günther 1861:267. Type by original designation (also monotypic). Valid (Clark Hubbs 1952:57 [ref. 2252]). Labrisomidae.

Moapa Hubbs & Miller 1948:1 [ref. 2258]. Fem. *Moapa coriacea* Hubbs & Miller 1948:8. Type by original designation (also monotypic). Valid. Cyprinidae.

Mobula Rafinesque 1810:48, 61 [ref. 3595]. Fem. *Mobula auriculata* Rafinesque 1810:48 (= *Raia mobular* Bonnaterre 1788:5).

Type by monotypy. Rafinesque's *auriculata* given as a substitute for *Raja mobula* of Lacepède (= *R. mobular* Bonnaterre). Valid (Krefft & Stehmann 1973:77 [ref. 7167], Nakaya in Masuda et al. 1984:16 [ref. 6441], Compagno 1986:135 [ref. 5648], Cappetta 1987:177 [ref. 6348], Paxton et al. 1989:51 [ref. 12442]). Mobulidae.

Mochokiella Howes 1980:165 [ref. 2221]. Fem. *Mochokiella paynei* Howes 1980:165. Type by original designation (also monotypic). Valid (Gosse 1986:116 [ref. 6194], Burgess 1989:197 [ref. 12860]). Mochokidae.

Mochokus Joannis 1835:Pl. 8 (3 pp.) [ref. 2355]. Masc. *Mochokus niloticus* Joannis 1835:Pl. 8 (3 pp.). Type by monotypy. *Mochocus* Günther 1864:217 [ref. 1974] is an unjustified emendation (see also Briggs 1961:163 [ref. 13439]). Valid (Gosse 1986:117 [ref. 6194]). Mochokidae.

Modicus Hardy 1983:864 [ref. 5339]. Masc. *Modicus minimus* Hardy 1983:865. Type by original designation. Gobiesocidae: Gobiesocinae.

Modigliania Perugia 1893:246 [ref. 3434]. Fem. *Modigliania papillosa* Perugia 1893:246. Type by monotypy. Synonym of *Noemacheilus* Kuhl & van Hasselt 1823 (Kottelat 1984:225 [ref. 5292] assuming *Noemacheilus* is available); synonym of *Nemacheilus* Bleeker 1863 (Roberts 1989:106 [ref. 6439], Kottelat 1990:20 [ref. 14137]). Balitoridae: Nemacheilinae.

Moebia Goode & Bean 1896:331 [ref. 1848]. Fem. *Bathynectes gracilis* Günther 1878:21. Type by monotypy. Ophidiidae: Neobythitinae.

Moema Costa 1989:223 [ref. 14270]. Fem. *Moerna piriana* Costa 1989:223. Type by original designation. Aplocheilidae: Rivulinae.

Moenkhausia Eigenmann 1903:145 [ref. 1218]. Fem. *Tetragonopterus xinguensis* Steindachner 1882:178. Type by original designation. Valid (Géry 1977:438 [ref. 1597]). Characidae.

Mogurnda Gill 1863:270 [ref. 1691]. Fem. *Eleotris mogurnda* Richardson 1844:4. Type by original designation (also monotypic and by tautonymy). Valid (Iwata et al. 1985:374 [ref. 6724], Allen & Hoese 1986 [ref. 6252], Birdsong et al. 1988:182 [ref. 7303]). Eleotridae.

Mohanga Boulenger 1911:261 [ref. 578]. Fem. *Haplochilus tanganicanus* Boulenger 1898:25. Type by monotypy. Objective synonym of *Lamprichthys* Regan 1911 [Regan's article preceded Boulenger's in same journal] (Parenti 1981:508 [ref. 7066], Wildekamp et al. 1986:191 [ref. 6198]). Cyprinodontidae: Aplocheilichthyinae.

Moharra Poey 1875:124 [ref. 3509]. Fem. *Gerres rhombeus* Cuvier in Cuvier & Valenciennes 1830:459. Type by monotypy. Synonym of *Gerres* Quoy & Gaimard 1824 (Roux 1986:325 [ref. 6209], Deckert & Greenfield 1987:184 [ref. 6778]). Gerreidae.

Mola Blyth 1860:164 [ref. 477]. Fem. *Mola buchanani* Blyth 1860:164 (= *Cyprinus mola* Hamilton 1822:334, 392). Type by original designation (also by absolute tautonymy of senior objective synonym—*mola* renamed *buchanani* by Blyth). Preoccupied by and objective synonym and homonym of *Mola* Heckel 1843; also preoccupied by *Mola* Koelreuter 1770. *Mola* Heckel replaced by *Amblypharyngodon* Bleeker 1869. Clearly intended as a new genus. Cyprinidae.

Mola Cuvier 1798:323 [ref. 5558]. Fem. *Tetraodon mola* Linnaeus 1758:334. Type by monotypy (also by absolute tautonymy). Perhaps not intended as an original description, the name appearing in earlier [uncited] works. Synonym of *Mola* Koelreuter 1770. Molidae.

Mola Heckel 1843:257 (Appendix) [ref. 2067]. Fem. *Cyprinus mola* Hamilton 1822:334, 392. Type by absolute tautonymy. Apparently appeared in Appendix to Ref. 2067; original not located. Preoccupied by Koelreuter 1770 and by Cuvier 1798, both in fishes; replaced by *Amblypharyngodon* Bleeker 1859. Objective synonym of *Amblypharyngodon* Bleeker 1859. Cyprinidae.

Mola Koelreuter 1770:337 [ref. 2654]. Fem. *Mola aculeata* Koelreuter 1770:ca. 337. Original not seen. Valid (Tortonese 1973:649 [ref. 7192], Tyler 1980:391 [ref. 4477], Matsuura in Masuda et al. 1984:366 [ref. 6441], Tortonese in Whitehead et al. 1986:1349 [ref. 13677], Heemstra 1986:908 [ref. 5660]). Molidae.

Mola Linck 1790:37 [ref. 4985]. Fem. *Tetraodon mola* Linnaeus 1758:334. Original not examined. Molidae.

Molacanthus Swainson 1839:195, 329 [ref. 4303]. Masc. *Molacanthus pallasii* Swainson 1829:329 (= *Diodon mola* Pallas 1770:39). Type by monotypy. Swainson included one species as "*M. Pallasii* Sw. Pall. Spec. zool. pl. 4." Swainson's *pallasii* is an unneeded substitute for *D. mola* Pallas. Synonym of *Mola* Koelreuter 1770 (Fraser-Brunner 1943:8 [ref. 1495]). Molidae.

Molaracana Le Danois 1961:304 [ref. 2731]. Fem. *Ostracion aculeata* Houttuyn 1764. Type by monotypy. Ostraciidae: Aracaninae.

Molarii Richardson 1848:79 [ref. 3740]. *Muraena ophis* of Rüppell 1838. Type by subsequent designation. Perhaps not available, apparently in plural form only, as a division in a key to species based on teeth. Latinized (*Molarius*) by Jordan 1919:223 [ref. 2410] and a type named; probably not available from Jordan (not used as a valid name); but accepted as *Molarii* in Jordan & Evermann 1896:402 [ref. 2443] where type was designated. In the synonymy of *Echidna* Forster 1777 (Böhlke et al. 1989:130 [ref. 13286]). Muraenidae: Muraeninae.

Molarius see *Molarii*. Muraenidae: Muraeninae.

Mollienesia Lesueur 1821:3 [ref. 2736]. Fem. *Mollienesia latipinna* Lesueur 1821:3. Type by monotypy. Originally as *Mollinesia* in text and *Molienisia* on Pl. 3; named after "Monsieur Mollien" so emended to *Mollienesia*. Variously misspelled *Mollienisia*, *Molinesia* (see Bailey & Miller 1950:318 [ref. 162]). Synonym of *Poecilia* (Rosen & Bailey 1963:44 [ref. 7067]); as a valid subgenus (Miller 1983 [ref. 6815]). Poeciliidae.

Mollisquama Dolganov 1984:1589 [ref. 5823]. *Mollisquama parini* Dolganov 1984:1589. Type by original designation (also monotypic). Squalidae.

Molochophrys Whitley 1931:310 [ref. 4672]. Fem. *Cestracion galeatus* Günther 1870:416. Type by original designation (also monotypic). Synonym of *Heterodontus* Blainville 1816 (Compagno 1984:155 [ref. 6474]). Heterodontidae.

Molva Lesueur 1819:159 [ref. 12573]. Fem. *Gadus molva* Linnaeus 1758:254. Text somewhat unclear; if *Gadus molva* was included on p. 160, then type is by absolute tautonymy. Also spelled *Molvia* and *Molua* in early literature. Valid (Svetovidov 1973:313 [ref. 7169], Fahay & Markle 1984:266 [ref. 13653], Svetovidov in Whitehead et al. 1986:702 [ref. 13676]). Lotidae.

Molvella Kaup 1858:90 [ref. 2576]. Fem. *Molvella borealis* Kaup 1858:90. Type by subsequent designation. Earliest subsequent designation not researched; type usually wrongly given as by monotypy. Synonym of *Ciliata* Couch 1832 (Svetovidov 1973:312 [ref. 7169]). Lotidae.

Momonatira Paulin 1986:357 [ref. 5326]. *Momonatira globosus* Paulin 1986:360. Type by original designation (also monotypic).

Valid. Moridae.

Monacanthus Oken (ex Cuvier) 1817:1183 [ref. 3303]. Masc. *Balistes chinensis* Osbeck 1765:147. Based on "Les Monacanthes" of Cuvier 1816:152. See Gill 1903:966 [ref. 5768]. First technical addition of species not researched. Valid (Matsuura 1979:164 [ref. 7019], Tyler 1980:176 [ref. 4477], Arai 1983:199 [ref. 14249], Aboussouan & Leis 1984:452 [ref. 13661], Matsuura in Masuda et al. 1984:359 [ref. 6441]). Monacanthidae.

Monacoa Whitley 1943:171 [ref. 4703]. Fem. *Opisthoproctus grimaldii* Zugmayer 1911:2. Type by being a replacement name. Replacement for *Grimaldia* Chapman 1942, preoccupied by Chevreux 1889 in Crustacea. Synonym of *Opisthoproctus* Vaillant 1888 (Cohen 1973:156 [ref. 6589]). Opisthoproctidae.

Monhoplichthys Fowler 1938:95 [ref. 1426]. Masc. *Monhoplichthys gregoryi* Fowler 1938:96. Type by original designation. Hoplichthyidae.

Moniana Girard 1856:199 [ref. 1810]. Fem. *Leuciscus lutrensis* Baird & Girard 1853:391. Type by subsequent designation. Type designated by Jordan & Gilbert 1877:91 [ref. 4907]. Synonym of *Notropis* Rafinesque 1818 (Gilbert 1978:15 [ref. 7042], Mayden 1987 [ref. 6630]); synonym of *Cyprinella* Girard 1857 (Mayden 1989:45 [ref. 12555]). Cyprinidae.

Monishia Smith 1959:206 [ref. 4122]. Fem. *Bathygobius william* Smith 1948:341. Type by original designation. Valid (Miller 1973:501 [ref. 6888], Goren 1985 [ref. 5179], Miller in Whitehead et al. 1986:1056 [ref. 13677], Hoese 1986:794 [ref. 5670], Maugé 1986:376 [ref. 6218], Birdsong et al. 1988:184, 186 [ref. 7303]). Gobiidae.

Monistiancistrus Fowler 1940:236 [ref. 1432]. Masc. *Monistiancistrus carachama* Fowler 1940:238. Type by original designation (also monotypic). Valid (Isbrücker 1980:57 [ref. 2303], Burgess 1989:429 [ref. 12860]); synonym of *Pseudorinelepis* Bleeker 1862 (Nijssen & Isbrücker 1987 [ref. 5993]). Loricariidae.

Monocentris Bloch & Schneider 1801:100 [ref. 471]. Fem. *Monocentris carinata* Bloch & Schneider 1801:100. Type by monotypy. Misspelled *Monocentrus* by authors. Valid (Shimizu in Masuda et al. 1984:109 [ref. 6441], Smith 1986:413 [ref. 5712], Paxton et al. 1989:364 [ref. 12442]). Monocentridae.

Monoceratias Gilbert 1915:379 [ref. 1632]. Masc. *Monoceratias acanthias* Gilbert 1915:379. Type by original designation (also monotypic). Valid (Pietsch 1974:33 [ref. 5332]). Oneirodidae.

Monoceros Bloch & Schneider 1801:180 [ref. 471]. Masc. *Monoceros biaculeatus* Bloch & Schneider 1801:180 (= *Chaetodon unicornis* Forsskål 1775:xiii, 63). Type by subsequent designation. Type designated by Jordan 1917:58 [ref. 2407]. Synonym of *Naso* Lacepède 1801 (Randall 1955:361 [ref. 13648]). Acanthuridae.

Monoceros Plumier in Lacepède 1798:357 (footnote) [ref. 2708]. Masc. Not available; Plumier manuscript name mentioned in passing under *Balistes sinensis*. See remarks under Opinion 89 in Appendix B. Not same as *Monoceros* Bloch & Schneider 1801. Monacanthidae.

Monochir Cuvier 1829:343 [ref. 995]. Fem. *Pleuronectes microchirus* Delaroche 1809:320. Type by monotypy. Other species doubtfully as synonyms in footnote. "N" for new not given by Cuvier, probably not intended as a new spelling. In the synonymy of *Monochirus* Oken 1817. Soleidae.

Monochirus Kaup 1858:101 [ref. 2578]. Masc. *Monochir maculipinnis* Agassiz 1829:88, Pl. 49. Type by monotypy. As "*Monochirus* Agass. nec. Cuv.", with description provided. Can be regarded as a new genus, dating to Kaup. Preoccupied by Rafinesque 1814 and Oken 1817 in fishes. Soleidae.

Monochirus Oken (ex Cuvier) 1817:1182a [ref. 3303]. Masc. *Pleuronectes microchirus* Delaroche 1809:320, 356. Type by monotypy. Based on "Monochires" Cuvier 1816:223 [ref. 993]. See Gill 1903:966 [ref. 5768]). Soleidae.

Monochirus Rafinesque 1814:17 [ref. 3582]. Masc. *Monochirus hispidus* Rafinesque 1814:17. Type by monotypy. Valid (Torchio 1973:633 [ref. 6892], Quéro et al. in Whitehead et al. 1986:1317 [ref. 13677], Heemstra & Gon 1986:871 [ref. 5665]). Soleidae.

Monocirrhus Heckel 1840:439 [ref. 2064]. Masc. *Monocirrhus polyacanthus* Heckel 1840:439. Type by monotypy. Valid. Nandidae: Nandinae.

Monodactylus Lacepède (ex Commerson) 1801:131 [ref. 2710]. Masc. *Monodactylus falciformis* Lacepède 1801:131, 132. Type by monotypy. Valid (Hayashi in Masuda et al. 1984:165 [ref. 6441], Desoutter 1986:338 [ref. 6212], Heemstra 1986:607 [ref. 5660]). Monodactylidae.

Monodichthys Chabanaud 1925:356 [ref. 780]. Masc. *Monodichthys proboscideus* Chabanaud 1925:356. Type by monotypy. Synonym of *Heteromycteris* Kaup 1858 (Desoutter 1986:430 [ref. 6212]). Soleidae.

Monognathus Bertin 1936:533 [ref. 292]. Masc. *Monognathus taningi* Bertin 1936:538. Type by subsequent designation. Described without type species after 1930 and not available from this author/date (Art. 13b); genus apparently can date to Myers 1940:141 [ref. 3119] where a type is designated; see Appendix A, Art. 13b. Treated as valid and dating to Bertin (Böhlke 1966:618 [ref. 5256], Bertelsen & Nielsen 1987 [ref. 6618], Bertelsen et al. 1989:652 [ref. 13293]). Monognathidae.

Monolene Goode 1880:337, 338 [ref. 1834]. *Monolene sessilicauda* Goode 1880:337, 338. Type by monotypy. Valid (Norman 1934:164 [ref. 6893], Ahlstrom et al. 1984:642 [ref. 13641], Hensley 1986:860 [ref. 5669], Hensley 1986:941). Bothidae: Bothinae.

Monomeropus (subgenus of *Monomitopus*) Garman 1899:157, 158 [ref. 1540]. Masc. *Monomeropus malispinosus* Garman 1899:157. Type by original designation (also monotypic). Type designation occurs on p. 157, no separate subgeneric description. Synonym of *Monomitopus* Alcock 1890 (Cohen & Nielsen 1978:35 [ref. 881]). Ophidiidae: Neobythitinae.

Monomitopus Alcock 1890:297 [ref. 83]. Masc. *Sirembo nigripinnis* Alcock 1889:384. Type by monotypy. Also appeared in Alcock 1896:304, 308 [ref. 91], with different type species. Valid (Nielsen 1973:551 [ref. 6885], Cohen & Nielsen 1978:35 [ref. 881], Machida in Masuda et al. 1984:100 [ref. 6441], Carter & Cohen 1985:86 [ref. 5145], Nielsen in Whitehead et al. 1986:1163 [ref. 13677], Nielsen & Cohen 1986:349 [ref. 5700]). Ophidiidae: Neobythitinae.

Monomitra Goode 1883:109 [ref. 1835]. Fem. *Amitra liparina* Goode 1880:478. Type by being a replacement name. Unneeded replacement for and objective synonym of *Amitra* Goode 1880, not preoccupied by *Amitrus* Schönherr in Coleoptera. Synonym of *Paraliparis* Collett 1878 (Stein 1978:38 [ref. 4203], Andriashev 1986:14 [ref. 12760], Kido 1988:230 [ref. 12287]). Cyclopteridae: Liparinae.

Monopenchelys Böhlke & McCosker 1982:127 [ref. 502]. Fem. *Uropterygius acutus* Parr 1930:16. Type by original designation (also monotypic). Valid (Böhlke et al. 1989:191 [ref. 13286]).

Muraenidae: Muraeninae.

Monoprion Poey 1860:123 [ref. 3499]. Masc. *Monoprion maculatus* Poey 1860:123. Type by subsequent designation. Type apparently first designated by Jordan & Evermann 1896:1106 [ref. 2443]. Preoccupied by Barrande 1850 in Coelenterata, apparently not replaced. Synonym of *Apogon* Lacepède 1801 (Fraser 1972:17 [ref. 5195]). Apogonidae.

Monopterhinus (subgenus of *Squalus*) Blainville 1816:121 [ref. 306]. Masc. *Squalus griseus* Bonnaterre 1788:9. Type by subsequent designation. Type apparently first designated by Jordan & Evermann 1896:18 [ref. 2443]. Objective synonym of *Hexanchus* Rafinesque 1810. Before ICZN. Synonym of *Hexanchus* Rafinesque 1810 (Boeseman 1973:8 [ref. 7161], Compagno 1984:19 [ref. 6474], Cappetta 1987:46 [ref. 6348]). Hexanchidae.

Monopterus Lacepède 1800:138 [ref. 2709]. Masc. *Monopterus javanensis* Lacepède 1800:138, 139. Type by monotypy. Rosen & Greenwood 1976:56 give *Muraena alba* Zuiew as the type of *Monopterus* (not an originally included species; Lacepède included only one species, *javanensis*, and it is the type by monotypy). Valid (Rosen & Greenwood 1976:56 [ref. 7094] and Jayaram 1981:309 [ref. 6497] with wrong type, Matsuura in Masuda et al. 1984:366 [ref. 6441], Daget 1986:291 [ref. 6203], Paxton et al. 1989:436 [ref. 12442], Kottelat 1989:16 [ref. 13605], Roberts 1989:183 [ref. 6439]). Synbranchidae.

Monosira Poey 1881:326 [ref. 3511]. *Monosira stahli* Poey 1881:326. Type by monotypy. Synonym of *Larimus* Cuvier 1830 (Chao 1978:31 [ref. 6983]). Sciaenidae.

Monostichodus Vaillant in Pellegrin 1900:352 [ref. 6253]. Masc. Apparently not available, appeared as name only in Vaillant in Riviere 1887 (not researched), and in synonymy in Vaillant in Pellegrin 1900:352, but apparently never used as valid name. Same as *Hemistichodus* Pellegrin 1900 (Daget & Gosse 1984 [ref. 6185]). Citharinidae: Distichodontinae.

Monotaxis Bennett 1830:688 [ref. 259]. Fem. *Monotaxis indica* Bennett 1830:603. Type by monotypy. Valid (Johnson 1980:11 [ref. 13553], Sato in Masuda et al. 1984:178 [ref. 6441], Smith 1986:599 [ref. 5712], Sato 1986:603 [ref. 5152]). Lethrinidae.

Monothrix Ogilby 1897:87 [ref. 3272]. Fem. *Monothrix polylepis* Ogilby 1897:88. Type by monotypy. Valid (Cohen & Nielsen 1978:60 [ref. 881], Paxton et al. 1989:317 [ref. 12442]). Bythitidae: Brosmophycinae.

Monotocheirodon Eigenmann & Pearson in Pearson 1924:34 [ref. 3396]. Masc. *Monotocheirodon pearsoni* Eigenmann in Pearson 1924:34. Type by monotypy. Valid (Géry 1977:547 [ref. 1597]). Characidae.

Monotretus Troschel (ex Bibron) 1856:88 [ref. 12559]. Fem. *Tetraodon cutcutia* Hamilton 1822:8, 362. Appeared first as *Monotréte* Bibron in Duméril 1855:280 [ref. 297]; latinized by Troschel 1856 as above, also by Hollard 1857:319 [ref. 2186] as *Monotreta*. First addition of species not researched; type above as given by Jordan 1919:263 [ref. 2410]. Synonym of *Tetraodon* Linneaus 1758 (Fraser-Brunner 1943:14 [ref. 1495], Arai 1983:207 [ref. 14249] as *Monotreta*); valid (Tyler 1980:341 [ref. 4477] and Kottelat 1985:276 [ref. 11441] as *Monotreta*). Tetraodontidae.

Montalbania (subgenus of *Etrumeus*) Fowler 1934:244 [ref. 1416]. Fem. *Etrumeus (Montalbania) albulina* Fowler 1934:244. Type by original designation (also monotypic). *Montalbiana* is a misspelling. Synonym of *Dussumieria* Valenciennes 1847 (Whitehead 1985:28 [ref. 5141]). Clupeidae.

Montereya Hubbs 1926:16 [ref. 2235]. Fem. *Blennicottus recalvus* Greeley 1899:9. Type by original designation (also monotypic). Synonym of *Clinocottus* Gill 1861 (Bolin 1944:76 [ref. 6379]). Cottidae.

Moojenichthys Miranda-Ribeiro [P.] 1956:546 [ref. 3729]. Masc. *Moojenichthys myersi* Miranda-Ribeiro 1956:546. Type by original designation (also monotypic). Valid (Géry 1977:343 [ref. 1597]). Characidae.

Moolgarda Whitley 1945:14 [ref. 4707]. Fem. *Moolgarda pura* Whitley 1945:15. Type by original designation. Mugilidae.

Mora Risso 1826:224 [ref. 3757]. Fem. *Mora mediterranea* Risso 1826:224. Type by monotypy. Valid (Cohen 1973:325 [ref. 6589], Paulin 1983:111 [ref. 5459], Fahay & Markle 1984:266 [ref. 13653], Cohen in Whitehead et al. 1986:721 [ref. 13676], Paxton et al. 1989:301 [ref. 12442]). Moridae.

Moralesia Fowler 1943:96 [ref. 1440]. Fem. *Anacyrtus tectifer* Cope 1870:565. Type by original designation (also monotypic). Apparently preoccupied by Espanol 1844 in Coleoptera [not researched], replaced by *Moralesicus* Fowler 1958. Synonym of *Charax* Scopoli 1777, as a valid subgenus (Géry 1977:307 [ref. 1597]). Characidae.

Moralesicus Fowler 1958:9 [ref. 1470]. Masc. *Anacyrtus tectifer* Cope 1870:565. Type by being a replacement name. Replacement for *Moralesia* Fowler 1943, preoccupied by Espanol 1844 in Coleoptera [not researched]. Characidae.

Morara Bleeker 1859:424 [ref. 370]. *Cyprinus (Chela) morar* Hamilton 1822:264, 384. Type by subsequent monotypy. Apparently appeared first in key, without included species. One species included by Bleeker 1860:212 [ref. 380]. Cyprinidae.

Mordacia Gray 1851:143 [ref. 4939]. Fem. *Petromyzon mordax* Richardson 1845:62. Type by monotypy. Also appeared in Gray 1853 [for 1851]:239 [ref. 1886]. Valid (Hubbs & Potter 1971:56 [ref. 13397], Pequeño 1989:6 [ref. 14125]). Petromyzontidae: Mordaciinae.

Morhua Fleming 1828:190 [ref. 1339]. Fem. *Gadus morhua* Linnaeus 1758:252. Type by absolute tautonymy. Several included species, one being *vulgaris* with *Gadus morhua* in synonymy. Synonym of *Gadus* Linnaeus 1758. Gadidae.

Moringua Gray 1831:Pl. 95 (v. 1) [ref. 1878]. *Moringua linearis* Gray 1831:Pl. 95. Type by monotypy. Appeared as above on 25 Jan. 1831; also in Gray 1831:9 [ref. 1879] which Fowler dates to Feb. 1831. Bleeker 1864:14 [ref. 4860] lists *M. raitaborua* Cantor as type. Gray 1831:9 credits species as "*Anguilla linearis*, Hardw. MSS." but species authorship should be Gray. See also Smith 1989:65 for nomenclatural comments. Valid (Asano in Masuda et al. 1984:21 [ref. 6441], Castle 1986:187 [ref. 5644], Paxton et al. 1989:111 [ref. 12442], Smith 1989:65 [ref. 13285]). Moringuidae.

Mormyra Browne 1789:446 [ref. 669]. Fem. Not available, published in a rejected work on Official Index (Opinion 89). Scaridae: Scarinae.

Mormyrodes Gill 1862:139 [ref. 1661]. Masc. *Mormyrus hasselquistii* Valenciennes in Cuvier & Valenciennes 1846:253. Type by monotypy. Synonym of *Mormyrus* Linnaeus 1758 (Taverne 1972:163 [ref. 6367], Gosse 1984:98 [ref. 6169]). Mormyridae.

Mormyrops Müller 1843:324 [ref. 3063]. Masc. *Mormyrus anguilloides* of Geoffroy St. Hilaire (= *Mormyrus anguilloides* Linnaeus 1758:327). Type by subsequent designation. Type designated by Gill 1862:139 [ref. 1661]. Mormyridae.

Mormyrostoma Miranda-Ribeiro 1912:192 [ref. 3716]. Neut.

Silurus carinatus Linnaeus 1766:504. Type by monotypy. Objective synonym of *Doras* Lacepède 1803. Doradidae.

Mormyrus Catesby 1771:2 [ref. 774]. Masc. Not available, published in a rejected work on Official Index (Opinion 89, Opinion 259). Gerreidae.

Mormyrus Linnaeus 1758:327 [ref. 2787]. Masc. *Mormyrus cyprinoides* Linnaeus 1758:327. Type by subsequent designation. Type designated by Jordan 1917:15 [ref. 2407], not *caschive* a pre-Linnaean name in synonymy and not available for type designation and not *anguilloides*; see Appendix A. On Official List (Opinion 77, Direction 56) with type correctly as *cyprinoides*. Valid (Lévêque & Bigorne 1985 [ref. 5947], Roberts 1989 [ref. 12832]). Mormyridae.

Mormyrynchus (subgenus of *Xiphostoma*) Swainson 1839:186, 291 [ref. 4303]. Masc. *Mormyrynchus gronovii* Swainson 1839:291 (= *Salmo anostomus* Linnaeus 1758:312). Type by monotypy. Misspelled *Mormorynchus* on p. 444 (index). Misspelled *Mormyrhunchus* by Jordan 1919:203 [ref. 2410]. Objective synonym of *Anostomus* Scopoli 1777; Swainson's *M. gronovii* is an unneeded substitute for *S. anostomus* Linnaeus. Objective synonym of *Anostomus* Scopoli 1777 (Winterbottom 1980:9 [ref. 4755] as *Mormyrhynchus*). Curimatidae: Anostominae.

Moroco Jordan & Hubbs 1925:180 [ref. 2486]. Masc. *Pseudaspius bergi* Jordan & Metz 1913:22. Type by original designation. Valid (Sawada in Masuda et al. 1984:57 [ref. 6441]); synonym of *Lagowskiella* Dybowski 1916 (Howes 1985:63 [ref. 5274]). Cyprinidae.

Morone Mitchill 1814:18 [ref. 3030]. Fem. *Morone rufa* Mitchill 1814:18. Type by subsequent designation. Gill 1860:111 [ref. 1793] restricted the genus but did not technically designate a type; Gill 1861:50 [ref. 1768] designated the type as *Morone americana* Gill, but that was not an originally-included species; first technical designation apparently by Bleeker 1876:263 [ref. 447] as "*Morone americana* Gill = *Morone rufa* Mitchill." Bleeker 1876:263 also serves as first reviser when *Morone* and *Roccus* are synonymized, selecting *Morone*. Moronidae.

Moronopsis Gill 1863:82 [ref. 1679]. Fem. *Dules marginatus* Cuvier in Cuvier & Valenciennes 1829:116. Type by monotypy. Misspelled *Moronophis* by Gill in Day 1875:67 [ref. 1080]. Synonym of *Kuhlia* Gill 1861 (Maugé 1986 [ref. 6218]). Kuhliidae.

Morrhua Oken (ex Cuvier) 1817:1182a [ref. 3303]. Fem. *Gadus morhua* Linnaeus 1758:252. Usually given as above, but we only find "Morr." on p. 1182a; based on "Les Morues" of Cuvier 1816:212 [ref. 993]. First subsequent latinization not researched. Also as *Marhua* in early literature. Synonym of *Gadus* Linnaeus 1758 (Svetovidov 1973:303 [ref. 7169]). Gadidae.

Morris Berkenhout 1789:65 [ref. 12437]. See Castle 1969:9 [ref. 12436]; not researched by us. Possibly never made available, no addition of species. Congridae: Congrinae.

Morua Risso 1826:225 [ref. 3757]. *Gadus capelanus* of Risso (= *Gadus capelanus* Lacepède 1800:366, 411). Type by monotypy. Synonym of *Trisopterus* Rafinesque 1814 (Svetovidov 1973:310 [ref. 7169]). Lotidae.

Morulius (subgenus of *Cyprinus*) Hamilton 1822:331, 391 [ref. 2031]. Masc. *Cyprinus (Morulius) morala* Hamilton 1822:331, 391. Type by subsequent designation. Type designated by Bleeker 1863:195 [ref. 397] and 1863:25 [ref. 4859]. Misspelled once as *Marulius* by Hamilton (p. 391). Synonym of *Labeo* Cuvier 1816 (see Böhlke 1984:75 [ref. 13621]); valid (Roberts 1989:45 [ref. 6439]). Cyprinidae.

Morwong Whitley 1957:65 [ref. 4727]. Masc. *Chilodactylus fuscus* Castelnau 1879:376. Type by original designation (also monotypic). Treated as masculine by author. Correct spelling of genus of type species is *Cheilodactylus*. Cheilodactylidae.

Moseleya Goode & Bean 1896:417 [ref. 1848]. Fem. *Coryphaenoides longifilis* Günther 1877:439. Type by monotypy. Preoccupied by Quelch 1884 in Colenterata, replaced by *Dolloa* Jordan 1900. Synonym of *Coryphaenoides* Gunner 1765 (Marshall 1973:294 [ref. 7194], Marshall & Iwamoto 1973:565 [ref. 6966]). Macrouridae: Macrourinae.

Motella Cuvier 1829:334 [ref. 995]. Fem. *Gadus mustela* Linnaeus 1758:255. Type by monotypy. Jordan 1917:131 [ref. 2407] regards as a replacement for *Mustela* Cuvier 1816, but there is no internal evidence that it was proposed technically as a replacement name. Synonym of *Gaidropsarus* Rafinesque 1810 (Svetovidov 1973:318 [ref. 7169], Svetovidov 1986 [ref. 8033]). Lotidae.

Moxostoma (subgenus of *Catostomus*) Rafinesque 1820:300 [ref. 5006]. Neut. *Catostomus anisurus* Rafinesque 1820:300. Type by subsequent designation. Also appeared in Rafinesque 1820 (Dec.):53 [ref. 3592]. Type designated by Bleeker 1863:190 [ref. 397] and 1863:23 [ref. 4859]. Spelled *Myxostoma* by Jordan 1877:348 [ref. 2373] (*Myxostoma* preoccupied by Troschel 1847 in Mollusca) and *Myostoma* by Meek 1904:34 [ref. 2958]. Valid (Robins & Raney 1956 [ref. 12222] and current authors). Catostomidae.

Mrigala Bleeker 1859:427 [ref. 370]. *Cirrhina bengalensis* Bleeker 1853:136. Type by subsequent monotypy. Apparently appeared first in key, without species; one species included by Bleeker 1859:259 [ref. 371] and 4 species (plus 2 with question) included by Bleeker 1860:225 [ref. 380]). Type not *mrigala* Hamilton. Correct spelling for genus of type species is *Cirrhinus*. Synonym of *Cirrhinus* Oken 1817. Cyprinidae.

Mucogobius McCulloch 1912:93 [ref. 2937]. Masc. *Gobius mucosus* Günther 1871:663. Type by original designation (also monotypic). Synonym of *Callogobius* Bleeker 1874 (Hoese 1986:784 [ref. 5670]). Gobiidae.

Mugil Linnaeus 1758:316 [ref. 2787]. Masc. *Mugil cephalus* Linnaeus 1758:316. Type by monotypy. On Official List (Opinion 75). *Mugie* Macklot 1830 on Official Index as an incorrect subsequent spelling (Direction 56). Valid (Trewavas 1973:567 [ref. 7201], de Sylva 1984 [ref. 13645], Yoshino & Senou in Masuda et al. 1984:119 [ref. 6441], Ben-Tuvia in Whitehead et al. 1986:1201 [ref. 13677], Smith & Smith 1986:718 [ref. 5717], Thomson 1986: 348 [ref. 6215], Kottelat 1989:18 [ref. 13605]). Mugilidae.

Mugilogobius (subgenus of *Gobius*) Smitt 1900:552 [ref. 4148]. Masc. *Ctenogobius abei* Jordan & Snyder 1901:55. Type by subsequent designation. No included species in 1900; Smitt in letter to Jordan in 1903 says that species was *Ctenogobius abei* Jordan & Snyder (Jordan 1920:487 [ref. 4905]); species added and type designated by Jordan, Tanaka & Snyder 1913:345 [ref. 6448]. Valid (Akihito in Masuda et al. 1984:268 [ref. 6441], Hoese 1986:795 [ref. 5670], Maugé 1986:376 [ref. 6218], Miller 1987:695 [ref. 6336], Birdsong et al. 1988:188 [ref. 7303], Kottelat 1989:19 [ref. 13605], Roberts 1989:168 [ref. 6439]). Gobiidae.

Mugiloides Lacepède 1803:393 [ref. 4930]. Masc. *Mugil chilensis* Molina 1782:222. Type by monotypy. This genus is evidently based on a mullet, family Mugilidae (Rosa & Rosa 1987 [ref. 6066]). This means that the family name Mugiloididae (or

Mugiloidae) no longer is used for the fishes known as sandperches; the oldest family name available for them is the Pinguipedidae. Mugilidae.

Mugilomorus Lacepède 1803:397 [ref. 4930]. Masc. *Mugilomorus annacarolina* Lacepède 1803:397, 398. Type by monotypy. Synonym of *Elops* Linnaeus 1766 (Daget 1984:30 [ref. 6170]). Elopidae.

Mugilops Meek & Hildebrand 1923:271 [ref. 2963]. Masc. *Mugilops cyanellus* Meek & Hildebrand 1923:271. Type by original designation. Synonym of *Melanorhinus* Metzlaar 1919. Atherinidae: Menidiinae.

Mugilostoma Hildebrand & Schroeder 1928:327 [ref. 2163]. Neut. *Mugilostoma gobio* Hildebrand & Schroeder 1928:327. Type by original designation (also monotypic). Synonym of *Evorthodus* Gill 1859 (Hoese, pers. comm.). Gobiidae.

Mulgoa Ogilby 1897:740 [ref. 3274]. *Eleotris coxii* Krefft 1864:183. Type by original designation (also monotypic). Synonym of *Gobiomorphus* Gill 1863 (Hoese, pers. comm.). Eleotridae.

Mulichthys Lloyd 1909:156 [ref. 2814]. Masc. *Mulichthys squamiceps* Lloyd 1909:158. Type by monotypy. Synonym of *Cubiceps* Lowe 1843 (Haedrich 1967:78 [ref. 5357]). Nomeidae.

Mullhypeneus Poey 1867:307 [ref. 3505]. Masc. *Mullus maculatus* Bloch 1793:348. Type by monotypy. As a section under *Upeneus* Cuvier. Synonym of *Pseudupeneus* Bleeker 1862. Mullidae.

Mulloides Bleeker 1849:6 [ref. 318]. Masc. *Mullus flavolineatus* Lacepède 1801:406. Type by subsequent designation. Type designated by Bleeker 1876:333 [ref. 448]. Preoccupied by *Mulloides* Richardson 1843 (made available by Whitley 1929 back to Richardson 1843 when Whitley treated as a senior homonym); replaced by *Mulloidichthys* Whitley 1929. Treated as valid (Ben-Tuvia 1986:610 [ref. 5641], Ben-Tuvia & Kissil 1988:2 [ref. 12819]), but apparently *Mulloidichthys* Whitley 1929 should be used. Mullidae.

Mulloides Richardson (ex Solander) 1843:16 [ref. 12502]. Masc. *Centropristes sapidissimus* Richardson 1843:16. Type by subsequent designation (also monotypic). First published in synonymy, but recognized as a senior homonym by Whitley 1929:122 [ref. 4665], who replaced *Mulloides* Bleeker 1849 (see Art. 11e). The type of *Mulloides* Richardson is the species designated by Whitley as *Centropristes sapidissimus* Richardson — the available species associated with *Mulloides* by Richardson. Synonym of *Arripis* Jenyns 1840. Arripidae.

Mulloidichthys Whitley 1929:122 [ref. 4665]. Masc. *Mullus flavolineatus* Lacepède 1802:406. Type by being a replacement name. Replacement for *Mulloides* Bleeker 1849; see *Mulloides* Richardson. On Official List (Opinion 846), but with Jordan 1917 as designator of type for *Mulloides* Bleeker. Should be valid, with *Mulloides* Bleeker 1849 an objective synonym [but not treated as such by Ben-Tuvia & Kissil 1988:2 [ref. 12819]). Valid (Yamakawa in Masuda et al. 1984:164 [ref. 6441]). Mullidae.

Mullus Linnaeus 1758:299 [ref. 2787]. Masc. *Mullus barbatus* Linnaeus 1758:299. Type by subsequent designation. Type probably designated by Bleeker 1876:334 [ref. 448] in designating this species as type of *Mullus* Klein 1749. On Official List (Opinion 77). Valid (Hureau 1973:402 [ref. 7197], Hureau in Whitehead et al. 1986:877 [ref. 13676], Ben-Tuvia & Kissil 1988:2 [ref. 12819]). Mullidae.

Munrogobius Whitley 1951:67 [ref. 4711]. Masc. *Paraphya semivestitus* Munro 1949:234. Type by being a replacement name. Unneeded replacement for *Paraphya* Munro 1949, not preoccupied by *Paraphia* or *Paraphyia* in Lepidoptera. Synonym of *Gobiopterus* Bleeker 1874 (Hoese, pers. comm.). Gobiidae.

Mupus Cocco 1840:20 [ref. 861]. *Mupus imperialis* Cocco 1840:20. Type by monotypy. Haedrich 1973:560 [ref. 7216] gives date as 1840, but Fowler (MS) cites a 1833 reference that if accurate causes *Mupus* to take precedence over *Schedophilus* [needs investigation]. Synonym of *Schedophilus* Cocco 1839 [?] (Haedrich 1967:59 [ref. 5357], Haedrich 1973:560 [ref. 7216]). Centrolophidae.

Muraena Linnaeus 1758:244 [ref. 2787]. Fem. *Muraena helena* Linnaeus 1758:244. Type by subsequent designation. Placed on Official List (Opinion 77) but later withdrawn. Type designated by Jordan & Gilbert 1883:355 [ref. 2476], as *helenae*, but Bleeker 1865:113 [ref. 409] is earlier with *anguilla*. *Murena* in s misspelling. Probably should be resubmitted to ICZN to fix type as *M. helena*. Valid (Blache et al. 1973:224 [ref. 7185], Bauchot in Whitehead et al. 1986:543 [ref. 13676], Paxton et al. 1989:132 [ref. 12442], Böhlke et al. 1989:194 [ref. 13286]). Muraenidae: Muraeninae.

Muraenesox McClelland 1844:408 [ref. 2927]. Masc. *Muraenesox hamiltoniae* McClelland 1844:409. Type by subsequent designation. Earliest type designation probably Bleeker 1864:19 [ref. 4860] as *M. bagio* Kaup = *M. hamiltoniae* McClelland; *tricuspidata* given as type by Jordan 1919:220 [ref. 2410]. Also in McClelland 1844:210 [ref. 2928]. Valid (Castle & Williamson 1975 [ref. 7115], Asano in Masuda et al. 1984:29 [ref. 6441], Bauchot & Saldanha in Whitehead et al. 1986:560 [ref. 13676], Castle 1986:188 [ref. 5644], Paxton et al. 1989:145 [ref. 12442], Smith 1989:436 [ref. 13285]). Muraenesocidae.

Muraenichthys Bleeker 1853:505 [ref. 336]. Masc. *Muraena gymnopterus* Bleeker 1853:52. Type by monotypy. Also spelled *Muraenichthijs* by Bleeker elsewhere. Valid (McCosker 1970 [ref. 2931], McCosker 1977:58 [ref. 6836], Asano in Masuda et al. 1984:30 [ref. 6441], McCosker & Castle 1986:180 [ref. 5690], Paxton et al. 1989:117 [ref. 12442]. McCosker et al. 1989:271 [ref. 13288]). Ophichthidae: Myrophinae.

Muraenoblenna Kaup 1856:67 [ref. 2572]. Fem. *Ichthyophis tigrinus* Lesson (not of Lacepède). Not intended as new; Kaup cites Lacepède as author of genus, but Lacepèdes *Muraenoblenna* is a myxinid; Kaup's *Muraenoblenna* is preoccupied by Lacepède 1803. Also appeared as name only in Kaup in Duméril 1856:200 [ref. 1154]. Muraenidae.

Muraenoblenna Lacepède (ex Commerson) 1803:652 [ref. 4930]. Fem. *Muraenoblenna olivacea* Lacepède 1803:652, 653. Type by monotypy. Synonym of *Myxine* Linnaeus 1758 (Fowler 1964:48 [ref. 7160]). Myxinidae: Myxininae.

Muraenoclinus Smith 1946:538 [ref. 4072]. Masc. *Clinus dorsalis* Castelnau in Bleeker 1860:54. Type by original designation (also monotypic). Synonym of *Clinus* Cuvier 1816 (Bennett 1983 [ref. 5299]); valid (Smith 1986:766 [ref. 5712]). Clinidae.

Muraenoides Lacepède 1800:324 [ref. 2709]. Masc. *Blennius sujef* Lacepède 1800:324 (= *Blennius muraenoides* Sujef 1779:195). Type by monotypy. *B. sujef* Lacepède is an unneeded replacement for *B. muraenoides* Sujef. Synonym of *Pholis* Scopoli 1777 (Makushok 1973:534 [ref. 6889], Yatsu 1981:169 [ref. 4814]). Pholidae.

Muraenolepis Günther 1880:17 [ref. 2011]. Fem. *Muraenolepis marmoratus* Günther 1880:18. Type by monotypy. Valid (Cohen 1984:263 [ref. 13646], Fahay & Markle 1984:266 [ref. 13653],

Inada in Nakamura et al. 1986:102 [ref. 14235]). Muraenolepididae.

Muraenophis Lacepède 1803:627 [ref. 4930]. Masc. *Muraena helena* Linnaeus 1758:244. Type by subsequent designation. Type designated by Jordan 1917:68 [ref. 2407], but *Muraenophis* is an unjustified emendation of *Murenophis* Cuvier 1798, with same type (see Norman 1922:297 [ref. 3211]). *Muraenopsis* Kaup 1856:46 [ref. 2573] is a misspelling. In the synonymy of *Muraena* Linnaeus 1758 (Blache et al. 1973:224 [ref. 7185], Böhlke et al. 1989:194 [ref. 13286]). Muraenidae: Muraeninae.

Muraenopsis Lesueur in Kaup 1856:46 [ref. 2572]. Fem. *Muraenophis ocellata* Lesueur 1825:108. Type by subsequent designation. Also appeared in Kaup 1856:11 [ref. 2573]. Treated by some authors as available and not same as *Muraenophis*; treated by others (e.g. Jordan, Norman, and McCosker) as a misspelling of *Muraenophis*. Synonym of *Ophichthus* Ahl 1789 (Blache et al. 1973:247 [ref. 7185], McCosker 1977:80 [ref. 6836]). Ophichthidae: Ophichthinae.

Muraenosaurus Osório 1909:14 [ref. 3317]. Masc. *Muraenosaurus guentheri* Osório 1909:14. Type by monotypy. Preoccupied by Seeley 1874 in Reptilia, replaced by *Osorina* Whitley 1951. Synonym of *Nettastoma* Rafinesque 1810 (Blache et al. 1973:236 [ref. 7185], Smith et al. 1981:538 [ref. 6158], Smith 1989:604 [ref. 13285]). Nettastomatidae.

Murasoius (subgenus of *Sebastes*) Matsubara 1943:235 [ref. 2905]. Masc. *Sebastes pachycephalus* Temminck & Schlegel 1843:47. Type by original designation (also monotypic). Synonym of *Sebastes* Cuvier 1829. Scorpaenidae: Sebastinae.

Murenophis Cuvier 1798:329 [ref. 5558]. Masc. *Muraena helena* Linnaeus 1758:244. Type by monotypy. Synonym of *Muraena* Linnaeus 1758 (Blache et al. 1973:224 [ref. 7185], Böhlke et al. 1989:194 [ref. 13286]). Muraenidae: Muraeninae.

Murmille Setna & Sarangdhar (ex Gistel) 1946:246, 251 [ref. 6848]. *Squalus mustelus* Linnaeus 1758:235. Type by monotypy. Authors cite Gistel as author of *Murmille* [not located by us]; genus apparently can date to Setna & Sarangdhar as above. Objective synonym of *Mustelus* Linck 1790. Triakidae: Triakinae.

Murrayia Castelnau 1872:61 [ref. 757]. Fem. *Murrayia guntheri* Castelnau 1872:61. Type by subsequent designation. Type designated by McCulloch 1929:141 [ref. 2948]. Misspelled *Murraya* by Bleeker 1876:267 [ref. 447]. Synonym of *Macquaria* Cuvier 1830 (Paxton et al. 1989:513 [ref. 12442]). Percichthyidae.

Musgravius (subgenus of *Pescadorichthys*) Whitley 1961:62 [ref. 4731]. *Pescadorichthys (Musgravius) laudandus* Whitley 1961:63. Type by original designation (also monotypic). Synonym of *Plagiotremus* Gill 1865, but as a valid subgenus (Smith-Vaniz 1976:108 [ref. 4144]). Blenniidae.

Mustel Oken (ex Cuvier) 1817:1183 [ref. 3303]. Fem. *Gadus mustela* Linnaeus 1758:255. Based on "Les Mustèles" of Cuvier 1816:215 [ref. 993] (see Gill 1903:966 [ref. 5768]). Technical addition of species not researched; type usually given as by tautonymy. Preoccupied by Linnaeus 1758 in Mammalia, *Motella* Cuvier 1829 is available with same type. Often written *Mustela*. Synonym of *Gaidropsarus* Rafinesque 1810 (Svetovidov 1973:318 [ref. 7169], Svetovidov 1986 [ref. 8033]). Lotidae.

Mustelichthys Tanaka 1917:201 [ref. 4330]. Masc. *Mustelichthys ui* Tanaka 1917:201. Type by monotypy. Serranidae: Anthiinae.

Mustellus Fischer von Waldheim 1813:78 [ref. 1331]. Masc. On Official Index as an incorrect subsequent spelling for *Mustelus* Linck 1790 (Direction 56). Original not seen. Triakidae: Triakinae.

Mustellus Risso 1826:126 [ref. 3757]. Masc. Presumably a misspelling for *Mustelus* Cuvier 1817. Synonym of *Mustelus* Linck 1790 (Compagno 1973:28 [ref. 7163]). Triakidae: Triakinae.

Mustelus Cuvier 1816:128 [ref. 993]. Masc. *Squalus mustelus* Linnaeus 1758:235. Type by monotypy (also by absolute tautonymy); perhaps described without knowledge of Linck. Homonym of and objective synonym of *Mustelus* Linck 1790 (Compagno 1973:28 [ref. 7163], Compagno 1988:219 [ref. 13488]). Triakidae: Triakinae.

Mustelus Linck 1790:31 [ref. 4985]. Masc. *Squalus mustelus* Linnaeus 1758:235. Type designated by ICZN. On Official List (Opinion 93). *Mustellus* Fischer von Waldheim 1813 is an incorrect subsequent spelling placed on Official Index (Direction 56); *Mustellus* Risso 1826 apparently also an incorrect subsequent spelling. See also Hubbs 1938 [ref. 5958]. Valid (Compagno 1973:28 [ref. 7163], Compagno 1984:397 [ref. 6846], Nakaya in Masuda et al. 1984:5 [ref. 6441], Bass et al. 1986:81 [ref 5639], Cappetta 1987:116 [ref. 6348], Herman et al. 1988:104 [ref. 13267], Paxton et al. 1989:82 [ref. 12442]). Triakidae: Triakinae.

Mustelus Valmont de Bomare 1768:746 [ref. 4507]. Masc. Not available, published in a rejected work on Official Index (Opinion 89, Direction 32). In the synonymy of *Mustelus* Linck 1790. Triakidae: Triakinae.

Myaka Trewavas, Green & Corbet 1972:59 [ref. 4460]. *Myaka myaka* Trewavas, Green & Corbet 1972:59. Type by original designation (also monotypic). Cichlidae.

Mycteroperca Gill 1862:236 [ref. 1664]. Fem. *Serranus olfax* Jenyns 1842:9. Type by monotypy. Valid (Smith 1971:171 [ref. 14102], Tortonese 1973:360 [ref. 7192], Kendall 1984:500 [ref. 13663]). Serranidae: Epinephelinae.

Myctophum Rafinesque 1810:35, 56 [ref. 3595]. Neut. *Myctophum punctatum* Rafinesque 1810:35. Type by monotypy. Valid (Krefft & Bekker 1973:171 [ref. 7181], Paxton 1979:15 [ref. 6440], Hulley in Whitehead et al. 1984:472 [ref. 13675], Moser et al. 1984:219 [ref. 13645], Fujii in Masuda et al. 1984:66 [ref. 6441], Hulley 1986:312 [ref. 5672], Paxton et al. 1989:266 [ref. 12442]). Myctophidae.

Myersglanis Hora & Silas 1952:19 [ref. 2218]. Masc. *Exostoma blythi* Day 1869:525. Type by original designation (also monotypic). Valid (Chu 1979:76 [ref. 831], Jayaram 1981:263 [ref. 6497], Burgess 1989:133 [ref. 12860]). Sisoridae.

Myersichthys Clark Hubbs 1952:103 [ref. 2252]. Masc. *Clinus guttulatus* Valenciennes in Cuvier & Valenciennes 1836:286. Type by original designation (also monotypic). Synonym of *Calliclinus* Gill 1860 (Stephens & Springer 1974:19 [ref. 7149]). Labrisomidae.

Myersina Herre 1934:89 [ref. 2108]. Fem. *Myersina macrostoma* Herre 1934:90. Type by original designation (also monotypic). Valid (Hoese & Lubbock 1982 [ref. 6551], Akihito & Meguro 1983 [ref. 5301], Akihito in Masuda et al. 1984:259 [ref. 6441], Birdsong et al. 1988:193 [ref. 7303]). Gobiidae.

Myersiscus Fowler 1934:361 [ref. 1416]. Masc. *Myersiscus obtusifrons* Fowler 1934:362. Type by original designation (also monotypic). Chiasmodontidae.

Mylacochromis (subgenus of *Gaurochromis*) Greenwood 1980:36 [ref. 1899]. Masc. *Haplochromis obtusidens* Trewavas 1928:95. Type by original designation. Cichlidae.

Mylacrodon Regan 1903:62 [ref. 3615]. Masc. *Mylacrodon goeldii*

Regan 1903:62. Type by monotypy. Haemulidae.

Myleocollops (subgenus of *Metynnis*) Eigenmann 1903:147 [ref. 1218]. Masc. *Metynnis goeldii* Eigenmann 1910:443 (= *Myletes lippencottianus* Ulrey, not Cope). Type by original designation (also monotypic). Synonym of *Metynnis* Cope 1878 (Géry 1976:50 [ref. 14199]). Characidae: Serrasalminae.

Mylesinus Valenciennes in Cuvier & Valenciennes 1849:234 [ref. 1014]. Masc. *Mylesinus schomburgkii* Valenciennes in Cuvier & Valenciennes 1849:235. Type by monotypy. Valid (Géry 1976:49 [ref. 14199], Géry 1977:275 [ref. 1597], Jégu & Dos Santos 1988 [ref. 12838]). Characidae: Serrasalminae.

Myletes Cuvier 1815:115 Masc. *Myletes rhomboidalis* Cuvier 1818. Needs more research. Paugy 1984:140 [ref. 6183] dates to Cuvier 1814:75 with type as *niloticus* Forsskål = *Salmo dentex* Linnaeus 1758 (see also Monod 1950: 49 [ref. 14468]). Type above from Jordan; Cuvier 1814:75 is Cuvier in Desmarest 1814, Bull. Soc. Philomath. (not investigated). Valid (Géry 1976:48 [ref. 14199] in Serrasalmidae); in the synonym of [the later, African] *Alestes* Müller & Troschel 1844 (Paugy 1984:140 [ref. 6183]). Alestiidae.

Myleus Müller & Troschel 1844:98 [ref. 3070]. Masc. *Myleus setiger* Müller & Troschel 1844:98. Type by subsequent designation. Type designated by Eigenmann 1910:443 [ref. 1224]. See also discussion of *Cartaba* Hilhouse 1825 in Whitehead 1973:6, footnote [ref. 13755]. Valid (Géry 1976:49 [ref. 14199], Géry 1977:259 [ref. 1597], Géry et al. 1987:446 [ref. 6001]). Characidae: Serrasalminae.

Mylio Commerson in Lacepède 1802:131 (footnote) [ref. 4929]. Apparently not available, see remarks under Opinion 89 in Appendix B. But if considered a name published in synonymy then it apparently was made available by Munro (1949) (not investigated). In the synonymy of *Acanthopagrus* Peters 1855. Sparidae.

Myliobates Agassiz 1843:Pl. D [ref. 13390]. Masc. Name only, not available; also preoccupied by Schinz 1822 in fishes if available. Myliobatidae.

Myliobates Schinz (ex Dumeril) 1822:234, 832 [ref. 3926]. Masc. *Raja aquila* Linnaeus 1758:232. Regarded as an incorrect subsequent spelling for *Myliobatis* Cuvier [appeared in latinized form in Cuvier 1816 [ref. 993]; Schinz work being a translation of Cuvier 1816]. Myliobatidae.

Myliobatis Cuvier (ex Duméril) 1816:137 [ref. 993]. Fem. *Raja aquila* Linnaeus 1758:232. Type by subsequent designation. Type designated first by Bory de Saint-Vincent, v. 14, 1828:449 [ref. 3853] (see Whitley 1935:137 [ref. 6396], but designated on p. 449 and not p. 499 as given by Whitley). Valid (Krefft & Stehmann 1973:74 [ref. 7167], Nakaya in Masuda et al. 1984:16 [ref. 6441], Compagno 1986:133 [ref. 5648], Cappetta 1987:172 [ref. 6348], Paxton et al. 1989:49 [ref. 12442]). Myliobatidae.

Myliobatis Geoffroy St. Hilaire 1817:Pl. 26 [ref. 4186]. Fem. *Myliobatis bovina* Geoffroy St. Hilaire 1817:Pl. 26. Type by subsequent designation. Plates 18-27 apparently published in 1817 (see Taylor 1985 [ref. 6640]). Type designated by Fowler 1911:84 [ref. 6398]. Myliobatidae.

Mylocheilus Agassiz 1855:229 [ref. 5839]. Masc. *Mylocheilus lateralis* Agassiz & Pickford in Agassiz 1855:231. Type by original designation ("new generic type") or by monotypy. Cyprinidae.

Mylochromis Regan 1920:45 [ref. 3669]. Masc. *Tilapia lateristriga* Günther 1864:312. Type by original designation (also monotypic). Cichlidae.

Myloleuciscus Garman 1912:116 [ref. 1544]. Masc. *Myloleuciscus atripinnis* Garman 1912:116. Type by monotypy (second species conditionally included). Synonym of *Mylopharyngodon* Peters 1880 (Howes 1981:41 [ref. 14200]). Cyprinidae.

Myloleucops Cockerell 1913:136 [ref. 870]. Masc. *Leuciscus aethiops* Basilewski 1855:233. Type by being a replacement name. Replacement for *Myloleucus* Günther 1873, preoccupied by Cope 1872 in fishes. Synonym of *Leuciscus* Cuvier 1816. Cyprinidae.

Myloleucus Cope 1872:475 [ref. 923]. Masc. *Myloleucus pulverulentus* Cope 1872:475. Type by monotypy. Synonym of *Mylopharyngodon* Peters 1880 (Howes 1981:41 [ref. 14200]). Cyprinidae.

Myloleucus Günther 1873:247 [ref. 2004]. Masc. *Leuciscus aethiops* Basilewski 1855:233. Type by original designation (also monotypic). Preoccupied by Cope 1872 in fishes, replaced by *Myloleucops* Cockerell 1913. Objective synonym of *Myloleucops* Cockerell 1913. Synonym of *Leuciscus* Cuvier 1816. Cyprinidae.

Mylopharodon Ayres 1855 [ref. 13428]. Masc. *Mylopharodon robustus* Ayres 1855:33. Type by monotypy. Read at meeting of 12 Mar. 1855; appeared first in "The Pacific" newspaper, v. 4 (16), 23 Mar. 1855, then in the Proceedings, p. 35 [ref. 159]. Valid (Uyeno 1961:338 [ref. 4479]). Cyprinidae.

Mylopharyngodon Peters 1880:925 [ref. 3455]. Masc. *Leuciscus aethiops* Basilewski 1855:233. Type by monotypy. Valid (Yang & Hwang 1964:9 [ref. 13497], Howes 1981:41 [ref. 14200], Sawada in Masuda et al. 1984:58 [ref. 6441], Chen & Li in Chu & Chen 1989:37 [ref. 13584], Kottelat 1989:9 [ref. 13605]). Cyprinidae.

Myloplus Gill 1896:214 [ref. 1740]. Masc. *Myletes asterias* Müller & Troschel 1844:98. Type by subsequent designation. Proposed by Gill for the subgenus *Myletes* as treated by Müller & Troschel 1844, not *Myletes* Cuvier; no type mentioned. First technical addition of species not researched; type as given by Jordan 1920:467 [ref. 4905]. Synonym of *Myleus* Müller & Troschel 1844, as a valid subgenus (Géry 1976:49 [ref. 14199]). Characidae: Serrasalminae.

Mylorhina Gill 1865:136 [ref. 1712]. Fem. *Rhinoptera lalandii* Müller & Henle 1841:182. Type by original designation (also monotypic). Synonym of *Rhinoptera* Cuvier 1829 (Cappetta 1987:173 [ref. 6348]). Myliobatidae.

Mylossoma Eigenmann & Kennedy 1903:530 [ref. 1260]. Neut. *Myletes albiscopus* Cope 1872:267. Type by monotypy. Also appeared in Eigenmann 1903 (Dec.):148 [ref. 1218]. Misspelled *Mylosoma* by Eigenmann 1910:444 [ref. 1224]. Valid (Géry 1976:50 [ref. 14199], Géry 1977:258 [ref. 1597], Géry et al. 1987:443 [ref. 6001]). Characidae: Serrasalminae.

Myocharax (subgenus of *Leporinus*) Fowler 1914:239 [ref. 1390]. Masc. *Leporinus desmotes* Fowler 1914:239. Type by original designation (also monotypic). Synonym of *Leporinus* Agassiz 1829, but as a valid subgenus (Géry 1977:158 [ref. 1597]). Curimatidae: Anostominae.

Myoglanis Eigenmann 1912:130, 159 [ref. 1227]. Masc. *Myoglanis potaroensis* Eigenmann 1912:159. Type by original designation. Genus and species appeared first as name only in Eigenmann 1910:384 [ref. 1224], available species questionably included, therefore not available from 1910. Valid (Stewart 1986:668 [ref. 5211], Burgess 1989:276 [ref. 12860]). Pimelodidae.

Myomyrus Boulenger 1898:9 [ref. 542]. Masc. *Myomyrus macrodon* Boulenger 1898:10. Type by monotypy. Valid (Taverne 1972:87 [ref. 6367]). Mormyridae.

Myoxocephalus Tilesius (ex Steller) 1811:273 [ref. 4408]. Masc. *Myoxocephalus stelleri* Tilesius 1811:273. Type by monotypy.

Valid (Neyelov 1973:597 [ref. 7219], Neyelov 1979:115, 120 [ref. 3152], Washington et al. 1984:443 [ref. 13660], Yabe in Masuda et al. 1984:326 [ref. 6441], Yabe 1985:111 [ref. 11522], Fedorov in Whitehead et al. 1986:1253 [ref. 13677]). Cottidae.

Myrichthys Girard 1859:58 [ref. 1821]. Masc. *Myrichthys tigrinus* Girard 1859:58. Type by monotypy. Valid (McCosker 1977:78 [ref. 6836], Asano in Masuda et al. 1984:31 [ref. 6441], McCosker & Castle 1986:181 [ref. 5690], Paxton et al. 1989:118 [ref. 12442], McCosker et al. 1989:372 [ref. 13288]). Ophichthidae: Ophichthinae.

Myriodon Brisout de Barneville 1847:133 [ref. 643]. Masc. *Scorpaena vaigiensis* Quoy & Gaimard 1824:324. Type by monotypy. Objective synonym of *Centrogenys* Richardson 1842. Centrogeniidae.

Myriolepis Lockington 1880:248 [ref. 2818]. Fem. *Myriolepis zonifer* Lockington 1880:248. Type by monotypy. Preoccupied by Egerton 1864 in fossil fishes, replaced by *Erilepis* Gill 1894. Objective synonym of *Erilepis* Gill 1894. Anoplopomatidae.

Myriosteon Gray 1864:164 [ref. 1888]. Neut. *Myriosteon higginsii* Gray 1864:164. Type by monotypy. Described as an echinoderm, but based on a tube from rostral cartilage of a *Pristis* (Jordan 1919:332 [ref. 4904]). Synonym of *Pristis* Linck 1790 (Cappetta 1987:158 [ref. 6348]). Pristidae.

Myripristis Cuvier 1829:150 [ref. 995]. Fem. *Myripristis jacobus* Cuvier 1829:150. Type by subsequent designation. Appeared first as above (Mar.) with genus latinized in footnote, then in Cuvier & Valenciennce (Apr.) 1829 [ref. 4879]. Type designated by Jordan & Evermann 1896:846 [ref. 2443]. Spelled *Myriopristis* by Gill 1863:87 [ref. 1679]). Valid (Woods & Sonoda 1973:368 [ref. 6899], Greenfield 1974 [ref. 7142], Randall & Guézé 1981 [ref. 6911], Shimizu in Masuda et al. 1984:112 [ref. 6441], Randall & Heemstra 1986:422 [ref. 5707], Paxton et al. 1989:376 [ref. 12442]). Holocentridae.

Myrmillo Gistel 1848:X [ref. 1822]. *Squalus mustelus* Linnaeus 1758:235. Type by being a replacement name. Replacement for *Mustelus* Cuvier 1816, not preoccupied by *Mustela* Linnaeus in Mammalia (but preoccupied by *Mustelus* Linck 1790); although Gistel lists species *vulgaris*, his names are regarded as replacement names taking the type of original genus. Objective synonym of *Mustelus* Linck 1790 (Compagno 1973:28 [ref. 7163], Compagno 1988:219 [ref. 13488]). Triakidae: Triakinae.

Myroconger Günther 1870:93 [ref. 1995]. Masc. *Myroconger compressus* Günther 1870:93. Type by monotypy. Appeared first without sufficient distinguishing features in Günther 1869:238 [ref. 13284] as "... the new genus *Myroconger* is of great interest, being a *Muraena* with pectoral fins."; species as name only (p. 369). Valid (Smith 1984 [ref. 6810], Smith 1989:98 [ref. 13285]). Myrocongridae.

Myrophis Lütken 1852:14 [ref. 2852]. Masc. *Myrophis punctatus* Lütken 1852:15. Type by monotypy. Valid (McCosker 1977:59 [ref. 6836], Karrer 1982:79 [ref. 5679], Asano in Masuda et al. 1984:30 [ref. 6441], McCosker et al. 1989:279 [ref. 13288]). Ophichthidae: Myrophinae.

Myropterura Ogilby 1897:247 [ref. 3273]. Fem. *Myropterura laticaudata* Ogilby 1897:247. Type by monotypy. Possibly published in 1898. Synonym of *Muraenichthys* Bleeker 1853 (McCosker 1970:509 [ref. 2931], McCosker 1977:58 [ref. 6836]). Ophichthidae: Myrophinae.

Myrus Kaup 1856:53 [ref. 2572]. Masc. *Muraena vulgaris* Kaup 1856:53 (= *Muraena myrus* Linnaeus 1758:245). Type by monotypy. Species *myrus* renamed *vulgaris* by Kaup. Also in Kaup 1856:31 [ref. 2573] and as name only in Kaup in Duméril 1856:198 [ref. 1154]. Synonym of *Echelus* Rafinesque 1810 (Blache et al. 1973:245 [ref. 7185], McCosker 1977:75 [ref. 6836]). Ophichthidae: Ophichthinae.

Mystacoleucus Günther 1868:206 [ref. 1990]. Masc. *Systomus (Capoeta) padangensis* Bleeker 1852:593. Type by original designation (also monotypic). Valid (Wu et al. 1977:272 [ref. 4807], Jayaram 1981:111 [ref. 6497], Kottelat 1985:264 [ref. 11441], Chu & Kottelat 1989:1 [ref. 12575], Roberts 1989:45 [ref. 6439], Chu & Cui in Chu & Chen 1989:225 [ref. 13584], Kottelat 1989:9 [ref. 13605]). Cyprinidae.

Mystaconurus (subgenus of *Macrurus*) Günther 1887:124, 139 [ref. 2013]. Masc. *Hymenocephalus italicus* Giglioli in Giglioli & Issel 1884:228. Type by subsequent designation. Type designated by Jordan & Evermann 1898:2580 [ref. 2445]. Objective synonym of *Hymenocephalus* Giglioli 1884 (Marshall 1973:289 [ref. 7194], Iwamoto 1979:140 [ref. 2311]). Macrouridae: Macrourinae.

Mystidens Whitley 1944:25 [ref. 4704]. Masc. *Mystidens innominatus* Whitley 1944:25. Type by original designation (also monotypic). Synonym of *Negaprion* Whitley 1940 (Compagno 1984:516 [ref. 6846], Compagno 1988:341 [ref. 13488]). Carcharhinidae.

Mystriophis Kaup 1856:45 [ref. 2572]. Masc. *Ophisurus rostellatus* Richardson 1848:105. Type by subsequent designation. Type designated by Bleeker 1864:35 [ref. 4860] and 1865:118 [ref. 409]. Also appeared in Kaup 1856:10 [ref. 2573] and as name only in Kaup in Duméril 1856:199 [ref. 1154]. Valid (McCosker 1977:79 [ref. 6836], Asano in Masuda et al. 1984:31 [ref. 6441], McCosker & Castle 1986:181 [ref. 5690], McCosker et al. 1989:299 [ref. 13288]). Ophichthidae: Ophichthinae.

Mystus Gray 1854:155 [ref. 1911]. Masc. *Mystus carolinensis* Gray 1854:156. Type by subsequent designation. Gray and not Gronow is apparently responsible for this description (see p. vi in Preface). Two included species; earliest type designation not researched. Apparently a synonym of *Bagre* Cloquet 1816 or *Ailurichthys* Baird & Girard 1854. Ariidae.

Mystus Gronow 1763:124 [ref. 1910]. Masc. Not available, published in a rejected work on Official Index (Opinion 261). See also *Myste* Bosc as discussed by Whitley 1936:190 [ref. 6397]. Bagridae.

Mystus Klein 1775:535 [ref. 2618]. Masc. Not available, published in a work that does not conform to the principle of binominal nomenclature. Not *Mystus* Gronow of Scopoli. In the synonymy of *Barbus* Cuvier 1816. Cyprinidae.

Mystus Lacepède 1803:466 [ref. 4930]. Masc. *Mystus clupeoides* Lacepède 1803:466 (= *Clupea mystus* Linnaeus 1758:319). Type by monotypy. Preoccupied by Scopoli 1777 in fishes. Synonym of *Coilia* Gray 1830 (Whitehead 1967:148 [ref. 6464], Whitehead et al. 1988:460 [ref. 5725]). Engraulidae.

Mystus Scopoli (ex Gronow) 1777:451 [ref. 3990]. Masc. *Bagrus halapensis* Valenciennes in Cuvier & Valenciennes 1839:413. Type by subsequent designation. Appeared first without species, earliest addition of species not researched; above type from literature. Valid (Jayaram 1977:20 [ref. 7005], Jayaram 1978 [ref. 7008], Jayaram 1981:195 [ref. 6497], Kottelat 1985:270 [ref. 11441], Burgess 1989:69 [ref. 12860], Kottelat 1989:13 [ref. 13605], Roberts 1989:120 [ref. 6439]). Bagridae.

Mytilophagus Gibbons 1854:1, col. 1 [ref. 6064]. Masc. *Mytilophagus fasciatus* Gibbons 1854:1, col. 1. Type by monotypy. Also in Gibbons 1854 (Oct.):125 [ref. 1610]. Synonym of *Amphistichus* Agassiz (17 May) 1854 (Tarp 1952:39 [ref. 12250]). Embiotocidae.

Myxine Linnaeus 1758:650 [ref. 2787]. Fem. *Myxine glutinosa* Linnaeus 1758:650. Type by monotypy. On Official List (Opinion 75). Valid (Vladykov 1973:6 [ref. 7159], Masuda & Kanayama in Masuda et al. 1984:1 [ref. 6441], Fernholm & Vladykov in Whitehead et al. 1984:68 [ref. 13675], Fernholm 1986:36 [ref. 6283]). Myxinidae: Myxininae.

Myxocephalus Steindachner in Steindachner & Döderlein 1887:281 [ref. 4249]. Masc. *Myxocephalus japonicus* Steindachner in Steindachner & Döderlein 1887:281. Type by monotypy. Synonym of *Diplacanthopoma* Günther 1887 (Cohen & Nielsen 1978:47 [ref. 881]). Bythitidae: Bythitinae.

Myxocyprinus Gill 1878:1574 [ref. 1719]. Masc. *Carpiodes asiaticus* Bleeker 1864:19. Type by monotypy. Original not examined. Also appeared as Gill in Jordan 1878:104, 217 [see under ref. 1719, examined] Catostomidae.

Myxodagnus Gill 1861:269 [ref. 1778]. Masc. *Myxodagnus opercularis* Gill 1861:270. Type by monotypy. Valid (Dawson 1982:69 [ref. 1072]). Dactyloscopidae.

Myxodes Cuvier 1829:238 [ref. 995]. Masc. *Myxodes viridis* Valenciennes in Cuvier & Valenciennes 1836:398. Type by subsequent designation. Appeared first without species; several species included by Valenciennes in Cuvier & Valenciennes 1836:397 [ref. 1005]. Type by subsequent designation, possibly first by Jordan 1917:129 [ref. 2407]. *Mixodes* is a misspelling. Valid (Clark Hubbs 1952:108 [ref. 2252], Stephens & Springer 1974 [ref. 7149]). Clinidae.

Myxonum Rafinesque 1815:88 [ref. 3584]. *Mugil chilensis* Molina 1782:222. Type by being a replacement name. As "*Myxonum* R. [Rafinesque] *Mugiloides* Lac." An available replacement name (unneeded) for and objective synonym of *Mugiloides* Lacepède 1803 (see Rosa & Rosa 1987:1049 [ref. 6066]). Mugilidae.

Myxus Günther 1861:466 [ref. 1964]. Masc. *Myxus elongatus* Günther 1861:466. Type by subsequent designation. Type designated by Jordan 1919:307 [ref. 2410]. Valid (Smith & Smith 1986:718 [ref. 5717], Thomson 1986:349 [ref. 6215]). Mugilidae.

Myzopsetta Gill 1861:51 [ref. 1766]. Fem. *Platessa ferruginea* Storer 1839:141. Type by subsequent designation. Type designated by Jordan & Evermann 1898:2644 [ref. 2445]. Synonym of *Limanda* Gottsche 1835. Pleuronectidae: Pleuronectinae.

Naevochromis Eccles & Trewavas 1989:197 [ref. 13547]. Masc. *Haplochromis chrysogaster* Trewavas 1935:103. Type by original designation (also monotypic). Cichlidae.

Nalbantichthys Schultz 1967:1 [ref. 3974]. Masc. *Nalbantichthys elongatus* Schultz 1967:2. Type by original designation (also monotypic). Valid (Anderson 1984:578 [ref. 13634]). Zoarcidae.

Nalbantius Maugé & Bauchot 1984:465 [ref. 6614]. Masc. *Chaetodon speculum* Kuhl & van Hasselt in Cuvier 1831:73. Type by original designation. Chaetodontidae.

Nandina Gray 1831:8 [ref. 1879]. Fem. *Nandina hamiltonii* Gray 1831:8 (= *Cyprinis nandina* Hamilton 1822:300, 388). Type by monotypy. Gray needlessly renamed Hamilton's species *nandina* as *hamiltonii*. Cyprinidae.

Nandopsis (subgenus of *Cichlasoma*) Gill 1862:238 [ref. 1664]. Fem. *Chromis tetracanthus* of Poey (= *Centrarchus tetracanthus* Valenciennes 1831:460). Type by monotypy. Cichlidae.

Nandopsis Meinken 1954:27 [ref. 2970]. Fem. *Nandopsis sheljuzhkoi* Meinken 1954:28. Type by original designation (also monotypic). Preoccupied by Gill 1862 in fishes, replaced by *Afronandus* Meinken 1955. Objective synonym of *Afronandus* Meinken 1955. Nandidae: Nandinae.

Nandus Valenciennes in Cuvier & Valenciennes 1831:481 [ref. 4881]. Masc. *Nandus marmoratus* Valenciennes in Cuvier & Valenciennes 1831:482 (= *Coius nandus* Hamilton 1822:96, 370). Type by monotypy. *Nandus marmoratus* Valenciennes is an unneeded substitute for *C. nandus* Hamilton. Valid (Jayaram 1981:334 [ref. 6497], Roberts 1989:164 [ref. 6439]). Nandidae: Nandinae.

Nangra Day 1876:493 [ref. 4886]. Fem. *Pimelodus nangra* Hamilton 1822:193, 378. Type by absolute tautonymy. Type not *N. punctata* Day as given by Jordan 1919:385 [ref. 4904]. Day's *N. buchanani* is an unneeded substitute for *P. nangra* Hamilton. Valid (Jayaram 1981:240 [ref. 6497]). Sisoridae.

Nanichthys Hubbs & Wisner 1980:530 [ref. 2267]. Masc. *Nanichthys simulans* Hubbs & Wisner 1980:531. Type by original designation (also monotypic). Valid (Collette et al. 1984:352 [ref. 11422], Parin in Whitehead et al. 1986:610 [ref. 13676], Smith 1986:387 [ref. 5712]). Scomberesocidae.

Nannacara Miranda-Ribeiro 1918:14 [ref. 3720]. *See Nannacara* Regan. Cichlidae.

Nannacara Regan 1905:344 [ref. 3623]. Fem. *Nannacara anomala* Regan 1905:344. Type by monotypy. Treated as feminine by author. *Nannacara* Miranda-Riberio 1918:14 [ref. 7320] sometimes cited as an original description (e.g. by Jordan 1920:564), but it is a use of *Nannacara* Regan [see p. 4 in Miranda-Ribeiro 1918]; see *Parvacara* Whitley. Valid (Kullander & Nijssen 1989:194 [ref. 14136]). Cichlidae.

Nannaethiops Günther 1872:669 [ref. 1997]. Masc. *Nannaethiops unitaeniatus* Günther 1872:670. Type by monotypy. Date may be 1871. Valid (Géry 1977:62 [ref. 1597], Vari 1979:340 [ref. 5490], Daget & Gosse 1984:200 [ref. 6185]). Citharinidae: Distichodontinae.

Nannapogon Fowler 1938:142 [ref. 1428]. Masc. *Nannapogon polynesiae* Fowler 1938:143. Type by original designation (also monotypic). Evidently based on a young pomacentrid (Randall in lit.). Pomacentridae.

Nannatherina Regan 1906:451 [ref. 6552]. Fem. *Nannatherina balstoni* Regan 1906:451. Type by monotypy. Family placement follows Johnson 1984:465 [ref. 9681]; see also Paxton et al. 1989. Valid (Kuiter & Allen 1986:109 [ref. 5213], Paxton et al. 1989:540 [ref. 12442]). Percichthyidae.

Nannobrachium Günther 1887:199 [ref. 2013]. Neut. *Nannobrachium nigrum* Günther 1887:199. Type by monotypy. Misspellings include *Nanobrachium, Nannobranchium* and *Nannabrachium*. Synonym of *Lampanyctus* Bonaparte 1840 (Bolin 1959:26 [ref. 503], Krefft & Bekker 1973:186 [ref. 7181], Paxton 1979:13 [ref. 6440]). Myctophidae.

Nannobrycon Hoedeman 1950:15, 22 [ref. 2175]. Masc. *Nannostomus eques* Steindachner 1876:126. Type by original designation (also monotypic). Synonym of *Nannostomus* Günther 1872 (Weitzman & Cobb 1975:3 [ref. 7134]); valid (Géry 1977:134 [ref. 1597]). Lebiasinidae: Pyrrhulininae.

Nannocampichthys Hora & Mukerji 1936:22 [ref. 2217]. Masc. *Nannocampichthys gigas* Hora & Mukerji 1936:23. Type by original designation (also monotypic). Syngnathidae: Syngnathinae.

Nannocampus Günther 1870:178 [ref. 1995]. Masc. *Nannocampus subosseus* Günther 1870:178. Type by monotypy. Valid (Dawson 1985:148 [ref. 6541], Dawson 1986:456 [ref. 5650], Paxton et al. 1989:426 [ref. 12442]). Syngnathidae: Syngnathinae.

Nannoceratias Regan & Trewavas 1932:112 [ref. 3682]. Masc. *Nannoceratias denticulatus* Regan & Trewavas 1932:112. Type by monotypy. Ceratioidei.

Nannocharax Günther 1867:112 [ref. 1989]. Masc. *Nannocharax fasciatus* Günther 1867:112. Type by monotypy. Valid (Géry 1977:74 [ref. 1597], Vari 1979:340 [ref. 5490], Vari 1983:5 [ref. 5419], Daget & Gosse 1984:200 [ref. 6185], Coenen & Teugels 1989 [ref. 13539]). Citharinidae: Distichodontinae.

Nannoglanis Boulenger 1887:278 [ref. 532]. Masc. *Nannoglanis fasciatus* Boulenger 1887:278. Type by monotypy. Synonym of *Heptapterus* Bleeker 1858 (Mees 1974:177 [ref. 2969], but see Buckup 1988 [ref. 6635]). Pimelodidae.

Nannoperca Günther 1861:116 [ref. 5749]. Fem. *Nannoperca australis* Günther 1861:116. Type by monotypy. Also appeared in Günther 1861 (June):490 [ref. 1965]; 1861:116 published 1 May according to Fowler (MS). Family placement follows Johnson 1984:465 [ref. 9681]. Valid (Kuiter & Allen 1986:109 [ref. 5213], Paxton et al. 1989:540 [ref. 12442]). Percichthyidae.

Nannopetersius (subgenus of *Phenacogrammus*) Hoedeman 1956:560 [ref. 6184]. Masc. *Petersius ansorgii* Boulenger 1910:543. Type by original designation. Appeared first in Hoedeman 1951:8 [ref. 2178] as a new subgenus of *Alestopetersius* but not available (no fixation of type species after 1930, Art. 13b). Apparently available as above (not seen). Valid (Poll 1967:116 [ref. 3529], Paugy 1984:178 [ref. 6183]). Alestiidae.

Nannorhamdia Regan 1913:467 [ref. 3656]. Fem. *Nannorhamdia spurrellii* Regan 1913:467. Type by monotypy. Synonym of *Imparfinis* Eigenmann & Norris 1900 (Mees 1974:167 [ref. 2969]); valid (see Stewart 1986:47 [ref. 5777], Stewart 1986:667 [ref. 5211]). Pimelodidae.

Nannosalarias Smith-Vaniz & Springer 1971:32 [ref. 4145]. Masc. *Blennius nativitatus* Regan 1909:404. Type by original designation (also monotypic). Valid (Yoshino in Masuda et al. 1984:299 [ref. 6441]). Blenniidae.

Nannostomus Günther 1872:146 [ref. 2000]. Masc. *Nannostomus beckfordi* Günther 1872:146. Type by monotypy. Valid (Weitzman & Cobb 1975 [ref. 7134], Géry 1977:130 [ref. 1597], Weitzman 1978 [ref. 7040], Fernandez & Weitzman 1987 [ref. 5981]). Lebiasinidae: Pyrrhulininae.

Nannothrissa Poll 1965:309 [ref. 3525]. Fem. *Microthrissa parva* Regan 1917:202. Type by monotypy. *Nanothrissa* is a misspelling. Valid (Poll et al. 1984:47 [ref. 6172], Grande 1985:247 [ref. 6466] as *Nanothrissa*, Whitehead 1985:144 [ref. 5141]). Clupeidae.

Nanochromis Pellegrin 1904:(163) 273 [ref. 3419]. Masc. *Pseudoplesiops nudiceps* Boulenger 1899:122. Type by being a replacement name. Replacement for *Pseudoplesiops* Boulenger 1899, preoccupied by Bleeker 1858 in fishes. Unjustifiably emended to *Nannochromis* by Boulenger 1915:375 [ref. 584]. Valid (Stewart & Roberts 1984 [ref. 6480], Greenwood 1987:180 [ref. 6166]). Cichlidae.

Nanognathus Boulenger 1895:2 [ref. 536]. Masc. *Nanognathus borellii* Boulenger 1895:3. Type by monotypy. Mention (Géry 1977:155 [ref. 1597]). In Characidiinae (P. Buckup, pers. comm. July 1990). Characidae: Characidiinae.

Nanostoma Putnam in Jordan 1877:6 [ref. 2374]. Neut. *Poecilichthys zonalis* Cope 1868:212. Type by original designation. Not preoccupied by *Nannostomus* Gunther 1872. Synonym of *Etheostoma* Rafinesque 1819, but as a valid subgenus (Page 1981:32 [ref. 3347], Page & Burr 1982 [ref. 5462]); as a synonym of subgenus *Etheostoma* (Bailey & Etnier 1988:12 [ref. 6873]). Percidae.

Nansenia Jordan & Evermann 1896:527, 528 [ref. 2443]. Fem. *Microstomus groenlandicus* Reinhardt 1841:LXXIV. Type by original designation (also monotypic). Type species originally as *grönlandicus*, correction in spelling mandatory. Valid (Cohen 1973:153 [ref. 6589], Cohen in Whitehead et al. 1984:390 [ref. 13675], Uyeno in Masuda et al. 1984:40 [ref. 6441], Ahlstrom et al. 1984:156 [ref. 13627], Cohen 1986:215 [ref. 5646], Lloris & Rucabado 1985 [ref. 6792], Matallanas 1986 [ref. 6755], Matallanas 1986 [ref. 8077], Paxton et al. 1989:167 [ref. 12442]). Microstomatidae.

Naqua (subgenus of *Sciaena*) Forsskål 1775:xvii [ref. 1351]. *Sciaena gibba* Forsskål 1775:lx, 46. Not available, regarded as non-latinized Arabic name, doubtfully tied to a species in text (see Jordan 1917:33-34 [ref. 2407]). In the synonymy of *Lutjanus* Bloch 1790. Lutjanidae.

Narcacion Bleeker (ex Klein) 1866:171 [ref. 420]. Neut. Several species mentioned; type listed by Jordan 1919:340 [ref. 4904] as *Raja torpedo* but that species not specifically mentioned by Bleeker. *Narcacion* Klein earlier made available by Gill 1861. Not intended by Bleeker as a new name. Synonym of *Torpedo* Houttuyn 1764. Torpedinidae.

Narcacion Gill (ex Klein) 1861:61 [ref. 1766]. *Torpedo occidentalis* Storer 1843:166. Type by monotypy. Apparently the first valid use of *Narcacion* Klein; only one species mentioned by Gill. Synonym of *Torpedo* Duméril 1806. Torpedinidae.

Narcacion Klein 1776:237 [ref. 4918]. Neut. Also in Klein 1777:726 [ref. 4920]. Not available, published in a work that does not conform to the principle of binominal nomenclature. Validly used by Gill 1861:61 and by Bleeker 1866:171 [ref. 420]. In the synonymy of *Torpedo* Houttuyn 1764. Torpedinidae.

Narcetes Alcock 1890:305 [ref. 83]. *Narcetes erimelas* Alcock 1890:305. Type by monotypy. Valid (Krefft 1973:91 [ref. 7166], Markle & Quéro in Whitehead et al. 1984:246 [ref. 13675], Okamura in Masuda et al. 1984:43 [ref. 6441], Markle 1986:221 [ref. 5687]). Alepocephalidae.

Narcine Henle 1834:31 [ref. 2092]. Fem. *Torpedo brasiliensis* Ölfers 1831:19. Type by subsequent designation. Type possibly designated by Bonaparte 1838:7 (of separate) [ref. 4979]. Valid (Cappetta 1987:162 [ref. 6348], Nakaya in Masuda et al. 1984:12 [ref. 6441], Paxton et al. 1989:60 [ref. 12442]). Narkidae.

Narcinops Whitley 1940:164 [ref. 4700]. Masc. *Narcine tasmaniensis* Richardson 1840:29. Type by original designation. Synonym of *Narcine* Henle 1834. Narkidae.

Narcobatus (subgenus of *Raia [Raja]*) Blainville 1816:121 [ref. 306]. Masc. *Raja torpedo* Linnaeus 1758:231. Type by subsequent designation. Type usually given as designated by Jordan 1917:95 [ref. 2407], but *torpedo* was not an originally-included species. Type should be selected from the 11 listed by Blainville. Also as *Narkobatus* and *Narcobatis* in early literature. Objective synonym of *Torpedo* Houttuyn 1764 (Krefft & Stehmann 1973:55 [ref. 7167], Cappetta 1987:161 [ref. 6348]). Torpedinidae.

Narke Kaup 1826:88 [ref. 2568]. Fem. *Raja capensis* Gmelin 1789:1512. Type by monotypy. Original not seen. Valid (Nakaya in Masuda et al. 1984:12 [ref. 6441], Compagno 1986:114 [ref. 5648]). Narkidae.

Narooma Whitley 1935:215 [ref. 4683]. *Narooma benefica* Whitley 1935:215. Type by original designation (also monotypic). Second species included with some doubt. Synonym of *Vinciguerria* Jordan & Evermann 1896 (Witzell 1973:121 [ref. 7172]). Gonostomatidae.

Naseus Commerson in Lacepède 1801:105 (footnote) [ref. 2710]. Masc. Probably not available; name mentioned in passing under *Naso fronticornis* Lacepède. See remarks under Opinion 89 in Appendix B. Perhaps can date to Cuvier 1829 as treated by Randall 1955:361 [ref. 13648]. In the synonymy of *Naso* Lacepède 1801 (Randall 1955:361 [ref. 13648]). Acanthuridae.

Nasisqualus Smith & Radcliffe in Smith 1912:681 [ref. 4042]. Masc. *Nasisqualus profundorum* Smith & Radcliffe in Smith 1912:681. Type by original designation (also monotypic). Synonym of *Deania* Jordan & Snyder 1902 (Compagno 1984:65 [ref. 6474]). Squalidae.

Nasistomias Koefoed 1956:11 [ref. 2653]. Masc. *Nasistomias curvatus* Koefoed 1956:11. Type by monotypy. Proposed somewhat conditionally as "*Nasistomias* n. g.?", but regarded as available (conditional proposal, but before 1961). Synonym of *Bathophilus* Giglioli 1882 (Morrow in Morrow & Gibbs 1964:456 [ref. 6962], Morrow 1973:135 [ref. 7175]). Melanostomiidae.

Naso Lacepède 1801:104 [ref. 2710]. *Naso fronticornis* Lacepède 1801:104, 105. Type by subsequent designation. Type designated by Jordan 1917:61 [ref. 2407]. Valid (Leis & Richards 1984:548 [ref. 13669], Kishimoto in Masuda et al. 1984:229 [ref. 6441], Randall 1986:819 [ref. 5706], Tyler et al. 1989:37 [ref. 13460]). Acanthuridae.

Nasocassis (subgenus of *Leiocassis*) Nichols 1925:1 [ref. 3180]. Fem. *Leiocassis longirostris* Günther 1864:87. Type by original designation (also monotypic). Bagridae.

Nasolamia Compagno & Garrick 1983:3 [ref. 5410]. Fem. *Carcharhinus velox* Gilbert in Jordan & Evermann 1898:2747. Type by original designation (also monotypic). Valid (Compagno 1984:515 [ref. 6846], Compagno 1988:337 [ref. 13488]). Carcharhinidae.

Nasolychnus (subgenus of *Myctophum*) Smith 1933:126 [ref. 4063]. Masc. *Myctophum (Nasolychnus) florentii* Smith 1933:126. Type by monotypy. Synonym of *Gymnoscopelus* Günther 1873, but as a valid subgenus (Paxton 1979:11 [ref. 6440], Moser et al. 1984:220 [ref. 13645], Hulley 1986:300 [ref. 5672]). Myctophidae.

Nasonus Rafinesque 1815:83 [ref. 3584]. *Chaetodon fronticornis* Lacepède 1802:104. Type by being a replacement name. As "*Nasonus* R. [Rafinesque] *Naso* Lac. [Lacepède]. Either an unneeded replacement for *Naso* Lacepède 1801 or an unavailable incorrect subsequent spelling of *Naso*; style in work favors the former. Objective synonym of *Naso* Lacepède 1801 (Randall 1955:361 [ref. 13648]). Acanthuridae.

Nasus Basilewski (ex Cuvier) 1855:234 [ref. 200]. Masc. *Cyprinus nasus* Linnaeus 1758:325. Type by absolute tautonymy. On Official List (Opinion 513). Objective synonym of *Chondrostoma* Agassiz 1832. Cyprinidae.

Natalichthys Winterbottom 1980:2 [ref. 4756]. Masc. *Natalichthys ori* Winterbottom 1980:3. Type by original designation. Valid (Winterbottom 1986:25 [ref. 5727], Winterbottom 1986:730 [ref. 5728]). Pseudochromidae: Congrogadinae.

Nauclerus Valenciennes in Cuvier & Valenciennes 1833:247 [ref. 1002]. Masc. *Nauclerus compressus* Valenciennes in Cuvier & Valenciennes 1833:249. Type by subsequent designation. Type apparently first designated by Jordan 1917:142 [ref. 2407]. Preoccupied by Vigors 1825 in Aves, not replaced. Synonym of *Naucrates* Rafinesque 1810 (Hureau & Tortonese 1973:377 [ref. 7198]). Carangidae.

Naucrates Rafinesque 1810:43 [ref. 3594]. Masc. *Centronotus conductor* Lacepède 1801:309 (= *Gasterosteus ductor* Linnaeus 1758:295). Type by subsequent designation. Type designated by Jordan & Gilbert 1883:443 [ref. 2476]. Valid (Hureau & Tortonese 1973:377 [ref. 7198], Smith-Vaniz 1984:524 [ref. 13664], Gushiken in Masuda et al. 1984:153 [ref. 6441], Smith-Vaniz 1986:653 [ref. 5718], Paxton et al. 1989:581 [ref. 12442]). Carangidae.

Naucratopsis Gill 1863:441 [ref. 1669]. Fem. *Seriola gigas* Günther 1860:466. Type by monotypy. *Seriola gigas* Günther preoccupied by Poey 1860; next available name for Günther's species is *S. hippos* Günther 1876 (Smith-Vaniz, pers. comm.). Synonym of *Seriola* Cuvier 1816. Carangidae.

Naurua Whitley & Colefax 1938:290 [ref. 4736]. *Naurua waitei* Whitley & Colefax 1938:290. Type by original designation (also monotypic). Serranidae: Anthiinae.

Nautichthys Girard 1858:74 [ref. 4911]. Masc. *Blepsias oculofasciatus* Girard 1857:202. Type by monotypy. Valid (Bolin 1944:102 [ref. 6379], Washington et al. 1984:443 [ref. 13660], Yabe in Masuda et al. 1984:323 [ref. 6441], Yabe 1985:123 [ref. 11522] in Hemitripteridae). Cottidae.

Nautiscus Jordan & Evermann 1898:1883, 2019 [ref. 2444]. Masc. *Nautichthys pribilovius* Jordan & Gilbert in Jordan & Evermann 1898:2019. Type by original designation (also monotypic). Synonym of *Nautichthys* Girard 1858. Cottidae.

Nautopaedium Jordan 1919:342 [ref. 2413]. Neut. *Porichthys plectrodon* Jordan & Gilbert 1882:291. Type by original designation. Type given as *Porichthys plectrodon* = *Batrachus porosissimus* Cuvier & Valenciennes. Synonym of *Porichthys* Girard 1854 (Walker & Rosenblatt 1988:888 [ref. 9284]). Batrachoididae.

Navarchus Filippi & Verany 1857:187 [ref. 1329]. Masc. *Navarchus sulcatus* Filippi & Verany 1857:187. Type by monotypy. Also appeared as "*Navarchus*, n. gen." in Doûmet 1864:425 [ref. 13456] but clearly based on Filippi & Verany and not a new genus description. Synonym of *Cubiceps* Lowe 1843 (Haedrich 1967:78 [ref. 5357], Haedrich 1973:562 [ref. 7216]). Nomeidae.

Navodon Whitley 1930:179 [ref. 5811]. Masc. *Balistes australis* Donovan 1824. Type by original designation. Name an anogram or Donovan. Synonym of *Meuschenia* Whitley 1929 (Hutchins 1977 [ref. 2283]); valid (Matsuura 1979:165 [ref. 7019], Tyler 1980:176 [ref. 4477], Arai 1983:199 [ref. 14249], Aboussouan & Leis 1984:452 [ref. 13661]). Monacanthidae.

Nazatexico Whitley 1931:334 [ref. 4672]. *Notropis orca* Woolman 1894:56. Type by being a replacement name. Replacement for two genera with same type; unneeded replacement for *Orcella* Jordan & Evermann (not preoccupied) but apparently can serve as a replacement for *Orcula* Jordan & Evermann, preoccupied by Held 1837 in Mollusca, Weisse 1846 in Protozoa, and Troschel 1846 in Echini. Objective synonym of *Orcella*; synonym of *Notropis* Rafinesque 1818. Cyprinidae.

Naziritor (subgenus of *Tor*) Mirza & Javed 1985:226 [ref. 5695]. Masc. *Tor zhobensis* Mirza 1967:54. Type by original designation (also monotypic). Cyprinidae.

Neacanthopsis Smith 1945:297 [ref. 4056]. Fem. *Neacanthopsis gracilentus* Smith 1945:297. Type by original designation (also monotypic). Valid (Kottelat 1989:13 [ref. 13605]). Cobitidae: Cobitinae.

Nealosa Herre & Myers 1931:235, 236 [ref. 2115]. Fem. *Chatoessus punctatus* Schlegel in Temminck & Schlegel 1846:240. Type by original designation (also monotypic). Objective synonym of *Konosirus* Jordan & Snyder 1900 (Whitehead 1985:240 [ref. 5141]). Clupeidae.

Nealotus Johnson 1865:434 [ref. 2359]. Masc. *Nealotus tripes* Johnson 1865:434. Type by monotypy. Also appeared as new in Johnson 1865 (Oct.):283 [ref. 5779]. Valid (Parin & Bekker 1973:458 [ref. 7206], Fuji in Uyeno et al. 1983:410 [ref. 14275], Collette et al. 1984:600 [ref. 11421], Nakamura in Masuda et al. 1984:226 [ref. 6441], Parin in Whitehead et al. 1986:970 [ref. 13676]). Gempylidae.

Neamia Smith & Radcliffe in Radcliffe 1912:441 [ref. 3576]. Fem. *Neamia octospina* Smith & Radcliffe in Radcliffe 1912:441. Type by original designation (also monotypic). Valid (Fraser 1972:12 [ref. 5195], Hayashi in Masuda et al. 1984:144 [ref. 6441], Gon 1986:556 [ref. 5657], Gon 1987 [ref. 6709], Paxton et al. 1989:555 [ref. 12442]). Apogonidae.

Neanis Gistel 1848:IX [ref. 1822]. Fem. *Labrus julis* Linnaeus 1758:284. Type by being a replacement name. Unneeded replacement for *Julis* "Lacep." [Cuvier 1814], not preoccupied by *Julus* Linnaeus 1758 in Myriapoda. Objective synonym of *Julis* Cuvier 1814; synonym of *Coris* Lacepède 1801. Labridae.

Neanthias Norman 1931:354 [ref. 3220]. Masc. *Neanthias accraensis* Norman 1931:354. Type by original designation (also monotypic). *Novanthias* Whitley 1937 is an unneeded replacement, not preoccupied by *Neoanthias* Castelnau 1879. Misspelled *Neoanthias* in Zoological Record for 1879. Serranidae: Anthiinae.

Neatypus Waite 1905:64 [ref. 4562]. Masc. *Neatypus obliquus* Waite 1905:65. Type by monotypy. Kyphosidae: Microcanthinae.

Neblinichthys Ferraris, Isbrücker & Nijssen 1986:70 [ref. 5988]. Masc. *Neblinichthys pilosus* Ferraris, Isbrücker & Nijssen 1986:70. Type by original designation (also monotypic). Valid (Burgess 1989:436 [ref. 12860]). Loricariidae.

Nebris Cuvier in Cuvier & Valenciennes 1830:149 [ref. 999]. Fem. *Nebris microps* Cuvier in Cuvier & Valenciennes 1830:149. Type by monotypy. Valid (Chao 1978:31 [ref. 6983], Uyeno & Sato in Uyeno et al. 1983:368 [ref. 14275]). Sciaenidae.

Nebrius Rüppell 1837:62 [ref. 3844]. Masc. *Nebrius concolor* Rüppell 1837:62. Type by monotypy. Valid (Compagno 1984:207 [ref. 6474], Nakaya & Shirai in Masuda et al. 1984:8 [ref. 6441], Bass 1986:65 [ref. 5635], Cappetta 1987:80 [ref. 6348], Paxton et al. 1989:90 [ref. 12442]). Ginglymostomatidae.

Nebrodes Garman 1913:56 [ref. 1545]. Masc. *Nebrius concolor* Rüppell 1835:62. Type by being a replacement name. Unneeded replacement for *Nebrius* Rüppell 1835, not preoccupied by *Nebria* Latreille 1802 in insects or *Nebris* Cuvier in fishes. Objective synonym of *Nebrius* Rüppell 1837 (Compagno 1984:207 [ref. 6474], Cappetta 1987:80 [ref. 6348]). Ginglymostomatidae.

Nectamia Jordan 1917:47 [ref. 2406]. Fem. *Apogon fuscus* Quoy & Gaimard 1824:345. Type by original designation (also monotypic). Synonym of *Apogon* Lacepède 1801, but as a valid subgenus (Fraser & Lachner 1985:4 [ref. 5215]); *Ostorhinchus* Lacepède 1801 replaces *Nectamia* as a subgenus of *Apogon* (Gon 1987:144 [ref. 6706]). Apogonidae.

Nectarges Myers & Wade 1942:126 [ref. 3134]. Masc. *Nectarges nepenthe* Myers 1942:130. Type by original designation. Synonym of *Atherinella* Steindachner 1875 (Chernoff 1986:240 [ref. 5847]); valid (Pequeño 1989:51 [ref. 14125]). Atherinidae: Menidiinae.

Nectoliparis Gilbert & Burke 1912:82 [ref. 1634]. Masc. *Nectoliparis pelagicus* Gilbert & Burke 1912:82. Type by original designation (also monotypic). Valid (Stein 1978:31 [ref. 4203], Kido in Masuda et al. 1984:340 [ref. 6441], Kido 1988:244 [ref. 12287]). Cyclopteridae: Liparinae.

Nector (subgenus of *Bairdiella*) Jordan & Evermann 1898:1432, 1436 [ref. 2444]. Masc. *Corvina chrysoleuca* Günther 1869:387, 427. Type by original designation. Synonym of *Stellifer* Oken 1817 (Chao 1978:40 [ref. 6983]). Sciaenidae.

Nedystoma Ogilby 1898:32 [ref. 5861]. Neut. *Hemipimelodus dayi* Ramsay & Ogilby 1866:16. Type by original designation (also monotypic). Valid (Burgess 1989:167 [ref. 12860]). Ariidae.

Neenchelys Bamber 1915:479 [ref. 172]. Fem. *Neenchelys microtretus* Bamber 1915:479. Type by monotypy. Valid (McCosker 1977:60 [ref. 6836], McCosker 1982:62 [ref. 2934], Paxton et al. 1989:119 [ref. 12442], McCosker et al. 1989:270 [ref. 13288]). Ophichthidae: Myrophinae.

Neetroplus Günther 1867:603 [ref. 1984]. Masc. *Neetroplus nematopus* Günther 1867:603. Type by monotypy. Also appeared in Günther (15 Sept.) 1868:469 [ref. 1994]. Valid (see Rogers 1981 [ref. 5502]). Cichlidae.

Negambassis Whitley 1935:360 [ref. 4684]. Fem. *Tetracentrum apogonoides* Macleay 1883:256. Type by being a replacement name. Unneeded replacement for and objective synonym of *Tetracentrum* Macleay, not preoccupied by *Tetracentron* Brauer 1865. Ambassidae.

Negaprion Whitley 1940:111 [ref. 4700]. Masc. *Aprionodon acutidens queenslandicus* Whitley 1939:233. Type by original designation (also monotypic). For purposes of the type species, the subspecies *queenslandicus* is elevated to the species level; type not *acutidens*. Valid (Compagno 1973:29 [ref. 7163], Compagno 1984:516 [ref. 6846], Nakaya in Masuda et al. 1984:7 [ref. 6441], Bass et al. 1986:83 [ref. 5638], Cappetta 1987:124 [ref. 6348], Compagno 1988:341 [ref. 13488], Paxton et al. 1989:83 [ref. 12442]). Carcharhinidae.

Negogaleus Whitley 1931:334 [ref. 4672]. Masc. *Hemigaleus microstoma* Bleeker 1852:46. Type by being a replacement name. Apparently an unneeded replacement for *Hemigaleus* Bleeker 1852, not preoccupied by *Hemigalea* (not investigated) or *Hemigalus* in Mammalia. Objective synonym of *Hemigaleus* Bleeker 1852 (Compagno 1984:438 [ref. 6846], Compagno 1988:262 [ref. 13488]). Hemigaleidae.

Negoscartes Whitley 1930:20 [ref. 4671]. Masc. *Salarias irroratus* Alleyne & Macleay 1877:337. Type by original designation (also monotypic). Synonym of *Salarias* Cuvier 1816 (Smith-Vaniz & Springer 1971:38 [ref. 4145]). Blenniidae.

Negostegastes Whitley 1929:225 [ref. 4666]. Masc. *Glyphisodon leucozona* Bleeker 1859:339. Type by original designation. Synonym of *Plectroglyphidodon* Fowler & Ball 1924 (Shen & Chan 1979:51 [ref. 6944]). Pomacentridae.

Negotirus (subgenus of *Synodus*) Whitley 1937:219 [ref. 4690]. Masc. *Synodus evermanni* Jordan & Bollman 1889:152. Type by original designation. Synonym of *Synodus* Scopoli 1777 (Anderson et al. 1966:47 [ref. 6977]). Synodontidae: Synodontinae.

Nelabrichthys Russell 1983:1 [ref. 5413]. Masc. *Labrus ornatus* Carmichael 1818:502. Type by original designation (also monotypic). Labridae.

Neleus Rafinesque 1815:91 [ref. 3584]. Not available, name only; presumably for a species of gymnotid. Gymnotidae.

Nelus Whitley 1930:179 [ref. 5811]. Masc. *Monacanthus vittatus* Richardson 1846:66. Type by original designation. *Nelusetta* Whitley 1939 is an unneeded replacement. *Nelusetta* treated as valid by Matsuura 1979:165 [ref. 7019]). Monacanthidae.

Nelusetta Whitley 1939:277 [ref. 4698]. Fem. *Monacanthus vittatus* Richardson 1846:66. Type by being a replacement name. Apparently an unneeded replacement for *Nelus* Whitley 1930 (14 Jan.), apparently not preoccupied by Sharp 1912 (Zoological Record, 1913:index p. 12) — a misspelling of *Nenus* Navás 1912 in Insecta [needs more investigation]. Valid (Matsuura 1979:165 [ref. 7019], Arai 1983:199 [ref. 14249]). Monacanthidae.

Nemabathytroctes (subgenus of *Bathytroctes*) Fowler 1934:252 [ref. 1416]. Masc. *Bathytroctes longifilis* Brauer 1902:277. Type by original designation (also monotypic). Valid (Parr 1951:4 [ref. 3380]). Alepocephalidae.

Nemacheilus Bleeker 1863:34 [ref. 400]. Masc. *Cobitis fasciata* Valenciennes in Cuvier & Valenciennes 1846:25. Type by original designation (also monotypic). May date to Bleeker 1863:364 or 1863, Pl. 103 in part 8 [ref. 4859]. *Noemacheilus* Kuhl & van Hasselt 1823 is considered a nomen nudum by Kottelat 1987 [ref. 5962] and 1990:20 [ref. 14137]. *Nemachilus* Günther 1868:347 [ref. 1990] is an unjustified emendation. *Nemacheilos* and *Nematocheilos* are misspellings. Valid as *Nemacheilus* (Kottelat 1989:12 [ref. 13605], Kottelat 1990:20 [ref. 14137]). Balitoridae: Nemacheilinae.

Nemachilichthys Day 1878:611 [ref. 4887]. Masc. *Cobitis ruppelli* Sykes 1841:366. Type by monotypy. Synonym of *Noemacheilus* Kuhl & van Hasselt 1823, but as a valid subgenus (Jayaram 1981:150 [ref. 6497], Menon 1987:158 [ref. 14149] as *Noemacheilichthys*); valid (Kottelat 1990:20 [ref. 14137]). Balitoridae: Nemacheilinae.

Nemaclinus Böhlke & Springer 1975:57 [ref. 615]. Masc. *Nemaclinus atelestos* Böhlke & Springer 1975:58. Type by original designation (also monotypic). Labrisomidae.

Nemacoclinus Smith 1937:195 [ref. 6553]. Masc. Not available; based on text and contents (p. 167) this is an obvious error for *Climacoporus* and not a replacement name or new genus. In the synonymy of *Climacoporus* Barnard 1935 (Bennett 1983 [ref. 5299]). Clinidae.

Nemadactylus Richardson 1839:98 [ref. 3732]. Masc. *Nemadactylus concinnus* Richardson 1839:97. Type by monotypy. *Nematodactylus* Gill 1862:114, 121 [ref. 1658] is an unjustified emendation. Cheilodactylidae.

Nemadoras Eigenmann 1925:359 [ref. 1244]. Masc. *Oxydoras elongatus* Boulenger 1898:424. Type by original designation. Valid (Burgess 1989:224 [ref. 12860]). Doradidae.

Nemalycodes Herzenstein 1896:14 [ref. 2151]. Masc. *Nemalycodes grigorjewi* Herzenstein 1896:14. Type by monotypy. Synonym of *Gymnelus* Reinhardt 1834 (Andriashev 1973:540 [ref. 7214], McAllister et al. 1981:835 [ref. 5431], Anderson 1982:28 [ref. 5520]). Zoarcidae.

Nemamyxine Richardson 1958:284 [ref. 3750]. Fem. *Nemamyxine elongata* Richardson 1958:284. Type by original designation (also monotypic). Valid. Myxinidae: Myxininae.

Nemanthias Smith 1954:4 [ref. 4090]. Masc. *Nemanthias carberryi* Smith 1954:4. Type by original designation (also monotypic). Subgroup of *Anthias* (Kendall 1984:500 [ref. 13663]); valid (Heemstra & Randall 1986:513 [ref. 5667]). Serranidae: Anthiinae.

Nemaperistedion Fowler 1938:126 [ref. 1426]. Neut. *Nemaperistedion orientale* Fowler 1938:127. Type by original designation (also monotypic). Triglidae: Peristediinae.

Nemaphoerus Kuhl & van Hasselt in Bleeker 1879:21 [ref. 457]. *Nemaphoerus maculosus* Kuhl & van Hasselt in Bleeker 1879:22. Type by monotypy. Not available, both genus and species appeared as name only in synonymy. Belontiidae.

Nemapontinus Fowler 1938:73 [ref. 1426]. Masc. *Nemapontinus tentacularis* Fowler 1938:73. Type by original designation (also monotypic). Synonym of *Pontinus* Poey 1860. Scorpaenidae: Scorpaeninae.

Nemapterois Fowler 1938:81 [ref. 1426]. *Nemapterois biocellatus* Fowler 1938:81. Type by original designation (also monotypic). Synonym of *Dendrochirus* Swainson 1839 (Eschmeyer & Randall 1975:275 [ref. 6389]). Scorpaenidae: Pteroinae.

Nemapteryx Ogilby 1908:3, 10 [ref. 3285]. Fem. *Arius stirlingi* Ogilby 1898:281. Type by original designation (also monotypic). Ariidae.

Nemasiluroides Fowler 1937:137 [ref. 1425]. Masc. *Nemasiluroides furcatus* Fowler 1937:137. Type by original designation. Synonym of *Platytropius* Hora 1937 (see Böhlke 1984:136 [ref. 13621]). Pangasiidae.

Nematabramis Boulenger 1894:249 [ref. 535]. Fem. *Nematabramis everetti* Boulenger 1894:250. Type by monotypy. Cyprinidae.

Nematagnus Gill 1861:113 [ref. 1774]. Masc. *Uranoscopus filibarbis* Cuvier in Cuvier & Valenciennes 1829:307. Type by monotypy. Valid (Mees 1960:47 [ref. 11931]); synonym of *Uranoscopus* Linnaeus 1758 (Pietsch 1989:295 [ref. 12541]). Uranoscopidae.

Nematalosa Regan 1917:312 [ref. 3665]. Fem. *Clupea nasus* Bloch 1795:116. Type by subsequent designation. Type designated by Jordan 1920:560 [ref. 4905]. *Nematolosa* is a misspelling. Valid (Uyeno & Sato in Masuda et al. 1984:20 [ref. 6441], Grande 1985:248 [ref. 6466], Whitehead 1985:241 [ref. 5141], Whitehead & Wongratana 1986:202 [ref. 6284], Paxton et al. 1989:155 [ref. 12442]). Clupeidae.

Nemateleotris Fowler 1938:131 [ref. 1426]. Fem. *Nemateleotris magnifica* Fowler 1938:132. Type by original designation (also monotypic). Species originally as *magnificus*, correctly emended to *magnifica*. Valid (Randall & Allen 1973 [ref. 7123], Akihito in Masuda et al. 1984:245 [ref. 6441], Hoese 1986:795 [ref. 5670], Birdsong et al. 1988:200 [ref. 7303]). Microdesmidae: Ptereleotrinae.

Nematistius Gill 1862:258 [ref. 4909]. Masc. *Nematistius pectoralis* Gill 1862:259. Type by monotypy. *Nemathistius* is a misspelling. Valid (Rosenblatt & Bell 1976 [ref. 7076], Smith-Vaniz 1984:529 [ref. 13664]). Nematistiidae.

Nematobalistes Fraser-Brunner 1935:659, 661 [ref. 1489]. Masc. *Balistes forcipatus* Gmelin 1788:1472. Type by original designation (also monotypic). Synonym of *Balistes* Linnaeus 1758 (Tyler 1980:123 [ref. 4477]). Balistidae.

Nematobrotula Gill 1863:252 [ref. 1688]. Fem. *Brotula ensiformis* Günther 1862:372. Type by original designation (also monotypic). Synonym of *Brotula* Cuvier 1829 (Cohen & Nielsen 1978:11 [ref. 881]). Ophidiidae: Brotulinae.

Nematobrycon Eigenmann 1911:215 [ref. 1225]. Masc. *Nemato-*

brycon palmeri Eigenmann 1911:215. Type by monotypy. Valid (Géry 1977:386 [ref. 1597]). Characidae.

Nematocentris Peters 1866:516 [ref. 3439]. Fem. *Nematocentris splendida* Peters 1866:516. Type by monotypy. Synonym of *Melanotaenia* Gill 1862 (Allen 1980:473 [ref. 99], Allen & Cross 1982:44 [ref. 6251]). Atherinidae: Melanotaeniinae.

Nematocharax Weitzman, Menezes & Britski 1986:335 [ref. 5984]. Masc. *Nematocharax venustus* Weitzman, Menezes & Britski 1986:336. Type by original designation (also monotypic). Characidae.

Nematochromis Weber 1913:264 [ref. 4602]. Masc. *Nematochromis annae* Weber 1913:265. Type by monotypy. Synonym of *Pseudoplesiops* Bleeker 1858 (T. Gill, pers. comm.). Pseudochromidae: Pseudoplesiopinae.

Nematogenys Girard 1855:198 [ref. 1819]. Fem. *Trichomycterus inermis* Guichenot in Gay 1848:312. Type by monotypy. Valid (Arratia et al. 1978:183 [ref. 144], Pinna 1989:27 [ref. 12630], Burgess 1989:321 [ref. 12860]). Trichomycteridae.

Nematogobius Boulenger 1910:560 [ref. 577]. Masc. *Nematogobius ansorgii* Boulenger 1910:560. Type by original designation (also monotypic). Proposed as "at least a subgenus", but genus unspecified; treated as a genus on p. 560. Valid (Maugé 1986:376 [ref. 6218], Birdsong et al. 1988:185 [ref. 7303]). Gobiidae.

Nematonurus (subgenus of *Macrurus*) Günther 1887:124, 150 [ref. 2013]. Masc. *Macrurus armatus* Hector 1875:81. Type by subsequent designation. Type designated by Jordan 1920:437 [ref. 4905]. Valid (Marshall 1973:297 [ref. 7194], Marshall 1973:585 [ref. 6965], Fahay & Markle 1984:274 [ref. 13653], Geistdoerfer in Whitehead et al. 1986:668 [ref. 13676]); synonym of *Coryphaenoides* Gunner 1761, but as a valid subgenus (Iwamoto & Sazonov 1988:42 [ref. 6228]). Macrouridae: Macrourinae.

Nematonus Günther 1887:114 [ref. 2013]. Masc. *Bathyonus pectoralis* Goode & Bean 1886:604. Type by monotypy. Synonym of *Bathyonus* Goode & Bean 1885 (Cohen & Nielsen 1978:27 [ref. 881]). Ophidiidae: Neobythitinae.

Nematoparodon (subgenus of *Parodon*) Fowler 1943:226 [ref. 1443]. Masc. *Parodon apolinari* Myers 1930:66. Type by original designation (also monotypic). Hemiodontidae: Parodontinae.

Nematopoma Gill 1858:428 [ref. 1750]. Neut. *Nematopoma searlesii* Gill 1858:429. Type by monotypy. Synonym of *Corynopoma* Gill 1858 (Weitzman & S. Fink 1985:2 [ref. 5203]). Characidae.

Nematoprora Gilbert 1905:587 [ref. 1631]. Fem. *Nematoprora polygonifera* Gilbert 1905:587. Type by original designation (also monotypic). Synonym of *Nemichthys* Richardson 1848 (Smith & Nielsen 1989:452 [ref. 13290]). Nemichthyidae.

Nematops Günther 1880:57 [ref. 2011]. Masc. *Nematops microstoma* Günther 1880:57. Type by monotypy. Valid (Norman 1934:394 [ref. 6893], Ahlstrom et al. 1984:643 [ref. 13641], Sakamoto 1984 [ref. 5273]). Pleuronectidae: Poecilopsettinae.

Nematosoma Eichwald 1831:60 [ref. 5562]. Neut. *Nematosoma ophidium* of Eichwald (not of Linnaeus) 1831 (= *Scyphius teres* Rathke 1837:21). Original not seen; possibly based on a misidentified type species; apparently not *Syngnathus ophidion* Linnaeus. Above from Fowler (MS). Synonym of *Nerophis* Rafinesque 1810 (Wheeler 1973:277 [ref. 7190]). Syngnathidae: Syngnathinae.

Nematostomias Zugmayer 1911:5 [ref. 6161]. Masc. *Nematostomias gladiator* Zugmayer 1911:5. Type by monotypy. Also appeared in Zugmayer 1911 (Dec.):76 [ref. 4846]. Synonym of *Leptostomias* Gilbert 1905 (Morrow in Morrow & Gibbs 1964:434 [ref. 6962], Morrow 1973:140 [ref. 7175]). Melanostomiidae.

Nematozebrias Chabanaud 1943:292 [ref. 799]. Masc. *Aesopia quagga* Kaup 1858. Type by original designation (also monotypic). Soleidae.

Nemichthys Richardson 1848:25 [ref. 3744]. Masc. *Nemichthys scolopacea* Richardson 1848:25. Type by monotypy. Valid (Larsen 1973:231 [ref. 7187], Karmovskaya 1982:155 [ref. 5204], Karrer 1982:102 [ref. 5679], Asano in Masuda et al. 1984:22 [ref. 6441], Nielsen in Whitehead et al. 1986:552 [ref. 13676], Castle 1986:193 [ref. 5644], Paxton et al. 1989:134 [ref. 12442], Smith & Nielsen 1989:452 [ref. 13290]). Nemichthyidae.

Nemipterus (subgenus of *Sparus*) Swainson 1839:172, 223 [ref. 4303]. Masc. *Dentex filamentosus* Valenciennes in Cuvier & Valenciennes 1830:244. Type by monotypy. Valid (Johnson 1980:11 [ref. 13553], Akazaki in Masuda et al. 1984:176 [ref. 6441], Russell 1986:600 [ref. 5708], Russell 1986 [ref. 5991]). Nemipteridae.

Nemipus Rafinesque 1815:84 [ref. 3584]. Not available, name only. Unplaced genera.

Nemobrama Valenciennes in Webb & Berthelot 1837:Pl. 8 [ref. 4502]. Fem. *Nemobrama webbii* Valenciennes in Webb & Berthelot 1837:Pl. 8. Type by monotypy. In text in 1843:40, plate published in 1837. Spelled *Nemabrama* by Jordan, Evermann & Clark 1930:234 [ref. 6476]. Synonym of *Polymixia* Lowe 1836 (Nielsen 1973:336 [ref. 6885], Woods & Sonoda 1973: 269 [ref. 6899] as *Nemabrama*). Polymixiidae.

Nemocampsis Rafinesque 1820:51 [ref. 7305]. Fem. *Lepomis flexuolaris* Rafinesque 1820:51. Type by original designation. Also appeared in Rafinesque 1820:31 [ref. 3592]. Synonym of *Micropterus* Lacepède 1802. Centrarchidae.

Nemochirus Rafinesque 1815:100, 105 [ref. 3583]. Masc. *Nemochirus erythropterus* Rafinesque 1815:100. Type by monotypy. Evidently still unplaced. Jordan 1917:86-87 [ref. 2407] gives a full reproduction of the description. Rafinesque 1815:91 [ref. 3584] placed near *Trachiurus*, Jordan indicated it had much in common with *Stylephorus cordatus* Shaw. Trachipteridae.

Nemophis Kaup 1858:168 [ref. 2577]. Masc. *Nemophis lessoni* Kaup 1858:168. Type by monotypy. Synonym of *Xiphasia* Swainson 1839 (Smith-Vaniz 1976:65 [ref. 4144]). Blenniidae.

Nemotherus Costa (ex Risso) 1834:fig. 9 [ref. 975]. Masc. Original not examined; perhaps intended for *Nemochirus* Rafinesque 1810. Trachipteridae.

Nemuroglanis Eigenmann & Eigenmann 1889:29 [ref. 1253]. Masc. *Nemuroglanis lanceolatus* Eigenmann & Eigenmann 1889:29. Type by original designation (also monotypic). Valid (Ferraris 1988 [ref. 6685], Burgess 1989:277 [ref. 12860]). Pimelodidae.

Neoachiropsetta Kotlyar 1978:809 [ref. 2665]. Fem. *Mancopsetta milfordi* Penrith 1965:181. Type by original designation (also monotypic). Spelled *Neoachirorsetta* in main heading on p. 809 [regarded as a mistake], otherwise as *Neoachiropsetta* throughout article. Synonym of *Mancopsetta* Gill 1881 (Hensley 1986:860 [ref. 5669], Hensley 1986:941 [ref. 6326]). Achiropsettidae.

Neoanthias Castelnau 1879:366 [ref. 764]. Masc. *Neoanthias guentheri* Castelnau 1879:367. Type by monotypy. Misspelled *Neanthias* in index (p. 7) to Zoological Record for 1879. Synonym of *Caprodon* Temminck & Schlegel 1843. Serranidae: Anthiinae.

Neoaploactis Eschmeyer & Allen 1978:444 [ref. 1276]. Fem. *Neoaploactis tridorsalis* Eschmeyer & Allen 1978:444. Type by original designation (also monotypic). Original description predated mention of this name in Poss & Eschmeyer 1978 [ref. 6387]). Valid (Washington et al. 1984:441 [ref. 13660] as *Neaploactis*, Paxton et al. 1989:460 [ref. 12442]). Aploactinidae.

Neoarius Castelnau 1878:237 [ref. 761]. Masc. *Arius curtisii* Castelnau 1878:236. Type by monotypy. Synonym of *Arius* Valenciennes 1840 based on placement of type species (Paxton et al. 1989:219 [ref. 12442]). Ariidae.

Neoatherina Castelnau 1875:31 [ref. 768]. Fem. *Neoatherina australis* Castelnau 1875:32. Type by monotypy. Synonym of *Melanotaenia* Gill 1862 (Allen 1980:474 [ref. 99], Allen & Cross 1982:44 [ref. 6251]). Atherinidae: Melanotaeniinae.

Neobagrus Bellotti 1892:100 [ref. 253]. Masc. *Neobagrus fuscus* Bellotti 1892:101. Type by monotypy. Synonym of *Liobagrus* Hilgendorf 1878. Amblycipitidae.

Neobarynotus Banarescu 1980:475 [ref. 216]. Masc. *Capoeta microlepis* Bleeker 1851:206. Type by original designation (also monotypic). Valid (Kottelat 1985:264 [ref. 11441], Kottelat 1989:9 [ref. 13605]); synonym of *Cyclocheilichthys* Bleeker 1859 (Roberts 1989:33 [ref. 6439]). Cyprinidae.

Neoblennius Castelnau 1875:26 [ref. 768]. Masc. *Neoblennius fasciatus* Castelnau 1875:26. Type by monotypy. Valid (Hoese 1976: 52 [ref. 7338], George & Springer 1980:7 [ref. 6935]). Clinidae.

Neobola Vinciguerra 1895:56 [ref. 4521]. Fem. *Neobola bottegoi* Vinciguerra 1895:57. Type by monotypy. Valid (Howes 1984:152 [ref. 5834], Lévêque & Daget 1984:325 [ref. 6186]). Cyprinidae.

Neoborus Boulenger 1899:78 [ref. 549]. Masc. *Neoborus ornatus* Boulenger 1899:78. Type by monotypy. Preoccupied by Distant 1884 in Hemiptera, replaced by *Phagoborus* Myers 1924. Synonym of *Ichthyborus* Günther 1864 (Daget & Gosse 1984:197 [ref. 6185]). Citharinidae: Distichodontinae.

Neobythites Goode & Bean 1885:600 [ref. 1842]. Masc. *Neobythites gilli* Goode & Bean 1885:601. Type by monotypy. *Tetranematopus* Günther 1887:100 [ref. 2013] is an unavailable manuscript name intended for *Neobythites* Goode & Bean 1886. Valid (Cohen & Nielsen 1978:36 [ref. 881], Machida in Masuda et al. 1984:100 [ref. 6441], Nielsen & Cohen 1986:349 [ref. 5700], Paxton et al. 1989:313 [ref. 12442]). Ophidiidae: Neobythitinae.

Neocarassius Castelnau 1872:236 [ref. 757]. Masc. *Neocarassius ventricosus* Castelnau 1872:237. Type by monotypy. As *Neocorassius* on p. 236 and 242, and *Neocarassuis* on p. 237, based on *Carassius* which Castelnau misspelled *Corassius*; corrected by McCulloch 1929:53 [ref. 2948]. Based on an introduced goldfish (Jordan 1919 [ref. 4904]). Synonym of *Carassius* Nilsson 1832. Cyprinidae.

Neocentropogon Matsubara 1943:429 [ref. 2905]. Masc. *Paracentropogon aeglefinus* Weber 1913:500. Type by original designation (also monotypic). Valid (Washington et al. 1984:440 [ref. 13660], Nakabo in Masuda et al. 1984:319 [ref. 6441], Klausewitz 1985 [ref. 5806], Paxton et al. 1989:444 [ref. 12442]). Scorpaenidae: Tetraroginae.

Neoceratias Pappenheim 1914:198 [ref. 3361]. Masc. *Neoceratias spinifer* Pappenheim 1914:198. Type by monotypy. Valid (Bertelsen & Pietsch 1983:93 [ref. 5335], Paxton et al. 1989:293 [ref. 12442]). Neoceratiidae.

Neoceratodus Castelnau 1876:130, 132 [ref. 760]. Masc. *Neoceratodus blanchardi* Castelnau 1876:133. Type by monotypy. Valid (Paxton et al. 1989:102 [ref. 12442]). Ceratodontidae.

Neochaetodon Castelnau 1873:130 [ref. 758]. Masc. *Neochaetodon vittatum [vittatus]* Castelnau 1873:130. Type by monotypy. Synonym of *Microcanthus* Swainson 1839. Kyphosidae: Microcanthinae.

Neochanna Günther 1867:306 [ref. 1987]. Fem. *Neochanna apoda* Günther 1867:306. Type by original designation (also monotypic). Valid (McDowall 1984:150 [ref. 11850]). Galaxiidae: Galaxiinae.

Neochela (subgenus of *Chela*) Silas 1958:64, 92 [ref. 4026]. Fem. *Laubuca dadyburjori* Menon 1952:1. Type by original designation (also monotypic). Species originally spelled two ways, *dadyburjori* is correct [see Dadyburjor, 1955, Bull. Bombay Aquar. Soc. v. 3 (1-2):12-13]. Synonym of *Chela* Hamilton 1822 (Roberts 1989:31 [ref. 6439]). Cyprinidae.

Neochromis Regan 1920:45 [ref. 3669]. Masc. *Tilapia simotes* Boulenger 1911:75. Type by original designation (also monotypic). Valid (Greenwood 1980:49 [ref. 1899]). Cichlidae.

Neocirrhilabrus Cheng & Wang 1979:73 [ref. 827]. Masc. *Neocirrhilabrus oxyurus* Cheng & Wang 1979:73. Type by original designation (also monotypic). Authors placed in Labroidei of uncertain family. Labridae.

Neocirrhites Castelnau 1873:101 [ref. 758]. Masc. *Neocirrhites armatus* Castelnau 1873:101. Type by monotypy. Valid (Araga in Masuda et al. 1984:199 [ref. 6441], Donaldson 1986:624 [ref. 6317]). Cirrhitidae.

Neoclinus Girard 1858:114 [ref. 4911]. Masc. *Neoclinus blanchardi* Girard 1858:114. Type by monotypy. Valid (Clark Hubbs 1953 [ref. 12698], Fukao 1980 [ref. 5257], Araga in Masuda et al. 1984:294 [ref. 6441], Fukao & Okazaki 1987 [ref. 6344], Fukao 1987 [ref. 6345]). Labrisomidae.

Neoconger Girard 1858:171 [ref. 1813]. Masc. *Neoconger mucronatus* Girard 1858:171. Type by monotypy. Valid (Paxton et al. 1989:112 [ref. 12442], Smith 1989:60 [ref. 13285]). Moringuidae.

Neocottus Sideleva 1982:31, 80 [ref. 14469]. Masc. *Abyssocottus werestschagini* Taliev 1935:39. Type apparently by original designation (alos monotypic) [not fully translated]. Cottocomephoridae.

Neocyema Castle 1978:70 [ref. 771]. Neut. *Neocyema erythrosoma* Castle 1978:70. Type by original designation (also monotypic). Author stated genus is feminine, but *cyema* is neuter. Valid (Castle 1986:193 [ref. 5644], Smith 1989:633 [ref. 13285]). Cyematidae.

Neocyttus Gilchrist 1906:153 [ref. 1647]. Masc. *Neocyttus rhomboidalis* Gilchrist 1906:153. Type by monotypy. Valid (Wheeler 1973:352 [ref. 7190], Karrer in Whitehead et al. 1986:775 [ref. 13676], Karrer 1986:439 [ref. 5680], James et al. 1988:309 [ref. 6639], Paxton et al. 1989:392 [ref. 12442]). Oreosomatidae.

Neoditrema Steindachner in Steindachner & Döderlein 1883:32 [ref. 4247]. Neut. *Neoditrema ransonnetii* Steindachner in Steindachner & Döderlein 1883:32. Type by monotypy. Valid (Tarp 1952:67 [ref. 12250], Nakabo in Masuda et al. 1984:191 [ref. 6441]). Embiotocidae.

Neoepinnula Matsubara & Iwai 1952:193 [ref. 2906]. Fem. *Epinnula orientalis* Gilchrist & von Bonde 1924:15. Type by original designation (also monotypic). Valid (Fujii in Uyeno et al. 1983:408 [ref. 14275], Collette et al. 1984:600 [ref. 11421], Nakamura in Masuda et al. 1984:226 [ref. 6441], Nakamura 1986:827 [ref. 5696]). Gempylidae.

Neoetropus Hildebrand & Schroeder 1928:174 [ref. 2163]. Masc. *Neoetropus macrops* Hildebrand & Schroeder 1928:174. Type by original designation (also monotypic). Valid (Norman 1934:283 [ref. 6893]). Pleuronectidae: Pleuronectinae.

Neoeucirrhichthys Banarescu & Nalbant 1968:349 [ref. 6554].

Masc. *Neoeucirrhichthys maydelli* Banarescu 1968:349. Type by original designation. Valid (Jayaram 1981:178 [ref. 6497], Sawada 1982:202 [ref. 14111]). Cobitidae: Cobitinae.

Neofundulus Myers 1924:9 [ref. 3091]. Masc. *Fundulus paraguayensis* Eigenmann & Kennedy 1903:530. Type by original designation (also monotypic). Valid (Parenti 1981:489 [ref. 7066], Costa 1988 [ref. 14292]). Aplocheilidae: Rivulinae.

Neogastromyzon Popta 1905:180 [ref. 3549]. Masc. *Neogastromyzon nieuwenhuisii* Popta 1905:181. Type by monotypy. Valid (Silas 1953:240 [ref. 4024], Sawada 1982:206 [ref. 14111], Roberts 1982:497 [ref. 6689], Roberts 1989:93 [ref. 6439]). Balitoridae: Balitorinae.

Neogobius Iljin 1927:135 [ref. 5613]. Masc. *Gobius fluviatilis* Pallas 1811:162. Type by monotypy. Iljin credits genus to Berg as a museum name, but name was made available by Iljin as above. Valid (Miller 1973:501 [ref. 6888], Miller in Whitehead et al. 1986:1057 [ref. 13677], Birdsong et al. 1988:202 [ref. 7303]). Gobiidae.

Neogunellus Castelnau 1875:27 [ref. 768]. Masc. *Neogunellus sulcatus* Castelnau 1875:27. Type by monotypy. Synonym of *Ophiclinus* Castelnau 1872 (George & Springer 1980:12 [ref. 6935]). Clinidae.

Neoharriotta Bigelow & Schroeder 1950:406 [ref. 302]. Fem. *Harriotta pinnata* Schnakenbeck 1931:40. Type by original designation (also monotypic). Valid (Compagno 1986:146 [ref. 5648]). Rhinochimaeridae.

Neohemilepidotus Sakamoto 1932:4 [ref. 3860]. Masc. *Neohemilepidotus japonicus* Sakamoto 1932:4. Type by monotypy. Synonym of *Hemilepidotus* Cuvier 1829, subgenus *Melletes* Bean 1880 (Peden 1978:39 [ref. 5530]). Cottidae.

Neoheterandria Henn 1916:117 [ref. 2093]. Fem. *Neoheterandria elegans* Henn 1916:118. Type by monotypy. Valid (Rosen & Bailey 1963:126 [ref. 7067], Parenti & Rauchenberger 1989:9 [ref. 13538]). Poeciliidae.

Neohispaniscus (subgenus of *Sebastes*) Matsubara 1943:226 [ref. 2905]. Masc. *Sebastes schlegeli* Hilgendorf 1880:171. Type by original designation. Synonym of *Sebastes* Cuvier 1829. Scorpaenidae: Sebastinae.

Neohomaloptera (subgenus of *Homaloptera*) Herre 1944:50 [ref. 2137]. Fem. *Homaloptera (Neohomaloptera) johorensis* Herre 1944:51. Type by original designation (also monotypic). Valid (Silas 1953:202 [ref. 4024], Roberts 1989:93 [ref. 6439]). Balitoridae: Balitorinae.

Neolabrus Steindachner 1875:461 [ref. 4222]. Masc. *Neolabrus fenestratus* Steindachner 1875:461. Type by monotypy. Labridae.

Neolaeops Amaoka 1969:148 [ref. 105]. Masc. *Laeops microphthalmus* von Bonde 1922:11. Type by original designation (also monotypic). Valid (Amaoka in Masuda et al. 1984:350 [ref. 6441], Ahlstrom et al. 1984:643 [ref. 13641], Hensley 1986:860 [ref. 5669], Hensley 1986:941 [ref. 6326]). Bothidae: Bothinae.

Neolamprologus Colombe & Allgayer 1985:14 [ref. 13457]. *Lamprologus tetracanthus* Boulenger 1899:118. Type by original designation. Valid (Poll 1986:55 [ref. 6136]). Cichlidae.

Neolebias Steindachner 1894:78 [ref. 4237]. Masc. *Neolebias unifasciatus* Steindachner 1894:78. Type by monotypy. Valid (Géry 1977:62 [ref. 1597], Vari 1979:340 [ref. 5490], Vari 1983:5 [ref. 5419], Daget & Gosse 1984:205 [ref. 6185]). Citharinidae: Distichodontinae.

Neolethrinus Castelnau 1875:11 [ref. 768]. Masc. *Neolethrinus similis* Castelnau 1875:12. Type by monotypy. Lethrinidae.

Neoliparis (subgenus of *Liparis*) Steindachner 1875:82 [ref. 4223]. Masc. *Liparis mucosus* Ayres 1855:22. Type by monotypy. Synonym of *Liparis* Scopoli 1777 (Kido 1988:165 [ref. 12287]). Cyclopteridae: Liparinae.

Neolissochilus Rainboth 1985:26 [ref. 5968]. Masc. *Barbus stracheyi* Day 1871:307. Type by original designation. Valid (Kottelat 1989:9 [ref. 13605]). Cyprinidae.

Neolumpenus Miki, Kanamaru & Amaoka 1987:128 [ref. 6704]. Masc. *Neolumpenus unocellatus* Miki, Kanamaru & Amaoka 1987:130. Type by original designation (also monotypic). Stichaeidae.

Neomaenis Girard 1858:167 [ref. 1813]. Fem. *Lobotes emarginatus* Baird & Girard 1855:332. Type by original designation (also monotypic). Synonym of *Lutjanus* Bloch 1790 (Allen 1985:33 [ref. 6843] and Allen & Talbot 1985:8 [ref. 6491] as *Neomaensis*). Lutjanidae.

Neomerinthe Fowler 1935:41 [ref. 1420]. *Neomerinthe hemingwayi* Fowler 1935:41. Type by original designation. Valid (Eschmeyer 1986:468 [ref. 5652], Paxton et al. 1989:444 [ref. 12442]). Scorpaenidae: Scorpaeninae.

Neomesoprion Castelnau 1875:8 [ref. 768]. Masc. *Neomesoprion unicolor* Castelnau 1875:8. Type by monotypy. Second species doubtfully included. Synonym of *Lutjanus* Bloch 1790 (Allen 1985:33 [ref. 6843], Allen & Talbot 1985:8 [ref. 6491]). Lutjanidae.

Neomordacia Castelnau 1872:232 [ref. 757]. Fem. *Neomordacia howittii* Castelnau 1872:232. Type by monotypy. Synonym of *Geotria* Gray 1851. Petromyzontidae: Geotriinae.

Neomugil Vaillant 1894:72 [ref. 4488]. Masc. *Neomugil digueti* Vaillant 1894:73. Type by monotypy. Synonym of *Agonostomus* Bennett 1832 (Thomson 1986:344 [ref. 6215]). Mugilidae.

Neomuraena Girard 1858:171 [ref. 1813]. Fem. *Neomuraena nigromarginata* Girard 1858:171. Type by monotypy. Synonym of *Gymnothorax* Bloch 1795 (Blache et al. 1973:226 [ref. 7185], Böhlke et al. 1989:145 [ref. 13286] but as a valid subgenus on p. 161). Muraenidae: Muraeninae.

Neomyripristis Castelnau 1873:98 [ref. 758]. Fem. *Neomyripristis amaenus* Castelnau 1873:99. Type by monotypy. Synonym of *Myripristis* Cuvier 1829 (Woods & Sonoda 1973:368 [ref. 6899]). Holocentridae.

Neomyxine Richardson 1953:380 [ref. 3749]. Fem. *Myxine biniplicata* Richardson & Jowett 1951:3. Type by original designation (also monotypic). Valid. Myxinidae: Myxininae.

Neomyxus (subgenus of *Myxus*) Steindachner 1878:384 [ref. 4226]. Masc. *Myxus (Neomyxus) sclateri* Steindachner 1878:384. Type by monotypy. Date might be 1879. Valid (Yoshino & Senou in Masuda et al. 1984:120 [ref. 6441]). Mugilidae.

Neonesthes Regan & Trewavas 1929:30 [ref. 3680]. Fem. *Neonesthes macrolychnus* Regan & Trewavas 1929:30. Type by monotypy; second species doubtfully included as, "*N. macrolychnus* may prove to be a synonym of *Astronesthes capensis*." Valid (Gibbs 1964:346 [ref. 6960], Gibbs & Morrow 1973:128 [ref. 7174], Gibbs in Whitehead et al. 1984:333 [ref. 13675], Kawaguchi & Moser 1984:171 [ref. 13642], Fujii in Masuda et al. 1984:50 [ref. 6441], Fink 1985:11 [ref. 5171], Gibbs 1986:233 [ref. 5655], Paxton et al. 1989:196 [ref. 12442]). Astronesthidae.

Neoniphon Castelnau 1875:4 [ref. 768]. Masc. *Neoniphon armatus* Castelnau 1875:5. Type by monotypy. *Neoniphon* De Vis

1885:537 [ref. 4899] not intended as a new genus (wrongly listed by Jordan 1919:378 [ref. 4904]). Valid (Randall & Heemstra 1985:2 [ref. 5144], Randall & Heemstra 1986:416 [ref. 5707], Paxton et al. 1989:378 [ref. 12442]). Holocentridae.

Neonoemacheilus Zhu & Guo 1985:321 [ref. 6100]. Masc. *Neonoemacheilus labiosus* Zhu & Guo 1985:321. Type by original designation (also monotypic). Valid (Kottelat 1989:12 [ref. 13605], Kottelat 1990:20 [ref. 14137]). Balitoridae: Nemacheilinae.

Neoodax Castelnau 1875:37 [ref. 768]. Masc. *Neoodax waterhousii* Castelnau 1875:37. Type by subsequent designation. Type designated by McCulloch 1929:323 [ref. 2948]; second species included, but text somewhat unclear if provisionally included or not. Valid ([J. K.] Scott 1976 [ref. 3996], Richards & Leis 1984:544 [ref. 13668], Gomon & Paxton 1986:27 [ref. 5656]). Odacidae.

Neoophorus Hubbs & Turner 1939:50 [ref. 2265]. Masc. *Zoogoneticus diazi* Meek 1902:93. Type by original designation (also monotypic). Name appeared first in Turner 1937:498 et seq. [ref. 6400], without clear differentiating characters. Valid (Uyeno et al. 1983:505 [ref. 6818]). Goodeidae.

Neoopisthopterus Hildebrand 1948:6 [ref. 2162]. Masc. *Odontognathus tropicus* Hildebrand 1946:94. Type by original designation. Valid (Grande 1985:244 [ref. 6466], Whitehead 1985:287 [ref. 5141]). Clupeidae.

Neopagetopsis Nybelin 1947:45 [ref. 3234]. Fem. *Neopagetopsis ionah* Nybelin 1947:46. Type by monotypy. Valid (Stevens et al. 1984:563 [ref. 13633], Iwami 1985:57 [ref. 13368]). Channichthyidae.

Neopangasius Popta 1904:180 [ref. 3547]. Masc. *Neopangasius nieuwenhuisii* Popta 1904:180. Type by monotypy. Synonym of *Pangasius* Valenciennes 1840 (Roberts 1989:131 [ref. 6439]). Pangasiidae.

Neoparascyllium (subgenus of *Parascyllium*) Whitley 1939:227 [ref. 4695]. Neut. *Parascyllium multimaculatum* Scott 1935:63. Type by original designation (also monotypic). Synonym of *Parascyllium* Gill 1862 (Compagno 1984:170 [ref. 6474]). Parascylliidae.

Neopataecus (subgenus of *Pataecus*) Steindachner 1884:1087 [ref. 4234]. Masc. *Pataecus maculatus* of Steindachner 1884 (= *Pataecus waterhousii* Castelnau 1872:244). Type by monotypy. Apparently based on a misidentified type species; *P. maculatus* of Steindachner not same as *P. maculatus* Günther 1861. Valid (Washington et al. 1984:440 [ref. 13660], Paxton et al. 1989:462 [ref. 12442]). Pataecidae.

Neopempheris Macleay 1881:517 [ref. 2869]. Fem. *Neopempheris ramsayi* Macleay 1881:517. Type by monotypy. Synonym of *Leptobrama* Steindachner 1878. Leptobramidae.

Neopercis Steindachner in Steindachner & Döderlein 1884:212 [ref. 4248]. Fem. *Percis ramsayi* Steindachner 1881:1072. Type by being a replacement name. Replacement for *Parapercis* Steindachner 1884, preoccupied by Bleeker 1863 in same family. Synonym of *Parapercis* Bleeker 1863. Pinguipedidae.

Neopharynx Poll 1948:97 [ref. 3519]. Masc. *Neopharynx schwetzi* Poll 1948:97. Type by monotypy. Cichlidae.

Neophos Myers 1932:61 [ref. 5027]. Neut. *Neophos nexilis* Myers 1932:61. Type by original designation (also monotypic). Synonym of *Thorophos* Bruun 1931 (Weitzman 1974:476 [ref. 5174], Ahlstrom et al. 1984:185 [ref. 13643]). Sternoptychidae: Maurolicinae.

Neophrynichthys Günther 1876:395 [ref. 2007]. Masc. *Psychrolutes latus* Hutton 1875:316. Type by monotypy. Also in Günther 1877:470 [ref. 5754]. Valid (Nelson 1977 [ref. 7034], Nelson 1982:1499 [ref. 5470], Washington et al. 1984:444 [ref. 13660], Yabe 1985:123 [ref. 11522]). Psychrolutidae.

Neoplatycephalus Castelnau 1872:87 [ref. 757]. Masc. *Neoplatycephalus grandis* Castelnau 1872:87. Type by monotypy. Synonym of *Platycephalus* Bloch 1795 (Paxton et al. 1989:469 [ref. 12442] based on placement of the type species). Platycephalidae.

Neoplecostomus (subgenus of *Plecostomus*) Eigenmann & Eigenmann 1888:171 [ref. 1249]. Masc. *Plecostomus microps* Steindachner 1876:688. Type by original designation. Valid (Isbrücker 1980:6 [ref. 2303], Burgess 1989:429 [ref. 12860]). Loricariidae.

Neoplotosus Castelnau 1875:45 [ref. 768]. Masc. *Neoplotosus waterhousii* Castelnau 1875:45. Type by monotypy. Plotosidae.

Neopoecilia Hubbs 1924:11 [ref. 2231]. Fem. *Neopoecilia holacanthus* Hubbs 1924:11. Type by original designation (also monotypic). Synonym of *Poecilia* Bloch & Schneider 1801 (Rosen & Bailey 1963:45 [ref. 7067]). Poeciliidae.

Neopomacentrus Allen 1975:39, 166 [ref. 97]. Masc. *Glyphisodon anabatoides* Bleeker 1847:28. Type by original designation. Valid (Shen & Chan 1978:213 [ref. 6945], Yoshino in Masuda et al. 1984:195 [ref. 6441], Allen 1986:678 [ref. 5631]). Pomacentridae.

Neoraja McEachran & Compagno 1982:422 [ref. 2952]. Fem. *Breviraja caerulea* Stehmann 1976:99. Type by original designation. Also described as a new subgenus. Valid (McEachran 1984:55 [ref. 5225] but with *B. stehmanni* as type, McEachran & Stehmann 1984 [ref. 5224], Hulley 1986:117 [ref. 5672], McEachran & Miyake 1987 [ref. 5973]). Rajidae.

Neorhombus Castelnau 1875:44 [ref. 768]. Masc. *Neorhombus unicolor* Castelnau 1875:45. Type by monotypy. Questionably a synonym of *Pseudorhombus* Bleeker 1862 (Norman 1934:89 [ref. 6893], Desoutter 1986:428 [ref. 6212]). Paralichthyidae.

Neorohita (subgenus of *Osteochilus*) Fowler 1937:180 [ref. 1425]. Fem. *Rohita hasseltii* Valenciennes in Cuvier & Valenciennes 1842:209. Type by original designation. Synonym of *Osteochilus* Günther 1868, but as a valid subgenus (Jayaram 1981:129 [ref. 6497]). Cyprinidae.

Neosalanx Wakiya & Takahasi 1937:282 [ref. 4571]. Masc. *Neosalanx jordani* Wakiya & Takahasi 1937:282. Type by original designation. Valid (Roberts 1984:210 [ref. 5318]). Salangidae.

Neoscombrops Gilchrist 1922:67 [ref. 1648]. Masc. *Neoscombrops annectens* Gilchrist 1922:68. Type by monotypy. Valid (Mochizuki in Masuda et al. 1984:125 [ref. 6441], Mochizuki & Sano 1984 [ref. 5188], Johnson 1984:464 [ref. 9681], Heemstra 1986:562 [ref. 5660]). Acropomatidae.

Neoscopelarchoides Chapman 1939:530 [ref. 817]. Masc. *Neoscopelarchoides dentatus* Chapman 1939:530. Type by original designation (also monotypic). Synonym of *Benthalbella* Zugmayer 1911 (Johnson 1974:61 [ref. 7050]). Scopelarchidae.

Neoscopelus Castelnau 1875:46 [ref. 768]. Masc. *Scopelus cephalotes* Castelnau 1875:46. Type by monotypy. Preoccupied by Johnson 1863 in fishes, replaced by *Scopelapogon* Whitley 1933 (see our Appendix A). Synonym of *Siphamia* Weber 1909 (Fraser 1972:14 [ref. 5195]). Apogonidae.

Neoscopelus Johnson 1863:44 [ref. 5021]. Masc. *Neoscopelus macrolepidotus* Johnson 1863:44. Type by monotypy. Valid (Nielsen 1973:170 [ref. 6885], Hulley in Whitehead et al. 1984:426 [ref. 13675], Okiyama 1984:207 [ref. 13644], Fujii in Masuda et al. 1984:75 [ref. 6441], Hulley 1986:321 [ref. 5672], Paxton et al. 1989:252 [ref. 12442]). Neoscopelidae.

Neoscorpis Smith 1931:150 [ref. 4062]. Fem. *Scorpis lithophilus* Gilchrist & Thompson 1908:162. Type by monotypy. Valid (Smith 1986:604 [ref. 5712]). Kyphosidae: Scorpidinae.

Neosebastes Guichenot 1867:83 [1] [ref. 1949]. Masc. *Scorpaena panda* Richardson 1842:216. Type by subsequent designation. Type designated by Bleeker 1876:3 [ref. 12248] and 1876:295 [ref. 450]; type apparently not *N. scorpaenodes* Guichenot; two originally included species, neither designated type. Valid (Shimizu in Masuda et al. 1984:315 [ref. 6441], Paxton et al. 1989:444 [ref. 12442]). Scorpaenidae: Neosebastinae.

Neosillago Castelnau 1875:16 [ref. 768]. Fem. *Neosillago marmorata* Castelnau 1875:16. Type by monotypy. Sillaginidae.

Neosilurus Castelnau 1878:238 [ref. 761]. Masc. *Neosilurus australis* Castelnau 1878:238. Type by monotypy. Apparently independently proposed; preoccupied by Steindachner 1867 in same family; replaced by *Cainosilurus* Macleay 1881. Synonym of *Neosilurus* Steindachner 1867 based on placement of type species (Paxton et al. 1989:224 [ref. 12442]). Plotosidae.

Neosilurus Steindachner 1867:14 [ref. 4214]. Masc. *Neosilurus hyrtlii* Steindachner 1867:14. Type by monotypy. Valid (Paxton et al. 1989:224 [ref. 12442]). Plotosidae.

Neosphyraena Castelnau 1872:96 [ref. 757]. Fem. *Neosphyraena multiradiata* Castelnau 1872:97. Type by monotypy. According to Fowler (MS), *Neosphyraena* was published 15 July 1872, *Dinolestes* in early 1872. Synonym of *Dinolestes* Klunzinger 1872 (Scott 1981:130 [ref. 5533], Paxton et al. 1989:560 [ref. 12442]). Dinolestidae.

Neostethus Regan 1916:2 [ref. 3667]. Masc. *Neostethus lankesteri* Regan 1916:2. Type by original designation, use of "gen. et sp. n." for one of two included new species before 1931 (Art. 68b(1)). Valid (White et al. 1984:360 [ref. 13655], Kottelat 1989:16 [ref. 13605], Parenti 1989:269 [ref. 13486]). Phallostethidae.

Neosteus Norman 1923:17 [ref. 3212]. Masc. *Pellona ditchela* Valenciennes in Cuvier & Valenciennes 1847:427. Type by subsequent designation. Type designated by Norman in Zoological Record for 1923:25. Synonym of *Pellona* Valenciennes 1847 (Whitehead 1967:105 [ref. 6464], Poll et al. 1984:48 [ref. 6172], Whitehead 1985:278 [ref. 5141]). Clupeidae.

Neostoma Filhol (ex Vaillant) 1884:184 [ref. 1326]. Neut. *Neostoma bathyphilum* Filhol (ex Vaillant) 1884:184. Type by monotypy. Synonym of *Gonostoma* Rafinesque 1810 (Witzell 1973:114 [ref. 7172]). Gonostomatidae.

Neostomias Gilchrist 1906:168 [ref. 1647]. Masc. *Neostomias filiferum* Gilchrist 1906:168. Type by monotypy. Synonym of *Eustomias* Vaillant 1888 (Gibbs in Morrow & Gibbs 1964:377 [ref. 6962], Morrow 1973:137 [ref. 7175]). Melanostomiidae.

Neosudis Castelnau 1873:118 [ref. 758]. Fem. *Neosudis vorax* Castelnau 1873:118. Type by monotypy. Synonym of *Chirocentrus* Cuvier 1816 (Bardack 1965:68 [ref. 6370] but spelled *Jeosudis*, Luther 1986:47 [ref. 6795]). Chirocentridae.

Neosynchiropus Nakabo 1982:92 [ref. 3139]. Masc. *Callionymus ocellatus* Pallas 1770:25. Type by original designation. Preoccupied by Nalbant 1979 in fishes (same family), apparently not replaced. Synonym of *Synchiropus* Gill 1859 (Fricke 1982:74 [ref. 5432]); valid (Houde 1984:637 [ref. 13674], Nakabo in Masuda et al. 1984:343 [ref. 6441]). Callionymidae.

Neosynchiropus Nalbant 1979:349 [ref. 3142]. Masc. *Neosynchiropus bacescui* Nalbant 1979:349. Type by original designation (also monotypic). Not *Neosynchiropus* Nakabo 1982, a junior homonym. Fricke says date is 1980 rather than 1979 [not investigated]. Valid (Fricke 1982:73 [ref. 5432]). Callionymidae.

Neotephraeops Castelnau 1872:68 [ref. 757]. Masc. *Crenidens zebra* Richardson 1846:70. Type by monotypy. *Neotephrops* is a misspelling. Objective synonym of *Girellichthys* Klunzinger 1872. Kyphosidae: Girellinae.

Neothunnus Kishinouye 1923:445 [ref. 2609]. Masc. *Thynnus macropterus* Temminck & Schlegel 1844:98. Type by subsequent designation. Type designated by Jordan & Hubbs 1925:218 [ref. 2486]). Synonym of *Thunnus* South 1845 (Gibbs & Collette 1967:97 [ref. 13640]). Scombridae.

Neotilapia Regan 1920:38 [ref. 3669]. Fem. *Chromis tanganicae* Günther 1893:630. Type by original designation. Cichlidae.

Neotoca Hubbs & Turner 1939:71 [ref. 2265]. Fem. *Characodon bilineatus* Bean 1887:371. Type by original designation (also monotypic). Name appeared first in Turner 1937:497 et seq. [ref. 6400], without clear differentiating characters. Synonym of *Skiffia* Meek 1902 (Miller & Fitzsimons 1971:10 [ref. 3019]); as a valid subgenus (Uyeno et al. 1983:505 [ref. 6818]). Goodeidae.

Neotriakis Smith 1957:262 [ref. 4114]. Fem. *Neotriakis sinuans* Smith 1957:262. Type by original designation. Synonym of *Eridacnis* Smith 1913 (Compagno 1984:372 [ref. 6846], Compagno 1988:185 [ref. 13488]). Proscylliidae.

Neotropius Kulkarni 1952:231 [ref. 2698]. Masc. *Neotropius khavalchor* Kulkarni 1952:232. Type by monotypy. Valid (Jayaram 1977:17 [ref. 7006], Jayaram 1981:218 [ref. 6497], Burgess 1989:98 [ref. 12860]). Schilbeidae.

Neotrygon Castelnau 1873:122 [ref. 758]. Fem. *Raja trigonoides* Castelnau 1873:121. Type by monotypy. Dasyatidae.

Neotylognathus (subgenus of *Tylognathus*) Kosswig 1950:409 [ref. 5022]. Masc. *Tylognathus (Neotylognathus) klatti* Kosswig 1950:409. Type by monotypy. Synonym of *Hemigrammocapoeta* Pellegrin 1927, but as a valid subgenus (Karaman 1971:236 [ref. 2560]). Cyprinidae.

Neozoarces Steindachner 1881:263 [ref. 4230]. Masc. *Neozoarces pulcher* Steindachner 1881:263. Type by monotypy. Valid (Amaoka in Masuda et al. 1984:304 [ref. 6441]). Zoarcidae.

Neptomenus Günther 1860:389 [ref. 1963]. Masc. *Neptomenus brama* Günther 1860:390. Type by monotypy. Misspelled *Neptonemus* by Castelnau 1872 and others. Synonym of *Seriolella* Guichenot 1848 (Haedrich 1967:69 [ref. 5357], McDowall 1981:110 [ref. 5356]). Centrolophidae.

Neptotichthys Hutton 1890:278 [ref. 2286]. Masc. *Ditrema violacea* Hutton 1873:261. Type by monotypy. Kyphosidae: Scorpidinae.

Nerophis Rafinesque 1810:37, 57 [ref. 3595]. Masc. *Syngnathus ophiodon* Linnaeus 1758:337. Type by subsequent designation. Type sometimes given (e.g. as by Wheeler 1973:277) as *Nerophis maculatus* Rafinesque 1810; Rafinesque included both *maculatus* (on p. 37) and *ophiodon* (on p. 57). Earliest designation found that of Jordan 1917:82 [ref. 2407] as above. Valid (Wheeler 1973:277 [ref. 7190], Dawson in Whitehead et al. 1986:632 [ref. 13676]). Syngnathidae: Syngnathinae.

Nes (subgenus of *Gobiosoma*) Ginsburg 1933:25 [ref. 1799]. *Gobiosoma longum* Nichols 1914:143. Type by original designation (also monotypic). Valid (Birdsong et al. 1988:189 [ref. 7303]). Gobiidae.

Nesiarchus Johnson 1862:173 [ref. 2357]. Masc. *Nesiarchus nasutus* Johnson 1862:173. Type by monotypy. Valid (Parin & Bekker 1973:459 [ref. 7206], Nakamura et al. 1981 [ref. 5477],

Nakamura et al. 1983 [ref. 5407], Collette et al. 1984:600 [ref. 11421], Nakamura in Masuda et al. 1984:227 [ref. 6441], Parin in Whitehead et al. 1986:971 [ref. 13676]). Gempylidae.

Nesiotes De Vis 1884:453 [ref. 1089]. Fem. *Nesiotes purpurascens* De Vis 1884:453. Type by monotypy. Preoccupied by Martens 1860 in Mollusca, Wollaston 1861 in Coleoptera, and Stål 1873 in insects; replaced by *Cypho* Myers 1940. Pseudochromidae: Pseudochrominae.

Nesochaetodon (subgenus of *Mesochaetodon*) Maugé & Bauchot 1984:478 [ref. 6614]. Masc. *Chaetodon trichrous* Günther 1874. Type by original designation (also monotypic). See account of *Mesochaetodon*; the new subgenus should have been described as a subgenus of *Corallochaetodon* Burgess 1978 and not a subgenus of *Mesochaetodon*. Chaetodontidae.

Nesocongrus Whitley 1935:219 [ref. 4683]. Masc. *Congermuraena howensis* McCulloch & Waite 1916:438. Type by original designation (also monotypic). Synonym of *Ariosoma* Swainson 1838 (Blache et al. 1973:241 [ref. 7185], Smith 1989:492 [ref. 13285]). Congridae: Bathymyrinae.

Nesogalaxias Whitley 1935:Pl. 3 legend [ref. 4686]. Masc. *Galaxias neocaledonicus* Weber & de Beaufort 1913:173. Type by original designation. Not available from this reference, no description after 1930 [Art. 13a(i)]; subsequent use in an available way not investigated. Treated as valid (McDowall 1984:151 [ref. 11850]). Galaxiidae: Galaxiinae.

Nesogobius Whitley 1929:62 [ref. 4664]. Masc. *Gobius hinsbyi* McCulloch & Ogilby (ex Johnston) 1919:215. Type by original designation (also monotypic). Valid (Hoese, pers. comm.). Gobiidae.

Nesogrammus Evermann & Seale 1907:61 [ref. 1285]. Masc. *Nesogrammus piersoni* Evermann & Seale 1907:61. Type by original designation (also monotypic). Synonym of *Grammatorycnus* Gill 1862 (Fowler MS). Scombridae.

Nessorhamphus Schmidt 1931:372 [ref. 3933]. Masc. *Leptocephalus ingolfianus* Schmidt 1912:49. Type by monotypy. Valid (Blache et al. 1973:246 [ref. 7185], Bauchot & Saldanha in Whitehead et al. 1986:576 [ref. 13676], Castle 1986:192 [ref. 5644], Paxton et al. 1989:124 [ref. 12442], Robins 1989:427 [ref. 13289]). Derichthyidae.

Nestis Valenciennes in Cuvier & Valenciennes 1836:166 [ref. 1005]. Fem. *Nestis cyprinoides* Valenciennes in Cuvier & Valenciennes 1836:167. Type by subsequent designation. Type designated by Jordan 1919:185 [ref. 2410]. Synonym of *Agonostomus* Bennett 1832 (Thomson 1986:344 [ref. 6215]). Mugilidae.

Nettastoma Rafinesque 1810:66 [ref. 3594]. Neut. *Nettastoma melanura* Rafinesque 1810:66. Type by monotypy. Valid (Blache et al. 1973:236 [ref. 7185], Smith, Böhlke & Castle 1981 [ref. 6158], Karrer 1982:62 [ref. 5679], Smith & Castle 1982:7 [ref. 5453], Asano in Masuda et al. 1984:29 [ref. 6441], Saldanha in Whitehead et al. 1986:563 [ref. 13676], Castle 1986:191 [ref. 5644], Paxton et al. 1989:113 [ref. 12442], Smith 1989:604 [ref. 13285]). Nettastomatidae.

Nettastomella Facciolà 1911:277 [ref. 7188]. Fem. *Nettastomella physonema* Facciolà 1914:47. Type by subsequent monotypy. Appeared first and dates to 1911, with reference to a description and with species *juxta* [apparently never described, not fully investigated]; subsequently Facciolà 1914:47 [ref. 1290] included *physonema*. Preoccupied by Carpenter 1865 in Mollusca; replaced by *Facciolella* Whitley 1938 who dated to 1914. Objective synonym of *Facciolella* Whitley 1938 (Blache et al. 1973:237 [ref. 7185], Smith 1989:596 [ref. 13285]). Nettastomatidae.

Nettastomops Steindachner 1906:299 [ref. 4241]. Masc. *Nettastomops barbatula* Steindachner 1906:299. Type by monotypy. Synonym of *Rhinomuraena* Garman 1888. Muraenidae: Muraeninae.

Nettenchelys Alcock 1898:149 [ref. 92]. Fem. *Nettenchelys taylori* Alcock 1898:150. Type by monotypy. Valid (Smith, Böhlke & Castle 1981 [ref. 6158], Smith & Castle 1982:12 [ref. 5453], Smith 1989:599 [ref. 13285], Brito 1989 [ref. 13509]). Nettastomatidae.

Nettodarus Whitley 1951:407 [ref. 4715]. *Nettastoma brevirostre* Facciolà 1887:166. Type by being a replacement name. Replacement for *Todarus* Grassi & Calandruccio 1896 [preoccupation not researched, Whitley provides no details]. Valid (Blache et al. 1973:237 [ref. 7185]); synonym of *Dysomma* Alcock 1889 (Robins & Robins 1976:256 [ref. 3784], Robins & Robins 1989:244 [ref. 13287]). Synaphobranchidae: Ilyophinae.

Nettophichthys Holt 1891:122 [ref. 2195]. Masc. *Nettophichthys retropinnatus* Holt 1891:123. Type by monotypy. Synonym of *Synaphobranchus* Johnson 1862 (Blache et al. 1973:252 [ref. 7185], Robins & Robins 1989:219 [ref. 13287]). Synaphobranchidae: Synaphobranchinae.

Netuma Bleeker 1858:62, 67, 93 [ref. 365]. Fem. *Bagrus netuma* Valenciennes in Cuvier & Valenciennes 1840:438. Type by absolute tautonymy. Also appeared on p. 23 et seq. Type apparently by tautonymy in ref. 365, not *N. thalassina* = *Netuma nasuta* as designated by Bleeker 1862:7 [ref. 393]. Valid (Higuchi et al. 1982:3 [ref. 11467], Inada in Nakamura et al. 1986:85 [ref. 14235], Taylor 1986:158 [ref. 6195]). Ariidae.

Newtonscottia (subgenus of *Synodus*) Whitley 1937:219 [ref. 4690]. Fem. *Synodus houlti* McCulloch 1921:165. Type by original designation. Synonym of *Synodus* Scopoli 1777. Synodontidae: Synodontinae.

Nexilarius Gilbert in Jordan & Evermann 1896:512 [ref. 2442]. Masc. *Euschistodus concolor* Gill 1862:145. Type by original designation (also monotypic). Misprinted initially as *Nexilaris*, corrected by Jordan & Evermann 1898:1559 [ref. 2444]. Synonym of *Abudefduf* Forsskål 1775. Pomacentridae.

Nexilosus Heller & Snodgrass 1903:204 [ref. 2089]. Masc. *Nexilosus albemarleus* Heller & Snodgrass 1903:204. Type by monotypy. Misspelled *Nelixosus* in Zoological Record for 1903. Valid (see Hensley 1986:857 [ref. 5734]). Pomacentridae.

Nezumia Jordan in Jordan & Starks 1904:620 [ref. 2526]. Fem. *Nezumia condylura* Jordan & Gilbert in Jordan & Starks 1904:620. Type by original designation (also monotypic). Valid (Marshall 1973:291 [ref. 7194], Marshall & Iwamoto 1973:624 [ref. 6966], Iwamoto 1979:156 [ref. 2311], Fahay & Markle 1984:274 [ref. 13653], Okamura in Masuda et al. 1984:95 [ref. 6441], Geistdoerfer in Whitehead et al. 1986:669 [ref. 13676], Iwamoto 1986:337 [ref. 5674], Paxton et al. 1989:328 [ref. 12442]). Macrouridae: Macrourinae.

Nibea (subgenus of *Sciaena*) Jordan & Thompson 1911:244, 246 [ref. 2539]. Fem. *Pseudotolithus mitsukurii* Jordan & Snyder 1901:356. Type by original designation. Type designated on p. 244; Jordan's style of type species in parentheses (also designated by Jordan 1920:539 [ref. 4905]). Valid (Trewavas 1977:375 [ref. 4459], Okamura in Masuda et al. 1984:162 [ref. 6441], Kinoshita & Fujita 1988 [ref. 6693], Kottelat 1989:17 [ref. 13605]). Sciaenidae.

Nicholsiculter Rendahl 1928:118 [ref. 3702]. Masc. *Hemiculter andrewsi* Nichols 1925. Type by original designation (also monotypic). Synonym of *Anabarilius* Cockerell 1923 (Yih & Wu 1964:71 [ref. 13499], Chen in Chu & Chen 1989:56 [ref. 13584]). Cyprinidae.

Nicholsicypris Chu 1935:10 [ref. 832]. Fem. *Aphyocypris normalis* Nichols & Pope 1927:376. Type by original designation (also monotypic). Valid (Yang & Hwang 1964:18 [ref. 13497]). Cyprinidae.

Nicholsina (subgenus of *Cryptotomus*) Fowler 1915:3 [ref. 1393]. Fem. *Cryptotomus beryllinus* Jordan & Swain 1884:101. Type by original designation. Valid (Richards & Leis 1984:544 [ref. 13668]). Scaridae: Sparisomatinae.

Nicholsopuntius (subgenus of *Barbus*) Pellegrin 1933:107 [ref. 3413]. Masc. *Barbus candens* Nichols & Griscom 1917:701. Type by original designation. Synonym of *Barbus* Cuvier & Cloquet 1816 (Lévêque & Daget 1984:218 [ref. 6186]). Cyprinidae.

Niger de Buen 1926:81 [ref. 5054]. As a "grupo" for 12 species of *Gobius*. Not available on basis of Art. 1b(6) [see de Buen's definition of "grupo" on p. 11]; see Appendix A. Gobiidae.

Nigracus Whitley 1953:135 [ref. 4718]. Masc. *Stigmatopora nigra* Kaup 1856:53. Type by being a replacement name. Replacement for *Pipettella* Whitley 1951, preoccupied by Haeckel 1887 in Radiolaria. Synonym of *Stigmatopora* Kaup 1853 (Dawson 1982:576 [ref. 5443], Dawson 1985:174 [ref. 6541]). Syngnathidae: Syngnathinae.

Nilotilapia Thys van den Audenaerde 1970:290, 291 [ref. 12518]. Fem. Not available, manuscript name taken from Trewavas; no included species and no description provided; as a subgroup of *Sarotherodon (Oreochromis)*. Cichlidae.

Nimbochromis Eccles & Trewavas 1989:282 [ref. 13547]. Masc. *Hemichromis livingstonii* Günther 1893:625. Type by original designation. Cichlidae.

Ninnia de Buen 1930:130, 132 [ref. 685]. Fem. *Gobius canestrini* Ninni 1883:276. Type by original designation. Preoccupied by Westerlund 1903 in Mollusca, replaced by *Ninnigobius* Whitley 1951. Synonym of *Pomatoschistus* Gill 1863 (Miller 1973:506 [ref. 6888]), Maugé 1986:380 [ref. 6218]). Gobiidae.

Ninnigobius Whitley 1951:68 [ref. 4711]. Masc. *Gobius canestrini* Ninni 1883:276. Type by being a replacement name. Replacement for *Ninnia* de Buen, preoccupied by Westerlund 1903 in Mollusca. Synonym of *Pomatoschistus* Gill 1863 (Miller 1973:506 [ref. 6888], Maugé 1986:380 [ref. 6218]). Gobiidae.

Niphon Cuvier in Cuvier & Valenciennes 1828:131 [ref. 997]. Masc. *Niphon spinosus* Cuvier in Cuvier & Valenciennes 1828:131. Type by monotypy. Valid (Johnson 1983 [ref. 5675], Kendall 1984:500 [ref. 13663], Katayama in Masuda et al. 1984:124 [ref. 6441] in Percichthyidae, Johnson 1988 [ref. 6691]). Placement in Serranidae follows Johnson (1983, 1988). Serranidae: Epinephelinae.

Nivicola (subgenus of *Etheostoma*) Jordan & Evermann 1896:1066, 68, 82 [ref. 2443]. Masc. *Poecilichthys boreale* Jordan 1884:477. Type by original designation (also monotypic). Apparently preoccupied by Hodgson 1893 in Aves, replaced by *Niviperca* Whitley 1951. Synonym of *Etheostoma* Rafinesque 1819 (Collette & Banarescu 1977:1456 [ref. 5845]). Percidae.

Niviperca Whitley 1951:68 [ref. 4711]. Fem. *Poecilichthys borealis* Jordan 1884:477. Type by being a replacement name. Replacement for *Nivicola* Jordan & Evermann 1896, apparently preoccupied by Hodgson 1893 in Aves. Synonym of *Etheostoma* Rafinesque 1819 (Collette & Banarescu 1977:1456 [ref. 5845]). Percidae.

Niwaella Nalbant 1963:362 [ref. 3140]. *Cobitis delicta* Niwa 1937. Type by original designation. Published as *Niwaëlla*. Valid (Sawada & Kim 1977 [ref. 6985], Sawada 1982:200 [ref. 14111], Sawada in Masuda et al. 1984:58 [ref. 6441]). Cobitidae: Cobitinae.

Nixiblennius Whitley 1930:20 [ref. 4671]. Masc. *Blennius snowi* Fowler 1928:431. Type by original designation (also monotypic). Synonym of *Rhabdoblennius* Whitley 1930 (Smith-Vaniz & Springer 1971:37 [ref. 4145]). Blenniidae.

Nocomis Girard 1856:190 [ref. 1810]. Masc. *Nocomis nebrascensis* Girard 1857:190. Type by monotypy. Treated as masculine by author. Valid (Lachner & Jenkins 1967 [ref. 7136]). Cyprinidae.

Nodogymnus Chabanaud 1928:39 [ref. 783]. Masc. *Gymnachirus fasciatus* Günther 1862:488. Type by original designation (also monotypic). Achiridae.

Noelius Rafinesque 1815:220 [ref. 3584]. In "Additions et Corrections" on p. 220 referring back to p. 93. As a replacement for *Lamnea*. Both *Lamnea* and *Noelius* are not available, name only. Lamnidae.

Noemacheilus Kuhl & van Hasselt in van Hasselt 1823:133 [ref. 4513]. Masc. *Noemacheilus fasciatus* Kuhl & van Hasselt in van Hasselt 1823:133. Type by monotypy. Genus and species description not diagnostic, both regarded by Kottelat 1987:371 [ref. 5962] as nomina nuda. Genus is available from Bleeker 1863 [ref. 400] as *Nemacheilus* and species by Valenciennes 1846. See *Nemacheilus*. Valid [*Noemacheilus* or *Nemcheilus*] (Jayaram 1981:147 [ref. 6497]), Sawada 1982:202 [ref. 14111], Kottelat 1984 [ref. 5292], Sawada in Masuda et al. 1984:59 [ref. 6441], Menon 1987:155 [ref. 14149], Zhu & Cao 1987:327 [ref. 14139]). Balitoridae: Nemacheilinae.

Nofua (subgenus of *Synanceja [Synanceia]*) Whitley 1930:24 [ref. 4671]. *Synanceja platyrhynchus* Bleeker 1874:11, 14. Type by original designation (also monotypic). Synonym of *Synanceia* Bloch & Schneider 1801 (Eschmeyer & Rama-Rao 1973:342 [ref. 6391]). Scorpaenidae: Synanceiinae.

Nomalus Gistel 1848:VIII [ref. 1822]. Fem. *Lonchurus ancylodon* Bloch & Schneider 1801:102. Type by being a replacement name. Replacement for *Ancylodon* Cuvier [Bosc 1816 or Oken (ex Cuvier) 1817], preoccupied; Gistel's name is unneeded — *Ancylodon* replaced earlier by *Macrodon* Schinz 1822. Objective synonym of *Macrodon* Schinz 1822 (Chao 1978:37 [ref. 6983]). Sciaenidae.

Nomeus Cuvier 1816:315 [ref. 993]. Masc. *Gobius gronovii* Gmelin 1789:1205. Type by subsequent designation. Type designated by Jordan & Gilbert 1883:449 [ref. 2476]. Valid (Haedrich 1967:81 [ref. 5357], Haedrich 1973:562 [ref. 7216], Horn 1984:628 [ref. 13637], Nakabo in Masuda et al. 1984:235 [ref. 6441], Haedrich in Whitehead et al. 1986:1185 [ref. 13677], Haedrich 1986:848 [ref. 5659]). Nomeidae.

Nominostomias (subgenus of *Eustomias*) Regan & Trewavas 1930:72, 82 [ref. 3681]. Masc. *Eustomias bibulbosus* Parr 1927:71. Type by original designation. Synonym of *Eustomias* Vaillant 1888 (Gibbs in Morrow & Gibbs 1964:377 [ref. 6962], Morrow 1973:137 [ref. 7175]); as a valid subgenus (Gibbs et al. 1983 [ref. 5269]). Melanostomiidae.

Nomoctes (subgenus of *Bathytroctes*) Parr 1952:266 [ref. 3381]. Masc. *Bathytroctes michaelsarsi* Koefoed 1910:48. Type by original designation (also monotypic). Valid (Anderson et al. 1985 [ref. 5164]). Alepocephalidae.

Nomorhamphus Weber & de Beaufort 1922:141 [ref. 4598]. Masc. *Nomorhamphus celebensis* Weber & de Beaufort 1922:141. Type by subsequent designation. Type designated by Jordan 1923:Index A, p. ii. [ref. 2421]. Misspelled *Nomarhamphus* by Jordan 1923:161 [ref. 2421]. Valid (Collette et al. 1984:352 [ref. 11422]). Hemiramphidae.

Norfolkia Fowler 1953:262 [ref. 1463]. Fem. *Norfolkia lairdi* Fowler 1953:264. Type by original designation (also monotypic). Valid (Hardy 1984:176 [ref. 5340], Holleman 1986:758 [ref. 5671], Kuiter 1986:91 [ref. 6026]). Tripterygiidae.

Noriona Strand 1942:401 [ref. 4289]. Fem. *Alepocephalus andersoni* Fowler 1834:246. Type by being a replacement name. Replacement for *Normania* Parr 1937, preoccupied by Brady 1866 in Crustacea, Bowerbank 1869 in sponges, and Boeck 1871 in Crustacea; but *Normania* Parr replaced earlier by *Proditor* Whitley 1940. Objective synonym of *Proditor* Whitley 1940. Alepocephalidae.

Normanetta Whitley 1931:322 [ref. 4672]. Fem. *Achirus poropterus* Bleeker 1851:410. Type by original designation (also monotypic). Synonym of *Pardachirus* Günther 1862 (Clark & George 1979:104 [ref. 6992]). Soleidae.

Normania Parr 1937:5, 9 [ref. 3376]. Fem. *Alepocephalus andersoni* Fowler 1934:246. Type by original designation (also monotypic). Preoccupied by Brady 1866 in Crustacea, Bowerbank 1869 in sponges, and Boeck 1871 in Crustacea; replaced by *Proditor* Whitley 1940 and by *Noriona* Strand 1942. Synonym of *Alepocephalus* Risso 1820 (Parr 1951:4 [ref. 3380]). Alepocephalidae.

Normanichthys Clark 1937:90 [ref. 840]. Masc. *Normanichthys crockeri* Clark 1937:90. Type by monotypy. Valid (Washington et al. 1984:443 [ref. 13660], Yabe 1985:123 [ref. 11522], Pequeño 1989:57 [ref. 14125]). Normanichthyidae.

Normichthys Parr 1951:17, 19 [ref. 3380]. Masc. *Normichthys operosa* Parr 1951:19. Type by original designation (also monotypic). Valid (Krefft 1973:97 [ref. 7166], Quéro et al. in Whitehead et al. 1984:263 [ref. 13675], Matsui & Rosenblatt 1986:224 [ref. 5688], Sazonov 1986 [ref. 6003]). Platytroctidae.

Notacanthus Bloch 1788:278 [ref. 466]. Masc. *Notacanthus chemnitzii* Bloch 1788:278. Type by monotypy. *Notacanthum* Rafinesque 1815:89 [ref. 3584] is an incorrect subsequent spelling. Valid (Uyeno in Masuda et al. 1984:32 [ref. 6441], Nakamura in Nakamura et al. 1986:60 [ref. 14235], Sulak in Whitehead et al. 1986:599 [ref. 13676], Sulak 1986:195 [ref. 5720], Paxton et al. 1989:150 [ref. 12442]). Notacanthidae.

Notarius Gill 1863:171 [ref. 1681]. Masc. *Arius grandicassis* Valenciennes in Cuvier & Valenciennes 1840:54. Type by monotypy. Ariidae.

Notastrape Whitley 1932:327 [ref. 4674]. *Notastrape macneilli* Whitley 1932:327. Type by original designation (also monotypic). Synonym of *Torpedo* Houttuyn 1764 (Cappetta 1987:161 [ref. 6348]). Torpedinidae.

Notemigonus Rafinesque 1819:420 [ref. 3590]. Masc. *Notemigonus auratus* Rafinesque 1819:421. Type by monotypy. Valid. Cyprinidae.

Notesthes Ogilby 1903:8, 17 [ref. 3280]. Fem. *Centropogon robustus* Günther 1860:128. Type by monotypy. Valid (Washington et al. 1984:440 [ref. 13660] as *Notestes*, Paxton et al. 1989:445 [ref. 12442]). Scorpaenidae: Tetraroginae.

Nothistium Herrmann 1804:305 [ref. 2146]. Neut. *Scomber gladius* Bloch 1793:81. Appeared first without species; first addition of species not researched; type apparently as above. Unjustifiably emended to *Notistium* by Agassiz 1845:42 [ref. 4889] and 1846:251 [ref. 64]. Synonym of *Istiophorus* Lacepède 1801 (de Sylva 1973:477 [ref. 7210], Nakamura 1983:276 [ref. 5371] as *Notistium*). Istiophoridae.

Nothobranchius Peters 1868:145 [ref. 7935]. Masc. *Cyprinodon orthonotus* Peters 1844:35. Type by monotypy. Also in Peters 1868:60 [ref. 3440]; above apparently earliest but not researched. Valid (Parenti 1981:479 [ref. 7066], Wildekamp et al. 1986:263 [ref. 6198], Wildekamp 1987 [ref. 5994]). Aplocheilidae: Aplocheilinae.

Nothonotus Putnam (ex Agassiz) 1863:3 [ref. 3567]. Masc. *Etheostoma maculatum* Kirtland 1840:276. Type by subsequent designation. Type designated by Jordan & Gilbert 1877:93 [ref. 4907]. Synonym of *Etheostoma* Rafinesque 1819, but as a valid subgenus (Collette & Banarescu 1977:1456 [ref. 5845], Page 1981:35 [ref. 3347], Bailey & Etnier 1988:24 [ref. 6873]). Percidae.

Notidanus Cuvier 1816:128 [ref. 993]. Masc. *Squalus griseus* Bonnaterre 1788:9. Type by monotypy. Objective synonym of *Hexanchus* Rafinesque 1810 (Boeseman 1973:8 [ref. 7161], Compagno 1984:19 [ref. 6474]). Hexanchidae.

Notiocampus Dawson 1979:482 [ref. 1068]. Masc. *Nannocampus ruber* Ramsay & Ogilby 1886:757. Type by original designation (also monotypic). Valid (Dawson 1985:152 [ref. 6541], Paxton et al. 1989:427 [ref. 12442]). Syngnathidae: Syngnathinae.

Notocetichthys Balushkin, Fedorov & Paxton 1989:155 [ref. 12557]. Masc. *Notocetichthys trunovi* Balushkin, Fedorov & Paxton 1989:156. Type by original designation (also monotypic). Valid (Paxton 1989:166 [ref. 13435]). Cetomimidae.

Notocheirus Clark 1937:88 [ref. 840]. Masc. *Notocheirus hubbsi* Clark 1937:89. Type by monotypy. Valid (Pequeño 1989:51 [ref. 14125]). Atherinidae: Notocheirinae.

Notoclinops Whitley 1930:20 [ref. 4671]. Masc. *Tripterygion segmentatum* McCulloch & Phillipps 1923:20. Type by original designation. Valid (Hardy 1987 [ref. 6027]). Tripterygiidae.

Notoclinus Gill 1893:119, 124 [ref. 1736]. Masc. *Trypterygion fenestratus* Forster (=*Blennius fenestratus* Bloch & Schneider 1801:173). Valid. Tripterygiidae.

Notogaleus Whitley 1931:310 [ref. 4672]. Masc. *Galeus australis* Macleay 1881:354. Type by original designation (also monotypic). Synonym of *Galeorhinus* Blainville 1816 (Compagno 1984:386 [ref. 6846], Cappetta 1987:115 [ref. 6348], Compagno 1988:247 [ref. 13488]). Carcharhinidae.

Notoglanidium Günther 1903:336 [ref. 2021]. Neut. *Notoglanidium walkeri* Günther 1903:337. Type by monotypy. Valid (Risch 1986:33 [ref. 6190], Burgess 1989:71 [ref. 12860]). Bagridae.

Notoglanis Günther 1864:136 [ref. 1974]. Masc. *Pimelodus multiradiatus* Kner 1857:414. Type by monotypy. Synonym of *Rhamdia* Bleeker 1858. Pimelodidae.

Notognidion Rafinesque 1810:46 [ref. 3594]. Neut. *Notognidion scirenga* Rafinesque 1810:46. Type by monotypy. Family placement uncertain. Serranidae.

Notogrammus Bean 1881:147 [ref. 223]. Masc. *Notogrammus rothrocki* Bean 1881:146. Type by monotypy. Stichaeidae.

Notograptus Günther 1867:63 [ref. 1988]. Masc. *Notograptus guttatus* Günther 1867:64. Type by monotypy. Valid. Notograptidae.

Notolabrus Russell 1988:12 [ref. 12549]. Masc. *Labrus fucicola*

Richardson 1840:26. Type by original designation. Labridae.

Notolepidomyzon (subgenus of *Pantosteus*) Fowler 1913:47 [ref. 1388]. Masc. *Pantosteus arizonae* Gilbert in Jordan & Evermann 1896:170. Type by original designation (also monotypic). Synonym of *Catostomus* Lesueur 1817. Catostomidae.

Notolepis Dollo 1908:60 [ref. 1136]. Fem. *Notolepis coatsi* Dollo 1908:60. Type by monotypy. Valid (Post 1973:208 [ref. 7182], Post in Whitehead et al. 1984:503 [ref. 13675], Okiyama 1984:207 [ref. 13644], Fujii in Masuda et al. 1984:76 [ref. 6441], Post 1986:276 [ref. 5705], Post 1987:100 [ref. 6225], Paxton et al. 1989:247 [ref. 12442]). Paralepididae.

Notoliparis Andriashev 1975:315 [ref. 119]. Masc. *Notoliparis kurchatovi* Andriashev 1975:315. Type by original designation. Cyclopteridae: Liparinae.

Notolychnus Fraser-Brunner 1949:1077 [ref. 1496]. Masc. *Myctophum valdiviae* Brauer 1904:398. Type by being a replacement name. Replacement for *Vestula* Bolin 1946, preoccupied by Stål 1865 in Hemiptera. Valid (Krefft & Bekker 1973:193 [ref. 7181], Paxton 1979:16 [ref. 6440], Hulley in Whitehead et al. 1984:475 [ref. 13675], Moser et al. 1984:219 [ref. 13645], Fujii in Masuda et al. 1984:67 [ref. 6441], Hulley 1986:315 [ref. 5672], Paxton et al. 1989:267 [ref. 12442]). Myctophidae.

Notolycodes Gosztonyi 1977:224 [ref. 6103]. Masc. *Notolycodes schmidti* Gosztonyi 1977:224. Type by original designation (also monotypic). Valid (Anderson 1984:578 [ref. 13634]). Zoarcidae.

Notomyxine Nani & Gneri 1951:195 [ref. 3143]. Fem. *Myxine tridentiger* Garman 1899:345. Type by original designation (also monotypic). Synonym of *Myxine* Linnaeus 1758 (Fowler 1964:48 [ref. 7160]). Myxinidae: Myxininae.

Notophthalmus Hyrtl 1859:17 [ref. 2291]. Masc. *Hypophthalmus marginatus* Valenciennes in Cuvier & Valenciennes 1859:17. Type by monotypy. Preoccupied by Rafinesque 1820 in Amphibia; apparently not replaced. Synonym of *Hypophthalmus* Cuvier 1829. Hypophthalmidae.

Notophtophis Castro-Aguirre & Suárez de los Cobos 1983:114 [ref. 5313]. Masc. *Notophtophis brunneus* Castro-Aguirre & Suárez de los Cobos 1983:114. Type by original designation (also monotypic). Synonym of *Echiophis* Kaup 1856 (McCosker et al. 1989:357 [ref. 13288]). Ophichthidae: Ophichthinae.

Notopodichthys (subgenus of *Bathophilus*) Regan & Trewavas 1930:65 [ref. 3681]. Masc. *Bathophilus brevis* Regan & Trewavas 1930:66. Type by monotypy. Synonym of *Bathophilus* Giglioli 1882, as a subgenus (Morrow in Morrow & Gibbs 1964:465 [ref. 6962). Melanostomiidae.

Notopogon Regan 1914:14 [ref. 3661]. Masc. *Notopogon lilliei* Regan 1914:14. Type by subsequent designation. Type not *N. schotei* Weber as designated by Jordan 1920:555 [ref. 4905]; *schotei* not an originally included species; *schotei* appears in this genus in article immediately following one containing the genus description. First subsequent type designation not researched. Valid (Nakamura et al. 1986:174 [ref. 14235], Heemstra 1986:460 [ref. 5660], Paxton et al. 1989:409 [ref. 12442]). Centriscidae: Macroramphosinae.

Notopterus Lacepède 1800:189 [ref. 2709]. Masc. *Gymnotus kapirat* Lacepède 1800:190 (= *Gymnotus notopterus* Pallas 1769:40). Type is the species *notopterus* by absolute tautonymy of senior objective synonym of *kapirat*; two included species, with *Gymnotus notopterus* Gmelin (validated by Pallas) included in synonymy of *kapirat*. Valid (Jayaram 1981:53 [ref. 6497], Kottelat 1989:4 [ref. 13605], Roberts 1989:24 [ref. 6439]). Notopteridae.

Notorabula Whitley 1934:154 [ref. 4681]. Fem. *Muraena callorhyncha* Günther 1870:122. Type by original designation (also monotypic). Synonym of *Gymnothorax* Bloch 1795 (Böhlke et al. 1989:145 [ref. 13286]). Muraenidae: Muraeninae.

Notoraja (subgenus of *Breviraja*) Ishiyama 1958:322 [ref. 2308]. Fem. *Raja tobitukai* Hiyama 1940:169. Type by original designation (also monotypic). Valid (Ishihara & Ishiyama 1986:272 [ref. 5142], Stehmann 1989 [ref. 13266]). Rajidae.

Notorynchus Ayres 1855:73 [ref. 159]. Masc. *Notorynchus maculatus* Ayres 1855:72. Type by monotypy. Spelled *Notorhynchus* by Gill 1864:149 [ref. 1697] and others. Valid (Compagno 1984:22 [ref. 6474], Nakaya & Shirai in Masuda et al. 1984:3 [ref. 6441], Bass et al. 1986:47 [ref. 5638], Cappetta 1987:48 [ref. 6348], Paxton et al. 1989:27 [ref. 12442]). Hexanchidae.

Notoscopelus (subgenus of *Scopelus*) Günther 1864:405, 415 [ref. 1974]. Masc. *Lampanyctus resplendens* Richardson 1845:42. Type by subsequent designation. In key (p. 405) as subgenus of *Scopelus* with corresponding species on pp. 415-416. Type designated by Goode & Bean 1896:82 [ref. 1848]. Valid (Krefft & Bekker 1973:194 [ref. 7181], Nafpaktitis 1975 [ref. 3137], Fujii & Uyeno 1976 [ref. 7014], Paxton 1979:16 [ref. 6440], Hulley in Whitehead et al. 1984:475 [ref. 13675], Moser et al. 1984:220 [ref. 13645], Fujii in Masuda et al. 1984:74 [ref. 6441], Hulley 1986:315 [ref. 5672], Paxton et al. 1989:267 [ref. 12442]). Myctophidae.

Notosema Goode & Bean 1883:192 [ref. 1838]. Neut. *Notosema dilecta* Goode & Bean 1883:193. Type by monotypy. Misspelled *Nothosema* in Zoological Record for 1882. Synonym of *Ancylopsetta* Gill 1864 (Norman 1934:124 [ref. 6893]). Paralichthyidae.

Notosudis Waite 1916:56 [ref. 4568]. Fem. *Notosudis hamiltoni* Waite 1916:57. Type by monotypy. Synonym of *Scopelosaurus* Bleeker 1860 (Krefft 1973:168 [ref. 7166], Bertelsen et al. 1976:31 [ref. 289]). Notosudidae.

Notothenia Richardson 1844:5 [ref. 3740]. Fem. *Notothenia coriiceps* Richardson 1844:5. Type by subsequent designation. Type designated by Jordan 1919:222 [ref. 2410]. Valid (Stevens et al. 1984:563 [ref. 13633], Andersen 1984:24 [ref. 13369] with species as *corriceps*). Nototheniidae.

Nototheniops Balushkin 1976:132 [ref. 170]. Masc. *Notothenia nybelini* Balushkin 1976:8. Type by original designation. Valid (Andersen 1984:24 [ref. 13369], Shandikov 1987 [ref. 6343]). Nototheniidae.

Nototropis Jordan 1877:342 [ref. 2373]. Masc. *Notropis atherinoides* Rafinesque 1818:204. Misspelling or unjustified emendation of *Notropis* Rafinesque 1818 [correct orthography would have been *Nototropis*]; see Gilbert 1978:16-17 [ref. 7042] who designates *N. stilbius* as type [but withdrew in unpublished "addenda"]. *Nototropis* is preoccupied by Costa 1853 in Crustacea. Objective synonym of *Notropis* Rafinesque 1818 (Gilbert 1978:16 [ref. 7042]). Cyprinidae.

Notropis Rafinesque 1818:204 [ref. 3585]. Masc. *Notropis atherinoides* Rafinesque 1818:204. Type by monotypy. On Official List (Opinion 1230); ruled masculine by ICZN. Valid (Gilbert 1978 [ref. 7042], Chernoff & Miller 1986 [ref. 6782], Mayden 1989:41 [ref. 12555]). Cyprinidae.

Notropocharax Marini, Nichols & La Monte 1933:6 [ref. 2889]. Masc. *Notropocharax difficilis* Marini, Nichols & La Monte 1933:6. Type by monotypy. Synonym of *Aphyocharax* Günther 1868 (Fowler MS). Characidae.

Notrullus Whitley 1951:67 [ref. 4711]. Masc. *Cynoglossus acaudatus* Gilchrist 1906:162. Type by being a replacement name. Replacement for *Cynoglossoides* Smith 1949, preoccupied by von Bonde 1922 in same family. Synonym of *Cynoglossus* Hamilton 1822 (Heemstra 1986:865 [ref. 5660] based on placement of type species). Cynoglossidae: Cynoglossinae.

Noturus Rafinesque 1818:41 [ref. 3589]. Masc. *Noturus flavus* Rafinesque 1818:41. Type by monotypy. Valid (Taylor 1969 [ref. 6555], Burgess 1989:34 [ref. 12860]). Ictaluridae.

Novacampus Whitley 1955:110 [ref. 4722]. Masc. *Syngnathus norae* Waite 1910:25. Type by original designation (also monotypic). Synonym of *Leptonotus* Kaup 1853 (Fritzsche 1980:190 [ref. 1511], Dawson 1982:40 [ref. 6764], Dawson 1985:111 [ref. 6541]). Syngnathidae: Syngnathinae.

Novacula Catesby 1771:18 [ref. 774]. Fem. Not available, published in a rejected work on Official Index (Opinion 89, Opinion 259). In the synonymy of *Scarus* Forsskål 1775. Scaridae: Scarinae.

Novacula Cuvier 1815:324 et seq. [ref. 1019]. Fem. *Coryphaena novacula* Linnaeus 1758:262. Type by monotypy (also by absolute tautonymy). Also in Cuvier 1816:265 [ref. 993]. Not preoccupied by Catesby 1771 (not available). Synonym of *Xyrichtys* Cuvier 1814 (Bauchot & Quignard 1973:442 [ref. 7204]). Labridae.

Novaculichthys Bleeker 1862:414 [ref. 382]. Masc. *Labrus taeniourus* Lacepède 1801:448. Type by original designation (also monotypic). Also appeared in Bleeker 1862:102 [ref. 386]. Valid (Randall 1981:98 [ref. 5447], Richards & Leis 1984:544 [ref. 13668], Yamakawa in Masuda et al. 1984:212 [ref. 6441], Randall 1986:699 [ref. 5706]). Labridae.

Novaculops Schultz 1960:(122) 143 [ref. 3972]. Masc. *Novaculichthys woodi* Jenkins 1900:52. Type by original designation (also monotypic). Valid (Yamakawa in Masuda et al. 1984:212 [ref. 6441]). Synonym of *Xyrichtys* Cuvier 1814 (Shen & Yeh 1987:64 [ref. 6419] based on placement of type species). Labridae.

Novanthias Whitley 1937:122 [ref. 4689]. Masc. *Neanthias accraensis* Norman 1931:354. Type by being a replacement name. Unneeded replacement for *Neanthias* Norman 1931, not preoccupied by *Neanthias* (Rye 1881, in Index to Zoological Record for 1879, an incorrect subsequent spelling of *Neoanthias* Castelnau). Serranidae: Anthiinae.

Noviricuzenius (subgenus of *Ricuzenius*) Bolin 1936:27 [ref. 505]. Masc. *Ricuzenius (Noviricuzenius) nudithorax* Bolin 1936:27. Type by original designation (also monotypic). Cottidae.

Novumbra Schultz 1929:76 [ref. 3950]. Fem. *Novumbra hubbsi* Schultz 1929:76. Type by original designation (also monotypic). Valid (Wilson & Veilleux 1982 [ref. 14203], Martin 1984:140 [ref. 13639]). Umbridae.

Nox Nalbant 1986:169 [ref. 6135]. Fem. *Hemitaurichthys thompsoni* Fowler 1923:384. Type by original designation (also monotypic). Chaetodontidae.

Nuchequula (subgenus of *Eubleekeria*) Whitley 1932:109 [ref. 4675]. Fem. *Equula blochii* Valenciennes in Cuvier & Valenciennes 1835:84. Type by original designation. Synonym of *Leiognathus* Lacepède 1802. Leiognathidae.

Nudagobioides Shaw 1929:1 [ref. 4016]. Masc. *Nudagobioides nankaii* Shaw 1929:2. Type by original designation (also monotypic). Misspelled *Nudogobioides* in Zoological Record for 1929. Valid. Gobiidae.

Nudiantennarius Schultz 1957:(55) 66 [ref. 3969]. Masc. *Antennarius subteres* Smith & Radcliffe 1912:205. Type by original designation (also monotypic). Valid (Pietsch 1984:36 [ref. 5380]). Antennariidae.

Nudipagellus (subgenus of *Pagellus*) Fowler 1925:4 [ref. 1401]. Masc. *Sparus centrodontus* Delaroche 1809:317, 345. Type by original designation (also monotypic). Synonym of *Pagellus* Valenciennes 1830 (Tortonese 1973:411 [ref. 7192]). Sparidae.

Nukta (subgenus of *Schismatorhynchus*) Hora 1942:13 [ref. 2213]. *Cyprinus nukta* Sykes 1838:159. Type by original designation (also monotypic and by absolute tautonymy). Synonym of *Schismatorhynchos* Bleeker 1855. Cyprinidae.

Nun Banarescu & Nalbant 1982:23 [ref. 174]. *Cobitis galilaea* Günther 1864:493. Type by original designation (also monotypic). Synonym of *Nemacheilus* Bleeker 1863 (Krupp & Schneider 1989:378 [ref. 13651]); valid (Kottelat 1990:20 [ref. 14137]). Balitoridae: Nemacheilinae.

Nuria Valenciennes in Cuvier & Valenciennes 1842:238 [ref. 1009]. Fem. *Nuria thermoicos* Valenciennes in Cuvier & Valenciennes 1842:238. Type by subsequent designation. Type apparently first designated by Jordan 1919:210 [ref. 2410]. Synonym of *Esomus* Swainson 1839. Cyprinidae.

Nyasalapia Thys van den Audenaerde 1970:290, 291 [ref. 12518]. Not available, no included species and no description; as a subgroup of *Oreochromis*. Cichlidae.

Nyassachromis Eccles & Trewavas 1989:75 [ref. 13547]. Masc. *Haplochromis breviceps* Regan 1922:694. Type by original designation. Cichlidae.

Nybelinella Nielsen 1972:53 [ref. 3196]. Fem. *Barathronus erikssoni* Nybelin 1957:308. Type by being a replacement name. Replacement for *Nybelinia* Nielsen 1969, preoccupied by Poche 1925 in tapeworms. Valid (Nielsen 1973:555 [ref. 6885], Nielsen in Whitehead et al. 1986:1170 [ref. 13677]). Aphyonidae.

Nybelinia Nielsen 1969:22 [ref. 3195]. Fem. *Barathronus erikssoni* Nybelin 1957:308. Type by original designation (also monotypic). Preoccupied by Poche 1925 in tapeworms (see Whitley 1976:48 [ref. 4735]). Whitley intended a new genus and provided a new family name Roachiidae; Whitley's new generic names were removed by the editor (see p. 50). (The name Roachiidae is unavailable, not based on an available generic name.) Objective synonym of *Nybelinella* Nielsen 1972, replacement for *Nybelinia* (Nielsen 1973:555 [ref. 6885], Cohen & Nielsen 1978:62 [ref. 881]). Aphyonidae.

Nyctimaster Jordan 1921:645 [ref. 2419]. Masc. *Lampanyctus jordani* Gilbert 1913:104. Type by original designation. Synonym of *Lampanyctus* Bonaparte 1840 (Bolin 1959:26 [ref. 503], Paxton 1979:13 [ref. 6440]). Myctophidae.

Nyctophus Cocco 1829:44 or 144 [ref. 857]. Masc. *Nyctophus rafinesquii* Cocco 1838:180. Type by monotypy. Misspelled *Nychtopus* by Cocco 1838:180 [ref. 865]. A substitute for *Myctophum* according to Jordan 1917:133 [ref. 2407]. Apparently treated by Paxton 1979:7 [ref. 6440] as a misspelling; in synonymy of *Diaphus* Eigenmann & Eigenmann 1890. Needs investigation; not in Cocco 1829:144 [ref. 857] where *Myctophum* is treated; possibly first in Cocco 1829, ref. 856 [not seen]. Myctophidae.

Nystactes Böhlke 1957:68 [ref. 598]. Masc. *Nystactes halis* Böhlke 1957:68. Type by original designation (also monotypic). Preoccupied by Gloger 1827 in Aves and Kaup 1829 in Mammalia; replaced by *Nystactichthys* Böhlke 1958. Synonym of *Heteroconger* Bleeker 1868 (Smith 1989:484 [ref. 13285]). Congridae: Heterocongrinae.

Nystactichthys Böhlke 1958:59 [ref. 600]. Masc. *Nystactes halis* Böhlke 1957:68. Type by being a replacement name. Replacement for *Nystactes* Böhlke 1957, preoccupied by Gloger 1827 in Aves and Kaup 1829 in Mammalia. Synonym of *Taenioconger* Herre 1923 (Blache & Bauchot 1976:427 [ref. 305]). Synonym of *Heteroconger* Bleeker 1868 (Smith 1989:485 [ref. 13285]). Congridae: Heterocongrinae.

Oblada Cuvier 1829:185 [ref. 995]. Fem. *Sparus melanurus* Linnaeus 1758:278. Type by monotypy. Spelled *Oblata* by Valenciennes in Cuvier & Valenciennes 1830:366 [ref. 996]. Valid (Tortonese 1973:410 [ref. 7192], Bauchot & Hureau in Whitehead et al. 1986:897 [ref. 13676]). Sparidae.

Obliquichthys Hardy 1987:52 [ref. 9092]. Masc. *Obliquichthys maryannae* Hardy 1987:53. Type by original designation (also monotypic). Tripterygiidae.

Obliquogobius Koumans 1941:219 [ref. 2677]. Masc. *Gobius cometes* Alcock 1890:208. Type by original designation (also monotypic). Valid (Hoese, pers. comm.). Gobiidae.

Obolarius Tilesius (ex Steller) 1810:225 Masc. *Obolarius aculeatus* Steller (MS). From Monod 1973; not investigated. Synonym of *Gasterosteus* Linnaeus 1758 (Monod 1973:280 [ref. 7193]). Gasterosteidae: Gasterosteinae.

Obtortiophagus Whitley 1933:91 [ref. 4677]. Masc. *Obtortiophagus koumansi* Whitley 1933:92. Type by original designation (also monotypic). Synonym of *Mars* Jordan & Seale 1906 (Yanagisawa 1978:278 [ref. 7028]); synonym of *Cryptocentrus* Valenciennes (ex Ehrenberg) 1837 (Hoese, pers. comm.). Gobiidae.

Occa Jordan & Evermann 1898:2032, 2043 [ref. 2444]. Fem. *Brachyopsis verrucosus* Lockington 1880:60. Type by original designation. Preoccupied by Chesnon 1835 in Aves; replaced by *Chesnonia* Iredale & Whitley 1969 (see Bailey & Gruchy 1970 [ref. 6508]). Synonym of *Occella* Jordan & Hubbs 1925. Agonidae.

Occella Jordan & Hubbs 1925:290, 291 [ref. 2486]. Fem. *Agonus dodecaedron* Tilesius 1813:Pl. 13. Type by original designation (also monotypic). Misspelled *Ocella* on p. 96 and 290, corrected on p. xvii; *Occella* with main description and with species on p. 291. Sometimes as *Ocella* in current literature. Valid (Bailey & Gruchy 1970 [ref. 6508], Washington et al. 1984:442 [ref. 13660], Kanayama in Masuda et al. 1984:331 [ref. 6441], Yabe 1985:123 [ref. 11522], Maeda & Amaoka 1988:73 [ref. 12616]). Agonidae.

Oceanomyzon Fowler 1908:461 [ref. 1378]. Masc. *Oceanomyzon wilsoni* Fowler 1908:462. Type by original designation (also monotypic). Synonym of *Petromyzon* Linnaeus 1758 (Hubbs & Potter 1971:42 [ref. 13397], Vladykov 1973:2 [ref. 7159]). Petromyzontidae: Petromyzontinae.

Oceanops Jordan & Seale 1906:277 [ref. 2497]. Masc. *Labrus latovittatus* Lacepède 1801:455, 526. Type by original designation (also monotypic). Synonym of *Malacanthus* Cuvier 1829 (Dooley 1978:54 [ref. 5499]). Malacanthidae: Malacanthinae.

Ochetobius Günther 1868:297 [ref. 1990]. Masc. *Opsarius elongatus* Kner 1865:358. Type by monotypy. Valid (Yang & Hwang 1964:44 [ref. 13497], Chen & Li in Chu & Chen 1989:43 [ref. 13584]). Cyprinidae.

Ochmacanthus Eigenmann 1912:213 [ref. 1227]. Masc. *Ochmacanthus flabelliferus* Eigenmann 1912:213. Type by original designation (also monotypic). Valid (Burgess 1989:324 [ref. 12860], Pinna 1989 [ref. 12630]). Trichomycteridae.

Ochotskia Schmidt 1915:612 [ref. 3935]. Fem. *Ochotskia armata* Schmidt 1915:612. Type by monotypy. Synonym of *Icelus* Krøyer 1845 (Nelson 1984:19 [ref. 5391]). Cottidae.

Ocosia Jordan & Starks 1904:162 [ref. 2527]. Fem. *Ocosia vespa* Jordan & Starks 1904:162. Type by original designation (also monotypic). Valid (Washington et al. 1984:440 [ref. 13660], Nakabo in Masuda et al. 1984:319 [ref. 6441], Poss & Eschmeyer 1975 [ref. 6388]). Scorpaenidae: Tetraroginae.

Ocotlanichthys (subgenus of *Chirostoma*) de Buen 1945:526 [ref. 691]. Masc. *Chirostoma sphyraena* Boulenger 1900:54. Type by original designation (also monotypic). Misspelled by Schultz 1948:30 [ref. 3966] as *Acotlanichthys*. Synonym of *Chirostoma* Swainson 1839. Atherinidae: Menidiinae.

Octocynodon (subgenus of *Halichoeres*) Fowler 1904:535 [ref. 1367]. Masc. *Julis miniatus* Valenciennes in Cuvier & Valenciennes 1839:460. Type by original designation. Synonym of *Halichoeres* Rüppell 1835 (Fowler MS). Labridae.

Octogrammus Bleeker 1874:370 [ref. 435]. Masc. *Labrax pallasi* Bleeker 1874 (= *Labrax octogrammus* Pallas 1811:283). Type by monotypy. Bleeker's *pallasi* is an unneeded substitute for *L. octogrammus* Schlegel, which is *octogrammus* Pallas. Synonym of *Hexagrammos* Steller 1809. Hexagrammidae: Hexagramminae.

Octonema Herzenstein in Herzenstein & Warpachowski 1887:47 [ref. 2152]. Neut. *Octonema pleskei* Herzenstein in Herzenstein & Warpachowski 1887:48. Type by monotypy. Preoccupied by Martens 1868 in fishes and by Haecker 1879 in Coelenterata, replaced by *Lefua* Herzenstein 1888. Objective synonym of *Lefua* Herzenstein 1888 (Kottelat 1990:19 [ref. 14137]). Balitoridae: Nemacheilinae.

Octonema (subgenus of *Homaloptera*) Martens 1868:608 [ref. 2896]. Neut. *Homaloptera (Octonema) rotundicauda* Martens 1868:608. Type by monotypy. Synonym of *Oreonectes* Günther 1868 (Kottelat 1990:20 [ref. 14137]). Balitoridae: Nemacheilinae.

Octonematichthys Bleeker 1858:60, 65 [ref. 365]. Masc. *Bagrus nigrita* Valenciennes in Cuvier & Valenciennes 1839:426. Type by monotypy. Synonym of *Clarotes* Kner 1855 (Risch 1986:27 [ref. 6190]). Bagridae.

Octonus Rafinesque 1810:29, 54 [ref. 3595]. Masc. *Octonus olosteon* Rafinesque 1810:29. Type by monotypy. Synonym of *Peristedion* Lacepède 1801 (Blanc & Hureau 1973:591 [ref. 7218]). Triglidae: Peristediinae.

Oculeus Commerson in Lacepède 1803:290 (footnote) [ref. 4930]. Masc. Not available; published as a footnote in synonymy of *Megalops* Lacepède. Commerson names in footnotes in this volume of Lacepède placed on Official Index of Rejected Works (see remarks under Opinion 89 in Appendix B). In the synonymy of *Megalops* Lacepède 1803 (Daget 1984:32 [ref. 6170]). Megalopidae.

Oculospinus Koefoed 1927:139 [ref. 2650]. Masc. *Oculospinus brevis* Koefoed 1927:139. Type by monotypy. Valid (Nielsen 1973:551 [ref. 6885]); synonym of *Cataetyx* Günther 1887 (Cohen & Nielsen 1978:46 [ref. 881], Hureau & Nielsen 1981:25 [ref. 5438], Nielsen in Whitehead et al. 1986:1154 [ref. 13677]). Bythitidae: Bythitinae.

Ocyanthias Jordan & Evermann 1896:1131, 1227 [ref. 2443]. Masc. *Aylopon martinicensis* Guichenot 1868:8. Type by original designation (also monotypic). Misspelled *Oxyanthias* in Zoological Record for 1896. Valid (Matsuura in Uyeno et al. 1983:312 [ref. 14275], Kendall 1984:500 [ref. 13663]); synonym of *Holanthias* Günther 1868 (Heemstra & Randall 1986:512 [ref. 5667]). Serranidae: Anthiinae.

Ocycrius Jordan & Hubbs 1925:226 [ref. 2486]. Masc. *Centrolophus japonicus* Döderlein in Steindachner & Döderlein 1885:183. Type by original designation. Synonym of *Hyperoglyphe* Günther 1859 (Haedrich 1967:55 [ref. 5357]). Centrolophidae.

Ocynectes Jordan & Starks 1904:306 [ref. 2528]. Masc. *Ocynectes maschalis* Jordan & Starks 1904:307. Type by original designation (also monotypic). Valid (Washington et al. 1984:443 [ref. 13660], Yabe in Masuda et al. 1984:329 [ref. 6441], Yabe 1985:111 [ref. 11522], Shiogaki 1987 [ref. 6708]). Cottidae.

Ocyurus Gill 1862:236, 237 [ref. 1664]. Masc. *Sparus chrysurus* Bloch 1791:28. Type by monotypy. Valid (Johnson 1980:10 [ref. 13553], Allen 1985:129 [ref. 6843]); as a valid subgenus of *Lutjanus* Bloch 1790 (Akazaki & Iwatsuki 1986 [ref. 6316]). Lutjanidae.

Odamphus Rafinesque 1815:89 [ref. 3584]. Not available, name only. Unplaced genera.

Odax Commerson in Lacepède 1801:70 (footnote) [ref. 2710]. Masc. Apparently not available; name mentioned in passing in footnote under *Scarus*. Not *Odax* Valenciennes 1840, a name in current use. See remarks under Opinion 89 in Appendix B. In the synonymy of *Scarus* Forsskål 1775. Scaridae: Scarinae.

Odax Valenciennes in Cuvier & Valenciennes 1840:299 [ref. 4882]. Masc. *Scarus pullus* Bloch & Schneider 1801:288. Type by subsequent designation. Appeared first in Cuvier 1829:266 [ref. 995] as "Les Odax"; based on style of text and contents, the name was apparently not intended as new but as a new use of *Odax* Commerson in Lacepède 1801 (not available) but in the vernacular. Probably dates to Valenciennes as above; type species and type designation not researched, usually given as above. Valid (Ayling & Paxton 1983 [ref. 5258], Richards & Leis 1984:544 [ref. 13668], Gomon & Paxton 1986:31 [ref. 5656]). Odacidae.

Odaxothrissa Boulenger 1899:64 [ref. 549]. Fem. *Odaxothrissa losera* Boulenger 1899:64. Type by monotypy. Valid (Poll et al. 1984:47 [ref. 6172], Grande 1985:247 [ref. 6466], Whitehead 1985:139 [ref. 5141]). Clupeidae.

Odondebuenia de Buen 1930:9 [ref. 684]. Fem. *Eleotris balearicus [balearica]* Pellegrin & Fage 1907:11. Type by original designation. Misspelled *Odonebyenia* in Zoological Record for 1930. Valid (Miller 1972:401 [ref. 3011], Miller 1973:505 [ref. 6888], Miller in Whitehead et al. 1986:1065 [ref. 13677]). Gobiidae.

Odontamblyopus Bleeker 1874:330 [ref. 437]. Masc. *Gobioides rubicundus* Hamilton 1822:37. Type by original designation (also monotypic). Valid (Larson & Hoese 1980:42 [ref. 2725], Birdsong et al. 1988:197 [ref. 7303]). Gobiidae.

Odontanthias Bleeker 1873:236 [ref. 12596]. Masc. *Serranus borbonius* Cuvier in Cuvier & Valenciennes 1828:263. Type by original designation. Apparently above is earliest. Jordan 1919:367 [ref. 4904] and Zoological Record for 1873 have incorrect references and type species. Synonym of *Holanthias* Günther 1868 (Heemstra & Randall 1986:512 [ref. 5667]); valid (Kendall 1984:500 [ref. 13663], Katayama in Masuda et al. 1984:134 [ref. 6441], Katayama & Yamamoto 1986 [ref. 6716]). Serranidae: Anthiinae.

Odontaspis Agassiz 1838:87 [ref. 13390]. Fem. *Carcharias ferox* Risso 1826:122 (= *Squalus ferox* Risso 1810:38). Type by monotypy. Type confirmed by ICZN, on Official List (Opinion 723); type equals *Squalus ferox* Risso 1810 (Compagno 1984:219 [ref. 6474]); *Odontaspis* to take precedence over *Carcharias* Rafinesque 1810 when considered synonyms (Opinion 1459). Valid (Springer 1973:11 [ref. 7162], Compagno 1984:219 [ref. 6474], Nakaya in Masuda et al. 1984:7 [ref. 6441], Bass & Compagno 1986:104 [ref. 5637], Cappetta 1987:88 [ref. 6348], Paxton et al. 1989:64 [ref. 12442]). Odontaspididae: Odontaspidinae.

Odonteleotris Gill 1863:270 [ref. 1691]. Fem. *Eleotris macrodon* Bleeker 1853:104. Type by original designation (also monotypic). Synonym of *Bostrychus* Lacepède 1801 (Maugé 1986:390 [ref. 6218]); valid (Birdsong et al. 1988:180 [ref. 7303]). Eleotridae.

Odontengraulis (subgenus of *Stolephorus*) Whitehead, Boeseman & Wheeler (ex Bleeker) 1966:12 [ref. 6860]. Fem. Cited as a name mentioned in a letter from Bleeker to Günther; not available, not used as a valid name by Whitehead, Boeseman & Wheeler. In the synonymy of *Lycothrissa* Günther 1868 (Whitehead et al. 1988 [ref. 5725]). Engraulidae.

Odontesthes Evermann & Kendall 1906:94 [ref. 1282]. Fem. *Odontesthes perugiae* Evermann & Kendall 1906:94. Type by original designation (also monotypic). Valid (White 1985:17 [ref. 13551], Crabtree 1987:861 [ref. 6771]). Atherinidae: Atherinopsinae.

Odontobutis Bleeker 1874:305 [ref. 437]. *Eleotris obscura* Schlegel in Temminck & Schlegel 1847:149. Type by original designation (also monotypic). Valid (Akihito in Masuda et al. 1984:241 [ref. 6441], Iwata et al. 1985 [ref. 6724], Birdsong et al. 1988:202 [ref. 7303]). Eleotridae.

Odontoclinus Reid 1935:164 [ref. 3683]. Masc. *Odontoclinus dendriticus* Reid 1935:165. Type by original designation (also monotypic). Synonym of *Labrisomus* Swainson 1839 (Hubbs 1953:117 [ref. 2253], Springer 1958:422 [ref. 10210]). Labrisomidae.

Odontogadus Gill 1863:248 [ref. 1688]. Masc. *Gadus euxinus* Nordmann 1840:526. Type by monotypy. Synonym of *Merlangius* Geoffroy 1767 (Svetovidov 1973:307 [ref. 7169]). Gadidae.

Odontoglyphis (subgenus of *Dentex*) Fowler 1904:527 [ref. 1367]. *Dentex tolu* Valenciennes in Cuvier & Valenciennes 1830:248. Type by original designation (also monotypic). Synonym of *Nemipterus* Swainson 1839. Nemipteridae.

Odontognathus Lacepède 1800:220 [ref. 2709]. Masc. *Odontognathus mucronatus* Lacepède 1800:220. Type by monotypy. Valid (Grande 1985:244 [ref. 6466], Whitehead 1985:297 [ref. 5141]). Clupeidae.

Odontogobius Bleeker 1874:323 [ref. 437]. Masc. *Gobius bynoensis* Richardson 1844:1. Type by original designation (also monotypic). Synonym of *Amblygobius* Bleeker 1874 (Maugé 1986:359 [ref. 6218]). Gobiidae.

Odontolabrax Bleeker 1873:149 [ref. 431]. Masc. *Odontolabrax typus* Bleeker 1873:150. Type by monotypy (also by use of *typus*). No recent treatment located; family placement follows Fowler (MS). Serranidae.

Odontolepis Fischer von Waldheim 1813:71, 78 [ref. 1331]. Fem. No included species; Jordan 1917:95 [ref. 2407] says type may be assumed as *Symphurus nigrescens* Rafinesque 1810; first technical addition of species not researched. Original not seen. Synonym of *Symphurus* Rafinesque 1810 (Torchio 1973:635 [ref. 6892]). Cynoglossidae: Symphurinae.

Odontolimia (subgenus of *Limia*) Rivas 1980:29 [ref. 3763]. Fem. *Limia grossidens* Rivas 1980:29. Type by original designation. Synonym of *Poecilia* Bloch & Schneider 1801, but as a valid subgenus (Parenti & Rauchenberger 1989:8 [ref. 13538]).

Poeciliidae.

Odontoliparis Stein 1978:33 [ref. 4203]. Masc. *Odontoliparis ferox* Stein 1978:33. Type by original designation (also monotypic). Cyclopteridae: Liparinae.

Odontomacrurus Norman 1939:49 [ref. 6556]. Masc. *Odontomacrurus murrayi* Norman 1939:49. Type by original designation. Valid (Marshall 1973:292 [ref. 7194], Marshall & Iwamoto 1973:534 [ref. 6963], Fahay & Markle 1984:274 [ref. 13653] as *Ondontomacrurus*, Geistdoerfer in Whitehead et al. 1986:671 [ref. 13676], Iwamoto & Sazonov 1988:39 [ref. 6228], Paxton et al. 1989:329 [ref. 12442]). Macrouridae: Macrourinae.

Odontonectes Günther 1859:265 [ref. 1961]. Masc. *Caesio erythrogaster* Cuvier (ex Kuhl & van Hasselt) in Cuvier & Valenciennes 1830:442. Type by monotypy. Synonym of *Caesio* Lacepède 1801, but as a valid subgenus (Carpenter 1987:15 [ref. 6430], Carpenter 1988:4 [ref. 9296]). Caesionidae.

Odontonema Weber 1913:148 [ref. 4602]. Neut. *Odontonema kerberti* Weber 1913:149. Type by monotypy. Synonym of *Kali* Lloyd 1909 (Krefft 1973:453 [ref. 7166], Johnson & Cohen 1974:34 [ref. 7133]). Chiasmodontidae.

Odontopholis (subgenus of *Percina*) Page 1974:84 [ref. 3346]. Fem. *Etheostoma cymatotaenia* Gilbert & Meek 1887:51. Type by original designation (also monotypic). Synonym of *Percina* Haldeman 1842, but as a valid subgenus (Page 1974:84 [ref. 3346], Collette & Banarescu 1977:1454 [ref. 5845]). Percidae.

Odontopsis van Hasselt 1823:131 [ref. 5963]. Fem. *Odontopsis armata* van Hasselt 1823:131. Type by monotypy. See Kottelat 1987:370 [ref. 5962]. Placement uncertain. Unplaced genera.

Odontopyxis Lockington 1880:328 [ref. 2815]. Fem. *Odontopyxis trispinosus* Lockington 1880:328. Type by monotypy. Valid (Washington et al. 1984:442 [ref. 13660], Yabe 1985:123 [ref. 11522]). Agonidae.

Odontorhamphus Weed 1933:47, 51 [ref. 6557]. Masc. *Odontorhamphus chancellori* Weed 1933:52. Type by original designation (also monotypic). Synonym of *Hyporhamphus* Gill 1859, subgenus *Reporhamphus* Whitley 1931 (Parin et al. 1980:52 [ref. 6895]). Hemiramphidae.

Odontoscion Gill 1862:18 [ref. 1657]. Masc. *Corvina dentex* Cuvier in Cuvier & Valenciennes 1830:139. Type by original designation (also monotypic). Valid (Chao 1978:39 [ref. 6983]). Sciaenidae.

Odontostilbe Cope 1870:566 [ref. 914]. Fem. *Odontostilbe fugitiva* Cope 1870:566. Type by monotypy. Synonym of *Cheirodon* Girard 1855 (Fink & Weitzman 1974:3 [ref. 7132]); valid (Géry 1977:554 [ref. 1597], Malabarba 1989:136 [ref. 14217]). Characidae.

Odontostoechus Gomes 1947:7 [ref. 1830]. Masc. *Odontostoechus lethostigmus* Gomes 1947:8. Type by original designation (also monotypic). Synonym of *Othonocheirodus* Myers 1927 (Géry 1977:559 [ref. 1597]). Characidae.

Odontostomias Norman 1930:309 [ref. 3219]. Masc. *Odontostomias micropogon* Norman 1930:310. Type by original designation. Valid (Morrow in Morrow & Gibbs 1964:354 [ref. 6962], Fink 1985:11 [ref. 5171]). Melanostomiidae.

Odontostomops (subgenus of *Evermannella*) Fowler 1934:322 [ref. 1416]. Masc. *Evermannella normalops* Parr 1928:164. Type by original designation (also monotypic). Valid (Johnson 1982:147 [ref. 5519], Johnson in Whitehead et al. 1984:492 [ref. 13675], Fujii in Masuda et al. 1984:78 [ref. 6441]). Evermannellidae.

Odontostomus Cocco 1838:192 [32] [ref. 865]. Masc. *Odontostomus hyalinus* Cocco 1838:192 [32]. Type by monotypy. Spelled *Odondostomus* on p. 192 [p. 32 of separate], correctly as *Odontostomus* on Pl. 4, fig. 11. Preoccupied by Beck 1837 in Mollusca, replaced by *Evermannella* Fowler 1901. Objective synonym of *Evermannella* Fowler 1901 (Johnson 1982:123 [ref. 5519]). Evermannellidae.

Odonus Gistel 1848:XI [ref. 1822]. *Xenodon niger* Rüppell 1837:53. Type by being a replacement name. Replacement for *Xenodon* Rüppell 1836, preoccupied; predates *Erythrodon* Rüppell 1852 and *Pyrodon* Kaup 1855. Valid (Matsuura 1980:33 [ref. 6943], Tyler 1980:120 [ref. 4477], Arai 1983:199 [ref. 14249], Aboussouan & Leis 1984:452 [ref. 13661], Matsuura in Masuda et al. 1984:358 [ref. 6441], Smith & Heemstra 1986:879 [ref. 5714]). Balistidae.

Oedalechilus (subgenus of *Liza*) Fowler 1903:748 [ref. 1361]. Masc. *Mugil labeo* Cuvier 1829:233. Type by original designation (also monotypic). *Oedachilus* is a misspelling. Valid (Trewavas 1973:573 [ref. 7201], Yoshino & Senou in Masuda et al. 1984:120 [ref. 6441], Ben-Tuvia in Whitehead et al. 1986:1203). Mugilidae.

Oedemognathus Myers 1936:115 [ref. 3114]. Masc. *Oedemognathus exodon* Myers 1936:115. Type by original designation (also monotypic). Valid (see Mago-Leccia 1978:14 [ref. 5489]). Gymnotidae: Gymnotinae.

Oelemaria (subgenus of *Guianacara*) Kullander & Nijssen 1989:92 [ref. 14136]. Fem. *Guianacara oelemariensis* Kullander & Nijssen 1989:126. Type by original designation (also monotypic). Cichlidae.

Ogcocephalus Fischer von Waldheim 1813:70, 78 [ref. 1331]. Masc. *Lophius vespertilio* Linnaeus 1758:236. Type by subsequent designation. Described with no type; first addition of species not researched; type apparently designated first by Jordan & Evermann 1896:511 [ref. 2442]. Spelled *Oncocephalus* by Jordan 1895:506 [ref. 2394] and *Onchocephalus* by Gill in Goode & Bean 1896:498 [ref. 1848] (see also Briggs 1961:163 [ref. 13439]). Original not seen. Valid (Bradbury 1980 [ref. 6538]). Ogcocephalidae.

Ogilamia (subgenus of *Galeolamna*) Whitley 1939:231 [ref. 4695]. Fem. *Carcharinus stevensi* Ogilby 1911:38. Type by monotypy. Correct spelling for genus of type species is *Carcharhinus*. Synonym of *Carcharhinus* Blainville 1816 (Garrick 1982:19 [ref. 5454], Compagno 1984:449 [ref. 6846], Cappetta 1987:121 [ref. 6348], Compagno 1988:308 [ref. 13488]). Carcharhinidae.

Ogilbia Jordan & Evermann in Evermann & Kendell 1898:132 [ref. 1281]. Fem. *Ogilbia cayorum* Evermann & Kendall 1898:133. Type by original designation (also monotypic). Valid (Cohen & Nielsen 1978:60 [ref. 881]). Bythitidae: Brosmophycinae.

Ogilbyina (subgenus of *Dampieria*) Fowler 1931:5, 19 [ref. 1407]. Fem. *Dampieria longipinnis* Ogilby 1908:34. Type by original designation (also monotypic). Valid (Gill, pers. comm.). Pseudochromidae: Pseudochrominae.

Ognichodes Swainson 1839:183, 278 [ref. 4303]. Masc. *Gobioides broussonnetii* Lacepède 1800:576. Type by monotypy. Objective synonym of *Gobioides* Lacepède 1800 (Maugé 1986:370 [ref. 6218]). Gobiidae.

Oidiphorus McAllister & Rees 1964:104 [ref. 2921]. Masc. *Maynea brevis* Norman 1937:108. Type by original designation (also monotypic). Valid (Gosztonyi 1977:227 [ref. 6103], Anderson 1984:578 [ref. 13634]). Zoarcidae.

Okamejei (subgenus of *Raja*) Ishiyama 1958:354 [ref. 2308]. Fem. *Raja fusca* Garman 1885:42. Type by original designation. Synonym of *Raja* Linnaeus 1758, but as a valid subgenus (Ishihara & Ishiyama 1986:274 [ref. 5142], Ishihara 1987:248 [ref. 6264]).

Rajidae.

Okkelbergia (subgenus of *Lampetra*) Creaser & Hubbs 1922:8 [ref. 990]. Fem. *Ammocoetes aepyptera* Abbott 1860:327. Type by original designation (also monotypic). Valid (Hubbs & Potter 1971:48 [ref. 13397]); synonym of *Lampetra* Gray 1851 (Vladykov & Kott 1976 [ref. 7095]); as a subgenus of *Lampetra* (Bailey 1980:1627 [ref. 5253]). Petromyzontidae: Petromyzontinae.

Oligancistrus Rapp Py-Daniel 1989:246 [ref. 13470]. Masc. *Chaetostomus punctatissimus* Steindachner 1882:119. Type by original designation (also monotypic, one species mentioned). Genus proposed somewhat conditionally but accepted as available (see also *Baryancistrus* Rapp Py-Daniel and Appendix A). Loricariidae.

Oliglyphisodon Fowler 1941:266 [ref. 1438]. Masc. *Glyphisodon imparipennis* Vaillant & Sauvage 1875:279. Type by original designation (also monotypic). Pomacentridae.

Oligobrycon Eigenmann 1915:57 [ref. 1231]. Masc. *Oligobrycon microstomus* Eigenmann 1915:58. Type by original designation (also monotypic). Valid (Géry 1977:587 [ref. 1597]). Characidae.

Oligocephalus Girard 1859:67 [ref. 1821]. Masc. *Boleosoma lepida* Baird & Girard 1853:388. Type by monotypy. Synonym of *Etheostoma* Rafinesque 1819, but as a valid subgenus (Collette & Banarescu 1977:1456 [ref. 5845], Page 1981:39 [ref. 3347], Bailey & Etnier 1988:25 [ref. 6873]). Percidae.

Oligocottus Girard 1856:132 [ref. 1809]. Masc. *Oligocottus maculosus* Girard 1856:133. Type by monotypy. Valid (Bolin 1944:61, 65 [ref. 6379], Washington et al. 1984:443 [ref. 13660], Yabe in Masuda et al. 1984:328 [ref. 6441], Yabe 1985:111 [ref. 11522], Washington 1986 [ref. 5202]). Cottidae.

Oligolepis (subgenus of *Stenogobius*) Bleeker 1874:318 [ref. 437]. Fem. *Gobius melanostigma* Bleeker 1849:32. Type by original designation (also monotypic). Valid (Akihito in Masuda et al. 1984:253 [ref. 6441], Hoese 1986:796 [ref. 5670], Maugé 1986:377 [ref. 6218], Birdsong et al. 1988:188 [ref. 7303], Kottelat 1989:19 [ref. 13605]). Gobiidae.

Oligoplites Gill 1863:166 [ref. 1681]. Masc. *Gasterosteus occidentalis* Linnaeus 1758:295. Type by subsequent designation. Gill refers to *Chorinemus occidentalis* Cuvier & Valenciennes [Valenciennes in Cuvier & Valenciennes 1832:393 [ref. 1000]] which is Valenciennes' unneeded replacement name: "*Chorinemus saltans*, nob.; *Gasterosteus occidentalis*, Linn." Type designated by Jordan & Gilbert 1883:447 [ref. 2476]. Based on a nomen dubium (see Smith-Vaniz et al. 1979:5 [ref. 12247], who regards type as *Chorinemus occidentalis* Günther). Valid (Smith-Vaniz & Staiger 1973:213 [ref. 7106]). Carangidae.

Oligopodes Cuvier (ex Risso) 1816:328 [ref. 993]. Masc. *Oligopus noir* Risso 1826. Type by monotypy. Type originally as "l'-Oligopode noir" of Risso, later named *Oligopodus noir*. Synonym of *Pteraclis* Gronow 1772. Bramidae.

Oligopodus Lacepède 1800:511 [ref. 2709]. Masc. *Coryphaena velifera* Pallas 1770:19. Type by monotypy. Spelled *Oligopus* by Risso 1810 [ref. 3755], but species included by Risso in a different family; *Oligopus* Risso regarded as available by Cohen 1964 [ref. 5145] with different type than *Oligopodus* Lacepède (contrary to Art. 33b(iii)); if *Oligopus* Risso is an unjustified emendation of *Oligopodus* then it is automatically a junior objective synonym of *Oligopodus*. Synonym of *Pteraclis* Gronow 1772 (Mead 1973:388 [ref. 7199]). Bramidae.

Oligopus Risso 1810:141 [ref. 3755]. Masc. *Coryphaena velifera* Pallas 1770:19. Apparently an unjustified emendation (or incorrect subsequent spelling) of *Oligopodus* Lacepède 1800 and type is as above (not *Oligopus ater* Risso 1810); Cohen's 1964:4-5 [ref. 6891] interpretation apparently incorrect. Synonym of *Pteraclis* in family Bramidae. Wrongly treated as valid (Cohen 1964 [ref. 6891], Nielsen 1973:551 [ref. 6885], Cohen & Nielsen 1978:49 [ref. 881], Machida in Masuda et al. 1984:101 [ref. 6441]). See *Grammonus* Gill 1896. Bramidae.

Oligorus Günther 1859:251 [ref. 1961]. Masc. *Grystes macquariensis* Cuvier in Cuvier & Valenciennes 1829:58. Type by monotypy, second species conditionally included. Preoccupied by Dejean 1834 in Coleoptera, replaced by *Maccullochella* Whitley 1929. Correct spelling of genus of type species is *Gristes*. Objective synonym of *Maccullochella* Whitley 1929 (Berra & Weatherley 1972:54 [ref. 7104], Paxton et al. 1989:511 [ref. 12442]). Percichthyidae.

Oligosarcus Günther 1864:353 [ref. 1974]. Masc. *Oligosarcus argenteus* Günther 1864:353. Type by monotypy. *Oligosargus* is a misspelling. Valid (Géry 1977:326 [ref. 1597], Malabarba 1989:137 [ref. 14217]). Characidae.

Oligoscorpaena Fowler 1939:1 [ref. 1430]. Fem. *Scorpaena bandanensis* Bleeker 1851:237. Type by original designation (also monotypic). Scorpaenidae: Scorpaeninae.

Olisthops Richardson 1850:74 [ref. 3745]. Masc. *Olisthops cyanomelas* Richardson 1850:75. Type by monotypy. *Olistherops* Günther 1862:243 [ref. 1969] is an unjustified emendation. Synonym of *Odax* Cuvier 1839 (Gomon & Paxton 1986:31 [ref. 5656]). Odacidae.

Olistus Cuvier 1829:209 [ref. 995]. Masc. *Olistus malabaricus* Cuvier in Cuvier & Valenciennes 1833:137. Type by subsequent designation. Appeared first without species as above; species added by Cuvier in Cuvier & Valenciennes 1833:137 et seq. [ref. 1002]. Type apparently first designated by Jordan 1917:129 [ref. 2407]. Apparently a senior synonym of the widely used *Carangoides* Bleeker 1851 (Smith-Vaniz, pers. comm., Nov. 1989). Carangidae.

Olivaichthys Arratia 1987:66 [ref. 5957]. Masc. *Diplomystes viedmensis* MacDonagh 1931. Type by original designation (also monotypic). Diplomystidae.

Oliverichthus Whitley & Phillipps 1939:236 [ref. 4737]. Masc. *Trachelochismus melobesia* Phillipps 1927:131. Type by original designation (also monotypic). Misspelled *Oliverichtus* in Zoological Record for 1939. Synonym of *Trachelochismus* Brisout de Barneville 1846 (Briggs 1955:18 [ref. 637] as *Oliverichtus*). Gobiesocidae: Gobiesocinae.

Ollentodon Hubbs & Turner 1939:70 [ref. 2265]. Masc. *Xenendum multipunctatum* Pellegrin 1901:205. Type by original designation (also monotypic). Name appeared first in Turner 1937:503, et seq. [ref. 6400], without clear differentiating characters. Synonym of *Skiffia* Meek 1902 (Miller & Fitzsimons 1971 [ref. 3019]), but as a valid subgenus (Uyeno et al. 1983:505 [ref. 6818]). Goodeidae.

Oloplotosus Weber 1913:521 [ref. 4603]. Masc. *Oloplotosus mariae* Weber 1913:522. Type by monotypy. Valid (Allen 1985 [ref. 6244], Burgess 1989:180 [ref. 12860]). Plotosidae.

Olssonichthys Fowler 1958:15 [ref. 1470]. Masc. *Hypsirhynchus hepaticus* Facciolà 1884:112. Type by being a replacement name. Unneeded replacement for *Hypsirhynchus* Facciolà 1884, preoccupied by Günther 1856 in Reptilia but replaced earlier by *Rhynchogadus* Tortonese 1948. Objective synonym of *Rhyn-*

chogadus Tortonese 1948. Moridae.

Olyra McClelland 1842:588 [ref. 2926]. Fem. *Olyra longicaudatus* McClelland 1842:588. Type by subsequent designation. Species as *longicaudatus* usually emended to *longicaudata*. Type apparently first designated by Jordan 1919:212 [ref. 2410]. Valid (Jayaram 1981:275 [ref. 6497], Burgess 1989:154 [ref. 12860], Kottelat 1989:15 [ref. 13605]). Olyridae.

Oman Springer 1985:92 [ref. 6107]. Fem. *Oman ypsilon* Springer 1985:92. Type by original designation (also monotypic). Blenniidae.

Omegophora Whitley 1934:160 [ref. 4681]. Fem. *Tetraodon armilla* Waite & McCulloch 1915:475. Type by original designation (also monotypic). Valid (Hardy & Hutchins 1981 [ref. 5582], Arai 1983:207 [ref. 14249]). Tetraodontidae.

Omobranchus Ehrenberg in Cuvier & Valenciennes 1836:287 [ref. 1005]. Masc. *Omobranchus fasciolatus* Valenciennes (ex Ehrenberg) in Cuvier & Valenciennes 1836:287. Generic and specific names first published in synonymy of *Blennechis fasciolatus* Valenciennes in Cuvier & Valenciennes; made available back to Valenciennes by Swainson 1839:274 [ref. 4303] [type species designation not researched by us]. Valid (Springer & Gomon 1975 [ref. 6083], Yoshino in Masuda et al. 1984:296 [ref. 6441], Springer 1985:91 [ref. 6107], Springer 1986:750 [ref. 5719]). Blenniidae.

Omochelys (subgenus of *Pisodonophis*) Fowler 1918:3 [ref. 1396]. Fem. *Pisodonophis cruentifer* Goode & Bean 1896:147, 166. Type by original designation (also monotypic). Synonym of *Pisodonophis* Kaup 1856 (Blache et al. 1973:250 [ref. 7185], McCosker 1977:80 [ref. 6836], Castle 1984:38 [ref. 6171]). Synonym of *Ophichthus* Ahl 1789 (McCosker et al. 1989:379 [ref. 13288]). Ophichthidae: Ophichthinae.

Omochetus (subgenus of *Hyperlophus*) Ogilby 1897:72 [ref. 3272]. Masc. *Hyperlophus copii* Ogilby 1897:72. Type by original designation (also monotypic). Synonym of *Hyperlophus* Ogilby 1892 (Whitehead 1985:187 [ref. 5141]). Clupeidae.

Omopomacentrus (subgenus of *Pomacentrus*) Fowler 1944:363 [ref. 1448]. Masc. *Pomacentrus acapulcoensis* Fowler 1944:363. Type by original designation (also monotypic). Synonym of *Pomacentrus* Lacepède 1802. Pomacentridae.

Omosudis Günther 1887:201 [ref. 2013]. Fem. *Omosudis lowii* Günther 1887:201. Type by monotypy. Valid (Maul 1973:202 [ref. 7171], Post in Whitehead et al. 1984:496 [ref. 13675], Okiyama 1984:207 [ref. 13644], Fujii in Masuda et al. 1984:77 [ref. 6441], Maul 1986:280 [ref. 5689], Paxton et al. 1989:250 [ref. 12442]). Omosudidae.

Omox Springer 1972:11 [ref. 4178]. Masc. *Omox biporos* Springer 1972:11. Type by original designation (also monotypic). Valid (Yoshino in Masuda et al. 1984:296 [ref. 6441], Springer 1985:92 [ref. 6107]). Blenniidae.

Ompax Castelnau 1879:165 [ref. 769]. Fem. *Ompax spatuloides* Castelnau 1879:165. Type by original designation (also monotypic). Perhaps mythical; based on a drawing that is probably a rough representation of *Epiceratodus* Teller, according to Jordan. A sketch based on a madeup fish and involving a hoax (Herald 1961:291 [ref. 13600]). Ceratodontidae.

Ompok Lacepède 1803:49 [ref. 4930]. Masc. *Ompok siluroides* Lacepède 1803:49, 50. Type by monotypy. Spelled *Ompolk*, *Ompock*, and *Ompocus* by early authors. Valid (Haig 1952:83, 103 [ref. 12607], Jayaram 1977:2 [ref. 7006], Jayaram 1981:207 [ref. 6497], Kottelat 1985:268 [ref. 11441], Burgess 1989:86 [ref. 12860], Kottelat 1989:14 [ref. 13605], Roberts 1989:150 [ref. 6439]). Siluridae.

Onar De Vis 1885:875 [ref. 1091]. Neut. *Onar nebulosum* De Vis 1885:875. Type by monotypy. Synonym of *Pseudochromis* Rüppell 1835. Pseudochromidae: Pseudochrominae.

Oncesthes Jordan & Hubbs 1925:319 [ref. 2486]. Fem. *Petroscirtes fluctuans* Weber 1909:146. Type by original designation (also monotypic). Synonym of *Aspidontus* Cuvier 1834 (Smith-Vaniz 1976:53 [ref. 4144]). Blenniidae.

Onchocottus Gill 1861:42 [ref. 1766]. Masc. *Cottus hexacornis* of Storer 1846 (= *Cottus hexacornis* Richardson 1823:726). Type by monotypy. Spelled *Oncocottus* by Gill 1862:13 [ref. 1654] in which type is stated by Gill (footnote, p. 13) to be *Cottus quadricornis* of Europe, but *quadricornis* not an included species with original description of genus. Synonym of *Myoxocephalus* Tilesius 1811 (Neyelov 1973:597 [ref. 7219]); synonym of *Triglopsis* Girard (Neyelov 1979:131 [ref. 3152] but with wrong type and as *Oncocottus*). Cottidae.

Oncobalistes Fowler 1946:213 [ref. 1456]. Masc. *Oncobalistes erythropterus* Fowler 1946:213. Type by original designation. Synonym of *Melichthys* Swainson 1839 (Matsuura 1980:40 [ref. 6943]). Balistidae.

Oncopterus Steindachner 1875:363 [ref. 4221]. Masc. *Oncopterus darwinii* Steindachner 1875:363. Type by being a replacement name. Not preoccupied by *Oncoptera* Lacordaire 1869, *Curioptera* Whitley 1951 is an unneeded replacement. Valid (Norman 1934:414 [ref. 6893], Ahlstrom et al. 1984:643 [ref. 13641], Sakamoto 1984 [ref. 5273], Inada in Nakamura et al. 1986:314 [ref. 14235]). Pleuronectidae: Rhombosoleinae.

Oncorhynchus (subgenus of *Salmo*) Suckley 1861:313 [ref. 4298]. Masc. *Salmo scouleri* Richardson 1836:158. Type by original designation. Valid (Svetovidov 1973:146 [ref. 7169], Svetovidov in Whitehead et al. 1984:377 [ref. 13675], Araga in Masuda et al. 1984:38 [ref. 6441], Kendall & Behnke 1984:144 [ref. 13638], Paxton et al. 1989:164 [ref. 12442]). Salmonidae: Salmoninae.

Oncotion Klein 1777:46 [ref. 4920]. Neut. Not available, published in a work that does not conform to the principle of binominal nomenclature. In the synonymy of *Cyclopterus* Linnaeus 1758. Cyclopteridae: Cyclopterinae.

Oneirodes Lütken 1871:57 et seq. [ref. 2853]. Masc. *Oneirodes eschrichtii* Lütken 1871:72. Type by monotypy. *Onirodes* and *Oneiroides* of authors are incorrect subsequent spellings. Valid (Maul 1973:670 [ref. 7171], Pietsch 1974:31 [ref. 5332], Bertelsen & Pietsch 1977:172 [ref. 7063], Bertelsen & Pietsch 1983:84 [ref. 5335], Amaoka in Masuda et al. 1984:106 [ref. 6441], Bertelsen in Whitehead et al. 1986:1392 [ref. 13677], Swinney & Pietsch 1988 [ref. 9285], Paxton et al. 1989:291 [ref. 12442]). Oneirodidae.

Onigocia Jordan & Thompson 1913:70 [ref. 2542]. Fem. *Platycephalus macrolepis* Bleeker 1854:76. Type by original designation (also monotypic). Valid (Ochiai in Masuda et al. 1984:321 [ref. 6441], Knapp 1986:483 [ref. 5683], Paxton et al. 1989:467 [ref. 12442]). Platycephalidae.

Onogadus de Buen 1934:500 [ref. 687]. Masc. *Motella ensis* Reinhardt 1837:116. Type by monotypy. Valid (Svetovidov 1973:319 [ref. 7169], Svetovidov in Whitehead et al. 1986:703 [ref. 13676]); probably a synonym of *Gaidropsarus* Rafinesque 1810 (Cohen & Russo 1979:99 [ref. 6975]); synonym of *Gaidropsarus* Rafinesque 1810 (Svetovidov 1986 [ref. 8033]). Lotidae.

Onopionus Rafinesque 1815:89 [ref. 3584]. Not available, name only. Unplaced genera.

Onos Risso 1826:214 [ref. 3757]. Masc. *Onos mustella* of Risso 1826 (= *Gadus mediterraneus* Linnaeus 1758:255). Type by subsequent designation. Type designated by Jordan 1917:119 [ref. 2407]. *Onus* Agassiz 1846:259 [ref. 64] is an unjustified emendation. Synonym of *Gaidropsarus* Rafinesque 1810 (Svetovidov 1973:318 [ref. 7169], Svetovidov 1986 [ref. 8033]). Lotidae.

Onouphrios Whitley 1951:68 [ref. 4711]. *Psalidostoma caudimaculatus* Kner 1865:99. Type by being a replacement name. Replacement for *Psalidostoma* Kner 1864 [details of preoccupation not researched]. Citharinidae: Distichodontinae.

Onus Rafinesque 1810:12 [ref. 3595]. Masc. *Gadus merluccius* Linnaeus 1758:254. Type by being a replacement name. Apparently predates *Merluccius* Rafinesque 1810:25 [ref. 3594]; *Merluccius* cited on 1810:12 in parentheses. On p. 67 Rafinesque says, "In vece di *Onus*, sp. 30. leggete *Merlangus*"; so *Merlangus* is a replacement for *Onus*. Synonym of *Merluccius* Rafinesque 1810 (Svetovidov 1973:300 [ref. 7169]). Merlucciidae: Merlucciinae.

Onuxodon Smith 1955:405 [ref. 4099]. Masc. *Carapus parvibrachium* Fowler 1927:31. Type by original designation (also monotypic). Valid (Trott 1981:625 [ref. 14205], Williams 1984:392 [ref. 5314], Olney & Markle 1986:353 [ref. 5701], Shen & Yeh 1987:47 [ref. 6418], Paxton et al. 1989:321 [ref. 12442]). Carapidae: Carapinae.

Onychodon Dybowski 1872:211 [ref. 1170]. Masc. *Cephalus mantschuricus* Basilewski 1855:235. Type by monotypy. Apparently preoccupied by Newman 1838 in Coleoptera (not investigated). Same as *Cephalus* Basilewsky 1855 (preoccupied). Synonym of *Hypophthalmichthys* Bleeker 1859 (Howes 1981:45 [ref. 14200]). Cyprinidae.

Onychognathus Troschel 1866:231 [ref. 4465]. Masc. *Onychognathus cautus* Troschel 1866:231. Type by monotypy. Preoccupied by Hartlaub 1859 in Aves, replaced by *Agripopa* Whitley 1928. Pomacentridae.

Onychostoma Günther 1896:211 [ref. 2019]. Neut. *Onychostoma laticeps* Günther 1896:211. Type by monotypy. Synonym of *Varicorhinus* Rüppell 1836 (Lévêque & Daget 1984:336 [ref. 6186]); as a valid subgenus (Wu et al. 1977:306 [ref. 4807], Chu & Cui in Chu & Chen 1989:213 [ref. 13584]); valid (Kottelat 1989:9 [ref. 13605], Chen 1989 [ref. 14144]). Cyprinidae.

Oonidus Rafinesque 1815:90 [ref. 3584]. Masc. Type by being a replacement name. As "*Oonidus* R. [Rafinesque] *Ovoide* Lac. [Lacepède]." Proposed as a replacement name but not for an available name; would apparently have to stand on its own with species subsequently added. *Ovoides* Cuvier 1800 is an earlier validation of "Les Ovoides" Lacepède. Tetraodontidae.

Oostethus Hubbs 1929:3 [ref. 2238]. Masc. *Doryichthys lineatus* Kaup 1856:59. Type by original designation (also monotypic). Treated as masculine by author. Valid (Dawson 1982:36 [ref. 6764], Araga in Masuda et al. 1984:86 [ref. 6441]); synonym of *Microphis* Kaup 1853, but as a valid subgenus (Dawson 1984:151 [ref. 5879], Dawson 1985:126, 127 [ref. 6541], Dawson 1986:284 [ref. 6201]). Syngnathidae: Syngnathinae.

Opaeophacus Bond & Stein 1984:522 [ref. 5310]. Masc. *Opaeophacus acrogeneius* Bond & Stein 1984:523. Type by original designation (also monotypic). Zoarcidae.

Opeatogenys Briggs 1955:24 [ref. 637]. Fem. *Mirbelia gracilis* Canestrini 1864:195. Type by original designation (also monotypic). Valid (Briggs 1973:656 [ref. 7222], Briggs in Whitehead et al. 1986:1358 [ref. 13677]). Gobiesocidae: Gobiesocinae.

Ophicardia McClelland 1844:175, 191, 218 [ref. 2928]. Fem. *Ophicardia phayriana* McClelland 1844:191, 218. Type by monotypy. Species apparently misspelled *phyariana* in main entry (p. 191); named after Capt. Phayre (mentioned twice on p. 191-192) and spelled *phayriana* on p. 204 (legend to Pl. 12) and on p. 218. Synonym of *Monopterus* Lacepède 1800 (Rosen & Greenwood 1976:56 [ref. 7094] but misspelled as *Ophiocardia*, species as *phyariana*). Synbranchidae.

Ophicephalus Bloch 1793:137 [ref. 4868]. Masc. *Ophicephalus punctatus* Bloch 1793:139. Type by subsequent designation. Earliest subsequent type designation not researched. Spelled *Ophiocephalus* by Hamilton 1822:59 [ref. 2031] (Briggs 1961:163 [ref. 13439]) and *Ophiocephalus* by Günther 1861:468 [ref. 1964]. Synonym of *Channa* Scopoli 1777 (see Teugels et al. 1986:288 [ref. 6202], Roberts 1989:169 [ref. 6439]). Channidae.

Ophichthus Ahl 1789:5 [ref. 80]. Masc. *Muraena ophis* Linnaeus 1758:244. Type by subsequent designation. Type designated by Bleeker 1864:43 [ref. 4860] with spelling *Ophichthys*; *Ophichthys* Swainson 1839 apparently independently described as indicated by Bleeker 1864:43. Valid (Blache et al. 1973:247 [ref. 7185], McCosker 1977:79 [ref. 6836], Karrer 1982:73 [ref. 5679], Asano in Masuda et al. 1984:31 [ref. 6441], McCosker & Castle 1986:182 [ref. 5690], Asano 1987 [ref. 6705], Paxton et al. 1989:119 [ref. 12442], McCosker et al. 1989:379 [ref. 13288]). Ophichthidae: Ophichthinae.

Ophichthys Swainson 1839:196, 336 [ref. 4303]. Masc. *Ophichthys punctatus* Swainson 1839:336 (= *Unibranchapertura cuchia* Hamilton 1822:16, 363). Type by monotypy. As *Ophicthys* on p. 196 and 441 (index). Swainson's *O. punctatus* is an unneeded substitute for *U. cuchia*. Objective synonym of *Cuchia* Hamilton (in Taylor) 1831; also predates *Amphipnous* Müller 1841 with same type. Synonym of *Monopterus* Lacepède 1800 (Rosen & Greenwood 1976:56 [ref. 7094], Daget 1986:291 [ref. 6203]). Synbranchidae.

Ophiclinops Whitley 1932:348 [ref. 4674]. Masc. *Ophiclinus pardalis* McCulloch & Waite 1918:58. Type by original designation (also monotypic). Misspelled *Ophioclinops* in Zoological Record for 1932. Valid (George & Springer 1980:9 [ref. 6935]). Clinidae.

Ophiclinus Castelnau 1872:246 [ref. 757]. Masc. *Ophiclinus antarcticus* Castelnau 1872:246. Type by monotypy. Spelled *Ophioclinus* by Castelnau 1873:69 [ref. 758]. Valid (George & Springer 1980:12 [ref. 6935]). Clinidae.

Ophidion Linnaeus 1758:259 [ref. 2787]. Neut. *Ophidion barbatum* Linnaeus 1758:259. Type by Linnaean tautonymy (also designated by Gill 1863:210 [ref. 1683]). *Ophidium* Linnaeus 1766:431 is an unjustified emendation placed on Official Index (Direction 56). *Ophidion* placed on Official List (Opinion 92). Valid (Nielsen 1973:553 [ref. 6885], Cohen & Nielsen 1978:16 [ref. 881], Machida in Masuda et al. 1984:99 [ref. 6441], Nielsen in Whitehead et al. 1986:1164 [ref. 13677], Nielsen & Cohen 1986:349 [ref. 5700], Paxton et al. 1989:313 [ref. 12442]). Ophidiidae: Ophidiinae.

Ophieleotris Aurich 1938:132 [ref. 152]. Fem. *Eleotris aporos* Bleeker 1854:59. Not available (Art. 13b), two included species, neither apparently designated as type [article not translated]. If not available from Aurich 1938, then it dates to treatment in Zoological Record for 1938 (see remarks on Art. 13b in Appendix A. Valid

(Akihito in Masuda et al. 1984:240 [ref. 6441], Birdsong et al. 1988:181 [ref. 7303]). Eleotridae.

Ophioblennius Gill 1860:103 [ref. 1765]. Masc. *Blennophis webbii* Valenciennes in Webb & Berthelot 1843:61. Type by being a replacement name. Replacement for *Blennophis* Valenciennes 1843, preoccupied by Swainson 1839. Valid (Smith-Vaniz & Springer 1971:35 [ref. 4145], Greenfield & Johnson 1981:71 [ref. 5580], Williams 1989:18 [ref. 13549]). Blenniidae.

Ophiocara Gill 1863:270 [ref. 1691]. Neut. *Eleotris ophiocephalus* Valenciennes in Cuvier & Valenciennes 1837:239. Type by original designation (also monotypic). Valid (Akihito in Masuda et al. 1984:239 [ref. 6441], Kottelat 1985:274 [ref. 11441], Hoese 1986:810 [ref. 5670], Maugé 1986:396 [ref. 6218], Birdsong et al. 1988:180 [ref. 7303], Kottelat 1989:18 [ref. 13605]). Eleotridae.

Ophiocephalops (subgenus of *Erythrinus*) Fowler 1906:293 [ref. 1373]. Masc. *Erythrinus unitaeniatus* Agassiz in Spix & Agassiz 1829:42. Type by original designation (also monotypic). Objective synonym of *Hoplerythrinus* Gill 1896. Erythrinidae.

Ophiodon Girard 1854:133 [ref. 1817]. Masc. *Ophiodon elongatus* Girard 1854:133. Type by monotypy. Valid (Washington et al. 1984:443 [ref. 13660]). Hexagrammidae: Ophiodontinae.

Ophioglossus Duméril 1856:218 [ref. 1154]. Masc. Incorrect subsequent spelling of *Ophiognathus* Harwood 1827 (Bauchot 1973:216 [ref. 7184]). Saccopharyngidae.

Ophiognathus Harwood 1827:51 [ref. 2046]. Masc. *Ophiognathus ampullaceus* Harwood 1827:52. Type by monotypy. Misprinted *Ophioglossus* by Duméril 1856:218 [ref. 1154]. On Official List (Opinion 1603). Synonym of *Saccopharynx* Mitchill 1824 (Böhlke 1966:618 [ref. 5256], Bauchot 1973:216 [ref. 7184], Nielsen & Bertelsen 1985:174 [ref. 5255], Eschmeyer & Robins 1988 [ref. 6886], Bertelsen et al. 1989:643 [ref. 13293]). Saccopharyngidae.

Ophiogobius Gill 1863:269 [ref. 1691]. Masc. *Gobius ophiocephalus* Jenyns 1842:97. Type by monotypy. Valid (Birdsong et al. 1988:189 [ref. 7303]). Gobiidae.

Ophiorrhinus Ogilby 1897:745 [ref. 3274]. Masc. *Eleotris grandiceps* Krefft 1864:183. Type by original designation. Synonym of *Philypnodon* Bleeker 1874 (Hoese, pers. comm.). Eleotridae.

Ophioscion Gill 1863:164 [ref. 1681]. Masc. *Ophioscion typicus* Gill 1884:165. Type by monotypy (also by use of *typicus*). Valid (Chao 1978:39 [ref. 6983]). Sciaenidae.

Ophis Turton 1807:82, 87 [ref. 12590]. *Ophis maculata* Turton 1807. Type by monotypy. Original not examined. Species apparently in reference to *Muraena meleagis* of Shaw. Synonym of *Ophichthus* Ahl 1789 (Blache et al. 1973:247 [ref. 7185], McCosker 1977:79 [ref. 6836], McCosker et al. 1989:379 [ref. 13288]). Ophichthidae: Ophichthinae.

Ophisichthys Osório 1917:129 [ref. 3318]. Masc. *Ophisichthys dubius* Osório 1917:130. Type by monotypy. Spelled *Ophisichtys* once on p. 130, *Ophisichthys* elsewhere (p. 105, 129). Synonym of *Panturichthys* Pellegrin 1913 (Blache et al. 1973:228 [ref. 7185]). Heterenchelyidae.

Ophisoma Swainson 1839:334, 396 [ref. 4303]. Neut. *Ophisoma acuta* Swainson 1839:334, 396. Type by subsequent designation. Described first as *Ariosoma* Swainson 1838:220 [ref. 4302], name changed to *Ophisoma* in 1839 [ref. 4303]. Type apparently designated first by Bleeker 1864:20 [not *O. obtusa* as designated by Swain 1883:287]. Objective synonym of *Ariosoma* Swainson 1838 (Blache et al. 1973:240 [ref. 7185], Smith 1989:491 [ref. 13285]). Congridae: Bathymyrinae.

Ophisomus Swainson 1839:73, 83, 183, 277 [ref. 4303]. Masc. *Blennius gunnellus* Linnaeus 1758:257. Proposed for *Gunnellus* of authors. Type by monotypy unless regarded as a replacement name. Objective synonym of *Gunnellus* Fleming 1828; synonym of *Pholis* Scopoli 1777 (Makushok 1973:534 [ref. 6889], Yatsu 1981:169 [ref. 4814]). Pholidae.

Ophisternon McClelland 1844:175, 196, 220 [ref. 2928]. Neut. *Ophisternon bengalensis [e]* McClelland 1844:197, 220. Type by subsequent designation. Type designated by Jordan 1919:220 [ref. 2410]. Valid (Rosen & Greenwood 1976:50 [ref. 7094], Jayaram 1981:310 [ref. 6497], Daget 1986:291 [ref. 6203], Paxton et al. 1989:436 [ref. 12442], Kottelat 1989:16 [ref. 13605]). Synbranchidae.

Ophisurapus Kaup 1856:52 [ref. 2572]. Masc. *Ophisurapus gracilis* Kaup 1856:52. Type by monotypy. Also in Kaup 1856:29 [ref. 2573] as *Ophisuraphis* and as name only in Kaup in Duméril 1856:199 [ref. 1154]. Synonym of *Apterichtus* Duméril 1806 (Blache et al. 1973:248 [ref. 7185], McCosker 1977:65 [ref. 6836], McCosker et al. 1989:318 [ref. 13288]). Ophichthidae: Ophichthinae.

Ophisurus Lacepède 1800:195 [ref. 2709]. Masc. *Muraena serpens* Linnaeus 1758:244. Type by subsequent designation. Two included species; type evidently designated first by Risso 1826 [ref. 3757], not *M. ophis* as designated by Bleeker 1864:64 [ref. 4860]. Valid (Blache et al. 1973:249 [ref. 7185], McCosker 1977:81 [ref. 6836], Asano in Masuda et al. 1984:32 [ref. 6441], Bauchot in Whitehead et al. 1986:583 [ref. 13676], McCosker & Castle 1986:184 [ref. 5690], Paxton et al. 1989:120 [ref. 12442], McCosker et al. 1989:299 [ref. 13288]). Ophichthidae: Ophichthinae.

Ophithorax McClelland 1844:212 [ref. 2928]. Masc. *Ophisurus ophis* Lacepède 1800:491. Type by subsequent designation. Earliest type designation found that of Jordan 1919:220 [ref. 2410]. Synonym of *Ophichthus* Ahl 1789 (McCosker 1977:79 [ref. 6836], McCosker et al. 1989:379 [ref. 13288]). Ophichthidae: Ophichthinae.

Ophthalmochromis Poll 1956:140 [ref. 12591]. Masc. *Paratilapia ventralis* Boulenger 1898:495. Type by monotypy. Synonym of *Ophthalmotilapia* Pellegrin 1904 (Liem 1981:191 [ref. 6897]). Cichlidae.

Ophthalmolepis Bleeker 1862:413 [ref. 382]. Fem. *Julis lineolatus* Valenciennes in Cuvier & Valenciennes 1839:436. Type by original designation (also monotypic). Valid (see Randall & Kuiter 1982:159 [ref. 5446]). Labridae.

Ophthalmolophus Gill 1860:104 [ref. 1765]. Masc. *Clinus latipennis* Valenciennes in Cuvier & Valenciennes 1836:394. Type by monotypy. Synonym of *Clinus* Cuvier 1816 (Bennett 1983 [ref. 5299], Smith 1986:761 [ref. 5712]). Clinidae.

Ophthalmolycus Regan 1913:243 [ref. 3651]. Masc. *Lycodes macrops* Günther 1880:21. Type by monotypy, second species tentatively included. Valid (Gosztonyi 1977:229 [ref. 6103], Anderson 1984:578 [ref. 13634], Anderson 1988:81 [ref. 7304]). Zoarcidae.

Ophthalmopelton Maul 1946:62 [ref. 2915]. *Ophthalmopelton macropus* Maul 1946:62. Type by original designation (also monotypic). Synonym of *Rhynchohyalus* Barnard 1925 (Cohen 1973:157 [ref. 6589]). Opisthoproctidae.

Ophthalmotilapia Pellegrin 1904:(165) 345 [ref. 3419]. Fem. *Tilapia boops* Boulenger 1901:5. Type by subsequent designation. Earliest type designation not researched; two included species. Valid (Liem 1981:192 [ref. 6897], Poll 1986:94 [ref. 6136]).

Cichlidae.

Opictus Rafinesque 1815:91 [ref. 3584]. Not available, name only. Unplaced genera.

Opisthanodus Ahl 1935:46 [ref. 79]. Masc. *Opisthanodus haerteli* Ahl 1935:47. Type by original designation (also monotypic). Valid (Géry 1977:431 [ref. 1597]). Characidae.

Opisthistius Gill 1862:245 [ref. 1665]. Masc. *Sciaena tahmel* Rüppell 1835:35. Type by subsequent designation. Earliest type designation not researched. Questionably a synonym of *Kyphosus* Lacepède 1801 (Desoutter 1973:420 [ref. 7203]). Kyphosidae: Kyphosinae.

Opisthocentrus Kner 1868:29 [ref. 6074]. Masc. *Centronotus quinquemaculatus* Kner 1868:29. Type by monotypy. Genus described as "*Centronotus quinquemaculatus* nov. sp. an et nov. gen.? *Opisthocentrus quinquemac.* nov. gen. et sp." Also appeared as new in Kner 1868:340-341 [ref. 2646]. Valid (Shiogaki 1984 [ref. 5309], Amaoka & Miki in Masuda et al. 1984:302 [ref. 6441]). Stichaeidae.

Opisthonema Gill 1861:37 [ref. 1767]. Neut. *Opisthonema thrissa* Gill 1861:37. Type by original designation (also monotypic). Gill lists type as *Opisthonema thrissa* Gill which was his style when placing an established species in his new genera; he had *Clupanodon thrissa* Lacepède [1803:470] in synonymy [which goes back to earlier authors] but not to *thrissa* Linnaeus. Whitehead 1985 lists type as *thrissa* Gill = *Megalops oglina* Lesueur 1818; based on Gill's style, type would by *thrissa* Lacepède. Valid (Grande 1985:250 [ref. 6466], Whitehead 1985:67 [ref. 5141]). Clupeidae.

Opisthoproctus Vaillant 1888:105 [ref. 4496]. Masc. *Opisthoproctus soleatus* Vaillant 1888:106. Type by monotypy. Valid (Cohen 1973:156 [ref. 6589], Cohen in Whitehead et al. 1984:396 [ref. 13675], Ahlstrom et al. 1984:156 [ref. 13627], Heemstra 1986:217 [ref. 5660], Paxton et al. 1989:170 [ref. 12442]). Opisthoproctidae.

Opisthopterus Gill 1861:38 [ref. 1767]. Masc. *Pristigaster tartoor* Valenciennes 1847:328. Type by original designation (also monotypic). Valid (Whitehead 1967:121 [ref. 6464], Grande 1985:244 [ref. 6466], Whitehead 1985:290 [ref. 5141], Kottelat 1989:4 [ref. 13605]). Clupeidae.

Opistocheilos Bleeker 1859:425 [ref. 370]. Masc. *Schizopyge plagiostomus* Heckel 1838:16. Type by subsequent designation. Apparently appeared first in key, without species, as *Opistocheilos*. Four species included by Bleeker 1860:115, 213 [ref. 380], two with question (also as *Opistocheilos*). Type perhaps not designated until Jordan 1919:287 [ref. 4904]. Spelled *Opistocheilus* by authors, including Bleeker 1863:196 [ref. 397]. Synonym of *Schizothorax* Heckel 1838 (Tsao 1964:139 [ref. 13501]). Cyprinidae.

Opistognathus Cuvier 1816:252 [ref. 993]. Masc. *Opistognathus sonneratii* Valenciennes in Cuvier & Valenciennes 1836:498. Type by monotypy. Original spelling *Opistognathus*, often misspelled *Opisthognathus*. Valid (Yoshino in Masuda et al. 1984:200 [ref. 6441], Smith-Vaniz & Yoshino 1985 [ref. 6721], Smith-Vaniz 1986:726 [ref. 5718]). Opistognathidae.

Opladelus (subgenus of *Ictalurus*) Rafinesque 1820:359 [ref. 7311]. Masc. *Silurus nebulosus* Rafinesque 1820:50. Type by monotypy. Also in Rafinesque 1820 (Dec):64-65 [ref. 3592]. Type species not *Pimelodus nebulosus* Lesueur 1819 or *olivaceus* Rafinesque. Spelled *Hopladelus* by Gill 1862:51 [ref. 1673], Bleeker 1862:12 [ref. 393]) and others. Synonym of *Pylodictis* Rafinesque 1819. Ictaluridae.

Oplegnathus Richardson 1840:27 [ref. 3733]. Masc. *Oplegnathus conwaii* Richardson 1840:27. Type by monotypy. Unjustifiably emended to *Hoplegnathus* by Richardson 1844:144 [ref. 13097] and *Hoplognathus* by Günther 1865:184 [ref. 1980]. Species originally as *conwaii*, sometimes spelled *conwayi*. Valid (Araga in Masuda et al. 1984:190 [ref. 6441], Heemstra 1986:632 [ref. 5660]). Oplegnathidae.

Oplichthys see *Hoplichthys*. Hoplichthyidae.

Oplopoma Girard 1856:135 [ref. 1809]. Neut. *Oplopoma pantherina* Girard 1856:135. Type by monotypy. Synonym of *Ophiodon* Girard 1854. Hexagrammidae: Ophiodontinae.

Oplopomops Smith 1959:189 [ref. 4122]. Masc. *Oplopomus diacanthus* Schultz 1943:242. Type by original designation (also monotypic). Type given as *Oplopomus diacanthus* Schultz 1943 = *atherinoides* Peters 1855. Valid (Akihito in Masuda et al. 1984:254 [ref. 6441], Goren 1984 [ref. 5178], Birdsong et al. 1988:193 [ref. 7303]). Gobiidae.

Oplopomus Valenciennes (ex Ehrenberg) 1837:66 [ref. 1006]. Masc. *Gobius oplopomus* Valenciennes in Cuvier & Valenciennes 1837:66. Appeared first as name in synonymy of *Gobius oplopomus*, as "*Oplopomus pulcher*. Ehrenb., Zool. pisc., pl. 9, fig. 6." Apparently made available by subsequent use by Steindacher 1860 (not investigated). Gobiidae.

Opostomias Günther 1887:208 [ref. 2013]. Masc. *Echiostoma micripnus* Günther 1878:180. Type by monotypy. Misspelled *Optostomias* in Zoological Record for 1887. Valid (Morrow in Morrow & Gibbs 1964:353 [ref. 6962], Kawaguchi & Moser 1984:171 [ref. 13642], Fujii in Masuda et al. 1984:50 [ref. 6441], Fink 1985:11 [ref. 5171], Gibbs 1986:242 [ref. 5655], Paxton et al. 1989:201 [ref. 12442]). Melanostomiidae.

Opsanus Rafinesque 1818:203 [ref. 3585]. Masc. *Opsanus cerapalus* Rafinesque 1818:204. Type by original designation (also monotypic). Valid. Batrachoididae.

Opsaridium Peters 1854:783 [ref. 13481]. Neut. *Leuciscus zambezensis* Peters 1852:682. Type by monotypy. Also spelled *Opsaridion* by Peters 1854:783. Original not examined. Valid (Lévêque & Daget 1984:327 [ref. 6186], Roberts 1989:30 [ref. 6439]). Cyprinidae.

Opsariichthys Bleeker 1863:203 [ref. 397]. Masc. *Leuciscus uncirostris* Temminck & Schlegel 1846:211. Type by monotypy. Also appeared in Bleeker 1863:263 [ref. 403] and 1863:28 [ref. 4859], with type designated [relative dates of publication not established]. Valid (Yang & Hwang 1964:40 [ref. 13497], Chen 1982:297 [ref. 824], Sawada in Masuda et al. 1984:57 [ref. 6441], Kuang in Chu & Chen 1989:30 [ref. 13584], Kottelat 1989:9 [ref. 13605] as *Opsarichthys*). Cyprinidae.

Opsarius McClelland 1839:295, 413 [ref. 2923]. Masc. *Opsarius maculatus* McClelland 1839:417. Type by subsequent designation. Also in McClelland 1939:944 [ref. 2924] without species. Earliest type designation not researched; not designated by Bleeker 1863:203 [ref. 397]; *maculatus* is given by Jordan 1919:195 [ref. 2410]). Synonym of *Barilius* Hamilton 1822 (Roberts 1989:30 [ref. 6439] with type as *barila* Hamilton). Cyprinidae.

Opsipseudochromis Fowler 1934:355 [ref. 1416]. Masc. *Opsipseudochromis grammodon* Fowler 1934:357. Type by original designation (also monotypic). Cepolidae.

Opsodentex (subgenus of *Dentex*) Fowler 1925:4 [ref. 1401]. Masc. *Sparus macrophthalmus* Bloch 1791:63. Type by original designation (also monotypic). Synonym of *Dentex* Cuvier 1814 (Tortonese 1973:407 [ref. 7192]). Sparidae.

Opsodoras Eigenmann 1925:306, 348 [ref. 1244]. Masc. *Opsodoras orthacanthus* Eigenmann 1925:351. Type by original designation. Valid (Burgess 1989:222 [ref. 12860]). Doradidae.

Opsopoea Jordan & Evermann 1896:247, 248, 249 [ref. 2443]. Fem. *Opsopoeodus bollmani* Gilbert 1889:226. Type by original designation (also monotypic). Type designated on p. 247 (name in parentheses). Synonym of *Notropis* Rafinesque 1818 (Gilbert 1978:18 [ref. 7042]). Cyprinidae.

Opsopoeodus Hay 1881:507 [ref. 2053]. Masc. *Opsopoeodus emiliae* Hay 1881:507. Type by monotypy. Synonym of *Notropis* Rafinesque 1818, but as a valid subgenus (Gilbert & Bailey 1972 [ref. 7153], Gilbert 1978:16 [ref. 7042]); valid genus (authors). Cyprinidae.

Optivus Whitley 1947:150 [ref. 4708]. Masc. *Trachichthys elongatus* Günther 1859:10. Type by original designation (also monotypic). Valid (Paulin 1979:70 [ref. 6918], Paxton et al. 1989:365 [ref. 12442]). Trachichthyidae.

Optonurus (subgenus of *Macrurus*) Günther 1887:124, 147 [ref. 2013]. Masc. *Macrurus denticulatus* Richardson 1846:53. Type by monotypy. Synonym of *Lepidorhynchus* Richardson 1846 (Scott 1979:107 [ref. 6995]). Macrouridae: Macrourinae.

Opua Jordan 1925:36 [ref. 2544]. *Opua nephodes* Jordan 1925:36. Type by original designation (also monotypic). Valid (Birdsong et al. 1988:193 [ref. 7303]). Gobiidae.

Orbidus Rafinesque 1815:90 [ref. 3584]. Masc. *Tetrodon spengleri* Bloch 1782:135. Type by being a replacement name. As "*Orbidus* R. [Rafinesque] *Spheroide* Lac. [Lacepède]." An available name latinizing "Les Spheroides" Lacepède but earlier published as *Spheroides* by Duméril 1806, and earlier as *Sphoeroides* Anonymous 1798. In the synonymy of *Spheroides* Duméril 1806 (Fraser-Brunner 1943:10 [ref. 1495]). Tetraodontidae.

Orbis Catesby 1771:28 [ref. 774]. Masc. Not available, published in a rejected work on Official Index (Opinion 89, Opinion 259). Tetraodontidae.

Orbis Fischer von Waldheim (ex Lacepède) 1813:70 [ref. 1331]. Masc. Original not seen. Synonym of *Tetraodon* Linnaeus 1758 (Fraser-Brunner 1943:14 [ref. 1495]). Tetraodontidae.

Orbis Müller 1766:141 [ref. 3055]. Not available, published in a rejected work on Official Index (Opinion 701). Diodontidae.

Orbonymus Whitley 1947:150 [ref. 4708]. Masc. *Callionymus (Calliurichthys) rameus* McCulloch 1926:201. Type by original designation (also monotypic). Synonym of *Synchiropus* Gill 1860, but as a valid subgenus (Fricke 1981:20 [ref. 1499], Fricke 1982:78 [ref. 5432]); valid genus (Nakabo 1982:100 [ref. 3139], Houde 1984:637 [ref. 13674]). Callionymidae.

Orcella (subgenus of *Notropis*) Jordan & Evermann 1896:254, 257, 289 [ref. 2443]. Fem. *Notropis orca* Woolman 1894:56. Type by original designation (also monotypic). Apparently not preoccupied by *Orcaella* or by *Orcella* Anderson 1871:142 [not researched], a misspelling of *Orcaella* Gray 1866 in Cetacea. Synonym of *Notropis* Rafinesque 1818 (Gilbert 1978:16 [ref. 7042]). Cyprinidae.

Orcula (subgenus of *Notropis*) Jordan & Evermann 1900:3140 [ref. 2446]. Fem. *Notropis orca* Woolman 1894:56. Type by being a replacement name. Unneeded replacement for *Orcella* Jordan & Evermann 1896, apparently not preoccupied by *Orcella* Anderson (misspelling for *Orcaella* Gray 1866 in Cetacea). Synonym of *Notropis* Rafinesque 1818, subgenus *Orcella* Jordan & Evermann 1896 (Gilbert 1978:16 [ref. 7042]). Cyprinidae.

Orcynopsis Gill 1862:125 [ref. 1659]. Fem. *Scomber unicolor* Geoffroy St. Hilaire 1809:Pl. 24. Type by original designation (also monotypic). Regarded as misspelled *Orycnopsis* in original description, based on *Orcynus* Cuvier, which Gill spelled as *Orycnus*. But Gill used the spelling *Orycnus* and the suffix *orycnus* in other genera, so it probably cannot be regarded as a misspelling, and these Gill's names would need to be submitted to the ICZN to conserve spelling as "orcy"]. Valid (Postel 1973:474 [ref. 7208], Collette et al. 1984:600 [ref. 11421]). Scombridae.

Orcynus Cuvier 1816:314 [ref. 993]. Masc. *Scomber germo* Lacepède 1801:1 (= *Scomber germon* Lacepède 1800:598). Type by subsequent designation. Type designated by Jordan 1888:180 [ref. 2389] as *Scomber germo* = *Scomber alatunga* (*alalonga*). Spelled *Orycnus* by Gill 1862:125 [ref. 1659]. Preoccupied by Rafinesque 1815 in fishes, replaced by *Germo* Jordan 1888. Synonym of *Thunnus* South 1845 (Gibbs & Collette 1967:97 [ref. 13640], Postel 1973:467 [ref. 7208]). Scombridae.

Orcynus Rafinesque 1815:84 [ref. 3584]. Masc. *Scomberoides noelii* Lacepède 1801:50. Type by being a replacement name. As "*Orcynus* R. [Rafinesque] *Scomberoides* Lac. [Lacepède]." An available (unneeded) replacement name for *Scomberoides* Lacepède 1801. Objective synonym of *Scomberoides* Lacepède 1801 (Smith-Vaniz & Staiger 1973:190 [ref. 7106], Daget & Smith-Vaniz 1986:316 [ref. 6207]). Carangidae.

Orectolobus (subgenus of *Scyllium*) Bonaparte 1834:puntata 39 [ref. 517]. Masc. *Squalus barbatus* Gmelin 1789:1493. Type by subsequent designation. Published in fasc. 7, puntata 39 under *Scyllium canicula*. Genus restricted by Gill 1896:211 [ref. 12504], but type not technically designated by him. Earliest technical designation not fully researched but possibly by Bonaparte 1838:11 (of separate, and see p. 2) [ref. 4979]. Valid (Compagno 1984:180 [ref. 6474], Nakaya & Shirai in Masuda et al. 1984:8 [ref. 6441]). Orectolobidae.

Oregonichthys Hubbs in Schultz 1929:47 [ref. 5039]. Masc. *Hybopsis crameri* Snyder 1908:181. Type by monotypy. No description, proposed for *Hybopsis crameri*. For nomenclatural history see Schultz & Hubbs 1961:477 [ref. 3949]. Valid (authors); in the synonymy of *Hybopsis* Agassiz 1854 (authors). Cyprinidae.

Oreias Sauvage 1874:334 [ref. 3873]. Masc. *Oreias dabryi* Sauvage 1874:334. Type by monotypy. Preoccupied by Kaup 1829 and Temminck 1839 in Aves. Valid (Kottelat 1990:20 [ref. 14137]). Balitoridae: Nemacheilinae.

Oreichthys Smith 1933:63 [ref. 4051]. Masc. *Oreichthys parvus* Smith 1933:63. Type by monotypy. Valid (Jayaram 1981:96 [ref. 6497], Kottelat 1989:9 [ref. 13605]). Cyprinidae.

Oreinus (subgenus of *Barbus*) McClelland 1839:273 [ref. 2923]. Masc. *Oreinus guttatus* McClelland 1839:273, 344. Type by subsequent designation. Also in McClelland 1939:943, 946 [ref. 2924]. Earliest type designation possibly Bleeker 1865:26 [ref. 4859]. Misspelled *Oreina* by Gistel 1848:X [ref. 1822]. *Englottogaster* Gistel 1848:X is an unneeded replacement, *Oreinus* not preoccupied by *Orena*. Synonym of *Schizothorax* Heckel 1838 (Tsao 1964:139 [ref. 13501], Jayaram 1981:67 [ref. 6497], Mo in Chu & Chen 1989:287 [ref. 13584]). Cyprinidae.

Oreochromis Günther 1889:70 [ref. 2015]. Masc. *Oreochromis hunteri* Günther 1889:70. Type by monotypy. Valid (Poll 1986:31 [ref. 6136], Krupp & Schneider 1989:396 [ref. 13651]). Cichlidae.

Oreodaimon Greenwood & Jubb 1967:19 [ref. 1901]. Neut. *Labeo quathlambae* Barnard 1938:525. Type by original designation (also monotypic). Valid (Lévêque & Daget 1984:330 [ref. 6186]). Cyprinidae.

Oreoglanis Smith 1933:70 [ref. 4051]. Masc. *Oreoglanis siamensis* Smith 1933:70. Type by original designation (also monotypic). Valid (Chu 1979:76 [ref. 831], Jayaram 1981:264 [ref. 6497], Burgess 1989:133 [ref. 12860], Kottelat 1989:15 [ref. 13605]). Sisoridae.

Oreogobius Boulenger 1899:125 [ref. 552]. Masc. *Oreogobius rosenbergii* Boulenger 1899:126. Type by monotypy. Gobiidae.

Oreoleuciscus Warpachowski 1897:263 [ref. 4515]. Masc. *Chondrostoma potanini* Kessler 1879:267. Type by subsequent designation. Earliest subsequent designation not researched. Valid (Bogutskaya 1987:936 [ref. 13521], Travers 1989:193 [ref. 13578]). Cyprinidae.

Oreonectes Günther 1868:369 [ref. 1990]. Masc. *Oreonectes platycephalus* Günther 1868:369. Type by monotypy. Valid (Banarescu & Nalbant 1968:339 [ref. 6554], Jayaram 1981:147 [ref. 6497], Zhu & Cao 1987:326 [ref. 14139], Kottelat 1990:20 [ref. 14137]). Balitoridae: Nemacheilinae.

Oreosoma Cuvier 1829:171 [ref. 995]. Neut. *Oreosoma atlanticum* Cuvier in Cuvier & Valenciennes 1829:515. Type by subsequent monotypy. Appeared first without species as above; one species included by Cuvier in Cuvier & Valenciennes 1829 (Nov.):515 [ref. 998]. Valid (Karrer 1986:439 [ref. 5680], James et al. 1988:302 [ref. 6639], Paxton et al. 1989:393 [ref. 12442]). Oreosomatidae.

Orestias Valenciennes in Cuvier & Valenciennes 1846:221 [ref. 1011]. Masc. *Orestias cuvieri* Valenciennes in Cuvier & Valenciennes 1846:225. Type by subsequent designation. Genus apparently appeared first in Valenciennes 1839 in "L'Institut", p. 1183 as name only (not investigated; from Fowler MS). Type designated by Bleeker 1864:140 [ref. 4859]. Valid (Parenti 1984 [ref. 5359]). Cyprinodontidae: Cyprinodontinae.

Orfus Fitzinger 1873:152, 163 [ref. 1337]. Masc. *Leuciscus virgo* Heckel 1852:69. Type by monotypy. Cyprinidae.

Orinocodoras Myers 1927:124 [ref. 3096]. Masc. *Orinocodoras eigenmanni* Myers 1927:124. Type by original designation (also monotypic). Valid (Burgess 1989:224 [ref. 12860]). Doradidae.

Orissagobius Herre 1945:402 [ref. 2141]. Masc. *Gobius cometes* Alcock 1890:208. Type by original designation (also monotypic). Synonym of *Obliquogobius* Koumans 1941 (Hoese, pers. comm.). Gobiidae.

Ornichthys (subgenus of *Trigla*) Swainson 1839:55, 179, 262 [ref. 4303]. Masc. *Prionotus punctatus* Bloch 1793:353. Type by subsequent designation. Type designated by Swain 1882:277 [ref. 5966]. Synonym of *Prionotus* Lacepède 1801. Triglidae: Triglinae.

Orqueta Jordan 1919:344 [ref. 2413]. *Micropteryx (Micropus) polycentrus* Kner 1868:29. Type by being a replacement name. Replacement for *Micropus* Kner 1868, four times preoccupied. Not a carangid, belongs in Latritidae (Smith-Vaniz, pers. comm., Nov. 1989). Latridae.

Orsinigobius Gandolfi, Marconato & Torricelli 1986:376 [ref. 6140]. Masc. *Gobius punctatissimus* Canestrini 1864:101. Type by monotypy. Valid. Gobiidae.

Orthagoriscus Cuvier 1816:148 [ref. 993]. Masc. *Tetraodon mola* Linnaeus 1758:334. Apparently an incorrect subsequent spelling of *Orthragoriscus* Bloch & Schneider 1801; Bloch & Schneider cited by Cuvier but their spelling not cited. Synonym of *Mola* Koelreuter 1770 (Tortonese 1973:649 [ref. 7192]). Molidae.

Ortheoleucos (subgenus of *Rutilus*) Derjavin 1937:71 [ref. 5035]. *Rutilus atropsatenus* Derjavin 1937:71, 77. Type by monotypy. Cyprinidae.

Orthichthys Gill 1862:234 [ref. 1663]. Masc. *Centriscus velitaris* Pallas 1770:36. Type by monotypy. Synonym of *Macroramphosus* Lacepède 1803 (Wheeler 1973:273 [ref. 7190]). Centriscidae: Macroramphosinae.

Orthochromis Greenwood 1954:402 [ref. 1893]. Masc. *Haplochromis malagaraziensis* David 1937. Type by original designation (also monotypic). Valid (Greenwood 1984:206 [ref. 5311], Poll 1986:42 [ref. 6136]). Cichlidae.

Orthocolus Gistel 1848:XI [ref. 1822]. Masc. *Salmo thymallus* Linnaeus 1758:311. Type by being a replacement name. Unneeded replacement for *Thymallus* Cuvier, not preoccupied by *Thymalus* Latreille 1803 in Coleoptera. Salmonidae: Thymallinae.

Orthocraeros Smith 1956:31 [ref. 4107]. *Makaira bermudae* Mowbray 1931:1 [unpagin.]. Type by original designation (also monotypic). Synonym of *Makaira* Lacepède 1802 (de Sylva 1973:479 [ref. 7210], Nakamura 1983:321 [ref. 5371]). Istiophoridae.

Orthodon Girard 1856:182 [ref. 1810]. Masc. *Gila microlepidota* Ayres 1854:21. Type by monotypy. Valid. Cyprinidae.

Orthomyleus (subgenus of *Myleus*) Eigenmann 1903:148 [ref. 1218]. Masc. *Myletes ellipticus* Günther 1864:375. Type by original designation. Synonym of *Myleus* Müller & Troschel 1844 (Géry 1976:49 [ref. 14199]). Characidae: Serrasalminae.

Orthonopias Starks & Mann 1911:11 [ref. 4199]. Masc. *Orthonopias triacis* Starks & Mann 1911:11. Type by monotypy. Misspelled *Orthopnias* in Zoological Record for 1911 and by Jordan 1920:541 [ref. 4905]. Valid (Bolin 1944:59 [ref. 6379], Washington et al. 1984:443 [ref. 13660], Yabe 1985:111 [ref. 11522]). Cottidae.

Orthophallus (subgenus of *Gambusia*) Rivas 1963:337 [ref. 3761]. Masc. *Gambusia lemaitrei* Fowler 1950. Type by original designation (also monotypic). Synonym of *Gambusia* Poey 1854 (Rosen & Bailey 1963:90 [ref. 7067]). Poeciliidae.

Orthopristis Girard 1858:167 [ref. 1813]. Fem. *Orthopristis duplex* Girard 1858:167. Type by monotypy. Valid (Johnson 1980:11 [ref. 13553], Matsuura in Uyeno et al. 1983:351 [ref. 14275]); synonym of *Pomadasys* Lacepède 1802 (Roux 1973:391 [ref. 7200], Roux 1986:328 [ref. 6209]). Haemulidae.

Orthopsetta Gill 1862:330 [ref. 1668]. Fem. *Psettichthys sordidus* Girard 1856:142. Type by monotypy. Also appeared in Gill 1864:196 [ref. 1701]. Synonym of *Citharichthys* Bleeker 1862 (Norman 1934:139 [ref. 6893], Desoutter 1986:428 [ref. 6212]). Paralichthyidae.

Orthospinus Reis 1989:42 [ref. 14219]. Masc. *Buritia cisalpinoi* Brant 1974:148. Type by being a replacement name. Replacement for *Buritia* Brant 1974, preoccupied by Young 1951 in Hemiptera. Characidae: Stethaprioninae.

Orthosternarchus Ellis 1913:144 [ref. 1271]. Masc. *Sternarchus tamandua* Boulenger 1898:427. Type by original designation (also monotypic). Valid (see Mago-Leccia 1978:14 [ref. 5489]). Gymnotidae: Apteronotinae.

Orthostoechus Gill 1862:255 [ref. 4909]. Masc. *Orthostoechus maculicauda* Gill 1862:255. Type by monotypy. Haemulidae.

Orthostomus Kner 1868:29 [ref. 6074]. Masc. *Orthostomus* *amblyopinus* Kner 1868:29. Type by monotypy. Also appeared as new in Kner 1868:329 [ref. 2646]. Apparently not preoccupied, *Stomogobius* Whitley is an unneeded replacement. Microdesmidae: Ptereleotrinae.

Orthragoriscus Bloch & Schneider 1801:510 [ref. 471]. Masc. *Tetraodon mola* Linnaeus 1758:334. Type by subsequent designation. Earliest type designation not researched. Spelled *Orthragoriascus* by early authors; original regarded as misprinted, but spelled *Orthragoriscus* on pp. lvii, 510, plate 97 and on p. 583. Objective synonym of *Mola* Koelreuter 1770 (Fraser-Brunner 1943:8 [ref. 1495], Tortonese 1973:649 [ref. 7192]). Molidae.

Orthragus Rafinesque 1810:17 [ref. 3594]. *Tetraodon mola* Linnaeus 1758:334. Type by subsequent designation. Type first designated by Bory de Saint-Vincent, v. 12, 1827:503 [ref. 3853] (see Whitley 1935:137 [ref. 6396]); although Bory de Saint Vincent spelled the genus as *Ostragus*, it is clear he was referring to Rafinesque's genus. Objective synonym of *Mola* Koelreuter 1770 (Fraser-Brunner 1943:8 [ref. 1495]). Molidae.

Orthrias Jordan & Fowler 1903:769 [ref. 2461]. Masc. *Orthrias oreas* Jordan & Fowler 1903:769. Type by original designation (also monotypic). Valid (Banarescu et al. 1982:3 [ref. 174]). Synonym of *Nemacheilus* Bleeker 1863 (Krupp & Schneider 1989:378 [ref. 13651]). Balitoridae: Nemacheilinae.

Orycnopsis see *Orcynopsis*. Scombridae.

Oryzias Jordan & Snyder 1906:289 [ref. 2520]. Masc. *Poecilia latipes* Temminck & Schlegel 1846:224. Type by original designation (also monotypic). Valid (Rosen & Parenti 1981 [ref. 5538], Collette et al. 1984:335 [ref. 11422], Uyeno & Arai in Masuda et al. 1984:83 [ref. 6441], Kottelat 1985:272 [ref. 11441], Sakaizumi 1985 [ref. 6790], Magtoon 1986 [ref. 6321], Uwa 1986 [ref. 6322], Uwa & Parenti 1988 [ref. 6852]). Adrianichthyidae: Oryziinae.

Osbeckia Jordan & Evermann 1896:424 [ref. 2442]. Fem. *Balistes scriptus* Osbeck 1757:144. Type by original designation (also monotypic). Monacanthidae.

Oshimia Jordan 1919:342 [ref. 2413]. Fem. *Micracanthus marchei* Sauvage 1880:96. Type by being a replacement name. Unneeded replacement for *Micracanthus* Sauvage 1880, not preoccupied by *Microcanthus* Swainson 1839 in fishes. Synonym of *Betta* Bleeker 1850 (Roberts 1989:171 [ref. 6439]). Belontiidae.

Osmerus Lacepède 1803:229 [ref. 4930]. Masc. *Salmo eperlanus* Linnaeus 1758:310. Type by subsequent designation. ICZN Direction 69 gives authorship of this genus to Linnaeus 1758; see also Whitley 1935:137 [ref. 6396] who regards Bory de Saint-Vincent, v. 6, 1824:204 [ref. 3853] as the first to designate the type for *Osmerus* Lacepède. Objective synonym of *Osmerus* Linnaeus as validated by ICZN. Osmeridae.

Osmerus (subgenus of *Salmo*) Linnaeus 1758:310 [ref. 2787]. Masc. *Salmo eperlanus* Linnaeus 1758:310. Originally as "Osmeri" a subgroup of *Salmo*; with two species; made available by ICZN (Opinion 77; Direction 69). Type designated by plenary powers; on Official List (Opinion 77). Valid (Kljukanov & McAllister 1973:158 [ref. 7178], Luey et al. 1982 [ref. 6822], McAllister in Whitehead et al. 1984:401 [ref. 13675], Uyeno in Masuda et al. 1984:33 [ref. 6441]). Osmeridae.

Osopsaron Jordan & Starks 1904:600 [ref. 2526]. Neut. *Pteropsaron verecundum* Jordan & Snyder 1902:472. Type by original designation (also monotypic). Valid (Okamura in Masuda et al. 1984:290 [ref. 6441], Kao & Shen 1985 [ref. 5229], Nelson 1982:7 [ref. 5469], Parin 1985 [ref. 6722], Heemstra & Nelson 1986:738 [ref. 6304]). Percophidae: Hemerocoetinae.

Osorina Whitley 1951:68 [ref. 4711]. Fem. *Muraenosaurus guentheri* Osório 1909:14. Type by being a replacement name. Replacement for *Muraenosaurus* Osorio 1909, preoccupied by Seeley 1874 in Reptilia. Synonym of *Nettastoma* Rafinesque 1810 (Blache et al. 1973:236 [ref. 7185], Smith et al. 1981:538 [ref. 6158], Smith 1989:604 [ref. 13285]). Nettastomatidae.

Osorioia (subgenus of *Scorpaena*) Fowler 1938:63 [ref. 1426]. Fem. *Scorpaena hemilepidota* Fowler 1938:63. Type by original designation (also monotypic). Scorpaenidae: Scorpaeninae.

Ospatulus Herre 1924:1569 [ref. 2120]. Masc. *Ospatulus truncatulus* Herre 1924:278. Type by original designation. Genus apparently published first as above, with 2 undefined species; species described and genus also described as new in Herre 1924:277 [ref. 2118] and 1924:706 [ref. 2119] where type was designated; dates of publication not fully investigated. Probably valid (Kornfield & Carpenter 1984:75 [ref. 5435] as *Ospatalus*). Cyprinidae.

Osphronemus Lacepède 1801:116 [ref. 2710]. Masc. *Osphronemus goramy* Lacepède 1801:116, 117. Type by subsequent designation. Type apparently designated by Bleeker 1879:16-17 [ref. 457], *goramy* in synonymy of *olfax*. *Osphromenus* is an unjustified emendation (e.g., by Günther 1861:382 [ref. 1964]). Valid (Jayaram 1981:385 [ref. 6497], Kottelat 1985:275 [ref. 11441], Kottelat 1989:20 [ref. 13605], Roberts 1989:177 [ref. 6439] as sole member of Osphronemidae). Osphronemidae.

Osphyolax Cope 1876:450 [ref. 936]. Masc. *Osphyolax pellucidus* Cope 1876:450. Type by monotypy. Indicated as masculine by author. Synonym of *Nerophis* Rafinesque 1810 or of *Entelurus* Duméril 1870. Syngnathidae: Syngnathinae.

Osteobagrus (subgenus of *Mystus*) Jayaram 1954:529, 547 [ref. 2336]. Masc. *Pimelodus aor* Hamilton 1822:205, 379. Type by original designation. Bagridae.

Osteobrama Heckel 1843:1033 [ref. 2066]. Fem. *Cyprinus cotio* Hamilton 1822:339, 393. Type by subsequent designation. Type apparently first designated by Jordan 1919:211 [ref. 2407]. Species spelled *cotio* in main entries in Hamilton, but *cotis* by Hamilton on Pl. 39 and by Heckel. Valid (Jayaram 1981:112 [ref. 6497], Kottelat 1989:9 [ref. 13605]). Cyprinidae.

Osteochilichthys (subgenus of *Osteochilus*) Hora 1942:8 [ref. 2213]. Masc. *Scaphiodon thomassi* Day 1877:551. Type by original designation. Synonym of *Osteochilus* Günther 1868, but as a valid subgenus (Jayaram 1981:128 [ref. 6497]). Cyprinidae.

Osteochilus Günther 1868:40 [ref. 1990]. Masc. *Rohita melanopleura* Bleeker 1852:430. Type by subsequent designation. Type designated by Jordan 1919:351 [ref. 4904]. Misspelled *Osteocheilus* by authors. Valid (Wu et al. 1977:348 [ref. 4807], Jayaram 1981:127 [ref. 6497], Kottelat 1985:264 [ref. 11441], Roberts 1989:45 [ref. 6439], Chu & Cui in Chu & Chen 1989:267 [ref. 13584], Kottelat 1989:9 [ref. 13605]). Cyprinidae.

Osteochromis Franz 1910:52 [ref. 1481]. Masc. *Osteochromis larvatus* Franz 1910:52. Type by monotypy. Type not *Chaetodon larvatus* Cuvier 1831. Synonym of *Chaetodon* Linnaeus 1758. Chaetodontidae.

Osteodiscus Stein 1978:24 [ref. 4203]. Masc. *Osteodiscus cascadiae* Stein 1978:24. Type by original designation (also monotypic). Valid (Kido 1988:248 [ref. 12287]). Cyclopteridae: Liparinae.

Osteogaster Cope 1894:102 [ref. 965]. Fem. *Corydoras eques* Steindachner 1876:140. Type by original designation. Misspelled *Osteogater* by Jordan 1920:464 [ref. 4905]. Synonym of *Corydoras* Lacepède 1803 (Nijssen & Isbrücker 1980:192 [ref. 6910]). Callichthyidae.

Osteogeneiosus Bleeker 1846:173 [ref. 5872]. Masc. *Arius militaris* Valenciennes in Cuvier & Valenciennes 1840:114. Type by subsequent designation. Also in Bleeker 1847:49 [ref. 313]. Type designated by Bleeker 1862:8 [ref. 393] and 1863:93 [ref. 401]. *Osteogeniosus* Günther 1864:181 [ref. 1974] apparently is an unjustified emendation; spelled *Ostogeneiosus* by Jordan 1919:278 [ref. 2410]. Valid (Jayaram & Dhanze 1979:48 [ref. 6800], Jayaram 1981:278 [ref. 6497] and Burgess 1989:167 [ref. 12860] as *Ostogeniosus* and type as *macrocephalus* Bleeker, Kottelat 1985:271 [ref. 11441], Kottelat 1989:15 [ref. 13605]). Ariidae.

Osteoglossum Agassiz in Spix & Agassiz 1829:46 [ref. 13]. Neut. *Osteoglossum bicirrhosum* Agassiz in Spix & Agassiz 1829:47. Type by monotypy. See account of *Osteoglossum* Cuvier 1829. If one regards the species names *bicirrhosum* and *vandelli* as name only in Cuvier, then the type of *Osteoglossum* Agassiz is *bicirrhosum* Agassiz by monotypy (as *vandelli* is not at that time available); if one regards *bicirrhosum* as available from Cuvier (as does Kottelat), then the type species authorship is Cuvier. See also Case pending 2659 in Appendix B. Synonym of *Osteoglossum* Cuvier 1829 (see Kottelat 1988:81). Osteoglossidae: Osteoglossinae.

Osteoglossum Basilewski 1855:244 [ref. 200]. Neut. *Osteoglossum prionostoma* Basilewski 1855:244. Type by monotypy. Preoccupied by Vandelli 1829 in fishes, apparently not replaced. Engraulidae.

Osteoglossum Cuvier (ex Vandelli) 1829:328 [ref. 995]. Neut. *Osteoglossum bicirrhosum* Agassiz in Spix & Agassiz 1829:47. Type by subsequent monotypy. Cuvier 1829 predates Spix and Agassiz 1829 [ref. 13] (Whitehead & Myers 1971 [ref. 6584] and Kottelat 1988:81 [ref. 13380]). Authorship of species above follows Whitehead & Myers (differing from Kottelat), but if one regards Cuvier's "*Osteoglossum Vandellii*, n., ou *Ischnosoma bicirrhosum*, Spix, xxxv" as a combined species description with the genus (rather than names only in Cuvier) then *vandelli* is type by monotypy (but *bicirrhosum* should be conserved). Valid. Osteoglossidae: Osteoglossinae.

Osteomugil Luther 1982:7 [ref. 2851]. Masc. *Mugil cunnesius* Valenciennes in Cuvier & Valenciennes 1836:114. Type by original designation (also monotypic). Appeared first in Luther 1975:107 [ref. 7300], but without clear differentiating characters and unavailable. Mugilidae.

Osteomystax Whitley 1940:242 [ref. 4660]. Masc. *Ceratocheilus osteomystax* Miranda-Ribeiro 1918:644. Type by being a replacement name. Replacement for *Ceratocheilus* Miranda-Ribeiro 1918, preoccupied by Wesché 1810 in Diptera. Synonym of *Auchenipterus* Valenciennes 1840 (Mees 1974:16 [ref. 2969]). Auchenipteridae.

Ostichthys Cuvier (ex Langsdorf) in Cuvier & Valenciennes 1829:174 [ref. 4879]. Masc. *Ostichthys japonicus* Cuvier in Cuvier & Valenciennes 1829:173. Mentioned in synonymy of *Myripristis*, with species *O. aureus* in synonymy of *Myripristis japonicus*. Treated as a valid subgenus by Jordan & Evermann 1896:846 [ref. 2443] and therefore dates to 1829 (Art. 11e) with authorship as Cuvier (Art. 50g) (see Appendix A); type by subsequent designation of Jordan & Evermann. Treated as valid by current workers, but with Jordan & Evermann as authors. Holocentridae.

Ostichthys (subgenus of *Myripristis*) Jordan & Evermann (ex Langsdorf) 1896:846 [ref. 2443]. Masc. *Myripristis japonicus* Cuvier in Cuvier & Valenciennes 1829:173. Type by original designation. Appeared first as Langsdorf (manuscript name) in synonymy in Cuvier & Valenciennes 1829:174 and probably dates to Cuvier (ex Langsdorf) 1829 and not Jordan & Evermann. Valid (Randall et al. 1982 [ref. 3602], Shimizu in Masuda et al. 1984:114 [ref. 6441], Randall & Heemstra 1986:425 [ref. 5707], Randall & Wrobel 1988 [ref. 12743], Paxton et al. 1989:379 [ref. 12442]). Holocentridae.

Ostophycephalus Ogilby 1899:155 [ref. 3279]. Masc. *Ostophycephalus duriceps* Ogilby 1899:156. Type by original designation (also monotypic). Synonym of *Cnidoglanis* Günther 1864 (Paxton et al. 1989:223 [ref. 12442]). Plotosidae.

Ostorhinchus Lacepède 1802:23 [ref. 4929]. Masc. *Ostorhinchus fleurieu* Lacepède 1802:23, 24. Type by monotypy. *Ostorincus* Rafinesque 1815:85 [ref. 3584] is an incorrect subsequent spelling. Questionably a synonym of *Apogon* Lacepède 1801 (Fraser 1972:17 [ref. 5195]); valid as a subgenus of *Apogon* (Gon 1987 [ref. 6706]). Apogonidae.

Ostracion Linnaeus 1758:330 [ref. 2787]. Neut. *Ostracion cubicus* Linnaeus 1758:332. Type by subsequent designation. Earliest type designation not resolved; Bleeker 1865:27 [ref. 416] lists *O. tetragonus* as type, and Jordan & Gilbert 1883:853 [ref. 2476] list *cubiceps* as type. Valid (Tyler 1980:239 [ref. 4477], Arai 1983:203 [ref. 14249], Matsuura in Masuda et al. 1984:362 [ref. 6441], Smith 1986:892 [ref. 5712]). Ostraciidae: Ostraciinae.

Ostracoberyx Fowler 1934:353 [ref. 1416]. Masc. *Ostracoberyx dorygenys* Fowler 1934:353. Type by original designation (also monotypic). Placed by Johnson 1984:465 as an incertae sedis family Ostracoberycidae in the suborder Percoidei. Valid (Katayama in Masuda et al. 1984:126 [ref. 6441]). Percoidei.

Ostreoblennius (subgenus of *Petroscirtes*) Whitley 1930:20 [ref. 4671]. Masc. *Petroscirtes (Ostreoblennius) steadi* Whitley 1930:20. Type by original designation (also monotypic). Synonym of *Petroscirtes* Rüppell 1830 (Smith-Vaniz 1976:23 [ref. 4144]). Blenniidae.

Ostreogobius Whitley 1930:122 [ref. 4669]. Masc. *Gillichthys australis* Ogilby 1894:367. Type by original designation (also monotypic). Synonym of *Redigobius* Herre 1927 (Miller 1987:698 [ref. 6336]). Gobiidae.

Ostreophilus Koumans 1940:163 [ref. 2676]. Masc. Not available; museum name mentioned by Koumans in synonymy of *Rhinogobius leftwichi* Ogilby 1910. Gobiidae.

Osurus Jordan & Evermann 1903:206 [ref. 2450]. Masc. *Parapercis schauinslandi* Steindachner 1900:175. Type by original designation. Synonym of *Parapercis* Bleeker 1863. Pinguipedidae.

Otakia Jordan & Snyder 1900:345 [ref. 2502]. Fem. *Otakia rasborina* Jordan & Snyder 1900:345. Type by original designation (also monotypic). Synonym of *Gnathopogon* Bleeker 1859 (Banarescu & Nalbant 1973:61 [ref. 173]). Cyprinidae.

Otalia de Buen 1945:528 [ref. 691]. Fem. *Chirostoma promelas* Jordan & Snyder 1900:136. Type by original designation (also monotypic). Synonym of *Chirostoma* Swainson 1839. Atherinidae: Menidiinae.

Othonias (subgenus of *Sciaena*) Jordan & Thompson 1911:244, 246, 257 [ref. 2539]. Masc. *Sciaena manchurica* Jordan & Thompson 1911:255. Type by original designation (also monotypic). Type designated on p. 257. Synonym of *Larimichthys* Jordan & Starks 1905 (Trewavas 1977:392 [ref. 4459]). Sciaenidae.

Othonocheirodus Myers 1927:113 [ref. 3096]. Masc. *Othonocheirodus eigenmanni* Myers 1927:114. Type by original designation (also monotypic). Valid (Géry 1977:559 [ref. 1597]). Characidae.

Othonophanes Eigenmann 1903:145 [ref. 1218]. *Brycon labiatus* Steindachner 1879:188. Type by original designation (also monotypic). Misspelled *Orthophanes* in Zoological Record for 1903. Mention (Géry 1977:335 [ref. 1597]); synonym of *Brycon* Müller & Troschel 1844 (Howes 1982:4 [ref. 14201]). Characidae.

Othonops Smith [= Rosa Smith Eigenmann] 1881:19 [ref. 4143]. Masc. *Othonops eos* Smith 1881:19. Type by original designation (also monotypic). Synonym of *Typhlogobius* Steindachner 1879. Gobiidae.

Othos Castelnau 1875:43 [ref. 768]. *Othos cephalotes* Castelnau 1875:44. Type by monotypy. Valid (Paxton et al. 1989:506 [ref. 12442] in Anthiinae). Serranidae: Anthiinae.

Otocinclus Cope 1871:112 [ref. 5775]. Masc. *Otocinclus vestitus* Cope 1872:283. Type by subsequent monotypy. Appeared first with brief description and without species as above; more complete description and species added in 1872:283 [ref. 921]. Valid (Isbrücker 1980:81 [ref. 2303], Burgess 1989:438 [ref. 12860], Malabarba 1989:150 [ref. 14217]). Loricariidae.

Otohime Jordan & Starks 1907:131 [ref. 2533]. Fem. *Trigla hemisticta* Schlegel 1843:36. Type by original designation (also monotypic). Triglidae: Triglinae.

Otolithes Oken (ex Cuvier) 1817:1182 [ref. 3303]. *Johnius ruber* Bloch & Schneider 1801:75. Type by subsequent designation. Earliest technical addition of species not researched. Type designated by Gill 1861:80 [ref. 1771]. Based on "Les Otolithes" of Cuvier 1816:299 [ref. 993] (see Gill 1903:966 [ref. 5768]). Written *Otolithus* by Cuvier 1829:172 [ref. 995] and authors. Valid (Trewavas 1977:347 [ref. 4459], Jayaram 1981:329 [ref. 6497], Daget & Trewavas 1986:334 [ref. 6211], Heemstra 1986:619 [ref. 5660], Kottelat 1989:17 [ref. 13605]). Sciaenidae.

Otolithoides Fowler 1933:364 [ref. 1414]. Masc. *Otolithus biauritus* Cantor 1850:1039. Type by original designation. Correct spelling for genus of type species is *Otolithes*. Valid (Trewavas 1977:296 [ref. 4459], Jayaram 1981:328 [ref. 6497], Kottelat 1989:17 [ref. 13605]). Sciaenidae.

Otoperca Boulenger 1915:130 [ref. 584]. Fem. *Larimus auritus* Valenciennes in Cuvier & Valenciennes 1831:501. Type by monotypy. Objective synonym of *Brachydeuterus* Gill 1862 (Roux 1973:392 [ref. 7200], Roux 1986:327 [ref. 6209]). Haemulidae.

Otopharynx Regan 1920:38 [ref. 3669]. Masc. *Tilapia auromarginata* Boulenger 1908:241. Type by original designation (also monotypic). Valid (Eccles & Trewavas 1989:154 [ref. 13547]). Cichlidae.

Otophidium Gill in Jordan 1885:914 [126] [ref. 2385]. Neut. *Genypterus omostigma* Jordan & Gilbert 1882:301. Type by original designation (also monotypic). Valid (Cohen & Nielsen 1978:16 [ref. 881]). Ophidiidae: Ophidiinae.

Otothyris Myers 1927:127 [ref. 3096]. Fem. *Otothyris canaliferus* Myers 1927:128. Type by original designation (also monotypic). Valid (Isbrücker 1980:85 [ref. 2303], Burgess 1989:439 [ref. 12860], Malabarba 1989:151 [ref. 14217]). Loricariidae.

Otrynter Jordan & Evermann 1896:388 [ref. 2442]. *Stenotomus caprinus* Bean 1882:426. Type by original designation (also monotypic). Synonym opf *Stenotomus* Gill 1865. Sparidae.

Ovoides Anonymous 1798:675 [ref. 13098]. Masc. *Ovoides fasciatus* Cuvier 1800. Type by subsequent monotypy. First latinization of "Les Ovoïdes" Lacepède 1798; also latinized by Cuvier 1800:1, tab. [ref. 994, not seen]. See also Whitley 1832:311 [ref. 4676]. Type apparently by subsequent monotypy [not researched]. Tetraodontidae.

Ovoides Lacepède 1798:521 [ref. 2708]. Masc. Not available, genus and species names not latinized. See second entry for *Ovoides*. Tetraodontidae.

Ovum Bloch & Schneider 1801:530 [ref. 471]. *Ovum commersoni* Bloch & Schneider 1801:530. Type by monotypy. Based on l'ovoide fascé of Lacepède. Tetraodontidae.

Owsianka Dybowski 1862:283 [ref. 1168]. Fem. *Aspius owsianka* Czernay 1851:281. Type by absolute tautonymy. Dybowski's *Owsianka czernayi* is as unneeded replacement for *A. owsianka* Czernay. Synonym of *Leucaspius* Heckel & Kner 1858. Cyprinidae.

Owstonia Tanaka 1908:46 [ref. 6032]. Fem. *Owstonia totomiensis* Tanaka 1908:47. Type by monotypy. Valid (Machida in Masuda et al. 1984:201 [ref. 6441], Smith-Vaniz 1986:727 [ref. 5718], Mok 1988:507 [ref. 12752]). Cepolidae.

Oxima Rafinesque 1815:86 [ref. 3584]. Not available, name only. Unplaced genera.

Oxleyana Whitley 1937:121 [ref. 4689]. Fem. *Syngnathus parviceps* Ramsay & Ogilby 1887:475. Type by original designation (also monotypic). Synonym of *Hippichthys* Bleeker 1849 (Dawson 1985:96 [ref. 6541], Dawson 1986:282 [ref. 6201]). Syngnathidae: Syngnathinae.

Oxuderces Eydoux & Souleyet 1850:181 [ref. 4501]. Masc. *Oxuderces dentatus* Eydoux & Souleyet 1850:182. Type by monotypy. Author not Valenciennes and date not 1842 as usually cited; see Bauchot et al. 1982:60 et seq. [ref. 6562]; see also Springer 1978:1 [ref. 6955]. Valid (Springer 1978 [ref. 6955], Birdsong et al. 1988:195 [ref. 7303], Kottelat 1989:19 [ref. 13605], Murdy 1989:19 [ref. 13628]). Gobiidae.

Oxybarbus Vaillant 1893:57 [ref. 4485]. Masc. *Barbus heteronema* Bleeker 1853:446. Type by monotypy. Synonym of *Cyclocheilichthys* Bleeker 1859 (Roberts 1989:33 [ref. 6439]). Cyprinidae.

Oxybeles Richardson 1846:73 [ref. 3740]. Masc. *Oxybeles homei* Richardson 1846:74. Type by monotypy. *Oxybelus* Bleeker 1851:278 [ref. 12505] is an incorrect subsequent spelling. Synonym of *Carapus* Rafinesque 1810 (Arnold 1956:260 [ref. 5315]). Carapidae: Carapinae.

Oxybrycon Géry 1964:15 [ref. 1580]. Masc. *Oxybrycon parvulus* Géry 1964:16. Type by original designation (also monotypic). Valid (Géry 1977:591 [ref. 1597]). Characidae.

Oxycephas Rafinesque 1810:31 [ref. 3594]. *Oxycephas scabrus* Rafinesque 1810:31. Type by monotypy. Synonym of *Trachyrincus* Giorna 1809 (Marshall 1973:287 [ref. 7194], Marshall & Iwamoto 1973:516 [ref. 6963]). Macrouridae: Trachyrincinae.

Oxychaetodon (subgenus of *Tetragonoptrus*) Bleeker 1876:306 [ref. 448]. Masc. *Chaetodon lineolatus* Cuvier (ex Quoy & Gaimard) in Cuvier & Valenciennes 1831:40. Type by original designation, also monotypic [in ref. 448]. Also appeared in Bleeker 1876:314 [ref. 451] and 1876:Pl. 377 [ref. 6835] (earliest not determined). Synonym of *Chaetodon* Linnaeus 1758, subgenus *Rabdophorus* Swainson 1839 (Burgess 1978:578 [ref. 700]). Synonym of *Rabdophorus* Swainson 1839 (Maugé & Bauchot 1984:468 [ref. 6614]). Chaetodontidae.

Oxycheilinus Gill 1862:143 [ref. 1662]. Masc. *Cheilinus arenatus* Valenciennes in Cuvier & Valenciennes 1839:101. Type by original designation (also monotypic). Type designated by Gill's style of one species in parentheses in key. Synonym of *Cheilinus* Lacepède 1801. Labridae.

Oxycirrhites Bleeker 1857:39 [ref. 356]. Masc. *Oxycirrhites typus* Bleeker 1857:40. Type by monotypy (also by use of *typus*). Valid (Araga in Masuda et al. 1984:199 [ref. 6441], Donaldson 1986:624 [ref. 6317]). Cirrhitidae.

Oxyconger Bleeker 1864:19 [ref. 4860]. Masc. *Conger leptognathus* Bleeker 1858:27. Type by original designation (also monotypic). Bleeker 1864:19 published 21 Sept. 1864, also in Bleeker 1865:116 [ref. 409]. Valid (Asano in Masuda et al. 1984:29 [ref. 6441], Paxton et al. 1989:145 [ref. 12442], Smith 1989:434 [ref. 13285]). Muraenesocidae.

Oxycottus Jordan & Evermann 1898:1883, 2015 [ref. 2444]. Masc. *Oligocottus acuticeps* Gilbert 1896:432. Type by original designation. Synonym of *Clinocottus* Gill 1861 (Bolin 1944:84 [ref. 6379]). Cottidae.

Oxydoras Kner 1855:142 [ref. 2629]. Masc. *Doras niger* Kner (not of Valenciennes) (= *Oxydoras kneri* Bleeker 1863:14). Type by subsequent designation. Type evidently a misidentified type species; *Doras (Oxydoras) niger* of Kner (renamed *O. kneri* by Bleeker), not *Doras niger* Valenciennes 1811. Type designated by Bleeker 1862:5 [ref. 393] and 1863:85 [ref. 401]. Valid (Burgess 1989:224 [ref. 12860]). Doradidae.

Oxyeleotris Bleeker 1874:302 [ref. 437]. Fem. *Eleotris marmorata* Bleeker 1852:424. Type by original designation (also monotypic). Synonym of *Bostrychus* Lacepède 1801 (Maugé 1986:389 [ref. 6218]); valid (Kottelat 1985:274 [ref. 11441], Allen & Hoese 1986:99 [ref. 6252], Birdsong et al. 1988:180 [ref. 7303], Kottelat 1989:18 [ref. 13605], Roberts 1989:166 [ref. 6439]). Eleotridae.

Oxygadus (subgenus of *Coelorhynchus*) Gilbert & Hubbs 1920:515 [ref. 1638]. Masc. *Macrurus parallelus* Günther 1877:439. Type by original designation. Synonym of *Caelorinchus* Giorna 1809 (Marshall 1973:293 [ref. 7194], Marshall & Iwamoto 1973:538 [ref. 6966]). Macrouridae: Macrourinae.

Oxygaster van Hasselt 1823:133 [ref. 5963]. Fem. *Oxygaster anomalura* van Hasselt 1823:133. Type by monotypy. Also in French version, van Hasselt 1824:377 [ref. 5104]. See Kottelat 1987:373 [ref. 5962]. Valid but as made available by Günther 1868 (Roberts 1989:55 [ref. 6439]); valid (Kottelat 1989:10 [ref. 13605]). Cyprinidae.

Oxygeneum Forbes 1885:136 [ref. 1344]. Neut. *Oxygeneum pulverulentum* Forbes 1885:136. Type by monotypy. Not avialable; apparently based on a hybrid between *Campostoma* and *Phoxinus* (see Hubbs & Bailey 1952 [ref. 12506]). Cyprinidae.

Oxyglanis Vinciguerra 1898:249 [ref. 4522]. Masc. *Oxyglanis sacchii* Vinciguerra 1898:250. Type by monotypy. Synonym of *Auchenoglanis* Günther 1865 (Risch 1986:2 [ref. 6190]). Bagridae.

Oxygymnocypris (subgenus of *Gymnocypris*) Tsao 1964:183 [ref. 13501]. Fem. *Schizopygopsis stewartii* Lloyd 1908. Type by original designation (also monotypic). Valid (Wu 1987:47 [ref. 12822]). Cyprinidae.

Oxyjulis Gill 1864:223 [ref. 1685]. Fem. *Halichoeres californicus* Günther 1861:386. Type by original designation (also monotypic). Type *Julis modestus* Girard 1854, not of Bleeker, *H. californicus* Günther is a species replacement name. Valid (Richards & Leis 1984:544 [ref. 13668]). Labridae.

Oxylabrax Bleeker 1876:264 [ref. 447]. Masc. *Sciaena undecimalis* Bloch 1792:60. Type by being a replacement name. Unneeded replacement for *Centropomus* Lacepède 1802. Objective synonym of *Centropomus* Lacepède 1802 (Rivas 1986:587 [ref. 5210]). Centropomidae: Centropominae.

Oxylapia Kiener & Maugé 1966:74 [ref. 2605]. Fem. *Oxylapia polli* Kiener & Maugé 1966:75. Type by original designation (also monotypic). Cichlidae.

Oxylebius Gill 1862:277 [ref. 1666]. Masc. *Oxylebius pictus* Gill 1862:278. Type by monotypy. Valid (Washington et al. 1984:443 [ref. 13660]). Hexagrammidae: Oxylebiinae.

Oxyloricaria Bleeker 1862:3 [ref. 393]. Fem. *Loricaria barbata* Kner 1854:87. Type by original designation (also monotypic). Synonym of *Sturisoma* Swainson 1838 (Isbrücker 1980:93 [ref. 2303]). Loricariidae.

Oxymacrurus Bleeker 1874:370 [ref. 435]. Masc. *Macrurus japonicus* Temminck & Schlegel 1846:256. Type by original designation (also monotypic). Synonym of *Caelorinchus* Giorna 1809 (Marshall 1973:293 [ref. 7194]). Macrouridae: Macrourinae.

Oxymetopon Bleeker 1861:258 [ref. 383]. Neut. *Oxymetopon typus* Bleeker 1861:259. Type by monotypy (also by use of *typus*). Valid (Klausewitz & Condé 1981 [ref. 5479], Birdsong et al. 1988:200 [ref. 7303]). Microdesmidae: Ptereleotrinae.

Oxymonacanthus Bleeker 1865:Pl. 224 [ref. 416]. Masc. *Monacanthus longirostris* Cuvier 1816. Apparently dates to Pl. 224 published in part 19 (1865), with type by monotypy; corresponding text (pp. 100, 137) published in part 21 (in 1869). May date to Bleeker 1865:183 [ref. 414] with type *Monacanthus chrysospilus* Bleeker by monotypy. Also in Bleeker 1866:13 [ref. 417]. Valid (Matsuura 1979:165 [ref. 7019], Tyler 1980:176 [ref. 4477], Arai 1983:200 [ref. 14249], Matsuura in Masuda et al. 1984:361 [ref. 6441], Hutchins 1986:884 [ref. 5673]). Monacanthidae.

Oxymormyrus Bleeker 1874:367 [ref. 435]. Masc. *Mormyrus zanclirostris* Günther 1867:115. Type by original designation (also monotypic). Gosse 1984:91 [ref. 6169] treats in synonymy of *Mormyrops* Müller 1843, but that genus with nomenclatural problems; see account of *Mormyrops* and *Marcusenius*. Mormyridae.

Oxymugil Whitley 1948:271 [ref. 4709]. Masc. *Mugil acutus* Valenciennes in Cuvier & Valenciennes 1836:140. Type by original designation (also monotypic). Mugilidae.

Oxynoemacheilus (subgenus of *Noemacheilus*) Banarescu & Nalbant 1966:153 [ref. 218]. Masc. *Cobitis persa* Heckel 1846:266. Type by original designation (also monotypic). Misspelled once as *Oxynolmacheilus* in Zoological Record for 1967. Synonym of *Nemacheilus* Bleeker 1863 (Krupp & Schneider 1989:378 [ref. 13651], Kottelat 1990:20 [ref. 14137]). Balitoridae: Nemacheilinae.

Oxynotus Rafinesque 1810:45, 60 [ref. 3595]. Masc. *Squalus centrina* Linnaeus 1758:233. Type by monotypy. Valid (Krefft & Tortonese 1973:35 [ref. 7165], Compagno 1984:124 [ref. 6474], Yano & Murofushi 1985 [ref. 5797], Bass et al. 1986:59 [ref. 5636], Cappetta 1987:59 [ref. 6348], Paxton et al. 1989:36 [ref. 12442]). Squalidae.

Oxyodon Brauer 1906:287 [ref. 632]. Masc. *Oxyodon macrops* Brauer 1906:288. Type by monotypy. Family placement uncertain, possibly an Epigoninae (Fraser 1972:42 [ref. 5195]); synonym of *Epigonus* Rafinesque 1810 (Mayer 1974:151 [ref. 6007]). Epigonidae.

Oxyodontichthys Poey 1880:254 [ref. 6524]. Masc. *Ophichthys macrurus* Poey 1867:256. Type by subsequent designation. Type designated by Jordan & Evermann 1896:381 [ref. 2442]. Synonym of *Ophichthus* Ahl 1789 (Blache et al. 1973:247 [ref. 7185], McCosker 1977:80 [ref. 6836] as *Oxydontichthys*, McCosker et al. 1989:379 [ref. 13288]). Ophichthidae: Ophichthinae.

Oxyporhamphus Gill 1864:273 [ref. 1693]. Masc. *Hemiramphus cuspidatus* Valenciennes in Cuvier & Valenciennes 1846:56. Type by original designation (also monotypic). Valid (Parin et al. 1980:145 [ref. 6895], Yoshino in Masuda et al. 1984:80 [ref. 6441], Collette et al. 1984:337 [ref. 11422], Collette 1986:391 [ref. 5647], Collette & Su 1986:286 [ref. 5998], Paxton et al. 1989:338 [ref. 12442]). Hemiramphidae.

Oxypristis Hoffmann 1912:334 [ref. 5070]. Fem. *Pristis cuspidatus* Latham 1794:279. Type by monotypy. Preoccupied by Signoret 1861 in Hemiptera, replaced by *Anoxypristis* White & Moy-Thomas 1941. Based on a Recent species but fossil species were included. Objective synonym of *Anoxypristis* White & Moy-Thomas 1941 (Cappetta 1987:157 [ref. 6348], Paxton et al. 1989:58 [ref. 12442]). Pristidae.

Oxyrhina Agassiz 1835:86 [feuil. ad. 5] [ref. 13390]. Fem. *Lamna oxyrhina* Valenciennes in Cuvier & Valenciennes (= *Isurus oxyrinchus* Rafinesque 1810:12). Type by monotypy (also by tautonymy). Although Agassiz stated, "Le type de ce genre est le Lamna de Spallanzani" [*Lamna spallanzanii* Rafinesque], he only included one species (*L. oxyrhina*) by name. *Oxyrhina* not preoccupied. Spelled *Oxyrrhina* in early literature. Synonym of *Isurus* Rafinesque 1810 (Springer 1973:14 [ref. 7162], Compagno 1984:242 [ref. 6474], Cappetta 1987:96 [ref. 6348]). Lamnidae.

Oxyrhynchus de Buen 1926:32 [ref. 5054]. As a "grupo" for 4 species of Rajidae. Not available on basis of Art. 1b(6) [see de Buen's definition of "grupo" on p. 11]; see Appendix A. Preoccupied by Leach 1818 in fishes. In the synonymy of *Raja* Linnaeus 1758. Rajidae.

Oxyrhynchus Leach in Tuckey 1818:410 [ref. 5023]. Masc. *Oxyrhynchus deliciosus* Leach in Tuckey 1818:410. Type by monotypy. Treated incorrectly as a nomen oblitum (forgotten name) by Gosse 1984:91 in synonymy of *Mormyrops* Müller 1843, *Mormyrops* also with problems; see account of *Mormyrops*. Original not seen; above from Fowler 1975 [ref. 9331]. Synonym of *Mormyrops* Müller 1843 (Taverne 1972:164 [ref. 6367]). Mormyridae.

Oxyropsis Eigenmann & Eigenmann 1889:39 [ref. 1253]. Fem. *Oxyropsis wrightiana* Eigenmann & Eigenmann 1889:39. Type by original designation (also monotypic). Synonym of *Hypoptopoma* Günther 1868 (Isbrücker 1980:86 [ref. 2303]). Loricariidae.

Oxystomus Rafinesque 1810:49, 62 [ref. 3595]. Masc. *Oxystomus hyalinus* Rafinesque 1810:62. Type by monotypy. Preoccupied by Fischer von Waldheim 1803 in Mammalia; replaced by *Bertinulus* Whitley 1948. Not a serrivomerid (Tighe 1989:618 [ref. 13291]). Ophichthidae: Ophichthinae.

Oxyurichthys Bleeker 1857:464 [ref. 6220]. Masc. *Gobius belosso* Bleeker 1854:316. Type by subsequent designation. Also appeared in Bleeker 1860:44 [ref. 379]. Misprinted once as *Oxyurichthus* by Bleeker 1874:324 [ref. 437]. Type designated by Bleeker 1874:324 [ref. 437]. Valid (Larson & Hoese 1980:43 [ref. 2725], Kurup & Samuel 1982 [ref. 6796], Akihito in Masuda et al. 1984:262 [ref. 6441], Hoese 1986:796 [ref. 5670], Maugé 1986:378 [ref. 6218], Miller in Whitehead et al. 1986:1066 [ref. 13677], Birdsong et al. 1988:188 [ref. 7303], Kottelat 1989:19 [ref. 13605]). Gobiidae.

Oxyurus Rafinesque 1810:19 [ref. 3594]. Masc. *Oxyurus vermiformis* Rafinesque 1810:19. Type by monotypy. Status uncertain, based on leptocephalus, probably of *Conger* (Castle 1969:9 [ref. 12436]). Congridae: Congrinae.

Oxyzygonectes (subgenus of *Fundulus*) Fowler 1916:425 [ref. 1394]. Masc. *Haplochilus dovii* Günther 1866:316. Type by original designation (also monotypic). Valid (Parenti 1981:504 [ref. 7066]). Anablepidae: Oxyzygonectinae.

Ozarka (subgenus of *Etheostoma*) Williams & Robison 1980:150 [ref. 4743]. Fem. *Poecilichthys punctulatus* Agassiz 1854:304. Type by original designation. Synonym of *Etheostoma* Rafinesque 1819, but as a valid subgenus (Page 1981:38 [ref. 3347], Bailey & Etnier 1988:26 [ref. 6873]). Percidae.

Ozodura Ranzani 1839:table [ref. 3605]. Fem. *Ozodura orsini* Ranzani 1839:table. Type by monotypy. Synonym of *Mola* Koelreuter 1770 (Fraser-Brunner 1943:8 [ref. 1495]). Molidae.

Ozorthe Jordan & Evermann 1898:2441 [ref. 2445]. *Stichaeus hexagrammus* Schlegel in Temminck & Schlegel 1845:136. Type by monotypy. Stichaeidae.

Pacamus Rafinesque 1815:82 [ref. 3584]. Not available, name only. Unplaced genera.

Pachycara Zugmayer 1911:12 [ref. 6161]. Neut. *Pachycara obesa* Zugmayer 1911:12. Type by monotypy. Also appeared in Zugmayer 1911 (Dec.):134 [ref. 4846]. *Pachychara* is a misspelling. Valid (Andriashev 1973:547 [ref. 7214], Markle & Sedberry 1978 [ref. 7031], Anderson 1984:578 [ref. 13634], Toyoshima 1985:144 [ref. 5722], Andriashev in Whitehead et al. 1986:1148 [ref. 13677], Anderson & Peden 1988 [ref. 7215], Anderson 1988:74 [ref. 7304], Anderson 1989 [ref. 13487]). Zoarcidae.

Pachycarichthys Whitley 1931:334 [ref. 4672]. Masc. *Pachycara obesa* Zugmayer 1911:12. Type by being a replacement name. Unneeded replacement for *Pachycara* Zugmayer 1911, not preoccupied by *Pachycarus* Solier 1835 in Coleoptera or by *Pachycare* Gould 1876 in Aves. Objective synonym of *Pachycara* Zugmayer 1911 (Markle & Sedberry 1978:22 [ref. 7031], Anderson 1989:223 [ref. 13487]). Zoarcidae.

Pachychilon (subgenus of *Leuciscus*) Steindachner 1882:71 [ref. 4233]. *Squalus pictus* Heckel & Kner 1858:196. Type by monotypy. Synonym of *Rutilus* Rafinesque 1820 (Howes 1981:46 [ref. 14200]). Cyprinidae.

Pachylabrus Gibbons 1854 [ref. 6065]. Masc. *Pachylabrus variegatus* Gibbons 1854. Type by monotypy. Appeared in newspaper, published 21 June 1854. Original not examined. Also appeared in Gibbons 1854 (Oct.):126 [ref. 1610]. Synonym of *Rhacochilus* Agassiz (17 May) 1854 (Tarp 1952:53 [ref. 12250]). Embiotocidae.

Pachymetopon Günther 1859:413, 424 [ref. 1961]. Neut. *Pachymetopon grande* Günther 1859:424. Type by monotypy. Valid (Smith & Smith 1986:588 [ref. 5710]). Sparidae.

Pachynathus (subgenus of *Capriscus*) Swainson 1839:194, 326 [ref. 4303]. Masc. *Pachynathus triangularis* Swainson 1839:326 (= *Balistes capistratus* Shaw 1804:417). Type by monotypy. Regarded as a misspelling for *Pachygnathus* (Opinion 29) and therefore preoccupied by Dugès 1834 in arachnids; replaced by *Sufflamen* Jordan 1916. Objective synonym of *Sufflamen* Jordan 1916 (Matsuura 1980:47 [ref. 6943]). Balistidae.

Pachypanchax Myers 1933:1 [ref. 3105]. Masc. *Haplochilus playfairii* Günther 1866:314. Type by original designation. Valid

(Parenti 1981:473 [ref. 7066], Wildekamp et al. 1986:274 [ref. 6198]). Aplocheilidae: Aplocheilinae.

Pachypops Gill 1861:87 [ref. 1771]. Masc. *Micropogon trifilis* Müller & Troschel 1848:622. Type by original designation (also monotypic). Valid (Chao 1978:42 [ref. 6983]). Sciaenidae.

Pachypterus Swainson 1838:346 et seq. [ref. 4302]. Masc. *Silurus atherinoides* Bloch 1794:48. Type by subsequent designation. Dates to 1838:346; also in Swainson 1839:189 and 306 [ref. 4303] (species added). Type designated by Swain 1882:281 [ref. 5966]. Apparently preoccupied by Lucas ?1846 in Coleoptera (Solier in Dijean 1834 a nomen nudum), not replaced. Synonym of *Pseudeutropius* Bleeker 1862. Schilbeidae.

Pachystomias Günther 1887:210 [ref. 2013]. Masc. *Echiostoma microdon* Günther 1878:180. Type by monotypy. Valid (Morrow in Morrow & Gibbs 1964:374 [ref. 6962], Kawaguchi & Moser 1984:171 [ref. 13642], Gibbs in Whitehead et al. 1984:361 [ref. 13675], Fujii in Masuda et al. 1984:51 [ref. 6441], Fink 1985:11 [ref. 5171], Gibbs 1986:242 [ref. 5655], Paxton et al. 1989:202 [ref. 12442]). Melanostomiidae.

Pachystomus Heckel 1843:1038 [ref. 2066]. Masc. *Cyprinus (Barilius) schacra* Hamilton 1822:271. Type by monotypy. Preoccupied by Latreille 1809 in Diptera; apparently not replaced. Species unjustifiably emended to or misspelled *schagra* by authors. Identical to *Shacra* Bleeker 1860:431 [ref. 380]. Synonym of *Barilius* Hamilton 1822 (Roberts 1989:30 [ref. 6439], Kuang in Chu & Chen 1989:19 [ref. 13584]). Cyprinidae.

Pachytrigla Fowler 1938:110 [ref. 1426]. Fem. *Pachytrigla marisinensis* Fowler 1938:111. Type by original designation (also monotypic). Synonym of *Lepidotrigla* Günther 1860 (Richards & Saksena 1977:209 [ref. 5285]). Triglidae: Triglinae.

Pachyula Ogilby 1898:33 [ref. 5861]. Fem. *Hemipimelodus crassilabris* Ramsay & Ogilby 1886:18. Type by original designation (also monotypic). Ariidae.

Pachyurus Agassiz in Spix & Agassiz 1831:125, 127 [ref. 13]. Masc. *Pachyurus squamipinnis* Agassiz in Spix & Agassiz 1829:128. Type by monotypy. For authorship and date see Kottelat 1988:78 [ref. 13380]. Valid (Chao 1978:42 [ref. 6983]). Synonym of *Lepipterus* Cuvier 1830. Sciaenidae.

Pachyurus Swainson 1839:335 [ref. 4303]. Masc. *Pachyurus linearis* Swainson 1839 (= *Moringua linearis* Gray 1831:9). Type by monotypy. Spelled *Pachiurus* by Swainson 1839:196 [ref. 4303]; technical first reviser not researched. Preoccupied by Agassiz 1831 in Recent fishes. Synonym of *Moringua* Gray 1831 (Smith 1989:65 [ref. 13285]). Moringuidae.

Pacificogramma Kharin 1983:116 [ref. 6258]. Neut. *Pacificogramma stepanenkoi* Kharin 1983:116. Type by original designation (also monotypic). Serranidae: Anthiinae.

Pacu Agassiz in Spix & Agassiz 1829:63 [ref. 13]. *Pacu argenteus* Agassiz in Spix & Agassiz 1829. Appeared first as a name published in synonymy of *Prochilodus* Agassiz 1829; apparently made available by Muller & Troschel 1844:84 (see Kottelat 1988:82 [ref. 13380]) back to Agassiz 1829. See account of *Pacu* Cuvier 1829. Preoccupied by *Pacu* Cuvier 1829 if one follows Kottelat's interpretation. If *Pacu* Cuvier 1829 was not made available before 1961, then *Pacu* Agassiz is available. In the synonymy of *Prochilodus* Agassiz 1829 (if one follows Kottelat 1988:82). Curimatidae: Prochilodontinae.

Pacu Cuvier 1829:309 [ref. 995]. Regarded by Kottelat 1988:82 [ref. 13380] as available from Cuvier 1829. However, *Pacu* Cuvier must be regarded as a name published in the synonymy of *Prochilodus*, and *Pacu* Cuvier [not *Pacu* Agassiz] apparently was not used as an available valid name or senior homonym before 1961 and is therefore unavailable. There were no originally-included species for *Pacu* Cuvier, and apparently none added until Kottelat 1988 [after 1961]. Curimatidae: Prochilodontinae.

Pacu Valenciennes 1847:9, Pl. 8 [ref. 5010]. *Pacu lineatus* Valenciennes 1847:9. Type by monotypy. Apparently not intended as a new name, Spix mentioned. Spelled two ways by Valenciennes: *Paca* in vernacular heading and *Pacu* with species *lineatus* (p. 9) and as *Paca lineatus* on Pl. 8 (names on plates normally latinized). Should be considered in analysis of validation of *Pacu* Agassiz (and Cuvier). In the synonymy of *Prochilodus* Agassiz 1829. Curimatidae: Prochilodontinae.

Padogobius Berg 1932 Masc. *Gobius martensii* Günther 1861:15. Original not traced. See also *Fluvicola* Iljin 1830 with same type. Gobiidae.

Paeneapocryptes (subgenus of *Parapocryptes*) Herre 1927:261 [ref. 2104]. Masc. *Parapocryptes (Paeneapocryptes) mindanensis* Herre 1927:262. Type by monotypy in subgenus. Synonym of *Oxyurichthys* Bleeker 1857 (Hoese, pers. comm.). Gobiidae.

Pagellus Valenciennes in Cuvier & Valenciennes 1830:169 [ref. 996]. Masc. *Sparus erythrinus* Linnaeus 1758:279. Type by subsequent designation. Appeared in Cuvier 1829:182 [ref. 995] but not fully written out in Latin (but as *Pagr.*). Type designated by Jordan & Fesler 1893:517 [ref. 2455]. *Pagelus* is a misspelling (e.g. by Griffith 1834:164 [ref. 1908]). Valid (Tortonese 1973:411 [ref. 7192], Bauchot & Hureau in Whitehead et al. 1986:898 [ref. 13676], Smith & Smith 1986:589 [ref. 5710]). Sparidae.

Pagetodes Richardson 1844:15 [ref. 3740]. Masc. *Pagetodes sp.*. No species named ("a cat carried it [specimen] away ... and ate it.") An available genus name with an original description and figure, but apparently no species has yet been referred to this genus. Perhaps an earlier name for *Cryodraco* Dollo (Fowler MS). Channichthyidae.

Pagetopsis Regan 1913:286 [ref. 3651]. Fem. *Champsocephalus macropterus* Boulenger 1903:3, Pl. 1. Type by monotypy. Valid (Stevens et al. 1984:563 [ref. 13633], Iwami 1985:57 [ref. 13368]). Channichthyidae.

Pagothenia Nichols & La Monte 1936:2 [ref. 3188]. Fem. *Pagothenia antarctica* Nichols & La Monte 1936:3. Type by original designation (also monotypic). Valid (Stevens et al. 1984:563 [ref. 13633], Andersen 1984:25 [ref. 13369]). Nototheniidae.

Pagrichthys Bleeker 1860:60 [ref. 373]. Masc. *Pagrichthys castelnaui* Bleeker 1860:61. Type by monotypy. Synonym of *Sparus* Linnaeus 1758. Sparidae.

Pagrosomus Gill 1893:97 [ref. 1736]. Masc. *Labrus auratus* Bloch & Schneider 1801:266 (= *Sciaena aurata* Forster). Type by monotypy. Called *Sparosomus* by error by Gill on pp. 116 and 123 (see Jordan 1920:461 [ref. 4905]). Sparidae.

Pagrus Cuvier 1816:272 [ref. 993]. Masc. *Sparus pagrus* Linnaeus 1758:279. Type by absolute tautonymy (species mentioned in footnote). Appeared first in Cuvier 1814:92 [ref. 4884] as "Les Pagres". Cuvier includes *S. pagrus* of Bloch 1791 (Pl. 267), which is *Sparus pagrus* Linnaeus. Not preoccupied by *Pagrus* Plumier in Lacepède 1802 [not available] in fishes. Synonym of *Sparus* Linnaeus 1758 (Tortonese 1973:405 [ref. 7192]); valid (Bianchi 1984 [ref. 5159], Akazaki in Masuda et al. 1984:177 [ref. 6441]).

Sparidae.

Pagrus Plumier in Lacepède 1802:293, footnote [ref. 4929]. Masc. *Bodianus vivanet* Lacepède 1802:293. Not available; Plumier manuscript name mentioned in passing in the synonymy of *Bodianus vivanet*. Not *Pagrus* Cuvier 1816. In the synonymy of *Lutjanus* Bloch 1790. Lutjanidae.

Palaenichthys (subgenus of *Trigla*) Kaup 1873:90 [ref. 2585]. Masc. *Trigla aspera* Cuvier in Cuvier & Valenciennes 1829:77. Type by subsequent designation. Type designated by Jordan 1919:370 [ref. 4904]. Objective synonym of *Lepidotrigla* Günther 1860 (Blanc & Hureau 1973:589 [ref. 7218], Richards & Saksena 1977:209 [ref. 5285]). Triglidae: Triglinae.

Palamita (subgenus of *Thynnus*) Bonaparte 1831:173 [ref. 4978]. Fem. *Scomber sarda* Bloch 1793:44. Type by being a replacement name. Appeared as a section under *Thynnus* as "3. *Palamita*, Nob. (*Pelamis*, Cuv. nec. Daud.). Replacement for *Pelamis* [= *Pelamys*] Cuvier 1831, preoccupied by Oken 1816 in Reptilia [Bonaparte regarded as preoccupied by Daudan]. Objective synonym of *Sarda* Cuvier 1829. Scombridae.

Palatogobius Gilbert 1971:30 [ref. 1641]. Masc. *Palatogobius paradoxus* Gilbert 1971:31. Type by original designation (also monotypic). Misspelled *Palatagobius* in Zoological Record for 1971. Valid (Gilbert 1977 [ref. 7041], Birdsong et al. 1988:191 [ref. 7303]). Gobiidae.

Paleatogobius Takagi 1957:117 [ref. 4310]. Masc. *Paleatogobius uchidai* Takagi 1957:118. Type by original designation (also monotypic). Valid (Hoese, pers. comm.). Gobiidae.

Paleolamprologus Colombe & Allgayer 1985:16 [ref. 13457]. Masc. *Lamprologus toae* Poll 1949:41 (Type by original designation (also monotypic).). Cichlidae.

Palinurichthys Bleeker 1859:xxii [ref. 371]. Masc. *Coryphaena perciformis* Mitchill 1819:244. Type by being a replacement name. Replacement for *Palinurus* DeKay 1842, preoccupied by Weber 1795 in Insecta and Fabricius 1798 in Crustacea. Apparently published Nov. 1859 (Fowler, MS), thereby predating *Palinurichthys* Gill in early 1860; but later than *Hyperoglyphe* See also *Pammelas* Günther 1860. Synonym of *Hyperoglyphe* Günther 1859 (June) (Haedrich 1967:55 [ref. 5357], Haedrich 1973:560 [ref. 7216]). Centrolophidae.

Palinurichthys Gill 1860:20 [ref. 1763]. Masc. *Coryphaena perciformis* Mitchill 1819:244. Type by being a replacement name. Unneeded replacement for *Palinurus* DeKay 1842, replaced earlier with exact name *Palinurichthys* by Bleeker 1859. Synonym of *Hyperoglyphe* Günther 1859, proposed about 5 months earlier (Haedrich 1967:55 [ref. 5357]). Centrolophidae.

Palinurus DeKay 1842:118 [ref. 1098]. Masc. *Coryphaena perciformis* Mitchill 1819:244. Type by subsequent designation. Preoccupied by Weber 1795 in insects after action by ICZN (Opinion 519) and by Fabricius 1798 in Crustacea. Placed on Official Index (Opinion 519). For two named species; earliest type designation not researched. Replaced by and an objective synonym of *Palinurichthys* Bleeker 1859. Synonym of *Hyperoglyphe* Günther 1859 (Haedrich 1967:54 [ref. 5357], Haedrich 1973:560 [ref. 7216]). Centrolophidae.

Pallasia Nardo 1840:111 [ref. 3149]. Fem. *Orthragoriscus hispidus* Bloch & Schneider 1801:511. Type by monotypy. Possibly appeared in 1839 with type as *pallasi* (not investigated). Synonym of *Mola* Koelreuter 1770 (Fraser-Brunner 1943:8 [ref. 1495]). Molidae.

Pallasina Cramer in Jordan & Starks 1895:815 [ref. 2522]. Fem. *Siphagonus barbatus* Steindachner 1876:188. Type by original designation (also monotypic). Valid (Washington et al. 1984:442 [ref. 13660], Kanayama in Masuda et al. 1984:332 [ref. 6441], Yabe 1985:123 [ref. 11522], Maeda & Amaoka 1988:80 [ref. 12616]). Agonidae.

Pallidogobius Herre 1953:184 [ref. 2143]. Masc. *Pallidogobius rigilius* Herre 1953:185. Type by original designation (also monotypic). Synonym of *Istigobius* Whitley 1932 (Murdy & Hoese 1985:5 [ref. 5237]). Gobiidae.

Palmichthys (subgenus of *Chirostoma*) de Buen 1945:527 [ref. 691]. Masc. *Chirostoma diazi* Jordan & Snyder 1900:137. Type by original designation (also monotypic). Synonym of *Chirostoma* Swainson 1839. Atherinidae: Menidiinae.

Paloa Herre 1927:56 [ref. 2104]. Fem. *Paloa polylepis* Herre 1927:56. Type by original designation (also monotypic). Eleotridae.

Palometa (subgenus of *Rhombus*) Jordan & Evermann 1896:965, 966 [ref. 2443]. Fem. *Stromateus palometa* Jordan & Bollman 1889 :156. Type by original designation (also by absolute tautonymy). Synonym of *Peprilus* Cuvier 1829 (Haedrich 1967:103 [ref. 5357]). Stromateidae.

Paludopanchax (subgenus of *Aphyosemion*) Radda 1977:211 [ref. 3580]. Masc. *Fundulus arnoldi* Boulenger 1908:29. Type by original designation. Synonym of *Fundulopanchax* Myers 1924, but as a valid subgenus (Parenti 1981:479 [ref. 7066]); synonym of *Aphyosemion* Myers 1924 (Wildekamp et al. 1986:197 [ref. 6198]). Aplocheilidae: Aplocheilinae.

Palunolepis Barnard 1927:69 [ref. 193]. Fem. *Chilodactylus grandis* Günther 1860:81. Type by original designation. Also appeared in Barnard 1927 (Oct.):456 [ref. 194]. Correct spelling for genus of type species is *Cheilodactylus*. Synonym of *Chirodactylus* Gill 1862 (Smith 1986:667 [ref. 5712]). Cheilodactylidae.

Palutrus Smith 1959:208 [ref. 4122]. Masc. *Palutrus reticularis* Smith 1959:208. Type by original designation (also monotypic, second species tentatively included). Gobiidae.

Pama Fowler 1933:360 [ref. 1414]. Fem. *Bola pama* Hamilton 1822:70, 368. Type by original designation (also by absolute tautonymy). Valid (Jayaram 1981:329 [ref. 6497]). Sciaenidae.

Pammelas Günther 1860:485 [ref. 1963]. *Coryphaena perciformis* Mitchill 1819:244. Type by being a replacement name. Unneeded replacement for *Palinurus* DeKay 1842, preoccupied by Weber 1795 in Insecta and Fabricius 1798 in Crustacea, but replaced earlier by *Palinurichthys* Bleeker 1859 (Nov.). Objective synonym of *Palinurichthys* Bleeker 1859; synonym of *Hyperoglyphe* Günther 1859 (Haedrich 1967:55 [ref. 5357], Haedrich 1973:560 [ref. 7216]). Centrolophidae.

Pampanoa (subgenus of *Trachinotus*) Fowler 1906:116 [ref. 1372]. *Chaetodon glaucus* Bloch 1787:102. Type by original designation (also monotypic). Synonym of *Trachinotus* Lacepède 1801 (Daget & Smith-Vaniz 1986:319 [ref. 6207] as *Pampano*). Carangidae.

Pamphoria Regan 1913:1003 [ref. 3653]. Fem. *Cnesterodon scalpridens* Garman 1875:45. Type by monotypy. Questionably a synonym of *Poecilia* Bloch & Schneider 1801 (Rosen & Bailey 1963:44 [ref. 7067]). Poeciliidae.

Pamphorichthys Regan 1913:1003 [ref. 3653]. Masc. *Heterandria minor* Garman 1895:92. Type by monotypy. Synonym of *Poecilia* Bloch & Schneider 1801, but as a valid subgenus (Rosen & Bailey 1963:44, 57 [ref. 7067], Parenti & Rauchenberger 1989:8 [ref.

13538]). Poeciliidae.

Pampus (subgenus of *Stromateus*) Bonaparte 1837:puntata 48 [ref. 517]. *Stromateus candidus* Valenciennes in Cuvier & Valenciennes 1833:391. Type by subsequent designation. Apparently appeared first in puntata 48, fasc. 9 under *Stromateus fiatola* without included species. First addition of species not researched. Fowler 1905:499 [ref. 1369] designated *S. candidus* as type. Valid (Haedrich 1967:108 [ref. 5357], Horn 1984:628 [ref. 13637], Nakabo in Masuda et al. 1984:235 [ref. 6441]). Stromateidae.

Panamichthys Hubbs 1924:8 [ref. 2231]. Masc. *Priapichthys panamensis* Meek & Hildebrand 1916:322. Type by original designation (also monotypic). Synonym of *Priapichthys* Regan 1913 (Rosen & Bailey 1963:120 [ref. 7067]). Poeciliidae.

Panaque Eigenmann & Eigenmann 1889:44 [ref. 1253]. *Chaetostomus nigrolineatus* Peters 1877:471. Type by original designation. Valid (Isbrücker 1980:74 [ref. 2303], Burgess 1989:437 [ref. 12860]). Loricariidae.

Panchax Valenciennes in Cuvier & Valenciennes 1846:380 [ref. 1011]. Masc. *Panchax buchanani* Valenciennes in Cuvier & Valenciennes 1842:383 (= *Esox panchax* Hamilton 1822:211, 380). Type is *panchax* by absolute tautonymy of senior objective synonym, Valenciennes' *P. buchanani* is an unneeded replacement for *E. panchax*. Not *lineatum* as designated by Bleeker 1864:140 [ref. 4859]. Synonym of *Aplocheilus* McClelland 1839 (Parenti 1981:471 [ref. 7066]). Aplocheilidae: Aplocheilinae.

Pandaka Herre 1927:196 [ref. 2104]. Fem. *Pandaka pusilla* Herre 1927:197. Type by original designation. Valid (Akihito in Masuda et al. 1984:275 [ref. 6441], Hoese 1986:798 [ref. 5670], Maugé 1986:379 [ref. 6218], Miller 1987:695 [ref. 6336], Birdsong et al. 1988:188 [ref. 7303]). Gobiidae.

Pangasianodon Chevey 1931:538 [ref. 830]. Masc. *Pangasianodon gigas* Chevey 1931:538. Type by monotypy. Synonym of *Pangasius* (Burgess 1989:105 [ref. 12860]); valid (Kottelat 1985:269 [ref. 11441], Fumihito 1989 [ref. 12578], Kottelat 1989:14 [ref. 13605]). Pangasiidae.

Pangasius Valenciennes in Cuvier & Valenciennes 1840:45 [ref. 1008]. Masc. *Pangasius buchanani* Valenciennes in Cuvier & Valenciennes 1840:45 (= *Pimelodus pangasius* Hamilton 1822:163, 376). Type by monotypy. Valenciennes' *buchanani* is an unneeded replacement for *P. pangasius*. Valid (Jayaram 1977:26 [ref. 7006], Jayaram 1981:226 [ref. 6497], Kottelat 1985:269 [ref. 11441], Burgess 1989:105 [ref. 12860], Kottelat 1989:14 [ref. 13605], Roberts 1989:131 [ref. 6439]). Pangasiidae.

Pangio Blyth 1860:169 [ref. 477]. *Cobitis cinnamomea* McClelland 1839:309, 435. Type by monotypy. Blyth treated *pangia* (spelled by him as *pangio*) Hamilton 1822 and *cinnamomea* McClelland 1839 as synonymous, using the latter name as valid. Synonym of *Acantophthalmus* van Hasselt 1823 (Roberts 1989:95 [ref. 6439]). Cobitidae: Cobitinae.

Panichthys (subgenus of *Peristedion*) Whitley 1933:97 [ref. 4677]. Masc. *Peristedion picturatum* McCulloch 1926:212. Type by original designation. Synonym of *Peristedion* Lacepède 1801. Triglidae: Peristediinae.

Panna Mohan 1969:296 [ref. 3034]. *Otolithus microdon* Bleeker 1849:10. Type by original designation (also monotypic). Correct spelling for genus of type species is *Otolithes*. Valid (Trewavas 1977:306 [ref. 4459]). Sciaenidae.

Panotus Rafinesque 1815:85 [ref. 3584]. Masc. *Taenianotus triacanthus* Lacepède 1802:303. Type by being a replacement name. As "*Panotus* R. [Rafinesque] *Taenianotus* Lac. [Lacepède]." Name only but an available (unneeded) replacement for *Taenianotus* Lacepède 1802. Objective synonym of *Taenianotus* Lacepède 1802. Scorpaenidae: Scorpaeninae.

Pantanodon Myers 1955:7 [ref. 3126]. Masc. *Pantanodon podoxys* Myers 1955:7. Type by monotypy. Valid (Parenti 1981:509 [ref. 7066], Wildekamp 1986:169 [ref. 6199]). Cyprinodontidae: Aplocheilichthyinae.

Pantodon Peters 1877:195 [ref. 3445]. Masc. *Pantodon buchholzi* Peters 1877:196. Type by monotypy. Also appeared in Gill 1877:clxvii [ref. 1715]. Valid (Gosse 1984:59 [ref. 6169]). Pantodontidae.

Pantolabus Whitley 1931:108 [ref. 4673]. Masc. *Caranx parasitus* Garman 1903:232. Type by original designation (also monotypic). Valid (Smith-Vaniz 1984:524 [ref. 13664], Gushiken 1988:443 [ref. 6697], Paxton et al. 1989:581 [ref. 12442]). Carangidae.

Pantonora Smith 1965:(713) 719 [ref. 4132]. Fem. *Ophichthys tenuis* Günther 1870:88. Type by original designation. Synonym of *Yirrkala* Whitley 1940 (McCosker 1977:69 [ref. 6836]). Ophichthidae: Ophichthinae.

Pantophos Jordan & Hubbs 1925:156 [ref. 2486]. *Diaphus glandulifer* Gilbert 1913:90. Type by original designation (also monotypic). *Panthophos* is a misspelling. Synonym of *Diaphus* Eigenmann & Eigenmann 1890 (Nafpaktitis 1968:22 [ref. 6979], Krefft & Bekker 1973:176 [ref. 7181], Paxton 1979:7 [ref. 6440]). Myctophidae.

Pantosteus Cope in Cope & Yarrow 1876:673 [ref. 968]. Masc. *Minomus platyrhynchus* Cope 1874:134. Type by subsequent designation. Type designated by Jordan & Gilbert 1877:95 [ref. 4907]. Valid (some authors); synonym of *Catostomus* Lesueur 1817. Catostomidae.

Panturichthys Pellegrin 1913:117 [ref. 3427]. Masc. *Panturichthys mauritanicus* Pellegrin 1913:118. Type by monotypy. Valid (Blache et al. 1973:228 [ref. 7185], Saldanha in Whitehead et al. 1986:545 [ref. 13676], Smith 1989:52 [ref. 13285], Klausewitz 1989:258 [ref. 13650]). Heterenchelyidae.

Papenua Herre 1935:430 [ref. 2109]. Fem. *Sicydium pugnans* Ogilvie-Grant 1884:160. Type by original designation (also monotypic). Gobiidae.

Papiliochromis Kullander 1977:253 [ref. 2699]. Fem. *Apistogramma ramirezi* Myers & Harry 1948:77. Type by original designation (also monotypic). Genus designated feminine by author. See comments under *Microgeophagus* Axelrod 1971. Objective synonym of *Microgeophagus* Axelrod 1971 (see Robins & Bailey 1982:209 [ref. 6548], Poll 1986:117 [ref. 6136]). Cichlidae.

Papillapogon Smith 1947:799 [ref. 4073]. Masc. *Apogon auritus* Valenciennes in Cuvier & Valenciennes 1831:443. Type by original designation (also monotypic). Objective synonym of *Fowleria* Jordan & Evermann 1903 (see Fraser 1972:11 [ref. 5195]). Apogonidae.

Papillocheilus Smith 1945:230 [ref. 4056]. Masc. *Papillocheilus ayuthiae* Smith 1945:231. Type by original designation (also monotypic). Synonym of *Cosmochilus* Sauvage 1878 (R. M. Bailey, pers. comm.). Cyprinidae.

Papilloculiceps Fowler & Steinitz 1956:283 [ref. 1478]. Neut. *Platycephalus grandidieri* Sauvage 1878:56. Type by original designation (also monotypic). Valid (Knapp 1986:484 [ref. 5683]). Platycephalidae.

Papuengraulis Munro 1964:150 [ref. 3058]. Fem. *Papuengraulis* *micropinna* Munro 1964:151. Type by monotypy. Valid (Whitehead et al. 1988:449 [ref. 5725]). Engraulidae.

Papuservus Whitley 1943:182 [ref. 4703]. Masc. *Therapon trimaculatus* Macleay 1883:259. Type by original designation (also monotypic). Synonym of *Hephaestus* De Vis 1884 (Vari 1978:279 [ref. 4514]); synonym of *Terapon* Cuvier 1816 (Mees & Kailola 1977:32 [ref. 5183]). Terapontidae.

Papyrichthys Smith 1934:93 [ref. 4064]. Masc. *Psenes pellucidus* Lütken 1880:516. Type by original designation (also monotypic). Synonym of *Psenes* Valenciennes 1833 (Haedrich 1967:84 [ref. 5357]). Stromateidae.

Papyrocephalus (subgenus of *Hymenocephalus*) Gilbert & Hubbs 1920:539 [ref. 1638]. Masc. *Hymenocephalus aterrimus* Gilbert 1905:666. Type by original designation. Macrouridae: Macrourinae.

Papyrocranus Greenwood 1963:401 [ref. 1897]. Masc. *Notopterus afer* Günther 1868:480. Type by monotypy. Valid (Daget 1984:61 [ref. 6170]). Notopteridae.

Parabagrus Bleeker 1862:11 [ref. 393]. Masc. *Pimelodus pusillus* Ranzani. Type by original designation (also monotypic). No details for type species located. Family placement may be incorrect. Pimelodidae.

Parabalistes (subgenus of *Balistes*) Bleeker 1865:Pl. 225 [ref. 416]. Masc. *Balistes chrysospilos* Bleeker 1853:94. Type by monotypy. Apparently dates to Pl. 225 in Atlas (1865); corresponding text (pp. 98, 110) not published until 1869; also in Bleeker 1866:10 [ref. 417]. A second species was figured with question on Pl. 231 on same date; type by monotypy (type also designated in 1866:10 [ref. 417] and in corresponding text in 1869). Original spelling of species is *chrysospilos*, subsequently changed by Bleeker to *chrysospilus*. Balistidae.

Parabarbus Franz 1910:8 [ref. 1481]. Masc. *Parabarbus habilis* Franz 1910:8. Type by monotypy. Cyprinidae.

Parabarilius Pellegrin & Fang 1940:117 [ref. 3418]. Masc. *Parabarilius laoensis* Pellegrin & Fang 1940:118. Type by monotypy. Valid (Kottelat 1982:524 [ref. 5400]). Cyprinidae.

Parabarossia Kotthaus 1976:59 [ref. 2672]. Fem. *Parabarossia lanceolata* Kotthaus 1976:60. Type by original designation (also monotypic). Kotthaus based name on "*Barossia* Smith 1952," but Smith spelled the genus *Barrosia*; *Parabarossia* perhaps can be corrected. Synonym of *Grammatonotus* Gilbert 1905 (T. Gill, pers. comm.). Callanthiidae.

Parabassogigas Nybelin 1957:298 [ref. 3235]. Masc. *Sirembo grandis* Günther 1877:437. Type by original designation. Valid (Nielsen 1973:552 [ref. 6885], Hubbs & Follett 1978 [ref. 7017], Cohen & Nielsen 1978:36 [ref. 881]); synonym of *Spectrunculus* Jordan & Thompson 1914 (Nielsen & Hureau 1980:153 [ref. 5585]). Ophidiidae: Neobythitinae.

Parabathophilus Matallanas 1984:558 [ref. 5831]. Masc. *Parabathophilus gloriae* Matallanas 1984:558. Type by original designation (also monotypic). Melanostomiidae.

Parabathymyrus Kamohara 1938:14 [ref. 2551]. Masc. *Parabathymyrus macrophthalmus* Kamohara 1938:14. Type by original designation (also monotypic). Valid (Smith & Kanazawa 1977:531 [ref. 4036], Karrer 1982:15 [ref. 5679], Asano in Masuda et al. 1984:27 [ref. 6441], Smith 1989:503 [ref. 13285]). Congridae: Bathymyrinae.

Parabatrachus Roux 1971:633 [ref. 3830]. Masc. *Batrachus elminensis* Bleeker 1863:98. Type by original designation. Type designated on p. 628. Preoccupied by Owen 1853 in fossil fishes, replaced by and objective synonym of *Perulibatrachus* Roux & Whitley 1971. Batrachoididae.

Parabelonichthys Fowler 1943:57 [ref. 1441]. Masc. *Parabelonichthys kellersi* Fowler 1943:58. Type by original designation (also monotypic). Synonym of *Microphis* Kaup 1853, subgenus *Belonichthys* Peters 1868 (Dawson 1984:136 [ref. 5879], Dawson 1985:126, 128 [ref. 6541], Dawson 1986:282 [ref. 6201]). Syngnathidae: Syngnathinae.

Parabembras Bleeker 1874:370 [ref. 435]. Fem. *Bembras curtus* Temminck & Schlegel 1843:42. Type by monotypy. Valid (Washington et al. 1984:441 [ref. 13660], Ochiai in Masuda et al. 1984:321 [ref. 6441], Knapp 1986:481 [ref. 5683]). Bembridae.

Parablennius Miranda-Ribeiro 1915:3 [ref. 3711]. Masc. *Blennius pilicornis* Valenciennes in Cuvier & Valenciennes 1836:254. Type by monotypy. Appears on p. 3 of section titled Blenniidae. Synonym of *Blennius* Linnaeus 1758 (Bath 1973:519 [ref. 7212]); valid (Springer 1986:751 [ref. 5719], Zander in Whitehead et al. 1986:1106 [ref. 13677], Bath & Hutchins 1986:168 [ref. 5151], Bath 1989 [ref. 13309], Bath 1989 [ref. 13310]). Blenniidae.

Parabodianus de Beaufort 1940:50 [ref. 239]. Masc. *Parabodianus rutteni* de Beaufort 1940:51. Type by monotypy. "Rectification" slip by author and bound between pp. x and xi indicates that this genus was based on a specimen of *Pentapus carinus*, not a new genus of labrids. Synonym of *Pentapus* Valenciennes 1830. Nemipteridae.

Parabothus Norman 1931:600 [ref. 3221]. Masc. *Arnoglossus polylepis* Alcock 1889:290. Type by original designation. Valid (Norman 1934:240 [ref. 6893], Amaoka 1969:120 [ref. 105], Ahlstrom et al. 1984:643 [ref. 13641], Amaoka in Masuda et al. 1984:348 [ref. 6441], Hensley 1986:941 [ref. 6326]). Bothidae: Bothinae.

Parabotia Guichenot in Dabry de Thiersant 1872:191 [ref. 12507]. Fem. *Parabotia fasciata* Guichenot in Dabry de Thiersant 1872:191. Type by monotypy. From Fowler manuscript, original not examined. Cobitidae: Botiinae.

Parabrachirus Matsubara 1943:346 [ref. 2905]. Masc. *Pterois heterura* Bleeker 1856:33. Type by original designation (also monotypic). Objective synonym of *Parapterois* Bleeker 1876. Scorpaenidae: Pteroinae.

Parabramis Bleeker 1865:21 [ref. 407]. Fem. *Abramis perkinensis* Basilewski 1865:239. Type by original designation (also monotypic). Valid (Yih & Wu 1964:115 [ref. 13499], Chen in Chu & Chen 1989:86 [ref. 13584]). Cyprinidae.

Parabranchioica Devincenzi & Vaz-Ferreira in Devincenzi 1939:36 (or 167) [ref. 1121]. Fem. *Parabranchioica teaguei* Devincenzi & Vaz-Ferreira in Devincenzi 1939:36 (or 167). Type by monotypy. Also appeared in Arch. Soc. Bio. Montev. v. 9:167 in 1939 [earliest not researched] . Authorship of ref. 1121 is Devincenzi alone, but see paragraph on p. 37, which might permit including Vaz-Ferreira as a second author. Trichomycteridae.

Parabrotula Zugmayer 1911:10 [ref. 6161]. Fem. *Parabrotula plagiophthalmus* Zugmayer 1911:10. Type by monotypy. Also appeared in Zugmayer 1911 (Dec.):129 [ref. 4846]. Often placed in its own family Parabrotulidae (including also *Leucobrotula*), with possible affinities with the Aphyonidae, e.g., by Nielsen and by Anderson. Valid (Nielsen 1973:548 [ref. 6885], Nielsen in Whitehead et al. 1986:1151 [ref. 13677], Anderson 1986:343 [ref. 5633]). Ophidiidae.

Paracaesio Bleeker 1875:38, footnote [ref. 443]. *Caesio xanthurus* Bleeker 1869:78. Type by monotypy. Possibly published in 1874. Valid (Johnson 1980:10 [ref. 13553], Raj & Seeto 1983 [ref. 6817], Yoshino in Masuda et al. 1984:168 [ref. 6441], Allen 1985:130 [ref. 6843], Anderson 1986:578 [ref. 5634], Akazaki & Iwatsuki 1986 [ref. 6316]). Lutjanidae.

Paracallionymus Barnard 1927:68 [ref. 193]. Masc. *Callionymus costatus* Boulenger 1898:9. Type by original designation (also monotypic). Also published in Barnard 1927 (Oct.):448 [ref. 194]. Valid (Nakabo 1982:90 [ref. 3139], Fricke 1982:73 [ref. 5432], Houde 1984:637 [ref. 13674], Fricke 1986:773 [ref. 5653]). Callionymidae.

Paracanthistius Bleeker 1874:3, 13 [ref. 5110]. Masc. *Holocentrus leopardus* Lacepède 1802:332, 367. Type by original designation. Also appeared in Bleeker 1875:25 and on legend p. 124 (1876) but not on accompanying plate 296 published in 1872 [ref. 4861]. Synonym of *Plectropomus* Oken 1817 (Randall & Hoese 1986:5 [ref. 6009]). Serranidae: Epinephelinae.

Paracanthobrama Bleeker 1865:23 [ref. 407]. Fem. *Paracanthobrama guichenoti* Bleeker 1865:24. Type by original designation (also monotypic). Valid subgenus of *Hemibrabus* Bleeker 1859 (Banarescu & Nalbant 1973:196 [ref. 173]); valid genus (Lu, Luo & Chen 1977:451 [ref. 13495]). Cyprinidae.

Paracanthochaetodon Schmidt & Lindberg 1930:469 [ref. 3940]. Masc. *Paracanthochaetodon modestus* Schmidt & Lindberg 1930:469. Type by original designation (also monotypic). Synonym of *Chaetodon* Linnaeus 1758, subgenus *Roa* Jordan 1923 (Burgess 1978:347 [ref. 700]). Chaetodontidae.

Paracanthopoma Giltay 1935:1 [ref. 1796]. Neut. *Paracanthopoma parva* Giltay 1935:1. Type by original designation (also monotypic). Valid (Burgess 1989:324 [ref. 12860], Pinna 1989:35 [ref. 12630]). Trichomycteridae.

Paracanthostracion Whitley 1933:105 [ref. 4677]. Neut. *Ostracion lindsayi* Phillipps 1932:233. Type by original designation (also monotypic). Ostraciidae: Ostraciinae.

Paracanthurus Bleeker 1863:252 [ref. 402]. Masc. *Teuthis hepatus* of Bloch & Schneider (not of Linnaeus) 1801. Type by monotypy. According to Fowler (MS) this is based on a misidentified type species, not *Teuthis hepatus* Linnaeus; Randall 1986 says based on *hepatus* Linnaeus in part. Valid (Kishimoto in Masuda et al. 1984:230 [ref. 6441], Randall 1986:817 [ref. 5706], Tyler et al. 1989:37 [ref. 13460]). Acanthuridae.

Paracara Bleeker 1878:193 [ref. 455]. Masc. *Paracara typus* Bleeker 1878:193. Type by monotypy (also by use of *typus*). Synonym of *Paratilapia* Bleeker 1868 [?1869]. Cichlidae.

Paracentropogon Bleeker 1876:5, 66 [ref. 12248]. Masc. *Apistus longispinis* Cuvier in Cuvier & Valenciennes 1829:408. Type by original designation. Type of *Hypodytes* Gistel 1848 was regarded as *A. longispinis* by Jordan 1919:235 [ref. 2410] such that *Hypodytes* is a senior objective synonym of *Paracentropogon*, but we interpret Gistel's *Hypodytes* to be a replacement of *Apistus* Cuvier 1829, with type *Apistus alatus*. Also appeared in Bleeker 1876 [ref. 450]. Valid (Washington et al. 1984:440 [ref. 13660], Paxton et al. 1989:446 [ref. 12442]). Scorpaenidae: Tetraroginae.

Paracentropristis Klunzinger 1884:16 [ref. 2625]. Fem. *Labrus hepatus* Linnaeus 1758:282. Type by monotypy. *Paracentropristes* as used by Jordan 1919:358 [ref. 4904] is an incorrect subsequent spelling. Synonym of *Serranus* Cuvier 1816 (Tortonese 1973:355 [ref. 7192]), as a valid subgenus (Klausewitz 1989:261 [ref. 13650]). Serranidae: Serraninae.

Paracentroscyllium Alcock 1889:379 [ref. 81]. Neut. *Paracentroscyllium ornatum* Alcock 1889:379. Type by monotypy. Synonym of *Centroscyllium* Müller & Henle 1841 (Compagno 1984:46 [ref. 6474]). Squalidae.

Paraceratias (subgenus of *Ceratias*) Tanaka 1908:18 [ref. 4321]. Masc. *Ceratias (Paraceratias) mitsukurii* Tanaka 1908:18. Type by monotypy. Synonym of *Cryptopsaras* Gill 1883 (Pietsch 1986:488 [ref. 5969]). Ceratiidae.

Paracetonurus Marshall 1973:615 [ref. 6965]. Masc. *Macrourus parvipes* Smith & Radcliffe 1924:124. Type by original designation. Valid (Iwamoto 1979:146 [ref. 2311], Fahay & Markle 1984:274 [ref. 13653], Iwamoto 1986:339 [ref. 5674]). Macrouridae: Macrourinae.

Paracetopsis Bleeker (ex Guichenot) 1862:16 [ref. 393]. Fem. *Paracetopsis bleekeri* Guichenot (? MS). The single species included by Bleeker apparently was never published in an available way; as name only in Bleeker, and not made available by Bleeker. Subsequent inclusion of species not researched. Cetopsidae.

Paracetopsis Eigenmann & Bean 1907:665 [ref. 1247]. Fem. *Cetopsis occidentalis* Steindachner 1880:47. Type by original designation (also monotypic). Preoccupied by Guichenot in Bleeker 1862:16 (if available), in same family; replaced by *Cetopsogiton* Eigenmann 1910. Objective synonym of *Cetopsogiton* Eigenmann & Bean 1910. Cetopsidae.

Parachaenichthys Boulenger 1902:176 [ref. 561]. Masc. *Parachaenichthys georgianus* Fischer 1885:50. Type by monotypy. Valid (DeWitt and Hureau 1979:782, 789 [ref. 1125], Stevens et al. 1984:563 [ref. 13633], Voskoboinikova 1988:45 [ref. 12756]). Bathydraconidae.

Parachaetodon Bleeker 1874:371 [ref. 435]. Masc. *Chaetodon oligacanthus* Bleeker 1845:520. Type by original designation (also monotypic). Valid (Burgess 1978:275 [ref. 700], Ida in Masuda et al. 1984:186 [ref. 6441], Maugé & Bauchot 1984:463 [ref. 6614], Nalbant 1986:170 [ref. 6135]). Chaetodontidae.

Parachaeturichthys Bleeker 1874:325 [ref. 437]. Masc. *Chaeturichthys polynema* Bleeker 1853:44. Type by original designation (also monotypic). Valid (Akihito in Masuda et al. 1984:269 [ref. 6441], Hoese 1986:798 [ref. 5670] but misprinted *Parachaeturichthyus*, Birdsong et al. 1988:193 [ref. 7303]). Gobiidae.

Parachanna Teugels & Daget 1984:1 [ref. 5158]. Fem. *Ophiocephalus obscurus* Günther 1861:476. Type by being a replacement name. Replacement for *Parophiocephalus* Senna 1924, preoccupied by Popta 1905 in fishes. Correct spelling for genus of type species is *Ophicephalus*. Valid (Teugels et al. 1986:288 [ref. 6202]). Channidae.

Paracheilinus Fourmanoir in Roux-Estève & Fourmanoir 1955:199 [ref. 5324]. Masc. *Paracheilinus octotaenia* Fourmanoir in Roux-Estève & Fourmanoir 1955:199. Type by original designation (also monotypic). Valid (Allen 1974 [ref. 7101], Randall & Harmelin-Vivien 1977 [ref. 5323], Randall & Lubbock 1981 [ref. 5544], Randall 1988:202 [ref. 14253]). Labridae.

Paracheilognathus Bleeker 1863:213 [ref. 397]. Masc. *Capoeta rhombea* Temminck & Schlegel 1846:204. Type by original designation (also monotypic). Also appeared in Bleeker 1863:264 [ref. 403] and 1863:33 [ref. 4859]; earliest publication not established. Valid (Wu 1964:208 [ref. 13503]); synonym of *Acheilognathus* Bleeker 1859 (Arai & Akai 1988:205 [ref. 6999]). Cyprinidae.

Paracheirodon Géry 1960:12 [ref. 1603]. Masc. *Hyphessobrycon* *innesi* Myers 1936:97. Type by original designation (also monotypic). Valid (Géry 1977:587 [ref. 1597], Weitzman & Fink 1983:353 [ref. 5383]). Characidae.

Parachela Steindachner 1881:404 [ref. 4232]. Fem. *Parachela breitensteinii* Steindachner 1881:404. Type by monotypy. Valid (Kottelat 1985:264 [ref. 11441], Kottelat 1989:10 [ref. 13605]); synonym of *Oxygaster* van Hasselt 1823 (*Parachela* based on specimen abnormally lacking pelvic fins). Cyprinidae.

Parachiloglanis Wu, He & Chu 1981:76, 79 [ref. 4809]. Masc. *Glyptosternum hodgarti* Hora 1923. Type by original designation (also monotypic). Correct spelling for genus of type species is *Glyptosternon*. Sisoridae.

Parachirus Matsubara & Ochiai 1963:93 [ref. 2908]. Masc. *Parachirus xenicus* Matsubara & Ochiai 1963:94. Type by original designation (also monotypic). Valid (Ochiai in Masuda et al. 1984:354 [ref. 6441], Heemstra & Gon 1986:871 [ref. 5665]). Soleidae.

Parachromis Agassiz 1859:408 [ref. 74]. Masc. *Parachromis gulosus* Agassiz 1859:408. Type by monotypy. Cichlidae.

Parachromis Regan 1922:251 [ref. 3674]. Masc. *Hemichromis sacer* Günther 1864:493. Type by original designation (also monotypic). Preoccupied by Agassiz 1859 in fishes; replaced by *Tristramella* Trewavas 1942. Cichlidae.

Paracirrhites Bleeker 1875:2, 5 [ref. 12526]. Masc. *Grammistes forsteri* Bloch 1801:191. Type by subsequent designation. Apparently appeared first as above, then in Bleeker 1875:93 [ref. 443]. Type designated by Bleeker 1876:314 [ref. 448]. Valid (Araga in Masuda et al. 1984:199 [ref. 6441], Randall 1986:666 [ref. 5706], Donaldson 1986:624 [ref. 6317]). Cirrhitidae.

Paracirrhites Steindachner in Steindachner & Döderlein 1883:25 [ref. 4247]. Masc. *Paracirrhites japonicus* Steindachner in Steindachner & Döderlein 1883:25. Type by monotypy. Preoccupied by Bleeker 1875 in fishes (same family), replaced by *Isobuna* Jordan 1907. Cirrhitidae.

Paracitharus Regan 1920:209 [ref. 3671]. Masc. *Arnoglossus macrolepis* Gilchrist 1905:12. Type by original designation (also monotypic). Synonym of *Citharoides* Hubbs 1915 (Norman 1934:170 [ref. 6893]). Citharidae: Citharinae.

Paraclinus Mocquard 1888:41 [ref. 3032]. Masc. *Acanthoclinus chaperi* Mocquard 1885:18. Type by being a replacement name. Replacement for *Acanthoclinus* Mocquard 1885, preoccupied by Jenyns 1842 in fishes. Valid (Clark Hubbs 1952:65 [ref. 2252], Greenfield & Johnson 1981:30 [ref. 5580]). Labrisomidae.

Paracobitis Bleeker 1863:37 [ref. 400]. Fem. *Cobitis malapterura* Valenciennes in Cuvier & Valenciennes 1846:67. Type by original designation (also monotypic). Also in Bleeker 1863 (after 24 Oct.):3 [ref. 4859] and possibly other Bleeker papers. Valid (Banarescu et al. 1982:3 [ref. 174], Kottelat 1990:20 [ref. 14137]). Balitoridae: Nemacheilinae.

Paraconger Kanazawa 1961:4 [ref. 2559]. Masc. *Echelus caudilimbatus* Poey 1867:249. Type by original designation. Valid (Blache et al. 1973:242 [ref. 7185], Blache & Bauchot 1976:380 [ref. 305], Bauchot & Saldanha in Whitehead et al. 1986:571 [ref. 13676], Smith 1989:506 [ref. 13285]). Congridae: Bathymyrinae.

Paraconodon Bleeker 1876:272 [ref. 447]. Masc. *Conodon pacifici* Günther 1864:23. Type by original designation (also monotypic). Haemulidae.

Paracoradion (subgenus of *Chaetodon*) Ahl 1923:47, 107 [ref. 5113]. Neut. *Chaetodon ocellipinnis* Macleay 1878:33. Type by monotypy. Described as a section of *Chaetodon*. Chaetodontidae.

Paracottus Taliev in Berg 1949:1330 [ref. 12882]. Masc. *Cottus kneri* Dybowski 1874:385. Type by subsequent designation. Appeared first without species as a quotation in Berg's Addenda and Corrigenda. Subsequent addition of species not researched. Valid (Sideleva 1982:28 [ref. 14469], Washington et al. 1984:443 [ref. 13660]). Cottocomephoridae.

Paracristiceps Herre 1939:321 [ref. 2128]. Neut. *Cristiceps filifer* Steindachner 1864:199. Type by original designation (also monotypic). Treated as in the genus *Cristiceps* Valenciennes 1836 (Shen 1971:697 [ref. 4017]), but Shen indicated that *filifer* may not even be a clinid; type specimens of *filifer* were lost. Clinidae.

Paracrossochilus Popta 1904:200 [ref. 3547]. Masc. *Paracrossochilus bicornis* Popta 1904:201. Type by monotypy. Spelled *Paracrossocheilus* by Jordan 1920:510 [ref. 4905]. Valid (Roberts 1989:57 [ref. 6439]). Cyprinidae.

Paracubiceps Belloc 1937:356 [ref. 251]. Neut. *Paracubiceps ledanoisi* Belloc 1937:356. Type by monotypy. Species misspelled *ledenoisi* in title, correctly *ledanoisi* on p. 356; named for Le Danois. Synonym of *Ariomma* Jordan & Snyder 1904 (Haedrich 1967:91 [ref. 5357]). Ariommatidae.

Paracyprichromis Poll 1986:146 [ref. 6136]. Masc. *Paratilapia nigripinnis* Boulenger 1901:3. Type by original designation. Cichlidae.

Paracypselurus (subgenus of *Cheilopogon*) Parin 1961:167 [ref. 3362]. Masc. *Parexocoetus papilio* Clark 1936:384. Type by original designation (also monotypic). Exocoetidae.

Paracyttopsis Gilchrist & von Bonde 1924:18 [ref. 1649]. Fem. *Paracyttopsis scutatus* Gilchrist & von Bonde 1924:18. Type by monotypy. Synonym of *Cyttopsis* Gill 1862 (Heemstra 1980:3 [ref. 14195]). Zeidae.

Paradanio Day 1865:219 [ref. 1074]. Masc. *Perilampus aurolineatus* Day 1865:306. Type by monotypy. We regard authorship as Day alone, in spite of remark in footnote. Synonym of *Danio* Hamilton 1822. Cyprinidae.

Paradanniops Yen 1978:125 [ref. 13511]. Masc. Apparently not available; see Kottelat 1989:1103 [ref. 14361]. Cyprinidae.

Paradentex Bleeker 1872:Pl. 308 [ref. 4861]. Masc. *Dentex microdon* Bleeker 1851:219. Type by monotypy. Probably dates to Pl. 308 in Atlas vol. 7 in 1872 as above. Subsequently (e.g. Bleeker 1877:95 [ref. 4862]) placed by Bleeker in the synonymy of *Gymnocranius*. Synonym of *Gymnocranius* Klunzinger 1870 (Sato 1986:605 [ref. 5152], Carpenter & Allen 1989:18 [ref. 13577]). Lethrinidae.

Paradicichthys Whitley 1930:13 [ref. 4671]. Masc. *Paradicichthys venenatus* Whitley 1930:13. Type by original designation (also monotypic). Family placement uncertain, not in Allen's 1985 [ref. 6843] lutjanid treatment. Lutjanidae.

Paradicrolene Alcock 1889:387 [ref. 81]. Masc. *Paradicrolene multifilis* Alcock 1889:387. Type by monotypy. Synonym of *Dicrolene* Goode & Bean 1883 (Cohen & Nielsen 1978:28 [ref. 881]). Ophidiidae: Neobythitinae.

Paradicula Whitley 1931:322 [ref. 4672]. Fem. *Synaptura setifer* Pardice & Whitley 1927:101. Type by being a replacement name. Replacement for *Whitleyia* Chabanaud 1930 (5 July), preoccupied by Fowler & Bean 1930 (early in same year). Soleidae.

Paradiodon Bleeker 1865:Pls. 206, 207,212 [ref. 416]. Masc. *Diodon hystrix* Linnaeus 1758:335. Type by subsequent designation. Apparently dates to Pls. 206, 207 and 212 published in part

18 (19 Apr. 1865), corresponding text pp. 49 and 56 published in part 19. *D. histryx* was figured in Pl. 207; type designation dates to p. 49. Synonym of *Diodon* Linnaeus 1758 (Fraser-Brunner 1943:17 [ref. 1495], Leis 1978:538 [ref. 5529]). Diodontidae.

Paradiplogrammus Nakabo 1982:95 [ref. 3139]. Masc. *Callionymus enneactis* Bleeker 1879:95. Type by original designation. Valid (Nakabo in Masuda et al. 1984:344 [ref. 6441], Nakabo 1984 [ref. 5343], Houde 1984:637 [ref. 13674]); synonym of *Callionymus* (Fricke 1982:58 [ref. 5432]). Callionymidae.

Paradiplomystes Bleeker 1862:8 [ref. 393]. Masc. *Pimelodus coruscans* Lichtenstein 1819:58. Type by original designation (also monotypic). Also in Bleeker 1863:92 [ref. 401]. *Paradiplomystax* Günther 1864:180 [ref. 1974] is an unjustified emendation. Valid (Burgess 1989:168 [ref. 12860]). Ariidae.

Paradiplospinus Andriashev 1960:244 [ref. 122]. Masc. *Paradiplospinus antarcticus* Andriashev 1960:245. Type by original designation (also monotypic). Valid (Collette et al. 1984:600 [ref. 11421], Nakamura in Nakamura et al. 1986:274 [ref. 14235], Nakamura 1986:827 [ref. 5696]). Gempylidae.

Paradiretmus Whitley 1948:83 [ref. 4710]. Masc. *Paradiretmus circularis* Whitley 1948:84. Type by original designation (also monotypic). Based on a larval specimen; not Diretmidae. Synonym of *Centropyge* Kaup 1860 (Allen et al. 1976:410 [ref. 13629]). Pomacanthidae.

Paradistichodus Pellegrin 1922:70 [ref. 5028]. Masc. *Paradistichodus elegans* Pellegrin 1922:72. Type by original designation. Type designated on pp. 65-66. Spelled *Paredistichodus* by Pellegrin 1926:163 [ref. 3404]. Valid (Géry 1977:74 [ref. 1597], Vari 1979:340 [ref. 5490], Vari 1983:5 [ref. 5419], Daget & Gosse 1984:209 [6185] with wrong type). Citharinidae: Distichodontinae.

Paradoxichthys Giglioli 1882:535 [ref. 1618]. Masc. *Notacanthus rissoanus* Filippi & Verany 1859:190. Type by monotypy. See also *Teratichthys* Giglioli 1882. Also proposed a species name *Paradoxichthys garibaldianus* for his specimen if it was found to differ from *rissoanus*, but no distinguishing features were given, and *garibaldianus* is unavailable. Objective synonym of *Polyacanthonotus* Bleeker 1874 (Wheeler 1973:257 [ref. 7190]). Notacanthidae.

Paradoxodacna Roberts 1989:160 [ref. 6439]. Fem. *Paradoxodacna piratica* Roberts 1989:160. Type by original designation (also monotypic). Ambassidae.

Paradules Bleeker 1863:257 [ref. 13458]. Masc. *Dules marginatus* Cuvier in Cuvier & Valenciennes 1829:116. Type by monotypy. Synonym of *Kuhlia* Gill 1861 (Maugé 1986:306 [ref. 6218]). Kuhliidae.

Paradules Klunzinger 1872:20 [ref. 2623]. Masc. *Paradules obscurus* Klunzinger 1872:20. Type by subsequent designation. Two included species; earliest type designation not researched; type above as given by Jordan 1919:366 [ref. 4904]. Treated by author as masculine. Preoccupied by Bleeker 1863 in fishes, not replaced. Synonym of *Nannoperca* Günther 1861. Percichthyidae.

Paragalaxias Scott 1935:41 [ref. 3991]. Masc. *Paragalaxias shannonensis* Scott 1935:41. Type by original designation (also monotypic). Second species doubtfully included (p. 45). Valid (McDowall & Fulton 1978 [ref. 7003], McDowall & Frankenberg 1981:569 [ref. 5500], McDowall 1984:150 [ref. 11850], Paxton et al. 1989:179 [ref. 12442]). Galaxiidae: Galaxiinae.

Paragaleus Budker 1935:107 [ref. 683]. Masc. *Paragaleus gruveli* Budker 1935:108. Type by monotypy. Valid (Compagno 1973:29 [ref. 7163], Compagno 1984:440 [ref. 6846], Compagno & Smale 1985 [ref. 5649], Bass et al. 1986:83 [ref. 5638], Cappetta 1987:118 [ref. 6348], Compagno 1988:258 [ref. 13488]). Hemigaleidae.

Paragambusia Meek 1904:133 [ref. 2958]. Fem. *Gambusia nicaraguensis* Günther 1866:336. Type by original designation (also monotypic). Synonym of *Gambusia* Poey 1854 (Rivas 1963:333 [ref. 3761], Rosen & Bailey 1963:90 [ref. 7067]). Poeciliidae.

Paragillellus Carvalho & Pinto 1965:112 [ref. 738]. Masc. *Paragillellus macropoma* Carvalho & Pinto 1965:112. Type by original designation. Synonym of *Dactyloscopus* Gill 1859 (Dawson 1982:19 [ref. 1072]). Dactyloscopidae.

Paraglyphidodon Bleeker 1877:116 [ref. 454]. Masc. *Paraglyphidodon oxycephalus* Bleeker 1877:116. Type by subsequent designation. Type designated by Jordan 1919:384 [ref. 4904]. Also appeared in Bleeker 1877:40 [ref. 452], and if this predates 1877:116 then type is *Glyphidodon melas* Kuhl & van Hasselt by monotypy. Also in Bleeker 1877:387 [ref. 452]. Relative dates of publication not established. Valid (Shen & Chan 1979:64 [ref. 6944], Yoshino in Masuda et al. 1984:198 [ref. 6441], Allen 1986:679 [ref. 5631]). Pomacentridae.

Paraglyptothorax (subgenus of *Glyptothorax*) Li 1986:524 [ref. 6132]. *Glyptothorax pallozonum* Lin 1934. Type by original designation. Sisoridae.

Paragobiodon Bleeker 1873:129 [ref. 431]. Masc. *Gobius echinocephalus* Rüppell 1830:136. Type by monotypy. Also appeared in Bleeker 1874:309 [ref. 437] with type as *Gobius melanosoma* Bleeker 1852:703. Valid (Yoshino & Yamamoto in Masuda et al. 1984:266 [ref. 6441], Hoese 1986:798 [ref. 5670], Maugé 1986:379 [ref. 6218], Birdsong et al. 1988:193 [ref. 7303]). Gobiidae.

Paragobioides Kendall & Goldsborough 1911:324 [ref. 2594]. Masc. *Paragobioides grandoculis* Kendall & Goldsborough 1911:324. Type by original designation (also monotypic). Microdesmidae: Microdesminae.

Paragobiopsis Koumans 1941:245 [ref. 2677]. Fem. *Gobius ostreicola* Chaudhuri 1916:105. Type by original designation (also monotypic). Gobiidae.

Paragobius Bleeker 1873:128, 152 [ref. 431]. Masc. *Paragobius sinensis* Bleeker 1873:128, 152. Type by subsequent designation. Two included species, *P. sinensis* and *Gobius knutteli* Bleeker 1858:16. Earliest type designation not researched. Synonym of *Cryptocentrus* Valenciennes (ex Ehrenberg) 1837. Gobiidae.

Paragoniates Steindachner 1876:117 [ref. 4225]. Masc. *Paragoniates alburnus* Steindachner 1876:117. Type by subsequent designation. Type designated by Eigenmann 1910:441 [ref. 1224]). Valid (Géry 1977:347 [ref. 1597]). Characidae.

Paragonus Gill 1861:167 [ref. 1775]. Masc. *Agonus acipenserinus* Tilesius 1811:422. Type by original designation (also monotypic). *Paragonus* dates to 22 Oct. Synonym of *Podothecus* Gill (14 May) 1861. Agonidae.

Paragonus Guichenot 1869:201 [ref. 1952]. Masc. *Paragonus sturioides* Guichenot 1869:202. Type by monotypy. Second species doubtfully included (see footnote, p. 202). Preoccupied by Gill 1861 in fishes (same family). Agonidae.

Paragonus Miranda-Ribeiro 1918:788 [ref. 3724]. Masc. *Paragonus sertorii* Miranda-Ribeiro 1918:788. Type by monotypy. Preoccupied by Gill 1861 and Guichenot 1869 in fishes, replaced by *Ribeiroa* Jordan 1920. Agonidae.

Paragunnellichthys Dawson 1967:74 [ref. 1064]. Masc. *Paragunnellichthys seychellensis* Dawson 1967:75. Type by original designation (also monotypic). Valid (Birdsong et al. 1988:200 [ref. 7303]). Microdesmidae: Microdesminae.

Parahalecula Fowler 1958:5 [ref. 1470]. Fem. *Etrumeus acuminatus* Gilbert 1890:56. Type by being a replacement name. Replacement for *Halecula* Jordan 1924, preoccupied by Facciolà 1891 [not researched]. Synonym of *Etrumeus* Bleeker 1853 (Whitehead 1985:30 [ref. 5141]). Clupeidae.

Paraheminodus Kamohara 1957:4 [ref. 2554]. Masc. *Satyrichthys laticephalus* Kamohara 1952:2. Type by original designation (also monotypic). Triglidae: Peristediinae.

Parahemiodon Bleeker 1862:373 [ref. 390]. Masc. *Parahemiodon typus* Bleeker 1862:373. Type by original designation (also monotypic and by use of *typus*). For information on type see Boeseman 1976:163 [ref. 6991]. Synonym of *Loricariichthys* Bleeker 1862 (Isbrücker 1980:125 [ref. 2303]). Loricariidae.

Parahollardia Fraser-Brunner 1941:427 [ref. 1493]. Fem. *Triacanthodes lineatus* Longley 1935. Type by original designation (also monotypic). Valid (Tyler 1968:73 [ref. 6438], Tyler 1980:56 [ref. 4477]). Triacanthodidae.

Paraholtbyrnia Krefft 1967:1 [ref. 2687]. Fem. *Paraholtbyrnia cyanocephala* Krefft 1967:2. Type by original designation (also monotypic). Synonym of *Holtbyrnia* Parr 1937 (Sazonov 1986 [ref. 6003]). Platytroctidae.

Parahucho (subgenus of *Hucho*) Vladykov 1963:478 [ref. 4526]. Masc. *Salmo perryi* Brevoort 1856:273. Type by monotypy. Also appeared as new in Vladykov & Gruchy 1972 [ref. 4527] with designated type species, but this was unneeded because when proposed in 1963, *H. perryi* was type by indication (monotypy). Synonym of *Hucho* Günther 1866, but as a valid subgenus (Kendall & Behnke 1984:144 [ref. 13638]). Salmonidae: Salmoninae.

Parahynnodus Barnard 1927:69 [ref. 193]. Masc. *Parahynnodus robustus* Barnard 1927:70. Type by monotypy. Also published in Barnard 1927 (Oct.):525 [ref. 194]. Synonym of *Epigonus* Rafinesque 1810 (Mayer 1974:151 [ref. 6007]). Epigonidae.

Parahypsos Bath 1982:220 [ref. 5640]. *Hypsoblennius piersoni* Gilbert & Starks 1984:191. Type by being a replacement name. Replacement for *Leptoblennius* Bath 1978, preoccupied by Gill 1961 in fishes. Valid (Bath 1987:324 [ref. 6305]). Blenniidae.

Parailia Boulenger 1899:105 [ref. 589]. Fem. *Parailia congica* Boulenger 1899:106. Type by monotypy. Valid (De Vos 1986:38 [ref. 6191], Burgess 1989:99 [ref. 12860]). Schilbeidae.

Parajulis Bleeker 1865:251 [ref. 412]. Fem. *Julis poecilopterus* Temminck & Schlegel 1845:169. Type by original designation. Listed as above by Jordan 1919:335 [ref. 4904] but name *Parajulis* not found in Bleeker 1865:251. Synonym of *Halichoeres* Rüppell 1835. Labridae.

Parakneria Poll 1965:7 [ref. 3526]. Fem. *Parakneria damasi* Poll 1965:9. Type by original designation. Valid (Penrith 1973 [ref. 7143], Poll 1984:131 [ref. 6180], see Howes 1985:286 [ref. 5148]). Kneriidae.

Parakuhlia Pellegrin 1913:1489 [ref. 3401]. Fem. *Parakuhlia boulengeri* Pellegrin 1913:1489. Type by original designation (also monotypic). Valid (Johnson 1980:12 [ref. 13553] in Haemulidae, Smith 1986:508 [ref. 5712] in Kuhliidae). Haemulidae.

Parakumba Trunov 1981:28 [ref. 4468]. Fem. *Parakumba maculisquama* Trunov 1981:30. Type by monotypy. Valid (Fahay & Markle 1984:274 [ref. 13653]). Macrouridae: Macrourinae.

Parakysis Herre 1940:11 [ref. 2130]. *Parakysis verrucosa* Herre 1940:12. Type by original designation (also monotypic). Valid (Burgess 1989:119 [ref. 12860]). Valid, in new family Parakysidae (Roberts 1989:142 [ref. 6439]). Parakysidae.

Paralabidochromis Greenwood 1956:327 [ref. 1894]. Masc. *Paralabidochromis victoriae* Greenwood 1956:328. Type by original designation (also monotypic). Valid (Greenwood 1980:67 [ref. 1899]). Cichlidae.

Paralabrax Girard 1856:131 [ref. 1809]. Masc. *Labrax nebulifer* Girard 1854:142. Type by subsequent designation. Type designated by Jordan & Eigenmann 1890:386 [ref. 2440]. Valid (Kendall 1984:500 [ref. 13663]). Serranidae: Serraninae.

Paralampanyctus Kotthaus 1972:13 [ref. 2671]. Masc. *Nannobrachium nigrum* Günther 1887:199. Type by original designation. Synonym of *Lampanyctus* Bonaparte 1840 (Paxton 1979:13 [ref. 6440]). Myctophidae.

Paralarimus Fowler & Bean 1923:18 [ref. 1474]. Masc. *Paralarimus patagonicus* Fowler & Bean 1923:18. Type by original designation (also monotypic). Synonym of *Cynoscion* Gill 1861 (Chao 1978:34 [ref. 6983]). Sciaenidae.

Paralaubuca Bleeker 1865:15 [ref. 406]. Fem. *Paralaubuca typus* Bleeker 1865:16. Type by monotypy (also by use of *typus*). Valid (Yih & Wu 1964:76 [ref. 13499], Kottelat 1985:265 [ref. 11441], Chen in Chu & Chen 1989:51 [ref. 13584], Kottelat 1989:10 [ref. 13605]). Cyprinidae.

Paralepidocephalus Tchang 1935:17 [ref. 4365]. Masc. *Paralepidocephalus yui* Tchang 1935:17. Type by monotypy. Valid (Nalbant 1963:367 [ref. 3140], Sawada 1982:201 [ref. 14111]). Cobitidae: Cobitinae.

Paralepis Cuvier 1816:xi, 289 [ref. 993]. Fem. *Paralepis coregonoides* Risso 1820:253. Type by subsequent designation. No included species, reference to Risso names. First addition of species evidently by Risso 1820; type usually given as by subsequent designation of Jordan 1917:104, 120 [ref. 2407]. If regarded as not latinized in Cuvier 1816, then dates to Bosc 1817:59. Valid (Post 1973:203 [ref. 7182], Post in Whitehead et al. 1984:503 [ref. 13675], Fujii in Masuda et al. 1984:76 [ref. 6441], Post 1986:277 [ref. 5705], Post 1987:109 [ref. 6225], Paxton et al. 1989:247 [ref. 12442]). Paralepididae.

Paraletharchus McCosker 1974:620 [ref. 2933]. Masc. *Letharchus pacificus* Osburn & Nichols 1916:146. Type by original designation. Valid (McCosker 1977:64 [ref. 6836], McCosker et al. 1989:296 [ref. 13288]). Ophichthidae: Ophichthinae.

Paraleucogobio Berg 1907:163 [ref. 267]. Masc. *Paraleucogobio notacanthus* Berg 1907:163. Type by monotypy. Synonym of *Gnathopogon* Bleeker 1859 (Banarescu & Nalbant 1973:61 [ref. 173]); valid (Lu, Luo & Chen 1977:455 [ref. 13495]). Cyprinidae.

Paralichthodes Gilchrist 1902:108 [ref. 1644]. Masc. *Paralichthodes algoensis* Gilchrist 1902:108. Type by monotypy. Valid (Norman 1934:398 [ref. 6893], Ahlstrom et al. 1984:643 [ref. 13641], Sakamoto 1984 [ref. 5273], Heemstra 1986:863 [ref. 5660]). Pleuronectidae: Paralichthodinae.

Paralichthys Girard 1858:146 [ref. 4911]. Masc. *Pleuronectes maculosus* Girard 1856:155. Type by monotypy. Valid (Norman 1934:69 [ref. 6893], Matsuura in Uyeno et al. 1983:459 [ref. 14275], Ahlstrom et al. 1984:642 [ref. 13641], Amaoka in Masuda et al. 1984:346 [ref. 6441], Pequeño & Plaza 1987 [ref. 6629]). Paralichthyidae.

Paralimanda Breder 1927:86 [ref. 635]. Fem. *Paralimanda inermis* Breder 1927:87. Type by monotypy. Synonym of *Poecilopsetta* Günther 1880 (Norman 1934:387 [ref. 6893]). Pleuronectidae: Poecilopsettinae.

Paraliparis Collett 1878:34 [ref. 885]. Masc. *Paraliparis bathybii* Collett 1878:32. Type by monotypy. Date for genus possibly 1879. Valid (Lindberg 1973:611 [ref. 7220], Stein 1978:37 [ref. 4203], Kido 1985 [ref. 6723], Stein & Able in Whitehead et al. 1986:1280 [ref. 13677], Andriashev 1986:14 [ref. 12760], Stein 1986:493 [ref. 6297], Kido 1988:229 [ref. 12287], Stein & Tompkins 1989 [ref. 12858], Paxton et al. 1989:479 [ref. 12442]). Cyclopteridae: Liparinae.

Paralipophrys Bath 1977:200 [ref. 208]. Fem. *Blennius trigloides* Valenciennes 1836:228. Type by original designation (also monotypic). Blenniidae.

Paralithoxus (subgenus of *Lithoxus*) Boeseman 1982:46 [ref. 492]. Masc. *Ancistrus bovallii* Regan 1906:96. Type by original designation. Misspelled *Paralithoides* in author's abstract (p. 41). Loricariidae.

Paralonchurus Bocourt 1869:21 [ref. 486]. Masc. *Paralonchurus petersii* Bocourt 1869:22. Type by monotypy. Valid (Chao 1978:38 [ref. 6983], Uyeno & Sato in Uyeno et al. 1983:376 [ref. 14275]). Sciaenidae.

Paraloricaria Isbrücker 1979:87, 90 [ref. 2302]. Fem. *Loricaria vetula* Valenciennes in Cuvier & Valenciennes 1840:466. Type by original designation. Valid (Isbrücker 1980:114 [ref. 2303], Isbrücker 1981:56 [ref. 5522], Burgess 1989:443 [ref. 12860]). Loricariidae.

Paralosa (subgenus of *Harengula*) Bleeker 1868:300 [ref. 423]. Fem. *Alausa melanura* Valenciennes in Cuvier & Valenciennes 1847:441. Type by monotypy. Appeared in list as "*Harengula (Paralosa) Valenciennesi* Blkr = *Har. melanurus* Blkr"; which is *A. melanura* Valenciennes 1847. Synonym of *Sardinella* Valenciennes 1847 (Whitehead 1985:90 [ref. 5141]). Clupeidae.

Paralosa Regan 1916:167 [ref. 12509]. Fem. *Alosa durbanensis* Regan 1906:4. Type by monotypy. Preoccupied by Bleeker 1868 in fishes, replaced by *Hilsa* Regan 1917. Objective synonym of *Hilsa* Regan 1917 (Whitehead 1985:220 [ref. 5141]), but see account of *Macroura* van Hasselt. Clupeidae.

Paralosa (subgenus of *Alosa*) Roule 1925:73 [ref. 5090]. Fem. *Clupea fallax* Lacepède 1803:424, 452. Type by subsequent designation. Preoccupied by Bleeker 1868 and Regan 1916 in fishes, apparently not replaced. Earliest subsequent designation of type not researched. Synonym of *Alosa* Linck 1790 (Svetovidov 1973:105 [ref. 7169], Whitehead 1985:191 [ref. 5141]). Clupeidae.

Paraluteres Bleeker 1865:Pl. 228 [ref. 416]. *Alutarius prionurus* Bleeker 1851:260. Apparently dates to Pl. 228 published in part 19 (1865) with type by monotypy; corresponding text (pp. 100, 138) published in part 21 (in 1869). Also in Bleeker 1866:14 [ref. 417]. Correct spelling for genus of type species is *Aluterus*. Valid (Matsuura 1979:165 [ref. 7019], Tyler 1980:176 [ref. 4477], Arai 1983:200 [ref. 14249], Matsuura in Masuda et al. 1984:361 [ref. 6441], Hutchins 1986:885 [ref. 5673]). Monacanthidae.

Paralycodes Bleeker 1874:369 [ref. 435]. Masc. *Lycodes variegatus* Günther 1862:322. Type by original designation (also monotypic). Zoarcidae.

Paramacrurus Bleeker 1874:370 [ref. 435]. Masc. *Lepidoleprus australis* Richardson 1839:100. Type by original designation (also monotypic). Synonym of *Caelorinchus* Giorna 1809 (Marshall 1973:293 [ref. 7194], Marshall & Iwamoto 1973:538 [ref. 6966]). Macrouridae: Macrourinae.

Parambassis Bleeker 1874:86, 102 [ref. 438]. Fem. *Ambassis apogonoides* Bleeker 1851:200. Type by original designation. Type designated on p. 86. Valid (Allen 1982:165 [ref. 5461], Paxton et al. 1989:486 [ref. 12442], Kottelat 1989:17 [ref. 13605], Roberts 1989:161 [ref. 6439]). Ambassidae.

Paramia Bleeker 1863:233 [ref. 398]. Fem. *Cheilodipterus quinquelineatus* Cuvier in Cuvier & Valenciennes 1828:167. Type by monotypy. Appeared above as "*Paramia quinquelineata* Blkr = *Cheilodipterus quinquelineatus* CV.") Synonym of *Cheilodipterus* Lacepède 1801 (Fraser 1972:16 [ref. 5195]). Apogonidae.

Paramicrophis Klausewitz 1955:325 [ref. 2611]. Masc. *Paramicrophis schmidti* Klausewitz 1955:326. Type by original designation (also monotypic). Synonym of *Microphis*, subgenus *Microphis* Kaup 1853 (Dawson 1984:143 [ref. 5879], Dawson 1985:126, 136 [ref. 6541], Dawson 1986:284 [ref. 6201]). Syngnathidae: Syngnathinae.

Paraminous Fowler 1943:68 [ref. 1441]. Masc. *Paraminous quincarinatus* Fowler 1943:69. Type by original designation (also monotypic). Synonym of *Minous* Cuvier 1829 (Eschmeyer et al. 1979:454 [ref. 1277]). Scorpaenidae: Minoinae.

Paramisgurnus Sauvage 1878:89 [ref. 3878]. Masc. *Paramisgurnus dabryanus* Sauvage 1878:90. Type by monotypy. Cobitidae: Cobitinae.

Paramonacanthus Bleeker 1865:Pls. 225, 227 [ref. 416]. Masc. *Monacanthus curtorhynchus* Bleeker 1855:430. Type by subsequent designation. Apparently dates to Pls. 225 and 227 published in part 19 (1865); corresponding text (pp. 99, 130) not published until 1869 in part 21. Also in Bleeker 1866:12 [ref. 417] to which type designation dates. Valid (Matsuura 1979:164 [ref. 7019], Tyler 1980:176 [ref. 4477], Arai 1983:199 [ref. 14249], Matsuura in Masuda et al. 1984:359 [ref. 6441], Hutchins 1986:885 [ref. 5673]). Monacanthidae.

Paramonacanthus (subgenus of *Monocanthus*) Steindachner 1867:591 [ref. 4213]. Masc. *Monacanthus knerii* Steindachner 1867:591. Type by monotypy. Preoccupied by Bleeker 1866 in fishes (same family); replaced by and objective synonym of *Laputa* Whitley 1930. Monacanthidae.

Paramormyrops Taverne, Thys van den Audenaerde & Heymer 1977:634 [ref. 4363]. Masc. *Paramormyrops gabonensis* Taverne, Thys van den Audenaerde & Heymer 1977:635. Type by original designation. Valid (Gosse 1984:107 [ref. 6169]). Mormyridae.

Paramphilius Pellegrin 1907:23 [ref. 3422]. Masc. *Paramphilius trichomycteroides* Pellegrin 1907:24. Type by original designation (also monotypic). Valid (Skelton & Teugels 1986:61 [ref. 6192], Burgess 1989:114 [ref. 12860], Skelton 1989:2 [ref. 14123]). Amphiliidae.

Paramphiprion Wang 1941:89 [ref. 4583]. Masc. *Paramphiprion hainanensis* Wang 1941:89. Type by original designation (also monotypic). Pomacentridae.

Paramyloplus Norman 1929:828 [ref. 3218]. Masc. *Paramyloplus ternetzi* Norman 1929:828. Type by monotypy. Synonym of *Myleus* Müller & Troschel 1844, as a valid subgenus (Géry 1976:49 [ref. 14199], Géry 1977:266 [ref. 1597]). Characidae: Serrasalminae.

Paramyomyrus Pellegrin 1927:297 [ref. 3407]. Masc. *Paramyomyrus aequipinnis* Pellegrin 1927:297. Type by original designation (also monotypic). Synonym of *Hippopotamyrus*

Pappenheim 1906 (Myers 1960:124 [ref. 3128], Taverne 1972:170 [ref. 6367], Gosse 1984:73 [ref. 6169]). Mormyridae.

Paramyrus Günther 1870:51 [ref. 1995]. Masc. *Conger cylindroideus* Ranzani 1840:80. Type by subsequent designation. Type designated by Jordan & Davis 1891:641 [ref. 2437]. Synonym of *Myrophis* Lütken 1852 (McCosker 1977:59 [ref. 6836]). Synonym of *Ophichthus* Ahl 1789 (McCosker et al. 1989:379 [ref. 13288]). Ophichthidae: Ophichthinae.

Paramyxine Dean 1904:14 [ref. 1094]. Fem. *Paramyxine atami* Dean 1904:14. Type by monotypy. Valid (Sato in Masuda et al. 1984:1 [ref. 6441]). Myxinidae: Eptatretinae.

Paramyxodagnus Carvalho & Pinto 1965:107, 108 [ref. 738]. *Paramyxodagnus moreirai* Carvalho & Pinto 1965:108. Type by original designation. Synonym of *Dactyloscopus* Gill 1859 (Dawson 1982:19 [ref. 1072]). Dactyloscopidae.

Paranandus Day 1865:130 [ref. 1074]. Masc. *Catopra malabarica* Günther 1864:375. Type by monotypy. Synonym of *Pristolepis* Jerdon 1849 (Roberts 1989:165 [ref. 6439]). Nandidae: Pristolepidinae.

Parananochromis Greenwood 1987:174 [ref. 6166]. Masc. *Pelmatochromis longirostris* Boulenger 1903:411. Type by original designation. Cichlidae.

Parancistrus Bleeker 1862:2 [ref. 393]. Masc. *Hypostomus aurantiacus* Castelnau 1855:43. Type by original designation (also monotypic). Valid (Isbrücker 1980:58 [ref. 2303], Heitmans et al. 1983 [ref. 5278], Burgess 1989:435 [ref. 12860], Rapp Py-Daniel 1989:236 [ref. 13470]). Loricariidae.

Paraneetroplus Regan 1905:436 [ref. 3622]. Masc. *Paraneetroplus bulleri* Regan 1905:436. Type by monotypy. Cichlidae.

Paranemachilus Zhu 1983:311 [313] [ref. 6667]. Masc. *Paranemachilus genilepis* Zhu 1983:311 [313]. Type by original designation (also monotypic). English summary on p. 313. Valid (Zhu & Cao 1987: 324 [ref. 14139] as *Paranoemacheilus*, Kottelat 1990:20 [ref. 14137]). Balitoridae: Nemacheilinae.

Paranibea Trewavas 1977:370 [ref. 4459]. Fem. *Corvina semiluctuosa* Cuvier 1830:97. Type by original designation (also monotypic). Sciaenidae.

Paranothobranchius Seegers 1985 [ref. 14269]. *Paranothobranchius ocellatus* Seegers 1985. Type by original designation. Not seen. Aplocheilidae: Aplocheilinae.

Paranotothenia Balushkin 1976:122, 124 [ref. 170]. Fem. *Gadus magellanicus* Forster in Bloch & Schneider 1801:10. Type by original designation (also monotypic). Valid (Andersen 1984:24 [ref. 13369]). Nototheniidae.

Paranotropis (subgenus of *Notropis*) Fowler 1904:245 [ref. 1366]. Fem. *Photogenis leuciodus* Cope 1868:164. Type by original designation. Fowler states that the type is *P. luciodus* and also states that *Episema* Jordan, based on *scabriceps*, is preoccupied; contrary to Jordan (1920:507 [ref. 4905]), we do not feel Fowler proposed this as a replacement for *Episema*. Synonym of *Notropis* Rafinesque 1818, subgenus *Hydrophlox* Jordan 1878 (Gilbert 1978:16 [ref. 7042]). Cyprinidae.

Paranthias (subgenus of *Anthias*) Guichenot 1868:87 [ref. 1936]. Masc. *Serranus furcifer* Valenciennes in Cuvier & Valenciennes 1828:264. Type by monotypy. Valid (Smith 1971:84 [ref. 14102], Randall et al. 1989:417 [ref. 12737], Kendall 1984:500 [ref. 13663]). Serranidae: Epinephelinae.

Paraoncorhynchus Glückman, Konovalov & Rassadnikov 1973:1473 [ref. 1825]. Masc. *Salmo tshawytscha* Walbaum 1792:71. Type by original designation. Synonym of *Oncorhynchus* Suckley 1861. Salmonidae: Salmoninae.

Parapegasus Duméril (ex Bleeker) 1870:492 [ref. 1147]. Masc. *Pegasus natans* Linnaeus 1766:418. Type by subsequent designation. Type designated by Jordan 1919:357 [ref. 4904]. Valid (Araga in Masuda et al. 1984:90 [ref. 6441]); synonym of *Pegasus* Linnaeus 1758 (Palsson & Pietsch 1989:18 [ref. 13536]). Pegasidae.

Parapelecus Günther 1889:227 [ref. 2016]. Masc. *Parapelecus argenteus* Günther 1889:227. Type by monotypy. Valid (Yih & Wu 1964:81 [ref. 13499]); synonym of *Pseudolaubuca* Bleeker 1864 (Chen in Chu & Chen 1989:48 [ref. 13584]). Cyprinidae.

Parapempheris von Bonde 1924:11 [ref. 521]. Fem. *Parapempheris argenteus* von Bonde 1924:11. Type by monotypy. Synonym of *Parapriacanthus* Steindachner 1870 (Heemstra 1986:669 [ref. 5660] based on placement of type species). Pempheridae.

Parapercichthys Whitley & Phillipps 1939:235 [ref. 4737]. Masc. *Enchelyopus colias* Forster in Bloch & Schneider 1801:54. Type by original designation (also monotypic). Synonym of *Parapercis* Bleeker 1863 (J. R. Paxton, pers. comm.). Pinguipedidae.

Parapercis Bleeker 1863:236 [ref. 398]. Fem. *Sciaena cylindrica* Bloch 1792:42. Type by monotypy. Appeared in list as, "*Parapercis cylindrica* Blkr. = *Percis cylindrica* CV." Species dates to Bloch. Valid (Randall 1984 [ref. 6067], Okamura and Yoshino in Masuda et al. 1984:290 [ref. 6441], Heemstra 1986:739 [ref. 5660]). Pinguipedidae.

Parapercis Steindachner 1884:1071 [ref. 4234]. Fem. *Parapercis ramsayi* Steindachner 1884:1072. Type by monotypy. Preoccupied by Bleeker 1864 in fishes (same family), replaced by *Neopercis* Steindachner 1884. Pinguipedidae.

Parapetenia (subgenus of *Cichlasoma*) Regan 1905:324 [ref. 3622]. Fem. *Acara adspersa* Günther 1862:282. Type by subsequent designation. Type designated by Eigenmann 1910:476 [ref. 1224]. Cichlidae.

Paraphago Boulenger 1899:76 [ref. 549]. *Paraphago rostratus* Boulenger 1899:76. Type by monotypy. Valid (Géry 1977:91 [ref. 1597], Vari 1979:340 [ref. 5490], Daget & Gosse 1984:209 [ref. 6185]). Citharinidae: Distichodontinae.

Paraphotichthys Whitley 1931:334 [ref. 4672]. Masc. *Gonostoma maderense* Johnson 1890:458. Type by being a replacement name. Unneeded replacement for *Manducus* Goode & Bean 1896, not preoccupied by *Manduca* Huebner 1806 in Lepidoptera. Synonym of *Diplophos* Günther 1873 (Witzell 1973:118 [ref. 7172]). Gonostomatidae.

Paraphoxinus Bleeker 1863:209 [ref. 397]. Masc. *Phoxinellus alepidotus* Heckel 1843:1040. Type by original designation (also monotypic). Also appeared in Bleeker 1863:31 [ref. 4859] and 1863:263 [ref. 403]; earliest publication not determined. Cyprinidae.

Paraphractura Boulenger 1902:47 [ref. 562]. Fem. *Paraphractura tenuicauda* Boulenger 1902:48. Type by monotypy. Synonym of *Phractura* Boulenger 1900 (Skelton & Teugels 1986:62 [ref. 6192]). Amphiliidae.

Paraphya Munro 1949:233 [ref. 3059]. Fem. *Paraphya semivestita* Munro 1949:234. Type by original designation (also monotypic). Synonym of *Gobiopterus* Bleeker 1874 (Hoese, pers. comm.). Gobiidae.

Paraphyosemion (subgenus of *Aphyosemion*) Kottelat 1976:24 [ref. 6566]. Neut. *Fundulus gardneri* Boulenger 1911:261. Appeared first as above, with a description to follow in the same journal, but this was not published (Kottelat, pers. comm., July 1990)]; no description in 1976 and unavailable (Art. 13a). Perhaps can date to Radda 1977:213 [ref. 3580], but needs more study. Synonym of *Fundulopanchax* Myers 1924, but as a valid subgenus (Parenti 1981:477 [ref. 7066]); synonym of *Aphyosemion* Myers 1924 (Wildekamp et al. 1986:196 [ref. 6198]). Aplocheilidae: Aplocheilinae.

Parapimelodus La Monte 1933:226 [ref. 2706]. Masc. *Pimelodus valenciennis* Krøyer 1874:200, 204. Type by original designation (also monotypic). Valid (Burgess 1989:280 [ref. 12860], Malabarba 1989:141 [ref. 14217]). Pimelodidae.

Paraplagusia Bleeker 1865:274 [ref. 415]. Fem. *Plagusia bilineata* Cantor 1849. Type by subsequent designation. Two included species, earliest subsequent type designation not researched; *bilineata* listed by Jordan 1919:336 [ref. 4904] as type. Valid (Menon 1980 [ref. 6798], Ahlstrom et al. 1984:643 [ref. 13641], Ochiai in Masuda et al. 1984:355 [ref. 6441], Heemstra 1986:867 [ref. 5660], Desoutter 1986:433 [ref. 6212], Chapleau 1988 [ref. 13819] as *Parapaglusia*). Cynoglossidae: Cynoglossinae.

Paraplesichthys Bleeker (ex Kaup) 1876:335 [ref. 448]. Masc. *Ancylodon parvipinnis* of Gill (= *Ancylodon parvipinnis* Cuvier 1830:84). Type by monotypy. Not available; published in the synonymy of *Isopisthus* Gill, and apparently never used as valid name or senior homonym. Type as given by Jordan 1919:383 [ref. 4904]. In the synonymy of *Isopisthus* Gill 1862 (Chao 1978:37 [ref. 6983]). Sciaenidae.

Paraplesiops Bleeker 1875:3 [ref. 444]. Masc. *Plesiops bleekeri* Günther 1861:364. Type by original designation (also monotypic). See Hoese & Kuiter 1984 [ref. 5300] and Paxton et al. 1989:525 [ref. 12442] for discussion of problems surrounding the names *Ruppelia, Bleeckeria* and *Lacepedia* as proposed by Castelnau 1873. Valid (Hoese & Kuiter 1984 [ref. 5300], Hutchins 1987 [ref. 12583], Paxton et al. 1989:525 [ref. 12442]). Plesiopidae.

Paraploactis Bleeker 1865:168 [ref. 411]. Fem. *Paraploactis trachyderma* Bleeker 1865:169. Type by original designation (also monotypic). Type designation established in the title. Valid (Poss & Eschmeyer 1978 [ref. 6387], Washington et al. 1984:441 [ref. 13660], Nakabo in Masuda et al. 1984:319 [ref. 6441], Paxton et al. 1989:460 [ref. 12442]). Aploactinidae.

Paraplotosus Bleeker 1862:100 [ref. 393]. Masc. *Plotosus albilabris* Valenciennes in Cuvier & Valenciennes 1840:427. Type by monotypy. Valid (Burgess 1989:180 [ref. 12860], Paxton et al. 1989:225 [ref. 12442]). Plotosidae.

Parapocryptes Bleeker 1874:299, 327 [ref. 437]. Masc. *Apocryptes macrolepis* Bleeker 1851:66. Type by original designation (also monotypic). Misspelled *Parapocrytes* by Jordan 1923:225 [ref. 2421]. Valid (Birdsong et al. 1988:195 [ref. 7303], Kottelat 1989:19 [ref. 13605], Murdy 1989:22 [ref. 13628]). Gobiidae.

Parapoecilia Hubbs 1924:11 [ref. 2231]. Fem. *Limia hollandi* Henn 1916:138. Type by original designation (also monotypic). Synonym of *Poecilia* Bloch & Schneider 1801 (Rosen & Bailey 1963:45 [ref. 7067]). Poeciliidae.

Parapomacentrus Bleeker 1877:65 [ref. 454]. Masc. *Pomacentrus polynema* Bleeker 1853:283. Type by subsequent designation. Also appeared in Bleeker 1877:39 [ref. 453], and if this predates 1877:65 then type is *Glyphisodon bankieri* Richardson by monotypy. Otherwise type designated by Jordan 1919:387 [ref. 4904]. Synonym of *Pomacentrus* Lacepède 1802 (Shen & Chan 1978:237 [ref. 6945]). Pomacentridae.

Parapriacanthus Steindachner 1870:623 [ref. 4218]. Masc. *Parapriacanthus ransonneti* Steindachner 1870:623. Type by monotypy. Valid (Scott 1983:196 [ref. 5346], Hayashi in Masuda et al. 1984:165 [ref. 6441], Heemstra 1986:668 [ref. 5660], Tominaga 1986:595 [ref. 6315]). Pempheridae.

Parapristella Géry 1964:41 [ref. 1582]. Fem. *Pristella aubynei* Eigenmann 1909:24. Type by original designation. Valid (Géry 1977:487 [ref. 1597]). Characidae.

Parapristipoma Bleeker 1873:21 [ref. 434]. Neut. *Perca trilineata* Thunberg 1793:55. Type by monotypy. Valid (Roux 1973:393 [ref. 7200], Johnson 1980:12 [ref. 13553], Akazaki in Masuda et al. 1984:171 [ref. 6441], Kimura 1985:345 [ref. 6262], Ben-Tuvia & McKay in Whitehead et al. 1986:859 [ref. 13676]). Haemulidae.

Parapristipomoides (subgenus of *Pristipomoides*) Kami 1973:557 [ref. 5616]. Masc. *Pristipomoides squamimaxillaris* Kami 1973:557. Type by original designation (also monotypic). Valid (Johnson 1980:10 [ref. 13553], Allen 1985:138 [ref. 6843], Akazaki & Iwatsuki 1986 [ref. 6316]). Lutjanidae.

Parapristurus (subgenus of *Pentanchus*) Fowler 1934:237 [ref. 1416]. Masc. *Catulus spongiceps* Gilbert 1905:579. Type by original designation. Misspelled *Parapristiurus* in Zoological Record for 1934. Valid (Springer 1979:97 [ref. 4175]); synonym of *Apristurus* Garman 1913 (Compagno 1984:257 [ref. 6846], Compagno 1988:163 [ref. 13488]). Scyliorhinidae.

Paraprocypris Fang 1936:707 [ref. 1304]. Fem. *Paraprocypris papillosolabiatus* Fang 1936:708. Type by original designation (also monotypic). Synonym of *Procypris* Lin 1933 (Chen & Huang 1977:398 [ref. 13496], Zhou in Chu & Chen 1989:326 [ref. 13584]). Cyprinidae.

Paraprotomyzon Pellegrin & Fang 1935:99 [ref. 3416]. Masc. *Paraprotomyzon multifasciatus* Pellegrin & Fang 1935:103. Type by original designation (also monotypic). Valid (Silas 1953:230 [ref. 4024], Chen 1980:111 [ref. 6901], Sawada 1982:205 [ref. 14111]). Balitoridae: Balitorinae.

Paraprotosalanx Fang 1934:233, 246 [ref. 1298]. Masc. *Paraprotosalanx andersoni* Fang (not of Rendahl 1923) 1934:246. Type by original designation (also monotypic). Type not *Protosalanx andersoni* Rendahl 1923 (Roberts 1984:205 [ref. 5318]), based on misidentified type species and should go to ICZN. Synonym of *Protosalanx* Regan 1908 (Roberts 1984:204 [ref. 5318]). Salangidae.

Parapsenes Smith 1949:847 [ref. 4080]. Masc. *Psenes rotundus* Smith 1949:307. Type by original designation (also monotypic). Synonym of *Psenes* Valenciennes 1833 (Haedrich 1967:84 [ref. 5357]). Nomeidae.

Parapsettus (subgenus of *Psettus*) Steindachner 1875:78 [ref. 4223]. Masc. *Psettus (Parapsettus) panamensis* Steindachner 1875:79. Type by monotypy. Valid (Johnson 1984:465 [ref. 9681], Smith 1986:605 [ref. 5712]). Ephippidae.

Parapseudecheneis Hora in Hora & Chabanaud 1930:216 [ref. 2215]. Fem. *Pseudecheneis paviei* Vaillant 1892?:126. Type by monotypy. Synonym of *Pseudecheneis* Blyth 1860 (Chu 1982 [ref. 5245]). Sisoridae.

Parapsilorhynchus Hora 1921:13 [ref. 2201]. Masc. *Psilorhynchus tentaculatus* Annandale 1919:128. Type by original designation. Type designated on p. 13, not *P. discophorus* of authors. Valid (Jayaram 1981:132 [ref. 6497]); synonym of *Garra* Hamilton 1822 (Roberts 1989:40 [ref. 6439]). Cyprinidae.

Parapterodoras Risso & Morra 1964:1 [ref. 5940]. Masc. *Parap-*

terodoras paranensis Risso & Morra 1964:2. Type by original designation (also monotypic). Doradidae.

Parapterois Bleeker 1876:296 [ref. 450]. Fem. *Pterois heterurus* Bleeker 1856:33. Type by original designation. Valid (Shimizu in Masuda et al. 1984:316 [ref. 6441], Eschmeyer 1986:466 [ref. 5652]). Scorpaenidae: Pteroinae.

Parapterygotrigla Matsubara 1937:266 [ref. 2904]. Fem. *Parapterygotrigla multiocellata* Matsubara 1937:266. Type by monotypy. Valid (Chen & Shao 1988:134 [ref. 6676]). Triglidae: Triglinae.

Parapuntius Karaman 1971:190 [ref. 2560]. Masc. *Barbus anema* Boulenger 1903:538. Type by original designation (also monotypic). Synonym of *Barbus* Cuvier & Cloquet 1816 (Lévêque & Daget 1984:219 [ref. 6186]). Cyprinidae.

Pararasbora Regan 1908:360 [ref. 3636]. Fem. *Pararasbora moltrechti* Regan 1908:360. Type by monotypy. Cyprinidae.

Parargyrops Tanaka 1916:141 [ref. 4326]. Masc. *Parargyrops edita* Tanaka 1916:141. Type by monotypy. Misspelled *Paragyrops* in Jordan 1920:560 [ref. 4905]. Synonym of *Argyrops* Swainson 1839. Sparidae.

Pararhodeus Berg 1907:160 [ref. 269]. Masc. *Rhodeus syriacus* Lortet 1883:168. Type by monotypy. Valid (Wu 1964:206 [ref. 13503], Coad 1981:2062 [ref. 5572]); synonym of *Pseudophoxinus* Bleeker 1859 (Lévêque & Daget 1984:331 [ref. 6186]). See also Krupp & Schneider 1989:375 [ref. 13651]. Cyprinidae.

Pararhynchobdella Bleeker 1874:368 [ref. 435]. Fem. *Rhynchobdella maculata* Cuvier (ex Reinhardt) in Cuvier & Valenciennes 1831:340. Type by original designation (also monotypic). Synonym of *Mastacembelus* Scopoli 1777 (Sufi 1956:105 [ref. 12498], Roberts 1989:180 [ref. 6439]). Mastacembelidae.

Pararius (subgenus of *Tachysurus*) Whitley 1940:409 [ref. 4699]. Masc. *Arius proximus* Ogilby 1898:280. Type by original designation. Ariidae.

Parartedius Hubbs 1926:3 [ref. 6069]. Masc. *Parartedius hankinsoni* Hubbs 1926:3. Type by original designation (also monotypic). Synonym of *Artedius* Girard 1856 (Bolin 1944:53 [ref. 6379], Begle 1989:646 [ref. 12739]). Cottidae.

Pararutilus (subgenus of *Rutilus*) Berg 1912:40, 43 [ref. 5874]. Masc. *Leuciscus frisii* Nordmann 1840:487. Type by original designation (also monotypic). Synonym of *Rutilus* Rafinesque 1820 (Howes 1981:46 [ref. 14200]). Cyprinidae.

Parasalanx Regan 1908:444 [ref. 3632]. Masc. *Parasalanx gracillimus* Regan 1908:446. Type by subsequent designation. Type designated by Jordan 1920:530 [ref. 4905]. Synonym of *Salanx* Cuvier 1816 (Roberts 1984:206 [ref. 5318]). Salangidae.

Parasalmo (subgenus of *Salmo*) Vladykov in Vladykov & Gruchy 1972:1632 [ref. 4527]. Masc. *Salmo clarkii* Richardson 1836:225. Type by original designation (also monotypic). Appeared first in Vladykov 1963 without designation of type species and therefore unavailable (Art. 13b). Published in an available way as above. Valid (Kendall & Behnke 1984:144 [ref. 13638]); synonym of *Oncorhynchus* Suckley 1861 (some authors). Salmonidae: Salmoninae.

Parascaphirhynchus Forbes & Richardson 1905:38 [ref. 1345]. Masc. *Parascaphirhynchus albus* Forbes & Richardson 1905:38. Type by monotypy. Misspelled *Parascaphirynchus* in Zoological Record for 1905. Synonym of *Scaphirhynchus* Heckel 1836 (Bailey & Cross 1954:174 [ref. 5358]). Acipenseridae: Scaphirhynchinae.

Paraschizothorax Bleeker 1863:262 [2] [ref. 403]. Masc. *Schizothorax huegelii* Heckel 1838:36. Type by original designation (also monotypic). On page 2 of separate. Cyprinidae.

Paraschizothorax Tsao 1964:168 [ref. 13501]. Masc. *Schizothorax oconneri* Lloyd 1908:343. Type by original designation (also monotypic). Preoccupied by Bleeker 1863 in same family. Species originally as *o'conneri*, emendation to *oconneri* mandatory. Cyprinidae.

Parasciadonus Nielsen 1984:39 [ref. 5156]. Masc. *Parasciadonus brevibrachium* Nielsen 1984:40. Type by original designation (also monotypic). Aphyonidae.

Parascolopsis Boulenger 1901:262 [ref. 560]. Fem. *Parascolopsis townsendi* Boulenger 1901:262. Type by monotypy. Also appeared in Boulenger 1902 (May):373 [ref. 5759]. Valid (Russell 1986:601 [ref. 5708], Russell 1986 [ref. 5992]). Nemipteridae.

Parascombrops Alcock 1889:296 [ref. 84]. Masc. *Parascombrops pellucidus* Alcock 1889:296. Type by monotypy. Acropomatidae.

Parascorpaena Bleeker 1876:295 [ref. 450]. Fem. *Scorpaena picta* Kuhl & van Hasselt in Cuvier & Valenciennes 1829:236. Type by original designation (also monotypic). Also in Bleeker 1876:4 [ref. 12248]. Valid (Eschmeyer 1986:469 [ref. 5652]). Scorpaenidae: Scorpaeninae.

Parascorpaenodes Smith 1957:63 [ref. 4112]. Masc. *Parascorpaenodes hirsutus* Smith 1957:63. Type by original designation. Synonym of *Scorpaenodes* Bleeker 1857. Scorpaenidae: Scorpaeninae.

Parascorpis Bleeker 1875:380 [ref. 441]. Fem. *Parascorpis typus* Bleeker 1875:381. Type by monotypy (also by use of *typus*). Valid (Heemstra 1986:602 [ref. 5660]). Parascorpididae.

Parascyllium Gill 1862:407, 408 [ref. 1783]. Neut. *Hemiscyllium variolatum* Duméril 1853:121. Type by original designation (also monotypic). Also in Gill 1862:412 [ref. 4910]. Valid (Compagno 1984:170 [ref. 6474], Paxton et al. 1989:91 [ref. 12442]). Parascylliidae.

Paraserranus Bleeker 1874:3, 6 [ref. 5110]. Masc. *Paraserranus hasseltii* Bleeker 1874:7. Type by monotypy. Also appeared in Bleeker 1875:22 [ref. 4861]. Synonym of *Diplectrum* Holbrook 1855. Serranidae: Serraninae.

Paraserrivomer Roule & Angel 1931:2 [ref. 3825]. Masc. *Gavialiceps hasta* Zugmayer 1911:86. Type by monotypy. Also appeared as new in Roule & Angel 1933:69 [ref. 3827]. Synonym of *Serrivomer* Gill & Ryder 1883 (Bauchot & Saldanha 1973:229 [ref. 7186], Tighe 1989:617 [ref. 13291]). Serrivomeridae.

Parasicydium Risch 1980:127 [ref. 3754]. Neut. *Parasicydium bandama* Risch 1980:128. Type by original designation (also monotypic). Valid (Maugé 1986:380 [ref. 6218]). Gobiidae.

Parasillago (subgenus of *Sillago*) McKay 1985:13 [ref. 5265]. Fem. *Sillago ciliata* Cuvier in Cuvier & Valenciennes 1829:415. Type by original designation. Sillaginidae.

Parasilurus Bleeker 1862:392, 394 [ref. 391]. Masc. *Silurus japonicus* Temminck & Schlegel 1846:226. Type by original designation (also monotypic). Also in Bleeker (26 Nov.) 1862:17 [ref. 393]. Synonym of *Silurus* Linnaeus 1758 (Haig 1952:97 [ref. 12607], Kobayakawa 1989:157 [ref. 13476]). Siluridae.

Parasinilabeo Wu 1939:106 [ref. 4805]. Masc. *Epalzeorhynchus [sic] mutabilis* Lin 1933:84. Type by original designation (also monotypic). Valid (Wu et al. 1977:366 [ref. 4807]). Cyprinidae.

Parasphaerichthys Prashad & Mukerji 1929:216 [ref. 3558]. Masc. *Parasphaerichthys ocellatus* Prashad & Mukerji 1929:217. Type by original designation (also monotypic). Valid (Jayaram 1981:382 [ref. 6497]). Belontiidae.

Parasphenanthias Gilchrist 1922:69 [ref. 1648]. Masc. *Parasphenanthias weberi* Gilchrist 1922:69. Type by monotypy. Misspelled *Parosphenanthias* by Jordan 1923:194 [ref. 2421]. Synonym of *Owstonia* Tanaka 1908 (Smith-Vaniz 1986:728 [ref. 5718] based on placement of type species). Cepolidae.

Parasphyraenops Bean 1912:124 [ref. 232]. Masc. *Parasphyraenops atrimanus* Bean 1912:124. Type by monotypy. Family placement uncertain (Fraser 1972:42 [ref. 5195]). Valid, in Serranidae (Johnson & Smith-Vaniz 1987 [ref. 9235]). Serranidae: Serraninae.

Paraspinibarbus Chu & Kottelat 1989:2 [ref. 12575]. Masc. *Spinibarbus macracanthus* Pellegrin & Chevey 1936:376. Type by original designation (also monotypic). Cyprinidae.

Parastathmonotus Chabanaud 1942:119 [ref. 798]. Masc. *Parastathmonotus sinuscalifornici* Chabanaud 1942:115. Type by original designation. Synonym of *Stathmonotus* Bean 1885, but as a valid subgenus (Springer 1955:74 [ref. 10208]). Labrisomidae.

Parastegophilus Miranda-Ribeiro 1946:12 [ref. 3025]. Masc. *Stegophilus maculatus* Steindachner 1879:25. Type by original designation (also monotypic). Valid (Pinna 1989 [ref. 12630], Burgess 1989:324 [ref. 12860] but may be a synonym of *Homodiaetus* Eigenmann & Ward 1907). Trichomycteridae.

Parastomias Roule & Angel 1931:4 [ref. 3825]. Masc. *Eustomias tetranema* Zugmayer 1913:2. Type by original designation. Type regarded as designated by "...et de former [*Eustomias tetranema*] un type générique distinct, que nous nommons *Parastomias*." Otherwise more than one species after 1930 without type and dates to Roule & Angel 1933:9 [ref. 3827]. Synonym of *Eustomias* Vaillant 1888 (Gibbs in Morrow & Gibbs 1964:377 [ref. 6962], Morrow 1973:138 [ref. 7175]). Melanostomiidae.

Parastremma Eigenmann 1912:20 [ref. 1228]. Neut. *Parastremma sadina* Eigenmann 1912:20. Type by monotypy. Valid (Géry 1977:538 [ref. 1597]). Characidae.

Parastrolytes Hubbs 1926:2 [ref. 6069]. Masc. *Artedius notospilotus* Girard 1856:134. Type by original designation (also monotypic). Synonym of *Artedius* Girard 1856 (Bolin 1944:48 [ref. 6379], Begle 1989:646 [ref. 12739]). Cottidae.

Parastromateus Bleeker 1865:174 [ref. 413]. Masc. *Stromateus niger* Bloch 1795:93. Type by monotypy. Valid (Smith-Vaniz 1984:526 [ref. 13664] who synonymizes Apolectidae (or Formionidae) into Carangidae, Gushiken in Masuda et al. 1984:157 [ref. 6441], Smith-Vaniz 1986:653 [ref. 5718], Yamada & Nakabo 1986 [ref. 6373], Gushiken 1988:443 [ref. 6697], Paxton et al. 1989:581 [ref. 12442]). Carangidae.

Parasturisoma Miranda-Ribeiro 1912:109 [ref. 3716]. Neut. *Loricaria (Rineloricaria) brevirostris* Eigenmann & Eigenmann 1889:35. Type by monotypy. Synonym of *Sturisoma* Swainson 1838 (Isbrücker 1980:93 [ref. 2303]). Loricariidae.

Parasudis Regan 1911:127 [ref. 3639]. Fem. *Chlorophthalmus truculentus* Goode & Bean 1896:61. Type by monotypy. Type designated on p. 128. Valid (Sulak 1977:53 [ref. 4299], Okiyama 1984:207 [ref. 13644], Hartel & Stiassny 1986 [ef. 5471]). Chlorophthalmidae: Chlorophthalminae.

Parasyngnathus (subgenus of *Syngnathus*) Duncker 1915:14, 29, 79 [ref. 6567]. Masc. *Syngnathus argyrostictus* Kaup 1856:33, 46. Type by original designation. Synonym of *Hippichthys* Bleeker 1849 (Dawson 1978:133 [ref. 7026], Dawson 1986:282 [ref. 6201]); as a valid subgenus (Dawson 1985:96 [ref. 6541], Dawson 1986:451 [ref. 5650]); valid (Araga in Masuda et al. 1984:86 [ref. 6441]). Syngnathidae: Syngnathinae.

Parataeniophorus Bertelsen & Marshall 1956:8 [ref. 290]. Masc. *Parataeniophorus gulosus* Bertelsen & Marshall 1956:8. Not available from Bertelsen & Marshall 1956, two included species but no type designated after 1930 (Art. 13b); probably can date to treatment in Zoological Record for 1956, p. 73 (see remarks in Appendix A on Art. 13b). Valid (Paxton 1973:213 [ref. 7183], Bertelsen in Whitehead et al. 1986:523 [ref. 13676], Bertelsen & Marshall 1984:380 [ref. 13657], Bertelsen 1986:406 [ref. 5642], Paxton et al. 1989:385 [ref. 12442], Shiganova 1989 [ref. 14115]). Mirapinnidae.

Parateleopus Smith & Radcliffe in Radcliffe 1912:139 [ref. 3578]. Masc. *Parateleopus microstomus* Smith & Radcliffe in Radcliffe 1912:140. Type by original designation (also monotypic). Ateleopodidae.

Paratheraps Werner & Stawikowski 1987:20 [ref. 13492]. *Paratheraps breidohri* Werner & Stawikowski 1987:20. Apparently not available from this publication as a second species was mentioned and no type designated. Name can date to these authors in 1989:10 [ref. 14232] (Kottelat, pers. comm. July 1990). See also this genus in Appendix A. Cichlidae.

Paratherina Aurich 1935:170 [ref. 150]. Fem. *Paratherina wolterecki* Aurich 1935:170. Four included species; if no type was designated then name is not available from this reference (after 1930 with no fixation of type, Art. 13b) [article not fully translated]. Atherinidae: Pseudomugilinae.

Parathunnus Kishinouye 1923:442 [ref. 2609]. Masc. *Thunnus mebachi* Kishinouye 1915:19. Type by monotypy. Kishinouye 1915 not examined. Synonym of *Thunnus* South 1845 (Gibbs & Collette 1967:97 [ref. 13640]); as a valid subgenus (Postel 1973:469 [ref. 7208]). Scombridae.

Paratilapia Bleeker 1868:308 [ref. 424]. Fem. *Paratilapia polleni* Bleeker 1868:307. Type by monotypy. Cichlidae.

Parator Wu, Yang, Yue & Huang 1963:91 [ref. 12576]. Masc. *Tor zonatus* Lin 1935:308. Type by monotypy. Valid (Wu et al. 1977:330 [ref. 4807], Chu & Kottelat 1989:1 [ref. 12575]); as a subgenus of *Tor* Gray 1833 (Chu & Cui in Chu & Chen 1989:137 [ref. 13584]). Cyprinidae.

Paratrachichthys Waite 1899:64 [ref. 4557]. Masc. *Trachichthys traillii* Hutton 1875:315. Type by monotypy. Valid (Woods & Sonoda 1973:322 [ref. 6899], Paulin 1979:70 [ref. 6918], Scott 1981:125 [ref. 5533], Yamakawa in Masuda et al. 1984:109 [ref. 6441], Paxton et al. 1989:365 [ref. 12442]). Trachichthyidae.

Paratrachinops (subgenus of *Trachinops*) Allen 1977:61 [ref. 98]. Masc. *Trachinops brauni* Allen 1977:62. Type by monotypy. Plesiopidae.

Paratractus Gill 1862:330 [ref. 1668]. Masc. *Caranx pisquetus* Cuvier in Cuvier & Valenciennes 1833:97. Type by original designation. Synonym of *Caranx* Lacepède 1801 (Daget & Smith-Vaniz 1986:310 [ref. 6207]). Carangidae.

Paratriacanthodes Fowler 1934:362 [ref. 1416]. Masc. *Paratriacanthodes retrospinis* Fowler 1934:363. Type by original designation (also monotypic). Valid (Tyler 1968:139 [ref. 6438], Tyler 1980:56 [ref. 4477]), Matsuura in Masuda et al. 1984:357 [ref. 6441], Tyler 1986:889 [ref. 5723]). Triacanthodidae.

Paratrigla Ogilby 1911:36, 56 [ref. 3290]. Fem. *Trigla pleuracanthica* Richardson 1845:23. Type by original designation (also monotypic). Synonym of *Lepidotrigla* Günther 1860 (Richards & Saksena 1977:209 [ref. 5285]). Triglidae: Triglinae.

Paratrimma Hoese & Brothers 1976:495 [ref. 2180]. Neut. *Paratrimma nigrimenta [um]* Hoese & Brothers 1976:496. Type by original designation. *Trimma* is neuter, species *nigrimenta* is correctly *nigrimentum* and *urospila* should be *urospilum*. Gobiidae.

Paratrygon Duméril 1865:594 [ref. 1150]. Fem. *Trygon aiereba* Muller & Henle 1841. Type by monotypy. Valid (Rosa et al. 1987:447 [ref. 5974]). Potamotrygonidae.

Paratylognathus Sauvage 1880:227 [ref. 3889]. Masc. *Paratylognathus davidi* Sauvage 1880:227. Type by monotypy. Synonym of *Schizothorax* Heckel 1838, subgenus *Schizopyge* Heckel 1943 (Tsao 1964:139 [ref. 13501], Mo in Chu & Chen 1989:287 [ref. 13584]). Cyprinidae.

Paratyntlastes Giltay 1935:11 [ref. 1797]. Masc. *Paratyntlastes africanus* Giltay 1935:12. Type by original designation. Gobiidae.

Parauchenipterus Bleeker 1862:7 [ref. 393]. Masc. *Silurus galeatus* Bloch (= *Silurus galeatus* Linnaeus 1766:503). Type by original designation (also monotypic). Valid (Mees 1974:38 [ref. 2969], Burgess 1989:242 [ref. 12860], Curran 1989 [ref. 12547]). Auchenipteridae.

Parauchenoglanis Boulenger 1911:364 [ref. 579]. Masc. *Pimelodus guttatus* Lönnberg 1895:184. Type by subsequent designation. Type designated by Jordan 1920:538 [ref. 4905]. Valid (Risch 1986:33 [ref. 6190], Burgess 1989:71 [ref. 12860]). Bagridae.

Paravandellia Miranda-Ribeiro 1912:28 [ref. 3718]. Fem. *Paravandellia oxyptera* Miranda-Ribeiro 1912:29. Type by monotypy. Valid (Burgess 1989:324 [ref. 12860], Pinna 1989:35 [ref. 12630]). Trichomycteridae.

Paravocettinops Kanazawa & Maul 1967:2 [ref. 5618]. Masc. *Paravocettinops trilinearis* Kanazawa & Maul 1967:3. Type by original designation (also monotypic). Valid (Larsen 1973:231 [ref. 7187]); synonym of *Nemichthys* Richardson 1848 (Smith & Nielsen 1976 [ref. 7084], Smith & Nielsen 1989:452 [ref. 13290]). Nemichthyidae.

Paraxenomystax Reid 1940:1 [ref. 3684]. Masc. *Paraxenomystax bidentatus* Reid 1940:3. Type by original designation. Synonym of *Xenomystax* Gilbert 1891 (Smith 1989:558 [ref. 13285]). Congridae: Congrinae.

Parazacco Chen 1982:293 [ref. 824]. *Aspius spilurus* Günther 1868:311. Type by original designation. Valid (Kuang in Chu & Chen 1989:28 [ref. 13584]). Cyprinidae.

Parazanclistius Hardy 1983:373 [ref. 5392]. Masc. *Parazanclistius hutchinsi* Hardy 1983:375. Type by original designation (also monotypic). Pentacerotidae.

Parazen Kamohara 1935:245, 247 [ref. 5617]. Masc. *Parazen pacificus* Kamohara 1935:245, 247. Type by original designation (also monotypic). Valid (Machida in Masuda et al. 1984:118 [ref. 6441], Paxton et al. 1989:386 [ref. 12442]). Parazenidae.

Parazenopsis Cligny 1909:874 [ref. 850]. Fem. *Parazenopsis argenteus* Cligny 1909:875. Type by original designation (also monotypic). Synonym of *Zenopsis* Gill 1862 (Wheeler 1973:349 [ref. 7190], Heemstra 1980:11 [ref. 14195]). Zeidae.

Parchrosomus Gasowska 1979:404 [ref. 1566]. Masc. *Chrosomus oreas* Cope 1868:233. Type by original designation (also monotypic). Synonym of *Phoxinus* Rafinesque 1820 (Howes 1985:66 [ref. 5274]). Cyprinidae.

Pardachirus Günther 1862:478 [ref. 1969]. Masc. *Achirus marmoratus* Lacepède 1802:658. Type by subsequent designation. Type designated by Jordan 1919:319 [ref. 4904]. Valid (Clark & George 1979 [ref. 6992], Ochiai in Masuda et al. 1984:354 [ref. 6441], Heemstra & Gon 1986:872 [ref. 5665], Chapleau & Keast 1988:2799 [ref. 12625]). Soleidae.

Pardiglanis Poll, Lanza & Romoli Sassi 1972:330 [ref. 3536]. Masc. *Pardiglanis tarabinii* Poll, Lanza & Romoli Sassi 1972:330. Type by original designation (also monotypic). Valid (Risch 1986:34 [ref. 6190], Burgess 1989:68 [ref. 12860]). Bagridae.

Parecbasis Eigenmann 1914:45 [ref. 1230]. Fem. *Parecbasis cyclolepis* Eigenmann 1914:45. Type by monotypy. Valid (Géry 1977:590 [ref. 1597]). Characidae.

Parectodus Poll 1942:351 [ref. 3516]. Masc. *Parectodus lestradei* Poll 1942:352. Type by original designation (also monotypic). Cichlidae.

Pareiodon Kner 1855:160 [ref. 2629]. Masc. *Pareiodon microps* Kner 1855:160. Type by monotypy. Misspelled *Nareiodon* in Fig. 2. Spelled *Pariodon* by Günther 1864:275 [ref. 1974]. Valid (Burgess 1989:323 [ref. 12860]). Trichomycteridae.

Pareiophus (subgenus of *Notoscopelus*) Nafpaktitis 1975:83 [ref. 3137]. Masc. *Notoscopelus (Pareiophus) bolini* Nafpaktitis 1975:83. Type by original designation (also monotypic). Synonym of *Notoscopelus* Günther 1864, but as a valid subgenus (Paxton 1979:16 [ref. 6440], Moser et al. 1984:220 [ref. 13645] as *Parieophus*). Myctophidae.

Pareiorhaphis Miranda-Ribeiro 1918:106 [ref. 3726]. Fem. *Hemipsilichthys calmoni* Steindachner 1907. Type by subsequent designation. Earliest type designation found is by Jordan 1923:153 [ref. 2421] as *Hemipsilichthys calmoni* Ribeiro. *Hemipsilichthys duseni* was designated type by Gosline 1947:102 [ref. 1857]. Although confusing, apparently *calmoni* of Miranda-Ribeiro is *calmoni* Steindachner, but more research needed. Treated as valid by Isbrücker 1980:13 [ref. 2303] and Burgess 1989:430 [ref. 12860] but with type as *duseni*; *calmoni* placed by Isbrücker in *Hemispilichthys*. Loricariidae.

Pareiorhina Gosline 1947:104 [ref. 1857]. Fem. *Rhinelepis rudolphi* Miranda-Ribeiro 1911:84. Type by original designation (also monotypic). Valid (Isbrücker 1980:15 [ref. 2303], Burgess 1989:430 [ref. 12860]). Loricariidae.

Paremblemaria Longley 1927:222 [ref. 5630]. Fem. *Paremblemaria aspera* Longley 1927:224. Type by original designation (also monotypic). Synonym of *Acanthemblemaria* Metzelaar 1919 (Stephens 1963:27 [ref. 4270]); as a valid subgenus (Acero P. 1984:41 [ref. 5534]). Chaenopsidae.

Parenchelyurus Springer 1972:12 [ref. 4178]. Masc. *Enchelyurus hepburni* Snyder 1908:110. Type by original designation (also monotypic). Valid (Yoshino in Masuda et al. 1984:296 [ref. 6441], Springer 1985:91 [ref. 6107]). Blenniidae.

Parenophrys Taranetz 1941:433 [ref. 5535]. Fem. *Cottus bubalis* Euphrasen 1786:65. Type by original designation. Objective synonym of *Taurulus* Gracianov 1907 (Neyelov 1973:600 [ref. 7219], Neyelov 1979:149 [ref. 3152]). Cottidae.

Parephippus Gill 1861:165 [ref. 1775]. Masc. *Ephippus gigas* Cuvier 1829:191. Type by original designation. Synonym of *Chaetodipterus* Lacepède 1802 (Desoutter 1986:340 [ref. 6212] but with wrong type). Ephippidae.

Parepinephelus Bleeker 1874:3 [ref. 5110]. Masc. *Serranus acutirostris* Cuvier in Cuvier & Valenciennes 1828:286. Type by original designation (also monotypic). Synonym of *Mycteroperca*

Gill 1862 (Smith 1971:171 [ref. 14102]). Serranidae: Epinephelinae.

Parepiplatys (subgenus of *Epiplatys*) Clausen 1967:28 [ref. 5926]. *Haplochilus grahami* Boulenger 1911:267. Type by original designation. Synonym of *Epiplatys* Gill 1862 (Parenti 1981:475 [ref. 7066], Wildekamp et al. 1986:244 [ref. 6198]). Aplocheilidae: Aplocheilinae.

Pareques Gill in Goode 1876:50 [ref. 1832]. Masc. *Grammistes acuminatus* Bloch & Schneider 1801:184. Type by monotypy. Valid (Chao 1978:28 [ref. 6983], Yueno & Sato in Uyeno et al. 1983:363 [ref. 14275], Miller & Woods 1988 [ref. 6633]). Sciaenidae.

Parequula Steindachner 1879:8 [ref. 4228]. Fem. *Parequula bicornis* Steindachner 1879:8. Type by monotypy. Gerreidae.

Paretroplus Bleeker 1868:311 [ref. 424]. Masc. *Paretroplus damii* Bleeker 1868:313. Type by monotypy. Cichlidae.

Pareuchiloglanis Pellegrin 1936:245 [ref. 3415]. Masc. *Pareuchiloglanis poilanei* Pellegrin 1936:246. Type by monotypy. Valid (Chu 1981:27, 30 [ref. 5249], Wu 1987:109 [ref. 12824], Kottelat 1989:15 [ref. 13605]). Sisoridae.

Pareustomias Bailly 1930:378 [ref. 163]. Masc. *Pareustomias chabanaudi* Bailly 1930:378. Type by monotypy. Synonym of *Eustomias* Vaillant 1888 (Gibbs in Morrow & Gibbs 1964:377 [ref. 6962], Morrow 1973:137 [ref. 7175]). Melanostomiidae.

Pareutropius Regan 1920:105 [ref. 3670]. Masc. *Pareutropius micristius* Regan 1920:105. Type by monotypy. Wrongly treated as a synonym of the later *Eutropiellus* Nichols & La Monte 1933, but as a valid subgenus (De Vos 1986:36 [ref. 6191]). Schilbeidae.

Parexocoetoides Fowler 1944:420 [ref. 1448]. Masc. *Parexocoetoides vanderbilti* Fowler 1944:421. Type by original designation (also monotypic). Synonym of *Cypselurus* Swainson 1838. Exocoetidae.

Parexocoetus Bleeker 1866:126 [ref. 418]. Masc. *Exocoetus mento* Valenciennes in Cuvier & Valenciennes 1847:124. Type by monotypy. A second species (*Exocoetus acutus* Valenciennes) somewhat doubtfully included. Valid (Parin 1973:266 [ref. 7191], Collette et al. 1984:338 [ref. 11422], Yoshino in Masuda et al. 1984:80 [ref. 6441], Parin in Whitehead et al. 1986:618 [ref. 13676], Heemstra & Parin 1986:395 [ref. 6293], Paxton et al. 1989:334 [ref. 12442]). Exocoetidae.

Parexoglossum Hubbs 1931:4 [ref. 2241]. Neut. *Parexoglossum laurae* Hubbs 1931:7. Type by original designation (also monotypic). *Exoglossops* Hubbs in Osburn, Wickliff & Trautman 1930:173 [ref. 5943] is a nomen nudum (and also apparently preoccupied). Synonym of *Exoglossum* Rafinesque 1818. Cyprinidae.

Parexostoma Regan 1905:182 [ref. 3625]. Neut. *Exostoma stoliczkae* Day 1876:782. Type by subsequent designation. Type apparently designated first by Jordan 1920:515 [ref. 4905]. Sisoridae.

Parhaplodactylus Thominot 1883:140 [ref. 4385]. Masc. *Haplodactylus lophodon* Günther 1859:435. Type by subsequent designation. Type apparently designated first by Jordan 1920:426 [ref. 4905]. Correct spelling for genus of type species is *Aplodactylus*. Objective synonym of *Crinodus* Gill 1862. Aplodactylidae.

Parhomaloptera Vaillant 1902:129 [ref. 4490]. Fem. *Parhomaloptera obscura* Vaillant 1902:130. Type by monotypy. Valid (Silas 1953:225 [ref. 4024]). Balitoridae: Balitorinae.

Pariah Böhlke 1969:2 [ref. 5128]. Masc. *Pariah scotius* Böhlke 1969:3. Type by original designation (also monotypic). Valid (Birdsong et al. 1988:189 [ref. 7303]). Gobiidae.

Paricelinus Eigenmann & Eigenmann 1889:130 [ref. 1251]. Masc. *Paricelinus hopliticus* Eigenmann & Eigenmann 1889:131. Type by monotypy. Valid (Bolin 1944:11 [ref. 6379], Washington et al. 1984:443 [ref. 13660]). Cottidae.

Parika Whitley 1955:111 [ref. 4722]. Fem. *Balistes scaber* Bloch & Schneider 1801:477. Type by original designation (also monotypic). Valid (Aboussouan & Leis 1984:452 [ref. 13661]). Monacanthidae.

Parinoberyx Kotlyar 1984:1592 [ref. 6644]. *Parinoberyx horridus* Kotlyar 1984:1592. Type by original designation (also monotypic). Trachichthyidae.

Parioglossus Regan 1912:302 [ref. 3643]. Masc. *Parioglossus taeniatus* Regan 1912:302. Type by monotypy. Misspelled *Pariglossus* by authors. Valid (Yoshino & Senou in Masuda et al. 1984:247 [ref. 6441], Rennis & Hoese 1985 [ref. 5859], Birdsong et al. 1988:200 [ref. 7303], Kottelat 1989:19 [ref. 13605]). Microdesmidae: Ptereleotrinae.

Pariolanthus (subgenus of *Lepidaplois*) Smith 1968:343 [ref. 4142]. Masc. *Lepidaplois (Pariolanthus) grandisquamis* Smith 1968:343. Type by original designation (also monotypic). Labridae.

Pariolius Cope 1872:289 [ref. 921]. Masc. *Pariolius armillatus* Cope 1872:289. Type by monotypy. Synonym of *Heptapterus* Bleeker 1858 (Mees 1974:177 [ref. 2969]); valid (Stewart 1986:47 [ref. 5777], Stewart 1986:669 [ref. 5211], Buckup 1988:642 [ref. 6635]). Pimelodidae.

Paristiopterus Bleeker 1876:268 [ref. 447]. Masc. *Richardsonia insignis* Castelnau 1872:112. Type by being a replacement name. Replacement for *Richardsonia* Castelnau 1872, preoccupied by Steindachner 1866 in fishes. Valid (Hardy 1983:188 [ref. 5385]). Pentacerotidae.

Parkia (subgenus of *Lutianus*) Fowler 1904:525 [ref. 1367]. Fem. *Lutianus furvicaudatus* Fowler 1904:525. Type by original designation. Synonym of *Lutjanus* Bloch 1790 (Allen 1985:33 [ref. 6843], Allen & Talbot 1985:8 [ref. 6491]). Lutjanidae.

Parkraemeria Whitley 1951:402 [ref. 4715]. Fem. *Parkraemeria ornata* Whitley 1951:403. Type by original designation (also monotypic). Valid (Hayashi in Masuda et al. 1984:287 [ref. 6441], Birdsong et al. 1988:193 [ref. 7303]). Gobiidae.

Parluciosoma Howes 1980:183, 194 [ref. 2223]. Neut. *Leuciscus argyrotaenia* Bleeker 1850:21. Type by original designation. Valid (Kottelat 1985:265 [ref. 11441]); synonym of *Rasbora* Bleeker 1859 (Roberts 1989:66 [ref. 6439]). Cyprinidae.

Parma Günther 1862:57 [ref. 1969]. Fem. *Parma microlepis* Günther 1862:57. Type by subsequent designation. Type designated by Jordan 1919:318 [ref. 4904]. Valid (Allen 1975:187 [ref. 97], Allen & Hoese 1975 [ref. 7097], Hensley 1986:857 [ref. 5734], Allen 1987 [ref. 6250]). Pomacentridae.

Parmaturus Garman 1906:203 [ref. 1542]. Masc. *Parmaturus pilosus* Garman 1906:204. Type by subsequent designation. Type designated by Jordan 1920:518 [ref. 4905]. Valid (Nakaya 1975:57 [ref. 7083], Springer 1979:99 [ref. 4175], Compagno 1984:339 [ref. 6846], Nakaya in Masuda et al. 1984:4 [ref. 6441], Compagno 1988:157 [ref. 13488]). Scyliorhinidae.

Parochusus Whitley 1930:16 [ref. 4671]. Masc. *Gerres profundus* Macleay 1878:350. Type by original designation. Synonym of *Gerres* Quoy & Gaimard 1824 (Roux 1986:325 [ref. 6209]). Leiognathidae.

Parocosia (subgenus of *Amblyapistus*) Whitley 1958:45 [ref. 4728].

Fem. *Amblyapistus (Parocosia) slacksmithi* Whitley 1958:45. Type by original designation (also monotypic). Scorpaenidae: Tetraroginae.

Parodax Scott 1976:367 [ref. 3996]. Masc. *Parodax caninis* Scott 1976:367. Type by original designation (also monotypic). Synonym of *Siphonognathus* Richardson 1858 (Gomon & Paxton 1986:41 [ref. 5656] with type as *caninus*). Odacidae.

Parodon Valenciennes in Cuvier & Valenciennes 1849:50 [ref. 1014]. Masc. *Parodon suborbitale* Valenciennes in Cuvier & Valenciennes 1849:51. Type by monotypy. Valid (Roberts 1974:433 [ref. 6872], Géry 1977:202 [ref. 1597], Vari 1983:5 [ref. 5419], Géry et al. 1987:406 [ref. 6001]). Hemiodontidae: Parodontinae.

Parodontops Schultz & Miles 1943:251 [ref. 3976]. Masc. *Parodon ecuadoriensis* Eigenmann & Henn in Eigenmann, Henn & Wilson 1914:12. Type by original designation (also monotypic). Synonym of *Parodon* Valenciennes 1849, but as a valid subgenus (Géry 1977:207 [ref. 1597]); synonym of *Saccodon* Kner 1863 (Roberts 1974:433 [ref. 6872]). Hemiodontidae: Parodontinae.

Paroligosarcus (subgenus of *Oligosarcus*) Amaral Campos & Trewavas 1949:157 [ref. 108]. Masc. *Oligosarcus pintoi* Amaral Campos 1945:456. Type by monotypy. Valid (Géry 1977:323 [ref. 1597]). Characidae.

Parona Berg 1895:39 [ref. 261]. Fem. *Paropsis signata* Jenyns 1841:66. Type by being a replacement name. Replacement for *Paropsis* Jenyns 1842, preoccupied by Olivier 1807 in Coleoptera. Valid (Smith-Vaniz & Staiger 1973:225 [ref. 7106], Smith-Vaniz 1984:524 [ref. 13664], Nakamura in Nakamura et al. 1986 [ref. 14235]). Carangidae.

Paroncheilus Smith 1964:621 [ref. 4130]. Masc. *Paroncheilus stauchi* Smith 1964:621. Type by original designation (also monotypic). Synonym of *Apogon* Lacepède 1801, but as a valid subgenus (Fraser & Lachner 1985:4 [ref. 5215]). Apogonidae.

Paroneirodes Alcock 1890:206 [ref. 82]. Masc. *Paroneirodes glomerulosus* Alcock 1890:206. Type by monotypy. Valid (Maul 1973:669 [ref. 7171]); synonym of *Diceratias* Günther 1887 (Uwate 1979:138 [ref. 7015]). Wrongly as a synonym of *Phrynichthys* Pietschmann 1926 (Bertelsen in Whitehead et al. 1986:1381 [ref. 13677]). Diceratiidae.

Paronescodes Smith 1958:177 [ref. 4120]. Masc. *Paronescodes asperrimus* Smith 1958:177. Type by original designation, second species included as possible senior synonym of type. Synonym of *Scorpaenodes* Bleeker 1857. Scorpaenidae: Scorpaeninae.

Parophidion Tortonese 1954:376 [ref. 4416]. Neut. *Ophidion vassali* Risso 1810:97. Type by original designation (also monotypic). Valid (Nielsen 1973:554 [ref. 6885], Cohen & Nielsen 1978:17 [ref. 881], Nielsen in Whitehead et al. 1986:1165 [ref. 13677]). Ophidiidae: Ophidiinae.

Parophiocephalus Popta 1905:184 [ref. 3549]. Masc. *Parophiocephalus unimaculatus* Popta 1905:184. Type by monotypy. Synonym of *Betta* Bleeker 1850 (Roberts 1989:171 [ref. 6439]). Belontiidae.

Parophiocephalus (subgenus of *Ophiocephalus*) Senna 1924:156 [ref. 4005]. Masc. *Ophiocephalus obscurus* Günther 1861:476. Type by subsequent designation. Apparently 3 included species (article not translated), with genus established for *obscurus* but type not designated. Preoccupied by Popta 1905 in fishes; replaced by *Parachanna* Teugels & Daget 1984 (see Teugels et al. 1986:288 [ref. 6202]). Correct spelling of genus of type species is *Ophicephalus*. Channidae.

Parophrys Girard 1854:139 [ref. 1817]. Fem. *Parophrys vetulus* Girard 1854:140. Type by monotypy. Valid (Norman 1934:328 [ref. 6893], Ahlstrom et al. 1984:643 [ref. 13641]); synonym of *Pleuronectes* Linnaeus 1758 (Sakamoto 1984:95 [ref. 5273]). Pleuronectidae: Pleuronectinae.

Paropsis Jenyns 1841:65 [ref. 2344]. Fem. *Paropsis signata* Jenyns 1841:66. Type by monotypy. Preoccupied by Olivier 1907 in Coleoptera, replaced by *Parona* Berg 1895. Objective synonym of *Parona* Berg 1895 (Smith-Vaniz & Staiger 1973:225 [ref. 7106]). Carangidae.

Paroreoglanis Pellegrin 1936:244 [ref. 3415]. Masc. *Paroreoglanis delacouri* Pellegrin 1936:244. Type by monotypy. Sisoridae.

Parosphromenus Bleeker 1879:19 [ref. 457]. Masc. *Osphromenus deissneri* Bleeker 1859:361, 376, 377. Type by monotypy. Correct spelling for genus of type species is *Osphronemus*. Valid (Kottelat 1989:20 [ref. 13605], Roberts 1989:174 [ref. 6439]). Belontiidae.

Parosteobrama Tchang 1930:50 [ref. 4366]. Fem. *Parosteobrama pellegrini* Tchang 1930:50. Type by monotypy. Cyprinidae.

Parotocinclus Eigenmann & Eigenmann 1889:41 [ref. 1253]. Masc. *Otocinclus maculicauda* Steindachner 1877:223. Type by monotypy. Valid (Isbrücker 1980:80 [ref. 2303], Schaefer 1988 [ref. 6236], Garavello 1988 [ref. 6853], Burgess 1989:438 [ref. 12860]). Loricariidae.

Paroxyurichthys Bleeker 1876:140 [ref. 449]. Masc. *Paroxyurichthys typus* Bleeker 1876:140. Type by monotypy (also by use of *typus*). Synonym of *Gobionellus* Girard 1858 (Maugé 1986 [ref. 6218]), but see *Ctenogobius*. Gobiidae.

Parrella Ginsburg 1938:116 [ref. 1802]. Fem. *Parrella maxillaris* Ginsburg 1938:116. Type by original designation (also monotypic). Valid (Birdsong et al. 1988:191 [ref. 7303]). Gobiidae.

Parrichthys Barbour 1942:84 [ref. 180]. Masc. *Parrichthys merrimani* Barbour 1942:84. Type by monotypy. Synonym of *Ceratias* Krøyer 1845 (Pietsch 1986:481 [ref. 5969]). Ceratiidae.

Parupeneus Bleeker 1863:234 [ref. 398]. Masc. *Mullus barberinus* Cuvier 1829 (= *Mullus barberinus* Lacepède 1802:406). Type by subsequent designation. On Official List (Opinion 846) but apparently with type wrongly as *bifasciatus* Lacepède in Buffon 1802 as designated by Jordan 1919:322 [ref. 4904]. Type designated by Bleeker 1876:334 [ref. 448] (ICZN did not use plenary powers to designate the type; see also Bauchot et al. 1985:4 [ref. 12595]). Valid (Ben-Tuvia 1986:611 [ref. 5641], Ben-Tuvia & Kissil 1988:4 [ref. 12819] but with wrong type; Yamakawa in Masuda et al. 1984:164 [ref. 6441]). Mullidae.

Parupygus Hoedeman 1962:58 [ref. 13556]. Masc. *Parupygus savannensis* Hoedeman 1962:58. Type by monotypy. Valid (see Mago-Leccia 1978:14 [ref. 5489]). Gymnotidae: Hypopominae.

Paruroconger Blache & Bauchot 1976:413 [ref. 305]. Masc. *Paruroconger drachi* Blache & Bauchot 1976:413. Type by original designation (also monotypic). Very close to *Uroconger* Kaup 1856 (Smith 1989:545 [ref. 13285]). Congridae: Congrinae.

Parvacara Whitley 1951:68 [ref. 4711]. Fem. *Acara dorsigera* Heckel 1840:343. Type by being a replacement name. Unneeded replacement for *Nannacara* Miranda-Ribeiro 1918 (not an original description), preoccupied by Regan 1905 in fishes. Perhaps *Parvacara* is not available from Whitley 1951 on technical grounds as it is not technically a replacement name and must stand on its own as a generic description. Synonym of *Aequidens* Eigenmann & Bray 1894. Cichlidae.

Parviclinus Fraser-Brunner 1932:827 [ref. 1487]. Masc. *Parviclinus spinosus* Fraser-Brunner 1932:828. Type by original designation, also monotypic. Type locality is given as North Wales, British coast, but references from that area apparently do not include this genus. Family my be incorrect. Labrisomidae.

Parvicrepis Whitley 1931:325 [ref. 4672]. Fem. *Diplocrepis parvipinnis* Waite 1906:202. Type by original designation. Valid (Briggs 1955:47 [ref. 637]). Gobiesocidae: Gobiesocinae.

Parvigobius Whitley 1930:122 [ref. 4669]. Masc. *Parvigobius immeritus* Whitley 1930:122. Type by original designation (also monotypic). Type *P. immeritus* (a replacement for *Gobius flavescens* De Vis 1884, preoccupied). Synonym of *Redigobius* Herre 1927 (Hoese, pers. comm.). Gobiidae.

Parvilux Hubbs & Wisner 1964:448 [ref. 2266]. Fem. *Parvilux ingens* Hubbs & Wisner 1964:451. Type by original designation. Synonym of *Lampanyctus* Bonaparte 1840, but as a valid subgenus (Paxton 1979:14 [ref. 6440]); valid genus (Moser et al. 1984:220 [ref. 13645], Paxton et al. 1984:241 [ref. 13625]). Myctophidae.

Parviparma Herre 1927:81 [ref. 2104]. Fem. *Parviparma straminea* Herre 1927:82. Type by original designation (also monotypic). Valid (Birdsong et al. 1988:202 [ref. 7303]). Eleotridae.

Paschalestes Gistel 1848:IX [ref. 1822]. Masc. *Macquaria australasica* Cuvier in Cuvier & Valenciennes 1830:377. Type by being a replacement name. Unneeded replacement for *Macquaria* Cuvier 1830, name not preoccupied or inappropriate. Misspelled *Paschaltestes* by Jordan 1919:339 [ref. 2409]. Objective synonym of *Macquaria* Cuvier 1830. Percichthyidae.

Passer Klein 1775:816 [ref. 2618]. Masc. Not available, published in a work that does not conform to the principle of binominal nomenclature; also preoccupied by Brisson 1760 in Aves. In the synonymy of *Platichthys* Girard 1854 (Norman 1934:376 [ref. 6893]). Pleuronectidae: Pleuronectinae.

Passer Valenciennes (ex Klein) 1846:tab., Pl. 9 [ref. 6165]. Masc. *Passer marchionessarum* Valenciennes 1846:tab, Pl. 9. Type by monotypy. First published in Atlas (1846) to which genus and species can date; description followed in text 1855 [ref. 4504]. Not available, preoccupied by Brisson 1760 in Aves; not replaced. Synonym of *Scophthalmus* Rafinesque 1810 (Norman 1934:262 [ref. 6893] but with different type). Scophthalmidae.

Pastinaca Swainson 1838:172 [ref. 4302]. Fem. *Pastinaca olivacea* Swainson 1839:312, 319 (= *Raja pastinaca* Linnaeus 1758:232). Type by subsequent designation. Species added in 1839:192, 319 [ref. 4303]. Could be considered a replacement name for *Himantura* based on footnote, p. 172. Type apparently first designated by Bigelow & Schroeder 1953:341 [ref. 6568] if not a replacement name. Synonym of *Dasyatis* Rafinesque 1810 (Krefft & Stehmann 1973:70 [ref. 7167], Compagno & Roberts 1984:4 [ref. 6167]). Dasyatidae.

Pastinacae Nardo 1827:11 [ref. 3146]. *Raja pastinaca* Linnaeus 1758:232. Not available, name given in plural only. Original not examined. Also in Isis, v. 20:476 [seen]. Dasyatidae.

Pastinachus Rüppell 1828:82 [ref. 3843]. Masc. *Raia sephen* Forsskål 1775:viii, 17. Original not examined. Appears to be a senior synonym of currently-recognized genus *Hypolophus* Müller & Henle 1837 (Paxton et al. 1989:43 [ref. 12442]). Dasyatidae.

Pataecus Richardson 1844:280 [ref. 3738]. Masc. *Pataecus fonto* Richardson 1844:280. Type by monotypy. Valid (Washington et al. 1984:440 [ref. 13660], Paxton et al. 1989:462 [ref. 12442]). Pataecidae.

Patagonina Eigenmann 1928:56 [ref. 1245]. Fem. *Menidia hatcheri* Eigenmann 1928:56. Type by monotypy. Spelled two ways originally: *Patagonina* (p. 56, 60, Pl. 12), *Patagonia* (p. 56); *Patagonia* evidently in error; White 1985:17 [ref. 13551] selected *Patagonina*. Synonym of *Odontesthes* Evermann & Kendall 1906 (White 1985:17 [ref. 13551]). Atherinidae: Atherinopsinae.

Patagonotothen Balushkin 1976:122, 126 [ref. 170]. *Notothenia tessellata* Richardson 1845:19. Type by original designation. Valid (Stevens et al. 1984:563 [ref. 13633], Andersen 1984:24 [ref. 13369], Nakamura in Nakamura et al. 1986:246 [ref. 14235]). Nototheniidae.

Paulicea Ihering 1898:108 [ref. 2292]. Fem. *Paulicea jahu* Ihering 1898:108. Type by monotypy. Valid (Stewart 1986:668 [ref. 5211] as *Paulicia*, Burgess 1989:282 [ref. 12860]). Pimelodidae.

Pauloscirtes Whitley 1935:351 [ref. 4684]. Masc. *Petroscirtes obliquus* Garman 1903:237. Type by original designation (also monotypic). Synonym of *Omobranchus* Ehrenberg in Cuvier & Valenciennes 1836 (Springer 1972:9 [ref. 4178], Springer & Gomon 1975:9 [ref. 6083]). Blenniidae.

Pavoclinus Smith 1946:545 [ref. 4072]. Masc. *Clinus pavo* Gilchrist & Thompson 1908:123. Type by original designation. Valid (Smith 1986:766 [ref. 5712], Heemstra & Wright 1986:6 [ref. 5997]). Clinidae.

Pavoraja Whitley 1939:254 [ref. 4695]. Fem. *Raja nitida* Günther 1880:27. Type by original designation. Valid (McEachran 1984:56 [ref. 5225], Paxton et al. 1989:56 [ref. 12442]). Rajidae.

Pawnurus (subgenus of *Malacocephalus*) Parr 1946:27 [ref. 3378]. Masc. *Malacocephalus occidentalis* Goode & Bean 1886:597. Type by original designation (also monotypic). Synonym of *Malacocephalus* Günther 1862, but as a valid subgenus. Macrouridae: Macrourinae.

Peaolopesia Smith 1949:370 [ref. 4079]. Fem. *Xiphochilus gymnogenys* Günther 1866:Pl. 12. Type by original designation (also monotypic). Correct spelling for genus of type species is *Xiphocheilus*. Valid (Yamakawa in Masuda et al. 1984:202 [ref. 6441]). Labridae.

Peckoltia Miranda-Ribeiro 1912:7 [ref. 3718]. Fem. *Chaetostomus vittatus* Steindachner 1882:115. Type by subsequent designation. Type designated by Gosline 1945:85 [ref. 13558]; see Isbrücker 1980:53 [ref. 2303]. See also *Peckoltichthys* Miranda-Ribero 1917. Correct spelling for genus of type species is *Chaetostoma*. Valid (Isbrücker 1980:53 [ref. 2303], Heitmans et al. 1983 [ref. 5278], Burgess 1989:434 [ref. 12860]). Loricariidae.

Peckoltichthys Miranda-Ribeiro 1917:49 [ref. 5742]. Masc. *Peckoltichthys filicaudatus* Miranda-Ribeiro 1917:49. Type by monotypy. Regarded by Isbrücker 1980:53 [ref. 2303] as an unneeded replacement for and objective synonym of *Peckoltia* Miranda-Ribeiro 1912 with type as *vittatus*, but there is no evidence in the proposal in 1917 that this was a replacement name; type is *filicaudatus* by monotypy. Loricariidae.

Pectenocypris Kottelat 1982:421 [ref. 2667]. Fem. *Pectenocypris korthausae* Kottelat 1982:421. Type by original designation (also monotypic). Relationships in Cyprinidae uncertain. Valid (Roberts 1989:57 [ref. 6439]). Cyprinidae.

Pectinantus Sazonov 1986:[96] [ref. 6003]. Masc. *Barbantus parini* Sazonov 1976:14. Type by original designation. On p. 96 of English summary. Platytroctidae.

Pedalibrycon Fowler 1943:314 [ref. 1444]. Masc. *Pedalibrycon felipponei* Fowler 1943:314. Type by original designation (also monotypic). Misspelled *Pedalibycon* by Neave 1950:202 [ref. 6512]. Synonym of *Cheirodon* Girard 1855 (see Böhlke 1984:46 [ref. 13621], Malabarba 1989:133 [ref. 14217] based on placement of type species). Characidae.

Pedalion Guilding in Swainson 1838:199 [ref. 4302]. Neut. *Pedalion gigas* Guilding in Swainson 1838:199. Type by monotypy. Without a description but with a figure in 1838; also in Swainson 1839:195, 329 [ref. 4303]. *Pedalion* Swainson [= Guilding in Swainson] 1838 placed on Official Index (Opinion 326) as a junior homonym of *Pedalion* Dillwyn 1817. Synonym of *Mola* Koelreuter 1770 (Fraser-Brunner 1943:8 [ref. 1495]). Molidae.

Pedites Gistel 1848:IX [ref. 1822]. Masc. *Macropodus viridiauratus* Lacepède 1801:416. Type by being a replacement name. Unneeded replacement for *Macropodus* Lacepède 1801, not preoccupied by *Macropus*. Belontiidae.

Pegasus Linnaeus 1758:338 [ref. 2787]. Masc. *Pegasus volitans* Linnaeus 1758:338. Type by monotypy. Valid (Araga in Masuda et al. 1984:90 [ref. 6441], Smith 1986:443 [ref. 5712], Paxton et al. 1989:434 [ref. 12442], Palsson & Pietsch 1989:18 [ref. 13536]). Pegasidae.

Pegedictis Rafinesque 1820:85 [ref. 3592]. Masc. *Pegedictis ictalops* Rafinesque 1820:85. Type by monotypy. Spelled *Pegedichthys* by Jordan 1876:97 [ref. 2370] and by Jordan & Copeland 1877:139 [ref. 5961]. Description poor. Usually regarded as a synonym of *Cottus* Linnaeus 1758. Cottidae.

Pegusa de Buen 1926:94 [ref. 5054]. As a "grupo" for 3 species of Soleidae. Not available on basis of Art. 1b(6) [see de Buen's definition of "grupo" on p. 11]; see Appendix A. Soleidae.

Pegusa (subgenus of *Solea*) Günther 1862:462, 467-468 [ref. 1969]. *Solea aurantiaca* Günther 1862:467. Described in key (p. 462) as section of *Solea* with 4 species (pp. 467-468). Type by subsequent designation, earliest found that of Jordan 1919:319 [ref. 4904]. Valid (Torchio 1973:628 [ref. 6892], Heemstra & Gon 1986:872 [ref. 5665], Desoutter 1986:430 [ref. 6212]). Soleidae.

Pelagocephalus Tyler & Paxton 1979:203 [ref. 4478]. Masc. *Pelagocephalus coheni* Tyler & Paxton 1979:203. Type by original designation (also monotypic). Valid (Heemstra & Smith 1981 [ref. 5415], Arai 1983:208 [ref. 14249], Smith & Heemstra 1986:901 [ref. 5714]). Tetraodontidae.

Pelagocyclus Lindberg & Legeza 1955:436 [ref. 2785]. Masc. *Pelagocyclus vitiazi* Lindberg & Legeza 1955:437. Type by original designation (also monotypic). Valid (Kido in Masuda et al. 1984:337 [ref. 6441]). Cyclopteridae: Cyclopterinae.

Pelamichthys Giglioli 1880:25 [ref. 1617]. Masc. *Scomber unicolor* Geoffroy St. Hilaire 1809:Pl. 24. Type by original designation. Objective synonym of *Orcynopsis* Gill 1862 (Postel 1973:474 [ref. 7208], Collette & Chao 1975:592 [ref. 5573]). Scombridae.

Pelamis Plumier in Lacepède 1801:55 (footnote) [ref. 2710]. Fem. Not available; Plumier non-binominal manuscript name mentioned in passing under *Scomberoides saltator*. See remarks under Opinion 89 in Appendix B. Carangidae.

Pelamys Cuvier in Cuvier & Valenciennes 1832:149 [ref. 1000]. Fem. *Scomber sarda* Bloch 1793:44. Type by subsequent designation. Earliest type designation not researched. Spelled *Pelamis* by Swainson 1839:238 [ref. 4303]. Objective synonym of *Sarda* Cuvier 1829 (Postel 1973:475 [ref. 7208], Collette & Chao 1975:597 [ref. 5573]). Scombridae.

Pelamys Klein 1775:176 [ref. 2618]. Fem. Not available, published in a work that does not conform to the principle of binominal nomenclature. In the synonymy of *Scomber* Linnaeus 1758. Scombridae.

Pelates Cuvier 1829:148 [ref. 995]. Masc. *Pelates quadrilineatus* Cuvier in Cuvier & Valenciennes 1829:146. Type by subsequent designation. One unavailable species listed in footnote; fuller description and 3 species in Cuvier & Valenciennes (Apr.) 1829:145-148 [ref. 4879]. Type apparently designated by Bleeker (not researched). Synonym of *T[h]erapon* Cuvier 1816 (Mees & Kailola 1977:32 [ref. 5183]); valid (Tortonese 1973:363 [ref. 7192], Vari 1978:249 [ref. 4514], Akazaki in Masuda et al. 1984:174 [ref. 6441] as *Pelatus*, Heemstra 1986:543 [ref. 5660], Paxton et al. 1989:534 [ref. 12442]). Terapontidae.

Pelecanichthys Gilbert & Cramer 1897:432 [ref. 1635]. Masc. *Pelecanichthys crumenalis* Gilbert & Cramer 1897:433. Type by monotypy. Valid (Norman 1934:252 [ref. 6893], Ahlstrom et al. 1984:643 [ref. 13641]); synonym of *Chascanopsetta* Alcock 1894 (Amaoka & Yamamoto 1984:202 [ref. 5632]). Bothidae: Bothinae.

Pelecinomimus Gilchrist 1922:56 [16] [ref. 1648]. Masc. *Pelecinomimus picklei* Gilchrist 1922:57. Type by monotypy. On p. 16 of separate. Synonym of *Cetomimus* Goode & Bean 1895 (Paxton 1989:177 [ref. 13435]). Cetomimidae.

Pelecus Agassiz 1835:39 [ref. 22]. Masc. *Cyprinus cultratus* Linnaeus 1758:326. Type by monotypy. Valid (Bogutskaya 1988:104 [ref. 12754]). Cyprinidae.

Pelia Schlegel in Bleeker 1863:128 [ref. 395]. Fem. *Sphagebranchus cephalopeltis* Bleeker 1863:128. Appeared as name in synonymy as, "*Sphagebranchus? cephalopeltis* Blkr./ Syn. *Pelis cephalopeltis* Schl., Mus. Lugd. bat." Apparently not used subsequently as a valid name or senior homonym; therefore not available. Synonym of *Dalophis* Rafinesque 1810 (Blache et al. 1973:249 [ref. 7185], McCosker 1977:71 [ref. 6836], Castle 1984:38 [ref. 6171]). Ophichthidae: Ophichthinae.

Pellegrinina Fowler 1907:442 [ref. 1374]. Fem. *Pellegrinina heterolepis* Fowler 1907:442. Type by original designation (also monotypic). Synonym of *Chalceus* Cuvier 1817 (see Böhlke 1984:48 [ref. 13621]). Characidae.

Pellisolus Parr 1951:17 [ref. 3380]. Masc. *Pellisolus facilis* Parr 1951:19. Type by original designation (also monotypic). Valid (Matsui & Rosenblatt 1986:224 [ref. 5688]); synonym of *Mentodus* Parr 1951 (Sazonov 1986 [ref. 6003]). Platytroctidae.

Pellochromis (subgenus of *Pomacentrus*) Fowler & Bean 1928:14 [ref. 1475]. Masc. *Pomacentrus trimaculatus* Rüppell 1828:39. Type by original designation. Genus masculine or feminine; treated by Fowler & Bean as masculine. Synonym of *Dascyllus* Cuvier 1829 (Randall & Allen 1977:351 [ref. 6482]). Pomacentridae.

Pellona Valenciennes in Cuvier & Valenciennes 1847:300 [ref. 1012]. Fem. *Pellona orbignyana* Valenciennes in Cuvier & Valenciennes 1847:302. Type by subsequent designation. Type designated by Gill 1861:38 [ref. 1767] (see Whitehead 1967:105 [ref. 6464]). Valid (Poll et al. 1984:48 [ref. 6172], Grande 1985:245 [ref. 6466], Whitehead 1985:278 [ref. 5141]), Whitehead & Wongratana 1986:202 [ref. 6284], Paxton et al. 1989:156 [ref. 12442]). Clupeidae.

Pellonula Günther 1868:82, 452 [ref. 1990]. Fem. *Pellonula vorax* Günther 1868:452. Type by monotypy. Valid (Poll et al. 1984:48 [ref. 6172], Grande 1985:247 [ref. 6466], Whitehead 1985:142 [ref. 5141]). Clupeidae.

Pellonulops Smith 1949:98 [ref. 4077]. Masc. *Spratelloides madagascariensis* Sauvage 1883:160. Type by original designation (also monotypic). See account of *Sauvagella* Bertin 1940. Objective synonym of *Sauvagella* Bertin 1940 (Poll et al. 1984:53 [ref. 6172], Whitehead 1985:169 [ref. 5141]). Clupeidae.

Pellucidus de Buen 1926:78 [ref. 5054]. As a "grupo" for *Crystallogobius*. Not available on basis of Art. 1b(6) [see de Buen's definition of "grupo" on p. 11]; see Appendix A. Gobiidae.

Pelmatia Browne 1789:450 [ref. 669]. Fem. Not available, published in a rejected work on Official Index (Opinion 89). In the synonymy of *Gobiomorus* Lacepède 1800. Eleotridae.

Pelmatochromis (subgenus of *Paratilapia*) Steindachner 1894:40 [ref. 4237]. Masc. *Paratilapia (Pelmatochromis) buettikoferi* Steindachner 1894:40. Type by subsequent designation. Type designated by Jordan 1920:465 [ref. 4905] and by Regan 1922:252 [ref. 3673]. Valid (Greenwood 1987:142 [ref. 6166]; fossils referred to this genus by van Couvering 1982:36 [ref. 2042]). Cichlidae.

Pelmatolapia Thys van den Audenaerde 1970:289, 290 [ref. 12518]. Fem. Not available; two species mentioned but no generic description provided and no type designated. Cichlidae.

Pelontrus Smith 1961:364 [ref. 3789]. *Pelontrus morgansi* Smith 1961:365. Type by original designation (also monotypic). Synonym of *Plectranthias* Bleeker 1873 (Robins & Starck 1961:297 [ref. 3789], Randall 1980:105 [ref. 6717]). Serranidae: Anthiinae.

Pelophiletor Ogilby 1906 Masc. Not available, name only; appeared in "Honorary Curator's Report" Amateur Fisherm. Assoc. Queensland, Ann. Rept. 1905-6:3-14 (not seen, from Hutchins 1976 [ref. 6971]). In the synonymy of *Batrachomoeus* Ogilby 1908 (Hutchins 1976:19 [ref. 6971]). Batrachoididae.

Pelopsia Facciolà 1883:145 [ref. 1289]. Fem. *Pelopsia candida* Facciolà 1883:145. Type by subsequent designation. Earliest designation of type apparently by Jordan 1920:423 [ref. 4905]. Synonym of *Chlorophthalmus* Bonaparte 1840 (Nielsen 1973:167 [ref. 6885]). Chlorophthalmidae: Chlorophthalminae.

Pelor Cuvier in Cuvier & Valenciennes 1829:427 [ref. 4879]. Neut. *Scorpaena didactyla* Pallas 1769:26. Type by subsequent designation. Appeared first as "Les Pélors" in Cuvier (Apr.) 1829 [ref. 995], not latinized ["*Pel. obscurum* in footnote not sufficient]. Preoccupied by Bonelli 1813 in Coleoptera, replaced by *Simopias* Gill 1905. Spelled *Pelors* by Gray 1835:Pl. 90. Type apparently first designated by Jordan 1917:127 [ref. 2407]. In the synonymy of *Inimicus* Jordan & Starks 1904 (Eschmeyer et al. 1979:483 [ref. 6385]). Scorpaenidae: Choridactylinae.

Peloria Cocco 1844:27 [ref. 866]. Fem. *Peloria heckelii* Cocco 1844:27. Type by subsequent designation. Two included species; earliest type designation not researched. Based on a larva. Doubtfully associated with *Arnoglossus* Bleeker 1862 (Norman 1934:173 [ref. 6893]) and with *Bothus* Rafinesque 1810 (Norman 1934:220 [ref. 6893]). Bothidae: Bothinae.

Peloropsis Gilbert 1905:630 [ref. 1631]. Fem. *Peloropsis xenops* Gilbert 1905:630. Type by original designation (also monotypic). Synonym of *Rhinopias* Gill 1905 (Eschmeyer et al. 1973:287 [ref. 6390]). Scorpaenidae: Scorpaeninae.

Pelotretis Waite 1911:50 [ref. 4567]. Masc. *Pelotretis flavilatus* Waite 1911:50. Type by monotypy. Valid (Norman 1934:418 [ref. 6893], Ahlstrom et al. 1984:643 [ref. 13641], Sakamoto 1984 [ref. 5273]). Pleuronectidae: Rhombosoleinae.

Pelotrophus Günther 1864:314 [ref. 1979]. Masc. *Pelotrophus macrocephalus* Günther 1864:314. Type by subsequent designation. First designation of type species not researched, possibly not as above; misspelled *Peletrophus* by Jordan 1919:333 [ref. 4904] and type given as *P. microlepis* Günther. Fowler (MS) lists type as above, but wrongly as by monotypy. Synonym of *Barilius* Hamilton 1822. Cyprinidae.

Pelsartia Whitley 1943:183 [ref. 4703]. Fem. *Therapon humeralis* Ogilby 1899:177. Type by original designation (also monotypic). Synonym of *Terapon* Cuvier 1816 (Mees & Kailola 1977:32 [ref. 5183]); valid (Vari 1978:264 [ref. 4514], Paxton et al. 1989:535 [ref. 12442]). Terapontidae.

Peltapleura (subgenus of *Curimata*) Fowler 1906:300 [ref. 1373]. Fem. *Salmo cyprinoides* Linnaeus 1766:514. Type by original designation (also monotypic). Synonym of *Curimata* Bosc 1817 (Vari 1989:6 [ref. 9189], Vari 1989:21 [ref. 13506]). Curimatidae: Curimatinae.

Peltatetraops (subgenus of *Anableps*) Fowler 1931:396 [ref. 1410]. Masc. *Anableps microlepis* Müller & Troschel 1844:(198) 266. Type by original designation (also monotypic). Synonym of *Anableps* Scopoli 1777 (Parenti 1981:501 [ref. 7066] as *Peltatetrops*). Anablepidae: Anablepinae.

Pelteobagrus Bleeker 1865:9 [ref. 405]. Masc. *Silurus calvarius* Basilewski 1855:241. Type by monotypy. Valid (Jayaram 1968:295 [ref. 5615], Sawada in Masuda et al. 1984:59 [ref. 6441], Burgess 1989:68 [ref. 12860], Roberts 1989:126 [ref. 6439]). Bagridae.

Peltharpadon (subgenus of *Harpadon*) Fowler 1934:281 [ref. 1416]. Masc. *Harpodon squamosus* Alcock 1891:127. Type by original designation (also monotypic). Synonym of *Harpadon* Lesueur 1825 (Sulak 1977:53 [ref. 4299]). Synodontidae: Harpadontinae.

Peltorhamphus Günther 1862:460 [ref. 1969]. Masc. *Peltorhamphus novaezeelandiae* Günther 1862:461. Type by monotypy. Valid (Norman 1934:427 [ref. 6893], James 1972 [ref. 7082], Ahlstrom et al. 1984:643 [ref. 13641], Sakamoto 1984 [ref. 5273]). Pleuronectidae: Rhombosoleinae.

Peltura Perugia 1892:972 [ref. 3433]. Fem. *Peltura bovei* Perugia 1892:972. Type by monotypy. Preoccupied by *Peltura* Agassiz 1846:278 [ref. 64], an unjustified emendation of *Peltoura* Milne-Edwards 1840 in trilobites; replaced by *Phractura* Boulenger 1900. Synonym of *Phractura* (Skelton & Teugels 1986:62 [ref. 6192]). Amphiliidae.

Pelvicachromis (subgenus of *Pelmatochromis*) Thys van den Audenaerde 1968:379 [ref. 4402]. Masc. *Pelmatochromis pulcher* Boulenger 1901:9. Type by original designation. Valid (Greenwood 1987:169 [ref. 6166]). Cichlidae.

Pempherichthys Klunzinger 1871:470 [ref. 2622]. Masc. *Pempherichthys guentheri* Klunzinger 1871:470. Type by monotypy. Synonym of *Parapriacanthus* Steindachner 1870 (Scott 1983:196 [ref. 5346]). Pempheridae.

Pempheris Cuvier 1829:195 [ref. 995]. Fem. *Pempheris touea* Cuvier 1829:195. Type by subsequent designation. Type designated by Bleeker 1876:312 [ref. 448]. Valid (Hayashi in Masuda et al. 1984:165 [ref. 6441], Heemstra 1986:669 [ref. 5660]; close to Glaucosomatidae (Tominaga 1986:595 [ref. 6315]). Pempheridae.

Penesilurus Herre 1924:1570 [ref. 2120]. Masc. *Penesilurus palavanensis* Herre 1924:1570. Type by original designation (also monotypic). Combined genus and species description; species described more fully in 1924:703 [ref. 2119] where genus was also described as new; exact dates of publication not fully investigated. Synonym of *Silurus* Linnaeus 1758 (Haig 1952:102 [ref. 12607]).

Siluridae.

Penetopteryx Lunel 1881:275 [ref. 2849]. Fem. *Penetopteryx taeniocephalus* Lunel 1881:275. Type by monotypy. Valid (Dawson & Allen 1978:393 [ref. 1073], Dawson 1982:13 [ref. 6764], Dawson 1985:153 [ref. 6541]). Syngnathidae: Syngnathinae.

Penicelinus (subgenus of *Icelinus*) Bolin 1936:156 [ref. 506]. Masc. *Icelinus fimbriatus* Gilbert 1891:50, 85, 87. Type by original designation. Synonym of *Icelinus* Jordan 1885 (Bolin 1944:31 [ref. 6379]). Cottidae.

Penicipelta Whitley 1947:150 [ref. 4708]. Fem. *Monacanthus guntheri* Macleay 1881. Type by original designation (also monotypic). Valid. Monacanthidae.

Pennaclinus de Buen 1962:82 [ref. 699]. Masc. *Pennaclinus racemarius* de Buen 1962:82. Type by original designation (also monotypic). Synonym of *Calliclinus* Gill 1860 (Stephens & Springer 1974:19 [ref. 7149]). Labrisomidae.

Pennahia (subgenus of *Johnius*) Fowler 1926:776 [ref. 1402]. Fem. *Otolithus macrophthalmus* Bleeker 1850:16. Type designated by ICZN; on Official List (Opinion 1237). Correct spelling for genus of type species is *Otolithes*. Valid (Trewavas 1977:313 [ref. 4459], Sasaki & Kailola 1988:263 [ref. 12553]). Sciaenidae.

Pennon Whitley 1941:32 [ref. 4701]. *Upeneoides filifer* Ogilby 1910:95. Type by original designation (also monotypic). Mullidae.

Penopus Goode & Bean 1896:335 [ref. 1848]. Masc. *Penopus macdonaldi* Goode & Bean 1896:336. Type by monotypy. Valid (Cohen & Nielsen 1978:37 [ref. 881], Carter & Sulak 1984:359 [ref. 8244], Nielsen & Cohen 1986:350 [ref. 5700], Séret 1988 [ref. 12835]). Ophidiidae: Neobythitinae.

Pentaceropsis Steindachner in Steindachner & Döderlein 1883:13 [ref. 4247]. Fem. *Histiopterus recurvirostris* Richardson 1845:34. Type by subsequent designation. Type designated by Jordan 1920:426 [ref. 4905]. Valid (Hardy 1983:194 [ref. 5385]). Pentacerotidae.

Pentaceros Cuvier in Cuvier & Valenciennes 1829:30 [ref. 4879]. Masc. *Pentaceros capensis* Cuvier in Cuvier & Valenciennes 1829:30. Type by monotypy. Not preoccupied by *Pentaceros* Schulze 1760 or Schröter 1782 in echinoderms, both being nonbinominal; see Follett & Dempster 1963:328 [ref. 6569]. Valid (Hardy 1983:197 [ref. 5385], Mochizuki in Masuda et al. 1984:189 [ref. 6441], Heemstra 1986:623 [ref. 5660], Parin & Kotlyar 1988 [ref. 13518]). Pentacerotidae.

Pentanchus Smith & Radcliffe in Smith 1912:490 [ref. 4041]. Masc. *Pentanchus profundicolus* Smith & Radcliffe in Smith 1912:490. Type by original designation (also monotypic). Valid (Nakaya 1975:7 [ref. 7083], Springer 1979:110 [ref. 4175], Compagno 1984:345 [ref. 6846] but as possible senior synonym of *Apristurus* Garman 1913, Compagno 1988:175 [ref. 13488]). Scyliorhinidae.

Pentanemus Günther 1860:330 [ref. 1963]. Masc. *Polynemus quinquarius* Linnaeus 1758:317. Type by monotypy. Valid (de Sylva 1984:540 [ref. 13667], Daget & Njock 1986:352 [ref. 6216]). Polynemidae.

Pentapodus Quoy & Gaimard (ex Cuvier) 1824:294 [ref. 3574]. Masc. *Pentapodus vitta* Quoy & Gaimard 1824:294. Type by monotypy. Valid (Johnson 1980:11 [ref. 13553], Akazaki in Masuda et al. 1984:175 [ref. 6441]). Nemipteridae.

Pentaprion Bleeker 1850:13 [ref. 322]. Masc. *Pentaprion gerreoides* Bleeker 1850:13. Type by monotypy. Valid (Akazaki & Juso in Masuda et al. 1984:161 [ref. 6441]). Gerreidae.

Pentapus Valenciennes in Cuvier & Valenciennes 1830:258 [ref. 996]. Masc. *Sparus vittatus* Bloch 1791:107. Type by subsequent designation. Type designated by Bleeker 1876:279 [ref. 447]. Nemipteridae.

Pentaroge Günther 1860:132 [ref. 1963]. Fem. *Apistus marmoratus* Cuvier in Cuvier & Valenciennes 1829:416. Type by monotypy. Objective synonym of *Gymnapistes* Swainson 1839. Scorpaenidae: Tetraroginae.

Pentherichthys (subgenus of *Dolopichthys*) Regan & Trewavas 1932:81 [ref. 3682]. Masc. *Dolopichthys atratus* Regan & Trewavas 1932:81. Not available from Regan & Trewavas 1932 (Art. 13b). Apparently available from Burton 1933 (in Zoological Record for 1932) where there is a citation to Regan & Trewavas and the type is designated. Valid (Maul 1973:672 [ref. 7171], Pietsch 1974:33 [ref. 5332], Bertelsen & Pietsch 1977:186 [ref. 7063], Bertelsen in Whitehead et al. 1986:1397 [ref. 13677] with authorship and date as Regan & Trewavas 1932). Oneirodidae.

Pentheroscion Trewavas 1962:170 [ref. 4455]. Masc. *Sciaena mbizi* Poll 1950:8. Type by original designation (also monotypic). Sciaenidae.

Peprilus Cuvier 1829:213 [ref. 995]. Masc. *Peprilus longipinnis* Mitchill 1815:366. Type by subsequent designation. Earliest type designation not established; Haedrich 1967 lists *Sternoptyx gardenii* Bloch & Schneider as type, designated by Gill 1862:126 [ref. 1659], but *gardenii* not an originally-included species; Jordan lists type as *P. crenulatus* Cuvier, but that species was listed without distinguishing features (unavailable) in Cuvier 1829. Valid (Haedrich 1967:103 [ref. 5357], Horn 1984:628 [ref. 13637]). Stromateidae.

Perca Linnaeus 1758:289 [ref. 2787]. Fem. *Perca fluviatilis* Linnaeus 1758:289. Type by subsequent designation. Type designated by Gill 1861:48 [ref. 1768]. On Official List (Opinion 77, Direction 56). Valid (Collette & Banarescu 1977:1451 [ref. 5845], Paxton et al. 1989:561 [ref. 12442]). Percidae.

Percalabrax Temminck & Schlegel 1842:2 [ref. 4370]. Masc. *Labrax japonicus* Cuvier in Cuvier & Valenciennes 1828:85. Type by monotypy. Appeared originally as *Perca-labrax* but must be corrected by removal of hyphen. Percichthyidae.

Percalates Ramsay & Ogilby 1887:182 [ref. 3598]. Masc. *Lates colonorum* Günther 1863:115. Type by monotypy. Synonym of *Macquaria* Cuvier 1830 (Paxton et al. 1989:513 [ref. 12442] based on placement of type species). Percichthyidae.

Percamia Bleeker 1876:260 [ref. 447]. Fem. *Microperca yarrae* Castelnau 1872:48. Type by being a replacement name. Replacement for *Microperca* Castelnau 1872, preoccupied by Putnam 1863 in fishes. Synonym of *Nannoperca* Günther 1861. Kuhliidae.

Percanthias Tanaka 1922:591 [ref. 4334]. Masc. *Callanthias japonicus* Franz 1910:40. Type by original designation (also monotypic). Type designated on p. 594. Synonym of *Callanthias* Lowe 1839 (Kendall 1984:500 [ref. 13663]). Callanthiidae.

Percaprionodes (subgenus of *Prionodes*) Fowler 1944:399 [ref. 1448]. Masc. *Prionodes macropus* Fowler 1944:399. Type by original designation (also monotypic). Synonym of *Lutjanus* Bloch 1790 (Heemstra 1974:23 [ref. 7125]). Lutjanidae.

Percarina Nordmann 1840:357 [ref. 3209]. Fem. *Percarina demidoffii* Nordmann 1840:357. Type by monotypy. Valid (Collette & Banarescu 1977:1454 [ref. 5845]). Percidae.

Perccottus Dybowski 1877:28 [ref. 1171]. Masc. *Perccottus glenii* Dybowski 1877:28. Type by monotypy. Misspelled *Percottus* by authors. Original not seen. Valid (Birdsong et al. 1988:183 [ref. 7303]). Eleotridae.

Percichthys Girard 1855:197 [ref. 1819]. Masc. *Perca chilensis* Girard 1855:197 (= *Perca trucha* Valenciennes 1833:429). Type by subsequent designation. Type designated by Gill 1861:51 [ref. 1768]. Girard's *Percichthys chilensis* is an unneeded substitute for *P. trucha* Guichenot in Gay = *P. trucha* Valenciennes. Valid (see Arratia 1982:8 [ref. 143]). Percichthyidae.

Percilia Girard 1855:197 [ref. 1819]. Fem. *Percilia gillissi* Girard 1855:197. Type by monotypy. Also in Girard 1855:236 [ref. 4912], but this may have appeared as a separate before ref. 1819. Sometimes placed in its own family (e.g., by Arratia 1982 [ref. 143]). Valid (Arratia 1982:26 [ref. 143]). Percichthyidae.

Percina (subgenus of *Perca*) Haldeman 1842:330 [ref. 2029]. Fem. *Perca (Percina) nebulosa* Haldeman 1842:330. Type by monotypy. Apparently predates *Pileoma* DeKay 1842, Haldeman was (5 July) 1842. Valid (subgenera defined by Page 1974 [ref. 3346] and Page 1981 [ref. 3347], Collette & Banarescu 1977 [ref. 5845]). Percidae.

Percis Bloch & Schneider 1801:179 (xxxvi) [ref. 471]. Fem. *Percis maculata* Bloch & Schneider 1801:179. Type by monotypy. Preoccupied by *Percis* Scopoli 1777. Synonym of *Parapercis* Bleeker 1863. Pinguipedidae.

Percis Klein 1776:45 [ref. 4918]. Fem. Not available, published in a work that does not conform to the principle of binominal nomenclature. Not *Percis* Scopoli. Percidae.

Percis Klein in Walbaum 1792:585 [ref. 4572]. Fem. Not available (Opinion 21). Preoccupied by *Percis* Scopoli 1777, not replaced. In the synonymy of *Gymnocephalus* Bloch 1793 (Collette & Banarescu 1977:1453 [ref. 5845]). Percidae.

Percis Scopoli 1777:454 [ref. 3990]. Fem. *Cottus japonicus* Pallas 1772:30. Type by monotypy. Valid (Washington et al. 1984:442 [ref. 13660], Kanayama in Masuda et al. 1984:331 [ref. 6441], Yabe 1985:123 [ref. 11522], Maeda & Amaoka 1988:58 [ref. 12616]). Agonidae.

Percocypris Chu 1935:12 [ref. 832]. Fem. *Leptobarbus pingi* Tchang 1930:84. Type by original designation (also monotypic). Valid (Wu et al. 1977:265 [ref. 4807], Chu & Cui in Chu & Chen 1989:177 [ref. 13584]). Cyprinidae.

Percophis Quoy & Gaimard (ex Cuvier) 1825:351 [ref. 3574]. Masc. *Percophis brasilianus* Quoy & Gaimard 1825:351. Type by monotypy. Valid (Nakamura in Nakamura et al. 1986:264 [ref. 14235]). Percophidae: Percophinae.

Percopsis Agassiz 1849:81 [ref. 65]. Fem. *Percopsis guttatus* Agassiz 1850:286. Type by subsequent monotypy. Appeared first without named species. Description begun on p. 80 (published Nov. 1848), name appears on p. 81 (published Mar. 1849); genus dates to Mar. 1849, with type by subsequent monotypy. Also appeared in Agassiz 1850:284 [ref. 66]. Valid. Percopsidae.

Percosoma Gill 1861:51 [ref. 1768]. Neut. *Percichthys melanops* Girard 1854:197. Type by original designation (also monotypic). Synonym of *Percichthys* Girard 1855. Percichthyidae.

Pereulixia Smith 1959:238 [ref. 4123]. Fem. *Salarias kosiensis* Regan 1908:254. Type by original designation (also monotypic). Valid (Springer 1986:752 [ref. 5719], Williams 1989:15 [ref. 13549]). Blenniidae.

Perilampus McClelland 1839:288, 388 [ref. 2923]. Masc. *Cyprinus devario* Hamilton 1822:341, 393. Type by subsequent designation. Earliest type designation not fully researched, probably by Bleeker 1865:33 [ref. 4859]. Also appeared in McClelland 1839:943, 947 [ref. 2924]. Preoccupied by Latrielle 1809 in Hymenoptera, apparently not replaced. Synonym of *Danio* Hamilton 1822. Cyprinidae.

Perioceps (subgenus of *Asquamiceps*) Parr 1954:5 [ref. 3383]. Neut. *Asquamiceps (Perioceps) pacificus* Parr 1954:6. Type by original designation (also monotypic). Synonym of *Asquamiceps* Zugmayer 1911 (Markle 1980:45 [ref. 6077]). Alepocephalidae.

Periophthalmodon Bleeker 1874:326 [ref. 437]. Masc. *Gobius schlosseri* Pallas 1770:1. Type by original designation (also monotypic). Valid (Birdsong et al. 1988:196 [ref. 7303], Kottelat 1989:19 [ref. 13605], Murdy 1989:25 [ref. 13628]). Gobiidae.

Periophthalmus Bloch & Schneider 1801:63 (xxvii) [ref. 471]. Masc. *Periophthalmus papilio* Bloch & Schneider 1801:63. Type by subsequent designation. Type apparently designated first by Bleeker 1874:326 [ref. 437]. Valid (Akihito in Masuda et al. 1984:286 [ref. 6441], Hoese 1986:799 [ref. 5670], Maugé 1986:399 [ref. 6218], Birdsong et al. 1988:196 [ref. 7303], Kottelat 1989:19 [ref. 13605], Murdy 1989:30 [ref. 13628]). Gobiidae.

Perioptera Gistel 1848:XI [ref. 1822]. Fem. *Hieroptera abredonensis* Fleming 1841:236. Type by being a replacement name. Apparently a replacement for *Peroptera* in fishes; according to Fowler 1969:537 [ref. 6832] it is an unneeded replacement for *Hieroptera* Fleming 1841; *Peroptera* as used by Gistel 1848:XI also regarded as an emendation or replacement. Synonym of *Raja* Linnaeus 1758 (according to Fowler). Rajidae.

Perissias Jordan & Evermann 1898:2608, 2667 [ref. 2445]. Masc. *Platophrys taeniopterus* Gilbert 1890:118. Type by original designation (also monotypic). Valid (Norman 1934:162 [ref. 6893], Ahlstrom et al. 1984:642 [ref. 13641], Hensley 1986:941 [ref. 6326]). Bothidae: Taeniopsettinae.

Perissodus Boulenger 1898:20 [ref. 547]. Masc. *Perissodus microlepis* Boulenger 1898:21. Type by monotypy. Valid (Liem & Stewart 1976 [ref. 7096], Poll 1986:149 [ref. 6136]). Cichlidae.

Peristedion Lacepède 1801:368 [ref. 2710]. Neut. *Peristedion malarmat* Lacepède 1801:368, 369 (= *Trigla cataphracta* Linnaeus 1758). Type by subsequent designation. Type designated by Bory de Saint-Vincent, v. 10, 1826:52 [ref. 3853] plus v. 16, 1830:270 (see Whitley 1935:137 [ref. 6396]); also by Jordan & Gilbert 1883:732 [ref. 2476]. Spelled *Peristethidion*, *Peristethion*, *Peristethium*, and *Peristhedion* in early literature. Valid (Blanc & Hureau 1973:591 [ref. 7218], Ochiai & Yatou in Masuda et al. 1984:335 [ref. 6441], Heemstra 1986:489 [ref. 5660], Chen & Shao 1988:131 [ref. 6676], Paxton et al. 1989:456 [ref. 12442]). Triglidae: Peristediinae.

Peristedium Jordan & Gilbert 1883:732 [ref. 2476]. Neut. Unjustified emendation of *Peristedion* Lacepède 1801. In the synonymy of *Peristedion* Lacepède 1801 (Blanc & Hureau 1973:591 [ref. 7218]). Triglidae: Peristediinae.

Peristethidium Agassiz 1846:280 [ref. 64]. Neut. Unjustified emendation of *Peristedion* Lacepède 1801. In the synonymy of *Peristedion* Lacepède 1801 (Blanc & Hureau 1973:591 [ref. 7218]). Triglidae: Peristediinae.

Peristethus Kaup 1858:336 [ref. 2580]. Masc. *Trigla cataphracta* Linnaeus 1758:300. Type by being a replacement name. Unneeded replacement for *Peristedion* Lacepède 1801, which Kaup felt was "wrongly formed." Also appeared in Kaup 1859:103 [ref. 2587]. Objective synonym of *Peristedion* Lacepède 1801 (Blanc & Hureau 1973:591 [ref. 7218]). Triglidae: Peristediinae.

Peristrominous Whitley 1952:25 [ref. 4716]. Masc. *Peristrominous dolosus* Whitley 1952:25. Type by original designation (also monotypic). Valid (Poss & Eschmeyer 1978:404 [ref. 6387], Washington et al. 1984:441 [ref. 13660], Paxton et al. 1989:461 [ref. 12442]). Aploactinidae.

Perkinsia Eigenmann 1891:153 [ref. 1268]. Fem. *Perkinsia othonops* Eigenmann 1891:153. Type by monotypy. Synonym of *Etrumeus* Bleeker 1853 (Whitehead 1985:30 [ref. 5141). Clupeidae.

Peronedys Steindachner 1884:1083 [ref. 4234]. Fem. *Peronedys anguillaris* Steindachner 1884:1083. Type by monotypy. Valid (George & Springer 1980:24 [ref. 6935]). Clinidae.

Peropus Lay & Bennett 1839:59 [ref. 2730]. Masc. *Blepsias bilobus* Cuvier 1829:279. Type by monotypy. Preoccupied [details not researched], replaced by *Histiocottus* Gill 1889. Objective synonym of *Histiocottus* Gill 1889; synonym of *Blepsias* Cuvier 1829 (Bolin 1944:99 [ref. 6379]). Cottidae.

Perrunichthys Schultz 1944:(188) 229 [ref. 3959]. Masc. *Perrunichthys perruno* Schultz 1944:230. Type by original designation (also monotypic). Valid (Burgess 1989:282 [ref. 12860]). Pimelodidae.

Perryena Whitley 1940:428 [ref. 4699]. Fem. *Congiopus leucometopon* Waite 1922:216. Type by original designation (also monotypic). Valid (Paulin & Moreland 1979:601 [ref. 6915], Washington et al. 1984:440 [ref. 13660], Paxton et al. 1989:475 [ref. 12442]). Congiopodidae.

Persparsia Parr 1951:17, 18 [ref. 3380]. Fem. *Persparsia taaningi* Parr 1951:18. Type by original designation (also monotypic). Valid (Matsui & Rosenblatt 1986:225 [ref. 5688], Sazonov 1986 [ref. 6003], Paxton et al. 1989:212 [ref. 12442]). Platytroctidae.

Pertica (subgenus of *Gerres*) Fowler 1904:530 [ref. 1367]. Fem. *Gerres filamentosus* Cuvier 1829:188. Type by original designation (also monotypic). Synonym of *Gerres* Quoy & Gaimard 1824 (Roux 1986:325 [ref. 6209]). Gerreidae.

Perugia Eigenmann & Norris 1900:355 [ref. 1264]. Fem. *Pirirampus agassizii* Steindachner 1875:607. Type by original designation (also monotypic). Correct spelling for genus of type species is *Pinirampus*. Synonym of *Pinirampus* Bleeker 1858 (Stewart 1986:669 [ref. 5211], Burgess 1989:275 [ref. 12860]). Pimelodidae.

Perulibatrachus Roux & Whitley 1972:349 [ref. 3832]. Masc. *Batrachus elminensis* Bleeker 1863:98. Type by being a replacement name. Replacement for *Parabatrachus* Roux 1970, preoccupied by Owen 1853 in fossil fishes. Valid (Hutchins 1986:360 [ref. 5673]). Batrachoididae.

Pervagor (subgenus of *Stephanolepis*) Whitley 1930:120 [ref. 4669]. Masc. *Monacanthus alternans* Ogilby 1899:741. Type by original designation (also monotypic). Valid (Matsuura 1979:164 [ref. 7019], Tyler 1980:176 [ref. 4477], Arai 1983:199 [ref. 14249], Matsuura in Masuda et al. 1984:360 [ref. 6441], Hutchins 1986:886 [ref. 5673]). Monacanthidae.

Pescadorichthys Tomiyama 1955:8 [ref. 4412]. Masc. *Salarias namiyei* Jordan & Evermann 1903:362. Type by original designation (also monotypic). Synonym of *Ecsenius* McCulloch 1923 (Smith-Vaniz & Springer 1971:22 [ref. 4145], Springer 1988:8 [ref. 6804]). Blenniidae.

Petacara Böhlke 1959:2 [ref. 601]. Neut. *Bunocephalus dolichurus* Delsman 1941:fasc. 21. Type by original designation (also monotypic). Valid (Mees 1988:91 [ref. 6401], Burgess 1989:304 [ref. 12860]). Aspredinidae: Bunocephalinae.

Petalichthys Regan 1904:129 [ref. 12514]. Masc. *Petalichthys capensis* Regan 1904:129. Type by monotypy. Regan's species not the same as *Belone capensis* Günther 1866. Valid (Collette et al. 1984:352 [ref. 11422], Collette 1986:386 [ref. 5647]). Belonidae.

Petalosoma Regan 1908:458 [ref. 3637]. Neut. *Petalosoma cultratum* Regan 1908:462. Type by monotypy. Preoccupied by Lewis 1903 in Coleoptera, replaced by *Petalurichthys* Regan 1912. Synonymy of *Alfaro* Meek 1912 (Rosen & Bailey 1963:42 [ref. 7067]). Poeciliidae.

Petalurichthys Regan 1912:494 footnote [ref. 3648]. Masc. *Petalosoma cultratum* Regan 1908:462. Type by being a replacement name. Replacement for *Petalosoma* Regan 1908, preoccupied by Lewis 1903 in Coleoptera. Objective synonym of *Afaro* Meek (Sept. 12) 1912; *Petalurichthys* published Nov. 1912. Synonym of *Alfaro* Meek 1912 (Rosen & Bailey 1963:42 [ref. 7067]). Poeciliidae.

Petenia Günther 1862:301 [ref. 1969]. Fem. *Petenia splendida* Günther 1862:301. Type by monotypy. Valid. Cichlidae.

Petersialestes (subgenus of *Alestopetersius*) Hoedeman 1951:8 (in key) [ref. 2178]. Masc. *Petersius xenurus* Boulenger 1920:17. Type by monotypy (one species, two subspecies). Synonym of *Alestopetersius* Hoedeman 1951 (or 1956) (Paugy 1984:160 [ref. 6183]). Alestiidae.

Petersius Hilgendorf 1894:172 [ref. 2169]. Masc. *Petersius conserialis* Hilgendorf 1894:173. Type by monotypy. Valid (Poll 1967:28 [ref. 3529], Géry 1977:50 [ref. 1597], Paugy 1984:179 [ref. 6183]). Alestiidae.

Petimbuabo Catesby 1771:18 [ref. 774]. Not available, published in a rejected work on Official Index (Opinion 89, Opinion 259). Fistulariidae.

Petitella Géry & Boutière 1964:474 [ref. 1599]. Fem. *Petitella georgiae* Géry & Boutière 1964:474. Type by original designation (also monotypic). Valid (Géry 1977:547 [ref. 1597]). Characidae.

Petraites Ogilby 1885:226 [ref. 3262]. Masc. *Petraites heptaeolus* Ogilby 1885:225. Type by subsequent designation. Earliest type designation not researched; two included species. Valid (Hoese 1976:52 [ref. 7338], Araga in Masuda et al. 1984:294 [ref. 6441]). Clinidae.

Petrocephalus Marcusen 1854:14 [ref. 2887]. Masc. *Mormyrus bane* Lacepède 1803:620, 622. Type by subsequent designation. Several included species; earliest type designation not researched; type above as given by Jordan 1919:334 [ref. 4904]. Valid (Taverne 1972:162 [ref. 6367], Gosse 1984:108 [ref. 6169]). Mormyridae.

Petrochromis Boulenger 1898:20 [ref. 547]. Masc. *Petrochromis polyodon* Boulenger 1898:20. Type by monotypy. Valid (Yamaoka 1983 [ref. 5363], Poll 1986:79 [ref. 6136]). Cichlidae.

Petrometopon Gill 1865:105 [ref. 1709]. Neut. *Serranus guttatus* of Poey (= *Sparus cruentatus* Lacepède 1803:52, 156). Type by monotypy. Type given as *Serranus guttatus* Poey, apparently a subsequent identification and not an original description; possibly goes back to *Perca guttata* Linnaeus, or based on a misidentified type species. Fowler (MS) gives type as above. Synonym of subgenus *Cephalopholis* Bloch & Schneider 1801 of genus *Epinephelus* Bloch 1793 (C. L. Smith 1971:92 [ref. 14102]). Serranidae: Epinephelinae.

Petromyzon Linnaeus 1758:230 [ref. 2787]. Masc. *Petromyzon marinus* Linnaeus 1758:230. Type by subsequent designation. Type designated by Jordan & Copeland 1877:161 [ref. 5961]. On

Official List (Opinion 1171). Valid (Hubbs & Potter 1971:42 [ref. 13397], Vladykov 1973:2 [ref. 7159], Vladykov in Whitehead et al. 1984:67 [ref. 13675]). Petromyzontidae: Petromyzontinae.

Petronason Swainson 1839:172, 226 [ref. 4303]. *Scarus psittacus* of Rüppell (= *Scarus psittacus* Forsskål 1775:x, 29). Type by subsequent designation. Type designated by Swain 1883:274 [ref. 5966]. Synonym of *Scarus* Forsskål 1775. Scaridae: Scarinae.

Petroschmidtia Taranetz & Andriashev 1934:507 [ref. 4338]. Fem. *Petroschmidtia albonotata* Taranetz & Andriashev 1934:507. Type by original designation (also monotypic). Valid (Toyoshima in Masuda et al. 1984:306 [ref. 6441], Toyoshima 1985:137 [ref. 5722]). Zoarcidae.

Petroscirtes Rüppell 1830:110 [ref. 3843]. Masc. *Petroscirtes mitratus* Rüppell 1830:111. Type by monotypy. *Petroscertes* Swainson 1839:79, 80 [ref. 4303] and *Petroskirtes* Valenciennes in Cuvier & Valenciennes 1836:293, 294 [ref. 1005] are incorrect subsequent spellings. Valid (Smith-Vaniz 1976 [ref. 4144], Yoshino in Masuda et al. 1984:297 [ref. 6441], Springer 1986:753 [ref. 5719], Smith-Vaniz 1987:1 [ref. 6404]). Blenniidae.

Petrotilapia Trewavas 1935:(67) 76 [ref. 4451]. Fem. *Petrotilapia tridentiger* Trewavas 1935:76. Type by monotypy. Valid (Ribbink et al. 1983:209 [ref. 13555]). Cichlidae.

Petrotyx Heller & Snodgrass 1903:222 [ref. 2089]. *Petrotyx hopkinsi* Heller & Snodgrass 1903:222. Type by monotypy. Valid (Cohen & Nielsen 1978:37 [ref. 881]). Ophidiidae: Neobythitinae.

Petruichthys (subgenus of *Noemacheilus*) Menon 1987:36, 181 [ref. 14149]. Masc. *Nemacheilus brevis* Boulenger 1893:203. Type by original designation (also monotypic). Synonym of *Yunnanilus* Nichols 1925 (Kottelat 1990:21 [ref. 14137]). Balitoridae: Nemacheilinae.

Petrus Smith 1938:302 [ref. 4067]. Masc. *Dentex rupestris* Valenciennes in Cuvier & Valenciennes 1830:231. Type by original designation (also monotypic). Valid (Smith & Smith 1986:589 [ref. 5710]). Sparidae.

Peyeria Whitley 1940:242 [ref. 4660]. Fem. *Ariopsis aegyptiacus* Peyer 1928:43. Type by being a replacement name. Replacement for *Ariopsis* Peyer 1928, preoccupied by Gill 1861 in fishes. *Peyeria* itself preoccupied by Weiler 1935 in fossil fishes. Ariidae.

Péromère Duméril 1856:170 [ref. 1154]. *Syngnathus rondeletii* Delaroche 1809:314, 324. Not available, French vernacular name only, apparently not later made available. Syngnathidae: Syngnathinae.

Pfrille Jordan 1924:71 [ref. 2424]. Fem. *Phoxinus neogaeus* Cope 1869:375. Type by original designation (also monotypic). Synonym of *Phoxinus* Rafinesque 1820 (Howes 1985:66 [ref. 5274]); as a valid subgenus (Gasowska 1979:403 [ref. 1566]). Cyprinidae.

Phaenodon Lowe 1852:250 [ref. 2835]. Masc. *Phaenodon ringens* Lowe 1852:251. Type by monotypy. Spelled *Phaenodus* by Goode & Bean 1896. Doubtful synonym of *Astronesthes* Richardson 1845 (Gibbs 1964:313 [ref. 6960]). Astronesthidae.

Phaenomonas Myers & Wade 1941:77 [ref. 3133]. Fem. *Phaenomonas pinnata* Myers & Wade 1941:77. Type by original designation (also monotypic). Valid (McCosker 1975 [ref. 7100], McCosker 1977:73 [ref. 6836], McCosker & Castle 1986:184 [ref. 5690], McCosker et al. 1989:351 [ref. 13288]). Ophichthidae: Ophichthinae.

Phaenopogon Herre 1935:122 [ref. 2111]. Masc. *Phaenopogon barbulifer* Herre 1935:123. Type by original designation (also monotypic). Synonym of *Cirrhigaleus* Tanaka 1912. Squalidae.

Phaeoptyx Fraser & Robins 1970:303 [ref. 1485]. Fem. *Amia conklini* Silvester 1915:215. Type by original designation. Valid (Fraser 1972:24 [ref. 5195]). Apogonidae.

Phaethonichthys Nichols 1923:1 [ref. 3176]. Masc. *Phaethonichthys tuberculatus* Nichols 1923:2. Type by monotypy. Apparently not preoccupied by Bleeker 1876 in fishes (name in synonymy); not replaced. Synonym of *Xiphias* Linnaeus 1758 (Nakamura 1983 [ref. 5371]). Xiphiidae.

Phaetonichthys Bleeker 1875:30 [ref. 4861]. Masc. Also in Bleeker 1876:256 [ref. 447]. Not available, name in synonymy [but possibly is a replacement name]; apparently never made available. Misspelled *Phaethonichthys* by Jordan 1919:382 [ref. 4904]; see *Uriphaeton* Swainson. In the synonymy of *Cephalopholis* Bloch & Schneider 1801. Serranidae: Epinephelinae.

Phago Günther 1865:209 [ref. 1981]. Masc. *Phago loricatus* Günther 1865:210. Type by monotypy. Also appeared in Günther's footnote in Zoological Record for 1864, p. 175 [after Mar. 1865:209] with description of group Phagonina. Valid (Géry 1977:91 [ref. 1597], Vari 1979:340 [ref. 5490], Daget & Gosse 1984:209 [ref. 6185]). Citharinidae: Distichodontinae.

Phagoborus Myers 1924:397 [ref. 3090]. Masc. *Neoborus ornatus* Boulenger 1899:78. Type by being a replacement name. Replacement for *Neoborus* Boulenger 1899, preoccupied by Distant 1884 in Hemiptera. Valid (Géry 1977:86 [ref. 1597]); synonym of *Ichthyborus* Günther 1864 (Vari 1979:339 [ref. 5490], Daget & Gosse 1984:197 [ref. 6185]). Citharinidae: Distichodontinae.

Phagorus McClelland 1844:225 [ref. 2928]. Masc. *Cossyphus ater* McClelland 1844:403. Type by monotypy. Type apparently a mutilated specimen of *Silurus batrachus* Linnaeus. Replacement for *Cossyphus* McClelland 1844, preoccupied; replacement name appeared in an "Errata" notice (p. 225). Synonym of *Clarias* Scopoli 1777 (Teugels 1986:11 [ref. 12548]). Clariidae.

Phagrus Marcusen 1864:111, 142 [ref. 2888]. Masc. *Mormyrus dorsalis* Geoffroy St. Hilaire 1809:276, Pl. 8. Type by monotypy. Defined as a subgenus but unnamed in Marcusen 1854:6, 14 [ref. 2887]. Synonym of *Hyperopisus* Gill 1862 (Gosse 1984:77 [ref. 6169]). Mormyridae.

Phalacromacrurus Maul & Koefoed 1950:971 [ref. 2919]. Masc. *Phalacromacrurus pantherius* Maul & Koefoed 1950:972. Type by monotypy. Synonym of *Odontomacrurus* Norman 1939 (Marshall 1973:292 [ref. 7194], Marshall & Iwamoto 1973:534 [ref. 6963]). Macrouridae: Macrourinae.

Phalacronotus Bleeker 1858:255, 257, 302 [ref. 365]. Masc. *Silurus phalacronotus* Bleeker 1851:428. Type by absolute tautonymy. Also on pp. 32 et seq.; *Phalacronotus phalacronotus* is included on p. 32, so type is by absolute tautonymy. Type not *S. leptonema* as designated by Bleeker 1862:395 [ref. 391] and 1862:18 [ref. 393]. Synonym of *Kryptopterus* Bleeker 1858 (Haig 1952:106 [ref. 12607], Roberts 1989:145 [ref. 6439]). Siluridae.

Phalangistes Pallas 1814:109 et seq. [ref. 3351]. Masc. *Cottus cataphractus* Linnaeus 1758:264. Type by subsequent designation. Type designated by Jordan & Evermann 1898:2064 [ref. 2444]. Objective synonym of *Agonus* Bloch & Schneider 1801 (Lindberg 1973:605 [ref. 7220]). Agonidae.

Phalerebus Whitley 1929:216 [ref. 4666]. Masc. *Amphiprion alkallopisos* Bleeker 1853:281. Type by original designation. Pomacentridae.

Phallichthys Hubbs 1924:10 [ref. 2231]. Masc. *Poeciliopsis* *isthmensis* Regan 1913:997. Type by original designation. Valid (Rosen & Bailey 1959:16 [ref. 12020], Rosen & Bailey 1963:139 [ref. 7067], Bussing 1979 [ref. 6946], Parenti & Rauchenberger 1989:10 [ref. 13538]). Poeciliidae.

Phalloceros Eigenmann 1907:427, 431 [ref. 1219]. Masc. *Girardinus caudimaculatus* Hensel 1868:362. Type by original designation (also monotypic). Valid (Rosen & Bailey 1963:69 [ref. 7067], Paxton et al. 1989:347 [ref. 12442], Parenti & Rauchenberger 1989:8 [ref. 13538], Malabarba 1989:161 [ref. 14217]). Poeciliidae.

Phallocottus Schultz 1938:187 [ref. 3951]. Masc. *Phallocottus obtusus* Schultz 1938:188. Type by original designation (also monotypic). Valid (Washington et al. 1984:443 [ref. 13660]). Cottidae.

Phalloptychus Eigenmann 1907:426, 430 [ref. 1219]. Masc. *Girardinus januarius* Hensel 1868:360. Type by original designation (also monotypic). Misspelled *Phalloptycus* by Eigenmann 1910:458 [ref. 1224]. Valid (Rosen & Bailey 1963:73 [ref. 7067], Parenti & Rauchenberger 1989:8 [ref. 13538], Malabarba 1989:161 [ref. 14217]). Poeciliidae.

Phallostethus Regan 1913:549 [ref. 3657]. Masc. *Phallostethus dunckeri* Regan 1913:550. Type by monotypy. Valid (White et al. 1984:360 [ref. 13655], Parenti 1984 [ref. 5379], Kottelat 1989:16 [ref. 13605], Parenti 1989:267 [ref. 13486]). Phallostethidae.

Phallotorynus Henn 1916:126 [ref. 2093]. Masc. *Phallotorynus fasciolatus* Henn 1916:129. Type by monotypy. Spelled *Phallatorhynchus* by Jordan 1920:559 [ref. 4905]. Valid (Rosen & Bailey 1963:66 [ref. 7067], Parenti & Rauchenberger 1989:8 [ref. 13538]). Poeciliidae.

Phanerobranchus Cocco 1846:63 [ref. 5016]. Masc. *Phanerobranchus kronhii* Cocco 1846:63. Type by monotypy. Preoccupied by Leuckart 1821 in Amphibia; not replaced. Based on an undetermined larva. Original not examined; spelling of species unconfirmed. Myctophiformes.

Phanerocephalus Gracianov 1906:403 [ref. 1869]. Masc. *Phanerocephalus ellioti* Gracianov 1906:403. Type by monotypy. Misspelled *Planerocephalus* on page 403; *Phanerocephalus* on page 400, 404. Synonym of *Gymnura* van Hasselt 1823. Gymnuridae.

Phanerodon Girard 1854:153 [ref. 5769]. Masc. *Phanerodon furcatus* Girard 1854:153. Type by monotypy. Valid (Tarp 1952:49 [ref. 12250]). Embiotocidae.

Phanerotokeus Duncker 1940:84 [ref. 1157]. Masc. *Phanerotokeus gohari* Duncker 1940:85. Type by original designation (also monotypic). Synonym of *Halicampus* Kaup 1856 (Dawson 1985:75 [ref. 6541]). Syngnathidae: Syngnathinae.

Phanops Rofen 1963:4 [ref. 3795]. Masc. *Scopelarchus michaelsarsi* Koefoed 1955:6. Type by original designation. Synonym of *Scopelarchus* Alcock 1896 (Yanagisawa 1978:153 [ref. 7028]). Scopelarchidae.

Pharopteryx Rüppell 1828:15 [ref. 3843]. Fem. *Pharopteryx nigricans* Rüppell 1828:15. Type by monotypy. Spelling *Pharopterix* in index ruled an incorrect original spelling by ICZN and placed on Official Index (Opinion 1082). Objective synonym of *Plesiops* Oken 1817. Plesiopidae.

Pharopteryx Rüppell 1852:16 [ref. 3846]. Fem. *Pharopteryx benoit* Rüppell 1852:16. Type by monotypy. Preoccupied by *Pharopteryx* Rüppell 1828 in fishes, not replaced. On Official Index as a junior homonym (Opinion 1082). Synonym of *Eretmophorus* Giglioli 1889 (Cohen 1973:322 [ref. 6589]). Moridae.

Pharyngochromis Greenwood 1979:310 [ref. 1898]. Masc. *Pelmatochromis darlingi* Boulenger 1911:377. Type by original designation (also monotypic). Cichlidae.

Phasmatocottus Bolin 1936:33 [ref. 505]. Masc. *Phasmatocottus ctenopterygius* Bolin 1936:33. Type by original designation (also monotypic). Valid (Yabe in Masuda et al. 1984:328 [ref. 6441]). Cottidae.

Phasmatostoma Myers 1940:141 [ref. 3119]. Neut. *Monognathus jesperseni* Bertin 1936:538. Type by original designation. See account of *Monognathus*. Valid (Böhlke 1966:618 [ref. 5256]); synonym of *Monognathus* Bertin 1936 (Bertelsen & Nielsen 1987:174 [ref. 6618], Bertelsen et al. 1989:652 [ref. 13293]). Monognathidae.

Phasmichthys Jordan & Hubbs 1925:119 [ref. 2486]. Masc. *Chimaera mitsukurii* Dean in Jordan & Snyder 1904:224. Type by original designation (also monotypic). Second species tentatively referred to genus. Species appeared first in Jordan & Snyder (23 Jan.) 1904 from Dean manuscript, then in Dean (15 Feb.) 1904:6. Synonym of *Hydrolagus* Gill 1862. Chimaeridae.

Phenablennius Springer & Smith-Vaniz 1972:66 [ref. 4180]. Masc. *Petroscirtes heyligeri* Bleeker 1859:340. Type by original designation (also monotypic). Also published in Springer 1972 [ref. 4178]. Date for above is 8 Mar. 1972. Valid (Smith-Vaniz 1975 [ref. 7074]). Blenniidae.

Phenacobius Cope 1867:96 [ref. 908]. Masc. *Phenacobius teretulus* Cope 1867:96. Type by subsequent designation. Type designated by Jordan & Gilbert 1877:94 [ref. 4907]. Valid. Cyprinidae.

Phenacobrycon Eigenmann 1922:147 [ref. 1243]. Masc. *Bryconamericus henni* Eigenmann in Eigenmann, Henn & Wilson 1914:6. Type by original designation. Valid (Roberts 1973:490 [ref. 3776], Géry 1977:358 [ref. 1597], Weitzman & S. Fink 1985:1 et seq. [ref. 5203]). Characidae: Glandulocaudinae.

Phenacogaster Eigenmann 1907:769 [ref. 1220]. Fem. *Tetragonopterus pectinatus* Cope 1870:560. Type by original designation (also monotypic). Valid (Géry 1977:527 [ref. 1597]). Characidae.

Phenacogrammus Eigenmann in Eigenmann & Ogle 1907:30 [ref. 1266]. Masc. *Micralestes interruptus* Boulenger 1899:88. Type by original designation (also monotypic). Valid (Poll 1967:53 [ref. 3529], Géry 1977:30 [ref. 1597], Paugy 1984:179 [ref. 6183]). Alestiidae.

Phenacorhamdia Dahl 1961:504 [ref. 1027]. Fem. *Phenacorhamdia macarenensis* Dahl 1961:504. Type by monotypy. Synonym of *Heptapterus* Bleeker 1858 (Mees 1974:177 [ref. 2969], but see Buckup 1988 [ref. 6635]). Pimelodidae.

Phenacoscorpius Fowler 1938:69 [ref. 1426]. Masc. *Phenacoscorpius megalops* Fowler 1938:70. Type by original designation (also monotypic). Valid (Eschmeyer 1965:522 [ref. 1273], Eschmeyer & Randall 1975:293 [ref. 6389], Eschmeyer 1986:470 [ref. 5652]). Scorpaenidae: Scorpaeninae.

Phenacostethus Myers 1928:6 [ref. 3101]. Masc. *Phenacostethus smithi* Myers 1928:6. Type by original designation (also monotypic). Valid (Kottelat 1985:272 [ref. 11441], Parenti 1986 [ref. 5192], Kottelat 1989:16 [ref. 13605], Parenti 1989:267 [ref. 13486]). Phallostethidae.

Phenagoniates Eigenmann & Wilson in Eigenmann, Henn & Wilson 1914:2 [ref. 1259]. Masc. *Phenagoniates wilsoni* Eigenmann in Eigenmann, Henn & Wilson 1914:2. Type by monotypy. Spelled *Phanagoniates* by Eigenmann 1915:43 [ref. 1231], also misspelled

Phaneagoniates. Valid (Fink & Weitzman 1974:30 [ref. 7132], Géry 1977:347 [ref. 1597]). Characidae.

Pherallodichthys Shiogaki & Dotsu 1983:115 [ref. 5396]. Masc. *Pherallodichthys meshimaenis* Shiogaki & Dotsu 1983:115. Type by original designation (also monotypic). Valid (Yoshino in Masuda et al. 1984:342 [ref. 6441]). Gobiesocidae: Gobiesocinae.

Pherallodiscus Briggs 1955:128 [ref. 637]. Masc. *Gobiesox funebris* Gilbert 1890:95. Type by original designation. Gobiesocidae: Gobiesocinae.

Pherallodus Briggs 1955:43 [ref. 637]. Masc. *Crepidogaster indicus* Weber 1913:525. Type by original designation. Valid (Yoshino in Masuda et al. 1984:341 [ref. 6441], Briggs 1986:380 [ref. 5643]). Gobiesocidae: Gobiesocinae.

Phillippsichthys Whitley 1937:143 [ref. 4689]. Masc. *Auchenopterus aysoni* Hector 1902:240. Type by original designation (also monotypic). Clinidae.

Philypnodon Bleeker 1874:301 [ref. 437]. Masc. *Eleotris nudiceps* Castelnau 1872:126. Type by original designation (also monotypic). Valid (Birdsong et al. 1988:182 [ref. 7303]). Eleotridae.

Philypnoides Bleeker 1849:19 [ref. 319]. Masc. *Philypnoides surakartensis* Bleeker 1849:19. Type by monotypy. Synonym of *Channa* Scopoli 1777 (Roberts 1989:169 [ref. 6439]). Channidae.

Philypnus Valenciennes in Cuvier & Valenciennes 1837:255 [ref. 1006]. Masc. *Platycephalus dormitator* Bloch & Schneider 1801:60. Type by monotypy. Valid (Kottelat 1989:18 [ref. 13605]). Eleotridae.

Phobetor Krøyer 1845:263 [ref. 2689]. Masc. *Cottus tricuspis* Reinhardt 1832:lii. Type by monotypy. Synonym of *Gymnocanthus* Swainson 1839 (Neyelov 1973:595 [ref. 7219]). Cottidae.

Phocaegadus Jensen 1948:140 [ref. 2343]. Masc. *Phocaegadus megalops* Jensen 1948:141. Type by monotypy. Synonym of *Arctogadus* Drjagin 1932 (Svetovidov 1973:304 [ref. 7169]). Gadidae.

Pholidapus Bean & Bean 1896:389 [ref. 233]. Masc. *Pholidapus grebnitzkii* Bean & Bean 1896:390. Type by monotypy. Valid (Shiogaki 1984 [ref. 5309]). Stichaeidae.

Pholidichthys Bleeker 1856:406 [ref. 353]. Masc. *Pholidichthys leucotaenia* Bleeker 1856:406. Type by monotypy. Valid (Springer & Freihofer 1976 [ref. 7108]). Pholidichthyidae.

Pholidus Rafinesque 1815:82 [ref. 3584]. Masc. Not available; name only and evidently an incorrect subsequent spelling of *Pholis* Gronow. Pholidae.

Pholioides Nielsen 1961:253 [ref. 3193]. Masc. *Pholioides thomaseni* Nielsen 1961:253. Type by original designation (also monotypic). Synonym of *Halidesmus* Günther 1872 (Winterbottom 1982:755 [ref. 5436]). Pseudochromidae: Congrogadinae.

Pholis Cuvier 1816:251 [ref. 993]. Fem. *Blennius pholis* Linnaeus 1758:257. Type by subsequent designation. Earliest type designation not researched. Preoccupied by *Pholis* Scopoli 1777. Synonym of *Blennius* Linnaeus 1758 (Bath 1973:519 [ref. 7212]); synonym of *Lipophrys* Gill 1896 (Bath 1977:190 [ref. 208]). Pholidae.

Pholis Gronow 1763:78 [ref. 1910]. Fem. Not available, published in a rejected work placed on Official Index (Opinion 261). In the synonymy of *Pholis* Scopoli 1777. Pholidae.

Pholis Röse 1793:116 [ref. 3833]. Fem. *Blennius pholis* Linnaeus 1758:257. Not *Pholis* Scopoli 1777. Synonym of *Blennius* Linnaeus 1758. Pholidae.

Pholis Scopoli (ex Gronow) 1777:456 [ref. 3990]. Fem. *Blennius gunnellus* Linnaeus 1758:259. Appeared first as name only; first addition of species and designation of type not researched. Valid (Makushok 1973:534 [ref. 6889], Yatsu 1981 [ref. 4814], Amaoka in Masuda et al. 1984:303 [ref. 6441], Makushok in Whitehead et al. 1986:1124 [ref. 13677]). Pholidae.

Phosichthys Hutton 1872:55 [ref. 2287]. Masc. *Phosichthys argenteus* Hutton 1872:56. Type by monotypy. *Photichthys* Hutton 1873:269, Pl. 15 [ref. 2285] is an incorrect subsequent spelling; Hutton p. 269 says,"...Dr. Günther suggests that the name...should be altered to *Photichthys*, a suggestion...I willingly adopt." The correct family is Phosichthyidae as used by Fowler 1974:256 [ref. 7156], not Photichthyidae of authors. Valid, but spelled *Photichthys* (Weitzman 1974:472 [ref. 5174], Schaefer et al. 1986:245 [ref. 5709], Paxton et al. 1989:188 [ref. 12442]). Phosichthyidae.

Photichthys see *Phosichthys*. Phosichthyidae.

Photoblepharon Weber 1902:108 [ref. 4608]. Neut. *Sparus palpebratus* Boddaert 1781:55. Type by monotypy. *Protobelpharon* is a misspelling. Valid (McCosker 1986:413 [ref. 6294], McCosker & Rosenblatt 1987:158 [ref. 6707], Johnson & Rosenblatt 1988 [ref. 6682]). Anomalopidae.

Photocorynus Regan 1925:393 [ref. 3678]. Masc. *Photocorynus spiniceps* Regan 1925:393. Type by monotypy. Linophrynidae.

Photogenis Cope 1868:163 [ref. 7316]. *Squalius photogenis* Cope 1864:280. Type by absolute tautonymy. Also appeared in Cope 1869:378 [ref. 910]; in 1868 paper Cope cites original as 1866:378 which is our Cope 1869 [ref. 910]. Reference 910 was read in 1866 and apparently published in 1869, but distribution of separates before 1869 not investigated. Synonym of *Notropis* Rafinesque 1818 (Gilbert 1978:15 [ref. 7042]); synonym of *Cyprinella* Girard 1857 (Mayden 1989:45 [ref. 12555]). [With type as above, genus is a synonym of *Notropis* Rafinesque 1818.] Cyprinidae.

Photonectes Günther 1887:212 [ref. 2013]. Masc. *Lucifer albipennis* Döderlein 1882:26. Type by being a replacement name. Replacement for *Lucifer* Döderlein 1882, preoccupied by Thompson 1830 in Crustacea and by Reichenbach 1849 in Aves. Valid (Morrow in Morrow & Gibbs 1964:486 [ref. 6962], Morrow 1973:140 [ref. 7175], Kawaguchi & Moser 1984:171 [ref. 13642], Gibbs in Whitehead et al. 1984:362 [ref. 13675], Fujii in Masuda et al. 1984:52 [ref. 6441], Fink 1985:11 [ref. 5171], Gibbs 1986:243 [ref. 5655], Paxton et al. 1989:202 [ref. 12442]). Melanostomiidae.

Photonectoides Koefoed 1956:11 [ref. 2653]. Masc. *Photonectoides paucidentatus* Koefoed 1956:11. Type by monotypy. Proposed somewhat conditionally as "*Photonectoides* n. g.?", but available (conditional proposal before 1961). Synonym of *Photonectes* Günther 1887 (Gibbs in Fink 1985:2 [ref. 5171]). Melanostomiidae.

Photonectops Chapman 1939:515 [ref. 817]. Masc. *Photonectops multipunctata* Chapman 1939:515. Type by original designation (also monotypic). Published 28 Apr. Synonym of *Tactostoma* Bolin (9 Mar.) 1939. Stomiidae.

Photostomias Collett 1889:291 [ref. 4875]. Masc. *Photostomias guernei* Collett 1889:291. Type by monotypy. Valid (Morrow 1964:525 [ref. 6958], Goodyear 1973:143 [ref. 7176], Kawaguchi & Moser 1984:171 [ref. 13642], Gibbs in Whitehead et al. 1984:370 [ref. 13675], Fujii in Masuda et al. 1984:53 [ref. 6441], Fink 1985:11 [ref. 5171]). Malacosteidae.

Photostylus Beebe 1933:163 [ref. 5873]. Masc. *Photostylus pycnopterus* Beebe 1933:163. Type by monotypy. Also in Beebe (Aug.)

1933:82 [ref. 245]. Valid (Wisner 1976 [ref. 6956], Markle & Quéro in Whitehead et al. 1984:247 [ref. 13675], Markle 1986:221 [ref. 5687], Paxton et al. 1989:210 [ref. 12442]). Alepocephalidae.

Phoxargyrea Fowler 1903:732 [ref. 1362]. Fem. *Phoxargyrea dayi* Fowler 1903:732. Type by original designation (also monotypic). Synonym of *Menidia* Bonaparte 1836 (Böhlke 1984:23 [ref. 13621]). Atherinidae: Menidiinae.

Phoxinellus Heckel 1843:1039 [ref. 2066]. Masc. *Phoxinellus zeregi* Heckel 1843:1063. Type by subsequent designation. Type apparently designated first by Bleeker 1863:209 [ref. 397], 1863:263 [ref. 403] and 1863:31 [ref. 4859]. Misspelled *Rhoxinellus* by Heckel 1843:1012. Valid (see Howes 1985:69 [ref. 5274]). Cyprinidae.

Phoxinopsis Regan 1907:262 [ref. 3630]. Fem. *Phoxinopsis typicus* Regan 1907:262. Type by monotypy (also by use of *typicus*). Mentioned (Géry 1977:607 [ref. 1597]). Characidae.

Phoxinus Agassiz 1835:37 [ref. 22]. Masc. *Cyprinus phoxinus* Linnaeus 1758:322. Type by absolute tautonymy. Species *phoxinus* needlessly renamed *laevis* by Agassiz. Regarded as a genus described independently of *Phoxinus* Rafinesque 1820. Objective synonym of *Phoxinus* Rafinesque 1820. Treated as valid (Yang & Hwang 1964:22 [ref. 13497] with Agassiz as author). Cyprinidae.

Phoxinus Rafinesque 1820:236 [ref. 7310]. Masc. *Cyprinus phoxinus* Linnaeus 1758:322. Type by subsequent tautonymy. Proposed for European species, but no species listed. First addition of species not researched. Also in Rafinesque (Dec.) 1820:46 [ref. 3592]. *Roxinus* is a misspelling. Valid (Howes 1985:66 [ref. 5274], Bogutskaya 1987:936 [ref. 13521], Starnes & Jenkins 1988 [ref. 6686], Travers 1989:198 [ref. 13578]). Cyprinidae.

Phoxiscus Oshima 1919:225 [ref. 3312]. Masc. *Phoxiscus kikuchii* Oshima 1919:226. Type by monotypy. Misspelled *Phosciscus* in Zoological Record for 1919. Cyprinidae.

Phoxocampus Dawson 1977:612 [ref. 1066]. Masc. *Ichthyocampus belcheri* Kaup 1856:117. Type by original designation. Valid (Araga in Masuda et al. 1984:88 [ref. 6441], Dawson 1985:155 [ref. 6541], Dawson 1986:456 [ref. 5650], Paxton et al. 1989:427 [ref. 12442]). Syngnathidae: Syngnathinae.

Phractocephalus Agassiz in Spix & Agassiz 1829:10, 22 [ref. 13]. Masc. *Phractocephalus bicolor* Agassiz in Spix & Agassiz 1829:23. Type by monotypy. For authorship and date see Kottelat 1988:78 [ref. 13380]; also see his analysis on p. 80, and see the account of *Pirarara* and Kottelat 1989 [ef. 14233]. Valid (Boeseman 1983:105 [ref. 5329], Lundberg et al. 1988 [ref. 6637], Burgess 1989:282 [ref. 12860], Kottelat 1989 [ref. 14233]). Pimelodidae.

Phractolaemus Boulenger 1901:6 [ref. 559]. Masc. *Phractolaemus ansorgii* Boulenger 1901:6. Type by monotypy. Valid (Thys van den Audenaerde 1984:136 [ref. 6181]). Phractolaemidae.

Phractura Boulenger 1900:527 [ref. 554]. Fem. *Peltura bovei* Perugia 1892:972. Type by being a replacement name. Replacement for *Peltura* Perugia 1892, preoccupied by *Peltura* Agassiz 1846:278 [ref. 64] (an unjustified emendation of *Peltoura* Edwards 1840 in trilobites). Valid (Skelton & Teugels 1986:62 [ref. 6192], Burgess 1989:114 [ref. 12860]). Amphiliidae.

Phreatichthys Vinciguerra 1924:240 [ref. 4523]. Masc. *Phreatichthys andruzzii* Vinciguerra 1924:240. Type by monotypy. Valid (Lévêque & Daget 1984:330 [ref. 6186]). Cyprinidae.

Phreatobius Goeldi 1905:545 [ref. 6570]. Masc. *Phreatobius cisternarum* Goeldi 1905:545. Type by monotypy. Misspelled *Phrenatobius* in Jordan 1920:480 [ref. 4905] and apparently with date wrongly as 1898. Original not seen. Valid (Stewart 1986:669 [ref. 5211]); synonym of *Heptapterus* Bleeker 1858 (Buckup 1988:643 [ref. 6635], Burgess 1989:282 [ref. 12860]). Pimelodidae.

Phricus Berg 1895:65 [ref. 261]. Masc. *Aphritis urvillii* Valenciennes in Cuvier & Valenciennes 1831:484. Type by being a replacement name. Replacement for *Aphritis* Valenciennes 1831, preoccupied by Latreille 1804 in Diptera. Synonym of *Pseudaphritis* Castelnau 1872 (Scott 1982:202 [ref. 5472]). Bovichtidae.

Phrynelox Whitley 1931:328 [ref. 4672]. Masc. *Lophius striatus* Shaw & Nodder 1794:Pl. 175. Type by original designation (also monotypic). Synonym of *Antennarius* Daudin 1816 (Pietsch 1984:33 [ref. 5380], Pietsch in Whitehead et al. 1986:1364 [ref. 13677]); valid (Araga in Masuda et al. 1984:102 [ref. 6441]). Antennariidae.

Phrynichthys Agassiz 1846:55, 288 [ref. 64]. Masc. *Scorpaena horrida* Linnaeus 1766:453. Type by being a replacement. Replacement for *Bufichthys* Swainson 1839. Predates *Phrynichthys* Pietschmann 1926. Objective synonym of *Synanceia* Bloch & Schneider 1801. Scorpaenidae: Synanceiinae.

Phrynichthys Pietschmann 1926:88 [ref. 3475]. Masc. *Phrynichthys wedli* Pietschmann 1926:88. Type by monotypy. Also appeared in Pietschmann 1930:419 [ref. 3476]. Preoccupied by *Phrynichthys* Agassiz 1846 in fishes; replaced by *Bufoceratias* Whitley 1931. Synonym of *Paroneirodes* Alcock 1890 (Maul 1973:669 [ref. 7171]). Incorrectly treated as valid (Uwate 1979:141 [ref. 7015], Bertelsen in Whitehead et al. 1986:1381 [ref. 13677], Pietsch 1986:377 [ref. 5704]). Diceratiidae.

Phrynorhombus Günther 1862:414 [ref. 1969]. Masc. *Rhombus unimaculatus* Risso 1826:252. Type by monotypy. Valid (Norman 1934:275 [ref. 6893], Nielsen 1973:617 [ref. 6885], Ahlstrom et al. 1984:640 [ref. 13641], Nielsen in Whitehead et al. 1986:1289 [ref. 13677]). Scophthalmidae.

Phrynotitan Gill 1885:255 [ref. 1653]. Masc. *Batrachus gigas* Günther 1869:131. Type by original designation. Synonym of *Promicrops* Poey (ex Gill) 1868; *Promicrops* a synonym of *Epinephelus* Bloch 1793 in latest treatments. Serranidae: Epinephelinae.

Phthanophaneron Johnson & Rosenblatt 1988:70 [ref. 6682]. Masc. *Photoblepharon harveyi* Rosenblatt & Montgomery 1976:510. Type by original designation (also monotypic). Anomalopidae.

Phtheirichthys Gill 1862:239 [ref. 1664]. Masc. *Echeneis lineata* Menzies 1791:187. Type by original designation (also monotypic). Type designated by Gill's style of type enclosed in parentheses in key. Valid (Lachner 1973:637 [ref. 7221], Okamura in Masuda et al. 1984:222 [ref. 6441], Lachner in Whitehead et al. 1986:1330 [ref. 13677], Heemstra 1986:662 [ref. 5660], Paxton et al. 1989:571 [ref. 12442]). Echeneidae.

Phucocoetes Jenyns 1842:168 [ref. 2344]. Masc. *Phucocoetes latitans* Jenyns 1842:168. Type by monotypy. *Phycocoetes* Jordan 1923:236 [ref. 2421] is an incorrect subsequent spelling. Valid (Gosztonyi 1977:233 [ref. 6103], Anderson 1984:578 [ref. 13634]). Zoarcidae.

Phycis Artedi in Walbaum 1792:575 [ref. 4572]. Fem. *Tinca marina* Walbaum 1792:575. Type by monotypy. Treated as earliest description of *Phycis* by authors. Valid (Svetovidov 1973:314 [ref. 7169], Fahay & Markle 1984:266 [ref. 13653], Svetovidov in

Whitehead et al. 1986:705 [ref. 13676]). Phycidae.

Phycis Bloch & Schneider 1801:56 [ref. 471]. Fem. *Blennius phycis* Linnaeus 1766:422. Type by absolute tautonymy. Apparently not an original description, but listed as such by Jordan. Bloch & Schneider 1801 renamed the species *phycis* as *tinca*. Preoccupied by Artedi 1792 in fishes and by Fabricus 1798 in Lepidoptera. Synonym of *Phycis* Artedi 1792. Phycidae.

Phycis Rafinesque 1810:26 [ref. 3594]. Fem. *Phycis punctatus* Rafinesque 1810:26. Type by subsequent designation. Earliest type designation found that of Jordan 1917:79 [ref. 2407]. Preoccupied by Artedi 1792 in fishes and Fabricius 1798 in Lepidoptera. Spelled *Physis* by Swainson 1838:322 [ref. 4302] and 1839:391-392 [ref. 4303] on Cuvier. Phycidae.

Phycis Röse 1793 [ref. 3833]. Fem. *Phycis tinca* Bloch & Schneider 1801:56. Original not examined. Synonym of *Phycis* Artedi 1792. Phycidae.

Phycodurus Gill 1896:159 [ref. 1743]. Masc. *Phyllopteryx eques* Günther 1865:327. Type by monotypy. Valid (Dawson 1985:157 [ref. 6541], Kuiter 1988 [ref. 6371], Paxton et al. 1989:427 [ref. 12442]). Syngnathidae: Syngnathinae.

Phyllichthys McCulloch 1916:66 [ref. 2944]. Masc. *Synaptura sclerolepis* Macleay 1878:363. Type by original designation. Valid (Chapleau & Keast 1988:2799 [ref. 13625]). Soleidae.

Phyllogobius Larson 1986:131 [ref. 6141]. Masc. *Cottogobius platycephalops* Smith 1964. Type by original designation, also monotypic. Gobiidae.

Phyllogramma Pellegrin 1934:46 [ref. 3414]. Neut. *Phyllogramma regani* Pellegrin 1934:47. Type by monotypy. Synonym of *Cynoponticus* Costa 1845 (Blache et al. 1973:235 [ref. 7185], Smith 1989:437 [ref. 13285]). Muraenesocidae.

Phyllonemus Boulenger 1906:552 [ref. 573]. Masc. *Phyllonemus typus* Boulenger 1906:552. Type by monotypy (also by use of *typus*). Valid (Bailey & Stewart 1984:16 [ref. 5232], Risch 1986:34 [ref. 6190], Risch 1987:29 [ref. 6751]). Bagridae.

Phyllophichthus Gosline 1951:316 [ref. 1858]. Masc. *Phyllophichthus xenodontus* Gosline 1951:316. Type by original designation (also monotypic). Valid (McCosker 1977:82 [ref. 6836], McCosker & Castle 1986:185 [ref. 5690], Paxton et al. 1989:120 [ref. 12442], McCosker et al. 1989:298 [ref. 13288]). Ophichthidae: Ophichthinae.

Phyllophorus Rafinesque 1815:90 [ref. 3584]. Masc. Not available, name only. Unplaced genera.

Phyllophryne Pietsch 1984:39 [ref. 5380]. Fem. *Histiophryne scortea* McCulloch & Waite 1918:74. Type by original designation (also monotypic). Valid (Paxton et al. 1989:280 [ref. 12442]). Antennariidae.

Phyllopteryx (subgenus of *Hippocampus*) Swainson 1839:332 [ref. 4303]. Fem. *Syngnathus foliatus* Shaw 1804:456. Type by monotypy. Authorship of type is Shaw; Swainson's fig. 102 apparently a retracing of Shaw's pl. 180. Valid (Dawson 1985:158 [ref. 6541], Kuiter 1988 [ref. 6371], Paxton et al. 1989:428 [ref. 12442]). Syngnathidae: Syngnathinae.

Phyllorhinichthys Pietsch 1969:365 [ref. 3471]. Masc. *Phyllorhinichthys micractis* Pietsch 1969:366. Type by original designation (also monotypic). Valid (Pietsch 1974:32 [ref. 5332], Bertelsen & Pietsch 1977:178 [ref. 7063], Bertelsen in Whitehead et al. 1986:1398 [ref. 13677]). Oneirodidae.

Phylogephyra Boulenger 1898:330 [ref. 544]. Fem. *Phylogephyra altaica* Boulenger 1898:330. Type by original designation (also monotypic). Misspelled *Phyllogephyra* by Jordan 1920:479 [ref. 4905]. Possibly valid; see comments in Travers 1989:191 [ref. 13578]. Salmonidae: Thymallinae.

Phymatophryne Le Danois 1964:115 [ref. 6571]. Fem. *Antennarius maculatus* Desjardins 1840:1. Type by original designation (also monotypic). Synonym of *Antennarius* Daudin 1816 (Pietsch 1984:34 [ref. 5380]). Antennariidae.

Physailia Boulenger 1901:445 [ref. 557]. Fem. *Physailia pellucida* Boulenger 1901:445. Type by monotypy. Second species doubtfully included. Synonym of *Parailia* Boulenger 1899 (De Vos 1986:38 [ref. 6191]); as a valid subgenus (Burgess 1989:98 [ref. 12860]). Schilbeidae.

Physiculus Kaup 1858:88 [ref. 2576]. Masc. *Physiculus dalwigki* Kaup 1858:88. Type by monotypy. Valid (Cohen 1973:325 [ref. 6589], Cohen 1979 [ref. 6950], Paulin 1983:96 [ref. 5459], Fahay & Markle 1984:266 [ref. 13653], Okamura in Masuda et al. 1984:91 [ref. 6441], Cohen in Whitehead et al. 1986:722 [ref. 13676], Cohen 1986:328 [ref. 5646], Paulin 1989:103 [ref. 9297], Paxton et al. 1989:301 [ref. 12442]). Moridae.

Physodon Valenciennes in Müller & Henle 1838:30 [ref. 3069]. Masc. *Carcharias (Physodon) muelleri* Valenciennes in Müller & Henle 1838:30. Type by monotypy. Also apparently appeared as Valenciennes in Bonaparte 1838:10 (of separate) [ref. 4979] with no species named. Synonym of *Scoliodon* Müller & Henle 1837 (Compagno 1984:533 [ref. 6846], Compagno 1988:284 [ref. 13488]). Carcharhinidae.

Physogaster (subgenus of *Tetrodon [=Tetraodon]*) Müller 1841:252 [ref. 3061]. Fem. *Tetraodon oblongus* Bloch 1796:505. Type by subsequent designation. Two species (*oblongus* and *lunaris*) mentioned; earliest subsequent designation perhaps is Bleeker 1865:46 [ref. 416] through objective synonym *Gastrophysus*; Jordan 1919:196 [ref. 2410] lists *lunaris* as type. Apparently preoccupied, replaced by *Gastrophysus* Müller 1832. Synonym of *Lagocephalus* Swainson 1839 (Shipp 1974:17 [ref. 7147]). Tetraodontidae.

Physopyxis Cope 1871:112 [ref. 5775]. Fem. *Physopyxis lyra* Cope 1871:112. Type by monotypy. More complete description in Cope 1872:273 [ref. 921]. Valid (Bailey & Baskin 1976:2 [ref. 161], Burgess 1989:223 [ref. 12860]). Doradidae.

Physoschistura Banarescu & Nalbant in Singh et al. 1982:208 [ref. 4030]. Fem. *Noemacheilus brunneanus* Annandale 1918:44. Type by original designation. Valid (Kottelat 1989:12 [ref. 13605], Kottelat 1990:20 [ref. 14137]). Balitoridae: Nemacheilinae.

Phytichthys Hubbs in Jordan 1923:234 [ref. 2421]. Masc. *Xiphister chirus* Jordan & Gilbert 1880:135. Type by being a replacement name. Replacement for *Xiphistes* Jordan & Starks 1895, preoccupied in insects [details not researched]. Valid (Robins et al. 1980:52 [ref. 7111], Yatsu 1986 [ref. 5150]). Stichaeidae.

Piabarchus Myers 1928:90 [ref. 3100]. Masc. *Piabina analis* Eigenmann 1914:8. Type by original designation (also monotypic). Valid (Géry 1977:395 [ref. 1597], Mahnert & Géry 1988:1 [ref. 6407]). Characidae.

Piabina Reinhardt 1866:49 [ref. 3694]. Fem. *Piabina argentea* Reinhardt 1866:50. Type by monotypy. Valid (Géry 1977:403 [ref. 1597]); synonym of *Creagrutus* Günther 1864 (Mahnert & Géry 1988:5 [ref. 6407]). Characidae.

Piabuca Müller & Troschel (ex Cuvier) 1844:85 [ref. 3070]. Fem. *Salmo argentinus* Linnaeus 1766:511. Type by monotypy. Made available earlier by Oken as *Piabucus*; objective synonym of *Piabucus* Oken 1817. Characidae.

Piabucidium (subgenus of *Piabucus*) Myers in Eigenmann & Myers 1929:496 [ref. 1263]. Neut. *Piabucus spilurus* Günther 1864:344. Type by original designation (also monotypic). Synonym of *Piabucus* Oken 1817. Characidae.

Piabucina Valenciennes in Cuvier & Valenciennes 1849:161 [ref. 1014]. Fem. *Piabucina erythrinoides* Valenciennes in Cuvier & Valenciennes 1849:161. Type by monotypy. Synonym of *Lebiasina* Valenciennes 1846 (Géry 1977:123 [ref. 1597]); valid (Weitzman & Cobb 1975:2 [ref. 7134]). Lebiasinidae: Lebiasininae.

Piabucus Oken (ex Cuvier) 1817:1183 [ref. 3303]. Masc. *Salmo argentinus* Linnaeus 1766:511. Type by subsequent designation. See Gill 1903:966 [ref. 5768]. Type designated by Eigenmann 1910:440 [ref. 1224]. Valid (Géry 1977:374 [ref. 1597], Vari 1977:1 [ref. 7037]). Characidae.

Piaractus Eigenmann 1903:148 [ref. 1218]. Masc. *Myletes brachypomus* Cuvier 1818:452. Type by original designation (also monotypic). Misspelled *Piarctus* by Eigenmann & Allen 1942:247 [ref. 1246]. Synonym of *Colossoma* Eigenmann & Kennedy 1903, as a valid subgenus (Géry 1976:50 [ref. 14199], Géry 1977:255 [ref. 1597]); valid (Géry 1986:97 [ref. 6012], Géry et al. 1987:441 [ref. 6001], Machado-Allison 1986:1 [ref. 12757]). Characidae: Serrasalminae.

Picorellus Rafinesque 1820:165 [ref. 7306]. Masc. *Esox vittatus* Rafinesque 1818:447. Also in Rafinesque 1820:70 (Dec.) [ref. 3592]. Based on a drawing in Rafinesque's notebook; apparently mythical (Jordan & Evermann 1896:625 [ref. 2443]). Synonym of *Esox* Linnaeus 1758. Esocidae.

Pictiblennius Whitley 1930:19 [ref. 4671]. Masc. *Blennius intermedius* Ogilby 1915:127. Type by original designation. Synonym of *Blennius* Linnaeus 1758 (Bath 1973:519 [ref. 7212]); synonym of *Parablennius* Miranda-Ribeiro 1915 (Bath 1982:219 [ref. 5640], Bath & Hutchins 1986:168 [ref. 5151]); valid (Yoshino in Masuda et al. 1984:295 [ref. 6441]). Blenniidae.

Pictilabrus Gill 1891:403 [ref. 1735]. Masc. *Labrus laticlavius* Richardson 1839:99. Type by monotypy. Valid (Russell 1988:35 [ref. 12549]). Labridae.

Piedrabuenia Gosztonyi 1977:235 [ref. 6103]. Fem. *Piedrabuenia ringueleti* Gosztonyi 1977:236. Type by original designation (also monotypic). Zoarcidae.

Piescephalus Rafinesque 1810:63 [ref. 3594]. Masc. *Piescephalus adherens* Rafinesque 1810:63. Type by monotypy. Synonym of *Lepadogaster* Goüan 1770 (Briggs 1955:33 [ref. 637], Briggs 1973:654 [ref. 7222]). Gobiesocidae: Gobiesocinae.

Pietschichthys Kharin 1989:158 [ref. 12556]. Masc. *Pietschichthys horridus* Kharin 1989:159. Type by original designation (also monotypic). Oneirodidae.

Pigus (subgenus of *Gardonus*) Bonaparte 1846:29 [ref. 519]. *Cyprinus pigus* Lacepède 1803:607, 610. Type by absolute tautonymy. Synonym of *Rutilus* Rafinesque 1820 (Howes 1981:45 [ref. 14200]). Cyprinidae.

Pikea Steindachner 1874:375 [ref. 4219]. Fem. *Grystes lunulatus* Guichenot 1863:4. Type by monotypy. Correct spelling for genus of type species is *Gristes*. Valid (Matsuura in Uyeno et al. 1983:315 [ref. 14275], Kendall 1984:501 [ref. 13663], Katayama in Masuda et al. 1984:133 [ref. 6441]); synonym of *Liopropoma* Gill 1861 (Randall & Taylor 1988:7 [ref. 6429]). Serranidae: Liopropomatinae.

Pileoma DeKay 1842:16 [ref. 1098]. *Pileoma semifasciatum* DeKay 1842:16. Type by monotypy. Synonym of subgenus *Percina* of genus *Percina* Haldeman 1842 (Collette & Banarescu 1977:1455 [ref. 5845]). Percidae.

Pillaia Yazdani 1972:134 [ref. 4815]. Fem. *Pillaia indica* Yazdani 1972:134. Type by original designation (also monotypic). Valid (Jayaram 1981:390 [ref. 6497]); synonym of *Chaudhuria* Annandale 1918 (Travers 1984:142 [ref. 5147]). Chaudhuriidae.

Pilodictis see *Pylodictis*. Ictaluridae.

Pimelenotus Gill 1858:387 [31] [ref. 1750]. Masc. *Pimelenotus wilsoni* Gill 1858:391. Type by subsequent designation. On p. 31 of separate. Type designated by Eigenmann & Eigenmann 1890:116 [ref. 12251]. Spelled *Pimelonotus* by Günther 1864:114 [ref. 1974]. Synonym of *Rhamdia* Bleeker 1858 (Mees 1974:152 [ref. 2969]). Pimelodidae.

Pimelepterus Lacepède 1802:429 [ref. 4929]. Masc. *Pimelepterus bosquii* Lacepède 1802:429, 430. Type by monotypy. Misspellings include *Pimelipterus* and *Pimelopterus*; species sometimes spelled *boscii*. Synonym of *Kyphosus* Lacepède 1801 (Desoutter 1973:420 [ref. 7203]). Kyphosidae: Kyphosinae.

Pimeletropis Gill 1859:196 [ref. 1756]. Fem. *Pimeletropis lateralis* Gill 1859:196. Type by monotypy. Spelled *Pimelotopsis* by Bleeker 1862:12 [ref. 393], Jordan 1919:289 [ref. 4904] and others. Synonym of *Calophysus* Müller & Troschel 1843. Pimelodidae.

Pimelodella Eigenmann & Eigenmann 1888:131 [ref. 1249]. Fem. *Pimelodus cristatus* Müller & Troschel 1848:628. Type by original designation. Valid (Mees 1974:142 [ref. 2969], Burgess 1989:280 [ref. 12860], Malabarba 1989:141 [ref. 14217]). Pimelodidae.

Pimelodina Steindachner 1876:149 [ref. 4225]. Fem. *Pimelodina flavipinnis* Steindachner 1876:150. Type by monotypy. Valid (Stewart 1986 [ref. 5211], Burgess 1989:277 [ref. 12860]). Pimelodidae.

Pimelodon Lesueur in Vaillant 1896:28 [ref. 13482]. Masc. *Pimelodon insignarius* Vaillant 1896:28. Type by monotypy. Appeared first in Lesueur 1819:155 [ref. 12589], but that regarded as probably a vernacular and nonbinomial; made available as above according to Taylor 1969:20 [ref. 6555]. Synonym of *Noturus* Rafinesque 1818 (Taylor 1969:20 [ref. 6555]). Ictaluridae.

Pimelodus Lacepède 1803:93 [ref. 4930]. Masc. *Pimelodus maculatus* Lacepède 1803:94, 103. Type by subsequent designation. Needs more research. Type perhaps designated first by Bleeker as *bagre* (Bleeker 1862:386 [391], 1862:8 [ref. 393]), and if this is the first designation than current usage would be upset. Type usually given as above. Valid (Mees 1974:130 [ref. 2969], Burgess 1989:279 [ref. 12860], Malabarba 1989:142 [ref. 14217]). Pimelodidae.

Pimelometopon Gill 1864:58 [ref. 1694]. Neut. *Labrus pulcher* Ayres 1854:3. Type by original designation. Synonym of *Semicossyphus* Günther 1861. Labridae.

Pimephales Rafinesque 1820:242 [ref. 7310]. Masc. *Pimephales promelas* Rafinesque 1820:242. Type by monotypy. Also appeared in Rafinesque 1820:52 (Dec.) [ref. 3592]; Rafinesque states name is from "Pimelecephales"; *Pimelocephales* Meek 1904:50 [ref. 2958] is an unjustified emendation of *Pimephales*. Valid (Mayden 1989:25 [ref. 12555]). Cyprinidae.

Pingalla Whitley 1955:45 [ref. 4724]. Fem. *Pingalla gilberti* Whitley 1955:46. Type by original designation. Synonym of *Terapon* Cuvier 1816 (Mees & Kailola 1977:32 [ref. 5183]); valid (Vari 1978:307 [ref. 4514], Allen & Merrick 1984 [ref. 6248], Paxton et al. 1989:535 [ref. 12442]). Terapontidae.

Pinguilabrum Hildebrand 1946:168 [ref. 2161]. Neut. *Epelytes punctatus* Evermann & Radcliffe 1917:71. Type by being a replacement name. Replacement for *Epelytes* Evermann & Radcliffe 1917, preoccupied in insects [details not researched]. Synonym of *Graus* Philippi 1887 (Johnson & Fritzsche 1989:2 [ref. 13513]). Kyphosidae: Girellinae.

Pinguipes Cuvier in Cuvier & Valenciennes 1829:277 [ref. 4879]. Masc. *Pinguipes brasilianus* Cuvier in Cuvier & Valenciennes 1829:277. Type by monotypy. Appeared first as "Les Pinguipes" in Cuvier (Mar.) 1829:153 [ref. 995], with "*Ping. Brasiliensis*" listed but without distinguishing features (unavailable); genus and species more fully described in Cuvier & Valenciennes (Apr.) 1829 to which both taxa date ["*Ping.*" as given by Cuvier 1829:153 is not sufficient to latinize *Pinguipes*]. Valid (Nakamura in Nakamura et al. 1986:266 [ref. 14235], Rosa & Rosa 1987 [ref. 6066]). Pinguipedidae.

Pinirampus Bleeker 1858:198, 205, 208 [ref. 365]. *Pimelodus pirinampu* Agassiz in Spix & Agassiz 1829. Type by monotypy. Species initially given by Bleeker as *pinirampus* Agassiz, but Bleeker's spelling was incorrect; species also later renamed *typus* by Bleeker. *Pirinampus* Günther 1864:135 [ref. 1974] is an unjustified emendation. Valid (Stewart 1986:665 [ref. 5211], Burgess 1989:278 [ref. 12860]). Pimelodidae.

Pinjalo Bleeker 1873:178 [ref. 13527]. *Caesio pinjalo* Bleeker 1850:10. Type by original designation. Appeared first without sufficient distinguishing features in Bleeker 1845:521 [ref. 312]. Type not *P. typus* Bleeker (name only). Genus apparently dates to Bleeker 1873 (see Randall et al. 1987:2 [ref. 6431]). Valid (Johnson 1980:10 [ref. 13553], Akazaki in Masuda et al. 1984:168 [ref. 6441], Allen 1985:139 [ref. 6843], Akazaki & Iwatsuki 1986 [ref. 6316], Randall et al. 1987 [ref. 6431]). Lutjanidae.

Pinnacorvina (subgenus of *Johnius*) Fowler 1925:4 [ref. 1401]. Fem. *Rhinoscion epipercus* Bleeker 1863:64. Type by original designation (also monotypic). Synonym of *Pseudotolithus* Bleeker 1863 (Daget & Trewavas 1986:335 [ref. 6211]). Sciaenidae.

Pinniwallago Gupta, Jayaram & Hajela 1981:291 [ref. 1959]. *Pinniwallago kanpurensis* Gupta, Jayaram & Hajela 1981:290. Type by original designation (also monotypic). Valid (Jayaram 1981:396 [ref. 6497]). Siluridae.

Pintoichthys Fowler 1954:316, 386 [ref. 1465]. Masc. *Biotodoma trifasciatus* Eigenmann & Kennedy 1903:536. Type by original designation (also monotypic). Synonym of *Apistogramma* Regan 1913 (Kullander 1980:21 [ref. 5526], Kullander 1986:155 [ref. 12439], Kullander & Nijssen 1989:74 [ref. 14136]). Cichlidae.

Pipettella (subgenus of *Stigmatopora*) Whitley 1951:62 [ref. 4711]. Fem. *Stigmatopora nigra* Kaup 1856:53. Type by original designation (also monotypic). Type species appeared first as a nomen nudum in Kaup 1853:233. Preoccupied by Haeckel 1887 in Radiolaria, replaced by and objective synonym of *Nigracus* Whitley 1953. Synonym of *Stigmatopora* Kaup 1853 (Dawson 1982:576 [ref. 5443], Dawson 1985:174 [ref. 6541]). Syngnathidae: Syngnathinae.

Pipidonia Smith 1931:39 [ref. 4047]. Fem. *Pipidonia quinquecincta* Smith 1931:39. Type by monotypy. Valid (Lachner & McKinney 1974:877 [ref. 2547]); synonym of *Gobiopsis* Steindachner 1861 (Lachner & McKinney 1978:10 [ref. 6603]). Gobiidae.

Piramutana Bleeker 1858:355, 357 [ref. 365]. *Bagrus piramuta* Kner 1857:382. Type by monotypy. Also in Bleeker 1862:11 [ref. 393]. Valid (Burgess 1989:281 [ref. 12860]). Pimelodidae.

Pirarara Agassiz in Spix & Agassiz 1829:23, pl. 6 [ref. 13]. *Silurus hemilopterus* Bloch & Schneider 1801. Type by monotypy. Appeared first as name in synonymy under *Phractocephalus* (see also legend for Pl. 6); made available by Bleeker 1862:11 [ref. 393] and 1863:100 [ref. 401] back to Agassiz; type perhaps *Phractocephalus bicolor* Agassiz in Spix & Agassiz, not *Silurus hemilopterus* Bloch & Schneider as given by Bleeker. See Kottelat 1988:78, 80 [ref. 13380]. Synonym of *Phractocephalus* Agassiz 1829 (Kottelat 1989 [ref. 14233]). Pimelodidae.

Piratia Rafinesque 1815:91 [ref. 3584]. Not available, name only. Unplaced genera.

Piratinga Bleeker 1858:357 [ref. 365]. Fem. *Bagrus reticulatus* Kner 1857:376. Type by subsequent designation. Also in Bleeker 1862:11 [ref. 393] where type is designated. Synonym of *Brachyplatystoma* Bleeker 1862 (Mees 1974:120 [ref. 2969]). Pimelodidae.

Pirellinus Whitley 1928:226 [ref. 4661]. Masc. *Oxybeles lumbricoides* Bleeker 1854:163. Type by being a replacement name. Replacement for *Helminthodes* Gill 1864 (late Nov. - early Dec.), preoccupied by Marsh 1864 (Nov.) in fossil worms. Synonym of *Carapus* Rafinesque 1810 (Arnold 1956:260 [ref. 5315]). Carapidae: Carapinae.

Pirene Gistel 1848:IX [ref. 1822]. *Chaetodon aruanus* Linnaeus 1758:275. Type by being a replacement name. Unneeded replacement for *Dascyllus* Cuvier, not preoccupied by *Dascillus*. *Pirene* is apparently itself preoccupied. Objective synonym of *Dascyllus* Cuvier 1829 (Randall & Allen 1977:351 [ref. 6482]). Pomacentridae.

Pirinampus Günther 1864:135 [ref. 1974]. See *Pinirampus* Bleeker 1858. Pimelodidae.

Pisciregia Abbott 1899:342 [ref. 1]. Fem. *Pisciregia beardsleei* Abbott 1899:1899. Type by monotypy. Synonym of *Basilichthys* Girard 1855 (White 1985:17 [ref. 13551]). Atherinidae: Atherinopsinae.

Pisinnicaesio (subgenus of *Pterocaesio*) Carpenter 1987:31 [ref. 6430]. Fem. *Caesio chrysozona* Cuvier (ex Kuhl & van Hasselt) in Cuvier & Valenciennes 1830:440. Type by original designation. Synonym of *Pterocaesio* Bleeker 1874, but as a valid subgenus (Carpenter 1988:4 [ref. 9296]). Caesionidae.

Pisodonophis Kaup 1856:47 [ref. 2572]. Masc. *Ophisurus cancrivorus* Richardson 1848:97. Type by subsequent designation. Type designated by Bleeker 1864:36 [ref. 409]. As *Pisoodonophis* in Kaup 1856:17 [ref. 2573]; unjustifiably emended to *Pisodontophis* by Günther 1870:55 [ref. 1995]. Fowler (MS) also lists a *Pisoodontus* Popta. Valid (Blache et al. 1973:250 [ref. 7185], McCosker 1977:82 [ref. 6836], Castle 1984:38 [ref. 6171], Asano in Masuda et al. 1984:31 [ref. 6441], McCosker & Castle 1986:185 [ref. 5690], Paxton et al. 1989:120 [ref. 12442], McCosker et al. 1989:298 [ref. 13288]). Ophichthidae: Ophichthinae.

Pithecocharax Fowler 1906:319 [ref. 1373]. Masc. *Salmo anostomus* Linnaeus 1758:312. Type by being a replacement name. Unneeded replacement for *Anostomus* Scopoli 1777, not preoccupied. Objective synonym of *Anostomus* Scopoli 1777 (Winterbottom 1980:9 [ref. 4755]). Curimatidae: Anostominae.

Pithecomyzon (subgenus of *Lipomyzon*) Fowler 1913:54 [ref. 1388]. Masc. *Chasmistes cujus* Cope 1883:149. Type by original designation (also monotypic). Synonym of *Chasmistes* Jordan 1878 (Robins et al. 1980:26 [ref. 7111]). Catostomidae.

Pituna Costa 1989:225 [ref. 14270]. Fem. *Pituna poranga* Costa

1989:226. Type by original designation (also monotypic). Aplocheilidae: Rivulinae.

Placidochromis Eccles & Trewavas 1989:108 [ref. 13547]. Masc. *Haplochromis longimanus* Trewavas 1935:108. Type by original designation. Cichlidae.

Placocheilus Wu in Wu, Lin, Chen, Chen & He 1977:382 [ref. 4807]. Masc. *Discognathus cardofasciatus* Pellegrin & Chevey 1936. Type by original designation (also monotypic). Misspelled *Placoheilus* in index (p. 593). Valid (Chu & Cui in Chu & Chen 1989:278 [ref. 13584]). Cyprinidae.

Placopharynx Cope 1870:467 [ref. 913]. Masc. *Placopharynx carinatus* Cope 1870:467. Type by monotypy. Synonym of *Moxostoma* Rafinesque 1820 (Robins & Raney 1956:6 [ref. 12222]). Catostomidae.

Plagiogeneion Forbes 1890:273 [ref. 1343]. Neut. *Therapon rubiginosus* Hutton 1876:209. Type by monotypy. Valid (Heemstra & Randall 1977:366 [ref. 7057], Heemstra 1986:638 [ref. 5660]). Emmelichthyidae.

Plagiognathops Berg 1907:419 [ref. 270]. Masc. *Plagiognathus jelskii* Dybowski 1872:216. Type by being a replacement name. Replacement for *Plagiognathus* Dybowski 1872, preoccupied by Fieber 1858 in Hemiptera. Valid (Yang 1964:127 [ref. 13500], Howes 1981:45 [ref. 14200] with wrong type, Li 1986:480 [ref. 6154]). Cyprinidae.

Plagiognathus Dybowski 1872:216 [ref. 1170]. Masc. *Plagiognathus jelskii* Dybowski 1872:216. Type by monotypy. Preoccupied by Fieber 1858 in Hemiptera, replaced by and objective synonym of *Plagiognathops* Berg 1907. Cyprinidae.

Plagiogrammus Bean 1894:699 [ref. 230]. Masc. *Plagiogrammus hopkinsii* Bean 1894:700. Type by monotypy. Valid (Follett & Powell 1988:150 [ref. 6234]). Stichaeidae.

Plagiopsetta Franz 1910:64 [ref. 1481]. Fem. *Plagiopsetta glossa* Franz 1910:64. Type by monotypy. Doubtful synonym of *Samariscus* Gilbert 1905 (Norman 1934:407 [ref. 6893]); valid (Sakamoto 1984 [ref. 5273], Sakamoto in Masuda et al. 1984:353 [ref. 6441]). Pleuronectidae: Samarinae.

Plagioscion Gill 1861:82 [ref. 1771]. Masc. *Sciaena squamosissima* Heckel 1840:433. Type by subsequent designation. Described by Gill 1861 without included species. First addition of species not researched. Type designated by Jordan and Eigenmann 1889:380 [ref. 2439]. Valid (Chao 1978:43 [ref. 6983]). Sciaenidae.

Plagiotremus Gill 1865:138 [ref. 1677]. Masc. *Plagiotremus spilistius* Gill 1865:140. Type by monotypy. Valid (Smith-Vaniz 1976:108 [ref. 4144], Yoshino in Masuda et al. 1984:297 [ref. 6441], Springer 1986:753 [ref. 5719], Smith-Vaniz 1987:46 [ref. 6404]). Blenniidae.

Plagiusa Rafinesque 1815:83 [ref. 3584]. Fem. As "*Plagiusa* R. sp. do.," meaning a new name for a species of the preceding genus (*Pleuronectes*). Not available, name only (apparently intended for *Pleuronectes plagusia* Linnaeus). Cynoglossidae: Symphurinae.

Plagopterus Cope 1874:130 [ref. 932]. Masc. *Plagopterus argentissimus* Cope 1874:130. Type by monotypy. Valid (Miller & Hubbs 1960:33 [ref. 11934]). Cyprinidae.

Plagusia Bonaparte 1833:puntata 27 [ref. 516]. Fem. *Plagusia lactea* Bonaparte 1833:puntata 27. Type by original designation. Described on unnumbered pp. 7-8 in puntata 27; apparently can be regarded as an original description, and with "Ci è sembrato opportuno il riguardarlo come tipo d'un genere da se, e per questo abbiamo adottato il nome *Plagusia*." Preoccupied by Latreille 1804 in Crustacea. Cynoglossidae: Symphurinae.

Plagusia Browne 1789:445 [ref. 669]. Fem. Not available, published in rejected work on Official Index (Opinion 89). Cynoglossidae: Symphurinae.

Plagusia Cuvier (ex Browne) 1816:224 [ref. 993]. Fem. *Pleuronectes plagusia* of Bloch & Schneider (not Linnaeus) 1801. Type not fully researched. Apparently not available, preoccupied by Latreille 1804 in Crustacea. Synonym of *Symphurus* Rafinesque 1810 (Torchio 1973:635 [ref. 6892]). Cynoglossidae: Symphurinae.

Plagusia Jarocki 1822:295 [ref. 4984]. On Official Index as a junior homonym of *Plagusia* Latreille 1804 (Opinion 712). Original not seen. Unplaced genera.

Plagyodontis Steller in Pallas 1814:383 [ref. 3351]. *Alepisaurus aesculapius* Bean 1883:661. Appeared without species; subsequent addition of species not researched. Type above as given by Jordan 1917:84 [ref. 2407]; Jordan spelled genus as *Plagyodus*, based on *Plagyodum* (used by Pallas on p. 384). See account of *Plagyodus* Günther 1867. Alepisauridae.

Plagyodus Günther (ex Steller in Pallas) 1867:185 [ref. 1985]. Masc. Type by subsequent designation. Jordan regarded *Plagyodus* as making available Pallas' *Plagyodentem* given in dative case, but Pallas (p. 383) used *Plagyodontis*. Günther's use probably can be regarded as an incorrect subsequent spelling of *Plagyodontis*, but Günther's treatment probably is the first addition of species (three) to *Platyodontis*; if so, subsequent designation needs to be established, and the type given for *Platyodontis* will change. Synonym of *Alepisaurus* Lowe 1833. Alepisauridae.

Planaltina Böhlke 1954:265 [ref. 594]. Fem. *Planaltina myersi* Böhlke 1954:267. Type by original designation (also monotypic). Valid (Géry 1977:358 [ref. 1597], Weitzman & S. Fink 1985:1 et seq. [ref. 5203], Weitzman et al. 1988:383 [ref. 13557]). Characidae: Glandulocaudinae.

Planctanthias Fowler 1935:385 [ref. 1421]. Masc. *Planctanthias praeopercularis* Fowler 1935:385. Type by original designation (also monotypic). Serranidae: Anthiinae.

Plancterus (subgenus of ***Fundulus***) Garman 1895:96 [ref. 1538]. Masc. *Fundulus kansae* Garman 1895:103. Type by monotypy. Valid (Parenti 1981:493 [ref. 7066]); synonym of *Fundulus* Lacepède 1803 (Poss & Miller 1983:55 [ref. 14470]). Cyprinodontidae: Fundulinae.

Planerocephalus see *Phanerocephalus*. Gymnuridae.

Planiliza (subgenus of ***Moolgarda***) Whitley 1945:17 [ref. 4707]. *Moolgarda (Planiliza) ordensis* Whitley 1945:17. Type by original designation (also monotypic). Mugilidae.

Planiloricaria (subgenus of ***Pseudohemiodon***) Isbrücker 1971:276 [ref. 2300]. Fem. *Pseudohemiodon (Planiloricaria) cryptodon* Isbrücker 1971:278. Type by original designation (also monotypic). Valid (Isbrücker 1980:122 [ref. 2303], Isbrücker & Nijssen 1986:103 [ref. 5212], Isbrücker & Nijssen 1986 [ref. 7321], Burgess 1989:444 [ref. 12860]). Loricariidae.

Planiprora Whitley 1931:327 [ref. 4672]. Fem. *Platycephalus fuscus* Cuvier in Cuvier & Valenciennes 1829:241. Type by original designation (also monotypic). Synonym of *Platycephalus* Bloch 1795 (Paxton et al. 1989:468 [ref. 12442] based on placement of the type species). Platycephalidae.

Plargyrus Rafinesque 1820:240 [ref. 7310]. Masc. *Rutilus plargyrus* Rafinesque 1820:240. Type by absolute tautonymy; also verified by ICZN in Opinion 33. Also appeared in Rafinesque

1820:50 (Dec.) [ref. 3592]. Synonym of *Notropis* Rafinesque 1818 (Gilbert 1978:15 [ref. 7042]); synonym of subgenus *Luxilus* Rafinesque 1820 of *Notropis* (authors); synonym of *Lyxilus* when treated as valid (e.g., as by Mayden 1989 [ref. 12555]. Cyprinidae.

Platacanthus Day 1865:296 [ref. 5295]. Masc. *Platacanthus agrensis* Day 1865:296. Type by monotypy. Also appeared in Day 1865:204 [ref. 1074]. Preoccupied by Waldeim 1850 [?1849] in fossil fishes; not replaced. Synonym of *Lepidocephalichthys* Bleeker 1863 (Roberts 1989:103 [ref. 6439]). Cobitidae: Cobitinae.

Platanichthys Whitehead 1968:479 [ref. 4659]. Masc. *Lile platana* Regan 1917:394. Type by original designation (also monotypic). Valid (Grande 1985:250 [ref. 6466], Whitehead 1985:121 [ref. 5141]). Clupeidae.

Plataplochilus Ahl 1928:116 [ref. 78]. Masc. *Haplochilichthys ngaensis* Ahl 1924:135. Type by original designation (also monotypic). Correct spelling for genus of type species is *Aplocheilichthys.* Valid (Parenti 1981:513 [ref. 7066], Wildekamp et al. 1986:191 [ref. 6198]). Cyprinodontidae: Aplocheilichthyinae.

Platax Cuvier 1816:334 [ref. 993]. Masc. *Chaetodon teira* Bloch & Schneider 1801 (= *Chaetodon teira* Forsskål 1775:xii, 60). Type by subsequent designation. Type designated by Bleeker 1876:309 [ref. 448]. Valid (Johnson 1984:465 [ref. 9681], Hayashi in Masuda et al. 1984:181 [ref. 6441], Smith 1986:605 [ref. 5712], Kishimoto et al. 1988 [ref. 13446]). Ephippidae.

Plataxoides Castelnau 1855:21 [ref. 766]. Masc. *Plataxoides dumerilii* Castelnau 1855:21. Type by monotypy. Synonym of *Pterophyllum* Heckel 1840 (Kullander 1986:210 [ref. 12439]). Cichlidae.

Platea Steindachner 1898:323 [ref. 4238]. Fem. *Platea insignis* Steindachner 1898:323. Type by monotypy. Preoccupied by Brisson 1760 in Aves, replaced by *Dadyanos* Whitley 1951. Objective synonym of *Dadyanos* Whitley 1951 (Gosztonyi 1977:210 [ref. 6103]). Zoarcidae.

Platessa Cuvier 1816:220 [ref. 993]. Fem. *Pleuronectes platessa* Linnaeus 1758:269. Type by absolute tautonymy. On Offical List (Direction 33). Objective synonym of *Pleuronectes* Linnaeus 1758 (Nielsen 1973:623 [ref. 6885]). Pleuronectidae: Pleuronectinae.

Platichthys Girard 1854:139 [ref. 1817]. Masc. *Platichthys rugosus* Girard 1854:139. Type by monotypy. Valid (Norman 1934:376 [ref. 6893], Nielsen 1973:626 [ref. 6885], Ahlstrom et al. 1984:643 [ref. 13641], Sakamoto 1984 [ref. 5273], Sakamoto in Masuda et al. 1984:353 [ref. 6441], Nielsen in Whitehead et al. 1986:1304 [ref. 13677]). Pleuronectidae: Pleuronectinae.

Platiglossus Klein 1776:300 [ref. 4919]. Masc. Not available, published in a work that does not conform to the principle of binominal nomenclature. In the synonymy of *Halichoeres* Rüppell 1835. Labridae.

Platipornax (subgenus of *Rhinobatos*) Whitley 1939:244 [ref. 4695]. *Rhinobatos thouin* Anonymous 1798:287, 677, 685. Type by monotypy. Synonym of *Rhinobatos* Linck 1790. Rhinobatidae: Rhinobatinae.

Platirostra Lesueur 1818:227 [ref. 2735]. Fem. *Platirostra edentula* Lesueur 1818:228. Type by monotypy. *Planirostra, Planinostra,* and *Platyrostra* are misspellings. Synonym of *Polyodon* Lacepède 1797. Polyodontidae.

Platistus Rafinesque 1815:89 [ref. 3584]. Masc. As "*Platistus* Bl. [Bloch]." Not available, name only; based on style in this work this name is regarded as an incorrect subsequent spelling of *Platystacus* Bloch 1794. Aspredinidae: Aspredininae.

Platophrys Swainson 1839:187, 302 [ref. 4303]. Fem. *Pleuronectes ocellatus* Agassiz in Spix & Agassiz 1829:85. Type by monotypy. Described as a genus on p. 187, as a subgenus of *Psetta* on p. 302. Synonym of *Bothus* Rafinesque 1810 (Norman 1934:220 [ref. 6893], Amaoka 1969:161 [ref. 105], Nielsen 1973:620 [ref. 6885]). Bothidae: Bothinae.

Platopterus Rafinesque 1815:93 [ref. 3584]. Masc. *Raja miraletus* Linnaeus 1758:232. Type by being a replacement name. As "*Platopterus* R. *Raja* L.," meaning a new name *Platopterus* Rafinesque for *Raja* Linnaeus. Based on style in this work, this is an available (unneeded) replacement name for and objective synonym of *Raja* Linnaeus 1758. Rajidae.

Platotichthys Nichols 1921:21 [ref. 3174]. Masc. *Platotichthys chartes* Nichols 1921:21. Type by original designation (also monotypic). Synonym of *Bothus* Rafinesque 1810 (Norman 1934:220 [ref. 6893]). Bothidae: Bothinae.

Platuronides Roule & Bertin 1924:64 [ref. 3828]. Masc. *Platuronides danae* Roule & Bertin 1924:64. Type by monotypy. Also appeared as new in Roule & Bertin 1929 [ref. 3829]. Valid (Asano in Masuda et al. 1984:30 [ref. 6441]); synonym of *Serrivomer* Gill & Ryder 1883 (Tighe 1989:617 [ref. 13291]). Serrivomeridae.

Platyallabes Poll 1977:129 [ref. 3533]. Fem. *Gymnallabes tihoni* Poll 1944:79. Type by original designation (also monotypic). Valid (Teugels 1986:100 [ref. 6193], Burgess 1989:147 [ref. 12860]). Clariidae.

Platybelone Fowler 1919:2 [ref. 1397]. Fem. *Belone platyura* Bennett 1831:168. Type by original designation. *Eucaulus* Ogilby 1909 (preoccupied) and *Tropidocaulus* Ogilby 1921 are objective synonyms. Valid (Parin 1973:259 [ref. 7191], Collette et al. 1984:352 [ref. 11422], Yoshino in Masuda et al. 1984:78 [ref. 6441], Collette & Parin in Whitehead et al. 1986:607 [ref. 13676], Paxton et al. 1989:342 [ref. 12442]). Belonidae.

Platyberyx Zugmayer 1911:8 [ref. 6161]. Masc. *Platyberyx opalescens* Zugmayer 1911:8. Type by monotypy. Also appeared in Zugmayer 1911 (Dec.):101 [ref. 4846]. Valid (Nielsen 1973:339 [ref. 6885], Post in Whitehead et al. 1986:748 [ref. 13676]). Caristiidae.

Platycanthus (subgenus of *Tetrosomus*) Swainson 1839:194, 324 [ref. 4303]. Masc. *Ostracion auritus* Shaw 1798:338. Type by monotypy. Ostraciidae: Ostraciinae.

Platycara McClelland 1839:246, 299, 427 [ref. 2923]. Neut. *Balitora brucei* Gray 1830. Type by being a replacement name. Also in McClelland 1839:944, 947 [ref. 2924]; as published in ref. 2924 it is less clear that it is a replacement name, and Jordan and Fowler both regard *P. nasuta* McClellan as type as first designated by Jordan 1919:195 [ref. 2410]. Synonym of *Garra* Hamilton 1822 (Karaman 1971:232 [ref. 2560], Lévêque & Daget 1984:301 [ref. 6186], Roberts 1989:40 [ref. 6439]). Cyprinidae.

Platycephaloides (subgenus of *Clarias*) Teugels 1982:11 [ref. 6670]. Masc. *Clarias platycephalus* Boulenger 1902. Type by original designation. Also appeared in Teugels 1982:736 [ref. 4377]. Synonym of *Clarias* Scopoli 1777 (Teugels 1986:69 [ref. 6193]). Clariidae.

Platycephalops Smith 1957:822 [ref. 4110]. Masc. *Eleotris polyzonatus* Klunzinger 1871:482. Type by original designation (also monotypic). Xenisthmidae.

Platycephalus Bloch 1795:96 [ref. 464]. Masc. *Platycephalus spathula* Bloch 1795:97 (= *Callionymus indicus* Linnaeus 1758:250). Type by monotypy. Valid (Hureau 1973:592 [ref. 7197], Ochiai in Masuda et al. 1984:322 [ref. 6441], Hureau in Whitehead et al. 1986:1241 [ref. 13677], Knapp 1986:484 [ref. 5683], Paxton et al. 1989:467 [ref. 12442]). Platycephalidae.

Platycephalus Miranda-Ribeiro 1902:3, 7 [ref. 3710]. Masc. *Sciaena undecimalis* Bloch 1792:60. Apparently not an original description. Miranda-Ribeiro used *Platycephalus* Bloch & Schneider 1801:58 [ref. 471] for *Centropomus undecimalis*, but *Platycephalus* Bloch 1795 (in Platycephalidae) predates use by Bloch & Schneider 1801. In the synonymy of *Centropomus* Lacepède 1802. Centropomidae: Centropominae.

Platychoerops Klunzinger 1880:399 [ref. 2624]. Masc. *Platychoerops muelleri* Klunzinger 1880:399. Type by original designation (also monotypic). Misspelled *Platychaerops* by Jordan 1919:404 [ref. 4904]. Species originally spelled *mülleri*, correction mandatory. On Official Index as a junior homonym of Charlesworth 1855 in mammals (Opinion 1123). Labridae.

Platyclarias Poll 1977:136 [ref. 3533]. Masc. *Platyclarias machadoi* Poll 1977:141. Type by original designation (also monotypic). Valid (Teugels 1986:100 [ref. 6193], Burgess 1989:147 [ref. 12860]). Clariidae.

Platydoras Bleeker 1862:5 [ref. 393]. Masc. *Silurus costatus* Linnaeus 1766:306. Type by original designation. Valid (Burgess 1989:224 [ref. 12860]). Doradidae.

Platygaster (subgenus of *Clupea*) Swainson 1838:278, 280 [ref. 4302]. Fem. *Clupea africana* Bloch 1795:45. Type by subsequent designation. Also in Swainson 1839:186, 294 [ref. 4303]. Type designated by Swain 1882:280 [ref. 5966]. Preoccupied by Latreille 1809 in Hymenoptera and Schilling 1829 in Hemiptera; not replaced. Synonym of *Ilisha* Richardson 1846 (Poll et al. 1984 [ref. 6172], Whitehead 1985:261 [ref. 5141]). Clupeidae.

Platygillellus Dawson 1974:40 [ref. 1065]. Masc. *Gillelus (sic) rubellulus* Kendall & Radcliffe 1912. Type by original designation. Valid (Dawson 1982:61 [ref. 1072]). Dactyloscopidae.

Platyglanis Daget 1979:821 [ref. 1026]. Masc. *Platyglanis depierrei* Daget 1979:821. Type by original designation (also monotypic). Valid (Risch 1986:35 [ref. 6190], Burgess 1989:71 [ref. 12860]). Bagridae.

Platyglossus Bleeker (ex Klein) 1862:411 [ref. 382]. Masc. *Julis annulatis* Valenciennes in Cuvier & Valenciennes 1839:482. Type by original designation (also monotypic). Also appeared in Bleeker 1862:99 [ref. 386]. Synonym of *Halichoeres* Rüppell 1835 (Fowler). Labridae.

Platygnathochromis Eccles & Trewavas 1989:228 [ref. 13547]. Masc. *Haplochromis melanonotus* Regan 1922:708. Type by original designation (also monotypic). Cichlidae.

Platygobio Gill 1863:178 [ref. 1674]. Masc. *Pogonichthys communis* Girard 1856:188. Type by monotypy. Synonym of *Hybopsis* Agassiz 1854 (authors); valid (authors). Cyprinidae.

Platygobius Bleeker 1874:316 [ref. 437]. Masc. *Gobius macrorhynchus* Bleeker 1867:403. Type by original designation (also monotypic). Synonym of *Chonophorus* Poey 1860 (Maugé 1986:363 [ref. 6218]), but see *Aqaous* Valenciennes 1837. Gobiidae.

Platyinius Gill 1862:236, 237 [ref. 1664]. Masc. *Mesoprion vorax* Poey 1861:154. Type by monotypy. Synonym of *Pristipomoides* Bleeker 1852 (Allen 1985:141 [ref. 6843]); as a valid subgenus (Akazaki & Iwatsuki 1986 [ref. 6316], Akazaki & Iwatsuki 1987:325 [ref. 6699]). Lutjanidae.

Platylepes (subgenus of *Seriola*) Swainson 1839:176, 247 [ref. 4303]. Fem. *Scomber lactarius* Bloch & Schneider 1801:31. Type by monotypy. Apparently described independently of *Lactarius* Valenciennes 1833. Lactariidae.

Platynematichthys Bleeker 1858:357 [ref. 365]. Masc. *Bagrus punctulatus* Kner 1857:380. Type by monotypy. Also in Bleeker 1862:11 [ref. 393]. Valid (Burgess 1989:281 [ref. 12860]). Pimelodidae.

Platypanchax Ahl 1928:116 [ref. 78]. Masc. *Haplochilus modestus* Pappenheim & Boulenger 1914:252. Type by original designation (also monotypic). Synonym of *Hypsopanchax* Myers 1924 (Parenti 1981:513 [ref. 7066]). Aplocheilidae: Aplocheilinae.

Platypharodon Herzenstein 1891:226 [ref. 4917]. Masc. *Platypharodon extremus* Herzenstein 1891:229. Type by subsequent designation. Type designated by Jordan 1920:442 [ref. 4905]. Valid (Tsao 1964:192 [ref. 13501], Wu 1987:46 [ref. 12822]). Cyprinidae.

Platypodon Gill 1862:401 [ref. 1783]. Masc. *Carcharias (Prionodon) menisorrah* Valenciennes in Müller & Henle 1841:46. Type by original designation (also monotypic). Synonym of *Carcharhinus* Blainville 1816 (Garrick 1982:19 [ref. 5454] but misspelled *Platyposdon*, Compagno 1984:449 [ref. 6846], Cappetta 1987:121 [ref. 6348], Compagno 1988:307 [ref. 13488]). Carcharhinidae.

Platypodus Lacepède 1804:211 [ref. 12515]. Masc. *Labrus furca* Lacepède 1802:429, 477. Type by monotypy. Belontiidae.

Platypoecilus Günther 1866:350 [ref. 1983]. Masc. *Platypoecilus maculatus* Günther 1866:350. Type by monotypy. Synonym of *Xiphophorus* Heckel 1848 (Rosen & Bailey 1963:62 [ref. 7067]). Poeciliidae.

Platypogon Starks 1913:28 [ref. 4197]. Masc. *Platypogon caerulorostris* Starks 1913:29. Type by monotypy. Valid (Burgess 1989:282 [ref. 12860]). Pimelodidae.

Platyptera Cuvier (ex Kuhl & van Hasselt) 1829:248 [ref. 995]. Fem. *Platyptera aspro* Cuvier (ex Kuhl & van Hasselt) 1837:321. Type by subsequent monotypy. *P. melanocephala* and *P. trigonocephala* mentioned with original description, but both were name only and unavailable [never made available]. First available species added by Cuvier in Cuvier & Valenciennes 1837:321 as above. Preoccupied by Meigen 1803 in Diptera, replaced by and objective synonym of *Rhyacichthys* Boulenger 1901. Rhyacichthyidae.

Platypterus (subgenus of *Apistes*) Swainson 1839:65, 180, 265 [ref. 4303]. Masc. *Apistes taenionotus* Cuvier 1828:168. Type by subsequent designation. *Platypterus* on p. 183 is a misspelling for *Platyptera* (p. 280). Earliest type designation not researched. Preoccupied by Chandoir 1838 in Coleoptera. Objective synonym of *Ablabys* Kaup 1873. Scorpaenidae: Apistinae.

Platyrhina Müller & Henle 1838:90 [ref. 3066]. Fem. *Raja sinensis* Bloch & Schneider 1801:34, 157. Type by original designation. Also in Müller & Henle 1838:85 [ref. 3068] and spelled *Platyrrhina* and in 1841:125 [ref. 3069] as *Platyrhina*. On Official List (Opinion 345). Unneeded replacement name *Analithis* Gistel 1848 also placed on Official Index. Valid (Nakaya in Masuda et al. 1984:12 [ref. 6441]). Platyrhinidae.

Platyrhinoidis Garman 1881:516, 522 [ref. 1529]. Fem. *Platyrhina triseriata* Jordan & Gilbert 1881:36. Type by monotypy. Platyrhinidae.

Platysalmo (subgenus of *Salmo*) Behnke 1969:2 [ref. 250]. Masc.

Salmo (Platysalmo) platycephalus Behnke 1969:2. Type by monotypy. Synonym of *Salmo* Linnaeus 1758, but as a valid subgenus (Kendall & Behnke 1984:144 [ref. 13638]). Salmonidae: Salmoninae.

Platysilurus Haseman 1911:320 [ref. 2047]. Masc. *Platysilurus barbatus* Haseman 1911:320. Type by monotypy. Pimelodidae.

Platysmacheilus Lu, Luo & Chen 1977:533 [ref. 13495]. Masc. *Saurogobio exiguus* Lin 1932:516. Type by original designation. Cyprinidae.

Platysomatichthys Bleeker 1862:425 [ref. 388]. Masc. *Pleuronectes pinguis* Fabricius 1824:40. Type by monotypy. Synonym of *Reinhardtius* Gill 1861 (Norman 1934:288 [ref. 6893], Nielsen 1973:627 [ref. 6885]). Pleuronectidae: Pleuronectinae.

Platysomatos Bloch 1797:115 [ref. 5123]. *Platystacus cotylephorus* Bloch 1794:54. Type by being a replacement name. According to Harry 1947 [ref. 14435], this name is an unexplained replacement for *Platystacus* Bloch 1794. Absolute synonym of *Platystacus* (Harry 1947 [ref. 14435]); synonym of *Asprtedo* Scopoli 1777. Aspredinidae: Aspredininae.

Platysome Liénard 1832:112 [ref. 12516]. Neut. *Dules caudavittatus* Cuvier in Cuvier & Valenciennes 1829 (= *Holocentrus caudavittatus* Lacepède 1802:332). Type by monotypy. Appeared as "..., [species] as the type of a new genus...*Platysome*:it is evidently the *Dules caudavittatus*, ..." If regarded as available, then *Platysoma* Scudder 1882:268 [ref. 6462] is an unjustified emendation (and preoccupied); action would be needed to conserve *Kuhlia* Gill 1861. An alternate view is that the type was not definitely referred and the description inadequate. *Platysoma* as a synonym of *Kuhlia* Gill 1861 (Maugé 1986:306 [ref. 6218]). Kuhliidae.

Platysomus Swainson 1839:176, 250 [ref. 4303]. Masc. *Vomer brownii* Cuvier in Cuvier & Valenciennes 1833:89. Type by being a replacement name. Apparently an unneeded replacement for *Vomer* Cuvier (see Swainson 1839:405 [ref. 4303]). Preoccupied by Agassiz 1835 in fossil fishes. Objective synonym of *Vomer* Cuvier 1816. Synonym of *Selene* Lacepède 1802 (Daget & Smith-Vaniz 1986:318 [ref. 6207]). Carangidae.

Platysqualus (subgenus of *Zygaena*) Swainson 1839:192, 318 [ref. 4303]. Masc. *Squalus tiburo* Linnaeus 1758:324. Type by monotypy. Synonym of *Sphyrna* Rafinesque 1810 (Compagno 1984:541 [ref. 6846], Cappetta 1987:127 [ref. 6348], Compagno 1988:362 [ref. 13488]). Sphyrnidae.

Platystacus Bloch 1794:52 [ref. 463]. Masc. *Platystacus cotylephorus* Bloch 1794:54. Type by subsequent designation. Earliest type designation not researched, possibly Bleeker 1863:118 [ref. 401]. *Platystachus* is a misspelling (see also Harry 1947 [ref. 14435]). Synonym of *Aspredo* Scopoli 1777 (Mees 1987:183 [ref. 11510]). Aspredinidae: Aspredininae.

Platystacus Klein 1779:52 [ref. 4924]. Masc. Not available, published in a work that does not conform to the principle of binominal nomenclature. Original not checked. In the synonymy of *Aspredo* Scopoli 1777. Aspredinidae: Aspredininae.

Platystethus Günther 1860:391 [ref. 1963]. Masc. *Cichla cultrata* Bloch & Schneider 1801:343. Type by monotypy. Preoccupied by Mannerheim 1831 in Coleoptera, replaced by *Bathystethus* Gill 1893. Objective synonym of *Bathystethus* Gill 1893 (Paxton et al. 1989:567 [ref. 12442]). Kyphosidae: Scorpidinae.

Platystoma Agassiz in Spix & Agassiz 1829:10, 23 [ref. 13]. Neut. *Silurus lima* Bloch & Schneider 1801:384. Type by subsequent designation. Type designated by Jordan 1917:131 [ref. 2407]. Preoccupied by Meigen 1803 in Diptera; *Abron* Gistel 1848 is a replacement (through *Platystoma* Valenciennes). Objective synonym of *Sorubim* Cuvier 1829 (see Kottelat 1988:80 [ref. 13380]). Pimelodidae.

Platystomatichthys Bleeker 1862:10 [ref. 393]. Masc. *Platystoma sturio* Kner 1857:395. Type by original designation (also monotypic). Valid (Burgess 1989:282 [ref. 12860]). Pimelodidae.

Platytaeniodus Boulenger 1906:451 [ref. 574]. Masc. *Platytaeniodus degeni* Boulenger 1906:451. Type by monotypy. Misspelled *Platyaeniodus* by Jordan 1920:517 [ref. 4905]. Valid (Greenwood 1980:75 [ref. 1899]). Cichlidae.

Platytroctegen Lloyd 1909:145 [ref. 2814]. Masc. *Platytroctegen mirus* Lloyd 1909:145. Type by monotypy. Valid (Krefft 1973:98 [ref. 7166], Quéro et al. in Whitehead et al. 1984:263 [ref. 13675], Sazonov 1986 [ref. 6003]). Platytroctidae.

Platytroctes Günther 1878:249 [ref. 2010]. Masc. *Platytroctes apus* Günther 1878:249. Type by monotypy. Valid (Krefft 1973:98 [ref. 7166], Quéro et al. in Whitehead et al. 1984:264 [ref. 13675], Sazonov 1986 [ref. 6003], Paxton et al. 1989:213 [ref. 12442]). Platytroctidae.

Platytropius Hora 1937:39 [ref. 2210]. Masc. *Pseudeutropius siamensis* Sauvage 1882:154. Type by monotypy. Valid (Burgess 1989:99 [ref. 12860], Kottelat 1989:14 [ref. 13605]). Schilbeidae.

Platyuraspis Fowler 1938:149 [ref. 1427]. Fem. *Uraspis heidi* Fowler 1938:150. Type by original designation (also monotypic). Synonym of *Uraspis* Bleeker 1855 (Smith-Vaniz, pers. comm.). Carangidae.

Plecodus Boulenger 1898:22 [ref. 547]. Masc. *Plecodus paradoxus* Boulenger 1898:22. Type by monotypy. Synonym of *Perissodus* Boulenger 1898 (Liem & Stewart 1976:336 [ref. 7096]); valid (Poll 1986:150 [ref. 6136]). Cichlidae.

Plecoglossus (subgenus of *Salmo*) Temminck & Schlegel 1846:229 [ref. 4374]. Masc. *Salmo (Plecoglossus) altivelis* Temminck & Schlegel 1846:229. Type by monotypy. Valid (Araga in Masuda et al. 1984:33 [ref. 6441], Howes & Sanford 1987:17 [ref. 12820] with suggested change in family placement, Nishida 1988 [ref. 12742]). Plecoglossidae.

Plecopodus Rafinesque 1815:87 [ref. 3584]. Masc. *Gobioides broussonnetii* Lacepède 1800:576, 580. Type by being a replacement name. As "*Plecopodus* R. [Rafinesque] *Gobioides* Lac. [Lacepède]." An available replacement name (unneeded) for *Gobioides* Lacepède 1800. Synonym of *Gobioides* (Maugé 1986 [ref. 6218]). Gobiidae.

Plecostomus Gronow 1763:127 [ref. 1910]. Masc. Not available, published in a rejected work on Official Index (Opinion 261). Loricariidae.

Plecostomus Gronow in Walbaum 1792:663 [ref. 4572]. Masc. *Acipenser plecostomus* Linnaeus 1758:238. Type by subsequent designation. Not available if considered as nonbinominal as reproduced by Walbaum; but recognized as the valid genus by Fowler (MS). Isbrücker 1980:17-18 [ref. 2303] mentions *Plecostomus* Gronow in Gray 1854 and Bleeker 1862, which he synonymizes in *Hypostomus* Lacepède 1803. See also *Plecostomus* Swainson 1839 as mentioned by Isbrücker on p. 125. Loricariidae.

Plecostomus Swainson (ex Gronow) 1839:304 [ref. 4303]. Masc. *Loricaria maculata* Bloch 1794:73. Type by monotypy. Apparently available, and if recognized as such it would replace *Loricariichthys* Bleeker 1862 according to Isbrücker 1980:125 [ref. 2303].

Loricariidae.

Plectobranchus Gilbert 1890:102 [ref. 1623]. Masc. *Plectobranchus evides* Gilbert 1890:102. Type by original designation (also monotypic). Valid. Stichaeidae.

Plectorhinchus Lacepède 1801:134 [ref. 2710]. Masc. *Plectorhinchus chaetodonoides* Lacepède 1801:134, 135. Type by monotypy. *Plectorhincus, Plectorincus, Plectorhynchus, Plectrorhynchus*, and *Plectorrhynchus* of early authors are emendations or incorrect subsequent spellings. Valid (Roux 1973:394 [ref. 7200], Johnson 1980:12 [ref. 13553], Akazaki in Masuda et al. 1984:172 [ref. 6441], Ben-Tuvia & McKay in Whitehead et al. 1986:861 [ref. 13676], Smith & McKay 1986:565 [ref. 5716], Roux 1986:327 [ref. 6209]). Haemulidae.

Plectorhynchus see *Plectorhinchus*. Haemulidae.

Plectranthias Bleeker 1873:238 [ref. 12596]. Masc. *Plectropoma anthioides* Günther 1871:655. Type by monotypy. Also in Bleeker 1875:21 [ref. 4861]. Valid (Randall 1980 [ref. 6717], Kendall 1984:501, 503 [ref. 13663], Katayama in Masuda et al. 1984:133 [ref. 6441], Heemstra & Randall 1986:514 [ref. 5667], Katayama & Yamamoto 1986 [ref. 6716], Paxton et al. 1989:506 [ref. 12442]). Serranidae: Anthiinae.

Plectrochilus Miranda-Ribeiro 1917:50 [ref. 5742]. Masc. *Plectrochilus machadoi* Miranda-Ribeiro 1917:50. Type by monotypy. Valid (Burgess 1989:324 [ref. 12860]). Trichomycteridae.

Plectrogenium Gilbert 1905:634 [ref. 1631]. Neut. *Plectrogenium nanum* Gilbert 1905:634. Type by original designation (also monotypic). Valid (Eschmeyer & Randall 1975:284 [ref. 6389], Amaoka in Masuda et al. 1984:316 [ref. 6441]). Scorpaenidae: Plectrogeninae.

Plectroglyphidodon Fowler & Ball 1924:271 [ref. 1471]. Masc. *Plectroglyphidodon johnstonianus* Fowler & Ball 1924:271. Type by original designation (also monotypic). Valid (Allen 1975:191 [ref. 97], Shen & Chan 1979:51 [ref. 6944], Yoshino in Masuda et al. 1984:197 [ref. 6441], Allen 1986:679 [ref. 5631]). Pomacentridae.

Plectromus Gill 1883:257 [ref. 1724]. Masc. *Plectromus suborbitalis* Gill 1883:258. Type by monotypy. Synonym of *Melamphaes* Günther 1864 (Maul 1973:343 [ref. 7171], Ebeling & Weed 1973:451 [ref. 6898]). Melamphaidae.

Plectroperca Peters 1864:121 [ref. 3438]. Fem. *Plectroperca berendtii* Peters 1864:121. Type by monotypy. Synonym of *Siniperca* Gill 1862. Percoidei.

Plectrophallus (subgenus of *Panamichthys*) Fowler 1932:384 [ref. 1411]. Masc. *Panamichthys tristani* Fowler 1932:384. Type by original designation (also monotypic). Synonym of *Brachyrhaphis* Regan 1913 (Rosen & Bailey 1963:81 [ref. 7067]). Poeciliidae.

Plectroplites Gill 1862:236 [ref. 1664]. Masc. *Datnia ambigua* Richardson 1845:25. Type by monotypy. Synonym of *Macquaria* Cuvier 1839 (Paxton et al. 1989:512 [ref. 12442] based on placement of type species). Percichthyidae.

Plectropoma Quoy & Gaimard (ex Cuvier) 1824:318 [ref. 3574]. Neut. *Plectropoma punctatum* Quoy & Gaimard 1824:318. Type by monotypy. Synonym of *Plectropomus* Oken 1817 (Randall & Hoese 1986:5 [ref. 6009]). Serranidae: Epinephelinae.

Plectropomus Oken (ex Cuvier) 1817:1182 [ref. 3303]. Masc. *Bodianus maculatus* Bloch 1790:48. Type by subsequent designation. Type designated by Jordan, Tanaka & Snyder 1913:152 [ref. 6448]. Based on "Plectropomes" Cuvier 1816:277 [ref. 993] (see Gill 1903:966 [ref. 5768]). Valid (Kendall 1984:500 [ref. 13663], Katayama in Masuda et al. 1984:126 [ref. 6441], Randall & Hoese 1986 [ref. 6009], Paxton et al. 1989:499 [ref. 12442] including discussion of nomenclature). Serranidae: Epinephelinae.

Plectrostethus Myers 1935:5 [ref. 3108]. Masc. *Plectrostethus palawanensis* Myers 1935:5. Type by original designation (also monotypic). Synonym of *Neostethus* Regan 1916 (Parenti 1989:269 [ref. 13486]). Phallostethidae.

Plectrypops Gill 1862:237 [ref. 1664]. Masc. *Holocentrum retrospinis* Guichenot 1853:35. Type by monotypy. Correct spelling for genus of type species is *Holocentrus*. Valid (Woods & Sonoda 1973:382 [ref. 6899], Shimizu in Masuda et al. 1984:114 [ref. 6441], Randall & Heemstra 1986:426 [ref. 5707], Paxton et al. 1989:379 [ref. 12442]). Holocentridae.

Plesienchelys Anderson 1988:268 [ref. 6334]. Fem. *Ophthalmolycus stehmanni* Gosztonyi 1977:230. Type by original designation (also monotypic). Zoarcidae.

Plesiolebias Costa 1989:193 [ref. 14436]. Masc. *Cynolebias xavantei* Costa, Lacerda & Tanizaki 1988. Type by original designation. Aplocheilidae: Rivulinae.

Plesiomyzon Zheng & Chen 1980:90 [99] [ref. 4838]. Masc. *Plesiomyzon baotingensis* Zheng & Chen 1980:90 [99]. Type by original designation (also monotypic). English description on p. 99. Valid (Chen 1980:96 [ref. 6901]). Balitoridae: Balitorinae.

Plesioperca Vaillant 1873:36 [ref. 4492]. Fem. *Plesioperca anceps* Vaillant 1873:37. Type by monotypy. Synonym of *Percina* Haldeman 1842, subgenus *Hadropterus* Agassiz 1854 (Collette & Banarescu 1977:1454 [ref. 5845]). Percidae.

Plesiops Oken (ex Cuvier) 1817:1182 [ref. 3303]. Masc. *Plesiops nigricans* Rüppell 1828:15. Type by subsequent designation. Based on "Les Plésiops" of Cuvier 1816:266 [ref. 993]. Type not named with original description; first addition of species not researched; type apparently by subsequent designation of Bleeker 1876:322 [ref. 448]. Valid (Hayashi in Masuda et al. 1984:140 [ref. 6441], Heemstra 1986:543 [ref. 5660], Paxton et al. 1989:526 [ref. 12442]). Plesiopidae.

Plesiotrygon Rosa, Castello & Thorson 1987:449 [ref. 5974]. Fem. *Plesiotrygon iwamae* Rosa, Castello & Thorson 1987:450. Type by original designation (also monotypic). Potamotrygonidae.

Plethodectes Cope 1870:563 [ref. 914]. Masc. *Plethodectes erythrurus* Cope 1870:563. Type by monotypy. Characidae.

Pleuracromylon Gill 1864:148 [ref. 1697]. *Mustelus laevis* Müller & Henle 1841:190. Type by monotypy. Synonym of *Mustelus* Linck 1790 (Compagno 1973:28 [ref. 7163], Compagno 1984:397 [ref. 6846], Cappetta 1987:116 [ref. 6348], Compagno 1988:219 [ref. 13488]). Triakidae: Triakinae.

Pleuragramma Boulenger 1902:187 [ref. 561]. Neut. *Pleuragramma antarcticum* Boulenger 1902:187. Type by monotypy. Valid (Stevens et al. 1984:563 [ref. 13633], Andersen 1984:25 [ref. 13369]). Nototheniidae.

Pleuranacanthus Bleeker (ex Bibron) 1865:59 et seq. [ref. 416]. Masc. Not available, manuscript name mentioned in passing in the synonymy of *Tetraodon*; apparently never made available later. In the synonymy of *Lagocephalus* Swainson 1839. Tetraodontidae.

Pleurogadus Bean in Jordan 1885:918 [130] [ref. 2385]. Masc. *Gadus gracilis* Tilesius 1810:354. Type by being a replacement name. Replacement for *Tilesia* Swainson 1839, preoccupied by Lamouroux 1821 in Bryozoa. Synonym of *Eleginus* Fischer von Waldheim 1813. Gadidae.

Pleurogobius Seale 1910:536 [ref. 4000]. Masc. No indication that this was being described as a new genus; a misspelling (lapsus) for *Pterogobius* (see Herre 1943:132 [ref. 11020]), as Seale center-headed new genera; Seale's species placed in new genus *Cingulogobius* by Herre 1927:202 [ref. 2104]. Sometimes treated as an available name with type as *P. boulengeri* Seale (e.g., by Tomiyama 1936:59 [ref. 4413]). Gobiidae.

Pleurogrammus Gill 1861:166 [ref. 1775]. Masc. *Labrax monopterygius* Pallas 1810:391. Type by monotypy. Valid (Washington et al. 1984:443 [ref. 13660], Amaoka in Masuda et al. 1984:321 [ref. 6441]). Hexagrammidae: Pleurogramminae.

Pleurolepis Putnam (ex Agassiz) 1863:5 [ref. 3567]. Fem. *Pleurolepis pellucidus* Agassiz in Putnam 1863:5. Type by monotypy. Preoccupied by Quenstedt 1852 in fossil fishes, replaced by *Vigil* Jordan 1919. Synonym of subgenus *Ammocrypta* of genus *Ammocrypta* Jordan 1877 (Collette & Banarescu 1977:1455 [ref. 5845]). Percidae.

Pleuronectes Linnaeus 1758:268 [ref. 2787]. Masc. *Pleuronectes platessa* Linnaeus 1758:269. Type by subsequent designation. Type designated first by Bory de Saint-Vincent, v. 14, 1828:58, 65 [ref. 3853] (see Whitley 1935:137 [ref. 6396]). On Official List (Direction 33). Valid (Norman 1934:348 [ref. 6893], Nielsen 1973:623 [ref. 6885], Ahlstrom et al. 1984:643 [ref. 13641], Sakamoto 1984 [ref. 5273], Sakamoto in Masuda et al. 1984:353 [ref. 6441], Nielsen in Whitehead et al. 1986:1305 [ref. 13677]). Pleuronectidae: Pleuronectinae.

Pleuronichthys Girard 1854:139 [ref. 1817]. Masc. *Pleuronichthys coenosus* Girard 1854:139. Type by monotypy. Valid (Norman 1934:317 [ref. 6893], Ahlstrom et al. 1984:643 [ref. 13641], Sakamoto 1984 [ref. 5273], Sakamoto in Masuda et al. 1984:352 [ref. 6441]). Pleuronectidae: Pleuronectinae.

Pleuroperca (subgenus of *Plectropomus*) Fowler & Bean 1930:195, 201 [ref. 1477]. Fem. *Plectropoma oligacanthus* Bleeker 1854:422. Type by original designation (also monotypic). Synonym of *Plectropomus* Oken 1817 (Randall & Hoese 1986:5 [ref. 6009]). Serranidae: Epinephelinae.

Pleurophysus Miranda-Ribeiro 1918:636 [ref. 3725]. Masc. *Pleurophysus hydrostaticus* Miranda-Ribeiro 1918:636. Type by monotypy. Valid (Burgess 1989:324 [ref. 12860]). Trichomycteridae.

Pleuroscopus Barnard 1927:67 [ref. 193]. Masc. *Pleuroscopus pseudodorsalis* Barnard 1927:67. Type by monotypy. Also appeared in Barnard 1927 (Oct.):437 [ref. 194]. Valid (Mees 1960:47 [ref. 11931], Heemstra 1986:735 [ref. 5660], Kishimoto et al. 1988 [ref. 6648], Pietsch 1989:293 [ref. 12541]). Uranoscopidae.

Pleurosicya Weber 1913:456 [ref. 4602]. Fem. *Pleurosicya boldinghi* Weber 1913:457. Type by monotypy. Valid (Larson & Hoese 1980:33 [ref. 2725], Yoshino in Masuda et al. 1984:283 [ref. 6441], Hoese 1986:800 [ref. 5670], Birdsong et al. 1988:193 [ref. 7303]). Gobiidae.

Pleurosicyops Smith 1959:217 [ref. 4122]. Masc. *Pleurosicyops timidus* Smith 1959:217. Type by original designation (also monotypic). Synonym of *Pleurosicya* Weber 1913 (Larson & Hoese 1980:33 [ref. 2725]). Gobiidae.

Pleurothyris Lowe 1843:64 [ref. 2833]. Fem. *Sternoptyx olfersii* Cuvier 1829:316. Type by monotypy. *Pleurothysis* is a misspelling. Synonym of *Argyropelecus* Cocco 1829 (Baird 1973:123 [ref. 7173] as *Pleurothysis*). Sternoptychidae: Sternoptychinae.

Plicomugil Schultz in Schultz et al. 1953:315, 320 [ref. 3975]. Masc. *Mugil labiosus* Valenciennes in Cuvier & Valenciennes 1836:125. Type by original designation (also monotypic). Mugilidae.

Pliosteostoma Norman 1923:21 [ref. 3212]. Neut. *Pristigaster lutipinnis* Jordan & Gilbert 1881:340. Type by monotypy. Valid (Grande 1985:245 [ref. 6466], Whitehead 1985:284 [ref. 5141]). Clupeidae.

Pliotrema Regan 1906:1 [ref. 3628]. Neut. *Pliotrema warreni* Regan 1906:1. Type by monotypy. Valid (Compagno 1984:132 [ref. 6474], Bass & Heemstra 1986:106 [ref. 5639], Cappetta 1987:65 [ref. 6348]). Pristiophoridae.

Plitops (subgenus of *Holacanthus*) Fraser-Brunner 1933:581 [ref. 671]. Masc. *Holacanthus clarionensis* Gilbert 1890:72. Not available from Fraser-Brunner, no type species designated or indicated after 1930, 2 included species (Art. 13b). Apparently can date to Burton 1934 in the Zoological Record for 1933 (see remarks on Art. 13b in Appendix A). Pomacanthidae.

Plotosus Lacepède 1803:129 [ref. 4930]. Masc. *Platystacus anguillaris* Bloch 1794:61. Type by monotypy. Variously spelled *Plotosis*, *Plotoseus*, and *Plotosius* in early literature. Valid (Jayaram 1981:284 [ref. 6497], Gomon & Taylor 1982 [ref. 8475], Sawada in Masuda et al. 1984:60 [ref. 6441], Gomon 1986:213 [ref. 6286], Taylor & Gomon 1986:160 [ref. 6196], Burgess 1989:180 [ref. 12860], Kottelat 1989:15 [ref. 13605], Paxton et al. 1989:225 [ref. 12442]). Plotosidae.

Pluchus Smith 1949:261 [ref. 5846]. Masc. *Plectorhynchus chubbi* Regan 1919:199. Type by original designation. Synonym of *Plectorhinchus* Lacepède 1801. Haemulidae.

Plumantennatus (subgenus of *Antennarius*) Schultz 1957:(59) 89 [ref. 3969]. Masc. *Antennarius asper* Macleay 1881:580. Type by original designation (also monotypic). Synonym of *Lophiocharon* Whitley 1933 (Pietsch 1984:38 [ref. 5380] but as *Plumantennarius*). Antennariidae.

Pluto Hubbs 1938:291 [ref. 2248]. *Pluto infernalis* Hubbs 1938:292. Type by original designation (also monotypic). Apparently preoccupied in Hymenoptera [details not researched], replaced by *Furmastix* Whitley 1951. Objective synonym of *Furmastix* Whitley 1951. Synonym of *Ophisternon* McClelland 1844 (Rosen & Greenwood 1976:50 [ref. 7094], Daget 1986:291 [ref. 6203]). Synbranchidae.

Pluviopsetta Tanaka 1916:141 [ref. 4326]. Fem. *Pluviopsetta taniguchi* Tanaka 1916:141. Type by monotypy. Pleuronectidae.

Pneumabranchus McClelland 1844:411 [ref. 2927]. Masc. *Pneumabranchus cinereus* McClelland 1844:411. Type by monotypy. Usually attributed to McClelland 1844 [1845]:175, 192 [ref. 2928] with type as *P. striatus*, but appeared first in McClelland 1844 as above with only one included species. Synonym of *Monopterus* Lacepède 1800 (Rosen & Greenwood 1976:56 [ref. 7094], Daget 1986:291 [ref. 6203]). Synbranchidae.

Pneumatophorus (subgenus of *Scomber*) Jordan & Gilbert 1883:593 [ref. 2473]. Masc. *Scomber pneumatophorus* Delaroche 1809:315, 334. Type by absolute tautonymy (or by monotypy). Apparently Gill intended *S. colias* also to go in this subgenus, but his text is unclear. Synonym of *Scomber* Linnaeus 1758, as a valid subgenus (Postel 1973:465 [ref. 7208]). Scombridae.

Pnictes Jordan 1919:343 [ref. 2413]. *Achiropsis asphyxiatus* Jordan & Goss 1889:94. Type by original designation (also monotypic). Achiridae.

Poblana de Buen 1945:495 [ref. 691]. Fem. *Poblana alchichica* de Buen 1945:495. Type by original designation. Valid (Chernoff

1986:189 [ref. 5847]). Atherinidae: Menidiinae.

Podabrus Richardson 1848:11 [ref. 3744]. Masc. *Podabrus centropomus* Richardson 1848:11. Type by subsequent designation. Two included species, earliest type designation not researched. Preoccupied by Gould (May) 1845 in Mammalia, replaced by *Vellitor* Jordan & Starks 1904. Cottidae.

Podager Gistel 1848:IX [ref. 1822]. Masc. *Gerres vaigiensis* Quoy & Gaimard 1824:292. Type by being a replacement name. Unneeded replacement for *Gerres* Cuvier 1824, not preoccupied by *Gerris* Fabricius 1794 in insects. *Podager* itself is preoccupied (see Jordan 1919:338 [ref. 2409]). Objective synonym of *Gerres* Quoy & Gaimard 1824. Gerreidae.

Podateles Boulenger 1902:403 [ref. 568]. *Ateleopus japonicus* Bleeker 1854:19. Type by being a replacement name. Unneeded replacement for and objective synonym of *Ateleopus* Schlegel 1846, not preoccupied by *Atelopus* Dumeril & Bibron 1841 in Reptilia. Ateleopodidae.

Podoleptus Rafinesque 1815:220 [ref. 3584]. Masc. *Leptopus peregrinus* Rafinesque 1814:16. Type by being a replacement name. In "Additions et Corrections" on p. 220, referring back to p. 86. Unneeded replacement for and objective synonym of *Leptopus* Rafinesque 1814, apparently not preoccupied in insects. Synonym of *Lophotus* Giorna 1809 (Palmer 1973:334 [ref. 7195]). Lophotidae.

Podonema Rass 1954:57 [ref. 3609]. Neut. *Laemonema longipes* Schmidt 1938:655. Type by monotypy. Preoccupied by Solier in Gay 1851 in Coleoptera and by Stimpson 1860 in Crustacea, replaced by *Podonematichthys* Whitley 1965. Objective synonym of *Podonematichthys* Whitley 1965. Moridae.

Podonematichthys Whitley 1965:25 [ref. 4733]. Masc. *Laemonema longipes* Schmidt 1938:655. Type by being a replacement name. Replacement for *Podonema* Rass 1954, preoccupied by Solier in Gay 1851 in Coleoptera and by Stimpson 1860 in Crustacea. Valid. Moridae.

Podothecus Gill 1861:77 [ref. 1770]. Masc. *Podothecus peristethus* Gill 1861:259. Type by subsequent monotypy. Proposed by Gill as above without included species, also as name only in Gill 1861:167 [ref. 1775]. More complete description with one species added by Gill 1861:259 [ref. 12597]. Valid (Ilyina 1978 [ref. 6914], Kanayama in Masuda et al. 1984:332 [ref. 6441], Yabe 1985:123 [ref. 11522], Maeda & Amaoka 1988:86 [ref. 12616]). Agonidae.

Poecilia Bloch & Schneider 1801:452 [ref. 471]. Fem. *Poecilia vivipara* Bloch & Schneider 1801:452. Type by subsequent designation. Type designated by Bleeker 1864:140 [ref. 4859]. Spelled *Paecilia* by McClelland 1839:300 [ref. 2923]. Valid (Rosen & Bailey 1963:43, 47 [ref. 7067], Parenti 1981:505 [ref. 7066], Paxton et al. 1989:347 [ref. 12442], Parenti & Rauchenberger 1989:7 [ref. 13538], Malabarba 1989:162 [ref. 14217]). Poeciliidae.

Poecilichthys Agassiz 1854:304, 305 [ref. 69]. Masc. *Etheostoma variatum* Kirtland 1838:168, 192. Type by being a replacement name. Replacement for *Poecilosoma* Agassiz 1850, preoccupied by Hübner 1819 in Lepidoptera and Newman 1838 in Coleoptera. Synonym of subgenus *Etheostoma* of genus *Etheostoma* Rafinesque 1819 (Collette & Banarescu 1977:1456 [ref. 5845]). Percidae.

Poeciliopsis Regan 1913:996 [ref. 3653]. Fem. *Poecilia presidionis* Jordan & Culver in Jordan 1895:413. Type by subsequent designation. Type designated by Henn 1916:119 [ref. 2093]. Misspelled *Poecilopsis* by Jordan 1920:550 [ref. 4905]. On Official List (Opinion 375). Valid (Rosen & Bailey 1963:131 [ref. 7067], Parenti & Rauchenberger 1989:9 [ref. 13538]). Poeciliidae.

Poecilistes Hubbs 1926:63, 68 [ref. 2233]. Masc. *Heterandria lutzi* Meek 1904:148. Type by original designation. Treated as a monotypic genus, but Hubbs designated a junior synonym as type. Synonym of *Poeciliopsis* Regan 1913 (Rosen & Bailey 1963:131 [ref. 7067]). Poeciliidae.

Poecilobrycon Eigenmann 1909:43 [ref. 1222]. Masc. *Poecilobrycon harrisoni* Eigenmann 1909:43. Type by original designation. Synonym of *Nannostomus* Günther 1872 (Weitzman & Cobb 1975:3 [ref. 7134], Géry 1977:131 [ref. 1597] as a valid subgenus). Lebiasinidae: Pyrrhulininae.

Poecilocephalus Kaup 1856:43 [ref. 2572]. Masc. *Poecilocephalus bonaparti* Kaup 1856:43. Type by monotypy. Also appeared in Kaup 1856:5 [ref. 2573] and as name only in Kaup in Duméril 1856:198 [ref. 1154]. Synonym of *Ophichthus* Ahl 1789 (Blache et al. 1973:247 [ref. 7185], McCosker 1977:79 [ref. 6836], McCosker et al. 1989:379 [ref. 13288]). Ophichthidae: Ophichthinae.

Poecilocharax Eigenmann 1909:34 [ref. 1222]. Masc. *Poecilocharax bovalii* Eigenmann 1909:34. Type by monotypy. Valid (Géry 1977:111 [ref. 1597]). Characidae.

Poeciloconger Günther 1872:673 [ref. 1997]. Masc. *Poeciloconger fasciatus* Günther 1872:673. Type by monotypy. Spelled *Poecilogonger* once on p. 673 (regarded as a typographical error), as *Poecilogonger* in main genus heading and on Pl. 68; misspelled *Poecilogconger* in Jordan 1923:131 [ref. 2421]. Valid (Smith 1989:511 [ref. 13285]). Congridae: Congrinae.

Poecilocypsilurus (subgenus of *Cypsilurus [Cypselurus]*) Bruun 1935:84 [ref. 5130]. Masc. *Exocoetus callopterus* Günther 1866:292. Type by original designation (also monotypic). Synonym of *Cypselurus* Swainson 1838, but as a valid subgenus (Collette et al. 1984:338 [ref. 11422]). Exocoetidae.

Poeciloides Steindachner 1863:176 [ref. 4208]. Masc. *Poeciloides bimaculatus* Steindachner 1863:176. Type by monotypy. Misspelled *Poecilodes* by Jordan 1919:329 [ref. 4904]. *P. bimaculatus* Steindachner is an original description, not *X. bimaculatus* Heckel [of which it is a subjective synonym]. Synonym of *Heterandria* Agassiz 1853 (Rosen & Bailey 1963:128 [ref. 7067]). Poeciliidae.

Poecilophis Kaup 1856:66 [ref. 2572]. Masc. *Gymnothorax catenatus* Bloch 1795:84. Type by subsequent designation. Type designated by Jordan 1919:272 [ref. 2410]. Also in Kaup 1856:98 [ref. 2573] and as name only in Kaup in Duméril 1856:200 [ref. 1154]. Synonym of *Echidna* Forster 1777 (Böhlke et al. 1989:130 [ref. 13286]). Muraenidae: Muraeninae.

Poecilopsetta Günther 1880:48 [ref. 2011]. Fem. *Poecilopsetta colorata* Günther 1880:48. Type by monotypy. Valid (Norman 1934:387 [ref. 6893], Ahlstrom et al. 1984:643 [ref. 13641], Sakamoto 1984 [ref. 5273], Sakamoto in Masuda et al. 1984:353 [ref. 6441], Heemstra 1986:864 [ref. 5660], Quéro et al. 1988 [ref. 12837]). Pleuronectidae: Poecilopsettinae.

Poecilosoma Agassiz 1850:299 [ref. 66]. Neut. *Etheostoma variatum* Kirtland 1838:168, 192. Type by subsequent designation. Type designated by Agassiz 1854:306 [ref. 69]. Preoccupied by Hübner 1819 in Lepidoptera and Newmann 1838 in Coleoptera [not by Stephens 1829 in Hemiptera (nomen nudum)]; replaced by *Poecilichthys* Agassiz 1854. Synonym of subgenus *Etheostoma* of genus *Etheostoma* Rafinesque 1819 (Collette & Banarescu 1977:1455 [ref. 5845]). Percidae.

Poecilosomatops (subgenus of *Characidium*) Fowler 1906:323 [ref. 1373]. Masc. *Characidium etheostoma* Cope 1872:259. Type by original designation (also monotypic). Synonym of *Characidium* Reinhardt 1866. Characidae: Characidiinae.

Poecilosomus Swainson 1839:183 [ref. 4303]. Masc. Apparently not available, description not diagnostic; evidently *Amblyopus* Valenciennes used instead of *Poecilosomus* by Swainson on p. 278. In the synonymy of *Amblyopus* Valenciennes 1837. Gobiidae.

Poecilothrissa Regan 1917:201 [ref. 3668]. Fem. *Poecilothrissa congica* Regan 1917:202. Type by monotypy. Valid (Poll et al. 1984:50 [ref. 6172], Grande 1985:247 [ref. 6466], Whitehead 1985:147 [ref. 5141]). Clupeidae.

Poecilurichthys Gill 1858:414, 417 [ref. 1750]. Masc. *Poecilurichthys brevoortii* Gill 1858:417. Type by subsequent designation. Type designated by Eigenmann 1910:432 [ref. 1224]. Synonym of *Astyanax* Baird & Girard 1854, as a valid subgenus (Géry 1977:426 [ref. 1597]). Characidae.

Pogonathus Lacepède (ex Commerson) 1803:120 [ref. 4930]. Masc. *Pogonathus courbina* Lacepède 1803:120, 121. Type by subsequent designation. Type apparently designated first by Jordan 1917:65 [ref. 2407]. Spelled *Pogonatus* in early literature.

Pogonognathus Agassiz 1846:301 [ref. 64] is an unjustified emendation. Synonym of *Pogonias* Lacepède 1801 (Chao 1978:34 [ref. 6983]). Sciaenidae.

Pogoneleotris Bleeker 1875:107 [ref. 440]. Fem. *Eleotris heterolepis* Günther 1869:445. Type by original designation (also monotypic). Valid (Hoese, pers. comm.). Eleotridae.

Pogonias Lacepède 1801:137 [ref. 2710]. Masc. *Pogonias fasciatus* Lacepède 1801:137, 138. Type by monotypy. Spelled *Pogonius* by Jarocki 1822:196 [ref. 4984]. Valid (Chao 1978:34 [ref. 6983]). Sciaenidae.

Pogonichthys Girard 1854:136 [ref. 1817]. Masc. *Pogonichthys inaequilobus* Baird & Girard in Girard 1854:136. Type by monotypy. Valid. Cyprinidae.

Pogonocharax Regan 1907:261 [ref. 3630]. Masc. *Pogonocharax rehi* Regan 1907:261. Type by monotypy. Based on an aquarium fish (probably from southern Asia), wrongly reported from Argentina and wrongly thought to be a characin (R. M. Bailey). Synonym of *Esomus* Swainson 1839. Cyprinidae.

Pogonoculius Fowler 1938:134 [ref. 1426]. Masc. *Pogonoculius zebra* Fowler 1938:134. Type by original designation (also monotypic). Synonym of *Ptereleotris* Gill 1863 (Randall & Hoese 1985 [ref. 5197]). Microdesmidae: Ptereleotrinae.

Pogonognathus Bleeker 1849:73 [ref. 316]. Masc. *Pogonognathus barbatus* Bleeker 1849. Type by monotypy. Monacanthidae.

Pogonogobius Smith 1931:37 [ref. 4047]. Masc. *Gobius planifrons* Day 1873:108. Type by monotypy. Synonym of *Gobiopsis* Steindachner 1860 (Lachner & McKinney 1978:10 [ref. 6603]). Gobiidae.

Pogonolycus Norman 1937:106 [ref. 3227]. Masc. *Pogonolycus elegans* Norman 1937:106. Type by original designation (also monotypic). Valid (Gosztonyi 1977:238 [ref. 6103], Anderson 1984:578 [ref. 13634], Pequeño 1989:49 [ref. 14125]). Zoarcidae.

Pogononemacheilus (subgenus of *Noemacheilus*) Fowler 1937:158 [ref. 1425]. Masc. *Noemacheilus masyae* Smith 1933:58. Type by original designation (also monotypic). Synonym of *Noemacheilus* Kuhl & van Hasselt 1823 (Kottelat 1984:225 [ref. 5292]); synonym of *Nemacheilus* Bleeker 1863 (Kottelat 1990:20 [ref. 14137]). Balitoridae: Nemacheilinae.

Pogonoperca Günther 1859:51, 169 [ref. 1961]. Fem. *Pogonoperca ocellata* Günther 1859:169. Type by monotypy. Valid (Kendall 1984:501 [ref. 13663], Katayama in Masuda et al. 1984:139 [ref. 6441]). Serranidae: Grammistinae.

Pogonophis Myers & Wade 1941:78 [ref. 3133]. Masc. *Pogonophis fossatus* Myers & Wade 1941:79. Type by original designation (also monotypic). Valid (McCosker 1977:83 [ref. 6836]); synonym of *Herpetoichthys* Kaup 1856 (McCosker et al. 1989:364 [ref. 13288]). Ophichthidae: Ophichthinae.

Pogonophryne Regan 1914:13 [ref. 3661]. Fem. *Pogonophryne scotti* Regan 1914:13. Type by monotypy. Valid (Andriashev 1967 [ref. 5205], Eakin 1981:138 [ref. 14216], Eakin 1981 [ref. 8609], Eakin 1981 [ref. 8610], Stevens et al. 1984:563 [ref. 13633], Eakin & Kock 1984 [ref. 13452], Eakin 1987 [ref. 6224], Eakin 1988 [ref. 9116], Eakin 1988 [ref. 6573], Balushkin 1988 [ref. 9291] in Artedidraconidae). Harpagiferidae.

Pogonopoma (subgenus of *Plecostomus*) Regan 1904:205 [ref. 3621]. Neut. *Plecostomus werthheimeri* Steindachner 1867:701. Type by subsequent designation. Type designated by Eigenmann 1910:407 [ref. 1224]. Valid (Isbrücker 1980:9 [ref. 2303], Burgess 1989:429 [ref. 12860]). Loricariidae.

Pogonopomoides Gosline 1947:109 [ref. 1857]. Masc. *Rhinelepis parahybae* Steindachner 1877:2. Type by original designation (also monotypic). Valid (Isbrücker 1980:15 [ref. 2303], Burgess 1989:430 [ref. 12860]). Loricariidae.

Pogonoscorpius Regan 1908:236 [ref. 3634]. Masc. *Pogonoscorpius seychellensis* Regan 1908:236. Type by monotypy. Possibly a synonym of *Rhinopias* Gill 1905 (Eschmeyer et al. 1973:287, 303 [ref. 6390]). Scorpaenidae: Scorpaeninae.

Pogonymus Gosline 1959:71 [ref. 1861]. Masc. *Pogonymus pogognathus* Gosline 1959:72. Type by original designation (also monotypic). Synonym of *Eleutherochir* Bleeker 1879 (Nakabo 1982:109 [ref. 3139]); synonym of *Draculo* Snyder 1911 (Fricke 1982:72 [ref. 5432], Fricke 1986:772 [ref. 5653]). Callionymidae.

Pogostoma Rafinesque 1818:445 [ref. 3587]. Neut. *Pogostoma leucops* Rafinesque 1818:447. Type by monotypy. Also appeared in Rafinesque 1820:54 (Feb.) [ref. 7305] and 1820:34 (Dec.) [ref. 3592]. *Pogonostoma* Agassiz 1846: 301 [ref. 64] is an unjustified emendation. Based on a drawing by Audubon, apparently mythical. Percidae.

Polemius Kaup 1858:333 [ref. 2580]. Masc. *Apistus alatus* Cuvier in Cuvier & Valenciennes 1829:392. Type by monotypy. Preoccupied by Leconte 1851 in Coleoptera. Objective synonym of *Apistus* Cuvier 1829. Scorpaenidae: Apistinae.

Polipturus Rafinesque 1815:84 [ref. 3584]. Masc. *Scomberomorus plumierii* Lacepède 1801:292. Type by being a replacement name. As "*Polipturus* R. [Rafinesque] *Scomberomorus* Lac. [Lacepède]." Spelled *Polypturus* and *Polypterurus* by authors. An available (unneeded) replacement for *Scomberomorus* Lacepède 1801. Objective synonym of *Scomberomorus* Lacepède 1801 (Postel 1973:473 [ref. 7208], Collette & Russo 1984:611 [ref. 5221]). Scombridae.

Polistonemus Gill 1861:277 [ref. 1779]. Masc. *Polynemus multifilis* Schlegel in Temminck & Schlegel 1843:29. Type by monotypy. Valid (de Sylva 1984:540 [ref. 13667]); synonym of *Polynemus* Linnaeus 1758 (Roberts 1989:166 [ref. 6439]). Polynemidae.

Polistotrema Gill in Jordan & Gilbert 1881:458 [ref. 12598]. Neut. *Gastrobranchus dombeyi* of Müller (= *Bdellostoma stouti* Lockington 1878:793). Type by monotypy. Appeared in list as "*Polistotrema dombeyi* (Muller) Gill," with *Bdellostoma polytrema* Girard and *B. stouti* Lockington as synonyms in footnote. Also in Jordan & Gilbert 1882:30 [ref. 2368]. Based on a misidentified type species; not *Gastrobranchus dombeyi* Shaw (ex Lacepède). Synonym of *Eptatretus* Cloquet 1819. Myxinidae: Eptatretinae.

Pollachius (subgenus of *Gadus*) Nilsson 1832:43 [ref. 3204]. Masc. *Gadus pollachius* Linnaeus 1758:254. Type by absolute tautonymy. Valid (Svetovidov 1973:308 [ref. 7169], Fahay & Markle 1984:267 [ref. 13653], Svetovidov in Whitehead et al. 1986:690 [ref. 13676]). Gadidae.

Pollichthys Grey 1959:167 [ref. 1904]. Masc. *Yarrella mauli* Poll 1953:59. Type by original designation (also monotypic). Valid (Witzell 1973:120 [ref. 7172], Weitzman 1974:472 [ref. 5174], Badcock in Whitehead et al. 1984:320 [ref. 13675], Ahlstrom et al. 1984:185 [ref. 13643], Fujii in Masuda et al. 1984:45 [ref. 6441], Schaefer et al. 1986:243 [ref. 5709]). Phosichthyidae.

Pollimyrus Taverne 1971:104, 108 [ref. 4349]. Masc. *Marcusenius isidori* Valenciennes in Cuvier & Valenciennes 1846:285. Type by original designation. Valid (Taverne 1972:171 [ref. 6367], Gosse 1984:114 [ref. 6169]). Mormyridae.

Polotus Blyth 1858:283 [ref. 476]. Masc. *Polotus nitidus* Blyth 1858:283. Type by monotypy. Synonym of *Pomadasys* Lacepède 1802 (Roux 1973:391 [ref. 7200], Roux 1986:328 [ref. 6209]). Haemulidae.

Polyacanthonotus Bleeker 1874:368 [ref. 435]. Masc. *Notacanthus rissoanus* Filippi & Verany 1859:190. Type by original designation (also monotypic). Valid (Wheeler 1973:256 [ref. 7190], Sulak et al. 1984 [ref. 5143], Uyeno in Masuda et al. 1984:32 [ref. 6441], Sulak in Whitehead et al. 1986:601 [ref. 13676], Sulak 1986:195 [ref. 5720]). Notacanthidae.

Polyacanthus Cuvier (ex Kuhl) 1829:227 [ref. 995]. Masc. *Chaetodon chinensis* Bloch 1790:5. Type by subsequent designation. Jordan 1917:129 [ref. 2407] listed *Trachopodus colisa* Hamilton as type; then in 1919:173 [ref. 2410] Jordan designated *Chaetodon chinensis* Bloch as type because of earlier restriction by Cuvier & Valenciennes; Cuvier in Cuvier & Valenciennes 1831:353-336 [ref. 4881] placed *colisa* in a new genus *Colisa*, but did not establish a type for *Polyacanthus*. If Jordan is the earliest to validly designate a type, then the type of *Polyacanthus* is *colisa*. Belontiidae.

Polyacantichthys Kaup 1873:82 [ref. 2585]. Masc. *Peristedion orientale* Temminck & Schlegel 1843:37. Type by monotypy. Triglidae: Peristediinae.

Polyamblyodon Norman 1935:21 [ref. 3224]. Masc. *Pachymetopon germanum* Barnard 1934:231. Type by original designation (also monotypic). Valid (Smith & Smith 1986:589 [ref. 5710]). Sparidae.

Polycanthus (subgenus of *Aulostoma*) Swainson 1839:175, 242 [ref. 4303]. Masc. *Gasterosteus spinachia* Linnaeus 1758:296. Type by monotypy. As a subgenus on p. 175, a genus on p. 242. Not *Polycanthus* [*Polyacanthus*] Swainson 1839:174, 236 (ex Kuhl), a subgenus of *Colisa*. Objective synonym of *Spinachia* Cuvier 1816 (Monod 1973:286 [ref. 7193]). Gasterosteidae: Gasterosteinae.

Polycaulus Günther 1860:175 [ref. 1963]. Masc. *Synanceia elongata* Cuvier in Cuvier & Valenciennes 1829:456. Type by monotypy. *Polycaulis* is a misspelling. Objective synonym of *Trachicephalus* Swainson 1839 (Eschmeyer & Rama-Rao 1973:372 [ref. 6391]). Scorpaenidae: Synanceiinae.

Polycentropsis Boulenger 1901:8 [ref. 559]. Fem. *Polycentropsis abbreviata* Boulenger 1901:8. Type by monotypy. Valid (Thys van den Audenaerde & Breine 1986:342 [ref. 6214]). Nandidae: Nandinae.

Polycentrus Müller & Troschel 1848:622 [ref. 3072]. Masc. *Polycentrus schomburgkii* Müller & Troschel 1848:622. Type by monotypy. Valid. Nandidae: Nandinae.

Polycirrhus Bocourt 1869:23 [ref. 486]. Masc. *Polycirrhus dumerilii* Bocourt 1869:23. Type by monotypy. *Polyclemus* Berg 1895 is an unneeded replacement, not preoccupied by *Polycirrus* Grube 1850 in Polychaeta. Synonym of *Paralonchurus* Bocourt 1869 (Chao 1978:38 [ref. 6983]). Sciaenidae.

Polyclemus Berg 1895:54 [ref. 261]. *Polycirrhus dumerili* Bocourt 1869:22. Type by being a replacement name. Unneeded replacement for *Polycirrhus* Bocourt 1869, not preoccupied by *Polycirrus* Grube 1850 in Polychaeta. Synonym of *Paralonchurus* Bocourt 1869 (Chao 1978:38 [ref. 6983]). Sciaenidae.

Polydactylus Lacepède 1803:419 [ref. 4930]. Masc. *Polydactylus plumierii* Lacepède 1803:419, 420. Type by monotypy. Synonym of *Polynemus* Linnaeus 1758 (Daget & Njock 1986:353 [ref. 6216]); valid (Matsuura in Uyeno et al. 1983:396 [ref. 14275], de Sylva 1984:540 [ref. 13667], Yoshino in Masuda et al. 1984:121 [ref. 6441], Smith 1986:721 [ref. 5712]). Polynemidae.

Polydatus Gistel 1848:105 [ref. 1822]. *Polydatus lucius* Gistel 1848 (= *Gadus merluccius* Linnaeus 1758:254). Type by monotypy. Described as "(*G. [Gadus] Merlucius* ober *Polydatus Lucius*, Nobis)" and apparently can be regarded as an available generic name, with *lucius* an unneeded species substitute for *merluccius*. Synonym of *Merluccius* Rafinesque 1810. Merlucciidae: Merlucciinae.

Polyipnus Günther 1887:170 [ref. 2013]. Masc. *Polyipnus spinosus* Günther 1887:170. Type by monotypy. Valid (Weitzman 1974:472 [ref. 5174], Badcock in Whitehead et al. 1984:312 [ref. 13675], Ahlstrom et al. 1984:185 [ref. 13643], Baird 1986:257 [ref. 6288], Paxton et al. 1989:192 [ref. 12442], Harold 1989 [ref. 13508]). Sternoptychidae: Sternoptychinae.

Polylepion Gomon 1977:622 [ref. 1831]. Neut. *Bodianus russelli* Gomon & Randall 1975:443. Type by original designation. Valid (Gomon & Randall 1978:45 [ref. 5481], Yamakawa in Masuda et al. 1984:202 [ref. 6441]). Labridae.

Polymetme McCulloch 1926:166 [ref. 2947]. Fem. *Polymetme illustris* McCulloch 1926:167. Type by original designation (also monotypic). Valid (Witzell 1973:120 [ref. 7172], Weitzman 1974:472 [ref. 5174], Badcock in Whitehead et al. 1984:321 [ref. 13675], Ahlstrom et al. 1984:185 [ref. 13643], Fujii in Masuda et al. 1984:44 [ref. 6441], Schaefer et al. 1986:245 [ref. 5709], Paxton et al. 1989:188 [ref. 12442]). Phosichthyidae.

Polymixia Lowe 1836:198 [ref. 2828]. Fem. *Polymixia nobilis* Lowe 1836:198. Type by monotypy. *Polymyxia* is a misspelling. Valid (Woods & Sonoda 1973:269 [ref. 6899], Nielsen 1973:336 [ref. 6885], Okamura in Masuda et al. 1984:115 [ref. 6441], Kotlyar 1984 [ref. 13450], Hureau in Whitehead et al. 1986:738 [ref. 13676], Heemstra 1986:432 [ref. 5660], Paxton et al. 1989:362 [ref. 12442]). Polymixiidae.

Polynemus Linnaeus 1758:317 [ref. 2787]. Masc. *Polynemus paradiseus* Linnaeus 1758:317. Type designated by ICZN. On Official List (Opinion 93). Valid (Jayaram 1981:347 [ref. 6497], de Sylva 1984:540 [ref. 13667], Daget & Njock 1986:353 [ref. 6216], Kottelat 1989:18 [ref. 13605], Roberts 1989:166 [ref. 6439]).

Polynemidae.

Polyodon Bloch & Schneider 1801:457 [ref. 471]. Masc. *Polyodon folium* Bloch & Schneider 1801:457. Type by monotypy. Objective synonym of *Polyodon* Lacepède 1797. Polyodontidae.

Polyodon Lacepède 1797:49 [ref. 2707]. Masc. *Polyodon feuille* Lacepède 1797:49. Type by monotypy. Valid. Polyodontidae.

Polypera Burke 1912:567 [ref. 701]. Fem. *Neoliparis greeni* Jordan & Starks 1895:829. Type by original designation (also monotypic). Synonym of *Liparis* Scopoli 1777 (Kido 1988:165 [ref. 12287]). Cyclopteridae: Liparinae.

Polyplacapros Fujii & Uyeno 1979:2 [ref. 1516]. Masc. *Polyplacapros tyleri* Fujii & Uyeno 1979:4. Type by original designation (also monotypic). Valid (Winterbottom & Tyler 1983:902 [ref. 5320]). Ostraciidae: Aracaninae.

Polyprion Oken (ex Cuvier) 1817:1182 [ref. 3303]. Masc. *Amphiprion americanus* Bloch & Schneider 1801:205. Subsequent addition of species not researched. Based on "Les Polyprions" Cuvier 1816:282 [ref. 993]. *Polyprium* is a misspelling. Valid (Tortonese 1973:361 [ref. 7192], Heemstra 1986:509 [ref. 5660], Paxton et al. 1989:514 [ref. 12442] in Percichthyidae with Schinz 1822 as author, Roberts 1989 [ref. 12441]). Polyprionidae.

Polyprosopus Couch 1862:67 [ref. 989]. Masc. *Squalus rashleighanus* Couch 1838:51. Type by subsequent designation. Gill gives date for Couch as 1861. Type designated by Gill 1862:398 [p. 32 of separate] [ref. 1783]. Original not seen. Synonym of *Cetorhinus* Blainville 1816 (Cappetta 1987:107 [ref. 6348]). Cetorhinidae.

Polypterichthys Bleeker 1853:608 [ref. 337]. Masc. *Polypterichthys valentini* Bleeker 1853:608. Type by monotypy. Spelled two ways when originally proposed: *Polypterichthys* (p. 597, 608) and *Polijpterichthys* (p. 608), *Polypterichthys* is correctly formed, the latter is a misspelling. Synonym of *Aulostomus* Lacepède 1803. Aulostomidae.

Polypterus Lacepède 1803:340 [ref. 4930]. Masc. *Polypterus bichir* Lacepède 1803:340. Type by subsequent monotypy. Extensive first description was given by Geoffroy St. Hilaire 1802 [1798]:97-98 [ref. 4183], but genus name given only in the vernacular; apparently latinized first by Lacepède 1803 as above, with one species. Valid (Gosse 1984:19 [ref. 6169], Gosse 1988 [ref. 6868]). Polypteridae.

Polyspina Hardy 1983:42 [ref. 5341]. Fem. *Torquigener piosae* Whitley 1955:56. Type by original designation (also monotypic). Valid (see Su et al. 1986:112 [ref. 12582]). Tetraodontidae.

Polysteganus (subgenus of *Dentex*) Klunzinger 1870:763 [ref. 2621]. Masc. *Polysteganus coeruleopunctatus* Klunzinger 1870:763. Type by subsequent designation. Type designated by Jordan 1919:359 [ref. 4904]. Valid (Smith 1978 [ref. 6936], Smith & Smith 1986:590 [ref. 5710]); subgenus of *Dentex* Cuvier 1814 (Bauchot & Hureau in Whitehead et al. 1986:886 [ref. 13676]). Sparidae.

Polytrema Girard 1855:251 [ref. 4912]. Neut. *Bdellostoma polytrema* Girard 1854:199. Type by monotypy by inference from text p. 251. Preoccupied by Rafinesque 1819 in Echini, Ferrusac 1822 in Crustacea, and D'Orbigny 1850 in Bryozoa; apparently not replaced. Myxinidae: Eptatretinae.

Polyuranodon Kaup 1856:65 [ref. 2572]. Masc. *Polyuranodon kuhli* Kaup 1856:65 (= *Muraena polyuranodon* Bleeker 1853:425). Type by monotypy. Bleeker's species needlessly renamed *Polyuranodon kuhli* by Kaup. Also appeared in Kaup 1856:96 [ref. 2573]. Synonym of *Lycodontis* McClelland 1844 (Blache et al. 1973:225 [ref. 7185]). Synonym of *Gymnothorax* Bloch 1795 (Böhlke et al. 1989:145 [ref. 13286]). Muraenidae: Muraeninae.

Pomacampsis (subgenus of *Perca*) Rafinesque 1820:371 [ref. 7308]. *Perca nigropunctata* Rafinesque 1820:371. Type by monotypy. Also in Rafinesque 1820:23 (Dec.) [ref. 3592]. Apparently mythical, description not agreeing with any genus in area, species a nomen dubium. Percidae.

Pomacanthis Rafinesque 1815:86 [ref. 3584]. Not available, name only. Unplaced genera.

Pomacanthodes Gill 1862:244 [ref. 1665]. Masc. *Pomacanthodes zonipectus* Gill 1862:244. Type by monotypy. Synonym of *Holacanthus* Lacepède 1802. Pomacanthidae.

Pomacanthops Smith 1955:383 [ref. 4098]. Masc. *Pomacanthops filamentosus* Smith 1955:383. Type by original designation. Synonym of *Pomacanthus* Lacepède 1802 (Smith & Heemstra 1986:625 [ref. 5714]). Pomacanthidae.

Pomacanthus Lacepède 1802:517 [ref. 4929]. Masc. *Chaetodon arcuatus* Linnaeus 1758:273. Type by subsequent designation. Type apparently designated first by Jordan & Gilbert 1883:615 [ref. 2476]. *Pomacantha* Rafinesque 1815:83 [ref. 3584] is an incorrect subsequent spelling. Valid (Matsuura in Uyeno et al. 1983:390 [ref. 14275], Araga in Masuda et al. 1984:187 [ref. 6441], Smith & Heemstra 1986:625 [ref. 5714]). Pomacanthidae.

Pomacentrus Lacepède 1802:505 [ref. 4929]. Masc. *Chaetodon pavo* Bloch 1787:60. Type by subsequent designation. Type apparently designated by Guichenot 1839:503 (not researched). Spelled *Pomatocentrus* by Gill 1890:9 (Cent. Dict., not researched). Valid (Allen 1975:202 [ref. 97], Shen & Chan 1978:236 [ref. 6945], Yoshino in Masuda et al. 1984:195 [ref. 6441], Allen 1986:680 [ref. 5631]). Pomacentridae.

Pomachromis Allen & Randall 1974:45 [ref. 100]. Masc. *Abudefduf richardsoni* Snyder 1909:600. Type by original designation. Valid (Allen 1975:223 [ref. 97], Shen & Chan 1978:210 [ref. 6945], Yoshino in Masuda et al. 1984:195 [ref. 6441]). Pomacentridae.

Pomadasyina (subgenus of *Pomadasys*) Fowler 1931:304 [ref. 1407]. Fem. *Anthias grunniens* Bloch & Schneider 1801:308. Type by original designation. Synonym of *Pomadasys* Lacepède 1802. Haemulidae.

Pomadasys Lacepède 1802:515 [ref. 4929]. Masc. *Sciaena argentea* Forsskål 1775:51. Type by monotypy. Spelled *Pomadasis* in early literature. Valid (Roux 1973:391 [ref. 7200], Johnson 1980:11 [ref. 13553], Akazaki in Masuda et al. 1984:173 [ref. 6441], Ben-Tuvia & McKay in Whitehead et al. 1986:862 [ref. 13676], Smith & McKay 1986:566 [ref. 5716], Roux 1986:328 [ref. 6209]). Haemulidae.

Pomagonus Rafinesque 1815:86 [ref. 3584]. Not available, name only. Unplaced genera.

Pomanotis Guichenot 1847:390 [ref. 1937]. Fem. *Pomanotis rubescens* Guichenot 1847:392. Type by original designation (also monotypic). Nandidae.

Pomataprion Gill 1863:216 [ref. 1684]. Masc. *Hypsypops dorsalis* Gill 1862:147. Type by subsequent designation. Type designated by Jordan 1919:324 [ref. 4904]. Synonym of *Microspathodon* Günther 1862. Pomacentridae.

Pomatias Bloch & Schneider 1801:559 [ref. 471]. Masc. *Triurus bougainvillianus* Lacepède 1800:200. Type by being a replacement name. For "Triure" of Lacepède; probably can be considered as an unneeded replacement for *Triurus* Lacepède 1800. Objective synonym of *Triurus* Lacepède 1800. Alepocephalidae.

Pomatomichthys Giglioli 1880:20 [ref. 1617]. Masc. *Pomatomichthys constanciae* Giglioli 1880:20. Type by monotypy. Synonym of *Epigonus* Rafinesque 1810 (Tortonese 1973:366 [ref. 7192], Mayer 1974:151 [ref. 6007], Mayer & Tortonese 1977:1 [ref. 7053]). Epigonidae.

Pomatomus Lacepède 1802:435 [ref. 4929]. Masc. *Pomatomus skib* Lacepède 1802:435, 436. Type by monotypy. *Pomatotomus* and *Pomatosus* are misspellings. Valid (Monod 1973:369 [ref. 7193], Tortonese in Whitehead et al. 1986:812 [ref. 13676], Smith & Smith 1986:564 [ref. 5717], Paxton et al. 1989:570 [ref. 12442]). Pomatomidae.

Pomatomus Risso 1810:301 [ref. 3755]. Masc. *Pomatomus telescopium* Risso 1810:261. Type by monotypy. Preoccupied by *Pomatomus* Lacepède 1802. Same as *Pomatomus* of Cuvier 1828. Synonym of *Epigonus* Rafinesque 1810 (Tortonese 1973:366 [ref. 7192]). Epigonidae.

Pomatopsetta Gill 1864:216 [ref. 1704]. Fem. *Platessa dentata* Storer 1839:143. Type by monotypy. Synonym of *Hippoglossoides* Gottsche 1835 (Norman 1934:294 [ref. 6893], Nielsen 1973:624 [ref. 6885]). Pleuronectidae: Pleuronectinae.

Pomatoschistus Gill 1863:263 [ref. 1690]. *Gobius minutus* Pallas 1770:4. Type by original designation (also monotypic). *Pomatochistus* is a misspelling. Valid (Miller 1973:506 [ref. 6888], Miller in Whitehead et al. 1986:1067 [ref. 13677], Maugé 1986:380 [ref. 6218], Birdsong et al. 1988:191 [ref. 7303]). Gobiidae.

Pomodon Boulenger 1895:144 [ref. 537]. Masc. *Plectropoma macrophthalmos* Tschudi 1845:6. Type by being a replacement name. Unneeded replacement for *Hemilutjanus* Bleeker 1876. Objective synonym of *Hemilutjanus* Bleeker 1876. Percoidei.

Pomolobus Rafinesque 1820:170 [ref. 7309]. Masc. *Pomolobus chrysochloris* Rafinesque 1820:171. Type by monotypy. Also appeared in Rafinesque 1820:38 (Dec.) [ref. 3592]. Valid (Grande 1985:249 [ref. 6466]); synonym of *Alosa* Linck 1790 (Whitehead 1985:191 [ref. 5141]). Clupeidae.

Pomotis Cuvier 1829:147 [ref. 995]. Fem. *Pomotis vulgaris* Cuvier 1829:147. Type by monotypy. Cuvier listed in footnote "*Pomotis vulgaris*, Nob., ou *Labrus auritus*, Lin., appelé...[with citation to Catesby]." Jordan 1917:126 [ref. 2407] indicates that Cuvier's *vulgaris* is *Perca gibbosa* Linnaeus and not *auritus*. Type perhaps best considered as *vulgaris* Cuvier 1829. Cuvier does not mention *Pomotis* Rafinesque 1819, and *Pomotis* Cuvier can be considered to be preoccupied by *Pomotis* Rafinesque. Synonym of *Lepomis* Rafinesque 1819. Centrarchidae.

Pomotis (subgenus of *Lepomis*) Rafinesque 1819:420 [ref. 3590]. Fem. *Labrus auritus* Linnaeus 1758:283. Type by subsequent designation. Type designated by Jordan 1917:110 [ref. 2407]. *Pomatotis* is an incorrect subsequent spelling. Objective synonym of *Lepomis* Rafinesque 1819. Centrarchidae.

Pomoxis Rafinesque 1818:417 [ref. 3588]. Masc. *Pomoxis annularis* Rafinesque 1818:417. Type by monotypy. Appeared in 1818:417 on 7 Nov.; appeared at same time (Nov.) in Rafinesque 1818:41 [ref. 3598], and in revised form in (Feb.) 1820:53 [ref. 7305] and (Dec.) 1820:33 [ref. 3592]. *Pomoxys* of Gill 1865:64 [ref. 12608] is an unjustified emendation. Valid. Centrarchidae.

Pompilus Lowe 1839:81 [ref. 2829]. *Centrolophus pompilus* Valenciennes in Cuvier & Valenciennes 1833:334. Type by absolute tautonymy of a cited synonym. Apparently preoccupied by Schneider 1784 in Mollusca, Fabricius 1798 in Hymenoptera, and Minding 1832 in fishes. Synonym of *Centrolophus* Lacepède 1802 (Haedrich 1967:62 [ref. 5357], Haedrich 1973:559 [ref. 7216]). Centrolophidae.

Pompilus Minding 1832:108 [ref. 3022]. Masc. *Gasterosteus ductor* Linnaeus 1758:295. Type by monotypy. Objective synonym of *Naucrates* Rafinesque 1810. Carangidae.

Ponerodon Alcock 1890:203 [ref. 82]. Masc. *Ponerodon vastator* Alcock 1890:203. Type by monotypy. Channichthyidae.

Ponticola Iljin 1927:134 [ref. 5613]. Masc. *Gobius ratan* Nordmann 1840:416. Type by subsequent designation. Type designated by Iljin 1930:59 [ref. 2297]. Synonym of *Neogobius* Iljin 1927 (Miller 1973:502 [ref. 6888]). Gobiidae.

Pontinus Poey 1860:172 [ref. 3499]. Masc. *Pontinus castor* Poey 1860:173. Type regarded as by monotypy since Poey only included one species with certainty (see also Eschmeyer 1965:527 [ref. 1273]). Valid (Blanc & Hureau 1973:582 [ref. 7218], Shimizu in Masuda et al. 1984:314 [ref. 6441], Hureau & Litvinenko in Whitehead et al. 1986:1213 [ref. 13677], Eschmeyer 1986:470 [ref. 5652]). Scorpaenidae: Scorpaeninae.

Pontosudis Rofen 1963:4 [ref. 3794]. Fem. *Pontosudis advena* Rofen 1963:4. Type by monotypy. Paralepididae.

Popondetta Allen 1980:468 [ref. 99]. Fem. *Pseudomugil furcatus* Nichols 1955:2. Type by original designation (also monotypic). Preoccupied by Woodward 1978 in Hemiptera; replaced by *Popondichthys* Allen 1987. Valid (Allen 1981:43 [ref. 5516], Allen & Cross 1982:116 [ref. 6251]); objective synonym of *Popondichthys* Allen 1987 after *Popondetta* was replaced. Synonym of *Pseudomugil* Kner 1866 (Saeed et al. 1989:720 [ref. 13533]). Atherinidae: Pseudomugilinae.

Popondichthys Allen 1987:409 [ref. 6713]. Masc. *Pseudomugil furcatus* Nichols 1955:2. Type by being a replacement name. Replacement for *Popondetta* Allen 1980, preoccupied by Woodward 1978 in Hemiptera. Synonym of *Pseudomugil* Kner 1866 (Saeed et al. 1989:779 [ref. 13533]). Atherinidae: Pseudomugilinae.

Poptella Eigenmann 1908:106 [ref. 1221]. Fem. *Tetragonopterus longipinnis* Popta 1901:85. Type by original designation (also monotypic). Valid (Géry 1977:367 [ref. 1597], Reis 1989:18 [ref. 14219]). Characidae: Stethaprioninae.

Porcostoma Smith 1938:270 [ref. 4067]. Neut. *Chrysophrys dentatus* Gilchrist & Thompson 1908:173. Type by original designation (also monotypic). Valid (Smith & Smith 1986:591 [ref. 5710]). Sparidae.

Porcus Geoffroy St. Hilaire 1808:Pl. 15 [ref. 4182]. Masc. *Silurus bajad* Forsskål 1775:66. Type by monotypy. Not available, suppressed under plenary powers for purposes of priority; on Official Index (Opinion 1402). Plate apparently appeared in 1808 (see Taylor 1985 [ref. 6640]). Original not seen. In the synonymy of *Bagrus* Bosc 1816. Bagridae.

Porichthys Girard 1854:141 [ref. 1818]. Masc. *Porichthys notatus* Girard 1854:141. Type by subsequent designation. Type designated by Jordan & Gilbert 1883:751 [ref. 2476]. Valid (Walker & Rosenblatt 1988 [ref. 9284]). Batrachoididae.

Poroalticus Fowler 1931:403 [ref. 1410]. Masc. *Poroalticus sewalli* Fowler 1931:403. Type by original designation (also monotypic). Synonym of *Omobranchus* Ehrenberg 1836 (Springer 1972:9 [ref. 4178], Springer & Gomon 1975:9 [ref. 6083]). Blenniidae.

Porobronchus Kaup 1860:272 [ref. 2582]. Masc. *Porobronchus linearis* Kaup 1860:273. Type by monotypy. Synonym of *Carapus* Rafinesque 1810 (Arnold 1956:260 [ref. 5315]). Carapidae:

Carapinae.

Porochilus Weber 1913:523 [ref. 4603]. Masc. *Porochilus obbesi* Weber 1913:523. Type by monotypy. Valid (Burgess 1989:180 [ref. 12860], Paxton et al. 1989:226 [ref. 12442]). Plotosidae.

Poroclinus Bean 1890:40 [ref. 229]. Masc. *Poroclinus rothrocki* Bean 1890:40. Type by monotypy. Valid (see Miki et al. 1987:131 [ref. 6704]). Stichaeidae.

Porocottus Gill 1859:166 [ref. 1760]. Masc. *Porocottus quadrifilis* Gill 1859:166. Type by monotypy. Valid (Neyelov 1979:115, 135 [ref. 3152], Washington et al. 1984:443 [ref. 13660], Yabe in Masuda et al. 1984:327 [ref. 6441], Yabe 1985:111 [ref. 11522]). Cottidae.

Poroderma (subgenus of *Scyllium*) Smith 1838:85 [ref. 4034]. Neut. *Squalus africanus* Gmelin 1789:1494. Type by subsequent designation. Type designated by Fowler 1908:53 [ref. 6847]. Valid (Springer 1979:112 [ref. 4175], Compagno 1984:346 [ref. 6846], Bass 1986:94 [ref. 5635], Compagno 1988:115 [ref. 13488]). Scyliorhinidae.

Porogadus Goode & Bean 1885:602 [ref. 1842]. Masc. *Porogadus miles* Goode & Bean 1885:602. Type by monotypy. Valid (Cohen & Nielsen 1978:38 [ref. 881], Carter & Sulak 1984 [ref. 8244], Machida in Masuda et al. 1984:101 [ref. 6441], Nielsen & Cohen 1986:350 [ref. 5700]). Ophidiidae: Neobythitinae.

Porogobius Bleeker 1874:321 [ref. 437]. Masc. *Gobius schlegelii* Günther 1861:46. Type by original designation (also monotypic). Valid (Maugé 1986:381 [ref. 6218], Birdsong et al. 1988:193 [ref. 7303]). Gobiidae.

Porogrammus Gilchrist & Thompson 1916:57 [ref. 5602]. Masc. *Porogrammus capensis* Gilchrist & Thompson 1916:57. Type by monotypy. Synonym of *Halidesmus* Günther 1872 (Winterbottom 1982:755 [ref. 5436]). Pseudochromidae: Congrogadinae.

Poromitra Goode & Bean 1883:214 [ref. 1838]. Fem. *Poromitra capito* Goode & Bean 1883:215. Type by monotypy. Valid (Maul 1973:344 [ref. 7171], Ebeling & Weed 1973:431 [ref. 6898], Ebeling 1975 [ref. 7105], Parin & Ebeling 1980 [ref. 5523], Fujii in Masuda et al. 1984:110 [ref. 6441], Maul in Whitehead et al. 1986:760 [ref. 13676], Ebeling 1986:429 [ref. 5651], Paxton et al. 1989:372 [ref. 12442]. Melamphaidae.

Poromitrella Zugmayer 1911:7 [ref. 6161]. Fem. *Poromitrella nigriceps* Zugmayer 1911:7. Type by monotypy. Also appeared in Zugmayer 1911 (Dec.):100 [ref. 4846]. Possibly a synonym of *Scopelogadus* Vaillant 1888 (Maul 1973:344 [ref. 7171]). Melamphaidae.

Poronotus Gill 1861:35 [ref. 1766]. Masc. *Rhombus triacanthus* Peck 1804:51. Type by monotypy. Synonym of *Peprilus* Cuvier 1829 (Haedrich 1967:103 [ref. 5357]). Stromateidae.

Poropanchax Clausen 1967:12, 36 [ref. 5926]. Masc. *Aplocheilichthys macrophthalmus* Meinken 1932:53. Type by original designation. Synonym of *Aplocheilichthys* Bleeker 1863 (Wildekamp et al. 1986:170 [ref. 6198]); as a valid subgenus (Parenti 1981:508 [ref. 7066]). Cyprinodontidae: Aplocheilichthyinae.

Poropuntius Smith 1931:14 [ref. 4047]. Masc. *Poropuntius normani* Smith 1931:15. Type by monotypy. Valid (Kottelat 1989:10 [ref. 13605]). Cyprinidae.

Porotergus Ellis in Eigenmann 1912:423, 440 [ref. 1227]. Masc. *Porotergus gymnotus* Ellis in Eigenmann 1912:441. Type by original designation. Valid (see Mago-Leccia 1978:14 [ref. 5489]). Gymnotidae: Apteronotinae.

Porteridia Fowler 1945:25 [ref. 5599]. Fem. *Parapercis chilensis* Norman 1937:62. Type by original designation (also monotypic). Pinguipedidae.

Porthmeus Valenciennes in Cuvier & Valenciennes 1833:255 [ref. 1002]. Masc. *Porthmeus argenteus* Valenciennes in Cuvier & Valenciennes 1833:256. Type by monotypy. *Porthmeus* Goüan 1770:42 [ref. 1863] is a nomen nudum. Synonym of *Lichia* Cuvier 1816 (Hureau & Tortonese 1973:377 [ref. 7198], Daget & Smith-Vaniz 1986:315 [ref. 6207]). Carangidae.

Potamalosa Ogilby 1897:504 [ref. 3271]. Fem. *Potamalosa novaehollandiae* of Ogilby 1897:504 (= *Clupea richmondia* Macleay 1879:380). Type by monotypy. Based on a misidentified type species, not *Meletta novaehollandiae* Valenciennes 1847; Ogilby 1897:70 [ref. 3272] says type is *P. antiqua* Ogilby; Paxton et al. 1989:156 [ref. 12442] list *C. richmondia* as type. Technically should be submitted to the ICZN; Whitehead regards Ogilby's specimens as = *P. richmondia*, and *richmondia* would be the best type. Valid (Grande 1985:247 [ref. 6466], Whitehead 1985:186 [ref. 5141], Paxton et al. 1989:156 [ref. 12442]). Clupeidae.

Potamarius Hubbs & Miller 1960:101 [ref. 2259]. Masc. *Conorhynchos nelsoni* Evermann & Goldsborough 1902. Type by original designation. Valid. Ariidae.

Potamocottus Gill 1861:40 [ref. 1785]. Masc. *Potamocottus punctulatus* Gill 1861:40. Type by subsequent designation. Type designated by Jordan & Gilbert 1877:93 [ref. 4907]. Synonym of *Cottus* Linnaeus 1758. Cottidae.

Potamophylax Myers & Carvalho in Myers 1955:7 [ref. 3126]. Masc. *Potamophylax pygmaeus* Myers & Carvalho in Myers 1955:7. Type by monotypy. Treated as masculine by authors. Preoccupied by Wallengren 1891 in Trichoptera, replaced by *Fluviphylax* Whitley 1965. Objective synonym of *Fluviphylax* Whitley 1965 (Parenti 1981:514 [ref. 7066]). Cyprinodontidae: Fluviphylacinae.

Potamorhina Cope 1878:685 [ref. 945]. Fem. *Curimatus (Anodus) pristigaster* Steindachner 1876:73. Type by monotypy. Unjustifiably emended to, or misspelled *Potamorrhina* by authors. Valid (Vari 1983:4 [ref. 5419], Vari 1984 [ref. 5307], see also Géry et al. 1987:433 [ref. 6001], Vari 1989:6 [ref. 9189]). Curimatidae: Curimatinae.

Potamorrhaphis (subgenus of *Belone*) Günther 1866:234, 256 [ref. 1983]. Fem. *Belone taeniata* Günther 1866:256. Type by subsequent designation. Described in key (p. 234) for 2 species on p. 256. Type designated by Jordan & Fordice 1887:359 [ref. 2456]. Misspelled *Pomatorrhaphis* by Bleeker 1871:43 and by others in different ways (see Collette 1982:717 [ref. 5467]). Valid (Collette 1982 [ref. 5467], Collette et al. 1984:352 [ref. 11422]). Belonidae.

Potamothrissa Regan 1917:203 [ref. 3668]. Fem. *Pellonula obtusirostris* Boulenger 1909:158. Type by subsequent designation. Type designated by Jordan 1920:563 [ref. 4905]). Valid (Poll et al. 1984:51 [ref. 6172], Grande 1985:247 [ref. 6466], Whitehead 1985:154 [ref. 5141]). Clupeidae.

Potamotrygon Garman 1877:210 [ref. 1528]. Fem. *Trygon hystrix* Müller & Henle 1841:167. Type by subsequent designation. Type given as *hystrix* as designated by Jordan 1919:389 [ref. 4904] by Séret & McEachran 1986:6 [ref. 9312]; Garman treated *histrix* as a synonym of *humboldtii*. Eigenmann 1910 says type is *humboldtii* Roulin [not investigated]. Valid (Rosa et al. 1987:447 [ref. 5974]). Potamotrygonidae.

Poutawa Griffin 1936:16 [ref. 1907]. Fem. *Congrus habenatus* Richardson 1848:109. Two included species, neither technically designated type, but clear from text that genus was intended for *habenatus*; unfortunately name is apparently unavailable (Art. 13b). Derivation of name not given; treated as feminine by author. Apparently can date to Zoological Record for 1936:72 where citation to Griffin is provided and a type is designated. Synonym of *Gnathophis* Kaup 1860 (Blache et al. 1973:242 [ref. 7185], Smith 1989:521 [ref. 13285]). Congridae: Congrinae.

Powellichthys Smith 1966:298 [ref. 4136]. Masc. *Powellichthys ventriosus* Smith 1966:299. Type by original designation (also monotypic). Valid (see Smith 1989:77 [ref. 13285]). Chlopsidae.

Poweria Bonaparte 1840:fasc. 27 [ref. 514]. Fem. *Gonostomus poweriae* Cocco 1838:167. Type by monotypy. Synonym of *Vinciguerria* Jordan & Evermann 1896 (Witzell 1973:121 [ref. 7172]). Phosichthyidae.

Praealticus Schultz & Chapman in Schultz et al. 1960:368 [ref. 3972]. Masc. *Salarias natalis* Regan 1909:405. Type by original designation. Valid (Smith-Vaniz & Springer 1971:36 [ref. 4145], Yoshino in Masuda et al. 1984:300 [ref. 6441]). Blenniidae.

Praeformosania Fang 1935:71 [ref. 1300]. Fem. *Praeformosania pingchowensis* Fang 1935:72. Type by original designation. Type species misspelled *pinchowensis* on p. 71. Valid (Silas 1953:227 [ref. 4024], Sawada 1982:205 [ref. 14111]); synonym of *Vanmanenia* Hora 1932 (Chen 1980:97 [ref. 6901]). Balitoridae: Balitorinae.

Prajadhipokia Fowler 1934:338 [ref. 1418]. Fem. *Prajadhipokia rex* Fowler 1934:339. Type by original designation (also monotypic). Synonym of *Heterobagrus* Bleeker 1864 (Jayaram 1968:369 [ref. 5615]). Bagridae.

Pranesella Whitley 1934:241 [ref. 4680]. Fem. *Pranesella endorae* Whitley 1934:241. Type by monotypy. Synonym of *Atherinosoma* Castelnau 1872 (Pavlov et al. 1988:392 [ref. 12285]). Atherinidae: Atherininae.

Pranesus Whitley 1930:9 [ref. 4671]. Masc. *Pranesus ogilbyi* Whitley 1930:9. Type by original designation (also monotypic). Valid (Kiener & Spillmann 1973:578 [ref. 7217]); synonym of *Atherinomorus* Fowler 1903 (Whitehead & Ivantsoff 1983:361 [ref. 5418], Ivantsoff 1986:382 [ref. 6292]); valid but spelled *Prasenus* (Kottelat 1989:16 [ref. 13605]). Atherinidae: Atherininae.

Premnas Cuvier 1816:345 [ref. 993]. Fem. *Chaetodon biaculaetus* Bloch 1790:11. Type by monotypy. Valid (Allen 1975:62 [ref. 97]). Pomacentridae.

Prenes Gistel 1848:X [ref. 1822]. *Chaetodon argus* Linnaeus 1766:464. Type by being a replacement name. Unneeded replacement for *Scatophagus* Cuvier 1831, not preoccupied by *Scatophaga*. Objective synonym of *Scatophagus* Cuvier 1831. Scatophagidae.

Priacanthichthys Day 1868:193 [ref. 1076]. Masc. *Priacanthichthys maderaspatensis* Day 1868:193. Type by monotypy. Synonym of *Epinephelus* Bloch 1793 (Smith 1971:103 [ref. 14102], Daget & Smith 1986:301 [ref. 6204]). Serranidae: Epinephelinae.

Priacanthopsis (subgenus of *Pempheris*) Fowler 1906:122 [ref. 1372]. Fem. *Pempheris muelleri* Poey in Klunzinger 1879:380. Type by original designation (also monotypic). Synonym of *Pempheris* Cuvier 1829. Pempheridae.

Priacanthus Oken (ex Cuvier) 1817:1182 [ref. 3303]. Masc. *Anthias macrophthalmus* Bloch 1792:115. Type by subsequent designation. Based on "Les Priacanthes" of Cuvier 1816:281 [ref. 993] (see Gill 1903:966 [ref. 5768]) and possibly Cuvier 1814:90. Cuvier included 2 species in a footnote; earliest subsequent designation appears to be Jordan 1917:104 [ref. 2407] and not Cuvier 1829 as given by Starnes 1988. Valid (Hureau 1973:364 [ref. 7197], Yoshino in Masuda et al. 1984:143 [ref. 6441], Heemstra 1986:545 [ref. 5660], Starnes 1988:154 [ref. 6978], Paxton et al. 1989:543 [ref. 12442]). Priacanthidae.

Priapella Regan 1913:992 [ref. 3653]. Fem. *Gambusia bonita* Meek 1904:132. Type by monotypy. Valid (Rosen & Bailey 1963:60 [ref. 7067], Parenti & Rauchenberger 1989:8 [ref. 13538]). Poeciliidae.

Priapichthys Regan 1913:991 [ref. 3653]. Masc. *Gambusia annectens* Regan 1907:259. Type by monotypy, 5 additional species "assumed" to be congeneric, so only one was referred to the genus with certainty; type also designated by Henn 1916:115 [ref. 2093]. Valid (Rosen & Bailey 1963:120 [ref. 7067], Parenti & Rauchenberger 1989:9 [ref. 13538]). Poeciliidae.

Pricus Rafinesque 1815:94 [ref. 3584]. Masc. As "*Prisca* R. sp. do.," meaning *Prisca* Rafinesque based on a species from a preceding genus [*Petromyzon*]. Not available, name only; probably intended for the pre-Linnaean name "pricka". Petromyzontidae: Petromyzontinae.

Prietella Carranza 1954:130 [ref. 734]. Fem. *Prietella phreatophila* Carranza 1954:132. Type by original designation (also monotypic). Valid (Burgess 1989:35 [ref. 12860]). Ictaluridae.

Prilonotus Richardson 1854:162 [ref. 3746]. Masc. *Prilonotus caudacacinctus* Richardson 1854:162. Type regarded as by monotypy, other species mentioned were ones included by Kaup (manuscript) as quoted by Richardson. Name quoted from Müller and from Kaup manuscript, but *Prilonotus* probably a slip for *Psilonotus* Swainson 1839 and not an original generic description. In the synonymy of *Canthigaster* Swainson 1839. Tetraodontidae.

Primospina Eigenmann & Beeson 1893:669 [ref. 1212]. Fem. *Sebastodes mystinus* Jordan & Gilbert 1880:455. Type by original designation (also monotypic). Synonym of *Sebastes* Cuvier 1829. Scorpaenidae: Sebastinae.

Prinodon Rafinesque 1815:88 [ref. 3584]. Masc. *Cyprinodon variegatus* Lacepède 1803:486, 487. Type by being a replacement name. As "*Prinodon* R. [Rafinesque] *Cyprinodon* Lac. [Lacepède]." An available replacement name (unneeded) for *Cyprinodon* Lacepède 1803. Objective synonym of *Cyprinodon* Lacepède 1803 (Parenti 1981:526 [ref. 7066]). Cyprinodontidae: Cyprinodontinae.

Priocharax Weitzman & Vari 1987:641 [ref. 6055]. Masc. *Priocharax ariel* Weitzman & Vari 1987:641. Type by original designation. Characidae.

Priodon Quoy & Gaimard (ex Cuvier) 1825:377 [ref. 3574]. Masc. *Priodon annulatus* Quoy & Gaimard 1825:377. Type by monotypy. Synonym of *Naso* Lacepède 1801 (Randall 1955:361 [ref. 13648]). Acanthuridae.

Priodonophis Kaup 1860:22 [ref. 2586]. Masc. *Gymnothorax ocellatus* Agassiz 1829:91. Type by monotypy. *Priodontophis* is a misspelling. Synonym of *Gymnothorax* Bloch 1795 (Blache et al. 1973:226 [ref. 7185], Böhlke et al. 1989:145 [ref. 13286]). Muraenidae: Muraeninae.

Priodontichthys Bonaparte 1831:175 [ref. 4978]. Masc. *Priodon annularis* Quoy & Gaimard 1824:377. Type by being a replacement name. Appeared as "*Priodontichthys*, Nob. (*Priodon*, Cuv.)". Replacement for *Priodon* Cuvier [= Quoy & Gaimard (ex Cuvier)]; preoccupation not researched. Synonym of *Naso* Lacepède 1801 (Randall 1955:361 [ref. 13648]). Acanthuridae.

Priolepis Bleeker (ex Ehrenberg) 1874:305 [ref. 437]. Fem. Name mentioned in passing in synonymy of *Asterropteryx* Rüppell; name made available earlier by Valenciennes (see separate entry). Gobiidae.

Priolepis Valenciennes (ex Ehrenberg) in Cuvier & Valenciennes 1837:67 [ref. 1006]. Fem. *Priolepis mica* Ehrenberg in Cuvier & Valenciennes 1837:67. Type by subsequent monotypy. Appeared as name in synonymy of *Gobius*, but used as a valid name before 1931 and therefore made available back to Valenciennes 1837. Valid (Larson & Hoese 1980:41 [ref. 2725], Akihito in Masuda et al. 1984:248 [ref. 6441], Hoese 1986:801 [ref. 5670], Birdsong et al. 1988:193 [ref. 7303], Greenfield 1989 [ref. 12545], Winterbottom & Burridge 1989 [ref. 14486]). Gobiidae.

Prionace Cantor 1849:1381 [399] [ref. 715]. Fem. *Squalus glaucus* Linnaeus 1758:235. Type designated by ICZN. On p. 399 of separate. On Official List (Opinion 723). Valid (Compagno 1973:30 [ref. 7163], Compagno 1984:521 [ref. 6846], Nakaya in Masuda et al. 1984:7 [ref. 6441], Bass et al. 1986:84 [ref. 5638], Cappetta 1987:125 [ref. 6348], Compagno 1988:346 [ref. 13488], Paxton et al. 1989:83 [ref. 12442]). Carcharhinidae.

Prionistius Bean 1884:355 [ref. 225]. Masc. *Prionistius macellus* Bean 1884:355. Type by monotypy. Synonym of *Triglops* Reinhardt 1831. Cottidae.

Prionobrama Fowler 1913:534 [ref. 1389]. Fem. *Prionobrama madeirae* Fowler 1913:535. Type by original designation (also monotypic). Valid (Géry 1977:347 [ref. 1597]). Characidae.

Prionobutis Bleeker 1874:305 [ref. 437]. *Eleotris dasyrhynchus* Günther 1868:265. Type by original designation (also monotypic). Valid (Hoese 1986:810 [ref. 5670], Maugé 1986:397 [ref. 6218], Birdsong et al. 1988:180 [ref. 7303], Kottelat 1989:18 [ref. 13605]). Eleotridae.

Prionodes Jenyns 1840:46 [ref. 2344]. Masc. *Prionodes fasciatus* Jenyns 1840:47. Type by monotypy. Serranidae: Serraninae.

Prionodon (subgenus of *Carcharias*) Müller & Henle 1838:35 [ref. 3069]. Masc. *Squalus glaucus* Linnaeus 1758:235. Type by subsequent designation. Not available, on Official Index (Opinion 723); preoccupied by Horsfield 1822 in fossil mammals. Type apparently designated first by Fowler 1911:74 [ref. 6398]. In the synonymy of *Prionace* Cantor 1849 if type is *glaucus*; Compagno 1988:307 [ref. 13488] treats in the synonymy of *Carcharhinus* Blainville 1816. Carcharhinidae.

Prionodraco Regan 1914:13 [ref. 3661]. Masc. *Prionodraco evansii* Regan 1914:13. Type by monotypy. Misspelled *Prinodraco* by Jordan 1920:554 [ref. 4905]. Valid (DeWitt & Hureau 1979:789 [ref. 1125], Stevens et al. 1984:563 [ref. 13633], Voskoboinikova 1988:45 [ref. 12756]). Bathydraconidae.

Prionolepis Smith 1931:145 [ref. 4062]. Fem. *Prionolepis hewitti* Smith 1931:145. Type by monotypy. Preoccupied by Egerton 1850 in fossil fishes, apparently not replaced. Synonym of *Naso* Lacepède 1801 (Randall 1955:362 [ref. 13648]). Acanthuridae.

Prionosparus (subgenus of *Austrosparus*) Smith 1942:280, 282 [ref. 4070]. Masc. *Austrosparus (Prionosparus) tricuspidens* Smith 1942:282. Type by monotypy. Synonym of *Rhabdosargus* Fowler 1933 (Smith 1979:702 [ref. 6940], Bauchot & Skelton 1986:332 [ref. 6210]). Sparidae.

Prionotus Lacepède 1801:336 [ref. 2710]. Masc. *Trigla evolans* Linnaeus 1766:498. Type by monotypy. Valid (Uyeno & Sato in Uyeno et al. 1983:443 [ref. 14275]). Triglidae: Triglinae.

Prionurus Lacepède 1804:(205) 211 [ref. 12515]. Masc. *Prionurus microlepidotus* Lacepède 1804:(205) 211. Type by monotypy. Latinized on p. 211. *Acanthocaulus* Waite 1900 apparently is an unneeded replacement. Valid (Kishimoto in Masuda et al. 1984:228 [ref. 6441], Tyler et al. 1989:37 [ref. 13460]). Acanthuridae.

Prionurus Otto 1821:5 [ref. 4987]. Masc. *Squalus prionurus* Otto 1821:5. Type by monotypy (also by absolute tautonymy). Preoccupied by Lacepède 1804 in fishes. Above from Fowler, original not seen. Questionably a synonym of *Galeus* Rafinesque 1810 (Cappetta 1987:111 [ref. 6348]). Scyliorhinidae.

Priopidichthys Whitley 1935:364 [ref. 4684]. Masc. *Pseudoambassis ramsayi* Macleay 1881:340. Type by original designation. Ambassidae.

Priopis Kuhl & van Hasselt in Cuvier & Valenciennes 1830:503 [ref. 996]. Fem. *Priopis argyrozona* Kuhl & van Hasselt in Cuvier & Valenciennes 1830:504. Type by monotypy. Ambassidae.

Pristella Eigenmann 1908:99 [ref. 1221]. Fem. *Holopristes riddlei* Meek in Eigenmann & Ogle 1907:13. Type by original designation (also monotypic). Correct spelling for genus of type species is *Holopristis*. Valid (Géry 1977:582 [ref. 1597]). Characidae.

Pristes Fleming 1822:376 [ref. 5063]. Masc. Original not seen. Unjustified emendation (or misspelling) of *Pristis* Linck 1790. In the synonymy of *Pristis* Linck 1790 (Cappetta 1987:158 [ref. 6348]). Pristidae.

Pristhoplichthys Fowler 1938:99 [ref. 1426]. Masc. *Hoplichthys platophrys* Gilbert 1905:642. Type by original designation (also monotypic). Bembridae.

Pristhoplotrigla (subgenus of *Lepidotrigla*) Fowler 1938:107 [ref. 1426]. Fem. *Trigla strauchii* Steindachner 1876:214. Type by original designation (also monotypic). Synonym of *Lepidotrigla* Günther 1860 (Richards & Saksena 1977:209 [ref. 5285]). Triglidae: Triglinae.

Pristiancistrus Fowler 1945:121 [ref. 1454]. Masc. *Pristiancistrus eustictus* Fowler 1945:121. Type by original designation (also monotypic). Synonym of *Ancistrus* Kner 1854 (Isbrücker 1980:66 [ref. 2303]). Loricariidae.

Pristiapogon (subgenus of *Apogon*) Klunzinger 1870:715 [ref. 2621]. Masc. *Apogon fraenatus* Valenciennes 1832:57. Type by monotypy. Synonym of *Apogon* Lacepède 1801, but as a valid subgenus (Fraser & Lachner 1985:4 [ref. 5215]). Apogonidae.

Pristibatis Blainville 1825:49 [ref. 4991]. Fem. *Pristibatis antiquorum* Latham 1794:277 (= *Squalus pristis* Linnaeus 1758:235). Type by subsequent designation. Jordan 1917:134 [ref. 2407] lists as above with author as Serville; see note under Blainville 1825 [ref. 4991]. Above use perhaps best considered an incorrect subsequent spelling of *Pristobatus* Blainville. In the synonymy of *Pristis* Linck 1790. Pristidae.

Pristicharax Fowler 1949:1 [ref. 1460]. Masc. *Pristicharax hanseni* Fowler 1949:2. Type by original designation (also monotypic). Synonym of *Hasemania* Ellis 1911 (see Weitzman & S. Fink 1985:2 [ref. 5203]). Characidae: Glandulocaudinae.

Pristicon (subgenus of *Apogon*) Fraser 1972:22 [ref. 5195]. Fem. *Apogon trimaculatus* Cuvier in Cuvier & Valenciennes 1828:115. Type by original designation. Synonym of *Apogon* Lacepède 1801, but as a valid subgenus (Fraser & Lachner 1985:4 [ref. 5215]). Apogonidae.

Pristidoryrhamphus Fowler 1944:158 [ref. 1451]. Masc. *Pristidoryrhamphus jacksoni* Fowler 1944:159. Type by original designation (also monotypic). Synonym of *Doryrhamphus* Kaup 1856 (Fritzsche 1980:187 [ref. 1511], Dawson 1981:2 [ref. 5511]).

Syngnathidae: Syngnathinae.

Pristidurus Bonaparte 1838:11 (of separate) [ref. 4979]. Masc. *Galeus melastomus* Rafinesque 1810:13. Described as "Nob.", but technically probably is an incorrect subsequent spelling of *Pristiurus* Bonaparte 1834. Fowler says Agassiz 1838 in fossil fishes is earlier than Bonaparte 1838. Objective synonym of *Galeus* Rafinesque 1810. Scyliorhinidae.

Pristigaster Cuvier 1816:176 [ref. 993]. Fem. *Pristigaster cayanus* Cuvier 1829:321. Type by subsequent designation. First appeared (1816:176 [ref. 993]) with description of 1 unnamed species; 2 species named in Cuvier 1829:321 [ref. 995], *P. cayanus* traceable to 1816:176 (as type); type also restricted by Gill 1861; see Whitehead 1967:100 [ref. 6464]. Spelled *Pristogaster* by Swainson 1838:266 [ref. 4302]. Valid (Grande 1985:245 [ref. 6466], Whitehead 1985:301 [ref. 5141]). Clupeidae.

Pristigenys Agassiz 1835:299 [ref. 13390]. Fem. *Chaetodon substriatus* Blainville 1818. Type by monotypy. Apparently available from Agassiz 1835 as new generic name in association with an established fossil species name; Recent species are assigned to it as well. Valid (Fritzsche & Johnson 1981 [ref. 5399], Yoshino in Masuda et al. 1984:143 [ref. 6441], Heemstra 1986:546 [ref. 5660], Taverne 1988 [ref. 6863], Starnes 1988:131 [ref. 6978], Paxton et al. 1989:543 [ref. 12442]). Priacanthidae.

Pristilepis Randall, Shimizu & Yamakawa 1982:4 [ref. 3602]. Fem. *Holotrachys oligolepis* Whitley 1941:28. Type by original designation (also monotypic). Valid (Shimizu in Masuda et al. 1984:114 [ref. 6441], Randall & Heemstra 1986:426 [ref. 5707], Paxton et al. 1989:379 [ref. 12442]). Holocentridae.

Pristiodon Dybowski 1877:26 [ref. 1171]. Masc. *Pristiodon siemionovi* Dybowski 1877:26. Type by monotypy. Preoccupied by Fitzinger 1843 in Reptilia; not replaced. Original not seen. Synonym of *Ctenopharyngodon* Steindachner 1866 (Howes 1981:40 [ref. 14200]). Cyprinidae.

Pristiophorus Müller & Henle 1837:116 [ref. 3067]. Masc. *Pristis cirratus* Latham 1794:281. Type by monotypy. Also in Müller & Henle 1939:97 [ref. 3069]. Spelled *Pristidophorus* by Bonaparte 1838:8 (of separate) [ref. 4979]. Valid (Compagno 1984:133 [ref. 6474], Nakaya & Shirai in Masuda et al. 1984:11 [ref. 6441], Cappetta 1987:65 [ref. 6348], Paxton et al. 1989:39 [ref. 12442]). Pristiophoridae.

Pristiopsis (subgenus of *Pristis*) Fowler 1905:459 [ref. 1370]. Fem. *Pristis perrotteti* Valenciennes in Müller & Henle 1841:106. Type by original designation (also monotypic). Synonym of *Pristis* Linck 1790 (Krefft & Stehmann 1973:51 [ref. 7167], Cappetta 1987:158 [ref. 6348]). Pristidae.

Pristipoma Quoy & Gaimard (ex Cuvier) 1824:320 [ref. 3574]. Neut. *Pristipoma sexlineatum* Quoy & Gaimard 1824:320. Type by monotypy. Name from "Les Pristipomes" Cuvier 1816:279, but earlier latinized by Oken 1817 as *Pristipomus*; apparently available with type as above. Also spelled *Pristapoma* in early literature. Also described as new in Cuvier 1829:176 [ref. 995]. Synonym of *Pristipomus* Oken 1817, which is a synonym of *Pomadasys* Lacepède 1802. Haemulidae.

Pristipomoides Bleeker 1852:574 [ref. 334]. Masc. *Pristipomoides typus* Bleeker 1852:575. Type by monotypy (also by use of *typus*). Valid (Johnson 1980:9 [ref. 13553], Allen 1985:141 [ref. 6843], Yoshino in Masuda et al. 1984:166 [ref. 6441], Anderson 1986:578 [ref. 5634], Akazaki & Iwatsuki 1986 [ref. 6316], Akazaki & Iwatsuki 1987 [ref. 6699]). Lutjanidae.

Pristipomus Oken (ex Cuvier) 1817:1182 [ref. 3303]. Fem. *Lutjanus hasta* Bloch 1790:109. Type by subsequent designation. Based on "Les Pristipomes" of Cuvier 1816:279 [ref. 993]. Type designated by Jordan 1817:103 [ref. 2407]. Spelled *Pristopoma* in early literature. Synonym of *Pomadasys* Lacepède 1802 (Roux 1973:391 [ref. 7200], Roux 1986:328 [ref. 6209]). Haemulidae.

Pristis Klein 1776:61 [ref. 4919]. Fem. Not available, published in a work that does not conform to the principle of binominal nomenclature. In the synonymy of *Pristis* Linck 1790. Pristidae.

Pristis Latham 1794:276 [ref. 2727]. Fem. *Squalus pristis* Linnaeus 1758:235. Type by tautonymy (five included species). Objective synonym of *Pristis* Linck 1790. Pristidae.

Pristis Linck 1790:31 [ref. 4985]. Fem. *Squalus pristis* Linnaeus 1758:235. Type by monotypy (also by absolute tautonymy). Valid (Krefft & Stehmann 1973:51 [ref. 7167], Nakaya in Masuda et al. 1984:12 [ref. 6441], Compagno 1986:110 [ref. 5648], Cappetta 1987:158 [ref. 6348], Kottelat 1989:4 [ref. 13605], Paxton et al. 1989:58 [ref. 12442]). Pristidae.

Pristiurus (subgenus of *Scyllium*) Bonaparte 1834:puntata 39 [ref. 517]. Masc. *Galeus melastomus* Rafinesque 1810:13. Type by monotypy. Appeared first in puntata 39, fasc. 7 under *Scyllium canicula* and under *Scyllium melanostomum*. Spelled *Pristidurus* by Bonaparte 1838:11 [ref. 4979, not investigated]. Objective synonym of *Galeus* Rafinesque 1810 (Springer 1973:20 [ref. 7162], Nakaya 1975:40 [ref. 7083], Springer 1979:48 [ref. 4175], Compagno 1984:306 [ref. 6846], Cappetta 1987:111 [ref. 6348], Compagno 1988:134 [ref. 13488]). Scyliorhinidae.

Pristobatus (subgenus of *Raia [Raja]*) Blainville 1816:121 [ref. 306]. Masc. *Pristis antiquorum* Latham 1794:277. Type by subsequent designation. Type designated by Fowler 1911:81 [ref. 6398]. Also spelled *Pristibatys* by Blainville 1818:27 [ref. 307] and *Pristibatis* by Blainville 1825:49 (not investigated). Synonym of *Pristis* Linck 1790 (Krefft & Stehmann 1973:51 [ref. 7167], Cappetta 1987:158 [ref. 6348]). Pristidae.

Pristobrycon Eigenmann 1915:245 [ref. 1232]. Masc. *Serrasalmo (Pygocentrus) calmoni* Steindachner 1908:361. Type by original designation. Synonym of *Serrasalmus* Lacepède 1803, as a valid subgenus (Géry 1976:52 [ref. 14199], Géry 1977:278 [ref. 1597]); valid (authors). Characidae: Serrasalminae.

Pristocantharus Gill 1862:256 [ref. 4909]. Masc. *Pristipoma cantharinum* Jenyns 1842:49. Type by original designation (also monotypic). Synonym of *Orthopristis* Girard 1858. Haemulidae.

Pristogaster Swainson 1838:266 et seq. [ref. 4302]. Fem. Also in Swainson 1839:186, 294 [ref. 4303]. Unjustified emendation or incorrect subsequent spelling of *Pristigaster* Cuvier 1816. Clupeidae.

Pristolepis Jerdon 1849:141 [ref. 2346]. Fem. *Pristolepis marginatus[a]* Jerdon 1849:141. Type by monotypy. Valid (Jayaram 1981:336 [ref. 6497], Kottelat 1985:273 [ref. 11441], Kottelat 1989:18 [ref. 13605], Roberts 1989:165 [ref. 6439]). Nandidae: Pristolepidinae.

Pristotis Rüppell 1838:128 [ref. 3844]. Fem. *Pristotis cyanostigma* Rüppell 1838:128. Type by monotypy. Valid (Allen 1975:227 [ref. 97], Shen & Chan 1978:211 [ref. 6945], Kawashima & Moyer 1982 [ref. 5451], Yoshino in Masuda et al. 1984:194 [ref. 6441]). Pomacentridae.

Proamblys Gill 1862:236 [ref. 1664]. Masc. *Diacope nigra* of Cuvier in Cuvier & Valenciennes 1828:415 (= *Sciaena niger* Forsskål 1775: xi, 47). Type by monotypy. Synonym of *Macolor*

Bleeker 1860 (Allen 1985:125 [ref. 6843] as *Promblys*, Kishimoto et al. 1987 [ref. 6061]). Lutjanidae.

Probarbus Sauvage 1880:232 [ref. 3889]. Masc. *Probarbus jullieni* Sauvage 1880:232. Type by monotypy. Valid (Kottelat 1985:265 [ref. 11441], Kottelat 1989:10 [ref. 13605]). Cyprinidae.

Probolodus Eigenmann 1911:164 [ref. 1226]. Masc. *Probolodus heterostomus* Eigenmann 1911:164. Type by original designation (also monotypic). Valid (Géry 1977:579 [ref. 1597]). Characidae.

Procatopus Boulenger 1904:20 [ref. 572]. Masc. *Procatopus nototaenia* Boulenger 1904:20. Type by monotypy. Valid (Parenti 1981:511 [ref. 7066], Wildekamp et al. 1986:193 [ref. 6198]). Cyprinodontidae: Aplocheilichthyinae.

Proceros Rafinesque 1820:87 [ref. 3592]. Masc. *Proceros maculatus* Rafinesque 1820:86. Type by subsequent designation. Type designated by Jordan & Gilbert 1877:87 [ref. 4907]. Description poor, second-hand; perhaps mythical. Usually regarded as a synonym of *Polyodon* Lacepède 1797. Polyodontidae.

Procetichthys Paxton 1989:151, 153 [ref. 13435]. Masc. *Procetichthys kreffti* Paxton 1989:153. Type by original designation (also monotypic). Cetomimidae.

Prochilodus Agassiz in Spix & Agassiz 1829:57, 62 [ref. 13]. Masc. *Prochilodus argenteus* Agassiz in Spix & Agassiz 1829:63. Type by subsequent designation. Type designated by Eigenmann 1910:424 [ref. 1224]. On Official List (Opinion 772). Kottelat 1988:82 [ref. 13380] states the *Prochilodus* was proposed as a replacement for *Pacu* Agassiz; see Appendix A. Valid (Roberts 1973:213 [ref. 7051], Géry 1977:218 [ref. 1597], Vari 1983:4 [ref. 5419], Géry et al. 1987:436 [ref. 6001], Malabarba 1989:125 [ref. 14217]). Curimatidae: Prochilodontinae.

Prochilus Bleeker (ex Klein) 1865:185 [ref. 414]. Masc. Type by subsequent designation. Validates *Prochilus* Klein 1778, not available. Preoccupied by Illiger 1811 in Mammalia, Cuvier 1816 in fishes, and Brullé 1835 in Orthoptera. Earliest subsequent type designation not researched; several species included by Bleeker. Objective synonym of *Amphiprion* Bloch & Schneider 1801. Pomacentridae.

Prochilus Cuvier 1816:294 [ref. 993]. Masc. *Sciaena macrolepidota* Bloch 1790:298. Type by subsequent designation. Type designated by Jordan 1917:104 [ref. 2407]. Preoccupied by Illiger 1811 in Mammalia. Synonym of *Dormitator* Gill 1861 (Maugé 1986:391 [ref. 6218]). Eleotridae.

Prochilus Klein 1775:1043 [ref. 2618]. Masc. Not available, published in a work that does not conform to the principle of binominal nomenclature. In the synonymy of *Amphiprion* Bloch & Schneider 1801. Pomacentridae.

Procottus Gracianov 1902:41 [ref. 1868]. Masc. *Cottus jeittelesi* Dybowski 1874:384. Type by subsequent designation. Type designated by Berg 1933:712 [ref. 279]. Original not seen. Valid (Sideleva 1982:31 [ref. 14469], Washington et al. 1984:443 [ref. 13660], Yabe 1985:123 [ref. 11522]). Cottocomephoridae.

Proctostegus Nardo 1827:18, 42 [ref. 3145]. Masc. *Proctostegus proctostegus* Nardo 1827:18, 42. Type by monotypy (also by absolute tautonymy). Original not seen. Synonym of *Luvarus* Rafinesque 1810 (Topp 1973:476 [ref. 7209]). Luvaridae.

Procypris Lin 1933:193 [ref. 5930]. Fem. *Procypris merus* Lin 1933:194. Type by original designation (also monotypic). Valid (Chen & Huang 1977:398 [ref. 13496], Wu 1987:44 [ref. 12822], Zhou in Chu & Chen 1989:326 [ref. 13584]). Cyprinidae.

Procypsilurus (subgenus of *Cypsilurus [Cypselurus]*) Bruun 1935:84 [ref. 5130]. Masc. *Exocoetus exsiliens* Linnaeus 1771:529. Type by original designation. Synonym of *Cheilopogon* Lowe 1841, but as a valid subgenus (Collette et al. 1984:338 [ref. 11422]). Exocoetidae.

Proditor Whitley 1940:407 [ref. 4699]. Masc. *Alepocephalus andersoni* Fowler 1934:246. Type by being a replacement name. Replacement for *Normania* Parr 1937, preoccupied by Brady 1866 in Crustacea, Bowerbank 1869 in sponges, and Boeck 1871 in Crustacea. Synonym of *Alepocephalus* Risso 1820 (Parr 1951:4 [ref. 3380]). Alepocephalidae.

Prodontocharax Eigenmann & Pearson in Pearson 1924:35 [ref. 3396]. Masc. *Prodontocharax melanotus* Pearson 1924:36. Type by monotypy. Valid (Géry 1977:590 [ref. 1597]). Characidae.

Proeutropiichthys Hora 1937:353 [ref. 6575]. Masc. *Eutropius macrophthalmus* Blyth 1860. Type by original designation (also monotypic). Valid (Jayaram 1977:16 [ref. 7006], Jayaram 1981:218 [ref. 6497], Burgess 1989:98 [ref. 12860]). Schilbeidae.

Proeutropius (subgenus of *Eutropius*) Fowler 1936:307 [ref. 1424]. Masc. *Silurus congensis* Leach 1818:409. Type by original designation (also monotypic). Synonym of *Eutropius* Müller & Troschel 1849 (De Vos 1986:41 [ref. 6191]). Schilbeidae.

Profundisudis (subgenus of *Notolepis*) Harry 1953:238 [ref. 2045]. Fem. *Arctozenus coruscans* Jordan & Gilbert 1881:411. Type by original designation. Synonym of *Notolepis* Dollo 1908 (Post 1973:208 [ref. 7182]). Synonym of *Arctozenus* Gill 1864 (Post 1987:79 [ref. 6225]). Paralepididae.

Profundulus Hubbs 1924:12 [ref. 2231]. Masc. *Fundulus punctatus* Günther 1866:320. Type by original designation. Valid (Parenti 1981:492 [ref. 7066]). Cyprinodontidae: Profundulinae.

Progastromyzon Hora & Jayaram 1952:191 [ref. 2216]. Masc. *Progastromyzon griswoldi* Hora & Jayaram 1952:192. Type by original designation (also monotypic). Valid (Silas 1953:239 [ref. 4024], Sawada 1982:206 [ref. 14111]). Balitoridae: Balitorinae.

Prognathochromis Greenwood 1980:14 [ref. 1899]. Masc. *Paratilapia prognatha* Pellegrin 1904:181. Type by original designation. Described as a genus on p. 14, as a subgenus on p. 19. Cichlidae.

Prognathodes Gill 1862:238 [ref. 1664]. Masc. *Chelmo pelta* Günther 1860:38. Type by monotypy. As *Prognathodus* in Bleeker 1876 [ref. 448]. Synonym of *Chaetodon* Linnaeus 1758, but as a valid subgenus (Burgess 1978:314 [ref. 700]); valid genus (Maugé & Bauchot 1984:464 [ref. 6614], Nalbant 1986:168 [ref. 6135], Randall & De Bruin 1988 [ref. 6861]). Chaetodontidae.

Prognichthys Breder 1928:14, 20 [ref. 636]. Masc. *Exocoetus gibbifrons* Valenciennes in Cuvier & Valenciennes 1847:118. Type by original designation. Valid (Collette et al. 1984:338 [ref. 11422], Yoshino in Masuda et al. 1984:82 [ref. 6441], Heemstra & Parin 1986:395 [ref. 6293]). Exocoetidae.

Prognurus Jordan & Gilbert in Jordan & Evermann 1898:2866 [ref. 2445]. Masc. *Prognurus cypselurus* Jordan & Gilbert in Jordan & Evermann 1898:2866. Type by original designation (also monotypic). Also in Jordan & Gilbert 1898:478 [ref. 1793]. Synonym of *Careproctus* Krøyer 1862 (Stein 1978:10 [ref. 4203], Kido 1988:193 [ref. 12287]). Cyclopteridae: Liparinae.

Progobiobotia (subgenus of *Gobiobotia*) Chen & Tsao 1977:551 [ref. 825]. Fem. *Gobiobotia abbreviata* Fang & Wang 1931. Type by original designation (also monotypic). Cyprinidae.

Prolabeo Norman 1932:182 [ref. 3222]. Masc. *Prolabeo batesi* Norman 1932:182. Type by original designation (also monotypic).

Valid (Lévêque & Daget 1984:330 [ref. 6186]). Cyprinidae.

Prolabeops Schultz 1941:85 [ref. 3954]. Masc. *Prolabeops cameroonensis* Schultz 1941:87. Type by original designation (also monotypic). Valid (Lévêque & Daget 1984:330 [ref. 6186]). Cyprinidae.

Prolatilus Gill 1866:67 [ref. 1708]. Masc. *Latilus jugularis* Valenciennes in Cuvier & Valenciennes 1833:500. Type by original designation (also monotypic). Valid (Randall 1984:41 [ref. 6067], Nakamura in Nakamura et al. 1986 [ref. 14235]). Pinguipedidae.

Promacheon Weber 1913:84 [ref. 4602]. *Promacheon sibogae* Weber 1913:85. Type by monotypy. Synonym of *Lampanyctus* Bonaparte 1840 (Paxton 1979:13 [ref. 6440]). Myctophidae.

Promecocephalus Troschel (ex Bibron) 1856:88 [ref. 12559]. Masc. *Tetraodon laevigatus* Linnaeus 1766:410. Type by subsequent designation. Appeared first as "Promécocéphale" Bibron in Duméril 1855:279 [ref. 297]; latinized by Troschel as above, also by Hollard 1857:319 [ref. 2186]. First technical addition of species not researched. Type above as given by Jordan 1919:262 [ref. 2410]. Synonym of *Lagocephalus* Swainson 1839 (Tortonese 1973:645 [ref. 7192], Shipp 1974:17 [ref. 7147]). Tetraodontidae.

Prometheus Lowe 1838:181 [ref. 2831]. Masc. *Prometheus atlanticus* Lowe 1838:181 (= *Gempylus prometheus* Cuvier 1831:213). Type by monotypy. Apparently preoccupied by Hübner 1824 [details not researched]; replaced by *Promethichthys* Gill 1893. In the synonymy of *Promethichthys* Gill 1893 (Parin & Bekker 1973:459 [ref. 7206]). Gempylidae.

Promethichthys Gill 1893:115, 123 [ref. 1736]. Masc. *Prometheus atlanticus* Lowe 1841:181 (= *Gempylus prometheus* Cuvier 1831:213). Type by being a replacement name. Replacement for *Prometheus* Lowe 1841, preoccupied by Hübner 1824 [details not researched]. Spelled *Prometheichthys* by Jordan, Tanaka & Snyder 1913:122 [ref. 6448]. Valid (Parin & Bekker 1973:459 [ref. 7206], Fujii in Uyeno et al. 1983:409 [ref. 14275], Collette et al. 1984:600 [ref. 11421], Nakamura in Masuda et al. 1984:227 [ref. 6441], Parin in Whitehead et al. 1986:971 [ref. 13676]). Gempylidae.

Promicrops Poey (ex Gill) 1868:287 [ref. 3505]. Masc. *Serranus guasa* Poey 1860:141, 354. Type by monotypy. Valid (Katayama in Masuda et al. 1984:132 [ref. 6441]); subgenus of *Epinephelus* Bloch 1793 (C. L. Smith 1971:152 [ref. 14102], Kendall 1984:501 [ref. 13663]); synonym of *Epinephelus* (Heemstra & Randall 1986:520 [ref. 5667]). Serranidae: Epinephelinae.

Promicropterus Gill 1861:31 [ref. 1766]. Masc. *Rypticus maculatus* Holbrook 1856:39. Type by monotypy. Synonym of *Rypticus* Cuvier 1829. Serranidae: Grammistinae.

Promyllantor Alcock 1890:310 [ref. 83]. Masc. *Promyllantor purpureus* Alcock 1890:310. Type by monotypy. Valid (Blache et al. 1973:243 [ref. 7185]). Congridae: Congrinae.

Pronothobranchius (subgenus of *Nothobranchius*) Radda 1969:162 [ref. 6078]. Masc. *Nothobranchius kiyawensis* Ahl 1928:601. Type by original designation (also monotypic). Synonym of *Nothobranchius* Peters 1868 (Parenti 1981:479 [ref. 7066]); valid (Wildekamp et al. 1986:276 [ref. 6198]). Aplocheilidae: Aplocheilinae.

Pronotogrammus Gill 1863:81 [ref. 1679]. Masc. *Pronotogrammus multifasciatus* Gill 1863:81. Type by monotypy. Valid (Fitch 1982:1 [ref. 5398], Matsuura in Uyeno et al. 1983:313 [ref. 14275], Kendall 1984:500 [ref. 13663]). Serranidae: Anthiinae.

Proodus Fowler 1944:183 [ref. 1448]. Masc. *Proodus xanthopterus* Fowler 1944:183. Type by original designation (also monotypic). Tetraodontidae.

Prophagorus Smith 1939:236 [ref. 4055]. Masc. *Clarias nieuhofi* Valenciennes in Cuvier & Valenciennes 1840:386. Type by original designation (also monotypic). Synonym of *Clarias* Scopoli 1777 (Teugels 1986:11 [ref. 12548]). Clariidae.

Propherallodus Shiogaki & Dotsu 1983:112 [ref. 5396]. Masc. *Propherallodus briggsi* Shiogaki & Dotsu 1983:113. Type by original designation. Valid (Yoshino in Masuda et al. 1984:341 [ref. 6441]). Gobiesocidae: Gobiesocinae.

Propoma Günther 1880:39 [ref. 2011]. Neut. *Propoma roseum* Günther 1880:39. Type by monotypy. Synonym of *Symphysanodon* Bleeker 1878 (Anderson 1970:326 [ref. 7662]). Symphysanodontidae.

Propseudecheneis Hora 1937:348 [ref. 2209]. Fem. *Propseudecheneis tchangi* Hora 1937:348. Type by original designation (also monotypic). Type designated on p. 349. Synonym of *Pseudecheneis* Blyth 1860 (Chu 1982 [ref. 5245]). Sisoridae.

Propterygia Otto 1821:111 [ref. 3321]. Fem. *Propterygia hyposticta* Otto 1821:112. Type by monotypy. Apparently based on a deformed specimen of *Raja batis*. Description and figure as given by Otto are reproduced in Fleming 1841:238 [ref. 1340], in which Fleming dates to Otto 1821 [original not seen; date not investigated]. Synonym of *Raja* Linnaeus 1758. Rajidae.

Proscyllium (subgenus of *Scyllium*) Hilgendorf 1904:39 [ref. 2170]. Neut. *Proscyllium habereri* Hilgendorf 1904:39. Type by monotypy. See also Nakaya 1983 [ref. 5697] for description of type. Valid (Compagno 1984:376 [ref. 6846], Nakaya in Masuda et al. 1984:5 [ref. 6441], Compagno 1988:189 [ref. 13488]). Proscylliidae.

Proscymnodon (subgenus of *Scymnodon*) Fowler 1934:239 [ref. 1416]. Masc. *Centrophorus plunketi* Waite 1909:38. Type by original designation (also monotypic). Synonym of *Centroscymnus* Bocage & Capello 1864 (Compagno 1984:53 [ref. 6474]). Squalidae.

Prosoarchus (subgenus of *Glossanodon*) Cohen 1958:155 [ref. 878]. Masc. *Glossanodon (Prosoarchus) pygmaeus* Cohen 1958:156. Type by original designation (also monotypic). Synonym of *Glossanodon* Guichenot 1867. Argentinidae.

Prosomyleus (subgenus of *Myleus*) Géry 1972:182 [ref. 1594]. Masc. *Myletes rhomboidalis* Cuvier 1818:449. Type by original designation (also monotypic). Synonym of *Myleus* Müller & Troschel 1844 (Géry 1976:49 [ref. 14199], Géry 1977:266 [ref. 1597]). Characidae: Serrasalminae.

Prosopium Jordan (ex Milner) 1878:361 [ref. 2376]. Neut. *Coregonus quadrilateralis* Richardson 1823:714. Type by subsequent designation. Type designated by Jordan & Gilbert 1883:297 [ref. 2476]. Valid (Kendall & Behnke 1984:144 [ref. 13638]). Salmonidae: Coregoninae.

Prosoplismus Waite 1903:59 [ref. 4560]. Masc. *Histiopterus recurvirostris* Richardson 1845:34. Type by original designation (also monotypic). Type designated on p. 56. Objective synonym of *Pentaceropsis* Steindachner 1883 (Hardy 1983:194 [ref. 5385]). Pentacerotidae.

Prosopodasys Cantor 1849:1026 [44] [ref. 715]. Fem. *Apistus alatus* Cuvier in Cuvier & Valenciennes 1829:392. Type by being a replacement name. Unneeded replacement for *Apistus* Cuvier 1829, not preoccupied by *Apista* or *Apistis*. On page 44 of separate. Bleeker 1876:6 [ref. 12248] and 1876:298 [ref. 450] lists type as *Apistus trachinoides* CV. Preoccupation by Hübner in Lepidoptera not investigated. Objective synonym of *Apistus* Cuvier 1829. Scorpaenidae: Apistinae.

Prosoproctus Poss & Eschmeyer 1979:11 [ref. 3552]. Masc. *Prosoproctus pataecus* Poss & Eschmeyer 1979:12. Type by original designation (also monotypic). Valid (Washington et al. 1984:441 [ref. 13660]). Aploactinidae.

Prososcopa Rass 1961:1858 [ref. 13630]. Fem. *Prososcopa stilbia* Rass 1961:1860. Type by original designation (also monotypic). Genus and species synonymized with *Xenophthalmichthys danae* Regan by Rass in 1962 [ref. 13631]. Microstomatidae.

Prospinus Poey 1861:364, 388 [ref. 3499]. Masc. *Plectropoma chloropterum* Cuvier in Cuvier & Valenciennes 1828:398. Type by subsequent designation. Also appeared as Poey in Gill 1862:236 [ref. 1664]. Earliest type designation found that of Jordan & Evermann 1896:1164 [ref. 2443]. Synonym of subgenus *Alphestes* Bloch & Schneider 1801 of genus *Epinephelus* Bloch 1793 (Smith 1971:162 [ref. 14102]). Serranidae: Epinephelinae.

Prostheacanthus Blyth 1860:167 [ref. 477]. Masc. *Prostheacanthus spectabilis* Blyth 1860:167. Type by monotypy. Synonym of *Acantopsis* van Hasselt 1823. Cobitidae: Cobitinae.

Protemblemaria Stephens 1963:15 [ref. 4270]. Fem. *Emblemaria bicirris* Hildebrand 1946:406. Type by original designation. Synonym of *Coralliozetus* Evermann & Marsh 1899 (Acero P. 1984 [ref. 5534]). Chaenopsidae.

Proteracanthus Günther 1859:413, 426 [ref. 1961]. Masc. *Crenidens sarissophorus* Cantor 1850:52. Type by monotypy. Valid (Johnson 1984:465 [ref. 9681] in Ephippididae). Ephippidae.

Proterorhinus (subgenus of *Gobius*) Smitt 1900:544 [ref. 4148]. Masc. *Gobius marmoratus* Pallas 1811:161. Type by monotypy. Valid (Miller 1973:511 [ref. 6888], Miller in Whitehead et al. 1986:1078 [ref. 13677]). Gobiidae.

Protistius Cope 1874:66 [ref. 933]. Masc. *Protistius semotilus* Cope 1874:66. Type by monotypy. Synonym of *Basilichthys* Girard 1855 (White 1985:17 [ref. 13551]). Atherinidae: Atherinopsinae.

Protocampus Günther 1870:193 [ref. 1995]. Masc. *Syngnathus hymenolomus* Richardson 1848:52. Type by monotypy. Same as *Hymenolomus* Duméril 1870; relative dates of publication not researched. Apparently an objective synonym of *Hymenolomus* Duméril 1870 of earlier date. Synonym of *Entelurus* Duméril 1870 (Wheeler 1973:278 [ref. 7190]). Syngnathidae: Syngnathinae.

Protogrammus Fricke 1985:294 [ref. 4952]. Masc. *Callionymus sousai* Maul 1972:1. Type by original designation (also monotypic). Valid (Fricke in Whitehead et al. 1986:1092 [ref. 13677]). Callionymidae.

Protomelas Eccles & Trewavas 1989:40 [ref. 13547]. Masc. *Chromis kirkii* Günther 1893:624. Type by original designation. Cichlidae.

Protomelus Hogg 1841:359 [ref. 2183]. Masc. *Lepidosiren annectens* Owen 1839:27. Type by being a replacement name. Unneeded replacement for *Protopterus* Owen 1839, which Hogg felt was inappropriate. Objective synonym of *Protopterus* Owen 1839 (Gosse 1984:8 [ref. 6169]). Lepidosirenidae: Protopterinae.

Protomugil (subgenus of *Liza*) Popov 1930:64 [ref. 6576]. Masc. *Mugil saliens* Risso 1810:345. Type by original designation (also monotypic). Valid (Trewavas 1973:572 [ref. 7201]). Mugilidae.

Protomyctophum (subgenus of *Electrona*) Fraser-Brunner 1949: 1045 [ref. 1496]. Neut. *Myctophum tenisoni* Norman 1930:321. Type by original designation. Valid (Krefft & Bekker 1973:196 [ref. 7181], Paxton 1979:17 [ref. 6440], Hulley in Whitehead et al. 1984:479 [ref. 13675], Moser et al. 1984:219 [ref. 13645], Fujii in Masuda et al. 1984:65 [ref. 6441], Hulley 1986:316 [ref. 5672], Paxton et al. 1989:268 [ref. 12442]). Myctophidae.

Protomyzon Hora 1932:306 [ref. 2208]. Masc. *Homaloptera whiteheadi* Vaillant 1894:92. Type by original designation (also monotypic). Valid (Silas 1953:237 [ref. 4024], Chen 1980:105 [ref. 6901], Sawada 1982:206 [ref. 14111]). Balitoridae: Balitorinae.

Protonibea Trewavas 1971:458 [ref. 6577]. Fem. *Lutjanus diacanthus* Lacepède 1802:240. Type by monotypy. Sciaenidae.

Protoporus Cope 1872:473 [ref. 923]. Masc. *Protoporus domninus* Cope 1872:473. Type by monotypy. Synonym of *Gila* Baird & Girard 1853. Cyprinidae.

Protopsetta (subgenus of *Hippoglossoides*) Schmidt 1904:230 [ref. 3946]. Fem. *Hippoglossoides herzensteini* Schmidt 1904:229. Type by monotypy. Not translated; perhaps two included species; type above as listed by Jordan 1920:511 [ref. 4905]. Synonym of *Cleisthenes* Jordan & Starks 1904 (Norman 1934:304 [ref. 6893]). Pleuronectidae: Pleuronectinae.

Protopterus Owen 1839:32 [ref. 3322]. Masc. *Lepidosiren annectens* Owen 1839:27. Type by monotypy. Type species described fully in Trans. Zool. Soc. London, v. 28 (1841):327-361, Pls. 23-27. Valid (Gosse 1984:8 [ref. 6169]). Lepidosirenidae: Protopterinae.

Protorestias Eigenmann & Allen 1942:353 [ref. 1246]. Masc. Not available, no description and no type species after 1930; name used to refer to a hypothetical ancestor of the genus *Orestias*, which makes in unavailable (Art. 1b(1)). Listed under genus *Orestias* Valenciennes (Parenti 1981:524 [ref. 7066]). Cyprinodontidae: Cyprinodontinae.

Protosalanx Regan 1908:444 [ref. 3632]. Masc. *Salanx hyalocranius* Abbott 1901:490. Type by monotypy. Valid (Roberts 1984:204 [ref. 5318]). Salangidae.

Prototroctes Günther 1864:382 [ref. 1974]. Masc. *Prototroctes maraena* Günther 1864:382. Type by monotypy. Valid (McDowall 1976:643 [ref. 7065], McDowall 1984:151 [ref. 11850], Paxton et al. 1989:174 [ref. 12442]). Retropinnidae: Prototroctinae.

Protoxotes Whitley 1950:244 [ref. 4712]. Fem. *Toxotes lorentzi* Weber 1911:232. Type by original designation (also monotypic). Toxotidae.

Protozygaena Whitley 1940:110 [ref. 4700]. Fem. *Physodon taylori* Ogilby 1915:117. Type by original designation (also monotypic). Synonym of *Rhizoprionodon* Whitley 1929 (Compagno 1984:524 [ref. 6846], Compagno 1988:294 [ref. 13488]). Carcharhinidae.

Prymnothonoides Whitley & Phillipps 1939:228 [ref. 4737]. Masc. *Prymnothonoides regani* Whitley & Phillipps 1939:228. Type by original designation (also monotypic). Doubtfully a synonym of *Notolepis* Dollo 1908 or *Paralepis* Cuvier 1816 (Post 1973:203, 208 [ref. 7182], Post 1987:100 [ref. 6225]). Paralepididae.

Prymnothonus Richardson 1845:51 [ref. 3740]. Masc. *Prymnothonus hookeri* Richardson 1845:51. Type by monotypy. Larval form, doubtfully a synonym of *Notolepis* Dollo 1908 or *Paralepis* Cuvier 1816 (Post 1973:203, 208 [ref. 7182], Post 1987:100 [ref. 6225]). Paralepididae.

Psalidodon Eigenmann 1911:165 [ref. 1226]. Masc. *Psalidodon gymnodontus* Eigenmann 1911:166. Type by original designation (also monotypic). Valid (Géry 1977:578 [ref. 1597]). Characidae.

Psalidostoma Kner 1864:99 [ref. 2639]. Neut. *Psalidostoma caudimaculatum* Kner 1864:100. Type by monotypy. Apparently preoccupied, replaced by *Onouphrios* Whitley 1951. Synonym of *Ichthyborus* Günther 1864 (Daget & Gosse 1984:197 [ref. 6185]).

Citharinidae: Distichodontinae.

Psalidostomus Minding 1832:121 [ref. 3022]. Masc. *Esox osseus* Linnaeus 1758:313. Misprinted on p. 121 as *Palidostomus*, corrected in corrigenda after p. 131. Name apparently not in current literature; an objective synonym of *Lepisosteus* Lacepède 1803. Lepisosteidae.

Psalisostomus Klein 1781:154 [ref. 4926]. Masc. Not available, published in a work that does not conform to the principle of binominal nomenclature. Original not checked. In the synonymy of *Lepisosteus* Lacepède 1803. Lepisosteidae.

Psallisostomus Klein in Walbaum 1792:581 [ref. 4572]. Masc. *Esox osseus* Linnaeus 1758:313. Type by subsequent designation. Not available (Opinion 21); probably can date to Fowler 1906:89 [ref. 7112, month uncertain] with type by monotypy (also Fowler 1906:81 [ref.1371, 26 July 1906]). In the synonymy of *Lepisosteus* Lacepède 1803. Lepisosteidae.

Psammichthys Regan 1908:246 [ref. 3634]. Masc. *Psammichthys nudus* Regan 1908:246. Type by monotypy. Synonym of *Kraemeria* Steindachner 1906 (Maugé 1986:375 [ref. 6218]). Kraemeriidae.

Psammobatis Günther 1870:470 [ref. 1995]. Fem. *Psammobatis rudis* Günther 1870:470. Type by monotypy. Valid (McEachran 1983 [ref. 5382]). Rajidae.

Psammochromis Greenwood 1980:53 [ref. 1899]. Masc. *Pelmatochromis riponianus* Boulenger 1911:69. Type by original designation. Cichlidae.

Psammodiscus Günther 1862:457 [ref. 1969]. Masc. *Psammodiscus ocellatus* Günther 1862:457. Type by monotypy. Valid (Norman 1934:415 [ref. 6893], Ahlstrom et al. 1984:643 [ref. 13641], Sakamoto 1984 [ref. 5273]). Pleuronectidae: Rhombosoleinae.

Psammogobius Smith 1935:215 [ref. 4066]. Masc. *Psammogobius knysnaensis* Smith 1935:215. Type by monotypy. Valid (Hoese 1986:801 [ref. 5670], Maugé 1986:381 [ref. 6218], Birdsong et al. 1988:190 [ref. 7303]). Gobiidae.

Psammoperca Richardson 1848:115 [ref. 3740]. Fem. *Psammoperca datnioides* Richardson 1848:116. Type by monotypy. Valid (Greenwood 1976:77 [ref. 14198], Katayama et al. 1977:52 [ref. 7052], Katayama in Masuda et al. 1984:123 [ref. 6441], Paxton et al. 1989:482 [ref. 12442]). Centropomidae: Latinae.

Psapharocetus (subgenus of *Cetomimus*) Harry 1952:59 [ref. 2044]. Masc. *Cetomimus kerdops* Parr 1934. Type by original designation (also monotypic). Synonym of *Cetomimus* Goode & Bean 1895 (Paxton 1989:177 [ref. 13435]). Cetomimidae.

Psectrogaster Eigenmann & Eigenmann 1889:7 [ref. 1252]. Fem. *Psectrogaster rhomboides* Eigenmann & Eigenmann 1889:7. Type by original designation. Also in Eigenmann & Eigenmann 1889 (Nov.):412 [ref. 1254]; 1889:7 published in April. Valid (Vari 1983:4 [ref. 5419], Géry et al. 1987:429 [ref. 6001], Vari 1989:6 [ref. 9189], Vari 1989 [ref. 13548]). Curimatidae: Curimatinae.

Psednoblennius Jenkins & Evermann 1889:156 [ref. 2342]. Masc. *Psednoblennius hypacanthus* Jenkins & Evermann 1889:156. Type by original designation (also monotypic). Synonym of *Emblemaria* Jordan & Gilbert 1883 (Stephens 1963:68 [ref. 4270]); as a valid subgenus (Acero P. 1984:41 [ref. 5534]). Chaenopsidae.

Psednos Barnard 1927:76 [ref. 193]. Masc. *Psednos micrurus* Barnard 1927:77. Type by monotypy. Also in Barnard 1927 (Oct.):927 [ref. 194]. Synonym of *Paraliparis* Collett 1878 (Stein 1979 [ref. 6799], Andriashev 1986:14 [ref. 12760]). Cyclopteridae: Liparinae.

Pselaphias Jordan & Seale 1906:406 [ref. 2497]. Masc. *Gobius ophthalmonemus* Bleeker 1856:208. Type by original designation (also monotypic). Synonym of *Oxyurichthys* Bleeker 1857 (Hoese, pers. comm.). Gobiidae.

Psellogrammus Eigenmann 1908:99 [ref. 1221]. Masc. *Hemigrammus kennedyi* Eigenmann in Eigenmann & Kennedy 1903:520. Type by original designation (also monotypic). Valid (Géry 1977:434 [ref. 1597]). Characidae.

Psenes Valenciennes in Cuvier & Valenciennes 1833:259 [ref. 1002]. Masc. *Psenes cyanophrys* Valenciennes in Cuvier & Valenciennes 1833:260. Type by subsequent designation. Type designated by Jordan 1917:142 [ref. 2407]. Valid (Haedrich 1967:84 [ref. 5357], Haedrich 1973:563 [ref. 7216], Horn 1984:628 [ref. 13637], Nakabo in Masuda et al. 1984:234 [ref. 6441], Haedrich in Whitehead et al. 1986:1186 [ref. 13677], Haedrich 1986:849 [ref. 5659]). Nomeidae.

Psenopsis Gill 1862:127 [ref. 1659]. Fem. *Trachinotus anomalus* Temminck & Schlegel 1844:107. Type by monotypy. Valid (Haedrich 1967:72 [ref. 5357], Horn 1984:628 [ref. 13637], Nakabo in Masuda et al. 1984:234 [ref. 6441], Haedrich 1986:844 [ref. 5659]). Centrolophidae.

Psephurus Günther 1873:250 [ref. 2004]. Masc. *Polyodon gladius* Martens 1861:476. Type by monotypy. Valid (Liu & Zeng 1988 [ref. 6414]). Polyodontidae.

Psetta Klein 1775:922 [ref. 2618]. Fem. Not available, published in a work that does conform to the principle of binominal nomenclature. In the synonymy of *Acanthurus* Forsskål 1775. Acanthuridae.

Psetta Swainson 1839:187, 302 [ref. 4303]. Fem. *Pleuronectes maximus* Linnaeus 1758:271. Type by monotypy. Synonym of *Scophthalmus* Rafinesque 1810 (Norman 1934:262 [ref. 6893]); valid (Nielsen 1973:618 [ref. 6885], Nielsen in Whitehead et al. 1986:1290 [ref. 13677]). Scophthalmidae.

Psettias Jordan in Jordan & Seale 1906:236 [ref. 2497]. Masc. *Psettus sebae* Valenciennes in Cuvier & Valenciennes 1831:189. Type by original designation (also monotypic). Monodactylidae.

Psettichthys Girard 1854:140 [ref. 1817]. Masc. *Psettichthys melanostictus* Girard 1854:140. Type by monotypy. Valid (Norman 1934:310 [ref. 6893], Ahlstrom et al. 1984:643 [ref. 13641], Sakamoto 1984 [ref. 5273]). Pleuronectidae: Pleuronectinae.

Psettina Hubbs 1915:456 [ref. 2224]. Fem. *Engyprosopon iijimae* Jordan & Starks 1904:626. Type by original designation (also monotypic). Valid (Norman 1934:199 [ref. 6893], Amaoka 1969:177 [ref. 105], Ahlstrom et al. 1984:643 [ref. 13641], Amaoka in Masuda et al. 1984:349 [ref. 6441], Hensley 1986:861 [ref. 5669], Hensley 1986:941 [ref. 6326], Fedorov & Foroshchuk 1988 [ref. 13478]). Bothidae: Bothinae.

Psettinella (subgenus of *Psettina*) Fedorov & Foroshchuk 1988:44 of translation [ref. 13478]. Fem. Apparenlty not available; described in key with 3 included species; no type designated (Art. 13b). Later use in an available way not researched. Bothidae: Bothinae.

Psettodes Bennett 1831:147 [ref. 5778]. Masc. *Psettodes belcheri* Bennett 1831:147. Apparently three included species; earliest subsequent designation not fully researched; type above as given by Jordan, but Bleeker 1862:423 [ref. 388] listed *Hippoglossus erumei* as type. Valid (Norman 1934:57 [ref. 6893], Ahlstrom et al. 1984:640 [ref. 13641], Heemstra 1986:853 [ref. 5660]). Psettodidae.

Psettus Commerson in Lacepède 1801:131 (footnote) [ref. 2710].

Masc. Not available, first word of non-binominal name mentioned in passing under *Monodactylus* Lacepède 1801; used validly by Cuvier 1829. See remarks under Opinion 89 in Appendix B. In the synonymy of *Monodactylus* Lacepède 1801. Monodactylidae.

Psettus Cuvier (ex Commerson) 1829:193 [ref. 995]. Masc. *Chaetodon rhombeus* Bloch & Schneider 1801:235. Type by subsequent designation. Appeared as "Les Psettus" with species mentioned in footnote, but without full latinization of *Psettus*; genus probably technically dates to a later work. Type designated by Jordan 1917:128 [ref. 2407]. Synonym of *Monodactylus* Lacepède 1801 (Desoutter 1986:338 [ref. 6212], Heemstra 1986:607 [ref. 5660]). Monodactylidae.

Psettyllis Alcock 1890:437 [ref. 86]. *Psettyllis pellucida* Alcock 1890:437. Type by subsequent designation. Earliest designation found that of Jordan 1920:450 [ref. 4905]. Spelled *Psettylis* by Jordan 1920:450 [ref. 4905], Zoological Record for 1890, and others. Synonym of *Bothus* Rafinesque 1810 (Norman 1934:220 [ref. 6893], Amaoka 1969:161 [ref. 105] but spelled *Psettylis*). Bothidae: Bothinae.

Pseudacanthicus Bleeker 1862:2 [ref. 393]. Masc. *Hypostomus serratus* Valenciennes in Cuvier & Valenciennes 1840:503. Type by original designation (also monotypic). Valid (Isbrücker 1980:76 [ref. 2303], Burgess 1989:438 [ref. 12860]). Loricariidae.

Pseudaesopia (subgenus of *Zebrias*) Chabanaud 1934:424, 433 [ref. 791]. Fem. *Synaptura regani* Gilchrist 1906. Type by monotypy. Valid (Ochiai in Masuda et al. 1984:355 [ref. 6441]). Soleidae.

Pseudageneiosus Bleeker 1862:14 [ref. 393]. Masc. *Ageneiosus brevifilis* Valenciennes in Cuvier & Valenciennes 1840:242. Type by original designation (also monotypic). Synonym of *Ageneiosus* Lacepède 1803. Ageneiosidae.

Pseudalectrias Popov 1933:ca. 150 [ref. 6535]. Masc. *Pseudalectrias tarasovi* Popov 1933:ca. 150. Original not seen. Valid (Miki et al. 1987 [ref. 12551]). Stichaeidae.

Pseudalphestes (subgenus of *Acanthistius*) Boulenger 1895:139 [ref. 537]. *Plectropoma pictum* Tschudi 1845:5. Type by monotypy. Synonym of *Acanthistius* Gill 1862. Serranidae: Serraninae.

Pseudalutarius Bleeker 1865:273 [ref. 415]. Masc. *Aluteres nasicornis* Schlegel in Temminck & Schlegel 1850:293. Type by monotypy. May date to Bleeker 1865:183 [ref. 414] with same type. Also in Bleeker 1869:100, 139 [ref. 416] with spelling *Paeudalutares*. Correct spelling for genus of type species is *Aluterus*. Valid (Matsuura 1979:165 [ref. 7019], Tyler 1980:176 [ref. 4477] as *Pseudaluteres*, Arai 1983:200 [ref. 14249], Abousouan & Leis 1984:452 [ref. 13661], Matsuura in Masuda et al. 1984:361 [ref. 6441], Hutchins 1986:886 [ref. 5673]). Monacanthidae.

Pseudambassis Bleeker 1874:86 [ref. 438]. Fem. *Chanda lala* Hamilton 1822:114, 371. Type by original designation (also monotypic). Synonym of *Parambassis* Bleeker 1874 (Roberts 1989:161 [ref. 6439]). Ambassidae.

Pseudamia Bleeker 1865:280 [284] [ref. 415]. Fem. *Chilodipterus polystigma* Bleeker (ex Castelnau) 1859:484. Type by monotypy. *Pseudoamia* is a misspelling. Correct spelling for genus of type species is *Cheilodipterus*. Valid (Randall et al. 1985 [ref. 9188], Hayashi in Masuda et al. 1984:150 [ref. 6441], Gon 1986:561 [ref. 5657], Paxton et al. 1989:556 [ref. 12442]). Apogonidae.

Pseudamiops Smith 1954:783 [ref. 4093]. Masc. *Pseudamiops pellucidus* Smith 1954:785. Type by original designation (also monotypic). Valid (Fraser 1972:31 [ref. 5195], Hayashi in Masuda et al. 1984:150 [ref. 6441], Gon 1986:561 [ref. 5657], Paxton et al. 1989:556 [ref. 12442]). Apogonidae.

Pseudanampses (subgenus of *Anampses*) Bleeker 1862:101 [ref. 4858]. *Anampses pterophthalmus* Bleeker 1862:102. Type by subsequent designation. Proposed by Bleeker for non-typical *Anampses* on basis of scale size and teeth; here regarded as a subgenus with Bleekers's first 2 of 7 species included in it. *A. pterophthalmus* here designated type. Synonym of *Anampses* Quoy & Gaimard 1824. Labridae.

Pseudancistrus Bleeker 1862:2 [ref. 393]. Masc. *Hypostomus barbatus* Valenciennes in Cuvier & Valenciennes 1840:506. Type by original designation (also monotypic). Valid (Isbrücker 1980:10 [ref. 2303], Isbrücker et al. 1988:16 [ref. 6409], Burgess 1989:429 [ref. 12860]). Loricariidae.

Pseudanos Winterbottom 1980:24 [ref. 4755]. *Schizodon trimaculatus* Kner 1859:161. Type by original designation. Curimatidae: Anostominae.

Pseudanthias Bleeker 1871:Pls. 287-288 [ref. 4861]. Masc. *Anthias pleurotaenia* Bleeker 1857:34. Type by subsequent designation. Apparently correctly dates to Pls. 287-288 in part 24 as above; corresponding legend (p. 124) published in 1876, corresponding text (p. 16) published in 1875. Also appeared in Bleeker 1873:158 [ref. 432] where type was designated. Synonym of *Anthias* Bloch 1792 (Heemstra & Randall 1986:511 [ref. 5667]); valid (Katayama in Masuda et al. 1984:136 [ref. 6441], Katayama & Amaoka 1986:219 [ref. 6680], Randall & Hutomo 1988 [ref. 6679], Randall & Allen 1989 [ref. 13389]). Serranidae: Anthiinae.

Pseudaphritis Castelnau 1872:92 [ref. 757]. Fem. *Pseudaphritis bassii* Castelnau 1872:72. Type by monotypy. Valid (Scott 1982: 202 [ref. 5472], Stevens et al. 1984:563 [ref. 13633] as *Pseudophrites*). Bovichtidae.

Pseudaphya Iljin 1930:46 [ref. 2297]. Fem. *Aphya ferreri* O. de Buen & Fage 1908:105. Type by original designation (also monotypic). The correct spelling for the genus of the type species is *Aphia*. Valid (Miller 1973:512 [ref. 6888], Miller in Whitehead et al. 1986:1079 [ref. 13677]). Gobiidae.

Pseudapocryptes Bleeker 1874:328 [ref. 437]. Masc. *Apocryptes lanceolatus* Cantor 1850 (= *Eleotris lanceolata* Bloch & Schneider 1801:67). Type by original designation (also monotypic). Valid (Birdsong et al. 1988:195 [ref. 7303], Kottelat 1989:19 [ref. 13605], Murdy 1989:45 [ref. 13628]). Gobiidae.

Pseudariodes Bleeker 1862:11 [ref. 393]. Masc. *Silurus clarias* Linnaeus 1758:306. Type by original designation (also monotypic). Type given as "*Pseudariodes clarias* = *Silurus clarias* Bl. [Bloch]." The possibility that this genus was based on a misidentified type species or deliberate use of a misidentification not investigated. Pimelodidae.

Pseudarius Bleeker 1862:8 [ref. 393]. Masc. *Pimelodus arius* Hamilton 1822:170, 376. Type by original designation. Dates to and type designated on p. 8 (in part 6), three species included in plates 49-51 (also part 6) and three included on p. 36 (part 7 in 1863). Objective synonym of *Arius* Valenciennes 1840 (Taylor 1986:153 [ref. 6195]). Ariidae.

Pseudaspius Dybowski 1869:953 [ref. 1169]. Masc. *Cyprinus leptocephalus* Pallas 1776:207, 703. Type by monotypy. Valid (Yang & Hwang 1964:34 [ref. 13497], Bogutskaya 1987:936 [ref. 13521]). Cyprinidae.

Pseudauchenipterus Bleeker 1862:6 [ref. 393]. Masc. *Silurus nodosus* Bloch 1794:35. Type by original designation (also monotypic). Valid (Burgess 1989:241 [ref. 12860], Curran 1989 [ref. 12547]). Auchenipteridae.

Pseudaustroglossus Chabanaud 1937:932 [ref. 794]. Masc. *Pseudaustroglossus annectens* Chabanaud 1937:933. Type by monotypy. Soleidae.

Pseudecheneis Blyth 1860:154 [ref. 477]. Fem. *Glyptosternon sulcatus* McClelland 1842:587. Type by monotypy. Valid (Jayaram 1981:267 [ref. 6497], Chu 1982 [ref. 5245], Burgess 1989:133 [ref. 12860], Kottelat 1989:15 [ref. 13605]). Sisoridae.

Pseudechidna Bleeker 1863:272 [ref. 399]. Fem. *Muraena brummeri* Bleeker 1858:137. Type by monotypy. Muraenidae: Muraeninae.

Pseudemblemaria Stephens 1961:3 [ref. 4269]. Fem. *Emblemaria signifer* Ginsburg 1942:367. Type by original designation (also monotypic). Valid (Stephens 1963:66 [ref. 4270]); synonym of *Emblemariopsis* Longley 1927 (Stephens 1970:283 [ref. 6994]). Chaenopsidae.

Pseudepapterus (subgenus of *Auchenipterus*) Steindachner 1915:82 [199] [ref. 4244]. Masc. *Auchenipterus (Pseudepapterus) hasemani* Steindachner 1915:82. Type by monotypy. On p. 199 of separate. Misspelled *Pseudepterus* by Jordan 1920:558 [ref. 4905]. Valid (Burgess 1989:241 [ref. 12860], Curran 1989 [ref. 12547]). Auchenipteridae.

Pseudepiplatys Clausen 1967:20, 30 [ref. 5926]. Masc. *Haplochilus annulatus* Boulenger 1915:203. Type by original designation (also monotypic). Misspelled once as *Pseudepiplatus* on p. 20. Synonym of *Epiplatys* Gill 1862 (Parenti 1981:475 [ref. 7066], Wildekamp et al. 1986:244 [ref. 6198]). Aplocheilidae: Aplocheilinae.

Pseuderythrinus Hoedeman 1950:80 [ref. 2176]. Masc. *Pseuderythrinus rosapinnis* Hoedeman 1950:82. Type by original designation (also monotypic). Characidae.

Pseudetroplus Bleeker 1862:125 [ref. 389]. Masc. *Etroplus coruchi* Cuvier in Cuvier & Valenciennes 1830:368. Type by original designation. Also appeared [perhaps first] as Bleeker in Günther 1862:266 [ref. 1969]. Günther cited Bleeker as intending to describe a new genus and provided Bleeker's diagnosis; Günther did not accept Bleeker's conclusion unless Bleeker had a third species or a very old specimen of *suratensis*. If 1862:266 was first, then *suratensis* is probably the type; see account in Günther where *suratensis* is the species associated with *Pseudetroplus*. Cichlidae.

Pseudeustomias Fowler 1934:261 [ref. 1416]. Masc. *Pseudeustomias myersi* Fowler 1934:262. Type by original designation (also monotypic). Synonym of *Stomias* Cuvier 1816 (Morrow 1964:292 [ref. 6967], Morrow 1973:132 [ref. 7175]). Stomiidae.

Pseudeutropichthys Koller 1926:74 [ref. 2658]. Masc. *Pseud)-eutropichthys multiradiatus* Koller 1926:74. Type by original designation (also monotypic). Also appeared in Koller 1927:29 [ref. 5622]. Cranoglanididae.

Pseudeutropius Bleeker 1862:398 [ref. 391]. Masc. *Eutropius brachypopterus* Bleeker 1858:169. Type by original designation (also monotypic). Also in Bleeker 1862:14, 74 [ref. 393]. Valid (Jayaram 1977:14 [ref. 7006], Jayaram 1981:216 [ref. 6497], Burgess 1989:99 [ref. 12860], Roberts 1989:128 [ref. 6439]). Schilbeidae.

Pseudexostoma Chu 1979:78, 81 [ref. 831]. Neut. *Glyptosternum yunnanensis* Tchang 1935. Type by original designation (also monotypic). Correct spelling for genus of type species is *Glyptosternon*. Sisoridae.

Pseudoambassis Castelnau 1878:43 [ref. 762]. Fem. *Pseudoambassis macleayi* Castelnau 1878:43. Type by subsequent designation. Earliest type designation not researched; Jordan 1919:393 [ref. 4905] lists type as above. Apparently preoccupied, replaced by *Blandowskiella* Iredale & Whitley 1932. Ambassidae.

Pseudoapistogramma Axelrod 1971:344 [ref. 5456]. Not available; name only, name mentioned in passing in synonymy of *Microgeophagus* Axelrod 1971 (see Robins & Bailey 1982:209 [ref. 6548]). Cichlidae.

Pseudobagrichthys Bleeker 1862:9, 49 [ref. 393]. Masc. *Bagroides macropterus* Bleeker 1853:515. Type by original designation. Dates to p. 9 and Pl. 67 (2 species) published in part 6 (26 Nov. 1862); text p. 49 published in part 7 (27 Jan. 1863). Also appeared as name only in Bleeker 1862:392 [ref. 391]. Synonym of *Bagrichthys* Bleeker 1858 (Jayaram 1968:378 [ref. 5615], Roberts 1989:111 [ref. 6439]). Bagridae.

Pseudobagrus Bleeker 1859:257 [ref. 371]. Masc. *Bagrus aurantiacus* Temminck & Schlegel 1846:227. Type by monotypy. Appeared first as name only in Bleeker 1858:34, 60 [ref. 365]; also in 1860:87 [ref. 374]; above apparently first. Valid (Jayaram 1968:325 [ref. 5615], Sawada in Masuda et al. 1984:59 [ref. 6441], Burgess 1989:68 [ref. 12860]). Bagridae.

Pseudobalistes (subgenus of *Balistes*) Bleeker 1865:Pls. 218, 225 [ref. 416]. Masc. *Balistes flavimarginatus* Bleeker 1865. Type by monotypy. Apparently dates to Pl. 218 and Pl. 225 (1865, in part 19), with type as *flavimarginatus* Bleeker; *viridescens* appears in Pl. 231 (part 20); corresponding text (99, 110) not published until 1869. Also in Bleeker 1866:11 [ref. 417] with type designated as *viridescens* (also 1869:99 [ref. 416]). Valid (Matsuura 1980:35 [ref. 6943], Tyler 1980:123 [ref. 4477], Arai 1983:199 [ref. 14249], Matsuura in Masuda et al. 1984:358 [ref. 6441], Smith & Heemstra 1986:880 [ref. 5714]. Balistidae.

Pseudobarbus (subgenus of *Barbus*) Smith 1841:Pl. 11 [ref. 4035]. Masc. *Barbus (Pseudobarbus) burchellii* Smith 1841:Pl. 11. Type by subsequent designation. Type designated by Jordan 1919:244 [ref. 2410]. Synonym of *Barbus* Cuvier & Cloquet 1816 (Lévêque & Daget 1984:218 [ref. 6186]); valid (Skelton 1988:263 [ref. 7302]). Cyprinidae.

Pseudobathylagus Kobyliansky 1986:43 [ref. 6002]. Masc. *Bathylagus milleri* Jordan & Gilbert in Jordan & Evermann 1895:2825. Type by original designation (also monotypic). Bathylagidae.

Pseudobatrachus Castelnau 1875:24 [ref. 768]. Masc. *Pseudobatrachus striatus* Castelnau 1875:24. Type by monotypy. Preoccupied by Peters 1873 in Amphibia. Synonym of *Batrachomoeus* Ogilby 1908 (Hutchins 1976:19 [ref. 6971]). Batrachoididae.

Pseudobetta Richter 1981:273 [ref. 6578]. Fem. *Betta pugnax* Cantor 1849:1066. Type by original designation (also monotypic). Synonym of *Betta* Bleeker 1850 (Roberts 1989:171 [ref. 6439]). Belontiidae.

Pseudoblennius Temminck & Schlegel 1850:313 [ref. 4375]. Masc. *Pseudoblennius percoides* Günther 1861:297. Type by subsequent monotypy. Original description without species; one species added by Günther 1861:297 [ref. 1964]. As *Pseudoclinus* on Temminck & Schlegel's caption to Pl. 79A; obviously a misprint differing from text and index. Valid (Washington et al. 1984:443 [ref. 13660], Yabe in Masuda et al. 1984:329 [ref. 6441], Yabe 1985:111 [ref. 11522], Kimura et al. 1988 [ref. 6692]). Cottidae.

Pseudobrama Bleeker 1870:253 [ref. 429]. Fem. *Pseudobrama dumerili* Bleeker 1871:60. Type by monotypy. Type species appeared as name only in Bleeker 1870:253, described in Bleeker 1871:60. If Bleeker's remarks on p. 253 are insufficient to validate the genus, then both genus and species date to Bleeker 1871:60 [ref. 6421]. Cyprinidae.

Pseudobythites Meek & Hildebrand 1928:968 [ref. 2964]. Masc. *Pseudobythites sanguineus* Meek & Hildebrand 1928:968. Type by original designation (also monotypic). Synonym of *Petrotyx* Heller & Snodgrass 1903 (Cohen & Nielsen 1978:38 [ref. 881]). Ophidiidae.

Pseudocalliurichthys Nakabo 1982:104 [ref. 3139]. Masc. *Callionymus variegatus* Temminck & Schlegel 1845:153. Type by original designation (also monotypic). Synonym of *Callionymus* Linnaeus 1758 (Fricke 1982:58 [ref. 5432]); valid (Houde 1984:637 [ref. 13674], Nakabo in Masuda et al. 1984:344 [ref. 6441]). Callionymidae.

Pseudocallophysus Bleeker 1862:12 [ref. 393]. Masc. *Pimelodus ctenodus* Agassiz 1829:21. Type by original designation (also monotypic). Also appeared as name only in Bleeker 1862:393 [ref. 391]. Synonym of *Calophysus* Müller & Troschel 1843. Pimelodidae.

Pseudocaranx Bleeker 1863:82 [ref. 395]. Masc. *Scomber dentex* Bloch & Schneider 1801:30. Type by subsequent designation. Possibly dates to an earlier Bleeker paper. Type designated by Fowler 1936:692 [ref. 6546]. Valid (Smith-Vaniz 1984:526 [ref. 13664], Gushiken in Masuda et al. 1984:155 [ref. 6441], Smith-Vaniz 1986:654 [ref. 5718], Gushiken 1988:443 [ref. 6697], Paxton et al. 1989:582 [ref. 12442]). Carangidae.

Pseudocarcharias (subgenus of *Carcharias*) Cadenat 1963:526 [ref. 709]. Masc. *Carcharias (Pseudocarcharias) pelagicus* Cadenat 1963:526. Type by original designation (also monotypic). Valid (Compagno 1984:225 [ref. 6474], Nakaya in Masuda et al. 1984:7 [ref. 6441], Bass 1986:103 [ref. 5635]). Odontaspididae: Pseudocharchariinae.

Pseudocentrophorus Chu, Meng & Liu 1981:100, 102 [ref. 835]. Masc. *Pseudocentrophorus isodon* Chu, Meng & Liu 1981:100, 102. Type by original designation (also monotypic). English description begins on p. 102. Squalidae.

Pseudocepola Kamohara 1935:135 [ref. 2549]. Fem. *Pseudocepola taeniosoma* Kamohara 1935:136. Type by original designation (also monotypic). Valid (Machida in Masuda et al. 1984:201 [ref. 6441], Mok 1988:507 [ref. 12752]). Cepolidae.

Pseudocetonurus Sazonov & Shcherbachev 1982:712 [ref. 3908]. Masc. *Pseudocetonurus septifer* Sazonov & Shcherbachev 1982:712. Type by original designation (also monotypic). Macrouridae: Macrourinae.

Pseudocetopsis Bleeker 1862:403 [ref. 392]. Fem. *Cetopsis gobioides* Kner 1857:407. Type by original designation (also monotypic). Also appeared in Bleeker 1862:16 [ref. 393] and 1863:112 [ref. 401]. Valid (Burgess 1989:291 [ref. 12860]). Cetopsidae.

Pseudochaenichthys Norman 1937:476 [ref. 3226]. Masc. *Pseudochaenichthys georgianus* Norman 1937:476. Type by original designation (also monotypic). Valid (Stevens et al. 1984:563 [ref. 13633], Iwami 1985:57 [ref. 13368]). Channichthyidae.

Pseudochaetodon Burgess 1978:298 [ref. 700]. Masc. *Sarothrodus nigrirostris* Gill 1863:243. Type by original designation (also monotypic). Objective synonym of *Johnrandallia* Nalbant 1974 (Maugé & Bauchot 1984:463 [ref. 6614]). Chaetodontidae.

Pseudochalceus Kner 1863:225 [ref. 5002]. Masc. *Pseudochalceus lineatus* Kner 1863:225. Type by monotypy. Also appeared as new in Kner & Steindachner 1864:31 [ref. 2649]. Valid (Géry 1977:414 [ref. 1597]). Characidae.

Pseudocheilinops Schultz in Schultz et al. 1960:128 [ref. 3972]. Masc. *Pseudocheilinops ataenia* Schultz in Schultz et al. 1960: 129. Type by original designation (also monotypic). Labridae.

Pseudocheilinus Bleeker 1862:409 [ref. 382]. Masc. *Cheilinus hexataenia* Bleeker 1857:84. Type by original designation (also monotypic). Also appeared in Bleeker 1862:95 [ref. 386]. Valid (Richards & Leis 1984:544 [ref. 13668], Yamakawa in Masuda et al. 1984:211 [ref. 6441], Randall 1986:700 [ref. 5706]). Labridae.

Pseudocheirodon Meek & Hildebrand 1916:275 [ref. 2962]. Masc. *Pseudocheirodon affinis* Meek & Hildebrand 1916:275. Type by original designation (also monotypic). Synonym of *Cheirodon* Girard 1855 (Fink & Weitzman 1974:3 [ref. 7132]), as a valid subgenus (Géry 1977:566 [ref. 1597]). Characidae.

Pseudochirocentrodon Miranda-Ribeiro 1920:8 [ref. 3727]. Masc. *Pseudochirocentrodon amazonicum* Miranda-Ribeiro 1920:8. Type by monotypy. Synonym of *Ilisha* Richardson 1846 (Poll et al. 1984:44 [ref. 6172], Whitehead 1985:261 [ref. 5141]). Clupeidae.

Pseudochromichthys Schmidt 1931:180 [ref. 3938]. Masc. *Pseudochromichthys riukianus* Schmidt 1931:180. Type by monotypy. Plesiopidae.

Pseudochromis Rüppell 1835:8 [ref. 3844]. Masc. *Pseudochromis olivaceus* Rüppell 1835:9. Type by subsequent designation. Type designated by Bleeker 1875:2 [ref. 444] and 1876:321 [ref. 448]. Valid (Lubbock 1977:2 [ref. 7039], Hayashi in Masuda et al. 1984:139 [ref. 6441], Smith 1986:540 [ref. 5712], Randall & Stanaland 1989 [ref. 12853], Paxton et al. 1989:519 [ref. 12442]). Pseudochromidae: Pseudochrominae.

Pseudocirrhites Mowbray in Breder 1927:48 [ref. 635]. Masc. *Pseudocirrhites pinos* Mowbray in Breder 1927:48. Type by monotypy. Synonym of *Amblycirritus* Gill 1862. Cirrhitidae.

Pseudocitharichthys Weber 1913:413 [ref. 4602]. Masc. *Pseudocitharichthys aureus* Day 1877:422. Type by monotypy. Doubtful synonym of *Bothus* Rafinesque 1810 (Norman 1934:220 [ref. 6893]). Bothidae: Bothinae.

Pseudoclinus Temminck & Schlegel 1850:Pl. LXXIXA [ref. 4375]. Masc. A misprint for *Pseudoblennius* Temminck & Schlegel 1850; see *Pseudoblennius*. Cottidae.

Pseudocoris Bleeker 1862:411 [ref. 382]. Fem. *Julis (Halichoeres) heteropterus* Bleeker 1857:78. Type by original designation (also monotypic). Also appeared in Bleeker 1862:97 [ref. 386]; earliest publication not established. Valid (see Randall & Kuiter 1982:159 [ref. 5446], Araga in Masuda et al. 1984:210 [ref. 6441]). Labridae.

Pseudocorynopoma Perugia 1891:646 [ref. 3431]. Neut. *Pseudocorynopoma doriae* Perugia 1891:646. Type by monotypy. Predates junior synonyms of same year; *Pseudocorynopoma* published 30 April, *Chalcinopelecus* Holmberg in June, *Bergia* Steindachner on 9 July. Valid (Géry 1977:359 [ref. 1597], Weitzman & S. Fink 1985:1 et seq. [ref. 5203], Weitzman et al. 1988:383 [ref. 13557], Malabarba 1989:138 [ref. 14217]). Characidae: Glandulocaudinae.

Pseudocrenilabrus Fowler 1934:462 [ref. 1419]. Masc. *Pseudocrenilabrus natalensis* Fowler 1934:463. Type by original designation (also monotypic). Valid (Greenwood 1984:213 [ref. 5311], Greenwood 1989 [ref. 14120]). Cichlidae.

Pseudoculter Bleeker 1859:432 [ref. 370]. Masc. *Culter pekinensis* Basilewski 1855:237. Type by subsequent designation. Apparently appeared first in key, without included species. Two species included by Bleeker 1860:282, 401 [ref. 380]. Type designated by Bleeker 1863:31 [ref. 4859] and 1863:210 [ref. 397]. Cyprinidae.

Pseudocurimata Fernández-Yépez 1948:45 [ref. 1316]. Fem. *Curimatus lineopunctatus* Boulenger 1911:213. Type by original designation. Valid (Vari 1989:6 [ref. 9189], Vari 1989:10 [ref. 13475]). Curimatidae: Curimatinae.

Pseudocyttus Gilchrist 1906:152 [ref. 1647]. Masc. *Pseudocyttus maculatus* Gilchrist 1906:153. Type by monotypy. Valid (Nakamura in Nakamura et al. 1986:172 [ref. 14235], Karrer 1986:440 [ref. 5680], James et al. 1988:293 [ref. 6639], Paxton et al. 1989:393 [ref. 12442]). Oreosomatidae.

Pseudodax Bleeker 1861:229 [ref. 381]. Masc. *Odax moluccanus* Valenciennes in Cuvier & Valenciennes 1839:395. Type by original designation. Also appeared in Bleeker 1862:409 [ref. 382] and 1862:96 [ref. 386]. Valid (see Randall 1981:100 [ref. 5447], Araga in Masuda et al. 1984:204 [ref. 6441] and Randall 1986:701 [ref. 5706] in its own subfamily). Labridae.

Pseudodiaphus Tåning 1918:71 [ref. 12242]. *Myctophum (Lampanyctus) dofleini* Zugmayer 1911:3. Type by subsequent designation. Type designated by Paxton 1979:15 [ref. 6440]. Original not examined. Synonym of *Lobianchia* Gatti 1904 (Paxton 1979:15 [ref. 6440]). Myctophidae.

Pseudodon Kessler 1874:40 [ref. 2596]. Masc. *Pseudodon longicauda* Kessler 1874:40. Type by monotypy. Original not translated. Apparently preoccupied by Gould 1845 in Mollusca; not replaced. Synonym of *Paracobitis* Bleeker 1863 (Kottelat 1990:20 [ref. 14137]). Balitoridae: Nemacheilinae.

Pseudodoras Bleeker 1858:53, 54 [ref. 365]. Masc. *Doras niger* Valenciennes 1811:184. Type by subsequent designation. Type designated by Eigenmann 1925:331 [ref. 1244]. Valid (Burgess 1989:224 [ref. 12860]). Doradidae.

Pseudogastromyzon (subgenus of *Hemimyzon*) Nichols 1925:1 [ref. 3177]. Masc. *Hemimyzon zebroidus* Nichols 1925:1. Type by monotypy. Valid (Silas 1953:231 [ref. 4024], Chen 1980:107 [ref. 6901], Sawada 1982:205 [ref. 14111]). Balitoridae: Balitorinae.

Pseudogeophagus Hoedeman 1974:1041 [ref. 5457]. Masc. *Apistogramma ramirezi* Myers & Harry 1948:77. Technically a name published in synonymy and unavailable; appeared as "This [differences from *Apistogramma*] was reason enough for Wickler (1963) to establish the genus *Pseudogeophagus* for this species." Wickler 1963 not listed in Hoedeman's literature cited; not treated as valid by Hoedeman. In the synonymy of *Microgeophagus* Axelrod 1971 (see Robins & Bailey 1982:209 [ref. 6548]). Cichlidae.

Pseudoginglymostoma Dingerkus 1986:240 [ref. 6118]. Neut. *Pseudoginglymostoma brevicaudatum* Günther in Playfair & Günther 1866:141. Type by original designation (also monotypic). Author placed in family Rhincodontidae as redefined to include Ginglmostomatinae. Ginglymostomatidae.

Pseudogobio Bleeker 1859:425 [ref. 370]. Masc. *Gobio esocinus* Temminck & Schlegel 1846:196. Type by subsequent monotypy. Apparently appeared first in key, without species; one species included by Bleeker 1860:115, 215 [ref. 380]. Valid (Banarescu & Nalbant 1973:229 [ref. 173], Lu, Luo & Chen 1977:512 [ref. 13495], Sawada in Masuda et al. 1984:56 [ref. 6441], Hosoya 1986:488 [ref. 6155]). Cyprinidae.

Pseudogobiodon Bleeker 1874:309 [ref. 437]. Masc. *Gobius citrinus* Rüppell 1835:139. Type by original designation (also monotypic). Apparently based on a misidentified type species; renamed *Pseudogobiodon macrochir* by Bleeker 1875:116 [ref. 12599]. Gobiidae.

Pseudogobiops (subgenus of *Pseudogobio*) Berg 1914:499, 500 [ref. 274]. Masc. *Gobio rivularis* Basilewski 1855:231. Type by original designation. Synonym of *Abbottina* Jordan & Fowler 1903 (Banarescu & Nalbant 1973:135 [ref. 173], Lu, Luo & Chen 1977:516 [ref. 13495], Chen & Li in Chu & Chen 1989:111 [ref. 13584]). Cyprinidae.

Pseudogobiopsis Koumans 1935:131 [ref. 2674]. Fem. *Gobiopsis oligactis* Bleeker 1875:113. Type by original designation. Valid (Birdsong et al. 1988:188 [ref. 7303], Kottelat 1989:19 [ref. 13605], Roberts 1989:168 [ref. 6439]). Gobiidae.

Pseudogobius Aurich 1938:158 [ref. 152]. Masc. *Gobius javanicus* Bleeker 1856:88. Type by original designation. Makes available *Pseudogobius* Koumans 1931 (on museum name of Bleeker published in synonymy); should not be credited to Aurich. Described independently of *Pseudogobius* Popta 1922, of which it is a synonym. See Appendix A. Treated as valid (Akihito in Masuda et al. 1984:268 [ref. 6441], Miller 1987:695 [ref. 6336] but on p. 698 indicates that it equals *Lizagobius* Whitley 1933, Roberts 1989:169 [ref. 6439]). See *Pseudogobius* of Popta and of Koumans. Gobiidae.

Pseudogobius Koumans (ex Bleeker) 1931:101 [ref. 5623]. Masc. *Gobius javanicus* Bleeker 1856:88. Museum name from Bleeker mentioned in synonymy of *Stigmatogobius* Bleeker 1874. See also *Pseudogobius* Aurich and *Pseudogobius* Popta. Aurich's treatment makes name available from Koumans 1931, with type by monotypy (*javanicus* the only available species name directly associated with *Pseudogobius* in Koumans 1931). See Appendix A. Gobiidae.

Pseudogobius Popta 1922:36 [ref. 3550]. Masc. Popta included two species, *penango* (described as new) and *javanicus* Bleeker—neither designated as type. Aurich 1938 independently described *Pseudogobius* (actually he made available *Pseudogobius* Koumans), and Aurich's designation of a type (*javanicus*) does not apply to *Pseudogobius* Popta. If Popta's *javanicus* is not misidentified, then it should be designated type of Popta's genus. *Pseudogobius* Popta should be recognized as valid. See Appendix A. Gobiidae.

Pseudogramma Bleeker 1875:2, 24 [ref. 444]. Neut. *Pseudochromis polyacanthus* Bleeker 1856:375. Type by original designation (also monotypic). Valid, in Pseudogrammatidae (Hayashi in Masuda et al. 1984:140 [ref. 6441], Smith 1986:542 [ref. 5712], Paxton et al. 1989:523 [ref. 12442]); in Grammistinae (Kendall 1984:501 [ref. 13663]). Serranidae: Grammistinae.

Pseudogyrinocheilus Fang 1933:255 [ref. 1297]. Masc. *Discognathus procheilus* Sauvage & Dabry de Thiersant 1874:8. Type by original designation. Synonym of *Semilabeo* Peters 1880 (Chu & Cui in Chu & Chen 1989:238 [ref. 13584]). Cyprinidae.

Pseudohelotes Guimarães 1882:222 [ref. 1953]. Fem. *Pseudohelotes guntheri* Guimarães (ex Capello) 1882:222. Type by monotypy. Originally as *Pseudo-Helotes*, correction mandatory. Synonym of *Plectorhinchus* Lacepède 1801 (Roux 1973:394 [ref. 7200], Roux 1986:327 [ref. 6209]). Haemulidae.

Pseudohemiculter (subgenus of *Hemiculter*) Nichols & Pope 1927:372 [ref. 5747]. *Hemiculter hainanensis* Nichols & Pope 1927:372. Type by original designation. Valid (Yih & Wu 1964:79 [ref. 13499], Chen in Chu & Chen 1989:77 [ref. 13584]). Cyprinidae.

Pseudohemiodon Bleeker 1862:3 [ref. 393]. Masc. *Hemiodon platy-*

cephalus Kner 1854:89. Type by original designation (also monotypic). Valid (Isbrücker 1980:120 [ref. 2303], Isbrücker & Nijssen 1986:103 [ref. 5212], Isbrücker & Nijssen 1986:40 [ref. 7321], Burgess 1989:444 [ref. 12860]). Loricariidae.

Pseudohistiophorus de Buen 1950:171 [ref. 692]. Masc. *Tetrapturus illingworthi* Jordan & Evermann 1926:32. Type by original designation. Synonym of *Tetrapturus* Rafinesque 1810 (de Sylva 1973:480 [ref. 7210], Nakamura 1983:294 [ref. 5371]). Istiophoridae.

Pseudohomaloptera Silas 1953:204 [ref. 4024]. Fem. *Homaloptera tateregani* Popta 1905:180. Type by original designation (also monotypic). Species originally *tate-regani*, removal of hyphen mandatory. Valid (Sawada 1982:205 [ref. 14111]). Balitoridae: Balitorinae.

Pseudohowella Fedoryako 1976:179 [ref. 1313]. Fem. *Pseudohowella intermedia* Fedoryako 1976:180. Type by original designation (also monotypic). Acropomatidae.

Pseudohypophthalmus Bleeker 1862:15 [ref. 393]. Masc. *Hypophthalmus fimbriatus* Kner 1857:444. Type by original designation (also monotypic). Synonym of *Hypophthalmus* Agassiz 1829. Hypophthalmidae.

Pseudoicichthys Parin & Permitin 1969:981 [ref. 3365]. Masc. *Icichthys australis* Haedrich 1966:201. Type by original designation (also monotypic). Synonym of *Icichthys* Jordan & Gilbert 1880 (McDowall 1981:130 [ref. 5356]); valid (Haedrich 1986:844 [ref. 5659]). Centrolophidae.

Pseudojulis Bleeker 1862:412 [ref. 382]. Fem. *Julis (Julis) girardi* Bleeker 1858:168. Type by original designation (also monotypic). Also appeared in Bleeker 1862:99 [ref. 386]; earliest not established. Probable synonym of *Halichoeres* Rüppell 1835 (Randall 1978 [ref. 5545]). Labridae.

Pseudojuloides Fowler 1949:119 [ref. 1462]. Masc. *Pseudojulis cerasina* Snyder 1904:528. Type by original designation (also monotypic). Valid (Ayling & Russell 1977 [ref. 7228], Randall & Randall 1981 [ref. 5494], Araga in Masuda et al. 1984:208 [ref. 6441], Randall 1986:701 [ref. 5706]). Labridae.

Pseudojulops Fowler 1941:271 [ref. 1438]. Masc. *Pseudojulis trifasciatus* Weber 1913:380. Type by original designation (also monotypic). Labridae.

Pseudolabrus Bleeker 1862:413 [ref. 382]. Masc. *Labrus rubiginosus* Temminck & Schlegel 1845:165. Type by original designation (also monotypic). Also appeared in Bleeker 1862:101 [ref. 386]. Type apparently preoccupied by Risso 1826 and not replaced; type apparently is a synonym of *Labrus japonicus* Houttuyn 1782. Valid (Russell & Randall 1981 [ref. 6392], Araga in Masuda et al. 1984:206 [ref. 6441], Russell 1988 [ref. 12549]). Labridae.

Pseudolaguvia Misra 1976:253 [ref. 3027]. Fem. *Glyptothorax tuberculatus* Prashad & Mukerji 1929:182. Type by original designation (also monotypic). Valid (Jayaram 1981:251 [ref. 6497], Burgess 1989:132 [ref. 12860]). Sisoridae.

Pseudolais Vaillant 1902:51 [ref. 4490]. Fem. *Pseudolais tetranema* Vaillant 1902:52. Type by monotypy. Synonym of *Pangasius* Valenciennes 1840 (Roberts 1989:131 [ref. 6439]). Pangasiidae.

Pseudolates Alleyne & Macleay 1877:262 [ref. 101]. Masc. *Pseudolates cavifrons* Alleyne & Macleay 1877:262. Type by monotypy. Synonym of *Lates* Cuvier 1828 (Paxton et al. 1989:482 based on placement of type species). Centropomidae: Latinae.

Pseudolaubuca Bleeker 1865:28 [ref. 407]. Fem. *Pseudolaubuca sinensis* Bleeker 1865:29. Type by monotypy. Valid (Chen in Chu & Chen 1989:48 [ref. 13584]). Cyprinidae.

Pseudolepidaplois Bauchot & Blanc 1961:53 [ref. 210]. *Pseudolepidaplois pfaffi* Bauchot & Blanc 1961:54. Type by monotypy. Valid (Bauchot & Quignard 1973:434 [ref. 7204], Quignard & Pras in Whitehead et al. 1986:930 [ref. 13676]). Labridae.

Pseudolioteres (subgenus of *Lioteres*) Smith 1958:156, 157 [ref. 4118]. Masc. *Lioteres (Pseudolioteres) simulans* Smith 1958:157. Type by original designation (also monotypic). Synonym of *Hetereleotris* Bleeker 1874 (Akihito & Meguro 1981:331 [ref. 5508], Hoese 1986:3 [ref. 5996]). Gobiidae.

Pseudoliparis (subgenus of *Careproctus*) Andriashev 1955:341 [ref. 121]. Masc. *Careproctus (Pseudoliparis) amblystomopsis* Andriashev 1955:341. Type by original designation (also monotypic). Cyclopteridae: Liparinae.

Pseudoloricaria Bleeker 1862:3 [ref. 393]. Fem. *Loricaria laeviuscula* Valenciennes in Cuvier & Valenciennes 1840:476. Type by original designation (also monotypic). Valid (Isbrücker & Nijssen 1976 [ref. 7075], Isbrücker 1980:124 [ref. 2303], Burgess 1989:444 [ref. 12860]). Loricariidae.

Pseudomancopsetta Evseenko 1984:710 [ref. 5978]. Fem. *Pseudomancopsetta andriashevi* Evseenko 1984:711. Type by original designation (also monotypic). Valid (Hensley 1986:941 [ref. 6326]). Achiropsettidae.

Pseudomola Cadenat 1959:1115 [ref. 708]. Fem. *Pseudomola lasserati* Cadenat 1959:1115. Type by monotypy. Molidae.

Pseudomonacanthus Bleeker 1865:Pl. 228 [ref. 416]. Masc. *Monacanthus macrurus* Bleeker 1857:226. Apparently dates to Pl. 228 published in part 19 (1865), with type by monotypy; corresponding text (pp. 99, 134) published in part 21 (in 1869). Also in Bleeker 1866:12 [ref. 417]. Valid (Matsuura 1979:165 [ref. 7019], Tyler 1980:183 [ref. 4477], Arai 1983:200 [ref. 14249]). Monacanthidae.

Pseudomonopterus Bleeker 1863:266 [ref. 12600]. Masc. *Gasterosteus volitans* Linnaeus 1758:296. Type by monotypy. Validates *Pseudomonopterus* Klein 1777. Synonym of *Pterois* Oken 1817. Scorpaenidae: Pteroinae.

Pseudomoringua Bleeker 1864:15 [ref. 4860]. Fem. *Moringua lumbricoidea* Richardson 1844:113. Type by original designation (also monotypic). Bleeker 1864:15 published 21 Sept. 1864; also in Bleeker 1865:114 [ref. 409]. Synonym of *Moringua* Gray 1831 (Smith 1989:95 [ref. 13285]). Moringuidae.

Pseudomugil Kner 1866:543 [1] [ref. 2636]. Masc. *Pseudomugil signifer* Kner 1866:543. Type by monotypy. Apparently appeared first as above; also described as new in Kner 1867:275 [ref. 2638]; reference 2638 published in parts in 1865-1867 - p. 275 apparently in 1867. On p. 1 of separate of ref. 2636. Valid (Allen & Cross 1982:124 [ref. 6251], Allen & Sarti 1983 [ref. 5354], Ivantsoff & Allen 1984 [ref. 6380], Allen & Ivantsoff 1986 [ref. 6246], Paxton et al. 1989:352 [ref. 12442], Saeed et al. 1989 [ref. 13533]). Atherinidae: Pseudomugilinae.

Pseudomulloides Miranda-Ribeiro 1915:4 [ref. 3711]. Masc. *Pseudomulloides carmineus* Miranda-Ribeiro 1915:4. Type by monotypy. Appears on p. 4 in section titled Mullidae. Mullidae.

Pseudomuraena Johnson 1862:167 [ref. 2357]. Fem. *Pseudomuraena maderensis* Johnson 1862:167. Type by monotypy. Synonym of *Gymnothorax* Bloch 1795 (Blache et al. 1973:226 [ref. 7185], Böhlke et al. 1989:145 [ref. 13286]). Muraenidae: Muraeninae.

Pseudomycterus Ogilby 1908:94 [ref. 3287]. Masc. *Pseudomycterus maccullochi* Ogilby 1908:96. Type by monotypy. Synonym of *Johnius*, subgenus *Johnius* Bloch 1793 (Trewavas 1977:406 [ref. 4459]). Sciaenidae.

Pseudomyrophis Wade 1946:199 [ref. 4542]. Masc. *Pseudomyrophis micropinna* Wade 1946:200. Type by original designation (also monotypic). Valid (McCosker 1977:61 [ref. 6836], McCosker et al. 1989:289 [ref. 13288]). Ophichthidae: Myrophinae.

Pseudomystus (subgenus of *Leiocassis*) Jayaram 1968:359 [ref. 5615]. Masc. *Bagrus stenomus* Valenciennes in Cuvier & Valenciennes 1839:307. Type by original designation. Questionably a synonym of *Leiocassis* Bleeker 1858 (Roberts 1989:116 [ref. 6439]). Bagridae.

Pseudonezumia Okamura 1970:38 [ref. 6580]. Fem. *Pseudonezumia japonicus* Okamura 1970:39. Type by original designation (also monotypic). Valid (Marshall & Iwamoto 1973:531 [ref. 6963], Fahay & Markle 1984:274 [ref. 13653], Okamura in Masuda et al. 1984:95 [ref. 6441]). Macrouridae: Macrourinae.

Pseudonus Garman 1899:169 [ref. 1540]. Masc. *Pseudonus acutus* Garman 1899:169. Type by monotypy. Valid (Cohen & Nielsen 1978:50 [ref. 881]). Bythitidae: Bythitinae.

Pseudopangasius Bleeker 1862:399 [ref. 391]. Masc. *Pangasius polyuranodon* Bleeker 1852:425. Type by original designation (also monotypic). Also in Bleeker 1862:14, 75 [ref. 393]; earliest publication not established. Synonym of *Pangasius* Valenciennes 1840 (Roberts 1989:131 [ref. 6439]). Pangasiidae.

Pseudopentaceros Bleeker 1876:270 [ref. 447]. Masc. *Pentaceros richardsoni* Smith 1849:Pl. 21. Type by original designation (also monotypic). Valid (Hardy 1983:206 [ref. 5385], Heemstra 1986:623 [ref. 5660], Humphreys & Tagami 1986 [ref. 6000], Humphreys et al. 1989 [ref. 9286]). Pentacerotidae.

Pseudopercis Miranda-Ribeiro 1903:41 [ref. 3709]. Fem. *Pseudopercis numida* Miranda-Ribeiro 1903:41. Type by subsequent designation. Type designated by Jordan 1920:506 [ref. 4905]. *Pseudopercis* Miranda-Ribeiro 1918 in family Cichlidae as given by Jordan (1920:564 [ref. 4905]) in error. Valid (Nakamura in Nakamura et al. 1986:268 [ref. 14235]). Pinguipedidae.

Pseudoperilampus Bleeker 1863:214 [ref. 397]. Masc. *Pseudoperilampus typus* Bleeker 1863:235. Type by original designation (also monotypic and by use of *typus*). Also in Bleeker 1863:264 [ref. 403] and 1863:33 [ref. 4859], earliest not established for genus or for species. Valid (Wu 1964:204 [ref. 13503], Sawada in Masuda et al. 1984:55 [ref. 6441]); synonym of *Acheilognathus* Bleeker 1859 (Arai & Akai 1988:205 [ref. 6999]); synonym of *Rhodeus* Agassiz 1835 (Chen & Li in Chu & Chen 1989:124 [ref. 13584]). Cyprinidae.

Pseudophallus Herald 1940:51 [ref. 2095]. Masc. *Siphostoma starksii* Jordan & Culver in Jordan 1895:416. Type by original designation (also monotypic). Valid (Dawson 1982:44 [ref. 6764], Dawson 1985:161 [ref. 6541]). Syngnathidae: Syngnathinae.

Pseudophichthys Roule 1915:283 [ref. 3817]. Masc. *Pseudophichthys latedorsalis* Roule 1915:283. Type by monotypy. Also appeared in Roule 1916:4 [ref. 3818]. Synonym of *Promyllantor* Alcock 1890 (Blache et al. 1973:243 [ref. 7185]); valid (Blache & Bauchot 1976:417 [ref. 305], Bauchot & Saldanha in Whitehead et al. 1986:572 [ref. 13676], Smith 1989:551 [ref. 13285]). Congridae: Congrinae.

Pseudophidium Gracianov 1907:420 [ref. 1871]. Neut. *Ophidium giganteum* Kittlitz 1858. Original not seen; from Zoological Record for 1907. Correct spelling for genus of type species is *Ophidion*. Not an Ophidiinae (R. N. Lea, pers. comm.). Ophidiiformes.

Pseudophoxinus Bleeker 1859:431 [ref. 370]. Masc. *Phoxinellus zeregi* Heckel 1843:1063. Type by subsequent monotypy. Apparently appeared first in key, without included species. One species included by Bleeker 1860:281, 395 [ref. 380]. Valid (Lévêque & Daget 1984:331 [ref. 6186], Krupp & Schneider 1989:375 [ref. 13651], but see Coad 1981:2062 [ref. 5572]). Cyprinidae.

Pseudophycis Günther 1862:350 [ref. 1969]. Fem. *Lota breviuscula* Richardson 1846:61. Type by monotypy. Valid (Paulin 1983:90 [ref. 5459], Fahay & Markle 1984:266 [ref. 13653], Paxton et al. 1989:302 [ref. 12442]). Moridae.

Pseudopimelodus Bleeker 1858:196, 204, 207 [ref. 365]. Masc. *Pimelodus raninus* Valenciennes in Cuvier & Valenciennes 1840:157. Type by subsequent designation. Type designated by Bleeker 1862:11 [ref. 393]. Valid (Mees 1974:187 [ref. 2969], Mees 1978:253 [ref. 5691], Stewart 1986:667 [ref. 5211], Burgess 1989:275 [ref. 12860]). Pimelodidae.

Pseudoplatichthys Hikita 1934:11, et. seq. [ref. 2160]. Masc. *Pseudoplatichthys oshorensis* Hikita 1934:11, et seq. Type by original designation (also monotypic). Pleuronectidae.

Pseudoplatystoma Bleeker 1862:10 [ref. 393]. Neut. *Silurus fasciatus* Linnaeus 1766:505. Type by original designation (also monotypic). Valid (Mees 1974:127 [ref. 2969], Burgess 1989:282 [ref. 12860]). Pimelodidae.

Pseudoplesiops Bleeker 1858:217 [ref. 362]. Masc. *Pseudoplesiops typus* Bleeker 1858:217. Type by monotypy (also by use of *typus*). Valid (Kishimoto in Masuda et al. 1984:141 [ref. 6441], Allen 1987 [ref. 6247], Paxton et al. 1989:521 [ref. 12442]). Pseudochromidae: Pseudoplesiopinae.

Pseudoplesiops Boulenger 1899:121 [ref. 589]. Masc. *Pseudoplesiops nudiceps* Boulenger 1899:122. Type by monotypy. Preoccupied by Bleeker 1858 in fishes, replaced by *Nanochromis* Pellegrin 1904. Cichlidae.

Pseudopleuronectes Bleeker 1862:428 [ref. 388]. Masc. *Platessa planus* Mitchill 1814:8. Type by monotypy. Valid (Norman 1934:342 [ref. 6893], Ahlstrom et al. 1984:643 [ref. 13641]). Pleuronectidae: Pleuronectinae.

Pseudopoecilia Regan 1913:995 [ref. 3653]. Fem. *Poecilia festae* Boulenger 1898:13. Type by monotypy. Synonym of *Priapichthys* Regan 1913 (Rosen & Bailey 1963:120 [ref. 7067]). Poeciliidae.

Pseudopomacentrus (subgenus of *Pomacentrus*) Bleeker 1877:39 [ref. 454]. Masc. *Pomacentrus littoralis* Cuvier (ex Kuhl & van Hasselt) in Cuvier & Valenciennes 1830:425. Type by subsequent designation. Also appeared in Bleeker 1877:39 [ref. 453, same page number 39]. Type designated by Fowler & Bean 1928:65 [ref. 1475]. Synonym of *Pomacentrus* Lacepède 1802 (Shen & Chan 1978:236 [ref. 6945]). Pomacentridae.

Pseudopriacanthus Bleeker 1869:241 [ref. 427]. Masc. *Priacanthus niphonius* Cuvier in Cuvier & Valenciennes 1829:107. Type by subsequent designation. Type designated by Morrison 1890 [ref. 6864]. Valid (Fitch & Crooke 1984 [ref. 4950]); synonym of fossil genus *Pristigenys* Agassiz (Fritzsche & Johnson 1981 [ref. 5399], Taverne 1988 [ref. 6863], Starnes 1988:131 [ref. 6978]). Priacanthidae.

Pseudopristella Géry 1960:18 [ref. 1605]. Fem. *Pseudopristella* *simulata* Géry 1960:18. Type by original designation (also monotypic). Valid (Géry 1977:582 [ref. 1597]). Characidae.

Pseudopristipoma Sauvage 1880:220 [ref. 3888]. Neut. *Pristipoma leucurum* Valenciennes in Cuvier & Valenciennes 1833:488. Type by monotypy. Synonym of *Plectorhinchus* Lacepède 1801 (Roux 1973:394 [ref. 7200], Roux 1986:327 [ref. 6209]). Haemulidae.

Pseudopsectrogaster Fernández-Yépez 1948:31 [ref. 1316]. Fem. *Psectrogaster curviventris* Eigenmann & Kennedy 1903:509. Type by original designation (also monotypic). Synonym of *Psectrogaster* Eigenmann & Eigenmann 1889 (Vari 1989:6 [ref. 9189], Vari 1989:12 [ref. 13548]). Curimatidae: Curimatinae.

Pseudopterus Bleeker (ex Klein) 1876:296 [ref. 450]. Masc. *Gasterosteus volitans* Linnaeus 1758:296. Also in Bleeker 1876:40 [ref. 12248]; published as a name in the synonymy of *Pseudomonopterus*. Apparently not available, not subsequently treated as a valid taxon or as a senior homonym. Type as listed by Jordan 1920:384 [ref. 4904]. In the synonymy of *Pterois* Oken 1817. Scorpaenidae: Pteroinae.

Pseudopterus Klein 1776:139 [ref. 4919]. Masc. Not available, published in a work that does not conform to the principle of binominal nomenclature. In the synonymy of *Pterois* Oken 1817. Scorpaenidae: Pteroinae.

Pseudopungtungia Mori 1935:164 [ref. 3043]. Fem. *Pseudopungtungia nigra* Mori 1935:164. Type by original designation (also monotypic). Valid (Banarescu & Nalbant 1973:35 [ref. 173]). Cyprinidae.

Pseudoraja Bigelow & Schroeder 1954:4 [ref. 5551]. Fem. *Pseudoraja fischeri* Bigelow & Schroeder 1954:4. Type by original designation (also monotypic). Rajidae.

Pseudorasbora Bleeker 1859:435 [ref. 370]. Fem. *Leuciscus pusillus* Temminck & Schlegel 1846:216. Type by subsequent monotypy. Appeared first in key, without species; one species (*pusillus*) included by Bleeker 1859:261 [ref. 380] and 1860:2, 97 [ref. 374]. Type apparently not *Leuscisus parvus* Temminck & Schlegel as designated by Bleeker 1863:212 [ref. 397] and 1863:32 [ref. 4859], although months of publication for pertinent Bleeker papers not established). Valid (Banarescu & Nalbatn 1973:20 [ref. 173], Lu, Luo & Chen 1977:462 [ref. 13495], Chen & Li in Chu & Chen 1989:103 [ref. 13584]). Cyprinidae.

Pseudorhamdia Bleeker 1862:11 [ref. 393]. Fem. *Pimelodus maculatus* Lacepède 1803:94, 107. Type by original designation (also monotypic). Also in Bleeker 1862:384 [ref. 390] and 1863:101 [ref. 401]; earliest publication not established. Type designated by Bleeker 1862:11 [ref. 393] if needed. Pimelodidae.

Pseudorhegma Schultz 1966:191 [ref. 3973]. Neut. *Pseudorhegma diagramma* Schultz 1966:193. Type by original designation. Serranidae: Grammistinae.

Pseudorhombus Bleeker 1862:426 [ref. 388]. Masc. *Rhombus polyspilos* Bleeker 1853:503. Type by monotypy. Valid (Norman 1934:89 [ref. 6893], Amaoka 1969:88 [ref. 105], Ahlstrom et al. 1984:642 [ref. 13641], Amaoka in Masuda et al. 1984:347 [ref. 6441], Hensley 1986:861 [ref. 5669], Desoutter 1986:428 [ref. 6212]). Paralichthyidae.

Pseudorinelepis Bleeker 1862:3 [ref. 393]. Fem. *Rinelepis genibarbis* Valenciennes in Cuvier & Valenciennes 1840:484. Type by original designation (also monotypic). Spelled *Pseudorhinelepis* in reprint edition index to Jordan 1917-23. Correct original spelling for genus of type species is *Rhinelepis*. Valid (Isbrücker 1980:8 [ref. 2303], Burgess 1989:429 [ref. 12860]). Loricariidae.

Pseudosawara (subgenus of *Scomberomorus*) Munro 1943:68 [ref. 3056]. *Cybium kuhlii* Valenciennes in Cuvier & Valenciennes 1831:178. Type by original designation. Synonym of *Scomberomorus* Lacepède 1801 (Collette & Russo 1984:611 [ref. 5221]). Scombridae.

Pseudoscaphirhynchus Nikolskii 1900:257 [ref. 3202]. Masc. *Pseudoscaphirhynchus rossikowi* Nikolskii 1900:258. Type by monotypy. On Official List (Opinion 971). Valid (Bailey & Cross 1954:173 [ref. 5358]). Acipenseridae: Scaphirhynchinae.

Pseudoscarus Bleeker 1861:230 [ref. 381]. Masc. *Scarus microrhinos* Bleeker 1854:200. Type by subsequent designation. Appeared first in Bleeker 1861:70 [ref. 12601] as "*Pseudoscarus psittacus* Blkr." name only; apparently Bleeker was referring to *Scarus psittacus*" of earlier authors. In 1861:240 [ref. 381] Bleeker referred to *Scarus psittacus* Cantor, while including 41 species in *Pseudoscarus*. If *Pseudoscarus* 1861:70 is regarded as available, then the type is *psittacus* by monotypy; otherwise, type designated by Jordan & Evermann 1898:1655 [ref. 2444]. Scaridae: Scarinae.

Pseudosciaena Bleeker 1863:142 [ref. 396]. Fem. *Pseudosciaena amblyceps* Bleeker 1863:142. Type by subsequent designation. Bleeker 1874:18 [ref. 12517] and 1876:329 [ref. 448] listed *Sciaena aquila* Risso [= Lacepède 1803] as type (accepted by Trewavas 1977:387 [ref. 4459]), but *aquila* was not a named included species. Type apparently validly designated first by Jordan 1919:321 [ref. 4904]. Synonym of *Argyrosomus* De la Pylaie 1835 (Trewavas 1973:397 [ref. 7201], Trewavas 1977:322 [ref. 4459], Daget & Trewavas 1986:333 [ref. 6211]); valid (Okamura in Masuda et al. 1984:162 [ref. 6441]). Sciaenidae.

Pseudoscopelus Lütken 1892:285 [ref. 2858]. Masc. *Pseudoscopelus scriptus* Lütken 1892:284. Type by monotypy. Misspelled *Pseudoseopelus* by Jordan 1923:230 [ref. 2421]. Valid (Krefft 1971 [ref. 7434], Krefft 1973:453 [ref. 7166], Uyeno & Aizawa in Uyeno et al. 1983:403 [ref. 14275], Uyeno in Masuda et al. 1984:221 [ref. 6441], Johnson & Keene in Whitehead et al. 1986:960 [ref. 13676]). Chiasmodontidae.

Pseudoscymnus Herre 1935:124 [ref. 2111]. Masc. *Pseudoscymnus boshuensis* Herre 1935:124. Type by original designation (also monotypic). Synonym of *Dalatias* Rafinesque 1810 (Compagno 1984:63 [ref. 6474]). Synonym of *Dalatias* or *Scymnorhinus* Bonaparte 1846 (Cappetta 1987:62 [ref. 6348]). Squalidae.

Pseudosebastes (subgenus of *Sebastes*) Sauvage 1878:120 [ref. 3880]. Masc. *Sebastes bougainvillei* Cuvier in Cuvier & Valenciennes 1829:349. Type by monotypy. May have appeared first in 1875 (Assoc. Français pour l'Advancement des Sciences, Lille, 1874, p. 470), but reference not yet examined. Synonym of *Neosebastes* Guichenot 1867. Scorpaenidae: Neosebastinae.

Pseudoserranus Klunzinger 1870:687 [ref. 2621]. Masc. *Perca louti* Forsskål 1775:40. Type by monotypy. Synonym of *Variola* Swainson 1839. Serranidae: Epinephelinae.

Pseudosetipinna Peng & Zhao 1988:355 [ref. 13758]. Fem. *Pseudosetipinna haizhouensis* Peng & Zhao 1988:355. Type by original designation (also monotypic). Engraulidae.

Pseudosilurus Bleeker 1858:254-256, 275 [ref. 365]. Masc. *Silurus bimaculatus* Bloch 1797:24. Type by subsequent designation. Also on pp. 24, 26, et seq. Earliest subsequent designation apparently Jordan 1919:279 [ref. 2410] but with species credited to Bleeker (also designated by Roberts 1989:151 [ref. 6439]). Synonym of *Ompok* Lacepède 1803 (Haig 1952:103 [ref. 12607], Roberts 1989:151 [ref. 6439]). Siluridae.

Pseudosimochromis Nelissen 1977:730 [ref. 3153]. Masc. *Simochromis curvifrons* Poll 1942:344. Type by original designation (also monotypic). Valid (Poll 1986:85 [ref. 6136]). Cichlidae.

Pseudosphromenus Bleeker 1879:2, 17 [ref. 457]. Masc. *Polyacanthus cupanus* Cuvier in Cuvier & Valenciennes 1831:267. Type by original designation (also monotypic). Type designated on p. 17, not *Osphromenus opercularis* Bleeker. Valid. Belontiidae.

Pseudostegophilus Eigenmann & Eigenmann 1889:54 [ref. 1253]. Masc. *Stegophilus nemurus* Günther 1868:429. Type by original designation (also monotypic). Valid (Burgess 1989:323 [ref. 12860], Pinna 1989 [ref. 12630]). Trichomycteridae.

Pseudosynanceia Day 1875:163 [ref. 1080]. Fem. *Pseudosynanceia melanostigma* Day 1875:163. Type by monotypy. Valid (Eschmeyer & Rama-Rao 1973:369 [ref. 6391], Washington et al. 1984:440 [ref. 13660]). Scorpaenidae: Synanceiinae.

Pseudosynodontis Bleeker 1862:6 [ref. 393]. Fem. *Synodontis serratus* Rüppell 1829:8. Type by original designation (also monotypic). Synonym of *Synodontis* Cuvier 1816 (Gosse 1986:117 [ref. 6194]). Mochokidae.

Pseudotaractes Abe 1961:94 [ref. 7]. Masc. *Brama saussuri* Lunel 1865:185. Type by original designation (also monotypic). Synonym of *Eumegistus* Jordan & Jordan 1922 (Mead 1972:8 [ref. 6976]). Bramidae.

Pseudotatia Mees 1974:105 [ref. 2969]. Fem. *Pseudotatia parva* Mees 1974:105. Type by original designation (also monotypic). Valid (Burgess 1989:241 [ref. 12860], Curran 1989 [ref. 12547]). Auchenipteridae.

Pseudothyrina Miranda-Ribeiro 1915:11 [ref. 3711]. Fem. *Pseudothyrina iheringi* Miranda-Ribeiro 1915:11. Type by monotypy. Appears on p. 11 in section titled Trematolepides. Synonym of *Odontesthes* Evermann & Kendall 1906 (White 1985:17 [ref. 13551]). Atherinidae: Atherinopsinae.

Pseudotocinclus Nichols 1919:534 [ref. 3172]. Masc. *Pseudotocinclus intermedius* Nichols 1919:534. Type by monotypy. Valid (Isbrücker 1980:86 [ref. 2303], Britski & Garavello 1984:226 [ref. 5166], Burgess 1989:439 [ref. 12860]). Loricariidae.

Pseudotolithus Bleeker 1863:59 [ref. 395]. Masc. *Pseudotolithus typus* Bleeker 1863:60. Type by use of *typus* (3 included species). Valid (Trewavas 1973:398 [ref. 7201], Daget & Trewavas 1986:335 [ref. 6211]). Sciaenidae.

Pseudotor Karaman 1971:229 [ref. 2560]. Masc. *Barbus fritschii* Günther 1874:231. Type by original designation. Synonym of *Barbus* Cuvier & Cloquet 1816 (Lévêque & Daget 1984:219 [ref. 6186]). Cyprinidae.

Pseudotothyris Britski & Garavello 1984:232 [ref. 5166]. Fem. *Otocinclus obtusus* Miranda-Ribeiro 1911:95. Type by original designation. Valid (Burgess 1989:439 [ref. 12860]). Loricariidae.

Pseudotrachinus Bleeker 1861:378 [ref. 384]. Masc. *Trachinus radiatus* Cuvier 1829:152. Type by subsequent designation. Two included species; first designation of type species apparently by Jordan 1919:301, 309 [ref. 4904]. Also appeared in Bleeker 1862:117 [ref. 385]. Synonym of *Trachinus* Linnaeus 1758 (Wheeler 1973:449 [ref. 7190]). Trachinidae.

Pseudotrematomus Balushkin 1982:9 [ref. 6042]. *Trematomus bernacchii* Boulenger 1902:181. Type by original designation. Valid (Balushkin & Tarakanov 1987 [ref. 6226]). Nototheniidae.

Pseudotriacanthus Fraser-Brunner 1941:(429) 430 [ref. 1493]. Masc. *Triacanthus strigilifer* Cantor 1849:1345. Type by original designation (also monotypic). Valid (Tyler 1968:290 [ref. 6438], Tyler 1980:98 [ref. 4477]). Triacanthidae.

Pseudotriakis Capello 1868:315 [ref. 718]. Fem. *Pseudotriakis microdon* Capello 1868:316. Type by monotypy. *Pseudotriacis* Günther 1870:395 [ref. 1995] is an unjustified emendation. Valid (Springer 1973:22 [ref. 7162], Taniuchi et al. 1984 [ref. 6732], Compagno 1984:378 [ref. 6846], Nakaya & Shirai in Masuda et al. 1984:5 [ref. 6441], Bass 1986:96 [ref. 5635], Compagno 1988:197 [ref. 13488]). Pseudotriakidae.

Pseudotrichonotus Yoshino & Araga in Masuda, Araga & Yoshino 1975:176 [ref. 2902]. Masc. *Pseudotrichonotus altivelis* Yoshino & Araga in Masuda, Araga & Yoshino 1977:176. Type by original designation (also monotypic). Valid (Machida in Masuda et al. 1984:60 [ref. 6441]). Pseudotrichonotidae.

Pseudotropheus Regan 1922:681 [ref. 3673]. Masc. *Chromis williamsi* Günther 1894:623. Type by original designation. Valid (Ribbink et al. 1983:157 [ref. 13555], Trewavas 1984 [ref. 5303], Meyer & Foerster 1984 [ref. 6645], Stauffer 1988 [ref. 6678]). Cichlidae.

Pseudotrypauchen Hardenberg 1931:418 [ref. 2036]. Masc. *Pseudotrypauchen multiradiatus* Hardenberg 1931:418. Type by monotypy. Misspelled *Pseudotrypanchen* in Zoological Record for 1932. Gobiidae.

Pseudotylosurus Fernández-Yépez 1948:72 [ref. 1317]. Masc. *Pseudotylosurus brasiliensis* Fernández-Yépez 1948:73. Type by monotypy. Misspelled *Pseudotilosurus* in title. Valid (Collette 1974 [ref. 7131], Collette et al. 1984:336 [ref. 11422]). Belonidae.

Pseudoxenomystax Breder 1927:6 [ref. 635]. Masc. *Pseudoxenomystax dubius* Breder 1927:6. Type by original designation (also monotypic). Valid (Cervigón et al. 1980 [ref. 5421]); synonym of *Rhechias* Jordan 1921 (Smith 1989:532 [ref. 13285]). Congridae: Congrinae.

Pseudoxiphophorus Bleeker 1859:440 [ref. 370]. Masc. *Xiphophorus bimaculatus* Heckel 1848:169. Appeared in key, without included species; also in other Bleeker papers in 1859-1860; earliest not established. Type by subsequent monotypy (possibly dating to Bleeker 1864:140 [ref. 4859]). Synonym of *Heterandria* Agassiz 1853 (Rosen & Bailey 1963:128 [ref. 7067]; as a valid subgenus (Miller 1974 [ref. 7119], Rosen 1979:315 [ref. 7020], Parenti & Rauchenberger 1989:9 [ref. 13538]). Poeciliidae.

Pseudoxygaster Banarescu 1967:306 [ref. 213]. Fem. *Cyprinus gora* Hamilton 1822:263, 384. Type by original designation (also monotypic). Cyprinidae.

Pseudoxymetopon Chu & Wu 1962:219 [ref. 834]. Neut. *Pseudoxymetopon sinensis* Chu & Wu 1962:219. Type by original designation (also monotypic). Trichiuridae.

Pseudupeneus Bleeker 1862:134 [ref. 389]. Masc. *Pseudupeneus prayensis* Cuvier in Cuvier & Valenciennes 1829:485. Type by monotypy. Also appeared in Bleeker 1863 (possibly 1862):56 [ref. 395]. Valid (Hureau 1973:403 [ref. 7197], Hureau in Whitehead et al. 1986:878 [ref. 13676]). Mullidae.

Psilocephalus Swainson 1839:194, 327 [ref. 4303]. Masc. *Balistes (Anacanthus) barbatus* Gray 1831:357. Type by monotypy. Valid (Tyler 1980:176 [ref. 4477], Arai 1983:200 [ref. 14249]). Monacanthidae.

Psilocranium Macleay 1884:439 [ref. 2873]. Neut. *Psilocranium coxii* Macleay 1884:440. Type by monotypy. Cirrhitidae.

Psilodraco Norman 1937:475 [ref. 3226]. Masc. *Psilodraco breviceps* Norman 1937:476. Type by original designation (also monotypic). Valid (DeWitt & Hureau 1979:789 [ref. 1125], Stevens et al. 1984:563 [ref. 13633], Voskoboinikova 1988:44 [ref. 12756]).

Bathydraconidae.

Psilogobius Baldwin 1972:125 [ref. 169]. Masc. *Psilogobius mainlandi* Baldwin 1972:126. Type by original designation (also monotypic). Valid (Birdsong et al. 1988:193 [ref. 7303]). Gobiidae.

Psiloides Fischer von Waldheim 1813:74 [ref. 1331]. Masc. Original not seen. Jordan 1917:85 [ref. 2407] treats as an unneeded substitute for *Bostrychoides* Lacepède 1801. Eleotridae.

Psilonotus Swainson 1839:328 [ref. 4303]. Masc. *Tetraodon rostratus* Bloch 1782:Pl. 146. Type by subsequent designation. As *Canthigaster* on p. 194, changed to *Psilonotus* on p. 328. Type designation not researched, first designation possibly by Bleeker 1865:45 [ref. 416]. Apparently preoccupied in Hymenoptera [not researched]. Objective synonym of *Canthigaster* Swainson 1839 (Allen & Randall 1977:478 [ref. 6714]). Tetraodontidae.

Psilopentapodus (subgenus of *Pentapodus*) Fowler 1933:71, 83 [ref. 1414]. Masc. *Pentapus dux* Valenciennes 1862:1203. Type by original designation. Synonym of *Pentapodus* Quoy & Gaimard 1824. Nemipteridae.

Psilorhynchus McClelland 1839:248, 300, 428 [ref. 2923]. Masc. *Cyprinus sucatio* Hamilton 1822:347. Type by subsequent designation. Also in McClelland 1839:944 [ref. 2924] without species. Type apparently designated first by Jordan 1919:195 [ref. 2410] but more investigation needed. Valid (Jayaram 1981:139 [ref. 6497] with type as *Cyprinus balitora* Hamilton, Rainboth 1983 [ref. 5429]). Psilorhynchidae.

Psilosomus Swainson 1839:183 [ref. 4303]. Masc. *Taenioides hermanni* Lacepède 1800:532. Type by being a replacement name. Changed by Swainson on p. 279 (footnote) from *Psilosoma* (sic) to *Amblyopus* Cuvier. Unneeded replacement for *Amblyopus*. Objective synonym of *Amblyopus* Valenciennes 1837. Synonym of *Taenioides* Lacepède 1800. Gobiidae.

Psilotris Ginsburg 1953:22 [ref. 1806]. Fem. *Psilotris alepis* Ginsburg 1953:22. Type by original designation (also monotypic). Valid (Birdsong et al. 1988:189 [ref. 7303]). Gobiidae.

Psilus Fischer von Waldheim 1813:74 [ref. 1331]. Masc. *Bostrychus sinensis* Lacepède 1801:141. Type by being a replacement name. Original not seen; apparently an unneeded replacement for *Bostrychus* Lacepède 1801. Objective synonym of *Bostrychus* Lacepède 1801 (Maugé 1986:389 [ref. 6218]). Eleotridae.

Psittacus Catesby 1771:29 [ref. 774]. Fem. Not available, published in a rejected work on Official Index (Opinion 89, Opinion 259). *Psittacus* Catesby of 1777 is on Official Index as a junior homonym of *Psittacus* Linnaeus 1758 (Direction 44). Scaridae: Scarinae.

Psychichthys (subgenus of *Hydrolagus*) Fowler 1907:419 [ref. 1377]. Masc. *Hydrolagus waitei* Fowler 1907:419. Type by original designation (also monotypic). Synonym of *Hydrolagus* Gill 1862 (Böhlke 1984:56 [ref. 13621] based on placement of type species). Chimaeridae.

Psychrolutes Günther 1861:516 [ref. 1964]. Masc. *Psychrolutes paradoxus* Günther 1861:516. Type by monotypy. Valid (Washington et al. 1984:444 [ref. 13660], Yabe in Masuda et al. 1984:330 [ref. 6441], Yabe 1985:123 [ref. 11522], Nelson et al. 1985 [ref. 5264], Fedorov & Nelson in Whitehead et al. 1986:1264 [ref. 13677], Nelson 1986:491 [ref. 5698], Paxton et al. 1989:478 [ref. 12442]). Psychrolutidae.

Psychromaster Jordan & Evermann 1896:1099 [ref. 2443]. Masc. *Etheostoma tuscumbia* Gilbert & Swain 1887:63. Type by original designation (also monotypic). Misspelled *Psychomaster* in Zoological Record for 1896. Synonym of *Etheostoma* Rafinesque 1819, but as a valid subgenus (Collette & Banarescu 1977:1456 [ref. 5845], Page 1981:30 [ref. 3347], Bailey & Etnier 1988:25 [ref. 6873]). Percidae.

Psychropoecilia (subgenus of *Mollienesia*) Myers 1935:311 [ref. 3110]. Fem. *Platypoecilus dominicensis* Evermann & Clark 1906:852. Type by original designation (also monotypic). Synonym of *Poecilia* Bloch & Schneider 1801 (Rosen & Bailey 1963:45 [ref. 7067]). Poeciliidae.

Ptarmus Smith 1947:816 [ref. 4073]. Masc. *Coccotropus jubatus* Smith 1935:223. Type by original designation. Valid (Washington et al. 1984:441 [ref. 13660], Poss 1986:480 [ref. 6296]). Aploactinidae.

Ptax Jordan & Evermann 1927:504 [ref. 2453]. *Dicrotus parvipinnis* Goode & Bean 1896:201. Type by original designation (also monotypic). Gempylidae.

Ptenichthys Müller 1843:312 [ref. 3063]. Masc. *Exocoetus furcatus* Mitchill 1815:449. Type by subsequent designation. Type designated by Jordan 1919:216 [ref. 2410]; type not initially named ("*Exocoetus* mit Barbfaden"). First addition of species not researched. Synonym of *Cheilopogon* Lowe 1841 (Parin 1973:264 [ref. 7191]), but as a valid subgenus (Collette et al. 1984:337 [ref. 11422]). Exocoetidae.

Ptenonotus Ogilby 1908:13 [ref. 3286]. Masc. *Exocoetus cirriger* Peters 1877:555. Type by original designation (also monotypic). Type designated on p. 2. Exocoetidae.

Pteracles Swainson 1838:41 [ref. 4302]. Also p. 20 and 1839:47, 178, 257 [ref. 4303]. Unjustified emendation of *Pteraclis* (on Cuvier), but not clear from text; if independently described then dates to 1838:41 with type *Pteraclis trichipterus* Cuvier. Synonym of *Pteraclis* Gronow 1772. Bramidae.

Pteraclidus Rafinesque 1815:82 [ref. 3584]. Masc. Not available; name only; apparently an incorrect subsequent spelling of *Pteraclis* Gronow with *Oligopodus* Lacepède apparently synonymized. In the synonymy of *Pteraclis* Gronow 1772 (Mead 1973:388 [ref. 7199]). Bramidae.

Pteraclis Gronow 1772:43 [ref. 12602]. Neut. *Coryphaena velifera* Pallas 1770:19. Type by monotypy. Original not seen. Valid (Mead 1972:104 [ref. 6976], Mead 1973:388 [ref. 7199], Mochizuki in Masuda et al. 1984:160 [ref. 6441], Smith 1986:634 [ref. 5712], Yatsu & Nakamura 1989:190 [ref. 13449]). Bramidae.

Pteragogus Peters 1855:451 [ref. 3449]. *Cossyphus opercularis* Peters 1855:451. Type by monotypy. Type species preoccupied by *Cossyphus opercularis* Guichenot 1847; replaced by *Pteragogus pelycus* Randall 1981:82 [ref. 5447]. Valid (Randall 1981 [ref. 5447], Richards & Leis 1984:544 [ref. 13668], Araga in Masuda et al. 1984:205 [ref. 6441], Randall 1986:701 [ref. 5706]). Labridae.

Pteranthias Weber 1913:208 [ref. 4602]. Masc. *Pteranthias longimanus* Weber 1913:209. Type by monotypy. Synonym of *Plectranthias* Bleeker 1873 (Randall 1980:105 [ref. 6717]). Serranidae: Anthiinae.

Pterapogon Koumans 1933:78 [ref. 2673]. Masc. *Pterapogon kauderni* Koumans 1933:78. Type by monotypy. Valid (Fraser 1972:26 [ref. 5195], Paxton et al. 1989:556 [ref. 12442]). Apogonidae.

Pterapon Gray 1835:Pl. 88 (v. 2) [ref. 1878]. Masc. *Pterapon trivittatus* Gray 1835:Pl. 88. Type by monotypy. Considered as a different spelling for *Terapon* Cuvier 1816, but no evidence in original to determine if an emendation or an intended new name. In the synonymy of *Terapon* Cuvier 1816 (Vari 1978:254 [ref. 4514],

Vari 1986:304 [ref. 6205]). Terapontidae.

Ptereleotris Gill 1863:271 [ref. 1691]. Fem. *Eleotris microlepis* Bleeker 1856:102. Type by original designation (also monotypic). Valid (Randall & Hoese 1985 [ref. 5197], Yoshino in Masuda et al. 1984:245 [ref. 6441], Hoese 1986:802 [ref. 5670], Birdsong et al. 1988:201 [ref. 7303]). Microdesmidae: Ptereleotrinae.

Pterengraulis (subgenus of *Engraulis*) Günther 1868:384, 398 [ref. 1990]. Fem. *Clupea atherinoides* Linnaeus 1766:523. Type by monotypy. Described in key (p. 398) as subgenus of *Engraulis* for 1 species treated on p. 398. Valid (Grande 1985:245 [ref. 6466], Whitehead et al. 1988:386 [ref. 5725]). Engraulidae.

Pterichthus Commerson in Lacepède 1803:403 (footnote) [ref. 4930]. Masc. *Exocoetus commersonii* Lacepède 1803:401, 403. Not available. Commerson names in footnotes in this volume of Lacepède placed on Official Index of Rejected Works (see remarks under Opinion 89 in Appendix B). In the synonymy of *Exocoetus* Linnaeus 1758. Exocoetidae.

Pterichthys (subgenus of *Apistes*) Swainson 1839:63, 180, 265 [ref. 4303]. Masc. *Scorpaena carinata* Bloch & Schneider 1801:193. Type by original designation on p. 63, not *Scorpaena carinata* as designated by Swain 1882:277 [ref. 5966]. Spelled *Ptericthys* on pp. 63, 64, *Plerichthys* on p. 65; *Pterichthys* on pp. 180, 265, 442 (index). Synonym of *Apistus* Cuvier 1829. Scorpaenidae: Apistinae.

Pteridium Filippi & Vérany 1859:11 (?195) [ref. 1329]. Neut. *Oligopus ater* Risso 1810:142. Type by being a replacement name. Apparently not an original description, but *ater* included in *Pteridium* Scopoli following Swainson. *Verater* Jordan 1919 proposed as a substitute for *Pteridium* Filippi & Verany [also as a substitute for *Gadopsis*]. Bythitidae: Bythitinae.

Pteridium Scopoli 1777:454 [ref. 3990]. Neut. *Coryphaena velifera* Pallas 1770:19. Type by monotypy. Apparently intended as a new name credited to himself, not a replacement for *Pteraclis*. Synonym of *Pteraclis* Gronow 1772 (Mead 1972:104 [ref. 6976], Mead 1973:388 [ref. 7199]). Bramidae.

Pterobrycon Eigenmann 1913:3 [ref. 1229]. Masc. *Pterobrycon landoni* Eigenmann 1913:3. Type by monotypy. Valid (Géry 1977:359 [ref. 1597], Weitzman & S. Fink 1985:1 et seq. [ref. 5203]). Characidae: Glandulocaudinae.

Pterobunocephalus (subgenus of *Bunocephalus*) Fowler 1943:1 [ref. 1442]. Masc. *Bunocephalus albifasciatus* Fowler 1943:2. Type by original designation. Synonym of *Dysichthys* Cope 1874 (Mees 1988:89 [ref. 6401]). Aspredinidae: Bunocephalinae.

Pterocaesio Bleeker 1876:153 [ref. 445]. Fem. *Caesio multiradiatus [a]* Steindachner 1861:175. Type by original designation (also monotypic). Also in Bleeker 1876:41 [ref. 4862]; earliest not determined. Valid (Johnson 1980:10 [ref. 13553], Smith 1986:579 [ref. 5712], Carpenter 1987:29 [ref. 6430], Carpenter 1988:50 [ref. 9296]). Caesionidae.

Pterocapoeta Günther 1902:446 [ref. 2020]. Fem. *Pterocapoeta maroccana* Günther 1902:446. Type by monotypy. Synonym of *Varicorhinus* Rüppell 1836 (Karaman 1971:231 [ref. 2560], Lévêque & Daget 1984:336 [ref. 6186]). Cyprinidae.

Pterocephalus Swainson 1838:170, 174 [ref. 4302]. Fem. *Raja giorna* Lacepède 1803:662. Type by being a replacement name. Dates to Swainson 1838:170, 174, with *P. massena* Swainson mentioned (= *Cephalopterus massena* Risso 1810) but technically a replacement name for *Cephalopterus* (see footnote p. 174). Spelled *Pterocephala* by Swainson 1839 [ref. 4303]. Synonym of *Mobula* Rafinesque 1810 (Krefft & Stehmann 1973:77 [ref. 7167] as *Pterocephala*, Cappetta 1987:177 [ref. 6348]). Mobulidae.

Pterochromis Trewavas 1973:11 [ref. 4458]. Masc. *Pelmatochromis congicus* Boulenger 1897:422. Type by original designation (also monotypic). Valid (Greenwood 1987:154 [ref. 6166]). Cichlidae.

Pterocryptis Peters 1861:712 [ref. 3451]. Fem. *Pterocryptis gangelica* Peters 1861:712. Type by monotypy. Species originally spelled *gangelica*; apparently misspelled *gangetica* in literature. Synonym of *Silurus* Linnaeus 1758 (Haig 1952:97 [ref. 12607]). Siluridae.

Pteroculiops Fowler 1938:133 [ref. 1426]. Masc. *Pteroculiops guttatus* Fowler 1938:133. Type by original designation (also monotypic). Synonym of *Amblyeleotris* Bleeker 1874 (Yanagisawa 1978:298 [ref. 7028]). Eleotridae.

Pterocyclosoma Fowler 1941:264 [ref. 1438]. Neut. *Glyphisodon sindonis* Jordan & Evermann 1903:188. Type by original designation (also monotypic). Pomacentridae.

Pterodicromita (subgenus of *Dicromita*) Fowler 1925:5 [ref. 1401]. Fem. *Sirembo oncerocephalus* Vaillant 1888:277. Type by original designation (also monotypic). Synonym of *Bassozetus* Gill 1883 (Cohen & Nielsen 1978:27 [ref. 881]). Ophidiidae: Neobythitinae.

Pterodiscus Eigenmann 1909:12 [ref. 1222]. Masc. *Pterodiscus levis* Eigenmann 1909:12. Type by original designation (also monotypic). Preoccupied by Pilsbry 1893 in Mollusca; not replaced (see Myers 1940:35 [ref. 3118]). Synonym of *Gasteropelecus* Scopoli 1777. Gasteropelecidae.

Pterodoras Bleeker 1862:5 [ref. 393]. Masc. *Doras granulosus* Valenciennes 1833:184. Type by original designation (also monotypic). Valid (Burgess 1989:224 [ref. 12860]). Doradidae.

Pteroglanis Eigenmann & Pearson in Pearson 1924:9 [ref. 3396]. Masc. *Pteroglanis manni* Eigenmann & Pearson in Pearson 1924:9. Type by monotypy. Valid (Burgess 1989:277 [ref. 12860]); synonym of *Sorubimichthys* Bleeker 1862 (Lundberg et al. 1989 [ref. 12544]). Pimelodidae.

Pteroglanis Fowler 1934:92 [ref. 1417]. Masc. *Pteroglanis horai* Fowler 1934:92. Type by original designation (also monotypic). Preoccupied by Eigenmann & Pearson 1924 in fishes, replaced by *Pteropsoglanis* Fowler 1934. Synonym of *Glyptothorax* Blyth 1860 (Li 1986:522 [ref. 6132]). Sisoridae.

Pterognathus (subgenus of *Neoclinus*) Girard in Jordan & Evermann 1898:2354, 2355 [ref. 2445]. Masc. *Neoclinus satiricus* Girard 1859:57. Type by original designation (also monotypic). Proposed somewhat hypothetically by Girard (1859:57) as a more appropriate generic name for a species he described in the genus *Neoclinus*; technically not available from Girard 1859 (name mentioned in passing and not used as a valid generic name). Published in an available way in Jordan & Evermann 1898, where the name was used for a subgenus of *Neoclinus*. See Appendix A. Synonym of *Neoclinus* Girard 1858 (Clark Hubbs 1953:12 [ref. 12698]). Labrisomidae.

Pterogobius Gill 1863:266 [ref. 1690]. Masc. *Gobius virgo* Temminck & Schlegel 1845:143. Type by monotypy. Valid (Akihito in Masuda et al. 1984:279 [ref. 6441], Birdsong et al. 1988:184 [ref. 7303]). Gobiidae.

Pterogymnus Smith 1938:257 [ref. 4067]. Masc. *Pagrus laniarius* Valenciennes in Cuvier & Valenciennes 1830:163. Type by original designation (also monotypic). Valid (Smith & Smith 1986:591 [ref. 5710]). Sparidae.

Pterohemiodus Fowler 1940:257 [ref. 1432]. Masc. *Pterohemiodus* *atranalis* Fowler 1940:258. Type by original designation (also monotypic). Synonym of *Hemiodus* Müller 1842 (Roberts 1974:432 [ref. 6872]); valid (Géry 1977:198 [ref. 1597]). Hemiodontidae: Hemiodontinae.

Pteroidichthys Bleeker 1856:33 [ref. 311]. Masc. *Pteroidichthys amboinensis* Bleeker 1856:34. Type by monotypy. Possibly valid (Eschmeyer et al. 1973:305 [ref. 6390]); valid (Rama-Rao 1980 [ref. 6797], Kishimoto in Masuda et al. 1984:317 [ref. 6441], Chen & Liu 1984 [ref. 13451], Paxton et al. 1989:446 [ref. 12442]). Scorpaenidae: Scorpaeninae.

Pteroidonus Günther 1887:106 [ref. 2013]. Masc. *Pteroidonus quinquarius* Günther 1887:106. Type by monotypy. Synonym of *Dicrolene* Goode & Bean 1883 (Cohen & Nielsen 1978:28 [ref. 881]). Ophidiidae: Neobythitinae.

Pterois Oken (ex Cuvier) 1817:1182 [ref. 3303]. Fem. *Scorpaena volitans* of Bloch (= *Gasterosteus volitans* Linnaeus 1758:296). Type by subsequent designation. Based on "Les Pterois" of Cuvier 1816 (see Gill 1903:966 [ref. 5768]). Technical addition of species not researched. Type apparently designated by Desmarest 1874:215 [not seen]; also see Whitley 1935:137 [ref. 6396]. Treated as feminine by most authors. Valid (Shimizu in Masuda et al. 1984:316 [ref. 6441], Eschmeyer 1986:466 [ref. 5652], Paxton et al. 1989:446 [ref. 12442]). Scorpaenidae: Pteroinae.

Pterolamia Springer 1950:7 [ref. 4172]. Fem. *Squalus longimanus* Poey 1861:338. Type by original designation (also monotypic). Second species doubtfully included. Preoccupied by Breuning 1942 in Coleoptera, replaced by *Pterolamiops* Springer 1951. On Official Index (Opinion 723). Synonym of *Carcharhinus* Blainville 1816 (Garrick 1982:19 [ref. 5454], Compagno 1984:450 [ref. 6846], Compagno 1988:308 [ref. 13488]). Carcharhinidae.

Pterolamiops Springer 1951:244 [ref. 4173]. Masc. *Squalus (Carcharias) longimanus* Poey 1861:338. Type by being a replacement name. Replacement for *Pterolamia* Springer 1950, preoccupied by Breuning 1942 in Coleoptera. On Official List (Opinion 723). Synonym of *Carcharhinus* Blainville 1816 (Compagno 1973:23 [ref. 7163], Garrick 1982:19 [ref. 5454], Compagno 1984:450 [ref. 6846], Compagno 1988:308 [ref. 13488]); valid (Cappetta 1987:125 [ref. 6348]). Carcharhinidae.

Pterolebias Garman 1895:141 [ref. 1538]. Masc. *Pterolebias longipinnis* Garman 1895:142. Type by monotypy. Valid (Parenti 1981:485 [ref. 7066], Costa 1988 [ref. 14438]). Aplocheilidae: Rivulinae.

Pteroleptus (subgenus of *Pterois*) Swainson 1839:180, 264 [ref. 4303]. Masc. *Pteroleptus longicauda* Swainson 1839:264. Type by monotypy. Synonym of *Pterois* Oken 1817. Scorpaenidae: Pteroinae.

Pteromugil Smith 1948:837 [ref. 4076]. Masc. *Mugil diadema* Gilchrist & Thompson 1911:29. Type by original designation (also monotypic). Synonym of *Liza* Jordan & Swain 1884 (Smith & Smith 1986:715 [ref. 5717]). Mugilidae.

Pteromylaeus Garman 1913:437 [ref. 1545]. Masc. *Myliobatis asperrimus* Gilbert in Jordan & Evermann 1898:2754. Type by subsequent designation. Type designated by Jordan 1920:548 [ref. 4905]. Valid (Krefft & Stehmann 1973:74 [ref. 7167], Compagno 1986:133 [ref. 5648]). Myliobatidae.

Pteronemus Van der Hoeven 1849:177 [ref. 2182]. Masc. *Cheilodactylus fasciatus* Lacepède 1803:6. Original not seen. Objective synonym of *Cheilodactylus* Lacepède 1803. Cheilodactylidae.

Pteronotropis (subgenus of *Erogala*) Fowler 1935:15 [ref. 1422]. Fem. *Alburnus formosus* Putnam 1863:9. Type by original designation (also monotypic). Type species preoccupied in *Notropis* by *Moniana formosa* Girard 1856; same as *Leuciscus hypselopterus* Günther 1868. Synonym of *Notropis* Rafinesque 1818, but as a valid subgenus (Gilbert 1978:16 [ref. 7042]); valid (Mayden 1989:30 [ref. 12555]). Cyprinidae.

Pteronotus Swainson 1839:190, 309 [ref. 4303]. Masc. *Heterobranchus sextentaculatus* Agassiz in Spix & Agassiz 1829:28. Type by monotypy. Preoccupied by Rafinesque 1815 in Mammalia, not replaced. Synonym of *Rhamdia* Bleeker 1858. Pimelodidae.

Pteropangasius Fowler 1937:142 [ref. 1425]. Masc. *Pangasius cultratus* Smith 1931:25. Type by original designation (also monotypic). Valid (Kottelat 1985:270 [ref. 11441], Kottelat 1989:14 [ref. 13605], Burgess 1989:105 [ref. 12860]). Pangasiidae.

Pteropelor Fowler 1938:77 [ref. 1426]. Neut. *Pteropelor noronhai* Fowler 1938:78. Type by original designation (also monotypic). Possibly valid (Eschmeyer et al. 1973:305 [ref. 6390]). Valid (Chen & Liu 1984:93 [ref. 13451]). Scorpaenidae: Scorpaeninae.

Pterophryne Gill 1863:90 [ref. 1680]. Fem. *Cheironectes laevigatus* Cuvier 1817:423. Type by original designation (also monotypic). Not preoccupied by *Pterophrynus* Lütken 1863 in Amphibia; *Pterophrynoides* Gill 1879 is an unneeded replacement. Correct spelling for genus of type species is *Chironectes*. Synonym of *Histrio* Fischer 1813 (Monod & Le Danois 1973:659 [ref. 7223], Pietsch 1984:37 [ref. 5380], Pietsch in Whitehead et al. 1986:1367 [ref. 13677]). Antennariidae.

Pterophrynoides Gill 1878:215 [ref. 5604]. Masc. *Cheironectes laevigatus* Cuvier 1817:423. Type by being a replacement name. Unneeded replacement (tentatively proposed) for *Pterophryne* Gill 1863, not preoccupied by *Pterophrynus* Lütken 1863 in Amphibia. Synonym of *Histrio* Fischer 1813 (Monod & Le Danois 1973:659 [ref. 7223], Pietsch 1984:37 [ref. 5380], Pietsch in Whitehead et al. 1986:1367 [ref. 13677]). Antennariidae.

Pterophyllum Heckel 1840:334 [ref. 2064]. Neut. *Platax scalaris* Cuvier in Cuvier & Valenciennes 1831:237 (= *Zeus scalaris* Lichtenstein 1823:14). Type by monotypy. Not preoccupied (see Myers 1940:36 [ref. 3118]). Species *scalaris* as senior objective synonym from Myers [ref. 3118], not verified. Valid (Kullander 1986:210 [ref. 12439]). Cichlidae.

Pteroplatea Müller & Henle 1837:117 [ref. 3067]. Fem. *Raja altavela* Linnaeus 1758:232. Type by subsequent designation (and subsequent monotypy). Also in Müller & Henle 1838:90 [ref. 3066] without species. Species added in Müller & Henle 1841:168 [ref. 3069] but apparently earlier by Bonaparte 1838:202 [ref. 4979] where *altavela* was designated type (see p. 2 of separate). Synonym of *Gymnura* van Hasselt 1823 (Krefft & Stehmann 1973:72 [ref. 7167], Cappetta 1987:165 [ref. 6348]). Gymnuridae.

Pteroplatytrygon (subgenus of *Dasyatis*) Fowler 1910:474 [ref. 1379]. Fem. *Trygon violacea* Bonaparte 1832:fasc. 1. Type by original designation (also monotypic). Synonym of *Dasyatis* Rafinesque 1810 (Krefft & Stehmann 1973:70 [ref. 7167]). Dasyatidae.

Pteropodus Eigenmann & Beeson 1893:670 [ref. 1212]. Masc. *Sebastodes maliger* Jordan & Gilbert 1880:322. Type by original designation. Synonym of *Sebastes* Cuvier 1829. Scorpaenidae: Sebastinae.

Pterops Rafinesque 1815:84, 91 [ref. 3584]. Masc. *Bostrychoides* *oculatus* Lacepède 1801:144. Type by being a replacement name. As "*Pterops* R. [Rafinesque] *Bostrychoides* Lac. [Lacepède]." An available (unneeded) replacement name for *Bostrychoides* Lacepède 1801. Objective synonym of *Bostrychoides* Lacepède 1801. Eleotridae.

Pteropsarion Günther 1868:284 [ref. 1990]. Neut. *Barilius bakeri* Day 1865:305. Type by subsequent designation. Type designated by Jordan 1919:351 [ref. 4904]. Synonym of *Barilius* Hamilton 1822. Cyprinidae.

Pteropsaron Jordan & Snyder 1902:470 [ref. 2513]. Neut. *Pteropsaron evolans* Jordan & Snyder 1902:471. Type by original designation (also monotypic). Valid (Nelson 1982 [ref. 5469], Okamura in Masuda et al. 1984:290 [ref. 6441], see Parin 1985:360 [ref. 6722], Heemstra & Nelson 1986:738 [ref. 6304]). Percophidae: Hemerocoetinae.

Pteropsoglanis Fowler 1934:351 [ref. 1418]. Masc. *Pteroglanis horai* Fowler 1934:92. Type by being a replacement name. Replacement for *Pteroglanis* Fowler 1934, preoccupied by Eigenmann & Pearson 1924 in fishes. Synonym of *Glyptothorax* Blyth 1860, based on placement of *Pteroglanis* in synonymy by Li 1986:522 [ref. 6132]). Sisoridae.

Pteropterus (subgenus of *Pterois*) Swainson 1839:180, 264 [ref. 4303]. Masc. *Scorpaena radiata* Cuvier in Cuvier & Valenciennes 1829:369. Type by monotypy. Synonym of *Pterois* Oken 1817. Scorpaenidae: Pteroinae.

Pterorhombus (subgenus of *Stromateus*) Fowler 1906:118 [ref. 1372]. Masc. *Fiatola fasciata* Risso 1826:289. Type by original designation (also monotypic). Synonym of *Stromateus* Linnaeus 1758 (Haedrich 1967:100 [ref. 5357], Haedrich 1973:565 [ref. 7216]). Stromateidae.

Pteroscion (subgenus of *Larimus*) Fowler 1925:4 [ref. 1401]. Masc. *Larimus peli* Bleeker 1863:63. Type by original designation (also monotypic). Sciaenidae.

Pterosmaris (subgenus of *Centracanthus*) Fowler 1925:4 [ref. 1401]. Fem. *Smaris melanurus* Valenciennes in Cuvier & Valenciennes 1830:318. Type by original designation (also monotypic). Valid (Tortonese et al. 1973:419 [ref. 7202], Johnson 1980:10 [ref. 13553], Tortonese in Whitehead et al. 1986:909 [ref. 13676]). Centracanthidae.

Pterosturisoma Isbrücker & Nijssen 1978:69 [ref. 2305]. Neut. *Harttia microps* Eigenmann & Allen 1942:211. Type by original designation (also monotypic). Valid (Isbrücker 1980:92 [ref. 2303], Burgess 1989:440 [ref. 12860]). Loricariidae.

Pterosynchiropus Nakabo 1982:93 [ref. 3139]. Masc. *Callionymus splendidus* Herre 1927:416. Type by original designation (also monotypic). Synonym of *Synchiropus* Gill 1859 (Fricke 1982:74 [ref. 5432]); valid (Houde 1984:637 [ref. 13674], Nakabo in Masuda et al. 1984:344 [ref. 6441]). Callionymidae.

Pterothrissus Hilgendorf 1877:127 [ref. 2165]. Masc. *Pterothrissus gissu* Hilgendorf 1877:127. Type by monotypy. Prior to and senior synonym of *Bathythrissa* Günther, 1 Nov. 1877, *Pterothrissus* dating to 3 Sept. 1877 (see Goode & Bean 1896:51 [ref. 1848]). Valid (Schwarzhans 1981:80 [ref. 3988] on fossil otoliths and in Pterothrissidae, Uyeno in Masuda et al. 1984:21 [ref. 6441], Smith 1986:157 [ref. 5712]); synonym of fossil genus *Istieus* Agassiz 1844 (Robins 1989:18 [ref. 13483]). Albulidae: Pterothrissinae.

Pterotolithus (subgenus of *Otolithes*) Fowler 1933:354, 359 [ref. 1414]. Masc. *Otolithus maculatus* Kuhl & van Hasselt in Cuvier & Valenciennes 1830:64. Type by original designation (also monotypic). Correct spelling for genus of type species is *Otolithes*. Valid (Trewavas 1977:354 [ref. 4459], Kottelat 1989:17 [ref. 13605]). Sciaenidae.

Pterozygus De la Pylaie 1835:530 [ref. 1086]. Masc. *Pterozygus bievrii* De la Pylaie 1835. Original not seen. Cobitidae: Cobitinae.

Ptertopomus (subgenus of *Holocentrus*) Cuvier in Goldfuss 1820:66 [ref. 1829]. Masc. *Holocentrus calcarifer* Bloch 1790:100. Type by monotypy. Name perhaps overlooked, not in current literature; apparently predates *Lates* Cuvier 1828 which apparently it should replace unless the ICZN is asked to set aside *Ptertopomus*. Centropomidae: Latinae.

Pterurus Rafinesque 1810:43, 59 [ref. 3595]. Masc. *Pterurus flexuosus* Rafinesque 1810:59. Type by monotypy. Perhaps preoccupied [not researched]. Synonym of *Dalophis* Rafinesque 1810 (Blache et al. 1973:249 [ref. 7185], McCosker 1977:71 [ref. 6836], Castle 1984:38 [ref. 6171]). Ophichthidae: Ophichthinae.

Pterurus (subgenus of *Anguilla*) Swainson 1839:196, 334 [ref. 4303]. Masc. *Pterurus maculatus* Swainson 1839:334 (= *Muraena raitaborua* Hamilton 1822:25, 364). Type by subsequent designation. Type designated by Swain 1882:283 [ref. 5966]. Preoccupied by Rafinesque 1810 in fishes, not replaced. Objective synonym of *Rataboura* Gray 1831, synonym of *Moringua* Gray 1831 (Smith 1989:65 [ref. 13285]). Moringuidae.

Pterycombus Fries 1837:15 [ref. 1501]. Masc. *Pterycombus brama* Fries 1837:15. Type by monotypy. Valid (Mead 1972:93 [ref. 6976], Mead 1973:387 [ref. 7199], Mochizuki in Masuda et al. 1984:160 [ref. 6441], Smith 1986:635 [ref. 5712], Yatsu & Nakamura 1989:190 [ref. 13449]). Bramidae.

Pterygiocottus Bean & Weed 1920:73 [ref. 221]. Masc. *Pterygiocottus macouni* Bean & Weed 1920:73. Type by original designation (also monotypic). Synonym of *Artedius* Girard 1856 (Bolin 1944:45 [ref. 6379], Begle 1989:646 [ref. 12739]). Cottidae.

Pterygoplichthys Gill 1858:408 [ref. 1750]. Masc. *Hypostomus duodecimalis* Valenciennes in Cuvier & Valenciennes 1840:498. Type by subsequent designation. Type designated by Bleeker 1862:2 [ref. 393] and 1863:78 [ref. 401] (with genus spelled *Pterygophlichtys*). Valid (Isbrücker 1980:39 [ref. 2303], Burgess 1989:433 [ref. 12860]). Loricariidae.

Pterygotrigla Waite 1899:28, 108 [ref. 4557]. Fem. *Trigla polyommata* Richardson 1839:96. Type by being a replacement name. Replacement for *Hoplonotus* Guichenot 1866, preoccupied by Schmidt 1846 in Coleoptera. Valid (Ochiai & Yatou in Masuda et al. 1984:334 [ref. 6441], Chen & Shao 1988:134 [ref. 6676], Paxton et al. 1989:456 [ref. 12442]). Triglidae: Triglinae.

Ptérure Duméril 1856:169 [ref. 1154]. *Syngnathus aequoreus* Linnaeus 1758:337. Not available, French vernacular. Syngnathidae: Syngnathinae.

Ptilichthys Bean 1881:157 [ref. 223]. Masc. *Ptilichthys goodei* Bean 1881:157. Type by monotypy. Valid. Ptilichthyidae.

Ptychidio Myers 1930:110 [ref. 5026]. Fem. *Ptychidio jordani* Myers 1930:112. Type by original designation (also monotypic). Valid (Wu et al. 1977:360 [ref. 4807], Chu & Cui in Chu & Chen 1989:234 [ref. 13584]). Cyprinidae.

Ptychobarbus Steindachner 1866:789 [ref. 5030]. Masc. *Ptychobarbus conirostris* Steindachner 1866:789. Type by monotypy. Synonym of *Diptychus* Steindachner 1866, but as a valid subgenus (Tsao 1964:170 [ref. 13501]); valid genus (Jayaram 1981:70 [ref. 6497], Wu 1987:47 [ref. 12822], Mo in Chu & Chen 1989:317 [ref. 13584]). Cyprinidae.

Ptychocheilus Agassiz 1855:227 [ref. 5839]. Masc. *Ptychocheilus gracilis* Agassiz 1855:229. Type by original designation. Type generally regarded as designated by Jordan & Gilbert 1877:90 [ref. 4907], but Agassiz (p. 229) says, "The predatory habits of the type of this genus...[gracilis]." Spelled *Ptychochilus* by Gill 1865:70 [ref. 12243]. Valid. Cyprinidae.

Ptychochromis Steindachner 1880:248 [ref. 4230]. Masc. *Tilapia oligacanthus* Bleeker 1868:309. Type by monotypy. Cichlidae.

Ptychochromoides Kiener & Maugé 1966:77 [ref. 2605]. Masc. *Tilapia betsileana* Boulenger 1899:139. Type by original designation. Cichlidae.

Ptycholepis (subgenus of *Leuciscus*) Richardson in Richardson & Gray 1843:218 [ref. 1885]. Fem. *Mugil salmoneus* Forster in Bloch & Schneider 1801:121. Type by monotypy. Preoccupied by Agassiz 1832 in fossil fishes. Synonym of *Chanos* Lacepède 1803. Chanidae.

Ptychostomus Agassiz 1855:88 [ref. 71]. Masc. *Catostomus aureolus* Lesueur 1817:95. Type by subsequent designation. Type designated by Bleeker 1863:23 [ref. 4859] or 1863:190 [ref. 397]. Objective synonym of *Teretulus* Rafinesque 1820; synonym of *Moxostoma* Rafinesque 1820. Catostomidae.

Ptyobranchus McClelland 1844:199, 221 [ref. 2928]. Masc. *Ptyobranchus arundinaceus* McClelland 1844:200, 221. Type by subsequent designation. Type apparently first designated by Jordan 1919:220 [ref. 2410]. Synonym of *Moringua* Gray 1831 (Smith 1989:65 [ref. 13285]). Moringuidae.

Ptyochromis Greenwood 1980:60 [ref. 1899]. Masc. *Ctenochromis sauvagei* Pfeffer 1896:15. Type by original designation. Cichlidae.

Ptyonotus Günther 1860:175 [ref. 1963]. Masc. *Triglopsis thompsonii* Girard 1851:19. Type by being a replacement name. Unneeded replacement for and objective synonym of *Triglopsis* Girard 1851, not preoccupied by *Triglops*. Synonym of *Triglopsis* Girard 1851 (Neyelov 1979:131 [ref. 3152]). Cottidae.

Puck Pietsch 1978:10 [ref. 3473]. Fem. *Puck pinnata* Pietsch 1978:11. Type by original designation (also monotypic). Oneirodidae.

Pugnaso Whitley 1948:75 [ref. 4710]. *Syngnathus curtirostris* Castelnau 1872:243. Type by original designation (also monotypic). Valid (Dawson 1985:162 [ref. 6541], Paxton et al. 1989:428 [ref. 12442]). Syngnathidae: Syngnathinae.

Pungitius Coste 1848:588 [ref. 5556]. Masc. *Gasterosteus pungitius* Linnaeus 1758:296. Type by subsequent designation or tautonymy. Appeared without named species; subsequent addition of species not researched; type above as given by Jordan 1923:174 [ref. 2421]. Type may involve *P. laevis*(see footnote in Monod 1973:283). Fowler (MS) credits genus to d'Annone 1760:302 [Act. Helvet., v. 4; not investigated]. Valid (Monod 1973:283 [ref. 7193], Takata et al. 1984 [ref. 6727], Ida in Masuda et al. 1984:83 [ref. 6441], Banister in Whitehead et al. 1986:641 [ref. 13676]). Gasterosteidae: Gasterosteinae.

Pungtungia Herzenstein 1892:231 [ref. 5037]. Fem. *Pungtungia herzi* Herzenstein 1892:231. Type by monotypy. Valid (Banarescu & Nalbant 1973:30 [ref. 173], Lu, Luo & Chen 1977:457 [ref. 13495], Sawada in Masuda et al. 1984:55 [ref. 6441]). Cyprinidae.

Pungu Trewavas, Green & Corbet 1972:65 [ref. 4460]. Masc. *Barombia maclareni* Trewavas 1962:184. Type by being a replacement name. Replacement for *Barombia* Trewavas 1962, apparently preoccupied in insects [not researched]. Cichlidae.

Puntazzo Bleeker 1876:284 [ref. 447]. *Sparus acutirostris* Delaroche 1809:348 (= *Sparus puntazzo* Cetti 1784). Type by being a replacement name. Based on Bleeker's style this is a replacement name for *Charax* Risso 1826, preoccupied by Scopoli 1877 in fishes. Valid (Tortonese 1973:413 [ref. 7192]). Sparidae.

Puntioplites Smith 1929:11 [ref. 4046]. Masc. *Puntius proctozysron* Bleeker 1865:200. Type by original designation (also monotypic). Valid (Chen & Huang 1977:396 [ref. 13496], Kottelat 1985:265 [ref. 11441], Wu 1987:44 [ref. 12822], Roberts 1989:59 [ref. 6439], Zhou in Chu & Chen 1989:323 [ref. 13584], Kottelat 1989:10 [ref. 13605]). Cyprinidae.

Puntius (subgenus of *Cyprinus*) Hamilton 1822:310, 388 [ref. 2031]. Masc. *Cyprinus sophore* Hamilton 1822:310, 389. Type by subsequent designation. Type designated by Bleeker 1863:27 [ref. 4859], 1863:263 [ref. 403] or 1863:199 [ref. 397]. Valid (Karaman 1971:189 [ref. 2560], Jayaram 1981:97 [ref. 6497], Roberts 1989:60 [ref. 6439], Kottelat 1989:10 [ref. 13605]). Cyprinidae.

Pusa Jordan & Gilbert 1879:374 [ref. 2465]. *Choerojulis grandisquamis* Gill 1863:206. Type by monotypy, one definitely-included species. Preoccupied by Scopoli 1777 in Mammalia [not investigated]. Synonym of *Halichoeres* Rüppell 1835. Labridae.

Pusichthys (subgenus of *Silurus*) Swainson 1838:348 et seq. [ref. 4302]. Masc. *Schilbe uranoscopus* Rüppell 1832:4. Type by monotypy. Also in Swainson 1839:189, 307 [ref. 4303]. Synonym of *Schilbe* Oken 1817 (De Vos 1986:41 [ref. 6191]). Schilbeidae.

Puzanovia Fedorov 1975:587 [ref. 1310]. Fem. *Puzanovia rubra* Fedorov 1975:589. Type by original designation (also monotypic). Valid (Fedorov 1982 [ref. 5252], Anderson 1984:578 [ref. 13634], Toyoshima in Masuda et al. 1984:306 [ref. 6441]). Zoarcidae.

Pycnochromis Fowler 1941:258 [ref. 1438]. Masc. *Pycnochromis vanderbilti* Fowler 1941:260. Type by original designation (also monotypic). Synonym of *Chromis* Cuvier 1814 (see Böhlke 1984:147 [ref. 13621]). Pomacentridae.

Pycnocraspedum Alcock 1889:386 [ref. 81]. Neut. *Pycnocraspedum squamipinne* Alcock 1889:386. Type by monotypy. Valid (Cohen & Nielsen 1978:38 [ref. 881], Machida in Masuda et al. 1984:101 [ref. 6441], Paxton et al. 1989:313 [ref. 12442]). Ophidiidae: Neobythitinae.

Pycnomma Rutter 1904:252 [ref. 3842]. Neut. *Pycnomma semisquamatum* Rutter 1904:252. Type by monotypy. Valid (Birdsong et al. 1988:189 [ref. 7303]). Gobiidae.

Pygidianops Myers 1944:592 [ref. 3123]. Masc. *Pygidianops eigenmanni* Myers 1944:592. Type by original designation (also monotypic). Valid (Burgess 1989:325 [ref. 12860], Pinna 1989 [ref. 12630], Pinna 1989:372 [ref. 13515]). Trichomycteridae.

Pygidium Meyen 1835:475 [ref. 2984]. Neut. *Pygidium fuscum* Meyen 1835:475. Type by monotypy. Valid. Trichomycteridae.

Pygocentrus Müller & Troschel 1844:94 [ref. 3070]. Masc. *Serrasalmo piraya* Cuvier 1820:368. Type by subsequent designation. Type designated by Eigenmann 1910:442 [ref. 1224]. Synonym of *Serrasalmus* Lacepède 1803, as a valid subgenus (Géry 1976:52 [ref. 14199], Géry 1977:290 [ref. 1597]); valid (current authors). Characidae: Serrasalminae.

Pygoplites Fraser-Brunner 1933:587 [ref. 671]. Masc. *Chaetodon diacanthus* Boddaert 1772:Pl. 9. Type by original designation (also monotypic). Valid (Araga in Masuda et al. 1984:188 [ref. 6441], Smith & Heemstra 1986:626 [ref. 5714]). Pomacanthidae.

Pygopristis Müller & Troschel 1844:95 [ref. 3070]. Fem. *Pygopristis fumarius* Müller & Troschel 1844:35. Type by subsequent designation. Type designated by Eigenmann 1910:441 [ref. 1224]. Synonym of *Serrasalmus* Lacepède 1803, as a valid subgenus (Géry 1976:52 [ref. 14199]); valid (current authors). Characidae: Serrasalminae.

Pygosteus Gill (ex Brevoort) 1861:39 [ref. 1766]. Masc. *Gasterosteus occidentalis* Cuvier in Cuvier & Valenciennes 1829:509. Type by subsequent designation. Type designated by Jordan & Gilbert 1877:93 [ref. 4907]. Synonym of *Pungitius* Coste 1848 (Monod 1973:283 [ref. 7193]). Gasterosteidae: Gasterosteinae.

Pylodictis Rafinesque 1819:422 [ref. 3590]. Masc. *Pylodictis limosus* Rafinesque 1819:422. Type by monotypy. Spelled *Pilodictis* by Rafinesque 1820:361 (July) [ref. 7311] and 1820:67 (Dec.) [ref. 3592] and *Pelodichthys* by Jordan 1877:10 [ref. 12244]. On Official List (Opinion 1584). Valid (Burgess 1989:35 [ref. 12860]). Ictaluridae.

Pyosicus Smith 1960:312 [ref. 4126]. Masc. *Pyosicus niger* Smith 1960:312. Type by original designation (also monotypic). Synonym of *Bathygobius* Bleeker 1878 (Maugé 1986:360 [ref. 6218]). Gobiidae.

Pyramodon Smith & Radcliffe in Radcliffe 1913:175 [ref. 3579]. Masc. *Pyramodon ventralis* Smith & Radcliffe in Radcliffe 1913:175. Type by original designation (also monotypic). Valid (Cohen & Nielsen 1978:6 [ref. 881], Williams 1983:848 [ref. 5367], Machida in Masuda et al. 1984:99 [ref. 6441], Olney & Markle 1986:354 [ref. 5701], Paxton et al. 1989:321 [ref. 12442]). Carapidae: Pyramodontinae.

Pyrenophorus (subgenus of *Chirolophius*) Le Danois 1975:75 [ref. 2732]. Masc. *Chirolophius kempi* Norman 1935:34. Not available from Le Danois, after 1930 without type designation (Art. 13b). Appeared in Zoological Record for 1975, Pisces, p. 508 (published in 1980) but with anonymous authorship. Probably dates to Pietsch et al. 1986:133 [ref. 6339] with type as above. For authorship, see discussion in Appendix A (Art. 13b); if that interpretation of the Code is correct, then the genus *Pyrenophorus* is Pietsch, Bauchot & Desoutter 1986. Lophiidae.

Pyrodon Kaup 1855:222 [ref. 2571]. Masc. *Balistes niger* Rüppell 1837:53. Type by being a replacement name. Unneeded replacement for *Xenodon* Rüppell 1835, twice replaced before Kaup. Objective synonym of *Odonus* Gistel 1848. Balistidae.

Pyrrhulina Valenciennes in Cuvier & Valenciennes 1846:535 [ref. 1011]. Fem. *Pyrrhulina filamentosa* Valenciennes in Cuvier & Valenciennes 1846:535. Type by monotypy. Valid (Géry 1977:138 [ref. 1597], Malabarba 1989:127 [ref. 14217]). Lebiasinidae: Pyrrhulininae.

Pythonichthys Poey 1867:265 [ref. 3503]. Masc. *Pythonichthys sanguineus* Poey 1867:265. Type by monotypy. Valid (Rosenblatt & Rubinoff 1972 [ref. 7124], McCosker & Phillips 1979 [ref. 6980], Smith 1989:52 [ref. 13285]). Heterenchelyidae.

Pyxichromis Greenwood 1980:24 [ref. 1899]. Masc. *Haplochromis parorthostoma* Greenwood 1967:103. Type by original designation. Cichlidae.

Pyxiloricaria Isbrücker & Nijssen 1984:163 [ref. 5279]. Fem. *Pyxiloricaria menezesi* Isbrücker & Nijssen 1984:164. Type by original designation (also monotypic). Valid (Isbrücker & Nijssen 1986:103 [ref. 5212], Isbrücker & Nijssen 1986:40 [ref. 7321], Burgess 1989:444 [ref. 12860]). Loricariidae.

Qinghaichthys (subgenus of *Triplophysa*) Zhu 1981:1063 [ref. 4840]. Masc. *Nemachilus alticeps* Herzenstein 1888:28. Type by original designation (also monotypic). Valid (Kottelat 1990:21 [ref. 14137]). Balitoridae: Nemacheilinae.

Quadrarius Jordan 1907:236 [ref. 2401]. Masc. *Pentaceros decacanthus* Günther 1859:213. Type by original designation (also monotypic). Synonym of *Pentaceros* Cuvier 1829 (Hardy 1983:197 [ref. 5385]). Pentacerotidae.

Quassilabia Jordan & Brayton in Jordan 1878:406 [ref. 2376]. Fem. *Lagochila lacera* Jordan & Brayton 1877:280. Type by being a replacement name. Appeared in Addenda (p. 406). Unneeded replacement for and objective synonym of *Lagochila* Jordan & Brayton 1877, not preoccupied. Catostomidae.

Quassiremus Jordan & Davis 1891:622 [ref. 2437]. Masc. *Ophichthys evionthas* Jordan & Bollman 1889:154. Type by original designation. Valid (McCosker 1977:83 [ref. 6836], McCosker et al. 1989:409 [ref. 13288]). Ophichthidae: Ophichthinae.

Quenselia (subgenus of *Monochirus*) Jordan in Jordan & Goss 1888:306 (in key) [ref. 2482]. Fem. *Pleuronectes ocellatus* Linnaeus 1758:269. Type by monotypy. Synonym of *Monochirus* Rafinesque 1814 and of *Dicologlossa* Chabanaud 1930 (Torchio 1973:631, 632; type evidently a composite). Soleidae.

Queriblennius (subgenus of *Blennius*) Whitley 1933:93 [ref. 4677]. Masc. *Blennius gaudichaudi* Whitley 1933:93. Type by original designation. Whitley's *gaudichaudi* a replacement for *Blennius punctatus* Quoy & Gaimard 1824, apparently preoccupied. Synonym of *Blennius* Linnaeus 1758 (Bath 1973:519 [ref. 7212]). Blenniidae.

Querigalaxias Whitley 1935:Pl. 3 legend [ref. 4686]. Masc. *Galaxias dissimilis* Regan 1906:383. Not available from this reference, no description after 1930 [Art. 13a(i)]; subsequent availability not investigated. Objective synonym of *Paragalaxias* Scott 1935 (Apr.), Whitley is July (McDowall & Frankenberg 1981:569 [ref. 5500]). Galaxiidae: Galaxiinae.

Querimana Jordan & Gilbert 1883:588 [ref. 2473]. *Myxus harengus* Günther 1861:467. Type by original designation (also monotypic). Mugilidae.

Quietula Jordan & Evermann in Jordan & Starks 1895:839 [ref. 2522]. Fem. *Gillichthys ycauda* Jenkins & Evermann 1888:147. Type by original designation (also monotypic). Valid (Birdsong et al. 1988:185, 187 [ref. 7303]). Gobiidae.

Quinca Mees 1966:83 [ref. 2968]. Fem. *Quinca mirifica* Mees 1966:83. Type by original designation (also monotypic). Synonym of *Pterapogon* Koumans 1933, but as valid subgenus (Fraser 1972:27 [ref. 5195]). Apogonidae.

Quincuncia (subgenus of *Coelorhynchus*) Gilbert & Hubbs 1920:432 [ref. 1638]. Fem. *Coelorhynchus argentatus* Smith & Radcliffe 1912:137. Type by original designation. Synonym of *Caelorinchus* Giorna 1809 (Marshall 1973:293 [ref. 7194], Marshall & Iwamoto 1973:538 [ref. 6966]). Macrouridae: Macrourinae.

Quinquarius Jordan 1907:236, 238 [ref. 2401]. Masc. *Pentaceros japonicus* Döderlein in Steindachner & Döderlein 1882:8. Type by original designation. Technically not proposed as a replacement for *Pentaceros* Cuvier 1829 although its preoccupation was noted by Jordan; described as a new genus with stated type as *Pentaceros japonicus* and with *capensis* included (p. 236). Synonym of *Pentaceros* Cuvier 1829 (Hardy 1983:197 [ref. 5385]). Pentacerotidae.

Quintana Hubbs 1934:2 [ref. 2244]. Fem. *Quintana atrizona* Hubbs 1934:4. Type by original designation (also monotypic). Valid (Rosen & Bailey 1963:112 [ref. 7067], Parenti & Rauchenberger 1989:9 [ref. 13538]). Poeciliidae.

Quirichthys Whitley 1951:63 [ref. 4711]. Masc. *Quiris stramineus*

Whitley 1950:239. Type by being a replacement name. Replacement for *Quiris* Whitley 1950, preoccupied by Pate 1946 in Hymenoptera. Valid (Paxton et al. 1989:359 [ref. 12442]). Atherinidae: Pseudomugilinae.

Quiris Whitley 1950:239 [ref. 4712]. Fem. *Quiris stramineus* Whitley 1950:239. Type by original designation (also monotypic). Preoccupied by Pate 1946 in Hymenoptera, replaced by *Quirichthys* Whitley 1951. Objective synonym of *Quirichthys* Whitley 1951 (Paxton et al. 1989:359 [ref. 12442]). Atherinidae: Pseudomugilinae.

Quisquilius Jordan & Evermann 1903:203 [ref. 2450]. Masc. *Quisquilius eugenius* Jordan & Evermann 1903:203. Type by original designation (also monotypic). Synonym of *Priolepis* Valenciennes 1837 (Greenfield 1989:397 [ref. 12545]). Gobiidae.

Ra Whitley 1931:334 [ref. 4672]. Fem. *Ichthyborus microlepis* Günther 1864:363. Type by being a replacement name. Unneeded replacement for *Ichthyborus* Günther 1864, not preoccupied. Objective synonym of *Ichthyborus* Günther 1864 (Daget & Gosse 1984:197 [ref. 6185]). Citharinidae: Distichodontinae.

Rabaulichthys Allen 1984:48 [ref. 6242]. Masc. *Rabaulichthys altipinnis* Allen 1984:48. Type by original designation (also monotypic). Valid (Randall & Pyle 1989 [ref. 14121]). Serranidae: Anthiinae.

Rabdophorus (subgenus of *Chaetodon*) Swainson 1839:170, 211 [ref. 4303]. Masc. *Chaetodon ephippium* Cuvier in Cuvier & Valenciennes 1831:80. Type by monotypy. Synonym of *Chaetodon* Linnaeus 1758, but as a valid subgenus (Burgess 1978:578 [ref. 700]); valid (Maugé & Bauchot 1984:467 [ref. 6614]). Chaetodontidae.

Rabida (subgenus of *Schilbeodes*) Jordan & Evermann 1896:144 [ref. 2443]. *Noturus furiosus* Jordan & Meek 1888:351. Type by original designation. Type designated on p. 144 (name in parentheses). Spelled *Rabidus* in Zoological Record for 1896 and by Jordan 1920:473 [ref. 4905]. Synonym of *Noturus* Rafinesque 1818, but as a valid subgenus (Taylor 1969:20, 128 [ref. 6555]). Ictaluridae.

Rabirubia (subgenus of *Lutjanus*) Jordan & Fesler 1893:432, 438 [ref. 2455]. Fem. *Mesoprion inermis* Peters 1869:705. Type by original designation (also monotypic). Misspelled *Rarirubia* in Zoological Record for 1893. Synonym of *Lutjanus* Bloch 1790, but as a valid subgenus (Akazaki & Iwatsuki 1986 [ref. 6316]). Lutjanidae.

Rabula (subgenus of *Gymnothorax*) Jordan & Davis 1891:589, 590 [ref. 2437]. Fem. *Muraena aquaedulcis* Cope 1872:589. Type by original designation. Apparently based on a misidentified type species (see McCosker & Rosenblatt 1975:422 [ref. 9341]). Synonym of *Gymnothorax* Bloch 1795 (Böhlke et al. 1989:145 [ref. 13286]). Muraenidae: Muraeninae.

Rachovia Myers 1927:119 [ref. 3098]. Fem. *Rivulus brevis* Regan 1912:504. Type by original designation. Valid (Taphorn & Thomerson 1978 [ref. 4337], Parenti 1981:486 [ref. 7066]). Aplocheilidae: Rivulinae.

Rachoviscus Myers 1926:1 [ref. 3094]. Neut. *Rachoviscus crassiceps* Myers 1926:1. Type by monotypy. Valid (Géry 1977:347 [ref. 1597], Weitzman et al. 1988:420 [ref. 13557]). Characidae.

Rachycentron Kaup 1826:col. 89 [ref. 2568]. Neut. *Rachycentron typus* Kaup 1826:col. 89. Type by monotypy (also by use of *typus*). Original not examined. Spelled *Rachycentrum* and *Rachicentron* by Kaup 1827:624 [not researched]. Valid (Monod 1973:371 [ref. 7193], Nakamura in Masuda et al. 1984:153 [ref. 6441], Tortonese in Whitehead et al. 1986:814 [ref. 13676], Smith 1986:661 [ref. 5712], Shaffer & Nakamura 1989 [ref. 13517]). Rachycentridae.

Racoma McClelland and Griffith in McClelland 1842:576 [ref. 2926]. Fem. *Racoma labiata* McClelland 1842:578. Type by subsequent designation. Attributed to McClelland and Griffith; Griffith provided specimens, drawings, and notes and evidently participated in the description; as a genus (p. 573), elsewhere as a subgenus of *Schizothorax*. Type apparently designated first by Bleeker 1863:198 [ref. 397] or 1863:26 [ref. 4859]. Synonym of *Schizothorax* Heckel 1838 (Tsao 1964:139 [ref. 13501], Mo in Chu & Chen 1989:287 [ref. 13584); valid (Wu 1987:46 [ref. 12822], Mirza & Saeed 1988:313 [ref. 13385]). Cyprinidae.

Raconda Gray 1831:9 [ref. 1879]. Fem. *Raconda russeliana* Gray 1831:9. Type by monotypy. Valid (Grande 1985:245 [ref. 6466], Whitehead 1985:302 [ref. 5141]). Clupeidae.

Racovitzia Dollo 1900:317 [ref. 1134]. Fem. *Racovitzia glacialis* Dollo 1900:318. Type by monotypy. Valid (DeWitt & Hureau 1979:789 [ref. 1125], Stevens et al. 1984:563 [ref. 13633], Voskoboinikova 1988:45 [ref. 12756]). Bathydraconidae.

Radcliffella Hubbs 1921:2 [ref. 2229]. Fem. *Garmannia spongicola* Radcliffe 1917:423. Type by original designation (also monotypic). Treated again by Hubbs 1923:1 [ref. 2230]. Gobiidae.

Raddabarbus Thys van den Audenaerde 1971:132 [ref. 4403]. Masc. *Raddabarbus camerunensis* Thys van den Audenaerde 1971:133. Type by original designation (also monotypic). Synonym of *Barboides* Brüning 1929 (Lévêque & Daget 1984:217 [ref. 6186]). Cyprinidae.

Raddaella (subgenus of *Aphyosemion*) Huber 1977:unnum. p. 10 [ref. 2268]. Fem. *Fundulus batesii* Boulenger 1911:261. Type by original designation. Synonym of *Fundulopanchax* Myers 1924, but as a valid subgenus (Parenti 1981:479 [ref. 7066]); synonym of *Aphyosemion* Myers 1924 (Wildekamp et al. 1986:196 [ref. 6198]). Aplocheilidae: Aplocheilinae.

Radiicephalus Osório 1917:113 [ref. 3318]. Masc. *Radiicephalus elongatus* Osório 1917:114. Type by monotypy. Valid (Palmer 1973:333 [ref. 7195], Olney 1984:369 [ref. 13656], Heemstra & Kannemeyer 1984:35 [ref. 5349], Palmer in Whitehead et al. 1986:733 [ref. 13676], Heemstra & Kannemeyer 1986:402 [ref. 5666]). Radiicephalidae.

Radulinellus (subgenus of *Radulinus*) Bolin 1950:197 [ref. 510]. Masc. *Radulinus (Radulinellus) vinculus* Bolin 1950:197. Type by original designation (also monotypic). Cottidae.

Radulinopsis Soldatov & Lindberg 1930:183 [ref. 4164]. Fem. *Radulinopsis derjavini* Soldatov & Lindberg 1930. Original not examined. Valid (Washington et al. 1984:443 [ref. 13660]). Cottidae.

Radulinus Gilbert 1890:88 [ref. 1623]. Masc. *Radulinus asprellus* Gilbert 1890:88. Type by original designation (also monotypic). Valid (Bolin 1944:37 [ref. 6379], Washington et al. 1984:443 [ref. 13660], Yabe 1985:111 [ref. 11522]). Cottidae.

Rafinesquiellus (subgenus of *Etheostoma*) Jordan & Evermann 1896:1066, 1068, 1082 [ref. 2443]. Masc. *Aplesion pottsii* Girard 1860:102. Type by original designation (also monotypic). Synonym of *Etheostoma* Rafinesque 1819 (Collette & Banarescu 1977:1456 [ref. 5845]). Percidae.

Raia See *Raja*. Rajidae.

Raiamas Jordan 1919:344 [ref. 2413]. *Cyprinus bola* Hamilton 1822:274, 385. Type by being a replacement name. Replacement for *Bola* Günther 1868, preoccupied by Hamilton 1822 in fishes. Valid (Lévêque & Daget 1984:332 [ref. 6186], Kottelat 1985:265 [ref. 11441], Kuang in Chu & Chen 1989:23 [ref. 13584], Kottelat 1989:11 [ref. 13605], Howes & Teugels 1989 [ref. 13624]); synonym of *Barilius* Hamilton 1822 (Roberts 1989:30 [ref. 6439]). Cyprinidae.

Rainfordia McCulloch 1923:119 [ref. 2946]. Fem. *Rainfordia opercularis* McCulloch 1923:120. Type by monotypy. Valid (Kendall 1984:500 [ref. 13663] in Liopropominae, Paxton et al. 1989:500 [ref. 12442] in Serranidae). Serranidae: Liopropomatinae.

Raizero (subgenus of *Lutjanus*) Jordan & Fesler 1893:432, 438 [ref. 2455]. *Mesoprion aratus* Günther 1864:145. Type by monotypy. Synonym of *Lutjanus* Bloch 1790 (Allen 1985:33 [ref. 6843], Allen & Talbot 1985:9 [ref. 6491]). Lutjanidae.

Raja Linnaeus 1758:231 [ref. 2787]. Fem. *Raja miraletus* Linnaeus 1758:231. Type by subsequent designation. Type designated by Bonaparte 1838:7 (of separate) [ref. 4979]. Spelled *Raia* by authors. Valid (Stehmann 1973:58 [ref. 7168], Nakaya in Masuda et al. 1984:13 [ref. 6441], Hulley 1986:118 [ref. 5672], Ishihara 1987 [ref. 6264], Cappetta 1987:143 [ref. 6348] including fossils, Paxton et al. 1989:56 [ref. 12442]). Rajidae.

Rajabatis De la Pylaie 1835:528 [ref. 1086]. *Raja mosaica* Lacepède 1800:675. Original not seen. Possibly not intended as a generic name (Jordan 1919:183 [ref. 2410]). Synonym of *Raja* Linnaeus 1758. Rajidae.

Rajella (subgenus of *Raja*) Stehmann 1970:151 [ref. 4202]. Fem. *Raja fyllae* Lütken 1888:1. Type by original designation. Synonym of *Raja* Linnaeus 1758, but as a valid subgenus (Stehmann 1978 [ref.6981]). Rajidae.

Rama Bleeker 1858:201, 205, 208 [ref. 365]. Fem. *Rama buchanani* Bleeker 1858:208 (= *Pimelodus rama* Hamilton 1822:176, 377). Type by monotypy unless other species are included in text (not translated), if other species then type is *rama* by tautonymy. *Rama buchanani* Bleeker is an unneeded substitute for *P. rama* Hamilton. Also in Bleeker 1862:8 [ref. 393]. Synonym of *Batasio* Blyth 1860 (Jayaram 1977:16 [ref. 7005], Jayaram 1981:191 [ref. 6497]). Bagridae.

Rambaibarnia (subgenus of *Danio*) Fowler 1934:341 [ref. 1418]. Fem. *Danio regina* Fowler 1934:342. Type by original designation. Synonym of *Danio* Hamilton 1822. Cyprinidae.

Ramirezella Fernández-Yépez 1949:1 [ref. 1319]. Fem. *Ramirezella newboldi* Fernández-Yépez 1949:2. Type by original designation (also monotypic). Mentioned (Géry 1977:487 [ref. 1597]). Characidae.

Ramnogaster Whitehead 1965:324 [ref. 4658]. Fem. *Clupea arcuata* Jenyns 1842:134. Type by original designation. Valid (Grande 1985:250 [ref. 6466], Whitehead 1985:123 [ref. 5141]). Clupeidae.

Ramphistoma see *Raphistoma*. Belonidae.

Ramularia Jordan & Evermann 1898:2606, 2663 [ref. 2445]. Fem. *Ancylopsetta dendritica* Gilbert 1891:121. Type by original designation (also monotypic). Synonym of *Ancylopsetta* Gill 1864 (Norman 1934:124 [ref. 6893]). Paralichthyidae.

Randallichthys Anderson, Kami & Johnson 1977:89 [ref. 115]. Masc. *Etelis filamentosus* Fourmanoir 1970:26. Type by original designation (also monotypic). Valid (Johnson 1980:9 [ref. 13553], Yoshino in Masuda et al. 1984:167 [ref. 6441], Allen 1985:156 [ref. 6843]). Synonym of *Etelis* Cuvier 1828, but as a valid subgenus (Akazaki & Iwatsuki 1986:600 [ref. 6316]). Lutjanidae.

Raneya Robins 1961:212 [ref. 3785]. Fem. *Lepophidium fluminense* Miranda-Ribeiro 1904. Type by original designation (also monotypic). Valid (Cohen & Nielsen 1978:17 [ref. 881], Inada in Nakamura et al. 1986:148 [ref. 14235]). Ophidiidae: Ophidiinae.

Raniceps Oken (ex Cuvier) 1817:1182a [ref. 3303]. Neut. *Gadus raninus* Müller 1788:15 (= *Blennius raninus* Linnaeus 1758:258). Based on "Les Raniceps" of Cuvier 1816:217 [ref. 993]. Technical addition of species after latinization by Oken not researched. Valid (Svetovidov 1973:315 [ref. 7169], Fahay & Markle 1984:266 [ref. 13653], Svetovidov in Whitehead et al. 1986:707 [ref. 13676]). Lotidae.

Ranipterois Whitley 1951:407 [ref. 4715]. Fem. *Brachypterois serrulifer* Fowler 1938:(51) 79. Type by being a replacement name. Unneeded replacement for *Brachypterois* Fowler 1938, not preoccupied by *Brachypterois* Jordan & Seale 1906, a misspelling for *Bathypterois* Günther. Objective synonym of *Brachypterois* Fowler 1938. Scorpaenidae: Pteroinae.

Ranulina Jordan & Starks 1906:522 [ref. 2531]. Fem. *Ranulina fimbriidens* Jordan & Starks 1906:523. Type by original designation (also monotypic). Synonym of *Lophogobius* Gill 1862 (Hoese, pers. comm.). Gobiidae.

Ranzania Nardo 1840:111 [ref. 3149]. Fem. *Ranzania typus* Nardo 1840. Type by monotypy (also by use of *typus*). Valid (Tortonese 1973:650 [ref. 7192], Tyler 1980:391 [ref. 4477], Matsuura in Masuda et al. 1984:366 [ref. 6441], Tortonese in Whitehead et al. 1986:1350 [ref. 13677], Heemstra 1986:908 [ref. 5660]). Molidae.

Raogobius Mukerji 1935:262 [ref. 3054]. Masc. *Raogobius andamanicus* Mukerji 1935:264. Type by original designation (also monotypic). Gobiidae.

Raphistoma Rafinesque 1815:89 [ref. 3584]. Neut. Type by being a replacement name. As "*Raphistoma* R. [Rafinesque] *Belone* Gr. [Gronow]." *Ramphistoma* Swainson 1838:295, 296 [ref. 4302] is an incorrect subsequent spelling. Not available, suppressed by ICZN; on Official Index (Opinion 225). In the synonymy of *Belone* Cuvier 1816 (Parin 1973:258 [ref. 7191] as *Ramphistoma*). Belonidae.

Rasbora Bleeker 1859:435 [ref. 370]. Fem. *Cyprinus rasbora* Hamilton 1822:329, 391. Apparently appeared first in key, without species. Many species in Bleeker 1859:154 [ref. 371] and 1860:285, 435 et seq. [ref. 380]. Type by subsequent absolute tautonymy (not *R. cephalotaenia* as designated by Bleeker 1863:202 [ref. 397] and 1863:28 [ref. 4859]). Valid (Brittan 1954 [ref. 646] and 1972 [ref. 12245], Jayaram 1981:83 [ref. 6497], Kottelat 1985:265 [ref. 11441], Kottelat & Chu 1987 [ref. 13493], Kottelat 1989:11 [ref. 13605], Roberts 1989:66 [ref. 6439]). Cyprinidae.

Rasborella Fowler & Bean 1923:7 [ref. 1474]. Fem. *Rasborella dubia* Fowler & Bean 1923:7. Type by original designation (also monotypic). Cyprinidae.

Rasborichthys Bleeker 1859:435 [ref. 370]. Masc. *Leuciscus helfrichii* Bleeker 1857:15. Type by subsequent monotypy. Apparently appeared first in key, without included species. One species included by Bleeker 1859:155 [ref. 371] and 1860:286, 456 [ref. 380]. Valid (Roberts 1989:77 [ref. 6439]). Cyprinidae.

Rasborinus Oshima 1920:130 [ref. 3313]. Masc. *Rasborinus takakii* Oshima 1920:130. Type by original designation. Valid (Yih & Wu 1964:69 [ref. 13499], Chen in Chu & Chen 1989:54 [ref. 13584], Kottelat 1989:11 [ref. 13605]). Cyprinidae.

Rasboroides (subgenus of *Rasbora*) Brittan 1954:199 [ref. 646].

Masc. *Rasbora vaterifloris* Deraniyagala 1930:28. Type by monotypy. Synonym of *Rasbora* Bleeker 1859, but as a valid subgenus (Jayaram 1981:83 [ref. 6497]). Cyprinidae.

Rastrelliger Jordan & Starks in Jordan & Dickerson 1908:607 [ref. 2438]. Masc. *Scomber brachysoma* Bleeker 1850:355, 356. Type by original designation. Valid (Collette & Nauen 1983:46 [ref. 5375], Collette et al. 1984:600 [ref. 11421], Nakamura in Masuda et al. 1984:224 [ref. 6441], Collette 1986:834 [ref. 5647]). Scombridae.

Rastrineobola (subgenus of *Engraulicypris*) Fowler 1936:296 [ref. 1424]. Fem. *Neobola argentea* Pellegrin 1904:184. Type by original designation (also monotypic). Valid (Howes 1984:173 [ref. 5834], Lévêque & Daget 1984:335 [ref. 6186] but as *Rastineobola*). Cyprinidae.

Rastrinus Jordan & Evermann 1896:437 [ref. 2442]. *Icelus scutiger* Bean 1890:41. Type by original designation (also monotypic). Valid (Nelson 1984:16 [ref. 5391]). Cottidae.

Rastrum (subgenus of *Alepes*) Fowler 1904:509 [ref. 1367]. Neut. *Alepes scitula* Fowler 1904:509. Type by original designation (also monotypic). Synonym of *Alepes* Swainson 1839 (Smith-Vaniz, pers. comm.). Carangidae.

Rataboura Gray 1831:Pl. 95 (v. 1) [ref. 1878]. Fem. *Rataboura hardwickii* Gray 1831:Pl. 95. Type by monotypy. Appeared as above on 25 Jan. 1831; also in Gray 1831:9 [ref. 1879] of apparently later date [Fowler MS says Feb. 1831] with two species. *Raitaborua* is a misspelling. Synonym of *Moringua* Gray 1831 (Smith 1989:65 [ref. 13285]). Moringuidae.

Ratabulus Jordan 1925:286 [ref. 2486]. Masc. *Thysanophrys megacephalus* Tanaka 1917:9. Type by original designation (also monotypic). Spelled *Rutabulus* on p. 96; first reviser not researched. Valid (Ochiai in Masuda et al. 1984:322 [ref. 6441], Paxton et al. 1989:470 [ref. 12442]). Platycephalidae.

Rathbunella Jordan & Evermann 1896:463 [ref. 2442]. Fem. *Bathymaster hypoplectus* Gilbert 1890:97. Type by original designation (also monotypic). Valid. Bathymasteridae.

Ratsirakia Maugé 1984:100 [ref. 5945]. Fem. *Eleotris legendrei* Pellegrin 1919:270. Type by original designation (also monotypic). Valid (Maugé 1986:398 [ref. 6218]). Eleotridae.

Recepoecilia Whitley 1951:68 [ref. 4711]. Fem. *Poecilia vivipara parae* Eigenmann 1894:629. Type by being a replacement name. For purposes of the type species, the subspecies *parae* is elevated to species level; type not *vivipara*. Unneeded replacement for *Micropoecilia* Hubbs 1926, not preoccupied by *Micropoecila* Kraatz 1880 in Coleoptera. Synonym of *Poecilia* Bloch & Schneider 1801 (Rosen & Bailey 1963:45 [ref. 7067]). Poeciliidae.

Rectoris Lin 1935:303 [ref. 2779]. *Rectoris posehensis* Lin 1935:304. Type by original designation (also monotypic). Valid (Wu et al. 1977:361 [ref. 4807]). Cyprinidae.

Redigobius Herre 1927:98 [ref. 2104]. Masc. *Gobius sternbergi* Smith 1902:169. Type by monotypy. Valid (Akihito in Masuda et al. 1984:269 [ref. 6441], Hoese 1986:801 [ref. 5670], Maugé 1986:382 [ref. 6218], Miller 1987:695 [ref. 6336], Birdsong et al. 1988:202 [ref. 7303], Kottelat 1989:19 [ref. 13605]). Gobiidae.

Regalecus Ascanius 1772:5 [ref. 5115]. Masc. *Regalecus glesne* Ascanius 1772:5, Pl. 11. Type by monotypy. Valid (Palmer 1973: 329 [ref. 7195], Scott 1983:169 [ref. 5346], Olney 1984:369 [ref. 13656], Fujii in Masuda et al. 1984:117 [ref. 6441], Palmer in Whitehead et al. 1986:727 [ref. 13676], Heemstra 1986:403 [ref. 5660], Paxton et al. 1989:401 [ref. 12442]). Regalecidae.

Regalecus Brünnich 1771:418 [ref. 675]. Masc. *Regalecus remipes* Brünnich 1771. Type by monotypy. Cited by Fowler (MS) for *Regalecus* [not investigated, see *Regalecus* Ascanius 1772]. Did appear in Brünnich 1788:414 in same journal and just following Brünnich 1788 [ref. 5131]. Regalecidae.

Reganella Eigenmann 1905:794 [ref. 5563]. Fem. *Hemiodon depressus* Kner 1853:91. Type by being a replacement name. Replacement for *Hemiodon* Kner 1854, preoccupied by Swainson 1840 in Mollusca. Valid (Isbrücker & Nijssen 1974:216 [ref. 7126], Isbrücker 1980:123 [ref. 2303], Burgess 1989:444 [ref. 12860]). Loricariidae.

Regania Jordan in Jordan & Starks 1904:602, 604 [ref. 2526]. Fem. *Regania nipponica* Jordan in Jordan & Starks 1904:605. Type by original designation (also monotypic). Synonym of *Bathygadus* Günther 1878 (Marshall 1973:288 [ref. 7194], Marshall & Iwamoto 1973:525 [ref. 6963]). Macrouridae: Bathygadinae.

Reganichthys Bigelow & Barbour 1944:10 [ref. 299]. Masc. *Reganichthys giganteus* Bigelow & Barbour 1944:10. Type by monotypy. Preoccupied by Ogilby 1915 in fishes, replaced by *Reganula* Bigelow & Barbour (June) 1944. Synonym of *Ceratias* Krøyer 1845 (Pietsch 1986:481 [ref. 5969]). Ceratiidae.

Reganichthys Ogilby 1915:123 [ref. 3293]. Masc. *Reganichthys magnificus* Ogilby 1915:123. Type by monotypy. Synonym of *Glaucosoma* Temminck & Schlegel 1843. Glaucosomatidae.

Reganina Fowler 1907:475 [ref. 1374]. Fem. *Myletes bidens* Agassiz in Spix & Agassiz 1829:75. Type by original designation (also monotypic). Synonym of *Colossoma* Eigenmann & Kennedy 1903 (Géry 1976:50 [ref. 14199]). Characidae: Serrasalminae.

Reganisalanx Fang 1934:508 [ref. 1299]. Masc. *Reganisalanx normani* Fang 1934:508. Type by original designation. Synonym of *Salanx* Cuvier 1816 (Roberts 1984:206 [ref. 5318]). Salangidae.

Reganochromis Whitley 1929:112 [ref. 4665]. Masc. *Paratilapia calliura* Boulenger 1901:2. Type by being a replacement name. Replacement for *Leptochromis* Regan 1920, preoccupied by Bleeker 1875 [or 1876] in fishes. Valid (Poll 1986:132 [ref. 6136]). Cichlidae.

Reganotilapia Whitley 1950:44 [ref. 4713]. Fem. *Tilapia buettikoferi* Hubrecht 1881:66. Type by being a replacement name. Replacement for *Heterotilapia* Regan 1920, apparently preoccupied [not researched]. Cichlidae.

Reganula Bigelow & Barbour 1944:123 [ref. 298]. Fem. *Reganichthys giganteus* Bigelow & Barbour 1944:10. Type by being a replacement name. Replacement for *Reganichthys* Bigelow & Barbour (14 Apr.) 1944, preoccupied by Ogilby 1915 in fishes; *Reganula* was published in June 1944. Synonym of *Ceratias* Krøyer 1845 (Pietsch 1986:481 [ref. 5969]). Ceratiidae.

Regificola Whitley 1931:316 [ref. 4672]. Masc. *Seriola grandis* Castelnau 1872:115. Type by original designation (also monotypic). Synonym of *Seriola* Cuvier 1816 (Smith-Vaniz, pers. comm., Nov. 1989). Carangidae.

Regilophotes Whitley 1933:72 [ref. 4677]. Fem. *Lophotes guntheri* Johnson 1883:142, 177. Type by original designation (also monotypic). Synonym of *Lophotus* Giorna 1809 (Palmer 1973:334 [ref. 7195]). Lophotidae.

Reicheltia Hardy 1982:16 [ref. 2038]. Fem. *Sphaeroides halsteadi* Whitley 1957:70. Type by original designation (also monotypic). For spelling of genus see *Sphoeroides*. Valid (see Su et al. 1986:112 [ref. 12582]). Tetraodontidae.

Reighardina (subgenus of *Ichthyomyzon*) Creaser & Hubbs 1922:4

[ref. 990]. Fem. *Ichthyomyzon fossor* Reighard & Cummins 1916:1. Type by original designation (also monotypic). Synonym of *Ichthyomyzon* Girard 1858 (Hubbs & Potter 1971:40 [ref. 13397]). Petromyzontidae: Petromyzontinae.

Reinhardtius Gill 1861:50 [ref. 1766]. Masc. *Pleuronectes cynoglossus* Fabricius 1780:163. Type by monotypy. Valid (Norman 1934:288 [ref. 6893], Nielsen 1973:627 [ref. 6885], Ahlstrom et al. 1984:643 [ref. 13641], Sakamoto 1984 [ref. 5273], Sakamoto in Masuda et al. 1984:351 [ref. 6441], Nielsen in Whitehead et al. 1986:1306 [ref. 13677]). Pleuronectidae: Pleuronectinae.

Relictogobius Ptchelina 1939:586 [ref. 3566]. Masc. *Relictogobius kryzhanovskii* Ptchelina 1939:587. Type by monotypy. Synonym of *Chromogobius* de Buen 1930 (Miller 1973:492 [ref. 6888]). Gobiidae.

Relictus Hubbs & Miller 1972:101 [ref. 2260]. Masc. *Relictus solitarius* Hubbs & Miller 1972:102. Type by original designation (also monotypic). Valid (Hubbs et al. 1974:180 [ref. 14477]). Cyprinidae.

Remilegia Gill 1862:239 [ref. 1664]. Fem. *Echeneis scutata* Günther 1860:401. Type by original designation (name in parentheses in key), also monotypic. Synonym of *Remora* Gill 1862 (Lachner 1973:638 [ref. 7221]). Echeneidae.

Remora Catesby 1771:26 [ref. 774]. Fem. Not available, published in a rejected work on Official Index (Opinion 89, Opinion 259). Echeneidae.

Remora Gill 1862:239 [ref. 1664]. Fem. *Echeneis remora* Linnaeus 1758:260. Type by original designation (name in parentheses in key). On Official List (Opinion 242); *Remora* Goüan 1770:183 and *Remora* Forster 1771:20 placed on Official Index. Valid (Lachner 1973:638 [ref. 7221], Okamura in Masuda et al. 1984:222 [ref. 6441], Lachner in Whitehead et al. 1986:1331 [ref. 13677], Heemstra 1986:663 [ref. 5660], Paxton et al. 1989:572 [ref. 12442]). Echeneidae.

Remorina (subgenus of *Remora*) Jordan & Evermann 1896:490 [ref. 2442]. Fem. *Echeneis albescens* Temminck & Schlegel 1850:272. Type by original designation (also monotypic). Valid (Lachner 1973:640 [ref. 7221], Okamura in Masuda et al. 1984:223 [ref. 6441], Lachner in Whitehead et al. 1986:1334 [ref. 13677], Paxton et al. 1989:572 [ref. 12442]). Echeneidae.

Remoropsis Gill 1863:88 [ref. 1679]. Fem. *Echeneis brachyptera* Lowe 1839:89. Type by original designation (also monotypic). Synonym of *Remora* Gill 1862 (Lachner 1973:638 [ref. 7221]). Echeneidae.

Rendahlia Chabanaud 1930:21 [ref. 784]. Fem. *Achirus jaubertensis* Rendahl 1923. Type by original designation (also monotypic). Misspelled *Rendhalia* at main entry (p. 21), *Rendahlia* in key (p. 21), and named for Rendahl so *Rendahlia* is correctly formed. Valid (Chapleau & Keast 1988:2799 [ref. 12625]). Soleidae.

Reniceps Gill 1862:403 [ref. 1783]. Neut. *Squalus tiburo* Linnaeus 1758:324. Type by original designation (also monotypic). Also in Gill 1862:412 [ref. 4910] where author of species is clear. Objective synonym of *Platysqualus* Swainson 1839. Synonym of *Sphyrna* Rafinesque 1810 (Compagno 1984:541 [ref. 6846], Cappetta 1987:127 [ref. 6348], Compagno 1988:362 [ref. 13488]). Sphyrnidae.

Repomucenus Whitley 1931:323 [ref. 4672]. Masc. *Callionymus calcaratus* Macleay 1881:628. Type by original designation (also monotypic). Synonym of *Callionymus* Linnaeus 1758 (Fricke 1982:58 [ref. 5432]); valid (Nakabo 1982:105 [ref. 3139], Houde 1984:637 [ref. 13674], Nakabo in Masuda et al. 1984:344 [ref. 6441], Nakabo et al. 1987 [ref. 6374]). Callionymidae.

Reporhamphus Whitley 1931:314 [ref. 4672]. Masc. *Hemirhamphus australis* Steindachner 1866:471. Type by original designation. Correct spelling for genus of type species is *Hemiramphus*. Synonym of *Hyporhamphus* Gill 1859, but as a valid subgenus (Parin et al. 1980:52 [ref. 6895], Collette et al. 1984:352 [ref. 11422], Collette 1986:390 [ref. 5647], Collette & Su 1986:252 [ref. 5998]). Hemiramphidae.

Repotrudis (subgenus of *Suggrundus*) Whitley 1930:27 [ref. 4671]. Fem. *Platycephalus macracanthus* Bleeker 1869:253. Type by original designation (also monotypic). As a subgenus, but somewhat unclear under which genus *Repotrudis* was proposed. Synonym of *Suggrundus* Whitley 1930 (Paxton et al. 1989:471 [ref. 12442] based on placement of the type species). Platycephalidae.

Retroculus Eigenmann & Bray 1894:614 [ref. 1248]. Masc. *Retroculus boulengeri* Eigenmann & Bray 1894:614. Type by monotypy. Cichlidae.

Retropinna Gill 1862:14 [ref. 1655]. Fem. *Argentina retropinna* Richardson 1845:121. Type by monotypy. Valid (McDowall 1979:90 [ref. 7021], McDowall 1984:151 [ref. 11850], Paxton et al. 1989:172 [ref. 12442]). Retropinnidae: Retropinninae.

Rewa Whitley 1950:245 [ref. 4712]. *Rewa hickingli* Whitley 1950:245. Type by original designation (also monotypic). Gobiidae.

Rexea Waite 1911:49 [ref. 4567]. Fem. *Rexea furcifera* Waite 1911:49. Type by original designation. Spelled *Rexia* by authors. Senior synonym of *Jordanidia* Snyder 1911, *Rexea* Waite published 18 Jan. 1911 as above (also in June 1911 in Records Cant. Mus.), *Jordanidia* published 24 June 1911. Valid (Collette et al. 1984:600 [ref. 11421], Nakamura in Masuda et al. 1984:226 [ref. 6441], Nakamura 1986:827 [ref. 5696], Parin 1989 [ref. 12753]). Gempylidae.

Rexichthys Parin & Astakhov 1987:149 [ref. 9146]. Masc. *Rexichthys johnpaxtoni* Parin & Astakhov 1987:149. Gempylidae.

Rhabdaethiops (subgenus of *Nannaethiops*) Fowler 1936:264 [ref. 1424]. Masc. *Nannaethiops tritaeniatus* Boulenger 1899:114. Type by original designation (also monotypic). Synonym of *Neolebias* Steindachner 1894 (Daget & Gosse 1984:205 [ref. 6185]). Citharinidae: Distichodontinae.

Rhabdalestes (subgenus of *Micralestes*) Hoedeman 1951:6 (in key) [ref. 2178]. Masc. *Petersius tangensis* Lönnberg 1907:2. Type by monotypy (one species, two subspecies). Synonym of *Hemigrammopetersius* Pellegrin 1926 (Géry 1977:39 [ref. 1597]); valid (Poll 1967:125 [ref. 3529], Paugy 1984:181 [ref. 6183]). Alestiidae.

Rhabdamia Weber 1909:165 [ref. 4600]. Fem. *Rhabdamia clupeiformis* Weber 1909:165. Type by subsequent designation. Type designated by Jordan 1920:534 [ref. 4905]. Valid (Fraser 1972:27 [ref. 5195], Hayashi in Masuda et al. 1984:150 [ref. 6441], Gon 1986:556 [ref. 5657], Allen 1987:4 [ref. 13387], Paxton et al. 1989:556 [ref. 12442]). Apogonidae.

Rhabdoblennius Whitley 1930:20 [ref. 4671]. Masc. *Blennius rhabdotrachelus* Fowler & Ball 1924:272. Type by original designation. Valid (Smith-Vaniz & Springer 1971:37 [ref. 4145], Yoshino in Masuda et al. 1984:298 [ref. 6441]). Blenniidae.

Rhabdolichops Eigenmann & Allen 1942:316 [ref. 1246]. Masc. *Rhabdolichops longicaudatus* Eigenmann & Allen 1942:317. Type by monotypy. Valid (Mago-Leccia 1978:17 [ref. 5489], Mago-Leccia & Zaret 1978 [ref. 5488]). Gymnotidae: Sternopyginae.

Rhabdopetersius (subgenus of *Alestopetersius*) Hoedeman 1951:8 (in key) [ref. 2178]. Masc. *Petersius leopoldianus* Boulenger 1899:90. Type by monotypy in subgenus, one species (two subspecies); nominate subspecies is type. Synonym of *Alestopetersius* Hoedeman (1951) 1956 (Paugy 1984:160 [ref. 6183]). Alestiidae.

Rhabdosargus (subgenus of *Diplodus*) Fowler 1933:175, 178 [ref. 1414]. Masc. *Sargus auriventris* Peters 1855:243. Type by original designation (also monotypic). Valid (Smith 1979 [ref. 6940], Smith & Smith 1986:592 [ref. 5710], Bauchot & Skelton 1986:332 [ref. 6210]). Sparidae.

Rhabdosebastes Fowler & Bean 1922:60 [ref. 1473]. Masc. *Sebastes stolickzae* Day 1877:149. Type by original designation (also monotypic). Objective synonym of *Gennadius* Jordan & Seale 1907, wrongly described as a genus of Scorpaenidae; synonym of *Centrogenys* Richardson 1842. Centrogeniidae.

Rhabdura Ogilby 1907:12 [ref. 3282]. Fem. *Muraena macrura* Bleeker 1854:354. Type by monotypy. Objective synonym of *Evenchelys* Jordan & Evermann 1902. Muraenidae: Muraeninae.

Rhachinotus Cantor 1849:1404 [422] [ref. 715]. Masc. *Raja africana* Bloch & Schneider 1801:307. Type by being a replacement name. Replacement for *Anacanthus* Ehrenberg in Van der Hoeven 1833, apparently preoccupied by Ehrenberg in Cuvier 1829, Gray 1831 in fishes, and Serville 1832 in Coleoptera. On page 422 of separate. Synonym of *Urogymnus* Müller & Henle 1837. Dasyatidae.

Rhacochilus Agassiz 1854:367 [ref. 70]. Masc. *Rhacochilus toxotes* Agassiz 1854:367. Type by monotypy. Spelled *Rhacocheilus* by Girard 1855:320 [ref. 1820]. Valid (Tarp 1952:53 [ref. 12250]). Embiotocidae.

Rhadinesthes Regan & Trewavas 1929:29 [ref. 3680]. Fem. *Astronesthes decimus* Zugmayer 1911:80. Type by monotypy. Valid (Gibbs 1964:343 [ref. 6960], Gibbs & Morrow 1973:128 [ref. 7174], Gibbs in Whitehead et al. 1984:334 [ref. 13675], Kawaguchi & Moser 1984:171 [ref. 13642], Fujii in Masuda et al. 1984:50 [ref. 6441], Fink 1985:11 [ref. 5171]). Astronesthidae.

Rhadinocentrus Regan 1914:280 [ref. 3660]. Masc. *Rhadinocentrus ornatus* Regan 1914:280. Type by monotypy. Valid (Allen & Cross 1982:108 [ref. 6251], White et al. 1984:360 [ref. 13655], Paxton et al. 1989:353 [ref. 12442]). Atherinidae: Melanotaeniinae.

Rhadinoloricaria Isbrücker & Nijssen 1974:73 [ref. 2304]. Fem. *Loricaria macromystax* Günther 1869:426. Type by original designation (also monotypic). Valid (Isbrücker & Nijssen 1986:103 [ref. 5212], Isbrücker & Nijssen 1986:40 [ref. 7321], Burgess 1989:444 [ref. 12860]). Loricariidae.

Rhamdella (subgenus of *Rhamdia*) Eigenmann & Eigenmann 1888:129 [ref. 1249]. Fem. *Rhamdella eriarcha* Eigenmann & Eigenmann 1888:129. Type by original designation. Valid (Burgess 1989:278 [ref. 12860], Malabarba 1989:143 [ref. 14217]). Pimelodidae.

Rhamdia Bleeker 1858:197, 204, 207,244 [ref. 365]. Fem. *Pimelodus sebae* Valenciennes in Cuvier & Valenciennes 1840:169. Type by subsequent designation. Type designated by Bleeker 1862:11 [ref. 393] and 1863:101 [ref. 401]. Valid (Mees 1974:152 [ref. 2969], Miller 1984 [ref. 5281], Burgess 1989:278 [ref. 12860]). Pimelodidae.

Rhamdioglanis Ihering 1907:16, 17 [ref. 2294]. Masc. *Rhamdioglanis frenatus* Ihering 1907:16, 17. Type by original designation (also monotypic). Synonym of *Imparfinis* Eigenmann & Norris 1900 (Mees 1974:167 [ref. 2969]). Pimelodidae.

Rhamdiopsis Haseman 1911:375 [ref. 2048]. Fem. *Rhamdiopsis moreirai* Haseman 1911:375. Type by monotypy. Valid (Burgess 1989:276 [ref. 12860]). Pimelodidae.

Rhamphichthys Müller & Troschel 1848:640 [ref. 3072]. Masc. *Gymnotus rostratus* Linnaeus 1766:428. Type by monotypy. Apparently appeared first as *Ramphichthys* without description in Müller 1844 [not researched], then in 1848 as above, then in 1849:15 [ref. 3073]. Valid (see Mago-Leccia 1978:14 [ref. 5489]). Gymnotidae: Rhamphichthyinae.

Rhamphobatis Gill 1862:408 [ref. 1783]. Fem. *Rhina ancylostoma* Bloch & Schneider 1801:352. Type by being a replacement name. Unneeded replacement for *Rhina* Bloch & Schneider 1801, not preoccupied by Klein 1742 [unavailable] in fishes. Objective synonym of *Rhina* Bloch & Schneider 1801. Rhinobatidae: Rhininae.

Rhamphoberyx Gill 1863:87 [ref. 1679]. Masc. *Rhamphoberyx poecilopus* Gill 1863:87. Type by subsequent designation. Type designated by Jordan & Evermann 1896:846 [ref. 2443]. Synonym of *Myripristis* Cuvier 1829 (Woods & Sonoda 1973:368 [ref. 6899]). Holocentridae.

Rhamphocetichthys Paxton 1989:151, 178 [ref. 13435]. Masc. *Rhamphocetichthys savagei* Paxton 1989:178. Type by original designation (also monotypic). Cetomimidae.

Rhamphochromis Regan 1922:724 [ref. 3673]. Masc. *Hemichromis longiceps* Günther 1864:313. Type by original designation. Valid (Ribbink et al. 1983:249 [ref. 13555], Eccles & Trewavas 1989:311 [ref. 13547]). Cichlidae.

Rhamphocottus Günther 1874:369 [ref. 2006]. Masc. *Rhamphocottus richardsoni* Günther 1874:369. Type by monotypy. Valid (Washington et al. 1984:443 [ref. 13660], Yabe in Masuda et al. 1984:323 [ref. 6441], Yabe 1985:122 [ref. 11522] in Rhamphocottidae, Saruwatari et al. 1987 [ref. 6702]). Cottidae.

Rhamphodermogenys (subgenus of *Dermogenys*) Fowler & Bean 1922:15 [ref. 1473]. Fem. *Dermogenys bakeri* Fowler & Bean 1922:15. Type by original designation (also monotypic). Hemiramphidae.

Rhamphosternarchus (subgenus of *Sternarchus*) Günther 1870:4 [ref. 1995]. Masc. *Sternarchus oxyrhynchus* Müller & Troschel 1849:16. Type by subsequent designation. Type designated by Jordan 1919:357 [ref. 4904]. Gymnotidae: Apteronotinae.

Rhaphiobelone Fowler 1934:322 [ref. 1416]. Fem. *Rhaphiobelone dammermani* Fowler 1934:323. Type by original designation (also monotypic). Belonidae.

Rhaphiodon Agassiz in Spix & Agassiz 1829:59, 76 [ref. 13]. Masc. *Rhaphiodon vulpinus* Agassiz in Spix & Agassiz 1829:76. Type by subsequent designation. Type designated by Eigenmann 1910:444 [ref. 1224]. *Raphiodon* is a misspelling. For authorship and date see Kottelat 1988:78 [ref. 13380]. Kottelat's interpretation (p. 83) is perhaps incorrect; see account of *Cynodon*. Valid (Géry 1977:299 [ref. 1597], Vari 1983:5 [ref. 5419], Géry 1986:63 [ref. 6019]). Cynodontidae.

Rhaphiodontichthys Amaral Campos 1945:473 [ref. 106]. Masc. *Cynodon vulpinus* Agassiz in Spix & Agassiz 1829:76. Type by original designation (also monotypic). Misspelled *Rhapiodontichthys* by Neave in Zoological Record for 1950. Synonym of *Raphiodon* Agassiz 1829 (Géry 1977:302 [ref. 1597] based on placement of type species). Cynodontidae.

Rhaphiolepis (subgenus of *Scomberoides*) Fowler 1905:59 [ref.

1369]. Fem. *Chorinemus tol* Cuvier in Cuvier & Valenciennes 1831:283. Type by original designation (also monotypic). Synonym of *Scomberoides* Lacepède 1801 (Smith-Vaniz & Staiger 1973:190 [ref. 7106], Daget & Smith-Vaniz 1986:316 [ref. 6207]). Carangidae.

Rhechias Jordan 1921:644 [ref. 2419]. Masc. *Rhechias armiger* Jordan 1921:644. Type by original designation (also monotypic). Valid (Smith & Kanazawa 1977:538 [ref. 4036], Karrer 1982:29 [ref. 5679], Asano in Masuda et al. 1984:28 [ref. 6441], Castle 1986:165 [ref. 5644], Smith 1989:532 [ref. 13285]). Congridae: Congrinae.

Rhectogramma Norman 1930:348 [ref. 3219]. Neut. *Rhectogramma sherborni* Norman 1930:348. Type by original designation (also monotypic). Synonym of *Howella* Ogilby 1899 (Tortonese 1973:366 [ref. 7192]). Percoidei.

Rhegma Gilbert in Jordan & Evermann 1900:3169 [ref. 2446]. Neut. *Rhegma thaumasium* Gilbert in Jordan & Evermann 1900:3170. Type by original designation. Synonym of *Pseudogramma* Bleeker 1875. Serranidae: Grammistinae.

Rhencus Jordan & Evermann 1896:387 [ref. 2442]. Masc. *Pristipoma panamense* Steindachner 1875:36. Type by original designation (also monotypic). Misspelled *Rhenchus* by Jordan & Evermann 1898:1329 [ref. 2444] in key. Synonym of *Pomadasys* Lacepède 1802 (Roux 1973:391 [ref. 7200], Roux 1986:328 [ref. 6209]). Haemulidae.

Rheocles Jordan & Hubbs in Jordan 1919:343 [ref. 2413]. Masc. *Eleotris sikorae* Sauvage 1891:521. Type by original designation (also monotypic). Valid (Maugé 1986:278 [ref. 6218]). Atherinidae: Bedotiinae.

Rheocloides Nichols & La Monte 1931:1 [ref. 3186]. Masc. *Rheocloides pellegrini* Nichols & La Monte 1931:1. Type by original designation (also monotypic). Valid (Maugé 1986:278 [ref. 6218]). Atherinidae: Bedotiinae.

Rheocrypta Jordan 1877:9 [ref. 2374]. Fem. *Rheocrypta copelandi* Jordan 1877:9. Type by monotypy. Synonym of *Cottogaster* Putnam 1863; as a subgenus of *Percina* Haldeman 1842 (Collette & Banarescu 1977:1455 [ref. 5845]). Percidae.

Rheoglanis Poll 1966:425 [ref. 3527]. Masc. *Rheoglanis dendrophorus* Poll 1966:425. Type by original designation (also monotypic). Valid (Risch 1986:35 [ref. 6190], Burgess 1989:68 [ref. 12860]). Bagridae.

Rheogobio (subgenus of *Gobio*) Banarescu 1961:330 [ref. 211]. Masc. *Cyprinus uranoscopus* Agassiz 1828:1047. Type by original designation. Valid subgenus of *Gobio* Cuvier 1816 (Banarescu & Nalbant 1973:136 [ref. 173]). Cyprinidae.

Rheohaplochromis (subgenus of *Haplochromis*) Thys van den Audenaerde 1963:145 [ref. 4404]. Masc. *Haplochromis polyacanthus* Boulenger 1899:124. Apparently not available as above, described after 1930 with two included species and no designation of a type species (Art 13b). Can date to treatment in Zoological Record for 1964 (see remarks on Art. 13b in Appendix A). Cichlidae.

Rheopresbe Jordan & Starks 1904:270 [ref. 2528]. *Rheopresbe fujiyamae* Jordan & Starks 1904:271. Type by original designation (also monotypic). Synonym of *Cottus* Linnaeus 1758. Cottidae.

Rhigophila DeWitt 1962:820 [ref. 1122]. Fem. *Rhigophila dearborni* DeWitt 1962:821. Type by original designation (also monotypic). Synonym of *Lycodichthys* Pappenheim 1911 (Anderson 1988:78 [ref. 7304]). Zoarcidae.

Rhina Bloch & Schneider 1801:352 [ref. 471]. Fem. *Rhina ancylostomus* Bloch & Schneider 1801:352. Type designated by indication under ICZN Opinion 6. On Official List; *Rhina* Schaeffer 1760, *Rhina* Walbaum 1792, and *Rhina* Rafinesque 1810 placed on Official Index (Opinion 345). Valid (Nakaya in Masuda et al. 1984:12 [ref. 6441], Compagno 1986:128 [ref. 5648], Paxton et al. 1989:53 [ref. 12442]). Rhinobatidae: Rhininae.

Rhina Gill (ex Klein) 1862:408 [ref. 1783]. Fem. *Rhina squatina* of Rafinesque (= *Squalus squatina* Linnaeus 1758:233). Preoccupied by *Rhina* Bloch & Schneider 1801 in fishes. In the synonymy of *Squatina* Duméril 1806. Squatinidae.

Rhina Klein 1776:587 [ref. 4918]. Fem. Not available, published in a work that does not conform to the principle of binominal nomenclature. In the synonymy of *Squatina* Duméril 1806. Squatinidae.

Rhina Rafinesque 1810:14 [ref. 3594]. Fem. *Squalus squatina* Linnaeus 1758:233. Type by monotypy. On Official Index (Opinion 345) as a junior homonym. Preoccupied by *Rhina* Bloch & Schneider 1801 in fishes. In the synonymy of *Squatina* Duméril 1806. Squatinidae.

Rhina Schaeffer 1760:20 [ref. 4989]. Fem. Not available, published in a rejected work on Official Index (Opinion 345). Not *Rhina* Bloch & Schneider 1801. Original not examined. In the synonymy of *Squatina* Duméril 1806 (Compagno 1984:138 [ref. 6474]). Squatinidae.

Rhincodon Smith 1829:433 [ref. 4976]. Masc. *Rhiniodon typus* Smith 1828:2. Type by monotypy (also by use of *typus*). On Official List (Opinion 1278). Misspelled *Rineodon, Rhiniodon, Rhinodon,* and *Rhinecodon*. *Rhiniodon* Smith 1828:2 on Official Index for purposes of priority (Opinion 1278). Appeared first as *Rhiniodon* Smith 1828 (see also Penrith 1972 [ref. 7140]), but not accepted by ICZN. Valid (Compagno 1984:209 [ref. 6474], Bass 1986:66 [ref. 5635], Wolfson 1986 [ref. 6150], Cappetta 1987:81 [ref. 6348], Paxton et al. 1989:94 [ref. 12442]). Rhincodontidae.

Rhinecanthus (subgenus of *Balistes*) Swainson 1839:194, 325 [ref. 4303]. Masc. *Balistes ornatissimus* Lesson 1830:119. Type by subsequent designation. Type designated by Swain 1882:282 [ref. 5966]. Valid (Tyler 1980:121 [ref. 4477], Randall & Steene 1983 [ref. 6023], Arai 1983:199 [ref. 14249], Matsuura in Masuda et al. 1984:358 [ref. 6441], Smith & Heemstra 1986:880 [ref. 5714], Matsuura & Shiobara 1989 [ref. 13563]). Balistidae.

Rhinechidna Barbour 1908:41 [ref. 177]. Fem. *Rhinomuraena eritima* Jordan & Seale 1906:196. Type by monotypy. Synonym of *Enchelycore* Kaup 1856 (Böhlke et al. 1989:134 [ref. 13286]). Muraenidae: Muraeninae.

Rhinelepis Agassiz in Spix & Agassiz 1829:2, 4 [ref. 13]. Fem. *Rhinelepis aspera* Agassiz in Spix & Agassiz 1829:4. Type by monotypy. Spelled *Rhinelepes* by Swainson 1839:304 [ref. 4303], *Rinelepis* by Valenciennes in Cuvier & Valenciennes 1840:480 [ref. 1008], and *Rhinolepis* by Borodin 1927:7 [ref. 12246]. Valid (Isbrücker 1980:7 [ref. 2303], Burgess 1989:429 [ref. 12860]). Loricariidae.

Rhinenchelys Blache & Bauchot 1972:718 [ref. 304]. Fem. *Sphagebranchus ophioneus* Evermann & Marsh 1902:73. Type by original designation (also monotypic). Synonym of *Ichthyapus* Brisout de Barneville 1847 (McCosker 1977:67 [ref. 6836], McCosker et al. 1989:322 [ref. 13288]). Ophichthidae: Ophichthinae.

Rhinesomus (subgenus of *Tetrosomus*) Swainson 1839:194, 324 [ref. 4303]. Masc. *Ostracion triqueter* Linnaeus 1758:330. Type by subsequent designation. Type designated by Swain 1882:282 [ref. 5966]. Valid (Tyler 1980:239 [ref. 4477], Arai 1983:203 [ref. 14249], Aboussouan & Leis 1984:452 [ref. 13661]). Ostraciidae: Ostraciinae.

Rhinhoplichthys Fowler 1938:100 [ref. 1426]. Masc. *Hoplichthys haswelli* McCulloch 1907:351. Type by original designation (also monotypic). Synonym of *Hoplichthys* Cuvier 1829 (Paxton et al. 1989:473 [ref. 12442] based on placement of the type species). Hoplichthyidae.

Rhinichthys Agassiz 1849:81 [ref. 65]. Masc. *Cyprinus atronasus* Mitchill 1815:460. Type by subsequent designation. Type designated by Jordan & Gilbert 1877:89 [ref. 4907]. Valid (Peden & Hughes 1988 [ref. 12855]). Cyprinidae.

Rhiniodon Smith 1828:2 [ref. 12603]. Masc. *Rhiniodon typus* Smith 1828:2. Type by monotypy (also by use of *typus*). *Rhiniodon* placed on Official Index for purposes of priority (Opinion 1278). See *Rhincodon* Smith. Rhincodontidae.

Rhinobagrus Bleeker 1865:7 [ref. 405]. Masc. *Rhinobagrus dumerili* Bleeker 1865:7. Type by monotypy. Synonym of *Leiocassis* Bleeker 1858 (Jayaram 1968:347 [ref. 5615]). Bagridae.

Rhinobatos Klein 1776:593 [ref. 4918]. Masc. Not available, published in a work that does not conform to the principle of binominal nomenclature. In the synonymy of *Rhinobatus* Bloch & Schneider 1801. Rhinobatidae: Rhinobatinae.

Rhinobatos Linck 1790:32 [ref. 4985]. Masc. *Raja rhinobatos* Linnaeus 1758:232. No included species; first technical addition of species not researched; type usually regarded as *R. rhinobatos* Linnaeus, assumed from tautonymy; technical subsequent designation not researched. Valid (Krefft & Stehmann 1973:53 [ref. 7167], Nakaya in Masuda et al. 1984:12 [ref. 6441], Compagno 1986:129 [ref. 5648], Paxton et al. 1989:53 [ref. 12442]). Rhinobatidae: Rhinobatinae.

Rhinobatus Bloch & Schneider 1801:353 [ref. 471]. Masc. *Raja rhinobatos* Linnaeus 1758:232. Type usually regarded as by tautonymy, but Linnaeus' spelling of the species was *rhinobatos*; earliest subsequent designation not researched. Synonym of *Rhinobatos* Linck 1790 (Krefft & Stehmann 1973:53 [ref. 7167]). Rhinobatidae: Rhinobatinae.

Rhinoberyx Gill 1862:237 [ref. 1664]. Masc. *Rhynchichthys brachyrhynchos* Bleeker 1853:107. Type by monotypy. Synonym of *Myripristis* Cuvier 1829 (Woods & Sonoda 1973:368 [ref. 6899]). Holocentridae.

Rhinobrycon Myers 1944:587 [ref. 3122]. Masc. *Rhinobrycon negrensis* Myers 1944:589. Type by original designation (also monotypic). Valid (Géry 1977:402 [ref. 1597]). Characidae.

Rhinochimaera Garman 1901:75 [ref. 1541]. Fem. *Harriotta pacifica* Mitsukuri 1895:97. Type by original designation (also monotypic). Valid (Krefft 1973:80 [ref. 7166], Inada & Garrick 1979 [ref. 7002], Stehmann & Bürkel in Whitehead et al. 1984:217 [ref. 13675], Nakaya in Masuda et al. 1984:17 [ref. 6441], Compagno 1986:146 [ref. 5648], Paxton et al. 1989:101 [ref. 12442]). Rhinochimaeridae.

Rhinocryptis Peters 1844:414 [ref. 3447]. Fem. *Rhinocryptis amphibia* Peters 1844:414. Type by monotypy. Synonym of *Protopterus* Owen 1839 (Gosse 1984:8 [ref. 6169]). Lepidosirenidae: Protopterinae.

Rhinodactylus Smith 1956:686 [ref. 4108]. Masc. *Rhinodactylus baixopindae* Smith 1956:686. Type by original designation (also monotypic). Synonym of *Naso* Lacepède 1801. Acanthuridae.

Rhinodoras Bleeker 1862:5 [ref. 393]. Masc. *Doras (Oxydoras) dorbignyi* Krøyer in Kner 1855:140. Type by original designation (also monotypic). Valid (Glodek et al. 1976 [ref. 7068], Burgess 1989:224 [ref. 12860]). Doradidae.

Rhinoglanis Günther 1864:216 [ref. 1974]. Masc. *Rhinoglanis typus* Günther 1864:216. Type by monotypy (also by use of *typus*). Synonym of *Mochokus* Joannis 1835. Mochokidae.

Rhinogobio Bleeker 1870:253 [ref. 429]. Masc. *Rhinogobio typus* Bleeker 1871:29. Type by subsequent monotypy (also by use of *typus*). Apparently appeared first as above without included available species (*typus* listed, p. 252). One species described in 1871:29 [ref. 6421]. If Bleeker's comments on p. 253 are insufficient to make available, then genus dates to Bleeker 1871:29 [ref. 6421]. Valid (Banarescu & Nalbant 1973:166 [ref. 173], Lu, Luo & Chen 1977:507 [ref. 13495], Hosoya 1986:488 [ref. 6155], Chen & Li in Chu & Chen 1989:107 [ref. 13584]). Cyprinidae.

Rhinogobioides (subgenus of *Gobio*) Rendahl 1928:83 [ref. 3702]. Masc. *Gobio longipinnis* Nichols 1925:5. Type by monotypy. Synonym of *Rhinogobio* Bleeker 1870 (Banarescu & Nalbant 1973:166 [ref. 173]). Cyprinidae.

Rhinogobiops Hubbs 1926:1 [ref. 2234]. Masc. *Gobius nicholsii* Bean 1881:469. Type by original designation (also monotypic). Synonym of *Coryphopterus* Gill 1863. Gobiidae.

Rhinogobius Gill 1859:145 [ref. 1762]. Masc. *Rhinogobius similis* Gill 1859:145. Type by monotypy. Valid (Miller 1973:515 [ref. 6888], Hayashi in Masuda et al. 1984:269 [ref. 6441], Birdsong et al. 1988:202 [ref. 7303], Kottelat 1989:19 [ref. 13605]). Gobiidae.

Rhinoliparis Gilbert 1896:445 [ref. 1628]. Masc. *Rhinoliparis barbulifer* Gilbert 1896:445. Type by original designation (also monotypic). Valid (Stein 1978:32 [ref. 4203], Kido & Kitagawa 1986 [ref. 5682], Kido 1988:230 [ref. 12287]). Cyclopteridae: Liparinae.

Rhinomugil Gill 1863:169 [ref. 1681]. Masc. *Mugil corsula* Hamilton 1822:221, 381. Type by monotypy. Valid (Jayaram 1981:345 [ref. 6497]). Mugilidae.

Rhinomuraena (subgenus of *Muraena*) Garman 1888:114 [ref. 1534]. Fem. *Rhinomuraena quaesita* Garman 1888:114. Type by monotypy. Date possibly 1889. *Rhinamuraena* is a misspelling. Valid (Hatooka in Masuda et al. 1984:25 [ref. 6441], Paxton et al. 1989:132 [ref. 12442], Böhlke et al. 1989:130 [ref. 13286]). Muraenidae: Muraeninae.

Rhinonemus Gill 1863:241 [ref. 1687]. Masc. *Gadus cimbrius* Linnaeus 1766:440. Type by subsequent designation. Type designated by Jordan & Evermann 1898:2560 [ref. 2445]; although somewhat unclear in original description, it has been interpreted that there were 2 included species. Valid (Svetovidov 1973:316 [ref. 7169] with *Enchelyopus* in synonymy by preoccupation, Svetovidov in Whitehead et al. 1986:707 [ref. 13676]); synonym of *Enchelyopus* Bloch & Schneider 1801 (Cohen & Russo 1979:101 [ref. 6975]). Lotidae.

Rhinopetitia Géry 1964:454 [ref. 1583]. Fem. *Rhinopetitia myersi* Géry 1964:454. Type by original designation (also monotypic). Valid (Géry 1977:402 [ref. 1597]). Characidae.

Rhinopias Gill 1905:225 [ref. 1789]. Masc. *Scorpaena frondosa* Günther 1891:483. Type by original designation (also monotypic). Valid (Eschmeyer et al. 1973 [ref. 6390], Dinesen & Nash 1982 [ref. 5487], Shimizu in Masuda et al. 1984:315 [ref. 6441], Eschmeyer 1986:470 [ref. 5652], Paxton et al. 1989:447 [ref. 12442]). Scorpaenidae: Scorpaeninae.

Rhinoplagusia (subgenus of *Paraplagusia*) Bleeker 1870:27 [ref. 428]. Fem. *Plagusia japonica* Temminck & Schlegel 1846:187. Type by monotypy. Synonym of *Paraplagusia* Bleeker 1865 (Menon 1980:12 [ref. 6798], Desoutter 1986:433 [ref. 6212]). Cynoglossidae: Cynoglossinae.

Rhinoprenes Munro 1964:179 [ref. 3058]. *Rhinoprenes pentanemus* Munro 1964:179. Type by original designation (also monotypic). Valid (Johnson 1984:465 [ref. 9681] in Ephippididae). Ephippidae.

Rhinoptera Cuvier 1829:401 [ref. 995]. Fem. *Myliobatis marginata* Geoffroy St. Hilaire 1809:334, Pl. 25. Type by subsequent designation. Type designated by Bonaparte 1828:6 (of separate) [ref. 4979], also by Hay 1902:321 [ref. 6281]. Appeared first as *Rhenoptera* van Hasselt 1823:318 [ref. 4513] and *Rhinoptera* van Hasselt 1824:90 [ref. 5104], regarded as nomina nuda. Cuvier's "Les Rhinoptera Kuhl" evidently sufficient to latinize; two included species. Valid (Krefft & Stehmann 1973:76 [ref. 7167], Compagno 1986:133 [ref. 5648], Cappetta 1987:173 [ref. 6348], Paxton et al. 1989:49 [ref. 12442]). Myliobatidae.

Rhinoptera van Hasselt 1824:90 [ref. 5104]. *Myliobatis marginata* Geoffroy St. Hilaire 1809:334. Type by subsequent designation. Not available, appeared without distinguishing features for two unnamed species. *Rhenoptera* van Hasselt 1823 also not available. Myliobatidae.

Rhinoraja Ishiyama 1952:24 [ref. 2307]. Fem. *Rhinoraja kujiensis* Tanaka 1916:173. Type by original designation. Valid (Nakaya in Masuda et al. 1984:14 [ref. 6441], Ishihara & Ishiyama 1986:272 [ref. 5142]). Rajidae.

Rhinosardinia Eigenmann 1912:444, 445 [ref. 1227]. Fem. *Rhinosardinia serrata* Eigenmann 1912:445. Type by original designation (also monotypic). Valid (Grande 1985:251 [ref. 6466], Whitehead 1985:125 [ref. 5141]). Clupeidae.

Rhinoscion Gill 1861:78 [ref. 1770]. Masc. *Amblodon saturnus* Girard 1858:98. Type by monotypy. Synonym of *Cheilotrema* Tschudi 1846. Sciaenidae.

Rhinoscopelus (subgenus of *Scopelus*) Lütken 1892:209 [ref. 13407]. Masc. *Scopelus coccoi* Cocco 1829:143. Type by subsequent designation. Appeared first in Lütkin 1892:209 as above (see Paxton 1979:11 [ref. 6440]). Also in Lütken 1892:236, 242 [ref. 2858]. Appeared first with one species (*andreae*) questionably included; three species in 1892 [ref. 2858], with *coccoi* designated type on p. 232. Synonym of *Gonichthys* Gistel 1850 (Bolin 1959:16 [ref. 503], Krefft & Bekker 1973:182 [ref. 7181], Paxton 1979:11 [ref. 6440]). Myctophidae.

Rhinoscymnus Gill 1865:264 [ref. 1705]. Masc. *Scymnus rostratus* Risso 1826:138. Type by monotypy. Synonym of *Somniosus* Lesueur 1818 (Compagno 1984:102 [ref. 6474], Cappetta 1987:62 [ref. 6348]). Squalidae.

Rhinosolea Fowler 1946:209 [ref. 1456]. Fem. *Rhinosolea microlepidota* Fowler 1946:211. Type by original designation (also monotypic). Valid (Ochiai in Masuda et al. 1984:355 [ref. 6441]). Soleidae.

Rhinotriacis Gill 1863:486 [ref. 1671]. Fem. *Rhinotriacis henlei* Gill 1862:486. Type by monotypy. Synonym of *Mustelus* Linck 1790 (Compagno 1984:397 [ref. 6846], Compagno 1988:219 [ref. 13488]). Synonym of *Triakis* Müller & Henle 1838 (Cappetta 1987:117 [ref. 6348]). Triakidae: Triakinae.

Rhizoiketicus Vaillant 1893:746 [ref. 4487]. Masc. *Rhizoiketicus carolinensis* Vaillant 1893:746. Type by monotypy. Synonym of *Carapus* Rafinesque 1810 (Arnold 1956:260 [ref. 5315]). Carapidae: Carapinae.

Rhizophryne (subgenus of *Linophryne*) Bertelsen 1982:92 [ref. 288]. Fem. *Linophryne arborifera* Regan 1925. Type by original designation (also monotypic). Linophrynidae.

Rhizoprion Ogilby 1915:132 [ref. 3294]. Masc. *Carcharias (Scoliodon) crenidens* Klunzinger 1880:426. Type by original designation (also monotypic). Preoccupied by Jourdan 1861 in Mammalia, replaced by *Rhizoprionodon* Whitley 1929. Objective synonym of *Rhizoprionodon* Whitley 1929 (Compagno 1984:524 [ref. 6846], Cappetta 1987:126 [ref. 6348], Compagno 1988:294 [ref. 13488], Paxton et al. 1989:83 [ref. 12442]). Carcharhinidae.

Rhizoprionodon Whitley 1929:354 [ref. 4668]. Masc. *Carcharias (Scoliodon) crenidens* Klunzinger 1879:426. Type by being a replacement name. Replacement for *Rhizoprion* Ogilby 1915, preoccupied by Jourdan 1861 in Mammalia. Valid (Compagno 1973:31 [ref. 7163], Compagno 1984:524 [ref. 6846], Nakaya in Masuda et al. 1984:5 [ref. 6441], Bass et al. 1986:85 [ref. 5638], Cappetta 1987:126 [ref. 6348], Compagno 1988:294 [ref. 13488], Paxton et al. 1989:83 [ref. 12442]). Carcharhinidae.

Rhizosomichthys Miles 1943:369 [ref. 2997]. Masc. *Pygidium totae* Miles 1942:55. Type by original designation (also monotypic). Valid (Pinna 1989:31 [ref. 12630]). Trichomycteridae.

Rhoadsia Fowler 1911:497 [ref. 1384]. Fem. *Rhoadsia altipinna* Fowler 1911:498. Type by original designation (also monotypic). Valid (Géry 1977:538 [ref. 1597], Böhlke 1984:42 [ref. 13621]). Characidae.

Rhodeoides Thominot 1884:149 [ref. 4387]. Masc. *Rhodeoides vaillanti* Thominot 1884:150. Type by monotypy. Described as a cyprinodontid; referred by Myers 1953:786 [index to Jordan's Genera reprinted in 1953] to the Characidae. Characiformes.

Rhodeops (subgenus of *Acheilognathus*) Fowler 1910:479 [ref. 1380]. Masc. *Acheilognathus brevianalis* Fowler 1910:479. Type by original designation. Synonym of *Acheilognathus* Bleeker 1859 (Arai & Akai 1988:205 [ref. 6999]). Cyprinidae.

Rhodeus Agassiz 1832:134 [ref. 1511]. Masc. *Cyprinus amarus* Bloch 1782:52. Also in Agassiz 1835:37 [ref. 22]. *Cyprinus amarus* and two fossil species were mentioned in Agassiz 1832, but the fossil species were as name only; type is *amarus* by monotypy (only one available spevies included). Valid (Wu 1964:200 [ref. 13503], Sawada in Masuda et al. 1984:55 [ref. 6441], Arai & Akai 1988:209 [ref. 6999], Chen & Li in Chu & Chen 1989:124 [ref. 13584], Kottelat 1989:11 [ref. 13605]). Cyprinidae.

Rhodichthys Collett 1878:99 [ref. 885]. Masc. *Rhodichthys regina* Collett 1878:99. Type by monotypy. Also appeared as new in Collett 1878:153 [ref. 887], but with citation to Collett 1878:99. Valid (Lindberg 1973:611 [ref. 7220], Stein & Able in Whitehead et al. 1986:1282 [ref. 13677]); synonym of *Paraliparis* Collett 1878 (Kido 1988:230 [ref. 12287). Cyclopteridae: Liparinae.

Rhodoniichthys Takagi 1966:39 [ref. 4311]. Masc. *Gobius laevis* Steindachner 1880:140. Type by original designation (also monotypic). Gobiidae.

Rhodopleuriscus Fowler 1944:52 [ref. 1445]. Masc. *Leuciscus vandoisulus* Valenciennes in Cuvier & Valenciennes 1844:317. Type by original designation (also monotypic). Synonym of *Leuciscus* Cuvier 1816. Cyprinidae.

Rhodymenichthys Jordan & Evermann 1896:474 [ref. 2442]. Masc. *Gunnellus ruberrimus* Valenciennes in Cuvier & Valenciennes 1839:440. Type by original designation. Valid (Yatsu 1981:181 [ref. 4814], Amaoka in Masuda et al. 1984:304 [ref. 6441], Yatsu

1985:281 [ref. 5149], Miki 1986:949 [ref. 6330]); synonym of *Pholis* Scopoli 1777 (Makushok in Whitehead et al. 1986:1124 [ref. 13677]). Pholidae.

Rhombatractus Gill 1894:709 [ref. 1738]. Masc. *Aristeus fitzroyensis* Castelnau 1878:111. Type by being a replacement name. Replacement for *Aristeus* Castelnau 1878, preoccupied by Duvernoy 1840 in Crustacea. Synonym of *Melanotaenia* Gill 1862 (Allen 1980:474 [ref. 99], Allen & Cross 1982:44 [ref. 6251]). Atherinidae: Melanotaeniinae.

Rhombiscus Jordan & Snyder 1901:379 [ref. 2502]. Masc. *Rhombus cinnamomeus* Temminck & Schlegel 1846:180. Type by original designation (also monotypic). Synonym of *Pseudorhombus* Bleeker 1862 (Norman 1934:89 [ref. 6893], Amaoka 1969:88 [ref. 105], Desoutter 1986:428 [ref. 6212]). Paralichthyidae.

Rhombochaetodon (subgenus of *Chaetodon*) Burgess 1978:390 [ref. 700]. Masc. *Chaetodon mertensii* Cuvier 1831:47. Type by original designation. Synonym of *Exornator* Nalbant 1971 [but see *Tifia* Jordan 1922], but as a valid subgenus (Maugé & Bauchot 1984:474 [ref. 6614]). Chaetodontidae.

Rhombochirus Gill 1863:88 [ref. 1679]. Masc. *Echeneis osteochir* Cuvier in Cuvier & Valenciennes 1829:348. Type by original designation (also monotypic). Synonym of *Remora* Gill 1862 (Lachner 1973:638 [ref. 7221]). Echeneidae.

Rhombocyttus Gill 1893:115, 123 [ref. 1736]. Masc. *Cyttus traversi* Hutton 1872:19. Type by monotypy. Synonym of *Cyttus* Günther 1860 (James 1976:495 [ref. 7081], Heemstra 1980:7 [ref. 14195]). Zeidae.

Rhomboida Browne 1789:455 [ref. 669]. Fem. Not available, published in a rejected work on Official Index (Opinion 89). In the synonymy of *Vomer* Cuvier 1817 (Hureau & Tortonese 1973:384 [ref. 7198]). Synonym of *Selene* (current authors). Carangidae.

Rhomboides Goldfuss 1820:73 [ref. 1829]. Masc. *Pleuronectes rhombus* Linnaeus 1758:271. Type by being a replacement name. Apparently an unneeded substitute for *Rhombus* Cuvier. Objective synonym of *Scophthalmus* Rafinesque 1810 (Norman 1934:262 [ref. 6893]). Scophthalmidae.

Rhomboidichthys Bleeker 1856:67 [ref. 352]. Masc. *Rhomboidichthys myriaster* Temminck & Schlegel 1846:181. Type by monotypy. Synonym of *Bothus* Rafinesque 1810 (Norman 1934:220 [ref. 6893], Amaoka 1969:161 [ref. 105], Nielsen 1973:620 [ref. 6885]). Bothidae: Bothinae.

Rhomboplites Gill 1862:236, 237 [ref. 1664]. Masc. *Centropristes aurorubens* Cuvier in Cuvier & Valenciennes 1829:45. Type by monotypy. Correct spelling for genus of type species is *Centropristis*. Valid (Johnson 1980:10 [ref. 13553], Allen 1985:157 [ref. 6843]). Lutjanidae.

Rhomboplitoides Fowler 1918:33 [ref. 1396]. Masc. *Rhomboplitoides megalops* Fowler 1918:33. Type by original designation (also monotypic). Synonym of *Lutjanus* Bloch 1790 (Allen 1985:33 [ref. 6843], Allen & Talbot 1985:8 [ref. 6491]). Lutjanidae.

Rhomboserranus Fowler 1943:59 [ref. 1441]. Masc. *Rhomboserranus gracilispinis* Fowler 1943:59. Type by original designation (also monotypic). Synonym of *Doederleinia* Steindachner 1883 (Johnson 1984:464 [ref. 9681]). Acropomatidae.

Rhombosolea Günther 1862:458 [ref. 1969]. Fem. *Rhombosolea monopus* Günther 1862:459. Type by subsequent designation. Type designated by Jordan 1919:319 [ref. 4904]. Valid (Norman 1934:429 [ref. 6893], Ahlstrom et al. 1984:643 [ref. 13641], Sakamoto 1984 [ref. 5273]). Pleuronectidae: Rhombosoleinae.

Rhombosoma Regan 1914:283 [ref. 3660]. Neut. *Nematocentris novaeguineae* Ramsay & Ogilby 1887:13. Type by subsequent designation. Type apparently designated first by Jordan 1920:554 [ref. 4905]. Synonym of *Melanotaenia* Gill 1862 (Allen 1980:474 [ref. 99], Allen & Cross 1982:44 [ref. 6251]). Atherinidae: Melanotaeniinae.

Rhomboteuthis (subgenus of *Teuthis*) Fowler 1944:109 [ref. 1448]. Fem. *Acanthurus coeruleus* Bloch & Schneider 1801:214. Type by original designation (also monotypic). Synonym of *Acanthurus* Forsskål 1775. Acanthuridae.

Rhombotides Bleeker (ex Klein) 1863:235 [ref. 398]. Masc. *Chaetodon triostegus* Linnaeus 1758:274. Type by subsequent designation. Appeared in list with four species; earliest subsequent designation not researched. Acanthuridae.

Rhombotides Klein 1775:922 [ref. 2618]. Masc. Not available, published in a work that does not conform to the principle of binominal nomenclature. In the synonymy of *Acanthurus* Forsskål 1775. Acanthuridae.

Rhombus Cuvier 1816:222 [ref. 993]. Masc. *Pleuronectes rhombus* Linnaeus 1758:271. Type by absolute tautonymy. Preoccupied by da Costa 1776 in Mollusca. Synonym of *Scophthalmus* Rafinesque 1810 (Norman 1934:262 [ref. 6893]). Scophthalmidae.

Rhombus Klein 1775:918 [ref. 2618]. Masc. Also in Klein 1779:88 [ref. 4924]. Not available, published in a work that does not conform to the principle of binominal nomenclature. In the synonymy of *Scophthalmus* Rafinesque 1810 (Norman 1934:262 [ref. 6893]). Scophthalmidae.

Rhombus Lacepède 1800:321 [ref. 2709]. Masc. *Chaetodon alepidotus* Linnaeus 1766:460. Type by monotypy. Preoccupied by Walbaum (ex Klein) 1792:582 [ref. 12604]; not replaced. Synonym of *Peprilus* Cuvier 1829. Stromateidae.

Rhombus Walbaum (ex Klein) 1792:582 [ref. 4572]. *Pleuronectes rhombus* Linnaeus 1758:271. Makes available *Rhombus* Klein. Addition of species not researched. Preoccupied by *Rhombus* da Costa 1776 in Mollusca. Synonym of *Scophthalmus* Rafinesque 1810 (Norman 1934:262 [ref. 6893]). Scophthalmidae.

Rhonciscus Jordan & Evermann 1896:387 [ref. 2442]. Masc. *Pristipoma crocro* Cuvier in Cuvier & Valenciennes 1830:264. Type by original designation. Synonym of *Pomadasys* Lacepède 1802 (Roux 1973:391 [ref. 7200], Roux 1986:328 [ref. 6209]). Haemulidae.

Rhothoeca (subgenus of *Etheostoma*) Jordan 1885:868 [80] [ref. 2385]. Fem. *Poecilichthys zonalis* Cope 1868:212. Type by being a replacement name. On page 80 of separate. Unneeded replacement for *Nanostoma* Putnam 1877, not preoccupied by *Nannostomus* Günther 1872. Synonym of *Etheostoma* Rafinesque 1819 (Collette & Banarescu 1977:1456 [ref. 5845]). Percidae.

Rhyacanthias Jordan 1921:646 [ref. 2419]. Masc. *Rhyacanthias carlsmithi* Jordan 1921:647. Type by original designation (also monotypic). Synonym of *Symphysanodon* Bleeker 1878 (Anderson 1970:326 [ref. 7662]). Symphysanodontidae.

Rhyacichthys Boulenger 1901:267 [ref. 558]. Masc. *Platyptera aspro* Cuvier in Cuvier & Valenciennes 1837:321. Type by being a replacement name. Replacement for *Platyptera* Cuvier (ex Kuhl & van Hasselt) 1829, preoccupied by Meigen 1803 in Diptera. Valid (Hayashi in Masuda et al. 1984:238 [ref. 6441], Birdsong et al. 1988:180 [ref. 7303]). Rhyacichthyidae.

Rhycherus Ogilby 1907:17 [ref. 3283]. Masc. *Rhycherus wildii*

Ogilby 1907:18. Type by monotypy. Valid (Pietsch 1984:40 [ref. 5380], Pietsch 1984 [ref. 5378], Paxton et al. 1989:280 [ref. 12442]). Antennariidae.

Rhynchactis Regan 1925:565 [ref. 3677]. Fem. *Rhynchactis leptonema* Regan 1925:566. Type by monotypy. Valid (Bertelsen et al. 1981:63 [ref. 5330]). Gigantactinidae.

Rhynchias Gill in Jordan & Evermann 1898:2841 [ref. 2445]. Masc. *Ammodytes septipinnis* Pallas 1811:11. Type by original designation (also monotypic). Hypoptychidae.

Rhynchichthys Valenciennes in Cuvier & Valenciennes 1831:503 [ref. 4881]. Masc. *Rhynchichthys pelamidis* Valenciennes in Cuvier & Valenciennes 1831:504. Type by monotypy. Synonym of *Myripristis* Cuvier 1829 (Woods & Sonoda 1973:368 [ref. 6899]). Holocentridae.

Rhynchobatis Philippi 1857:271 [ref. 3462]. Fem. *Tarsistes philippii* Jordan 1919:343. Type by subsequent monotypy. Jordan 1919:343 [ref. 4904] provided a new name *Tarsistes* (regarding *Rhynchobatis* as preoccupied by *Rhynchobatus*) and a species, *T. philippii*. Probably available, with type by subsequent monotypy. Based on a dried head of a ray. Rhinobatidae: Rhinobatinae.

Rhynchobatus Müller & Henle 1837:116 [ref. 3067]. Masc. *Rhinobatus laevis* Bloch & Schneider 1801:354. Type by monotypy. Also in Müller & Henle 1841:111 [ref. 3069]. *Rhinchobatis* is a misspelling. Valid (Nakaya in Masuda et al. 1984:12 [ref. 6441], Compagno 1986:131 [ref. 5648], Cappetta 1987:134 [ref. 6348], Paxton et al. 1989:54 [ref. 12442]). Rhinobatidae: Rhynchobatinae.

Rhynchobdella Bloch & Schneider 1801:478 (liv) [ref. 471]. Fem. *Rhynchobdella orientalis* Bloch & Schneider 1801:478 (= *Ophidium aculeatum* Bloch 1786:72). Type by subsequent designation. Type designated by Jordan 1917:59 [ref. 2407]. Travers (1984:142) gives type as *Rhynchobdella sinensis* Bleeker 1870. Misspelled *Rynchobdella* by Bloch & Schneider on p. liv [p. wrongly typeset as xliv]. Valid (Travers 1984:142 [ref. 5147]); synonym of *Macrognathus* Lacepède 1800 (Sufi 1956:99 [ref. 12498], Roberts 1986:98 [ref. 5802], Roberts 1989:178 [ref. 6439]). Mastacembelidae.

Rhynchoceratias Regan 1925:566 [ref. 3677]. Masc. *Rhynchoceratias brevirostris* Regan 1925:566. Type by subsequent designation. Type designated by Fowler 1936:1348 [ref. 6546]. Synonym of *Himantolophus* Reinhardt 1837 (Bertelsen & Krefft 1988:35 [ref. 6615]). Himantolophidae.

Rhynchoconger Jordan & Hubbs 1925:192, 196 [ref. 2486]. Masc. *Leptocephalus ectenurus* Jordan & Richardson 1909:171. Type by original designation (also monotypic). Valid (Asano in Masuda et al. 1984:28 [ref. 6441], Paxton et al. 1989:142 [ref. 12442], Smith 1989:525 [ref. 13285]). Congridae: Congrinae.

Rhynchocymba Jordan & Hubbs 1925:192, 195 [ref. 2486]. Fem. *Leptocephalus nystromi* Jordan & Snyder 1901:853. Type by original designation. Synonym of *Gnathophis* Kaup 1860 (Blache et al. 1973:242 [ref. 7185], Smith 1989:521 [ref. 13285]). Congridae: Congrinae.

Rhynchocypris Günther 1889:225 [ref. 2016]. Fem. *Rhynchocypris variegata* Günther 1889:225. Type by monotypy. Valid (Howes 1985:60 [ref. 5274], Travers 1989:198 [ref. 13578]); formerly regarded as a synonym of *Phoxinus* Rafinesque 1820. Cyprinidae.

Rhynchodoras Klausewitz & Rössel 1961:45 [ref. 2617]. Masc. *Rhynchodoras xingui* Klausewitz & Rössel 1961:46. Type by original designation (also monotypic). Valid (Glodek 1976 [ref. 7080], Burgess 1989:225 [ref. 12860] as *Rhyncodoras*). Doradidae.

Rhynchogadus Tortonese 1948:38 [ref. 4415]. Masc. *Hypsirhynchus hepaticus* Facciolà 1884:112. Type by being a replacement name. Replacement for *Hypsirhynchus* Facciola 1884, preoccupied by Günther 1858 in Reptilia. *Olssonichthys* Fowler 1958 is an unneeded replacement for *Hypsirhynchus*. Valid (Cohen 1973:326 [ref. 6589], Fahay & Markle 1984:266 [ref. 13653], Cohen in Whitehead et al. 1986:722 [ref. 13676]). Moridae.

Rhynchohyalus Barnard 1925:130 [ref. 192]. Masc. *Hyalorhynchus natalensis* Gilchrist & von Bonde 1924:4. Type by being a replacement name. Replacement for *Hyalorhynchus* Gilchrist & von Bonde 1924, preoccupied by Ogilby 1910 in fishes. Valid (Cohen 1973:157 [ref. 6589], Cohen in Whitehead et al. 1984:398 [ref. 13675], Ahlstrom et al. 1984:156 [ref. 13627], Fujii in Masuda et al. 1984:41 [ref. 6441], Heemstra 1986:217 [ref. 5660], Paxton et al. 1989:170 [ref. 12442]). Opisthoproctidae.

Rhynchopelates (subgenus of *Pelates*) Fowler 1931:358, 363 [ref. 1407]. Masc. *Therapon oxyrhynchus* Schlegel in Temminck & Schlegel 1842:16. Type by original designation (also monotypic). Valid (Vari 1978:267 [ref. 4514] and Akazaki in Masuda et al. 1984:173 [ref. 6441] but as *Rhyncopelates*). Terapontidae.

Rhynchorhamphus (subgenus of *Hemirhamphus (sic)*) Fowler 1928:75 [ref. 5596]. Masc. *Hemiramphus georgii* Valenciennes in Cuvier & Valenciennes 1847:37. Type by original designation (also monotypic). Valid (Collette 1976 [ref. 7107], Parin et al. 1980:99 [ref. 6895], Collette et al. 1984:337 [ref. 11422] as *Rhychorhamphus*, Collette & Su 1986:287 [ref. 5998], Paxton et al. 1989:339 [ref. 12442]). Hemiramphidae.

Rhynchostomias (subgenus of *Eustomias*) Regan & Trewavas 1930: 72, 94 [ref. 3681]. Masc. *Eustomias parri* Regan & Trewavas 1930:94. Type by original designation (also monotypic). Synonym of *Eustomias* Vaillant 1888 (Gibbs in Morrow & Gibbs 1964:377 [ref. 6962], Morrow 1973:137 [ref. 7175]). Melanostomiidae.

Rhynchostracion Fraser-Brunner 1935:316, 319 [ref. 1490]. Neut. *Ostracion nasus* Bloch 1785:118. Type by original designation. Valid (Tyler 1980:239 [ref. 4477], Arai 1983:203 [ref. 14249]). Ostraciidae: Ostraciinae.

Rhynchotes Troschel (ex Bibron) 1856:88 [ref. 12559]. Masc. *Tetraodon gronovii* Cuvier 1829:369. Appeared first as *Rhynchote* Bibron in Duméril 1855:280 [ref. 297]; latinized by Troschel 1856 as above, also by Hollard 1857:319 [ref. 2186] as *Rhynchotus*. First technical addition of species and subsequent type designation not researched. Type above as given by Jordan 1919:263 [ref. 2410]. Synonym of *Canthigaster* Swainson 1839 (Allen & Randall 1977:478 [ref. 6714]). Tetraodontidae.

Rhytejulis (subgenus of *Stethojulis*) Fowler & Bean 1928:232, 241 [ref. 1475]. Fem. *Labrus trilineatus* Bloch & Schneider 1801:253. Type by original designation. Synonym of *Stethojulis* Günther 1861. Labridae.

Rhytidostomus Heckel 1843:1023 [ref. 2066]. Masc. *Catostomus elongatus* Lesueur 1817:103. Type by subsequent designation. Type designated by Jordan & Evermann 1896:168 [ref. 2442]. Synonym of *Cycleptus* Rafinesque 1819. Catostomidae.

Rhytiodus Kner 1858:78 [ref. 13404]. Masc. *Rhytiodus microlepis* Kner 1858:78. Type by subsequent designation. Also appeared in Kner 1859:165 [ref. 2631]. Type designated by Eigenmann 1910:425 [ref. 1224]. Valid (Géry 1977:178 [ref. 1597], Winterbottom 1980:2 [ref. 4755], Vari 1983:5 [ref. 5419], Géry 1987 [ref.

6739]). Curimatidae: Anostominae.

Ribeiroa Jordan 1920:564, 571 [ref. 4905]. Fem. *Paragonus sertorii* Miranda-Ribeiro 1918:788. Type by being a replacement name. Replacement for *Paragonus* Miranda-Ribeiro 1918, preoccupied by Gill 1861 and Guichenot 1869 in fishes. Agonidae.

Ribeiroclinus Pinto 1965:15 [ref. 3480]. Masc. *Ribeiroclinus santanensis* Pinto 1965:15. Type by original designation (also monotypic). Valid (see Stephens & Springer 1974:4 [ref. 7149]). Clinidae.

Richardsonia Castelnau 1872:112 [ref. 757]. Fem. *Richardsonia insignis* Castelnau 1872:112. Type by monotypy. Preoccupied by Steindachner 1866 in fishes, replaced by *Paristiopterus* Bleeker 1876 and by *Macullochia* Waite 1910. Objective synonym of *Paristiopterus* Bleeker 1876 (Hardy 1983:188 [ref. 5385]). Pentacerotidae.

Richardsonia Steindachner 1866:469 [ref. 4210]. Fem. *Argentina retropinna* Richardson 1845:121. Type by monotypy. Objective synonym of *Retropinna* Gill 1862 (McDowall 1979:90 [ref. 7021]). Retropinnidae: Retropinninae.

Richardsonichthys Smith 1958:169 [ref. 4120]. Masc. *Apistus leucogaster* Richardson 1848:5. Type by original designation (also monotypic). Valid (Washington et al. 1984:440 [ref. 13660], Paxton et al. 1989:447 [ref. 12442]). Scorpaenidae: Tetraroginae.

Richardsonius Girard 1856:201 [ref. 1810]. Masc. *Abramis balteatus* Richardson 1836:301. Type by subsequent designation. Type designated by Jordan & Gilbert 1877:91 [ref. 4907]. Valid. Cyprinidae.

Richia Coker 1926:106 [ref. 5553]. Fem. *Richia brevispina* Coker 1926:106. Type by original designation (also monotypic). Preoccupied by Grote 1887 in Lepidoptera, replaced by *Richiella* Coker 1927. Synonym of subgenus *Catonotus* Agassiz 1854 of genus *Etheostoma* Rafinesque 1819 (Collette & Banarescu 1977:1456 [ref. 5845], Braasch & Mayden 1985:3 [ref. 6874]). Percidae.

Richiella Coker 1927:18 [ref. 882]. Fem. *Richia brevispina* Coker 1926:106. Type by being a replacement name. Replacement for *Richia* Coker 1926, preoccupied by Grote 1887 in Lepidoptera. Synonym of subgenus *Catonotus* Agassiz 1854 of genus *Etheostoma* Rafinesque 1819 (Collette & Banarescu 1977:1457 [ref. 5845], Braasch & Mayden 1985:3 [ref. 6874]). Percidae.

Ricola Isbrücker & Nijssen 1978:182 [ref. 2306]. Masc. *Loricaria macrops* Regan 1904:290. Type by original designation (also monotypic). Valid (Isbrücker 1980:114 [ref. 2303], Isbrücker 1981:56 [ref. 5522], Burgess 1989:443 [ref. 12860]). Loricariidae.

Rictugobius Koumans in Smith 1932:258 [ref. 4050]. Masc. Not available, name mentioned in passing in synonymy of *Mahidolia* Smith. In the synonymy of *Waitea* Jordan & Seale 1906 (Maugé 1986:386 [ref. 6218]). Gobiidae.

Ricuzenius Jordan & Starks 1904:242 [ref. 2528]. Masc. *Ricuzenius pinetorum* Jordan & Starks 1904:243. Type by original designation (also monotypic). Valid (Washington et al. 1984:443 [ref. 13660], Yabe in Masuda et al. 1984:324 [ref. 6441], Yabe 1985:111 [ref. 11522]). Cottidae.

Riekertia Smith 1952:(315) 325 [ref. 4084]. Fem. *Riekertia ellisi* Smith 1952:325. Type by original designation. Valid (Hutchins 1986:360 [ref. 5673]). Batrachoididae.

Rimicola Jordan & Evermann in Jordan 1896:231 [ref. 2395]. Masc. *Gobiesox muscarum* Meek & Pierson 1895:571. Type by original designation. Valid (Briggs 1955:75 [ref. 637], Allen [L. G.] 1984:629 [ref. 13673]). Gobiesocidae: Gobiesocinae.

Rincoxus Rafinesque 1815:93 [ref. 3584]. Not available, name only; for an eel. Anguilliformes.

Rineloricaria Bleeker 1862:3 [ref. 393]. Fem. *Loricaria lima* Kner 1854:89. Type by original designation (also monotypic). Spelled *Rhineloricaria* by Eigenmann 1910:413 [ref. 1224]. Valid (Isbrücker 1980:103 [ref. 2303], Reis 1983 [ref. 12857], Isbrücker & Nijssen 1984 [ref. 9845], Burgess 1989:441 [ref. 12860], Malabarba 1989:155 [ref. 14217]). Loricariidae.

Rinoctes Parr 1952:263 [ref. 3381]. Masc. *Bathytroctes nasutus* Koefoed 1927:50. Type by original designation (also monotypic). Valid (Markle & Merrett 1980 [ref. 6948], Markle & Quéro in Whitehead et al. 1984:248 [ref. 13675], Anderson et al. 1985 [ref. 5164], Markle 1986:221 [ref. 5687]). Alepocephalidae.

Rioraja Whitley 1939:254 [ref. 4695]. Fem. *Uraptera agassizii* Müller & Henle 1841:155. Type by being a replacement name. Replacement for *Uraptera* Müller & Henle 1837, preoccupied by Billberg 1820 in Lepidoptera. Synonym of *Raja* Linnaeus 1758. Rajidae.

Risor (subgenus of *Garmannia*) Ginsburg 1933:56 [ref. 1799]. Masc. *Garmannia binghami* Parr 1930:124. Type by original designation, also monotypic (2 additional species questionably included). Valid (Birdsong et al. 1988:189 [ref. 7303]). Gobiidae.

Rissola Jordan & Evermann 1896:483 [ref. 2442]. Fem. *Ophidium marginatum* DeKay 1842:315. Type by original designation (also monotypic). Correct spelling for genus of type species is *Ophidion*. Synonym of *Ophidion* Linnaeus 1758 (Cohen & Nielsen 1978:16 [ref. 881]). Ophidiidae: Ophidiinae.

Rita Bleeker 1853:122 [ref. 341]. Fem. *Rita buchanani* Bleeker 1853:123 (= *Pimelodus rita* Hamilton 1822:165, 376). Type by monotypy. *R. buchanani* Bleeker is an unneeded substitute for *Pimelodus rita* Hamilton. Valid (Jayaram 1977:12 [ref. 7005], Jayaram 1981:190 [ref. 6497], Burgess 1989:66 [ref. 12860] but dating to Bleeker 1859). Bagridae.

Riukiuia Fowler 1946:200 [ref. 1456]. Fem. *Riukiuia poecila* Fowler 1946:201. Type by original designation (also monotypic). Synonym of *Hetereleotris* Bleeker 1874 (Akihito & Meguro 1981:331 [ref. 5508], Hoese 1986:3 [ref. 5996]). Gobiidae.

Rivasella Fernández-Yépez 1948:56 [ref. 1316]. Fem. *Curimatus (Steindachnerina) melaniris* Fowler 1940:253. Type by original designation. Synonym of *Steindachnerina* Fowler 1906 (Vari 1989:6 [ref. 9189]). Curimatidae: Curimatinae.

Riverina Castelnau 1872:64 [ref. 757]. Fem. *Riverina fluviatilis* Castelnau 1872:64. Type by monotypy. Synonym of *Macquaria* Cuvier 1830 (Paxton et al. 1989:513 [ref. 12442]). Percichthyidae.

Rivulichthys Myers 1927:118 [ref. 3098]. Masc. *Rivulus rondoni* Miranda-Ribeiro 1920:7. Type by original designation (also monotypic). Synonym of *Trigonectes* Myers 1925 (Parenti 1981:484 [ref. 7066]). Aplocheilidae: Rivulinae.

Rivulus Poey 1860:307 [ref. 3499]. Masc. *Rivulus cylindraceus* Poey 1860:308, 383. Type by monotypy. Valid (Parenti 1981:481 [ref. 7066], Costa 1989 [ref. 14319]). Aplocheilidae: Rivulinae.

Roa Jordan 1923:63 [ref. 2420]. Fem. *Loa excelsa* Jordan 1922:652. Type by being a replacement name. Replacement for *Loa* Jordan 1922, preoccupied by Stiles 1902 in worms. Synonym of *Chaetodon* Linnaeus 1758, but as a valid subgenus (Burgess 1978:347 [ref. 700], Maugé & Bauchot 1984:471 [ref. 6614]). Chaetodontidae.

Roaops Maugé & Bauchot 1984:476 [ref. 6614]. Masc. *Chaetodon burgessi* Allen & Starck 1973:17. Type by original designation.

Valid (Pyle 1988 [ref. 6613]). Chaetodontidae.

Robia Pietsch 1979:12 [ref. 3474]. Fem. *Robia legula* Pietsch 1979:13. Type by original designation (also monotypic). Caulophrynidae.

Robinsia Böhlke & Smith 1967:2 [ref. 612]. Fem. *Robinsia catherinae* Böhlke & Smith 1967:3. Type by original designation (also monotypic). Valid (Smith 1989:80 [ref. 13285]). Chlopsidae.

Robinsichthys Birdsong 1988:438 [ref. 6572]. Masc. *Robinsichthys arrowsmithensis* Birdsong 1988:439. Type by original designation (also monotypic). Gobiidae.

Roccus Mitchill 1814:24 [ref. 3030]. Masc. *Roccus striatus* Mitchill 1814:24. Type by subsequent designation. Gill 1860:112 [ref. 1793] redefined the genus but did not fix the type; Gill 1898:vii [ref. 7956] stated, "*Roccus* was revived as a generic name [by Gill, 1860] but restricted to the typical species and another closely related one unknown to Mitchill," but that does not technically fix the type either. Type designation may date to Jordan 1917:86 [ref. 2407]. Synonym of *Morone* Mitchill 1814 when regarded as congeneric (see Whitehead & Wheeler 1966:76 [ref. 14481]). Moronidae.

Roeboexodon Géry 1959:346 [ref. 1579]. Masc. *Exodon guyanensis* Puyo 1948:78. Type by original designation (also monotypic). Valid (Géry 1977:322 [ref. 1597]). Characidae.

Roeboides (subgenus of *Anacyrtus*) Günther 1864:345, 347-348 [ref. 1974]. Masc. *Epicyrtus microlepis* Reinhardt 1849:46. Type by subsequent designation. Described in key (p. 345) as a section or subgenus of *Anacyrtus* with corresponding species on p. 347-348. Type designated by Eigenmann 1910:445 [ref. 1224](not by Jordan 1919:333 [4904]). Spelled *Rhaeboides* by Berg 1899:94 [not investigated]. Valid (Géry 1977:315 [ref. 1597]). Characidae.

Roestes (subgenus of *Anacyrtus*) Günther 1864:345, 347 [ref. 1974]. *Cynopotamus molossus* Kner 1860:51. Type by monotypy. Described in key (p. 345) as a section or subgenus of *Anacyrtus* with corresponding single species on p. 347. Same as *Lycodon* Kner 1860 (preoccupied) but Günther does not indicate he was providing a replacement name. Valid (Menezes 1974 [ref. 7129], Géry 1977:311 [ref. 1597]). Characidae.

Rogadius Jordan & Richardson 1908:630 [ref. 2491]. Masc. *Platycephalus asper* Cuvier in Cuvier & Valenciennes 1829:257. Type by original designation. Valid (Knapp 1979:48 [ref. 14196], Ochiai in Masuda et al. 1984:321 [ref. 6441], Paxton et al. 1989:470 [ref. 12442]). Platycephalidae.

Rogenia Valenciennes in Cuvier & Valenciennes 1847:340 [ref. 1012]. Fem. *Clupea alba* Yarrell 1829:137. Type by monotypy. Synonym of *Clupea* Linnaeus 1758 (Svetovidov 1973:99 [ref. 7169], Whitehead 1967:17 [ref. 6464], Whitehead 1985:115 [ref. 5141]). Clupeidae.

Rohanus Chu 1935:12 [ref. 832]. Masc. *Ischikauia transmontana* Nichols 1925:7. Type by original designation (also monotypic). Valid (Yih & Wu 1964:70 [ref. 13499]); synonym of *Anabarilius* Cockerel 1923 (Chen in Chu & Chen 1989:56 [ref. 13584]). Cyprinidae.

Rohita Valenciennes in Cuvier & Valenciennes 1842:242 [ref. 1009]. Fem. *Cyprinus rohita* Hamilton 1822:301, 388. Type by absolute tautonymy. Type not *Rohita nandina* Valenciennes as designated by Bleeker 1863:25 [ref. 4859]. Synonym of *Labeo* Cuvier 1816. Cyprinidae.

Rohitichthys Bleeker 1859:424 [ref. 370]. Masc. *Labeo senegalensis* Valenciennes in Cuvier & Valenciennes 1842:486. Type by subsequent monotypy. Apparently appeared first in key, without included species. One species included by Bleeker 1860:114, 191 [ref. 380]. Synonym of *Labeo* Cuvier 1816 (Lévêque & Daget 1984:305 [ref. 6186]). Cyprinidae.

Rohitodes (subgenus of *Rohita*) Bleeker 1860:159, 162 [ref. 380]. Masc. *Labeo cephalus* Valenciennes in Cuvier & Valenciennes 1842:265. Type by monotypy. Cyprinidae.

Rohtee Sykes 1839:58 [ref. 4306]. *Rohtee ogilbii* Sykes 1839:58. Type by subsequent designation. Signature for v. 4, no. 21, dated Sept. 1839. Also appeared as Sykes 1840 (? month):364. Type designated by Bleeker 1863:201 [ref. 397] and 1863:28 [ref. 4859]. Valid (Jayaram 1981:111 [ref. 6497], Chu & Kottelat 1989:1 [ref. 12575]). Cyprinidae.

Rohteichthys Bleeker 1859:431 [ref. 370]. Masc. *Barbus microlepis* Bleeker 1850:12. Type by subsequent monotypy. Apparently appeared first in key, without included species. One species included by Bleeker 1860:281, 395 [ref. 380]. Not to be confused with *Rohitichthys* Bleeker. Valid (Roberts 1989:78 [ref. 6439]). Cyprinidae.

Roloffia Clausen 1966:338 [ref. 844]. Fem. *Aphyosemion occidentale* Clausen 1966:331. Type by original designation. Not available; on Official Index (Opinion 1010) as a junior objective synonym of *Callopanchax* Myers 1933. In the synonymy of *Aphyosemion* Myers 1924 (Wildekamp et al. 1986:196 [ref. 6198]). Aplocheilidae: Aplocheilinae.

Romanichthys Dumitrescu, Banarescu & Stoica 1957:225 [ref. 1155]. Masc. *Romanichthys valsanicola* Dumitrescu, Banarescu, Stoica 1957:230. Type by original designation (also monotypic). Valid (Collette & Banarescu 1977:1459 [ref. 5845]). Percidae.

Romanogobio (subgenus of *Gobio*) Banarescu 1961:332 [ref. 211]. Masc. *Gobio kessleri* Dybowski 1862:71. Type by original designation. Also in Banarescu 1962 [ref. 212]. Valid subgenus of *Gobio* Cuvier 1816 (Banarescu & Nalbant 1973:143 [ref. 173]). Cyprinidae.

Roncador Jordan & Gilbert 1880:28 [ref. 2466]. *Corvina stearnsii* Steindachner 1875:50. Type by original designation (also monotypic). Proposed as the type of "a distinct genus or subgenus [of *Sciaenops*]..." Valid. Sciaenidae.

Ronchifex Gistel 1848:VIII [ref. 1822]. *Bodianus bodianus* Bloch 1790:24. Type by being a replacement name. Replacement for *Cossyphus* Valenciennes 1839, preoccupied by Olivier 1791 in Coleoptera and by Rafinesque 1815 and Dumont 1823 in Aves. Synonym of *Bodianus* Bloch 1790. Labridae.

Rondeletia Goode & Bean 1895:454 [ref. 5767]. Fem. *Rondeletia bicolor* Goode & Bean 1895:454. Type by monotypy. Also as new in Goode & Bean 1896:68 [ref. 1848]. Valid (Uyeno in Masuda et al. 1984:115 [ref. 6441], Paxton in Whitehead et al. 1986:526 [ref. 13676], Paxton & Bray 1986:434 [ref. 5703], Paxton et al. 1989:382 [ref. 12442]). Rondeletiidae.

Ronquilus Jordan & Starks 1895:838 [ref. 2522]. Masc. *Bathymaster jordani* Gilbert 1888:554. Type by monotypy. Valid. Bathymasteridae.

Rooseveltia Jordan & Evermann in Jordan & Seale 1906:265 [ref. 2497]. Fem. *Serranus brighami* Seale 1901:7. Type by original designation. Synonym of *Pristipomoides* Bleeker 1852 (Allen 1985:141 [ref. 6843], Akazaki & Iwatsuki 1987:326 [ref. 6699], but with type as *R. aloha* Jordan & Snyder). Lutjanidae.

Rooseveltiella Eigenmann 1915:240 [ref. 1232]. Fem. *Pygocentrus nattereri* Kner 1858:166. Type by original designation. Preoccupied by Fox in Siphonaptera [not investigated]; replaced by

Taddyella Ihering 1928. Synonym of subgenus *Taddyella* of genus *Serrasalmus* Lacepède 1803 (Géry 1976:52 [ref. 14199]). Characidae: Serrasalminae.

Rosanthias Tanaka 1917:198 [ref. 4330]. Masc. *Rosanthias amoenus* Tanaka 1917:198. Type by monotypy. Appeared first in Japanese (15 July), English version (28 Nov.) 1918:503 [ref. 6037]. Species as *amaenus* in 1917 a misprint for *amoenus* (see synonymy in 1918:503). Serranidae: Anthiinae.

Rosaura Tucker 1954:167 [ref. 4470]. Fem. *Rosaura rotunda* Tucker 1954:167. Type by monotypy. Valid (Johnson 1984:199 [ref. 13623], Johnson 1986:273 [ref. 5677], Paxton et al. 1989:245 [ref. 12442]). Giganturidae.

Rosenblattia Mead & De Falla 1965:263 [ref. 2955]. Fem. *Rosenblattia robusta* Mead & De Falla 1965:263. Type by original designation (also monotypic). Valid (Johnson 1984:464 [ref. 9681], Gon 1986:560 [ref. 5657], Paxton et al. 1989:557 [ref. 12442]). Epigonidae.

Rosenblattichthys Johnson 1974:451 [ref. 2361]. Masc. *Phanops volucris* Rofen 1966:595. Type by original designation. Valid (Johnson 1974:95 [ref. 7050], Johnson in Whitehead et al. 1984:485 [ref. 13675], Johnson 1986:266 [ref. 5677], Okiyama & Johnson 1986 [ref. 5191], Paxton et al. 1989:233 [ref. 12442]). Scopelarchidae.

Rosicola (subgenus of *Sebastodes*) Jordan & Evermann 1896:429 [ref. 2442]. Masc. *Sebastosomus pinniger* Gill 1864:147. Type by original designation. Synonym of *Sebastes* Cuvier 1829. Scorpaenidae: Sebastinae.

Rostrogobio Taranetz 1937:114 [ref. 4340]. Masc. *Rostrogobio amurensis* Taranetz 1937:114. Type by monotypy. Synonym of *Microphysogobio* Mori 1934 (Banarescu & Nalbant 1973:244 [ref. 173]); valid (Lu, Luo & Chen 1977:529 [ref. 13495]). Cyprinidae.

Rostroraja (subgenus of *Raja*) Hulley 1972:77 [ref. 5611]. Fem. *Raja alba* Lacepède 1803:661. Type by original designation (also monotypic). Synonym of *Raja* Linnaeus 1758, but as a valid subgenus (Stehmann 1973:66 [ref. 7168], Stehmann 1976:170 [ref. 7085]). Rajidae.

Rotuma Springer 1988:531 [ref. 6683]. Masc. *Rotuma lewisi* Springer 1988:535. Type by original designation (also monotypic). Genus stated to be masculine by author (p. 535). Xenisthmidae.

Roughleyia Whitley 1931:318 [ref. 4672]. Fem. *Chrysophrys australis* Günther 1859:494. Type by original designation. Synonym of *Sparus* Linnaeus 1758. Sparidae.

Rouleina (subgenus of *Eurypharynx*) Fowler 1925:2 [ref. 1401]. Fem. *Eurypharynx richardi* Roule 1914:1821. Type by original designation (also monotypic). Preoccupied by Jordan 1923 in fishes, replaced by *Jordanites* Fowler 1925. Synonym of *Eurypharynx* Vaillant 1882 (Böhlke 1966:610 [ref. 5256], Bauchot 1973:218 [ref. 7184], Bertelsen et al. 1989:649 [ref. 13293]). Eurypharyngidae.

Rouleina Jordan 1923:122 [ref. 2421]. Fem. *Xenodermichthys guentheri* Alcock 1892:359. Type by original designation (also monotypic). Valid (Krefft 1973:91 [ref. 7166], Uyeno & Kishida 1977 [ref. 7016], Markle 1978 [ref. 7030], Markle & Quéro in Whitehead et al. 1984:248 [ref. 13675], Machida in Masuda et al. 1984:43 [ref. 6441], Markle 1986:221 [ref. 5687], Paxton et al. 1989:210 [ref. 12442] Alepocephalidae.

Roxasella Fowler 1943:87 [ref. 1441]. Fem. *Roxasella fusiforme* Fowler 1943:87. Type by original designation (also monotypic). Preoccupied by Merino 1936 in insects, replaced by *Cirrinasus* Schultz 1960. Synonym of *Matsubaraea* Taki 1953 (Iwamoto 1980:113 [ref. 6933]). Percophidae: Hemerocoetinae.

Ruanoho Hardy 1986:157 [ref. 6139]. *Trypterigium decemdigitatus* Clarke 1879:292. Type by original designation. Correct spelling for genus of type species is *Trypterygion*. Tripterygiidae.

Rubellus Fitzinger 1873:152, 162 [ref. 1337]. Masc. *Cyprinus rutilus* Linnaeus 1758:324. Type by subsequent designation. Two included species (p. 152); earliest type designation found that of Jordan 1919:369 [ref. 4904]). Objective synonym of *Rutilus* Rafinesque 1820 (Howes 1981:46 [ref. 14200]). Cyprinidae.

Ruboralga Whitley 1931:326 [ref. 4672]. Fem. *Scorpaena jacksoniensis* Steindachner 1866:438. Type by original designation. Scorpaenidae: Scorpaeninae.

Rubusqualus (subgenus of *Echinorhinus*) Whitley 1931:311 [ref. 4672]. Masc. *Echinorhinus (Rubusqualus) mccoyi* Whitley 1931: 311. Type by original designation (also monotypic). Synonym of *Echinorhinus* Blainville 1816 (Compagno 1984:25 [ref. 6474]). Echinorhinidae.

Rudarius Jordan & Fowler 1902:270 [ref. 2457]. Masc. *Rudarius ercodes* Jordan & Fowler 1902:270. Type by original designation (also monotypic). Valid (Hutchins 1977:49 [ref. 2283], Matsuura 1979:165 [ref. 7019], Tyler 1980:176 [ref. 4477], Arai 1983:200 [ref. 14249], Aboussouan & Leis 1984:452 [ref. 13661], Matsuura in Masuda et al. 1984:361 [ref. 6441], Matsuura 1989 [ref. 12751]). Monacanthidae.

Rugogymnocypris Yeuh & Hwang 1964 [ref. 12823]. Fem. *Rugogymnocypris tibetanus* Yueh & Hwang 1964. Original not seen. Synonym of *Gymnocypris* Günther 1868 (Wu 1987:43 [ref. 12822]). Cyprinidae.

Runcinatus Whitley 1929:356 [ref. 4668]. Masc. *Solegnathus dunckeri* Whitley 1927:293. Type by original designation (also monotypic). Synonym of *Solegnathus* Swainson 1839 (Dawson 1982:140 [ref. 5442]); as a valid subgenus (Dawson 1985:169 [ref. 6541]). Syngnathidae: Syngnathinae.

Runula Jordan & Bollman 1890:171 [ref. 2433]. Fem. *Runula azalea* Jordan & Bollman 1890:171. Type by original designation (also monotypic). Synonym of *Plagiotremus* Gill 1865, but as a valid subgenus (Smith-Vaniz 1976:108 [ref. 4144]). Blenniidae.

Runulops (subgenus of *Petroscirtes*) Ogilby 1910:55 [ref. 3288]. Masc. *Blennechis fasciatus* Jenyns 1842:84. Type by subsequent designation. Perhaps proposed as a genus and not a subgenus based on style of key. Described without species, "...founded on two South American species described by Jenyns." First addition of species and type designation not researched. Synonym of *Hypsoblennius* Gill 1861 (Bath 1977:186 [ref. 208]). Blenniidae.

Rupiscartes (subgenus of *Salaris*) Swainson 1839:79, 182, 275 [ref. 4303]. Masc. *Salarias alticus* Valenciennes in Cuvier & Valenciennes 1836:337. Type by monotypy. Synonym of *Alticus* Commerson 1800 (Smith-Vaniz & Springer 1971:14 [ref. 4145], Bath 1986:355 [ref. 6217]). Blenniidae.

Rupisuga Swainson 1839:147, 339 [ref. 4303]. Fem. *Rupisuga nicensis* Swainson 1839:339 (= *Lepodogaster balbis* Risso 1810:73). Type by monotypy. Appeared without distinguishing features in Swainson 1838:216, 224 [ref. 4302]. Swainson's *R. nicensis* is an unneeded substitute for *L. balbis* Risso. Synonym of *Gouania* Nardo 1833 (Briggs 1955:22 [ref. 637], Briggs 1973:653 [ref. 7222]). Gobiesocidae: Gobiesocinae.

Ruppelia Castelnau 1873:51 [ref. 758]. Fem. *Ruppelia prolongata* Castelnau 1873:1873 (51). Type by monotypy. See account of

Bleeckeria Castelnau. Regarded as misspelled, emended to *Ruppellia* and therefore preoccupied by Swainson 1839 in Gobiidae; not replaced. Synonym of *Paraplesiops* Bleeker 1875 (Hoese & Kuiter 1984:9 [ref. 5300]). Plesiopidae.

Ruppellia Swainson 1839:184, 281 [ref. 4303]. Fem. *Gobius echinocephalus* Rüppell 1830:136. Type by monotypy. Spelled *Ruppelia* on p. 184, *Rupellia* on p. 281. Corrected to *Ruppellia* by ICZN (Opinion 27). Synonym of *Paragobiodon* Bleeker 1873 (Maugé 1986:379 [ref. 6218] as *Ruppelia*). Gobiidae.

Ruscariops Hubbs 1926:12 [ref. 6069]. Masc. *Ruscariops creaseri* Hubbs 1926:12. Type by original designation (also monotypic). Synonym of *Artedius* Girard 1856 (Bolin 1944:43 [ref. 6379]). Cottidae.

Ruscarius Jordan & Starks 1895:805 [ref. 2522]. Masc. *Ruscarius meanyi* Jordan & Starks 1895:805. Type by original designation (also monotypic). Valid (Begle 1989:646 [ref. 12739]). Cottidae.

Rusciculus Greeley 1901:13 [ref. 1889]. Masc. *Rusciculus rimensis* Greeley 1901:13. Type by monotypy. Synonym of *Oligocottus* Girard 1856 (Bolin 1944:62 [ref. 6379]). Cottidae.

Rusichthys Winterbottom 1979:298 [ref. 4754]. Masc. *Rusichthys plesiomorphus* Winterbottom 1979:299. Type by original designation (also monotypic). Valid (Winterbottom 1986:27 [ref. 5727]). Pseudochromidae: Congrogadinae.

Rusulus Starks & Mann 1911:13 [ref. 4199]. Masc. *Rusulus saburrae* Starks & Mann 1911:14. Type by monotypy. Synonym of *Clinocottus* Gill 1861. Cottidae.

Rutilus Rafinesque 1820:240 [ref. 7310]. Masc. *Leuciscus rutilus* Linnaeus 1758:324. Type by original designation (also by absolute tautonymy). Also appeared in Rafinesque 1820:50 (Dec.) [ref. 3592]. Valid (Yang & Hwang 1964:12 [ref. 13497], Howes 1981:45 [ref. 14200], Bogutskaya 1987:936 [ref. 13521]). Cyprinidae.

Ruvettus Cocco 1829:21 Masc. *Ruvettus pretiosus* Cocco 1829:21. Type by monotypy. Usually dated to 1833 in different reference; above from Fowler as Giorn. Sci. Lett. Art. Sicil. Palermo, v. 17:21 (not investigated). *Rovettus* and *Rovetus* are misspellings. Valid (Parin & Bekker 1973:460 [ref. 7206], Collette et al. 1984:600 [ref. 11421], Nakamura in Masuda et al. 1984:227 [ref. 6441], Parin in Whitehead et al. 1986:972 [ref. 13676], Nakamura 1986:828 [ref. 5696]). Gempylidae.

Rynchana Richardson 1845:44 [ref. 3740]. Fem. *Rynchana greyi* Richardson 1845:45. Type by monotypy. Originally (1845) spelled *Rynchana* and that spelling should stand; spelled *Rhynchana* by Richardson on p. v. published in 1848, where Richardson referred genus to *Gonorhynchus*. Synonym of *Gonorynchus* Scopoli 1777. Gonorynchidae.

Rypticus Cuvier 1829:144 [ref. 995]. Masc. *Anthias saponaceus* Bloch & Schneider 1801:310. Type by subsequent designation. Type designated by Bleeker 1876:258 [ref. 447]. *Rhypticus* Agassiz 1846:326, 328 [ref. 64] is an unjustified emendation. Valid (Kendall 1984:501 [ref. 13663]). Serranidae: Grammistinae.

Sabanejewia Vladykov 1929:86 [ref. 4525]. Fem. *Cobitis balcanica* Karaman 1922. Type by original designation. Valid (Nalbant 1963:361 [ref. 3140], Sawada 1982:200 [ref. 14111] as *Sabajenewia*, Vasil'yeva & Vasil'ev 1988 [ref. 13477]). Cobitidae: Cobitinae.

Saccarius Günther 1861:183 [ref. 1964]. Masc. *Saccarius lineatus* Günther 1861:183. Type by monotypy. Synonym of *Antennarius* Daudin 1816 (Pietsch 1984:33 [ref. 5380]). Antennariidae.

Saccobranchus Valenciennes in Cuvier & Valenciennes 1840:399 [ref. 1008]. Masc. *Silurus singio* Hamilton 1822:147, 374. Type by monotypy. Synonym of *Heteropneustes* Müller 1840. Heteropneustidae.

Saccoderma Schultz 1944:314 [ref. 3960]. Neut. *Saccoderma melanostigma* Schultz 1944:315. Type by original designation. Valid (Fink & Weitzman 1974:33 [ref. 7132], Géry 1977:558 [ref. 1597]). Characidae.

Saccodon Kner 1863:225 [ref. 5002]. Masc. *Saccodon wagneri* Kner 1863:225. Type by monotypy. Also appeared as new in Kner & Steindachner 1864:31 [ref. 2649]. Valid (Roberts 1974:433 [ref. 6872], Géry 1977:207 [ref. 1597], Vari 1983:5 [ref. 5419]). Hemiodontidae: Parodontinae.

Saccogaster Alcock 1889:389 [ref. 81]. Fem. *Saccogaster maculatus* Alcock 1889:389. Type by monotypy. Valid (Cohen 1972 [ref. 7157], Cohen & Nielsen 1978:50 [ref. 881], Cohen 1981 [ref. 5586], Okamura in Masuda et al. 1984:101 [ref. 6441], Cohen 1987 [ref. 6040]). Bythitidae: Bythitinae.

Saccopharynx Mitchill 1824:86 [ref. 3031]. Masc. *Saccopharynx flagellum* Cuvier 1829:355. Type by being a replacement name. Proposed as a replacement for *Stylephorus* Swainson; see Eschmeyer & Robins 1988 [ref. 6886]; validated by ICZN as a separate genus and placed on Official List (Opinion 1603). Valid (Böhlke 1966:618 [ref. 5256], Bauchot 1973:216 [ref. 7184], Nielsen & Bertelsen 1985 [ref. 5255], Bertelsen & Nielsen in Whitehead et al. 1986:530 [ref. 13676], Paxton et al. 1989:110 [ref. 12442], Bertelsen et al. 1989:643 [ref. 13293]). Saccopharyngidae.

Saccostoma Sauvage (ex Guichenot) 1882:171 [ref. 3894]. Neut. *Saccostoma gulosum* Sauvage (ex Guichenot) 1882:171. Type by monotypy. Species originally *S. gulosus*, corrected to *gulosum* to agree in gender with genus. Both genus and species attributed by Sauvage to "Guichenot in collect." but we assume Sauvage was responsible for the descriptions and is the author. Apparently preoccupied [details not investigated]. Synonym of *Chasmichthys* Jordan 1901. Gobiidae.

Sachsdoras Fernández-Yépez 1968:66 [ref. 1325]. Masc. *Sachsdoras apurensis* Fernández-Yépez 1968:66. Type by original designation (also monotypic). Valid (Burgess 1989:224 [ref. 12860]). Doradidae.

Sacrestinus (subgenus of *Aphareus*) Jordan, Evermann & Tanaka 1927:670 [ref. 2454]. Masc. *Aphareus flavivultus* Jenkins 1901: 390. Type by original designation (also monotypic). Synonym of *Aphareus* Cuvier 1830 (Allen 1985:163 [ref. 6843] based on placement of type species; genus not treated by Allen). Lutjanidae.

Sacura (subgenus of *Anthias*) Jordan & Richardson 1910:468 [ref. 2494]. Fem. *Anthias margaritaceus* Hilgendorf 1879:78. Type by original designation (also monotypic). Valid (Heemstra & Randall 1979 [ref. 6938], Kendall 1984:500 [ref. 13663], Katayama in Masuda et al. 1984:135 [ref. 6441]). Serranidae: Anthiinae.

Safole Jordan 1912:655 [ref. 2403]. *Dules taeniurus* Cuvier in Cuvier & Valenciennes 1829:114. Type by being a replacement name. Replacement for *Boulengerina* Fowler 1906, preoccupied by Dollo 1886 in Ophidia. Synonym of *Kuhlia* Gill 1861 (Maugé 1986:306 [ref. 6218]). Kuhliidae.

Sagamia Jordan & Snyder 1901:100 [ref. 2509]. Fem. *Sagamia russula* Jordan & Snyder 1901:100. Type by original designation (also monotypic). Valid (Akihito in Masuda et al. 1984:279 [ref. 6441], Birdsong et al. 1988:184 [ref. 7303]). Gobiidae.

Sagamichthys Parr 1953:1 [ref. 3382]. Masc. *Sagamichthys abei*

Parr 1953:6. Type by original designation (also monotypic). Valid (Krefft 1973:97 [ref. 7166], Quéro et al. in Whitehead et al. 1984:265 [ref. 13675], Uyeno in Masuda et al. 1984:43 [ref. 6441], Matsui & Rosenblatt 1986:223 [ref. 5688], Sazonov 1986 [ref. 6003]). Platytroctidae.

Sagenichthys Berg 1895:52 [ref. 261]. Masc. *Lonchurus ancylodon* Bloch & Schneider 1801:102. Type by being a replacement name. Unneeded replacement for *Ancylodon* Bosc 1816 or Oken (Cuvier) 1817, already replaced by *Macrodon* Schinz 1822 and *Nomalus* Gistel 1848. Objective synonym of *Macrodon* Schinz 1822 (Chao 1978:37 [ref. 6983]). Sciaenidae.

Sagenocephalus Kaup 1873:83 [ref. 2585]. Masc. *Prionotus japonicus* Bleeker 1857:398. Type by subsequent designation. Type designated by Whitley 1933:97 [ref. 4677]. Synonym of *Lepidotrigla* Günther 1860 (Richards & Saksena 1977:209 [ref. 5285]). Triglidae: Triglinae.

Sagittabarilius (subgenus of *Barilius*) Fowler 1936:293 [ref. 1424]. Masc. *Barilius salmolucius* Nichols & Griscom 1917:702. Type by original designation (also monotypic). Second species questionably included. Synonym of *Raiamas* Jordan 1919 (Lévêque & Daget 1984:332 [ref. 6186]). Synonym of *Barilius* Hamilton 1822 (Roberts 1989:30 [ref. 6439]). Cyprinidae.

Salangichthys Bleeker 1860:101 [ref. 374]. Masc. *Salanx microdon* Bleeker 1860:101. Type by monotypy. Valid (Roberts 1984:210 [ref. 5318]). Salangidae.

Salanx Cuvier 1816:185 [ref. 993]. Masc. *Leucosoma reevesi* Gray 1831:4. Type apparently by subsequent designation. Usually dated to Oken (ex Cuvier) 1817:1183. Appeared first without species as "Les Salanx" in Cuvier 1816:185, but in footnote (1) is the latinized *Salanx* which can only refer to "Les Salanx" based on Cuvier's style. Two species included by Valenciennes in Cuvier & Valenciennes 1850:360 [ref. 1014]. Type possibly first designated by Jordan 1917:99. Valid (Roberts 1984:206 [ref. 5318]; Zhang 1985 [ref. 12818] with comments on type [not translated]). Salangidae.

Salar Valenciennes in Cuvier & Valenciennes 1848:314 [ref. 1013]. Masc. *Salar ausonii* Valenciennes in Cuvier & Valenciennes 1848:319. Type by subsequent designation. Type designated by Berg 1916:34 [type cannot be *salar*, not mentioned by Valenciennes in original description]. Synonym of *Salmo* Linnaeus 1758 (Behnke 1984:125 [ref. 6177]). Salmonidae: Salmoninae.

Salaria Forsskål 1775:x, 22 [ref. 1351]. Fem. *Blennius basiliscus* Valenciennes in Cuvier & Valenciennes 1836. Type by subsequent designation. Appeared first without included species. Earliest addition of species not researched (see remarks on type in Krupp & Schneider 1989:405 [ref. 13651]). Genus apparently needs more study. Synonym of *Blennius* Linnaeus 1758 (Bath 1973:519 [ref. 7212]); valid (Bath 1977:208 [ref. 208], Bath 1986:356 [ref. 6217], Krupp & Schneider 1989:405 [ref. 13651]). Blenniidae.

Salarias Cuvier 1816:251 [ref. 993]. Masc. *Salarias quadripennis* Cuvier 1816:251. Type by subsequent designation. Type designated by Jordan 1917:101 [ref. 2407]. Not *Salaria* Forsskål 1775. *Salaris* is a misspelling. Valid (Yoshino in Masuda et al. 1984:298 [ref. 6441], Springer 1986:754 [ref. 5719]). Blenniidae.

Salarichthys Guichenot 1867:96 [14] [ref. 1951]. Masc. *Salarias vomerinus* Valenciennes in Cuvier & Valenciennes 1836:349. Type by original designation. Guichenot misspelled name once as *Salarichtys* on p. 100. On p. 14 of separate. *Salariichthys* is an incorrect subsequent spelling. Synonym of *Entomacrodus* Gill 1859 (Smith-Vaniz & Springer 1971:23 [ref. 4145]). Blenniidae.

Salarigobius Pfeffer 1893:141 [ref. 3461]. Masc. *Salarigobius stuhlmanni* Pfeffer 1893:141. Type by monotypy. Gobiidae.

Salema (subgenus of *Archosargus*) Jordan & Evermann 1896:390 [ref. 2442]. Fem. *Perca unimaculata* Bloch 1792:75. Type by original designation. Sparidae.

Salilota Günther 1887:95 [ref. 2013]. Fem. *Haloporphyrus australis* Günther 1878:19. Type by monotypy. Valid (Fahay & Markle 1984:266 [ref. 13653], Nakamura in Nakamura et al. 1986:104 [ref. 14235], Paulin 1989:127 [ref. 9297]). Moridae.

Salius Minding 1832:86 [ref. 3022]. Masc. *Salius halticus* Minding 1832:86. Type by monotypy. Name not in current literature, needs study. Unplaced genera.

Salminus (subgenus of *Hydrocyon*) Agassiz in Spix & Agassiz 1829:76 [ref. 13]. Masc. *Hydrocyon brevidens* Cuvier 1819:364. Type by monotypy. For authorship and date see Kottelat 1988:78 [ref. 13380]. Valid (Géry 1977:331 [ref. 1597], Vari 1983:5 [ref. 5419], Malabarba 1989:138 [ref. 14217]). Characidae.

Salmo Linnaeus 1758:308 [ref. 2787]. Masc. *Salmo salar* Linnaeus 1758:308. Type by subsequent designation. Type designated by Jordan & Gilbert 1883:309 [ref. 2476]. On Official List (Opinion 77, Direction 56). *Salmus* is a misspelling. Valid (Svetovidov 1973:145 [ref. 7169], Svetovidov in Whitehead et al. 1984:380 [ref. 13675], Kendall & Behnke 1984:144 [ref. 13638], Behnke 1984:125 [ref. 6177], Araga in Masuda et al. 1984:38 [ref. 6441], Paxton et al. 1989:164 [ref. 12442]). Salmonidae: Salmoninae.

Salmoperca Thompson 1850:163 [ref. 4392]. Fem. *Salmoperca pellucida* Thompson 1850:164. Type by monotypy. Genus and species proposed as new, although conditionally as the same as *Percopsis*; species described under the heading *Percopsis pellucida* (see Appendix A). Synonym of *Percopsis* Agassiz 1849. Percopsidae.

Salmophasia (subgenus of *Cyprinus*) Swainson 1839:284 [ref. 4303]. Fem. *Cyprinus oblonga* Swainson 1839:284 (= *Cyprinus bacaila* Hamilton 1822:384). Type by subsequent designation. *Salmostoma* on p. 184, changed to *Salmophasia* on p. 284. Type designated by Swain 1882:279 [ref. 5966]. Jordan 1919:202 [ref. 2410] apparently is first reviser, selecting *Salmophasia*. *C. oblonga* Swainson is an unneeded substitute for *C. bacaila*. Cyprinidae.

Salmosaurus Minding 1832:120 [ref. 3022]. Masc. *Salmosaurus lacerata* Minding 1832:120. Name not in current literature, needs study. Perhaps same as *Saurus*. Synodontidae: Synodontinae.

Salmostoma Swainson 1839:184 [ref. 4303]. Neut. *Cyprinus oblonga* Swainson 1839:284 (= *Cyprinus bacaila* Hamilton 1822:384). Type by subsequent designation. On p. 284 Swainson replaces with *Salmophasia*. Type designated by Swain 1882:279 through *Salmophasia*. Jordan 1919:202 [ref. 2410] apparently serves as first reviser selecting *Salmophasia* over *Salmostoma*. Valid (Jayaram 1981:73 [ref. 6497], Kottelat 1989:11 [ref. 13605]). Cyprinidae.

Salmothymus Berg 1908:502, 503 [ref. 271]. Masc. *Salmo obtusirostris* Heckel 1852:367. Type by monotypy. Valid (some authors); synonym of *Salmo* Linnaeus 1758, but as a valid subgenus (Behnke 1969:11 [ref. 250], Kendall & Behnke 1984:144 [ref. 13638]). Salmonidae: Salmoninae.

Saloptia Smith 1964:719 [ref. 4131]. Fem. *Saloptia powelli* Smith 1964:719. Type by original designation (also monotypic). Valid (Katayama in Masuda et al. 1984:127 [ref. 6441]). Serranidae: Epinephelinae.

Salpa Catesby 1771:17 [ref. 774]. Fem. Not available, Catesby 1771 is a rejected work on Official Index (Opinion 89, Opinion 259).

Salpa Edwards in Catesby placed on Official Index for purposes of both priority and homonymy. Lutjanidae.

Saltatrix Catesby 1771:14 [ref. 774]. Fem. Not available, published in a rejected work on Official Index (Opinion 89, Opinion 259). In the synonymy of *Pomatomus* Lacepède 1802 (Monod 1973:369 [ref. 7193]). Pomatomidae.

Salvelinus (subgenus of *Salmo*) Richardson (ex Nilsson) 1836:169 [ref. 3731]. Masc. *Salmo salvelinus* Linnaeus 1758:308. Mentioned under *Salmo alipes* Richardson, as "Sub-genus, *Salvelinus*. Nilsson" and in text (p. 169) as a sub-group "Salvelini." Species included are those on Richardson's p. 139 as Salvelini (not an absolute direct association perhaps, see Art. 67(l) and Appendix A); type by absolute tautonymy. Valid (Svetovidov 1973:147 [ref. 7169], Araga in Masuda et al. 1984:36 [ref. 6441], Kendall & Behnke 1984:144 [ref. 13638], Paxton et al. 1989:165 [ref. 12442]). Salmonidae: Salmoninae.

Samaris Gray 1831:4 [ref. 1880]. Fem. *Samaris cristatus* Gray 1831:5. Type by monotypy. Valid (Norman 1934:402 [ref. 6893], Ahlstrom et al. 1984:643 [ref. 13641], Sakamoto 1984 [ref. 5273], Sakamoto in Masuda et al. 1984:354 [ref. 6441], Heemstra 1986:864 [ref. 5660], Quéro et al. 1989 [ref. 12826]). Pleuronectidae: Samarinae.

Samariscus Gilbert 1905:682 [ref. 1631]. Masc. *Samariscus corallinus* Gilbert 1905:682. Type by original designation (also monotypic). Valid (Norman 1934:407 [ref. 6893], Ahlstrom et al. 1984:643 [ref. 13641], Sakamoto 1984 [ref. 5273], Sakamoto in Masuda et al. 1984:354 [ref. 6441], Heemstra 1986:865 [ref. 5660], Quéro et al. 1989 [ref. 12826]). Pleuronectidae: Samarinae.

Sanagia Holly 1926:155 [ref. 5038]. Fem. *Sanagia velifera* Holly 1926:155. Type by original designation (also monotypic). Also published in Holly 1927:139 [ref. 2188]. Valid (Lévêque & Daget 1984:336 [ref. 6186]). Cyprinidae.

Sandakanus (subgenus of *Neostethus*) Herre 1942:151 [ref. 2134]. Masc. *Neostethus borneensis* Herre 1939:143. Type by original designation. Synonym of *Neostethus* Regan 1916 (Parenti 1989:269 [ref. 13486]). Phallostethidae.

Sandat Bory de Saint-Vincent 1828:204 [ref. 3853]. Masc. *Perca lucioperca* Linnaeus 1758:289. Original not seen. Synonym of *Stizostedion* Rafinesque 1820. Percidae.

Sandat Cloquet 1827:126, 173 [ref. 853]. Masc. *Perca lucioperca* Linnaeus 1758:289. Type apparently designated by Jordan 1917:122 [ref. 2407]. Synonym of *Stizostedion* Rafinesque 1820 (Collette & Banarescu 1977:1457 [ref. 5845]). Percidae.

Sandelia Castelnau 1861:36 [ref. 767]. Fem. *Sandelia bainsii* Castelnau 1861:37. Type by monotypy. Valid (Gosse 1986:413 [ref. 6194]). Anabantidae.

Sander Oken (ex Cuvier) 1817:1182 [ref. 3303]. Masc. *Perca lucioperca* of Bloch (= *Perca lucioperca* Linnaeus 1758:289). Type by subsequent monotypy. Technical addition of species after latinization not investigated. Based on "Les Sandres" of Cuvier 1816:294 [ref. 993] (see Gill 1903:966 [ref. 5768]). Synonym of *Stizostedion* Rafinesque 1820. Percidae.

Sandrus Stark 1828:465 [ref. 4193]. Masc. *Perca lucioperca* Linnaeus 1758:289. Type by subsequent designation. Type designated by Jordan 1917:123 [ref. 2407]. Synonym of *Stizostedion* Rafinesque 1820 (Collette & Banarescu 1977:1457 [ref. 5845]). Percidae.

Sanopus Smith 1952:314 [ref. 4084]. Masc. *Opsanus barbatus* Meek & Hildebrand 1928:917. Type by original designation (also monotypic). Valid (Collette 1974 [ref. 5218], Collette 1983 [ref. 5219]). Batrachoididae.

Sapa Kazanskii 1928:16 [ref. 14268]. Fem. *Cyprinus sapa* Pallas 1811:328. Original not examined; from Berg 1949:768 [ref. 12882]. Synonym of *Abramis* Cuvier 1816 (Berg 1949:768 [ref. 12882]. Cyprinidae.

Saraca Steindachner 1875:125 [ref. 4220]. Fem. *Saraca opercularis* Steindachner 1875:125. Type by monotypy. Preoccupied by Walker 1865 in Lepidoptera, replaced by *Biotoecus* Eigenmann & Kennedy 1903. Cichlidae.

Sarchirus Rafinesque 1818:418 [ref. 3588]. Masc. *Sarchirus vittatus* Rafinesque 1818:419. Type by monotypy. Rafinesque 1818:418 published 7 Nov.; also appeared in Nov. in Rafinesque 1818:41 [ref. 3589]. Synonym of *Lepisosteus* Lacepède 1803 (Suttkus 1963:69 [ref. 7110], Wiley 1976:41 [ref. 7091]). Lepisosteidae.

Sarcidium Cope 1871:440 [ref. 922]. Neut. *Sarcidium scopiferum* Cope 1871:440. Type by monotypy. Synonym of *Phenacobius* Cope 1867. Cyprinidae.

Sarcocara (subgenus of *Diplacanthopoma*) Smith and Radcliffe in Radcliff 1913:167 [ref. 3579]. Neut. *Diplacanthopoma (Sarcocara) brunnea* Smith & Radcliffe in Radcliffe 1913:167. Type by monotypy. Synonym of *Diplacanthopoma* Günther 1887 (Cohen & Nielsen 1978:47 [ref. 881]). Bythitidae: Bythitinae.

Sarcocheilichthys Bleeker 1859:435 [ref. 370]. Masc. *Leuciscus variegatus* Temminck & Schlegel 1846:213. Type by subsequent monotypy. Apparently appeared first in key, without included species. One species included by Bleeker 1860:285, 426-427 [ref. 380] (as *Sarcoheilichthys* on p. 426). Unjustifiably emended to *Sarcochilichthys* by Günther 1868:175 [ref. 1990]. Evidently *Acrocheilichthys* in Jordan 1923:142 [ref. 2421] is a misprint. Valid (Banarescu & Nalbant 1973:39 [ref. 173], Lu, Luo & Chen 1977:467 [ref. 13495], Sawada in Masuda et al. 1984:55 [ref. 6441]). Cyprinidae.

Sarcodaces Günther 1864:352 [ref. 1974]. Masc. *Salmo odoe* Bloch 1794:122. Type by monotypy. Objective synonym of *Hepsetus* Swainson 1838 (Géry 1977:17 [ref. 1597], Roberts 1984:138 [ref. 6182]). Hepsetidae.

Sarcogenys Bleeker (ex Kuhl & van Hasselt) 1858:96 [ref. 365]. Fem. *Sarcogenys rostratus* Kuhl and van Hasselt (MS). Manuscript name mentioned in synonymy or *Netuma nasuta*; apparently never later made available. Ariidae.

Sarcoglanis Myers & Weitzman 1966:279 [ref. 3136]. Masc. *Sarcoglanis simplex* Myers & Weitzman 1966:279. Type by original designation (also monotypic). Valid (Burgess 1989:325 [ref. 12860], Pinna 1989:23 [ref. 12630]). Trichomycteridae.

Sarda Cuvier 1829:199 [ref. 995]. Fem. *Scomber sarda* Bloch 1793:44. Type by monotypy (also by absolute tautonymy). Valid (Postel 1973:475 [ref. 7208], Collette et al. 1984:600 [ref. 11421], Nakamura in Masuda et al. 1984:225 [ref. 6441], Collette 1986:834 [ref. 5647]). Scombridae.

Sarda Gronow in Gray 1854:119 [ref. 1911]. Fem. *Sarda immaculata* Gronow in Gray 1854:119 (= *Scomber pelagicus* Linnaeus 1758:299). Type by subsequent designation. Earliest designation of type not researched. Synonym of *Coryphaena* Linnaeus 1758. Coryphaenidae.

Sarda Plumier in Lacepède 1802:141 (footnote) [ref. 4929]. Fem. Not available, non binominal manuscript name mentioned in passing in footnote. See remarks under Opinion 89 in Appendix B. Not

Sarda Cuvier 1829 or Gray 1854. In the synonymy of *Ocyurus* Gill 1862. Lutjanidae.

Sardina Antipa 1904:302 [ref. 129]. Fem. *Sardina dobrogica* Antipa 1904:302. Type needs more research. Also in Antipa 1906 [ref. 6859]. On Official List (Opinion 799). In Opinion 799 type is given as by monotypy, but it is stated (p. 302) that *Sardina dobrogica* differs from *Sardina pilchardus*...; *pilchardus* is listed as type by Jordan 1920:512 [ref. 4905] and by Fowler. Misspelled once (p. 303) as *Sardinia*. Valid (Svetovidov 1973:102 [ref. 7169], Grande 1985:251 [ref. 6466], Whitehead 1985:55 [ref. 5141]). Clupeidae.

Sardinella Valenciennes in Cuvier & Valenciennes 1847:261 [ref. 1012]. Fem. *Sardinella aurita* Valenciennes in Cuvier & Valenciennes 1847:263. Type by subsequent designation. Type designation by Gill 1861:35 [ref. 1767] (see Whitehead 1967:36 [ref. 6464]). Valid (Svetovidov 1973:102 [ref. 7169], Poll et al. 1984:52 [ref. 6172], Uyeno & Sato in Masuda et al. 1984:19 [ref. 6441], Grande 1985:251 [ref. 6466], Whitehead 1985:90 [ref. 5141], Whitehead & Wongratana 1986:202 [ref. 6284], Paxton et al. 1989:156 [ref. 12442]). Clupeidae.

Sardinia Poey 1860:311 [ref. 3499]. Fem. *Sardina pseudohispanica* Poey 1860:311. Type by monotypy. Synonym of *Sardinella* Valenciennes 1847 (Whitehead 1985:90 [ref. 5141]). Clupeidae.

Sardinops Hubbs 1929:264 [ref. 2239]. Masc. *Meletta caerulea* Girard 1854:138. Type by original designation. Valid (Uyeno & Sato in Masuda et al. 1984:19 [ref. 6441], Grande 1985:251 [ref. 6466], Whitehead 1985:57 [ref. 5141], Whitehead & Wongratana 1986:204 [ref. 6284], Paxton et al. 1989:157 [ref. 12442]). Clupeidae.

Sargocentron (subgenus of *Holocentrus*) Fowler 1904:235 [ref. 1365]. Neut. *Holocentrum leo* Cuvier in Cuvier & Valenciennes 1829:204. Type by original designation (also monotypic). Correct spelling for genus of type species is *Holocentrus*. Valid (Shimizu in Masuda et al. 1984:111 [ref. 6441], Randall & Heemstra 1985:5 [ref. 5144], Ben-Tuvia in Whitehead et al. 1986:753 [ref. 13676], Randall & Heemstra 1986:417 [ref. 5707], Paxton et al. 1989:380 [ref. 12442]). Holocentridae.

Sargochromis Regan 1920:45 [ref. 3669]. Masc. *Paratilapia codringtoni* Boulenger 1908:495. Type by original designation (also monotypic). Synonym of *Serranochromis* Regan 1920, but as a valid subgenus (Greenwood 1984:216 [ref. 5311]). Cichlidae.

Sargosomus Agassiz (L.) in A. Agassiz 1861:129 [ref. 11]. Masc. *"Sargosomus fluviatilis"* Agassiz (L.) in A. Agassiz 1861:130. Not available, manuscript name published in synonymy, and apparently never later made available. In the synonymy of *Hysterocarpus* Gibbons 1854 (Tarp 1952:77 [ref. 12250]). Embiotocidae.

Sargus Cuvier 1816:272 [ref. 993]. Masc. *Sparus sargus* Linnaeus 1758:278. Type by absolute tautonymy. Appeared as "Les Sargues" in Cuvier 1814:91 [ref. 4884]. Preoccupied by Fabricius 1798 in Diptera (and not by Plumier in Lacepède 1802 [or 1803] in fishes); replaced by *Denius* Gistel 1848. Sparidae.

Sargus Klein 1775:966 [ref. 2618]. Masc. Not available, published in a work that does not conform to the principle of binominal nomenclature. In the synonymy of *Diplodus* Rafinesque 1810 (Tortonese 1973:408 [ref. 7192]). Sparidae.

Sargus Plumier in Lacepède 1802:167 (footnote) [ref. 4929]. Masc. Not available, nonbinominal manuscript name mentioned in passing under *Dipterodon plumieri*. See remarks under Opinion 89 in Appendix B. Not *Sargus* Cuvier 1816. Lutjanidae.

Sarotherodon Rüppell 1852:21 [ref. 3846]. Masc. *Sarotherodon melanotheron* Rüppell 1852:21. Type by monotypy. Type species conserved and genus name placed on Official List (Opinion 1548). Synonym of *Tilapia* Smith 1840 (authors); valid (Trewavas et al. 1972:48 [ref. 4460], see Trewavas 1987 [ref. 6377], Krupp & Schneider 1989:398 [ref. 13651]; fossil species included by van Couvering 1982:82 [ref. 2042]). Cichlidae.

Sarothrodus Gill 1861:99 [ref. 1772]. Masc. *Chaetodon capistratus* Linnaeus 1758:275. Type by being a replacement name. Unneeded replacement (see footnote on p. 99) for *Chaetodon* Linnaeus 1758. Objective synonym of *Chaetodon* Linnaeus 1758 (Burgess 1978:653 [ref. 700]). Chaetodontidae.

Sarpa (subgenus of *Box*) Bonaparte 1831:171 [ref. 4978]. *Sparus salpa* Linnaeus 1758:280. Appeared as name only; as a section under *Box* as "96. *Box*, Cuv. (Boops, Riss.). 1. Box, Nob. 2. Sarpa, Nob." Subsequent use in an available way not investigated. Treated as valid (Tortonese 1973:413 [ref. 7192], Bauchot & Hureau in Whitehead et al. 1986:905 [ref. 13676], Smith & Smith 1986:593 [ref. 5710]). Sparidae.

Sarritor Cramer in Jordan & Evermann 1896:448 [ref. 2442]. Masc. *Odontopyxis frenatus* Gill 1896:435. Type by original designation. Valid (Washington et al. 1984:442 [ref. 13660], Kanayama in Masuda et al. 1984:332 [ref. 6441], Yabe 1985:123 [ref. 11522], Maeda & Amaoka 1988:100 [ref. 12616]). Agonidae.

Sartor Myers & Carvalho 1959:148 [ref. 3130]. Masc. *Sartor respectus* Myers & Carvalho 1959:149. Type by original designation (also monotypic). Valid (Géry 1977:186 [ref. 1597], Winterbottom 1980:31 [ref. 4755]). Curimatidae: Anostominae.

Satan Hubbs & Bailey 1947:4 [ref. 2254]. Masc. *Satan eurystomus* Hubbs & Bailey 1947:8. Type by original designation (also monotypic). Valid (Burgess 1989:35 [ref. 12860]). Ictaluridae.

Satanoperca Günther 1862:312 [ref. 1969]. Fem. *Geophagus daemon* Heckel 1840:389. Type by subsequent designation. Type designated by Jordan & Evermann 1898:1542 [ref. 2444]. Valid (Kullander 1986:146 [ref. 12439], Kullander & Ferreira 1988 [ref. 12825], Kullander & Nijssen 1989:66 [ref. 14136]). Cichlidae.

Satsuma Smith & Pope 1906:472 [ref. 4058]. *Satsuma macrops* Smith & Pope 1906:472. Type by original designation (also monotypic). Preoccupied by Adams 1868 in Mollusca and by Murray 1874 in Lepidoptera, not replaced. Synonym of *Malakichthys* Döderlein 1883. Acropomatidae.

Satulinus Smith 1958:160 [ref. 4118]. Masc. *Satulinus zanzibarensis* Smith 1958:160. Type by original designation (also monotypic). Synonym of *Hetereleotris* Bleeker 1874 (Akihito & Meguro 1981:331 [ref. 5508], Hoese 1986:3 [ref. 5996]). Gobiidae.

Satyrichthys Kaup 1873:82 [ref. 2585]. Masc. *Peristethus rieffeli* Kaup 1859:82. Type by monotypy. Valid (Ochiai & Yatou in Masuda et al. 1984:335 [ref. 6441], Heemstra 1986:489 [ref. 5660], Chen & Shao 1988:130 [ref. 6676], Paxton et al. 1989:457 [ref. 12442]). Triglidae: Peristediinae.

Saurenchelys Peters 1864:397 [ref. 3437]. Fem. *Saurenchelys cancrivora* Peters 1864:397. Type by monotypy. Valid (Blache et al. 1973:237 [ref. 7185], Smith & Castle 1982:19 [ref. 5453], Asano in Masuda et al. 1984:29 [ref. 6441], Saldanha in Whitehead et al. 1986:564 [ref. 13676], Paxton et al. 1989:114 [ref. 12442], Smith 1989:590 [ref. 13285]). Nettastomatidae.

Saurida Valenciennes in Cuvier & Valenciennes 1849:499 [ref. 1014]. Fem. *Salmo tumbil* Bloch 1795:112. Type by subsequent designation. Type designated by Jordan, Tanaka & Snyder 1913:53

[ref. 6448]. Valid (Anderson et al. 1966:84 [ref. 6977], Nielsen 1973:162 [ref. 6885], Sulak 1977:53 [ref. 4299], Waples 1981 [ref. 5491], Sulak in Whitehead et al. 1984:408 [ref. 13675], Okiyama 1984:207 [ref. 13644], Machida in Masuda et al. 1984:61 [ref. 6441], Cressey 1986:271 [ref. 6289], Paxton et al. 1989:242 [ref. 12442]). Synodontidae: Harpadontinae.

Sauridichthys Bleeker 1858:2 [ref. 364]. Masc. *Saurus ophiodon* Cuvier 1829:314. Type by monotypy. Synonym of *Harpadon* Lesueur 1825. Synodontidae: Harpadontinae.

Saurogobio Bleeker 1870:253 [ref. 429]. Masc. *Saurogobio dumerili* Bleeker 1871:25. Type by monotypy. Appeared as above without available species (2 unavailable ones listed); two species described in Bleeker 1871:25 [ref. 6421], neither designated type. First subsequent designation not located. If comments on 1870:253 [ref. 429] are insufficient to validate, then genus dates to Bleeker 1871:25 [ref. 6421]. Valid (Banarescu & Nalbant 1973:282 [ref. 173], Lu, Luo & Chen 1977:537 [ref. 13495], Hosoya 1986:488 [ref. 6155], Chen & Li in Chu & Chen 1989:116 [ref. 13584]). Cyprinidae.

Sauromuraenesox Alcock 1889:457 [ref. 81]. Masc. *Sauromuraenesox vorax* Alcock 1889:458. Type by monotypy. Misspelled *Sauromuraenesax* in Zoological Record for 1889. Valid (Talwar 1977 [ref. 6954]). Muraenesocidae.

Saurus Browne 1789:452 [ref. 669]. Masc. Not available, published in a rejected work on Official Index (Opinion 89). Not *Saurus* Cuvier. Carangidae.

Saurus Catesby 1771:2 [ref. 774]. Masc. Not available, published in a rejected work on Official Index (Opinion 89, Opinion 259). Synodontidae: Synodontinae.

Saurus Cuvier 1816:169 [ref. 993]. Masc. *Salmo saurus* Linnaeus 1758:310. Type by absolute tautonymy. Synonym of *Synodus* Scopoli 1777 (Anderson et al. 1966:47 [ref. 6977]). Synodontidae: Synodontinae.

Sauvagea Jordan & Seale 1906:420 [ref. 2497]. Fem. *Lepidoblennius caledonicus* Sauvage 1874:338. Type by being a replacement name. Replacement for *Lepidoblennius* Sauvage 1874, preoccupied by Steindachner 1867 in fishes. Tripterygiidae.

Sauvagella Bertin 1940:300 [ref. 293]. Fem. *Spratelloides madagascariensis* Sauvage 1883:160. Type by subsequent designation. Not available from Bertin 1940, no designation of a type after 1930 (Art. 13b). Genus can date to Trewavas 1945 (in Zoological Record for 1944) where a citation to Bertin is given and a type designated. See Art. 13b in Appendix A. Valid (Poll et al. 1984:53 [ref. 6172], Whitehead 1985:169 [ref. 5141] with author as Bertin). Clupeidae.

Sawara Jordan & Hubbs 1925:214 [ref. 2486]. Fem. *Cybium niphonium* Valenciennes in Cuvier & Valenciennes 1831:180. Type by original designation (also monotypic). Synonym of *Scomberomorus* Lacepède 1801 (Collette & Russo 1984:611 [ref. 5221]). Scombridae.

Sawbwa Annandale 1918:48 [ref. 127]. *Sawbwa resplendens* Annandale 1918:48. Type by original designation (also monotypic). Misspelled *Sambwa* in Zoological Record for 1918. Valid (Jayaram 1981:97 [ref. 6497], Kottelat 1989:11 [ref. 13605]). Cyprinidae.

Saxilaga Scott 1936:105 [ref. 3994]. Fem. *Galaxias cleaveri* Scott 1934:41. Type by original designation. Also described as a new subgenus in same work. Synonym of *Galaxias* Cuvier 1816 (McDowall & Frankenberg 1981:455 [ref. 5500], McDowall 1984:126 [ref. 6178]). Galaxiidae: Galaxiinae.

Sayonara Jordan & Seale 1906:145 [ref. 2496]. *Sayonara satsumae* Jordan & Seale 1906:145. Type by original designation (also monotypic). Synonym of *Plectranthias* Bleeker 1873 (Randall 1980:105 [ref. 6717]); valid (Paxton et al. 1989:507 [ref. 12442]). Serranidae: Anthiinae.

Sayris Rafinesque 1810:60 [ref. 3594]. *Sayris recurvirostra* Rafinesque 1810:61. Type by subsequent designation. Type designated by Jordan 1917:81 [ref. 2407]. Synonym of *Scomberesox* Lacepède 1803 (Parin 1973:261 [ref. 7191]). Scomberesocidae.

Scaeops Jordan & Starks 1904:627 [ref. 2526]. Masc. *Rhombus grandisquama* Temminck & Schlegel 1846:183. Type by original designation. Synonym of *Engyprosopon* Günther 1862 (Norman 1934:203 [ref. 6893], Amaoka 1969:142 [ref. 105]). Bothidae: Bothinae.

Scaevius Whitley 1947:142 [ref. 4708]. Masc. *Scaevius nicanor* Whitley 1947:142. Type by original designation (also monotypic). Nemipteridae.

Scalanago Whitley 1935:217 [ref. 4683]. Masc. *Scalanago lateralis* Whitley 1935:218. Type by original designation (also monotypic). Valid (Paxton et al. 1989:143 [ref. 12442], Smith 1989:511 [ref. 13285]). Congridae: Congrinae.

Scalantarus Smith 1965:535 [ref. 4133]. Masc. *Anthias chrysostictus* Günther 1871:655. Type by original designation (also monotypic). Synonym of *Holanthias* Günther 1868 (Heemstra & Randall 1986:412 [ref. 5667]). Serranidae: Anthiinae.

Scalicus Jordan 1923:216 [ref. 2421]. Masc. *Peristedion amiscus* Jordan & Starks 1904:593. Type by original designation (also monotypic). Synonym of *Peristedion* Lacepède 1801. Triglidae: Peristediinae.

Scapasaurus Marwick 1942 Not available, name only; taken from Compagno 1984 (original not seen and reference not cited by Compagno). In the synonymy of *Cetorhinus* Blainville 1816 (Compagno 1984:234 [ref. 6474]). Cetorhinidae.

Scaphesthes Oshima 1919:208 [ref. 3312]. Fem. *Scaphesthes tamusuiensis* Oshima 1919:209. Type by original designation (also monotypic). Misspelled *Scaphestes* in Zoological Record for 1919. Synonym of *Varicorhinus* Rüppell 1836, but as a valid subgenus (Wu et al. 1977:298 [ref. 4807], Chu & Cui in Chu & Chen 1989:213 [ref. 13584]). Synonym of *Onychostoma* Günther 1898 (Chen 1989:119 [ref. 14144]). Cyprinidae.

Scaphiodon Heckel 1843:1020 [ref. 2066]. Masc. *Scaphiodon tinca* Heckel 1843:1021. Type by subsequent designation. Type designated by Bleeker 1863:196 [ref. 397] and 1863:26 [ref. 4859]. Misspelled once as *Scapiodon* by Heckel p. 1020 and as *Scaphioidon* p. 1060, but not for example pp. 1056-1059; *Scaphioidon* corrected to *Scaphiodon* in Corrigenda accompanying separate. Synonym of *Varicorhinus* Rüppell 1836 (Lévêque & Daget 1984:336 [ref. 6186]). Synonym of *Capoeta* Valenciennes 1842 (Krupp & Schneider 1989:364 [ref. 13651]). Cyprinidae.

Scaphiodonichthys Vinciguerra 1890:285 [ref. 4520]. Masc. *Scaphiodonichthys burmanicus* Vinciguerra 1890:285. Type by monotypy. Synonym of *Cyprinion* Heckel 1843 (Howes 1982:331 [ref. 14202]); valid (Jayaram 1981:96 [ref. 6497], Chen 1989:118 [ref. 14144]). Cyprinidae.

Scaphiodontella Oshima 1920:125 [ref. 3313]. Fem. *Scaphiodontella alticorpus* Oshima 1920:126. Type by original designation (also monotypic). Synonym of *Onychostoma* Günther 1896 (Chen 1989:119 [ref. 14144]). Cyprinidae.

Scaphiodontopsis Fowler 1934:117 [ref. 1417]. Fem. *Scaphiodontopsis acanthopterus* Fowler 1934:118. Type by original designation (also monotypic). Synonym of *Cyprinion* Heckel 1843 (Howes 1982:331 [ref. 14202]); apparently a synonym of *Cyprinion* Heckel 1843 (Kottelat 1989:7 [ref. 13605]). Cyprinidae.

Scaphirhynchus Heckel 1836:71 [ref. 2062]. Masc. *Acipenser rafinesquii* Heckel 1836:72. Type by monotypy. Appeared twice (earliest not researched); as above and as Heckel in Müller 1836:77, footnote [ref. 3060]. Several variant spellings and misprints. *Scaphirhynchops* Gill 1863 is an unneeded replacement, *Scaphirhynchus* not preoccupied. Valid (Bailey & Cross 1954 [ref. 5358]). Acipenseridae: Scaphirhynchinae.

Scaphognathops Smith 1945:208 [ref. 4056]. Masc. *Scaphognathus stejnegeri* Smith 1931:22. Type by being a replacement name. Replacement for *Scaphognathus* Smith 1931, preoccupied by Wagner 1861 in Reptilia. Valid (Kottelat 1985:266 [ref. 11441], Kottelat 1989:11 [ref. 13605]). Cyprinidae.

Scaphognathus Smith 1931:21 [ref. 4047]. Masc. *Scaphognathus stejnegeri* Smith 1931:22. Type by monotypy. Preoccupied by Wagner 1861 in Reptilia, replaced by *Scaphognathops* Smith 1945. Cyprinidae.

Scaphyrhynchops Gill 1863:178 [ref. 1674]. Masc. *Acipenser platorynchus* Rafinesque 1820:80. Type by being a replacement name. Appeared as "*Scaphyrhynchops platyrhynchus*, Gill (*Scaphrhynchus rafinesquii*, Heckel.)" Apparently an unneeded replacement for *Scaphirhynchus* Heckel 1836 (not preoccupied by *Scaphorhynchus* Wied 1831 in Aves), but this is unclear from text (see also *Platygobio*, apparently not proposed as a replacement name in the same list). If a replacement name then type is *rafinesquei* Heckel. See Bailey & Cross 1954:174 [ref. 5358] for variant spellings. Acipenseridae: Scaphirhynchinae.

Scaradon Temminck & Schlegel 1844:89 [ref. 4372]. Masc. *Scaradon fasciatus* Temminck & Schlegel 1844:89. Type by subsequent designation. Type designated by Jordan 1919:223 [ref. 2410], but genus misspelled *Scarodon*. Synonym of *Oplegnathus* Richardson 1840. Oplegnathidae.

Scarcina Rafinesque 1810:20 [ref. 3594]. Fem. *Scarcina argyrea* Rafinesque 1810:20. Type by subsequent designation. Type designated by Jordan 1917:79 [ref. 2407]. Synonym of *Lepidopus* Goüan 1770 (Parin & Bekker 1973:464 [ref. 7206]). Trichiuridae: Lepidopinae.

Scardiniopsis Jaeckel 1864:64 [ref. 2338]. Fem. *Scardiniopsis anceps* Jaeckel 1864:64. Type by monotypy. Apparently based on a hybrid between *Rutilus* and *Scardinius*. Cyprinidae.

Scardinius (subgenus of *Leuciscus*) Bonaparte 1837:puntata 96 [ref. 4893]. Masc. *Leuciscus scardafa* Bonaparte 1837:puntata 96. Type by original designation. Apparently appeared first in puntata 96, fasc. 19 under *Leuciscus scardafa* [species misspelled once as *scarpata*]. Synonym of *Rutilus* Rafinesque 1820 (Howes 1981:45 [ref. 14200]); valid (Bogutskaya 1987:936 [ref. 13521]). Cyprinidae.

Scarichthys Bleeker 1859:xvii, 106 [ref. 371]. Masc. *Scarus naevius* Valenciennes in Cuvier & Valenciennes 1839:212. Type by subsequent designation. Earliest type designation not established. Also appeared in Bleeker 1859:334 [ref. 368] as name with one described species; type by monotypy if ref. 368 was published before ref. 371. Also in Bleeker 1861:243 [ref. 381]. Synonym of *Leptoscarus* Swainson 1839 (Bruce & Randall 1985 [ref. 5234]). Scaridae: Sparisomatinae.

Scaridea Jenkins 1903:468 [ref. 2341]. Fem. *Scaridea zonarcha* Jenkins 1903:468. Type by original designation (also monotypic). Synonym of *Calotomus* Gilbert 1890 (Bruce & Randall 1985:7 [ref. 5234]). Scaridae: Sparisomatinae.

Scarops Schultz 1958:17, 18 [ref. 3970]. Masc. *Scarus rubroviolaceus* Bleeker 1849:52. Type by original designation. Species misspelled *rubroviolaceous* on p. 18, correctly on p. 21. Scaridae: Scarinae.

Scarostoma Kner 1867:715 [ref. 2645]. Neut. *Scarostoma insigne* Kner 1867:715. Type by monotypy. Synonym of *Oplegnathus* Richardson 1840. Oplegnathidae.

Scartelaos Swainson 1839:183, 279 [ref. 4303]. Masc. *Gobius viridis* Hamilton 1822:42, 366. Type by monotypy. Valid (Jayaram 1981:368 [ref. 6497], Akihito in Masuda et al. 1984:286 [ref. 6441], Birdsong et al. 1988:195 [ref. 7303], Kottelat 1989:19 [ref. 13605] as *Scarteleos*, Murdy 1989:49 [ref. 13628]). Gobiidae.

Scartella Jordan 1886:50 [ref. 2386]. Fem. *Blennius microstomus* Poey 1861:288. Type by original designation (also monotypic). Type designated on p. 51. Synonym of *Blennius* Linnaeus 1758 (Bath 1973:519 [ref. 7212]); valid (Greenfield & Johnson 1981:72 [ref. 5580], Yoshino in Masuda et al. 1984:296 [ref. 6441], Zander in Whitehead et al. 1986:1112 [ref. 13677]). Blenniidae.

Scartes Jordan & Evermann 1896:471 [ref. 2442]. Masc. *Salarias rubropunctatus* Valenciennes in Cuvier & Valenciennes 1836:348. Type by original designation (also monotypic). Preoccupied by Swainson 1835 in Mammalia, replaced by *Scartichthys* Jordan & Evermann 1898. Objective synonym of *Scartichthys* Jordan & Evermann 1898 (Smith-Vaniz & Springer 1971:39 [ref. 4145], Williams 1989:21 [ref. 13549]). Blenniidae.

Scartichthys Jordan & Evermann 1898:2346, 2395 [ref. 2445]. Masc. *Salarias rubropunctatus* Valenciennes in Cuvier & Valenciennes 1836:348. Type by being a replacement name. Replacement for *Scartes* Jordan & Evermann 1896, preoccupied by Swainson 1835 in Mammalia. Valid (Smith-Vaniz & Springer 1971:39 [ref. 4145], Williams 1989:21 [ref. 13549]). Blenniidae.

Scartoblennius Fowler 1946:174 [ref. 1456]. Masc. *Blennius ellipes* Jordan & Starks 1906:702. Type by original designation (also monotypic). Synonym of *Rhabdoblennius* Whitley 1930 (Smith-Vaniz & Springer 1971:37 [ref. 4145]). Blenniidae.

Scartomyzon (subgenus of *Moxostoma*) Fowler 1913:59 [ref. 1388]. Masc. *Ptychostomus cervinus* Cope 1868:236. Type by original designation (also monotypic). Synonym of *Moxostoma* Rafinesque 1820 (Robins & Raney 1956:5 [ref. 12222]). Catostomidae.

Scarus Bleeker 1849:4, 9, 42, 44 [ref. 317]. Masc. *Labrus cretensis* Linnaeus 1758:282. On p. 9 as "*Scarus*. Vide sub genere Scaro"; otherwise as a genus. Type above as given by Jordan, but that species apparently not mentioned by Bleeker. Not *Scarus* of Gronow 1763 or Forsskål 1775. In the synonymy of *Sparisoma* Swainson 1839 (Monod 1973:444 [ref. 7193]). Scaridae: Sparisomatinae.

Scarus Forsskål 1775:x, 25 [ref. 1351]. Masc. *Scarus psittacus* Forsskål (not of Linnaeus) 1775:x, 29. Type by subsequent designation. Type designated by Swain 1883:274 [ref. 5966]. Not preoccupied by *Scarus* Gronow (not available). Valid (Randall & Choat 1980 [ref. 5543], Randall & Bruce 1983:8 [ref. 5412], Richards & Leis 1984:544 [ref. 13668], Kishimoto in Masuda et al. 1984:218 [ref. 6441], Randall 1986:709 [ref. 5706], Bellwood & Choat 1989:16 et seq. [ref. 13494]). Scaridae: Scarinae.

Scarus Gronow 1763:67 [ref. 1910]. Masc. Not available, published in a rejected work on Official Index (Opinion 261). Labridae.

Scatharus Valenciennes in Cuvier & Valenciennes 1830:375 [ref. 996]. Masc. *Scatharus graecus* Valenciennes in Cuvier & Valenciennes 1830:376. Type by monotypy. Misspelled *Scathurus* by Swainson 1839:223 [ref. 4303]. Kyphosidae: Girellinae.

Scatophagus Cuvier in Cuvier & Valenciennes 1831:136 [ref. 4881]. Masc. *Chaetodon argus* Linnaeus 1766:464. Type by subsequent designation. Type designated by Jordan 1917:136 [ref. 2407]. *Prenes* Gistel 1848 and *Cacodoxus* Cantor 1849 are unneeded replacements, *Scatophagus* not preoccupied. Valid (Ida in Masuda et al. 1984:182 [ref. 6441], Gosline 1985:355 [ref. 5283], Arnoult 1986:341 [ref. 6213], Heemstra 1986:604 [ref. 5660]). Scatophagidae.

Scepterias Jordan & Jordan 1922:44 [ref. 2487]. Masc. *Scepterias fragilis* Jordan & Jordan 1922:45. Type by original designation (also monotypic). Synonym of *Epigonus* Rafinesque 1810 (Mayer 1974:151 [ref. 6007]). Epigonidae.

Schacra Günther 1868:294 [ref. 1990]. *Cyprinus shacra* Hamilton 1822:271. Type by monotypy. Objective synonym of *Shacra* Bleeker 1860. Cyprinidae.

Schedophilopsis Steindachner 1881:396 [ref. 4232]. Fem. *Schedophilopsis spinosus* Steindachner 1881:396. Type by monotypy. Synonym of *Icosteus* Lockington 1880. Icosteidae.

Schedophilus Cocco 1839:30, 57 [ref. 858]. Masc. *Schedophilus medusophagus* Cocco 1839:57. Type by monotypy. Original not examined. Fowler (MS) cites the date of *Schedophilus* as 1834 and for *Mupus* Cocco as 1833 [needs investigation]. Valid (Haedrich 1967:59 [ref. 5357], Haedrich 1973:560 [ref. 7216], McAllister & Randall 1975 [ref. 7079], McDowall 1980 [ref. 6931], McDowall 1981:123 [ref. 5356], Horn 1984:628 [ref. 13637], Haedrich in Whitehead et al. 1986:1180 [ref. 13677], Haedrich 1986:844 [ref. 5659]). Centrolophidae.

Scheponopodus see *Skeponopodus*. Istiophoridae.

Schilbe Oken (ex Cuvier) 1817:1183 [ref. 3303]. Masc. *Silurus mystus* Linnaeus 1758:305. Type by monotypy. First appeared as "Les Schilbé" in Cuvier 1816:202 [ref. 993]; latinized by Oken (see Gill 1903:966 [ref. 5768]). Spelled *Schilbeus*, *Schilbea* and *Schilba* in early literature. Spelled *Schillee* by Jerdon 1849:335 [ref. 4902]. Valid (De Vos 1986:41 [ref. 6191], Burgess 1989:99 [ref. 12860]). Schilbeidae.

Schilbeichthys Bleeker 1858:255, 256 [ref. 365]. Masc. *Silurus garua* Hamilton 1822:156, 375. Type by monotypy. Objective synonym of *Clupisoma* Swainson 1838. Schilbeidae.

Schilbeodes Bleeker 1858:258 [ref. 365]. Masc. *Silurus gyrinus* Mitchill 1817:282. Type by monotypy. Spelled *Schilbeoides* in early literature [not investigated]. Synonym of *Noturus* Rafinesque 1818, but as a valid subgenus (Taylor 1969:20, 32 [ref. 6555]). Ictaluridae.

Schilus Jarocki 1822:224 [ref. 4984]. Masc. *Perca lucioperca* Linnaeus 1758:289. Type by monotypy. *Schilum* is a misspelling. Original not seen. Synonym of *Stizostedion* Rafinesque 1820 (Collette & Banarescu 1977:1457 [ref. 5845]). Percidae.

Schilus Krynicki 1832:441 [ref. 5624]. Masc. *Schilus pallasi* Krynicki 1832:441 (*Perca volgensis* Pallas 1776:461). Type by subsequent designation. Original not examined. Type designated by Jordan 1919:176 [ref. 2410]. Synonym of *Stizostedion* Rafinesque 1820 (Collette & Banarescu 1977:1457 [ref. 5845]). Percidae.

Schindleria Giltay 1934:8 [ref. 13409]. Fem. *Hemirhamphus praematurus* Schindler 1931:7. Type by original designation. Correct spelling for genus of type species is *Hemiramphus*. D. G. Johnson (oral presentation, June 1990) demonstrates that this genus belongs near the suborder Gobioidei and does not show relationships to the ammodytoids. Valid (Bruun 1940 [ref. 13410], Ozawa & Matsui 1979 [ref. 6990], Watson et al. 1984 [ref. 13670], Ida in Masuda et al. 1984:309 [ref. 6441]). Schindleriidae.

Schismatogobius de Beaufort 1912:139 [ref. 235]. Masc. *Schismatogobius bruynisi* de Beaufort 1912:139. Type by original designation (also monotypic). Type designated on p. 139. Valid (Akihito in Masuda et al. 1984:263 [ref. 6441], Kottelat & Pethiyagoda 1989 [ref. 14143]). Gobiidae.

Schismatorhynchos Bleeker 1855:258, 269 [ref. 351]. Neut. *Lobocheilus heterorhynchos* Bleeker 1853:524. Type by monotypy. Spelled two ways when proposed: *Schismatorhijnchos* (p. 258) and *Schismatorhynchos* (p. 260, 269), the latter correctly formed. Subsequently spelled *Schismatorhynchus* by Bleeker 1863:193 [ref. 397] and 1863:25 [ref. 4859]. Valid (Jayaram 1981:115 [ref. 6497] as *Schismatorhynchus*, Roberts 1989:79 [ref. 6439]). Cyprinidae.

Schismorhynchus McCosker 1970:509 [ref. 2931]. Masc. *Muraenichthys labialis* Seale 1917:79. Type by original designation (also monotypic). Name given as neuter in original description; changed to masculine in 1977 [ref. 6836]. Valid (McCosker 1977:61 [ref. 6836], Paxton et al. 1989:121 [ref. 12442]. McCosker et al. 1989:271 [ref. 13288]). Ophichthidae: Myrophinae.

Schistoperca Fowler 1943:61 [ref. 1441]. Fem. *Schistoperca macrobrachium* Fowler 1943:62. Type by original designation (also monotypic). Synonym of *Bathysphyraenops* Parr 1933. Percoidei.

Schistorus Gill 1862:236, 237 [ref. 1664]. Masc. *Serranus mystacinus* Poey 1862:52. Type by monotypy. Synonym of *Epinephelus* Bloch 1793 (C. L. Smith 1971:103 [ref. 14102], Daget & Smith 1986:301 [ref. 6204]). Serranidae: Epinephelinae.

Schistura (subgenus of *Cobitis*) McClelland 1839:306, 439 [ref. 2923]. Fem. *Cobitis rupecula [rupicula]* McClelland 1839:309, 441. Type by subsequent designation. Also (possibly first) in McClelland 1839:944, 947 [ref. 2924] (which Kottelat 1990:21 dates to 1838). Species as *rupecula*, corrected to *rupicola* in bound errata sheet. Type apparently first designated by Jordan 1919:195 [ref. 2410]. Valid (Mirza et al. 1981 [ref. 5390], Kottelat 1989:12 [ref. 13605], Kottelat 1990:21 [ref. 14137]); as a subgenus of *Noemacheilus* Kuhl & van Hasselt 1823 (Jayaram 1981:151 [ref. 6497], Menon 1987:37 [ref. 14149]). Balitoridae: Nemacheilinae.

Schizochirus Waite 1904:241 [ref. 13443]. Masc. *Schizochirus insolens* Waite 1904:242. Type by monotypy. Valid (Nelson 1985 [ref. 5154]). Creediidae.

Schizocypris Regan 1914:262 [ref. 3663]. Fem. *Schizocypris brucei* Regan 1914:262. Type by monotypy. Valid (Tsao 1964:168 [ref. 13501]). Cyprinidae.

Schizodon Agassiz in Spix & Agassiz 1829:58, 66 [ref. 13]. Masc. *Schizodon fasciatus* Agassiz in Spix & Agassiz 1829:66. Type by monotypy. For authorship and date see Kottelat 1988:78 [ref. 13380]. Valid (Géry 1977:151 [ref. 1597], Winterbottom 1980:2 [ref. 4755], Vari 1983:5 [ref. 5419], Géry et al. 1987:375 [ref. 6001], Malabarba 1989:126 [ref. 14217]). Curimatidae: Anostominae.

Schizodontopsis (subgenus of *Anostomus*) Garman 1890:16, 18 [ref. 1535]. Fem. *Schizodontopsis proximus* Garman 1890:19. Type by subsequent designation. Type apparently first designated by Jordan 1920:451 [ref. 4905]. Synonym of *Laemolyta* Cope 1872. Curimatidae: Anostominae.

Schizolecis Britski & Garavello 1984:228 [ref. 5166]. *Microlepidogaster guntheri* Miranda-Ribeiro 1918:634. Type by original designation (also monotypic). Valid (Burgess 1989:439 [ref. 12860]). Loricariidae.

Schizophallus (subgenus of *Gambusia*) Hubbs 1926:25, 40 [ref. 2233]. Masc. *Gambusia holbrookii* Girard 1860:61. Type by original designation. Synonym of *Gambusia* Poey 1854 (Rivas 1963:333 [ref. 3761], Rosen & Bailey 1963:90 [ref. 7067]). Poeciliidae.

Schizopyge Heckel 1847:285 [ref. 2068]. Fem. *Schizothorax curvifrons* Heckel 1838:25. Type by subsequent designation. Type designated by Bleeker 1863:196 [ref. 397] and 1863:26 [ref. 4859]. Original not examined. Synonym of *Schizothorax* Heckel 1838 (Mo in Chu & Chen 1989:287 [ref. 13584]); as a valid subgenus (Tsao 1964:139 [ref. 13501]); valid genus (Jayaram 1981:63 [ref. 6497], Mirza & Saeed 1988:313 [ref. 13385]). Cyprinidae.

Schizopygopsis Steindachner 1866:785 [ref. 5030]. Fem. *Schizopygopsis stoliczkae* Steindachner 1866:786. Type by monotypy. Valid (Tsao 1964:184 [ref. 13501], Tchang & Yueh 1964 [ref. 3504], Jayaram 1981:68 [ref. 6497], Wu 1987:47 [ref. 12822], Wu 1987:111 [ref. 12824]). Cyprinidae.

Schizothoraichthys Misra 1962:48 [ref. 3026]. Masc. *Schizothorax esocinus* Heckel 1838:48. Type by original designation. Synonym of *Schizopyge* Heckel 1847 (Jayaram 1981:63 [ref. 6497]); synonym of *Schizothorax* Heckel 1838 (Mo in Chu & Chen 1989:287 [ref. 13584]). Cyprinidae.

Schizothorax Heckel 1838:11 [ref. 2063]. Masc. *Schizothorax plagiostomus* Heckel 1838:16. Type by subsequent designation. Type apparently first designated by Bleeker 1863:196 [ref. 397], 1863:26 [ref. 4859] and 1863:262 [ref. 403], not *cavifrons* designated by Günther 1868. Original not seen. Valid (Tsao 1964:139 [ref. 13501], Karaman 1971:191 [ref. 2560], Jayaram 1981:67 [ref. 6497], Terashima 1984 [ref. 6729], Wu 1987:44 [ref. 12822], Mirza & Saeed 1988 [ref. 13385], Mo in Chu & Chen 1989:287 [ref. 13584]). Cyprinidae.

Schmidtia Jordan & Starks 1904:237 [ref. 2528]. Fem. *Schmidtia misakia* Jordan & Starks 1904:237. Type by original designation (also monotypic). Preoccupied [details not researched]; replaced by *Schmidtina* Jordan & Starks 1904. Cottidae.

Schmidtina Jordan & Starks 1904:961 [ref. 2529]. Fem. *Schmidtia misakia* Jordan & Starks 1904:237. Type by being a replacement name. Replacement for *Schmidtia* Jordan & Starks 1904, preoccupied [details not researched]. Cottidae.

Schour (subgenus of *Sciaena*) Forsskål 1775:44 [ref. 1351]. *Sciaena nebulosa* Forsskål 1775:xii, 52. Not available, regarded as non-latinized Arabic name (see Jordan 1917:33-34 [ref. 2407]). In the synonymy of *Lethrinus* Cuvier 1829. Lethrinidae.

Schraitzer Schaeffer 1761:38 [ref. 3910]. Not available, published in a rejected work on Official Index (Opinion 345). Original not examined. In the synonymy of *Gymnocephalus* Bloch 1793 (Collette & Banarescu 1977:1453 [ref. 5845]). Percidae.

Schroederichthys Springer 1966:604 [ref. 4174]. Masc. *Schroederichthys maculatus* Springer 1966:605. Type by original designation. Valid (Springer 1979:115 [ref. 4175], Uyeno & Sasaki in Uyeno et al. 1983:52 [ref. 14275], Compagno 1984:351 [ref. 6846], Compagno 1988:107 [ref. 13488] in new subfamily Schroederichthyinae). Scyliorhinidae.

Schroederobatis (subgenus of *Anacanthobatis*) Hulley 1973:154 [ref. 2275]. Fem. *Anacanthobatis americanus* Bigelow & Schroeder 1962:217. Type by original designation (also monotypic). Synonym of *Anacanthobatis* von Bonde and Swart 1923, but as a valid subgenus (Hulley 1986:127 [ref. 5672], Séret 1986:322 [ref. 6753]). Anacanthobatidae.

Schubotzia Boulenger 1914:258 [ref. 582]. Fem. *Schubotzia eduardiana* Boulenger 1914:258. Type by monotypy. Valid (Greenwood 1980:85 [ref. 1899]). Cichlidae.

Schuettea Steindachner 1866:449 [ref. 4210]. Fem. *Schuettea scalaripinnis* Steindachner 1866:449. Type by monotypy. Monodactylidae.

Schultzea Woods 1958:249 [ref. 4761]. Fem. *Schultzea campechanus* Woods 1958:250. Type by original designation (also monotypic). Not preoccupied by *Shultzea* Zachvatkin 1941 in Arachnida; *Schultzetta* Whitley 1965 is an unneeded replacement. Valid (Robins et al. 1980:38 [ref. 7111], Kendall 1984:500 [ref. 13663]). Serranidae: Serraninae.

Schultzetta Whitley 1965:26 [ref. 4733]. Fem. *Schultzea campechanus* Woods 1958:250. Type by being a replacement name. Unneeded replacement for *Schultzea* Woods 1958, not preoccupied by *Shultzea* Zachvatkin 1941 in Arachnida. Objective synonym of *Schultzea* Woods 1958. Serranidae: Serraninae.

Schultzichthys Dahl 1960:312 [ref. 5836]. Masc. *Schultzichthys gracilis* Dahl 1960:312. Type by monotypy. Trichomycteridae.

Schultzidia (subgenus of *Muraenichthys*) Gosline 1951:309 [ref. 1858]. Fem. *Muraenichthys johnstonensis* Schultz & Woods 1949:172. Type by original designation (also monotypic). Second species doubtfully included. Valid (McCosker 1977:61 [ref. 6836], McCosker et al. 1989:271 [ref. 13288]). Ophichthidae: Myrophinae.

Schultzites Géry 1964:31 [ref. 1582]. Masc. *Schultzites axelrodi* Géry 1964:32. Type by original designation (also monotypic). Valid (Géry 1977:450 [ref. 1597]). Characidae.

Schwetzochromis Poll 1948:99 [ref. 3519]. Masc. *Schwetzochromis neodon* Poll 1948:99. Type by monotypy. Cichlidae.

Sciadeichthys Bleeker 1858:62, 66 [ref. 365]. Masc. *Bagrus (Sciades) emphysetus* Müller & Troschel 1849:8. Type by monotypy. Type not *pictus* as designated by Bleeker 1863:10 [ref. 393]. Objective synonym of *Sciades* Müller & Troschel 1849. Ariidae.

Sciadeoides (subgenus of *Sciades*) Eigenmann & Eigenmann 1888:136 [ref. 1249]. Masc. *Sciades marmoratus* Gill 1870:55. Type by monotypy. Type of this species included by Stewart 1986:668 [ref. 5211] in *Leiarius* Bleeker 1862. Pimelodidae.

Sciadeops (subgenus of *Sciades*) Fowler 1944:211 [ref. 1448]. Masc. *Sciades troschelii* Gill 1863:171. Type by original designation (also monotypic). Ariidae.

Sciades (subgenus of *Bagrus*) Müller & Troschel 1849:6 [ref. 3073]. *Bagrus (Sciades) emphysetus* Müller & Troschel 1849:8. Type by subsequent designation. Type apparently designated first by Bleeker 1862:8 [ref. 393], not *Bagrus pictus* designated by Eigenmann 1910:390 [ref. 1224]. Unfortunately, Bleeker 1858:62, 66 used *Sciades* for *B. pictus*, but his 1858 treatment does not constitute type designation for *Sciades*. Therefore, *Sciades* should be treated in the Ariidae, and as a senior synonym of *Sciadeichthys*. Ariidae.

Sciadonus Garman 1899:171 [ref. 1540]. Masc. *Sciadonus pedicellaris* Garman 1899:172. Type by monotypy. Valid (Nielsen 1969:62 [ref. 3195], Cohen & Nielsen 1978:62 [ref. 881], Nielsen in Whitehead et al. 1986:1171 [ref. 13677], Pequeño 1989:49 [ref. 14125]). Aphyonidae.

Sciaena Linnaeus 1758:288 [ref. 2787]. Fem. *Sciaena umbra* Linnaeus 1758:289. Type designated by ICZN (Opinion 988, supersedes Opinion 93); name placed on Official List. *Sciaena* Cuvier in Cuvier & Valenciennes 1830:28 regarded as a new definition but not an original description. Valid (Trewavas 1973:396 [ref. 7201], Chao 1978:28 [ref. 6983]). Sciaenidae.

Sciaenochromis Eccles & Trewavas 1989:231 [ref. 13547]. Masc. *Haplochromis ahli* Trewavas 1935:101. Type by original designation. Cichlidae.

Sciaenoides Blyth 1860:139 [ref. 477]. Masc. *Otolithus biauritus* Cantor 1849:347. Type by subsequent designation. Type designated by Bleeker 1876:330 [ref. 448]. Apparently not preoccupied by Richardson 1843 in fishes (name in synonymy); *Otolithoides* Fowler 1933 is an unneeded replacement. Correct spelling for genus of type species is *Otolithes*. Sciaenidae.

Sciaenoides Richardson (ex Solander) 1850:62 [ref. 3745]. Masc. *Sciaenoides abdominalis* Solander (manuscript) (= *Sciaena macroptera* Forster). Not available, name in synonymy; apparently never made available. Might have appeared in 1843 (see Whitley 1935:235 [ref. 4683]). Species *macroptera* appeared in Bloch & Schneider 1801:342. In the synonymy of *Dactylosparus* Gill 1862. Cheilodactylidae.

Sciaenops Gill 1863:30 [ref. 1678]. Masc. *Perca ocellata* Linnaeus 1766:483. Type by monotypy. Valid (Chao 1978:34 [ref. 6983]). Sciaenidae.

Sciaenus Commerson in Lacepède 1803:682 (footnote) [ref. 4930]. Masc. Non-binominal Commerson name mentioned in passing under *Caranxomorus sacrestinus*. Commerson footnotes in this volume are on the Official Index of Rejected Works; see remarks under Opinion 89 in Appendix B. Lutjanidae.

Scianectes Alcock 1889:284 [ref. 85]. Masc. *Scianectes lophoptera* Alcock 1889:284. Type by monotypy. Type not *S. macrophthalmus* as given by Norman 1934:252 [ref. 6893]). Synonym of *Laeops* Günther 1880 (Norman 1934:252 [ref. 6893], Amaoka 1969:204 [ref. 105]). Bothidae: Bothinae.

Scidorhombus Tanaka 1915:567 [ref. 4324]. Masc. *Scidorhombus pallidus* Tanaka 1915:567. Type by monotypy. Synonym of *Arnoglossus* Bleeker 1862 (Amaoka 1969:186 [ref. 105]). Bothidae: Bothinae.

Scimnus S. D. W. 1837 [ref. 12605]. Whitley 1955 [ref. 4724] discusses this name (*Thinnus* also included). Perhaps can be regarded as an unjustified emendation of *Scymnus* Cuvier. Original not examined. Synonym of *Dalatias* Rafinesque 1810 (Compagno 1984:63 [ref. 6474]). Squalidae.

Scissor Günther 1864:331 [ref. 1974]. Masc. *Scissor macrocephalus* Günther 1864:331. Type by monotypy. Valid (Géry 1977:323 [ref. 1597]). Characidae.

Sclerocottus Fischer 1885:58 [ref. 1333]. Masc. *Sclerocottus schraderi* Fischer 1885:58. Type by monotypy. Synonym of *Gymnocanthus* Swainson 1839 (Neyelov 1973:595 [ref. 7219]). Cottidae.

Sclerognathus Valenciennes in Cuvier & Valenciennes 1844:472 [ref. 1010]. Masc. *Catostomus cyprinus* Lesueur 1817:91. Type by subsequent designation. Genus restricted by Günther 1868:22-23 [ref. 1990] but type not technically designated; type apparently first designated by Jordan & Gilbert 1877:89 [ref. 4907]. Synonym of *Carpiodes* Rafinesque 1820. Catostomidae.

Scleromystax (subgenus of *Callichthys*) Günther 1864:225, 229 [ref. 1974]. Masc. *Callichthys barbatus* Quoy & Gaimard 1824:234. Type by monotypy. Described as a subgenus in key (p. 225) with species on p. 229. Synonym of *Corydoras* Lacepède 1803 (Nijssen & Isbrücker 1980:192 [ref. 6910]). Callichthyidae.

Scleronema Eigenmann 1917:691 [ref. 1237]. Neut. *Scleronema operculatum* Eigenmann 1917:691. Type by original designation (also monotypic). Valid (Burgess 1989:321 [ref. 12860], Pinna 1989:31 [ref. 12630], Malabarba 1989:145 [ref. 14217]). Trichomycteridae.

Scleropages Günther 1864:196 [ref. 1978]. Masc. *Scleropages leichardti* Günther 1864:196. Type by monotypy. See Berra 1989 [ref. 13530] for comments on spelling of specific name. Valid (Paxton et al. 1989:103 [ref. 12442], Kottelat 1989:4 [ref. 13605], Roberts 1989:23 [ref. 6439]). Osteoglossidae: Osteoglossinae.

Scleropteryx Waite 1906:209 [ref. 6937]. *Ophioclinus [sic] devisi* Ogilby 1894:373. Type by original designation. Appeared first as a "Museum name" credited to De Vis and mentioned in synonymy of *Ophiclinus* Castelnau by Ogilby 1894:372 [ref. 3267]; published in an available way as above. If regarded as a name first published in synonymy, then genus dates to Ogilby 1894. Synonym of *Peronedys* Steindachner 1884 (George & Springer 1980:24 [ref. 6935]). Clinidae.

Sclerotis Hubbs in Ortenburger & Hubbs 1926:138 [ref. 3306]. *Lepomis miniatus* Jordan 1877:26. Type by original designation (also monotypic). Synonym of *Lepomis* Rafinesque 1819. Centrarchidae.

Scobatus (subgenus of *Rhinobatos*) Whitley 1939:244 [ref. 4695]. Masc. *Rhinobatos granulatus* Blainville 1816. Type by original designation, also monotypic, used for 2 species treated by Norman, but only one species mentioned by name. Synonym of *Rhinobatos* Linck 1790. Rhinobatidae: Rhinobatinae.

Scobinancistrus Isbrücker & Nijssen 1989:542 [ref. 13622]. Masc. *Scobinancistrus pariolispos* Isbrücker & Nijssen 1989:542. Type by original designation (also monotypic). Loricariidae.

Scobinichthys Whitley 1931:332 [ref. 4672]. Masc. *Balistes granulata* White (or Shaw) 1790:295. Type by original designation (also monotypic). Valid (Matsuura 1979:165 [ref. 7019], Tyler 1980:178 [ref. 4477], Arai 1983:200 [ref. 14249]). Monacanthidae.

Scolecenchelys Ogilby 1897:246 [ref. 3273]. Fem. *Muraenichthys australis* Macleay 1882:272. Type by monotypy. Spelled *Scolenchelys* in Zoological Record for 1897 and by Jordan 1920:477 [ref. 4905]. Synonym of *Muraenichthys* Bleeker 1853 (McCosker 1970:509 [ref. 2931], McCosker 1977:58 [ref. 6836]). Ophichthidae: Myrophinae.

Scolecosoma Girard 1858:384 [ref. 4911]. Neut. *Ammocoetes concolor* Kirtland 1838. Type by subsequent designation. Type designated by Jordan & Gilbert 1877:92 [ref. 4907]. Correct spelling for genus of type species is *Ammocoetus*. Synonym of *Ichthyomyzon* Girard 1858 (Hubbs & Potter 1971:40 [ref. 13397]). Petromyzontidae: Petromyzontinae.

Scolichthys Rosen 1967:2 [ref. 3808]. Masc. *Scolichthys greenwayi* Rosen 1967:4. Type by original designation. Valid (Parenti & Rauchenberger 1989:8 [ref. 13538]). Poeciliidae.

Scoliodon Müller & Henle 1837:114 [ref. 3067]. Masc. *Carcharias (Scoliodon) laticaudus* Müller & Henle 1838:28 [first p. 28]. Type apparently by subsequent monotypy in Müller & Henle 1838:28 [ref. 3069], also in Bonaparte 1838:10 of separate [ref. 4979]. Also without description in Müller & Henle 1838:84 [ref. 3068]. Valid

(Compagno 1984:533 [ref. 6846], Nakaya in Masuda et al. 1984:5 [ref. 6441], Compagno 1988:284 [ref. 13488]). Carcharhinidae.

Scoliophis Anonymous 1817 From Compagno 1984:234 [ref. 6474], not investigated. Doubtful synonym of *Cetorhinus* Blainville 1816 (Compagno 1984:234 [ref. 6474]). Cetorhinidae.

Scoliostomus Rüppell 1828:17 [ref. 3843]. Masc. *Lutodeira indica* van Hasselt 1823:333. Type by subsequent designation. Type apparently first designated by Jordan 1919:122 [ref. 2407]; type may be *Mugil chanos* Linnaeus by monotypy. Synonym of *Chanos* Lacepède 1803 (Arnoult 1984:128 [ref. 6179]). Chanidae.

Scolopacichthys Regan 1914:21 [ref. 3662]. Masc. *Centriscus armatus* Sauvage 1879:36. Type by monotypy. Centriscidae: Macroramphosinae.

Scoloplax Bailey & Baskin 1976:5 [ref. 161]. Fem. *Scoloplax dicra* Bailey & Baskin 1976:7. Type by original designation (also monotypic). Valid (Isbrücker 1980:130 [ref. 2303], Burgess 1989:450 [ref. 12860], Schaefer et al. 1989 [ref. 13514]). Scoloplacidae.

Scolopsides Cuvier 1829:178 [ref. 995]. Masc. *Scolopsides kurita* Cuvier 1929:178. Type by subsequent designation. Type apparently designated first by Jordan 1917:128 [ref. 2407]; *kurita* is available from 1829 by reference to Russell. Earlier called *Scolopsis* by Cuvier. Synonym of *Scolopsis* Cuvier 1814. Nemipteridae.

Scolopsis Cuvier 1814:90 [ref. 4884]. Fem. *Scolopsides kate* Cuvier 1829:178. Type by subsequent monotypy. Usually dated to Cuvier 1815:361 [ref. 1019]. In 1816:280 [ref. 993], Cuvier mentiones only "le *kurite*" and "*botche*" as figured by Russell. By 1829:178 [ref. 995] Cuvier had adopted the name *Scolopsides*; first addition of available species in *Scolopsis* of 1814 not researched, possibly by Bleeker 1876:270 [ref. 447] who designated *Scolopsis [Scolopsides] kate* Cuvier 1829 as type. Valid (Akazaki in Masuda et al. 1984:175 [ref. 6441], Russell 1986:601 [ref. 5708]). Nemipteridae.

Scomber Linnaeus 1758:297 [ref. 2787]. Masc. *Scomber scombrus* Linnaeus 1758:297. Type by subsequent designation. Type designated by Gill 1862:125 [ref. 1659]. On Official List (Opinion 77, Direction 56). Valid (Postel 1973:465 [ref. 7208], Collette & Nauen 1983:55 [ref. 5375], Collette et al. 1984:600 [ref. 11421], Nakamura in Masuda et al. 1984:224 [ref. 6441], Collette 1986:835 [ref. 5647]). Scombridae.

Scomberesox Lacepède 1803:344 [ref. 4930]. Masc. *Scomberesox camperii* Lacepède 1803:344, 345. Type by monotypy. *Scombresox* and *Scombrisox* of early authors are misspellings or incorrect subsequent spellings. Valid (Parin 1973:261 [ref. 7191], Hubbs & Wisner 1980 [ref. 2267], Collette et al. 1984:336 [ref. 11422], Parin in Whitehead et al. 1986:611 [ref. 13676], Smith 1986:388 [ref. 5712], Paxton et al. 1989:345 [ref. 12442]). Scomberesocidae.

Scomberoides Lacepède 1801:50 [ref. 2710]. Masc. *Scomberoides noelii* Lacepède 1801:50, 51. Type by subsequent designation. Type designated by Jordan & Gilbert 1883:446 [ref. 2476]; can be *commersonnianus* Lacepède 1801:50,53 as designated by Jordan 1917:60 [ref. 2407], if *noelii* is a nomen dubium (see Smith-Vaniz et al. 1979:6 [ref. 12247]. Valid (Smith-Vaniz & Staiger 1973:190 [ref. 7106], Smith-Vaniz 1984:524 [ref. 13664], Gushiken in Masuda et al. 1984:153 [ref. 6441], Smith-Vaniz 1986:654 [ref. 5718], Paxton et al. 1989:582 [ref. 12442]). Carangidae.

Scomberomorus Lacepède 1801:292 [ref. 2710]. Masc. *Scomberomorus plumierii* Lacepède 1801:292, 293. Type by monotypy. Valid (Postel 1973:473 [ref. 7208], Collette et al. 1984:600 [ref. 11421], Collette & Russo 1984 [ref. 5221], Nakamura in Masuda et al. 1984:225 [ref. 6441], Kottelat 1985:273 [ref. 11441], Collette & Russo 1985 [ref. 5217], Collette 1986:835 [ref. 5647]). Scombridae.

Scomberopsis see *Scombrocypris*. Cyprinidae.

Scombrocottus Peters 1872:568 [ref. 3452]. Masc. *Scombrocottus salmoneus* Peters 1872:569. Type by monotypy. Synonym of *Anoplopoma* Ayres 1859. Anoplopomatidae.

Scombrocypris Günther 1889:226 [ref. 2016]. Fem. *Scombrocypris styani* Günther 1889:226. Type by monotypy. Jordan 1920:446 [ref. 4905] lists a *Scomberopsis* Günther 1889:226, with type as *styani*, but this is in error; Jordan lists *Scombrocypris* correctly. Synonym of *Elopichthys* Bleeker 1859. Cyprinidae.

Scombrolabrax Roule 1921:1534 [ref. 3819]. Masc. *Scombrolabrax heterolepis* Roule 1921:1534. Type by monotypy. Also appeared in Roule 1922:498 [ref. 3820] and Roule 1922:1 et seq. [ref. 3819]. Placement follows Collette et al 1984:591 [ref. 11421]; Johnson 1986 [ref. 5676] removes from the Scombroidei. Valid (Parin & Bekker 1973:461 [ref. 7206], Collette et al. 1984:600 [ref. 11421], Nakamura in Masuda et al. 1984:224 [ref. 6441], Parin in Whitehead et al. 1986:974 [ref. 13676], Nakamura 1986:825 [ref. 5696]). Scombrolabracidae.

Scombrops Temminck & Schlegel 1845:118 [ref. 4373]. Masc. *Scombrops cheilodipteroides* Bleeker 1853:9. Type by subsequent monotypy. Original description without species; one species added by Bleeker 1853:9 [ref. 340] and 1857:58 [ref. 357]. Valid (Mochizuki in Masuda et al. 1984:152 [ref. 6441], Heemstra 1986:563 [ref. 5660]). Scombropidae.

Scombrosphyraena Fourmanoir 1970:28 [ref. 1356]. Fem. *Scombrosphyraena oceanica* Fourmanoir 1970:27. Type by monotypy. Synonym of *Sphyraenops* Gill 1860 (Suda & Tominaga 1983:291 [ref. 5795]). Epigonidae.

Scopaeocharax Weitzman & Fink 1985:56 [ref. 5203]. Masc. *Tyttocharax rhinodus* Böhlke 1958:320. Type by original designation. Characidae: Glandulocaudinae.

Scopas (subgenus of *Teuthis*) Bonaparte 1831:175 [ref. 4978]. *Acanthurus scopas* Valenciennes in Cuvier & Valenciennes 1835:196. Type by subsequent designation. Apparently not available, appeared with no included species or distinguishing features; type presumed and designated by Jordan 1919:175 [ref. 2410]; apparently published in an available way by Kner 1865. In the synonymy of *Zebrasoma* Swainson 1839 (Randall 1955:363 [ref. 13648]). Acanthuridae.

Scopas Kner (ex Bonaparte) 1865:212 [ref. 2638]. *Acanthurus scopas* Valenciennes in Cuvier & Valenciennes 1835:196. Appeared first without species. Addition of species and type fixation not researched; type as given by Jordan 1919:175 [ref. 2410]. Acanthuridae.

Scopelapogon (subgenus of *Adenapogon*) Whitley 1933:74 [ref. 4677]. Masc. *Scopelus cephalotes* Castelnau 1875:46. Type by being a replacement name. Possibly can be regarded as a replacement for *Scopelus* Castelnau 1875, preoccupied by Johnson 1863 in fishes; Whitley named *Adenapogon woodi* as type; see discussion in Appendix A). Synonym of *Siphamia* Weber 1909 (Fraser 1972:14 [ref. 5195]). Apogonidae.

Scopelarchoides Parr 1929:14 [ref. 3369]. Masc. *Scopelarchoides nicholsi* Parr 1929:16. Type by original designation (also monotypic). Valid (Johnson 1974:116 [ref. 7050], Johnson 1982:165 [ref. 5519], Johnson 1986:266 [ref. 5677], Paxton et al.

1989:233 [ref. 12442]). Scopelarchidae.

Scopelarchus Alcock 1896:306 [ref. 91]. Masc. *Scopelarchus guentheri* Alcock 1896:307. Type by monotypy. Valid (Maul 1973:199 [ref. 7171], Johnson 1974 [ref. 2361], Johnson 1982:169 [ref. 5519], Johnson in Whitehead et al. 1984:486 [ref. 13675], Okiyama 1984:207 [ref. 13644], Fujii in Masuda et al. 1984:63 [ref. 6441], Johnson 1986:267 [ref. 5677], Paxton et al. 1989:234 [ref. 12442]). Scopelarchidae.

Scopelengys Alcock 1890:302 [ref. 83]. *Scopelengys tristis* Alcock 1890:303. Type by monotypy. Misprinted *Scopelogenys* in Zoological Record for 1890 and in Jordan 1920:449 [ref. 4905]. Valid (Nielsen 1973:170 [ref. 6885], Hulley in Whitehead et al. 1984:428 [ref. 13675], Okiyama 1984:207 [ref. 13644], Fujii in Masuda et al. 1984:75 [ref. 6441], Hulley 1986:322 [ref. 5672]). Neoscopelidae.

Scopeloberyx Zugmayer 1911:8 [ref. 6161]. Masc. *Scopeloberyx opercularis* Zugmayer 1911:8. Type by monotypy. Also appeared in Zugmayer 1911 (Dec.):103 [ref. 4846]. Valid (Maul 1973:346 [ref. 7171], Ebeling & Weed 1973:444 [ref. 6898], Fujii in Masuda et al. 1984:110 [ref. 6441], Maul in Whitehead et al. 1986:762 [ref. 13676], Ebeling 1986:430 [ref. 5651], Paxton et al. 1989:372 [ref. 12442]). Melamphaidae.

Scopelogadus Vaillant 1888:141 [ref. 4496]. Masc. *Scopelogadus cocles* Vaillant 1888:143. Type by monotypy. Valid (Maul 1973:344 [ref. 7171], Ebeling & Weed 1973:422 [ref. 6898], Fujii in Masuda et al. 1984:110 [ref. 6441], Maul in Whitehead et al. 1986:765 [ref. 13676], Ebeling 1986:431 [ref. 5651], Paxton et al. 1989:372 [ref. 12442]). Melamphaidae.

Scopelopsis Brauer 1906:146 [ref. 632]. Fem. *Scopelopsis multipunctatus* Brauer 1906:146. Type by monotypy. Valid (Paxton 1979:17 [ref. 6440], Moser et al. 1984:220 [ref. 13645], Paxton et al. 1984:241 [ref. 13625], Hulley 1986:318 [ref. 5672], Paxton et al. 1989:268 [ref. 12442]). Myctophidae.

Scopelosaurus Bleeker 1860:12 [ref. 378]. Masc. *Scopelosaurus hoedti* Bleeker 1860:13. Type by monotypy. Valid (Krefft 1973:168 [ref. 7166], Bertelsen et al. 1976:31 [ref. 289], Krefft in Whitehead et al. 1984:423 [ref. 13675], Okiyama 1984:207 [ref. 13644], Fujii in Masuda et al. 1984:63 [ref. 6441], Krefft 1986:268 [ref. 5684], Paxton et al. 1989:229 [ref. 12442]). Notosudidae.

Scopelus Cuvier 1816:169 [ref. 993]. Masc. *Serpe [= Gasteropelecus] humboldti* Risso 1810:358. Type by subsequent designation. Possibly based on a misidentified type species. Type evidently first designated by Goode & Bean 1896:70 [ref. 1848] as *humboldti* of Risso = *Myctophum punctatus* Rafinesque 1810. Whitley 1953 [ref. 4718] says type is *M. humboldti* of Waite 1911 but not of Risso. Synonym of *Myctophum* Rafinesque 1810 (Krefft & Bekker 1973:171 [ref. 7181], Paxton 1979:15 [ref. 6440]). Myctophidae.

Scopelus (subgenus of *Myctophum*) Fraser-Brunner 1949:1054 [ref. 1496]. Masc. *Gasteropelecus humboldti* Risso (= *Myctophus boops* Richardson, fide Bolin). Apparently not an original description; attributed to Cuvier by Fraser-Brunner, with stated type as *G. humboldti* Risso (but evidently misidentified). In the synonymy of *Symbolophorus* Bolin & Wisner (Krefft & Bekker 1973:197 [ref. 7181]). Myctophidae.

Scophthalmus Rafinesque 1810:14, 53 [ref. 3595]. Masc. *Pleuronectes rhombus* Linnaeus 1758:271. Type by subsequent designation. Type designated by Jordan 1917:82 [ref. 2407]. Valid (Norman 1934:262 [ref. 6893], Nielsen 1973:616 [ref. 6885], Ahlstrom et al. 1984:640 [ref. 13641], Nielsen in Whitehead et al. 1986:1291 [ref. 13677]). Scophthalmidae.

Scopularia de Buen 1959:95 [ref. 696]. Fem. *Scopularia rubra* de Buen 1959:95. Type by original designation (also monotypic). Synonym of *Hypoplectrodes* Gill 1862 (Anderson & Heemstra 1989:1003 [ref. 13526]). Serranidae: Anthiinae.

Scorpaena Linnaeus 1758:266 [ref. 2787]. Fem. *Scorpaena porcus* Linnaeus 1758:266. Type by subsequent designation. Type designated by Bleeker 1876:3 [ref. 12248] and 1876:295 [ref. 450]. On Official List (Opinion 77, Direction 56). Valid (Blanc & Hureau 1973:579 [ref. 7218], Shimizu in Masuda et al. 1984:314 [ref. 6441], Hureau & Litvinenko in Whitehead et al. 1986:1214 [ref. 13677], Eschmeyer 1986:471 [ref. 5652], Paxton et al. 1989:447 [ref. 12442]). Scorpaenidae: Scorpaeninae.

Scorpaenella Fowler 1938:83 [ref. 1426]. Fem. *Scorpaenella cypho* Fowler 1938:83. Type by original designation (also monotypic). Synonym of *Setarches* Johnson 1862 (Eschmeyer & Collette 1966:355 [ref. 6485]). Scorpaenidae: Setarchinae.

Scorpaenichthys Bleeker 1856:385, 402 [ref. 353]. Masc. *Perca gibbosa* Bloch & Schneider 1801:192. Type by subsequent designation. Type apparently first designated by Jordan 1919:267 [ref. 2410]. Preoccupied by Girard 1854 in fishes, not replaced. Synonym of *Scorpaenopsis* Heckel 1837 (Eschmeyer & Randall 1975:296 [ref. 6389]). Scorpaenidae: Scorpaeninae.

Scorpaenichthys Girard 1854:131 [ref. 1817]. Masc. *Hemitripteras marmoratus* Ayres 1854:174. Type by monotypy. See Lea & Eschmeyer 1988 [ref. 12249] and Opinion 1583 in Appendix B); genus name on Official List with type species as given above. Correct spelling of the genus of the type species is *Hemitripterus*. Valid (Washington et al. 1984:443 [ref. 13660], Yabe 1985:111 [ref. 11522]). Cottidae.

Scorpaenodes Bleeker 1857:371 [ref. 358]. Masc. *Scorpaena polylepis* Bleeker 1851:173. Type by monotypy. Valid (Blanc & Hureau 1973:583 [ref. 7218], Shimizu in Masuda et al. 1984:314 [ref. 6441], Hureau & Litvinenko in Whitehead et al. 1986:1221 [ref. 13677], Eschmeyer 1986:471 [ref. 5652], Paxton et al. 1989:449 [ref. 12442]). Scorpaenidae: Scorpaeninae.

Scorpaenopsella Fowler 1938:67 [ref. 1426]. Fem. *Scorpaenopsella armata* Fowler 1938:68. Type by original designation (also monotypic). Scorpaenidae: Scorpaeninae.

Scorpaenopsis Heckel 1837:158 [ref. 2079]. Fem. *Scorpaena nesogalica* Cuvier in Cuvier & Valenciennes 1829:315. Type by subsequent designation. Type designated by Bleeker 1876:4 and 28 [ref. 12248]; Bleeker designated *Scorpaena gibbosa* Bloch as type (not an included species) but on p. 28 treated *nesogalica* and *gibbosa* as synonyms, therefore *nesogalica* is type (Art. 69 (v)). Valid (Eschmeyer 1986:473 [ref. 5652], Paxton et al. 1989:450 [ref. 12442]). Scorpaenidae: Scorpaeninae.

Scorpichthes (subgenus of *Cottus*) Bonaparte 1846:62 [ref. 519]. Masc. *Cottus scorpius* Linnaeus 1758:265. Type by subsequent designation. Apparently not available, plural form only in parallel with "Cotti" as two subgroups of *Cottus*. In the synonymy of *Myoxocephalus* Tilesius 1811. Cottidae.

Scorpiodoras Eigenmann 1925:305, 324 [ref. 1244]. Masc. *Doras heckelii* Kner 1855:125. Type by original designation (also monotypic). Valid (Burgess 1989:224 [ref. 12860]). Doradidae.

Scorpis Valenciennes in Cuvier & Valenciennes 1832:503 [ref. 1000]. Fem. *Scorpis georgianus* Valenciennes in Cuvier & Valenciennes 1832:503. Type by monotypy. Valid. Kyphosidae: Scorpidinae.

Scorpius Plumier in Lacepède 1801:282 (footnote) [ref. 2710].

Masc. Not available, nonbinominal name mentioned in passing under *Scorpaena plumieri*; also name used by other earlier workers. See remarks under Opinion 89 in Appendix B. Scorpaenidae: Scorpaeninae.

Scortum Whitley 1943:183 [ref. 4703]. Neut. *Therapon parviceps* Macleay 1883:201. Type by original designation. Synonym of *Terapon* Cuvier 1816 (Mees & Kailola 1977:32 [ref. 5183]); valid (Vari 1978:301 [ref. 4514], Paxton et al. 1989:536 [ref. 12442]). Terapontidae.

Scriptaphyosemion (subgenus of *Aphyosemion*) Radda & Pürzl 1987:8 [ref. 14231]. Neut. *Aphyosemion geryi* Lambert 1958:52. Type by original designation. Aplocheilidae: Aplocheilinae.

Scrofaria Gistel 1848:VIII [ref. 1822]. Fem. *Ausonia cuvieri* Risso 1826:342. Type by being a replacement name. Unneeded replacement for *Ausonia* Risso 1826, apparently not preoccupied. Spelled *Scafaria* by authors. Synonym of *Luvarus* Rafinesque 1810 (Topp 1973:476 [ref. 7209]). Luvaridae.

Scrophicephalus (subgenus of *Mormyrus*) Swainson 1838:309 [ref. 4302]. Masc. *Scrophicephalus longispinnis* Swainson 1838:308-309. Type by monotypy. Dates to Swainson 1838:309 with one species mentioned. Also in Swainson 1839:187 [ref. 4303] without species and as a subgenus of *Mormyrus*; also as a subgenus in 1838:309 based on text. Synonym of *Mormyrus* Linnaeus 1758 (Taverne 1972:163 [ref. 6367]). Mormyridae.

Scurrilichthys (subgenus of *Arotrolepis*) Fraser-Brunner 1941:184 [ref. 1494]. Masc. *Arotrolepis (Scurrilichthys) barbarae* Fraser-Brunner 1941:187. Type by original designation (also monotypic). Monacanthidae.

Scutengraulis Jordan & Seale 1925:30 [ref. 2499]. Fem. *Clupea hamiltonii* Gray 1835:Pl. 92. Type by original designation (also monotypic). Synonym of *Thryssa* Cuvier 1829 (Whitehead 1967:140 [ref. 6464], Whitehead et al. 1988:421 [ref. 5725]). Engraulidae.

Scutica (subgenus of *Uropterygius*) Jordan & Evermann 1896:403, 404 [ref. 2443]. Fem. *Gymnomuraena nectura* Jordan & Gilbert 1882:356. Type by original designation (also monotypic). Synonym of *Uropterygius* Rüppell 1838 (Böhlke et al. 1989:126 [ref. 13286]). Muraenidae: Uropterygiinae.

Scuticaria Jordan & Snyder 1901:886 [ref. 2508]. Fem. *Ichthyophis tigrinus* Lesson 1829:399. Type by original designation (also monotypic). Valid (Böhlke et al. 1989:117 [ref. 13286]). Muraenidae: Uropterygiinae.

Scyliorhinus (subgenus of *Squalus*) Blainville 1816:121 [ref. 306]. Masc. *Squalus canicula* Linnaeus 1758:234. Type by subsequent designation. Type designated by Gill 1862:407 [ref. 1783]. Misspelled or unjustifiably emended to *Scylliorhinus*, *Scyliorhynchus*, and *Scyliorhynus* by authors. Valid (Springer 1973:19 [ref. 7162], Nakaya 1975:14 [ref. 7083], Springer 1979:123 [ref. 4175], Compagno 1984:355 [ref. 6846], Nakaya in Masuda et al. 1984:4 [ref. 6441], Bass 1986:95 [ref. 5635], Cappetta 1987:113 [ref. 6348], Compagno 1988:119 [ref. 13488]). Scyliorhinidae.

Scylliogaleus Boulenger 1902:51 [ref. 566]. Masc. *Scylliogaleus quecketti* Boulenger 1902:51. Type by monotypy. Valid (Compagno 1984:426 [ref. 6846], Bass et al. 1986:85 [ref. 5638], Herman et al. 1988:105 [ref. 13267], Compagno 1988:226 [ref. 13488]). Triakidae: Triakinae.

Scyllium Cuvier 1816:124 [ref. 993]. Neut. *Squalus canicula* Linnaeus 1758:234. Type by subsequent designation. Type designated first by Bory de Saint-Vincent, v. 14, 1828:708 [ref. 3853] (see Whitley 1935:137 [ref. 6396]). Spelled *Scylium* by Minding 1832:47 [ref. 3022]. Objective synonym of *Scyliorhinus* Blainville 1816 (Springer 1973:19 [ref. 7162], Springer 1979:123 [ref. 4175], Compagno 1984:355 [ref. 6846], Cappetta 1987:113 [ref. 6348], Compagno 1988:119 [ref. 13488]). Scyliorhinidae.

Scymnium Valenciennes in Cuvier 1838:legend to Pl. 115 [ref. 4980]. *Squalus licha* Bonnaterre 1788:12. Type by subsequent designation. Perhaps a lapus, for *Scymnus* treated on p. 567; on legend page as *Scymium nicense* under genus *Scymnius*; could be treated as a name in synonymy; appeared as above in Fowler 1969:484 [ref. 9321]. Probably not available. Synonym of *Dalatias* Rafinesque 1810 (Compagno 1984:63 [ref. 6474]). Squalidae.

Scymnodalatias Garrick 1956:564 [ref. 1546]. Masc. *Scymnodon sherwoodi* Archey 1921:195. Type by original designation (also monotypic). Valid (Compagno 1984:96 [ref. 6474], Taniuchi & Garrick 1986:120 [ref. 5721], Kukuyev & Konovalenko 1988 [ref. 9290]). Squalidae.

Scymnodon Bocage & Capello 1864:263 [ref. 479]. Masc. *Scymnodon ringens* Bocage & Capello 1864:263. Type by monotypy. Synonym of *Centroscymnus* Bocage & Capello 1864 (Bass et al. 1986:52). Valid (Krefft & Tortonese 1973:44 [ref. 7165], Compagno 1984:97 [ref. 6474], Taniuchi & Garrick 1986:119 [ref. 5721], Cappetta 1987:60 [ref. 6348], Paxton et al. 1989:36 [ref. 12442]). Squalidae.

Scymnorhinus Bonaparte 1846:16 [ref. 519]. Masc. *Squalus lichia* of Bonaparte 1846:16 (= *Squalus lichia* Bonnaterre 1788:12). Type by monotypy. *Scymnus* Cuvier and *Dalatias* Raf "p". [= part] in synonymy; but apparently not proposed as a replacement name for *Scymnus* Cuvier 1816, preoccupied by Kugelmann 1794 in Coleoptera. Valid (Krefft & Tortonese 1973:46 [ref. 7165], Bass et al. 1986:60 [ref. 5636], Cappetta 1987:62 [ref. 6348] with *Dalatias* questionably in synonymy); synonym of *Dalatias* Rafinesque 1810 (Compagno 1984:63 [ref. 6474]). Squalidae.

Scymnus Cuvier 1816:130 [ref. 993]. Masc. *Squalus americanus* Gmelin 1789:1503. Type by subsequent designation. Additional species were mentioned in footnote, so type requires subsequent designation; Whitley 1935:137 [ref. 6396] determined that the type was first designated by Lesson, v. 15, 1829:598 [ref. 13391]. Preoccupied by Kugelmann 1794 in Coleoptera. Replaced by *Scymnorhinus* Bonaparte 1846. Synonym of *Dalatias* Rafinesque 1810 (Compagno 1984:63 [ref. 6474], Cappetta 1987:62 [ref. 6348]). Squalidae.

Scyphius Risso 1826:185 [ref. 3757]. Masc. *Scyphius fasciatus* Risso 1826:185. Type by subsequent designation [details not researched], five included species. Synonym of *Nerophis* Rafinesque 1810 (Wheeler 1973:277 [ref. 7190]). Syngnathidae: Syngnathinae.

Scyris Cuvier 1829:209 [ref. 995]. Fem. *Gallus alexandrinus* Geoffroy St. Hilaire 1817:Pl. 22. Type by subsequent designation. Appeared in 1829 with species cited as "Le Gal d'Alexandrie." First technical addition of species cited by scientific name apparently was in Cuvier & Valenciennes 1833:145-153 [ref. 1002] (*S. indica* and *S. alexandrina*). Earliest technical subsequent designation not established. Valid (Hureau & Tortonese 1973:378 [ref. 7198]); synonym of *Alectis* Rafinesque 1815 (Daget & Smith-Vaniz 1986:308 [ref. 6207]). Carangidae.

Scytalichthys (subgenus of *Mystriophis*) Jordan & Davis 1891:634 [ref. 2437]. Masc. *Ophichthys miurus* Jordan & Gilbert 1882:357. Type by original designation (also monotypic). Valid (McCosker

1977:84 [ref. 6836], McCosker et al. 1989:299 [ref. 13288]). Ophichthidae: Ophichthinae.

Scytalina Jordan & Gilbert 1880:266 [ref. 2367]. Fem. *Scytalina cerdale* Jordan & Gilbert 1880:267. Type by monotypy. *Scytaliscus* Jordan & Gilbert 1883 is an unneeded replacement. Valid. Scytalinidae.

Scytaliscus Jordan & Gilbert 1883:111 [ref. 2477]. Masc. *Scytalina cerdale* Jordan & Gilbert 1880:267. Type by being a replacement name. Unneeded replacement for *Scytalina* Jordan & Gilbert, not preoccupied by *Scytalinus* Erichson 1840 in Coleoptera. Objective synonym of *Scytalina* Jordan & Gilbert 1880. Scytalinidae.

Scytallurus Duméril (ex Kaup) 1856:199 [ref. 1154]. Masc. *Sphagebranchus imberbis* Delaroche 1809:360. Type by monotypy. Appeared as *Scytallurus imberbis* in list of genera and species taken from Kaup manuscript, but without description or indication; author of species inferred. Synonym of *Dalophis* Rafinesque 1810 (Blache et al. 1973:249 [ref. 7185], McCosker 1977:71 [ref. 6836], Castle 1984:38 [6171]). Ophichthidae: Ophichthinae.

Scytalophis Kaup 1856:46 [ref. 2572]. Masc. *Scytalophis magnioculis* Kaup 1856:46. Type by subsequent designation. Type designated by Jordan 1919:347 [ref. 4904]. Also appeared in Kaup 1856:13 [ref. 2573] and as name only in Kaup in Duméril 1856:199 [ref. 1154]. Synonym of *Ophichthus* Ahl 1789 (Blache et al. 1973:247 [ref. 7185], McCosker 1977:80 [ref. 6836], McCosker et al. 1989:379 [ref. 13288]). Ophichthidae: Ophichthinae.

Sealeina Fowler 1907:478 [ref. 1374]. Fem. *Myletes lippincottianus* Cope 1870:561. Type by original designation (also monotypic). Misspelled *Sealina* in Zoological Record for 1906, correctly spelled in 1907. Synonym of *Metynnis* Cope 1878 (Géry 1976:50 [ref. 14199]). Characidae: Serrasalminae.

Searsia Parr 1937:8, 12 [ref. 3376]. Fem. *Searsia koefoedi* Parr 1937:16. Type by original designation. *Searsea* is a misspelling. Valid (Krefft 1973:95 [ref. 7166], Quéro et al. in Whitehead et al. 1984:266 [ref. 13675], Matsui & Rosenblatt 1979:68 [ref. 7024], Sazonov 1986 [ref. 6003]). Platytroctidae.

Searsioides Sazonov 1977:55 [ref. 3905]. Masc. *Searsioides multispinus* Sazonov 1977:56. Type by original designation (also monotypic). Species misspelled once as *multispinis*. Synonym of *Searsia* Parr 1937 (Matsui & Rosenblatt 1979:68 [ref. 7024]); valid (Sazonov 1986 [ref. 6003]). Platytroctidae.

Sebastapistes Gill in Streets 1877:62 [ref. 4290]. Masc. *Sebastes strongia* Valenciennes in Cuvier & Valenciennes 1829:323. Type by subsequent designation. Three included species, first designation of type not researched. Valid (Blanc & Hureau 1973:585 [ref. 7218], Eschmeyer 1986:475 [ref. 5652]). Scorpaenidae: Scorpaeninae.

Sebastella Tanaka 1917:10 [ref. 4329]. Fem. *Sebastella littoralis* Tanaka 1918:10. Type by monotypy. Synonym of *Scorpaenodes* Bleeker 1857. Scorpaenidae: Scorpaeninae.

Sebastes Cuvier 1829:166 [ref. 995]. Masc. *Perca norvegica* Müller 1776. Type by subsequent designation. Type designated by Bleeker 1876:2 [ref. 12248] and 1876:294 [ref. 450]; species may go back to Ascanius 1772:7 (see Fernholm & Wheeler 1983:240 [ref. 14214]). Valid (Blanc & Hureau 1973:583 [ref. 7218], Barsukov 1981 [ref. 5306], Washington et al. 1984:440 [ref. 13660], Amaoka in Masuda et al. 1984:310 [ref. 6441], Hureau & Litvinenko in Whitehead et al. 1986:1224 [ref. 13677]). Scorpaenidae: Sebastinae.

Sebastichthys Gill 1862:278 [ref. 1666]. Masc. *Sebastes nigrocinctus* Ayres 1859:25, 217. Type by subsequent designation. Type designated by Bleeker 1876:2 [ref. 12248] and 1876:294 [ref. 450]. Synonym of *Sebastes* Cuvier 1829. Scorpaenidae: Sebastinae.

Sebastiscus Jordan & Starks 1904:124 [ref. 2527]. Masc. *Sebastes marmoratus* Cuvier in Cuvier & Valenciennes 1829:345. Type by original designation (type in parentheses). Synonym of *Sebastes* Cuvier 1829, but as a valid subgenus (Barsukov & Chen 1978 [ref. 7010], Barsukov 1981 [ref. 5306]); valid genus (Washington et al. 1984:440 [ref. 13660], Shimizu and Amaoka in Masuda et al. 1984:313 [ref. 6441]). Scorpaenidae: Sebastinae.

Sebastocarus Jordan & Evermann 1927:507 [ref. 2453]. Masc. *Sebastichthys serriceps* Jordan & Gilbert 1880:38. Type by original designation (also monotypic). Synonym of *Sebastes* Cuvier 1829. Scorpaenidae: Sebastinae.

Sebastocles (subgenus of *Sebastes*) Jordan & Hubbs 1925:260 [ref. 2486]. Masc. *Sebastichthys hubbsi* Matsubara 1937:57. Type designated by ICZN; on Official List (Opinion 1235). Synonym of *Sebastes* Cuvier 1829. Scorpaenidae: Sebastinae.

Sebastodes Gill 1861:165 [ref. 1775]. Masc. *Sebastes paucispinis* Ayres 1854:6. Type by monotypy. Synonym of *Sebastes* Cuvier 1829. Scorpaenidae: Sebastinae.

Sebastolobus Gill 1881:375 [ref. 1721]. Masc. *Sebastes macrochir* Günther 1880:65. Type by monotypy. Valid (Washington et al. 1984:440 [ref. 13660], Amaoka in Masuda et al. 1984:315 [ref. 6441]). Scorpaenidae: Sebastolobinae.

Sebastomus Gill 1864:147 [ref. 1696]. Masc. *Sebastes rosaceus* Girard 1854:146. Type by monotypy. Synonym of *Sebastes* Cuvier 1829. Scorpaenidae: Sebastinae.

Sebastoplus Gill 1863:208 [ref. 1682]. Masc. *Scorpaena kuhlii* Bowdich 1825:123. Type by original designation. Synonym of *Pontinus* Poey 1860 (Blanc & Hureau 1973:582 [ref. 7218]). Scorpaenidae: Scorpaeninae.

Sebastopsis Gill 1862:278 [ref. 1666]. Fem. *Scorpaena polylepis* Bleeker 1851:173. Type by monotypy. Objective synonym of *Scorpaenodes* Bleeker 1857. Scorpaenidae: Scorpaeninae.

Sebastopsis Sauvage 1873:1 [ref. 3870]. Fem. *Sebastes minutus* Cuvier in Cuvier & Valenciennes 1829:255, 348. Type by original designation. Preoccupied by and synonym of *Sebastopsis* Gill 1863 in fishes. Synonym of *Scorpaenodes* Bleeker 1857. Scorpaenidae: Scorpaeninae.

Sebastopyr Jordan & Evermann 1927:506 [ref. 2453]. Neut. *Sebastodes ruberrimus* Cramer 1895:597. Type by original designation (also monotypic). Synonym of *Sebastes* Cuvier 1829. Scorpaenidae: Sebastinae.

Sebastosemus Gill 1905:220 [ref. 1788]. Masc. *Neosebastes entaxis* Jordan & Snyder 1904:120. Type by original designation (also monotypic). Synonym of *Neosebastes* Guichenot 1867. Scorpaenidae: Neosebastinae.

Sebastosomus Gill 1864:59, 147 [ref. 1696]. Masc. *Sebastes melanops* Girard 1856:130. Type by original designation. Synonym of *Sebastes* Cuvier 1829. Scorpaenidae: Sebastinae.

Sectator (subgenus of *Kyphosus*) Jordan & Fesler 1893:533, 534, 536 [ref. 2455]. Masc. *Pimelepterus ocyurus* Jordan & Gilbert 1903:185. Type by original designation (also monotypic). Synonym of *Kyphosus* Lacepède 1801 (Desoutter 1973:420 [ref. 7203]); valid (Araga in Masuda et al. 1984:166 [ref. 6441]). Kyphosidae: Kyphosinae.

Securicula (subgenus of *Chela*) Günther 1868:332 [ref. 1990]. Fem. *Cyprinus gora* Hamilton 1822:263, 384. Type by subsequent designation. Type apparently first designated by Jordan 1919:351 [ref. 4904]. Valid (Jayaram 1981:73 [ref. 6497]). Cyprinidae.

Secutor Gistel 1848:IX [ref. 1822]. Masc. *Zeus insidiator* Bloch 1787:41. Type by being a replacement name. Unexplained replacement for *Equula* Cuvier 1815 (see Jordan 1919:336 [ref. 2409]). Valid (James 1985:397 [ref. 12861], Smith 1986:621 [ref. 5712], Kottelat 1989:17 [ref. 13605]). Leiognathidae.

Segutilum Whitley 1931:319 [ref. 4672]. Neut. *Pimelepterus sydneyanus* Günther 1886:368. Type by original designation (also monotypic). Synonym of *Kyphosus* Lacepède 1801. Kyphosidae: Kyphosinae.

Selache Cuvier 1816:129 [ref. 993]. *Squalus maximus* Gunnerus 1765:33. Type by subsequent designation. Type apparently first designated by Bonaparte 1838:9 (of separate) [ref. 4979]. *Selanche* Jarocki 1822 and *Selachus* Minding 1832 evidently are misspellings. Objective synonym of *Cetorhinus* Blainville 1816 (Springer 1973:16 [ref. 7162], Compagno 1984:234 [ref. 6474]). Cetorhinidae.

Selachophidium Gilchrist 1903:209 [ref. 1645]. Neut. *Selachophidium guentheri* Gilchrist 1903:209. Type by monotypy. Valid (Cohen & Nielsen 1978:39 [ref. 881], Hureau & Nielsen 1981:21 [ref. 5438], Nielsen & Cohen 1986:350 [ref. 5700]). Ophidiidae: Neobythitinae.

Selanonius Fleming 1828:169 [ref. 1339]. Masc. *Selanonius walkeri* Fleming 1828:169 (= *Squalus selanoneus* Walker in Leach 1818). Type by monotypy. *S. walkeri* Fleming is an unneeded substitute for *S. selanoneus* Walker. Synonym of *Lamna* Cuvier 1816 (Springer 1973:13 [ref. 7162], Compagno 1984:246 [ref. 6474]). Lamnidae.

Selar Bleeker 1851:343, 352, 359 [ref. 326]. *Caranx boops* Cuvier in Cuvier & Valenciennes 1833:46. Type by subsequent designation. Type apparently designated first by Jordan and Evermann 1896:916 [ref. 2443] or by Fowler 1918:14 [ref. 1396]; type not *S. hasseltii* Bleeker. Valid (Hureau & Tortonese 1973:379 [ref. 7198], Smith-Vaniz 1984:526 [ref. 13664], Gushiken in Masuda et al. 1984:154 [ref. 6441], Smith-Vaniz 1986:655 [ref. 5718], Gushiken 1988:443 [ref. 6697], Paxton et al. 1989:583 [ref. 12442]). Carangidae.

Selaroides Bleeker 1851:343, 352 [ref. 326]. Masc. *Caranx leptolepis* Cuvier (ex Kuhl & van Hasselt) in Cuvier & Valenciennes 1833:63. Type by monotypy. *Leptaspis* Bleeker 1852 is an unneeded substitute. Valid (Smith-Vaniz 1984:526 [ref. 13664], Gushiken in Masuda et al. 1984:155 [ref. 6441], Kijima et al. 1986:841 [ref. 6320], Gushiken 1988:443 [ref. 6697], Paxton et al. 1989:583 [ref. 12442]). Carangidae.

Seleima Bowdich 1825:xii, 238 [ref. 590]. Fem. *Seleima aurata* Bowdich 1825:237. Type by monotypy. Also involves fig. 37 opposite p. 238 in conjunction with p. xii. Synonym of *Kyphosus* Lacepède 1801 (Desoutter 1973:420 [ref. 7203]). Kyphosidae: Kyphosinae.

Selenanthias Tanaka 1918:516 [ref. 4331]. Masc. *Selenanthias analis* Tanaka 1918:516. Type by original designation (also monotypic). Type designated on p. 520. Valid (Kendall 1984:500 [ref. 13663], Katayama in Masuda et al. 1984:133 [ref. 6441], Paxton et al. 1989:507 [ref. 12442]). Serranidae: Anthiinae.

Selenaspis Bleeker 1858:62, 66 [ref. 365]. Fem. *Silurus herzbergii* Bloch 1794:33. Type by subsequent designation. Six included species, three with question [earliest type designation not researched]. Ariidae.

Selene Lacepède 1802:560 [ref. 4929]. Fem. *Selene argentea* Lacepède 1802:560, 562 (= *Zeus vomer* Linnaeus 1758:286). Type by subsequent designation. Type designated by Jordan & Gilbert 1883:439 [ref. 2476]. On Official List (Opinion 569). Valid (Smith-Vaniz 1984:526 [ref. 13664], Smith-Vaniz 1986:656 [ref. 5718], Daget & Smith-Vaniz 1986:318 [ref. 6207], Gushiken 1988:443 [ref. 6697]). Carangidae.

Selenia Bonaparte 1846:75 [ref. 519]. Fem. *Caranx luna* Geoffroy St. Hilaire 1809:182; Pl. 23. Type by monotypy. Preoccupied by Hubner 1816 in Coleoptera, replaced by *Longirostrum* Wakiya 1924. Synonym of *Pseudocaranx* Bleeker 1863. Carangidae.

Seleniolycus Anderson 1988:68 [ref. 7304]. Masc. *Oidiphorus laevifasciatus* Torno, Tomo & Marschoff 1977:4. Type by original designation (also monotypic). Zoarcidae.

Selenotoca Myers 1936:84 [ref. 3113]. Fem. *Scatophagus multifasciatus* Richardson 1846:57. Type by original designation (also monotypic). Synonym of *Scatophagus* Cuvier 1831 (Arnoult 1986:341 [ref. 6213]). Scatophagidae.

Sema Jordan 1878:399 [ref. 2378]. Neut. *Sema signifer* Jordan 1878:399. Type by monotypy. Synonym of *Embiotoca* Agassiz 1853 (Follett in Tarp 1952:74, footnote [ref. 12250]). Embiotocidae.

Semablennius Fowler 1954:1 [ref. 1466]. Masc. *Semablennius gallowayi* Fowler 1954:2. Type by original designation (also monotypic). Synonym of *Lupinoblennius* Herre 1942 (Bath 1977:194 [ref. 208]). Blenniidae.

Semachlorella (subgenus of *Novaculichthys*) Fowler & Bean 1928: 367 [ref. 1475]. Fem. *Julis bifer* Lay & Bennett 1839:64. Type by original designation (also monotypic). Synonym of *Novaculichthys* Bleeker 1862 (Fowler, MS). Labridae.

Semadascyllus Fowler 1941:257 [ref. 1438]. Masc. *Dascyllus albisella* Gill 1862:149. Type by original designation (also monotypic). Synonym of *Dascyllus* Cuvier 1829 (Randall & Allen 1977:351 [ref. 6482]). Pomacentridae.

Semapagrus (subgenus of *Pagrus*) Fowler 1925:4 [ref. 1401]. Masc. *Pagrus auriga* Valenciennes 1843:34. Type by original designation (also monotypic). Sparidae.

Semaprochilodus Fowler 1941:171 [ref. 1437]. Masc. *Semaprochilodus squamilentus* Fowler 1941:172. Type by original designation. Valid (Roberts 1973:213 [ref. 7051], Géry 1977:215 [ref. 1597], Vari 1983:5 [ref. 5419], Castro 1988 [ref. 6684]). Curimatidae: Prochilodontinae.

Semathunnus Fowler 1933:163 [ref. 1415]. Masc. *Semathunnus guildi* Fowler 1933:164. Type by original designation (also monotypic). Synonym of *Thunnus* South 1845 (Gibbs & Collette 1967:97 [ref. 13640], Böhlke 1984:152 [ref. 13621]). Scombridae.

Semelcarinata Fernández-Yépez 1948:59 [ref. 1316]. Fem. *Curimatus isognathus* Eigenmann & Eigenmann 1889:428. Type by original designation (also monotypic). Synonym of *Psectrogaster* Eigenmann & Eigenmann 1889 (Vari 1989:6 [ref. 9189] with wrong type, Vari 1989:12 [ref. 13548]). Curimatidae: Curimatinae.

Semicossyphus Günther 1861:384 [ref. 1967]. Masc. *Cossyphus reticulatus* Valenciennes in Cuvier & Valenciennes 1839:100. Type by subsequent designation. Earliest type designation not researched. Valid (Richards & Leis 1984:544 [ref. 13668], Yamakawa in Masuda et al. 1984:204 [ref. 6441]). Labridae.

Semiculter Chu 1935:4 [ref. 832]. Masc. *Nicholsiculter rendahli* Wu 1830:74. Type by original designation (also monotypic). Cyprinidae.

Semilabeo Peters 1880:1032 [ref. 3456]. Masc. *Semilabeo notabilis* Peters 1880:1032. Type by monotypy. Valid (Wu et al. 1977:368 [ref. 4807], Chu & Cui in Chu & Chen 1989:238 [ref. 13584]). Cyprinidae.

Semiplotus Bleeker 1859:424 [ref. 370]. Masc. *Cyprinus semiplotus* McClelland 1939:274, 346. Type by subsequent monotypy (also by absolute tautonymy). Apparently appeared first in key, without included species. One species included by Bleeker 1860:115 [ref. 380]. Synonym of *Cyprinion* Heckel 1843 (Howes 1982:331 [ref. 14202]); valid (Jayaram 1981:95 [ref. 6497], Chen 1989:118 [ref. 14144]). Cyprinidae.

Semitapicis (subgenus of *Curimatus*) Eigenmann & Eigenmann 1889:417 [ref. 1254]. Masc. *Charax planirostris* Gray 1854:154. Type by subsequent designation. Type designated by Eigenmann 1910:422 [ref. 1224]. Type belongs in *Curimata cyprinoides* complex (see discussion in Vari 1984:14-16 [ref. 5307]). *Semitapiscis* Braga & Azpelicueta 1983:139, footnote on p. 140 [ref. 5308] is an unjustified emendation. Valid (Braga & Azpelicueta 1983:139 [ref. 5308]; synonym of *Curimata* Bosc 1817 (Vari 1989:6 [ref. 9189], Vari 1989:21 [ref. 13506]). Curimatidae: Curimatinae.

Semotilus Rafinesque 1820:239 [ref. 7310]. Masc. *Semotilus dorsalis* Rafinesque 1820:239. Type by subsequent designation. Also in Rafinesque 1820:49 (Dec.) [ref. 3592]. Bleeker 1863:211 [ref. 397] and 1863:32 [ref. 4859] wrongly designated *L. pulchellus* Girard [not an included species] as type under genus but designated *S. dorsalis* under the subgenus *Semotilus*; Bleeker 1863:264 [ref. 403] designated *dorsalis* as type. Valid. Cyprinidae.

Sephenia Rafinesque 1815:93 [ref. 3584]. Not available, name only; for a ray. Torpediniformes.

Septobranchus Hardenberg 1941:223 [ref. 2037]. Masc. *Septobranchus johannae* Hardenberg 1941:223. Type by monotypy. Ariidae.

Sericagobioides Herre 1927:335 [ref. 2104]. Masc. *Sericagobioides lighti* Herre 1927:336. Type by monotypy (second species questionably included). Gobiidae.

Seriola Cuvier 1816:315 [ref. 993]. Fem. *Caranx dumerili* Risso 1810:175. Type by original designation (Opinion 461). On Official List (Opinion 461). Valid (Hureau & Tortonese 1973:379 [ref. 7198], Smith-Vaniz 1984:524 [ref. 13664], Smith-Vaniz 1986:656 [ref. 5718], Paxton et al. 1989:584 [ref. 12442]). Carangidae.

Seriolella Guichenot 1848:238 [ref. 1939]. Fem. *Seriolella porosa* Guichenot 1848:239. Type by subsequent designation. Type designated by Jordan 1923:238 [ref. 2421]. Valid (Haedrich 1967:69 [ref. 5357], McDowall 1981:110 [ref. 5356], Horn 1984:628 [ref. 13637], Inada in Nakamura et al. 1986:284 [ref. 14235]). Centrolophidae.

Seriolichthys Bleeker 1854:195 [ref. 342]. Masc. *Seriola bipinnulata* Quoy & Gaimard 1824:363. Type by monotypy. Synonym of *Elagatis* Bennett 1840 (Hureau & Tortonese 1973:376 [ref. 7198]). Carangidae.

Seriolina Wakiya 1924:222, 230 [ref. 4570]. Fem. *Seriola intermedia* Temminck & Schlegel 1845:116. Type by original designation (also monotypic). Valid (Smith-Vaniz 1984:524 [ref. 13664], Gushiken in Masuda et al. 1984:153 [ref. 6441], Smith-Vaniz 1986:657 [ref. 5718], Paxton et al. 1989:585 [ref. 12442]). Carangidae.

Seriolophus Guichenot 1867:90 [ref. 1950]. Masc. *Seriolophus carangoides* Guichenot 1867:90 [10]. Type by monotypy. Preoccupied by Swainson 1837 in Aves, not replaced. Synonym of *Nematistius* Gill 1862. Nematistiidae.

Seriphus Ayres 1860:80 [ref. 158]. Masc. *Seriphus politus* Ayres 1860:80. Type by monotypy. Apparently not preoccupied [details not researched], but replaced by *Kroseriphus* Whitley 1950. Valid. Sciaenidae.

Serpa Cloquet 1827:190 [ref. 853]. Masc. *Serpa crocodilus* Cloquet 1827:190 (= *Gasteropelecus crocodilus* Risso 1810:357). Type by subsequent designation. Investigation incomplete. May date to Cloquet as above. Type designated by Whitley 1933:64 [ref. 4677]. Genus credited to Whitley 1933 by authors. Synonym of *Lampanyctus* Bonaparte 1840, with authorship of *Serpa* credited to Whitley 1933 (Krefft & Bekker 1973:186 [ref. 7181], Paxton 1979:13 [ref. 6440]). Should go to ICZN to suppress the earlier *Serpa* Cloquet 1827 if available. Myctophidae.

Serrabrycon Vari 1986:329 [ref. 5989]. Masc. *Serrabrycon magoi* Vari 1986:329. Type by original designation (also monotypic). Characidae.

Serranellus (subgenus of *Serranus*) Jordan in Jordan & Eigenmann 1890:399, 404 [ref. 2440]. Masc. *Perca scriba* Linnaeus 1758:292. Type by original designation. Type designated on p. 399; two included species on p. 404. Synonym of *Serranus* Cuvier 1816 (Tortonese 1973:355 [ref. 7192]). Serranidae: Serraninae.

Serranguilla Whitley & Phillipps 1939:228 [ref. 4737]. Fem. *Gymnothorax prionodon* Ogilby 1895:720. Type by original designation (also monotypic). Synonym of *Gymnothorax* Bloch 1795 (Böhlke et al. 1989:145 [ref. 13286]). Muraenidae: Muraeninae.

Serranichthys Bleeker 1855:344 [ref. 349]. Masc. *Serranus altivelis* Cuvier in Cuvier & Valenciennes 1828:324. Type by monotypy. Objective synonym of *Chromileptes* Swainson 1839. Serranidae: Epinephelinae.

Serraniculus Ginsburg 1952:86 [ref. 1805]. Masc. *Serraniculus pumilio* Ginsburg 1952:88. Type by original designation (also monotypic). Valid (Kendall 1984:500 [ref. 13663]). Serranidae: Serraninae.

Serranochromis Regan 1920:45 [ref. 3669]. Masc. *Chromys thumbergi* Castelnau 1861:13. Type by original designation. Valid (Ribbink et al. 1983:249 [ref. 13555], Greenwood 1984:216 [ref. 5311]). Cichlidae.

Serranocirrhitus Watanabe 1949:17 [ref. 6581]. Masc. *Serranocirrhitus latus* Watanabe 1949:18. Type by original designation (also monotypic). Described originally as a cirrhitid. Valid (Randall & Heemstra 1978 [ref. 6993], Kendall 1984:500 [ref. 13663], Katayama in Masuda et al. 1984:135 [ref. 6441], Paxton et al. 1989:508 [ref. 12442]). Serranidae: Anthiinae.

Serranops Regan 1914:15 [ref. 3661]. Masc. *Serranops maculicauda* Regan 1914:15. Type by monotypy. Synonym of *Plectranthias* Bleeker 1873 (Randall 1980:105 [ref. 6717]). Serranidae: Anthiinae.

Serranus Cuvier 1816:276 [ref. 993]. Masc. *Perca cabrilla* Linnaeus 1758:294. Type designated by ICZN; on Official List (Opinion 93). Valid (Tortonese 1973:355 [ref. 7192], Kendall 1984:500 [ref. 13663], Heemstra & Randall 1986:536 [ref. 5667]). Serranidae: Serraninae.

Serraria Gilbert 1884:205 [ref. 1622]. Fem. *Hadropterus scierus* Swain 1883:252. Type by original designation (also monotypic). Synonym of *Percina* Haldeman 1842, subgenus *Hadropterus* Agassiz 1854 (Collette & Banarescu 1977:1454 [ref. 5845]). Percidae.

Serrasalmo Duméril 1806:146, 342 [ref. 1151]. Masc. *Salmo rhombeus* Linnaeus 1766:514. Type by subsequent designation. Latinized on p. 342. Type designated by Fowler 1950:279 [not researched]. Perhaps not intended as a new name — *Serrasalmo* Lacepède in parentheses; apparently can be regarded as an incorrect subsequent spelling. Objective synonym of *Serrasalmus* Lacepède 1803. Characidae: Serrasalminae.

Serrasalmus Lacepède 1803:283 [ref. 4930]. Masc. *Salmo rhombeus* Linnaeus 1766:514. Type by monotypy. *Serrasalmo* is a misspelling or unjustified emendation. Valid (Géry 1976:52 [ref. 14199], Géry 1977:278 [ref. 1597], Géry et al. 1987:449 [ref. 6001]). Characidae: Serrasalminae.

Serrichromis Fowler 1943:77 [ref. 1441]. Masc. *Dascyllus pomacentroides* Kendall & Goldsborough 1911:298. Type by original designation (also monotypic). Pomacentridae.

Serrihastaperca Fowler 1944:384 [ref. 1448]. Fem. *Serrihastaperca exsul* Fowler 1944:385. Type by original designation (also monotypic). Based on postlarval specimen. Probably a species of *Epinephelus* Bloch 1793 (Heemstra 1974:25 [ref. 7125]). Serranidae: Epinephelinae.

Serrivomer Gill & Ryder 1883:260 [ref. 1746]. Masc. *Serrivomer beanii* Gill & Ryder 1883:261. Type by monotypy. Appeared as name only in Gill 1883:255 [ref. 1724]. Valid (Bauchot & Saldanha 1973:229 [ref. 7186], Karrer 1982:56 [ref. 5679], Ida in Masuda et al. 1984:30 [ref. 6441], Bauchot in Whitehead et al. 1986:548 [ref. 13676], Castle 1986:191 [ref. 5644], Paxton et al. 1989:125 [ref. 12442], Tighe 1989:617 [ref. 13291]). Serrivomeridae.

Seserinus Oken (ex Cuvier) 1817:1182 [ref. 3303]. Masc. *Seserinus rondeletii* Cuvier 1839:Pl. 63. Type by subsequent designation. Type designated by Jordan 1917:106 [ref. 2407]. Based on "Les Seserinus" of Cuvier 1816:342 [ref. 993], species *seserinus* Rondelet 257. See also Gill 1903:966 [ref. 5768]). Technical addition of species after latinization not researched. Synonym of *Stromateus* Linnaeus 1758 (Haedrich 1967:99 [ref. 5357], Haedrich 1973:565 [ref. 7216]). Stromateidae.

Setarches Johnson 1862:177 [ref. 2357]. Masc. *Setarches guentheri* Johnson 1862:177. Type by monotypy. Valid (Blanc & Hureau 1973:584 [ref. 7218], Eschmeyer & Collette 1966:355 [ref. 6485], Amaoka in Masuda et al. 1984:317 [ref. 6441], Eschmeyer 1986:478 [ref. 5652], Hureau & Litvinenko in Whitehead et al. 1986:1227 [ref. 13677], Paxton et al. 1989:451 [ref. 12442]). Scorpaenidae: Setarchinae.

Setipinna (subgenus of *Elops*) Swainson 1839:186, 292 [ref. 4303]. Fem. *Setipinna megalura* Swainson 1839:292 (= *Clupea phasa* Hamilton 1822:240, 382). Type by subsequent designation. Type designated by Swain 1882:280 [ref. 5966] (see Whitehead 1967:145 [ref. 6464]). Misspelled *Setifinna* by Swainson 1839:447 (index) [ref. 4303]. Valid (Grande 1985:245 [ref. 6466], Whitehead et al. 1988:451 [ref. 5725], Paxton et al. 1989:160 [ref. 12442], Kottelat 1989:6 [ref. 13605], Roberts 1989:26 [ref. 6439]). Engraulidae.

Sewellia Hora 1932:315 [ref. 2208]. Fem. *Balitora lineolata* Valenciennes in Cuvier & Valenciennes 1849:99. Type by original designation (also monotypic). Valid (Silas 1953:230 [ref. 4024], Sawada 1982:205 [ref. 14111], Kottelat 1989:13 [ref. 13605]). Balitoridae: Balitorinae.

Seychellea Smith 1957:726 [ref. 4109]. Fem. *Seychellea hectori* Smith 1957:726. Type by original designation (also monotypic). Second species tentatively included. Synonym of *Amblygobius* Bleeker 1874 (Hoese, pers. comm.). Gobiidae.

Sgairhynchus Costa 1849:62 [ref. 976]. Masc. *Ammodytes cicerellus* Rafinesque 1810:21. Type by subsequent designation. Not available, appeared as name only; type affixed by Fowler 1936:1029 [ref. 6546] but as name in synonymy and not used as a valid taxon. In the synonymy of *Ammodytes* Linnaeus 1758. Ammodytidae.

Shacra (subgenus of *Opsarus*) Bleeker 1860:287 [ref. 370]. *Cyprinus (Barilius) shacra* Hamilton 1822:271. Type by subsequent absolute tautonymy. Apparently appeared first as name only in Bleeker 1859:436 [ref. 370]. Many species included by Bleeker 1860:287 [ref. 380]. Same as *Pachystomus* Heckel 1843. Synonym of *Barilius* Hamilton 1822 (Roberts 1989:30 [ref. 6439]). Cyprinidae.

Sheardichthys (subgenus of *Neoodax*) Whitley 1947:146 [ref. 4708]. Masc. *Malacanthus radiatus* Quoy & Gaimard 1834:717. Type by original designation (also monotypic). Valid (Gomon & Paxton 1986:41 [ref. 5656]). Odacidae.

Shipa (subgenus of *Acipenser*) Brandt 1869:113 [ref. 618]. *Acipenser shipa* of Güldenstädt. Type by subsequent designation. As a subgenus of *Acipenser* with 2 species: *A. shipa* of Güldenstädt (not of Brandt and Ratzeburg) and *Acipenser nudiventris* Lovetski. Jordan 1919:354 [ref. 4904] gives type as *A. schypa* Eichwald = *A. nudiventris* Lovetski; Jordan misspells genus as *Schipa*. Synonym of *Acipenser* Linnaeus 1758. Acipenseridae: Acipenserinae.

Shippofugu (subgenus of *Sphoeroides*) Abe 1949:90 (in key) [ref. 3]. Masc. *Tetraodon hypselogeneion* Bleeker 1852:300. Type by monotypy. Synonym of *Amblyrhynchotes* Troschel 1856 (Masuda et al. 1984:364 [ref. 6441]). Tetraodontidae.

Shipwayia Whitley 1954:155 [ref. 4719]. Fem. *Eleotris aurea* Shipway 1950:75. Type by monotypy. Synonym of *Hypseleotris* Gill 1863 (Hoese, pers. comm.). Eleotridae.

Shosaifugu (subgenus of *Sphoeroides*) Abe 1950:199 [ref. 5588]. Masc. *Tetraodon vermicularis* Temminck & Schlegel 1850:278. Appeared in Abe 1949:92 (in key) [ref. 3] with 4 included species but no definite type fixation; therefore not available from Abe 1949. Type fixed by Abe 1950:199 with bibliographic reference to Abe 1949; name dates to Abe 1950. Synonym of *Takifugu* Abe 1949 (Masuda et al. 1984:363 [ref. 6441]). Tetraodontidae.

Siaja (subgenus of *Cyclocheilichthys*) Bleeker 1859:149 [ref. 371]. Fem. *Capoeta siaja* Bleeker 1851:432. Type by absolute tautonymy. Appeared as name only in Bleeker 1859:431 [ref. 370]. Apparently dates to 1859 as above; with many included species, one of which is *siaja*. Type not *Capoeta microlepis*. Also in Bleeker 1863:27 [ref. 4859] and 1863:199 [ref. 397]. Synonym of *Cyclocheilichthys* Bleeker 1859 (Roberts 1989:33 [ref. 6439] with type as *microlepis*). Cyprinidae.

Sibogapistus de Beaufort 1949:68 [ref. 241]. Masc. *Paracentropogon cynocephalus* Weber 1913:501. Type by original designation. Scorpaenidae: Tetraroginae.

Siboma Girard 1856:209 [ref. 1810]. Fem. *Lavinia crassicauda* Baird & Girard in Girard 1854:137. Type by subsequent designation. Type designated by Bleeker 1863:29 [ref. 4859] and 1863:205 [ref. 397]. Synonym of *Gila* Baird & Girard 1853. Cyprinidae.

Sicamugil Fowler 1939:9 [ref. 5597]. Masc. *Mugil hamiltonii* Day 1869:614. Type by original designation (also monotypic). Valid (Jayaram 1981:344 [ref. 6497]). Mugilidae.

Sicya (subgenus of *Cotylopus*) Jordan & Evermann 1896:456 [ref. 2442]. Fem. *Sicydium gymnogaster* Ogilvie-Grant 1884:159. Type by original designation. Gobiidae.

Sicyases Müller & Troschel in Müller 1843:298 [ref. 3063]. Masc. *Sicyases sanguineus* Müller & Troschel in Müller 1843:298. Type by monotypy. Valid (Briggs 1955:54 [ref. 637], Pequeño 1989:41 [ref. 14125]). Gobiesocidae: Gobiesocinae.

Sicydiops (subgenus of *Sicyopterus*) Bleeker 1874:314 [ref. 437]. Masc. *Sicydium xanthurus* Bleeker 1853. Type by original designation (also monotypic). Synonym of *Sicyopterus* Gill 1860 (Maugé 1986:383 [ref. 6218]). Gobiidae.

Sicydium Valenciennes in Cuvier & Valenciennes 1837:167 [ref. 1006]. Neut. *Gobius plumieri* Bloch 1786:125. Type by subsequent designation. Type designated by Gill 1861:101. Valid (Akihito & Meguro 1979 [ref. 6996], Maugé 1986:382 [ref. 6218], Birdsong et al. 1988:198 [ref. 7303]). Gobiidae.

Sicyodon Fourmanoir 1966:956 [ref. 1355]. Masc. *Sicyodon albus* Fourmanoir 1966:957. Type by monotypy. Synonym of *Lobulogobius* Koumans 1944 (Larson & Hoese 1980:38 [ref. 2725]). Gobiidae.

Sicyogaster Brisout de Barneville 1846:144 [ref. 9183]. Fem. *Gobiesox marmoratus* Jenyns 1842:140. Type by monotypy. Synonym of *Gobiesox* Lacepède 1800 (Briggs 1955:87 [ref. 637]). Gobiesocidae: Gobiesocinae.

Sicyogaster Gill 1860:101 [ref. 1764]. Fem. *Sicyogaster concolor* Gill 1860:101. Type by original designation (also monotypic). Preoccupied by de Brisout de Barneville 1846 in fishes, replaced by *Lentipes* Günther 1861. Gobiidae.

Sicyopterus (subgenus of *Sicydium*) Gill 1860:101 [ref. 1764]. Masc. *Sicydium (Sicyopterus) stimpsoni* Gill 1860:101. Type by original designation (also monotypic). Valid (Akihito & Meguro 1979 [ref. 6996], Akihito in Masuda et al. 1984:285 [ref. 6441], Maugé 1986:383 [ref. 6218], Klausewitz & Henrich 1986:117 [ref. 5214], Birdsong et al. 1988:198 [ref. 7303]). Gobiidae.

Sicyopus Gill 1863:262 (footnote) [ref. 1690]. *Sicydium zosterophorum* Bleeker 1857:296. Type by subsequent designation. Type designated by Bleeker 1874:311 [ref. 437]. Valid (Akihito in Masuda et al. 1984:284 [ref. 6441], Klausewitz & Henrich 1986 [ref. 5214], Birdsong et al. 1988:198 [ref. 7303]). Gobiidae.

Sicyosus (subgenus of *Cotylopus*) Jordan & Evermann 1898:2867 [ref. 2445]. Masc. *Sicydium gymnogaster* Ogilvie-Grant 1884:158. Type by being a replacement name. Replacement for *Sicya* Jordan & Evermann 1896, apparently preoccupied in Lepidoptera [details not investigated]. Gobiidae.

Sidera Kaup in Duméril 1856:200 [ref. 1154]. Not available, name only as "*Sidera pantherina*," without description or indication in list of genera and species taken from Kaup manuscript by Duméril; see *Siderea* Kaup 1856. Muraenidae: Muraeninae.

Siderea Kaup 1856:58 [ref. 2572]. Fem. *Siderea pfeifferi* Bleeker 1853:(154) 173. Type by subsequent designation. Type designated by Jordan 1919:271 [ref. 2410]. Also in Kaup 1856:70 [ref. 2573] as *Sidera* (incorrect subsequent spelling) and as name only in Kaup in Dumeril 1856:200 [ref. 1154]. Valid (Castle & McCosker 1986:173 [ref. 5645], Paxton et al. 1989:133 [ref. 12442], Böhlke et al. 1989:130 [ref. 13286]). Muraenidae: Muraeninae.

Sierra (subgenus of *Scomberomorus*) Fowler 1905:766 [ref. 1368]. Fem. *Cybium cavalla* Cuvier 1829:200. Type by original designation (also monotypic). Synonym of *Scomberomorus* Lacepède 1801 (Collette & Russo 1984:611 [ref. 5221]). Scombridae.

Sierrathrissa Thys van den Audenaerde 1969:386 [ref. 6582]. Fem. *Sierrathrissa leonensis* Thys van den Audenaerde 1969:386. Type by original designation (also monotypic). Valid (Poll et al. 1984:54 [ref. 6172], Grande 1985:247 [ref. 6466], Whitehead & Teugels 1985 [ref. 5726], Whitehead 1985:162 [ref. 5141]). Clupeidae.

Siganites (subgenus of *Teuthis*) Fowler 1904:546 [ref. 1367]. Masc. *Chaetodon canaliculatus* Mungo Park 1797:33. Type by original designation (also monotypic). Synonym of *Siganus* Forsskål 1775. Siganidae.

Siganus Forsskål 1775:x, 25 [ref. 1351]. Masc. *Scarus rivulatus* Forsskål 1775:x, 25. Type by monotypy. Original description confusing, proposed as a new genus (p. x) within new genus *Scarus*. Valid (Tortonese 1973:456 [ref. 7192], Leis & Richards 1984:548 [ref. 13669], Kishimoto in Masuda et al. 1984:232 [ref. 6441], Ben-Tuvia in Whitehead et al. 1986:964 [ref. 13676], Woodland 1986:824 [ref. 6299], see Tyler et al. 1989:37 [ref. 13460]). Siganidae.

Sigmistes Rutter in Jordan & Evermann 1898:2863 [ref. 2445]. Masc. *Sigmistes caulias* Rutter in Jordan & Evermann 1898:2863. Type by original designation (also monotypic). Misspelled *Sigmites* in Zoological Record for 1898. Valid (Washington et al. 1984:443 [ref. 13660]). Cottidae.

Sigmops Gill 1883:256 [ref. 1724]. Masc. *Sigmops stigmaticus* Gill 1883:256. Type by monotypy. Synonym of *Gonostoma* Rafinesque 1810 (Witzell 1973:114 [ref. 7172]). Gonostomatidae.

Sigmurus (subgenus of *Ophioscion*) Gilbert in Jordan & Evermann 1898:1446,-47,-52 [ref. 2444]. Masc. *Corvina vermicularis* Günther 1868:387, 427. Type by original designation (also monotypic). Synonym of *Ophioscion* Gill 1863 (Chao 1978:39 [ref. 6983]). Sciaenidae.

Signalosa Evermann & Kendall 1898:127 [ref. 1281]. Fem. *Signalosa atchafalayae* Evermann & Kendall 1898:127. Type by original designation (also monotypic). Valid (Grande 1985:249 [ref. 6466]); synonym of *Dorosoma* Rafinesque 1820 (Whitehead 1985:232 [ref. 5141]). Clupeidae.

Signigobius Hoese & Allen 1977:199 [ref. 2179]. Masc. *Signigobius biocellatus* Hoese & Allen 1977:200. Type by original designation (also monotypic). Valid (Birdsong et al. 1988:193 [ref. 7303]). Gobiidae.

Sikukia Smith 1931:138 [ref. 4049]. Fem. *Sikukia stejnegeri* Smith 1931:138. Type by monotypy. Valid (Kottelat 1985:266 [ref. 11441], Kottelat 1985 [ref. 5288], Chu & Cui in Chu & Chen 1989:166 [ref. 13584], Kottelat 1989:11 [ref. 13605]). Cyprinidae.

Silhouettea Smith 1959:213 [ref. 4122]. Fem. *Silhouettea insinuans* Smith 1959:214. Type by original designation (also monotypic). Valid (Yoshino in Masuda et al. 1984:254 [ref. 6441], Hoese 1986:803 [ref. 5670], Miller in Whitehead et al. 1986:1080 [ref. 13677], Maugé 1986:384 [ref. 6218], Larson & Miller 1986 [ref. 5803], Miller & Fouda 1986 [ref. 12844], Birdsong et al. 1988:193 [ref. 7303]). Gobiidae.

Sillaginichthys Bleeker 1874:63 [ref. 12517]. Masc. *Sillago domina* Cuvier in Cuvier & Valenciennes 1829:415. Type by subsequent designation. Probably not available, name in synonymy; also in Bleeker 1876:332 [448] as name in synonymy and "[Bleeker] 1859 sed diagnosi nulla"; use by Bleeker 1859 not yet located. Fowler 1933:432 [ref. 1414] designated a type but still used the name only in synonymy. Treated as available by McKay (1985:47 [ref. 5265]). Objective synonym of *Sillaginopsis* Gill 1862. Sillaginidae.

Sillaginodes Gill 1862:504 [ref. 1780]. Masc. *Sillago punctata* Cuvier in Cuvier & Valenciennes 1829:413. Type by original designation (also monotypic). Valid (McKay 1985:46 [ref. 5265], Paxton et al. 1989:562 [ref. 12442]). Sillaginidae.

Sillaginopodys (subgenus of *Sillago*) Fowler 1933:416, 430 [ref. 1414]. *Sillago chondropus* Bleeker 1849:61. Type by original designation (also monotypic). Synonym of *Sillago* Cuvier 1816, but as a valid subgenus (McKay 1985:5 [ref. 5265]). Sillaginidae.

Sillaginopsis Gill 1862:505 [ref. 1780]. Fem. *Sillago domina* Cuvier in Cuvier & Valenciennes 1829:415. Type by original designation (also monotypic). Valid (McKay 1985:47 [ref. 5265]). Sillaginidae.

Sillago Cuvier 1816:258 [ref. 993]. Fem. *Sillago acuta* Cuvier 1816:258. Type by subsequent designation. Type designated by Gill 1861:503 [ref. 1780] as *Sillago sihama* Rüppell, with *acuta* in synonymy; *sihama* not mentioned by Cuvier. *Silago* is a misspelling. Valid (Sano & Mochizuki 1984 [ref. 5216], Mochizuki in Masuda et al. 1984:151 [ref. 6441], McKay 1985:5 [ref. 5265], McKay 1986:615 [ref. 6300], Paxton et al. 1989:562 [ref. 12442]). Sillaginidae.

Silonia (subgenus of *Ageneious*) Swainson 1838:345 et seq. [ref. 4302]. Fem. *Silonia lurida* Swainson 1838:306 (= *Pimelodus silondia* Hamilton 1822:160, 345). Type by monotypy in Swainson 1838:345; *S. lurida* Swainson is an unneeded substitute for *P. silondia* Hamilton. Also in Swainson 1839:189, 305 [ref. 4303]. Valid (Jayaram 1977:23 [ref. 7006], Jayaram 1981:224 [ref. 6497], Burgess 1989:105 [ref. 12860]). Schilbeidae.

Silonopangasius Hora 1937 [ref. 6575]. Masc. *Ageneiosus childreni* Sykes 1835:165. Type by original designation (also monotypic). Synonym of *Silonia* Swainson 1838. Schilbeidae.

Silundia Valenciennes in Cuvier & Valenciennes 1840:48 [ref. 1008]. Fem. *Silundia gangetica* Valenciennes in Cuvier & Valenciennes 1840:49 (= *Pimelodus silondia* Hamilton 1822:160, 345). Type by subsequent designation. Type designated by Bleeker 1862:399 [ref. 391]. Valenciennes' *gangetica* is an unneeded substitute for *Pimelodus silondia* Hamilton. *Silondia* Günther 1864:65 [ref. 1974] is an unjustified emendation. Objective synonym of *Silonia* Swainson 1838. Schilbeidae.

Siluranodon Bleeker 1858:253, 255, 256 [ref. 365]. Masc. *Silurus auritus* Geoffroy St. Hilaire 1809:Pl. 11. Type by monotypy. Valid (De Vos 1986:53 [ref. 6191], Burgess 1989:99 [ref. 12860]). Schilbeidae.

Silurichthys Bleeker 1856:417, 418 [ref. 5118]. Masc. *Silurus phaiosoma* Bleeker 1851:428. Type by monotypy. Valid (Haig 1952:67 [ref. 12607], Kottelat 1985:269 [ref. 11441], Burgess 1989:85 [ref. 12860], Kottelat 1989:14 [ref. 13605], Roberts 1989:151 [ref. 6439]). Siluridae.

Silurodes Bleeker 1858:255, 256, 271 [ref. 365]. Masc. *Silurus hypophthalmus* Bleeker 1846:149. Type by subsequent designation. Type designated by Bleeker 1862:394 [ref. 391], 1862:17 [ref. 393] and 1863:115 [ref. 401]. Synonym of *Ompok* Lacepède 1803 (Haig 1952:103 [ref. 12607], Roberts 1989:150 [ref. 6439]). Siluridae.

Silurodon Kner 1866:546 [4] [ref. 2636]. Masc. *Silurodon hexanema* Kner 1866:546. Type by monotypy. On p. 4 of separate. Also described as new in Kner 1867:305 [ref. 2638]. Questionably a synonym of *Silurus* Linnaeus 1758 (Haig 1952:101 [ref. 12607]). Siluridae.

Silurus Linnaeus 1758:304 [ref. 2787]. Masc. *Silurus glanis* Linnaeus 1758:304. Type by subsequent designation. Type usually given as by Linnaean tautonymy, but "Silurus" occurs with 4 of 14 species. Earliest type designation found is Bleeker 1862:393 [ref. 391]. On Official List (Opinion 77, Direction 56). Valid (Haig 1952:71, 97 [ref. 12607], Jayaram 1977:7 [ref. 7006], Jayaram 1981:210 [ref. 6497], Sawada in Masuda et al. 1984:59 [ref. 6441], Kottelat 1985:269 [ref. 11441], Burgess 1989:85 [ref. 12860], Kobayakawa 1989 [ref. 13476], Kottelat 1989:14 [ref. 13605]). Siluridae.

Silus Reinhardt 1833:11 [ref. 3690]. Masc. *Salmo silus* Ascanius 1763:24. Type by absolute tautonymy. Synonym of *Argentina* Linnaeus 1758 (Cohen 1973:152 [ref. 6589]). Argentinidae.

Silvaichthys Fernández-Yépez 1973:3 (unnum.) [ref. 14284]. Masc. *Silvaichthys aguilerae* Fernándes-Yépez 1973:4 (unnum.). Type by original designation (also monotypic). Auchenipteridae.

Silvesterina Fowler 1934:274 [ref. 1416]. Fem. *Silvesterina parvibranchialis* Fowler 1934:275. Type by original designation (also monotypic). Valid (Smith 1989:512 [ref. 13285]). Congridae: Congrinae.

Simenchelys Gill in Goode & Bean 1879:27 [ref. 5605]. Fem. *Simenchelys parasiticus* Gill in Goode & Bean 1879:27. Type by monotypy. *Simenchelis* is a misspelling. Valid (Bauchot et al. 1973:223 [ref. 7185], Asano in Masuda et al. 1984:26 [ref. 6441], Saldanha & Bauchot in Whitehead et al. 1986:590 [ref. 13676], Castle 1986:190 [ref. 5644], Paxton et al. 1989:108 [ref. 12442], Robins & Robins 1989:214 [ref. 13287]). Synaphobranchidae: Simenchelyinae.

Similiparma Hensley 1986:858 [ref. 5734]. Fem. *Glyphidodon (Parma) hermani* Steindachner 1887:230. Type by original designation (also monotypic). Correct spelling for genus of type species is *Glyphisodon*. Pomacentridae.

Simobrama Fowler 1944:2 [ref. 1447]. Fem. *Seserinus xanthurus* Quoy & Gaimard 1824:384. Type by original designation (also monotypic). Synonym of *Peprilus* Cuvier 1829 (Haedrich 1967:103 [ref. 5357]). Stromateidae.

Simocampus (subgenus of *Bryx*) Fritzsche 1980:193 [ref. 1511]. Masc. *Siphostoma arctum* Jenkins & Evermann 1888:137. Type by original designation. Synonym of *Cosmocampus* Dawson 1979 (Dawson 1982:120 [ref. 6764], Dawson 1985:47 [ref. 6541]). Syngnathidae: Syngnathinae.

Simocantharus (subgenus of *Spondyliosoma*) Fowler 1933:182, 185 [ref. 1414]. Masc. *Cantharus aeneus* Gilchrist & Thompson 1908:166. Type by original designation. Synonym of *Pachymetopon* Günther 1859 (Smith & Smith 1986 [ref. 5710] based on placement of type species). Sparidae.

Simochromis Boulenger 1898:19 [ref. 547]. Masc. *Chromis diagramma* Günther 1893:632. Type by original designation (also monotypic). Valid (Axelrod & Harrison 1978 [ref. 7009], Poll 1986:77 [ref. 6136]). Cichlidae.

Simopias Gill 1905:224 [ref. 1789]. Masc. *Scorpaena didactyla* Pallas 1769:26. Type by being a replacement name. Replacement for *Pelor* Cuvier 1829, preoccupied by Bonelli 1813 in Coleoptera. Treated as a subgenus of *Inimicus*, but Gill wrongly thought *filamentosum* was type species of *Pelor*. Synonym of *Inimicus* Jordan & Starks 1904 (Eschmeyer et al. 1979:483 [ref. 6385]). Scorpaenidae: Choridactylinae.

Simosyngnathus Fowler 1940:12 [ref. 1435]. Masc. *Siphostoma crinigerum* Bean & Dresel 1884:99. Type by original designation (also monotypic). Objective synonym of *Anarchopterus* Hubbs 1935 (Dawson 1982:33 [ref. 6764]). Syngnathidae: Syngnathinae.

Simpsonichthys Carvalho 1959:2 [ref. 736]. Masc. *Simpsonichthys boitonei* Carvalho 1959:5. Type by original designation (also monotypic). Synonym of *Cynolebias* Steindachner 1876 (Parenti

1981:490 [ref. 7066], Costa 1989:183 [ref. 14323]). Aplocheilidae: Rivulinae.

Sindoscopus Dawson 1977:150 [ref. 1067]. Masc. *Gillellus australis* Fowler & Bean 1923:23. Type by original designation (also monotypic). Valid (Dawson 1982:83 [ref. 1072]). Dactyloscopidae.

Sineleotris Herre 1940:293 [ref. 2132]. Fem. *Sineleotris saccharae* Herre 1940:293. Type by original designation (also monotypic). Eleotridae.

Sinibarbus Sauvage 1874:335 [ref. 3873]. Masc. *Sinibarbus vittatus* Sauvage 1874:335. Type by monotypy. Cyprinidae.

Sinibotia (subgenus of *Botia*) Fang 1936:6, 19 [ref. 1302]. Fem. *Botia (Hymenophysa) superciliaris* Günther 1892:250. Type by original designation (also monotypic). Synonym of *Botia* Gray 1831, but as a valid subgenus (Nalbant 1963:359 [ref. 3140], Banarescu & Nalbant 1968:341 [ref. 6554]). Cobitidae: Botiinae.

Sinibrama Wu 1939:115 [ref. 4805]. Fem. *Chanodichthys wui* Lin 1932:105. Type by monotypy. Valid (Yih & Wu 1964:109 [ref. 13499], Chen in Chu & Chen 1989:52 [ref. 13584]). Cyprinidae.

Sinigobio Chu 1935:11 [ref. 832]. Masc. *Gobio sihuensis* Chu 1932:22. Type by original designation (also monotypic). Synonym of *Gnathopogon* Bleeker 1859 (Lu, Luo & Chen 1977:478 [ref. 13495]); synonym of *Squalidus* Dybowski 1872 (Banarescu & Nalbant 1973:80 [ref. 173], Chen & Li in Chu & Chen 1989:105 [ref. 13584]). Cyprinidae.

Siniichthys Banarescu 1970:161 [ref. 214]. Masc. *Siniichthys brevirostris* Banarescu 1970:161. Type by original designation (also monotypic). Cyprinidae.

Sinilabeo Rendahl 1932:81 [ref. 3703]. Masc. *Varicorhinus tungting* Nichols 1925:3. Type by original designation (also monotypic). Valid (Wu et al. 1977:333 [ref. 4807], Chu & Cui in Chu & Chen 1989:252 [ref. 13584]). Cyprinidae.

Siniperca Gill 1862:16 [ref. 1656]. Fem. *Perca chuatsi* Basilewski 1855:218. Type by original designation (also monotypic). Type species spelled *chua-tsi* and *chuan-tsi*. Placement in classification follows Johnson 1984:465 [ref. 9681]. Valid (Zhou et al. 1986:965 [ref. 6332]). Percoidei.

Sinobatis (subgenus of *Anacanthobatis*) Hulley 1973:153 [ref. 2275]. Fem. *Anacanthobatis borneensis* Chan 1965:47. Type by original designation (also monotypic). Second species tentatively included. Synonym of *Anacanthobatis* von Bonde & Swart 1923, but as a valid subgenus (Hulley 1986:127 [ref. 5672], Séret 1986:322 [ref. 6753]). Anacanthobatidae.

Sinocrossocheilus Wu in Wu, Lin, Chen, Chen & He 1977:359 [ref. 4807]. Masc. *Sinocrossocheilus guizhouensis* Wu in Wu, Lin, Chen, Chen & He 1977:360. Type by original designation (also monotypic). Valid (Cui & Chu 1986 [ref. 9822], Chu & Cui in Chu & Chen 1989:246 [ref. 13584]). Cyprinidae.

Sinocyclocheilus Fang 1936:588 [ref. 1303]. Masc. *Sinocyclocheilus tingi* Fang 1936:590. Type by original designation (also monotypic). Genus misspelled *Sinocyclocheils* once on p. 588. Valid (Wu et al. 1977:261 [ref. 4807], Chu & Cui in Chu & Chen 1989:169 [ref. 13584]). Cyprinidae.

Sinogastromyzon Fang 1930:35 [ref. 1296]. Masc. *Sinogastromyzon wui* Fang 1930:36. Type by original designation (also monotypic). Valid (Silas 1953:214 [ref. 4024], Chen 1978:341 [ref. 6900], Sawada 1982:204 [ref. 14111], Kottelat & Chu 1988:195 [ref. 13491]). Balitoridae: Balitorinae.

Sinogobius (subgenus of *Gobius*) Liu 1940:215 [ref. 2790]. Masc. *Gobius (Sinogobius) szechuanensis* Liu 1940:213. Type by original designation (also monotypic). Gobiidae.

Sinohomaloptera (subgenus of *Homaloptera*) Fang 1930:26 [ref. 1296]. Fem. *Homaloptera kwangsiensis* Fang 1930:27. Type by original designation (also monotypic). Valid (Silas 1953:209 [ref. 4024], Chen 1978:336 [ref. 6900], Sawada 1982:204 [ref. 14111]); synonym of *Balitora* Gray 1830 (Kottelat 1988:489 [ref. 13379], Kottelat & Chu 1988:189 [ref. 13491]). Balitoridae: Balitorinae.

Sinomyrus Lin 1933:93 [ref. 2783]. Masc. *Sinomyrus angustus* Lin 1933:94. Type by original designation (also monotypic). Synonym of *Dysomma* Alcock 1889 (Robins & Robins 1976:256 [ref. 3784], Robins & Robins 1989:244 [ref. 13287]). Synaphobranchidae: Ilyophinae.

Sinopangasius Chang & Wu 1965:11, 13 [ref. 811]. Masc. *Sinopangasius semicultratus* Chang & Wu 1965:11, 13. Type by original designation (also monotypic). Synonym of *Pangasius* Valenciennes 1840 (Roberts, pers. comm.). Pangasiidae.

Sinosturio Jaekel 1929:25 [ref. 2320]. Masc. *Acipenser (Antaceus) dabryanus* Duméril 1868:98. Type by original designation. Original not seen. Synonym of *Acipenser* Linnaeus 1758. Acipenseridae: Acipenserinae.

Sio Moss 1962:4 [ref. 3047]. *Melamphaes nordenskjoldii* Lönnberg 1905:58. Type by original designation (also monotypic). Valid (Ebeling 1986:431 [ref. 5651], Paxton et al. 1989:372 [ref. 12442]). Melamphaidae.

Siokunichthys Herald in Schultz et al. 1953:254 [ref. 3975]. Masc. *Siokunichthys herrei* Herald in Schultz et al. 1953:254. Type by original designation (also monotypic). Valid (Dawson 1983 [ref. 5351], Dawson 1985:165 [ref. 6541], Paxton et al. 1989:428 [ref. 12442]). Syngnathidae: Syngnathinae.

Siphagonus Steindachner 1876:188 [ref. 4225]. Masc. *Agonus segaliensis* Tilesius. Type by subsequent designation. Type designated by Jordan 1919:387 [ref. 4904]. Agonidae.

Siphamia Weber 1909:168 [ref. 4600]. Fem. *Siphamia tubifer* Weber 1909:168. Type by monotypy. *Beanea* Steindachner 1902 suppressed for priority in favor of *Siphamia*; *Siphamia* placed on Official List (Opinion 1481). Valid (Fraser 1972:14 [ref. 5195], Hayashi in Masuda et al. 1984:144 [ref. 6441], Gon 1986:557 [ref. 5657], Paxton et al. 1989:557 [ref. 12442]). Apogonidae.

Siphateles Cope 1883:146 [ref. 951]. Masc. *Siphateles vittatus* Cope 1883:146. Type by monotypy. Synonym of *Gila* Baird & Girard 1853. Cyprinidae.

Siphonochromis Fowler 1946:143 [ref. 1456]. Masc. *Siphonochromis lepidostethicus* Fowler 1946:145. Type by original designation (also monotypic). Synonym of *Chromis* Cuvier 1814 (see Böhlke 1984:146 [ref. 13621]). Pomacentridae.

Siphonognathus Richardson 1858:237 [ref. 3748]. Masc. *Siphonognathus argyrophanes* Richardson 1858:238. Type by monotypy. Valid (Gomon & Paxton 1986:41 [ref. 5656]). Odacidae.

Siphonostoma Kaup 1856:48 Neut. Not examined. Fowler (MS) treats as an emendation of *Siphostoma* Rafinesque, with different type. Agassiz 1846 used this spelling earlier; see *Siphostoma* Rafinesque. Syngnathidae: Syngnathinae.

Siphostoma Rafinesque 1810:18 [ref. 3594]. Neut. *Syngnathus pelagicus* Linnaeus 1758:337. Type by subsequent designation. Apparently first type designation is by Jordan & Evermann 1896:761 [ref. 2443]. Spelled *Siphonostomus* and *Siphonostoma* by authors; *Siphonostoma* Agassiz 1846:342 [ref. 64] is an unjustified emendation. Synonym of *Syngnathus* Linnaeus 1758 (Wheeler 1973:274 [ref. 7190], Fritzsche 1980:198 [ref. 1511], Dawson 1982:55 [ref. 6764], Dawson 1985:181 [ref. 6541]). Syngnathidae: Syngnathinae.

Sirembo Bleeker 1858:22 [ref. 360]. *Brotula imberbis* Temminck & Schlegel 1846:253. Type by monotypy. Valid (Cohen & Nielsen 1978:19 [ref. 881], Machida in Masuda et al. 1984:100 [ref. 6441], Cohen & Robins 1986 [ref. 5254], Paxton et al. 1989:313 [ref. 12442]). Ophidiidae: Neobythitinae.

Sisor Hamilton 1822:208, 379 [ref. 2031]. Masc. *Sisor rabdophorus* Hamilton 1822:208, 379. Type by monotypy. Species misspelled or unjustifiably emended to *rhabdophorus* by authors. Treated by author as masculine. Valid (Jayaram 1981:268 [ref. 6497], Burgess 1989:132 [ref. 12860]). Sisoridae.

Skagerakia Nybelin 1947:4 [ref. 3233]. Fem. *Skagerakia nilssoni* Nybelin 1947:4. Type by monotypy. Valid (Nielsen 1973:165 [ref. 6885]); synonym of subgenus *Benthosaurus* Goode & Bean 1886 of genus *Bathypterois* Günther 1878 (Sulak 1977:76 [ref. 4299]). Chlorophthalmidae: Ipnopinae.

Skeponopodus Nardo 1833:? [ref. 3147]. Masc. *Skeponopodus typus* Nardo 1833. Original not examined. Type apparently by use of *typus*. *Scheponopodus* is a misspelling or unjustified emendation. Synonym of *Istiophorus* Lacepède 1801 (de Sylva 1973:477 [ref. 7210] and Nakamura 1983:277 [ref. 5371] with type as *guebucu*; both also place in the synonymy of *Tetrapterus* with type as "typus"). Istiophoridae.

Skiffia Meek 1902:102 [ref. 2957]. Fem. *Skiffia lermae* Meek 1902:102. Type by original designation. Valid (Miller & Fitzsimons 1971:10 [ref. 3019], Uyeno et al. 1983:505 [ref. 6818]). Goodeidae.

Sladenia Regan 1908:250 [ref. 3634]. Fem. *Sladenia gardineri* Regan 1908:251. Type by monotypy. Valid (Caruso & Bullis 1976 [ref. 5167], Caruso 1985:874 [ref. 5170]). Lophiidae.

Slatinia Werner 1906:326 [ref. 4625]. Fem. *Slatinia mongallensis* Werner 1906:327. Type by monotypy. Synonym of *Andersonia* Boulenger 1900 (Skelton & Teugels 1986:59 [ref. 6192]). Amphiliidae.

Smaragdus Poey 1860:279 [ref. 3499]. Fem. *Smaragdus valenciennesi* Poey 1860:280 (= *Gobius smaragdus* Valenciennes 1837:173). Type by absolute tautonymy of cited objective synonym. Poey's *S. valenciennesi* is an unneeded substitute for *G. smaragdus* Valenciennes in Cuvier & Valenciennes. Synonym of *Gobionellus* Girard 1858. Gobiidae.

Smaris Cuvier 1814:92 [ref. 4884]. Fem. *Sparus smaris* Linnaeus 1758:278. Type by absolute tautonymy. Also appeared in Cuvier 1815:111 [ref. 5017] and 1816:269 [ref. 993]. Preoccupied by Latreille 1796 in Arachnida, replaced by *Marsis* Barnard 1927. Placed on Official Index because of preoccupation (Opinion 960). Synonym of *Spicara* Rafinesque 1810 (Tortonese et al. 1973:417 [ref. 7202]). Centracanthidae.

Smecticus Valenciennes 1855:305 [ref. 4504]. Masc. *Rypticus bicolor* Valenciennes 1846:tab., Pl.2. Type by monotypy. As *Rypticus bicolor* in Ichthyologie Pl. 2 (1846) [ref. 6165] which preceded text where genus name was changed to *Smecticus*; species dates to 1846. Synonym of *Rypticus* Cuvier 1829. Serranidae: Grammistinae.

Smiliogaster Bleeker 1859:438 [ref. 370]. Fem. *Leuciscus belangeri* Valenciennes in Cuvier & Valenciennes 1843:99. Type by subsequent monotypy. Apparently appeared first in key, without included species. One species included by Bleeker 1860:296, 467 [ref. 380]. Type also designated by Bleeker 1863:214 [ref. 397] and 1863:33 [ref. 4859]). Synonym of *Rohtee* Sykes 1839. Cyprinidae.

Smilogobius Herre 1934:88 [ref. 2108]. Masc. *Smilogobius inexplicatus* Herre 1934:88. Type by original designation. Synonym of *Cryptocentrus* Valenciennes (ex Ehrenberg) 1837 (Polunin & Lubbock 1977:92 [ref. 3540], Yanagisawa 1978:271 [ref. 7028]). Gobiidae.

Smithichthys Clark Hubbs 1952:107 [ref. 2252]. Masc. *Clinus fucorum* Gilchrist & Thompson 1908:121. Type by original designation (also monotypic). Valid (Smith 1986:768 [ref. 5712]). Clinidae.

Snellius Koumans 1953:183 [ref. 2679]. Masc. *Snellius boschmai* Koumans 1953:184. Type by original designation (also monotypic). Sternoptychidae: Sternoptychinae.

Snyderichthys Miller 1945:28 [ref. 3015]. Masc. *Squalius copei* Jordan & Gilbert 1880:461. Type by original designation (also monotypic). Synonym of *Gila* Baird & Girard 1853, as a valid subgenus. Cyprinidae.

Snyderidia Gilbert 1905:654 [ref. 1631]. Fem. *Snyderidia canina* Gilbert 1905:655. Type by original designation (also monotypic). Valid (Cohen & Nielsen 1978:7 [ref. 881], Williams 1983:850 [ref. 5367], Arai in Uyeno et al. 1983:237 [ref. 14275]). Carapidae: Pyramodontinae.

Snyderina Jordan & Starks 1901:381 [ref. 2523]. Fem. *Snyderina yamanokami* Jordan & Starks 1901:381. Type by monotypy. Misspelled *Snyderia* (and species *jamanokami*) in Zoological Record for 1901. Valid (Yamakawa 1976 [ref. 6969], Washington et al. 1984:440 [ref. 13660], Nakabo in Masuda et al. 1984:319 [ref. 6441]). Scorpaenidae: Tetraroginae.

Soarus Linck 1790:38 [ref. 4985]. Masc. Appeared without included species; probably a misprint for *Saurus* (see Gill 1903:962 [ref. 4983]). In the synonymy of *Synodus* Scopoli 1777 (Nielsen 1973:161 [ref. 6885], see Anderson et al. 1966:46 [ref. 6977]). Synodontidae: Synodontinae.

Sokodara (subgenus of *Ventrifossa*) Iwamoto 1979:153 [ref. 2311]. Fem. *Coryphaenoides misakius* Jordan & Gilbert 1904:611. Type by original designation (also monotypic). One or two undescribed species also included in subgenus. Macrouridae: Macrourinae.

Solagmedens Bauchot & Blanc 1963:53 [ref. 6583]. Fem. *Oligoplites africana* Delsman 1941:52. Type by original designation (also monotypic). Synonym of *Campogramma* Regan 1903 (Smith-Vaniz & Staiger 1973:246 [ref. 7106]). Carangidae.

Soldatovia Taranetz 1937:153 [ref. 13384]. Fem. *Blennius polyactocephalus* Pallas 1811:179. Type by monotypy. Valid (Miki & Maruyama 1986:404 [ref. 5694]). Stichaeidae.

Solea Catesby 1771:27 [ref. 774]. Fem. Not available, published in a rejected work on Official Index (Opinion 89, Opinion 259). Bothidae: Bothinae.

Solea Cuvier 1816:223 [ref. 993]. Fem. *Pleuronectes solea* Linnaeus 1758:270. Type by absolute tautonymy. Synonym of *Solea* Quensel 1806. Soleidae.

Solea Klein 1776:115 [ref. 4919]. Fem. Not available, published in a work that does not conform to the principle of binominal nomenclature. Soleidae.

Solea Quensel 1806:53 [ref. 3569]. Fem. *Solea vulgaris* Quensel 1806:54 (= *Pleuronectes solea* Linnaeus 1758:270). Type by monotypy. Linnaeus' species *solea* needlessly renamed *vulgaris* by Quensel. Valid (Torchio 1973:628 [ref. 6892], Quéro et al. in

Whitehead et al. 1986:1318 [ref. 13677], Heemstra & Gon 1986:873 [ref. 5665], Desoutter 1986:431 [ref. 6212]). Soleidae.

Solea Rafinesque 1810:14, 52 [ref. 3595]. Fem. *Solea buglossa* Rafinesque 1810 (= *Pleuronectes solea* Linnaeus 1758:270). Type is *solea* by absolute tautonymy; Rafinesque's *S. buglossa* is an unneeded replacement for *P. solea* Linnaeus. In the synonymy of *Solea* Quensel 1806. Soleidae.

Solegnathus (subgenus of *Syngnathus*) Swainson 1839:195, 333 [ref. 4303]. Masc. *Syngnathus hardwickii* Gray 1830:Pl. 89. Type by monotypy. *Solenognathus* Agassiz 1846:343, 344 [ref. 64] is an unjustified emendation; this spelling also used by early authors (e.g. Bleeker). Valid (Dawson 1982 [ref. 5442], Araga in Masuda et al. 1984:89 [ref. 6441], Dawson 1985:169 [ref. 6541], Paxton et al. 1989:429 [ref. 12442]). Syngnathidae: Syngnathinae.

Soleichthys Bleeker 1860:14 [ref. 379]. Masc. *Solea heterorhinos* Bleeker 1856:64. Type by monotypy. Valid (Ochiai in Masuda et al. 1984:355 [ref. 6441], Chapleau & Keast 1988:2799 [ref. 12625]). Soleidae.

Solenichthys Bleeker 1865:183 [ref. 414]. Masc. *Fistularia paradoxa* Pallas 1770:32. Type by being a replacement name. Replacement for *Solenostoma [us]* Lacepède 1803, not preoccupied by Gronow 1763, Walbaum 1792 or Klein 1778 in fishes [rejected works]. Later spelled *Solenostomichthys* by Bleeker 1873:126 and *Solenostomatichthys* 1874:76. Synonym of *Solenostomus* Lacepède 1803 (Fritzsche 1986:459 [ref. 6295]). Solenostomidae.

Solenoides Kaup 1858:96 [ref. 2578]. Name only, attributed to Bleeker, in synonymy of *Synaptura* Cantor. Not available; apparently never made available. In the synonymy of *Synaptura* Cantor 1849. Soleidae.

Solenomormyrus Bleeker 1874:368 [ref. 435]. Masc. *Centriscus niloticus* Bloch & Schneider 1801:113. Type by original designation (also monotypic). Misspelled *Selenomormyrus* in Zoological Record for 1874. Synonym of *Mormyrus* Linnaeus 1758 (Taverne 1972:163 [ref. 6367], Gosse 1984:98 [ref. 6169]). Mormyridae.

Solenophallus Aurich 1937:264 [ref. 151]. Not available; two included species after 1931, neither designated type (Art. 13b). Apparently can date to Herre 1953 (see remarks on Art. 13b in Appendix A). In the synonymy of *Neostethus* Regan 1916 (Parenti 1989:269 [ref. 13486]). Phallostethidae.

Solenophallus Herre (ex Aurich) 1953:242 [ref. 151]. Masc. *Solenophallus thessa* Aurich 1937:264. Type by original designation (also monotypic). Not available from Aurich 1937:264, no designation of type after 1930 (Art. 13b). Herre (1939:142, 144) reassigned one of Aurich's 2 included species to his *Ctenophallus* and left the second in *Solenophallus*. Herre (1953:242) clearly indicates a type for *Solenophallus*, and in absence of other information, the genus can date to Herre 1953. Valid (White et al. 1984:360 [ref. 13655]); synonym of *Neostethus* Regan 1916 (Parenti 1989:269 [ref. 13486]). Phallostethidae.

Solenostoma Duméril (ex Gronow) 1806:106, 138 [ref. 1151]. Neut. Synonym of *Aulostomus* Lacepède 1803 (Fowler, MS). Aulostomidae.

Solenostomatichthys Bleeker 1875:76 [ref. 443]. Masc. *Fistularia paradoxa* Pallas 1770:32. Type by being a replacement name. Replacement for or incorrect subsequent spelling of *Solenichthys* Bleeker 1865; but appears to be a replacement for *Solenostoma* or *Solenostomus*; apparently Bleeker changed his *Solenichthys* to the spelling *Solenostomatichthys*. Possibly published in 1874. Objective synonym of *Solenichthys* Bleeker 1865 and of *Solenostomus* Lacepède 1803. Solenostomidae.

Solenostomus Browne 1789:441 [ref. 669]. Masc. Not available, published in a rejected work on Official Index (Opinion 89). Fistulariidae.

Solenostomus Gill (ex Gronow) 1861:38 [ref. 1766]. Masc. *Fistularia tabacaria* of Storer (= *Fistularia tabacaria* Linnaeus 1758:312). Type by subsequent designation. Type perhaps designated first by Jordan 1919:302 [ref. 4904]. Synonym of *Fistularia* Linnaeus 1758. Fistulariidae.

Solenostomus Gray (ex Klein and Gronow) 1854:146 [ref. 1911]. Masc. *Fistularia chinensis* Linnaeus 1766:515. Type by monotypy. Second species treated under *Flagellaria*. Synonym of *Aulostomus* Lacepède 1803. Aulostomidae.

Solenostomus Gronow 1763:119 [ref. 1910]. Masc. Not available, published in a rejected work on Official Index (Opinion 261). Fistulariidae.

Solenostomus Klein 1778:32 [ref. 4922]. Masc. Not available, published in a work that does not conform to the principle of binominal nomenclature. Not *Solenostomus* Lacepède 1803. Original not checked. In the synonymy of *Fistularia* Linnaeus 1758. Fistulariidae.

Solenostomus Lacepède 1803:360 [ref. 4930]. Masc. *Fistularia paradoxa* Pallas 1770:32. Type by subsequent designation. Type designated by Jordan, Tanaka & Snyder 1913:93 [ref. 6448]. Not preoccupied by Gronow 1763, Klein 1778, Walbaum 1792, or Browne 1789 — all are unavailable, and if they were subsequently made available then this occurred after 1803. Valid (Araga in Masuda et al. 1984:85 [ref. 6441], Fritzsche 1984 [ref. 13658], Fritzsche 1986:459 [ref. 6295], Paxton et al. 1989:411 [ref. 12442]). Solenostomidae.

Soleonasus Eigenmann 1912:526, 528 [ref. 1227]. Masc. *Soleonasus finis* Eigenmann 1912:528. Type by original designation (also monotypic). Achiridae.

Soleotalpa Günther 1862:489 [ref. 1969]. Fem. *Soleotalpa unicolor* Günther 1862:489. Type by monotypy. Achiridae.

Solivomer Miller 1947:81 [ref. 3017]. Masc. *Solivomer arenidens* Miller 1947:84. Type by original designation (also monotypic). Valid (Okiyama 1984:207 [ref. 13644]). Neoscopelidae.

Somersia Beebe & Tee-Van 1934:1 [ref. 248]. Fem. *Somersia furcata* Beebe & Tee-Van 1934:1. Type by original designation (also monotypic). Blenniidae.

Somileptes (subgenus of *Canthophrys*) Swainson 1839:(190) 311 [ref. 4303]. Masc. *Somileptes bispinosa* Swainson 1839:311 (= *Cobitis gongota* Hamilton 1822:351, 394). Type by subsequent designation. Type designated by Bleeker 1863:3 [ref. 4859] as *S. gongota* Hamilton 1822 (for which *S. bispinosa* Swainson is an unneeded substitute). Swainson spelled as *Somileptus* on pp. 190 and 443 (first reviser not researched); *Somileptus* perhaps the correct name as used by Nalbant 1963. Valid (Nalbant 1963:364 [ref. 3140], Jayaram 1981:179 [ref. 6497], Sawada 1982:200 [ref. 14111]). Cobitidae: Cobitinae.

Somniosus Lesueur 1818:222 [ref. 2735]. Masc. *Somniosus brevipinna* Lesueur 1818:222. Type by monotypy. Proposed as a "subgenus, allied to the genus *Aiguillats* (Spix, Cuv.)." *Somnolentus* Swainson 1838:146 [ref. 4302] is regarded as an incorrect subsequent spelling. Valid (Krefft & Tortonese 1973:46 [ref. 7165], Compagno 1984:102 [ref. 6474], Bass et al. 1986:60 [ref. 5636], Cappetta 1987:62 [ref. 6348]). Squalidae.

Somnispinax (subgenus of *Centrophorus*) Whitley 1940:146 [ref. 4700]. *Centrophorus nilsoni* Thompson 1930:276. Type by original designation (also monotypic). Misspelled *Somnisphinax* by Neave 1950:252 [ref. 6512]. Synonym of *Centrophorus* Müller & Henle 1837 (Compagno 1984:35 [ref. 6474]). Squalidae.

Sonoda Grey 1959:180 [ref. 1904]. Fem. *Sonoda megalophthalma* Grey 1959:181. Type by original designation (also monotypic). Valid (Weitzman 1974:472 [ref. 5174], Ahlstrom et al. 1984:185 [ref. 13643], Weitzman 1986:254 [ref. 6287]). Sternoptychidae: Maurolicinae.

Sonorolux Trewavas 1977:389 [ref. 4459]. Fem. *Sonorolux fluminis* Trewavas 1977:390. Type by original designation (also monotypic). Sciaenidae.

Soranus Rafinesque 1815:88 [ref. 3584]. Not available, name only. Unplaced genera.

Sorgentinia Risso & Risso 1953:12 [ref. 5938]. Fem. *Atherina incisa* Jenyns 1842:79. Type by monotypy. Name apparently not in current literature. Objective synonym of *Austroatherina* Marrero 1950 (not available). Synonym of *Odontesthes* Evermann & Kendall 1906 (B. Dyer, pers. comm.). Atherinidae: Atherinopsinae.

Sorosichthys Whitley 1945:22 [ref. 4707]. Masc. *Sorosichthys ananassa* Whitley 1945:22. Type by original designation (also monotypic). Valid (Paxton et al. 1989:367 [ref. 12442]). Trachichthyidae.

Sorsogona Herre 1934:67 [ref. 2108]. Fem. *Sorsogona serrulata* Herre 1934:67. Type by original designation (also monotypic). Valid (Knapp 1979:50 [ref. 14196], Knapp 1986:484 [ref. 5683], Paxton et al. 1989:470 [ref. 12442]). Platycephalidae.

Sorubim Agassiz in Spix & Agassiz 1829:24 [ref. 13]. *Silurus lima* Bloch & Schneider 1801:384. Type by subsequent designation (and monotypy). First appeared in synonymy in Spix and Agassiz as above, but made available back to that authorship and date because of use as a valid name by Bleeker 1862:10 [ref. 393]; Bleeker included one species *lima* and designated it type. Valid (Stewart 1986:668 [ref. 5211], Burgess 1989:282 [ref. 12860]). See Kottelat 1988:80 who dates to Cuvier 1829. Pimelodidae.

Sorubim Cuvier 1829:293 [ref. 995]. *Silurus lima* Bloch & Schneider 1801:384. Type by subsequent designation. See analysis by Kottelat 1988:78, 80 [ref. 13380] who indicates that *Sorubim* Cuvier predates *Sorubim* Agassiz 1829. Kottelat regards the type as designated by Bleeker 1862:10, but perhaps technically that is incorrect since Bleeker was designating the type for *Sorubim* "Spix" [= Agassiz]; subsequent type designation for *Sorubim* Cuvier perhaps first dates to Kottelat 1988. Pimelodidae.

Sorubimichthys Bleeker 1862:10 [ref. 393]. Masc. *Sorubim jandia* Agassiz in Spix & Agassiz 1829:26. Type by original designation (also monotypic). Bleeker designated the type as "*Sorubim jandia* Spix"; this corresponds to *Sorubim spatula* Agassiz in text (p. 26) (See Whitehead & Myers 1971 [ref. 6584]; also Lundberg et al. 1989:333 [ref. 12544]). Technically, *jandia* was a Spix name first published in synonymy (and on pl. 14, if not considered a vernacular), but it was validated to Agassiz 1829 by its use as a valid name by Bleeker. Valid (Lundberg et al. 1989 [ref. 12544], Burgess 1989:282 [ref. 12860]). Pimelodidae.

Sosia Vaillant 1902:81 [ref. 4490]. Fem. *Sosia chamaeleon* Vaillant 1902:82. Type by monotypy. Synonym of *Acrochordonichthys* Bleeker 1858 (Roberts 1989:137 [ref. 6439]). Akysidae.

Sovichthys Schultz 1944:(185) 190 [ref. 3959]. Masc. *Sovichthys abuelo* Schultz 1944:191. Type by original designation (also monotypic). Synonym of *Cheirocerus* Eigenmann 1917 (Stewart & Pavlik 1985:357 [ref. 5240]). Pimelodidae.

Spaniblennius Bath & Wirtz 1989:278 [ref. 13307]. Masc. *Blennius riodourensis* Metzelaar 1919:291. Type by original designation. Blenniidae.

Spanius Gistel 1848:IX [ref. 1822]. Masc. *Leptosoma atra* Nardo 1827. Type by being a replacement name. Replacement for *Leptosoma* Nardo 1827, preoccupied by Leach 1819 in Crustacea. Soleidae.

Sparactodon Rochebrune 1880:162 [ref. 3790]. Masc. *Sparactodon nalnal* Rochebrune 1880:162. Type by monotypy. Misspelled *Sparaetodon* in Zoological Record for 1880. Synonym of *Pomatomus* Lacepède 1802 (Monod 1973:369 [ref. 7193]). Pomatomidae.

Sparidentex Munro 1948:276 [ref. 3057]. Masc. *Dentex hasta* Valenciennes in Cuvier & Valenciennes 1830:189 (= *Chrysophrys cuvieri* Day 1875:141). Type by original designation (also monotypic). Specific name *hasta* preoccupied by *Sparus hasta* Bloch & Schneider 1801, replaced by *C. cuvieri* Day 1875. Synonym of *Sparus* Linnaeus 1758. Sparidae.

Sparisoma (subgenus of *Petronason*) Swainson 1839:172, 227 [ref. 4303]. Neut. *Scarus abildgaardii* Bloch 1791:22, Pl. 259. Type by monotypy. *Sparisomus* is a misspelling. Valid (Monod 1973:444 [ref. 7193], Richards & Leis 1984:544 [ref. 13668], Quignard & Pras in Whitehead et al. 1986:943 [ref. 13676]). Scaridae: Sparisomatinae.

Sparodon Smith 1938:249 [ref. 4067]. Masc. *Sargus durbanensis* Castelnau 1861:18. Type by original designation (also monotypic). Valid (Smith & Smith 1986:593 [ref. 5710]). Sparidae.

Sparopsis Kner 1868:27 [ref. 6074]. Fem. *Sparopsis latifrons* Kner 1868:27. Type by monotypy. Also appeared as new in Kner 1868:302 [ref. 2646], where Kner changed the species name to *elongatus* (an objective synonym of *latifrons*). Nemipteridae.

Sparosomus Gill 1893:116, 123 [ref. 1736]. Masc. *Chrysophrys unicolor* Quoy & Gaimard 1824:299. Type by monotypy. Apparently in error for *Pagrosomus* Gill (same publication, p. 97). Sparidae.

Sparus Linnaeus 1758:277 [ref. 2787]. Masc. *Sparus aurata* Linnaeus 1758:277. Type by subsequent designation. Type designated by Bleeker 1876:281 [ref. 447]. On Official List (Direction 34, supplement to Opinion 69). Valid (Tortonese 1973:405 [ref. 7192], Akazaki in Masuda et al. 1984:178 [ref. 6441], Bauchot & Hureau in Whitehead et al. 1986:906 [ref. 13676]). Sparidae.

Spathodus Boulenger 1900:152 [ref. 555]. Masc. *Spathodus erythrodon* Boulenger 1900:152. Type by monotypy. Valid (Poll 1986:89 [ref. 6136]). Cichlidae.

Spatularia Shaw 1804:362 [ref. 4015]. Fem. *Spatularia reticulata* Shaw 1804:362. Type by monotypy. Synonym of *Polyodon* Lacepède 1797. Polyodontidae.

Spatuloricaria Schultz 1944:287, 334 [ref. 3959]. Fem. *Spatuloricaria phelpsi* Schultz 1944:335. Type by original designation (also monotypic). Valid (Isbrücker 1980:112 [ref. 2303], Burgess 1989:443 [ref. 12860]). Loricariidae.

Spectracanthicus Nijssen & Isbrücker 1987:93 [ref. 5993]. Masc. *Spectracanthicus murinus* Nijssen & Isbrücker 1987:94. Type by original designation (also monotypic). Valid (Burgess 1989:445 [ref. 12860] as *Spectracanthus*). Loricariidae.

Spectrunculus Jordan & Thompson 1914:301 [ref. 2543]. Masc. *Spectrunculus radcliffei* Jordan & Thompson 1914:301. Type by monotypy. Valid (Cohen & Nielsen 1978:39 [ref. 881], Nielsen & Hureau 1980 [ref. 5585], Hureau & Nielsen 1981:23 [ref. 5438], Machida in Masuda et al. 1984:101 [ref. 6441], Nielsen in Whitehead et al. 1986:1165 [ref. 13677], Nielsen & Cohen 1986:350 [ref. 5700], Machida et al. 1987 [ref. 6621]). Ophidiidae: Neobythitinae.

Speleogobius Zander & Jelinek 1976:275 [ref. 4828]. Masc. *Speleogobius trigloides* Zander & Jelinek 1976:275. Type by original designation (also monotypic). Valid (Miller in Whitehead et al. 1986:1080 [ref. 13677]). Gobiidae.

Speoplatyrhinus Cooper & Kuehne 1974:487 [ref. 904]. Masc. *Speoplatyrhinus poulsoni* Cooper & Kuehne 1974:491. Type by original designation (also monotypic). Amblyopsidae.

Sperata Holly 1939:143 [ref. 2191]. Fem. *Bagrus lamarrii* Valenciennes in Cuvier & Valenciennes 1840:407. Type by being a replacement name. Intended as a replacement for *Macrones* Duméril 1856, preoccupied by Newman 1841 in Coleoptera; but Holly designated *vittata* Bloch as type; if *Macrones* is considered a French vernacular, then *Sperata* apparently can stand on its own with type as *vittata*. See also *Aoria* Jordan 1917, *Aorichthys* Wu 1939, and *Macronichthys* White & Moy-Thomas 1940. Synonym of *Mystus* Scopoli 1777 (Roberts 1989:120 [ref. 6439]). Bagridae.

Sphaeramia (subgenus of *Amia*) Fowler & Bean 1930:25, 29 [ref. 1477]. Fem. *Apogon nematoptera* Bleeker 1856:35. Type by original designation. Valid (Fraser 1972:26 [ref. 5195], Allen 1975 [ref. 7098], Hayashi in Masuda et al. 1984:149 [ref. 6441], Gon 1986:557 [ref. 5657]). Apogonidae.

Sphaerichthys Canestrini 1860:707 [ref. 713]. Masc. *Sphaerichthys osphromenoides* Canestrini 1860:707. Type by monotypy, additional species apparently questionably included. Valid (Kottelat 1989:20 [ref. 13605], Roberts 1989:175 [ref. 6439]). Belontiidae.

Sphaerodon Rüppell 1838:112 [ref. 3844]. Masc. *Sciaena grandoculis* Forsskål 1775:53. Type by monotypy. Synonym of *Monotaxis* Bennett 1830 (Sato 1986:603 [ref. 5152]). Lethrinidae.

Sphaerophysa Cao & Zhu 1988:405 [ref. 14140]. Fem. *Sphaerophysa dianchiensis* Cao & Zhu 1988:406. Type by original designation (also monotypic). Valid (Kottelat 1990:21 [ref. 14137]). Balitoridae: Nemacheilinae.

Sphagebranchus Bloch 1795:88 [ref. 464]. Masc. *Sphagebranchus rostratus* Bloch 1795:88. Type by monotypy. Synonym of *Caecula* Vahl 1794 (Böhlke & McCosker 1975 [ref. 607], McCosker 1977:66 [ref. 6836], McCosker et al. 1989:323 [ref. 13288]). Ophichthidae: Ophichthinae.

Sphagemacrurus (subgenus of *Macruroplus*) Fowler 1925:3 [ref. 1401]. Masc. *Macrurus hirundo* Collett 1896:72. Type by original designation (also monotypic). Valid (Marshall 1973:291 [ref. 7194], Marshall 1973:621 [ref. 6965], Fahay & Markle 1984:274 [ref. 13653], Geistdoerfer in Whitehead et al. 1986:672 [ref. 13676], Iwamoto 1986:339 [ref. 5674]). Macrouridae: Macrourinae.

Sphagomorus Cope 1869:407 [ref. 910]. Masc. *Pleuronectes erumei* Bloch & Schneider 1801:150. Type by monotypy. Synonym of *Psettodes* Bennett 1831 (Norman 1934:57 [ref. 6893]). Psettodidae.

Sphenanthias Weber 1913:210 [ref. 4602]. Masc. *Sphenanthias sibogae* Weber 1913:211. Type by monotypy. Synonym of *Owstonia* Tanaka 1908 (Smith-Vaniz 1986:728 [ref. 5718]). Cepolidae.

Sphenentogobius Fowler 1940:396 [ref. 1433]. Masc. *Sphenentogobius vanderbilti* Fowler 1940:396. Type by original designation (also monotypic). Synonym of *Redigobius* Herre 1927 (Miller 1987:698 [ref. 6336]). Gobiidae.

Sphenosargus (subgenus of *Salema*) Fowler 1940:1 [ref. 1434]. Masc. *Salema atkinsoni* Fowler 1940:1. Type by original designation (also monotypic). Synonym of *Salema* Jordan & Evermann 1896. Sparidae.

Spheroides Duméril 1806:342 [ref. 1152]. Masc. *Tetraodon spengleri* Bloch 1782:135. Based on *Sphéroides* Lacepède 1798 (table). Synonym of *Sphoeroides* Anonymous 1798. Tetraodontidae.

Spheroides Lacepède 1800:22 [ref. 2709]. Masc. Not available, genus and species not latinized. Validated by Duméril 1806 [ref. 1152], but see account of *Spheroides* Duméril and *Sphoeroides* Anonymous 1798. Valid but with spellings both as *Sphoeroides* and *Spheroides* and authorship as Anonymous (current authors); correctly *Sphoeroides* Anonymous 1798. Tetraodontidae.

Sphoerodon Rüppell 1838:112 [ref. 3844]. Masc. *Sciaena grandoculis* Forsskål 1775:53. Type by monotypy. Lethrinidae.

Sphoeroides Anonymous [Lacepède] 1798:676 [ref. 13098]. Masc. *Tetrodon [sic] spengleri* Bloch 1782:135. Apparently the first latinization of *Sphéroïdes* Lacepède 1798:table. Tortonese 1973:646 cites Lacepède as author. Type as given by Jordan for *Spheroides* Duméril; see also Jordan 1923:240 [ref. 2421]. Technical addition of species not researched. Valid (Tortonese 1973:646 [ref. 7192], Arai 1983:207 [ref. 14249], Matsuura in Masuda et al. 1984:364 [ref. 6441], Smith & Heemstra 1986:902 [ref. 5714], Tortonese in Whitehead et al. 1986:1344 [ref. 13677]). Tetraodontidae.

Sphyra Van der Hoeven 1858:68 [ref. 2182]. Fem. *Squalus zygaena* Linnaeus 1758:234. Original not seen. Apparently an unjustified emendation or incorrect subsequent spelling of *Sphyrna* Rafinesque 1810. In the synonymy of *Sphyrna* Rafinesque 1810 (Gilbert 1973:32 [ref. 7164], Compagno 1984:541 [ref. 6846], Cappetta 1987:127 [ref. 6348], Compagno 1988:362 [ref. 13488]). Sphyrnidae.

Sphyraena Bloch & Schneider 1801:109 [ref. 471]. Fem. *Esox sphyraena* Linnaeus 1758:313. Type by absolute tautonymy. Objective synonym of *Sphyraena* Röse 1793. Sphyraenidae.

Sphyraena Klein 1778:464 [ref. 4922]. Fem. Not available, published in a work that does not conform to the principle of binominal nomenclature. Original not checked. In the synonymy of *Sphyraena* Röse 1793. Sphyraenidae.

Sphyraena Röse 1793:52, 112 [ref. 3833]. Fem. *Esox sphyraena* Linnaeus 1758:313. Type by absolute tautonymy. Spelled *Sphyrena* by Rafinesque 1810:34 and *Sphaerina* by Swainson 1839:175 (242) [ref. 4303]. Original not seen. Apparently oldest available name for genus; authors also date to Bloch & Schneider 1801. Valid (de Sylva 1975 [ref. 6302], de Sylva 1984:534 [ref. 13666], Yoshino in Masuda et al. 1984:121 [ref. 6441], de Sylva & Williams 1986:722 [ref. 6301], Daget 1986:35 [ref. 6203], Lin & Shao 1987 [ref. 6420], Johnson 1986:32 [ref. 5676]). Sphyraenidae.

Sphyraenella Smith 1956:38 [ref. 4105]. Fem. *Sphyraena flavicauda* Rüppell 1835:100. Type by original designation. Synonym of *Sphyraena* Röse 1793 (de Sylva 1975:76 [ref. 6302], Daget 1986:350 [ref. 6203]); as a subgenus (de Sylva 1984:534 [ref. 13666]). Sphyraenidae.

Sphyraenocharax (subgenus of *Acestrorhynchus*) Fowler 1907:460

[ref. 1374]. Masc. *Xiphorhamphus abbreviatus* Cope 1876:687. Type by original designation. Characidae.

Sphyraenops Gill in Poey 1860:349 [ref. 3499]. Masc. *Sphyraenops bairdianus* Poey 1860:350. Type by monotypy. Valid (Suda & Tominaga 1983:291 [ref. 5795], Johnson 1984:469 [ref. 9681], Paxton et al. 1989:514 [ref. 12442] in Percichthyidae). Epigonidae.

Sphyrichthys Thienemann 1828:408 [ref. 4990]. Masc. *Squalus zygaena* Linnaeus 1758:234. Type by being a replacement name. Unneeded replacement for *Sphyrna* Rafinesque 1810, not preoccupied. Original not examined. Objective synonym of *Sphyrna* Rafinesque 1810 (Gilbert 1973:32 [ref. 7164], Compagno 1984: 541 [ref. 6846], Cappetta 1987:127 [ref. 6348], Compagno 1988:362 [ref. 13488]). Sphyrnidae.

Sphyrna Rafinesque 1810:46, 60 [ref. 3595]. Fem. *Squalus zygaena* Linnaeus 1758:234. Type by subsequent designation. Type designated by Bonaparte 1838:10 (of separate, see also p. 2)[ref. 4979]; also designated by Jordan & Gilbert 1883:26 [ref. 2476]. Valid (Gilbert 1973:32 [ref. 7164], Compagno 1984:541 [ref. 6846], Nakaya in Masuda et al. 1984:7 [ref. 6441], Bass 1986:96 [ref. 5635], Cappetta 1987:127 [ref. 6348], Compagno 1988:362 [ref. 13488], Paxton et al. 1989:86 [ref. 12442]). Sphyrnidae.

Sphyrnias Rafinesque 1815:93 [ref. 3584]. Masc. Not available, incorrect subsequent spelling (or unjustified emendation) for *Sphyrna* Rafinesque 1810. In the synonymy of *Sphyrna* Rafinesque 1810 (Gilbert 1973:32 [ref. 7164], Compagno 1984:541 [ref. 6846], Cappetta 1987:127 [ref. 6348]). Sphyrnidae.

Spicara Rafinesque 1810:51 [ref. 3594]. Neut. *Spicara flexuosa* Rafinesque 1810:51. Type by monotypy. On Official List (Opinion 960). Valid (Tortonese et al. 1973:417 [ref. 7202], Johnson 1980:10 [ref. 13553], Tortonese in Whitehead et al. 1986:909 [ref. 13676], Heemstra 1986:594 [ref. 5660]). Centracanthidae.

Spicomacrurus (subgenus of *Hymenogadus*) Okamura 1970:63 [ref. 6580]. Masc. *Hymenocephalus kuronumai* Kamohara 1938:70. Type by original designation (also monotypic). Spelled *Spicomacrurus* on pp. 3, 61, 64, 215; *Spicomacurus* on p. 63 (main account) is regarded as a misspelling. Macrouridae: Macrourinae.

Spilostomias (subgenus of *Eustomias*) Regan & Trewavas 1930:72, 77 [ref. 3681]. Masc. *Eustomias braueri* Zugmayer 1911:5. Type by original designation. Synonym of *Eustomias* Vaillant 1888 (Gibbs in Morrow & Gibbs 1964:377 [ref. 6962], Morrow 1973:137 [ref. 7175]). Melanostomiidae.

Spilotichthys (subgenus of *Plectorhinchus*) Fowler 1904:528 [ref. 1367]. Masc. *Holocentrus radjabau* Lacepède 1802:372. Type by original designation (also monotypic). Synonym of *Plectorhinchus* Lacepède 1801 (Roux 1986:327 [ref. 6209]). Haemulidae.

Spinachia Cuvier 1816:320 [ref. 993]. Fem. *Gasterosteus spinachia* Linnaeus 1758:296. Type by monotypy (also by absolute tautonymy). Valid (Monod 1973:286 [ref. 7193], Banister in Whitehead et al. 1986:643 [ref. 13676]). Gasterosteidae: Gasterosteinae.

Spinachia Fleming 1828:219 [ref. 1339]. Fem. *Spinachia vulgaris* Fleming 1828:219 (= *Gasterosteus spinachia* Linnaeus 1758:296). Type by monotypy. *Spinachia vulgaris* an unneeded substitute for *G. spinachia*. Preoccupied by and an absolute synonym of *Spinachia* Cuvier 1816. Gasterosteidae: Gasterosteinae.

Spinapsaron Okamura & Kishida 1963:43 [ref. 3302]. Neut. *Spinapsaron barbatum* Okamura & Kishida 1963:43. Type by monotypy. Valid (Nelson 1982:6 [ref. 5469], Okamura in Masuda et al. 1984:290 [ref. 6441]). Percophidae: Hemerocoetinae.

Spinax Cuvier 1816:129 [ref. 993]. *Squalus spinax* Linnaeus 1758:233. Type by absolute tautonymy. According to Whitley 1935:136 [ref. 6396], Bosc published this name first [not investigated]. Synonym of *Etmopterus* Rafinesque 1810 (Krefft & Tortonese 1973:42 [ref. 7165], Compagno 1984:69 [ref. 6474], Cappetta 1987:58 [ref. 6348]). Squalidae.

Spinax Cuvier in Cuvier & Valenciennes (ex Commerson) 1832:333 [ref. 1000]. Not available, nonbinominal Commerson name mentioned in passing; also preoccupied. In the synonymy of *Rachycentron* Kaup 1826. Rachycentridae.

Spinibarbichthys Oshima 1926:11 [ref. 3314]. Masc. *Spinibarbichthys denticulatus* Oshima 1926:11. Type by original designation. Synonym of *Spinibarbus* Oshima 1919 (Chu & Cui in Chu & Chen 1989:149 [ref. 13584]). Cyprinidae.

Spinibarbus Oshima 1919:217 [ref. 3312]. Masc. *Spinibarbus hollandi* Oshima 1919:218. Type by original designation (also monotypic). Valid (Chu & Kottelat 1989:1 [ref. 12575], Chu & Cui in Chu & Chen 1989:149 [ref. 13584]). Cyprinidae.

Spinicapitichthys (subgenus of *Callionymus*) Fricke 1981:60 [ref. 1500]. Masc. *Callionymus spiniceps* Regan 1908:249. Type by original designation. Synonym of *Callionymus* Linnaeus 1758, but as a valid subgenus (Fricke 1982:58 [ref. 5432]); valid genus (Houde 1984:637 [ref. 13674], Nakabo 1982:106 [ref. 3139], Nakabo in Masuda et al. 1984:345 [ref. 6441]). Callionymidae.

Spinicephalus Lesueur in Vaillant 1896:29 [ref. 13482]. Masc. *Spinicephalus fibulatus* Lesueur in Vaillant 1896:26. Type by monotypy. Synonym of *Pimephales* Rafinesque 1820. Cyprinidae.

Spinipegasus (subgenus of *Pegasus*) Rendahl 1930:56 [ref. 6880]. Masc. *Pegasus laternarius* Cuvier 1816:364. Type by original designation (also monotypic). Synonym of *Pegasus* Linnaeus 1758 (Palsson & Pietsch 1989:18 [ref. 13536]). Pegasidae.

Spinipercina Fowler 1944:245 [ref. 1448]. Fem. *Spinipercina grayi* Fowler 1944:245. Type by original designation (also monotypic). Based on a postlarval specimen. Synonym of *Conodon* Cuvier 1830 (Heemstra 1974:21 [ref. 7125]). Haemulidae.

Spiniphryne Bertelsen 1951:122 [ref. 287]. Fem. *Dolopichthys gladisfenae* Beebe 1932:86. Type by monotypy. *Bertelsenna* Whitley 1954 apparently is an unneeded replacement. Valid (Bertelsen & Pietsch 1975 [ref. 7062]). Oneirodidae.

Spiniraja (subgenus of *Raja*) Whitley 1939:251 [ref. 4695]. Fem. *Raja (Spiniraja) ogilbyi* Whitley 1939:251. Type by monotypy. Synonym of *Raja* Linnaeus 1758. Rajidae.

Spinirhombus Oshima 1927:187 [ref. 3315]. Masc. *Spinirhombus ctenosquamis* Oshima 1927:187. Type by original designation. Synonym of *Pseudorhombus* Bleeker 1862 (Norman 1934:89 [ref. 6893], Amaoka 1969:88 [ref. 105], Desoutter 1986:428 [ref. 6212]). Paralichthyidae.

Spinivomer Gill & Ryder 1883:261 [ref. 1746]. Masc. *Spinivomer goodei* Gill & Ryder 1883:261. Type by monotypy. Appeared first as name only in Gill 1883:255 [ref. 1724]. Synonym of *Serrivomer* Gill & Ryder 1883 (Bauchot & Saldanha 1973:229 [ref. 7186], Tighe 1989:617 [ref. 13291] with question). Serrivomeridae.

Spinoblennius Herre 1935:435 [ref. 2109]. Masc. *Spinoblennius spiniger* Herre 1935:435. Type by original designation (also monotypic). Synonym of *Hypsoblennius* Gill 1861 (Bath 1977:186 [ref. 208]). Blenniidae.

Spinophoxinellus (subgenus of *Phoxinellus*) Karaman 1972:120 [ref. 2561]. Masc. *Phoxinellus anatolicus* Hanko 1925:141. Type by monotypy in subgenus. Cyprinidae.

Spintherobolus Eigenmann 1911:167 [ref. 1226]. Masc. *Spintherobolus papilliferus* Eigenmann 1911:167. Type by original designation (also monotypic). Mention (Géry 1977:607 [ref. 1597]). Characidae.

Spirinchus (subgenus of *Osmerus*) Jordan & Evermann (ex Jonston) 1896:522 [ref. 2443]. Masc. *Osmerus thaleichthys* Ayres 1860:62. Type by original designation. Valid (Uyeno in Masuda et al. 1984:33 [ref. 6441]). Osmeridae.

Spirlinus Fatio 1882:389 [ref. 1308]. Masc. *Cyprinus bipunctatus* Bloch 1782:50. Type by monotypy. Misspelled *Spirlingus* by Jordan 1920:450 [ref. 4905]. Cyprinidae.

Spirobranchus Cuvier 1829:229 [ref. 995]. Masc. *Spirobranchus capensis* Cuvier in Cuvier & Valenciennes 1831:392. Type by subsequent monotypy. Species name listed with original description but without distinguishing features. Preoccupied by Owen 1881 in Vermes. Synonym of *Sandelia* Castelnau 1861 (Gosse 1986:413 [ref. 6194]). Anabantidae.

Spixostoma Whitley 1951:407 [ref. 4715]. Neut. *Xiphostoma cuvieri* Agassiz in Spix & Agassiz 1829:78. Type by being a replacement name. Replacement for *Xiphostoma* Agassiz 1829, preoccupied by Kirby & Spence 1818 in Hemiptera. Synonym of *Boulengerella* Eigenmann 1903, but as a valid subgenus (Géry 1977:106 [ref. 1597]). Ctenoluciidae.

Spondyliosoma Cantor 1849:1032 [50] [ref. 715]. Neut. *Sparus cantharus* Linnaeus 1758:280. Type by being a replacement name. Replacement for *Cantharus* Cuvier 1816, preoccupied by Bolton 1798 and by Monfort 1808. On page 50 of separate. Valid (Tortonese 1973:414 [ref. 7192], Bauchot & Hureau in Whitehead et al. 1986:907 [ref. 13676], Smith & Smith 1986:594 [ref. 5710]). Sparidae.

Spottobrotula Cohen & Nielsen 1978:40 [ref. 881]. Fem. *Spottobrotula mahodadi* Cohen & Nielsen 1978:40. Type by original designation. Valid (Cohen & Nielsen 1982 [ref. 5406], Paxton et al. 1989:314 [ref. 12442]). Ophidiidae: Neobythitinae.

Spratella Valenciennes in Cuvier & Valenciennes 1847:356 [ref. 1012]. Fem. *Spratella pumila* Valenciennes in Cuvier & Valenciennes 1846:357 (= *Clupea sprattus* Linnaeus 1758:318). Type by subsequent designation. Type designated by Gill 1861:36 [ref. 1767]. Synonym of *Sprattus* Girgensohn 1846 (Svetovidov 1973:104 [ref. 7169], Whitehead 1985:45 [ref. 5141], Whitehead et al. 1985:263 [ref. 6542]; see also Whitehead 1967:18 [ref. 6464]). Clupeidae.

Spratellicypris Herre & Myers 1931:239 [ref. 2115]. Fem. *Barbodes palata* Herre 1924:2569. Type by original designation (also monotypic). Probably valid (Kornfield & Carpenter 1984:75 [ref. 5435]). Cyprinidae.

Spratelloides Bleeker 1851:214 [ref. 330]. Masc. *Clupea argyrotaenia* Bleeker 1849:72. Type by monotypy. Apparently appeared first as "*Spratelloïdes argyrotaenia* Blkr. = *Clupea argyrotaenia* Blkr. Makassar." Valid (Uyeno & Sato in Masuda et al. 1984:19 [ref. 6441], Grande 1985:248 [ref. 6466], Whitehead 1985:33 [ref. 5141], Whitehead & Wongratana 1986:204 [ref. 6284], Paxton et al. 1989:157 [ref. 12442]). Clupeidae.

Spratellomorpha Bertin in Angel, Bertin & Guibé 1946:474 [ref. 125]. Fem. *Sauvagella madagascariensis bianalis* Bertin 1940:300. Type by monotypy. Proposed as a replacement for "*Sauvagella* Bertin 1943" (not 1940). For purposes of the type species, the subspecies *bianalis* is raised to the species level; type not *S. madagascariensis*. Valid (Poll et al. 1984:54 [ref. 6172], Grande 1985:247 [ref. 6466], Whitehead 1985:170 [ref. 5141]). Clupeidae.

Sprattus Girgensohn 1846:534 [ref. 12458]. Masc. *Sprattus haleciformis* Girgensohn 1846 (= *Clupea sprattus* Linnaeus 1758:318). Type by monotypy. Original not seen. Valid (Svetovidov 1973:104 [ref. 7169], Whitehead 1985:45 [ref. 5141], Whitehead et al. 1985:263 [ref. 6542], Paxton et al. 1989:158 [ref. 12442]). Clupeidae.

Springeratus Shen 1971:700 [ref. 4017]. *Clinus xanthosoma* Bleeker 1857:340. Type by original designation (also monotypic). Valid (Araga in Masuda et al. 1984:294 [ref. 6441]). Clinidae.

Springeria Bigelow & Schroeder 1951:111 [ref. 303]. Fem. *Springeria folirostris* Bigelow & Schroeder 1951:112. Type by original designation. Synonym of *Anacanthobatis* von Bonde & Swart 1923, but as a valid subgenus (Hulley 1986:127 [ref. 5672], Séret 1986:321 [ref. 6753]); valid genus (Zhu et al. 1981:105 [ref. 4841]). Anacanthobatidae.

Springeria Carvalho & Pinto 1965:113 [ref. 738]. Fem. *Springeria santosi* Carvalho & Pinto 1965:113. Type by original designation. Original not examined. Preoccupied by Bigelow & Schroeder 1951 in fishes, replaced by *Jopaica* Pinto 1970. Synonym of *Dactyloscopus* Gill 1859 (Dawson 1982:19 [ref. 1072]). Dactyloscopidae.

Spurco Cuvier (ex Commerson) in Cuvier & Valenciennes 1829:452 [ref. 998]. *Scorpaena brachio* Cuvier in Cuvier & Valenciennes 1829:447. Not available, name mentioned in passing in synonymy of *Synanceia*, and species in synonymy of *S. brachio*. Type "designated" by Fowler 1936:930 [ref. 6546] but *Spurco* was not used by Fowler as a valid name. In the synonymy of *Synanceia* Bloch & Schneider 1801. Scorpaenidae: Synanceiinae.

Squalalburnus Berg 1932:482 [ref. 278]. Masc. *Alburnoides oblongus* Bulgakov 1923:227. Type by original designation. Cyprinidae.

Squalidus Dybowski 1872:215 [ref. 1170]. Masc. *Squalidus chankaensis* Dybowski 1872:215. Type by monotypy. Synonym of *Gnathopogon* Bleeker 1859 (Lu, Luo & Chen 1977:478 [ref. 13495]); valid (Banarescu & Nalbant 1973:80 [ref. 173], Sawada in Masuda et al. 1984:56 [ref. 6441], Hosoya 1986:488 [ref. 6155], Chen & Li in Chu & Chen 1989:105 [ref. 13584]). Cyprinidae.

Squaliobarbus Günther 1868:297 [ref. 1990]. Masc. *Leuciscus curriculus* Richardson 1845:299. Type by monotypy. Valid (Yang & Hwang 1964:52 [ref. 13497], Howes 1981:41 [ref. 14200], Chen & Li in Chu & Chen 1989:42 [ref. 13584]). Cyprinidae.

Squaliolus Smith & Radcliffe in Smith 1912:684 [ref. 4042]. Masc. *Squaliolus laticaudus* Smith & Radcliffe 1912:684. Type by original designation (also monotypic). Misspelled *Squalidus* by Regan 1912:81 [ref. 3650]. Valid (Krefft & Tortonese 1973:48 [ref. 7165], Seigel 1978 [ref. 6987], Compagno 1984:108 [ref. 6474], Nakaya & Shirai in Masuda et al. 1984:11 [ref. 6441], Sasaki & Uyeno 1987 [ref. 6700], Paxton et al. 1989:36 [ref. 12442]). Squalidae.

Squalioscardinus Kolombatovic 1907:6 [ref. 6586]. Masc. Proposed for a specimen intermediate between *Scardinus erythrophthalmus* and *Squalius illyricus* (see p. 5). According to Fowler (MS), name is based on a hybrid between them. No species named by Kolombatovic; apparently not available for lack of subsequent addition of species. Cyprinidae.

Squalius (subgenus of *Leuciscus*) Bonaparte 1837:fasc. 19 [ref. 4893]. Masc. *Leuciscus squalus* Bonaparte 1837:fasc. 19. Type by subsequent designation. Occurred in puntata 96, fasc. 19 under *Leuciscus squalus* and two additional species; also in later fascicles. Type evidently designated first by Jordan 1919:187 [ref. 2410]. Synonym of *Leuciscus* Cuvier 1816. Cyprinidae.

Squalogadus Gilbert & Hubbs 1916:156 [ref. 1636]. Masc. *Squalogadus modificatus* Gilbert & Hubbs 1916:156. Type by original designation (also monotypic). Valid (Marshall & Iwamoto 1973: 517 [ref. 6963], Fahay & Markle 1984:274 [ref. 13653], Okamura in Masuda et al. 1984:93 [ref. 6441] in Macrouroididae). Macrouridae: Macrouroidinae.

Squalomugil Ogilby 1908:3, 28 [ref. 3285]. Masc. *Mugil nasutus* De Vis 1883:621. Type by original designation (also monotypic). Synonym of *Rhinomugil* Gill 1863. Mugilidae.

Squalraia De la Pylaie 1835:526 [ref. 1086]. Fem. *Squalraia acephala* De la Pylaie 1829:394 (= *Squalus squatina* Linnaeus 1758:233). Original not seen. Synonym of *Squatina* Duméril 1806 (Compagno 1984:138 [ref. 6474], Cappetta 1987:68 [ref. 6348]) as *Squaloraja*. Squatinidae.

Squalus Linnaeus 1758:233 [ref. 2787]. Masc. *Squalus acanthias* Linnaeus 1758:233. Type by subsquent designation of Gill 1862:39 (of separate) [ref. 1783]. [Bonaparte 1838:10 (of separate, and see p. 2 [ref. 4979]) designated *S. carcharias* earlier—needs investigation.] Spelled *Squallus* by Scopoli 1777:464 [ref. 3990]. Valid (Krefft & Tortonese 1973:37 [ref. 7165], Compagno 1984:28 [ref. 6474], Compagno 1984:109 [ref. 6474], Nakaya & Shirai in Masuda et al. 1984:9 [ref. 6441], Bass et al. 1986:60 [ref. 5636], Cappetta 1987:58 [ref. 6348], Paxton et al. 1989:37 [ref. 12442], Muñoz-Chápuli & Ramos 1989 [ref. 12577]). Squalidae.

Squamicreedia Rendahl 1921:20 [ref. 3700]. Fem. *Squamicreedia obtusa* Rendahl 1921:21. Type by monotypy. Valid (Nelson 1982:8 [ref. 5469]). Percophidae: Hemerocoetinae.

Squamosicaesio (subgenus of *Pterocaesio*) Carpenter 1987:35 [ref. 6430]. *Pterocaesio marri* Schultz 1953:545. Type by original designation. Synonym of *Pterocaesio* Bleeker 1876, but as a valid subgenus (Carpenter 1988:4 [ref. 9296]). Caesionidae.

Squatina Duméril 1806:102, 342 [ref. 1151]. Fem. *Squatina angelus* Duméril 1808 (= *Squalus squatina* Linnaeus 1758:233). Type generally regarded as *S. squatina*, implied by tautonymy. Apparently Duméril applied the species name *angelus* in 1808 [not investigated], with *S. angelus* an unneeded substitute for *S. squatina*. Compagno 1984:138 [ref. 6474] indicates that the type is *S. vulgaris* Risso 1810 by subsequent monotypy. Valid (Krefft 1973:49 [ref. 7166], Compagno 1984:138 [ref. 6474], Bass 1986:107 [ref. 5635], Cappetta 1987:68 [ref. 6348], Paxton et al. 1989:62 [ref. 12442]). Squatinidae.

Squatina Risso 1810:45 [ref. 3755]. Fem. *Squatina vulgaris* Risso 1810 (= *Squalus squatina* Linnaeus 1758:233). Type by monotypy. *S. vulgaris* Risso is an unneeded substitute for *S. squatina* Linnaeus. Risso cites Duméril so genus may not have been an original description, but may be the first addition of species for Duméril's *Squatina*. Synonym of *Squatina* Duméril 1806 (Krefft 1973:49 [ref. 7166]). Squatinidae.

Squatinoraja Nardo 1824:61 [ref. 3144]. Fem. *Squatinoraja colonna* Nardo 1824. Type by monotypy. Original not located; not in ref. 3144. *Squatiniraja* Agassiz 1846:350 [ref. 64] is an unjustified emendation. Synonym of *Rhinobatos* Linck 1790. Rhinobatidae: Rhinobatinae.

Stagonotrigla (subgenus of *Lepidotrigla*) Fowler 1938:107 [ref. 1426]. Fem. *Lepidotrigla macrobrachium* Fowler 1938:109. Type by original designation. Synonym of *Lepidotrigla* Günther 1860 (Richards & Saksena 1977:209 [ref. 5285]). Triglidae: Triglinae.

Stalix Jordan & Snyder 1902:495 [ref. 2513]. Fem. *Stalix histrio* Jordan & Snyder 1902:495. Type by original designation (also monotypic). Valid (Smith-Vaniz 1974 [ref. 12815], Yoshino in Masuda et al. 1984:200 [ref. 6441], Klausewitz 1985 [ref. 5986], Smith-Vaniz & Yoshino 1985:18 [ref. 6721], Smith-Vaniz 1989 [ref. 13438]). Opistognathidae.

Stanulus Smith 1959:246 [ref. 4123]. Masc. *Stanulus seychellensis* Smith 1959:246. Type by original designation (also monotypic). Valid (Smith-Vaniz & Springer 1971:40 [ref. 4145], Yoshino in Masuda et al. 1984:299 [ref. 6441], Williams 1989:14 [ref. 13549]). Blenniidae.

Stappersetta Whitley 1950:44 [ref. 4713]. Fem. *Stappersia singularis* Boulenger 1914:445. Type by being a replacement name. Replacement for *Stappersia* Boulenger 1914, apparently preoccupied [details not researched]. Cichlidae.

Stappersia Boulenger 1914:445 [ref. 583]. Fem. *Stappersia singularis* Boulenger 1914:445. Type by monotypy. Apparently preoccupied [details not researched], replaced by *Stappersetta* Whitley 1950. Cichlidae.

Starksia Jordan & Evermann in Jordan 1896:231 [ref. 2395]. Fem. *Labrosomus cremnobates* Gilbert 1890:100. Type by original designation (also monotypic). Correct spelling for genus of type species is *Labrisomus*. Valid (Clark Hubbs 1952:95 [ref. 2252], Rosenblatt & Taylor 1971:452 [ref. 3811], Greenfield 1979 [ref. 7013], Greenfield & Johnson 1981:36 [ref. 5580]). Labrisomidae.

Starksina Fowler 1907:476 [ref. 1374]. Fem. *Myletes herniarius* Cope 1872:268. Type by original designation (also monotypic). Synonym of *Mylossoma* Eigenmann & Kennedy 1903 (Géry 1976;50 [ref. 14199]). Characidae: Serrasalminae.

Stathmonotus Bean 1885:191 [ref. 226]. Masc. *Stathmonotus hemphillii* Bean 1885:191. Type by monotypy. Valid (Springer 1955 [ref. 10208], Greenfield & Johnson 1981:44 [ref. 5580]). Labrisomidae.

Stauroglanis Pinna 1989:6 [ref. 12630]. Masc. *Stauroglanis gouldingi* Pinna 1989:7. Type by original designation (also monotypic). Trichomycteridae.

Stearopterus Minding 1832:116 [ref. 3022]. Masc. *Stearopterus bagre* Minding 1832:116. Type by monotypy. Name not in current literature, and needs study; apparently same as *Bagre* Cloquet. Ariidae.

Steatocranus Boulenger 1899:52 [ref. 548]. Masc. *Steatocranus gibbiceps* Boulenger 1899:52. Type by monotypy. Cichlidae.

Steatogenys Boulenger 1898:428 [ref. 543]. Fem. *Rhamphichthys (Brachyrhamphichthys) elegans* Steindachner 1880:89. Type by monotypy. Valid (Schwassmann 1984 [ref. 5345]). Gymnotidae: Hypopominae.

Steeneichthys Allen & Randall 1985:186 [ref. 6106]. Masc. *Steeneichthys plesiopsus* Allen & Randall 1985:187. Type by original designation (also monotypic). Valid (Allen 1987 [ref. 13386], Paxton et al. 1989:526 [ref. 12442]). Plesiopidae.

Stegastes Jenyns 1840:62 [ref. 2344]. Masc. *Stegastes imbricatus* Jenyns 1840:63. Type by monotypy. Valid (Shen & Chan 1978:220 [ref. 6945], Emery & Allen 1980 [ref. 6917], Allen & Woods 1980 [ref. 6919], Richards & Leis 1984:544 [ref. 13668], Yoshino in Masuda et al. 1984:194 [ref. 6441], Allen & Emery 1985 [ref. 5236], Allen 1986:682 [ref. 5631]). Pomacentridae.

Stegophilus Reinhardt 1859:83 [ref. 3693]. Masc. *Stegophilus insidiosus* Reinhardt 1859:83. Type by monotypy. Valid (Burgess 1989:323 [ref. 12860]). Trichomycteridae.

Stegostoma Müller & Henle 1837:112 [ref. 3067]. Neut. *Squalus fasciatus* Bloch 1785:19 (= *Squalus fasciatus* Hermann 1783). Type by original designation (also monotypic). *Stegostonea* is a misspelling. Valid (Compagno 1984:200 [ref. 6474], Nakaya & Shirai in Masuda et al. 1984:8 [ref. 6441], Bass 1986:65 [ref. 5635], Paxton et al. 1989:92 [ref. 12442]). Stegostomatidae.

Steindachnerella Eigenmann 1897:159 [ref. 1215]. Fem. *Steindachneria argentea* Goode & Bean 1896:419. Type by being a replacement name. Unneeded replacement for *Steindachneria* Goode & Bean (Apr.) 1888, not preoccupied by Eigenmann & Eigenmann (18 July) 1897 in fishes. Objective synonym of *Steindachneria* Goode & Bean 1888. Merlucciidae: Steindachneriinae.

Steindachneria Eigenmann & Eigenmann 1888:137 [ref. 1249]. Fem. *Steindachneria amblyurua* Eigenmann & Eigenmann 1888:137. Type by original designation. Preoccupied by Goode & Bean (Apr.) 1888 in fishes, replaced by *Steindachneridion* Eigenmann & Eigenmann 1919. Pimelodidae.

Steindachneria Goode & Bean in Agassiz 1888:26 [ref. 1845]. Fem. *Steindachneria argentea* Goode & Bean 1896:419. Type by subsequent monotypy. Appeared with short diagnosis but no included species; one species added by Goode & Bean 1896:419 [ref. 1848]. Predates *Steindachneria* Eigenmann & Eigenmann (18 July) 1888 in catfishes. *Steindachnerella* Eigenmann 1897 is an unneeded replacement for *Steindachneria* Goode & Bean. Valid (Cohen 1984:263 [ref. 13646], Fahay & Markle 1984:267 [ref. 13653]). Merlucciidae: Steindachneriinae.

Steindachneridion Eigenmann & Eigenmann 1919:525 [ref. 1257]. Neut. *Steindachneria amblyura* Eigenmann & Eigenmann 1888:137. Type by being a replacement name. Replacement for *Steindachneria* Eigenmann & Eigenmann 1888, preoccupied by Goode & Bean 1888 in fishes. Valid (Burgess 1989:282 [ref. 12860]). Pimelodidae.

Steindachnerina (subgenus of *Curimata*) Fowler 1906:298 [ref. 1373]. Fem. *Curimatus trachystethus* Cope 1878:684. Type by original designation. Valid (Vari 1989:6 [ref. 9189], Vari & Williams Vari 1989 [ref. 12508], Malabarba 1989:125 [ref. 14217]). Curimatidae: Curimatinae.

Steinegeria Jordan & Evermann 1887:467 [ref. 2441]. Fem. *Steinegeria rubescens* Jordan & Evermann 1887:467. Type by original designation (also monotypic). Synonym of *Taractes* Lowe 1843 (Mead 1972:16 [ref. 6976], Mead 1973:386 [ref. 7199]). Bramidae.

Stelgidonotus Gilbert & Thompson 1905:977 [ref. 1640]. Masc. *Stelgidonotus latifrons* Gilbert & Thompson 1905:977. Type by original designation (also monotypic). Synonym of *Oligocottus* Girard 1856 (Bolin 1944:62 [ref. 6379]). Cottidae.

Stelgis Cramer in Jordan & Starks 1895:821 [ref. 2522]. Fem. *Agonus vulsus* Jordan & Gilbert 1880:330. Type by original designation (also monotypic). Preoccupied by Pomel 1872 in sponges, replaced by *Ganoideus* Whitley 1950 and by *Acanthostelgis* Fowler 1958. Synonym of *Agonopsis* Gill 1861 (Lea & Dempster 1982:250 [ref. 14236]). Agonidae.

Stelgistrops Hubbs 1926:15 [ref. 6069]. Masc. *Stelgistrum beringianum* Gilbert & Burke 1912:52. Type by original designation (also monotypic). Synonym of *Stelgistrum* Jordan & Gilbert 1898. Cottidae.

Stelgistrum Jordan & Gilbert in Jordan & Evermann 1898:1881, 1921 [ref. 2444]. Neut. *Stelgistrum stejnegeri* Jordan & Gilbert in Jordan & Evermann 1898:1921. Type by original designation (also monotypic). Valid (Washington et al. 1984:443 [ref. 13660], Yabe in Masuda et al. 1984:324 [ref. 6441], Yabe 1985:111 [ref. 11522]). Cottidae.

Stellerina Cramer in Jordan & Evermann 1896:447 [ref. 2442]. Fem. *Brachyopsis xyosternus* Jordan & Gilbert 1880:152. Type by original designation (also monotypic). Valid (Washington et al. 1984:442 [ref. 13660], Yabe 1985:123 [ref. 11522]). Agonidae.

Stellicarens (subgenus of *Stellifer*) Gilbert in Jordan & Evermann 1898:1439, 1840, 1445 [ref. 2444]. *Stellifer zestocarus* Gilbert in Jordan & Evermann 1898:1445. Type by original designation (also monotypic). Synonym of *Stellifer* Oken 1817 (Chao 1978:40 [ref. 6983]). Sciaenidae.

Stellifer Oken (ex Cuvier) 1817:1182 [ref. 3303]. Masc. *Bodianus stellifer* Bloch 1790:55. Type by monotypy. Based on "Les Stellifères" of Cuvier 1816:283 [ref. 993] (see Gill 1903:966 [ref. 5768]). Valid (Chao 1978:40 [ref. 6983], Uyeno & Sato in Uyeno et al. 1983:377 [ref. 14275]). Sciaenidae.

Stelliferus Stark 1828:459 [ref. 4193]. Masc. *Stelliferus capensis* Stark 1828 (= *Bodianus stellifer* Bloch 1790:55). Type by monotypy. *S. capensis* Stark is an unneeded substitute for *B. stellifer* Bloch. Objective synonym of *Stellifer* Oken 1817 (Chao 1978:40 [ref. 6983]). Sciaenidae.

Stellistius Jordan & Tanaka 1927:389 [ref. 2537]. Masc. *Stellistius katsukii* Jordan & Tanaka 1927:389. Type by original designation (also monotypic). Valid (Amaoka in Masuda et al. 1984:321 [ref. 6441]). Hexagrammidae: Hexagramminae.

Stemonidium Gilbert 1905:586 [ref. 1631]. Neut. *Stemonidium hypomelas* Gilbert 1905:586. Type by original designation, name in parentheses (also monotypic). Valid (Asano in Masuda et al. 1984:30 [ref. 6441], Clarke 1984 [ref. 6814], Karrer 1982:60 [ref. 5679], Tighe 1989:625 [ref. 13291]). Serrivomeridae.

Stemonosudis Harry 1951:32 [ref. 2043]. Fem. *Macroparalepis intermedius* Ege 1933. Type by original designation. Valid (Okiyama 1984:207 [ref. 13644], Fujii in Masuda et al. 1984:77 [ref. 6441], Post 1986:277 [ref. 5705], Paxton et al. 1989:248 [ref. 12442]). Paralepididae.

Stenatherina Schultz 1948:(7) 20 [ref. 3966]. Fem. *Atherina temminckii* Bleeker 1853:506 (= *Atherina panatela* Jordan & Richardson 1908:243). Type by original designation. Apparently based on a misidentified type species, not *temminckii* of Bleeker (see Paxton et al. 1989:360 [ref. 12442]). Valid (White et al. 1984:360 [ref. 13655], Paxton et al. 1989:360 [ref. 12442]). Atherinidae: Atherininae.

Stenesthes Jordan 1917:87 [ref. 2408]. Fem. *Sparus argyrops* Linnaeus 1766:471. Type by being a replacement name. Unneeded replacement for *Stenotomus* Gill 1865, not preoccupied by *Stenotoma*. Sparidae.

Stenobrachius (subgenus of *Myctophum*) Eigenmann & Eigenmann 1890:5 [ref. 1256]. Masc. *Myctophum (Stenobrachius) leucopsarum* Eigenmann & Eigenmann 1890:5. Type by original designation (also monotypic). Proposed as a subgenus, but in text "... as a subgeneric or generic name for this species ..." Valid (Paxton 1979:17 [ref. 6440], Moser et al. 1984:220 [ref. 13645], Paxton et al. 1984:241 [ref. 13625], Fujii in Masuda et al. 1984:69 [ref. 6441]). Myctophidae.

Stenocaulus (subgenus of *Tylosurus*) Ogilby 1908:91 [ref. 3287].

Masc. *Belone krefftii* Günther 1866:250. Type by original designation (also monotypic). Apparently intended as a subgenus, but text unclear. Belonidae.

Stenodus Richardson 1836:521 [ref. 3730]. Masc. *Salmo mackenzii* Richardson 1823:707. Type by monotypy. Original not examined. Valid (Svetovidov 1973:151 [ref. 7169], Svetovidov in Whitehead et al. 1984:384 [ref. 13675], Kendall & Behnke 1984:144 [ref. 13638]). Salmonidae: Coregoninae.

Stenogobius Bleeker 1874:317 [ref. 437]. Masc. *Gobius gymnopomus* Bleeker 1853:270. Type by original designation. Valid (Akihito in Masuda et al. 1984:271 [ref. 6441], Hoese 1986:804 [ref. 5670], Maugé 1986:384 [ref. 6218], Birdsong et al. 1988:188 [ref. 7303]). Gobiidae.

Stenometopus Troschel (ex Bibron) 1856:88 [ref. 12559]. Masc. *Tetraodon testudineus* Linnaeus 1758:332. Type by subsequent designation. Appeared first as "Sténométope" Bibron in Duméril 1855:278 [ref. 297]; latinized by Troschel as above; also by Hollard 1857:319 [ref. 2186]. First technical addition of species not researched. Type as given by Jordan 1919:263 [ref. 2410]. Synonym of *Spheroides* Duméril 1806 (Fraser-Brunner 1943:10 [ref. 1495]). Tetraodontidae.

Stenophus Castelnau 1875:26 [ref. 768]. Masc. *Stenophus marmoratus* Castelnau 1875:27. Type by subsequent designation. Type designated by Jordan 1919:378 [ref. 4904]. Synonym of *Congrogadus* Günther 1862 (George & Springer 1980:6 [ref. 6935], Winterbottom et al. 1984:1607 [ref. 5140]). Pseudochromidae: Congrogadinae.

Stenotomus Gill 1865:266 [ref. 1707]. Masc. *Sparus argyrops* Linnaeus 1766:471. Text unclear, but apparently Gill proposed to unite three species under *argyrops* and provide a new name, therefore type by monotypy. Valid. Sparidae.

Stephanoberyx Gill 1883:258 [ref. 1724]. Masc. *Stephanoberyx monae* Gill 1883:258. Type by monotypy. Valid (Ebeling & Weed 1973:417 [ref. 6898]). Stephanoberycidae.

Stephanolepis Gill 1861:78 [ref. 1770]. Fem. *Monacanthus setifer* Bennett 1831:112. Type by original designation (also monotypic). Valid (Tortonese 1973:643 [ref. 7192], Matsuura 1979:164 [ref. 7019], Tyler 1980:176 [ref. 4477], Arai 1983:199 [ref. 14249], Aboussouan & Leis 1984:452 [ref. 13661], Matsuura in Masuda et al. 1984:359 [ref. 6441], Tortonese in Whitehead et al. 1986:1338 [ref. 13677]). Monacanthidae.

Stephanophryne (subgenus of *Linophryne*) Bertelsen 1982:92 [ref. 288]. Fem. *Aceratias macrorhinus indicus* Brauer 1902:296. Type by original designation (also monotypic). For purposes of the type species, the subspecies *indicus* is elevated to the species level; type not *macrorhinus*. Linophrynidae.

Stereolepis Ayres 1859:28 [ref. 155]. Fem. *Stereolepis gigas* Ayres 1859:28. Type by monotypy. Valid (Katayama in Masuda et al. 1984:124 [ref. 6441]). Polyprionidae.

Stereolepoides Fowler 1923:382 [ref. 1398]. Masc. *Stereolepoides thompsoni* Fowler 1923:382. Type by original designation (also monotypic). Synonym of *Epinephelus* Bloch 1793 (Randall, pers. comm., June 1990). Serranidae: Epinephelinae.

Sterleta Güldenstädt 1772:533 [ref. 5066]. Fem. *Acipenser ruthenus* Linnaeus 1758:237. Type by subsequent designation. Type listed by Jordan 1919:168 [ref. 2410] as above, but as nonbinomial. Actual is: "*Sterleta*: *Acipenser* rostro fubulato, recto, diametro oris quadruplo longiore; cirris vix ori propioribus; labiis integris." Two other similar taxa (*Schypa* and *Seuruga*) also appear on p. 533. Probably not available (non-binomial work), but only pp. 533-534 in this publication were examined. In the synonymy of *Acipenser* Linnaeus 1758. Acipenseridae: Acipenserinae.

Sterletus Brandt & Ratzeburg 1833:3, 349 [ref. 619]. Masc. *Acipenser ruthenus* Linnaeus 1758:237. Type by monotypy. Original not examined; apparently as "Sterletae" (vernacular), a group within *Acipenser*; subsequent availability not researched. Preoccupied by Rafinesque 1820 in fishes. Also spelled *Sterleta* and *Sterledus*. Acipenseridae: Acipenserinae.

Sterletus (subgenus of *Accipenser [sic]*) Rafinesque 1820:248 [ref. 5088]. Masc. *Accipenser [sic] serotinus* Rafinesque 1820:248. Type by subsequent designation. Type designated by Jordan & Gilbert (see note) Jordan 1917:113 [ref. 2407]. Also appeared in Rafinesque 1820:80 (Dec.) [ref. 3592]. Rafinesque's use of the spelling *Accipenser* is an unjustified emendation or misspelling. Synonym of *Acipenser* Linnaeus 1758. Acipenseridae: Acipenserinae.

Sternarchella Eigenmann in Eigenmann & Ward 1905:163 [ref. 1267]. Fem. *Sternarchus schotti* Steindachner 1868:252. Type by original designation. Misspelled *Sternachella* in Zoological Record for 1905. Valid (see Mago-Leccia 1978:14 [ref. 5489]). Gymnotidae: Apteronotinae.

Sternarchogiton Eigenmann in Eigenmann & Ward 1905:164 [ref. 1267]. Masc. *Sternarchus nattereri* Steindachner 1868:251. Type by original designation. Valid (see Mago-Leccia 1978:14 [ref. 5489]). Gymnotidae: Apteronotinae.

Sternarchorhamphus Eigenmann in Eigenmann & Ward 1905:165 [ref. 1267]. Masc. *Sternarchus (Rhamphosternarchus) muelleri* Steindachner 1881:15. Type by original designation. Valid (see Mago-Leccia 1978:14 [ref. 5489]). Gymnotidae: Apteronotinae.

Sternarchorhynchus Castelnau 1855:95 [ref. 766]. Masc. *Sternarchus oxyrhynchus* Müller & Troschel 1849:16. Type by monotypy. *Stenarchus oxyrhynchus* Müller & Troschel renamed *Stenarchorhynchus mulleri* by Castelnau. Valid (Mago-Leccia 1978:14 [ref. 5489], but misspelled *Sternarchorchynchus*). Gymnotidae: Apteronotinae.

Sternarchus Bloch & Schneider 1801:497 [ref. 471]. Masc. *Gymnotus albifrons* Linnaeus 1766:428. Type by subsequent designation. Type designated by Eigenmann 1910:448 [ref. 1224]. Synonym of *Apteronotus* Lacepède 1800. Gymnotidae: Apteronotinae.

Sternias Jordan & Evermann 1898:1881, 1926 [ref. 2444]. Masc. *Triglops xenostethus* Gilbert 1895:429. Type by original designation (also monotypic). Valid (Washington et al. 1984:443 [ref. 13660]). Cottidae.

Sternoptychides Ogilby 1888:1313 [ref. 3265]. Masc. *Sternoptychides amabilis* Ogilby 1888:1313. Type by monotypy. Sternoptychidae: Sternoptychinae.

Sternoptyx Hermann 1781:8, 33 [ref. 2145]. Fem. *Sternoptyx diaphana* Herrmann 1781:33. Type by monotypy. *Sternoptrix* and *Sternoptix* (see Jordan 1917:44 [ref. 2407]) are misspellings. Valid (Baird 1973:123 [ref. 7173], Weitzman 1974:472 [ref. 5174], Badcock in Whitehead et al. 1984:314 [ref. 13675], Ahlstrom et al. 1984:185 [ref. 13643], Fujii in Masuda et al. 1984:48 [ref. 6441], Baird 1986:258 [ref. 6288], Paxton et al. 1989:193 [ref. 12442]). Sternoptychidae: Sternoptychinae.

Sternopygus Müller & Troschel 1848:639 [ref. 3072]. Masc. *Gymnotus macrurus* Bloch & Schneider 1801:522. Type by subsequent designation. According to Fowler 1975 [ref. 9333], appeared first in Müller 1846:194 [ref. 13283] (not investigated); then in 1848 as above. Valid (Mago-Leccia 1978:28 [ref. 5489]). Gymnotidae: Sternopyginae.

Sternotremia Nelson 1876:39 [ref. 3154]. Fem. *Sternotremia isolepis* Nelson 1876:39. Type by monotypy. *Asternotremia* Jordan 1877:52 [ref. 2374] technically is a misspelling. Synonym of *Aphredoderus* Lesueur 1833. Aphredoderidae.

Stethaprion Cope 1870:562 [ref. 914]. Masc. *Stethaprion erythrops* Cope 1870:562. Type by monotypy. Valid (Géry 1977:370 [ref. 1597], Reis 1989:47 [ref. 14219]). Characidae: Stethaprioninae.

Stethochaetus Gronow in Gray 1854:174 [ref. 1911]. Masc. *Stethochaetus biguttatus* Gronow in Gray 1854:174. Type by monotypy. Synonym of *Setipinna* Swainson 1839. Engraulidae.

Stethojulis Günther 1861:386 [ref. 1967]. Fem. *Julis strigiventer* Bennett 1832:184. Type by subsequent designation. Type designated by Jordan 1919:308 [ref. 4904]. Also appeared in Günther 1862:140 [ref. 1969]. Valid (Richards & Leis 1984:544 [ref. 13668], Araga in Masuda et al. 1984:207 [ref. 6441], Randall 1986:702 [ref. 5706]). Labridae.

Stethopristes Gilbert 1905:622 [ref. 1631]. Masc. *Stethopristes eos* Gilbert 1905:622. Type by original designation (also monotypic). Valid (Pequeño 1989:54 [ref. 14125]). Zeidae.

Stethopterus (subgenus of *Ophisurus*) Bleeker 1853:24 [ref. 339]. Masc. *Ophisurus vimineus* Richardson 1845:107. Type by monotypy. Appeared on p. 24 as a subgroup of *Ophisurus* without included species; first addition of species not located; *O. vimineus* Richardson 1845 listed as type by Jordan 1919:252 [ref. 2410]. *Leiuranus* and *Stethopterus* appeared in same publication and are regarded as synonyms; Bleeker 1865:119 [ref. 409] apparently serves as first reviser selecting *Leiuranus* over *Stethopterus*. Synonym of *Leiuranus* Bleeker 1853 (McCosker 1977:77 [ref. 6836]). Ophichthidae: Ophichthinae.

Stevardia Gill 1858:423 [ref. 1750]. Fem. *Stevardia albipinnis* Gill 1858:425. Type by monotypy. Synonym of *Corynopoma* Gill 1858 by action of first reviser (Günther 1864:287 [ref. 1974]); see Weitzman & S. Fink 1985:2 [ref. 5203]). Characidae: Glandulocaudinae.

Sthenopus Richardson 1848:10 [ref. 3744]. Masc. *Sthenopus mollis* Richardson 1848:10. Type by monotypy. Not preoccupied (see Whitley 1933:101 [ref. 4677]); *Trichopleura* Kaup 1858 is an unneeded replacement. Valid (Poss & Eschmeyer 1978:404 [ref. 6387], Washington et al. 1984:441 [ref. 13660]). Aploactinidae.

Stichaeopsis Kner in Steindachner & Kner 1870:441 [ref. 4250]. Fem. *Stichaeopsis nana* Kner in Steindachner & Kner 1870:441. Type by monotypy. Valid (Amaoka & Miki in Masuda et al. 1984:302 [ref. 6441], see Follett & Powell 1988 [ref. 6234]). Stichaeidae.

Stichaeus Reinhardt 1837:CX [ref. 6587]. Masc. *Blennius punctatus* Fabricius 1780:153. Article examined but not translated; two species, *B. punctatus* Fabricius and *S. unimaculatus* mentioned; type designation not established. Valid (Amaoka & Miki in Masuda et al. 1984:302 [ref. 6441], see Miki & Maruyama 1986:401 [ref. 5694]). Stichaeidae.

Sticharium Günther 1867:63 [ref. 1988]. Neut. *Sticharium dorsale* Günther 1867:63. Type by monotypy. Valid (George & Springer 1980:27 [ref. 6935]). Clinidae.

Stichonodon Eigenmann 1903:146 [ref. 1218]. Masc. *Luetkenia insignis* Steindachner 1876:86. Type by being a replacement name. Replacement for *Luetkenia* [original *Lütkenia*] Steindachner 1877, perhaps preoccupied by *Lutkenia* Claus 1864 in Crustacea [original spelling not investigated]. Misspelled *Stichanodon* by Eigenmann 1910:441 [ref. 1224]. Valid (Géry 1977:534 [ref. 1597]). Characidae.

Stictorhinus Böhlke & McCosker 1975:5 [ref. 607]. Masc. *Stictorhinus potamius* Böhlke & McCosker 1975:5. Type by original designation (also monotypic). Valid (McCosker 1977:69 [ref. 6836], McCosker et al. 1989:325 [ref. 13288]). Ophichthidae: Ophichthinae.

Stigmatochromis Eccles & Trewavas 1989:173 [ref. 13547]. Masc. *Haplochromis woodi* Regan 1922:702. Type by original designation. Cichlidae.

Stigmatogobius Bleeker 1874:323 [ref. 437]. Masc. *Gobius pleurostigma* Bleeker 1849:28. Type by original designation (also monotypic). Valid (Birdsong et al. 1988:203 [ref. 7303], Kottelat 1989:19 [ref. 13605], Roberts 1989:169 [ref. 6439]). Gobiidae.

Stigmatonotus Peters 1877:838 [ref. 3454]. Masc. *Stigmatonotus australis* Peters 1877:838. Type by monotypy. Type lost; apparently based on a juvenile anthiine serranid (Johnson 1984:465 [ref. 9681]). Serranidae: Anthiinae.

Stigmatopora Kaup 1853:233 [ref. 2569]. Fem. *Syngnathus argus* Richardson 1840:29. Type by monotypy, second species unavailable. Subsequent spellings include *Stigmatophora* and *Stigmatophota*. Valid (Dawson 1982 [ref. 5443], Dawson 1985:174 [ref. 6541], Paxton et al. 1989:430 [ref. 12442]). Syngnathidae: Syngnathinae.

Stilbe DeKay 1842:204 [ref. 1098]. Fem. *Cyprinus crysoleucas* Mitchill 1814:23. Type by monotypy. Synonym of *Notemigonus* Rafinesque 1819. Cyprinidae.

Stilbiscus Jordan & Bollman 1889:549 [ref. 2432]. Masc. *Stilbiscus edwardsi* Jordan & Bollman 1889:549. Type by original designation (also monotypic). Synonym of *Moringua* Gray 1831 (Smith 1989:65 [ref. 13285]). Moringuidae.

Stilbius Gill 1865:260 [ref. 1707]. Masc. *Cyprinus crysoleucas* Mitchill 1814:23. Type by being a replacement name. Text unclear, but apparently proposed as a replacement for *Stilbe* DeKay 1842, used in Botany [but not thereby preoccupied in Zoology]; type not *C. americanus*. Synonym of *Notemigonus* Rafinesque 1819. Cyprinidae.

Stipecampus Whitley 1948:75 [ref. 4710]. Masc. *Ichthyocampus cristatus* McCulloch & Waite 1918:40. Type by original designation (also monotypic). Valid (Dawson 1977:646 [ref. 1066], Dawson 1985:178 [ref. 6541], Paxton et al. 1989:430 [ref. 12442]). Syngnathidae: Syngnathinae.

Stiphodon Weber 1895:269 [ref. 4607]. Masc. *Stiphodon semoni* Weber 1895:274. Original not seen. Valid (Akihito in Masuda et al. 1984:285 [ref. 6441], Ryan 1986:655 [ref. 6318], Birdsong et al. 1988:198 [ref. 7303]). Gobiidae.

Stizostedion (subgenus of *Perca*) Rafinesque 1820:371 [ref. 7308]. Neut. *Perca salmonea* Rafinesque 1818:354. Type by original designation (also monotypic). Also in Rafinesque 1820:23 (Dec.) [ref. 3592]. *Stizostethidium* Agassiz 1846:353 [ref. 64] is an unjustified emendation. Spelled *Stizostedium* by Cope 1865:82, 85 [ref. 907], and *Stizostethium* by Jordan 1877:43 [ref. 2374]. Valid, with review of synonymy (Collette & Banarescu 1977:1457 [ref. 5845]). Percidae.

Stlegicottus Bolin 1936:36 [ref. 505]. Masc. *Stlegicottus xenogrammus* Bolin 1936:36. Type by original designation (also monotypic). Valid (Washington et al. 1984:443 [ref. 13660]). Cottidae.

Stlengis Jordan & Starks 1904:236 [ref. 2528]. Fem. *Stlengis osensis* Jordan & Starks 1904:236. Type by original designation (also monotypic). Valid (Washington et al. 1984:443 [ref. 13660], Yabe in Masuda et al. 1984:325 [ref. 6441], Fricke & Brunken 1984 [ref. 5262], Yabe 1985:111 [ref. 11522], Nelson 1985 [ref. 5155]). Cottidae.

Stoasodon Cantor 1849:1416 [434] [ref. 715]. Masc. *Raja narinari* Euphrasen 1790:217. Type by being a replacement name. Unneeded replacement for *Aetobatis* Müller & Henle 1838. On page 434 of separate. Synonym of *Aetobatus* Blainville 1816 (Cappetta 1987:170 [ref. 6348]). Myliobatidae.

Stokellia Whitley 1955:110 [ref. 4722]. Fem. *Retropinna anisodon* Stokell 1941:371. Type by original designation (also monotypic). Valid (McDowall 1979:109 [ref. 7021], McDowall 1984:150 [ref. 11850]). Retropinnidae: Retropinninae.

Stolephorus Lacepède 1803:381 [ref. 4930]. Masc. *Stolephorus commersonnii* Lacepède 1803:381, 382. Type designated by ICZN and name placed on Official List (Opinion 93 and 749). Valid (see discussion in Whitehead 1967:135-136 [ref. 6464], Uyeno & Sato in Masuda et al. 1984:20 [ref. 6441], Grande 1985:246 [ref. 6466], Whitehead & Wongratana 1986:205 [ref. 6284], Whitehead et al. 1988:401 [ref. 5725], Kottelat 1989:6 [ref. 13605], Paxton et al. 1989:160 [ref. 12442]). Engraulidae.

Stolothrissa Regan 1917:206 [ref. 3668]. Fem. *Stolothrissa tanganicae* Regan 1917:206. Type by monotypy. Valid (Poll et al. 1984:54 [ref. 6172], Grande 1985:247 [ref. 6466], Whitehead 1985:158 [ref. 5141]). Clupeidae.

Stomatepia Trewavas 1962:181 [ref. 4456]. Fem. *Paratilapia mariae* Holly 1930:206. Type by original designation (also monotypic). Valid (Trewavas et al. 1972:68 [ref. 4460]). Cichlidae.

Stomatorhinus Boulenger 1898:9 [ref. 542]. Masc. *Mormyrus walkeri* Günther 1867:116. Type by subsequent designation. Type designated by Jordan 1920:478 [ref. 4905] [author indicates genus was established for *walkeri* but not sufficient for original designation; two included species]. Valid (Taverne 1972:105, 169 [ref. 6367], Gosse 1984:120 [ref. 6169]). Mormyridae.

Stomianodon Bleeker 1849:10 [ref. 321]. Masc. *Stomianodon chrysophekadion* Bleeker 1849:10. Type by monotypy. Synonym of *Astronesthes* Richardson 1845 (Gibbs 1964:313 [ref. 6960]). Astronesthidae.

Stomias Cuvier 1816:184 [ref. 993]. Masc. *Esox boa* Risso 1810: 330. Type by monotypy. Valid (Morrow 1964:291 [ref. 6967], Morrow 1973:132 [ref. 7175], Gibbs in Whitehead et al. 1984:339 [ref. 13675], Fujii in Masuda et al. 1984:49 [ref. 6441], Fink 1985:11 [ref. 5171], Gibbs 1986:229 [ref. 5655], Fink & Fink 1986 [ref. 5176], Paxton et al. 1989:207 [ref. 12442]). Stomiidae.

Stomiasunculus Kaup 1860:270 [ref. 2582]. Masc. *Stomiasunculus barbatus* Kaup 1860:270. Type by monotypy. Synonym of *Stomias* Cuvier 1816 (Morrow 1964:291 [ref. 6967], Morrow 1973:132 [ref. 7175]). Stomiidae.

Stomiatella Roule & Angel 1930:13 et seq. [ref. 6884]. Fem. *Stomiatella "A"*. Not available, no species listed by scientific name and no type species designation after 1930. Also could be considered as unavailable by being an artificial category. Specimens evidently belong in several melanostomiid genera (see Morrow 1973 [ref. 7175]). Melanostomiidae.

Stomioides Parr 1933:177 [ref. 3374]. Masc. *Stomioides nicholsi* Parr 1933:177. Type by original designation (also monotypic). Synonym of *Stomias* Cuvier 1816 (Morrow 1964:291 [ref. 6967], Morrow 1973:132 [ref. 7175]). Stomiidae.

Stomocatus Bonaparte 1839:puntata 129 [ref. 514]. *Cyprinus catostomus* Forster 1773:158. Type by subsequent designation. For the "Catostomi" of Lesueur. No included species. Technical addition of species not researched; type as given by Jordan 1919:206 [ref. 2410]. Objective synonym of *Catostomus* Lesueur 1817. Catostomidae.

Stomodon Mitchill 1814:7 [ref. 3030]. Masc. *Stomodon bilinearis* Mitchill 1814:7. Type by monotypy. Synonym of *Merluccius* Rafinesque 1810. Merlucciidae: Merlucciinae.

Stomogobius Whitley 1931:334 [ref. 4672]. Masc. *Orthostomus amblyopinus* Kner 1868:29. Type by being a replacement name. Unneeded replacement for *Orthostomus* Kner 1868, not preoccupied by *Orthostoma* or *Orthostomum*. Microdesmidae: Ptereleotrinae.

Stoneiella Fowler 1914:271 [ref. 1390]. Fem. *Stoneiella leopardus* Fowler 1914:271. Type by original designation (also monotypic). Misspelled *Stoniella* by Jordan 1920:553 [ref. 4905]. Synonym of *Pseudacanthicus* Bleeker 1862 (Isbrücker 1980:76 [ref. 2303]). Loricariidae.

Stonogobiops Polunin & Lubbock 1977:73 [ref. 3540]. Masc. *Stonogobiops dracula* Polunin & Lubbock 1977:74. Type by original designation (also monotypic). Valid (Hoese & Randall 1982 [ref. 5297], Akihito in Masuda et al. 1984:259 [ref. 6441], Birdsong et al. 1988:194 [ref. 7303]). Gobiidae.

Storrsia Dawson 1982:78 [ref. 1072]. Fem. *Storrsia olsoni* Dawson 1982:79. Type by original designation (also monotypic). Dactyloscopidae.

Strabo Kner & Steindachner 1867:372 [ref. 2640]. Masc. *Strabo nigrofasciatus* Kner & Steindachner 1867:373. Type by monotypy. Synonym of *Melanotaenia* Gill 1862 (Allen 1980:473 [ref. 99], Allen & Cross 1982:44 [ref. 6251]). Atherinidae: Melanotaeniinae.

Strabozebrias Chabanaud 1943:293 [ref. 799]. Masc. *Synaptura cancellata* McCulloch 1916:60. Type by original designation. Soleidae.

Strandichthys Whitley 1937:140 [ref. 4689]. Masc. *Synaptura muelleri* Steindachner 1879:4. Type by original designation (also monotypic). Synonym of *Dexillus* Chabanaud 1930 (Chabanaud 1943:291 [ref. 799]). Soleidae.

Strangomera (subgenus of *Clupea*) Whitehead 1965:323 [ref. 4658]. *Clupea bentincki* Norman 1936:491. Type by original designation (also monotypic). Valid (Grande 1985:251 [ref. 6466], Whitehead 1985:130 [ref. 5141]). Clupeidae.

Strephon Gistel 1848:VIII [ref. 1822]. *Brontes prenadilla* Valenciennes in Cuvier & Valenciennes 1840:343. Type by being a replacement name. Replacement for *Brontes* Valenciennes 1840, preoccupied by Fabricius 1801 in Coleoptera, de Montfort 1810 in Mollusca, and Goldfuss 1839 in Trilobites. Astroblepidae.

Strializa Smith 1948:839 [ref. 4076]. Fem. *Mugil canaliculatus* Smith 1935:587. Type by original designation, also monotypic (second species doubtfully included). Synonym of *Liza* Jordan & Swain 1884 (Trewavas 1973:572 [ref. 7201], Smith & Smith 1986:715 [ref. 5717], Thomson 1986:345 [ref. 6215]). Mugilidae.

Strinsia Rafinesque 1810:12, 51 [ref. 3595]. Fem. *Strinsia tinca* Rafinesque 1810:51. Type by monotypy. Species spelled *tinea* on p. 12 and *tinca* on p. 52; technical first reviser not researched. Lotidae.

Stromateoides Bleeker 1851:368 [ref. 326]. Masc. *Stromateus cinereus* Bloch 1793:90. Type by subsequent designation. Type designated by Gill 1862:126 [ref. 1659]. Also appeared in Bleeker 1852:75 [ref. 332]. Synonym of *Pampus* Bonaparte 1837 (Haedrich 1967:109 [ref. 5357]). Stromateidae.

Stromateus Linnaeus 1758:248 [ref. 2787]. Masc. *Stromateus fiatola* Linnaeus 1758:248. Type by Linnaean tautonymy. Type also designated by Gill 1862:126 [ref. 1659]. Valid (Haedrich 1967:99 [ref. 5357], Haedrich 1973:565 [ref. 7216], Horn 1984:628 [ref. 13637], Haedrich in Whitehead et al. 1986:1192 [ref. 13677], Haedrich 1986:846 [ref. 5659]). Stromateidae.

Stromatoidea Castelnau 1861:44 [ref. 767]. Fem. *Stromatoidea layardi* Castelnau 1861:44. Type by monotypy. Synonym of *Monodactylus* Lacepède 1801 (Desoutter 1986:338 [ref. 6212]). Monodactylidae.

Strongylochaetodon (subgenus of *Mesochaetodon*) Maugé & Bauchot 1984:477 [ref. 6614]. Masc. *Chaetodon melannotus* Bloch & Schneider 1801:224. Type by original designation. See account of *Mesochaetodon*. Should have been described as a subgenus of *Corallochaetodon* Burgess 1978. Chaetodontidae.

Strongylura van Hasselt 1824:374 [ref. 5964]. Fem. *Strongylura caudimaculata* van Hasselt 1823:374. Type by monotypy. Valid (Yoshino in Masuda et al. 1984:78 [ref. 6441], Collette et al. 1984:336 [ref. 11422], Paxton et al. 1989:342 [ref. 12442], Kottelat 1989:16 [ref. 13605]). Belonidae.

Strophidon McClelland 1844:187, 203, 214 [ref. 2928]. Masc. *Lycodontis longicaudata* McClelland 1844:187, 215. Type by subsequent designation. Appeared in "Errata" (p. 202) as substitute for *Lycodontis* used earlier in article. Regarded as spelled in two ways (Art. 32i); first reviser is Bleeker who mentioned both names and used *Strophidon* as valid. *Lycodontis* is thus regarded as an incorrect original spelling. Valid (Hatooka in Masuda et al. 1984:22 [ref. 6441], Böhlke et al. 1989:130 [ref. 13286]). Apparently a senior synonym of *Thyrsoidea* Kaup 1856 (Castle, pers. comm.). Muraenidae: Muraeninae.

Strophiurichthys Fraser-Brunner 1935:316, 318 [ref. 1490]. Masc. *Strophiurichthys inermis* Fraser-Brunner 1935:318. Type by original designation (also monotypic). Valid (Tyler 1980:205 [ref. 4477], Winterbottom & Tyler 1983:902 [ref. 5320], Arai 1983:202 [ref. 14249], Smith 1986:893 [ref. 5712]). Ostraciidae: Aracaninae.

Stupens Whitley 1954:30 [ref. 4721]. *Curimatus simulatus* Eigenmann & Eigenmann 1889:430. Type by being a replacement name. Replacement for *Camposichthys* Whitley 1953, preoccupied by Travassos 1946 in fishes. Synonym of *Curimata* Bosc 1817 (Vari 1989:6 [ref. 9189], Vari 1989:21 [ref. 13506]). Characidae.

Stupidogobius Aurich 1938:149 [ref. 152]. Masc. *Stupidogobius flavipinnis* Aurich 1938:149. Type by monotypy. Gobiidae.

Sturio Müller 1836:77 [ref. 3060]. Masc. Original not examined; needs more study. Apparently no included species. Synonym of *Acipenser* Linnaeus 1758. Acipenseridae: Acipenserinae.

Sturio Rafinesque 1810:41, 58 [ref. 3595]. Masc. *Sturio vulgaris* Rafinesque 1810 (= *Acipenser sturio* Linnaeus 1758:237). Type by monotypy. Rafinesque's *vulgaris* is an unneeded substitute for *sturio* Linnaeus. Objective synonym of *Acipenser* Linnaeus 1758. Acipenseridae: Acipenserinae.

Sturisoma Swainson 1838:333 et seq. [ref. 4302]. Neut. *Loricaria rostrata* Spix in Spix & Agassiz 1829:5. Type by monotypy. Also in Swainson 1839:189, 304 [ref. 4303]. Valid (Isbrücker 1980:93 [ref. 2303], Burgess 1989:440 [ref. 12860]). Loricariidae.

Sturisomatichthys Isbrücker & Nijssen in Isbrücker 1979:91 [ref. 2302]. Masc. *Oxyloricaria leightoni* Regan 1912:669. Type by original designation. Valid (Isbrücker 1980:92 [ref. 2303], Burgess 1989:440 [ref. 12860]). Loricariidae.

Stygichthys Brittan & Böhlke 1965:1 [ref. 647]. Masc. *Stygichthys typhlops* Brittan & Böhlke 1965:2. Type by original designation (also monotypic). Valid (Géry 1977:535 [ref. 1597]). Characidae.

Stygicola Gill 1863:252 [ref. 1688]. Masc. *Lucifuga dentatus* Poey 1860:102. Type by original designation (also monotypic). Synonym of *Lucifuga* Poey 1858 (Cohen & Nielsen 1978:54 [ref. 881]). Bythitidae: Brosmophycinae.

Stygnobrotula Böhlke 1957:1 [ref. 597]. Fem. *Stygnobrotula latebricola* Böhlke 1957:2. Type by original designation (also monotypic). Valid (Cohen & Nielsen 1978:51 [ref. 881]). Bythitidae: Bythitinae.

Stygogenes Günther 1864:223 [ref. 1974]. Masc. *Cyclopium humboldtii* Swainson 1838:343. Type by subsequent designation. Type designated by Jordan 1919:332 [ref. 4904]. Synonym of *Astroblepus* Humboldt 1805. Astroblepidae.

Stylephorus Shaw 1791:90 [ref. 4012]. Masc. *Stylephorus chordatus* Shaw 1791:90. Type by monotypy. Spelled *Stylophonus* in Bloch & Schneider 1801:519 [ref. 471]; *Stylophorus* Günther 1861:306 [ref. 1964] is an unjustified emendation. On Official List (Opinion 1603). Valid (Nielsen 1973:335 [ref. 6885], Pietsch 1978 [ref. 5322], Olney 1984:369 [ref. 13656], Johnson & Berman in Whitehead et al. 1986:736 [ref. 13676], Hulley 1986:404 [ref. 5672], Eschmeyer & Robins 1988 [ref. 6886]). Stylephoridae.

Stylophthalmoides Mazzarelli 1912:4 [ref. 12985]. Masc. *Stylophthalmus lobiancoi* Mazzarelli 1909:187. Type by subsequent designation. Type designated by Tåning 1932 [ref. 5031], according to Paxton 1979:15 [ref. 6440]. Also appeared in Sanzo 1915 [ref. 12984, not seen]. [Original description and reference not examined, taken from Paxton 1979.] Synonym of *Myctophum* Rafinesque 1810 (Paxton 1979:15 [ref. 6440]). Myctophidae.

Stylophthalmus Brauer 1902:298 [ref. 631]. Masc. *Stylophthalmus paradoxus* Brauer 1902:298. Type by monotypy. Synonym of *Idiacanthus* Peters 1877 (Gibbs 1964:513 [ref. 6961], Krueger 1973:144 [ref. 7177]). Idiacanthidae.

Stypodon Garman 1881:90 [ref. 1530]. Masc. *Stypodon signifer* Garman 1881:90. Type by monotypy. Valid. Cyprinidae.

Suareus Dardignac & Vincent in Furnestin et al. 1958:444 [ref. 1517]. Masc. *Caranx suareus* Risso in Cuvier & Valenciennes 1833:33. Type by original designation. Synonym of *Trachurus* Rafinesque 1810 (Hureau & Tortonese 1973:380 [ref. 7198] and Berry & Cohen 1974:184 [ref. 7489] with type as *S. furnestini*). Carangidae.

Sudis Cuvier 1816:180 [ref. 993]. Fem. *Sudis gigas* Cuvier 1829:327. Appeared without species. Earliest addition of species probably by Cuvier 1829:327 [ref. 995]. Preoccupied by *Sudis* Rafinesque 1810 in fishes. *Vastres* Valenciennes 1846 later used for *Sudis* Cuvier. In the synonymy of *Arapaima* Müller 1843. Osteoglossidae: Heterotidinae.

Sudis Rafinesque 1810:60 [ref. 3594]. Fem. *Sudis hyalina* Rafinesque 1810:60. Type by monotypy. Valid (Post 1973:209 [ref. 7182], Post in Whitehead et al. 1984:507 [ref. 13675], Okiyama 1984:207 [ref. 13644], Post 1986:278 [ref. 5705]). Paralepididae.

Sueviota Winterbottom & Hoese 1988:3 [ref. 9274]. Fem. *Sueviota lachneri* Winterbottom & Hoese 1988:9. Type by original designation. Gobiidae.

Suezia Smith 1957:100, 106 [ref. 4113]. Fem. *Labrichthys caudovittatus* Steindachner 1898:783. Type by original designation (also monotypic). Apparently preoccupied in Crustacea [details not researched], replaced by *Suezichthys* Smith 1958. Objective synonym of *Suezichthys* Smith 1958 (Russell 1985:3 [ref. 5235]). Labridae.

Suezichthys Smith 1958:319 [ref. 4117]. Masc. *Labrichthys caudovittatus* Steindachner 1898:783. Type by being a replacement name. Replacement for *Suezia* Smith 1957, apparently preoccupied in Crustacea [details not researched]. Valid (Araga in Masuda et al. 1984:206 [ref. 6441], Russell 1985 [ref. 5235], Russell 1986 [ref. 5990]). Labridae.

Sufflamen Jordan 1916:27 [ref. 2405]. *Balistes capistratus* Shaw 1804:417. Type by being a replacement name. Replacement for *Pachynathus* Swainson 1839 in fishes (ruled in Opinion 29 of the ICZN to be a typographical error for *Pachygnathus*; preoccupied by Dugès 1834 in arachnids). Valid (Matsuura 1980:47 [ref. 6943], Tyler 1980:123 [ref. 4477], Arai 1983:199 [ref. 14249], Abousouan & Leis 1984:452 [ref. 13661], Matsuura in Masuda et al. 1984:358 [ref. 6441], Smith & Heemstra 1986:881 [ref. 5714]). Balistidae.

Sufflogobius Smith 1956:714 [ref. 4106]. Masc. *Gobius bibarbatus* von Bonde 1924:28. Type by original designation (also monotypic). Valid (Hoese 1986:804 [ref. 5670], Maugé 1986:377 [ref. 6218]). Gobiidae.

Suggrundus Whitley 1930:26 [ref. 4671]. Masc. *Platycephalus rudis* Günther 1880:66. Type by being a replacement name. Replacement for *Insidiator* Oken 1842, apparently preoccupied [details not researched]. Valid (Ochiai in Masuda et al. 1984:321 [ref. 6441], Paxton et al. 1989:471 [ref. 12442]). Platycephalidae.

Suiboga Pinto 1960:1 [ref. 3479]. Fem. *Suiboga travassosi* Pinto 1960:2. Type by original designation (also monotypic). Gobiidae.

Suillus Catesby 1771:15 [ref. 774]. Masc. Not available, published in a rejected work on Official Index (Opinion 89, Opinion 259). In the synonymy of *Lachnolaimus* Cuvier 1829. Labridae.

Sundagagata Boeseman 1966:243 [ref. 489]. Fem. *Sundagagata robusta* Boeseman 1966:243. Type by original designation (also monotypic). Second species tentatively referred to genus (p. 246). Valid (Burgess 1989:133 [ref. 12860]); synonym of *Glyptothorax* Blyth 1860 (Kottelat, pers. comm. June 1990). Sisoridae.

Sundasalanx Roberts 1981:297 [ref. 6588]. Masc. *Sundasalanx praecox* Roberts 1981:300. Type by original designation. Placement of this genus in the Salangidae follows Fink 1964:204 [ref. 13636]. Valid (Roberts 1984:213 [ref. 5318], Kottelat 1989:16 [ref. 13605], Roberts 1989:27 [ref. 6439]). Salangidae.

Superglyptothorax (subgenus of *Glyptothorax*) Li 1986:524 [ref. 6132]. Masc. *Glyptothorax coheni* Ganguly, Datta & Sen 1972:342. Type by original designation. Sisoridae.

Suprasinelepichthys Fernández-Yépez 1948:35 [ref. 1316]. Masc. *Curimatus laticeps* Valenciennes in Cuvier & Valenciennes 1849:21. Type by original designation (also monotypic). Synonym of *Potamorhina* Cope 1878 (Vari 1984:11 [ref. 5307], Vari 1989:6 [ref. 9189]). Curimatidae: Curimatinae.

Suruga Jordan & Snyder 1901:96 [ref. 2509]. Fem. *Suruga fundicola* Jordan & Snyder 1901:96. Type by original designation (also monotypic). Valid (Akihito in Masuda et al. 1984:279 [ref. 6441], Birdsong et al. 1988:184 [ref. 7303]). Gobiidae.

Sutorectus Whitley 1939:228 [ref. 4695]. Masc. *Crossorhinus tentaculatus* Peters 1864:123. Type by original designation (also monotypic). Synonym of *Orectolobus* Bonaparte 1834 (Compagno 1984:180 [ref. 6474]); valid (Paxton et al. 1989:92 [ref. 12442]). Orectolobidae.

Suttonia Smith 1953:556 [ref. 4086]. Fem. *Suttonia suttoni* Smith 1953:556. Type by original designation (also monotypic). Valid (Kendall 1984:501 [ref. 13663]). Serranidae: Grammistinae.

Svetovidovia Cohen 1973:326 [ref. 6589]. Fem. *Gargilius lucullus* Jensen in Koefoed 1953:11. Type by original designation (also monotypic). "Replacement" for *Gargilius* Jensen 1953, preoccupied by Faimaire 1891 in Insecta. See account of *Gargilius*; see Appendix A. Valid (Markle 1982:3428 [ref. 5439], Fahay & Markle 1984:266 [ref. 13653], Cohen in Whitehead et al. 1986:723 [ref. 13676]). Moridae.

Swainia (subgenus of *Hypohomus*) Jordan & Evermann 1896:1039, 1040 [ref. 2443]. Fem. *Etheostoma (Hadropterus) squamatus* Gilbert & Swain in Gilbert 1887:50. Type by original designation (also monotypic). Synonym of *Percina* Haldeman 1842, but as a valid subgenus (Page 1974:83 [ref. 3346], Collette & Banarescu 1977:1454 [ref. 5845]). Percidae.

Syacium Ranzani 1842:18 [ref. 3606]. Neut. *Syacium micrurum* Ranzani 1842:18. Type by monotypy. Valid (Norman 1934:129 [ref. 6893], Matsuura in Uyeno et al. 1983:456 [ref. 14275], Ahlstrom et al. 1984:642 [ref. 13641], Hensley 1986:863 [ref. 5669]). Paralichthyidae.

Syletophis Whitley 1950:44 [ref. 4713]. Masc. *Pisodonophis cruentifer* Good & Bean 1896:147. Type by being a replacement name. Replacement for *Syletor* Jordan 1919, preoccupied by Tschitscherin 1899 in Coleoptera. Synonym of *Ophichthus* Ahl 1789 (McCosker 1977:80 [ref. 6836], McCosker et al. 1989:379 [ref. 13288]). Ophichthidae: Ophichthinae.

Syletor Jordan 1919:343 [ref. 2413]. Masc. *Pisodonophis cruentifer* Goode & Bean 1896:147. Type by original designation (also monotypic). Preoccupied by Tschitscherin 1899 in Coleoptera, replaced by *Syletophis* Whitley 1950. As *Styletor* in Jordan, Evermann & Clark 1930:86 [ref. 6476]. Objective synonym of *Omochelys* Fowler 1918. Synonym of *Ophichthus* Ahl 1789 (McCosker 1977:80 [ref. 6836], McCosker et al. 1989:379 [ref. 13288]); synonym of *Pisodonophis* Kaup 1856 (Blache et al. 1973:250 [ref. 7185], Castle 1984:38 [ref. 6171]). Ophichthidae: Ophichthinae.

Symbolophorus Bolin & Wisner in Bolin 1959:11 [ref. 503]. Masc. *Myctophum californiense* Eigenmann & Eigenmann 1889:124. Type by original designation. Valid (Krefft & Bekker 1973:197 [ref. 7181], Paxton 1979:17 [ref. 6440], Hulley in Whitehead et al. 1984:480 [ref. 13675], Fujii in Masuda et al. 1984:67 [ref. 6441], Hulley 1986:319 [ref. 5672], Paxton et al. 1989:269 [ref. 12442]). Myctophidae.

Symboulichthys Chabanaud 1927:76 [ref. 5135]. Masc. *Platophrys maculifer* Jordan & Goss 1889:267. Type by monotypy. Synonym of *Bothus* Rafinesque 1810 (Norman 1934:220 [ref. 6893], Amaoka 1969:161 [ref. 105]). Bothidae: Bothinae.

Symbranchus See *Synbranchus*. Synbranchidae.

Symmetrurus Jordan 1878:788 [ref. 2377]. Masc. *Pogonichthys argyreiosus* Girard 1854:153. Type by original designation (also monotypic). Type designated in footnote. Synonym of *Pogonichthys* Girard 1854. Cyprinidae.

Symphocles Rafinesque 1815:91 [ref. 3584]. Masc. *Trichiurus lepturus* Linnaeus 1758:246. Type by subsequent designation. Appeared as name only in synonymy of *Trachiurus* Linnaeus. Fowler 1936:641 [ref. 6546] named a type but did not validly use the taxon; apparently not available. In the synonymy of *Trichiurus* Linnaeus

1758. Trichiuridae: Trichiurinae.

Symphodus Rafinesque 1810:41 [ref. 3594]. Masc. *Symphodus fulvescens* Rafinesque 1810:41. Type by subsequent designation. Whitley 1935:138 [ref. 6396] determined that the type was designated first by Lesson, v. 15, 1829:728 [ref. 13391]. Valid (Bauchot & Quignard 1973:434 [ref. 7204], Richards & Leis 1984:544 [ref. 13668], Quignard & Pras in Whitehead et al. 1986:931 [ref. 13676]). Labridae.

Symphorichthys Munro 1967:310 [ref. 6844]. Masc. *Symphorus spilurus* Günther 1872:439. Type by monotypy. Proposed for *Symphorus* of authors (not of Günther), with one included species (*spilurus*). Valid (Johnson 1980:10 [ref. 13553], Yoshino in Masuda et al. 1984:168 [ref. 6441], Allen 1985:158 [ref. 6843] but with type as *S. nematophorus* Bleeker). Lutjanidae.

Symphorus Günther 1872:438 [ref. 2002]. Masc. *Symphorus taeniolatus* Günther 1872:439. Type by monotypy. Valid (Johnson 1980:10 [ref. 13553], Akazaki in Masuda et al. 1984:168 [ref. 6441], Allen 1985:160 [ref. 6843]). Lutjanidae.

Symphurus Rafinesque 1810:13, 52 [ref. 3595]. Masc. *Symphurus nigrescens* Rafinesque 1810:13, 52. Type by monotypy. Valid (Torchio 1973:635 [ref. 6892], Menezes & Benvegnú Ahlstrom et al. 1984:643 [ref. 13641], Ochiai in Masuda et al. 1984:356 [ref. 6441], Quéro et al. in Whitehead et al. 1986:1327 [ref. 13677], Heemstra 1986:868 [ref. 5660], Chapleau 1988 [ref. 13819]). Cynoglossidae: Symphurinae.

Symphysanodon Bleeker 1878:60 [ref. 456]. Masc. *Symphysanodon typus* Bleeker 1878:61. Type by monotypy (also by use of *typus*). Also appeared as new in Bleeker 1880:28 [ref. 461]. Misspelled *Symphisanodon* in Zoological Record for 1880. Placed in its own family Symphysanodontidae by Katayama and by Lee. Valid (Katayama 1967 [ref. 7141], Anderson 1970 [ref. 7662], Johnson 1980:68 [ref. 13553], Katayama in Masuda et al. 1984:138 [ref. 6441], Lee 1989 [ref. 14122]). Symphysanodontidae.

Symphysodon Heckel 1840:332 [ref. 2064]. Masc. *Symphysodon discus* Heckel 1840:332. Type by monotypy. Valid (Kullander 1986:226 [ref. 12439]). Cichlidae.

Symphysoglyphus Miranda-Ribeiro 1915:43 [ref. 3711]. Masc. *Otolithus bairdii* Steindachner 1879:40. Type by monotypy. Appears on p. 43 in section titled Sciaenidae. Correct spelling for genus of type species is *Otolithes*. Synonym of *Cynoscion* Gill 1861 (Chao 1978:34 [ref. 6983]). Sciaenidae.

Sympodoichthys Facciolà 1888:167, 169 [ref. 1293]. Masc. *Sympodoichthys fasciatus* Facciolà 1888:167. Type by monotypy. Doubtfully the same as *Rhynchogadus* Tortonese 1948 (Cohen 1973:326 [ref. 6589]). Moridae.

Symproptopterus Cocco in Facciolà 1885:294 Masc. First appeared as *Synproptopterurus* Cocco in Bonaparte 1846:35 [ref. 519] as a name in synonymy of *Paralepis coregonoides*. Appearance in Facciolà not examined or evaluated (apparently Nat. Sicil., v. 5). In the synonymy of *Paralepis* Cuvier 1816. Paralepididae.

Sympterichthys Gill 1878:222 [ref. 1717]. Masc. *Lophius laevis* Lacepède 1803. Type by original designation (also monotypic). Species not located in Lacepède 1803. Brachionichthyidae.

Sympterygia Müller & Henle 1837:117 [ref. 3067]. Fem. *Sympterygia bonapartii* Müller & Henle 1841:155. Type by subsequent monotypy. Also in Müller & Henle 1838:90 [ref. 3069] without species. One species added by Müller & Henle 1841:155 [ref. 3069]. Valid (McEachran 1982 [ref. 5381]). Rajidae.

Synagris Bleeker (ex Klein) 1876:278 [ref. 447]. Fem. *Dentex vulgaris* Cuvier 1817:273. Type by original designation (also monotypic). Based on *Synagris* Klein 1775, not available. Synonym of *Dentex* Cuvier 1814. Nemipteridae.

Synagris Günther 1859:373 [ref. 1961]. Fem. *Dentex furcosus* Valenciennes in Cuvier & Valenciennes 1830:244. Type by subsequent designation. Type designated by Jordan 1919:291 [ref. 4904]. Not preoccupied by Klein 1775 or Klein in Walbaum 1792 (not available). Synonym of *Nemipterus* Swainson 1839. Nemipteridae.

Synagris Klein 1775:442 [ref. 2618]. Fem. Not available; published in a work that does not conform to the principle of binominal nomenclature. Sparidae.

Synagris Klein in Walbaum 1792:586 [ref. 4572]. Fem. Not available (Opinion 21). In the synonymy of *Dentex* Cuvier 1814. Sparidae.

Synagrops Günther 1887:16 [ref. 2013]. Masc. *Melanostoma japonicum* Döderlein in Steindachner & Döderlein 1884:5. Type by being a replacement name. Replacement for *Melanostoma* Döderlein in Steindachner & Döderlein 1883, preoccupied by Schiner 1860 in Diptera and Stål in Hemiptera 1872. Valid (Mochizuki in Masuda et al. 1984:124 [ref. 6441], Mochizuki & Sano 1984 [ref. 6730], Heemstra 1986:562 [ref. 5660] in Acropomatidae, Paxton et al. 1989:514 [ref. 12442] and Mochizuki & Gultneh 1989 [ref. 13505] in Percichthyidae). Acropomatidae.

Synanceia Bloch & Schneider 1801:194 (xxxvii) [ref. 471]. Fem. *Scorpaena horrida* Linnaeus 1766:453. Type by subsequent designation. Type designated by Desmarest 1874:215 [not seen] (or by Jordan 1917:58 [ref. 2407]). Spelled originally *Synanceia* (p. xxxvii), *Synanceja* (p. 194), and *Synanceia* (Pl. 45), but p. 174 corrected to *Synanceia* in corrigenda (p. 573). *Synancia* Agassiz 1846:358 [ref. 64] is an unjustified emendation. Valid (Eschmeyer & Rama-Rao 1973 [ref. 6391], Shimizu in Masuda et al. 1984:318 [ref. 6441], Eschmeyer 1986:478 [ref. 5652], Paxton et al. 1989:452 [ref. 12442]). Scorpaenidae: Synanceiinae.

Synanceichthys Bleeker 1863:234 [ref. 398]. Masc. *Synanceia verrucosa* Bloch & Schneider 1801:195. Type by monotypy. Appeared as "*Synanceichthys verrucosus* Blkr. = *Synanceia brachio* CV." Synonym of *Synanceia* Bloch & Schneider 1801 (Eschmeyer & Rama-Rao 1973:341 [ref. 6391]). Scorpaenidae: Synanceiinae.

Synanchia Swainson 1839:180, 268 [ref. 4303]. Fem. Unjustified emendation or misspelling of *Synanceia*; *Synanchia* Bleeker (on Swainson) 1874:1 also not available (see Eschmeyer & Rama Rao 1973:342 [ref. 6391]). Swainson's subgenus *Synanchia* (p. 268) is in the synonymy of *Erosa*. Scorpaenidae: Synanceiinae.

Synancidium Müller 1843:302 [ref. 3063]. Neut. *Scorpaena horrida* Linnaeus 1766:453. Type by subsequent designation. Appeared first without included species. First addition of species not researched. Type designated by Swain 1883:277 [ref. 5966]. *Synancydium* by Agassiz 1845:63 [ref. 4889] and 1846:358 [ref. 64] is an unjustified emendation. Objective synonym of *Synanceia* Bloch & Schneider 1801 (see Eschmeyer & Rama-Rao 1973:342-343 [ref. 6391]). Scorpaenidae: Synanceiinae.

Synaphobranchus Johnson 1862:169 [ref. 2357]. Masc. *Synaphobranchus kaupii* Johnson 1862:169. Type by monotypy. Valid (Blache et al. 1973:252 [ref. 7185], Karrer 1982:84 [ref. 5679], Asano in Masuda et al. 1984:26 [ref. 6441], Saldanha & Bauchot in Whitehead et al. 1986:591 [ref. 13676], Castle 1986:190 [ref. 5644], Paxton et al. 1989:108 [ref. 12442], Robins & Robins 1989:219 [ref. 13287]). Synaphobranchidae: Synaphobranchinae.

Synapteretmus (subgenus of *Bathypterois*) Goode & Bean 1896:64 (in key) [ref. 1848]. Masc. *Bathypterois quadrifilis* Günther 1878:184. Type by subsequent designation. Type designated by Jordan & Evermann 1896:545 [ref. 2443]. Chlorophthalmidae: Ipnopinae.

Synaptolaemus Myers & Fernández-Yépes in Myers 1950:190 [ref. 3124]. Masc. *Synaptolaemus cingulatus* Myers & Fernández-Yépes in Myers 1950:190. Type by original designation (also monotypic). Valid (Géry 1977:186 [ref. 1597], Winterbottom 1980:33 [ref. 4755], Vari 1983:5 [ref. 5419]). Curimatidae: Anostominae.

Synaptura Cantor 1849:1204 [222] [ref. 715]. Fem. *Pleuronectes orientalis* Swainson 1839 (= *Pleuronectes orientalis* Bloch & Schneider 1801). Type by being a replacement name. Replacement for *Brachirus* Swainson 1839 [p. 303, not p. 71, a scorpaenid], not preoccupied by ***Brachyurus*** [but preoccupied by *Brachirus* Swainson in Scorpaenidae]. On page 222 of separate. Valid (Torchio 1973:634 [ref. 6892], Ochiai in Masuda et al. 1984:354 [ref. 6441], Heemstra & Gon 1986:873 [ref. 5665], Quéro et al. in Whitehead et al. 1986:1323 [ref. 13677], Desoutter 1986:431 [ref. 6212], Kottelat 1989:20 [ref. 13605]). Soleidae.

Synapturichthys Chabanaud 1927:11 [ref. 781]. Masc. *Synaptura savignyi* Kaup 1858:97. Type by monotypy. Synonym of *Solea* Quensel 1806 (Torchio 1973:628 [ref. 6892]); valid (Heemstra & Gon 1986:873 [ref. 5665]). Soleidae.

Synbranchus Bloch 1795:86 [ref. 464]. Masc. *Synbranchus marmoratus* Bloch 1795:87. Type by subsequent designation. Type designated by Bleeker 1865:117 [ref. 4860]. *Symbranchus* is apparently a misspelling. Valid (Rosen & Greenwood 1976:53 [ref. 7094], Malabarba 1989:162 [ref. 14217]). Synbranchidae.

Synchiropus Gill 1859:129 [ref. 1761]. Masc. *Callionymus lateralis* Richardson 1844:65. Type by subsequent designation. Type designated by Bleeker 1879:80 [ref. 458]. Valid (Fricke 1981:18 [ref. 1499], Nakabo 1982:98 [ref. 3139], Houde 1984:637 [ref. 13674], Zaiser & Fricke 1985 [ref. 5267], Fricke in Whitehead et al. 1986:1093 [ref. 13677], Fricke 1986:773 [ref. 5653].). Callionymidae.

Synchirus Bean 1890:641 [ref. 228]. Masc. *Synchirus gilli* Bean 1890:642. Type by monotypy. Valid (Washington et al. 1984:443 [ref. 13660], Yabe 1985:111 [ref. 11522]). Cottidae.

Synchismus Gill 1862:407, 408 [ref. 1783]. *Squalus tuberculatus* Bloch & Schneider 1801:137. Type by original designation (also monotypic). Also in Gill 1862:413 [ref. 4910]. Synonym of *Chiloscyllium* Müller & Henle 1837 (Compagno 1984:189 [ref. 6474], Kharin 1987:364 [ref. 6227], Cappetta 1987:72 [ref. 6348]). Hemiscylliidae.

Synclidopus Chabanaud 1943:291 [ref. 799]. Masc. *Solea macleayana* Ramsay 1881:462. Type by original designation. Soleidae.

Syncomistes Vari 1978:311 [ref. 4514]. Masc. *Syncomistes butleri* Vari 1978:311. Type by original designation. Valid (Paxton et al. 1989:536 [ref. 12442]). Terapontidae.

Syncrossus Blyth 1860:166 [ref. 477]. Masc. *Syncrossus berdmorei* Blyth 1860:166. Type by subsequent designation. Two included species; earliest subsequent designation not researched. Synonym of *Botia* Gray 1831 (Roberts 1989:101 [ref. 6439]). Cobitidae: Botiinae.

Synechoglanis Gill 1859:39 [ref. 1752]. Masc. *Synechoglanis beadlei* Gill 1859:40. Type by monotypy, second species questionably included. Synonym of *Ictalurus* Rafinesque 1820. Ictaluridae.

Synechogobius Gill 1863:46, 266 [ref. 1690]. Masc. *Gobius hasta* Temminck & Schlegel 1845:144. Type by monotypy. Appeared first in passing in Gill 1859:46 [ref. 1754] without mention of species. Valid (Birdsong et al. 1988:194 [ref. 7303] as *Synochogobius*). Gobiidae.

Synechopterus Norman 1935:61 [ref. 3225]. Masc. *Synechopterus caudovittatus* Norman 1935:62. Type by original designation (also monotypic). Ambassidae.

Syngnathoides Bleeker 1851:231, 259 [ref. 331]. Masc. *Syngnathoides blochii* Bleeker 1851:259. Type by monotypy. Valid (Araga in Masuda et al. 1984:89 [ref. 6441], Dawson 1985:179 [ref. 6541], Dawson 1986:456 [ref. 5650], Paxton et al. 1989:431 [ref. 12442]). Syngnathidae: Syngnathinae.

Syngnathus Linnaeus 1758:336 [ref. 2787]. Masc. *Syngnathus acus* Linnaeus 1758:337. Type by subsequent designation. Type designated by Fowler 1906:93 [ref. 1371], predating Jordan 1912:103 as given by ICZN; on Official List (Opinion 77, Direction 56); *Syngnathus* Rafinesque 1810 placed on Official Index (Direction 56). Valid (Wheeler 1973:274 [ref. 7190], Fritzsche 1980:198 [ref. 1511], Dawson 1982:55 [ref. 6764], Araga in Masuda et al. 1984:87 [ref. 6441], Dawson 1985:181 [ref. 6541], Dawson 1986:287 [ref. 6201], Dawson 1986:457 [ref. 5650]). Syngnathidae: Syngnathinae.

Synistius Gill 1862:238 [ref. 1664]. Masc. *Gerres longirostris* Günther (ex Rapp) 1861:142. Type by monotypy. Not *Labrus longirostris* Lacepède 1802. Günther's *longirostris* the basis for *Gerres rappi* Barnard 1927. Synonym of *Gerres* Quoy & Gaimard 1824 (Roux 1986:325 [ref. 6209]). Gerreidae.

Synnema Haast 1873:274 [ref. 2025]. Neut. *Uranoscopus monopterygius* Bloch & Schneider 1801:49. Type by monotypy. Haast states "... because he [Hutton] finds a filament in the mouth, so that the generic name *Anema* of Günther (without filament) would be quite inappropriate." Haast only removed this one species from *Anema*, so *Synnema* is not regarded as a replacement for *Anema*. Synonym of *Genyagnus* Gill 1861 (Mees 1960:47 [ref. 11931], Pietsch 1989:296 [ref. 12541]). Uranoscopidae.

Synodontis Cuvier 1816:203 [ref. 993]. Fem. *Silurus clarias* Linnaeus 1758:306. Type by subsequent designation. Type designated by Bleeker 1862:6 [ref. 393]. Apparently *Synodontes* Minding 1832:116 is the same. Valid (Gosse 1986:117 [ref. 6194], Paugy 1987 [ref. 6738], Burgess 1989:195 [ref. 12860]). Mochokidae.

Synodus Bloch & Schneider 1801:396 (xlix) [ref. 471]. Masc. *Esox synodus* Linnaeus 1758:313. Type by absolute tautonymy. Objective synonym of *Synodus* Scopoli 1777. Synodontidae: Synodontinae.

Synodus Gronow 1763:112 [ref. 1910]. Masc. Not available, published in a rejected work on Official Index (Opinions 20, 89, 261). In the synonymy of *Synodus* Scopoli 1777 (see Anderson et al. 1966:46 [ref. 6977]). Synodontidae: Synodontinae.

Synodus Scopoli (ex Gronow) 1777:449 [ref. 3990]. Masc. *Esox synodus* Linnaeus 1758:313. Type by subsequent designation. Described without species, first addition of species and subsequent designator not researched. Valid (Anderson et al. 1966:46 [ref. 6977], Cressey 1981 [ref. 5574], Sulak in Whitehead et al. 1984:409 [ref. 13675], Okiyama 1984:207 [ref. 13644], Machida in Masuda et al. 1984:60 [ref. 6441], Cressey 1986:271 [ref. 6289], Waples & Randall 1988 [ref. 9187], Paxton et al. 1989:237 [ref. 12442]). Synodontidae: Synodontinae.

Sypterus Eichwald 1831:69 [ref. 5562]. Masc. *Sypterus pallasii* Eichwald 1831:69 (= *Scomber sypterus* Pallas 1814:220). Type by monotypy. Original not seen. Synonym of *Pomatomus* Lacepède 1802 (Monod 1973:369 [ref. 7193]). Pomatomidae.

Syrictes Jordan & Evermann 1927:504 [ref. 2453]. *Syngnathus fuscus* Storer 1839:162. Type by original designation (also monotypic). Described as a new genus of Syngnathidae, but they also state, "This subgenus includes.." Synonym of *Syngnathus* Linnaeus 1758 (Fritzsche 1980:198 [ref. 1511], Dawson 1982:55 [ref. 6764], Dawson 1985:181 [ref. 6541]). Syngnathidae: Syngnathinae.

Syrraxis Bonaparte (ex Jourdan) 1841:puntata 160 [ref. 512]. Masc. *Narcine indica* Henle 1834:35. Type by monotypy. Apparently appeared first in puntata 160, fasc. 30 under *Torpedo narce*. *Syrrhaxis* Agassiz 1846:359 [ref. 64] is an unjustified emendation. Synonym of *Narcine* Henle 1834 (Cappetta 1987:162 [ref. 6348]). Narkidae.

Syrrhina (subgenus of ***Rhinobatus***) Müller & Henle 1841:113 [ref. 3069]. Fem. ***Rhinobatus columnae*** Bonaparte 1836:17. Type by subsequent designation. Type apparently first designated by Jordan & Evermann 1896:61 [ref. 2443], not *S. brevirostris* Müller & Henle; five included species in 1841:113. Synonym of *Rhinobatos* Linck 1790 (Krefft & Stehmann 1973:53 [ref. 7167]). Rhinobatidae: Rhinobatinae.

Syrrhothonus Chabanaud 1933:1249 [ref. 788]. Masc. *Syrrhothonus charrieri* Chabanaud 1933:1249. Type by monotypy. Also appeared as Chabanaud (Dec. 31) 1933:172 [ref. 789]. Synonym of *Pomatoschistus* Gill 1863 (Miller 1973:506 [ref. 6888], Maugé 1986:380 [ref. 6218]). Gobiidae.

Systomus McClelland 1839:284, 379 [ref. 2923]. Masc. *Systomus immaculatus* McClelland 1839:284, 380. Type by subsequent designation. Earliest type designation not researched; several included species. Also appeared in McClelland 1839:943 [ref. 2924] without species. Spelled *Systoma* by Valenciennes in Cuvier & Valenciennes 1842:381 [ref. 1009]. Synonym of *Barbus* Cuvier & Cloquet 1816. Cyprinidae.

Taaningichthys Bolin 1959:25 [ref. 503]. Masc. *Lampadena bathyphila* Tåning 1928:63. Type by original designation (also monotypic). Valid (Krefft & Bekker 1973:197 [ref. 7181], Paxton 1979:18 [ref. 6440], Hulley in Whitehead et al. 1984:481 [ref. 13675], Moser et al. 1984:220 [ref. 13645], Fujii in Masuda et al. 1984:68 [ref. 6441], Hulley 1986:320 [ref. 5672], Paxton et al. 1989:269 [ref. 12442]). Myctophidae.

Tachysurus Lacepède 1803:150 [ref. 4930]. Masc. *Tachysurus sinensis* Lacepède 1803:150, 151. Type by monotypy. Spelled *Tachisurus* by Eigenmann & Eigenmann 1890:41 [ref. 12251]. Valid in Ariidae (Jayaram 1981:278 [ref. 6497]). Status uncertain, not an ariid (Taylor 1986:211 [ref. 6195]). Siluriformes.

Tactostoma Bolin 1939:39 [ref. 507]. Neut. *Tactostoma macropus* Bolin 1939:39. Type by original designation (also monotypic). Valid (Morrow in Morrow & Gibbs 1964:353 [ref. 6962], Kawaguchi & Moser 1984:171 [ref. 13642], Fujii in Masuda et al. 1984:52 [ref. 6441], Fink 1985:11 [ref. 5171]). Melanostomiidae.

Taddyella Ihering 1928:45 [ref. 5011]. Fem. *Pygocentrus nattereri* Kner 1858:166. Type by being a replacement name. Replacement for *Rooseveltiella* Eigenmann 1915, preoccupied by Fox 1914 in Siphonaptera. Synonym of *Pygocentrus* Müller & Troschel 1844 (authors); synonym of *Serrasalmus* Lacepède 1803, as a valid subgenus (Géry 1976:52 [ref. 14199], Géry 1977:291 [ref. 1597]). Characidae: Serrasalminae.

Taenia Röse 1793:114 [ref. 3833]. Fem. *Cepola taenia* Linnaeus 1766:455. Type by monotypy. Original not examined. Preoccupied by Linnaeus 1758 in worms; not replaced. Objective synonym of *Cepola* Linnaeus 1766. Cepolidae.

Taeniacara Myers 1935:11 [ref. 3109]. Fem. *Taeniacara candidi* Myers 1935:11. Type by original designation (also monotypic). Valid. Cichlidae.

Taenianotus Lacepède 1802:303 [ref. 4929]. Masc. *Taenianotus triacanthus* Lacepède 1802:303, 306. Type by subsequent designation. Type designated by Cuvier in Cuvier & Valenciennes 1829:317 [ref. 998]. *Taenionotus* Agassiz 1846 [ref. 64] is an unjustified emendation. Valid (Eschmeyer & Randall 1975:285 [ref. 6389], Nakabo in Masuda et al. 1984:317 [ref. 6441], Eschmeyer 1986:476 [ref. 5652], Paxton et al. 1989:452 [ref. 12442]). Scorpaenidae: Scorpaeninae.

Taeniochromis Eccles & Trewavas 1989:73 [ref. 13547]. Masc. *Haplochromis holotaenia* Regan 1922:697. Type by original designation (also monotypic). Cichlidae.

Taenioconger Herre 1923:152 [ref. 2117]. Masc. *Taenioconger chapmani* Herre 1923:152. Type by original designation (also monotypic). Misspelled *Taeniconger* by Jordan 1923:131 [ref. 2421]. Valid (Blache & Bauchot 1976:423 [ref. 305], Bauchot & Saldanha in Whitehead et al. 1986:573 [ref. 13676]); synonym of *Heteroconger* Bleeker 1868 (Smith 1989:484 [ref. 13285]). Congridae: Heterocongrinae.

Taeniodon Döderlein in Steindachner & Döderlein 1883:235 [ref. 4246]. Masc. *Taeniodon maculatus* Döderlein in Steindachner & Döderlein 1883:235. Not available, name mentioned in passing in synonymy of *Pikea*. In the synonymy of *Liopropoma* Gill 1861 (Randall & Taylor 1988:7 [ref. 6429]). Serranidae: Liopropomatinae.

Taenioides Lacepède 1800:532 [ref. 2709]. Masc. *Taenioides hermannii* Lacepède 1800:532. Type by monotypy. Valid (Akihito in Masuda et al. 1984:288 [ref. 6441], Hoese 1986:804 [ref. 5670], Maugé 1986:385 [ref. 6218], Birdsong et al. 1988:197 [ref. 7303], Kottelat 1989:19 [ref. 13605]). Gobiidae.

Taeniolabrus Steindachner 1867:713 [ref. 6393]. Masc. *Taeniolabrus filamentosus* Steindachner 1867:713. Type by monotypy. Synonym of *Trichonotus* Bloch & Schneider 1801 (Nelson 1986:1 [ref. 5153]). Trichonotidae.

Taeniolethrinops Eccles & Trewavas 1989:261 [ref. 13547]. Masc. *Haplochromis praeorbitalis* Regan 1922:717. Type by original designation. Cichlidae.

Taeniomembras Ogilby 1898:41 [ref. 5861]. Fem. *Atherina microstoma* Günther 1861:401. Type by original designation (also monotypic). Synonym of *Atherinosoma* Castelnau 1872 (Prince et al. 1982:64 [ref. 5417], Pavlov et al. 1988:392 [ref. 12285]). Atherinidae: Atherininae.

Taenionema (subgenus of *Brachyplatystoma*) Eigenmann & Bean 1907:662 [ref. 1247]. Neut. *Taenionema steerei* Eigenmann & Bean 1907:662. Type by original designation. Preoccupied by Banks 1905 in Plecoptera and by Bolivar 1906 in Orthoptera; replaced by *Goslinia* Myers 1941. Pimelodidae.

Taenionotus Agassiz 1846:360 [ref. 64]. Masc. See *Taenianotus*. Scorpaenidae: Scorpaeninae.

Taeniophis Kaup 1860:suppl. 1 [ref. 2586]. Masc. *Taeniophis westphali* Kaup 1860:suppl. 1. Type by subsequent designation. Type designated by Jordan & Davis 1891:589 [ref. 2437] if accepted; also by Jordan 1919:297 [ref. 4904]. Synonym of *Lycodontis* McClelland 1844 (Blache et al. 1973:225 [ref. 7185]). Synonym of *Gymnothorax* Bloch 1795 (Böhlke et al. 1989:145 [ref. 13286] but as a valid subgenus on p. 176). Muraenidae: Muraeninae.

Taeniophorus Bertelsen & Marshall 1956:6 [ref. 290]. Masc. *Taeniophorus festivus* Bertelsen & Marshall 1956:6. Type by monotypy. Preoccupied by Linnavuori 1952 in Insecta, replaced by *Eutaeniophorus* Bertelsen & Marshall 1958. Objective synonym of *Eutaeniophorus* Bertelsen & Marshall 1958 (Paxton 1973:213 [ref. 7183]). Mirapinnidae.

Taeniopsetta Gilbert 1905:680 [ref. 1631]. Fem. *Taeniopsetta radula* Gilbert 1905:680. Type by original designation (type in parentheses), also monotypic (second species doubtfully included). Valid (Norman 1934:122 [ref. 6893], Amaoka 1969:115 [ref. 105], Ahlstrom et al. 1984:642 [ref. 13641], Amaoka in Masuda et al. 1984:348 [ref. 6441], Hensley 1986:941 [ref. 6326]). Bothidae: Taeniopsettinae.

Taeniotoca Agassiz 1861:133 [ref. 11]. Fem. *Embiotoca lateralis* Agassiz 1854:366. Type by monotypy. Synonym of *Embiotoca* Agassiz 1853 (Tarp 1952:59 [ref. 12250]). Embiotocidae.

Taeniura Müller & Henle 1837:117 [ref. 3067]. Fem. *Trygon ornatum* Gray 1832:Pl. 99. Type by monotypy. Also in Müller & Henle 1938:90 [ref. 3066] and as new in Müller & Henle 1841:171 [ref. 3069]. Valid (Krefft & Stehmann 1973:73 [ref. 7167], Nakaya in Masuda et al. 1984:16 [ref. 6441], Compagno 1986:140 [ref. 5648], Paxton et al. 1989:43 [ref. 12442]). Dasyatidae.

Taeniurops (subgenus of *Taeniura*) Garman 1913:399 [ref. 1545]. Masc. *Taeniura meyeni* Müller & Henle 1841:172. Type by subsequent designation. Type apparently designated first by Fowler 1941:397 [ref. 6536]. Synonym of *Taeniura* Müller & Henle 1837. Dasyatidae.

Tagusa Herre 1935:434 [ref. 2109]. Fem. *Tagusa delicata* Herre 1935:435. Type by original designation (also monotypic). Tripterygiidae.

Tahhmel Forsskål 1775:45 [ref. 1351]. *Sciaena tahhmel* Forsskål 1775:53. Not available, regarded as non-latinized Arabic name (see Jordan 1917:33 [ref. 2407]). Same as *Opisthistius* Gill 1862; in the synonymy of *Kyphosus* Lacepède 1801. Kyphosidae: Kyphosinae.

Tahuantinsuyoa Kullander 1986:308 [ref. 12439]. Fem. *Tahuantinsuyoa macantzatza* Kullander 1986:309. Type by original designation (also monotypic). Cichlidae.

Taius Jordan & Thompson 1912:570 [ref. 2541]. Masc. *Chrysophrys tumifrons* Temminck & Schlegel 1843:70. Type by original designation (also monotypic). Sparidae.

Takenokius (subgenus of *Sebastes*) Matsubara 1943:233 [ref. 2905]. Masc. *Sebastes oblongus* Günther 1880:64. Type by original designation (also monotypic). Synonym of *Sebastes* Cuvier 1829. Scorpaenidae: Sebastinae.

Takifugu (subgenus of *Sphoeroides*) Abe 1949:90 (in key) [ref. 3]. Masc. *Tetrodon oblongus* Bloch 1786:6. Type by monotypy. Appeared first in Abe 1939:336 [ref. 5589] for several species; no type designated; not available (Art. 13b). For technical reasons (see Art. 13b in Appendix A) the genus apparently can date to Marshall & Palmer 1950 (in Zoological Record for 1949, were a citation to Abe is given and a type is designated). Valid (Matsuura in Masuda et al. 1984:362 [ref. 6441], Smith & Heemstra 1986:902 [ref. 5714], Su et al. 1986:112 [ref. 12582], Kottelat 1989:21 [ref. 13605]). Tetraodontidae.

Talismania (subgenus of *Bathytroctes*) Goode & Bean 1896:41, 43 [ref. 1848]. Fem. *Bathytroctes homopterus* Vaillant 1888:153. Type by subsequent designation. Type designated by Jordan 1920:467 [ref. 4905]. Valid (Markle & Quéro in Whitehead et al. 1984:250 [ref. 13675], Okamura in Masuda et al. 1984:43 [ref. 6441], Markle 1986:222 [ref. 5687], Paxton et al. 1989:211 [ref. 12442]). Alepocephalidae.

Tamandareia Carvalho & Pinto 1965:114 [ref. 738]. Fem. *Tamandareia oliveirai* Carvalho & Pinto 1965:115. Type by original designation. Synonym of *Dactyloscopus* Gill 1859 (Dawson 1982:20 [ref. 1072]). Dactyloscopidae.

Tamanka Herre 1927:220 [ref. 2104]. Fem. *Tamanka siitensis* Herre 1927:220. Type by original designation. Valid (Birdsong et al. 1988:188 [ref. 7303]). Gobiidae.

Tambra (subgenus of *Hypselobarbus*) Bleeker 1860:275, 311, 312 [ref. 380]. *Cyprinus abramioides* Sykes 1838:158. Type by monotypy. Appeared first as name only in Bleeker 1859:430 [ref. 370]. Description dates to Bleeker 1860 as above, with one species included in subgenus. Cyprinidae.

Tanakia Jordan & Thompson 1914:231 [ref. 2543]. Fem. *Rhodeus oryzae* Jordan & Seale 1906:144. Type by original designation. Valid (Sawada in Masuda et al. 1984:55 [ref. 6441], Arai & Akai 1988:204 [ref. 6999]). Cyprinidae.

Tanakius (subgenus of *Dexistes*) Hubbs 1918:370 [ref. 2228]. Masc. *Microstomus kitaharai* Jordan & Starks 1904:625. Type by original designation (also monotypic). Species originally as *kitaharae*, but named after a male so corrected to *kitaharai*. Valid (Ahlstrom et al. 1984:643 [ref. 13641], Sakamoto 1984 [ref. 5273], Sakamoto in Masuda et al. 1984:353 [ref. 6441]). Pleuronectidae: Pleuronectinae.

Tandanus (subgenus of *Plotosus*) Mitchell 1838:95 [ref. 3029]. Masc. *Plotosus (Tandanus) tandanus* Mitchell 1838:44, 95. Type by monotypy (also by absolute tautonymy). Valid (Allen 1985 [ref. 6244], Burgess 1989:180 [ref. 12860], Paxton et al. 1989:226 [ref. 12442]). Plotosidae.

Tandya Whitley 1930:19 [ref. 4671]. *Opisthognathus maculatus* Alleyne & Macleay 1877:280. Type by original designation. Correct spelling for genus of type species is *Opistognathus*. Opistognathidae.

Tangachromis Poll 1981:169 [ref. 3534]. Masc. *Limnochromis dhanisi* Poll 1949:18. Type by original designation (also monotypic). Valid (Poll 1986:138 [ref. 6136]). Cichlidae.

Tanganicodus Poll 1950:297 [ref. 3520]. Masc. *Tanganicodus irsacae* Poll 1950:297. Type by monotypy. Valid (Poll 1986:90 [ref. 6136]). Cichlidae.

Tanganikallabes Poll 1943:127 [ref. 3517]. Fem. *Tanganikallabes mortiauxi* Poll 1943:131. Type by monotypy. Valid (Poll 1977:147 [ref. 3533], Teugels 1986:100 [ref. 6193], Burgess 1989:147 [ref. 12860]). Clariidae.

Tangia Chan 1970:19 [ref. 808]. Fem. *Tangia carnolabrum* Chan 1970:20. Type by original designation (also monotypic). Preoccupied by Stål 1859 in Hemiptera (see Whitley 1976:49 [ref. 4735]), replaced by *Lipocheilus* Anderson, Talwar & Johnson 1977 (see Yoshino & Sata 1981 [ref. 5506]). Objective synonym of *Lipocheilus* Anderson, Talwar & Johnson 1977 (Yoshino & Sata 1981 [ref. 5506], Allen 1985:32 [ref. 6843]). Lutjanidae.

Tangus Rafinesque 1815:91 [ref. 3584]. As "*Tangus* R. *Heptaca* R." Based on style in this work *Tangus* is a replacement name for *Heptaca* Rafinesque, but the latter unknown. Unavailable. Unplaced genera.

Tanichthys Lin 1932:379 [ref. 2780]. Masc. *Tanichthys albonubes* Lin 1932:379. Type by monotypy. Valid (Yang & Hwang 1964:17 [ref. 13497]). Cyprinidae.

Tantalisor Whitley 1947:146 [ref. 4708]. Masc. *Tantalisor pauciradiatus* Whitley 1947:147. Type by original designation (also monotypic). Balistidae.

Tapirisolea Ramsay 1883:17, 44 [ref. 6592]. Fem. Not available, name only. In the synonymy of *Ammotretis* Günther 1862 (Norman 1934:419 [ref. 6893]). Pleuronectidae: Rhombosoleinae.

Taractes Lowe 1843:82 [ref. 2832]. Masc. *Taractes asper* Lowe 1843:83. Type by monotypy. Valid (Mead 1972:16 [ref. 6976], Mead 1973:386 [ref. 7199], Mochizuki in Masuda et al. 1984:159 [ref. 6441], Smith 1986:635 [ref. 5712], Yatsu & Nakamura 1989:190 [ref. 13449]). Bramidae.

Taractichthys (subgenus of *Taractes*) Mead & Maul 1958:407, 408 [ref. 2956]. Masc. *Brama longipinnis* Lowe 1843:82. Type by original designation. Valid (Mead 1972:25 [ref. 6976], Mead 1973:387 [ref. 7199], Mochizuki in Masuda et al. 1984:160 [ref. 6441], Smith 1986:635 [ref. 5712], Yatsu & Nakamura 1989:190 [ref. 13449]). Bramidae.

Tarandichthys Jordan & Evermann in Jordan 1896:225 [ref. 2395]. Masc. *Icelinus filamentosus* Gilbert 1890:85. Type by original designation (also monotypic). Described as "... a subgenus or genus distinct from *Icelinus*." Synonym of *Icelinus* Jordan 1885 (Bolin 1944:23 [ref. 6379]). Cottidae.

Taranetzella Andriashev 1952:415 [ref. 6593]. Fem. *Taranetzella lyoderma* Andriashev 1952:416. Type by original designation (also monotypic). Valid (Anderson 1984:578 [ref. 13634], Toyoshima 1985:144 [ref. 5722]). Zoarcidae.

Taratretis Last 1978:22 [ref. 2726]. *Taratretis derwentensis* Last 1978:23. Type by original designation (also monotypic). Valid (Sakamoto 1984 [ref. 5273]). Pleuronectidae: Rhombosoleinae.

Tarletonbeania Eigenmann & Eigenmann 1890:6 [ref. 1256]. Fem. *Tarletonbeania tenua* Eigenmann & Eigenmann 1890:7. Type by original designation (also monotypic). Second species questionably referred to genus. Valid (Paxton 1979:18 [ref. 6440], Moser et al. 1984:219 [ref. 13645], Paxton et al. 1984:241 [ref. 13625], Fujii in Masuda et al. 1984:67 [ref. 6441]). Myctophidae.

Tarphops Jordan & Thompson 1914:307 [ref. 2543]. Masc. *Pseudorhombus oligolepis* Bleeker 1859:8. Type by monotypy. Valid (Norman 1934:118 [ref. 6893], Amaoka 1969:107 [ref. 105], Ahlstrom et al. 1984:642 [ref. 13641], Amaoka in Masuda et al. 1984:347 [ref. 6441]). Paralichthyidae.

Tarpon Jordan & Evermann 1896:408, 409 [ref. 2443]. Masc. *Megalops atlanticus* Valenciennes in Cuvier & Valenciennes 1846:398. Type by original designation (also monotypic). Synonym of *Megalops* Lacepède 1803 (authors); valid (Daget 1984:33 [ref. 6170], Hureau in Whitehead et al. 1984:226 [ref. 13675]). Megalopidae.

Tarsistes Jordan 1919:344 [ref. 2413]. Masc. *Tarsistes philippii* Jordan 1919:344. Type by being a replacement name. Apparently an unneeded replacement for *Rhynchobatis* Philippi 1858, not preoccupied by *Rhynchobatus* Müller & Henle 1837 [but perhaps preoccupied by an unjustified emendation of it as *Rhynchobatis* - not investigated]. Rhinobatidae: Rhinobatinae.

Tasica Rafinesque 1815:84 [ref. 3584]. Not available, name only. Unplaced genera.

Tasmanogobius Scott 1935:55 [ref. 3992]. Masc. *Tasmanogobius lordi* Scott 1935:56. Type by original designation (also monotypic). Valid (Hoese & Larson 1987:43 [ref. 6609]). Gobiidae.

Tateichthys La Monte 1929:1 [ref. 3039]. Masc. *Tateichthys duidae* La Monte 1929:1. Type by monotypy. Synonym of *Steatogenys* Boulenger 1898 (Schwassmann 1984:102 [ref. 5345]). Gymnotidae: Hypopominae.

Tateurndina Nichols 1955:4 [ref. 3184]. Fem. *Tateurndina ocellicauda* Nichols 1955:5. Type by monotypy. Valid (Birdsong et al. 1988:202 [ref. 7303]). Eleotridae.

Tathicarpus Ogilby 1907:19 [ref. 3283]. Masc. *Tathicarpus butleri* Ogilby 1907:20. Type by subsequent designation. Type designated by Jordan 1920:526 [ref. 4905], possibly designated earlier by McCulloch (not researched). Valid (Pietsch 1984:40 [ref. 5380], Paxton et al. 1989:281 [ref. 12442]). Antennariidae.

Tatia Miranda-Ribeiro 1912:360 [ref. 3716]. Fem. *Centromochlus intermedius* Steindachner 1876:664. Type by subsequent designation. Type designated by Jordan 1920:545 [ref. 4905]. Valid (Mees 1974:55 [ref. 2969], Mees 1988 [ref. 13382], Burgess 1989:242 [ref. 12860], Curran 1989 [ref. 12547]). Auchenipteridae.

Taumakoides (subgenus of *Acanthoclinus*) Whitley 1955:111 [ref. 4722]. Masc. *Acanthoclinus trilineatus* Griffin 1933:330. Type by original designation (also monotypic). Valid (Hardy 1985:364 [ref. 5184]). Acanthoclinidae.

Taunayia Miranda-Ribeiro 1918:642 [ref. 3725]. Fem. *Taunayia marginata* Miranda-Ribeiro 1918:624. Type by monotypy. Misspelled *Tannayia* by Jordan 1920:564 [ref. 4905] and 1923:146 [ref. 2421]. Valid (Burgess 1989:242 [ref. 12860], Curran 1989:409 [ref. 12547]). Auchenipteridae.

Taunis Rafinesque 1815:82 [ref. 3584]. Not available, name only. Unplaced genera.

Tauphysa (subgenus of *Nemacheilus*) Rendahl 1933:22 [ref. 3704]. Fem. *Nemacheilus kungessanus* Kessler 1878:286. Type by original designation (also monotypic). Synonym of *Triplophysa* Rendahl 1933 (Kottelat 1990:21 [ref. 14137]). Balitoridae: Nemacheilinae.

Tauredophidium Alcock 1890:212 [ref. 82]. Neut. *Tauredophidium hextii* Alcock 1890:213. Type by monotypy. Valid (Cohen & Nielsen 1978:20 [ref. 881]). Ophidiidae: Neobythitinae.

Taurichthys Cuvier 1829:192 [ref. 995]. Masc. *Taurichthys varius* Cuvier 1829:192. Type by subsequent designation. Type designated by Bleeker 1876:304 [ref. 448]. Synonym of *Heniochus* Cuvier 1816 (Burgess 1978:218 [ref. 700]). Chaetodontidae.

Tauridea Jordan & Rice in Jordan 1878:252, 255 [ref. 2376]. Fem. *Uranidea spilota* Cope 1865:82. Type by monotypy. Cottidae.

Taurocottus Soldatov & Pavlenko 1915:149 [ref. 4165]. Masc. *Taurocottus bergii* Soldatov & Pavlenko 1915:149. Type by original designation (also monotypic). Valid (Neyelov 1979:115, 142 [ref. 3152], Washington et al. 1984:443 [ref. 13660], Yabe in Masuda et al. 1984:326 [ref. 6441, Yabe 1985:111 [ref. 11522]]). Cottidae.

Taurulus (subgenus of *Myoxocephalus*) Gracianov 1907:296 [ref. 1871]. Masc. *Cottus bubalis* Euphrasen 1786:65. Type by monotypy. Original not seen. Valid (Neyelov 1973:600 [ref. 7219], Neyelov 1979:116, 149 [ref. 3152], Yabe 1985:111 [ref. 11522], Fedorov in Whitehead et al. 1986:1255 [ref. 13677]). Cottidae.

Tautoga Mitchill 1814:23 [ref. 3030]. Fem. *Tautoga niger* Mitchill 1814:23. Type by subsequent designation. Earliest subsequent type designation not researched; two included species plus 3 additional varities; possibly designated first by Bonaparte 1841:puntata

156, fasc. 30 [ref. 516]. Valid (Richards & Leis 1984:544 [ref. 13668]). Labridae.

Tautogolabrus (subgenus of *Ctenolabrus*) Günther 1862:89, 90 [ref. 1969]. Masc. *Ctenolabrus burgall* Günther 1862:90. Type by monotypy, one species with synonyms and one variety. As a section of *Ctenolabrus* for American species. Species credited to Günther, on "Burgall" Schöpf (but more investigation needed). Valid (Richards & Leis 1984:544 [ref. 13668]). Labridae.

Teixeirichthys Smith 1953:13 [ref. 4087]. Masc. *Teixeirichthys mossambicus* Smith 1953:14. Type by original designation (also monotypic). Valid (Shen & Chan 1978:207 [ref. 6945], Yoshino in Masuda et al. 1984:194 [ref. 6441], Allen 1986:682 [ref. 5631]). Pomacentridae.

Tekla Nichols 1922:69 [ref. 3175]. Fem. *Cremnobates fasciatus* Steindachner 1876:224. Type by original designation (also monotypic). Synonym of *Paraclinus* Mocquard 1888 (Clark Hubbs 1952:66 [ref. 2252]). Labrisomidae.

Telara Valenciennes 1848:54 [ref. 1013]. Fem. *Clupea telara* Hamilton 1822:241, 382. Type by absolute tautonymy. Name should be credited to Valenciennes and not to Günther 1868 (see Whitehead 1967:145 [ref. 6464]). Synonym of *Setipinna* Swainson 1839 (Whitehead et al. 1988:451 [ref. 5725], Roberts 1989:26 [ref. 6439]). Engraulidae.

Teleocichla Kullander 1988:196 [ref. 6232]. Fem. *Teleocichla centrarchus* Kullander 1988:198. Type by original designation. Cichlidae.

Teleogramma Boulenger 1899:53 [ref. 548]. Neut. *Teleogramma gracile* Boulenger 1899:53. Type by monotypy. Described as a labrid; Myers 1939 [ref. 14271] places as a possible synonym of the cichlid *Leptolamprologus* Pellegrin 1927. Cichlidae.

Teleotrema Regan & Trewavas 1932:92 [ref. 3682]. Neut. *Teleotrema microphthalmus* Regan & Trewavas 1932:93. Type by monotypy. Synonym (males) of *Gigantactis* Brauer 1902 (Bertelsen et al. 1981:24 [ref. 5330]). Gigantactinidae.

Telescopias Jordan & Snyder 1901:909 [ref. 2511]. Masc. *Telescopias gilberti* Jordan & Snyder 1901:909. Type by original designation (also monotypic). Epigonidae.

Telescops Bleeker 1876:261 [ref. 447]. Masc. *Pomatomus telescopium [us]* Risso 1810:261. Type by monotypy. Based on *Pomatomus* of Cuvier (not of Lacepède). Synonym of *Epigonus* Rafinesque 1810 (Mayer 1974:151 [ref. 6007]). Epigonidae.

Telestes (subgenus of *Leuciscus*) Bonaparte 1837:puntata 146 [ref. 4893]. *Telestes muticellus* Bonaparte 1837:puntata 146. Type by original designation. Apparently appeared first in puntata 146, fasc. 27 under *Telestes savigny*. Synonym of *Leuciscus* Cuvier 1816. Cyprinidae.

Telipomis Rafinesque 1820:375 [ref. 7308]. Fem. *Lepomis cyanellus* Rafinesque 1819:420. Type by subsequent designation. Type designated by Jordan & Copeland 1876:138 [ref. 5961]. Also appeared in Rafinesque 1820:27 (Dec.) [ref. 3592]. Objective synonym of *Apomotis* Rafinesque 1819; synonym of *Lepomis* Rafinesque 1819. Centrarchidae.

Tellia Gervais 1853:15 [ref. 1575]. Fem. *Tellia apoda* Gervais 1853:15. Type by monotypy. Synonym of *Aphanius* Nardo 1827 (Parenti 1981:521 [ref. 7066], Wildekamp et al. 1986:165 [ref. 6198]). Cyprinodontidae: Cyprinodontinae.

Telmatherina Boulenger 1897:428 [ref. 539]. Fem. *Telmatherina celebensis* Boulenger 1897:428. Type by monotypy. Valid (White et al. 1984:360 [ref. 13655], Saeed et al. 1989:720 [ref. 13533]. Atherinidae: Pseudomugilinae.

Telmatochromis Boulenger 1898:10 [ref. 547]. Masc. *Telmatochromis temporalis* Boulenger 1898:11. Type by subsequent designation. Type designated by Regan (Jan.) 1920:51 [ref. 3669]; not *T. vittatus* Boulenger as designated by Jordan (Aug.) 1920:479 [ref. 4905]. Valid (Poll 1986:67 [ref. 6136], Louisy 1989 [ref. 9293]). Cichlidae.

Telotrematocara Poll 1986:122 [ref. 6136]. Neut. *Trematocara macrostoma* Poll 1952:3. Type by original designation (also monotypic). Cichlidae.

Temeculina (subgenus of *Richardsonius*) Cockerell 1909:216 [ref. 868]. Fem. *Phoxinus (Tigoma) orcutti* Eigenmann & Eigenmann 1890:3. Type by monotypy. Synonym of *Gila* Baird & Girard 1853. Cyprinidae.

Temera Gray 1831:7 [ref. 1879]. *Temera hardwickii* Gray 1831:7. Type by monotypy. Also in Gray 1834:Pl. 102 [ref. 1878]. Narkidae.

Temnistia Richardson 1836:59 [ref. 3731]. Fem. *Blepsias ventricosus* Eschscholtz 1829:4. Type by monotypy. Synonym of *Hemilepidotus* Cuvier 1829 (Bolin 1944:13 [ref. 6379], Peden 1978:23 [ref. 5530]). Cottidae.

Temnocara Burke 1930:146 [ref. 702]. Neut. *Careproctus candidus* Gilbert & Burke 1912:77. Type by original designation (also monotypic). Synonym of *Careproctus* Krøyer 1862 (Kido 1988:193 [ref. 12287], but spelled *Temnocora*). Cyclopteridae: Liparinae.

Temnodon Schinz (ex Cuvier) 1822:547 [ref. 3926]. Masc. *Cheilodipterus heptacanthus* Lacepède 1801:542. Type by monotypy. Based on "Les Temnodons" Cuvier 1816:346 [ref. 993]. Latinized by Schinz 1822. Synonym of *Pomatomus* Lacepède 1802 (Monod 1973:369 [ref. 7193]). Pomatomidae.

Tenacigobius Larson & Hoese 1980:39 [ref. 2725]. Masc. *Cottogobius yongei* Davis & Cohen 1969:749. Type by original designation. Synonym of *Bryaninops* Smith 1959 (Larson 1985:59 [ref. 5186]); valid (Yoshino in Masuda et al. 1984:284 [ref. 6441], Birdsong et al. 1988:194 [ref. 7303]). Gobiidae.

Tengujei (subgenus of *Raja*) Ishiyama 1958:354, 377 [ref. 2308]. Fem. *Raja tengu* Jordan & Fowler 1903:654. Type by original designation. Synonym of *Raja* Linnaeus 1758, subgenus *Dipterus* Rafinesque 1810 (see Ishihara & Ishiyama 1986:274 [ref. 5142]). Rajidae.

Tentaculus Rao & Dutt 1966:455 [ref. 3607]. Masc. *Tentaculus waltairiensis* Rao & Dutt 1966:455. Type by original designation (also monotypic). Synonym of *Halidesmus* Günther 1872 (Winterbottom 1982:755 [ref. 5436]). Pseudochromidae: Congrogadinae.

Tentoriceps Whitley 1948:94 [ref. 4710]. Neut. *Trichiurus cristatus* Klunzinger 1884:120. Type by original designation (also monotypic). Valid (Collette et al. 1984:600 [ref. 11421], Nakamura in Masuda et al. 1984:228 [ref. 6441], Nakamura 1986:830 [ref. 5696]). Trichiuridae: Trichiurinae.

Tenualosa (subgenus of *Hilsa*) Fowler 1934:246 [ref. 1416]. Fem. *Alosa reevesii* Richardson 1846:305. Type by original designation. Misspelled *Tennalosa* in Zoological Record for 1934. Valid (Grande 1985:251 [ref. 6466], Whitehead 1985:222 [ref. 5141], Kottelat 1989:4 [ref. 13605]). Clupeidae.

Tephraeops Günther 1859:413, 431 [ref. 1961]. Masc. *Crenidens tephraeops* Richardson 1846:69. Type by absolute tautonymy. Species *tephraeops* needlessly renamed *T. richardsoni* by Günther; second species also included. Kyphosidae: Girellinae.

Tephrinectes Günther 1862:475 [ref. 1971]. Masc. *Pleuronectes sinensis* Lacepède 1802:595, 638. Type by being a replacement name. Replacement for *Tephritis* Günther 1862, preoccupied by Fabricius 1794 in Diptera; *Velifracta* Jordan 1907 is a later replacement name. Valid (Norman 1934:62 [ref. 6893], Ahlstrom et al. 1984:642 [ref. 13641]). Paralichthyidae.

Tephritis Günther 1862:406 [ref. 1969]. Fem. *Pleuronectes sinensis* Lacepède 1802:595, 638. Type by monotypy. Preoccupied by Fabricius 1794 in Diptera, replaced by *Tephrinectes* Günther 1862 and later by *Velifracta* Jordan 1907. Objective synonym of *Tephrinectes* Günther 1862 (Norman 1934:62 [ref. 6893]). Paralichthyidae.

Teramulus Smith 1965:619 [ref. 4135]. Masc. *Teramulus kieneri* Smith 1965:619. Type by original designation. Valid (Maugé 1986:279 [ref. 6218]). Atherinidae: Atherininae.

Terapon Cuvier 1816:295 [ref. 993]. Masc. *Holocentrus servus* Bloch 1790:80. Type by subsequent designation. Type designated by Bleeker 1876:267 [ref. 447] as *jarbua* = *servus* [*jarbua* not originally included]; Bory de Saint-Vincent, v. 13, 1828:204 [ref. 3853] not valid. Vari (1978:255 [ref. 4514]) treats *Terapon* as an incorrect transliteration, and not to be emended to *Therapon* as by Cloquet (1819) and others. Valid (Mees & Kailola 1977 [ref. 5183] as *Therapon*, Vari 1978:255 [ref. 4514], Akazaki in Masuda et al. 1984:174 [ref. 6441], Heemstra 1986:544 [ref. 5660], Paxton et al. 1989:537 [ref. 12442]). Terapontidae.

Teratichthys Giglioli 1882:535 [ref. 1618]. Masc. Name technically published in synonymy, as an alternate name for *Paradoxichthys* "should that term be pre-occupied." Apparently never made available. Also preoccupied by König 1825 in fossil fishes. In the synonymy of *Polyacanthonotus* Bleeker 1874 (Wheeler 1973:257 [ref. 7190]). Notacanthidae.

Teratorhombus Macleay 1881:126 [ref. 4931]. Masc. *Teratorhombus excisiceps* Macleay 1881:126. Type by monotypy. Synonym of *Pseudorhombus* Bleeker 1862 (Norman 1934:89 [ref. 6893], Desoutter 1986:428 [ref. 6212] with type species misspelled). Paralichthyidae.

Teretulus (subgenus of *Catostomus*) Rafinesque 1820:302 [304] [ref. 5006]. Masc. *Catostomus aureolus* Lesueur 1817:95. Type by subsequent designation. Type designated by Jordan & Copeland 1877:157 [ref. 5961]. Also appeared in Rafinesque 1820:57 (Dec.) [ref. 3592]. Synonym of *Moxostoma* Lesueur 1817. Catostomidae.

Terpolepis (subgenus of *Anguilla*) McClelland 1844:225 [ref. 2928]. Fem. *Anguilla brevirostris* McClelland 1844:177, 208. Type by subsequent designation. Proposed somewhat conditionally in a "Note" on p. 225 as a subgenus for Bengal species of the genus *Anguilla*, which includes more than one species mentioned on p. 208. Subsequent designation is by Blache 1973:220 [ref. 7185] according to Smith 1989:32 [ref. 13285]; genus not treated by Jordan. Synonym of *Anguilla* Schrank 1798 (Blache et al. 1973:220 [ref. 7185], Castle 1984:34 [ref. 6171], Smith 1989:32 [ref. 13285]). Anguillidae.

Terranatos Taphorn & Thomerson 1978:384 [ref. 4337]. *Austrofundulus dolichopterus* Weitzman & Wourms 1967:95. Type by original designation (also monotypic). Synonym of *Cynolebias* Steindachner 1876 (Parenti 1981:490 [ref. 7066] as *Terranotus*). Aplocheilidae: Rivulinae.

Tetrabrachium Günther 1880:44 [ref. 2011]. Neut. *Tetrabrachium ocellatum* Günther 1880:45. Type by monotypy. Valid (Pietsch 1981 [ref. 5540], Paxton et al. 1989:281 [ref. 12442]). Tetrabrachiidae.

Tetrabranchus Bleeker 1851:69 [ref. 327]. Masc. *Tetrabranchus microphthalmus* Bleeker 1851:69. Type by monotypy. Synonym of *Ophisternon* McClelland 1844 (Rosen & Greenwood 1976:50 [ref. 7094], Daget 1986:291 [ref. 6203]). Synbranchidae.

Tetracentrum Macleay 1883:256 [ref. 2872]. Neut. *Tetracentrum apogonoides* Macleay 1883:256. Type by monotypy. *Negambassis* Whitley 1935 is an unneeded replacement, apparently not preoccupied by *Tetracentron* Brauer 1865 (see Schultz 1945:117, footnote [ref. 3962]). Ambassidae.

Tetrachaetodon (subgenus of *Chaetodon*) Weber & de Beaufort 1936:53, 56 [ref. 4606]. Masc. *Chaetodon plebeius* Cuvier in Cuvier & Valenciennes 1831:68. Type by original designation (also monotypic). Synonym of *Chaetodon* Linnaeus 1758, but as a valid subgenus (Burgess 1978:446 [ref. 700]); synonym of *Megaprotodon* Guichenot 1848 (Maugé & Bauchot 1984:465 [ref. 6614]). Chaetodontidae.

Tetractenos Hardy 1983:8 [ref. 5341]. Neut. *Tetraodon hamiltoni* Gray & Richardson 1843:226. Type by original designation. Valid (see Su et al. 1986:112 [ref. 12582]). Tetraodontidae.

Tetracuspidatus de Buen 1926:85 [ref. 5054]. As a "grupo" for 2 species of *Callionymus*. Not available on basis of Art. 1b(6) [see de Buen's definition of "grupo" on p. 11]; see Appendix A. Callionymidae.

Tetrades Bleeker 1865:145 [ref. 410]. Listed by Jordan as in this reference on p. 145 as a lapsus for *Tetradrachmum*, but *Tetrades* apparently not in this reference. In the synonymy of *Tetradrachmum* Cantor 1849, which is a synonym of *Dascyllus* Cuvier 1829. Pomacentridae.

Tetradrachmum Cantor 1849:1223 [240] [ref. 715]. *Chaetodon aruanus* Linnaeus 1758:275. Type by being a replacement name. Unneeded replacement for *Dascyllus* Cuvier 1829, not preoccupied by *Dascylus* Latreille 1796 in Coleoptera. *Pirene* Gistel 1848 is an earlier unneeded replacement. On page 240 of separate. *Tetrades* Bleeker 1865 apparently a mistake. Objective synonym of *Dascyllus* Cuvier 1829 (Randall & Allen 1977:351 [ref. 6482]). Pomacentridae.

Tetragonopterus Bleeker 1863:234 [ref. 398]. Bleeker adopted *Tetragonoptrus* of Klein (unavailable) in Chaetodontidae and used it in many publications in the 1860s (as *Tetragonopterus*, sometimes as *Tetragonoptrus*); above use may not be earliest, but genus can date to Bleeker. As above with 17 species listed; type perhaps not yet established, not *capistratus* as listed by Jordan 1919:348 [ref. 4904] if above was first. Preoccupied by *Tetragonopterus* Cuvier 1816. Synonym of *Chaetodon* Linnaeus 1758. Chaetodontidae.

Tetragonopterus Cuvier 1816:166 [ref. 993]. Masc. *Tetragonopterus argenteus* Cuvier 1816:166. Type by monotypy. Appeared first without latinization in Cuvier 1815:114 [ref. 5017]. Valid (Géry 1977:450 [ref. 1597]). Characidae.

Tetragonoptrus Klein 1776:153 [ref. 4919]. Not available, published in a work that does not conform to the principle of binominal nomenclature. Made available by Bleeker, apparently as *Tetragonopterus*. In the synonymy of *Chaetodon* Linnaeus 1758 (Burgess 1978:653 [ref. 700]). Chaetodontidae.

Tetragonoptrus Walbaum (ex Klein) 1792:342 [ref. 4572]. *Chaetodon striatus* Linnaeus 1758:275. Type by subsequent designation. Apparently not available, non-binominal as appearing in Walbaum. Subsequent availability not researched. Fowler (MS) lists type as above, as designated by Bleeker 1876; see also *Tetragonopterus* Bleeker 1863. In the synonymy of *Chaetodon* Linnaeus 1758. Chaetodontidae.

Tetragonurus Risso 1810:347 [ref. 3755]. Masc. *Tetragonurus cuvieri* Risso 1810:347. Type by monotypy. Valid (Haedrich 1967:96 [ref. 5357], Haedrich 1973:564 [ref. 7216], Aboussouan 1983:21 [ref. 12850], Horn 1984:628 [ref. 13637], Nakabo in Masuda et al. 1984:234 [ref. 6441], Haedrich in Whitehead et al. 1986:1189 [ref. 13677], Haedrich 1986:851 [ref. 5659]). Tetragonuridae.

Tetranematichthys Bleeker 1858:357, 359 [ref. 365]. Masc. *Ageneiosus quadrifilis* Kner 1857:442. Type by monotypy. Also in Bleeker 1862:14 [ref. 393]. Valid; tentatively in family Ageneiosidae, not Auchenipteridae (Curran 1989:412 [ref. 12547], Burgess 1989:286 [ref. 12860]). Ageneiosidae.

Tetranematopus Günther 1887:100 [ref. 2013]. Masc. Manuscript name intended for *Neobythites* Goode & Bean, mentioned by Günther in passing. In the synonymy of *Neobythites* Goode & Bean 1885 (Cohen & Nielsen 1978:36 [ref. 881]). Ophidiidae: Neobythitinae.

Tetranesodon Weber 1913:545 [ref. 4603]. Masc. *Tetranesodon conorhynchus* Weber 1913:546. Type by monotypy. Valid (Burgess 1989:168 [ref. 12860]). Ariidae.

Tetraodon Linnaeus 1758:332 [ref. 2787]. Masc. *Tetraodon lineatus* Linnaeus 1758:333. Type by subsequent designation. Type designated by Lesson, v. 16, 1830:198-199 [ref. 13391] (see Whitley 1935:138 [ref. 6396]). *Tetrodon* of authors is a misspelling or incorrect subsequent spelling (see Briggs 1961:164 [ref. 13439]). Valid (Tyler 1980:341 [ref. 4477], Arai 1983:207 [ref. 14249], Roberts 1986:434 [ref. 6223], Kottelat 1989:21 [ref. 13605], Roberts 1989:188 [ref. 6439]). Tetraodontidae.

Tetrapleurodon (subgenus of *Entosphenus*) Creaser & Hubbs 1922:6 [ref. 990]. Masc. *Lampetra spadiceus* Bean 1887:374. Type by original designation (also monotypic). Valid (Hubbs & Potter 1971:47 [ref. 13397]); as a subgenus of *Lampetra* (Bailey 1980:1627 [ref. 5253]). Petromyzontidae: Petromyzontinae.

Tetrapturus Cuvier in Cuvier & Valenciennes 1832:286 [ref. 1000]. Masc. *Tetrapturus indicus* Cuvier in Cuvier & Valenciennes 1832:286. Type by monotypy. Not *Tetrapturus* Rafinesque 1810. Synonym of *Makaira* Lacepède 1802 (de Sylva 1973:479 [ref. 7210]). Istiophoridae.

Tetrapturus Rafinesque 1810:54 [ref. 3594]. Masc. *Tetrapturus belone* Rafinesque 1810:54. Type by monotypy. *Tetrapterus*, *Tetrapterurus*, *Tetraplurus* and *Tetraperus* are misspellings or unjustified emendations (see de Sylva 1973:479-480 [ref. 7210]). Valid (de Sylva 1973:479 [ref. 7210], Nakamura 1983:294 [ref. 5371], Collette et al. 1984:600 [ref. 11421], Nakamura in Masuda et al. 1984:223 [ref. 6441], Heemstra 1986:840 [ref. 5660]). Istiophoridae.

Tetraroge Günther 1860:132 [ref. 1963]. Fem. *Apistus barbatus* Cuvier in Cuvier & Valenciennes 1829:413. Type by subsequent designation. Type designated by Jordan 1919:296 [ref. 4904]. Valid (Washington et al. 1984:440 [ref. 13660], Shimizu in Masuda et al. 1984:317 [ref. 6441], Paxton et al. 1989:452 [ref. 12442]). Scorpaenidae: Tetraroginae.

Tetronarce Gill 1862:387 [ref. 1783]. Fem. *Torpedo occidentalis* Storer 1843:166. Type by original designation as name in parentheses in key (also monotypic). Spelled *Tetranarce* by Jordan 1919:307 [ref. 4904], who regarded the original *Tetronarce* as a misspelling. *Tetronarcine* Tanaka 1908:2 is a misspelling. Synonym of *Torpedo* Houttuyn 1764 (Cappetta 1987:161 [ref. 6348]). Torpedinidae.

Tetronarcine Tanaka 1908:2 [ref. 6032]. Clear from text that this is a misspelling of *Tetronarce* Gill 1861 and not intended as a new genus. In the synonymy of *Torpedo* Houttuyn 1764 (Cappetta 1987:161 [ref. 6348]). Torpedinidae.

Tetroras Rafinesque 1810:11 [ref. 3594]. *Tetroras angiova* Rafinesque 1810:11. Type by monotypy. Later spelled *Tetraoras* by Rafinesque. Nomen dubium, perhaps referring to *Cetorhinus maximus* (Jordan 1917:77 [ref. 2407]). Doubtful synonym of *Cetorhinus* Blainville 1816 (Compagno 1984:234 [ref. 6474]). Cetorhinidae.

Tetrosomus Swainson 1839:194, 323 [ref. 4303]. Masc. *Ostracion turritus* Forsskål 1775:xiv, 75. Type by monotypy. Valid (Tyler 1980:239 [ref. 4477], Arai 1983:203 [ref. 14249], Matsuura in Masuda et al. 1984:362 [ref. 6441], Smith 1986:893 [ref. 5712]). Ostraciidae: Ostraciinae.

Tetrostichodon Tchang, Yueh & Hwang 1964:273 [ref. 4364]. Masc. *Schizothorax oconnori* Lloyd 1908:343. Type by original designation (also monotypic). Cyprinidae.

Teuthis Browne 1789:454 [ref. 669]. Fem. Not available, published in a rejected work on Official Index (Opinion 89). Acanthuridae.

Teuthis Linnaeus 1766:507 [ref. 2786]. Fem. *Teuthis hepatis or T. javus* Linnaeus 1766:507. Apparently under review by ICZN; see Taylor 1970 [ref. 6162] and Woodland 1972 [ref. 6163] and 1973 [ref. 6164]; at one time on Official List (Opinion 93). As *Theuthys*, *Teutis*, *Teuthys*, and *Theuthis* in early literature. *Teuthys* Linck 1790 on Official Index as an incorrect subsequent spelling (supplement to Opinion 56). Synonym of *Acanthurus* Forsskål 1775 (Randall 1955:363 [ref. 13648], Desoutter 1973:455 [ref. 7203]). Acanthuridae.

Tewara Griffin 1933:174 [ref. 1906]. *Tewara cranwelli* Griffin 1933:174. Type by monotypy. Valid (Nelson 1985 [ref. 5154]). Creediidae.

Thaerodontis McClelland 1844:154, 174, 187 [ref. 2928]. *Thaerodontis reticulata* McClelland 1844:188, 216. Type by subsequent designation. Type designated by Jordan & Evermann 1896:392 [ref. 2443]. On pp. 216-217 McClelland includes 7 species, so type not by monotypy on p. 188. Synonym of *Lycodontis* McClelland 1844 (Blache et al. 1973:225 [ref. 7185]); synonym of *Gymnothorax* Bloch 1795 (Böhlke et al. 1989:145 [ref. 13286]). Muraenidae: Muraeninae.

Thaigobiella Smith 1931:35 [ref. 4047]. Fem. *Thaigobiella sua* Smith 1931:35. Type by monotypy. Synonym of *Brachygobius* Bleeker 1874 (Miller 1987:699 [ref. 6336]). Gobiidae.

Thalasseleotris Hoese & Larson 1987:44 [ref. 6609]. Fem. *Thalasseleotris adela* Hoese & Larson 1987:45. Type by original designation (also monotypic). Eleotridae.

Thalassenchelys Castle & Raju 1975:8 [ref. 772]. Fem. *Thalassenchelys foliaceus* Castle & Raju 1975:8. Type by original designation (also monotypic). Placement uncertain (Lavenberg 1988:253 [ref. 6617]). Anguilliformes.

Thalassinus Moreau 1881:319, 320 (v. 1) [ref. 3040]. Masc. *Squalus rondeletii* Risso 1810:27. Type by monotypy. Objective synonym of *Thalassorhinus* Valenciennes 1838; synonym of *Prionace* Cantor 1849 (Compagno 1973:30 [ref. 7163], Compagno 1984:521 [ref. 6846], Compagno 1988:346 [ref. 13488]). Carcharhinidae.

Thalassobathia Cohen 1963:1 [ref. 880]. Fem. *Thalassobathia pelagica* Cohen 1963:3. Type by original designation (also monotypic). Valid (Nielsen 1973:552 [ref. 6885], Cohen & Nielsen 1978:51 [ref. 881], Nielsen in Whitehead et al. 1986:1156 [ref. 13677]). Bythitidae: Bythitinae.

Thalassogobius Herre 1953:182, 183 [ref. 2143]. Masc. *Thalassogobius corallinus* Herre 1953:183. Type by original designation (also monotypic). Species misspelled *corrallinus* once on p. 183. Synonym of ***Fusigobius*** Whitley 1930 (Hoese, pers. comm.). Gobiidae.

Thalassoklephtes Gistel 1848:VIII [ref. 1822]. Masc. *Caninoa chiereghini* Nardo 1841:312. Type by being a replacement name. Unneeded replacement for *Caninoa* Nardo 1841; see *Caninoa* Nardo; Gistel felt name was inappropriate (see Jordan 1919:337 [ref. 2409]). Squaliformes.

Thalassoma (subgenus of *Zyrichthys*) Swainson 1839:172, 224 [ref. 4303]. Neut. *Scarus purpureus* Forsskål 1775:x, 27. Type by monotypy. Valid (Bauchot & Quignard 1973:441 [ref. 7204], Richards & Leis 1984:544 [ref. 13668], Araga in Masuda et al. 1984:205 [ref. 6441], Randall 1986:703 [ref. 5706], Quignard & Pras in Whitehead et al. 1986:940 [ref. 13676]). Labridae.

Thalassophryne Günther 1861:174 [ref. 1964]. Fem. *Thalassophryne maculosa* Günther 1861:175. Type by monotypy. Valid (Collette 1966:849 [ref. 14192]). Batrachoididae.

Thalassorhinus Valenciennes in Bonaparte 1838:204? [10] [ref. 4895]. Masc. *Squalus rondeletii* Risso 1810:27. Type by subsequent designation. Apparently above is first (p. 10 of separate); also as Valenciennes in Müller & Henle 1839:62 [ref. 3069]. As above the single species mentioned by Bonapate (*vulpecula*) was not yet available; two species (with *rondelettii* renamed *vulpecula*) in Valenciennes 1839:62. Type apparently designated first by Gill 1862:402 [ref. 1783]. In the synonymy of *Prionace* Cantor 1849 (Compagno 1973:30 [ref. 7163], Compagno 1984:521 [ref. 6846], Compagno 1988:346 [ref. 13488]). Carcharhinidae.

Thalassosteus Jordan, Evermann & Tanaka 1927:651 [ref. 2454]. Masc. *Belone appendiculata* Klunzinger 1871:580. Type by original designation (also monotypic). Belonidae.

Thalassothia Berg 1895:67 [ref. 261]. Fem. *Thalassophryne montevidensis* Berg 1895:67. Type by monotypy. Synonym of *Thalassophryne* Günther 1861 (Collette 1966:849 [ref. 14192]). Batrachoididae.

Thaleichthys Girard 1858:325 [ref. 4911]. Masc. *Thaleichthys stevensi* Girard 1858:325. Type by monotypy. Valid. Osmeridae.

Thalliurus (subgenus of *Crenilabrus*) Swainson 1839:230 [ref. 4303]. Masc. *Labrus blochii* Swainson 1839:230. Type by monotypy. Labridae.

Thamnaconus Smith 1949:404 [ref. 5846]. Masc. *Cantherines arenaceus* Barnard 1927:78. Type by original designation. Valid (Matsuura in Masuda et al. 1984:360 [ref. 6441], Hutchins & Matsuura 1984 [ref. 7092], Hutchins 1986:886 [ref. 5673]). Monacanthidae.

Tharbacus Smith 1952:333 [ref. 4084]. Fem. *Tharbacus vanecki* Smith 1952:333. Type by original designation. Synonym of *Chatrabus* Smith 1949 (Hutchins 1986:359 [ref. 5673]). Batrachoididae.

Thaumastomias Alcock 1890:220 [ref. 82]. Masc. *Thaumastomias atrox* Alcock 1890:220. Type by monotypy. Synonym of *Photostomias* Collett 1889 (Morrow 1964:525 [ref. 6958]). Malacosteidae.

Thaumatichthys Smith & Radcliffe 1912:579 [ref. 4057]. Masc. *Thaumatichthys pagidostomus* Smith & Radcliffe 1912:580. Type by monotypy. Valid (Bertelsen & Struhsaker 1977 [ref. 5331]). Thaumatichthyidae.

Thayeria Eigenmann 1908:94 [ref. 1221]. Fem. *Thayeria obliquus [obliqua]* Eigenmann 1908:94. Type by original designation (also monotypic). Type species originally spelled *obliquus* but emended by Eigenmann 1910:437 to *obliqua* to agree in gender with genus. Valid (Géry 1977:514 [ref. 1597]). Characidae.

Thecapteryx Fowler 1948:1 [ref. 1459]. Fem. *Thecapteryx lioderma* Fowler 1948:2. Type by original designation (also monotypic). Synonym of *Sphoeroides* Anonymous 1798. Tetraodontidae.

Thecopsenes Fowler 1944:63 [ref. 1448]. Masc. *Psenes chapmani* Fowler 1906:119. Type by original designation (also monotypic). Synonym of *Psenes* Valenciennes 1833 (Haedrich 1967:84 [ref. 5357]). Nomeidae.

Thecopterus Smith 1904:163 [ref. 4040]. Masc. *Thecopterus aleuticus* Smith 1904:163. Type by monotypy. Misspelled *Theocopterus* in Zoological Record for 1904. Presumed valid (Nelson 1982:1499 [ref. 5470]); valid in Cottidae (Washington et al. 1984:443 [ref. 13660]). Psychrolutidae.

Themistocles (subgenus of *Prionobutis*) Whitley 1939:296 [ref. 4697]. Masc. *Prionobutis (Themistocles) wardi* Whitley 1939:296. Type by original designation (also monotypic). Synonym of *Prionobutis* Bleeker 1874 (Hoese, pers. comm.). Eleotridae.

Theragra Lucas in Jordan & Evermann 1898:2535 [ref. 2445]. Fem. *Gadus chalcogrammus* Pallas 1811:198. Type by monotypy. Valid (Svetovidov 1973:309 [ref. 7169], Fahay & Markle 1984:267 [ref. 13653], Okamura in Masuda et al. 1984:92 [ref. 6441], Svetovidov in Whitehead et al. 1986:691 [ref. 13676]). Gadidae.

Therapaina Kaup 1860:140 [ref. 2583]. Fem. *Chaetodon strigatus* Cuvier (ex Langsdorf) in Cuvier & Valenciennes 1831:25. Type by monotypy. Objective synonym of *Microcanthus* Swainson 1839. Kyphosidae: Microcanthinae.

Therapon Cloquet 1819:299 [ref. 852]. Masc. See *Terapon*. Terapontidae.

Theraps Günther 1862:284 [ref. 1969]. Masc. *Theraps irregularis* Günther 1862:284. Type by monotypy. Synonym of *Cichlasoma* Swainson 1839 (authors). Cichlidae.

Thermarces Rosenblatt & Cohen 1986:72 [ref. 5198]. Masc. *Thermarces cerberus* Rosenblatt & Cohen 1986:74. Type by original designation. Valid (Arnulf et al. 1987 [ref. 6744]). Zoarcidae.

Therobromus Lucas in Jordan & Gilbert 1899:440 [ref. 2478]. Masc. *Therobromus callorhini* Lucas in Jordan & Gilbert 1898:440. Type by monotypy. Synonym of *Bathylagus* Günther 1878 (Ahlstrom et al. 1984:156 [ref. 13627], Kobyliansky 1986:38 [ref. 6002]). Bathylagidae.

Thetaraia (subgenus of *Raja*) Leigh-Sharpe 1924:568, 577 [ref. 5748]. Fem. *Raja eatoni* Günther 1876:390. Type by original designation (also monotypic). As a "Pseudogenus" of *Raia* [=*Raja*]. Not available [Art. 1b (6)], used as an artificial category (see Leigh-Sharpe 1928 [ref. 6152]). Rajidae.

Theutis Bonnaterre 1788:lv, 156 [ref. 4940]. *Theutis hepatus* Linnaeus 1766. Type by subsequent designation. Earliest type designation not researched; 2 included species. Synonym of *Acanthurus* Forsskål 1775 (Desoutter 1973:455 [ref. 7203]). Acanthuridae.

Theutys Goüan 1770:105 [ref. 1863]. *Teuthis hepatus* Linnaeus 1766. Type by subsequent designation. Appeared without species, type as given by Fowler & Bean 1929:207 [ref. 1476]. Perhaps (on

p. 105) just a misspelling for *Teuthis* Linnaeus as used by Goüan on p. 163 where the description of *Theutys* would have appeared. Synonym of *Acanthurus* Forsskål 1775 (Desoutter 1973:455 [ref. 7203]). Acanthuridae.

Thinnus S. D. W. 1837:108 [ref. 12605]. Masc. Discussed by Whitley 1955:51-52 [ref. 4724]; treated by Whitley as an emendation; appeared with initials "S. D. W." only [apparently S. D. Wood]. Suppressed under plenary powers for purposes of priority but not homonymy and placed on the Official Index (Opinion 809). In the synonymy of *Thunnus* South 1845 (Gibbs & Collette 1967:97 [ref. 13640]). Scombridae.

Thoburnia Jordan & Snyder in Jordan 1917:88 [ref. 2408]. Fem. *Catostomus rhothoecus* Thoburn in Jordan & Evermann 1896:181. Type by original designation (also monotypic). Synonym of *Moxostoma* Rafinesque 1820 (Robins et al. 1980:27 [ref. 7111]; valid (Buth 1979 [ref. 6941]). Catostomidae.

Tholichthys Günther 1868:457 [ref. 1993]. Masc. *Tholichthys osseus* Günther 1868:457. Type by original designation (also monotypic). Synonym of *Chaetodon* Linnaeus 1758, based on a larval specimen. Chaetodontidae.

Thoracatherina Fowler 1941:249 [ref. 1438]. Fem. *Atherina insularum* Jordan & Evermann 1903:170. Type by original designation (also monotypic). Synonym of *Atherinomorus* Fowler 1903. Atherinidae: Atherininae.

Thoracocharax (subgenus of *Gasteropelecus*) Fowler 1907:452 [ref. 1374]. Masc. *Gasteropelecus stellatus* Kner 1860:17. Type by original designation (also monotypic). Valid (Géry 1977:246 [ref. 1597], Géry et al. 1987:439 [ref. 6001]). Gasteropelecidae.

Thoracochromis Greenwood 1979:290 [ref. 1898]. Masc. *Paratilapia wingatii* Boulenger 1902:264. Type by original designation. Valid (Greenwood 1984:189 [ref. 5311]). Cichlidae.

Thorichthys Meek 1904:222 [ref. 2958]. Masc. *Thorichthys ellioti* Meek 1904:223. Type by original designation. As a group of *Cichlasoma* (Miller & Taylor 1984:933 [ref. 6809]). Cichlidae.

Thorogobius Miller 1969:839 [ref. 3010]. Masc. *Gobius ephippiatus* Lowe 1839:84. Type by original designation. Valid (Miller 1973:512 [ref. 6888], Miller 1984:382 [ref. 6338], Miller in Whitehead et al. 1986:1081 [ref. 13677], Birdsong et al. 1988:190 [ref. 7303]). Gobiidae.

Thorophos Bruun 1931:288 [ref. 672]. *Thorophos euryops* Bruun 1931:288. Type by original designation (also monotypic). Valid (Weitzman 1974:472 [ref. 5174], Ahlstrom et al. 1984:185 [ref. 13643], Weitzman 1986:254 [ref. 6287]). Sternoptychidae: Maurolicinae.

Thrattidion Roberts 1972:2 [ref. 3775]. Neut. *Thrattidion noctivagus* Roberts 1972:4. Type by original designation (also monotypic). Valid (Poll et al. 1984:55 [ref. 6172], Grande 1985:247 [ref. 6466], Whitehead 1985:162 [ref. 5141]). Clupeidae.

Threpterius Richardson 1850:68 [ref. 3745]. Masc. *Threpterius maculosus* Richardson 1850:70. Type by monotypy. In family Chironemidae in Jordan, in Aplodactylidae in Fowler (MS); no recent use of name located. Aplodactylidae.

Thrichomycterus Humboldt 1805:35 [ref. 2278]. *Eremophilus mutisii* Humboldt 1805:35. Type by monotypy. Taken from Fowler (MS). Apparently mentioned in association with *Eremophilus* Humboldt; original not examined. Whether this affects *Trichomycterus* Valenciennes needs investigation. Trichomycteridae.

Thrissa Cuvier 1816:176 [ref. 993]. Fem. *Clupea mystus* Linnaeus 1758:319. Type by subsequent designation. Type designated by Bory de St. Vincent, v. 4, 1823:231 [ref. 3853] (see Whitehead et al. 1988:421 [ref. 5725] and Whitley 1937:137 [ref. 6396]). Preoccupied by *Thrissa* Rafinesque 1815, *Thryssa* Cuvier 1829 next available. Spelled *Thryssa* by Swainson 1838:279 [ref. 4302]. Treated as valid (Grande 1985:246 [ref. 6466], Whitehead et al. 1988:421 [ref. 5725]). Engraulidae.

Thrissa Rafinesque 1815:88 [ref. 3584]. Fem. *Clupea thrissa* Linnaeus 1758:318. Type by being a replacement name. As "*Thrissa* R. [Rafinesque] *Clupanodon* Lac. [Lacepède]." Available replacement name for and objective synonym of *Clupanodon* Lacepède 1803. Synonym of *Clupanodon* Lacepède 1803 (Whitehead 1985:238 [ref. 5141]). Clupeidae.

Thrissina Jordan & Seale 1925:30 [ref. 2499]. Fem. *Clupea baelama* Forsskål 1775:72. Type by original designation (also monotypic). Valid (Whitehead 1967:139 [ref. 6464], Nelson 1982 [ref. 5486], Grande 1985:246 [ref. 6466]); synonym of *Thryssa* Cuvier 1829 (Whitehead et al. 1988:421 [ref. 5725]). Engraulidae.

Thrissobrycon Böhlke 1953:168 [ref. 593]. Masc. *Thrissobrycon pectinifer* Böhlke 1953:169. Type by original designation (also monotypic). Valid (Géry 1977:594 [ref. 1597]). Characidae.

Thrissocharax Myers 1926:174 [ref. 3095]. Masc. *Nannocharax ocellicauda* Boulenger 1907:485. Type by original designation (also monotypic). Objective synonym of *Hemigrammocharax* Pellegrin 1923 (Daget & Gosse 1984:194 [ref. 6185]). Citharinidae: Distichodontinae.

Thrissochromis Fowler 1941:262 [ref. 1438]. Masc. *Chromis velox* Jenkins 1901:393. Type by original designation (also monotypic). Pomacentridae.

Thrissocles Jordan & Evermann in Jordan 1917:98 [ref. 2407]. Masc. *Clupea setirostris* Broussonet 1782:unnumbered. Type by being a replacement name. Replacement for *Thrissa* Cuvier 1816. Synonym of *Thryssa* Cuvier 1829 (see Whitehead 1967:140 [ref. 6464], Whitehead & Wongratana 1986:206 [ref. 6284], Whitehead et al. 1988:421 [ref. 5725]). Engraulidae.

Thrissomimus (subgenus of *Leucichthys*) Gill in Jordan & Evermann 1911:3, 4 [ref. 2452]. Masc. *Coregonus artedi* Lesueur 1818:231. Type by original designation. Synonym of *Coregonus* Linnaeus 1758. Salmonidae: Coregoninae.

Thrycomycterus Humboldt & Valenciennes 1811 [ref. 5612]. Masc. *Thrycomycterus nigricans* Humboldt & Valenciennes 1811. Listed as above by Jordan 1919:170 [ref. 2410] but not included by Fowler (MS). Jordan gave no page number for the genus and we are unable to locate it in the work cited by Jordan. See also *Thrichomycterus* and *Trichomycterus*. Synonym of *Eremophilus* Humboldt 1805, according to Evermann (fide Jordan). Trichomycteridae.

Thryssa Cuvier 1829:323 [ref. 995]. Fem. *Clupea mystus* Linnaeus 1758:319. Apparently a new spelling for *Thrissa* Cuvier 1816, preoccupied by *Thrissa* Rafinesque 1815 in fishes (see Whitehead 1967:140 [ref. 6464]), and if regarded as such then type is same as for *Thrissa* Cuvier. Valid (Grande 1985:246 [ref. 6466], Whitehead & Wongratana 1986:206 [ref. 6284], Kottelat 1989:6 [ref. 13605], Paxton et al. 1989:161 [ref. 12442]). Engraulidae.

Thryssocypris Roberts & Kottelat 1984:142 [ref. 5352]. Fem. *Thryssocypris smaragdinus* Roberts & Kottelat 1984:146. Type by original designation. Valid (Kottelat 1985:267 [ref. 11441], Kottelat 1989:12 [ref. 13605], Roberts 1989:79 [ref. 6439]). Cyprinidae.

Thunnus South 1845:620 [ref. 4170]. Masc. *Scomber thynnus* Linnaeus 1758:297. Type by being a replacement name. Replacement for *Thynnus* Cuvier 1816, preoccupied by Fabricius 1775 in Hymenoptera. On Official List (Opinion 809); *Thynnus* Cuvier 1816:313 on Official Index; *Thinnus* S. D. W.[Wood] also placed on Official Index (Opinion 809). Valid (Gibbs & Collette 1967:97 [ref. 13640], Postel 1973:467 [ref. 7208], Collette & Nauen 1983:80 [ref. 5375], Collette et al. 1984:600 [ref. 11421], Nakamura in Masuda et al. 1984:226 [ref. 6441], Collette 1986:836 [ref. 5647]). Scombridae.

Thymalloides (subgenus of *Thymallus*) Berg 1908:503 [ref. 271]. Masc. *Salmo arcticus* Pallas 1776:35, 50. Type by original designation. Synonym of *Thymallus* Linck 1790. Salmonidae: Thymallinae.

Thymallus Cuvier 1829:306 [ref. 995]. Masc. *Salmo thymallus* Linnaeus 1758:311. Type by absolute tautonymy. Treated by Cuvier as a new name. Spelled *Thymalus* by Valenciennes in Cuvier & Valenciennes 1848:426 [ref. 1013]. Objective synonym of *Thymallus* Linck 1790. Salmonidae: Thymallinae.

Thymallus Linck 1790:35 [ref. 4985]. Masc. *Salmo thymallus* Linnaeus 1758:311. Appeared without species; subsequent use and addition of species not researched. Valid (Kendall & Behnke 1984:144 [ref. 13638]). Salmonidae: Thymallinae.

Thynnichthyina (subgenus of *Thynnichthys*) Fowler 1937:177 [ref. 1425]. Fem. *Thynnichthys thai* Fowler 1937:177. Type by original designation (also monotypic). Second species mentioned would be nominate species of subgenus *Thynnichthys*. Synonym of *Thynnichthys* Bleeker 1859. Cyprinidae.

Thynnichthys Bleeker 1859:433 [ref. 370]. Masc. *Leuciscus thynnoides* Bleeker 1852:599. Type by subsequent designation. Apparently appeared first in key, without included species. Two species included by Bleeker 1859:153-154 [ref. 371]; six species (3 with question) included by Bleeker 1860:283, 406-407 [ref. 380]. Type designated by Bleeker 1863:201 [ref. 397] and 1863:28 [ref. 4859]. Valid (Jayaram 1981:114 [ref. 6497], Kottelat 1985:267 [ref. 11441], Kottelat 1989:12 [ref. 13605], Roberts 1989:80 [ref. 6439]). Cyprinidae.

Thynnichthys Giglioli 1880:25 [ref. 1617]. Masc. *Thynnus thunnina* Cuvier 1829. Type by subsequent designation. Preoccupied by Bleeker 1859 in fishes, replaced by *Wanderer* Whitley 1937 (see also Appendix A). Synonym of *Euthynnus* Lütken in Jordan & Gilbert 1883 (Postel 1973:470 [ref. 7208]). Scombridae.

Thynnus Browne 1789:451 [ref. 669]. Masc. Not available, name published in a rejected work on Official Index (Opinion 89). Scombridae.

Thynnus Cuvier 1816:313 [ref. 993]. Masc. *Scomber thynnus* Linnaeus 1758:297. Type by monotypy (also by absolute tautonymy). Preoccupied by *Thynnus* Fabricius 1775; on Official Index (Opinion 809). *Albacora* Jordan 1888 is an unneeded replacement. In the synonymy of *Thunnus* South 1845 (Gibbs & Collette 1967:97 [ref. 13640], Postel 1973:467 [ref. 7208]). Scombridae.

Thynnus Gronow in Gray 1854:121 [ref. 1911]. Masc. *Thynnus moluccensis* Gronow in Gray 1854:121. Type by subsequent designation. Subsequent designation not researched. Preoccupied by Fabricius 1775, also by Cuvier 1816 in fishes. Carangidae.

Thyreoconger Wade 1946:188 [ref. 4542]. Masc. *Thyreoconger hemiaspidus* Wade 1946:189. Type by original designation (also monotypic). Synonym of *Ariosoma* Swainson 1838 (Blache et al. 1973:241 [ref. 7185], Smith 1989:492 [ref. 13285]). Congridae: Bathymyrinae.

Thyrina Jordan & Culver in Jordan 1895:419 [ref. 2394]. Fem. *Thyrina evermanni* Jordan & Culver in Jordan 1895:419. Type by original designation. Preoccupied by Poujade 1886 in Lepidoptera, replaced by *Atherthyrina* Fowler 1958. Synonym of *Atherinella* Steindachner 1875 (Chernoff 1986:240 [ref. 5847]). Atherinidae: Menidiinae.

Thyrinops Hubbs 1918:306 [ref. 2226]. Masc. *Atherinichthys pachylepis* Günther 1864:25. Type by original designation (also monotypic). Synonym of *Atherinella* Steindachner 1875 (Chernoff & Miller 1984:1 [ref. 8175], Chernoff 1986:240 [ref. 5847]). Atherinidae: Menidiinae.

Thyris Goode 1880:337, 344 [ref. 1834]. Fem. *Thyris pellucidus* Goode 1880:337, 344. Type by monotypy. Preoccupied by Laspeyres 1803 and Ochsenheimer 1808 in Lepidoptera, replaced by *Delothyris* Goode 1883. Synonym of *Monolene* Goode 1880 (Norman 1934:164 [ref. 6893]). Bothidae: Bothinae.

Thyriscus Gilbert & Burke 1912:43 [ref. 1634]. Masc. *Thyriscus anoplus* Gilbert & Burke 1912:43. Type by original designation (also monotypic). Valid (Washington et al. 1984:443 [ref. 13660], Yabe 1985:111 [ref. 11522]). Cottidae.

Thyrsites Cuvier in Cuvier & Valenciennes 1832:196 [ref. 1000]. Masc. *Scomber atun* Euphrasen 1791:315. Type by subsequent designation. Appeared first as "Les Thyrsites" in Cuvier 1829:200 [ref. 995]. Dates to 1832 as above, with type designated by Gill 1862:126 [ref. 1659]. Apparently named independently and earlier by Lesson 1831 [ref. 2776]. Synonym and homonym of *Thyrsites* Lesson 1831. Gempylidae.

Thyrsites Lesson 1831:158 [ref. 2776]. *Thyrsites lepidopodea* Lesson (ex Cuvier) 1831:158. Type by monotypy. Predates *Thyrsites* Cuvier 1832. Valid (Collette et al. 1984:600 [ref. 11421], Nakamura in Nakamura et al. 1986:270 [ref. 14235], Nakamura 1986:828 [ref. 5696]). Gempylidae.

Thyrsitoides Fowler 1929:255 [ref. 1403]. Masc. *Thyrsitoides marleyi* Fowler 1929:255. Type by original designation (also monotypic). Valid (Nakamura 1980 [ref. 5478], Collette et al. 1984:600 [ref. 11421], Nakamura in Masuda et al. 1984:227 [ref. 6441], Nakamura 1986:828 [ref. 5696]). Gempylidae.

Thyrsitops Gill 1862:125 [ref. 1659]. Masc. *Thyrsites lepidopoides* Valenciennes in Cuvier & Valenciennes 1831:205. Type by original designation (also monotypic). Valid (Collette et al. 1984:600 [ref. 11421], Nakamura et al. 1986:272 [ref. 14235]); status uncertain (see Collette & Russo 1986 [ref. 6324] as *Thryisitops*). Gempylidae.

Thyrsoidea Kaup 1856:60 [ref. 2572]. Fem. *Muraena thyrsoidea* Richardson 1844:111. Type by absolute tautonymy of an included synonym. *Muraena thyrsoidea* Richardson needlessly renamed *Thyrsoidea arenata* by Kaup. Also in Kaup 1856:74 [ref. 2573] and as name only in Kaup in Duméril 1856:200 [ref. 1154]. Valid (Castle & McCosker 1986:174 [ref. 5645], Ajiad 1987 [ref. 6752] and Paxton et al. 1989:133 [ref. 12442] with type as *T. longissima* Kaup 1856, Böhlke et al. 1989:130 [ref. 13286]). Muraenidae: Muraeninae.

Thysanactis Regan & Trewavas 1930:57 [ref. 3681]. Fem. *Thysanactis dentex* Regan & Trewavas 1930:58. Type by monotypy. Valid (Morrow in Morrow & Gibbs 1964:446 [ref. 6962], Kawaguchi & Moser 1984:171 [ref. 13642], Fujii in Masuda et al. 1984:51 [ref. 6441], Fink 1985:11 [ref. 5171], Paxton et al. 1989:203 [ref. 12442]). Melanostomiidae.

Thysanichthys Jordan & Starks 1904:122 [ref. 2527]. Masc. *Thysanichthys crossotus* Jordan & Starks 1904:123. Type by original designation (also monotypic). Valid (Shimizu in Masuda et al. 1984:313 [ref. 6441]). Scorpaenidae: Scorpaeninae.

Thysanocara (subgenus of *Xenocara*) Regan 1906:96 [ref. 3627]. Neut. *Hypostomus cirrhosus* Valenciennes in Cuvier & Valenciennes 1840:511. Type by monotypy. Proposed for *Xenocara cirrhosum* and its allies; *X. brevispinnis* also described, but whether Regan placed it in the subgenus *Thysanocara* is unclear from text. Objective synonym of *Ancistrus* Kner 1854 (Isbrücker 1980:66 [ref. 2303]). Loricariidae.

Thysanocheilus Kner 1864:185 [ref. 2637]. Masc. *Thysanocheilus ornatus* Kner 1864:185. Type by monotypy. Also in Kner 1865:4 [ref. 6174] and as Anonymous 1865:77 [ref. 6173]; assume above published in 1864. *Thysanochilus* is an unjustified emendation or misspelling. Not preoccupied by Philippi 1857. Synonym of *Labrichthys* Bleeker 1854 (Randall & Springer 1973:283 [ref. 3603]). Labridae.

Thysanochilus Philippi 1857:268, footnote [ref. 3462]. Masc. *Thysanochilus valdivianus* Philippi 1857:268. Type by monotypy. Apparently editor (Troschel) did not accept this Philippi name as valid, but still published it in the footnote. [Article not translated; status unclear but probably unavailable; authorship perhaps Troschel in Philippi.] Synonym of *Geotria* Gray 1851. Petromyzontidae: Geotriinae.

Thysanophrys Ogilby 1898:40 [ref. 5861]. Fem. *Platycephalus cirronasus* Richardson 1848:114. Type by original designation (also monotypic). Valid (Hureau 1973:592 [ref. 7197], Ochiai in Masuda et al. 1984:322 [ref. 6441], Knapp 1986:485 [ref. 5683], Paxton et al. 1989:471 [ref. 12442]). Platycephalidae.

Thysanopsetta Günther 1880:22 [ref. 2011]. Fem. *Thysanopsetta naresi* Günther 1880:22. Type by monotypy. Valid (Norman 1934:64 [ref. 6893], Ahlstrom et al. 1984:642 [ref. 13641]). Paralichthyidae.

Thysia Loiselle & Welcomme 1972:40 [ref. 2821]. Fem. *Pelmatochromis ansorgii* Boulenger 1901:8. Type by original designation. Preoccupied by Thomson 1860 in Coleoptera (see Whitley 1976:49 [ref. 4735]); replaced by *Thysochromis* Daget 1988. Valid (Greenwood 1987:160 [ref. 6166] before replacement by *Thysochromis*). Cichlidae.

Thysochromis Daget 1988:97 [ref. 6734]. Masc. *Pelmatochromis ansorgii* Boulenger 1901:8. Type by being a replacement name. Replacement for *Thysia* Loiselle & Welcomme 1972, preoccupied by Thomson 1860 in Coleoptera. Valid (see *Thysia*). Cichlidae.

Tiaroga Girard 1856:204 [ref. 1810]. Fem. *Tiaroga cobitis* Girard 1856:204. Type by monotypy. Valid (authors); synonym of *Rhinichthys* Agassiz 1849 (Coburn & Cavender, pers. comm.). Cyprinidae.

Tifia Jordan in Jordan & Jordan 1922:60 [ref. 2487]. Fem. *Chaetodon corallicola* Snyder 1904:53. Type by original designation (also monotypic). Maugé & Bauchot 1984:473 place *Tifia* in the synonymy of the much later *Exornator* Nalbant 1971. Synonym of *Chaetodon* Linnaeus 1758 (Burgess 1978:653 [ref. 700]). Chaetodontidae.

Tigoma Girard 1856:205 [ref. 1810]. Fem. *Gila pulchella* Baird & Girard 1854:29. Type by subsequent designation. Type designated by Jordan & Gilbert 1877:91 [ref. 4907]. Synonym of *Gila* Baird & Girard 1853. Cyprinidae.

Tigrigobius (subgenus of *Gobiosoma*) Fowler 1931:401 [ref. 1410]. Masc. *Gobiosoma macrodon* Beebe & Tee-Van 1928:226. Type by original designation (also monotypic). Synonym of *Elacatinus* Jordan 1904 (Hoese, pers. comm.). Gobiidae.

Tilapia Smith 1840:Pl. 5 [ref. 4035]. Fem. *Tilapia sparrmanii* Smith 1840:Pl. 5. Type by original designation (also monotypic). Valid (Uyeno & Fujii in Masuda et al. 1984:190 [ref. 6441], Poll 1986:28 [ref. 6136], Krupp & Schneider 1989:399 [ref. 13651]). Cichlidae.

Tilesia Swainson 1838:318 [ref. 4302]. Fem. *Gadus gracilis* Tilesius 1810:354. Type by monotypy. Also in Swainson 1839:188, 300 [ref. 4303]. Preoccupied by Lamouroux 1821 in Bryozoa, replaced by *Pleurogadus* Bean 1887. Objective synonym of *Pleurogadus* Bean 1885; synonym of *Eleginus* Fischer von Waldheim 1813. Gadidae.

Tilesina Schmidt 1904:134 [ref. 3946]. Fem. *Tilesina gibbosa* Schmidt 1904:135. Type by monotypy. Apparently appeared first as name only in Schmidt 1903:518 [ref. 3945]). Valid (Washington et al. 1984:442 [ref. 13660], Kanayama in Masuda et al. 1984:332 [ref. 6441], Yabe 1985:123 [ref. 11522], Maeda & Amaoka 1988:71 [ref. 12616]). Agonidae.

Tilodon Thominot (ex Guichenot) 1881:140 [ref. 4384]. Masc. *Tilodon australis* Thominot (ex Guichenot) 1881:140. Type by monotypy. Kyphosidae: Scorpidinae.

Tilurella Roule 1911:734 [ref. 3813]. Fem. *Tilurella gaussiana* Pappenheim 1914:187. Type by subsequent monotypy. No type named; based on larval specimen. See synonymy in Smith & Nielsen 1989:454 [ref. 13290] for possible subsequent addition of species. If above is first addition of species, then name is a synonym of *Nemichthys*. In the synonymy of *Nemichthys* Richardson 1848 (Larsen 1973:231 [ref. 7187]). Nemichthyidae.

Tiluropsis Roule 1911:734 [ref. 3813]. Fem. Apparently not available, described without species and none referred to it subsequently; based on a larva. *Tiluropsis* used by Smith 1989:957 [ref. 13285] for reference for unidentified larva in Notacanthiformes. Notacanthidae.

Tilurus Kölliker 1854:100 [ref. 2680]. Masc. *Tilurus gegenbauri* Kölliker 1854:101 (= *Leptocephalus trichiurus* Cocco). Type by monotypy. Valid, as larval Notacanthiformes (Smith 1989:956 [ref. 13285]). Notacanthidae.

Tinca Cuvier 1816:193 [ref. 993]. Fem. *Cyprinus tinca* Linnaeus 1758:321. Type by absolute tautonymy. Valid (Yang & Hwang 1964:10 [ref. 13497], Jayaram 1981:115 [ref. 6497]). Cyprinidae.

Tinimogaster Bonaparte (ex Cocco) 1846:68 [ref. 519]. Fem. Apparently not available, name in synonymy under *Pharopteryx* as "(*Gastronemus* vel *Tinimogaster*? Cocco)". Synonym of *Mora* Risso 1826. Moridae.

Tiphle Rafinesque 1810:18 [ref. 3594]. Fem. *Tiphle hexagonus* Rafinesque 1810:18 (= *Syngnathus typhle* Linnaeus 1758:336). Type by subsequent designation. Apparently earliest type designation is by Jordan 1917:78 [ref. 2407]. Genus spelled *Tiphle* and Linnaeus' species misspelled *tiphle* instead of *typhle*, so no tautonymy. Not preoccupied by *Typhle* Lacepède 1800 in mammals. Synonym of *Syngnathus* Linnaeus 1758 (Wheeler 1973:274 [ref. 7190], Dawson 1982:55 [ref. 6764], Dawson 1985:181 [ref. 6541]). Syngnathidae: Syngnathinae.

Tiricoris Whitley 1955:111 [ref. 4722]. Fem. *Cymolutes sandeyeri* Hector 1884:323. Type by original designation (also monotypic). Labridae.

Tirodon Hay 1882:68 [ref. 2054]. Masc. *Tirodon amnigenus* Hay 1882:68. Type by monotypy. Synonym of *Hybognathus* Agassiz 1855. Cyprinidae.

Tirus Rafinesque 1810:56 [ref. 3594]. Masc. *Tirus marmoratus*

Rafinesque 1810:56. Type by monotypy. Synonym of *Synodus* Scopoli 1777 (Nielsen 1973:161 [ref. 6885], Anderson et al. 1966:47 [ref. 6977]). Synodontidae: Synodontinae.

Tlaloc Alvarez & Carranza 1951:40 [ref. 103]. Masc. *Tlaloc mexicanus* Alvarez & Carranza 1951:41. Type by original designation (also monotypic). Synonym of *Profundulus* Hubbs 1924 (Parenti 1981:492 [ref. 7066] with type as *labialis* Günther). Cyprinodontidae: Profundulinae.

Tobinia Whitley 1933:47 [ref. 6595]. Fem. *Tobinia paragaudata* Whitley 1933:47. Type by monotypy. Not available from this date, no separate generic description, and combined description does not meet requirements of Art. 13(c). Subsequent publication in an available way not investigated. Balistidae.

Tocantinsia Mees 1974:108 [ref. 2969]. Fem. *Tocantinsia depressa* Mees 1974:108. Type by original designation (also monotypic). Valid (Mees 1984 [ref. 5692], Burgess 1989:241 [ref. 12860], Curran 1989 [ref. 12547]). Auchenipteridae.

Tocichthys (subgenus of *Hyperprosopon*) Hubbs 1918:12 [ref. 2227]. Masc. *Hyperprosopon agassizii* Gill 1862:276. Type by original designation (also monotypic). Synonym of *Hyperprosopon* Gibbons 1854 (Tarp 1952:31 [ref. 12250]). Embiotocidae.

Todarus Grassi & Calandruccio 1896:349 [ref. 1877]. Masc. *Nettastoma brevirostre* Facciolà 1887:166. Type by monotypy. Apparently preoccupied [details not researched], replaced by *Nettodarus* Whitley 1951. Objective synonym of *Nettodarus* Whitley 1951 (Blache et al. 1973:238 [ref. 7185]). Synonym of *Dysomma* Alcock 1889 (Robins & Robins 1976:256 [ref. 3784], Robins & Robins 1989:244 [ref. 13287]). Synaphobranchidae: Ilyophinae.

Toledia Miranda-Ribeiro 1915:5 [ref. 3711]. Fem. *Toledia macrophthalma* Miranda-Ribeiro 1915:5. Type by monotypy. Appears on p. 5 in section titled Stromateidae. Synonym of *Hyperoglyphe* Günther 1859 (Haedrich 1967:55 [ref. 5357]). Centrolophidae.

Tometes Valenciennes in Cuvier & Valenciennes 1849:225 [ref. 1014]. Masc. *Tometes trilobatus* Valenciennes in Cuvier & Valenciennes 1849:226. Type by subsequent designation. Type apparently first designated by Jordan 1919:242 [ref. 2410]. Synonym of *Myleus* Müller & Troschel 1844 (Géry 1976:49 [ref. 14199]). Characidae: Serrasalminae.

Tomeurus Eigenmann 1909:53 [ref. 1222]. Masc. *Tomeurus gracilis* Eigenmann 1909:53. Type by monotypy. Valid (Rosen & Bailey 1963:36 [ref. 7067], Parenti & Rauchenberger 1989:6 [ref. 13538]). Poeciliidae.

Tomicodon Brisout de Barneville 1846:144 [ref. 9183]. Masc. *Tomicodon chilensis* Brisout de Barneville 1846:144. Type by subsequent designation. Type designated by Jordan 1919:228 [ref. 2410]. Valid (Briggs 1955:57 [ref. 637], Pequeño 1989:41 [ref. 14125]). Gobiesocidae: Gobiesocinae.

Tomiyamichthys Smith 1956:553 [ref. 4103]. Masc. *Cryptocentrus oni* Tomiyama 1936:82. Type by original designation (also monotypic). Valid (Yanagisawa 1978:295 [ref. 7028], Akihito in Masuda et al. 1984:260 [ref. 6441], Birdsong et al. 1988:194 [ref. 7303]); synonym of *Flabelligobius* Smith 1956 (Hoese, pers. comm.). Gobiidae.

Tomocichla Regan 1908:463 [ref. 3637]. Fem. *Herichthys underwoodi* Regan 1908:30. Type by monotypy; only one definitely-included species. Synonym of *Cichlasoma* Swainson 1839 (authors). Cichlidae.

Tongaichthys Nakamura & Fujii 1983:174 [ref. 5409]. Masc. *Tongaichthys robustus* Nakamura & Fujii 1983:174. Type by original designation (also monotypic). Valid (Collette et al. 1984:600 [ref. 11421]); presumed valid (see Collette & Russo 1986 [ref. 6324]). Gempylidae.

Tor Gray 1834:Pl. 96 (v. 2) [ref. 1878]. Masc. *Tor hamiltonii* Gray 1834:Pl. 96 (= *Cyprinus tor* Hamilton 1822:305, 338). Type by monotypy. Species as "[Pl.] 96. Fig. 1. Dr. Hamilton's Tor Carp. *Tor hamiltonii*." Gray's *T. hamiltoni* is an unneeded substitute for *Cyprinus tor* Hamilton. Valid (Karaman 1971:224 [ref. 2560], Wu et al. 1977:322 [ref. 4807], Jayaram 1981:123 [ref. 6497], Chen & Chu 1985 [ref. 5250], Roberts 1989:80 [ref. 6439], Chu & Cui in Chu & Chen 1989:136 [ref. 13584], Kottelat 1989:12 [ref. 13605]). Cyprinidae.

Torafugu Abe 1950:199 [ref. 5588]. Masc. *Tetraodon rubripes* Temminck & Schlegel 1850:283. Type by original designation and monotypy (in 1950). Appeared first in Abe 1939:336 [ref. 5589] without type designation (Art. 13b); not available. In 1950:199 [ref. 558], Abe listed the type as *Tetraodon rubripes* Temminck & Schlegel 1850 with bibliographic reference to Abe 1939. In 1954:122 [ref. 5] Abe indicated that *Fugu* should replace *Torafugu* Abe. Available from Abe 1950 with type as *rubripes*. In the synonymy of *Takifugu* Abe 1949. Tetraodontidae.

Torictus Parr 1951:10 [ref. 3380]. Masc. *Alepocephalus edentulus* Alcock 1892:358. Type by original designation (also monotypic). Valid (Krefft 1973:92 [ref. 7166]). Alepocephalidae.

Torpedo Duméril 1806:102, 343 [ref. 1151]. Fem. *Raja torpedo* Linnaeus 1758:231. Type by subsequent monotypy. Appeared without species, first addition of species probably by Bonaparte 1838:7 (of separate) [ref. 4979]. Objective synonym of *Torpedo* Houttuyn 1764. Torpedinidae.

Torpedo Forsskål 1775:16 [ref. 1351]. Fem. Misidentification; wrongly described the electric catfish of the Nile under the electric ray, *Torpedo*. Malapteruridae.

Torpedo Houttuyn 1764:453 [ref. 2219]. Fem. *Raja torpedo* Linnaeus 1758:231. Apparently type by subsequent monotypy or tautonymy [original not seen]. Valid (Krefft & Stehmann 1973:55 [ref. 7167], Nakaya in Masuda et al. 1984:12 [ref. 6441], Compagno 1986:112 [ref. 5648], Cappetta 1987:161 [ref. 6348], Paxton et al. 1989:61 [ref. 12442]). Torpedinidae.

Torpedo Rafinesque 1810:48, 60 [ref. 3595]. Fem. *Raja torpedo* Linnaeus 1758:231. Type by absolute tautonymy. *Raja torpedo* Linnaeus renamed by Rafinesque as *T. ocellata*; two additional "*R. torpedo* var. Linn." were also renamed by Rafinesque. Synonym of *Torpedo* Houttuyn 1764. Torpedinidae.

Torquigener Whitley 1930:31 [ref. 4671]. Masc. *Spheroides tuberculiferus* Ogilby 1912:61. Type by original designation (also monotypic). Valid (Tyler 1980:341 [ref. 4477], Hardy 1983 [ref. 5341], Hardy 1983 [ref. 5342], Arai 1983:207 [ref. 14249], Smith & Heemstra 1986:902 [ref. 5714], Su et al. 1986:112 [ref. 12582]). Tetraodontidae.

Torrentaria (subgenus of *Etheostoma*) Jordan & Evermann 1896: 1066,-68,-80 [ref. 2443]. Fem. *Etheostoma australe* Jordan 1889: 362. Type by original designation. Reportedly preoccupied by Hodgson in Gray 1863 in Aves (under current rules Gray's name is probably unavailable), replaced by *Austroperca* Hubbs 1936 but this name probably not needed. Synonym of *Etheostoma* Rafinesque 1819, subgenus *Austroperca* Hubbs 1936 (Collette & Banarescu 1977:1456 [ref. 5845]); subgenus *Oligocephalus* Girard 1859 (Bailey & Etnier 1988:25 [ref. 6873]). Percidae.

Torresia Castelnau 1875:36 [ref. 768]. Fem. *Torresia australis*

Sauvage 1875:36. Type by monotypy. Synonym of *Choerodon* Bleeker 1849. Labridae.

Tosana Smith & Pope 1906:470 [ref. 4058]. Fem. *Tosana niwae* Smith & Pope 1906:470. Type by original designation (also monotypic). Valid (Kendall 1984:500 [ref. 13663], Katayama in Masuda et al. 1984:135 [ref. 6441]). Serranidae: Anthiinae.

Tosanoides Kamohara 1953:3 [ref. 2553]. Masc. *Tosanoides filamentosus* Kamohara 1953:3. Type by original designation (also monotypic). Valid (Kendall 1984:500 [ref. 13663], Katayama in Masuda et al. 1984:135 [ref. 6441]). Serranidae: Anthiinae.

Tosarhombus Amaoka 1969:128 [64] [ref. 105]. Masc. *Tosarhombus octoculatus* Amaoka 1969:129 [65]. Type by original designation (also monotypic). Valid (Ahlstrom et al. 1984:643 [ref. 13641], Amaoka in Masuda et al. 1984:348 [ref. 6441], Hensley 1986:941 [ref. 6326]). Bothidae: Bothinae.

Toshia Whitley 1933:60 [ref. 4677]. Fem. *Dasyatis fluviorum* Ogilby 1908:6. Type by original designation (also monotypic). Synonym of *Dasyatis* Rafinesque 1810. Dasyatidae.

Totoaba Villamar 1980:130 [ref. 6596]. Fem. *Cynoscion macdonaldi* Gilbert 1890:64. Type by original designation (also monotypic). Sciaenidae.

Toxabramis Günther 1873:249 [ref. 2004]. Fem. *Toxabramis swinhonis* Günther 1873:250. Type by monotypy. Valid (Yih & Wu 1964:84 [ref. 13499], Chen in Chu & Chen 1989:83 [ref. 13584]). Cyprinidae.

Toxotes Cuvier 1816:338 [ref. 993]. Fem. *Labrus jaculator* of Shaw 1803:485 (? = *Sciaena jaculator* Pallas 1767). Type by monotypy. See Whitley 1935:136 for possible earlier date. Valid (Allen 1978 [ref. 6922], Jayaram 1981:331 [ref. 6497], Roberts 1989:165 [ref. 6439]). Toxotidae.

Toxus Eigenmann 1903:226 [ref. 1217]. Masc. *Toxus riddlei* Eigenmann 1903:226. Type by original designation (also monotypic). Synonym of *Girardinus* Poey 1854 (Rosen & Bailey 1963:109 [ref. 7067]). Poeciliidae.

Trachelochismus Brisout de Barneville 1846:212 [ref. 642]. Masc. *Cyclopterus pinnulatus* Forster 1844:301. Type by monotypy. Valid (Briggs 1955:18 [ref. 637], Allen [L. G.] 1984:629 [ref. 13673]). Gobiesocidae: Gobiesocinae.

Trachelocirrhus Doûmet 1863:220 [ref. 1138]. Masc. *Trachelocirrhus mediterraneus* Doûmet 1863:222. Type by monotypy. Misspelled *Trachelocirrus* by Jordan 1919:323 [ref. 4904]. Synonymized with *Navarchus sulcatus* by Doûmet 1864 [ref. 13456]. Synonym of *Cubiceps* Lowe 1843 (Haedrich 1967:78 [ref. 5357] and Haedrich 1973:562 [ref. 7216]). Nomeidae.

Trachelyichthys Mees 1974:111 [ref. 2969]. Masc. *Trachelyichthys decaradiatus* Mees 1974:112. Type by original designation (also monotypic). Valid (Greenfield & Glodek 1977 [ref. 7054], Burgess 1989:241 [ref. 12860], Curran 1989 [ref. 12547]). Auchenipteridae.

Trachelyopterichthys Bleeker 1862:402 [ref. 392]. Masc. *Trachelyopterus taeniatus* Kner 1857:434. Type by original designation (also monotypic). Also appeared in Bleeker 1862:14 [ref. 393]. Spelled *Tracheliopterichthys* by Miranda-Ribeiro 1911:375 [not researched]. Valid (Ferraris & Fernandez 1987 [ref. 6805], Burgess 1989:242 [ref. 12860], Curran 1989 [ref. 12547]). Auchenipteridae.

Trachelyopterus Valenciennes in Cuvier & Valenciennes 1840:220 [ref. 1008]. Masc. *Trachelyopterus coriaceus* Valenciennes in Cuvier & Valenciennes 1840:220. Type by monotypy. Spelled *Tracheliopterus* by Valenciennes on Pl. 438. Valid (Burgess 1989:242 [ref. 12860], Curran 1989 [ref. 12547]). Auchenipteridae.

Trachicephalus (subgenus of *Synanchia*) Swainson 1839:181, 268 [ref. 4303]. Masc. *Synanceia elongata* Cuvier in Cuvier & Valenciennes 1829:456. Type by monotypy. Not preoccupied by *Trachycephalus* Tschudi 1838 in Reptilia. See account of *Trichophasia* Swainson 1839. Valid (Eschmeyer & Rama-Rao 1973:372 [ref. 6391], Washington et al. 1984:440 [ref. 13660]). Scorpaenidae: Synanceiinae.

Trachichthodes Gilchrist 1903:203 [ref. 1645]. Masc. *Trachichthodes spinosus* Gilchrist 1903:204. Type by monotypy. Synonym of *Centroberyx* Gill 1862 (Scott 1981:115 [ref. 5533], Heemstra 1986:410 [ref. 5660]). Berycidae.

Trachichthys Shaw in Shaw & Nodder 1799:Pl. 378 [ref. 4013]. Masc. *Trachichthys australis* Shaw 1799:Pl. 378. Type by monotypy. Also in Shaw 1803:630 [ref. 4014]. *Trachychthis* Rafinesque 1815:85 [ref. 3584] is an incorrect subsequent spelling. Original not seen. Valid (Paulin 1979:69 [ref. 6918], Paxton et al. 1989:367 [ref. 12442]). Trachichthyidae.

Trachidermis Heckel 1837:159 [ref. 2079]. Fem. *Trachidermis fasciatus* Heckel 1837:168. Type by subsequent designation. Subsequent designation not researched. Apparently not preoccupied by *Trachyderma* or *Trachidermus*; *Aphobus* Gistel 1848 is an unneeded replacement. Species spelled "*efasciatus*" in main heading (p. 160) but otherwise as *fasciatus*. Valid (Washington et al. 1984:443 [ref. 13660] and Yabe in Masuda et al. 1984:326 [ref. 6441] and Yabe 1985:111 [ref. 11522] as *Trachydermus*). Cottidae.

Trachinocephalus Gill 1861:53 [ref. 1766]. Masc. *Salmo myops* Forster in Bloch & Schneider 1801:421. Type by monotypy. Valid (Anderson et al. 1966:37 [ref. 6977], Sulak 1977:53 [ref. 4299], Okiyama 1984:207 [ref. 13644], Machida in Masuda et al. 1984:61 [ref. 6441], Cressey 1986:273 [ref. 6289], Paxton et al. 1989:239 [ref. 12442]). Synodontidae: Synodontinae.

Trachinoides Borodin 1934:119 [ref. 529]. Masc. *Trachinoides moroccanus* Borodin 1934:120. Type by monotypy. Synonym of *Merluccius* Rafinesque 1810 (Svetovidov 1973:300 [ref. 7169]). Merlucciidae: Merlucciinae.

Trachinops Günther 1861:366 [ref. 1964]. Masc. *Trachinops taeniatus* Günther 1861:366. Type by monotypy. Valid (Allen 1977 [ref. 98], Hoese & Kuiter 1984:8 [ref. 5300], Paxton et al. 1989:526 [ref. 12442]). Plesiopidae.

Trachinostomias (subgenus of *Photonectes*) Parr 1927:105 [ref. 3367]. Masc. *Echiostoma margarita* Goode & Bean 1896:109. Type by subsequent designation. "*P. marginata*... and...*P. flagellatus*... may be regarded as the type species"; therefore no type designated. Earliest type designation not researched. Synonym of *Photonectes* Günther 1887, but as a valid subgenus (Morrow in Morrow & Gibbs 1964:488, 489 [ref. 6962]). Melanostomiidae.

Trachinotus Lacepède 1801:78 [ref. 2710]. Masc. *Scomber falcatus* Forsskål 1775:57. Type by monotypy. *Trachynotus* Agassiz 1846:373, 374 [ref. 64] and authors is an unjustified emendation; as emended is apparently preoccupied by Latreille 1829 in Coleoptera and Gravenhorst 1829 in Hymenoptera. Type species also preoccupied; next available name is *Caesiomorus blochii* Lacepède 1801. Valid (Hureau & Tortonese 1973:383 [ref. 7198] as *Trachynotus*, Gushiken in Masuda et al. 1984:154 [ref. 6441], Smith-Vaniz 1986:658 [ref. 5718], Daget & Smith-Vaniz 1986:319 [ref. 6207]). Carangidae.

Trachinus Linnaeus 1758:250 [ref. 2787]. Masc. *Trachinus draco* Linnaeus 1758:250. Type by monotypy. *Trachynus* Minding 1832:87 [ref. 3022] is an incorrect subsequent spelling. On Official List (Opinion 75). Valid (Wheeler 1973:449 [ref. 7190], Bentivegna & Fiorito 1983 [ref. 12849], Tortonese in Whitehead et al. 1986:952 [ref. 13676]). Trachinidae.

Trachinus Swainson 1839:247, 249 [ref. 4303]. Four species mentioned; genus appears to be a mixture of species now assigned to other genera. Subsequent type designation not researched. Not available, preoccupied by Linnaeus 1758. Treated by Swain 1883:276 [ref. 5966] as "Evidently a misprint for *Trachurus*." Carangidae.

Trachipterus Goüan 1770:104, 153 [ref. 1863]. Masc. *Cepola trachyptera* Gmelin 1789:1187. Appeared first without included species. Spelled *Trachyterus* by Bloch & Schneider 1801:480 [ref. 471], and *Trachypterus* by Cuvier 1816:235 [ref. 993]. Valid (Palmer 1973:330 [ref. 7195], Scott 1983:172 [ref. 5346], Olney 1984:369 [ref. 13656], Heemstra & Kannemeyer 1984:17 [ref. 5349], Fujii in Masuda et al. 1984:117 [ref. 6441], Palmer in Whitehead et al. 1986:729 [ref. 13676], Heemstra & Kannemeyer 1986:400 [ref. 5666], Paxton et al. 1989:400 [ref. 12442]). Trachipteridae.

Trachonurus (subgenus of *Macrurus*) Günther 1887:124, 142 [ref. 2013]. Masc. *Coryphaenoides villosus* Günther 1877:441. Type by monotypy. Valid (Marshall 1973:290 [ref. 7194], Marshall 1973:619 [ref. 6965], Fahay & Markle 1984:274 [ref. 13653], Okamura in Masuda et al. 1984:95 [ref. 6441], Geistdoerfer in Whitehead et al. 1986:674 [ref. 13676], Iwamoto 1986:340 [ref. 5674], Paxton et al. 1989:329 [ref. 12442]). Macrouridae: Macrourinae.

Trachurops Gill 1862:238 [ref. 1664]. Masc. *Scomber plumieri* Bloch 1793:77. Type by monotypy. Type not *Scomber crumenophthalmus* as given by Gill 1863:432 [ref. 1669]. Proposed in 1862:238 with only *Caranx plumieri* mentioned. Synonym of *Selar* Bleeker 1851. Carangidae.

Trachurus Gronow in Gray 1854:124 [ref. 1911]. Masc. *Trachurus trachurus* Linnaeus 1766:494. Type by absolute tautonymy, *trachurus* included by Gronow in synonymy of *T. europaeus* Gronow on p. 125. Type not *Trachurus cordyla* Gronow 1854 as given by Jordan 1919:259 [ref. 2410]. In the synonymy of *Trachurus* Rafinesque 1810. Carangidae.

Trachurus Plumier in Lacepède 1801:84 (footnote) [ref. 2710]. Masc. Not available; Plumier manuscript name mentioned in passing under *Caranxomorus plumierianus*. See remarks under Opinion 89 in Appendix B. In the synonymy of *Trachurus* Rafinesque 1810. Carangidae.

Trachurus Rafinesque 1810:41 [ref. 3594]. Masc. *Trachurus saurus* Rafinesque 1810:41. Type by subsequent designation. Type not *Scomber trachurus* Linnaeus 1758, not an included species or cited synonym; Whitley 1935:137 [ref. 6396] determined that Lesson, v. 16, 1830:328 [ref. 13391] first designated *saurus* as type (see Berry & Cohen 1974:184-185 [ref. 7489]). *Trachyurus* Agassiz 1846:374 [ref. 64] is an unjustified emendation. Valid (Hureau & Tortonese 1973:380 [ref. 7198], Smith-Vaniz 1986:659 [ref. 5718], Ben Salem 1988 [ref. 6736], Paxton et al. 1989:586 [ref. 12442]). Carangidae.

Trachyberyx Roule 1929:2 [ref. 3822]. Masc. *Trachyberyx barretoi* Roule 1929:2. Type by monotypy. Synonym of *Taractes* Lowe 1843 (Mead 1972:16 [ref. 6976], Mead 1973:386 [ref. 7199]). Bramidae.

Trachybrama Bleeker 1863:210 [ref. 397]. Fem. *Acanthobrama marmid* Heckel 1843:1075. Not available, name published in synonymy of *Acanthobrama* Heckel; apparently never made available. Cyprinidae.

Trachycephalus De Vis 1884:455 [ref. 1089]. Masc. *Trachycephalus bankiensis* De Vis 1884:456. Type by monotypy. Preoccupied by Tschudi 1838 in batrachians, apparently not replaced. Synonym of *Caracanthus* Krøyer 1845. Caracanthidae.

Trachycorystes Bleeker 1858:200, 205, 208 [ref. 365]. Masc. *Auchenipterus trachycorystes* Valenciennes in Cuvier & Valenciennes 1840:214. Type by absolute tautonymy. Valid (Mees 1974:26 [ref. 2969], Burgess 1989:242 [ref. 12860], Curran 1989 [ref. 12547]). Auchenipteridae.

Trachydoras Eigenmann 1925:306, 337 [ref. 1244]. Masc. *Trachydoras atripes* Eigenmann 1925:339. Type by original designation. Valid (Burgess 1989:223 [ref. 12860]). Doradidae.

Trachyglanis Boulenger 1902:48 [ref. 562]. Masc. *Trachyglanis minutus* Boulenger 1902:49. Type by monotypy. Valid (Skelton & Teugels 1986:64 [ref. 6192], Burgess 1989:114 [ref. 12860]). Amphiliidae.

Trachymochlus Hoedeman 1961:137 [ref. 11969]. Masc. *Trachymochlus cupido* Hoedeman 1961:137. Type by monotypy. Placement uncertain, not an auchenipterid; perhaps with wrong locality (see Mees 1974:14 [ref. 2969]). Auchenipteridae.

Trachypoma Giebel 1871:97 [ref. 1616]. Neut. *Trachypoma marmoratum* Geibel 1871:97. Type by original designation (also monotypic). Preoccupied by Günther 1859 in fishes; not replaced. Synonym of *Eremophilus* Humboldt 1805. Trichomycteridae.

Trachypoma Günther 1859:167 [ref. 1961]. Neut. *Trachypoma macracanthus* Günther 1859:167. Type by monotypy. Valid (Paxton et al. 1989:500 [ref. 12442]). Serranidae.

Trachypterophrys Franz 1910:60 [ref. 1481]. Fem. *Trachypterophrys raptator* Franz 1910:60. Type by monotypy. Synonym of *Chascanopsetta* Alcock 1894 (Norman 1934:249 [ref. 6893], Amaoka & Yamamoto 1984:202 [ref. 5632]). Bothidae: Bothinae.

Trachypterus Bloch & Schneider 1801:480 [ref. 471]. Masc. *Trachypterus taenia* Bloch & Schneider 1801:480. Type by subsequent designation. Apparently not an original description, as Goüan is cited; best regarded as an incorrect subsequent spelling of *Trachipterus* Goüan. Synonym of *Trachipterus* Goüan 1770 (see Scott 1983:172 [ref. 5346]). Trachipteridae.

Trachyrhamphus Kaup 1853:231 [ref. 2569]. Masc. *Syngnathus serratus* Temminck & Schlegel 1850:272. Type by monotypy - only one available species among three included. As *Trachyrhynchus* Kaup 1856:25 (name only). Spelled *Trachyrrhamphus* by Duncker 1902:232 [not researched]. Valid (Dawson 1984 [ref. 5291], Araga in Masuda et al. 1984:88 [ref. 6441], Dawson 1985:190 [ref. 6541], Dawson 1986:457 [ref. 5650], Paxton et al. 1989:431 [ref. 12442]). Syngnathidae: Syngnathinae.

Trachyrincus Giorna 1809:179 [ref. 1808]. Masc. *Lepidoleprus trachyrincus* Risso 1810:197. Type by subsequent designation. Giorna's species "Trachyrinque-Anonyme" not latinized and unavailable; Risso 1810:197 named it *Lepidoleprus trachyrincus* but technically did not fix type; included species may date to Günther 1864:152 [ref. 2013]; type designation may date to Jordan 1917:74 [ref. 2407]. Spelled *Trachyrhynchus* by authors. Valid (Marshall 1973:287 [ref. 7194], Marshall & Iwamoto 1973:516 [ref. 6963], Iwamoto 1986:340 [ref. 5674], Paxton et al. 1989:329 [ref. 12442]).

Macrouridae: Trachyrincinae.

Trachyscorpia Ginsburg 1953:23, 57 [ref. 1807]. Fem. *Scorpaena cristulata* Goode & Bean 1896:246. Type by original designation. Valid (Blanc & Hureau 1973:585 [ref. 7218], Washington et al. 1984:440 [ref. 13660], Hureau & Litvinenko in Whitehead et al. 1986:1228 [ref. 13677], Eschmeyer 1986:477 [ref. 5652]). Scorpaenidae: Sebastolobinae.

Trachystoma Ogilby 1888:614 [ref. 3264]. Neut. *Trachystoma multidens* Ogilby 1888:614. Type by monotypy. Mugilidae.

Tragulichthys Whitley 1931:125 [ref. 4673]. Masc. *Diodon jaculiferus* Cuvier 1818:130. Type by original designation (also monotypic). Synonym of *Diodon* Linnaeus 1758, but as a valid subgenus (Fraser-Brunner 1943:17 [ref. 1495]); valid genus (Leis 1984:448 [ref. 13659]). Diodontidae.

Tramitichromis Eccles & Trewavas 1989:256 [ref. 13547]. Masc. *Tilapia brevis* Boulenger 1908:248. Type by original designation. Cichlidae.

Travancoria Hora 1941:228 [ref. 2212]. Fem. *Travancoria jonesi* Hora 1941:230. Type by original designation (also monotypic). Valid (Silas 1953:203 [ref. 4024], Jayaram 1981:143 [ref. 6497], Sawada 1982:205 [ref. 14111], Menon 1987:236 [ref. 14149]). Balitoridae: Balitorinae.

Trematocara Boulenger 1899:89 [ref. 550]. Neut. *Trematocara marginatum* Boulenger 1899:89. Type by monotypy. Valid (Bailey & Stewart 1977:24 [ref. 7230], Poll 1986:120 [ref. 6136]). Cichlidae.

Trematochromis Poll 1987:168 [ref. 6746]. Masc. *Trematochromis schreyeni* Poll 1987:169. Type by original designation (also monotypic). Cichlidae.

Trematocranus Trewavas 1935:(68) 113 [ref. 4451]. Masc. *Trematocranus microstoma* Trewavas 1935:114. Type by original designation. Valid (see Stauffer & McKaye 1988:448 [ref. 6412], Eccles & Trewavas 1989:188 [ref. 13547]). Cichlidae.

Trematomus Boulenger 1902:177 [ref. 561]. Masc. *Trematomus newnesi* Boulenger 1920:177. Type by subsequent designation. Earliest type designation not researched; genus not treated by Jordan. Valid (Andersen 1984:24 [ref. 13369]). Nototheniidae.

Trematopsis Ranzani 1839:table [ref. 3605]. Fem. *Trematopsis willughbei* Ranzani 1839:table. Type by monotypy. Synonym of *Mola* Koelreuter 1770 (Fraser-Brunner 1943:8 [ref. 1495]). Molidae.

Trematorhynchus Regan & Trewavas 1932:91 [ref. 3682]. Masc. *Rhynchoceratias leucorhinus* Regan 1925. Type by subsequent designation. Not available from Regan & Trewavas 1932 (Art. 13b). Can date to treatment in the Zoological Record for 1932 where a type was designated (see remarks for Art. 13b in Appendix A). Oneirodidae.

Trewavasia (subgenus of *Tilapia*) Thys van den Audenaerde 1970:290 [ref. 12518]. Fem. Not available, name only; subsequent publication not researched; not made available by Trewavas 1973:15 [ref. 4458]. Also preoccupied by White & Moy-Thomas 1941 in fossil fishes. Cichlidae.

Triacanthodes Bleeker 1858:37 [ref. 360]. Masc. *Triacanthus anomalus* Temminck & Schlegel 1850:295. Type by original designation (also monotypic). Valid (Tyler 1968:114 [ref. 6438], Tyler 1980:56 [ref. 4477], Matsuura in Masuda et al. 1984:357 [ref. 6441], Tyler 1986:889 [ref. 5723]). Triacanthodidae.

Triacanthurodes Fowler 1944:332 [ref. 1448]. Masc. *Naseus laticlavius* Valenciennes 1846:Pl. 7, fig.2. Type by original designation (also monotypic). Synonym of *Prionurus* Lacepède 1804 (Randall 1955:362 [ref. 13648]). Acanthuridae.

Triacanthus Oken (ex Cuvier) 1817:1183 [ref. 3303]. Masc. *Balistes biaculeatus* Bloch 1786:17. Type by monotypy. Based on "Les Triacanthes" Cuvier 1816:153 [ref. 995]. See Gill 1903:966 [ref. 5768]. Valid (Tyler 1968:253 [ref. 6438], Tyler 1980:98 [ref. 4477], Matsuura in Masuda et al. 1984:357 [ref. 6441], Kottelat 1989:21 [ref. 13605]). Triacanthidae.

Triacis Agassiz 1846:375 [ref. 64]. Fem. Unjustified emendation of *Triakis* Müller & Henle 1939. Triakidae: Triakinae.

Triaenodon Müller & Henle 1837:113 [ref. 3067]. Masc. *Carcharias obesus* Rüppell 1837:64. Type by subsequent monotypy. Appeared first without species as above, one species added by Bonaparte 1838:212 (p. 11 of separate) [ref. 4979] and species apparently designated type (see p. 2 of separate). Also appeared in Müller & Henle 1839:55 [ref. 3069]. Valid (Compagno 1984:535 [ref. 6846], Nakaya in Masuda et al. 1984:6 [ref. 6441], Bass et al. 1986:86 [ref. 5638], Compagno 1988:351 [ref. 13488], Paxton et al. 1989:84 [ref. 12442]). Carcharhinidae.

Triaenophorichthys Gill 1859:195 [ref. 1758]. Masc. *Triaenophorus trigonocephalus* Gill 1858:17. Type by being a replacement name. Replacement for *Triaenophorus* Gill 1859, preoccupied by Rudolphi 1793 in helminths. Synonym of *Tridentiger* Gill 1859. Gobiidae.

Triaenophorus Gill 1859:17 [ref. 1753]. Masc. *Triaenophorus trigonocephalus* Gill 1859:17. Type by monotypy. Preoccupied by Rudolphi 1793 in helminths, replaced by *Triaenophorichthys* Gill 1859. Synonym of *Tridentiger* Gill 1859. Gobiidae.

Triaenopogon Bleeker 1874:312 [ref. 437]. Masc. *Triaenophorichthys barbatus* Günther 1861:194. Type by original designation (also monotypic). Synonym of *Tridentiger* Gill 1859 (Hoese, pers. comm.). Gobiidae.

Triakis Müller & Henle 1838:36 [ref. 3066]. Fem. *Triakis scyllium* Müller & Henle 1839:63. Type by subsequent monotypy. Appeared first without species, species added in Müller & Henle 1939:63 [ref. 3069]; also one species [perhaps first] in Bonaparte 1838:10 (of separate) [ref. 4979]. *Triacis* Agassiz 1846:375 [ref. 64] and Gill 1862 are unjustified emendations. Valid (Compagno 1984:428 [ref. 6846], Nakaya in Masuda et al. 1984:5 [ref. 6441], Bass et al. 1986:86 [ref. 5638], Cappetta 1987:117 [ref. 6348], Herman et al. 1988:100 [ref. 13267], Compagno 1988:212 [ref. 13488]). Triakidae: Triakinae.

Trianectes McCulloch & Waite 1918:53 [ref. 2950]. Masc. *Trianectes bucephalus* McCulloch & Waite 1918:53. Type by original designation (also monotypic). Valid. Tripterygiidae.

Triantennatus (subgenus of *Phrynelox*) Schultz 1957:(56) 74 [ref. 3969]. Masc. *Antennarius zebrinus* Schultz 1957:75. Type by original designation. Synonym of *Antennarius* Daudin 1816 (Pietsch 1984:34 [ref. 5380]). Antennariidae.

Triarcus Waite 1910:387 [ref. 4566]. Masc. *Maurolicus australis* Hector 1875:250. Type by monotypy. Misspelled *Triareus* by Jordan 1920:537 [ref. 4905] and *Tricarus* in Zoological Record for 1910. Synonym of *Maurolicus* Cocco 1838 (Witzell 1973:119 [ref. 7172]). Sternoptychidae: Maurolicinae.

Triathalassothia Fowler 1943:330 [ref. 1444]. Fem. *Triathalassothia devincenzii* Fowler 1943:330. Type by original designation (also monotypic). Valid (Greenfield & Greenfield 1973 [ref. 7128]). Batrachoididae.

Tribolodon Sauvage 1883:149 [ref. 3896]. Masc. *Tribolodon punctatus* Sauvage 1883:149. Type by monotypy. Valid (Sawada in

Masuda et al. 1984:56 [ref. 6441], Bogutskaya 1987:936 [ref. 13521]). Cyprinidae.

Tribranchus Müller 1844:193 [ref. 13283]. Masc. *Tribranchus anguillaris* Müller 1846:193. Type by monotypy. Original not seen. Synonym of *Anguilla* Schrank 1798 (Blache et al. 1973:220 [ref. 7185], Castle 1984:34 [ref. 6171], Smith 1989:32 [ref. 13285]). Anguillidae.

Trichidion Gill (ex Klein) 1861:40 [ref. 1766]. Neut. *Polynemus americanus* of Storer (= *Polynemus virginicus* Linnaeus 1758:317). Type by monotypy. Synonym of *Polynemus* Linnaeus 1758 (Daget & Njock 1986:353 [ref. 6216]). Polynemidae.

Trichidion Klein 1776:592 [ref. 4919]. Neut. Not available, published in a work that does not conform to the principle of binominal nomenclature. In the synonymy of *Polynemus* Linnaeus 1758 (Daget & Njock 1986:353 [ref. 6216]). Polynemidae.

Trichis Plumier in Lacepède 1803:448 [ref. 4930]. Fem. *Trichis bellonii* Plumier in Lacepède 1803:448. Not available, name without description published under *Clupea alosa*. See remarks under Opinion 89 in Appendix B. In the synonymy of *Alosa* Linck 1790. Clupeidae.

Trichiurus Linnaeus 1758:246 [ref. 2787]. Masc. *Trichiurus lepturus* Linnaeus 1758:246. Type by monotypy. Valid (Collette et al. 1984:600 [ref. 11421], Nakamura in Masuda et al. 1984:228 [ref. 6441], Parin in Whitehead et al. 1986:979 [ref. 13676], Nakamura 1986:830 [ref. 5696]). Trichiuridae: Trichiurinae.

Trichobrachirus Chabanaud 1943:292 [ref. 799]. Masc. *Synaptura villosa* Weber 1908. Type by original designation (also monotypic). Soleidae.

Trichochirus (subgenus of *Bathophilus*) Regan & Trewavas 1930:65 [ref. 3681]. Masc. *Bathophilus pawneei* Parr 1927:88. Type by subsequent designation. Type designated in Zoological Record for 1930 (Pisces):47. Stomiidae.

Trichocottus Soldatov & Pavlenko 1915:151 [ref. 4165]. Masc. *Trichocottus brashnikovi* Soldatov & Pavlenko 1915:152. Type by original designation (also monotypic). Valid (Neyelov 1979:115, 143 [ref. 3152], Yabe 1985:111 [ref. 11522]). Cottidae.

Trichocyclus Günther 1870:316 [ref. 1995]. Masc. *Trichocyclus erinaceus* Günther 1870:316. Type by monotypy. Synonym of *Diodon* Linnaeus 1758 (Fraser-Brunner 1943:17 [ref. 1495], Leis 1978:538 [ref. 5529]). Diodontidae.

Trichoderma (subgenus of *Monocanthus (sic)*) Swainson 1839:194, 328 [ref. 4303]. Neut. *Balistes scapus* Lacepède 1798:Pl. 18. Type by subsequent designation. Type designated by Swain 1882:283 [ref. 5966]. Synonym of *Amanses* Gray 1835 (Randall 1964:333 [ref. 3148]). Monacanthidae.

Trichodiodon Bleeker 1865:49 [ref. 416]. Masc. *Diodon pilosus* Mitchill 1815:471. Type by original designation (also monotypic). Also in Bleeker 1866:18 [ref. 417]. Synonym of *Diodon* Linnaeus 1758 (Fraser-Brunner 1943:17 [ref. 1495], Leis 1978:538 [ref. 5529]). Diodontidae.

Trichodon Tilesius (ex Steller) 1813:468 [ref. 13413]. Masc. *Trachinus trichodon* Tilesius (ex Steller) 1813:Pl. 15. Type by subsequent monotypy. Appeared as a name first published in synonymy of *Trachinus*; made available back to this date by later use as a valid taxon. Appeared under heading "*Trachinus gasteropelecus* vel *Trichodon Stelleri*" on p. 466; species as *Drachinus trichodon* on p. 406, and as *Trachinus trichodon* on P. 15. First subsequent valid use and technical addition of species probably by Cuvier 1829:149 [ref. 995]. Steller extensively quoted; authorship perhaps could be Steller. Valid. Trichodontidae.

Trichogaster Bloch & Schneider 1801:164 [ref. 471]. Fem. *Trichogaster fasciatus* Bloch & Schneider 1801:164. Type by subsequent designation. Two originally-included species are *fasciatus* and *trichopterus*; type not designated by Cuvier in Cuvier & Valenciennes; earliest subsequent designation not researched; *fasciatus* listed by Jordan 1917:58 [ref. 2407]. Myer's 1923:112 [ref. 12875] analysis of type apparently in error. Treated as valid (Kottelat 1985:275 [ref. 11441], Kottelat 1989:20 [ref. 13605], Roberts 1989:177 [ref. 6439] with type as *trichopterus*). Belontiidae.

Trichogenes Britski & Ortega 1983:211 [ref. 5408]. *Trichogenes longipinnis* Britski & Ortega 1983:212. Type by original designation (also monotypic). Valid (Burgess 1989:323 [ref. 12860], Pinna 1989:27 [ref. 12630]). Trichomycteridae.

Trichomycterus (subgenus of *Eremophilus*) Valenciennes in Humboldt 1833:348 [ref. 4503]. Masc. *Trichomycterus nigricans* Valenciennes in Cuvier & Valenciennes 1846:494. Type by monotypy. Original not seen. Spelled once (p. 485) as *Thrychomycterus* by Valenciennes in Cuvier & Valenciennes 1846:485 [ref. 1011], and as *Thrichomycterus* in early literature. Valid (Arratia et al. 1978 [ref. 144] with type as *areolatus*, Pinna 1989:31 [ref. 12630], Burgess 1989:321 [ref. 12860], Malabarba 1989:146 [ref. 14217]). Trichomycteridae.

Trichonotops Schultz in Schultz et al. 1960:276 [ref. 3972]. Masc. *Taeniolabrus marleyi* Smith 1936:4. Type by original designation (also monotypic). Synonym of *Trichonotus* Bloch & Schneider 1801 (Nelson 1986:1 [ref. 5153]). Trichonotidae.

Trichonotus Bloch & Schneider 1801:179 [ref. 471]. Masc. *Trichonotus setiger* Bloch & Schneider 1801:179. Type by monotypy. Valid (Shimada & Yoshino 1984 [ref. 6733], Yoshino & Shimada in Masuda et al. 1984:292 [ref. 6441], Heemstra 1986:736 [ref. 5660], Nelson 1986:1 [ref. 5153]). Trichonotidae.

Trichonotus Rafinesque 1815:88 [ref. 3584]. Masc. *Mugilomorus annacarolina* Lacepède 1803:397. Type by being a replacement name. As "*Trichonotus* R. [Rafinesque] *Mugiliomorus* Lac. [Lacepède]." An available replacement (unneeded) for *Mugliomorus* Lacepède 1803. Preoccupied by Bloch & Schneider 1801 in fishes. Objective synonym of *Mugilomorus* Lacepède 1803. Synonym of *Elops* Linnaeus 1766 (Daget 1984:30 [ref. 6170]). Elopidae.

Trichopharynx Ogilby 1898:769 [ref. 3275]. Masc. *Gobius crassilabris* Günther 1861:63. Type by original designation (also monotypic). Synonym of *Chonophorus* Poey 1860 (Maugé 1986:363 [ref. 6218]). A synonym of *Awaous* Valenciennes 1837; see remarks under *Chonophorus*. Gobiidae.

Trichophasia Swainson 1839:61 [ref. 4303]. Fem. *Synanceia elongata* Cuvier in Cuvier & Valenciennes 1829:456. Type implied from text, *Trichophasia* and *Trachicephalus* were both used by Swainson for same taxon; Gill (1905:224 [ref. 1789]) acts as first reviser, selecting *Trachicephalus*. Objective synonym of *Trachicephalus* Swainson 1839 (Eschmeyer & Rama-Rao 1973:372 [ref. 6391]). Scorpaenidae: Synanceiinae.

Trichophryne McCulloch & Waite 1918:68 [ref. 2950]. Fem. *Antennarius mitchellii* Morton 1897:98. Type by original designation (also monotypic). Valid (Pietsch 1984:39 [ref. 5380], Paxton et al. 1989:281 [ref. 12442]); synonym of *Echinophryne* McCulloch & Waite 1918 (Pietsch & Kuiter 1984:23 [ref. 5194]). Antennariidae.

Trichopleura Kaup 1858:338 [ref. 2580]. Fem. *Sthenopus mollis*

Richardson 1848:10. Type by being a replacement name. Unneeded replacement for *Sthenopus* Richardson 1848 (see Whitley 1933:101 [ref.4677]). Objective synonym of *Sthenopus* Richardson 1848 (Poss & Eschmeyer 1978:404 [ref. 6387]). Aploactinidae.

Trichopodus Lacepède 1801:125 [ref. 2710]. Masc. *Labrus trichopterus* Pallas 1770:45. Type by subsequent designation. Apparently type is *Labrus trichopterus* Pallas as designated by Bleeker 1879:21 [ref. 457] in text and not *T. mentum* of Lacepède. Spelled *Trichopus* by Shaw 1803:388 [ref. 4014]. See also Myers 1923:112 [ref. 12875]). Synonym of *Osphronemus* Lacepède 1801 if type is *mentum*; otherwise synonym of *Trichogaster* Bloch & Schneider 1801 in Belontiidae. Belontiidae.

Trichopsetta Gill 1889:601 [ref. 1730]. Fem. *Citharichthys ventralis* Goode & Bean 1886:592. Type by original designation (also monotypic). Valid (Norman 1934:160 [ref. 6893], Matsuura in Uyeno et al. 1983:454 [ref. 14275], Ahlstrom et al. 1984:642 [ref. 13641], Hensley 1986:941 [ref. 6326]). Bothidae: Taeniopsettinae.

Trichopsis Canestrini (ex Kner) 1860:708 [ref. 713]. Fem. *Trichopsis striatus* Bleeker 1850:106. Type by monotypy. Valid (Kottelat 1985:275 [ref. 11441], Kottelat 1989:20 [ref. 13605]). Belontiidae.

Trichopterus Gronow in Gray 1854:162 [ref. 1911]. Masc. *Trichopterus indicus* Gray 1854:162. Type by monotypy. Cheilodactylidae.

Trichopus Shaw 1803:392 [ref. 4014]. Masc. *Trichopus pallasii* Shaw 1803:392 (= *Labrus trichopterus* Pallas 1770:45). Type by subsequent designation. Earliest designation of type found that of Jordan 1917:73 [ref. 2407]. *Trichopus pallasii* is an unneeded substitute for *L. trichopterus*; perhaps genus just an emendation of *Trichopodus* Lacepède (see Myers 1923:112 [ref. 12875]). Synonym of *Osphronemus* Lacepède 1801 or of *Trichogaster* Bloch & Schneider 1801; see account of *Trichogaster*. Belontiidae.

Trichosoma Swainson 1838:281 et seq. [ref. 4302]. Neut. *Colisa hamiltonii* Gray 1831:9. Type by monotypy. Also in Swainson 1839:186 and 292 [ref. 4303] (as a subgenus of *Osteoglossum*). Not *Trichosomus* Swainson 1839:65 and 71 (misspelled *Trichosoma*), 180, 265. Preoccupied by Rudolphi 1819 in Vermes, Rambur 1833 in Lepidoptera. Synonym of *Thryssa* Cuvier 1829 (Whitehead et al. 1988:421 [ref. 5725]). Engraulidae.

Trichosomus (subgenus of *Apistes*) Swainson 1839:180, 265 [ref. 4303]. Masc. *Apistus trachinoides* Cuvier in Cuvier & Valenciennes 1829:401. Type by subsequent designation. Misspelled *Trichosoma* on p. 65, 71 (not same as the engraulid *Trichosoma* Swainson 1838). Type designated by Swain 1882:277 [ref. 5966]. Scorpaenidae: Apistinae.

Trichostomias Zugmayer 1911:6 [ref. 6161]. Masc. *Trichostomias vaillanti* Zugmayer 1911:6. Type by monotypy. Also appeared in Zugmayer 1911 (Dec.):78 [ref. 4846]. Synonym of *Bathophilus* Giglioli 1882 (Morrow in Morrow & Gibbs 1964:456 [ref. 6962], Morrow 1973:135 [ref. 7175]). Melanostomiidae.

Triclonostomias (subgenus of *Eustomias*) Regan & Trewavas 1930:73, 95 [ref. 3681]. Masc. *Eustomias drechseli* Regan & Trewavas 1930:95. Type by original designation. Synonym of *Eustomias* Vaillant 1888 (Gibbs in Morrow & Gibbs 1964:377 [ref. 6962], Morrow 1973:138 [ref. 7175]). Melanostomiidae.

Tricropterus Rafinesque 1810:41 [ref. 3594]. Masc. *Scomber carangus* Bloch 1793:69. Type by subsequent designation. Originally without species, species added and type designated by Jordan 1917:79 [ref. 2407]. Spelled *Trichopterus* by Agassiz 1845: 66 [ref. 4889] on Rafinesque 1815. Objective synonym of *Caranx* Lacepède 1801 (Daget & Smith-Vaniz 1986:310 [ref. 6207]). Carangidae.

Tricuspidalestes Poll 1967:142 [ref. 3529]. Masc. *Phenacogrammus caeruleus* Matthes 1964:53. Type by original designation (also monotypic). Valid (Géry 1977:38 [ref. 1597], Paugy 1984:183 [ref. 6183]). Alestiidae.

Tricuspidatus de Buen 1926:86 [ref. 5054]. As a "grupo" for 2 species of *Callionymus*. Not available on basis of Art. 1b(6) [see de Buen's definition of "grupo" on p. 11]; see Appendix A. Callionymidae.

Tridens Eigenmann & Eigenmann 1889:53 [ref. 1253]. Masc. *Tridens melanops* Eigenmann & Eigenmann 1889:53. Type by original designation. Valid (Burgess 1989:325 [ref. 12860]). Trichomycteridae.

Tridensimilis Schultz 1944:(257) 266 [ref. 3959]. Masc. *Tridensimilis venezuelae* Schultz 1944:267. Type by original designation. Valid (Burgess 1989:325 [ref. 12860], Pinna 1989 [ref. 12630]). Trichomycteridae.

Tridentiger Gill 1859:16 [ref. 1753]. Masc. *Sicydium obscurum* Temminck & Schlegel 1845:145. Type by original designation. See also *Trigonocephalus* Okada 1961. Valid (Akihito in Masuda et al. 1984:271 [ref. 6441], Birdsong et al. 1988:203 [ref. 7303], Akihito & Sakamoto 1989 [ref. 14124]). Gobiidae.

Tridentopsis Myers 1925:84 [ref. 3093]. Fem. *Tridentopsis pearsoni* Myers 1925:84. Type by original designation. Valid (Burgess 1989:325 [ref. 12860], Pinna 1989 [ref. 12630]). Trichomycteridae.

Tridontochromis (subgenus of *Prognathochromis*) Greenwood 1980: 20 [ref. 1899]. Masc. *Haplochromis tridens* Regan & Trewavas 1928:226. Type by original designation. Cichlidae.

Trifarcius Poey 1860:305 [ref. 3499]. Masc. *Trifarcius riverendi* Poey 1860:306. Type by monotypy. Synonym of *Cyprinodon* Lacepède 1803 (Parenti 1981:526 [ref. 7066]). Cyprinodontidae: Cyprinodontinae.

Trifissus Jordan & Snyder 1900:373 [ref. 2502]. Masc. *Trifissus ioturus* Jordan & Snyder 1900:373. Type by original designation (also monotypic). Synonym of *Tridentiger* Gill 1859 (Akihito & Sakamoto 1989:101 [ref. 14124]). Gobiidae.

Trigla Linnaeus 1758:300 [ref. 2787]. Fem. *Trigla lyra* Linnaeus 1758:300. Type by subsequent designation. Type designated by Jordan & Gilbert 1883:733 [ref. 2476]. Valid (Blanc & Hureau 1973:586 [ref. 7218], Hureau in Whitehead et al. 1986:1235 [ref. 13677], Heemstra 1986:488 [ref. 5660]). Triglidae: Triglinae.

Triglachromis Poll & Thys van den Audenaerde 1974:128 [ref. 3539]. Masc. *Limnochromis otostigma* Regan 1920:152. Type by original designation (also monotypic). Valid (Poll 1981:167 [ref. 3534], Poll 1986:135 [ref. 6136]). Cichlidae.

Triglochis Müller & Henle 1837:113 [ref. 3067]. *Carcharias taurus* Rafinesque 1810:10. Type by monotypy. Suppressed for purposes of priority but not homonymy and placed on Official List (Opinion 723). Synonym of *Carcharias* Rafinesque 1810 (see account of *Odontaspis*). Apparently wrongly treated as a synonym of *Synodontaspis* by Cappetta 1987:90 [ref. 6348]). Odontaspididae: Odontaspidinae.

Trigloporus (subgenus of *Trigla*) Smith 1934:333 [ref. 4065]. Masc. *Trigla africana* Smith 1934:334. Type by original designation. Valid (Blanc & Hureau 1973:589 [ref. 7218], Heemstra 1982:294 [ref. 5416], Hureau in Whitehead et al. 1986:1237 [ref. 13677],

Heemstra 1986:488 [ref. 5660]). Triglidae: Triglinae.

Triglops Reinhardt 1831:18 [ref. 6533]. Masc. *Triglops pingeli* Reinhardt 1831. Type by monotypy. Original not examined. May have appeared a second time as 1832:52. Valid (Neyelov 1973:601 [ref. 7219], Washington et al. 1984:443 [ref. 13660], Yabe in Masuda et al. 1984:325 [ref. 6441], Yabe 1985:111 [ref. 11522], Fedorov in Whitehead et al. 1986:1256 [ref. 13677]). Cottidae.

Triglopsis Girard 1851:18 [ref. 1816]. Fem. *Triglopsis thompsonii* Girard 1851:19. Type by monotypy. *Ptyonotus* Günther 1860 is an unneeded replacement. Synonym of *Myoxocephalus* Tilesius 1811 (authors); valid (Neyelov 1979:115, 131 [ref. 3152], Fedorov in Whitehead et al. 1986:1259 [ref. 13677]). Cottidae.

Trigonectes Myers 1925:371 [ref. 5744]. Masc. *Trigonectes strigabundus* Myers 1925:371. Type regarded as by monotypy; possible synonyms mentioned. Also appeared in more detail in Myers 1927:128-129 [ref. 3098]. Valid (Parenti 1981:484 [ref. 7066]). Aplocheilidae: Rivulinae.

Trigonocephalus Okada 1961:265 [ref. 6363]. Masc. Not available, no type designated. Apparently a mistake for *Tridentiger* (see Hubbs 1962:238 [ref. 6362] and Whitley 1967:49 [ref. 4735]). Gobiidae.

Trigonolampa Regan & Trewavas 1930:55 [ref. 3681]. Fem. *Trigonolampa miriceps* Regan & Trewavas 1930:55. Type by monotypy. Valid (Morrow in Morrow & Gibbs 1964:371 [ref. 6962], Morrow 1973:141 [ref. 7175], Kawaguchi & Moser 1984:171 [ref. 13642], Gibbs in Whitehead et al. 1984:364 [ref. 13675], Fink 1985:11 [ref. 5171], Gibbs 1986:243 [ref. 5655], Paxton et al. 1989:203 [ref. 12442]). Melanostomiidae.

Trigonophallus Hubbs 1926:48 [ref. 2233]. Masc. *Trigonophallus punctifer* Hubbs 1926:49. Type by original designation (also monotypic). Synonym of *Brachyrhaphis* Regan 1913 (Rosen & Bailey 1963:81 [ref. 7067]). Poeciliidae.

Trigrammnus Gracianov 1907:418 [ref. 1871]. Masc. *Ernogrammus storoshi* Schmidt 1904:193. Type by original designation. Original not seen. Spelled *Trigrammus* by Jordan (perhaps correct) and species *stroshi*; *Trigrammnus* and species *storoshi* in Zoological Record for 1907. Stichaeidae.

Trikeras Harless 1850:841 [ref. 5068]. *Myliobates marginata* Geoffroy St. Hilaire 1809. Original not translated; apparently not available. In the synonymy of *Rhinoptera* Cuvier 1829 (Cappetta 1987:173 [ref. 6348]). Myliobatidae.

Triloburus Gill 1861:30 [ref. 1766]. Masc. *Centropristis trifurca* of Storer 1846 (= *Perca trifurca* Linnaeus 1766:489). Type by monotypy. Synonym of *Centropristis* Cuvier 1829. Serranidae: Serraninae.

Trimma Jordan & Seale 1906:391 [ref. 2497]. Neut. *Trimma caesiura* Jordan & Seale 1906:391. Type by original designation (also monotypic). Valid (Yoshino & Shimada in Masuda et al. 1984:244 [ref. 6441], Winterbottom 1984 [ref. 5321], Hoese 1986:805 [ref. 5670], Birdsong et al. 1988:194 [ref. 7303]). Gobiidae.

Trimmatom Winterbottom & Emery 1981:140 [ref. 4757]. Masc. *Trimmatom nanus* Winterbottom & Emery 1981:143. Type by original designation. Valid (Winterbottom 1989 [ref. 14487]). Gobiidae.

Trinectes Rafinesque 1832:20 [ref. 3593]. Masc. *Trinectes scabra* Rafinesque 1832:20. Type by monotypy. Valid. Achiridae.

Trinematichthys (subgenus of *Luciosoma*) Bleeker 1860:283, 412, 416 [ref. 380]. Masc. *Leuciscus trinema* Bleeker 1852:600. Appeared first as name only as a subgenus of *Luciosoma* in Bleeker 1859:433 [ref. 370]; apparently dates to Bleeker 1860:283 as above, with type by monotypy in subgenus. Synonym of *Luciosoma* Bleeker 1855 (Roberts 1989:42 [ref. 6439]). Cyprinidae.

Triodon Cuvier 1829:370 [ref. 995]. Masc. *Triodon macropterus* Lesson 1830:103. Type by monotypy. *Triodon bursarius* Reinwardt is mentioned by Cuvier in parentheses in passing; *T. macropterus* the only available species included. Valid (see Tyler 1980:243 et seq. [ref. 4477], Matsuura in Masuda et al. 1984:362 [ref. 6441], Smith 1986:894 [ref. 5712]). Triodontidae.

Triorus Jordan & Hubbs 1925:256 [ref. 2486]. Masc. *Lactophrys tritropis* Snyder 1911:535. Type by original designation (also monotypic). Type designated as *L. tritropis* Snyder = *Ostracion stellifer* Bloch; type clearly is *tritropis* (see also Jordan & Hubbs p. 96). Ostraciidae: Ostraciinae.

Tripennata de Buen 1926:77 [ref. 5054]. As a "grupo" for 1 species of *Tripterygium*. Not available on basis of Art. 1b(6) [see de Buen's definition of "grupo" on p. 11]; see Appendix A. Tripterygiidae.

Triphoturus (subgenus of *Lampanyctus*) Fraser-Brunner 1949:1083 [ref. 1496]. Masc. *Myctophum (Lampanyctus) micropterum* Brauer 1906:239. Type by original designation. Valid (Paxton 1979:18 [ref. 6440], Moser et al. 1984:220 [ref. 13645], Fujii in Masuda et al. 1984:71 [ref. 6441], Hulley 1986:321 [ref. 5672], Paxton et al. 1989:269 [ref. 12442]). Myctophidae.

Triplophos Brauer 1902:282 [ref. 631]. Masc. *Triplophos elongatus* Brauer 1902:282. Type by monotypy. Valid (Weitzman 1974:472 [ref. 5174], Ahlstrom et al. 1984:185 [ref. 13643], Schaefer et al. 1986:253 [ref. 5709]). Gonostomatidae.

Triplophysa (subgenus of *Nemacheilus*) Rendahl 1933:21 [ref. 3704]. Fem. *Nemacheilus (Triplophysa) hutjertjuensis* Rendahl 1933:28. Type by original designation (also monotypic). Synonym of *Noemacheilus* Kuhl & van Hasselt 1823 (Jayaram 1981:159 [ref. 6497]); valid (Menon 1987:197 [ref. 14149], Wu 1987:110 [ref. 12824], Kottelat 1990:21 [ref. 14137]). Balitoridae: Nemacheilinae.

Tripodichthys Tyler 1968:298 [ref. 6438]. Masc. *Triacanthus blochi* Bleeker 1852:81. Type by original designation. Valid (Tyler 1980:98 [ref. 4477]). Triacanthidae.

Triportheus Cope 1872:263 [ref. 921]. Masc. *Triportheus albus* Cope 1872:264. Type by subsequent designation. Type designated by Jordan 1919:363 [ref. 4904]. Valid (Géry 1977:343 [ref. 1597]). Characidae.

Tripterodon Playfair in Playfair & Günther 1866:42 [ref. 3490]. Masc. *Tripterodon orbis* Playfair in Playfair & Günther 1866:42. Type by monotypy. Valid (Johnson 1984:464 [ref. 9681], Smith 1986:606 [ref. 5712]). Ephippidae.

Tripteronotus Lacepède 1803:47 [ref. 4930]. Masc. *Tripteronotus hautin* Lacepède 1803:47, 48. Type by monotypy. Synonym of *Coregonus* Linnaeus 1758. Salmonidae: Coregoninae.

Tripterophycis Boulenger 1902:335 [ref. 564]. Fem. *Tripterophycis gilchristi* Boulenger 1902:335. Type by monotypy. Also published in Boulenger 1903 (28 Feb.):168 [ref. 5757]. Valid (Paulin 1983:104 [ref. 5459], Fahay & Markle 1984:266 [ref. 13653], Cohen 1986:328 [ref. 5646], Sazonov & Shcherbachev 1986 [ref. 8047], Paxton et al. 1989:302 [ref. 12442]). Moridae.

Tripterygion Risso 1826:241 [ref. 3757]. Neut. *Tripterygion nasus* Risso 1826:241. Type by monotypy. Spelled *Tripterygium* and *Trypterygium* by early workers. Valid (Wheeler 1973:531 [ref. 7190], Yoshino in Masuda et al. 1984:294 [ref. 6441], Zander in

Whitehead et al. 1986:1118 [ref. 13677]). Tripterygiidae.

Triradulifer (subgenus of *Paratriacanthodes*) Fraser-Brunner 1941: 427 [ref. 1493]. Masc. *Paratriacanthodes herrei* Myers 1934:9. Type by original designation. Synonym of *Paratriacanthodes* Fowler 1934 (Tyler 1968:140 [ref. 6438]). Triacanthodidae.

Triscurrichthys Whitley 1931:327, 328 [ref. 4672]. Masc. *Trigla carolina* Linnaeus 1771:528. Type by being a replacement name. Unneeded replacement for *Merulinus* Jordan & Evermann 1898, not preoccupied by *Merulina* Ehrenberg 1834 in Coelenterata. Synonym of *Prionotus* Lacepède 1801. Triglidae: Triglinae.

Trismegistus Jordan & Snyder 1904:238 [ref. 2519]. Masc. *Trismegistus owstoni* Jordan & Snyder 1904:238. Type by monotypy. Misspelled *Trimegistus* in Zoological Record for 1904. Synonym of *Liparis* Scopoli 1777. Cyclopteridae: Liparinae.

Triso Randall, Johnson & Lowe 1989:415 [ref. 12737]. Masc. *Serranus dermopterus* Temminck & Schlegel 1842:10. Type by original designation (also monotypic). Serranidae: Epinephelinae.

Trisopterus Rafinesque 1814:16 [ref. 3582]. Masc. *Gadus capelanus* Lacepède 1800:366, 411 (= *Gadus minutus* Linnaeus 1758:253). Type by monotypy. Valid (Svetovidov 1973:309 [ref. 7169], Fahay & Markle 1984:267 [ref. 13653], Svetovidov in Whitehead et al. 1986:692 [ref. 13676]). Gadidae.

Trisotropis Gill 1865:104 [ref. 1710]. Fem. *Johnius guttatus* Bloch & Schneider 1801:77. Type by original designation. Valid (Kendall 1984:500 [ref. 13663], Katayama in Masuda et al. 1984:132 [ref. 6441]); synonym of *Mycteroperca* Gill 1862 (Smith 1971:171 [ref. 14102], Randall et al. 1989:414 [ref. 12737]). Serranidae: Epinephelinae.

Tristichodus Boulenger 1920:19 [ref. 587]. Masc. *Tristichodus christyi* Boulenger 1920:20. Type by monotypy. Synonym of *Microstomatichthyoborus* Nichols & Griscom 1917 (Daget & Gosse 1984:199 [ref. 6185]). Citharinidae: Distichodontinae.

Tristramella Trewavas 1942:532 [ref. 4452]. Fem. *Hemichromis sacra* Günther 1864:493. Type by being a replacement name. Replacement for *Parachromis* Regan 1922, preoccupied by Agassiz 1859. Misspelled *Tristamella* on p. 532, spelled *Tristramella* throughout article. Valid (Krupp & Schneider 1989:401 [ref. 13651]). Cichlidae.

Triurobrycon Eigenmann 1909:33 [ref. 1222]. Masc. *Brycon lundii* Reinhardt in Lütken 1874:135. Type by original designation (also monotypic). Synonym of *Brycon* Müller & Troschel 1844 (Howes 1982:4 [ref. 14201]). Characidae.

Triurus Lacepède 1800:200 [ref. 2709]. Masc. *Triurus bougainvillianus* Lacepède 1800:200. Type by monotypy. Perhaps unidentifiable; Jordan placed in Clupeidae and also in Alepocephalidae; Fowler 1974:13 [ref. 7180] placed in Alepocephalidae; Fraser-Brunner 1943:7 [ref. 1495] treated as a synonym of *Ranzania* (Molidae) without comment. Renamed *Pomatias* by Bloch & Schneider 1801. Alepocephalidae.

Triurus (subgenus of *Laurida*) Swainson 1839:185, 288 [ref. 4303]. Masc. *Triurus microcephalus* Swainson 1839:288. Type by monotypy. Preoccupied by Lacepède 1800 in fishes; not replaced. Synonym of *Harpadon* Lesueur 1825. Synodontidae: Harpadontinae.

Trixiphichthys (subgenus of *Triacanthus*) Fraser-Brunner 1941:430 [ref. 1493]. Masc. *Triacanthus weberi* Chaudhuri 1910. Type by original designation (also monotypic). Valid (Tyler 1968:283 [ref. 6438], Tyler 1980:98 [ref. 4477]). Triacanthidae.

Trochocopus Günther 1862:100 [ref. 1969]. Masc. *Trochocopus opercularis* Günther 1862:100. Type by monotypy. Type by subsequent designation of Jordan 1919:318 [ref. 4904]. Synonym of *Bodianus* Bloch 1790, as a valid subgenus (Gomon & Madden 1981:122 [ref. 5482]). Labridae.

Troglichthys Eigenmann 1899:250 [ref. 1216]. Masc. *Typhlichthys rosae* Eigenmann 1898:231. Type by monotypy. Synonym of *Amblyopsis* DeKay 1842. Amblyopsidae.

Troglocobitis (subgenus of *Noemacheilus*) Parin 1983:83 Fem. *Noemacheilus starstini* Parin 1983:83. Type by original designation (also monotypic). Valid (Kottelat 1990:21 [ref. 14137]). Balitoridae: Nemacheilinae.

Trogloglanis Eigenmann 1919:397 [ref. 1241]. Masc. *Trogloglanis pattersoni* Eigenmann 1919:399. Type by monotypy. Valid (Lundberg 1982 [ref. 5450], Burgess 1989:35 [ref. 12860]). Ictaluridae.

Trompe Gistel 1848:XI [ref. 1822]. *Sciaena jaculatrix* Pallas 1767:186. Type by being a replacement name. Unexplained and unneeded replacement for *Toxotes* Cuvier 1816. Objective synonym of *Toxotes* Cuvier 1816 (Allen 1978:358 [ref. 6922]). Toxotidae.

Tropheops (subgenus of *Melanochromis*) Trewavas 1984:102 [ref. 5303]. Masc. *Pseudotropheus tropheops* Regan 1921:683. Type by original designation (also by absolute tautonymy). Cichlidae.

Tropheus Boulenger 1898:17 [ref. 547]. Masc. *Tropheus moorii* Boulenger 1898:18. Type by monotypy. Valid (Poll 1986:75 [ref. 6136]). Cichlidae.

Tropidichthys Bleeker 1854:500 [ref. 344]. Masc. *Tropidichthys margaritatus* Rüppell 1828:501. Type by subsequent designation. Also misspelled *Tropidichthjs* in original account. Earliest type designation not researched; *marginatus* Bleeker listed as type by Jordan 1919:256 [ref. 2410]. Synonym of *Canthigaster* Swainson 1839 (Allen & Randall 1977:478 [ref. 6714]). Tetraodontidae.

Tropidinius Poey (ex Gill) 1868:296 [ref. 3505]. Masc. *Mesoprion arnillo* Poey 1861:154. Type by monotypy. Synonym of *Pristipomoides* Bleeker 1852 (Allen 1985:141 [ref. 6843]); synonym of subgenus *Platyinius* Gill 1862 (Akazaki & Iwatsuki 1986 [ref. 6316]); valid genus (Yoshino in Masuda et al. 1984:167 [ref. 6441]). Lutjanidae.

Tropidocaulus Ogilby 1919:45 [ref. 3300]. Masc. *Belone platyura* Bennett 1831:168. Type by being a replacement name. Replacement for *Eurycaulus* Ogilby 1909, preoccupied by Fairmaire 1868 in Coleoptera. Objective synonym of *Platybelone* Fowler 1919. Belonidae.

Tropidodus Gill 1863:489, 490 [ref. 1671]. Masc. *Cestracion pantherinus* Valenciennes 1846:350. Type by original designation (also monotypic). Type designated in footnote on p. 489. Synonym of *Heterodontus* Blainville 1816 (Compagno 1984:155 [ref. 6474]). Heterodontidae.

Tropidophoxinellus Stephanidis 1974:245 [ref. 4268]. Masc. *Rutilus spartiaticus* Stephanidis 1971:176. Type by original designation. Cyprinidae.

Tropidostethops Schultz 1950:150 [ref. 3977]. Masc. *Tropidosteth-Mus rhothophilus* Ogilby 1895:323. Type by being a replacement name. Replacement for *Tropidostethus* Ogilby 1895, preoccupied by Philippi 1863 in Orthoptera. Synonym of *Iso* Jordan & Starks 1901 (Smith 1965:603 [ref. 4135]). Atherinidae: Notocheirinae.

Tropidostethus Ogilby 1895:322 [ref. 3268]. Masc. *Tropidostethus rhothophilus* Ogilby 1895:323. Type by monotypy. Preoccupied by Philippi 1863 in Orthoptera, replaced by *Tropidostethops*

Schultz 1950. Synonym of *Iso* Jordan & Starks 1901. Atherinidae: Notocheirinae.

Trudis Whitley 1931:327 [ref. 4672]. Fem. *Platycephalus bassensis* Cuvier in Cuvier & Valenciennes 1829:247. Type by original designation (also monotypic). Synonym of *Platycephalus* Bloch 1795 (Paxton et al. 1989:468 [ref. 12442] based on placement of the type species). Platycephalidae.

Trulla Kaup 1858:109 [ref. 2579]. Fem. *Plagusia trulla* Cantor 1949:1213. Type by absolute tautonymy. Two included species; one is *Trulla cantori* Kaup, an unneeded replacement for *P. trulla* Cantor; the latter is the type. Synonym of *Cynoglossus* Hamilton 1822 (Menon 1977:16 [ref. 7071], Desoutter 1986:432 [ref. 6212]). Cynoglossidae: Cynoglossinae.

Trutta Geoffroy St. Hilaire 1767:399 [ref. 1570]. Fem. *Salmo trutta* Linnaeus 1758:308. Type by monotypy or absolute tautonymy; original not seen. Synonym of *Salmo* Linnaeus 1758 (Svetovidov 1973:145 [ref. 7169], Behnke 1984:125 [ref. 6177]). Salmonidae: Salmoninae.

Truttae (subgenus of *Salmo*) Linnaeus 1758:308 [ref. 2787]. Not available; appeared as pleural "Truttae" as a subgroup of *Salmo*; not later made available, although the ICZN made available "Coregoni" (as *Coregonus*) and "Osmeri" (as *Osmerus*), both proposed in same way by Linnaeus. In the synonymy of *Salmo* Linnaeus 1758 (Svetovidov 1973:145 [ref. 7169]). Salmonidae: Salmoninae.

Trycera Koch in Döderlein 1884:242 [ref. 5073]. Fem. Not available; manuscript name as *Trycera typica* from Koch published in synonymy of *Rhinoptera marginata* and apparently never made available. In the synonymy of *Rhinoptera* Cuvier 1829. Myliobatidae.

Trycherodon Forbes in Jordan & Gilbert 1883:247 [ref. 2476]. Masc. *Trycherodon megalops* Forbes in Jordan & Gilbert 1883:248. Type by original designation (also monotypic). Synonym of *Notropis* Rafinesque 1818, subgenus *Opsopoeodus* Hay 1881 (Gilbert & Bailey 1972:3 [ref. 7153], Gilbert 1978:16 [ref. 7042]). Cyprinidae.

Trygon Cuvier (ex Adanson) 1816:136 [ref. 993]. Fem. *Raja pastinaca* Linnaeus 1758:232. Type by subsequent designation. Type apparently designated first by Bory de Saint-Vincent, v. 13, 1828:99 [ref. 3853] (see Whitley 1935:138 [ref. 6396]). Synonym of *Dasyatis* Rafinesque 1810 (Krefft & Stehmann 1973:70 [ref. 7167], Compagno & Roberts 1984:4 [ref. 6167], Cappetta 1987: 163 [ref. 6348]). Dasyatidae.

Trygon Geoffroy St. Hilaire 1827:218 Fem. *Trygon grabatus* Geoffroy St. Hilaire 1827:218, Pl. 25. Original not seen; cited from Jordan 1917:120 [ref. 2407]. Preoccupied by *Trygon* Cuvier 1816. Apparently a synonym of *Taeniura* Müller & Henle 1837. Dasyatidae.

Trygonobatis (subgenus of *Raja*) Blainville 1825:35 [ref. 4991]. Fem. *Raja pastinaca* Linnaeus 1758:232. Type by monotypy. As a section of *Raja*; apparently only one species mentioned by name. Perhaps best considered an unjustified emendation of or new spelling for *Trygonobatus* Blainville 1818. In the synonymy of *Dasyatis* Rafinesque 1810. Dasyatidae.

Trygonobatus (subgenus of *Raia [Raja]*) Blainville 1816:112 [= 120] [ref. 306]. Masc. *Raja pastinaca* Linnaeus 1758:232. Type by subsequent designation. Type designated by Lesson, v. 16, 1830:374 [ref. 13391] (see Whitley 1935:137 [ref. 6396]); Lesson's spelling was *Trigonobatus*. Synonym of *Dasyatis* Rafinesque 1810 (Krefft & Stehmann 1973:70 [ref. 7167], Compagno & Roberts 1984:4 [ref. 6167]). Dasyatidae.

Trygonoptera Müller & Henle 1841:174 [ref. 3069]. Fem. *Trygonoptera testacea* Müller & Henle (ex Banks) 1841:174. Type by monotypy. Synonym of *Urolophus* Müller & Henle 1837 (Cappetta 1987:165 [ref. 6348]). Urolophidae.

Trygonorrhina Müller & Henle 1838:90 [ref. 3066]. Fem. *Trygonorhina fasciata* Müller & Henle 1841:124. Type by monotypy. Appeared first and spelled *Trygonorrhina* in Müller & Henle 1838:90 [ref. 3066]; as name only in 1838:85 [ref. 3068]; also in 1841:124 [ref. 3069] and spelled *Trygonorhina* (p. 124, p. xvii). Valid (Scott 1981:102 [ref. 5533] and Paxton et al. 1989:54 [ref. 12442] as *Trygonorrhina*). Rhinobatidae: Rhinobatinae.

Trypauchen Valenciennes in Cuvier & Valenciennes 1837:152 [ref. 1006]. *Gobius vagina* Bloch & Schneider 1801:73. Type by monotypy. Valid (Hoese 1986:805 [ref. 5670], Birdsong et al. 1988:197 [ref. 7303], Kottelat 1989:19 [ref. 13605]). Gobiidae.

Trypauchenichthys Bleeker 1860:4, 63 [ref. 377]. Masc. *Trypauchenichthys typus* Bleeker 1860:63. Type by monotypy (also by use of typus). Valid (Birdsong et al. 1988:197 [ref. 7303], Kottelat 1989:19 [ref. 13605]). Gobiidae.

Trypauchenophrys Franz 1910:68 [ref. 1481]. Fem. *Trypauchenophrys anotus* Franz 1910:68. Type by monotypy. Gobiidae.

Trypauchenopsis Volz 1903:554 [ref. 4531]. Fem. *Trypauchenopsis intermedius* Volz 1903:555. Type by monotypy. Treated by author as masculine, *opsis* is feminine. Gobiidae.

Tubbia Whitley 1943:178 [ref. 4703]. Fem. *Tubbia tasmanica* Whitley 1943:179. Type by original designation (also monotypic). Synonym of *Schedophilus* Cocco 1839 (Haedrich 1967:59 [ref. 5357]); valid (McDowall 1979 [ref. 6953], McDowall 1981:133 [ref. 5356], Horn 1984:628 [ref. 13637], Haedrich 1986:846 [ref. 5659]). Centrolophidae.

Tukugobius Herre 1927:119 [ref. 2104]. Masc. *Rhinogobius carpenteri* Herre 1927:122. Type by original designation. Valid (Birdsong et al. 1988:203 [ref. 7303]). Gobiidae.

Tulelepis Smith 1954:869 [ref. 4094]. Fem. *Tulelepis canis* Smith 1954:869. Type by original designation (also monotypic). Synonym of *Grammistops* Schultz 1953 (Randall 1986:538 [ref. 5706]). Serranidae: Grammistinae.

Tupa de Buen 1953:48 [ref. 694]. Fem. *Atherinichthys platensis* Berg 1895:27. Type by monotypy. Synonym of *Odontesthes* Evermann & Kendall 1906 (Dyer, pers. comm.). Atherinidae: Atherinopsinae.

Turcinoemacheilus Banarescu & Nalbant 1964:178 [ref. 217]. Masc. *Turcinoemacheilus kosswigi* Banarescu & Nalbant 1964:178. Type by original designation (also monotypic). Valid (Kottelat 1990:21 [ref. 14137]). Balitoridae: Nemacheilinae.

Turdus Catesby 1771:9 [ref. 774]. Masc. Not available, published in a rejected work on Official Index (Opinion 89, Opinion 259). Lutjanidae.

Turrum Whitley 1932:337 [ref. 4674]. *Turrum emburyi* Whitley 1932:337. Type by original designation (also monotypic). Synonym of *Carangoides* Bleeker 1851 (Smith-Vaniz, pers. comm., Nov. 1989). Carangidae.

Tydemania Weber 1913:570 [ref. 4602]. Fem. *Tydemania navigatoris* Weber 1913:571. Type by monotypy. Valid (Tyler 1968:183 [ref. 6438], Tyler 1980:56 [ref. 4477], Matsuura in Masuda et al. 1984:357 [ref. 6441], Tyler 1986:890 [ref. 5723]). Triacanthodidae.

Tylerius Hardy 1984:33 [ref. 5182]. Masc. *Spheroides spinosissimus* Regan 1908:253. Type by original designation (also monotypic). Valid (Smith & Heemstra 1986:903 [ref. 5714], see Su et al. 1986:112 [ref. 12582]). Tetraodontidae.

Tylobronchus Eigenmann 1912:253, 271 [ref. 1227]. Masc. *Tylobronchus maculosus* Eigenmann 1912:272. Type by monotypy. Misspelled *Tylobranchus* by Jordan 1920:542 [ref. 4905]. Curimatidae: Chilodontinae.

Tylochromis Regan 1920:37 [ref. 3669]. Masc. *Pelmatochromis jentinkii* Steindachner 1895:43. Type by original designation. Valid (Poll 1986:44 [ref. 6136]). Cichlidae.

Tylognathoides (subgenus of *Tylognathus*) Tortonese 1937:15 [ref. 10283]. *Tylognathus festai* Tortonese 1937:13. Type by monotypy. Date may be 1938. Valid (Karaman 1971:239 [ref. 2560]). Cyprinidae.

Tylognathus Heckel 1843:1027 [ref. 2066]. Masc. *Varicorhinus diplostomus* Heckel 1838:67. Type by subsequent designation. Type designated by Bleeker 1863:194 [ref. 397] or 1863:25 [ref. 4859]. Synonym of *Crossocheilus* Kuhl & van Hasselt 1823 (Karaman 1971:236 [ref. 2560]). Cyprinidae.

Tylometopon Bleeker 1873:133 [ref. 431]. Neut. *Brama dussumieri* Valenciennes in Cuvier & Valenciennes 1831:219. Type by original designation. Synonym of *Brama* Bloch & Schneider 1801 (Mead 1972:25 [ref. 6976], Mead 1973:386 [ref. 7199]). Bramidae.

Tylosurus Cocco 1833:18 [ref. 859]. Masc. *Tylosurus cantrainei* Cocco 1833:18. Type by monotypy. Species spelled *cantraine* (p. 18) and *cantrainei* (p. 21), earliest first reviser not researched; later spelled *cantraini* by Cocco. Valid (Parin 1973:260 [ref. 7191], Yoshino in Masuda et al. 1984:78 [ref. 6441], Collette et al. 1984:336 [ref. 11422], Collette & Parin in Whitehead et al. 1986:608 [ref. 13676], Paxton et al. 1989:343 [ref. 12442]). Belonidae.

Tympanomium Ranzani 1839:table [ref. 3605]. Neut. *Tympanomium planci* Ranzani 1839. Type by monotypy. Synonym of *Mola* Koelreuter 1770 (Fraser-Brunner 1943:8 [ref. 1495]). Molidae.

Tympanopleura Eigenmann 1912:203 [ref. 1227]. Fem. *Tympanopleura piperata* Eigenmann 1912:203. Type by original designation (also monotypic). Valid (Burgess 1989:286 [ref. 12860]). Ageneiosidae.

Tyntlastes (subgenus of *Amblyopus*) Günther 1862:194 [ref. 1970]. Masc. *Amblyopus sagitta* Günther 1862:193. Type by monotypy. As a section of *Amblyopus*. Synonym of *Gobioides* Lacepède 1800 (Maugé 1986:370 [ref. 6218]). Gobiidae.

Typhlachirus Hardenberg 1931:415 [ref. 2036]. Masc. *Typhlachirus caecus* Hardenberg 1931:415. Type by monotypy. Valid (Kottelat 1989:20 [ref. 13605]). Soleidae.

Typhleotris Petit 1933:347 [ref. 3457]. Fem. *Typhleotris madagascariensis* Petit 1933:347. Type by monotypy. Valid (Maugé 1986:398 [ref. 6218]). Eleotridae.

Typhlias Hubbs 1938:287 [ref. 2248]. Masc. *Typhlias pearsei* Hubbs 1938:291. Type by original designation (also monotypic). Apparently preoccupied [details not researched], replaced by *Typhliasina* Whitley 1951. Synonym of *Ogilbia* Jordan & Evermann 1898 (Cohen & Nielsen 1978:60 [ref. 881]). Bythitidae: Brosmophycinae.

Typhliasina Whitley 1951:67 [ref. 4711]. Fem. *Typhlias pearsei* Hubbs 1938:291. Type by being a replacement name. Replacement for *Typhlias* Hubbs 1938, apparently preoccupied [details not researched]. Synonym of *Ogilbia* Jordan & Evermann 1898 (Cohen & Nielsen 1978:60 [ref. 881]). Bythitidae: Brosmophycinae.

Typhlichthys Girard 1859:63 [ref. 1821]. Masc. *Typhlichthys subterraneus* Girard 1859:63. Type by monotypy. Valid (Mayden & Cross 1983 [ref. 6632]). Amblyopsidae.

Typhlinus Rafinesque 1815:90 [ref. 3584]. Masc. As "*Typhlinus* R. sp. do.," meaning a new name for a species formerly in the preceding genus *Syngnathus*. Not available, name only; perhaps intended for *Typhle* or *Tiphle*. Misspelled *Tiphlinus* in Jordan 1917:91 [ref. 2407]. Syngnathidae: Syngnathinae.

Typhlobagrus Miranda-Ribeiro 1907:[1] [ref. 3713]. Masc. *Typhlobagrus kronei* Miranda-Ribeiro 1907:[1]. Type by monotypy. On unnumbered p. 1. Valid (Burgess 1989:280 [ref. 12860]). Pimelodidae.

Typhlobarbus Chu & Chen 1982:383 [ref. 836]. Masc. *Typhlobarbus nudiventris* Chu & Chen 1982:383. Type by monotypy. Valid (Chu & Cui in Chu & Chen 1989:223 [ref. 13584]). Cyprinidae.

Typhlobelus Myers 1944:593 [ref. 3123]. Masc. *Typhlobelus ternetzi* Myers 1944:593. Type by original designation (also monotypic). Valid (Burgess 1989:325 [ref. 12860], Pinna 1989 [ref. 12630], Pinna 1989:372 [ref. 13515]). Trichomycteridae.

Typhlobranchus Bloch & Schneider 1801:537 [ref. 471]. Masc. *Typhlobranchus spurius* Bloch & Schneider 1801:537. Type by monotypy. Synonym of *Synbranchus* Bloch 1795 (Rosen & Greenwood 1976:53 [ref. 7094]). Synbranchidae.

Typhloceratias Barbour 1942:78 [ref. 180]. Masc. *Typhloceratias firthi* Barbour 1942:78. Type by monotypy. Synonym of *Ceratias* Krøyer 1845 (Pietsch 1986:481 [ref. 5969]). Ceratiidae.

Typhlogarra Trewavas 1955:552 [ref. 4454]. Fem. *Typhlogarra widdowsoni* Trewavas 1955:553. Type by original designation (also monotypic). Cyprinidae.

Typhlogobius Steindachner 1879:141 [ref. 4229]. Masc. *Typhlogobius californiensis* Steindachner 1879:142. Type by monotypy. Valid (Birdsong et al. 1988:185 [ref. 7303]). Gobiidae.

Typhlonarke Waite 1909:146 [ref. 4564]. Fem. *Astrape aysoni* Hamilton 1902:224. Type by monotypy. Narkidae.

Typhlonus Günther 1878:21 [ref. 2010]. Masc. *Typhlonus nasus* Günther 1878:21. Type by monotypy. Valid (Cohen & Nielsen 1978:41 [ref. 881], Hureau & Nielsen 1981:24 [ref. 5438]). Ophidiidae: Neobythitinae.

Typhlosynbranchus Pellegrin 1922:884 [ref. 3402]. Masc. *Typhlosynbranchus boueti* Pellegrin 1922:885. Type by monotypy. *Typhlosymbranchus* is a misspelling. Synonym of *Monopterus* Lacepède 1800 (Rosen & Greenwood 1976:56 [ref. 7094], Daget 1986:291 [ref. 6203]). Synbranchidae.

Typhlotes Fischer von Waldheim 1813:75 [ref. 1331]. Fem. *Caecilia branderiana* Lacepède 1800:135 (= *Muraena coeca* Linnaeus 1758:245). Type by being a replacement name. Replacement for *Caecilia* Lacepède 1800, preoccupied by Linnaeus 1758 in Amphibia. Original not seen. Synonym of *Apterichtus* Duméril 1806 (Blache et al. 1973:248 [ref. 7185], McCosker 1977:65 [ref. 6836], McCosker et al. 1989:318 [ref. 13288]). Ophichthidae: Ophichthinae.

Typhlus Duméril (ex Bibron) 1870:540 [ref. 1147]. Masc. Not available, name from Bibron manuscript mentioned in synonymy under *Ichthyocampus ponticerianus* Kaup. Syngnathidae: Syngnathinae.

Typlopsaras Gill 1883:284 [ref. 1723]. *Typlopsaras shufeldti* Gill 1883:284. Type by monotypy. Spelled *Typhlosparas* by Regan

1926:37 [ref. 3679] and *Typhlopsarus* by Barbour 1942:78 [ref. 180]. Synonym of *Ceratias* Krøyer 1845 (Pietsch 1986:481 [ref. 5969]). Ceratiidae.

Tyrannochromis Eccles & Trewavas 1989:97 [ref. 13547]. Masc. *Haplochromis macrostoma* Regan 1922:719. Type by original designation. Cichlidae.

Tyrannophryne Regan & Trewavas 1932:83 [ref. 3682]. Fem. *Tyrannophryne pugnax* Regan & Trewavas 1932:83. Type by monotypy. Valid (Pietsch 1974:32 [ref. 5332]). Oneirodidae.

Tyson Springer 1983:5 [ref. 5365]. Masc. *Tyson belos* Springer 1983:6. Type by original designation (also monotypic). Valid (Springer 1988:536 [ref. 6683], Birdsong et al. 1988:183 [ref. 7303]). Xenisthmidae.

Tyttobrycon Géry 1973:117 [ref. 1596]. Masc. *Tyttobrycon xeruini* Géry 1973:126. Type by original designation. Valid (Géry 1977:603 [ref. 1597]). Characidae.

Tyttocharax Fowler 1913:563 [ref. 1389]. Masc. *Tyttocharax madeirae* Fowler 1913:564. Type by original designation (also monotypic). Valid (Géry 1977:362 [ref. 1597], Weitzman & S. Fink 1985:1 et seq. [ref. 5203]). Characidae: Glandulocaudinae.

Uaru Heckel 1840:330 [ref. 2064]. Masc. *Uaru amphiacanthoides* Heckel 1840:331. Type by monotypy. Valid. Cichlidae.

Ubidia Miles 1945:461 [ref. 2998]. Fem. *Ubidia magdalenensis* Miles 1945:461. Type by original designation (also monotypic). Valid (see Mago-Leccia 1978:14 [ref. 5489]). Gymnotidae: Apteronotinae.

Uegitglanis Gianferrari 1923:1 [ref. 1608]. Masc. *Uegitglanis zammaranoi* Gianferrari 1923:1. Type by original designation (also monotypic). Valid (Poll 1977:145 [ref. 3533], Teugels 1986:101 [ref. 6193], Burgess 1989:147 [ref. 12860]). Clariidae.

Ulaema Jordan & Evermann in Jordan 1895:471 [ref. 2394]. Neut. *Diapterus lefroyi* Goode 1874:123. Type by original designation (name in parentheses), also monotypic. Synonym of *Eucinostomus* Baird & Girard 1855 (Roux 1986:325 [ref. 6209]); valid (Deckert & Greenfield 1987:184 [ref. 6778]). Gerreidae.

Ulapiscis Whitley 1933:78 [ref. 4677]. Masc. *Ulapiscis kennedyi* Whitley 1933:78. Type by original designation (also monotypic). Synonym of *Aphareus* Cuvier 1830 (Whitley 1976:49 [ref. 4735]). Lutjanidae.

Ulaula (subgenus of *Pristipomoides*) Jordan & Thompson 1911:459, 460 [ref. 2540]. Fem. *Chaetopterus sieboldii* Bleeker 1857:20. Type by being a replacement name. P. 459, "... new subgenus; type, *Bowersia ulaula* Jordan & Evermann; substitute for *Chaetopterus*, preoccupied." P. 460, "*Ulaula* = *Chaetopterus*, name preoccupied):" On p. 462 *ulaula* is synonymized with *sieboldii*. *Ulaula* is considered to be a replacement name and type must be *sieboldii*. Synonym of *Pristipomoides* Bleeker 1852 (Allen 1985:141 [ref. 6843], Akazaki & Iwatsuki 1987:326 [ref. 6699]). Lutjanidae.

Ulca Jordan & Evermann in Jordan 1896:227 [ref. 2395]. Fem. *Hemitripterus marmoratus* Bean 1891:43. Type by monotypy. Treated as feminine by authors. Synonym of *Hemitripterus* Cuvier 1829. Cottidae.

Ulcigobius (subgenus of *Drombus*) Fowler 1918:69 [ref. 1396]. Masc. *Drombus maculipinnis* Fowler 1918:69. Type by original designation (also monotypic). Second species tentatively included. Synonym of *Callogobius* Bleeker 1874 (Hoese, pers. comm.). Gobiidae.

Ulcina (subgenus of *Aspidophoroides*) Cramer in Jordan & Evermann 1896:449 [ref. 2442]. Fem. *Aspidophoroides olrikii* Lütken 1876:386. Type by original designation (also monotypic). Valid (Lindberg 1973:606 [ref. 7220], Andriashev in Whitehead et al. 1986:1267 [ref. 13677]). Agonidae.

Ulocentra Jordan 1878:218, 223 [ref. 2376]. Fem. *Arlina atripinnis* Jordan 1877:10. Type by monotypy. Synonym of *Etheostoma* Rafinesque 1819, but as a valid subgenus (Collette & Banarescu 1977:1456 [ref. 5845], Bailey & Etnier 1988:16 [ref. 6873]). Percidae.

Ultimostomias Beebe 1933:174 [ref. 246]. Masc. *Ultimostomias mirabilis* Beebe 1933:174. Type by monotypy. Synonym of *Photostomias* Collett 1889 (Morrow 1964:528 [ref. 6958], Fink 1985:2 [ref. 5171]). Malacosteidae.

Ulua Jordan & Snyder 1908:39 [ref. 2521]. *Ulua richardsoni* Jordan & Snyder 1908:39. Type by original designation (also monotypic). Valid (Smith-Vaniz 1984:526 [ref. 13664], Smith-Vaniz 1986:660 [ref. 5718], Gushiken 1988:443 [ref. 6697], Paxton et al. 1989:586 [ref. 12442]). Carangidae.

Ulvaria Jordan & Evermann 1896:475 [ref. 2442]. Fem. *Pholis subbifurcatus* Storer 1839:63. Type by original designation (also monotypic). Misspelled *Ulvarius* by Jordan & Evermann 1898:2349 (in key) [ref. 2445]. Stichaeidae.

Ulvicola Gilbert & Starks in Gilbert 1897:455 [ref. 1629]. Masc. *Ulvicola sanctaerosae* Gilbert & Starks in Gilbert 1897:455. Type by monotypy. Synonym of *Apodichthys* Girard 1854 (Yatsu 1981:182 [ref. 4814]); valid (some recent authors). Pholidae.

Umalius Herre & Herald 1950:310 [ref. 2114]. Masc. *Umalius philippinus* Herre & Herald 1950:312. Type by original designation (also monotypic). Synonym of *Sirembo* Bleeker 1858 (Cohen & Nielsen 1978:19 [ref. 881]). Ophidiidae: Neobythitinae.

Umbla Catesby 1771:1 [ref. 774]. Not available, published in a rejected work on Official Index (Opinion 89, Opinion 259). Sphyraenidae.

Umbla Rapp 1854:171 [ref. 3608]. *Salmo umbla* Linnaeus 1758:310. Type by absolute tautonymy. Apparently available; not preoccupied by *Umbla* Catesby 1771 in fishes (a rejected work). Synonym of *Salvelinus* Richardson 1836 (Svetovidov 1973:147 [ref. 7169]). Salmonidae: Salmoninae.

Umbra Kramer in Scopoli 1777:450 [ref. 3990]. Fem. *Cyprinodon krameri* Walbaum 1792:657. Type apparently by subsequent monotypy. First appeared in Gronow 1763, as unavailable (rejected work); published in an available way as above. Valid (Wilson & Veilleux 1982 [ref. 14203], Martin 1984:140 [ref. 13639]). Umbridae.

Umbrina Cuvier 1816:297 [ref. 993]. Fem. *Sciaena cirrosa* Linnaeus 1758:289. Type by monotypy, only one species definitely included. On Official List (Opinion 988). Valid (Trewavas 1973:399 [ref. 7201], Trewavas 1977:278 [ref. 4459], Chao 1978:29 [ref. 6983], Heemstra 1986:619 [ref. 5660], de Lucena 1988 [ref. 12613]). Sciaenidae.

Umbrula (subgenus of *Menticirrhus*) Jordan & Eigenmann 1889:423, 426 [ref. 2439]. Fem. *Umbrina littoralis* Holbrook 1855:142. Type by original designation. Type designated on p. 413 (name in parentheses). Synonym of *Menticirrhus* Gill 1861 (Chao 1978:30 [ref. 6983]). Sciaenidae.

Unagius Jordan 1919:343 [ref. 2413]. Masc. *Cryptophthalmus robustus* Franz 1910:15. Type by being a replacement name. Replacement for *Cryptophthalmus* Franz 1910, preoccupied by Rafinesque 1814 in Crustacea and Ehrenberg 1831 in Mollusca. Family placement uncorfirmed; apparently not in current literature.

Synbranchidae.

Uncisudis Maul 1956:91 [ref. 2917]. Fem. *Uncisudis longirostra* Maul 1956:91. Type by monotypy. Valid (Post 1973:209 [ref. 7182], Post in Whitehead et al. 1984:508 [ref. 13675], Okiyama 1984:207 [ref. 13644]). Paralepididae.

Undecimus Whitley 1934:unpaginated [ref. 4682]. Masc. *Quinquarius hendecacanthus* McCulloch 1915:144. Type by original designation (also monotypic). Synonym of *Pentaceros* Cuvier 1829 (Hardy 1983:197 [ref. 5385]). Pentacerotidae.

Uniantennatus (subgenus of *Lophiocharon*) Schultz 1957:(57) 83 [ref. 3969]. Masc. *Antennarius horridus* Bleeker 1853:83. Type by original designation. Synonym of *Antennarius* Daudin 1816 (Pietsch 1984:34 [ref. 5380]). Antennariidae.

Unibranchapertura Lacepède 1803:656 [ref. 4930]. Fem. *Symbranchus marmoratus* Bloch 1795:87. Type by subsequent designation. Type designated by Jordan 1917:68 [ref. 2407]. Spelled *Unibranchaperturus* and *Unibranchapterura* in early literature; and as *Unipertura* by Duméril 1856:201 [ref. 1154]. Correct spelling for genus of type species is *Synbranchus*. Synonym of *Synbranchus* Bloch 1795 (Rosen & Greenwood 1976:53 [ref. 7094]). Synbranchidae.

Unicornis Catesby 1771:19 [ref. 774]. Masc. Not available, published in a rejected work on Official Index (Opinion 89, Opinion 259). Monacanthidae.

Unipennata de Buen 1926:73 [ref. 5054]. As a "grupo" for 14 species of Blenniidae. Not available on basis of Art. 1b(6) [see de Buen's definition of "grupo" on p. 11]; see Appendix A. Blenniidae.

Unipertura Duméril 1856:201 [ref. 1154]. Fem. *Synbranchus marmoratus* Bloch 1795. Type by being a replacement name. Unjustified emendation (abridgment) for *Unibranchapertura* Lacepède 1803 and taking same type; analysis by Rosen & Greenwood 1976:50-51 [ref. 7094] apparently in error [type of *Unipertura* not *U. laevis* and not "designated" as such]. In the synonymy of *Synbranchus* Bloch 1795. Synbranchidae.

Upeneichthys Bleeker 1855:7 [ref. 346]. Masc. *Upeneus porosus* Cuvier in Cuvier & Valenciennes 1829:455. Type by monotypy. Appeared without description but reference to Cuvier species makes available. *Hypeneichthys* Ogilby 1893:33 [ref. 12519] is an unjustified emendation. Valid (Ben-Tuvia 1986 [ref. 6314]). Mullidae.

Upeneoides Bleeker 1849:62, 63 [ref. 318]. Masc. *Mullus vittatus* of Bleeker (= *Mullus vittatus* Forsskål 1775:x, 31). Type by subsequent designation. Type apparently designated first by Jordan 1919:240 [ref. 2410]. *Hypeneoides* Ogilby 1886:17 [ref. not seen] and 1893:33 [ref. 12519] is an unjustified emendation. Objective synonym of *Upeneus* Cuvier 1829 (Hureau 1973:403 [ref. 7197]). Mullidae.

Upeneus Cuvier 1829:157 [ref. 995]. Masc. *Mullus vittatus* Forsskål 1775:31. Type by subsequent designation. Type designated by Bleeker 1876:333 [ref. 448]. Also appeared as Cuvier in Cuvier & Valenciennes 1829:448 [ref. 4879]. *Hypeneus* Agassiz 1846:190, 384 [ref. 64] is an unjustified emendation. Valid (Hureau 1973:403 [ref. 7197], Yamakawa in Masuda et al. 1984:163 [ref. 6441], Hureau in Whitehead et al. 1986:880 [ref. 13676], Ben-Tuvia 1986:612 [ref. 5641], Ben-Tuvia & Kissil 1988:10 [ref. 12819]). Mullidae.

Upselonphorus Gill 1861:113 [ref. 1774]. Masc. *Uranoscopus y-graecum* Cuvier in Cuvier & Valenciennes 1829:308. Type by subsequent designation. Type designation Kirsch 1889:262 [ref. 12542]. Spelled *Upsilonphorus* by Kirsch 1889:262 (as an incorrect subsequent spelling or mistake) and misspelled *Hypselophorus* in Zoological Record for 1876. Synonym of *Astroscopus* Brevoort 1860 (Mees 1960:47 [ref. 11931], Pietsch 1989:297 [ref. 12541]). Uranoscopidae.

Upsilodus Miranda-Ribeiro 1924:365 [ref. 3728]. Masc. *Upsilodus victori* Miranda-Ribeiro 1924:366. Type by monotypy. Valid (Isbrücker 1980:14 [ref. 2303], Burgess 1989:430 [ref. 12860]). Loricariidae.

Upsilonognathus Fowler 1946:4 [ref. 1455]. Masc. *Upsilonognathus chaplini* Fowler 1946:5. Type by original designation (also monotypic). Synonym of *Opistognathus* Cuvier 1816. Opistognathidae.

Uradia Kamohara 1938:52 [ref. 2551]. Fem. *Uradia macrolepidota* Kamohara 1938:53. Type by original designation (also monotypic). Triglidae: Triglinae.

Uraleptus Costa 1846:39 [ref. 976]. Masc. *Gadus maraldi* Risso 1810:123. Type by monotypy. Synonym of *Gadella* Lowe 1843 (Cohen 1973:323 [ref. 6589], Paulin 1989:95 [ref. 9297]). Moridae.

Uranga Whitley 1943:115 [ref. 4702]. Fem. *Uranga nasuta* Whitley 1943:115. Type by original designation (also monotypic). Synonym of *Carcharhinus* Blainville 1816 (Garrick 1982:19 [ref. 5454], Compagno 1984:449 [ref. 6846], Compagno 1988:308 [ref. 13488]). Carcharhinidae.

Uranganops (subgenus of *Galeolamna*) Whitley 1943:117 [ref. 4702]. Masc. *Galeolamna (Uranganops) fitzroyensis* Whitley 1943:117. Type by original designation (also monotypic). Synonym of *Carcharhinus* Blainville 1816 (Garrick 1982:19 [ref. 5454], Compagno 1984:449 [ref. 6846], Compagno 1988:308 [ref. 13488]). Carcharhinidae.

Uranichthys Poey 1867:256 [ref. 3503]. Masc. *Muraena hauanensis* Bloch & Schneider 1801:491. Type by subsequent designation. Type designated by Jordan & Davis 1891:624 [ref. 2437] if accepted, else by Jordan 1919:347 [ref. 4904]. Species spelled *hauanensis* by Bloch & Schneider; perhaps *havanensis* was intended. Synonym of *Ophichthus* Ahl 1789 (Blache et al. 1973:247 [ref. 7185], McCosker 1977:80 [ref. 6836], McCosker et al. 1989:379 [ref. 13288]). Ophichthidae: Ophichthinae.

Uranidea DeKay 1842:61 [ref. 1098]. Fem. *Uranidea quiescens* DeKay 1842:61. Type by monotypy. Synonym of *Cottus* Linnaeus 1758. Cottidae.

Uranoblepus Gill 1861:5 [ref. 1766]. Masc. *Synanceia elongata* Cuvier in Cuvier & Valenciennes 1829:456. Type by being a replacement name. Unneeded replacement for *Trachicephalus* Swainson 1839, not preoccupied by *Trachycephalus* Tschudi 1838 in Reptilia. Objective synonym of *Trachicephalus* Swainson 1839 (Eschmeyer & Rama-Rao 1973:372 [ref. 6391]). Scorpaenidae: Synanceiinae.

Uranoconger Fowler 1934:274 [ref. 1416]. Masc. *Uranoconger odontostomus* Fowler 1934:274. Type by original designation (also monotypic). Synonym of *Bathycongrus* Ogilby 1898 (Castle, pers. comm.); valid, mentioned in passing (Smith 1989:512 [ref. 13285]). Congridae: Congrinae.

Uranoscopus Gronow 1763:57 [ref. 1910]. Masc. Not available, published in a rejected work on Official Index (Opinion 261). In the synonymy of *Cottus* Linnaeus 1758. Cottidae.

Uranoscopus Linnaeus 1758:250 [ref. 2787]. Masc. *Uranoscopus* *scaber* Linnaeus 1758:250. Type by monotypy. On Official List (Opinion 75). Valid (Mees 1960:46 [ref. 11931], Wheeler 1973:451 [ref. 7190], Kishimoto in Masuda et al. 1984:293 [ref. 6441], Heemstra 1986:735 [ref. 5660], Hureau in Whitehead et al. 1986:955 [ref. 13676], Kishimoto 1987 [ref. 6062], Pietsch 1989:295 [ref. 12541]). Uranoscopidae.

Uranostoma Bleeker (ex Bibron) 1865:59 [ref. 416]. Neut. Not available; manuscript name mentioned in passing in the synonymy of *Tetraodon*; apparently never made available. Questionably in the synonymy of *Spheroides* Duméril 1806 (Fraser-Brunner 1943:11 [ref. 1495]). Tetraodontidae.

Uraptera Müller & Henle 1837:117 [ref. 3067]. Fem. *Uraptera agassizii* Müller & Henle 1841:155. Type by subsequent monotypy. Also in Müller & Henle 1838:90 [ref. 3066] without species. Species added in Müller & Henle 1841:155 [ref. 3069]. Apparently preoccupied by Billberg 1838 in Lepidoptera. Rajidae.

Uraspis Bleeker 1855:417, 418 [ref. 350]. Fem. *Uraspis carangoides* Bleeker 1855:418. Type by subsequent designation. Type designated by Jordan & Evermann 1896:916 [ref. 2443]. Valid (Smith-Vaniz 1984:526 [ref. 13664], Gushiken in Masuda et al. 1984:155 [ref. 6441], Smith-Vaniz 1986:660 [ref. 5718], Gushiken 1988:443 [ref. 6697], Paxton et al. 1989:587 [ref. 12442]). Carangidae.

Urichthys (subgenus of *Zyrichthys*) Swainson 1839:172, 224 [ref. 4303]. Masc. *Labrus lunulatus* Forsskål 1775:37. Type by subsequent designation. Spelled *Uricthys* on p. 172. Type designated by Swain 1882:274 [ref. 5966]. Synonym of *Cheilinus* Lacepède 1801. Labridae.

Urinophilus Eigenmann 1918:358 [ref. 1239]. Masc. *Vandellia sanguinea* Eigenmann 1917:70. Type by subsequent designation. Species referred and type designated by Eigenmann 1920:441 [ref. 12609]; originally described without clear indication of included species. Synonym of *Plectrochilus* Miranda-Ribeiro 1917. Trichomycteridae.

Uriphaeton (subgenus of *Eteles*) Swainson 1839:168, 202 [ref. 4303]. *Serranus phaeton* Cuvier in Cuvier & Valenciennes 1828:309. Type by monotypy. A made-up fish, a *Cephalopholis* with the tail of a *Fistularia* attached (see Bleeker 1875:31, footnote [ref. 4861], also Jordan 1919:198 [ref. 2410]). In the synonymy of *Cephalopholis* Bloch & Schneider 1801. Serranidae: Epinephelinae.

Urobatis Garman 1913:401 [ref. 1545]. Fem. *Leiobatus sloani* Blainville 1816:121. Type by original designation. Synonym of *Urolophus* Müller & Henle 1837 (Cappetta 1987:165 [ref. 6348]). Urolophidae.

Urocampus Günther 1870:179 [ref. 1995]. Masc. *Urocampus nanus* Günther 1870:179. Type by monotypy. Valid (Dawson 1980 [ref. 6909], Araga in Masuda et al. 1984:88 [ref. 6441], Dawson 1985:194 [ref. 6541], Paxton et al. 1989:431 [ref. 12442]). Syngnathidae: Syngnathinae.

Urocentrus Kner 1868:30 [ref. 6074]. Masc. *Urocentrus pictus* Kner 1868:30. Type by monotypy. Also appeared as new in Kner 1868:342 [ref. 2646]. Synonym of *Pholis* Scopoli 1777 (Yatsu 1981:169 [ref. 4814], Makushok in Whitehead et al. 1986:1124 [ref. 13677]). Pholidae.

Uroconger Kaup 1856:71 [ref. 2572]. Masc. *Uroconger lepturus* Richardson 1844:106. Type by monotypy. Also in Kaup 1856:110 [ref. 2573]. Valid (Karrer 1982:27 [ref. 5679], Asano in Masuda et al. 1984:29 [ref. 6441], Castle 1986:165 [ref. 5644], Smith 1989:545 [ref. 13285]). Congridae: Congrinae.

Urogymnus Müller & Henle 1837:434 [ref. 13421]. Masc. *Raja asperrima* Bloch & Schneider 1801:367. Type by being a replacement name. Replacement for *Gymnura* Müller & Henle 1837, preoccupied by van Hasselt 1823 in fishes. Valid (Compagno 1986:141 [ref. 5648], Paxton et al. 1989:43 [ref. 12442]). Dasyatidae.

Urolophoides Lindberg in Soldatov & Lindberg 1930:24 [ref. 4164]. Masc. *Urolophoides giganteus* Lindberg in Soldatov & Lindberg 1930:26. Type by original designation (also monotypic). Dasyatidae.

Urolophus Müller & Henle 1837:117 [ref. 3067]. Masc. *Raja cruciata* Lacepède 1804:201, 210. Type by original designation (also monotypic). Can date to Müller & Henle 1837:117 as above; also 1838:90 [ref. 3066]. See also Müller & Henle 1841:173 [ref. 3069]. Misspelled *Usolophus* by Müller & Henle 1838:85 [ref. 3066]. Valid (Nakaya in Masuda et al. 1984:15 [ref. 6441], Cappetta 1987:165 [ref. 6348], Paxton et al. 1989:46 [ref. 12442]). Urolophidae.

Uronectes Günther 1862:325 [ref. 1969]. Masc. *Ophidium parrii* Ross 1826:109. Type by monotypy. Preoccupied by Brown 1850 in Crustacea, replaced by *Lycocara* Gill 1884. Correct spelling for genus of type species is *Ophidion*. Synonym of *Liparis* Scopoli 1777 (Andriashev & McAllister 1978 [ref. 6988] and not a zoarcid). Cyclopteridae: Liparinae.

Urophycis Gill 1863:240 [ref. 1687]. Fem. *Blennius regius* Walbaum 1792:186. Type by monotypy. Valid (Svetovidov 1973:316 [ref. 7169], Musick 1973 [ref. 7144], Fahay & Markle 1984:266 [ref. 13653], Svetovidov in Whitehead et al. 1986:708 [ref. 13676]). Phycidae.

Uropsetta Gill 1862:330 [ref. 1668]. Fem. *Hippoglossus californicus* Ayres 1859:29. Type by monotypy. Synonym of *Paralichthys* Girard 1858 (Norman 1934:69 [ref. 6893], Amaoka 1969:85 [ref. 105]). Paralichthyidae.

Uropterygius Rüppell 1838:83 [ref. 3844]. Masc. *Uropterygius concolor* Rüppell 1838:83. Type by monotypy. Valid (McCosker et al. 1984 [ref. 6725], Hatooka in Masuda et al. 1984:26 [ref. 6441], Castle & McCosker 1986:174 [ref. 5645], Paxton et al. 1989:133 [ref. 12442], Böhlke et al. 1989:126 [ref. 13286]). Muraenidae: Uropterygiinae.

Urostomias (subgenus of *Eustomias*) Regan & Trewavas 1930:72, 78 [ref. 3681]. Masc. *Eustomias macrurus* Regan & Trewavas 1930:78. Type by original designation. Synonym of *Eustomias* Vaillant 1888 (Gibbs in Morrow & Gibbs 1964:377 [ref. 6962], Morrow 1973:137 [ref. 7175]). Melanostomiidae.

Urotrygon Gill 1863:173 [ref. 1681]. Fem. *Urotrygon mundus* Gill 1863:173. Type by monotypy. Valid (Nakaya in Masuda et al. 1984:15 [ref. 6441], Compagno 1986:141 [ref. 5648], Miyake & McEachran 1986:291 [ref. 6153], Miyake & McEachran 1988 [ref. 12878]). Urolophidae.

Uroxis Rafinesque 1810:48, 61 [ref. 3595]. *Dasyatis ujo* Rafinesque 1810:16. Type by monotypy. Objective synonym of *Dasyatis* Rafinesque 1810 (Krefft & Stehmann 1973:70 [ref. 7167]). Dasyatidae.

Uroxys Rafinesque 1815:93 [ref. 3584]. Not available, name only. Rajidae.

Urumara Miranda-Ribeiro 1920:6 [ref. 3727]. Fem. *Urumara rondoni* Miranda-Ribeiro 1920:9. Type by monotypy. *Urumaria* is a misspelling. Synonym of *Gymnorhamphichthys* Ellis 1912

(Nijssen et al. 1976:40 [ref. 7078], Schwassmann 1989 [ref. 13745]). Gymnotidae: Rhamphichthyinae.

Usa (subgenus of *Caranx*) Whitley 1927:299 [ref. 4662]. Fem. *Caranx luna* Geoffroy St. Hilaire 1809:Pl. 23. Type by being a replacement name. Unneeded replacement for *Longirostrum* Wakiya 1924, apparently not preoccupied by *Longirostris*. Whitley says type is *Caranx cordylaoides* Meuschen (not researched). Synonym of *Pseudocaranx* Bleeker 1863. Carangidae.

Usacaranx Whitley 1931:316 [ref. 4672]. Masc. *Caranx nobilis* Macleay 1881:532. Type by original designation. Synonym of *Pseudocaranx* Bleeker 1863 (Smith-Vaniz, pers. comm., Nov. 1989). Carangidae.

Usinostia Jordan & Snyder 1900:380 [ref. 2502]. Fem. *Plagusia japonica* Temminck & Schlegel 1850:187. Type by monotypy. Misspelled *Usinosta* in Zoological Record for 1901. Synonym of *Paraplagusia* Bleeker 1865 (Menon 1980:12 [ref. 6798], Desoutter 1986:433 [ref. 6212]). Cynoglossidae: Cynoglossinae.

Ussuria Nikolskii 1903:362 [ref. 3203]. Fem. *Ussuria leptocephala* Nikolskii 1903:362. Type by monotypy. Cobitidae: Cobitinae.

Utiaritichthys Miranda-Ribeiro 1937:58 [ref. 5025]. Masc. *Utiaritichthys sennaebragai* Miranda-Ribeiro 1937:56. Type by monotypy. Misspelled *Utiaritichlys* on p. 56. Species originally *sennae-bragai* (correction mandatory). Valid (Géry 1976:51 [ref. 14199], Géry 1977:267 [ref. 1597]). Characidae: Serrasalminae.

Vacuoqua Jordan & Evermann 1927:506 [ref. 2453]. *Corvina macrops* Steindachner 1875:52. Type by original designation (also monotypic). Tentatively a synonym of *Bairdiella* Gill 1861 (Chao 1978:38 [ref. 6983]). Sciaenidae.

Vadesuma Whitley 1933:94 [ref. 4677]. *Paracentropogon scorpio* Whitley 1910:115. Type by original designation (also monotypic). Scorpaenidae: Tetraroginae.

Vailima Jordan & Seale 1906:398 [ref. 2497]. Fem. *Vailima stevensoni* Jordan & Seale 1906:398. Type by original designation (also monotypic). Gobiidae.

Vaillantella Fowler 1905:474 [ref. 1370]. Fem. *Nemacheilus euepipterus* Vaillant 1902:137. Type by original designation (also monotypic). Valid (Nalbant & Banarescu 1977 [ref. 7045], Kottelat 1989:13 [ref. 13605], Roberts 1989:109 [ref. 6439], Kottelat 1990:21 [ref. 14137]). Balitoridae: Nemacheilinae.

Vaillantia Jordan in Jordan & Brayton 1878:89 [ref. 2436]. Fem. *Boleosoma camurum* Forbes in Jordan 1878:40. Type by original designation (also monotypic). Synonym of *Etheostoma* Rafinesque 1819, but as a valid subgenus (Collette & Banarescu 1977:1456 [ref. 5845], Page 1981:35 [ref. 3347], Bailey & Etnier 1988:23 [ref. 6873]). Percidae.

Vaimosa Jordan & Seale 1906:395 [ref. 2497]. Fem. *Vaimosa fontinalis* Jordan & Seale 1906:395. Type by original designation. Synonym of *Mugilogobius* Smitt 1900 [or 1899] (Maugé 1986:376 [ref. 6218], Miller 1987:695 [ref. 6336]). Gobiidae.

Valamugil Smith 1948:841 [ref. 4076]. Masc. *Mugil crenilabis seheli* Forsskål 1775:14, 73. Type by original designation. For purposes of the type species, the subspecies *seheli* is elevated to species level; type not *crenilabis*. Valid (Jayaram 1981:343 [ref. 6497], Yoshino & Senou in Masuda et al. 1984:120 [ref. 6441], Smith & Smith 1986:719 [ref. 5717], Kottelat 1989:18 [ref. 13605]). Mugilidae.

Valencia Myers 1928:8 [ref. 3099]. Fem. *Fundulus hispanicus* Valenciennes in Cuvier & Valenciennes 1846:214. Type by original designation (also monotypic). Valid (Parenti 1981:500 [ref. 7066] in new family Valenciidae, Bianco 1987:210 [ref. 6750], Bianco & Miller 1989 [ref. 13541]). Cyprinodontidae: Valenciinae.

Valenciennea Bleeker 1856:412 [ref. 353]. Fem. *Eleotris hasselti* Bleeker 1851:253. Type by monotypy. See discussion in Jordan 1919:373 [ref. 4904]. Valid (Yoshino in Masuda et al. 1984:242 [ref. 6441], Hoese 1986:806 [ref. 5670], Birdsong et al. 1988:194 [ref. 7303]). Gobiidae.

Valenciennellus Jordan & Evermann in Goode & Bean 1896:513 [ref. 1848]. Masc. *Maurolicus tripunctulatus* Esmark 1870:488. Type by monotypy. Also appeared in Jordan & Evermann 1896 (3 Oct.):577 [ref. 2443]. Valid (Witzell 1973:121 [ref. 7172], Weitzman 1974:472 [ref. 5174], Badcock in Whitehead et al. 1984:316 [ref. 13675], Ahlstrom et al. 1984:185 [ref. 13643], Fujii in Masuda et al. 1984:46 [ref. 6441], Weitzman 1986:254 [ref. 6287], Paxton et al. 1989:193 [ref. 12442]). Sternoptychidae: Maurolicinae.

Valenciennesia Bleeker 1874:307 [ref. 437]. Fem. *Eleotris strigata* Valenciennes in Cuvier & Valenciennes (= *Gobius strigatus* Broussonet 1782:1). Type by original designation (also monotypic). Also appeared in Bleeker 1874:372 [ref. 436]. Apparently a variant spelling for *Valenciennea* Bleeker but unclear from text; it also may stand on its own as a genus description (see discussion by Jordan 1919:373 [ref. 4904]). Gobiidae.

Vallicola (subgenus of *Oreochromis*) Trewavas 1983:27, 29 [ref. 6597]. Masc. *Tilapia amphimelas* Hilgendorf 1905:405. Type by original designation (also monotypic). Cichlidae.

Vanacampus (subgenus of *Parasyngnathus*) Whitley 1951:62 [ref. 4711]. Masc. *Syngnathus vercoi* Waite & Hale 1921:298. Type by original designation (also monotypic). Valid (Dawson 1985:197 [ref. 6541], Paxton et al. 1989:432 [ref. 12442]). Syngnathidae: Syngnathinae.

Vandellia Valenciennes in Cuvier & Valenciennes 1846:386 [ref. 1011]. Fem. *Vandellia cirrhosa* Valenciennes in Cuvier & Valenciennes 1846:386. Type by monotypy. Valid (Schmidt 1987 [ref. 6780], Burgess 1989:324 [ref. 12860]). Trichomycteridae.

Vandellius Shaw 1803:199 [ref. 4014]. Masc. *Vandellius lusitanicus* Shaw 1803:199. Type by monotypy. *Vandillia* is a misspelling. Synonym of *Lepidopus* Goüan 1770 (Parin & Bekker 1973:464 [ref. 7206]). Trichiuridae: Lepidopinae.

Vanderbiltella (subgenus of *Barbus*) Fowler 1936:273 [ref. 1424]. Fem. *Barbus lepidura* Fowler 1936:274. Type by original designation. Synonym of *Barbus* Cuvier & Cloquet 1816 (Lévêque & Daget 1984:218 [ref. 6186]). Cyprinidae.

Vanderhorstia Smith 1949:103 [ref. 4077]. Fem. *Gobius delagoae* Barnard 1937:62. Type by original designation (also monotypic). Valid (Polunin & Lubbock 1977:68 [ref. 3540], Yanagisawa 1978:286 [ref. 7028], Akihito in Masuda et al. 1984:260 [ref. 6441], Hoese 1986:806 [ref. 5670], Birdsong et al. 1988:194 [ref. 7303]). Gobiidae.

Vanmanenia Hora 1932:309 [ref. 2208]. Fem. *Homalosoma (sic) stenosoma* Boulenger 1901:270. Type by original designation (also monotypic). Second species referred to genus with question. Boulenger's *Homalosoma* apparently a mistake for *Homaloptera*. Valid (Silas 1953:225 [ref. 4024], Chen 1980:97 [ref. 6901], Sawada 1982:205 [ref. 14111]). Balitoridae: Balitorinae.

Vanneaugobius Brownell 1978:135 [ref. 670]. Masc. *Vanneaugobius dollfusi* Brownell 1978:136. Type by original designation (also monotypic). Valid (Miller in Whitehead et al. 1986:1083 [ref. 13677], Birdsong et al. 1988:190 [ref. 7303]). Gobiidae.

Vanstraelenia Chabanaud 1950:9 [ref. 801]. Fem. *Vanstraelenia insignis* Chabanaud 1950:10. Type by monotypy. Soleidae.

Variabilichromis Colombe & Allgayer 1985:12 [ref. 13457]. Masc. *Lamprologus moorei* Boulenger 1898:494. Type by original designation (also monotypic). Cichlidae.

Varicogobio Lin 1931:74 [ref. 4019]. Masc. *Varicogobio kaa* Lin 1931:74. Type by monotypy. Synonym of *Ptychidio* Myers 1930. Cyprinidae.

Varicorhinus Rüppell 1836:20 [ref. 3845]. Masc. *Varicorhinus beso* Rüppell 1836:21. Type by monotypy. Valid (Karaman 1971:231 [ref. 2560], Wu et al. 1977:298 [ref. 4807], Lévêque & Daget 1984:336 [ref. 6186], Banister 1984 [ref. 5282], Chu & Cui in Chu & Chen 1989:212 [ref. 13584], Chen 1989:109 [ref. 14144]). Cyprinidae.

Varicus Robins & Böhlke 1961:46 [ref. 3787]. Masc. *Varicus bucca* Robins & Böhlke 1961:47. Type by original designation (also monotypic). Valid (Greenfield 1981 [ref. 6826], Williams & Gilbert 1983 [ref. 5369], Birdsong et al. 1988:189 [ref. 7303]). Gobiidae.

Variola (subgenus of *Serranus*) Swainson 1839:168, 202 [ref. 4303]. Fem. *Variola longipinna* Swainson 1839:202 (= *Perca louti* Forsskål 1775:xi, 40). Type by monotypy. Swainson's *V. longipinna* apparently is an unneeded substitute for *S. louti* of Rüppell which is *Perca louti* Forsskål 1775. Valid (Kendall 1984:500 [ref. 13663], Katayama in Masuda et al. 1984:126 [ref. 6441], Paxton et al. 1989:500 [ref. 12442]). Serranidae: Epinephelinae.

Vastres Valenciennes in Cuvier & Valenciennes 1847:433 [ref. 4883]. *Vastres cuvieri* Valenciennes in Cuvier & Valenciennes 1847:441 (= *Sudis gigas* Cuvier 1829). Type by subsequent designation. Earliest type designation not researched. Objective synonym of *Arapaima* Müller 1843. Osteoglossidae: Heterotidinae.

Vauclusella Whitley 1931:324 [ref. 4672]. Fem. *Tripterygium annulatum* Ramsay & Ogilby 1888:1021. Type by original designation (also monotypic). Correct spelling for genus of type species is *Tripterygion*. Valid. Tripterygiidae.

Vegetichthys Tanaka 1917:7 [ref. 4329]. Masc. *Vegetichthys tumidus* Tanaka 1917:7. Type by monotypy. Synonym of *Paracaesio* Bleeker 1875 (Allen 1985:130 [ref. 6843]). Lutjanidae.

Velambassis Whitley 1935:365 [ref. 4684]. Fem. *Pseudoambassis jacksoniensis* Macleay 1881:340. Type by original designation (also monotypic). Ambassidae.

Velasia Gray 1851:143 [ref. 4939]. Fem. *Velasia chilensis* Gray 1851:143. Type by monotypy. Also in Gray 1853 [for 1851]:239 [ref. 1886]. Synonym of *Geotria* Gray 1851. Petromyzontidae: Geotriinae.

Velesionymus Whitley 1934:unpaginated [ref. 4682]. Masc. *Callionymus liniceps* Ogilby 1908:35. Type by original designation (also monotypic). Synonym of *Callionymus* Linnaeus 1758 (Fricke 1982:58 [ref. 5432]); synonym of *Repomucenus* Whitley 1931 (Nakabo 1982:105 [ref. 3139]). Callionymidae.

Velifer Temminck & Schlegel 1850:312 [ref. 4375]. Masc. *Velifer hypselopterus* Bleeker 1879:16. Type by subsequent monotypy. Original description without species; one species added by Bleeker 1879:16 [ref. 460]; Bleeker's species is name only but regarded as available by reference to "*Velifer* Schl." Valid (Olney 1984:369 [ref. 13656], Fujii in Masuda et al. 1984:116 [ref. 6441], Heemstra 1986:399 [ref. 5660] but credited to Bleeker, Paxton et al. 1989:397 [ref. 12442]). Veliferidae.

Velifracta Jordan 1907:239 [ref. 2401]. *Pleuronectes sinensis* Lacepède 1802:595, 638. Type by being a replacement name. Unneeded replacement for *Tephritis* Günther 1862, preoccupied by Fabricius 1794 in Diptera and by Latreille 1804, but earlier replaced by *Tephrinectes* Günther 1862. Objective synonym of *Tephrinectes* Günther 1862 (Norman 1934:62 [ref. 6893]). Paralichthyidae.

Vellitor Jordan & Starks 1904:318 [ref. 2528]. Masc. *Podabrus centropomus* Richardson 1848:11. Type by being a replacement name. Replacement for *Podabrus* Richardson 1848, preoccupied by Gould (May) 1845 in Mammalia, apparently also by Fischer in Coleoptera [not researched]. Valid (Iwata 1983 [ref. 5794], Washington et al. 1984:443 [ref. 13660], Yabe in Masuda et al. 1984:329 [ref. 6441], Yabe 1985:111 [ref. 11522]). Cottidae.

Venefica Jordan & Davis 1891:651 [ref. 2437]. Fem. *Nettastoma procerum* Goode & Bean 1883:224. Type by original designation. Valid (Blache et al. 1973:237 [ref. 7185], Karrer 1982:66 [ref. 5679], Smith & Castle 1982:41 [ref. 5453], Asano in Masuda et al. 1984:29 [ref. 6441], Saldanha in Whitehead et al. 1986:565 [ref. 13676], Castle 1986:191 [ref. 5644], Smith 1989:609 [ref. 13285]). Nettastomatidae.

Ventrifossa Gilbert & Hubbs 1920:543 [ref. 1638]. Fem. *Coryphaenoides garmani* Jordan & Gilbert in Jordan & Starks 1904:610. Type by original designation. Valid (Marshall 1973:653 [ref. 6965], Iwamoto 1979:151 [ref. 2311], Fahay & Markle 1984:274 [ref. 13653], Okamura in Masuda et al. 1984:94 [ref. 6441], Iwamoto 1986:340 [ref. 5674], Paxton et al. 1989:329 [ref. 12442]). Macrouridae: Macrourinae.

Veraequa Jordan & Starks 1904:625 [ref. 2526]. *Veraequa achne* Jordan & Starks 1904:625. Type by original designation (also monotypic). Synonym of *Microstomus* Gottsche 1835 (Norman 1934:355 [ref. 6893]). Pleuronectidae: Pleuronectinae.

Verasper Jordan & Gilbert in Jordan & Evermann 1898:2606, 2618 [ref. 2445]. Masc. *Verasper moseri* Jordan & Gilbert in Jordan & Evermann 1898:2619. Type by original designation (also monotypic). Valid (Norman 1934:311 [ref. 6893], Ahlstrom et al. 1984:643 [ref. 13641], Sakamoto 1984 [ref. 5273], Sakamoto in Masuda et al. 1984:351 [ref. 6441]). Pleuronectidae: Pleuronectinae.

Verater Jordan 1919:343 [ref. 2413]. Masc. *Oligopus ater* Risso 1810:142. Type by being a replacement name. Replacement for *Pteridium* Filippi & Verany 1859, apparently not an original description but inclusion of a species in *Pteridium* Scopoli 1777 following Swainson. Apparently *Verater* may stand with type as *O. ater*. See also second entry for *Verater* Jordan 1919. Objective synonym of *Grammonus* Gill 1896; also see account of *Oligopus* Risso 1810. Bythitidae: Bythitinae.

Verater Jordan 1919:265 [ref. 2410]. *Oligopus ater* Risso 1810:142. Type by being a replacement name. This name technically used first by Jordan 1919 (Apr.) as a replacement for *Pteridium* Filippi & Vernay 1859. See account of *Grammonus* Gill 1896. Bythitidae: Bythitinae.

Verconectes Whitley 1931:324 [ref. 4672]. Masc. *Trianectes bucephalus* McCulloch & Waite 1918:53. Type by being a replacement name. Unneeded replacement for *Trianectes* McCulloch & Waite 1918, not preoccupied by *Trinectes* Rafinesque 1832 in fishes. Tripterygiidae.

Verdithorax Whitley 1931:311 [ref. 4672]. Masc. *Muraena prasina* Richardson 1848:93. Type by original designation. Synonym of *Lycodontis* McClelland 1844 (Blache et al. 1973:225 [ref. 7185]). Synonym of *Gymnothorax* Bloch 1795 (Böhlke et al. 1989:145 [ref. 13286]). Muraenidae: Muraeninae.

Verecundum Jordan 1891:330 [ref. 2391]. *Verecundum rasile* Jordan 1891:330. Type by monotypy. Synonym of *Xystreurys* Jordan & Gilbert 1880 (Norman 1934:119 [ref. 6893]); valid (Ahlstrom et al. 1984:642 [ref. 13641], Nakamura in Nakamura et al. 1986:302 [ref. 14235]). Paralichthyidae.

Verilus Poey 1860:124 [ref. 3499]. Masc. *Verilus sordius* Poey 1860:125. Type by monotypy. Valid (Johnson 1980:66 [ref. 13553], Johnson 1984:464 [ref. 9681]). Acropomatidae.

Verma Jordan & Evermann 1896:372, 374 [ref. 2443]. Fem. *Sphagebranchus kendalli* Gilbert 1891:310. Type by original designation (also monotypic). Valid (Blache et al. 1973:250 [ref. 7185], McCosker 1977:65 [ref. 6836]); synonym of *Apterichtus* Duméril 1806 (McCosker et al. 1989:318 [ref. 13288]). Ophichthidae: Ophichthinae.

Verreo Jordan & Snyder 1902:619 [ref. 2514]. *Cossyphus oxycephalus* Bleeker 1862:129. Type by original designation (also monotypic). Synonym of *Bodianus* Bloch 1790 (Gomon & Randall 1978 [ref. 5481]). Labridae.

Verriculus Jordan & Evermann 1903:191 [ref. 2450]. Masc. *Verriculus sanguineus* Jordan & Evermann 1903:191. Type by original designation (also monotypic). Synonym of *Bodianus* Bloch 1790, subgenus *Trochocopus* Günther 1862 (Gomon & Madden 1981:122 [ref. 5482]). Labridae.

Verrugato Jordan 1923:195 [ref. 2421]. *Lobotes pacificus* Jordan in Jordan & Evermann 1898:2857. Type by original designation (also monotypic). Synonym of *Lobotes* Cuvier 1830. Lobotidae.

Verrunculus (subgenus of *Balistes*) Jordan 1924:82 [ref. 2425]. Masc. *Balistes polylepis* Steindachner 1876:69. Type by original designation (also monotypic). Described as "a distinct subgenus or genus under *Balistes*." Synonym of *Balistes* Linnaeus 1758 (Tyler 1980:123 [ref. 4477]). Balistidae.

Verulux (subgenus of *Rhabdamia*) Fraser 1972:28 [ref. 5195]. Fem. *Rhabdamia cypselurus* Weber 1909:167. Type by original designation (also monotypic). Presumed valid as a subgenus of *Rhabdamia* Weber 1909 (see Gon 1987:15 [ref. 6378]). Apogonidae.

Vesicatrus Eigenmann 1911:174 [ref. 1226]. *Vesicatrus tegatus* Eigenmann 1911:174. Type by original designation (also monotypic). Valid (Géry 1977:530 [ref. 1597]). Characidae.

Vespicula Jordan & Richardson 1910:52 [ref. 6598]. Fem. *Prosopodasys gogorzae* Jordan & Seale 1906:792. Type by original designation (also monotypic). Valid (Washington et al. 1984:440 [ref. 13660], Kottelat 1989:17 [ref. 13605]). Scorpaenidae: Tetraroginae.

Vesposus Jordan 1921:649 [ref. 2419]. Masc. *Vesposus egregius* Jordan 1921:650. Type by original designation (also monotypic). Synonym of *Grammicolepis* Poey 1873. Grammicolepididae.

Vestula Bolin 1946:144 [ref. 509]. Fem. *Myctophum valdiviae* Brauer 1904:398. Type by original designation (also monotypic). Preoccupied by Stål 1865 in Hemiptera, replaced by *Notolychnus* Fraser-Brunner 1949. Type species misspelled as *valcidiae* in Zoological Record for 1946. Objective synonym of *Notolychnus* Fraser-Brunner 1949 (Paxton 1979:16 [ref. 6440]). Myctophidae.

Veternio Snyder 1904:516 [ref. 4149]. *Veternio verrens* Snyder 1904:516. Type by original designation (also monotypic). Synonym of *Conger* Oken 1817 (Smith 1989:513 [ref. 13285]). Congridae: Congrinae.

Vexillicaranx (subgenus of *Caranx*) Fowler 1905:76 [ref. 1369]. Masc. *Caranx africanus* Steindachner 1884:1108. Type by original designation (also monotypic). Synonym of *Caranx* Lacepède 1801 (Daget & Smith-Vaniz 1986:310 [ref. 6207]). Carangidae.

Vexillifer Gasco 1870:59 [ref. 1547]. Masc. *Vexillifer dephilippii* Gasco 1870:59. Type by monotypy. Original not seen. Synonym of *Carapus* Rafinesque 1810 (Arnold 1956:260 [ref. 5315], Wheeler 1973:557 [ref. 7190]). Carapidae: Carapinae.

Vexillitrigla Whitley 1931:327 [ref. 4672]. Fem. *Prionotus militaris* Goode & Bean 1896:464. Type by being a replacement name. Unneeded replacement for and objective synonym of *Bellator* Jordan & Evermann 1896, not preoccupied by *Bellatrix* Boie 1831 in Aves. Triglidae: Triglinae.

Victor Whitley 1951:68 [ref. 4711]. Masc. *Gerres filamentosus* Cuvier 1829:188. Type by being a replacement name. Replacement for *Pertica* Fowler 1904, preoccupied [details not researched]. Leiognathidae.

Vieja Fernández-Yépez 1969:[5] [ref. 9186]. Fem. *Vieja panamensis* Fernández-Yépez 1969:[5]. Type by original designation. Treated as feminine by author. Synonym of *Cichlasoma* Swainson 1839. Cichlidae.

Vigil Jordan 1919:344 [ref. 2413]. Masc. *Pleurolepis pellucidus* Agassiz in Putnam 1863:5. Type by being a replacement name. Replacement for *Pleurolepis* Putnam (ex Agassiz) 1863, preoccupied by Quenstedt 1862 in fossil fishes. Synonym of subgenus *Ammocrypta* of genus *Ammocrypta* Jordan 1877. Percidae.

Villarius Rutter 1896:256 [ref. 3841]. Masc. *Villarius pricei* Rutter 1896:257. Type by subsequent designation. Type designated by Jordan & Evermann 1898:2789 [ref. 2445]. Synonym of *Ictalurus* Rafinesque 1820. Ictaluridae.

Villora Hubbs & Cannon 1935:11 [ref. 2255]. Fem. *Villora edwini* Hubbs & Cannon 1935:13. Type by original designation (also monotypic). Synonym of *Etheostoma* Rafinesque 1819, but as a valid subgenus (Collette & Banarescu 1977:1456 [ref. 5845], Page 1981:37 [ref. 3347], Bailey & Etnier 1988:27 [ref. 6873]). Percidae.

Vimba Fitzinger 1873:152, 159 [ref. 1337]. Fem. *Cyprinus vimba* Linnaeus 1758:325. Type by absolute tautonymy, two included species, one *vimba*. Synonym of *Abramis* Cuvier 1816 (Howes 1981:46 [ref. 14200]); valid (Bogutskaya 1987:936 [ref. 13521]). Cyprinidae.

Vincentia Castelnau 1872:245 [ref. 757]. Fem. *Vincentia waterhousii* Castelnau 1872:245. Type by monotypy. Valid (Fraser 1972:12 [ref. 5195], Allen 1987:6 [ref. 13387], Paxton et al. 1989:559 [ref. 12442]). Apogonidae.

Vinciguerria Jordan & Evermann in Goode & Bean 1896:513 [ref. 1848]. Fem. *Maurolicus attenuatus* Cocco 1838:193. Type by monotypy. Also appeared in Jordan & Evermann 1896 (3 Oct.):577 [ref. 2443]. Valid (Witzell 1973:121 [ref. 7172], Weitzman 1974:472 [ref. 5174], Johnson & Feltes 1984 [ref. 5348], Badcock in Whitehead et al. 1984:322 [ref. 13675], Ahlstrom et al. 1984:185 [ref. 13643], Fujii in Masuda et al. 1984:45 [ref. 6441], Schaefer et al. 1986:245 [ref. 5709], Paxton et al. 1989:188 [ref. 12442]). Phosichthyidae.

Vinculum McCulloch 1914:110 [ref. 2940]. Neut. *Chaetodon sexfasciatus* Richardson 1842:26. Type by monotypy. Kyphosidae: Microcanthinae.

Vipera Edwards (ex Catesby) 1771:9, appendix [ref. 774]. Fem. The appendix by Edwards is available, but Catesby is a rejected work on Official Index (Opinion 89, Opinion 259). But *Vipera* Edwards not intended as a generic name (see Jordan 1917:32 [ref. 2407]). In the synonymy of *Chauliodus* Bloch & Schneider 1801. Chauliodontidae.

Vireosa Jordan & Snyder 1901:34, 38 [ref. 2509]. Fem. *Vireosa hanae* Jordan & Snyder 1901:38. Type by original designation (also monotypic). Valid (Yanagisawa 1978:315 [ref. 7028]); synonym of *Eleotris* Gill 1863 (Randall & Hoese 1985 [ref. 5197]). Microdesmidae: Ptereleotrinae.

Virididentex (subgenus of *Dentex*) Poll 1971:9 [ref. 3531]. Masc. *Dentex acromegalus* Osório 1909:61. Type by original designation (also monotypic). Sparidae.

Virilia Roberts 1967:253 [ref. 3771]. Fem. *Phenacogrammus pabrensis* Roman 1966:71. Type by original designation. Synonym of *Phenacogrammus* Eigenmann 1907 (Paugy 1984:179 [ref. 6183]). Alestiidae.

Vitiaziella Rass 1955:330 [ref. 3610]. Fem. *Vitiaziella cubiceps* Rass 1955:331. Type by original designation (also monotypic). Valid (Myers & Freihofer 1966:193 [ref. 3088]). Megalomycteridae.

Vitraria Jordan & Evermann 1903:205 [ref. 2450]. Fem. *Vitraria clarescens* Jordan & Evermann 1903:205. Type by original designation (also monotypic). Valid (Birdsong et al. 1988:203 [ref. 7303]). Gobiidae.

Vitreola Jordan & Seale 1906:393 [ref. 2497]. Fem. *Vitreola sagitta* Jordan & Seale 1906:393. Type by original designation (also monotypic). Synonym of *Kraemeria* Steindachner (12 July) 1906, *Vitreola* published 15 Dec. 1906. Kraemeriidae.

Vivero (subgenus of *Epinephelus*) Jordan & Evermann 1927:505 [ref. 2453]. Masc. *Epinephelus morio* Cuvier in Cuvier & Valenciennes 1828:285. Type by original designation (also monotypic). Synonym of *Epinephelus* Bloch 1793 (Smith 1971:103 [ref. 14102], Daget & Smith 1986:301 [ref. 6204]). Serranidae: Epinephelinae.

Vogmarus Reid 1849:456 [ref. 3687]. Masc. *Bogmarus islandicus* Bloch & Schneider 1801:518. Original not seen. Apparently not intended as a new genus; see *Vogmarus* Reinhardt 1832. In the synonymy of *Trachipterus* Goüan 1770 (Palmer 1973:330 [ref. 7195]). Trachipteridae.

Vogmarus Reinhardt 1832:xviii [ref. 6533]. Masc. *Bogmarus islandicus* Bloch & Schneider 1801:518. Original not examined. Apparently an unneeded replacement for, or misspelling of *Bogmarus* Bloch & Schneider 1801. Name usually attributed to Reid 1849:456, but Reinhardt earlier. Synonym of *Trachipterus* Goüan 1770. Trachipteridae.

Volcanus Gosline 1954:78 [ref. 1860]. Masc. *Volcanus lineatus* Gosline 1954:79. Type by original designation (also monotypic). Synonym of *Luciobrotula* Smith & Radcliffe 1913 (Cohen 1974:109 [ref. 7139], Cohen & Nielsen 1978:35 [ref. 881]). Ophidiidae: Neobythitinae.

Volgiolus (subgenus of *Parvicrepis*) Whitley 1931:325 [ref. 4672]. Masc. *Diplocrepis costatus* Ogilby 1885:270. Type by original designation (also monotypic). Synonym of *Aspasmogaster* Waite 1907 (Briggs 1955:49 [ref. 637], Scott 1976:182 [ref. 7055]). Gobiesocidae: Gobiesocinae.

Vomer Cuvier 1816:316, 318 [ref. 993]. Masc. *Vomer brownii* Cuvier 1816:238. Type by subsequent designation. Type designated by Jordan & Gilbert 1883:440 [ref. 2476]. Also in Oken 1817:1182 (= p. 1782) [ref. 3303] (see Gill 1903:966 [ref. 5768]). Valid (Hureau & Tortonese 1973:384 [ref. 7198]); synonym of *Selene* Lacepède 1802 (Daget & Smith-Vaniz 1986:318 [ref. 6207]). Carangidae.

Vomeridens DeWitt & Hureau 1979:787 [ref. 1125]. Masc. *Racovitzia infuscipinnis* DeWitt 1964:502. Type by original designation (also monotypic). Valid (Stevens et al. 1984:563 [ref. 13633], Voskoboinikova 1988:45 [ref. 12756]). Bathydraconidae.

Vomerivulus (subgenus of *Rivulus*) Fowler 1944:244 [ref. 1452]. Masc. *Rivulus leucurus* Fowler 1944:244. Type by original designation (also monotypic). Synonym of *Rivulus* Poey 1860 (Parenti 1981:481 [ref. 7066]). Aplocheilidae: Rivulinae.

Vomerogobius Gilbert 1971:35 [ref. 1641]. Masc. *Vomerogobius flavus* Gilbert 1971:35. Type by original designation (also monotypic). Valid (Birdsong et al. 1988:203 [ref. 7303]). Gobiidae.

Vulpecula Garman (ex Valmont de Bomare) 1913:30 [ref. 1545]. Fem. *Vulpecula marina* Garman 1913:30. Type by monotypy. *Vulpecula* Valmont 1768 is unavailable (published in a rejected work). *Vulpecula* Garman is available, and described independently of Jarocki 1822. Garman recognized one species, based on pre-Linnaean *marina*, which can date to Garman. Synonym of *Alopias* Rafinesque 1810 (Compagno 1984:229 [ref. 6474]). Alopiidae.

Vulpecula Jarocki (ex Valmont de Bomare) 1822 [ref. 4984]. Fem. Original not seen. Synonym of *Alopias* Rafinesque 1810. Alopiidae.

Vulpecula Valmont de Bomare 1768:740 [ref. 4507]. Fem. Not available, published in a rejected work on Official Index (Opinion 89, Direction 32). Synonym of *Alopias* Rafinesque 1810 (Compagno 1984:229 [ref. 6474]). Alopiidae.

Vulpis Catesby 1771:1 [ref. 774]. Not available, published in a rejected work on Official Index (Opinion 89, Opinion 259). In the synonymy of *Albula* Scopoli 1777 (see Whitehead 1986:215 [ref. 5733]). Albulidae: Albulinae.

Vulsiculus Jordan & Evermann 1896:489 [ref. 2442]. Masc. *Peristedion imberbe* Poey 1861:367, 387. Type by original designation (also monotypic). Triglidae: Peristediinae.

Vulsus Günther 1861:151 [ref. 1964]. Masc. *Callionymus dactylopus* Bennett in Valenciennes in Cuvier & Valenciennes 1837:310. Type by being a replacement name. Unneeded replacement for and objective synonym of *Dactylopus* Gill 1860, not preoccupied by *Dactulopus* (see Fricke 1982:70 [ref. 5432]). Callionymidae.

Waitea Jordan & Seale 1906:407 [ref. 2497]. Fem. *Gobius mystacinus* Valenciennes in Cuvier & Valenciennes 1837:124. Type by original designation (also monotypic). Apparently based on a misidentified type species, specimen later renamed *Waitea stomias* by Smith 1941:411. Valid (Maugé 1986:386 [ref. 6218]). Gobiidae.

Waiteina (subgenus of *Colossoma*) Fowler 1907:473 [ref. 1374]. Fem. *Myletes nigripinnis* Cope 1878:693. Type by original designation (also monotypic). Synonym of *Colossoma* Eigenmann & Kennedy 1903 (Géry 1976:50 [ref. 14199] as *Wateina*). Characidae: Serrasalminae.

Waiteopsis Whitley 1930:122 [ref. 4669]. Fem. *Waiteopsis paludis* Whitley 1930:122. Type by original designation (also monotypic). Synonym of *Mugilogobius* Smitt 1900 (Hoese, pers. comm.). Gobiidae.

Wak Lin 1938:378 [ref. 6599]. *Bola coitor* Hamilton 1822:75, 368. Type by being a replacement name. Unneeded substitute for *Bola* Hamilton 1822. Synonym of *Johnius*, subgenus *Johnius* Bloch 1793 (Trewavas 1977:406 [ref. 4459]); valid (Tagawa in Masuda et al. 1984:162 [ref. 6441] as *Waku*). Sciaenidae.

Wakiyus Jordan & Hubbs 1925:286 [ref. 2486]. Masc. *Platycephalus spinosus* Temminck & Schlegel 1843:40. Type by original designation (also monotypic). Synonym of *Onigocia* Jordan & Thompson 1913 (Paxton et al. 1989:467 [ref. 12442] based on placement of the type species). Platycephalidae.

Walbaunina Fernández-Yépez 1948:24 [ref. 1316]. Fem. *Curimatus dorsalis* Eigenmann & Eigenmann 1889:420. Type by original designation (also monotypic). Synonym of *Curimatella* Eigenmann & Eigenmann 1889 (Vari 1989:6 [ref. 9189]). Curimatidae: Curimatinae.

Wallago Bleeker 1851:265 [ref. 325]. *Silurus muelleri* Bleeker 1846:289. Type by subsequent designation. Also in Bleeker 1851:198, 202 [ref. 329]. Bleeker 1862:394 [ref. 391] and 1862:17 [393] has type as *Wallago attu* Bleeker (*wallagoo* and *muelleri* originally included); Myers 1938:98 [ref. 3116] and 1948:19-20 [ref. 12606] missed 1851:265 description and erred in his analysis. Earliest valid designation probably by Haig 1952:101; see Appendix A. Valid (Haig 1952:79 [ref. 12607], Jayaram 1977:6 [ref. 7005] 1981:209 [ref. 6497], Roberts 1982 [ref. 6808], Burgess 1989:86 [ref. 12860], Roberts 1989:151 [ref. 6439]). Siluridae.

Wallagonia Myers 1938:98 [ref. 3116]. Fem. *Wallago leerii* Bleeker 1851:427. Type by original designation. Synonym of *Wallago* Bleeker 1851 (Haig 1952:101 [ref. 12607], Roberts 1982:890 [ref. 6808], Roberts 1989:151 [ref. 6439]). Siluridae.

Wamizichthys Smith 1954:205 [ref. 4091]. Masc. *Wamizichthys bibulus* Smith 1954:205. Type by original designation (also monotypic). Synonym of *Chlidichthys* Smith 1953 (Lubbock 1977: 12 [ref. 7039]). Pseudochromidae: Pseudoplesiopinae.

Wanderer Whitley 1937:229 [ref. 4690]. Masc. *Thynnus thunnina* Cuvier 1829. Type by being a replacement name. If regarded as a replacement for *Thynnichthys* Giglioli 1880 (preoccupied by Bleeker 1859 in fishes), then type is as above. Whitley named the type as *Wanderer wallisi* Whitley and that is type if regarded as a new genus; see Appendix A. Objective synonym of *Euthynnus* Lütken 1883 with type as *thunnina*. Scombridae.

Wangia Fowler 1954:54 [ref. 1467]. Fem. *Pomacentrus formosanus* Fowler & Bean 1922:46. Type by original designation (also monotypic). Preoccupied by Chen 1943 in Mollusca, replaced by *Wangietta* Whitley 1965. Pomacentridae.

Wangietta Whitley 1965:26 [ref. 4733]. Fem. *Pomacentrus formosanus* Fowler & Bean 1922:46. Type by being a replacement name. Replacement for *Wangia* Fowler 1954, preoccupied by Chen 1943 in Mollusca. Pomacentridae.

Warreenula (subgenus of *Astronesthes*) Whitley 1941:5 [ref. 4701]. Fem. *Astronesthes (Warreenula) lupina* Whitley 1941:5. Type by original designation (also monotypic). Based on a larva. Doubtful synonym of *Astronesthes* Richardson 1845 (Gibbs 1964:313 [ref. 6960]). Astronesthidae.

Watasea Jordan & Snyder 1901:765 [ref. 2504]. Fem. *Watasea sivicola* Jordan & Snyder 1901:765. Type by original designation. Synonym of *Neobythites* Goode & Bean 1885 (Cohen & Nielsen 1978:36 [ref. 881]). Ophidiidae: Neobythitinae.

Wattsia Chan & Chilvers 1974:85 [ref. 809]. Fem. *Gnathodentex mossambicus* Smith 1957:122. Type by monotypy. Valid (Sato in Masuda et al. 1984:179 [ref. 6441], Smith 1986:599 [ref. 5712], Sato 1986:604 [ref. 5152]). Lethrinidae.

Weberogobius Koumans 1953:172 [ref. 2678]. Masc. *Gobius amadi* Weber 1913:211. Type by original designation (also monotypic). Valid (Miller 1987:695 [ref. 6336]). Gobiidae.

Weerutta Scott 1962:310 [ref. 6608]. Fem. *Weerutta ovalis* Scott 1962:310. Type by monotypy. Synonym of *Eubalichthys* Whitley 1930 (Hutchins 1977:55 [ref. 2283]). Monacanthidae.

Wertheimeria Steindachner 1876:659 [101] [ref. 4224]. Fem. *Wertheimeria maculata* Steindachner 1876:660. Type by monotypy. Appeared first as name only in Steindachner 1876:191 [ref. 12584]. On p. 101 of separate. Valid (Burgess 1989:242 [ref. 12860]), but doubtfully in the Auchenipteridae (Curran 1989:414 [ref. 12547]). Auchenipteridae.

Wetmorella Fowler & Bean 1928:211 [ref. 1475]. Fem. *Wetmorella philippina* Fowler & Bean 1928:211. Type by original designation (also monotypic). Valid (Randall 1983 [ref. 5360], Yamakawa in Masuda et al. 1984:212 [ref. 6441]). Labridae.

Wheelerigobius Miller 1981:275 [ref. 3013]. Masc. *Eleotris maltzani* Steindachner 1882:40. Type by original designation (also monotypic). Valid (Maugé 1986:386 [ref. 6218]). Gobiidae.

Whitleyia Chabanaud 1930:16 [ref. 784]. Fem. *Synaptura setifer* Pardice & Whitley 1927:101. Type by original designation (also monotypic). See also *Whitleyia* Fowler & Bean 1930. Soleidae.

Whitleyia (subgenus of *Ambassis*) Fowler & Bean 1930:148, 163 [ref. 1477]. Fem. *Ambassis wolffi* Bleeker 1850:3, 9. Type by original designation (also monotypic). Spelled *Whitleyia* on pp. 2 and 148, as *Whitleyina* on pp. vii (contents), 163 (main account) and index (p. 334). *Whitleyina* would appear to be the intended form, but Fraser-Brunner 1955 [ref. 1498] serves as first reviser and selected *Whitleyia*. *Whitleyia* is preoccupied by Chabanaud 1930 in recent fishes. Synonym of *Parambassis* Bleeker 1874 (Roberts 1989:161 [ref. 6439] as *Whitleyina*). Ambassidae.

Whitleyidea (subgenus of *Alepocephalus*) Fowler 1934:247 [ref. 1416]. Fem. *Alepocephalus niger* Günther 1878:248. Type by original designation (also monotypic). Alepocephalidae.

Whitleyina See *Whitleyia* Fowler & Bean. Ambassidae.

Wilkesina (subgenus of *Harengula*) Fowler & Bean 1923:3 [ref. 1474]. Fem. *Harengula fijiense* Fowler & Bean 1923:3. Type by original designation. Synonym of *Sardinella* Valenciennes 1847 (Whitehead 1985:90 [ref. 5141]). Clupeidae.

Winteria Brauer 1901:126 [ref. 630]. Fem. *Winteria telescopa* Brauer 1901:126. Type by monotypy. Valid (Ahlstrom et al. 1984:156 [ref. 13627], Fujii in Masuda et al. 1984:42 [ref. 6441], Heemstra 1986:218 [ref. 5660]). Opisthoproctidae.

Woodsia Grey 1959:174 [ref. 1904]. Fem. *Photichthys nonsuchae* Beebe 1932:61. Type by original designation (also monotypic). Valid (Krefft 1973 [ref. 7146], Weitzman 1974:472 [ref. 5174], Ahlstrom et al. 1984:185 [ref. 13643], Fujii in Masuda et al. 1984:45 [ref. 6441], Schaefer et al. 1986:246 [ref. 5709], Paxton et al. 1989:189 [ref. 12442]). Phosichthyidae.

Wuia (subgenus of *Heterodontus*) Fowler 1934:233 [ref. 1416]. Fem. *Centracion zebra* Gray 1831:5. Type by original designation (also monotypic). Objective synonym of *Centracion* Gray 1831; synonym of *Heterodontus* Blainville 1816 (Compagno 1984:155 [ref. 6474]). Heterodontidae.

Xanclorhynchus See *Zanclorhynchus* Günther. Congiopodidae.

Xanothon Smith 1956:4 [ref. 4104]. Masc. *Callyodon bipallidus* Smith 1955:936. Type by original designation. Synonym of *Scarus* Forsskål 1775. Scaridae: Scarinae.

Xanthichthys Kaup in Richardson 1856:313 [ref. 3747]. Masc. *Balistes curassavicus* Gmelin 1788:1472. Type by monotypy. Valid (Randall, Matsuura & Zama 1978 [ref. 5532], Matsuura

1980:59 [ref. 6943], Tyler 1980 [ref. 4477], Arai 1983:199 [ref. 14249], Aboussouan & Leis 1984:452 [ref. 13661], Matsuura in Masuda et al. 1984:359 [ref. 6441], Smith & Heemstra 1986:881 [ref. 5714]). Balistidae.

Xantocles Jordan 1917:88 [ref. 2408]. Masc. *Zaniolepis frenatus* Eigenmann 1889:147. Type by original designation (also monotypic). Synonym of *Zaniolepis* Girard 1858. Hexagrammidae: Zaniolepidinae.

Xarifania Klausewitz & Eibl-Eibesfeldt 1959:137 [ref. 2616]. Fem. *Xarifania hassi* Klausewitz & Eibl-Eibesfeldt 1959:138. Type by original designation. Valid (Klausewitz & von Hentig 1975 [ref. 7093]); synonym of *Heteroconger* Bleeker 1868 (Smith 1989:485 [ref. 13285]). Congridae: Heterocongrinae.

Xenagoniates Myers 1942:90 [ref. 3121]. Masc. *Xenagoniates bondi* Myers 1942:90. Type by original designation (also monotypic). Valid (Géry 1977:347 [ref. 1597]). Characidae.

Xenambassis Schultz 1945:115 [ref. 3962]. Fem. *Xenambassis honessi* Schultz 1945:118. Type by original designation. Synonym of *Synechopterus* Norman 1935. Ambassidae.

Xenanthias Regan 1908:223 [ref. 3634]. Masc. *Xenanthias gardineri* Regan 1908:223. Type by monotypy. Synonym of *Plectranthias* Bleeker 1873 (Randall 1980:105 [ref. 6717]). Serranidae: Anthiinae.

Xenaploactis Poss & Eschmeyer 1980:288 [ref. 3553]. Fem. *Prosopodasys asperrimus* Günther 1860:140. Type by original designation. Valid (Washington et al. 1984:441 [ref. 13660]). Aploactinidae.

Xenatherina Regan 1907:64 [ref. 3629]. Fem. *Menidia lisa* Meek 1904:182. Type by original designation (also monotypy). Synonym of *Atherinella* Steindachner 1875 (Chernoff & Miller 1984:1 [ref. 8175], Chernoff 1986:240 [ref. 5847]). Atherinidae: Menidiinae.

Xenendum Jordan & Snyder 1899:127 [ref. 2501]. Neut. *Xenendum caliente* Jordan & Snyder 1900:127. Type by original designation. Goodeidae.

Xenengraulis Jordan & Seale 1925:29 [ref. 2499]. Fem. *Xenengraulis spinidens* Jordan & Seale 1925:29. Type by original designation (also monotypic). Synonym of *Thryssa* Cuvier 1829 (Whitehead et al. 1988:421 [ref. 5725]). Engraulidae.

Xenentodon Regan 1911:332 [ref. 3641]. Masc. *Belone cancila* Hamilton 1822:213, 380. Type by subsequent designation. Type designated by Jordan 1920:540 [ref. 4905]. Valid (Jayaram 1981:291 [ref. 6497], Collette et al. 1984:336 [ref. 11422], Kottelat 1989:16 [ref. 13605], Roberts 1989:152 [ref. 6439]). Belonidae.

Xeneretmus Gilbert in Jordan 1903:360 [ref. 2399]. Masc. *Xenochirus triacanthus* Gilbert 1890:91. Type by being a replacement name. Replacement for *Xenochirus* Gilbert 1890, preoccupied by Gloger 1842 in Mammalia. Valid (Washington et al. 1984:442 [ref. 13660], Yabe 1985:123 [ref. 11522], Leipertz 1985 [ref. 5243]). Agonidae.

Xenichthys Gill 1863:81 [ref. 1679]. Masc. *Xenichthys xanti* Gill 1863:82. Type by monotypy. Valid (Johnson 1980:11 [ref. 13553]). Haemulidae.

Xenisma Jordan 1876:142 [ref. 10443]. Neut. *"Fundulus" stelliferus* Jordan 1876:142. Type by subsequent designation. Proposed as a genus "or perhaps the sub-genus of *Fundulus*", with two species (*X. stellifera* Jordan MSS and *catenata* Storer); description of *stellifera* as *F. stelliferus* in footnote (p. 142) validates *stellifera* (see also Jordan 1877:322 [ref. 2373]). "Typified by" not precise enough; type designated by Jordan 1877:322 [ref. 2373]. Synonym of *Fundulus* Lacepède 1803 (Parenti 1981:494 [ref. 7066]); as a valid subgenus (Cashner et al. 1988 [ref. 6681]). Cyprinodontidae: Fundulinae.

Xenisthmus Snyder 1908:105 [ref. 4150]. Masc. *Xenisthmus proriger* Snyder 1908:105. Type by original designation (also monotypic). Valid (Springer 1983:1 [ref. 5365], Akihito in Masuda et al. 1984:241 [ref. 6441], Hoese 1986:811 [ref. 5670], Springer 1988:536 [ref. 6683], Birdsong et al. 1988:183 [ref. 7303]). Xenisthmidae.

Xenistius Jordan & Gilbert 1883:920 [ref. 2476]. Masc. *Xenichthys californiensis* Steindachner 1875:31. Type by original designation (also monotypic). Spelled *Xenisteus* by Neave 1940:666 [ref. 12569] and in Zoological Record for 1883. Valid (Johnson 1980:11 [ref. 13553]). Haemulidae.

Xenobalistes Matsuura 1981:191 [ref. 2910]. Masc. *Xenobalistes tumidipectoris* Matsuura 1981:192. Type by original designation (also monotypic). Valid (Heemstra & Smith 1983 [ref. 5414], Smith & Heemstra 1986:881 [ref. 5714]). Balistidae.

Xenobarbus Norman 1923:694 [ref. 3213]. Masc. *Xenobarbus loveridgei* Norman 1923:695. Type by monotypy. Valid (Lévêque & Daget 1984:342 [ref. 6186]). Cyprinidae.

Xenobrama Yatsu & Nakamura 1989:190 [ref. 13449]. *Xenobrama microlepis* Yatsu & Nakamura 1989:192. Type by original designation (also monotypic). Bramidae.

Xenobuglossus Chabanaud 1950:13 [ref. 801]. Masc. *Xenobuglossus elongatus* Chabanaud 1950:13. Type by monotypy. Soleidae.

Xenobythites Smith & Radcliffe in Radcliffe 1913:173 [ref. 3579]. Masc. *Xenobythites armiger* Smith & Radcliffe in Radcliffe 1913:173. Type by original designation (also monotypic). Synonym of *Bellottia* Giglioli 1883 (Cohen & Nielsen 1978:45 [ref. 881]). Bythitidae: Bythitinae.

Xenocara Regan 1904:195, 251 [ref. 3621]. Neut. *Chaetostomus latifrons* Günther 1869:426. Type by subsequent designation. Type designated by Eigenmann 1910:410 [ref. 1224]. Correct spelling for genus of type species is *Chaetostoma*. Synonym of *Ancistrus* Kner 1854 (Isbrücker 1980:66 [ref. 2303]). Loricariidae.

Xenocephalus Kaup 1858:85 [ref. 2576]. Masc. *Xenocephalus armatus* Kaup 1858:85. Type by monotypy. Family placement uncertain, based on young. Xenocephalidae.

Xenoceratias Regan & Trewavas 1932:54 [ref. 3682]. Masc. *Xenoceratias longirostris* Regan & Trewavas 1932:54. Not available from Regan & Trewavas 1932 (Art. 13b). Subsequent publication in an available way not researched; not made available in the Zoological Record for 1932. Synonym of *Melanocetus* Günther 1864 (Pietsch & Van Duzer 1980:70 [ref. 5333]). Melanocetidae.

Xenocharax Günther 1867:114 [ref. 1989]. Masc. *Xenocharax spilurus* Günther 1867:114. Type by monotypy. Valid (Géry 1977:62 [ref. 1597], Vari 1979:340 [ref. 5490], Daget & Gosse 1984:210 [ref. 6185]). Citharinidae: Distichodontinae.

Xenocheilichthys Smith 1934:304 [ref. 4052]. Masc. *Xenocheilichthys gudgeri* Smith 1934:305. Type by monotypy. Synonym of *Sikukia* Smith 1931 (Kottelat 1985:954 [ref. 5288], Chu & Cui in Chu & Chen 1989:166 [ref. 13584]). Cyprinidae.

Xenochirus Gilbert 1890:90 [ref. 1623]. Masc. *Xenochirus triacanthus* Gilbert 1890:91. Type by original designation. Preoccupied by Gloger 1842 in Mammalia, replaced by *Xeneretmus* Gilbert 1903. Objective synonym of *Xeneretmus* Gilbert 1903. Agonidae.

Xenochromis Boulenger 1899:125 [ref. 589]. Masc. *Xenochromis* *hecqui* Boulenger 1899:125. Type by original designation (also monotypic). Type designated on p. 126. Synonym of *Perissodus* Boulenger 1898 (Liem & Stewart 1976 [ref. 7096]); valid (Poll 1986:152 [ref. 6136]). Cichlidae.

Xenoclarias Greenwood 1958:321 [ref. 1895]. Masc. *Clarias eupogon* Norman 1928:105. Type by original designation. Valid (Poll 1977:147 [ref. 3533], Teugels 1986:101 [ref. 6193], Burgess 1989:147 [ref. 12860]). Clariidae.

Xenoconger Regan 1912:301 [ref. 3643]. Masc. *Xenoconger fryeri* Regan 1912:301. Type by monotypy. Valid (Smith 1989:77 [ref. 13285]). Chlopsidae.

Xenocyprioides Chen 1982:425 [427] [ref. 826]. Masc. *Xenocyprioides parvulus* Chen 1982:425 [427]. Type by original designation (also monotypic). English description on p. 427. Cyprinidae.

Xenocypris Günther 1868:205 [ref. 1990]. Fem. *Xenocypris argentea* Günther 1868:205. Type by monotypy. Valid (Yang 1964:121 [ref. 13500], Howes 1981:45 [ref. 14200], Li 1986:480 [ref. 6154], Bogutskaya 1987:936 [ref. 13521], Chen & Li in Chu & Chen 1989:93 [ref. 13584]). Cyprinidae.

Xenocys Jordan & Bollman 1890:160 [ref. 2433]. Fem. *Xenocys jessiae* Jordan & Bollman 1890:160. Type by original designation (also monotypic). Valid (Johnson 1980:12 [ref. 13553]). Haemulidae.

Xenocyttus Abe 1957:225 [ref. 6]. Masc. *Xenocyttus nemotoi* Abe 1957:228. Type by original designation (also monotypic). Synonym of *Pseudocyttus* Gilchrist 1906 (Karrer 1986:440 [ref. 5680], James et al. 1988:293 [ref. 6639]). Oreosomatidae.

Xenodermichthys Günther 1878:250 [ref. 2010]. Masc. *Xenodermichthys nodulosus* Günther 1878:250. Type by monotypy. Valid (Krefft 1973:92 [ref. 7166], Markle & Quéro in Whitehead et al. 1984:252 [ref. 13675], Machida in Masuda et al. 1984:43 [ref. 6441], Markle 1986:223 [ref. 5687], Carvalho & Almeida 1988 [ref. 6862], Paxton et al. 1989:211 [ref. 12442]). Alepocephalidae.

Xenodexia Hubbs 1950:8 [ref. 2250]. Fem. *Xenodexia ctenolepis* Hubbs 1950:9. Type by original designation (also monotypic). Valid (Rosen & Bailey 1963:142 [ref. 7067], Parenti & Rauchenberger 1989:10 [ref. 13538]). Poeciliidae.

Xenodon Rüppell 1836:52 [ref. 3844]. Masc. *Xenodon niger* Rüppell 1837:53. Type by monotypy. Spelled *Zenodon* by Swainson 1839:194, 325 [ref. 4303]. Genus is in the part published in 1836, species in 1837. Preoccupied by Boie 1827 in Amphibia; replaced by *Odonus* Gistel 1848, *Erythrodon* Rüppell 1852, and *Pyrodon* Kaup 1853. Type based on "Baliste noir" Lacepède 1798; Günther 1870 renamed *niger* Rüppell as *Balistes erythrodon*; not *Balistes niger* Bloch 1786. Synonym of *Odonus* Gistel 1848 (Matsuura 1980:33 [ref. 6943]). Balistidae.

Xenognathus Gilbert 1915:311 [ref. 1632]. Masc. *Xenognathus profundorum* Gilbert 1915:311. Type by original designation (also monotypic). Alepocephalidae.

Xenogobius Metzelaar 1919:140 [ref. 2982]. Masc. *Xenogobius weberi* Metzelaar 1919:140. Type by monotypy. Also appeared as new in Metzelaar 1922:141 [ref. 5741]. Synonym of *Microgobius* Poey 1876 (Birdsong 1981:268 [ref. 5425]). Gobiidae.

Xenogramma Waite 1904:157 [ref. 4561]. Neut. *Xenogramma carinatum* Waite 1904:158. Type by original designation (also monotypic). Synonym of *Lepidocybium* Gill 1862 (Parin & Bekker 1973:458 [ref. 7206], Nakamura 1986:826 [ref. 5696]). Gempylidae.

Xenojulis de Beaufort 1939:415 [ref. 238]. Fem. *Xenojulis montillai* de Beaufort 1939:417. Type by original designation. Type designated on p. 419. Valid (Randall & Adamson 1982 [ref. 5445]). Labridae.

Xenolepidichthys Gilchrist 1922:73 [ref. 1648]. Masc. *Xenolepidichthys dalgleishi* Gilchrist 1922:73. Type by monotypy. Valid (Shimizu in Uyeno et al. 1983:291 [ref. 14275], Machida in Masuda et al. 1984:118 [ref. 6441], Karrer & Heemstra 1986:440 [ref. 5681], Paxton et al. 1989:391 [ref. 12442]). Grammicolepididae.

Xenomedea Rosenblatt & Taylor 1971:444 [ref. 3811]. Fem. *Xenomedea rhodopyga* Rosenblatt & Taylor 1971:445. Type by original designation (also monotypic). Labrisomidae.

Xenomelaniris Schultz 1948:(13) 33 [ref. 3966]. Fem. *Atherina brasiliensis* Quoy & Gaimard 1825:332. Type by original designation. Synonym of *Atherinella* Steindachner 1875, but as a valid subgenus (Chernoff 1986:241 [ref. 5847]). Atherinidae: Menidiinae.

Xenomugil Schultz 1946:(380) 386 [ref. 3965]. Masc. *Mugil thoburni* Jordan & Starks in Jordan & Evermann 1896:812. Type by original designation (also monotypic). Mugilidae.

Xenomystax Gilbert 1891:348 [ref. 1625]. Masc. *Xenomystax atrarius* Gilbert 1891:348. Type by original designation (also monotypic). Also appeared in Gilbert in Jordan & Davis 1891 (month uncertain):648 [ref. 2437]. Valid (Smith 1989:558 [ref. 13285]). Congridae: Congrinae.

Xenomystus (subgenus of *Notopterus*) Günther 1868:479, 481 [ref. 1990]. Masc. *Notopterus nigri* Günther 1868:481. Type by monotypy. Described in key (p. 479) for one species treated on p. 481. Valid (Daget 1984:61 [ref. 6170]). Notopteridae.

Xenomystus Lütken 1874:217, 220 [ref. 2854]. Masc. *Xenomystus gobio* Lütken 1874:217, 220. Type by original designation (also monotypic). Preoccupied by Günther 1868 in fishes, replaced by *Hemipsilichthys* Eigenmann & Eigenmann 1889. Objective synonym of *Hemipsilichthys* Eigenmann & Eigenmann 1889 (Isbrücker 1980:11 [ref. 2303]). Loricariidae.

Xenoophorus Hubbs & Turner 1939:51 [ref. 2265]. Masc. *Goodea captiva* Hubbs 1924:4. Type by original designation. Name appeared first in Turner 1937:496 et seq. [ref. 6400], without clear differentiating characters and no fixation of type species. Valid (Uyeno et al. 1983:507 [ref. 6818]). Goodeidae.

Xenophallus Hubbs 1924:10 [ref. 2231]. Masc. *Gambusia umbratilis* Meek 1912:70. Type by original designation (also monotypic). Synonym of *Neoheterandria* Henn 1916 (Rosen & Bailey 1963:126 [ref. 7067]); valid (Radda & Meyer 1981:115 [ref. 5875]). Poeciliidae.

Xenophrynichthys (subgenus of *Antennatus*) Schultz 1957:(55) 81 [ref. 3969]. Masc. *Antennarius cryptacanthus* Weber 1913:564. Type by original designation (also monotypic). Objective synonym of *Golem* Whitley 1957 (apparently published earlier in 1957). Synonym of *Histiophryne* Gill 1863 (Pietsch 1984:40 [ref. 5380]). Antennariidae.

Xenophthalmichthys Regan 1925:59 [ref. 3676]. Masc. *Xenophthalmichthys danae* Regan 1925:59. Type by monotypy. Valid (Ahlstrom et al. 1984:156 [ref. 13627]). Microstomatidae.

Xenophysogobio (subgenus of *Gobiobotia*) Chen & Tsao 1977:567 [ref. 825]. Masc. *Gobiobotia boulengeri* Tchang 1929:307. Type by original designation (also monotypic). Cyprinidae.

Xenopoclinops (subgenus of *Xenopoclinus*) Smith 1961:352, 354 [ref. 4127]. Masc. *Xenopoclinops leprosus* Smith 1961:354. Type by original designation (also monotypic). Clinidae.

Xenopoclinus Smith 1948:732 [ref. 4075]. Masc. *Xenopoclinus kochi* Smith 1948:732. Type by original designation (also monotypic). Valid (Smith 1986:768 [ref. 5712]). Clinidae.

Xenopoecilus Regan 1911:374 [ref. 5762]. Masc. *Haplochilus sarasinorum* Popta 1905:239. Type by monotypy. Valid (Collette et al. 1984:352 [ref. 11422]). Adrianichthyidae: Adrianichthyinae.

Xenopomichthys Pellegrin 1905:145 [ref. 3420]. Masc. *Xenopomichthys auriculatus* Pellegrin 1905:146. Type by monotypy. *Xenopomatichthys* Boulenger 1909 is an unjustified emendation or misspelling. Synonym of *Kneria* Steindachner 1866 (Poll 1984:129 [ref. 6180]). Kneriidae.

Xenopterus Troschel (ex Bibron) 1856:88 [ref. 12559]. Masc. *Xenopterus [sic] bellengeri* Bibron in Duméril 1855:281 (= *Tetraodon naritus* Richardson 1848). Appeared first as "Xénoptère" Bibron in Duméril 1855:281 [ref. 297]; latinized by Troschel as above, also by Hollard 1856:319 [ref. 2186]. Addition of species not researched; type as given by Jordan 1919:263 [ref. 2410]. Perhaps an objective synonym of *Chonerhinos* Bleeker 1854, but not currently so treated. Valid (Fraser-Brunner 1943:16 [ref. 1495], Tyler 1980:341 [ref. 4477], Jayaram 1981:393 [ref. 6497], Arai 1983:208 [ref. 14249], Kottelat 1989:21 [ref. 13605]). Tetraodontidae.

Xenopyxis (subgenus of *Xeneretmus*) Gilbert 1915:345 [ref. 1632]. *Xenochirus latifrons* Gilbert 1890:92. Type by original designation. Described in key; type designated in footnote. Agonidae.

Xenorhynchichthys Regan 1908:461 [ref. 3637]. Masc. *Joturus stipes* Jordan & Gilbert 1882:373. Type by original designation (also monotypic). Misspelled *Xenorhychichthys* by Jordan 1920:530 [ref. 4905]. Mugilidae.

Xenoscarops (subgenus of *Scarops*) Schultz 1958:16, 23 [ref. 3970]. Masc. *Scarus perrico* Jordan & Gilbert 1881:357. Type by original designation (also monotypic). Scaridae: Scarinae.

Xenoscarus Evermann & Radcliffe 1917:129 [ref. 1284]. Masc. *Xenoscarus denticulatus* Evermann & Radcliffe 1917:129. Type by original designation (also monotypic). Scaridae: Sparisomatinae.

Xenotaenia Turner 1946:6 [ref. 4471]. Fem. *Xenotaenia resolanae* Turner 1946:7. Type by original designation (also monotypic). Valid (Uyeno et al. 1983:507 [ref. 6818]). Goodeidae.

Xenotilapia Boulenger 1899:92 [ref. 550]. Fem. *Xenotilapia sima* Boulenger 1899:92. Type by monotypy. Valid (Poll 1986:109 [ref. 6136]). Cichlidae.

Xenotis Jordan 1877:76 [ref. 2372]. Fem. *Pomotis fallax* Baird & Girard 1854:24. Type by original designation. Synonym of *Lepomis* Rafinesque 1819. Centrarchidae.

Xenotoca Hubbs & Turner 1939:41 [ref. 2265]. Fem. *Characodon variatus* Bean 1887:370. Type by original designation (also monotypic). Name appeared first in Turner 1937:508 et seq. [ref. 6400], without clear differentiating characters. Valid (Fitzsimons 1972:739 [ref. 7117], Uyeno et al. 1983:507 [ref. 6818]). Goodeidae.

Xenurobrycon Myers & Miranda-Ribeiro 1945:2 [ref. 3131]. Masc. *Xenurobrycon macropus* Myers & Miranda-Ribeiro 1945:5. Type by original designation (also monotypic). Valid (Weitzman & S. Fink 1985:1 et seq. [ref. 5203], Weitzman 1987 [ref. 5982]). Characidae: Glandulocaudinae.

Xenurocharax Regan 1913:463 [ref. 3656]. Masc. *Xenurocharax spurrellii* Regan 1913:463. Type by monotypy. Apparently a synonym of *Argopleura* Eigenmann (June) 1913, *Xenurocharax* published in Nov. Characidae: Glandulocaudinae.

Xererpes Jordan & Gilbert in Jordan & Starks 1895:846 [ref. 2522]. *Apodichthys fucorum* Jordan & Gilbert 1880:139. Type by monotypy. Synonym of *Apodichthys* Girard 1854 (Yatsu 1981:182 [ref. 4814]); valid (some recent authors). Pholidae.

Xesurus Jordan & Evermann 1896:421 [ref. 2442]. Masc. *Prionurus punctatus* Gill 1862:242. Type by original designation. Synonym of *Prionurus* Lacepède 1804 (Randall 1955:362 [ref. 13648]). Acanthuridae.

Xiphasia Swainson 1839:179, 259 [ref. 4303]. Fem. *Xiphasia setifer* Swainson 1839:259. Type by monotypy. "*Z. setifer*" in original description (p. 259) in error for *X. setifer*. Valid (Smith-Vaniz 1976:65 [ref. 4144], Yoshino in Masuda et al. 1984:297 [ref. 6441], Springer 1986:754 [ref. 5719], Smith-Vaniz 1987:4 [ref. 6404]). Blenniidae.

Xiphias Linnaeus 1758:248 [ref. 2787]. Masc. *Xiphias gladius* Linnaeus 1758:248. Type by monotypy. *Xyphias*, *Ziphias*, and *Ziphius* are misspellings or unjustified emendations. On Official List (Opinion 75). Valid (Tortonese 1973:482 [ref. 7192], Nakamura 1983:263 [ref. 5371], Collette et al. 1984:600 [ref. 11421], Nakamura in Masuda et al. 1984:224 [ref. 6441], Heemstra 1986:839 [ref. 5660]). Xiphiidae.

Xiphichthys (subgenus of *Gymnetrus*) Swainson 1839:46, 178, 259 [ref. 4303]. Masc. *Gymnetrus russellii* Swainson 1839 (?= *Gymnetrus russelli* Cuvier 1816.). Type by monotypy. Appeared as *Xiphichthis* on p. 46 (regarded as a misspelling) and *Xiphichthys* on 178, 259, and 445 (index). Synonym of *Regalecus* Ascanius 1772. Regalecidae.

Xiphidion Girard 1858:119 [ref. 4911]. Neut. *Xiphidion mucosum* Girard 1858:119. Type by monotypy. Apparently not preoccupied by *Xiphidium* Serville 1831 in Orthoptera; probably should be used instead of replacement *Xiphister* in current literature [if Fowler MS is correct]. Possibly published ion 1859. Stichaeidae.

Xiphister Jordan 1880:241 [ref. 2381]. Masc. *Xiphidion mucosum* Girard 1858:119. Type by being a replacement name. Apparently an unneeded replacement for *Xiphidion* Girard 1858, not preoccupied by *Xiphidium* Serville 1831 in Orthoptera. Valid (Yatsu 1986 [ref. 5150]). Stichaeidae.

Xiphistes Jordan & Starks 1895:847 [ref. 2522]. Masc. *Xiphister chirus* Jordan & Gilbert 1880:135. Type by original designation. Preoccupied in Hemiptera [details not investigated], replaced by *Phytichthys* Hubbs 1923. Objective synonym of *Phytichthys* Hubbs 1923. Stichaeidae.

Xiphiurus Smith 1847:Pl. 31 [ref. 4035]. Masc. *Xiphiurus capensis* Smith 1847:Pl. 31. Type by monotypy. Placed on Official Index for purposes of priority to conserve *Genypterus* Philippi 1857 (Opinion 1200). Ophidiidae: Ophidiinae.

Xiphocharax Fowler 1914:251 [ref. 1390]. Masc. *Xiphocharax ogilviei* Fowler 1914:252. Type by original designation (also monotypic). Synonym of *Roestes* Günther 1864 (Menezes 1974:221 [ref. 7129]). Characidae.

Xiphocheilus Bleeker 1856:223 [ref. 354]. Masc. *Xiphocheilus typus* Bleeker 1856:224. Type by monotypy. Spelled *Xiphochilus* by authors. Labridae.

Xiphogadus Günther 1862:374 [ref. 1969]. Masc. *Xiphasia setifer* Swainson 1839:(179) 259. Type by being a replacement name. Unneeded substitute for *Xiphasia* Swainson 1839. Objective synonym of *Xiphasia* Swainson 1839 (Smith-Vaniz 1976:65 [ref. 4144]). Blenniidae.

Xiphophorus Heckel 1848:291 [ref. 2069]. Masc. *Xiphophorus helleri* Heckel 1848:291. Type by subsequent designation. Type designated by Bleeker 1864:140 [ref. 4859], also by Günther 1866:349 [ref. 1983]. Valid (Rosen & Bailey 1963:63 [ref. 7067], Rosen 1979:332 [ref. 7020], Paxton et al. 1989:347 [ref. 12442], Parenti & Rauchenberger 1989:8 [ref. 13538]). Poeciliidae.

Xiphorhamphus Müller & Troschel 1844:92 [ref. 3070]. Masc. *Salmo falcatus* Bloch 1794:120. Type by being a replacement name. Replacement for *Xiphorhynchus* Agassiz 1829, preoccupied by Swainson 1827 in Aves. *Xiphorhamphus* itself preoccupied by Blyth 1843 in Aves; replaced by *Acestrorhynchus* Eigenmann & Kennedy 1903. Characidae.

Xiphorhynchus (subgenus of *Hydrocyon*) Agassiz in Spix & Agassiz 1829:76 [ref. 13]. Masc. *Salmo falcatus* Bloch 1794:120. Type by subsequent designation. Type designated by Jordan 1917:132 [ref. 2407]. Preoccupied by Swainson 1827 in Aves, replaced first by *Xiphorhamphus* Müller & Troschel 1845 (itself preoccupied) then by *Acestrorhynchus* Eigenmann & Kennedy 1903. For authorship and date see Kottelat 1988:78 [ref. 13380]. Objective synonym of *Acestrorhynchus* Eigenmann & Kennedy 1903. Characidae.

Xiphostoma Agassiz in Spix & Agassiz 1829:60, 78 [ref. 13]. Neut. *Xiphostoma cuvieri* Agassiz in Spix & Agassiz 1829:78. Type by monotypy. Preoccupied by Kirby & Spence 1818 in Hemiptera, replaced by *Spixostoma* Whitley 1951. Spelled *Xiphostomus* by Swainson 1839:290 [ref. 4303], also *Xyphostoma* by authors. For authorship and date see Kottelat 1988:78 [ref. 13380]. Synonym of *Boulengerella* Eigenmann 1903. Ctenoluciidae.

Xiphypops Jordan in Jordan & Jordan 1922:64 [ref. 2487]. Masc. *Holacanthus fisheri* Snyder 1904:532. Type by original designation (also monotypic). Spelled *Xiphipops* in Weber & de Beaufort 1936:159 [ref. 4606]. Pomacanthidae.

Xurel Jordan & Evermann 1927:505 [ref. 2453]. Masc. *Caranx vinctus* Jordan & Gilbert 1881:349. Type by original designation (also monotypic). Synonym of *Carangoides* Bleeker 1851 (Smith-Vaniz, pers. comm.). Carangidae.

Xyelacyba Cohen 1961:288 [ref. 879]. Fem. *Xyelacyba myersi* Cohen 1961:289. Type by original designation (also monotypic). Valid (Cohen & Nielsen 1978:20 [ref. 881], Machida 1989 [ref. 12579]). Ophidiidae: Neobythitinae.

Xyliphius Eigenmann 1912:10 [ref. 1228]. Masc. *Xyliphius magdalenae* Eigenmann 1912:10. Type by monotypy. Spelled two ways in original description: *Xyliphius* and *Xiliphius*. *Xiliphius* used by Jordan 1920:543 [ref. 4905]. Valid (Mees 1988:90 [ref. 6401], Burgess 1989:303 [ref. 12860]). Aspredinidae: Bunocephalinae.

Xypterus Rafinesque 1810:43, 59 [ref. 3595]. Masc. *Xypterus imperati* Rafinesque 1810:43, 59. Type by monotypy. Synonym of *Regalecus* Ascanius 1772. Regalecidae.

Xyrauchen Eigenmann & Kirsch in Kirsch 1889:556 [ref. 2608]. Masc. *Catostomus cypho* Lockington 1880:237. Type by original designation (also monotypic). Valid. Catostomidae.

Xyrias Jordan & Snyder 1901:868 [ref. 2508]. Masc. *Xyrias revulsus* Jordan & Snyder 1901:869. Type by original designation (also monotypic). Valid (McCosker 1977:84 [ref. 6836], Asano in Masuda et al. 1984:31 [ref. 6441], McCosker et al. 1989:299 [ref. 13288]). Ophichthidae: Ophichthinae.

Xyrichtys Cuvier 1814:87 [ref. 4884]. Masc. *Coryphaena novacula* Linnaeus 1758:262. Type by subsequent designation. Apparently dates to Cuvier 1814:87 as "...de nouveau nom générique de XYRICHTE (*Xyrichlys* [sic])." Type designation not researched, technically not monotypy. As *Xirichthys* in Cuvier 1829:262 [ref. 995] and *Xyrichthys* by authors. Valid (Bauchot & Quignard 1973:442 [ref. 7204], Richards & Leis 1984:544 [ref. 13668], Yamakawa in Masuda et al. 1984:211 [ref. 6441], Randall 1986:705 [ref. 5706], Shen & Yeh 1987 [ref. 6419]). Labridae.

Xyrocharax (subgenus of *Curimatus*) Fowler 1914:673 [ref. 1391]. Masc. *Curimatus stigmaturus* Fowler 1914:673. Type by original designation. Synonym of *Cyphocharax* Fowler 1906 (Vari 1989:6 [ref. 9189]). Curimatidae: Curimatinae.

Xyrula Jordan 1890:656 [ref. 2392]. Fem. *Xyrichthys jessiae* Jordan 1887:698. Type by original designation (also monotypic). Correct spelling for genus of type species is *Xyrichtys*. Labridae.

Xystaema Jordan & Evermann in Jordan 1895:471 [ref. 2394]. Neut. *Mugil cinereus* Walbaum 1792:228. Type by original designation (also monotypic). Synonym of *Gerres* Quoy & Gaimard 1824 (Roux 1986:325 [ref. 6209] as *Xistaema*). Gerreidae.

Xyster Lacepède (ex Commerson) 1803:484 [ref. 4930]. Masc. *Xyster fuscus* Lacepède 1803:484, 485. Type by monotypy. Synonym of *Kyphosus* Lacepède 1801 (Desoutter 1973:420 [ref. 7203]). Kyphosidae: Kyphosinae.

Xysterus Rafinesque 1815:88 [ref. 3584]. Masc. Not available, name only. Regarded as an incorrect subsequent spelling for *Xyster* Lacepède 1803 based on Rafinesque style in this work. In the synonymy of *Kyphosus* Lacepède 1801 (Desoutter 1973:420 [ref. 7203]). Kyphosidae: Kyphosinae.

Xystes Jordan & Starks 1895:824 [ref. 2522]. Masc. *Xystes axinophrys* Jordan & Starks 1895:824. Type by monotypy. Agonidae.

Xystichromis Greenwood 1980:46 [ref. 1899]. Masc. *Chromis nuchisquamulatus* Hilgendorf 1888:76. Type by original designation. Cichlidae.

Xystodus Ogilby 1910:5 [ref. 3288]. Masc. *Xystodus banfieldi* Ogilby 1910:6. Type by original designation (also monotypic). Type designated on p. 1. Synonym of *Synodus* Scopoli 1777 (Sulak 1977:53 [ref. 4299]). Synodontidae: Synodontinae.

Xystophorus Richardson 1845:52 [ref. 3740]. Masc. *Gasterosteus ductor* Linnaeus 1758:295. Type by subsequent designation. Appeared without species; Fowler 1936:681 [ref. 6546] applied a species and named it as type but did not treat *Xystophorus* as a valid name. Synonym of *Naucrates* Rafinesque 1810. Carangidae.

Xystramia Jordan 1917:46 [ref. 2406]. Fem. *Glossamia pandionis* Goode & Bean 1881:160. Type by original designation (also monotypic). Synonym of *Epigonus* Rafinesque 1810 (Mayer 1974:151 [ref. 6007]). Epigonidae.

Xystreurys Jordan & Gilbert 1880:34 [ref. 2467]. *Xystreurys liolepis* Jordan & Gilbert 1880:34. Type by monotypy. Valid (Norman 1934:119 [ref. 6893], Ahlstrom et al. 1984:642 [ref. 13641]). Paralichthyidae.

Xystrias Jordan & Starks 1904:623 [ref. 2526]. Masc. *Hippoglossus grigorjewi* Herzenstein 1891:56. Type by original designation (also monotypic). Synonym of *Eopsetta* Jordan & Goss 1885 (Norman 1934:307 [ref. 6893]). Pleuronectidae: Pleuronectinae.

Xystroperca (subgenus of *Mycteroperca*) Jordan & Evermann 1896:1169, 70, 81 [ref. 2443]. Fem. *Mycteroperca pardalis* Gilbert 1891:551. Type by original designation (also monotypic). Synonym of *Mycteroperca* Gill 1862 (Smith 1971:171 [ref. 14102]). Serranidae: Epinephelinae.

Xystroplites Jordan in Cope 1877:66 [ref. 939]. Masc. *Xystroplites longimanus* Cope 1877:66. Type by monotypy. Published on 10

July 1877 as above; also in Jordan 1877:24 [ref. 2374], apparently of a slightly later date; if published first in ref. 2374 then type is *X. gillii* Jordan 1877 by original designation (also monotypic). Synonym of *Lepomis* Rafinesque 1819. Centrarchidae.

Xystrosus Jordan & Snyder 1899:123 [ref. 2501]. Masc. *Xystrosus popoche* Jordan & Snyder 1899:123. Type by original designation (also monotypic). Synonym of *Algansea* Girard 1856 (Barbour & Miller 1978:8 [ref. 7033]). Cyprinidae.

Yabotichthys Herre 1945:3 [ref. 2138]. Masc. *Yabotichthys nocturnus* Herre 1945:3. Type by original designation (also monotypic). Synonym of *Amblygobius* Bleeker 1874 (Hoese, pers. comm.). Gobiidae.

Yaci de Buen 1953:51 [ref. 694]. Fem. *Yaci retropinnis* de Buen 1953:52. Type by monotypy. Synonym of *Odontesthes* Evermann & Kendall 1906 (White 1985:18 [ref. 13551]). Atherinidae: Atherinopsinae.

Yacius Whitley 1970:245 [ref. 6601]. Masc. *Acanthodes fragilis* Fourmanoir & Crosnier 1964:23. Type by being a replacement name. Replacement for *Acanthodes* Fourmanoir & Crosnier 1964, preoccupied (but not available). Scorpaenidae: Scorpaeninae.

Yaoshanicus Lin 1931:50 [ref. 4019]. Masc. *Yaoshanicus arcus* Lin 1931:50. Original not translated, type apparently by monotypy. Valid (Yang & Hwang 1964:42 [ref. 13497]). Cyprinidae.

Yarica Whitley 1930:12 [ref. 4671]. Fem. *Apogon hyalosoma var. torresiensis* Castelnau 1875:9. Type by original designation (also monotypic). For purposes of the type species, the variety *torresiensis* is elevated to species level; type not *hyalosoma*. Synonym of *Apogon* Lacepède 1801, but as a valid subgenus (Fraser & Lachner 1985:4 [ref. 5215]). Apogonidae.

Yarra Castelnau 1872:231 [ref. 757]. Fem. *Yarra singularis* Castelnau 1872:231. Type by monotypy. In the synonymy of *Geotria* Gray 1851. Petromyzontidae: Geotriinae.

Yarrella Goode & Bean 1896:103 [ref. 1848]. Fem. *Yarrella blackfordi* Goode & Bean 1896:103. Type by monotypy. Valid (Weitzman 1974:472 [ref. 5174], Ahlstrom et al. 1984:185 [ref. 13643] as *Yarella*, Schaefer et al. 1986:243 [ref. 5709]). Phosichthyidae.

Yerutius Whitley 1931:115 [ref. 4673]. Masc. *Callionymus apricus* McCulloch 1926:209. Type by original designation. Synonym of *Synchiropus* Gill 1860, but as a valid subgenus (Fricke 1981:18 [ref. 1499], Fricke 1982:74 [ref. 5432]); synonym of *Foetorepus* Whitley 1931 (Nakabo 1982:87 [ref. 3139]). Callionymidae.

Yirrkala Whitley 1940:410 [ref. 4699]. Fem. *Yirrkala chaselingi* Whitley 1940:410. Type by original designation. Valid (McCosker 1977:69 [ref. 6836], McCosker & Castle 1986:185 [ref. 5690], Paxton et al. 1989:121 [ref. 12442], McCosker et al. 1989:297 [ref. 13288]). Ophichthidae: Ophichthinae.

Yoga (subgenus of *Ctenogobius*) Whitley 1954:25 [ref. 4721]. Fem. *Ctenogobius (Yoga) pyrops* Whitley 1954:26. Type by original designation (also monotypic). Synonym of *Amoya* Herre 1927 (Hoese, pers. comm.). Gobiidae.

Yongeichthys Whitley 1932:302 [ref. 4676]. Masc. *Gobius criniger* Valenciennes in Cuvier & Valenciennes 1837:82. Type by original designation. Valid (Akihito in Masuda et al. 1984:255 [ref. 6441], Hoese 1986:807 [ref. 5670], Maugé 1986:387 [ref. 6218], Birdsong et al. 1988:194 [ref. 7303], Kottelat 1989:19 [ref. 13605]). Gobiidae.

Yozia Jordan & Snyder 1901:8 [ref. 2510]. Fem. *Yozia wakanourae* Jordan & Snyder 1902:8. Type by original designation. Synonym of *Trachyrhamphus* Kaup 1853 (Dawson 1984:165 [ref. 5291], Dawson 1985:190 [ref. 6541]). Syngnathidae: Syngnathinae.

Ypsigramma Schultz in Schultz et al. 1953:372 [ref. 3975]. Neut. *Ypsigramma lineata* Schultz in Schultz et al. 1953:375. Type by original designation. Probably a synonym of *Chorististium* Fowler & Bean 1930 (see Morgans 1982:30 [ref. 5411]); synonym of *Liopropoma* Gill 1861 (Randall & Taylor 1988:7 [ref. 6429]). Serranidae: Liopropomatinae.

Ypsiscarus (subgenus of *Scarus*) Schultz 1958:33, 47 [ref. 3970]. Masc. *Callyodon oedema* Snyder 1909:603. Type by original designation (also monotypic). Synonym of *Scarus* Forsskål 1775. Scaridae: Scarinae.

Yssichromis Greenwood 1980:22 [ref. 1899]. Masc. *Haplochromis fusiformis* Greenwood & Gee 1969:32. Type by original designation. Cichlidae.

Yunnanilus (subgenus of *Nemacheilus*) Nichols 1925:1 [ref. 3178]. Masc. *Nemacheilus pleurotaenia* Regan 1904:192. Technically type is by subsequent designation (apparently first in Zoological Record for 1925), but clearly Nichols intended *pleurotaenia* to be the type. Valid (Kottelat & Chu 1988 [ref. 13392], Kottelat 1989:13 [ref. 13605], Kottelat 1990:21 [ref. 14137]). Balitoridae: Nemacheilinae.

Yuriria Jordan & Evermann 1896:314, 315, 321 [ref. 2443]. Fem. *Hudsonius altus* Jordan 1879:301. Type by original designation (also monotypic). Valid (Coburn & Cavender, pers. comm.). Cyprinidae.

Zabidius Whitley 1930:17 [ref. 4671]. Masc. *Platax novemaculeatus* McCulloch 1916:188. Type by original designation (also monotypic). Valid (Smith 1986:605 [ref. 5712]). Ephippidae.

Zabulon Whitley 1928:296 [ref. 4663]. *Heliastes roseus* Günther 1880:45. Type by original designation (also monotypic). Pomacentridae.

Zacallanthias Katayama 1963:27 [ref. 5620]. Masc. *Zacallanthias sagamiensis* Katayama 1963:27. Type by original designation (also monotypic). Original not seen. Synonym of *Plectranthias* Bleeker 1873 (Randall 1980:105 [ref. 6717]). Serranidae: Anthiinae.

Zacalles Jordan & Snyder 1902:448 [ref. 2516]. *Zacalles bryope* Jordan & Snyder 1902:448. Type by original designation (also monotypic). Apparently preoccupied by Foerster 1869 in Ichneumonidae (Insecta), replaced by *Calliblennius* Barbour 1912. Synonym of *Neoclinus* Girard 1858 (Clark Hubbs 1953:12 [ref. 12698]). Labrisomidae.

Zacco Jordan & Evermann 1902:322 [ref. 2447]. *Leuciscus platypus* Temminck & Schlegel 1846:207. Type by original designation. Valid (Yang & Hwang 1964:45 [ref. 13497], Chen 1982:295 [ref. 824], Sawada in Masuda et al. 1984:57 [ref. 6441], Kuang in Chu & Chen 1989:29 [ref. 13584]). Cyprinidae.

Zaclemus (subgenus of *Paralonchurus*) Gilbert in Jordan & Evermann 1896:401 [ref. 2442]. *Paralonchurus goodei* Gilbert in Jordan & Evermann 1896:401. Type by original designation (also monotypic). Synonym of *Paralonchurus* Bocourt 1869 (Chao 1978:38 [ref. 6983]). Sciaenidae.

Zaireichthys Roberts 1967:124 [ref. 3770]. Masc. *Zaireichthys zonatus* Roberts 1967:124. Type by original designation (also monotypic). Often placed in the Bagridae. Valid (Risch 1986:35 [ref. 6190], Bailey & Stewart 1984:9 [ref. 5232] in Amphiliidae, Burgess 1989:68 [ref. 12860] as *Zairichthys*). Amphiliidae.

Zalanthias (subgenus of *Pseudanthias*) Jordan & Richardson 1910:470 [ref. 2494]. Masc. *Pseudanthias kelloggi* Jordan &

Evermann 1903:179. Type by original designation. Synonym of *Plectranthias* Bleeker 1873 (Randall 1980:105 [ref. 6717]). Serranidae: Anthiinae.

Zalarges Jordan & Williams in Jordan & Starks 1895:793 [ref. 2522]. Masc. *Zalarges nimbarius* Jordan & Williams in Jordan & Starks 1895:793. Type by monotypy. Synonym of *Vinciguerria* Jordan & Evermann 1896 (Witzell 1973:121 [ref. 7172]). Phosichthyidae.

Zalembius Jordan & Evermann 1896:403 [ref. 2442]. Masc. *Cymatogaster rosaceus* Jordan & Gilbert 1880:303. Type by original designation (also monotypic). Valid (Tarp 1952:69 [ref. 12250]). Embiotocidae.

Zalescopus Jordan & Hubbs 1925:312 [ref. 2486]. Masc. *Zalescopus tosae* Jordan & Hubbs 1925:312. Type by original designation. Synonym of *Uranoscopus* Linnaeus 1758 (Mees 1960:47 [ref. 11931], Pietsch 1989:295 [ref. 12541]). Uranoscopidae.

Zalieutes Jordan & Evermann 1896:511 [ref. 2442]. Masc. *Malthe elater* Jordan & Gilbert 1881:365. Type by original designation (also monotypic). Valid. Ogcocephalidae.

Zalises Jordan & Snyder 1901:2 [ref. 2510]. *Zalises umitengu* Jordan & Snyder 1901:2. Type by original designation (also monotypic). Only one species mentioned by name but more implied. Valid (Araga in Masuda et al. 1984:90 [ref. 6441]); synonym of *Eurypegasus* Bleeker 1863 (Palsson & Pietsch 1989:7 [ref. 13536]). Pegasidae.

Zalocys Jordan & McGregor in Jordan & Evermann 1898:2848 [ref. 2445]. Fem. *Zalocys stilbe* Jordan & McGregor in Jordan & Evermann 1898:2848. Type by original designation (also monotypic). Also appeared in Jordan & McGregor 1899:276 [ref. 2488]. Synonym of *Trachinotus* Lacepède 1801 (Daget & Smith-Vaniz 1986:319 [ref. 6207]). Carangidae.

Zalopyr (subgenus of *Sebastodes*) Jordan & Evermann 1898:1795 [ref. 2445]. Neut. *Sebastodes aleutianus* Jordan & Evermann 1898:1795. Type by original designation (also monotypic). Type designated in text on p. 1795. Synonym of *Sebastes* Cuvier 1829. Scorpaenidae: Sebastinae.

Zalypnus Jordan & Evermann 1896:459 [ref. 2442]. Masc. *Gobius emblematicus* Jordan & Gilbert 1881:330. Type by original designation. Synonym of *Microgobius* Poey 1876 (Birdsong 1981:268 [ref. 5425]). Gobiidae.

Zameus Jordan & Fowler 1903:632 [ref. 2460]. Masc. *Centrophorus squamulosus* Günther 1877:433. Type by original designation (also monotypic). Valid (Taniuchi & Garrick 1986:119 [ref. 5721]); synonym of *Scymnodon* Bocage & Capello 1864 (Compagno 1984: 97 [ref. 6474]). Squalidae.

Zamora Whitley 1931:108 [ref. 4673]. Fem. *Caranx hullianus* McCulloch 1909:319. Type by original designation (also monotypic). Preoccupied by Roewer 1928 in arachnids, replaced by *Bassetina* Whitley 1931. Synonym of *Uraspis* Bleeker 1855 (Smith-Vaniz, pers. comm.). Carangidae.

Zanchus Commerson in Lacepède 1802:472 (footnote) [ref. 4929]. Masc. Apparently not available; name from Commerson manuscript mentioned under *Chaetodon cornutus* as *Zanchus* (but apparently *Zanclus* in original Commerson manuscript). See remarks under Opinion 89 in Appendix B. In the synonymy of *Zanclus* Cuvier 1831. Zanclidae.

Zanclistius Jordan 1907:236 [ref. 2401]. Masc. *Histiopterus elevatus* Ramsay & Ogilby 1888:1311. Type by original designation (also monotypic). Valid (Hardy 1983:183 [ref. 5385], Hardy 1983:373 [ref. 5392]). Pentacerotidae.

Zanclorhynchus Günther 1880:15 [ref. 2011]. Masc. *Zanclorhynchus spinifer* Günther 1880:15. Type by monotypy. Spelled *Zanclorrhynchus*, *Xanclorhynchus* and *Xanchlorhynchus* by authors (last two by Moreland 1960:241, 242 [ref. 3041]). Valid (Paulin & Moreland 1979:601 [ref. 6915], Washington et al. 1984:440 [ref. 13660] as *Zanchlorynchus*). Congiopodidae.

Zanclurus Swainson 1839:175, 239 [ref. 4303]. Masc. *Zanclurus indicus* Swainson 1839:240. Type by monotypy. Synonym of *Istiophorus* Lacepède 1801 (de Sylva 1973:477 [ref. 7210], Nakamura 1983:277 [ref. 5371]). Istiophoridae.

Zanclus Cuvier (ex Commerson) in Cuvier & Valenciennes 1831: (92) 102 [ref. 4881]. Masc. *Chaetodon cornutus* Linnaeus 1758: 273. Type by monotypy. Valid (Leis & Richards 1984:548 [ref. 13669], Araga in Masuda et al. 1984:228 [ref. 6441], Heemstra & Smith 1986:823 [ref. 5668], see Tyler et al. 1989 [ref. 13460]). Zanclidae.

Zaniolepis Girard 1858:202 [ref. 1811]. Fem. *Zaniolepis latipinnis* Girard 1858:202. Type by monotypy. Misquoted *Zaniodermis* in synonymy by Günther 1860:94 [ref. 1963]. Valid (Washington et al. 1984:443 [ref. 13660]). Hexagrammidae: Zaniolepidinae.

Zanobatus Garman 1913:291 [ref. 1545]. Masc. *Platyrhina schoenleinii* Müller & Henle 1841:125. Type by monotypy. Platyrhinidae.

Zanotacanthus Gill 1876:883 [ref. 12520]. Masc. *Notacanthus rissoanus* Filippi & Verany 1859:190. Type by monotypy. Original not seen. Objective synonym of *Polyacanthonotus* Bleeker 1874 (Wheeler 1973:256 [ref. 7190]). Notacanthidae.

Zantecla Castelnau 1873:88 [ref. 758]. Fem. *Zantecla pusilla* Castelnau 1873:88. Type by monotypy. Synonym of *Melanotaenia* Gill 1862 (Allen 1980:473 [ref. 99], Allen & Cross 1982:44 [ref. 6251]). Atherinidae: Melanotaeniinae.

Zaphotias Goode & Bean in Jordan & Evermann 1898:2826 [ref. 2445]. Masc. *Bonapartia pedaliota* Goode & Bean 1896:102. Type by being a replacement name. Replacement for *Bonapartia* Goode & Bean 1896, preoccupied by Buettikofer 1896 in Aves. Date of Goode & Bean after July 20, 1896 (Cohen 1963 [ref. 6883]) and Buettikofer evidently June 1896. Probably should replace *Bonapartia* Goode & Bean in current use; now treated as a synonym of *Bonapartia* (e.g. Witzell 1973:116 [ref. 7172]). Gonostomatidae.

Zapogon (subgenus of *Apogon*) Fraser 1972:23 [ref. 5195]. Masc. *Apogon evermanni* Jordan & Snyder 1904:123. Type by original designation. Synonym of *Apogon* Lacepède 1801, but as a valid subgenus (Fraser & Lachner 1985:4 [ref. 5215]). Apogonidae.

Zappa Murdy 1989:53 [ref. 13628]. Masc. *Pseudapocryptes confluentus* Roberts 1978:68. Type by monotypy. Gobiidae.

Zaprora Jordan 1896:202 [ref. 2395]. Fem. *Zaprora silenus* Jordan 1896:202. Type by original designation (also monotypic). Valid (Amaoka in Masuda et al. 1984:304 [ref. 6441]). Zaproridae.

Zapteryx Jordan & Gilbert 1880:53 [ref. 2468]. Fem. *Platyrhina exasperata* Jordan & Gilbert 1880:32. Type by original designation (also monotypic). Valid. Rhinobatidae: Rhinobatinae.

Zastomias Gilbert 1915:322 [ref. 1632]. Masc. *Zastomias scintillans* Gilbert 1915:322. Type by original designation (also monotypic). Synonym of *Aristostomias* Zugmayer 1913 (Morrow 1964:531 [ref. 6958]). Malacosteidae.

Zathorax Cope 1871:112 [ref. 5775]. Masc. *Zathorax monitor* Cope 1872:272. Type by subsequent monotypy. Appeared first with brief description and no species; more complete description in Cope

1872:271 [ref. 921] with one species. Valid (Burgess 1989:223 [ref. 12860]). Doradidae.

Zeablennius Whitley 1930:20 [ref. 4671]. Masc. *Blennius laticlavius* Griffin 1926:542. Type by original designation (also monotypic). Synonym of *Parablennius* Miranda-Ribeiro 1915 (Bath 1977:196 [ref. 208]). Blenniidae.

Zearaja Whitley 1939:254 [ref. 4695]. Fem. *Raja nasuta* Müller & Henle (ex Banks) 1841:150. Type by original designation (also monotypic). Synonym of *Raja* Linnaeus 1758. Rajidae.

Zebrasoma (subgenus of *Acanthurus*) Swainson 1839:178, 256 [ref. 4303]. Neut. *Acanthurus velifer* Bloch 1795:106, pl. 427. Type by monotypy. Valid (Leis & Richards 1984:548 [ref. 13669], Kishimoto in Masuda et al. 1984:230 [ref. 6441], Randall 1986:817 [ref. 5706], Tyler et al. 1989:37 [ref. 13460]). Acanthuridae.

Zebreleotris Herre 1953:191 [ref. 2144]. Fem. *Zebreleotris fasciata* Herre 1953:191. Type by original designation (also monotypic). Synonym of *Amblyeleotris* Bleeker 1874 (Yanagisawa 1978:298 [ref. 7028]). Gobiidae.

Zebrias Jordan & Snyder 1900:380 [ref. 2502]. Masc. *Solea zebrina* Temminck & Schlegel 1846:185. Type by original designation (also monotypic). Valid (Ochiai in Masuda et al. 1984:355 [ref. 6441], Heemstra & Gon 1986:874 [ref. 5665], Chapleau & Keast 1988:2799 [ref. 13819]). Soleidae.

Zebricium Rafinesque 1815:93 [ref. 3584]. Not available, name only; for an eel. Anguilliformes.

Zebrus (subgenus of *Gobius*) de Buen 1930:135 [ref. 685]. Masc. *Gobius zebrus* Risso 1826:282. Type by original designation (also by absolute tautonymy). Valid (Miller 1973:513 [ref. 6888], Miller in Whitehead et al. 1986:1084 [ref. 13677]). Gobiidae.

Zeluco Whitley 1931:317 [ref. 4672]. *Otolithus atelodus* Günther 1867:60. Type by original designation (also monotypic). Correct spelling for genus of type species is *Otolithes*. Synonym of *Atractoscion* Gill 1862 (Trewavas 1977:282 [ref. 4459]). Sciaenidae.

Zen Jordan 1903:694 [ref. 2398]. *Cyttopsis itea* Jordan & Fowler 1902:519. Type by original designation (also monotypic). Synonym of *Cyttopsis* Gill 1862 (Heemstra 1980:3 [ref. 14195]). Zeidae.

Zenarchopterus Gill 1864:273 [ref. 1693]. Masc. *Hemiramphus dispar* Valenciennes in Cuvier & Valenciennes 1846:58. Type by original designation (also monotypic). Valid (Collette 1982 [ref. 5497], Collette et al. 1984:337 [ref. 11422], Yoshino in Masuda et al. 1984:80 [ref. 6441], Kottelat 1985:272 [ref. 11441], Collette 1986:163 [ref. 6197], Collette & Su 1986:290 [ref. 5998], Paxton et al. 1989:339 [ref. 12442], Kottelat 1989:16 [ref. 13605]). Hemiramphidae.

Zenion Jordan & Evermann 1896:418 [ref. 2442]. Neut. *Cyttus hololepis* Goode & Bean 1896:225. Type by original designation (also monotypic). Heemstra 1986 [ref. 5660] places in family Zeniontidae. This apparently should be Zeniidae, but Macrourocyttidae is an older family-group name (see Paxton et al. 1989:387 [ref. 12442]). Valid (Machida in Masuda et al. 1984:118 [ref. 6441], Heemstra 1986:441 [ref. 5660], Paxton et al. 1989:387 [ref. 12442]). Macrurocyttidae.

Zenodon (subgenus of *Capriscus*) Swainson 1839:194, 325 [ref. 4303]. Masc. Generally regarded as a misspelling for *Xenodon* Rüppell; see *Xenodon* Rüppell. In the synonymy of *Odonus* Gistel 1848 (Matsuura 1980:33 [ref. 6943]). Balistidae.

Zenopsis Gill 1862:126 [ref. 1659]. Fem. *Zeus nebulosus* Temminck & Schlegel 1845:123. Type by original designation (also monotypic). Valid (Wheeler 1973:349 [ref. 7190], Heemstra 1980:11 [ref. 14195], Machida in Masuda et al. 1984:118 [ref. 6441], Quéro in Whitehead et al. 1986:770 [ref. 13676], Heemstra 1986:437 [ref. 5660], Paxton et al. 1989:389 [ref. 12442], Parin 1898 [ref. 14116]). Zeidae.

Zeodrius Castelnau 1879:377 [ref. 764]. Masc. *Zeodrius vestitus* Castelnau 1879:351, 377. Type by subsequent designation. Two included species, *Z. vestitus* Castelnau and *Chilodactylus vittatus* Garrett 1864 [which Castelnau misprinted as *vestitus*]; type apparently designated first by McCulloch 1929 [ref. 2948]. Synonym of subgenus *Goniistius* Gill 1862 of genus *Cheilodactylus* Lacepède 1803 (Randall 1983:2 [ref. 5361]). Cheilodactylidae.

Zesticelus Jordan & Evermann 1896:443 [ref. 2442]. Masc. *Acanthocottus profundorum* Gilbert 1896:423. Type by original designation (also monotypic). Valid (Bolin 1944:94 [ref. 6379], Neyelov 1979:116, 160 [ref. 3152], Washington et al. 1984:443 [ref. 13660], Yabe 1985:111 [ref. 11522]). Cottidae.

Zestichthys Jordan & Hubbs 1925:321 [ref. 2486]. Masc. *Zestichthys tanakae [tanakai]* Jordan & Hubbs 1925:321. Type by original designation (also monotypic). Species name emended to *tanakai*, named after Mr. Tanaka, a male. Valid (Toyoshima in Masuda et al. 1984:309 [ref. 6441]). Zoarcidae.

Zestidium (subgenus of *Stellifer*) Gilbert in Jordan & Evermann 1898:1439, 1442 [ref. 2444]. Neut. *Stellifer illecebrosus* Gilbert in Jordan & Evermann 1898:1442. Type by original designation (also monotypic). Synonym of *Stellifer* Oken 1817 (Chao 1978:40 [ref. 6983]). Sciaenidae.

Zestis (subgenus of *Stellifer*) Gilbert in Jordan & Evermann 1898:1439, 1440 [ref. 2444]. Fem. *Sciaena oscitans* Jordan & Gilbert 1881:312. Type by original designation. Synonym of *Stellifer* Oken 1817 (Chao 1978:40 [ref. 6983]). Sciaenidae.

Zetaraia (subgenus of *Raja*) Leigh-Sharpe 1924:568, 575 [ref. 5748]. Fem. *Raja brachyura* Günther 1880:20. Type by original designation (also monotypic). As a "pseudogenus" of *Raia* [= *Raja*]. Not available [Art. 1b (6)], used as an artifical category (see Leigh-Sharpe 1928 [ref. 6152]). In the synonymy of *Bathyraja* Ishiyama 1958. Rajidae.

Zeugopterus Gottsche 1835:178 [ref. 1862]. Masc. *Pleuronectes hirtus* Abildgaard in Müller 1788:36. Type by monotypy. Valid (Norman 1934:279 [ref. 6893], Nielsen 1973:619 [ref. 6885], Ahlstrom et al. 1984:640 [ref. 13641], Nielsen in Whitehead et al. 1986:1292 [ref. 13677]). Scophthalmidae.

Zeus Linnaeus 1758:266 [ref. 2787]. Masc. *Zeus faber* Linnaeus 1758:267. Type by subsequent designation. Type designated by Gill 1862:126 [ref. 1659] for *Zeus* (Artedi). On Official List (Opinion 77, Direction 56). Valid (Wheeler 1973:349 [ref. 7190], Heemstra 1980:8 [ref. 14195], Machida in Masuda et al. 1984:118 [ref. 6441], Quéro in Whitehead et al. 1986:771 [ref. 13676], Heemstra 1986:437 [ref. 5660], Paxton et al. 1989:389 [ref. 12442]). Zeidae.

Zev Whitley 1927:289 [ref. 4662]. *Cirrhoscyllium expolitum* Smith & Radcliffe in Smith 1913:568. Type by being a replacement name. Unneeded replacement for *Cirrhoscyllium* Smith & Radcliffe 1913, not preoccupied by *Cirriscyllium* Ogilby 1908 in same family. Objective synonym of *Cirrhoscyllium* Smith & Radcliffe 1913 (Compagno 1984:167 [ref. 6474]). Parascylliidae.

Zevaia Chabanaud 1943:291 [ref. 799]. Fem. *Solea vulgaris azevia* Capello in Steindachner 1868:720. Type by original designation (also monotypic). For purposes of the type species, the variety *azevia* is elevated to species level; type not *vulgaris*. Synonym of *Microchirus* Bonaparte 1833 (Torchio 1973:632 [ref. 6892]). Soleidae.

Zezera Jordan & Fowler 1903:837 [ref. 2463]. Fem. *Sarcocheilichthys hilgendorfi* Ishikawa in Jordan & Fowler 1903:837. Type by original designation (also monotypic). Synonym of *Pungtungia* Herzenstein 1892 (Banarescu & Nalbant 1973:30 [ref. 173], Lu, Luo & Chen 1977:457 [ref. 13495]). Cyprinidae.

Zingel Cloquet 1817:240 (v. 4) [ref. 852]. *Perca zingel* Linnaeus 1766:482. Type by absolute tautonymy. Also appeared in Oken (Cuvier) 1817:1782 [=1182] [ref. 3303] (see Gill 1903:966 [ref. 5768]) and in Jarocki 1822:223 [ref. 4984]. Based on "Les Cingels" of Cuvier 1816:296 [ref. 993]. Valid (Collette & Banarescu 1977:1459 [ref. 5845]). Percidae.

Ziphotheca Montagu 1811:81 [ref. 3038]. Fem. *Ziphotheca tetradens* Montagu 1811:82. Type by monotypy. Spelled *Xiphotheca* by Jordan, Evermann & Clark 1930:262 [ref. 6476], *Zyphothyca* by Swainson 1839:239 [ref. 4303], and *Xipotheca* by Jordan 1917:84 [ref. 2407]. Synonym of *Lepidopus* Goüan 1770 (Parin & Bekker 1973:464 [ref. 7206] as *Ziphotheca*). Trichiuridae: Lepidopinae.

Zisius Oken 1816:ii, 151 From Whitley, not yet investigated. Synonym of *Xiphias* Linnaeus 1758 (see Whitley 1976:50 [ref. 4735]). Xiphiidae.

Zoarces Cuvier 1829:240 [ref. 995]. Masc. *Blennius viviparus* Linnaeus 1758:258. Type by subsequent designation. Earliest subsequent designation not researched. Spelled *Zoarcaeus*, *Zoarcus*, and *Zoarchus* by early authors. Valid (Andriashev 1973:540 [ref. 7214], Anderson 1984:578 [ref. 13634], Andriashev in Whitehead et al. 1986:1149 [ref. 13677]). Zoarcidae.

Zoarchias Jordan & Snyder 1902:480 [ref. 2516]. Masc. *Zoarchias veneficus* Jordan & Snyder 1902:480. Type by original designation (also monotypic). Valid (Amaoka in Masuda et al. 1984:304 [ref. 6441]). Zoarcidae.

Zoarcites Zugmayer 1914:3 [ref. 4848]. Masc. *Zoarcites pardalis* Zugmayer 1914:3. Type by monotypy. Also appeared in Zugmayer 1940:210 [ref. 4850]. Cryptacanthodidae.

Zonichthys (subgenus of *Trachinus*) Swainson 1839:39, 176, 248 [ref. 4303]. Masc. *Scomber fasciatus* Bloch 1793:73. Type by subsequent designation. Misspelled *Zonicthys* on p. 39; description dates to p. 176. Type designated by Swain 1882:276 [ref. 5966]. Synonym of *Seriola* Cuvier 1816 (Smith-Vaniz, pers. comm., Nov. 1989). Carangidae.

Zonogobius Bleeker 1874:323 [ref. 437]. Masc. *Gobius semifasciatus* Kner 1868:326. Type by original designation (also monotypic). Synonym of *Priolepis* Valenciennes 1837 (Hoese, pers. comm.). Gobiidae.

Zononothobranchius (subgenus of *Nothobranchius*) Radda 1969: 162 [ref. 6078]. Masc. *Nothobranchius rubroreticulatus* Blache & Miton 1960:214. Type by original designation. Synonym of *Nothobranchius* Peters 1868 (Parenti 1981:479 [ref. 7066] as *Zonothobranchius*, Wildekamp et al. 1986:263 [ref. 6198]). Aplocheilidae: Aplocheilinae.

Zonophichthus Whitley 1930:250 [ref. 4670]. Masc. *Ophichthys cephalozona* Bleeker 1864:49. Type by original designation. Synonym of *Ophichthus* Ahl 1789 (Blache et al. 1973:247 [ref. 7185], McCosker 1977:80 [ref. 6836], McCosker et al. 1989:379 [ref. 13288]). Ophichthidae: Ophichthinae.

Zonoscion (subgenus of *Paralonchurus*) Jordan & Evermann 1896:401 [ref. 2442]. Masc. *Polycirrhus rathbuni* Jordan & Bollman 1889:162. Type by original designation (also monotypic). Synonym of *Paralonchurus* Bocourt 1869 (Chao 1978:38 [ref. 6983]). Sciaenidae.

Zoogoneticus Meek 1902:91 [ref. 2957]. Masc. *Poecilia quitzeonensis* Bean 1899:540. Type by original designation. Valid (Uyeno et al. 1983:507 [ref. 6818]). Goodeidae.

Zopa Fitzinger 1873:152, 158 [ref. 1337]. Fem. *Cyprinus sapa* Pallas 1811:328. Type by subsequent designation. Two included species "(*Abr. Ballerus* und *Sapa*)"; type apparently first designated by Jordan 1919:368 [ref. 4904] as *sopa*). Howes lists *Sapa* Kasansky 1928 in the synonymy of *Abramis* [not investigated]. Synonym of *Abramis* Cuvier 1816 (Howes 1981:46 [ref. 14200]). Cyprinidae.

Zophendum Jordan 1878:786 [ref. 2377]. *Hyborhynchus siderius* Cope 1875:670. Type by original designation (also monotypic). Synonym of *Agosia* Girard 1856. Cyprinidae.

Zoramia Jordan 1917:46 [ref. 2406]. Fem. *Apogon graeffii* Günther 1873:22. Type by original designation (also monotypic). Synonym of *Apogon* Lacepède 1801, but as a valid subgenus (Fraser & Lachner 1985:4, 33 [ref. 5215]). Apogonidae.

Zostericola Iljin 1927:130, 135 [ref. 5613]. Masc. *Gobius ophiocephalus* Pallas 1811:153. Type by monotypy. Preoccupied by Ashby 1919 in Mollusca, replaced by *Zosterisessor* Whitley 1935. Objective synonym of *Zosterisessor* Whitley 1935 (Miller 1973:513 [ref. 6888]). Gobiidae.

Zosterisessor Whitley 1935:250 [ref. 4683]. Masc. *Gobius ophiocephalus* Pallas 1811:153. Type by being a replacement name. Replacement for *Zostericola* Iljin 1927, preoccupied by Ashby 1919 in Mollusca. Valid (Miller 1973:513 [ref. 6888], Miller in Whitehead et al. 1986:1085 [ref. 13677]). Gobiidae.

Zu Walters & Fitch 1960:445 [ref. 4580]. Masc. *Trachypterus cristatus* Bonelli 1820:487. Type by original designation (also monotypic). Valid (Palmer 1973:331 [ref. 7195], Scott 1983:188 [ref. 5346], Olney 1984:369 [ref. 13656], Heemstra & Kannemeyer 1984:23 [ref. 5349], Fujii in Masuda et al. 1984:116 [ref. 6441], Palmer in Whitehead et al. 1986:731 [ref. 13676], Heemstra & Kannemeyer 1986:401 [ref. 5666], Paxton et al. 1989:400 [ref. 12442]). Trachipteridae.

Zunasia Jordan & Metz 1913:7 [ref. 2490]. Fem. *Pristigaster chinensis* Basilewski 1855:243. Type by original designation (also monotypic). Synonym of *Ilisha* Richardson 1846 (Poll et al. 1984:44 [ref. 6172], Whitehead 1985:261 [ref. 5141]). Clupeidae.

Zungaro Bleeker 1858:196, 204, 207 [ref. 365]. *Pimelodus zungaro* Humboldt 1833:170. Type by monotypy, also by absolute tautonymy. Synonym of *Pseudopimelodus* Bleeker 1858 (Mees 1974:187 [ref. 2969]). Pimelodidae.

Zungaropsis Steindachner 1908:67 [ref. 13415]. Fem. *Zungaropsis multimaculatus* Steindachner 1908:67. Type by monotypy. Valid (Burgess 1989:278 [ref. 12860]). Pimelodidae.

Zygaena (subgenus of *Squalus*) Cuvier 1816:127 [ref. 993]. Fem. *Squalus zygaena* Linnaeus 1758:234. Type by monotypy (also by absolute tautonymy). Misspelled or unjustifiably emended to *Zygana* by Swainson 1838:139 [ref. 4302] and 1839:192, 318 [ref. 4303]. Preoccupied by Fabricius 1775 in Lepidoptera. Objective synonym of *Sphyrna* Rafinesque 1810 (Gilbert 1973:32 [ref. 7164], Compagno 1984:541 [ref. 6846], Cappetta 1987:127 [ref. 6348], Compagno 1988:362 [ref. 13488]). Sphyrnidae.

Zygana Swainson 1838:133, 139 [ref. 4302]. Also in Swainson 1839:192, 318 [ref. 4303]. Misspelling or unjustified emendation of *Zygaena* Cuvier 1816, Swainson specifically referring to "*Zygana* Antiq." (pre-Linnaean authors spelled it *Zygaena* as did Cuvier). In the synonymy of *Sphyrna* Rafinesque 1810 (Gilbert 1973:32 [ref. 7164], Compagno 1988:362 [ref. 13488]). Sphyrnidae.

Zygoena Risso 1826:125 [ref. 3757]. *Squalus zygaena* Linnaeus 1758:234. Apparently a misspelling of *Zygaena* Cuvier 1816, but perhaps independently described. Synonym of *Sphyrna* Rafinesque 1810 (Gilbert 1973:32 [ref. 7164], Compagno 1984:541 [ref. 6846], Compagno 1988:362 [ref. 13488]). Sphyrnidae.

Zygogaster Eigenmann 1913:22 [ref. 1229]. Fem. *Zygogaster filifurus* Eigenmann 1913:23. Type by original designation (also monotypic). Synonym of *Astyanax* Baird & Girard 1854, as a valid subgenus (Géry 1977:430 [ref. 1597]). Characidae.

Zygonectes Agassiz 1854:353 [ref. 69]. Masc. *Poecilia olivacea* Storer 1845:51. Type by subsequent designation. Appeared first in Agassiz 1853:135 [ref. 67] without adequate description and no included species, described more fully in 1854. Type designated by Jordan & Gilbert 1877 [ref. 4907]. Synonym of *Fundulus* Lacepède 1803 (Parenti 1981:494 [ref. 7066]). Cyprinodontidae: Fundulinae.

Zyphothyca Swainson 1839:174, 239 [ref. 4303]. Fem. *Gempylus coluber* Cuvier in Cuvier & Valenciennes 1831:211. Type by monotypy. Synonym of *Gempylus* Cuvier 1829 (Parin & Bekker 1973:457 [ref. 7206]). Gempylidae.

PART II

GENERA IN A CLASSIFICATION

William N. Eschmeyer

CLASS MYXINI

ORDER MYXINIFORMES

FAM. MYXINIDAE (Hagfishes)

Subfam. Myxininae
Anopsus Rafinesque 1815
Gastrobranchus Bloch 1791
Muraenoblenna Lacepède (ex Commerson) 1803
Myxine Linnaeus 1758
Nemamyxine Richardson 1958
Neomyxine Richardson 1953
Notomyxine Nani & Gneri 1951

Subfam. Eptatretinae
Bdellostoma Müller 1836
Dodecatrema Fowler 1947
Eptatretus Cloquet (ex Duméril) 1819
Heptatrema Duméril in Voigt 1832
Heptatremus Swainson 1839
Heptatretus Regan 1912
Heterotrema Girard 1855
Hexabranchus Schultze 1836
Hexatrema Girard 1855
Homea Fleming 1822
Paramyxine Dean 1904
Polistotrema Gill in Jordan & Gilbert 1881
Polytrema Girard 1855

CLASS CEPHALASPIDOMORPHI

ORDER PETROMYZONTIFORMES

FAM. PETROMYZONTIDAE (Lampreys)
Chilopterus Philippi 1858

Subfam. Petromyzontinae
Agnathomyzon Gracianov 1906
Ammocoetus Duméril (ex d'Hallois) 1812
Bathymyzon Gill 1883
Caspiomyzon Berg 1906
Entosphenus Gill 1862
Eudontomyzon Regan 1911
Haploglossa Gracianov 1906
Ichthyomyzon Girard 1858
Lampetra Gray 1851
Lampetra Bonnaterre 1788
Lampreda Rafinesque 1815
Lethenteron Creaser & Hubbs 1922
Oceanomyzon Fowler 1908
Okkelbergia Creaser & Hubbs 1922
Petromyzon Linnaeus 1758
Pricus Rafinesque 1815
Reighardina Creaser & Hubbs 1922
Scolecosoma Girard 1858
Tetrapleurodon Creaser & Hubbs 1922

Subfam. Geotriinae
Dionisia Lahille 1915
Exodomegas Gill 1883
Exomegas Gill 1883
Geotria Gray 1851
Macrophthalmia Plate 1897
Neomordacia Castelnau 1872
Thysanochilus Philippi 1857
Velasia Gray 1851
Yarra Castelnau 1872

Subfam. Mordaciinae
Caragola Gray 1851
Mordacia Gray 1851

CLASS ELASMOBRANCHII
Epinotus Rafinesque 1815

ORDER HEXANCHIFORMES

FAM. HEXANCHIDAE (Cow Sharks) Heptranchidae incl.
Heptanchus Müller & Henle 1841
Heptranchias Rafinesque 1810
Hexanchus Rafinesque 1810
Monopterhinus Blainville 1816
Notidanus Cuvier 1816
Notorynchus Ayres 1855

FAM. CHLAMYDOSELACHIDAE (Frill Sharks)
Chlamydoselachus Garman 1884

ORDER HETERODONTIFORMES

FAM. HETERODONTIDAE (Bullhead and Horn Sharks)
Centracion Gray 1831
Cestracion Oken (ex Cuvier) 1817
Gyropleurodus Gill 1862
Heterodontus Blainville 1816
Molochophrys Whitley 1931
Tropidodus Gill 1863
Wuia Fowler 1934

ORDER ORECTOLOBIFORMES

FAM. RHINCODONTIDAE (Whale Sharks) = Rhiniodontidae
Micristodus Gill 1865
Rhincodon Smith 1829
Rhiniodon Smith 1828

FAM. PARASCYLLIIDAE
Cirrhoscyllium Smith & Radcliffe in Smith 1913
Neoparascyllium Whitley 1939
Parascyllium Gill 1862
Zev Whitley 1927

FAM. BRACHYAELURIDAE
Brachaelurus Ogilby 1907
Brachaelurus Ogilby 1908
Cirriscyllium Ogilby 1908
Heteroscyllium Regan 1908

FAM. ORECTOLOBIDAE (Carpet or Nurse Sharks)
Crossorhinus Müller & Henle 1837
Eucrossorhinus Regan 1908
Orectolobus Bonaparte 1834
Sutorectus Whitley 1939

FAM. HEMISCYLLIIDAE
Chiloscyllium Müller & Henle 1837
Hemiscyllium Müller & Henle 1838
Synchismus Gill 1862

FAM. STEGOSTOMATIDAE
Stegostoma Müller & Henle 1837

FAM. GINGLYMOSTOMATIDAE
Ginglymostoma Müller & Henle 1837
Nebrius Rüppell 1837
Nebrodes Garman 1913
Pseudoginglymostoma Dingerkus 1986

ORDER LAMNIFORMES

FAM. ODONTASPIDIDAE (Sand Tiger Sharks) = Carchariidae

Subfam. Odontaspidinae (Sand Sharks)
Carcharias Rafinesque 1810
Eugomphodus Gill 1861
Odontaspis Agassiz 1838
Triglochis Müller & Henle 1837

Subfam. Mitsukurininae (Goblin Sharks)
Mitsukurina Jordan 1898

Subfam. Pseudocharchariinae
Pseudocarcharias Cadenat 1963

FAM. LAMNIDAE (Mackerel sharks)
= Carcharodontidae; Isuridae included
Carcharodon Smith in Müller & Henle 1838
Exoles Gistel 1848
Isuropsis Gill 1862
Isurus Rafinesque 1810
Lamia Risso 1826
Lamiostoma Glückman 1964
Lamna Cuvier 1816
Lymnea Rafinesque 1815
Noelius Rafinesque 1815
Oxyrhina Agassiz 1835
Selanonius Fleming 1828

FAM. MEGACHASMIDAE
Megachasma Taylor, Compagno & Struhsaker 1983

FAM. CETORHINIDAE (Basking Sharks)
Cetorhinus Blainville 1816
Halsydrus Fleming (ex Neil) in Brewster 1817
Polyprosopus Couch 1862
Scapasaurus Marwick 1942
Scoliophis Anonymous 1817
Selache Cuvier 1816
Tetroras Rafinesque 1810

FAM. ALOPIIDAE (Thresher Sharks)
Alopecias Müller & Henle 1837
Alopias Rafinesque 1810
Vulpecula Valmont de Bomare 1768
Vulpecula Garman (ex Valmont de Bomare) 1913
Vulpecula Jarocki (ex Valmont de Bomare) 1822

ORDER CARCHARINIFORMES

FAM. SCYLIORHINIDAE (Cat Sharks)
Alphascyllium Leigh-Sharpe 1926
Apristurus Garman 1913
Asymbolus Whitley 1939
Atelomycterus Garman 1913
Aulohalaelurus Fowler 1934
Betascyllium Leigh-Sharpe 1926
Bythaelurus Compagno 1988
Campagnoia Springer 1979
Catulus Valmont de Bomare 1768
Catulus Smith (ex Willoughby) 1838
Catulus Garman (ex Valmont) 1913
Cephaloscyllium Gill 1862
Cephalurus Bigelow & Schroeder 1941
Compagnoia see *Campagnoia*
Conoporoderma Fowler 1934
Deltascyllium Leigh-Sharpe 1926
Dichichthys Chan 1966
Figaro Whitley 1928
Galeus Rafinesque 1810
Gammascyllium Leigh-Sharpe 1926
Halaelurus Gill 1862
Haploblepharus Garman 1913
Holohalaelurus Fowler 1934
Juncrus Whitley 1939
Parapristurus Fowler 1934
Parmaturus Garman 1906
Pentanchus Smith & Radcliffe in Smith 1912
Poroderma Smith 1838
Prionurus Otto 1821
Pristidurus Bonaparte 1838
Pristiurus Bonaparte 1834
Schroederichthys Springer 1966
Scyliorhinus Blainville 1816
Scyllium Cuvier 1816

FAM. PROSCYLLIIDAE (Finbacked Cat-sharks)
Calliscyllium Tanaka 1912
Ctenacis Compagno 1973
Eridacnis Smith 1913
Gollum Compagno 1973
Neotriakis Smith 1957
Proscyllium Hilgendorf 1904

FAM. PSEUDOTRIAKIDAE (False Cat-sharks)
Pseudotriakis Capello 1868

FAM. LEPTOCHARIIDAE (Barbeled Houndsharks)
Leptocarcharias Günther 1870
Leptocarias Müller & Henle (ex Smith) 1839
Leptocharias Smith in Müller & Henle 1838

FAM. TRIAKIDAE (Houndsharks)
= Triakididae

Subfam. Triakinae
Allomycter Guitart 1972
Cazon de Buen 1959
Cynias Gill 1903
Emissola Jarocki 1822
Galeus Leach 1818
Galeus Garman 1913
Murmille Setna & Sarangdhar (ex Gistel) 1946
Mustellus Fischer von Waldheim 1813
Mustellus Risso 1826
Mustelus Valmont de Bomare 1768
Mustelus Linck 1790
Mustelus Cuvier 1816
Myrmillo Gistel 1848
Pleuracromylon Gill 1864
Rhinotriacis Gill 1863
Scylliogaleus Boulenger 1902
Triacis Agassiz 1846
Triakis Müller & Henle 1838

Subfam. Galeorhininae
Eugaleus Gill 1864
Fur Whitley 1943
Furgaleus Whitley 1951
Galeorhinus Blainville 1816
Galeus Cuvier 1816
Galeus Schaeffer 1760
Gogolia Compagno 1973
Hemitriakis Herre 1923
Hypogaleus Smith 1957
Iago Compagno & Springer 1971

FAM. HEMIGALEIDAE (Weasel Sharks)
Chaenogaleus Gill 1862
Dirrhizodon Klunzinger 1871
Hemigaleus Bleeker 1852
Hemipristis Agassiz 1843
Heterogaleus Gohar & Mazhar 1964
Negogaleus Whitley 1931
Paragaleus Budker 1935

FAM. CARCHARHINIDAE (Requiem Sharks)
Alopecula Valenciennes in Moreau 1881
Aprion Müller & Henle 1839
Aprionodon Gill 1861
Bogimba Whitley 1943
Boreogaleus Gill 1862
Carcharhinus Blainville 1816
Carcharias Cuvier 1816
Cynocephalus Klein 1777
Cynocephalus Gill (ex Klein) 1862
Eulamia Gill 1862
Galeocerdo Müller & Henle 1837
Galeolamna Owen 1853
Galeolamnoides Whitley 1934
Galeus Valmont de Bomare 1768
Gillisqualus Whitley 1934
Glyphis Agassiz 1843
Gymnorhinus Hilgendorf in Hemprich & Ehrenberg 1899
Hemigaleops Schultz & Welander in Schultz et al. 1953
Hypoprion Müller & Henle 1838
Hypoprionodon Gill 1862
Isogomphodon Gill 1862
Isoplagiodon Gill 1862
Lamiopsis Gill 1862
Lamnarius Whitley 1943
Longmania Whitley 1939
Loxodon Müller & Henle 1838
Mapolamia Whitley 1934
Mystidens Whitley 1944
Nasolamia Compagno & Garrick 1983
Negaprion Whitley 1940
Notogaleus Whitley 1931
Ogilamia Whitley 1939
Physodon Valenciennes in Müller & Henle 1838
Platypodon Gill 1862
Prionace Cantor 1849
Prionodon Müller & Henle 1838
Protozygaena Whitley 1940
Pterolamia Springer 1950
Pterolamiops Springer 1951
Rhizoprion Ogilby 1915
Rhizoprionodon Whitley 1929
Scoliodon Müller & Henle 1837
Thalassinus Moreau 1881
Thalassorhinus Valenciennes in Bonaparte 1838
Triaenodon Müller & Henle 1837
Uranga Whitley 1943
Uranganops Whitley 1943

FAM. SPHYRNIDAE (Hammerhead Sharks)
Cestracion Klein 1776
Cestracion Gill (ex Klein) 1862
Cestracion Ogilby (ex Walbaum after Klein) 1916
Cestrorhinus Blainville 1816
Eusphyra Gill 1862
Mesozygaena Compagno 1988
Platysqualus Swainson 1839
Reniceps Gill 1862
Sphyra Van der Hoeven 1858
Sphyrichthys Thienemann 1828

Sphyrna Rafinesque 1810
Sphyrnias Rafinesque 1815
Zygaena Cuvier 1816
Zygana Swainson 1838
Zygoena Risso 1826

ORDER SQUALIFORMES

Caninoa Nardo 1841
Caninotus Nardo 1844
Thalassoklephtes Gistel 1848

FAM. SQUALIDAE (Dogfish Sharks) Dalatiinae and Oxynotinae included

Acanthias Risso 1826
Acanthias Bonaparte 1846
Acanthias Leach 1818
Acanthidium Lowe 1839
Acanthorhinus Blainville 1816
Aculeola de Buen 1959
Atractophorus Gilchrist 1922
Borborodes Gistel 1848
Brevisomniosus Quéro 1976
Carcharias Gistel 1848
Centrina Cuvier 1816
Centrophorus Müller & Henle 1837
Centroscyllium Müller & Henle 1841
Centroscymnus Bocage & Capello 1864
Centroselachus Garman 1913
Cirrhigaleus Tanaka 1912
Dalatias Rafinesque 1810
Deania Jordan & Snyder 1902
Deaniops Whitley 1932
Encheiridiodon Smith 1967
Entoxychirus Gill 1863
Etmopterus Rafinesque 1810
Euprotomicroides Hulley & Penrith 1966
Euprotomicrus Gill 1865
Flakeus Whitley 1939
Gaboa Whitley 1940
Heteroscymnoides Fowler 1934
Heteroscymnus Tanaka 1912
Isistius Gill 1865
Koinga Whitley 1939
Laemargus Müller & Henle 1837
Leiodon Wood 1846
Leius Kner 1864
Lepidorhinus Bonaparte 1838
Machephilus Johnson 1868
Mollisquama Dolganov 1984
Nasisqualus Smith & Radcliffe in Smith 1912
Oxynotus Rafinesque 1810
Paracentroscyllium Alcock 1889
Phaenopogon Herre 1935
Proscymnodon Fowler 1934
Pseudocentrophorus Chu, Meng & Liu 1981
Pseudoscymnus Herre 1935
Rhinoscymnus Gill 1865
Scimnus S. D. W. 1837
Scymnium Valenciennes in Cuvier 1838
Scymnodalatias Garrick 1956
Scymnodon Bocage & Capello 1864
Scymnorhinus Bonaparte 1846
Scymnus Cuvier 1816
Somniosus Lesueur 1818
Somnispinax Whitley 1940
Spinax Cuvier 1816
Squaliolus Smith & Radcliffe in Smith 1912
Squalus Linnaeus 1758
Zameus Jordan & Fowler 1903

FAM. ECHINORHINIDAE (Bramble Sharks)

Echinorhinus Blainville 1816
Goniodus Agassiz 1836
Rubusqualus Whitley 1931

ORDER PRISTIOPHORIFORMES

FAM. PRISTIOPHORIDAE (Saw Sharks)

Pliotrema Regan 1906
Pristiophorus Müller & Henle 1837

ORDER SQUATINIFORMES

FAM. SQUATINIDAE (Angel Sharks)

Rhina Klein 1776
Rhina Rafinesque 1810
Rhina Gill (ex Klein) 1862
Rhina Schaeffer 1760
Squalraia De la Pylaie 1835
Squatina Duméril 1806
Squatina Risso 1810

ORDER PRISTIFORMES

FAM. PRISTIDAE (Sawfishes)

Anoxypristis White & Moy-Thomas 1941
Myriosteon Gray 1864
Oxypristis Hoffmann 1912
Pristes Fleming 1822
Pristibatis Blainville 1825
Pristiopsis Fowler 1905
Pristis Klein 1776
Pristis Linck 1790
Pristis Latham 1794
Pristobatus Blainville 1816

ORDER TORPEDINIFORMES

Apturus Rafinesque 1815
Megabatus Rafinesque 1815
Sephenia Rafinesque 1815

FAM. TORPEDINIDAE (Electric Rays)

Crassinarke Takagi 1951
Eunarce Fowler 1910
Fimbriotorpedo Fritsch 1884
Gymnotorpedo Fritsch 1884
Hypnarce Waite 1902
Hypnos Duméril 1852
Narcacion Klein 1776
Narcacion Bleeker (ex Klein) 1866
Narcacion Gill (ex Klein) 1861
Narcobatus Blainville 1816
Notastrape Whitley 1932
Tetronarce Gill 1862
Tetronarcine Tanaka 1908
Torpedo Duméril 1806
Torpedo Rafinesque 1810
Torpedo Houttuyn 1764

FAM. NARKIDAE

Astrape Müller & Henle 1837
Bengalichthys Annandale 1909
Benthobatis Alcock 1898
Cyclonarce Gill 1862
Diplobatis Bigelow & Schroeder 1948
Discopyge Heckel in Tschudi 1846
Gonionarce Gill 1862
Heteronarce Regan 1921
Narcine Henle 1834
Narcinops Whitley 1940
Narke Kaup 1826
Syrraxis Bonaparte (ex Jourdan) 1841
Temera Gray 1831
Typhlonarke Waite 1909

ORDER RAJIFORMES (Skates and Rays)

FAM. RHINOBATIDAE (Guitarfishes)

Subfam. Rhinobatinae

Acroteriobatus Giltay 1929
Aptychotrema Norman 1926
Glaucostegus Bonaparte 1846
Leiobatus Rafinesque 1810
Platipornax Whitley 1939
Rhinobatos Klein 1776
Rhinobatos Linck 1790
Rhinobatus Bloch & Schneider 1801
Rhynchobatis Philippi 1857
Scobatus Whitley 1939
Squatinoraja Nardo 1824
Syrrhina Müller & Henle 1841
Tarsistes Jordan 1919
Trygonorrhina Müller & Henle 1838
Zapteryx Jordan & Gilbert 1880

Subfam. Rhynchobatinae

Rhynchobatus Müller & Henle 1837

Subfam. Rhininae

Demiurga Gistel 1848
Rhamphobatis Gill 1862
Rhina Bloch & Schneider 1801

FAM. PLATYRHINIDAE (Thornbacks)

Analithis Gistel 1848
Discobatus Garman 1881
Platyrhina Müller & Henle 1838
Platyrhinoidis Garman 1881
Zanobatus Garman 1913

FAM. RAJIDAE (Skates)

Alpharaia Leigh-Sharpe 1924
Amblyraja Malm 1877
Arctoraja Ishiyama 1958
Argoraja Whitley 1940
Arhynchobatis Waite 1909

Atlantoraja Menni 1972
Bathyraja Ishiyama 1958
Batis Bonaparte 1838
Betaraia Leigh-Sharpe 1924
Breviraja Bigelow & Schroeder 1948
Cephaleutherus Rafinesque 1810
Clavata de Buen 1926
Cruriraja Bigelow & Schroeder 1948
Dactylobatus Bean & Weed 1909
Dasybatis Blainville 1825
Dasybatus Bonaparte 1834
Dasybatus Blainville 1816
Deltaraia Leigh-Sharpe 1924
Dentiraja Whitley 1940
Dipturus Rafinesque 1810
Eleutherocephalus Agassiz 1846
Epsilonraia Leigh-Sharpe 1925
Etaraia Leigh-Sharpe 1924
Fenestraja McEachran & Compagno 1982
Gammaraia Leigh-Sharpe 1924
Gurgesiella de Buen 1959
Hieroptera Fleming 1841
Iotaraia Leigh-Sharpe 1924
Irolita Whitley 1931
Kapparaia Leigh-Sharpe 1926
Laeviraja Bonaparte 1834
Laevirajae Nardo 1827
Leiobatus Klein 1775
Leucoraja Malm 1877
Malacobatis Gracianov 1907
Malacoraja Stehmann 1970
Malacorhina Garman 1877
Neoraja McEachran & Compagno 1982
Notoraja Ishiyama 1958
Okamejei Ishiyama 1958
Oxyrhynchus de Buen 1926
Pavoraja Whitley 1939
Perioptera Gistel 1848
Platopterus Rafinesque 1815
Propterygia Otto 1821
Psammobatis Günther 1870
Pseudoraja Bigelow & Schroeder 1954
Raia see *Raja*
Raja Linnaeus 1758
Rajabatis De la Pylaie 1835
Rajella Stehmann 1970
Rhinoraja Ishiyama 1952
Rioraja Whitley 1939
Rostroraja Hulley 1972
Spiniraja Whitley 1939
Sympterygia Müller & Henle 1837
Tengujei Ishiyama 1958
Thetaraia Leigh-Sharpe 1924
Uraptera Müller & Henle 1837
Uroxys Rafinesque 1815
Zearaja Whitley 1939
Zetaraia Leigh-Sharpe 1924

FAM. ANACANTHOBATIDAE (Smooth skates)

Anacanthobatis von Bonde & Swart 1923
Leiobatis von Bonde & Swart 1923
Schroederobatis Hulley 1973
Sinobatis Hulley 1973
Springeria Bigelow & Schroeder 1951

ORDER MYLIOBATIFORMES

FAM. DASYATIDAE (Stingrays)

Amphotistius Garman 1913
Anacanthus Cuvier (ex Ehrenberg) 1829
Anacanthus Ehrenberg in Van der Hoeven 1833
Bathytoshia Whitley 1933
Brachioptera Gracianov 1906
Dasyatis Rafinesque 1810
Dasybatus Klein 1775
Dasybatus Garman (ex Klein) 1885
Discobatis Miklukho-Maclay & Macleay 1886
Discotrygon Fowler 1910
Gymnura Müller & Henle 1837
Hemitrygon Müller & Henle 1838
Himantura Müller & Henle 1837
Hypanus Rafinesque 1818
Hypolophus Müller & Henle 1837
Neotrygon Castelnau 1873
Pastinaca Swainson 1838
Pastinacae Nardo 1827
Pastinachus Rüppell 1828
Pteroplatytrygon Fowler 1910
Rhachinotus Cantor 1849
Taeniura Müller & Henle 1837
Taeniurops Garman 1913
Toshia Whitley 1933
Trygon Cuvier (ex Adanson) 1816
Trygon Geoffroy St. Hilaire 1827
Trygonobatis Blainville 1825
Trygonobatus Blainville 1816
Urogymnus Müller & Henle 1837
Urolophoides Lindberg in Soldatov & Lindberg 1930
Uroxis Rafinesque 1810

FAM. GYMNURIDAE (Butterfly Rays)

Aetoplatea Valenciennes in Müller & Henle 1841
Dasyatis Gray 1851
Gymnura van Hasselt 1823
Phanerocephalus Gracianov 1906
Planerocephalus see *Phanerocephalus*
Pteroplatea Müller & Henle 1837

FAM. MYLIOBATIDAE (Eagle Rays and Cow-Nosed Rays)

Aetobatus Blainville 1816
Aetomylaeus Garman 1908
Goniobatus Agassiz 1858
Holorhinus Gill 1862
Ictaetus Rafinesque 1815
Indomanta Whitley 1936
Micromesus Gill 1865
Myliobates Agassiz 1843
Myliobates Schinz (ex Dumeril) 1822
Myliobatis Cuvier (ex Duméril) 1816
Myliobatis Geoffroy St. Hilaire 1817
Mylorhina Gill 1865
Pteromylaeus Garman 1913
Rhinoptera Cuvier 1829
Rhinoptera van Hasselt 1824
Stoasodon Cantor 1849
Trikeras Harless 1850
Trycera Koch in Döderlein 1884

FAM. UROLOPHIDAE (Round Stingrays)

Leiobatus Blainville 1816
Trygonoptera Müller & Henle 1841
Urobatis Garman 1913
Urolophus Müller & Henle 1837
Urotrygon Gill 1863

FAM. POTAMOTRYGONIDAE (River Stingrays)

Disceus Garman 1877
Elipesurus Schomburgk 1843
Paratrygon Duméril 1865
Plesiotrygon Rosa, Castello & Thorson 1987
Potamotrygon Garman 1877

FAM. MOBULIDAE (Manta Rays and Devil Rays)

Aodon Lacepède 1798
Apterurus Rafinesque 1810
Brachioptilon Hamilton in Newman 1849
Cephaloptera Cuvier (ex Duméril) 1816
Cephalopterus Risso (ex Duméril) 1810
Ceratobatis Boulenger 1897
Ceratoptera Müller & Henle 1837
Daemomanta Whitley 1932
Deratoptera Krefft 1868
Diabolicthys Holmes 1856
Dicerobatis Blainville 1825
Dicerobatus Blainville 1816
Manta Bancroft 1829
Mobula Rafinesque 1810
Pterocephalus Swainson 1838

FAM. HEXATRYGONIDAE (Sixgill Stingrays)

Hexatrematobatis Chu & Meng in Zhu et al. 1981
Hexatrygon Heemstra & Smith 1980

CLASS HOLOCEPHALI

ORDER CHIMAERIFORMES

FAM. CALLORHYNCHIDAE (Plownose Chimaeras)

Callorhinchus Lacepède (ex Gronow) 1798
Callorhyncus Fleming 1822
Callorynchus Gronow 1763
Callorynchus Cuvier (ex Gronow) 1816

FAM. CHIMAERIDAE (Shortnose Chimaeras)

Bathyalopex Collett 1904
Chimaera Linnaeus 1758
Hydrolagus Gill 1862
Phasmichthys Jordan & Hubbs 1925
Psychichthys Fowler 1907

FAM. RHINOCHIMAERIDAE (Longnose Chimaeras)

Anteliochimaera Tanaka 1909
Harriotta Goode & Bean 1895
Neoharriotta Bigelow & Schroeder 1950
Rhinochimaera Garman 1901

CLASS ACTINOPTERYGII = Osteichthyes

ORDER ACIPENSERIFORMES

FAM. ACIPENSERIDAE (Sturgeons)

Subfam. Acipenserinae
Acipenser Linnaeus 1758
Acipenses Linck 1790
Antacea Bory de Saint-Vincent 1822
Antaceus Heckel & Fitzinger 1836
Dinoctus Rafinesque 1818
Ellops Gistel 1848
Gladostomus Holly 1936
Helops Brandt & Ratzeburg 1833
Huso Brandt & Ratzeburg 1833
Ichthyocolla Geoffroy St. Hilaire 1767
Lioniscus Heckel & Fitzinger 1836
Lioniscus Bonaparte (ex Heckel & Fitzinger) 1846
Shipa Brandt 1869
Sinosturio Jaekel 1929
Sterleta Güldenstädt 1772
Sterletus Rafinesque 1820
Sterletus Brandt & Ratzeburg 1833
Sturio Rafinesque 1810
Sturio Müller 1836

Subfam. Scaphirhynchinae
Hemiscaphirhynchus Berg 1911
Kessleria Boghdanov 1882
Parascaphirhynchus Forbes & Richardson 1905
Pseudoscaphirhynchus Nikolskii 1900
Scaphirhynchus Heckel 1836
Scaphyrhynchops Gill 1863

FAM. POLYODONTIDAE (Paddlefishes)
Megarhinus Rafinesque 1820
Platirostra Lesueur 1818
Polyodon Lacepède 1797
Polyodon Bloch & Schneider 1801
Proceros Rafinesque 1820
Psephurus Günther 1873
Spatularia Shaw 1804

ORDER POLYPTERIFORMES

FAM. POLYPTERIDAE (Bichirs)
Calamoichthys Smith 1866
Erpetoichthys Smith 1865
Polypterus Lacepède 1803

ORDER LEPISOSTEIFORMES

FAM. LEPISOSTEIDAE (Gars)
Acus Catesby 1771
Atractosteus Rafinesque 1820
Cylindrosteus Rafinesque 1820
Lepisosteus Lacepède 1803
Litholepis Rafinesque 1818
Psalidostomus Minding 1832
Psalisostomus Klein 1781
Psallisostomus Klein in Walbaum 1792
Sarchirus Rafinesque 1818

ORDER AMIIFORMES

FAM. AMIIDAE (Bowfins)
Amia Linnaeus 1766
Amiatus Rafinesque 1815

ORDER OSTEOGLOSSIFORMES

SUBORDER OSTEOGLOSSOIDEI

FAM. OSTEOGLOSSIDAE (Bonytongues and Arapaimas)

Subfam. Heterotidinae
Arapaima Müller 1843
Clupisudis Swainson 1839
Helicobranchus Hyrtl 1854
Heterotis Rüppell (ex Ehrenberg) 1828
Sudis Cuvier 1816
Vastres Valenciennes in Cuvier & Valenciennes 1847

Subfam. Osteoglossinae
Delsmania Fowler 1934
Ischnosoma Agassiz in Spix & Agassiz 1829
Osteoglossum Cuvier (ex Vandelli) 1829
Osteoglossum Agassiz in Spix & Agassiz 1829
Scleropages Günther 1864

FAM. PANTODONTIDAE
Pantodon Peters 1877

SUBORDER NOTOPTEROIDEI

FAM. HIODONTIDAE (Mooneyes)
Amphiodon Rafinesque 1819
Clodalus Rafinesque 1820
Elattonistius Gill & Jordan in Jordan 1877
Glossodon Rafinesque 1818
Hiodon Lesueur 1818

FAM. NOTOPTERIDAE (Knifefishes or Featherbacks)
Chitala Fowler 1934
Glanis Gronow in Gray 1854
Notopterus Lacepède 1800
Papyrocranus Greenwood 1963
Xenomystus Günther 1868

SUBORDER MORMYROIDEI

FAM. MORMYRIDAE (Elephantfishes)
Boulengeromyrus Taverne & Géry 1968
Brevimyrus Taverne 1971
Brienomyrus Taverne 1971
Campylomormyrus Bleeker 1874
Cyphomyrus Myers 1960
Genyomyrus Boulenger 1898
Gnathonemus Gill 1863
Heteromormyrus Steindachner 1866
Hippopotamyrus Pappenheim 1906
Hyperopisus Gill 1862
Isichthys Gill 1863
Ivindomyrus Taverne & Géry 1975
Marcusenius Gill 1862
Mormyrodes Gill 1862
Mormyrops Müller 1843
Mormyrus Linnaeus 1758
Myomyrus Boulenger 1898
Oxymormyrus Bleeker 1874
Oxyrhynchus Leach in Tuckey 1818
Paramormyrops Taverne, Thys van den Audenaerde & Heymer 1977
Paramyomyrus Pellegrin 1927
Petrocephalus Marcusen 1854
Phagrus Marcusen 1864
Pollimyrus Taverne 1971
Scrophicephalus Swainson 1838
Solenomormyrus Bleeker 1874
Stomatorhinus Boulenger 1898

FAM. GYMNARCHIDAE
Gymnarchus Cuvier 1829

ORDER ELOPIFORMES

FAM. ELOPIDAE (Tenpounders)
Alloelops Nybelin 1979
Ellops Minding 1832
Elops Linnaeus 1766
Gularus Whitley 1940
Helops Agassiz 1846
Mugilomorus Lacepède 1803
Trichonotus Rafinesque 1815

FAM. MEGALOPIDAE (Tarpons)
Amia Browne 1789
Brisbania Castelnau 1878
Megalops Lacepède 1803
Oculeus Commerson in Lacepède 1803
Tarpon Jordan & Evermann 1896

ORDER ALBULIFORMES

FAM. ALBULIDAE (Bonefishes)

Subfam. Albulinae
Albula Gronow 1763
Albula Scopoli (ex Gronow) 1777
Albula Bloch & Schneider (ex Gronow) 1801
Atopichthys Garman 1899
Butyrinus Lacepède (ex Commerson) 1803
Conorynchus Nozemann 1758
Dixonina Fowler 1911
Esunculus Kaup 1856
Glossodonta Cuvier 1815
Glossodus Agassiz in Spix & Agassiz 1829
Vulpis Catesby 1771

Subfam. Pterothrissinae
Bathythrissa Günther 1877
Pterothrissus Hilgendorf 1877

ORDER NOTOCANTHIFORMES

FAM. HALOSAURIDAE (Halosaurs)
Aldrovandia Goode & Bean 1896
Halosaurichthys Alcock 1889

Halosauropsis Collett 1896
Halosaurus Johnson 1864

FAM. NOTACANTHIDAE (Spiny Eels)

Acanthonotus Bloch & Schneider 1801
Campilodon Cuvier 1829
Campylodon Fabricius 1793
Gigliolia Goode & Bean 1895
Gnathonotacanthus Fowler 1934
Macdonaldia Goode & Bean 1895
Notacanthus Bloch 1788
Paradoxichthys Giglioli 1882
Polyacanthonotus Bleeker 1874
Teratichthys Giglioli 1882
Tiluropsis Roule 1911
Tilurus Kölliker 1854
Zanotacanthus Gill 1876

FAM. LIPOGENYIDAE

Lipogenys Goode & Bean 1895

ORDER ANGUILLIFORMES

Rincoxus Rafinesque 1815
Thalassenchelys Castle & Raju 1975
Zebricium Rafinesque 1815

SUBORDER ANGUILLOIDEI

FAM. ANGUILLIDAE (Freshwater Eels)

Anguilla Schrank 1798
Terpolepis McClelland 1844
Tribranchus Müller 1844

FAM. HETERENCHELYIDAE

Heterenchelys Regan 1912
Lophenchelys Ben-Tuvia 1953
Ophisichthys Osório 1917
Panturichthys Pellegrin 1913
Pythonichthys Poey 1867

FAM. MORINGUIDAE (Spaghetti Eels)

Anguillichthys Mowbray in Breder 1927
Aphthalmichthys Kaup 1856
Aphthalmoichthys Kaup in Duméril 1856
Chrinorhinus Howell Rivero 1932
Mayerina Silvester 1915
Merinthichthys Howell Rivero 1934
Moringua Gray 1831
Neoconger Girard 1858
Pachyurus Swainson 1839
Pseudomoringua Bleeker 1864
Pterurus Swainson 1839
Ptyobranchus McClelland 1844
Rataboura Gray 1831
Stilbiscus Jordan & Bollman 1889

SUBORDER MURAENOIDEI

FAM. CHLOPSIDAE (False Morays) = Xenocongridae

Arenichthys Beebe & Tee-Van 1938
Brachyconger Norman 1922
Catesbya Böhlke & Smith 1968
Chilorhinus Lütken 1852
Chlopsis Rafinesque 1810
Endeconger Jordan 1923
Garmanichthys Seale 1917
Kaupichthys Schultz 1943
Powellichthys Smith 1966
Robinsia Böhlke & Smith 1967
Xenoconger Regan 1912

FAM. MYROCONGRIDAE

Myroconger Günther 1870

FAM. MURAENIDAE (Morays) Heteromyridae included

Heteromyrus Pietschmann 1935
Muraenoblenna Kaup 1856

Subfam. Uropterygiinae

Anarchias Jordan & Starks in Jordan & Seale 1906
Chamomuraena Kaup in Duméril 1856
Channomuraena Richardson 1848
Ichthyophis Lesson 1828
Scutica Jordan & Evermann 1896
Scuticaria Jordan & Snyder 1901
Uropterygius Rüppell 1838

Subfam. Muraeninae

Aemasia Jordan & Snyder 1901
Ahynnodontophis Fowler 1912
Arndha Deraniyagala 1931
Chasmenchelys Fowler 1944
Echidna Forster 1777
Enchelycore Kaup 1856
Enchelycotte Kaup in Duméril 1856
Enchelynassa Kaup 1855
Eurymyctera Kaup 1856
Evenchelys Jordan & Evermann 1902
Fimbrinares Whitley 1948
Gymnomuraena Lacepède 1803
Gymnopsis Rafinesque 1815
Gymnothorax Bloch 1795
Leihala Jordan 1925
Limmamuraena Kaup in Duméril 1856
Limomuraena Kaup 1856
Lycodontis McClelland 1844
Megaderus Rafinesque 1815
Molarii Richardson 1848
Molarius see *Molarii*
Monopenchelys Böhlke & McCosker 1982
Muraena Linnaeus 1758
Muraenophis Lacepède 1803
Murenophis Cuvier 1798
Neomuraena Girard 1858
Nettastomops Steindachner 1906
Notorabula Whitley 1934
Poecilophis Kaup 1856
Polyuranodon Kaup 1856
Priodonophis Kaup 1860
Pseudechidna Bleeker 1863
Pseudomuraena Johnson 1862
Rabula Jordan & Davis 1891
Rhabdura Ogilby 1907
Rhinechidna Barbour 1908
Rhinomuraena Garman 1888
Serranguilla Whitley & Phillipps 1939
Sidera Kaup in Duméril 1856
Siderea Kaup 1856
Strophidon McClelland 1844
Taeniophis Kaup 1860
Thaerodontis McClelland 1844
Thyrsoidea Kaup 1856
Verdithorax Whitley 1931
Voltella Grassi 1913

SUBORDER CONGROIDEI

FAM. SYNAPHOBRANCHIDAE (Cutthroat Eels)

Subfam. Ilyophinae (Arrowtooth Eels)

Atractodenchelys Robins & Robins 1970
Dysomma Alcock 1889
Dysommina Ginsburg 1951
Dysommopsis Alcock 1891
Ilyophis Gilbert 1891
Linkenchelys Smith 1989
Meadia Böhlke 1951
Nettodarus Whitley 1951
Sinomyrus Lin 1933
Todarus Grassi & Calandruccio 1896

Subfam. Synaphobranchinae (Cutthroat Eels)

Diastobranchus Barnard 1923
Haptenchelys Robins & Martin in Robins & Robins 1976
Histiobranchus Gill 1883
Nettophichthys Holt 1891
Synaphobranchus Johnson 1862

Subfam. Simenchelyinae (Pugnose Eels)

Conchognathus Collett 1889
Gymnosimenchelys Tanaka 1908
Simenchelys Gill in Goode & Bean 1879

FAM. OPHICHTHIDAE (Snake Eels and Worm Eels)

Colubrina Lacepède 1803

Subfam. Myrophinae

Ahlia Jordan & Davis 1891
Aotea Phillipps 1926
Asarcenchelys McCosker 1985
Benthenchelys Fowler 1934
Glenoglossa McCosker 1982
Hesperomyrus Myers & Storey 1939
Holopterura Cope 1871
Leptoconger Poey 1880
Mixomyrophis McCosker 1985
Muraenichthys Bleeker 1853
Myrophis Lütken 1852
Myropterura Ogilby 1897
Neenchelys Bamber 1915
Pseudomyrophis Wade 1946
Schismorhynchus McCosker 1970
Schultzidia Gosline 1951
Scolecenchelys Ogilby 1897

Subfam. Ophichthinae

Acanthenchelys Norman 1922
Achirophichthys Bleeker 1864
Allips McCosker 1972
Anepistomon Gistel 1848
Anguisurus Kaup 1856
Antobrantia Pinto 1970
Aplatophis Böhlke 1956
Aprognathodon Böhlke 1967

Apterichthys Kaup in Duméril 1856
Apterichtus Duméril 1806
Auchenichthys Kaup in Duméril 1856
Bascanichthys Jordan & Davis 1891
Bertinulus Whitley 1948
Brachycheirophis Fowler 1944
Brachysomophis Kaup 1856
Branderius Rafinesque 1815
Caecilia Lacepède 1800
Caecula Vahl 1794
Calamuraena Whitley 1944
Callechelys Kaup 1856
Caralophia Böhlke 1955
Centrurophis Kaup 1856
Chlevastes Jordan & Snyder 1901
Cirrhimuraena Kaup 1856
Cirricaecula Schultz in Schultz et al. 1953
Coecilophis Kaup 1856
Cogrus Rafinesque 1810
Crotalopsis Kaup 1860
Cryptopterenchelys Fowler 1925
Cryptopterus Kaup 1860
Cryptopterygium Ginsburg 1951
Cyclophichthys Whitley 1951
Dalophis Rafinesque 1810
Dendrophis Kaup in Duméril 1856
Echelus Rafinesque 1810
Echiophis Kaup 1856
Elapsopis Kaup 1856
Ethadophis Rosenblatt & McCosker 1970
Evips McCosker 1972
Giscenchelys Fowler 1944
Gordiichthys Jordan & Davis 1891
Hemerorhinus Weber & de Beaufort 1916
Herpetoichthys Kaup 1856
Hyphalophis McCosker & Böhlke 1982
Ichthyapus Brisout de Barneville 1847
Innominado Parra 1787
Jenkinsiella Jordan & Evermann 1905
Kertomichthys McCosker & Böhlke 1982
Lamnostoma Kaup 1856
Leiuranus Bleeker 1853
Leiurus Kaup in Duméril 1856
Leptenchelys Myers & Wade 1941
Leptognathus Swainson 1838
Leptorhinophis Kaup 1856
Leptorhynchus Smith 1840
Letharchus Goode & Bean 1882
Lethogoleos McCosker & Böhlke 1982
Leuropharus Rosenblatt & McCosker 1970
Machaerenchelys Fowler 1938
Macrodonophis Poey 1868
Malvoliophis Whitley 1934
Microdonophis Kaup 1856
Microrhynchus Blache & Bauchot 1972
Muraenopsis Lesueur in Kaup 1856
Myrichthys Girard 1859
Myrus Kaup 1856
Mystriophis Kaup 1856
Notophtophis Castro-Aguirre & Suárez de los Cobos 1983
Omochelys Fowler 1918
Ophichthus Ahl 1789
Ophis Turton 1807
Ophisurapus Kaup 1856
Ophisurus Lacepède 1800
Ophithorax McClelland 1844
Oxyodontichthys Poey 1880
Oxystomus Rafinesque 1810
Pantonora Smith 1965
Paraletharchus McCosker 1974
Paramyrus Günther 1870
Pelia Schlegel in Bleeker 1863
Phaenomonas Myers & Wade 1941
Phyllophichthus Gosline 1951
Pisodonophis Kaup 1856
Poecilocephalus Kaup 1856
Pogonophis Myers & Wade 1941
Pterurus Rafinesque 1810
Quassiremus Jordan & Davis 1891
Rhinenchelys Blache & Bauchot 1972
Scytalichthys Jordan & Davis 1891
Scytallurus Duméril (ex Kaup) 1856
Scytalophis Kaup 1856
Sphagebranchus Bloch 1795
Stethopterus Bleeker 1853
Stictorhinus Böhlke & McCosker 1975
Syletophis Whitley 1950
Syletor Jordan 1919
Typhlotes Fischer von Waldheim 1813
Uranichthys Poey 1867
Verma Jordan & Evermann 1896
Xyrias Jordan & Snyder 1901
Yirrkala Whitley 1940
Zonophichthus Whitley 1930

FAM. COLOCONGRIDAE

Ascomana Castle 1967
Coloconger Alcock 1889

FAM. CONGRIDAE (Conger Eels)

Subfam. Congrinae

Acromycter Smith & Kanazawa 1977
Astroconger Jordan & Hubbs 1925
Bassanago Whitley 1948
Bathycongrus Ogilby 1898
Bathyuroconger Fowler 1934
Blachea Karrer & Smith 1980
Conger Klein 1775
Conger Oken (ex Cuvier) 1817
Conger Bosc (ex Cuvier) 1817
Congerodon Kaup 1856
Congrhynchus Fowler 1934
Congrina Jordan & Hubbs 1925
Congriscus Jordan & Hubbs 1925
Congrosoma Garman 1899
Congrus Richardson 1845
Diploconger Kotthaus 1968
Euleptocephalus Strömman 1896
Fimbriceps Whitley 1946
Forskalichthys Whitley 1935
Gnathophis Kaup 1860
Helmictis Rafinesque 1810
Hildebrandia Jordan & Evermann 1927
Isognatha Gill (ex DeKay) 1861
Japonoconger Asano 1958
Lemkea Kotthaus 1968
Leptocephalichthys Bleeker 1856
Leptocephalus Scopoli (ex Gronow) 1777
Leptocephalus Gronow 1763
Lumiconger Castle & Paxton 1984
Macrocephenchelys Fowler 1934
Microcephalocongrus Fowler 1934
Microconger Fowler 1912
Morris Berkenhout 1789
Oxyurus Rafinesque 1810
Paraxenomystax Reid 1940
Paruroconger Blache & Bauchot 1976
Poeciloconger Günther 1872
Poutawa Griffin 1936
Promyllantor Alcock 1890
Pseudophichthys Roule 1915
Pseudoxenomystax Breder 1927
Rhechias Jordan 1921
Rhynchoconger Jordan & Hubbs 1925
Rhynchocymba Jordan & Hubbs 1925
Scalanago Whitley 1935
Silvesterina Fowler 1934
Uranoconger Fowler 1934
Uroconger Kaup 1856
Veternio Snyder 1904
Xenomystax Gilbert 1891

Subfam. Bathymyrinae

Alloconger Jordan & Hubbs 1925
Anago Jordan & Hubbs 1925
Ariosoma Swainson 1838
Bathymyrus Alcock 1889
Chiloconger Myers & Wade 1941
Congermuraena Kaup 1856
Congrellus Ogilby 1898
Diaphanichthys Peters 1864
Helmichthys Costa 1844
Nesocongrus Whitley 1935
Ophisoma Swainson 1839
Parabathymyrus Kamohara 1938
Paraconger Kanazawa 1961
Thyreoconger Wade 1946

Subfam. Heterocongrinae (Garden Eels)

Gorgasia Meek & Hildebrand 1923
Heteroconger Bleeker 1868
Nystactes Böhlke 1957
Nystactichthys Böhlke 1958
Taenioconger Herre 1923
Xarifania Klausewitz & Eibl-Eibesfeldt 1959

FAM. MURAENESOCIDAE (Pike Conger Eels)

Brachyconger Bleeker 1865
Cheiromuroenesox Fowler 1944
Congresox Gill 1890
Cynoponticus Costa 1845
Gavialiceps Alcock (ex Wood-Mason) 1889
Muraenesox McClelland 1844
Oxyconger Bleeker 1864
Phyllogramma Pellegrin 1934
Sauromuraenesox Alcock 1889

FAM. DERICHTHYIDAE (Longneck Eels)

Derichthys Gill 1884
Grammatocephalus Norman 1930
Nessorhamphus Schmidt 1931

FAM. NEMICHTHYIDAE (Snipe Eels)

Avocettina Jordan & Davis 1891
Avocettinops Roule & Bertin 1924
Belonopsis Brandt 1854
Borodinula Whitley 1931
Cercomitus Weber 1913

Investigator Goode in Goode & Bean 1896
Labichthys Gill & Ryder 1883
Leptorhynchus Lowe 1852
Nematoprora Gilbert 1905
Nemichthys Richardson 1848
Paravocettinops Kanazawa & Maul 1967
Tilurella Roule 1911

FAM. SERRIVOMERIDAE (Sawtooth Eels)

Alcockidia Gilbert 1905
Paraserrivomer Roule & Angel 1931
Platuronides Roule & Bertin 1924
Serrivomer Gill & Ryder 1883
Spinivomer Gill & Ryder 1883
Stemonidium Gilbert 1905

FAM. NETTASTOMATIDAE (Duckbill Eels)

Dietrichthys Whitley 1935
Facciolella Whitley 1938
Hoplunnis Kaup 1860
Hyoprorus Kölliker 1853
Metopomycter Gilbert 1905
Muraenosaurus Osório 1909
Nettastoma Rafinesque 1810
Nettastomella Facciolà 1911
Nettenchelys Alcock 1898
Osorina Whitley 1951
Saurenchelys Peters 1864
Venefica Jordan & Davis 1891

ORDER SACCOPHARYNGIFORMES

FAM. CYEMATIDAE (Bobtail Eels) = Cyemidae

Cyema Günther 1878
Neocyema Castle 1978

FAM. SACCOPHARYNGIDAE (Swallowers or Whiptail Gulpers)

Ophioglossus Duméril 1856
Ophiognathus Harwood 1827
Saccopharynx Mitchill 1824

FAM. EURYPHARYNGIDAE (Umbrella-mouth Gulpers)

Eurypharynx Vaillant 1882
Gastrostomus Gill & Ryder 1883
Jordanites Fowler 1925
Macropharynx Brauer 1902
Megalopharynx Brauer in Chun 1900
Rouleina Fowler 1925

FAM. MONOGNATHIDAE (Monognathids)

Monognathus Bertin 1936
Phasmatostoma Myers 1940

ORDER CLUPEIFORMES

FAM. DENTICIPITIDAE (Denticle Herrings)

Acanthothrissa Gras 1961
Denticeps Clausen 1959
Igborichthys Clausen 1959

FAM. CLUPEIDAE (Herrings, Shads, Sardines and allies)

Alausa Valenciennes in Cuvier & Valenciennes 1847
Alausella Gill 1861
Alosa Linck 1790
Amblygaster Bleeker 1849
Anodontostoma Bleeker 1849
Antu de Buen 1958
Apterogasterus De la Pylaie 1835
Apterygia Gray 1835
Arengus Cornide 1788
Brevoortia Gill 1861
Caspialosa Berg 1915
Chatoessus Cuvier 1829
Chirocentrodon Günther 1868
Clupalosa Bleeker 1849
Clupanodon Lacepède 1803
Clupea Linnaeus 1758
Clupeichthys Bleeker 1855
Clupeoides Bleeker 1851
Clupeonella Kessler 1877
Clupeonia Valenciennes in Cuvier & Valenciennes 1847
Congothrissa Poll 1964
Corica Hamilton 1822
Cynothrissa Regan 1917
Dascillus Gronow in Gray 1854
Dayella Talwar & Whitehead 1971
Dorosoma Rafinesque 1820
Dussumieria Valenciennes in Cuvier & Valenciennes 1847
Ehirava Deraniyagala 1929
Escualosa Whitley 1940
Ethmalosa Regan 1917
Ethmidium Thompson 1916
Etrumeus Bleeker 1853
Euplatygaster Fowler 1934
Filialosa Fowler 1944
Fimbriclupea Whitley 1940
Fiscina Whitley 1940
Fluvialosa Whitley 1943
Fluviatilis de Buen 1926
Fusiclupea Whitley 1940
Gilchristella Fowler 1935
Gnathobolus Bloch & Schneider 1801
Gonialosa Regan 1917
Gonostoma van Hasselt 1823
Gudusia Fowler 1911
Halecula Jordan 1925
Harengula Valenciennes in Cuvier & Valenciennes 1847
Harengus Geoffroy St. Hilaire 1767
Harengus Catesby 1771
Harengus Klein 1775
Heringia Fowler 1911
Herklotsella Fowler 1934
Herklotsichthys Whitley 1951
Hilsa Regan 1917
Hyalosprattus Whitley 1936
Hyperlophus Ogilby 1892
Hyrtlinus Fowler 1958
Ilisha Richardson (ex Gray) 1846
Indialosa Herre & Myers 1931
Jenkinsia Jordan & Evermann 1896
Konosirus Jordan & Snyder 1900
Kowala Valenciennes in Cuvier & Valenciennes 1847
Laeviscutella Poll, Whitehead & Hopson 1965
Laomeda Rafinesque 1815
Leptoclupea Whitehead, Boeseman & Wheeler (ex Bleeker) 1966
Leptogaster Bleeker 1870
Lile Jordan & Evermann 1896
Limnothrissa Regan 1917
Macrura van Hasselt 1823
Macrura Fowler 1941
Marinus de Buen 1926
Maugeclupea Whitley 1932
Medipellona Jordan & Seale 1926
Meletta Valenciennes in Cuvier & Valenciennes 1847
Microthrissa Boulenger 1902
Montalbania Fowler 1934
Nannothrissa Poll 1965
Nealosa Herre & Myers 1931
Nematalosa Regan 1917
Neoopisthopterus Hildebrand 1948
Neosteus Norman 1923
Odaxothrissa Boulenger 1899
Odontognathus Lacepède 1800
Omochetus Ogilby 1897
Opisthonema Gill 1861
Opisthopterus Gill 1861
Parahalecula Fowler 1958
Paralosa Bleeker 1868
Paralosa Regan 1916
Paralosa Roule 1925
Pellona Valenciennes in Cuvier & Valenciennes 1847
Pellonula Günther 1868
Pellonulops Smith 1949
Perkinsia Eigenmann 1891
Platanichthys Whitehead 1968
Platygaster Swainson 1838
Pliosteostoma Norman 1923
Poecilothrissa Regan 1917
Pomolobus Rafinesque 1820
Potamalosa Ogilby 1897
Potamothrissa Regan 1917
Pristigaster Cuvier 1816
Pristogaster Swainson 1838
Pseudochirocentrodon Miranda-Ribeiro 1920
Raconda Gray 1831
Ramnogaster Whitehead 1965
Rhinosardinia Eigenmann 1912
Rogenia Valenciennes in Cuvier & Valenciennes 1847
Sardina Antipa 1904
Sardinella Valenciennes in Cuvier & Valenciennes 1847
Sardinia Poey 1860
Sardinops Hubbs 1929
Sauvagella Bertin 1940
Sierrathrissa Thys van den Audenaerde 1969
Signalosa Evermann & Kendall 1898
Spratella Valenciennes in Cuvier & Valenciennes 1847
Spratelloides Bleeker 1851
Spratellomorpha Bertin in Angel, Bertin & Guibé 1946
Sprattus Girgensohn 1846
Stolothrissa Regan 1917
Strangomera Whitehead 1965

Tenualosa Fowler 1934
Thrattidion Roberts 1972
Thrissa Rafinesque 1815
Trichis Plumier in Lacepède 1803
Wilkesina Fowler & Bean 1923
Zunasia Jordan & Metz 1913

FAM. ENGRAULIDIDAE (Anchovies) = Engraulididae

Alpismaris Swainson 1838
Amazonsprattus Roberts 1984
Amentum Whitley 1940
Amplova Jordan & Seale 1925
Anchoa Jordan & Evermann 1927
Anchovia Jordan & Evermann in Jordan 1895
Anchoviella Fowler 1911
Anchovietta Nelson 1986
Austranchovia Whitley 1931
Cetengraulis Günther 1868
Chaetomus McClelland 1844
Choetomus see *Chaetomus*
Coilia Gray 1830
Demicoilia Jordan & Seale 1925
Encrasicholina Fowler 1938
Encrasicholus Commerson in Lacepède 1803
Encrasicholus Fleming 1828
Engraulis Cuvier 1816
Heterothrissa Günther 1868
Hildebrandichthys Schultz 1949
Jurengraulis Whitehead, Nelson & Wongratana 1988
Leptonurus Bleeker 1849
Lycengraulis Günther 1868
Lycothrissa Günther 1868
Menidia Browne 1789
Mystus Lacepède 1803
Odontengraulis Whitehead, Boeseman & Wheeler (ex Bleeker) 1966
Osteoglossum Basilewski 1855
Papuengraulis Munro 1964
Pseudosetipinna Peng & Zhao 1988
Pterengraulis Günther 1868
Scutengraulis Jordan & Seale 1925
Setipinna Swainson 1839
Stethochaetus Gronow in Gray 1854
Stolephorus Lacepède 1803
Telara Valenciennes 1848
Thrissa Cuvier 1816
Thrissina Jordan & Seale 1925
Thrissocles Jordan & Evermann in Jordan 1917
Thryssa Cuvier 1829
Trichosoma Swainson 1838
Xenengraulis Jordan & Seale 1925

FAM. CHIROCENTRIDAE (Wolf Herrings)

Chirocentrus Cuvier 1816
Neosudis Castelnau 1873

ORDER GONORYNCHIFORMES

FAM. CHANIDAE (Milkfishes)

Chanos Lacepède 1803
Lutodeira van Hasselt 1823
Ptycholepis Richardson in Richardson & Gray 1843
Scoliostomus Rüppell 1828

FAM. GONORYNCHIDAE

Gonorynchus Gronow 1763
Gonorynchus Scopoli (ex Gronow) 1777
Rynchana Richardson 1845

FAM. KNERIIDAE

Angola Myers 1928
Cromeria Boulenger 1901
Grasseichthys Géry 1964
Kneria Steindachner 1866
Parakneria Poll 1965
Xenopomichthys Pellegrin 1905

FAM. PHRACTOLAEMIDAE

Phractolaemus Boulenger 1901

ORDER CYPRINIFORMES

Aperioptus Richardson 1848
Caucus Bory de Saint-Vincent 1823

FAM. CYPRINIDAE (Minnows and Carps) No subfamilies are recognized

Abbottina Jordan & Fowler 1903
Abramidopsis Siebold 1863
Abramis Cuvier 1816
Abramocephalus Steindachner 1869
Abrostomus Smith 1841
Acahara Jordan & Hubbs 1925
Acanthalburnus Berg 1916
Acanthobrama Heckel 1843
Acanthogobio Herzenstein 1892
Acanthonotus Tickell in Day 1888
Acanthorhodeus Bleeker 1871
Acanthorutilus Berg 1912
Acapoeta Cockerell 1910
Acheilognathus Bleeker 1859
Acra Bleeker 1860
Acrocheilichthys see *Sarcocheilichthys*
Acrocheilus Agassiz 1855
Acrossocheilus Oshima 1919*Adamacypris* Fowler 1934
Afropuntio Karaman 1971
Ageneiogarra Garman 1912
Agenigobio Sauvage 1878
Agosia Girard 1856
Agrammobarbus Pellegrin 1935
Albulichthys Bleeker 1859
Alburnellus Girard 1856
Alburnoides Jeitteles 1861
Alburnops Girard 1856
Alburnus Rafinesque 1820
Algansea Girard 1856
Algoma Girard 1856
Allochela Silas 1958
Allodanio Smith 1945
Altigena Lin 1933
Amblypharyngodon Bleeker 1859
Amblyrhynchichthys Bleeker 1859
Amplolabrius Lin 1933
Anabarilius Cockerell 1923
Anaecypris Collares-Pereira 1983
Ancherythroculter Yih & Wu 1964
Anchovicypris Fowler 1936
Anematichthys Bleeker 1859
Aphyocyprioides Tang 1942
Aphyocypris Günther 1868
Apocope Cope 1872
Argyreus Heckel 1843
Aristichthys Oshima 1919
Armatogobio Taranetz 1937
Aspidoparia Heckel 1847
Aspiobarbus Berg 1932
Aspiolucius Berg 1907
Aspiopsis Zugmayer 1912
Aspiorhynchus Kessler 1879
Aspiostoma Nikolskii 1897
Aspius Agassiz 1832
Atrilinea Chu 1935
Aturius Dubalen 1878
Aulopyge Heckel 1841
Azteca Jordan & Evermann 1896
Aztecula Jordan & Evermann 1898
Balantiocheilos Bleeker 1859
Ballerus Heckel 1843
Bangana Hamilton 1822
Barbellion Whitley 1931
Barbichthys Bleeker 1859
Barbodes Bleeker 1860
Barbodon Dybowski 1872
Barboides Brüning 1929
Barbopsis Caporiacco 1926
Barbus Cuvier & Cloquet 1816
Barilius Hamilton 1822
Barynotus Günther 1868
Bathystoma Fitzinger 1873
Beirabarbus Herre 1936
Belligobio Jordan & Hubbs 1925
Bendilisis Bleeker 1860
Bengana Gray 1832
Bertinichthys Whitley 1953
Bertinius Fang 1943
Biwia Jordan & Fowler 1903
Blicca Heckel 1843
Bliccopsis Heckel 1843
Bola Günther 1868
Brachydanio Weber & de Beaufort 1916
Brachygramma Day 1865
Brama Klein 1775
Brama Bleeker (ex Klein) 1863
Brevigobio Tanaka 1916
Bungia Keyserling 1861
Cabdio Hamilton 1822
Cachius Günther 1868
Caecobarbus Boulenger 1921
Caecocypris Banister & Bunni 1980
Campostoma Agassiz 1855
Candidia Jordan & Richardson 1909
Capoeta Valenciennes in Cuvier & Valenciennes 1842
Capoetobrama Berg 1916
Carasobarbus Karaman 1971
Caraspius Nichols 1925
Carassioides Oshima 1926
Carassius Nilsson 1832
Carinozacco Zhu, Wang & Yong 1982
Carpio Heckel 1843
Carpionichthys Bleeker 1863
Catla Valenciennes in Cuvier & Valenciennes 1844
Catlocarpio Boulenger 1898
Cenisophius Bonaparte 1846
Cephalakompsus Herre 1924
Cephalopsis Fitzinger 1873
Cephalus Bonaparte 1846

Cephalus Basilewski 1855
Ceratichthys see *Ceraticthys*
Ceraticthys Baird & Girard 1853
Chagunius Smith 1938
Chalcalburnus Berg 1933
Chanodichthys Bleeker 1859
Chedrus Swainson 1839
Cheilobarbus Smith 1841
Cheilonemus Storer (ex Baird) 1855
Chela Hamilton 1822
Chelaethiops Boulenger 1899
Cheonda Girard 1856
Chilogobio Berg 1914
Chilonemus Baird 1851
Chondrochilus Heckel 1843
Chondrorhynchus Heckel 1843
Chondrostoma Agassiz 1832
Chriope Jordan 1878
Chrosomus Rafinesque 1820
Chrysophekadion Bleeker 1859
Chuanchia Herzenstein 1891
Cirrhinichthys Bleeker 1863
Cirrhinus Oken (ex Cuvier) 1817
Clarkina Jordan & Evermann 1927
Clinostomus Girard 1856
Cliola Girard 1856
Clypeobarbus Fowler 1936
Coccogenia Cockerell & Callaway 1909
Coccotis Jordan 1882
Cochlognathus Baird & Girard 1854
Codoma Girard 1856
Coliscus Cope 1871
Coptostomabarbus David & Poll 1937
Coreius Jordan & Starks 1905
Coreoleuciscus Mori 1935
Coripareius Garman 1912
Cosmochilus Sauvage 1878
Couesius Jordan 1878
Crossocheilichthys Bleeker 1860
Crossocheilus Kuhl & van Hasselt in van Hasselt 1823
Ctenopharyngodon Steindachner 1866
Culter Basilewski 1855
Culticula Abbott 1901
Cultrichthys Smith 1938
Cultriculus Oshima 1919
Cultrops Smith 1938
Cyclocheilichthys Bleeker 1859
Cyprinella Girard 1856
Cyprinion Heckel 1843
Cyprinopsis Fitzinger 1832
Cyprinopsis Blanchard 1866
Cyprinus Linnaeus 1758
Cyrene Heckel 1843
Czekanowskiella Dybowski 1916
Dangila Valenciennes in Cuvier & Valenciennes 1842
Danio Hamilton 1822
Danioides Chu 1935
Danionella Roberts 1986
Daniops Smith 1945
Devario Heckel 1843
Dillonia Heckel 1847
Dionda Girard 1856
Diplocheilichthys Bleeker 1859
Diplocheilos Bleeker 1860
Diplocheilus van Hasselt 1823
Diptychus Steindachner 1866
Discherodontus Rainboth 1989
Discognathichthys Bleeker 1859
Discognathus Heckel 1843
Discogobio Lin 1931
Discolabeo Fowler 1937
Distoechodon Peters 1880
Dobula Rafinesque 1820
Eilichthys Pellegrin 1929
Eirmotus Schultz 1959
Elopichthys Bleeker 1859
Endemichthys Hopkirk 1974
Englottogaster Gistel 1848
Engraulicypris Günther 1894
Enteromius Cope 1869
Epalzeorhynchos Bleeker 1855
Episema Cope & Jordan in Jordan 1877
Eremichthys Hubbs & Miller 1948
Ericymba Cope 1865
Erimonax Jordan 1924
Erimystax Jordan 1882
Erinemus Jordan 1876
Eritrema Cope & Yarrow 1875
Erogala Jordan in Jordan & Brayton 1878
Erythroculter Berg 1909
Esomus Swainson 1839
Estevea Whitley 1953
Eulinneela Dybowski 1916
Eupallasella Dybowski 1916
Eustira Günther 1868
Evarra Woolman 1894
Exoglossops Fowler & Bean 1920
Exoglossops Hubbs in Osburn et al. 1930
Exoglossum Rafinesque 1818
Extrarius Jordan 1919
Falcula Jordan & Snyder 1899
Falcularius Jordan & Snyder 1903
Filirasbora Fowler 1937
Folifer Wu in Wu, Lin, Chen, Chen & He 1977
Fundulichthys Bleeker 1859
Fusania Jordan & Starks 1905
Fustis Lin 1932
Gardonus Bonaparte 1846
Garra Hamilton 1822
Genghis Howes 1984
Georgichthys Nichols 1918
Gibelion Heckel 1843
Gila Baird & Girard 1853
Glabrobarbus Fowler 1930
Glossodon Heckel 1843
Glossognathus Rafinesque 1818
Gnathendalia Castelnau 1861
Gnathopogon Bleeker 1859
Gobio Cuvier 1816
Gobiobarbus Dybowski 1869
Gobiobotia Kreyenberg 1911
Gobiocypris Ye & Fu 1983
Gobionichthys Bleeker 1859
Gobiosoma Dybowski 1872
Gonoproktopterus Bleeker 1860
Gonorhynchus McClelland 1839
Grandisquamachela Fowler 1934
Graodus Günther 1868
Gymnocypris Günther 1868
Gymnodiptychus Herzenstein 1892
Gymnognathus Sauvage 1884
Gymnostomus Heckel 1843
Habrolepis Fitzinger 1873
Hainania Koller 1927
Hampala Kuhl & van Hasselt in van Hasselt 1823
Hampala Bleeker 1860
Heegerius Bonaparte 1846
Hemibarboides Wang 1935
Hemibarbus Bleeker 1859
Hemiculter Bleeker 1859
Hemiculterella Warpachowski 1887
Hemigarra Karaman 1971
Hemigrammocapoeta Pellegrin 1927
Hemigrammocapoeta Estève 1952
Hemigrammocypris Fowler 1910
Hemigrammopuntius Pellegrin 1923
Hemiplus Rafinesque 1820
Hemitremia Cope 1870
Henicorhynchus Smith 1945
Herzensteinia Chu 1935
Hesperoleucus Snyder 1913
Heterolenciscus Sauvage 1874
Holotylognathus Fowler 1934
Horadandia Deraniyagala 1943
Horalabiosa Silas 1954
Hudsonius Girard 1856
Huigobio Fang 1938
Hybognathus Agassiz 1855
Hybopsis Agassiz 1854
Hyborhynchus Agassiz 1855
Hydrophlox Jordan in Jordan & Brayton 1878
Hypargyrus Forbes in Gilbert 1884
Hypophthalmichthys Bleeker 1859
Hypselobarbus Bleeker 1859
Hypsolepis Agassiz (ex Baird) 1854
Iberocypris Doadrio 1980
Idus Heckel 1843
Incisilabeo Fowler 1937
Inlecypris Howes 1980
Iotichthys Jordan & Evermann 1896
Iranocypris Bruun & Kaiser 1944
Ischikauia Jordan & Snyder 1900
Isocephalus Heckel 1843
Kalimantania Banarescu 1980
Kantaka Hora 1942
Kendallia Evermann & Shaw 1927
Klamathella Miller 1945
Kosswigobarbus Karaman 1971
Labeo Cuvier 1816
Labeobarbus Rüppell 1836
Labiobarbus van Hasselt 1823
Ladigesocypris Karaman 1972
Ladislavia Dybowski 1869
Lagowskiella Dybowski 1916
Laichowcypris Yen 1978
Lanceabarbus Fowler 1936
Laubuca Bleeker 1859
Lavinia Girard 1854
Lepidomeda Cope 1874
Lepidopygopsis Raj 1941
Leptobarbus Bleeker 1859
Leptocephalus Basilewski (ex Pallas) 1855
Leptocypris Boulenger 1900
Leucabramis Smitt 1895
Leucalburnus Berg 1916
Leucaspius Heckel & Kner 1858
Leucidius Snyder 1917
Leucisculus Oshima 1920
Leuciscus Klein 1775

Leuciscus Cuvier (ex Klein) 1816
Leucogobio Günther 1896
Leucos Heckel 1843
Leucosomus Heckel 1843
Liparus Schulze 1890
Lissochilichthys Oshima 1920
Lissochilus Weber & de Beaufort 1916
Lissorhynchus Bleeker 1859
Lobocheilos Bleeker 1853
Lobocheilus Kuhl & van Hasselt in van Hasselt 1823
Longiculter Fowler 1937
Longurio Jordan & Starks 1905
Luciobarbus Heckel 1843
Luciobrama Bleeker 1870
Luciocyprinus Vaillant 1904
Luciosoma Bleeker 1855
Luxilinus Jordan 1885
Luxilus Rafinesque 1820
Lythrurus Jordan 1876
Machaerochilus Fitzinger 1873
Macrhybopsis Cockerell & Allison 1909
Macrochirichthys Bleeker 1859
Malayochela Banarescu 1968
Mandibularca Herre 1924
Mannichthys Schultz 1942
Margariscus Cockerell 1909
Masticbarbus Tang 1942
Matsya Day 1889
Maxillingua Rafinesque 1818
Mayoa Day 1870
Mearnsella Seale & Bean 1907
Meda Girard 1856
Megagobio Kessler 1876
Megalobrama Dybowski 1872
Megarasbora Günther 1868
Mekongina Fowler 1937
Mesobola Howes 1984
Mesocyprinus Cheng 1950
Mesocyprinus Fang 1936
Mesogobio Banarescu & Nalbant 1973
Mesopotamichthys Karaman 1971
Metallites Schulze 1890
Metzia Jordan & Thompson 1914
Micraspius Dybowski 1869
Microbarbus Géry 1957
Microlepis Bonaparte 1846
Microphysogobio Mori 1934
Microrasbora Annandale 1918
Miniellus Jordan 1888
Minnilus Rafinesque 1820
Mirogrex Goren, Fishelson & Trewavas 1973
Moapa Hubbs & Miller 1948
Mola Heckel 1843
Mola Blyth 1860
Moniana Girard 1856
Morara Bleeker 1859
Moroco Jordan & Hubbs 1925
Morulius Hamilton 1822
Mrigala Bleeker 1859
Mylocheilus Agassiz 1855
Myloleuciscus Garman 1912
Myloleucops Cockerell 1913
Myloleucus Cope 1872
Myloleucus Günther 1873
Mylopharodon Ayres 1855
Mylopharyngodon Peters 1880
Mystacoleucus Günther 1868
Mystus Klein 1775
Nandina Gray 1831
Nasus Basilewski (ex Cuvier) 1855
Nazatexico Whitley 1931
Naziritor Mirza & Javed 1985
Nematabramis Boulenger 1894
Neobarynotus Banarescu 1980
Neobola Vinciguerra 1895
Neocarassius Castelnau 1872
Neochela Silas 1958
Neolissochilus Rainboth 1985
Neorohita Fowler 1937
Neotylognathus Kosswig 1950
Nicholsiculter Rendahl 1928
Nicholsicypris Chu 1935
Nicholsopuntius Pellegrin 1933
Nocomis Girard 1856
Notemigonus Rafinesque 1819
Nototropis Jordan 1877
Notropis Rafinesque 1818
Nukta Hora 1942
Nuria Valenciennes in Cuvier & Valenciennes 1842
Ochetobius Günther 1868
Onychodon Dybowski 1872
Onychostoma Günther 1896
Opistocheilos Bleeker 1859
Opsaridium Peters 1854
Opsariichthys Bleeker 1863
Opsarius McClelland 1839
Opsopoea Jordan & Evermann 1896
Opsopoeodus Hay 1881
Orcella Jordan & Evermann 1896
Orcula Jordan & Evermann 1900
Oregonichthys Hubbs in Schultz 1929
Oreichthys Smith 1933
Oreinus McClelland 1839
Oreodaimon Greenwood & Jubb 1967
Oreoleuciscus Warpachowski 1897
Orfus Fitzinger 1873
Ortheoleucos Derjavin 1937
Orthodon Girard 1856
Ospatulus Herre 1924
Osteobrama Heckel 1843
Osteochilichthys Hora 1942
Osteochilus Günther 1868
Otakia Jordan & Snyder 1900
Owsianka Dybowski 1862
Oxybarbus Vaillant 1893
Oxygaster van Hasselt 1823
Oxygeneum Forbes 1885
Oxygymnocypris Tsao 1964
Pachychilon Steindachner 1882
Pachystomus Heckel 1843
Papillocheilus Smith 1945
Parabarbus Franz 1910
Parabarilius Pellegrin & Fang 1940
Parabramis Bleeker 1865
Paracanthobrama Bleeker 1865
Paracheilognathus Bleeker 1863
Parachela Steindachner 1881
Paracrossochilus Popta 1904
Paradanio Day 1865
Paradanniops Yen 1978
Paralaubuca Bleeker 1865
Paraleucogobio Berg 1907
Paranotropis Fowler 1904
Parapelecus Günther 1889
Paraphoxinus Bleeker 1863
Paraprocypris Fang 1936
Parapsilorhynchus Hora 1921
Parapuntius Karaman 1971
Pararasbora Regan 1908
Pararhodeus Berg 1907
Pararutilus Berg 1912
Paraschizothorax Bleeker 1863
Paraschizothorax Tsao 1964
Parasinilabeo Wu 1939
Paraspinibarbus Chu & Kottelat 1989
Parator Wu, Yang, Yue & Huang 1963
Paratylognathus Sauvage 1880
Parazacco Chen 1982
Parchrosomus Gasowska 1979
Parexoglossum Hubbs 1931
Parluciosoma Howes 1980
Parosteobrama Tchang 1930
Pectenocypris Kottelat 1982
Pelecus Agassiz 1835
Pelotrophus Günther 1864
Percocypris Chu 1935
Perilampus McClelland 1839
Pfrille Jordan 1924
Phenacobius Cope 1867
Photogenis Cope 1868
Phoxinellus Heckel 1843
Phoxinus Rafinesque 1820
Phoxinus Agassiz 1835
Phoxiscus Oshima 1919
Phreatichthys Vinciguerra 1924
Pigus Bonaparte 1846
Pimephales Rafinesque 1820
Placocheilus Wu in Wu, Lin, Chen, Chen & He 1977
Plagiognathops Berg 1907
Plagiognathus Dybowski 1872
Plagopterus Cope 1874
Plargyrus Rafinesque 1820
Platycara McClelland 1839
Platygobio Gill 1863
Platypharodon Herzenstein 1891
Platysmacheilus Lu, Luo & Chen 1977
Pogonichthys Girard 1854
Pogonocharax Regan 1907
Poropuntius Smith 1931
Pristiodon Dybowski 1877
Probarbus Sauvage 1880
Procypris Lin 1933
Progobiobotia Chen & Tsao 1977
Prolabeo Norman 1932
Prolabeops Schultz 1941
Protoporus Cope 1872
Pseudaspius Dybowski 1869
Pseudobarbus Smith 1841
Pseudobrama Bleeker 1870
Pseudoculter Bleeker 1859
Pseudogobio Bleeker 1859
Pseudogobiops Berg 1914
Pseudogyrinocheilus Fang 1933
Pseudohemiculter Nichols & Pope 1927
Pseudolaubuca Bleeker 1865
Pseudoperilampus Bleeker 1863
Pseudophoxinus Bleeker 1859
Pseudopungtungia Mori 1935
Pseudorasbora Bleeker 1859

Pseudotor Karaman 1971
Pseudoxygaster Banarescu 1967
Pterocapoeta Günther 1902
Pteronotropis Fowler 1935
Pteropsarion Günther 1868
Ptychidio Myers 1930
Ptychobarbus Steindachner 1866
Ptychocheilus Agassiz 1855
Pungtungia Herzenstein 1892
Puntioplites Smith 1929
Puntius Hamilton 1822
Racoma McClelland and Griffith in McClelland 1842
Raddabarbus Thys van den Audenaerde 1971
Raiamas Jordan 1919
Rambaibarnia Fowler 1934
Rasbora Bleeker 1859
Rasborella Fowler & Bean 1923
Rasborichthys Bleeker 1859
Rasborinus Oshima 1920
Rasboroides Brittan 1954
Rastrineobola Fowler 1936
Rectoris Lin 1935
Relictus Hubbs & Miller 1972
Rheogobio Banarescu 1961
Rhinichthys Agassiz 1849
Rhinogobio Bleeker 1870
Rhinogobioides Rendahl 1928
Rhodeops Fowler 1910
Rhodeus Agassiz 1832
Rhodopleuriscus Fowler 1944
Rhynchocypris Günther 1889
Richardsonius Girard 1856
Rohanus Chu 1935
Rohita Valenciennes in Cuvier & Valenciennes 1842
Rohitichthys Bleeker 1859
Rohitodes Bleeker 1860
Rohtee Sykes 1839
Rohteichthys Bleeker 1859
Romanogobio Banarescu 1961
Rostrogobio Taranetz 1937
Rubellus Fitzinger 1873
Rugogymnocypris Yeuh & Hwang 1964
Rutilus Rafinesque 1820
Sagittabarilius Fowler 1936
Salmophasia Swainson 1839
Salmostoma Swainson 1839
Sanagia Holly 1926
Sapa Kazanskii 1928
Sarcidium Cope 1871
Sarcocheilichthys Bleeker 1859
Saurogobio Bleeker 1870
Sawbwa Annandale 1918
Scaphesthes Oshima 1919
Scaphiodon Heckel 1843
Scaphiodonichthys Vinciguerra 1890
Scaphiodontella Oshima 1920
Scaphiodontopsis Fowler 1934
Scaphognathops Smith 1945
Scaphognathus Smith 1931
Scardiniopsis Jaeckel 1864
Scardinius Bonaparte 1837
Schacra Günther 1868
Schismatorhynchos Bleeker 1855
Schizocypris Regan 1914
Schizopyge Heckel 1847
Schizopygopsis Steindachner 1866
Schizothoraichthys Misra 1962
Schizothorax Heckel 1838
Scomberopsis see *Scombrocypius*
Scombrocypris Günther 1889
Securicula Günther 1868
Semiculter Chu 1935
Semilabeo Peters 1880
Semiplotus Bleeker 1859
Semotilus Rafinesque 1820
Shacra Bleeker 1860
Siaja Bleeker 1859
Siboma Girard 1856
Sikukia Smith 1931
Sinibarbus Sauvage 1874
Sinibrama Wu 1939
Sinigobio Chu 1935
Siniichthys Banarescu 1970
Sinilabeo Rendahl 1932
Sinocrossocheilus Wu in Wu, Lin, Chen, Chen & He 1977
Sinocyclocheilus Fang 1936
Siphateles Cope 1883
Smiliogaster Bleeker 1859
Snyderichthys Miller 1945
Spinibarbichthys Oshima 1926
Spinibarbus Oshima 1919
Spinicephalus Lesueur in Vaillant 1896
Spinophoxinellus Karaman 1972
Spirlinus Fatio 1882
Spratellicypris Herre & Myers 1931
Squalalburnus Berg 1932
Squalidus Dybowski 1872
Squaliobarbus Günther 1868
Squalioscardinus Kolombatovic 1907
Squalius Bonaparte 1837
Stilbe DeKay 1842
Stilbius Gill 1865
Stypodon Garman 1881
Symmetrurus Jordan 1878
Systomus McClelland 1839
Tambra Bleeker 1860
Tanakia Jordan & Thompson 1914
Tanichthys Lin 1932
Telestes Bonaparte 1837
Temeculina Cockerell 1909
Tetrostichodon Tchang, Yueh & Hwang 1964
Thryssocypris Roberts & Kottelat 1984
Thynnichthyina Fowler 1937
Thynnichthys Bleeker 1859
Tiaroga Girard 1856
Tigoma Girard 1856
Tinca Cuvier 1816
Tirodon Hay 1882
Tor Gray 1834
Toxabramis Günther 1873
Trachybrama Bleeker 1863
Tribolodon Sauvage 1883
Trinematichthys Bleeker 1860
Tropidophoxinellus Stephanidis 1974
Trycherodon Forbes in Jordan & Gilbert 1883
Tylognathoides Tortonese 1937
Tylognathus Heckel 1843
Typhlobarbus Chu & Chen 1982
Typhlogarra Trewavas 1955
Vanderbiltella Fowler 1936
Varicogobio Lin 1931
Varicorhinus Rüppell 1836
Vimba Fitzinger 1873
Xenobarbus Norman 1923
Xenocheilichthys Smith 1934
Xenocyprioides Chen 1982
Xenocypris Günther 1868
Xenophysogobio Chen & Tsao 1977
Xystrosus Jordan & Snyder 1899
Yaoshanicus Lin 1931
Yuriria Jordan & Evermann 1896
Zacco Jordan & Evermann 1902
Zezera Jordan & Fowler 1903
Zopa Fitzinger 1873
Zophendum Jordan 1878

FAM. PSILORHYNCHIDAE

Psilorhynchus McClelland 1839

FAM. COBITIDAE (Loaches)

Subfam. Botiinae

Botia Gray 1831
Diacantha Swainson 1839
Hymenphysa McClelland 1839
Leptobotia Bleeker 1870
Parabotia Guichenot in Dabry de Thiersant 1872
Sinibotia Fang 1936
Syncrossus Blyth 1860

Subfam. Cobitinae

Acanestrinia Bacescu 1962
Acanthophthalmus see *Acantophthalmus*
Acanthopsis Agassiz 1832
Acanthopsoides Fowler 1934
Acantophthalmus van Hasselt 1823
Acantopsis van Hasselt 1823
Apua Blyth 1860
Bicanestrinia Bacescu 1962
Canthophrys Swainson 1838
Cobitichthys Bleeker 1859
Cobitinula Hanko 1924
Cobitis Linnaeus 1758
Cobitophis Myers 1927
Enobarbichthys Whitley 1931
Enobarbus Whitley 1928
Eucirrhichthys Perugia 1892
Iberocobitis Bacescu 1962
Jerdonia Day 1871
Lepidocephalichthys Bleeker 1863
Lepidocephalus Bleeker 1859
Madrasia Nalbant 1963
Mesomisgurnus Fang 1935
Misgurnus Lacepède 1803
Neacanthopsis Smith 1945
Neoeucirrhichthys Banarescu & Nalbant 1968
Niwaella Nalbant 1963
Pangio Blyth 1860
Paralepidocephalus Tchang 1935
Paramisgurnus Sauvage 1878
Platacanthus Day 1865
Prostheacanthus Blyth 1860
Pterozygus De la Pylaie 1835
Sabanejewia Vladykov 1929
Somileptes Swainson 1839
Ussuria Nikolskii 1903

FAM. BALITORIDAE (Hillstream Loaches)
= Homalopteridae

Subfam. Nemacheilinae
Aborichthys Chaudhuri 1913
Acanthocobitis Peters 1861
Acoura Swainson 1839
Acourus see *Acoura*
Adiposia Annandale & Hora 1920
Barbatula Linck 1790
Barbucca Roberts 1989
Deuterophysa Rendahl 1933
Didymophysa Whitley 1950
Diplophysa Kessler 1874
Diplophysoides Fowler 1958
Ellopostoma Vaillant 1902
Elxis Jordan & Fowler 1903
Eonemachilus Berg 1938
Hedinichthys Rendahl 1933
Heminoemacheilus Zhu & Cao 1987
Homatula Nichols 1925
Indoreonectes Rita & Banarescu in Rita, Banarescu & Nalbant 1978
Infundibulatus Menon 1987
Lefua Herzenstein 1888
Mesonoemacheilus Banarescu & Nalbant in Singh et al. 1982
Micronemacheilus Rendahl 1944
Modigliania Perugia 1893
Nemacheilus Bleeker 1863
Nemachilichthys Day 1878
Neonoemacheilus Zhu & Guo 1985
Noemacheilus Kuhl & van Hasselt in van Hasselt 1823
Nun Banarescu & Nalbant 1982
Octonema Martens 1868
Octonema Herzenstein in Herzenstein & Warpachowski 1887
Oreias Sauvage 1874
Oreonectes Günther 1868
Orthrias Jordan & Fowler 1903
Oxynoemacheilus Banarescu & Nalbant 1966
Paracobitis Bleeker 1863
Paranemachilus Zhu 1983
Petruichthys Menon 1987
Physoschistura Banarescu & Nalbant in Singh et al. 1982
Pogononemacheilus Fowler 1937
Pseudodon Kessler 1874
Qinghaichthys Zhu 1981
Schistura McClelland 1839
Sectoria Kottelat 1990
Sphaerophysa Cao & Zhu 1988
Tauphysa Rendahl 1933
Triplophysa Rendahl 1933
Troglocobitis Parin 1983
Tuberoschistura Kottelat 1989
Turcinoemacheilus Banarescu & Nalbant 1964
Vaillantella Fowler 1905
Yunnanilus Nichols 1925

Subfam. Balitorinae
= Homalopterinae; Gastromyzontinae included
Annamia Hora 1932
Balitora Gray 1830
Balitoropsis Smith 1945
Beaufortia Hora 1932
Bhavania Hora 1920
Chopraia Prashad & Mukerji 1929
Crossostoma Sauvage 1878
Formosania Oshima 1919
Gastromyzon Günther 1874
Glaniopsis Boulenger 1899
Helgia Vinciguerra 1890
Hemimyzon Regan 1911
Homaloptera van Hasselt 1823
Homalopteroides Fowler 1905
Homalopterula Fowler 1940
Homalosoma Boulenger 1901
Hypergastromyzon Roberts 1989
Jinshaia Kottelat & Chu 1988
Lepidoglanis Vaillant 1889
Lepturichthys Regan 1911
Liniparhomaloptera Fang 1935
Metahomaloptera Chang 1944
Neogastromyzon Popta 1905
Neohomaloptera Herre 1944
Paraprotomyzon Pellegrin & Fang 1935
Parhomaloptera Vaillant 1902
Plesiomyzon Zheng & Chen 1980
Praeformosania Fang 1935
Progastromyzon Hora & Jayaram 1952
Protomyzon Hora 1932
Pseudogastromyzon Nichols 1925
Pseudohomaloptera Silas 1953
Sewellia Hora 1932
Sinogastromyzon Fang 1930
Sinohomaloptera Fang 1930
Travancoria Hora 1941
Vanmanenia Hora 1932

FAM. GYRINOCHEILIDAE (Algae Eaters)
Gyrinocheilops Fowler 1937
Gyrinocheilus Vaillant 1902

FAM. CATOSTOMIDAE (Suckers)
Acomus Girard 1856
Amblodon Rafinesque 1819
Bubalichthys Agassiz 1855
Carpiodes Rafinesque 1820
Catostomus Lesueur 1817
Chasmistes Jordan 1878
Cycleptus Rafinesque 1819
Decactylus Rafinesque 1820
Deltistes Seale 1896
Erimyzon Jordan 1876
Eurystomus Rafinesque 1820
Hylomyzon Agassiz 1855
Hypentelium Rafinesque 1818
Ictiobus Rafinesque 1820
Ictiorus see *Ictiobus*
Lagochila Jordan & Brayton 1877
Lipomyzon Cope 1881
Megastomatobus Fowler 1913
Minomus Girard 1856
Minytrema Jordan 1878
Moxostoma Rafinesque 1820
Myxocyprinus Gill 1878
Notolepidomyzon Fowler 1913
Pantosteus Cope in Cope & Yarrow 1876
Pithecomyzon Fowler 1913
Placopharynx Cope 1870
Ptychostomus Agassiz 1855
Quassilabia Jordan & Brayton in Jordan 1878
Rhytidostomus Heckel 1843
Scartomyzon Fowler 1913
Sclerognathus Valenciennes in Cuvier & Valenciennes 1844
Stomocatus Bonaparte 1839
Teretulus Rafinesque 1820
Thoburnia Jordan & Snyder in Jordan 1917
Xyrauchen Eigenmann & Kirsch in Kirsch 1889

ORDER CHARACIFORMES
Characini Linnaeus 1758
Rhodeoides Thominot 1884

FAM. CITHARINIDAE
Distichodontidae included

Subfam. Distichodontinae
Belonophago Giltay 1929
Champsoborus Boulenger 1909
Congocharax Matthes 1964
Distichodina Fowler 1935
Distichodomicrura Fowler 1936
Distichodura Fowler 1936
Distichodus Müller & Troschel 1844
Dundocharax Poll 1967
Eugnathichthys Boulenger 1898
Gavialocharax Pellegrin 1927
Hemigrammocharax Pellegrin 1923
Hemigrammonannocharax Holly 1930
Hemistichodus Pellegrin 1900
Ichthyborus Günther 1864
Lepinannocharax Fowler 1936
Mesoborus Pellegrin 1900
Micraethiops Daget 1965
Microdistichodus Pellegrin 1926
Microstomatichthyoborus Nichols & Griscom 1917
Monostichodus Vaillant in Pellegrin 1900
Nannaethiops Günther 1872
Nannocharax Günther 1867
Neoborus Boulenger 1899
Neolebias Steindachner 1894
Onouphrios Whitley 1951
Paradistichodus Pellegrin 1922
Paraphago Boulenger 1899
Phago Günther 1865
Phagoborus Myers 1924
Psalidostoma Kner 1864
Ra Whitley 1931
Rhabdaethiops Fowler 1936
Thrissocharax Myers 1926
Tristichodus Boulenger 1920
Xenocharax Günther 1867

Subfam. Citharininae
Citharidium Boulenger 1902
Citharinoides Daget 1962
Citharinops Daget 1962
Citharinus Cuvier 1816

FAM. ALESTIIDAE (African Tetras)
Includes all African "Characidae"
Alestes Müller & Troschel 1844
Alestiops Hoedeman 1951
Alestobrycon Hoedeman 1951

Alestogrammus Hoedeman 1956
Alestopetersiini Hoedeman 1951
Alestopetersius Hoedeman 1951
Arnoldichthys Myers 1926
Bathyaethiops Fowler 1949
Brachyalestes Günther 1864
Brachypetersius Hoedeman 1956
Brycinus Valenciennes in Cuvier & Valenciennes 1849
Bryconaethiops Günther 1873
Bryconalestes Hoedeman 1951
Clupeocharax Pellegrin 1926
Clupeopetersius Pellegrin 1928
Duboisialestes Poll 1967
Hemigrammalestes Pellegrin 1926
Hemigrammopetersius Pellegrin 1926
Hydrocionichthys Travassos 1952
Hydrocynus Cuvier 1816
Hydrocyon Cuvier 1819
Ladigesia Géry 1968
Lepidarchus Roberts 1966
Micralestes Boulenger 1899
Microlepidalestes Hoedeman 1951
Myletes Cuvier 1815
Nannopetersius Hoedeman 1956
Petersialestes Hoedeman 1951
Petersius Hilgendorf 1894
Phenacogrammus Eigenmann in Eigenmann & Ogle 1907
Rhabdalestes Hoedeman 1951
Rhabdopetersius Hoedeman 1951
Tricuspidalestes Poll 1967
Virilia Roberts 1967

FAM. HEPSETIDAE

Hepsetus Swainson 1838
Hydrocyonoides Castelnau 1861
Sarcodaces Günther 1864

FAM. HEMIODONTIDAE

Subfam. Parodontinae
Apareiodon Eigenmann 1916
Nematoparodon Fowler 1943
Parodon Valenciennes in Cuvier & Valenciennes 1849
Parodontops Schultz & Miles 1943
Saccodon Kner 1863

Subfam. Hemiodontinae
Anisitsia Eigenmann & Kennedy in Eigenmann 1903
Anodus Agassiz in Spix & Agassiz 1829
Anodus Cuvier 1829
Argonectes Böhlke & Myers 1956
Atomaster Eigenmann & Myers 1927
Bivibranchia Eigenmann 1912
Eigenmannina Fowler 1906
Elopomorphus Gill 1878
Hemiodopsis Fowler 1906
Hemiodus Müller 1842
Micromischodus Roberts 1971
Pterohemiodus Fowler 1940

FAM. CURIMATIDAE

Subfam. Curimatinae (Curimatas)
Acuticurimata Fowler 1941
Allenina Fernández-Yépez 1948
Apolinarella Fernández-Yépez 1948
Bitricarinata Fernández-Yépez 1948
Bondia Fernández-Yépez 1948
Bondichthys Whitley 1953
Camposella Fernández-Yépez 1948
Camposichthys Whitley 1953
Cruxentina Fernández-Yépez 1948
Curimata Walbaum 1792
Curimata Bosc 1817
Curimatella Eigenmann & Eigenmann 1889
Curimatichthys Fernández-Yépez 1948
Curimatoides Fowler 1940
Curimatopsis Steindachner 1876
Curimatorbis Fernández-Yépez 1948
Curimatus Oken (ex Cuvier) 1817
Cyphocharax Fowler 1906
Gasterotomus Eigenmann 1910
Hamatichthys Fernández-Yépez 1948
Hemicurimata Myers 1929
Lambepiedra Fernández-Yépez 1948
Lepipinna Fernández-Yépez 1948
Peltapleura Fowler 1906
Potamorhina Cope 1878
Psectrogaster Eigenmann & Eigenmann 1889
Pseudocurimata Fernández-Yépez 1948
Pseudopsectrogaster Fernández-Yépez 1948
Rivasella Fernández-Yépez 1948
Semelcarinata Fernández-Yépez 1948
Semitapicis Eigenmann & Eigenmann 1889
Steindachnerina Fowler 1906
Suprasinelepichthys Fernández-Yépez 1948
Walbaunina Fernández-Yépez 1948
Xyrocharax Fowler 1914

Subfam. Prochilodontinae
Chilomyzon Fowler 1906
Ichthyoelephas Posada 1909
Pacu Agassiz in Spix & Agassiz 1829
Pacu Valenciennes 1847
Pacu Cuvier 1829
Prochilodus Agassiz in Spix & Agassiz 1829
Semaprochilodus Fowler 1941

Subfam. Anostominae
Abramites Fowler 1906
Anostomoides Pellegrin 1909
Anostomos Gronow 1763
Anostomus Scopoli (ex Gronow) 1777
Anostomus Cuvier (ex Gronow) 1816
Garmanina Fowler 1906
Gnathodolus Myers 1927
Histiodromus Gistel 1848
Hypomasticus Borodin 1929
Laemolyta Cope 1872
Lahilliella Eigenmann & Kennedy in Eigenmann 1903
Leporellus Lütken 1875
Leporinodus Eigenmann 1922
Leporinops Géry 1960
Leporinus Agassiz in Spix & Agassiz 1829
Mormyrynchus Swainson 1839
Myocharax Fowler 1914
Pithecocharax Fowler 1906
Pseudanos Winterbottom 1980
Rhytiodus Kner 1858
Sartor Myers & Carvalho 1959
Schizodon Agassiz in Spix & Agassiz 1829
Schizodontopsis Garman 1890
Synaptolaemus Myers & Fernández-Yépes in Myers 1950

Subfam. Chilodontinae
Caenotropus Günther 1864
Chilodus Müller & Troschel 1844
Microdus Kner 1858
Tylobronchus Eigenmann 1912

FAM. ERYTHRINIDAE (Trahiras)

Erythrichthys Bonaparte 1831
Erythrinus Gronow 1763
Erythrinus Scopoli (ex Gronow) 1777
Hetererythrinus Günther 1864
Hoplerythrinus Gill 1896
Hoplias Gill 1903
Macrodon Müller 1843
Ophiocephalops Fowler 1906

FAM. LEBIASINIDAE

Subfam. Lebiasininae
Lebiasina Valenciennes in Cuvier & Valenciennes 1846
Piabucina Valenciennes in Cuvier & Valenciennes 1849

Subfam. Pyrrhulininae
Archicheir Eigenmann 1909
Copeina Fowler 1906
Copella Myers 1956
Holotaxis Cope 1870
Nannobrycon Hoedeman 1950
Nannostomus Günther 1872
Poecilobrycon Eigenmann 1909
Pyrrhulina Valenciennes in Cuvier & Valenciennes 1846

FAM. GASTEROPELECIDAE (Freshwater Hatchetfishes)

Carnegiella Eigenmann 1909
Gasteropelecus Scopoli (ex Gronow) 1777
Gastropelecys Agassiz 1846
Pterodiscus Eigenmann 1909
Thoracocharax Fowler 1907

FAM. CTENOLUCIIDAE (Pike-Characids) = Xiphostomidae

Belonocharax Fowler 1907
Boulengerella Eigenmann 1903
Ctenolucius Gill 1861
Luciocharax Steindachner 1878
Spixostoma Whitley 1951
Xiphostoma Spix in Spix & Agassiz 1829

FAM. CYNODONTIDAE

Cynodon Agassiz in Spix & Agassiz 1829
Hydrolycus Müller & Troschel 1844
Rhaphiodon Agassiz in Spix & Agassiz 1829
Rhaphiodontichthys Amaral Campos 1945

FAM. CHARACIDAE (Characins)
New World Characins
Some subfamilies are below

Acanthocharax Eigenmann 1912
Acestrocephalus Eigenmann 1910
Acestrorhamphus Eigenmann & Kennedy 1903

Acestrorhynchus Eigenmann & Kennedy 1903
Aequidens Steindachner 1915
Agoniates Müller & Troschel 1845
Amblystilbe Fowler 1940
Anacyrtus Günther 1864
Anoptichthys Hubbs & Innes 1936
Aphyocharacidium Géry 1960
Aphyocharax Günther 1868
Aphyocheirodon Eigenmann 1915
Aphyodite Eigenmann 1912
Apodastyanax Fowler 1911
Asiphonichthys Cope 1894
Astyanacinus Eigenmann 1907
Astyanax Baird & Girard 1854
Atopomesus Myers 1927
Aulixidens Böhlke 1952
Autanichthys Fernández-Yépez 1950
Axelrodia Géry 1965
Bario Myers 1940
Bergia Steindachner 1891
Bertoniolus Fowler 1918
Bleptonema Eigenmann 1914
Boehlkea Géry 1966
Bramocharax Gill 1877
Brittanichthys Géry 1965
Brycochandus Eigenmann 1908
Brycon Müller & Troschel 1844
Bryconacidnus Myers in Eigenmann & Myers 1929
Bryconamericus Eigenmann in Eigenmann, McAtee & Ward 1907
Bryconella Géry 1965
Bryconexodon Géry 1980
Bryconodon Eigenmann 1903
Bryconops Kner 1858
Camposichthys Travassos 1946
Carlana Strand 1928
Carlastyanax Géry 1972
Carlia Meek 1914
Catabasis Eigenmann & Norris 1900
Ceratobranchia Eigenmann in Eigenmann, Henn & Wilson 1914
Chalceus Cuvier 1817
Chalcinopelecus Holmberg 1891
Chalcinopsis Kner 1863
Chalcinus Valenciennes in Cuvier & Valenciennes 1849
Characinus Lacepède 1803
Characinus Cuvier 1816
Charax Gronow 1763
Charax Scopoli (ex Gronow) 1777
Charaxodon Fernández-Yépez 1947
Cheirodon Girard 1855
Cheirodontops Schultz 1944
Chilobrycon Géry & de Rham 1981
Chorimycterus Cope 1894
Clupeacharax Pearson 1924
Compsura Eigenmann 1915
Coptobrycon Géry 1966
Coscinoxyron Fowler 1907
Creagrudite Myers 1927
Creagrutops Schultz 1944
Creagrutus Günther 1864
Creatochanes Günther 1864
Crenuchus Günther 1863
Ctenobrycon Eigenmann 1908
Ctenocharax Regan 1907
Cynocharax Fowler 1907
Cynopotamus Valenciennes in Cuvier & Valenciennes 1849
Cyrtocharax Fowler 1907
Dermatocheir Durbin 1909
Deuterodon Eigenmann in Eigenmann, McAtee & Ward 1907
Distoechus Gomes 1947
Ectrepopterus Fowler 1943
Engraulisoma Castro 1981
Entomolepis Eigenmann 1917
Epicyrtus Müller & Troschel 1844
Eretmobrycon Fink 1976
Eucynopotamus Fowler 1904
Evenichthys Whitley 1935
Evermannella Eigenmann 1903
Evermannolus Eigenmann in Eigenmann & Ogle 1907
Exodon Müller & Troschel 1844
Galeocharax Fowler 1910
Genycharax Eigenmann 1912
Gilbertella Eigenmann 1903
Gilbertolus Eigenmann in Eigenmann & Ogle 1907
Gnathocharax Fowler 1913
Gnathoplax Myers 1960
Grammabrycon Fowler 1941
Grundulus Valenciennes in Cuvier & Valenciennes 1846
Gymnocharacinus Steindachner 1903
Gymnocorymbus Eigenmann 1908
Gymnotichthys Fernández-Yépez 1950
Hasemania Ellis 1911
Hemibrycon Günther 1864
Hemigrammus Gill 1858
Henochilus Garman 1890
Heterocharax Eigenmann 1912
Hollandichthys Eigenmann 1910
Holobrycon Eigenmann 1909
Holoprion Eigenmann 1903
Holopristis Eigenmann 1903
Holoshesthes Eigenmann 1903
Hoplocharax Géry 1966
Hybocharax Géry & Vu-Tân-Tuê 1963
Hydropardus Reinhardt 1849
Hyphessobrycon Durbin in Eigenmann 1908
Hystricodon Günther 1864
Iguanobrycon Géry 1970
Iguanodectes Cope 1872
Inpaichthys Géry & Junk 1977
Joinvillea Steindachner 1908
Knodus Eigenmann 1911
Lamprocheirodon Géry 1960
Leptagoniates Boulenger 1887
Leptobrycon Eigenmann 1915
Lobodeuterodon Fowler 1945
Lonchogenys Myers 1927
Luetkenia Steindachner 1876
Lycodon Kner 1860
Macropsobrycon Eigenmann 1915
Markiana Eigenmann 1903
Megalamphodus Eigenmann 1915
Megalobrycon Günther 1870
Microgenys Eigenmann 1913
Microschemobrycon Eigenmann 1915
Mixobrycon Eigenmann 1915
Moenkhausia Eigenmann 1903
Monotocheirodon Eigenmann & Pearson in Pearson 1924
Moojenichthys Miranda-Ribeiro [P.] 1956
Moralesia Fowler 1943
Moralesicus Fowler 1958
Nematobrycon Eigenmann 1911
Nematocharax Weitzman, Menezes & Britski 1986
Nematopoma Gill 1858
Notropocharax Marini, Nichols & La Monte 1933
Odontostilbe Cope 1870
Odontostoechus Gomes 1947
Oligobrycon Eigenmann 1915
Oligosarcus Günther 1864
Opisthanodus Ahl 1935
Othonocheirodus Myers 1927
Othonophanes Eigenmann 1903
Oxybrycon Géry 1964
Paracheirodon Géry 1960
Paragoniates Steindachner 1876
Parapristella Géry 1964
Parastremma Eigenmann 1912
Parecbasis Eigenmann 1914
Paroligosarcus Amaral Campos & Trewavas 1949
Pedalibrycon Fowler 1943
Pellegrinina Fowler 1907
Petitella Géry & Boutière 1964
Phenacogaster Eigenmann 1907
Phenagoniates Eigenmann & Wilson in Eigenmann, Henn & Wilson 1914
Phoxinopsis Regan 1907
Piabarchus Myers 1928
Piabina Reinhardt 1866
Piabuca Müller & Troschel (ex Cuvier) 1844
Piabucidium Myers in Eigenmann & Myers 1929
Piabucus Oken (ex Cuvier) 1817
Plethodectes Cope 1870
Poecilocharax Eigenmann 1909
Poecilurichthys Gill 1858
Priocharax Weitzman & Vari 1987
Prionobrama Fowler 1913
Pristella Eigenmann 1908
Probolodus Eigenmann 1911
Prodontocharax Eigenmann & Pearson in Pearson 1924
Psalidodon Eigenmann 1911
Psellogrammus Eigenmann 1908
Pseuderythrinus Hoedeman 1950
Pseudochalceus Kner 1863
Pseudocheirodon Meek & Hildebrand 1916
Pseudopristella Géry 1960
Rachoviscus Myers 1926
Ramirezella Fernández-Yépez 1949
Rhinobrycon Myers 1944
Rhinopetitia Géry 1964
Rhoadsia Fowler 1911
Roeboexodon Géry 1959
Roeboides Günther 1864
Roestes Günther 1864
Saccoderma Schultz 1944
Salminus Agassiz in Spix & Agassiz 1829
Schultzites Géry 1964
Scissor Günther 1864
Serrabrycon Vari 1986
Sphyraenocharax Fowler 1907
Spintherobolus Eigenmann 1911
Stichonodon Eigenmann 1903
Stupens Whitley 1954

Stygichthys Brittan & Böhlke 1965
Tetragonopterus Cuvier 1816
Thayeria Eigenmann 1908
Thrissobrycon Böhlke 1953
Triportheus Cope 1872
Triurobrycon Eigenmann 1909
Tyttobrycon Géry 1973
Vesicatrus Eigenmann 1911
Xenagoniates Myers 1942
Xiphocharax Fowler 1914
Xiphorhamphus Müller & Troschel 1844
Xiphorhynchus Agassiz in Spix & Agassiz 1829
Zygogaster Eigenmann 1913

Subfam. Glandulocaudinae
Acrobrycon Eigenmann & Pearson in Pearson 1924
Argopleura Eigenmann 1913
Coelurichthys Miranda-Ribeiro 1908
Corynopoma Gill 1858
Corynopomops Fowler 1943
Diapoma Cope 1894
Gephyrocharax Eigenmann 1912
Glandulocauda Eigenmann 1911
Hysteronotus Eigenmann 1911
Iotabrycon Roberts 1973
Landonia Eigenmann & Henn in Eigenmann, Henn & Wilson 1914
Microbrycon Eigenmann & Wilson in Eigenmann, Henn & Wilson 1914
Microcaelurus Miranda-Ribeiro 1939
Mimagoniates Regan 1907
Phenacobrycon Eigenmann 1922
Planaltina Böhlke 1954
Pristicharax Fowler 1949
Pseudocorynopoma Perugia 1891
Pterobrycon Eigenmann 1913
Scopaeocharax Weitzman & Fink 1985
Stevardia Gill 1858
Tyttocharax Fowler 1913
Xenurobrycon Myers & Miranda-Ribeiro 1945
Xenurocharax Regan 1913

Subfam. Serrasalminae (Piranhas and allies)
Acnodon Eigenmann 1903
Catoprion Müller & Troschel 1844
Colossoma Eigenmann & Kennedy 1903
Gastropristis Eigenmann 1915
Melloina Amaral Campos 1946
Metynnis Cope 1878
Myleocollops Eigenmann 1903
Mylesinus Valenciennes in Cuvier & Valenciennes 1849
Myleus Müller & Troschel 1844
Myloplus Gill 1896
Mylossoma Eigenmann & Kennedy 1903
Orthomyleus Eigenmann 1903
Paramyloplus Norman 1929
Piaractus Eigenmann 1903
Pristobrycon Eigenmann 1915
Prosomyleus Géry 1972
Pygocentrus Müller & Troschel 1844
Pygopristis Müller & Troschel 1844
Reganina Fowler 1907
Rooseveltiella Eigenmann 1915
Sealeina Fowler 1907
Serrasalmo Duméril 1806
Serrasalmus Lacepède 1803
Starksina Fowler 1907
Taddyella Ihering 1928
Tometes Valenciennes in Cuvier & Valenciennes 1849
Utiaritichthys Miranda-Ribeiro 1937
Waiteina Fowler 1907

Subfam. Characidiinae
Ammocryptocharax Weitzman & Kanazawa 1976
Characidium Reinhardt 1866
Elachocharax Myers 1927
Geisleria Géry 1971
Jobertina Pellegrin 1909
Klausewitzia Géry 1965
Microcharax Eigenmann 1909
Nanognathus Boulenger 1895
Poecilosomatops Fowler 1906

Subfam. Stethaprioninae
Brachychalcinus Boulenger 1892
Buritia Brant 1974
Ephippicharax Fowler 1913
Fowlerina Eigenmann 1907
Orthospinus Reis 1989
Poptella Eigenmann 1908
Stethaprion Cope 1870

ORDER SILURIFORMES

Tachysurus Lacepède 1803
Trachymochlus Hoedeman 1961

FAM. DIPLOMYSTIDAE (Diplomystid Catfishes)
Diplomystax Günther (ex Duméril) 1864
Diplomyste Duméril 1856
Diplomystes Bleeker (ex Duméril) 1858
Olivaichthys Arratia 1987

FAM. ICTALURIDAE (North American Freshwater Catfishes or Bullhead Catfishes)
Ameiurus Rafinesque 1820
Amiurus see *Ameiurus*
Bagre Catesby 1771
Elliops Rafinesque 1820
Gronias Cope 1864
Hopladelus see *Opladelus*
Ictalurus Rafinesque 1820
Ilictis Rafinesque 1820
Istlarius Jordan & Snyder 1899
Leptops Rafinesque 1820
Noturus Rafinesque 1818
Opladelus Rafinesque 1820
Pilodictis see *Pylodictis*
Pimelodon Lesueur in Vaillant 1896
Prietella Carranza 1954
Pylodictis Rafinesque 1819
Rabida Jordan & Evermann 1896
Satan Hubbs & Bailey 1947
Schilbeodes Bleeker 1858
Synechoglanis Gill 1859
Trogloglanis Eigenmann 1919
Villarius Rutter 1896

FAM. BAGRIDAE (Bagrid Catfishes)
Amarginops Nichols & Griscom 1917
Aoria Jordan 1919
Aorichthys Wu 1939
Aspidobagrus Bleeker 1862
Auchenaspis Bleeker 1858
Auchenoglanis Günther 1865
Austroglanis Skelton, Risch & de Vos 1984
Bagrichthys Bleeker 1858
Bagroides Bleeker 1851
Bagrus Bosc 1816
Batasio Blyth 1860
Bathybagrus Bailey & Stewart 1984
Brachymystus Fowler 1937
Chandramara Jayaram 1972
Chrysichthys Bleeker 1858
Chrysobagrus Boulenger 1899
Clarotes Kner 1855
Coreobagrus Mori 1936
Dermocassis Nichols 1925
Duxordia Tickell in Day 1888
Fluvidraco Jordan & Fowler 1903
Gephyroglanis Boulenger 1899
Gnathobagrus Nichols & Griscom 1917
Gogrius Day 1867
Gonocephalus Kner 1855
Hemibagrus Bleeker 1862
Heterobagrus Bleeker 1864
Horabagrus Jayaram 1955
Hypselobagrus Bleeker 1862
Leiocassis Bleeker 1858
Liauchenoglanis Boulenger 1916
Lophiobagrus Poll 1942
Macrones Duméril 1856
Macronichthys White & Moy-Thomas 1940
Macronoides Hora 1921
Macropterobagrus Nichols 1925
Melanodactylus Bleeker 1858
Mystus Gronow 1763
Mystus Scopoli (ex Gronow) 1777
Nasocassis Nichols 1925
Notoglanidium Günther 1903
Octonematichthys Bleeker 1858
Osteobagrus Jayaram 1954
Oxyglanis Vinciguerra 1898
Parauchenoglanis Boulenger 1911
Pardiglanis Poll, Lanza & Romoli Sassi 1972
Pelteobagrus Bleeker 1865
Phyllonemus Boulenger 1906
Platyglanis Daget 1979
Porcus Geoffroy St. Hilaire 1808
Prajadhipokia Fowler 1934
Pseudobagrichthys Bleeker 1862
Pseudobagrus Bleeker 1859
Pseudomystus Jayaram 1968
Rama Bleeker 1858
Rheoglanis Poll 1966
Rhinobagrus Bleeker 1865
Rita Bleeker 1853
Sperata Holly 1939

FAM. CRANOGLANIDIDAE (Armorhead Catfishes)
Cranoglanis Peters 1880
Pseudeutropichthys Koller 1926

FAM. SILURIDAE (Sheatfishes)
Anopleutropius Vaillant 1893
Apodoglanis Fowler 1905
Belodontichthys Bleeker 1858
Callichrous Hamilton 1822
Ceratoglanis Myers 1938
Cryptopterella Fowler 1944

Diastatomycter Vaillant 1891
Glanis Agassiz 1857
Hemisilurus Bleeker 1858
Herklotsella Herre 1933
Hito Herre 1924
Hitoichthys Herre 1924
Kryptopterichthys Bleeker 1858
Kryptopterus Bleeker 1858
Micronema Bleeker 1858
Ompok Lacepède 1803
Parasilurus Bleeker 1862
Penesilurus Herre 1924
Phalacronotus Bleeker 1858
Pinniwallago Gupta, Jayaram & Hajela 1981
Pseudosilurus Bleeker 1858
Pterocryptis Peters 1861
Silurichthys Bleeker 1856
Silurodes Bleeker 1858
Silurodon Kner 1866
Silurus Linnaeus 1758
Wallago Bleeker 1851
Wallagonia Myers 1938

FAM. SCHILBEIDAE (Schilbeid Catfishes)

Acanthonotus Gray 1830
Ailia Gray 1830
Ailiichthys Day 1872
Ansorgia Boulenger 1912
Ansorgiichthys Whitley 1935
Clupisoma Swainson 1838
Eutropiellus Nichols & La Monte 1933
Eutropiichthys Bleeker 1862
Eutropius Müller & Troschel 1849
Irvineia Trewavas 1943
Laides Jordan 1919
Lais Bleeker 1858
Neotropius Kulkarni 1952
Pachypterus Swainson 1838
Parailia Boulenger 1899
Pareutropius Regan 1920
Physailia Boulenger 1901
Platytropius Hora 1937
Proeutropiichthys Hora 1937
Proeutropius Fowler 1936
Pseudeutropius Bleeker 1862
Pusichthys Swainson 1838
Schilbe Oken (ex Cuvier) 1817
Schilbeichthys Bleeker 1858
Silonia Swainson 1838
Silonopangasius Hora 1937
Silundia Valenciennes in Cuvier & Valenciennes 1840
Siluranodon Bleeker 1858

FAM. PANGASIIDAE (Pangasid Catfishes)

Helicophagus Bleeker 1858
Nemasiluroides Fowler 1937
Neopangasius Popta 1904
Pangasianodon Chevey 1931
Pangasius Valenciennes in Cuvier & Valenciennes 1840
Pseudolais Vaillant 1902
Pseudopangasius Bleeker 1862
Pteropangasius Fowler 1937
Sinopangasius Chang & Wu 1965

FAM. AMBLYCIPITIDAE (Torrent Catfishes)

Amblyceps Blyth 1858
Branchiosteus Gill 1861
Liobagrus Hilgendorf 1878
Neobagrus Bellotti 1892

FAM. AMPHILIIDAE (Loach Catfishes)

Amphilius Günther 1864
Andersonia Boulenger 1900
Anoplopterus Pfeffer 1889
Belonoglanis Boulenger 1902
Chimarrhoglanis Vaillant 1897
Doumea Sauvage 1879
Leptoglanis Boulenger 1902
Paramphilius Pellegrin 1907
Paraphractura Boulenger 1902
Peltura Perugia 1892
Phractura Boulenger 1900
Slatinia Werner 1906
Trachyglanis Boulenger 1902
Zaireichthys Roberts 1967

FAM. AKYSIDAE (Stream Catfishes)

Acrochordonichthys Bleeker 1858
Akysis Bleeker 1858
Breitensteinia Steindachner 1881
Sosia Vaillant 1902

FAM. PARAKYSIDAE (Parakysid Catfishes)

Parakysis Herre 1940

FAM. SISORIDAE (Sisorid Catfishes)

Aglyptosternon Bleeker 1862
Bagarius Bleeker 1853
Callomystax Günther 1864
Chimarrichthys Sauvage 1874
Conta Hora 1950
Coraglanis Hora & Silas 1952
Erethistes Müller & Troschel 1849
Erethistoides Hora 1950
Euchiloglanis Regan 1907
Euclyptosternum Günther 1864
Euglyptosternum Day (ex Bleeker) 1877
Exostoma Blyth 1860
Gagata Bleeker 1858
Glaridoglanis Norman 1925
Glyptosternon McClelland 1842
Glyptothorax Blyth 1860
Hara Blyth 1860
Laguvia Hora 1921
Myersglanis Hora & Silas 1952
Nangra Day 1876
Oreoglanis Smith 1933
Parachiloglanis Wu, He & Chu 1981
Paraglyptothorax Li 1986
Parapseudecheneis Hora in Hora & Chabanaud 1930
Pareuchiloglanis Pellegrin 1936
Parexostoma Regan 1905
Paroreoglanis Pellegrin 1936
Propseudecheneis Hora 1937
Pseudecheneis Blyth 1860
Pseudexostoma Chu 1979
Pseudolaguvia Misra 1976
Pteroglanis Fowler 1934
Pteropsoglanis Fowler 1934
Sisor Hamilton 1822
Sundagagata Boeseman 1966
Superglyptothorax Li 1986

FAM. CLARIIDAE (Airbreathing and Labyrinth Catfishes)

Allabenchelys Boulenger 1902
Anguilloclarias Teugels 1982
Bathyclarias Jackson 1959
Brevicephaloides Teugels 1982
Channallabes Günther 1873
Clariallabes Boulenger 1900
Clarias Gronow 1763
Clarias Scopoli (ex Gronow) 1777
Clarioides David in David & Poll 1937
Cossyphus McClelland 1844
Dinotopteroides Fowler 1930
Dinotopterus Boulenger 1906
Dolichallabes Poll 1942
Encheloclarias Herre & Myers 1937
Gymnallabes Günther 1867
Heterobranchoides David 1935
Heterobranchus Geoffroy St. Hilaire 1808
Horaglanis Menon 1950
Macropteronotus Lacepède 1803
Phagorus McClelland 1844
Platyallabes Poll 1977
Platycephaloides Teugels 1982
Platyclarias Poll 1977
Prophagorus Smith 1939
Tanganikallabes Poll 1943
Uegitglanis Gianferrari 1923
Xenoclarias Greenwood 1958

FAM. HETEROPNEUSTIDAE (Airsac Catfishes)

Clarisilurus Fowler 1937
Heteropneustes Müller 1840
Saccobranchus Valenciennes in Cuvier & Valenciennes 1840

FAM. CHACIDAE (Squarehead or Angler Catfishes)

Brachystacus Van der Hoeven 1849
Chaca Gray 1831
Chaca Valenciennes 1832

FAM. OLYRIDAE (Olyrid Catfishes)

Olyra McClelland 1842

FAM. MALAPTERURIDAE (Electric Catfishes)

Anacanthus Minding 1832
Malapterurus Lacepède 1803
Torpedo Forsskål 1775

FAM. ARIIDAE (Sea Catfishes)

Aelurichthys see *Ailurichthys*
Ailurichthys Baird & Girard 1854
Ancharius Steindachner 1881
Anemanotus Fowler 1944
Ariodes Müller & Troschel 1849
Ariopsis Gill 1861
Arius Valenciennes in Cuvier & Valenciennes 1840
Aspistor Jordan & Evermann 1898
Bagre Cloquet 1816
Batrachocephalus Bleeker 1846
Breviceps Swainson 1838
Brustiarius Herre 1935
Catastoma Kuhl & van Hasselt in Cuvier & Valenciennes 1840

Cathorops Jordan & Gilbert 1882
Cephalocassis Bleeker 1858
Cinetodus Ogilby 1898
Cochlefelis Whitley 1941
Doiichthys Weber 1913
Eopeyeria Whitley 1947
Felichthys Swainson 1839
Galeichthys Valenciennes in Cuvier & Valenciennes 1840
Genidens Castelnau 1855
Glanide Agassiz in Spix & Agassiz 1829
Glanis Agassiz in Spix & Agassiz 1829
Guiritinga Bleeker 1858
Hemiarius Bleeker 1862
Hemipimelodus Bleeker 1858
Hexanematichthys Bleeker 1858
Ketengus Bleeker 1847
Leptarius Gill 1863
Mystus Gray 1854
Nedystoma Ogilby 1898
Nemapteryx Ogilby 1908
Neoarius Castelnau 1878
Netuma Bleeker 1858
Notarius Gill 1863
Osteogeneiosus Bleeker 1846
Pachyula Ogilby 1898
Paradiplomystes Bleeker 1862
Pararius Whitley 1940
Peyeria Whitley 1940
Potamarius Hubbs & Miller 1960
Pseudarius Bleeker 1862
Sarcogenys Bleeker (ex Kuhl & van Hasselt) 1858
Sciadeichthys Bleeker 1858
Sciadeops Fowler 1944
Sciades Müller & Troschel 1849
Selenaspis Bleeker 1858
Septobranchus Hardenberg 1941
Stearopterus Minding 1832
Tetranesodon Weber 1913

FAM. PLOTOSIDAE (Eeltail catfishes)

Anodontiglanis Rendahl 1922
Anyperistius Ogilby 1908
Cainosilurus Macleay 1881
Choeroplotosus Kner 1866
Cnidoglanis Günther 1864
Copidoglanis Günther 1864
Deportator Gistel 1848
Endorrhis Ogilby 1898
Eumeda Castelnau 1878
Euristhmus Ogilby 1899
Exilichthys Whitley 1933
Lambertia Perugia 1894
Lambertichthys Whitley 1938
Neoplotosus Castelnau 1875
Neosilurus Steindachner 1867
Neosilurus Castelnau 1878
Oloplotosus Weber 1913
Ostophycephalus Ogilby 1899
Paraplotosus Bleeker 1862
Plotosus Lacepède 1803
Porochilus Weber 1913
Tandanus Mitchell 1838

FAM. MOCHOKIDAE (Squeakers and Upside-down Catfishes)

Acanthocleithron Nichols & Griscom 1917
Atopochilus Sauvage 1879
Brachysynodontis Bleeker 1862
Chiloglanis Peters 1868
Euchilichthys Boulenger 1900
Hemisynodontis Bleeker 1862
Leiosynodontis Bleeker 1862
Microsynodontis Boulenger 1903
Mochokiella Howes 1980
Mochokus Joannis 1835
Pseudosynodontis Bleeker 1862
Rhinoglanis Günther 1864
Synodontis Cuvier 1816

FAM. DORADIDAE (Thorny Catfishes)

Acanthodoras Bleeker 1862
Agamyxis Cope 1878
Amblydoras Bleeker 1862
Anadoras Eigenmann 1925
Anduzedoras Fernández-Yépez 1968
Apuredoras Fernández-Yépez 1950
Astrodoras Bleeker 1862
Autanadoras Fernández-Yépez 1950
Cataphractus Catesby 1771
Centrochir Agassiz in Spix & Agassiz 1829
Centrodoras Eigenmann 1925
Deltadoras Fernández-Yépez 1968
Doraops Schultz 1944
Doras Lacepède 1803
Franciscodoras Eigenmann 1925
Hassar Eigenmann & Eigenmann 1888
Hemidoras Bleeker 1858
Hildadoras Fernández-Yépez 1968
Hoplodoras Eigenmann 1925
Hypodoras Eigenmann 1925
Laimumena Sauvage 1884
Leptodoras Boulenger 1898
Lithodoras Bleeker 1862
Megalodoras Eigenmann 1925
Mormyrostoma Miranda-Ribeiro 1912
Nemadoras Eigenmann 1925
Opsodoras Eigenmann 1925
Orinocodoras Myers 1927
Oxydoras Kner 1855
Parapterodoras Risso & Morra 1964
Physopyxis Cope 1871
Platydoras Bleeker 1862
Pseudodoras Bleeker 1858
Pterodoras Bleeker 1862
Rhinodoras Bleeker 1862
Rhynchodoras Klausewitz & Rössel 1961
Sachsdoras Fernández-Yépez 1968
Scorpiodoras Eigenmann 1925
Trachydoras Eigenmann 1925
Zathorax Cope 1871

FAM. AUCHENIPTERIDAE (Auchenipterid Catfishes)

Asterophysus Kner 1858
Auchenipterichthys Bleeker 1862
Auchenipterus Valenciennes in Cuvier & Valenciennes 1840
Centromochlus Kner 1858
Ceratocheilus Miranda-Ribeiro 1918
Entomocorus Eigenmann 1917
Epapterus Cope 1878
Euanemus Müller & Troschel in Müller 1842
Gelanoglanis Böhlke 1980
Gephyromochlus Hoedeman 1961
Glanidium Lütken 1874
Liosomadoras Fowler 1940
Osteomystax Whitley 1940
Parauchenipterus Bleeker 1862
Pseudauchenipterus Bleeker 1862
Pseudepapterus Steindachner 1915
Pseudotatia Mees 1974
Silvaichthys Fernández-Yépez 1973
Tatia Miranda-Ribeiro 1912
Taunayia Miranda-Ribeiro 1918
Tocantinsia Mees 1974
Trachelyichthys Mees 1974
Trachelyopterichthys Bleeker 1862
Trachelyopterus Valenciennes in Cuvier & Valenciennes 1840
Trachycorystes Bleeker 1858
Wertheimeria Steindachner 1876

FAM. PIMELODIDAE (Long-wiskered Catfishes)

Abron Gistel 1848
Acentronichthys Eigenmann & Eigenmann 1889
Aguarunichthys Stewart 1986
Bagropsis Lütken 1874
Batrochoglanis Gill 1858
Bergiaria Eigenmann & Norris 1901
Bergiella Eigenmann & Norris 1900
Brachyglanis Eigenmann 1912
Brachyplatystoma Bleeker 1862
Brachyrhamdia Myers 1927
Breviglanis Eigenmann 1910
Caecorhamdella Borodin 1927
Caecorhamdia Norman 1926
Calophysus Müller & Troschel in Müller 1843
Cephalosilurus Haseman 1911
Cetopsorhamdia Eigenmann & Fisher in Eigenmann 1916
Chasmocephalus Eigenmann 1910
Chasmocranus Eigenmann 1912
Cheirocerus Eigenmann 1917
Conorhynchos Bleeker 1858
Conostome Duméril 1856
Duopalatinus Eigenmann & Eigenmann 1888
Ginesia Fernández-Yépez 1951
Gladioglanis Ferraris & Mago-Leccia 1989
Goeldiella Eigenmann & Norris 1900
Goslinia Myers 1941
Hemiplatystoma Bleeker 1862
Hemisorubim Bleeker 1862
Heptapterus Bleeker 1858
Horiomyzon Stewart 1986
Iheringichthys Eigenmann & Norris 1900
Imparales Schultz 1944
Imparfinis Eigenmann & Norris 1900
Leiarius Bleeker 1862
Leptoglanis Eigenmann 1912
Leptorhamdia Eigenmann 1918
Lophiosilurus Steindachner 1876
Luciopimelodus Eigenmann & Eigenmann 1888
Malacobagrus Bleeker 1862
Medemichthys Dahl 1961
Megalonema Eigenmann 1912
Merodontotus Britski 1981
Microglanis Eigenmann 1912
Myoglanis Eigenmann 1912
Nannoglanis Boulenger 1887

Nannorhamdia Regan 1913
Nemuroglanis Eigenmann & Eigenmann 1889
Notoglanis Günther 1864
Parabagrus Bleeker 1862
Parapimelodus La Monte 1933
Pariolius Cope 1872
Paulicea Ihering 1898
Perrunichthys Schultz 1944
Perugia Eigenmann & Norris 1900
Phenacorhamdia Dahl 1961
Phractocephalus Agassiz in Spix & Agassiz 1829
Phreatobius Goeldi 1905
Pimelenotus Gill 1858
Pimeletropis Gill 1859
Pimelodella Eigenmann & Eigenmann 1888
Pimelodina Steindachner 1876
Pimelodus Lacepède 1803
Pinirampus Bleeker 1858
Piramutana Bleeker 1858
Pirarara Agassiz in Spix & Agassiz 1829
Piratinga Bleeker 1858
Pirinampus Günther 1864
Platynematichthys Bleeker 1858
Platypogon Starks 1913
Platysilurus Haseman 1911
Platystoma Agassiz in Spix & Agassiz 1829
Platystomatichthys Bleeker 1862
Pseudariodes Bleeker 1862
Pseudocallophysus Bleeker 1862
Pseudopimelodus Bleeker 1858
Pseudoplatystoma Bleeker 1862
Pseudorhamdia Bleeker 1862
Pteroglanis Eigenmann & Pearson in Pearson 1924
Pteronotus Swainson 1839
Rhamdella Eigenmann & Eigenmann 1888
Rhamdia Bleeker 1858
Rhamdioglanis Ihering 1907
Rhamdiopsis Haseman 1911
Sciadeoides Eigenmann & Eigenmann 1888
Sorubim Agassiz in Spix & Agassiz 1829
Sorubim Cuvier 1829
Sorubimichthys Bleeker 1862
Sovichthys Schultz 1944
Steindachneria Eigenmann & Eigenmann 1888
Steindachneridion Eigenmann & Eigenmann 1919
Taenionema Eigenmann & Bean 1907
Typhlobagrus Miranda-Ribeiro 1907
Zungaro Bleeker 1858
Zungaropsis Steindachner 1908

FAM. AGENEIOSIDAE (Bottlenose or Barbelless Catfishes)

Ageneiosus Lacepède 1803
Ceratorhynchus Agassiz in Spix & Agassiz 1829
Davalla Bleeker 1858
Pseudageneiosus Bleeker 1862
Tetranematichthys Bleeker 1858
Tympanopleura Eigenmann 1912

FAM. HELOGENEIDAE (Helogeneid Catfishes)

Helogenes Günther 1863
Leyvaichthys Dahl 1960

FAM. CETOPSIDAE (Whalelike Catfishes)

Cetopsis Agassiz in Spix & Agassiz 1829
Cetopsogiton Eigenmann & Bean in Eigenmann 1910
Hemicetopsis Bleeker 1862
Paracetopsis Bleeker (ex Guichenot) 1862
Paracetopsis Eigenmann & Bean 1907
Pseudocetopsis Bleeker 1862

FAM. HYPOPHTHALMIDAE (Loweye Catfishes)

Hypophthalmus Agassiz in Spix & Agassiz 1829
Hypophthalmus Cuvier 1829
Notophthalmus Hyrtl 1859
Pseudohypophthalmus Bleeker 1862

FAM. ASPREDINIDAE (Banjo Catfishes)

Subfam. Bunocephalinae

Agmus Eigenmann 1910
Amaralia Fowler 1954
Aspredo Swainson 1838
Bunocephalichthys Bleeker 1858
Bunocephalus Kner 1855
Dupouyichthys Schultz 1944
Dysichthys Cope 1874
Ernstichthys Fernández-Yépez 1953
Hoplomyzon Myers 1942
Petacara Böhlke 1959
Pterobunocephalus Fowler 1943
Xyliphius Eigenmann 1912

Subfam. Aspredininae

Aspredinichthys Bleeker 1858
Aspredo Gronow 1763
Aspredo Scopoli (ex Gronow) 1777
Chamaigenes Eigenmann 1910
Cotylephorus Swainson 1838
Platistus Rafinesque 1815
Platysomatos Bloch 1797
Platystacus Bloch 1794
Platystacus Klein 1779

FAM. TRICHOMYCTERIDAE (Parasitic Catfishes and Candirus)

Acanthopoma Lütken 1892
Apomatoceros Eigenmann 1922
Astemomycterus Guichenot 1860
Bathophilus Miles 1942
Bathypygidium Whitley 1947
Branchioica Eigenmann 1917
Bullockia Arratia, Chang, Menu-Marque & Rojas 1978
Centrophorus Kner 1855
Cobitiglanis Fowler 1914
Eremophilus Humboldt 1805
Glanapteryx Myers 1927
Gyrinurus Miranda-Ribeiro 1912
Haemomaster Myers 1927
Hatcheria Eigenmann 1909
Henonemus Eigenmann & Ward in Eigenmann, McAtee & Ward 1907
Homodiaetus Eigenmann & Ward in Eigenmann, McAtee & Ward 1907
Listrura de Pinna 1988
Malacoglanis Myers & Weitzman 1966
Miuroglanis Eigenmann & Eigenmann 1889
Nematogenys Girard 1855
Ochmacanthus Eigenmann 1912
Parabranchioica Devincenzi & Vaz-Ferreira in Devincenzi 1939
Paracanthopoma Giltay 1935
Parastegophilus Miranda-Ribeiro 1946
Paravandellia Miranda-Ribeiro 1912
Pareiodon Kner 1855
Plectrochilus Miranda-Ribeiro 1917
Pleurophysus Miranda-Ribeiro 1918
Pseudostegophilus Eigenmann & Eigenmann 1889
Pygidianops Myers 1944
Pygidium Meyen 1835
Rhizosomichthys Miles 1943
Sarcoglanis Myers & Weitzman 1966
Schultzichthys Dahl 1960
Scleronema Eigenmann 1917
Stauroglanis Pinna 1989
Stegophilus Reinhardt 1859
Thrichomycterus Humboldt 1805
Thrycomycterus Humboldt & Valenciennes 1811
Trachypoma Giebel 1871
Trichogenes Britski & Ortega 1983
Trichomycterus Valenciennes in Humboldt 1833
Tridens Eigenmann & Eigenmann 1889
Tridensimilis Schultz 1944
Tridentopsis Myers 1925
Typhlobelus Myers 1944
Urinophilus Eigenmann 1918
Vandellia Valenciennes in Cuvier & Valenciennes 1846

FAM. CALLICHTHYIDAE (Callichthyid Armored Catfishes)

Aspidoras Ihering 1907
Brochis Cope 1871
Callichthys Scopoli (ex Gronow) 1777
Callichthys Gronow 1763
Callichthys Linck 1790
Callichthys Meuschen 1778
Cascadura Ellis 1913
Cataphractops Fowler 1915
Cataphractus Bloch 1794
Chaenothorax Cope 1878
Cordorinus Rafinesque 1815
Corydoras Lacepède 1803
Decapogon Eigenmann & Eigenmann 1888
Dianema Cope 1871
Ellisichthys Miranda-Ribeiro 1920
Gastrodermus Cope 1878
Hoplisoma Swainson 1838
Hoplosternum Gill 1858
Microcorydoras Myers 1953
Osteogaster Cope 1894
Scleromystax Günther 1864

FAM. LORICARIIDAE (Suckermouth Armored Catfishes)

Acanthicus Agassiz in Spix & Agassiz 1829
Acanthodemus Marschall (ex Castelnau) 1873
Acestra Kner 1853
Acestridium Haseman 1911
Ancistrus Kner 1854
Aphanotorulus Isbrücker & Nijssen 1983
Apistoloricaria Isbrücker & Nijssen 1986
Aposturisoma Isbrücker, Britski, Nijssen & Ortega 1983
Aristommata Holmberg 1893

Baryancistrus Rapp Py-Daniel 1989
Brochiloricaria Isbrücker & Nijssen in Isbrücker 1979
Canthopomus Eigenmann 1910
Carinotus La Monte 1933
Chaetostoma Heckel in Tschudi 1846
Cheiridodus Eigenmann 1922
Cochliodon Heckel in Kner 1854
Cordylancistrus Isbrücker 1980
Corymbophanes Eigenmann 1909
Crossoloricaria Isbrücker 1979
Cteniloricaria Isbrücker & Nijssen in Isbrücker 1979
Dasyloricaria Isbrücker & Nijssen in Isbrücker 1979
Dekeyseria Rapp Py-Daniel 1985
Delturus Eigenmann & Eigenmann 1889
Dentectus Martín Salazar, Isbrücker & Nijssen 1982
Diapeltoplites Fowler 1915
Dolichancistrus Isbrücker 1980
Euacanthagenys Fowler 1945
Exastilithoxus Isbrücker & Nijssen in Isbrücker 1979
Farlowella Eigenmann & Eigenmann 1889
Furcodontichthys Rapp Py-Daniel 1981
Fusiloricaria Fowler 1940
Harttia Steindachner 1876
Harttiella Boeseman 1971
Hemiancistrus Bleeker 1862
Hemiloricaria Bleeker 1862
Hemiodon Kner 1853
Hemiodontichthys Bleeker 1862
Hemipsilichthys Eigenmann & Eigenmann 1889
Hisonotus Eigenmann & Eigenmann 1889
Hopliancistrus Isbrücker & Nijssen 1989
Hypocolpterus Fowler 1943
Hypopostomatinum Günther 1868
Hypoptopoma Günther 1868
Hypostomus Lacepède 1803
Isorineloricaria Isbrücker 1980
Ixinandria Isbrücker & Nijssen in Isbrücker 1979
Kronichthys Miranda-Ribeiro 1908
Lamontichthys Miranda-Ribeiro 1939
Lasiancistrus Regan 1904
Leporacanthicus Isbrücker & Nijssen 1989
Leptoancistrus Meek & Hildebrand 1916
Limatulichthys Isbrücker & Nijssen in Isbrücker 1979
Lipopterichthys Norman 1935
Liposarcus Günther 1864
Lithoxancistrus Isbrücker, Nijssen & Cala 1988
Lithoxus Eigenmann 1910
Loricaria Linnaeus 1758
Loricariichthys Bleeker 1862
Megalancistrus Isbrücker 1980
Metaloricaria Isbrücker 1975
Microlepidogaster Eigenmann & Eigenmann 1889
Monistiancistrus Fowler 1940
Neblinichthys Ferraris, Isbrücker & Nijssen 1986
Neoplecostomus Eigenmann & Eigenmann 1888
Oligancistrus Rapp Py-Daniel 1989
Otocinclus Cope 1871
Otothyris Myers 1927
Oxyloricaria Bleeker 1862
Oxyropsis Eigenmann & Eigenmann 1889
Panaque Eigenmann & Eigenmann 1889
Parahemiodon Bleeker 1862
Paralithoxus Boeseman 1982
Paraloricaria Isbrücker 1979
Parancistrus Bleeker 1862
Parasturisoma Miranda-Ribeiro 1912
Pareiorhaphis Miranda-Ribeiro 1918
Pareiorhina Gosline 1947
Parotocinclus Eigenmann & Eigenmann 1889
Peckoltia Miranda-Ribeiro 1912
Peckoltichthys Miranda-Ribeiro 1917
Planiloricaria Isbrücker 1971
Plecostomus Gronow in Walbaum 1792
Plecostomus Gronow 1763
Plecostomus Swainson (ex Gronow) 1839
Pogonopoma Regan 1904
Pogonopomoides Gosline 1947
Pristiancistrus Fowler 1945
Pseudacanthicus Bleeker 1862
Pseudancistrus Bleeker 1862
Pseudohemiodon Bleeker 1862
Pseudoloricaria Bleeker 1862
Pseudorinelepis Bleeker 1862
Pseudotocinclus Nichols 1919
Pseudotothyris Britski & Garavello 1984
Pterosturisoma Isbrücker & Nijssen 1978
Pterygoplichthys Gill 1858
Pyxiloricaria Isbrücker & Nijssen 1984
Reganella Eigenmann 1905
Rhadinoloricaria Isbrücker & Nijssen 1974
Rhinelepis Agassiz in Spix & Agassiz 1829
Ricola Isbrücker & Nijssen 1978
Rineloricaria Bleeker 1862
Schizolecis Britski & Garavello 1984
Scobinancistrus Isbrücker & Nijssen 1989
Spatuloricaria Schultz 1944
Spectracanthicus Nijssen & Isbrücker 1987
Stoneiella Fowler 1914
Sturisoma Swainson 1838
Sturisomatichthys Isbrücker & Nijssen in Isbrücker 1979
Thysanocara Regan 1906
Upsilodus Miranda-Ribeiro 1924
Xenocara Regan 1904
Xenomystus Lütken 1874

FAM. SCOLOPLACIDAE

Scoloplax Bailey & Baskin 1976

FAM. ASTROBLEPIDAE (Astroblepid Catfishes)

Arges Valenciennes in Cuvier & Valenciennes 1840
Astroblepus Humboldt 1805
Brontes Valenciennes in Cuvier & Valenciennes 1840
Cyclopium Swainson 1838
Lithogenes Eigenmann 1909
Strephon Gistel 1848
Stygogenes Günther 1864

ORDER GYMNOTIFORMES

FAM. GYMNOTIDAE (Knifefishes)

Dameus Rafinesque 1815
Neleus Rafinesque 1815

Subfam. Sternopyginae

Archolaemus Korringa 1970
Distocyclus Mago-Leccia 1978
Eigenmannia Jordan & Evermann 1896
Guichthys Fernández-Yépez 1968
Hildatia Fernández-Yépez 1968
Rhabdolichops Eigenmann & Allen 1942
Sternopygus Müller & Troschel 1848

Subfam. Rhamphichthyinae

Altona Kaup in Duméril 1856
Gymnorhamphichthys Ellis in Eigenmann 1912
Rhamphichthys Müller & Troschel 1848
Urumara Miranda-Ribeiro 1920

Subfam. Hypopominae

Brachyrhamphichthys Günther 1870
Hypopomus Gill 1864
Hypopygus Hoedeman 1962
Microsternarchus Fernández-Yépez 1968
Parupygus Hoedeman 1962
Steatogenys Boulenger 1898
Tateichthys La Monte 1929

Subfam. Apteronotinae

Adontosternarchus Ellis in Eigenmann 1912
Apteronotus Lacepède 1800
Memarchus Kaup in Duméril 1856
Orthosternarchus Ellis 1913
Porotergus Ellis in Eigenmann 1912
Rhamphosternarchus Günther 1870
Sternarchella Eigenmann in Eigenmann & Ward 1905
Sternarchogiton Eigenmann in Eigenmann & Ward 1905
Sternarchorhamphus Eigenmann in Eigenmann & Ward 1905
Sternarchorhynchus Castelnau 1855
Sternarchus Bloch & Schneider 1801
Ubidia Miles 1945

Subfam. Gymnotinae (Nakedback Knifefishes)

Carapo Oken 1817
Carapus Cuvier 1816
Cryptops Eigenmann 1894
Giton Kaup in Duméril 1856
Gymnotes Gill 1864
Gymnotus Linnaeus 1758
Oedemognathus Myers 1936

Subfam. Electrophorinae (Electric Knifefishes)

Electrophorus Gill 1864

ORDER SALMONIFORMES

SUBORDER ESOCOIDEI

FAM. ESOCIDAE (Pikes)

Esox Linnaeus 1758
Kenoza Jordan & Evermann 1896
Lucius Geoffroy St. Hilaire 1767
Lucius Klein 1776
Lucius Rafinesque 1810
Mascalongus Jordan 1878
Picorellus Rafinesque 1820

FAM. UMBRIDAE (Mudminnows)
Dallia Bean 1880
Melanura Agassiz 1853
Novumbra Schultz 1929
Umbra Kramer in Scopoli 1777

SUBORDER ARGENTINOIDEI
Halaphya Günther 1889

FAM. ARGENTINIDAE (Argentines)
Acantholepis Krøyer 1846
Argentina Linnaeus 1758
Glossanodon Guichenot 1867
Goniosoma Costa 1844
Prosoarchus Cohen 1958
Silus Reinhardt 1833

FAM. BATHYLAGIDAE (Deepsea Smelts)
Bathylagichthys Kobyliansky 1986
Bathylagoides Whitley 1951
Bathylagus Günther 1878
Dolicholagus Kobyliansky 1986
Leuroglossus Gilbert 1890
Lipolagus Kobyliansky 1986
Melanolagus Kobyliansky 1986
Pseudobathylagus Kobyliansky 1986
Therobromus Lucas in Jordan & Gilbert 1899

FAM. OPISTHOPROCTIDAE (Spookfishes or Barreleyes)
Bathylychnops Cohen 1958
Dolichopteryx Brauer 1901
Grimaldia Chapman 1942
Hyalorhynchus Gilchrist & von Bonde 1924
Macropinna Chapman 1939
Monacoa Whitley 1943
Ophthalmopelton Maul 1946
Opisthoproctus Vaillant 1888
Rhynchohyalus Barnard 1925
Winteria Brauer 1901

FAM. ALEPOCEPHALIDAE (Slickheads)
Alcockella Fowler 1934
Alepocephalus Risso 1820
Aleposomus Gill 1884
Aleposomus Roule (ex Brauer) 1915
Anomalopterichthys Whitley 1940
Anomalopterus Vaillant 1886
Asquamiceps Zugmayer 1911
Auchenalepoceps Fowler 1943
Aulastomatomorpha Alcock 1890
Bajacalifornia Townsend & Nichols 1925
Bathylaco Goode & Bean 1896
Bathyprion Marshall 1966
Bathypropteron Fowler 1934
Bathytroctes Günther 1878
Bellocia Parr 1951
Benthosphyraena Cockerell 1919
Binghamia Parr 1937
Binghamichthys Whitley 1941
Brunichthys Parr 1951
Caudania Roule 1935
Conocara Goode & Bean 1896
Einara Parr 1951
Ericara Gill & Townsend 1897
Grimatroctes Parr 1952
Halisauriceps Fowler 1934
Herwigia Nielsen 1972
Lepogenys Parr 1951
Leptoderma Vaillant 1886
Lloydiella Parr 1952
Macromastax Beebe 1933
Megalepocephalus Fowler 1934
Microphotolepis Sazonov & Parin 1977
Mirognathus Parr 1951
Mirorictus Parr 1947
Mitchillina Jordan & Evermann 1896
Narcetes Alcock 1890
Nemabathytroctes Fowler 1934
Nomoctes Parr 1952
Noriona Strand 1942
Normania Parr 1937
Perioceps Parr 1954
Photostylus Beebe 1933
Pomatias Bloch & Schneider 1801
Proditor Whitley 1940
Rinoctes Parr 1952
Rouleina Jordan 1923
Talismania Goode & Bean 1896
Torictus Parr 1951
Triurus Lacepède 1800
Whitleyidea Fowler 1934
Xenodermichthys Günther 1878
Xenognathus Gilbert 1915

FAM. PLATYTROCTIDAE (Tubeshoulders) = Searsiidae
Barbantus Parr 1951
Holtbyrnia Parr 1937
Krefftia Parr 1960
Maulisia Parr 1960
Mentodus Parr 1951
Normichthys Parr 1951
Paraholtbyrnia Krefft 1967
Pectinantus Sazonov 1986
Pellisolus Parr 1951
Persparsia Parr 1951
Platytroctegen Lloyd 1909
Platytroctes Günther 1878
Sagamichthys Parr 1953
Searsia Parr 1937
Searsioides Sazonov 1977

FAM. LEPTOCHILICHTHYIDAE (Leptochilichthyids)
Leptochilichthys Garman 1899

SUBORDER LEPIDOGALAXIOIDEI

FAM. LEPIDOGALAXIIDAE
Lepidogalaxias Mees 1961

SUBORDER SALMONOIDEI

FAM. OSMERIDAE (Smelts)
Allosmerus Hubbs 1925
Eperlanio Jordan 1919
Eperlanus Gaimard 1851
Eperlanus Basilewski 1855
Eperlanus Rutty 1772
Hypomesus Gill 1862
Mallotus Cuvier 1829
Mesopus Gill 1862
Osmerus Lacepède 1803
Osmerus Linnaeus 1758
Spirinchus Jordan & Evermann (ex Jonston) 1896
Thaleichthys Girard 1858

FAM. PLECOGLOSSIDAE (Ayu Fishes)
Plecoglossus Temminck & Schlegel 1846

FAM. SALANGIDAE (Icefishes or Noodlefishes)
Sundasalangidae included
Albula Osbeck 1762
Hemisalanx Regan 1908
Leucosoma Gray 1831
Metasalanx Wakiya & Takahasi 1937
Neosalanx Wakiya & Takahasi 1937
Paraprotosalanx Fang 1934
Parasalanx Regan 1908
Protosalanx Regan 1908
Reganisalanx Fang 1934
Salangichthys Bleeker 1860
Salanx Cuvier 1816
Sundasalanx Roberts 1981

FAM. RETROPINNIDAE (New Zealand Smelts)

Subfam. Retropinninae (Southern Smelts)
Jenynsella Ogilby 1908
Retropinna Gill 1862
Richardsonia Steindachner 1866
Stokellia Whitley 1955

Subfam. Prototroctinae (Southern Graylings)
Prototroctes Günther 1864

FAM. GALAXIIDAE (Galaxiids)

Subfam. Aplochitoninae
Aplochiton Jenyns 1842
Farionella Valenciennes in Cuvier & Valenciennes 1849
Haplochiton Agassiz 1846
Lovettia McCulloch 1915

Subfam. Galaxiinae
Agalaxis Scott 1936
Austrocobitis Ogilby 1899
Brachygalaxias Eigenmann 1928
Galaxias Cuvier 1816
Galaxiella McDowall 1978
Lixagasa Scott 1936
Lyragalaxias Whitley 1935
Mesites Jenyns 1842
Neochanna Günther 1867
Nesogalaxias Whitley 1935
Paragalaxias Scott 1935
Querigalaxias Whitley 1935
Saxilaga Scott 1936

FAM. SALMONIDAE (Salmonids)

Subfam. Coregoninae (Whitefishes)
Allosomus Jordan 1878
Argyrosomus Agassiz 1850
Cisco Jordan & Evermann 1911

Coregonus Lacepède 1803
Coregonus Linnaeus 1758
Coregonus Jarocki 1822
Irillion Jordan 1919
Leucichthys Dybowski 1874
Luciotrutta Günther 1866
Prosopium Jordan (ex Milner) 1878
Stenodus Richardson 1836
Thrissomimus Gill in Jordan & Evermann 1911
Tripteronotus Lacepède 1803

Subfam. Thymallinae (Graylings)
Choregon Minding 1832
Orthocolus Gistel 1848
Phylogephyra Boulenger 1898
Thymalloides Berg 1908
Thymallus Linck 1790
Thymallus Cuvier 1829

Subfam. Salmoninae (Salmons, Trouts and Chars)
Acantholingua Hadzisce 1960
Baione DeKay 1842
Brachymystax Günther 1866
Cristivomer Gill & Jordan in Jordan 1878
Epitomynis Schulze 1890
Fario Valenciennes in Cuvier & Valenciennes 1848
Hucho Günther 1866
Hypsifario Gill 1862
Oncorhynchus Suckley 1861
Parahucho Vladykov 1963
Paraoncorhynchus Glückman, Konovalov & Rassadnikov 1973
Parasalmo Vladykov in Vladykov & Gruchy 1972
Platysalmo Behnke 1969
Salar Valenciennes in Cuvier & Valenciennes 1848
Salmo Linnaeus 1758
Salmothymus Berg 1908
Salvelinus Richardson (ex Nilsson) 1836
Trutta Geoffroy St. Hilaire 1767
Truttae Linnaeus 1758
Umbla Rapp 1854

ORDER STOMIIFORMES

FAM. GONOSTOMATIDAE (Bristlemouths)
Bonapartia Goode & Bean 1896
Cyclothone Goode & Bean 1883
Diplophos Günther 1873
Gonostoma Rafinesque 1810
Manducus Goode & Bean 1896
Margrethia Jespersen & Tåning 1919
Narooma Whitley 1935
Neostoma Filhol (ex Vaillant) 1884
Paraphotichthys Whitley 1931
Sigmops Gill 1883
Triplophos Brauer 1902
Zaphotias Goode & Bean in Jordan & Evermann 1898

FAM. STERNOPTYCHIDAE (Marine Hatchetfishes)

Subfam. Maurolicinae
Araiophos Grey 1961
Argyripnus Gilbert & Cramer 1897
Danaphos Bruun 1931
Lychnopoles Garman 1899
Maurolicus Cocco 1838
Neophos Myers 1932
Sonoda Grey 1959
Thorophos Bruun 1931
Triarcus Waite 1910
Valenciennellus Jordan & Evermann in Goode & Bean 1896

Subfam. Sternoptychinae (Marine Hatchetfishes)
Acanthopolyipnus Fowler 1934
Argyropelecus Cocco 1829
Melanictis Rafinesque 1815
Pleurothyris Lowe 1843
Polyipnus Günther 1887
Snellius Koumans 1953
Sternoptychides Ogilby 1888
Sternoptyx Hermann 1781

FAM. PHOSICHTHYIDAE (Lightfishes) = Photichthyidae
Coccia Günther 1864
Ichthyococcus Bonaparte 1840
Phosichthys Hutton 1872
Photichthys see *Phosichthys*
Pollichthys Grey 1959
Polymetme McCulloch 1926
Poweria Bonaparte 1840
Vinciguerria Jordan & Evermann in Goode & Bean 1896
Woodsia Grey 1959
Yarrella Goode & Bean 1896
Zalarges Jordan & Williams in Jordan & Starks 1895

FAM. CHAULIODONTIDAE (Viperfishes)
Chauliodus Bloch & Schneider 1801
Leptodes Swainson 1838
Vipera Edwards (ex Catesby) 1771

FAM. STOMIIDAE (Scaly Dragonfishes)
Bathyembryx Beebe 1934
Dolichostomias Parr 1927
Macrostomias Brauer 1902
Microchirichthys Regan & Trewavas 1930
Microdontostomias Fowler 1934
Photonectops Chapman 1939
Pseudeustomias Fowler 1934
Stomias Cuvier 1816
Stomiasunculus Kaup 1860
Stomioides Parr 1933
Trichochirus Regan & Trewavas 1930

FAM. ASTRONESTHIDAE (Snaggletooths)
Astronesthes Richardson 1845
Bathylychnus Brauer 1902
Borostomias Regan 1908
Cryptostomias Gibbs & Weitzman 1965
Diplolychnus Regan & Trewavas 1929
Elapterostomias Fowler 1934
Heterophotus Regan & Trewavas 1929
Neonesthes Regan & Trewavas 1929
Phaenodon Lowe 1852
Rhadinesthes Regan & Trewavas 1929
Stomianodon Bleeker 1849
Warreenula Whitley 1941

FAM. MELANOSTOMIIDAE (Scaleless Black Dragonfishes)
Achirostomias Regan & Trewavas 1930
Bathophilus Giglioli 1882
Bathysphaera Beebe 1932
Biradiostomias Gomon & Gibbs 1985
Chirostomias Regan & Trewavas 1930
Dactylostomias Garman 1899
Dinematochirus Regan & Trewavas 1930
Diplostomias Kotthaus 1967
Echiostoma Lowe 1843
Eustomias Filhol 1884
Eustomias Vaillant 1888
Flagellostomias Parr 1927
Gnathostomias Pappenheim 1914
Grammatostomias Goode & Bean 1896
Haploclonus Regan & Trewavas 1930
Haplostomias Regan & Trewavas 1930
Hyperchoristus Gill 1883
Lamprotoxus Holt & Bryne 1913
Leptostomias Gilbert 1905
Lucifer Döderlein 1882
Melanonectes Regan & Trewavas 1930
Melanostomias Brauer 1902
Nasistomias Koefoed 1956
Nematostomias Zugmayer 1911
Neostomias Gilchrist 1906
Nominostomias Regan & Trewavas 1930
Notopodichthys Regan & Trewavas 1930
Odontostomias Norman 1930
Opostomias Günther 1887
Pachystomias Günther 1887
Parabathophilus Matallanas 1984
Parastomias Roule & Angel 1931
Pareustomias Bailly 1930
Photonectes Günther 1887
Photonectoides Koefoed 1956
Rhynchostomias Regan & Trewavas 1930
Spilostomias Regan & Trewavas 1930
Stomiatella Roule & Angel 1930
Tactostoma Bolin 1939
Thysanactis Regan & Trewavas 1930
Trachinostomias Parr 1927
Trichostomias Zugmayer 1911
Triclonostomias Regan & Trewavas 1930
Trigonolampa Regan & Trewavas 1930
Urostomias Regan & Trewavas 1930

FAM. MALACOSTEIDAE (Loosejaws)
Aristostomias Zugmayer 1913
Malacosteus Ayres 1848
Photostomias Collett 1889
Thaumastomias Alcock 1890
Ultimostomias Beebe 1933
Zastomias Gilbert 1915

FAM. IDIACANTHIDAE (Black Dragonfishes)
Bathyophis Günther 1878
Idiacanthus Peters 1877
Stylophthalmus Brauer 1902

ORDER AULOPIFORMES

SUBORDER AULOPOIDEI

FAM. AULOPIDAE (Aulopus)
Aulopus Cuvier 1816
Aulopus Cloquet (ex Cuvier) 1816
Hime Starks 1924
Latropiscis Whitley 1931

FAM. CHLOROPHTHALMIDAE (Greeneyes)

Subfam. Chlorophthalminae (Greeneyes)
Bathysauropsis Regan 1911
Chlorophthalmus Bonaparte 1840
Hyphalonedrus Goode 1881
Parasudis Regan 1911
Pelopsia Facciolà 1883

Subfam. Ipnopinae
Bathycygnus Sulak 1977
Bathymicrops Hjort & Koefoed in Murray & Hjort 1912
Bathypterois Günther 1878
Bathysaurops Fowler 1938
Bathytyphlops Nybelin 1957
Belonopterois Roule 1916
Benthosaurus Goode & Bean 1886
Discoverichthys Merrett & Nielsen 1987
Hemipterois Regan 1911
Ipnoceps Fowler 1943
Ipnops Günther 1878
Lychnoculus Murray 1877
Macrias Gill & Townsend 1901
Macristiella Berry & Robins 1967
Skagerakia Nybelin 1947
Synapteretmus Goode & Bean 1896

FAM. SCOPELARCHIDAE (Pearleyes)
Benthalbella Zugmayer 1911
Dissomma Brauer 1902
Neoscopelarchoides Chapman 1939
Phanops Rofen 1963
Rosenblattichthys Johnson 1974
Scopelarchoides Parr 1929
Scopelarchus Alcock 1896

FAM. NOTOSUDIDAE (Paperbones or Waryfishes)
Ahliesaurus Bertelsen, Krefft & Marshall 1976
Luciosudis Fraser-Brunner 1931
Notosudis Waite 1916
Scopelosaurus Bleeker 1860

SUBORDER ALEPISAUROIDEI
Alepichthys Facciolà 1882

FAM. SYNODONTIDAE

Subfam. Synodontinae (Lizardfishes)
Allouarnia Whitley 1937
Austrotirus Whitley 1937
Esosynodus Whitley 1937
Exotirichthys Whitley 1937
Goodella Ogilby 1897
Laurida Swainson 1838
Negotirus Whitley 1937
Newtonscottia Whitley 1937
Salmosaurus Minding 1832
Saurus Catesby 1771
Saurus Cuvier 1816
Soarus Linck 1790
Synodus Gronow 1763
Synodus Scopoli (ex Gronow) 1777
Synodus Bloch & Schneider 1801
Tirus Rafinesque 1810
Trachinocephalus Gill 1861
Xystodus Ogilby 1910

Subfam. Harpadontinae (Bombay Ducks)
Harpadon Lesueur 1825
Harpodon Cuvier 1829
Peltharpadon Fowler 1934
Saurida Valenciennes in Cuvier & Valenciennes 1849
Sauridichthys Bleeker 1858
Triurus Swainson 1839

Subfam. Bathysaurinae
Bathysaurus Günther 1878
Macristium Regan 1903

FAM. GIGANTURIDAE (Telescopefishes)
Bathyleptus Walters 1961
Gigantura Brauer 1901
Rosaura Tucker 1954

FAM. PARALEPIDIDAE (Barracudinas)
Arctozenus Gill 1864
Bathysudis Parr 1928
Dolichosudis Post 1969
Lestidiops Hubbs 1916
Lestidium Gilbert 1905
Lestrolepis Harry 1953
Longisudis Maul 1965
Macroparalepis Ege 1933
Maculisudis Kotthaus 1967
Magnisudis Harry 1953
Maulichthys Rofen 1963
Notolepis Dollo 1908
Paralepis Cuvier 1816
Pontosudis Rofen 1963
Profundisudis Harry 1953
Prymnothonoides Whitley & Phillipps 1939
Prymnothonus Richardson 1845
Stemonosudis Harry 1951
Sudis Rafinesque 1810
Symproptopterus Cocco in Facciolà 1885
Uncisudis Maul 1956

FAM. ANOTOPTERIDAE (Daggertooths)
Anotopterus Zugmayer 1911

FAM. EVERMANNELLIDAE (Sabertooth Fishes)
Coccorella Roule 1929
Evermannella Fowler 1901
Odontostomops Fowler 1934
Odontostomus Cocco 1838

FAM. OMOSUDIDAE (Omosudids)
Omosudis Günther 1887

FAM. ALEPISAURIDAE (Lancetfishes)
Alepisaurus Lowe 1833
Caulopus Gill 1862
Eugnathosaurus Regan 1913
Plagyodontis Steller in Pallas 1814
Plagyodus Günther (ex Steller in Pallas) 1867

FAM. PSEUDOTRICHONOTIDAE
Pseudotrichonotus Yoshino & Araga in Masuda, Araga & Yoshino 1975

ORDER MYCTOPHIFORMES
Cyrtorhynchus Costa 1855
Phanerobranchus Cocco 1846

FAM. NEOSCOPELIDAE (Blackchins)
Neoscopelus Johnson 1863
Scopelengys Alcock 1890
Solivomer Miller 1947

FAM. MYCTOPHIDAE (Lanternfishes)
Aethoprora Goode & Bean 1896
Alysia Lowe 1839
Benthosema Goode & Bean 1896
Bolinichthys Paxton 1972
Catablemella Eigenmann & Eigenmann 1890
Cavelampus Whitley 1933
Centrobranchus Fowler 1904
Ceratoscopelus Günther 1864
Collettia Goode & Bean 1896
Ctenoscopelus Fraser-Brunner 1949
Cyphoscopelus Fowler 1925
Dasyscopelus Günther 1864
Diaphus Eigenmann & Eigenmann 1890
Diogenichthys Bolin 1939
Dorsadena Coleman & Nafpaktitis 1972
Elampa Fraser-Brunner 1949
Elampadena Whitley 1953
Electrona Goode & Bean 1896
Gonichthys Gistel 1850
Gymnoscopelus Günther 1873
Hierops Fraser-Brunner 1949
Hintonia Fraser-Brunner 1949
Hygophum Bolin (ex Tåning) 1939
Hyperphotops Fraser-Brunner 1949
Idiolychnus Nafpaktitis & Paxton 1978
Krefftichthys Hulley 1981
Lampadena Goode & Bean in Gill 1893
Lampanyctodes Fraser-Brunner 1949
Lampanyctus Bonaparte 1840
Lampichthys Fraser-Brunner 1949
Lamprossa Jordan & Hubbs 1925
Lepidophanes Fraser-Brunner 1949
Lobianchia Gatti 1904
Loweina Fowler 1925
Lychnophora Fraser-Brunner 1949
Macrostoma Risso 1826
Metelectrona Wisner 1963
Myctophum Rafinesque 1810
Nannobrachium Günther 1887
Nasolychnus Smith 1933
Notolychnus Fraser-Brunner 1949
Notoscopelus Günther 1864
Nyctimaster Jordan 1921
Nyctophus Cocco 1829
Pantophos Jordan & Hubbs 1925

Paralampanyctus Kotthaus 1972
Pareiophus Nafpaktitis 1975
Parvilux Hubbs & Wisner 1964
Promacheon Weber 1913
Protomyctophum Fraser-Brunner 1949
Pseudodiaphus Tåning 1918
Rhinoscopelus Lütken 1892
Scopelopsis Brauer 1906
Scopelus Cuvier 1816
Scopelus Fraser-Brunner 1949
Serpa Cloquet 1827
Stenobrachius Eigenmann & Eigenmann 1890
Stylophthalmoides Mazzarelli 1912
Symbolophorus Bolin & Wisner in Bolin 1959
Taaningichthys Bolin 1959
Tarletonbeania Eigenmann & Eigenmann 1890
Triphoturus Fraser-Brunner 1949
Vestula Bolin 1946

ORDER PERCOPSIFORMES

FAM. PERCOPSIDAE (Trout-Perches)
Columatilla Whitley 1940
Columbia Eigenmann & Eigenmann 1892
Percopsis Agassiz 1849
Salmoperca Thompson 1850

FAM. APHREDODERIDAE (Pirate Perches)
Aphododerus see *Aphredoderus*
Aphredoderus Lesueur in Cuvier & Valenciennes 1833
Asternotremia Nelson in Jordan 1877
Sternotremia Nelson 1876

FAM. AMBLYOPSIDAE (Cavefishes)
Amblyopsis DeKay 1842
Chologaster Agassiz 1853
Forbesella Jordan & Evermann 1927
Forbesichthys Jordan 1929
Speoplatyrhinus Cooper & Kuehne 1974
Troglichthys Eigenmann 1899
Typhlichthys Girard 1859

ORDER GADIFORMES

Leptogadus Gill 1863

FAM. MURAENOLEPIDIDAE
Muraenolepis Günther 1880

FAM. BREGMACEROTIDAE (Codlets)
Asthenurus Tickell 1865
Bregmaceros Thompson 1840
Calloptilum Richardson 1845

FAM. EUCLICHTHYIDAE
Euclichthys McCulloch 1926

FAM. MACROURIDAE (Grenadiers or Rat-tails)
Macruroplus Bleeker 1874

Subfam. Bathygadinae
Bathygadus Günther 1878
Gadomus Regan 1903
Melanobranchus Regan 1903
Regania Jordan in Jordan & Starks 1904

Subfam. Macrouroidinae
Macrouroides Smith & Radcliffe in Radcliffe 1912
Squalogadus Gilbert & Hubbs 1916

Subfam. Trachyrincinae
Idiolophorhynchus Sazonov 1981
Lepidoleprus Risso 1810
Lepidosoma Swainson 1839
Oxycephas Rafinesque 1810
Trachyrincus Giorna 1809

Subfam. Macrourinae
Abyssicola Goode & Bean 1896
Albatrossia Jordan & Gilbert in Jordan & Evermann 1898
Asthenomacrurus Sazonov & Shcherbachev 1982
Ateleobrachium Gilbert & Burke 1912
Atherodus Gilbert & Hubbs 1920
Bogoslovius Jordan & Evermann 1898
Caelorinchus Giorna 1809
Cariburus Parr 1946
Cetonurichthys Sazonov & Shcherbachev 1982
Cetonurus Günther 1887
Chalinura Goode & Bean 1883
Chalinurus see *Chalinura*
Coccolus Bonaparte 1846
Coelocephalus Gilbert & Cramer 1897
Coelorinchus see *Caelorinchus*
Coryphaenoides Gunner 1765
Cynomacrurus Dollo 1909
Dolloa Jordan 1900
Echinomacrurus Roule 1916
Fuyangia Whitley 1931
Garichthys Whitley 1934
Grenurus Parr 1946
Haplomacrourus Trunov 1980
Hemimacrurus Fraser-Brunner 1935
Hymenocephalus Giglioli in Giglioli & Issel 1884
Hymenogadus Gilbert & Hubbs 1920
Hyomacrurus Gilbert & Hubbs 1920
Hyostomus Jordan (ex Gilbert & Hubbs) 1920
Krohnius Cocco 1844
Kumba Marshall 1973
Kuronezumia Iwamoto 1974
Lepidorhynchus Richardson 1846
Lepturus Gronow in Gray 1854
Lionurus Günther 1887
Lucigadella Gilbert & Hubbs 1920
Lucigadus Gilbert & Hubbs 1920
Macrosmia Merritt, Sazonov & Shcherbachev 1983
Macrourus Bloch 1786
Macrurus see *Macrourus*
Mahia McCann & McKnight 1980
Malacocephalus Günther 1862
Mataeocephalus Berg 1898
Mesobius Hubbs & Iwamoto 1977
Moseleya Goode & Bean 1896
Mystaconurus Günther 1887
Nematonurus Günther 1887
Nezumia Jordan in Jordan & Starks 1904
Odontomacrurus Norman 1939
Optonurus Günther 1887
Oxygadus Gilbert & Hubbs 1920
Oxymacrurus Bleeker 1874
Papyrocephalus Gilbert & Hubbs 1920
Paracetonurus Marshall 1973
Parakumba Trunov 1981
Paramacrurus Bleeker 1874
Pawnurus Parr 1946
Phalacromacrurus Maul & Koefoed 1950
Pseudocetonurus Sazonov & Shcherbachev 1982
Pseudonezumia Okamura 1970
Quincuncia Gilbert & Hubbs 1920
Sokodara Iwamoto 1979
Sphagemacrurus Fowler 1925
Spicomacrurus Okamura 1970
Trachonurus Günther 1887
Ventrifossa Gilbert & Hubbs 1920

FAM. MORIDAE (Deepsea Cods)
Antimora Günther 1878
Asellus Valenciennes in Webb & Berthelot 1838
Asellus Minding 1832
Auchenoceros Günther 1889
Austrophycis Ogilby 1897
Brosmiculus Vaillant 1888
Calloptilum Hutton 1873
Eeyorius Paulin 1986
Eretmophorus Giglioli 1889
Gadella Lowe 1843
Gargilius Jensen in Koefoed 1953
Gastronemus Bonaparte (ex Cocco) 1846
Guttigadus Taki 1953
Halargyreus Günther 1862
Haloporphyrus Günther in Johnson 1862
Hypsirhynchus Facciolà 1884
Laemonema Günther in Johnson 1862
Laemonemodes Gilchrist 1903
Lepidion Swainson 1838
Leptophycis Garman 1899
Lotella Kaup 1858
Microlepidium Garman 1899
Momonatira Paulin 1986
Mora Risso 1826
Olssonichthys Fowler 1958
Pharopteryx Rüppell 1852
Physiculus Kaup 1858
Podonema Rass 1954
Podonematichthys Whitley 1965
Pseudophycis Günther 1862
Rhynchogadus Tortonese 1948
Salilota Günther 1887
Svetovidovia Cohen 1973
Sympodoichthys Facciolà 1888
Tinimogaster Bonaparte (ex Cocco) 1846
Tripterophycis Boulenger 1902
Uraleptus Costa 1846

FAM. MELANONIDAE (Melanonids)
Melanonosoma Gilchrist 1902
Melanonus Günther 1878

FAM. GADIDAE (Cods and Haddocks)
Aeglefinus Malm 1877
Algoa Castelnau 1861
Arctogadus Drjagin 1932
Boreogadus Günther 1862
Brachygadus Gill 1862
Brachymesistius Gill 1863
Callarias Klein 1777
Cephus Swainson 1838

Cerdo Gistel 1848
Eleginus Fischer von Waldheim 1813
Gadiculus Guichenot 1850
Gadulus Malm 1877
Gadus Linnaeus 1758
Melanogrammus Gill 1862
Merlangius Geoffroy St. Hilaire 1767
Merlangus Oken (ex Cuvier) 1817
Microgadus Gill 1865
Micromesistius Gill 1863
Minutus de Buen 1926
Morhua Fleming 1828
Morrhua Oken (ex Cuvier) 1817
Odontogadus Gill 1863
Phocaegadus Jensen 1948
Pleurogadus Bean in Jordan 1885
Pollachius Nilsson 1832
Theragra Lucas in Jordan & Evermann 1898
Tilesia Swainson 1838
Trisopterus Rafinesque 1814

FAM. LOTIDAE (Hakes and Burbots)

Antonogadus Wheeler 1969
Batracocephalus Hollberg 1819
Brosma Schinz 1822
Brosme Oken (ex Cuvier) 1817
Brosme Rafinesque 1815
Brosmerus Lesueur 1819
Brosmius Cuvier 1829
Brosmus Stark 1828
Brosmus Fleming 1828
Ciliata Couch 1832
Couchia Thompson 1856
Dropsarus Rafinesque 1815
Enchelyopus Bloch & Schneider 1801
Enchura Minding 1832
Gaidropsarus Rafinesque 1810
Haustor Jordan & Evermann 1896
Hypsiptera Günther 1860
Lota Oken (ex Cuvier) 1817
Lotta Risso 1826
Molva Lesueur 1819
Molvella Kaup 1858
Morua Risso 1826
Motella Cuvier 1829
Mustel Oken (ex Cuvier) 1817
Onogadus de Buen 1934
Onos Risso 1826
Raniceps Oken (ex Cuvier) 1817
Rhinonemus Gill 1863
Strinsia Rafinesque 1810

FAM. PHYCIDAE

Emphycus Jordan & Evermann 1898
Phycis Röse 1793
Phycis Bloch & Schneider 1801
Phycis Rafinesque 1810
Phycis Artedi in Walbaum 1792
Urophycis Gill 1863

FAM. MERLUCCIIDAE (Merluccid Hakes)

Subfam. Merlucciinae
Macruroninae included

Epicopus Günther 1860
Homalopomus Girard 1856
Huttonichthys Whitley 1937
Hydronus Minding 1832
Lyconodes Gilchrist 1922
Lyconus Günther 1887
Macruronus Günther 1873
Merlangus Rafinesque 1810
Merluccius Rafinesque 1810
Merlucius Gronow in Gray 1854
Merlus Guichenot 1848
Onus Rafinesque 1810
Polydatus Gistel 1848
Stomodon Mitchill 1814
Trachinoides Borodin 1934

Subfam. Steindachneriinae

Steindachnerella Eigenmann 1897
Steindachneria Goode & Bean in Agassiz 1888

ORDER OPHIDIIFORMES

Pseudophidium Gracianov 1907

FAM. OPHIDIIDAE (Cuskeels)

Brotulophis Kaup 1858
Eretmichthys Garman 1899
Leptobrotula Nielsen 1986
Leucobrotula Koefoed 1952
Parabrotula Zugmayer 1911
Pseudobythites Meek & Hildebrand 1928

Subfam. Brotulinae

Brotula Cuvier 1829
Geneiates Tickell in Day 1888
Nematobrotula Gill 1863

Subfam. Brotulotaeniinae

Brotulotaenia Parr 1933

Subfam. Ophidiinae

Brotuloides Robins 1961
Cherublemma Trotter 1926
Chilara Jordan & Evermann 1896
Genypterus Philippi 1857
Hoplophycis Kaup 1858
Lepophidium Gill 1895
Leptophidium Gill 1863
Ophidion Linnaeus 1758
Otophidium Gill in Jordan 1885
Parophidion Tortonese 1954
Raneya Robins 1961
Rissola Jordan & Evermann 1896
Xiphiurus Smith 1847

Subfam. Neobythitinae

Abyssobrotula Nielsen 1977
Acanthonus Günther 1878
Alcockia Goode & Bean 1896
Apagesoma Carter 1983
Barathrites Zugmayer 1911
Barathrodemus Goode & Bean 1883
Bassobythites Brauer 1906
Bassogigas Goode & Bean (ex Gill) 1896
Bassozetus Gill 1883
Bathynectes Günther 1878
Bathyonus Goode & Bean 1885
Benthocometes Goode & Bean 1896
Brachydicrolene Norman 1939
Brotella Kaup 1858
Celema Goode & Bean 1896
Dannevigia Whitley 1941
Dermatorus Alcock 1890
Dicrolene Goode & Bean 1883
Dicromita Goode & Bean 1896
Enchelybrotula Smith & Radcliffe in Radcliffe 1913
Epetriodus Cohen & Nielsen 1978
Glyptophidium Alcock 1889
Grimaldichthys Roule 1913
Holcomycteronus Garman 1899
Homostolus Smith & Radcliffe in Radcliffe 1913
Hoplobrotula Gill 1863
Hypopleuron Smith & Radcliffe in Radcliffe 1913
Itatius Matsubara 1943
Lamprogrammus Alcock 1891
Leucicorus Garman 1899
Luciobrotula Smith & Radcliffe in Radcliffe 1913
Mastigopterus Smith & Radcliffe in Radcliffe 1913
Mixonus Günther 1887
Moebia Goode & Bean 1896
Monomeropus Garman 1899
Monomitopus Alcock 1890
Nematonus Günther 1887
Neobythites Goode & Bean 1885
Parabassogigas Nybelin 1957
Paradicrolene Alcock 1889
Penopus Goode & Bean 1896
Petrotyx Heller & Snodgrass 1903
Porogadus Goode & Bean 1885
Pterodicromita Fowler 1925
Pteroidonus Günther 1887
Pycnocraspedum Alcock 1889
Selachophidium Gilchrist 1903
Sirembo Bleeker 1858
Spectrunculus Jordan & Thompson 1914
Spottobrotula Cohen & Nielsen 1978
Tauredophidium Alcock 1890
Tetranematopus Günther 1887
Typhlonus Günther 1878
Umalius Herre & Herald 1950
Volcanus Gosline 1954
Watasea Jordan & Snyder 1901
Xyelacyba Cohen 1961

FAM. CARAPIDAE

Subfam. Carapinae (Pearlfishes)

Carapus Rafinesque 1810
Diaphasia Lowe 1843
Disparichthys Herre 1935
Echiodon Thompson 1837
Encheliophiops Reid 1940
Encheliophis Müller 1842
Fierasfer Oken (ex Cuvier) 1817
Helminthodes Gill 1864
Helminthostoma Günther (ex Cocco) 1870
Jordanicus Gilbert 1905
Lefroyia Jones 1874
Leptofierasfer Meek & Hildebrand 1928
Onuxodon Smith 1955
Oxybeles Richardson 1846
Pirellinus Whitley 1928
Porobronchus Kaup 1860
Rhizoiketicus Vaillant 1893
Vexillifer Gasco 1870

Subfam. Pyramodontinae (Pyramodontines)
Cynophidium Regan 1914
Pyramodon Smith & Radcliffe in Radcliffe 1913
Snyderidia Gilbert 1905

FAM. BYTHITIDAE (Livebearing Brotulas)

Subfam. Bythitinae
Abythites Nielsen & Cohen 1973
Barbuliceps Chan 1966
Bathystorreus Howell Rivero 1934
Bellottia Giglioli 1883
Bythites Reinhardt 1835
Calamopteryx Böhlke & Cohen 1966
Cataetyx Günther 1887
Diplacanthopoma Günther 1887
Eutyx Heller & Snodgrass 1903
Gadopsis Filippi 1855
Grammonoides Smith 1948
Grammonus Gill in Goode & Bean 1896
Hephthocara Alcock 1892
Microbrotula Gosline 1953
Myxocephalus Steindachner in Steindachner & Döderlein 1887
Oculospinus Koefoed 1927
Pseudonus Garman 1899
Pteridium Filippi & Vérany 1859
Saccogaster Alcock 1889
Sarcocara Smith and Radcliffe in Radcliff 1913
Stygnobrotula Böhlke 1957
Thalassobathia Cohen 1963
Verater Jordan 1919 (1)
Verater Jordan 1919 (2)
Xenobythites Smith & Radcliffe in Radcliffe 1913

Subfam. Brosmophycinae
Bidenichthys Barnard 1934
Brosmodorsalis Paulin & Roberts 1989
Brosmophyciops Schultz in Schultz et al. 1960
Brosmophycis Gill 1861
Brotulina Fowler 1946
Caecogilbia Poll & Leleup 1965
Calcarbrotula Fowler 1946
Dermatopsis Ogilby 1896
Dermatopsoides Smith 1948
Diancistrus Ogilby 1899
Dinematichthys Bleeker 1855
Dipulus Waite 1905
Gunterichthys Dawson 1966
Halias Ayres 1860
Lucifuga Poey 1858
Melodichthys Nielsen & Cohen 1986
Monothrix Ogilby 1897
Ogilbia Jordan & Evermann in Evermann & Kendell 1898
Stygicola Gill 1863
Typhlias Hubbs 1938
Typhliasina Whitley 1951

FAM. APHYONIDAE (Aphyonids)
Alexeterion Vaillant 1888
Aphyonus Günther 1878
Barathronus Goode & Bean 1886
Leucochlamys Zugmayer 1911
Meteoria Nielsen 1969
Nybelinella Nielsen 1972
Nybelinia Nielsen 1969
Parasciadonus Nielsen 1984
Sciadonus Garman 1899

ORDER BATRACHOIDIFORMES

FAM. BATRACHOIDIDAE (Toadfishes)
Amphichthys Swainson 1839
Aphos Hubbs & Schultz 1939
Austrobatrachus Smith 1949
Barchatus Smith 1952
Bathybatrachus Gilchrist & von Bonde 1924
Batrachichthys Agassiz 1846 see *Batrictius* Rafinesque 1815.
Batrachoides Lacepède 1800
Batrachomoeus Ogilby 1908
Batrachus Bloch & Schneider 1801
Batrichthys Smith 1934
Batrictius Rafinesque 1815
Chatrabus Smith 1949
Coryzichthys Ogilby 1908
Daector Jordan & Evermann 1898
Gymnobatrachus Smith 1949
Halobatrachus Ogilby 1908
Halophryne Gill 1863
Marcgravia Jordan 1887
Marcgravichthys Miranda-Ribeiro 1915
Nautopaedium Jordan 1919
Opsanus Rafinesque 1818
Parabatrachus Roux 1971
Pelophiletor Ogilby 1906
Perulibatrachus Roux & Whitley 1972
Porichthys Girard 1854
Pseudobatrachus Castelnau 1875
Riekertia Smith 1952
Sanopus Smith 1952
Thalassophryne Günther 1861
Thalassothia Berg 1895
Tharbacus Smith 1952
Triathalassothia Fowler 1943

ORDER LOPHIIFORMES (Anglerfishes)

SUBORDER LOPHIOIDEI

FAM. LOPHIIDAE (Goosefishes or monkfishes)
Batrachus Klein 1776
Chirolophius Regan 1903
Conomus Rafinesque 1815
Discolophius Fowler 1943
Lophidius Rafinesque 1815
Lophiodes Goode & Bean 1896
Lophioides Minding 1832
Lophiomus Gill 1883
Lophiopside(s) see *Lophiopsis*
Lophiopsis Guichenot 1867
Lophius Linnaeus 1758
Pyrenophorus Le Danois 1975
Sladenia Regan 1908

SUBORDER ANTENNARIOIDEI

FAM. ANTENNARIIDAE (Frogfishes)
Abantennarius Schultz 1957
Allenichthys Pietsch 1984
Antennarius Commerson in Lacepède 1798
Antennarius Cuvier (ex Commerson) 1816
Antennarius Daudin 1816
Antennatus Schultz 1957
Batrachopus Goldfuss 1820
Capellaria Gistel 1848
Chironectes Cuvier 1817
Chironectes Rafinesque 1814
Echinophryne McCulloch & Waite 1918
Fowlerichthys Barbour 1941
Golem Whitley 1957
Histiophryne Gill 1863
Histrio Fischer von Waldheim 1813
Kanazawaichthys Schultz 1957
Kuiterichthys Pietsch 1984
Lophiocharon Whitley 1933
Nudiantennarius Schultz 1957
Phrynelox Whitley 1931
Phyllophryne Pietsch 1984
Phymatophryne Le Danois 1964
Plumantennatus Schultz 1957
Pterophryne Gill 1863
Pterophrynoides Gill 1878
Rhycherus Ogilby 1907
Saccarius Günther 1861
Tathicarpus Ogilby 1907
Triantennatus Schultz 1957
Trichophryne McCulloch & Waite 1918
Uniantennatus Schultz 1957
Xenophrynichthys Schultz 1957

FAM. TETRABRACHIIDAE
Tetrabrachium Günther 1880

FAM. LOPHICHTHYIDAE
Lophichthys Boeseman 1964

FAM. BRACHIONICHTHYIDAE (Warty Anglerfishes)
Brachionichthys Bleeker 1855
Sympterichthys Gill 1878

SUBORDER CHAUNACIOIDEI

FAM. CHAUNACIDAE (Sea Toads)
Bathychaunax Caruso 1989
Chaunax Lowe 1846

SUBORDER OGCOCEPHALIOIDEI

FAM. OGCOCEPHALIDAE (Batfishes)
Astrocanthus Swainson 1839
Coelophrys Brauer 1902
Dibranchichthys Garman 1899
Dibranchopsis Garman 1899
Dibranchus Peters 1876
Halicmetus Alcock 1891
Halieutaea Valenciennes in Cuvier & Valenciennes 1837
Halieutella Goode & Bean 1885
Halieutichthys Poey in Gill 1863
Halieutopsis Garman 1899
Malthe Cuvier 1816
Malthopsis Alcock 1891

Ogcocephalus Fischer von Waldheim 1813
Zalieutes Jordan & Evermann 1896

SUBORDER CERATIOIDEI (Deepsea Anglerfishes)

Anomalophryne Regan & Trewavas 1932
Bathyceratias Beebe 1934
Cryptolychnus Regan & Trewavas 1932
Diabolidium Beebe 1926
Nannoceratias Regan & Trewavas 1932

FAM. CAULOPHRYNIDAE

Caulophryne Goode & Bean 1896
Ceratocaulophryne Roule & Angel 1932
Robia Pietsch 1979

FAM. NEOCERATIIDAE

Neoceratias Pappenheim 1914

FAM. MELANOCETIDAE

Centrocetus Regan & Trewavas 1932
Liocetus Günther 1887
Lyocetus Günther 1887
Melanocetus Günther 1864
Xenoceratias Regan & Trewavas 1932

FAM. HIMANTOLOPHIDAE (Footballfishes)

Aegaeonichthys Clarke 1878
Corynolophus Gill 1878
Corynophorus Osório 1912
Himantolophus Reinhardt 1837
Lipactis Regan 1925
Rhynchoceratias Regan 1925

FAM. DICERATIIDAE

Aeschynichthys Ogilby 1907
Bufoceratias Whitley 1931
Diceratias Günther 1887
Paroneirodes Alcock 1890
Phrynichthys Pietschmann 1926

FAM. ONEIRODIDAE

Bertella Pietsch 1973
Bertelsenna Whitley 1954
Caranactis Regan & Trewavas 1932
Chaenophryne Regan 1925
Chirophryne Regan & Trewavas 1932
Ctenochirichthys Regan & Trewavas 1932
Danaphryne Bertelsen 1951
Dermatias Smith & Radcliffe in Radcliffe 1912
Dolopichthys Garman 1899
Leptacanthichthys Regan & Trewavas 1932
Lophodolos Lloyd 1909
Microlophichthys Regan & Trewavas 1932
Monoceratias Gilbert 1915
Oneirodes Lütken 1871
Pentherichthys Regan & Trewavas 1932
Phyllorhinichthys Pietsch 1969
Pietschichthys Kharin 1989
Puck Pietsch 1978
Spiniphryne Bertelsen 1951
Trematorhynchus Regan & Trewavas 1932
Tyrannophryne Regan & Trewavas 1932

FAM. THAUMATICHTHYIDAE

Amacrodon Regan & Trewavas 1932
Galatheathauma Bruun 1953
Lasiognathus Regan 1925
Thaumatichthys Smith & Radcliffe 1912

FAM. CENTROPHRYNIDAE

Centrophryne Regan & Trewavas 1932

FAM. CERATIIDAE (Seadevils)

Ceratias Krøyer 1845
Cryptopsaras Gill 1883
Mancalias Gill 1878
Miopsaras Gilbert 1905
Paraceratias Tanaka 1908
Parrichthys Barbour 1942
Reganichthys Bigelow & Barbour 1944
Reganula Bigelow & Barbour 1944
Typhloceratias Barbour 1942
Typlopsaras Gill 1883

FAM. GIGANTACTINIDAE (Whipnoses)

Gigantactis Brauer 1902
Laevoceratias Parr 1927
Rhynchactis Regan 1925
Teleotrema Regan & Trewavas 1932

FAM. LINOPHRYNIDAE

Acentrophryne Regan 1926
Aceratias Brauer 1902
Allector Heller & Snodgrass 1903
Borophryne Regan 1925
Edriolychnus Regan 1925
Haplophryne Regan 1912
Hyaloceratias Koefoed 1944
Linophryne Collett 1886
Photocorynus Regan 1925
Rhizophryne Bertelsen 1982
Stephanophryne Bertelsen 1982

ORDER GOBIESOCIFORMES

FAM. GOBIESOCIDAE (Clingfishes)

Subfam. Gobiesocinae (Clingfishes)

Acyrtops Schultz 1951
Acyrtus Schultz 1944
Apepton Gistel 1848
Apletodon Briggs 1955
Arbaciosa Jordan & Evermann in Jordan 1896
Arcos Schultz 1944
Aspasma Jordan & Fowler 1902
Aspasmichthys Briggs 1955
Aspasmodes Smith 1957
Aspasmogaster Waite 1907
Athaena Castelnau 1861
Bryssetaeres Jordan & Evermann in Jordan 1896
Bryssophilus Jordan & Evermann 1898
Caularchus Gill 1862
Caulistius Jordan & Evermann 1896
Chorisochismus Brisout de Barneville 1846
Cochleoceps Whitley 1943
Conidens Briggs 1955
Coronichthys Herre 1942
Cotylichthys Jordan 1919
Cotylis Müller & Troschel in Müller 1843
Creocele Briggs 1955
Crepidogaster Günther 1861
Dellichthys Briggs 1955
Derilissus Briggs 1969
Diademichthys Pfaff 1942
Diplecogaster Fraser-Brunner 1938
Diplocrepis Günther 1861
Discotrema Briggs 1976
Eckloniaichthys Smith 1943
Gastrocyathus Briggs 1955
Gastrocymba Briggs 1955
Gastroscyphus Briggs 1955
Gobiesox Lacepède 1800
Gouania Nardo 1833
Gymnoscyphus Böhlke & Robins 1970
Haplocylix Briggs 1955
Infratridens Schultz 1944
Kopua Hardy 1984
Lecanogaster Briggs 1957
Lepadichthys Waite 1904
Lepadogaster Goüan 1770
Lepadogasterus Duméril 1806
Leptopterygius Troschel 1860
Liobranchia Briggs 1955
Lissonanchus Smith 1966
Megaphalus Rafinesque 1815
Mirbelia Canestrini 1864
Modicus Hardy 1983
Oliverichthus Whitley & Phillipps 1939
Opeatogenys Briggs 1955
Parvicrepis Whitley 1931
Pherallodichthys Shiogaki & Dotsu 1983
Pherallodiscus Briggs 1955
Pherallodus Briggs 1955
Piescephalus Rafinesque 1810
Propherallodus Shiogaki & Dotsu 1983
Rimicola Jordan & Evermann in Jordan 1896
Rupisuga Swainson 1839
Sicyases Müller & Troschel in Müller 1843
Sicyogaster Brisout de Barneville 1846
Tomicodon Brisout de Barneville 1846
Trachelochismus Brisout de Barneville 1846
Volgiolus Whitley 1931

Subfam. Cheilobranchinae
= Alabetidae

Alabes Cloquet 1816
Cheilobranchus Richardson 1845

ORDER ATHERINIFORMES

FAM. ATHERINIDAE (Silversides)

Subfam. Atherinopsinae

Atherinops Steindachner 1875
Atherinopsis Girard 1854
Austroatherina Marrero 1950
Austromenidia Hubbs 1918
Bachmannia Nani in Szidat & Nani 1951
Basilichthys Girard 1855
Cauque Eigenmann 1928
Colpichthys Hubbs 1918
Gastropterus Cope 1878
Hubbsiella Breder 1936
Kronia Miranda-Ribeiro 1915
Leuresthes Jordan & Gilbert 1880
Odontesthes Evermann & Kendall 1906
Patagonina Eigenmann 1928
Pisciregia Abbott 1899

Protistius Cope 1874
Pseudothyrina Miranda-Ribeiro 1915
Sorgentinia Risso & Risso 1953
Tupa de Buen 1953
Yaci de Buen 1953

Subfam. Menidiinae
Adenops Schultz 1948
Allomastax Chernoff 1986
Archomenidia Jordan & Hubbs 1919
Argyrea DeKay 1842
Atherinella Steindachner 1875
Atherinichthys Bleeker 1853
Atherinoides Bleeker 1853
Atherthyrina Fowler 1958
Charalia de Buen 1945
Chirostoma Swainson 1839
Coleotropis Myers & Wade 1942
Eslopsarum Jordan & Evermann 1896
Euryarges Myers & Wade 1942
Eurystole Jordan & Evermann in Jordan 1895
Heterognathus Girard 1855
Hubbesia Jordan 1919
Ischnomembras Fowler 1903
Kirtlandia Jordan & Evermann 1896
Labidesthes Cope 1870
Lethostole Jordan & Evermann 1896
Melaniris Meek 1902
Melanorhinus Metzelaar 1919
Membras Bonaparte 1836
Menidia Bonaparte 1836
Menidiella Schultz 1948
Mugilops Meek & Hildebrand 1923
Nectarges Myers & Wade 1942
Ocotlanichthys de Buen 1945
Otalia de Buen 1945
Palmichthys de Buen 1945
Phoxargyrea Fowler 1903
Poblana de Buen 1945
Thyrina Jordan & Culver in Jordan 1895
Thyrinops Hubbs 1918
Xenatherina Regan 1907
Xenomelaniris Schultz 1948

Subfam. Notocheirinae
Isonidae included
Iso Jordan & Starks 1901
Notocheirus Clark 1937
Tropidostethops Schultz 1950
Tropidostethus Ogilby 1895

Subfam. Atherioninae
Atherion Jordan & Starks 1901

Subfam. Atherininae
Alepidomus Hubbs 1944
Allanetta Whitley 1943
Atherina Linnaeus 1758
Atherinason Whitley 1934
Atherinomorus Fowler 1903
Atherinosoma Castelnau 1872
Craterocephalus McCulloch 1912
Hepsetia Bonaparte 1836
Hypoatherina Schultz 1948
Kestratherina Pavlov, Ivantsoff, Last & Crowley 1988
Leptatherina Pavlov, Ivantsoff, Last & Crowley 1988
Pranesella Whitley 1934
Pranesus Whitley 1930
Stenatherina Schultz 1948
Taeniomembras Ogilby 1898
Teramulus Smith 1965
Thoracatherina Fowler 1941

Subfam. Bedotiinae
Bedotia Regan 1903
Rheocles Jordan & Hubbs in Jordan 1919
Rheocloides Nichols & La Monte 1931

Subfam. Dentatherininae
Dentatherina Patten & Ivantsoff 1983

Subfam. Pseudomugilinae
Telmatherinidae included
Kiunga Allen 1983
Paratherina Aurich 1935
Popondetta Allen 1980
Popondichthys Allen 1987
Pseudomugil Kner 1866
Quirichthys Whitley 1951
Quiris Whitley 1950
Telmatherina Boulenger 1897

Subfam. Melanotaeniinae (Rainbowfishes)
Aida Castelnau 1875
Aidaprora Whitley 1935
Amneris Whitley 1935
Anisocentrus Regan 1914
Aristeus Castelnau 1878
Cairnsichthys Allen 1980
Centratherina Regan 1914
Charisella Fowler 1939
Chilatherina Regan 1914
Glossolepis Weber 1907
Iriatherina Meinken 1974
Lomanetia Whitley 1936
Melanotaenia Gill 1862
Nematocentris Peters 1866
Neoatherina Castelnau 1875
Rhadinocentrus Regan 1914
Rhombatractus Gill 1894
Rhombosoma Regan 1914
Strabo Kner & Steindachner 1867
Zantecla Castelnau 1873

FAM. PHALLOSTETHIDAE
Neostethidae included

Acanthostethus Herre 1939
Ceratostethus Myers 1937
Ctenophallus Herre 1939
Gulaphallus Herre 1925
Manacopus Herre 1940
Mirophallus Herre 1926
Neostethus Regan 1916
Phallostethus Regan 1913
Phenacostethus Myers 1928
Plectrostethus Myers 1935
Sandakanus Herre 1942
Solenophallus Herre (ex Aurich) 1953
Solenophallus Aurich 1937

ORDER CYPRINODONTIFORMES

FAM. APLOCHEILIDAE (Rivulines)

Subfam. Aplocheilinae (Old World Rivulines)
Adamas Huber 1979
Adiniops Myers 1924
Aphyobranchius Wildekamp 1977
Aphyoplatys Clausen 1967
Aphyosemion Myers 1924
Aplocheilus McClelland 1839
Archiaphyosemion Radda 1977
Callopanchax Myers 1933
Chromaphyosemion Radda 1971
Diapteron Huber & Seegers 1977
Epiplatys Gill 1862
Episemion Radda & Pürzl 1987
Foerschichthys Scheel & Romand 1981
Fundulopanchax Myers 1924
Fundulosoma Ahl 1924
Gularopanchax Radda 1977
Haplochilus see *Aplocheilus*
Kathetys Huber 1977
Lycocyprinus Peters 1868
Mesoaphyosemion Radda 1977
Nothobranchius Peters 1868
Pachypanchax Myers 1933
Paludopanchax Radda 1977
Panchax Valenciennes in Cuvier & Valenciennes 1846
Paranothobranchius Seegers 1985
Paraphyosemion Kottelat 1976
Parepiplatys Clausen 1967
Platypanchax Ahl 1928
Pronothobranchius Radda 1969
Pseudepiplatys Clausen 1967
Raddaella Huber 1977
Roloffia Clausen 1966
Scriptaphyosemion Radda & Pürzl 1987
Zononothobranchius Radda 1969

Subfam. Rivulinae (New World Rivulines)
Austrofundulus Myers 1932
Campellolebias Vaz-Ferreira & Sierra 1974
Cynodonichthys Meek 1904
Cynolebias Steindachner 1876
Cynopoecilus Regan 1912
Leptolebias Myers 1952
Moema Costa 1989
Neofundulus Myers 1924
Pituna Costa 1989
Plesiolebias Costa 1989
Pterolebias Garman 1895
Rachovia Myers 1927
Rivulichthys Myers 1927
Rivulus Poey 1860
Simpsonichthys Carvalho 1959
Terranatos Taphorn & Thomerson 1978
Trigonectes Myers 1925
Vomerivulus Fowler 1944

FAM. CYPRINODONTIDAE (Killifishes)

Subfam. Cyprinodontinae
Alpismaris Risso 1826
Anatolichthys Kosswig & Sözer 1945
Aphaniops Hoedeman 1951
Aphanius Nardo 1827
Cualac Miller 1956
Cyprinodon Lacepède (ex Bosc) 1803
Encrates Gistel 1848
Floridichthys Hubbs 1926
Garmanella Hubbs 1936
Jordanella Goode & Bean in Goode 1879

Kosswigichthys Sözer 1942
Lebia Oken (ex Cuvier) 1817
Lebias of authors
Megupsilon Miller & Walters 1972
Micromugil Gulia 1861
Orestias Valenciennes in Cuvier & Valenciennes 1846
Prinodon Rafinesque 1815
Protorestias Eigenmann & Allen 1942
Tellia Gervais 1853
Trifarcius Poey 1860

Subfam. Valenciinae
Valencia Myers 1928

Subfam. Aplocheilichthyinae
Andreasenius Clausen 1959
Aplocheilichthys Bleeker 1863
Atopocheilichthys Boulenger 1915
Congopanchax Poll 1971
Cynopanchax Ahl 1928
Hylopanchax Poll & Lambert 1965
Hypsopanchax Myers 1924
Laciris Huber 1981
Lacustricola Myers 1924
Lamprichthys Regan 1911
Micropanchax Myers 1924
Mohanga Boulenger 1911
Pantanodon Myers 1955
Plataplochilus Ahl 1928
Poropanchax Clausen 1967
Procatopus Boulenger 1904

Subfam. Profundulinae
Profundulus Hubbs 1924
Tlaloc Alvarez & Carranza 1951

Subfam. Fundulinae
Adinia Girard 1859
Borborys Goode & Bean (ex Broussonet/Linnaeus) 1885
Chriopeops Fowler 1916
Fontinus Jordan & Evermann 1896
Fundulus Lacepède 1803
Galasaccus Fowler 1916
Gambusinus Jordan & Evermann 1896
Hydrargira Lacepède 1803
Leptolucania Myers 1924
Lucania Girard 1859
Micristius Gill 1865
Plancterus Garman 1895
Xenisma Jordan 1876
Zygonectes Agassiz 1854

Subfam. Cubanichthyinae
Chriopeoides Fowler 1939
Cubanichthys Hubbs 1926

Subfam. Fluviphylacinae
Fluviphylax Whitley 1965
Potamophylax Myers & Carvalho in Myers 1955

Subfam. Empetrichthyinae
Crenichthys Hubbs 1932
Empetrichthys Gilbert 1893

FAM. GOODEIDAE (Goodeids)
Allodontichthys Hubbs & Turner 1939
Alloophorus Hubbs & Turner 1939
Allotoca Hubbs & Turner 1939
Ameca Miller & Fitzsimmons 1971
Ataeniobius Hubbs & Turner 1939
Balsadichthys Hubbs 1926
Chapalichthys Meek 1902
Characodon Günther 1866
Girardinichthys Bleeker 1860
Goodea Jordan 1880
Hubbsina de Buen 1940
Ilyodon Eigenmann 1907
Lermichthys Hubbs 1926
Limnurgus Günther 1866
Neoophorus Hubbs & Turner 1939
Neotoca Hubbs & Turner 1939
Ollentodon Hubbs & Turner 1939
Skiffia Meek 1902
Tapatia Alvarez & Arriola-Longoria 1972
Xenendum Jordan & Snyder 1899
Xenoophorus Hubbs & Turner 1939
Xenotaenia Turner 1946
Xenotoca Hubbs & Turner 1939
Zoogoneticus Meek 1902

FAM. POECILIIDAE (Livebearers)
Acanthophacelus Eigenmann 1907
Acropoecilia Hilgendorf 1889
Alazon Gistel 1848
Alfaro Meek 1912
Allodontium Howell Rivero & Rivas 1944
Allogambusia Hubbs 1924
Alloheterandria Hubbs 1924
Allophallus Hubbs 1936
Allopoecilia Hubbs 1924
Arizonichthys Nichols 1940
Arthrophallus Hubbs 1926
Aulophallus Hubbs 1926
Belonesox Kner 1860
Brachyrhaphis Regan 1913
Carlhubbsia Whitley 1951
Cnesterodon Garman 1895
Curtipenis Rivas & Myers 1950
Dactylophallus Howell Rivero & Rivas 1944
Darienichthys Hubbs 1924
Dicerophallus Alvarez 1952
Diphyacantha Henn 1916
Flexipenis Hubbs in Rivas 1963
Furcipenis Hubbs 1931
Gambusia Poey 1854
Girardinus Poey 1854
Glaridichthys Garman 1896
Glaridodon Garman 1895
Gulapinnus Langer 1913
Hemixiphophorus Bleeker 1859
Heterandria Agassiz 1853
Heterophallina Hubbs 1926
Heterophallus Regan 1914
Hubbsichthys Schultz 1949
Lebistes Filippi 1861
Lembesseia Fowler 1949
Leptorhaphis Regan 1913
Limia Poey 1854
Micropoecilia Hubbs 1926
Mollienesia Lesueur 1821
Neoheterandria Henn 1916
Neopoecilia Hubbs 1924
Odontolimia Rivas 1980
Orthophallus Rivas 1963
Pamphoria Regan 1913
Pamphorichthys Regan 1913
Panamichthys Hubbs 1924
Paragambusia Meek 1904
Parapoecilia Hubbs 1924
Petalosoma Regan 1908
Petalurichthys Regan 1912
Phallichthys Hubbs 1924
Phalloceros Eigenmann 1907
Phalloptychus Eigenmann 1907
Phallotorynus Henn 1916
Platypoecilus Günther 1866
Plectrophallus Fowler 1932
Poecilia Bloch & Schneider 1801
Poeciliopsis Regan 1913
Poecilistes Hubbs 1926
Poeciloides Steindachner 1863
Priapella Regan 1913
Priapichthys Regan 1913
Pseudopoecilia Regan 1913
Pseudoxiphophorus Bleeker 1859
Psychropoecilia Myers 1935
Quintana Hubbs 1934
Recepoecilia Whitley 1951
Schizophallus Hubbs 1926
Scolichthys Rosen 1967
Tomeurus Eigenmann 1909
Toxus Eigenmann 1903
Trigonophallus Hubbs 1926
Xenodexia Hubbs 1950
Xenophallus Hubbs 1924
Xiphophorus Heckel 1848

FAM. ANABLEPIDAE

Subfam. Anablepinae (Four-eyed Fishes)
Anableps Gronow 1763
Anableps Scopoli (ex Gronow) 1777
Anableps Bloch (ex Gronow) 1794
Peltatetraops Fowler 1931

Subfam. Jenynsiinae (Jenynsiids)
Fitzroyia Günther 1866
Jenynsia Günther 1866

Subfam. Oxyzygonectinae
Oxyzygonectes Fowler 1916

ORDER BELONIFORMES

SUBORDER ADRIANICHTHYOIDEI

FAM. ADRIANICHTHYIDAE

Subfam. Oryziinae (Medakas or Ricefishes)
Oryzias Jordan & Snyder 1906

Subfam. Adrianichthyinae (Adrianichthyids)
Adrianichthys Weber 1913
Xenopoecilus Regan 1911

Subfam. Horaichthyinae
Horaichthys Kulkarni 1940

SUBORDER EXOCOETOIDEI

FAM. SCOMBERESOCIDAE (Sauries)

Cololabis Gill 1895
Elassichthys Hubbs & Wisner 1980
Grammiconotus Costa 1862
Nanichthys Hubbs & Wisner 1980
Sayris Rafinesque 1810
Scomberesox Lacepède 1803

FAM. BELONIDAE (Needlefishes)

Ablennes Jordan & Fordice 1887
Acus Müller [P. L. S.] 1774
Athlennes Jordan & Fordice 1887
Belone Cuvier 1816
Belonion Collette 1966
Busuanga Herre 1930
Deltatylosurus Martin 1954
Djulongius Whitley 1935
Dorybelone Fowler 1944
Eurycaulus Ogilby 1908
Lewinichthys Whitley 1933
Mastaccembelus Klein 1776
Petalichthys Regan 1904
Platybelone Fowler 1919
Potamorrhaphis Günther 1866
Pseudotylosurus Fernández-Yépez 1948
Ramphistoma see *Raphistoma*
Raphistoma Rafinesque 1815
Rhaphiobelone Fowler 1934
Stenocaulus Ogilby 1908
Strongylura van Hasselt 1824
Thalassosteus Jordan, Evermann & Tanaka 1927
Tropidocaulus Ogilby 1919
Tylosurus Cocco 1833
Xenentodon Regan 1911

FAM. HEMIRAMPHIDAE (Halfbeaks)

Ardeapiscis Whitley 1931
Arrhamphus Günther 1866
Chriodorus Goode & Bean 1882
Dermogenys Kuhl & van Hasselt in van Hasselt 1823
Eulepidorhamphus Fowler 1919
Euleptorhamphus Gill 1859
Farhians Whitley 1930
Grecarchopterus Mohsen 1962
Hemiramphus Cuvier 1816
Hemirhamphodon Bleeker 1866
Hyporhamphus Gill 1859
Ichthyacus Fernández-Yépez 1948
Labidorhamphus Fowler 1905
Loligorhamphus Whitley 1931
Melapedalion Fowler 1934
Nomorhamphus Weber & de Beaufort 1922
Odontorhamphus Weed 1933
Oxyporhamphus Gill 1864
Reporhamphus Whitley 1931
Rhamphodermogenys Fowler & Bean 1922
Rhynchorhamphus Fowler 1928
Zenarchopterus Gill 1864

FAM. EXOCOETIDAE (Flyingfishes)

Abeichthys Parin 1961
Cheilopogon Lowe 1841
Cypselurus Swainson 1838
Cypsilurus see *Cypselurus*
Danichthys Bruun 1934
Eucypsilurus Bruun 1935
Evolantia Heller & Snodgrass 1903
Exocoetus Linnaeus 1758
Exonautes Jordan & Evermann 1896
Fodiator Jordan & Meek 1885
Halocypselus Weinland 1858
Hemiexocoetus Fowler 1901
Hirundichthys Breder 1928
Hirundo Catesby 1771
Lhotskia Whitley 1933
Maculocoetus Whitley & Colefax 1938
Paracypselurus Parin 1961
Parexocoetoides Fowler 1944
Parexocoetus Bleeker 1866
Poecilocypsilurus Bruun 1935
Procypsilurus Bruun 1935
Prognichthys Breder 1928
Ptenichthys Müller 1843
Ptenonotus Ogilby 1908
Pterichthus Commerson in Lacepède 1803

ORDER LAMPRIFORMES = Lampridiformes

SUBORDER LAMPROIDEI

FAM. LAMPRIDAE (Opahs)

Chrysotosus Lacepède 1802
Echemythes Gistel 1848
Lampris Retzius 1799

SUBORDER VELIFEROIDEI

FAM. VELIFERIDAE (Velifers)

Metavelifer Walters 1960
Velifer Temminck & Schlegel 1850

SUBORDER TRACHIPTEROIDEI

FAM. LOPHOTIDAE (Crestfishes)

Eumecichthys Regan 1907
Leptopus Rafinesque 1814
Lophotes Bosc 1817
Lophotopsis Barnard 1925
Lophotus Giorna 1809
Podoleptus Rafinesque 1815
Regilophotes Whitley 1933

FAM. RADIICEPHALIDAE (Tapertails)

Radiicephalus Osório 1917

FAM. TRACHIPTERIDAE (Ribbonfishes)

Argyctius Rafinesque 1810
Bogmarus Bloch & Schneider 1801
Cephalepis Rafinesque 1810
Desmodema Walters & Fitch 1960
Epidesmus Ranzani 1818
Gymnogaster Brünnich 1788
Nemochirus Rafinesque 1815
Nemotherus Costa (ex Risso) 1834
Trachipterus Goüan 1770
Trachypterus Bloch & Schneider 1801
Vogmarus Reid 1849
Vogmarus Reinhardt 1832
Zu Walters & Fitch 1960

FAM. REGALECIDAE (Oarfishes)

Agrostichthys Phillipps 1924
Gymnetrus Bloch 1795
Regalecus Brünnich 1771
Regalecus Ascanius 1772
Xiphichthys Swainson 1839
Xypterus Rafinesque 1810

SUBORDER STYLEPHOROIDEI

FAM. STYLEPHORIDAE (Tube-Eyes or Thread-Tails)

Stylephorus Shaw 1791

SUBORDER ATELEOPODOIDEI

FAM. ATELEOPODIDAE

Anodontus Cervigón 1961
Ateleopus Temminck & Schlegel 1846
Guentherus Osório 1917
Ijimaia Sauter 1905
Melanogloea Barnard 1941
Parateleopus Smith & Radcliffe in Radcliffe 1912
Podateles Boulenger 1902

SUBORDER MIRAPINNATOIDEI

FAM. MIRAPINNIDAE (Hairyfish and ribbontails) Eutaeniophoridae included

Eutaeniophorus Bertelsen & Marshall 1958
Mirapinna Bertelsen & Marshall 1956
Parataeniophorus Bertelsen & Marshall 1956
Taeniophorus Bertelsen & Marshall 1956

SUBORDER MEGALOMYCTEROIDEI

FAM. MEGALOMYCTERIDAE (Largenose fishes)

Ataxolepis Myers & Freihofer 1966
Cetomimoides Koefoed 1955
Megalomycter Myers & Freihofer 1966
Vitiaziella Rass 1955

ORDER BERYCIFORMES

SUBORDER BERCOIDEI

FAM. MONOCENTRIDAE (Pinecone Fishes)

Cleidopus De Vis 1882
Ericius Tilesius 1809
Lepicantha Rafinesque 1815
Lepisacanthus Lacepède 1801
Monocentris Bloch & Schneider 1801

FAM. TRACHICHTHYIDAE (Slimeheads)

Aulohoplostethus Fowler 1938

Aulotrachichthys Fowler 1938
Gephyroberyx Boulenger 1902
Hoplostethus Cuvier in Cuvier & Valenciennes 1829
Korsogaster Parr 1933
Leiogaster Weber 1913
Macrohoplostethus Kotlyar 1986
Optivus Whitley 1947
Paratrachichthys Waite 1899
Parinoberyx Kotlyar 1984
Sorosichthys Whitley 1945
Trachichthys Shaw in Shaw & Nodder 1799

FAM. ANOMALOPIDAE (Lanterneye Fishes)
Anomalops Kner 1868
Heterophthalmus Bleeker 1856
Kryptophanaron Silvester & Fowler 1926
Photoblepharon Weber 1902
Phthanophaneron Johnson & Rosenblatt 1988

FAM. DIRETMIDAE (Spinyfins)
Campbellina Fowler 1958
Diretmoides Post & Quero 1981
Diretmus Johnson 1864
Discus Campbell 1879
Gyrinomene Vaillant 1888

FAM. ANOPLOGASTRIDAE (Fangtooths)
Anoplogaster Günther 1859
Caulolepis Gill 1883

FAM. BERYCIDAE (Berycids or Alfonsinos)
Actinoberyx Roule 1923
Austroberyx McCulloch 1911
Beryx Cuvier 1829
Centroberyx Gill 1862
Trachichthodes Gilchrist 1903

FAM. HOLOCENTRIDAE (Squirrelfishes and Soldierfishes)
Adioryx Starks 1908
Archaeomyripristis Greenfield 1974
Beloholocentrus Fowler 1944
Cephalofarer Whitley 1933
Corniger Agassiz in Spix & Agassiz 1831
Dispinus Li in Li, Wang & Wu 1981
Erythrinus Plumier in Lacepède 1802
Faremusca Whitley 1933
Farer Forsskål 1775
Flammeo Jordan & Evermann 1898
Harpage De Vis 1884
Holocentrus Gronow 1763
Holocentrus Scopoli (ex Gronow) 1777
Holocentrus Bloch 1790
Holotrachys Günther 1874
Kutaflammeo Whitley 1933
Myripristis Cuvier 1829
Neomyripristis Castelnau 1873
Neoniphon Castelnau 1875
Ostichthys Cuvier (ex Langsdorf) in Cuvier & Valenciennes 1829
Ostichthys Jordan & Evermann (ex Langsdorf) 1896
Plectrypops Gill 1862
Pristilepis Randall, Shimizu & Yamakawa 1982
Rhamphoberyx Gill 1863
Rhinoberyx Gill 1862
Rhynchichthys Valenciennes in Cuvier & Valenciennes 1831
Sargocentron Fowler 1904

SUBORDER STEPHANOBERYCOIDEI

FAM. STEPHANOBERYCIDAE (Pricklefishes)
Acanthochaenus Gill 1884
Malacosarcus Günther 1887
Stephanoberyx Gill 1883

FAM. HISPIDOBERYCIDAE
Hispidoberyx Kotlyar 1981

FAM. MELAMPHAIDAE (Bigscales) = Melamphaeidae
Lophocephalus Osório 1906
Melamphaes Günther 1864
Metopias Lowe 1843
Plectromus Gill 1883
Poromitra Goode & Bean 1883
Poromitrella Zugmayer 1911
Scopeloberyx Zugmayer 1911
Scopelogadus Vaillant 1888
Sio Moss 1962

FAM. GIBBERICHTHYIDAE
Gibberichthys Parr 1933
Kasidoron Robins & De Sylva 1965

SUBORDER POLYMIXIOIDEI

FAM. POLYMIXIIDAE (Beardfishes)
Dinemus Poey 1860
Nemobrama Valenciennes in Webb & Berthelot 1837
Polymixia Lowe 1836

ORDER CETOMIMIFORMES

FAM. RONDELETIIDAE (Redmouth Whalefishes)
Rondeletia Goode & Bean 1895

FAM. BARBOURISIIDAE (Velvet Whalefishes)
Barbourisia Parr 1945

FAM. CETOMIMIDAE (Whalefishes)
Cetichthys Paxton 1989
Cetomimus Goode & Bean 1895
Cetostoma Zugmayer 1914
Danacetichthys Paxton 1989
Ditropichthys Parr 1934
Gyrinomimus Parr 1934
Notocetichthys Balushkin, Fedorov & Paxton 1989
Pelecinomimus Gilchrist 1922
Procetichthys Paxton 1989
Psapharocetus Harry 1952
Rhamphocetichthys Paxton 1989

ORDER ZEIFORMES

FAM. PARAZENIDAE
Parazen Kamohara 1935

FAM. MACRUROCYTTIDAE Zeniidae included
Cyttula Weber 1913
Macrurocyttus Fowler 1934
Zenion Jordan & Evermann 1896

FAM. ZEIDAE (Dories)
Capromimus Gill 1893
Cyttoides Smith 1947
Cyttoidops Smith 1949
Cyttomimus Gilbert 1905
Cyttopsis Gill 1862
Cyttus Günther 1860
Microzeus Blyth 1860
Paracyttopsis Gilchrist & von Bonde 1924
Parazenopsis Cligny 1909
Rhombocyttus Gill 1893
Stethopristes Gilbert 1905
Zen Jordan 1903
Zenopsis Gill 1862
Zeus Linnaeus 1758

FAM. OREOSOMATIDAE (Oreos)
Allocyttus McCulloch 1914
Crassispinus Maul 1948
Cyttosoma Gilchrist 1904
Neocyttus Gilchrist 1906
Oreosoma Cuvier 1829
Pseudocyttus Gilchrist 1906
Xenocyttus Abe 1957

FAM. GRAMMICOLEPIDIDAE (Diamond Dories)
Daramattus Smith 1960
Grammicolepis Poey 1873
Vesposus Jordan 1921
Xenolepidichthys Gilchrist 1922

FAM. CAPROIDAE (Boarfishes)
Antigonia Lowe 1843
Caprophonus Müller & Troschel 1849
Capros Lacepède 1802
Hypsinotus Temminck & Schlegel 1844

ORDER GASTEROSTEIFORMES

FAM. HYPOPTYCHIDAE (Sand-Eels)
Hypoptychus Steindachner 1881
Rhynchias Gill in Jordan & Evermann 1898

FAM. GASTEROSTEIDAE (Sticklebacks and Tubesnouts)

Subfam. Gasterosteinae (Sticklebacks)
Apeltes DeKay 1842
Culaea Whitley 1950
Eucalia Jordan 1876
Gasteracanthus Pallas 1814
Gasterostea Sauvage 1874
Gasterosteus Linnaeus 1758
Gastraea Sauvage 1874

Gladiunculus Jordan & Evermann 1927
Leiurus Swainson 1839
Obolarius Tilesius (ex Steller) 1810
Polycanthus Swainson 1839
Pungitius Coste 1848
Pygosteus Gill (ex Brevoort) 1861
Spinachia Cuvier 1816
Spinachia Fleming 1828

Subfam. Aulorhynchinae (Tubesnouts)
Aulichthys Brevoort in Gill 1862
Auliscops Peters 1866
Aulorhynchus Gill 1861

FAM. INDOSTOMIDAE
Indostomus Prashad & Mukerji 1929

FAM. PEGASIDAE (Seamoths)
Acanthopegasus McCulloch 1915
Cataphractus Gronow 1763
Eurypegasus Bleeker 1863
Leptopegasus Bleeker 1873
Parapegasus Duméril (ex Bleeker) 1870
Pegasus Linnaeus 1758
Spinipegasus Rendahl 1930
Zalises Jordan & Snyder 1901

ORDER SYNGNATHIFORMES

SUBORDER AULOSTOMOIDEI

FAM. AULOSTOMIDAE (Trumpetfishes)
Aulostomus Lacepède 1803
Polypterichthys Bleeker 1853
Solenostoma Dumèril (ex Gronow) 1806
Solenostomus Gray (ex Klein and Gronow) 1854

FAM. FISTULARIIDAE (Cornetfishes)
Aulus Commerson in Lacepède 1803
Cannorynchus Cantor 1849
Fistularia Linnaeus 1758
Flagellaria Gronow in Gray 1854
Petimbuabo Catesby 1771
Solenostomus Gronow 1763
Solenostomus Klein 1778
Solenostomus Browne 1789
Solenostomus Gill (ex Gronow) 1861

FAM. CENTRISCIDAE

Subfam. Macroramphosinae (Snipefishes)
Centriscus Cuvier 1816
Limiculina Fowler 1907
Macrognathus Gronow in Gray 1854
Macroramphosus Lacepède 1803
Notopogon Regan 1914
Orthichthys Gill 1862
Scolopacichthys Regan 1914

Subfam. Centriscinae (Shrimpfishes)
Acentrachme Gill 1862
Aeoliscus Jordan & Starks 1902
Amphisile Cuvier 1816
Amphisilen Klein 1775
Centriscops Gill 1862
Centriscus Linnaeus 1758

SUBORDER SYNGNATHOIDEI

FAM. SOLENOSTOMIDAE (Ghost Pipefishes)
Solenichthys Bleeker 1865
Solenostomatichthys Bleeker 1875
Solenostomus Lacepède 1803

FAM. SYNGNATHIDAE (Pipefishes and Seahorses)
Haliichthys Gray 1859

Subfam. Syngnathinae (Pipefishes)
Acanthognathus Duncker 1912
Acentronura Kaup 1853
Acestra Bonaparte (ex Jardine) 1846
Acmonotus Philippi 1896
Acus Müller 1766
Acus Valmont de Bomare 1791
Acus Swainson (ex Willoughby) 1839
Amphelikturus Parr 1930
Anarchopterus Hubbs 1935
Apterygocampus Weber 1913
Atelurus Duméril 1870
Belonichthys Peters 1868
Bhanotia Hora 1926
Bhanotichthys Parr 1930
Bombonia Herre 1927
Bryx Herald 1940
Bulbonaricus Herald in Schultz et al. 1953
Campichthys Whitley 1931
Castelnauina Fowler 1908
Choeroichthys Kaup 1856
Coelonotus Peters 1855
Corythoichthys Kaup 1853
Cosmocampus Dawson 1979
Dentirostrum Herald & Randall 1972
Dermatostethus Gill 1862
Doryichthys Kaup 1853
Doryrhamphinarum Kaup 1856
Doryrhamphus Kaup 1856
Dunckerocampus Whitley 1933
Enchelyocampus Dawson & Allen 1978
Enneacampus Dawson 1981
Entelurus Duméril 1870
Festucalex Whitley 1931
Filicampus Whitley 1948
Gasterotokeus Heckel in Kaup 1853
Halicampoides Fowler 1956
Halicampus Kaup 1856
Hemimarsupium Kaup 1853
Hemithylacus Kaup 1856
Heraldia Paxton 1975
Hippichthys Bleeker 1849
Histiogamphelus McCulloch 1914
Hymenolomus Duméril 1870
Hypselognathus Whitley 1948
Ichthyocampus Kaup 1853
Idiotropiscis Whitley 1947
Kaupia Smith 1963
Kaupus Whitley 1951
Kimblaeus Dawson 1980
Larvicampus Whitley 1948
Leptoichthys Kaup 1853
Leptonotus Kaup 1853
Lissocampus Waite & Hale 1921
Lophocampus Dawson 1984
Mannarichthys Dawson 1977
Maroubra Whitley 1948
Micrognathus Duncker 1912
Microphis Kaup 1853
Microsyngnathus Herald 1959
Minyichthys Herald & Randall 1972
Mitotichthys Whitley 1948
Nannocampichthys Hora & Mukerji 1936
Nannocampus Günther 1870
Nematosoma Eichwald 1831
Nerophis Rafinesque 1810
Nigracus Whitley 1953
Notiocampus Dawson 1979
Novacampus Whitley 1955
Oostethus Hubbs 1929
Osphyolax Cope 1876
Oxleyana Whitley 1937
Parabelonichthys Fowler 1943
Paramicrophis Klausewitz 1955
Parasyngnathus Duncker 1915
Penetopteryx Lunel 1881
Péromère Duméril 1856
Phanerotokeus Duncker 1940
Phoxocampus Dawson 1977
Phycodurus Gill 1896
Phyllopteryx Swainson 1839
Pipettella Whitley 1951
Pristidoryrhamphus Fowler 1944
Protocampus Günther 1870
Pseudophallus Herald 1940
Ptérure Duméril 1856
Pugnaso Whitley 1948
Runcinatus Whitley 1929
Scyphius Risso 1826
Simocampus Fritzsche 1980
Simosyngnathus Fowler 1940
Siokunichthys Herald in Schultz et al. 1953
Siphonostoma Kaup 1856
Siphostoma Rafinesque 1810
Solegnathus Swainson 1839
Stigmatopora Kaup 1853
Stipecampus Whitley 1948
Syngnathoides Bleeker 1851
Syngnathus Linnaeus 1758
Syrictes Jordan & Evermann 1927
Tiphle Rafinesque 1810
Trachyrhamphus Kaup 1853
Typhlinus Rafinesque 1815
Typhlus Duméril (ex Bribron) 1870
Urocampus Günther 1870
Vanacampus Whitley 1951
Yozia Jordan & Snyder 1901

Subfam. Hippocampinae (Seahorses)
Farlapiscis Whitley 1931
Hippocampus Rafinesque 1810
Hippocampus Leach 1814
Hippocampus Cuvier 1816
Hippocampus Perry 1810
Hippohystrix Whitley 1940
Jamsus Ginsburg 1937
Macleayina Fowler 1907

ORDER SYNBRANCHIFORMES

FAM. SYNBRANCHIDAE (Swamp-Eels)
Amphipnous Müller 1841
Anommatophasma Mees 1962
Apterigia Basilewski 1852
Cryptophthalmus Franz 1910
Cuchia Hamilton in Taylor 1831
Fluta Bloch & Schneider 1801
Furmastix Whitley 1951
Macrotrema Regan 1912
Monopterus Lacepède 1800
Ophicardia McClelland 1844
Ophichthys Swainson 1839
Ophisternon McClelland 1844
Pluto Hubbs 1938
Pneumabranchus McClelland 1844
Symbranchus
Synbranchus Bloch 1795
Tetrabranchus Bleeker 1851
Typhlobranchus Bloch & Schneider 1801
Typhlosynbranchus Pellegrin 1922
Unagius Jordan 1919
Unibranchapertura Lacepède 1803
Unipertura Duméril 1856

FAM. MASTACEMBELIDAE (Spiny-eels)
Aethiomastacembelus Travers 1988
Afromastacembelus Travers 1984
Bdellorhynchus Jordan & Tanaka 1927
Caecomastacembelus Poll 1958
Gyrinostomus Rochebrune 1885
Macrognathus Lacepède 1800
Mastacembelus Gronow 1763
Mastacembelus Scopoli (ex Gronow) 1777
Pararhynchobdella Bleeker 1874
Rhynchobdella Bloch & Schneider 1801

FAM. CHAUDHURIIDAE
Chaudhuria Annandale 1918
Garo Yazdani & Talwar 1981
Pillaia Yazdani 1972

ORDER SCORPAENIFORMES

SUBORDER SCORPAENOIDEI

FAM. SCORPAENIDAE (Scorpionfishes and Stonefishes)

Subfam. Sebastinae (Rockfishes and Rockcods)
Acutomentum Eigenmann & Beeson 1893
Allosebastes Hubbs 1951
Auctospina Eigenmann & Beeson 1893
Emmelas Jordan & Evermann 1898
Eosebastes Jordan & Evermann 1896
Eusebastes Sauvage 1878
Hatumeus Matsubara 1943
Helicolenus Goode & Bean 1896
Hispaniscus Jordan & Evermann 1896
Hozukius Matsubara 1934
Mebarus Matsubara 1943
Murasoius Matsubara 1943
Neohispaniscus Matsubara 1943
Primospina Eigenmann & Beeson 1893
Pteropodus Eigenmann & Beeson 1893
Rosicola Jordan & Evermann 1896
Sebastes Cuvier 1829
Sebastichthys Gill 1862
Sebastiscus Jordan & Starks 1904
Sebastocarus Jordan & Evermann 1927
Sebastocles Jordan & Hubbs 1925
Sebastodes Gill 1861
Sebastomus Gill 1864
Sebastopyr Jordan & Evermann 1927
Sebastosomus Gill 1864
Takenokius Matsubara 1943
Zalopyr Jordan & Evermann 1898

Subfam. Scorpaeninae (Scorpionfishes)
Acanthodes Fourmanoir & Crosnier 1964
Crossoscorpaena Fowler 1938
Dendroscorpaena Smith 1957
Hipposcorpaena Fowler 1938
Holoscorpaena Fowler 1944
Hoplosebastes Schmidt 1929
Hypomacrus Evermann & Seale 1907
Idiastion Eschmeyer 1965
Iracundus Jordan & Evermann 1903
Kantapus Smith 1947
Merinthe Snyder 1904
Metzelaaria Jordan 1923
Nemapontinus Fowler 1938
Neomerinthe Fowler 1935
Oligoscorpaena Fowler 1939
Osorioia Fowler 1938
Panotus Rafinesque 1815
Parascorpaena Bleeker 1876
Parascorpaenodes Smith 1957
Paronescodes Smith 1958
Peloropsis Gilbert 1905
Phenacoscorpius Fowler 1938
Pogonoscorpius Regan 1908
Pontinus Poey 1860
Pteroidichthys Bleeker 1856
Pteropelor Fowler 1938
Rhinopias Gill 1905
Ruboralga Whitley 1931
Scorpaena Linnaeus 1758
Scorpaenichthys Bleeker 1856
Scorpaenodes Bleeker 1857
Scorpaenopsella Fowler 1938
Scorpaenopsis Heckel 1837
Scorpius Plumier in Lacepède 1801
Sebastapistes Gill in Streets 1877
Sebastella Tanaka 1917
Sebastoplus Gill 1863
Sebastopsis Gill 1862
Sebastopsis Sauvage 1873
Taenianotus Lacepède 1802
Taenionotus Agassiz 1846
Thysanichthys Jordan & Starks 1904
Yacius Whitley 1970

Subfam. Sebastolobinae (Thornyheads)
Adelosebastes Eschmeyer, Abe & Nakano 1979
Mesoscorpia Eschmeyer 1969
Sebastolobus Gill 1881
Trachyscorpia Ginsburg 1953

Subfam. Plectrogeninae
Plectrogenium Gilbert 1905

Subfam. Pteroinae (Turkeyfishes and Lionfishes)
Brachirus Swainson 1839
Brachypterois Fowler 1938
Brachyrus Swainson 1839
Dendrochirus Swainson 1839
Ebosia Jordan & Starks 1904
Macrochirus Swainson 1839
Nemapterois Fowler 1938
Parabrachirus Matsubara 1943
Parapterois Bleeker 1876
Pseudomonopterus Bleeker 1863
Pseudopterus Klein 1776
Pseudopterus Bleeker (ex Klein) 1876
Pterois Oken (ex Cuvier) 1817
Pteroleptus Swainson 1839
Pteropterus Swainson 1839
Ranipterois Whitley 1951

Subfam. Setarchinae
Bathysebastes Döderlein in Steindachner & Döderlein 1884
Ectreposebastes Garman 1899
Lioscorpius Günther 1880
Lythrichthys Jordan & Starks 1904
Macroscorpius Fowler 1938
Scorpaenella Fowler 1938
Setarches Johnson 1862

Subfam. Neosebastinae
Cristula de Buen 1961
Maxillicosta Whitley 1935
Neosebastes Guichenot 1867
Pseudosebastes Sauvage 1878
Sebastosemus Gill 1905

Subfam. Apistinae
Apistes Cuvier in Cuvier & Valenciennes 1829
Apistops Ogilby 1911
Apistus Cuvier in Cuvier & Valenciennes 1829
Cheroscorpaena Mees 1964
Hypodytes Gistel 1848
Platypterus Swainson 1839
Polemius Kaup 1858
Prosopodasys Cantor 1849
Pterichthys Swainson 1839
Trichosomus Swainson 1839

Subfam. Tetraroginae (Waspfishes)
Abcichthys Whitley 1927
Ablabys Kaup 1873
Amblyapistus Bleeker 1876
Centropogon Günther 1860
Coccotropsis Barnard 1927
Cottapistus Bleeker 1876
Daia Ogilby 1903
Gadapistus de Beaufort 1949
Glyptauchen Günther 1860
Gymnapistes Swainson 1839
Liocranium Ogilby 1903
Neocentropogon Matsubara 1943
Notesthes Ogilby 1903
Ocosia Jordan & Starks 1904
Paracentropogon Bleeker 1876
Parocosia Whitley 1958
Pentaroge Günther 1860
Richardsonichthys Smith 1958

Sibogapistus de Beaufort 1949
Snyderina Jordan & Starks 1901
Tetraroge Günther 1860
Vadesuma Whitley 1933
Vespicula Jordan & Richardson 1910

Subfam. Minoinae
Corythobatus Cantor 1849
Decterias Jordan & Starks 1904
Lysodermus Smith & Pope 1906
Minous Cuvier in Cuvier & Valenciennes 1829
Paraminous Fowler 1943

Subfam. Choridactylinae
Choridactylodes Gilchrist 1902
Choridactylus Richardson 1848
Chorismodactylus see *Choridactylus*
Chorismopelor Chevey 1927
Inimicus Jordan & Starks 1904
Pelor Cuvier in Cuvier & Valenciennes 1829
Simopias Gill 1905

Subfam. Synanceiinae (Stonefishes and allies)
Barffianus Curtiss 1844
Bufichthys Swainson 1839
Dampierosa Whitley 1932
Deleastes Seale 1906
Emmydrichthys Jordan & Rutter in Jordan 1896
Erosa Swainson 1839
Leptosynanceia Bleeker 1874
Nofua Whitley 1930
Phrynichthys Agassiz 1846
Polycaulus Günther 1860
Pseudosynanceia Day 1875
Spurco Cuvier (ex Commerson) in Cuvier & Valenciennes 1829
Synanceia Bloch & Schneider 1801
Synanceichthys Bleeker 1863
Synanchia Swainson 1839
Synancidium Müller 1843
Trachicephalus Swainson 1839
Trichophasia Swainson 1839
Uranoblepus Gill 1861

FAM. CARACANTHIDAE (Coral Crouchers)
Amphiprionichthys Bleeker 1855
Caracanthus Krøyer 1845
Centropus Kner 1860
Crossoderma Guichenot 1869
Micropus Gray 1831
Trachycephalus De Vis 1884

FAM. APLOACTINIDAE (Velvetfishes)
Acanthosphex Fowler 1938
Adventor Whitley 1952
Aniculerosa Whitley 1933
Aploactis Temminck & Schlegel 1843
Aploactisoma Castelnau 1872
Aploactoides Fowler 1938
Bathyaploactis Whitley 1933
Cocotropus Kaup 1858
Erisphex Jordan & Starks 1904
Eschmeyer Poss & Springer 1983
Haploactis see *Aploactis*
Haploactisoma see *Aploactisoma*
Insopiscis Whitley 1933
Kanekonia Tanaka 1915
Karumba Whitley 1966
Kleiwegia de Beaufort 1952
Membracidichthys Whitley 1933
Neoaploactis Eschmeyer & Allen 1978
Paraploactis Bleeker 1865
Peristrominous Whitley 1952
Prosoproctus Poss & Eschmeyer 1979
Ptarmus Smith 1947
Sthenopus Richardson 1848
Trichopleura Kaup 1858
Xenaploactis Poss & Eschmeyer 1980

FAM. PATAECIDAE (Prowfishes)
Aetapcus Scott 1936
Neopataecus Steindachner 1884
Pataecus Richardson 1844

FAM. GNATHANACANTHIDAE (Red Velvetfishes)
Beridia Castelnau 1878
Gnathanacanthus Bleeker 1855
Holoxenus Günther 1876

FAM. CONGIOPODIDAE (Horsefishes)
Agriopus Cuvier in Cuvier & Valenciennes 1829
Alertichthys Moreland 1960
Cephalinus Gronow in Gray 1854
Congiopodus Perry 1811
Congiopus see *Congiopodus*
Perryena Whitley 1940
Xanclorhynchus
Zanclorhynchus Günther 1880

FAM. TRIGLIDAE (Searobins or Gurnards)

Subfam. Triglinae (Searobins)
Aoyagichthys Whitley 1958
Aspitrigla Fowler 1925
Bellator Jordan & Evermann 1896
Bovitrigla Fowler 1938
Chelidonichthys Kaup 1873
Chriolax Jordan & Gilbert 1879
Colotrigla Gill 1905
Corystion Klein 1776
Currupiscis Whitley 1931
Dinichthys Kaup 1873
Dixiphichthys Fowler 1938
Dixiphistes Fowler 1938
Dixiphistops Fowler 1938
Eutrigla Fraser-Brunner 1938
Exolissus Jordan 1923
Fissala Gill 1905
Gurnardus Jordan & Evermann 1898
Hatha Whitley 1959
Hoplonotus Guichenot 1866
Lepidotrigla Günther 1860
Lyrichthys Kaup 1873
Marubecula Whitley 1950
Merulinus Jordan & Evermann 1898
Microtrigla Kaup 1873
Ornichthys Swainson 1839
Otohime Jordan & Starks 1907
Pachytrigla Fowler 1938
Palaenichthys Kaup 1873
Parapterygotrigla Matsubara 1937
Paratrigla Ogilby 1911
Prionotus Lacepède 1801
Pristhoplotrigla Fowler 1938
Pterygotrigla Waite 1899
Sagenocephalus Kaup 1873
Stagonotrigla Fowler 1938
Trigla Linnaeus 1758
Trigloporus Smith 1934
Triscurrichthys Whitley 1931
Uradia Kamohara 1938
Vexillitrigla Whitley 1931

Subfam. Peristediinae (Armored Gurnards)
Acanthostedion Fowler 1943
Garariscus Smith 1917
Gargariscus Smith 1917
Heminodus Smith 1917
Nemaperistedion Fowler 1938
Octonus Rafinesque 1810
Panichthys Whitley 1933
Paraheminodus Kamohara 1957
Peristedion Lacepède 1801
Peristedium Jordan & Gilbert 1883
Peristethidium Agassiz 1846
Peristethus Kaup 1858
Polyacantichthys Kaup 1873
Satyrichthys Kaup 1873
Scalicus Jordan 1923
Vulsiculus Jordan & Evermann 1896

SUBORDER DACTYLOPTEROIDEI

FAM. DACTYLOPTERIDAE (Helmet Gurnards or Flying Gurnards) = Cephalacanthidae
Cephacandia Rafinesque 1815
Cephalacanthia Agassiz 1846
Cephalacanthus Lacepède 1801
Dactylophorus Swainson 1839
Dactyloptena Jordan & Richardson 1908
Dactylopterus Lacepède 1801
Daicocus Jordan & Richardson 1908
Ebisinus Jordan & Richardson 1908
Gonocephalus Gronow in Gray 1854
Mastigophorus Kaup 1873

SUBORDER PLATYCEPHALOIDEI

FAM. PLATYCEPHALIDAE (Flatheads)
Cacumen Whitley 1931
Calliomorus Lacepède 1800
Centranodon Lacepède 1803
Cociella Whitley 1940
Cocius Jordan & Hubbs 1925
Colefaxia Whitley 1935
Cumbel Whitley 1952
Cymbacephalus Fowler 1938
Elates Jordan & Seale 1907
Grammoplites Fowler 1904
Hyalorhynchus Ogilby 1910
Inegocia Jordan & Thompson 1913
Insidiator Jordan & Snyder 1900
Kumococius Matsubara & Ochiai 1955
Levanaora Whitley 1933
Leviprora Whitley 1931

Longitrudis Whitley 1931
Neoplatycephalus Castelnau 1872
Onigocia Jordan & Thompson 1913
Papilloculiceps Fowler & Steinitz 1956
Planiprora Whitley 1931
Platycephalus Bloch 1795
Ratabulus Jordan 1925
Repotrudis Whitley 1930
Rogadius Jordan & Richardson 1908
Sorsogona Herre 1934
Suggrundus Whitley 1930
Thysanophrys Ogilby 1898
Trudis Whitley 1931
Wakiyus Jordan & Hubbs 1925

FAM. BEMBRIDAE (Deepwater Flatheads)
Bambradon Jordan & Richardson 1908
Bembradium Gilbert 1905
Bembras Cuvier in Cuvier & Valenciennes 1829
Brachybembras Fowler 1938
Parabembras Bleeker 1874
Pristhoplichthys Fowler 1938

FAM. HOPLICHTHYIDAE (Spiny Flatheads)
Acanthoplichthys Fowler 1943
Hoplichthys Cuvier in Cuvier & Valenciennes 1829
Monhoplichthys Fowler 1938
Oplichthys see *Hoplichthys*
Rhinhoplichthys Fowler 1938

SUBORDER ANOPLOPOMATOIDEI

FAM. ANOPLOPOMATIDAE (Sablefishes and Skilfishes)
Anoplopoma Ayres 1859
Ebisus Jordan & Snyder 1901
Erilepis Gill 1894
Myriolepis Lockington 1880
Scombrocottus Peters 1872

SUBORDER HEXAGRAMMOIDEI

FAM. HEXAGRAMMIDAE (Greenlings)

Subfam. Hexagramminae (Greenlings)
Acantholebius Gill 1861
Agrammus Günther 1860
Chiropsis Girard 1858
Chirus Pallas (ex Steller) 1814
Decagrammus Hubbs 1928
Grammatopleurus Gill 1861
Hexagrammoides Gracianov 1907
Hexagrammos Steller in Tilesius 1809
Labrax Pallas 1810
Lebius Pallas (ex Steller) 1814
Octogrammus Bleeker 1874
Stellistius Jordan & Tanaka 1927

Subfam. Pleurogramminae (Atka Mackerels)
Pleurogrammus Gill 1861

Subfam. Ophiodontinae (Lingcods)
Ophiodon Girard 1854
Oplopoma Girard 1856

Subfam. Oxylebiinae (Painted Greenlings)
Oxylebius Gill 1862

Subfam. Zaniolepidinae (Combfishes)
Xantocles Jordan 1917
Zaniolepis Girard 1858

SUBORDER COTTOIDEI

FAM. NORMANICHTHYIDAE
Normanichthys Clark 1937

FAM. EREUNIIDAE
Ereunias Jordan & Snyder 1901
Marukawichthys Sakamoto 1931

FAM. COTTIDAE (Sculpins)
Acanthocottus Girard 1850
Agonocottus Pavlenko 1910
Ainocottus Jordan & Starks 1904
Alcichthys Jordan & Starks 1904
Alcidea Jordan & Evermann 1898
Allartedius Hubbs 1926
Allocottus Hubbs 1926
Alloricuzenius Matsubara & Iwai 1951
Antipodocottus Bolin 1952
Aphobus Gistel 1848
Archaulus Gilbert & Burke 1912
Archistes Jordan & Gilbert in Jordan & Evermann 1898
Argyrocottus Herzenstein 1892
Artediellichthys Taranetz 1941
Artediellina Taranetz 1937
Artedielliscus Fedorov 1973
Artedielloides Soldatov 1922
Artediellops Neelov 1979
Artediellus Jordan 1885
Artedius Girard 1856
Ascelichthys Jordan & Gilbert 1880
Asemichthys Gilbert 1912
Aspicottus Girard 1854
Astrocottus Bolin 1936
Astrolytes Jordan & Starks 1895
Atopocottus Bolin 1936
Axyrias Starks 1896
Bero Jordan & Starks 1904
Blennicottus Gill 1861
Blepsias Cuvier 1829
Boreocottus Gill 1859
Bunocottus Kner 1868
Calycilepidotus Ayres 1855
Centridermichthys Richardson 1844
Cephalocottus Gracianov 1907
Ceratocottus Gill 1859
Chitonotus Lockington 1881
Clinocottus Gill 1861
Clypeocottus Ayres 1854
Cottiusculus Schmidt 1904
Cottopsis Girard 1850
Cottus Linnaeus 1758
Crossias Jordan & Starks 1904
Daruma Jordan & Starks 1904
Dialarchus Greeley 1901
Elanura Gilbert 1896
Elaphichthys Jordan & Starks 1904
Elaphocottus Sauvage 1878
Enophrys Swainson 1839
Evermanniana Taranetz 1935
Eximia Greeley 1901
Furcina Jordan & Starks 1904
Greeleya Jordan 1920
Gymnacanthus see *Gymnocanthus*
Gymnocanthus Swainson 1839
Hemilepidotus Cuvier 1829
Hemitripterus Cuvier 1829
Histiocottus Gill 1889
Hoplocottus Kaup 1858
Icelichthys Schmidt 1935
Icelinus Jordan 1885
Icelopsis Taranetz 1936
Icelus Krøyer 1845
Jordania Starks 1895
Leiocottus Girard 1856
Leptocottus Girard 1854
Littocottus Neelov 1979
Medicelinus Bolin 1936
Megalocottus Gill 1861
Melletes Bean 1880
Mesocottus Gracianov 1907
Micrenophrys Andriashev 1954
Microcottus Schmidt 1940
Montereya Hubbs 1926
Myoxocephalus Tilesius (ex Steller) 1811
Nautichthys Girard 1858
Nautiscus Jordan & Evermann 1898
Neocottus Sideleva 1982
Neohemilepidotus Sakamoto 1932
Noviricuzenius Bolin 1936
Ochotskia Schmidt 1915
Ocynectes Jordan & Starks 1904
Oligocottus Girard 1856
Onchocottus Gill 1861
Orthonopias Starks & Mann 1911
Oxycottus Jordan & Evermann 1898
Parartedius Hubbs 1926
Parastrolytes Hubbs 1926
Parenophrys Taranetz 1941
Paricelinus Eigenmann & Eigenmann 1889
Pegedictis Rafinesque 1820
Penicelinus Bolin 1936
Peropus Lay & Bennett 1839
Phallocottus Schultz 1938
Phasmatocottus Bolin 1936
Phobetor Krøyer 1845
Podabrus Richardson 1848
Porocottus Gill 1859
Potamocottus Gill 1861
Prionistius Bean 1884
Pseudoblennius Temminck & Schlegel 1850
Pseudoclinus Temminck & Schlegel 1850
Pterygiocottus Bean & Weed 1920
Ptyonotus Günther 1860
Radulinellus Bolin 1950
Radulinopsis Soldatov & Lindberg 1930
Radulinus Gilbert 1890
Rastrinus Jordan & Evermann 1896
Rhamphocottus Günther 1874
Rheopresbe Jordan & Starks 1904
Ricuzenius Jordan & Starks 1904
Ruscariops Hubbs 1926
Ruscarius Jordan & Starks 1895
Rusciculus Greeley 1901
Rusulus Starks & Mann 1911
Schmidtia Jordan & Starks 1904

Schmidtina Jordan & Starks 1904
Sclerocottus Fischer 1885
Scorpaenichthys Girard 1854
Scorpichthes Bonaparte 1846
Sigmistes Rutter in Jordan & Evermann 1898
Stelgidonotus Gilbert & Thompson 1905
Stelgistrops Hubbs 1926
Stelgistrum Jordan & Gilbert in Jordan & Evermann 1898
Sternias Jordan & Evermann 1898
Stlegicottus Bolin 1936
Stlengis Jordan & Starks 1904
Synchirus Bean 1890
Tarandichthys Jordan & Evermann in Jordan 1896
Tauridea Jordan & Rice in Jordan 1878
Taurocottus Soldatov & Pavlenko 1915
Taurulus Gracianov 1907
Temnistia Richardson 1836
Thyriscus Gilbert & Burke 1912
Trachidermis Heckel 1837
Trichocottus Soldatov & Pavlenko 1915
Triglops Reinhardt 1831
Triglopsis Girard 1851
Ulca Jordan & Evermann in Jordan 1896
Uranidea DeKay 1842
Uranoscopus Gronow 1763
Vellitor Jordan & Starks 1904
Zesticelus Jordan & Evermann 1896

FAM. COTTOCOMEPHORIDAE

Abyssocottus Berg 1906
Asprocottus Berg 1906
Baicalocottus Berg 1903
Batrachocottus Berg 1903
Cottinella Berg 1907
Cottocomephorus Pellegrin 1900
Leocottus Taliev 1955
Limnocottus Berg 1906
Metacottus Taliev 1946
Paracottus Taliev in Berg 1949
Procottus Gracianov 1902

FAM. COMEPHORIDAE (Baikal Oilfishes)

Comephorus Lacepède 1800
Elaeorhous Pallas 1814

FAM. PSYCHROLUTIDAE (Fatheads)

Besnardia Lahille 1913
Cottunculoides Barnard 1927
Cottunculus Collett 1875
Dasycottus Bean 1890
Ebinania Sakamoto 1932
Eurymen Gilbert & Burke 1912
Gilbertidia Berg 1898
Gilbertina Jordan & Starks 1895
Japanopsychrolutes Nojima 1936
Malacocottus Bean 1890
Neophrynichthys Günther 1876
Psychrolutes Günther 1861
Thecopterus Smith 1904

FAM. AGONIDAE (Poachers)

Acanthostelgis Fowler 1958
Agonomalus Guichenot 1866
Agonopsis Gill 1861
Agonus Bloch & Schneider 1801
Anoplagonus Gill 1861
Aspidophoroides Lacepède 1801
Aspidophorus Lacepède 1801
Asterotheca Gilbert 1915
Averruncus Jordan & Starks 1895
Bathyagonus Gilbert 1890
Bothragonus Gill in Jordan & Gilbert 1883
Brachyopsis Gill 1861
Canthirhynchus Swainson 1839
Cataphractus Klein 1777
Cataphractus Fleming 1828
Cheiragonus Herzenstein 1890
Chesnonia Iredale & Whitley 1969
Draciscus Jordan & Snyder 1901
Ganoideus Whitley 1950
Hippocephalus Swainson 1839
Hypsagonus Gill 1861
Iburiella Jordan & Hubbs 1925
Iburina Jordan & Hubbs 1925
Leptagonus Gill 1861
Occa Jordan & Evermann 1898
Occella Jordan & Hubbs 1925
Odontopyxis Lockington 1880
Pallasina Cramer in Jordan & Starks 1895
Paragonus Gill 1861
Paragonus Guichenot 1869
Paragonus Miranda-Ribeiro 1918
Percis Scopoli 1777
Phalangistes Pallas 1814
Podothecus Gill 1861
Ribeiroa Jordan 1920
Sarritor Cramer in Jordan & Evermann 1896
Siphagonus Steindachner 1876
Stelgis Cramer in Jordan & Starks 1895
Stellerina Cramer in Jordan & Evermann 1896
Tilesina Schmidt 1904
Ulcina Cramer in Jordan & Evermann 1896
Xeneretmus Gilbert in Jordan 1903
Xenochirus Gilbert 1890
Xenopyxis Gilbert 1915
Xystes Jordan & Starks 1895

FAM. CYCLOPTERIDAE (Snailfishes) Liparidae included

Subfam. Cyclopterinae (Lumpsuckers)

Aptocyclus De la Pylaie 1835
Cyclocottus Popov in Soldatov & Lindberg 1930
Cyclolumpus Tanaka 1912
Cyclopsis Popov 1930
Cyclopterichthys Steindachner 1881
Cyclopterocottus Popov 1930
Cyclopteroides Garman 1892
Cyclopteropsis Soldatov & Popov 1929
Cyclopterus Linnaeus 1758
Elephantichthys Hubbs & Schultz 1934
Eumicrotremus Gill 1862
Lethotremus Gilbert 1896
Liparius Rafinesque 1815
Liparoides Lloyd 1909
Lumpus Rafinesque 1815
Lumpus Oken (ex Cuvier) 1817
Oncotion Klein 1777
Pelagocyclus Lindberg & Legeza 1955

Subfam. Liparinae (Snailfishes)

Acantholiparis Gilbert & Burke 1912
Actinochir Gill 1864
Allinectes Jordan & Evermann 1898
Allochir Jordan & Evermann 1896
Allurus Jordan & Evermann 1896
Amitra Goode 1881
Amitrichthys Jordan & Evermann 1896
Bathyphasma Gilbert 1896
Careliparis Garman 1892
Caremitra Jordan & Evermann 1896
Careproctus Krøyer 1862
Crystallias Jordan & Snyder 1902
Crystallichthys Jordan & Gilbert in Jordan & Evermann 1898
Cyclogaster Gronow 1763
Elassodiscus Gilbert & Burke 1912
Enantioliparis Vaillant 1888
Eutelichthys Tortonese 1959
Genioliparis Andriashev & Neelov 1976
Gymnolycodes Vaillant 1888
Gyrinichthys Gilbert 1896
Hilgendorfia Goode & Bean 1896
Liparis Scopoli (ex Artedi) 1777
Liparis Röse 1793
Lipariscus Gilbert 1915
Liparops Garman 1892
Lycocara Gill 1884
Lyoliparis Jordan & Evermann 1896
Massaria Gistel 1848
Monomitra Goode 1883
Nectoliparis Gilbert & Burke 1912
Neoliparis Steindachner 1875
Notoliparis Andriashev 1975
Odontoliparis Stein 1978
Osteodiscus Stein 1978
Paraliparis Collett 1878
Polypera Burke 1912
Prognurus Jordan & Gilbert in Jordan & Evermann 1898
Psednos Barnard 1927
Pseudoliparis Andriashev 1955
Rhinoliparis Gilbert 1896
Rhodichthys Collett 1878
Temnocara Burke 1930
Trismegistus Jordan & Snyder 1904
Uronectes Günther 1862

ORDER PERCIFORMES

SUBORDER PERCOIDEI
Incertae sedis genera

Actenolepis Dybowski 1872
Bathysphyraenops Parr 1933
Caesioscorpis Whitley 1945
Coreosiniperca Fang & Chong 1932
Galeagra Heller & Snodgrass 1903
Hapalogenys Richardson 1844
Hemilutjanus Bleeker 1876
Howella Ogilby 1899
Lateolabrax Bleeker 1857
Ostracoberyx Fowler 1934
Plectroperca Peters 1864
Pomodon Boulenger 1895
Rhectogramma Norman 1930
Schistoperca Fowler 1943
Siniperca Gill 1862

FAM. CENTROPOMIDAE

Subfam. Centropominae (Snooks)
Centropomus Lacepède 1802
Macrocephalus Browne 1789
Macrocephalus Bleeker (ex Browne) 1876
Oxylabrax Bleeker 1876
Platycephalus Miranda-Ribeiro 1902

Subfam. Latinae
Cnidon Müller & Troschel 1849
Hypopterus Gill 1861
Lates Cuvier in Cuvier & Valenciennes 1828
Luciolates Boulenger 1914
Psammoperca Richardson 1848
Pseudolates Alleyne & Macleay 1877
Ptertopomus Cuvier in Goldfuss 1820

FAM. AMBASSIDAE
= Chandidae

Acanthoperca Castelnau 1878
Ambassis Cuvier in Cuvier & Valenciennes 1828
Austrochanda Whitley 1935
Blandowskiella Iredale & Whitley 1932
Bogoda Bleeker 1853
Chanda Hamilton 1822
Denariusa Whitley 1948
Gymnochanda Fraser-Brunner 1955
Gymnochanda Boeseman 1957
Hamiltonia Swainson 1839
Konopickia Whitley 1937
Negambassis Whitley 1935
Paradoxodacna Roberts 1989
Parambassis Bleeker 1874
Priopidichthys Whitley 1935
Priopis Kuhl & van Hasselt in Cuvier & Valenciennes 1830
Pseudambassis Bleeker 1874
Pseudoambassis Castelnau 1878
Synechopterus Norman 1935
Tetracentrum Macleay 1883
Velambassis Whitley 1935
Whitleyia Fowler & Bean 1930
Whitleyina see *Whitleyia*
Xenambassis Schultz 1945

FAM. PERCICHTHYIDAE (Temperate Basses)
Perciliidae included

Acroperca Myers 1933
Bostockia Castelnau 1873
Coreoperca Herzenstein 1896
Ctenolates Günther 1871
Deuteropterus Gill 1861
Edelia Castelnau 1873
Gadopsis Richardson 1848
Homodemus De Vis 1884
Maccullochella Whitley 1929
Macquaria Cuvier in Cuvier & Valenciennes 1830
Murrayia Castelnau 1872
Nannatherina Regan 1906
Nannoperca Günther 1861
Oligorus Günther 1859
Paradules Klunzinger 1872
Paschalestes Gistel 1848
Percalabrax Temminck & Schlegel 1842
Percalates Ramsay & Ogilby 1887
Percichthys Girard 1855
Percilia Girard 1855
Percosoma Gill 1861
Plectroplites Gill 1862
Riverina Castelnau 1872

FAM. ACROPOMATIDAE (Lanternbellies)
Acanthocephalus Döderlein in Steindachner & Döderlein 1883
Acropoma Temminck & Schlegel 1843
Apogonops Ogilby 1896
Brephostoma Alcock 1889
Corusculus Jordan & Snyder 1901
Doederleinia Steindachner in Steindachner & Döderlein 1883
Eteliscus Jordan & Snyder 1900
Hypoclydonia Goode & Bean 1896
Macculochina Jordan in Jordan & Jordan 1922
Malakichthys Döderlein in Steindachner & Döderlein 1883
Melanostoma Döderlein in Steindachner & Döderlein 1883
Neoscombrops Gilchrist 1922
Parascombrops Alcock 1889
Pseudohowella Fedoryako 1976
Rhomboserranus Fowler 1943
Satsuma Smith & Pope 1906
Synagrops Günther 1887
Verilus Poey 1860

FAM. MORONIDAE
Chrysoperca Fowler 1907
Dicentrarchus Gill 1860
Labrax Cuvier in Cuvier & Valenciennes 1828
Labrax Klein 1776
Labrax Klein in Walbaum 1792
Lepibema Rafinesque 1820
Morone Mitchill 1814
Roccus Mitchill 1814

FAM. POLYPRIONIDAE (Wreckfishes)
Hectoria Castelnau 1873
Megaperca Hilgendorf 1878
Polyprion Oken (ex Cuvier) 1817
Stereolepis Ayres 1859

FAM. DINOPERCIDAE (Cavebasses)
Centrarchops Fowler 1923
Dinoperca Boulenger 1895

FAM. SERRANIDAE (Sea Basses and Groupers)
Bryttosus Jordan & Snyder 1900
Notognidion Rafinesque 1810
Odontolabrax Bleeker 1873
Trachypoma Günther 1859

Subfam. Serraninae
Acanthistius Gill 1862
Atractoperca Gill 1861
Bullisichthys Rivas 1971
Callidulus Fowler 1907
Centropristis Cuvier 1829
Chelidoperca Boulenger 1895
Cratinus Steindachner 1878
Diplectrum Holbrook 1855
Dules Cuvier in Cuvier & Valenciennes 1829
Dulichthys Bonaparte 1831
Eudulus Fowler 1907
Gonioperca Gill 1862
Haliperca Gill 1862
Hepatus Röse 1793
Hypoplectrus Gill 1861
Mentiperca Gill 1862
Paracentropristis Klunzinger 1884
Paralabrax Girard 1856
Paraserranus Bleeker 1874
Parasphyraenops Bean 1912
Prionodes Jenyns 1840
Pseudalphestes Boulenger 1895
Schultzea Woods 1958
Schultzetta Whitley 1965
Serranellus Jordan in Jordan & Eigenmann 1890
Serraniculus Ginsburg 1952
Serranus Cuvier 1816
Triloburus Gill 1861

Subfam. Anthiinae
Anthias Bloch 1792
Anthiasicus Ginsburg 1952
Aylopon Rafinesque 1810
Caesioperca Castelnau 1872
Caprodon Temminck & Schlegel 1843
Centristhmus Garman 1899
Chenia Fowler 1958
Colpognathus Klunzinger 1880
Dactylanthias Bleeker 1871
Ellerkeldia Whitley 1927
Emmelanthias Smith 1955
Entonanthias Jordan & Tanaka 1927
Epinephelides Ogilby 1899
Franzia Jordan & Thompson 1914
Giganthias Katayama 1954
Gilbertella Waite 1902
Gilbertia Jordan in Jordan & Eigenmann 1890
Hemanthias Steindachner 1874
Holanthias Günther 1868
Hypoplectrodes Gill 1862
Isobuna Jordan in Jordan & Herre 1907
Lacepedia Castelnau 1873
Lepidoperca Regan 1914
Leptanthias Tanaka 1918
Luzonichthys Herre 1936
Mirolabrichthys Herre 1927
Mustelichthys Tanaka 1917
Naurua Whitley & Colefax 1938
Neanthias Norman 1931
Nemanthias Smith 1954
Neoanthias Castelnau 1879
Novanthias Whitley 1937
Ocyanthias Jordan & Evermann 1896
Odontanthias Bleeker 1873
Othos Castelnau 1875
Pacificogramma Kharin 1983
Pelontrus Smith 1961
Planctanthias Fowler 1935
Plectranthias Bleeker 1873
Pronotogrammus Gill 1863
Pseudanthias Bleeker 1871
Pteranthias Weber 1913
Rabaulichthys Allen 1984
Rosanthias Tanaka 1917
Sacura Jordan & Richardson 1910
Sayonara Jordan & Seale 1906

Scalantarus Smith 1965
Scopularia de Buen 1959
Selenanthias Tanaka 1918
Serranocirrhitus Watanabe 1949
Serranops Regan 1914
Stigmatonotus Peters 1877
Tosana Smith & Pope 1906
Tosanoides Kamohara 1953
Xenanthias Regan 1908
Zacallanthias Katayama 1963
Zalanthias Jordan & Richardson 1910

Subfam. Epinephelinae (Groupers)
Aethaloperca Fowler 1904
Alphestes Bloch & Schneider 1801
Altiserranus Whitley 1947
Anyperodon Günther 1859
Archoperca Jordan & Evermann 1896
Brachyrhinus Gill 1862
Cephalopholis Bloch & Schneider 1801
Cerna Bonaparte 1833
Cernua Costa 1849
Chromileptes Swainson 1839
Chrysomelanus Plumier in Lacepède 1802
Creolus Jordan & Gilbert 1883
Cugupuguacu Catesby 1771
Cynichthys Swainson 1839
Daba Forsskål 1775
Dermatolepis Gill 1861
Enneacentrus Gill 1865
Enneistus Jordan & Evermann 1896
Epinephelus Bloch 1793
Garrupa Jordan in Jordan & Eigenmann 1890
Gonioplectrus Gill 1862
Gracila Randall 1964
Homalogrystes Alleyne & Macleay 1877
Hyporthodus Gill 1861
Hyposerranus Klunzinger 1884
Itaiara Vaillant & Bocourt 1878
Labroperca Gill 1862
Lioperca Gill 1862
Louti Forsskål 1775
Menephorus Poey 1871
Merou Bonaparte (ex Cuvier) 1831
Merus Poey (ex Cuvier) 1871
Mycteroperca Gill 1862
Niphon Cuvier in Cuvier & Valenciennes 1828
Paracanthistius Bleeker 1874
Paranthias Guichenot 1868
Parepinephelus Bleeker 1874
Petrometopon Gill 1865
Phaetonichthys Bleeker 1875
Phrynotitan Gill 1885
Plectropoma Quoy & Gaimard (ex Cuvier) 1824
Plectropomus Oken (ex Cuvier) 1817
Pleuroperca Fowler & Bean 1930
Priacanthichthys Day 1868
Promicrops Poey (ex Gill) 1868
Prospinus Poey 1861
Pseudoserranus Klunzinger 1870
Saloptia Smith 1964
Schistorus Gill 1862
Serranichthys Bleeker 1855
Serrihastaperca Fowler 1944
Stereolepoides Fowler 1923
Triso Randall, Johnson & Lowe 1989
Trisotropis Gill 1865
Uriphaeton Swainson 1839
Variola Swainson 1839
Vivero Jordan & Evermann 1927
Xystroperca Jordan & Evermann 1896

Subfam. Liopropomatinae
Bathyanthias Günther 1880
Chorististium Gill 1862
Flagelloserranus Kotthaus 1970
Jeboehlkia Robins 1967
Labracopsis Steindachner & Döderlein 1883
Liopropoma Gill 1861
Pikea Steindachner 1874
Rainfordia McCulloch 1923
Taeniodon Döderlein in Steindachner & Döderlein 1883
Ypsigramma Schultz in Schultz et al. 1953

Subfam. Grammistinae (Soapfishes)
Pseudogrammatidae included
Aporops Schultz 1943
Aulacocephalus Temminck & Schlegel 1842
Belonoperca Fowler & Bean 1930
Caribrhegma Breder 1927
Diploprion Cuvier (ex Kuhl & van Hasselt) in Cuvier & Valenciennes 1828
Eleutheractis Cope 1870
Grammistes Bloch & Schneider 1801
Grammistops Schultz in Schultz et al. 1953
Pogonoperca Günther 1859
Promicropterus Gill 1861
Pseudogramma Bleeker 1875
Pseudorhegma Schultz 1966
Rhegma Gilbert in Jordan & Evermann 1900
Rypticus Cuvier 1829
Smecticus Valenciennes 1855
Suttonia Smith 1953
Tulelepis Smith 1954

FAM. SYMPHYSANODONTIDAE
Propoma Günther 1880
Rhyacanthias Jordan 1921
Symphysanodon Bleeker 1878

FAM. CENTROGENIIDAE
Centrogenys Richardson 1842
Gennadius Jordan & Seale 1907
Myriodon Brisout de Barneville 1847
Rhabdosebastes Fowler & Bean 1922

FAM. PSEUDOCHROMIDAE (Dottybacks)

Subfam. Pseudochrominae
Assiculus Richardson 1846
Bartschina Fowler 1931
Cichlops Müller & Troschel 1849
Cypho Myers 1940
Dampieria Castelnau 1875
Devisina Fowler 1931
Klunzingerina Fowler 1931
Labracinus Schlegel 1858
Labristoma Swainson 1839
Leptochromis Bleeker 1875
Malacocanthus Tickell in Day 1888
Nesiotes De Vis 1884
Ogilbyina Fowler 1931
Onar De Vis 1885
Pseudochromis Rüppell 1835

Subfam. Pseudoplesiopinae
Chlidichthys Smith 1953
Nematochromis Weber 1913
Pseudoplesiops Bleeker 1858
Wamizichthys Smith 1954

Subfam. Anisochrominae
Anisochromis Smith 1954

Subfam. Congrogadinae (Eelblennies)
Blennodesmus Günther 1872
Congrogadoides Borodin 1933
Congrogadus Günther 1862
Halidesmus Günther 1872
Halimuraena Smith 1952
Halimuraenoides Maugé & Bardach 1985
Haliophis Rüppell 1829
Hierichthys Jordan & Fowler 1902
Machaerium Richardson 1843
Natalichthys Winterbottom 1980
Pholioides Nielsen 1961
Porogrammus Gilchrist & Thompson 1916
Rusichthys Winterbottom 1979
Stenophus Castelnau 1875
Tentaculus Rao & Dutt 1966

FAM. GRAMMATIDAE (Basslets) = Grammidae
Gramma Poey 1868
Lipogramma Böhlke 1960

FAM. CALLANTHIIDAE
Anogramma Ogilby 1899
Callanthias Lowe 1839
Grammatonotus Gilbert 1905
Parabarossia Kotthaus 1976
Percanthias Tanaka 1922

FAM. PLESIOPIDAE (Roundheads)
Acanthogonia Ogilby 1918
Assessor Whitley 1935
Barrosia Smith 1952
Bleeckeria Castelnau 1873
Calloplesiops Fowler & Bean 1930
Cirrhiptera Kuhl & van Hasselt in Bleeker 1853
Fraudella Whitley 1935
Paraplesiops Bleeker 1875
Paratrachinops Allen 1977
Pharopteryx Rüppell 1828
Plesiops Oken (ex Cuvier) 1817
Pseudochromichthys Schmidt 1931
Ruppelia Castelnau 1873
Steeneichthys Allen & Randall 1985
Trachinops Günther 1861

FAM. ACANTHOCLINIDAE (Spiny Basslets)
Acanthoclinus Jenyns 1841
Acanthoplesiops Regan 1912
Beliops Hardy 1985
Belonepterygion McCulloch 1915
Calliblennius Aoyagi 1954
Ernogrammoides Chen & Liang 1948
Taumakoides Whitley 1955

FAM. GLAUCOSOMATIDAE

Brachyglaucosoma Fowler 1934
Breviperca Castelnau 1875
Glaucosoma Temminck & Schlegel 1843
Reganichthys Ogilby 1915

FAM. TERAPONTIDAE (Grunters or Tiger-fishes) = Therapontidae

Amniataba Whitley 1943
Amphitherapon Whitley 1943
Archeria Nichols 1949
Archerichthys Whitley 1951
Autisthes De Vis 1884
Bidyanus Whitley 1943
Djabub Forsskål 1775
Eutherapon Fowler 1904
Hannia Vari 1978
Helotes Cuvier 1829
Hephaestus De Vis 1884
Lagusia Vari 1978
Leiopotherapon Fowler 1931
Madigania Whitley 1945
Mesopristes Bleeker 1873
Mesopristes Fowler (ex Bleeker) 1918
Papuservus Whitley 1943
Pelates Cuvier 1829
Pelsartia Whitley 1943
Pingalla Whitley 1955
Pterapon Gray 1835
Rhynchopelates Fowler 1931
Scortum Whitley 1943
Syncomistes Vari 1978
Terapon Cuvier 1816
Therapon Cloquet 1819

FAM. BANJOSIDAE

Anoplus Temminck & Schlegel 1842
Banjos Bleeker 1876

FAM. KUHLIIDAE (Flagtails or Aholeholes)

Boulengerina Fowler 1906
Herops De Vis 1884
Kuhlia Gill 1861
Microperca Castelnau 1872
Moronopsis Gill 1863
Paradules Bleeker 1863
Percamia Bleeker 1876
Platysome Liénard 1832
Safole Jordan 1912

FAM. CENTRARCHIDAE (Sunfishes and Freshwater Basses)

Acantharchus Gill 1864
Allotis Hubbs in Ortenburger & Hubbs 1926
Ambloplites Rafinesque 1820
Aplesion Rafinesque 1820
Aplites Rafinesque 1820
Apomotis Rafinesque 1819
Archoplites Gill 1861
Bartramiolus Fowler 1945
Bryttus Valenciennes in Cuvier & Valenciennes 1831
Calliurus Rafinesque 1819
Centrarchus Cuvier 1829
Chaenobryttus Gill 1864
Copelandia Jordan in Jordan & Copeland 1877
Dioplites Rafinesque 1820
Enneacanthus Gill 1864
Erichaeta Jordan in Klippart 1877
Eucentrarchus Gill 1864
Eupomotis Gill & Jordan in Gill 1877
Glossoplites Jordan 1876
Gristes Cuvier 1829
Grystes see *Gristes*
Helioperca Jordan 1877
Hemioplites Cope 1868
Hoplites see *Aplites*
Huro Cuvier in Cuvier & Valenciennes 1828
Hyperistius Gill 1864
Icthelis Rafinesque 1820
Lepomis Rafinesque 1819
Mesogonistius Gill 1864
Micropterus Lacepède 1802
Nemocampsis Rafinesque 1820
Pomotis Rafinesque 1819
Pomotis Cuvier 1829
Pomoxis Rafinesque 1818
Sclerotis Hubbs in Ortenburger & Hubbs 1926
Telipomis Rafinesque 1820
Xenotis Jordan 1877
Xystroplites Jordan in Cope 1877

FAM. ELASSOMATIDAE (Pygmy Sunfishes)

Elassoma Jordan 1877

FAM. PERCIDAE (Perches and Darters)

Acerina Güldenstädt 1774
Acerina Cuvier 1816
Allohistium Bailey in Bailey & Gosline 1955
Alvordius Girard 1859
Ammocrypta Jordan 1877
Anemoces Jordan 1929
Aplocentrus Rafinesque 1819
Arlina Girard 1859
Asper Schaeffer 1761
Asperulus Schaeffer 1761
Asperulus Klein 1776
Asperulus Gill (ex Klein) 1861
Aspro Cuvier in Cuvier & Valenciennes 1828
Asproperca Heckel in Canestrini 1860
Astatichthys Vaillant 1873
Austroperca Hubbs 1936
Belophlox Fowler 1947
Boleichthys Girard 1859
Boleosoma DeKay 1842
Catonotus Agassiz 1854
Cephimnus Rafinesque 1815
Cernua Schaeffer 1761
Cernua Fleming 1828
Cingla Fleming 1822
Claricola Jordan & Evermann 1896
Copelandellus Jordan & Evermann 1896
Cottogaster Putnam 1863
Crystallaria Jordan & Gilbert in Jordan 1885
Cynoperca Gill & Jordan in Jordan 1877
Diplesion Rafinesque 1820
Doration Jordan 1929
Epitrachys Schulze 1890
Ericosma Jordan & Copeland in Jordan 1877
Estrella Girard 1859
Etheostoma Rafinesque 1819
Fuscatelum Page 1981
Gremilla Gistel 1848
Gymnocephalus Bloch 1793
Hadropterus Agassiz 1854
Hololepis Putnam (ex Agassiz) 1863
Hyostoma Agassiz 1854
Hypohomus Cope 1870
Imostoma Jordan 1877
Ioa Jordan & Brayton 1878
Leptoperca Gill 1862
Leucops Rafinesque 1819
Litocara Bailey 1948
Lucioperca Cuvier in Cuvier & Valenciennes 1828
Lucioperca Schinz 1822
Lucioperca Fleming 1822
Microperca Putnam 1863
Mimoperca Gill & Jordan in Jordan 1877
Nanostoma Putnam in Jordan 1877
Nivicola Jordan & Evermann 1896
Niviperca Whitley 1951
Nothonotus Putnam (ex Agassiz) 1863
Odontopholis Page 1974
Oligocephalus Girard 1859
Ozarka Williams & Robison 1980
Perca Linnaeus 1758
Percarina Nordmann 1840
Percina Haldeman 1842
Percis Klein 1776
Percis Klein in Walbaum 1792
Pileoma DeKay 1842
Plesioperca Vaillant 1873
Pleurolepis Putnam (ex Agassiz) 1863
Poecilichthys Agassiz 1854
Poecilosoma Agassiz 1850
Pogostoma Rafinesque 1818
Pomacampsis Rafinesque 1820
Psychromaster Jordan & Evermann 1896
Rafinesquiellus Jordan & Evermann 1896
Rheocrypta Jordan 1877
Rhothoeca Jordan 1885
Richia Coker 1926
Richiella Coker 1927
Romanichthys Dumitrescu, Banarescu & Stoica 1957
Sandat Cloquet 1827
Sandat Bory de Saint-Vincent 1828
Sander Oken (ex Cuvier) 1817
Sandrus Stark 1828
Schilus Krynicki 1832
Schilus Jarocki 1822
Schraitzer Schaeffer 1761
Serraria Gilbert 1884
Stizostedion Rafinesque 1820
Swainia Jordan & Evermann 1896
Torrentaria Jordan & Evermann 1896
Ulocentra Jordan 1878
Vaillantia Jordan in Jordan & Brayton 1878
Vigil Jordan 1919
Villora Hubbs & Cannon 1935
Zingel Cloquet 1817

FAM. PRIACANTHIDAE (Bigeyes)

Abuhamrur Forsskål 1775
Bogoda Blyth 1860
Boops Gronow in Gray 1854
Cookeolus Fowler 1928
Heteropriacanthus Fitch & Crooke 1984
Priacanthus Oken (ex Cuvier) 1817
Pristigenys Agassiz 1835
Pseudopriacanthus Bleeker 1869

FAM. KURTIDAE (Nurseryfishes)

Kurtus Bloch 1786

FAM. APOGONIDAE (Cardinalfishes)

Acanthapogon Fowler 1938
Adenapogon McCulloch 1921
Amia Gronow 1763
Amia Gronow in Gray 1854
Amiichthys Poey in Jordan 1887
Amioides Smith & Radcliffe in Radcliffe 1912
Apogon Lacepède 1801
Apogonichthyoides Smith 1949
Apogonichthys Bleeker 1854
Apogonoides Bleeker 1849
Archamia Gill 1863
Asperapogon Smith 1961
Aspiscis Whitley 1930
Aspro Commerson in Lacepède 1802
Astrapogon Fowler 1907
Australaphia Whitley 1936
Beanea Steindachner 1902
Bentuviaichthys Smith 1961
Brephamia Jordan in Jordan & Jordan 1922
Cercamia Randall & Smith 1988
Cheilodipterops Schultz 1940
Cheilodipterus Lacepède 1801
Clodipterus Rafinesque 1815
Coranthus Smith 1961
Desmoamia Fowler & Bean 1930
Dipterodon Lacepède 1802
Foa Jordan & Evermann in Jordan & Seale 1905
Fodifoa Whitley 1936
Fowleria Jordan & Evermann 1903
Glossamia Gill 1863
Gronovichthys Whitley 1930
Gulliveria Castelnau 1878
Gymnapogon Regan 1905
Henicichthys Tanaka 1915
Holapogon Fraser 1973
Ioamia Fowler & Bean 1930
Jadamga Schultz 1940
Jaydia Smith 1961
Kurandapogon Whitley 1939
Lachneria Smith 1954
Lepidamia Gill 1863
Lovamia Whitley 1930
Macrolepis Rafinesque 1815
Mionorus Krefft 1867
Monoprion Poey 1860
Neamia Smith & Radcliffe in Radcliffe 1912
Nectamia Jordan 1917
Neoscopelus Castelnau 1875
Ostorhinchus Lacepède 1802
Papillapogon Smith 1947
Paramia Bleeker 1863
Paroncheilus Smith 1964
Phaeoptyx Fraser & Robins 1970
Pristiapogon Klunzinger 1870
Pristicon Fraser 1972
Pseudamia Bleeker 1865
Pseudamiops Smith 1954
Pterapogon Koumans 1933
Quinca Mees 1966
Rhabdamia Weber 1909
Scopelapogon Whitley 1933
Siphamia Weber 1909
Sphaeramia Fowler & Bean 1930
Verulux Fraser 1972
Vincentia Castelnau 1872
Yarica Whitley 1930
Zapogon Fraser 1972
Zoramia Jordan 1917

FAM. EPIGONIDAE

Brinkmannella Parr 1933
Epigonus Rafinesque 1810
Florenciella Mead & De Falla 1965
Hynnodus Gilbert 1905
Microichthys Rüppell 1852
Oxyodon Brauer 1906
Parahynnodus Barnard 1927
Pomatomichthys Giglioli 1880
Pomatomus Risso 1810
Rosenblattia Mead & De Falla 1965
Scepterias Jordan & Jordan 1922
Scombrosphyraena Fourmanoir 1970
Sphyraenops Gill in Poey 1860
Telescopias Jordan & Snyder 1901
Telescops Bleeker 1876
Xystramia Jordan 1917

FAM. DINOLESTIDAE

Dinolestes Klunzinger 1872
Lanioperca Günther 1872
Neosphyraena Castelnau 1872

FAM. SILLAGINIDAE (Sillagos)

Isosillago Macleay 1878
Neosillago Castelnau 1875
Parasillago McKay 1985
Sillaginichthys Bleeker 1874
Sillaginodes Gill 1862
Sillaginopodys Fowler 1933
Sillaginopsis Gill 1862
Sillago Cuvier 1816

FAM. MALACANTHIDAE (Tilefishes)

Subfam. Malacanthinae (Sand Tilefishes)

Dikellorhynchus Smith 1956
Malacanthus Cuvier 1829
Oceanops Jordan & Seale 1906

Subfam. Latilinae
= Branchiosteginae

Asymmetrurus Clark & Ben-Tuvia 1973
Branchiostegus Rafinesque 1815
Caulolatilus Gill 1862
Coryphaena Houttuyn 1782
Coryphaenoides Lacepède 1801
Dekaya Cooper 1863
Hoplolatilus Günther 1887
Latilus Cuvier in Cuvier & Valenciennes 1830
Lopholatilus Goode & Bean 1879

FAM. LACTARIIDAE (False Trevallies)

Lactarius Valenciennes in Cuvier & Valenciennes 1833
Platylepes Swainson 1839

FAM. SCOMBROPIDAE (Gnomefishes)

Latebrus Poey 1860
Scombrops Temminck & Schlegel 1845

FAM. POMATOMIDAE (Bluefishes)

Chromis Gronow in Gray 1854
Gonenion Rafinesque 1810
Lopharis Rafinesque 1810
Pomatomus Lacepède 1802
Saltatrix Catesby 1771
Sparactodon Rochebrune 1880
Sypterus Eichwald 1831
Temnodon Schinz (ex Cuvier) 1822

FAM. RACHYCENTRIDAE (Cobias)

Elacate Cuvier in Cuvier & Valenciennes 1832
Meladerma Swainson 1839
Rachycentron Kaup 1826
Spinax Cuvier in Cuvier & Valenciennes (ex Commerson) 1832

FAM. ECHENEIDAE (Remoras)
= Echeneididae

Echeneis Linnaeus 1758
Leptecheneis Gill 1864
Phtheirichthys Gill 1862
Remilegia Gill 1862
Remora Catesby 1771
Remora Gill 1862
Remorina Jordan & Evermann 1896
Remoropsis Gill 1863
Rhombochirus Gill 1863

FAM. CARANGIDAE (Jacks, Amberjacks, Pompanos)

Absalom Whitley 1937
Acanthinion Lacepède 1802
Alectis Rafinesque 1815
Alepes Swainson 1839
Apolectus Cuvier in Cuvier & Valenciennes 1832
Argyreiosus Lacepède 1802
Atropus Oken (ex Cuvier) 1817
Atule Jordan & Jordan 1922
Baillonus Rafinesque 1815
Bassetina Whitley 1941
Blepharichthys Gill 1861
Blepharis Cuvier 1816
Bothrolaemus Holbrook 1855
Branchialepes Fowler 1938
Buphthalmus Smith 1959
Caesiomorus Lacepède 1801
Campogramma Regan 1903
Carangichthys Bleeker 1852
Carangoides Bleeker 1851
Carangops Gill 1862
Carangulus Jordan & Evermann 1927
Carangus Griffith 1834
Carangus Girard 1858
Caranx Lacepède 1801
Centronotus Lacepède 1801
Chloroscombrus Girard 1858
Chorinemus Cuvier in Cuvier & Valenciennes 1832
Citula Cuvier 1816
Decapterus Bleeker 1851
Decaptus Poey 1861
Doliodon Girard 1858
Elagatis Bennett 1840
Elaphrotoxon Fowler 1905
Eleria Jordan & Seale 1905
Eustomatodus Gill 1862
Evepigymnus Gill 1862

Ferdauia Jordan, Evermann & Wakiya in Jordan, Evermann & Tanaka 1927
Formio Whitley in McCulloch 1929
Gallichtys Cuvier in Cuvier & Valenciennes 1833
Gallus Lacepède 1802
Glaucus Klein 1775
Glaucus Bleeker (ex Klein) 1863
Glaucus Fowler (ex Klein in Walbaum) 1906
Glaucus Jordan & Hubbs (ex Klein) 1917
Glaucus Klein in Walbaum 1792
Gnathanodon Bleeker 1851
Guaperva Plumier in Lacepède 1802
Gymnepignathus Gill 1862
Halatractus Gill 1863
Hemicaranx Bleeker 1862
Hildebrandella Nichols 1950
Hynnis Cuvier in Cuvier & Valenciennes 1833
Hypacantha Lacepède 1810
Hypacantus Rafinesque 1810
Hypocaranx Klunzinger 1884
Hypodis Rafinesque 1810
Irex Valenciennes 1862
Kaiwarinus Suzuki 1962
Laterosculatus de Buen 1926
Laterosquamatus de Buen 1926
Leioglossus Bleeker 1851
Leptaspis Bleeker 1852
Leptoligoplites Fowler 1944
Leucoglossa Jordan & Evermann in Jordan, Evermann & Tanaka 1927
Lichia Cuvier 1816
Longirostrum Wakiya 1924
Megalaspis Bleeker 1851
Micropteryx Agassiz in Spix & Agassiz 1831
Nauclerus Valenciennes in Cuvier & Valenciennes 1833
Naucrates Rafinesque 1810
Naucratopsis Gill 1863
Oligoplites Gill 1863
Olistus Cuvier 1829
Orcynus Rafinesque 1815
Pampanoa Fowler 1906
Pantolabus Whitley 1931
Parastromateus Bleeker 1865
Paratractus Gill 1862
Parona Berg 1895
Paropsis Jenyns 1841
Pelamis Plumier in Lacepède 1801
Platysomus Swainson 1839
Platyuraspis Fowler 1938
Pompilus Minding 1832
Porthmeus Valenciennes in Cuvier & Valenciennes 1833
Pseudocaranx Bleeker 1863
Rastrum Fowler 1904
Regificola Whitley 1931
Rhaphiolepis Fowler 1905
Rhomboida Browne 1789
Saurus Browne 1789
Scomberoides Lacepède 1801
Scyris Cuvier 1829
Selar Bleeker 1851
Selaroides Bleeker 1851
Selene Lacepède 1802
Selenia Bonaparte 1846
Seriola Cuvier 1816
Seriolichthys Bleeker 1854
Seriolina Wakiya 1924
Solagmedens Bauchot & Blanc 1963
Suareus Dardignac & Vincent in Furnestin et al. 1958
Thynnus Gronow in Gray 1854
Trachinotus Lacepède 1801
Trachinus Swainson 1839
Trachurops Gill 1862
Trachurus Plumier in Lacepède 1801
Trachurus Rafinesque 1810
Trachurus Gronow in Gray 1854
Tricropterus Rafinesque 1810
Turrum Whitley 1932
Ulua Jordan & Snyder 1908
Uraspis Bleeker 1855
Usa Whitley 1927
Usacaranx Whitley 1931
Vexillicaranx Fowler 1905
Vomer Cuvier 1816
Xurel Jordan & Evermann 1927
Xystophorus Richardson 1845
Zalocys Jordan & McGregor in Jordan & Evermann 1898
Zamora Whitley 1931
Zonichthys Swainson 1839

FAM. NEMATISTIIDAE (Roosterfishes)

Nematistius Gill 1862
Seriolophus Guichenot 1867

FAM. CORYPHAENIDAE (Dolphins or Dolphinfishes)

Caranxomorus Lacepède 1801
Coryphaena Linnaeus 1758
Coryphus Commerson in Lacepède 1801
Ectenias Jordan & Thompson 1914
Hippurus Klein 1779
Lampugus Valenciennes in Cuvier & Valenciennes 1833
Lepimphis Rafinesque 1810
Sarda Gronow in Gray 1854

FAM. MENIDAE (Moonfishes)

Mene Lacepède 1803
Meneus Rafinesque 1815

FAM. LEIOGNATHIDAE (Ponyfishes or Slipmouths)

Argylepes Swainson 1839
Aurigequula Fowler 1918
Deveximentum Fowler 1904
Equula Cuvier 1815
Equulites Fowler 1904
Eubleekeria Fowler 1904
Gazza Rüppell 1835
Halex Commerson in Lacepède 1803
Leiognathus Lacepède 1802
Macilentichthys Whitley 1932
Nuchequula Whitley 1932
Parochusus Whitley 1930
Secutor Gistel 1848
Victor Whitley 1951

FAM. BRAMIDAE (Pomfrets)

Amblytoxotes Bleeker 1876
Argo Döderlein in Steindachner & Döderlein 1883
Bentenia Jordan & Snyder 1901
Brama Bloch & Schneider 1801
Centropholis Hilgendorf 1878
Centropholoides Smith 1949
Collybus Snyder 1904
Eumegistus Jordan & Jordan 1922
Lepidotus Asso 1801
Lepodus Rafinesque 1810
Oligopodes Cuvier (ex Risso) 1816
Oligopodus Lacepède 1800
Oligopus Risso 1810
Pseudotaractes Abe 1961
Pteracles Swainson 1838
Pteraclidus Rafinesque 1815
Pteraclis Gronow 1772
Pteridium Scopoli 1777
Pterycombus Fries 1837
Steinegeria Jordan & Evermann 1887
Taractes Lowe 1843
Taractichthys Mead & Maul 1958
Trachyberyx Roule 1929
Tylometopon Bleeker 1873
Xenobrama Yatsu & Nakamura 1989

FAM. CARISTIIDAE (Veilfins or Manefishes)

Caristius Gill & Smith 1905
Elephenor Jordan 1919
Platyberyx Zugmayer 1911

FAM. ARRIPIDAE (Australian Salmon)

Arripis Jenyns 1840
Homodon Brisout de Barneville 1847
Lepidomegas Thominot 1880
Mulloides Richardson (ex Solander) 1843

FAM. EMMELICHTHYIDAE (Rovers)

Boxaodon Guichenot 1848
Emmelichthys Richardson 1845
Erythrichthys Temminck & Schlegel 1845
Erythrocles Jordan 1919
Plagiogeneion Forbes 1890

FAM. LUTJANIDAE (Snappers)

Aetiasis Barnard 1937
Anthea Catesby 1771
Aphareus Cuvier in Cuvier & Valenciennes 1830
Aprion Valenciennes in Cuvier & Valenciennes 1830
Apsilus Valenciennes in Cuvier & Valenciennes 1830
Arnillo Jordan, Evermann & Tanaka 1927
Bennettia Fowler 1904
Bowersia Jordan & Evermann 1903
Chaetopterus Schlegel in Temminck & Schlegel 1844
Deuteracanthus Fowler 1944
Diacope Cuvier 1815
Elastoma Swainson 1839
Erythrobussothen Parr 1933
Etelides Jordan & Thompson 1905
Etelinus Jordan in Jordan & Thompson 1911
Etelis Cuvier in Cuvier & Valenciennes 1828
Evoplites Gill 1862
Fares Jordan, Evermann & Tanaka 1927
Genyoroge Cantor 1849
Glabrilutjanus Fowler 1931
Hesperanthias Lowe 1843
Hobar Forsskål 1775

Hoplopagrus Gill 1861
Humefordia Whitley 1931
Hypoplites Gill 1862
Jordanichthys Evermann & Clark 1928
Lipocheilus Anderson, Talwar & Johnson 1977
Loxolutjanus Fowler 1931
Lutianus see *Lutjanus*
Lutjanus Bloch 1790
Macolor Bleeker 1860
Macrops Duméril 1856
Mesoprion Cuvier in Cuvier & Valenciennes 1828
Naqua Forsskål 1775
Neomaenis Girard 1858
Neomesoprion Castelnau 1875
Ocyurus Gill 1862
Pagrus Plumier in Lacepède 1802
Paracaesio Bleeker 1875
Paradicichthys Whitley 1930
Parapristipomoides Kami 1973
Parkia Fowler 1904
Percaprionodes Fowler 1944
Pinjalo Bleeker 1873
Platyinius Gill 1862
Pristipomoides Bleeker 1852
Proamblys Gill 1862
Rabirubia Jordan & Fesler 1893
Raizero Jordan & Fesler 1893
Randallichthys Anderson, Kami & Johnson 1977
Rhomboplites Gill 1862
Rhomboplitoides Fowler 1918
Rooseveltia Jordan & Evermann in Jordan & Seale 1906
Sacrestinus Jordan, Evermann & Tanaka 1927
Salpa Catesby 1771
Sarda Plumier in Lacepède 1802
Sargus Plumier in Lacepède 1802
Sciaenus Commerson in Lacepède 1803
Symphorichthys Munro 1967
Symphorus Günther 1872
Tangia Chan 1970
Tropidinius Poey (ex Gill) 1868
Turdus Catesby 1771
Ulapiscis Whitley 1933
Ulaula Jordan & Thompson 1911
Vegetichthys Tanaka 1917

FAM. CAESIONIDAE (Fusiliers)

Caesio Lacepède 1801
Clupeolabrus Nichols 1923
Dipterygonotus Bleeker 1849
Flavicaesio Carpenter 1987
Gymnocaesio Bleeker 1876
Liocaesio Bleeker 1876
Odontonectes Günther 1859
Pisinnicaesio Carpenter 1987
Pterocaesio Bleeker 1876
Squamosicaesio Carpenter 1987

FAM. LOBOTIDAE (Tripletails)

Coius Hamilton 1822
Datnioides Bleeker 1853
Datnioides Canestrini 1860
Lobotes Cuvier in Cuvier & Valenciennes 1830
Verrugato Jordan 1923

FAM. GERREIDAE (Mojarras)

Catochaenum Cantor 1849
Chthamalopteryx Ogilby 1888
Clara Gill 1862
Diapterus Ranzani 1842
Eucinostomus Baird & Girard in Baird 1855
Eugerres Jordan & Evermann 1927
Gerreomorpha Alleyne & Macleay 1877
Gerres Quoy & Gaimard (ex Cuvier) 1824
Moharra Poey 1875
Mormyrus Catesby 1771
Parequula Steindachner 1879
Pentaprion Bleeker 1850
Pertica Fowler 1904
Podager Gistel 1848
Synistius Gill 1862
Ulaema Jordan & Evermann in Jordan 1895
Xystaema Jordan & Evermann in Jordan 1895

FAM. HAEMULIDAE (Grunts)
= Pomadasyidae; Plectrorhynchidae included

Anarmostus Putnam (ex Scutter) 1863
Anisotremus Gill 1861
Anomalodon Bowdich 1825
Apostata Heckel in Canestrini 1860
Bathystoma Scudder in Putnam 1863
Boridia Cuvier in Cuvier & Valenciennes 1830
Brachydeuterus Gill 1862
Brachygenys Poey (ex Scutter) 1868
Cheironebris Fowler 1944
Cheiroxenichthys Fowler 1930
Cheloniger Plumier in Lacepède 1801
Cilus Delfin 1900
Conodon Cuvier in Cuvier & Valenciennes 1830
Dacymba Jordan & Hubbs 1917
Diabasis Desmarest 1823
Diagramma Oken (ex Cuvier) 1817
Diagrammella Pellegrin 1912
Euelatichthys Fowler 1904
Evapristis Jordan & Evermann 1896
Gaterin Forsskål 1775
Genyatremus Gill 1862
Haemulon Cuvier 1829
Haemulopsis Steindachner 1869
Isacia Jordan & Fesler 1893
Isaciella Jordan & Fesler 1893
Isaciops Miles 1953
Leitectus Smith 1952
Lepidopristis Fowler 1944
Lepthaemulon Fowler & Bean 1923
Lythrulon Jordan & Swain 1884
Microlepidotus Gill 1862
Mylacrodon Regan 1903
Orthopristis Girard 1858
Orthostoechus Gill 1862
Otoperca Boulenger 1915
Paraconodon Bleeker 1876
Parakuhlia Pellegrin 1913
Parapristipoma Bleeker 1873
Plectorhinchus Lacepède 1801
Plectorhynchus see *Plectorhinchus*
Pluchus Smith 1949
Polotus Blyth 1858
Pomadasyina Fowler 1931
Pomadasys Lacepède 1802
Pristipoma Quoy & Gaimard (ex Cuvier) 1824
Pristipomus Oken (ex Cuvier) 1817
Pristocantharus Gill 1862
Pseudohelotes Guimarães 1882
Pseudopristipoma Sauvage 1880
Rhencus Jordan & Evermann 1896
Rhonciscus Jordan & Evermann 1896
Spilotichthys Fowler 1904
Spinipercina Fowler 1944
Xenichthys Gill 1863
Xenistius Jordan & Gilbert 1883
Xenocys Jordan & Bollman 1890

FAM. INERMIIDAE (Bonnetmouths)

Emmelichthyops Schultz 1945
Inermia Poey 1860

FAM. SPARIDAE (Porgys and Seabreams)

Acanthopagrus Peters 1855
Allotaius Whitley 1937
Archosargus Gill 1865
Argyrops Swainson 1839
Argyrozona Smith 1938
Aurata Catesby 1771
Aurata Oken (ex Cuvier) 1817
Aurata Risso 1826
Austrosparus Smith 1938
Axineceps Smith 1938
Boopsoidea Castelnau 1861
Caeso Gistel 1848
Calamus Swainson 1839
Cantharus Cuvier 1816
Cantharusa Strand 1928
Caranthus Barnard 1927
Charax Risso 1826
Cheimerius Smith 1938
Chryseis Schinz 1822
Chrysoblephus Swainson 1839
Chrysophris Cuvier 1829
Chrysophrys Quoy & Gaimard 1824
Crenidens Valenciennes in Cuvier & Valenciennes 1830
Cymatoceps Smith 1938
Cynaedus Gronow 1763
Cynedus Scopoli (ex Gronow) 1777
Daurada Stark 1828
Denius Gistel 1848
Dentex Cuvier 1814
Diplodus Rafinesque 1810
Dorada Jarocki 1822
Dulosparus Fowler 1933
Eudynama Gistel 1848
Eusalpa Fowler 1925
Evynnis Jordan & Thompson 1912
Grammateus Poey 1872
Gymnocrotaphus Günther 1859
Labeo Bowdich 1825
Labeova Whitley 1950
Lagodon Holbrook 1855
Leptometopon Smith 1940
Lithognathus Swainson 1839
Mimocubiceps Fowler 1944
Mylio Commerson in Lacepède 1802
Nudipagellus Fowler 1925
Oblada Cuvier 1829
Opsodentex Fowler 1925
Otrynter Jordan & Evermann 1896
Pachymetopon Günther 1859
Pagellus Valenciennes in Cuvier & Valenciennes 1830
Pagrichthys Bleeker 1860

Pagrosomus Gill 1893
Pagrus Cuvier 1816
Parargyrops Tanaka 1916
Petrus Smith 1938
Polyamblyodon Norman 1935
Polysteganus Klunzinger 1870
Porcostoma Smith 1938
Prionosparus Smith 1942
Pterogymnus Smith 1938
Puntazzo Bleeker 1876
Rhabdosargus Fowler 1933
Rhamnubia Whitley 1951
Roughleyia Whitley 1931
Salema Jordan & Evermann 1896
Sargus Klein 1775
Sargus Cuvier 1816
Sarpa Bonaparte 1831
Semapagrus Fowler 1925
Simocantharus Fowler 1933
Sparidentex Munro 1948
Sparodon Smith 1938
Sparosomus Gill 1893
Sparus Linnaeus 1758
Sphenosargus Fowler 1940
Spondyliosoma Cantor 1849
Stenesthes Jordan 1917
Stenotomus Gill 1865
Synagris Klein 1775
Synagris Klein in Walbaum 1792
Taenarichthys Whitley 1953
Taenarus Whitley 1951
Taius Jordan & Thompson 1912
Viridentex Poll 1971

FAM. CENTRACANTHIDAE

Boops Cuvier 1814
Box Valenciennes in Cuvier & Valenciennes 1830
Centracantha
Centracanthus Rafinesque 1810
Coleosmaris Norman 1931
Maena Cuvier 1829
Maenas Klein 1776
Maenas Bleeker (ex Klein) 1876
Marsis Barnard 1927
Merolepis Rafinesque 1810
Pterosmaris Fowler 1925
Smaris Cuvier 1814
Spicara Rafinesque 1810

FAM. LETHRINIDAE (Emperors)

Gnathodentex Bleeker 1873
Gymnocranius Klunzinger 1870
Lethrinella Fowler 1904
Lethrinichthys Jordan & Thompson 1912
Lethrinus Cuvier 1829
Maina Gistel 1848
Monotaxis Bennett 1830
Neolethrinus Castelnau 1875
Paradentex Bleeker 1872
Schour Forsskål 1775
Sphaerodon Rüppell 1838
Sphoerodon Rüppell 1838
Wattsia Chan & Chilvers 1974

FAM. NEMIPTERIDAE (Threadfin Breams and Spinycheeks) Scolopsidae included

Anemura Fowler 1904
Ctenoscolopsis Fowler 1931
Euthyopteroma Fowler 1904
Ghanan Forsskål 1775
Heterodon Bleeker 1845
Heterognathodon Bleeker 1848
Leiopsis Bennett 1830
Leptoscolopsis Tanaka 1915
Lunicauda Whitley 1947
Lycogenis Cuvier (ex Kuhl & van Hasselt) in Cuvier & Valenciennes 1830
Maenoides Richardson 1843
Nemipterus Swainson 1839
Odontoglyphis Fowler 1904
Parabodianus de Beaufort 1940
Parascolopsis Boulenger 1901
Pentapodus Quoy & Gaimard (ex Cuvier) 1824
Pentapus Valenciennes in Cuvier & Valenciennes 1830
Psilopentapodus Fowler 1933
Scaevius Whitley 1947
Scolopsides Cuvier 1829
Scolopsis Cuvier 1814
Sparopsis Kner 1868
Synagris Günther 1859
Synagris Bleeker (ex Klein) 1876

FAM. SCIAENIDAE (Croakers and Drums)

Afroscion Trewavas 1977
Alburnus Catesby 1771
Amblyscion Gill 1863
Ancylodon Oken (ex Cuvier) 1817
Anomiolepis Gill 1861
Apeches Gistel 1848
Aplodinotus Rafinesque 1819
Apseudobranchus Gill 1862
Archoscion Gill 1862
Argyrosomus De la Pylaie 1835
Aspericorvina Fowler 1934
Asperina Ostroumoff 1896
Atractoscion Gill 1862
Atrobucca Chu, Lo & Wu 1963
Attilus Gistel 1848
Austronibea Trewavas 1977
Bahaba Herre 1935
Bairdiella Gill 1861
Blythia Talwar 1971
Blythsciaena Talwar 1975
Boesemania Trewavas 1977
Bola Hamilton 1822
Buccone Jordan & Evermann 1896
Callaus Jordan & Evermann 1889
Cantor Talwar 1970
Cestreus Gronow in Gray 1854
Cheilotrema Tschudi 1846
Chromis Plumier in Lacepède 1801
Chrysochir Trewavas & Yazdani 1966
Cirrimens Gill 1862
Collichthys Günther 1860
Coracinus Pallas 1814
Corvina Cuvier 1829
Corvula Jordan & Eigenmann 1889
Cromis Browne 1789
Ctenosciaena Fowler & Bean 1923
Cynoscion Gill 1861
Daysciaena Talwar 1970
Dendrophysa Trewavas 1964
Dhoma Talwar & Joglekar 1970
Diplolepis Steindachner 1863
Elattarchus Jordan & Evermann 1896
Eques Bloch 1793
Equetus Rafinesque 1815
Eriscion Jordan & Evermann 1927
Eutychelithus Jordan 1876
Excursor Gistel 1848
Fonticulus Trewavas 1962
Genyonemus Gill 1861
Haploidonotus see *Aplodinotus*
Hemisciaena Bleeker 1863
Homoprion Holbrook 1855
Hostia Trewavas 1962
Isopisthus Gill 1862
Johnieops Mohan 1972
Johnius Bloch 1793
Kalthala Mohan 1969
Kathala Mohan 1969
Kroseriphus Whitley 1950
Larimichthys Jordan & Starks 1905
Larimodon Bleeker (ex Kaup) 1876
Larimus Cuvier in Cuvier & Valenciennes 1830
Leiostomus Lacepède 1802
Lepipterus Cuvier in Cuvier & Valenciennes 1830
Lonchurus Bloch 1793
Macrodon Schinz 1822
Macrospinosa Mohan 1969
Megalonibea Chu, Lo & Wu 1963
Melantha Gistel 1848
Menticirrhus Gill 1861
Micropogon Cuvier in Cuvier & Valenciennes 1830
Micropogonias Bonaparte 1831
Miichthys Lin 1938
Miracorvina Trewavas 1962
Monosira Poey 1881
Nebris Cuvier in Cuvier & Valenciennes 1830
Nector Jordan & Evermann 1898
Nibea Jordan & Thompson 1911
Nomalus Gistel 1848
Odontoscion Gill 1862
Ophioscion Gill 1863
Othonias Jordan & Thompson 1911
Otolithes Oken (ex Cuvier) 1817
Otolithoides Fowler 1933
Pachypops Gill 1861
Pachyurus Agassiz in Spix & Agassiz 1831
Pama Fowler 1933
Panna Mohan 1969
Paralarimus Fowler & Bean 1923
Paralonchurus Bocourt 1869
Paranibea Trewavas 1977
Paraplesichthys Bleeker (ex Kaup) 1876
Pareques Gill in Goode 1876
Pennahia Fowler 1926
Pentheroscion Trewavas 1962
Pinnacorvina Fowler 1925
Plagioscion Gill 1861
Pogonathus Lacepède (ex Commerson) 1803
Pogonias Lacepède 1801
Polycirrhus Bocourt 1869
Polyclemus Berg 1895
Protonibea Trewavas 1971
Pseudomycterus Ogilby 1908
Pseudosciaena Bleeker 1863
Pseudotolithus Bleeker 1863
Pteroscion Fowler 1925
Pterotolithus Fowler 1933

Rhinoscion Gill 1861
Roncador Jordan & Gilbert 1880
Sagenichthys Berg 1895
Sciaena Linnaeus 1758
Sciaenoides Blyth 1860
Sciaenops Gill 1863
Seriphus Ayres 1860
Sigmurus Gilbert in Jordan & Evermann 1898
Sonorolux Trewavas 1977
Stellicarens Gilbert in Jordan & Evermann 1898
Stellifer Oken (ex Cuvier) 1817
Stelliferus Stark 1828
Symphysoglyphus Miranda-Ribeiro 1915
Totoaba Villamar 1980
Umbrina Cuvier 1816
Umbrula Jordan & Eigenmann 1889
Vacuoqua Jordan & Evermann 1927
Wak Lin 1938
Zaclemus Gilbert in Jordan & Evermann 1896
Zeluco Whitley 1931
Zestidium Gilbert in Jordan & Evermann 1898
Zestis Gilbert in Jordan & Evermann 1898
Zonoscion Jordan & Evermann 1896

FAM. MULLIDAE (Goatfishes)

Atahua Phillipps 1941
Barbupeneus Whitley 1931
Brachymullus Bleeker 1876
Caprupeneus Whitley 1931
Hogbinia Whitley 1929
Hypeneus Agassiz 1846
Megalepis Bianconi 1857
Mullhypeneus Poey 1867
Mulloides Bleeker 1849
Mulloidichthys Whitley 1929
Mullus Linnaeus 1758
Parupeneus Bleeker 1863
Pennon Whitley 1941
Pseudomulloides Miranda-Ribeiro 1915
Pseudupeneus Bleeker 1862
Upeneichthys Bleeker 1855
Upeneoides Bleeker 1849
Upeneus Cuvier 1829

FAM. PEMPHERIDAE (Sweepers)

Catalufa Snyder 1911
Liopempheris Ogilby 1913
Parapempheris von Bonde 1924
Parapriacanthus Steindachner 1870
Pempherichthys Klunzinger 1871
Pempheris Cuvier 1829
Priacanthopsis Fowler 1906

FAM. LEPTOBRAMIDAE (Beachsalmon)

Leptobrama Steindachner 1878
Neopempheris Macleay 1881

FAM. BATHYCLUPEIDAE (Bathyclupeids)

Bathyclupea Alcock 1891

FAM. TOXOTIDAE (Archerfishes)

Protoxotes Whitley 1950
Toxotes Cuvier 1816
Trompe Gistel 1848

FAM. CORACINIDAE (Galjoens)

Coracinus Gronow 1763

Dichistius Gill 1888
Dipterodon Cuvier 1829
Drepanoscorpis Fowler 1934

FAM. KYPHOSIDAE (Sea Chubs)

Cridorsa Whitley 1938

Subfam. Girellinae (Nibblers)

Aplodon Thominot (ex Duméril) 1883
Camarina Ayres 1860
Doidyxodon Valenciennes 1846
Doydixodon see *Doidyxodon*
Epelytes Evermann & Radcliffe 1917
Exocallus De la Pylaie 1835
Girella Gray 1835
Girellichthys Klunzinger 1872
Girellipiscis Whitley 1931
Girellops Regan 1913
Glyphodes Guichenot 1864
Graus Philippi 1887
Guichenotia Whitley 1950
Incisidens Gill 1862
Iredalella Whitley 1931
Melambaphes Günther 1863
Melanychthys Temminck & Schlegel 1844
Neotephraeops Castelnau 1872
Pinguilabrum Hildebrand 1946
Scatharus Valenciennes in Cuvier & Valenciennes 1830
Tephraeops Günther 1859

Subfam. Kyphosinae (Rudderfishes)

Dorsuarius Lacepède (ex Commerson) 1803
Hermosilla Jenkins & Evermann 1889
Kyphosus Lacepède 1801
Leptokyphosus Whitley 1931
Opisthistius Gill 1862
Pimelepterus Lacepède 1802
Sectator Jordan & Fesler 1893
Segutilum Whitley 1931
Seleima Bowdich 1825
Tahhmel Forsskål 1775
Xyster Lacepède (ex Commerson) 1803
Xysterus Rafinesque 1815

Subfam. Scorpidinae (Halfmoons)
Labracoglossidae included

Agenor Castelnau 1879
Atypus Günther 1860
Bathystethus Gill 1893
Caesioma Kaup 1864
Caesiosoma Bleeker (ex Kaup) 1876
Cypselichthys Steindachner & Döderlein 1883
Juvenella Whitley 1948
Labracoglossa Peters 1866
Medialuna Jordan & Fesler 1893
Neoscorpis Smith 1931
Neptotichthys Hutton 1890
Platystethus Günther 1860
Scorpis Valenciennes in Cuvier & Valenciennes 1832
Tilodon Thominot (ex Guichenot) 1881

Subfam. Microcanthinae

Atypichthys Günther 1862
Helotosoma Kaup 1863
Microcanthus Swainson 1839

Neatypus Waite 1905
Neochaetodon Castelnau 1873
Therapaina Kaup 1860
Vinculum McCulloch 1914

FAM. PARASCORPIDIDAE (Jutjaws)

Atyposoma Boulenger 1899
Parascorpis Bleeker 1875

FAM. DREPANIDAE (Sicklefishes)

Cryptosmilia Cope 1869
Drepane Cuvier in Cuvier & Valenciennes 1831
Drepanichthys Bonaparte 1831
Enixe Gistel 1848
Harpochris Cantor 1849

FAM. EPHIPPIDAE (Spadefishes, Batfishes and Scats)
= Chaetodipterinae; Rhinoprenidae and Platacinae included

Chaetodipterus Lacepède 1802
Ephippus Cuvier 1816
Ilarches Cantor 1849
Parapsettus Steindachner 1875
Parephippus Gill 1861
Platax Cuvier 1816
Proteracanthus Günther 1859
Rhinoprenes Munro 1964
Tripterodon Playfair in Playfair & Günther 1866
Zabidius Whitley 1930

FAM. MONODACTYLIDAE (Moonies)

Acanthopodus Lacepède 1802
Bramichthys Waite 1905
Centropodus Lacepède 1801
Monodactylus Lacepède (ex Commerson) 1801
Psettias Jordan in Jordan & Seale 1906
Psettus Commerson in Lacepède 1801
Psettus Cuvier (ex Commerson) 1829
Schuettea Steindachner 1866
Stromatoidea Castelnau 1861

FAM. SCATOPHAGIDAE (Scats)

Cacodoxus Cantor 1849
Desmoprenes Fowler & Bean 1929
Prenes Gistel 1848
Scatophagus Cuvier in Cuvier & Valenciennes 1831
Selenotoca Myers 1936

FAM. CHAETODONTIDAE (Butterflyfishes)

Acanthotaurichthys Burgess 1978
Amphichaetodon Burgess 1978
Anisochaetodon Klunzinger 1884
Apporetochaetodon Maugé & Bauchot 1984
Aspilurochaetodon Maugé & Bauchot 1984
Bauchotia Nalbant 1965
Burgessius Maugé & Bauchot 1984
Byssochaetodon Maugé & Bauchot 1984
Chaetodon Linnaeus 1758
Chaetodontops Bleeker 1876
Chelmon Cloquet 1817
Chelmonops Bleeker 1876
Citharoedus Kaup 1860
Coradion Kaup 1860
Corallochaetodon Burgess 1978
Diphreutes Cantor 1849

Discochaetodon Nalbant 1971
Eteira Kaup 1860
Exornator Nalbant 1971
Forcipiger Jordan & McGregor in Jordan & Evermann 1898
Gonochaetodon Bleeker 1876
Hemichaetodon Bleeker 1876
Heminigellus Nalbant 1984
Hemitaurichthys Bleeker 1876
Heniochus Cuvier 1816
Heterochaetodon Maugé & Bauchot 1984
Johnrandallia Nalbant 1974
Lepidochaetodon Bleeker 1876
Linophora Kaup 1860
Loa Jordan 1921
Megaprotodon Guichenot 1848
Mesochaetodon Maugé & Bauchot 1984
Nalbantius Maugé & Bauchot 1984
Nesochaetodon Maugé & Bauchot 1984
Nox Nalbant 1986
Osteochromis Franz 1910
Oxychaetodon Bleeker 1876
Paracanthochaetodon Schmidt & Lindberg 1930
Parachaetodon Bleeker 1874
Paracoradion Ahl 1923
Prognathodes Gill 1862
Pseudochaetodon Burgess 1978
Rabdophorus Swainson 1839
Rhombochaetodon Burgess 1978
Roa Jordan 1923
Roaops Maugé & Bauchot 1984
Sarothrodus Gill 1861
Strongylochaetodon Maugé & Bauchot 1984
Taurichthys Cuvier 1829
Tetrachaetodon Weber & de Beaufort 1936
Tetragonopterus Bleeker 1863
Tetragonoptrus Klein 1776
Tetragonoptrus Walbaum (ex Klein) 1792
Tholichthys Günther 1868
Tifia Jordan in Jordan & Jordan 1922

FAM. POMACANTHIDAE (Angelfishes)

Acanthochaetodon Bleeker 1876
Angelichthys Jordan & Evermann 1896
Apolemichthys Fraser-Brunner 1933
Arusetta Fraser-Brunner 1933
Centropyge Kaup 1860
Chaetodontoplus Bleeker 1876
Desmoholacanthus Fowler 1941
Euxiphipops Fraser-Brunner 1934
Genicanthus Swainson 1839
Heteropyge Fraser-Brunner 1933
Holacanthus Lacepède 1802
Paradiretmus Whitley 1948
Plitops Fraser-Brunner 1933
Pomacanthodes Gill 1862
Pomacanthops Smith 1955
Pomacanthus Lacepède 1802
Pygoplites Fraser-Brunner 1933
Xiphypops Jordan in Jordan & Jordan 1922

FAM. ENOPLOSIDAE (Oldwives)

Enoplosus Lacepède 1802

FAM. PENTACEROTIDAE (Armorheads)

Evistias Jordan 1907
Evistiopterus Whitley 1932
Gilchristia Jordan 1907
Glauertichthys Whitley 1945
Griffinetta Whitley & Phillipps 1939
Histiopterus Temminck & Schlegel 1844
Macullochia Waite 1910
Parazanclistius Hardy 1983
Paristiopterus Bleeker 1876
Pentaceropsis Steindachner in Steindachner & Döderlein 1883
Pentaceros Cuvier in Cuvier & Valenciennes 1829
Prosoplismus Waite 1903
Pseudopentaceros Bleeker 1876
Quadrarius Jordan 1907
Quinquarius Jordan 1907
Richardsonia Castelnau 1872
Undecimus Whitley 1934
Zanclistius Jordan 1907

FAM. NANDIDAE (Leaffishes)

Pomanotis Guichenot 1847

Subfam. Nandinae

Afronandus Meinken 1955
Bedula Gray 1835
Monocirrhus Heckel 1840
Nandopsis Meinken 1954
Nandus Valenciennes in Cuvier & Valenciennes 1831
Polycentropsis Boulenger 1901
Polycentrus Müller & Troschel 1848

Subfam. Pristolepidinae

Catopra Bleeker 1851
Paranandus Day 1865
Pristolepis Jerdon 1849

Subfam. Badinae

Badis Bleeker 1853

FAM. OPLEGNATHIDAE (Knifejaws)

Ichthyorhamphos Castelnau 1861
Oplegnathus Richardson 1840
Scaradon Temminck & Schlegel 1844
Scarostoma Kner 1867

FAM. CICHLIDAE (Cichlids)

Acara Heckel 1840
Acarichthys Eigenmann 1912
Acaronia Myers 1940
Acaropsis Steindachner 1875
Acharnes Müller & Troschel 1848
Aequidens Eigenmann & Bray 1894
Alcolapia Thys van den Audenaerde 1970
Allochromis Greenwood 1980
Alticorpus Stauffer & McKaye 1988
Altolamprologus Poll 1986
Amphilophus Agassiz 1859
Anomalochromis Greenwood 1985
Apistogramma Regan 1913
Apistogrammoides Meinken 1965
Archocentrus Gill 1877
Aristochromis Trewavas 1935
Asprotilapia Boulenger 1901
Astatheros Pellegrin 1904
Astatoreochromis Pellegrin 1904
Astatotilapia Pellegrin 1904
Astronotus Swainson 1839
Aulonocara Regan 1922
Aulonocranus Regan 1920
Baileychromis Poll 1986
Baiodon Agassiz 1859
Barombia Trewavas 1962
Bathybates Boulenger 1898
Batrachops Heckel 1840
Bayonia Boulenger 1911
Benthochromis Poll 1986
Biotodoma Eigenmann & Kennedy 1903
Biotoecus Eigenmann & Kennedy 1903
Boggiania Perugia 1897
Boulengerochromis Pellegrin 1904
Buccochromis Eccles & Trewavas 1989
Bujurquina Kullander 1986
Callochromis Regan 1920
Callopharynx Poll 1948
Caprichromis Eccles & Trewavas 1989
Caquetaia Fowler 1945
Cardiopharynx Poll 1942
Chaetobranchopsis Steindachner 1875
Chaetobranchus Heckel 1840
Chaetolabrus Swainson 1839
Chalinochromis Poll 1974
Champsochromis Boulenger 1915
Cheilochromis Eccles & Trewavas 1989
Chetia Trewavas 1961
Chilochromis Boulenger 1902
Chilotilapia Boulenger 1908
Christyella Trewavas 1935
Chromichthys Guichenot in Duméril 1859
Chromidotilapia Boulenger 1898
Chromis Günther 1862
Chuco Fernández-Yépez 1969
Cichla Bloch & Schneider 1801
Cichlasoma Swainson 1839
Cichlaurus Swainson 1839
Cichlosoma see *Cichlasoma*
Cleithracara Kullander & Nijssen 1989
Cleptochromis Greenwood 1980
Clinodon Regan 1920
Cnestrostoma Regan 1920
Copadichromis Eccles & Trewavas 1989
Copora Fernández-Yépez 1969
Coptodon Gervais 1853
Corematodus Boulenger 1897
Crenacara see *Crenicara*
Crenicara Steindachner 1875
Crenicichla Heckel 1840
Ctenochromis Pfeffer 1893
Ctenopharynx Eccles & Trewavas 1989
Cunningtonia Boulenger 1906
Curraichthys Fernández-Yépez 1969
Cyathochromis Trewavas 1935
Cyathopharynx Regan 1920
Cyclopharynx Poll 1948
Cynotilapia Regan 1922
Cyphotilapia Regan 1920
Cyprichromis Scheuermann 1977
Cyrtocara Boulenger 1902
Dagetia Thys van den Audenaerde 1970
Danakilia Thys van den Audenaerde 1970
Dicrossus Steindachner (ex Agassiz) 1875
Dimidiochromis Eccles & Trewavas 1989
Diplotaxodon Trewavas 1935
Docimodus Boulenger 1897
Eclectochromis Eccles & Trewavas 1989

Ectodus Boulenger 1898
Enantiopus Boulenger 1906
Enterochromis Greenwood 1980
Eretmodus Boulenger 1898
Erythrichthus Meek 1907
Etroplus Cuvier in Cuvier & Valenciennes 1830
Exochochromis Eccles & Trewavas 1989
Fossorochromis Eccles & Trewavas 1989
Gaurochromis Greenwood 1980
Genyochromis Trewavas 1935
Geophagus Heckel 1840
Gephyrochromis Boulenger 1901
Gnathochromis Poll 1981
Gobiochromis Poll 1939
Gobiocichla Kanazawa 1951
Grammatotria Boulenger 1899
Greenwoodochromis Poll 1983
Guianacara Kullander & Nijssen 1989
Gymnogeophagus Miranda-Ribeiro 1918
Haligenes Günther 1859
Haplochromis Hilgendorf 1888
Haplotaxodon Boulenger 1906
Harpagochromis Greenwood 1980
Hemibates Regan 1920
Hemichromis Peters 1858
Hemihaplochromis Wickler 1963
Hemitaeniochromis Eccles & Trewavas 1989
Hemitilapia Boulenger 1902
Herichthys Baird & Girard 1854
Heros Heckel 1840
Herotilapia Pellegrin 1904
Heterochromis Regan 1922
Heterogramma Regan 1906
Heterotilapia Regan 1920
Hoplarchus Kaup 1860
Hoplotilapia Hilgendorf 1888
Hygrogonus Günther 1862
Hypselecara Kullander 1986
Hypsophrys Agassiz 1859
Iodotropheus Oliver & Loiselle 1972
Iranocichla Coad 1982
Julidochromis Boulenger 1898
Konia Trewavas, Green & Corbet 1972
Krobia Kullander & Nijssen 1989
Labeotropheus Ahl 1926
Labidochromis Trewavas 1935
Labrochromis Daget 1952
Labrochromis Regan 1920
Laetacara Kullander 1986
Lamprologus Schilthuis 1891
Lepidiolamprologus Pellegrin 1904
Lepidochromis Poll 1981
Leptochromis Regan 1920
Leptolamprologus Pellegrin 1927
Leptotilapia Pellegrin 1928
Lestradea Poll 1943
Lethrinops Regan 1922
Lichnochromis Trewavas 1935
Limbochromis Greenwood 1987
Limnochromis Regan 1920
Limnotilapia Regan 1920
Lipochromis Regan 1920
Lobochilotes Boulenger 1915
Loruwiala Thys van den Audenaerde 1970
Macropleurodus Regan 1922
Maravichromis Eccles & Trewavas 1989
Maylandia Meyer & Foerster 1984
Melanochromis Trewavas 1935
Melanogenes Bleeker 1863
Mesonauta Günther 1862
Mesops Günther 1862
Microchromis Johnson 1975
Microdontochromis Poll 1986
Microgaster Swainson 1839
Microgeophagus Axelrod 1971
Myaka Trewavas, Green & Corbet 1972
Mylacochromis Greenwood 1980
Mylochromis Regan 1920
Naevochromis Eccles & Trewavas 1989
Nandopsis Gill 1862
Nannacara Regan 1905
Nannacara Miranda-Ribeiro 1918
Nanochromis Pellegrin 1904
Neetroplus Günther 1867
Neochromis Regan 1920
Neolamprologus Colombe & Allgayer 1985
Neopharynx Poll 1948
Neotilapia Regan 1920
Nilotilapia Thys van den Audenaerde 1970
Nimbochromis Eccles & Trewavas 1989
Nyasalapia Thys van den Audenaerde 1970
Nyassachromis Eccles & Trewavas 1989
Oelemaria Kullander & Nijssen 1989
Ophthalmochromis Poll 1956
Ophthalmotilapia Pellegrin 1904
Oreochromis Günther 1889
Orthochromis Greenwood 1954
Otopharynx Regan 1920
Oxylapia Kiener & Maugé 1966
Paleolamprologus Colombe & Allgayer 1985
Papiliochromis Kullander 1977
Paracara Bleeker 1878
Parachromis Regan 1922
Parachromis Agassiz 1859
Paracyprichromis Poll 1986
Paralabidochromis Greenwood 1956
Parananochromis Greenwood 1987
Paraneetroplus Regan 1905
Parapetenia Regan 1905
Paratheraps Werner & Stawikowski 1987
Paratilapia Bleeker 1868
Parectodus Poll 1942
Paretroplus Bleeker 1868
Parvacara Whitley 1951
Pelmatochromis Steindachner 1894
Pelmatolapia Thys van den Audenaerde 1970
Pelvicachromis Thys van den Audenaerde 1968
Perissodus Boulenger 1898
Petenia Günther 1862
Petrochromis Boulenger 1898
Petrotilapia Trewavas 1935
Pharyngochromis Greenwood 1979
Pintoichthys Fowler 1954
Placidochromis Eccles & Trewavas 1989
Plataxoides Castelnau 1855
Platygnathochromis Eccles & Trewavas 1989
Platytaeniodus Boulenger 1906
Plecodus Boulenger 1898
Prognathochromis Greenwood 1980
Protomelas Eccles & Trewavas 1989
Psammochromis Greenwood 1980
Pseudetroplus Bleeker 1862
Pseudoapistogramma Axelrod 1971
Pseudocrenilabrus Fowler 1934
Pseudogeophagus Hoedeman 1974
Pseudoplesiops Boulenger 1899
Pseudosimochromis Nelissen 1977
Pseudotropheus Regan 1922
Pterochromis Trewavas 1973
Pterophyllum Heckel 1840
Ptychochromis Steindachner 1880
Ptychochromoides Kiener & Maugé 1966
Ptyochromis Greenwood 1980
Pungu Trewavas, Green & Corbet 1972
Pyxichromis Greenwood 1980
Reganochromis Whitley 1929
Reganotilapia Whitley 1950
Retroculus Eigenmann & Bray 1894
Rhamphochromis Regan 1922
Rheohaplochromis Thys van den Audenaerde 1963
Saraca Steindachner 1875
Sargochromis Regan 1920
Sarotherodon Rüppell 1852
Satanoperca Günther 1862
Schubotzia Boulenger 1914
Schwetzochromis Poll 1948
Sciaenochromis Eccles & Trewavas 1989
Serranochromis Regan 1920
Simochromis Boulenger 1898
Spathodus Boulenger 1900
Stappersetta Whitley 1950
Stappersia Boulenger 1914
Steatocranus Boulenger 1899
Stigmatochromis Eccles & Trewavas 1989
Stomatepia Trewavas 1962
Symphysodon Heckel 1840
Taeniacara Myers 1935
Taeniochromis Eccles & Trewavas 1989
Taeniolethrinops Eccles & Trewavas 1989
Tahuantinsuyoa Kullander 1986
Tangachromis Poll 1981
Tanganicodus Poll 1950
Teleocichla Kullander 1988
Teleogramma Boulenger 1899
Telmatochromis Boulenger 1898
Telotrematocara Poll 1986
Theraps Günther 1862
Thoracochromis Greenwood 1979
Thorichthys Meek 1904
Thysia Loiselle & Welcomme 1972
Thysochromis Daget 1988
Tilapia Smith 1840
Tomocichla Regan 1908
Tramitichromis Eccles & Trewavas 1989
Trematocara Boulenger 1899
Trematochromis Poll 1987
Trematocranus Trewavas 1935
Trewavasia Thys van den Audenaerde 1970
Tridontochromis Greenwood 1980
Triglachromis Poll & Thys van den Audenaerde 1974
Tristramella Trewavas 1942
Tropheops Trewavas 1984
Tropheus Boulenger 1898
Tylochromis Regan 1920
Tyrannochromis Eccles & Trewavas 1989
Uaru Heckel 1840
Vallicola Trewavas 1983
Variabilichromis Colombe & Allgayer 1985
Vieja Fernández-Yépez 1969
Xenochromis Boulenger 1899

Xenotilapia Boulenger 1899
Xystichromis Greenwood 1980
Yssichromis Greenwood 1980

FAM. EMBIOTOCIDAE (Surfperches)

Abeona Girard 1855
Amphigonopterus Hubbs 1918
Amphistichus Agassiz 1854
Brachyistius Gill 1862
Bramopsis Agassiz (L.) in A. Agassiz 1861
Crossochir Hubbs 1933
Cymatogaster Gibbons 1854
Dacentrus Jordan 1878
Damalichthys Girard 1855
Ditrema Temminck & Schlegel 1844
Embiotoca Agassiz 1853
Ennichthys Girard 1855
Holconotus Agassiz 1854
Hyperprosopon Gibbons 1854
Hypocritichthys Gill 1862
Hypsurus Agassiz 1861
Hysterocarpus Gibbons 1854
Maenichthys Bleeker (ex Kaup) 1876
Metrogaster Agassiz 1861
Micrometrus Gibbons 1854
Mytilophagus Gibbons 1854
Neoditrema Steindachner in Steindachner & Döderlein 1883
Pachylabrus Gibbons 1854
Phanerodon Girard 1854
Rhacochilus Agassiz 1854
Sargosomus Agassiz (L.) in A. Agassiz 1861
Sema Jordan 1878
Taeniotoca Agassiz 1861
Tocichthys Hubbs 1918
Zalembius Jordan & Evermann 1896

FAM. POMACENTRIDAE (Damselfishes and Anemonefishes)

Abudefduf Forsskål 1775
Acanthochromis Gill 1863
Actinicola Fowler 1904
Actinochromis Bleeker 1877
Agripopa Whitley 1928
Amblyglyphidodon Bleeker 1877
Amblypomacentrus Bleeker 1877
Amphiprion Bloch & Schneider 1801
Ayresia Cooper 1863
Azurella Jordan 1919
Azurina Jordan & McGregor in Jordan & Evermann 1898
Belochromis Fowler 1944
Brachypomacentrus Bleeker 1877
Centrochromis Norman 1922
Cheiloprion Weber 1913
Chromanthias Whitley 1935
Chromis Cuvier 1814
Chromis Oken (ex Cuvier) 1817
Chrysiptera Swainson 1839
Ctenoglyphidodon Fowler 1918
Dascyllus Cuvier 1829
Daya Bleeker 1877
Demoisellea Whitley 1928
Dischistodus Gill 1863
Dorychromis Fowler & Bean 1928
Eupomacentrus Bleeker 1877
Euschistodus Gill 1862
Furcaria Poey 1860
Glyphidodontops Bleeker 1877
Glyphisodon Lacepède 1802
Heliases Cuvier in Cuvier & Valenciennes 1830
Heliastes Lowe 1838
Hemiglyphidodon Bleeker 1877
Heptadecanthus Alleyne & Macleay 1877
Hoplochromis Fowler 1918
Hypsypops Gill 1861
Indoglyphidodon Fowler 1944
Iredaleichthys Whitley 1928
Labrodascyllus Caporiacco 1947
Lepicephalochromis Fowler 1943
Lepidochromis Fowler & Bean 1928
Lepidopomacentrus Allen 1975
Lepidozygus Günther 1862
Mecaenichthys Whitley 1929
Microspathodon Günther 1862
Nannapogon Fowler 1938
Negostegastes Whitley 1929
Neopomacentrus Allen 1975
Nexilarius Gilbert in Jordan & Evermann 1896
Nexilosus Heller & Snodgrass 1903
Oliglyphisodon Fowler 1941
Omopomacentrus Fowler 1944
Onychognathus Troschel 1866
Paraglyphidodon Bleeker 1877
Paramphiprion Wang 1941
Parapomacentrus Bleeker 1877
Parma Günther 1862
Pellochromis Fowler & Bean 1928
Phalerebus Whitley 1929
Pirene Gistel 1848
Plectroglyphidodon Fowler & Ball 1924
Pomacentrus Lacepède 1802
Pomachromis Allen & Randall 1974
Pomataprion Gill 1863
Premnas Cuvier 1816
Pristotis Rüppell 1838
Prochilus Klein 1775
Prochilus Bleeker (ex Klein) 1865
Pseudopomacentrus Bleeker 1877
Pterocyclosoma Fowler 1941
Pycnochromis Fowler 1941
Semadascyllus Fowler 1941
Serrichromis Fowler 1943
Similiparma Hensley 1986
Siphonochromis Fowler 1946
Stegastes Jenyns 1840
Teixeirichthys Smith 1953
Tetrades Bleeker 1865
Tetradrachmum Cantor 1849
Thrissochromis Fowler 1941
Wangia Fowler 1954
Wangietta Whitley 1965
Zabulon Whitley 1928

FAM. CIRRHITIDAE (Hawkfishes)

Acanthocirrhitus Fowler 1938
Amblycirrhitus Gill 1862
Cirrhitichthys Bleeker 1857
Cirrhitoidea Jenkins 1903
Cirrhitops Smith 1951
Cirrhitopsis Gill 1862
Cirrhitus Lacepède 1803
Cyprinocirrhites Tanaka 1917
Dactylophora De Vis 1883
Gymnocirrhites Smith 1951
Hughichthys Schultz 1943
Isocirrhitus Randall 1963
Neocirrhites Castelnau 1873
Oxycirrhites Bleeker 1857
Paracirrhites Bleeker 1875
Paracirrhites Steindachner in Steindachner & Döderlein 1883
Pseudocirrhites Mowbray in Breder 1927
Psilocranium Macleay 1884

FAM. CHIRONEMIDAE (Kelpfishes)

Chironemus Cuvier 1829

FAM. APLODACTYLIDAE

Aplodactylus Valenciennes in Cuvier & Valenciennes 1832
Crinodus Gill 1862
Dactylosargus Gill 1862
Parhaplodactylus Thominot 1883
Threpterius Richardson 1850

FAM. CHEILODACTYLIDAE (Fingerfins or Morwongs)

Acantholatris Gill 1862
Cheilodactylus Lacepède 1803
Chirodactylus Gill 1862
Dactylopagrus Gill 1862
Dactylosparus Gill 1862
Goniistius Gill 1862
Gregoryina Fowler & Ball 1924
Morwong Whitley 1957
Nemadactylus Richardson 1839
Palunolepis Barnard 1927
Pteronemus Van der Hoeven 1849
Sciaenoides Richardson (ex Solander) 1850
Trichopterus Gronow in Gray 1854
Zeodrius Castelnau 1879

FAM. LATRIDAE (Trumpeters) = Latrididae

Evistius Gill 1893
Latridopsis Gill 1862
Latris Richardson 1839
Melbanella Whitley 1937
Mendosoma Guichenot 1848
Micropus Kner 1868
Orqueta Jordan 1919

FAM. CEPOLIDAE (Bandfishes) Owstoniidae included

Acanthocepola Bleeker 1874
Cepola Linnaeus 1766
Loxopseudochromis Fowler 1934
Opsipseudochromis Fowler 1934
Owstonia Tanaka 1908
Parasphenanthias Gilchrist 1922
Pseudocepola Kamohara 1935
Sphenanthias Weber 1913
Taenia Röse 1793

FAM. OPISTOGNATHIDAE (Jawfishes)

Gnathypops Gill 1862
Lonchistium Myers 1935
Lonchopisthus Gill 1862
Merogymnoides Whitley 1966
Merogymnus Ogilby 1908

Opistognathus Cuvier 1816
Stalix Jordan & Snyder 1902
Tandya Whitley 1930
Upsilonognathus Fowler 1946

FAM. NOTOGRAPTIDAE

Blanchardia Castelnau 1875
Notograptus Günther 1867

SUBORDER MUGILOIDEI

FAM. MUGILIDAE (Mullets)

Aeschrichthys Macleay 1883
Agonostomus Bennett 1832
Albula Catesby 1771
Aldrichetta Whitley 1945
Arnion Gistel 1848
Cephalus Lacepède (ex Plumier) 1800
Cestraeus Valenciennes in Cuvier & Valenciennes 1836
Cestreus Klein 1777
Chaenomugil Gill 1863
Chelon Röse 1793
Crenimugil Schultz 1946
Dajaus Valenciennes in Cuvier & Valenciennes 1836
Ello Gistel 1848
Ellochelon Whitley 1930
Gonostomyxus Macdonald 1869
Gracilimugil Whitley 1941
Heteromugil Schultz 1946
Joturus Poey 1860
Liza Jordan & Swain 1884
Moolgarda Whitley 1945
Mugil Linnaeus 1758
Mugiloides Lacepède 1803
Myxonum Rafinesque 1815
Myxus Günther 1861
Neomugil Vaillant 1894
Neomyxus Steindachner 1878
Nestis Valenciennes in Cuvier & Valenciennes 1836
Oedalechilus Fowler 1903
Osteomugil Luther 1982
Oxymugil Whitley 1948
Planiliza Whitley 1945
Plicomugil Schultz in Schultz et al. 1953
Protomugil Popov 1930
Pteromugil Smith 1948
Querimana Jordan & Gilbert 1883
Rhinomugil Gill 1863
Sicamugil Fowler 1939
Squalomugil Ogilby 1908
Strializa Smith 1948
Trachystoma Ogilby 1888
Valamugil Smith 1948
Xenomugil Schultz 1946
Xenorhynchichthys Regan 1908

SUBORDER POLYNEMOIDEI

FAM. POLYNEMIDAE (Threadfins)

Clodactylus Rafinesque 1815
Eleutheronema Bleeker 1862
Filimanus Myers 1936
Galeoides Günther 1860
Pentanemus Günther 1860
Polistonemus Gill 1861
Polydactylus Lacepède 1803
Polynemus Linnaeus 1758
Trichidion Klein 1776
Trichidion Gill (ex Klein) 1861

SUBORDER LABROIDEI

FAM. LABRIDAE (Wrasses)

Acantholabrus Valenciennes in Cuvier & Valenciennes 1839
Acarauna Sevastianoff 1802
Achoerodus Gill 1863
Amorphocephalus Bowdich 1825
Ampheces Jordan & Snyder 1902
Anampses Quoy & Gaimard (ex Cuvier) 1824
Anchichoerops Barnard 1927
Antonichthys Bauchot & Blanc 1961
Artisia de Beaufort 1939
Aspiurochilus Fowler 1956
Austrolabrus Steindachner 1884
Aygula Rafinesque 1815
Bermudichthys Nichols 1920
Bodianus Bloch 1790
Centrolabrus Günther 1861
Chaeropsodes Gilchrist & Thompson 1909
Cheilinoides Bleeker 1851
Cheilinus Lacepède 1801
Cheilio Lacepède 1802
Cheiliopsis Steindachner 1863
Cheilolabrus Alleyne & Macleay 1877
Chloricthys Swainson 1839
Choerodon Bleeker 1849
Choerodonoides Kamohara 1958
Choerojulis Gill 1862
Choerops Rüppell 1852
Cicla Klein 1776
Cicla Röse 1793
Cirrhilabrichthys Klausewitz 1976
Cirrhilabrus Temminck & Schlegel 1845
Clepticus Cuvier 1829
Conniella Allen 1983
Coris Lacepède (ex Commerson) 1801
Corycus Cuvier 1814
Cossyphodes Bleeker 1860
Cossyphus Valenciennes in Cuvier & Valenciennes 1839
Crassilabrus Swainson 1839
Crenilabrus Oken (ex Cuvier) 1817
Ctenocorissa Whitley 1931
Ctenolabrus Valenciennes in Cuvier & Valenciennes 1839
Cymolutes Günther 1861
Cynaedus Swainson 1839
Datnia Cuvier 1829
Decodon Günther 1861
Diastodon Bowdich 1825
Dimalacocentrus Gill 1863
Diproctacanthus Bleeker 1862
Doratonotus Günther 1861
Dotalabrus Whitley 1930
Duohemipteronotus Fowler 1956
Duymaeria Bleeker 1856
Elops Commerson in Lacepède 1801
Elops Bonaparte (ex Commerson) 1831
Emmeekia Jordan & Evermann 1896
Epibulus Cuvier 1815
Euhypsocara Gill 1863
Eupemis Swainson 1839
Eupetrichthys Ramsay & Ogilby 1888
Fowlerella Smith 1957
Frontilabrus Randall & Condé 1989
Gomphosus Lacepède 1801
Guentheria Bleeker 1862
Gymnopropoma Gill 1863
Halichoeres Rüppell 1835
Halinanodes Whitley 1931
Harpe Lacepède 1802
Helops Browne 1789
Hemicoris Bleeker 1862
Hemigymnus Günther 1861
Hemipteronotus Lacepède 1801
Hemitautoga Bleeker 1862
Hemiulis Swainson 1839
Heterochoerops Steindachner 1866
Hiatula Lacepède 1800
Hinalea Jordan & Jordan 1922
Hologymnosus Lacepède 1801
Hospilabrus Whitley 1931
Hypsigenys Günther 1861
Ichthycallus Swainson 1839
Iniistius Gill 1862
Iridio Jordan & Evermann 1896
Julichthys De Vis 1885
Julidio Jordan & Evermann 1896
Julis Cuvier 1814
Labrastrum Guichenot 1860
Labrichthys Bleeker 1854
Labroides Bleeker 1851
Labropsis Schmidt 1930
Labrus Linnaeus 1758
Lachnolaimus Cuvier 1829
Lappanella Jordan 1890
Larabicus Randall & Springer 1973
Lepidaplois Gill 1862
Leptojulis Bleeker 1862
Lienardella Fowler & Bean 1928
Lunolabrus Whitley 1933
Macrochoerodon Fowler & Bean 1928
Macropharyngodon Bleeker 1862
Malacocentrus Gill 1862
Malapterus Valenciennes in Cuvier & Valenciennes 1839
Marzapanus Facciolà 1916
Micropodus Rafinesque 1815
Minilabrus Randall & Dor 1980
Neanis Gistel 1848
Nelabrichthys Russell 1983
Neocirrhilabrus Cheng & Wang 1979
Neolabrus Steindachner 1875
Notolabrus Russell 1988
Novacula Cuvier 1815
Novaculichthys Bleeker 1862
Novaculops Schultz 1960
Octocynodon Fowler 1904
Ophthalmolepis Bleeker 1862
Oxycheilinus Gill 1862
Oxyjulis Gill 1864
Paracheilinus Fourmanoir in Roux-Estève & Fourmanoir 1955
Parajulis Bleeker 1865
Pariolanthus Smith 1968
Peaolopesia Smith 1949

Pictilabrus Gill 1891
Pimelometopon Gill 1864
Platiglossus Klein 1776
Platychoerops Klunzinger 1880
Platyglossus Bleeker (ex Klein) 1862
Polylepion Gomon 1977
Pseudanampses Bleeker 1862
Pseudocheilinops Schultz in Schultz et al. 1960
Pseudocheilinus Bleeker 1862
Pseudocoris Bleeker 1862
Pseudodax Bleeker 1861
Pseudojulis Bleeker 1862
Pseudojuloides Fowler 1949
Pseudojulops Fowler 1941
Pseudolabrus Bleeker 1862
Pseudolepidaplois Bauchot & Blanc 1961
Pteragogus Peters 1855
Pusa Jordan & Gilbert 1879
Rhytejulis Fowler & Bean 1928
Ronchifex Gistel 1848
Scarus Gronow 1763
Semachlorella Fowler & Bean 1928
Semicossyphus Günther 1861
Stethojulis Günther 1861
Suezia Smith 1957
Suezichthys Smith 1958
Suillus Catesby 1771
Symphodus Rafinesque 1810
Tautoga Mitchill 1814
Tautogolabrus Günther 1862
Thalassoma Swainson 1839
Thalliurus Swainson 1839
Thysanocheilus Kner 1864
Tiricoris Whitley 1955
Torresia Castelnau 1875
Trochocopus Günther 1862
Urichthys Swainson 1839
Verreo Jordan & Snyder 1902
Verriculus Jordan & Evermann 1903
Wetmorella Fowler & Bean 1928
Xenojulis de Beaufort 1939
Xiphocheilus Bleeker 1856
Xyrichtys Cuvier 1814
Xyrula Jordan 1890

FAM. ODACIDAE

Coregonoides Richardson 1843
Coridodax Günther 1862
Haletta Whitley 1947
Heteroscarus Castelnau 1872
Neoodax Castelnau 1875
Odax Valenciennes in Cuvier & Valenciennes 1840
Olisthops Richardson 1850
Parodax Scott 1976
Sheardichthys Whitley 1947
Siphonognathus Richardson 1858

FAM. SCARIDAE (Parrotfishes)

Subfam. Scarinae

Aper Lacepède (ex Plumier) 1803
Bolbometopon Smith 1956
Calliodon Bloch & Schneider (ex Gronow) 1801
Callyodon Gronow 1763
Callyodon Scopoli (ex Gronow) 1777
Callyodon Bloch 1788
Cetoscarus Smith 1956
Chlorurus Swainson 1839
Erychthys Swainson 1839
Hemistoma Swainson 1839
Hipposcarus Smith 1956
Loro Jordan & Evermann 1896
Margaritodon Smith 1956
Mormyra Browne 1789
Novacula Catesby 1771
Odax Commerson in Lacepède 1801
Petronason Swainson 1839
Pseudoscarus Bleeker 1861
Psittacus Catesby 1771
Scarops Schultz 1958
Scarus Forsskål 1775
Xanothon Smith 1956
Xenoscarops Schultz 1958
Ypsiscarus Schultz 1958

Subfam. Sparisomatinae

Callyodontichthys Bleeker 1861
Calotomus Gilbert 1890
Cryptotomus Cope 1870
Euscarus Jordan & Evermann 1896
Leptoscarus Swainson 1839
Nicholsina Fowler 1915
Scarichthys Bleeker 1859
Scaridea Jenkins 1903
Scarus Bleeker 1849
Sparisoma Swainson 1839
Xenoscarus Evermann & Radcliffe 1917

SUBORDER ZOARCOIDEI

FAM. BATHYMASTERIDAE (Ronquils)

Bathymaster Cope 1873
Rathbunella Jordan & Evermann 1896
Ronquilus Jordan & Starks 1895

FAM. ZOARCIDAE (Eelpouts)

Aiakas Gosztonyi 1977
Allolepis Jordan & Hubbs 1925
Andriashevia Fedorov & Neyelov 1978
Apodolycus Andriashev 1979
Aprodon Gilbert 1890
Austrolycichthys Regan 1913
Austrolycus Regan 1913
Bandichthys Parin 1979
Bergeniana Popov 1931
Bilabria Schmidt 1936
Bothrocara Bean 1890
Bothrocarichthys Schmidt 1938
Bothrocarina Suvorov 1935
Bothrocaropsis Garman 1899
Caneolepis Lahille 1908
Cepolophis Kaup 1856
Commandorella Taranetz & Andriashev 1935
Crossolycus Regan 1913
Crossostomus Lahille 1908
Dadyanos Whitley 1951
Davidijordania Popov 1931
Derepodichthys Gilbert 1896
Derjuginia Popov 1931
Dieidolycus Anderson 1988
Embryx Jordan & Evermann 1898
Enchelyopus Gronow 1760
Eucryphycus Anderson 1988
Exechodontes DeWitt 1977
Furcella Jordan & Evermann 1896
Furcimanus Jordan & Evermann 1898
Gengea Katayama 1943
Gymnelichthys Fischer 1885
Gymnelopsis Soldatov 1922
Gymnelus Reinhardt 1834
Hadropareia Schmidt 1904
Hadropogonichthys Fedorov 1982
Hypolycodes Hector 1881
Iluocoetes Jenyns 1842
Krusensterniella Schmidt 1904
Lacrimolycus Andriashev & Fedorov 1986
Letholycus Anderson 1988
Leurynnis Lockington 1880
Lycenchelys Gill 1884
Lycias Jordan & Evermann 1898
Lyciscus Evermann & Goldsborough 1907
Lycodalepis Bleeker 1874
Lycodapus Gilbert 1890
Lycodes Reinhardt 1831
Lycodichthys Pappenheim 1911
Lycodonus Goode & Bean 1883
Lycodophis Vaillant 1888
Lycodopsis Collett 1879
Lycogramma Gilbert 1915
Lycogrammoides Soldatov & Lindberg 1929
Lyconema Gilbert 1896
Lycozoarces Popov 1935
Macrozoarces Gill 1863
Maynea Cunningham 1871
Melanostigma Günther 1881
Nalbantichthys Schultz 1967
Nemalycodes Herzenstein 1896
Neozoarces Steindachner 1881
Notolycodes Gosztonyi 1977
Oidiphorus McAllister & Rees 1964
Opaeophacus Bond & Stein 1984
Ophthalmolycus Regan 1913
Pachycara Zugmayer 1911
Pachycarichthys Whitley 1931
Paralycodes Bleeker 1874
Petroschmidtia Taranetz & Andriashev 1934
Phucocoetes Jenyns 1842
Piedrabuenia Gosztonyi 1977
Platea Steindachner 1898
Plesienchelys Anderson 1988
Pogonolycus Norman 1937
Puzanovia Fedorov 1975
Rhigophila DeWitt 1962
Seleniolycus Anderson 1988
Taranetzella Andriashev 1952
Thermarces Rosenblatt & Cohen 1986
Zestichthys Jordan & Hubbs 1925
Zoarces Cuvier 1829
Zoarchias Jordan & Snyder 1902

FAM. STICHAEIDAE (Pricklebacks)

Abryois Jordan & Snyder 1902
Acantholumpenus Makushok 1958
Alectrias Jordan & Evermann 1898
Alectridium Gilbert & Burke 1912
Allolumpenus Hubbs & Schultz 1932
Anisarchus Gill 1864
Anoplarchus Gill 1861
Azygopterus Andriashev & Makushok 1955
Blenniops Nilsson 1855
Bryolophus Jordan & Snyder 1902

Bryozoichthys Whitley 1931
Carelophus Krøyer 1845
Cebidichthys Ayres 1855
Centroblennius Gill 1861
Chirolophis Swainson 1838
Ctenodon Nilsson 1855
Dictyosoma Temminck & Schlegel 1845
Dinogunellus Herzenstein 1890
Epigeichthys Hubbs 1927
Ernogrammus Jordan & Evermann 1898
Eulophias Smith 1902
Eumesogrammus Gill 1864
Gillias Evermann & Marsh 1900
Gymnoclinus Gilbert & Burke 1912
Kasatkia Soldatov & Pavlenko 1916
Leptoblennius Gill 1860
Leptoclinus Gill 1861
Leptogunnellus Ayres 1855
Leptostichaeus Miki 1985
Lumpenella Hubbs 1927
Lumpenopsis Soldatov 1916
Lumpenus Reinhardt 1837
Neolumpenus Miki, Kanamaru & Amaoka 1987
Notogrammus Bean 1881
Opisthocentrus Kner 1868
Ozorthe Jordan & Evermann 1898
Pholidapus Bean & Bean 1896
Phytichthys Hubbs in Jordan 1923
Plagiogrammus Bean 1894
Plectobranchus Gilbert 1890
Poroclinus Bean 1890
Pseudalectrias Popov 1933
Soldatovia Taranetz 1937
Stichaeopsis Kner in Steindachner & Kner 1870
Stichaeus Reinhardt 1837
Trigrammnus Gracianov 1907
Ulvaria Jordan & Evermann 1896
Xiphidion Girard 1858
Xiphister Jordan 1880
Xiphistes Jordan & Starks 1895

FAM. CRYPTACANTHODIDAE (Wrymouths)

Cryptacanthodes Storer 1839
Cryptacanthoides Lindberg in Soldatov & Lindberg 1930
Delolepis Bean 1882
Lyconectes Gilbert 1896
Zoarcites Zugmayer 1914

FAM. PHOLIDAE (Gunnels) = Pholididae

Allopholis Yatsu 1981
Apodichthys Girard 1854
Askoldia Pavlenko 1910
Asternopteryx Günther (ex Rüppell) 1861
Azuma Jordan & Snyder 1902
Blenniophidium Boulenger 1893
Bryostemma Jordan & Starks 1895
Centronotus Bloch & Schneider 1801
Dactyleptus Rafinesque 1815
Enedrias Jordan & Gilbert in Jordan & Evermann 1898
Gunnellops Bleeker 1874
Gunnellus Fleming 1828
Muraenoides Lacepède 1800
Ophisomus Swainson 1839
Pholidus Rafinesque 1815
Pholis Gronow 1763
Pholis Scopoli (ex Gronow) 1777
Pholis Röse 1793
Pholis Cuvier 1816
Rhodymenichthys Jordan & Evermann 1896
Ulvicola Gilbert & Starks in Gilbert 1897
Urocentrus Kner 1868
Xererpes Jordan & Gilbert in Jordan & Starks 1895

FAM. ANARHICHADIDAE (Wolffishes)

Anarhichas Linnaeus 1758
Anarrhichas see *Anarhichas*
Anarrhichthys Ayres 1855
Anarrichas see *Anarhichas*
Latargus Klein 1775
Lycichthys Gill 1877

FAM. PTILICHTHYIDAE (Quillfishes)

Ptilichthys Bean 1881

FAM. ZAPRORIDAE (Prowfishes)

Zaprora Jordan 1896

FAM. SCYTALINIDAE (Graveldivers)

Scytalina Jordan & Gilbert 1880
Scytaliscus Jordan & Gilbert 1883

SUBORDER NOTOTHENIOIDEI

FAM. BOVICHTIDAE (Bovichtids) = Bovichthyidae

Aphritis Valenciennes in Cuvier & Valenciennes 1831
Aurion Waite 1916
Bovichtus Valenciennes in Cuvier & Valenciennes 1831
Cottoperca Steindachner 1875
Phricus Berg 1895
Pseudaphritis Castelnau 1872

FAM. NOTOTHENIIDAE (cod icefishes)

Aethotaxis DeWitt 1962
Cryothenia Daniels 1981
Dissostichus Smitt 1898
Eleginops Gill 1862
Eleginus Cuvier in Cuvier & Valenciennes 1830
Gelidus Whitley 1937
Gobionotothen Balushkin 1976
Gvozdarus Balushkin 1989
Indonotothenia Balushkin 1984
Lepidonotothen Balushkin 1976
Lindbergia Balushkin 1976
Lindbergichthys Balushkin 1979
Macronotothen Gill 1862
Notothenia Richardson 1844
Nototheniops Balushkin 1976
Pagothenia Nichols & La Monte 1936
Paranotothenia Balushkin 1976
Patagonotothen Balushkin 1976
Pleuragramma Boulenger 1902
Pseudotrematomus Balushkin 1982
Trematomus Boulenger 1902

FAM. HARPAGIFERIDAE (Plunderfishes)

Artedidraco Lönnberg 1905
Dolloidraco Roule 1913
Harpagifer Richardson 1844
Histiodraco Regan 1914
Pogonophryne Regan 1914

FAM. BATHYDRACONIDAE (Antarctic Dragonfishes)

Aconichthys Waite 1916
Akarotaxis DeWitt & Hureau 1979
Bathydraco Günther 1878
Cygnodraco Waite 1916
Gerlachea Dollo 1900
Gymnodraco Boulenger 1902
Parachaenichthys Boulenger 1902
Prionodraco Regan 1914
Psilodraco Norman 1937
Racovitzia Dollo 1900
Vomeridens DeWitt & Hureau 1979

FAM. CHANNICHTHYIDAE (Crocodile Icefishes)

Chaenichthys Richardson 1844
Chaenocephalus Regan 1913
Chaenodraco Regan 1914
Champsocephalus Gill 1862
Channichthys Richardson 1844
Chionobathyscus Andriashev & Neelov 1978
Chionodraco Lönnberg 1906
Cryodraco Dollo 1900
Dacodraco Waite 1916
Neopagetopsis Nybelin 1947
Pagetodes Richardson 1844
Pagetopsis Regan 1913
Ponerodon Alcock 1890
Pseudochaenichthys Norman 1937

SUBORDER TRACHINOIDEI

FAM. XENOCEPHALIDAE

Xenocephalus Kaup 1858

FAM. CHIASMODONTIDAE (Swallowers)

Chiasmodon Johnson 1864
Chiasmodus Günther 1864
Dolichodon Parr 1931
Dysalotus MacGilchrist 1905
Gargaropteron Smith 1965
Hemicyclodon Parr 1931
Kali Lloyd 1909
Myersiscus Fowler 1934
Odontonema Weber 1913
Pseudoscopelus Lütken 1892

FAM. CHAMPSODONTIDAE (Gapers)

Champsodon Günther 1867

FAM. TRICHODONTIDAE (Sandfishes)

Arctoscopus Jordan & Evermann 1896
Chaetichthys Gistel 1848
Trichodon Tilesius (ex Steller) 1813

FAM. AMMODYTIDAE (Sand Lances)

Ammodytes Linnaeus 1758
Ammodytoides Duncker & Mohr 1939
Argyrotaenia Gill 1861
Bleekeria Günther 1862
Embolichthys Jordan & Evermann in Jordan 1903
Gymnammodytes Duncker & Mohr 1935

Herklotsina Fowler 1931
Hyperoplus Günther 1862
Sgairhynchus Costa 1849

FAM. TRACHINIDAE (Weeverfishes)
Corystion Rafinesque 1810
Echiichthys Bleeker 1861
Pseudotrachinus Bleeker 1861
Trachinus Linnaeus 1758

FAM. URANOSCOPIDAE (Stargazers)
Agnus Günther 1860
Anema Günther 1860
Ariscopus Jordan & Snyder 1902
Astroscopus Brevoort in Gill 1860
Benthoscopus Longley & Hildebrand 1940
Cathetostoma see *Kathetostoma*
Centropercis Ogilby 1895
Execestides Jordan & Thompson 1905
Genyagnus Gill 1861
Gnathagnoides Whitley & Phillipps 1939
Gnathagnus Gill 1861
Ichthyscopus Swainson 1839
Kathetostoma Günther 1860
Nematagnus Gill 1861
Pleuroscopus Barnard 1927
Synnema Haast 1873
Upselonphorus Gill 1861
Uranoscopus Linnaeus 1758
Zalescopus Jordan & Hubbs 1925

FAM. TRICHONOTIDAE (Sand Divers)
Lesueurina Fowler 1908
Taeniolabrus Steindachner 1867
Trichonotops Schultz in Schultz et al. 1960
Trichonotus Bloch & Schneider 1801

FAM. CREEDIIDAE (Sand Burrowers)
Apodocreedia de Beaufort 1948
Chalixodytes Schultz 1943
Creedia Ogilby 1898
Crystallodytes Fowler 1923
Limnichthys Waite 1904
Schizochirus Waite 1904
Tewara Griffin 1933

FAM. LEPTOSCOPIDAE
Crapatalus Günther 1861
Leptoscopus Gill 1859

FAM. PERCOPHIDAE (Duckbills)

Subfam. Percophinae
Percophis Quoy & Gaimard (ex Cuvier) 1825

Subfam. Bembropinae
Bathypercis Alcock 1893
Bembrops Steindachner 1876
Chriomystax Ginsburg 1955
Chrionema Gilbert 1905
Hypsicometes Goode 1880

Subfam. Hemerocoetinae
Acanthaphritis Günther 1880
Branchiopsaron McKay 1971
Cirrinasus Schultz in Schultz et al. 1960
Enigmapercis Whitley 1936
Hemerocoetes Valenciennes in Cuvier & Valenciennes 1837
Matsubaraea Taki 1953
Osopsaron Jordan & Starks 1904
Pteropsaron Jordan & Snyder 1902
Roxasella Fowler 1943
Spinapsaron Okamura & Kishida 1963
Squamicreedia Rendahl 1921

FAM. PINGUIPEDIDAE (Sandperches) = Parapercidae
Cheimarrichthys Haast 1874
Chilias Ogilby 1910
Kochia Kamohara 1960
Kochichthys Kamohara 1961
Neopercis Steindachner in Steindachner & Döderlein 1884
Osurus Jordan & Evermann 1903
Parapercichthys Whitley & Phillipps 1939
Parapercis Bleeker 1863
Parapercis Steindachner 1884
Percis Bloch & Schneider 1801
Pinguipes Cuvier in Cuvier & Valenciennes 1829
Porteridia Fowler 1945
Prolatilus Gill 1866
Pseudopercis Miranda-Ribeiro 1903

SUBORDER PHOLIDICHTHYOIDEI

FAM. PHOLIDICHTHYIDAE (Convict-Blennies)
Pholidichthys Bleeker 1856

SUBORDER BLENNIOIDEI

FAM. TRIPTERYGIIDAE (Threefin Blennies)
Apopterygion Kuiter 1986
Axoclinus Fowler 1944
Bellapiscis Hardy 1987
Blennodon Hardy 1987
Brachynectes Scott 1957
Ceratobregma Holleman 1987
Cremnochorites Holleman 1982
Cryptichthys Hardy 1987
Enneanectes Jordan & Evermann in Jordan 1895
Enneapterygius Rüppell 1835
Forsterygion Whitley & Phillipps 1939
Gilloblennius Whitley & Phillipps 1939
Helcogramma McCulloch & Waite 1918
Karalepis Hardy 1984
Lepidoblennius Steindachner 1867
Lepidoblennius Sauvage 1874
Norfolkia Fowler 1953
Notoclinops Whitley 1930
Notoclinus Gill 1893
Obliquichthys Hardy 1987
Ruanoho Hardy 1986
Sauvagea Jordan & Seale 1906
Tagusa Herre 1935
Trianectes McCulloch & Waite 1918
Tripennata de Buen 1926
Tripterygion Risso 1826
Vauclusella Whitley 1931
Verconectes Whitley 1931

FAM. LABRISOMIDAE (Labrisomids)
Acanthoclinus Mocquard 1885
Acteis Jordan 1904
Alloclinus Hubbs 1927
Anchenionchus see *Auchenionchus*
Andracanthus Longley 1927
Auchenionchus Gill 1860
Auchenistius Evermann & Marsh 1900
Auchenopterus Günther 1861
Brannerella Gilbert 1900
Brockius Clark Hubbs 1953
Calliblennius Barbour 1912
Calliclinus Gill 1860
Chalacoclinus de Buen 1962
Corallicola Jordan & Evermann 1898
Cremnobates Günther 1861
Crockeridius Clark 1936
Cryptotrema Gilbert 1890
Ctenichthys Howell Rivero 1936
Dialommus Gilbert 1891
Emmnion Jordan in Gilbert 1897
Ericteis Jordan 1904
Exerpes Jordan & Evermann in Jordan 1896
Flabelliclinus de Buen 1962
Gobioclinus Gill 1860
Haptoclinus Böhlke & Robins 1974
Histioclinus Metzelaar 1919
Labrisomus Swainson 1839
Lepisoma DeKay 1842
Malacoctenus Gill 1860
Mnierpes Jordan & Evermann 1896
Myersichthys Clark Hubbs 1952
Nemaclinus Böhlke & Springer 1975
Neoclinus Girard 1858
Odontoclinus Reid 1935
Paraclinus Mocquard 1888
Parastathmonotus Chabanaud 1942
Parviclinus Fraser-Brunner 1932
Pennaclinus de Buen 1962
Pterognathus Girard in Jordan & Evermann 1898
Starksia Jordan & Evermann in Jordan 1896
Stathmonotus Bean 1885
Tekla Nichols 1922
Xenomedea Rosenblatt & Taylor 1971
Zacalles Jordan & Snyder 1902

FAM. CLINIDAE (Clinids and Klipfishes)
Blakea Steindachner 1876
Blenniculus Facciolà 1911
Blennioclinus Gill 1860
Blenniomimus Smith 1946
Blennophis Swainson 1839
Breona Scott 1967
Caboclinus Smith 1966
Cancelloxus Smith 1961
Cirrhibarbis Valenciennes in Cuvier & Valenciennes 1836
Climacoporus Barnard 1935
Clinitrachus Swainson 1839
Clinoides Gilchrist & Thompson 1908
Clinoporus Barnard 1927
Clinus Cuvier 1816
Cologrammus Gill 1893
Cristiceps Valenciennes in Cuvier & Valenciennes 1836
Ericentrus Gill 1893
Eucentronotus Ogilby 1898

Fucomimus Smith 1946
Gibbonsia Cooper 1864
Gynutoclinus Smith 1946
Heteroclinus Castelnau 1872
Heterostichus Girard 1854
Labroclinus Smith 1946
Muraenoclinus Smith 1946
Myxodes Cuvier 1829
Nemacoclinus Smith 1937
Neoblennius Castelnau 1875
Neogunellus Castelnau 1875
Ophiclinops Whitley 1932
Ophiclinus Castelnau 1872
Ophthalmolophus Gill 1860
Paracristiceps Herre 1939
Pavoclinus Smith 1946
Peronedys Steindachner 1884
Petraites Ogilby 1885
Phillippsichthys Whitley 1937
Ribeiroclinus Pinto 1965
Scleropteryx Waite 1906
Smithichthys Clark Hubbs 1952
Springeratus Shen 1971
Sticharium Günther 1867
Xenopoclinops Smith 1961
Xenopoclinus Smith 1948

FAM. CHAENOPSIDAE (Pikeblennies)

Acanthemblemaria Metzelaar 1919
Chaenopsis Poey in Gill 1865
Coralliozetus Evermann & Marsh 1899
Ekemblemaria Stephens 1963
Emblemaria Jordan & Gilbert 1883
Emblemariopsis Longley 1927
Hemiemblemaria Longley & Hildebrand 1940
Lucaya Böhlke 1957
Lucayablennius Böhlke 1958
Lucioblennius Gilbert 1890
Mccoskerichthys Rosenblatt & Stephens 1978
Paremblemaria Longley 1927
Protemblemaria Stephens 1963
Psednoblennius Jenkins & Evermann 1889
Pseudemblemaria Stephens 1961

FAM. DACTYLOSCOPIDAE (Sand Stargazers)

Cokeridia Meek & Hildebrand 1928
Congrammus Fowler 1906
Dactylagnus Gill 1863
Dactyloscopus Gill 1859
Esloscopus Jordan & Evermann 1896
Gillellus Gilbert 1890
Heteristius Myers & Wade 1946
Jopaica Pinto 1970
Leurochilus Böhlke 1968
Myxodagnus Gill 1861
Paragillellus Carvalho & Pinto 1965
Paramyxodagnus Carvalho & Pinto 1965
Platygillellus Dawson 1974
Sindoscopus Dawson 1977
Springeria Carvalho & Pinto 1965
Storrsia Dawson 1982
Tamandareia Carvalho & Pinto 1965

FAM. BLENNIIDAE (Blennies)

Adonis Gronow in Gray 1854
Aidablennius Whitley 1947
Alloblennius Smith-Vaniz & Springer 1971
Allomeiacanthus Smith-Vaniz 1976
Alticops Smith 1948
Alticus Lacepède (ex Commerson) 1800
Alticus Valenciennes (ex Commerson) in Cuvier & Valenciennes 1836
Andamia Blyth 1858
Antennablennius Fowler 1931
Anthiiblennius Starck 1969
Aspidontus Cuvier in Quoy & Gaimard 1834
Atopoclinus Vaillant 1894
Atrosalarias Whitley 1933
Basilisciscartes Fowler 1939
Bathyblennius Bath 1977
Bipennata de Buen 1926
Blennechis Valenciennes in Cuvier & Valenciennes 1836
Blenniella Reid 1943
Blenniolus Jordan & Evermann 1898
Blennitrachus Swainson 1839
Blennius Linnaeus 1758
Blennophis Valenciennes in Webb & Berthelot 1843
Blennus Klein 1779
Chalaroderma Norman 1943
Chasmodes Valenciennes in Cuvier & Valenciennes 1836
Cirripectes Swainson 1839
Cirrisalarias Springer 1976
Coryphoblennius Norman 1943
Cremnotekla Whitley 1940
Crenalticus Whitley 1930
Croaltus Smith 1959
Crossosalarias Smith-Vaniz & Springer 1971
Cruantus Smith 1959
Cyneichthys Ogilby 1910
Cynoscartes Norman 1943
Damania Smith 1959
Dasson Jordan & Hubbs 1925
Dodekablennos Springer & Spreitzer 1978
Dubiblennius Whitley 1930
Ecsenius McCulloch 1923
Enchelyurus Peters 1868
Entomacrodops Fowler 1944
Entomacrodus Gill 1859
Erpicthys Swainson 1839
Escadotus Smith 1959
Exallias Jordan & Evermann 1905
Fallacirripectes Schultz & Chapman in Schultz et al. 1960
Giffordella Fowler 1932
Gloriella Schultz 1941
Glyptoparus Smith 1959
Graviceps Fowler 1903
Halmablennius Smith 1948
Haptogenys Springer 1972
Hepatoscartes Fowler 1944
Hirculops Smith 1959
Holomeiacanthus Smith-Vaniz 1976
Homesthes Gilbert in Jordan & Evermann 1898
Hypleurochilus Gill 1861
Hypsoblenniops Schultz 1941
Hypsoblennius Gill 1861
Ichthyocoris Bonaparte 1840
Isesthes Jordan & Gilbert 1883
Istiblennius Whitley 1943
Labroblennius Borodin 1928
Laiphognathus Smith 1955
Lembeichthys Herre 1936
Leoblennius Reid 1943
Leptoblennius Bath 1978
Lioblennius Svetovidov 1958
Lipophrys Gill 1896
Litanchus Smith 1959
Litobranchus Smith-Vaniz & Springer 1971
Lophalticus Smith 1957
Lupinoblennius Herre 1942
Macrurrhynchus Ogilby 1896
Medusablennius Springer 1966
Meiacanthus Norman 1943
Mimoblennius Smith-Vaniz & Springer 1971
Musgravius Whitley 1961
Nannosalarias Smith-Vaniz & Springer 1971
Negoscartes Whitley 1930
Nemophis Kaup 1858
Nixiblennius Whitley 1930
Oman Springer 1985
Omobranchus Ehrenberg in Cuvier & Valenciennes 1836
Omox Springer 1972
Oncesthes Jordan & Hubbs 1925
Ophioblennius Gill 1860
Ostreoblennius Whitley 1930
Parablennius Miranda-Ribeiro 1915
Parahypsos Bath 1982
Paralipophrys Bath 1977
Parenchelyurus Springer 1972
Pauloscirtes Whitley 1935
Pereulixia Smith 1959
Pescadorichthys Tomiyama 1955
Petroscirtes Rüppell 1830
Phenablennius Springer & Smith-Vaniz 1972
Pictiblennius Whitley 1930
Plagiotremus Gill 1865
Poroalticus Fowler 1931
Praealticus Schultz & Chapman in Schultz et al. 1960
Queriblennius Whitley 1933
Rhabdoblennius Whitley 1930
Runula Jordan & Bollman 1890
Runulops Ogilby 1910
Rupiscartes Swainson 1839
Salaria Forsskål 1775
Salarias Cuvier 1816
Salarichthys Guichenot 1867
Scartella Jordan 1886
Scartes Jordan & Evermann 1896
Scartichthys Jordan & Evermann 1898
Scartoblennius Fowler 1946
Semablennius Fowler 1954
Somersia Beebe & Tee-Van 1934
Spaniblennius Bath & Wirtz 1989
Spinoblennius Herre 1935
Stanulus Smith 1959
Unipennata de Buen 1926
Xiphasia Swainson 1839
Xiphogadus Günther 1862
Zeablennius Whitley 1930

SUBORDER ICOSTEOIDEI

FAM. ICOSTEIDAE (Ragfishes)

Acrotus Bean 1888
Icosteus Lockington 1880
Schedophilopsis Steindachner 1881

SUBORDER CALLIONYMOIDEI

FAM. CALLIONYMIDAE (Dragonets)

Amora see *Anaora*
Anaora Gray 1835
Anaoroides Fricke 1981
Bathycallionymus Nakabo 1982
Bicuspidatus de Buen 1926
Brachycallionymus Herre & Myers in Herre 1936
Callimucenus Whitley 1934
Callionymus Linnaeus 1758
Calliurichthys Jordan & Fowler 1903
Calymmichthys Jordan & Thompson 1914
Chalinops Smith 1963
Charibarbitus Smith 1963
Clathropus Smith 1966
Climacogrammus Smith 1963
Dactylopus Gill 1859
Dermosteira Schultz 1943
Dicallionymus Fowler 1941
Diplogrammoides Smith 1963
Diplogrammus Gill 1865
Draculo Snyder 1911
Eleutherochir Bleeker 1879
Eocallionymus Nakabo 1982
Foetorepus Whitley 1931
Minysynchiropus Nakabo 1982
Neosynchiropus Nakabo 1982
Neosynchiropus Nalbant 1979
Orbonymus Whitley 1947
Paracallionymus Barnard 1927
Paradiplogrammus Nakabo 1982
Pogonymus Gosline 1959
Protogrammus Fricke 1985
Pseudocalliurichthys Nakabo 1982
Pterosynchiropus Nakabo 1982
Repomucenus Whitley 1931
Spinicapitichthys Fricke 1981
Synchiropus Gill 1859
Tetracuspidatus de Buen 1926
Tricuspidatus de Buen 1926
Velesionymus Whitley 1934
Vulsus Günther 1861
Yerutius Whitley 1931

FAM. DRACONETTIDAE

Centrodraco Regan 1913
Draconetta Jordan & Fowler 1903
Liopsaron McKay 1972

SUBORDER SCHINDLERIOIDEI

FAM. SCHINDLERIIDAE

Schindleria Giltay 1934

SUBORDER GOBIOIDEI

FAM. RHYACICHTHYIDAE (Loach Gobies)

Platyptera Cuvier (ex Kuhl & van Hasselt) 1829
Rhyacichthys Boulenger 1901

FAM. ELEOTRIDAE (Sleepers) = Eleotrididae

Alexurus Jordan 1895
Alvarius Girard 1859
Asellus Plumier in Lacepède 1800
Austrogobio Ogilby 1898
Batanga Herre 1946
Belobranchus Bleeker 1856
Boroda Herre 1927
Borodamirus Whitley 1935
Bostrichthys Duméril 1806
Bostrictis Rafinesque 1815
Bostrychus Lacepède 1801
Bunaka Herre 1927
Butis Bleeker 1856
Callieleotris Fowler 1934
Calumia Smith 1958
Carassiops Ogilby 1897
Caulichthys Ogilby 1898
Cestreus McClelland 1842
Culius Bleeker 1856
Diaphoroculius Fowler 1938
Dormitator Gill 1861
Eleotris Bloch & Schneider 1801
Epiphthalmus Rafinesque 1815
Erotelis Poey 1860
Euleptoeleotris Hildebrand 1938
Fagasa Schultz 1943
Gigantogobius Fowler 1905
Giuris Sauvage 1880
Gobiomoroides Lacepède 1800
Gobiomorphus Gill 1863
Gobiomorus Lacepède 1800
Grahamichthys Whitley 1956
Guavina Bleeker 1874
Gymnobutis Bleeker 1874
Hanno Herre 1946
Hannoichthys Herre 1950
Hemieleotris Meek & Hildebrand 1916
Hypseleotris Gill 1863
Ictiopogon Rafinesque 1815
Incara Rao 1971
Kieneria Maugé 1984
Kimberleyeleotris Hoese & Allen 1987
Krefftius Ogilby 1897
Kribia Herre 1946
Lairdina Fowler 1953
Lembus Günther 1859
Leptophilypnus Meek & Hildebrand 1916
Lindemanella Whitley 1935
Lizettea Herre 1936
Meuschenula Whitley 1931
Microeleotris Meek & Hildebrand 1916
Micropercops Fowler & Bean 1920
Microphilypnus Myers 1927
Milyeringa Whitley 1945
Mogurnda Gill 1863
Mulgoa Ogilby 1897
Odonteleotris Gill 1863
Odontobutis Bleeker 1874
Ophieleotris Aurich 1938
Ophiocara Gill 1863
Ophiorrhinus Ogilby 1897
Oxyeleotris Bleeker 1874
Paloa Herre 1927
Parviparma Herre 1927
Pelmatia Browne 1789
Perccottus Dybowski 1877
Philypnodon Bleeker 1874
Philypnus Valenciennes in Cuvier & Valenciennes 1837
Pogoneleotris Bleeker 1875
Prionobutis Bleeker 1874
Prochilus Cuvier 1816
Psiloides Fischer von Waldheim 1813
Psilus Fischer von Waldheim 1813
Pteroculiops Fowler 1938
Pterops Rafinesque 1815
Ratsirakia Maugé 1984
Shipwayia Whitley 1954
Sineleotris Herre 1940
Tateurndina Nichols 1955
Thalasseleotris Hoese & Larson 1987
Themistocles Whitley 1939
Typhleotris Petit 1933

FAM. GOBIIDAE (Gobies)

Aboma Jordan & Starks in Jordan 1895
Abranches Smith 1947
Acanthogobius Gill 1859
Acentrogobius Bleeker 1874
Actinogobius Bleeker 1874
Agunia Fowler 1946
Ainosus Jordan & Snyder 1901
Alepideleotris Herre 1935
Alepidogobius Bleeker 1874
Allogobius Waite 1904
Aloricatogobius Munro 1964
Amblycentrus Goren 1979
Amblychaeturichthys Bleeker 1874
Amblyeleotris Bleeker 1874
Amblygobius Bleeker 1874
Amblyopus Valenciennes in Cuvier & Valenciennes 1837
Amblyotrypauchen Hora 1924
Amoya Herre 1927
Anatirostrum Iljin 1930
Aparrius Jordan & Richardson 1908
Aphia Risso 1826
Aphyogobius Whitley 1931
Apocryptes Osbeck 1762
Apocryptes Valenciennes in Cuvier & Valenciennes 1837
Apocryptichthys Day 1876
Apocryptodon Bleeker 1874
Apollonia Iljin 1927
Aprolepis Hubbs 1921
Arenigobius Whitley 1930
Aruma Ginsburg 1933
Aspidophilus Koumans 1931
Asra Iljin 1941
Asterropteryx Rüppell 1830
Astrabe Jordan & Snyder 1901
Atuona Herre 1935
Aulopareia Smith 1945
Aurigobius Whitley 1959
Austrogobius de Buen 1950
Austrolethops Whitley 1935
Awaous Steindachner 1860
Awaous Valenciennes in Cuvier & Valenciennes 1837
Babka Iljin 1927
Barbatogobius Koumans 1941
Barbulifer Eigenmann & Eigenmann 1888
Barbuligobius Lachner & McKinney 1974
Bathygobius Bleeker 1878
Batman Whitley 1956
Batracheleotris Fowler 1938
Benthophiloides Beling & Iljin 1927

Benthophilus Eichwald 1831
Berowra Whitley 1928
Biat Seale 1910
Bikinigobius Herre 1953
Boleophthalmus Valenciennes in Cuvier & Valenciennes 1837
Boleops Gill 1863
Bollmannia Jordan in Jordan & Bollman 1890
Boreogobius Gill 1863
Brachyamblyopus Bleeker 1874
Brachyeleotris Bleeker 1874
Brachygobius Bleeker 1874
Brachyochirus Nardo 1841
Bryanina Fowler 1932
Bryaninops Smith 1959
Bubyr Iljin 1930
Buenia Iljin 1930
Butigobius Whitley 1930
Cabillus Smith 1959
Cabotia de Buen 1930
Cabotichthys Whitley 1940
Caffrogobius Smitt 1900
Calamiana Herre 1945
Calleleotris Gill 1863
Callogobius Bleeker 1874
Caragobioides Smith 1945
Caragobius Smith & Seale 1906
Caspiosoma Iljin 1927
Cassigobius Whitley 1931
Cayennia Sauvage 1880
Centrogobius Bleeker 1874
Cephalogobius Bleeker 1874
Chaenogobius Gill 1859
Chaeturichthys Richardson 1844
Chaparrudo de Buen 1931
Chasmias Jordan & Snyder 1901
Chasmichthys Jordan & Snyder 1901
Chiramenu Rao 1971
Chlamydes Jenkins 1903
Chlamydogobius Whitley 1930
Chloea Jordan & Snyder 1901
Chloeichthys Whitley 1940
Chonophorus Poey 1860
Chriolepidops Smith 1958
Chriolepis Gilbert 1892
Chromogobius de Buen 1930
Cingulogobius Herre 1927
Clariger Jordan & Snyder 1901
Clevelandia Eigenmann & Eigenmann 1888
Colonianus de Buen 1926
Congruogobius Ginsburg 1953
Corcyrogobius Miller 1972
Coronogobius Herre 1945
Coryogalops Smith 1958
Coryphopterus Gill 1863
Cottogobius Koumans 1941
Cotylopus Guichenot 1864
Creisson Jordan & Seale 1907
Cremornea Whitley 1962
Cristatogobius Herre 1927
Croilia Smith 1955
Crossogobius Koumans 1931
Cryptocentroides Popta 1922
Cryptocentrops Smith 1958
Cryptocentrus Valenciennes (ex Ehrenberg) in Cuvier & Valenciennes 1837
Crystallogobius Gill 1863
Ctenogobiops Smith 1959
Ctenogobius Gill 1858
Ctenotrypauchen Steindachner 1867
Cyclogobius Steindachner 1860
Cyprinogobius Koumans 1937
Dactyleleotris Smith 1958
Deltentosteus Gill 1863
Didogobius Miller 1966
Dilepidion Ginsburg 1933
Diogenides Koumans 1931
Discordipinna Hoese & Fourmanoir 1978
Doliichthys Sauvage 1874
Doryptena Snyder 1908
Drombus Jordan & Seale 1905
Ebomegobius Herre 1946
Economidichthys Bianco, Bullock, Miller & Roubal 1987
Egglestonichthys Miller & Wongrat 1979
Eichwaldia Smitt 1900
Eichwaldiella Whitley 1930
Eilatia Klausewitz 1974
Elacatinus Jordan 1904
Eleotrica Ginsburg 1933
Eleotriculus Ginsburg 1938
Eleotriodes Bleeker 1857
Ellerya Castelnau 1873
Ellogobius Whitley 1933
Engrauligobius Iljin 1930
Enypnias Jordan & Evermann 1898
Euchoristopus Gill 1863
Euctenogobius Gill 1859
Eucyclogobius Gill 1862
Eugnathogobius Smith 1931
Eutaeniichthys Jordan & Snyder 1901
Evermannia Jordan 1895
Evermannichthys Metzelaar 1920
Eviota Jenkins 1903
Eviotops Smith 1957
Evorthodus Gill 1859
Expedio Snyder 1909
Exyrias Jordan & Seale 1906
Fagea de Buen 1940
Favonigobius Whitley 1930
Feia Smith 1959
Fereleotris Smith 1958
Flabelligobius Smith 1956
Fluvicola Iljin 1930
Fusigobius Whitley 1930
Galera Herre 1927
Gammogobius Bath 1971
Garmannia Jordan & Evermann in Jordan 1895
Gergobius Whitley 1930
Gerhardinus Meek & Hildebrand 1928
Gillia Günther 1865
Gillichthys Cooper 1863
Ginsburgellus Böhlke & Robins 1968
Gladiogobius Herre 1933
Glossogobius Gill 1859
Gnathogobius Smith 1945
Gnatholepis Bleeker 1874
Gobatinus Ginsburg 1953
Gobatus Ginsburg 1932
Gobica Ginsburg 1932
Gobicula Ginsburg 1944
Gobiculina Ginsburg 1944
Gobidus Ginsburg 1953
Gobiella Smith 1931
Gobiex Ginsburg 1932
Gobiichthys Klunzinger 1871
Gobileptes Swainson 1839
Gobileptes Bleeker (ex Swainson) 1874
Gobio Klein 1779
Gobiodon Bleeker (ex Kuhl & van Hasselt) 1856
Gobiodonella Lindberg 1934
Gobiohelpis Ginsburg 1944
Gobioides Lacepède 1800
Gobiolepis Ginsburg 1944
Gobionellus Girard 1858
Gobiopsis Steindachner 1860
Gobiopterus Bleeker 1874
Gobiopus Gill 1874
Gobiosoma Girard 1858
Gobius Linnaeus 1758
Gobiusculus Duncker 1928
Gobulus Ginsburg 1933
Gorogobius Miller 1978
Gunnamatta Whitley 1928
Gymneleotris Bleeker 1874
Gymnogobius Gill 1863
Gymnurus Rafinesque 1815
Hazeus Jordan & Snyder 1901
Hemigobius Bleeker 1874
Herrea Whitley 1930
Herreogobius Koumans 1940
Hetereleotris Bleeker 1874
Heterogobius Bleeker 1874
Heteroplopomus Tomiyama 1936
Hexacanthus Nordmann 1838
Hoplopomus see *Oplopomus*
Hypogymnogobius Bleeker 1874
Hyrcanogobius Iljin 1928
Iljinia de Buen 1930
Illana Smith & Seale 1906
Ilypnus Jordan & Evermann 1896
Innoculus Whitley 1952
Intonsagobius Herre 1943
Inu Snyder 1909
Iotogobius Smith 1959
Isthmogobius Koumans (ex Bleeker) 1931
Istigobius Whitley 1932
Itbaya Herre 1927
Kelloggella Jordan & Seale in Jordan & Evermann 1905
Knipowitschia Iljin 1927
Koumansetta Whitley 1940
Koumansiasis Visweswara Rao 1968
Latrunculodes Collett 1874
Latrunculus Günther 1861
Lebetus Winther 1877
Lebistes Smitt 1900
Leioeleotris Fowler 1934
Leme De Vis 1883
Lentipes Günther 1861
Lepidogobius Gill 1859
Leptogobius Bleeker 1874
Lesueuri de Buen 1926
Lesueuria Duncker 1928
Lesueurigobius Whitley 1950
Lethops Hubbs 1926
Leucopsarion Hilgendorf 1880
Lioteres Smith 1958
Lizagobius Whitley 1933
Lobulogobius Koumans in Blegvad & Løppenthin 1944

Lophiogobius Günther 1873
Lophogobius Gill 1862
Lotilia Klausewitz 1960
Lubricogobius Tanaka 1915
Luciogobius Gill 1859
Luposicya Smith 1959
Lythrypnus Jordan & Evermann 1896
Macgregorella Seale 1910
Macrodontogobius Herre 1936
Macrogobius de Buen 1930
Mahidolia Smith 1932
Mangarinus Herre 1943
Mapo Smitt 1900
Mars Jordan & Seale 1906
Mauligobius Miller 1984
Mesogobius Bleeker 1874
Metagobius Whitley 1930
Micrapocryptes Hora 1923
Microgobius Poey 1876
Microgobius Koumans (ex Bleeker) 1931
Microsicydium Bleeker 1874
Millerigobius Bath 1973
Mindorogobius Herre 1945
Minictenogobiops Goren 1978
Minutus de Buen 1926
Mirogobius Herre 1927
Mistichthys Smith 1902
Monishia Smith 1959
Mucogobius McCulloch 1912
Mugilogobius Smitt 1900
Mugilostoma Hildebrand & Schroeder 1928
Munrogobius Whitley 1951
Myersina Herre 1934
Nematogobius Boulenger 1910
Neogobius Iljin 1927
Nes Ginsburg 1933
Nesogobius Whitley 1929
Niger de Buen 1926
Ninnia de Buen 1930
Ninnigobius Whitley 1951
Nudagobioides Shaw 1929
Obliquogobius Koumans 1941
Obtortiophagus Whitley 1933
Odondebuenia de Buen 1930
Odontamblyopus Bleeker 1874
Odontogobius Bleeker 1874
Ognichodes Swainson 1839
Oligolepis Bleeker 1874
Ophiogobius Gill 1863
Oplopomops Smith 1959
Oplopomus Valenciennes (ex Ehrenberg) 1837
Opua Jordan 1925
Oreogobius Boulenger 1899
Orissagobius Herre 1945
Orsinigobius Gandolfi, Marconato & Torricelli 1986
Ostreogobius Whitley 1930
Ostreophilus Koumans 1940
Othonops Smith 1881
Oxuderces Eydoux & Souleyet 1850
Oxyurichthys Bleeker 1857
Padogobius Berg 1932
Paeneapocryptes Herre 1927
Palatogobius Gilbert 1971
Paleatogobius Takagi 1957
Pallidogobius Herre 1953
Palutrus Smith 1959
Pandaka Herre 1927
Papenua Herre 1935
Parachaeturichthys Bleeker 1874
Paragobiodon Bleeker 1873
Paragobiopsis Koumans 1941
Paragobius Bleeker 1873
Paraphya Munro 1949
Parapocryptes Bleeker 1874
Parasicydium Risch 1980
Paratrimma Hoese & Brothers 1976
Paratyntlastes Giltay 1935
Pariah Böhlke 1969
Parkraemeria Whitley 1951
Paroxyurichthys Bleeker 1876
Parrella Ginsburg 1938
Parvigobius Whitley 1930
Pellucidus de Buen 1926
Periophthalmodon Bleeker 1874
Periophthalmus Bloch & Schneider 1801
Phyllogobius Larson 1986
Pipidonia Smith 1931
Platygobius Bleeker 1874
Plecopodus Rafinesque 1815
Pleurogobius Seale 1910
Pleurosicya Weber 1913
Pleurosicyops Smith 1959
Poecilosomus Swainson 1839
Pogonogobius Smith 1931
Pomatoschistus Gill 1863
Ponticola Iljin 1927
Porogobius Bleeker 1874
Priolepis Bleeker (ex Ehrenberg) 1874
Priolepis Valenciennes (ex Ehrenberg) in Cuvier & Valenciennes 1837
Proterorhinus Smitt 1900
Psammogobius Smith 1935
Pselaphias Jordan & Seale 1906
Pseudaphya Iljin 1930
Pseudapocryptes Bleeker 1874
Pseudogobiodon Bleeker 1874
Pseudogobiopsis Koumans 1935
Pseudogobius Aurich 1938
Pseudogobius Koumans (ex Bleeker) 1931
Pseudogobius Popta 1922
Pseudolioteres Smith 1958
Pseudotrypauchen Hardenberg 1931
Psilogobius Baldwin 1972
Psilosomus Swainson 1839
Psilotris Ginsburg 1953
Pterogobius Gill 1863
Pycnomma Rutter 1904
Pyosicus Smith 1960
Quietula Jordan & Evermann in Jordan & Starks 1895
Quisquilius Jordan & Evermann 1903
Radcliffella Hubbs 1921
Ranulina Jordan & Starks 1906
Raogobius Mukerji 1935
Redigobius Herre 1927
Relictogobius Ptchelina 1939
Rewa Whitley 1950
Rhinogobiops Hubbs 1926
Rhinogobius Gill 1859
Rhodoniichthys Takagi 1966
Rictugobius Koumans in Smith 1932
Risor Ginsburg 1933
Riukiuia Fowler 1946
Robinsichthys Birdsong 1988
Ruppellia Swainson 1839
Saccostoma Sauvage (ex Guichenot) 1882
Sagamia Jordan & Snyder 1901
Salarigobius Pfeffer 1893
Satulinus Smith 1958
Scartelaos Swainson 1839
Schismatogobius de Beaufort 1912
Sericagobioides Herre 1927
Seychellea Smith 1957
Sicya Jordan & Evermann 1896
Sicydiops Bleeker 1874
Sicydium Valenciennes in Cuvier & Valenciennes 1837
Sicyodon Fourmanoir 1966
Sicyogaster Gill 1860
Sicyopterus Gill 1860
Sicyopus Gill 1863
Sicyosus Jordan & Evermann 1898
Signigobius Hoese & Allen 1977
Silhouettea Smith 1959
Sinogobius Liu 1940
Smaragdus Poey 1860
Smilogobius Herre 1934
Speleogobius Zander & Jelinek 1976
Sphenentogobius Fowler 1940
Stenogobius Bleeker 1874
Stigmatogobius Bleeker 1874
Stiphodon Weber 1895
Stonogobiops Polunin & Lubbock 1977
Stupidogobius Aurich 1938
Sueviota Winterbottom & Hoese 1988
Sufflogobius Smith 1956
Suiboga Pinto 1960
Suruga Jordan & Snyder 1901
Synechogobius Gill 1863
Syrrhothonus Chabanaud 1933
Taenioides Lacepède 1800
Tamanka Herre 1927
Tasmanogobius Scott 1935
Tenacigobius Larson & Hoese 1980
Thaigobiella Smith 1931
Thalassogobius Herre 1953
Thorogobius Miller 1969
Tigrigobius Fowler 1931
Tomiyamichthys Smith 1956
Triaenophorichthys Gill 1859
Triaenophorus Gill 1859
Triaenopogon Bleeker 1874
Trichopharynx Ogilby 1898
Tridentiger Gill 1859
Trifissus Jordan & Snyder 1900
Trigonocephalus Okada 1961
Trimma Jordan & Seale 1906
Trimmatom Winterbottom & Emery 1981
Trypauchen Valenciennes in Cuvier & Valenciennes 1837
Trypauchenichthys Bleeker 1860
Trypauchenophrys Franz 1910
Trypauchenopsis Volz 1903
Tukugobius Herre 1927
Tyntlastes Günther 1862
Typhlogobius Steindachner 1879
Ulcigobius Fowler 1918
Vailima Jordan & Seale 1906
Vaimosa Jordan & Seale 1906
Valenciennea Bleeker 1856

Valenciennesia Bleeker 1874
Vanderhorstia Smith 1949
Vanneaugobius Brownell 1978
Varicus Robins & Böhlke 1961
Vitraria Jordan & Evermann 1903
Vomerogobius Gilbert 1971
Waitea Jordan & Seale 1906
Waiteopsis Whitley 1930
Weberogobius Koumans 1953
Wheelerigobius Miller 1981
Xenogobius Metzelaar 1919
Yabotichthys Herre 1945
Yoga Whitley 1954
Yongeichthys Whitley 1932
Zalypnus Jordan & Evermann 1896
Zappa Murdy 1989
Zebreleotris Herre 1953
Zebrus de Buen 1930
Zonogobius Bleeker 1874
Zostericola Iljin 1927
Zosterisessor Whitley 1935

FAM. KRAEMERIIDAE (Sand Darts)
Gobitrichinotus Fowler 1943
Kraemeria Steindachner 1906
Psammichthys Regan 1908
Vitreola Jordan & Seale 1906

FAM. MICRODESMIDAE

Subfam. Microdesminae (Wormfishes)
Cerdale Jordan & Gilbert 1882
Clarkichthys Smith 1958
Gunnellichthys Bleeker 1858
Leptocerdale Weymouth 1910
Microdesmus Günther 1864
Paragobioides Kendall & Goldsborough 1911
Paragunnellichthys Dawson 1967

Subfam. Ptereleotrinae
= Oxymetopontinae
Aioliops Rennis & Hoese 1987
Andameleotris Herre 1939
Encaeura Jordan & Hubbs 1925
Gracileotris Herre 1953
Herrea Smith 1931
Herreichthys Koumans 1931
Herreolus Smith 1931
Ioglossus Bean in Jordan & Gilbert 1882
Laccoeleotris Fowler 1935
Nemateleotris Fowler 1938
Orthostomus Kner 1868
Oxymetopon Bleeker 1861
Parioglossus Regan 1912
Pogonoculius Fowler 1938
Ptereleotris Gill 1863
Stomogobius Whitley 1931
Vireosa Jordan & Snyder 1901

FAM. XENISTHMIDAE
Allomicrodesmus Schultz in Schultz et al. 1966
Gignimentum Whitley 1933
Kraemericus Schultz in Schultz et al. 1966
Luzoneleotris Herre 1938
Platycephalops Smith 1957
Rotuma Springer 1988
Tyson Springer 1983
Xenisthmus Snyder 1908

SUBORDER ACANTHUROIDEI

FAM. SIGANIDAE (Rabbitfishes)
Amphacanthus Bloch & Schneider 1801
Amphiscarus Swainson 1839
Buro Lacepède (ex Commerson) 1803
Buronus Rafinesque 1815
Centrogaster Houttuyn 1782
Lo Seale 1906
Siganites Fowler 1904
Siganus Forsskål 1775

FAM. LUVARIDAE (Luvars)
Astrodermus Cuvier (ex Bonnelli) 1829
Ausonia Risso 1826
Diana Risso 1826
Luvarus Rafinesque 1810
Proctostegus Nardo 1827
Scrofaria Gistel 1848

FAM. ZANCLIDAE (Moorish Idols)
Gnathocentrum Guichenot 1866
Gonopterus Gronow in Gray 1854
Zanchus Commerson in Lacepède 1802
Zanclus Cuvier (ex Commerson) in Cuvier & Valenciennes 1831

FAM. ACANTHURIDAE (Surgeonfishes and Unicornfishes)
Acanthocaulus Waite 1900
Acanthurus Forsskål 1775
Acanthus Bloch 1795
Acronurus Gronow in Gray 1854
Acronurus Günther (ex Gronow) 1861
Aspisurus Lacepède 1802
Atulonotus Smith 1955
Axinurus Cuvier 1829
Burobulla Whitley 1931
Callicanthus Swainson 1839
Colocopus Gill 1884
Ctenochaetus Gill 1884
Ctenodon Bonaparte 1831
Ctenodon Swainson 1839
Ctenodon Klunzinger 1871
Cyphomycter Fowler & Bean 1929
Dasyacanthurus Fowler 1944
Europus Klein 1775
Harpurina Fowler & Bean 1929
Harpurus Forster 1778
Hepatus Gronow 1763
Keris Valenciennes in Cuvier & Valenciennes 1835
Laephichthys Ogilby 1916
Monoceros Bloch & Schneider 1801
Naseus Commerson in Lacepède 1801
Naso Lacepède 1801
Nasonus Rafinesque 1815
Paracanthurus Bleeker 1863
Priodon Quoy & Gaimard (ex Cuvier) 1825
Priodontichthys Bonaparte 1831
Prionolepis Smith 1931
Prionurus Lacepède 1804
Psetta Klein 1775
Rhinodactylus Smith 1956
Rhomboteuthis Fowler 1944
Rhombotides Klein 1775
Rhombotides Bleeker (ex Klein) 1863
Scopas Bonaparte 1831
Scopas Kner (ex Bonaparte) 1865
Teuthis Linnaeus 1766
Teuthis Browne 1789
Theutis Bonnaterre 1788
Theutys Goüan 1770
Triacanthurodes Fowler 1944
Xesurus Jordan & Evermann 1896
Zebrasoma Swainson 1839

SUBORDER SPHYRAENOIDEI

FAM. SPHYRAENIDAE (Barracudas)
Acus Plumier in Lacepède 1803
Agrioposphyraena Fowler 1903
Australuzza Whitley 1947
Callosphyraena Smith 1956
Indosphyraena Smith 1956
Sphyraena Klein 1778
Sphyraena Röse 1793
Sphyraena Bloch & Schneider 1801
Sphyraenella Smith 1956
Umbla Catesby 1771

SUBORDER SCOMBROIDEI
Lepidosarda Kishinouye 1926

FAM. SCOMBROLABRACIDAE (Black Mackerels)
Scombrolabrax Roule 1921

FAM. GEMPYLIDAE (Snake Mackerels)
Acantoderma Cantraine 1835
Acinacea Bory de Saint-Vincent 1804
Aplurus Lowe 1838
Bipinnula Jordan & Evermann 1896
Dicrotus Günther 1860
Diplogonurus Noronha 1926
Diplospinus Maul 1948
Epinnula Poey 1854
Escolar Jordan & Evermann in Goode & Bean 1896
Gempylus Cuvier 1829
Jordanidia Snyder 1911
Leionura Bleeker 1860
Lemnisoma Lesson 1831
Lepidocybium Gill 1862
Lucoscombrus Van der Hoeven 1855
Machaerope Ogilby 1899
Mimasea Kamohara 1936
Nealotus Johnson 1865
Neoepinnula Matsubara & Iwai 1952
Nesiarchus Johnson 1862
Paradiplospinus Andriashev 1960
Prometheus Lowe 1838
Promethichthys Gill 1893
Ptax Jordan & Evermann 1927
Rexea Waite 1911
Rexichthys Parin & Astakhov 1987
Ruvettus Cocco 1829
Thyrsites Cuvier in Cuvier & Valenciennes 1832
Thyrsites Lesson 1831
Thyrsitoides Fowler 1929
Thyrsitops Gill 1862
Tongaichthys Nakamura & Fujii 1983
Xenogramma Waite 1904
Zyphothyca Swainson 1839

FAM. TRICHIURIDAE (Cutlassfishes, Scabbardfishes)

Pseudoxymetopon Chu & Wu 1962

Subfam. Aphanopodinae

Aphanopus Lowe 1839
Benthodesmus Goode & Bean 1882

Subfam. Lepidopinae

Assurger Whitley 1933
Eupleurogrammus Gill 1862
Evoxymetopon Gill 1863
Lepidopus Goüan 1770
Scarcina Rafinesque 1810
Vandellius Shaw 1803
Ziphotheca Montagu 1811

Subfam. Trichiurinae

Diepinotus Rafinesque 1815
Enchelyopus Klein 1775
Enchelyopus Bleeker 1862
Gymnogaster Gronow 1763
Lepturacanthus Fowler 1905
Lepturus Gill 1861
Symphocles Rafinesque 1815
Tentoriceps Whitley 1948
Trichiurus Linnaeus 1758

FAM. XIPHIIDAE (Swordfishes)

Phaethonichthys Nichols 1923
Xiphias Linnaeus 1758
Zisius Oken 1816

FAM. ISTIOPHORIDAE (Billfishes and Marlins)

Eumakaira Hirasaka & Nakamura 1947
Guebucus Rafinesque 1815
Histiophorus Cuvier in Cuvier & Valenciennes 1832
Istiompax Whitley 1931
Istiophorus Lacepède 1801
Kajikia Hirasaka & Nakamura 1947
Lamontella Smith 1956
Makaira Lacepède 1802
Marlina Hirasaka & Nakamura 1947
Marlina Grey 1928
Nothistium Herrmann 1804
Orthocraeros Smith 1956
Pseudohistiophorus de Buen 1950
Scheponopodus see *Skeponopodus*
Skeponopodus Nardo 1833
Tetrapturus Rafinesque 1810
Tetrapturus Cuvier in Cuvier & Valenciennes 1832
Zanclurus Swainson 1839

FAM. SCOMBRIDAE (Mackerels, Tunas and Bonitos)
Gasterochismatinae included

Acanthocybium Gill 1862
Albacora Jordan 1888
Allothunnus Serventy 1948
Apodontis Bennett 1832
Apolectus Bennett 1831
Auxis Cuvier 1829
Chenogaster Lahille 1903
Chriomitra Lockington 1879
Cordylus Gronow in Gray 1854
Creotroctes Gistel 1848
Cybiosarda Whitley 1935
Cybium Cuvier 1829
Euthynnus Lütken in Jordan & Gilbert 1883
Gasterochisma Richardson 1845
Germo Jordan 1888
Grammatorycnus Gill 1862
Gymnosarda Gill 1862
Indocybium Munro 1943
Katsuwonus Kishinouye 1915
Kishinoella Jordan & Hubbs 1925
Lepidothynnus Günther 1889
Macrorhyncus Lacepède in Duméril 1806
Neothunnus Kishinouye 1923
Nesogrammus Evermann & Seale 1907
Orcynopsis Gill 1862
Orcynus Cuvier 1816
Orycnopsis see *Orcynopsis*
Palamita Bonaparte 1831
Parathunnus Kishinouye 1923
Pelamichthys Giglioli 1880
Pelamys Klein 1775
Pelamys Cuvier in Cuvier & Valenciennes 1832
Pneumatophorus Jordan & Gilbert 1883
Polipturus Rafinesque 1815
Pseudosawara Munro 1943
Rastrelliger Jordan & Starks in Jordan & Dickerson 1908
Sarda Cuvier 1829
Sawara Jordan & Hubbs 1925
Scomber Linnaeus 1758
Scomberomorus Lacepède 1801
Semathunnus Fowler 1933
Sierra Fowler 1905
Thinnus S. D. W. 1837
Thunnus South 1845
Thynnichthys Giglioli 1880
Thynnus Browne 1789
Thynnus Cuvier 1816
Wanderer Whitley 1937

SUBORDER STROMATEOIDEI

FAM. AMARSIPIDAE (Amarsipids)

Amarsipus Haedrich 1969

FAM. CENTROLOPHIDAE (Medusafishes)

Acentrolophus Nardo 1827
Bathyseriola Alcock 1890
Centrolophodes Gilchrist & von Bonde 1923
Centrolophus Lacepède 1802
Coroplopus Smith 1966
Crius Valenciennes in Webb & Berthelot 1839
Eucrotus Bean 1912
Eurumetopos Morton 1888
Gymnocephalus Cocco 1838
Hoplocoryphis Gill 1862
Hyperoglyphe Günther 1859
Icichthys Jordan & Gilbert 1880
Leirus Lowe 1833
Mupus Cocco 1840
Neptomenus Günther 1860
Ocycrius Jordan & Hubbs 1925
Palinurichthys Bleeker 1859
Palinurichthys Gill 1860
Palinurus DeKay 1842
Pammelas Günther 1860
Pompilus Lowe 1839
Psenopsis Gill 1862
Pseudoicichthys Parin & Permitin 1969
Schedophilus Cocco 1839
Seriolella Guichenot 1848
Toledia Miranda-Ribeiro 1915
Tubbia Whitley 1943

FAM. NOMEIDAE (Flotsamfishes or Driftfishes)

Alepidichthys Torres-Orozco & Castro-Aguirre 1982
Atimostoma Smith 1845
Caristioides Whitley 1948
Cubiceps Lowe 1843
Icticus Jordan & Thompson 1914
Mandelichthys Nichols & Murphy 1944
Mulichthys Lloyd 1909
Navarchus Filippi & Verany 1857
Nomeus Cuvier 1816
Parapsenes Smith 1949
Psenes Valenciennes in Cuvier & Valenciennes 1833
Thecopsenes Fowler 1944
Trachelocirrhus Doûmet 1863

FAM. ARIOMMATIDAE (Ariommatids)

Ariomma Jordan & Snyder 1904
Paracubiceps Belloc 1937

FAM. TETRAGONURIDAE (Squaretails)

Ctenodax Macleay 1886
Tetragonurus Risso 1810

FAM. STROMATEIDAE (Butterfishes)

Chondroplites Gill 1862
Chrysostromus Lacepède 1802
Fiatola Cuvier 1816
Fiatola Risso 1826
Lepipterus Rafinesque 1815
Lepterus Rafinesque 1810
Leptolepis Guichenot (ex van Hasselt MS) 1867
Palometa Jordan & Evermann 1896
Pampus Bonaparte 1837
Papyrichthys Smith 1934
Peprilus Cuvier 1829
Poronotus Gill 1861
Pterorhombus Fowler 1906
Rhombus Lacepède 1800
Seserinus Oken (ex Cuvier) 1817
Simobrama Fowler 1944
Stromateoides Bleeker 1851
Stromateus Linnaeus 1758

SUBORDER ANABANTOIDEI

FAM. ANABANTIDAE (Climbing Gouramies)

Anabas Cloquet (ex Cuvier) 1816
Ctenopoma Peters 1844
Sandelia Castelnau 1861
Spirobranchus Cuvier 1829

FAM. BELONTIIDAE (Gouramies and allies)

Anostoma van Hasselt in Bleeker 1859
Belontia Myers 1923
Betta Bleeker 1850
Colisa Cuvier in Cuvier & Valenciennes 1831
Ctenops McClelland 1845

Deschauenseeia Fowler 1934
Lithulcus Gistel 1848
Macropodus Lacepède 1801
Malpulutta Deraniyagala 1937
Micracanthus Sauvage 1879
Nemaphoerus Kuhl & van Hasselt in Bleeker 1879
Oshimia Jordan 1919
Parasphaerichthys Prashad & Mukerji 1929
Parophiocephalus Popta 1905
Parosphromenus Bleeker 1879
Pedites Gistel 1848
Platypodus Lacepède 1804
Polyacanthus Cuvier (ex Kuhl) 1829
Pseudobetta Richter 1981
Pseudosphromenus Bleeker 1879
Sphaerichthys Canestrini 1860
Trichogaster Bloch & Schneider 1801
Trichopodus Lacepède 1801
Trichopsis Canestrini (ex Kner) 1860
Trichopus Shaw 1803

FAM. HELOSTOMATIDAE (Kissing Gouramies)

Helostoma Cuvier (ex Kuhl) 1829

FAM. OSPHRONEMIDAE (Giant Gouramies)

Osphronemus Lacepède 1801

SUBORDER LUCIOCEPHALOIDEI

FAM. LUCIOCEPHALIDAE (Pikeheads)

Diplopterus Gray 1830
Luciocephalus Bleeker 1851

SUBORDER CHANNOIDEI = Ophiocephaliformes

FAM. CHANNIDAE (Snakeheads)

Bostrychoides Lacepède 1801
Channa Gronow 1763
Channa Scopoli (Gronow) 1777
Ophicephalus Bloch 1793
Parachanna Teugels & Daget 1984
Parophiocephalus Senna 1924
Philypnoides Bleeker 1849

ORDER PLEURONECTIFORMES

Buglossa Bertrand 1763

SUBORDER PSETTOIDEI

FAM. PSETTODIDAE (Psettodids)

Psettodes Bennett 1831
Sphagomorus Cope 1869

SUBORDER PLEURONECTOIDEI

FAM. CITHARIDAE

Subfam. Brachypleurinae
Brachypleura Günther 1862
Laiopteryx Weber 1913
Lepidoblepharon Weber 1913

Subfam. Citharinae
Brachypleurops Fowler 1934
Chopinopsetta Whitley 1931
Citharoides Hubbs 1915
Citharus Röse 1793
Citharus Bleeker 1862
Eucitharus Gill 1889
Paracitharus Regan 1920

FAM. SCOPHTHALMIDAE

Lepidorhombus Günther 1862
Lophopsetta Gill 1861
Passer Valenciennes (ex Klein) 1846
Phrynorhombus Günther 1862
Psetta Swainson 1839
Rhomboides Goldfuss 1820
Rhombus Klein 1775
Rhombus Cuvier 1816
Rhombus Walbaum (ex Klein) 1793
Scophthalmus Rafinesque 1810
Zeugopterus Gottsche 1835

FAM. PARALICHTHYIDAE

Ancylopsetta Gill 1864
Aramaca Jordan & Goss in Jordan 1885
Azevia Jordan in Jordan & Goss 1889
Cephalopsetta Dutt & Rao 1965
Chaenopsetta Gill 1861
Citharichthys Bleeker 1862
Cyclopsetta Gill 1889
Etropus Jordan & Gilbert 1882
Gastropsetta Bean 1895
Hemirhombus Bleeker 1862
Hippoglossina Steindachner 1876
Istiorhombus Whitley 1931
Lioglossina Gilbert 1890
Metoponops Gill 1864
Neorhombus Castelnau 1875
Notosema Goode & Bean 1883
Orthopsetta Gill 1862
Paralichthys Girard 1858
Pseudorhombus Bleeker 1862
Ramularia Jordan & Evermann 1898
Rhombiscus Jordan & Snyder 1901
Spinirhombus Oshima 1927
Syacium Ranzani 1842
Tarphops Jordan & Thompson 1914
Tephrinectes Günther 1862
Tephritis Günther 1862
Teratorhombus Macleay 1881
Thysanopsetta Günther 1880
Uropsetta Gill 1862
Velifracta Jordan 1907
Verecundum Jordan 1891
Xystreurys Jordan & Gilbert 1880

FAM. BOTHIDAE (Lefteye Flounders)

Subfam. Taeniopsettinae
Engyophrys Jordan & Bollman 1890
Perissias Jordan & Evermann 1898
Taeniopsetta Gilbert 1905
Trichopsetta Gill 1889

Subfam. Bothinae
Anticitharus Günther 1880
Arnoglossus Bleeker 1862
Asterorhombus Tanaka 1915
Bascanius Schiødte 1868
Bothus Rafinesque 1810
Caulopsetta Gill 1893
Charybdia Facciolà 1885
Chascanopsetta Alcock 1894
Crossobothus Fowler 1934
Crossolepis Norman 1927
Crossorhombus Regan 1920
Delothyris Goode 1883
Dollfusetta Whitley 1950
Dollfusina Chabanaud 1933
Dorsopsetta Nielsen 1963
Engyprosopon Günther 1862
Grammatobothus Norman 1926
Japonolaeops Amaoka 1969
Kamoharaia Kuronuma 1940
Kyleia Chabanaud 1931
Laeops Günther 1880
Laeoptichthys Hubbs 1915
Lambdopsetta Smith & Pope 1906
Leptolaeops Fowler 1934
Lophonectes Günther 1880
Lophorhombus Macleay 1882
Monolene Goode 1880
Neolaeops Amaoka 1969
Parabothus Norman 1931
Pelecanichthys Gilbert & Cramer 1897
Peloria Cocco 1844
Platophrys Swainson 1839
Platotichthys Nichols 1921
Psettina Hubbs 1915
Psettinella Fedorov & Foroshchuk 1988
Psettyllis Alcock 1890
Pseudocitharichthys Weber 1913
Rhomboidichthys Bleeker 1856
Scaeops Jordan & Starks 1904
Scianectes Alcock 1889
Scidorhombus Tanaka 1915
Solea Catesby 1771
Symboulichthys Chabanaud 1927
Thyris Goode 1880
Tosarhombus Amaoka 1969
Trachypterophrys Franz 1910

FAM. ACHIROPSETTIDAE

Achiropsetta Norman 1930
Apterygopectus Ojeda R. 1978
Lepidopsetta Günther 1880
Mancopsetta Gill 1881
Neoachiropsetta Kotlyar 1978
Pseudomancopsetta Evseenko 1984

FAM. PLEURONECTIDAE (Righteye Flounders)

Pluviopsetta Tanaka 1916
Pseudoplatichthys Hikita 1934

Subfam. Poecilopsettinae
Alaeops Jordan & Starks 1904
Boopsetta Alcock 1896
Marleyella Fowler 1925
Nematops Günther 1880
Paralimanda Breder 1927
Poecilopsetta Günther 1880

Subfam. Rhombosoleinae
Adamasoma Whitley & Phillipps 1939
Ammotretis Günther 1862

Apsetta Kyle 1901
Azygopus Norman 1926
Bowenia Haast 1873
Colistium Norman 1926
Curioptera Whitley 1951
Oncopterus Steindachner 1875
Pelotretis Waite 1911
Peltorhamphus Günther 1862
Psammodiscus Günther 1862
Rhombosolea Günther 1862
Tapirisolea Ramsay 1883
Taratretis Last 1978

Subfam. Samarinae
Plagiopsetta Franz 1910
Samaris Gray 1831
Samariscus Gilbert 1905

Subfam. Pleuronectinae
Acanthopsetta Schmidt 1904
Araias Jordan & Starks 1904
Atheresthes Jordan & Gilbert 1880
Brachyprosopon Bleeker 1862
Citharus Reinhardt 1838
Cleisthenes Jordan & Starks 1904
Clidoderma Bleeker 1862
Cynicoglossus Bonaparte 1837
Cynoglossa Bonaparte 1846
Cynopsetta Jordan & Starks (ex Schmidt) 1906
Dexistes Jordan & Starks 1904
Drepanopsetta Gill 1861
Embassichthys Jordan & Evermann 1896
Eopsetta Jordan & Goss in Jordan 1885
Errex Jordan 1919
Euchalarodus Gill 1864
Flesus Moreau 1881
Gareus Hubbs 1915
Glyptocephalus Gottsche 1835
Heteroprosopon Bleeker 1862
Hippoglossoides Gottsche 1835
Hippoglossus Cuvier 1816
Hypsopsetta Gill 1862
Inopsetta Jordan & Goss in Jordan 1885
Isopsetta Lockington in Jordan & Gilbert 1883
Kareius Jordan & Snyder 1900
Lepidopsetta Gill 1862
Limanda Gottsche 1835
Limandella Jordan & Starks 1906
Liopsetta Gill 1864
Lyopsetta Jordan & Goss in Jordan 1885
Microstomus Gottsche 1835
Myzopsetta Gill 1861
Neoetropus Hildebrand & Schroeder 1928
Parophrys Girard 1854
Passer Klein 1775
Platessa Cuvier 1816
Platichthys Girard 1854
Platysomatichthys Bleeker 1862
Pleuronectes Linnaeus 1758
Pleuronichthys Girard 1854
Pomatopsetta Gill 1864
Protopsetta Schmidt 1904
Psettichthys Girard 1854
Pseudopleuronectes Bleeker 1862
Reinhardtius Gill 1861
Tanakius Hubbs 1918
Veraequa Jordan & Starks 1904
Verasper Jordan & Gilbert in Jordan & Evermann 1898
Xystrias Jordan & Starks 1904

Subfam. Paralichthodinae
Paralichthodes Gilchrist 1902

FAM. ACHIRIDAE
Achiropsis Steindachner 1876
Achirus Lacepède 1802
Anathyridium Chabanaud 1928
Aprionichthys Kaup 1858
Baiostoma Bean in Goode & Bean 1882
Catathyridium Chabanaud 1928
Grammichthys Kaup 1858
Gymnachirus Kaup 1858
Hypoclinemus Chabanaud 1928
Nodogymnus Chabanaud 1928
Pnictes Jordan 1919
Soleonasus Eigenmann 1912
Soleotalpa Günther 1862
Trinectes Rafinesque 1832

FAM. SOLEIDAE (Soles)
Achiroides Bleeker 1851
Achlyopa Whitley 1947
Aesopia Kaup 1858
Amate Jordan & Starks 1906
Anisochirus Günther 1862
Aseraggodes Kaup 1858
Austroglossus Regan 1920
Barbourichthys Chabanaud 1934
Barnardichthys Chabanaud 1927
Bathysolea Roule 1916
Beaufortella Chabanaud 1943
Brachirus Swainson 1839
Buglossidium Chabanaud 1930
Buglossus Günther 1862
Capartella Chabanaud 1950
Chabanaudetta Whitley 1931
Coryphaesopia Chabanaud 1930
Coryphillus Chabanaud 1931
Dagetichthys Stauch & Blanc 1964
Dexillichthys Whitley 1931
Dexillus Chabanaud 1930
Dicologlossa Chabanaud 1927
Echinosolea Chabanaud 1927
Euryglossa Kaup 1858
Eurypleura Kaup 1858
Eusolea Roule 1919
Haplozebrias Chabanaud 1943
Heterobuglossus Chabanaud 1931
Heteromycteris Kaup 1858
Holonodus Chabanaud 1936
Leptosoma Nardo 1827
Liachirus Günther 1862
Microbuglossus Günther 1862
Microchiropsis Chabanaud 1956
Microchirus Bonaparte 1833
Mischommatus Chabanaud 1938
Monochir Cuvier 1829
Monochirus Rafinesque 1814
Monochirus Oken (ex Cuvier) 1817
Monochirus Kaup 1858
Monodichthys Chabanaud 1925
Nematozebrias Chabanaud 1943
Normanetta Whitley 1931
Parachirus Matsubara & Ochiai 1963
Paradicula Whitley 1931
Pardachirus Günther 1862
Pegusa Günther 1862
Pegusa de Buen 1926
Phyllichthys McCulloch 1916
Pseudaesopia Chabanaud 1934
Pseudaustroglossus Chabanaud 1937
Quenselia Jordan in Jordan & Goss 1888
Rendahlia Chabanaud 1930
Rhinosolea Fowler 1946
Solea Klein 1776
Solea Quensel 1806
Solea Rafinesque 1810
Solea Cuvier 1816
Soleichthys Bleeker 1860
Solenoides Kaup 1858
Spanius Gistel 1848
Strabozebrias Chabanaud 1943
Strandichthys Whitley 1937
Synaptura Cantor 1849
Synapturichthys Chabanaud 1927
Synclidopus Chabanaud 1943
Trichobrachirus Chabanaud 1943
Typhlachirus Hardenberg 1931
Vanstraelenia Chabanaud 1950
Whitleyia Chabanaud 1930
Xenobuglossus Chabanaud 1950
Zebrias Jordan & Snyder 1900
Zevaia Chabanaud 1943

FAM. CYNOGLOSSIDAE (Tonguefishes)

Subfam. Symphurinae
Acedia Jordan 1888
Ammopleurops Günther 1862
Aphoristia Kaup 1858
Bibronia Cocco 1844
Eupnoea Gistel 1848
Euporista Gistel 1848
Glossichthys Gill 1861
Odontolepis Fischer von Waldheim 1813
Plagiusa Rafinesque 1815
Plagusia Browne 1789
Plagusia Cuvier (ex Browne) 1816
Plagusia Bonaparte 1833
Symphurus Rafinesque 1810

Subfam. Cynoglossinae
Arelia Kaup 1858
Areliscus Jordan & Snyder 1900
Cantoria Kaup 1858
Cantorusia Whitley 1940
Compsomidiama Chabanaud 1951
Cynoglossoides von Bonde 1922
Cynoglossoides Smith 1949
Cynoglossus Hamilton 1822
Dexiourius Chabanaud 1947
Dollfusichthys Chabanaud 1931
Icania Kaup 1858
Notrullus Whitley 1951
Paraplagusia Bleeker 1865
Rhinoplagusia Bleeker 1870
Trulla Kaup 1858
Usinostia Jordan & Snyder 1900

ORDER TETRAODONTIFORMES

SUBORDER BALISTOIDEI

FAM. TRIACANTHODIDAE (Spikefishes)

Atrophacanthus Fraser-Brunner 1950
Bathyphylax Myers 1934
Halimochirurgus Alcock 1899
Hollardia Poey 1861
Johnsonina Myers 1934
Macrorhamphosodes Fowler 1934
Mephisto Tyler 1966
Parahollardia Fraser-Brunner 1941
Paratriacanthodes Fowler 1934
Triacanthodes Bleeker 1858
Triradulifer Fraser-Brunner 1941
Tydemania Weber 1913

FAM. TRIACANTHIDAE (Triplespines)

Pseudotriacanthus Fraser-Brunner 1941
Triacanthus Oken (ex Cuvier) 1817
Tripodichthys Tyler 1968
Trixiphichthys Fraser-Brunner 1941

FAM. BALISTIDAE (Triggerfishes)

Abalistes Jordan & Seale 1906
Allomonacanthus Fraser-Brunner 1941
Balistapus Tilesius 1820
Balistes Linnaeus 1758
Balistoides Fraser-Brunner 1935
Canthidermis Swainson 1839
Capriscus Klein 1777
Capriscus Röse 1793
Capriscus Rafinesque 1810
Chalisoma Swainson 1839
Epimonus Rafinesque 1815
Erythrodon Rüppell 1852
Hanomanctus Smith 1949
Hemibalistes Fraser-Brunner 1935
Leiurus Swainson 1839
Liocornus Tortonese 1939
Melichthys Swainson 1839
Nematobalistes Fraser-Brunner 1935
Odonus Gistel 1848
Oncobalistes Fowler 1946
Pachynathus Swainson 1839
Parabalistes Bleeker 1865
Pseudobalistes Bleeker 1865
Pyrodon Kaup 1855
Rhinecanthus Swainson 1839
Sufflamen Jordan 1916
Tantalisor Whitley 1947
Tobinia Whitley 1933
Verrunculus Jordan 1924
Xanthichthys Kaup in Richardson 1856
Xenobalistes Matsuura 1981
Xenodon Rüppell 1836
Zenodon Swainson 1839

FAM. MONACANTHIDAE (Filefishes)

Acanthaluteres Bleeker 1865
Acreichthys Fraser-Brunner 1941
Aleuteres see *Aluterus*
Aleuterius see *Aluterus*
Alutera Oken (ex Cuvier) 1817
Aluterus Cloquet 1816
Amanses Gray 1835
Anacanthus Gray 1830
Arotrolepis Fraser-Brunner 1941
Bigener Hutchins 1977
Blandowskius Whitley 1931
Brachaluteres Bleeker 1865
Cantherhines Swainson 1839
Cantheschenia Hutchins 1977
Ceratacanthus Gill 1861
Chaetoderma see *Chaetodermis*
Chaetodermis Swainson 1839
Colurodontis Hutchins 1977
Davidia Miranda-Ribeiro 1915
Eubalichthys Whitley 1930
Laputa Whitley 1930
Leprogaster Fraser-Brunner 1941
Liomonacanthus Bleeker 1865
Meuschenia Whitley 1929
Monacanthus Oken (ex Cuvier) 1817
Monoceros Plumier in Lacepède 1798
Navodon Whitley 1930
Nelus Whitley 1930
Nelusetta Whitley 1939
Osbeckia Jordan & Evermann 1896
Oxymonacanthus Bleeker 1865
Paraluteres Bleeker 1865
Paramonacanthus Bleeker 1865
Paramonacanthus Steindachner 1867
Parika Whitley 1955
Penicipelta Whitley 1947
Pervagor Whitley 1930
Pogonognathus Bleeker 1849
Pseudalutarius Bleeker 1865
Pseudomonacanthus Bleeker 1865
Psilocephalus Swainson 1839
Rudarius Jordan & Fowler 1902
Scobinichthys Whitley 1931
Scurrilichthys Fraser-Brunner 1941
Stephanolepis Gill 1861
Thamnaconus Smith 1949
Trichoderma Swainson 1839
Unicornis Catesby 1771
Weerutta Scott 1962

FAM. OSTRACIIDAE (Boxfishes) = Ostraciontidae

Subfam. Aracaninae

Acarana Gray 1833
Anoplocapros Kaup 1855
Aracana Gray 1838
Aracanostracion Smith 1949
Caprichthys McCulloch & Waite 1915
Capropygia Kaup 1855
Kentrocapros Kaup 1855
Molaracana Le Danois 1961
Polyplacapros Fujii & Uyeno 1979
Strophiurichthys Fraser-Brunner 1935

Subfam. Ostraciinae

Acanthostracion Bleeker 1865
Chapinus Jordan & Evermann 1896
Cibotion Kaup 1855
Gonodermus Rafinesque 1815
Lactophrys Swainson 1839
Lactoria Jordan & Fowler 1902
Ostracion Linnaeus 1758
Paracanthostracion Whitley 1933
Platycanthus Swainson 1839
Rhinesomus Swainson 1839
Rhynchostracion Fraser-Brunner 1935
Tetrosomus Swainson 1839
Triorus Jordan & Hubbs 1925

SUBORDER TETRAODONTOIDEI

FAM. TRIODONTIDAE (Threetooth Puffers)

Triodon Cuvier 1829

FAM. TETRAODONTIDAE (Puffers) Canthigastrinae included

Akamefugu Abe 1954
Amblyrhynchote Bibron in Duméril 1855
Amblyrhynchotes Troschel (ex Bibron) 1856
Anchisomus Richardson (ex Kaup) 1854
Anosmius Peters 1855
Aphanacanthus Troschel (ex Bibron) 1856
Apsicephalus Hollard 1857
Arothron Müller 1841
Batrachops Bibron in Duméril 1855
Boesemanichthys Abe 1952
Brachycephalus Hollard 1857
Canthigaster Swainson 1839
Carinotetraodon Benl 1957
Catophorhynchus Troschel (ex Bibron) 1856
Cheilichthys Müller 1841
Chelonodon Müller 1841
Chelonodontops Smith 1958
Chonerhinos Bleeker 1854
Cirrhisomus Swainson 1839
Colomesus Gill 1884
Contusus Whitley 1947
Crayracion Klein 1777
Crayracion Bleeker (ex Klein) 1865
Crayracion Walbaum (ex Klein) 1792
Cyprichthys Whitley 1936
Dichotomycter Troschel (ex Bibron) 1856
Dilobomycter Troschel (ex Bibron) 1856
Ephippion Bibron in Duméril 1855
Epipedorhynchus Troschel (ex Bibron) 1856
Eumycterias Jenkins 1901
Feroxodon Su, Hardy & Tyler 1986
Fugu Abe 1952
Gastrophysus Müller 1843
Geneion Bibron in Duméril 1855
Guentheridia Gilbert & Starks 1904
Hemiconiatus Günther 1870
Higanfugu Abe 1949
Holacanthus Gronow in Gray 1854
Javichthys Hardy 1985
Kanduka Hora 1925
Lagocephalus Swainson 1839
Leiodon Swainson 1839
Leisomus Swainson 1839
Lepidorbidus Fowler 1929
Liosaccus Günther 1870
Lucubrapiscis Whitley 1931
Marilyna Hardy 1982
Monotretus Troschel (ex Bibron) 1856
Omegophora Whitley 1934
Oonidus Rafinesque 1815
Orbidus Rafinesque 1815
Orbis Catesby 1771
Orbis Fischer von Waldheim (ex Lacepède) 1813

Ovoides Anonymous 1798
Ovoides Lacepède 1798
Ovum Bloch & Schneider 1801
Pelagocephalus Tyler & Paxton 1979
Physogaster Müller 1841
Pleuranacanthus Bleeker (ex Bibron) 1865
Polyspina Hardy 1983
Prilonotus Richardson 1854
Promecocephalus Troschel (ex Bibron) 1856
Proodus Fowler 1944
Psilonotus Swainson 1839
Reicheltia Hardy 1982
Rhynchotes Troschel (ex Bibron) 1856
Shippofugu Abe 1949
Shosaifugu Abe 1950
Spheroides Lacepède 1800
Spheroides Duméril 1806
Sphoeroides Anonymous [Lacepède] 1798
Stenometopus Troschel (ex Bibron) 1856
Takifugu Abe 1949
Tetractenos Hardy 1983
Tetraodon Linnaeus 1758
Thecapteryx Fowler 1948
Torafugu Abe 1950
Torquigener Whitley 1930
Tropidichthys Bleeker 1854
Tylerius Hardy 1984
Uranostoma Bleeker (ex Bibron) 1865
Xenopterus Troschel (ex Bibron) 1856

FAM. DIODONTIDAE (Porcupinefishes and Burrfishes)

Allomycterus McCulloch 1921
Atinga Le Danois 1954
Atopomycterus Bleeker (ex Verreaux) 1865
Cephalopsis Rafinesque 1815
Chilomycterus Brisout de Barneville (ex Bibron) 1846
Cyanichthys Kaup 1855
Cyclichthys Kaup 1855
Dicotylichthys Kaup 1855
Diodon Linnaeus 1758
Euchilomycterus Waite 1900
Lophodiodon Fraser-Brunner 1943
Lyosphaera Evermann & Kendall 1898
Orbis Müller 1766
Paradiodon Bleeker 1865
Tragulichthys Whitley 1931
Trichocyclus Günther 1870
Trichodiodon Bleeker 1865

FAM. MOLIDAE (Molas or Ocean Sunfishes)

Acanthosoma DeKay 1842
Aledon Castelnau 1861
Centaurus Kaup 1855
Cephalus Shaw 1804
Diplanchias Rafinesque 1810
Masturus Gill 1884
Mola Koelreuter 1770
Mola Linck 1790
Mola Cuvier 1798
Molacanthus Swainson 1839
Orthagoriscus Cuvier 1816
Orthragoriscus Bloch & Schneider 1801
Orthragus Rafinesque 1810
Ozodura Ranzani 1839
Pallasia Nardo 1840
Pedalion Guilding in Swainson 1838
Pseudomola Cadenat 1959
Ranzania Nardo 1840
Trematopsis Ranzani 1839
Tympanomium Ranzani 1839

CLASS SARCOPTERYGII

ORDER COELACANTHIFORMES

FAM. LATIMERIIDAE (Coelacanths)

Latimeria Smith 1939
Malania Smith 1953

ORDER CERATODONTIFORMES

FAM. CERATODONTIDAE (Australian Lungfishes)

Epiceratodus Teller 1891
Neoceratodus Castelnau 1876
Ompax Castelnau 1879

ORDER LEPIDOSIRENIFORMES

FAM. LEPIDOSIRENIDAE

Subfam. Lepidosireninae (South American Lungfishes)

Amphibichthys Hogg 1841
Lepidosiren Fitzinger 1837

Subfam. Protopterinae (African Lungfishes)

Protomelus Hogg 1841
Protopterus Owen 1839
Rhinocryptis Peters 1844

UNPLACED GENERA

Acanthopus Oken 1816
Acaramus Rafinesque 1815
Acarauna Catesby 1771
Bathysidus Beebe 1934
Belone Oken 1816
Ceracantha Rafinesque 1815
Cerictius Rafinesque 1810
Cyrtus Minding 1832
Dipurus Rafinesque 1815
Draco Goüan 1770
Edomus Rafinesque 1815
Eleuthurus Rafinesque 1815
Gasterodon Rafinesque 1815
Gastrogonus Rafinesque 1815
Gobio Bertrand 1763
Gonipus Rafinesque 1815
Gonurus Rafinesque 1815
Guaris Rafinesque 1815
Homolenus Rafinesque 1815
Ictias Rafinesque 1815
Lepomus Rafinesque 1815
Maturacus Rafinesque 1815
Mesopodus Rafinesque 1815
Nemipus Rafinesque 1815
Odamphus Rafinesque 1815
Odontopsis van Hasselt 1823
Onopionus Rafinesque 1815
Opictus Rafinesque 1815
Oxima Rafinesque 1815
Pacamus Rafinesque 1815
Phyllophorus Rafinesque 1815
Piratia Rafinesque 1815
Plagusia Jarocki 1822
Pomacanthis Rafinesque 1815
Pomagonus Rafinesque 1815
Salius Minding 1832
Soranus Rafinesque 1815
Tangus Rafinesque 1815
Tasica Rafinesque 1815
Taunis Rafinesque 1815

Index to Higher Taxa of Part II

PART III

LITERATURE CITED

William N. Eschmeyer

ABBOTT, J. F. 1899 (22 Aug. - 8 Sept.) **[ref. 1]**. The marine fishes of Peru. Proc. Acad. Nat. Sci. Phila. 1899 [v. 51]: 324-364. [Pages 324-336 published 22 Aug., 337-352 on 29 Aug., 353-364 on 8 Sept.]

——. 1901 (25 Feb.) **[ref. 2]**. List of fishes collected in the river Pei-Ho, at Tien-Tsin, China, by Noah Fields Drake, with descriptions of seven new species. Proc. U. S. Natl. Mus. v. 23 (no. 1221): 483-491.

ABE, T. 1939 (May) **[ref. 5589]**. Notes on *Sphoeroides xanthopterus* (Temminck & Schlegel) (Tetraodontidae, Teleostei). Zool. Mag. (Tokyo) v. 51 (no. 5): 334-337.

——. 1949 (26 Dec.) **[ref. 3]**. Taxonomic studies on the puffers (Tetraodontidae, Teleostei) from Japan and adjacent regions — V. Synopsis of the puffers from Japan and adjacent regions. Bull. Biogeogr. Soc. Jpn. v. 14 (no. 13): 89-140, Pls. 1-2.

——. 1950 (30 Dec.) **[ref. 5588]**. Taxonomic studies on the puffers (Tetraodontidae, Teleostei) from Japan and adjacent regions — VI. Variation of pectoral fin. Jpn. J. Ichthyol. v. 1 (no. 3): 198-206 + table.

——. 1952 (29 Feb.) **[ref. 4]**. Taxonomic studies on the puffers (Tetraodontidae, Teleostei) from Japan and adjacent regions — VII. Concluding remarks, with the introduction of two new genera, *Fugu* and *Boesemanichthys*. Jpn. J. Ichthyol. v. 2 (no. 1): 35-44.

——. 1954 (30 June) **[ref. 5]**. Taxonomic studies on the puffers from Japan and adjacent regions - Corrigenda and addenda. Part I. Jpn. J. Ichthyol. v. 3 (nos. 3/4/5): 121-128, 1 col. pl.

——. 1957 (June) **[ref. 6]**. Notes on fishes from the stomachs of whales taken in the Antarctic. I. *Xenocyttus nemotoi*, a new genus and new species of zeomorph fish of the subfamily Oreosominae Goode and Bean, 1895. Sci. Rep. Whales Res. Inst. Tokyo No. 12: 225-233, 2 pls.

——. 1961 (31 July) **[ref. 7]**. Notes on some fishes of the subfamily Braminae, with the introduction of a new genus *Pseudotaractes*. Jpn. J. Ichthyol. v. 8 (nos. 3/4): 92-99.

ABE, T., AND T. IWAMI. 1989 **[ref. 13580]**. Notes on fishes from the stomachs of whales taken in the Antarctic. II. On *Dissostichus* and *Ceratias*, with an appendix (Japanese names of important Antarctic fishes). Proc. Natl. Inst. Polar Res. Symp. Polar Biol. v. 2: 78-82.

ABLE, K. W., AND D. E. MCALLISTER. 1980 **[ref. 6908]**. Revision of the snailfish genus *Liparis* from Arctic Canada. Can. Bull. Fish. Aquatic Sci. No. 208: i-viii + 1-52.

ABOUSSOUAN, A. 1983 (31 Dec.) **[ref. 12850]**. Contribution à l'étude des larves pélagiques du sousordre des Stromateoidei (Pisces, Perciformes). Cybium v. 7 (no. 4): 1-24.

——. 1988 (30 Mar.) **[ref. 12841]**. Description des larves d'-*Eucitharus macrolepidotus* (Bloch, 1787) et quelques commentaires sur leurs affinités phylogénétiques (Pleuronectiformes, Citharidae). Cybium v. 12 (no. 1): 59-66.

ABOUSSOUAN, A., AND J. M. LEIS. 1984 **[ref. 13661]**. Balistoidei: development. Am. Soc. Ichthyol. Herpetol. Spec. Publ. No. 1: 450-459.

ABRAMOV, A. A. 1987 **[ref. 13520]**. A new *Epigonus* species (Perciformes, Epigonidae) from the southern Pacific. Voprosy Ikhtiol. v. 27 (no. 6): 1010-1013. [In Russian. English translation in J. Ichthyol. v. 28 (no. 3): 102-106.]

ACERO P., A. 1984 **[ref. 5534]**. The chaenopsine blennies of the southwestern Caribbean (Pisces: Clinidae: Chaenopsinae). 1. Systematic analysis and zoogrography. An. Inst. Invest. Mar. Punta Betin v. 14: 29-46.

——. 1984 **[ref. 8191]**. A new species of *Emblemaria* (Pisces: Clinidae: Chaenopsinae) from the southwestern Caribbean with comments on two other species of the genus. Bull. Mar. Sci. v. 35 (no. 2): 187-194.

AGAFONOVA, T. B. 1988 **[ref. 13479]**. New data on the taxonomy and distribution of cigarfishes (*Cubiceps*, Nomeidae) of the Indian Ocean. Voprosy Ikhtiol. v. 28 (no. 4): 541-555. [In Russian. English translation in J. Ichthyol. (1989) v. 28 (no. 6): 46-61.]

AGASSIZ, A. 1861 (June-July) **[ref. 11]**. Notes on the described species of Holconoti, found on the western coast of North America. Proc. Boston Soc. Nat. Hist. v. 8 (1861 to 1862): 122-134.

——. 1888 **[ref. 1845]**. Three cruises of the United States coast and geodetic survey steamer "Blake." [Chapter xv. Sketches of the characteristic deep-sea types.—Fishes, pp. 21-36, figs. 195-224 is by Goode & Bean.] Bull. Mus. Comp. Zool. Harvard v. 15 (in 2 vols.): i-xxii + 1-314 and 1-220.

AGASSIZ, L. 1832 **[ref. 5111]**. Untersuchungen über die fossilen Süsswasser-Fische der tertiären Formationen. Neues Jahrb. Mineral. Geol. Petrefaktenk. v. 3: 129-138.

——. 1833-43 **[ref. 13390]**. Recherches sur les poissons fossiles. Neuchâtel, Switzerland. 5 vols. with atlas.

——. 1835 **[ref. 22]**. Description de quelques espèces de cyprins du lac de Neuchatel, qui sont encore inconnues aux naturalistes. Mem. Soc. Neuchatel. Sci. Nat. v. 1: 33-48.

——. 1845 **[ref. 4889]**. Nomenclator zoologicus... Nomina systematica generum Piscium, tam viventium quam fossilium... Soloduri. i-vi + 1-69 + 1-8 pp. [Published in 1845, Addenda et Corrigenda (pp. 1-8) possibly published later.]

——. 1846 **[ref. 64]**. Nomenclatoris Zoologici. Index universalis, continens nomina systematica classium, ordinum, familiarum et generum animalius omnium, tam viventium quam fossilius, secundum ordinem alphabeticum unicum disposita... Soloduri. i-viii + 1-393. [Also 1848 edition, pp. i-x + 1-1135.]

——. 1848-49 **[ref. 65]**. [Two new fishes from Lake Superior.] Proc. Boston Soc. Nat. Hist. v. 3 (1848 to 1851): 80-81. [Based on signature dates, p. 80 published Nov. 1848, p. 81 in Mar. 1849.]

——. 1850 **[ref. 66]**. Lake Superior: its physical character, vegetation, and animals, compared with those of other similar regions. By Louis Agassiz. With a narrative of the tour, by J. Elliott Cabot. And contributions by other scientific gentlemen. Boston. i-x + 9-428, frontispiece + Pls. 1-8. [Fishes treated in Chapter VI, pp. 246-378.]

——. 1853 (July) **[ref. 67]**. Recent researches of Prof. Agassiz. [Extract from letter to J. D. Dana dated Cambridge, June 9, 1853.] Am. J. Sci. Arts (Ser. 2) v. 16 (no. 46): 134-136.

——. 1853 (Nov.) **[ref. 68]**. Extraordinary fishes from California, constituting a new family, described by L. Agassiz. Am. J. Sci. Arts (Ser. 2) v. 16 (no. 48): 380-390.

——. 1854 (Mar./May) **[ref. 69]**. Notice of a collection of fishes from the southern bend of the Tennessee River, in the State of Alabama. Am. J. Sci. Arts (Ser. 2) v. 17: 297-308, 353-365.

——. 1854 (May) **[ref. 70]**. Additional notes on the *Holconoti*. [Appendix to ref. 69.] Am. J. Sci. Arts (Ser. 2) v. 17: 365-369.

——. 1855 (Jan.) **[ref. 71]**. Art. XII. Synopsis of the ichthyological fauna of the Pacific slope of North America, chiefly from the collections made by the U. S. Expl. Exped. under the command of Captain C. Wilkes, with recent additions and comparisons with eastern types. Am. J. Sci. Arts (Ser. 2) v. 19 (no. 55): 71-99.

——. 1855 (Mar.) **[ref. 5839]**. Art. XXII.—Synopsis of the ichthyological fauna of the Pacific slope of North America, chiefly from the collections made by the U. S. Expl. Exped. under the command of Capt. C. Wilkes, with recent additions and comparisons with eastern types. Am. J. Sci. Arts (Ser. 2) v. 19 (no. 56): 215-231 (con't from p. 99).

———. 1857 **[ref. 72]**. [Habits of the *Glanis* of Aristotle.] Proc. Am. Philos. Soc. v. 3: 325-333.

———. 1858 (Oct.) **[ref. 73]**. [A new species of skate from the Sandwich Islands.] Proc. Boston Soc. Nat. Hist. v. 6 (1856 to 1859): 385.

———. 1859 (Jan.) **[ref. 74]**. [Remarks on new fishes from Lake Nicaragua.] Proc. Boston Soc. Nat. Hist. v. 6 (1856 to 1859): 407-408.

AHL, E. 1923 (May) **[ref. 5113]**. Zur Kenntnis der Knochenfischfamilie Chaetodontidae insbesondere der Unterfamilie Chaetodontinae. Arch. Naturgeschichte v. 89 Abt. A, Heft 5: 1-205, 2 pls.

———. 1924 (20 June) **[ref. 76]**. Zur Systematik der altweltlichen Zahnkarpfen der Unterfamilie Fundulinae. Zool. Anz. v. 60 (art. 4): 49-55.

———. 1926 (30 July) **[ref. 77]**. Einige neue Fische der Familie Cichlidae aus dem Nyassa-See. Sitzungsber. Ges. Naturf. Freunde Berlin 1926: 51-62.

———. 1928 (1 Nov.) **[ref. 78]**. Beiträge zur Systematik der afrikanischen Zahnkarpfen. Zool. Anz. v. 79 (pt 3/4): 113-123.

———. 1935 (19 Mar.) **[ref. 79]**. Beschreibung eines neuen Characiniden aus Südamerika. Sitzungsber. Ges. Naturf. Freunde Berlin 1935: 46-49.

AHL, J. N. 1789 **[ref. 80]**. Specimen ichthyologicum de Muraena et Ophichtho. Upsala. 1-14, 2 pls. [Also published in 1801 as Dissertationes Academicae Upsalae, pp. 1-12, 2 pls. Not seen.]

AHLSTROM, E. H., K. AMAOKA, HENSLEY, D. A., MOSER, H. G. AND B. Y. SUMIDA. 1984 **[ref. 13641]**. Pleuronectiformes: development. Am. Soc. Ichthyol. Herpetol. Spec. Publ. No. 1: 640-670.

AHLSTROM, E. H., H. G. MOSER AND D. M. COHEN. 1984 **[ref. 13627]**. Argentinoidei: development and relationships. Am. Soc. Ichthyol. Herpetol. Spec. Publ. No. 1: 155-169.

AHLSTROM, E. H., W. J. RICHARDS AND S. H. WEITZMAN. 1984 **[ref. 13643]**. Families Gonostomatidae, Sternoptychidae, and associated stomiiform groups: development and relationships. Am. Soc. Ichthyol. Herpetol. Spec. Publ. No. 1: 184-198.

AJIAD, A. M. 1987 (31 Mar.) **[ref. 6752]**. First record of *Thyrsoidea macrura* (Teleostei: Muraenidae) from the Red Sea. Cybium v. 11 (no. 1): 102-103.

AJIAD, A. M., AND A. H. EL-ABSY. 1986 (30 Sept.) **[ref. 6758]**. First record of *Lycodontis elegans* (Pisces, Muraenidae) from the Red Sea. Cybium v. 10 (no. 3): 297-298.

AJIAD, A. M., AND D. M. MAHASNEH. 1986 (30 June) **[ref. 6760]**. Redescription of *Ariomma brevimanus* (Klunzinger, 1884), a rare stromateoid from the Gulf of Aquba (Red Sea). Cybium v. 10 (no. 2): 135-142, 2 col. pls.

AKAZAKI, M. 1972 (25 Dec.) **[ref. 7148]**. A critical study of the serranid fishes of the genus *Chelidoperca* found in Japan. Jpn. J. Ichthyol. v. 19 (no. 4): 174-282.

AKAZAKI, M., AND Y. IWATSUKI. 1986 (30 May) **[ref. 6316]**. Generic relationships in four subfamilies of the Lutjanidae. Pp. 600-601. In: Uyeno et al. (eds.) 1986 [ref. 6147].

———. 1987 (10 Dec.) **[ref. 6699]**. Classification of the lutjanid fish genus *Pristipomoides* (Percoidei). Jpn. J. Ichthyol. v. 34 (no. 3): 324-333.

AKIHITO, PRINCE, AND K. MEGURO. 1977 **[ref. 7043]**. First record of the goby *Mangarinus waterousi* from Japan. Jpn. J. Ichthyol. v. 24 (no. 3): 223-226.

———. 1979 **[ref. 6996]**. On the differences between the genera *Sicydium* and *Sicyopterus* (Gobiidae). Jpn. J. Ichthyol. v. 26 (no. 2): 192-202.

———. 1980 (30 Nov.) **[ref. 6920]**. On the six species of the genus *Bathygobius* found in Japan. Jpn. J. Ichthyol. v. 27 (no. 3): 215-236.

———. 1981 (30 Nov.) **[ref. 5508]**. A gobiid fish belonging to the genus *Hetereleotris* collected in Japan. Jpn. J. Ichthyol. v. 28 (no. 3): 329-339.

———. 1983 (10 Mar.) **[ref. 5301]**. *Myersina nigrivirgata*, a new species of goby from Okinawa Prefecture in Japan. Jpn. J. Ichthyol. v. 29 (no. 4): 343-348.

———. 1988 (25 Feb.) **[ref. 6694]**. Two new species of goby of the genus *Astrabe* from Japan. Jpn. J. Ichthyol. v. 34 (no. 4): 409-420.

AKIHITO, PRINCE, AND K. SAKAMOTO. 1989 **[ref. 14124]**. Reexamination of the status of the striped goby. Jpn. J. Ichthyol. v. 36 (no. 1): 100-112, 1 col pl.

ALCOCK, A. W. 1889 (Nov./Dec.) **[ref. 81]**. Natural history notes from H. M. Indian marine survey steamer 'Investigator,' Commander Alfred Carpenter, R. N., D. S. O., commanding.—No. 13. On the bathybial fishes of the Bay of Bengal and neighbouring waters, obtained during the seasons 1885-1889. Ann. Mag. Nat. Hist. (Ser. 6) v. 4 (no. 23): 376-399 (Nov.); (no. 24): 450-461 (Dec.).

———. 1889 **[ref. 84]**. Natural history notes from H. M.'s Indian marine survey steamer 'Investigator,' ... —No. 12. Descriptions of some new and rare species of fishes from the Bay of Bengal, obtained during the season of 1888-89. J. Asiat. Soc. Bengal v. 58 (pt 2, no. 3): 296-305, Pl. 22.

———. 1889 **[ref. 85]**. Natural history notes from H. M. Indian marine survey steamer 'Investigator,' ... —No. 10. List of the Pleuronectidae obtained in the Bay of Bengal in 1888 and 1889, with descriptions of new and rare species. J. Asiat. Soc. Bengal v. 57: 279-295; 293-305, Pls. 16-18.

———. 1890 (Sept.) **[ref. 82]**. Natural history notes from H. M. Indian marine survey steamer 'Investigator,' Commander R. F. Hoskyn, R. N., commanding.—No. 16. On the bathybial fishes collected in the Bay of Bengal during the season 1889-1890. Ann. Mag. Nat. Hist. (Ser. 6) v. 6 (no. 33): 197-222, Pls. 8-9.

———. 1890 (Oct.) **[ref. 83]**. Natural history notes from H. M. Indian marine survey steamer 'Investigator,' Commander R. F. Hoskyn, R. N., commanding.—No. 18. On the bathybial fishes of the Arabian Sea, obtained during the season 1889-1890. Ann. Mag. Nat. Hist. (Ser. 6) v. 6 (no. 34): 295-311.

———. 1890 (Dec.) **[ref. 86]**. Natural history notes from H. M. Indian marine survey steamer 'Investigator,' Commander R. F. Hoskyn, R. N., commanding.—No. 20. On some undescribed shore-fishes from the Bay of Bengal. Ann. Mag. Nat. Hist. (Ser. 6) v. 6 (no. 34): 425-443.

———. 1891 (July-Aug.) **[ref. 87]**. Class Pisces. In: II.—Natural history notes from H. M. Indian marine survey steamer 'Investigator,' Commander R. F. Hoskyn, R. N., commanding.—Series II., No. 1. On the results of deep-sea dredging during the season 1890-91. Ann. Mag. Nat. Hist. (Ser. 6) v. 8 (no. 43/44): 16-34 (July); 119-138 (Aug.), Pls. 7-8. [Authorship of article beginning on p. 16 and 119 is Wood-Mason & Alcock; authorship of Pisces (p. 19 et seq.) is Alcock.]

———. 1892 (Nov.) **[ref. 88]**. Natural history notes from H. M. Indian marine survey steamer 'Investigator,' Lieut. G. S. Gunn, R. N., commanding.—Series II, No. 5. On the bathybial fishes collected during the season of 1891-92. Ann. Mag. Nat. Hist. (Ser. 6) v. 10 (no. 59): 345-365, Pl. 18.

———. 1893 **[ref. 89]**. Natural history notes from H. M. Indian marine survey steamer, 'Investigator,' Commander C. F. Oldham, R. N., commanding. Series II., No. 9. An account of the deep sea collection made during the season of 1892-93. J. Asiat. Soc. Bengal v. 62 (pt 2, no. 4): 169-184, Pls. 8-9.

———. 1894 **[ref. 90]**. Natural history notes from H. M. Indian marine survey steamer 'Investigator,'... Series II., No. 11. An account of a recent collection of bathybial fishes from the Bay of Bengal and from the Laccadive Sea. J. Asiat. Soc. Bengal v. 63 (pt 2): 115-137, Pls. 6-7.

———. 1896 **[ref. 91]**. Natural history notes from H. M. Indian marine survey steamer 'Investigator,' Commander C. F. Oldham, R. N., commanding. Series II. No. 23. A supplementary list of the marine fishes of India, with descriptions of two new genera and eight new species. J. Asiat. Soc. Bengal v. 65 (pt 2, no. 3): 301-338.

———. 1898 (Aug.) **[ref. 92]**. Natural history notes from H. M. Indian marine survey ship 'Investigator,' Commander T. H. Heming, R. N., commanding.—Series II., No. 25. A note on the deep-sea fishes, with descriptions of some new genera and species, including another probably viviparous ophidioid. Ann. Mag. Nat. Hist. (Ser. 7) v. 2 (no. 8): 136-156.

———. 1899 **[ref. 93]**. [*Halimochirurgus centriscoides*, a new deep-sea fish from the Gulf of Manár.] Proc. Asiatic Soc. Bengal 1899: 78.

———. 1899 **[ref. 5114]**. A descriptive catalogue of the Indian deep-sea fishes in the Indian Museum. Being a revised account of the deep-sea fishes collected by the Royal Indian marine survey ship 'Investigator.' Calcutta. i-iii + 1-211 + i-viii. [New genera appearing in this work appeared first in J. Asiatic Soc Bengal and Ann. Mag. Nat. Hist.]

Allen, G. R. 1974 **[ref. 7101]**. A review of the labrid genus *Paracheilinus*, with the description of a new species from Melanesia. Pac. Sci. v. 28 (no. 4): 449-455.

———. 1975 **[ref. 97]**. Damselfishes of the south seas. T.F.H. Publ., Inc., Neptune City, New Jersey. 1-240, col. pls.

———. 1975 **[ref. 7098]**. The biology and taxonomy of the cardinalfish, *Sphaeramia orbicularis* (Pisces; Apogonidae). J. R. Soc. West. Aust. v. 58 (pt 3): 86-92.

———. 1977 **[ref. 98]**. A revision of the plesiopid fish genus *Trachinops*, with the description of a new species from Western Australia. Rec. West. Aust. Mus. v. 5 (no. 1): 59-72.

———. 1978 (31 Dec.) **[ref. 6922]**. A review of the archerfishes (family Toxotidae). Rec. West. Aust. Mus. v. 6 (no. 4): 355-378.

———. 1980 **[ref. 99]**. A generic classification of the rainbowfishes (family Melanotaeniidae). Rec. West. Aust. Mus. v. 8 (no. 3): 449-490.

———. 1981 (2 Nov.) **[ref. 5514]**. A new species of *Glossolepis* (Pisces: Melanotaeniidae) from fresh waters of Papua New Guinea. Rec. West. Aust. Mus. v. 9 (no. 3): 301-306.

———. 1981 (2 Nov.) **[ref. 5515]**. A revision of the rainbowfish genus *Chilatherina* (Melanotaeniidae). Rec. West. Aust. Mus. v. 9 (no. 3): 279-299.

———. 1981 (25 Sept.) **[ref. 5516]**. *Popondetta connieae*, a new species of rainbowfish (Melanotaeniidae) from Papua New Guinea. Rev. Fr. Aquariol. v. 8 (no. 2): 43-46.

———. 1982 (16 Apr.) **[ref. 5461]**. *Parambassis altipinnis*, a new species of freshwater glassfish from western New Guinea (Pisces, Ambassidae). Bull. Zool. Mus. Univ. Amst. v. 8 (no. 20): 165-169.

———. 1983 (Oct.) **[ref. 5350]**. *Kiunga ballochi*, a new genus and species of rainbowfish (Melanotaeniidae) from Papua New Guinea. Trop. Fish Hobby. v. 32 (no. 2): 72-77.

———. 1983 (1 Sept.) **[ref. 5355]**. A new genus and species of wrasse (Pisces: Labridae) from Rowley Shoals, Western Australia. Rev. Fr. Aquariol. v. 10 (no. 2): 43-46.

———. 1984 (15 Nov.) **[ref. 6242]**. A new genus and species of anthiid fish from Papua New Guinea. Rev. Fr. Aquariol. v. 11 (no. 2): 47-50.

———. 1984 **[ref. 6243]**. A new species of freshwater grunter (Pisces: Teraponidae) from New Guinea. Rec. West. Aust. Mus. v. 11 (no. 4): 393-397.

———. 1985 **[ref. 6244]**. Descriptions of two new species of freshwater catfishes (Plotosidae) from Papua New Guinea. Rec. West. Aust. Mus. v. 12 (no. 3): 247-256.

———. 1985 (15 Dec.) **[ref. 6245]**. Three new rainbowfishes (Melanotaeniidae) from Irian Jaya and Papua New Guinea. Rev. Fr. Aquariol. v. 12 (no. 2): 53-62.

———. 1985 (Dec.) **[ref. 6843]**. FAO species catalogue. Vol. 6. Snappers of the world. An annotated and illustrated catalogue of lutjanid species known to date. FAO Fish. Synop. No. 125, v. 6: 1-208.

———. 1986 **[ref. 5631]**. Family 219: Pomacentridae (pp. 670-682). In: Smiths' Sea Fishes (Smith & Heemstra 1986 [ref. 5715]).

———. 1986 (Apr.) **[ref. 6208]**. Lutjanidae (pp. 323-324). In: Daget et al. 1986 [ref. 6189].

———. 1987 (25 Feb.) **[ref. 5995]**. *Chrysiptera sinclairi*, a new species of damselfish from the tropical western Pacific Ocean. Rev. Fr. Aquariol. v. 13 (no. 4): 107-110.

———. 1987 **[ref. 6247]**. Descriptions of three new pseudochromid fishes of the genus *Pseudoplesiops* from Australia and surrounding regions. Rec. West. Aust. Mus. v. 13 (no. 2): 249-261.

———. 1987 **[ref. 6250]**. A new species of pomacentrid fish with notes on other damselfishes of the Kermadec Islands. Rec. West. Aust. Mus. v. 13 (no. 2): 263-273.

———. 1987 (20 Feb.) **[ref. 6713]**. *Popondichthys*, a replacement name for the melanotaeniid fish genus *Popondetta*. Jpn. J. Ichthyol. v. 33 (no. 4): 409.

———. 1987 **[ref. 13386]**. New Australian fishes. Part. 4. A new species of *Steeneichthys* (Plesiopidae). Mem. Mus. Victoria v. 48 (no. 1): 13-14.

———. 1987 **[ref. 13387]**. New Australian fishes. Part 2. Four new species of Apogonidae. Mem. Mus. Victoria v. 48 (no. 1): 3-8.

Allen, G. R., and A. M. Ayling. 1987 **[ref. 13388]**. New Australian fishes. Part 5. A new species of *Acanthurus* (Acanthuridae). Mem. Mus. Victoria v. 48 (no. 1): 15-16.

Allen, G. R., and N. J. Cross. 1982 **[ref. 6251]**. Rainbowfishes of Australia and Papua New Guinea. T.F.H. Publications Inc., New Jersey. 1-141.

Allen, G. R., and A. R. Emery. 1985 (Jan.) **[ref. 5236]**. A review of the pomacentrid fishes of the genus *Stegastes* from the Indo-Pacific, with descriptions of two new species. Indo-Pac. Fishes No. 3: 1-31, 3 col. pls.

Allen, G. R., and D. F. Hoese. 1975 **[ref. 7097]**. A review of the pomacentrid fish genus *Parma*, with descriptions of two new species. Rec. West. Aust. Mus. v. 3 (no. 4): 261-293.

———. 1980 **[ref. 5517]**. A collection of fishes form the Jardine River, Cape York Peninsula, Australia. J. R. Soc. West. Aust. v. 63 (no. 2): 53-61.

———. 1986 (8 Sept.) **[ref. 6252]**. The eleotrid fishes of Lake Lutubu, Papua New Guinea with descriptions of four new species. Rec. West. Aust. Mus. v. 13 (pt 1): 79-100.

Allen, G. R., D. F. Hoese, J. R. Paxton, J. E. Randall, B. C. Russell, W. A. Starck II, F. H. Talbot and G. P. Whitley. 1976 **[ref. 13629]**. Annotated checklist of the fishes of Lord Howe Island. Rec. Aust. Mus. v. 30: 365-454.

Allen, G. R., and W. Ivantsoff. 1986 (1 Feb.) **[ref. 6246]**. Deux nouvelles espèce de blue-eyes (*Pseudomugil*: Melanotaeniidae) de Nouvelle-Guinée. Rev. Fr. Aquariol. v. 12 (no. 3): 85-88.

Allen, G. R., and R. H. Kuiter. 1989 (30 Nov.) **[ref. 13504]**. *Hoplolatilus luteus*, a new species of malacanthid fish from Indonesia. Rev. Fr. Aquariol. v. 16 (no. 2): 39-41.

Allen, G. R., and J. R. Merrick. 1984 (9 Mar.) **[ref. 6248]**. A new species of freshwater grunter (Pisces: Teraponidae) from Northern Australia. Beagle (Occ. Pap. No. Terr. Mus. Arts Sci.) v. 1 (no. 8): 75-80.

Allen, G. R., and J. T. Moyer. 1980 **[ref. 6925]**. *Ellerkeldia wilsoni*, a new species of serranid fish from southwestern Australia. Jpn. J. Ichthyol. v. 26 (no. 4): 329-333.

Allen, G. R., and J. E. Randall. 1974 (May) **[ref. 100]**. Five new species and a new genus of damselfishes (family Pomacentridae) from the South Pacific Ocean. Trop. Fish Hobby. v. 22 (no. 9): 36-46, 48-49.

———. 1977 **[ref. 6714]**. Review of the sharpnose pufferfishes (subfamily Canthigasterinae) of the Indo-Pacific. Rec. Aust. Mus. v. 30 (no. 17): 475-517, 7 col figs.

———. 1985 **[ref. 6106]**. A new genus and species of plesiopid fish from Western Australia and the central-south Pacific Ocean. Rec. West. Aust. Mus. v. 12 (no. 2): 185-191.

Allen, G. R., and N. Sarti. 1983 (1 Sept.) **[ref. 5354]**. *Pseudomugil cyanodorsalis*, une nouvelle espèce de blue-eye (Melanotaeniidae) d'Australie nord-occidentale. Rev. Fr. Aquariol. v. 10 (no. 2): 47-50.

ALLEN, G. R., AND F. H. TALBOT. 1985 **[ref. 6491]**. Review of the snappers of the genus *Lutjanus* (Pisces: Lutjanidae) from the Indo-Pacific, with the description of a new species. Indo-Pac. Fishes No. 11: 1-86.

ALLEN, G. R., AND L. P. WOODS. 1980 (30 June) **[ref. 6919]**. A review of the damselfish genus *Stegastes* from the eastern Pacific with the description of a new species. Rec. West. Aust. Mus. v. 8 (no. 2): 171-198.

ALLEN, L. G. 1984 **[ref. 13673]**. Gobiesociformes: development and relationships. Am. Soc. Ichthyol. Herpetol. Spec. Publ. No. 1: 629-636.

ALLEYNE, H. G., AND W. MACLEAY. 1877 (Feb.-Mar.) **[ref. 101]**. The ichthyology of the Chevert expedition. Proc. Linn. Soc. N. S. W. v. 1 (pts 3-4): 261-281, 321-359, Pls. 3-9, 10-17.

ALVAREZ, J. 1952 **[ref. 102]**. Dicerophallini nueva tribu de Poeciliidae de Chiapas (Pisc., Cyprinodont.). Ciencia (Mex. City) v. 12 (nos. 3/4): 95-97.

ALVAREZ, J., AND J. CARRANZA. 1951 (15 Feb.) **[ref. 103]**. Descripcion de un genero y especie nuevos de peces Ciprinodontidos procedentes de Chiapas (Mexico). Ciencia (Mex. City) v. 11: 40-42.

AMAOKA, K. 1969 (Nov.) **[ref. 105]**. Studies on the sinistral flounders found in the waters around Japan.—Taxonomy, anatomy and phylogeny. J. Shimonoseki Coll. Fish. v. 18 (no. 2): 65-340.

AMAOKA, K., AND T. KANAYAMA. 1981 (15 Feb.) **[ref. 5579]**. Additional specimens of *Minous longimanus* from the western Indian Ocean, distinct from *M. inermis*. Jpn. J. Ichthyol. v. 27 (no. 4): 330-332.

AMAOKA, K., K. SAKAMOTO AND K. ABE. 1981 (25 May) **[ref. 5578]**. First record of the deep-sea sole, *Embassichthys bathybius*, from Japan. Jpn. J. Ichthyol. v. 28 (no. 1): 86-90.

AMAOKA, K., AND E. YAMAMOTO. 1984 (Nov.) **[ref. 5632]**. Review of the genus *Chascanopsetta*, with the description of a new species. Bull. Fac. Fish. Hokkaido Univ. v. 35 (no. 4): 201-224.

AMARAL CAMPOS, A. 1945 (10 Nov.) **[ref. 106]**. Contribuição ao conhecimento das espécies brasileiras do gênero *Hydrocynus* e afins. Arq. Zool. Estado Sao Paulo v. 4 (art. 12): 467-484, 3 unnum. pls.

———. 1946 **[ref. 107]**. Novo gênero e novas espécies de Caracídios do baixo amazonas. Pap. Avulsos Dep. Zool. (Sao Paulo) v. 7 (no. 17): 217-220, 1 pl.

AMARAL CAMPOS, A., AND E. TREWAVAS. 1949 (17 June) **[ref. 108]**. *Oligosarcus* Günther, a genus of South American characid fishes, and *Paroligosarcus*, subgen. nov. Ann. Mag. Nat. Hist. (Ser. 12) v. 2 (no. 14): 157-160.

ANDERSEN, N. C. 1984 (10 Apr.) **[ref. 13369]**. Genera and subfamilies of the family Nototheniidae (Pisces, Perciformes) from the Antarctic and subantarctic. Steenstrupia v. 10 (no. 1): 1-34.

ANDERSON, M. E. 1982 **[ref. 5520]**. Revision of the fish genera *Gymnelus* Reinhardt and *Gymnelopsis* Soldatov (Zoarcidae), with two new species and comparative osteology of *Gymnelus viridis*. Natl. Mus. Can. Publ. Zool. No. 17: i-iv + 1-76.

———. 1984 **[ref. 13634]**. Zoarcidae: development and relationships. Am. Soc. Ichthyol. Herpetol. Spec. Publ. No. 1: 578-582.

———. 1986 **[ref. 5633]**. Family 94: Zoarcidae (pp. 342-343), Family 95: Parabrotulidae (pp. 343-344). In: Smiths' Sea Fishes (Smith & Heemstra 1986 [ref. 5715]).

———. 1988 (5 Feb.) **[ref. 6021]**. *Eucryphycus*, a new genus of California eelpout (Teleostei: Zoarcidae) based on *Maynea californica* Starks and Mann, 1911. Proc. Calif. Acad. Sci. v. 45 (no. 5): 89-96.

———. 1988 (12 Apr.) **[ref. 6334]**. Studies on the Zoarcidae (Teleostei: Perciformes) of the Southern Hemisphere. II. Two new genera and a new species from temperate South America. Proc. Calif. Acad. Sci. v. 45 (no. 11): 267-276.

———. 1988 (Oct.) **[ref. 7304]**. Biology of the Antarctic Seas 19. Studies on the Zoarcidae (Teleostei: Perciformes) of the Southern Hemisphere. I. The Antarctic and Subantarctic regions. Antarctic Res. Ser. v. 47: 59-113. [Month of publication from author.]

———. 1989 **[ref. 13419]**. Records of rare eelpouts of the genus *Lycodapus* Gilbert in the North and southeastern Pacific Ocean, with an addition to the California marine fish fauna. Calif. Fish Game v. 75 (no. 3): 148-153.

———. 1989 (20 Dec.) **[ref. 13487]**. Review of the eelpout genus *Pachycara* Zugmayer, 1911 (Teleostei: Zoarcidae), with descriptions of six new species. Proc. Calif. Acad. Sci. v. 46 (no. 10): 221-242.

ANDERSON, M. E., R. E. CRABTREE, H. J. CARTER, K. J. SULAK, AND M. D. RICHARDSON. 1985 **[ref. 5164]**. Distribution of demersal fishes of the Caribbean Sea found below 2,000 meters. Bull. Mar. Sci. v. 37 (no. 3): 794-807.

ANDERSON, M. E., AND C. L. HUBBS. 1981 (15 May) **[ref. 5476]**. Redescription and osteology of the northeastern Pacific fish *Derepodichthys alepidotus* (Zoarcidae). Copeia 1981 (no. 2): 341-352.

ANDERSON, M. E., AND A. E. PEDEN. 1988 (7 Dec.) **[ref. 7215]**. The eelpout genus *Pachycara* (Teleostei: Zoarcidae) in the northeastern Pacific Ocean, with descriptions of two new species. Proc. Calif. Acad. Sci. v. 46 (no. 3): 83-94.

ANDERSON, W. D., JR. 1970 **[ref. 7662]**. Revision of the genus *Symphysanodon* (Pisces: Lutjanidae) with descriptions of four new species. U. S. Natl. Mar. Fish. Serv. Fish. Bull. v. 68 (no. 2): 325-346.

———. 1981 (29 Dec.) **[ref. 5433]**. A new species of Indo-West Pacific *Etelis* (Pisces: Lutjanidae), with comments on other species of the genus. Copeia 1981 (no. 4): 820-825.

———. 1986 **[ref. 5634]**. Family 181: Lutjanidae (pp. 572-579). In: Smiths' Sea Fishes (Smith & Heemstra 1986 [ref. 5715]).

ANDERSON, W. D., JR., AND P. FOURMANOIR. 1975 (28 Feb.) **[ref. 6028]**. The status of *Erythrobussothen gracilis*, a percoid fish. Copeia 1975 (no. 1): 181-182.

ANDERSON, W. D., JR., AND P. C. HEEMSTRA. 1980 (1 Feb.) **[ref. 5434]**. Two new species of western Atlantic *Anthias* (Pisces: Serranidae), redescription of *A. asperilinguis* and review of *Holanthias martinicensis*. Copeia 1980 (no. 1): 72-87.

———. 1989 (19 Dec.) **[ref. 13526]**. *Ellerkeldia*, a junior synonym of *Hypoplectrodes*, with redescriptions of the type species of the genera (Pisces: Serranidae: Anthiinae). Proc. Biol. Soc. Wash. v. 102 (no. 4): 1001-1017.

ANDERSON, W. D., JR., H. T. KAMI AND G. D. JOHNSON. 1977 (16 June) **[ref. 115]**. A new genus of Pacific Etelinae (Pisces: Lutjanidae) with redescription of the type-species. Proc. Biol. Soc. Wash. v. 90 (no. 1): 89-98.

ANDERSON, W. D., JR., J. F. MCKINNEY AND W. A. ROUMILLAT. 1975 (31 Dec.) **[ref. 7056]**. Review of the scorpaenid genus *Idiastion*. Copeia 1975 (no. 4): 780-782.

ANDERSON, W. D., JR., P. K. TALWAR AND G. D. JOHNSON. 1977 (24 Jan.) **[ref. 116]**. A replacement name for *Tangia* Chan (Pisces: Perciformes: Lutjanidae) with redescriptions of the genus and type species. Proc. Biol. Soc. Wash. v. 89 (no. 44): 509-517.

ANDERSON, W. W., J. W. GEHRINGER AND F. H. BERRY. 1966 **[ref. 6977]**. Family Synodontidae (pp. 30-102). In: Fishes of the Western North Atlantic. Mem. Sears Found. Mar. Res. No. 1 (pt. 5).

ANDRIASHEV, A. P. 1952 **[ref. 6593]**. [A new deep-sea fish of the eelpout family (Pisces, Zoarcidae) from the Bering Sea.] Tr. Zool. Inst. Akad. Nauk SSSR v. 12: 415-417. [In Russian. Proofed from 1963 translation.]

———. 1954 **[ref. 6547]**. [Fishes of the northern seas of the U.S.S.R.] Izv. Akad. Nauk SSSR. Moskwa — Leningrad. 1-566. [In Russian; English translation 1964, Israel Program for Scientific Translation.]

———. 1955 **[ref. 121]**. New liparid caught at a depth of 7 klm. Tr. Inst. Okeanol. v. 12: 340-344. [In Russian.]

———. 1960 **[ref. 122]**. Families of fishes new to the Antarctic. 1. *Paradiplospinus antarcticus* gen. et sp. n. (Pisces, Trichiuridae). Zool. Zh. v. 39 (no. 2): 244-249. [In Russian, English summ.]

———. 1967 **[ref. 5205]**. A review of the plunder fishes of the genus *Pogonophryne* Regan (Pisces, Harpagiferidae) with descriptions of five new species from the East Atlantic and South Orkney Islands. Studies of marine fauna IV (XII). Biol. Rep. Soviet Antarct. Exped. (1955-1958) v. 3: 289-412, 5 pls. [In Russian. Also a translation published by the National Science Foundation, pp. 399-425.]

———. 1973 **[ref. 7214]**. Zoarcidae (pp. 540-547). In: Hureau & Monod 1973 [ref. 6590].

———. 1975 **[ref. 119]**. A new ultra-abyssal fish, *Notoliparis kurchatovi* gen. et sp. n. (Liparidae) from the South-Orkney Trench (Antarctic). Tr. Inst. Okeanol. v. 103: 313-319. [In Russian, English summ.]

———. 1979 **[ref. 120]**. On the occurrence of fishes belonging to the families Zoarcidae and Liparidae off the Kerguelen Island. Biol. Morya (Vladivost.) v. 1979 (no. 6): 28-34. [In Russian, English summ.]

———. 1986 **[ref. 12760]**. Review of the snailfish genus *Paraliparis* (Scorpaeniformes: Liparididae) of the southern Ocean. Theses Zool., Koeltz Sci. Books v. 7: i-iv + 1-204.

Andriashev, A. P., and V. V. Fedorov. 1986 **[ref. 6133]**. First discovery of Zoarcidae in New Zealand waters. Voprosy Ikhtiol. v. 26 (no. 1): 24-32. [In Russian. English translation in J. Ichthyol. v. 26 (no. 1): 136-144.]

Andriashev, A. P., and V. M. Makushok. 1955 **[ref. 6465]**. *Azygopterus corallinus* (Pisces, Blennioidei) - a new fish without paired fins. Voprosy Ikhtiol. No. 3: 50-53. [In Russian. English translation by Ichthyol. Lab., NMFS, U. S. National Museum.]

Andriashev, A. P., and D. E. McAllister. 1978 (28 Dec.) **[ref. 6988]**. Status of the presumed zoarcid fish *Ophidium parrii* and its identity with *Liparis koefoedi*, Liparidae. Copeia 1978 (no. 4): 710-712.

Andriashev, A. P., and A. V. Neelov. 1976 **[ref. 124]**. *Genioliparis lindbergi*, gen. et sp. n. - a new fish of the family of sea snail fishes (Liparidae) from the bathyal depths of western Antarctica. Pp. 68-77. In: Korovina, V. M. (ed.) [Zoogeography and Systematics of Fishes.] Akad. Nauk. USSR, Zool. Inst. Acad. Sci. Leningrad. 5-195. [In Russian. English translation by D. Stein in files at California Academy of Sciences.]

———. 1978 **[ref. 123]**. A new whiteblooded fish (*Chionobathyscus dewitti*, gen. et sp. n., fam. Channichthyidae) from the continental slope of the east Antarctic. Pp. 5-12 in Skarlato, O. A., et al. (eds.) [Morphology and systematics of fish (Collection of scientific works.)] Zool. Inst. Akad. Sci. SSSR. 1-90. [In Russian.]

Angel, F., L. Bertin and J. Guibé. 1946 **[ref. 125]**. Note relative a la nomenclature d'un amphibien et d'un poisson. Bull. Mus. Natl. Hist. Nat. (Ser. 2) v. 18 (no. 6): 473-474.

Annandale, N. 1909 (May) **[ref. 126]**. Report on the fishes taken by the Bengal fisheries steamer "Golden Crown." Part I, Batoidei. Mem. Indian Mus. v. 2 (no. 1): 1-60, Pls. 1-5.

———. 1918 (9 May) **[ref. 127]**. Fish and fisheries of the Inlé Lake. Rec. Indian Mus. (Calcutta) v. 14: 33-64, Pls. 1-7.

Annandale, N., and S. L. Hora. 1920 (15 Sept.) **[ref. 128]**. The fish of Seistan. Rec. Indian Mus. (Calcutta) v. 18 (pt 4): 151-203, Pls. 15-17.

Anonymous. 1798 **[ref. 13098]**. Review of Tome I of 'Histoire naturelle des poissons' by Lacepède (1798). Allgemeine Literatur-Zeitung No. 287: columns 673-678. [Presented at meeting of 24 September. Apparently the first latinization of a few Lacepède genera.]

———. 1865 (Jan.) **[ref. 6173]**. Descriptions of some new fishes. By Prof. Kner. [An English synopsis of the original paper [our ref. 2637]; author of synopsis not given.] Ann. Mag. Nat. Hist. (Ser. 3) v. 15 (no. 85): 77-78.

Antipa, G. 1904 **[ref. 129]**. Die Clupeinen des westlichen Teiles des Schwarzen Meeres und der Donaumündungen. [Technically, a summary presented by Steindachner of Antipa's work that was published in 1906 as ref. 6859.] Anz. Akad. Wiss. Wien v. 41: 299-303. [Full text is Antipa 1906 [ref. 6859]. Article above perhaps should be cited as Antipa in Steindachner.]

———. 1906 **[ref. 6859]**. Die Clupeinen des westlichen Teiles des Schwarzen Meeres und der Donaumündungen. Denkschr. Akad. Wiss. Wien v. 78: 1-56.

Aoyagi, H. 1954 **[ref. 130]**. Description of one new genus and three new species of Blenniidae from the Riu-Kiu Islands. Zool. Mag. (Tokyo) v. 63: 213-217. [In Japanese, English summ.]

Arai, R. 1983 **[ref. 14249]**. Karyological osteological approach to phylogenetic systematics of tetraodontiform fishes. Bull. Nat. Sci. Mus. Tokyo, Ser. A (Zool.) v. 9 (no. 4): 175-210.

Arai, R., and Y. Akai. 1988 (22 Dec.) **[ref. 6999]**. *Acheilognathus melanogaster*, a senior synonym of *A. moriokae*, with a revision of the genera of the subfamily Acheilognathinae (Cypriniformes, Cyprinidae). Bull. Natl. Sci. Mus. (Ser. A) (Zool.) v. 14 (no. 4): 199-213.

Arnold, D. C. 1956 (Nov.) **[ref. 5315]**. A systematic revision of the fishes of the teleost family Carapidae (Percomorphi, Blennioidea), with descriptions of two new species. Bull. Br. Mus. (Nat. Hist.) Zool. v. 4 (no. 6): 245-307.

Arnoult, J. 1984 (Feb.) **[ref. 6179]**. Chanidae (p. 128). In: Daget et al. 1984 [ref. 6168].

———. 1986 (Apr.) **[ref. 6213]**. Scatophagidae (p. 341). In: Daget et al. 1986 [ref. 6189].

Arnulf, I., F. J. Meunier and P. Geistdoerfer. 1987 (30 June) **[ref. 6744]**. Ostéologie de *Thermarces cerberus* Rosenblatt et Cohen 1986, Zoarcidae des sources hydrothermales du Pacifique Est, suivie d'une discussion sur sa classification. Cybium v. 11 (no. 2): 141-158, 1 col pl.

Arratia, G. 1982 (15 Sept.) **[ref. 143]**. A review of freshwater percoids from South America (Pisces, Osteichthyes, Perciformes, Percichthyidae, and Perciliidae). Abh. Senckenb. Naturforsch. Ges. No. 540: 1-52.

———. 1987 **[ref. 5957]**. Description of the primitive family Diplomystidae (Siluriformes, Teleostei, Pisces): morphology, taxonomy and phylogenetic implications. Bonn. Zool. Monogr. No. 24: 1-120.

———. 1987 (30 Dec.) **[ref. 6740]**. Sexual dimorphism in the caudal skeleton of *Cheirodon* (Characidae, Teleostei). Cybium v. 11 (no. 4): 375-387.

Arratia, G., A. Chang G., S. Menu-Marque and G. Rojas M. 1978 **[ref. 144]**. About *Bullockia* gen. nov., *Trichomycterus mendozensis* n. sp. and revision of the family Trichomycteridae (Pisces, Siluriformes). Stud. Neotrop. Fauna Environ. v. 13 (nos. 3-4): 157-194.

Arratia, G., and S. Menu-Marque. 1981 **[ref. 6024]**. Revision of the freshwater catfishes of the genus *Hatcheria* (Siluriformes, Trichomycteridae) with commentaries on ecology and biogeography. Zool. Anz. Jena v. 207 (no. 1/2): 88-111.

Asano, H. 1958 **[ref. 146]**. Studies on the congrid eels of Japan. III. Description of a new genus *Japonoconger* typed by *Arisoma sivicola* Matsubara and Ochiai, with consideration to the related genera. Zool. Mag. (Tokyo) v. 67: 316-321. [In Japanese, English summ.]

———. 1987 (10 Sept.) **[ref. 6705]**. A new ophichthid eel, *Ophichthus megalops*, from the Kumano-nada, Japan. Jpn. J. Ichthyol. v. 34 (no. 2): 135-137.

Ascanius, P. 1772 **[ref. 5115]**. Icones rerum naturalium, ou figures enluminées d'histoire naturelle du Nord. Copenhagen, 1772-1806. Cayer 2: 1-8, Pls. 11-20.

Asso, I. de. 1801 **[ref. 6523]**. Introduccion á la ichthyologia oriental de España. An. Cienc. Nat. Inst. José Acosta, Madrid v. 4 (no. 10): 28-52.

Aurich, H. 1935 (15 Nov.) **[ref. 150]**. Mitteilungen der Wallacea-Expedition Woltereck. Mitteilung XIV. Fische II. Zool. Anz. v. 112 (no. 7/8): 161-177.

———. 1937 **[ref. 151]**. Die Phallostethiden (Unterordnung *Phallostethoidea* Myers). Int. Rev. Hydrobiol. Leipzig v. 34 (no. 3/5): 263-286.

———. 1938 **[ref. 152]**. Die Gobiiden (Ordnung: Gobioidea). (Mitteilung XXVIII der Wallacea-Expedition Woltereck.) Int. Rev. Hydrobiol. Leipzig v. 38: 125-183.

Axelrod, G. S., and J. A. Harrison. 1978 (15 Dec.) **[ref. 7009]**. *Simochromis margaretae*, a new species of cichlid fish from Lake

Tanganyika. J. L. B. Smith Inst. Ichthyol. Spec. Publ. No. 19: 1-16.

Axelrod, H. R. 1971 **[ref. 5456]**. Breeding aquarium fishes. Book 2. T.F.H. Publications, Inc. Ltd., Hong Kong. 1-352.

Ayling, A. M., and J. R. Paxton. 1983 (10 Feb.) **[ref. 5258]**. *Odax cyanoallix*, a new species of odacid fish from northern New Zealand. Copeia 1983 (no. 1): 95-101.

Ayling, A. M., and B. C. Russell. 1977 **[ref. 7228]**. The labrid fish genus *Pseudojuloides*, with a description of a new species. Aust. Zool. v. 19 (no. 2): 169-178.

Ayres, W. O. 1848 (Nov.) **[ref. 154]**. [On a very curious fish.] Proc. Boston Soc. Nat. Hist. v. 3 (1848 to 1851): 69-70.

———. 1849 **[ref. 5864]**. Description of a new genus of fishes, *Malacosteus*. Proc. Boston Soc. Nat. Hist. v. 6 (no. 1): 53-63. [Not seen.]

———. 1854 **[ref. 157]**. [Description of new fishes from California.] The Pacific v. 3: Several articles. [Also as Proc. Calif. Acad. Sci. v. 1: 3-22 (22 Sept. 1854). Reprinted in 2nd ed. of Academy's Proceedings, 1873.]

———. 1855 **[ref. 159]**. [Description of new species of Californian fishes.] A number of short notices read before the Society at several meetings in 1855. Proc. Calif. Acad. Nat. Sci. v. 1 [1854]: 25-27, 31-32, 33-35, 58-59, 72-73, 75-77. [Reprinted in 2nd ed. of Academy's Proceedings, 1873; some articles appeared first in "The Pacific" (see genera accounts)]

———. 1855 **[ref. 13428]**. [Description of new fishes from California.] The Pacific v. 4: Several articles. [Also appeared in Proc. Calif. Acad. Sci. v. 1 [see Ayres ref. 159].]

———. 1859 **[ref. 155]**. [On new fishes of the Californian coast.] Proc. Calif. Acad. Sci. v. 2 (sig. 2): 25-32. [Read at meeting of 17 Oct. 1859, assume published in 1859.]

———. 1860 **[ref. 158]**. [Description of fishes.] Proc. Calif. Acad. Nat. Sci. v. 2: 77-81, 81-86. [Pp. 77-81 read at meeting of 5 Nov. 1860, pp. 81-86 on 3 Dec. 1860; assume published in 1860 but perhaps later.]

———. 1860 **[ref. 156]**. [On new fishes of the Californian coast.] Proc. Calif. Acad. Sci. v. 2 (sig. 4): 52-59. [Read at meeting of 2 July 1860, assume published in 1860.]

Bacescu, M. 1962 **[ref. 6454]**. Contribution à la systématique du genre *Cobitis*. Description d'une espèce nouvelle, *Cobitis calderoni*, provenant de l'Espagne. Rev. Biol. Bucarest v. 6 (no. 4) [1961]: 435-448, Pl. 1.

Bailey, R. M. 1948 (30 June) **[ref. 160]**. Status, relationships, and characters of the percid fish, *Poecilichthys sagitta* Jordan and Swain. Copeia 1948 (no. 2): 77-85, Pl. 1.

———. 1951 (31 Aug.) **[ref. 5587]**. The authorship of names proposed in Cuvier and Valenciennes' "Histoire Naturelle des Poissons." Copeia 1951 (no. 3): 249-251.

———. 1957 (19 Dec.) **[ref. 6478]**. *Cichlaurus* versus *Cichlasoma* as the name for a genus of perciform fishes. Copeia 1967 (no. 4): 303-304.

———. 1957 (Dec.) **[ref. 13430]**. Request for a ruling determining the authorship to be attributed to the various portions of the work entitled "Histoire Naturelle des Poissons" written partly by Cuvier and partly by Valenciennes and published in the period 1828-1850. Bull. Zool. Nomencl. v. 13 (pt 10/11): 309-312.

———. 1969 (Jan.) **[ref. 14234]**. Comment on the proposed suppression of *Elipesurus spinicauda* Schomburgk (Pisces). Z.N.(S.) 1825. Bull. Zool. Nomencl. v. 25 (pts 4/5): 133-134.

———. 1980 **[ref. 5253]**. Comments on the classification and nomenclature of lampreys — an alternative view. Can. J. Fish. Aquat. Sci. v. 37 (no. 11): 1626-1629.

Bailey, R. M., and J. N. Baskin. 1976 (1 Sept.) **[ref. 161]**. *Scoloplax dicra*, a new armored catfish from the Bolivian Amazon. Occas. Pap. Mus. Zool. Univ. Mich. No. 674: 1-14.

Bailey, R. M., and F. B. Cross. 1954 **[ref. 5358]**. River sturgeons of the American genus *Scaphirhynchus*: characters, distribution, and synonymy. Pap. Mich. Acad. Sci. Arts Lett. v. 39: 169-208.

Bailey, R. M., and W. N. Eschmeyer. 1988 (Mar.) **[ref. 6624]**. *Ictiobus* Rafinesque, 1820 (Osteichthyes, Cypriniformes): proposed conservation. Bull. Zool. Nomencl. v. 45 (pt 1): 36-37.

Bailey, R. M., and D. A. Etnier. 1988 (16 Dec.) **[ref. 6873]**. Comments on the subgenera of darters (Percidae) with descriptions of two new species of *Etheostoma (Ulocentra)* from southeastern United States. Misc. Publ. Mus. Zool. Univ. Mich. No. 175: i-iv + 1-48, Pl. 1.

Bailey, R. M., and W. A. Gosline. 1955 (28 Sept.) **[ref. 6833]**. Variation and systematic significance of vertebral counts in the American fishes of the family Percidae. Misc. Publ. Mus. Zool. Univ. Mich. No. 93: 1-44.

Bailey, R. M., and C. G. Gruchy. 1970 (May) **[ref. 6508]**. *Occella* to supersede *Occa* for a genus of agonid fishes. J. Fish. Res. Board Can. v. 27 (no. 5): 981-983.

Bailey, R. M., and C. L. Hubbs. 1949 (25 Feb.) **[ref. 11647]**. The black basses (*Micropterus*) of Florida, with description of a new species. Occas. Pap. Mus. Zool. Univ. Mich. No. 516: 1-40, Pls. 1-2.

Bailey, R. M., and R. R. Miller. 1950 (22 Dec.) **[ref. 162]**. *Mollienesia* versus *Mollienisia* as the name for a genus of poeciliid fishes. Copeia 1950 (no. 4): 318.

Bailey, R. M., and W. J. Richards. 1963 (31 Dec.) **[ref. 6029]**. Identification of the "etheostomid" fish *Alvarius lateralis* Girard as an eleotrid, *Gobiomorus dormitor*. Copeia 1963 (no. 4): 702-703.

Bailey, R. M., and C. R. Robins. 1988 (June) **[ref. 6610]**. Changes in North American fish names, especially as related to the International Code of Zoological Nomenclature. Bull. Zool. Nomencl. v. 45 (pt 2): 92-103.

———. 1988 (June) **[ref. 6626]**. *Ameiurus* Rafinesque, 1820 (Osteichthyes, Siluriformes): proposed designation of *Silurus lividus* Rafinesque, 1820 (= *Pimelodus natalis* Lesueur, 1819) as the type species. Bull. Zool. Nomencl. v. 45 (pt 2): 135-137.

Bailey, R. M., C. R. Robins and P. H. Greenwood. 1980 (Dec.) **[ref. 6875]**. *Chromis* Cuvier in Desmarest, 1814 (Osteichthyes, Perciformes, Pomacantridae): proposal to place on Official List of Generic Names in Zoology, and that generic names ending in *-chromis* by ruled to be masculine. Z.N.(S.) 2329. Bull. Zool. Nomencl. v. 37 (pt 4): 247-255.

Bailey, R. M., and D. J. Stewart. 1977 (5 Aug.) **[ref. 7230]**. Cichlid fishes from Lake Tanganyika: additions to the Zambian fauna including two new species. Occas. Pap. Mus. Zool. Univ. Mich. No. 679: 1-30.

———. 1983 **[ref. 5242]**. *Bagrus* Bosc, 1816 (Pisces, Siluriformes): Proposal to place on the Official List. Z.N.(S.)2371. Bull. Zool. Nomencl. v. 40 (pt 3): 167-172.

———. 1984 (6 Sept.) **[ref. 5232]**. Bagrid catfishes from Lake Tanganyika, with a key and descriptions of new taxa. Misc. Publ. Mus. Zool. Univ. Mich. No. 168: i-iv + 1-41.

Bailey, R. M., and E. O. Wiley. 1976 (12 Oct.) **[ref. 7090]**. Identification of the American cyprinodontid fish *Hydrargira swampina* Lacépède. Proc. Biol. Soc. Wash. v. 89 (no. 41): 477-480.

Bailly, P. 1930 (May) **[ref. 163]**. Description d'un Stomatiatide nouveau de la région des Iles Canaries. Bull. Mus. Natl. Hist. Nat. (Ser. 2) v. 2 (no. 4): 378-380.

Baird, R. C. 1973 **[ref. 7173]**. Sternoptychidae (pp. 123-125). In: Hureau & Monod 1973 [ref. 6590].

———. 1986 **[ref. 6288]**. Tribe Sternoptychini (pp. 255-259). In: Smiths' Sea Fishes (Smith & Heemstra 1986 [ref. 5715]).

Baird, S. F. 1851 **[ref. 5033]**. Outlines of general zoology ... Fishes, by Spencer F. Baird. Pp. 197-243. Reprinted from the Iconographic Encyclopedia of Science, Literature and Art. New York. [Overall work is i-xxi + 1-502 + i-xvi.]

———. 1855 **[ref. 164]**. Report on the fishes observed on the coast of New Jersey and Long Island during the summer of 1854. Smithson. Inst. Annu. Rep. for 1854: 317-352 + 2nd 337. [Apparently first as a separate (dated June 1855): 1-39 + 1 p. index.]

Baird, S. F., and C. F. Girard. 1853 (ca. 5 Sept.) **[ref. 165]**. Descriptions of new species of fishes, collected by captains R. B. Marcy, and Geo. B. M'Clellan, in Arkansas. Proc. Acad. Nat. Sci. Phila. 1853

[v. 6] (no. 10): 390-392.
——. 1853 (ca. 5 Sept.) **[ref. 166]**. Descriptions of some new fishes form the River Zuni. Proc. Acad. Nat. Sci. Phila. 1853 [v. 6] (no. 9): 368-369.
——. 1854 (ca. 20 May) **[ref. 168]**. Descriptions of new species of fish collected in Texas, New Mexico and Sonora, by Mr. John H. Clark, on the U. S. and Mexican Boundary Survey, and in Texas by Capt. Stewart Van Vliet, U. S. A. Proc. Acad. Nat. Sci. Phila. 1854 [v. 7] (no. 2): 24-29.
——. 1854 (ca. 20 Oct.) **[ref. 167]**. Notice of a new genus of Cyprinidae. Proc. Acad. Nat. Sci. Phila. 1854 [v. 7] (no. 4): 158.
BALDWIN, W. J. 1972 (Jan.) **[ref. 169]**. A new genus and new species of Hawaiian gobiid fish. Pac. Sci. v. 26 (no. 1): 125-128.
BALTZ, D. M., AND P. B. MOYLE. 1981 (15 May) **[ref. 6827]**. Morphometric analysis of tule perch (*Hysterocarpus traski*) populations in three isolated drainages. Copeia 1981 (no. 2): 305-311.
BALUSHKIN, A. V. 1976 **[ref. 170]**. A short revision of notothenids (*Notothenia* Richardson and related species) from the family Nototheniidae. Pp. 118-134. In: Skarlato, O. A. [ed.] Zoogeography and systematics of fish. Akad. Nauk USSR, Zool. Inst., Leningrad. 1-195. [In Russian.]
——. 1979 **[ref. 171]**. *Lindbergichthys* (Nototheniidae) — a new generic name for *Lindbergia* Balushkin, 1976 non Riedel, 1959. Voprosy Ikhtiol. v. 19 (no. 5): 930-931. [In Russian. English translation in J. Ichthyol. v. 19 (no. 5): 144-145.]
——. 1982 **[ref. 6042]**. Classification of Antarctic Trematomine fishes. In: Biology of the shelf zones of the world ocean. Vol. 2. Vladivostok 9-10. [In Russian.]
——. 1984 **[ref. 6138]**. Morphological bases of the systematics and phylogeny of the nototheniid fish. Acad. Sci. SSSR, Zool. Inst., Leningrad 1984: 1-140. [In Russian.]
——. 1988 **[ref. 9291]**. A new species of toad beardfish, *Pogonophryne curtilemma* sp. n. (Artedidraconidae), from western Antarctica. Voprosy Ikhtiol. v. 28 (no. 2): 319-322. [In Russian. English translation in J. Ichthyol. v. 28 (no. 1): 127-130.]
——. 1989 **[ref. 13490]**. *Gvozdarus svetovidovi* gen. et sp. n. (Pisces, Nototheniidae) from the Ross Sea (Antarctic). Zool. Zh. v. 68 (no. 1): 83-88. [In Russian, English summ.]
BALUSHKIN, A. V., AND I. A. CHERESHNEV. 1982 **[ref. 5251]**. On the systematic study of the genus *Dallia* (family Umbridae, Esociformes). Proc. Zool. Inst. Acad. Sci. USSR v. 114: 36-56. [In Russian.]
BALUSHKIN, A. V., V. V. FEDOROV AND J. R. PAXTON. 1989 **[ref. 12557]**. *Notocetichthys trunovi* gen. et sp. nov. (Cetomimidae) from the Lazarev Sea (Antarctic). Voprosy Ikhtiol. v. 29 (no. 1): 155-157. [In Russian.]
BALUSHKIN, A. V., AND E. A. TARAKANOV. 1987 **[ref. 6226]**. Taxonomic status of *Pseudotrematomus cantronotus* (Regan, 1914) (Nototheniidae). Voprosy Ikhtiol. v. 27 (no. 3): 355-361. [In Russian. English translation in J. Ichthyol. v. 27 (no. 4): 56-62.]
BAMBER, R. C. 1915 (30 Sept.) **[ref. 172]**. Reports on the marine biology of the Sudanese Red Sea, from collections made by Cyril Crossland, M.A., D.Sc., F.L.S. XXII. The Fishes. J. Linn. Soc. Lond. Zool. v. 31 (no. 210): 477-485, Pl. 46.
BANARESCU, P. 1961 **[ref. 211]**. Weitere systematische Studien über die Gattung *Gobio* (Pisces, Cyprinidae), insbesondere im Donaubecken. Vestn. Ceskosl. Zool. Spolec. v. 25 (no. 4): 318-346, 4 pls.
——. 1962 (Feb.) **[ref. 212]**. Phylletische Beziehungen der Arten und Artbildung bei der Gattung *Gobio* (Pisces, Cyprinidae). Vestn. Ceskosl. Zool. Spolec. v. 26 (no. 1): 38-64.
——. 1967 **[ref. 213]**. Studies on the systematics of Cultrinae (Pisces, Cyprinidae) with description of a new genus. Rev. Roum. Biol. Ser. Zool. v. 12 (no. 5): 297-308.
——. 1968 (30 Feb.) **[ref. 215]**. Remarks on the genus *Chela* Hamilton-Buchanan (Pisces, Cyprinidae) with description of a new subgenus. Ann. Mus. Civ. Stor. Nat. 'Giacomo Doria' v. 77: 53-64.
——. 1970 **[ref. 214]**. *Siniichthys brevirostris* nov. gen., nov. sp., nouveau cyprinidé de Chine (Pisces, Cyprinidae). Bull. Mus. Natl. Hist. Nat. (Ser. 2) v. 42 (no. 1): 161-164.
——. 1977 **[ref. 14138]**. Position zoogéographic de l'ichthyofaune d'eau douce d'Asie Occidentale. Cybium (Ser. 3) v. 1: 33-55.
——. 1980 **[ref. 216]**. *Kalimantania* and *Neobarynotus*, two new Indonesian genera of minnows (Pisces, Cyprinidae). Trav. Mus. Hist. Nat. 'Grigore Antipa' v. 22 (no. 2): 471-478.
BANARESCU, P., AND T. T. NALBANT. 1964 (Mar.) **[ref. 217]**. Süsswasserfische der Türkei. 2. Teil Cobitidae. Mitt. Hamb. Zool. Mus. Inst. v. 61: 159-201, Pls. 5-8.
——. 1966 **[ref. 218]**. The 3rd Danish Expedition to central Asia. Zoological results 34. Cobitidae (Pisces) from Afghanistan and Iran. Vidensk. Medd. Dansk Naturh. Foren. Kjob. v. 129: 149-186, Pls. 9-11.
——. 1968 (May) **[ref. 6554]**. Cobitidae (Pisces, Cypriniformes) collected by the German India expedition. Mitt. Hamb. Zool. Mus. Inst. v. 65: 327-351, Pls. 1-2.
——. 1973 (Sept.) **[ref. 173]**. Pisces, Teleostei Cyprinidae (Gobioninae). Das Tierreich v. 93: i-vii + 1-304.
BANARESCU, P., T. T. NALBANT AND M. GOREN. 1982 **[ref. 174]**. The noemacheiline loaches from Israel (Pisces: Cobitidae: Noemacheilinae). Isr. J. Zool. v. 31 (nos. 1-2): 1-25.
BANCROFT, E. N. 1829 **[ref. 5051]**. On the fish known in Jamaica as the sea devil. Zool. J. v. 4: 444-457.
BANISTER, K. E. 1984 (25 Oct.) **[ref. 5282]**. Three new species of *Varicorhinus* (Pisces, Cyprinidae) from Africa. Bull. Br. Mus. (Nat. Hist.) Zool. v. 47 (no. 5): 273-282.
BANISTER, K. E., AND M. K. BUNNI. 1980 (29 May) **[ref. 175]**. A new blind cyprinid fish from Iraq. Bull. Br. Mus. (Nat. Hist.) Zool. v. 38 (no. 3): 151-158.
BARBOUR, C. D. 1973 (16 Mar.) **[ref. 5967]**. The systematics and evolution of the genus *Chirostoma* Swainson (Pisces, Atherinidae). Tulane Stud. Zool. Bot. v. 18 (no. 3): 97-141.
BARBOUR, C. D., AND R. R. MILLER. 1978 (4 Aug.) **[ref. 7033]**. A revision of the Mexican cyprinid fish genus *Algansea*. Occas. Pap. Mus. Zool. Univ. Mich. No. 155: 1-72.
BARBOUR, T. 1908 (29 Feb.) **[ref. 177]**. Notes on *Rhinomuraena*. Proc. Biol. Soc. Wash. v. 21: 39-42.
——. 1912 (24 Dec.) **[ref. 178]**. Two preoccupied names. Proc. Biol. Soc. Wash. v. 25: 187.
——. 1941 (22 Dec.) **[ref. 179]**. Notes on pediculate fishes. Proc. New England Zool. Club v. 19: 7-14, Pls. 2-7.
——. 1942 (10 Dec.) **[ref. 180]**. More concerning ceratioid fishes. Proc. New England Zool. Club v. 21: 77-86, Pls. 9-15.
BARDACK, D. 1965 (1 Dec.) **[ref. 6370]**. Anatomy and evolution of chirocentrid fishes. Paleontol. Contrib. Univ. Kansas Vertebrata Art. 10: 1-88, Pls. 1-2.
BARNARD, K. H. 1923 (Sept.) **[ref. 191]**. Diagnoses of new species of marine fishes from South African waters. Ann. S. Afr. Mus. v. 13 (pt 8, no. 14): 439-445.
——. 1925 (June) **[ref. 192]**. A monograph of the marine fishes of South Africa. Part 1. (Amphioxus, Cyclostomata, Elasmobranchii, and Teleostei — Isospondyli to Heterosomata.) Ann. S. Afr. Mus. v. 21 (pt 1): 1-418, Pls. 1-17.
——. 1927 (July) **[ref. 193]**. Diagnoses of new genera and species of South African marine fishes. Ann. Mag. Nat. Hist. (Ser. 9) v. 20 (no. 115): 66-79. [New genera also appeared in Barnard 1927 (Oct.) [ref. 194].]
——. 1927 (Oct.) **[ref. 194]**. A monograph of the marine fishes of South Africa. Part II. (Teleostei—Discocephali to end. Appendix.) Ann. S. Afr. Mus. v. 21 (pt 2): 419-1065, Pls. 18-38. [Several genera described as new were first diagnosed in (and date to) Barnard 1927 (July) [ref. 193].]
——. 1934 (Feb.) **[ref. 195]**. New records and descriptions of two new species of South African marine fishes. Ann. Mag. Nat. Hist. (Ser. 10) v. 13 (no. 74): 228-235.
——. 1935 (Feb.) **[ref. 196]**. Notes on South African marine fishes. Ann. S. Afr. Mus. v. 30 (pt 5, no. 20): 645-658, Pls. 23-25.
——. 1937 (Mar.) **[ref. 197]**. Further notes on South African marine

fishes. Ann. S. Afr. Mus. v. 32 (pt 2, no. 6): 41-67, Pls. 6-8.

——. 1941 [**ref. 198**]. Departmental reports. Department of Fishes and marine invertebrates. Rep. So. Afr. Mus. for 1940: 10-11, 1 pl.

——. 1950 (Oct.) [**ref. 6080**]. The date of issue of the "Illustrations of the Zoology of South Africa" and the "Marine Investigations in South Africa." J. Soc. Bibliogr. Nat. Hist. v. 2 (pt 6): 187-189.

Barsukov, V. V. 1973 [**ref. 7154**]. The species composition of the genus *Helicolenus* (Sebastinae, Scorpaenidae, Pisces) and a description of a new species. Voprosy Ikhtiol. v. 13 (no. 2): 195-201. [In Russian. English translation in J. Ichthyol. v. 13 (no. 2): 161-167.]

——. 1973 [**ref. 7213**]. Anarhichadidae (pp. 528-529). In: Hureau & Monod 1973 [ref. 6590].

——. 1981 [**ref. 5306**]. A brief review of the subfamily Sebastinae. Voprosy Ikhtiol. v. 21 (no. 1): 1-27. [In Russian. English translation in J. Ichthyol. v. 21.]

Barsukov, V. V., and L.-C. Chen. 1978 [**ref. 7010**]. Review of the subgenus *Sebastiscus* (*Sebastes*, Scorpaenidae) with a description of a new species. Voprosy Ikhtiol. v. 18 (no. 2): 195-210. [In Russian. English translation in J. Ichthyol. v. 18.]

Barsukov, V. V., and V. V. Fedorov. 1975 [**ref. 7011**]. Species of the genus *Hozukius* (Scorpaenidae, Sebastinae) from the guyots of the Hawaiian Submarine Ridge. Voprosy Ikhtiol. [In Russian. English translation in J. Ichthyol. v. 15 (no. 6): 869-876.]

Basilewski, S. 1855 [**ref. 200**]. Ichthyographia Chinae Borealis. Nouv. Mem. Soc. Imp. Natur. Moscou v. 10: 215-263, Pls. 1-9. [Apparently published in 1855, 1852 on cover.]

Bass, A. J. 1986 [**ref. 5635**]. [Various elasmobranch families] Family No. 3 (p. 47), No. 4 (p. 48), No. 7 (pp. 64-65), No. 11 (pp. 88-95), No. 12 (p. 96), No. 13 (p. 96-97), No. 14 (pp. 98-99), No. 15 (p. 101), No. 16 (p. 101), No. 18 (p. 103), No. 21 (p. 107). In: Smiths' Sea Fishes (Smith & Heemstra 1986 [ref. 5715]).

Bass, A. J., and L. J. V. Compagno. 1986 [**ref. 5637**]. Family No. 6: Echinorhinidae (p. 63), Family No. 10: Proscylliidae (pp. 87-88), Family No. 17: Mitsukurinidae (p. 103), Family No. 19: Odontaspididae (pp. 104-105). In: Smiths' Sea Fishes (Smith & Heemstra 1986 [ref. 5715]).

Bass, A. J., L. J. V. Compagno and P. C. Heemstra. 1986 [**ref. 5636**]. Family No. 5: Squalidae (pp. 49-62). In: Smiths' Sea Fishes (Smith & Heemstra 1986 [ref. 5715]).

Bass, A. J., and P. C. Heemstra. 1986 [**ref. 5639**]. Family No. 20: Pristiophoridae (p. 106). In: Smiths' Sea Fishes (Smith & Heemstra 1986 [ref. 5715]).

Bass, A. J., P. C. Heemstra and L. J. V. Compagno. 1986 [**ref. 5638**]. Family No. 2: Hexanchidae (pp. 45-47), Family No. 9: Carcharhinidae (pp. 67-86). In: Smiths' Sea Fishes (Smith & Heemstra 1986 [ref. 5715]).

Bath, H. 1971 (19 Nov.) [**ref. 206**]. *Gammogobius steinitizi* n. gen. n. sp. aus dem westlichen Mittelmeer (Pisces: Gobioidei: Gobiidae). Senckenb. Biol. v. 52 (no. 3/5): 201-210.

——. 1973 (21 Dec.) [**ref. 207**]. Wiederbeschreibung der Grundelart *Gobius macrocephalus* Kolombatovic aus dem Mittelmeer und Aufstellung einer neuen Gattung *Millerigobius* (Teleostei: Gobioidea: Gobiinae). Senckenb. Biol. v. 54 (no. 4/6): 303-310.

——. 1973 [**ref. 7212**]. Blenniidae (pp. 519-527). In: Hureau & Monod 1973 [ref. 6590].

——. 1977 (29 Apr.) [**ref. 208**]. Revision der Blenniini (Pisces: Blenniidae). Senckenb. Biol. v. 57 (no. 4/6): 167-234.

——. 1978 (19 Oct.) [**ref. 209**]. Ergänzungen zur Revision der Blenniini mit zwei neuen Gattungen (Pisces: Blenniidae). Senckenb. Biol. v. 59 (no. 3/4): 183-190.

——. 1982 (15 Sept.) [**ref. 5640**]. Beitrag zur Revalidation von *Parablennius ruber* (Valenciennes 1836) mit kritischen Bemerkungen zur Gültigkeit der Gattung *Pictiblennius* Whitley 1930 (Pisces: Blenniidae). Senckenb. Biol. v. 62 (no. 4/6): 211-224.

——. 1983 (30 Nov.) [**ref. 5393**]. Revision der Gattung *Antennablennius* Fowler 1931 mit Beschreibung einer neuen Art und Untersuchung der taxonomischen Stellung von *Antennablennius anuchalis* Springer & Spreitzer 1978. Senckenb. Biol. v. 64 (no. 1/3): 47-80.

——. 1983 (30 Apr.) [**ref. 5420**]. *Lipophrys sabry* n. sp. von der Mittelmeerküste Libyens (Pisces: Blenniidae). Senckenb. Biol. v. 63 (no. 3/4): 153-160.

——. 1986 (Apr.) [**ref. 6217**]. Blenniidae (pp. 355-357). In: Daget et al. 1986 [ref. 6189].

——. 1987 [**ref. 6305**]. *Hypsoblennius minutus* Meek & Hildebrand, 1928: ein Larvenstadium von *Parahypsos piersoni* (Gilbert & Starks, 1904) (Teleostei, Blenniidae). Zool. Anz. v. 219 (no. 5/6): 324-330.

——. 1989 (21 Aug.) [**ref. 13309**]. Die Arten der Gattung *Parablennius* Ribeiro 1915 im Roten Meer, Indischen und NW des Pazifischen Ozeans. Senckenb. Biol. v. 69 (no. 4/6): 301-343.

——. 1989 (21 Aug.) [**ref. 13310**]. Eine weitere Unterart von *Parablennius tasmanianus* (Richardson 1849). Senckenb. Biol. v. 69 (no. 4/6): 293-300.

Bath, H., and J. B. Hutchins. 1986 (2 May) [**ref. 5151**]. Die Blenniini des australischen Raums und Neuseelands mit Beschreibung einer neuen Art und einer neuen Unterart (Pisces: Blenniidae). Senckenb. Biol. v. 66 (no. 4/6): 167-213.

Bath, H., and P. Wirtz. 1989 (21 Aug.) [**ref. 13307**]. *Spaniblennius clandestinus* n. g., n. sp. der Tribus Blenniini van W-Afrika und ihre Beziehungen zur Gattung *Blennius* Linnaeus 1758. Senckenb. Biol. v. 69 (no. 4/6): 277-291.

Bauchot, M.-L. 1973 [**ref. 7184**]. Saccopharyngidae (pp. 216-217), Eurypharyngidae (pp. 218-129). In: Hureau & Monod 1973 [ref. 6590].

Bauchot, M.-L., and M. Blanc. 1961 (20 May) [**ref. 210**]. Poissons marins de l'Est Atlantique tropical. I. Labroidei (Téléostéens Perciformes). Atl. Rep. No. 6: 1-64.

——. 1963 (15 May) [**ref. 6583**]. Poissons marins de l'Est Atlantic tropical. II. Percoidei (Téléostéens Perciformes). 2e partie. Atl. Rep. No. 7: 37-61.

Bauchot, M.-L., J. Daget, J.-C. Hureau and T. Monod. 1970 [**ref. 12759**]. Le problème des 'auteurs secondaires' en taxionomie. Bull. Mus. Natn. Hist. Nat. (Ser. 2) v. 42 (no. 2): 301-304.

Bauchot, M.-L., and M. Desoutter. 1987 [**ref. 6382**]. Catalogue critique des types de poissons du Muséum national d'Histoire naturelle. (Suite) (Famille des Sciaenidae). Bull. Mus. Natl. Hist. Nat. Sect. A Zool. Biol. Ecol. Anim. v. 9 (no. 3, suppl.): 1-43.

Bauchot, M.-L., M. Desoutter and J. E. Randall. 1985 [**ref. 12595**]. Catalogue critique des types de poissons du Muséum national d'-Histoire naturelle. Bull. Mus. Natl. Hist. Nat. Sect. A Zool. Biol. Ecol. Anim. v. 7 (no. 2, suppl.): 1-25.

Bauchot, M.-L., and J. P. Quignard. 1973 [**ref. 7204**]. Labridae (pp. 426-443). In: Hureau & Monod 1973 [ref. 6590].

Bauchot, M.-L., and L. Saldanha. 1973 [**ref. 7186**]. Serrivomeridae (pp. 229-230), Cyemidae (p. 234). In: Hureau & Monod 1973 [ref. 6590].

Bauchot, M.-L., and P. H. Skelton. 1986 (Apr.) [**ref. 6210**]. Sparidae (pp. 331-332). In: Daget et al. 1986 [ref. 6189].

Bauchot, M.-L., P. J. P. Whitehead and T. Monod. 1982 [**ref. 6562**]. Date of publication and authorship of the fish names in Eydoux & Souleyet's zoology of *La Bonite*, 1841-1852. Cybium v. 6 (no. 3): 59-73.

Bean, B. A. 1895 (11 May) [**ref. 231**]. Descriptions of two new flounders, *Gastropsetta frontalis*, and *Cyclopsetta chittendeni*. No. XXXIII. In: Scientific results of explorations by the U. S. Fish Commission steamer *Albatross*. Proc. U. S. Natl. Mus. v. 17 (no. 1030): 633-636.

——. 1908 (4 Mar.) [**ref. 5014**]. On *Ctenolucius* Gill, a neglected genus of characin fishes, with notes on the typical species. Proc. U. S. Natl. Mus. v. 33 (no. 1588): 701-703.

Bean, B. A., and A. C. Weed. 1909 (27 May) [**ref. 220**]. Description of a new skate (*Dactylobatus armatus*) from deep water off the southern Atlantic coast of the United States. Proc. U. S. Natl. Mus. v. 36 (no. 1682): 459-461, Pl. 36.

——. 1920 [**ref. 221**]. Notes on a collection of fishes from Vancouver Island, B. C. Trans. R. Soc. Can. (Ser. 3) v. 13 [1919]: 69-83,

Pls. 1-4.

BEAN, T. H. 1880 (8 Apr.) **[ref. 222]**. Descriptions of some genera and species of Alaskan fishes. Proc. U. S. Natl. Mus. v. 2 [no. 100]: 353-359.

———. 1880 (8-10 July) **[ref. 6452]**. Check-list of duplicates of North American fishes distributed by the Smithsonian Institution in behalf of the United States National Museum, 1877-1880. Proc. U. S. Natl. Mus. v. 3 [no. 127]: 75-116.

———. 1881 (18 July) **[ref. 223]**. Descriptions of new fishes from Alaska and Siberia. Proc. U. S. Natl. Mus. v. 4 [no. 210]: 144-159.

———. 1882 (before 16 Aug.) **[ref. 224]**. Notes on a collection of fishes made by Captain Henry E. Nichols, U. S. N., in British Columbia and southern Alaska, with descriptions of new species and a new genus (*Delolepis*). Proc. U. S. Natl. Mus. v. 4 [no. 255]: 463-474.

———. 1884 (18 Jan.) **[ref. 225]**. Notes on collection of fishes made in 1882 and 1883 by Capt. Henry E. Nichols, U. S. N., in Alaska and British Columbia, with a description of a new genus and species, *Prionistius macellus*. Proc. U. S. Natl. Mus. v. 6 [no. 387]: 353-361.

———. 1885 (29 June) **[ref. 226]**. On *Stathmonotus*, a new genus of fishes related to *Muraenoides*, from Florida. Proc. U. S. Natl. Mus. v. 8 [no. 508]: 191-192, Pl. 13.

———. 1888 (19 Sept.) **[ref. 227]**. Description of a new genus and species of fish, *Acrotus willoughbyi*, from Washington Terratory. Proc. U. S. Natl. Mus. v. 10 [no. 672]: 631-632.

———. 1890 (4 Mar.) **[ref. 228]**. No. VIII.—Description of a new cottoid fish from British Columbia. In: Scientific results of explorations by the U. S. Fish Commission steamer *Albatross*. Proc. U. S. Natl. Mus. v. 12 (no. 787): 641-642. [Advance sheets issued 4 March 1890.]

———. 1890 (1 July) **[ref. 229]**. New fishes collected off the coast of Alaska and the adjacent region southward. No. XI. In: Scientific results of explorations by the U. S. Fish Commission steamer *Albatross*. Proc. U. S. Natl. Mus. v. 13 (no. 795): 37-45.

———. 1894 (10 Feb.) **[ref. 230]**. Description of a new blennioid fish from California. Proc. U. S. Natl. Mus. v. 16 (no. 967): 699-701.

———. 1912 (31 July) **[ref. 232]**. Descriptions of new fishes of Bermuda. Proc. Biol. Soc. Wash. v. 25: 121-126.

BEAN, T. H., AND B. A. BEAN. 1896 (30 Dec.) **[ref. 233]**. Notes on fishes collected in Kamchatka and Japan by Leonhard Stejneger and Nikolai A. Grebnitski, with a description of a new blenny. Proc. U. S. Natl. Mus. v. 19 (no. 1112): 381-392, Pls. 34-35.

BEAUFORT, L. F. DE. See de Beaufort, L. F.

BECKHAM, E. C., III. 1980 (28 Mar.) **[ref. 5464]**. *Percina gymnocephala*, a new percid fish of the subgenus *Alvordius*, from the New River in North Carolina, Virginia, and West Virginia. Occas. Pap. Mus. Zool. La. State Univ. No. 57: 1-11.

BEEBE, W. 1926 **[ref. 244]**. A new ceratioid fish. Bull. N. Y. Zool. Soc. v. 29 (no. 2): 80.

———. 1932 **[ref. 5015]**. A new deep-sea fish. Bull. N. Y. Zool. Soc. v. 35 (no. 5): 175-177.

———. 1933 (Aug.) **[ref. 245]**. Deep-sea fishes of the Bermuda oceanographic expeditions. No. I—Introduction. No. 2—Family Alepocephalidae. No. 3—Family Argentinidae. Zoologica (N. Y.) v. 16 (nos. 1-3): 1-147.

———. 1933 (27 Dec.) **[ref. 246]**. Deep-sea stomiatoid fishes. One new genus and eight new species. Copeia 1933 (no. 4): 160-175.

———. 1933 (25 July) **[ref. 5873]**. Deep-sea isospondylous fishes. Two new genera and four new species. Zoologica (N. Y.) v. 13 (no. 9): 159-167.

———. 1934 **[ref. 247]**. Three new deep-sea fish seen from the bathysphere. Bull. N. Y. Zool. Soc. v. 37 (no. 6): 190-193.

BEEBE, W., AND J. CRANE. 1947 (21 Feb.) **[ref. 6539]**. Eastern Pacific expeditions of the New York Zoological Society. XXXVII. Deep-sea ceratioid fishes. Zoologica (N. Y.) v. 31 (pt 4): 151-181, Pls. 1-3.

BEEBE, W., AND J. TEE-VAN. 1934 (6 June) **[ref. 248]**. A new genus and species of scaleless blenny, *Somersia furcata*, from Bermuda. Am. Mus. Novit. No. 730: 1-3.

———. 1938 (28 Sept.) **[ref. 249]**. Eastern Pacific expeditions of the New York Zoological Society, XV. Seven new marine fishes from Lower California. Zoologica (N. Y.) v. 23 (pt 3): 299-312, Pls. 1-3.

BEGLE, D. P. 1989 (8 Aug.) **[ref. 12739]**. Phylogenetic analysis of the cottid genus *Artedius* (Teleostei: Scorpaeniformes). Copeia 1989 (no. 3): 642-652.

BEHNKE, R. J. 1969 (Dec.) **[ref. 250]**. A new subgenus and species of trout, *Salmo (Platysalmo) platycephalus*, from southcentral Turkey, with comments on the classifikation of the subfamily Salmoninae. Mitt. Hamb. Zool. Mus. Inst. v. 66: 1-15.

———. 1984 (Feb.) **[ref. 6177]**. Salmonidae (pp. 125-126). In: Daget et al. 1984 [ref. 6168].

BELING, D., AND B. S. ILJIN. 1927 **[ref. 7211]**. *Benthophiloides brauneri* n. g., n. sp. Ein für das Schwarzmeerbassin neuer Vertreter der Familie der Gobiidae. Travaux Sta. Biol. Dniepre, Acad. Sci. Ukraine v. 3, livr. 7, no. 2: 309-325, 2 pls.

BELLOC, G. 1937 **[ref. 251]**. Note sur un poisson comestible nouveau de la côte occidentale d'Afrique (*Paracubiceps ledenoisi* nov. gen., nov. sp.). Rev. Trav. Off. Peches Marit. Paris v. 10: 353-356.

BELLOTTI, C. 1892 **[ref. 253]**. Un nuova siluroide giapponese. Atti Soc. Ital. Sci. Nat. v. 34: 99-101.

BELLWOOD, D. R., AND J. H. CHOAT. 1989 **[ref. 13494]**. A description of the juvenile phase colour patterns of 14 parrotfish species (family Scaridae) from the Great Barrier Reef, Australia. Rec. Aust. Mus. v. 41 (no. 1): 1-41.

BEN SALEM, M. 1988 (30 Mar.) **[ref. 6736]**. Taxinomie numérique des espèces du genre *Trachurus* Rafinesque, 1810 (Poissons Téléstéens, Carangidae). Cybium v. 12 (no. 1): 45-58.

BEN-TUVIA, A. 1953 (Aug.) **[ref. 257]**. Mediterranean fishes of Israel. Bull. Sea Fish. Res. Sta. Israel No. 8: 1-40.

———. 1986 **[ref. 5641]**. Family 196: Mullidae (pp. 610-613). In: Smiths' Sea Fishes (Smith & Heemstra 1986 [ref. 5715]).

———. 1986 (30 May) **[ref. 6314]**. Taxonomic status of *Upeneichthys lineatus* (Bloch) in Australian and New Zealand waters. Pp. 590-594. In: Uyeno et al. (eds.) 1986 [ref. 6147].

BEN-TUVIA, A., AND G. W. KISSIL. 1988 (Dec.) **[ref. 12819]**. Fishes of the family Mullidae in the Red Sea, with a key to the species in the Red Sea and the eastern Mediterranean. Ichthyol. Bull. J. L. B. Smith Inst. Ichthyol. No. 52: 1-16.

BENL, G. 1957 (1 July) **[ref. 258]**. *Carinotetraodon chlupatyi* nov. gen., nov. spec., ein Kugelfisch mit Kamm und Kiel [Pisces, Fam. Tetraodontidae]. Opusc. Zool. No. 5: 1-4.

BENNETT, B. A. 1983 (Nov.) **[ref. 5299]**. *Clinus spatulatus*, a new species of clinid fish (Perciformes: Blennoidei) from South Africa, with a modified definition of the genus *Clinus*. J. L. B. Smith Inst. Ichthyol. Spec. Publ. No. 29: 1-9.

BENNETT, E. T. 1830 **[ref. 259]**. Catalogue of the fishes of Sumatra. In: Memoir of the Life and Public Services of Sir Stamford Raffles, edited by Lady Raffles. London. 694 pp. [Not seen.]

———. 1831 (6 Dec.) **[ref. 5778]**. Observations on a collection of fishes from Mauritius, with characters of new genera and species. Proc. Zool. Soc. Lond. 1830-31 (pt 1): 145-148.

———. 1832 (2 Mar.) **[ref. 4944]**. Observations on a collection of fishes from the Mauritius with characters of new genera and species. Proc. Zool. Soc. Lond. 1830-31 (pt 1): 165-169. [Article appeared in 3 parts, 1831-1832, this part 1832.]

BENNETT, F. D. 1840 **[ref. 260]**. Narrative of a whaling voyage round the globe, from the year 1833 to 1836. London. v. 2: 1-395.

BENTIVEGNA, F., AND G. FIORITO. 1983 (31 Dec.) **[ref. 12849]**. Numerical taxonomic techniques confirm the validity of two genera in Trachinidae. Cybium v. 7 (no. 4): 51-56.

BERG, C. 1895 **[ref. 261]**. Enumeración sistemática y sinonímica de los peces de las costas Argentina y Uruguaya. An. Mus. Nac. Hist. Nat. B. Aires v. 4: 1-120, 1 pl.

———. 1898 (17 Dec.) **[ref. 262]**. Substitución de nombres genéricos. II. Comun. Mus. Nac. Buenos Aires v. 1 (no. 2): 41-43.

BERG, L. S. 1903 **[ref. 263]**. On the systematics of the Cottidae from

Lake Baikal. Ann. Mus. Zool. Acad. Imp. Sci. St. Petersburg v. 8: 99-114. [In Russian.]

———. 1906 **[ref. 264]**. Übersicht der Marsipobranchii des russischen Reiches. Bull. Acad. Imp. Sci. St. Petersburg (Ser. 5) v. 24 (no. 3): 169-183.

———. 1906 (Nov.) **[ref. 265]**. Üebersicht der Cataphracti (Fam. Cottidae, Cottocomephoridae und Comephoridae) des Baikalsees. Zool. Anz. v. 30 (no. 26): 906-911.

———. 1907 **[ref. 266]**. Die Cataphracti des Baikal-Sees (Fam. Cottidae, Cottocomephoridae und Comephoridae). Beiträge zur Osteologie und Systematik. Wiss. Ergebn. Zool. Exped. Baikal-See, 3rd ed. St. Petersburg & Berlin. 1-75, Pls. 1-5.

———. 1907 (Feb.) **[ref. 267]**. Description of a new cyprinoid fish, *Paraleucogobio notacanthus*, from N. China. Ann. Mag. Nat. Hist. (Ser. 7) v. 19 (no. 110): 163-164.

———. 1907 **[ref. 268]**. Verzeichnis der Fische von Russisch-Turkestan. Ann. Mus. Zool. Acad. Imp. Sci. St. Petersburg v. 10 (no. 3-4): 316-332.

———. 1907 (Feb.) **[ref. 269]**. Description of a new cyprinoid fish, *Acheilognathus signifer*, from Korea, with a synopsis of all the known Rhodeinae. Ann. Mag. Nat. Hist. (Ser. 7) v. 19 (no. 110): 159-163.

———. 1907 **[ref. 270]**. Beschreibungen einiger neuer Fische aus dem Stromgebiete des Amur. Ann. Mus. Zool. Acad. Imp. Sci. St. Petersburg v. 12: 418-423.

———. 1908 **[ref. 271]**. Vorläufige Bemerkungen über die europäisch-asiatischen Salmoninen, insbesondere die Gattung *Thymallus*. Ann. Mus. Zool. Acad. Imp. Sci. St. Petersburg v. 12: 500-514.

———. 1909 **[ref. 5116]**. Ichthyologia amurensis. Mem. Acad. Sci. St. Petersb. v. 24 (no. 8): 1-270, Pls. 1-3. [In Russian.]

———. 1911 **[ref. 272]**. Faune de la Russie et des pays limitrophes. Poissons (Marsipobranchii et Pisces). Vol. 1. Marsipobranchii, Selachii et Chondrostei. St. Petersburg 1-337, Pls. 1-8. [In Russian.]

———. 1912 **[ref. 5874]**. Fauna de la Russie et des pays limitrophes. Poissons (Marsipobranchii et Pisces). Vol. III. Ostariophysi. Part 1. St. Petersbourg. 1-336, Pls. 1-2.

———. 1913 **[ref. 273]**. A review of the clupeoid fishes of the Caspian Sea, with remarks on the herring-like fishes of the Russian empire. Ann. Mag. Nat. Hist. (Ser. 8) v. 11 (no. 65): 472-480.

———. 1914 **[ref. 274]**. Faune de la Russie et des Pays limitropes. Poissons, Marsipobranchii et Pisces. Vol. III. Ostariophysi, Part 2. St. Petersburg. 337-704, Pls. 3-5.

———. 1915 **[ref. 276]**. Compte-rendu préliminaire sur les harénges collectionnés dans la mer Caspienne par l'Expédition Caspienne de l'année 1913. Mat. Pozn. Russk. Rybolov v. 4 (no. 6): 1-8, 3 pls. [Not seen.]

———. 1916 **[ref. 277]**. Les Poissons des eaux douces de la Russie. Moscow. i-xxvii + 1-563. [In Russian.]

———. 1932 **[ref. 278]**. Les poissons des eaux douces de l'U.R.S.S. et des pays limitrophes. 3-e édition, revue et augmentée. Leningrad. Part 1: 1-554. [In Russian.]

———. 1933 **[ref. 279]**. Les poissons des eaux douces de l'U.R.S.S et des pays limitrophes. 3-e édition, revue et augmentée. Leningrad. Part 2: 545-903. [In Russian.]

———. 1933 **[ref. 5569]**. Faune de l'U.R.S.S. et des pays limitrophes fondée principalement sur les collections de l'Institut zoologique de l'Académie de Sciences de l'U.R.S.S. Poissons. Marsipobranchii et Pisces. Volume 3. Ostariophysi. Leningrad. Part 3: 705-846. [In Russian.]

———. 1938 **[ref. 281]**. On some South China loaches (Cobitidae, Pisces). Bull. Soc. Nat. Moscou Sect. Biol. (n. s.) v. 47 (no. 5-6): 314-318. [In Russian and English.]

———. 1948-1949 **[ref. 12882]**. Fresh-water fishes of Soviet Union and adjacent countries. I. II. III. Guide Fauna U.S.S.R. Nos. 27, 29, 30: 1-466, 467-925, 927-1382. [In Russian. Translations available, 1962-1965, Smithson. Instit. by Israel Prog. Sci. Transl.]

BERKENHOUT, J. 1789 **[ref. 12437]**. Synopsis of the natural history of Great Britain and Ireland. Containing a systematic arrangement... of all the animals... in these kingdoms. 2nd ed. London. v. 1: 1-19 + 1-334. [Not seen.]

BERRA, T. M. 1989 **[ref. 13528]**. The significance of William Bartram (1739-1823) to North American ichthyology. Amer. Midl. Natural. v. 122: 214-227.

———. 1989 **[ref. 13530]**. *Scleropages leichardti* Günther (Osteoglossiformes): the case of the missing h. Bull. Aust. Soc. Limnol. v. 12: 15-19.

BERRA, T. M., AND G. R. ALLEN. 1989 **[ref. 13529]**. Clarification of the differences between *Galaxiella nigrostriata* (Shipway, 1953) and *Galaxiella munda* McDowall, 1978 (Pisces: Galaxiidae) from Western Australia. Rec. West. Aust. Mus. v. 14 (no. 3): 293-297.

———. 1989 **[ref. 13531]**. Burrowing, emergence, behavior, and functional morphology of the Australian salamanderfish, *Lepidogalaxias salamandroides*. Fisheries v. 14 (no. 5): 2-10 + cover.

BERRA, T. M., AND A. H. WEATHERLEY. 1972 (8 Mar.) **[ref. 7104]**. A systematic study of the Australian freshwater serranid fish genus *Maccullochella*. Copeia 1972 (no. 1): 53-64.

BERRY, F. H., AND D. M. COHEN. 1974 **[ref. 7489]**. Synopsis of the species of *Trachurus* (Pisces, Carangidae). Q. J. Fla. Acad. Sci. v. 35 (no. 4): 177-211.

BERRY, F. H., AND C. R. ROBINS. 1967 (20 Mar.) **[ref. 286]**. *Macristiella perlucens*, a new clupeiform fish from the Gulf of Mexico. Copeia 1967 (no. 1): 46-50.

BERTELSEN, E. 1951 (18 Dec.) **[ref. 287]**. The ceratioid fishes. Ontogeny, taxonomy, distribution and biology. Dana Rep. No. 39: 1-276, 1 pl.

———. 1980 (20 Feb.) **[ref. 6927]**. Notes on Linophrynidae V: A revision of the deepsea anglerfishes of the *Linophryne arborifera*-group (Pisces, Ceratioidei). Steenstrupia v. 6 (no. 6): 29-70.

———. 1982 (20 May) **[ref. 288]**. Notes on Linophrynidae VIII. A review of the genus *Linophryne*, with new records and descriptions of two new species. Steenstrupia v. 8 (no. 3): 49-104.

———. 1986 **[ref. 5642]**. Family No. 125: Mirapinnidae (pp. 406-407). In: Smiths' Sea Fishes (Smith & Heemstra 1986 [ref. 5715]).

BERTELSEN, E., AND G. KREFFT. 1988 (30 June) **[ref. 6615]**. The ceratioid family Himantolophidae (Pisces, Lophiiformes). Steenstrupia v. 14 (no. 2): 9-89.

BERTELSEN, E., G. KREFFT AND N. B. MARSHALL. 1976 **[ref. 289]**. The fishes of the family Notosudidae. Dana Rep. No. 86: 1-114, 1 pl.

BERTELSEN, E., AND N. B. MARSHALL. 1956 (1 July) **[ref. 290]**. The Miripinnati, a new order of teleost fishes. Dana Rep. No. 42: 1-34, Pl. 1.

———. 1958 (1 July) **[ref. 291]**. Notes on Miripinnati (an addendum to Dana Report no. 42). A change of name and further records. Dana Rep. No. 45: 9-10.

———. 1984 **[ref. 13657]**. Mirapinnatoidei: development and relationships. Am. Soc. Ichthyol. Herpetol. Spec. Publ. No. 1: 380-383.

BERTELSEN, E., AND J. G. NIELSEN. 1987 (10 Dec.) **[ref. 6618]**. The deep sea eel family Monognathidae (Pisces, Anguilliformes). Steenstrupia v. 13 (no. 4): 141-198.

BERTELSEN, E., J. G. NIELSEN AND D. G. SMITH. 1989 **[ref. 13293]**. Suborder Saccopharyngoidei (pp. 636-655). In: Böhlke, E. B. (ed.) 1989 [ref. 13282].

BERTELSEN, E., AND T. W. PIETSCH. 1975 (Aug.) **[ref. 7062]**. Results of the research cruises of FRV "Walther Herwig" to South America. XXXVIII. Osteology and relationships of the ceratioid anglerfish genus *Spiniphryne* (family Oneirodidae). Arch. FischereiWiss. v. 26 (no. 1): 1-11.

———. 1977 (Mar.) **[ref. 7063]**. Results of the research cruises of FRV "Walther Herwig" to South America. XLVII. Ceratioid anglerfishes of the family Oneirodidae collected by the FRV "Walther Herwig." Arch. FischereiWiss. v. 27 (no. 3): 171-189.

———. 1983 **[ref. 5335]**. The ceratioid anglerfishes of Australia. Rec. Aust. Mus. v. 35: 77-99.

BERTELSEN, E., T. W. PIETSCH AND R. J. LAVENBERG. 1981 (20 Feb.) **[ref. 5330]**. Ceratioid anglerfishes of the family Gigantactinidae: morphology, systematics, and distribution. Contrib. Sci. (Los Ang.) No. 332: 1-74.

BERTELSEN, E., AND P. J. STRUHSAKER. 1977 **[ref. 5331]**. The ceratoid fishes of the genus *Thaumatichthys*: osteology, relationships, distribution and biology. Galathea Rep. v. 14: 7-40.

BERTIN, L. 1936 **[ref. 292]**. Un nouveau genre de poissons apodes caractérisé par l'absence de machoire supérieure. Bull. Soc. Zool. Fr. v. 61 [1936]: 533-540.

———. 1940 **[ref. 293]**. Catalogue des types de poissons du Muséum National d'Histoire Naturelle. 2e partie. Dipneustes, Chondrostéens, Holostèens, Isospondyles. Bull. Mus. Natl. Hist. Nat. (Ser. 2) v. 12 (no. 6): 244-322.

BERTRAND, E. 1763 **[ref. 6405]**. Dictionnaire universel des fossiles propres et des fossiles accidentels. [Non-binomial work on Official Index (Opinion 592). Original not seen.]

BIANCHI, G. 1984 (31 Dec.) **[ref. 5159]**. Study on the morphology of five Mediterranean and Atlantic sparid fishes with a reinstatement of the genus *Pagrus* Cuvier 1817. Cybium v. 8 (no. 4): 31-56.

BIANCO, P. G. 1987 (30 June) **[ref. 6750]**. Précision sur la distribution de *Cobitis taenia* Linnaeus, 1758 (Cobitidae) et de *Valencia hispanica* (Valenciennes, 1846) (Cyprinodontidae) dans les eaux douces d'Ilalie. Cybium v. 11 (no. 2): 207-212.

BIANCO, P. G., A. M. BULLOCK, P. J. MILLER AND F. R. ROUBAL. 1987 **[ref. 6337]**. A unique teleost dermal organ in a new European genus of fishes (Teleostei: Gobioidei). J. Fish Biol. v. 31: 797-803.

BIANCO, P. G., AND R. R. MILLER. 1989 (31 Dec.) **[ref. 13541]**. First record of *Valencia leptourneuxi* (Sauvage, 1880) in Peloponnese (Greece) and remarks on the Mediterranean family Valenciidae (Cyprinodontiformes). Cybium v. 13 (no. 4): 385-387.

BIANCONI, G. G. 1850-1870 **[ref. 295]**. Specimina zoologica Mosambicana quibus vel novae vel minus notae animalium species illustrantur. Bononiae. [Fascicles x (1855), xii (1857), xiii (1859) involve fishes.] Rec. Acad. Sci. Bologna. 1-363, 48 col pls. [Not seen. According to Dean 1916 [ref. 13327], abstracts with diagnoses were published earlier.]

BIGELOW, H. B., AND T. BARBOUR. 1944 (14 Apr.) **[ref. 299]**. A new giant ceratioid fish. Proc. New England Zool. Club v. 23: 9-15, Pls. 4-6.

———. 1944 (30 June) **[ref. 298]**. *Reganula gigantea* to replace *Reganichthys giganteus*. Copeia 1944 (no. 2): 123.

BIGELOW, H. B., AND W. C. SCHROEDER. 1941 (8 July) **[ref. 300]**. *Cephalurus*, a new genus of scyliorhinid shark with redescription of the genotype, *Catulus cephalus* Gilbert. Copeia 1941 (no. 2): 73-76.

———. 1948 **[ref. 301]**. New genera and species of batoid fishes. J. Mar. Res. v. 7: 543-566.

———. 1950 (June) **[ref. 302]**. New and little known cartilaginous fishes from the Atlantic. Bull. Mus. Comp. Zool. v. 103 (no. 7): 385-408, Pls. 1-7.

———. 1951 **[ref. 303]**. A new genus and species of anacanthobatid skate from the Gulf of Mexico. J. Wash. Acad. Sci. v. 41 (no. 3): 110-113.

———. 1953 **[ref. 6568]**. Fishes of the western North Atlantic. Part two. Sawfishes, guitarfishes, skates and rays. Mem. Sears Found. Mar. Res. Memoir 1 (pt 2): 1-514.

———. 1954 (27 Jan.) **[ref. 5551]**. A new family, a new genus, and two new species of batoid fishes from the Gulf of Mexico. Breviora No. 24: 1-16.

BIRDSONG, R. S. 1981 **[ref. 5425]**. A review of the gobiid fish genus *Microgobius* Poey. Bull. Mar. Sci. v. 31 (no. 2): 267-306.

———. 1988 (23 Aug.) **[ref. 6572]**. *Robinsichthys arrowsmithensis*, a new genus and species of deep-dwelling gobiid fish from the western Caribbean. Proc. Biol. Soc. Wash. v. 101 (no. 2): 438-443.

BIRDSONG, R. S., E. O. MURDY AND F. L. PEZOLD. 1988 **[ref. 7303]**. A study of the vertebral column and median fin osteology in gobioid fishes with comments on gobioid relationships. Bull. Mar. Sci. v. 42 (no. 2): 174-214.

BLACHE, J., AND M.-L. BAUCHOT. 1972 **[ref. 304]**. Contribution à la connaissance des poissons Anguilliformes de la côte occidentale d'Afrique. 13e note: les genres *Verma, Apterichthus, Ichthyapus, Hemerorhinus, Caecula, Dalophis* avec la description de deux genres nouveaux (Fam. des Ophichthidae). Bull. Inst. Fr. Afr. Noire (Ser. A) Sci. Nat. v. 34 (no. 3): 692-773.

———. 1976 **[ref. 305]**. Contribution à la connaissance des poissons Anguilliformes de la côte occidentale d'Afrique. 16e note: les familles des Congridae et des Cologongridae. Bull. Inst. Fr. Afr. Noire (Ser. A) Sci. Nat. v. 38 (no.2): 369-444.

BLACHE, J., M.-L. BAUCHOT AND L. SALDANHA. 1973 **[ref. 7185]**. [Several family accounts of anguilliform fishes.] In: Hureau & Monod 1973 [ref. 6590].

BLAINVILLE, H. M. DE. 1816 **[ref. 306]**. Prodrome d'une nouvelle distribution systématique du règne animal. Bull. Soc. Philomath. Paris v. 8: 105-112 [sic for 113-120] +121-124.

———. 1818 **[ref. 307]**. Sur les ichthyolites ou les poissons fossiles. [Nouveau Dictionnaire d'Histoire Naturelle, appliquée aux arts, àl'economie rurale et domestique, à la Medicine, etc.] Deterville, Paris. (Nouv. edit) 27: 310-395.

———. 1825 (Apr.) **[ref. 4991]**. Vertébrës. Class V. Poissons. In: L. P. Vieillot, et al., Faune Française; ou histoire naturelle, générale et particulière des animaux qui se trouvent en France... Paris, 1820-1830. Livr. 13 & 14: 1-96, Pls. 1-24. [For dates of parts see Sherborn & Woodward 1907 [ref. 13429]. Jordan 1917:134 [ref. 2407] has author as Serville.]

BLANC, M., AND J.-C. HUREAU. 1973 **[ref. 7218]**. Scorpaenidae (pp. 579-585), Triglidae (pp. 586-590), Peristediidae (p. 591). In: Hureau & Monod 1973 [ref. 6590].

BLANCHARD, E. 1866 **[ref. 310]**. Les poissons des eaux douces de la France. Paris. i-xvi + 1-656.

BLEEKER, P. 1845 **[ref. 312]**. Bijdragen tot de geneeskundige Topographie van Batavia. Generisch overzicht der Fauna. Natuur. Geneesk. Arch. Neerl.-Ind. v. 2: 505-528. [Continuation from v. 1: 551-553]

———. 1846 **[ref. 5872]**. Overzigt der siluroieden, wilke te Batavia voorkomen. Natuur. Geneesk. Arch. Neerl.-Ind. v. 2: 135-184.

———. 1847 **[ref. 313]**. Siluroideorum bataviensium conspectus diagnosticus. Verh. Batav. Genootsch. Kunst. Wet. v. 21: 1-60.

———. 1847 **[ref. 314]**. Pharyngognathorum Siluroideorumque species novae Javanenses. Natuur. Geneesk. Arch. Neerl.-Ind. v. 4 (no. 2): 155-169.

———. 1848 **[ref. 315]**. A contribution to the ichthyological fauna of Sumbawa. J. Indian Arch. & E. Asia v. 2 (no. 9): 632-639.

———. 1849 **[ref. 316]**. A contribution to the knowledge of the ichthyological fauna of Celebes. J. Indian Arch. & E. Asia v. 3: 65-74.

———. 1849 **[ref. 317]**. Overzigt der te Batavia voorkomende Gladschubbige Lipvisschen, met beschrijvning van 11 nieuwe species. Verh. Batav. Genootsch. Kunst. Wet. v. 22: 1-64.

———. 1849 **[ref. 318]**. Bijdrage tot de kennis der Percoïden van den Malayo-Molukschen Archipel, met beschrijving van 22 nieuwe soorten. Verh. Batav. Genootsch. Kunst. Wet. v. 22: 1-64.

———. 1849 **[ref. 319]**. Bijdrage tot de kennis der Blennioïden en Gobioïden van der Soenda-Molukschen Archipel, met beschrijving van 42 nieuwe soorten. Verh. Batav. Genootsch. Kunst. Wet. v. 22: 1-40.

———. 1849 **[ref. 320]**. Bijdrage tot de kennis der ichthyologische fauna van het eiland Madura, met beschrijving van eenige neiuwe soorten. Verh. Batav. Genootsch. Kunst. Wet. v. 22: 1-16.

———. 1849 **[ref. 321]**. Bijdrage tot de kennis der ichthyologische fauna van het eiland Bali, met beschrijving van eenige nieuwe species. Verh. Batav. Genootsch. Kunst. Wet. v. 22: 1-11.

———. 1850 **[ref. 322]**. Bijdrage tot de kennis der Maenoïden van den Soenda-Molukschen Archipel. Verh. Batav. Genootsch. Kunst. Wet. v. 23: 1-13.

———. 1850 **[ref. 323]**. Bijdrage tot de kennis der Visschen met doolhofvormige kieuwen van den Soenda-Molukschen Archipel.

Verh. Batav. Genootsch. Kunst. Wet. v. 23: 1-15.
———. 1851 **[ref. 324]**. Visschen van Banka. Natuurkd. Tijdschr. Neder.-Indië v. 1: 159-161.
———. 1851 **[ref. 325]**. Nieuwe bijdrage tot de kennis der ichthyologische fauna van Borneo, met beschrijving van eenige nieuwe soorten van zoetwatervisschen. Natuurkd. Tijdschr. Neder.-Indië v. 1: 259-275.
———. 1851 **[ref. 326]**. Over eenige nieuwe geslachten en soorten van Makreelachtige visschen van den Indischen Archipel. Natuurkd. Tijdschr. Neder.-Indië v. 1: 341-372.
———. 1851 **[ref. 327]**. Derde bijdrage tot de kennis der ichthyologische fauna van Borneo, met beschrijving van eenige nieuwe soorten van zoetwatervisschen. Natuurkd. Tijdschr. Neder.-Indië v. 2: 57-70.
———. 1851 **[ref. 328]**. *Cheilinoïdes* een nieuw geslacht van gladschubbige Labroïden van Batavia. Natuurkd. Tijdschr. Neder.-Indië v. 2: 71-72.
———. 1851 **[ref. 329]**. Vierde bijdrage tot de kennis der ichthyologische fauna van Borneo, met beschrijving van eenige nieuwe soorten van zoetwatervisschen. Natuurkd. Tijdschr. Neder.-Indië v. 2: 193-208.
———. 1851 **[ref. 330]**. Nieuwe bijdrage tot de kennis der ichthyologische fauna van Celebes. Natuurkd. Tijdschr. Neder.-Indië v. 2: 209-224.
———. 1851 **[ref. 331]**. Bijdrage tot de kennis der ichthyologische fauna van de Banda-eilanden. Natuurkd. Tijdschr. Neder.-Indië v. 2: 225-261.
———. 1851 **[ref. 6831]**. Over eenige nieuwe soorten van Pleuronectoïden van den Indischen Archipel. Natuurkd. Tijdschr. Neder.-Indië v. 1: 401-416. [Also as a separate, pp. 1-16.]
———. 1851 **[ref. 12505]**. *Oxybelus brandesii* Blkr, eene nieuwe soort van Ophidini van Banda neira. Natuurkd. Tijdschr. Neder.-Indië v. 1: 276-278, 1 pl.
———. 1852 **[ref. 332]**. Bijdrage tot de kennis der Makreelachtige visschen van den Soenda-Molukschen Archipel. Verh. Batav. Genootsch. Kunst. Wet. v. 24 (art. 5): 1-93.
———. 1852 **[ref. 333]**. Bijdrage tot de kennis der Plagiostomen van den Indischen Archipel. Verh. Batav. Genootsch. Kunst. Wet. v. 24 (art. 12): 1-92, Pls. 1-4.
———. 1852 **[ref. 334]**. Diagnostische beschrijvingen van nieuwe of weinig bekende vischsoorten van Sumatra. Tiental I - IV. Natuurkd. Tijdschr. Neder.-Indië v. 3: 569-608.
———. 1852 **[ref. 335]**. Derde bijdrage tot de kennis der ichthyologische fauna van Celebes. Natuurkd. Tijdschr. Neder.-Indië v. 3: 739-782.
———. 1853 **[ref. 336]**. Diagnostische beschrijvingen van nieuwe of weinig bekende vischsoorten van Batavia. Tiental I-VI. Natuurkd. Tijdschr. Neder.-Indië v. 4: 451-516.
———. 1853 **[ref. 337]**. Nieuwe bijdrage tot de kennis de ichthyologische fauna van Ternate en Halmaheira (Gilolo). Natuurkd. Tijdschr. Neder.-Indië v. 4: 595-610.
———. 1853 **[ref. 338]**. Zevende bijdrage tot de kennis der ichthyologische fauna van Borneo. Zoetwatervisschen van Sambas, Pontianak en Pangaron. Natuurkd. Tijdschr. Neder.-Indië v. 5: 427-462.
———. 1853 **[ref. 339]**. Bijdrage tot de kennis der Muraenoïden en Symbranchoïden van den Indischen Archipel. Verh. Batav. Genootsch. Kunst. Wet. v. 25: 1-76. [Written Sept.-Dec. 1853, so perhaps not published until 1854.]
———. 1853 **[ref. 340]**. Nalezingen op de ichthyologie van Japan. Verh. Batav. Genootsch. Kunst. Wet. v. 25: 1-56.
———. 1853 **[ref. 341]**. Nalezingen op de ichthyologische fauna van Bengalen en Hindostan. Verh. Batav. Genootsch. Kunst. Wet. v. 25: 1-164, 1 pl. [+ 6 pls. in v. 26, Aanhangsel. Maart 1854, p. 165-166. Text as a separate in 1854 but dated 1853.]
———. 1853 **[ref. 5117]**. Vierde bijdrage tot de kennis der ichthyologische fauna van Amboina. Natuurkd. Tijdschr. Neder.-Indië v. 5: 317-352.
———. 1853 **[ref. 5965]**. Nieuwe tientallen diagnostische beschrijvingen van nieuwe of weinig bekende vischsoorten van Sumatra. Natuurkd. Tijdschr. Neder.-Indië v. 5: 495-534.
———. 1853 **[ref. 12580]**. Diagnostische beschrijvingen van nieuwe of weinig bekende vischsoorten van Sumatra. Tiental V-X. Natuurkd. Tijdschr. Neder.-Indië v. 4: 243-302.
———. 1854 **[ref. 342]**. Speciés piscium bataviensium novae vel minus cognitae. Natuurkd. Tijdschr. Neder.-Indië v. 6: 191-202.
———. 1854 **[ref. 343]**. Bijdrage tot de kennis der ichthyologische fauna van het eiland Floris. Natuurkd. Tijdschr. Neder.-Indië v. 6: 311-338.
———. 1854 **[ref. 344]**. Vijfde bijdrage tot de kennis der ichthyologische fauna van Amboina. Natuurkd. Tijdschr. Neder.-Indië v. 6: 455-508.
———. 1854 **[ref. 345]**. Vijfde bijdrage tot de kennis der ichthyologische fauna van Celebes. Natuurkd. Tijdschr. Neder.-Indië v. 7: 225-260.
———. 1854-57 **[ref. 357]**. Nieuwe nalezingen op de ichthyologie van Japan. Verh. Batav. Genootsch. Kunst. Wet. v. 26: 1-132, Pls. 1-8.
———. 1855 **[ref. 346]**. Over eenige visschen van van Diemensland. Versl. Akad. Amsterdam v. 2: 1-30, 1 pl.
———. 1855 **[ref. 347]**. Derde bijdrage tot de kennis der ichthyologische fauna van de Kokos-eilanden. Natuurkd. Tijdschr. Neder.-Indië v. 8: 169-180.
———. 1855 **[ref. 348]**. Bijdrage tot de kennis der ichthyologische fauna van de Batoe Eilanden. Natuurkd. Tijdschr. Neder.-Indië v. 8: 305-328.
———. 1855 **[ref. 349]**. Visschen van de Duizendeilanden. Natuurkd. Tijdschr. Neder.-Indië v. 8: 344.
———. 1855 **[ref. 350]**. Zesde bijdrage tot de kennis der ichthyologische fauna van Amboina. Natuurkd. Tijdschr. Neder.-Indië v. 8: 391-434.
———. 1855 **[ref. 351]**. Nalezingen op de vischfauna van Sumatra. Visschen van Lahat en Sibogha. Natuurkd. Tijdschr. Neder.-Indië v. 9: 257-280.
———. 1856 **[ref. 352]**. Beschrijvingen van nieuwe of weinig bekende vischsoorten van Manado en Makassar grootendeels verzameld op eene reis naar den Molukschen Archipel in het gevolg van den Gouverneur Generaal Duymaer van Twist. Acta Soc. Sci. Indo-Neerl. v. 1: 1-80.
———. 1856 **[ref. 353]**. Bijdrage tot de kennis der ichthyologische fauna van het eiland Boeroe. Natuurkd. Tijdschr. Neder.-Indië v. 11: 383-414.
———. 1856 **[ref. 354]**. Bijdrage tot de kennis der ichthyologische fauna van Nias. Natuurkd. Tijdschr. Neder.-Indië v. 12: 211-228.
———. 1856 **[ref. 355]**. Nieuwe bijdrage tot de kennis der ichthyologische fauna van Bali. Natuurkd. Tijdschr. Neder.-Indië v. 12: 291-302.
———. 1856 **[ref. 311]**. Beschrijvningen van nieuwe en weinig bekende vischsoorten van Amboina, versameld op eene reis door den Molukschen Archipel gedaan in het gevolg van den Gouverneur-Generaal Duymaer van Twist, in September en Oktober 1855. Acta Soc. Sci. Indo-Neerl. v. 1: 1-76. [Also as a separate, Batavia, 1856.]
———. 1856 **[ref. 5118]**. Verslag van eenige verzamelingen van zee-en zoetwatervisschen van het eiland Banka. Natuurkd. Tijdschr. Neder.-Indië v. 11: 415-420. [Also as a separate, Batavia, 1856.]
———. 1857 **[ref. 356]**. Achtste bijdrage tot de kennis der vischfauna van Amboina. Acta Soc. Sci. Indo-Neerl. v. 2: 1-102.
———. 1857 **[ref. 358]**. Bijdrage tot de kennis der ichthyologische fauna van de Sangi-eilanden. Natuurkd. Tijdschr. Neder.-Indië v. 13: 369-380.
———. 1857 **[ref. 6220]**. Index descriptionum specierum piscium bleekerianarum in voluminibus I ad XIV diarii societatis scientiarum indo-Batavae. Natuurkd. Tijdschr. Neder.-Indië v. 14: 447-486.
———. 1858 **[ref. 359]**. Zesde bijdrage tot de kennis der vischfauna van Sumatra. Visschen van Padang, Troessan, Priaman, Sibogha en Palembang. Acta Soc. Sci. Indo-Neerl. v. 3: 1-50.
———. 1858 **[ref. 360]**. Vierde bijdrage tot de kennis der ich-

thyologische fauna van Japan. Acta Soc. Sci. Indo-Neerl. v. 3 (art. 10): 1-46. [Written Jan. 1857. Vol. is for 1858-59, year published is uncertain.]

——. 1858 **[ref. 361]**. Tiende bijdrage tot de kennis der vischfauna van Celebes. Acta Soc. Sci. Indo-Neerl. v. 3: 1-16. [Possibly published in 1857. Written Feb. 1857.]

——. 1858 **[ref. 362]**. Bijdrage tot de kennis der vischfauna van den Goram-Archipel. Natuurkd. Tijdschr. Neder.-Indië v. 15: 197-218.

——. 1858 **[ref. 363]**. Vierde bijdrage tot de kennis der vischfauna van Biliton. Natuurkd. Tijdschr. Neder.-Indië v. 15: 219-240.

——. 1858 **[ref. 364]**. Twaalfde bijdrage tot de kennis der vischfauna van Borneo. Visschen van Sinkawang. Acta Soc. Sci. Indo-Neerl. v. 5 (art. 7): 1-10. [Written Oct. 1857 and Mar. 1858. Published in vol. for 1858-59, year uncertain.]

——. 1858 **[ref. 365]**. De visschen van den Indischen Archipel. Siluri. Acta Soc. Sci. Indo-Neerl. [Also published as a separate: Ichthyologiae Archipelagi Indici Prodromus. Vol 1. Siluri. Batavia. i-xii + 1-370.]

——. 1859 **[ref. 366]**. [Over de geslachten der Cobitinen.] Natuurkd. Tijdschr. Neder.-Indië v. 16: 302-304.

——. 1859 **[ref. 367]**. [Vischsoorten gevangen bij Japara, verzameld door S. A. Thurkow.] Natuurkd. Tijdschr. Neder.-Indië v. 16: 406-409.

——. 1859 **[ref. 368]**. Over eenige vischsoorten van de Zuidkustwateren van Java. Natuurkd. Tijdschr. Neder.-Indië v. 19: 329-352.

——. 1859 **[ref. 369]**. [Vischsoorten van Siam, verzameld door Fr. de Castelnau.] Natuurkd. Tijdschr. Neder.-Indië v. 20: 101-102.

——. 1859 **[ref. 370]**. Conspectus systematis Cyprinorum. Natuurkd. Tijdschr. Neder.-Indië v. 20: 421-441. [Date may be 1860.]

——. 1859 **[ref. 371]**. Enumeratio specierum piscium hucusque in Archipelago indico observatarum, adjectis habitationibus citationibusque, ubi descriptiones earum recentiores reperiuntur, nec non speciebus Musei Bleekeriani Bengalensibus, Japonicis, Capensibus Tasmanicisque. Acta Soc. Sci. Indo-Neerl. v. 6: i-xxxvi + 1-276. [Date may be 1860.]

——. 1860 **[ref. 373]**. Over eenige vischsoorten van de Kaap de Goede Hoop. Natuurkd. Tijdschr. Neder.-Indië v. 21: 49-80.

——. 1860 **[ref. 374]**. Zesde bijdrage tot de kennis der vischfauna van Japan. Acta Soc. Sci. Indo-Neerl. v. 8: 1-104.

——. 1860 **[ref. 375]**. Achtste bijdrage tot de kennis der vischfauna van Sumatra (Visschen van Benkoelen, Priaman, Tandjong, Palembang en Djambi). Acta Soc. Sci. Indo-Neerl. v. 8 (art. 2): 1-88. [Written Aug. 1859.]

——. 1860 **[ref. 376]**. Negende bijdrage tot de kennis der vischfauna van Sumatra (Visschen uit de Lematang-Enim en van Benkoelen). Acta Soc. Sci. Indo-Neerl. v. 8 (art. 3): 1-12. [Written Feb.-Mar. 1860]

——. 1860 **[ref. 377]**. Dertiende bijdrage tot de kennis der vischfauna van Borneo. Acta Soc. Sci. Indo-Neerl. v. 8 (art. 4): 1-64. [Written Sept. 1859.]

——. 1860 **[ref. 378]**. Elfde bijdrage tot de kennis der vischfauna van Amboina. Acta Soc. Sci. Indo-Neerl. v. 8 (art. 5): 1-14. [Written Feb.-Sept. 1859.]

——. 1860 **[ref. 379]**. Dertiende bijdrage tot de kennis der vischfauna van Celebes (Visschen van Bonthain, Badjoa, Sindjai, Lagoesi en Pompenoea). Acta Soc. Sci. Indo-Neerl. v. 8 (art. 7): 1-60. [Written June 1860.]

——. 1860 **[ref. 380]**. De visschen van den Indischen Archipel, Beschreven en Toegelicht. Deel II. [Also:Ichthyologiae Archipelagi Indici Prodromus, Auct., Volumen II]. Cyprini. Ordo Cyprini. Karpers.] Acta Soc. Sci. Indo-Neerl. v. 7 (n. s., v. 2): 1-492 + i-xiii. [Also as a separate, Lange & Co., 1860.]

——. 1861 **[ref. 381]**. Iets over de geslachten der Scaroïden en hunne Indisch-archipelagische soorten. Versl. Akad. Amsterdam v. 12: 228-244.

——. 1861 **[ref. 383]**. Zesde bijdrage tot de kennis der vischfauna van Timor. Natuurkd. Tijdschr. Neder.-Indië v. 22: 247-261.

——. 1861 **[ref. 384]**. Notice sur le genre *Trachinus* (Artedi) et ses espèces. Ann. Sci. Nat. (Zool.) (Ser. 4) v. 16: 375-382. [Also as Bleeker 1862, Versl. Akad. Amsterdam v. 14: 113-122 [ref. 385].]

——. 1861 **[ref. 12601]**. Iets over de vischfauna van het eiland Pinang. Versl. Akad. Amsterdam v. 12: 64-80.

——. 1862 (Apr. 1862) **[ref. 382]**. Conspectus generum Labroideorum analyticus. Proc. Zool. Soc. Lond. 1861 (pt 3): 408-418. [Also appeared in different format as Bleeker 1862: 94-109 [ref. 386].]

——. 1862 **[ref. 385]**. Notice sur le genre *Trachinus* Art. et ses espèces. Versl. Akad. Amsterdam v. 14: 113-122. [Also as Bleeker 1861, Ann. Sci. Nat. 4 (Zool.) 16:375-382 [ref. 384].]

——. 1862 **[ref. 386]**. Conspectus generum Labroideorum analyticus. Versl. Akad. Amsterdam v. 13: 94-109. [Appeared in different format (apparently earlier) as Bleeker 1862 [ref. 382]; both articles written in Nov. 1861.]

——. 1862 **[ref. 387]**. Sixième memoire sur la fauna ichthyologique de l'île Batjan. Versl. Akad. Amsterdam v. 14: 99-112.

——. 1862 **[ref. 388]**. Sur quelques genres de la famille des Pleuronectoïdes. Versl. Akad. Amsterdam v. 13: 422-429.

——. 1862 **[ref. 389]**. Notices ichthyologiques (I-X). Versl. Akad. Amsterdam v. 14: 123-141.

——. 1862 **[ref. 390]**. Descriptions de quelques espèces nouvelles de Silures de Surinam. Versl. Akad. Amsterdam v. 14: 371-389.

——. 1862 **[ref. 391]**. Notice sur les genres *Parasilurus*, *Eutropiichthys*, *Pseudeutropius*, et *Pseudopangasius*. Versl. Akad. Amsterdam v. 14: 390-399.

——. 1862 **[ref. 392]**. Notice sur les genres *Trachelyopterichthys*, *Hemicetopsis* et *Pseudocetopsis*. Versl. Akad. Amsterdam v. 14: 400-403.

——. 1862-63 **[ref. 393]**. Atlas ichthyologique des Indes Orientales Néêrlandaises, publié sous les auspices du Gouvernement colonial néêrlandais. Tome II. Siluroïdes, Chacoïdes et Hétérobranchoïdes. Amsterdam. 1-112, Pls. 49-101. [Text published 1862-1863, plates published 1862-1863 (see Boeseman 1983: 4 [ref. 12564]).]

——. 1862-63 **[ref. 4858]**. Atlas ichthyologique des Indes Orientales Néêrlandaises, publié sous les auspices du Gouvernement colonial néêrlandais. Tome I. Scaroïdes et Labroïdes. Nos. 1-6 and 9: i-xxi + 1-168, Pls. 1-48. [Text published in 1862-1863, plates published in 1862 (see Boeseman 1983:4 [ref. 12564]).]

——. 1863 **[ref. 395]**. Mémoire sur les poissons de la côte de Guinée. Natuurk. Verh. Holland. Maatsch. Wet. Haarlem (Ser. 2) v. 18: 1-136, col. Pls. 1-28. [Also published as a separate, with date of 1862. Written Jan. 1862.]

——. 1863 **[ref. 396]**. Description de quelques espèces de poissons, nouvelles ou peu connues de Chine, envoyées au Musée de Leide par M.-G. Schlegel. Neder. Tijdschr. Dierk. v. 1: 135-150.

——. 1863 **[ref. 397]**. Systema Cyprinoideorum revisum. Neder. Tijdschr. Dierk. v. 1: 187-218. [Also as separate, pp. 1-32.]

——. 1863 **[ref. 398]**. Onzième notice sur la faune ichthyologique de l'île de Ternate. Neder. Tijdschr. Dierk. v. 1: 228-238.

——. 1863 **[ref. 399]**. Septième mémoire sur la faune ichthyologique de l'île de Timor. Neder. Tijdschr. Dierk. v. 1: 262-276.

——. 1863 **[ref. 400]**. Sur les genres de la famille des Cobitioïdes. Versl. Akad. Amsterdam v. 15: 32-44. [Also published in Ned. Tijdschr. Dierk, 1863, v. 1: 361-368.]

——. 1863 **[ref. 401]**. Systema Silurorum revisum. Neder. Tijdschr. Dierk. v. 1: 77-122.

——. 1863 **[ref. 402]**. Deuxième notice sur la faune ichthyologique de l'île de Flores. Neder. Tijdschr. Dierk. v. 1: 248-252.

——. 1863 **[ref. 403]**. Notice sur les noms de quelques genres de la famille des Cyprinoïdes. Versl. Akad. Amsterdam v. 15: 261-264.

——. 1863 **[ref. 12572]**. Beschrijving en afbeelding van eene nieuwe soort van Brama (*Abramis*). Versl. Akad. Amsterdam v. 15: 235-238, 1 col pl. [Also as Neder. Tijdschr. Dierk. v. 1:373-380.]

——. 1863 **[ref. 12600]**. Dixième notice sur la faune ichthyologique de l'île de Ternate. Versl. Akad. Amsterdam v. 15: 265-266.

——. 1863 **[ref. 13458]**. Septième notice sur la faune ichthyologi-

que de l'île de Céram. Neder. Tijdschr. Dierk. v. 1: 153-261.
———. 1863-64 [**ref. 4859**]. Atlas ichthyologique des Indes Orientales Néerlandaises, publiés sous les auspices du Gouvernement colonial néerlandais. Tome III. Cyprins. Nos. 11-14: 1-150, Pls. 102-144 (in parts 9-12). [Text published 1863-1864, plates published 1863-1864 (see Boeseman 1983: 4 [ref. 12564]).]
———. 1864 [**ref. 404**]. Notice sur la faune ichthyologique de Siam. Versl. Akad. Amsterdam v. 16: 352-358, 1 pl.
———. 1864-65 [**ref. 4860**]. Atlas ichthyologique des Indes Orientales Néêrlandaises, publié sous les auspices du Gouvernement colonial néêrlandaises. Tome IV. Murènes, Synbranches, Leptocéphales. 1-150, Pls. 145-193. [Text published 1864-1865, plates published 1864-1865 (see Boeseman 1983: 4 [ref. 12564]).]
———. 1865 [**ref. 405**]. *Rhinobagrus* et *Pelteobagrus*, deux genres nouveaux de Siluroïdes de Chine. Neder. Tijdschr. Dierk. v. 2: 7-10.
———. 1865 [**ref. 406**]. *Paralaubuca*, un genre nouveau de Cyprinoïdes de Siam. Neder. Tijdschr. Dierk. v. 2: 15-17.
———. 1865 [**ref. 407**]. Notices sur quelques genres et espèces de Cyprinoïdes de Chine. Neder. Tijdschr. Dierk. v. 2: 18-29.
———. 1865 [**ref. 408**]. Poissons inédits indo-archipélagiques de l'ordre des Murènes. Neder. Tijdschr. Dierk. v. 2: 38-54.
———. 1865 [**ref. 409**]. Systema Muraenorum revisum. Neder. Tijdschr. Dierk. v. 2: 113-122.
———. 1865 [**ref. 410**]. Quatrième notice sur la faune ichthyologique de l'île de Bouro. Neder. Tijdschr. Dierk. v. 2: 141-151.
———. 1865 [**ref. 411**]. Notice sur le genre *Paraploactis* et description de son espèce type. Neder. Tijdschr. Dierk. v. 2: 168-170.
———. 1865 [**ref. 412**]. Description de quelques espèces de poissons du Japon, du Cap de Bonne Espérance et de Suriname, conservées au Musée de Leide. Neder. Tijdschr. Dierk. v. 2: 250-269.
———. 1865 [**ref. 413**]. Sixième notice sur la faune ichthyologique de Siam. Neder. Tijdschr. Dierk. v. 2: 171-176.
———. 1865 [**ref. 414**]. Enumération des espèces de poissons actuellement connues de l'île de Céram. Neder. Tijdschr. Dierk. v. 2: 182-193.
———. 1865 [**ref. 415**]. Enumération des espèces de poissons actuellement connues de l'île d'Amboine. Neder. Tijdschr. Dierk. v. 2: 270-276, 273-293 [four pages repeated].
———. 1865-69 [**ref. 416**]. Atlas ichthyologique des Indes Orientales Néêrlandaises, publié sous les auspices du Gouvernement colonial néêrlandais. Tome V. Baudroies, Ostracions, Gymnodontes, Balistes. 1-152, Pls. 194-231. [Text published 1865-1869, plates published in 1865 (see Boeseman 1983: 4 [ref. 12564]).]
———. 1866 [**ref. 417**]. Systema Balistidorum, Ostracionidorum, Gymnodontidorumque revisum. Neder. Tijdschr. Dierk. v. 3: 8-19. [As separate, pp. 1-12. Note: Not same paper as Bleeker 1866 "Synonyma Balistidorum..."]
———. 1866 [**ref. 418**]. Sur les espèces d'Exocet de l'Inde Archipélagique. Neder. Tijdschr. Dierk. v. 3: 105-129.
———. 1866 [**ref. 419**]. Révision des Hémirhamphes de l'Inde archipélagique. Neder. Tijdschr. Dierk. v. 3: 136-170.
———. 1866 [**ref. 420**]. Description du *Narcacion Polleni*, espèce inédite des mers de l'île de la Réunion. Neder. Tijdschr. Dierk. v. 3: 171-173.
———. 1868 [**ref. 421**]. Troisème notice sur la faune ichthyologique de l'île d'Obi. Versl. Akad. Amsterdam (Ser. 2) v. 2: 275.
———. 1868 [**ref. 422**]. Cinquième notice sur la faune ichthyologique de l'île de Solor. Versl. Akad. Amsterdam (Ser. 2) v. 2: 283-288.
———. 1868 [**ref. 423**]. Notice sur la faune ichthyologique de l'île Waigiou. Versl. Akad. Amsterdam (Ser. 2) v. 2: 295-301.
———. 1868 [**ref. 424**]. Description de trois espèces inédites de Chromidöides de Madagascar. Versl. Akad. Amsterdam (Ser. 2) v. 2: 307-314.
———. 1868 [**ref. 425**]. Description de trois espèces inédites des poissons des îles d'Amboine et de Waigiou. Versl. Akad. Amsterdam (Ser. 2) v. 2: 331-335, 1 pl.
———. 1869 [**ref. 426**]. Description de deux espèces inédites s'-Alticus de Madagascar. Versl. Akad. Amsterdam (Ser. 2) v. 3: 234-236.
———. 1869 [**ref. 427**]. Neuvième notice sur la faune ichthyologique du Japon. Versl. Akad. Amsterdam (Ser. 2) v. 3: 237-252.
———. 1870 [**ref. 429**]. Mededeeling omtrent eenige nieuwe vischsoorten van China. Versl. Akad. Amsterdam (Ser. 2) v. 4: 251-253.
———. 1870 [**ref. 5871**]. Description d'une espèce inédite de *Botia* de Chine et figures du *Botia elongata* et du *Botia modesta*. Versl. Akad. Amsterdam (Ser. 2) v. 4: 254-256.
———. 1870-75 [**ref. 428**]. Atlas ichthyologique des Indes Orientales Néêrlandaises, publiés sous les auspices du Gouvernement colonial néêrlandais. Tome VI. Pleuronectes, Scombrésoces, Clupées, Clupésoces, Chauliodontes, Saurides. 1-170, Pls. 232-278. [Text published 1870-1875, plates published 1865-1871 (see Boeseman 1983: 4 [ref. 12564]).]
———. 1871 [**ref. 6421**]. Mémoire sur les cyprinoïdes de Chine. Verh. Akad. Amsterdam v. 12: 1-91. [Also as a separate, 1871.]
———. 1871-76 [**ref. 4861**]. Atlas ichthyologique des Indes Orientales Néêrlandaises, publié sous les auspices du Gouvernement colonial néêrlandais. Tome VII. Percoides I, Priacanthiformes, Serraniformes, Grammisteiformes, Percaeformes, Datniaeformes. 1-126, Pls. 279-320. [Text published 1875-1876, plates published 1871-1875 (see Boeseman 1983: 4 [ref. 12564]).]
———. 1873 [**ref. 431**]. Mémoire sur la faune ichthyologique de Chine. Neder. Tijdschr. Dierk. v. 4: 113-154.
———. 1873 [**ref. 432**]. Révision des espèces indo-archipélagiques du groupe des Anthianini. Neder. Tijdschr. Dierk. v. 4: 155-169.
———. 1873 [**ref. 433**]. Mededeelingen omtrent eene herziening der Indisch-Archipelagische soorten van *Epinephelus*, *Lutjanus*, *Dentex* en verwante geslachten. Versl. Akad. Amsterdam (Ser. 2) v. 7: 40-46.
———. 1873 [**ref. 434**]. Sur le genre *Parapristipoma* et sur l'identité spécifique des *Perca trilineata* Thunb., *Pristipoma japonicum* CV. et *Diagramma japonicum* Blkr. Arch. Neerl. Sci. Nat., Haarlem v. 8: 19-24, 1 col. pl.
———. 1873 [**ref. 12588**]. Révision des espèces insulindiennes du genre *Therapon*. Neder. Tijdschr. Dierk. v. 4: 372-393.
———. 1873 [**ref. 12596**]. Sur les especès indo-archipélagiques d'*Odontanthias* et de *Pseudopriacanthus*. Neder. Tijdschr. Dierk. v. 4: 235-240. [Also as a separate, pp. 1-6, possibly published in 1872.]
———. 1873 [**ref. 13527**]. Révision des espèces indo-archipélagiques du genre *Caesio* et de quelques genres voisins. Arch. Néerl. Sc. Nat. v. 8: 155-182.
———. 1874 [**ref. 435**]. Typi nonnulli generici piscium neglecti. Versl. Akad. Amsterdam (Ser. 2) v. 8: 367-371.
———. 1874 [**ref. 436**]. Notice sur les genres *Amblyeleotris*, *Valenciennesia* et *Brachyeleotris*. Versl. Akad. Amsterdam (Ser. 2) v. 8: 372-376.
———. 1874 [**ref. 437**]. Esquisse d'un système naturel des Gobioïdes. Arch. Neerl. Sci. Nat., Haarlem v. 9: 289-331.
———. 1874 [**ref. 438**]. Révision des espèces d'*Ambassis* et de *Parambassis* de l'Inde archipélagique. Natuurk. Verh. Holland. Maatsch. Wet. Haarlem (Ser. 3) v. 2 (no. 2): 83-106. [Also as a separate, pp. 1-23.]
———. 1874 [**ref. 439**]. Révision des espèces insulindiennes de la famille des Synancéoïdes. Natuurk. Verh. Holland. Maatsch. Wet. Haarlem (Ser. 3) v. 2 (no. 3): 1-22, Color pls. 1-4.
———. 1874 [**ref. 5110**]. Révision des espèces indo-archipélagiques du groupe des Epinephelini et de quelques genres voisins. Verh. Akad. Amsterdam v. 14: 1-134.
———. 1874 [**ref. 5120**]. Révision des espèces indo-archipélagiques du groupe des Apogonini. Natuurk. Verh. Holland. Maatsch. Wet. Haarlem (Ser. 3) v. 2 (no. 1): 1-82.
———. 1874 [**ref. 12517**]. Mémoire sur les Sciénoïdes et les Sillaginoïdes de l'Inde archipélagique. Verh. Akad. Amsterdam v. 14: 1-76.
———. 1875 [**ref. 440**]. Notice sur les Eleotriformes et description de trois espèces nouvelles. Arch. Neerl. Sci. Nat., Haarlem v. 10:

101-112.
——. 1875 **[ref. 441]**. Description du genre *Parascorpis* et du son espèce type. Arch. Neerl. Sci. Nat., Haarlem v. 10: 380-382.
——. 1875 **[ref. 443]**. Poissons de Madagascar et de l'Ile la Réunion des collections de MM. Pollen et Van Dam. In: Recherches sur la faune de Madagascar et de ses dépendances d'après les découvertes de François P. L. Pollen et D. C. van Dam. Leide. Part 4: 1-104 + 2 p. index. [Date of 1874 on cover of copy at California Academy of Sciences.]
——. 1875 **[ref. 444]**. Sur la famille des Pseudochromidoïdes et révision de ses espèces insulindiennes. Versl. Akad. Amsterdam v. 15: 1-32.
——. 1875 **[ref. 12526]**. Sur les espèces insulindiennes de la famille des Cirrhitéoïdes. Verh. Akad. Amsterdam v. 15: 1-20. [Date of 1874 on cover of separate.]
——. 1875 **[ref. 12599]**. Gobioideorum species insulindicae novae. Arch. Néerl. Sc. Nat. v. 10: 113-134.
——. 1875-76 **[ref. 4862]**. Atlas ichthyologique des Indes Orientales Néêrlandaises, publié sous les auspices du Gouvernement colonial néêrlandais. Tome VIII. Percoides II, (Spariformes), Bogodoides, Cirrhitéoides. 1-156, Pls. 321-354, 361-362. [Text published 1875-1876, plates published 1875-1876 (see Boeseman 1983: 4 [ref. 12564]).]
——. 1875-78 **[ref. 6835]**. Atlas ichthyologique des Indes Orientales Néêrlandaises, publié sous les auspices du Gouvernement colonial néêrlandais. Tome IX. Toxotoidei, Pempheridoidei, Chaetodontoidei, Nandoidei, etc. v. 9: 1-80, Pls. 355-360, 363-420. [Text published 1877-1878, plates published 1875-1878 (see Boeseman 1983: 4 [ref. 12564]).]
——. 1876 **[ref. 442]**. Révision des Sicydiini et Latrunculini de l'Insulinde. Versl. Akad. Amsterdam (Ser. 2) v. 9: 271-293.
——. 1876 **[ref. 445]**. Notice sur les genres *Gymnocaesio*, *Pterocaesio*, *Paracaesio* et *Lioceasio*. Versl. Akad. Amsterdam (Ser. 2) v. 9: 149-154.
——. 1876 **[ref. 447]**. Systema Percarum revisum. Pars I. Arch. Neerl. Sci. Nat., Haarlem v. 11: 247-288.
——. 1876 **[ref. 448]**. Systema Percarum revisum. Pars II. Arch. Neerl. Sci. Nat., Haarlem v. 11: 289-340.
——. 1876 **[ref. 449]**. Description de quelques espèces insulindiennes inédites des genres *Oxyurichthys*, *Paroxyurichthys* et *Cryptocentrus*. Versl. Akad. Amsterdam (Ser. 2) v. 9: 138-148.
——. 1876 **[ref. 450]**. Genera familiae Scorpaenoideorum conspectus analyticus. Versl. Akad. Amsterdam (Ser. 2) v. 9: 294-300.
——. 1876 **[ref. 451]**. Notice sur les genres et sur les espèces des Chétodontoïdes de la sous-famille des Taurichthyiformes. Versl. Akad. Amsterdam (Ser. 2) v. 10: 308-320.
——. 1876 **[ref. 12248]**. Mémoire sur les espèces insulidiennes de la famille des Scorpénoïdes. Versl. Akad. Amsterdam v. 16: 1-100.
——. 1877 **[ref. 452]**. Description de quelques espèces inédites de Pomacentroïdes de l'Inde archipélagique. Versl. Akad. Amsterdam (Ser. 2) v. 10: 384-391. [Written Dec. 1876, assume published in 1877, but 1876 on jacket to volume.]
——. 1877 **[ref. 453]**. Notice sur les espèces nominales de Pomacentroïdes de l'Inde archipélagique. Arch. Neerl. Sci. Nat., Haarlem v. 12: 38-41 [in extract as 22-25].
——. 1877 **[ref. 454]**. Mémoire sur les chromides marins ou pomacentroïdes de l'Inde archipélagique. Natuurk. Verh. Holland. Maatsch. Wet. Haarlem (Ser. 3) v. 2 (no. 6): 1-166. [Several genera attributed to this work may be predated by Bleeker 1877: 38-41 [ref. 453].]
——. 1878 **[ref. 455]**. Sur deux espèces inédites de Cichloides de Madagascar. Versl. Akad. Amsterdam (Ser. 2) v. 12: 192-198, Pl. 3.
——. 1878 **[ref. 456]**. Quatrième mémoire sur la faune ichthyologique de la Nouvelle-Guinée. Arch. Neerl. Sci. Nat., Haarlem v. 13: 35-66, Pls. 1-2.
——. 1879 **[ref. 457]**. Mémoire sur les poissons à pharyngiens labyrinthiformes de l'Inde archipélagique. Versl. Akad. Amsterdam v. 19: 1-56.
——. 1879 **[ref. 458]**. Révision des espèces insulindiennes de la famille des Callionymoïdes. Versl. Akad. Amsterdam (Ser. 2) v. 14: 79-107.
——. 1879 **[ref. 459]**. Sur quelques espèces inédites ou peu connues de poissons de Chine appartenant au Muséum de Hambourg. Versl. Akad. Amsterdam v. 18: 1-17.
——. 1879 **[ref. 460]**. Énumerátion des espèces de poissons actuellement connues du Japon et description de trois espèces inédites. Versl. Akad. Amsterdam v. 18: 1-33, Pls. 1-3.
——. 1880 **[ref. 461]**. Musei Hamburgensis. Species piscium novas minusque cognitas descripsit et depingi curavit. Abh. Geb. Naturwiss. Ver. Hamburg v. 7 (Abt. 1): 25-30, Pl. 5.
Blegvad, H., and B. Løppenthin. 1944 **[ref. 462]**. Fishes of the Iranian Gulf. Danish Scient. Invest. Iran, Einar Munksgaard, Copenhagen. 1-247, Pl. 1-11.
Bloch, M. E. 1785 **[ref. 4866]**. Naturgeschichte der ausländischen Fische. Berlin. v. 1: i-viii + 1-136, Pls. 109-144. [Also a combined edition of two volumes, v. 1-4 in I, 5-9 in II.]
——. 1785-95 **[ref. 5123]**. Naturgeschichte der ausländischen Fische. Berlin. Parts 1-9 + Atlas. Also issued as parts 4-12 as "Allgemeine Naturgeschichte der Fische." [v. 1 (1785), v. 2 (1786), v. 3 (1787), v. 4 (1790), v. 5 (1791), v. 6 (1792), v. 7 (1793), v. 8 (1794), v. 9 (1795).]
——. 1786 **[ref. 465]**. Naturgeschichte der ausländischen Fische. Berlin. v. 2: i-viii + 1-160, Pls. 145-180.
——. 1787 **[ref. 468]**. Naturgeschichte der ausländischen Fische. Berlin. v. 3: i-xii + 1-146, Pls. 181-216.
——. 1788 **[ref. 466]**. Ueber zwey merkwürdige Fischarten. Abh. Böhm. Ges. Wissen. v. 3 [for 1787]: 278-282, 2 pls. [Apparently published in 1788.]
——. 1788 **[ref. 467]**. Charactere und Beschreibung des Geschelechts der Papageyfische, *Callyodon*. Abh. Böhm. Ges. Wissen. v. 4: 242-248, 3 pls.
——. 1790 **[ref. 469]**. Naturgeschichte der ausländischen Fische. Berlin. v. 4: i-xii + 1-128, Pls. 217-252.
——. 1791 **[ref. 4867]**. Naturgeschichte der ausländischen Fische. Berlin. v. 5: i-viii + 1-152, Pls. 253-288.
——. 1791 **[ref. 6882]**. Sur les Gastrobranchus, nouveau genre de poisson. Schr. Ges. Naturf. Freunde Berlin v. 10: 1-26. [Abstract by Cuvier & Valenciennes 1791 in Bull. Soc. Philom. Paris, v. 1: 26.]
——. 1792 **[ref. 470]**. Naturgeschichte der ausländischen Fische. Berlin. v. 6: i-xii + 1-126, Pls. 289-323.
——. 1793 **[ref. 4868]**. Naturgeschichte der ausländischen Fische. Berlin. v. 7: i-xiv + 1-144, Pls. 325-360.
——. 1794 **[ref. 463]**. Naturgeschichte der ausländischen Fische. Berlin. v. 8: i-iv + 1-174, Pls. 361-396.
——. 1795 **[ref. 464]**. Naturgeschichte der ausländischen Fische. Berlin. v. 9: i-ii + 1-192, Pls. 397-429.
Bloch, M. E., and J. G. Schneider. 1801 **[ref. 471]**. M. E. Blochii, Systema Ichthyologiae iconibus cx illustratum. Post obitum auctoris opus inchoatum absolvit, correxit, interpolavit Jo. Gottlob Schneider, Saxo. Berolini. Sumtibus Austoris Impressum et Bibliopolio Sanderiano Commissum. i-lx + 1-584, Pls. 1-110.
Blyth, E. 1858 **[ref. 476]**. Report of the Curator, Zoological Department, for May, 1858. J. Asiat. Soc. Bengal v. 27 (no. 3): 267-290. [Fishes are discussed on pp. 270-272 and 281-290.]
——. 1860 **[ref. 477]**. Report on some fishes received chiefly from the Sitang River and its tributary streams, Tenasserim Provinces. J. Asiat. Soc. Bengal v. 29 (no. 2): 138-174.
Bocage, J. V. B. du, and F. de B. Capello. 1864 (Nov.) **[ref. 479]**. Sur quelque espèces inédites de Squalidae de la tribu Acanthiana, Gray, qui fréquentent les côtes du Portugal. Proc. Zool. Soc. Lond. pt. 2: 260-263. [ZR 1864 gives June 14 as date.]
Bocourt, F. 1869 **[ref. 486]**. Descriptions de quelques reptiles et poissons nouveaux appartenant à la faune tropicale de l'Amérique. Nouv. Arch. Mus. Natl. Hist. Nat. Paris v. 5: 19-24. [Checked from reprint. Date may be 1868.]
Boeseman, M. 1957 (29 May) **[ref. 487]**. On a collection of East

Asian fishes. Zool. Meded. (Leiden) v. 35 (no. 7): 69-78, Pl. 3.

——. 1964 **[ref. 488]**. Notes on the fishes of western New Guinea II. *Lophichthys boschmai*, a new genus and species from the Arafoera Sea. Zool. Meded. (Leiden) v. 39: 12-18, Pl. 1.

——. 1966 **[ref. 489]**. A new sisorid catfish from Java, *Sundagagata robusta* gen. et spec. nov. Proc. K. Ned. Akad. Wet. (Ser. C, Zool.) v. 69 (no. 2): 242-247 + table.

——. 1971 (12 July) **[ref. 490]**. The "comb-toothed" Loricariinae of Surinam, with reflections on the phylogenetic tendencies within the family Loricariidae (Siluriformes, Siluroidei). Zool. Verh. (Leiden) No. 116: 1-56, Pls. 1-8.

——. 1973 **[ref. 7161]**. Hexanchidae (pp. 8-9), Chlamydoselachidae (p. 10). In: Hureau & Monod 1973 [ref. 6590].

——. 1976 (29 Dec.) **[ref. 6991]**. A short review of the Surinam Loricariinae; with additional information on Surinam Harttiinae, including the description of a new species (Loricariidae, Siluriformes). Zool. Meded. (Leiden) v. 50 (no. 11): 153-177, Pls. 1-8.

——. 1982 (22 Mar.) **[ref. 492]**. The South American mailed catfish genus *Lithoxus* Eigenmann, 1910, with the description of three new species from Surinam and French Guyana and records of related species (Siluriformes, Loricariidae). Proc. K. Ned. Akad. Wet. (Ser. C) Biol. Med. Sci. v. 85 (no.1): 41-58.

——. 1983 (30 Sept.) **[ref. 5329]**. Some remarks on the South American pimelodid catfish usually known by the name of *Phractocephalus hemiliopterus* (Bloch & Schneider) (Pimelodidae, Siluriformes). Zool. Meded. (Leiden) v. 57 (no. 12): 105-114.

——. 1983 **[ref. 12564]**. Introduction (pp. 1-12). In: Atlas Ichthyologique des Indes Orientales Néêrlandaises, par M.- P. Bleeker. (Reproduction for the first time of plates originally prepared for unpublished Tomes XI-XIV.) Smithsonian Institution Press. 1-22, col. Pls. 421-575.

Boewe, C. 1982 **[ref. 6030]**. Fitzpatrick's Rafinesque: A sketch of his life with bibliography. Revised and enlarged by Charles Boewe. M & S Press, Weston, Massachusetts. i-vi + 1-327.

Boghdanov, M. N. 1882 **[ref. 499]**. [Sketch of the expeditions and natural history investigations in the Aral-Caspian region from 1720 to 1874.] [Not seen.]

Bogutskaya, N. G. 1987 **[ref. 13521]**. Morphological characters of some groups of genera of the subfamily Leuciscinae. Voprosy Ikhtiol. v. 27 (no. 6): 936-944. [In Russian. English translation in J. Ichthyol. 1988, v. 28 (no. 3): 26-34.]

——. 1988 **[ref. 12754]**. The limits and morphological features of cyprinid subfamily Leuciscinae. Proc. Zool. Inst. Leningrad; Syst. Morph. Ecol. Fishes v. 181: 96-113. [In Russian, brief English Summ.]

Böhlke, E. B. 1984 **[ref. 13621]**. Catalog of type specimens in the ichthyological colletion of the Academy of Natural Sciences of Philadelphia. Acad. Nat. Sci. Philad. Spec. Publ. 14: i-viii + 1-246.

——. 1989 (Sept.) **[ref. 13282]**. (ed.) Volume One: Orders Anguilliformes and Saccopharyngiformes. Volume Two: Leptocephali. Fishes of the Western North Atlantic. Number 1. Sears Found. Mar. Res., Yale Univ. Part 9: v. 1:i-xvii + 1-655; 2:i-vii + 657-1055.

Böhlke, E. B., and J. E. McCosker. 1982 (30 Dec.) **[ref. 502]**. *Monopenchelys*, a new eel genus, and redescription of the type species, *Uropterygius acutus* Parr (Pisces: Muraenidae). Proc. Acad. Nat. Sci. Phila. v. 134: 127-134.

Böhlke, E. B., J. E. McCosker and J. E. Böhlke. 1989 **[ref. 13286]**. Family Muraenidae (pp. 104-206). In: Böhlke, E. B. (ed.) 1989 [ref. 13282].

Böhlke, J. E. 1951 (27 Dec.) **[ref. 591]**. *Meadia*, a new genus for the West Pacific dysommid eel, *Dysomma abyssale* Kamohara. Stanford Ichthyol. Bull. v. 4 (no. 1): 6.

——. 1952 (Aug.) **[ref. 592]**. Studies on fishes of the family Characidae. No. 1. A new genus of Cheirodontine characids from the Canal de Casiquiare and adjacent waters in Venezuela and northern Brazil. Ann. Mag. Nat. Hist. (Ser. 12) v. 5 (no. 56): 775-777.

——. 1952 **[ref. 13618]**. Studies on fishes of the family Characidae. No. 2. The identity of the South American characid fish genus *Distoechus* Gomez. Ann. Mag. Nat. Hist. (Ser. 12) v. 5: 793-795.

——. 1953 (31 July) **[ref. 593]**. A minute new herring-like characid fish genus adapted for plankton feeding, from the Rio Negro. Stanford Ichthyol. Bull. v. 5: 168-170.

——. 1954 (23 Aug.) **[ref. 594]**. Studies on fishes of the family Characidae. No. 7. A new genus and species of glandulocaudine characids from Central Brazil. Stanford Ichthyol. Bull. v. 4 (no. 4): 265-274.

——. 1955 (19 Oct.) **[ref. 595]**. A new genus and species of ophichthid eels from the Bahamas. Not. Nat. (Phila.) No. 282: 1-7.

——. 1956 (3 Oct.) **[ref. 596]**. A small collection of new eels from western Puerto Rico. Not. Nat. (Phila.) No. 289: 1-13.

——. 1957 (12 Apr.) **[ref. 597]**. A new shallow-water brotulid fish from the Great Bahama Bank. Not. Nat. (Phila.) No. 295: 1-8.

——. 1957 (26 July) **[ref. 598]**. On the occurrence of garden eels in the western Atlantic, with a synopsis of the Heterocongrinae. Proc. Acad. Nat. Sci. Phila. v. 109: 59-79, Pl. 4.

——. 1957 (26 July) **[ref. 599]**. A review of the blenny genus *Chaenopsis*, and the description of a related new genus from the Bahamas. Proc. Acad. Nat. Sci. Phila. v. 109: 81-103, Pls. 5-6.

——. 1958 (21 Feb.) **[ref. 600]**. Substitute names for *Nystactes* Böhlke and *Lucaya* Böhlke, preoccupied. Copeia 1958 (no. 1): 59.

——. 1959 (29 May) **[ref. 601]**. Results of the Catherwood Foundation Peruvian Amazon Expedition. *Petacara*, a new genus for the bunocephalid catfish, *Bunocephalus dolichurus* Delsman. Not. Nat. (Phila.) No. 318: 1-6. [Also in Copeia 1958, pp. 318-325]

——. 1960 (25 Mar.) **[ref. 5941]**. Comments on serranoid fishes with disjunct lateral lines, with the description of a new one from the Bahamas. Not. Nat. (Phila.) No. 330: 1-11.

——. 1966 **[ref. 5256]**. Order Lyomeri (pp 603-628). In: Fishes of the Western North Atlantic. Mem. Sears Found. Mar. Res. No. 1 (pt 5).

——. 1967 (27 Jan.) **[ref. 602]**. The descriptions of three new eels from the tropical west Atlantic. Proc. Acad. Nat. Sci. Phila. v. 118: 91-108.

——. 1968 (8 July) **[ref. 604]**. The descriptions of three new stargazers (Dactyloscopidae) from the tropical west Atlantic. Not. Nat. (Phila.) No. 414: 1-16.

——. 1969 (5 June) **[ref. 5128]**. *Pariah scotius*, a new sponge-dwelling gobiid fish from the Bahamas. Not. Nat. (Phila.) No. 421: 1-7.

——. 1970 (31 Dec.) **[ref. 7150]**. A new species of the doradid catfish genus *Leptodoras*, with comments on related forms. Proc. Calif. Acad. Sci. v. 38 (no. 3): 53-62.

——. 1980 (19 Dec.) **[ref. 605]**. *Gelanoglanis stroudi*: a new catfish from the Rio Meta system in Colombia (Siluriformes, Doradidae, Auchenipterinae). Proc. Acad. Nat. Sci. Phila. v. 132: 150-155.

Böhlke, J. E., and D. M. Cohen. 1966 (30 Dec.) **[ref. 606]**. A new shallow-water ophidioid fish from the tropical west Atlantic. Not. Nat. (Phila.) No. 396: 1-7.

Böhlke, J. E., and J. E. McCosker. 1975 (28 Apr.) **[ref. 607]**. The status of the ophichthid eel genera *Caecula* Vahl and *Sphagebranchus* Bloch, and the description of a new genus and species from fresh waters in Brazil. Proc. Acad. Nat. Sci. Phila. v. 127 (no. 1): 1-11.

Böhlke, J. E., and N. A. Menezes. 1977 (25 Nov.) **[ref. 5524]**. The ophichthid eel, *Antobrantia ribeiroi* Pinto 1970 a synonym of *Ophichthus ophis* (Linnaeus 1758). Copeia 1977 (no. 4): 786.

Böhlke, J. E., and G. S. Myers. 1956 (23 May) **[ref. 608]**. Studies on fishes of the family Characidae.—No. 11. A new genus and species of hemiodontins from the Rio Orinoco in Venezuela. Not. Nat. (Phila.) No. 286: 1-6.

Böhlke, J. E., and C. H. Robins. 1974 (29 July) **[ref. 611]**. Description of new genus and species of clinid fish from the western Caribbean, with comments on the families of the Blennioidea. Proc. Acad. Nat. Sci. Phila. v. 126 (no. 1): 1-8.

Böhlke, J. E., and C. R. Robins. 1968 (9 July) **[ref. 609]**. Western Atlantic seven-spined gobies, with descriptions of ten new species and a new genus, and comments on Pacific relatives. Proc. Acad. Nat. Sci. Phila. v. 120: 45-174.

——. 1970 (22 Dec.) **[ref. 610]**. A new genus and species of deep-dwelling clingfish from the Lesser Antilles. Not. Nat. (Phila.) No. 434: 1-12.

Böhlke, J. E., and W. G. Saul. 1975 (15 Oct.) **[ref. 7109]**. The characid fish genus *Creagrudite* Myers a synonym of *Creagrutus* Günther, with the description of a new species from Amazonian Ecuador. Proc. Acad. Nat. Sci. Phila. v. 127 (no. 3): 25-28.

Böhlke, J. E., and D. G. Smith. 1967 (22 Nov.) **[ref. 612]**. A new xenocongrid eel from the western Indian and western Atlantic oceans. Not. Nat. (Phila.) No. 408: 1-6.

——. 1968 (26 June) **[ref. 614]**. A new xenocongrid eel from the Bahamas, with notes on other species in the family. Proc. Acad. Nat. Sci. Phila. v. 120: 25-43.

Böhlke, J. E., and V. G. Springer. 1975 (28 Oct.) **[ref. 615]**. A new genus and species of fish (*Nemaclinus atelestos*) from the western Atlantic (Perciformes: Clinidae). Proc. Acad. Nat. Sci. Phila. v. 127 (no. 7): 57-61.

Bolin, R. L. 1936 (15 June) **[ref. 504]**. Two new cottid fishes from the western Pacific, with a revision of the genus *Stlengis* Jordan & Starks. Proc. U. S. Natl. Mus. v. 83 (no. 2987): 325-334, Pl. 34.

——. 1936 (10 Oct.) **[ref. 505]**. New cottid fishes from Japan and Bering Sea. Proc. U. S. Natl. Mus. v. 84 (no. 3000): 25-38.

——. 1936 (15 Nov.) **[ref. 506]**. A revision of the genus *Icelinus* Jordan. Copeia 1936 (no. 3): 151-159.

——. 1939 (9 Mar.) **[ref. 507]**. A new stomiatoid fish from California. Copeia 1939 (no. 1): 39-41.

——. 1939 (24 May) **[ref. 508]**. A review of the myctophid fishes of the Pacific coast of the United States and of Lower California. Stanford Ichthyol. Bull. v. 1 (no. 4): 89-156.

——. 1944 (27 Oct.) **[ref. 6379]**. A review of the marine cottid fishes of California. Stanford Ichthyol. Bull. v. 3 (no. 1): 1-135.

——. 1946 (31 May) **[ref. 509]**. Lantern fishes from "Investigator" station 670, Indian Ocean. Stanford Ichthyol. Bull. v. 3 (no. 2): 137-152. [Copy received by Calif. Academy of Sciences, 23 May.]

——. 1950 (5 Sept.) **[ref. 510]**. Remarks on cottid fishes occasioned by the capture of two species new to California. Copeia 1950 (no. 3): 195-202.

——. 1952 **[ref. 511]**. Description of a new genus and species of cottid fish from the Tasman Sea, with a discussion of its derivation. Vidensk. Medd. Dansk Naturh. Foren. Kjob. v. 114: 431-441.

——. 1959 (July) **[ref. 503]**. Iniomi. Myctophidae from the "Michael Sars" North Atlantic deep-sea expedition 1910. Scient. Results M. Sars N. Atlant. Deep-Sea Exped., 1910 v. 4 (pt 2) (no. 7): 1-45.

Bonaparte, C. L. 1831-32 **[ref. 4978]**. Saggio di una distribuzione metodica degli animali vertebrati, (1831) 78 pp. Saggio d'una distribuzione... vertebrati a sangue freddo, (1832) 86 pp. Giornale Arcadico di Scienze Lettere ed Arti, vol. 52 (1831): with fishes on pp. 155-189. Also an edition in 1832 with fishes on pp. 89-123. [Pagination in all 4 works differs. We give those in 'Giornale Arcadico' v. 52 — often cited but perhaps not earliest.]

——. 1832-41 **[ref. 515]**. Iconografia delle fauna italica per le quattro classi degli animali vertebrati. Tomo III. Pesci. Roma. [Issued in puntate, without pagination; total of 556 pp., 78 pls. Also reorganized in book form without pagination but with table of contents. Fasc. 1, puntate 1-6, 2 pls. [published in 1832]. [For dates see Hureau & Monod 1973, v. 2: 324 [ref. 6590].]

——. 1833 **[ref. 516]**. Iconografia della fauna italica per le quattro classi degli animali vertebrati. Tomo III. Pesci. Roma. Fasc. 2-5, puntate 7-28, 12 pls.

——. 1834 **[ref. 517]**. Iconografia della fauna italica per le quattro classi degli animali vertebrati. Tomo III. Pesci. Roma. Fasc. 6-11, puntate 29-58, 12 pls.

——. 1835 **[ref. 518]**. Iconografia della fauna italica per le quattro classi degli animali vertebrati. Tomo III. Pesci. Roma. Fasc. 12-14, puntate 59-79, 12 pls.

——. 1836 **[ref. 4892]**. Iconografia della fauna italica per le quattro classi degli animali vertebrati. Tomo III. Pesci. Roma. Fasc. 15-18, puntate 80-93, 10 pls.

——. 1837 **[ref. 4893]**. Icongrafia della fauna italica per le quattro classi degli animali vertebrati. Tomo III. Pesci. Roma. Fasc. 19-21, puntate 94-103, 105-109, 5 pls.

——. 1838 **[ref. 4894]**. Iconografia della fauna italica per le quattro classi degli animali vertebrati. Tomo III. Pesci. Roma. Fasc. 22-23, puntate 104, 110-120, 2 pls.

——. 1838 **[ref. 4979]**. Selachorum tabula analytica. Nuovi Ann. Sci. Nat. v. 2: 195-214. [Also as separate, Rome, 1839, pp. 1-16, including "Systema ichthyologicum" (pp. 13-16).]

——. 1839 **[ref. 4895]**. Iconografia della fauna italica per le quattro classi degli animali vertebrati. Tomo III. Pesci. Roma. Fasc. 24-26, puntate 121-135, 8 pls.

——. 1840 **[ref. 514]**. Iconografia della fauna italica per le quattro classi degli animali vertebrati. Tomo III. Pesci. Roma. Fasc. 27-29, puntate 136-154, 10 pls.

——. 1841 **[ref. 512]**. Iconografia della fauna italica per le quattro classi degli animali vertebrati. Tomo III. Pesci. Roma. Fasc. 30, puntate 155-160, 5 pls.

——. 1845 **[ref. 13472]**. Catalogo metodico dei Ciprinidi d'Europe, e rilievi sul volume XVII della storia naturale dei pesci del Sign. Valenciennes. Milano. 20 pp. [Not seen.]

——. 1846 **[ref. 519]**. Catalogo metodico dei pesci europei. Atti Soc. Ital. Sci. Nat. 1846: 1-95. [Issued as separate, Napoli, 1846, 97 pp. Date of original possibly 1845. Proofed from separate, original not examined.]

Bond, C. E., and D. L. Stein. 1984 (17 Aug.) **[ref. 5310]**. *Opaeophacus acrogeneius*, a new genus and species of Zoarcidae (Pisces: Osteichthyes) from the Bering Sea. Proc. Biol. Soc. Wash. v. 97 (no. 3): 522-525.

Bonnaterre, J. P. 1788 **[ref. 4940]**. Tableau encyclopédique et méthodique des trois règnes de la nature... Ichthyologie. Paris. i-lvi + 1-215, Pls. A-B + 1-100.

Bornbusch, A. H., and J. G. Lundberg. 1989 (23 May) **[ref. 12543]**. A new species of *Hemisilurus* (Siluriformes, Siluridae) from the Mekong River, with comments on its relationships and historical biogeography. Copeia 1989 (no. 2): 434-444.

Borodin, N. A. 1927 (31 Mar.) **[ref. 525]**. A new blind catfish from Brazil. Am. Mus. Novit. No. 263: 1-5.

——. 1927 (20 Apr.) **[ref. 12246]**. Some new catfishes from Brazil. Am. Mus. Novit. No. 266: 1-7.

——. 1928 **[ref. 526]**. Scientific results of the yacht "Ara" Expedition during the years 1926 to 1928, while in command of William K. Vanderbilt. Fishes. Bull. Vanderbilt Oceanogr. Mus. v. 1 (art. 1): 1-37, Pls. 1-5.

——. 1929 (Apr.) **[ref. 527]**. Notes on some species and subspecies of the genus *Leporinus* Spix. Mem. Mus. Comp. Zool. v. 50 (pt 3): 269-290, Pls. 1-17.

——. 1933 (15 Oct.) **[ref. 528]**. A new Australian fish. Copeia 1933 (no. 3): 141-142.

——. 1934 **[ref. 529]**. Fishes. In: Scientific results of the yacht "Alva" Mediterranean cruise, 1933, in command of William K. Vanderbilt. Bull. Vanderbilt Mar. Mus. v. 1 (art. 4): 103-123, Pls. 1-2.

Bortone, S. A. 1977 (June) **[ref. 7059]**. Osteological notes on the genus *Centropristis* (Pisces: Serranidae). Northeast Gulf Sci. v. 1 (no. 1): 23-33.

——. 1977 (Sept.) **[ref. 7064]**. Revision of the sea basses of the genus *Diplectrum* (Pisces: Serranidae). NOAA Tech. Rep. NMFS Circ. No. 404: i-v + 1-49.

Bory de Saint-Vincent, J. B. G. M. 1804 **[ref. 6460]**. Voyages dans les quartre principales îles de mers d'Afrique. Paris. [Not seen.]

——. 1822-31 **[ref. 3853]**. [Pisces accounts.] In: Dictionnaire Classique d'Histoire Naturelle. Vols. 1-17. [Not seen. See Whitley 1935:136 [ref. 6396].]

Bosc, L. A. G. 1816-19 **[ref. 5126]**. [Pisces accounts.] In: Nouveau

Dictionnaire d'Histoire Naturelle, Nouv. Ed. [Not seen. See Whitley 1935 [ref. 6396] and Whitley 1936 [ref. 6397].]

Boulenger, G. A. 1887 (Aug.) **[ref. 532]**. An account of the fishes collected by Mr. C. Buckley in eastern Ecuador. Proc. Zool. Soc. Lond. 1887 (pt 2): 274-283, Pls. 20-24.

——. 1892 (July) **[ref. 533]**. On some new or little-known fishes obtained by Dr. J. W. Evans and Mr. Spencer Moore during their recent expedition to the Province of Matto Grosso, Brazil. Ann. Mag. Nat. Hist. (Ser. 6) v. 10 (no. 55): 9-12, Pls. 1-2.

——. 1893 (Apr.) **[ref. 534]**. Description of a new blennioid fish from Kamtschatka. Proc. Zool. Soc. Lond. 1892 (pt 4): 583-585.

——. 1894 (Mar.) **[ref. 535]**. Descriptions of new freshwater fishes from Borneo. Ann. Mag. Nat. Hist. (Ser. 6) v. 13 (no. 75): 245-251.

——. 1895 (18 Feb.) **[ref. 536]**. Viaggio del dottor Alfredo Borelli nella Repubblica Argentina e nel Paraguay. XII. Poissons. Boll. Mus. Zool. Anat. Comp. Torino v. 10 (no. 196): 1-3.

——. 1895 **[ref. 537]**. Catalogue of the fishes in the British Museum. Catalogue of the perciform fishes in the British Museum. Second edition. Vol. I. i-xix + 1-394, Pls. 1-15.

——. 1897 (Apr.) **[ref. 538]**. Descriptions of new fishes from the Upper Shiré River, British Central Africa, collected by Dr. Percy Rendall, and presented to the British Museum by Sir Harry H. Johnston, K. C. B. Proc. Zool. Soc. Lond. 1896 (pt 4): 915-920, Pl. 47.

——. 1897 (Aug.) **[ref. 539]**. An account of the fresh water fishes collected in Celebes by Drs. P. & F. Sarasin. Proc. Zool. Soc. Lond. 1897 (pt 2): 426-429, Pl. 28.

——. 1897 (Aug.) **[ref. 540]**. Description of a new ceratopterine eagle-ray from Jamaica. Ann. Mag. Nat. Hist. (Ser. 6) v. 20 (no. 116): 227-228.

——. 1898 (June) **[ref. 541]**. Description of a new genus of cyprinoid fishes from Siam. Ann. Mag. Nat. Hist. (Ser. 7) v. 1 (no. 6): 450-451.

——. 1898 **[ref. 542]**. Matériaux pour la faune du Congo. Poissons nouveaux du Congo. Première Partie. Mormyres. Ann. Mus. Congo (Ser. Zool.) v. 1: 1-20, Pls. 1-9.

——. 1898 (Aug.) **[ref. 543]**. On a collection of fishes from the Rio Jurua, Brazil. Trans. Zool. Soc. Lond. v. 14 (pt 7, no. 2): 421-428, Pls. 39-42.

——. 1898 (Apr.) **[ref. 544]**. On a new genus of salmonoid fishes from the Altai mountains. Ann. Mag. Nat. Hist. (Ser. 7) v. 1 (no. 4): 329-331.

——. 1898 (Dec.) **[ref. 545]**. Descriptions of two new siluroid fishes from Brazil. Ann. Mag. Nat. Hist. (Ser. 7) v. 2 (no. 12): 477-478.

——. 1898 (Aug.) **[ref. 546]**. A revision of the African and Syrian fishes of the family Cichlidae.—Part I. Proc. Zool. Soc. Lond. 1898 (pt 2): 132-152, Pl. 19.

——. 1898 (Dec.) **[ref. 547]**. Report on the collection of fishes made by Mr. J. E. S. Moore in Lake Tanganyika during his expedition, 1895-96. Trans. Zool. Soc. Lond. v. 15 (pt 1, no. 1): 1-30, Pls. 1-8. [Abstract in Proc. Zool. Soc. London 1898: 494-497.]

——. 1898 (Dec.) **[ref. 4864]**. Matériaux pour la faune du Congo. Poissons nouveaux du Congo. Deuxième Partie. Elopes, Characins, Cyprins. Ann. Mus. Congo (Ser. Zool.) v. 1: 21-38, Pls. 10-19.

——. 1899 (Apr.) **[ref. 548]**. Matériaux pour la faune du Congo. Poissons nouveaux du Congo. Troisième Partie. Silures, Acanthoptérygiens, Mastacembles, Plectognathes. Ann. Mus. Congo (Ser. Zool.) v. 1: 39-58, Pls. 20-29.

——. 1899 (Sept.) **[ref. 549]**. Matériaux pour la faune du Congo. Poissons nouveaux du Congo. Quatrième Partie. Polyptères, Clupes, Mormyres, Characins. Ann. Mus. Congo (Ser. Zool.) v. 1: 59-96, Pls. 30-39.

——. 1899 (Dec.) **[ref. 589]**. Matériaux pour la faune du Congo. Poissons nouveaux du Congo. Cinquième Partie. Cyprins, Silures, Cyprinodontes, Acanthoptérygiens. Ann. Mus. Congo (Ser. Zool.) v. 1: 97-128, Pls. 40-47.

——. 1899 (Dec.) **[ref. 550]**. Second contribution to the ichthyology of Lake Tanganyika.—On the fishes obtained by the Congo Free State Expedition under Lieut. Lemaire in 1898. Trans. Zool. Soc. Lond. v. 15 (pt 4, no. 1): 87-96, Pls. 18-20.

——. 1899 **[ref. 551]**. Description of a new genus of perciform fishes from the Cape of Good Hope. Ann. S. Afr. Mus. v. 1 (art. 10): 379-380, Pl. 9.

——. 1899 (Aug.) **[ref. 552]**. Description of a new genus of gobioid fishes from the Andes of Ecuador. Ann. Mag. Nat. Hist. (Ser. 7) v. 4 (no. 20): 125-126.

——. 1899 (Sept.) **[ref. 553]**. Descriptions of two new homalopteroid fishes from Borneo. Ann. Mag. Nat. Hist. (Ser. 7) v. 4 (no. 21): 228-229.

——. 1900 (Dec.) **[ref. 554]**. On some little-known African silurid fishes of the subfamily Doradinae. Ann. Mag. Nat. Hist. (Ser. 7) v. 6 (no. 36): 520-529.

——. 1900 (Dec.) **[ref. 555]**. Matériaux pour la faune du Congo. Poissons nouveaux du Congo. Sixième Partie. Mormyres, Characins, Cyprins, Silures, Acanthoptérygiens, Dipneustes. Ann. Mus. Congo (Ser. Zool.) v. 1: 129-164, Pls. 48-56.

——. 1901 (Oct.) **[ref. 556]**. Third contribution to the ichthyology of Lake Tanganyika.—Report on the collection of fishes made by Mr. J. E. S. Moore in lakes Tanganyika and Kivu during his second expedition, 1899-1900. Trans. Zool. Soc. Lond. v. 16 (pt 3, no. 1): 137-178, Pls. 12-20.

——. 1901 (Nov.) **[ref. 557]**. Diagnoses of new fishes discovered by Mr. W. L. S. Loat in the Nile. Ann. Mag. Nat. Hist. (Ser. 7) v. 8 (no. 47): 444-446.

——. 1901 (Oct.) **[ref. 558]**. Notes on the classification of teleostean fishes.—I. On the Trachinidae and their allies. Ann. Mag. Nat. Hist. (Ser. 7) v. 8: 261-271.

——. 1901 (June) **[ref. 559]**. On the fishes collected by Dr. W. J. Ansorge in the Niger delta. Proc. Zool. Soc. Lond. 1901, v. I (pt I): 4-10, Pls. 2-4.

——. 1901 (Mar.) **[ref. 560]**. On some deep-sea fishes collected by Mr. F. W. Townsend in the sea of Oman. Ann. Mag. Nat. Hist. (Ser. 7) v. 7 (no. 39): 261-263, Pl. 6. [Also in Boulenger 1902 (24 May), J. Bombay Nat. Hist. Soc. v. 14: 372-374, pl.]

——. 1901 (Aug.) **[ref. 5127]**. Descriptions of new freshwater fishes discovered by Mr. F. W. Styan at Ningpo, China. Proc. Zool. Soc. Lond. 1901, v. 1 (pt 2): 268-271, Pls. 23-24.

——. 1901 (Jan.) **[ref. 5758]**. Diagnoses of new fishes discovered by Mr. J. E. S. Moore in lakes Tanganyika and Kivu. Ann. Mag. Nat. Hist. (Ser. 7) v. 7 (no. 37): 1-6. [New genera also repeated later in Boulenger 1901 (Oct.) [ref. 556].]

——. 1902 **[ref. 561]**. Pisces. Report on the collections of natural history made in the Antarctic regions during the voyage of the "Southern Cross." Rep. "Southern Cross," Brit. Mus. (Nat. Hist.). Pt 5: 174-189, Pls. 11-18.

——. 1902 (Mar.) **[ref. 562]**. Additions à la faune ichthyologique de bassin du Congo. Matériaux pour la faune du Congo. Ann. Mus. Congo (Ser. Zool.) v. 2 (fasc. 2): 19-57, Pls. 7-16.

——. 1902 (Feb.) **[ref. 563]**. Descriptions of new characinid fish discovered by Dr. W. J. Ansorge in southern Nigeria. Ann. Mag. Nat. Hist. (Ser. 7) v. 9 (no. 50): 144-145, Pl. 3.

——. 1902 (May) **[ref. 564]**. Description of a new deep-sea gadid fish from South Africa. Ann. Mag. Nat. Hist. (Ser. 7) v. 9 (no. 53): 335-336.

——. 1902 (Mar.) **[ref. 565]**. Notes on the classification of teleostean fishes. Ann. Mag. Nat. Hist. (Ser. 7) v. 9 (no. 51): 197-204.

——. 1902 (July) **[ref. 566]**. Description of a new South-African galeid selachian. Ann. Mag. Nat. Hist. (Ser. 7) v. 10 (no. 55): 51-52, Pl. 4.

——. 1902 (July) **[ref. 567]**. Diagnoses of new cichlid fishes discovered by Mr. J. E. S. Moore in Lake Nyassa. Ann. Mag. Nat. Hist. (Ser. 7) v. 10 (no. 55): 69-71.

——. 1902 (Nov.) **[ref. 568]**. On the genus *Ateleopus* of Schlegel. Ann. Mag. Nat. Hist. (Ser. 7) v. 10 (no. 59): 402-403.

——. 1902 (1 Aug.) **[ref. 569]**. Contributions to the ichthyology of the Congo.—I. On some new fishes from the French Congo. Proc.

Zool. Soc. Lond. 1902, v. I (pt 2): 234-237, Pls. 22-24.

——. 1902 (24 May) **[ref. 5759]**. On some deep-sea fishes collected by Mr. F. W. Townsend in the Sea of Oman. J. Bombay Nat. Hist. Soc. v. 14 (pt 2) (art. 11): 372-374, 1 pl.

——. 1903 (June) **[ref. 570]**. On the fishes collected by Mr. G. L. Bates in southern Cameroon. Proc. Zool. Soc. Lond. 1903, v. 1 (pt 1): 21-29, Pls. 1-5.

——. 1903 (28 Feb.) **[ref. 5757]**. Descriptions of two new deep-sea fishes from South Africa. Mar. Invest. So. Afr. v. 2 (no. 11): 167-169.

——. 1904 (July) **[ref. 572]**. Descriptions of new west-African freshwater fishes. Ann. Mag. Nat. Hist. (Ser. 7) v. 14 (no. 79): 16-20.

——. 1906 (Oct.) **[ref. 573]**. Fourth contribution to the ichthyology of Lake Tanganyika.—Report on the collection of fishes made by Dr. W. A. Cunnington during the Third Tanganyika Expedition, 1904-1905. Trans. Zool. Soc. Lond. v. 17 (pt 6, no. 1): 537-619, Pls. 30-41.

——. 1906 (May) **[ref. 574]**. Descriptions of new fishes discovered by Mr. E. Degen in Lake Victoria. Ann. Mag. Nat. Hist. (Ser. 7) v. 17 (no. 101): 433-452.

——. 1907 **[ref. 6510]**. Zoology of Egypt: The fishes of the Nile. Hugh Rees, Ltd., London Text: i-li + 1-578; Pls. 1-97.

——. 1908 (Sept.) **[ref. 575]**. Diagnoses of new fishes discovered by Capt. E. L. Rhoades in Lake Nyassa. Ann. Mag. Nat. Hist. (Ser. 8) v. 2 (no. 9): 238-243.

——. 1909 (Sept.) **[ref. 576]**. Descriptions of new freshwater fishes discovered by Mr. G. L. Bates in south Cameroon. Ann. Mag. Nat. Hist. (Ser. 8) v. 4 (no. 21): 186-188.

——. 1910 (Dec.) **[ref. 577]**. On a large collection of fishes made by Dr. W. J. Ansorge in the Quanza and Bengo rivers, Angola. Ann. Mag. Nat. Hist. (Ser. 8) v. 6 (no. 36): 537-561.

——. 1911 (Aug.) **[ref. 578]**. Descriptions of new African cyprinodont fishes. Ann. Mag. Nat. Hist. (Ser. 8) v. 8 (no. 44): 260-268.

——. 1911 **[ref. 579]**. Catalogue of the fresh-water fishes of Africa in the British Museum (Natural History). London. v. 2: i-xii + 1-529.

——. 1911 **[ref. 580]**. On a third collection of fishes made by Dr. E. Bayon in Uganda, 1909-1910. Collezioni zoologiche fatte nell'-Uganda dal Dott. E. Bayon. XII. Ann. Mus. Civ. Stor. Nat. Genova (Ser. 3a). 64-78, Pls. 1-3.

——. 1912 (July) **[ref. 581]**. Poissons recueillis dans la Région du Bas-Congo par M. le Dr. W. J. Ansorge. Zoologie.—Série I: Poissons, Batraciens et Reptiles. Matériaux pour la Faune du Congo. Ann. Mus. Congo Belge (Ser. 1) v. 2 (fasc. 3): 1-25, Pls. 17-22.

——. 1914 **[ref. 582]**. Unterordnung: Acanthopterygii. Fam. Cichlidae. In: Pappenheim & Boulenger. Lief. 2: Fische. Wiss. Ergebn. Deutsch. Zent. Afrika-Exped., 1907-1908 v. 5 (Zool. no. 3): 253-259.

——. 1914 (25 May) **[ref. 583]**. Mission Stappers au Tanganyika-Moero. Diagnoses de poissons nouveaux. I. Acanthoptérygiens, Opisthomes, Cyprinodontes. Rev. Zool. Afr. v. 3 (pt 3): 442-447.

——. 1915 **[ref. 584]**. Catalogue of the fresh-water fishes of Africa in the British Museum (Natural History). London. v. 3: i-xii + 1-526.

——. 1916 **[ref. 585]**. Catalogue of the fresh-water fishes of Africa in the British Museum (Natural History). London. v. 4: i-xxvii + 1-392.

——. 1920 (Jan.) **[ref. 587]**. Poissons recueillis au Congo Belge par l'expédition du Dr. C. Christy. Zoologie. — Série I. Matériaux pour la Faune du Congo. Ann. Mus. Congo Belge (Ser. 1) v. 2 (fasc. 4): 1-38, Pls. 23-25.

——. 1921 (15 Dec.) **[ref. 588]**. Description d'un Poisson aveugle découvert par M. G. Geerts dans la grotte de Thysville (Bas-Congo). Rev. Zool. Afr. v. 9 (pt 3): 252-253.

Bowdich, S. L. 1825 **[ref. 590]**. Fishes of Madeira. Pp. 121-125 and 233-238. In: T. E. Bowdich. Excursions in Madeira and Porto Santo during the autumn of 1823, while on his third voyage to Africa. London. i-xii + 1-278, 11 pls. + 10 pls. [New genera available from figure captions (p. xii) for consecutive figures on unnumbered plates, and see pp. 237-238.]

Braasch, M. E., and R. L. Mayden. 1985 **[ref. 6874]**. Review of the subgenus *Catonotus* (Percidae) with descriptions of two new darters of the *Etheostoma squamiceps* species group. Occas. Pap. Mus. Nat. Hist. Univ. Kans. No. 119: 1-53.

Bradbury, M. G. 1980 (2 July) **[ref. 6538]**. A revision of the fish genus *Ogcocephalus* with descriptions of new species from the western Atlantic Ocean (Ogcocephalidae; Lophiiformes). Proc. Calif. Acad. Sci. v. 42 (no. 7): 229-285.

——. 1986 **[ref. 6291]**. Family 104: Ogcocephalidae (pp. 370-373). In: Smiths' Sea Fishes (Smith & Heemstra 1986 [ref. 5715]).

——. 1988 (31 May) **[ref. 6428]**. Rare fishes of the deep-sea genus *Halieutopsis*: a review with descriptions of four new species (Lophiiformes: Ogcocephalidae). Fieldiana Zool. (n. s.) No. 44: i-iii + 1-22.

Braga, L., and M. Azpelicueta. 1983 **[ref. 5308]**. *Semitapiscis squamoralevis* sp. nov. (Osteichthyes: Curimatidae), con consideraciones sobre el género. Stud. Neotrop. Fauna Environ. v. 18: 139-150.

Brandt, J. F. 1854 **[ref. 617]**. Remarques sur le Mémoire de Mr. Lowe, suivies d'une planche représentant le nouveau genre de poissons. Mem. Acad. Sci. St. Petersb. v. 7: 174-175, Pl. 8.

——. 1869 **[ref. 618]**. Einige Worte über die europäisch-asiatischen Störarten (Sturnionides). Mélanges Biol. v. 7: 110-116. [Also in Bull. Acad. Sci. St. Petersburg v. 14: 171-176 (1870).]

Brandt, J. F., and J. C. T. Ratzeburg. 1833 **[ref. 619]**. Medizinische Zoologie, oder getreue Darstellung und Beschreibung der Thiere, die in der Arzneimittellehre in betracht kommen, in systematischer folge herausgegeben. v. 2: i-iv + 1-364, Pls. 1-36 + 1.

Brant, V. 1974 **[ref. 628]**. Ictiofauna de Minas Gerais. VII - Um novo serrasalmídeo do estado de Minas Gerais, Brasil (Actinopterygii, Cypriniformes). Arq. Mus. Hist. Nat. Univ. Fed. Minas Gerais v. 1: 147-152, 1 separate fig. [English summ. Date of 1974 on cover, 1971 on article.]

Brauer, A. 1900 **[ref. 629]**. Aus der Tiefen des Weltmeeres. In: C. Chun. Schilderung von der deutschen Tiefsee-Expedition. Jena. 1-549.

——. 1901 (July) **[ref. 630]**. Über einige von der Valdivia-Expedition gesammelte Tiefseefische und ihre Augen. Sitzungsber. Ges. Naturw. Marburg No. 8: 115-130.

——. 1902 **[ref. 631]**. Diagnosen von neuen Tiefseefischen, welche von der Valdivia-Expedition gesammelt sind. Zool. Anz. v. 25 (no. 668): 277-298.

——. 1906 (? 17 Apr.) **[ref. 632]**. Die Tiefsee-Fische. I. Systematischer Teil. In: C. Chun. Wissenschaftl. Ergebnisse der deutschen Tiefsee-Expedition "Valdivia," 1898-99. Jena. v. 15: 1-432, Pls. 1-18.

Breder, C. M., Jr. 1927 (19 Oct.) **[ref. 635]**. Scientific results of the first oceanographic expedition of the "Pawnee" 1925. Fishes. Bull. Bingham Oceanogr. Collect. Yale Univ. v. 1 (art. 1): 1-90.

——. 1928 (Mar.) **[ref. 636]**. Scientific results of the second oceanographic expedition of the "Pawnee" 1926. Nematognathii, Apodes, Isospondyli, Synentognathi, and Thoracostraci from Panama to Lower California with a generic analysis of the Exocoetidae. Bull. Bingham Oceanogr. Collect. Yale Univ. v. 2 (art. 2): 1-25.

——. 1936 (Jan.) **[ref. 634]**. Scientific results of the second oceanographic expedition of the "Pawnee" 1926. Heterosomata to Pediculati from Panama to Lower California. Bull. Bingham Oceanogr. Collect. Yale Univ. v. 2 (art. 3): 1-56.

Briggs, J. C. 1955 (21 Sept.) **[ref. 637]**. A monograph of the clingfishes (Order Xenopterygii). Stanford Ichthyol. Bull. v. 6: i-iv + 1-224.

——. 1957 (26 Aug.) **[ref. 638]**. A new genus and two new species of eastern Atlantic clingfishes. Copeia 1957 (no. 3): 204-208, Pl. 1.

——. 1961 (19 June) **[ref. 13439]**. Emendated generic names in Berg's classification of fishes. Copeia 1961 (no. 2): 161-166.

——. 1969 (3 June) **[ref. 639]**. A new genus and species of clingfish (family Gobiesocidae) from the Bahama Islands. Copeia 1969 (no. 2): 332-334.

———. 1973 **[ref. 7222]**. Gobiesocidae (pp. 651-656). In: Hureau & Monod 1973 [ref. 6590].

———. 1976 (17 May) **[ref. 640]**. A new genus and species of clingfish from the western Pacific. Copeia 1976 (no. 2): 339-341.

———. 1986 **[ref. 5643]**. Family No. 110: Gobiesocidae (pp. 378-380). In: Smiths' Sea Fishes (Smith & Heemstra 1986 [ref. 5715]).

Brisout de Barneville, C. N. F. 1846 **[ref. 296]**. Note sur les Diodoniens. Rev. Zool. 1846: 136-143.

———. 1846 **[ref. 641]**. Supplément à une note sur le groupe des Gobiésoces. Rev. Zool. 1846: 209-212.

———. 1846 **[ref. 9183]**. Note sur le groupe des Gobiésoces. Rev. Zool. 1846: 143-146.

———. 1846 **[ref. 642]**. Note sur un nouveau genre de la famille des Discoboles. Rev. Zool. 1846: 212-213.

———. 1847 **[ref. 643]**. Note sur le genre *Centropriste* de Cuvier. Rev. Zool. 1847: 130-134.

———. 1847 **[ref. 644]**. Note sur un nouveau genre d'Anguilliformes. Rev. Zool. 1847: 219-220.

Brito, A. 1989 (27 Dec.) **[ref. 13509]**. *Nettenchelys dionisi*, a new species of nettastomatid eel (Pisces: Anguilliformes) from the Canary Islands. Copeia 1989 (no. 4): 876-880.

Britski, H. A. 1981 (24 Apr.) **[ref. 645]**. Sobre um novo gênero e espécie de Sorubiminae da Amazônia (Pisces, Siluriformes). Pap. Avulsos Dep. Zool. (São Paulo) v. 34 (no. 7): 109-114.

Britski, H. A., and J. C. Garavello. 1984 (28 Dec.) **[ref. 5166]**. Two new southeastern Brazilian genera of Hypoptopomatinae and a redescription of *Pseudotocinclus* Nichols, 1919 (Ostariophysi, Loricariidae). Pap. Avulsos Dep. Zool. (São Paulo) v. 35 (no. 21): 225-241.

Britski, H. A., and H. Ortega. 1983 (30 Apr.) **[ref. 5408]**. *Trichogenes longipinnis*, novo gênero e espéce de Trichomycterinae do sudeste do Brazil (Pisces, Siluriformes). Rev. Bras. Zool. v. 1 (no. 3): 211-216.

Brittan, M. R. 1954 **[ref. 646]**. A revision of the Indo-Malayan fresh-water fish genus *Rasbora*. Monogr. Inst. Sci. Tech. Manila Monogr. 3: 1-224.

———. 1972 **[ref. 12245]**. A revision of the Indo-Malayan fresh-water fish genus *Rasbora*. T. F. H. Publications. 1-224, Unnum. col. pls.

Brittan, M. R., and J. E. Böhlke. 1965 (28 Oct.) **[ref. 647]**. A new blind characid fish from southeastern Brazil. Not. Nat. (Phila.) No. 380: 1-4.

Brown, B. A., and C. J. Ferraris, Jr. 1988 (11 Feb.) **[ref. 6806]**. Comparative osteology of the Asian catfish family Chacidae, with the description of a new species from Burma. Am. Mus. Novit. No. 2907: 1-16.

Browne, P. 1789 **[ref. 669]**. The civil and natural history of Jamaica. Second edition. i-viii + 1-490, 49 pls. [A slightly revised reprint of the first edition of 1756. Fishes are on pp. 440-459. A rejected work.]

Brownell, C. L. 1978 (May) **[ref. 670]**. *Vanneaugobius dollfusi*, a new genus and species of small gobiid with divided ventrals from Morocco (Pisces: Gobiodei). Trans. R. Soc. S. Aust. v. 43 (pt 2): 135-145.

Bruce, R. W., and J. E. Randall. 1985 (Feb.) **[ref. 5234]**. Revision of the Indo-Pacific parrotfish genera *Calotomus* and *Leptoscarus*. Indo-Pac. Fishes No. 5: 1-32, Pls. 1-3.

Brüning, C. 1929 **[ref. 6187]**. Der Clou und der Pipifax. Wschr. Aquar.-u. Terrarienk v. 26 (no. 51): 758-759.

Brünnich, M. T. 1771 **[ref. 675]**. Collectio Nova Scriptorum Societatis Scientiarum Hafnensis. [Not seen.]

———. 1788 **[ref. 5131]**. Om den islandske fisk, bogmeren, *Gymnogaster arcticus*. K. Danske Selskab. Skrift. Kjöbenhavn v. 3: 408-413, Pl. B.

Bruun, A. F. 1931 **[ref. 672]**. On some new fishes of the family Gonostomatidae. Preliminary note. Vidensk. Medd. Dansk Naturh. Foren. Kjob. v. 92: 285-291, Pl. 8.

———. 1934 (14 June) **[ref. 5129]**. Notes on the Linnaean type-specimens of flying-fishes (Exocoetidae). J. Linn. Soc. Lond. v. 39 (no. 263): 133-135.

———. 1935 (5 Aug.) **[ref. 5130]**. Flying-fishes (Exocoetidae) of the Atlantic. Systematic and biological studies. Dana Rep. No. 6: 1-106, Pls. 1-7.

———. 1940 (14 June) **[ref. 13410]**. A study of a collection of the fish *Schindleria* from South Pacific waters. Dana-Rep. No. 21: 1-12.

———. 1953 **[ref. 6265]**. Dybhavets dyreliv. Pp. 153-192. In: Galatheas jordomsejling 1950-1952. København. [Not seen.]

Bruun, A. F., and E. W. Kaiser. 1944 **[ref. 674]**. *Iranocypris typhlops* n. g., n. sp., the first true cave-fish from Asia. Danish Scient. Invest. Iran Part 4: 1-8.

Buckup, P. A. 1988 (3 Aug.) **[ref. 6635]**. The genus *Heptapterus* (Teleostei, Pimelodidae) in southern Brazil and Uruguay, with the description of a new species. Copeia 1988 (no. 3): 641-653.

Budker, P. 1935 **[ref. 683]**. Description d'un genre nouveau de la famille des Carcharinidés. Bull. Mus. Natl. Hist. Nat. (Ser. 2) v. 7 (no. 2): 107-112.

Buen, F. de. See de Buen, F.

Burgess, G. H., and S. Springer. 1986 (30 May) **[ref. 6149]**. The hook-tooth shark, *Aculeaola nigra* DeBuen (family Squalidae) of the eastern South Pacific. Pp. 189-196. In: Uyeno et al. (eds.) 1986 [ref. 6147].

Burgess, W. E. 1978 **[ref. 700]**. Butterflyfishes of the world, a monograph of the family Chaetodontidae. T.F.H. Publ., Inc. Ltd., Neptune City, New Jersey, U.S.A. 1-832.

———. 1989 **[ref. 12860]**. An atlas of freshwater and marine catfishes. A preliminary survey of the Siluriformes. T.F.H. Publications, Neptune City, New Jersey, U.S.A. 1-784, col. Pls. 1-285.

Burke, C. V. 1912 (12 Dec.) **[ref. 701]**. A new genus and six new species of the family Cyclogasteridae. Proc. U. S. Natl. Mus. v. 43 (no. 1941): 567-574.

———. 1930 (27 May) **[ref. 702]**. Revision of the fishes of the family Liparidae. Bull. U. S. Natl. Mus. No. 150: i-xii + 1-204.

Burr, B. M. 1976 (30 Mar.) **[ref. 7118]**. A review of the Mexican stoneroller, *Campostoma ornatum* Girard (Pisces: Cyprinidae). Trans. San Diego Soc. Nat. Hist. v. 18 (no. 7): 127-143.

———. 1978 (31 July) **[ref. 7035]**. Systematics of the percid fishes of the subgenus *Microperca*, genus *Etheostoma*. Bull. Alabama Mus. Nat. Hist. No. 4: 1-53.

Bussing, W. A. 1978 **[ref. 6973]**. Taxonomic status of the atherinid fish genus *Melaniris* in lower Central America, with the description of three new species. Rev. Biol. Trop. v. 26 (no. 2): 391-413.

———. 1979 (16 Mar.) **[ref. 6946]**. A new fish of the genus *Phallichthys* (Family Poeciliidae) from Costa Rica. Contrib. Sci. (Los Ang.) No. 301: 1-8.

———. 1980 **[ref. 6904]**. *Liopropoma fasciatum*, a new serranid fish and only known member of the genus from the tropical eastern Pacific Ocean. Rev. Biol. Trop. v. 28 (no. 1): 147-151.

Bussing, W. A., and M. I. López S. 1977 **[ref. 7001]**. *Guentherus altivela* Osorio, the first ateleopodid fish reported from the eastern Pacific Ocean. Rev. Biol. Trop. v. 25 (no. 2): 179-190.

Buth, D. G. 1979 **[ref. 6941]**. Genetic relationships among the torrent suckers, genus *Thoburnia*. Biochem. Syst. Ecol. v. 7: 311-316.

———. 1980 (1 May) **[ref. 6942]**. Evolutionary genetics and systematic relationships in the catostomid genus *Hypentelium*. Copeia 1980 (no. 2): 280-290.

Cadenat, J. 1959 **[ref. 708]**. Notes d'Ichtyologie ouest-africaine. XXIV. Molidae ouest-africains avec description d'une espèce nouvelle: *Pseudomola lassarati* de Côte d'Ivoire. Bull. Inst. Fr. Afr. Noire (Ser. A) Sci. Nat. v. 21 (no.3): 112-122, 4 unnum. pls.

———. 1963 (Apr.) **[ref. 709]**. Notes d'ichtyologie ouest-africaine. XXXIX.—Notes sur les Requins de la famille des Carchariidae et formes apparentées de l'Atlantique ouest-africain (avec la description d'une espèce nouvelle: *Pseudocarcharias pelagicus*....) Bull. Inst. Fr. Afr. Noire (Ser. A) Sci. Nat. v. 25 (no. 2): 526-543.

Campbell, W. D. 1879 (May) **[ref. 711]**. On a new fish. Trans. Proc. N. Z. Inst. v. 11: 297-298.

CANESTRINI, G. 1860 **[ref. 712]**. Zur Systematik der Percoiden. Verh. K.-K. Zool.-Bot. Ver. Ges. Wien v. 10: 291-314.

———. 1860 **[ref. 713]**. Zur systematik und charakteristik der Anabatinen. Verh. Akad. Wiss. Wien. 697-712.

———. 1864 **[ref. 714]**. Studi sui *Lepadogaster* del Mediterraneo. Arch. Zool. Anat. Fisiol. (Genova) v. 3, fasc. 1: 177-196, Pl. 3.

CANTOR, T. E. 1849 **[ref. 715]**. Catalogue of Malayan fishes. J. R. Asiat. Soc. Bengal v. 18 (no. 2): i-xii + 981-1143, Pls. 1-14. [Also as a separate, J. Thomas, Calcutta, i-xii + 1-461. Often cited with date as 1850.]

CANTRAINE, F. J. 1835 **[ref. 7207]**. Sur un poisson nouveau, trouvé dans le canal de Messine en janvier 1833. Bull. Acad. R. Belge Cl. Sci. v. 2 (no. 1): 23-24.

———. 1837 **[ref. 716]**. Memoire sur un poisson nouveau trouvé dans le canal de Messine en janvier 1833. J. Bruxelles v. 10: 1-19, 2 pls. [Not seen.]

CAO, W.-X., AND S.-Q. ZHU. 1988 **[ref. 14140]**. A new genus and species of Nemacheilinae from Dianchi Lake, Yunnan Provincein in China. Acta Zool. Sin. v. 13: 405-408. [In Chinese, English summ.]

CAPELLO, F. DE B. 1868 **[ref. 718]**. Descripção de dos peixes novos provenientes dos mares de Portugal. J. Sci. Math. Phys. Nat. Lisboa No. 1: 314-317, Pl. 5.

CAPORIACCO, L. DI. 1926 **[ref. 720]**. Un nuovo genere di Ciprinide somalo delle acque di pozzo. Monit. Zool. Ital. v. 37 (no. 1-2): 23-25.

———. 1947 **[ref. 721]**. Miscellanea ichthyologica. Boll. Pesca Piscic. Idrobiol. v. 23: 193-205.

CAPPETTA, H. 1987 **[ref. 6348]**. Chondrichthys II. Handbook of Paleoichthyology. Vol. 3B. Gustav Fischer Verlag, Stuttgart and New York. i-vii + 1-193.

CARPENTER, K. E. 1987 (Sept.) **[ref. 6430]**. Revision of the Indo-Pacific fish family Caesionidae (Lutjanoidea), with descriptions of five new species. Indo-Pac. Fishes No. 15: 1-56, col. Pls. 1-7.

———. 1988 **[ref. 9296]**. FAO species catalog. Vol. 8. Fusilier fishes of the World. An annotated and illustrated catalogue of caesionid species known to date. FAO Fish. Synop. No. 125, v. 8: i-iv + 1-75, Pls. 1-5.

CARPENTER, K. E., AND G. R. ALLEN. 1989 **[ref. 13577]**. FAO species catalogue. Vol. 9. Emperor fishes and large-eye breams of the world (family Lethrinidae). An annotated and illustrated catalogue of lethrinid species known to date. FAO Fish. Synop. No. 125, v. 9: i-v + 1-118, col. Pls. 1-8.

CARRANZA, J. 1954 (15 Dec.) **[ref. 734]**. Descripción del primer bagre anoftalmo y depigmentado encontrado en aguas mexicanas. Ciencia (Mex. City) v. 14 (nos. 7-8): 129-136, Pl. 1.

CARTER, H. J. 1983 **[ref. 5165]**. *Apagesoma edentatum*, a new genus and species of ophidiid fish from the western North Atlantic. Bull. Mar. Sci. v. 33 (no. 1): 94-101.

CARTER, H. J., AND D. M. COHEN. 1985 **[ref. 5145]**. *Monomitopus magnus*, a new species of deep-sea fish (Ophidiidae) from the western North Atlantic. Bull. Mar. Sci. v. 36 (no. 1): 86-95.

CARTER, H. J., AND J. A. MUSICK. 1985 (11 Feb.) **[ref. 6791]**. Sexual dimorphism in the deep-sea fish *Barathrodemus manatinus* (Ophidiidae). Copeia 1985 (no. 1): 69-73.

CARTER, H. J., AND K. J. SULAK. 1984 **[ref. 8244]**. A new species and a review of the deep-sea fish genus *Porogadus* (Ophidiidae) from the western North Atlantic. Bull. Mar. Sci. v. 34 (no. 3): 358-379.

CARUSO, J. H. 1981 (26 Aug.) **[ref. 5169]**. The systematics and distribution of the lophiid anglerfishes: I. A revision of the genus *Lophiodes* with the description of two new species. Copeia 1981 (no. 3): 522-549.

———. 1983 (10 Feb.) **[ref. 5168]**. The systematics and distribution of the lophiid anglerfishes: II. Revisions of the genera *Lophiomus* and *Lophius*. Copeia 1983 (no. 1): 11-30.

———. 1985 (10 Dec.) **[ref. 5170]**. The systematics and distribution of the lophiid anglerfishes: III. Intergeneric relationships. Copeia 1985 (no. 4): 870-875.

———. 1986 **[ref. 6290]**. Family No. 101: Lophiidae (pp. 363-366). In: Smiths' Sea Fishes (Smith & Heemstra 1986 [ref. 5715]).

———. 1989 (27 Feb.) **[ref. 9287]**. Systematics and distribution of Atlantic chaunacid anglerfishes (Pisces: Lophiiformes). Copeia 1989 (no. 1): 153-165.

———. 1989 **[ref. 14230]**. A review of the Indo-Pacific members of the deep-water chaunacid anglerfish genus *Bathychaunax*, with the description of a new species from the eastern Indian Ocean (Pisces: Lophiiformes). Bull. Mar. Sci. v. 45 (no. 3): 574-579.

CARUSO, J. H., AND H. R. BULLIS, JR. 1976 **[ref. 5167]**. A review of the lophiid angler fish genus *Sladenia* with a description of a new species from the Caribbean Sea. Bull. Mar. Sci. v. 26 (no. 1): 59-64.

CARVALHO, A. L. DE. 1959 (11 May) **[ref. 736]**. Novo gênero e nova espécie de peixe anual de Brasília, com uma nota sôbre os peixes anuais da Baixada Fluminense, Brasil (Pisces - Cyprinodontidae-Fundulinae.) Bol. Mus. Nac. Rio de J. Zool. (n. s.) No. 201: 1-10.

CARVALHO, F. P., AND A. J. ALMEIDA. 1988 (30 June) **[ref. 6862]**. Notes on *Xenodermichthys copei* (Gill, 1884) (Pisces: Alepocephalidae). Cybium v. 12 (no. 2): 161-166.

CARVALHO, J. DE P., AND S. Y. PINTO. 1965 (Dec.) **[ref. 738]**. Novos dactiloscopídeos da Costa Brasileira (Actinopterygii-Perciformes). Arq. Estac. Biol. Mar. Univ. Ceara v. 5 (no. 2): 107-117.

CASCIOTTA, J. R. 1987 (9 Dec.) **[ref. 6772]**. *Crenicichla celidochilus* n. sp. from Uruguay and a multivariate analysis of the *lacustris* group (Perciformes, Cichlidae). Copeia 1987 (no. 4): 883-891.

CASHNER, R. C., B. M. BURR AND J. S. ROGERS. 1989 (27 Feb.) **[ref. 13576]**. Geographic variation of the mud sunfish, *Acantharchus pomotis* (family Centrarchidae). Copeia 1989 (no. 1): 129-141.

CASHNER, R. C., AND R. E. JENKINS. 1982 (10 Aug.) **[ref. 5463]**. Systematics of the Roanoke Bass, *Ambloplites cavifrons*. Copeia 1982 (no. 3): 581-594.

CASHNER, R. C., J. S. ROGERS AND J. M. GRADY. 1988 (3 Aug.) **[ref. 6681]**. *Fundulus bifax*, a new species of the subgenus *Xenisma* from the Tallapoosa and Coosa river systems of Alabama and Georgia. Copeia 1988 (no. 3): 674-683.

CASTELNAU, F. L. 1855 **[ref. 766]**. Expédition dans les parties centrales de l'Amérique du Sud, de Rio de Janeiro a Lima, et de Lima à Para; executee par ordre du gouvernement Français pendant les années 1843 a 1847. Septième partie, Zoology. Poissons. P. Bertrand, Paris v. 2: i-xii + 1-112, col. Pls. 1-50.

———. 1861 **[ref. 767]**. Mémoire sur les poissons de l'Afrique australe. Paris. i-vii + 1-78.

———. 1872 (15 July) **[ref. 757]**. Contribution to the ichthyology of Australia. No. 1.—The Melbourne fish market (pp. 29-242). No. II.—Note on some South Australian fishes (pp. 243-247). Proc. Zool. Acclim. Soc. Victoria v. 1: 29-248. [Also as part of a separate, Melbourne, 1872.]

———. 1873 **[ref. 758]**. Contribution to the ichthyology of Australia. Nos. III thru IX. Proc. Zool. Acclim. Soc. Victoria v. 2: 37-153. [Also as part of a separate, Melbourne, 1872.]

———. 1873 **[ref. 759]**. Notes on the edible fishes of Victoria. Intern. Exhib. Essays, 1872-3. No. 5: 1-17.

———. 1875 **[ref. 768]**. Researches on the fishes of Australia. Philadelphia Centennial Expedition of 1876. Intercolonial Exhibition Essays, 1875-6. Intercol. Exhib. Essays No. 2: 1-52.

———. 1876 **[ref. 760]**. Mémoire sur les poissons appelés barramundi par les aborigènes du nord-est de l'Australie. J. Zool. (Gervais) v. 5: 129-136.

———. 1878 (May) **[ref. 761]**. Australian fishes. New or little known species. Proc. Linn. Soc. N. S. W. v. 2 (pt 3): 225-248, Pls. 2-3.

———. 1878 (Sept.) **[ref. 762]**. Notes on the fishes of the Norman River. Proc. Linn. Soc. N. S. W. v. 3 (pt 1): 41-51.

———. 1878 (Dec.) **[ref. 763]**. On several new Australian (chiefly) fresh-water-fishes. Proc. Linn. Soc. N. S. W. v. 3 (pt 2): 140-144.

———. 1879 (May) **[ref. 764]**. Essay on the ichthyology of Port Jackson. Proc. Linn. Soc. N. S. W. v. 3 (pt 4): 347-402.

———. 1879 **[ref. 769]**. On a new ganoid fish from Queensland. Proc. Linn. Soc. N. S. W. v. 3 (pt 3): 164-165, Pl. 19.

CASTLE, P. H. J. 1967 (Aug.) **[ref. 770]**. Two remarkable eel-larvae from off southern Africa. Spec. Publ. Dep. Ichthyol. Rhodes Univ. No. 1: 1-12, Pls. 1-2.

———. 1969 (Dec.) **[ref. 12436]**. An index and bibliography of eel larvae. J. L. B. Smith Inst. Ichthyol. Spec. Publ. No. 7: 1-121.

———. 1972 **[ref. 6968]**. The eel genus *Benthenchelys* (Fam. Ophichthidae) in the Indo-Pacific. Dana Rep. No. 82: 1-32.

———. 1977 (25 Aug.) **[ref. 9301]**. The congrid genus *Fimbriceps*, a synonym of *Gnathophis*. Copeia 1977 (no. 3): 581-582.

———. 1978 **[ref. 771]**. Results of the research cruises of FRV "Walther Herwig" to South America. L. A new genus and species of bobtail eel (Anguilliformes, Cyemidae) from the South Atlantic. Arch. FischereiWiss. v. 28 (no. 2-3): 69-76. [Cover dated Dec. 1977, but Castle 1986: 193 [ref. 5644] uses date of 1978.]

———. 1984 (Feb.) **[ref. 6171]**. Anguillidae (pp. 34-37), Ophichthidae (pp. 38-39). In: Daget et al. 1984 [ref. 6168].

———. 1986 **[ref. 5644]**. [Various anguilliform families]. Family No. 39 (pp. 160-161), 40 (pp. 161-164), 43 (pp. 186-187), 44 (pp. 187-188), 45 (p. 188), 46 (pp. 188-190), 47 (pp. 190-191), 48 (191), 49 (pp. 191-192), 50 (pp. 192-193), 51 (pp. 193-194). In: Smiths' Sea Fishes (Smith & Heemstra 1986 [ref. 5715]).

Castle, P. H. J., and J. E. McCosker. 1986 **[ref. 5645]**. Family No. 41: Muraenidae (pp. 165-176). In: Smiths' Sea Fishes (Smith & Heemstra 1986 [ref. 5715]).

Castle, P. H. J., and J. R. Paxton. 1984 (23 Feb.) **[ref. 5259]**. A new genus and species of luminescent eel (Pisces: Congridae) from the Arafura Sea, northern Australia. Copeia 1984 (no. 1): 72-81.

Castle, P. H. J., and N. S. Raju. 1975 **[ref. 772]**. Some rare leptocephali from the Atlantic and Indo-Pacific oceans. Dana Rep. No. 85: 1-25, 1 pl.

Castle, P. H. J., and G. R. Williamson. 1975 (May) **[ref. 7115]**. Systematics and distribution of eels of the *Muraenesox* group (Anguilliformes, Muraenesocidae). J. L. B. Smith Inst. Ichthyol. Spec. Publ. No. 15: 1-9.

Castro, D. M. 1984 (June) **[ref. 5296]**. Hallazgo del bagre *Merodontotus tigrinus* en la Amazonia Colombiana. Bol. Fac. Biol. Mar. No. 3: 1-8.

Castro, R. M. C. 1981 (24 Apr.) **[ref. 773]**. *Engraulisoma taeniatum*, um novo gênero e espécie de Characidae da bacia do Rio Paraguai (Pisces, Ostariophysi). Pap. Avulsos Dep. Zool. (São Paulo) v. 34 (no. 11): 135-139.

———. 1988 (13 Sept.) **[ref. 6684]**. *Semiprochilodus varii*, a new species of prochilodontid fish (Ostariophysi: Characiformes) from the Marowijne River, Surinam. Proc. Biol. Soc. Wash. v. 101 (no. 3): 503-508.

Castro-Aguirre, J. L., and S. Suárez de los Cobos. 1983 **[ref. 5313]**. *Notophtophis brunneus*, nuevo género y especie de la familia Ophichthidae, (Pisces: Angnilliformes [sic]) hallado en la Bahía de Acapulco, Guerrero, México. An. Esc. Nac. Cienc. Biol. Mex. v. 27: 113-128.

Catesby, M. 1771 **[ref. 774]**. The natural history of Carolina, Florida and the Bahama Islands; containing the figures of birds, beasts, fishes, serpents ... with their descriptions in English and French, etc. 3rd. ed. 2 vols. London. [A rejected work on the Official Index, ICZN Opinions 89 and 259 (but not appendix by Edwards).]

Cervigón, F. 1961 (July) **[ref. 777]**. Descripción de *Anodontus mauritanicus* nov. gen. nov. sp. (orden Ateleopiformes) y *Cottunculus costae-canariae* nov. sp. (familia Cottidae) de las costas occidentales de Africa. Invest. Pesq. v. 29: 119-128.

Cervigón, F., G. Pequeño and I. Kong. 1980 **[ref. 5421]**. Presencia de *Pseudoxenomystax albescens* (Barnard, 1923) y *Xenomystax atrarius* Gilbert, 1891, en las costas de Chile (Teleostomi, Congridae). Bol. Mus. Nac. Hist. Nat. Chile v. 37: 317-321.

Chabanaud, P. 1925 **[ref. 780]**. *Monodichthys proboscideus* (gen. nov. et spec. nova) et remarques sur divers autres poissons Soléiformes. Bull. Mus. Natl. Hist. Nat. (Ser. 1) v. 31 (no. 5)[1925]: 356-361.

———. 1927 (25 Aug.) **[ref. 781]**. Observations morphologiques et remarques sur la systématique des poissons Hétérosomes Soléiformes. Bull. Inst. Oceanogr. (Monaco) No. 500: 1-15.

———. 1927 (5 Mar.) **[ref. 782]**. Les soles de l'Atlantique Oriental nord et des mers adjacentes. Bull. Inst. Oceanogr. (Monaco) No. 488: 1-67.

———. 1927 **[ref. 5135]**. Sur quelques poissons heterosomes de la Martinique. Bull. Soc. Zool. Fr. v. 52: 74-84.

———. 1928 (5 Sept.) **[ref. 783]**. Revision des poissons Hétérosomes de la sous-famille des Achirinae, d'après les types de Kaup, de Günther et de Steindachner. Bull. Inst. Oceanogr. (Monaco) No. 523: 1-53.

———. 1930 (5 July) **[ref. 784]**. Les genres de poissons Hétérosomates [Pisces Heterosomata] appartenant à la sous-famille des Soleinae. Bull. Inst. Oceanogr. (Monaco) No. 555: 1-21.

———. 1931 **[ref. 785]**. Sur divers poissons soléiformes de la région indo-pacifique. Bull. Soc. Zool. Fr. v. 56: 291-305.

———. 1931 (27 Oct.) **[ref. 6057]**. Sur la ceinture et quelques autres éléments morphologiques des poissons hétérosomates. Importance phylogénétique des caractères observés. Bull. Soc. Zool. Fr. v. 56: 386-398.

———. 1933 (30 Apr.) **[ref. 787]**. Poissons hétérosomes recueillis par M. le Professeur A. Gruvel et par MM. R.-Ph. Dollfus et J. Liouville sur la côte du Maroc. Mem. Soc. Sci. Nat. Maroc No. 35: 1-111, Pls. 1-2.

———. 1933 (20 Nov.) **[ref. 788]**. Un nouveau type de poissons de la famille de Gobiidés (*Syrrhothonus Charrieri*, n. g., n. sp.). C. R. Hebd. Seances Acad. Sci. v. 197: 1249-1251.

———. 1933 (31 Dec.) **[ref. 789]**. Description d'un poisson inédit de la famille des Gobiidés originaire de la côte Marocaine (Tanger) du détroit de Gibraltar. Bull. Soc. Sci. Nat. Maroc v. 13 (no. 7-8): 171-180.

———. 1934 **[ref. 790]**. Description d'un nouveau Soléidé, originaire de Zanzibar. Bull. Soc. Zool. Fr. v. 58: 388-396.

———. 1934 **[ref. 791]**. Les soléidés du groupe *Zebrias*. Définition d'un sous-genre nouveau et description d'une sous-espèce nouvelle. Bull. Soc. Zool. Fr. v. 59: 420-436.

———. 1936 **[ref. 792]**. Sur divers soléidés apparentés au genre *Zebrias*. Bull. Soc. Zool. Fr. v. 61: 382-404, Pl. 6.

———. 1937 (15 Nov.) **[ref. 794]**. Zoologie.—Sur un nouveau Téléostéen de la famille des Soléidés, *Pseudaustroglossus annectens*. C. R. Hebd. Seances Acad. Sci. v. 205: 932-934.

———. 1938 **[ref. 795]**. Contribution a la morphologie et la systématique des téléostéens dyssymétriques. Arch. Mus. Natl. Hist. Nat. Paris (Ser. 6) v. 15: 59-139, Pls. 1-9.

———. 1942 **[ref. 798]**. Contribution a la morphologie de Téléostéens appartenant a diverses familles de l'ordre des Blennoidea. Description d'une espèce et d'un genre inédits. Bull. Soc. Zool. Fr. v. 67: 111-120.

———. 1943 **[ref. 799]**. Notules ichthyologiques. (Sixième série). XX.—L'habitat du Soléidé *Pegusa lascaris* (Risso) ne serait-il pas circumafricain. XXI.—Le genre *Dexillus* Chabanaud. XXII.—Nouveaux genres de la famille des Soleidae. Bull. Mus. Natl. Hist. Nat. (Ser. 2) v. 15 (no. 5): 289-293. [Publication date possibly 1944.]

———. 1947 **[ref. 800]**. Notules ichthyologiques. XXXIII.—Définition d'un genre inédit, appartenant à la famille des Cynoglossidae. Bull. Mus. Natl. Hist. Nat. (Ser. 2) v. 19: 443.

———. 1950 (Dec.) **[ref. 801]**. Description de nouveaux Soleidae, capturés au cours de l'Expédition océanographique belge dans les eaux africaines de l'Atlantique Sud (1948-1949). Bull. Inst. R. Sci. Nat. Belg. v. 26 (no. 55): 1-19.

———. 1951 (30 Oct.) **[ref. 802]**. Description d'une espèce nouvelle, type d'un genre inédit, appartenant à la famille des Cynoglossidae, sous-famille des Cynoglossinae. Beaufortia No. 7: 1-10.

———. 1956 **[ref. 803]**. Rectifications afférentes à la nomenclature et à la systématique des Pleuronectiformes du sous-ordre des Soleoidei. Bull. Mus. Natl. Hist. Nat. (Ser. 2) v. 27 (no. 6): 447-452.

Chan, W. L. 1966 **[ref. 806]**. New sharks from the South China Sea. J. Zool. (Lond.) v. 148: 218-237, Pls. 1-3.

———. 1966 (20 Aug.) **[ref. 807]**. A new genus and species of deep-sea brotulid from the South China Sea. Jpn. J. Ichthyol. v. 14 (no. 1/3): 4-8.

——. 1970 (Oct.) **[ref. 808]**. A new genus and two new species of commercial snappers from Hong Kong. Hong Kong Fish. Bull. No. 1: 19-38.

Chan, W. L., and R. M. Chilvers. 1974 **[ref. 809]**. A revision of the Indo-Pacific spariform percoids of the Monotaxinae, with the description of a new genus *Wattsia*. Hong Kong Fish. Bull. No. 4: 85-95.

Chang, H.-W. 1944 (Dec.) **[ref. 5136]**. Notes of the fishes of western Szechwan and eastern Sikang. Sinensia v. 15 (nos. 1-6): 27-60.

Chang, Y.-W., and C.-T. Wu. 1965 **[ref. 811]**. A new pangasid cat-fish, *Sinopangasius semicultratus* gen. et sp. nov., found in China. Acta Zootaxon. Sin. v. 2: 11-14. [In Chinese and English.]

Chao, L. N. 1978 (Sept.) **[ref. 6983]**. A basis for classifying western Atlantic Sciaenidae (Teleostei: Perciformes). NOAA Tech. Rep. NMFS Circ. No. 415: i-v + 1-64.

Chapleau, F. 1988 **[ref. 13819]**. Comparative osteology and intergeneric relationships of the tongue soles (Pisces; Pleuronectiformes; Cynoglossidae). Can. J. Zool. v. 66: 1214-1232.

Chapleau, F., and A. Keast. 1988 (23 Oct.) **[ref. 12625]**. A phylogenetic reassessment of the monophyletic status of the family Soleidae, with comments on the suborder Soleoidei (Pisces: Pleuronectiformes). Can. J. Zool. v. 66: 2797-2810.

Chapman, W. M. 1939 (28 Apr.) **[ref. 817]**. Eleven new species and three new genera of oceanic fishes collected by the International Fisheries Commission from the northeastern Pacific. Proc. U. S. Natl. Mus. v. 86 (no. 3062): 501-542.

——. 1942 (Apr.) **[ref. 818]**. The osteology and relationship of the bathypelagic fish *Macropinna microstoma*, with notes on its visceral anatomy. Ann. Mag. Nat. Hist. (Ser. 11) v. 9 (no. 52): 272-304.

Chaudhuri, B. L. 1913 (Sept.) **[ref. 819]**. Zoological results of the Abor Expedition, 1911-12. XVIII. Fish. Rec. Indian Mus. (Calcutta) v. 8 (pt 3): 243-257, Pls. 7-9.

Chen, J. T. F., and Y.-S. Liang. 1948 (July) **[ref. 823]**. A new genus and species of the family Acanthoclinidae. Q. J. Taiwan Mus. (Taipei) v. 1 (no. 3): 31-34.

Chen, L.-C. 1985 (1 Dec.) **[ref. 6543]**. A study of the *Sebastes inermis* species complex, with delimitation of the subgenus *Membarus*. J. Taiwan Mus. v. 38 (no. 2): 23-37.

Chen, L.-C., and W.-Y. Liu. 1984 **[ref. 13451]**. *Pteroidichthys amboinensis*, a scorpaenid fish new to Taiwan, with a description of the species and a discussion of its validity. J. Taiwan Mus. v. 37 (no. 2): 93-95.

Chen, M.-H., and K.-T. Shao. 1988 (30 June) **[ref. 6676]**. Fish of Triglidae (Scorpaenoidei) from Taiwan. J. Taiwan Mus. v. 41 (no. 1): 127-138.

Chen, X.-L., and H.-Q. Huang. 1977 **[ref. 13496]**. Cyprinidae. Pp. 395-438. In: Wu et al. 1977 [ref. 12558].

Chen, Y. 1982 (May) **[ref. 824]**. A revision of opsariichthine cyprinid fishes. Oceanol. Limnol. Sin. v. 13 (no. 3): 293-299. [In Chinese, shorter version in English (p. 299).]

Chen, Y.-R., and X.-L. Chu. 1985 (Feb.) **[ref. 5250]**. Systematic study of the genus *Tor* (Pisces: Cyprinidae) with description of a new species. Zool. Res. v. 6 (no. 1): 79-86.

Chen, Y.-Y. 1978 (Dec.) **[ref. 6900]**. Systematic studies on the fishes of the family Homalopteridae of China. I. Classification of the fishes of the subfamily Homalopterinae. Acta Hydrobiol. Sin. v. 6 (no. 3): 331-348. [In Chinese, English Summ.]

——. 1980 (May) **[ref. 6901]**. Systematic studies of the fishes of the family Homalopteridae of China II. Classification of the fishes of the subfamily Gastormyzoninae. Acta Hydrobiol. Sin. v. 7 (no. 1): 95-120. [In Chinese, English Abstract and summary of new taxa.]

——. 1982 (Oct.) **[ref. 826]**. Description of a new genus and species of cyprinid fish. Acta Zootaxon. Sin. v. 7 (no. 4): 425-427. [In Chinese, English summ.]

——. 1989 (May) **[ref. 14144]**. Anatomy and phylogeny of the cyprinid fish genus *Onychostoma* Günther, 1896. Bull. Br. Mus. (Nat. Hist.) Zool. v. 55 (no. 1): 109-121.

Chen, Y.-Y., and W.-H. Tsao. 1977 **[ref. 825]**. Gobiobotinae. Pp. 550-570. In: Wu et al. 1977 [ref. 12558]. [In Chinese.]

Cheng, C.-T. 1950 **[ref. 828]**. Description d'un genre nouveau du Yunnan, Chine, appartenant a la sous-famille des Cyprininés, s. str. Bull. Mus. Natl. Hist. Nat. (Ser. 2) v. 22 (no. 5): 568-570.

Cheng, C.-T., and C.-X Wang (T. H. Wang). 1979 (Jan.) **[ref. 827]**. Description of a new genus and a new species of a labroid fish of China. Oceanol. Limnol. Sin. v. 10 (no. 1): 73-76. [In Chinese, with shorter English version (pp. 75-76).]

Chernoff, B. 1981 (29 Dec.) **[ref. 6824]**. Taxonomy of the Mexican atherinid fish genus *Archomenidia*. Copeia 1981 (no. 4): 913-914.

——. 1986 **[ref. 5847]**. Phylogenetic relationships and reclassification of Menidiinae silverside fishes with emphasis on the tribe Membradini. Proc. Acad. Nat. Sci. Phila. v. 138 (no. 1): 189-249.

——. 1986 **[ref. 5848]**. Systematics of American atherinid fishes of the genus *Atherinella*. I. The subgenus *Atherinella*. Proc. Acad. Nat. Sci. Phila. v. 138 (no. 1): 86-188.

Chernoff, B., J. V. Conner and C. F. Bryan. 1981 (15 May) **[ref. 5466]**. Systematics of the *Menidia beryllina* complex (Pisces: Atherinidae) from the Gulf of Mexico and its tributaries. Copeia 1981 (no. 2): 319-336.

Chernoff, B., and R. R. Miller. 1982 **[ref. 8494]**. Mexican freshwater silversides (Pisces: Atherinidae) of the genus *Archomenidia*, with the description of a new species. Proc. Biol. Soc. Wash. v. 95 (no. 3): 428-439.

——. 1984 (10 Oct.) **[ref. 8175]**. *Atherinella ammophila*, a new atherinid fish from eastern Mexico. Not. Nat. (Phila.) No. 462: 1-12.

——. 1986 (10 Feb.) **[ref. 6782]**. Fishes of the *Notropis calientis* complex with a key to the southern shiners of Mexico. Copeia 1986 (no. 1): 170-183.

Chernova, N. V. 1987 **[ref. 6341]**. Fishes of the family Liparididae of the Barents Sea and adjoining waters. Report II. *Liparis liparis* L. and *L. montagui* (Donovan). USSR Acad. Sci., Proc. Zool. Inst. Leningrad v. 162: 81-94. [In Russian, English summ.]

——. 1988 **[ref. 13480]**. Fishes of the family Liparididae of the Barents Sea and adjacent waters. I. Specific composition of the genus *Liparis*. Voprosy Ikhtiol. 1988 (no. 4): 556-561. [In Russian. English translation in J. Ichthyol. 1988, v. 28 (no. 6): 62-67.]

Chevey, P. 1927 **[ref. 829]**. Sur un genre nouveau de Scorpenidae du Tonkin. Bull. Mus. Natl. Hist. Nat. (Ser. 1) v. 33 [1927]: 222-223.

——. 1931 (3 Mar.) **[ref. 830]**. Sur un nouveau Silure Géant du Bassin du Mékong *Pangasianodon gigas* nov. g., nov. sp. Bull. Soc. Zool. Fr. v. 55 (for 1930): 536-542, Pl. 1.

Chirichigno-F., N. 1987 (May) **[ref. 12856]**. *Medialuna ancietae* nov. sp. Un pez nuevo del mar peruano. Biologia Lima No. 51: 89-95.

Chu, X.-L. 1979 (Feb.) **[ref. 831]**. Systematics and evolutionary pedigree of the glyptosternoid fishes (family Sisoridae). Acta Zootaxon. Sin. v. 4 (no. 1): 72-82. [In Chinese, English summ.]

——. 1981 (May) **[ref. 5248]**. A preliminary revision of fishes of the genus *Danio* from China. Zool. Res. v. 2 (no. 2): 145-156. [In Chinese, English summ.]

——. 1981 (Feb.) **[ref. 5249]**. Taxonomic revision of the genera *Pareuchiloglanis* and *Euchiloglanis*. Zool. Res. v. 2 (no. 1): 25-31. [In Chinese, English summ.]

——. 1982 (Oct.) **[ref. 5245]**. Phylogeny of the genus *Pseudecheneis* (Siluriformes: Sisoridae), with descriptions of two new species. Acta Zootaxon. Sin. v. 7 (no. 4): 428-437. [In Chinese, English summ.]

Chu, X.-L., and Y.-R. Chen. 1982 (Dec.) **[ref. 836]**. A new genus and species of blind cyprinid fish from China with special reference to its relationships. Acta Zool. Sin. v. 28 (no. 4): 383-388. [In Chinese, English abst.]

——. 1989 **[ref. 13584]**. (eds.) The fishes of Yunnan, China. Part 1 Cyprinidae. Science Press, Beijing, China. i-vii + 1-377.

Chu, X.-L., and M. Kottelat. 1989 (28 June) **[ref. 12575]**. *Paraspinibarbus*, a new genus of cyprinid fishes from the Red River

Basin. Jpn. J. Ichthyol. v. 36 (no. 1): 1-5.

CHU, X.-L., AND T. R. ROBERTS. 1985 (29 Aug.) **[ref. 5244]**. *Cosmochilus cardinalis*, a new cyprinid fish from the Lancang-Jiang or Mekong River in Yunnan Province, China. Proc. Calif. Acad. Sci. v. 44 (no. 1): 1-7.

CHU, Y.-T. 1935 (Jan.) **[ref. 832]**. Comparative studies on the scales and on the pharyngeals and their teeth in Chinese cyprinids, with particular reference to taxonomy and evolution. Biol. Bull. St. John's Univ. Shanghai No. 2: i-x + 1-225, Pls. 1-30.

CHU, Y.-T., Y.-L. LO AND H.-L. WU. 1963 **[ref. 833]**. A study on the classification of the sciaenoid fishes of China, with description of new genera and species. Monographs of fishes of China. Publ. Shanghai Fish. Inst. i-ii, 1-100, 40 pls. [In Chinese, English resumé (pp. 83-94).]

CHU, Y.-T., C.-W. MENG AND J.-X. LIU. 1981 (Jan.) **[ref. 835]**. Description of a new genus and a new species of Squalidae of China. Acta Zootaxon. Sin. v. 6 (no. 1): 100-103. [In Chinese, English summ.]

CHU, Y.-T., AND H.-L. WU. 1962 **[ref. 834]**. Description of a new genus and a new species of a trichiuroid fish of China. Acta Zool. Sin. v. 14: 219-223. [In Chinese and English (pp. 222-223).]

CLARK, E., AND A. BEN-TUVIA. 1973 **[ref. 838]**. Red Sea fishes of the family Branchiostegidae with a description of a new genus and species *Asymmetrurus oreni*. Bull. Sea Fish. Res. Sta. Israel No. 60: 63-74.

CLARK, E., AND A. GEORGE. 1979 **[ref. 6992]**. Toxic soles, *Pardachirus marmoratus* from the Red Sea and *P. pavoninus* from Japan, with notes on other species. Environ. Biol. Fishes v. 4 (no. 2): 103-123.

CLARK, H. W. 1936 (12 Aug.) **[ref. 839]**. New and noteworthy fishes. The Templeton Crocker expedition of the California Academy of Sciences, 1932. Proc. Calif. Acad. Sci. (Ser. 4) v. 21 (no. 29): 383-396.

———. 1937 (18 Aug.) **[ref. 840]**. New fishes from the Templeton Crocker expedition of 1934-35. Copeia 1937 (no. 2): 88-91.

CLARK HUBBS. See Hubbs, Clark

CLARKE, F. E. 1878 (May) **[ref. 841]**. On two new fishes. Trans. Proc. N. Z. Inst. v. 10 (for 1877): 243-246, Pl. 6.

CLARKE, T. A. 1984 (1 Aug.) **[ref. 6811]**. Diet and morphological variation in snipefishes, presently recognized as *Macrorhamphosus scolopax*, from southeast Australia: evidence for two sexually dimorphic species. Copeia 1984 (no. 3): 595-608.

———. 1984 (23 Feb.) **[ref. 6814]**. Ecology and sexual dimorphism of the pelagic eel, *Stemonidium hypomelas* (Serrivomeridae). Copeia 1984 (no. 1): 249-252.

CLAUSEN, H. S. 1959 **[ref. 842]**. Denticipitidae, a new family of primitive Isospondylous teleosts from West African fresh-water. Vidensk. Medd. Dansk Naturh. Foren. Kjob. v. 121: 141-151, Pls. 1-2.

———. 1959 **[ref. 843]**. Description of two subgenera and six new species of *Procatopus* Boul., a little-known West African genus of cyprinodont fishes. Vidensk. Medd. Dansk Naturh. Foren. Kjob. v. 121: 261-291.

———. 1966 (30 Dec.) **[ref. 844]**. Definition of a new cyprinodont genus and description of a 'new' but well-known West African cyprinodont, with a clarification of the terms '*sjöstedti*,' *Aphyosemion sjöstedti* (Lönnberg), and *Aphyosemion coeruleum* (Boulenger). Rev. Zool. Bot. Afr. v. 74 (pts 3-4): 331-341.

———. 1967 **[ref. 5926]**. Tropical Old World cyprinodonts. Reflections on the taxonomy of tropical Old World cyprinodonts, with remarks on their biology and distribution. Akad. Forlag, København. 1-64.

CLIGNY, A. 1909 **[ref. 850]**. Sur un nouveau genre de Zeidés. C. R. Hebd. Seances Acad. Sci. v. 148: 873-874.

CLOQUET, H. 1816 **[ref. 12560]**. [Pisces accounts.] In: Dictionnaire des sciences naturelles. v. 2, suppl.: 35-36.

———. 1816-30 **[ref. 852]**. [Pisces accounts.] In: Dictionnaire des sciences naturelles. Volumes 1-60. [Initials after accounts correspond to authors given in Vol. 1; fish accounts by Lacepède (L. L.), Duméril (C. D.), Daudin (F. M. D.) and Cloquet (H. C.)]. [Dates for volumes are given by Cassini 1834, *Opuscles Phytologiques, p. 47.]*

———. 1827 **[ref. 853]**. Nouveax Dictionnaire d'Histoire Naturelle: Nouvelle Edition, XXX. [For dates see Sherborn 1922, Index Animalium, ed. 2, pt 1, p. xliv.]

COAD, B. W. 1981 **[ref. 5572]**. *Pseudophoxinus persidis*, a new cyprinid fish from Fars, southern Iran. Can. J. Zool. v. 59 (no. 11): 2058-2063.

———. 1982 (23 Feb.) **[ref. 854]**. A new genus and species of cichlid endemic to southern Iran. Copeia 1982 (no. 1): 28-37.

———. 1982 (Nov.) **[ref. 5430]**. A re-description and generic re-assignment of *Kosswigobarbus kosswigi* (Ladiges, 1960), a cyprinid fish from Turkey and Iran. Mitt. Hamb. Zool. Mus. Inst. v. 79: 263-265.

———. 1984 **[ref. 5347]**. *Acanthobrama centisquama* Heckel and the validity of the genus *Micogrex* Goren, Fishelson and Trewavas (Osteichthyes: Cyprinidae). Hydrobiologia v. 109: 275-278.

———. 1988 **[ref. 11814]**. *Aphanius vladykovi*, a new species of tooth-carp from the Zagros mountains of Iran. Environ. Biol. Fishes v. 23 (no. 1-2): 115-125.

COAD, B. W., AND G. B. DELMASTRO. 1985 (30 Nov.) **[ref. 6495]**. Notes on a sisorid catfish from the Black Sea drainage of Turkey. Cybium v. 9 (no. 3): 221-224.

COCCO, A. 1829 **[ref. 857]**. Su alcuni nuovi pesci del mar di Messina. Giorn. Sci. Lett. Art. Sicilia v. 26 (no. 77): 138-147.

———. 1829 **[ref. 858]**. Sullo *Schedophilus medusophagus*. Giorn. Gabin. Litt. Messina v. 1: 30-32. [Also quoted as Innom. Messina Ann. 3: 57. Neither seen.]

———. 1833 **[ref. 859]**. Su di alcuni pesci de' mari di Messina Lettere di Anastasio Cocco al sig. A. Risso. Giorn. Sci. Lett. Art. Sicilia v. 42 (no. 124): 9-21, 1 pl.

———. 1833 **[ref. 861]**. Osservationes Peloritani. [Not seen.]

———. 1838 **[ref. 865]**. Su di alcuni salmonidi del mare di Messina; littera del Prof. Anastasio Cocco al Ch. D. Carlo Luciano Bonaparte. Nuovi Ann. Sci. Nat. v. 2 (fasc. 9): 161-194, Pls. 1-4. [Also as a separate, pp. 1-34.]

———. 1838 **[ref. 6499]**. [Title uncertain.] Nuovi. Ann. Sci. Nat. Bologna v. 2: e.g. 26. [Not seen.]

———. 1844 **[ref. 866]**. Intorno ad alcuni nuovi pesci del mare di Messina. Lettera del Prof. Anastasio Cocco al Signor Augusto Krohn. Messina. Giorn. Gabin. Lett. Messina Anno. 3, Tome 5: 21-30, Pl. 2. [Also as a separate, pp. 1-10, 1 pl. Reissued with corrections in 1888 in Naturalista Siciliano, e.g. 101-104, 125-128.]

———. 1846 **[ref. 5016]**. [Title uncertain.] Giorn. Gabin. Lett. Messina Ann. [Not seen.]

COCKERELL, T. D. A. 1909 (31 Dec.) **[ref. 868]**. The nomenclature of the American fishes usually called *Leuciscus* and *Rutilus*. Proc. Biol. Soc. Wash. v. 22: 215-217.

———. 1910 (2 Sept.) **[ref. 869]**. The scales of the African cyprinid fishes, with a discussion of related Asiatic and European species. Proc. Biol. Soc. Wash. v. 23: 141-152, Pl. 3.

———. 1913 (25 Oct.) **[ref. 870]**. Observations on fish scales. Bull. Bur. Fish. v. 32 (for 1912): 117-174, Pls. 32-40.

———. 1919 (24 Apr.) **[ref. 872]**. Some American Cretaceous fish scales, with notes on the classification and distribution of Cretaceous fishes. U. S. Geol. Survey, Prof. Papers No. 120-I: 165-188, Pls. 31-37.

———. 1923 (5 Dec.) **[ref. 13498]**. The scales of the cyprinid genus *Barilius*. Bull. Am. Mus. Nat. Hist. v. 48 (art. 14): 531-532.

COCKERELL, T. D. A., AND E. M. ALLISON. 1909 (28 July) **[ref. 875]**. The scales of some American Cyprinidae. Proc. Biol. Soc. Wash. v. 22: 157-163.

COCKERELL, T. D. A., AND O. CALLAWAY. 1909 (8 Dec.) **[ref. 876]**. Observations on the fishes of the genus *Notropis*. Proc. Biol. Soc. Wash. v. 22: 189-196.

COENEN, E. J., AND G. G. TEUGELS. 1989 (31 Dec.) **[ref. 13539]**. A new species of *Nannocharax* (Pisces, Distichodontidae) from southeast Nigeria and west Cameroun, with comments on the taxonomic status of *Hemigrammocharax polli* Roman, 1966. Cybium v. 13 (no. 4): 311-318.

COGGER, H. G. 1987 **[ref. 13912]**. Classification and nomenclature. Chapter 12A. Pp. 266-285. Fauna of Australia.

COHEN, D. M. 1958 (31 July) **[ref. 877]**. *Bathylychnops exilis*, a new genus and species of argentinoid fish from the North Pacific. Stanford Ichthyol. Bull. v. 7 (no. 3): 47-52.

——. 1958 (2 July) **[ref. 878]**. A revision of the fishes of the subfamily Argentininae. Bull. Fla. State Mus. Biol. Sci. v. 3 (no. 3): 93-172.

——. 1958 (18 June) **[ref. 13649]**. A nomenclatural discussion of the argentinid fish *Microstoma microstoma* (Risso) with new records from the eastern Pacific, and comments on the possible identity of the genus *Halaphya* Günther. Copeia 1958 (no. 2): 133-134.

——. 1961 (22 Sept.) **[ref. 879]**. A new genus and species of deepwater ophidioid fish from the Gulf of Mexico. Copeia 1961 (no. 3): 288-292.

——. 1963 (31 Dec.) **[ref. 880]**. A new genus and species of bathypelagic ophidioid fish from the western North Atlantic. Breviora No. 196: 1-8.

——. 1963 **[ref. 6883]**. The publication dates of Goode and Bean's *Oceanic Ichthyology*. J. Soc. Bibliogr. Nat. Hist. v. 4 (no. 3): 162-166.

——. 1964 **[ref. 6891]**. A review of the ophidioid fish genus *Oligopus* with the description of a new species from west Africa. Proc. U. S. Natl. Mus. v. 116 (no. 3494): 1-22.

——. 1972 (30 Dec.) **[ref. 7157]**. A review of the viviparous ophidioid fishes of the genus *Saccogaster*. Proc. Biol. Soc. Wash. v. 85 (no. 39): 445-468.

——. 1973 **[ref. 6589]**. Argentinidae (pp. 152-154), Bathylagidae (p. 155), Opisthoproctidae (pp. 156-157), Bregmacerotidae (p. 321), Eretmophoridae (pp. 322-326), Melanonidae (p. 327). In: Hureau & Monod 1973 [ref. 6590].

——. 1973 **[ref. 7137]**. The gadoid fish genus *Halargyreus* (family Eretmophoridae) in the Southern Hemisphere. J. R. Soc. N. Z. v. 3 (no. 4): 629-634.

——. 1973 (28 Sept.) **[ref. 7138]**. Viviparous ophidioid fish genus *Calamopteryx*: new species from western Atlantic and Galapagos. Proc. Biol. Soc. Wash. v. 86 (no. 28): 339-350.

——. 1974 **[ref. 6890]**. A review of the pelagic ophidioid fish genus *Brotulataenia* [sic] with descriptions of two new species. Zool. J. Linn. Soc. v. 55 (no. 2): 119-149.

——. 1974 **[ref. 7139]**. The ophidioid fish genus *Luciobrotula* in the Hawaiian Islands. Pac. Sci. v. 28 (no. 2): 109-110.

——. 1979 (15 Dec.) **[ref. 6950]**. Notes on the morid fish genera *Lotella* and *Physiculus* in Japanese waters. Jpn. J. Ichthyol. v. 26 (no. 3): 225-230.

——. 1981 (20 July) **[ref. 5586]**. *Saccogaster melanomycter* (Ophidiiformes: Bythitidae), a new fish species from the Caribbean. Proc. Biol. Soc. Wash. v. 94 (no. 2): 374-377.

——. 1982 **[ref. 5521]**. The deepsea fish genus *Enchelybrotula* (Ophidiidae): description of new species, notes on distribution, and osteology. Bull. Mar. Sci. v. 32 (no. 1): 99-111.

——. 1984 **[ref. 13646]**. Gadiformes: overview. Am. Soc. Ichthyol. Herpetol. Spec. Publ. No. 1: 259-265.

——. 1986 **[ref. 5646]**. Family No. 61: Argentinidae (pp. 215-216), Family 62: Bathylagidae (p. 216), Family 88: Gadidae (p. 324), Family 89: Merlucciidae (pp. 324-326), Family 90: Moridae (pp. 326-328), Family 91: Melanonidae (pp. 328-329), Family 98: Bythitidae (pp. 354-356). In: Smiths' Sea Fishes (Smith & Heemstra 1986 [ref. 5715]).

——. 1987 (18 June) **[ref. 6040]**. Notes on the bythitid fish genus *Saccogaster* with a new species from the Gulf of Mexico. Contrib. Sci. (Los Ang.) No. 385: 1-4.

——. 1989 (30 Mar.) **[ref. 13632]**. (Ed.) Papers on the systematics of gadiform fishes. Sci. Ser., Nat. Hist. Mus. Los Angeles Co. No. 32: i-ix + 1-262.

COHEN, D. M., AND J. G. NIELSEN. 1978 (Dec.) **[ref. 881]**. Guide to the identification of genera of the fish order Ophidiiformes with a tentative classification of the order. NOAA Tech. Rep. NMFS Circ. No. 417: 1-72.

——. 1982 (10 Aug.) **[ref. 5406]**. *Spottobrotula amaculata*, a new ophidiid fish from the Philippines. Copeia 1982 (no. 3): 497-500.

COHEN, D. M., AND C. R. ROBINS. 1986 (May) **[ref. 5254]**. A review of the ophidiid fish genus *Sirembo* with a new species from Australia. Mem. Queensl. Mus. v. 22 (pt 2): 253-263, 2 pls.

COHEN, D. M., AND J. L. RUSSO. 1979 **[ref. 6975]**. Variation in the fourbeard rockling, *Enchelyopus cimbrius*, a North Atlantic gadid fish, with comments on the genera of rocklings. U. S. Natl. Mar. Fish. Serv. Fish. Bull. v. 77 (no. 1): 91-104.

COHEN, D. M., AND J. P. WOURMS. 1976 (25 June) **[ref. 7046]**. *Microbrotula randalli*, a new viviparous ophidioid fish from Samoa and New Hebrides, whose embryos bear trophotaeniae. Proc. Biol. Soc. Wash. v. 89 (no. 5): 81-98.

COKER, R. E. 1926 (17 Aug.) **[ref. 5553]**. New genus of darter from western North Carolina. Bull. Bur. Fish. v. 42 (for 1926): 105-108.

——. 1927 **[ref. 882]**. *Richiella* to replace *Richia* as name for genus of darter. Copeia No. 162: 17-18.

COLEMAN, L. R., AND B. G. NAFPAKTITIS. 1972 (2 Mar.) **[ref. 883]**. *Dorsadena yaquinae*, a new genus and species of myctophid fish from the eastern North Pacific Ocean. Contrib. Sci. (Los Ang.) No. 225: 1-11.

COLLARES-PEREIRA, M. J. 1983 **[ref. 6668]**. Les phoxinelles circum-méditerraneéns (avec la description d'*Anaecypris* n. gen.) (Poissons, Cyprinidae). Cybium (Ser. 3) v. 7 (no. 3): 1-7.

COLLETT, R. 1875 **[ref. 884]**. Norges fiske, med bemaerkninger om deres Udbredelse. Christiania. 1-240, 2 pls. + map.

——. 1875 **[ref. 6521]**. Bidrage til Kundskaben om Norges Gobier. Forh. Vidensk. Selsk. Christiania 1875: 151-179, 1 pl.

——. 1878 **[ref. 885]**. Fiske fra Nordhavs-expeditionens sidste togt, sommeren 1878. Forh. Vidensk. Selsk. Christiania v. 14: 1-106. [Date may be 1879. Also as a separate.]

——. 1879 (Aug.) **[ref. 886]**. On a new fish of the genus *Lycodes* from the Pacific. Proc. Zool. Soc. Lond. 1879 (pt 2): 381-382.

——. 1880 **[ref. 887]**. Den Norske Nordhavs Expedition, 1876-1878. Zoologi. Fiske. Grøndahl & Son, Christiania. 1-164, 5 pls. [In Norwegian and English.]

——. 1886 (Aug.) **[ref. 888]**. On a new pediculate fish from the sea off Madeira. Proc. Zool. Soc. Lond. 1886 (pt 2): 138-143, Pl. 15.

——. 1889 **[ref. 889]**. Diagnoses de poissons nouveaux provenant des campagnes de "L'Hirondelle." I.—Sur un genre nouveau de la famille des Muraenidae. Bull. Soc. Zool. Fr. v. 14: 123-125.

——. 1889 **[ref. 4875]**. Diagnoses des poissons nouveaux provenant des campagnes de "L'Hirondelle."—II. Sur un genre nouveau de la famille des Stomiatidae. Bull. Soc. Zool. Fr. v. 14: 291-293 (continued from p. 125).

——. 1896 **[ref. 890]**. Poissons provenant des campagnes du Yacht "L'Hirondelle" (1885-1888). Résultats des campagnes scientifiques accomplies sur son yacht par Albert I, Prince Souverain de Monaco. Résultats des campagnes scientifiques du Prince de Monaco. Fasc. 10: i-viii + 1-198, 6 pls.

——. 1904 **[ref. 9338]**. Diagnoses of four hitherto undescribed fishes from the depths south of the Faroe Islands. Forh. Vidensk. Selsk. Christiania No. 9: 1-7.

COLLETTE, B. B. 1962 (Sept.) **[ref. 4554]**. *Hemiramphus bermudensis*, a new halfbeak from Bermuda, with a survey of endemism in Bermudian shore fishes. Bull. Mar. Sci. Gulf Caribb. v. 12 (no. 3): 432-449.

——. 1963 (31 Dec.) **[ref. 6459]**. The subfamilies, tribes, and genera of the Percidae (Teleostei). Copeia 1963 (no. 4): 615-623.

——. 1966 (19 Dec.) **[ref. 892]**. *Belonion*, a new genus of freshwater needlefishes from South America. Am. Mus. Novit. No. 2274: 1-22.

——. 1966 (23 Dec.) **[ref. 14192]**. A review of the venomous toadfishes, subfamily Thalassophryninae. Copeia 1966 (no. 4): 846-864.

——. 1974 (22 Oct.) **[ref. 5218]**. A review of the coral toadfishes of the genus *Sanopus* with descriptions of two new species from Cozumel Island, Mexico. Proc. Biol. Soc. Wash. v. 87 (no. 18): 185-204, Pl. 1.

——. 1974 (24 Oct.) **[ref. 7131]**. South American freshwater needlefishes (Belonidae) of the genus *Pseudotylosurus*. Zool. Meded. v. 48 (no. 16): 169-186.

——. 1976 (Jan.) **[ref. 7107]**. Indo-West Pacific halfbeaks (Hemiramphidae) of the genus *Rhynchorhamphus* with descriptions of two new species. Bull. Mar. Sci. v. 26 (no. 1): 72-98.

——. 1982 (20 Dec.) **[ref. 5467]**. South American freshwater needlefishes of the genus *Potamorrhaphis* (Beloniformes: Belonidae). Proc. Biol. Soc. Wash. v. 95 (no. 4): 714-747.

——. 1982 (28 May) **[ref. 5497]**. Two new species of freshwater halfbeaks (Pisces: Hemiramphidae) of the genus *Zenarchopterus* from New Guinea. Copeia 1982 (no. 2): 265-276.

——. 1983 (29 Dec.) **[ref. 5219]**. Two new species of coral toadfishes, family Batrachoididae, genus *Sanopus*, from Yucatan, Mexico, and Belize. Proc. Biol. Soc. Wash. v. 96 (no. 4): 719-724.

——. 1983 (29 Dec.) **[ref. 5220]**. Recognition of two species of double-lined mackerels (*Grammatorcynus*: Scombridae). Proc. Biol. Soc. Wash. v. 96 (no. 4): 715-718.

——. 1986 **[ref. 5647]**. Family No. 113: Belonidae (pp. 385-387), Family No. 115: Hemiramphidae (pp. 388-391), Family No. 249: Scombridae (pp. 831-838). In: Smiths' Sea Fishes (Smith & Heemstra 1986 [ref. 5715]).

——. 1986 (Apr.) **[ref. 6197]**. Hemiramphidae (pp. 163-164). In: Daget et al. 1986 [ref. 6189].

Collette, B. B., and P. Banarescu. 1977 (Oct.) **[ref. 5845]**. Systematics and zoogeography of the fishes of the family Percidae. J. Fish. Res. Board Can. v. 34 (no. 10): 1450-1463.

Collette, B. B., and L. N. Chao. 1975 **[ref. 5573]**. Systematics and morphology of the bonitos (*Sarda*) and their relatives (Scombridae, Sardini). U. S. Natl. Mar. Fish. Serv. Fish. Bull. v. 73 (no. 3): 516-625.

Collette, B. B., G. E. McGowen, N. V. Parin, and S. Mito. 1984 **[ref. 11422]**. Beloniformes: Development and relationships. In: Ontogeny and systematics of fishes. Am. Soc. Ichthyol. Herpetol. Spec. Publ. No. 1: 335-354.

Collette, B. B., and C. E. Nauen. 1983 **[ref. 5375]**. FAO species catalogue. Vol. 2. Scombrids of the world. An annotated and illustrated catalogue of tunas, mackerels, bonitos and related species known to date. FAO Fish. Synop. No. 125: i-vii + 1-137.

Collette, B. B., T. Potthoff, W. J. Richards, S. Uyanagi, J. L. Russo, and Y. Nishikawa. 1984 **[ref. 11421]**. Scombroidei: Development and Relationships. In: Ontogeny and Systematics of fishes. Am. Soc. Ichthyol. Herpetol. Spec. Publ. No. 1: 591-620.

Collette, B. B., and J. L. Russo. 1981 **[ref. 5575]**. A revision of the scaly toadfishes, genus *Batrachoides*, with descriptions of two new species from the eastern Pacific. Bull. Mar. Sci. v. 31 (no. 2): 197-233.

——. 1984 **[ref. 5221]**. Morphology, systematics, and biology of the Spanish mackerels (*Scomberomorus*, Scombridae). U. S. Natl. Mar. Fish. Serv. Fish. Bull. v. 82 (no. 4): 545-692.

——. 1985 **[ref. 5217]**. Interrelationships of the Spanish mackerels (Pisces: Scombridae: *Scomberomorus*) and their copepod parasites. Cladistics v. 1 (no. 2): 141-158.

——. 1986 (30 May) **[ref. 6324]**. Systematic status of the suborder Scombroidei [Abstract]. P. 938. In: Uyeno et al. (eds.) 1986 [ref. 6147].

Collette, B. B., and J.-X. Su. 1986 **[ref. 5998]**. The halfbeaks (Pisces, Beloniformes, Hemiramphidae) of the Far East. Proc. Acad. Nat. Sci. Phila. v. 138 (no. 1): 250-302.

Colombe, J., and R. Allgayer. 1985 (MAy) **[ref. 13457]**. Description de *Variabilchromis*, *Neolamprologus* et *Paleolamprologus* genres nouveaux du Lac Tanganyika, avec redescription des genres *Lamprologus* Schilthuis, 1891 et *Lepidiolamprologus* Pellegrin, 1904. Rev. Franc. Cichlidophiles No. 49: 9-28.

Compagno, L. J. V. 1973 (9 July) **[ref. 897]**. *Ctenacis* and *Gollum*, two new genera of sharks (Selachii; Carcharhinidae). Proc. Calif. Acad. Sci. (Ser. 4) v. 39 (no. 14): 257-272.

——. 1973 (24 Oct.) **[ref. 898]**. *Gogolia filewoodi*, a new genus and species of shark from New Guinea (Carcharhiniformes: Triakidae), with a redefinition of the family Triakidae and a key to triakid genera. Proc. Calif. Acad. Sci. (Ser. 4) v. 39 (no. 19): 383-410.

——. 1973 **[ref. 7163]**. Carcharhinidae (pp. 23-31). In: Hureau & Monod 1973 [ref. 6590].

——. 1984 **[ref. 6474]**. FAO species catalogue. Vol. 4. Sharks of the world. An annotated and illustrated catalogue of shark species known to date. Part 1 - Hexanchiformes to Lamniformes. i-viii + 1-249.

——. 1984 **[ref. 6846]**. FAO species catalogue. Vol. 4. Sharks of the world. An annotated and illustrated catalogue of shark species known to date. Part 2. Charcharhiniformes. FAO Fish. Synop. No. 125, v. 4 (pt 2): 251-655.

——. 1986 **[ref. 5648]**. [Various elasmobranch and chimaeriform families.] Family No. 22 (pp. 110-111), 23 (pp. 112-113), 24 (pp. 113-114), 27 (pp. 128-131), 28 (pp. 132-134), 29 (pp. 134-135), 30 (pp. 135-142), 32 (pp. 144-145), 33 (pp. 146-147), 34 (p. 147). In: Smiths' Sea Fishes (Smith & Heemstra 1986 [ref. 5715]).

——. 1988 **[ref. 13488]**. Sharks of the order Carcharhiniformes. Princeton Univ. Press, Princeton, N. J. i-xxii + 1-486 + separate figs., Pls. 1-35.

Compagno, L. J. V., and J. A. F. Garrick. 1983 (Aug.) **[ref. 5410]**. *Nasolamia*, new genus, for the shark *Carcharhinus velox* Gilbert, 1898 (Elasmobranchii: Carcharhinidae). Zool. Publ. Victoria Univ. Wellington No. 76: 1-16.

Compagno, L. J. V., and T. R. Roberts. 1984 **[ref. 6167]**. Dasyatidae (pp. 4-5). In: Daget et al. 1984 [ref. 6168].

Compagno, L. J. V., and M. J. Smale. 1985 (Apr.) **[ref. 5649]**. *Paragaleus leucolomatus*, a new shark from South Africa, with notes on the systematics of hemigaleid sharks (Carcharhiniformes: Hemigaleidae). J. L. B. Smith Inst. Ichthyol. Spec. Publ. No. 37: 1-21.

Compagno, L. J. V., and S. Springer. 1971 **[ref. 899]**. *Iago*, a new genus of carcharhinid sharks, with a redescription of *I. omanensis*. U. S. Natl. Mar. Fish. Serv. Fish. Bull. v. 69 (no. 3): 615-626.

Contreras-Balderas, S., and J. Verduzco-Martínez. 1977 (27 July) **[ref. 7058]**. *Dionda mandibularis*, a new cyprinid fish endemic to the Upper Rio Verde, San Luis Potosi, Mexico, with comments on related species. Trans. San Diego Soc. Nat. Hist. v. 18 (no. 16): 259-266.

Cooper, J. E., and R. A. Kühne. 1974 (13 June) **[ref. 904]**. *Speoplatyrhinus poulsoni*, a new genus and species of subterranean fish from Alabama. Copeia 1974 (no. 2): 486-493.

Cooper, J. G. 1863 (Nov.) **[ref. 905]**. On new genera and species of California fishes—I. Proc. Calif. Acad. Sci. (Ser. 1) v. 3 (sig. 5): 70-77.

——. 1864 (Jan.-Mar.) **[ref. 4877]**. On new genera and species of Californian fishes—No. III. Proc. Calif. Acad. Sci. (Ser. 1) v. 3 (sigs. 7-8): 108-114. [Pp. 113-114 in signature 8, Mar. 1864.]

Cope, E. D. 1864 (before 12 Dec.) **[ref. 906]**. On a blind silurid, from Pennsylvania. Proc. Acad. Nat. Sci. Phila. v. 16 (no. 4): 231-233.

——. 1865 (before 7 Aug.) **[ref. 907]**. Partial catalogue of the cold-blooded Vertebrata of Michigan. Part II. Proc. Acad. Nat. Sci. Phila. v. 17 (no. 2): 78-88.

——. 1867 (before 1 Nov.) **[ref. 908]**. Description of a new genus of cyprinoid fishes from Virginia. Proc. Acad. Nat. Sci. Phila. v. 19 (no. 3): 95-97.

——. 1868 (Dec.) **[ref. 909]**. On the distribution of fresh-water fishes in the Allegheny region of southwestern Virginia. J. Acad. Nat. Sci. Philadelphia (Ser. 2) v. 6 (art. 5): 207-247, Pls. 26-28 [wrongly as 22-24]. [Fowler (MS) gives date as Jan. 1869 [not confirmed].]

———. 1868 **[ref. 7316]**. On the genera of fresh-water fishes *Hypsilepis* Baird and *Photogenis* Cope, their species and distribution. Proc. Acad. Nat. Sci. Phila. v. 19: 156-166.

———. 1869 **[ref. 910]**. Synopsis of the Cyprinidae of Pennsylvania. Also includes: Supplement on some new species of American and African fishes (pp. 400-407). Supplementary synopsis of the esoces of Middle North America (pp.407-410). Trans. Am. Philos. Soc. v. 13 (pt 2, art. 13): 351-410, Pls. 10-13. [Read in 1866, published in 1869 but distribution of separates before 1869 not investigated.]

———. 1870 **[ref. 913]**. Partial synopsis of the fresh-water fishes of North Carolina. Proc. Am. Philos. Soc. v. 11: 448-495. [Reissued as second edition in 1877 with notes added.]

———. 1870 **[ref. 914]**. Contribution to the ichthyology of the Marañon. Proc. Am. Philos. Soc. v. 11: 559-570.

———. 1871 **[ref. 920]**. Contribution to the ichthyology of the Lesser Antilles. Trans. Am. Philos. Soc. (n. s.) v. 14 (pt 1, art. 5): 445-483.

———. 1871 **[ref. 922]**. On the fishes of the Tertiary shales of Green River, Wyoming Territory. Geol. Surv. Territ. Ann. Rept. 4 (for 1870): 425-431.

———. 1871 (11 July) **[ref. 5775]**. [Untitled report] "Some anatomical points of importance in the classification of the siluroids of the Amazon." Proc. Acad. Nat. Sci. Phila. v. 23: 112-113.

———. 1872 (16 Jan.- 13 Feb.) **[ref. 921]**. On the fishes of the Ambyiacu River. Proc. Acad. Nat. Sci. Phila. v. 23: 250-294, pls. 3-17.

———. 1872 **[ref. 923]**. Report on the recent reptiles and fishes of the survey, collected by Campbell Carrington and C. M. Dawes. U. S. Geol. Surv. Territ. Ann. Rept. for 1872 v. 5 (pt. 4): 467-476.

———. 1873 **[ref. 929]**. A contribution to the ichthyology of Alaska. Proc. Am. Philos. Soc. v. 13: 24-32.

———. 1874 (29 Sept.) **[ref. 931]**. On some bratrachia and nematognathi brought from the upper Amazon by Prof. Orton. Proc. Acad. Nat. Sci. Phila. v. 26: 120-137.

———. 1874 (13 Apr.) **[ref. 932]**. On the Plagoterinae and the ichthyology of Utah. Trans. Am. Philos. Soc. v. 14: 122-139. [Also as separate, 13 Apr. 1874.]

———. 1874 (10 May) **[ref. 933]**. Description of some species of reptiles obtained by Dr. John F. Bransford, Assistant Surgeon United States Navy, while attached to the Nicaraguan surveying expedition in 1873. Proc. Acad. Nat. Sci. Phila. v. 26: 64-72.

———. 1876 (11 Jan.) **[ref. 936]**. On a new genus of Lophobranchiate fishes. Proc. Acad. Nat. Sci. Phila. v. 27: 450, pl. 25.

———. 1877 (10 July) **[ref. 939]**. On some new and little known reptiles and fishes from the Austroriparian region. Proc. Am. Philos. Soc. v. 17: 63-68.

———. 1878 (16 or 27 June) **[ref. 945]**. Synopsis of the fishes of the Peruvian Amazon, obtained by Professor Orton during his expeditions of 1873 and 1877. Proc. Am. Philos. Soc. v. 17 (no. 101): 673-701.

———. 1881 (Jan.) **[ref. 949]**. A new genus of Catostomidae. Am. Nat. v. 15 (no. 1): 59.

———. 1883 (24 July - 7 Aug.) **[ref. 951]**. On the fishes of the Recent and Pliocene lakes of the western part of the Great Basin, and of the Idaho Pliocene lake. Proc. Acad. Nat. Sci. Phila. v. 35: 134-166, 1 map. [Pages 134-136 published 24 July, remainder on 7 Aug. 1883]

———. 1894 (before 6 Mar.) **[ref. 965]**. On the fishes obtained by the Naturalist Expedition in Rio Grande do Sul. Proc. Am. Philos. Soc. v. 33: 84-108, Pls. 4-9.

———. 1894 (Jan.) **[ref. 966]**. On three new genera of Characinidae. Am. Nat. v. 28 (no. 325): 67.

Cope, E. D., and H. C. Yarrow. 1876 **[ref. 968]**. Report upon the collections of fishes made in portions of Nevada, Utah, California, Colorado, New Mexico, and Arizona, during the years 1871, 1872, 1873, and 1874. U. S. Geol. Surv. West 100. Meridian v. 5 (Zool.) Chapter 6: 635-703, Pls. 26-32.

Cornide, J. 1788 **[ref. 5057]**. Ensayo de una historia de los peces y otras producciones marinas de la costa de Galicia, arreglado al sistema del Caballero Cárlos Linneo. Con un tratado de las diversas pescas, y de las redes y aparejos con que se practican. i-xxxviii + 1-263.

Costa, A. 1862 **[ref. 4852]**. Di un novello genere di pesci Esocetidei. Ann. Mus. Zool. Univ. Napoli v. 1: 54-57.

Costa, O. G. 1829-57 **[ref. 976]**. Fauna del regno di Napoli, ossia enumerazione di tutti gli animali che abitano le diverse regioni di questo regno e le acque che le bagnano, etc. Pesci. Part 1 (1829-53): 511 pp. (variously paginated); part 2 (1842-53): 148 pp., 69 pls.; part 3 (1837-57): 101 pp., 17 pls. [For dates see Sherborn 1937 [ref. 13381].]

———. 1834 **[ref. 975]**. Cenni zoologici, ossia descrizione sommaria delle specie nuovi di animali discoperti in diverse contrade del regno, nell' anno 1834. Napoli. [Not seen.]

———. 1837-57 **[ref. 4897]**. Fauna del regno di Napoli, ossia enumerazione di tutti gli animali che abitano le diverse regioni di questo regno e le acque che le bagnano, etc. Pesci. v. 3 (pt 3): 101 pp. [variously paginated], 17 pls. [For dates of sections see Sherborn 1937 [ref. 13381]. Not seen.]

———. 1842-53 **[ref. 980]**. Fauna del regno di Napoli, ossia enumerazione di tutti gli animali che abitano le diverse regioni di questo regno e le acque che le bagnano, etc. Pesci. v. 3 (pt 2): 148 pp. [variously paginated], 69 pls. [Not seen. For dates of sections see Sherborn 1937 [ref. 13381].]

Costa, W. J. E. M. 1988 (Feb.) **[ref. 14292]**. Sistemática e distribuição do gênero *Neofundulus* (Cyprinodontiformes, Rivulidae). Rev. Brasil Biol. v. 48 (no. 2): 103-111.

———. 1988 **[ref. 14438]**. A new species of the neotropical annual fish genus *Pterolebias* (Cyprinodontiformes, Rivulidae), from central Brazil. J. Zool. (Lond.) v. 215: 657-662.

———. 1989 **[ref. 14270]**. Descrição e relações filogenéticas de dois gêneros novos e trés espéces novas de peixes anuais neotropicais (Cyprinodontiformes, Rivulidae). Rev. Bras. Biol. v. 49 (no. 1): 221-230. [English abst.]

———. 1989 (20 Oct.) **[ref. 14319]**. Descrição de cinco novas espécies de *Rivulus* das bacias dos rios Paraná e São Francisco (Cypridontiformes, Rivulidae). Rev. Bras. Zool. v. 6 (no. 3): 423-534.

———. 1989 **[ref. 14323]**. Redescrição do gênero *Cynolebias* (Cyprinodontiformes, Rivulinae), com a descrição de uma nova espéce da Bacia do Rio Tocantins. Comun. Mus. Ciênc. PUCRS, Sér. Zool. Porto Alegre v. 2 (no. 9): 181-190.

———. 1989 **[ref. 14436]**. Descrição de um gênero e duas espécies novas de peixes anuais do centro da América do sul (Cyprinodontiformes, Rivulinae). Comun. Mus. Ciênc. PUCRS, Sér. Zool. Porto Alegre v.2 (no. 10): 191-202.

Costa, W. J. E. M., M. T. C. Lacerda and G. Campello Brasil. 1989 (15 Feb.) **[ref. 9292]**. Systématique et distribution du genre néotropical *Campellolebias* (Cyprinodontiformes, Rivulidae), avec description de deux nouvelles espèces. Rev. Fr. Aquariol. v. 15 (no. 3): 65-72.

Costa, W. J. E. M., M. T. C. Lacerda and K. Tanizaki. 1988 (15 Jan.) **[ref. 6372]**. Description d'une nouvelle espèce de *Cynolebias* du Brésil central (Cyprinodontiformes, Rivulinae). Rev. Fr. Aquariol. v. 14 (no. 4): 123-126.

Coste, P. 1848 **[ref. 5556]**. Nidification des épinoches et des épinochettes. Mem. Pres. Div. Savants Acad. Sci. Inst. Natl. Fr. (Ser. 2) v. 10: 574-588, 1 col pl.

Couch, J. 1832 **[ref. 5557]**. Fishes new to the British fauna, contained in Couch's "History of the Fishes of Cornwall." Mag. Nat. Hist. v. 5 (art. 4): 15-24.

———. 1862 **[ref. 989]**. A history of the fishes of the British islands. I. Chondrichthys, percoides, and sparoids. London. i-vii + 1-245, 57 col. pls. [Gill 1982 [ref. 1783] gives date for Couch as 1861. Date on cover of edition proofed is 1868. 1862 edition not seen.]

Cowan, C. F. 1969 **[ref. 6858]**. Cuvier's Régne Animal, first edition. J. Soc. Bibliogr. Nat. Hist. v. 5 (pt 3): 219.

———. 1976 **[ref. 13372]**. On the Disciples' edition of Cuvier's 'Regne Animal.' J. Soc. Bibliogr. Nat. Hist. v. 8 (no. 1): 32-64.

CRABTREE, C. B. 1987 (9 Dec.) **[ref. 6771]**. Allozyme evidence for the phylogenetic relationships within the silverside subfamily Atherinopsinae. Copeia 1987 (no. 4): 860-867.

———. 1989 (8 Aug.) **[ref. 12738]**. A new silverside of the genus *Colpichthys* (Atheriniformes: Atherinidae) from the Gulf of California, Mexico. Copeia 1989 (no. 3): 558-568.

CRABTREE, C. B., AND D. G. BUTH. 1987 (9 Dec.) **[ref. 6770]**. Biochemical systematics of the catostomid genus *Catostomus*: assessment of *C. clarki, C. plebeius*, and *C. discobolus* including the zuni sucker, *C. d. yarrowi*. Copeia 1987 (no. 4): 843-854.

CREASER, C. W., AND C. L. HUBBS. 1922 (6 July) **[ref. 990]**. A revision of the Holarctic lampreys. Occas. Pap. Mus. Zool. Univ. Mich. No. 120: 1-14, Pl. 1.

CRESSEY, R. F. 1981 (15 Dec.) **[ref. 5574]**. Revision of Indo-West Pacific lizardfishes of the genus *Synodus* (Pisces: Synodontidae). Smithson. Contrib. Zool. No. 342: i-iii + 1-53.

———. 1986 **[ref. 6289]**. Family No. 79: Synodontidae (pp. 270-273). In: Smiths' Sea Fishes (Smith & Heemstra 1986 [ref. 5715]).

CROSSMAN, E. J. 1978 **[ref. 6974]**. Taxonomy and distribution of North American esocids. Am. Fish. Soc. Spec. Publ. No. 11: 13-26.

CROWLEY, L. E. L. M., AND W. IVANTSOFF. 1988 **[ref. 12286]**. A new species of Australian *Craterocephalus* (Pisces: Atherinidae) and redescription of four other species. Rec. West. Aust. Mus. v. 14 (no. 2): 151-169.

CUI, G.-H., AND X.-L. CHU. 1986 **[ref. 8097]**. Systematic status of the genus *Luciocyprinus* and its specific differentiation (Pisces: Cyprinidae). Zool. Res. v. 7 (no. 1): 79-84. [In Chinese, English Summ.]

———. 1986 **[ref. 9822]**. New material for the Chinese cyprinid genus *Sinocrossocheilus*. Acta Zootaxon. Sin. v. 11 (no. 4): 425-428. [In Chinese, English summ. (p. 428).]

CUNNINGHAM, R. O. 1871 **[ref. 992]**. Notes on the reptiles, amphibia, fishes, mollusca, and crustacea obtained during the voyage of H. M. S. *Nassau* in the years 1866-69. Trans. Linn. Soc. London v. 27: 465-502, Pls. 58-59.

CURRAN, D. J. 1989 (23 May) **[ref. 12547]**. Phylogenetic relationships among the catfish genera of the family Auchenipteridae (Teleostei: Siluroidea). Copeia 1989 (no. 2): 408-419.

CURTISS, A. 1944 **[ref. 12574]**. Further notes on the zoology of Tahiti. [Follows: A short zoology of Tahiti in the Society Islands, privately published in 1938.] [Original not seen. Author's views on systematics were unconventional (Wheeler, in litt., 1985).]

CUVIER, G. 1798 **[ref. 5558]**. Tableau élémentaire de l'Histoire Naturélle des animaux. Paris. i-xvi + 1-710. [Poissons on pp. 303-371.]

———. 1800 **[ref. 994]**. Leçons d'anatomie comparée recueilles et publiées sous ses yeux par C. Duméril... [Not seen.]

———. 1814 **[ref. 4884]**. Observations et recherches critiques sur différentes poissons de la Méditerranée et, à leur occasion, sur des Poissons des autres mers plus ou moins liés avec eux; par M. G. Cuvier. [In a report by A.D. = A. G. Desmarets.] Bull. Soc. Philomath. Paris 1814: 80-92. [Sometimes cited as Cuvier in Desmarets, or apud A. D. [= A. G. Desmarets].]

———. 1815 **[ref. 1019]**. Observations et recherches critiques sur différentes poissons de la Méditerranée, et à leur occasion sur des Poissons d'autres mers, plus ou moins liés avec eux. [Second through fourth parts as "Suite des observations et recherches critiques."] Mem. Mus. Natl. Hist. Nat. v. 1: 226-241, 312-330 + Pl. 16, 353-363, 451-466.

———. 1815 **[ref. 5017]**. Mémoire sur la composition de la mâchoire supérieure des poissons, et sur le parti que l'on peut en tirer pour la distribution méthodique de ces animaux. Mem. Mus. Natl. Hist. Nat. v. 1: 102-114.

———. 1816 (Nov.) **[ref. 993]**. Le Régne Animal distribué d'après son organisation pour servir de base à l'histoire naturelle des animaux et d'introduction à l'anatomie comparée. Les reptiles, les poissons, les mollusques et les annélides. Edition 1. v. 2: i-xviii + 1-532. [Before Dec. 1916 (see Roux 1976 [ref. 6031], Whitehead 1967 [ref. 6464], 1967 [ref. 13373] and Cowan 1969 [ref. 6858]).]

———. 1817 **[ref. 1015]**. Sur le genre *Chironectes* Cuv. (*Antennarius* Commers.). Mem. Mus. Natl. Hist. Nat. v. 3: 418-435, Pls. 16-18.

———. 1817 **[ref. 1016]**. Sur les poissons du sous-genre Mylètes. Mem. Mus. Natl. Hist. Nat. v. 4: 444-456, Pls. 21-22.

———. 1819 **[ref. 1017]**. Sur les poissons du sous-genre *Hydrocyon*, sur deux nouvelles espèces de *Chalceus*, sur trois nouvelles espèces du *Serrasalmes*, et sur l'*Argentina glossodonta* de Forskahl, qui est l'*Albula gonorhynchus* de Bloch. Mem. Mus. Natl. Hist. Nat. v. 5: 351-379, Pls. 26-28.

———. 1829 (Mar.) **[ref. 995]**. Le Règne Animal, distribué d'après son organisation, pour servir de base à l'histoire naturelle des animaux et d'introduction à l'anatomie comparée. Edition 2. v. 2: i-xviii + 1-532. [For date of publication see Fowler 1907: 264 [ref. 1376].]

———. 1836-49 **[ref. 4980]**. Le règne animal distribué d'après son organisation, pour servir de base à l'histoire naturelle des animaux et d'introduction à l'anatomie comparée. 3rd ed. 23 vols. Paris, 1836-1849. "Les poissons, par A. Valenciennes" is vols. 4 and 5. [Vols. 4 and 5 published in 1836-43. See Cowan 1976 [ref. 13372].]

CUVIER, G., AND A. VALENCIENNES. 1828 (Oct.) **[ref. 4880]**. Histoire naturelle des poissons. Tome premier. Livre premièr. Tableau historique des progrès de l'ichthyologie, depuis son origine jusqu'a nos jours. Livre deuxième. Idée générale de la nature et de l'organisation des poissons. v. 1: i-xvi + 1-573 + 3 pp., Pls. 1-8 [double]. [Cuvier authored volume. See Bailey 1957 [ref. 13430] for authorships and dates. i-xiv + 1-422 in Strasbourg edition.]

———. 1828 (Oct.) **[ref. 997]**. Histoire naturelle des poissons. Tome second. Livre Troisième. Des poissons de la famille des perches, ou des percoïdes. v. 2: i-xxi + 2 pp. + 1-490, Pls. 9-40. [Cuvier authored volume. i-xvii + 1-317 in Strasbourg edition.]

———. 1829 (Apr.) **[ref. 4879]**. Histoire naturelle des poissons. Tome troisième. Suite du Livre troisième. Des percoïdes a dorsale unique a sept rayons branchiaux et a dents en velours ou en cardes. v. 3: i-xxviii + 2 pp. + 1-500, Pls. 41-71. [Cuvier authored volume. i-xxii + 1-368 in Strasbourg edition.]

———. 1829 (Nov.) **[ref. 998]**. Histoire naturelle des poissons. Tome quatrième. Livre quatrième. Des acanthoptérygiens à joue cuirassée. v. 4: i-xxvi + 2 pp. + 1-518, Pls. 72-99, 97 bis. [Cuvier authored volume. i-xx + 1-379 in Strasbourg edition.]

———. 1830 (July) **[ref. 999]**. Histoire naturelle des poissons. Tome cinquième. Livre cinquième. Des Sciénoïdes. v. 5: i-xxviii + 1-499 + 4 pp., Pls. 100-140. [Cuvier authored volume. i-xx + 1-374 in Strasbourg edition.]

———. 1830 (Sept.) **[ref. 996]**. Historie naturelle des poissons. Tome Sixième. Livre sixième. Partie I. Des Sparoïdes; Partie II. Des Ménides. v. 6: i-xxiv + 6 pp. + 1-559, Pls. 141-169. [Valenciennes author of pp. 1-425, 493-559; Cuvier 426-491. i-xviii + 1-470 in Strasbourg ed.]

———. 1831 (Apr.) **[ref. 4881]**. Histoire naturelle des poissons. Tome septième. Livre septième. Des Squamipennes. Livre huitième. Des poissons à pharyngiens labyrinthiformes. v. 7: i-xxix + 1-531, Pls. 170-208. [Cuvier authored pp. 1-440, Valenciennes 441-531. i-xxii + 1-399 in Strasbourg edition.]

———. 1832 (Jan.) **[ref. 1000]**. Histoire naturelle des poissons. Tome huitième. Livre neuvième. Des Scombéroïdes. v. 8: i-xix + 5 pp. + 1-509, Pls. 209-245. [Cuvier authored pp. 1-470; Valenciennes 471-509. Date of 1831 on title page. i-xv + 1-375 in Strasbourg edition.]

———. 1833 (Mar.) **[ref. 1002]**. Histoire naturelle des poissons. Tome neuvième. Suite du livre neuvième. Des Scombéroïdes. v. 9: i-xxix + 3 pp. + 1-512, Pls. 246-279. [Cuvier authored pp. 1-198, 330-359, 372-427; Valenciennes the balance. i-xxiv + 1-379 in Strasbourg edition.]

———. 1835 (Sept.) **[ref. 1004]**. Histoire naturelle des poissons. Tome dixième. Suite du livre neuvième. Scombéroïdes. Livre dixième. De la famille des Teuthyes. Livre onzième. De la famille des Taenioïdes. Livre douzième. Des Athérines. v. 10: i-xxiv +

1-482 + 2 pp., Pls. 280-306. [Valenciennes authored volume. i-xix + 1-358 in Strasbourg edition.]
——. 1836 (July) **[ref. 1005]**. Histoire naturelle des poissons. Tome onzième. Livre treizeìme. De la famille des Mugiloïdes. Livre quatorzième. De la famille des Gobioïdes. v. 11: i-xx + 1-506 + 2 pp., Pls. 307-343. [Valenciennes authored volume. i-xv + 1-373 in Strasbourg edition.]
——. 1837 (Mar.) **[ref. 1006]**. Histoire naturelle des poissons. Tome douzième. Suite du livre quatorzième. Gobioïdes. Livre quinzième. Acanthoptérygiens à pectorales pédiculées. v. 12: i-xxiv + 1-507 + 1 p., Pls. 344-368. [Valenciennes authored volume. i-xx + 1-377 in Strasbourg edition.]
——. 1839 (Apr.) **[ref. 1007]**. Histoire naturelle des poissons. Tome treizième. Livre seizième. Des Labroïdes. v. 13: i-xix + 1-505 + 1 p., Pls. 369-388. [Valenciennes authored volume. i-xvii + 1-370 in Strasbourg edition.]
——. 1840 (Jan.) **[ref. 4882]**. Histoire naturelles des poissons. Tome quatorzième. Suite du livre seizième. Labroïdes. Livre dix-septième. Des Malacoptérygiens. v. 14: i-xxii + 2 pp. + 1-464 + 4 pp., Pls. 389-420. [Valenciennes authored volume. i-xx + 1-344 in Strasbourg edition. Published as 1839.]
——. 1840 (Nov.) **[ref. 1008]**. Histoire naturelle des poissons. Tome quinzième. Suite du livre dix-septième. Siluroïdes. v. 15: i-xxxi + 1-540, Pls. 421-455. [Valenciennes authored volume. i-xxiv + 1-397 in Strasbourg edition.]
——. 1842 (Aug.) **[ref. 1009]**. Histoire naturelle des poissons. Tome seizième. Livre dix-huitième. Les Cyprinoïdes. v. 16: i-xx + 1-472, Pls. 456-487. [Valenciennes authored volume. i-xviii + 1-363 in Strasbourg edition.]
——. 1844 (July) **[ref. 1010]**. Histoire naturelle des poissons. Tome dix-septième. Suite du livre dix-huitième. Cyprinoïdes. v. 17: i-xxiii + 1-497 + 2 pp., Pls. 487-519. [Valenciennes authored volume. i-xx + 1-370 in Strasbourg edition.]
——. 1846 (Aug. (or Sept.)) **[ref. 1011]**. Histoire naturelle des poissons. Tome dix-huitième. Suite du livre dix-huitième. Cyprinoïdes. Livre dix-neuvième. Des Ésoces ou Lucioïdes. v. 18: i-xix + 2 pp. + 1-505 + 2 pp., Pls. 520-553. [Valenciennes authored volume. i-xviii + 1-375 in Strasbourg edition.]
——. 1847 (May) **[ref. 4883]**. Histoire naturelles des poissons. Tome dix-neuvième. Suite du livre dix-neuvième. Brochets ou Lucioïdes. Livre vingtième. De quelques familles de Malacoptérygiens, intermédiaires entre les Brochets et les Clupes. v. 19: i-xix + 1-544 + 6 pp., Pls. 554-590. [Valenciennes authored volume. Published as 1846. i-xv + 1-391 in Strasbourg edition.]
——. 1847 (Nov.) **[ref. 1012]**. Histoire naturelle des poissons. Tome vingtième. Livre vingt et unième. De la famille des Clupéoïdes. v. 20: i-xviii + 1 p. + 1-472, Pls. 591-606. [Valenciennes authored volume. i-xiv + 1-346 in Strasbourg edition.]
——. 1848 (Sept.) **[ref. 1013]**. Histoire naturelle des poissons. Tome vingt et unième. Suite du livre vingt et unième et des Clupéoïdes. Livre vingt-deuxième. De la famille des Salmonoïdes. v. 21: i-xiv + 1 p. + 1-536, pls. 607-633. [Valenciennes authored volume. i-xiii [+ iii] + 1-391 in Strasbourg edition.]
——. 1850 (Jan.) **[ref. 1014]**. Histoire naturelle des poissons. Tome vingt-deucième. Suite du livre vingt-deuxième. Suite de la famille des Salmonoïdes. Table génèrale de l'Histoire Naturelle des Poissons (pp. 1-91). v. 22: i-xx + 1 p. + 1-532 + 1-91, Pls. 634-650. [Valenciennes authored volume. Published as 1849. i-xvi + 1-395, index 1-81 (+ 1) in Strasbourg edition.]
Dabry de Thiersant, P. 1872 **[ref. 12507]**. La pisciculture et la peche en Chine. Paris. 1-192, 50 pls. [Not seen.]
Daget, J. 1952 (Jan.) **[ref. 1023]**. Description d'un Cichlidé pétricole du Niger *Labrochromis polli*, n. gen., sp. n. Bull. Inst. Fr. Afr. Noire v. 14: 226-228.
——. 1962 (29 Sept.) **[ref. 1024]**. Le genre *Citharinus* (Poissons, Characiformes). Rev. Zool. Bot. Afr. v. 66 (no. 1-2): 81-106.
——. 1965 (30 Sept.) **[ref. 1025]**. Les genres *Nannaethiops* et *Neolebias* (Poissons Characiformes). Rev. Zool. Bot. Afr. v. 72 (pts 1-2): 1-24.
——. 1979 (30 Sept.) **[ref. 1026]**. Description de *Platyglanis depierrei* n. gen., n. sp. (Pisces, Bagridae) du Sanaga (Sud Cameroun). Bull. Mus. Natl. Hist. Nat. Sect. A Zool. Biol. Ecol. Anim. v. 1 (no. 3) [1978]: 821-825.
——. 1984 (Feb.) **[ref. 6170]**. Elopidae (pp. 30-31), Megalopidae (pp. 32-33), Denticipitidae (p. 40), Osteoglossidae (pp. 57-58), Notopteridae (pp. 61-62), Citharinidae (pp. 212-216). In: Daget et al. 1984 [ref. 6168].
——. 1986 (Apr.) **[ref. 6203]**. Synbranchidae (pp. 291-292), Centropomidae (pp. 293-296), Sphyraenidae (pp. 350-351). In: Daget et al. 1986 [ref. 6189].
——. 1988 (30 Mar.) **[ref. 6734]**. Mutanda Ichthyologica: *Thysochromis* nom. nov. en replacement de *Thysia* (Pisces, Cichlidae). Cybium v. 12 (no. 1): 97.
Daget, J., and J.-P. Gosse. 1984 (Feb.) **[ref. 6185]**. Distichodontidae (pp. 184-211). In: Daget et al. 1984 [ref. 6168].
Daget, J., J.-P. Gosse and D. F. E. Thys van den Audenaerde [eds.]. 1984 (Feb.) **[ref. 6168]**. Check-list of the freshwater fishes of Africa. CLOFFA ORSTOM Paris, MRAC Tervuren v. 1: i-xviii + 1-410.
——. 1986 (Apr.) **[ref. 6189]**. Check-list of the freshwater fishes of Africa. CLOFFA. ISNB Bruxelles, MRAC Tervuren, ORSTOM Paris v. 2: i-xiv + 1-520.
——. 1986 (Nov.) **[ref. 13560]**. Check-list of the freshwater fishes of Africa. ISNB Bruxelles, MRAC Tervuren, ORSTOM Paris v. 3: 1-273.
Daget, J., and A. Iltis. 1965 **[ref. 13626]**. Poissons de Côte d'Ivoire (eaux douces et saumâtres). Mem. I.F.A.N. v. 74: 1-385, 4 pls. [Not seen.]
Daget, J., and J. C. Njock. 1986 (Apr.) **[ref. 6216]**. Polynemidae (pp. 352-354). In: Daget et al. 1986 [ref. 6189].
Daget, J., and C. L. Smith. 1986 (Apr.) **[ref. 6204]**. Serranidae (Serranidae s. str. + Moronidae) (pp. 299-303). In: Daget et al. 1986 [ref. 6189].
Daget, J., and W. F. Smith-Vaniz. 1986 (Apr.) **[ref. 6207]**. Carangidae (pp. 308-322). In: Daget et al. 1986 [ref. 6189].
Daget, J., and E. Trewavas. 1986 (Apr.) **[ref. 6211]**. Sciaenidae (pp. 333-337). In: Daget et al. 1986 [ref. 6189].
Dahl, G. 1960 (30 Aug.) **[ref. 5836]**. Nematognathus fishes collected during the Macarena Expedition 1959. Part I: Helogenidae, Cetopsidae, Ageniosidae, Pygidiidae. Novedades Colombianas v. 1 (no. 5): 302-317.
——. 1961 (1 Sept.) **[ref. 1027]**. Nematognathous fishes collected during the Macarena Expedition 1959. Dedicated to the memory of the Colombian ichthyologist, Dr. Ricardo Lozano. Decd May 23rd, 1959. Part II: Pimelodidae, Callophysidae. Novedades Colombianas v. 1 (no. 6): 483-514.
Daniels, R. A. 1981 (26 Aug.) **[ref. 1034]**. *Cryothenia peninsulae*, a new genus and species of nototheniid fish from the Antarctic Peninsula. Copeia 1981 (no. 3): 558-562.
Daudin, F. M. 1816 (Dec.) **[ref. 6445]**. *Antennarius*. In: Dictionaire des sciences naturelles. [See discussion under Cloquet 1816 [ref. 852]].
David, L. 1935 (21 Dec.) **[ref. 5559]**. Die Entwicklung der Clariiden und ihre Verbreitung. Eine anatomisch-systematische Untersuchung. Rev. Zool. Bot. Afr. v. 28 (pt 1): 77-147 + 5 foldout tables.
David, L., and M. Poll. 1937 (May) **[ref. 1043]**. Contribution à la faune ichthyologique du Congo Belge. Collections du Dr. H. Schouteden (1924-1926) et d'autres récolteurs. Ann. Mus. Congo Belge (Ser. 1) v. 3 (fasc. 5): 189-294, Pl. 12.
Dawson, C. E. 1966 (15 Aug.) **[ref. 1063]**. *Gunterichthys longipenis*, a new genus and species of ophidioid fish from the northern Gulf of Mexico. Proc. Biol. Soc. Wash. v. 79: 205-214.
——. 1967 (24 Mar.) **[ref. 1064]**. *Paragunnellichthys seychellensis*, a new genus and species of gobioid fish (Microdesmidae) from the western Indian Ocean. Proc. Biol. Soc. Wash. v. 80: 73-81.
——. 1974 (28 Mar.) **[ref. 1065]**. Studies on eastern Pacific sand

stargazers (Pisces: Dactyloscopidae) 1. *Platygillelus* new genus, with descriptions of new species. Copeia 1974 (no. 1): 39-55.

———. 1974 (13 June) **[ref. 7122]**. A review of the Microdesmidae (Pisces: Gobioidea). 1. *Cerdale* and *Clarkichthys* with descriptions of three new species. Copeia 1974 (no. 2): 409-448.

———. 1975 (30 June) **[ref. 7121]**. Studies on eastern Pacific sand stargazers (Pisces: Dactyloscopidae). 2. Genus *Dactyloscopus*, with descriptions of new species and subspecies. Nat. Hist. Mus. Los Ang. Cty. Sci. Bull. No. 22: 1-61.

———. 1977 **[ref. 1066]**. Synopsis of syngnathine pipefishes usually referred to the genus *Ichthyocampus* Kaup, with description of new genera and species. Bull. Mar. Sci. v. 27 (no. 4): 595-650.

———. 1977 (15 Apr.) **[ref. 1067]**. Studies on eastern Pacific sand stargazers (Pisces: Dactyloscopidae). 4. *Gillellus*, *Sindoscopus* new genus, and *Heteristius* with description of new species. Proc. Calif. Acad. Sci. v. 41 (no. 2): 125-160.

———. 1977 (24 Jan.) **[ref. 7047]**. Review of the Indo-Pacific pipefish genus *Lissocampus* (Syngnathidae). Proc. Biol. Soc. Wash. v. 89 (no. 53): 599-620.

———. 1977 (25 May) **[ref. 7048]**. Review of the pipefish genus *Corythoichthys* with description of three new species. Copeia 1977 (no. 2): 295-338.

———. 1978 (29 Aug.) **[ref. 7025]**. Review of the Indo-Pacific genus *Bhanotia*, with description of *B. nuda* n. sp. Proc. Biol. Soc. Wash. v. 91 (no. 2): 392-407.

———. 1978 (3 May) **[ref. 7026]**. Review of the Indo-Pacific pipefish genus *Hippichthys* (Syngnathidae). Proc. Biol. Soc. Wash. v. 91 (no. 1): 132-157.

———. 1979 (18 Oct.) **[ref. 1068]**. The Indo-Pacific pipefish genera *Notiocampus* gen. nov. and *Nannocampus* Günther. Proc. Biol. Soc. Wash. v. 92 (no. 3): 482-493.

———. 1979 (16 Nov.) **[ref. 1069]**. Notes on western Atlantic pipefishes with description of *Syngnathus caribbaeus* n. sp. and *Cosmocampus* n. gen. Proc. Biol. Soc. Wash. v. 92 (no. 4): 671-676.

———. 1979 (18 May) **[ref. 6947]**. A new wormfish (Pisces: Microdesmidae) from the eastern tropical Atlantic. Copeia 1979 (no. 2): 203-205.

———. 1980 **[ref. 1070]**. *Kimblaeus*, a new pipefish genus (Syngnathiformes: Syngnathidae) from Australia, with a key to genera of pipefishes with continuous superior ridges. Aust. J. Mar. Freshwater Res. v. 31 (no. 4): 517-523.

———. 1980 (6 Nov.) **[ref. 6909]**. The Indo-Pacific pipefish genus *Urocampus* (Syngnathidae). Proc. Biol. Soc. Wash. v. 93 (no. 3): 830-844.

———. 1981 (20 July) **[ref. 1071]**. Notes on west African pipefishes (Syngnathidae), with description of *Enneacampus*, n. gen. Proc. Biol. Soc. Wash. v. 94 (no. 2): 464-478.

———. 1981 (Nov.) **[ref. 5511]**. Review of the Indo-Pacific pipefish genus *Doryrhamphus* Kaup (Pisces, Syngnathidae), with descriptions of a new species and a new subspecies. Ichthyol. Bull. J. L. B. Smith Inst. Ichthyol. No. 44: 1-27.

———. 1981 (25 May) **[ref. 5527]**. Review of the Indo-Pacific doryrhamphine pipefish genus *Doryichthys*. Jpn. J. Ichthyol. v. 28 (no. 1): 1-18.

———. 1982 **[ref. 1072]**. Atlantic sand stargazers (Pisces: Dactyloscopidae), with description of one new genus and seven new species. Bull. Mar. Sci. v. 32 (no. 1): 14-85.

———. 1982 **[ref. 5440]**. Descriptions of *Cosmocampus retropinnis* sp. n., *Minyichthys sentus* sp. n. and *Amphelikturus* sp. (Pisces, Syngnathidae) from the eastern Atlantic region. Zool. Scr. v. 11 (no. 2): 135-140.

———. 1982 (20 Dec.) **[ref. 5441]**. Review of the genus *Micrognathus* Duncker (Pisces: Syngnathidae), with description of *M. natans*, n. sp. Proc. Biol. Soc. Wash. v. 95 (no. 4): 657-687.

———. 1982 (15 Aug.) **[ref. 5442]**. Synopsis of the Indo-Pacific genus *Solegnathus* (Pisces: Syngnathidae). Jpn. J. Ichthyol. v. 29 (no. 2): 139-161.

———. 1982 (Dec. (author stamp)) **[ref. 5443]**. Review of the Indo-Pacific pipefish genus *Stigmatopora* (Syngnathidae). Rec. Aust. Mus. v. 34 (no. 13): 575-605.

———. 1982 **[ref. 6764]**. Family Syngnathidae. In: Fishes of the Western North Atlantic. Mem. Sears Found. Mar. Res. Mem. 1 (pt 8): 1-172.

———. 1983 (14 Oct.) **[ref. 5351]**. Synopsis of the Indo-Pacific pipefish genus *Siokunichthys* (Syngnathidae), with description of *S. nigrolineatus* n. sp. Pac. Sci. v. 37 (no. 1): 49-63.

———. 1984 (1 Aug.) **[ref. 5275]**. *Bulbonaricus* Herald (Pisces: Syngnathidae), a senior synonym of *Enchelyocampus* Dawson and Allen, with description of *Bulbonaricus brucei* n. sp. from eastern Africa. Copeia 1984 (no. 3): 565-571.

———. 1984 (1 Aug.) **[ref. 5276]**. A new pipefish (Syngnathidae) from Western Australia, with remarks on the subgenera of *Acentronura*. Jpn. J. Ichthyol. v. 31 (no. 2): 156-160.

———. 1984 (15 Feb.) **[ref. 5290]**. *Festucalex prolixus*, a new species of pipefish (Syngnathidae) from the western Indo-Pacific region. Jpn. J. Ichthyol. v. 30 (no. 4): 371-373.

———. 1984 **[ref. 5291]**. Review of the Indo-Pacific pipefish genus *Trachyrhamphus* (Syngnathidae). Micronesica v. 18: 163-191.

———. 1984 **[ref. 5879]**. Revision of the genus *Microphis* Kaup (Pisces, Syngnathidae). Bull. Mar. Sci. v. 35 (no. 2): 117-181.

———. 1985 (Jan.) **[ref. 6541]**. Indo-Pacific pipefishes (Red Sea to the Americas). Gulf Coast Res. Lab., Ocean Springs, Mississippi. i-vi + 1-230.

———. 1986 **[ref. 5650]**. Family No. 145: Syngnathidae (pp. 445-458). In: Smiths' Sea Fishes (Smith & Heemstra 1986 [ref. 5715]).

———. 1986 (Apr.) **[ref. 6201]**. Syngnathidae (pp. 281-287). In: Daget et al. 1986 [ref. 6189].

Dawson, C. E., and G. R. Allen. 1978 (31 Dec.) **[ref. 1073]**. Synopsis of the 'finless' pipefish genera (*Penetopteryx*, *Apterygocampus* and *Enchelyocampus*, gen. nov.). Rec. West. Aust. Mus. v. 6 (no. 4): 391-411.

Dawson, C. E., and C. J. M. Glover. 1982 (11 Aug.) **[ref. 5444]**. *Hypselognathus horridus*, a new species of pipefish (Syngnathidae) from South Australia. Proc. Biol. Soc. Wash. v. 95 (no. 2): 403-407.

Day, F. 1865 **[ref. 1074]**. The fishes of Malabar. London. i-xxxii + 1-293, 20 pls.

———. 1865 (June) **[ref. 5295]**. On the fishes of Cochin, on the Malabar Coast of India. Proc. Zool. Soc. Lond. 1865 (pt 1): 286-318.

———. 1867 (Oct.) **[ref. 1075]**. On some new or imperfectly known fishes of Madras. Proc. Zool. Soc. Lond. 1867 (pt 2): 558-565.

———. 1868 (May) **[ref. 1076]**. On some new fishes from Madras. Proc. Zool. Soc. Lond. 1868 (pt 1): 192-199.

———. 1870 (Apr.) **[ref. 1077]**. Remarks on some fishes in the Calcutta Museum — Part II. Proc. Zool. Soc. Lond. 1869 (pt 3): 511-527, 548-560, 611-614.

———. 1871 (Apr.) **[ref. 1078]**. On the fishes of the Andaman Islands. Proc. Zool. Soc. Lond. 1870 (pt 3): 667-705.

———. 1872 (2 May) **[ref. 1079]**. On the freshwater siluroids of India and Burma. Proc. Zool. Soc. Lond. 1871 (pt 3): 703-721. [Date of Apr. given by Duncan 1937 [ref. 13606]; 2 May from Fowler MS.]

———. 1875 (Aug.) **[ref. 1080]**. The fishes of India; being a natural history of the fishes known to inhabit the seas and fresh waters of India, Burma, and Ceylon. London. part 1: 1-168, pls. 1-40. [For dates of publication of parts of this work see Menon & Rama Rao 1974 [ref. 7114].]

———. 1876 (Aug.) **[ref. 1081]**. The fishes of India; being a natural history of the fishes known to inhabit the seas and fresh waters of India, Burma, and Ceylon. Part 2: 169-368, Pls. 41-78.

———. 1877 (Aug.) **[ref. 4886]**. The fishes of India; being a natural history of the fishes known to inhabit the seas and fresh waters of India, Burma, and Ceylon. Part 3: 369-552, Pls. 79-138.

———. 1878 **[ref. 4887]**. The fishes of India; being a natural history of the fishes known to inhabit the seas and fresh waters of India, Burma, and Ceylon. Part 4: i-xx + 553-779, Pls. 139-195.

———. 1888 (Oct.) **[ref. 1082]**. The fishes of India; being a natural history of the fishes known to inhabit the seas and fresh waters of

India, Burma, and Ceylon. Supplement. 4 to. 779-816. [See Myers 1961 [ref. 13464] for comments on Tickell names mentioned by Day.]

——. 1889 **[ref. 1083]**. Fishes. In: W. T. Blanford (ed.). The fauna of British India, including Ceylon and Burma. v. 1: i-xviii + 1-548.

——. 1889 **[ref. 4888]**. Fishes. In: W. T. Blanford (ed.). The fauna of British India, including Ceylon and Burma. v. 2: i-xiv + 1-509.

de Beaufort, L. F. 1912 (30 Jan.) **[ref. 235]**. On some new Gobiidae from Ceram and Waigen [sic, Waigeu]. Zool. Anz. v. 39 (no. 3): 136-143.

——. 1939 **[ref. 237]**. On some Indo-Pacific genera of Labroid fishes, with the description of a new genus and species. Bijdr. Dierkd. Leiden v. 27: 14-18.

——. 1939 (5 Aug.) **[ref. 238]**. *Xenojulis*, a new genus of labroid fishes. Philipp. J. Sci. v. 69 (no. 4): 415-421.

——. 1940 **[ref. 239]**. The fishes of the Indo-Australian Archipelago. VIII. Percomorphi (continued). Cirrhitoidea, Labriformes, Pomacentriformes. E. J. Brill, Leiden. v. 8: i-xv + 1-508 pp.

——. 1948 **[ref. 240]**. On a new genus of fishes of the family Creediidae from South Africa, with remarks on its geographical distribution. Trans. R. Soc. S. Aust. v. 31 (pt 5): 475-478.

——. 1949 (15 Apr.) **[ref. 241]**. Two new genera of scorpaenoid fishes. Copeia 1949 (no. 1): 68.

——. 1952 (2 June) **[ref. 234]**. A new generic name for the scleropareid fish *Cocotropus de zwaani* from the Indian Ocean. Copeia 1952 (no. 1): 44-45.

de Beaufort, L. F., and J. C. Briggs. 1962 **[ref. 242]**. The fishes of the Indo-Australian Archipelago. XI. Scleroparei, Hypostomides, Pediculati, Plectognathi, Opisthomi, Discocephali, Xenopterygii. E. J. Brill, Leiden v. 11: i-xi + 1-481.

de Buen, F. 1926 **[ref. 5054]**. Catálogico ictiológico del Mediterráneo español y de Marruecos recopilando lo publicado sobre peces de las costas Mediterránea y próximas del Atlántico (Mar de España). Result. Campan. Real. Acuerd. Int. Madrid v. 2: 1-221.

——. 1930 (8 Nov.) **[ref. 684]**. *Lebetus* Whinter [sic] 1877, *Odondebuenia* nov. gen. y *Cabotia* nov. gen. (Gobiidae de Europa). Trab. Inst. Esp. Oceanogr. No. 5: 1-30.

——. 1930 **[ref. 685]**. Sur une collection de Gobiinae provenant du Maroc. Essai de synopsis des espèces de l'Europe. Bull. Soc. Sci. Nat. Maroc v. 10: 120-147.

——. 1931 (24 Nov.) **[ref. 686]**. Notas a la familia Gobiidae. Observaciones sobre algunos géneros y sinopsis de las especies ibéricas. Notas Résum. Inst. Espan. Oceanogr. Madrid Ser. 2 (no. 54): 1-76, Pl. 1.

——. 1934 **[ref. 687]**. Notas sobre los Gaidropsaridae (Peces). Un nuovo género (*Onogadus* nov. gen.) y una nueva especie (*Gaidropsarus barbatus* nov. sp.). Bol. Soc. Espan. Hist. Nat. v. 34: 499-504.

——. 1940 **[ref. 688]**. Un nuevo género de la familia Goodeidae perteneciente a la fauna ictiológica mexicana. An. Esc. Nac. Cienc. Biol. Mex. v. 2 (no. 2/3): 133-141, Pl. 10.

——. 1940 (15 June) **[ref. 689]**. Les Gobiidae pélagiques ou vivant sur les fonds d'algues calcaires de l'Europe occidentale. Bull. Inst. Oceanogr. (Monaco) No. 790: 1-16.

——. 1945 **[ref. 691]**. Investigaciones sobre ictiologia mexicana. I. Atherinidae de aguas continentales de México. An. Inst. Biol. Mex. v. 16 (no. 2): 475-532.

——. 1950 (Nov.) **[ref. 692]**. Contribuciones a la Ictiología. III. La familia Istiophoridae y descripción de una especie uruguaya (*Makaira perezi* de Buen). Publ. Cient., Serv. Oceanogr. Pesca, Minist. Ind. Montevideo No. 5: 163-178.

——. 1950 (May) **[ref. 13462]**. El mar de Solís y su fauna de peces (2.a parte). Publ. Cient., Serv. Oceanogr. Pesca, Minist. Ind. Montevideo No. 2: 45-144.

——. 1951 **[ref. 693]**. Contribuciones a la Ictiología. V-VI. Sôbre algunas especies de Gobiidae de la coleccion del Laboratorio Aragó (Banyuls-sur-Mer, Francia) y descripcion de un nuevo genero (*Austrogobius*) sudamericano. Bol. Inst. Oceanogr. S. Paulo v. 2 (Fasc. 2): 55-69, Pl. 1.

——. 1953 **[ref. 694]**. Los pejerrey (familia Atherinidae) en la fauna Uruguaya, con descripcion de nuevas especies. Bol. Inst. Oceanogr. S. Paulo v. 4 (no. 1-2): 3-80.

——. 1958 (Sept.) **[ref. 695]**. Peces de la superfamilia Clupeoidae en aguas de Chile. Rev. Biol. Mar., Valparaiso v. 8 (nos. 1-3): 83-110.

——. 1959 (Sept.) **[ref. 696]**. Lampreas, tiburones, rayas y peces en la Estacion de Biologia Marina de Montemar, Chile. (Primera contribucion). Rev. Biol. Mar., Valparaiso v. 9 (nos. 1-3): 3-200.

——. 1959 (14 July) **[ref. 697]**. Notas preliminares sobre la fauna marina preabismal de Chile, con descripción de una familia de rayas, dos géneros y siete especies nuevos. Bull. Mus. Natl. Hist. Nat. Santiago v. 27 (no. 3): 171-201.

——. 1961 (Sept.) **[ref. 698]**. Peces Chilenos. Familias Alepocephalidae, Muraenidae, Sciaenidae, Scorpaenidae, Liparidae y Bothidae. Montemar, Revista Biol. Mar. No. 1: 1-90.

——. 1962 (Apr.) **[ref. 699]**. Fauna Chilena. Peces de la familia Clinidae. Montemar, Revista Biol. Mar. No. 2: 53-96.

de Lucena, Z. M. S. 1988 **[ref. 12613]**. Discussão dos caracteres morfológicos dos gêneros *Umbrina* Cuvier, 1816 e *Ctenosciaena* Fowler & Bean, 1923. (Pisces; Perciformes; Sciaenidae). Comun. Mus. Cienc. PUCRGS Ser. Zool. v. 1 (no. 4/5): 49-122.

de Pinna, M. C. C. 1988 (Apr.) **[ref. 5999]**. A new genus of trichomycterid catfish (Siluroidei, Glanapteryginae), with comments on its phylogenetic relationships. Rev. Suisse Zool. v. 95 (no. 1): 113-128.

de Sylva, D. P. 1973 **[ref. 7210]**. Istiophoridae (pp. 477-481). In: Hureau & Monod 1973 [ref. 6590].

——. 1975 **[ref. 6302]**. Barracudas (Pisces: Sphyraenidae) of the Indian Ocean and adjacent seas — a preliminary review of their systematics and ecology. J. Mar. Biol. Assoc. India v. 15 (no. 1)[1973]: 74-94. [Published 1875, author's notation on reprint.]

——. 1984 **[ref. 13665]**. Mugiloidei: development and relationships. Am. Soc. Ichthyol. Herpetol. Spec. Publ. No. 1: 530-533.

——. 1984 **[ref. 13666]**. Sphyraenoidei: development and relationships. Am. Soc. Ichthyol. Herpetol. Spec. Publ. No. 1: 534-540.

——. 1984 **[ref. 13667]**. Polynemidae: development and relationships. Am. Soc. Ichthyol. Herpetol. Spec. Publ. No. 1: 540-541.

de Sylva, D. P., and W. N. Eschmeyer. 1977 (18 Aug.) **[ref. 5936]**. Systematics and biology of the deep-sea fish family Gibberichthyidae, a senior synonym of the family Kasidoroidae. Proc. Calif. Acad. Sci. v. 41 (no. 6): 215-231.

de Sylva, D. P., and F. Williams. 1986 **[ref. 6301]**. Family No. 224: Sphyraenidae (pp. 721-726). In: Smiths' Sea Fishes (Smith & Heemstra 1986 [ref. 5715]).

De Vis, C. W. 1882 (22 Oct.) **[ref. 1087]**. Descriptions of some new Queensland fishes. Proc. Linn. Soc. N. S. W. v. 7 (pt 3): 367-371.

——. 1883 (17 July) **[ref. 1088]**. Description of new genera and species of Australian fishes. Proc. Linn. Soc. N. S. W. v. 8 (pt 2): 283-289.

——. 1884 (21 Feb.) **[ref. 1089]**. Fishes from South Sea islands. Proc. Linn. Soc. N. S. W. v. 8 (pt 4): 445-457.

——. 1884 (19 Aug.) **[ref. 1090]**. New Australian fishes in the Queensland Museum. Proc. Linn. Soc. N. S. W. v. 9 (pt 2): 389-400. [1885 on cover, publ. Aug. 1884.]

——. 1885 (4 Mar.) **[ref. 1091]**. New Australian fishes in the Queensland Museum. No. 5. Proc. Linn. Soc. N. S. W. v. 9 (pt 4): 869-887.

——. 1885 (29 Nov.) **[ref. 4899]**. New fishes in the Queensland Museum. Proc. Linn. Soc. N. S. W. v. 9 (pt 3): 537-547.

De Vos, L. 1984 **[ref. 5157]**. Note on the species of the genus *Eutropius* (Pisces, Schilbeidae) from the Quanza and Bengo rivers (Angola) with description of *Eutropius angolensis* spec. nov. Cybium v. 8 (no. 2): 3-18.

——. 1986 (Apr.) **[ref. 6191]**. Schilbeidae (pp. 36-53). In: Daget et al. 1986 [ref. 6189].

Dean, B. 1904 **[ref. 1094]**. Notes on Japanese myxinoids. A new genus *Paramyxine* and a new species *Homea okinoseana*. Reference also to their eggs. J. Coll. Sci. Imp. Univ. Tokyo v. 19 (art. 2): 1-25, Pl. 1.

———. 1916 **[ref. 13327]**. A bibliography of fishes. American Museum of Natural History, New York v. 1 (A-K): i-xii + 1-718.

———. 1917 **[ref. 13431]**. A bibliography of fishes. American Museum of Natural History, New York v. 2 (L-Z): 1-702.

———. 1923 **[ref. 13432]**. A bibliography of fishes. American Museum of Natural History, New York v. 3: i-xiii + 1-707.

DECKERT, G. D., AND D. W. GREENFIELD. 1987 (11 Feb.) **[ref. 6778]**. A review of the western Atlantic species of the genera *Diapterus* and *Eugerres* (Pisces: Gerreidae). Copeia 1987 (no. 1): 182-194.

DEKAY, J. E. 1842 **[ref. 1098]**. Zoology of New-York; or the New-York fauna; comprising detailed descriptions of all the animals hitherto observed within the state of New-York, with brief notices of those occasionally found near its borders... In: Natural History of New York. Part iv. Fishes: 1-415, Fishes Pls. 1-79.

DELFIN, F. T. 1900 **[ref. 1099]**. Nota del Ictiolojia. El nuevo jéero *Cilus*. Acta Soc. Sci. Chile v. 10: 53-60.

DERANIYAGALA, P. E. P. 1929 (21 Mar.) **[ref. 1115]**. Ceylon sardines. Spolia Zeylan. (Ceylon J. Sci., Sec. B-Zool. Geol.) v. 15 (pt 1): 31-47, Pls. 13-18.

———. 1931 (8 Aug.) **[ref. 1116]**. Further notes on the anguilliform fishes of Ceylon. Spolia Zeylan. (Ceylon J. Sci., Sec. B-Zool. Geol.) v. 16 (pt 2): 131-137, Pls. 31-32.

———. 1937 (4 Aug.) **[ref. 1117]**. *Malpulutta kretseri*—a new genus and species of fish from Ceylon. Ceylon J. Sci. Sect. B Zool. v. 20 (pt 3): 351-353.

———. 1943 **[ref. 1118]**. A new cyprinoid fish from Ceylon. J. Ceylon Branch R. Asiatic Soc. v. 35 (no. 96, pt 4): ? 158-159. [Also as a separate, pp. 1-2; proofed from separate.]

DERJAVIN, A. 1937 **[ref. 5035]**. A new species of roach *Rutilus* (*Orthroleucos*) *atropatenus* nov. sp. from Azerbaidjan. Trudy Azerbaidzhanskogo Filiala, Acad. Sci. USSR v. 20: 71-78. [In Russian, English summ. (p. 77).]

DESMAREST, A. G. 1814 **[ref. 6876]**. See Cuvier 1814 [ref. 4884]. Bull. Soc. Philomath. Paris.

———. 1823 **[ref. 1120]**. Première Décade Ichthyologique, ou description complète de dix espèces de poissons nouvelles ou imparfaitement connues, habitant la mer qui baigne les côtes de l'ile de Cuba. Mem. Soc. Linn. Paris v. 2: 1-50, 6 [7] col. pls. [Also as a separate, Paris, 50 pp., 6 [7] pls.]

DESOUTTER, M. 1973 **[ref. 7203]**. Kyphosidae (pp. 420-421), Acanthuridae (p. 455). In: Hureau & Monod 1973 [ref. 6590].

———. 1986 (Apr.) **[ref. 6212]**. Monodactylidae (pp. 338-339), Ephippidae (p. 340), Bothidae (pp. 428-429), Soleidae (pp. 430-431), Cynoglossidae (pp. 432-433). In: Daget et al. 1986 [ref. 6189].

———. 1987 (30 Dec.) **[ref. 6742]**. Statut de *Microchirus boscanion* Chabanaud, 1926 et *Buglossidium luteum* (Risso, 1810) (Pisces, Pleuronectiformes, Soleidae). Cybium v. 11 (no. 4): 427-439.

DEVINCENZI, G. J. 1939 **[ref. 1121]**. Peces del Uruguay. Notas complementarias, III. Ann. Mus. Montev. (Ser. 2) v. 4 (no. 13): 1-37.

DEWITT, H. H. 1962 (31 Dec.) **[ref. 1122]**. A new genus and species of zoarcid fish from McMurdo Sound, Antarctica. Copeia 1962 (no. 4): 819-826.

———. 1962 (31 Dec.) **[ref. 1123]**. A new Antarctic nototheniid fish with notes on two recently described Nototheniiformes. Copeia 1962 (no. 4): 826-833.

———. 1977 **[ref. 1124]**. A new genus and species of eelpout (Pisces, Zoarcidae) from the Gulf of Mexico. U. S. Natl. Mar. Fish. Serv. Fish. Bull. v. 75 (no. 4): 789-793.

———. 1985 (30 Nov.) **[ref. 5161]**. A review of the genus *Bathydraco* Günther (Family Bathydraconidae). Cybium v. 9 (no. 3): 295-314.

DEWITT, H. H., AND J.-C. HUREAU. 1979 **[ref. 1125]**. Fishes collected during "Hero" cruise 72-2 in the Palmer Archipelago, Antarctica, with the description of two new genera and three new species. Bull. Mus. Natl. Hist. Nat. Sect. A Zool. Biol. Ecol. Anim. v. 1 (no. 3): 775-820.

DICK, M. M. 1974 **[ref. 7044]**. A review of the fishes of the family Bathyclupeidae. J. Mar. Biol. Assoc. India v. 14 (no. 2)[1972]: 539-544.

DINESEN, Z. D., AND W. J. NASH. 1982 (Aug. 15) **[ref. 5487]**. The scorpionfish *Rhinopias aphanes* Eschmeyer from Australia. Jpn. J. Ichthyol. v. 29 (no. 2): 179-184.

DINGERKUS, G. 1986 (30 May) **[ref. 6118]**. Interrelationships of orectolobiform sharks (Chondrichthyes: Selachii). Pp. 227-245. In: Uyeno et al. (eds.) 1986 [ref. 6147].

DINGERKUS, G., AND T. C. DEFINO. 1983 (19 Dec.) **[ref. 5386]**. A revision of the orectolobiform shark family Hemiscyllidae (Chondrichthyes, Selachii). Bull. Am. Mus. Nat. Hist. v. 176 (art. 1): 1-94.

DOADRIO, I. 1980 **[ref. 1129]**. Descripción de un nuevo género y de una nueva especie *Iberocypris palaciosi* n. gen. n. sp. (Pisces, Cyprinidae). Doñana Acta Vert. v. 7 (no. 1): 5-17.

DÖDERLEIN, L. 1882 **[ref. 1139]**. Ein Stomiatide aus Japan. Arch. Naturgeschichte v. 48 (bd 1): 26-31, Pl. 3.

DODERLEIN, P. 1884 **[ref. 5073]**. Elasmobranchi, Bonap. (Continuazione). Batoidei. Manuale ittiologico del Mediterraneo. Palermo, 1881-1891. v. 3: 121-256.

DOLGANOV, V. N. 1984 **[ref. 5823]**. A new shark from the family Squalidae caught on the Naska submarine ridge. Zool. Zh. v. 63 (no. 10): 1589-1591. [In Russian, English summ.]

DOLLO, L. 1900 **[ref. 1132]**. *Cryodraco antarcticus* poisson abyssal nouveaux recueilli par l'Expédition Antarctique Belge. Communicaton préliminaire. Bull. Acad. R. Belg. Cl. Sci. 1900, No. 2: 128-137. [Also as a separate.]

———. 1900 **[ref. 1133]**. *Gerlachea australis*, poisson abyssal nouveau recueilli par l'Expédition Antarctique Belge. Communication préliminaire. Bull. Acad. R. Belg. Cl. Sci. 1900, No. 3: 194-206. [Also as a separate.]

———. 1900 **[ref. 1134]**. *Racovitzia glacialis*, poisson abyssal nouveau, recueilli par cette Expédition. Expédition Antarctique Belge. Communication Préliminaire. Bull. Acad. R. Belg. Cl. Sci. 1900, No. 4: 316-327. [Also as a separate.]

———. 1908 (10 Jan.) **[ref. 1136]**. *Notolepis coatsi*, poisson pélagique nouveau recueilli par l'Expédition Antarctique Nationale Ecossaise. Note préliminaire. Proc. R. Soc. Edinb. v. 28 (pt 1, no. 5): 58-65. [Separates issued 10 Jan.]

———. 1909 **[ref. 1137]**. *Cynomacrurus piriei*, poisson abyssal nouveau recueilli par l'Expédition Antarctique Nationale Ecossaise. Note préliminaire. Proc. R. Soc. Edinb. v. 29 (pt 4, no. 18): 316-326.

DONALDSON, T. J. 1986 (30 May) **[ref. 6317]**. Distribution and species richness patterns of Indo-West Pacific Cirrhitidae: support for Woodland's hypothesis. Pp. 623-628. In: Uyeno et al. (eds.) 1986 [ref. 6147].

DOOLEY, J. K. 1978 (Apr.) **[ref. 5499]**. Systematic revision and comparative biology of the tilefishes (Perciformes: Branchiostegidae and Malacanthidae). NOAA Tech. Rep. NMFS Circ. No. 411: 1-78.

———. 1981 (Oct.) **[ref. 5496]**. A new species of tilefish (Pisces: Branchiostegidae) from Bermuda, with a brief discussion of the genus *Caulolatilus*. Northeast Gulf Sci. v. 5 (no. 1): 39-44.

DOOLEY, J. K., AND P. J. KAILOLA. 1988 **[ref. 7299]**. Four new tilefishes from the northeastern Indian Ocean, with a review of the genus *Branchiostegus*. Jpn. J. Ichthyol. v. 35 (no. 3): 247-260.

DOOLEY, J. K., AND J. R. PAXTON. 1975 **[ref. 7419]**. A new species of tilefish (family Branchiostegidae) from eastern Australia. Proc. Linn. Soc. N. S. W. v. 99 (no. 3): 151-156.

DOR, M. 1976 (June) **[ref. 6422]**. The dates of publication of Günther's "Andrew Garrett's Fische der Südsee." Isr. J. Zool. v. 24 (for 1975): 192.

DOUGLAS, M. E., W. L. MINCKLEY AND H. M. TYUS. 1989 (8 Aug.) **[ref. 12740]**. Qualitative characters, identification of Colorado River chubs (Cyprinidae: genus *Gila*) and the "art of seeing well." Copeia 1989 (no. 3): 653-662.

DOÛMET, P. N. 1863 **[ref. 1138]**. Description d'un nouveaux genre de poissons de la Méditerannée. Rev. Mag. Zool. v. 15: 212-223, Pl. 15. [Author same as Doûmet-Adanson.]

——. 1864 **[ref. 13456]**. Complément à la description du *Trachelocirrhus mediterraneus* (*Navarchus sulcatus*). Rev. Mag. Zool. v. 15 (for 1863): 425-432.

DRJAGIN, P. A. 1932 **[ref. 1140]**. *Arctogadus*, eine neue Gadidengattung aus Nordostsibirien. Zool. Anz. v. 98 (no. 5/6): 151-154.

DUBALEN. 1878 **[ref. 1141]**. Note sur un poisson mal connu du bassin de l'Adour. Bull. Soc. Borda, Dax. [Also issued as a separate. Not seen.]

DUGGINS, C. F., JR., A. A. KARLIN AND K. G. REYLEA. 1983 (6 May) **[ref. 6819]**. Electrophoretic variation in the killifish genus *Lucania*. Copeia 1983 (no. 2): 564-570.

DUMÉRIL, A. H. A. 1852 **[ref. 1148]**. Monographie de la famille des torpédiniens, ou poissons plagiostomes électriques, comprenant la description d'un genre nouveau, de 3 espèces nouvelles, et de 2 espèces nommées dans le Musée de Paris, mais non encore décrites. Rev. Mag. Zool. v. 4: 176-189, 227-244, 270-285. [Also as separate, Paris, 1852.]

——. 1855 **[ref. 297]**. Note sur un travail inédit de Bibron relatif aux poissons Plectognathes Gymnodontes (Diodons et Tétrodons). Rev. Mag. Zool. v. 8: 274-282.

——. 1858-61 **[ref. 1149]**. Reptiles et poissons de l'Afrique occidentale. Etude précédée de considérations générales sur leur distribution géographique. Arch. Mus. Natl. Hist. Nat. (Paris) v. 10: 137-268, 4 pls. [Not seen.]

——. 1865 **[ref. 1150]**. Histoire naturelle des poissons ou ichthyologie générale. Vol. I. Elasmobranches. Plagiostomes et holocéphales ou chimères. Parts 1-2: 1-720.

——. 1870 **[ref. 1147]**. Histoire naturelle des poissons, ou ichthyologie générale. Tome Second. Ganoïdes, Dipnés, Lophobranches. Paris. v. 2: 1-624.

DUMÉRIL, A. M. C. 1806 **[ref. 1151]**. Zoologie analytique, ou méthode naturelle de classification des animaux. Paris. i-xxxiii + 1-344. [Genera are latinized in "Table Latine" on pp. 331-344.]

——. 1806 **[ref. 1152]**. Dictionnaire des sciences naturelles.

——. 1812 **[ref. 1153]**. Dissertation sur la famille des poissons cyclostomes, pour démontrer leurs rapports avec les animaux sans vertèbres. Paris. 1-54.

——. 1856 **[ref. 1154]**. Ichthyologie analytique ou classification des poissons, suivant la méthode naturelle, à l'aide de tableaux synoptiques. Mem. Acad. Sci. Paris v. 27 (no. 1): 1-507. [Also as a separate, Paris, 1856, with slightly different title.]

DUMITRESCU, M., P. BANARESCU AND N. STOICA. 1957 **[ref. 1155]**. *Romanichthys valsanicola* nov. gen. nov. sp. (Pisces, Percidae). Trav. Mus. Hist. Nat. 'Grigore Antipa' v. 1: 225-244. [In German; Romanian & Russian summs.]

DUNCAN, F. M. 1937 (Apr.) **[ref. 13606]**. On the dates of publication of the Society's 'Proceedings,' 1859-1926. With an appendix containing the dates of publication of 'Proceedings,' 1830-1858, compiled by the late F. H. Waterhouse, and of the 'Transactions,' 1833-1869 ... Proc. Zool. Soc. Lond. v. 107 (pt 1) (A): 71-84.

DUNCKER, G. 1912 (22 Nov.) **[ref. 1156]**. Die Gattungen der Syngnathidae. Mitt. Naturhist. Mus. Hamburg v. 29: 219-240.

——. 1915 **[ref. 6567]**. Revision der Syngnathidae. Erster teil. Mitt. Naturhist. Mus. Hamburg v. 32: 9-120.

——. 1928 **[ref. 6525]**. Teleostei Physoclisti. 9. Gobiiformes. In: G. Grimpe & E. Wagler, Die Tierwelt der Nord- und Ostsee. v. 12 (no. 12): g121-g148.

——. 1940 **[ref. 1157]**. Ueber einige Syngnathidae aus dem Roten Meer. Publ. Mar. Biol. Stn. Al Ghardaqa No. 3: 83-88.

DUNCKER, G., AND E. MOHR. 1935 (15 May) **[ref. 5561]**. Die nordeuropäischen *Ammodytes*-Arten des Hamburger Zoologischen Museums. Zool. Anz. v. 110 (pt 7/8): 216-220.

——. 1939 (2 May) **[ref. 1158]**. Revision der Ammodytidae. Mitt. Zool. Mus. Berl. Bd. 24, Heft 1: 8-31.

DURBIN, M. L. 1909 (Aug.) **[ref. 1166]**. Reports on the expedition to British Guiana of the Indiana University and the Carnegie Museum, 1908. Report No. 2. A new genus and twelve new species of tetragonopterid characins. Ann. Carnegie Mus. v. 6 (no. 1): 55-72.

DUTT, S., AND K. H. RAO. 1965 **[ref. 1167]**. A new bothid flatfish *Cephalopsetta ventrocellatus* gen. et sp. nov. from Bay of Bengal. Proc. Indiana Acad. Sci. Sect. B v. 62 (no. 4): 180-187.

DYBOWSKI, B. I. 1862 **[ref. 1168]**. Versuch einer Monographie der Cyprinoiden Livlands, nebst einer synoptischen Aufzählung der europäischen Arten dieser Familie. Arch. Nat. Biol. Dorpat (Ser. 2) v. 6: 133-362, Pls. 1-7. [Apparently separates published in 1862; journal in 1864 (Jordan 1919: 313 [ref. 4904]).]

——. 1869 **[ref. 1169]**. Vorläufige Mittheilungen über die Fischfauna des Ononflusses und des Ingoda in Transbaikalien. Verh. K.-K. Zool.-Bot. Ver. Ges. Wien v. 19: 945-958.

——. 1872 **[ref. 1170]**. Zur Kenntniss der Fischfauna des Amurgebietes. Verh. K.-K. Zool.-Bot. Ver. Ges. Wien 1872: 209-222.

——. 1874 **[ref. 1172]**. Die Fische des Baikal-Wassersystemes. Verh. K.-K. Zool.-Bot. Ver. Ges. Wien v. 24 (no. 3-4): 383-394.

——. 1877 **[ref. 1171]**. [Fishes of the Amur water system.] Isvest. Sibirskogo Otd. Russ. Geor. Obshch. v. 8 (nos. 1-2): 1-29. [Not seen.]

——. 1916 **[ref. 6519]**. [Title unknown.] Pamietnik Fizyjograficzny, Warsaw v. 23: 100-102. [Not seen.]

EAKIN, R. R. 1981 **[ref. 8609]**. Biology of the Antarctic Seas IX. Reports on fishes from the University of Maine Antarctic Biological Research Program. 1. Genus *Pogonophryne* (Pisces, Harpagiferidae) from the South Orkney Islands. Antarct. Res. Ser. v. 31: 155-159.

——. 1981 **[ref. 8610]**. Biology of the Antarctic Seas IX. Two new species of *Pogonophryne* (Pisces, Harpagiferidae) from the Ross Sea, Antarctica. Antarct. Res. Ser. v. 31: 149-154.

——. 1981 **[ref. 14216]**. Biology of the Antarctic Seas IX. Osteology and relationships of the fishes of the Antarctic family Harpagiferidae (Pisces, Notothenioidei). Antarc. Res. Ser. v. 31: 81-147.

——. 1987 (Dec.) **[ref. 6224]**. Two new species of *Pogonophryne* (Pisces, Harpagiferidae) from the Weddell Sea, Antarctica. Arch. FischereiWiss. v. 38 (no. 1/2): 57-74.

——. 1988 (23 Aug.) **[ref. 6573]**. A new species of *Pogonophryne* (Pisces: Artedidraconidae) from the South Shetland Islands, Antarctica. Proc. Biol. Soc. Wash. v. 101 (no. 2): 434-437.

——. 1988 **[ref. 9116]**. A new species of *Pogonophryne* (Pisces, Artedidraconidae) from Queen Maud Land, Antarctica. J. L. B. Smith Inst. Ichthyol. Spec. Publ. No. 45: 1-4.

EAKIN, R. R., AND K.-H. KOCK. 1984 (Sept.) **[ref. 13452]**. Fishes of the genus *Pogonophryne* (Pisces, Harpagiferidae) collected during cruises of the Federal Republic of Germany (1975-1981) in west Antarctica and in the Weddell Sea. Arch. FischereiWiss. v. 35 (no. 1/2): 17-42.

EBELING, A. W. 1975 (23 May) **[ref. 7105]**. A new Indo-Pacific bathypelagic-fish species of *Poromitra* and a key to the genus. Copeia 1975 (no. 2): 306-315.

——. 1986 **[ref. 5651]**. Family No. 133: Melamphaidae (pp. 427-431). In: Smiths' Sea Fishes (Smith & Heemstra 1986 [ref. 5715]).

EBELING, A. W., AND W. H. WEED, III. 1973 **[ref. 6898]**. Order Xenoberyces (Stephanoberyciformes). In: Fishes of the Western North Atlantic. Mem. Sears Found. Mar. Res. Mem. 1 (pt 6): 397-478.

ECCLES, D. H., AND D. S. C. LEWIS. 1977 (Sept.) **[ref. 7049]**. A taxonomic study of the genus *Lethrinops* Regan (Pisces: Cichlidae) from Lake Malawi. Part 1. Ichthyol. Bull. J. L. B. Smith Inst. Ichthyol. No. 36: 1-12.

——. 1978 (Mar.) **[ref. 7012]**. A taxonomic study of the genus *Lethrinops* Regan (Pisces: Cichlidae) from Lake Malawi. Part 2. Ichthyol. Bull. J. L. B. Smith Inst. Ichthyol. No. 37: 1-11.

——. 1979 (Oct.) **[ref. 6939]**. A taxonomic study of the genus *Lethrinops* Regan (Pisces: Cichlidae) from Lake Malawi. Part 3. Ichthyol. Bull. J. L. B. Smith Inst. Ichthyol. No. 38: 1-25.

ECCLES, D. H., AND E. TREWAVAS. 1989 **[ref. 13547]**. Malawaian cichlid fishes. The classification of some Haplochromine genera. Lake Fish Movies, H. W. Dieckhoff, West Germany. 1-334.

ECHELLE, A. A., AND D. T. MOSIER. 1982 (10 Aug.) **[ref. 6821]**.

Menidia clarkhubbsi, n. sp. (Pisces: Atherinidae), an all-female species. Copeia 1982 (no. 3): 533-540.

Economidis, P. S. 1986 (31 Mar.) **[ref. 5163]**. *Chalcalburnus belvica* (Karman, 1924) (Pisces, Cyprinidae), nouvelle combinaison taxinomique pour la population provenenat du lac Petit Prespa (Macedoine, Grèce). Cybium v. 10 (no. 1): 85-90.

Ege, V. 1933 **[ref. 1186]**. On some new fishes of the families Sudidae and Stomiatidae. Preliminary note. Vidensk. Medd. Dansk Naturh. Foren. Kjob. v. 94: 223-236.

Ehrenberg, C. G. 1834 **[ref. 5036]**. Das Leuchten des Meeres. Neue Beobachtungen nebst Übersicht der Hauptmomente der geschichtlichen Entwicklung dieses merkwürdigen Phänomens. Abh. Dtsch. Akad. Wiss. Berl. 1834: 411-575, 2 pls. [Read 17 April 1834, publication date uncertain, 1836 in Daget et al. 1986 [ref. 6189].]

Eichwald, C. E. von. 1831 **[ref. 5562]**. Zoologia specialis quam expositis animalibus tum vivis, tum fossilibus potissimum Rossiae, in universam, et Poloniae in specie ... Wilna. [Not seen. Evidently 3 pts. in 2 vols., 1829-31.]

Eigenmann, C. H. 1892 (21 Oct.) **[ref. 1213]**. The Percopsidae on the Pacific slope. Science v. 20 (no. 507): 233-234.

———. 1894 (Feb.) **[ref. 1214]**. Notes on some South American fishes. Ann. N. Y. Acad. Sci. v. 7 (art. 5): 625-637.

———. 1897 **[ref. 1215]**. *Steindachneria*. Am. Nat. v. 31: 158-159.

———. 1899 (14 Oct.) **[ref. 1216]**. A case of convergence. Proc. Indiana Acad. Sci. 1899: 247-251. [Abstract in Science v. 9:217. Date of 14 Oct. on separate.]

———. 1903 (20 July) **[ref. 1217]**. The fresh-water fishes of western Cuba. Bull. U. S. Fish Comm. v. 22 [1902]: 211-236, Pls. 20-21.

———. 1903 (9 Dec.) **[ref. 1218]**. New genera of South American fresh-water fishes, and new names for old genera. Smithson. Misc. Collect. (Quarterly) v. 45: 144-148. [Some included genera with Eigenmann & Kennedy as authors.]

———. 1905 (19 May) **[ref. 5563]**. The mailed catfishes of South America. Science (n. s.) v. 21 (no. 542): 792-795.

———. 1907 (23 May) **[ref. 1219]**. The poeciliid fishes of Rio Grande do Sul and the La Plata Basin. Proc. U. S. Natl. Mus. v. 32 (no. 1532): 425-433.

———. 1907 (Dec.) **[ref. 1220]**. Fowler's "Heterognathus Fishes" with a note on the Stethaprioninae. Am. Nat. v. 41 (no. 492): 767-772.

———. 1908 (Dec.) **[ref. 1221]**. Preliminary descriptions of new genera and species of tetragonopterid characins. (Zoölogical Results of the Thayer Brazilian expedition.) Bull. Mus. Comp. Zool. v. 52 (no. 6): 91-106.

———. 1909 (Aug.) **[ref. 1222]**. Reports on the expedition to British Guiana of the Indiana University and the Carnegie Museum, 1908. Report no. 1. Some new genera and species of fishes from British Guiana. Ann. Carnegie Mus. v. 6 (no. 1): 4-54.

———. 1909 **[ref. 1223]**. The fresh-water fishes of Patagonia and an examination of the Archiplata-Archhelenis theory. In: Reports of the Princeton University expeditions to Patagonia 1896-1899. Zoology v. 3 (no. 1, pt 3): 225-374, Pls. 30-37.

———. 1910 (12 Feb.) **[ref. 1224]**. Catalogue of the fresh-water fishes of tropical and south temperate America. In: Reports of the Princeton University expeditions to Patagonia 1896-1899. Zoology v. 3 (pt 4): 375-511. [Also as a separate, issued 12 Feb. 1910 as: Catalog and bibliography of ...; Contr. Zool. Lab Indiana Univ. No. 76 (2).]

———. 1911 (Feb.) **[ref. 1225]**. Descriptions of two new tetragonopterid fishes in the British Museum. Ann. Mag. Nat. Hist. (Ser. 8) v. 7 (no. 38): 215-216.

———. 1911 (Dec.) **[ref. 1226]**. New characins in the collection of the Carnegie Museum. Ann. Carnegie Mus. v. 8 (no. 1): 164-181, Pls. 4-9.

———. 1912 (June) **[ref. 1227]**. The freshwater fishes of British Guiana, including a study of the ecological grouping of species, and the relation of the fauna of the plateau to that of the lowlands. Mem. Carnegie Mus. v. 5 (no. 1): i-xxii + 1-578, Pls. 1-103.

———. 1912 (23 Oct.) **[ref. 1228]**. Some results from an ichthyological reconnaissance of Colombia, South America. Part I. (Contrib. Zool. Lab. Ind. Univ. No. 127.) Ind. Univ. Studies No. 16 [sic No. 8]: 1-27. [Cover date Sept. 1912, issued 23 Oct. 1912, No. 8 on cover, is No. 16.]

———. 1913 (June) **[ref. 1229]**. Some results from an ichthyological reconnaissance of Colombia, South America. Part II. [Includes 5 separate subtitles.] (Contrib. Zool. Lab. Ind. Univ. No. 131) Ind. Univ. Studies No. 18: 1-32. [Cover date March 1913, issue date June 1913.]

———. 1914 (25 Apr.) **[ref. 1230]**. IV. New genera and species of South American fishes. Pp. 45-48. In: Some results from studies of South American fishes. (Contrib. Zool. Lab. Ind. Univ. No. 135) Ind. Univ. Studies.

———. 1915 (Dec.) **[ref. 1231]**. The Cheirodontinae, a subfamily of minute characid fishes of South America. Mem. Carnegie Mus. v. 7 (no. 1): 1-99, Pls. 1-17.

———. 1915 (Mar.) **[ref. 1232]**. The Serrasalminae and Mylinae. Ann. Carnegie Mus. v. 9 (nos. 3-4): 226-272, Pls. 44-58.

———. 1916 (Jan.) **[ref. 1233]**. New and rare fishes from South American rivers. Ann. Carnegie Mus. v. 10 (nos. 1-2): 77-86, Pls. 13-16.

———. 1916 (Jan.) **[ref. 1234]**. On *Apareiodon*, a new genus of characid fishes. Ann. Carnegie Mus. v. 10 (nos. 1-2): 71-76, Pls. 11-12.

———. 1917 (Oct.) **[ref. 1235]**. New and rare species of South American Siluridae in the Carnegie Museum. Ann. Carnegie Mus. v. 11 (nos. 3-4): 398-404, Pls. 39-41.

———. 1917 (Aug.) **[ref. 1236]**. The American Characidae [Part 1]. Mem. Mus. Comp. Zool. v. 43 (pt 1): 1-102, Pls. 1-8, 12, 14-16, 95, 98, 100-101.

———. 1917 **[ref. 1237]**. Descriptions of sixteen new species of Pygidiidae. Proc. Am. Philos. Soc. v. 56: 690-703.

———. 1918 (Sept.) **[ref. 1239]**. The Pygidiidae, a family of South American catfishes. Mem. Carnegie Mus. v. 7 (no. 5): 259-398, Pls. 36-56.

———. 1918 (Jan.) **[ref. 1240]**. The American Characidae [Part 2]. Mem. Mus. Comp. Zool. v. 43 (pt 2): 103-208, Pls. 9-11, 13, 17-29, 33, 78-80, 93.

———. 1919 **[ref. 1241]**. *Trogloglanis pattersoni* a new blind fish from San Antonio, Texas. Proc. Am. Philos. Soc. v. 58 (no. 6): 397-400.

———. 1920 (Apr.) **[ref. 12609]**. Limits of the genera *Vandellia* and *Urinophilus*. Science (n. s.) v. 51 (no. 1322): 441.

———. 1922 **[ref. 1242]**. On a new genus and two new species of Pygidiidae, a family of South American nematognaths. Bijdr. Dierkd. v. 22: 113-114, Pls. 3-4.

———. 1922 (Oct.) **[ref. 1243]**. The fishes of western South America, Part I. The fresh-water fishes of northwestern South America, including Colombia, Panama, and the Pacific slopes of Ecuador and Peru, together with an appendix upon the fishes of the Rio Meta in Colombia. Mem. Carnegie Mus. v. 9 (no. 1): 1-346, Pls. 1-38.

———. 1925 **[ref. 1244]**. A review of the Doradidae, a family of South American Nematognathi, or catfishes. Trans. Am. Philos. Soc. (n. s.) v. 22 (pt 5): 280-365, Pls. 1-27.

———. 1928 **[ref. 1245]**. The freshwater fishes of Chile. Mem. Natl. Acad. Sci. Wash. v. 22 (mem. 2): 1-63, Pls. 1-16. [Date of publication not confirmed; date on cover is 1927, most authors use 1928.]

Eigenmann, C. H., and W. R. Allen. 1942 **[ref. 1246]**. Fishes of western South America. I. The intercordilleran and Amazonian lowlands of Peru. II.- The high pampas of Peru, Bolivia, and northern Chile. With a revision of the Peruvian Gymnotidae, and of the genus *Orestias*. Univ. Kentucky, Lexington, Kentucky. i-xv + 1-494, Pls. 1-22.

Eigenmann, C. H., and B. A. Bean. 1907 (16 Jan.) **[ref. 1247]**. An account of Amazon River fishes collected by J. B. Steere; with a note on *Pimelodus clarias*. Proc. U. S. Natl. Mus. v. 31 (no. 1503): 659-668.

Eigenmann, C. H., and C. H. Beeson. 1893 (July) **[ref. 1212]**.

Preliminary note on the relationship of the species usually united under the generic name *Sebastodes*. Am. Nat. v. 27 (no. 319): 668-671.

EIGENMANN, C. H., AND W. L. BRAY. 1894 (Jan.) **[ref. 1248]**. A revision of the American Cichlidae. Ann. N. Y. Acad. Sci. v. 7 (art. 4): 607-624.

EIGENMANN, C. H., AND R. S. EIGENMANN. 1888 (18 July) **[ref. 1249]**. Preliminary notes on South American Nematognathi. I. Proc. Calif. Acad. Sci. (Ser. 2) v. 1 (pt 2): 119-172. [Issued as separate, 18 July 1888.]

———. 1888 (25 Jan.) **[ref. 1250]**. A list of American species of Gobiidae and Callionymidae, with notes on the specimens contained in the Museum of Comparative Zoölogy, at Cambridge, Massachusetts. Proc. Calif. Acad. Sci. (Ser. 2) v. 1 (pt 1): 51-78.

———. 1889 (9 Nov.) **[ref. 1251]**. Notes from the San Diego Biological Laboratory. The fishes of Cortez Banks. [Continued with additional subtitles.] West. Amer. Sci. v. 6: 123-132.

———. 1889 (Apr.) **[ref. 1258]**. Description of new nematognathoid fishes from Brazil. West. Amer. Sci. v. 6 (no. 42): 8-10.

———. 1889 (Apr.) **[ref. 1252]**. Preliminary description of new species and genera of Characinidae. West. Amer. Sci. v. 6 (no. 42): 7-8.

———. 1889 (18 Aug.) **[ref. 1253]**. Preliminary notes on South American Nematognathi. II. Proc. Calif. Acad. Sci. (Ser. 2) v. 2: 28-56. [Separate issued 18 Aug. 1889.]

———. 1889 (Nov.) **[ref. 1254]**. A revision of the Curimatinae. XVIII. A revision of the edentulous genera of Curimatinae. Ann. N. Y. Acad. Sci. v. 4: 409-440. [Also as a separate, pp. 1-32.]

———. 1889 **[ref. 12497]**. A review of the Erythrininae. Proc. Calif. Acad. Sci. v. 2: 100-116, Pl. 1.

———. 1890 (24 Mar.) **[ref. 1256]**. Additions to the fauna of San Diego. Proc. Calif. Acad. Sci. (Ser. 2) v. 3: 1-24. [Separate issued 24 Mar. 1890.]

———. 1890 **[ref. 12251]**. A revision of the South American Nematognathi or cat-fishes. Occas. Pap. Calif. Acad. Sci. No. 1: 1-508 + errata and map.

———. 1891 (16 July) **[ref. 12252]**. A catalogue of the fresh-water fishes of South America. Proc. U. S. Natl. Mus. v. 14 (no. 842): 1-81.

———. 1919 (5 Dec.) **[ref. 1257]**. *Steindachneridion*. Science (n. s.) v. 50 (no. 1301): 525-526.

EIGENMANN, C. H., A. W. HENN AND C. WILSON. 1914 (16 Jan.) **[ref. 1259]**. New fishes from western Colombia, Ecuador, and Peru. (Contrib. Zool. Lab. Ind. Univ. No. 133.) Ind. Univ. Studies No. 19: 1-15.

EIGENMANN, C. H., AND C. H. KENNEDY. 1903 (4-29 Sept.) **[ref. 1260]**. On a collection of fishes from Paraguay, with a synopsis of the American genera of cichlids. Proc. Acad. Nat. Sci. Phila. v. 50 (for 1903): 497-537. [Pages 497-528 published 4 Sept., pp. 529-537 on 29 Sept.]

EIGENMANN, C. H., W. L. MCATEE AND D. P. WARD. 1907 (July) **[ref. 1261]**. On further collections of fishes from Paraguay. Ann. Carnegie Mus. v. 4 (no. 2): 110-157, Pls. 31-45.

EIGENMANN, C. H., AND G. S. MYERS. 1927 (Aug.) **[ref. 1262]**. A new genus of Brazilian characin fishes allied to *Bivibranchia*. Proc. Natl. Acad. Sci. U. S. A. v. 13 (no. 8): 565-566.

———. 1929 (Sept.) **[ref. 1263]**. The American Characidae [Part 5, and incl. Supplement by G. S. Myers, pp. 516-550]. Mem. Mus. Comp. Zool. v. 43 (pt 5): 429-558, Pls. 57, 63, 70-74, 81-83, 94.

EIGENMANN, C. H., AND A. A. NORRIS. 1900 **[ref. 1264]**. Sobre alguns peixes de S. Paulo, Brazil. (Contr. Lab. Zool. Univ. Indiana, n. 33.) Rev. Mus. Paulista v. 4: 349-362.

———. 1901 (18 Mar.) **[ref. 1265]**. *Bergiaria*. Comun. Mus. Nac. Buenos Aires v. 1 (no. 8): 272.

EIGENMANN, C. H., AND F. OGLE. 1907 (10 Sept.) **[ref. 1266]**. An annotated list of characin fishes in the United States National Museum and the museum of Indiana University, with descriptions of new species. Proc. U. S. Natl. Mus. v. 33 (no. 1556): 1-36.

EIGENMANN, C. H., AND D. P. WARD. 1905 (20 June) **[ref. 1267]**. The Gymnotidae. Proc. Wash. Acad. Sci. v. 7: 159-188, Pls. 7-11.

EIGENMANN, R. S. 1891 (Feb.) **[ref. 1268]**. New California fishes. Am. Nat. v. 25 (no. 290): 153-156.

ELLIS, M. D. 1911 (Dec.) **[ref. 1269]**. II. On the species of *Hasemania*, *Hyphessobrycon*, and *Hemigrammus* collected by J. D. Haseman for the Carnegie Museum. Ann. Carnegie Mus. v. 8 (no. 1): 148-163, Pls. 1-3.

———. 1913 (Mar.) **[ref. 1270]**. The plated nematognaths. Ann. Carnegie Mus. v. 8 (nos. 3-4): 384-413, Pls. 25-31.

ELLIS, M. M. 1913 (Aug.) **[ref. 1271]**. The gymnotid eels of tropical America. Mem. Carnegie Mus. v. 6 (no. 3): 109-195, Pls. 15-23.

ELVIRA, B. 1987 (30 June) **[ref. 6743]**. Taxonomic revision of the genus *Chondrostoma* Agassiz, 1835 (Pisces, Cyprinidae). Cybium v. 11 (no. 2): 111-140.

EMERY, A. R. 1980 **[ref. 6928]**. The osteology of *Lepidozygus tapeinosoma* (Pisces: Pomacentridae). Bull. Mar. Sci. v. 30: 213-236.

———. 1983 **[ref. 5437]**. Geographic variation in the Indo-Pacific damselfish genus *Lepidozygus* (Pisces: Pomacentridae). Can. J. Zool. v. 61 (no. 6): 1326-1338.

EMERY, A. R., AND G. R. ALLEN. 1980 (30 June) **[ref. 6917]**. *Stegastes*; a senior synonym for the damselfish genus *Eupomacentrus*; osteological and other evidence, with comments on other genera. Rec. West. Aust. Mus. v. 8 (no. 2): 199-206.

ESCHMEYER, W. N. 1965 (Sept.) **[ref. 1273]**. Three new scorpionfishes of the genera *Pontinus*, *Phenacoscorpus* and *Idiastion* from the western Atlantic Ocean. Bull. Mar. Sci. v. 15 (no. 3): 521-534.

———. 1969 **[ref. 1274]**. A systematic review of the scorpionfishes of the Atlantic Ocean (Pisces: Scorpaenidae). Occas. Pap. Calif. Acad. Sci No. 79: i-iv + 1-143.

———. 1986 **[ref. 5652]**. Family No. 149: Scorpaenidae (pp. 463-478), Family No. 159: Caracanthidae (p. 490). In: Smiths' Sea Fishes (Smith & Heemstra 1986 [ref. 5715]).

ESCHMEYER, W. N., T. ABE AND S. NAKANO. 1979 (20 Feb.) **[ref. 1275]**. *Adelosebastes latens*, a new genus and species of scorpionfish from the North Pacific Ocean (Pisces, Scorpaenidae). Uo (Jpn. Soc. Ichthyol.) No. 30: 77-84, Pl. 1.

ESCHMEYER, W. N., AND G. R. ALLEN. 1978 **[ref. 1276]**. *Neoaploactis tridorsalis*, a new genus and species of fish from the Great Barrier Reef, Australia (Scorpaeniformes: Aploactinidae). Rec. West. Aust. Mus. v. 6 (no. 4): 443-448.

ESCHMEYER, W. N., AND B. B. COLLETTE. 1966 (June) **[ref. 6485]**. The scorpionfish subfamily Setarchinae, including the genus *Ectreposebastes*. Bull. Mar. Sci. v. 16 (no. 2): 349-375.

ESCHMEYER, W. N., L. E. HALLACHER AND K. V. RAMA-RAO. 1979 (24 Jan.) **[ref. 1277]**. The scorpionfish genus *Minous* (Scorpaenidae, Minoinae) including a new species from the Indian Ocean. Proc. Calif. Acad. Sci. v. 41 (no. 20): 453-473.

ESCHMEYER, W. N., AND E. S. HERALD. 1983 **[ref. 9277]**. A field guide to Pacific Coast fishes of North America. Peterson Field Guide Series No. 28: i-xii + 1-336, Pls. 1-48.

ESCHMEYER, W. N., Y. HIROSAKI AND T. ABE. 1973 (9 Aug.) **[ref. 6390]**. Two new species of the scorpionfish genus *Rhinopias*, with comments on related genera and species. Proc. Calif. Acad. Sci. v. 39 (no. 16): 285-310.

ESCHMEYER, W. N., AND S. G. POSS. 1976 (Oct.) **[ref. 5468]**. Review of the scorpionfish genus *Maxillicosta* (Pisces: Scorpaenidae), with a description of three new species from the Australian-New Zealand region. Bull. Mar. Sci. v. 26 (no. 4): 433-449.

ESCHMEYER, W. N., AND K. V. RAMA-RAO. 1973 (24 Oct.) **[ref. 6391]**. Two new stonefishes (Pisces, Scorpaenidae) from the Indo-West Pacific, with a synopsis of the subfamily Synanceiinae. Proc. Calif. Acad. Sci. v. 39 (no. 18): 337-382.

———. 1978 (20 Dec.) **[ref. 6386]**. A new scorpionfish, *Ebosia falcata* (Scorpaenidae, Pteroinae), from the western Indian Ocean, with comments on the genus. Matsya No. 3 [for 1977]: 64-71.

ESCHMEYER, W. N., K. V. RAMA-RAO AND L. E. HALLACHER. 1979 (24 Jan.) **[ref. 6385]**. Fishes of the scorpionfish subfamily Choridactylinae from the western Pacific and the Indian Ocean. Proc. Calif. Acad. Sci. v. 41 (no. 21): 475-500.

ESCHMEYER, W. N., AND J. E. RANDALL. 1975 (3 Oct.) **[ref. 6389]**. The scorpaenid fishes of the Hawaiian Islands, including new species and new records (Pisces: Scorpaenidae). Proc. Calif. Acad. Sci. v. 40 (no. 11): 265-334.

ESCHMEYER, W. N., AND C. R. ROBINS. 1988 (Sept.) **[ref. 6886]**. *Saccopharynx* Mitchill, 1824 (Osteichthyes, Saccopharyngiformes): proposed conservation. Bull. Zool. Nomencl. v. 45 (pt 3): 204-206.

ESTÈVE, R. 1952 **[ref. 5564]**. Poissons de Mauritanie et du Sahara oriental. Un nouveau sous-genre de *Barbus*. Bull. Mus. Natl. Hist. Nat. (Ser. 2) v. 24 (no. 2): 176-179.

EVERMANN, B. W., AND H. W. CLARK. 1928 (28 Feb.) **[ref. 5565]**. Descriptions of two new species of fishes from off Cape San Lucas, Lower California. Proc. Calif. Acad. Sci. (Ser. 4) v. 16 (no. 22): 685-688, Pls. 27-28.

EVERMANN, B. W., AND E. L. GOLDSBOROUGH. 1907 **[ref. 6532]**. The fishes of Alaska. Bull. Bur. Fish. v. 26 (for 1906): 219-360, Pls. 14-42.

EVERMANN, B. W., AND W. C. KENDALL. 1898 **[ref. 1281]**. Descriptions of new or little-known genera and species of fishes from the United States. Bull. U. S. Fish Comm. v. 17 [1897](art. 5): 125-133, Pls. 6-9.

———. 1906 (25 July) **[ref. 1282]**. Notes on a collection of fishes from Argentina, South America, with descriptions of three new species. Proc. U. S. Natl. Mus. v. 31 (no. 1482): 67-108.

EVERMANN, B. W., AND M. C. MARSH. 1900 **[ref. 1283]**. Descriptions of new genera and species of fishes from Puerto Rico. Rep. U. S. Fish Comm. v. 24 [1899]: 351-362.

EVERMANN, B. W., AND L. RADCLIFFE. 1917 (1 Aug.) **[ref. 1284]**. The fishes of the west coast of Peru and the Titicaca Basin. Bull. U. S. Natl. Mus. No. 95: i-xi + 1-166, Pls. 1-14.

EVERMANN, B. W., AND A. SEALE. 1907 (11 Jan.) **[ref. 1285]**. Fishes of the Philippine Islands. Bull. Bur. Fish. v. 26 (for 1906): 49-110.

EVERMANN, B. W., AND T. SHAW. 1927 (31 Jan.) **[ref. 1286]**. Fishes from eastern China, with descriptions of new species. Proc. Calif. Acad. Sci. (Ser. 4) v. 16 (no. 4): 97-122.

EVSEENKO, S. A. 1984 **[ref. 5978]**. A new genus and species of lefteye flounder, *Pseudomancopsetta andriashevi*, and their position in the suborder Pleuronectoidei. Voprosy Ikhtiol. v. 24 (no. 5): 709-717. [In Russian. English translation in J. Ichthyol. v. 25 (no. 1): 1-9.]

———. 1987 **[ref. 9289]**. A review of "armless" flounders of the genus *Achiropsetta* (Pleuronectoidei) with description of a new species, *Achiropsetta heterolepis* sp nov. Voprosy Ikhtiol. v. 27 (no. 5): 771-783. [In Russian. English translation in J. Ichthyol. v. 28 (no. 1): 10-21.]

EYDOUX, J. F. T., AND F. A. SOULET. 1850 **[ref. 4501]**. Poissons. Pp. 155-216. In: Voyage autour du monde exécuté pendant les années 1836 et 1837 sur la corvette La Bonite, commandée par M. Vaillant. Zoologie, Vol. 1 (pt 2). Paris. [For authorship and date of publication see Bauchot et al. 1982 [ref. 6562].]

FABRICIUS, O. 1793 **[ref. 1288]**. Beskrivelse over 2de sieldne Grønlandske fiske: bugte-tanden (campylodon), og den tornefulde rognkald (*Cyclopterus spinosus*). Skr. Naturh. Selsk. Kjobenhavn v. 4 (no. 2): 21-33. [Not seen.]

FACCIOLÀ, L. 1882 **[ref. 1291]**. Pesci nuovi o poco noti dello stretto di Messina. Nat. Sicil. v. 1: 166-168.

———. 1883 **[ref. 1289]**. Note sui pesci dello stretto di Messina. I. Su di alcune specie nuove o poco note. Nat. Sicil. v. 2 (no. 7): 145-148.

———. 1884 **[ref. 1292]**. Note sui pesci dello stretto di Messina. Nat. Sicil. v. 3: 111-114, Pl. 2. [Also as a separate, pp. 1-4.]

———. 1885 **[ref. 1295]**. Su di alcuni rari Pleuronettidi del mar di Messina. Nota preliminare. Nat. Sicil. v. 4: 261-266. [Also as a separate, pp. 1-6.]

———. 1888 **[ref. 1293]**. Annunzio ittiologico. Nat. Sicil. v. 7: 167-169.

———. 1911 **[ref. 7188]**. Generi dei vertebrati ittioidi del mare di Messina. Boll. Soc. Zool. Ital. (Ser. 2) v. 12: 268-287.

———. 1914 **[ref. 1290]**. Su di un nuovo tipo dei Nettastomidi. Boll. Soc. Zool. Ital. (Ser. 3) v. 3: 39-47.

———. 1916 **[ref. 5566]**. I Labroidi del mare di Messina. Monit. Zool. Ital. v. 27 (no. 7): 140-152.

FAHAY, M. P., AND D. F. MARKLE. 1984 **[ref. 13653]**. Gadiformes: development and relationships. Am. Soc. Ichthyol. Herpetol. Spec. Publ. No. 1: 265-283.

FANG, P. W. 1930 (Mar.) **[ref. 1296]**. New homalopterin loaches from Kwangsi, China. With supplementary note on basipterigia and ribs. Sinensia v. 1 (no. 3): 25-42, Pls. 1-2.

———. 1933 (Apr.) **[ref. 1297]**. Notes on a new cyprinoid genus, *Pseudogyrinocheilus* & *P. prochelus* (Sauvage & Dabry) from western China. Sinensia v. 3 (no. 10): 255-264 + table.

———. 1934 **[ref. 1298]**. Study on the fishes referring to Salangidae of China. Sinensia v. 4 (no. 9): 231-268.

———. 1934 **[ref. 1299]**. Supplementary notes on the fishes referring to Salangidae of China. Sinensia v. 5 (nos. 5 & 6): 505-511.

———. 1935 (Feb.) **[ref. 1300]**. Study on the crossostomoid fishes of China. Sinensia v. 6 (no. 1): 44-97.

———. 1935 **[ref. 1301]**. On *Mesomisgurnus*, gen. nov. & *Paramisgurnus*, Sauvage, with descriptions of three rarely known species & synopsis of Chinese cobitoid genera. Sinensia v. 6 (no. 2): 128-146.

———. 1936 (Feb.) **[ref. 1302]**. Study on the botoid fishes of China. Sinensia v. 7 (no. 1): 1-49.

———. 1936 **[ref. 1303]**. *Sinocyclocheilus tingi*, a new genus and species of Chinese barbid fishes from Yunnan. Sinensia v. 7 (no. 5): 588-593.

———. 1936 **[ref. 1304]**. Chinese fresh-water fishes referring to Cyprininae (sen. str.). Sinensia v. 7 (no. 6): 686-712.

———. 1938 (5 Aug.) **[ref. 1305]**. On *Huigobio chenhsiensis*, gen. & sp. nov. Bull. Fan Memorial Inst. Biol. Peiping (Zool. Ser.) v. 8 (no. 3): 237-243, Pl. 16.

———. 1943 **[ref. 1306]**. Sur certains types peu connus de Cyprinidés des collections du muséum de Paris (III). Bull. Mus. Natl. Hist. Nat. (Ser. 2) v. 15 (no. 6): 399-405.

FANG, P. W., AND L. T. CHONG. 1932 (June) **[ref. 1307]**. Study on the fishes referring to *Siniperca* of China. Sinensia v. 2 (no. 12): 137-200.

FATIO, V. 1882-90 **[ref. 1308]**. Faune des vertébrés de la Suisse. Vol. 4. Histoire Naturelle des Poissons. i-xiv + 1-786, Pls. 1-5.

FECHHELM, J. D., AND J. D. MCEACHRAN. 1984 (3 Dec. 1984) **[ref. 5227]**. A revision of the electric ray genus *Diplobatis* with notes on the interrelationships of Narcinidae (Chondrichthyes, Torpediniformes). Bull. Fla. State Mus. v. 29 (no. 5): 171-209.

FEDOROV, V. V. 1973 **[ref. 5567]**. A list of Bering Sea fishes. Izv. Tikhookean. Nauchno-Issled. Inst. Rybn. Khoz. Okeanogr. v. 87: 42-71. [In Russian. English translation by Natl. Mar. Fish. Serv.]

———. 1973 **[ref. 13393]**. Ichthyofauna of the continental slope of the Bering Sea and some aspects of its origin and formation. Izv. Tikhookean. Nauchno-Issled. Inst. Rybn. Khoz. Okeanogr. v. 87: 3-41. [In Russian. English translation by Natl. Mar. Fish. Serv.]

———. 1975 **[ref. 1310]**. A description of a new genus and species of a zoarcid fish *Puzanovia rubra*, gen. et sp. n. (Pisces, Zoarcidae) from the northern part of the Pacific Ocean. Voprosy Ikhtiol. v. 15 (no. 4): 587-591. [In Russian. English translation in J. Ichthyol. v. 15 (no. 4): 527-541.]

———. 1982 **[ref. 1311]**. A new eelpout, *Hadropogonichthys lindbergi* Fedorov, gen. et sp. nov. (Zoarcidae), from the bathyal depths of the Fourth Kuril Strait. Voprosy Ikhtiol. v. 22 (no. 5): 722-729. [In Russian. English translation in J. Ichthyol. v. 22 (no. 5): 16-23.]

———. 1982 **[ref. 5252]**. [Description of a new species of the zoarcid fishes, *Puzanovia virgata* sp. n. (Osteichthyes: Zoarcidae) from a region of the northern Kuril Islands.] Proc. Zool. Inst. Acad. Sci. USSR v. 114: 77-84. [In Russian.]

FEDOROV, V. V., AND V. P. FOROSHCHUK. 1988 **[ref. 13478]**. A new flounder, *Psettina multisquamea*, sp. nova (Bothidae) from Saya-de-Mal'ya Bank, Indian Ocean. Voprosy Ikhtiol. v. 28 (no. 4): 531-540.

[In Russian. English translation in J. Ichthyol. v. 28 (no. 6): 36-45.]

Fedorov, V. V., and A. V. Neyelov. 1978 **[ref. 1312]**. A new genus and species of eelpout *Andreiashevia aptera* gen. et sp. nov. (Perciformes, Zoarcidae). Voprosy Ikhtiol. v. 18 (no. 5): 952-955. [In Russian. English translation in J. Ichthyol. v. 18 (no. 5): 846-849.]

Fedorov, V. V., and B. A. Sheiko. 1988 **[ref. 12755]**. A second capture of *Andriashevia aptera* (Zoarcidae) off Japanese coasts. Proc. Zool. Inst. Leningrad; Syst. Morph. Ecol. Fishes v. 181: 117-120. [In Russian, brief English Summ.]

Fedoryako, B. I. 1976 **[ref. 1313]**. Materials on the systematics and distribution of the "oceanic Cheilodipteridae." Tr. Inst. Okeanol. v. 104: 156-190. [In Russian, English summ.]

Feibel, C. S. 1987 (Jan.) **[ref. 6113]**. Fossil fish nests from the Koobi Fora Formation (Plio-Pleistocene) of northern Kenya. J. Paleontol. v. 61 (no. 1): 130-134.

Fernandez, J. M., and S. H. Weitzman. 1987 (25 Feb.) **[ref. 5981]**. A new species of *Nannostomus* (Teleostei: Lebiasinidae) from near Puerto Ayacucho, Río Orinoco drainage, Venezuela. Proc. Biol. Soc. Wash. v. 100 (no. 1): 164-172.

Fernández-Yépez, A. 1947 (May) **[ref. 4817]**. *Charaxodon*, a new genus of characid fishes from South America. Publ. Establ. Venez. Cienc. Nat. Caracas, Evencias. (Ser. 1) No. 3: 3 unnum. pp.

———. 1948 **[ref. 1316]**. Los Curimatidos (Peces fluviales de Sur América). Catalogo descriptivo con nuevas adiciones genericas y especificas. Bol. Taxon. Lab. Pesqueria Caiguire Caracas No. 1: 1-79 + table + index.

———. 1948 **[ref. 1317]**. El *Pseudotilosurus brasilensis*, nuevo genero y nueva especie de pez, procedente del Brasil. Mem. Soc. Cienc. Nat. La Salle v. 8 (no. 21): 72-73.

———. 1948 **[ref. 1318]**. *Ichthyacus breederi* nuevo género y especie de pez Synentognatho, de los ríos de Sur América. Evencias No. 4: 3 unnum. pp.

———. 1949 (Mar.) **[ref. 1319]**. *Ramirezella newboldi* nuevo género y especie de pez Tetragonopteridae colectado en Venezuela. Evencias No. 6: 1-3.

———. 1950 (15 July) **[ref. 1323]**. Algunos peces del Rio Autana. Noved. Cient. Mus. Hist. Nat. La Salle (Ser. Zool.) No. 2: 1-18, 3 pls.

———. 1950 **[ref. 1321]**. Un nuevo pez de la familia Doradidae. Mem. Soc. Cienc. Nat. La Salle v. 10 (no. 27): 195-198.

———. 1951 **[ref. 14283]**. *Ginensia cunaguaro*, nuevo pez para la Ciencia colectado en el Río Apure, Venezuela. Evencias No. 10: 4 unnumbered.

———. 1953 (Oct.) **[ref. 1322]**. Algunas notas sobre los peces Asprediformes con descripción de *Ernstichthys anduzei*, nuevo e interesante bunocephalido. Noved. Cient. Mus. Hist. Nat. La Salle (Ser. Zool.) No. 11: 1-6, 1 pl.

———. 1968 **[ref. 1325]**. Contribucion al conocimiento de la familia Doradidae en Venezuela. Bol. Inst. Oceanogr. Univ. Oriente Cumana v. 7 (no. 1): 7-72.

———. 1968 (15 Oct.) **[ref. 7318]**. Contribución al conocimiento de los peces Gymnotiformes. Evencias No. 20: 7 unnum., 5 pls.

———. 1969 **[ref. 9186]**. Contribucion al conocimiento de los cichlidos. Evencias No. 22: 7 unnum. pp. + 10 figures.

———. 1973 (Dec.) **[ref. 14284]**. Contribucion al conocimiento de Auchenipteridae. Evencias No. 29: 1-7 (unnum.).

Fernholm, B. 1986 **[ref. 6283]**. Family No. 1: Myxinidae (pp. 35-36). In: Smiths' Sea Fishes (Smith & Heemstra 1986 [ref. 5715]).

Fernholm, B., and A. Wheeler. 1983 (July) **[ref. 14214]**. Linnaean fish specimens in the Swedish Museum of Natural History, Stockholm. Zool. J. Linn. Soc. v. 78: 199-286.

Ferraris, C. J., Jr. 1988 (13 Sept.) **[ref. 6685]**. Relationships of the neotropical catfish genus *Nemuroglanis*, with a description of a new species (Osteichthyes: Siluriformes: Pimelodidae). Proc. Biol. Soc. Wash. v. 101 (no. 3): 509-516.

Ferraris, C. J., Jr., and J. Fernandez. 1987 (19 May) **[ref. 6805]**. *Trachelyopterichthys anduzei*, a new species of auchenipterid catfish from the Upper Río Orinoco of Venezuela with notes on *T. taeniatus* (Kner). Proc. Biol. Soc. Wash. v. 100 (no. 2): 257-261.

Ferraris, C. J., Jr., J. H. Isbrücker and H. Nijssen. 1986 (15 Nov.) **[ref. 5988]**. *Neblinichthys pilosus*, a new genus and species of mailed catfish from the Rio Baria system, southern Venezuela (Pisces, Siluriformes, Loricariidae). Rev. Fr. Aquariol. v. 13 (no. 3): 69-72.

Ferraris, C. J., Jr., and F. Mago-Leccia. 1989 (27 Feb.) **[ref. 9288]**. A new genus and species of pimelodid catfish from the Río Negro and Río Orinoco drainages of Venezuela (Siluriformes: Pimelodidae). Copeia 1989 (no. 1): 166-171.

Filhol, H. 1884 **[ref. 1326]**. Explorations sous-marines: voyage du "Talisman." La Nature, Paris 1884: 161-164, 182-186, 198-202. [Not seen.]

Filippi, F. de. 1855 **[ref. 1327]**. Ueber die Schwimmblase des *Oligopus ater* Risso. [Aus einem Schreiben des Prof. Filippo de Filippi in Turin an A. Kölliker.] Zeitschr. Wiss. Zool. v. 7: 170-171. [Date may be 1856.]

———. 1861 **[ref. 1328]**. Note Zoologiche. IV. *Lebistes* nuovo genere di pesce della famiglia dei Ciprinodonti. Arch. Zool. Anat. Fisiol. v. 1: 69-70, Pl. 4.

Filippi, F. de, and G. B. Verany. 1857 **[ref. 1329]**. Sopra alcuni pesci nuovi o poco noti del Mediterraneo. Nota. Mem. Accad. Sci. Torino, (Ser. 2) v. 18: 187-199, 1 Pl. [Also as a separate, pp. 1-15. Separate dated 1857 (assumed correct); perhaps not published in journal until 1859.]

Fink, W. L. 1976 (22 Jan.) **[ref. 1330]**. A new genus and species of characid fish from the Bayano River Basin, Panama (Pisces: Cypriniformes). Proc. Biol. Soc. Wash. v. 88 (no. 30): 331-344.

———. 1979 (28 Nov.) **[ref. 6949]**. *Hildatia* Fernandez-Yepez, a synonym of the gymnotoid genus *Sternopygus* Müller and Troschel. Copeia 1979 (no. 4): 751-752.

———. 1984 **[ref. 13636]**. Basal Euteleosts: relationships. Am. Soc. Ichthyol. Herpetol. Spec. Publ. No. 1: 202-206.

———. 1985 (31 Dec.) **[ref. 5171]**. Phylogenetic interrelationships of the stomiid fishes (Teleostei: Stomiiformes). Misc. Publ. Mus. Zool. Univ. Mich. No. 171: i-vii + 1-127.

Fink, W. L., and S. V. Fink. 1986 (9 May) **[ref. 5176]**. A phylogenetic analysis of the genus *Stomias*, including the synonymization of *Macrostomias*. Copeia 1986 (no. 2): 494-503.

Fink, W. L., and S. H. Weitzman. 1974 (4 Sept.) **[ref. 7132]**. The so-called Cheirodontin fishes of Central America with descriptions of two new species (Pisces: Characidae). Smithson. Contrib. Zool. No. 172: i-iii + 1-46.

———. 1982 (12 Jan.) **[ref. 5177]**. Relationships of the stomiiform fishes (Teleostei), with a description of *Diplophos*. Bull. Mus. Comp. Zool. v. 150 (no. 2): 31-93.

Fischer, E. A. 1980 (5 Dec.) **[ref. 6905]**. Speciation in the hamlets (*Hypoplectrus*: Serranidae)—a continuing enigma. Copeia 1980 (no. 4): 649-659.

Fischer, J. G. 1885 **[ref. 1333]**. I. Über Fische von Süd-Georgien (pp. 49-65). In: Ichthyologische und herpetologische Bemerkungen. Jahrb. Wiss. Anst. Hamburg v. 2: 49-121, Pls. 1-4.

Fischer von Waldheim, G. 1813 **[ref. 1331]**. Zoognosia, tabulis synopticus illustrata in usum praelectionum Academiae Imperialis Medico-Chirurgicae Mosquensis. 3. edit. v. 1: i-xii + 1-466. [Not seen.]

———. 1813 **[ref. 1332]**. Recherches Zoologiques. Mem. Soc. Imp. Natural. Moscou v. 4: 237-275 of second edition. [First published in 1813 (not seen); second edition in 1830 (see Gill 1891: 303-304 [ref. 1734]).]

Fitch, J. E. 1982 (5 Feb.) **[ref. 5398]**. Revision of the eastern North Pacific anthiin basses (Pisces: Serranidae). Contrib. Sci. (Los Ang.) No. 339: 1-8.

Fitch, J. E., and S. J. Crooke. 1984 (11 Dec.) **[ref. 4950]**. Revision of eastern Pacific catalufas (Pisces: Priacanthidae) with description of a new genus and discussion of the fossil record. Proc. Calif. Acad. Sci. v. 43 (no. 19): 301-315.

Fitzinger, L. J. F. J. 1832 **[ref. 5019]**. Ueber die Ausarbeitung einer

Fauna des Erzherzogthums Oesterreich, nebst einer systematischen Aufzählung der in diesem Lande vorkommenden Säugethiere, Reptilien und Fische. Beitr. Landesk. Oesterreich. v. 1: 1-280 [see also p. 334]. [Not seen.]

——. 1837 **[ref. 1338]**. Vorläufiger Bericht über eine höchst interessante Entdeckung Dr. Natteres in Brasil. Isis (Oken) 1837: 379-380. [Not seen.]

——. 1873 **[ref. 1337]**. Die Gattungen der europäischen Cyprinen nach ihren äusseren Merkmalen. Sitzungsber. Akad. Wiss. Wien, Math.-Nat. Kl. v. 68 (1 Abt.): 145-170. [Also as a separate, Wien, 1874. Possibly first published in 1874.]

FITZSIMONS, J. M. 1972 (29 Dec.) **[ref. 7117]**. A revision of two genera of goodeid fishes (Cyprinodontiformes, Osteichthyes) from the Mexican Plateau. Copeia 1972 (no. 4): 728-756.

FLEMING, J. 1822 **[ref. 5063]**. The philosophy of zoology: or a general view of the structure, functions, and classification of animals. Archibald Constable & Co., Edinburgh. v. 2: 1-618. [Not seen.]

——. 1828 **[ref. 1339]**. A history of British animals, exhibiting the descriptive characters and systematical arrangement of the genera and species of quadrupeds, birds, reptiles, fishes, mollusca, and radiata of the United Kingdom... Edinburgh & London. Vol. I. i-xxiii + 1-565. [Second edition 1842, same pagination. Fishes on pp. 161-222.]

——. 1841 **[ref. 1340]**. Description of a new species of skate new to the British fauna. Edinburgh New Philos. J. v. 31: 236-238, Pls. 4-5.

FOLLETT, W. I., AND D. M. COHEN. 1958 (June) **[ref. 12570]**. Request for a ruling as to the species to be accepted as the type species of the nominal genus "*Bathylagus*" Günther (A. C. L. G.), 1878 (Class Pisces). Bull. Zool. Nomencl. v. 16 (pt 2): 73-78.

FOLLETT, W. I., AND L. J. DEMPSTER. 1963 **[ref. 6569]**. Relationships of the percoid fish *Pentaceros richardsoni* Smith, with description of a specimen from the coast of California. Proc. Calif. Acad. Sci. (Ser. 4) v. 32 (no. 10): 315-338.

——. 1965 (31 Dec.) **[ref. 13619]**. Ichthyological and herpetological names and works on which the International Commission on Zoological Nomenclature has ruled since the publication (in 1958) of the several official lists and indexes. Copeia 1965 (no. 4): 518-523.

FOLLETT, W. I., AND D. C. POWELL. 1988 (5 Feb.) **[ref. 6234]**. *Ernogrammus walkeri*, a new species of prickleback (Pisces: Stichaeidae) from south-central California. Copeia 1988 (no. 1): 135-152.

FORBES, H. O. 1890 (May) **[ref. 1343]**. On a new genus of fishes of the family Percidae, from New Zealand. Trans. Proc. N. Z. Inst. v. 22 (art. 30): 273-275. [Is 5th volume of new series.]

FORBES, S. A. 1885 **[ref. 1344]**. Description of new Illinois fishes. Bull. Illinois State Lab. Nat. Hist. v. 2 (art. 2): 135-139.

FORBES, S. A., AND R. E. RICHARDSON. 1905 (May) **[ref. 1345]**. On a new shovelnose sturgeon from the Mississippi River. Bull. Illinois State Lab. Nat. Hist. v. 7 (art. 4): 37-44, Pls. 4-7.

FORSSKÅL, P. 1775 **[ref. 1351]**. Descriptiones animalium avium, amphibiorum, piscium, insectorum, vermium; quae in itinere orientali observavit. Post mortem auctoris edidit Carsten Niebuhr. Hauniae. 1-20 + i-xxxiv + 1-164, 43 pls. [Pisces on pp. x-xix and 22-76. See Hureau & Monod 1973, v. 2: 322 [ref. 6590] for spelling of author's name.]

FORSTER, J. R. 1777 **[ref. 1353]**. Icones Ineditae. Bibliotheca Banksiae. [Not seen.]

——. 1778 **[ref. 1354]**. Enchiridion historiae naturali inserviens, quo, termini et delineationes ad avium, piscium, insectorum et plantarum adumbrationes intelligendas et concinnandas, secundum methodum systematis Linnaeani continentur. Halae. [Not seen.]

FOURMANOIR, P. 1966 **[ref. 1355]**. Trois nouvelles espèces de poissons du Vietnam: *Sicyodon albus* nov. gen., nov. sp., et *Lubricogobius ornatus*, nov. sp. (Gobiidae), et *Parupeneus aurantius* nov. sp. (Mullidae). Bull. Mus. Natl. Hist. Nat. (Ser. 2) v. 37 (no. 6): 956-961.

——. 1970 **[ref. 1356]**. Notes ichthyologiques (1). Cah. ORSTOM Ser. Oceanogr. v. 8 (no. 2): 19-33.

——. 1988 (30 Sept.) **[ref. 6870]**. *Acropoma lecorneti*, une nouvelle espèce de Nouvelle-Calédonie (Pisces, Perciformes, Acropomatidae). Cybium v. 12 (no. 3): 259-263.

FOURMANOIR, P., AND A. CROSNIER. 1964 **[ref. 5568]**. Deuxième liste complémentaire des poissons du canal de Mozambique. Diagnoses préliminaire de 11 espèces nouvelles. Trav. Centre Océanogr. Pêches Nosy-Bé—Cah. ORSTOM No. 6 (1963): 2-32, Pls. A, 13-16.

FOWLER, H. W. 1901 (7 June) **[ref. 1358]**. Description of a new hemiramphid. Proc. Acad. Nat. Sci. Phila. v. 53 (for 1901): 293-294.

——. 1901 (7 May) **[ref. 1359]**. Note on the Odontostomidae. Proc. Acad. Nat. Sci. Phila. v. 53 (for 1901): 211-212.

——. 1903 (4 June) **[ref. 1360]**. Descriptions of several fishes from Zanzibar Island, two of which are new. Proc. Acad. Nat. Sci. Phila. v. 55 (for 1903): 161-176, Pls. 6-8.

——. 1903 (16 Dec.) **[ref. 1361]**. New and little known Muglidae and Sphyraenidae. Proc. Acad. Nat. Sci. Phila. v. 55 (for 1903): 743-752, Pls. 45-46.

——. 1903 (16 Dec.) **[ref. 1362]**. Descriptions of new, little known, and typical Atherinidae. Proc. Acad. Nat. Sci. Phila. v. 55 (for 1903): 727-742, Pls. 41-44. [Fowler (Fishes World manuscript) gives date as 13 Jan. 1904, date on reverse of title page for volume is 16 Dec. 1903.]

——. 1904 (15 Jan.) **[ref. 1363]**. Description of a new lantern fish. Proc. Acad. Nat. Sci. Phila. v. 55 (for 1903): 754-755.

——. 1904 (7 Mar.) **[ref. 1364]**. Note on the Characinidae. Proc. Acad. Nat. Sci. Phila. v. 56 (for 1904): 119.

——. 1904 (7 Apr.) **[ref. 1365]**. New, little known and typical berycoid fishes. Proc. Acad. Nat. Sci. Phila. v. 56 (for 1904): 222-238.

——. 1904 (7 Apr.) **[ref. 1366]**. Notes on fishes from Arkansas, Indian Territory and Texas. Proc. Acad. Nat. Sci. Phila. v. 56 (for 1904): 242-249.

——. 1904 (ca. 10 June) **[ref. 1367]**. A collection of fishes from Sumatra. J. Acad. Nat. Sci. Phila. (Ser. 2) v. 12 (pt 4): 495-560, Pls. 7-28. [Extra copies were printed for author on 10 June 1904, distribution date probably about on that date.]

——. 1905 (16-31 Jan.) **[ref. 1368]**. New, rare or little known scombroids. I. Proc. Acad. Nat. Sci. Phila. v. 56 (for 1904): 757-771. [Pages 757-760 published 16 Jan., pp. 761-771 on 31 Jan.]

——. 1905 (31 Mar.) **[ref. 1369]**. New, rare or little known scombroids. No. II. Proc. Acad. Nat. Sci. Phila. v. 57 (for 1905): 56-88.

——. 1905 (14 Aug.) **[ref. 1370]**. Some fishes from Borneo. Proc. Acad. Nat. Sci. Phila. v. 57 (for 1905): 455-523.

——. 1906 (29 May) **[ref. 1371]**. Some cold-blooded vertebrates of the Florida Keys. Proc. Acad. Nat. Sci. Phila. v. 58 (for 1906): 77-113, Pls. 3-4.

——. 1906 (20 June) **[ref. 1372]**. New, rare or little known scombroids, No. 3. Proc. Acad. Nat. Sci. Phila. v. 58 (for 1906): 114-122.

——. 1906 (25 Sept.) **[ref. 1373]**. Further knowledge of some heterognathus fishes. Part I. Proc. Acad. Nat. Sci. Phila. v. 58 (for 1906): 293-351.

——. 1906 **[ref. 7112]**. The fishes of New Jersey. Rept. New Jersey State Mus. Part II: 35-477, Pls. 1-103.

——. 1907 (7-16 Jan.) **[ref. 1374]**. Further knowledge of some heterognathous fishes. Part II. Proc. Acad. Nat. Sci. Phila. v. 58 (for 1906): 431-483. [Pages 431-460 published 7 Jan., pp. 461-483 on 16 Jan.]

——. 1907 (19 Feb.) **[ref. 1375]**. Some new and little-known percoid fishes. Proc. Acad. Nat. Sci. Phila. v. 58 (for 1906): 510-528.

——. 1907 (16 Aug.) **[ref. 1376]**. Notes on Serranidae. Proc. Acad. Nat. Sci. Phila. v. 59 (for 1907): 249-269.

——. 1907-08 (4 Dec. 07-17 Jan.08) **[ref. 1377]**. A collection of fishes from Victoria, Australia. Proc. Acad. Nat. Sci. Phila. v. 59 (for 1907): 419-444. [Pages 419-432 published 4 Dec. 1907, pp.

433-444 on 17 Jan. 1908.]
——. 1908 (27 Jan.) **[ref. 1378]**. Notes on lancelets and lampreys. Proc. Acad. Nat. Sci. Phila. v. 59 (for 1907): 461-466.
——. 1908 (22 July) **[ref. 6847]**. Notes on sharks. Proc. Acad. Nat. Sci. Phila. v. 60 (for 1908): 52-70.
——. 1910 (17 Aug.) **[ref. 1379]**. Notes on batoid fishes. Proc. Acad. Nat. Sci. Phila. v. 62 (for 1910): 468-475.
——. 1910 (17 Aug.) **[ref. 1380]**. Descriptions of four new cyprinoids (Rhodeinae). Proc. Acad. Nat. Sci. Phila. v. 62 (for 1910): 476-486.
——. 1910 (20 May) **[ref. 4994]**. The proper restriction of *Eucynopotamus*. Science (n. s.) v. 31 (no. 803): 790.
——. 1911 (27 Jan.) **[ref. 1381]**. A new albuloid fish from Santo Domingo. Proc. Acad. Nat. Sci. Phila. v. 62 (for 1910): 651-654.
——. 1911 (24 May) **[ref. 1382]**. Notes on clupeoid fishes. Proc. Acad. Nat. Sci. Phila. v. 63 (for 1911): 204-221.
——. 1911 (27 July - 15 Aug.) **[ref. 1383]**. Some fishes from Venezuela. Proc. Acad. Nat. Sci. Phila. v. 63 (for 1911): 419-437. [Pages 419-424 published 27 July, pp. 425-437 on 15 Aug.]
——. 1911 (28 Oct. - 6 Nov.) **[ref. 1384]**. New fresh-water fishes from western Ecuador. Proc. Acad. Nat. Sci. Phila. v. 63 (for 1911): 493-520. [Pages 493-508 published 28 Oct., pp. 509-520 on 6 Nov.]
——. 1911 **[ref. 6398]**. A description of the fossil fish remains of the Cretaceous, Eocene and Miocene formations of New Jersey [with a chapter on the geology by Henry B. Kümmel]. Bull. Geol. Surv. New Jersey 1911 (no. 4): 1-192.
——. 1912 (3 Apr.) **[ref. 1385]**. Descriptions of nine new eels, with notes on other species. Proc. Acad. Nat. Sci. Phila. v. 64 (for 1912): 8-33.
——. 1913 (11 July) **[ref. 1387]**. *Fowlerina* Eigenmann a preoccupied generic name. Science (n. s.) v. 38 (no. 967): 51.
——. 1913 (4 Apr.) **[ref. 1388]**. Notes on catostomoid fishes. Proc. Acad. Nat. Sci. Phila. v. 65 (for 1913): 45-60.
——. 1913 (19-22 Nov.) **[ref. 1389]**. Fishes from the Madeira River, Brazil. Proc. Acad. Nat. Sci. Phila. v. 65 (for 1913): 517-579. [Pages 517-552 published 19 Nov., pp. 553-579 on 11 Nov.]
——. 1914 (3 June) **[ref. 1390]**. Fishes from the Rupununi River, British Guiana. Proc. Acad. Nat. Sci. Phila. v. 66 (for 1914): 229-284.
——. 1914 (28 Jan.) **[ref. 1391]**. *Curimatus spilurus* Cope, a wrongly identified characin. Proc. Acad. Nat. Sci. Phila. v. 65 (for 1913): 673-675.
——. 1915 (28 May) **[ref. 1392]**. Notes on nematognathous fishes. Proc. Acad. Nat. Sci. Phila. v. 67 (for 1915): 203-243.
——. 1915 (25 Jan.) **[ref. 1393]**. The genus *Cryptotomus* Cope. Copeia No. 14: 3.
——. 1916 (14-30 Aug.) **[ref. 1394]**. Notes on fishes of the orders Haplomi and Microcyprini. Proc. Acad. Nat. Sci. Phila. v. 68 (for 1916): 415-439. [Pages 415-426 published 14 Aug., pp. 427-439 on 30 Aug.]
——. 1918 (6 Sept.) **[ref. 1395]**. A new characin from Paraguay. Proc. Acad. Nat. Sci. Phila. v. 70 (for 1918): 141-143.
——. 1918 (11 Apr. - 28 May) **[ref. 1396]**. New or little-known fishes from the Philippine Islands. Proc. Acad. Nat. Sci. Phila. v. 70 (for 1918): 2-71. [Pages 2-64 published 11 April, pp. 65-71 on 28 May]
——. 1919 (20 May) **[ref. 1397]**. Notes on synentognathous fishes. Proc. Acad. Nat. Sci. Phila. v. 71 (for 1919): 2-15.
——. 1923 **[ref. 1398]**. New or little-known Hawaiian fishes. Occas. Pap. Bernice P. Bishop Mus. v. 8 (no. 7): 375-392.
——. 1923 (31 Dec.) **[ref. 1399]**. New fishes obtained by the American Museum Congo Expedition 1909-1915. Am. Mus. Novit. No. 103: 1-6.
——. 1925 (19 Nov.) **[ref. 1400]**. On two preoccupied fish names *Rouelina* and *Eusalpa*. Copeia No. 147: 75-76.
——. 1925 (31 Mar.) **[ref. 1401]**. New taxonomic names of West African marine fishes. Am. Mus. Novit. No. 162: 1-5.
——. 1925 (20 Nov.) **[ref. 5570]**. Fishes from Natal, Zululand and Portuguese East Africa. Proc. Acad. Nat. Sci. Phila. v. 77 (for 1925): 187-268.
——. 1926 (1 Nov.) **[ref. 1402]**. Notes on fishes from Bombay. J. Bombay Nat. Hist. Soc. v. 31 (pt 3): 770-779.
——. 1928 **[ref. 5596]**. The fishes of Oceania. Mem. Bishop Mus. Honolulu No. 10: i-iii + 1-540, Pls. 1-49.
——. 1929 **[ref. 1403]**. New and little-known fishes from the Natal coast. Ann. Natal Mus. v. 6 (pt 2): 245-264.
——. 1930 (15 Jan.) **[ref. 1404]**. Notes on Japanese and Chinese fishes. Proc. Acad. Nat. Sci. Phila. v. 81 (for 1929): 589-616.
——. 1930 **[ref. 1405]**. Notes on percoid and related fishes. Proc. Acad. Nat. Sci. Phila. v. 81 (for 1929): 633-657.
——. 1930 (11 Apr.) **[ref. 1406]**. The freshwater fishes obtained by the Gray African expedition—1929. With notes on other species in the Academy collection. Proc. Acad. Nat. Sci. Phila. v. 82 (for 1930): 27-83.
——. 1931 (21 Mar.) **[ref. 1407]**. Contributions to the biology of the Philippine Archipelago and adjacent regions. The fishes of the families Pseudochromidae... and Teraponidae, collected by... steamer "Albatross," chiefly in Philippine seas and adjacent waters. Bull. U. S. Natl. Mus. No. 100, v. 11: i-xi + 1-388.
——. 1931 (4 Nov.) **[ref. 1408]**. Studies of Hong Kong fishes—No. 2. Hong Kong Nat. v. 2 (no. 4): 287-317.
——. 1931 (15 May) **[ref. 1409]**. The fishes obtained by the De Schauensee South African expedition.—1930. Proc. Acad. Nat. Sci. Phila. v. 83 (for 1931): 233-249.
——. 1931 (11 Aug.) **[ref. 1410]**. Fishes obtained by the Barber Asphalt Company in Trinidad and Venezuela in 1930. Proc. Acad. Nat. Sci. Phila. v. 83 (for 1931): 391-410.
——. 1932 (18 Aug.) **[ref. 1411]**. Notes on fresh water fishes from Central America. Proc. Acad. Nat. Sci. Phila. v. 84 (for 1932): 379-385.
——. 1932 (16 Feb.) **[ref. 1412]**. The fishes obtained by the Pinchot South Seas expedition of 1929, with description of one new genus and three new species. Proc. U. S. Natl. Mus. v. 80 (no. 2906): 1-16.
——. 1932 **[ref. 1413]**. Fresh-water fishes from the Marquesas and Society Islands. Occas. Pap. Bernice P. Bishop Mus. v. 9 (no. 25): 1-11.
——. 1933 (19 May) **[ref. 1414]**. Contributions to the biology of the Philippine Archipelago and adjacent regions. The fishes of the families Banjosidae...Enoplosidae collected by the United States Bureau of Fisheries steamer "Albatross," chiefly in Philippine seas and adjacent waters. Bull. U. S. Natl. Mus. No. 100, v. 12: i-vi + 1-465.
——. 1933 (21 July) **[ref. 1415]**. Description of a new long-finned tuna (*Semathunnus guildi*), from Tahiti. Proc. Acad. Nat. Sci. Phila. v. 85 (for 1933): 163-164, Pl. 12.
——. 1934 (20 Jan.) **[ref. 1416]**. Descriptions of new fishes obtained 1907 to 1910, chiefly in the Philippine Islands and adjacent seas. Proc. Acad. Nat. Sci. Phila. v. 85 (for 1933): 233-367.
——. 1934 (30 Apr.) **[ref. 1417]**. Zoological results of the third De Schauensee Siamese Expedition, Part I.—Fishes. Proc. Acad. Nat. Sci. Phila. v. 86 (for 1934): 67-163, Pl. 12.
——. 1934 (25 June) **[ref. 1418]**. Zoological results of the third De Schauensee Siamese Expedition, Part V.—Additional fishes. Proc. Acad. Nat. Sci. Phila. v. 86 (for 1934): 335-352.
——. 1934 (6 Nov.) **[ref. 1419]**. Fishes obtained by Mr. H. W. Bell-Marley chiefly in Natal and Zululand in 1929 to 1932. Proc. Acad. Nat. Sci. Phila. v. 86 (for 1934): 405-514.
——. 1935 (23 Apr.) **[ref. 1420]**. Description of a new scorpaenoid fish (*Neomerinthe hemingwayi*) from off New Jersey. Proc. Acad. Nat. Sci. Phila. v. 87 (for 1935): 41-43.
——. 1935 (1 Nov.) **[ref. 1421]**. South African fishes received from Mr. H. W. Bell-Marley in 1935. Proc. Acad. Nat. Sci. Phila. v. 87 (for 1935): 361-408.
——. 1935 **[ref. 1422]**. Notes on South Carolina fresh-water fishes. Contrib. Charleston Mus. v. 7: 1-28, 11 unnumbered pls.
——. 1935 (21 Feb.) **[ref. 1423]**. Scientific results of the Vernay-

Lang Kalahari expedition, March to September, 1930. Fresh-water fishes. Ann. Transvaal Mus. v. 16 (pt 2): 251-293, Pls. 6-9.

———. 1936 (9 July) **[ref. 1424]**. Zoological results of the George Vanderbilt African expedition of 1934. Part III,—The fresh water fishes. Proc. Acad. Nat. Sci. Phila. v. 88 (for 1936): 243-335.

———. 1936 (21 Jan.) **[ref. 6545]**. The marine fishes of West Africa based on the collection of the American Museum Congo expedition, 1909-1915. Part 1. Bull. Am. Mus. Nat. Hist. v. 70: 1-605.

———. 1936 (18 Nov.) **[ref. 6546]**. The marine fishes of West Africa based on the collection of the American Museum Congo expedition, 1909-1915. Part II. Bull. Am. Mus. Nat. Hist. v. 70: 607-1493.

———. 1937 (19 May) **[ref. 1425]**. Zoological results of the third De Schauensee Siamese expedition. Part VIII,—Fishes obtained in 1936. Proc. Acad. Nat. Sci. Phila. v. 89 (for 1937): 125-264.

———. 1938 (23 May) **[ref. 1426]**. Descriptions of new fishes obtained by the United States Bureau of Fisheries Steamer "Albatross," chiefly in Philippine seas and adjacent waters. Proc. U. S. Natl. Mus. v. 85 (no. 3032): 31-135.

———. 1938 (24 Oct.) **[ref. 1427]**. Descriptions of a new carangid fish from New Jersey. Proc. Acad. Nat. Sci. Phila. v. 90 (for 1938): 149-151.

———. 1938 (14 Oct.) **[ref. 1428]**. The fishes of the George Vanderbilt South Pacific expedition, 1937. Monogr. Acad. Nat. Sci. Phila. No. 2: 1-349, Pls. 1-12.

———. 1939 (14 Aug.) **[ref. 1429]**. Zoological results of the Denison-Crockett South Pacific expedition for the Academy of Natural Sciences of Philadelphia, 1937-1938. Part III.—The fishes. Proc. Acad. Nat. Sci. Phila. v. 91 (for 1939): 77-96. [Publication date in contents misprinted 14 Aug. 1940 instead of 1939.]

———. 1939 (31 Aug.) **[ref. 1430]**. New subfamilies, genera and subgenera of fishes. Not. Nat. (Phila.) No. 26: 1-2.

———. 1939 (13 Nov.) **[ref. 1431]**. Notes on fishes from Jamaica with descriptions of three new species. Not. Nat. (Phila.) No. 35: 1-16.

———. 1939 (7 July) **[ref. 5597]**. A collection of fishes from Rangoon, Burma. Not. Nat. (Phila.) No. 17: 1-12.

———. 1940 (20 Feb.) **[ref. 1432]**. A collection of fishes obtained by Mr. William C. Morrow in the Ucayali River Basin, Peru. Proc. Acad. Nat. Sci. Phila. v. 91 (for 1939): 219-289.

———. 1940 (24 May) **[ref. 1433]**. Zoological results of the George Vanderbilt Sumatran expedition, 1936-1939. Part II.—The fishes. Proc. Acad. Nat. Sci. Phila. v. 91 (for 1939): 369-398.

———. 1940 (27 June) **[ref. 1434]**. Description of a new sparoid fish from off southern New Jersey. Not. Nat. (Phila.) No. 49: 1-4.

———. 1940 (3 Oct.) **[ref. 1435]**. A collection of fishes obtained on the west coast of Florida by Mr. and Mrs. C. G. Chaplin. Proc. Acad. Nat. Sci. Phila. v. 92 (for 1940): 1-22, Pl. 1.

———. 1940 (22 Oct.) **[ref. 1436]**. Zoological results of the second Bolivian expedition for the Academy of Natural Sciences of Philadelphia, 1936-1937. Part I.—The fishes. Proc. Acad. Nat. Sci. Phila. v. 92 (for 1940): 43-103.

———. 1941 (10 Oct.) **[ref. 1437]**. A collection of fresh-water fishes obtained in eastern Brazil by Dr. Rodolpho von Ihering. Proc. Acad. Nat. Sci. Phila. v. 93 (for 1941): 123-199.

———. 1941 (7 Nov.) **[ref. 1438]**. The George Vanderbilt Oahu survey—the fishes. Proc. Acad. Nat. Sci. Phila. v. 93 (for 1941): 247-279.

———. 1941 (8 Apr.) **[ref. 1439]**. New fishes of the family Callionymidae, mostly Philippine, obtained by the United States Bureau of Fisheries steamer, "Albatross." Proc. U. S. Natl. Mus. v. 90 (no. 3106): 1-31.

———. 1941 (10 Mar.) **[ref. 6536]**. Contributions to the biology of the Philippine archipelago and adjacent regions. The fishes of the groups Elasmocephalii, Holocephali, Isospondyli, and Ostariophysi obrained by the United States..."Albatross" in 1907 to 1910... Bull. U. S. Natl. Mus. No. 100, v. 13: i-x + 1-879.

———. 1943 **[ref. 1440]**. Los peces del Peru. Catálogo sistemático de los peces que habitan en aguas peruanas. Bol. Mus. Hist. Nat. "Javier Prado" Lima v. 7 (nos. 24-25): 96-124.

———. 1943 (19 July) **[ref. 1441]**. Contributions to the biology of the Philippine Archipelago and adjacent regions. Descriptions and figures of new fishes obtained in Philippine seas and adjacent waters by the United States Bureau of Fisheries steamer "Albatross." Bull. U. S. Natl. Mus. No. 100, v. 14 (pt 2): i-iii + 53-91.

———. 1943 (1 Apr.) **[ref. 1442]**. Zoological results of the second Bolivian expedition for the Academy of Natural Sciences of Philadelphia, 1936-1937. Part II.—Additional new fishes. Not. Nat. (Phila.) No. 120: 1-7.

———. 1943 (17 Dec.) **[ref. 1443]**. A collection of fresh-water fishes from Colombia, obtained chiefly by Brother Nicéforo Maria. Proc. Acad. Nat. Sci. Phila. v. 95 (for 1943): 223-266.

———. 1943 (31 Dec.) **[ref. 1444]**. Notes and descriptions of new or little known fishes from Uruguay. Proc. Acad. Nat. Sci. Phila. v. 95 (for 1943): 311-334.

———. 1944 **[ref. 1445]**. Notes on Pennsylvania fishes obtained in 1940, 1941 and 1942 with an account of a new genus of rosy-sided dace. Bienn. Rep. Bd. Fish. Comm. Pennsylvania for 1942: 50-55.

———. 1944 (30 June) **[ref. 1447]**. Description of a new genus and a new species of American stromateid fishes. Not. Nat. (Phila.) No. 142: 1-4.

———. 1944 (25 Aug.) **[ref. 1448]**. Results of the fifth George Vanderbilt expedition (1941) (Bahamas, Caribbean Sea, Panama, Galapagos Archipelago and Mexican Pacific islands). The Fishes. Monogr. Acad. Nat. Sci. Phila. No. 6: 57-529, Pls. 1-20.

———. 1944 (8 Sept.) **[ref. 1451]**. Fishes obtained in the New Hebrides by Dr. Edward L. Jackson. Proc. Acad. Nat. Sci. Phila. v. 96 (for 1944): 155-199.

———. 1944 (20 Sept.) **[ref. 1452]**. Fresh-water fishes from northwestern Colombia. Proc. Acad. Nat. Sci. Phila. v. 96 (for 1944): 227-248.

———. 1944 (28 Apr.) **[ref. 1446]**. Description of a new genus and species of apogonid fish from New Jersey. Not. Nat. (Phila.) No. 130: 1-4.

———. 1944 (Sept.) **[ref. 5598]**. A new glass catfish from Borneo. Fish Culturist v. 24 (no. 1): 1-2.

———. 1944 (Dec.) **[ref. 6513]**. A new demoiselle fish from the tropical Indian Ocean. Fish Culturist v. 24 (no. 4): 25-27.

———. 1945 (25 Oct.) **[ref. 1453]**. A study of the fishes of the southern Piedmont and coastal plain. Monogr. Acad. Nat. Sci. Phila. No. 7: i-vi + 1-408, 313 figs. on 73 unnum. pls.

———. 1945 (30 Nov.) **[ref. 1454]**. Colombian zoological survey. Pt. I.—The freshwater fishes obtained in 1945. Proc. Acad. Nat. Sci. Phila. v. 97 (for 1945): 93-135.

———. 1945 **[ref. 5599]**. Description of a new genus of parapercid fishes from Chile. Rev. Chil. Hist. Nat. v. 48 (for 1944): 51-53.

———. 1946 (28 June) **[ref. 1455]**. Notes on Bahama fishes with a description of a new jaw fish (Opisthognathidae). Not. Nat. (Phila.) No. 181: 1-8.

———. 1946 (6 Nov.) **[ref. 1456]**. A collection of fishes obtained in the Riu Kiu Islands by Captain Ernest R. Tinkham, A. U. S. Proc. Acad. Nat. Sci. Phila. v. 98 (for 1946): 123-218.

———. 1947 (28 Mar.) **[ref. 1457]**. Description of a new species and genus of darter from the Cape Fear River basin of North Carolina. Not. Nat. (Phila.) No. 191: 1-3.

———. 1947 (21 Feb.) **[ref. 1458]**. New taxonomic names of fish-like vertebrates. Not. Nat. (Phila.) No. 187: 1-16.

———. 1948 (16 Apr.) **[ref. 1459]**. Description of a new swell-fish from off New Jersey. Not. Nat. (Phila.) No. 208: 1-4.

———. 1949 (5 May) **[ref. 1460]**. Description of a new genus and species of characin (*Pristicharax hanseni*) from Goiaz, Brazil. Not. Nat. (Phila.) No. 216: 1-4.

———. 1949 (10 Nov.) **[ref. 1461]**. Results of the two Carpenter African expeditions, 1946-1948. Pt. II—The fishes. Proc. Acad. Nat. Sci. Phila. v. 101: 233-275.

———. 1949 **[ref. 1462]**. The fishes of Oceania—Supplement 3. Mem. Bishop Mus. Honolulu Mem. 12 (no. 2): 37-186.

———. 1953 (Sept.) **[ref. 1463]**. On a collection of fishes made by

Dr. Marshall Laird at Norfolk Island. Trans. R. Soc. N. Z. v. 81 (pt 2): 257-267.

———. 1953 (Dec.) **[ref. 1464]**. Two new gobioid fishes from Oceania. Trans. R. Soc. N. Z. v. 81 (pt 3): 385-388.

———. 1954 **[ref. 1465]**. Os peixes de água doce do Brasil. Arq. Zool. (Sao Paulo) v. 9: i-ix + 1-400.

———. 1954 (29 Nov.) **[ref. 1466]**. Description of a new blenniioid fish from southwest Florida. Not. Nat. (Phila.) No. 265: 1-3.

———. 1954 (June) **[ref. 1467]**. A synopsis of the fishes of China. Part VII. The perch-like fishes (continued). Q. J. Taiwan Mus. (Taipei) v. 7: 1-110.

———. 1956 **[ref. 1468]**. Fishes of the Red Sea and southern Arabia. I. Branchiostomida to Polynemida. Weizmann Sci. Press, Jerusalem 1-240. [Date on cover 1956, possibly published in 1957.]

———. 1956 **[ref. 1469]**. A synopsis of the fishes of China. Part VII. The perch like fishes (completed). Q. J. Taiwan Mus. (Taipei) v. 9 (no. 3 & 4): 161-354.

———. 1958 (22 Aug.) **[ref. 1470]**. Some new taxonomic names of fishlike vertebrates. Not. Nat. (Phila.) No. 310: 1-16.

———. 1964 **[ref. 7160]**. A catalog of World fishes [Part I]. Q. J. Taiwan Mus. (Taipei) v. 17 (nos. 3/4): 1-62.

———. 1965 **[ref. 9313]**. A catalog of World fishes [Part II]. Q. J. Taiwan Mus. (Taipei) v. 28 (nos. 1/2): 137-202 [catalog pp. 63-128].

———. 1965 **[ref. 9314]**. A catalog of World fishes (III). Q. J. Taiwan Mus. (Taipei) v. 28 (nos. 3/4): 341-397 [catalog pp. 129-185].

———. 1966 **[ref. 9315]**. A catalog of World fishes (IV). Q. J. Taiwan Mus. (Taipei) v. 19 (nos. 1/2): 75-139 [catalog pp. 186-250].

———. 1966 **[ref. 9316]**. A catalog of World fishes (V). Q. J. Taiwan Mus. (Taipei) v. 29 (nos. 3/4): 303-371 [catalog pp. 251-319].

———. 1967 **[ref. 9317]**. A catalog of World fishes (VI). Q. J. Taiwan Mus. (Taipei) v. 10 (nos. 1/2): 79-148 [catalog pp. 320-389].

———. 1967 **[ref. 9318]**. A catalog of World fishes (VII). Q. J. Taiwan Mus. (Taipei) v. 20 (nos. 3/4): 341-366 [catalog pp. 390-415].

———. 1968 **[ref. 9319]**. A catalog of World fishes (VIII). Q. J. Taiwan Mus. (Taipei) v. 21 (nos. 1/2): 53-211 [catalog pp. 416-472].

———. 1968 **[ref. 9320]**. A catalog of World fishes (IX). Q. J. Taiwan Mus. (Taipei) v. 21 (nos. 3/4): 181-211 [catalog pp. 442-472].

———. 1969 **[ref. 9321]**. A catalog of World fishes (X). Q. J. Taiwan Mus. (Taipei) v. 22 (nos. 1/2): 57-84 [catalog pp. 473-500].

———. 1969 **[ref. 6832]**. A catalog of World fishes (XI). Q. J. Taiwan Mus. (Taipei) v. 22 (nos. 3/4): 125-190 [catalog pp. 501-566].

———. 1970 **[ref. 7313]**. A catalog of World fishes (XII). Q. J. Taiwan Mus. (Taipei) v. 23 (nos. 1/2): 39-126 [catalog pp. 567-654].

———. 1970 **[ref. 9322]**. A catalog of World fishes (XIII). Q. J. Taiwan Mus. (Taipei) v. 23 (nos. 3/4): 151-199 [catalog pp. 655-703].

———. 1971 **[ref. 9323]**. A catalog of World fishes. Volume II. Q. J. Taiwan Mus. (Taipei) v. 23 (nos. 3/4): 201-251 [catalog v. 2, pp. 1-51].

———. 1971 **[ref. 9324]**. A catalog of World fishes (XIV). Q. J. Taiwan Mus. (Taipei) v. 24 (nos. 1/2): 1-58 [catalog v. 2, pp. 52-109].

———. 1971 **[ref. 9325]**. A catalog of World fishes (XV). Q. J. Taiwan Mus. (Taipei) v. 24 (nos. 3/4): 365-409 [catalog v. 2, pp. 110-154].

———. 1972 **[ref. 9326]**. A catalog of World fishes (XVI). Q. J. Taiwan Mus. (Taipei) v. 25 (nos. 1/2): 1-40 [catalog v. 2, pp. 155-194].

———. 1972 **[ref. 9327]**. A catalog of World fishes (XVII). Q. J. Taiwan Mus. (Taipei) v. 25 (nos. 3/4): 157-198 [catalog v. 2, pp. 195-236].

———. 1973 **[ref. 9328]**. A catalog of World fishes (XVIII). Q. J. Taiwan Mus. (Taipei) v. 26 (nos. 1/2): 1-111 [catalog v. 2, pp. 237-347].

———. 1973 **[ref. 9329]**. A catalog of World fishes (XIX). Q. J. Taiwan Mus. (Taipei) v. 26 (nos. 3/4): 217-346 [catalog v. 2, pp. 349-478].

———. 1974 **[ref. 7180]**. A catalog of World fishes (XX). Q. J. Taiwan Mus. (Taipei) v. 27 (nos. 1/2): 1-132 [catalog v. 2, pp. 479-610].

———. 1974 **[ref. 7156]**. A catalog of World fishes (XXI). Q. J. Taiwan Mus. (Taipei) v. 27 (nos. 3/4): 239-388 [catalog v. 2, pp. 611-760].

———. 1975 **[ref. 9331]**. A catalog of World fishes (XXII). Volume III. Q. J. Taiwan Mus. (Taipei) v. 28 (nos. 1/2): 1-124 [catalog v. 3, pp. 1-124].

———. 1975 **[ref. 9333]**. A catalog of World fishes (XXIII). Q. J. Taiwan Mus. (Taipei) v. 28 (nos. 3/4): 277-401 [catalog v. 3, pp. 125-249].

———. 1976 **[ref. 7323]**. A catalog of World fishes (XXIV). Q. J. Taiwan Mus. (Taipei) v. 29 (nos. 1/2): 1-110 [catalog v. 3, pp. 250-359].

———. 1976 **[ref. 9335]**. A catalog of World fishes (XXV). Q. J. Taiwan Mus. (Taipei) v. 29 (nos. 3/4): 277-396 [catalog v. 3, pp. 360-479].

———. 1977 **[ref. 9336]**. A catalog of World fishes (XXVI). Q. J. Taiwan Mus. (Taipei) v. 30 (nos. 1/2): 1-88 [catalog v. 3, pp. 480-566].

FOWLER, H. W., AND S. C. BALL. 1924 (1 Nov.) **[ref. 1471]**. Descriptions of new fishes obtained by the Tanager expedition of 1923 in the Pacific islands west of Hawaii. Proc. Acad. Nat. Sci. Phila. v. 76 (for 1924): 269-274.

FOWLER, H. W., AND B. A. BEAN. 1920 (3 Nov.) **[ref. 1472]**. A small collection of fishes from Soochow, China, with descriptions of two new species. Proc. U. S. Natl. Mus. v. 58 (no. 2338): 307-321.

———. 1922 (28 Jan.) **[ref. 1473]**. Fishes from Formosa and the Philippine Islands. Proc. U. S. Natl. Mus. v. 62 (no. 2448): 1-73.

———. 1923 (22 Dec.) **[ref. 1474]**. Descriptions of eighteen new species of fishes from the Wilkes exploring expedition, preserved in the United States National Museum. Proc. U. S. Natl. Mus. v. 63 (no. 2488): 1-27.

———. 1928 (17 Apr.) **[ref. 1475]**. Contributions to the biology of the Philippine Archipelago and adjacent regions. The fishes of the families Pomacentridae, Labridae, and Callyodontidae, collected by the... steamer "Albatross," chiefly in Philippine seas and adjacent waters. Bull. U. S. Natl. Mus. No. 100, v. 7: i-viii + 1-525, Pls. 1-49.

———. 1929 (11 Mar.) **[ref. 1476]**. Contributions to the biology of the Philippine Archipelago and adjacent waters. The fishes of the series Capriformes, Ephippiformes, and Squamipennes, collected by the United States Bureau of Fisheries steamer "Albatross" chiefly in Philippine Seas and adjacent waters. Bull. U. S. Natl. Mus. No. 100, v. 8: i-xi + 1-352.

———. 1930 (21 Mar.) **[ref. 1477]**. Contributions to the biology of the Philippine Archipelago and adjacent regions. The fishes of the families Amiidae ... and Serranidae, obtained by the United States Bureau of Fisheries steamer "Albatross" in 1907 to 1910... adjacent seas. Bull. U. S. Natl. Mus. No. 100, v. 10: i-ix + 1-334.

FOWLER, H. W., AND H. STEINITZ. 1956 **[ref. 1478]**. Fishes from Cyprus, Iran, Iraq, Israel and Oman. Bull. Res. Counc. Isr. v. 5B (no. 3-4): 260-292.

FRANZ, V. 1910 **[ref. 1481]**. Die Japanischen Knochenfische der Sammlungen Haberer und Döflein. (Beiträge zur Naturgeschichte Ostasiens.) Abh. Akad. Wiss. Munchen Math.-Phys. Kl. v. 4 (Suppl.) (no. 1): 1-135, 11 pls.

FRASER, T. H. 1972 (June) **[ref. 5195]**. Comparative osteology of the shallow water cardinal fishes [Perciformes: Apogonidae] with reference to the systematics and evolution of the family. Ichthyol. Bull. J. L. B. Smith Inst. Ichthyol. No. 34: i-v + 1-105, Pls. 1-44.

———. 1973 (24 Apr.) **[ref. 1483]**. Evolutionary significance of *Holapogon*, a new genus of cardinal fishes (Apogonidae), with a redescription of its type-species, *Apogon maximus*. J. L. B. Smith Inst. Ichthyol. Spec. Publ. No. 10: 1-7.

FRASER, T. H., AND E. A. LACHNER. 1985 (16 May) **[ref. 5215]**. A revision of the cardinalfish subgenera *Pristiapogon* and *Zoramia* (genus *Apogon*) of the Indo-Pacific region (Teleostei: Apogonidae). Smithson. Contrib. Zool. No. 412: 1-47.

FRASER, T. H., AND C. R. ROBINS. 1970 (Dec.) **[ref. 1485]**. The R/V Pillsbury deep-sea biological expedition to the Gulf of Guinea, 1964-65. 18. A new Atlantic genus of cardinalfishes with comments on some species from the Gulf of Guinea. Stud. Trop. Oceanogr. No. 4 (pt 2): 302-315.

FRASER-BRUNNER, A. 1931 (Sept.) **[ref. 1486]**. Some interesting West African fishes, with descriptions of a new genus and two new species. Ann. Mag. Nat. Hist. (Ser. 10) v. 8 (no. 45): 217-225.

———. 1932 **[ref. 1487]**. A new genus of blennioid fishes from the British coast. Proc. Zool. Soc. Lond. 1932 (pt 4) (no. 40): 827-828.

———. 1933 (20 Sept.) **[ref. 671]**. A revision of the chaetodont fishes of the subfamily Pomacanthinae. Proc. Zool. Soc. Lond. 1933 (art. 30): 543-599, Pl. 1.

———. 1934 (31 Dec.) **[ref. 1488]**. Substitute name for *Hateropyge* Fraser-Brunner, a genus of chaetodont fishes. Copeia 1934 (no. 4): 192.

———. 1935 (June) **[ref. 1489]**. Notes on the Plectognath fishes.—I. A synopsis of the genera of the family Balistidae. Ann. Mag. Nat. Hist. (Ser. 10) v. 15 (no. 90): 658-663.

———. 1935 (Aug.) **[ref. 1490]**. Notes on the Plectognath fishes.—II. A synopsis of the genera of the family Ostraciontidae. Ann. Mag. Nat. Hist. (Ser. 10) v. 16 (no. 92): 313-320.

———. 1935 **[ref. 1491]**. New of rare fishes from the Irish Atlantic Slope. Proc. R. Ir. Acad. Sect. B Biol. Geol. Chem. Sci. v. 42: 319-326.

———. 1938 (Nov.) **[ref. 1492]**. Notes on the classification of certain British fishes. Ann. Mag. Nat. Hist. (Ser. 11) v. 2 (no. 11): 410-416.

———. 1941 (May) **[ref. 1493]**. Notes on the plectognath fishes.—V. The families of triacanthiform fishes, with a synopsis of the genera and description of a new species. Ann. Mag. Nat. Hist. (Ser. 11) v. 7 (no. 41): 420-430.

———. 1941 (Sept.) **[ref. 1494]**. Notes on the plectognath fishes.—VI. A synopsis of the genera of the family Aluteridae, and descriptions of seven new species. Ann. Mag. Nat. Hist. (Ser. 11) v. 8 (no. 45): 176-199.

———. 1943 (Jan.) **[ref. 1495]**. Notes on the plectognath fishes.—VIII. The classification of the suborder Tetraodontoidea, with a synopsis of the genera. Ann. Mag. Nat. Hist. (Ser. 11) v. 10 (no. 61): 1-18.

———. 1949 (Feb.) **[ref. 1496]**. A classification of the fishes of the family Myctophidae. Proc. Zool. Soc. Lond. v. 118 (pt 4): 1019-1106, Pl. 1.

———. 1950 (20 Nov.) **[ref. 1497]**. Studies in plectognath fishes from the "Dana"-Expeditions. I. An interesting new genus of triacanthodid fishes from the Celebes Sea. Dana Rep. No. 35: 1-8.

———. 1955 **[ref. 1498]**. A synopsis of the centropomid fishes of the subfamily Chandinae, with descriptions of a new genus and two new species. Bull. Raffles Mus. No. 25 (Dec. 1954): 185-213. [1955 in small print on cover.]

FREY, H. 1957 **[ref. 5455]**. Das Aquarium von A bis Z. 1st Ed. Neuman Verlag, Leipzig. 1-370.

FRICKE, R. 1981 **[ref. 1499]**. Revision of the genus *Synchiropus* (Teleostei: Callionymidae). Theses Zool. v. 1: 1-194.

———. 1981 (23 Apr.) **[ref. 1500]**. Neue Fundorte und noch nicht beschriebene Geschlechtsunterschiede einiger Arten der Gattung *Callionymus* (Pisces, Perciformes, Callionymidae), mit Bemerkungen zur Systematik innerhalb dieser Gattung und Beschreibung einer neuen Untergattung und einer neuen Art. Ann. Mus. Civ. Stor. Nat. 'Giacomo Doria' v. 83: 57-105.

———. 1982 (15 July) **[ref. 5432]**. Nominal genera and species of dragonets (Teleostei: Callionymidae, Draconettidae). Ann. Mus. Civ. Stor. Nat. Genova v. 84: 53-92.

———. 1985 (28 Nov.) **[ref. 4952]**. *Protogrammus*, a new genus of callionymid fishes, with a redescription of *P. sousai* from the eastern Atlantic. Jpn. J. Ichthyol. v. 32 (no. 3): 294-298.

———. 1986 **[ref. 5653]**. Family No. 239: Callionymidae (pp. 770-774). In: Smiths' Sea Fishes (Smith & Heemstra 1986 [ref. 5715]).

FRICKE, R., AND H. BRUNKEN. 1984 **[ref. 5262]**. A new cottid fish of the genus *Antipodocottus* (Teleostei: Scorpaeniformes) from eastern Australia, with a key to the species of the genera *Stlengis* and *Antipodocottus*. J. Nat. Hist. v. 18: 41-46.

FRICKE, R., AND M. J. ZAISER. 1982 (25 Nov.) **[ref. 5452]**. Redescription of *Diplogrammus xenicus* (Teleostei: Callionymidae) from Miyake-jima, Japan, with ecological notes. Jpn. J. Ichthyol. v. 29 (no. 3): 253-259.

FRIES, B. F. 1837 **[ref. 1501]**. *Pterycombus*, ett nytt fisk-slägte från Ishafvet. K. Sven. Vetenskapsakad. Handl. 1837: 14-22. [Also in Arch. Nat. (5 Jahrg.) pt. 1: 19-26.]

FRIIS, I., AND M. THULIN. 1984 (Nov.) **[ref. 5595]**. The spelling of Pehr Forsskål's family name. Taxon v. 33 (no. 4): 668-672.

FRITSCH, G. T. 1884 **[ref. 1510]**. Ergebnisse der Vergleichungen an den elektrischen Organen der Torpedineen. Stizber. Akad. Wiss. Berlin for 1884: 445-456. [Also published in Arch. Anat. Physiol., v. for 1886: 358-370.]

FRITZSCHE, R. A. 1976 (Apr.) **[ref. 7102]**. A review of the cornetfishes, genus *Fistularia* (Fistulariidae), with a discussion of intrageneric relationships and zoogeography. Bull. Mar. Sci. v. 26 (no. 2): 196-204.

———. 1980 (2 July) **[ref. 1511]**. Revision of the eastern Pacific Syngnathidae (Pisces: Syngnathiformes), including both recent and fossil forms. Proc. Calif. Acad. Sci. v. 42 (no. 6): 181-227.

———. 1984 **[ref. 13658]**. Gasterosteiformes: development and relationships. Am. Soc. Ichthyol. Herpetol. Spec. Publ. No. 1: 398-405.

———. 1986 **[ref. 6295]**. Family No. 146: Solenostomidae (p. 459). In: Smiths' Sea Fishes (Smith & Heemstra 1986 [ref. 5715]).

FRITZSCHE, R. A., AND G. D. JOHNSON. 1981 (15 May) **[ref. 5399]**. *Pseudopriacanthus* Bleeker, a synonym of the priacanthid genus *Pristigenys* Agassiz. Copeia 1981 (no. 2): 490-492.

FUJII, E., AND T. UYENO. 1976 **[ref. 7014]**. On three species of the myctophid genus *Notoscopelus* found in western North Pacific. Jpn. J. Ichthyol. v. 22 (no. 4): 227-233.

———. 1979 (15 June) **[ref. 1516]**. *Polyplacapros tyleri*, a new genus and species of ostraciid trunkfish from off eastern Australia and Norfolk Ridge. Jpn. J. Ichthyol. v. 26 (no. 1): 1-10.

FUKAO, R. 1980 (Feb.) **[ref. 5257]**. Review of Japanese fishes of the genus *Neoclinus* with description of two new species and notes on habitat preference. Publ. Seto Mar. Biol. Lab. v. 25 (no. 1/4): 175-209, Pls. 1-2.

———. 1984 (1 Aug.) **[ref. 6726]**. Review of Japanese fishes of the genus *Cirripectes* (Blenniidae) with description of a new species. Jpn. J. Ichthyol. v. 31 (no. 2): 105-121.

———. 1987 (10 Dec.) **[ref. 6345]**. Fishes of *Neoclinus bryope* species complex from Shirahama, Japan, with description of two new species. Jpn. J. Ichthyol. v. 34 (no. 3): 291-308.

FUKAO, R., AND T. OKAZAKI. 1987 (10 Dec.) **[ref. 6344]**. A study on the divergence of Japanese fishes of the genus *Neoclinus*. Jpn. J. Ichthyol. v. 34 (no. 3): 309-323.

FUMIHITO, A. 1989 (28 June) **[ref. 12578]**. Morphological comparison of the Mekong giant catfish, *Pangasianodon gigas*, with other pangasiid species. Jpn. J. Ichthyol. v. 36 (no. 1): 113-119.

FURNESTIN, J. 1958 **[ref. 1517]**. Données nouvelles sur les poissons du Maroc atlantique. Rev. Trav. Off. Peches Marit. Paris v. 22: 381-487.

GAIMARD, J. P. 1851 **[ref. 1523]**. Voyage de la commission scientifique du Nord. Voyage en Skandinavie, en Laponie, au Spitzberg et aux Feröe. Paris. Sect. VII. Zoologie. [Not seen.]

GANDOLFI, G., A. MARCONATO AND P. TORRICELLI. 1986 **[ref. 6140]**. Posizione sistematica e biologica di un ghiozzo delle acque dolci italiane: *Orsinigobius* (gen. nov.) *punctatissimus* (Canestrini, 1864) (Pisces: Gobiidae). Boll. Mus. Civ. Stor. Nat. Verona v. 12 (for 1985): 367-380.

GARAVELLO, J. C. 1988 **[ref. 6853]**. Three new species of *Parotocinclus* Eigenmann & Eigenmann, 1889 with comments on their geographical distribution (Pisces, Loricariidae). Naturalia v. 13: 117-128.

——. 1988 **[ref. 14272]**. A new species of the genus *Leporinus* Spix from the Rio Meta, Colombia, South America (Pisces, Ostariophysi, Anostomidae). Proc. Acad. Nat. Sci. Phila. v. 140 (no. 2): 143-149.

——. 1989 (31 May) **[ref. 14273]**. *Leporinus microphthalmus* sp. n. da bacia do rio Raranaíba, also Paraná (Pisces, Anostomidae). Rev. Bras. Biol. v. 49 (no. 2): 497-501.

Garavello, J. C., and H. A. Britski. 1987 **[ref. 6851]**. Duas novas espécies do género *Leporinus* Spix, 1829, da bacia do alto Paraná (Teleostei, Anostomidae). Comun. Mus. Cienc. PUCRGS No. 44: 153-165.

Garman, S. 1877 (Nov.) **[ref. 1528]**. On the pelvis and external sexual organs of selachians, with especial references to the new genera *Potamotrygon* and *Disceus* (with descriptions). Proc. Boston Soc. Nat. Hist. v. 19: 197-215.

——. 1881 (23 Feb.) **[ref. 1529]**. Synopsis and descriptions of the American Rhinobatidae. Proc. U. S. Natl. Mus. v. 3 [no. 180]: 516-523.

——. 1881 (Feb.) **[ref. 1530]**. New and little-known reptiles and fishes in the museum collections. Bull. Mus. Comp. Zool. v. 8 (no. 3): 85-93.

——. 1884 (17 Jan.) **[ref. 1531]**. New sharks, *Chlamydoselachus anguineus. Heptranchias pectorosus*. [With subsections: An extraordinary shark (pp. 3-11), A species of *Heptranchias* supposed to be new (pp. 13-14)]. Bull. Essex Inst. v. 16: 3-14, 1 pl.

——. 1885 (24 July) **[ref. 1532]**. The generic name of the Pastinacas, or "sting rays." Proc. U. S. Natl. Mus. v. 8 [no. 514]: 221-224.

——. 1888 **[ref. 1534]**. On an eel from the Marshall Islands. Bull. Essex Inst. v. 20: 114-116. [Possibly published in 1889.]

——. 1890 **[ref. 1535]**. On the species of the genus *Anostomus*. Bull. Essex Inst. v. 22 (nos. 1-3): 15-23.

——. 1890 **[ref. 1536]**. On a genus and species of the characines (*Henochilus wheatlandii*, gen. n. et sp. n.). Bull. Essex Inst. v. 22: 49-52, Pl. 1. [Also as separate, pp. 1-4, 1 pl.]

——. 1892 (Apr.) **[ref. 1537]**. The Discoboli. Cyclopteridae, Liparopsidae, and Liparididae. Mem. Mus. Comp. Zool. v. 14 (pt 2): 1-96, Pls. 1-13.

——. 1895 (July) **[ref. 1538]**. The cyprinodonts. Mem. Mus. Comp. Zool. v. 19 (pt 1): 1-179, Pls. 1-12.

——. 1896 (Mar.) **[ref. 1539]**. Cross fertilization and sexual rights and lefts among vertebrates. Am. Nat. v. 30: 232.

——. 1899 (Dec.) **[ref. 1540]**. The Fishes. In: Reports of an exploration of the west coasts of Mexico, Central and South America, and off the Gaplapagos Islands ... by the U. S. Fish Commission steamer "Albatross," during 1891 ... No. XXVI. Mem. Mus. Comp. Zool. v. 24: Text: 1-431, Atlas: Pls. 1-97.

——. 1901 (2 Nov.) **[ref. 1541]**. Genera and families of the chimaeroids. Proc. New England Zool. Club v. 2: 75-77.

——. 1906 (Jan.) **[ref. 1542]**. New Plagiostomia. Bull. Mus. Comp. Zool. v. 46 (no. 11): 203-208.

——. 1908 (Feb.) **[ref. 1543]**. New Plagiostomia and Chismopnea. Bull. Mus. Comp. Zool. v. 51 (no. 9): 249-256.

——. 1912 (Aug.) **[ref. 1544]**. Pisces. In: Some Chinese vertebrates. Mem. Mus. Comp. Zool. v. 40 (pt 4): 111-123.

——. 1913 (Sept.) **[ref. 1545]**. The Plagiostomia (sharks, skates, and rays). Mem. Mus. Comp. Zool. v. 36: 1-515, Also Atlas: 77 pls.

Garrick, J. A. F. 1956 (Jan.) **[ref. 1546]**. Studies on New Zealand Elasmobranchii. Part V. *Scymnodalatias* n. g. Based on *Scymnodon sherwoodi* Archey, 1921 (Selachii). Trans. R. Soc. N. Z. v. 83 (pt 3): 555-571.

——. 1982 (May) **[ref. 5454]**. Sharks of the genus *Carcharhinus*. NOAA Tech. Rep. NMFS Circ. No. 445: 1-194.

——. 1985 (Nov.) **[ref. 5654]**. Additions to a revision of the shark genus *Carcharhinus*: synonymy of *Aprionodon* and *Hypoprion*, and description of a new species of *Carcharhinus* (Carcharhinidae). NOAA Tech. Rep. NMFS 34: i-iii + 1-26.

Gasco, F. 1870 **[ref. 1547]**. Intorno ad un nuovo genere di pesci, etc. Bull. Assoc. Nat. Med. Napol. 1870: 59-61. [Not seen.]

Gasowska, M. 1979 (15 Sept.) **[ref. 1566]**. Osteological revision of the genus *Phoxinus* Raf., sensu Banarescu 1964, with description of a new genus, *Parchrosomus* gen. n. (Pisces, Cyprinidae). Ann. Zool. (Warsaw) v. 34 (no. 12): 371-413, Pls. 1-2. [In English; Polish and Russian summaries.]

Gatti, M. 1904 **[ref. 6529]**. Ricerche sugli organi luminosi dei pesci. Ann. Agric. Roma No. 233 (1903): 7-126, 1 pl.

Geoffroy St. Hilaire, E. L. 1767 **[ref. 1570]**. Descriptions, vertus et usages de 719 Plantes et de 134 animaux... 5 vols. Paris. 1-472. [Not seen.]

——. 1802 **[ref. 4183]**. Description d'un nouveau genre de poisson, de l'ordre des abdominaux. Bull. Soc. Philomath. Paris v. 3 (6th yr) (no.61): 97-98, Pl. 5. [Sometimes date is given as 1798 [not researched]. Authorship appears as C. E. Geoffroy.]

——. 1808-09 **[ref. 4182]**. Poissons du Nil, de la mer Rouge et de la Méditerranée. In: Description de l'Egypte ... Histoire Naturelle. Paris, 1809-30. v. 1 (pt 1): 1-52, Poissons Pls. 1-17. [Text published 1809 (see Tollitt 1986 [ref. 6634]); plates in 1808 or 1809 (see Taylor 1985 [ref. 6640]). Not seen.]

Geoffroy St. Hilaire, I. 1817 **[ref. 4186]**. Poissons du Nil, de la mer Rouge et de la Méditerranée. In: Description de l'Egypte ... Histoire Naturelle. v. 1: Pls. 18-27. [See Taylor 1985 [ref. 6640] for dates of plates 1-17 and 18-27. Not seen.]

George, A., and V. G. Springer. 1980 (13 June) **[ref. 6935]**. Revision of the clinid fish tribe Ophiclinini, including five new species, and definition of the family Clinidae. Smithson. Contrib. Zool. No. 307: i-iii + 1-31.

Gervais, F. L. P. 1853 **[ref. 1575]**. Remarques sur les poissons fluviatiles de l'Algérie, et description de deux genres nouveaux sous les noms de *Coptodon* et *Tellia*. Ann. Sci. Nat. (Zool.) (Ser. 3) v. 19: 5-17.

Géry, J. 1957 **[ref. 2024]**. Notes d'aquariologie ouest-africaine. XI - A propos du genre *Barbus*. L'Aquarium v. 7 (no. 5-6): 5-32.

——. 1959 **[ref. 1579]**. Contributions a l'étude des Poissons Characoides (Ostariophysi) (II.) *Roeboexodon* gen. n. de Guyane, redescription de *R. guyanensis* (Puyo, 1948) et relations probables avec les formes voisnes. Bull. Mus. Natl. Hist. Nat. (Ser. 2) v. 31 (no. 4): 345-352.

——. 1960 (Oct.) **[ref. 1603]**. Contributions to the study of characoid fishes. 11. The generic position of *Hyphessobrycon innesi* and *Chairodon axelrodi*, with a review of the morphological affinities of some Cheirodontinae (Pisces - Cypriniformes). Bull. Aquat. Biol. v. 2 (no. 12): 1-18.

——. 1960 **[ref. 1604]**. Contributions a l'étude des poissons Characoïdes (No. 8). Un nouveau sous-genre de *Leporinus* (Erythrinidae, Anostominae): *Leporinops*, type *Leporinus moralesi* Fowler. Bull. Mus. Natl. Hist. Nat. (Ser. 2) v. 32 (no. 4): 308-313.

——. 1960 (30 Apr.) **[ref. 1605]**. Contributions to the study of the characoid fishes, No. 6. New Cheirodontinae from French Guiana. Senckenb. Biol. v. 41 (no. 1/2): 15-39, Pl. 2.

——. 1964 **[ref. 1580]**. Poissons characoïdes de l'Amazonie péruvienne. Beitr. Neotrop. Fauna v. 4 (no. 1): 1-44.

——. 1964 (21 Dec.) **[ref. 1581]**. Une nouvelle famille de Poissons dulcaquicoles africaines: les Grasseichthyidae. C. R. Hebd. Seances Acad. Sci. v. 259: 4805-4807.

——. 1964 **[ref. 1582]**. Preliminary description of seven new species and two new genera of characoid fishes from the Upper Rio Meta in Colombia. Trop. Fish Hobby. v. 13 (no. 4, Jan.): 25-32, 41-48.

——. 1964 **[ref. 1583]**. Poissons characoïdes nouveaux ou non signalés de l'Ilha do Bananal, Brésil. Vie Milieu Suppl. No. 17: 447-471, Pls. 1-4.

——. 1965 (26 Mar.) **[ref. 1584]**. Poissons characoïdes sud-américains du Senckenberg Muséum, II. Characidae et Crenuchidae de l'Igarapé Préto (Haute Amazonie). Senckenb. Biol. v. 46 (no. 1): 11-45, Pls. 1-4.

——. 1965 **[ref. 1585]**. A new genus from Brazil—*Brittanichthys*. Trop. Fish Hobby. v. 13 (no. 6, Feb.): 13-24, 61-69.

———. 1965 (12 July) **[ref. 1586]**. Poissons characoïdes sud-américaines du Senckenberg Muséum, II. Characidae et Crenuchidae de l'Igarapé Préto (Haute Amazonie). [Fin] Senckenb. Biol. v. 46 (no. 3): 195-218, Pls. 18, 18a.

———. 1966 **[ref. 1587]**. *Axelrodia riesei*, a new characoid fish from Upper Rio Méta in Colombia. (With remarks concerning the genus *Axelrodia* and a description of a similar, sympatric, *Hyphessobrycon*-species.) Ichthyol. Aquarium J. v. 37 (no. 3): 111-120.

———. 1966 **[ref. 1588]**. A review of certain Tetragonopterinae (Characoidei), with the description of two new genera. Ichthyol. Aquarium J. v. 37 (no. 5): 211-236.

———. 1966 **[ref. 1589]**. *Hoplocharax goethei*, a new genus and species of South American characoid fishes, with a review of the sub-tribe Heterocharacini. Ichthyol. Aquarium J. v. 38 (no. 3): 281-296.

———. 1968 (Apr.) **[ref. 1591]**. *Ladigesia roloffi*, a new genus and species of African characoid fishes. Trop. Fish Hobby. v. 16 (no. 8, Apr.): 78-87, 2 col. figs.

———. 1970 (Dec.) **[ref. 1592]**. Le genre *Iguanodectes* Cope (Pisces, Characoidei). Amazoniana v. 2 (no. 4): 417-433.

———. 1971 **[ref. 1593]**. Une sous-famille nouvelle de poissons Characoides Sud-Américains: les Geisleriinae. Vie Milieu (Ser. C) v. 22 (no. 1): 153-166. [English and German summs.]

———. 1972 (19 Dec.) **[ref. 1594]**. Poissons characoïdes des Guyanes. 1. Généralités. 2. Famille des Serrasalmidae. Zool. Verh. (Leiden) No. 122: 1-250, 16 pls.

———. 1972 **[ref. 1595]**. Contribution à l'étude des poissons characoïdes de l'Équateur. Avec une révision du genre *Pseudochalceus* et la description d'une nouveaux genre endémique du Rio Cauca en Colombie. Acta Humboldt. (Ser. Geol. Palaeontol. Biol.) No. 2: 1-110, 8 pls.

———. 1973 **[ref. 1596]**. New and little-known Aphyoditeina (Pisces, Characoidei) from the Amazon basin. Stud. Neotrop. Fauna v. 8: 81-137. [Spanish summ.]

———. 1976 (18 Mar.) **[ref. 14199]**. Les genres de Serrasalmidae (Pisces, Characoidei). Bull. Zool. Mus. Univ. Amst. v. 5 (no. 6): 47-54.

———. 1977 **[ref. 1597]**. Characoids of the world. T. F. H. Publications, Neptune City, New Jersey. 1-672.

———. 1980 (21 Apr.) **[ref. 1598]**. Un nouveau Poisson characoïde occupant la niche des mangeurs d'écailles dans le haut rio Tapajoz, Brésil: *Bryconexodon juruenae* n. g. sp. Rev. Fr. Aquariol. v. 7 (no. 1): 1-8.

———. 1986 (21 July) **[ref. 6012]**. Notes de Characologie néotropicale 1. Progrès dans la systématique des genres *Colossoma* et *Piaractus*. Rev. Fr. Aquariol. v. 12 (no. 4): 97-102.

———. 1986 (15 Nov.) **[ref. 6019]**. Notes de Characologie néotropicale 2. Progrès récents dans la connaissance des cynodontinés (characidés). Rev. Fr. Aquariol. v. 13 (no. 3): 61-68.

———. 1987 (30 Dec.) **[ref. 6739]**. Description d'une nouvelle espèce de poisson anostomidé (Ostariophysi, Characoidei) du rio Mamoré, Bolivie: *Rhytiodus lauzannei* sp. n. Cybium v. 11 (no. 4): 365-373.

———. 1989 (31 July) **[ref. 13422]**. Sur quelques noms du groupe-famille chez les Poissons. Revue Fr. Aquariol. v. 16 (no. 1): 5-6.

GÉRY, J., AND H. BOUTIÈRE. 1964 **[ref. 1599]**. *Petitella georgiae* gen. et sp. nov. (Pisces, Cypriniformes, Characoidei). Vie Milieu Suppl. No. 17: 473-484, tab. 1.

GÉRY, J., AND W. J. JUNK. 1977 (Sept.) **[ref. 1601]**. *Inpaichthys kerri* n. g. n. sp., um novo peixe caracídeo do alto rio Aripuanã, Mato Grosso, Brasil. Acta Amazonica v. 7 (no. 3): 417-422 + foldout table.

GÉRY, J., AND V. MAHNERT. 1988 (Mar.) **[ref. 6881]**. *Hydrolycus* Müller & Troschel, 1844 (Osteichthyes, Cypriniformes): confirmation proposée de *Hydrocyon scomberoides* Cuvier, 1819 comme espèce-type. Case 2556. Bull. Zool. Nomencl. v. 45 (pt 1): 38-40.

GÉRY, J., V. MAHNERT AND C. DLOUHY. 1987 (July) **[ref. 6001]**. Poissons characoïdes non Characidae du Paraguay (Pisces, Ostariophysi). Rev. Suisse Zool. v. 94 (no. 2): 357-464.

GÉRY, J., P. PLANQUETTE AND P. Y. LE BAIL. 1988 (4 May) **[ref. 6408]**. Un nouveau Tetragonopterinae (Pisces, Characoidei, Characidae) de la Guyane: *Astyanax leopoldi* sp. n. Rev. Fr. Aquariol. v. 15 (no. 1): 9-12.

GÉRY, J., AND J.-F. RENNO. 1989 (31 July) **[ref. 13420]**. Un nouveau poisson characiforme (Ostariophysaires) de la Guyana: *Creagrutus planquettei* sp. n. Rev. Fr. Aquariol. v. 16 (no. 1): 1-5.

GÉRY, J., AND P. DE RHAM. 1981 (26 June) **[ref. 1600]**. Un nouveau Poisson characidé endémique du bassin du Rio Tumbés au nord du Pérou, *Chilobrycon deuterodon* n. g. sp. (Characoidei). Rev. Fr. Aquariol. v. 8 (no. 1): 7-12.

GÉRY, J., AND VU-TÂN-TUÊ. 1963 **[ref. 1602]**. Définitions de *Cynopotamus* Val. et genres voisins (Pisces, Characoidei) (Suite). Bull. Mus. Natl. Hist. Nat. (Ser. 2) v. 35 (no. 3): 238-246.

GIANFERRARI, L. 1923 **[ref. 1608]**. *Uegitglanis zammaronoi* un nuovo siluride cieco africano. Atti Soc. Ital. Sci. Nat. Milano v. 62: 1-3, Pl. 1.

GIBBONS, W. P. 1854 (ca. 20 Oct.) **[ref. 1610]**. Description of new species of viviparous marine and fresh-water fishes, from the bay of San Francisco, and from the river and lagoons of the Sacramento. Proc. Acad. Nat. Sci. Phila. 1854 [v. 7] (no. 4): 122-126. [Most genera appeared first as Gibbons 1854 (18 May); also as Arch. Naturgesch. v. 21 (1): 331-341.]

———. 1854 (18 May) **[ref. 5207]**. Description of four new species of viviparous fish, read before the California Academy of Natural Sciences, Monday evening, May 15, 1854. Daily Placer Times and Transcript for Wednesday, May 18, 1854. P. 2 [newspaper]. [Also published in Gibbons 1854 (Oct.) [ref. 1610].]

———. 1854 (30 May) **[ref. 6064]**. A paper describing two new species of viviparous fish, from the Bay of San Francisco. Read Monday evening, May 22nd, 1854, before the California Academy of Natural Sciences. Daily Placer Times and Transcript for May 30, 1854. p. 1.

———. 1854 **[ref. 6065]**. Daily Placer Times and Transcript for June 21, 1854. [Not seen.]

GIBBS, R. H., JR. 1964 **[ref. 6960]**. Family Astronesthidae (pp. 311-350). In: Fishes of the Western North Atlantic. Mem. Sears Found. Mar. Res. No. 1 (pt 4) .

———. 1964 **[ref. 6961]**. Family Idiacanthidae (pp. 512-522). In: Fishes of the Western North Atlantic. Mem. Sears Found. Mar. Res. No. 1 (pt 4).

———. 1986 **[ref. 5655]**. Family No. 67: Stomiidae (pp. 229-230), Family No. 68: Chauliodontidae (p. 230), Family No. 69: Astronesthidae (pp. 231-234), Family No. 72: Melanostomiidae (pp. 236-242). In: Smiths' Sea Fishes (Smith & Heemstra 1986 [ref. 5715]).

GIBBS, R. H., JR., T. A. CLARKE AND J. R. GOMON. 1983 (20 Sept.) **[ref. 5269]**. Taxonomy and distribution of the stomioid fish genus *Eustomias* (Melanostomiidae), I: subgenus *Nominostomias*. Smithson. Contrib. Zool. No. 380: i-iv + 1-139.

GIBBS, R. H., JR., AND B. B. COLLETTE. 1967 **[ref. 13640]**. Comparative anatomy and systematics of the tunas, genus *Thunnus*. Fish. Bull. v. 66 (no. 1): 65-130.

GIBBS, R. H., JR., AND J. F. MCKINNEY. 1988 (5 Apr.) **[ref. 6628]**. High-count species of the stomiid fish genus *Astronesthes* from the southern subtropical convergence region: two new species and redescription of *Cryptostomias* (= *Astronesthes*) *psychrolutes*. Smithson. Contrib. Zool. No. 460: i-iii + 1-25.

GIBBS, R. H., JR., AND J. E. MORROW, JR. 1973 **[ref. 7174]**. Astronesthidae (pp. 126-129). In: Hureau & Monod 1973 [ref. 6590].

GIBBS, R. H., JR., AND S. H. WEITZMAN. 1965 **[ref. 1612]**. *Cryptostomias psychrolutes*, a new genus and species of astronesthid fish from the southwestern Pacific Ocean. (Papers from the "Dana" Oceanographical Collections No. 56.) Vidensk. Medd. Dansk Naturh. Foren. Kjob. v. 128: 265-271.

GIEBEL, C. G. A. 1871 **[ref. 1616]**. [*Trachypoma marmoratum*, ein neuer Wels aus dem Amazonenstrome.] Z. Ges. Naturw. Berlin (n.f., 3) v. 37: 97.

GIGLIOLI, E. H. 1880 **[ref. 1617]**. Elenco dei mammiferi, degli uccelli e dei rettili ittiofagi appartenenti alla fauna italica e catalogo degli

anfibi e dei pesci italiani. Firenze. 1-55. [Pisces, pp. 18-55.]
———. 1882 (ca. 6 Apr.) **[ref. 1618]**. New and very rare fish from the Mediterranean. Nature (Lond.) v. 25 (no. 649): 535.
———. 1882 (28 Dec.) **[ref. 1620]**. New deep-sea fish from the Mediterranean. Nature (Lond.) v. 27: 198-199. [Sometimes cited as 1883; possibly not published until early 1883.]
———. 1883 (7 May) **[ref. 1619]**. Intorno a due nuovi pesci dal golfo di Napoli. Zool. Anz. v. 6 (no. 144): 397-400.
———. 1889 (Oct.) **[ref. 1621]**. On a supposed new genus and species of pelagic gadoid fishes from the Mediterranean. Proc. Zool. Soc. Lond. 1889 (pt 3): 328-332, Pl. 34.
GIGLIOLI, E. H., AND A. ISSEL. 1884 **[ref. 5325]**. Pelagos. Saggi sulla vita e sui prodotti del mare. Esplorazione talassografica del Mediterraneo. Pp. 198-270. Istituto de' Sordo-muti, Genova.
GILBERT, C. H. 1884 (1 Sept.) **[ref. 1622]**. A list of fishes collected in the east fork of the White River, Indiana, with descriptions of two new species. Proc. U. S. Natl. Mus. v. 7 [no. 423]: 199-205.
———. 1890 (1 July) **[ref. 1623]**. No. XII.—A preliminary report on the fishes collected by the steamer "Albatross" on the Pacific Coast of North America during the year 1889, with descriptions of twelve new genera and ninety-two new species. Proc. U. S. Natl. Mus. v. 13 (no. 797): 49-126.
———. 1891 (29 May) **[ref. 1624]**. No. XIX.—A supplementary list of fishes collected at Galapagos Islands and Panama, with descriptions of one new genus and three new species. Scientific results of explorations by the U. S. Fish Commission steamer "Albatross." Proc. U. S. Natl. Mus. v. 13 (no. 840): 449-455.
———. 1891 (8 Sept.) **[ref. 1625]**. No. XXI.—Descriptions of apodal fishes from the tropical Pacific. Scientific results of explorations by the U. S. Fish Commission steamer "Albatross." Proc. U. S. Natl. Mus. v. 14 (no. 856): 347-352.
———. 1892 (28 Mar.) **[ref. 1626]**. No. XXII.—Descriptions of thirty-four new species of fishes collected in 1888 and 1889, principally among the Santa Barbara Islands and in the Gulf of California. Scientific results of explorations by the U. S. Fish Commission steamer "Albatross." Proc. U. S. Natl. Mus. v. 14 (no. 880): 539-566.
———. 1893 (31 May) **[ref. 1627]**. Report on the fishes of the Death Valley expedition, collected in southern California and Nevada in 1891, with descriptions of new species. North American Fauna No. 7: 229-234, Pls. 5-6.
———. 1896 (9 Dec.) **[ref. 1628]**. The ichthyological collections of the steamer "Albatross" during the years 1890 and 1891. Rep. U. S. Fish Comm. v. 19 [1893]: 393-476, Pls. 20-34.
———. 1897 (5 Feb.) **[ref. 1629]**. Descriptions of twenty-two new species of fishes collected by the steamer "Albatross," of the United States Fish Commission. Proc. U. S. Natl. Mus. v. 19 (no. 1115): 437-457, Pls. 49-55.
———. 1900 (20 Aug.) **[ref. 1630]**. Results of the Branner-Agassiz expedition to Brazil. III. The fishes. Proc. Wash. Acad. Sci. v. 2: 161-184, Pl. 9.
———. 1905 (5 Aug.) **[ref. 1631]**. II. The deep-sea fishes of the Hawaiian Islands. In: The aquatic resources of the Hawaiian Islands. Bull. U. S. Fish Comm. v. 23 (pt 2) [1903]: 577-713, Pls. 66-101.
———. 1912 **[ref. 9276]**. A new genus and species of cottoid fish from Departure Bay, Vancouver Island. Contr. Canadian Biol., Marine Biol. Sta. 1906-1910: 215-216.
———. 1915 (28 Jan.) **[ref. 1632]**. Fishes collected by the United States fisheries steamer "Albatross" in southern California in 1904. Proc. U. S. Natl. Mus. v. 48 (no. 2075): 305-380, Pls. 14-22.
GILBERT, C. H., AND C. V. BURKE. 1912 (6 May) **[ref. 1634]**. Fishes from Bering Sea and Kamchatka. Bull. Bur. Fish. v. 30 (for 1910): 31-96.
GILBERT, C. H., AND F. CRAMER. 1897 (5 Feb.) **[ref. 1635]**. Report on the fishes dredged in deep water near the Hawaiian Islands, with descriptions and figures of twenty-three new species. Proc. U. S. Natl. Mus. v. 19 (no. 1114): 403-435, Pls. 36-48.
GILBERT, C. H., AND C. L. HUBBS. 1916 (28 Oct.) **[ref. 1636]**. Report on the Japanese macruroid fishes collected by the United States Fisheries steamer "Albatross" in 1906, with a synopsis of the genera. Proc. U. S. Natl. Mus. v. 51 (no. 2149): 135-214, Pls. 8-11.
———. 1920 (5 Oct.) **[ref. 1638]**. Contributions to the biology of the Philippine Archipelago and adjacent regions. The macrouroid fishes of the Philippine Islands and the East Indies. Bull. U. S. Natl. Mus. No. 100, v. 1 (pt 7): 369-588.
GILBERT, C. H., AND E. C. STARKS. 1904 **[ref. 1639]**. The fishes of Panama Bay. Mem. Calif. Acad. Sci. v. 4: 1-304, Pls. 1-33.
GILBERT, C. H., AND J. C. THOMPSON. 1905 (8 Aug.) **[ref. 1640]**. Notes on the fishes of Puget Sound. Proc. U. S. Natl. Mus. v. 28 (no. 1414): 973-987.
GILBERT, C. R. 1971 (8 Mar.) **[ref. 1641]**. Two new genera and species of western Atlantic gobiid fishes with vomerine teeth. Copeia 1971 (no. 1): 27-38.
———. 1973 **[ref. 7164]**. Sphyrnidae (pp. 32-34). In: Hureau & Monod 1973 [ref. 6590].
———. 1977 (June) **[ref. 7041]**. The gobiid fish *Palatogobius paradoxus* in the northern Gulf of Mexico. Northeast Gulf Sci. v. 1 (no. 1): 48-51.
———. 1978 **[ref. 7042]**. Type catalogue of the North American cyprinid fish genus *Notropis*. Bull. Fla. State Mus. Biol. Sci. v. 23 (no. 1): 1-104.
GILBERT, C. R., AND R. M. BAILEY. 1972 (9 Mar.) **[ref. 7153]**. Systematics and zoogeography of the American cyprinid fish *Notropis (Opsopoeodus) emiliae*. Occas. Pap. Mus. Zool. Univ. Mich. No. 664: 1-35, Pls. 1-2.
GILBERT, C. R., AND G. H. BURGESS. 1986 (10 Feb.) **[ref. 5949]**. Variation in western Atlantic gobiid fishes of the genus *Evermannichthys*. Copeia 1986 (no. 1): 157-165.
GILBERT, C. R., AND J. E. RANDALL. 1979 (June) **[ref. 6929]**. Two new western Atlantic species of the gobiid fish genus *Gobionellus*, with remarks on characteristics of the genus. Northeast Gulf Sci. v. 3 (no. 1): 27-47.
GILCHRIST, J. D. F. 1902 (7 Oct.) **[ref. 1644]**. South African fishes. Mar. Invest. So. Afr. v. 2: 101-113, Pls. 5-10.
———. 1903 (8 July) **[ref. 1645]**. Descriptions of new South African fishes. Mar. Invest. So. Afr. v. 2: 203-211, Pls. 13-18.
———. 1904 (1 Mar.) **[ref. 1646]**. Descriptions of new South African fishes. Mar. Invest. So. Afr. v. 3: 1-16, Pls. 19-25.
———. 1906 (30 Oct.) **[ref. 1647]**. Descriptions of fifteen new South African fishes, with notes on other species. Mar. Invest. So. Afr. v. 4: 143-171, Pls. 37-51. [Sometimes cited as 1908, "published 30th October, 1906" on reprint at CAS.]
———. 1922 **[ref. 1648]**. Deep-sea fishes procured by the S.S. "Pickle" (Part I). Fish. Mar. Biol. Surv., Union So. Afr. Rep. No. 2 (art. 3): 41-79, Pls. 7-12. [Also as separate, pp. 1-39, Pls. 7-12.]
GILCHRIST, J. D. F., AND C. VON BONDE. 1923 (25 Aug.) **[ref. 5931]**. The Stromateidae (butter-fishes) collected by the S. S. "Pickle." Fish. Mar. Biol. Surv., Union S. Afr. Rep. no. 3, for 1922, Spec. Rep. no. 4: 1-12, Pls. 17-19.
———. 1924 (25 Feb.) **[ref. 1649]**. Deep-sea fishes procured by the S.S. "Pickle" (Part II). Rep. Fish. Mar. Biol. Surv. Union So. Afr. Rept. 3 (no. 7): 1-24, Pls. 1-6.
GILCHRIST, J. D. F., AND W. W. THOMPSON. 1908 (31 Dec.) **[ref. 5840]**. The Blenniidae of South Africa. Ann. S. Afr. Mus. v. 6 (pt 2, no. 2): 97-143.
———. 1909 (30 Sept.) **[ref. 1650]**. Descriptions of fishes from the coast of Natal (Part II.). Ann. S. Afr. Mus. v. 6 (pt 3, no. 5): 213-279.
———. 1916 **[ref. 5602]**. Description of four new S. African fishes. Mar. Biol. Rep. So. Afr. 1914-1918 (pt. 3): 56-61.
GILL, T. N. 1858 **[ref. 1750]**. Synopsis of the fresh water fishes of the western portion of the island of Trinidad, W. I. Ann. Lyc. Nat. Hist. N. Y. v. 6 (nos. 10-13): 363-430. [Also appeared as a separate, pp. 1-70.]
———. 1859 **[ref. 1751]**. Prodromus descriptionis subfamiliae Gobinarum squamis cycloideis piscium, cl. W. Stimpsono in mare Pacifico acquisitorum. Ann. Lyc. Nat. Hist. N. Y. v. 6 (nos. 1-3): 12-16.

———. 1859 **[ref. 1752]**. Description of a new genus of Pimelodinae from Canada. Ann. Lyc. Nat. Hist. N. Y. v. 7 (nos. 1-3): 39-42.

———. 1859 **[ref. 1753]**. Prodromus descriptionis familiae Gobioidaeum duorum generum novorum. Ann. Lyc. Nat. Hist. N. Y. v. 7 (nos. 1-3): 16-19.

———. 1859 **[ref. 1754]**. Description of a new generic form of Gobinae from the Amazon River. Ann. Lyc. Nat. Hist. N. Y. v. 7 (nos. 1-3): 45-48. [Fowler (MS) records date for this publication as 1862 (not investigated).]

———. 1859 (before 18 Oct.) **[ref. 1755]**. Description of a new genus of Salarianae, from the West Indies. Proc. Acad. Nat. Sci. Phila. v. 11: 168-169.

———. 1859 (18 Oct.) **[ref. 1756]**. Description of new South American type of siluroids, allied to *Callophysus*. Proc. Acad. Nat. Sci. Phila. v. 11: 196-197.

———. 1859 (before 18 Oct.) **[ref. 1757]**. Description of a third genus of Hemirhamphinae. Proc. Acad. Nat. Sci. Phila. v. 11: 155-157.

———. 1859 (18 Oct.) **[ref. 1758]**. Description of a type of gobioids intermediate between Solinae and Tridentigerinae. Proc. Acad. Nat. Sci. Phila. v. 11: 195-196.

———. 1859 (ca. 10 May) **[ref. 1759]**. Description of *Hyporhamphus*, a new genus of fishes allied to *Hemirhamphus*, Cuv. Proc. Acad. Nat. Sci. Phila. v. 11: 131-132.

———. 1859 (before 18 Oct.) **[ref. 1760]**. Description of new generic types of cottoids, from the collection of the North Pacific exploring expedition under Com. John Rodgers. Proc. Acad. Nat. Sci. Phila. v. 11: 165-166.

———. 1859 (ca. 10 May) **[ref. 1792]**. On *Dactyloscopus* and *Leptoscopus*, two new genera of the family of Uranoscopidae. Proc. Acad. Nat. Sci. Phila. v. 11: 132-133.

———. 1859 (ca. 10 May) **[ref. 1761]**. On the genus *Callionymus* of authors. Proc. Acad. Nat. Sci. Phila. 1859 [v. 11]: 128-130.

———. 1859 (May or June) **[ref. 1762]**. Notes on a collection of Japanese fishes, made by Dr. J. Morrow. Proc. Acad. Nat. Sci. Phila. 1859 [v. 11]: 144-150.

———. 1860 (before 21 Mar.) **[ref. 1763]**. Notes on the nomenclature of North American fishes. Proc. Acad. Nat. Sci. Phila. 1860 [v. 12]: 19-21.

———. 1860 (before July) **[ref. 1764]**. Conspectus piscium in expeditione ad oceanum Pacificum septentrionalem, C. Ringold et J. Rodgers ducibus, a Gulielmo Stimpson collectorum. Sicydianae. Proc. Acad. Nat. Sci. Phila. 1860 [v. 12]: 100-102.

———. 1860 (before 17 July) **[ref. 1765]**. Monograph of the genus *Labrosomus* Sw. Proc. Acad. Nat. Sci. Phila. 1860 [v. 12]: 102-108.

———. 1860 (before 17 July) **[ref. 1793]**. Monograph of the genus *Labrax*, of Cuvier. Proc. Acad. Nat. Sci. Phila. 1860 [v. 12]: 108-119.

———. 1861 (Feb.) **[ref. 1766]**. Catalogue of the fishes of the eastern coast of North America, from Greenland to Georgia. Proc. Acad. Nat. Sci. Phila. 1860 [v.13] (Suppl.): 1-63.

———. 1861 (19 Mar. or 1 Apr.) **[ref. 1767]**. Synopsis of the subfamily of Clupeinae, with descriptions of a new genera. Proc. Acad. Nat. Sci. Phila. 1861 [v. 13]: 33-38.

———. 1861 (19 Mar. or 2 Apr.) **[ref. 1768]**. Synopsis of the subfamily of Percinae. Proc. Acad. Nat. Sci. Phila. 1861 [v. 13]: 44-52.

———. 1861 (19 Mar. or 2 Apr.) **[ref. 1769]**. Synopsis generum Rhyptici et affinium. Proc. Acad. Nat. Sci. Phila. 1861 [v. 13]: 52-54.

———. 1861 (14 May) **[ref. 1770]**. On several new generic types of fishes contained in the museum of the Smithsonian Institution. Proc. Acad. Nat. Sci. Phila. 1861 [v. 13]: 77-78.

———. 1861 (14 May) **[ref. 1771]**. Revision of the genera of North American Sciaeninae. Proc. Acad. Nat. Sci. Phila. 1861 [v. 13]: 79-89.

———. 1861 (before 22 Oct.) **[ref. 1772]**. Two new species of marine fishes. Proc. Acad. Nat. Sci. Phila. 1861 [v. 13]: 98-99.

———. 1861 (before 22 Oct.) **[ref. 1773]**. On the Haploidonotinae. Proc. Acad. Nat. Sci. Phila. 1861 [v. 13]: 100-105.

———. 1861 (before 22 Oct.) **[ref. 1774]**. Synopsis of the uranoscopoids. Proc. Acad. Nat. Sci. Phila. 1861 [v. 13]: 108-117.

———. 1861 (22 Oct.) **[ref. 1775]**. Notes on some genera of fishes of the western coast of North America. Proc. Acad. Nat. Sci. Phila. 1861 [v. 13]: 164-168.

———. 1861 (22 Oct.) **[ref. 1776]**. On a new typs [sic] of aulostomatoids, found in Washington Territory. Proc. Acad. Nat. Sci. Phila. 1861 [v. 13]: 168-170.

———. 1861 (19 Nov.) **[ref. 1777]**. Description of a new generic type of blennioids. Proc. Acad. Nat. Sci. Phila. 1861 [v. 13]: 261-263.

———. 1861 (19 Nov.) **[ref. 1778]**. Monograph of the tridigitate uranoscopoids. Proc. Acad. Nat. Sci. Phila. 1861 [v. 13]: 263-271.

———. 1861 (15 Nov.) **[ref. 1779]**. Synopsis of the polynematoids. Proc. Acad. Nat. Sci. Phila. 1861 [v. 13]: 271-282.

———. 1861 (Apr.) **[ref. 1785]**. Observations on the genus *Cottus*, and descriptions of two new species (abridged from the forthcoming report of Capt. J. H. Simpson). Proc. Boston Soc. Nat. Hist. v. 8 (1861 to 1862): 40-42.

———. 1861 (Apr.) **[ref. 1673]**. Synopsis of the genera of the subfamily of Pimelodinae. Proc. Boston Soc. Nat. Hist. v. 8 (1861 to 1862): 46-55.

———. 1861 **[ref. 12597]**. On the genus *Podothecus*. Proc. Acad. Nat. Sci. Phila. 1861 [v. 13]: 258-261.

———. 1862 (before 31 Mar.) **[ref. 1780]**. Synopsis of the silaginoids. Proc. Acad. Nat. Sci. Phila. 1861 [v. 13]: 501-505.

———. 1862 (before 31 Mar.) **[ref. 1781]**. Synopsis of the chaenichthyoids. Proc. Acad. Nat. Sci. Phila. 1861 [v. 13]: 507-510.

———. 1862 (before 31 Mar.) **[ref. 1782]**. Synopsis of the notothenioids. Proc. Acad. Nat. Sci. Phila. 1861 [v. 13]: 512-522.

———. 1862 **[ref. 1783]**. Analytical synopsis of the order of Squali; and revision of the nomenclature of the genera. [Genera date to this article, also treated in Gill 1862:409-413 [ref. 4910]. Both articles combined as separate, pp. 1-42.] Ann. Lyc. Nat. Hist. N. Y. v. 7: 367-*370*, 371-408. [Pp. 367-370 duplicated in preceding article. Read 16 Dec. 1861, probably published early 1862.]

———. 1862 (before 25 Apr.) **[ref. 1654]**. Notice of a new species of *Hemilepidotus* and remarks on the group (Temnistiae) of which it is a member. Proc. Acad. Nat. Sci. Phila. 1862 [v. 14]: 13-14.

———. 1862 (before 25 Apr.) **[ref. 1655]**. On the subfamily Argentininae. Proc. Acad. Nat. Sci. Phila. 1862 [v. 14] (no. 1-2): 14-15.

———. 1862 (before 25 Apr.) **[ref. 1656]**. Appendix to the synopsis of the subfamily Percinae. Proc. Acad. Nat. Sci. Phila. 1862 [v. 14] (no. 1-2): 15-16.

———. 1862 (before 25 Apr.) **[ref. 1657]**. Note on the sciaenoids of California. Proc. Acad. Nat. Sci. Phila. 1862 [v. 14] (no. 1-2): 16-18.

———. 1862 (before 27 May) **[ref. 1658]**. Synopsis of the family of cirrhitoids. Proc. Acad. Nat. Sci. Phila. 1862 [v. 14] (no. 3-4): 102-124.

———. 1862 (before 27 May) **[ref. 1659]**. On the limits and arrangement of the family of scombroids. Proc. Acad. Nat. Sci. Phila. 1862 [v. 14] (no. 3-4): 124-127.

———. 1862 (before 27 May) **[ref. 1660]**. Descriptions of new species of Alepidosauroidae. Proc. Acad. Nat. Sci. Phila. 1862 [v. 14] (no. 3-4): 127-132.

———. 1862 (before 27 May) **[ref. 1661]**. On the West African genus *Hemichromis* and descriptions of new species in the museums of the Academy and Smithsonian Institution. Proc. Acad. Nat. Sci. Phila. 1862 [v. 14] (no. 3-4): 134-139.

———. 1862 (before 27 May) **[ref. 1662]**. Catalogue of the fishes of Lower California in the Smithsonian Institution, collected by Mr. J. Xantus. Proc. Acad. Nat. Sci. Phila. 1862 [v. 14] (no. 3-4): 140-151.

———. 1862 (about June) **[ref. 1663]**. On a new genus of fishes allied to *Aulorhynchus* and on the affinities of the family Aulorhynchoidae, to which it belongs. Proc. Acad. Nat. Sci. Phila. 1862 [v. 14] (no. 5): 233-235.

———. 1862 (about June) **[ref. 1664]**. Remarks on the relations of the genera and other groups of Cuban fishes. Proc. Acad. Nat. Sci. Phila. 1862 [v. 14] (no. 5): 235-242.

——. 1862 (about June) **[ref. 1665]**. Catalogue of the fishes of Lower California, in the Smithsonian Institution, collected by Mr. J. Xantus. Part II. Proc. Acad. Nat. Sci. Phila. 1862 [v. 14] (no. 5): 242-246.

——. 1862 (before 1 Aug.) **[ref. 1666]**. Notice of a collection of the fishes of California presented to the Smithsonian Institution by Mr. Samuel Hubbard. Proc. Acad. Nat. Sci. Phila. 1862 [v. 14] (no. 6): 274-282.

——. 1862 (before 1 Aug.) **[ref. 1667]**. Synopsis of the species of lophobranchiate fishes of western North America. Proc. Acad. Nat. Sci. Phila. 1862 [v. 14] (no. 6): 282-284.

——. 1862 (28 Oct.) **[ref. 1668]**. Note on some genera of fishes of western North America. Proc. Acad. Nat. Sci. Phila. 1862 [v. 14] (no. 7-9): 329-332.

——. 1862 (about June) **[ref. 4909]**. Catalogue of the fishes of Lower California, in the Smithsonian Institution, collected by Mr. J. Xantus. Part III. Proc. Acad. Nat. Sci. Phila. 1862 [v. 14] (no. 5): 249-262.

——. 1862 **[ref. 4910]**. Squalorum generum novorum descriptiones diagnosticae. Ann. Lyc. Nat. Hist. N. Y. v. 8: 409-413.

——. 1862 **[ref. 4974]**. Squalorum generum novorum descriptiones diagnosticae. Ann. Lyc. Nat. Hist. N. Y. v. 7: 409-413. [Follows Gill 1862: 367-408 [ref. 1783]; genera date to earlier article. Also separate, pp. 43-47 [with ref. 1783].]

——. 1863 (before 12 Jan.) **[ref. 1669]**. Synopsis of the carangoids of the eastern coast of North America. Proc. Acad. Nat. Sci. Phila. 1862 [v. 14] (no. 9): 430-443. [Probably published in late 1862; no. 9 is the second no. 9 through error in numbering.]

——. 1863 (before 12 Jan.) **[ref. 1670]**. Description of a new generic type of mormyroids and note on the arrangement of the genus. Proc. Acad. Nat. Sci. Phila. 1862 [v. 14] (no. 9): 443-445. [Probably published late 1862; no. 9 is second no. 9 through error in numbering.]

——. 1863 (before 26 Feb.) **[ref. 1671]**. On the classification of the families and genera of the Squali of California. Proc. Acad. Nat. Sci. Phila. 1862 [v.14] (no. 10-12): 483-501.

——. 1863 (before 26 Feb.) **[ref. 1672]**. On the limits and affinity of the family of Leptoscopoids. Proc. Acad. Nat. Sci. Phila. 1862 [v. 14] (no.10-12): 501-506.

——. 1863 **[ref. 1674]**. Fishes (p. 178). In: On the geology and natural history of the upper Missouri. Trans. Am. Philos. Soc. (n. s.) v. 12 (pt 1): 1-218, 1 map. [Gill authorship assumed from literature; overall authorship is Hayden.]

——. 1863 **[ref. 1678]**. Catalogue of the North American sciaenoid fishes. Proc. Acad. Nat. Sci. Phila. 1863 [v. 15] (no. 1): 28-32.

——. 1863 (before 8 June) **[ref. 1679]**. Catalogue of the fishes of Lower California, in the Smithsonian Institution, collected by Mr. J. Xantus. Part IV. Proc. Acad. Nat. Sci. Phila. 1863 [v. 15] (no. 2): 80-88.

——. 1863 (before 8 June) **[ref. 1680]**. Descriptions of some new species of Pediculati, and on the classification of the group. Proc. Acad. Nat. Sci. Phila. 1863 [v. 15] (no. 2): 88-92.

——. 1863 (before 27 Oct.) **[ref. 1681]**. Descriptive enumeration of a collection of fishes from the western coast of Central America, presented to the Smithsonian Institution by Captain John M. Dow. Proc. Acad. Nat. Sci. Phila. 1863 [v. 15] (no. 4): 162-180.

——. 1863 (28 Nov.) **[ref. 1682]**. On an unnamed generic type allied to *Sebastes*. Proc. Acad. Nat. Sci. Phila. 1863 [v. 15] (no. 5): 207-209.

——. 1863 (before 28 Nov.) **[ref. 1683]**. Description of a new generic type of ophidioids. Proc. Acad. Nat. Sci. Phila. 1863 [v. 15] (no. 5): 209-211.

——. 1863 (before 28 Nov.) **[ref. 1684]**. Synopsis of the pomacentroids of the western coast of North and Central America. Proc. Acad. Nat. Sci. Phila. 1863 [v. 15] (no. 5): 213-221.

——. 1863 (before 28 Nov.) **[ref. 1685]**. Notes on the labroids of the western coast of North America. Proc. Acad. Nat. Sci. Phila. 1863 [v. 15] (no. 5): 221-224.

——. 1863 (before 28 Nov.) **[ref. 1686]**. Synopsis of the family of lepturoids, and description of a remarkable new generic type. Proc. Acad. Nat. Sci. Phila. 1863 [v. 15] (no. 5): 224-229.

——. 1863 (before 28 Nov.) **[ref. 1687]**. Synopsis of the North American gadoid fishes. Proc. Acad. Nat. Sci. Phila. 1863 [v. 15] (no. 5): 229-242.

——. 1863 (before 28 Nov.) **[ref. 1688]**. Descriptions of the genera of gadoid and brotuloid fishes of western North America. Proc. Acad. Nat. Sci. Phila. 1863 [v. 15] (no. 5): 242-254.

——. 1863 (before 28 Nov.) **[ref. 1689]**. Synopsis of the family of Lycodoidae. Proc. Acad. Nat. Sci. Phila. 1863 [v. 15] (no. 5): 254-262.

——. 1863 (before Nov. 28) **[ref. 1690]**. Descriptions of the gobioid genera of the western coast of temperate North America. Proc. Acad. Nat. Sci. Phila. 1863 [v. 15] (no. 5): 262-267.

——. 1863 (before 28 Nov.) **[ref. 1691]**. On the gobioids of the eastern coast of the United States. Proc. Acad. Nat. Sci. Phila. 1863 [v. 15] (no. 5): 267-271.

——. 1863 (before 27 Nov.) **[ref. 1692]**. On the genus *Periophthalmus* of Schneider. Proc. Acad. Nat. Sci. Phila. 1863 [v. 15] (no. 5): 271-272.

——. 1863-64 (28 Nov. - 27 Jan.) **[ref. 1693]**. Note on the genera of Hemirhamphinae. Proc. Acad. Nat. Sci. Phila. 1863 [v. 15] (no. 5-6): 272-273. [Page 272 (in no. 5) published before 28 Nov. 1863, p. 273 (in no. 6) published before 27 Jan. 1864.]

——. 1864 (before 30 June) **[ref. 1694]**. Description of a new labroid genus allied to *Trochocopus* Gthr. Proc. Acad. Nat. Sci. Phila. 1864 [v. 16] (no. 2): 57-59.

——. 1864 (before 30 June) **[ref. 1695]**. Notes on the nomenclature of genera and species of the family Echeneidoidae. Proc. Acad. Nat. Sci. Phila. 1864 [v. 16] (no. 2): 59-61.

——. 1864 (before 30 Sept.) **[ref. 1696]**. Critical remarks on the genera *Sebastes* and *Sebastodes* of Ayres. Proc. Acad. Nat. Sci. Phila. 1864 [v. 16] (no. 3): 145-147.

——. 1864 (before 30 Sept.) **[ref. 1697]**. Second contribution to the selachology of California. Proc. Acad. Nat. Sci. Phila. v. 16 (no. 3): 147-151.

——. 1864 (before 30 Sept.) **[ref. 1698]**. Several points in ichthyology and conchology. Proc. Acad. Nat. Sci. Phila. 1864 [v. 16] (no. 3): 151-152.

——. 1864 (before 12 Dec.) **[ref. 1699]**. Note on the paralepidoids and microstomatoids, and on some peculiarities of Arctic ichthyology. Proc. Acad. Nat. Sci. Phila. 1864 [v. 16] (no. 4): 187-189.

——. 1864 (before 12 Dec.) **[ref. 1700]**. Synopsis of the cyclopteroids of eastern North America. Proc. Acad. Nat. Sci. Phila. 1864 [v. 16] (no. 4): 189-194.

——. 1864 (before 12 Dec.) **[ref. 1701]**. Synopsis of the pleuronectoids of California and north-western America. Proc. Acad. Nat. Sci. Phila. v. 16 (no. 4): 194-198.

——. 1864 (before 12 Dec.) **[ref. 1702]**. On the affinity of several doubtful British fishes. Proc. Acad. Nat. Sci. Phila. 1864 [v. 16] (no. 4): 199-208. [Also in Ann. Mag. Nat. Hist. (Ser. 3) v. 15: 40-48.]

——. 1864 (before 12 Dec.) **[ref. 1703]**. Note on the family of stichaeoids. Proc. Acad. Nat. Sci. Phila. 1864 [v. 16] (no. 4): 208-211.

——. 1864 (before 12 Dec.) **[ref. 1704]**. Synopsis of the pleuronectoids of the eastern coast of North America. Proc. Acad. Nat. Sci. Phila. v. 16 (no. 4): 214-220.

——. 1864 **[ref. 1706]**. Review of Holbrook's Ichthyology of South Carolina. Am. J. Sci. Arts (Ser. 2) v. 37 (art. 10): 89-94.

——. 1864 (before 12 Dec.) **[ref. 5770]**. Description of a new generic type of pleuronectoids in the collection of the Geological Survey of California. Proc. Acad. Nat. Sci. Phila. 1864 [v. 16] (no. 4): 198-199.

——. 1864 (before 12 Dec.) **[ref. 5773]**. Descriptions of new genera and species of eastern American pleuronectoids. Proc. Acad. Nat. Sci. Phila. 1864 [v. 16] (no. 4): 220-224.

——. 1865 (May) **[ref. 1676]**. On a new family type of fishes related

to the blennioids. Ann. Lyc. Nat. Hist. N. Y. v. 8 (art. 15): 141-144.
——. 1865 (May) **[ref. 1677]**. On a remarkable new type of fishes allied to *Nemophis*. Ann. Lyc. Nat. Hist. N. Y. v. 8 (art. 14): 138-141, Pl. 3.
——. 1865 (before 13 Feb.) **[ref. 1705]**. Synopsis of the eastern American sharks. Proc. Acad. Nat. Sci. Phila. 1864 [v. 16] (no. 5): 258-265.
——. 1865 **[ref. 1707]**. Synopsis of the fishes of the Gulf of St. Lawrence and Bay of Fundy. Can. Nat. v. 2 (Aug. 1865): 244-266. [Also appeared as a separate, pp. 1-24.]
——. 1865 (before 7 Aug.) **[ref. 1708]**. On the genus *Caulolatilus*. Proc. Acad. Nat. Sci. Phila. 1865 [v. 17] (no. 2): 66-68.
——. 1865 (before 7 Aug.) **[ref. 1709]**. On the cranial characters of *Gadus proximus* Grd. Proc. Acad. Nat. Sci. Phila. 1865 [v. 17] (no. 2): 69.
——. 1865 (before 7 Aug.) **[ref. 1710]**. On a new genus of Serraninae. Proc. Acad. Nat. Sci. Phila. 1865 [v. 17] (no. 2): 104-106.
——. 1865 (before 26 Dec.) **[ref. 1711]**. On a new generic type of sharks. Proc. Acad. Nat. Sci. Phila. 1865 [v. 17] (no. 4): 177.
——. 1865 (May) **[ref. 1712]**. Note on the family of *Myliobatoids*, and on a new species of *Aëtobatis*. Ann. Lyc. Nat. Hist. N. Y. v. 8 (art. 13): 135-138.
——. 1865 **[ref. 12243]**. Note on several genera of cyprinoids. Proc. Acad. Nat. Sci. Phila. 1865 [v. 17]: 69-70.
——. 1865 **[ref. 12608]**. Synopsis of the genus *Pomoxys*. Proc. Acad. Nat. Sci. Phila. 1865 [v. 17]: 64-66.
——. 1874 (Aug.) **[ref. 1713]**. On the identity of *Esox lewini* with the *Dinolestes mülleri* of Klunzinger. Ann. Mag. Nat. Hist. (Ser. 4) v. 14 (no. 80): 159-160.
——. 1876 **[ref. 12520]**. [Account of *Zanotacanthus*.] Johnson's Universal Cyclopaedia v. 3: 883. [Not seen.]
——. 1877 (10-17 July) **[ref. 1714]**. Synopsis of the fishes of Lake Nicaragua. Proc. Acad. Nat. Sci. Phila. 1877 [v. 29]: 175-191.
——. 1877 **[ref. 1715]**. Vertebrate zoology. Pp. clxvi-clxxiv. General summary of scientific and industrial progress during the year 1876. In: Annual Record of Industry and Science for 1876.
——. 1877 **[ref. 1745]**. The scientific names of our common sunfishes. Field & Forest v. 2 (May) no. 11: 188-190.
——. 1878 (July) **[ref. 1716]**. On a remarkable new generic type of characins. Ann. Mag. Nat. Hist. (Ser. 5) v. 2 (no. 7): 112. [Appeared first in Field & Forest, 1878 (May) v. 3: 167-169 [ref. 5755].]
——. 1878 (18 Dec.) **[ref. 1717]**. Note on the Antennariidae. Proc. U. S. Natl. Mus. v. 1 [no. 31]: 221-222.
——. 1878 (23 Dec.) **[ref. 1718]**. Note on the Ceratiidae. Proc. U. S. Natl. Mus. v. 1 [no. 33]: 227-231.
——. 1878 **[ref. 1719]**. [Account of *Myxocyprinis*.] In: Johnson's Cyclopaedia. p. 1574. [Not seen. See also Gill in Jordan 1878: 217 [ref. 12254].]
——. 1878 (18 Dec.) **[ref. 5604]**. Synopsis of the pediculate fishes of the eastern coast of extratropical North America. Proc. U. S. Natl. Mus. v. 1 [no. 30]: 215-221.
——. 1878 (21 May) **[ref. 5755]**. On a remarkable new generic type of characins. Field & Forest For March/April: 167-168. [Also published as Gill 1878 (July), Ann. Mag. Nat. Hist. (Ser. 5) 2: 112 [ref. 1716].]
——. 1878 (23 Dec.) **[ref. 12021]**. Note on the Maltheidae. Proc. U. S. Natl. Mus. v. 1 [no. 34]: 231-232.
——. 1880 (15 Sept.) **[ref. 5766]**. On the identity of the genus *Leurynnis*, Lockington, with *Lycodopsis*, Collett. Proc. U. S. Natl. Mus. v. 3 [no. 139]: 247-248.
——. 1881 **[ref. 1721]**. A deep-sea rock-fish. Smithson. Inst. Annu. Rep. for 1880: 373.
——. 1881 **[ref. 5954]**. Pleuronectids without pectorals. Smithson. Inst. Annu. Rep. for 1880: 372.
——. 1883 (3 Apr.) **[ref. 1722]**. Supplementary note on the Pediculati. Proc. U. S. Natl. Mus. v. 5 [no. 316]: 551-556.
——. 1883 (Nov.) **[ref. 1723]**. Deep-sea fishing fishes. Forest & Stream Nov. 8, 1883: 284.
——. 1883 (5 Dec.) **[ref. 1724]**. Diagnosis of new genera and species of deep-sea fish-like vertebrates. Proc. U. S. Natl. Mus. v. 6 [no. 380]: 253-260. [Also as a separate, Washington (1884).]
——. 1883 (3 Apr.) **[ref. 4941]**. Note on the petromyzontids. Proc. U. S. Natl. Mus. v. 5 [no. 310]: 521-525.
——. 1884 (12-19 Aug.) **[ref. 1725]**. On the anacanthine fishes. Proc. Acad. Nat. Sci. Phila. 1884 [v. 36]: 167-183.
——. 1884 (19 Sept.) **[ref. 1726]**. Synopsis of the genera of the superfamily Teuthidoidea (families Teuthididae and Siganidae). Proc. U. S. Natl. Mus. v. 7 [no. 435]: 275-281.
——. 1884 (9-18 Oct.) **[ref. 1727]**. Synopsis of the plectognath fishes. Proc. U. S. Natl. Mus. v. 7 [no. 448]: 411-427.
——. 1884 (Apr.) **[ref. 1728]**. Three new families of fishes added to the deep-sea fauna in a year. Am. Nat. v. 18 (no. 4, Apr.): 433.
——. 1885 **[ref. 1653]**. Lower Vertebrates. Chapter Acanthopterygians. Chapter 3. In: J. S. Kingsley (ed.) Riverside Natural History. [Not seen.]
——. 1888 (8 Nov.) **[ref. 1732]**. Notes on the genus *Dipterodon*. Proc. U. S. Natl. Mus. v. 11 [no. 684]: 67-68.
——. 1889 (25 Sept.) **[ref. 1729]**. On the classification of the mail-cheeked fishes. Proc. U. S. Natl. Mus. v. 11 [no. 756]: 567-592.
——. 1889 (25 Sept.) **[ref. 1730]**. Gleanings among the pleuronectids, and observations on the name *Pleuronectes*. Proc. U. S. Natl. Mus. v. 11 [no. 757]: 593-606.
——. 1890 (16 Sept.) **[ref. 1733]**. Osteological characteristics of the family Muraenesocidae. Proc. U. S. Natl. Mus. v. 13 (no. 815): 231-234.
——. 1891 (27 Aug.) **[ref. 1734]**. On *Eleginus* of Fischer, otherwise called *Tilesia* or *Pleurogadus*. Proc. U. S. Natl. Mus. v. 14 (no. 853): 303-305.
——. 1891 (8 Sept.) **[ref. 1735]**. On the genera *Labrichthys* and *Pseudolabrus*. Proc. U. S. Natl. Mus. v. 14 (no. 861): 395-404.
——. 1893 **[ref. 1736]**. A comparison of antipodal faunas. Mem. Natl. Acad. Sci. Wash. v. 6 (mem. 5): 91-124.
——. 1894 (26 Jan.) **[ref. 1737]**. (*Erilepis*.) Science v. 23 (no. 573): 52.
——. 1894 (Aug.) **[ref. 1738]**. An Australasian sub-family of fresh-water atherinoid fishes. Am. Nat. v. 28 (no. 322): 708-709.
——. 1895 (Feb.) **[ref. 1742]**. The genus *Leptophidium*. Am. Nat. v. 29 (no. 338): 167-168.
——. 1895 **[ref. 6957]**. The families of synentognathous fishes and their nomenclature. Proc. U. S. Natl. Mus. v. 18 (no. 1051): 167-178.
——. 1895 (16 Apr.) **[ref. 12504]**. Notes on *Orectolobus* or *Crossorhinus*, a genus of sharks. Proc. U. S. Natl. Mus. v. 18 (no. 1057): 211-212.
——. 1896 (23 Apr.) **[ref. 1739]**. The differential characters of characinoid and erythrinoid fishes. Proc. U. S. Natl. Mus. v. 18 (no. 1056): 205-209.
——. 1896 (16 Apr.) **[ref. 1740]**. Note on the fishes of the genus *Characinus*. Proc. U. S. Natl. Mus. v. 18 (no. 1058): 213-215.
——. 1896 (23 Apr.) **[ref. 1743]**. The differential characters of the syngnathid and hippocampid fishes. Proc. U. S. Natl. Mus. v. 18 (no. 1049): 153-159.
——. 1896 **[ref. 1744]**. *Lipophrys* a substitute for *Pholis*. Am. Nat. v. 30: 498.
——. 1898 **[ref. 7956]**. Report in part of Samuel L. Mitchill, M.D., Professor of natural history, etc., on the fishes of New York. Edited by Theodore Gill. Washington: "printed for the editor, 1898." [Contains an analysis and reproduction of the original rare Mitchill 1814.] i-x + 1-30.
——. 1903 (6 July) **[ref. 1786]**. Note on the fish genera named *Macrodon*. Proc. U. S. Natl. Mus. v. 26 (no. 1349): 1015-1016.
——. 1903 (11 July) **[ref. 4983]**. On some neglected genera of fishes. Proc. U. S. Natl. Mus. v. 26 (no. 1344): 959-962.
——. 1903 (11 July) **[ref. 5768]**. On some fish genera of the first edition of Cuvier's Règne Animal and Oken's names. Proc. U. S. Natl. Mus. v. 26 (no. 1346): 965-967.
——. 1904 (5 Oct.) **[ref. 6606]**. *Labracinus* the proper name for the

fish genus *Cichlops*. Proc. U. S. Natl. Mus. v. 28 (no. 1384): 119.

——. 1905 (15 Feb.) **[ref. 1788]**. The scorpaenoid fish, *Neosebastes entaxis*, as the type of a distinct genus. Proc. U. S. Natl. Mus. v. 28 (no. 1393): 219-220.

——. 1905 (23 Feb.) **[ref. 1789]**. Note on the genera of synanceine and pelorine fishes. Proc. U. S. Natl. Mus. v. 28 (no. 1394): 221-225.

——. 1905 (15 Feb.) **[ref. 1790]**. On the generic characteristics of *Prionotus stearnsii*. Proc. U. S. Natl. Mus. v. 28 (no. 1396): 339-342.

Gill, T. N., and J. A. Ryder. 1883 (5 Dec.) **[ref. 1746]**. Diagnosis of new genera of nemoichthyoid eels. Proc. U. S. Natl. Mus. v. 6 [no. 381]: 260-262.

——. 1883 (5-20 Dec.) **[ref. 1747]**. On the anatomy and relations of the Eurypharyngidae. Proc. U. S. Natl. Mus. v. 6 [no. 382]: 262-273. [Pp. 262-272 published 5 Dec., p. 273 on 20 Dec.]

Gill, T. N., and H. M. Smith. 1905 (9 Dec.) **[ref. 1748]**. A new family of jugular acanthopterygians. Proc. Biol. Soc. Wash. v. 18: 249-250.

Gill, T. N., and C. H. Townsend. 1897 (17 Sept.) **[ref. 1749]**. Diagnosis of new species of fishes found in Bering Sea. Proc. Biol. Soc. Wash. v. 11: 231-234.

——. 1901 (13 Dec.) **[ref. 1791]**. The largest deep-sea fish. Science (n. s.) v. 14 (no. 363): 937-938.

Gilmore, R. G., and R. S. Jones. 1988 (May) **[ref. 12879]**. *Lipogramma flavescens*, a new grammid fish from the Bahama Islands, with description and descriptive and distributional notes on *L. evides* and *L. anabantoides*. Bull. Mar. Sci. v. 42 (no. 3): 435-445.

Giltay, L. 1929 (25 Oct.) **[ref. 1795]**. Un Characide nouveau du Congo belge (*Belonophago hutsebouti*, n. g., n. sp.) de la sous-famille des Ichthyoborinae. Rev. Zool. Bot. Afr. v. 18 (pt 2): 271-276.

——. 1929 **[ref. 5065]**. Notes ichthyologiques. II.— Une espèce nouvelle de *Rhinobatus* du Congo belge (*Rhinobatus congolensis*, nov. sp.). Ann. Soc. R. Zool. Belg. v. 59: 21-27. [Dated 1928, evidently appeared in 1929.]

——. 1934 (Mar.) **[ref. 13409]**. Notes ichthyologiques. VIII.—Les larves de Schindler sont-elles des Hemirhamphidae? Bull. Mus. R. Hist. Nat. Belg. v. 10 (no. 13): 1-10.

——. 1935 (Aug.) **[ref. 1796]**. Notes ichthyologiques. X.—Description d'une espèce nouvelle de Trichomycteridae. Bull. Mus. R. Hist. Nat. Belg. v. 11 (no. 27): 1-3.

——. 1935 (Dec.) **[ref. 1797]**. Note sur quelques poissons marins du Congo belge. Bull. Mus. R. Hist. Nat. Belg. v. 11 (no. 36): 1-15.

Ginsburg, I. 1932 (Mar.) **[ref. 1798]**. A revision of the genus *Gobionellus* (family Gobiidae). Bull. Bingham Oceanogr. Collect. Yale Univ. v. 4 (art. 2): 1-51.

——. 1933 (Dec.) **[ref. 1799]**. A revision of the genus *Gobiosoma* (family Gobiidae) with an account of the genus *Garmannia*. Bull. Bingham Oceanogr. Collect. Yale Univ. v. 4 (art. 5): 1-59.

——. 1933 (19 May) **[ref. 1800]**. Descriptions of new and imperfectly known species and genera of gobioid and pleuronectid fishes in the United States National Museum. Proc. U. S. Natl. Mus. v. 82 (no. 2961): 1-23.

——. 1937 (18 Jan.) **[ref. 1801]**. Review of the seahorses (*Hippocampus*) found on the coasts of the American continents and of Europe. Proc. U. S. Natl. Mus. v. 83 (no. 2997): 497-594.

——. 1938 (15 June) **[ref. 1802]**. Eight new species of gobioid fishes from the American Pacific coast. Allan Hancock Pac. Exped. v. 2 (no. 7): 109-121.

——. 1944 **[ref. 1803]**. A description of a new gobiid fish from Venezuela, with notes on the genus *Garmannia*. J. Wash. Acad. Sci. v. 34 (no. 11): 375-380.

——. 1951 (30 Sept.) **[ref. 1804]**. The eels of the northern Gulf Coast of the United States and some related species. Tex. J. Sci. v. 3 (no. 3): 431-485.

——. 1952 **[ref. 1805]**. Eight new fishes from the Gulf coast of the United States, with two new genera and notes on geographic distribution. J. Wash. Acad. Sci. v. 42 (no. 3): 84-101.

——. 1953 **[ref. 1806]**. Ten new American gobioid fishes in the United States National Museum, including additions to a revision of *Gobionellus*. J. Wash. Acad. Sci. v. 43 (no. 1): 18-26.

——. 1953 (28 May) **[ref. 1807]**. Western Atlantic scorpionfishes. Smithson. Misc. Collect. v. 121 (no. 8): 1-103.

——. 1955 (13 Oct.) **[ref. 5606]**. Fishes of the family Percophididae from the coasts of eastern United States and the West Indies, with descriptions of four new species. Proc. U. S. Natl. Mus. v. 104 (no. 3347): 623-639.

Giorna, M. E. 1803-08 **[ref. 1808]**. Mémoire sur des poissons d'espèces nouvelles et de genres nouveaux. Plus: Suite et conclusion du mémoire (pp. 177-180). Mem. Accad. Imp. Sci. Lit. Beaux-arts., Turin v. 9 (pt. 1): 1-19, 177-180, Pls. 1-2. [Date uncertain, often cited as 1805; 'Suite' which includes the new genera probably published in 1809.]

Girard, C. F. 1850 (Mar.) **[ref. 1814]**. On the genus *Cottus* auct. Proc. Boston Soc. Nat. Hist. v. 3 (1848 to 1851): 183-190.

——. 1850 (Nov.) **[ref. 1815]**. [Some additional observations on the nomenclature and classification of the genus *Cottus*.] Proc. Boston Soc. Nat. Hist. v. 3 (1848 to 1851): 302-305.

——. 1851 **[ref. 1816]**. A new genus of American cottoids. Proc. Boston Soc. Nat. Hist. v. 4 (1851 to 1854): 18-19.

——. 1854 (before 20 Oct.) **[ref. 1817]**. Descriptions of new fishes, collected by Dr. A. L. Heermann, naturalist attached to the survey of the Pacific railroad route, under Lieut. R. S. Williamson, U. S. A. Proc. Acad. Nat. Sci. Phila. 1854 [v. 7] (no. 4): 129-140.

——. 1854 (ca. 20 Oct.) **[ref. 1818]**. Enumeration of the species of marine fishes, collected at San Francisco, California, by Dr. C. B. R. Kennerly, naturalist attached to the survey of the Pacific railroad route, under Lieut. A. W. Whipple. Proc. Acad. Nat. Sci. Phila. 1854 [v. 7] (no. 4): 141-142.

——. 1854 (ca. 20 Oct.) **[ref. 5769]**. Observations upon a collection of fishes made on the Pacific coast of the United States, by Lieut. W. P. Trowbridge, U. S. A., for the museum of the Smithsonian Institution. Proc. Acad. Nat. Sci. Phila. 1854 [v. 7] (no. 4): 142-156.

——. 1855 (ca. 13 Apr.) **[ref. 1819]**. Abstract of a report to Lieut. Jas. M. Gilliss, U. S. N., upon the fishes collected during the U. S. N. Astronomical Expedition to Chili. Proc. Acad. Nat. Sci. Phila. 1854 [v. 7] (no. 6): 197-199. [Soemtimes given as 1854.]

——. 1855 (ca. 15 June) **[ref. 1820]**. Notice upon the viviparous fishes inhabiting the Pacific coast of North America, with an enumeration of the species observed. Proc. Acad. Nat. Sci. Phila. 1854 [v. 7] (no. 8): 318-323. [Signature dated Feb. 1855. Also appeared as Arch. Naturgesch. v. 21: 342-354.]

——. 1855 **[ref. 4912]**. Contributions to the fauna of Chile. Report to Lieut. James M. Gilliss, U. S. N., upon the fishes collected by the U. S. Naval Astronomical Expedition to the southern hemisphere during the years 1849-50-51-52. Washington. 1858, 2 vols., 42 pls. Fishes in v. 2: 230-253, Pls. 29-34. [First published as a separate, pp. 1-58, that was possibly published earlier than 1855.]

——. 1856 (ca. 18 June) **[ref. 1809]**. Contributions to the ichthyology of the western coast of the United States, from specimens in the museum of the Smithsonian Institution. Proc. Acad. Nat. Sci. Phila. 1856 [v. 8] (no. 3): 131-137.

——. 1856 (late 1856) **[ref. 1810]**. Researches upon the cyprinoid fishes inhabiting the fresh waters of the United States of America, west of the Mississippi Valley, from specimens in the museum of the Smithsonian Institution. Proc. Acad. Nat. Sci. Phila. 1856 [v. 8] (no. 5): 165-213. [Separate also issued, probably late in 1856. Often cited as 1857.]

——. 1858 (about 1 May) **[ref. 1811]**. Notice upon new genera and new species of marine and fresh-water fishes from western North America. Proc. Acad. Nat. Sci. Phila. 1857 [v. 9] (no. 15): 200-202.

——. 1858 **[ref. 1813]**. Notes upon various new genera and new species of fishes, in the museum of the Smithsonian Institution, and collected in connection with the United States and Mexican boundary survey: Major William Emory, Commissioner. Proc. Acad. Nat. Sci. Phila. 1858 [v. 10] (sig. 12): 167-171. [Apparently published in late 1858.]

——. 1858 **[ref. 4911]**. Fishes of North America, observed on a survey for a railroad route from the Mississippi River to the Pacific Ocean. Washington. i-xiv + 1-400, 21 pls. [Also 1859 [ref. 1812] in U. S. Senate Misc. Doc. no. 78 (33rd. Congress, 2nd. Session): i-xiv + 1-400, 27 pls.]

——. 1859 (probably mid-1859) **[ref. 1821]**. Ichthyological notices. Proc. Acad. Nat. Sci. Phila. 1859 [v. 11] (sigs. 4, 8, 9): 56-68, 100-104, 113-122.

——. 1859 **[ref. 1812]**. Fishes. In: General report upon zoology of the several Pacific railroad routes, 1857. U. S. Senate Misc. Doc. No. 78 (33rd Congress, 2nd session). i-xiv + 1-400, 27 pls. [Also published separately (see Girard 1858 [ref. 4911]).]

Girgensohn, O. G. L. 1846 **[ref. 12458]**. Anatomie und physiologie des Fisch-nervensystems. Mem. Pres. Acad. Imp. Sci. St. Petersbourg Div. Sav. v. 5: 275-589, Pls. 1-15. [Not seen.]

Gistel, J. 1848 **[ref. 1822]**. Naturgeschichte des Thierreichs, für höhere Schulen. Stuttgart. I-XVI + 1-216, Pls. 1-32. [See also Jordan 1919 [ref. 2409].]

——. 1850 **[ref. 5020]**. [Title uncertain.] Isis (Munich) v. 5: 71. [Not seen.]

Glodek, G. S. 1976 (12 Mar.) **[ref. 7080]**. *Rhynchodoras woodsi*, a new catfish from eastern Ecuador (Siluriformes: Doradidae) with a redefinition of *Rhynchodoras*. Copeia 1976 (no. 1): 43-46.

Glodek, G. S., and H. J. Carter. 1978 (23 Feb.) **[ref. 6159]**. A new helogeneid catfish from eastern Ecuador (Pisces, Siluriformes, Helogeneidae). Fieldiana Zool. v. 72 (no. 6): 75-82.

Glodek, G. S., G. L. Whitmire and G. Orces V. 1976 (16 Nov.) **[ref. 7068]**. *Rhinodoras boehlkei*, a new catfish from eastern Ecuador (Osteichthyes, Siluroidei, Doradidae). Fieldiana Zool. v. 70 (no. 1): 1-11.

Glückman, L. S. 1964 **[ref. 1824]**. Akuly paleogena i ikh stratigraficheskoe znachenie. [The sharks of the Paleogene and their stratigraphical importance.] Izd. 'Nauka', Moskva, Leningrad 1-229, 31 pls. [Not seen.]

Glückman, L. S., S. M. Konovalov and O. A. Rassadnikov. 1973 **[ref. 1825]**. Direction of the evolutionary development of the chondrocranium of the Salmonidae genera *Salvelinus*, *Salmo* and *Oncorhynchus*. Dokl. Akad. Nauk SSSR v. 211 (no. 6): 1472-1474. [In Russian.]

Godkin, C. M., and R. Winterbottom. 1985 **[ref. 5233]**. Phylogeny of the family Congrogadidae (Pisces: Perciformes) and its placement as a subfamily of the Pseudochromidae. Bull. Mar. Sci. v. 36 (no. 3): 633-671.

Goeldi, E. A. 1905 **[ref. 6570]**. Nova zoologica aus der Amazonas-Region. Neue Wirbeltiere. C. R. 6. Congr. Internat. Zool. Berne 1905: 542-549.

Gohar, H. A. F., and F. M. Mazhar. 1964 **[ref. 1827]**. The elasmobranchs of the north-western Red Sea. Publ. Mar. Biol. Stn. Al Ghardaqa No. 13: 1-144, Pls. 1-16 + map.

Golani, D., and A. Ben-Tuvia. 1986 (30 Sept.) **[ref. 6757]**. New records of fishes from the Mediterranean coast of Israel including Red Sea immigrants. Cybium v. 10 (no. 3): 285-291.

Goldfuss, G. A. 1820 **[ref. 1829]**. Handbuch der Zoologie. Nürnberg. v. 3 (pt 2): i-xxiv + 1-510, Pls. 1-4.

Golvan, Y.-J. 1962 **[ref. 13459]**. Catalogue systématic des noms de genres de poissons actuels. Ann. Parasito. Hum. Comp. v. 37 (no. 6) suppl.: 1-227.

Gomes, A. L. 1947 (28 Nov.) **[ref. 1830]**. A small collection of fishes from Rio Grande do Sul, Brazil. Misc. Publ. Mus. Zool. Univ. Mich. No. 67: 1-39, 1-3.

Gomon, J. R. 1986 **[ref. 6286]**. Family No. 60: Plotosidae (p. 213). In: Smiths' Sea Fishes (Smith & Heemstra 1986 [ref. 5715]).

Gomon, J. R., and R. H. Gibbs, Jr. 1985 (14 June) **[ref. 5268]**. Taxonomy and distribution of the stomioid fish genus *Eustomias* (Melanostomiidae), II: *Biradiostomias*, new subgenus. Smithson. Contrib. Zool. No. 409: 1-58.

Gomon, J. R., and W. R. Taylor. 1982 **[ref. 8475]**. *Plotosus nkunga*, a new species of catfish from South Africa, with a redescription of *Plotosus limbatus* Valenciennes and key to the species of *Plotosus* (Siluriformes: Plotosidae). J. L. B. Smith Inst. Ichthyol. Spec. Publ. No. 22: 1-16.

Gomon, M. F. 1974 (22 Oct.) **[ref. 7103]**. A new eastern Pacific labrid (Pisces), *Decodon melasma*, a geminate species of the western Atlantic *D. puellaris*. Proc. Biol. Soc. Wash. v. 87 (no. 19): 205-216.

——. 1977 (24 Jan.) **[ref. 1831]**. A new genus and eastern Pacific species of Bodianine labrid fish. Proc. Biol. Soc. Wash. v. 89 (no. 54): 621-629.

——. 1979 **[ref. 5480]**. A revision of the labrid genus *Bodianus*, with an analysis of the relationships of other members of the tribe Hypsigenyini. Disseration, Univ. of Miami, 1979.

Gomon, M. F., and W. D. Madden. 1981 (1 Mar.) **[ref. 5482]**. Comments on the labrid fish subgenus *Bodianus* (*Trochocopus*) with a description of a new species from the Indian and Pacific oceans. Rev. Fr. Aquariol. v. 7 (no. 4): 121-126.

Gomon, M. F., and J. R. Paxton. 1986 (24 Feb.) **[ref. 5656]**. A review of the Odacidae, a temperate Australian-New Zealand labroid fish family. Indo-Pac. Fishes No. 8: 1-57, Color Pls. 1-6. [Date on Cover is October 1985, stamped inside is Feb. 24, 1986.]

Gomon, M. F., and J. E. Randall. 1978 **[ref. 5481]**. Review of the Hawaiian fishes of the labrid tribe Bodianini. Bull. Mar. Sci. v. 28 (no. 1): 32-48.

Gon, O. 1986 **[ref. 5657]**. Family No. 175: Apogonidae (pp. 546-561). In: Smiths' Sea Fishes (Smith & Heemstra 1986 [ref. 5715]).

——. 1987 (Aug.) **[ref. 6268]**. The fishes of the genus *Bathylagus* of the Southern Ocean. J. L. B. Smith Inst. Ichthyol. Spec. Publ. No. 43: 1-22.

——. 1987 (Mar.) **[ref. 6378]**. The cardinal fishes (Perciformes; Apogonidae) collected in the Maldive Islands during the Xarifa expedition (1957/58). J. L. B. Smith Inst. Ichthyol. Spec. Publ. No. 42: 1-18.

——. 1987 (10 Sept.) **[ref. 6706]**. Redescription of *Apogon (Ostorhinchus) fleurieu* (Lacepède, 1802) with notes on its synonymy. Jpn. J. Ichthyol. v. 34 (no. 2): 138-145.

——. 1987 (10 June) **[ref. 6709]**. *Apogon sphenurus* Klunzinger, 1884, a senior synonym of *Neamia octospina* Smith et Radcliffe, 1912. Jpn. J. Ichthyol. v. 34 (no. 1): 91-95.

Gon, O., and P. C. Heemstra. 1987 (30 June) **[ref. 6748]**. *Mendosoma lineatum* Guichenot 1848, first record in the Atlantic Ocean, with a re-evaluation of the taxonomic status of other species of the genus *Mendosoma* (Pisces, Latridae). Cybium v. 11 (no. 2): 183-193.

Goode, G. B. 1876 **[ref. 1832]**. Catalogue of the fishes of the Bermudas. Based chiefly upon the collection of the United States National Museum. Bull. U. S. Natl. Mus. No. 5: 1-82.

——. 1879 (about 19 Sept.) **[ref. 1836]**. A preliminary catalogue of the fishes of the St. Johns River and the east coast of Florida. Proc. U. S. Natl. Mus. v. 2 [no. 73]: 108-121.

——. 1880 (30 Dec.) **[ref. 1834]**. Descriptions of seven new species of fishes from deep soundings on the southern New England coast, with diagnoses of two undescribed genera of flounders and a genus related to *Merlucius*. Proc. U. S. Natl. Mus. v. 3 [no. 165]: 337-350.

——. 1881 (25 Feb.) **[ref. 1833]**. Fishes from the deep water on the south coast of New England obtained by the United States Fish Commission in the summer of 1880. Proc. U. S. Natl. Mus. v. 3 [no. 177]: 467-486.

——. 1883 (2 Aug.) **[ref. 1835]**. The generic names *Amitra* and *Thyris* replaced. Proc. U. S. Natl. Mus. v. 6 [no. 350]: 109.

——. 1886 **[ref. 12455]**. The beginnings of natural history in America. Proc. Biol. Soc. Wash. v. 3: 35-105.

Goode, G. B., and T. H. Bean. 1879 (12 Nov. - 17 Dec.) **[ref. 1837]**. Description of a new genus and species of fish, *Lopholatilus chamaeleonticeps*, from the south coast of New England. Proc. U. S. Natl. Mus. v. 2 [no. 77]: 205-209.

——. 1879 **[ref. 5605]**. A catalogue of the fishes of Essex County, Massachusetts, including the fauna of Massachusetts Bay and the contiguous deep waters. Bull. Essex Inst. v. 11: 1-38.

——. 1882 (13 Apr.) **[ref. 1839]**. *Benthodesmus*, a new genus of deep-sea fishes, allied to *Lepidopus*. Proc. U. S. Natl. Mus. v. 4 [no. 241]: 379-383.

——. 1882 (16 Sept. - 11 Nov.) **[ref. 1840]**. Descriptions of twenty-five new species of fish from the southern United States, and three new genera, *Letharchus*, *Ioglossus*, and *Chriodorus*. Proc. U. S. Natl. Mus. v. 5 [no. 297]: 412-437. [Pp. 412-416 published 16 Sept., 417-437 on 11 Nov.]

——. 1883 **[ref. 1838]**. Reports on the results of dredging under the supervision of Alexander Agassiz, on the east coast of the United States, during the summer of 1880, by the U. S. coast survey steamer "Blake," Commander J. R. Bartlett, U. S. N., commanding. Bull. Mus. Comp. Zool. v. 10 (no. 5): 183-226. [Often wrongly cited as 1882.]

——. 1885 (29 June) **[ref. 1841]**. On the American fishes in the Linnaean collection. Proc. U. S. Natl. Mus. v. 8 [no. 510]: 193-208.

——. 1885 (21 Nov.) **[ref. 1842]**. Description of new fishes obtained by the United States Fish Commission mainly from deep water off the Atlantic and Gulf coasts. Proc. U. S. Natl. Mus. v. 8 [no. 543]: 589-605. [Also as separate, Washington (1886).]

——. 1885 (10 Apr. 1884) **[ref. 1843]**. Description of a new genus and species of Pediculate fishes (*Halieutella lappa*). Proc. Biol. Soc. Wash. v. 2: 88. [Separates of adjoining papers published 10 Apr. 1884.]

——. 1886 (July) **[ref. 1844]**. Reports on the results of dredging ... in the Gulf of Mexico (1877-78) and in the Caribbean Sea (1879-80), by the U.S. Coast survey steamer "Blake," ... XXVIII.—Description of thirteen species and two new genera of fishes form the "Blake" collection. Bull. Mus. Comp. Zool. v. 12 (no. 5): 153-170.

——. 1895 (26 Jan.) **[ref. 1846]**. On *Harriotta*, a new type of chimaeroid fish from the deeper waters of the northwestern Atlantic. Scientific results of exploration by the U. S. Fish Commission Steamer "Albatross." No. XXX. Proc. U. S. Natl. Mus. v. 17 (no. 1014): 471-473, Pl. 19.

——. 1895 (26 Jan.) **[ref. 1847]**. A revision of the order Heteromi, deep-sea fishes, with a description of the new generic types *Macdonaldia* and *Lipogenys*. Scientific results of explorations by the U. S. Fish Commission steamer "Albatross." No. XXIX. Proc. U. S. Natl. Mus. v. 17 (no. 1013): 455-470, Pl. 18.

——. 1895 (26 Jan.) **[ref. 5767]**. On Cetomimidae and Rondeletiidae, two new families of bathybial fishes from the northwestern Atlantic. Scientific results of explorations by the U. S. Fish Commission steamer "Albatross." No. XXVIII. Proc. U. S. Natl. Mus. v. 17 (no. 1012): 451-454, Pl. 17.

——. 1896 (23 Aug.) **[ref. 1848]**. Oceanic Ichthyology, a treatise on the deep-sea and pelagic fishes of the world, based chiefly upon the collections made by the steamers Blake, Albatross, and Fish Hawk in the northwestern Atlantic, with an atlas containing 417 figures. Spec. Bull. U. S. Nat. Mus. No. 2: Text: i-xxxv + 1-26 + 1-553, Atlas: i-xxiii, 1-26, 123 pls. [Also Mem. Mus. Comp. Zool. Harv. Coll. v. 22. Date from Jordan & Evermann 1898:2843 [ref. 2445], Cohen 1963 [ref. 6883].]

GOODYEAR, R. H. 1973 **[ref. 7176]**. Malacosteidae (pp. 142-143). In: Hureau & Monod 1973 [ref. 6590].

GOODYEAR, R. H., AND R. H. GIBBS, JR. 1986 **[ref. 5658]**. Family No. 71: Malacosteidae (pp. 235-236). In: Smiths' Sea Fishes (Smith & Heemstra 1986 [ref. 5715]).

GOREN, M. 1978 (19 Oct.) **[ref. 1851]**. A new gobiid genus and seven new species from Sinai coasts (Pisces: Gobiidae). Senckenb. Biol. v. 59 (no. 3/4): 191-203.

——. 1979 (15 Aug.) **[ref. 1852]**. The Gobiinae of the Red Sea (Pisces: Gobiidae). Senckenb. Biol. v. 60 (no. 1-2): 13-64.

——. 1979 **[ref. 6902]**. Red Sea fishes assigned to the genus *Calliogobius* Bleeker with a description of a new species (Teleostei: Gobiidae). Isr. J. Zool. v. 28: 209-217.

——. 1979 **[ref. 6952]**. A new gobioid species *Coryogalops sufensis* from the Red Sea (Pisces, Gobiidae). Cybium (Ser. 3) No. 6: 91-95.

——. 1984 (15 Nov.) **[ref. 5178]**. A new species of *Oplopomops* Smith 1959 from Elat, northern Red Sea (Pisces: Gobiidae). Senckenb. Biol. v. 65 (no. 1/2): 19-23.

——. 1985 (11 Apr.) **[ref. 5179]**. A review of the gobiid fish genus *Monishia* Smith, 1949, from the western Indian Ocean and Red Sea, with description of a new species. Contrib. Sci. (Los Ang.) No. 360: 1-9.

——. 1987 **[ref. 6611]**. *Kraeneria nudum* (Regan) — first record of the family Kraemeriidae in the Red Sea. Isr. J. Zool. v. 34 (1986/87): 149-153.

——. 1988 **[ref. 6612]**. Redescription of *Bathygobius albopunctatus* (Valenciennes, 1837) and a note on its distribution. Cybium v. 12 (no. 1): 37-43.

GOREN, M., L. FISHELSON AND E. TREWAVAS. 1973 (7 Mar.) **[ref. 1853]**. The cyprinid fishes of *Acanthobrama* Heckel and related genera. Bull. Br. Mus. (Nat. Hist.) Zool. v. 24 (no. 6): 293-315.

GOREN, M., AND I. KARPLUS. 1980 (4 Mar.) **[ref. 6903]**. *Fowleria abocellata*, a new cardinal fish from the Gulf of Elat — Red Sea (Pisces, Apogonidae). Zool. Meded. v. 55 (no. 20): 231-234, Pl. 1.

GOSLINE, W. A. 1940 (23 Dec.) **[ref. 6489]**. A revision of the neotropical catfishes of the family Callichthyidae. Stanford Ichthyol. Bull. v. 2 (no. 1): 1-11.

——. 1945 (10 Mar.) **[ref. 13558]**. Catálogo dos nematognatos de ágya-doce da América do sul e central. Bol. Mus. Nac., n. s. Zool. No. 33: 1-138.

——. 1947 (16 Oct.) **[ref. 1857]**. Contributions to the classification of the loricariid catfishes. Arq. Mus. Nac. Rio de J. v. 41: 79-134, Pls. 1-9. [Distribution date given as 16 Oct. 1947.]

——. 1951 (Oct.) **[ref. 1858]**. The osteology and classification of the ophichthid eels of the Hawaiian Islands. Pac. Sci. v. 5: 298-320.

——. 1953 (27 Nov.) **[ref. 1859]**. Hawaiian shallow-water fishes of the family Brotulidae, with the description of a new genus and notes on brotulid anatomy. Copeia 1953 (no. 4): 215-225.

——. 1954 (Jan.) **[ref. 1860]**. Fishes killed by the 1950 eruption of Mauna Loa. II. Brotulidae. Pac. Sci. v. 8 (no. 1): 68-83.

——. 1959 (1 Jan.) **[ref. 1861]**. Four new species, a new genus, and a new suborder of Hawaiian fishes. Pac. Sci. v. 13 (no. 1): 67-77.

——. 1985 (20 Feb.) **[ref. 5283]**. Relationships among some relatively deep-bodied percoid fish groups. Jpn. J. Ichthyol. v. 31 (no. 4): 351-357.

GOSSE, J.-P. 1975 **[ref. 7029]**. Révision du genre *Geophagus* (Pisces Cichlidae). Acad. R. Sci. Outre-Mer, Cl. Sci. Nat. Méd. (n. s.) v. 19 (no. 3): 1-173, Pls. 1-5.

——. 1984 (Feb.) **[ref. 6169]**. Protopteridae (pp. 8-17), Polypteridae (pp. 18-29), Pantodontidae (pp. 59-60), Mormyridae (pp. 63-122), Gymnarchidae (pp. 123-124). In: Daget et al. 1984 [ref. 6168].

——. 1986 (Apr.) **[ref. 6194]**. Malapteruridae (pp. 102-104), Mochokidae (pp. 105-152), Anabantidae (pp. 402-414). In: Daget et al. 1986 [ref. 6189].

——. 1988 (30 Sept.) **[ref. 6868]**. Révision systématique de deux espèces du genre *Polypterus* (Pisces, Polypteridae). Cybium v. 12 (no. 3): 239-245.

GOSZTONYI, A. E. 1977 (Mar.) **[ref. 6103]**. Results of the research cruises FRV "Walther Herwig" to South America. XLVIII. Revision of the South American Zoarcidae (Osteichthyes, Blennioidei) with the description of three new genera and five new species. Arch. FischereiWiss. v. 27 (no. 3): 191-249.

GOTTSCHE, C. M. 1835 **[ref. 1862]**. Die seeländischen Pleuronectes-Arten. Arch. Naturgeschichte v. 2: 133-185.

GOÜAN, A. 1770 **[ref. 1863]**. Historia piscium, sistens ipsorum anatomen externam, internam, atque genera in classes et ordines redacta. Also: Histoire des poissons, contenant la déscription anatomique de leurs parties externes et internes, & le caractère des divers genres rangés par classes & par ordres. Strasbourg. i-xviii + 1-252 (twice), Pls. 1-4. [Text in Latin and French, on opposite pages with same page number.]

GOULD, S. J. 1990 (Feb.) **[ref. 14276]**. Bully for *Brontosaurus*. Nat. Hist. Feb. 1990: 16-24. [Also reproducted in Bull. Zool. Nomencl. June 1990, v. 47 (no. 2):88-96.]

GOURÈNE, G., AND G. G. TEUGELS. 1988 (30 Dec.) **[ref. 12839]**. A new species of herring-like fish *Microthrissa* (Pisces, Clupeidae, Pellonulinae) from the Zaire basin, Central Africa. Cybium v. 12 (no. 4): 357-363.

GRACIANOV, V. 1902 **[ref. 1868]**. Die Ichthyo-fauna des Baikalsees. Dnevn. Zool. Otd. Obsc. Liub. Jest. Moskva v. 3 (no. 3): 18-61. [In Russian.]

———. 1906 (17 July) **[ref. 1869]**. Über eine besondere Gruppe der Rochen. Zool. Anz. v. 30 (no. 13/14): 399-406.

———. 1906 **[ref. 1870]**. Die Neunaugen des russischen Reiches. Dnevn. Zool. Otd. Obsc. Liub. Jest. Moskva v. 3 (no. 7-8): 18. [Not seen. Text in Russian. Dated December 1906; perhaps published in 1907 (date used by Fowler, MS).]

———. 1907 **[ref. 1871]**. [A synoptic essay of the taxonomy and geography of the fishes of the Russian Empire.] Trudy Otdela Ichtiol. Russ. Obsc. Akklimat. Zhiv. Moskva. v. 4: i-xxx + 1-567. [Not seen. Text in Russian. Author's name also spelled Gratsianov and Gratzianov.]

———. 1907 **[ref. 1872]**. Übersicht de Süsswassercottiden des russischen Reiches. Zool. Anz. v. 31: 654-660.

GRANDE, L. 1985 (29 Oct.) **[ref. 6466]**. Recent and fossil clupeomorph fishes with materials for revision of the subgroups of clupeoids. Bull. Am. Mus. Nat. Hist. v. 181 (art. 2): 231-372.

GRANDE, L., AND J. T. EASTMAN. 1986 **[ref. 6054]**. A review of Antarctic ichthyofaunas in the light of new fossil discoveries. Palaeontol. (Lond.) v. 29 (pt 1): 113-137.

GRAS, R. 1961 (30 Jan.) **[ref. 1876]**. Contribution a l'étude des poissons du Bas-Dahomey. Description de quatre espèces nouvelles. Bull. Mus. Natl. Hist. Nat. (Ser. 2) v. 32 (no. 5): 401-410.

GRASSI, G. B., AND S. CALANDRUCCIO. 1896 **[ref. 1877]**. Sullo sviluppo dei murenoidi. Accad. Nazionale Lincei, Cl. Sci. Fisiche, Matemat. Natur. v. 5 (no. 1): 348-349.

GRAY, J. E. 1830-35 **[ref. 1878]**. Illustrations of Indian zoology; chiefly selected from the collection of Major-General Hardwicke. 20 parts in 2 vols. Pls. 1-202. [For dates of parts see Sawyer 1953 [ref. 6842].]

———. 1831 **[ref. 1879]**. Description of twelve new genera of fish, discovered by Gen. Hardwicke, in India, the greater part in the British Museum. Zool. Misc. 1831: 7-10.

———. 1831 **[ref. 1880]**. Description of three new species of fish, including two undescribed genera discovered by John Reeves, Esq., in China. Zool. Misc. 1831 (art. 6): 4-5.

———. 1831 **[ref. 1881]**. Description of a new genus of percoid fish, discovered by Samuel Stutchbury, in the Pacific sea, and now in the British Museum. Zool. Misc. 1831: 20.

———. 1838 (Apr.) **[ref. 1884]**. Notes on the fish. [Remarks accompanying: Notices accompanying a collection of quadrupeds and fishes from Van Diemen's Land. With Notes and descriptions of the new species.] Ann. Mag. Nat. Hist. (n. s.) v. 1 (no. 2): 109-111.

———. 1851 (25 July) **[ref. 4939]**. List of the specimens of fish in the collection of the British Museum. Part I.—Chondropterygii. London. i-x + 1-160, Pls. 1-2.

———. 1853 (26 July) **[ref. 1886]**. Description of a new form of lamprey from Australia, with a synopsis of the family. Proc. Zool. Soc. Lond. Part 19 (1851): 235-241, Pls. 4-5. [Published in volume for 1851 but actual date 26 July 1853. Also in Ann. Mag. Nat. Hist. (Ser. 2) v. 13 (1854):58-65]

———. 1854 **[ref. 1911]**. Catalogue of fish collected and described by Laurence Theodore Gronow, now in the British Museum. London. i-vii + 1-196.

———. 1859 (Feb.-June) **[ref. 1887]**. Description of a new genus of lophobranchiate fishes from Western Australia. Proc. Zool. Soc. Lond. 1859 (pt 1): 38-39. [Also in Ann. Mag. Nat. Hist. (Ser. 3) v. 4: 309-311, 1 pl.]

———. 1864 (Nov.) **[ref. 1888]**. Notice of a portion of new form of animal (*Myriosteon higginsi*) probably indicating a new group of echinodermata. Proc. Zool. Soc. Lond. 1864 (pt 2): 163-166.

GREELEY, A. W. 1901 **[ref. 1889]**. Notes on the tide-pool fishes of California, with a description of four new species. Bull. U. S. Fish Comm. v. 19 [1899]: 7-20.

GREENFIELD, D. W. 1966 **[ref. 1890]**. Systematics and zoogeography of *Myripristis* Cuvier (Pisces: Holocentridae). Diss. Abstr. Int. B Sci. Eng. v. 27: 2185. [Also as authorized facsimili, Univ. Microfilms Intl., 1985. 218 pp.]

———. 1974 (30 June) **[ref. 7142]**. A revision of the squirrelfish genus *Myripristis* Cuvier (Pisces: Holocentridae). Nat. Hist. Mus. Los Ang. Cty. Sci. Bull. No. 19: 1-54.

———. 1979 (28 Feb.) **[ref. 7013]**. A review of the western Atlantic *Starksia ocellata*-complex (Pisces: Clinidae) with the description of two new species and proposal of superspecies status. Fieldiana Zool. v. 73 (no. 2): 9-48.

———. 1981 (15 May) **[ref. 6826]**. *Varicus imswe*, a new species of gobiid fish from Belize. Copeia 1981 (no. 2): 269-272.

———. 1988 (18 May) **[ref. 6413]**. A review of the *Lythrypnus mowbrayi* complex (Pisces: Gobiidae), with the description of a new species. Copeia 1988 (no. 2): 460-469.

———. 1989 (23 May) **[ref. 12545]**. *Priolepis dawsoni* n. sp. (Pisces: Gobiidae), a third Atlantic species of *Priolepis*. Copeia 1989 (no. 2): 397-401.

GREENFIELD, D. W., AND G. S. GLODEK. 1977 (19 Dec.) **[ref. 7054]**. *Trachelyichthys exilis*, a new species of catfish (Pisces: Auchenipteridae) from Peru. Fieldiana Zool. v. 72 (no. 3): 47-58.

GREENFIELD, D. W., AND T. GREENFIELD. 1973 (28 Aug.) **[ref. 7128]**. *Triathalassothia gloverensis*, a new species of toadfish from Belize (= British Honduras) with remarks on the genus. Copeia 1973 (no. 3): 560-565.

GREENFIELD, D. W., AND R. K. JOHNSON. 1981 (5 Oct.) **[ref. 5580]**. The blennioid fishes of Belize and Honduras, Central America, with comments on their systematics, ecology, and distribution (Blenniidae, Chaenopsidae, Labrisomidae, Tripterygiidae). Fieldiana Zool. (n. s.) No. 8: i-viii + 1-106.

GREENFIELD, D. W., AND L. P. WOODS. 1980 (5 Dec.) **[ref. 5581]**. Review of the deep-bodied species of *Chromis* (Pisces: Pomacentridae) from the eastern Pacific, with descriptions of three new species. Copeia 1980 (no. 4): 626-641.

GREENWOOD, P. H. 1954 (June) **[ref. 1893]**. On two species of cichlid fishes from the Malagarazi River (Tanganyika), with notes on the pharyngeal apophysis in species of the *Haplochromis* group. Ann. Mag. Nat. Hist. (Ser. 12) v. 7 (no. 78): 401-414.

———. 1956 (Feb.) **[ref. 1894]**. The monotypic genera of cichlid fishes in Lake Victoria. Bull. Br. Mus. (Nat. Hist.) Zool. v. 3 (no. 7): 295-333.

———. 1958 (12 Nov.) **[ref. 1895]**. A new genus and species of cat-fish (Pisces, Clariidae) from the deeper waters of Lake Victoria. Ann. Mag. Nat. Hist. (Ser. 13) v. 1 (no. 5): 321-325.

———. 1963 (Dec.) **[ref. 1897]**. The swimbladder in African Notopteridae (Pisces) and its bearing on the taxonomy of the family. Bull. Br. Mus. (Nat. Hist.) Zool. v. 11 (no. 5): 377-412, Pls. 1-4.

———. 1965 (27 Apr.) **[ref. 5765]**. The status of *Acanthothrissa* Gras, 1961 (Pisces, Clupeidae). Ann. Mag. Nat. Hist. (Ser. 13) v. 7 (no. 78): 337-338.

———. 1976 **[ref. 14198]**. A review of the family Centropomidae (Pisces, Perciformes). Bull. Br. Mus. (Nat. Hist.) Zool. v. 29 (no. 1): 1-81.

———. 1979 **[ref. 1898]**. Towards a phyletic classification of the 'genus' *Haplochromis* (Pisces, Cichlidae) and related taxa. Part 1. Bull. Br. Mus. (Nat. Hist.) Zool. v. 35 (no. 4): 265-322.

———. 1980 (30 Oct.) **[ref. 1899]**. Towards a phyletic classification of the 'genus' *Haplochromis* (Pisces, Cichlidae) and related taxa. Part 2; the species from lakes Victoria, Nabugabo, Edward, George and Kivu. Bull. Br. Mus. (Nat. Hist.) Zool. v. 39 (no. 1): 1-101.

———. 1983 (25 Aug.) **[ref. 5364]**. On *Macropleurodus*, *Chilotilapia* (Teleostei, Cichlidae), and the interrelationships of African cichlid species flocks. Bull. Br. Mus. (Nat. Hist.) Zool. v. 45 (no. 4): 209-231.

———. 1984 (27 Sept.) **[ref. 5311]**. The haplochromine species

(Teleostei, Cichlidae) of the Cunene and certain other Angolan rivers. Bull. Br. Mus. (Nat. Hist.) Zool. v. 47 (no. 4): 187-239.

———. 1985 (19 Dec.) **[ref. 4951]**. The generic status and affinities of *Paratilapia thomasi* Blgr 1915 (Teleostei, Cichlidae). Bull. Br. Mus. (Nat. Hist.) Zool. v. 49 (no. 2): 257-272.

———. 1987 (26 Nov.) **[ref. 6166]**. The genera of pelmatochromine fishes (Teleostei, Cichlidae). A phylogenetic review. Bull. Br. Mus. (Nat. Hist.) Zool. v. 53 (no. 3): 139-203.

———. 1989 (Sept.) **[ref. 14120]**. The taxonomic status and phylogenetic relationships of *Pseudocrenilabrus* Fowler (Teleostei, Cichlidae). Ichthyol. Bull. J. L. B. Smith Inst. Ichthyol. No. 54: 1-16.

Greenwood, P. H., and R. A. Jubb. 1967 (10 Mar.) **[ref. 1901]**. The generic identity of *Labeo quathlambae* Barnard (Pisces, Cyprinidae). Ann. Cape Prov. Mus. Nat. Hist. v. 6 (pt 2): 17-37.

Grey, M. 1959 (July) **[ref. 1904]**. Three new genera and one new species of the family Gonostomatidae. Bull. Mus. Comp. Zool. v. 121 (no. 4): 167-184.

———. 1961 (July) **[ref. 1905]**. Fishes killed by the 1950 eruption of Mauna Loa. Part V. Gonostomatidae. Pac. Sci. v. 15 (no. 3): 462-476.

Grey, Z. 1928 **[ref. 6540]**. Big game fishing in New Zealand seas. Nat. Hist. v. 28 (no. 1): 46-52.

Griffin, L. T. 1933 (28 Feb.) **[ref. 1906]**. Descriptions of New Zealand fishes. Trans. Proc. N. Z. Inst. v. 63 (pt 2): 171-177, Pls. 24-25.

———. 1936 (June) **[ref. 1907]**. Revision of the eels of New Zealand. Trans. Proc. R. Soc. N. Z. v. 66 (pt 1): 12-26, Pls. 5-6.

Griffith, E. 1834 **[ref. 1908]**. The class Pisces, arranged by the Baron Cuvier, with supplementary additions, by Edward Griffith, F.R.S., &c. and Lieut.-Col. Charles Hamilton Smith, F.R., L.S.S., &c. &c. London. 1-680, Pls. 1-62 + 3. [Published as vol. X of Cuvier's Animal Kingdom. London, 1827-35. Griffith perhaps responsible only for portions.]

Gronow, L. T. 1760 **[ref. 13466]**. Animalium in Belgio habitantium centuria prima. Acta Helvetica v. 4: 243-270. [Not checked.]

———. 1763 **[ref. 1910]**. Zoophylacii Gronoviani fasciculus primus exhibens animalia quadrupeda, amphibia atque pisces, quae in museo suo adservat, rite examinavit, systematice disposuit, descripsit atque iconibus illustravit Laur. Theod. Gronovius, J.U.D... Lugduni Batavorum. 1-136, 14 pls. [See Wheeler 1958 [ref. 13434].]

———. 1772 **[ref. 12602]**. Animalium rariorum fasciculus. Pisces. Acta Helvetica v. 7: 43-52, Pls. 2-3. [Not seen.]

———. 1854. See Gray, J. T. 1854.

Gudger, E. W. 1924 (28 July) **[ref. 5927]**. The sources of the material for Hamilton-Buchanan's fishes of the Ganges, the fate of his collections, drawings and notes, and the use made of his data. J. Proc. Asiatic Soc. Bengal (n. s.) v. 29 (no. 4): 121-136.

Guichenot, A. 1847 **[ref. 1937]**. Notice sur un nouveau genre de Percoïdes, voisin des *Centrarchus*, des *Pomotis* et des *Bryttes*. Rev. Zool. v. 10: 390-394.

———. 1848 **[ref. 1938]**. Notice sur l'établissement d'un nouveau genre de Chétodons. Rev. Zool. v. 11 [1848]: 12-14.

———. 1848 **[ref. 1939]**. Fauna Chilena. Pisces. Pp. 137-370. In: C. Gay, Historia fisica y politica de Chile. Zoologia. Tomo segundo. Paris & Santiago.

———. 1850 **[ref. 1940]**. Histoire naturelle des reptiles et poissons. Pp. i-iv + 31-138, Pls. 1-8. In: Exploration scientique de l'Algérie. Paris. Vol. 3. Zoologie.

———. 1860 **[ref. 1941]**. Notice sur un nouveau Poisson du genre des *Trichomyctères*. Rev. Mag. Zool. (Ser. 2) v. 12 (no. 12): 525-527.

———. 1860 **[ref. 1942]**. Notice sur un nouveau poisson du groupe des *Cténolabres*. Rev. Mag. Zool. (Ser. 2) v. 12 (no. 4): 152-154.

———. 1864 **[ref. 1943]**. Fauna ichthiologique. Annexe C. Pp. C1-C32. In: L. Maillard, Notes sur l'ile de la Réunion (Bourbon). Paris. Tome II.

———. 1866 **[ref. 1944]**. Ichthyologie. I. Le Trigle Polyommate, nouveau genre de poissons de la famille des Trigloïdes. Ann. Soc. Linn. Maine-et-Loire v. 9: 1-4. [Original not seen, date may be 1867, pages may differ from separate examined.]

———. 1866 **[ref. 1945]**. Ichthyologie. II. Le Zancle Centrognathe, nouveau genre de Chétodons. Ann. Soc. Linn. Maine-et-Loire v. 9: 4-7. [Original not seen, pp. 4-7 in separate examined; date may be 1867.]

———. 1866 **[ref. 1947]**. Notice sur un nouveau genre de la famille des Cottoides, du muséum de Paris. Mem. Soc. Imp. Sci. Nat. Cherbourg v. 12 (Ser. 2, v. 2): 253-256, Pl. 9.

———. 1867 **[ref. 1946]**. Ichthyologie. III. L'Argentine *Léioglosse*, nouveau genre de Salmonoïdes. Ann. Soc. Linn. Maine-et-Loire v. 9: 7-9. [Original not seen, pp. 7-9 in separate examined; date may be 1866.]

———. 1867 **[ref. 1948]**. Notice sur le *Lophiopside*, nouveau genre de poisson de la famille de Lophioides, et description de l'espèce type. Mem. Soc. Sci. Nat. Cherbourg v. 13: 101-106. [Also as separate, pp. 19-24. Date may be 1868.]

———. 1867 **[ref. 1949]**. Notice sur le *Néosébaste*, nouveau genre de poissons de la famille des Scorpènoides, et description d'une nouvelle espèce. Mem. Soc. Sci. Nat. Cherbourg v. 13: 83-89. [Also as separate, pp. 1-7. Date may be 1868.]

———. 1867 **[ref. 1950]**. Notice sur le *Sériolophe*, nouveau genre de poissons de la famille des Scombéroides, et description d'une nouvelle espèce. Mem. Soc. Sci. Nat. Cherbourg v. 13: 90-95. [Also as separate, pp. 8-13. Date may be 1868.]

———. 1867 **[ref. 1951]**. Notice sur le *Salarichthys*, nouveau genre de poissons de la famille des Blennoides, et description de l'espèce type. Mem. Soc. Sci. Nat. Cherbourg v. 13: 96-100. [Also as separate, pp. 14-18. Date may be 1868.]

———. 1868 **[ref. 1936]**. Index generum ac specierum Anthiadidorum hucusque in Museo Parisiensi observatorum. Ann. Soc. Linn. Maine-et-Loire v. 10: 80-87.

———. 1869 **[ref. 1952]**. Notice sur quelques poissons inédits de Madagascar et de la Chine. Nouv. Arch. Mus. Natl. Hist. Nat. Paris v. 5 (fasc. 3): 193-206, Pl. 12.

Guimarães, A. R. P. 1882 **[ref. 1953]**. Description d'un nouveau poisson du Portugal. J. Acad. Sci. Lisboa v. 8 (no. 31): 222-224. [Dated Dec. 1881 but apparently published in 1882.]

Guitart, D. J. 1972 (4 July) **[ref. 1954]**. Un nuevo género y especie de tiburón de la familia Triakidae. Poeyana, Inst. Zool. Acad. Sci. Cuba No. 99: 1-4.

Güldenstädt, A. J. von. 1772 **[ref. 5066]**. [Title not examined.] Novi Comment. Acad. Sci. Imp. Petropol. [Only pp. 533-534 examined.]

———. 1774 **[ref. 1955]**. *Acerina*; piscis, ad Percae genus pertinens, descriptus. Novi Comment. Acad. Sci. Imp. Petropol. v. 19: 455-462, Pl. 11. [Plate not examined.]

Gulia, G. 1861 **[ref. 1956]**. Tentamen ichthyologiae Melitensis sistens methodo naturali stirpium objectis nonnullis observationibus genera ac species, a recentioribus de re zoologica scriptoribus admissas piscium insularum Melitae. [Includes: Discorso sulla ittiologia di Malta.] Melitae: 1-71 + i-iv + 2 pp. Errata. [In Latin (pp. 1-32) and Italian; also apparently in Maltese as Catalogu tal hut ta Malta [not seen].]

Gunner [Gunnerus], J. E. 1765 **[ref. 1958]**. Efterretning om Berglaxen, en rar Norsk fisk, som kunde kaldes: *Coryphaenoides rupestris*. Trontheim Gesell. Schrift. v. 3: 50-58, Pl. 3.

Günther, A. 1859 (10 Dec.) **[ref. 1961]**. Catalogue of the fishes in the British Museum. Catalogue of the acanthopterygian fishes in the collection of the British Museum. Gasterosteidae, Berycidae, Percidae, Aphredoderidae, Pristipomatidae, Mullidae, Sparidae. v. 1: i-xxxi + 1-524.

———. 1859 **[ref. 1962]**. On the reptiles and fishes collected by the Rev. H. B. Tristram in northern Africa. Proc. Zool. Soc. Lond. 1859 (pt 3): 469-474, Pl. 9. [Dated by Duncan 1937 [ref. 13606] as issued between Oct. 1859 and Feb. 1860.]

———. 1860 (13 Oct.) **[ref. 1963]**. Catalogue of the fishes in the British Museum. Catalogue of the acanthopterygian fishes.

Squamipinnes, Cirrhitidae, Triglidae, Trachinidae, Sciaenidae, Polynemidae, Sphyraenidae, Trichiuridae, Scombridae, Carangidae, Xiphiidae. v. 2: i-xxi + 1-548.

——. 1861 (14 Dec.) **[ref. 1964]**. Catalogue of the fishes in the British Museum. Catalogue of the acanthopterygian fishes in the collection of the British Museum. Gobiidae ...[thru]... Notacanthi. v. 3: i-xxv + 1-586 + i-x.

——. 1861 (June) **[ref. 1965]**. On a new genus of Australian freshwater fishes. Ann. Mag. Nat. Hist. (Ser. 3) v. 7 (no. 42): 490-491. [Also earlier as Proc. Zool. Soc. London 1861: 116-117 [ref. 5749].]

——. 1861 (Feb.) **[ref. 1966]**. On three new trachinoid fishes. Ann. Mag. Nat. Hist. (Ser. 3) v. 7 (no. 38): 85-90, Pl. 10.

——. 1861 (Nov.) **[ref. 1967]**. A preliminary synopsis of the labroid genera. Ann. Mag. Nat. Hist. (Ser. 3) v. 8 (no. 47): 382-389.

——. 1861 **[ref. 1968]**. On a collection of fishes sent by Capt. Dow from the Pacific Coast of Central America. Proc. Zool. Soc. Lond. 1861 (pt 3): 370-376. [Also in Ann. Mag. Nat. Hist. (Ser. 3) v. 9: 326-331.]

——. 1861 (1 May) **[ref. 5749]**. On a new genus of Australian freshwater fishes. Proc. Zool. Soc. Lond. 1861 (pt 1): 116-117, Pl. 19.

——. 1862 (8 Nov.) **[ref. 1969]**. Catalogue of the fishes in the British Museum. Catalogue of the Acanthopterygii Pharyngognathi and Anacanthini in the collection of the British Muesum. v. 4: i-xxi + 1-534.

——. 1862 (Sept.) **[ref. 1970]**. Descriptions of new species of reptiles and fishes in the collection of the British Museum. Proc. Zool. Soc. Lond. 1862 (pt 2): 188-194, Pls. 25-27. [Also in Ann. Mag. Nat. Hist. (Ser. 3) v. 11: 134-140.]

——. 1862 (Dec.) **[ref. 1971]**. Note on *Pleuronectes sinensis* Lacép. Ann. Mag. Nat. Hist. (Ser. 3) v. 10 (no. 60): 475.

——. 1863 (Feb.) **[ref. 1972]**. On new species of fishes from Victoria, South Australia. Ann. Mag. Nat. Hist. (Ser. 3) v. 11 (no. 62): 114-117.

——. 1863 (Dec.) **[ref. 1973]**. On new species of fishes from the Essequibo. Ann. Mag. Nat. Hist. (Ser. 3) v. 12 (no. 72): 441-443.

——. 1864 (10 Dec.) **[ref. 1974]**. Catalogue of the fishes in the British Museum. Catalogue of the Physostomi, containing the families Siluridae, Characinidae, Haplochitonidae, Sternoptychidae, Scopelidae, Stomiatidae in the collection of the British Museum. v. 5: i-xxii + 1-455.

——. 1864 (Sept.) **[ref. 1976]**. On some new species of Central-American fishes. Ann. Mag. Nat. Hist. (Ser. 3) v. 14 (no. 81): 227-232. [Appeared earlier in Günther 1864: 23-27 [ref. 5752].]

——. 1864 (Sept.) **[ref. 1978]**. On a new generic type of fishes discovered by the late Dr. Leichardt in Queensland. Ann. Mag. Nat. Hist. (Ser. 3) v. 14 (no. 81): 195-197, Pl. 7.

——. 1864 (Nov.) **[ref. 1979]**. Report on a collection of reptiles and fishes made by Dr. Kirk in the Zambesi and Nyassa regions. Proc. Zool. Soc. Lond. 1864 (pt 2): 303-314, Pls. 26-27.

——. 1864 (Nov.) **[ref. 5750]**. On a new genus of pediculate fish from the Sea of Madeira. Proc. Zool. Soc. Lond. 1864 (pt 2): 301-303, Pl. 25. [Also in Günther 1865: 332-334 [ref. 1977].]

——. 1864 (July) **[ref. 5752]**. On some new species of Central-American fishes. Proc. Zool. Soc. Lond. 1864 (pt 1): 23-27, Pls. 3-4. [Also as Günther 1864 (Sept.): 227-232 [ref. 1976].]

——. 1865 (Mar.) **[ref. 1977]**. On a new genus of pediculate fish from the Sea of Madeira. Ann. Mag. Nat. Hist. (Ser. 3) v. 15 (no. 88): 332-334. [Appeared earlier in Günther 1864: 301-303 [ref. 5750].]

——. 1865 **[ref. 1980]**. Pisces. Zool. Record for 1864: 133-188.

——. 1865 (Mar.) **[ref. 1981]**. Description of a new characinoid genus of fish from West Africa. Ann. Mag. Nat. Hist. (Ser. 3) v. 15 (no. 87): 209-210, Pl. 5.

——. 1866 (13 Oct.) **[ref. 1983]**. Catalogue of fishes in the British Museum. Catalogue of the Physostomi, containing the families Salmonidae, Percopsidae, Galaxidae, Mormyridae, Gymnarchidae, Esocidae, Umbridae, Scombresocidae, Cyprinodontidae, in the collection of the British Museum. v. 6: i-xv + 1-368.

——. 1867 (Apr.) **[ref. 1984]**. On the fishes of the states of Central America, founded upon specimens collected in fresh and marine waters of various parts of that country by Messrs. Salvin, Godman and Capt. J. M. Dow. Proc. Zool. Soc. Lond. 1866 (pt 3): 600-604.

——. 1867 (Mar.) **[ref. 1985]**. On the identity of *Alepisaurus* (Lowe) with *Plagyodus* (Steller). Ann. Mag. Nat. Hist. (Ser. 3) v. 19 (no. 111): 185-187.

——. 1867 (May) **[ref. 1986]**. Description of some new or little-known species of fishes in the collection of the British Museum. Proc. Zool. Soc. Lond. 1867 (pt. 1): 99-104, Pl. 10.

——. 1867 (Nov.) **[ref. 1987]**. On a new form of mudfish from New Zealand. Ann. Mag. Nat. Hist. (Ser. 3) v. 20 (no. 119): 305-309, Pl. 7.

——. 1867 (July) **[ref. 1988]**. Additions to the knowledge of Australian reptiles and fishes. Ann. Mag. Nat. Hist. (Ser. 3) v. 20 (no. 115): 45-68.

——. 1867 (Aug.) **[ref. 1989]**. New fishes from the Gaboon and Gold Coast. Ann. Mag. Nat. Hist. (Ser. 3) v. 20 (no. 116): 110-117, Pls. 2-3.

——. 1868 (14 Mar.) **[ref. 1990]**. Catalogue of the fishes in the British Museum. Catalogue of the Physostomi, containing the families Heteropygii, Cyprinidae, Gonorhynchidae, Hyodontidae, Osteoglossidae, Clupeidae, Chirocentridae, Alepocephalidae, Notopteridae, Halosauridae, in B. Mus. v. 7: i-xx + 1-512.

——. 1868 (Sept.) **[ref. 1991]**. Report on a collection of fishes made at St. Helena by J. C. Melliss, Esq. Proc. Zool. Soc. Lond. 1868 (pt 2) (art. 4): 225-228, Pls. 18-19.

——. 1868 (June) **[ref. 1992]**. Diagnoses of some new freshwater fishes from Surinam and Brazil, in the collection of the British Museum. Ann. Mag. Nat. Hist. (Ser. 4) v. 1 (no. 6): 475-481. [Also appeared as Günther 1868 (Sept.) [ref. 5756].]

——. 1868 (June) **[ref. 1993]**. Additions to the ichthyological fauna of Zanzibar. Ann. Mag. Nat. Hist. (Ser. 4) v. 1 (no. 6): 457-459.

——. 1868 (15 Sept.) **[ref. 1994]**. An account of the fishes of the states of Central America, based on collections made by Capt. J. M. Dow, F. Godman, Esq., and O. Salvin, Esq. Trans. Zool. Soc. Lond. v. 6 (pt 7, no. 14): 377-494, Pls. 63-87.

——. 1868 (Sept.) **[ref. 5756]**. Descriptions of freshwater fishes from Surinam and Brazil. Proc. Zool. Soc. Lond. 1868 (pt 2) (art. 5): 229-247, Pls. 20-22.

——. 1869 (Sept.) **[ref. 13284]**. Report of a second collection of fishes made at St. Helena by J. C. Mellis, Esq. Proc. Zool. Soc. Lond. 1869 (pt 2): 238-239, Pl. 16.

——. 1870 (25 June) **[ref. 1995]**. Catalogue of the fishes in the British Museum. Catalogue of the Physostomi, containing the families Gymnotidae, Symbranchidae, Muraenidae, Pegasidae, and of the Lophobranchii, Plectognathi, Dipnoi, Ganoidei, Chondropterygii, Leptocardii, in the B. Mus. v. 8: i-xxv + 1-549.

——. 1870 (Apr.) **[ref. 5780]**. Descriptions of some species of fishes from the Peruvian Amazons. Proc. Zool. Soc. Lond. 1869 (pt 3) (art. 4): 423-429.

——. 1871 (Aug.) **[ref. 1996]**. Description of new percoid fish from the Macquarie River. Proc. Zool. Soc. Lond. 1871 (pt 2) (art 4): 320, Pl. 33.

——. 1872 (2 May) **[ref. 1997]**. Report on several collections of fishes recently obtained for the British Museum. Proc. Zool. Soc. Lond. 1871 (pt 3): 652-675, Pls. 53-70.

——. 1872 (June) **[ref. 2000]**. On a new genus of characinoid fishes from Demerara. Proc. Zool. Soc. Lond. 1872 (pt 1) (art. 5): 146.

——. 1872 (Sept.) **[ref. 2001]**. Description of two new fishes from Tasmania. Ann. Mag. Nat. Hist. (Ser. 4) v. 10 (no. 57): 183-184.

——. 1872 (June) **[ref. 2002]**. Notice on two new fishes (*Symphorus taeniolatus*, *Mugil meyeri*) from Celebes. Ann. Mag. Nat. Hist. (Ser. 4) v. 9 (no. 54): 438-440.

——. 1873 **[ref. 1999]**. Pisces. Zool. Record for 1871: 89-112.

——. 1873 (Aug.) **[ref. 2003]**. New fishes from Angola. Ann. Mag.

Nat. Hist. (Ser. 4) v. 12 (no. 68): 142-144.
———. 1873 (Sept.) **[ref. 2004]**. Report on a collection of fishes from China. Ann. Mag. Nat. Hist. (Ser. 4) v. 12 (no. 69): 239-250.
———. 1873 **[ref. 6423]**. Erster ichthyologischer Beitrag nach Exemplaren aus dem Museum Godeffroy. J. Mus. Godeffroy 1873, heft 2: 97-103. [Also as a separate, pp. 1-7.]
———. 1873 **[ref. 6424]**. Zweiter ichthyologischer Beitrag nach Exemplaren aus dem Museum Godeffroy. J. Mus. Godeffroy 1873, heft 4: 89-92. [Also as a separate, pp. 9-12.]
———. 1873-75 **[ref. 2005]**. Andrew Garrett's Fische der Südsee, beschrieben und redigirt von A. C. L. G. Günther. Band I. J. Mus. Godeffroy. 1-128, Pls. 1-83. [For dates of publication of fascicles for all three volumes of this work see Dor 1976 [ref. 6422].]
———. 1874 (Nov.) **[ref. 2006]**. Descriptions of new species of fishes in the British Museum. Ann. Mag. Nat. Hist. (Ser. 4) v. 14 (no. 83): 368-371.
———. 1874 (Dec.) **[ref. 5753]**. Descriptions of new species of fishes in the British Museum. [Continued from p. 371] Ann. Mag. Nat. Hist. (Ser. 4) v. 14 (no. 84): 453-455.
———. 1876 (May) **[ref. 2007]**. Remarks on fishes, with descriptions of new species in the British Museum, chiefly from southern seas. Ann. Mag. Nat. Hist. (Ser. 4) v. 17 (no. 101): 389-402.
———. 1877 (Nov.) **[ref. 2009]**. Preliminary notes on new fishes collected in Japan during the expedition of H. M. S. 'Challenger.' Ann. Mag. Nat. Hist. (Ser. 4) v. 20 (no. 119): 433-446.
———. 1877 **[ref. 5754]**. Remarks on New Zealand fishes. Trans. N. Z. Inst. v. 9 (art. 63): 469-472.
———. 1878 (July/Aug./Sept.) **[ref. 2010]**. Preliminary notices of deep-sea fishes collected during the voyage of H. M. S. 'Challenger.' Ann. Mag. Nat. Hist. (Ser. 5) v. 2 (nos. 7/8/9): 17-28 (July), 179-187 (Aug.), 248-251 (Sept.).
———. 1880 **[ref. 2011]**. Report on the shore fishes procured during the voyage of H. M. S. Challenger in the years 1873-1876. In: Report on the scientific results of the voyage of H. M. S. Challenger during the years 1873-76. Zoology. v. 1 (pt 6): 1-82, Pls. 1-32.
———. 1881 (June) **[ref. 2012]**. Reptiles, batrachians, and fishes (pp. 18-22). In: Account of the zoological collections made during the survey of H. M. S. 'Alert' in the Straits of Magellan and on the coast of Patagonia. Proc. Zool. Soc. Lond. 1881 (pt 1): 2-141, Pls. 1-2 (fishes). [Günther's article also as a separate.]
———. 1887 **[ref. 2013]**. Report on the deep-sea fishes collected by H. M. S. Challenger during the years 1873-76. In: Report on the Scientific Results of the voyage of H. M. S. Challenger during the years 1873-76. Zoology. v. 22 (pt 57): i-lxv + 1-268, Pls. 1-73.
———. 1887 (Oct.) **[ref. 2014]**. Descriptions of two new species of fishes from Mauritius. Proc. Zool. Soc. Lond. 1887 (pt 3) (art. 8): 550-551, Pls. 48-49.
———. 1889 (June) **[ref. 2015]**. On some fishes from Kilima-Njaro District. Proc. Zool. Soc. Lond. 1889 (pt 1): 70-72, Pl. 8.
———. 1889 (Sept.) **[ref. 2016]**. Third contribution to our knowledge of reptiles and fishes from the Upper Yangtsze-Kiang. Ann. Mag. Nat. Hist. (Ser. 6) v. 4 (no. 21): 218-229.
———. 1889 **[ref. 2017]**. Report on the pelagic fishes collected by H. M. S. Challenger during the years 1873-76. In: Report on the scientific results of the voyage of H. M. S. Challenger during the years 1873-76. v. 31 (pt 78): 1-47, Pls. 1-6.
———. 1894 (Apr.) **[ref. 2018]**. Second report on the reptiles, batrachians, and fishes transmitted by Mr. H. H. Johnston, C. B., from British Central Africa. Proc. Zool. Soc. Lond. 1893 (pt 4): 616-628, Pls. 53-57.
———. 1896 **[ref. 2019]**. Report on the collections of reptiles, batrachians, and fishes made by Messrs. Potanin & Berezowski in the Chinese provinces Kansu and Sze-Chuen. Ann. Acad. St. Petersburg 1896: 199-219, Pls. 1-2.
———. 1902 (July) **[ref. 2020]**. Third notice of new species of fishes from Morocco. Novitat. Zool. (Tring.) v. 9: 446-448, Pls. 22-23.
———. 1903 (Apr.) **[ref. 2021]**. Last account of fishes collected by Mr. R. B. N. Walker, C. M. Z. S., on the Gold Coast. Proc. Zool. Soc. Lond. 1902, v. 2 (pt 2): 330-339, Pls. 30-33.
Gupta, S. K., K. C. Jayaram and K. P. Hajela. 1981 (28 Mar.) **[ref. 1959]**. On a new silurid cat-fish from Uttar Pradesh, India. J. Bombay Nat. Hist. Soc. v. 77 (pt 2): 290-291.
Gushiken, S. 1988 (25 Feb.) **[ref. 6697]**. Phylogenetic relationships of the perciform genera of the family Carangidae. Jpn. J. Ichthyol. v. 34 (no. 4): 443-461.
Haast, J. F. J. von. 1873 **[ref. 2025]**. Notes on some undescribed fishes of New Zealand. Trans. Proc. N. Z. Inst. v. 5: 272-278, Pl. 16.
———. 1874 (June) **[ref. 2026]**. On *Cheimarrichthys forsteri*, a new genus belonging to the New Zealand freshwater fishes. Trans. Proc. N. Z. Inst. v. 6: 103-104, Pl. 18.
Hadley Hansen, P. E. 1986 (Mar.) **[ref. 5810]**. Revision of the tripterygiid fish genus *Helcogramma*, including descriptions of four new species. Bull. Mar. Sci. v. 38 (no. 2): 313-354.
Hadzisce, S. 1960 **[ref. 13406]**. Zur Kenntnis der Gattung *Salmothymus* Berg. Publ. Zavoda za ribarsivo NRM — Skopje. v. 3 (no. 2): 39-52.
———. 1961 (July) **[ref. 13566]**. Zur Kenntnis des *Salmothymus ohridanus* (Steindachner) (Pisces, Salmonidae). Verh. Internat. Verein. Limnol. v. 14: 785-791.
Haedrich, R. L. 1967 (Jan.) **[ref. 5357]**. The stromateoid fishes: systematics and a classification. Bull. Mus. Comp. Zool. v. 135 (no. 2): 31-139.
———. 1969 **[ref. 2028]**. A new family of aberrant stromateoid fishes from the equatorial Indo-Pacific. Dana Rep. No. 76: 1-14.
———. 1973 **[ref. 7216]**. Centrolophidae (pp. 559-561), Nomeidae (pp. 562-563), Tetragonuridae (p. 564), Stromateidae (p. 565). In: Hureau & Monod 1973 [ref. 6590].
———. 1986 **[ref. 5659]**. Suborder Stromateoidei (pp. 842-851). In: Smiths' Sea Fishes (Smith & Heemstra 1986 [ref. 5715]).
Haig, J. 1952 **[ref. 12607]**. Studies on the classification of the catfishes of the Oriental and Palaearctic family Siluridae. Rec. Indian Mus. (Calcutta) v. 48 (pts 3-4): 59-116. [Dated 1950, apparently published in 1952.]
Haldeman, S. S. 1842 (28 Oct.) **[ref. 2029]**. Description of two new species of the genus *Perca*, from the Susquehannah River. J. Acad. Nat. Sci. Phila. v. 8 (pt 2): 330.
Hamilton, F. [Buchanan]. 1822 **[ref. 2031]**. An account of the fishes found in the river Ganges and its branches. Edinburgh & London. i-vii + 1-405, Pls. 1-39. [Often as Hamilton-Buchanan or Buchanan-Hamilton; in work as Hamilton [formerly Buchanan]. See Gudger 1924 [ref. 5927].]
Hanko, B. 1924 (29 Dec.) **[ref. 2035]**. Fische aus Klein-Asien. Ann. Hist. Nat. Mus. Natl. Hung. v. 21: 137-158, Pl. 3.
Hardenberg, J. D. F. 1931 (Dec.) **[ref. 2036]**. Some new or rare fishes of the Indo-Australian Archipelago. Treubia Buitenzorg v. 13 (no. 3-4): 411-419. [Date may be 1832, but Dec. 1831 on cover of separate.]
———. 1941 (Dec.) **[ref. 2037]**. Fishes of New Guinea. Treubia Buitenzorg v. 18 (pt 2): 217-231.
Hardy, G. S. 1982 (June) **[ref. 2038]**. Two new generic names for some Australian pufferfishes (Tetraodontiformes: Tetraodontidae), with species redescriptions and osteological comparisons. Aust. Zool. v. 21 (pt 1): 1-26.
———. 1983 (14 Dec.) **[ref. 5339]**. A new genus and two new species of clingfishes (Gobiesocidae) from New Zealand. Copeia 1983 (no. 4): 863-868.
———. 1983 **[ref. 5341]**. Revision of Australian species of *Torquigener* Whitley (Tetraodontiformes: Tetraodontidae), and two new generic names for Australian puffer fishes. J. R. Soc. N. Z. v. 13 (no. 1/2): 1-48.
———. 1983 **[ref. 5342]**. The status of *Torquigener hypselogeneion* (Bleeker) (Tetraodontiformes: Tetraodontidae) and some related species, including a new species from Hawaii. Pac. Sci. v. 37 (no. 1): 65-74.
———. 1983 **[ref. 5385]**. A revision of the fishes of the family Pentacerotidae (Perciformes). N. Z. J. Zool. v. 10: 177-220.

———. 1983 (30 Sept.) **[ref. 5392]**. A new genus and species of boarfish (Perciformes: Pentacerotidae) from Western Australia. Rec. West. Aust. Mus. v. 10 (pt 4): 373-380.

———. 1984 **[ref. 5182]**. *Tylerius*, a new generic name for the Indo-Pacific pufferfish, *Spheroides spinosissimus* Regan, 1908 (Tetraodontiformes: Tetraodontidae) and comparisons with *Amblyrhynchotes* (Bibron) Duméril. Bull. Mar. Sci. v. 35 (no. 1): 32-37.

———. 1984 **[ref. 5338]**. A new genus and species of deepwater clingfish (family Gobiesocidae) from New Zealand. Bull. Mar. Sci. v. 34 (no. 2): 244-247.

———. 1984 (4 June) **[ref. 5340]**. A new genus and species of triplefin (Pisces: family Tripterygiidae) from New Zealand. Natl. Mus. N. Z. Rec. v. 2 (no. 16): 175-180.

———. 1985 **[ref. 5184]**. Revision of the Acanthoclinidae (Pisces: Perciformes), with descriptions of a new genus and five new species. N. Z. J. Zool. v. 11: 357-393. [Dated 1984, published 1985.]

———. 1985 **[ref. 5185]**. A new genus and species of pufferfish (Tetraodontidae) from Java. Bull. Mar. Sci. v. 36 (no. 1): 145-149.

———. 1986 **[ref. 6139]**. Redescription of *Gilloblennius* Whitley and Phillipps, 1939 (Pisces: Tripterygiidae), and a description of a new genus and two new species from New Zealand. J. R. Soc. N. Z. v. 16 (no. 2): 145-168.

———. 1986 (30 May) **[ref. 6325]**. The status of some species in the family Tripterygiidae from New Zealand [Abstract]. P. 940. In: Uyeno et al. (eds.) 1986 [ref. 6147].

———. 1987 (11 June) **[ref. 5959]**. A new genus for *Trypterigium dorsalis* Clarke, 1879, an unusual triplefin (Pisces: Tripterygiidae) from New Zealand. J. R. Soc. N. Z. v. 17 (no. 2): 157-164.

———. 1987 (Sept.) **[ref. 5960]**. Revision of some triplefins (Pisces: Tripterygiidae) from New Zealand and Australia, with descriptions of two new genera and two new species. J. R. Soc. N. Z. v. 17 (no. 3): 253-274.

———. 1987 (June) **[ref. 6027]**. Revision of *Notoclinops* Whitley, 1930 (Pisces: Tripterygiidae), and description of a new species from New Zealand. J. R. Soc. N. Z. v. 17 (no. 2): 165-176.

———. 1987 (23 Nov.) **[ref. 9092]**. Descriptions of a new genus and two new species of tripterygiid fishes from New Zealand. Natl. Mus. N. Z. Rec. v. 3 (no. 5): 47-58, 1 col. fig.

———. 1989 **[ref. 12485]**. The genus *Forsterygion* Whitley & Phillipps, 1939 (Pisces: Tripterygiidae) in New Zealand and Australia, with descriptions of two new species. J. Nat. Hist. v. 23 (no. 3): 491-512.

Hardy, G. S., and J. B. Hutchins. 1981 (20 July) **[ref. 5582]**. On the validity of the pufferfish genus *Omegophora* Whitley (Tetraodontiformes: Tetraodontidae) with the description of a new species. Rec. West. Aust. Mus. v. 9 (no. 2): 187-201.

Harless, E. 1850 **[ref. 5068]**. Ueber den Zahnbau von *Myliobates* und dem verwandten Rochen Trikeras. Abh. Bayer. Akad. Wiss. v. 5 (no. 3): 841-876, Pls. 1-3.

Harold, A. S. 1989 (27 Dec.) **[ref. 13508]**. A new species of *Polyipnus* (Stomiiformes: Sternoptychidae) from the Coral Sea, with a revised key to the species of the *P. spinosus* complex. Copeia 1989 (no. 4): 871-876.

Harrisson, C. M. H. 1973 **[ref. 7189]**. Halosauridae (pp. 254-255). In: Hureau & Monod 1973 [ref. 6590].

Harry, R. R. 1947 (12 Sept.) **[ref. 14435]**. *Platysomatos*, a neglected name for a genus of aspredinid catfishes. Copeia.

———. 1951 (20 Apr.) **[ref. 2043]**. Deep-sea Fishes of the Bermuda oceanographic expeditions. Family Paralepididae. Zoologica (N. Y.) v. 36 (pt 1): 17-35.

———. 1952 (30 June) **[ref. 2044]**. Deep-sea fishes of the Bermuda oceanographic expeditions. Families Cetomimidae and Rondeletiidae. Zoologica (N. Y.) v. 37 (pt. 1): 55-72, Pl. 1.

———. 1953 (Apr.) **[ref. 2045]**. Studies on the bathypelagic fishes of the family Paralepididae. 1. Survey of the genera. Pac. Sci. v. 7 (no. 2): 219-249.

Hartel, K. E., and L. J. Stiassny. 1986 (29 Aug.) **[ref. 5471]**. The identification of larval *Parasudis* (Teleostei, Chlorophthalmidae); with notes on the anatomy and relationships of aulopiform fishes. Breviora No. 487: 1-23.

Harwood, J. 1827 **[ref. 2046]**. On a newly discovered genus of serpentiform fishes. Philos. Trans. R. Soc. Lond. 1827 (art. 5): 49-57, Pl. 7.

Haseman, J. D. 1911 (Oct.) **[ref. 2047]**. Descriptions of some new species of fishes and miscellaneous notes on others obtained during the expedition of the Carnegie Museum to central South America. Ann. Carnegie Mus. v. 7 (nos. 3-4)(17): 315-328, Pls. 46-52.

———. 1911 (Oct.) **[ref. 2048]**. Some new species of fishes from the Rio Iguassú. Ann. Carnegie Mus. v. 7 (nos. 3-4)(19): 374-387, Pls. 50, 58, 73-83.

Hastings, P. A., and S. A. Bortone. 1981 (20 July) **[ref. 5426]**. *Chriolepis vespa*, a new species of gobiid fish from the northeastern Gulf of Mexico. Proc. Biol. Soc. Wash. v. 94 (no. 2): 427-436.

Hay, O. P. 1881 (23 Feb.) **[ref. 2053]**. On a collection of fishes from eastern Mississippi. Proc. U. S. Natl. Mus. v. 3 [no. 179]: 488-515.

———. 1882 (before 6 Oct.) **[ref. 2054]**. On a collection of fishes from the lower Mississippi Valley. Bull. U. S. Fish Comm. v. 2 [1882]: 57-75.

———. 1902 **[ref. 6281]**. Bibliography and catalogue of the fossil vertebrata of North America. Bull. U. S. Geol. Surv. No. 179: 1-868.

Hays, A. N. 1952 **[ref. 9281]**. David Starr Jordan. A bibliography of his writings 1871-1931. Stanford Univ. Publ., Univ. Ser., Library Stud. v. 1: i-xv + 1-195.

Heckel, J. J. 1836 **[ref. 2062]**. *Scaphirhynchus*, eine neue Fischgattung aus der Ordnung der Chondropterygier mit freien Kiemen. Ann. Wien. Mus. Naturges. v. 1: 68-78, Pl. 8. [Possibly published in 1835. Also as a separate.]

———. 1837 **[ref. 2079]**. Ichthyologische Beiträge zu den Familien der Cottoiden, Scorpaenoiden, Gobioiden und Cyprinoiden. Ann. Wien. Mus. Naturges. v. 2: 143-164, 2 pls. [Date of 1837 from Paxton et al. 1989: 450 [ref. 12442].]

———. 1838 **[ref. 2063]**. Fische aus Caschmir gesammelt und herausgegeben von Carl Freiherrn von Hügel, beschrieben von J. J. Heckel. Wien. 1-112, 13 pls. [Not seen.]

———. 1840 **[ref. 2064]**. Johann Natterer's neue Flussfische Brasilien's nach den Beobachtungen und Mittheilungen des Entdeckers beschrieben. Abth. 1, Die Labroiden. Ann. Wien. Mus. Naturges. v. 2: 325-471, Pls. 29-30.

———. 1841 **[ref. 2065]**. Ueber eine neue Gattung (Genus) von Süsswasserfischen in Europa. Aus einem Schreiben an den Akademiker Dr. Brandt. Bull. Imp. Acad. Sci. St. Petersburg v. 8: 384.

———. 1843 **[ref. 2066]**. Ichthyologie [von Syrien]. In: J. von Russegger. Reisen in Europa, Asien und Africa, mit besonderer Rücksicht auf die naturwissenschaftlichen Verhältnisse der betreffenden Länder unternommen in den Jahren 1835 bis 1841, etc. Stuttgart. v. 1 (pt 2): 990-1099. [Date may be late 1842. Heckel ref. 2067 below is a separate with subtitles and dated 1843.]

———. 1843 **[ref. 2067]**. Abbildungen und Beschreibungen der Fische Syriens, nebst einer neuen Classification und Characteristik sämmtlicher Gattungen der Cyprinen (pp. 991-1044). Süsswasser-Fische Syriens (pp. 1044-1099). Stuttgart. From Russegger's Reisen, v. 1 (pt 2)]. [As separate, pp. 1-109, with original pagination in parentheses.]

———. 1847 **[ref. 2068]**. Ichthyologie (von Syrien). In: Russegger, J. von: Reisen in Europa, Asien und Africa... unternommen in den Jahren 1835 bis 1841. [Not seen; apparently a second part, after refs. 2067-2068. Fowler MS dates to 1847.]

———. 1848 **[ref. 2069]**. Eine neue Gattung von Poecilien mit rochenartigem Anklammerungs-Organe. Sitzungsber. Akad. Wiss. Wien v. 1 (pt 1-5) [1848]: 289-303, Pls. 8-9.

Heckel, J. J., and L. J. F. J. Fitzinger. 1836 **[ref. 2077]**. Monographische Darstellung der Gattung *Acipenser*. Ann. Wien. Mus. Naturges. v. 1: 261-326.

Heckel, J. J., and R. Kner. 1858 **[ref. 2078]**. Die Süsswasserfische der Österreichischen Monarchie, mit Rücksicht auf die angränzenden

Länder. Leipzig. i-xii + 1-388.

HECTOR, J. 1881 (Apr.) **[ref. 2080]**. Notice of a new fish. Trans. Proc. N. Z. Inst. v. 13: 194-195.

HEEMSTRA, P. C. 1974 (2 Dec.) **[ref. 7125]**. On the identity of certain eastern Pacific and Caribbean post-larval fishes (Perciformes) described by Henry Fowler. Proc. Acad. Nat. Sci. Phila. v. 126 (no. 3): 21-26.

———. 1980 (Jan.) **[ref. 14195]**. A revision of the zeid fishes (Zeiformes: Zeidae) of South Africa. Ichthyol. Bull. J. L. B. Smith Inst. Ichthyol. No. 41: i-iii + 1-18, Pls. 1-2.

———. 1982 (28 May) **[ref. 5416]**. Taxonomic notes on some triglid and peristediid fishes (Pisces: Scorpaeniformes) from southern Africa. Copeia 1982 (no. 2): 291-295.

———. 1984 (May) **[ref. 5298]**. *Apolemichthys kingi*, a new species of angelfish (Pomacanthidae) from South Africa, with comments on the classification of angelfishes and a checklist of the pomacanthids of the western Indian Ocean. J. L. B. Smith Inst. Ichthyol. Spec. Publ. No. 35: 1-17.

———. 1986 **[ref. 5660]**. [Numerous family accounts]. In: Smiths' Sea Fishes (Smith & Heemstra 1986 [ref. 5715]).

HEEMSTRA, P. C., AND W. D. ANDERSON, JR. 1986 **[ref. 5664]**. Family No. 168: Calanthiidae (pp. 538-539). In: Smiths' Sea Fishes (Smith & Heemstra 1986 [ref. 5715]).

HEEMSTRA, P. C., AND O. GON. 1986 **[ref. 5665]**. Family No. 262: Soleidae (pp. 868-874). In: Smiths' Sea Fishes (Smith & Heemstra 1986 [ref. 5715]).

HEEMSTRA, P. C., AND T. HECHT. 1986 (Jan.) **[ref. 5971]**. Dinopercidae, a new family for the percoid marine fish genera *Dinoperca* Boulenger and *Centrarchops* Fowler (Pisces: Perciformes). Ichthyol. Bull. J. L. B. Smith Inst. Ichthyol. No. 51: 1-20.

HEEMSTRA, P. C., AND S. X. KANNEMEYER. 1984 (June) **[ref. 5349]**. The families Trachipteridae and Radiicephalidae (Pisces, Lampriformes) and a new species of *Zu* from South Africa. Ann. S. Afr. Mus. v. 94 (pt 2): 13-39.

———. 1986 **[ref. 5666]**. Family No. 119: Trachipteridae (pp. 399-402), Family 120: Radiicephalidae (p. 402). In: Smiths' Sea Fishes (Smith & Heemstra 1986 [ref. 5715]).

HEEMSTRA, P. C., AND T. J. MARTIN. 1986 **[ref. 6298]**. Family No. 163: Ambassidae (pp. 507-508). In: Smiths' Sea Fishes (Smith & Heemstra 1986 [ref. 5715]).

HEEMSTRA, P. C., AND J. S. NELSON. 1986 **[ref. 6304]**. Family No. 233: Percophidae (pp. 737-739). In: Smiths' Sea Fishes (Smith & Heemstra 1986 [ref. 5715]).

HEEMSTRA, P. C., AND N. V. PARIN. 1986 **[ref. 6293]**. Family No. 116: Exocoetidae (pp. 391-396). In: Smiths' Sea Fishes (Smith & Heemstra 1986 [ref. 5715]).

HEEMSTRA, P. C., AND J. E. RANDALL. 1977 **[ref. 7057]**. A revision of the Emmelichthyidae (Pisces: Perciformes). Aust. J. Mar. Freshwater Res. v. 28: 361-396.

———. 1979 (Nov.) **[ref. 6938]**. A revision of the anthiine fish genus *Sacura* (Perciformes: Serranidae) with descriptions of two new species. J. L. B. Smith Inst. Ichthyol. Spec. Publ. No. 20: 1-13.

———. 1986 **[ref. 5667]**. Family No. 166: Serranidae (pp. 509-537). In: Smiths' Sea Fishes (Smith & Heemstra 1986 [ref. 5715]).

HEEMSTRA, P. C., AND M. M. SMITH. 1980 (17 Oct.) **[ref. 2081]**. Hexatrygonidae, a new family of stingrays (Myliobatiformes: Batoidea) from South Africa, with comments on the classification of batoid fishes. Ichthyol. Bull. J. L. B. Smith Inst. Ichthyol. No. 43: 1-17.

———. 1981 **[ref. 5415]**. *Pelagocephalus marki*, a new species of puffer fish (Tetraodontidae) from South Africa. Bull. Mar. Sci. v. 31 (no. 4): 911-915.

———. 1983 (Jan.) **[ref. 5414]**. A new species of the triggerfish genus *Xenobalistes* Matsuura (Tetraodontiformes: Balistidae) from South Africa. J. L. B. Smith Inst. Ichthyol. Spec. Publ. No. 26: 1-5.

———. 1986 **[ref. 5668]**. Family No. 85: Alepisauridae (pp. 280-281), Family No. 244: Zanclidae (pp. 823-824). In: Smiths' Sea Fishes (Smith & Heemstra 1986 [ref. 5715]).

HEEMSTRA, P. C., AND J. E. WRIGHT. 1986 (July) **[ref. 5997]**. Two new species of clinid fishes (Perciformes: Clinidae) from South Africa. J. L. B. Smith Inst. Ichthyol. Spec. Publ. No. 40: 1-11, Pl. 1.

HEITMANS, W. R. B., H. NIJSSEN AND I. J. H. ISBRÜCKER. 1983 **[ref. 5278]**. The mailed catfish genus *Lasiancistrus* Regan, 1904, from French Guiana and Surinam, with descriptions of two new species (Pisces, Siluriformes, Loricariidae). Bijdr. Dierkd. v. 53 (no. 1): 33-48.

HELLER, E., AND R. E. SNODGRASS. 1903 (12 Sept.) **[ref. 2089]**. Papers from the Hopkins Stanford Galapagos expedition, 1898-1899. XV. New fishes. Proc. Wash. Acad. Sci. v. 5: 189-229, Pls. 2-20.

HEMPRICH, F. G., AND C. G. EHRENBERG. 1899 **[ref. 4977]**. Symbolae physicae, seu icones adhue ineditae corporum naturalium novorum aut minus cognitorum quae ex itineribus per Libyam, AEgyptiam, Nubiam, Dongolam, Syriam, Arabiam et Habessiniam publico institutis sumptu ... studio annis MDCCCXX - MDCCCXXV redierunt. Zoologica. Berlin. [A posthumous series of plates, the fishes published under the editorship of F. Hilgendorf. Not seen.]

HENLE, F. G. J. 1834 **[ref. 2092]**. Sur le *Narcine*, nouveaux genre de raies électriques, suivi d'un synopsis des raies électriques en géneral. [Also as: Ueber *Narcine*, eine neue Gattung electrischer Rochen nebst einer Synopsis der electrischen Rochen.] Ann. Sci. Nat. [Also as a separate in German, Berlin, pp. 1-44, Pls. 1-4. Only separate examined.]

HENN, A. W. 1916 (Jan.) **[ref. 2093]**. On various South American poeciliid fishes. Ann. Carnegie Mus. v. 10 (nos. 1-2) (9): 93-142, Pls. 18-21.

HENSLEY, D. A. 1985 (10 Dec.) **[ref. 6783]**. *Eptatretus mendozai*, a new species of hagfish (Myxinidae) from off the southwest coast of Puerto Rico. Copeia 1985 (no. 4): 865-869.

———. 1986 **[ref. 5669]**. Family No. 259: Bothidae (pp. 854-863). In: Smiths' Sea Fishes (Smith & Heemstra 1986 [ref. 5715]).

———. 1986 (23 Dec.) **[ref. 5734]**. A new damselfish genus from the Cape Verde Archipelago based on *Gliphidodon (Parma) hermani* Steindachner, 1887 (Pisces: Pomacentridae). Copeia 1986 (no. 4): 857-863.

———. 1986 (30 May) **[ref. 6326]**. Current research on Indo-Pacific bothids [Abstract]. P. 941. In: Uyeno et al. (eds.) 1986 [ref. 6147]).

HERALD, E. S. 1940 (24 June) **[ref. 2095]**. A key to the pipefishes of the Pacific American coasts with descriptions of new genera and species. Rep. Allan Hancock Pacific Exped. 1932-1938 v. 9 (no. 3): 51-64.

———. 1959 (29 May) **[ref. 2096]**. From pipefish to seahorse—a study of phylogenetic relationships. Proc. Calif. Acad. Sci. (Ser. 4) v. 24 (no. 13): 465-473.

———. 1961 **[ref. 13600]**. Living fishes of the World. Chanticleer Press. Doubleday & Company, Inc., Garden City, N. Y. 1-304.

HERALD, E. S., AND J. E. RANDALL. 1972 (27 Dec.) **[ref. 2097]**. Five new Indo-Pacific pipefishes. Proc. Calif. Acad. Sci. (Ser. 4) v. 39 (no. 11): 121-140.

HERMAN, J., M. HOVESTADT-EULER AND D. C. HOVESTADT. 1988 **[ref. 13267]**. Contributions to the study of the comparative morphology of teeth and other relevant ichthyodorulites in living supraspecific taxa of chondrichthyan fishes. Part A: Selachii. No. 2a: Order: Carcharhiniformes - Family: Triakidae. Bull. Inst. R. Sci. Nat. Belg. v. 58: 99-126.

HERMANN, J. 1781 **[ref. 2145]**. Schreiben über eine neues americanisches Fischgeschlecht, *Sternoptyx diaphana*, der durchsichtige Brustfalten-Fisch. Naturforscher v. 16: 8-36, 1 pl.

———. 1804 **[ref. 2146]**. Observationes zoologicae, quibus novae complures, aliaeque animalium species describuntur et illustrantur. Opus posthumum edidit Fridericus Ludovicus Hammer. Argentorati. i-viii + 1-332. [Pisces on pp. 290-328.]

HERRE, A. W. 1923 (9 July) **[ref. 2116]**. Notes on Philippine sharks, I. Philipp. J. Sci. v. 23 (no. 1): 67-73, Pl. 1.

———. 1923 (8 Aug.) **[ref. 2117]**. A review of the eels of the Philippine Archipelago. Philipp. J. Sci. v. 23 (no. 2): 123-236, Pls. 1-11.

——. 1924 (28 Apr.) **[ref. 2118]**. Distribution of the true fresh-water fishes in the Philippines. I. The Philippine Cyprinidae. Philipp. J. Sci. v. 24 (no. 3): 249-307, Pls. 1-2.
——. 1924 (30 July) **[ref. 2119]**. Distribution of the true fresh-water fishes in the Philippines, II. The Philippine Labyrinthici, Clariidae, and Siluridae. Philipp. J. Sci. v. 24 (no. 6): 683-709, Pls. 1-2.
——. 1924 **[ref. 2120]**. The distribution of true fresh-water fishes in the Philippines and its significance. Proc. Pan-Pac. Sci. Congr. Melbourne v. 2: 1561-1570.
——. 1925 (5 Sept.) **[ref. 2121]**. Two strange new fishes from Luzon. Philipp. J. Sci. v. 27 (no. 4): 507-513, Pls. 1-2.
——. 1926 (15 Dec.) **[ref. 2122]**. Four new Philippine fishes. Philipp. J. Sci. v. 31 (no. 4): 533-543, Pls. 1-3.
——. 1927 (17 Mar.) **[ref. 2102]**. A new genus and three new species of Philippine fishes. Philipp. J. Sci. v. 32 (no. 3): 413-419, Pls. 1-2.
——. 1927 (14 Dec.) **[ref. 2103]**. Four new fishes from Lake Taal (Bombon). Philipp. J. Sci. v. 34 (no. 3): 273-279, Pls. 1-3.
——. 1927 (15 Sept.) **[ref. 2104]**. Gobies of the Philippines and the China Sea. Monogr. Bur. Sci. Manila Monogr. 23: 1-352, frontispiece + Pls. 1-30.
——. 1930 (31 Jan.) **[ref. 2105]**. *Busuanga* Herre, new genus. Science (n. s.) v. 71 (no. 1831): 132.
——. 1933 (3 Apr.) **[ref. 2106]**. Twelve new Philippine fishes. Copeia 1933 (no. 3): 17-25.
——. 1934 **[ref. 2107]**. *Herklotsella anomala.*—A new fresh water cat-fish from Hong Kong. Hong Kong Nat. v. 4 (no. 2): 179-180. [Dated Dec. 1833 but perhaps published in early 1934.]
——. 1934 (10 Mar.) **[ref. 2108]**. Notes on fishes in the Zoological Museum of Stanford University. I. The fishes of the Herre Philippine expedition of 1931. The fishes of the Herre 1931 Philippine expedition with descriptions of 17 new species. Newspaper Enterprise Ltd., Hong Kong. 1-106. [Original limited to 120 copies, reprinted through efforts of G. S. Myers, 1972, N. K. Gregg Publ., Kentfield, Calif.]
——. 1935 (15 Feb.) **[ref. 2109]**. New fishes obtained by the Crane Pacific expedition. Field Mus. Nat. Hist. Publ. Zool. Ser. v. 18 (pt 12, no. 335): 383-438.
——. 1935 (4 Oct.) **[ref. 2110]**. A new sciaenid from southeastern China. Lingnan Sci. J. Canton v. 14 (no. 4): 603-604.
——. 1935 (15 Oct.) **[ref. 2111]**. Notes on fishes in the Zoological Museum of Stanford University. II. Two new genera and species of Japanese sharks and a Japanese species of *Narcetes*. Copeia 1935 (no. 3): 122-127.
——. 1936 (9 Mar.) **[ref. 2124]**. Notes on fishes in the Zoological Museum of Stanford University. IV. A new catostomid from Mexico and a new callionymid from Celebes and the Philippines. Proc. Biol. Soc. Wash. v. 49: 11-13.
——. 1936 (22 Aug.) **[ref. 2112]**. A new cyprinid genus and species and a new characin from Portuguese East Africa. Proc. Biol. Soc. Wash. v. 49: 99-101.
——. 1936 (12 May) **[ref. 2125]**. Fishes in the Zoölogical Museum of Stanford University, III. New genera and species of gobies and blennies and a new *Myxus*, from the Pelew Islands and Celebes. Philipp. J. Sci. v. 59 (no. 2): 275-287, Pl. 1.
——. 1936 (17 June) **[ref. 5609]**. Notes on fishes in the Zoölogical Museum of Stanford University, V. New or rare Philippine fishes from the Herre 1933 Philippine expedition. Philipp. J. Sci. v. 59 (no. 3): 357-373, Pls. 1-2.
——. 1938 (20 June) **[ref. 2126]**. *Luzoneleotris*, a new genus of eleotrid fishes from Luzon. Stanford Ichthyol. Bull. v. 1 (no. 2): 59-60.
——. 1939 (Dec.) **[ref. 2127]**. On a collection of littoral and freshwater fishes from the Andaman Islands. Rec. Indian Mus. (Calcutta) v. 41 (pt 4): 327-372.
——. 1939 (23 Dec.) **[ref. 2128]**. The Philippine blennies. Philipp. J. Sci. v. 70 (no. 4): 315-373, Pls. 1-5.
——. 1939 (11 Oct.) **[ref. 2129]**. The genera of Phallostethidae. Proc. Biol. Soc. Wash. v. 52: 139-144.
——. 1940 (July) **[ref. 2130]**. New species of fishes from the Malay Peninsula and Borneo. Bull. Raffles Mus. No. 16: 5-26, Pls. 1-20.
——. 1940 (23 Dec.) **[ref. 2132]**. Notes on fishes in the Zoölogical Museum of Stanford University, VIII. A new genus and two new species of Chinese gobies with remarks on some other species. Philipp. J. Sci. v. 73 (no. 3): 293-299, Pl. 1.
——. 1940 (28 July) **[ref. 5781]**. *Manacopus*, a new name for a genus of Phallostethidae. Copeia 1940 (no. 2): 141.
——. 1942 (24 Aug.) **[ref. 2133]**. A new genus and species of Gobiesocidae from the Philippines. Stanford Ichthyol. Bull. v. 2 (no. 4): 120-122.
——. 1942 (31 Aug.) **[ref. 2134]**. New and little known phallostethids, with keys to the genera and Philippine species. Stanford Ichthyol. Bull. v. 2 (no. 5): 137-156. [Copy received by Calif. Academy of Sciences 27 Aug.]
——. 1942 (18 Mar.) **[ref. 2135]**. Notes on a collection of fishes from Antigua and Barbados, British West Indies. Stanford Univ. Publ., Univ. Ser., Biol. Sci. v. 7 (no. 2): 286-305.
——. 1943 (1 Oct.) **[ref. 2136]**. Notes on fishes in the Zoological Museum of Stanford University. XI. Two new genera and species. With key to the genera of gobies with vomerine teeth. Proc. Biol. Soc. Wash. v. 56: 91-95.
——. 1943 **[ref. 11020]**. On *Pleurogobius*, a typographical error. Copeia 1943 (no. 2): 132.
——. 1944 (31 Oct.) **[ref. 2137]**. Notes on fishes in the Zoological Museum of Stanford University. XVII. New fishes from Johore and India. Proc. Biol. Soc. Wash. v. 57: 45-51.
——. 1945 (31 Mar.) **[ref. 2138]**. Two new genera and four new gobies from the Philippines and India. Copeia 1945 (no. 1): 1-6.
——. 1945 (21 Mar.) **[ref. 2139]**. Notes on fishes in the Zoological Museum of Stanford University. XIV.—A new genus and three new species of gobies from the Philippines. Proc. Biol. Soc. Wash. v. 58: 11-15.
——. 1945 (30 June) **[ref. 2140]**. Notes on fishes in the Zoological Museum of Stanford University. XIX.—Two new Philippine gobies, with key to the genera of gobies with vomerine teeth. Proc. Biol. Soc. Wash. v. 58: 77-81.
——. 1945 (29 Dec.) **[ref. 2141]**. Notes on fishes in the Zoological Museum of Stanford University. XX, New fishes from China and India, a new genus, and a new Indian record. J. Wash. Acad. Sci. v. 35 (no. 12): 399-404.
——. 1946 (25 Oct.) **[ref. 2142]**. New genera of Eleotridae and Gobiidae and one new species from West Africa. Proc. Biol. Soc. Wash. v. 59: 121-126.
——. 1950 (21 Aug.) **[ref. 2113]**. A new name for *Hanno*, a genus of African gobies. Stanford Ichthyol. Bull. v. 3 (no. 4): 198.
——. 1953 (14 Nov.) **[ref. 2143]**. Tropical Pacific gobies with vomerine teeth. Philipp. J. Sci. v. 82 (no. 2): 181-188.
——. 1953 (14 Nov.) **[ref. 2144]**. The tropical Pacific Eleotridae with vomerine teeth with descriptions of two new genera and two new species from the Marshall Islands. Philipp. J. Sci. v. 82 (no. 2): 189-192.
——. 1953 **[ref. 5594]**. Check list of Philippine fishes. U. S. Fish Wildl. Serv. Res. Rep. No. 20: 1-977.
Herre, A. W., and E. S. Herald. 1950 (13 Aug.) **[ref. 2114]**. Noteworthy additions to the Philippine fish fauna with descriptions of a new genus and species. Philipp. J. Sci. v. 79 (no. 3): 309-340.
Herre, A. W., and G. S. Myers. 1931 **[ref. 2115]**. Fishes from southeastern China and Hainan. Lingnan Sci. J. Canton v. 10 (nos. 2-3): 233-254.
——. 1937 (Aug.) **[ref. 2123]**. A contribution to the ichthyology of the Malay Peninsula. Bull. Raffles Mus. No. 13: 5-75, Pls. 1-7.
Herzenstein, S. M. 1888 **[ref. 2147]**. Fische. In: Wissenschaftliche Resultate der von N. M. Przewalski nach Central-Asien unternommenen Reisen. Zoologischr. Theil. Band 3 (2 abt.) (1): i-vi + 1-91, pls. 1-8. [In Russian and German. For continuation see Herzenstein 1888 (ref. 2148) and 1891 (ref. 4917).]
——. 1888 **[ref. 2148]**. Fische. In: Wissenschaftliche Resultate der

von N. M. Przewalski nach Central-Asien unternommenen Reisen. Zool. 3 (2 abt.) (2): 91-180, Pls. 9-12. [In Russian and German.]

———. 1890 **[ref. 2149]**. Ichthyologische Bemerkungen aus dem Zoologischen Museum der Kaiserlichen Akademie der Wissenschaften. Mélanges Biol., Bull. Acad. Imp. Sci. St. Petersburg v. 13: 113-125. [Article continues in additional parts.]

———. 1891 (25 Sept.) **[ref. 4917]**. Fische. In: Wissenschaftliche Resultate der von N. M. Przewalski nach Central-Asien unternommenen Reisen. Zoologischer Theil. v. 3 (abt. 2)(3): 181-262, Pls. 14-25. [Continued from Herzenstein 1888 (ref. 2148)]

———. 1892 **[ref. 5037]**. Ichthyologische Bemerkungen aus dem Zoologischen Museum der Kaiserlichen Akademie Wissenschaften. III. Mélanges Biol., Bull. Acad. Imp. Sci. St. Petersburg v. 13 (pt. 2): 219-235. [See also Bull. Acad. Sci. St. Petersburg (Ser. 2) v. 3: 49-65.]

———. 1896 **[ref. 2151]**. Über einige neue und seltene Fische des Zoologischen Museums der Kaiserlichen Museums der Kaiserlichen Akademie der Wissenschaften. Ann. Mus. Zool. Acad. Imp. Sci. St. Petersburg v. 1 (no. 1896): 1-14.

HERZENSTEIN, S. M., AND N. A. WARPACHOWSKI. 1887 **[ref. 2152]**. Notizen über die Fischfauna des Amur-Beckens und der angrenzenden Gebiete. Tr. St. Petersburg Nat. v. 18 (no. 7): 1-58, 1 pl. [In Russian, German summ.]

HIGUCHI, H., E. G. REIS AND F. G. ARAÚJO. 1982 **[ref. 11467]**. Uma nova espécie de bagre marinho do litoral do Rio Grande do sul e consideracões sobre o género nominal *Netuma* Bleeker, 1858 no Atlántico sul ocidental (Siluriformes, Ariidae). Atlantica, Rio Grande v. 5: 1-15.

HIKITA, T. 1934 **[ref. 2160]**. Flatfishes found in northern Japan. Bull. School Fish. Hokkaido v. 4: 187-296 + 10-15, Pls. 1-29. [In Japanese, English summ. (pp. 10-15).]

HILDEBRAND, S. F. 1928 (28 Sept.) **[ref. 11966]**. A new catalogue of the fresh-water fishes of Panama. Field Mus. Nat. Hist. Publ. Zool. Ser. v. 22 (pt 4): 217-359.

———. 1946 (26 Feb.) **[ref. 2161]**. A descriptive catalog of the shore fishes of Peru. Bull. U. S. Natl. Mus. No. 189: i-xi + 1-530.

———. 1948 (28 July) **[ref. 2162]**. A new genus and five new species of American fishes. Smithson. Misc. Collect. v. 110 (no. 9): 1-15.

HILDEBRAND, S. F., AND W. C. SCHROEDER. 1928 **[ref. 2163]**. Fishes of Chesapeake Bay. Bull. Bur. Fish. v. 43 (1927, pt 1): 1-366.

HILGENDORF, F. M. 1877 **[ref. 2165]**. *Pterothrissus*, eine neue Clupeidengattung. Acta Soc. Leopoldina v. 13: 127-128.

———. 1878 **[ref. 2171]**. Über das Vorkommen einer *Brama*-Art und einer neuen Fischgattung *Centropholis* aus der Nachbarschaft des Genus *Brama* in den japanischen Meeren. Sitzungsber. Ges. Naturf. Freunde Berlin 1878 (for 15 Jan.): 1-2.

———. 1878 **[ref. 2166]**. Einige neue japanische Fischgattungen. Sitzungsber. Ges. Naturf. Freunde Berlin 1878: 155-157. [Also as separate, pp. 1-2.]

———. 1880 (5 Apr.) **[ref. 2167]**. Über eine neue bemerkenswerthe Fischgattung *Leucopsarion* aus Japan. Monatsb. Konigl. Ak. Wiss. Berlin 1880: 339-341.

———. 1888 **[ref. 2168]**. Fische aus dem Victoria-Nyanza (Ukerewe-See), gesammelt von dem verstorbenen Dr. G. A. Fischer. Sitzungsber. Ges. Naturf. Freunde Berlin 1888: 75-79.

———. 1889 **[ref. 2164]**. Über eine Fischsammlung von Haiti, welche 2 neue Arten, *Poecilia* (subg. n. *Acropoecilia*) *tridens* und *Eleotris maltzani*, enthält. Sitzungsber. Ges. Naturf. Freunde Berlin 1889 (19 Feb.): 51-55.

———. 1894 **[ref. 2169]**. Eine neue Characinidengattung, *Petersius*, aus dem Kinganiflusse in Deutsch-Ostafrika, und sprach über die sonstigen von Dr. Stuhlmann dort gesammelten Fische. Sitzungsber. Ges. Naturf. Freunde Berlin 1894: 172-173.

———. 1904 **[ref. 2170]**. Ein neuer *Scyllium*-artiger Haifisch, *Proscyllium habereri*, nov. subgen., n. spec. von Formosa. Sitzungsber. Ges. Naturf. Freunde Berlin 1904 (no. 2): 39-41.

HIRASAKA, K., AND H. NAKAMURA. 1947 (June) **[ref. 2174]**. On the Formosan spear-fishes. Bull. Oceanogr. Inst. Taiwan No. 3: 9-24, Pls. 1-3.

HOEDEMAN, J. J. 1950 (14 Apr.) **[ref. 2175]**. Rediagnosis of the characid-nannostomine fish genera *Nannostomus* and *Poecilobrycon*. Amsterdam Nat. (Bull. Zool. Mus. Amsterdam) v. 1 (no. 1): 11-27, Pls. 8-9.

———. 1950 (23 Oct.) **[ref. 2176]**. A new characid-erythrinine fish (*Pseuderythrinus rosapinnis* gen. et. sp. nov.). Amsterdam Nat. (Bull. Zool. Mus. Amsterdam) v. 1 (no. 3): 79-91.

———. 1951 (5 Mar.) **[ref. 2177]**. Rediagnosis of the Old World cyprinodont genus *Aphanius*. Beaufortia No. 1: 1-6.

———. 1951 (10 May) **[ref. 2178]**. Studies on African characid fishes. I. The tribe Alestidi. Beaufortia No. 3: 1-8.

———. 1956 **[ref. 6184]**. Aquariumvissen Encyclopedie. De Bezige Bij. Amsterdam. v. 2: 530-728. [Not seen. New generic-group names may date to 1859 edition.]

———. 1961 **[ref. 11969]**. Notes on the ichthyology of Surinam and other Guianas. 8. Additional records of siluriform fishes (2). Bull. Aquat. Biol. v. 2 (no. 23): 129-139.

———. 1962 (July) **[ref. 12585]**. Notes on the ichthyology of Surinam and other Guianas. 11. New gymnotoid fishes from Surinam and French Guiana, with additional records and a key to the groups and species from Guiana. Bull. Aquat. Biol. v. 3 (no. 30): 97-108.

———. 1962 (Apr.) **[ref. 13556]**. Notes on the ichthyology of Surinam and other Guianas. 9. New records of gymnotid fishes. Bull. Aquat. Biol. v. 3 (no. 26): 53-60.

———. 1974 **[ref. 5457]**. Naturalists' guide to fresh-water aquarium fish. Sterling Publ. Co., Inc. New York. 1-1152.

HOESE, D. F. 1975 (6 June) **[ref. 5294]**. A revision of the gobiid fish genus *Kelloggella*. Rec. Aust. Mus. v. 29 (no. 17): 473-484, Pls. 1-3.

———. 1976 **[ref. 7338]**. A redescription of *Heteroclinus adelaidae* Castelnau (Pisces: Clinidae), with description of a related new species. Aust. Zool. v. 19 (no. 1): 51-67.

———. 1986 **[ref. 5670]**. Family No. 240: Gobiidae (pp. 774-807), Family No. 241: Eleotridae (pp. 807-811), Family No. 242: Kraemeriidae (p. 811). In: Smiths' Sea Fishes (Smith & Heemstra 1986 [ref. 5715]).

———. 1986 (Sept.) **[ref. 5996]**. Descriptions of two new species of *Hetereleotris* (Pisces: Gobiidae) from the western Indian Ocean, with discussion of related species. J. L. B. Smith Inst. Ichthyol. Spec. Publ. No. 41: 1-25.

HOESE, D. F., AND G. R. ALLEN. 1977 (31 Mar.) **[ref. 2179]**. *Signigobius biocellatus*, a new genus and species of sand-dwelling coral reef gobiid fish from the western tropical Pacific. Jpn. J. Ichthyol. v. 23 (no. 4): 199-207.

———. 1987 **[ref. 6604]**. New Australian fishes part 10. A new genus and two new species of freshwater eleotridid fishes (Gobioidei) from the Kimberley region of Western Australia. Mem. Mus. Victoria v. 48 (no. 1): 35-42.

HOESE, D. F., AND E. B. BROTHERS. 1976 (20 Aug.) **[ref. 2180]**. *Paratrimma*, a new genus of gobiid fishes and two new species. Copeia 1976 (no. 3): 494-497.

HOESE, D. F., AND P. FOURMANOIR. 1978 (26 June) **[ref. 2181]**. *Discordipinna griessingeri*, a new genus and species of gobiid fish from the tropical Indo-West Pacific. Jpn. J. Ichthyol. v. 25 (no. 1): 19-24.

HOESE, D. F., AND R. H. KUITER. 1984 **[ref. 5300]**. A revision of the Australian plesiopid fish genus *Paraplesiops*, with notes on other Australian genera. Rec. Aust. Mus. v. 36: 7-18.

HOESE, D. F., AND H. K. LARSON. 1985 (3 May) **[ref. 6787]**. Revision of the eastern Pacific species of the genus *Barbulifer* (Pisces: Gobiidae). Copeia 1985 (no. 2): 333-339.

———. 1987 **[ref. 6609]**. New Australian fishes. Part 11. A new genus and species of eleotridid (Gobioidei) from southern Australia with a discussion of relationships. Mem. Mus. Victoria v. 48 (no. 1): 43-50.

HOESE, D. F., AND R. LUBBOCK. 1982 **[ref. 6551]**. A review of the genus *Myersina* (Pisces: Gobiidae), with the description of a new species. Aust. Zool. v. 21 (pt 1): 47-54.

HOESE, D. F., AND Y. OBIKA. 1988 (15 Dec.) **[ref. 12745]**. A new gobiid fish, *Fusigobius signipinnis*, from the western tropical Pacific. Jpn. J. Ichthyol. v. 35 (no. 3): 282-288.

HOESE, D. F., AND J. E. RANDALL. 1982 (1 Nov.) **[ref. 5297]**. Revision of the gobiid fish genus *Stonogobiops*. Indo-Pac. Fishes No. 1: 1-18, Pls. 1-3.

HOESE, D. F., AND R. WINTERBOTTOM. 1979 (28 Feb.) **[ref. 7022]**. A new species of *Lioteres* (Pisces, Gobiidae) from Kwazulu, with a revised checklist of South African gobies and comments on the generic relationships and endemism of western Indian Ocean gobioids. R. Ont. Mus. Life Sci. Occas. Pap. No. 31: 1-13.

HOFFMANN, L. 1912 **[ref. 5070]**. Zur Kenntnis des Neurocraniums der Pristiden und Pristiophoriden. Zool. Jb. (Anat.) v. 33: 239-360, Pls. 13-24.

HOGG, J. 1841 **[ref. 2183]**. On the existence of branchiae in the young Caeciliae; and on a modification and extension of the branchial classification of the Amphibia. Ann. Mag. Nat. Hist. (n. s.) v. 7 (no. 45): 353-363.

HOLBROOK, J. E. 1855 **[ref. 2184]**. Ichthyology of South Carolina. Charleston. 1-182, 27 pls. [Issued in parts; much of this edition destroyed by fire; see Gill 1864 [ref. 1706]. Second edition published in 1860.]

———. 1860 **[ref. 2185]**. Ichthyology of South Carolina. (Second Edition) 1-205, plates. [See Holbrook 1855 [ref. 2184].]

HOLLARD, H. L. G. M. 1857 **[ref. 2186]**. Études sur les gymnodontes et en particulier sur leur ostéologie et sur les indications qu'elle peut fournir pour leur classification. Ann. Sci. Nat. (Zool.) (Ser. 4) v. 8 (no. 5): 275-328, Pls. 5-6.

HOLLBERG, L. 1819 **[ref. 6468]**. Beskrifning öfver Bohuslanske fiskarne. I Häftet. Göteborgs K. Vetensk.-o. Vitter. Samh. Handl. v. 3: 1-54.

HOLLEMAN, W. 1982 (29 Oct.) **[ref. 2187]**. Three new species and a new genus of tripterygiid fishes (Blenniodei) from the Indo-West Pacific Ocean. Ann. Cape Prov. Mus. Nat. Hist. v. 14 (pt 4): 109-137.

———. 1986 **[ref. 5671]**. Family No. 236: Tripterygiidae (pp. 755-769). In: Smiths' Sea Fishes (Smith & Heemstra 1986 [ref. 5715]).

———. 1987 (30 June) **[ref. 6747]**. Description of a new genus and species of tripterygiid fish (Perciformes: Blennioidei) from the Indo-Pacific, and the reallocation of *Vauclusella acanthops* Whitley, 1965. Cybium v. 11 (no. 2): 173-181.

HOLLY, M. 1926 **[ref. 5038]**. Einige neue Fischformen aus Kamerun. Anz. Akad. Wiss. Wien v. 63 (no. 18): 155-157.

———. 1927 **[ref. 2188]**. Mormyriden, Characiniden und Cypriniden aus Kamerun. Sitzungsber. Akad. Wiss. Wien v. 136 (no. 3-4): 115-150.

———. 1930 **[ref. 2190]**. Synopsis der Süsswasserfische Kameruns. Sitzungsber. Akad. Wiss. Wien v. 139 (1. Abt.) (3-4): 195-281, Pls. 1-2.

———. 1936 **[ref. 6492]**. Pisces 4, Ganoidei. Das Tierreich, Leipzig v. 67: i-xiv + 1-65. [Not seen.]

———. 1939 **[ref. 2191]**. Zur Nomenklatur der Siluridengattung *Macrones* C. Duméril. Zool. Anz. v. 125: 143.

HOLMBERG, E. L. 1891 **[ref. 2192]**. Sobre algunos peces nuevos ó poco conocidos de la República Argentina. Rev. Argent. Hist. Nat. Buenos Aires v. 1: 180-193.

———. 1893 **[ref. 2193]**. Nombres vulgares de peces Argentinos con sus equivalencias científicas. Rev. Jardin Zool. Buenos Aires v. 1 (no. 3): 85-96.

———. 1893 **[ref. 5977]**. El nuevo género *Aristommata*, Holmb. Rev. Jardin Zool. Buenos Aires v. 1 (no. 3): 96.

HOLMES, F. S. 1856 **[ref. 2194]**. Contributions to the natural history of the American devil fish, with descriptions of a new genus from the harbour of Charleston, South Carolina. Proc. Elliott Soc. Nat. Hist. v. 1: 39-46.

HOLT, E. W. L. 1891 **[ref. 2195]**. Survey of fishing grounds, west coast of Ireland. Preliminary note on the fish obtained during the cruise of the SS "Fingal," 1890. Sci. Proc. R. Dublin Soc. (n. s.) v. 7 (pt 2): 121-123.

HOLT, E. W. L., AND L. W. BYRNE. 1908 **[ref. 6487]**. Second report on the fishes of the Irish Atlantic slope. Fish. Ireland Sci. Invest. No. 5 (1906): 1-63, Pls. 1-5.

———. 1910 (Sept.) **[ref. 2196]**. Preliminary diagnosis of a new stomiatoid fish from south-west of Ireland. Ann. Mag. Nat. Hist. (Ser. 8) v. 6 (no. 33): 294-297.

———. 1913 **[ref. 2197]**. Sixth report on the fishes of the Irish Atlantic slope. The families Stomiatidae, Sternoptychidae and Salmonidae. Fish. Ireland Sci. Invest. 1912 (no. 1): 1-28, Pls. 1-2.

HOLTHUIS, L. B., AND M. BOESEMAN. 1977 **[ref. 6877]**. Notes on C. S. Rafinesque Schmaltz's (1810) 'Caratteri di alcuni nuovi generi e nuove specie di animali e piante della Sicilia.' J. Soc. Bibliogr. Nat. Hist. v. 8 (no. 3): 231-234.

HOPKIRK, J. D. 1968 **[ref. 2198]**. Endemism in fishes of the Clear Lake region. Diss. Abstr. Int. B Sci. Eng. v. 29 (no. 1): 414.

———. 1974 (28 Mar.) **[ref. 2199]**. Endemism in fishes of the Clear Lake region of central California. Univ. Calif. Publ. Zool. v. 96: 1-135, Pls. 1-4. [Publication date not 30 Nov. 1973 but 28 Mar. 1974, established through correspondence by W. I. Follett.]

———. 1988 **[ref. 13463]**. Fish evolution and the late Pleistocene and Holocene history of Clear Lake, California. Pp. 183-193. In: J. D. Sims (ed.), Late Quaternary climate, tectonism, and sedimentation in Clear Lake, northern California coast ranges. Spec. Pap., Geol. Soc. Amer.

HORA, S. L. 1920 (21 Dec.) **[ref. 2200]**. Revision of the Indian Homalopteridae and of the genus *Psilorhynchus* (Cyprinidae). Rec. Indian Mus. (Calcutta) v. 19 (pt 5): 195-215, Pls. 10-11.

———. 1921 (Apr.) **[ref. 2201]**. Notes on fishes in the Indian Museum. I. On a new genus of fish closely resembling *Psilorhynchus*, McClelland. Rec. Indian Mus. (Calcutta) v. 22 (pt 1): 13-17.

———. 1921 (Oct.) **[ref. 2202]**. Fish and fisheries of Manipur with some observations on those of the Naga Hills. Rec. Indian Mus. (Calcutta) v. 22 (pt 3, no. 19): 165-214, Pls. 9-12.

———. 1921 (Dec.) **[ref. 2203]**. On some new or rare species of fish from the eastern Himalayas. Rec. Indian Mus. (Calcutta) v. 22 (pt 5, no. 33): 731-744, Pl. 29.

———. 1923 **[ref. 2204]**. Fauna of the Chilka Lake. Fish, part V. Mem. Indian Mus. v. 5: 737-769.

———. 1924 **[ref. 2205]**. Notes on fishes in the Indian Museum. VI. On a new genus of gobioid fishes (subfamily Trypaucheninae) with notes on related forms. Rec. Indian Mus. (Calcutta) v. 26 (pt 2): 155-163.

———. 1925 **[ref. 2206]**. Notes on fishes in the Indian Museum. VII. On a new genus of "Globe-fishes" (fam. Tetraodontidae). Rec. Indian Mus. (Calcutta) v. 26 (pt 6): 579-582, Pl. 34.

———. 1926 **[ref. 2207]**. Notes on fishes in the Indian Museum. IX-XIV. Rec. Indian Mus. (Calcutta) v. 27 (pt 6): 453-469, Pl. 11.

———. 1932 (Dec.) **[ref. 2208]**. Classification, bionomics and evolution of homalopterid fishes. Mem. Indian Mus. v. 12 (no. 2): 263-330, Pls. 10-12.

———. 1937 (Dec.) **[ref. 2209]**. Notes on fishes in the Indian Museum. XXXVI.—On a new genus of Chinese catfishes allied to *Pseudecheneis* Blyth. Rec. Indian Mus. (Calcutta) v. 39 (pt 4): 348-350.

———. 1937 (Nov.) **[ref. 2210]**. A new genus of Siamese catfishes. J. Siam Soc. Nat. Hist. Suppl. v. 11 (no. 1): 39-46, Pl. 2.

———. 1937 **[ref. 6575]**. Geogographical distribution of Indian freshwater fishes and its bearing on the probable land connections between India and the adjacent countries. Curr. Sci. v. 5 (no. 7): 351-356.

———. 1941 (June) **[ref. 2212]**. Homalopterid fishes from peninsular India. Rec. Indian Mus. (Calcutta) v. 43 (pt 2): 221-232, Pl. 8.

———. 1942 (Mar.) **[ref. 2213]**. Notes on fishes in the Indian Museum. XII. On the systematic position of the Indian species of *Scaphiodon* Heckel. XIII. On the systematic position of *Cyprinus nukta* Sykes. Rec. Indian Mus. (Calcutta) v. 44 (pt 1): 1-14.

———. 1950 **[ref. 2214]**. Siluroid fishes of India, Burma and Ceylon.

XIII. Fishes of the genera *Erethistes* Müller and Troschel, *Hara* Blyth and of two new allied genera. Rec. Indian Mus. (Calcutta) v. 47 (pt 2): 183-202, Pls. 1-2.

HORA, S. L., AND P. CHABANAUD. 1930 **[ref. 2215]**. The siluroid fish *Pseudecheneis* and an allied new genus. Rec. Indian Mus. (Calcutta) v. 32 (pt 3): 215-221.

HORA, S. L., AND K. C. JAYARAM. 1952 **[ref. 2216]**. On two new gastromyzonid fishes from Borneo. Rec. Indian Mus. (Calcutta) v. 49 (pt 2): 191-195.

HORA, S. L., AND D. D. MUKERJI. 1936 (Mar.) **[ref. 2217]**. Notes on the fishes in the Indian Museum. XXVII.—On two collections of fish from Maungmagan, Tavoy District, Lower Burma. Rec. Indian Mus. (Calcutta) v. 38 (pt 1): 15-39, Pls. 1-2.

HORA, S. L., AND E. G. SILAS. 1952 **[ref. 2218]**. Notes on fishes in the Indian Museum. XLVII.—Revision of the glyptosternoid fishes of the family Sisoridae, with descriptions of new genera and species. Rec. Indian Mus. (Calcutta) v. 49 (pt 1): 5-29, Pl. 1.

HORN, M. L. 1984 **[ref. 13637]**. Stromateoidei: development and relationships. Am. Soc. Ichthyol. Herpetol. Spec. Publ. No. 1: 620-628.

HOSOYA, K. 1986 (30 May) **[ref. 6155]**. Interrelationships of the Gobioninae (Cyprinidae). Pp. 484-501. In: Uyeno et al. (eds.) 1986 [ref. 6147].

HOUDE, E. D. 1984 **[ref. 13654]**. Bregmacerotidae: development and relationships. Am. Soc. Ichthyol. Herpetol. Spec. Publ. No. 1: 300-308.

———. 1984 **[ref. 13674]**. Callionymidae: development and relationships. Am. Soc. Ichthyol. Herpetol. Spec. Publ. No. 1: 637-640.

HOUTTUYN, M. 1764 **[ref. 2219]**. Natuurlyke historie of uitvoerige beschryving der dieren, planten en mineraalen, volgens het samenstel van den Heer Linnaeus. Met naauwkeurige afbeeldingen. 3 vols. in 37 parts. Amsterdam, 1761-85. [Fishes, pts. 7 & 8. Not seen.]

———. 1782 **[ref. 2220]**. Beschryving van eenige Japanse visschen, en andere zee-schepzelen. Verh. Holl. Maatsch. Wet. Haarlem v. 20 (pt 2): 311-350.

HOWELL RIVERO, L. 1932 (2 Apr.) **[ref. 3765]**. The apodal fishes of Cuba. Proc. New England Zool. Club v. 13: 3-26.

———. 1934 (July) **[ref. 3766]**. Nuevo genero de peces para Cuba. Mem. Soc. Cubana Hist. Nat. -Felipe Poey- v. 8 (no. 2): 69-72, Pl. 7.

———. 1934 (Dec.) **[ref. 3767]**. Some new and rare Cuban eels. Mem. Soc. Cubana Hist. Nat. -Felipe Poey- v. 8 (no. 6): 339-344.

———. 1936 (Feb.) **[ref. 12257]**. Some new, rare and little-known fishes from Cuba. Proc. Boston Soc. Nat. Hist. v. 41 (no. 4): 41-76, Pls. 9-13.

HOWELL RIVERO, L., AND L. R. RIVAS. 1944 (31 May) **[ref. 7312]**. Studies of cyprinodont fishes. Two new genera of the tribe Girardinini, from Cuba. Torreia No. 12: 1-14, Pls. 1-2.

HOWES, G. J. 1980 (29 May) **[ref. 2221]**. A new catfish from Sierra Leone. Bull. Br. Mus. (Nat. Hist.) Zool. v. 38 (no. 3): 165-170.

———. 1980 (29 May) **[ref. 2222]**. A new genus of cheline cyprinid fishes. Bull. Br. Mus. (Nat. Hist.) Zool. v. 38 (no. 3): 171-173.

———. 1980 (31 Jan.) **[ref. 2223]**. The anatomy, phylogeny, and classification of bariliine cyprinid fishes. Bull. Br. Mus. (Nat. Hist.) Zool. v. 37 (no. 3): 129-198.

———. 1981 (27 Aug.) **[ref. 14200]**. Anatomy and phylogeny of the Chinese major carps *Ctenopharyngodon* Steind., 1866 and *Hypophthalmichthys* Blkr., 1860. Bull. Br. Mus. (Nat. Hist.) Zool. v. 41 (no. 1): 1-52.

———. 1982 (29 July) **[ref. 14201]**. Review of the genus *Brycon* (Teleostei: Characoidei). Bull. Br. Mus. (Nat. Hist.) Zool. v. 43 (no. 1): 1-47.

———. 1982 (24 June) **[ref. 14202]**. Anatomy and evolution of the jaws in the semiplotine carps with a review of the genus *Cyprinion* Heckel, 1843 (Teleostei: Cyprinidae). Bull. Br. Mus. (Nat. Hist.) Zool. v. 42 (no. 4): 299-335.

———. 1984 (25 Oct.) **[ref. 5312]**. Phyletics and biogeography of the aspinine cyprinid fishes. Bull. Br. Mus. (Nat. Hist.) Zool. v. 47 (no. 5): 283-303.

———. 1984 (30 Aug.) **[ref. 5834]**. A review of the anatomy, taxonomy, phylogeny and biogeography of the African neoboline cyprinid fishes. Bull. Br. Mus. (Nat. Hist.) Zool. v. 47 (no. 3): 151-185.

———. 1985 (19 Dec.) **[ref. 5148]**. Cranial muscles of gonorynchiform fishes, with comments on generic relationships. Bull. Br. Mus. (Nat. Hist.) Zool. v. 49 (no. 2): 273-303.

———. 1985 (28 Feb.) **[ref. 5274]**. A revised synonymy of the minnow genus *Phoxinus* Rafinesque, 1820 (Teleostei: Cyprinidae) with comments on its relationships and distribution. Bull. Br. Mus. (Nat. Hist.) Zool. v. 48 (no. 1): 57-74.

HOWES, G. J., AND C. P. J. SANFORD. 1987 (May) **[ref. 12820]**. The phylogenetic position of the Plecoglossidae (Teleostei, Salmoniformes), with comments on the Osmeridae and Osmeroidei. Pp. 17-30. In: Kullander & Fernholm (eds.), Proceedings Fifth Congress of European Ichthyologists (1985). Stockholm.

HOWES, G. J., AND G. G. TEUGELS. 1989 **[ref. 13624]**. New bariliin cyprinid fishes from West Africa, with a consideration of their biogeography. J. Nat. Hist. v. 23: 873-902.

HUBBS, C. L. 1915 (20 Mar.) **[ref. 2224]**. Flounders and soles from Japan collected by the United States Bureau of Fisheries steamer "Albatross" in 1906. Proc. U. S. Natl. Mus. v. 48 (no. 2082): 449-496, Pls. 25-27.

———. 1916 (17 Mar.) **[ref. 2225]**. Notes on the marine fishes of California. Univ. Calif. Publ. Zool. v. 16 (no. 13): 153-169, Pls. 18-20.

———. 1918 (1 Feb.) **[ref. 2226]**. *Colpichthys*, *Thyrinops* and *Austromenidia*, new genera of atherinoid fishes from the New World. Proc. Acad. Nat. Sci. Phila. v. 69 (for 1917): 305-308.

———. 1918 (16 May) **[ref. 2227]**. A revision of the viviparous perches. Proc. Biol. Soc. Wash. v. 31: 9-14.

———. 1918 (after 15 Oct.) **[ref. 2228]**. Supplementary notes on flounders from Japan with remarks on the species of *Hippoglossoides*. Annot. Zool. Jpn. v. 9 (pt 4): 369-376.

———. 1921 (9 Apr.) **[ref. 2229]**. Description of a new genus and species of goby from California with notes on related species. Occas. Pap. Mus. Zool. Univ. Mich. No. 99: 1-5.

———. 1923 (21 Dec.) **[ref. 2230]**. A note on the species of *Evermannichthys*, a genus of sponge-inhabiting gobies. Occas. Pap. Mus. Zool. Univ. Mich. No. 144: 1-2.

———. 1924 (18 Jan.) **[ref. 2231]**. Studies of the fishes of the order Cyprinodontes. Misc. Publ. Mus. Zool. Univ. Mich. No. 13: 1-31, Pls. 1-4.

———. 1925 (12 Mar.) **[ref. 2232]**. A revision of the osmerid fishes of the North Pacific. Proc. Biol. Soc. Wash. v. 38: 49-56.

———. 1926 (9 July) **[ref. 2233]**. Studies of the fishes of the order Cyprinodontes. VI. Misc. Publ. Mus. Zool. Univ. Mich. No. 16: 1-86, Pls. 1-4.

———. 1926 (17 Feb.) **[ref. 2234]**. Notes on the gobioid fishes of California, with descriptions of two new genera. Occas. Pap. Mus. Zool. Univ. Mich. No. 169: 1-6, Pl. 1.

———. 1926 (20 Feb.) **[ref. 2235]**. A revision of the fishes of the subfamily Oligocottinae. Occas. Pap. Mus. Zool. Univ. Mich. No. 171: 1-18.

———. 1926 (20 Feb.) **[ref. 6069]**. Descriptions of new genera of cottoid fishes related to *Artedius*. Occas. Pap. Mus. Zool. Univ. Mich. No. 170: 1-16.

———. 1926 (7 July) **[ref. 12022]**. A check-list of the fishes of the Great Lakes and tributary waters, with nomenclatorial notes and analytical keys. Misc. Publ. Mus. Zool. Univ. Mich. No. 15: 1-77, Pls. 1-4.

———. 1927 (Apr.) **[ref. 2236]**. Notes on the blennioid fishes of western North America. Pap. Mich. Acad. Sci. Arts Lett. v. 7 [1926]: 351-394.

———. 1928 (July-Sept.) **[ref. 2237]**. A check [sic] of the marine fishes of Oregon and Washington. J. Pan-Pac. Res. Inst. v. 3 (no. 3): 9-16.

———. 1929 (7 June) **[ref. 2238]**. *Oostethus*: a new generic name for a doryrhamphine pipefish. Occas. Pap. Mus. Zool. Univ. Mich. No. 199: 1-4.

———. 1929 (5 Apr.) **[ref. 2239]**. The generic relationships and nomenclature of the Californian sardine. Proc. Calif. Acad. Sci. (Ser. 4) v. 18 (no. 11): 261-265.

———. 1930 (30 Apr.) **[ref. 5590]**. Materials for a revision of the catostomid fishes of eastern North America. Misc. Publ. Mus. Zool. Univ. Mich. No. 20: 1-47.

———. 1931 (12 Oct.) **[ref. 2240]**. Studies of the fishes of the order Cyprinodontes. IX. A new and primitive genus of Poeciliidae from Central America. Occas. Pap. Mus. Zool. Univ. Mich. No. 230: 1-3.

———. 1931 (30 Nov.) **[ref. 2241]**. *Parexoglossum laurae*, a new cyprinid fish from the Upper Kanawha River system. Occas. Pap. Mus. Zool. Univ. Mich. No. 234: 1-12, Pls. 1-2.

———. 1932 (26 Oct.) **[ref. 2242]**. Studies of the fishes of the order Cyprinodontes. XII. A new genus related to *Empetrichthys*. Occas. Pap. Mus. Zool. Univ. Mich. No. 252: 1-5, Pl. 1.

———. 1933 (7 June) **[ref. 2243]**. *Crossochir koelzi*: a new Californian surf-fish of the family Embiotocidae. Proc. U. S. Natl. Mus. v. 82 (no. 2962): 1-9, 1 pl.

———. 1934 (26 Nov.) **[ref. 2244]**. Studies of the fishes of the order Cyprinodontes. XIII. *Quintana atrizona*, a new poeciliid. Occas. Pap. Mus. Zool. Univ. Mich. No. 301: 1-8, Pl. 1.

———. 1935 (26 July) **[ref. 2245]**. *Anarchopterus*, a new genus of syngnathid fishes from the western Atlantic. Occas. Pap. Mus. Zool. Univ. Mich. No. 320: 1-3.

———. 1935 (30 Jan.) **[ref. 5593]**. The scientific name of two sunfishes, *Helioperca macrochira* (Rafinesque) and *Eupomotis microlophus* (Günther). Occas. Pap. Mus. Zool. Univ. Mich. No. 305: 1-12.

———. 1935 (16 July) **[ref. 6467]**. [Review of] Half mile down. By William Beebe. Copeia 1935 (no. 2): 105.

———. 1936 (26 Aug.) **[ref. 2246]**. *Austroperca*, a new name to replace *Torrentaria*, for a genus of Mexican fishes. Occas. Pap. Mus. Zool. Univ. Mich. No. 341: 1-3.

———. 1936 (5 Feb.) **[ref. 2247]**. XVII. Fishes of the Yucatan Peninsula. Carnegie Inst. Wash. Publ. No. 457: 157-287, Pls. 1-15.

———. 1938 (15 June) **[ref. 2248]**. Fishes from the caves of Yucatan. Carnegie Inst. Wash. Publ. No. 491: 261-295, Pls. 1-4.

———. 1938 (26 May) **[ref. 5958]**. The scientific names of the American "smooth dogfish," *Mustelus canis* (Mitchill), and of the related European species. Occas. Pap. Mus. Zool. Univ. Mich. No. 374: 1-19.

———. 1939 (9 Sept.) **[ref. 5012]**. *Hepsetus* to replace *Hydrocyonoides* and *Sarcodaces* for a genus of African fresh-water fishes. Copeia 1939 (no. 3): 168.

———. 1944 (2 Sept.) **[ref. 2249]**. Relationships of *Alepidomus*, a new genus of atherinine fishes from the fresh waters of Cuba. Occas. Pap. Mus. Zool. Univ. Mich. No. 488: 1-10.

———. 1950 (28 Dec.) **[ref. 2250]**. Studies of cyprinodont Fishes. XX. A new subfamily from Guatemala, with ctenoid scales and a unilateral pectoral clasper. Misc. Publ. Mus. Zool. Univ. Mich. No. 78: 1-28, Pls. 1-4.

———. 1951 (19 Nov.) **[ref. 2251]**. *Allosebastes*, new subgenus for *Sebastodes sinensis*, scorpaenid fish of the Gulf of California. Proc. Biol. Soc. Wash. v. 64: 129-130.

———. 1962 (11 Apr.) **[ref. 6362]**. Review of: Studies on the freshwater fishes of Japan. By Y. Okada. Copeia 1962 (no. 1): 237-238.

———. 1971 (30 Apr.) **[ref. 7683]**. *Lampetra (Entosphenus) lethophaga*, new species, the nonparasitic derivative of the Pacific lamprey. Trans. San Diego Soc. Nat. Hist. v. 16 (no. 6): 125-163.

Hubbs, C. L., and R. M. Bailey. 1940 (27 July) **[ref. 12253]**. A revision of the black basses (*Micropterus* and *Huro*) with descriptions of four new forms. Occas. Pap. Mus. Zool. Univ. Mich. No. 48: 1-51, Pls. 1-6, 2 maps.

———. 1947 (28 Apr.) **[ref. 2254]**. Blind catfishes from artesian waters of Texas. Occas. Pap. Mus. Zool. Univ. Mich. No. 499: 1-15, Pl. 1.

———. 1952 (Aug.) **[ref. 12506]**. Identification of *Oxygeneum pulverulentum* Forbes, from Illinois, as a hybrid cyprinid fish. Pap. Mich. Acad. Sci. Arts Lett. v. 37 [1951]: 143-152, Pl. 1.

Hubbs, C. L., and J. D. Black. 1947 **[ref. 10851]**. Revision of Ceratichthys, a genus of American cyprinid fishes. Misc. Publ. Mus. Zool. Univ. Mich. No. 66: 1-56.

Hubbs, C. L., and M. D. Cannon. 1935 (9 Oct.) **[ref. 2255]**. The darters of the genera *Hololepis* and *Villora*. Misc. Publ. Mus. Zool. Univ. Mich. No. 30: 1-93, Pls. 1-3.

Hubbs, C. L., and W. I. Follett. 1978 (28 Dec.) **[ref. 7017]**. Anatomical notes on an adult male of the deep-sea ophidiid fish *Parabassogigas grandis* from off California. Proc. Calif. Acad. Sci. v. 41 (no. 17): 389-399.

Hubbs, C. L., and W. T. Innes. 1936 (17 Dec.) **[ref. 2256]**. The first known blind fish of the family Characidae: a new genus from Mexico. Occas. Pap. Mus. Zool. Univ. Mich. No. 342: 1-7, Pl. 1.

Hubbs, C. L., and T. Iwamoto. 1977 (18 Aug.) **[ref. 2257]**. A new genus (*Mesobius*), and three new bathypelagic species of Macrouridae (Pisces, Gadiformes) from the Pacific Ocean. Proc. Calif. Acad. Sci. v. 41 (no. 7): 233-251.

Hubbs, C. L., and R. R. Miller. 1948 (20 May) **[ref. 2258]**. Two new relict genera of cyprinid fishes from Nevada. Occas. Pap. Mus. Zool. Univ. Mich. No. 507: 1-30, Pls. 1-3.

———. 1960 (29 June) **[ref. 2259]**. *Potamarius*, a new genus of ariid catfishes from the fresh waters of Middle America. Copeia 1960 (no. 2): 101-112, Pl. 1.

———. 1965 (30 Sept.) **[ref. 9217]**. Studies of Cyprinodont fishes. XXII. Variation in *Lucania parva*, its establishment in western United States, and description of a new species from an interior basin in Coahuila, México Misc. Publ. Mus. Zool. Univ. Mich. No. 127: 1-104, Pls. 1-3.

———. 1972 (29 Sept.) **[ref. 2260]**. Diagnoses of new cyprinid fishes of isolated waters in the Great Basin of western North America. Trans. San Diego Soc. Nat. Hist. v. 17 (no. 8): 101-106.

———. 1977 (2 Sept.) **[ref. 7060]**. Six distinctive cyprinid fish species referred to *Dionda* inhabiting segments of the Tampico embayment drainage of Mexico. Trans. San Diego Soc. Nat. Hist. v. 18 (no. 17): 267-336.

Hubbs, C. L., R. R. Miller and L. C. Hubbs. 1974 (8 Feb.) **[ref. 14477]**. Hydrographic history and relict fishes of the north-central Great Basin. Mem. Calif. Acad. Sci. v. 7: i-v + 1-259.

Hubbs, C. L., and I. C. Potter. 1971 **[ref. 13397]**. Distribution, phylogeny and taxonomy. Pp. 1-65. In: Hardisty, M. W., and I. C. Potter (eds.), The Biology of Lampreys. Academic Press, New York.

Hubbs, C. L., and L. P. Schultz. 1932 **[ref. 2261]**. A new blenny from British Columbia with records of two other fishes new to the region. Contrib. Can. Biol. Fish. (n. s.) v. 7: 319-324. [(Also No. 25, Ser. A, General, no. 22)]

———. 1934 (24 Apr.) **[ref. 5610]**. *Elephantichthys copeianus*, a new cyclopterid fish from Alaska. Copeia 1934 (no. 1): 21-26 + insert fig.

———. 1939 (29 Apr.) **[ref. 2263]**. A revision of the toadfishes referred to *Porichthys* and related genera. Proc. U. S. Natl. Mus. v. 86 (no. 3060): 473-496.

Hubbs, C. L., and C. L. Turner. 1939 (9 Nov.) **[ref. 2265]**. Studies of the fishes of the order Cyprinodontes. XVI. A revision of the Goodeidae. Misc. Publ. Mus. Zool. Univ. Mich. No. 42: 1-80, Pls. 1-5.

Hubbs, C. L., and R. L. Wisner. 1964 (17 Jan.) **[ref. 2266]**. *Parvilux*, a new genus of myctophid fishes from the northeastern Pacific, with two new species. Zool. Meded. (Leiden) v. 39: 445-463, Pl. 25.

———. 1980 **[ref. 2267]**. Revision of the sauries (Pisces, Scomberesocidae) with descriptions of two new genera and one new species. U. S. Natl. Mar. Fish. Serv. Fish. Bull. v. 77 (no. 3): 521-566.

Hubbs, Clark. 1952 (15 Apr.) **[ref. 2252]**. A contribution to the classification of the blennoid fishes of the family Clinidae, with a partial revision of eastern Pacific forms. Stanford Ichthyol. Bull. v. 4 (no. 2): 41-165.

———. 1953 (25 Nov.) **[ref. 2253]**. Revision of the eastern Pacific fishes of the clinid genus *Labrisomus*. Zoologica (N. Y.) v. 38 (pt 3, no. 9): 113-136.

———. 1953 **[ref. 12698]**. Revision and systematic position of the blenniid fishes of the genus *Neoclinus*. Copeia 1953 (no. 1): 11-23.

HUBER, J. H. 1977 **[ref. 2268]**. Liste nominale annotée de *Aphyosemion* Myers, avec description de *Raddaella* et *Kathetys* deux nouveaux sous-genres nouveaux à la biologie originale. Killi Revue v. 4 (no. 4)(suppl.): 16 unnumbered pages. [Photocopied, but apparently new names are available.]

———. 1979 (26 Mar.) **[ref. 2269]**. Cyprinodontidés de la cuvette congolaise (*Adamas formosus* n. gen., n. sp. et nouvelle description de *Aphyosemion splendidum*). Rev. Fr. Aquariol. v. 6 (no. 1): 5-10. [A translated version appeared in Huber 1979 [ref. 2270].]

———. 1979 **[ref. 2270]**. Cyprinodonts of the Congo Basin. (*Adamas formosus* new genus, new species; with a new description of *Aphyosemion splendidum*). J. Am. Killifish Assoc. v. 12 (no. 6): 165-174. [Appeared first in French as Huber 1979 [ref. 2269].]

———. 1981 (Nov.) **[ref. 2271]**. A review of cyprinodont fauna of the coastal plain in Rio Muni, Gabon, Congo, Cabinda and Zaire with taxonomic shifts in *Aphyosemion*, *Epiplatys* and West African procatopodins. British Killifish Assoc. Publ. 1-46. [Possibly not distributed until Mar. 1982.]

HUBER, J. H., AND L. SEEGERS. 1977 **[ref. 2273]**. Vorläufige Beschreibung von *Diapteron*, nov. subgen. DKG-Jour. v. 9 (no. 9): 146-148.

———. 1978 (Mar.) **[ref. 2272]**. *Diapteron*, nouveau sous-genre de *Aphyosemion* Myers. Rev. Fr. Aquariol. v. 4 (no. 4): 115-116.

HULLEY, P. A. 1972 **[ref. 5611]**. The origin, interrelationships and distribution of southern African Rajidae (Chondrichthyes, Batoidei). Ann. S. Afr. Mus. v. 60 (pt 1): 1-103.

———. 1973 (Nov.) **[ref. 2275]**. Interrelationships within the Anacanthobatidae (Chondrichthyes, Rajoidea), with a description of the lectotype of *Anacanthobatis marmoratus* von Bonde & Swart, 1923. Ann. S. Afr. Mus. v. 62 (pt 4): 131-158.

———. 1981 (31 June) **[ref. 2276]**. Results of the research cruises of FRV "Walther Herwig" to South America. LVIII. Family Myctophidae (Osteichthyes, Myctophiformes). Arch. FischereiWiss. v. 31 (Beih. 1): 1-303.

———. 1986 **[ref. 5672]**. Family No. 25: Rajidae (pp. 115-127), 26: Acanthobatidae (p. 127), 70: Idiacanthidae (pp. 234-235), 82: Anotopteridae (p. 278), 86: Myctophidae (pp. 282-321), 87: Neoscopelidae (pp. 321-322), 123: Stylephoridae (p. 404), 131: Anoplogastridae (p. 415). In: Smiths' Sea Fishes (Smith & Heemstra 1986 [ref. 5715]).

———. 1989 (Feb.) **[ref. 12284]**. Lanternfishes of the southern Benguela region. Part 2. *Gymnoscopelus (Gymnoscopelus) bolini* Andriashev in South African waters, with comments on the distribution of subantarctic myctophids in the eastern South Atlantic. Ann. S. Afr. Mus. v. 98 (pt. 8): 221-240.

HULLEY, P. A., AND M. J. PENRITH. 1966 (June) **[ref. 2277]**. *Euprotomicroides zantedeschia*, a new genus and species of pigmy dalatiid shark from South Africa. Bull. Mar. Sci. v. 16 (no. 2): 222-229.

HUMBOLDT, F. H. A. VON. 1805 **[ref. 2278]**. Ueber den *Eremophilus* und den *Astroblepus*, zwei neue Fisch-Gattungen. Observationes Zoologicae. [Orig. not seen; Fowler dates to 1805 as Voy. Inter. Amer., Obser. Zool.; sometimes genera dated as 1806.]

———. 1833 **[ref. 4503]**. Nouvelles observations sur l'*Eremophilus*. Recueil d'Observ. Zool. [Not seen. See also Humboldt and Valenciennes 1811.]

HUMBOLDT, F. H. A. VON, AND A. VALENCIENNES. 1812 **[ref. 5612]**. Recherches sur les poissons fluviatiles de l'Amérique Équinoxiale. Pp. 145-216. Pls. 45-48. In: Homboldt & Bonpland, Recueil d'observations de zoologie ... dans l'océan Atlantic, dans l'intéieur du nouveau continent ... pendant les années 1799, 1800, 1801, 1802 et 1803. Zool. v. 2. [Later edition; the original in 1806. See Sherborn 1899, Ann. Mag. Nat. Hist. (Ser. 7) v. 3: 428 for dates.]

HUMPHREYS, R. L., JR., AND D. T. TAGAMI. 1986 (Sept.) **[ref. 6000]**. Review and current status of research on the biology and ecology of the genus *Pseudopentaceros*. NOAA Tech. Rep. NMFS 43: 55-62.

HUMPHREYS, R. L., JR., G. A. WINANS AND D. T. TAGAMI. 1989 (27 Feb.) **[ref. 9286]**. Synonymy and life history of the North Pacific armorhead, *Pseudopentaceros wheeleri* Hardy (Pisces: Pentacerotidae). Copeia 1989 (no. 1): 142-153.

HUREAU, J.-C. 1973 **[ref. 7197]**. Priacanthidae (p. 364), Mullidae (pp. 402-404), Platycephalidae (p. 592). In: Hureau & Monod 1973 [ref. 6590].

HUREAU, J.-C., J. LOUIS, A. TOMO AND C. OZOUF. 1980 **[ref. 6932]**. Application de l'analyse canonique discriminante à la révision du genre *Harpagifer* (Téléostéens, Notothéniiformes). Vie Milieu Ser. AB Biol. Mar. Oceanogr. v. 28-29 (fasc. 2): 287-306.

HUREAU, J.-C., AND T. MONOD. 1973 **[ref. 6590]**. Check-list of the fishes of the north-eastern Atlantic and of the Mediterranean. Unesco, Paris CLOFNAM I: i-xxii + 1-683; CLOFNAM II: 1-331.

HUREAU, J.-C., AND J. G. NIELSEN. 1981 (30 Sept.) **[ref. 5438]**. Les poissons Ophidiiformes des campagnes du N. O. "Jean Charcot" dans l'Atlantic et la Méditerranée. Cybium (Ser. 3) v. 5 (no. 3): 3-27.

HUREAU, J.-C., AND E. TORTONESE. 1973 **[ref. 7198]**. Carangidae (pp. 373-384). In: Hureau & Monod 1973 [ref. 6590].

HUTCHINS, J. B. 1974 **[ref. 6970]**. *Halophryne ocellatus*, a new species of frogfish (Batrachoididae) from Western Australia. Rec. West. Aust. Mus. v. 3 (no. 2): 115-120.

———. 1976 **[ref. 6971]**. A revision of the Australian frogfishes (Batrachoididae). Rec. West. Aust. Mus. v. 4 (no. 1): 3-43.

———. 1977 **[ref. 2283]**. Descriptions of three new genera and eight new species of monacanthid fishes from Australia. Rec. West. Aust. Mus. v. 5 (no. 1): 3-58.

———. 1981 (30 Jan.) **[ref. 5583]**. Description of a new species of serranid fish from Western Australia, with a key to the Australian species of *Acanthistius*. Rec. West. Aust. Mus. v. 8 (no. 4): 491-499.

———. 1981 (15 May) **[ref. 6830]**. Nomenclatural status of the toadfishes of India. Copeia 1981 (no. 2): 336-341.

———. 1983 (14 Nov.) **[ref. 5374]**. Redescription of the clingfish *Cochleoceps spatula* (Gobiesocidae) from Western Australia and South Australia, with the description of a new species from Victoria and Tasmania. Rec. West. Aust. Mus. v. 11 (no. 1): 33-47.

———. 1984 (19 Apr.) **[ref. 5230]**. Description of a new gobiesocid fish from south-western Australia, with a key to the species of *Aspasmogaster*. Rec. West. Aust. Mus. v. 11 (no. 2): 129-140.

———. 1986 **[ref. 5673]**. Family No. 100: Batrachoididae (pp. 358-361), Family No. 264: Monacanthidae (pp. 882-887). In: Smiths' Sea Fishes (Smith & Heemstra 1986 [ref. 5715]).

———. 1987 (13 Apr.) **[ref. 12583]**. Description of a new plesiopid fish from south-western Australia, with a discussion of the zoogeography of *Paraplesiops*. Rec. West. Aust. Mus. v. 13 (pt 2): 231-240.

HUTCHINS, J. B., AND R. H. KUITER. 1982 (13 Dec.) **[ref. 5373]**. A new species of *Acanthistius* (Pisces: Serranidae) from eastern Australia. Rec. West. Aust. Mus. v. 10 (no. 2): 127-131.

HUTCHINS, J. B., AND K. MATSUURA. 1984 **[ref. 7092]**. Description of a new monacanthid fish of the genus *Thamnaconus* from Fiji. Rec. West. Aust. Mus. v. 11 (no. 4): 387-391.

HUTCHINS, J. B., AND J. E. RANDALL. 1982 **[ref. 5372]**. *Cantherhines longicaudus*, a new filefish from Oceania, with a review of the species of the *C. fronticinctus* complex. Pac. Sci. v. 36 (no. 2): 175-185.

HUTCHINS, J. B., AND R. SWAINSTON. 1985 (2 Apr.) **[ref. 5231]**. Revision of the monacanthid fish genus *Brachaluteres*. Rec. West. Aust. Mus. v. 12 (no. 1): 57-78.

HUTTON, F. W. 1872 **[ref. 2287]**. Fishes of New Zealand. Catalogue with diagnoses of the species [Followed by an article by J. Hector, Notes on the edible fishes, pp. 95-133]. Colonial Mus. & Geol Surv. Dept., Wellington. 1-93 + 95-133, Pls. 1-12. [Plates used for both articles; new taxa by Hutton.]

——. 1873 **[ref. 2285]**. Contributions to the ichthyology of New Zealand. Trans. Proc. N. Z. Inst. v. 5 (art. 28): 259-272, Pls. 7-12.

——. 1890 (May) **[ref. 2286]**. List of New Zealand fishes. Trans. Proc. N. Z. Inst. v. 22 [1889]: 275-285.

Hyrtl, C. J. 1854 **[ref. 2290]**. Beitrag zur Anatomie von *Heterotis ehrenbergii* C. V. Denkschr. Akad. Wiss. Wien v. 8: 73-88, 3 pls. [Abstract in Sitzungsber. Akad. Wiss. Wien v. 12: 396-399. Also as separate, 1855, 16 pp.]

——. 1859 **[ref. 2291]**. Anatomische Untersuchung des *Clarotes (Gonocephalus) heuglini* Kner. Mit einer Abbildung und einer osteologischen Tabelle der Siluroiden. Denkschr. Akad. Wiss. Wien v. 16: 1-18, 1 pl.

Ihering, H. von. 1898 (5 Apr.) **[ref. 2292]**. Contributions to the herpetology of São Paulo.—1. Proc. Acad. Nat. Sci. Phila. 1898 [v. 50]: 101-109.

——. 1907 **[ref. 2294]**. Diversas especies novas de peixes nemathognathas do Brazil. Notas preliminares. Rev. Mus. Paulista (n. s.) v. 1 (fasc. 1): 13-39. [In English and Portuguese.]

——. 1928 (9 June) **[ref. 5011]**. *Taddyella* nom. nov. pro. *Roosveltiella* Eig. 1915. Bol. Biol., Trab. Lab. Parasit. Fac. Med., S. Paulo v. 12 (no. 47): 45.

Iljin, B. S. 1927 **[ref. 5613]**. [Definitions of gobies (Fam. Gobiidae) of the Sea of Azov and the Black Sea. Preliminary communication.] Abh. Wiss. Fisch. Exped. Asowsch. Schwarzen Meer. Lief. 2: 128-143, Pls. 1-2. [In Russian.]

——. 1928 **[ref. 2296]**. Two new genera and a new species of Gobiidae from the Caspian Sea. Rep. Astrakhan Sci. Fish. Stat. v. 6 (no. 3): 39-48, 1 pl. [In Russian, English summ. Possibly not published until 1929.]

——. 1930 (30 Mar.) **[ref. 2297]**. Le système des Gobiidés. Trab. Inst. Esp. Oceanogr. v. 2: 1-63.

——. 1941 **[ref. 2298]**. *Asra turcomanus*, a new genus and species of gobies (Gobiidae) from the Caspian Sea. Bull. Acad. Sci. U.R.S.S., Ser. Biol. v. 1941 (no. 3): 385-390. [In Russian and in English.]

Ilyina, M. B. 1978 **[ref. 6914]**. On the systematic status of the genus *Podothecus* Gill in the family Agonidae. Pp. 5-12. In: Morphology and systematics of fish. Acad. Sci. Leningrad. [In Russian.]

Inada, T., and J. A. F. Garrick. 1979 (15 Feb.) **[ref. 7002]**. *Rhinochimaera pacifica*, a long-snouted Chimaera (Rhinochimaeridae), in New Zealand waters. Jpn. J. Ichthyol. v. 25 (no. 4): 235-243.

Inada, T., and I. Nakamura. 1975 (Nov.) **[ref. 7099]**. A comparative study of two populations of the gadoid fish *Micromesistius australis* from the New Zealand and Patagonian-Falkland regions. Bull. Far Seas Fish. Res. Lab. (Shimizu) Bull. 13: 1-26.

Iredale, T., and G. P. Whitley. 1932 (8 Aug.) **[ref. 2299]**. Blandowski. Victorian Nat. Melbourne v. 49: 90-96.

——. 1969 (24 Apr.) **[ref. 6763]**. Chesnon's "Essai sur l'histoire naturelle," 1835. Proc. R. Zool. Soc. N. S. W. v. for 1967-68: 43-45.

Isbrücker, I. J. H. 1971 (3 Feb.) **[ref. 2300]**. *Pseudohemiodon (Planiloricaria) cryptodon*, a new species and subgenus from Peru (Pisces, Siluriformes, Loricariidae). Bonn. Zool. Beitr. v. 21 (heft 3/4): 274-283, 7 pls. ["Issued Febr 3 1971" stamped on cover of reprint.]

——. 1975 **[ref. 2301]**. *Metaloricaria paucidens*, a new species and genus of mailed catfish from French Guiana (Pisces, Siluriformes, Loricariidae). Bull. Inst. R. Sci. Nat. Belg. Biol. v. 50 (no. 4): 1-9, Pls. 1-3. [Date on cover is 30 Dec. 1974, date of 1975 from Isbrücker & Nijssen 1982 [ref. 5277].]

——. 1979 (30 Jan.) **[ref. 2302]**. Descriptions préliminaries de nouveaux taxa de la famille des Loricariidae, poissons-chats cuirassés néotropicaux, avec un catalogue critique de la sous-famille nominale (Pisces, Siluriformes). Rev. Fr. Aquariol. v. 5 (no. 4): 86-117.

——. 1980 (3 Mar.) **[ref. 2303]**. Classification and catalogue of the mailed Loricariidae (Pisces, Siluriformes). Versl. Tech. Gegevens No. 22: 1-181.

——. 1981 (30 Oct.) **[ref. 5522]**. Revision of *Loricaria* Linnaeus, 1758 (Pisces, Siluriformes, Loricariidae). Beaufortia v. 31 (no. 3): 51-96.

Isbrücker, I. J. H., H. A. Britski, H. Nijssen and H. Ortega. 1983 (1 Sept.) **[ref. 5388]**. *Aposturisoma myriodon*, une espèce et un genre nouveaux de Poisson-Chat cuirassé, tribu Farlowellini Fowler, 1958 du Bassin du Rio Ucayali, Pérou (Pisces, Siluriformes, Loricariidae). Rev. Fr. Aquariol. v. 10 (no. 2): 33-42.

Isbrücker, I. J. H., and H. Nijssen. 1974 (31 July) **[ref. 2304]**. *Rhadinoloricaria* gen. nov. and *Planiloricaria*, two genera of South American mailed catfishes (Pisces, Siluriformes, Loricariidae). Beaufortia v. 22 (no. 290): 67-81.

——. 1974 (20 Dec.) **[ref. 7126]**. On *Hemiodontichthys acipenserinus* and *Reganella depressa*, two remarkable mailed catfishes from South America (Pisces, Siluriformes, Loricariidae). Beaufortia v. 22 (no. 294): 193-222.

——. 1976 (17 Nov.) **[ref. 7075]**. The South American mailed catfishes of the genus *Pseudoloricaria* Bleeker, 1862 (Pisces, Siluriformes, Loricariidae). Beaufortia v. 25 (no. 325): 107-129.

——. 1978 **[ref. 2305]**. The neotropical mailed catfishes of the genera *Lamontichthys* P. de Miranda Ribeiro, 1939 and *Pterosturisoma* n. gen., including the description of *Lamontichthys stibaros* n. sp. from Ecuador (Pisces, Siluriformes, Loricariidae). Bijdr. Dierkd. v. 48 (no. 1): 57-80.

——. 1978 (18 June) **[ref. 2306]**. Two new species and a new genus of neotropical mailed catfishes of the subfamily Loricariinae Swainson, 1838 (Pisces, Siluriformes, Loricariidae). Beaufortia v. 27 (no. 339): 177-206.

——. 1982 **[ref. 5277]**. New data on *Metaloricaria paucidens* from French Guiana and Surinam (Pisces, Siluriformes, Loricariidae). Bijdr. Dierkd. v. 52 (no. 2): 155-168.

——. 1983 (1 Mar.) **[ref. 5389]**. *Aphanotorulus frankei*, une espèce et un genre nouveaux de Poissons-Chats cuirassés du Bassin du Rio Ucayali au Pérou (Pisces, Siluriformes, Loricariidae). Rev. Fr. Aquariol. v. 9 (no. 4): 105-110.

——. 1984 **[ref. 5279]**. *Pyxiloricaria menezesi*, a new genus and species of mailed catfish from Rio Miranda and Rio Cuiabá, Brazil (Pisces, Siluriformes, Loricariidae). Bijdr. Dierkd. v. 54 (no. 2): 163-168.

——. 1984 (14 Nov.) **[ref. 9845]**. *Rineloricaria castroi*, a new species of mailed catfish from Rio Trombetas, Brazil (Pisces, Siluriformes, Loricariidae). Beaufortia v. 34 (no. 3): 93-99.

——. 1986 (21 July) **[ref. 5212]**. *Apistoloricaria condei*, nouveau genre et nouvelle espèce de Poisson-Chat cuirassé, tribu Loricariini Bonaparte, 1831, du bassin du Rio Napo, haute Amazone, Equateur (Pisces, Siluriformes, Loricariidae). Rev. Fr. Aquariol. v. 12 (no. 4): 103-108.

——. 1986 **[ref. 7321]**. New records of the mailed catfish *Planiloricaria cryptodon* from the Upper Amazon in Peru, Brazil and Bolivia, with a key to the genera of the Planiloricariina. Bijdr. Dierkd. v. 56 (no. 1): 39-46.

——. 1988 (30 Sept.) **[ref. 7319]**. Review of the South American characiform fish genus *Chilodus*, with description of a new species, *C. gracilis* (Pisces, Characiformes, Chilodontidae). Beaufortia v. 38 (no. 3): 47-56.

——. 1988 **[ref. 7320]**. *Acanthicus adonis*, ein neuer Harnischwels aus dem Rio Tocantins, Brasilien (Pisces, Siluriformes, Loricariidae). Aquar. Terrar. Z. v. 41 (no. 6): 164-167.

——. 1989 **[ref. 13622]**. Diagnose dreier neuer Harnischwelsgattungen mit fünf neuen Arten aus Brasilien (Pisces, Siluriformes, Loricariidae). Aquar. Terrar. Z. v. 42 (no. 9): 541-547.

Isbrücker, I. J. H., H. Nijssen and P. Cala. 1988 (4 May) **[ref. 6409]**. *Lithoxancistrus orinoco*, nouveau genre et espèce de poisson-chat cuirassé du Rio Orinoco en Colombie (Pisces, Siluriformes, Loricariidae). Rev. Fr. Aquariol. v. 15 (no. 1): 13-16.

Ishida, M., and K. Amaoka. 1986 **[ref. 11443]**. *Sebastiscus triacanthus* Fowler a junior synonym of *Hozukius emblemarius* (Jordan et Starks). Jpn. J. Ichthyol. v. 33 (no. 3): 323-325.

ISHIHARA, H. 1987 (10 Dec.) **[ref. 6264]**. Revision of the western North Pacific species of the genus *Raja*. Jpn. J. Ichthyol. v. 34 (no. 3): 241-285.

ISHIHARA, H., AND R. ISHIYAMA. 1985 (30 Aug.) **[ref. 5799]**. Two new North Pacific skates (Rajidae) and a revised key to *Bathyraja* in the area. Jpn. J. Ichthyol. v. 32 (no. 2): 143-179.

——. 1986 (30 May) **[ref. 5142]**. Systematics and distribution of the skates of the North Pacific (Chondrichthyes, Rajoidei). Pp. 269-280. In: Uyeno et al. (eds.) 1986 [ref. 6147].

ISHIYAMA, R. 1952 (July) **[ref. 2307]**. Studies on the rays and skates belonging to the family *Rajidae*, found in Japan and adjacent regions. 4. A revision of three genera of Japanese rajids with descriptions of one new genus and four new species mostly occured in northern Japan. J. Shimonoseki Coll. Fish. v. 2 (no. 2): 1-34, Pls. 1-4.

——. 1958 (July) **[ref. 2308]**. Studies on the rajid fishes (Rajidae) found in the waters around Japan. J. Shimonoseki Coll. Fish. v. 7 (no. 2,3): 193-394, Pls. 1-3.

ISHIYAMA, R., AND C. L. HUBBS. 1968 (5 June) **[ref. 2309]**. *Bathyraja*, a genus of Pacific skates (Rajidae) regarded as phyletically distinct from the Atlantic genus *Breviraja*. Copeia 1968 (no. 2): 407-410.

ISHIYAMA, R., AND H. ISHIHARA. 1977 (15 Sept.) **[ref. 5401]**. Five new species of skates in the genus *Bathyraja* from the western North Pacific, with reference to their interspecific relationships. Jpn. J. Ichthyol. v. 24 (no. 2): 71-90.

IVANTSOFF, W. 1986 **[ref. 6292]**. Family No. 111: Atherinidae (pp. 381-384), Family No. 112: Notocheiridae (p. 384). In: Smiths' Sea Fishes (Smith & Heemstra 1986 [ref. 5715]).

IVANTSOFF, W., AND G. R. ALLEN. 1984 (Dec.) **[ref. 6380]**. Two new species of *Pseudomugil* (Pisces: Melanotaeniidae) from Irian Jaya and New Guinea. Aust. Zool. v. 21 (no. 5): 479-489.

IVANTSOFF, W., L. E. L. M. CROWLEY AND G. R. ALLEN. 1987 **[ref. 6229]**. Descriptions of three new species and one subspecies of freshwater hardyhead (Pisces: Atherinidae: *Craterocephalus*) from Australia. Rec. West. Aust. Mus. v. 13 (pt 2): 171-188.

IVANTSOFF, W., AND M. KOTTELAT. 1988 (20 Sept.) **[ref. 6856]**. Redescription of *Hypoatherina valenciennei* and its relationships to other species of Atherinidae in the Pacific and Indian oceans. Jpn. J. Ichthyol. v. 35 (no. 2): 142-149.

IVANTSOFF, W., B. SAID AND A. WILLIAMS. 1987 (5 Aug.) **[ref. 6230]**. Systematic position of the family Dentatherinidae in relationship to Phallostethidae and Atherinidae. Copeia 1987 (no. 3): 649-658.

IWAMI, T. 1985 (Mar.) **[ref. 13368]**. Osteology and relationships of the family Channichthyidae. Mem. Natl. Inst. Polar Res. (Ser. E) No. 36: 1-69.

IWAMI, T., AND T. ABE. 1980 (27 Dec.) **[ref. 6894]**. Records of adults of some scopelarchid fishes from the western North Pacific and the Southern Ocean, with osteological notes on five species of the genus *Benthalbella*. Uo (Jpn. Soc. Ichthyol.) No. 31: 1-20, Pl. 1.

IWAMOTO, T. 1974 (27 June) **[ref. 2310]**. *Nezumia (Kuronezumia) bubonis*, a new subgenus and species of grenadier (Macrouridae: Pisces) from Hawaii and the western North Atlantic. Proc. Calif. Acad. Sci. (Ser. 4) v. 39 (no. 22): 507-516.

——. 1979 (22 Dec.) **[ref. 2311]**. Eastern Pacific macrourine grenadiers with seven branchiostegal rays (Pisces: Macrouridae). Proc. Calif. Acad. Sci. v. 42 (no. 5): 135-179.

——. 1980 **[ref. 6933]**. *Matsubaraea* Taki, a senior synonym of *Cirrinasus* Schultz (Percophididae). Jpn. J. Ichthyol. v. 27 (no. 2): 111-114.

——. 1986 **[ref. 5674]**. Family No. 93: Macrouridae (pp. 330-341). In: Smiths' Sea Fishes (Smith & Heemstra 1986 [ref. 5715]).

IWAMOTO, T., AND T. ARAI. 1987 (11 Feb.) **[ref. 6779]**. A new grenadier *Malacocephalus okamurai* (Pisces: Gadiformes: Macrouridae) from the western Atlantic. Copeia 1987 (no. 1): 204-208.

IWAMOTO, T., J. E. MCCOSKER AND O. BARTON. 1976 **[ref. 7089]**. Alepocephalid fishes of the genera *Herwigia* and *Bathylaco*, with the first Pacific record of *H. kreffti*. Jpn. J. Ichthyol. v. 23 (no. 1): 55-59.

IWAMOTO, T., AND YU. I. SAZONOV. 1988 (5 Feb.) **[ref. 6228]**. A review of the southeastern Pacific *Coryphaenoides* (sensu lato) (Pisces, Gadiformes, Macrouridae). Proc. Calif. Acad. Sci. v. 45 (no. 3): 35-82.

IWAMOTO, T., AND J. C. STAIGER. 1976 (Oct.) **[ref. 7072]**. Percophidid fishes of the genus *Chrionema* Gilbert. Bull. Mar. Sci. v. 26 (no. 4): 488-498.

IWATA, A. 1983 (15 May) **[ref. 5794]**. A revision of the cottid fish genus *Vellitor*. Jpn. J. Ichthyol. v. 30 (no. 1): 1-9.

IWATA, A., S.-R. JEON, N. MIZUNO AND K.-C. CHOI. 1985 (20 Feb.) **[ref. 6724]**. A revision of the eleotrid goby genus *Odontobutis* in Japan, Korea and China. Jpn. J. Ichthyol. v. 31 (no. 4): 373-388.

IWATSUKI, Y., H. SENOU AND T. SUZUKI. 1989 (15 Mar.) **[ref. 12750]**. A record of the lutjanid fish, *Lutjanus ehrenbergii*, from Japan with reference to its related species. Jpn. J. Ichthyol. v. 35 (no. 4): 469-478.

JÄCKEL, A. J. 1864 **[ref. 2338]**. Die Fische Bayerns. Ein Beitrag zur Kenntniss der deutschen Süsswasserfische. Abh. Zool. Min. Ver. Regensburg v. 9 (1864): 1-101. [Also as a separate, 1864, 1-101 + index.]

JACKSON, P. B. N. 1959 (Jan.) **[ref. 2312]**. Revision of the clariid catfishes of Nyasaland, with a description of a new genus and seven new species. Proc. Zool. Soc. Lond. v. 132 (pt 1): 109-128.

JAEKEL, O. 1929 **[ref. 2320]**. Morphogenie der ältesten Wirbeltiere. Mon. Geol. Pal. Berlin v. 3: 1-198, 14 pls. [Not seen.]

JAMES, G. D. 1972 (8 June) **[ref. 7082]**. Revision of the New Zealand flatfish genus *Peltorhamphus* with descriptions of two new species. Copeia 1972 (no. 2): 345-355.

——. 1976 **[ref. 7081]**. *Cyttus traversi* Hutton: juvenile form of *C. ventralis* Barnard and Davies (Pisces: Zeidae). J. R. Soc. N. Z. v. 6 (no. 4): 493-498.

JAMES, G. D., T. INADA AND I. NAKAMURA. 1988 **[ref. 6639]**. Revision of the oreosomatid fishes (family Oreosomatidae) from the southern oceans, with a description of a new species. N. Z. J. Zool. v. 15: 291-326.

JAMES, P. S. B. R. 1978 (Mar.) **[ref. 5317]**. A systematic review of the fishes of the family Leiognathidae. J. Mar. Biol. Assoc. India v. 17 (no. 1): 138-172, Pls. 1-3. [Volume for Apr. 1975, issued Mar. 1978.]

——. 1985 **[ref. 12861]**. Comparative osteology of the fishes of the family Leiognathidae. Part II. Relationships among the genera and the species. Indian J. Fish. v. 32 (no. 4): 395-416.

JAROCKI, F. 1822 **[ref. 4984]**. Zoologiia. [Not seen. Discussed by Whitehead 1982 [ref. 9738].]

JAYARAM, K. C. 1954 **[ref. 2336]**. Siluroid fishes of India, Burma and Ceylon. XIV.—Fishes of the genus *Mystus* Scopoli. Rec. Indian Mus. (Calcutta) v. 51 (pt 4): 527-558, Pl. 19.

——. 1955 **[ref. 5614]**. The Palaearctic element in the fish fauna of peninsular India. Bull. Natl. Inst. Sci. India No. 7: 260-263.

——. 1968 **[ref. 5615]**. Contributions to the study of bagrid fishes (Siluroidea: Bagridae). 3. A systematic account of the Japanese, Chinese, Malayan and Indonesian genera. Treubia, Mus. Zool. Borgoriense v. 27 (pt 203): 287-386.

——. 1972 **[ref. 2337]**. Contributions to the study of bagrid fishes (Siluroidea: Bagridae). 10. Systematic position of *Pimelodus chandramara* Hamilton with description of a new genus. Int. Rev. Gesamten Hydrobiol. v. 57 (no. 5): 815-820.

——. 1977 **[ref. 7005]**. Aid to identification of siluroid fishes of India, Burma, Sri Lanka, Pakistan and Bangladesh. 1. Bagridae. Rec. Zool. Surv. India, Misc. Publ., Occas. Pap. No. 8: 1-41.

——. 1977 **[ref. 7006]**. Aid to identification of siluroid fishes of India, Burma, Sri Lanka, Pakistan and Bangladesh. 2. Siluridae, Schilbeidae, Pangasidae, Amblycipitidae, Akysidae. Rec. Zool. Surv. India, Misc. Publ., Occas. Pap. No. 10: 1-33.

——. 1977 **[ref. 7007]**. Contributions to the study of bagrid fishes. 12. The correct family position of *Batsio* Blyth (Siluroidea). Newsl. Zool. Surv. India v. 3 (no 4): 242-245.

——. 1978 **[ref. 7008]**. Contributions to the study of bagrid fishes 14. The systematic postion of the species of *Mystus* Scopoli known from China. Proc. Indian Acad. Sci. Sect. B v. 87 (no. 9): 221-228.

———. 1981 (Dec.) **[ref. 6497]**. The freshwater fishes of India, Pakistan, Bangladesh, Burma and Sri Lanka—a handbook. Zool. Surv. India. i-xxii + 1-475, Pls. 1-13.

JAYARAM, K. C., AND J. R. DHANZE. 1979 (20 Dec.) **[ref. 6800]**. Siluroid fishes of India, Berma and Ceylon. 22. A preliminary review of the genera of the family Ariidae (Pisces: Siluroidea). Matsya No. 4 [for 1978]: 42-51A.

JEFFREY, C. 1977 **[ref. 13543]**. Biological nomenclature. Second edition. Crane, Russak & Co., Inc. New York. i-viii + 1-72.

JÉGU, M., AND G. M. DOS SANTOS. 1988 (30 Dec.) **[ref. 12838]**. Une nouvelle espèce du genre *Mylesinus* (Pisces, Serrasalmidae), *M. paucisquamatus*, décrite du bassin du Rio Tocantins (Amazonie, Brésil). Cybium v. 12 (no. 4): 331-341.

JEITTELES, L. H. 1861 **[ref. 2339]**. Zoologische Mittheilungen. I. Ueber zwei für die Fauna Ungarns neue Fische, *Lucioperca volgensis* Cuv. Val. und *Alburnus maculatus* Kessler. Verh. K.-K. Zool.-Bot. Ver. Ges. Wien v. 11: 323-326.

JENKINS, O. P. 1901 **[ref. 2340]**. Descriptions of fifteen new species of fishes from the Hawaiian Islands. Bull. U. S. Fish Comm. v. 19 [1899]: 387-404.

———. 1903 (23 July) **[ref. 2341]**. Report on collections of fishes made in the Hawaiian Islands, with descriptions of new species. Bull. U. S. Fish Comm. v. 22 [1902]: 415-511, Pls. 1-4.

JENKINS, O. P., AND B. W. EVERMANN. 1889 (5 Jan.) **[ref. 2342]**. Description of eighteen new species of fishes from the Gulf of California. Proc. U. S. Natl. Mus. v. 11 (no. 698): 137-158.

JENSEN, A. S. 1948 **[ref. 2343]**. Contributions to the ichthyofauna of Greenland 8-24. Spolia Zool. Mus. Haun. v. 9: 1-182, Pls. 1-4.

JENYNS, L. J. 1840-42 **[ref. 2344]**. Pisces. In: The zoology of the voyage of H. M. S. Beagle, under the command of Captain Fitzroy, R. N., during the years 1832 to 1836. London (in 4 parts): i-xvi + 1-172, Pls. 1-29. [Sherborn 1897 [ref. 13554] dates to Jan. 1840 (pp. 1-32), June 1840 (33-64), Apr. 1841 (65-96), Apr. 1842 (97-172).]

JERDON, T. C. 1849 **[ref. 2346]**. On the fresh-water fishes of southern India. Madras J. Lit. Sci. v. 15 (pt 1): 139-149.

———. 1849 **[ref. 4902]**. On the fresh-water fishes of southern India. (Continued from p. 149.) Madras J. Lit. Sci. v. 15 (pt 2): 302-346.

JESPERSEN, P., AND A. V. TÅNING. 1919 **[ref. 2350]**. Some Mediterranean and Atlantic Sternoptychidae. Preliminary note. Vidensk. Medd. Dansk Naturh. Foren v. 70: 215-226, Pl. 17.

JEWETT, S. L., AND E. A. LACHNER. 1983 (29 Dec.) **[ref. 5368]**. Seven new species of the Indo-Pacific genus *Eviota* (Pisces: Gobiidae). Proc. Biol. Soc. Wash. v. 96 (no. 4): 780-806.

JOANNIS, L. DE. 1835 **[ref. 2355]**. Observations sur les poissons du Nil, et description de plusieurs espèces nouvelles. [Also includes: Tableau des poissons du Nil.] Mag. Zool. 1835 (5 anneé): 53 pp. numbered as Classe IV, Pls. 1-15. ["Classe IV" misprinted Classe III or Cl. III on some page headings.]

JOHNSON, D. S. 1975 **[ref. 2356]**. More new Malawi cichlids. Today's Aquarist v. 2 (no. 1): 15-26.

JOHNSON, G. D. 1980 **[ref. 13553]**. The limits and relationships of the Lutjanidae and associated families. Bull. Scripps Inst. Oceanogr. v. 24: 1-114.

———. 1983 (16 Aug.) **[ref. 5675]**. *Niphon spinosus*: a primitive epinepheline serranid, with comments on the monophyly and interrelationships of the Serranidae. Copeia 1983 (no. 3): 777-787.

———. 1984 **[ref. 9681]**. Percoidei: development and relationships. Pp. 464-498. In: Ontogeny and Systematics of Fishes. Am. Soc. Ichthyol. Herpetol. Spec. Publ. No. 1.

———. 1986 **[ref. 5676]**. Scombroid phylogeny: an alternative hypothesis. Bull. Mar. Sci. v. 39 (no. 1): 1-41.

———. 1988 (25 May) **[ref. 6691]**. *Niphon spinosus*, a primitive Epinepheline serranid: corroborative evidence from the larvae. Jpn. J. Ichthyol. v. 35 (no. 1): 7-18.

JOHNSON, G. D., AND E. B. BROTHERS. 1989 (19 Dec.) **[ref. 13532]**. *Acanthemblemaria paula*, a new diminutive chaenopsid (Pisces: Blennioidei) from Belize, with comments on life history. Proc. Biol. Soc. Wash. v. 102 (no. 4): 1018-1030.

JOHNSON, G. D., AND R. A. FRITZSCHE. 1989 (30 Nov.) **[ref. 13513]**. *Graus nigra*, an omnivorous girellid, with comparative osteology and comments on relationships of the Girellidae (Pisces: Perciformes). Proc. Acad. Nat. Sci. Phila. v. 141: 1-27.

JOHNSON, G. D., AND R. H. ROSENBLATT. 1988 (Sept.) **[ref. 6682]**. Mechanisms of light organ occlusion in flashlight fishes, family Anomalopidae (Teleostei: Beryciformes), and the evolution of the group. Zool. J. Linn. Soc. v. 94 (no. 1): 65-96.

JOHNSON, G. D., AND W. F. SMITH-VANIZ. 1987 **[ref. 9235]**. Redescription and relationships of *Parasphyraenops atrimanus* Bean (Pisces: Serranidae), with discussion of other Bermudian fishes known only from stomach contents. Bull. Mar. Sci. v. 40 (no. 1): 48-58.

JOHNSON, J. Y. 1862 (Sept.) **[ref. 2357]**. Descriptions of some new genera and species of fishes obtained at Madeira. Proc. Zool. Soc. Lond. 1862 (pt 2): 167-180, Pls. 22-23.

———. 1862 (Sept.) **[ref. 5804]**. Notes on rare and little-known fishes taken at Madeira. No. I. Ann. Mag. Nat. Hist. (Ser. 3) v. 10 (no. 57): 161-172.

———. 1863 (May) **[ref. 5021]**. Description of five new species of fishes obtained at Madeira. Proc. Zool. Soc. Lond. 1863 (pt 1): 36-46, Pl. 7.

———. 1864 (July) **[ref. 2358]**. Description of three new genera of marine fishes obtained at Madeira. Ann. Mag. Nat. Hist. (Ser. 3) v. 14 (no. 79): 70-78, 1 pl. [Appeared earlier as Johnson 1864: 403-410, 1 pl. [ref. 5751].]

———. 1864 (Apr.) **[ref. 5751]**. Description of three new genera of marine fishes obtained at Madeira. Proc. Zool. Soc. Lond. 1863 (pt 3): 403-410. [Also in Johnson 1864: 70-78 [ref. 2358]. Date of Apr. 1864 from Duncan 1937: 72 [ref. 13606].]

———. 1865 (Oct.) **[ref. 2359]**. Description of new genus of trichuroid fishes obtained at Madeira, with remarks on the genus *Dicrotus*, Günther, and on some allied genera of Trichiuridae. Proc. Zool. Soc. Lond. 1865 (pt 2) (art. 5): 434-437.

———. 1865 (Oct.) **[ref. 5779]**. Description of a new genus of trichiuroid fishes obtained at Madeira, with remarks on the genus *Dicrotus*, Günther, and on some allied genera of Trichiuridae. Ann. Mag. Nat. Hist. (Ser. 3) v. 16 (no. 94): 283-286.

———. 1868 (Apr.) **[ref. 2360]**. Description of a new genus of Spinacidae, founded on a shark obtained at Madeira. Proc. Zool. Soc. Lond. 1867 (pt 3) (art. 6): 713-715.

JOHNSON, R. K. 1974 (13 June) **[ref. 2361]**. Five new species and a new genus of alepisauroid fishes of the Scopelarchidae (Pisces: Myctophiformes). Copeia 1974 (no. 2): 449-457.

———. 1974 (31 Dec.) **[ref. 7050]**. A revision of the alepisauroid family Scopelarchidae (Pisces: Myctophiformes). Fieldiana Zool. v. 66: i-ix + 1-249.

———. 1974 (31 Dec.) **[ref. 7135]**. A *Macristium* larva from the Gulf of Mexico with additional evidence for the synonymy of *Macristium* with *Bathysaurus* (Myctophiformes: Bathysauridae). Copeia 1974 (no. 4): 973-977.

———. 1982 (18 Aug.) **[ref. 5519]**. Fishes of the families Evermannellidae and Scopelarchidae: systematics, morphology, interrelationships, and zoogeography. Fieldiana Zool. (n. s.) No. 12: i-xiii + 1-252.

———. 1984 **[ref. 13623]**. Giganturidae: development and relationships. Am. Soc. Ichthyol. Herpetol. Spec. Publ. No. 1: 199-201.

———. 1986 **[ref. 5677]**. Family No. 77: Scopelarchidae (pp. 265-267), Family No. 80: Giganturidae (pp. 273-274), Family No. 83: Evermannellidae (pp. 278-280). In: Smiths' Sea Fishes (Smith & Heemstra 1986 [ref. 5715]).

JOHNSON, R. K., AND D. M. COHEN. 1974 (Sept.) **[ref. 7133]**. Results of the research cruises of FRV "Walther Herwig" to South America. XXX. Revision of the chiasmodontid fish genera *Dysalotus* and *Kali*, with descriptions of two new species. Arch. FischereiWiss. v. 25 (no. 1/2): 13-46.

JOHNSON, R. K., AND R. M. FELTES. 1984 (29 Feb.) **[ref. 5348]**. A new species of *Vinciguerria* (Salmoniformes: Photichthyidae) from the Red Sea and Gulf of Aquba, with comments on the depauperacy of the Red Sea mesopelagic fish fauna. Fieldiana Zool. (n. s.) No. 22: i-vi + 1-35.

JOHNSON, R. K., AND M. J. KEENE. 1986 **[ref. 6303]**. Family No. 228: Chiasmodontidae (pp. 734-735). In: Smiths' Sea Fishes (Smith & Heemstra 1986 [ref. 5715]).

JONES, J. M. 1874 (Jan.) **[ref. 2362]**. A new fish. Zoologist (Ser. 2) v. 9: 3837-3838.

JORDAN, D. S. 1876 (Apr.) **[ref. 2370]**. Concerning the fishes of the Ichthyologia Ohiensis. Bull. Buffalo Soc. Nat. Hist. v. 3 (no. 3, art. 8): 91-97.

——. 1876 **[ref. 2371]**. Class V.—Pisces. (The fishes.) Pp. 199-362. In: Manual of the vertebrates of the northern United States, including the district east of the Mississippi River and north of North Carolina and Tennessee, exclusive of marine species. Chicago. [Later editions 1878 et seq.]

——. 1876 **[ref. 10443]**. Checklist of the fishes of the fresh waters of North America. Bull. Buffalo Soc. Nat. Sci. v. 3 (no. 4): 133-164. [Signature date is December 1876; possibly pages after 136 published Feb. 1877 (see Hays 1952: 95 [ref. 9281]).]

——. 1877 (17 Apr.) **[ref. 2372]**. On the fishes of northern Indiana. Proc. Acad. Nat. Sci. Phila. 1877 [v. 29]: 42-82.

——. 1877 (June) **[ref. 2373]**. A partial synopsis of the fishes of upper Georgia; with supplementary papers on fishes of Tennessee, Kentucky, and Indiana. Ann. Lyc. Nat. Hist. N. Y. v. 11 (no. 11-12) (29): 307-377. [Jacket to Nos. 11-12 dated June 1877.]

——. 1877 **[ref. 2374]**. Contributions to North American ichthyology based primarily on the collections of the United States National Museum. No. 2. A.—Notes on Cottidae ... Hyodontidae, with revisions of the genera and descriptions of new or little known species. Added title page: Bull. U. S. Natl. Mus. No. 10: 5-68.

——. 1877 **[ref. 2375]**. Catalogue of fishes of Ohio. Pp. 44-56. In: Klippart, J. H., First Annual Report of the Ohio State Fish Commission, to the Governor of the State of Ohio, for the years 1875 and 1876. Columbus.

——. 1877 **[ref. 12244]**. Contributions to North American Ichthyology based primarily on the collections of the United States National Museum. I. Review of Rafinesque's memoirs on North American fishes. Bull. U. S. Natl. Mus. No. 9: 1-53.

——. 1878 **[ref. 2376]**. Manual of the vertebrates of the northern United States, including the district east of the Mississippi River and north of North Carolina and Tennessee, exclusive of marine species. Chicago. 2nd. edition, revised and enlarged. 1-407.

——. 1878 (Dec.) **[ref. 2377]**. Report on the collection of fishes made by Dr. Elliott Coues U. S. A. in Dakoda and Montana during the seasons of 1873 and 1874. Bull. U. S. Geol. Geogr. Surv. Terr. v. 4 (no. 4, art. 33): 777-779.

——. 1878 (3 May) **[ref. 2378]**. Notes on a collection of fishes from the Rio Grande, at Brownsville, Texas. Bull. U. S. Geol. Geogr. Surv. Terr. v. 4 (no. 2, art. 17): 397-406. [Continued as pp. 663-667 of same volume.]

——. 1878 (3 May) **[ref. 2379]**. A catalogue of fishes of the fresh waters of North America. Bull. U. S. Geol. Geogr. Surv. Terr. v. 4 (no. 2, art. 18): 407-442.

——. 1878 **[ref. 2380]**. (Notes on fishes of Ohio.) Second Report Ohio Fish Commission; John H. Klippart, Commissioner. [Not seen.]

——. 1878 (29 July) **[ref. 5860]**. Notes on a collection of fishes from the Rio Grande, at Brownsville, Texas—continued. U. S. Geol. Geogr. Surv. Terr. v. 4 (no. 3, art. 27): 663-667. [Continued from p. 406.]

——. 1878 **[ref. 12254]**. A synopsis of the family Catostomidae. Bull. U. S. Natl. Mus. No. 12: 97-237.

——. 1880 (3 Feb.) **[ref. 2381]**. Description of new species of North American fishes. Proc. U. S. Natl. Mus. v. 2 [no. 84]: 235-241.

——. 1880 (30 Mar.) **[ref. 2382]**. Note on a collection of fishes obtained in the streams of Guanajuato and in Chapala Lake, Mexico, by Prof. A. Dugès. Proc. U. S. Natl. Mus. v. 2 [no. 94]: 298-301.

——. 1882 (Dec.) **[ref. 2383]**. Report on the fishes of Ohio. Rep. Geol. Surv. Ohio v. 4: 737-1002.

——. 1885 (19 June) **[ref. 2384]**. Identification of the species of Cyprinidae and Catostomidae, described by Dr. Charles Girard, in the Proceedings of the Academy of Natural Sciences of Philadelphia for 1856. Proc. U. S. Natl. Mus. v. 8 [no. 500]: 118-127.

——. 1885 (2 Oct.) **[ref. 2385]**. A catalogue of the fishes known to inhabit the waters of North America, north of the Tropic of Cancer, with notes on species discovered in 1883 and 1884. Rep. U. S. Fish Comm. v. 13 [1885]: 789-973. [Report published in 1887, separate in 1885.]

——. 1886 (17 Sept.) **[ref. 2386]**. List of fishes collected at Havana, Cuba, in December, 1883, with notes and descriptions. Proc. U. S. Natl. Mus. v. 9 [no. 551]: 31-55.

——. 1887 (14-24 Feb.) **[ref. 2387]**. Notes on typical specimens of fishes described by Cuvier and Valenciennes and preserved in the Musée d'Histoire Naturelle in Paris. Proc. U. S. Natl. Mus. v. 9 [no. 593]: 525-546.

——. 1887 (24 Feb.) **[ref. 2388]**. A preliminary catalog of the fishes of the West Indies. Proc. U. S. Natl. Mus. v. 9 [no. 595]: 554-608.

——. 1888 (7 Aug.) **[ref. 2389]**. On the generic name of the tunny. Proc. Acad. Nat. Sci. Phila. 1888 [v. 40]: 180.

——. 1888 **[ref. 2390]**. A manual of vertebrate animals of the northern United States, including the district north and east of the Ozark mountains, south of the Laurentian hills, north of ... Virginia, and east of the Missouri River; inclusive of marine species. 5th edition. Chicago. i-iii + 1-375. [Also published in 1890.]

——. 1890 **[ref. 2392]**. A review of the labroid fishes of America and Europe. Rep. U. S. Fish Comm. v. 15 [1887]: 559-699, Pls. 1-11. [Published as a separate in 1890, in "Report" in 1891.]

——. 1891 (8 Apr.) **[ref. 2391]**. No. XVIII.—List of fishes collected in the Harbor of Bahia, Brazil, and in adjacent waters. Scientific results of explorations by the U. S. Fish Commission steamer "Albatross." Proc. U. S. Natl. Mus. v. 13 (no. 829): 313-336.

——. 1895 (8 Apr.) **[ref. 2393]**. Description of *Evermannia*, a new genus of gobioid fishes. Proc. Calif. Acad. Sci. (Ser. 2) v. 4: 592.

——. 1895 (15 Aug.) **[ref. 2394]**. The fishes of Sinaloa. Proc. Calif. Acad. Sci. (Ser. 2) v. 5: 377-514, Pls. 26-55. [Separate issued 15 Aug. 1895. Reprinted in Contrib. Biol. Hopkins Seaside Lab. v. 3: 1-71, Pls. 26-55.]

——. 1896 (19 June) **[ref. 2395]**. Notes on fishes little known or new to science. Proc. Calif. Acad. Sci. (Ser. 2) v. 6: 201-244, Pls. 20-43. [Reprint in Contrib. Biol. Hopkins Seaside Lab. 5: 1-48. Plates XX - XLIII.]

——. 1898 (15 Jan.) **[ref. 2396]**. Description of a species of fish (*Mitsukurina owstoni*) from Japan, the type of a distinct family of lamnoid sharks. Proc. Calif. Acad. Sci. (Ser. 3) v. 1 (no. 6): 199-202, Pls. 11-12. [Date of separate 15 Jan. 1898.]

——. 1900 (Nov.) **[ref. 2397]**. Notes on recent fish literature. Am. Nat. v. 34 (no. 407, Nov.): 897-899.

——. 1903 (9 Apr.) **[ref. 2398]**. Supplementary note on *Bleekeria mitsukurii*, and on certain Japanese fishes. Proc. U. S. Natl. Mus. v. 26 (no. 1328): 693-696.

——. 1903 (May) **[ref. 2399]**. [Generic names of fishes.] Am. Nat. v. 37 (no. 437, May): 360.

——. 1904 (19 Jan.) **[ref. 2400]**. Notes on the fishes collected in the Tortugas Archipelago. Bull. U. S. Fish Comm. v. 22 [1902]: 539-544, Pls. 1-2.

——. 1907 (12 Mar.) **[ref. 2401]**. A review of the fishes of the family Histiopteridae, found in the waters of Japan; with a note on *Tephritis* Günther. Proc. U. S. Natl. Mus. v. 32 (no. 1423): 235-239.

——. 1912 (29 Aug.) **[ref. 2403]**. Note on the generic name *Safole*, replacing *Boulengerina*, for a genus of kuhliid fishes. Proc. U. S. Natl. Mus. v. 42 (no. 1922): 655.

——. 1916 (12 Apr.) **[ref. 2405]**. The nomenclature of American fishes as affected by the opinions of the International Commission on Zoological Nomenclature. Copeia No. 29: 25-28.

——. 1917 (24 May) **[ref. 2406]**. Notes on *Glossamia* and related genera of cardinal fishes. Copeia No. 44: 46-47.

——. 1917 (Aug.) **[ref. 2407]**. The genera of fishes, from Linnaeus to Cuvier, 1758-1833, seventy-five years, with the accepted type of each. A contribution to the stability of scientific nomenclature. (Assisted by Barton Warren Evermann.) Leland Stanford Jr. Univ. Publ., Univ. Ser. No. 27: 1-161.

——. 1917 (4 Oct.) **[ref. 2408]**. Changes in names of American fishes. Copeia No. 49: 85-89.

——. 1917-20 **[ref. 4906]**. The genera of fishes... In four parts: Stanford University, University Series. [See individual citations for dates, titles, and pagination.]

——. 1919 **[ref. 2409]**. Note on Gistel's genera of fishes. Proc. Acad. Nat. Sci. Phila. v. 70 (for 1918): 335-340.

——. 1919 (July) **[ref. 2410]**. The genera of fishes, part II, from Agassiz to Bleeker, 1833-1858, twenty-six years, with the accepted type of each. A contribution to the stability of scientific nomenclature. Leland Stanford Jr. Univ. Publ., Univ. Ser. No. 36: i-ix + 163-284 + i-xiii.

——. 1919 (15 Dec.) **[ref. 2411]**. On *Elephenor*, a new genus of fishes from Japan. Ann. Carnegie Mus. v. 12 (nos. 3-4) (4): 329-343, Pls. 54-58.

——. 1919 (10 Apr.) **[ref. 2413]**. New genera of fishes. Proc. Acad. Nat. Sci. Phila. v. 70 (for 1918): 341-344.

——. 1919 (26 Apr.) **[ref. 2415]**. On certain genera of atherine fishes. Proc. U. S. Natl. Mus. v. 55 (no. 2273): 309-311.

——. 1919 (Oct.) **[ref. 4904]**. The genera of fishes, part III, from Guenther to Gill, 1859-1880, twenty-two years, with the accepted type of each. A contribution to the stability of scientific nomenclature. Leland Stanford Jr. Univ. Publ., Univ. Ser. No. 39: 285-410. [Also includes Index to Part III, i-xv.]

——. 1920 (Aug.) **[ref. 4905]**. The genera of fishes, part IV, from 1881 to 1920, thirty-nine years, with the accepted type of each. A contribution to the stability of scientific nomenclature. Leland Stanford Jr. Univ. Publ., Univ. Ser. No. 43: 411-576 + i-xviii.

——. 1921 (14 Oct.) **[ref. 2419]**. Description of deep-sea fishes from the coast of Hawaii, killed by a lava flow from Mauna Loa. Proc. U. S. Natl. Mus. v. 59 (no. 2392): 643-656.

——. 1923 (20 May) **[ref. 2420]**. *Roa*.—A genus of chaetodont fishes. Copeia No. 118: 63.

——. 1923 (Jan.) **[ref. 2421]**. A classification of fishes including families and genera as far as known. Stanford Univ. Publ., Univ. Ser., Biol. Sci. v. 3 (no. 2): 77-243 + i-x. [Reprinted in 1934 and 1963.]

——. 1924 (31 May) **[ref. 2423]**. Concerning the genus *Hybopsis* of Agassiz. Copeia No. 130: 51-52.

——. 1924 (15 July) **[ref. 2424]**. Concerning the American dace allied to the genus *Leuciscus*. Copeia No. 132: 70-72.

——. 1924 (1 Sept.) **[ref. 2425]**. Rare species of fishes from the coast of southern California. Copeia No. 134: 81-82.

——. 1925 **[ref. 2428]**. The fossil fishes of the Miocene of southern California. Contribution no. VIII. [With sections: A. Species from the diatom beds at Lompoc; B. Fossil fishes from Los Angeles County, California; C. Fishes from a quarry in Monterey County near San Miguel.] Stanford Univ. Publ., Univ. Ser., Biol. Sci. v. 4 (no. 1): 1-51, Pls. 1-21.

——. 1925 (20 May) **[ref. 5077]**. Subdivisions of the genus *Raja* Linnaeus. Copeia No. 142: 37-39.

——. 1929 (19 July) **[ref. 2431]**. *Forbesichthys* for *Forbesella*. Science (n. s.) v. 70 (no. 1803): 68.

——. 1929 **[ref. 6443]**. Manual of the vertebrate animals of the northeastern United States inclusive of marine species. Thirteenth Edition [with an introduction by Barton Warren Evermann]. World Book Co., Yonkers-on-Hudson, N. Y. i-xxxi + 1-446.

Jordan, D. S., and C. H. Bollman. 1889 (20 Sept.) **[ref. 2432]**. List of fishes collected at Green Turtle Cay, in the Bahamas, by Charles L. Edwards, with descriptions of three new species. Proc. U. S. Natl. Mus. v. 11 [no. 752]: 549-553.

——. 1890 (5 Feb.) **[ref. 2433]**. Descriptions of new species of fishes collected at the Galapagos Islands and along the coast of the United States of Colombia, 1887-'88. In: Scientific results of explorations by the U. S. Fish Commission steamer *Albatross*. Proc. U. S. Natl. Mus. v. 12 (no. 770): 149-183.

Jordan, D. S., and A. W. Brayton. 1877-78 (9 Oct. - 1 Jan. 1878) **[ref. 2435]**. On *Lagochila*, a new genus of catostomoid fishes. Proc. Acad. Nat. Sci. Phila. 1877 [v. 29]: 280-283. [Page 280 published 9 Oct. 1877, pp. 281-283 on 1 Jan. 1878. Genus dates to 9 Oct. 1877.]

——. 1878 **[ref. 2436]**. Contributions to North American ichthyology. No. 3. A. On the distribution of the fishes of the Allegany region of South Carolina, Georgia, and Tennessee, with descriptions of new or little known species. Bull. U. S. Natl. Mus. No. 12: 3-95.

Jordan, D. S., and H. E. Copeland. 1877 (Feb.) **[ref. 5961]**. Check list of the fishes of the fresh waters of North America. Bull. Buffalo Soc. Nat. Sci. v. 3: 133-164. [Date of Feb. 1877 comes from Hays (1952), possibly published in Dec. 1876, pp. 133-136 possibly earlier.]

Jordan, D. S., and B. M. Davis. 1891 **[ref. 2437]**. A preliminary review of the apodal fishes or eels inhabiting the waters of America and Europe. Rep. U. S. Fish Comm. v. 16 [1888]: 581-677, Pls. 73-80. [As a separate in 1891, in the volume in June 1892 (Hays 1952: 119 [ref. 9281]).]

Jordan, D. S., and M. C. Dickerson. 1908 (14 Sept.) **[ref. 2438]**. On a collection of fishes from Fiji, with notes on certain Hawaiian fishes. Proc. U. S. Natl. Mus. v. 34 (no. 1625): 603-617.

Jordan, D. S., and C. H. Eigenmann. 1887 (14 Feb.) **[ref. 8016]**. A review of the Gobiidae of North America. Proc. U. S. Natl. Mus. v. 9 [no. 587]: 477-518.

——. 1889 **[ref. 2439]**. A review of the Sciaenidae of America and Europe. Rep. U. S. Fish Comm. v. 14 [1886]: 343-446, Pls. 1-4. [Also as separate with index.]

——. 1890 **[ref. 2440]**. A review of the genera and species of Serranidae found in the waters of America and Europe. Bull. U. S. Fish Comm. v. 8 [1888](art. 9): 329-441, Pls. 60-69. [Separate issued in 1890.]

Jordan, D. S., and B. W. Evermann. 1887 (14 Feb.) **[ref. 2441]**. Description of six new species of fishes from the Gulf of Mexico, with notes on other species. Proc. U. S. Natl. Mus. v. 9 [no. 586]: 466-476.

——. 1896 (28 Dec.) **[ref. 2442]**. A check-list of the fishes and fish-like vertebrates of North and Middle America. Rep. U. S. Fish Comm. v. 21 [1895] Append. 5: 207-584.

——. 1896 (3 Oct.) **[ref. 2443]**. The fishes of North and Middle America: a descriptive catalogue of the species of fish-like vertebrates found in the waters of North America, north of the Isthmus of Panama. Part I. Bull. U. S. Natl. Mus. No. 47: i-lx + 1-1240.

——. 1898 (3 Oct.) **[ref. 2444]**. The fishes of North and Middle America: a descriptive catalogue of the species of fish-like vertebrates found in the waters of North America, north of the Isthmus of Panama. Part II. Bull. U. S. Natl. Mus. No. 47: i-xxx + 1241-2183.

——. 1898 (26 Nov.) **[ref. 2445]**. The fishes of North and Middle America: a descriptive catalogue of the species of fish-like vertebrates found in the waters of North America north of the Isthmus of Panama. Part III. Bull. U. S. Natl. Mus. No. 47: i-xxiv + 2183a-3136.

——. 1900 (26 June) **[ref. 2446]**. The fishes of North and Middle America: a descriptive catalogue of the species of fish-like vertebrates found in the waters of North America, north of the Isthmus of Panama. Part IV. Bull. U. S. Natl. Mus. No. 47: i-ci + 3137-3313, Pls. 1-392.

——. 1902 (24 Sept.) **[ref. 2447]**. Notes on a collection of fishes from the island of Formosa. Proc. U. S. Natl. Mus. v. 25 (no. 1289): 315-368.

——. 1903 (9 July) **[ref. 2449]**. Description of a new genus and two new species of fishes from the Hawaiian Islands. Bull. U. S. Fish Comm. v. 22 [1902]: 209-210.

——. 1903 (11 Apr.) **[ref. 2450]**. Descriptions of new genera and species of fishes from the Hawaiian Islands. Bull. U. S. Fish Comm.

v. 22 [1902]: 161-208.
——. 1905 (29 July) **[ref. 2451]**. The aquatic resources of the Hawaiian Islands. Part I.—The shore fishes of the Hawaiian Islands, with a general account of the fish fauna. Bull. U. S. Fish Comm. v. 23 (pt 1) [1903]: i-xxviii + 1-574, Pls. 1-65, color Pls. 1-73.
——. 1911 (7 Feb.) **[ref. 2452]**. A review of the salmonoid fishes of the Great Lakes, with notes on the whitefishes of other regions. Bull. Bur. Fish. v. 29 (for 1909): 1-41, Pls. 1-7.
——. 1927 (27 Apr.) **[ref. 2453]**. New genera and species of North American Fishes. Proc. Calif. Acad. Sci. (Ser. 4) v. 16 (no. 15): 501-507.
JORDAN, D. S., B. W. EVERMANN AND H. W. CLARK. 1930 (Feb.) **[ref. 6476]**. Check list of the fishes and fishlike vertebrates of North and Middle America north of the northern boundary of Venezuela and Colombia. Rep. U. S. Comm. Fish. for 1928. Pt 2: 1-670.
JORDAN, D. S., B. W. EVERMANN AND S. TANAKA. 1927 (14 Nov.) **[ref. 2454]**. Notes on new or rare fishes from Hawaii. Proc. Calif. Acad. Sci. (Ser. 4) v. 16 (no. 20): 649-680, Pls. 22-24.
JORDAN, D. S., AND B. FESLER. 1893 (28 Oct.) **[ref. 2455]**. A review of the sparoid fishes of America and Europe. Rep. U. S. Fish Comm. v. 27 [1889-91]: 421-544, Pls. 28-62. [Issued as a separate, U.S. Fish Commission Document No. 219, 28 Oct. 1893.]
JORDAN, D. S., AND M. W. FORDICE. 1887 (10 Feb.) **[ref. 2456]**. A review of the American species of Belonidae. Proc. U. S. Natl. Mus. v. 9 [no. 575]: 339-361.
JORDAN, D. S., AND H. W. FOWLER. 1902 (17 Sept.) **[ref. 2457]**. A review of the trigger-fishes, file-fishes, and trunk-fishes of Japan. Proc. U. S. Natl. Mus. v. 25 (no. 1287): 251-286.
——. 1902 (19 Sept.) **[ref. 2458]**. A review of the cling-fishes (Gobiesocidae) of the waters of Japan. Proc. U. S. Natl. Mus. v. 25 (no. 1291): 413-415.
——. 1902 (2 Dec.) **[ref. 2459]**. A review of the ophidioid fishes of Japan. Proc. U. S. Natl. Mus. v. 25 (no. 1303): 743-766.
——. 1903 (30 Mar.) **[ref. 2460]**. A review of the elasmobranchiate fishes of Japan. Proc. U. S. Natl. Mus. v. 26 (no. 1324): 593-674, Pls. 26-27.
——. 1903 (9 Apr.) **[ref. 2461]**. A review of the Cobitidae, or loaches, of the rivers of Japan. Proc. U. S. Natl. Mus. v. 26 (no. 1332): 765-774.
——. 1903 (9 May) **[ref. 2462]**. A review of the dragonets (Callionymidae) and related fishes of the waters of Japan. Proc. U. S. Natl. Mus. v. 25 (no. 1305): 939-959.
——. 1903 (6 July) **[ref. 2463]**. A review of the cyprinoid fishes of Japan. Proc. U. S. Natl. Mus. v. 26 (no. 1334): 811-862.
——. 1903 (7 July) **[ref. 2464]**. A review of the siluroid fishes or catfishes of Japan. Proc. U. S. Natl. Mus. v. 26 (no. 1338): 897-911.
JORDAN, D. S., AND C. H. GILBERT. 1877 (17 Apr.) **[ref. 4907]**. On the genera of North American freshwater fishes. Proc. Acad. Nat. Sci. Phila. 1877 [v. 29]: 83-104.
——. 1879 (17-25 Mar.) **[ref. 2465]**. Notes on the fishes of Beaufort Harbor, North Carolina. Proc. U. S. Natl. Mus. v. 1 [no. 55]: 365-388. [Pp. 365-384 published 17 Mar., pp. 385-388 on 25 Mar. Also in Smithson. Misc. Coll. 1880, v. 19 (art. 1).]
——. 1880 (ca. 18 May) **[ref. 2466]**. Notes on a collection of fishes from San Diego, California. Proc. U. S. Natl. Mus. v. 3 [no. 106]: 23-34.
——. 1880 (18 May) **[ref. 2467]**. Description of a new flounder (*Xystreurys liolepis*), from Santa Catalina Island, California. Proc. U. S. Natl. Mus. v. 3 [no. 107]: 34-36.
——. 1880 (18 May) **[ref. 2366]**. Description of a new flounder (*Pleuronichthys verticalis*) from the coast of California, with notes on other species. Proc. U. S. Natl. Mus. v. 3 [no. 117]: 49-51.
——. 1880 (18 May) **[ref. 2468]**. On the generic relations of *Platyrhina exasperata*. Proc. U. S. Natl. Mus. v. 3 [no. 119]: 53.
——. 1880 (22 Sept.) **[ref. 2367]**. Descriptions of two new species of fishes, *Ascelichthys rhodorus* and *Scytalina cerdale*, from Neah Bay, Washington Territory. Proc. U. S. Natl. Mus. v. 3 [no. 144]: 264-268.
——. 1880 (18 Oct.) **[ref. 2469]**. Description of a new species of deep-water fish (*Icichthys lockingtoni*), from the coast of California. Proc. U. S. Natl. Mus. v. 3 [no. 154]: 305-308.
——. 1881 (22 Apr. - 9 May) **[ref. 2368]**. Notes on the fishes of the Pacific coast of the United States. Proc. U. S. Natl. Mus. v. 4 [no. 191]: 29-70. [Pp. 29-48 published 22 Apr., 49-64 on 9 May, 65-70 on 10 May.]
——. 1881 (4 Feb.) **[ref. 12598]**. List of the fishes of the Pacific coast of the United States, with a table showing the distribution of the species. Proc. U. S. Natl. Mus. v. 3 [no. 173]: 452-458.
——. 1882 (6 Apr.) **[ref. 2470]**. Description of thirty-three new species of fishes from Mazatlan, Mexico. Proc. U. S. Natl. Mus. v. 4 [no. 137]: 338-365.
——. 1882 (23 May-9 June) **[ref. 2471]**. Descriptions of nineteen new species of fishes from the Bay of Panama. Bull. U. S. Fish Comm. v. 1 [1881]: 306-335.
——. 1882 (16-22 Aug.) **[ref. 2472]**. Notes on fishes observed about Pensacola, Florida, and Galveston, Texas, with description of new species. Proc. U. S. Natl. Mus. v. 5 [no. 282]: 241-307. [Pp. 241-272 published 16 Aug., 273-307 on 22 Aug.]
——. 1883 (28 Apr. - 22 May) **[ref. 2473]**. Notes on a collection of fishes from Charleston, South Carolina, with descriptions of three new species. Proc. U. S. Natl. Mus. v. 5 [no. 328]: 580-620. [Pp. 580-592 published 28 Apr., 593-620 on 22 May.]
——. 1883 (22-29 May) **[ref. 2474]**. List of fishes now in the museum of Yale College, collected by Prof. Frank H. Bradley, at Panama, with descriptions of three new species. Proc. U. S. Natl. Mus. v. 5 [no. 329]: 620-632. [Pp. 620-624 published 22 May, 625-632 on 29 May.]
——. 1883 (25 Sept.-6 Oct.) **[ref. 2475]**. A review of the siluroid fishes found on the Pacific coast of tropical America, with descriptions of three new species. Bull. U. S. Fish Comm. v. 2 [1882]: 34-54.
——. 1883 (early Apr.) **[ref. 2476]**. Synopsis of the fishes of North America. Bull. U. S. Natl. Mus. No. 16: i-liv + 1-1018. [Often cited as 1882. Hays [ref. 9281] uses 1883, in part based on contemporary statement by Bean 1883: 161 [ref. 9282].]
——. 1883 (2 Aug.) **[ref. 2477]**. Notes on the nomenclature of certain North American fishes. Proc. U. S. Natl. Mus. v. 6 [no. 352]: 110-111.
——. 1899 **[ref. 2478]**. The fishes of Bering Sea. In: Jordan, D. S., Fur seals, and fur-seal islands of the North Pacific Ocean. Part III. Washington. Art. 18: 433-492, Pls. 43-85.
JORDAN, D. S., AND D. K. GOSS. 1889 **[ref. 2482]**. A review of the flounders and soles (Pleuronectidae) of America and Europe. Rep. U. S. Fish Comm. v. 14 [1886]: 225-342, Pls. 1-9. [Also as a separate, 1889.]
JORDAN, D. S., AND A. W. HERRE. 1907 (23 Oct.) **[ref. 2483]**. A review of the cirrhitoid fishes of Japan. Proc. U. S. Natl. Mus. v. 33 (no. 1562): 157-167.
JORDAN, D. S., AND C. L. HUBBS. 1917 (Oct.) **[ref. 2484]**. Notes on a collection of fishes from Port Said, Egypt. Ann. Carnegie Mus. v. 11 (nos. 3-4) (18): 461-468, Pls. 46-47.
——. 1919 (18 Dec.) **[ref. 2485]**. Studies in ichthyology. A monographic review of the family of Atherinidae or silversides. Leland Stanford Jr. Univ. Publ., Univ. Ser. [1919]: 1-87, Pls. 1-12.
——. 1925 (27 June) **[ref. 2486]**. Record of fishes obtained by David Starr Jordan in Japan, 1922. Mem. Carnegie Mus. v. 10 (no. 2): 93-346, Pls. 5-12.
JORDAN, D. S., AND E. K. JORDAN. 1922 (1 Dec.) **[ref. 2487]**. A list of the fishes of Hawaii, with notes and descriptions of new species. Mem. Carnegie Mus. v. 10 (no. 1): 1-92, Pls. 1-4.
JORDAN, D. S., AND R. C. MCGREGOR. 1899 **[ref. 2488]**. List of fishes collected at the Revillagigedo Archipelago and neighboring islands. Rep. U. S. Fish Comm. v. 24 [1898]: 271-284, Pls. 4-7.
JORDAN, D. S., AND S. E. MEEK. 1885 (6 May) **[ref. 2489]**. A review of the American species of flying fishes (*Exocoetus*). Proc. U. S. Natl. Mus. v. 8 [no. 483]: 44-67.

JORDAN, D. S., AND C. W. METZ. 1913 (Aug.) **[ref. 2490]**. A catalog of the fishes known from the waters of Korea. Mem. Carnegie Mus. v. 6 (no. 1): 1-65, Pls. 1-10.

JORDAN, D. S., AND R. E. RICHARDSON. 1908 (28 Feb.) **[ref. 2491]**. A review of the flat-heads, gurnards, and other mail-cheeked fishes of the waters of Japan. Proc. U. S. Natl. Mus. v. 33 (no. 1581): 629-670.

——. 1908 (16 Dec.) **[ref. 2492]**. Fishes from islands of the Philippine Archipelago. Bull. Bur. Fish. v. 27 (for 1907): 233-287.

——. 1909 **[ref. 2493]**. A catalogue of the fishes of the island of Formosa, or Taiwan, based on the collections of Dr. Hans Sauter. Mem. Carnegie Mus. v. 4 (no. 4): 159-204, Pls. 63-74.

——. 1910 (19 Jan.) **[ref. 2494]**. A review of the Serranidae or sea bass of Japan. Proc. U. S. Natl. Mus. v. 37 (no. 1714): 421-474.

——. 1910 (20 Jan.) **[ref. 6598]**. Check-list of the species of fishes known from the Philippine Archipelago. Philippine Is., Bur. Science Publ. no. 1: 1-78.

JORDAN, D. S., AND A. SEALE. 1905 (3 July) **[ref. 2495]**. List of fishes collected by Dr. Bashford Dean on the island of Negros, Philippines. Proc. U. S. Natl. Mus. v. 28 (no. 1407): 769-803.

——. 1906 (4 Apr.) **[ref. 2496]**. Descriptions of six new species of fishes from Japan. Proc. U. S. Natl. Mus. v. 30 (no. 1445): 143-148.

——. 1906 (15 Dec.) **[ref. 2497]**. The fishes of Samoa. Description of the species found in the archipelago, with a provisional check-list of the fishes of Oceania. Bull. Bur. Fish. v. 25 (for 1905): 173-455, Pls. 33-53. [Also as a separate. See also Hays 1952: 138 [ref. 9281].]

——. 1907 (11 Jan.) **[ref. 2498]**. Fishes of the islands of Luzon and Panay. Bull. Bur. Fish. v. 26 (for 1906): 1-48.

——. 1925 (30 Apr.) **[ref. 2499]**. Analysis of the genera of anchovies or Engraulidae. Copeia No. 141: 27-32. [Second author name misprinted Alvin "Steele".]

——. 1926 (May) **[ref. 2500]**. Review of the Engraulidae, with descriptions of new and rare species. Bull. Mus. Comp. Zool. v. 67 (no. 11): 355-418.

JORDAN, D. S., AND J. O. SNYDER. 1899 (30 Aug.) **[ref. 2501]**. Notes on a collection of fishes from the rivers of Mexico, with description of twenty new species. Bull. U. S. Fish Comm. v. 19 [1899]: 115-147.

——. 1900 (10 Dec.) **[ref. 2502]**. A list of fishes collected in Japan by Keinosuke Otaki, and by the United States Fish Commission steamer "Albatross," with descriptions of fourteen new species. Proc. U. S. Natl. Mus. v. 23 (no. 1213): 335-380, Pls. 9-20.

——. 1901 (22 Apr.) **[ref. 2503]**. Descriptions of two new genera of fishes (*Ereunias* and *Draciscus*) from Japan. Proc. Calif. Acad. Sci. (Ser. 3) v. 2 (nos. 7-8): 377-380, Pls. 18-19.

——. 1901 (2 July) **[ref. 2504]**. List of fishes collected in 1883 and 1885 by Pierre Louis Jouy and preserved in the United States National Museum, with descriptions of six new species. Proc. U. S. Natl. Mus. v. 23 (no. 1235): 740-769, Pls. 21-28.

——. 1901 (3 Apr.) **[ref. 2505]**. A preliminary check list of the fishes of Japan. Annot. Zool. Jpn. v. 3 (pts 2 & 3): 31-159.

——. 1901 **[ref. 2506]**. Descriptions of nine new species of fishes contained in museums of Japan. J. Coll. Sci. Imp. Univ. Tokyo v. 15 (pt 2): 301-311, Pls. 15-17.

——. 1901 (Nov.) **[ref. 2507]**. Fishes of Japan. Am. Nat. v. 35 (no. 419, Nov.): 941.

——. 1901 (28 Aug.) **[ref. 2508]**. A review of the apodal fishes or eels of Japan, with descriptions of nineteen new species. Proc. U. S. Natl. Mus. v. 23 (no. 1239): 837-890.

——. 1901 (25 Sept.) **[ref. 2509]**. A review of the gobioid fishes of Japan, with descriptions of twenty-one new species. Proc. U. S. Natl. Mus. v. 24 (no. 1244): 33-132.

——. 1901 (27 Sept.) **[ref. 2510]**. A review of the Hypostomide and Lophobranchiate fishes of Japan. Proc. U. S. Natl. Mus. v. 24 (no. 1241): 1-20, Pls. 1-12.

——. 1901 (12 Oct.) **[ref. 2511]**. A review of the cardinal fishes of Japan. Proc. U. S. Natl. Mus. v. 23 (no. 1240): 891-913, Pls. 43-44.

——. 1902 (10 Feb.) **[ref. 2512]**. A review of the discobolous fishes of Japan. Proc. U. S. Natl. Mus. v. 24 (no. 1259): 343-351.

——. 1902 (28 Mar.) **[ref. 2513]**. A review of the trachinoid fishes and their supposed allies found in the waters of Japan. Proc. U. S. Natl. Mus. v. 24 (no. 1263): 461-497.

——. 1902 (2 May) **[ref. 2514]**. A review of the labroid fishes and related forms found in the waters of Japan. Proc. U. S. Natl. Mus. v. 24 (no. 1266): 595-662.

——. 1902 (2 Sept.) **[ref. 2515]**. Description of two new species of squaloid sharks from Japan. Proc. U. S. Natl. Mus. v. 25 (no. 1279): 79-81.

——. 1902 (26 Sept.) **[ref. 2516]**. A review of the blennioid fishes of Japan. Proc. U. S. Natl. Mus. v. 25 (no. 1293): 441-504.

——. 1902 (4 Nov.) **[ref. 2517]**. On certain species of fishes confused with *Bryostemma polyactocephalum*. Proc. U. S. Natl. Mus. v. 25 (no. 1300): 613-618.

——. 1904 (2 June) **[ref. 2518]**. Notes on collections of fishes from Oahu Island and Laysan Island, Hawaii, with descriptions of four new species. Proc. U. S. Natl. Mus. v. 27 (no. 1377): 939-948.

——. 1904 (11 Apr.) **[ref. 2519]**. On a collection of fishes made by Mr. Alan Owston in the deep waters of Japan. Smithson. Misc. Collect. v. 45: 230-240, 58-63.

——. 1906 (10 Sept.) **[ref. 2520]**. A review of the Poeciliidae or killifishes of Japan. Proc. U. S. Natl. Mus. v. 31 (no. 1486): 287-290.

——. 1908 (1 Apr.) **[ref. 2521]**. Descriptions of three new species of carangoid fishes from Formosa. Mem. Carnegie Mus. v. 4 (no. 2): 37-40, Pls. 51-53.

JORDAN, D. S., AND E. C. STARKS. 1895 (14 Dec.) **[ref. 2522]**. The fishes of Puget Sound. Proc. Calif. Acad. Sci. (Ser. 2) v. 5: 785-855, Pls. 76-104. [Also as a separate as Contr. Biol. Hopkins Seaside Lab. 3: 1-71, Plates 76-104.]

——. 1901 (22 Apr.) **[ref. 2523]**. Descriptions of three new species of fishes from Japan. Proc. Calif. Acad. Sci. (Ser. 3) v. 2 (nos. 7-8): 381-386, Pls. 20-21. [Separate dated 22 Apr. 1901.]

——. 1901 (4 Oct.) **[ref. 2524]**. A review of the atherine fishes of Japan. Proc. U. S. Natl. Mus. v. 24 (no. 1250): 199-206.

——. 1902 (2 Dec.) **[ref. 2525]**. A review of the hemibranchiate fishes of Japan. Proc. U. S. Natl. Mus. v. 26 (no. 1308): 57-73.

——. 1904 (13 Aug.) **[ref. 2526]**. List of fishes dredged by the steamer Albatross off the coast of Japan in the summer of 1900, with descriptions of new species and a review of the Japanese Macrouridae. Bull. U. S. Fish Comm. v. 22 [1902]: 577-630, Pls. 1-8.

——. 1904 (22 Jan.) **[ref. 2527]**. A review of the scorpaenoid fishes of Japan. Proc. U. S. Natl. Mus. v. 27 (no. 1351): 91-175, Pls. 1-2.

——. 1904 (28 Jan.) **[ref. 2528]**. A review of the Cottidae or sculpins found in the waters of Japan. Proc. U. S. Natl. Mus. v. 27 (no. 1358): 231-335.

——. 1904 (27 June) **[ref. 2529]**. *Schmidtina*, a new genus of Japanese sculpins. Proc. U. S. Natl. Mus. v. 27 (no. 1381): 961.

——. 1905 (23 Feb.) **[ref. 2530]**. On a collection of fishes made in Korea, by Pierre Louis Jouy, with descriptions of new species. Proc. U. S. Natl. Mus. v. 28 (no. 1391): 193-212.

——. 1906 (8 Oct.) **[ref. 2531]**. Notes on a collection of fishes from Port Arthur, Manchuria, obtained by James Francis Abbott. Proc. U. S. Natl. Mus. v. 31 (no. 1493): 515-526.

——. 1906 (10 Sept.) **[ref. 2532]**. A review of the flounders and soles of Japan. Proc. U. S. Natl. Mus. v. 31 (no. 1484): 161-246.

——. 1907 (8 Feb.) **[ref. 2533]**. Note on *Otohime*, a new genus of gurnards. Proc. U. S. Natl. Mus. v. 32 (no. 1517): 131-133.

JORDAN, D. S., AND J. SWAIN. 1884 (19 Sept.) **[ref. 2535]**. A review of the American species of marine Mugilidae. Proc. U. S. Natl. Mus. v. 7 [no. 434]: 261-275.

——. 1884 (19-27 Sept.) **[ref. 2536]**. A review of the species of the genus *Haemulon*. Proc. U. S. Natl. Mus. v. 7 [no. 436]: 281-317. [Pp. 281-304 published 19 Sept., pp. 305-317 on 27 Sept.]

——. 1884 (3-9 Oct.) **[ref. 9337]**. A review of the American species of *Epinephelus* and related genera. Proc. U. S. Natl. Mus. v. 7 [no. 447]: 358-410. [Pp. 358-384 published 3 Oct., pp. 385-410 on 9 Oct.]

JORDAN, D. S., AND S. TANAKA. 1927 (27 Jan.) **[ref. 2537]**. Notes on new and rare fishes of the fauna of Japan. Ann. Carnegie Mus. v. 17 (nos. 3-4) (12): 385-392, Pl. 34.

JORDAN, D. S., S. TANAKA AND J. O. SNYDER. 1913 **[ref. 6448]**. A catalogue of the fishes of Japan. J. Coll. Sci. Imp. Univ. Tokyo v. 33 (art. 1): 1-497.

JORDAN, D. S., AND J. C. THOMPSON. 1905 (3 May) **[ref. 2538]**. The fish fauna of the Tortugas Archipelago. Bull. Bur. Fish. v. 24 (for 1904): 229-256.

JORDAN, D. S., AND W. F. THOMPSON. 1911 (30 Jan.) **[ref. 2539]**. A review of the sciaenoid fishes of Japan. Proc. U. S. Natl. Mus. v. 39 (no. 1787): 241-261.

———. 1911 (30 Jan.) **[ref. 2540]**. A review of the fishes of the families Lobotidae and Lutianidae, found in the waters of Japan. Proc. U. S. Natl. Mus. v. 39 (no. 1792): 435-471.

———. 1912 (22 Jan.) **[ref. 2541]**. A review of the Sparidae and related families of perch-like fishes found in the waters of Japan. Proc. U. S. Natl. Mus. v. 41 (no. 1875): 521-601.

———. 1913 (23 Aug.) **[ref. 2542]**. Notes on a collection of fishes from the island of Shikoku in Japan, with a description of a new species, *Gnathypops iyonis*. Proc. U. S. Natl. Mus. v. 46 (no. 2011): 65-72.

———. 1914 (Sept.) **[ref. 2543]**. Record of the fishes obtained in Japan in 1911. Mem. Carnegie Mus. v. 6 (no. 4): 205-313, Pls. 24-42.

JORDAN, E. K. 1925 (22 Sept.) **[ref. 2544]**. Notes on the fishes of Hawaii, with descriptions of six new species. Proc. U. S. Natl. Mus. v. 66 (no. 2570): 1-43, Pls. 1-2.

KAEDING, L. R., B. D. BURDICK, P. A. SCHRADER, AND W. R. NOONAN. 1986 (23 Dec.) **[ref. 6781]**. Recent capture of a bonytail (*Gila elegans*) and observations on this nearly extinct cyprinid from the Colorado River. Copeia 1986 (no. 4): 1021-1023.

KAILOLA, P. J. 1986 (30 May) **[ref. 6312]**. Ariidae systematics: comparison of the giant sea catfishes *Arius thalassinus* and *A. bilineatus* of the Indo-Pacific. Pp. 540-549. In: Uyeno et al. (eds.) 1986 [ref. 6147].

KAMI, H. T. 1973 (28 Aug.) **[ref. 5616]**. A new subgenus and species of *Pristipomoides* (family Lutjanidae) from Easter Island and Rapa. Copeia 1973 (no. 3): 557-559.

KAMOHARA, T. 1935 (15 June) **[ref. 2549]**. On the Owstoniidae of Japan. Annot. Zool. Jpn. v. 15 (no. 1): 130-138.

———. 1935 (15 Apr.) **[ref. 5617]**. On a new fish of the Zeidae from Kochi, Japan. Dobutsugaku Zasshi [Zool. Mag. Tokyo] v. 47 (no. 558): 245-247. [In Japanese, with English description on p. 247.]

———. 1936 **[ref. 2550]**. Supplementary note on the fishes collected in the vicinity of Kôchi-shi (X). Zool. Mag. (Tokyo) v. 48 (no. 11): 929-935. [In Japanese, English summary of new taxa on p. 929.]

———. 1938 (30 Oct.) **[ref. 2551]**. On the offshore bottom-fishes of Prov. Tosa, Shikoku, Japan. Maruzen Kobushiki Kaisha, Tokyo. 1-86.

———. 1953 (June) **[ref. 2553]**. Marine fishes newly found in Prov. Tosa, Japan, with descriptions of a new genus and species. Res. Rep. Kôchi Univ. v. 2 (no. 11): 1-10, 2 pls.

———. 1957 **[ref. 2554]**. Notes on twenty additions to the marine fish fauna of Prov. Tosa, Japan, including one new genus (Family Peristediidae). Res. Rep. Kôchi Univ. v. 6 (no. 5): 1-6.

———. 1958 (Nov.) **[ref. 2555]**. A review of the labrid fishes found in the waters of Kochi Prefecture, Japan. Rep. Usa Mar. Biol. Stn. v. 5 (no. 2): 1-20, Pls. 1-8.

———. 1960 (Oct.) **[ref. 2556]**. A review of the fishes of the family Parapercidae found in the waters of Japan. Rep. Usa Mar. Biol. Stn. v. 7 (no. 2): 1-14, Pls. 1-2.

———. 1961 **[ref. 2557]**. Additional records of marine fishes from Kochi Prefecture, Japan, including one new genus of the parapercid. Rep. Usa Mar. Biol. Stn. v. 8 (no. 1): 1-9.

KAN, T. T. 1986 (30 May) **[ref. 6313]**. Occurrences of *Masturus lanceolatus* (Molidae) in the western Pacific Ocean. Pp. 550-554. In: Uyeno et al. (eds.) 1986 [ref. 6147].

KANAYAMA, T. 1981 **[ref. 5539]**. Scorpaenid fishes from the Emperor Seamount Chain. Res. Inst. N. Pac. Fish., Hokkaido Univ., Spec. Vol. 119-129.

KANAYAMA, T., AND K. AMAOKA. 1981 (15 Aug.) **[ref. 5584]**. First record of the scorpaenid fish *Brachypterois serrulatus* from Japan, with a key to Japanese genera of the Pteroinae. Jpn. J. Ichthyol. v. 28 (no. 2): 181-183.

KANAZAWA, R. H. 1951 (Apr.) **[ref. 2558]**. Description of a new genus of cichlid fish, *Gobiocichla*, from the French Sudan. Ann. Mag. Nat. Hist. (Ser. 12) v. 4 (no. 40): 378-381.

———. 1961 (26 Jan.) **[ref. 2559]**. *Paraconger*, a new genus with three new species of eels (family Congridae). Proc. U. S. Natl. Mus. v. 113 (no. 3450): 1-14, 2 pls.

KANAZAWA, R. H., AND G. E. MAUL. 1967 (2 May) **[ref. 5618]**. Description of a new genus and species of the eel family Nemichthyidae from the eastern Atlantic. Bocagiana (Funchal) No. 12: 1-6, Pls. 1-2.

KAO, H. W., AND S.-C. SHEN. 1985 (June) **[ref. 5229]**. A new percophidid fish, *Osopsaron formosensis* (Percophidae: Hermerocoetinae) from Taiwan. J. Taiwan Mus. v. 38 (no. 1): 175-178.

KARAMAN, M. S. 1969 **[ref. 7823]**. Revision der kleinasiatischen und vorderasiatischen arten des genus *Capoeta* (*Varicorhinus*, partim). Mitt. Hamb. Zool. Mus. Inst. v. 66: 17-54.

———. 1971 **[ref. 2560]**. Süsswasserfische der Türkei. 8. Teil. Revision der Barben Europas, Vorderasiens und Nordafrikas. Mitt. Hamb. Zool. Mus. Inst. v. 67: 175-254.

———. 1972 (Dec.) **[ref. 2561]**. Süsswasserfische der Türkei. 9. Teil. Revision einiger kleinwüchsiger Cyprinidengattungen *Phoxinellus*, *Leucaspius*, *Acanthobrama* usw. aus Südeuropa, Kleinasien, Vorder-Asien und Nordafrika. Mitt. Hamb. Zool. Mus. Inst. v. 69: 115-155, Pl. 1.

KARMOVSKAYA, E. S. 1982 **[ref. 5204]**. Systematics and some aspects of ecology of the family Nemichthyidae. Proc. P. P. Shirshov Inst. Oceanol. v. 118: 151-161. [In Russian, English summ.]

KARRER, C. 1982 **[ref. 5679]**. Anguilliformes du Canal de Mozambique (Pisces, Teleostei). Fauna Trop. v. 23: 1-116.

———. 1984 (31 Dec.) **[ref. 12817]**. Notes on the synonymies of *Ariomma brevimanum* and *A. luridum* and the presence of the latter in the Atlantic (Teleostei, Perciformes, Ariommatidae). Cybium v. 8 (no. 4): 94-95.

———. 1986 **[ref. 5680]**. Family No. 139: Oreosomatidae (pp. 438-440). In: Smiths' Sea Fishes (Smith & Heemstra 1986 [ref. 5715]).

———. 1986 (31 Mar.) **[ref. 6762]**. Occurrence of the barrelfish, *Hyperoglyphe perciformis* (Teleostei, Perciformes, Stromateoidei), in the Mediterranean Sea and off Portugal. Cybium v. 10 (no. 1): 77-83.

KARRER, C., AND P. C. HEEMSTRA. 1986 **[ref. 5681]**. Family No. 140: Grammicolepididae (pp. 440-441). In: Smiths' Sea Fishes (Smith & Heemstra 1986 [ref. 5715]).

KARRER, C., AND D. G. SMITH. 1980 (5 Dec.) **[ref. 2566]**. A new genus and species of congrid eel from the Indo-west Pacific. Copeia 1980 (no. 4): 642-648.

KATAYAMA, E., E. YAMAMOTO AND T. YAMAKAWA. 1982 (27 Feb.) **[ref. 5397]**. A review of the serranid fish genus *Grammatonotus*, with description of a new species. Jpn. J. Ichthyol. v. 28 (no. 4): 368-374.

KATAYAMA, M. 1943 (June) **[ref. 2567]**. On two new ophidioid fishes from the Japan Sea. Annot. Zool. Jpn. v. 22 (no. 2): 101-104.

———. 1954 (31 Jan.) **[ref. 5619]**. A new serranid fish found in Japan. Jpn. J. Ichthyol. v. 3 (no. 2): 56-61.

———. 1963 **[ref. 5620]**. A new genus and species of anthinid fish from Sagami Bay, Japan. Bull. Fac. Educ. Yamaguchi Univ. v. 13 (no. 2): 27-33. [Not seen.]

———. 1967 **[ref. 7141]**. Notes on the osteology and systematic position of *Symphysanodon typus* Bleeker. Bull. Fac. Educ. Yamaguchi Univ. v. 17 (pt 2): 105-111.

KATAYAMA, M., T. ABE AND T.-T. NGUYEN. 1977 (Aug.) **[ref. 7052]**. Notes on some Japanese and Australian fishes of the family Centropomidae. Bull. Tohoku Reg. Fish. Res. Lab. No. 90: 45-57.

KATAYAMA, M., AND K. AMAOKA. 1986 (1 Nov.) **[ref. 6680]**. Two new anthiine fishes form the eastern tropical Pacific. Jpn. J. Ichthyol. v. 33 (no. 3): 213-222.

KATAYAMA, M., T. YAMAKAWA AND K. SUZUKI. 1980 (24 Dec.) **[ref. 5548]**. *Grammatonotus surugaensis*, a new serranid fish from Suruga Bay and the Straits of Osumi, Japan. Bull. Biogeogr. Soc. Jpn. v. 35 (No. 4): 45-48.

KATAYAMA, M., AND E. YAMAMOTO. 1986 (15 Mar.) **[ref. 6716]**. The anthiine fishes, *Odontanthias dorsomaculatus* sp. nov. and *Plectranthias bauchotae* Randall, from the western Indian Ocean. Jpn. J. Ichthyol. v. 32 (no. 4): 387-391.

KAUP, J. J. 1826 **[ref. 2568]**. Beiträge zur Amphibiologie und Ichthyologie. Isis (Oken) v. 19: 87-90.

———. 1853 **[ref. 2569]**. Uebersicht der Lophobranchier. Arch. Naturgeschichte v. 19 (no. 1): 226-234.

———. 1855 **[ref. 2570]**. *Enchelynassa*, neue Gattung aus der Familie der Aale. Arch. Naturgeschichte v. 21 (no. 1): 213-214, Pl. 10.

———. 1855 **[ref. 2571]**. Uebersicht über die Species einiger Familien der Sclerodermen. Arch. Naturgeschichte v. 21 (no. 1): 215-233.

———. 1856 **[ref. 2572]**. Uebersicht der Aale. Arch. Naturgeschichte v. 22 (no. 1): 41-77. [Many genera appeared here first, then in Kaup 1856, ref. 2573.]

———. 1856 **[ref. 2573]**. Catalogue of the apodal fish in the collection of the British Museum. London. 1-163, 19 pls. [Many new genera appeared first in Kaup 1856, ref. 2572. Date possibly 1857, as used by Whitley.]

———. 1856 **[ref. 2574]**. Einiges über die Unterfamilie Ophidinae. Arch. Naturgeschichte v. 22 (no. 1): 93-100.

———. 1856 **[ref. 2575]**. Catalogue of the lophobranchiate fish in the collection of the British Museum. London. i-iv + 1-76, Pls. 1-4.

———. 1858 **[ref. 2576]**. Uebersicht der Familie Gadidae. Arch. Naturgeschichte v. 24 (no. 1): 85-93.

———. 1858 (13 July) **[ref. 2577]**. On *Nemophis*, a new genus of riband-shaped fishes. Proc. Zool. Soc. Lond. Part 26 (1858): 168-169. [Also in Ann. Mag. Nat. Hist. (Ser. 3) v. 2: 301-303.]

———. 1858 **[ref. 2578]**. Uebersicht der Soleinae, der vierten Subfamilie der Pleuronectidae. Arch. Naturgeschichte v. 24 (no. 1): 94-104.

———. 1858 **[ref. 2579]**. Uebersicht der Plagusinae, der fünften Subfamilie der Pleuronectidae. Arch. Naturgeschichte v. 24 (no. 1): 105-110.

———. 1858 **[ref. 2580]**. Einiges über die Acanthopterygiens à joue cuirassée Cuv. Arch. Naturgeschichte v. 24 (no. 1): 329-343.

———. 1859 (Feb.-June) **[ref. 2587]**. Description of a new species of fish, *Peristethus rieffeli*. Proc. Zool. Soc. Lond. 1859 (pt 1): 103-107, Pl. 8. [Also in Ann. Mag. Nat. Hist. 1859 (Ser. 3) v. 5: 64-68.]

———. 1860 **[ref. 2586]**. Neue aalaehnliche Fische des Hamburger Museums. Abh. Naturwiss. Ver. Hamburg v. 4 (no. 2): 1-29 + suppl. 1-4, Pls. 1-5. [Possibly published as separate in 1859.]

———. 1860 **[ref. 2581]**. *Hoplarchus*, neues Genus der Familie Labridae. Arch. Naturgeschichte v. 26 (no. 1): 128-133, Pl. 6.

———. 1860 (Oct.) **[ref. 2582]**. On some new genera and species of fishes collected by Drs. Keferstein and Heckel at Messina. Ann. Mag. Nat. Hist. (Ser. 3) v. 6 (no. 34): 270-273, Pl. 3.

———. 1860 **[ref. 2583]**. Ueber die Chaetodontidae. Arch. Naturgeschichte v. 26 (no. 1): 133-156.

———. 1863 **[ref. 2584]**. Ueber einige japanische Fische. Neder. Tijdschr. Dierk. v. 1: 161-162. [Not seen.]

———. 1873 **[ref. 2585]**. Ueber die Familie Triglidae, nebst einigen Worten über die Classification. Arch. Naturgeschichte v. 39 (1 Bd.): 71-94.

KAWAGUCHI, K., AND H. G. MOSER. 1984 **[ref. 13642]**. Stomiatoidea: development. Am. Soc. Ichthyol. Herpetol. Spec. Publ. No. 1: 169-181.

KAWASHIMA, N., AND J. T. MOYER. 1982 (25 Nov.) **[ref. 5451]**. Two pomacentrid fishes, *Pristotis jerdoni* and *Pomacentrus vaiuli*, from the Ryukyu Islands. Jpn. J. Ichthyol. v. 29 (no. 3): 260-266.

KAZANSKII, V. I. 1928 **[ref. 14268]**. [On the morphology and taxonomy of the larval cyprinids of the Vobla (*Rutilus rutilus caspicus* Jak.) type.] Trudy Astrakhanskoi rybokhozyaistvennoi stansii v. 6 (no. 3): 1-18. [Not seen. Taken from Berg 1949 [ref. 12882].]

KENDALL, A. W., JR. 1984 **[ref. 13663]**. Serranidae: development and relationships. Am. Soc. Ichthyol. Herpetol. Spec. Publ. No. 1: 499-510.

KENDALL, A. W., JR., AND R. J. BEHNKE. 1984 **[ref. 13638]**. Salmonidae: development and relationships. Am. Soc. Ichthyol. Herpetol. Spec. Publ. No. 1: 142-149.

KENDALL, W. C., AND E. L. GOLDSBOROUGH. 1911 (Feb.) **[ref. 2594]**. The shore fishes. In: Reports on the scientific results of the expedition to the tropical Pacific, in charge of Alexander Agassiz, by the U.S. Fish Commission steamer "Albatross," from August, 1899, to March, 1900... No. XIII. Mem. Mus. Comp. Zool. v. 26 (pt 7): 239-344, Pls. 1-7.

KESSLER, K. T. 1874 **[ref. 2596]**. Pisces. In: Fedtschensko's Expedition to Turkestan. Zoogeographical Researches. Bull. Soc. Sci. Moscou v. 11: i-iv + 1-63, Pls. 1-8. [In Russian (some descriptions in Latin). Apparently also as a separate, 1874, Moscow.]

———. 1876 **[ref. 2595]**. Description of fishes collected by Col. Prejevalsky in Mongolia. In: N. Prejevalsky. Mongolia i Strana Tangutov. v. 2 (pt 4): 1-36, 3 pls. [In Russian. Not seen.]

———. 1877 **[ref. 2597]**. The Aralo-Caspian Expedition. IV. Fishes of the Aralo-Caspio-Pontine region. St. Petersburg. 1-360. [Not seen.]

———. 1879 **[ref. 2598]**. Beiträge zur Ichthyologie von Central-Asien. Bull. Imp. Acad. Sci. St. Petersburg v. 25: 282-310. [Also apparently as Mél. Biol. Bull. Acad. Sci. St. Petersburg 1879, v. 10: 233-272 (not seen).]

KEYSERLING, E. VON. 1861 **[ref. 2601]**. Neue Cypriniden aus Persien. Z. Ges. Naturw. Berlin v. 17: 1-24. [Not seen. Also apparently as a separate, Berlin 1861.]

KHARIN, V. E. 1983 **[ref. 6258]**. A new genus and species of grammid perch from the waters of Lower California (Osteichthyes, Grammidae). Izvestia Tinro v. 107: 116-119.

———. 1987 **[ref. 6227]**. New and lesser known species of carpet shark (Orectolobidae) from Vietnamese waters with a note on species composition of the genus *Chiloscyllium* Muller et Henle, 1837. Voprosy Ikhtiol. v. 27 (no. 3): 362-368. [In Russian. English translation in J. Ichthyol. v. 27 (no. 4): 63-70.]

———. 1989 **[ref. 12556]**. A new genus and a new species of deepsea anglers of the family Oneirodidae from the northwest Pacific. Voprosy Ikhtiol. v. 29 (no. 1): 158-160. [In Russian.]

KIDO, K. 1984 (15 May) **[ref. 6731]**. The third specimen of cyclopterid fish, *Eumicrotremus barbatus*, from Japan. Jpn. J. Ichthyol. v. 31 (no. 1): 83-85.

———. 1985 (30 May) **[ref. 6720]**. New and rare species of the genus *Careproctis* (Liparididae) from the Bering Sea. Jpn. J. Ichthyol. v. 32 (no. 1): 6-17.

———. 1985 (20 Feb.) **[ref. 6723]**. New and rare species of the genus *Paraliparis* (family Liparididae) from southern Japan. Jpn. J. Ichthyol. v. 31 (no. 4): 362-368.

———. 1988 (Dec.) **[ref. 12287]**. Phylogeny of the family Liparididae, with the taxonomy of the species found around Japan. Mem. Fac. Fish. Hokkaido Univ. v. 35 (no. 2): 125-256.

KIDO, K., AND D. KITAGAWA. 1986 **[ref. 5682]**. Development of larvae and juveniles of *Rhinoliparis barbulifer* (Liparididae). Pp. 697-702. In: Indo-Pac. Fish. Biol., Ichthyol. Soc. Japan.

KIENER, A., AND M. MAUGÉ. 1966 **[ref. 2605]**. Contributions à l'étude systématique et écologique des poissons Cichlidae endémiques de Madagascar. Mem. Mus. Natl. Hist. Nat. (Ser. A) Zool. v. 40 (no. 2): 51-99, 4 pls.

KIENER, A., AND J. SPILLMANN. 1973 **[ref. 7217]**. Atherinidae (pp. 576-578). In: Hureau & Monod 1973 [ref. 6590].

KIJIMA, A., N. TANIGUCHI AND A. OCHIAI. 1986 (30 May) **[ref. 6320]**. Genetic relationships in the family Carangidae. Pp. 840-848. In: Uyeno et al. (eds.) 1986 [ref. 6147].

KIM, I.-S. 1986 (30 May) **[ref. 6327]**. Taxonomy and zoogeography of the genus *Cobitis* (Pisces, Cobitididae) from Korea [Abstract]. P. 945. In: Uyeno et al. (eds.) 1986 [ref. 6147].

KIMURA, S. 1985 **[ref. 6262]**. *Diagramma aporognathus*, a junior synonym of *Parapristipoma trilineatum*. Jpn. J. Ichthyol. v. 32 (no. 3): 345-346.

KIMURA, S., K. TSUMOTO AND K. MORI. 1988 (25 May) **[ref. 6692]**. Development of the cottid fish, *Pseudoblennius percoides*, reared in the laboratory, with brief descriptions of juvenile *P. marmoratus* and *P. zonostigma*. Jpn. J. Ichthyol. v. 35 (no. 1): 19-24.

KING, R. P. 1989 (31 Mar.) **[ref. 12831]**. Distribution, abundance, size and feeding habits of *Brienomyrus brachyistius* (Gill, 1862) (Teleostei: Mormyridae) in a Nigerian rainforest stream. Cybium v. 13 (no. 1): 25-36.

KINOSHITA, I., AND S. FUJITA. 1988 (25 May) **[ref. 6693]**. Larvae and juveniles of blue drum, *Nibea mitsukurii*, occurring in the surf zone of Tosa Bay, Japan. Jpn. J. Ichthyol. v. 35 (no. 1): 25-30.

———. 1988 (25 Feb.) **[ref. 6698]**. Larvae and juveniles of temperate bass, *Lateolabrax latus*, occurring in the surf zones of Tosa Bay, Japan. Jpn. J. Ichthyol. v. 34 (no. 4): 468-475.

KIRSCH, P. H. 1889 (20 Sept.) **[ref. 2608]**. Notes on a collection of fishes obtained in the Gila River, at Fort Thomas, Arizona, by Lieut. W. L. Carpenter, U. S. Army. Proc. U. S. Natl. Mus. v. 11 [no. 754]: 555-558.

———. 1889 **[ref. 12542]**. A review of the European and American Uranoscopidae or star-gazers. Proc. Acad. Nat. Sci. Phila. 1889 [v. 41]: 258-265.

KISHIMOTO, H. 1987 (10 June) **[ref. 6062]**. A new stargazer, *Uranoscopus flacipinnis*, from Japan and Taiwan with redescription and neotype designation of *U. japonicus*. Jpn. J. Ichthyol. v. 34 (no. 1): 1-14.

———. 1989 (20 Dec.) **[ref. 13562]**. A new species and a new subspecies of the stargazer genus *Gnathagnus* from northwestern Australia. Jpn. J. Ichthyol. v. 36 (no. 3): 303-314.

KISHIMOTO, H., K. AMAOKA, H. KOHNO AND T. HAMAGUCHI. 1987 (10 Sept.) **[ref. 6061]**. A revision of the black-and-white snappers, genus *Macolor* (Perciformes: Lutjanidae). Jpn. J. Ichthyol. v. 34 (no. 2): 146-156.

KISHIMOTO, H., M. HAYASHI, H. KOHNO AND O. MORIYAMA. 1988 (Dec.) **[ref. 13446]**. Revision of Japanese batfishes, genus *Platax*. Sci. Rept. Yokosuka City Mus. No. 36: 19-38, Pls. 3-4. [In Japanese, English abst.]

KISHIMOTO, H., P. R. LAST, E. FUJII AND M. F. GOMON. 1988 (20 Sept.) **[ref. 6648]**. Revision of a deep-sea stargazer genus *Pleuroscopus*. Jpn. J. Ichthyol. v. 35 (no. 2): 150-158.

KISHINOUYE, K. 1923 (30 Mar.) **[ref. 2609]**. Contributions to the comparative study of the so-called scombroid fishes. J. Coll. Agric. Imp. Univ. Tokyo v. 8 (no. 3): 293-475, Pls. 13-34.

———. 1926 (May) **[ref. 2610]**. A new aberrant form of the Cybiidae from Japan. J. Coll. Agric. Imp. Univ. Tokyo v. 7 (no. 4): 377-382.

KLAUSEWITZ, W. 1955 (1 Dec.) **[ref. 2611]**. *Paramicrophis schmidti*, eine neue Seenadel aus Indien (Pisces, Syngnathidae). Senckenb. Biol. v. 36 (no. 5/6): 325-327.

———. 1960 (15 Sept.) **[ref. 2613]**. Fische aus dem Roten Meer. IV. Einige systematisch und ökologisch bemerkenswerte Meergrundeln (Pisces, Gobiidae). Senckenb. Biol. v. 41 (no. 3/4): 149-162, Pl. 21.

———. 1974 (23 Dec.) **[ref. 2614]**. *Eilatia latruncularia* n. gen. n. sp. und *Vanderhorstia mertensi* n. sp. vom Golf von Aqaba (Pisces: Gobiidae: Gobiinae). Senckenb. Biol. v. 55 (no. 4/6): 205-212.

———. 1976 (31 May) **[ref. 2615]**. *Cirrhilabrichthys filamentosus* n. gen., n. sp., aus der Javasee (Pisces: Labridae). Senckenb. Biol. v. 57 (no. 1/3): 11-14.

———. 1983 (30 Nov.) **[ref. 6011]**. Tiefenwasser-und Tiefseefische aus dem Roten Meer. VII. *Harpadon erythraeus* n. sp. aus der Tiefsee des zentralen Roten Meeres (Pisces: Teleostei: Scopelomorpha: Myctophiformes: Harpadontidae). Senckenb. Biol. v. 64 (no. 1/3): 34-45.

———. 1985 (31 Oct.) **[ref. 5806]**. Tiefenwasser-und Tiefseefische aus dem Roten Meer. XI. *Neocentropogon mesedai* n. sp. aus dem Mesobenthos. Senckenb. Marit. v. 17 (no. 1/3): 15-23.

———. 1985 (2 Sept.) **[ref. 5986]**. Fische aus dem Roten Meer. XVII. A new species of the genus *Stalix* from the Gulf of Aquba, Red Sea (Pisces: Teleostei: Perciformes: Opistognathidae). Rev. Fr. Aquariol. v. 12 (no. 1): 17-22.

———. 1989 (29 Dec.) **[ref. 13650]**. Deepsea and deep water fish of the eastern Mediterranean, collected during the METEOR-expedition 1987. Senckenb. Marit. v. 20 (no. 5/6): 251-263.

KLAUSEWITZ, W., AND B. CONDÉ. 1981 (25 Nov.) **[ref. 5479]**. *Oxymetopon cyanoctenosum* n. sp., un nouvel eléotride des Philippines, avec une étude comparée du genre (Pisces, Perciformes, Gobioidei, Eleotridae). Rev. Fr. Aquariol. v. 8 (no. 3): 67-76.

KLAUSEWITZ, W., AND I. EIBL-EIBESFELDT. 1959 (1 Sept.) **[ref. 2616]**. Neue Röhrenaale von den Maldiven und Nikobaren (Pisces, Apodes, Heterocongridae). Senckenb. Biol. v. 40 (no. 3/4): 135-153.

KLAUSEWITZ, W., AND S. HENRICH. 1986 (21 July) **[ref. 5214]**. *Sicyopus jonklaasi* n. sp., a new freshwater goby from Sri Lanka (Pisces, Perciformes, Gobioidei, Gobiidae, Sicydiaphiinae). Rev. Fr. Aquariol. v. 12 (no. 4): 117-121.

KLAUSEWITZ, W., J. E. MCCOSKER, J. E. RANDALL AND H. ZETZSCHE. 1978 (30 Nov.) **[ref. 5337]**. *Hoplolatilus chlupatyi* n. sp., un nouveau poisson marin des Philippines (Pisces, Perciformes, Percoidei, Branchiostegidae). Rev. Fr. Aquariol. v. 5 (no. 2): 41-48.

KLAUSEWITZ, W., AND F. RÖSSEL. 1961 (5 Feb.) **[ref. 2617]**. *Rhynchodoras xingui*, ein bemerkenswerter neuer Wels aus Brasilien (Pisces, Siluroidea, Doradidae). Senckenb. Biol. v. 42 (no. 1/2): 45-48.

KLAUSEWITZ, W., AND R. VON HENTIG. 1975 (14 Nov.) **[ref. 7093]**. *Xarfania hassi* und *Gorgasia maculata*, zwei Neunachweise für die Komoren. Senckenb. Biol. v. 56 (no. 4/6): 209-216.

KLEIN, J. T. 1775 **[ref. 2618]**. Neuer Schauplatz der Natur, nach den Richtigsten Beobachtungen und Versuchen, in alphabetischer Ordnung, vorgestellt durch eine Gesellschaft von Gelehrten. Weidmann, Leipzig. [= "Gesellschaft Schauplatz"; see Jordan 1917:34-37 [ref. 2407]] v. 1: i-xiv + 1-1044. [Klein's "Gesellschaft Schauplatz" is regarded as unavailable (non binominal) but not on Official Index.]

———. 1776 **[ref. 4918]**. Gesellschaft Schauplatz (see Klein 1775 [ref. 2618]). v. 2: 1-842.

———. 1776 **[ref. 4919]**. Gesellschaft Schauplatz (see Klein 1775 [ref. 2618]). v. 3: 1-836.

———. 1777 **[ref. 4920]**. Gesellschaft Schauplatz (see Klein 1775 [ref. 2618]). v. 4: 1-874.

———. 1777 **[ref. 4921]**. Gesellschaft Schauplatz (see Klein 1775 [ref. 2618]). v. 5: 1-840.

———. 1778 **[ref. 4922]**. Gesellschaft Schauplatz (see Klein 1775 [ref. 2618]). v. 6: 1-5 + 1-782.

———. 1779 **[ref. 4923]**. Gesellschaft Schauplatz (see Klein 1775 [ref. 2618]). v. 7: 1-820.

———. 1779 **[ref. 4924]**. Gesellschaft Schauplatz (see Klein 1775 [ref. 2618]). v. 8: 1-824.

———. 1780 **[ref. 4925]**. Gesellschaft Schauplatz (see Klein 1775 [ref. 2618]). v. 9: 1-832.

———. 1781 **[ref. 4926]**. Gesellschaft Schauplatz (see Klein 1775 [ref. 2618]). v. 10: 1-604.

KLIPPART, J. H. 1877. See Jordan 1877 [ref. 2375].

KLJUKANOV, V. A., AND D. E. MCALLISTER. 1973 **[ref. 7178]**. Osmeridae (pp. 158-159). In: Hureau & Monod 1973 [ref. 6590].

KLUNZINGER, C. B. 1870 **[ref. 2621]**. Synopsis der Fische des Rothen Meeres. I. Theil. Percoiden-Mugiloiden. Verh. K.-K. Zool.-Bot. Ver. Ges. Wien v. 20: 669-834. [Also as "Systematische Uebersicht der Fische des Rothen Meeres, als Anhang und Register zur Synopsis." Wien, 1871.]

———. 1871 **[ref. 2622]**. Synopsis der Fische des Rothen Meeres. II. Theil. Verh. K.-K. Zool.-Bot. Ver. Ges. Wien v. 21: 441-688. [Continuation of ref. 2621. See note with part 1, above.]

———. 1872 **[ref. 2623]**. Zur Fischfauna von Süd-Australien. Arch. Naturgeschichte v. 38 (pt 1): 17-47.

———. 1880 **[ref. 2624]**. Die von Müller'sche Sammlung australischer Fische in Stuttgart. Sitzungsber. Akad. Wiss. Wien v. 80 (1. Abt.) (3-4): 325-430, Pls. 1-8. [Also as a separate, pp. 1-206, Pls. 1-8, with original pagination in brackets.]

——. 1884 **[ref. 2625]**. Die Fische des Rothen Meeres. Eine kritische Revision mit Bestimmungstabellen. I. Teil. Acanthopteri veri Owen. Stuttgart. i-ix + 1-133, Pls. 1-13.

KNAPP, L. W. 1979 (July) **[ref. 14196]**. Fische des Indischen Ozeans. Ergebnisse der ichthyologischen Untersuchungen während des Expedition des Forschungsschiffes "Meteor" in den Indischen Ozean, Oktober 1964 bis 1965. A. Systematischer Teil, XXII. Scorpaeniformes (4). "Meteor Forsch.-Ergebnisse D (no. 29): 48-54. [In English.]

——. 1986 **[ref. 5683]**. Family No. 154: Bembridae (pp. 481-482), Family No. 155: Platycephalidae (pp. 482-486). In: Smiths' Sea Fishes (Smith & Heemstra 1986 [ref. 5715]).

KNER, R. 1853 **[ref. 2627]**. Die Panzerwelse des K.K. Hof-naturalien-Cabinetes zu Wien. I. Abtheilung. Loricarinae. Denkschr. Akad. Wiss. Wien v. 6: 65-98, Pls. 1-8. [Also as Separate, Wien, pp. 1-98, Pls. 1-8. Abstract in Sitzungsber. Akad. Wiss. Wien 1853, v. 10: 113-116.]

——. 1854 **[ref. 2628]**. Die Hypostomiden. Zweite Hauptgruppe der Familie der Panzerfische. (Loricata vel Goniodontes). Denkschr. Akad. Wiss. Wien v. 7: 251-286, Pls. 1-5. [Abstract in Sitzungsber. Akad. Wiss. Wien 1853, v. 10: 279-282. Also as separate, pp. 1-36.]

——. 1855 **[ref. 2629]**. Ichthyologische Beiträge. Sitzungsber. Math-naturw. Classe Akad. Wiss. Wien v. 17 (s. 92): 92-162, Pls. 1-6. [Also as separate, pp. 1-73.]

——. 1855 **[ref. 12581]**. Über ein neues genus aus der familie der Welse, Siluroidei. Sitzungsber. Math-naturw. Classe Kais. Akad. Wiss. Wien v. 17: 313-316, 2 pls. [Also as a separate, pp. 1-6, 2 pls., with original pagination in brackets.]

——. 1858 **[ref. 2630]**. Ichthyologische Beiträge. II. Abtheilung. Sitzungsber. Akad. Wiss. Wien v. 26 (s. 373): 373-448, Pls. 1-9. [Also as a separate, pp. 1-78.]

——. 1858 **[ref. 13404]**. Beiträge zur Familie der Characinen. Sitzungsber. Math-Naturw. Classe Akad. Wiss. Wien v. 30: 75-80. [Synopsis predating Kner 1859 [ref. 2631]; published in 1858 according to Fowler (MS).]

——. 1858-59 **[ref. 2631]**. Zur Familie der Characinen. III. Folge der Ichthyologischen Beiträge. Denkschr. Math-Nat. Classe Kaiserlichen. Akad. Wiss. Wien v. 17: 137-182, Pls. 1-8. [Cont. in 1860, v. 18: 9-62. Abst. in Sitzungsber. Akad. Wiss. Wien v. 30: 75-80, v. 32:163-169. Also separate, 46 pp.]

——. 1860 **[ref. 2632]**. Über *Belonesox belizanus*, nov. gen. et spec., aus der Familie der Cyprinodonten. Sitzungsber. Akad. Wiss. Wien v. 40: 419-422, 1 pl.

——. 1860 **[ref. 2633]**. Über einige noch unbeschriebene Fische. Sitzungsber. Akad. Wiss. Wien v. 39: 531-547, 1 pl.

——. 1860 **[ref. 7130]**. Zur Familie der Characinen. III. Folge. Der Ichthyologische Beiträge. Denkschr. Akad. Wiss. Wien v. 18: 9-62, Pls. 1-8.

——. 1863 **[ref. 5002]**. Uebersicht der ichthyologischen Ausbeute des Herrn Professors Dr. Mor. Wagner in Central-Amerika. Sitzungsber. Koningl. Bayer. Akad. Wiss. Muenchen 1863 (Band 2): 221-230.

——. 1864 **[ref. 2637]**. [Untitled, headed by "Als neue Gattungen werden vorgeführt:..." Anz. Akad. Wiss. Wien v. 1: 185-187. [Notice in Anonymous 1865 [ref. 6173]. Date [read ?] of 10 Nov. 1864 given in that notice which appeared in Jan. 1865.]

——. 1865 **[ref. 2639]**. *Psalidostoma*, eine neue Characinen-Gattung aus dem weissen Nil. Sitzungsber. Akad. Wiss. Wien v. 50: 99-102, 1 pl. [Notice in Ann. Mag. Nat. Hist. (Ser. 3) v. 14: 399.]

——. 1865 **[ref. 6174]**. Fische aus dem Naturhistorischen Museum der Hrn. J. C. Godeffroy & Sohn in Hamburg. Denkschr. Akad. Wiss. Wien v. 24: 1-12, Pls. 1-4.

——. 1865-67 **[ref. 2638]**. Reise der öesterreichischen Fregatte "Novara" um die Erde in de*r* Jahren 1857-59, unter den Befehlen des Commodore B. von Wüllerstorf-Urbain. Wien. Zool. Theil, Fische. 1-3 Abth.: 1-433, Pls. 1-16. [Pp. 1-109, pl. 1-5 (1865); 111-272, pls. 6-11 (1865); 273-433, pls. 12-16 (1867).]

——. 1866 **[ref. 2636]**. Specielles Verzeichniss der während der Reise der kaiserlichen Fregatte "Novara" gesammelten Fische. III. und Schlussabtheilung. Sitzungsber. Akad. Wiss. Wien v. 53: 543-550. [Also as a separate, pp. 1-8.]

——. 1867 **[ref. 2645]**. Neue Fische aus dem Museum der Herren J. Cäs. Godeffroy & Sohn in Hamburg. Sitzungsber. Akad. Wiss. Wien v. 56: 709-728, 4 pls. [Also as a separate, 1867, pp. 1-20, Pls. 1-4.]

——. 1868 **[ref. 2646]**. IV. Folge neuer Fische aus dem Museum der Herren Joh. Cäs. Godeffroy und Sohn in Hamburg. Sitzungsber. Akad. Wiss. Wien v. 58: 293-356, Pls. 1-9. [Also as a separate, pp. 1-64, Pls. 1-9. Possibly published in 1869. "New" genera appeared first in Kner 1868, ref. 6074.]

——. 1868 **[ref. 6074]**. Über neue Fische aus dem Museum der Herren Johann Cäsar Godeffroy & Sohn in Hamburg. (IV. Folge). Sitzungsberg. Akad. Wiss. Wien v. 58: 26-31. [More expanded treatment in Kner 1868 [ref. 2646].]

KNER, R., AND F. STEINDACHNER. 1864 **[ref. 2649]**. Neue Gattungen und Arten von Fischen aus Central-Amerika; gesammelt von Prof. Moritz Wagner. Abh. Bayer. Akad. Wiss. v. 10 (1. abth.): 1-61, Pls. 1-6. [Dates vary, 1864, 1866, 1870, but 1864 on title page of reprint, new genera date to 1863 [ref. 5002].]

——. 1867 (4 Sept.) **[ref. 2640]**. Neue Fische aus dem Museum der Herren J. Cäs. Godeffroy & Sohn in Hamburg. Sitzungsber. Akad. Wiss. Wien v. 54: 356-395, Pls. 1-5. [Also as a separate, Hamburg, 1867, pp. 1-40, Pls. 1-5. Date from Fowler (MS).]

KOBAYAKAWA, M. 1989 (28 Sept.) **[ref. 13476]**. Systematic revision of the catfish genus *Silurus*, with description of a new species from Thailand and Burma. Jpn. J. Ichthyol. v. 36 (no. 2): 155-186.

KOBYLIANSKY, S. H. 1986 **[ref. 6002]**. Materials for a revision of the family Bathylagidae (Teleostei, Salmoniformes). Trans. Shirshov Inst. Oceanol. v. 121: 6-50. [In Russian, English summ.]

KOEFOED, E. 1927 (May) **[ref. 2650]**. Fishes from the sea-bottom. Scient. Results M. Sars N. Atlant. Deep-Sea Exped., 1910 v. 4 (pt 1): 1-148, Pls. 1-6.

——. 1944 (Apr.) **[ref. 2651]**. Pediculati from the "Michael Sars" North Atlantic deep-sea expedition 1910. Scient. Results M. Sars N. Atlant. Deep-Sea Exped. 1910 v. 4 (pt 2, no. 1): 1-18, Pls. 1-3.

——. 1952 (8 Oct.) **[ref. 2652]**. Zeomorphi, Percomorphi, Plectognathi from the "Michael Sars" North Atlantic deep-sea expedition 1910. Scient. Results M. Sars N. Atlant. Deep-Sea Exped. 1910 v. 4 (pt 2, no. 2): 1-27, Pls. 1-3.

——. 1953 **[ref. 6486]**. Synentognathi, Solenichthyes, Anacanthini, Berycomorphi, Xenoberyces from the "Michael Sars" North Atlantic deep-sea expedition 1910. Scient. Results M. Sars N. Atlant. Deep-Sea Exped. 1910 v. 4 (pt 2, no. 3): 1-39, Pls. 1-4.

——. 1955 (Apr.) **[ref. 5621]**. Iniomi (Myctophidae exclusive), Lyomeri, Apodes from the "Michael Sars" North Atlantic deep-sea expedition 1910. Scient. Results M. Sars N. Atlant. Deep-Sea Exped. 1910 v. 4 (pt 2, no. 4): 1-16, Pls. 1-2.

——. 1956 **[ref. 2653]**. Isospondyli. 1. Gymnophotodermi and Lepidophotodermi from the "Michael Sars" North Atlantic deep-sea expedition 1910. Scient. Results M. Sars N. Atlant. Deep-Sea Exped. 1910 v. 4 (pt 2, no. 5): 1-21, Pls. 1-3.

KOELREUTER, J. G. 1770 **[ref. 2654]**. Piscium variorum e Museo Petropolitano excerptorum descriptiones. Novi Comment. Acad. Petropol. v. 8 (for 1761): 404-430. [Not seen.]

KOHNO, H. 1984 (20 Nov.) **[ref. 5796]**. Osteology and systematic position of the butterfly mackerel, *Gasterochisma melampus*. Jpn. J. Ichthyol. v. 31 (no. 3): 268-286.

KOLLER, O. 1926 **[ref. 2658]**. Einige neue Fischformen von der Insel Hainan. Anz. Akad. Wiss. Wien v. 63 (no. 9): 74-77.

——. 1927 **[ref. 5622]**. Fische von der Insel Hai-nan. Ann. Naturhist. Mus. Wien 41 (1927): 25-49, Pl. 1.

KÖLLIKER, R. A. VON. 1853 **[ref. 2680]**. Weitere Bemerkungen über die Helmichthyiden. Verh. Phys. Med. Ges. Wurz. v. 4 (heft 1):

100-102.

KOLOMBATOVIC, J. 1907 **[ref. 6586]**. Contribuzioni alla fauna dei vertebrati della Dalmazia. Glasnika Hrvatskoga Narav. Drustva, Zagreb v. 19: 1-24.

KORNFIELD, I., AND K. E. CARPENTER. 1984 **[ref. 5435]**. Cyprinids of Lake Lanao, Philippines: taxonomic validity, evolutionary rates and speciation scenarios. Pp. 69-84. In: Evolution of fish species flocks. A. A. Echelle & I. Kornfield (eds). Oklahoma State Univ. Press. i-x + 1-257.

KORRINGA, M. 1970 (31 Dec.) **[ref. 2662]**. A new gymnotoid fish from the Rio Tocantins, Brazil. Proc. Calif. Acad. Sci. (Ser. 4) v. 38 (no. 13): 265-271.

KOSAKI, R. K. 1989 (27 Dec.) **[ref. 13510]**. *Centropyge nahackyi*, a new species of angelfish from Johnston Atoll (Teleostei: Pomacanthidae). Copeia 1989 (no. 4): 880-886.

KOSSWIG, C. 1950 **[ref. 5022]**. Die Gattung *Tylognathus* in Vorderasien. Zool. Anz. v. 145: 406-415.

KOSSWIG, C., AND F. SÖZER. 1945 **[ref. 2664]**. Nouveaux Cyprinodontides de l'Anatolie centrale. Rev. Fac. Sci. Univ. Istanbul (Ser. B) v. 10 (f. 2): 77-83.

KOTLYAR, A. N. 1978 **[ref. 2665]**. A contribution to the taxonomy of the "armless" flounders (Pisces, Bothidae) from southwestern Atlantic. Voprosy Ikhtiol. v. 18 (no. 5): 799-813. [In Russian. English translation in J. Ichthyol. v. 18 (no. 5): 708-721.]

———. 1981 **[ref. 2666]**. A new family, genus and species of beryciform fishes, Hispidoberycidae fam. n. *Hispidoberyx ambagiosus* gen. et sp. n. (Beryciformes). Voprosy Ikhtiol. v. 21 (no. 3): 411-416. [In Russian. English translation in J. Ichthyol. v. 21 (no. 3): 9-13.]

———. 1984 **[ref. 6644]**. A new genus and species of fishes (Beryciformes, Trachichthyidae) from the Pacific. Zool. Zh. v. 63 (no. 10): 1591-1594. [In Russian, English summ.]

———. 1984 **[ref. 13450]**. Systematics and the distribution of fishes of the family Polymixidae (Polymixioidei, Beryciformes). Voprosy Ikhtiol. v. 24 (no. 5): 691-708. [In Russian. English translation in J. Ichthyol. v. 24 (no. 6): 1-20.]

———. 1986 **[ref. 6004]**. Systematics and distribution of species of the genus *Hoplostethus* Cuvier (Beryciformes, Trachichthyidae). Trans. Shirshov Inst. Oceanol. v. 121: 97-140. [In Russian, English summ.]

———. 1987 **[ref. 13522]**. Classification and distribution of fishes of the family Diretmidae (Beryciformes). Voprosy Ikhtiol. v. 27 (no. 6): 883-897. [In Russian. English translation in J. Ichthyol. 1988, v. 28 (no. 2): 1-15.]

KOTLYAR, A. N., AND N. V. PARIN. 1986 **[ref. 5850]**. Two new species of *Chlorophthalmus* (Osteichthyes, Myctophiformes, Chlorophthalmidae) from submarine mountain ridges in the south-eastern part of the Pacific Ocean. Zool. Zh. v. 65 (no. 3): 369-377. [In Russian, brief English summ.]

KOTTELAT, M. 1976 **[ref. 6566]**. Modifications taxonomiques au sein des super-espèces *Aphyosemion gardneri* (Blgr., 1911) et *A. walkeri* (Blgr., 1911) avec une espèce et une sous-espèce "nouvelle" mais connues et un sous-genre nouveau. Aquarama v. 10 (no. 36, Oct.): 23-28.

———. 1982 (June) **[ref. 2667]**. A small collection of fresh-water fishes from Kalimantan, Borneo, with descriptions of one new genus and three new species of Cyprinidae. Rev. Suisse Zool. v. 89 (no. 2): 419-437.

———. 1982 **[ref. 5400]**. Notes d'Ichthyologie asiatique. Bull. Mus. Natl. Hist. Nat. Sect. A Zool. Biol. Ecol. Anim. v. 4 (no. 3-4): 523-529.

———. 1983 **[ref. 5289]**. A new species of *Erethistes* Müller & Troschel from Thailand and Burma (Osteichthyes: Siluriformes: Sisoridae). Hydrobiologia v. 107: 71-74.

———. 1983 (Nov.) **[ref. 6013]**. Status of *Luciocyprinus* and *Fustis* (Osteichthyes: Cyprinidae). Zool. Res. v. 4 (no. 4): 383-386.

———. 1984 (20 Nov.) **[ref. 5292]**. Revision of the Indonesian and Malaysian loaches of the subfamily Noemacheilinae. Jpn. J. Ichthyol. v. 31 (no. 3): 225-260.

———. 1985 (23 Jan.) **[ref. 5288]**. Notulae ichthyologiae orientalis. V. A synopsis of the oriental cyprinid genus *Sikukia*. VI. Status of the Kampuchea cyprinid *Albulichthys krempfi*. Rev. Suisse Zool. v. 91 (no. 4): 953-958. [Date on cover is Dec. 1984, author stamp on reprint 23 Jan. 1985.]

———. 1985 **[ref. 11441]**. Fresh-water fishes of Kampuchea. Hydrobiologia v. 121: 249-279.

———. 1987 (20 Feb.) **[ref. 5962]**. Nomenclatural status of the fish names created by J. C. van Hasselt (1823) and of some cobitoid genera. Jpn. J. Ichthyol. v. 33 (no. 4): 368-375.

———. 1988 (June) **[ref. 13379]**. Indian and Indochinese species of *Balitora* (Osteichthyes: Cypriniformes) with descriptions of two new species and comments on the family-group names Balitoridae and Homalopteridae. Rev. Suisse Zool. v. 95 (no. 2): 487-504.

———. 1988 (15 July) **[ref. 13380]**. Authorship, dates of publication, status and types of Spix and Agassiz's Brazilian fishes. Spixiana v. 11 (no. 1): 69-93.

———. 1989 (26 May) **[ref. 13605]**. Zoogeography of the fishes from Indochinese inland waters with an annotated check-list. Bull. Zool. Mus. Univ. Amst. v. 12 (no. 1): 1-55.

———. 1989 (29 Dec.) **[ref. 14233]**. On the validity of *Phractocephalus* Agassiz, 1829, vs. *Pirarara* Agassiz, 1829 (Osteichthyes: Pimelodidae). Spixiana (Muench.) v. 12 (no. 3): 321.

———. 1989 (27 Dec.) **[ref. 14361]**. [Review of] Identification of the fresh-water fishes of North Viet Nam. Copeia 1989 (no. 4): 1102-1104.

———. 1990 (Apr.) **[ref. 14137]**. Indochinese nemacheilines. A revision of nemacheiline loaches (Pisces: Cypriniformes) of Thailand, Burma, Laos, Cambodia and southern Viet Nam. Verlag Dr. Friedrich Pfeil, München. 1-262.

KOTTELAT, M., AND X.-L. CHU. 1987 (Dec.) **[ref. 13493]**. Two new species of *Rasbora* Bleeker, 1860 from southern Yunnan and northern Thailand. Spixiana v. 10 (no. 3): 313-318.

———. 1988 (30 June) **[ref. 12840]**. The genus *Homaloptera* (Osteichthyes, Cypriniformes, Homalopteridae) in Yunnan, China. Cybium 1988 (no. 2): 103-106.

———. 1988 **[ref. 13392]**. Revision of *Yunnanilus* with descriptions of a miniature species flock and six new species from China (Cypriniformes: Homalopteridae). Environ. Biol. Fishes v. 23 (no. 1-2): 65-93.

———. 1988 (Apr.) **[ref. 13491]**. A synopsis of Chinese balitorine loaches (Osteichthyes: Homalopteridae) with comments on their phylogeny and description of a new genus. Rev. Suisse Zool. v. 95 (no. 1): 181-201.

KOTTELAT, M., AND R. PETHIYAGODA. 1989 (29 Dec.) **[ref. 14143]**. *Schismatogobius deraniyagalai*, a new goby from Sri Lanka: description and field observations (Osteichthyes, Gobiidae). Spixiana (München) v. 12 (no. 3): 315-320.

KOTTHAUS, A. 1967 **[ref. 2668]**. Fische des Indischen Ozeans. Meteor Forschungsergeb. Reihe D Biol. No. 1: 1-84.

———. 1968 **[ref. 2669]**. Fische des Indischen Ozeans. A. Systematischer Teil. III. Ostariophysi und Apodes. Meteor Forschungsergeb. Reihe D Biol. No. 3: 14-56.

———. 1970 **[ref. 2670]**. *Flagelloserranus*, a new genus of serranid fishes with the description of two new species (Pisces, Percomorphi). Dana Rep. No. 78: 1-32.

———. 1972 (June) **[ref. 2671]**. Die meso- und bathypelagischen Fische der "Meteor"-Rossbreiten-Expedition 1970 (2. und 3. Fahrtabschnitt). Meteor Forschungsergeb. Reihe D Biol. No. 11: 1-28, 6 unnum. pls.

———. 1976 (May) **[ref. 2672]**. Fische des Indischen Ozeans. Ergebnisse der ichthyologischen Untersuchungen während der Expedition des Forschungsschiffes "Meteor" in den indischen Ozean, Oktober 1964 bis Mai 1965. A. Systematischer Teil, XVII. Percomorphi (7). Meteor Forschungsergeb. Reihe D Biol. No. 23: 45-61.

KOUMANS, F. P. 1931 (4 Dec.) **[ref. 5623]**. A preliminary revision of the genera of the gobioid fishes with united ventral fins.

Proefschrift, Lisse. 1-174.
———. 1933 **[ref. 2673]**. On a new genus and species of Apogonidae. Zool. Meded. (Leiden) v. 16 (no. 1-2): 78, Pl. 1.
———. 1935 **[ref. 2674]**. Notes on Gobioid fishes. 6. On the synonymy of some species from the Indo-Australian Archipelago. Zool. Meded. (Leiden) v. 18: 121-150.
———. 1937 **[ref. 2675]**. Notes on gobioid fishes. 9. Notes on the synonymy (continuation of Note 8). Zool. Meded. (Leiden) v. 20: 11-23.
———. 1940 **[ref. 2676]**. Results of a reexamination of types and specimens of gobioid fishes, with notes on the fishfauna (sic) of the surroundings of Batavia. Zool. Meded. (Leiden) v. 22: 121-210.
———. 1941 (July) **[ref. 2677]**. Gobioid fishes of India. Mem. Indian Mus. v. 13 (pt 3): 205-329.
———. 1953 **[ref. 2678]**. Gobioidea. In: Weber and de Beaufort. Fishes of the Indo-Australian Archipelago. E. J. Brill, Leiden. v. 10: i-xiii + 1-423.
———. 1953 **[ref. 2679]**. Biological results of the Snellius expedition. XVI. The Pisces and Leptocardii of the Snellius expedition. Temminckia v. 9: 177-275.
KRASYUKOVA, Z. V., AND A. V. GUSEV. 1987 **[ref. 6340]**. Description of the new species *Gyrinocheilus monchadskii* sp. n. (Gyrinocheilidae) and the new species of its parasitic monogenean *Dactylogyrus lindbergi* sp. n. (Dactylogyridae, Dactylogyridea). USSR Acad. Sci., Proc. Zool. Inst. Leningrad v. 162: 67-72, 1 pl. [In Russian, English summ.]
KREFFT, G. 1967 (July) **[ref. 2687]**. *Paraholtbyrnia cyanocephala* gen. nov., spec. nov. (Pisces, Salmoniformes, Alepocephaloidei), ein neuer Searside aus dem tropischen Atlantik. Arch. FischereiWiss. v. 18 (no. 1): 1-11.
———. 1971 **[ref. 7434]**. Ergebrisse der Forschungsreisen des FFS "Walther Herwig" nach Südamerika. XVIII. *Pseudoscopelus scutatus* spec. nov. (Pisces, Perciformes, Trachinoidei, Chiasmodontidae), ein neuer Kreuzzahnbarsch aus dem tropischen Atlantik. Arch. FischereiWiss. v. 22 (no. 3): 165-174.
———. 1973 (Aug.) **[ref. 7146]**. Ergebnisse der Forschungsreisen des FFS "Walther Herwig" nach Südaneruka. XXVIII. *Woodsia meyerwaardeni* spec. nov., ein neuer Gonostomatide aus dem Südatlantik. Arch. FischereiWiss. v. 24 (no. 1-3): 129-139.
———. 1973 **[ref. 7166]**. Squatinidae (pp. 49-50), Chimaeridae (pp. 78-79), Rhinochimaeridae (p.80), Alepocephalidae (pp. 86-93), Bathyprionidae (p. 94), Searsiidae (pp. 95-98), Scopelosauridae (pp. 168-169), Caproidae (pp. 353-354), Chiasmodontidae (pp. 452-454). In: Hureau & Monod 1973 [ref. 6590].
———. 1986 **[ref. 5684]**. Family No. 78: Notosudidae (pp. 268-270). In: Smiths' Sea Fishes (Smith & Heemstra 1986 [ref. 5715]).
KREFFT, G., AND V. E. BEKKER. 1973 **[ref. 7181]**. Myctophidae (pp. 171-198). In: Hureau & Monod 1973 [ref. 6590].
KREFFT, G., AND M. STEHMANN. 1973 **[ref. 7167]**. Pristidae (pp. 51-52), Rhinobatidae (pp. 53-54), Torpedinidae (pp. 55-57), Dasyatidae (pp. 70-73), Myliobatidae (pp. 74-75), Rhinopteridae (p. 76), Mobulidae (p. 77). In: Hureau & Monod 1973 [ref. 6590].
KREFFT, G., AND E. TORTONESE. 1973 **[ref. 7165]**. Oxynotidae (pp. 35-36), Squalidae (pp. 37-48). In: Hureau & Monod 1973 [ref. 6590].
KREFFT, J. L. G. 1868 (Apr.) **[ref. 2686]**. Descriptions of some new Australian freshwater fishes. Proc. Zool. Soc. Lond. 1867 (pt 3): 942-944.
———. 1868 **[ref. 5074]**. [Title unknown.] Illust. Sydney News v. 5: 3, 9. [Not seen.]
KREYENBERG, M. 1911 **[ref. 2688]**. Eine neue Cobitinen-Gattung aus China. Zool. Anz. v. 38: 417-419.
KRØYER, H. N. 1845 **[ref. 2689]**. Ichthyologiske Bidrag. Naturhist. Tidsskr. Kjøbenhavn (n. s.) v. 1: 213-282. [Includes 9 numbered articles treating genera and species.]
———. 1845 **[ref. 2692]**. Ichthyologiske Bidrag. 10. *Ceratis hollbölli*. Naturhist. Tidsskr. Kjøbenhavn (n. s.) v. 1: 639-649. [Continuation of Ref. 2689.]
———. 1846 **[ref. 2693]**. Danmarks Fiske. Kjøbenhavn. v. 3: 1-640. [Entire series 1838-1853, 4 vols.]
———. 1862 **[ref. 2694]**. Nogle Bidrag tel Nordisk ichthyologi [with subsections under separate titles]. Naturhist. Tidsskr. Kjøbenhavn (Ser. 3) v. 1: 233-310. [Date apparently 1862, sometimes given as 1861.]
KRUEGER, W. H. 1973 **[ref. 7177]**. Idiacanthidae (p. 144). In: Hureau & Monod 1973 [ref. 6590].
KRUPP, F. 1985 (31 May) **[ref. 6394]**. A new species of *Chondrostoma* from the Orontes River drainage basin of Turkey and Syria. Senckenb. Biol. v. 66 (no. 1/3): 27-33.
———. 1985 **[ref. 6403]**. Rehabilitation of *Barbus lorteti* Sauvage, 1882, and comments on the validity of the generic names *Bertinius* Fang, 1943, and *Bertinichthys* Whitley, 1953 (Pisces: Cyprinidae). Hydrobiologia v. 120: 63-68.
KRUPP, F., AND W. SCHNEIDER. 1989 **[ref. 13651]**. The fishes of the Jordan River drainage basin and Azraq Oasis. Fauna Saudi Arabia v. 10: 347-416.
KRYNICKI, J. 1832 **[ref. 5624]**. Schilus pallasii descriptus et icone illustratus. Nouv. Mem. Soc. Imp. Natur. Moscou. [Not seen.]
KUITER, R. H. 1986 (15 Nov.) **[ref. 6020]**. A new species of butterflyfish, *Chelmonops curiosus*, from Australia's south coast. Rev. Fr. Aquariol. v. 13 (no. 3): 73-78.
———. 1986 (1 Feb.) **[ref. 6026]**. A new genus and three new species of tripterygiid fishes of Australia's south coast. Rev. Fr. Aquariol. v. 12 (no. 3).: 89-96.
———. 1988 (15 Jan.) **[ref. 6371]**. Note sur les soins parentaux, l'éclosion et l'élevage des dragons de mer (Syngnathidae). Rev. Fr. Aquariol. v. 14 (no. 4): 113-122.
KUITER, R. H., AND G. R. ALLEN. 1986 (21 July) **[ref. 5213]**. A synopsis of the Australian pygmy perches (Percichthyidae), with the description of a new species. Rev. Fr. Aquariol. v. 12 (no. 4): 109-116.
KUKUYEV, E. I., AND I. I. KONOVALENKO. 1988 **[ref. 9290]**. Two new species of sharks of the genus *Scymnodalatias* (Dalatiidae) from the North Atlantic and southeastern Pacific oceans. Voprosy Ikhtiol. v. 28 (no. 2): 315-319. [In Russian. English translation in J. Ichthyol. 1988, v. 28 (no. 1): 122-124.]
KULKARNI, C. V. 1940 (June) **[ref. 2697]**. On the systematic position, structural modifications, bionomics and development of a remarkable new family of cyprinodont fishes from the province of Bombay. Rec. Indian Mus. (Calcutta) v. 42 (pt 2): 379-423.
———. 1952 **[ref. 2698]**. A new genus of schilbeid catfishes from the Deccan. Rec. Indian Mus. (Calcutta) v. 49 (pts 3-4): 231-238.
KULLANDER, S. O. 1977 **[ref. 2699]**. *Papiliochromis* gen. n., a new genus of South American cichlid fish (Teleostei, Perciformes). Zool. Scr. v. 6 (no. 3): 253-254.
———. 1980 **[ref. 5526]**. A taxonomical study of the genus *Apistogramma* Regan, with a revision of Brazilian and Peruvian species (Teleostei: Percoidei: Cichlidae). Bonn. Zool. Monogr. No. 14: 1-152.
———. 1983 **[ref. 8319]**. A revision of the South American cichlid genus *Cichlasoma* (Teleostei: Cichlidae). Naturhistoriska Riksmuseet, Stockholm. 1-296.
———. 1983 **[ref. 14221]**. Comment on the availability of "*Microgeophagus* Axelrod". Buntbarsche Bull. No. 99: 10. [Not seen.]
———. 1986 (21 Nov.) **[ref. 12439]**. Cichlid fishes of the Amazon River drainage of Peru. Swedish Museum of Natural History. 1-431, Pls. 1-38.
———. 1987 (30 June) **[ref. 6749]**. Cichlid fishes from the La Plata Basin. Part VI. Description of a new *Bujurquina* species from Bolivia. Cybium v. 11 (no. 2): 195-205.
———. 1987 **[ref. 9163]**. A new *Apistogramma* species (Teleostei, Cichlidae) from the Rio Negro in Brazil and Venezuela. Zool. Scr. v. 16 (no. 3): 259-270.
———. 1988 (5 Feb.) **[ref. 6232]**. *Teleocichla*, a new genus of South American rheophilic cichlid fishes with six new species (Teleostei: Cichlidae). Copeia 1988 (no. 1): 196-230.

KULLANDER, S. O., AND E. J. G. FERREIRA. 1988 **[ref. 12825]**. A new *Satanoperca* species (Teleostei, Cichlidae) from the Amazon River basin in Brazil. Cybium v. 12 (no. 4): 343-355.

KULLANDER, S. O., AND H. NIJSSEN. 1989 **[ref. 14136]**. The cichlids of Surinam. Teleostei: Labroidei. E. J. Brill, Leiden. i-xxxii + 1-256.

KULLANDER, S. O., AND W. STAECK. 1988 (30 Sept.) **[ref. 6866]**. Description of a new *Apistogramma* species (Teleostei, Cichlidae) from the Rio Negro in Brazil. Cybium v. 12 (no. 3): 189-201.

KURONUMA, K. 1940 (Mar.) **[ref. 2701]**. The heterosomate fishes collected in deep waters of Japan. I. Bull. Biogeogr. Soc. Jpn. v. 10 (no. 3): 29-61.

KURUP, B. M., AND C. T. SAMUEL. 1982 (2 May) **[ref. 6796]**. On the occurrence of *Oxyurichthys nijsseni* Menon and Govindan (Pisces: Gobiidae) in Vembanad Lake, south India. Matsya No. 7 [for 1981]: 91-94.

KYLE, H. M. 1901 (Apr.) **[ref. 2704]**. On a new genus of flat-fishes from New Zealand. Proc. Zool. Soc. Lond. 1900 (pt 4): 986-992.

LA MONTE, F. 1929 (28 Sept.) **[ref. 3039]**. Two new fishes from Mt. Duida, Venezuela. Am. Mus. Novit. No. 373: 1-4.

———. 1933 (23 Jan.) **[ref. 2705]**. A new subgenus of *Plecostomus* from Brazil. Am. Mus. Novit. No. 591: 1-2.

———. 1933 (27 Dec.) **[ref. 2706]**. *Pimelodus valenciennis* Kr. the type of a new genus. Copeia 1933 (no. 4): 226.

LACEPÈDE, B. G. E. 1797 **[ref. 2707]**. Mémoire sur le polyodon feuille. Bull. Soc. Philomath. Paris v. 1 (pt 2, no. 7): 49. [Also apparently in: Magasin Encyclop. (Millin) 1797, v. 3 (pt. 4): 13-14 [not seen].]

———. 1798 **[ref. 2708]**. Histoire naturelle des poissons. v. 1: 1-8 + i-cxlvii + 1-532, Pls. 1-25, 1 table. [For dates see Hureau & Monod 1973, v. 2: 323 [ref. 6590].]

———. 1800 **[ref. 2709]**. Histoire naturelle des poissons. v. 2: i-lxiv + 1-632, Pls. 1-20.

———. 1801 **[ref. 2710]**. Histoire naturelle des poissons. v. 3: i-lxvi + 1-558, Pls. 1-34.

———. 1802 **[ref. 4929]**. Histoire naturelle des poissons. v. 4: i-xliv + 1-728, Pl. 1-16.

———. 1803 **[ref. 4930]**. Histoire naturelle des poissons. v. 5: i-xlviii + 1-803, Pls. 1-21.

———. 1804 (May) **[ref. 12515]**. Mémoire sur plusieurs animaux de la Nouvelle Hollande dont la description n'a pas encore été publiée. Ann. Mus. Hist. Nat. Paris v. 4: 184-211, 4 pls.

LACHNER, E. A. 1973 **[ref. 7221]**. Echeneididae (pp. 637-640). In: Hureau & Monod 1973 [ref. 6590].

LACHNER, E. A., AND R. E. JENKINS. 1967 (1 Sept.) **[ref. 7136]**. Systematics, distribution, and evolution of the chub genus *Nocomis* (Cyprinidae) in the southwestern Ohio River Basin, with the description of a new species. Copeia 1967 (no. 3): 557-580.

LACHNER, E. A., AND S. J. KARNELLA. 1980 (28 Oct.) **[ref. 6916]**. Fishes of the Indo-Pacific genus *Eviota* with descriptions of eight new species (Teleostei: Gobiidae). Smithson. Contrib. Zool. No. 315: i-iii + 1-127.

LACHNER, E. A., AND J. F. MCKINNEY. 1974 (31 Dec.) **[ref. 2547]**. *Barbuligobius boehlkei*, a new Indo-Pacific genus and species of Gobiidae (Pisces), with notes on the genera *Callogobius* and *Pipidonia*. Copeia 1974 (no. 4): 869-879.

———. 1978 (24 May) **[ref. 6603]**. A revision of the Indo-Pacific fish genus *Gobiopsis* with descriptions of four new species (Pisces: Gobiidae). Smithson. Contrib. Zool. No. 262: i-iii + 1-52, Pls. 1-10.

———. 1979 (14 Sept.) **[ref. 7018]**. Two new gobiid fishes of the genus *Gobiopsis* and a redescription of *Feia nympha* Smith. Smithson. Contrib. Zool. No. 299: i-iii + 1-18.

LAHILLE, F. 1903 **[ref. 2711]**. Nota sobre un género nuevo de Escómbrido. An. Mus. Nac. Hist. Nat. B. Aires (Ser. 3) v. 2: 375-376.

———. 1908 **[ref. 5869]**. Nota sobre los zoarcidos Argentinos. An. Mus. Nac. Hist. Nat. B. Aires (Ser. 3) v. 9: 403-441, Pls. 6-7.

———. 1913 (1 Mar.) **[ref. 2712]**. Nota sobre siete peces de las costas Argentinas. An. Mus. Nac. Hist. Nat. B. Aires v. 24: 1-24, Pls. 1-7.

———. 1915 **[ref. 5625]**. Apuntes sobre las Lampreas Argentinas y los acraniotas. An. Mus. Nac. Hist. Nat. B. Aires v. 26: 361-382, Pls. 12-13.

LANGER, W. F. 1913 **[ref. 2717]**. Beiträge zur Morphologie der viviparen Cyprinodontiden. Morph. Jahrb. Leipzig v. 47 (nos. 1-2): 193-307.

LAROCHE, W. A., W. F. SMITH-VANIZ AND S. L. RICHARDSON. 1984 **[ref. 13525]**. Carangidae: Development. Pp. 510-522. In: Ontogeny and Systematics of Fishes. Spec. Publ. No. 1, Amer. Soc. Ichthyol. Herp.

LARSEN, V. 1973 **[ref. 7187]**. Nemichthyidae (pp. 231-232). In: Hureau & Monod 1973 [ref. 6590].

LARSON, H. K. 1985 **[ref. 5186]**. A revision of the gobiid genus *Bryaninops* (Pisces), with a description of six new species. Beagle, Occ. Pap. Northern Terr. Mus. Arts Sci. v. 2 (no. 1): 57-93.

———. 1986 **[ref. 6141]**. *Phyllogobius*, a new generic name for *Cottogobius platycephalops* Smith (Pisces: Gobiidae), and a redescription of the species. Beagle v. 3 (no. 1): 131-136.

———. 1986 (30 May) **[ref. 6328]**. The species of the commensal goby genus *Bryaninops* and related genera [Abstract]. P. 947. In: Uyeno et al. (eds.) 1986 [ref. 6147].

LARSON, H. K., AND D. F. HOESE. 1980 (Dec.) **[ref. 2725]**. Fische des Indischen Ozeans. Ergebnisse der ichthyologischen Untersuchungen während der Expedition des Forschungsschiffes "Meteor" in den Indischen Ozean, Oktober 1964 bis Mai 1965. A. Systematischer Teil, XXIII. Gobiidae. Meteor Forschungsergeb. Reihe D Biol. No. 32: 33-43. [In English.]

LARSON, H. K., AND P. J. MILLER. 1986 (15 Aug.) **[ref. 5803]**. Two new species of *Silhouettea* (Gobiidae) from Northern Australia. Jpn. J. Ichthyol. v. 33 (no. 2): 110-118.

LAST, P. R. 1978 (Aug.) **[ref. 2726]**. A new genus and species of flounder (f. Pleuronectidae) with notes on other Tasmanian species. Pap. Proc. R. Soc. Tasmania v. 112: 21-28.

LATHAM, J. F. 1794 **[ref. 2727]**. An essay on the various species of sawfish. Trans. Linn. Soc. London v. 2 (art. 25): 273-282, Pls. 26-27.

LAVENBERG, R. J. 1988 **[ref. 6617]**. Chlopsid eels of the eastern Pacific with a new species and descriptions of larval forms. Bull. Mar. Sci. v. 42 (no. 2): 253-264.

LAY, G. T., AND E. T. BENNETT. 1839 **[ref. 2730]**. Fishes. Pp. 41-75, Pls. 15-23. In: The zoology of Captain Beechey's voyage... to the Pacific and Behring's Straits... in 1825-28. London.

LE DANOIS, Y. 1954 (14 June) **[ref. 6451]**. Sur le dimorphisme sexuel des poissons de la famille des Diodontides. C. R. Seanc. Acad. Sci. Paris v. 238 (no. 24): 2354-2356.

———. 1961 **[ref. 2731]**. Remarques sur les poissons orbiculates du sous-ordre des Ostracioniformes [with several parts]. Mem. Mus. Natl. Hist. Nat. (Ser. A) Zool. v. 19 (no. 2): 207-338.

———. 1964 **[ref. 6571]**. Étude anatomique et systématique des Antennaires de l'ordre des Pédiculates. Mem. Mus. Natl. Hist. Nat. (Ser. A) Zool. v. 31 (no. 1): 1-162.

———. 1975 **[ref. 2732]**. Étude ostéo-myologique et révision systématique de la famille des Lophiidae (pédiculates haplo-ptérygiens). Mem. Mus. Natl. Hist. Nat. (Ser. A) Zool. v. 91: 1-127. [Dated 1874, apparently published in 1875.]

———. 1979 (20 Feb.) **[ref. 6972]**. Révision systématique de la famille des Chaunacidae (Pisces Pediculati). Uo (Jpn. Soc. Ichthyol.) No. 30: 1-76 + 2 tables.

———. 1984 (30 June) **[ref. 12846]**. Description d'une nouvelle espèce de Chaunacidae, *Chaunax latipunctatus*, des îles Galapagos. Cybium v. 8 (no. 2): 95-101.

LEA, R. N. 1987 **[ref. 6376]**. On the second record of *Barbourisia rufa*, the velvet whalefish, from California. Calif. Fish Game v. 73 (no. 2): 124.

LEA, R. N., AND L. J. DEMPSTER. 1982 **[ref. 14236]**. Status and nomenclatural history of *Agonus vulsus* Jordan and Gilbert, 1880 (Pisces—Family Agonidae). Calif. Fish Game v. 69 (no. 4): 249-252.

LEA, R. N., AND W. N. ESCHMEYER. 1988 (June) **[ref. 12249]**. *Scorpaenichthys marmoratus* Girard, 1854 (Osteichthyes, Scorpaeniformes): proposed conservation of the specific name and confirmation of authorship. Bull. Zool. Nomencl. v. 45 (pt 2): 132-134.

Leach, W. E. 1814 **[ref. 2738]**. Zoological miscellany; being descriptions of new or interesting animals. London. v. 1: 103-105. [Not seen.]

———. 1818 **[ref. 12565]**. Some observations on the genus *Squalus* of Linné, with descriptions and outline figures of two British species. Mem. Wernerian Nat. Hist. Soc. Edinburgh v. 2: 61-66, Pl. 2.

Lee, S.-C. 1989 **[ref. 14122]**. Fish of the family Symphysanodontidae of Taiwan. Bull. Inst. Zool. Acad. Sin. (Taipei) v. 28 (no. 1): 69-71.

Legendre, V. 1942 **[ref. 2740]**. Redécouverte après un siècle et reclassification d'une espèce de Catostomidé. Nat. Can. (Que.) v. 69 (nos. 10-11): 227-233.

Leiby, M. M. 1984 **[ref. 12859]**. Leptocephalus larvae of the tribe Callechelyini (Anguilliformes, Ophichthidae, Ophichthinae) in the western North Atlantic. Bull. Mar. Sci. v. 34 (no. 3): 398-423.

Leigh-Sharpe, W. H. 1924 (5 Dec.) **[ref. 5076]**. The comparative morphology of the secondary sexual characters of elasmobranch fishes. The claspers, clasper siphons, and clasper glands. Memoir VI. J. Morph. Physiol. Phila. v. 39 (no. 2): 553-566.

———. 1924 (5 Dec.) **[ref. 5748]**. Comparative morphology of the secondary sexual characters of the elasmobranch fishes. The Claspers, clasper siphons, and clasper glands. Memoir VII. J. Morph. Physiol. Phila. v. 39 (no. 2): 567-577.

———. 1926 (5 June) **[ref. 5627]**. The comparative morphology of the secondary sexual characters of elasmobranch fishes. The claspers, clasper siphons, and clasper glands. Memoirs VIII-X. J. Morph. Physiol. Phila. v. 42 (no. 1): 307-320, 321-334, 335-348.

———. 1926 (5 June) **[ref. 5628]**. The comparative morphology of the secondary sexual characters of elasmobranch fishes. The claspers, clasper siphons, and clasper glands, together with a dissertation on the Cowper's glands of *Homo*. Memoir XI. J. Morph. Physiol. Phila. v. 42 (no. 1): 349-358.

———. 1928 (28 June) **[ref. 6152]**. Pseudogenera. Copeia No. 167: 32-33.

Leipertz, S. L. 1985 (29 Aug.) **[ref. 5243]**. A review of the fishes of the agonid genus *Xeneretmus* Gilbert. Proc. Calif. Acad. Sci. v. 44 (no. 3): 17-40.

———. 1988 (5 Feb.) **[ref. 6233]**. The rockhead poacher, *Bothragonus swani* (Teleostei: Agonidae): selected osteology, with comments on phylogeny. Copeia 1988 (no. 1): 64-71.

Leipertz, S. L., and T. W. Pietsch. 1987 (13 May) **[ref. 5972]**. A new species of ceratioid anglerfish of the genus *Dolopichthys* (Pisces: Lophiiformes) from the western North Atlantic Ocean. Copeia 1987 (no. 2): 406-409.

Leis, J. M. 1978 (July) **[ref. 5529]**. Systematics and zoogeography of the porcupinefishes (*Diodon*, Diodontidae, Tetraodontiformes), with comments on egg and larval development. U. S. Natl. Mar. Fish. Serv. Fish. Bull. v. 76 (no. 3): 535-567.

———. 1984 **[ref. 13659]**. Tetraodontoidei: development. Am. Soc. Ichthyol. Herpetol. Spec. Publ. No. 1: 447-450.

———. 1986 **[ref. 5686]**. Family No. 269: Diodontidae (pp. 903-907). In: Smiths' Sea Fishes (Smith & Heemstra 1986 [ref. 5715]).

Leis, J. M., and M.-L. Bauchot. 1984 **[ref. 12539]**. Catalogue critique des types de Poissons du Muséum national d'Histoire naturelle. (Suite) (Famille des Diodontidae). Bull. Mus. Natl. Hist. Nat. Sect. A Zool. Biol. Ecol. Anim. v. 6 (no. 3): 83-101.

Leis, J. M., and W. J. Richards. 1984 **[ref. 13669]**. Acanthuroidei: development and relationships. Am. Soc. Ichthyol. Herpetol. Spec. Publ. No. 1: 547-551.

Leslie, A. J., Jr., and D. J. Stewart. 1986 (10 Feb.) **[ref. 5948]**. Systematics and distributional ecology of *Etropus* (Pisces, Bothidae) on the Atlantic Coast of the United States with description of a new species. Copeia 1986 (no. 1): 140-156.

Lesson, R. P. 1828 **[ref. 2775]**. Description du nouveau genre *Ichthyophis* et de plusieurs espèces inédites ou peu connues de poissons, recueillis dans le voyage autour du monde de la Corvette "La Coquille." Mem. Soc. Nat. Hist. Paris v. 4: 397-412. [Abstract in Bull. Sci. Nat. (Férussac) 17: 299-301, and Isis (Oken) v. 5: 487-488 [both not seen].]

———. 1929-30 **[ref. 13391]**. Pisces accounts. In: "Dictionnaire classique histoire naturelle." [See also Bory de Saint Vincent [ref. 3853].]

———. 1830-31 **[ref. 2776]**. Poissons. In: L. I. Duperrey. Voyage autour du monde... sur la corvette de La Majesté La Coquille, pendant les années 1822, 1823, 1824 et 1825... Zoologie. Zool. v. 2 (pt 1): 66-238, Atlas: Pls. 1-38. [For dates see Sherborn & Woodward 1909, Ann. Mag. Nat. Hist. (Ser. 7) v. 17: 335-336.]

Lesueur, C. A. 1817 (Sept./Oct.) **[ref. 2734]**. A new genus of fishes, of the order Abdominales, proposed, under the name of *Catostomus*; and the characters of this genus, with those of its species, indicated. J. Acad. Nat. Sci. Phila. v. 1 (pt 5/6): 88-96, 102-111. [Pp. 88-96 published in Sept., pp. 102-111 in Oct.]

———. 1818 (May/Sept.) **[ref. 2735]**. Description of several new species of North American fishes. J. Acad. Nat. Sci. Phila. v. 1 (pt 2): 222-235; 359-368. [Pp. 222-235 published in May, pp. 359-368 in Sept.]

———. 1819 **[ref. 12573]**. Notice de quelques poissons découverts dans les lacs du Haut-Canada, durant l'été de 1816. Mem. Mus. Natl. Hist. Nat. Paris v. 5: 148-161, 2 pls.

———. 1821 (Jan. 1821) **[ref. 2736]**. Description of a new genus, and of several new species of fresh water fish indigenous to the United States. J. Acad. Nat. Sci. Phila. v. 2 (pt 1): 2-8, Pls. 1-3.

———. 1825 (Aug.) **[ref. 5024]**. Description of a new fish of the genus *Salmo*. J. Acad. Nat. Sci. Phila. v. 5: 48-51.

Lévêque, C. 1989 (30 June) **[ref. 12829]**. Remarques taxinomiques sur quelques petits *Barbus* (Pisces, Cyprinidae) d'Afrique de l'Ouest (première parte). Cybium v. 13 (no. 2): 165-180.

———. 1989 (30 Sept.) **[ref. 13471]**. Remarques taxinomiques sur quelques petits *Barbus* (Pisces, Cyprinidae) d'Afrique de l'Ouest (deuxième partie). Cybium 1989, v. 13 (no. 3): 197-212.

Lévêque, C., and R. Bigorne. 1985 (30 June) **[ref. 5160]**. Le genre *Hippopotamyrus* (Pisces, Mormyridae) en Afrique de l'Ouest, avec la description d'*Hippopotamyrus paugyi* n. sp. Cybium v. 9 (no. 2): 175-192.

———. 1985 (31 Dec.) **[ref. 5947]**. Répartition et variabilité des charactères méristiques et métriques des espèces du genre *Mormyrus* (Pisces - Mormyridae) en Afrique de l'Ouest. Cybium v. 9 (no. 4): 325-340.

Lévêque, C., and J. Daget. 1984 (Feb.) **[ref. 6186]**. Cyprinidae (pp. 217-342). In: Daget et al. 1984 [ref. 6168].

Lévêque, C., G. G. Teugels and D. F. E. Thys van den Audenaerde. 1988 (30 Sept.) **[ref. 6865]**. Description de trois nouvelles espèces de *Barbus* d'Afrique de l'Ouest. Cybium v. 12 (no. 3): 179-187.

Li, C.-S. 1986 (30 May) **[ref. 6329]**. Studies on the Chinese swellfishes of the genus *Lagocephalus* (Teleostomi, Tetraodontidae) [Abstract]. P. 948. In: Uyeno et al. (eds.) 1986 [ref. 6147].

Li, S.-H., H.-M. Wang and Y.-M. Wu. 1981 **[ref. 6437]**. Observations on the osteology of some holocentrid fishes. Trans. Chinese Ichthyol. Soc. No. 2 (1981): 73-80. [In Chinese, English summ.]

Li, S.-S. 1986 (30 May) **[ref. 6132]**. Systematics, distribution and evolution of *Glyptothorax* (Siluriformes: Sisoridae). Pp. 521-528. In: Uyeno et al. (eds.) 1986 [ref. 6147].

Li, S.-Z. 1986 (30 May) **[ref. 6154]**. Discussion on the geographical distribution of the Xenocypridinae in China. Pp. 480-483. In: Uyeno et al. (eds.) 1986 [ref. 6147].

Liem, K. F. 1981 (6 Feb.) **[ref. 6897]**. A phyletic study of the Lake Tanganyika cichlid genera *Asprotilapia, Ectodus, Lestradea, Cunningtonia, Ophthalmochromis,* and *Ophthalmotilapia*. Bull. Mus. Comp. Zool. v. 149 (no. 3): 191-214.

Liem, K. F., and D. J. Stewart. 1976 (12 Feb.) **[ref. 7096]**. Evolution of the scale-eating cichlid fishes of Lake Tanganyika: a generic revision with a description of a new species. Bull. Mus. Comp. Zool. v. 147 (no. 7): 319-350, Pls. 1-2.

Liénard, E. 1832 (14 Aug.) **[ref. 12516]**. [As part of an extract read to the Committee of Science of the Zoological Society of London;

untitled.] In: Deshardins, M. J., Analyse des Travaux de la Société d'Histoire Naturelle de l'Ile Maurice, pendant la 2de Année. Proc. Zool. Soc. Lond. Part II (1832): 111-112.

Lin, L.-H., and K.-T. Shao. 1987 (31 Dec.) **[ref. 6420]**. Fishes of the family Sphyraenidae of Taiwan. J. Taiwan Mus. v. 40 (no. 2): 73-79.

Lin, S.-Y. 1931 (Apr.) **[ref. 4019]**. Carps and carp-like fishes of Kwangtung and adjacent islands. 1-167. [In Chinese.]

———. 1932 (22 July) **[ref. 2780]**. New cyprinid fishes from White Cloud Mountain, Canton. Lingnan Sci. J. Canton v. 11 (no. 3): 379-383.

———. 1932 (15 Nov.) **[ref. 2781]**. On new fishes from Kweuchow Province, China. Lingnan Sci. J. Canton v. 11 (no. 4): 515-519.

———. 1933 **[ref. 2782]**. Contribution to a study of Cyprinidae of Kwangtung and adjacent provinces. Lingnan Sci. J. Canton v. 12 (no. 1): 75-91, Pl. 4. [Article continues in same journal, pp. 197-215, 337-348, 489-505.]

———. 1933 **[ref. 2783]**. A new genus and three new species of marine fish from Hainan Island. Lingnan Sci. J. Canton v. 12 (no. 1): 93-96.

———. 1933 **[ref. 5930]**. A new genus of cyprinid fish from Kwangsi, China. Lingnan Sci. J. Canton v. 12 (no. 2): 193-195.

———. 1933 **[ref. 5932]**. Contribution to a study of Cyprinidae of Kwangtung and adjacent provinces. Lingnan Sci. J. Canton v. 12 (no. 3): 337-348. [Continued from Lingnan Sci. J. v. 12 (no. 2), p. 215.]

———. 1935 **[ref. 2779]**. Notes on a new genus, three new and two little known species of fishes from Kwantung and Kwangsi Provinces. Lingnan Sci. J. Canton v. 14 (no. 2): 303-313.

———. 1938 (16 June) **[ref. 12501]**. Further notes on the sciaenid fishes of China. Lingnan Sci. J. Canton v. 17 (no. 2): 161-173.

———. 1938 **[ref. 6599]**. Further notes on sciaenid fishes of China. Lingnan Sci. J. Canton v. 17 (no. 3): 367-381.

Linck, H. F. 1790 **[ref. 4985]**. Versuch einer Eintheilung der Fische nach den Zähnen. Mag. Neuste Phys. Naturgesch. Gotha v. 6 (no. 3): 28-38. [Discussion and an outline of included classification given by Gill 1903: 959-960 [ref. 4983]. Date may be 1789.]

Lindberg, G. U. 1934 **[ref. 6496]**. Description of a new genus and species *Gobiodonella macrops* (Gobiidae, Pisces) from Misaki, Japan. C. R. Acad. Sci. U.R.S.S. Leningrad, n. s. v. 2 (no. 7): 436-440. [In Russian, English synopsis on p. 440.]

———. 1973 **[ref. 7220]**. Agonidae (pp. 605-606), Cyclopteridae (pp. 607-608), Liparidae (pp. 609-612). In: Hureau & Monod 1973 [ref. 6590].

Lindberg, G. U., and M. I. Legeza. 1955 **[ref. 2785]**. A review of the genera and species of the subfamily Cyclopterinae (Pisces). Tr. Zool. Inst. Akad. Nauk SSSR v. 18: 389-458. [In Russian. Translation by Israel Program for Scientific Translations, 1964.]

Linnaeus, C. 1758 (1 Jan.) **[ref. 2787]**. Systema Naturae, Ed. X. (Systema naturae per regna tria naturae, secundum classes, ordines, genera, species, cum characteribus, differentiis, synonymis, locis. Tomus I. Editio decima, reformata.) Holmiae. v. 1: i-ii + 1-824. [Nantes and Pisces in Tom. 1, pp. 230-338. Date fixed by ICZN, Code Article 3.]

———. 1766 **[ref. 2786]**. Systema naturae sive regna tria naturae, secundum classes, ordines, genera, species, cum characteribus, differentiis, synonymis, locis. Laurentii Salvii, Holmiae. 12th Ed., vol. 1, pt. 1. 1-532. [Nantes and Pisces on pp. 394-532.]

Liu, C. K. 1940 (Apr.) **[ref. 2790]**. On two new fresh-water gobies. Sinensia v. 11 (no. 3-4): 213-219.

Liu, C.-H., and S.-C. Shen. 1985 (1 Dec.) **[ref. 8144]**. *Centroberyx rubricaudus*, a new berycoid fish (family Berycidae) from Taiwan. J. Taiwan Mus. v. 38 (no. 2): 1-7.

Liu, C.-H., and Y.-J. Zeng. 1988 (18 May) **[ref. 6414]**. Notes on the Chinese paddlefish, *Psephurus gladius* (Martens). Copeia 1988 (no. 2): 482-484.

Lloris, D., and J. A. Rucabado. 1985 (11 Feb.) **[ref. 6792]**. A new species of *Nansenia* (*N. problematica*) (Salmoniformes: Bathylagidae) from the southeast Atlantic. Copeia 1985 (no. 1): 141-145.

Lloyd, R. E. 1909 (Aug.) **[ref. 2814]**. A description of the deep-sea fish caught by the R. I. M. S. ship 'Investigator' since the year 1900, with supposed evidence of mutation in *Malthopsis*. [Including: Illustrations of the Zoology of the ...Investigator ... Fishes—Pt. X, Pls. XLIV—L.] Mem. Indian Mus. v. 2 (no. 3): 139-180, Pls. 44-50.

Lobel, P. S. 1981 **[ref. 5536]**. *Bodianus prognathus* (Labridae, Pisces), a new longnose hogfish from the central Pacific. Pac. Sci. v. 35 (no. 1): 45-50.

Lockington, W. N. 1879 (13 May) **[ref. 2816]**. On a new genus and species of Scombridae. Proc. Acad. Nat. Sci. Phila. 1879 [v. 31]: 133-136.

———. 1880 (31 Mar.) **[ref. 2815]**. Descriptions of new genera and species of fishes from the coast of California. Proc. U. S. Natl. Mus. v. 2 [no. 97]: 326-332.

———. 1880 (18 May - 8 July) **[ref. 2817]**. Description of new genus and some new species of California fishes (*Icosteus anigmaticus* and *Osmerus attenuatus*). Proc. U. S. Natl. Mus. v. 3 [no. 123]: 63-68. [Pp. 63-64 published on 18 May, pp. 65-68 on 8 July.]

———. 1880 (15 Sept.) **[ref. 2818]**. Description of a new chiroid fish, *Myriolepis zonifer*, from Monterey Bay, California. Proc. U. S. Natl. Mus. v. 3 [no. 140]: 248-251.

———. 1881 (18 July) **[ref. 2819]**. Description of a new genus and species of Cottidae. Proc. U. S. Natl. Mus. v. 4 [no. 209]: 141-144.

Loiselle, P. V., and R. L. Welcomme. 1972 (31 Mar.) **[ref. 2821]**. Description of a new genus of cichlid fish from West Africa. Rev. Zool. Bot. Afr. v. 85 (no. 1-2): 37-58.

Longley, W. H. 1927 (Dec.) **[ref. 5630]**. Observations upon the ecology of Tortugas fishes with notes upon the taxonomy of species new or little known. (Definition of three new genera and two species). Carnegie Inst. Wash. Year Book No. 26: 222-224.

Longley, W. H., and S. F. Hildebrand. 1940 (14 Sept.) **[ref. 2822]**. New genera and species of fishes from Tortugas, Florida. Pap. Tortugas Lab. Carnegie Instn. v. 32: 223-285, Pl. 1.

Lönnberg, A. J. E. 1905 **[ref. 2839]**. The fishes of the Swedish South Polar Expedition. Wiss. Ergebn. Schwed. Südpolar-Exp. v. 5 (no. 6): 1-72, Pls. 1-5.

———. 1906 **[ref. 12988]**. Contributions to the fauna of South Georgia. I. Taxonomic and biological notes on vertebrates. Handl. Svensk Vet Akad. v. 40: 1-104, Pls. 1-12. [Fishes on pp. 91-100, no plates.]

López, M. I. 1981 **[ref. 5187]**. Los "roncadores" del género *Pomadasys* (*Haemulopsis*) [Pisces: Haemulidae] de la costa Pacífica de Centro América. Rev. Biol. Trop. v. 29 (no. 1): 83-94.

Louisy, P. 1989 (15 Feb.) **[ref. 9293]**. Description de *Telmatochromis brichardi* (Pisces, Cichlidae, Lamprologini), espèce nouvelle du lac Tanganyika. Rev. Fr. Aquariol. v. 15 (no. 3): 79-85.

Lowe, R. T. 1833 (10 Oct.) **[ref. 2825]**. Description of a new genus of acanthopterygian fishes, *Alepisaurus ferox*. Proc. Zool. Soc. Lond. Part 1 (1833): 104.

———. 1834 (16 Apr.) **[ref. 2826]**. Characters of a new genus *Leirus*, and of several new species of fishes from Madeira. Proc. Zool. Soc. Lond. Part 1 (1833): 142-144.

———. 1838 **[ref. 2828]**. Piscium Maderensium species quaedam novae, vel minus rite cognitae breviter descriptae, etc. Trans. Cambridge Philos. Soc. v. 6: 195-202, 5 col. pls.

———. 1838 (5 Dec.) **[ref. 2831]**. A synopsis of the fishes of Madeira; with the principal synonyms, Portuguese names, and characters of the new genera and species. Trans. Zool. Soc. Lond. v. 2 (pt 3, art. 14): 173-200. [Date from Duncan 1937: 83 [ref. 13606]; Fowler (MS) cites as 1839, others use 1841 (date of last part of volume).]

———. 1839 (Oct.) **[ref. 2829]**. A supplement to a synopsis of the fishes of Madeira. Proc. Zool. Soc. Lond. Part 7 (1839): 76-92. [Also in Ann. Mag. Nat. Hist. v. 4: 405-424; Trans. Zool. Soc. London 3: 1-20; Isis (Oken) 1844: 759-764.]

———. 1841 (Jan.) **[ref. 2830]**. On new species of fishes from Madeira. Proc. Zool. Soc. Lond. Part 8 (1840) (89): 36-39. [Also in Ann. Mag. Nat. Hist. v. 7: 92-94.]

——. 1843 (Dec.) **[ref. 2832]**. Notices of fishes newly observed or discovered in Madeira during the years 1840, 1841,and 1842. Proc. Zool. Soc. Lond. Part 11 (1843): 81-95. [Also in Ann. Mag. Nat. Hist. 1844, v. 13: 390-403.]

——. 1843 **[ref. 2833]**. A history of the fishes of Madeira, with original figures from nature of all the species, by Hon. C. E. C. Norton and M. Young. London, 1843-60. 1-196, 27 pls. [Pt 1, July 1843:i-xvi + 1-20, Pls. I-IV; pt 2, Sept. 1843:21-52, Pls. V-VII; pt 3, Nov. 1843:53-84, Pls. IX-XII; pt 4, Jan. 1844:85-116, Pls. XIII-XVII; pt 5, Oct. 1860:117-196.]

——. 1846 (Nov.) **[ref. 2834]**. On a new genus of the family Lophidae (les pectorales pediculées, Cuv.) discovered in Madeira. Proc. Zool. Soc. Lond. Part 14 (1846): 81-83. [Also apparently in Trans. Zool. Soc. London v. 3: 339-344, 1 pl.; Ann. Mag. Nat. Hist. v. 18: 416-418.]

——. 1852 (24 Jan.) **[ref. 2835]**. An account of fishes discovered or observed in Madeira since the year 1842. Proc. Zool. Soc. Lond. Part 18 (1850): 247-253. [Published as 1850, but date is 24 Jan. 1852 [see Proc. Zool. Soc. London 1893: 439]. Also in Lowe 1852 [ref. 2836].]

——. 1852 (July) **[ref. 2836]**. An account of fishes discovered or observed in Madeira since the year 1842. Ann. Mag. Nat. Hist. (Ser. 2) v. 10 (no. 55): 49-55. [Published first in Lowe 1852 [ref. 2835].]

——. 1854 **[ref. 9184]**. Description d'un nouveau genre de poisson de la famille des Murénoïdes, rapporté de Madère par son Altesse Impériale le duc Maximilien de Leuchtenberg. Mem. Acad. Sci. St. Petersb. v. 7: 171-174.

LOZANO, I. J., AND A. BRITO. 1989 (30 June) **[ref. 12828]**. First record of *Corniger spinosus* Agassiz, 1829 (Pisces: Beryciformes: Holocentridae) from the eastern Atlantic (Canary Islands). Cybium v. 13 (no. 2): 131-137.

LU, Y.-L., P.-Q. LUO AND Y.-Y. CHEN. 1977 **[ref. 13495]**. Gobioninae. Pp. 439-549. In: Wu et al. 1977 [ref. 12558].

LUBBOCK, R. 1977 (Apr.) **[ref. 7039]**. Fishes of the family Pseudochromidae (Perciformes) in the western Indian Ocean. Ichthyol. Bull. J. L. B. Smith Inst. Ichthyol. No. 35: 1-28, Pls. 1-5.

LUCENA, C. A. S. DE. 1989 (20 May) **[ref. 12852]**. Trois nouvelles espèces du genre *Charax* Scopoli, 1777 pour la région Nord du Brésil (Characiformes, Characidae, Characinae). Rev. Fr. Aquariol. v. 15 (no. 4): 97-104.

LUEY, J. E., C. C. KREUGER AND D. R. SCHREINER. 1982 (10 Aug.) **[ref. 6822]**. Genetic relationships among smelt, genus *Osmerus*. Copeia 1982 (no. 3): 725-728.

LUNDBERG, J. G. 1982 (3 Dec.) **[ref. 5450]**. The comparative anatomy of the toothless blindcat, *Trogloglanis pattersoni* Eigenmann, with a phylogenetic analysis of the ictalurid catfishes. Misc. Publ. Mus. Zool. Univ. Mich. No. 163: 1-85.

LUNDBERG, J. G., O. J. LINARES, M. E. ANTONIO AND P. NASS. 1988 (June) **[ref. 6637]**. *Phractocephalus hemiliopterus* (Pimelodidae, Siluriformes) from the Upper Miocene Urumaco Formation, Venezuela: a further case of evolutionary stasis and local extinction among South American fishes. J. Vertebr. Paleontol. v. 8 (no. 2): 131-138.

LUNDBERG, J. G., AND L. A. MCDADE. 1986 (17 Oct.) **[ref. 5731]**. On the South American catfish *Brachyrhamdia imitator* Myers (Siluriformes, Pimelodidae), with phylogenetic evidence for a large intrafamilial lineage. Not. Nat. (Phila.) No. 463: 1-24.

LUNDBERG, J. G., P. NASS AND F. MAGO-LECCIA. 1989 (23 May) **[ref. 12544]**. *Pteroglanis manni* Eigenmann and Pearson, a juvenile of *Sorubimichthys planiceps* (Agassiz), with a review of *Sorubimichthys* (Pisces: Pimelodidae). Copeia 1989 (no. 2): 332-344.

LUNEL, G. 1881 **[ref. 2849]**. Mélanges ichthyologiques. Liste de quelques espèces de poissons, nouvelles pour la faune de l'île Maurice. Mem. Soc. Phys. Hist. Nat. Geneve v. 27 (pt 2): 266-303, 1 pl.

LUTHER, G. 1975 **[ref. 7300]**. New characters for consideration in the taxonomic appraisal of grey mullets. Aquaculture v. 5 (no. 1): 107.

——. 1982 (July) **[ref. 2851]**. New characters for consideration in the taxonomic appraisal of grey mullets. J. Mar. Biol. Assoc. India v. 19 (nos. 1-2): 1-9. [For 1977, issued July 1982.]

——. 1986 (20 Aug.) **[ref. 6795]**. Studies on the biology and fishery of the fishes of the *Chirocentrus* Cuvier. I. Taxonomy. Matsya No. 11 [for 1985]: 46-55.

LÜTKEN, C. F. 1852 **[ref. 2852]**. Nogle bemaerkinger om naeseborenes stiling hos de i gruppe med *Ophisurus* staaende slaegter af aalefamilien. Vidensk. Medd. Dansk Naturh. Foren. Kjob. 1851 (nos. 1-2): 1-21, Pl. 1. [Also in Arch. Naturgesch. (Wiegmann) v. 18 (1): 254-276 [not seen]. Fowler (MS) uses date of 1852.]

——. 1871 **[ref. 2853]**. *Oneirodes eschrichtii* Ltk., en ny grønlandsk Tudsefisk. Overs. Danske Vidensk. Selsk. Forhandl Kjobenhavn 1871 (no. 2): 56-74 + 9-17, Pl. 2. [Also in Ann. Mag. Nat. Hist. 1872 (Ser. 4) v. 9: 329-344. In Danish, French resumé (pp. 9-17).]

——. 1874 **[ref. 2854]**. Ichthyographiske bidrag. I. Nogle nye eller mindre fuldstaendigt kjendte Pandsermaller, isaer fra det nordlige Sydamerica. Vidensk. Medd. Dansk Naturh. Foren. Kjob. (for 1873) No. 13-14: 202-220, Pl. 4. [Resumé in Vidensk. Medd. Dansk Naturh. Foren. Kjob. 1874 [1875]: 26-27.]

——. 1874 **[ref. 2855]**. Siluridae novae Brasiliae centralis a clarissimo J. Reinhardt in provincia Minas-geraës circa oppidulum Lagoa Santa, praecipue in flumine Rio das Velhas et affluentibus collectae, secundum caracteres essentiales, breviter descriptae. Overs. Danske Vidensk. Selsk. Kjobenhavn 1873 (no. 3): 29-36.

——. 1875 **[ref. 2856]**. Characinae novae Brasiliae centralis a clarissimo J. Reinhardt in provincia Minas-Geraes circa oppidulum Lagoa Santa in lacu ejusdem nominis, flumine Rio das Velhas et rivulis affluentibus collectae, secundum caracteres essentiales breviter descriptae. Overs. Danske Vidensk. Selsk. Forhandl Kjobenhavn 1874 (no. 3): 127-143.

——. 1892 **[ref. 2857]**. Om en med stegophiler og tricomycterer beslaegtet sydamerikansk mallefisk (*Acanthopoma annectens* Ltk. n. g. & sp.?). Vidensk. Medd. Dansk Naturh. Foren. Kjob. For 1891: 53-60.

——. 1892 **[ref. 2858]**. Spolia Atlantica. Scopelini Musei zoologici Universitatis Hauniensis. Bidrag til Kundskab om det aabne Havs Laxesild eller Scopeliner. Med et tillaeg om en anden pelagisk fiskeslaegt. Dansk. Vid. Selsk. Skr. (Ser. 6) v. 7: 221-297, Pls. 1-3. [French resumé. Also issued as a separate.]

——. 1892 **[ref. 13407]**. Korte Bidrag til nordisk Ichthyographi. VIII. Nogle nordiske Laxesild (Scopeliner). Vidensk. Medd. Dansk Naturh. Foren. Kjob. for 1891 [v. 43]: 203-233. [Also as a separate, pp. 1-31.]

MACDONALD, J. D. 1869 (June) **[ref. 2866]**. On the characters of a type of a proposed new genus of Mugilidae inhabiting the fresh waters of Viti Levu, Feejee group; with a brief account of the native mode of capturing it. Proc. Zool. Soc. Lond. 1869 (pt 1): 38-40, Pl. 1.

MACGILCHRIST, A. C. 1905 (Mar.) **[ref. 2953]**. Natural history notes from the R. I. M. S. 'Investigator,' Capt. T. H. Heming, R. N. (retired), commanding.—Series III., No. 8. On a new genus of teleostean fish closely allied to *Chiasmodus*. Ann. Mag. Nat. Hist. (Ser. 7) v. 15 (no. 87): 268-270.

MACHADO-ALLISON, A. 1986 (Oct.) **[ref. 12757]**. Osteología comparada del neurocráneo y branquicráneo en los géneros de la subfamilia Serrasalminae (Teleostei - Characidae). Acta Biol. Venez. v. 12 (no. 2) Suppl.: 1-75.

MACHIDA, Y. 1982 (Mar.) **[ref. 5473]**. Record of *Luciobrotula bartschi* from the Okinawa Trough off Kyushu, Japan. Mem. Fac. Sci. Kochi Univ. (Ser. D) (Biol.) v. 3: 71-77.

——. 1988 (Dec.) **[ref. 13418]**. An additional specimen of imperfectly known bythitid fish, *Diplacanthopoma japonicum* (Bythitidae, Ophidiiformes). Rep. Usa Mar. Biol. Inst. Kochi Univ. No. 10: 69-73.

——. 1989 (28 June) **[ref. 12579]**. First record of the deep-sea fish *Xyelacyba myersi* (Ophidiidae, Ophidiiformes) from Japan. Jpn. J. Ichthyol. v. 36 (no. 1): 120-125.

——. 1989 (28 Sept.) **[ref. 13417]**. A new deep-sea ophidiid fish,

Bassozetus levistomatus, from the Izu-Bonin Trench, Japan. Jpn. J. Ichthyol. v. 36 (no. 2): 187-189.

Machida, Y., S. Ohta and O. Okamura. 1987 (Dec.) **[ref. 6621]**. Newly obtained specimens and information on a deep-sea fish *Spectrunculus grandis* (Günther) (Ophidiidae, Ophidiiformes) from Japan. Rep. Usa Mar. Biol. Inst. Kochi Univ. No. 9: 189-200.

Machida, Y., O. Okamura and S. Ohta. 1988 (25 May) **[ref. 6623]**. Notes on *Halosauropsis macrochir* (Halosauridae: Notacanthiformes) from Japan. Jpn. J. Ichthyol. v. 35 (no. 1): 78-82.

Machida, Y., and M. Shiogaki. 1988 (25 May) **[ref. 6622]**. *Leptochilichthys microlepis*, a new species of the family Leptochilichthyidae, Salmoniformes, from Aomori, northern Japan. Jpn. J. Ichthyol. v. 35 (no. 1): 1-6.

Machida, Y., and Y. Tachibana. 1986 (15 Mar.) **[ref. 6620]**. A new record of *Bassozetus zenkevitchi* (Ophidiidae, Ophidiiformes) from Japan. Jpn. J. Ichthyol. v. 32 (no. 4): 437-439.

Machida, Y., and T. Yoshino. 1984 (Mar.) **[ref. 5362]**. First record of *Brosmophyciops pautzkei* (Bythitidae, Ophidiiformes) from Japan. Mem. Fac. Sci. Kochi Univ. (Ser. D) (Biol.) v. 5: 37-41.

Macleay, W. 1878 (Sept.) **[ref. 2868]**. Description of some new fishes from Port Jackson and King George's Sound. Proc. Linn. Soc. N. S. W. v. 3 (pt 1): 33-37, 4 pls.

——. 1881 (20 May) **[ref. 2869]**. Descriptive catalogue of the fishes of Australia. Part II. Proc. Linn. Soc. N. S. W. v. 5 (pt 4): 510-629, 2 pls. [All parts combined and printed in two bound volumes in 1884, including Supplement [date on cover 1881].]

——. 1881 (July) **[ref. 4931]**. Descriptive catalogue of the fishes of Australia. Part III. Proc. Linn. Soc. N. S. W. v. 6 (pt 1): 1-138. [Continues on pp. 202-387 [ref. 6222].]

——. 1881 (12 Sept.) **[ref. 6222]**. A descriptive catalogue of Australian fishes. Part IV. Proc. Linn. Soc. N. S. W. v. 6 (pt 2): 202-387.

——. 1882 (May) **[ref. 2870]**. Notes on the Pleuronectidae of Port Jackson, with descriptions of two hitherto unobserved species. Proc. Linn. Soc. N. S. W. v. 7 (pt 1): 11-15.

——. 1883 (19 June) **[ref. 2871]**. On a new and remarkable fish of the family Mugilidae from the interior of New Guinea. Proc. Linn. Soc. N. S. W. v. 8 (pt 1): 2-6.

——. 1883 (17 July) **[ref. 2872]**. Contributions to a knowledge of the fishes of New Guinea, No. 4. Proc. Linn. Soc. N. S. W. v. 7: 224-250, 351-366, 585-598. [Continues as v. 8 (pt 2):252-280.]

——. 1884 (21 Feb.) **[ref. 2873]**. On a new genus of fishes from Port Jackson. Proc. Linn. Soc. N. S. W. v. 8 (pt 4): 439-441, Pl. 22.

——. 1884 (23 May) **[ref. 4932]**. Supplement to the descriptive catalogue of the fishes of Australia. Proc. Linn. Soc. N. S. W. v. 9 (pt 1): 2-64. [Also published with "Descriptive catalogue" in two bound volumes, 1884.]

——. 1886 (3 Apr.) **[ref. 2874]**. A remarkable fish from Lord Howe Island. Proc. Linn. Soc. N. S. W. v. 10 (pt 4): 718-720, Pl. 47.

Maeda, K., and K. Amaoka. 1988 (Mar.) **[ref. 12616]**. Taxonomic study of larvae and juveniles of agonid fishes in Japan. Mem. Fac. Fish. Hokkaido Univ. v. 35 (no. 1): 47-124.

Mago-Leccia, F. 1978 **[ref. 5489]**. Los peces de la familia Sternopygidae de Venezuela. Acta Cient. Venez. v. 29 (suppl. 1): 1-89.

Mago-Leccia, F., J. G. Lundberg and J. N. Baskin. 1985 (11 Apr.) **[ref. 5732]**. Systematics of the South American freshwater fish genus *Adontosternarchus* (Gymnotiformes, Apteronotidae). Contrib. Sci. (Los Ang.) No. 358: 1-19.

Mago-Leccia, F., and T. M. Zaret. 1978 **[ref. 5488]**. The taxonomic status of *Rhabdolichops troscheli* (Kaup, 1856), and speculations on gymnotiform evolution. Environ. Biol. Fishes v. 3 (no. 4): 379-384.

Magtoon, W. 1986 (30 May) **[ref. 6321]**. Distribution and phyletic relationships of *Oryzias* fishes in Thailand. Pp. 859-866. In: Uyeno et al. (eds.) 1986 [ref. 6147].

Mahnert, V., and J. Géry. 1988 (4 May) **[ref. 6407]**. Les genres *Piabarchus* Myers et *Creagrutus* Günther du Paraguay, avec la description de deux nouvelles espèces (Pisces, Ostariophysi, Characidae). Rev. Fr. Aquariol. v. 15 (no. 1): 1-8.

Maisey, J. G. 1985 (11 Feb.) **[ref. 6793]**. Relationships of the megamouth shark, *Megachasma*. Copeia 1985 (no. 1): 228-231.

Makushok, V. M. 1958 **[ref. 2878]**. The morphology and classification of the northern blennioid fishes (Stichaeidae, Blennioidei, Pisces). Tr. Zool. Inst. Akad. Nauk SSSR v. 25: 3-129. [In Russian. English translation in 1959 by Ichthyological Laboratory, U. S. Fish & Wildlife Service.]

——. 1973 **[ref. 6889]**. Stichaeidae (pp. 532-533), Pholidae (pp. 534-535), Lumpenidae (pp. 536-539). In: Hureau & Monod 1973 [ref. 6590].

Malabarba, L. R. 1989 **[ref. 14217]**. Histórico sistemático e lista comentada das espécies de peixes de ägua doce do sistema da Laguna dos Patos, Rio Grande do Sul, Brasil. Comun. Mus. Cienc. PUCRS, Ser. Zool. Porto Alegre v. 2 (no. 8): 107-179.

Malm, A. W. 1877 **[ref. 2881]**. Göteborgs och Bohusläns fauna, Ryggradsdjuren. Göteborg. 1-674, Pls. 1-9.

Marcusen, J. 1854 **[ref. 2887]**. Vorläufige Mittheilung aus einer Abhandlung über die Familie der Mormyren. Bull. Cl. Physico-Math. Imp. Acad. Sci. St. Petersburg (no. 265) v. 12 (no. 1): 1-14. [Apparently also in Mél. Biol. v. 2 (no. 1): 33-51 (not seen).]

——. 1864 **[ref. 2888]**. Die Familie der Mormyren. Eine anatomisch-zoologische Abhandlung. Mem. Acad. Sci. St. Petersb. (Ser. 7) v. 7 (no. 4): 1-162, Pls. 1-5. [Also as a separate, Leipzig, 1864.]

Marini, T. L., J. T. Nichols and F. R. La Monte. 1933 (9 May) **[ref. 2889]**. Six new eastern South American fishes examined in the American Museum of Natural History. Am. Mus. Novit. No. 618: 1-7.

Marino, R. P., and J. K. Dooley. 1982 **[ref. 5498]**. Phylogenetic relationships of the tilefish family Branchiostegidae (Perciformes) based on comparative myology. J. Zool. (Lond.) v. 196: 151-163.

Markle, D. F. 1978 **[ref. 7030]**. Taxonomy and distribution of *Rouleina attrita* and *Rouleina maderensis* (Pisces: Alepocephalidae). U. S. Natl. Mar. Fish. Serv. Fish. Bull. v. 76 (no. 1): 79-87.

——. 1980 **[ref. 6077]**. A new species and review of the deep-sea fish genus *Asquamiceps* (Salmoniformes, Alepocephalidae). Bull. Mar. Sci. v. 30 (no. 1): 45-53.

——. 1982 **[ref. 5439]**. Identification of larval and juvenile Canadian Atlantic gadoids with comments on the systematics of gadid subfamilies. Can. J. Zool. v. 60 (no. 12): 3420-3438.

——. 1986 **[ref. 5687]**. Family No. 64: Alepocephalidae (pp. 218-223), Family No. 66: Leptochilichthyidae (pp. 225-226). In: Smiths' Sea Fishes (Smith & Heemstra 1986 [ref. 5715]).

Markle, D. F., and G. Krefft. 1985 (3 May) **[ref. 6789]**. A new species and review of *Bajacalifornia* (Pisces: Alepocephalidae) with comments on the hook jaw of *Narcetes stomias*. Copeia 1985 (no. 2): 345-356.

Markle, D. F., and R. Melandez C. 1988 (28 Dec.) **[ref. 9283]**. A new species of *Laemonema* from off Chile, with a redescription of *L. globiceps* Gilchrist (Pisces: Moridae). Copeia 1988 (no. 4): 871-876.

Markle, D. F., and N. R. Merrett. 1980 **[ref. 6948]**. The abyssal alepocephalid, *Rinoctes nasutus* (Pisces: Salmoniformes), a redescription and an evaluation of its systematic position. J. Zool. (Lond.) v. 190: 225-239.

Markle, D. F., and G. R. Sedberry. 1978 (10 Feb.) **[ref. 7031]**. A second specimen of the deep-sea fish, *Pachycara obesa*, with a discussion and a checklist of other Zoarcidae off Virginia. Copeia 1978 (no. 1): 22-25.

Marrero, A. G. 1950 **[ref. 5939]**. Flechas de Plata, Atherínidos argentinos. Pejerreyes y Laterinos. Historia-biologia-sistematica-zoografia. Buenos Aires. 1-157. [Not seen.]

Marschall, A. de. 1873 **[ref. 6455]**. Nomenclator Zoologicus. Continens nomina systematica generum animalium tam viventium quam fossilium, secondum ordinem alphabeticum disposita. Vindobonae. i-iv + 1-482.

Marshall, N. B. 1966 **[ref. 2894]**. *Bathyprion danae* a new genus and species of alepocephaliform fishes. Dana Rep. No. 68: 1-10.

——. 1973 **[ref. 6965]**. [Several genera accounts in family Macrouridae.] In: Fishes of the Western North Atlantic. Mem. Sears Found. Mar. Res. No. 1 (pt 6).

——. 1973 **[ref. 7194]**. Macrouridae (pp. 287-299). In: Hureau & Monod 1973 [ref. 6590].

Marshall, N. B., and T. Iwamoto. 1973 **[ref. 6963]**. Family Macrouridae (pp. 496-537). In: Fishes of the Western North Atlantic. Mem. Sears Found. Mar. Res. No. 1 (pt 6).

——. 1973 **[ref. 6966]**. Genus *Coelorhynchus* (pp. 538-563), Genus *Coryphaenoides* (pp. 565-580), Genus *Hymenocephalus* (pp. 601-612), Genus *Nezumia* (pp. 624-649). In: Fishes of the Western North Atlantic. Mem. Sears Found. Mar. Res. No. 1 (pt 6).

Martens, E. von. 1868 **[ref. 2896]**. Über eine neue Art und Untergattung der Cyprinoiden, *Homaloptera (Octonema) rotundicauda*, über einige neue Crustaceen und über die neuholländischen Süsswasserkrebse. Monatsb. Akad. Wiss. Berlin for 1868: 607-620. [Possibly published in 1869.]

Martin, F. 1954 (July) **[ref. 2897]**. Un nuevo genero y especie de los peces Beloniformes, Berg 1940. Noved. Cient. Mus. Hist. Nat. La Salle (Ser. Zool.) No. 14: 1-8.

Martin, F. D. 1984 **[ref. 13639]**. Escooidei: development and relationships. Am. Soc. Ichthyol. Herpetol. Spec. Publ. No. 1: 140-142.

Martín Salazar, F. J., I. J. H. Isbrücker and H. Nijssen. 1982 (31 Dec.) **[ref. 2900]**. *Dentectus barbarmatus*, a new genus and species of mailed catfish from the Orinoco Basin of Venezuela (Pisces, Siluriformes, Loricariidae). Beaufortia v. 32 (no. 8): 125-137.

Masuda, H., K. Amaoka, C. Araga, T. Uyeno and T. Yoshino. 1984 **[ref. 6441]**. The fishes of the Japanese Archipelago. Tokai Univ. Press. Text: i-xxii + 1-437, Atlas: Pls. 1-370.

Masuda, H., C. Araga and T. Yoshino. 1975 **[ref. 2902]**. Coastal fishes of southern Japan. Tokai University Press, Tokyo. 1-379, 142 col. pls. (on pp. 9-151). [In English & Japanese.]

Masuda, S., T. Ozawa and O. Tabeta. 1986 (15 Mar.) **[ref. 5801]**. *Bregmaceros neonectabanus*, a new species of the family Bregmacerotidae, Gadiformes. Jpn. J. Ichthyol. v. 32 (no. 4): 392-399.

Matallanas, J. 1984 (Dec.) **[ref. 5831]**. Descripción de *Parabathophilus*, n. gen. de Melanostomiatidae (Pisces, Salmoniformes) y de *P. gloriae*, su especie tipo. Invest. Pesq. v. 48 (no. 3): 557-562.

——. 1984 (31 Mar.) **[ref. 12848]**. A new species for the Mediterranean and Spanish ichthyofauna: *Dicologoglosa hexophthalma* Bennett, 1831 (Pisces, Soleidae) from Catalan waters. Cybium v. 8 (no. 1): 95.

——. 1986 (31 Dec.) **[ref. 6755]**. Notes ostéologiques sur *Nansenia problematica* Lloris et Rucabado, 1985, avec discussion de son statut générique. Cybium v. 10 (no. 4): 389-394.

——. 1986 (30 June) **[ref. 8077]**. *Nansenia iberica*, a new species of Microstomatidae (Pisces, Salmoniformes). Cybium (Ser. 3) v. 10 (no. 2): 193-198.

Matarese, A. C., E. G. Stevens and W. Watson. 1984 **[ref. 13672]**. Icosteoidei: development and relationships. Am. Soc. Ichthyol. Herpetol. Spec. Publ. No. 1: 576-577.

Matheson, Jr., R. E., and J. D. McEachran. 1984 (18 Dec.) **[ref. 5228]**. Taxonomic studies of the *Eucinostomus argenteus* complex (Pisces: Gerridae): preliminary studies of external morphology. Copeia 1984 (no. 4): 893-902.

Matsubara, K. 1937 (July) **[ref. 2904]**. Studies on the deep-sea fishes of Japan. V. Diagnosis of a new mail-cheeked fish, *Parapterygotrigla multiocellata* n. g., n. sp., belonging to Triglidae. Zool. Mag. (Tokyo) v. 49 (no. 7): 266-267.

——. 1943 (Dec.) **[ref. 2903]**. Studies on the scorpaenoid fishes of Japan. I. Descriptions of one new genus and five new species. J. Imp. Fish. Inst. Tokyo v. 30 (no. 3): 199-210.

——. 1943 (Aug.) **[ref. 2905]**. Studies on the scorpaenoid fishes of Japan (II). Trans. Sigenkagaku Kenkyusyo, Tokyo No. 2: 171-486, Pls. 1-4.

——. 1943 **[ref. 6514]**. Ichthyological annotations from the depth of the Sea of Japan, I-VII. Trans. Sigenkagaku Kenkyusyo, Tokyo v. 1 (no. 1): 37-82.

Matsubara, K., and T. Iwai. 1951 (Feb.) **[ref. 2909]**. A new cottid fish found in Toyama Bay. Misc. Rep. Res. Inst. Nat. Resourc. (Tokyo) Nos. 19-20: 86-93.

——. 1952 (July) **[ref. 2906]**. Studies on some Japanese fishes of the family Gempylidae. Pac. Sci. v. 6 (no. 3): 193-212.

Matsubara, K., and A. Ochiai. 1955 (Feb.) **[ref. 2907]**. A revision of the Japanese fishes of the family Platycephalidae (the flatheads). Mem. Coll. Agric. Kyoto Univ. No. 68: 1-109, Pls. 1-3.

——. 1963 (25 Mar.) **[ref. 2908]**. Report on the flatfish collected by the Amami Islands expedition in 1958. Bull. Misaki Mar. Biol. Inst. Kyoto Univ. No. 4: 83-105.

Matsubara, K., A. Ochiai, K. Amaoka and I. Nakamura. 1964 (25 Mar.) **[ref. 7061]**. Revisional study of the trachinoid fishes of the family Champsodontidae from the waters around Japan, and Tonking Bay. Bull. Misaki Mar. Biol. Inst. Kyoto Univ. No. 6: 1-20.

Matsui, T., and R. H. Rosenblatt. 1979 **[ref. 7024]**. Two new searsid fishes of the genera *Maulisia* and *Searsia* (Pisces: Salmoniformes). Bull. Mar. Sci. v. 29 (no. 1): 62-78.

——. 1986 **[ref. 5688]**. Family No. 65: Platytroctidae (pp. 223-225). In: Smiths' Sea Fishes (Smith & Heemstra 1986 [ref. 5715]).

Matsuura, K. 1979 (Mar.) **[ref. 7019]**. Phylogeny of the superfamily Balistoidea (Pisces: Tetraodontiformes). Mem. Fac. Fish. Hokkaido Univ. v. 26 (no. 1/2): 49-169.

——. 1980 (22 Mar.) **[ref. 6943]**. A revision of Japanese balistoid fishes. I. Family Balistidae. Bull. Natl. Sci. Mus. (Ser. A) (Zool.) v. 6 (no. 1): 27-69.

——. 1981 (22 Dec.) **[ref. 2910]**. *Xenobalistes tumidipectoris*, a new genus and species of triggerfish (Tetraodontiformes, Balistidae) from the Marianas Islands. Bull. Natl. Sci. Mus. (Ser. A) (Zool.) v. 7 (no. 4): 191-200.

——. 1986 (1 Nov.) **[ref. 6715]**. A new sharpnose pufferfish, *Canthigaster flavoreticulata*, collected from the South Pacific. Jpn. J. Ichthyol. v. 33 (no. 3): 223-224.

——. 1987 (10 June) **[ref. 6710]**. First record of a triacanthodid fish, *Macrorhamphosodes uradoi* from New Zealand. Jpn. J. Ichthyol. v. 34 (no. 1): 105-107.

——. 1989 (15 Mar.) **[ref. 12751]**. First record of an extremely small filefish *Rudarius excelsus* from the North Pacific. Jpn. J. Ichthyol. v. 35 (no. 4): 482-483.

Matsuura, K., and T. Shimizu. 1982 (30 June) **[ref. 5503]**. The squirrelfish genus *Adioryx*, a junior synonym of *Sargocentron*. Jpn. J. Ichthyol. v. 29 (no. 1): 93-94.

Matsuura, K., and Y. Shiobara. 1989 (20 Dec.) **[ref. 13563]**. A new triggerfish, *Rhinecanthus abyssus*, from the Ryukyu Islands. Jpn. J. Ichthyol. v. 36 (no. 3): 315-317.

Matsuura, K., and M. Toda. 1981 (25 May) **[ref. 5537]**. First records of two pufferfishes, *Arothron mappa* and *A. reticularis*, from Japan. Jpn. J. Ichthyol. v. 28 (no. 1): 91-93.

Matsuura, K., and T. Yamakawa. 1982 (30 June) **[ref. 5504]**. Rare boxfishes, *Kentrocapros flavofasciatus* and *K. rosapinto*, with notes on their relationships. Jpn. J. Ichthyol. v. 29 (no. 1): 31-42.

Matthes, H. 1964 **[ref. 2911]**. Les poissons du lac Tumba et de la region d'Ikela. Étude systématique et écologique. Koninklijk Mus. Midden-Afr. Tervuren No. 126: 1-204, map, table, Pls. 1-6.

Matthews, W. J. 1987 (5 Aug.) **[ref. 6774]**. Geographic variation in *Cyprinella lutrensis* (Pisces: Cyprinidae) in the United States, with notes on *Cyprinella lepida*. Copeia 1987 (no. 3): 616-637.

Maugé, A. L. 1984 (31 Dec.) **[ref. 5945]**. Diagnoses préliminaires d'Eleotridae des eaux douces de Madagascar. Cybium v. 8 (no. 4): 98-100.

——. 1986 (Apr.) **[ref. 6218]**. Atherinidae (pp. 277-279), Kuhliidae (pp. 306-307), Gobiidae (pp. 358-388), Eleotridae (pp. 389-398), Periophthalmidae (pp. 399-401). In: Daget et al. 1986 [ref. 6189].

Maugé, A. L., and J. E. Bardach. 1985 (31 Dec.) **[ref. 5162]**. Congrogadinae de Madagascar (Pisces, Pseudochromidae) description d'*Halimuraenoides isostigma* n. g. et. n. sp. Cybium v. 9 (no.

4): 375-384.

MAUGÉ, A. L., AND R. BAUCHOT. 1984 **[ref. 6614]**. Les genres et sous-genre de Chaetodontidés étudiés par une méthode d'analyse numérique. Bull. Mus. Natl. Hist. Nat. Sect. A Zool. Biol. Ecol. Anim. v. 6 (no. 2): 453-485.

MAUL, G. E. 1946 (Oct.) **[ref. 2915]**. Um novo género e espécie dos Macropinídeos. Bol. Mus. Munic. Funchal No. 2 (art. 3): 62-65. [In French and English.]

———. 1948 (May) **[ref. 2916]**. Quatro peixes novos dos mares da Madeira. Bol. Mus. Munic. Funchal No. 3 (art. 6): 41-55.

———. 1956 (Dec.) **[ref. 2917]**. Additions to the previously revised orders or families of fishes of the Museu Municipal do Funchal (Stomiatidae, Astronesthidae, Paralepididae). Bol. Mus. Munic. Funchal No. 9 (art. 24): 75-96.

———. 1965 **[ref. 2918]**. On a new genus and species of paralepidid from Madeira. Bol. Mus. Munic. Funchal No. 19 (art. 81): 55-61.

———. 1973 **[ref. 7171]**. [Many deepsea family accounts.] In: Hureau & Monod 1973 [ref. 6590].

———. 1986 **[ref. 5689]**. Family No. 84: Omosudidae (p. 280). In: Smiths' Sea Fishes (Smith & Heemstra 1986 [ref. 5715]).

MAUL, G. E., AND E. KOEFOED. 1950 (Nov.) **[ref. 2919]**. On a new genus and species of macrourid fish, *Phalacromacrurus pantherinus*. Ann. Mag. Nat. Hist. (Ser. 12) v. 3 (no. 35): 970-976.

MAYDEN, R. L. 1985 **[ref. 6631]**. Nuptial structures in the subgenus *Catonotus*, genus *Etheostoma* (Percidae). Copeia 1985 (no. 3): 580-583.

———. 1987 (5 Aug.) **[ref. 6630]**. Identification of *Moniana tristis* Girard (Cypriniformes: Cyprinidae). Copeia 1987 (no. 3): 790-792.

———. 1988 (5 Feb.) **[ref. 6235]**. Systematics of the *Notropis zonatus* species group, with description of a new species from the interior highlands of North America. Copeia 1988 (no. 1): 153-173.

———. 1989 (1 June) **[ref. 12555]**. Phylogenetic studies of North American minnows, with emphasis on the genus *Cyprinella* (Teleostei: Cyprinidormes). Univ. Kansas Mus. Nat. Hist., Misc. Publ. No. 80: 1-189, Pls. 1-2.

MAYDEN, R. L., AND F. B. CROSS. 1983 **[ref. 6632]**. Reevaluation of Oklahoma records of the southern cavefish, *Typhlichthys subterraneus* Girard (Amblyopsidae). Southwest. Nat. v. 28 (no. 4): 471-473.

MAYDEN, R. L., AND L. M. PAGE. 1979 (1 Aug.) **[ref. 6989]**. Systematics of *Percina roanoka* and *P. crassa*, with comparisons to *P. peltata* and *P. notogramma* (Pisces: Percidae). Copeia 1979 (no. 3): 413-426.

MAYER, G. F. 1974 (19 Sept.) **[ref. 6007]**. A revision of the cardinalfish genus *Epigonus* (Perciformes, Apogonidae), with descriptions of two new species. Bull. Mus. Comp. Zool. v. 146 (no. 3): 147-203.

MAYER, G. F., AND E. TORTONESE. 1977 (27 May) **[ref. 7053]**. *Epigonus trewavasae* Poll, a junior synonym of *Epigonus constanciae* (Giglioli) (Perciformes, Apogonidae). Breviora No. 443: 1-13.

MAYR, E. 1969 **[ref. 13542]**. Principles of systematic zoology. McGraw-Hill Book Co., New York. i-xi + 1-428.

MAZZARELLI, G. 1912 **[ref. 12985]**. Studi sui pesci batipelagici dello Stretto di Messina, I, Larve stiloftalmoidi ("periscopiche" di Holt e Byrne) di Scopelidi e loro metamorfosi iniziale. Rivist. Mensil Pesca Idrobiologia (Pavia). (14) v. 7 (no. 1-3): 1-26, 4 pls. [Not seen.]

MCALLISTER, D. E., M. E. ANDERSON AND J. G. HUNTER. 1981 **[ref. 5431]**. Deep-water eelpouts, Zoarcidae, from Arctic Canada and Alaska. Can. J. Fish. Aquat. Sci. v. 38 (no. 7): 821-839.

MCALLISTER, D. E., AND J. E. RANDALL. 1975 **[ref. 7079]**. A new species of centrolophid fish from Easter Island and Rapa Iti Island in the South Pacific. Natl. Mus. Can. Publ. Biol. Oceanogr. No. 8: i-ix + 1-7.

MCALLISTER, D. E., AND E. I. S. REES. 1964 (Mar.) **[ref. 2921]**. A revision of the eelpout genus *Melanostigma* with a new genus and with comments on *Maynea*. Bull. Natl. Mus. Can. No. 199: 85-110. [Date on cover is December, 1963; hand corrected by D. E. M. to March 1964. Also as Stud. Fish. Res. Bd. Canada, No. 826.]

MCCANN, C., AND D. G. MCKNIGHT. 1980 **[ref. 2922]**. The marine fauna of New Zealand: macrourid fishes (Pisces: Gadida). N. Z. Oceanogr. Inst. Mem. 61: 1-91.

MCCLELLAND, J. 1839 **[ref. 2923]**. Indian Cyprinidae. Asiatic Researches v. 19 (pt 2): 217-471, Pls. 37-55. [Also as McClelland 1841 [ref. 6175]. See note under McClelland 1839 [ref. 2924]. Also spelled M'Clelland.]

———. 1839 **[ref. 2924]**. Observations on six new species of Cyprinidae, with an outline of a new classification of the family. J. Asiat. Soc. Bengal v. 7 (for Nov. 1838): 941-948, Pls. 55-56. [Apparently published in 1839 (perhaps after Ref. 2923 since McClelland cites plates from ref. 2923 in ref. 2924).]

———. 1841 (Sept., Oct., Nov.) **[ref. 6175]**. Indian Cyprinidae. Ann. Mag. Nat. Hist. (n. s.) v. 8: 35-46, 108-121, 192-203. [New taxa appeared earlier in McClelland 1839 [ref. 2923].]

———. 1842 **[ref. 2925]**. Remarks on a new genus of thoracic percoid fishes. J. Nat. Hist. Calcutta v. 2: 150-152.

———. 1842 (Jan.) **[ref. 2926]**. On the fresh-water fishes collected by William Griffith, Esq., F. L. S. Madras Medical Service, during his travels under the orders of the Supreme Government of India, from 1835 to 1842. J. Nat. Hist. Calcutta v. 2 (no. 8): 560-589, Pls. 15, 18, 20, 21. [Cover dated January, 1842.]

———. 1844 **[ref. 2927]**. Description of a collection of fishes made at Chusan and Ningpo in China, by Dr. G. R. Playfair, Surgeon of the Phlegethon, war steamer, during the late military operations in that country. J. Nat. Hist. Calcutta v. 4 (for 1843): 390-413, Pls. 21-25.

———. 1844 (5 July) **[ref. 2928]**. Apodal fishes of Bengal. J. Nat. Hist. Calcutta v. 5 (no. 18) July: 151-226, Pls. 5-14. [Date of 5 July 1844 from Fowler (MS), but perhaps incorrect; usually cited as 1845 in recent literature.]

———. 1845 **[ref. 2929]**. Description of four species of fishes from the rivers at the foot of the Boutan Mountains. J. Nat. Hist. Calcutta v. 5 (no. 18): 274-282. [Issue for July 1844, possibly published in 1844.]

MCCOSKER, J. E. 1970 (Oct.) **[ref. 2931]**. A review of the eel genera *Leptenchelys* and *Muraenichthys*, with the descriptions of a new genus, *Schismorhynchus*, and a new species *Muraenichthys chilensis*. Pac. Sci. v. 24 (no. 4): 506-516.

———. 1972 (27 Dec.) **[ref. 2932]**. Two new genera and two new species of western Pacific snake-eels (Apodes: Ophichthidae). Proc. Calif. Acad. Sci. (Ser. 4) v. 39 (no. 10): 111-119.

———. 1974 (18 Oct.) **[ref. 2933]**. A revision of the ophichthid eel genus *Letharchus*. Copeia 1974 (no. 3): 619-629.

———. 1975 **[ref. 7100]**. The eel genus *Phaenomonas* (Pisces, Ophichthidae). Pac. Sci. v. 29 (no. 4): 361-363.

———. 1977 (15 Feb.) **[ref. 6836]**. The osteology, classification, and relationships of the eel family Ophichthidae. Proc. Calif. Acad. Sci. (Ser. 4) v. 41 (no. 1): 1-123.

———. 1982 (4 Nov.) **[ref. 2934]**. A new genus and two new species of remarkable Pacific worm eels (Ophichthidae, subfamily Myrophinae). Proc. Calif. Acad. Sci. v. 43 (no. 5): 59-66.

———. 1985 (29 Aug.) **[ref. 5238]**. Two new genera and two new species of deepwater western Atlantic worm eels (Pisces: Ophichthidae). Proc. Calif. Acad. Sci. v. 44 (no. 2): 9-15.

———. 1986 **[ref. 6294]**. Family No. 129: Anomalopidae (pp. 413-414). In: Smiths' Sea Fishes (Smith & Heemstra 1986 [ref. 5715]).

MCCOSKER, J. E., E. B. BÖHLKE AND J. E. BÖHLKE. 1989 **[ref. 13288]**. Family Ophichthidae (pp. 254-412). In: Böhlke, E. B. (ed.) 1989 [ref. 13282].

MCCOSKER, J. E., AND J. E. BÖHLKE. 1982 (30 Dec.) **[ref. 2935]**. Three new genera and two new species of deepwater western Atlantic snake-eels (Pisces: Ophichthidae). Proc. Acad. Nat. Sci. Phila. v. 134: 113-121.

———. 1984 (28 Dec.) **[ref. 5316]**. A review of the snake eel genera *Gordiichthys* and *Ethadophis*, with descriptions of new species and comments on related Atlantic bascanichthyins (Pisces: Ophichthidae). Proc. Acad. Nat. Sci. Phila. v. 136: 32-44.

McCosker, J. E., and P. H. J. Castle. 1986 **[ref. 5690]**. Family No. 42: Ophichthidae (pp. 176-187). In: Smiths' Sea Fishes (Smith & Heemstra 1986 [ref. 5715]).

McCosker, J. E., K. Hatooka, K. Sasaki and J. T. Moyer. 1984 (20 Nov.) **[ref. 6725]**. Japanese moray eels of the genus *Uropterygius*. Jpn. J. Ichthyol. v. 31 (no. 3): 261-267.

McCosker, J. E., and M. D. Lagios. 1979 (22 Dec.) **[ref. 6998]**. The biology and physiology of the living Coelacanth. Occas. Pap. Calif. Acad. Sci No. 134: 1-175.

McCosker, J. E., and P. C. Phillips. 1979 **[ref. 6980]**. Occurrence of the heterenchelyid eel *Pythonichthys asodes* at Costa Rica and El Salvador. Bull. Mar. Sci. v. 29 (no. 4): 599-600.

McCosker, J. E., and R. H. Rosenblatt. 1975 (3 Oct.) **[ref. 9341]**. The moray eels (Pisces: Muraenidae) of the Galapagos Islands, with new records and synonymies of extralimital species. Proc. Calif. Acad. Sci. (Ser. 4) v. 40 (no. 13): 417-427.

———. 1987 (10 Sept.) **[ref. 6707]**. Notes on the biology, taxonomy, and distribution of the flashlight fishes (Beryciformes: Anomalopidae). Jpn. J. Ichthyol. v. 34 (no. 2): 157-164.

McCulloch, A. R. 1911 (22 Dec.) **[ref. 2936]**. Report on the fishes obtained by the F. I. S. "Endeavour," on the coasts of New South Wales, Victoria, South Australia and Tasmania. Part I. Biol. Results "Endeavour" 1909 [v. 1] (pt 1): 1-87, Pls. 1-16.

———. 1912 **[ref. 2937]**. Notes on some Western Australian fishes. Rec. West. Aust. Mus. v. 1 (pt 2): 78-97, Pls. 9-13.

———. 1912 (29 Aug.) **[ref. 2938]**. Notes on some Australian Atherinidae. Proc. R. Soc. Queensl. v. 24: 47-53, Pl. 1.

———. 1914 (13 June) **[ref. 2939]**. Notes on some Australian pipe-fishes. Aust. Zool. v. 1 (pt 1): 29-31.

———. 1914 (3 July) **[ref. 2940]**. Report on some fishes obtained by the F. I. S. "Endeavour" on the coasts of Queensland, New South Wales, Victoria, Tasmania, South and South-western Australia. Part II. Biol. Results "Endeavour" 1909-14 v. 2 (pt 3): 77-165, Pls. 13-34.

———. 1915 (21 Apr.) **[ref. 2941]**. Report on some fishes obtained by the F. I. S. "Endeavour" on the coasts of Queensland, New South Wales, Victoria, Tasmania, South and South-Western Australia, Part III. Biol. Results "Endeavour" 1909 v. 3 (pt 3): 97-170, Pls. 13-37.

———. 1915 (15 Sept.) **[ref. 2942]**. Notes on, and descriptions of Australian fishes. Proc. Linn. Soc. N. S. W. v. 40 (pt 2): 259-277, Pls. 35-37.

———. 1915 (28 Jan.) **[ref. 2943]**. Notes and illustrations of Queensland fishes. Mem. Queensl. Mus. v. 3: 47-56, Pls. 16-18.

———. 1916 (10 July) **[ref. 2944]**. Ichthyological items. Mem. Queensl. Mus. v. 5: 58-69, Pls. 7-9.

———. 1921 (12 Apr.) **[ref. 2945]**. Studies in Australian fishes. No. 7. Rec. Aust. Mus. v. 13 (no. 4): 123-142, Pls. 21-24.

———. 1923 (10 Dec.) **[ref. 2946]**. Fishes from Australia and Lord Howe Island. No. 2. Rec. Aust. Mus. v. 14 (no. 2): 113-125, Pls. 14-16.

———. 1926 (8 June) **[ref. 2947]**. Report on some fishes obtained by the F. I. S. "Endeavour" on the coasts of Queensland, New South Wales, Victoria, Tasmania, South and South-Western Australia. Part V. Biol. Results "Endeavour" 1909 v. 5 (pt 4): 157-216, Pls. 43-16.

———. 1929-30 **[ref. 2948]**. A check-list of the fishes recorded from Australia. Parts I-IV. Mem. Aust. Mus. Memoir 5: 1-534. [Pt I: 1-144 published 29 June, II: 145-329 on 10 Sept., III: 329-436 on 28 Nov. 1929, IV: 437-534 on 26 May 1930.]

McCulloch, A. R., and E. R. Waite. 1915 **[ref. 2949]**. A revision of the genus *Aracana* and its allies. Trans. R. Soc. S. Aust. v. 39: 477-493, Pls. 16-25.

———. 1918 (24 May) **[ref. 2950]**. Some new and little-known fishes from South Australia. Rec. Aust. Mus. v. 1 (no. 1): 39-78, Pls. 2-7.

McDowall, R. M. 1975 (22 Sept.) **[ref. 7113]**. A revision of the New Zealand species of *Gobiomorphus* (Pisces: Eleotridae). Natl. Mus. N. Z. Rec. v. 1 (no. 1): 1-32.

———. 1976 **[ref. 7065]**. Fishes of the family Prototroctidae (Salmoniformes). Aust. J. Mar. Freshwater Res. v. 27: 641-649.

———. 1978 **[ref. 2951]**. A new genus and species of galaxiid fish from Australia (Salmoniformes: Galaxiidae). J. R. Soc. N. Z. v. 8 (no. 1): 115-124.

———. 1979 (28 Nov.) **[ref. 6953]**. The centrolophid genus *Tubbia* (Pisces: Stromateoidei). Copeia 1979 (no. 4): 733-738.

———. 1979 **[ref. 7021]**. Fishes of the family Retropinnidae (Pisces: Salmoniformes) — a taxonomic revision and synopsis. J. R. Soc. N. Z. v. 9 (no. 1): 85-121.

———. 1980 **[ref. 6931]**. First adults of *Schedophilus maculatus* Günther, 1860 (Stromateoidei: Centrolophidae). J. R. Soc. N. Z. v. 10 (no. 2): 145-151.

———. 1981 **[ref. 5356]**. The centrolophid fishes of New Zealand (Pisces: Stromateoidei). J. R. Soc. N. Z. v. 12 (no. 2): 103-142.

———. 1984 (Feb.) **[ref. 6178]**. Galaxiidae (pp. 126-127). In: Daget et al. 1984 [ref. 6168].

———. 1984 **[ref. 11850]**. Southern Hemisphere freshwater salmoniforms: development and relationships. Am. Soc. Ichthyol. Herpetol. Spec. Publ. No. 1: 150-154.

McDowall, R. M., and R. S. Frankenberg. 1981 **[ref. 5500]**. The galaxiid fishes of Australia. Rec. Aust. Mus. v. 33 (no. 10): 443-605.

McDowall, R. M., and W. Fulton. 1978 **[ref. 7003]**. A further new species of *Paragalaxias* Scott (Salmoniformes: Galaxiidae) from Tasmania with a revised key to the species. Aust. J. Mar. Freshwater Res. v. 29: 659-665.

McDowall, R. M., and K. Nakaya. 1987 (10 Dec.) **[ref. 6701]**. Identity of the galaxioid fishes of the genus *Aplochiton* Jenyns from southern Chile. Jpn. J. Ichthyol. v. 34 (no. 3): 377-383.

———. 1988 (5 Feb.) **[ref. 6237]**. Morphological divergence in the two species of *Aplochiton* Jenyns (Salmoniformes: Aplochitonidae): a generalist and a specialist. Copeia 1988 (no. 1): 233-236.

McDowall, R. M., and B. J. Pusey. 1983 **[ref. 6522]**. *Lepidogalaxias salamandroides* Mees — a redescription, with natural history notes. Rec. West. Aust. Mus. v. 11 (no. 1): 11-23.

McEachran, J. D. 1982 (21 Dec.) **[ref. 5381]**. Revision of the South American skate genus *Sympterygia* (Elasmobranchii: Rajiformes). Copeia 1982 (no. 4): 867-890.

———. 1983 (July) **[ref. 5382]**. Results of the research cruises of FRV "Walther Herwig" to South America. LXI. Revision of the South American skate genus *Psammobatis* Günther, 1870 (Elasmobranchii: Rajiformes, Rajidae). Arch. FischereiWiss. v. 34 (no. 1): 23-80.

———. 1984 (23 Feb.) **[ref. 5225]**. Anatomical investigations of the New Zealand skates *Bathyraja asperula* and *B. spinifera*, with an evaluation of their classification within the Rajoidei (Chondrichthyes). Copeia 1984 (no. 1): 45-58.

McEachran, J. D., and L. J. V. Compagno. 1979 **[ref. 5226]**. A further description of *Gurgesiella furvescens* with comments on the interrelationships of Gurgesiellidae and Pseudorajidae (Pisces, Rajoidei). Bull. Mar. Sci. v. 29 (no. 4): 530-553.

———. 1980 (July) **[ref. 6896]**. Results of the research cruises of FRV "Walther Herwig" to South America. LVI. A new species of skate from the southwestern Atlantic *Gurgesiella dorsalifera* sp. nov. (Chondrichyes, Rajoidei). Arch. FischereiWiss. v. 31 (no. 1): 1-14.

———. 1982 **[ref. 2952]**. Interrelationships of and within *Breviraja* based on anatomical structures (Pisces: Rajoidei). Bull. Mar. Sci. v. 32 (no. 2): 399-425.

McEachran, J. D., and T. Miyake. 1987 (13 May) **[ref. 5973]**. A new species of skate of the genus *Breviraja* from off Nova Scotia, with comments on the status of *Breviraja* and *Neoraja* (Chondrichthys, Rajoidei). Copeia 1987 (no. 2): 409-417.

McEachran, J. D., and M. Stehmann. 1984 (31 Dec.) **[ref. 5224]**. A new species of skate, *Neoraja carolinensis*, from off the southeastern United States (Elasmobranchii: Rajoidei). Proc. Biol. Soc. Wash. v. 97 (no. 4): 724-735.

McKay, R. J. 1972 (July) **[ref. 2954]**. Two new genera and five new species of percophidid fishes (Pisces: Percophididae) from Western Australia. J. R. Soc. West. Aust. v. 54 (pt 2): 40-46.

———. 1985 (Feb.) **[ref. 5265]**. A revision of the fishes of the family Sillaginidae. Mem. Queensl. Mus. v. 22 (pt 1): 1-73.

——. 1986 **[ref. 6300]**. Family No. 198: Sillaginidae (pp. 615-616). In: Smiths' Sea Fishes (Smith & Heemstra 1986 [ref. 5715]).

McKinney, J. F., and V. G. Springer. 1976 (28 Sept.) **[ref. 7087]**. Four new species of the fish genus *Ecsenius* with notes on other species of the genus (Blenniidae: Salariini). Smithson. Contrib. Zool. No. 236: i-iii + 1-27.

Mead, G. W. 1972 **[ref. 6976]**. Bramidae. Dana Rep. No. 81: 1-166, Pls. 1-9.

——. 1973 **[ref. 7199]**. Bramidae (pp. 386-388). In: Hureau & Monod 1973 [ref. 6590].

Mead, G. W., and J. E. De Falla. 1965 (30 Nov.) **[ref. 2955]**. New oceanic cheilodipterid fishes from the Indian Ocean. Bull. Mus. Comp. Zool. v. 134 (no. 7): 261-274.

Mead, G. W., and G. E. Maul. 1958 (Oct.) **[ref. 2956]**. *Taractes asper* and the systematic relationships of the Steinegeriidae and Trachyberycidae. Bull. Mus. Comp. Zool. v. 119 (no. 6): 393-417, 1 pl.

Meek, S. E. 1902 (May) **[ref. 2957]**. A contribution to the ichthyology of Mexico. Field Columbian Mus. Zool. Ser. v. 3 (no. 6): 63-128, Pls. 14-31.

——. 1904 (Aug.) **[ref. 2958]**. The fresh-water fishes of Mexico north of the isthmus of Tehuantepec. Field Columbian Mus. Zool. Ser. v. 5: i-lxiii + 1-252, Pls. 1-17.

——. 1907 (July) **[ref. 2959]**. Synopsis of the fishes of the great lakes of Nicaragua. Field Columbian Mus. Zool. Ser. v. 7 (no. 4): 97-132.

——. 1912 (18 Sept.) **[ref. 2960]**. New species of fishes from Costa Rica. Field Mus. Nat. Hist. Publ. Zool. Ser. v. 10 (pt 7): 69-75.

——. 1914 (30 Mar.) **[ref. 2961]**. An annotated list of fishes known to occur in the fresh-waters of Costa Rica. Field Mus. Nat. Hist. Publ. Zool. Ser. v. 10 (pt 10): 101-134.

Meek, S. E., and S. F. Hildebrand. 1916 (28 Dec.) **[ref. 2962]**. The fishes of the fresh waters of Panama. Field Mus. Nat. Hist. Publ. Zool. Ser. v. 10 (pt 15): 1-374, Pls. 6-32.

——. 1923 (20 Dec.) **[ref. 2963]**. The marine fishes of Panama. Part I. Field Mus. Nat. Hist. Publ. Zool. Ser. v. 15 (publ. 215): i-xi + 1-330, Pls. 1-24.

——. 1925 (15 Apr.) **[ref. 13609]**. The marine fishes of Panama. Part II. Field Mus. Nat. Hist. Publ. Zool. Ser. v. 15 (publ. 226): i-xix + 331-707, Pls. 25-71.

——. 1928 (1 Sept.) **[ref. 2964]**. The marine fishes of Panama. Part III. Field Mus. Nat. Hist. Publ. Zool. Ser. v. 15 (publ. 249): i-xxxi + 709-1045, Pls. 72-102.

Mees, G. F. 1960 **[ref. 11931]**. The Uranoscopidae of Western Australia (Pisces, Perciformes). J. R. Soc. West. Aust. v. 43 (pt 2): 46-58.

——. 1961 **[ref. 2965]**. Description of a new fish of the family Galaxiidae from Western Australia. J. R. Soc. West. Aust. v. 44 (pt 2): 33-38, Pls. 1-2.

——. 1962 **[ref. 2966]**. The subterranean freshwater fauna of Yardie Creek Station, North West Cape, Western Australia. J. R. Soc. West. Aust. v. 45 (pt 1): 24-32.

——. 1964 (18 Feb.) **[ref. 2967]**. A new fish of the family Scorpaenidae from New Guinea. Zool. Meded. (Leiden) v. 40 (no. 1): 1-4, Pl. 1.

——. 1966 (23 Dec.) **[ref. 2968]**. A new fish of the family Apogonidae from tropical Western Australia. J. R. Soc. West. Aust. v. 49 (pt 3): 83-84.

——. 1974 (28 June) **[ref. 2969]**. The Auchenipteridae and Pimelodidae of Suriname (Pisces, Nematognathi). Zool. Verh. (Leiden) No. 132: 1-256, Pls. 1-15. [Date of publication from author (not 24 July).]

——. 1978 (20 Dec.) **[ref. 5691]**. Two new species of Pimelodidae from northwestern South America (Pisces, Nematognathi). Zool. Meded. v. 53 (no. 23): 253-261, Pls. 1-3.

——. 1984 (Dec.) **[ref. 5692]**. A note on the genus *Tocantinsia* (Pisces, Nematognathi, Auchenipteridae). Amazoniana v. 9 (no. 1): 31-34.

——. 1986 (29 Sept.) **[ref. 5693]**. Records of Auchenipteridae and Pimelodidae from French Guiana (Pisces, Nematognathi). Proc. Konink. Neder. Akad. Wetensch. v. 89 (no. 3): 311-325.

——. 1987 (18 Dec.) **[ref. 6619]**. A new species of *Heptapterus* from Venezuela (Pisces, Nematognathi, Pimelodidae). Proc. Konink. Neder. Akad. Wetensch. (Ser. C.) v. 90 (no. 4): 451-456.

——. 1987 (22 June) **[ref. 11510]**. The members of the subfamily Aspredininae, family Aspredinidae in Suriname (Pisces, Nematognathi). Proc. Konink. Neder. Akad. Wetensch. (Ser. C) v. 90 (no. 2): 173-192.

——. 1988 (28 Mar.) **[ref. 6401]**. The genera of the subfamily Bunocephalinae (Pisces, Nematognathi, Aspredinidae). Proc. Konink. Neder. Akad. Wetensch. (Ser. C) v. 91 (no. 1): 85-102.

——. 1988 (19 Dec.) **[ref. 13382]**. Notes on the genus *Tatia* (Pisces, Nematognathi, Auchenipteridae). Proc. Konink. Neder. Akad. Wetensch. (Ser. C) v. 91 (no. 4): 405-414.

——. 1989 (19 June) **[ref. 13383]**. Notes on the genus *Dysichthys*, subfamily Bunocephalidae, family Aspridinidae (Pisces, Nematognathi). Proc. Konink. Neder. Akad. Wetensch. (Ser. C) v. 92 (no. 2): 189-250.

Mees, G. F., and P. Cala. 1989 (25 Sept.) **[ref. 14277]**. Two new species of *Imparfinis* from northern South America (Pisces, Nematognathi, Pimelodidae). Proc. Konink. Neder. Akad. Wetensch. (Ser. C) v. 92 (no. 3): 379-394.

Mees, G. F., and P. J. Kailola. 1977 (15 Aug.) **[ref. 5183]**. The freshwater Therapontidae of New Guinea. Zool. Verh. (Leiden) No. 153: 1-89.

Meinken, H. 1954 **[ref. 2970]**. Mitteilungen der Fischbestimmungsstelle des VDA. XVIII. Ein neuer Nandide aus Westafrika. Aquar. Terrar. Z. v. 7 (Feb.) (no. 2): 27-29.

——. 1955 (Mar.) **[ref. 2971]**. Mitteilungen der Fischbestimmungsstelle des VDA. XIX. *Afronandus sheljuzhkoi* Meinken 1955. Aquar. Terrar. Z. v. 8 (no. 3): 59.

——. 1965 (26 Mar.) **[ref. 2972]**. Über eine neue Gattung und Art der Familie Cichlidae aus Peru (Pisces, Percoidea, Cichlidae). Senckenb. Biol. v. 46 (no. 1): 47-53.

——. 1974 (Jan.) **[ref. 2973]**. Aus Neu-Guinea kommt eine neue Gattung und Art der Ährenfische (Pisces, Atherinidae). Aquarium Aqua Terra v. 8 (no. 55): 9-11.

——. 1975 (Mar.) **[ref. 2974]**. A new atherinid fish from New Guinea. Trop. Fish Hobby. v. 23 (no. 8, Apr.): 60-65, 2 col. figs.

Melville, R. V., and J. D. D. Smith [eds.]. 1987 **[ref. 13620]**. Official lists and indexes of names and works in zoology. The International Trust for Zoological Nomenclature. 1-366.

Menezes, N. A. 1974 (29 Jan.) **[ref. 7129]**. Redescription of the genus *Roestes* (Pisces, Characidae). Pap. Avulsos Dep. Zool. (São Paulo) v. 27 (no. 17): 219-225.

——. 1976 (12 Nov.) **[ref. 7073]**. On the Cynopotaminae, a new subfamily of Characidae (Osteichthyes, Ostariophysi, Characoidei). Arq. Zool. (São Paulo) v. 28 (fasc. 2): 1-91.

——. 1977 (20 Jan.) **[ref. 7070]**. *Acestrocephalus boehlkei*, a new and disjunct cynopotamine from Ecuadorean and Peruvian Amazon (Osteichthyes, Ostariophysi, Characidae). Pap. Avulsos Dep. Zool. (São Paulo) v. 30 (no. 13): 185-193.

Menezes, N. A., and G. de Q. Benvegnú. 1976 (30 Dec.) **[ref. 7069]**. On the species of the genus *Symphurus* from the Brazilian coast, with description of two new species (Osteichthyes, Pleuronectiformes, Cynoglossidae). Pap. Avulsos Dep. Zool. (São Paulo) v. 30 (no. 11): 137-170.

Menni, R. C. 1972 **[ref. 2979]**. *Raja ("Atlantoraja")* subgen. nov. y lista critica de los "Rajidae" Argentinos (Chondrichthyes, Rajiformes). Rev. Mus. La Plata Secc. Zool. v. 11 (no. 103): 165-173. [English summ.]

Menon, A. G. K. 1950 **[ref. 2980]**. On a remarkable blind siluroid fish of the family Clariidae from Kerala (India). Rec. Indian Mus. (Calcutta) v. 48 (pt 1): 59-66, 1 pl.

——. 1977 (25 Apr.) **[ref. 7071]**. A systematic monograph of the tongue soles of the genus *Cynoglossus* Hamilton-Buchanan (Pisces:

Cynoglossidae). Smithson. Contrib. Zool. No. 238: i-iv + 1-129, Pls. 1-21.

——. 1980 (24 Mar.) **[ref. 6798]**. A revision of the fringe-lip tongue soles of the genus *Paraplagusia* Bleeker, 1865 (Family Cynoglossidae). Matsya No. 5 [for 1979]: 11-22.

——. 1984 (30 June) **[ref. 12845]**. *Noemacheilus (Mesonoemacheilus) petrubanarescui*, a new loach from Dharmasthala, Karnataka State, India (Pisces, Cobitidae). Cybium v. 8 (no. 2): 45-49.

——. 1987 (May) **[ref. 14149]**. The fauna of India and the adjacent countries. Pisces. Vol. IV. Teleostei - Cobitoidea. Part 1. Homalopteridae. Zoological Survey of India, Calcutta. i-x + 1-259, Pls. 1-16.

Menon, A. G. K., B. V. Gobind and K. V. Rajagopal. 1978 (20 Dec.) **[ref. 6801]**. Taxonomic assessment of the torrential fish of the genus *Balitora* Gray (Family Homalopteridae) from the Indian peninsula. Matsya No. 3 [for 1977]: 31-34.

Menon, A. G. K., and K. V. Rama Rao. 1974 **[ref. 7114]**. On the dates of the parts of Day's 'Fishes of India.' J. Soc. Bibliogr. Nat. Hist. v. 7 (no. 1): 143.

Merrett, N. R. 1989 (8 Aug.) **[ref. 12741]**. Revised key to the eastern North Atlantic species of the rattail subgenus *Chalinura* (Pisces: Macrouridae) having 8-9 pelvic-fin rays. Copeia 1989 (no. 3): 742-744.

Merrett, N. R., and J. G. Nielsen. 1987 **[ref. 6058]**. A new genus and species of the family Ipnopidae (Pisces, Teleostei) from the eastern North Atlantic, with notes on its ecology. J. Fish Biol. v. 31: 451-464.

Merrett, N. R., Yu. I. Sazonov and Yu. N. Shcherbachev. 1983 **[ref. 6672]**. A new genus and species of rattail fish (Macrouridae) from the eastern North Atlantic and eastern Indian Ocean, with notes on its ecology. J. Fish Biol. v. 22 (no. 5): 549-561.

Metzelaar, J. 1919 **[ref. 2982]**. Report on the fishes, collected by Dr. J. Boeke in the Dutch West Indies 1904-1905, with comparative notes on marine fishes of tropical West Africa. F. J. Belanfante, 's-Gravenhage. 1-314. [Also as Over tropisch Atlantische visschen. A. H. Kruyt, Amsterdam.]

——. 1922 **[ref. 5741]**. On a collection of marine fishes from the Lesser Antilles. Bijdr. Dierkd. v. 22: 133-141.

Meyen, J. 1835 **[ref. 2984]**. Reise in Peru. I. [Not seen.]

Meyer, M. K., and W. Foerster. 1984 (20 Mar.) **[ref. 6645]**. Un nouveau *Pseudotropheus* du lac Malawi avec des remarques sur le complexe *Pseudotropheus-Melanochromis* (Pisces, Perciformes, Cichlidae). Rev. Fr. Aquariol. v. 10 (no. 4): 107-112.

Miki, T. 1985 (30 Aug.) **[ref. 5798]**. New genus and species of the family Stichaeidae from Hokkaido, Japan. Jpn. J. Ichthyol. v. 32 (no. 2): 137-142.

——. 1986 (30 May) **[ref. 6330]**. Geographic variation of meristics in a pholidid fish, *Rhodymenichthys dolichogaster*, around Hokkaido [Abstract]. Pp. 949-950. In: Uyeno et al. (eds.) 1986 [ref. 6147].

Miki, T., S. Kanamaru and K. Amaoka. 1987 (10 Sept.) **[ref. 6704]**. *Neolumpenus unocellatus*, a new genus and species of stichaeid fish from Japan. Jpn. J. Ichthyol. v. 34 (no. 2): 128-134.

Miki, T., and S. Maruyama. 1986 (15 Mar.) **[ref. 5694]**. New and rare stichaeid fishes from the Okhotsk Sea. Jpn. J. Ichthyol. v. 32 (no. 4): 400-408.

Miki, T., H. Yoshida and K. Amaoka. 1987 (Feb.) **[ref. 12551]**. Rare stichaeid fish, *Pseudalectrias tarasovi* (Popov), from Japan and its larvae and juveniles. Bull. Fac. Fish. Hokkaido Univ. v. 38 (no. 1): 1-13.

Miklukho-Maclay, N., and W. Macleay. 1886 (3 Apr.) **[ref. 2996]**. Plagiostomata of the Pacific. Part III. Proc. Linn. Soc. N. S. W. v. 10 (pt 4): 673-678, Pls. 45-46.

Miles, C. 1942 (1 Aug.) **[ref. 12429]**. Descripcion sistematica del "pez graso" del Lago de Tota (Boyacá). Caldasia No. 5: 55-58.

——. 1943 **[ref. 2997]**. On three recently described species and a new genus of pygidiid fishes from Colombia. Rev. Acad. Colomb. Cienc. Exactas Fis. Nat. v. 5 (no. 19): 367-369.

——. 1945 (1 Dec.) **[ref. 2998]**. Some newly recorded fishes from the Magdalena River system. Caldasia v. 3 (no. 15): 453-464.

——. 1953 (20 Mar.) **[ref. 2999]**. A new pomadasid fish from the Colombian Caribbean. J. Linn. Soc. Lond. Zool. v. 42 (no. 285): 273-275.

Miller, D. J., and R. N. Lea. 1972 **[ref. 13613]**. Guide to the coastal marine fishes of California. Fish Bull. Dept. Fish Game Calif. No. 157: 1-235.

Miller, G. C., and L. P. Woods. 1988 **[ref. 6633]**. A new species of sciaenid fish, *Pareques iwamotoi*, from the western Atlantic, with color descriptions of prejuvenile and juvenile *Pareques acuminatus* and *Pareques umbrosus*. Bull. Mar. Sci. v. 43 (no. 1): 88-92.

Miller, P. J. 1966 (20 Jan.) **[ref. 3009]**. A new genus and species of gobiid fish from the eastern Mediterranean. Ann. Mag. Nat. Hist. (Ser. 13) v. 8 (nos. 87/88): 162-172, Pls. 4-5.

——. 1969 **[ref. 3010]**. Systematics and biology of the leopard-spotted goby, *Gobius ephippiatus* [Teleostei: Gobiidae], with description of a new genus and notes on the identity of *G. macrolepis* Kolombatovic. J. Mar. Biol. Assoc. U. K. v. 49: 831-855, col. Pl. 1.

——. 1972 **[ref. 3011]**. Generic status and redescription of the Mediterranean fish *Gobius liechtensteini* Kolombatovic, 1891 (Telostei: Gobioidea), and its affinities with certain American and Indo-Pacific gobies. J. Nat. Hist. v. 6 (no. 4): 395-407.

——. 1973 **[ref. 6888]**. Gobiidae (pp. 483-518). In: Hureau & Monod 1973 [ref. 6590].

——. 1978 (Sept.) **[ref. 3012]**. The status of the west African fish *Gobius nigricinctus* with reference to New World autochthones and an Old World colour-analogue. Zool. J. Linn. Soc. v. 64 (no. 1): 27-39.

——. 1981 (Nov.) **[ref. 3013]**. The systematic position of a west African gobioid fish, *Eleotris maltzani* Steindachner. Zool. J. Linn. Soc. v. 73 (no. 3): 273-286.

——. 1981 **[ref. 6219]**. Gobiidae (pp. 1-8). In: FAO species identification sheets for fishery purposes. Eastern Central Atlantic. Vol. II. [Individual family accounts separately paginated.]

——. 1984 **[ref. 6338]**. The gobiid fishes of temperate Macaronesia (eastern Atlantic). J. Zool. (Lond.) v. 204: 363-412.

——. 1987 **[ref. 6336]**. Affinities, origin and adaptive features of the Australian desert goby *Chlamydogobius eremius* (Zietz, 1896) (Teleostei: Gobiidae). J. Nat. Hist. v. 21: 687-705.

——. 1989 (31 Dec.) **[ref. 13540]**. The classification of bumble-bee gobies (*Brachygobius* and associated genera) (Teleostei: Gobiidae). Cybium v. 13 (no. 4): 375-383.

Miller, P. J., and M. M. Fouda. 1986 (31 Dec.) **[ref. 12844]**. Notes on the biology of a Red Sea goby, *Silhouetta awgyptia* (Chabanaud, 1933) (Teleostei: Gobiidae). Cybium v. 10 (no. 4): 395-409.

Miller, P. J., and P. Wongrat. 1979 (14 Nov.) **[ref. 3014]**. A new goby (Teleostei: Gobiidae) from the South China Sea and its significance for gobioid classification. Zool. J. Linn. Soc. v. 67 (no. 3): 239-257.

Miller, R. R. 1945 (20 Jan.) **[ref. 3015]**. *Snyderichthys*, a new generic name for the leatherside chub of the Bonneville and Upper Snake drainages in western United States. J. Wash. Acad. Sci. v. 35 (no. 1): 28.

——. 1945 (30 June) **[ref. 3016]**. A new cyprinid fish from southern Arizona, and Sonora, Mexico, with the description of a new subgenus of *Gila* and a review of related species. Copeia 1945 (no. 2): 104-110, Pl. 1.

——. 1947 (18 July) **[ref. 3017]**. A new genus and species of deep-sea fish of the family Myctophidae from the Philippine Islands. Proc. U. S. Natl. Mus. v. 97 (no. 3211): 81-90.

——. 1956 (21 Dec.) **[ref. 3018]**. A new genus and species of cyprinodontid fish from San Luis Potosi, Mexico, with remarks on the subfamily Cyprinodontinae. Occas. Pap. Mus. Zool. Univ. Mich. No. 581: 1-17, Pls. 1-2.

——. 1974 (28 June) **[ref. 7119]**. Mexican species of the genus *Heterandria*, subgenus *Pseudoxiphophorus* (Pisces: Poeciliidae). Trans. San Diego Soc. Nat. Hist. v. 17 (no. 17): 235-250.

——. 1976 (Aug.) **[ref. 7032]**. Four new pupfishes of the genus *Cyprinodon* from Mexico, with a key to the *C. eximius* complex.

Bull. South. Calif. Acad. Sci. v. 75 (pt 2): 68-75.
——. 1983 (16 Aug.) **[ref. 6815]**. Checklist and key to the mollies of Mexico (Pisces: Poeciliidae: *Poecilia*, subgenus *Mollienesia*). Copeia 1983 (no. 3): 817-822.
——. 1984 (18 Jan.) **[ref. 5281]**. *Rhamdia redelli*, new species, the first blind pimelodid catfish from Middle America, with a key to the Mexican species. Trans. San Diego Soc. Nat. Hist. v. 20 (no. 8): 135-144.
MILLER, R. R., AND J. M. FITZSIMONS. 1971 (8 Mar.) **[ref. 3019]**. *Ameca splendens*, a new genus and species of goodeid fish from western Mexico, with remarks on the classification of the Goodeidae. Copeia 1971 (no. 1): 1-13.
MILLER, R. R., AND C. L. HUBBS. 1960 (5 July) **[ref. 11934]**. The spiny-rayed cyprinid fishes (Plagopterini) of the Colorado River system. Misc. Publ. Mus. Zool. Univ. Mich. No. 115: 1-39, Pls. 1-3.
MILLER, R. R., AND G. R. SMITH. 1981 (7 May) **[ref. 5465]**. Distribution and evolution of *Chasmistes* (Pisces: Catostomidae) in western North America. Occas. Pap. Mus. Zool. Univ. Mich. No. 696: 1-46.
MILLER, R. R., AND J. N. TAYLOR. 1984 (18 Dec.) **[ref. 6809]**. *Cichlasoma socolofi*, a new species of cichlid fish of the *Thorichthys* group from northern Chiapas, Mexico. Copeia 1984 (no. 4): 933-940.
MILLER, R. R., AND T. UYENO. 1980 (24 Apr.) **[ref. 5576]**. *Allodontichthys hubbsi*, a new species of goodeid fish from southwestern Mexico. Occas. Pap. Mus. Zool. Univ. Mich. No. 692: 1-13.
MILLER, R. R., AND V. WALTERS. 1972 (17 Oct.) **[ref. 3020]**. A new genus of cyprinodontid fish from Nuevo Leon, Mexico. Contrib. Sci. (Los Ang.) No. 233: 1-13.
MILLIKEN, D. M., AND E. D. HOUDE. 1984 **[ref. 8132]**. A new species of Bregmacerotidae (Pisces), *Bregmaceros cantori*, from the western Atlantic Ocean. Bull. Mar. Sci. v. 35 (no. 1): 11-19.
MINDING, J. 1832 **[ref. 3022]**. Lehrbuch der Naturgeschichte der Fische. Berlin. i-xii + 1-132, 6 pls. on one foldout.
MIRANDA-RIBEIRO, A. DE. 1902 **[ref. 3710]**. Oito especies de peixes do Rio Pomba. Bol. Soc. Nac. Agric., Rio de Janeiro 1902: 1-8. [Pages cited above may be from separate and may differ from the original pagination.]
——. 1903 (23 Oct.) **[ref. 3709]**. Pescas do "Annie." Bol. Soc. Nac. Agric., Rio de Janeiro 1903 (nos. 4-7): 1-53 + p. 50a. [Pages listed may be from separate (publ. 1904) and not the original pages.]
——. 1907 **[ref. 3713]**. Uma novidade ichthyologica. Kosmos, Rio de Janeiro v. 4 (no. 1): 3 unnum. pp.
——. 1908 **[ref. 3715]**. Peixes da Ribeira, resultados de excursão do Sr. Ricardo Krone, membro correspondente do Museu Nacional do Rio de Janeiro. Kosmos, Rio de Janeiro [Rev. Art. Sci. Litt.] v. 5 (no. 2): 5 unnum. pp.
——. 1912 **[ref. 3716]**. Fauna brasiliense. Peixes. Tomo IV (A) [Eleutherobranchios Aspirophoros]. Arq. Mus. Nac. Rio de J. v. 16 (for 1911): 1-504, Pls. 22-54.
——. 1912 (Sept.) **[ref. 3718]**. Loricariidae, Callichthyidae, Doradidae, e Trichomycteridae. In: Commissão de Linhas Telegraphicas Estrategicas de Matto-Grosso ao Amazonas. Annexo no. 5: 1-31, 1 pl.
——. 1915 **[ref. 3711]**. Fauna brasiliense. Peixes. Tomo V. [Eleutherobranchios Aspirophoras]. Physoclisti. Arq. Mus. Nac. Rio de J. v. 17: 1-[ca. 600], pls. [Not continuously paginated, plates not numbered, no index.]
——. 1917 **[ref. 5742]**. De scleracanthis. Fluvio "Solimões" anno MCMVIII a cl. F. Machado da Silva duce brasiliense invertis et in Museu Urbis "Rio de Janeiro" servatis. Rev. Soc. Sci. Rio de Janeiro v. 1: 49-52.
——. 1918 **[ref. 3720]**. Historia Natural. Zoologia. Cichlidae. In: Commissão de Linhas Telegraphicas Estrategicas de Matto-Grosso ao Amazonas. Publ. 46 (Annexo 5): 1-18, Pls. 1-16.
——. 1918 **[ref. 3724]**. Dous generos e tres especies novas de peixes Brasileiros determinados nas collecções do Museu Paulista. Rev. Mus. Paulista v. 10: 787-791, 1 pl.
——. 1918 **[ref. 3725]**. Tres generos e dezesete especies novas de peixes Brasilieros. Rev. Mus. Paulista v. 10: 631-646, 2 pls.
——. 1918 **[ref. 3726]**. *Hemipsilichthys*, Eignm. & Eignm., e generos alliados. Rev. Soc. Sci. Rio de Janeiro v. 2: 101-107, Pls. 1-7.
——. 1920 **[ref. 3727]**. Peixes (excl. Characinidae). In: Commissão de Linhas Telegraphicas Estrategicas de Matto-Grosso ao Amazonas. Historia Natural. Zoologia. No. 58 (Annexo 5): 1-15, 17 pls.
——. 1924 **[ref. 3728]**. Ainda "Hemipsilichthys" e generos alliados. Bol. Mus. Nac. Rio de Janeiro v. 1 (no. 5): 365-366.
——. 1937 **[ref. 5025]**. Sobre uma collecçao de vertebrados do nordeste brasileiro. Primeira parte: Peixes e batrachios. O Campo Rio de Janeiro No. 1: 54-56. [Not seen.]
——. 1939 (30 Oct.) **[ref. 3023]**. Alguns novos dados ictiológicos da nossa fauna. Bol. Biol. Sao Paulo (n. s.) v. 4 (no. 3): 358-363.
MIRANDA-RIBEIRO, P. DE. 1939 **[ref. 3024]**. Sobre o gênero *Harttia*, Steind. (Peixes: Loricariidae). Bol. Biol. São Paulo (n. s.) v. 4 (no. 1): 11-13, Pl. 2.
——. 1946 (20 Mar.) **[ref. 3025]**. Notas paro o estudo dos Pygidiidae Brasileiros (Pisces - Pygidiidae - Stegophilinae). Bol. Mus. Nac. Rio de J. Zool. (n. s.) No. 58: 1-20, foldout table, Pls. 1-7.
——. 1956 **[ref. 3729]**. On a new genus and a new species of South American fishes. Int. Congr. Zool. v. 14 (1953): 546-547.
MIRZA, M. R., AND M. N. JAVED. 1985 **[ref. 5695]**. A note on the mahseers of Pakistan with the description of *Naziritor*, new subgenus (Pisces: Cyprinidae). Pak. J. Zool. v. 17 (no. 3): 225-227.
MIRZA, M. R., T. T. NALBANT AND P. M. BANARESCU. 1981 **[ref. 5390]**. A review of the genus *Schistura* in Pakistan with description of new species and subspecies (Pisces, Cobitidae, Noemacheilinae). Bijdr. Dierkd. v. 51 (no. 1): 105-130.
MIRZA, M. R., AND T. SAEED. 1988 **[ref. 13385]**. A note on the systematics of the genus *Schizothorax* Heckel, 1938 (Pisces: Cyprinidae). Pak. J. Zool. v. 20 (no. 2): 312-314.
MISRA, K. S. 1962 (31 Aug.) **[ref. 3026]**. An aid to the identification of the common commercial fishes of India and Pakistan. Rec. Indian Mus. (Calcutta) v. 57 (pts 1-4): 1-320.
——. 1976 **[ref. 3027]**. Teleostomi: Cypriniformes; Siluri. Fauna India (Pisces, 2nd Edition) v. 3: i-xxi + 1-367, Pls. 1-5.
MITCHELL, J. 1838 **[ref. 3029]**. Three expeditions into the interior of eastern Australia, with descriptions of recently explored regions of Australia Felix and the present colony of New South Wales. London. v. 1: 1-351. [Original not seen.]
MITCHILL, S. L. 1814 (1 Jan.) **[ref. 3030]**. Report in part of Samuel L. Mitchill, M. D., on the fishes of New-York. New York. 1-28. [See Gill 1898 [ref. 7956] for review and discussion and for a reproduction of original.]
——. 1824 **[ref. 3031]**. Description of an extraordinary fish, resembling the *Stylephorus* of Shaw. Ann. Lyc. Nat. Hist. N. Y. v. 1 (pt 1): 82-86.
MITSUKURI, K. 1895 (June) **[ref. 5935]**. On a new genus of the chimaeroid group *Hariotta*. Zool. Mag. (Tokyo) v. 7 (no. 80): 2 pp., Pl. 16.
MIYAKE, T., AND J. D. MCEACHRAN. 1986 (30 May) **[ref. 6153]**. Taxonomy of the stingray genus *Urotrygon* (Myliobatiformes: Urolophidae): preliminary results based on external morphology. Pp. 291-302. In: Uyeno et al. (eds.) 1986 [ref. 6147].
——. 1988 (May) **[ref. 12878]**. Three new species of the stingray genus *Urotrygon* (Myliobatiformes: Urolophidae) from the eastern Pacific. Bull. Mar. Sci. v. 42 (no. 3): 366-375.
MOCHIZUKI, K., AND S. GULTNEH. 1989 **[ref. 13505]**. Redescription of *Synagrops spinosus* (Percichthyidae) with its first record from the west Pacific. Jpn. J. Ichthyol. v. 35 (no. 4): 421-427.
MOCHIZUKI, K., AND M. SANO. 1984 (15 Feb.) **[ref. 5188]**. A new percichthyid fish *Neoscombrops atlanticus* from the Caribbean Sea. Jpn. J. Ichthyol. v. 30 (no. 4): 335-340.
——. 1984 (15 May) **[ref. 6730]**. A new percichthyid fish *Synagrops trispinosus* from the Caribbean Sea and its adjacent waters. Jpn. J. Ichthyol. v. 31 (no. 1): 1-4.

MOCHIZUKI, K., AND K. SHIRAKIHARA. 1983 **[ref. 8302]**. A new and a rare apogonid species of the genus *Epigonus* from Japan. Jpn. J. Ichthyol. v. 30 (no. 3): 199-207.

MOCQUARD, F. 1885 **[ref. 3033]**. Sur un nouveau genre de Blenniidae voisin des *Clinus*. Bull. Soc. Philomath. Paris (Ser. 7) v. 10: 18-20.

———. 1888 **[ref. 3032]**. Révision des *Clinus* de la collection du Museum. Bull. Soc. Philomath. Paris (Ser. 8) v. 1 (no. 1): 40-46. [Also as separate, pp. 1-7.]

MOHAN, R. S. L. 1969 (20 June) **[ref. 3034]**. On three new genera of sciaenid fishes (Pisces: Sciaenidae) from India. Curr. Sci. v. 38: 295-296.

———. 1972 (July) **[ref. 5743]**. A synopsis of the Indian genera of the fishes of the family Sciaenidae. Indian J. Fish. v. 16 (nos. 1-2) [1969]: 82-98.

MOHSEN, T. 1962 (Sept.) **[ref. 3035]**. Un nouveau genre d'Hémirhamphidés: *Grecarchopterus* nov. gen., basé sur des caractères particuliers du système uro-génital. Bull. Aquat. Biol. v. 3 (no. 31): 109-120.

MOK, H.-K. 1988 (25 Feb.) **[ref. 12752]**. Osteological evidence for the monophyly of Cepolidae and Owstoniidae. Jpn. J. Ichthyol. v. 35 (no. 4): 507-508.

MONOD, T. 1950 **[ref. 14468]**. Notes d'ichthyologie ouest-africaine. Bull. Inst. Fr. Afr. Noire v. 12 (no. 1): 48-71.

———. 1973 **[ref. 7193]**. [Many family accounts.] In: Hureau & Monod 1973 [ref. 6590].

MONOD, T., AND Y. LE DANOIS. 1973 **[ref. 7223]**. Lophiidae (pp. 659-660), Antennariidae (pp. 661-664). In: Hureau & Monod 1973 [ref. 6590].

MONTAGU, G. 1811 **[ref. 3038]**. An account of five rare species of British fishes. Mem. Wernerian Nat. Hist. Soc. Edinburgh v. 1 [1809]: 79-101, Pls. 2-5.

MOREAU, E. 1881 **[ref. 3040]**. Histoire naturelle des poissons de la France. v. 1: i-vii + 1-480; v. 2: 1-572; v. 3: 1-697; supplement in 1891: 1-144.

MORELAND, J. M. 1960 (Feb.) **[ref. 3041]**. A new genus and species of congiopodid fish from southern New Zealand. Rec. Dom. Mus. (Wellington) v. 3 (pt 3): 241-246.

MORGANS, J. F. C. 1982 (May) **[ref. 5411]**. Serranid fishes of Tanzania and Kenya. Ichthyol. Bull. J. L. B. Smith Inst. Ichthyol. No. 46: 1-44, Pls. 1-7.

MORI, T. 1933 **[ref. 7968]**. On the classifications of cyprinoid fishes, *Microphysogobio*, n. gen. and *Saurogobio*. Zool. Mag. Tokyo [Nippon Dobutsu Z.] v. 45: 114-115. [In Japanese.]

———. 1934 (Oct.) **[ref. 3042]**. The fresh water fishes of Jehol. Rep. First Sci. Exped. Manchoukuo, Tokyo Sec. 5 (Zool.) Pt 1: 1-61, Pls. 1-21.

———. 1935 (15 Dec.) **[ref. 3043]**. Descriptions of two new genera and seven new species of Cyprinidae from Chosen. Annot. Zool. Jpn. v. 15 (no. 2): 161-181, Pls. 11-13.

———. 1936 **[ref. 3044]**. Descriptions of one new genus and three new species of Siluroidea from Chosen. Zool. Mag. (Tokyo) v. 48 (nos. 8-10): 671-675, Pl. 24. [In Japanese and English.]

MORRISON, W. L. 1890 **[ref. 6864]**. A review of the American species of Priacanthidae. Proc. Acad. Nat. Sci. Phila. 1889: 159-163.

MORROW, J. E., JR. 1964 **[ref. 6958]**. Family Malacosteidae. Pp. 523-549. In: Fishes of the Western North Atlantic. Mem. Sears Found. Mar. Res. No. 1 (pt 4).

———. 1964 **[ref. 6967]**. Family Stomiatidae (pp. 290-310). In: Fishes of the Western North Atlantic. Mem. Sears Found. Mar. Res. No. 1 (pt 4).

———. 1973 **[ref. 7175]**. Chauliodontidae (pp. 130-131), Stomiatidae (pp. 132-133), Melanostomiatidae (pp. 134-141). In: Hureau & Monod 1973 [ref. 6590].

MORROW, J. E., JR., AND R. H. GIBBS, JR. 1964 **[ref. 6962]**. Family Melanostomiatidae (pp. 351-511). In: Fishes of the Western North Atlantic. Mem. Sears Found. Mar. Res. No. 1 (pt 4).

MORTON, A. 1888 **[ref. 3046]**. Description of two new fishes. Pap. Proc. R. Soc. Tasmania (for 1887): 77-78, 1 pl.

MOSER, H. G., E. H. AHLSTROM AND J. R. PAXTON. 1984 **[ref. 13645]**. Myctophidae: development. Am. Soc. Ichthyol. Herpetol. Spec. Publ. No. 1: 218-244.

MOSS, S. A. 1962 **[ref. 3047]**. Melamphaidae II. A new melamphaid genus, *Sio*, with a redescription of *Sio nordenskjöldii* (Lönnberg). Dana Rep. No. 56: 1-10.

MUKERJI, D. D. 1935 (Sept.) **[ref. 3054]**. Notes on some rare and interesting fishes form the Andaman Islands, with descriptions of two new freshwater gobies. Rec. Indian Mus. (Calcutta) v. 37 (pt 3): 259-277, Pl. 6.

MÜLLER, J. 1836 **[ref. 3060]**. Vergleichende Anatomie der Myxinoiden, der Cyclostomen mit durchbohrten Gaumen. Erster Theil. Osteologie und Myologie. Abh. Dtsch. Akad. Wiss. Berl. 1834: 65-340, Pls. 1-9.

———. 1840 **[ref. 12523]**. Arch. Anat. Physiol. [Not seen.]

———. 1841 **[ref. 3061]**. Vergleichende Anatomie der Myxinoiden. Dritte Fortsetzung. Über das Gefässystem. Abh. Dtsch. Akad. Wiss. Berl. 1839: 175-304, Pls. 1-5. [Read 11 Nov. and 9 Dec. 1839; apparently published in 1841. Abstract in Ber. Akad. Wiss. Berlin 1839: 184-186.]

———. 1842 **[ref. 3062]**. Über die Schwimmblase der Fische, mit Bezug auf einige neue Fishgattungen. Khonigl. Akad. Wiss. Berlin 1842: 202-210.

———. 1843 **[ref. 3063]**. Beiträge zur Kenntniss der natürlichen Familien der Fische. Arch. Naturgeschichte v. 9: 292-330.

———. 1844 **[ref. 13283]**. Über den Bau und die Grenzen der Ganoiden und das naturliche System der Fische. Abhandl. Preuss. Akad Wiss. Berlin 1844: 117-216. [Not seen.]

MÜLLER, J., AND F. G. J. HENLE. 1837 **[ref. 3067]**. Gattungen der Haifische und Rochen nach einer von ihm mit Hrn. Henle unternommenen gemeinschaftlichen Arbeit über die Naturgeschichte der Knorpelfische. Ber. Akad. Wiss. Berlin 1837: 111-118. [Presented 31 July 1837, assume published late 1837. A synopsis appeared in L'Institut 1837 [?1838]: 63-65.]

———. 1837 **[ref. 13421]**. Ueber die Gattungen der Plagiostomen. Arch. Naturgeschichte 1837: 394-401, 434 [Nachträgliche Bemerkung]. [Same as Müller & Henle 1837, ref. 3067 in content.]

———. 1838 **[ref. 3066]**. On the generic characters of cartilaginous fishes, with descriptions of new genera. Mag. Nat. Hist. (n. s.) v. 2: 33-37; 88-91. [See also: Arch. Anat. (Müller), 1842: 414-417.]

———. 1838 **[ref. 3068]**. Ueber die Gattungen der Plagiostomen. Arch. Naturgeschichte Berlin v. 4: 83-85.

———. 1838-41 **[ref. 3069]**. Systematische Beschreibung der Plagiostomen. Berlin. i-xxii + 1-200, 60 pls. [Pp. 1-28 published in 1838, reset pp. 27-28, 29-102 in 1839, i-xxii + 103-200 in 1841.]

MÜLLER, J., AND F. H. TROSCHEL. 1844 **[ref. 3070]**. Synopsis generum et specierum familiae Characinorum. (Prodromus descriptionis novorum generum et specierum). Arch. Naturgeschichte v. 10 (pt. 1): 81-99 + add. p. 99 (foldout).

———. 1845 **[ref. 3071]**. Horae Ichthyologicae. Beschreibung und Abbildung neuer Fische. Die Familie der Characinen. Erstes und Zweites Heft. Berlin. Nos. 1 & 2: 1-40, Pls. 1-11.

———. 1848 **[ref. 3072]**. Fische (pp. 618-644). In: Reisen in Britisch-Guiana in den Jahren 1840-44. Im Auftrag Sr. Mäjestat des Königs von Preussen ausgeführt von Richard Schomburgk. [Versuch einer Fauna und Flora von Britisch-Guiana.] v. 3. Berlin.

———. 1849 **[ref. 3073]**. Horae Zoologicae. Beschreibung und Abbildung neuer Fische; die Familie Characinen. Berlin. v. 3: 1-27 + additional p. 24, Pls. 1-5.

MÜLLER, P. L. S. 1766 **[ref. 3055]**. Deliciae Naturae. [Not seen.] [Issued in 3 volumes, ed. 1 in 1766, ed. 2 in 1778, Dutch trans. 1771; all works rejected for nomenclatural purposes.]

———. 1773-76 **[ref. 6461]**. Des Ritters Carl von Linné vollständiges Natursystem nach der 12ten Ausgabe, und nach Anleitung Houttynischen Werkes, mit einer ausfügrkucgeb Erklärung ausgefertigt. 6 vols. Nürnberg. [Not seen.]

MULLER, S. 1989 (Dec.) **[ref. 13512]**. Description de deux nouvelles espèces paraguayennes du genre *Ancistrus* Kner, 1854 (Pisces,

Siluriformes, Loricariidae). Revue Suisse Zool. v. 96 (no. 4): 885-904.

MUÑOZ-CHÁPULI, R., AND F. RAMOS. 1989 **[ref. 12577]**. Morphological comparison of *Squalus blainvillei* and *S. megalops* in the eastern Atlantic, with notes on the genus. Jpn. J. Ichthyol. v. 36 (no. 1): 6-21.

———. 1989 (31 Mar.) **[ref. 12834]**. Review of the *Centrophorus* sharks (Elasmobranchii, Squalidae) of the eastern Atlantic. Cybium v. 13 (no. 1): 65-81.

MUNRO, I. S. R. 1943 (6 Nov.) **[ref. 3056]**. Revision of Australian species of *Scomberomorus*. Mem. Queensl. Mus. v. 12 (pt 2): 65-95, Pls. 6-8.

———. 1948 (31 Dec.) **[ref. 3057]**. *Sparidentex hasta* (Valenciennes), a new name for *Chrysophrys cuvieri* Day. Copeia 1948 (no. 4): 275-280.

———. 1949 (22 June) **[ref. 3059]**. A new genus and species of transparent gobioid fish from Australia. Ann. Mag. Nat. Hist. (Ser. 12) v. 2 (no. 15): 229-240.

———. 1964 **[ref. 3058]**. Additions to the fish fauna of New Guinea. Papua New Guinea Agric. J. v. 16 (no. 4): 141-186.

———. 1967 **[ref. 6844]**. The fishes of New Guinea. Port Moresby, New Guinea, Dept. Agric., Stock and Fisheries. i-xxxvii + 1-650, Pls. 1-78.

MURDY, E. O. 1989 (31 Aug.) **[ref. 13628]**. A taxonomic revision and cladistic analysis of the oxudercine gobies (Gobiidae: Oxudercinae). Rec. Aust. Mus. Suppl. no. 11: 1-93.

MURDY, E. O., AND D. F. HOESE. 1984 (23 Feb.) **[ref. 5377]**. The monotypic gobiid fish genus *Macrodontogobius*, including synonymization of *Gnatholepis hendersoni*. Copeia 1984 (no. 1): 227-229.

———. 1985 (Jan.) **[ref. 5237]**. Revision of the gobiid fish genus *Istigobius*. Indo-Pac. Fishes No. 4: 1-41, Color Pls. 1-3.

MURRAY, J. 1877 **[ref. 6531]**. [Title unknown.] Science Lectures for the People (Ser. 9) v. 4: 132. [Not seen. See ICZN Opinion 1333.]

MUSICK, J. A. 1973 **[ref. 7144]**. A meristic and morphometric comparison of the hakes, *Urophycis chuss* and *U. tenuis* (Pisces, Gadidae). U. S. Natl. Mar. Fish. Serv. Fish. Bull. v. 71 (no. 2): 479-488.

MYERS, G. S. 1923 (20 May) **[ref. 3089]**. Notes on the nomenclature of certain anabantids and a new generic name proposed. Copeia No. 118: 62-63.

———. 1923 (20 Nov.) **[ref. 12875]**. Further notes on anabantids. Copeia No. 124: 111-113.

———. 1924 (1 Aug.) **[ref. 3090]**. Mutanda Ichthyologica. *Neoborus* Boulenger and *Barbus rubripinnis* Nichols and Griscom. Rev. Zool. Afr. v. 12 (pt 3): 397.

———. 1924 (6 June) **[ref. 3091]**. A new poeciliid fish from the Congo, with remarks on funduline genera. Am. Mus. Novit. No. 116: 1-9.

———. 1924 (20 May) **[ref. 3092]**. New genera of African poeciliid fishes. Copeia No. 129: 41-45.

———. 1925 (25 Nov.) **[ref. 3093]**. *Tridentopsis pearsoni* a new pygidiid catfish from Bolivia. Copeia No. 148: 83-86.

———. 1925 (April) **[ref. 5744]**. Results of some recent studies on the American killifishes. Fish Culturist v. 4 (no. 8): 370-371.

———. 1926 **[ref. 3094]**. Eine neue Characinidengattung der Unterfamilie Cheirodontinae aus Rio de Janeiro, Brasilien. Bl. Aquarien-Terranienfunde, Stuttgart v. 37 (no. 24): 1-2.

———. 1926 (1 Mar.) **[ref. 3095]**. Two new genera of African characin fishes. Rev. Zool. Afr. v. 13 (no. 3-4): 174-175.

———. 1927 (July) **[ref. 3096]**. Descriptions of new South American fresh-water fishes collected by Dr. Carl Ternetz. Bull. Mus. Comp. Zool. v. 68 (no. 3): 107-135.

———. 1927 (20 Apr.) **[ref. 3097]**. *Puntius streeteri*, a new cyprinoid fish from Borneo, and *Cobitophis*, a new genus of Bornean Cobitidae. Am. Mus. Novit. No. 265: 1-4.

———. 1927 (Jan.) **[ref. 3098]**. IX.—An analysis of the genera of neotropical killifishes allied to *Rivulus*. Ann. Mag. Nat. Hist. (Ser. 9) v. 19 (no. 109): 115-129.

———. 1928 (23 Mar.) **[ref. 3099]**. Two new genera of fishes. Copeia No. 166: 7-8.

———. 1928 (July) **[ref. 3100]**. New fresh-water fishes from Peru, Venezuela, and Brazil. Ann. Mag. Nat. Hist. (Ser. 10) v. 2 (no. 7): 83-90.

———. 1928 (1 Feb.) **[ref. 3101]**. The systematic position of the phallostethid fishes, with diagnosis of a new genus from Siam. Am. Mus. Novit. No. 295: 1-12.

———. 1929 (June) **[ref. 3102]**. On curimatid characin fishes having an incomplete lateral line, with a note on the peculiar sexual dimorphism of *Curimatopsis macrolepis*. Ann. Mag. Nat. Hist. (Ser. 10) v. 3 (no. 18): 618-621.

———. 1930 (31 Dec.) **[ref. 5026]**. *Ptychidio jordani*, an unusual new cyprinoid fish from Formosa. Copeia 1930 (no. 4): 110-113.

———. 1932 (27 Sept.) **[ref. 3103]**. A new genus of funduline cyprinodont fishes from the Orinoco Basin, Venezuela. Proc. Biol. Soc. Wash. v. 45: 159-162.

———. 1932 (1 July) **[ref. 5027]**. A new gonostomatid fish, *Neophos nexilis*, from the Philippines. Copeia 1932 (no. 2): 61-62.

———. 1933 (27 Dec.) **[ref. 3104]**. The genera of Indo-Malayan and African cyprinodont fishes related to *Panchax* and *Nothobranchius*. Copeia 1933 (no. 4): 180-185.

———. 1933 (23 Jan.) **[ref. 3105]**. *Pachypanchax*, a new genus of cyprinodont fishes from the Seychelles Islands and Madagascar. Am. Mus. Novit. No. 592: 1 p.

———. 1933 (1 Apr.) **[ref. 3106]**. A new genus of Chinese fresh-water serranid fishes. Hong Kong Nat. v. 4 (no. 1): 76.

———. 1934 (2 Apr.) **[ref. 3107]**. Three new deep-water fishes from the West Indies. Smithson. Misc. Collect. v. 91 (no. 9): 1-12, Pl. 1.

———. 1935 (6 Feb.) **[ref. 3108]**. A new phallostethid fish from Palawan. Proc. Biol. Soc. Wash. v. 48: 5-6.

———. 1935 (6 Feb.) **[ref. 3109]**. Four new fresh-water fishes from Brazil, Venezuela and Paraguay. Proc. Biol. Soc. Wash. v. 48: 7-14.

———. 1935 (29 Nov.) **[ref. 3110]**. An annotated list of the cyprinodont fishes of Hispaniola, with descriptions of two new species. Zoologica (N. Y.) v. 10 (no. 3): 301-316.

———. 1935 (24 Dec.) **[ref. 3111]**. A new genus of opisthognathid fishes. Smithson. Misc. Collect. v. 91 (no. 23): 1-5.

———. 1936 (15 Sept.) **[ref. 3112]**. Ichthyology.—A new polynemid fish collected in the Sadong River, Sarawak, by D. William T. Hornaday, with notes on the genera of Polynemidae. J. Wash. Acad. Sci. v. 26 (no. 9): 376-382.

———. 1936 (3 July) **[ref. 3113]**. On the Indo-Australian fishes of the genus *Scatophagus*, with description of a new genus, *Selenotoca*. Proc. Biol. Soc. Wash. v. 49: 83-85.

———. 1936 (22 Aug.) **[ref. 3114]**. A new genus of gymnotid eels from the Peruvian Amazon. Proc. Biol. Soc. Wash. v. 49: 115-116.

———. 1937 (6 Jan.) **[ref. 3115]**. Notes on phallostethid fishes. Proc. U. S. Natl. Mus. v. 84 (no. 3007): 137-143.

———. 1938 (30 June) **[ref. 3116]**. Notes on *Ansorgia*, *Clarisilurus*, *Wallago*, and *Ceratoglanis*, four genera of African and Indo-Malayan catfishes. Copeia 1938 (no. 2): 98.

———. 1939 (24 May) **[ref. 14271]**. The possible identity of the Congo fish *Teleogramma* with the cichlid genus *Leptolamprolodus*. Stanford Ichthyol. Bull. v. 1 (no. 4): 160.

———. 1940 (7 Feb.) **[ref. 3117]**. Suppression of *Acaropsis* and *Chalcinus*, two preoccupied generic names of South American fresh-water fishes. Stanford Ichthyol. Bull. v. 1 (no. 5): 170.

———. 1940 (23 Dec.) **[ref. 3118]**. Suppression of some preoccupied generic names of fishes (*Kessleria*, *Entomolepis*, *Pterodiscus* and *Nesiotes*), with a note on *Pterophyllum*. Stanford Ichthyol. Bull. v. 2 (no. 1): 35-36.

———. 1940 (28 July) **[ref. 3119]**. A note on *Monognathus*. Copeia 1940 (no. 2): 141.

———. 1941 (27 Nov.) **[ref. 3120]**. A new name for *Taenionema*, a genus of Amazonian siluroid fishes. Stanford Ichthyol. Bull. v. 2 (no. 3): 88.

———. 1942 (24 Aug.) **[ref. 3121]**. Studies on South American fresh-water fishes. I. Stanford Ichthyol. Bull. v. 2 (no. 4): 89-114.

———. 1944 (22 Aug.) **[ref. 3122]**. *Rhinobrycon negrensis*, a new genus and species of characid fishes from the Rio Negro, Brazil. Proc. Calif. Acad. Sci. (Ser. 4) v. 23 (no. 39): 587-590.

———. 1944 (7 Nov.) **[ref. 3123]**. Two extraordinary new blind nematognath fishes from the Rio Negro, representing a new subfamily of Pygidiidae, with a rearrangement of the genera of the family, and illustrations of some previously described genera and species from Venezuela and Brazil. Proc. Calif. Acad. Sci. (Ser. 4) v. 23 (no. 40): 591-602, Pls. 52-56.

———. 1948 **[ref. 12606]**. Note on two generic names of Indo-Malayan silurid fishes, *Wallago* and *Wallagonia*. Proc. Calif. Zool. Club v. 1 (no. 4): 19-20.

———. 1950 (21 Aug.) **[ref. 3124]**. Studies on South American fresh-water fishes. II. The genera of anostomine characids. Stanford Ichthyol. Bull. v. 3 (no. 4): 184-198.

———. 1951 (27 Dec.) **[ref. 13464]**. Some forgotten but available names for Indian fishes. Stanford Ichthyol. Bull. v. 4 (no. 1): 26.

———. 1952 (ca. July) **[ref. 3125]**. Annual fishes. Aquarium J. v. 23 (no. 7): 125-141.

———. 1953 (Nov.) **[ref. 5745]**. A note on the habits and classification of *Corydoras hastatus*. Aquarium J. v. 24 (no. 11): 268-270.

———. 1955 (Mar.) **[ref. 3126]**. Notes on the classification and names of cyprinodont fishes. Trop. Fish Mag. Mar. 1955: 7.

———. 1956 (30 Aug.) **[ref. 3127]**. *Copella*, a new genus of pyrrhulinin characid fishes from the Amazon. Stanford Ichthyol. Bull. v. 7 (no. 2): 12-13.

———. 1960 (28 Oct.) **[ref. 3128]**. The mormyrid genera *Hippopotamyrus* and *Cyphomyrus*. Stanford Ichthyol. Bull. v. 7 (no. 4): 123-125.

———. 1960 (28 Oct.) **[ref. 3129]**. The South American characid genera *Exodon*, *Gnathoplax* and *Roeboexodon*, with notes on the ecology and taxonomy of characid fishes. Stanford Ichthyol. Bull. v. 7 (no. 4): 206-211.

Myers, G. S., and J. E. Böhlke. 1956 (30 Aug.) **[ref. 5937]**. The xenurobryconini, a group of minute South American characid fishes with teeth outside the mouth. Stanford Ichthyol. Bull. v. 7 (no. 2): 6-12.

Myers, G. S., and W. C. Freihofer. 1966 (7 Oct.) **[ref. 3088]**. Megalomycteridae, a previously unrecognized family of deep-sea cetomimiform fishes based on two new genera from the North Atlantic. Stanford Ichthyol. Bull. v. 8 (no. 3): 193-207.

Myers, G. S., and R. R. Harry. 1948 (1 Aug.) **[ref. 5458]**. *Apistogramma ramirezi*, a cichlid fish from Venezuela. Proc. Calif. Zool. Club v. 1 (no. 1): 1-8.

Myers, G. S., and A. Leitão de Carvalho. 1959 (24 July) **[ref. 3130]**. A remarkable new genus of anostomin characid fishes from the Upper Rio Xingú in central Brazil. Copeia 1959 (no. 2): 148-152.

Myers, G. S., and P. Miranda-Ribeiro. 1945 (25 Jan.) **[ref. 3131]**. A remarkable new genus of sexually dimorphic characid fishes from the Rio Paraguay Basin in Matto Grosso. Bol. Mus. Nac. Rio de J. Zool. (n. s.) No. 32: 1-7.

Myers, G. S., and M. H. Storey. 1939 (24 May) **[ref. 3132]**. *Hesperomyrus fryi*, a new genus and species of echelid eels from California. Stanford Ichthyol. Bull. v. 1 (no. 4): 156-159.

Myers, G. S., and C. B. Wade. 1941 (25 June) **[ref. 3133]**. Four new genera and ten new species of eels from the Pacific coast of tropical America. Allan Hancock Pac. Exped. v. 9 (no. 4): 65-111, Pls. 7-16.

———. 1942 (30 Mar.) **[ref. 3134]**. The Pacific American atherinid fishes of the genera *Eurystole*, *Nectarges*, *Coleotropis* and *Melanorhinus*. Allan Hancock Pac. Exped. v. 9 (no. 5): 113-149, Pls. 17-19.

———. 1946 (16 Dec.) **[ref. 3135]**. New fishes of the families Dactyloscopidae, Microdesmidae, and Antennariidae from the west coast of Mexico and the Galapagos Islands, with a brief account of the use of rotenone fish poisons in ichthyological collecting. Allan Hancock Pac. Exped. v. 9 (no. 6): 151-179, Pls. 20-23.

Myers, G. S., and S. H. Weitzman. 1966 **[ref. 3136]**. Two remarkable new trichomycterid catfishes from the Amazon basin in Brazil and Colombia. J. Zool. (Lond.) v. 149: 277-287.

Naffaktitis, B. G. 1968 **[ref. 6979]**. Taxonomy and distribution of the lanternfishes, genera *Lobianchia* and *Diaphus*, in the North Atlantic. Dana Rep. No. 73: 1-131.

———. 1975 (Jan.) **[ref. 3137]**. Review of the lanternfish genus *Notoscopelus* (family Myctophidae) in the North Atlantic and the Mediterranean. Bull. Mar. Sci. v. 25 (no. 1): 75-87.

Naffaktitis, B. G., and J. R. Paxton. 1978 (10 Aug.) **[ref. 3138]**. *Idiolychnus*, a new genus of Myctophidae based on *Diaphus urolampus*. Copeia 1978 (no. 3): 492-497.

Nakabo, T. 1982 (Mar.) **[ref. 3139]**. Revision of genera of the dragonets (Pisces: Callionymidae). Publ. Seto Mar. Biol. Lab. v. 27 (no. 1/3): 77-131.

———. 1982 (27 Feb.) **[ref. 5507]**. Revision of the family Draconettidae. Jpn. J. Ichthyol. v. 28 (no. 4): 355-367.

———. 1984 (1 Aug.) **[ref. 5343]**. A new species of the genus *Paradiplogrammus* (Callionymidae) from the western Pacific. Jpn. J. Ichthyol. v. 32 (no. 2): 150-155.

———. 1987 (20 Feb.) **[ref. 6375]**. A new species of the genus *Foetorepus* (Callionymidae) from southern Japan with a revised key to the Japanese species of the genus. Jpn. J. Ichthyol. v. 33 (no. 4): 335-341.

Nakabo, T., S.-R. Jeon and S.-Z. Li. 1987 (10 Dec.) **[ref. 6374]**. A new species of the genus *Repomucenus* (Callionymidae) from the Yellow Sea. Jpn. J. Ichthyol. v. 34 (no. 3): 286-290.

Nakamura, I. 1980 (15 Feb.) **[ref. 5478]**. New record of a rare gempylid, *Thyrsitoides marleyi*, from the Sea of Japan. Jpn. J. Ichthyol. v. 26 (no. 4): 357-360.

———. 1983 (Dec.) **[ref. 5371]**. Systematics of the billfishes (Xiphiidae and Istiophoridae). Publ. Seto Mar. Biol. Lab. v. 28 (no. 5/6): 255-396.

———. 1986 **[ref. 5696]**. Family No. 246: Scombrolabracidae (p. 825), Family No. 247: Gempylidae (pp. 825-830), Family No. 248: Trichiuridae (pp. 829-830). In: Smiths' Sea Fishes (Smith & Heemstra 1986 [ref. 5715]).

Nakamura, I., and E. Fujii. 1983 **[ref. 5409]**. A new genus and species of Gempylidae (Pisces: Perciformes) from Tonga Ridge. Publ. Seto Mar. Biol. Lab. v. 27 (no. 4/6): 173-191.

Nakamura, I., E. Fujii and T. Arai. 1983 (10 Mar.) **[ref. 5407]**. The gempylid, *Nesiarchus nasutus* from Japan and the Sulu Sea. Jpn. J. Ichthyol. v. 29 (no. 4): 408-415.

Nakamura, I., T. Inada, Takeda, M. and H. Hatanaka. 1986 (Feb.) **[ref. 14235]**. Important fishes trawled off Patagonia. Japan Mar. Fish. Resource Research Center. 1-369, Color figs. [In Japanese and English.]

Nakamura, I., B. F. Webb and G. A. Tunnicliffe. 1981 (Sept.) **[ref. 5477]**. First record of a rare gempylid fish, *Nesiarchus nasutus*, (Teleostei; Gempylidae) from New Zealand. Rec. Canterbury Mus. v. 9 (no. 7): 337-344.

Nakaya, K. 1975 (Dec.) **[ref. 7083]**. Taxonomy, comparative anatomy and phylogeny of Japanese catsharks, Scyliorhinidae. Mem. Fac. Fish. Hokkaido Univ. v. 23 (no. 1): 1-94.

———. 1983 (10 Mar.) **[ref. 5697]**. Redescription of the holotype of *Proscyllium habereri* (Lamniformes, Triakidae). Jpn. J. Ichthyol. v. 29 (no. 4): 469-473.

———. 1986 (30 May) **[ref. 6323]**. Revisional study of Japanese species of the genus *Apristurus* (Scyliorhinidae, Lamniformes) [Abstract]. P. 931. In: Uyeno et al. (eds.) 1986 [ref. 6147].

———. 1988 (25 Feb.) **[ref. 6696]**. Morphology and taxonomy of *Apristurus longicephalus* (Lamniformes, Scyliorhinidae). Jpn. J. Ichthyol. v. 34 (no. 4): 431-442.

———. 1988 (20 Sept.) **[ref. 6855]**. Records of *Apristurus herklotsi* (Lamniformes, Scyliorhinidae) and discussion of its taxonomic relationships. Jpn. J. Ichthyol. v. 35 (no. 2): 133-141.

Nalbant, T. T. 1963 **[ref. 3140]**. A study of the genera of Botiinae and Cobitinae (Pisces, Ostariophysi, Cobitidae). Trav. Mus. Hist. Nat. 'Grigore Antipa' v. 4 (art. 11): 343-379, Pls. 1-4.

———. 1965 **[ref. 3141]**. Sur les Chaetodons de l'Atlantique, avec la description d'un nouveau genre *Bauchotia* (Pisces Chaetodontidae). Bull. Mus. Natl. Hist. Nat. (Ser. 2) v. 36 (no. 5): 584-589, Pl. 1.

———. 1971 (28 May) **[ref. 6642]**. On butterfly fishes from the Atlantic, Indian and Pacific oceans (Pisces, Perciformes, Chaetodontidae). Steenstrupia v. 1 (no. 20): 207-228.

———. 1974 **[ref. 6641]**. Some osteological characters in butterfly fishes with special references to their phylogeny and evolution (Pisces, Perciformes, Chaetodontidae). Trav. Mus. Hist. Nat. 'Grigore Antipa' v. 15: 303-314, 5 pls. [Romanian and Russian summs.]

———. 1979 **[ref. 3142]**. Studies on the reef fishes of Tanzania. II. *Neosynchiropus bacescui* gen. n., sp. n., an interesting dragonet fish from Makatumbe coral reefs (Pisces, Perciformes, Callionymidae). Trav. Mus. Hist. Nat. 'Grigore Antipa' v. 20 (no. 1): 349-352.

———. 1984 **[ref. 5855]**. Studies on chaetodont fishes. II. *Heminigelus*, a new genus of butterflyfishes (Pisces, Chaetodontidae). Trav. Mus. Hist. Nat. 'Grigore Antipa' v. 26: 239-240.

———. 1986 **[ref. 6135]**. Studies on chaetodont fishes. III. Redescription of the genus *Roaops* Maugé & Bauchot, 1984, and some problems on the phylogeny and evolution of butterflyfishes (Pisces, Chaetodontidae). Trav. Mus. Hist. Nat. 'Grigore Antipa' v. 28: 163-176, 6 pls.

Nalbant, T. T., and P. Banarescu. 1977 (26 Oct.) **[ref. 7045]**. Vaillantellinae, a new subfamily of Cobitidae (Pisces, Cypriniformes). Zool. Meded. v. 52 (no. 8): 99-105.

Nani, A., and F. S. Gneri. 1951 **[ref. 3143]**. Introduccion al estudio de los Mixinoideos Sudamericanos. I. Un nuevo genero de "Babosa de mar," *Notomyxine* (classe Myxini, familia Myxinidae). Rev. Inst. Invest. Mus. Argent. Cienc. Nat. Zool. v. 2 (no. 4): 183-224, Pls. 1-31. [Perhaps not published until 1952.]

Nardo, G. D. 1824 **[ref. 3144]**. Osservazione ed aggiunte all' Adriatica ittiologia pubblicata dal Sig. Cav. Fortunata Luigi Naccari. Giorn. Fisica Chimica Storia Nat. Med. Arti, Pavia v. 7: 222-234; 249-263.

———. 1827 **[ref. 3145]**. De Proctostego, novo piscium genere specimen ichthyologicum anatomicum. Patavii. 17 pp., 1 pl. [Not seen. Possibly in Diario Chem. Hist. Nat. Ticino, v. 1.]

———. 1827 **[ref. 3146]**. Prodromus observationum et disquisitionum Adriaticae ichthyologiae. [Not seen and confused. Possibly in: Giorn. Fisica Nat. Pavia 1827 v. 10; summarized in Isis (Oken) 1827, v. 20:474-488.]

———. 1833 **[ref. 3147]**. De Skeponopodo, novo piscium genere, et de *Guebucu marcgravii*, species illi cognata. Isis (Oken) 1833: 416-420. [Not seen; possible appeared in two publications.]

———. 1833 **[ref. 5746]**. Eine neue Art von *Lepadogaster* (*L. piger*). Isis (Oken). 549-549. [Not seen.]

———. 1840 **[ref. 3149]**. Considerazioni sulla famiglia dei pesci *Mola*, e sui caratteri che li distinguono. Ann. Soc. R. Lombardo-Veneto, Padova v. 10: 105-112. [See also Rev. Zool. 1840: 29.]

———. 1841 **[ref. 3150]**. Proposizione per la formazioni di un nuovo generi di pesci, intitolato *Brachyochirus*. Ann. Soc. R. Lombardo-Veneto, Padova v. 11: 1?. [Not seen.]

———. 1841 **[ref. 13424]**. Atti Riuione Sci. Ital. [Not seen.]

———. 1844 **[ref. 3151]**. Proposizione per la formazione di un nuovo genere di Selachi chiamato *Caninoa* o *Caninotus* che costituirebbe una nuova sotto-famiglia prossima ai Natidani. Ann. Sci. Regno Lombardo-Veneto, Padova v. 13: 8-9.

Neave, S. A. 1939-40 **[ref. 12569]**. Nomenclator Zoologiscus. A list of the names of genera and subgenera in zoology from the tenth edition of Linnaeus 1758 to the end of 1935. 1939: v. 1 (A-C): i-xiv + 1-957; 1940: v. 2 (D-L): 1-1025, v. 3 (M-P): 1-1065, v. 4 (Q-Z and suppl.): 1-758. Zoological Society of London.

———. 1950 **[ref. 6512]**. Nomenclator Zoologist. Zoological Society of London. v.5 (1936-1945): 1-308. [Also series continues with v. 6 in 1966 and v. 7 in 1975.]

Nelissen, M. H. J. 1977 (30 Sept.) **[ref. 3153]**. *Pseudosimochromis*, a new genus of the family Cichlidae (Pisces) from Lake Tanganyika. Rev. Zool. Afr. v. 91 (no. 3): 730-731.

Nelson, D. W. 1984 (17 Jan.) **[ref. 5391]**. Systematics and distribution of cottid fishes of the genera *Rastrinus* and *Icelus*. Occas. Pap. Calif. Acad. Sci No. 138: 1-58.

———. 1986 **[ref. 5808]**. Two new species of the cottid genus *Artediellus* from the western North Pacific Ocean and the Sea of Japan. Proc. Acad. Nat. Sci. Phila. v. 138 (no. 1): 33-45.

Nelson, E. W. 1876 **[ref. 3154]**. A partial catalogue of the fishes of Illinois. Bull. Illinois Mus. Nat. Hist. No. 1: 33-52.

Nelson, G. J. 1982 (30 June) **[ref. 5486]**. A second Indo-Pacific species of *Thrissina*. Jpn. J. Ichthyol. v. 29 (no. 1): 99-101.

———. 1983 (10 Feb.) **[ref. 5189]**. *Anchoa argentivittata*, with notes on other eastern Pacific anchovies and the Indo-Pacific genus *Encrasicholina*. Copeia 1983 (no. 1): 48-54.

———. 1984 (1 May) **[ref. 5190]**. Identity of the anchovy *Hildebrandichthys setiger* with notes on relationships and biogeography of the genera *Engraulis* and *Cetengraulis*. Copeia 1984 (no. 2): 422-427.

———. 1986 (23 Dec.) **[ref. 5735]**. Identity of the Anchovy *Engraulis clarki* with notes on the species-groups of *Anchoa*. Copeia 1986 (no. 4): 891-902.

Nelson, J. S. 1969 **[ref. 7145]**. Geographic variation in the brook stickleback, *Culaea inconstans*, and notes on nomenclature and distribution. J. Fish. Res. Board Can. v. 26 (no. 9): 2431-2447.

———. 1977 **[ref. 7034]**. Fishes of the Southern Hemisphere genus *Neophrynichthys* (Scorpaeniformes: Cottidei), with descriptions of two new species from New Zealand and Macquarie Island. J. R. Soc. N. Z. v. 7 (no. 4): 485-511.

———. 1978 (Oct.) **[ref. 7023]**. *Bembrops morelandi*, a new percophidid fish from New Zealand, with notes on other members of the genus. Natl. Mus. N. Z. Rec. v. 1 (no. 14): 237-241.

———. 1979 **[ref. 6951]**. Revision of the fishes of the New Zealand genus *Hemerocoetes* (Perciformes: Percophididae), with descriptions of two new species. N. Z. J. Zool. v. 6: 587-599.

———. 1982 (Nov.) **[ref. 5469]**. *Pteropsaron heemstrai* and *Osopsaron natalensis* (Perciformes: Percophidae), new fish species from South Africa, with comments on *Squamicreedia obtusa* from Australia and on the classification of the subfamily Hemerocoetinae. J. L. B. Smith Inst. Ichthyol. Spec. Publ. No. 25: 1-11.

———. 1982 **[ref. 5470]**. Two new South Pacific fishes of the genus *Ebinania* and contributions to the systematics of Psychrolutidae (Scorpaeniformes). Can. J. Zool. v. 60 (no. 6): 1470-1504.

———. 1983 (25 Mar.) **[ref. 5272]**. *Creedia alleni* and *Creedia partimsquamigera* (Perciformes: Creediidae), two new marine fish species from Australia, with notes on other Australian creediids. Proc. Biol. Soc. Wash. v. 96 (no. 1): 29-37.

———. 1984 **[ref. 13596]**. Fishes of the World. 2nd edition. John Wiley & Sons. i-xv + 1-523.

———. 1985 (28 Nov.) **[ref. 5154]**. On the interrelationships of the genera of Creediidae (Perciformes: Trachinoidei). Jpn. J. Ichthyol. v. 32 (no. 3): 283-293.

———. 1985 (Aug.) **[ref. 5155]**. On the relationships of the New Zealand marine fish *Antipodocottus galatheae* with the Japanese *Stlengis misakia* (Scorpaeniformes: Cottidae). N. Z. Oceanogr. Inst. v. 5 (no. 1): 1-12.

———. 1986 (28 May) **[ref. 5153]**. Some characters of Trichonotidae, with emphasis to those distinguishing it from Creediidae (Perciformes: Trachinoidei). Jpn. J. Ichthyol. v. 33 (no. 1): 1-6.

———. 1986 **[ref. 5698]**. Family No. 160: Psychrolutidae (pp. 491-492), Family No. 232: Creediidae (pp. 736-737). In: Smiths' Sea Fishes (Smith & Heemstra 1986 [ref. 5715]).

———. 1989 (23 May) **[ref. 12546]**. *Cottunculus nudus*, a new psychrolutid fish from New Zealand (Scorpaeniformes: Cottoidei). Copeia 1989 (no. 2): 401-408.

Nelson, J. S., N. Chirichigno and F. Balbontín. 1985 **[ref. 5264]**. New material of *Psychrolutes sio* (Scorpaeniformes, Psychrolutidae) from the eastern Pacific of South America and comments on the taxonomy of *Psychrolutes inermis* and *Psychrolutes macrocephalus* from the eastern Atlantic. Can. J. Zool. v. 63 (no. 2): 444-451.

Nelson, J. S., and J. E. Randall. 1985 (16 May) **[ref. 5271]**. *Crystallodytes pauciradiatus* (Perciformes), a new creedid fish species from Easter Island. Proc. Biol. Soc. Wash. v. 98 (no. 2): 403-410.

NELVA, A. 1988 (30 Dec.) **[ref. 12836]**. Origine et biogéographie des deux Chondrostomes français: *Chondrostoma nasus* et *C. toxostoma* (Pisces, Cyprinidae). Cybium v. 12 (no. 4): 287-299.

NEWMAN, E. 1849 **[ref. 3169]**. Enormous undescribed fish, apparently allied to the Raiidae, killed off California. Zoologist (Lond.) v. 7 (for 1849): 2357-2358.

NEYELOV, A. V. 1973 **[ref. 7219]**. Cottidae (pp. 593-602), Cottunculidae (pp. 603-604). In: Hureau & Monod 1973 [ref. 6590].

——. 1979 **[ref. 3152]**. Seismosensory system and classification of cottidae fishes (Cottidae: Myoxocephalinae, Artediellinae). Akad. Nauka, Leningrad. 1-208. [In Russian. Author also as Neelov.]

NICHOLS, J. T. 1918 (16 May) **[ref. 3171]**. New Chinese fishes. Proc. Biol. Soc. Wash. v. 31: 15-20.

——. 1919 **[ref. 3172]**. Una novo genero de cascudos da familia Loricariidae. Rev. Mus. Paulista v. 11: 533-535, 539-540. [Separate, pp. 3-5, in Portugese, separate pp. 9-10 is same article in English.]

——. 1920 (24 July) **[ref. 3173]**. A contribution to the ichthyology of Bermuda. Proc. Biol. Soc. Wash. v. 33: 59-64.

——. 1921 (22 Mar.) **[ref. 3174]**. A list of Turk Islands fishes, with a description of a new flatfish. Bull. Am. Mus. Nat. Hist. v. 44 (art. 3): 21-24, Pl. 3.

——. 1922 (15 Sept.) **[ref. 3175]**. *Tekla*, a new genus of blennies, and other notes. Copeia No. 110: 67-69.

——. 1923 (19 Oct.) **[ref. 3176]**. Two new fishes from the Pacific Ocean. Am. Mus. Novit. No. 94: 1-3.

——. 1925 (22 Apr.) **[ref. 3177]**. A new homalopterin loach from Fukien. Am. Mus. Novit. No. 167: 1-2.

——. 1925 (26 May) **[ref. 3178]**. *Nemacheilus* and related loaches in China. Am. Mus. Novit. No. 171: 1-7.

——. 1925 (20 June) **[ref. 3179]**. Some Chinese fresh-water fishes. I.—Loaches of the genus *Botia* in the Yangtze Basin. II.—A new minnow-like carp from Szechwan. III.—The Chinese sucker, *Myxocyprinus*. Am. Mus. Novit. No. 177: 1-9.

——. 1925 (25 Sept.) **[ref. 3180]**. Some Chinese fresh-water fishes. X.—Subgenera of bagrin catfishes. XI.—Certain apparently undescribed carps from Fukien. XII.—A small goby from the central Yangtze. XIII.—A new minnow referred to *Leucogobio*. XIV.—Two apparently undescribed fishes from Yunnan. Am. Mus. Novit. No. 185: 1-7.

——. 1940 (11 Oct.) **[ref. 3181]**. Results of the Archbold expeditions. No. 28. A new tooth-carp from Arizona. Am. Mus. Novit. No. 1084: 1-2.

——. 1949 (7 Nov.) **[ref. 3182]**. Results of the Archbold expeditions. No. 62. Fresh-water fishes from Cape York, Australia. Am. Mus. Novit. No. 1433: 1-8.

——. 1950 (30 Mar.) **[ref. 3183]**. *Hildebrandella*, a new generic name for a carangid fish from the Philippines. Copeia 1950 (no. 1): 19-21.

——. 1955 (10 June) **[ref. 3184]**. Results of the Archbold expeditions. No. 71. Two new fresh-water fishes from New Guinea. Am. Mus. Novit. No. 1735: 1-6.

NICHOLS, J. T., AND L. GRISCOM. 1917 (26 Nov.) **[ref. 3185]**. Fresh-water fishes of the Congo basin obtained by the American Museum Congo expedition, 1909-1915. Bull. Am. Mus. Nat. Hist. v. 37 (art. 25): 653-756, Pls. 64-83.

NICHOLS, J. T., AND F. R. LA MONTE. 1931 (9 Dec.) **[ref. 3186]**. *Rheocloides*, a new atherinid fish from Madagascar. Am. Mus. Novit. No. 508: 1-2.

——. 1933 (8 Sept.) **[ref. 3187]**. New fishes from the Kasai district of the Belgian Congo. Am. Mus. Novit. No. 656: 1-6.

——. 1936 (10 Apr.) **[ref. 3188]**. *Pagothenia*, a new Antarctic fish. Am. Mus. Novit. No. 839: 1-4.

NICHOLS, J. T., AND R. C. MURPHY. 1944 (1 Aug.) **[ref. 3189]**. A collection of fishes from the Panama Bight, Pacific Ocean. Bull. Am. Mus. Nat. Hist. v. 83 (art. 4): 217-260, Pls. 15-18.

NICHOLS, J. T., AND C. H. POPE. 1927 (12 Sept.) **[ref. 5747]**. The fishes of Hainan. Bull. Am. Mus. Nat. Hist. v. 54 (art. 2): 321-394, Pl. 26.

NIELSEN, J. G. 1961 **[ref. 3193]**. On some fishes from Karachi and Bombay with description of a new genus and species of the Haliophidae. Vidensk. Medd. Dansk Naturh. Foren. Kjob. v. 123: 249-256.

——. 1963 **[ref. 3194]**. Notes on some Heterosomata (Pisces) from n.-w. South America with the description of a new genus and species and a new subspecies of Paralichthinae. Vidensk. Medd. Dansk Naturh. Foren. Kjob. v. 125: 375-400, Pls. 13-15.

——. 1969 **[ref. 3195]**. Systematics and biology of the Aphyonidae (Pisces, Ophidioidea). Galathea Rep. v. 10: 7-90, Pls. 1-4.

——. 1972 **[ref. 3196]**. Rare northeast Atlantic aphyonid fishes (Ophidioidei). Meteor Forschungsergeb. Reihe D Biol. No. 12: 52-55.

——. 1972 (June) **[ref. 3197]**. Ergebnisse de Forschungsreisen des FFS "Walther Herwig" nach Südamerika. XX. Additional notes on Atlantic Bathylaconidae (Pisces, Isospondyli) with a new genus. Arch. FischereiWiss. v. 23 (no. 1): 29-36. [German summ.]

——. 1973 **[ref. 6885]**. [Many individual family accounts.] In: Hureau & Monod 1973 [ref. 6590].

——. 1977 **[ref. 3198]**. The deepest living fish *Abyssobrotula galatheae*. A new genus and species of oviparous ophidioids (Pisces, Brotulidae). Galathea Rep. v. 14: 41-48.

——. 1980 (20 Feb.) **[ref. 6926]**. *Holcomycteronus* Garman, 1899: an ophidiid genus distinct from *Bassogigas* Goode & Bean, 1896 (Pisces, Ophidiiformes). Steenstrupia v. 6 (no. 4): 17-20.

——. 1984 (31 Mar.) **[ref. 5156]**. *Parasciadonus brevibrachium* n. gen. et sp.— an abyssal aphyonid from the central Atlantic (Pisces, Ophidiiformes). Cybium v. 8 (no. 1): 39-44.

——. 1984 (1 Aug.) **[ref. 5286]**. Two new, abyssal *Barathronus* spp. from the North Atlantic (Pisces: Aphyonidae). Copeia 1984 (no. 3): 579-584.

——. 1986 (10 Feb.) **[ref. 3199]**. *Leptobrotula breviventralis*, a new bathyal fish genus and species from the Indo-West Pacific (Ophidiiformes, Ophidiidae). Copeia 1986 (no. 1): 166-170.

——. 1986 **[ref. 5699]**. Family No. 99: Aphyonidae (pp. 356-357). In: Smiths' Sea Fishes (Smith & Heemstra 1986 [ref. 5715]).

NIELSEN, J. G., AND E. BERTELSEN. 1985 (10 Oct.) **[ref. 5255]**. The gulper-eel family Saccopharyngidae (Pisces, Anguilliformes). Steenstrupia v. 11 (no. 6): 157-206.

NIELSEN, J. G., E. BERTELSEN AND Å. JESPERSEN. 1989 **[ref. 14467]**. The biology of *Eurypharynx pelecanoides* (Pisces, Eurypharyngidae). Acta Zool. (Stockholm) v. 70 (no. 3): 187-197.

NIELSEN, J. G., AND D. M. COHEN. 1973 (27 Dec.) **[ref. 3200]**. A review of the viviparous ophidioid fishes of the genera *Bythites* Reinhardt and *Abythites* new (Pisces, Ophidioidei). Steenstrupia v. 3 (no. 8): 71-88.

——. 1986 **[ref. 5700]**. Family No. 96: Ophidiidae (pp. 345-350). In: Smiths' Sea Fishes (Smith & Heemstra 1986 [ref. 5715]).

——. 1986 **[ref. 6039]**. *Melodichthys*, a new genus with two new species of upper bathyal bythitids (Pisces, Ophidiiformes). Cybium v. 10 (no. 4): 381-387.

NIELSEN, J. G., AND S. A. EVSEENKO. 1989 (31 Mar.) **[ref. 12830]**. Larval stages of *Benthocometes robustus* (Ophidiidae) from the Mediterranean. Cybium v. 13 (no. 1): 7-12.

NIELSEN, J. G., AND J.-C. HUREAU. 1980 (5 Sept.) **[ref. 5585]**. Revision of the ophidiid genus *Spectrunculus* Jordan & Thompson, 1914, a senior synonym of *Parabassogigas* Nybelin, 1957 (Pisces, Ophidiiformes). Steenstrupia v. 6 (no 10 [= 11]): 149-169.

NIELSEN, J. G., AND Y. MACHIDA. 1985 (30 May) **[ref. 5222]**. Notes on *Barathronus maculatus* (Aphyonidae) with two records from off Japan. Jpn. J. Ichthyol. v. 32 (no. 1): 1-5.

——. 1988 (15 Dec.) **[ref. 12746]**. Revision of the Indo-Pacific bathyal fish genus *Glyptophidium* (Ophidiiformes, Ophidiidae). Jpn. J. Ichthyol. v. 35 (no. 3): 289-319.

NIJSSEN, H., AND I. J. H. ISBRÜCKER. 1976 **[ref. 7077]**. The South American plated catfish genus *Aspidoras* R. von Ihering, 1907, with descriptions of nine new species from Brazil (Pisces, Siluriformes,

Callichthyidae). Bijdr. Dierkd. v. 46 (no. 1): 107-131.

NIJSSEN, H., I. J. H. ISBRÜCKER AND J. GÉRY. 1976 [**ref. 7078**]. On the species of *Gymnorhamphichthys* Ellis, 1912, translucent sand-dwelling gymnotid fishes from South America (Pisces, Cypriniformes, Gymnotoidei). Stud. Neotrop. Fauna Environ. v. 11: 37-63.

NIJSSEN, H., AND I. J. H. ISBRÜCKER. 1980 [**ref. 6910**]. A review of the genus *Corydoras* Lacépède, 1803 (Pisces, Siluriformes, Callichthyidae). Bijdr. Dierkd. v. 50 (no. 1): 190-220.

——. 1980 [**ref. 6921**]. *Aspidoras virgulatus* n. sp., a plated catfish from Espírto Santo, Brazil (Pisces, Siluriformes, Callichthyidae). Bull. Zool. Mus. Univ. Amst. v. 7 (no. 13): 133-139.

——. 1983 [**ref. 5387**]. *Brochis britskii*, a new species of plated catfish from the Upper Rio Paraguai system, Brazil (Pisces, Siluriformes, Callichthyidae). Bull. Zool. Mus. Univ. Amst. v. 9 (no. 2): 177-186.

——. 1985 [**ref. 9706**]. *Lasiancistrus scolymus*, a new species of mailed catfish from Rio Aripuanã, est. Mato Grosso do Sul, Brazil (Pisces, Siluriformes, Loricariidae). Bijdr. Dierkd. v. 55 (no. 2): 242-248.

——. 1986 [**ref. 6010**]. Review of the genus *Corydoras* from Peru and Ecuador (Pisces, Siluriformes, Callichthyidae). Stud. Neotrop. Fauna Environ. v. 21 (no. 1-2): 1-68.

——. 1987 (25 Feb.) [**ref. 5993**]. *Spectracanthicus murinus*, nouveaux genre et espèce de poisson-chat cuirassédu Rio Tapajós, Est. Pará, Brésil, avec des remarques sur d'autres genres de Loricariidés (Pisces, Siluriformes, Loricariidae). Rev. Fr. Aquariol. v. 13 (no. 4): 93-98.

——. 1988 (21 Nov.) [**ref. 7322**]. Trois nouvelles espèces du genre *Apistoloricaria* de Colombie et du Périy, avec illustration du dimorphisme sexuel secondaire des lèvres de *A. condei* (Pisces, Siluriformes, Loricariidae). Rev. Fr. Aquariol. v. 15 (no. 2): 33-38.

NIKOLSKII, A. M. 1897 [**ref. 3201**]. Reptiles, amphibiens, and fishes collected by N. A. Zarundy in eastern Persia. Ann. Mus. Zool. Acad. Imp. Sci. St. Petersburg 1897: 306-348, Pls. 17-19. [In Russian.]

——. 1900 [**ref. 3202**]. *Pseudoscaphirhynchus rossikowi* n. gen. et spec. Ann. Mus. Zool. Acad. Imp. Sci. St. Petersburg v. 4: 257-260. [In Russian.]

——. 1903 [**ref. 3203**]. Espèces nouvelles de poissons de l'Asie orientale. Ann. Mus. Zool. Acad. Imp. Sci. St. Petersburg v. 8 (for 1903): 356-363. [In Russian. Possibly not published until 1904.]

NILSSON, S. 1832 [**ref. 3204**]. Prodromus ichthyologiae Scandinavicae. Lundae. i-iv + 1-124.

——. 1855 [**ref. 3205**]. Skandinavisk fauna. Fjerde Delen: Fiskarna. Första Häftet. Lund. 1-280. [Date on jacket is 1852. In parts, total as i-xxxiv + 1-768.]

NISHIDA, K., AND K. NAKAYA. 1988 (15 Dec.) [**ref. 12554**]. *Dasyatis izuensis*, a new stingray from the Izu Peninsula, Japan. Jpn. J. Ichthyol. v. 35 (no. 3): 227-235.

NISHIDA, M. 1988 (15 Dec.) [**ref. 12742**]. A new subspecies of the Ayu, *Plecoglossus altivelis*, (Plecoglossidae) from the Ryukyu Islands. Jpn. J. Ichthyol. v. 35 (no. 3): 236-242.

NISHIMOTO, R. T., AND J. M. FITZSIMONS. 1986 (30 May) [**ref. 6319**]. Courtship, territoriality, and coloration in the endemic Hawaiian freshwater goby, *Lentipes concolor*. Pp. 811-817. In: Uyeno et al. (eds.) 1986 [ref. 6147].

NOJIMA, S. 1936 (Dec.) [**ref. 3207**]. Description of a new genus and species of Cottidae from the western coast of Hokkaido. Trans. Sapporo Nat. Hist. Soc. v. 14 (pt 4): 246-248.

NOLAN, R. S., AND R. H. ROSENBLATT. 1975 (28 Feb.) [**ref. 6266**]. A review of the deep-sea angler fish genus *Lasiognathus* (Pisces: Thaumatichthyidae). Copeia 1975 (no. 1): 60-66.

NORDMANN, A. VON. 1838 [**ref. 3208**]. Bericht an die Kaiserliche Akademie der Wissenschaften über eine neue Fischgattung (Genus) aus der Familie der Gobioiden. Bull. Imp. Acad. Sci. St. Petersburg v. 3: 328-332.

——. 1840 [**ref. 3209**]. Observations sur la fauna pontique. In: A. de Démidoff. Voyage dans la Russie méridionale et la Crimée. Vol. III. Paris. 355-635, Atlas: 32 col. pls. [1842].

NORMAN, J. R. 1922 (Aug.) [**ref. 3210**]. Two new fishes from New Britain and Japan. Ann. Mag. Nat. Hist. (Ser. 9) v. 10 (no. 56): 217-218.

——. 1922 (Sept.) [**ref. 3211**]. A new eel from Tobago. Ann. Mag. Nat. Hist. (Ser. 9) v. 10 (no. 57): 296-297.

——. 1922 (May) [**ref. 6475**]. Fishes from Tobago. Ann. Mag. Nat. Hist. (Ser. 9) v. 9: 533-536.

——. 1923 (Jan.) [**ref. 3212**]. A revision of the clupeid fishes of the genus *Ilisha* and allied genera. Ann. Mag. Nat. Hist. (Ser. 9) v. 11 (no. 61): 1-22.

——. 1923 (Dec.) [**ref. 3213**]. A new cyprinoid fish from Tanganyika Territory, and two new fishes from Angola. Ann. Mag. Nat. Hist. (Ser. 9) v. 12 (no. 72): 694-696.

——. 1925 (May) [**ref. 6493**]. Two new fishes from Tonkin, with notes on the siluroid genera *Glyptosternum, Exostoma*, etc. Ann. Mag. Nat. Hist. (Ser. 9) v. 15: 570-575.

——. 1926 (Oct.) [**ref. 3214**]. A new blind catfish from Trinidad, with a list of the blind cave-fishes. Ann. Mag. Nat. Hist. (Ser. 9) v. 18 (no. 106): 324-331.

——. 1926 (Dec.) [**ref. 3215**]. A synopsis of the rays of the family Rhinobatidae, with a revision of the genus *Rhinobatus*. Proc. Zool. Soc. Lond. 1926 (pt 4) (no. 48): 941-982.

——. 1926 (15 June) [**ref. 3216**]. A report on the flatfishes (Heterosomata) collected by the F.I.S. "Endeavour," with a synopsis of the flatfishes of Australia and a revision of the subfamily Rhombosoleinae. Biol. Results "Endeavour" 1909-14. v. 5 (pt 5): 219-308.

——. 1927 (Apr.) [**ref. 3217**]. The flatfishes (Heterosomata) of India, with a list of the specimens in the Indian Museum. Part I. Rec. Indian Mus. (Calcutta) v. 29 (pt 1): 7-48, Pls. 2-7.

——. 1929 (Jan.) [**ref. 3218**]. The South American characid fishes of the subfamily Serrasalmoninae, with a revision of the genus *Serrasalmus*, Lacepède. Proc. Zool. Soc. Lond. 1928 (pt 4) (no. 30): 781-829, Pl. 1.

——. 1930 (Nov.) [**ref. 3219**]. Oceanic fishes and flatfishes collected in 1925-1927. Discovery Reps. v. 2: 261-370, Pl. 2.

——. 1931 (Apr.) [**ref. 3220**]. Four new fishes from the Gold Coast. Ann. Mag. Nat. Hist. (Ser. 10) v. 7 (no. 40): 352-359.

——. 1931 (Dec.) [**ref. 3221**]. Notes on flatfishes (Heterosomata).—III. Collections from China, Japan, and the Hawaiian Islands. Ann. Mag. Nat. Hist. (Ser. 10) v. 8 (no. 48): 597-604.

——. 1932 (Aug.) [**ref. 3222**]. A collection of fishes from Sierra Leone. Ann. Mag. Nat. Hist. (Ser. 10) v. 10 (no. 56): 180-185.

——. 1934 [**ref. 6893**]. A systematic monograph of the flatfishes (Heterosomata). Vol. I. Psettodidae, Bothidae, Pleuronectidae. British Mus. (Nat. Hist.). i-viii + 1-459.

——. 1935 (June) [**ref. 3223**]. Description of a new loricariid catfish from Ecuador. Ann. Mag. Nat. Hist. (Ser. 10) v. 15 (no. 90): 627-629.

——. 1935 (June) [**ref. 3224**]. The European and South African sea breams of the genus *Spondyliosoma* and related genera; with notes on *Dichistius* and *Tripterodon*. Ann. S. Afr. Mus. v. 32 (pt 1, no. 2): 5-22, Pl. 2.

——. 1935 (16 July) [**ref. 3225**]. A new percoid fish from Papua. Copeia 1935 (no. 2): 61-63.

——. 1937 (Oct.) [**ref. 3226**]. Diagnoses of new nototheniiform fishes collected by the 'Discovery' expedition. Ann. Mag. Nat. Hist. (Ser. 10) v. 20 (no. 118): 475-476.

——. 1937 (Feb.) [**ref. 3227**]. Coast fishes. Part II. The Patagonian region. Discovery Reps. v. 16: 1-150, Pls. 1-5.

——. 1938 (25 May) [**ref. 7314**]. Notes on the dates etc. of the "Memorias," "Repertorio," "Synopsis" and "Enumeratorio" of Felipe Poey. J. Soc. Bibliogr. Nat. Hist. v. 1 (pt 5): 135-137.

——. 1939 (25 Nov.) [**ref. 6556**]. Fishes. The John Murray Expedition 1933-34. Sci. Reports, John Murray Exped. v. 7 (no. 1): 1-116.

——. 1943 (Dec.) [**ref. 3228**]. Notes on the blennioid fishes.—I. A provisional synopsis of the genera of the family Blenniidae. Ann. Mag. Nat. Hist. (Ser. 11) v. 10 (no. 72): 793-812.

——. 1966 [**ref. 13535**]. A draft synopsis of the orders, families and genera of Recent fishes and fish-like vertebrates. Trustees Brit. Mus. (Nat. Hist.) London. 1-649. [Technically not an available publication for nomenclatural purposes.]

NORONHA, A. C. DI. 1926 (10 Apr.) **[ref. 3229]**. Description of a new genus and species of deep water gempyloid fish, *Diplogonurus maderensis*. Ann. Carnegie Mus. v. 16 (no. 3-4) (12): 381-383.

NORRIS, S. M., R. J. MILLER AND M. E. DOUGLAS. 1988 (18 May) **[ref. 6415]**. Distribution of *Ctenopoma muriei* and the status of *Ctenopoma ctenotis* (Pisces: Anabantidae). Copeia 1988 (no. 2): 487-491.

NOZEMAN, C. 1758 **[ref. 13433]**. Beschrijving van een zeldzamen. Uitgez. Verh. Amst. v. 3: 381-386. [Orig. not examined.]

NYBELIN, O. 1947 **[ref. 3233]**. Notice préliminaire sur quelques espèces nouvelles de poissons. Ark. Zool. v. 38 B (no. 2): 1-6.

———. 1947 **[ref. 3234]**. Antarctic fishes. Sci. Res. Norweg. Ant. Exped. 1927-1928. Oslo v. 2 (no. 26): 1-76, Pls. 1-6.

———. 1957 **[ref. 3235]**. Deep-sea bottom fishes. Rep. Swed. Deep-Sea Exped. 1947-48 v. 2 (Zool.)(no. 20): 247-345, Pls. 1-7.

———. 1979 **[ref. 3239]**. Contributions to taxonomy and morphology of the genus *Elops* (Pisces, Teleostei). Acta Regiae Soc. Sci. Litt. Gothob. Zool. Zoologica 12: 1-37, Pls. 1-3.

OGILBY, J. D. 1885 (31 July) **[ref. 3262]**. Notes and descriptions of some rare Port Jackson fishes. Proc. Linn. Soc. N. S. W. v. 10 (pt 2): 199-123, 225-232, 445-447.

———. 1888 (Apr.) **[ref. 3263]**. On a new genus of Percidae. Proc. Zool. Soc. Lond. 1887 (pt 4, art 5): 616-618.

———. 1888 (Apr.) **[ref. 3264]**. On a new genus and species of Australian Mugilidae. Proc. Zool. Soc. Lond. 1887 (pt 4, art. 4): 614-616.

———. 1888 (7 Dec.) **[ref. 3265]**. Description of a new genus and species of deep-sea fish from Lord Howe Island. Proc. Linn. Soc. N. S. W. (Ser. 2) v. 3 (pt 3): 1313.

———. 1892 (Aug.) **[ref. 3266]**. On some undescribed reptiles and fishes from Australia. Rec. Aust. Mus. v. 2 (no. 2): 23-26.

———. 1893 **[ref. 12519]**. Edible fishes and crustaceans of New South Wales. Published by the Authority of the New South Wales Commissioners for the World's Columbian Exposition, Chicago, 1893. Charles Potter, Government Printer, Sydney. i-ii + 1-212, Pls. 1-51.

———. 1894 (10 Dec.) **[ref. 3267]**. Description of five new species from the Australasian region. Proc. Linn. Soc. N. S. W. (Ser. 2) v. 9 (pt 2): 367-374.

———. 1895 (18 Nov.) **[ref. 3268]**. On two new genera and species of fishes from Australia. Proc. Linn. Soc. N. S. W. (Ser. 2) v. 10 (pt 2): 320-324.

———. 1896 (16 July) **[ref. 3269]**. On a new genus and species of fishes from Maroubra Bay. Proc. Linn. Soc. N. S. W. v. 21 (pt 1): 23-25.

———. 1896 (23 Sept.) **[ref. 3270]**. Descriptions of two new genera and species of Australian fishes. Proc. Linn. Soc. N. S. W. v. 21 (pt 2): 136-142.

———. 1897 (31 May) **[ref. 3271]**. [Rough-backed herrings, in "Notes and Exhibits" section]. Proc. Linn. Soc. N. S. W. v. 21 (pt 4): 504-505.

———. 1897 (17 Sept.) **[ref. 3272]**. New genera and species of Australian fishes. Proc. Linn. Soc. N. S. W. v. 22 (pt 1): 62-95.

———. 1897 (25 Oct.) **[ref. 3273]**. Some new genera and species of fishes. Proc. Linn. Soc. N. S. W. v. 22 (pt 2): 245-251.

———. 1897 (4 June) **[ref. 3274]**. On some Australian Eleotrinae. Proc. Linn. Soc. N. S. W. v. 22 (pt 4): 725-757.

———. 1898 (4 June) **[ref. 3275]**. A contribution to the zoology of New Caledonia. Proc. Linn. Soc. N. S. W. v. 22 (pt 4): 762-770.

———. 1898 (9 Dec.) **[ref. 3276]**. New genera and species of fishes. Proc. Linn. Soc. N. S. W. v. 23 (pt 3): 280-299 (continued from p. 41).

———. 1898 (4 June) **[ref. 3278]**. On some Australian Eleotrinae. Proc. Linn. Soc. N. S. W. v. 22 (pt 4): 783-893.

———. 1898 (23 June) **[ref. 5861]**. New genera and species of fishes. Proc. Linn. Soc. N. S. W. v. 23 (pt 1): 32-41.

———. 1899 (19 May) **[ref. 3277]**. Additions to the fauna of Lord Howe Island. Proc. Linn. Soc. N. S. W. v. 23 (pt 4): 730-745.

———. 1899 (8 Aug.) **[ref. 3279]**. Contributions to Australian ichthyology. Proc. Linn. Soc. N. S. W. v. 24 (pt 1): 154-186.

———. 1905 (8 Sept.) **[ref. 3280]**. Studies in the ichthyology of Queensland. Proc. R. Soc. Queensl. v. 18: 7-27. [Issue date from author's handwriting on separate.]

———. 1907 (1 Feb.) **[ref. 3281]**. Notes on exhibits. Proc. R. Soc. Queensl. v. 20: 27-30.

———. 1907 (1 Feb.) **[ref. 3282]**. Symbranchiate and apodal fishes new to Australia. Proc. R. Soc. Queensl. v. 20: 1-15.

———. 1907 (1 Feb.) **[ref. 3283]**. Some new pediculate fishes. Proc. R. Soc. Queensl. v. 20: 17-25.

———. 1908 (14 Oct.) **[ref. 3284]**. Revision of the Batrachoididae of Queensland. Ann. Queensl. Mus. No. 9 (pt 2): 43-57.

———. 1908 (14 Oct.) **[ref. 3285]**. New or little known fishes in the Queensland Museum. Ann. Queensl. Mus. No. 9 (pt 1): 1-41.

———. 1908 (25 Aug.) **[ref. 3286]**. On new genera and species of fishes. Proc. R. Soc. Queensl. v. 21: 1-26. [Separate issued 25 Aug. 1908.]

———. 1908 (25 Aug.) **[ref. 3287]**. Descriptions of new Queensland fishes. Proc. R. Soc. Queensl. v. 21: 87-98. [Separate issued 25 Aug. 1908.]

———. 1910 (7 Nov.) **[ref. 3288]**. On new or insufficiently described fishes. Proc. R. Soc. Queensl. v. 23: 1-55.

———. 1910 (10 Dec.) **[ref. 3289]**. On some new fishes from the Queensland coast. Endeavour Series, I. Was to have appeared as Proc. R. Soc. Queensland v. 23: 85-139. [Withdrawn and privately published.]

———. 1911 (1 Nov.) **[ref. 3290]**. Descriptions of new or insufficiently described fishes from Queensland waters. Ann. Queensl. Mus. No. 10: 36-58.

———. 1913 (10 Dec.) **[ref. 3291]**. Edible fishes of Queensland. Part I.—Family Pempheridae. Part II.—The gadopseiform percoids. Mem. Queensl. Mus. v. 2: 60-80, Pls. 18-20.

———. 1915 (28 Jan.) **[ref. 3293]**. On some new or little-known Australian fishes. Mem. Queensl. Mus. v. 3: 117-129, Pls. 29-30.

———. 1915 (28 Jan.) **[ref. 3294]**. Ichthyological notes (no. 2). Mem. Queensl. Mus. v. 3: 130-136.

———. 1916 (10 July) **[ref. 3295]**. Check-list of the Cephalochordates, Selachians, and fishes of Queensland. Mem. Queensl. Mus. v. 5: 70-99.

———. 1916 (10 July) **[ref. 3297]**. Edible fishes of Queensland. Parts IV through IX. Mem. Queensl. Mus. v. 5: 127-177, Pls. 14-23.

———. 1918 (19 Dec.) **[ref. 3298]**. Edible fishes of Queensland. Parts X through XIV. Mem. Queensl. Mus. v. 6: 45-90, Pls. 16-26.

———. 1919 (4 Aug.) **[ref. 3300]**. Alteration of generic name. Proc. R. Soc. Queensl. v. 31 (no. 5): 45.

OJEDA R., F. P. 1978 (Nov.) **[ref. 3301]**. *Apterygopectus avilesi* nuevo género y nueva especie de lenguado para aguas australes chilenas (Pisces: Pleuronectiformes). Notic. Mens. Mus. Nac. Hist. Nat. Chile v. 23 (no. 267): 3-10. [English summ.]

OKADA, Y. 1961 **[ref. 6363]**. Studies on the freshwater fishes of Japan. Prefectural University of Mei, Tsu, Mie Prefecture, Japan. "1959-1960." 1-860, Pls. 1-62. [Published in 1961 (see Hubbs 1962 [ref. 6362]).]

OKAMURA, O. 1970 **[ref. 6580]**. Fauna Japonica. Macrourina (Pisces). Academic Press of Japan. 1-216, Pls. 1-44.

OKAMURA, O., AND S. KISHIDA. 1963 (25 Mar.) **[ref. 3302]**. A new genus and species of the bembroid fish collected from the Bungo Channel, Japan. Bull. Misaki Mar. Biol. Inst. Kyoto Univ. No. 4: 43-48.

OKAMURA, O., Y. MACHIDA, K. MOCHIZUKI AND T. YAMAKAWA. 1987 (Dec.) **[ref. 6850]**. First record of the deep-sea batfish *Halieutopsis stellifera* from Japan. Rep. Usa Mar. Biol. Inst. Kochi Univ. No. 9: 201-205.

OKEN, L. 1815-16 **[ref. 6406]**. Okens Lehrbuch der Naturgeschichte. [Rejected work on Official Index (Opinion 417).]

———. 1817 **[ref. 3303]**. V. Kl. Fische. In: Isis oder Encyclopädische Zeitung. v. 8 (no. 148): 1779-1782 [for 1179-1182 + [1182a]]. [See Gill 1903: 965-967 [ref. 5768] for discussion of pagination and Cuvier's French "generic" names latinized by Oken.]

OKIYAMA, M. 1984 **[ref. 13644]**. Myctophiformes: development. Am. Soc. Ichthyol. Herpetol. Spec. Publ. No. 1: 206-218.

OKIYAMA, M., AND R. K. JOHNSON. 1986 (15 Mar.) **[ref. 5191]**. *Rosenblattichthys nemotoi*, a new species of Scopelarchidae, from the south Indian Ocean subtropical submergence zone. Jpn. J. Ichthyol. v. 32 (no. 4): 409-412.

OKIYAMA, M., AND Y. TSUKAMOTO. 1989 (20 Dec.) **[ref. 13564]**. Sea whip goby, *Bryaninops yongei*, collected from outer shelf off Miyakojima, East China Sea. Jpn. J. Ichthyol. v. 36 (no. 3): 369-370.

OLIVER, M. K., AND P. V. LOISELLE. 1972 (30 June) **[ref. 3305]**. A new genus and species of cichlid of the mbuna group (Pisces: Cichlidae) from Lake Malawi. Rev. Zool. Bot. Afr. v. 85 (no. 3-4): 309-320.

OLNEY, J. E. 1984 **[ref. 13656]**. Lampriformes: development and relationships. Am. Soc. Ichthyol. Herpetol. Spec. Publ. No. 1: 368-379.

OLNEY, J. E., AND D. F. MARKLE. 1986 **[ref. 5701]**. Family No. 97: Carapidae (pp. 350-354). In: Smiths' Sea Fishes (Smith & Heemstra 1986 [ref. 5715]).

ORTENBURGER, A. I., AND C. L. HUBBS. 1926 (1 Jan.) **[ref. 3306]**. A report on the fishes of Oklahoma, with descriptions of new genera. Proc. Okla. Acad. Sci. Pt. 1, v. 6 (art. 19): 123-141.

OSBECK, P. 1762 **[ref. 3311]**. Reise nach Ostindien und China... Deutsche Übersetzung von J. G. Georgius. Rostock. [Only 1765 version examined.]

OSBURN, R. C., E. L. WICKLIFF AND M. B. TRAUTMAN. 1930 (May) **[ref. 5943]**. A revised list of the fishes of Ohio. Ohio J. Sci. v. 30 (no. 3): 169-176.

OSHIMA, M. 1919 **[ref. 3312]**. III. Contributions to the study of the fresh water fishes of the island of Formosa. Ann. Carnegie Mus. v. 12 (nos. 2-4): 169-328, Pls. 48-53.

———. 1920 (12 July) **[ref. 3313]**. Notes on freshwater fishes of Formosa, with descriptions of new genera and species. Proc. Acad. Nat. Sci. Phila. v. 72: 120-135, Pls. 3-5.

———. 1926 (1 Feb.) **[ref. 3314]**. Notes on a collection of fishes from Hainan, obtained by Prof. S. F. Light. Annot. Zool. Jpn. v. 11 (no. 1): 1-25.

———. 1927 (31 Mar.) **[ref. 3315]**. List of flounders and soles found in the waters of Formosa, with descriptions of hitherto unrecorded species. Jpn. J. Zool. v. 1 (no. 5): 177-204.

OSÓRIO, B. 1906 **[ref. 3316]**. Description d'un poisson des profondeurs appartenant à un genre nouveau et trouvé sur les côtes du Portugal. J. Acad. Sci. Lisboa (Ser. 2) v. 7: 172-174, 1 pl.

———. 1909 **[ref. 3317]**. Contribuição para o conhecimento da fauna bathypelagica visinha das costas de Portugal. Mem. Mus. Bocage, Lisboa Fasc. 1: i-xlii + 1-35, Pls. 1-3.

———. 1909 **[ref. 13412]**. Appendice ämemoria intitulada Contribuição para o conhecimento da fauna bathypelagica visinha das costas de Portugal. Mem. Mus. Bocage, Lisboa Fasc. 1: 37-49, Pls. 1-2.

———. 1912 **[ref. 6481]**. Nova contribuição para o conhecimento da fauna bathypelagica visinha das costas de Portugal. Mem. Mus. Bocage, Lisboa v. 4: 89-93, 1 pl.

———. 1917 **[ref. 3318]**. Nota sobre algumas especies de peixes que vivem no Atlântico ocidental. Arq. Univ. Lisboa v. 1917 (no. 4): 103-131, Pls. 29-36.

OSTROUMOFF, A. A. 1896 **[ref. 3320]**. Zwei neue Relicten-Gattungen im Azow'schen Meere. Zool. Anz. v. 19 (no. 493): 30.

OTTO, A. W. 1821 **[ref. 3321]**. Ueber eine neue Roche und eine gleichfalls neue Molluske. Nova Acta Acad. Leop.-Carol. v. 10: 111-126, 2 pls. [Not seen.]

———. 1821 **[ref. 4987]**. Conspectus animalium quorundam maritimorum, etc. Inaug. Dissert. Vratislaviae. 20 pp. [Not seen.]

OWEN, R. 1839 **[ref. 3322]**. On a new species of the genus *Lepidosiren* of Fitzinger and Natterer. Proc. Linn. Soc. Lond. 1839 [v. 1]: 27-32. [Also apparently in Ann. Sci. Nat. (Zool.) (Ser. 2) v. 11: 371-378; Notizen (Froriep) v. 11: 19-23]

———. 1853 **[ref. 4988]**. Descriptive catalogue of the osteological series contained in the Museum of the Royal College of Surgeons of England. Vol. 1. Pisces, Reptilia, Aves, Marsupialia. London. 350 pp. [Not seen.]

OYARZÚN, C., AND P. W. CAMPOS. 1987 **[ref. 12877]**. *Dissostichus eleginoides* Smitt 1898; consideraciones sobre su determinación taxonómica e implicancias biogeográficas (Pisces, Perciformes, Nototheniidae). Rev. Biol. Mar., Valparaiso v. 23 (no. 2): 173-192.

OZAWA, T., AND S. MATSUI. 1979 **[ref. 6990]**. First record of the schindlerid fish, *Schindleria praematura*, from southern Japan and the South China Sea. Jpn. J. Ichthyol. v. 25 (no. 4): 283-285.

PAGE, L. M. 1974 (28 Mar.) **[ref. 3346]**. The subgenera of *Percina* (Percidae: Etheostomatinae). Copeia 1974 (no. 1): 66-86.

———. 1981 (28 May) **[ref. 3347]**. The genera and subgenera of darters (Percidae, Etheostomatini). Occas. Pap. Mus. Nat. Hist. Univ. Kans. No. 90: 1-69.

PAGE, L. M., AND B. M. BURR. 1982 (18 June) **[ref. 5462]**. Three new species of darters (Percidae, *Etheostoma*) of the subgenus *Nanostoma* from Kentucky and Tennessee. Occas. Pap. Mus. Nat. Hist. Univ. Kans. No. 101: 1-20.

PALLAS, P. S. 1810 **[ref. 3350]**. Labraces, novum genus piscium, oceani orientalis. Mem. Acad. Sci. St. Petersb. v. 2: 382-398, Pls. 22-23.

———. 1814 **[ref. 3351]**. Zoographia Rosso-Asiatica, sistens omnium animalium in extenso Imperio Rossico et adjacentibus maribus observatorum recensionem, domicilia, mores et descriptiones, anatomen atque icones plurimorum. 3 vols [1811-1814]. Petropoli. v. 3: i-vii + 1-428 + index (I-CXXV), plates. [For dates of publication see Svetovidov 1978 [ref. 6025]. Also appeared in 1931 edition. Vol. 3 published in 1814.]

PALMER, G. 1973 **[ref. 7195]**. Lamprididae (p. 328), Regalecidae (p. 329), Trachipteridae (pp. 330-332), Radiicephalidae (p. 333), Lophotidae (p. 334). In: Hureau & Monod 1973 [ref. 6590].

PALSSON, W. A., AND T. W. PIETSCH. 1989 (Dec.) **[ref. 13536]**. Revision of the acanthopterygian fish family Pegasidae (Order Gasterosteiformes). Indo-Pac. Fishes No. 18: 1-38, col. Pl. 1.

PAPACONSTANTINOU, C. A. 1984 (30 June) **[ref. 12847]**. Occurrence of *Bellottia apoda* (Fam. Brotulidae) in the Greek seas. Cybium v. 8 (no. 2): 103-104.

PAPPENHEIM, P. 1906 (Dec.) **[ref. 3360]**. Neue und ungenügend bekannte elektrische Fische (Fam. Mormyridae) aus den deutschafrikanischen Schutzgebieten. Sitzungsber. Ges. Naturf. Freunde Berlin 1906 (no. 10): 260-264.

———. 1911 **[ref. 6534]**. Neue antarktische Fische. Nach dem Material der Deutschen Südpolarexpedition 1901-1903. Sitzungsber. Ges. Naturf. Freunde Berlin v. 8: 382-383.

———. 1914 **[ref. 3361]**. II. Die Tiefseefische. Pp. 161-200, Pls. 9-10. In: Die Fische der deutschen Südpolar Expedition, 1901-1903. Dtsch. Sudpolar-Exped. 1901-1903.

PARENTI, L. R. 1981 (3 Sept.) **[ref. 7066]**. A phylogenetic and biogeographic analysis of cyprinodontiform fishes (Teleostei, Atherinomorpha). Bull. Am. Mus. Nat. Hist. v. 168 (art. 4): 335-557.

———. 1982 (5 Oct.) **[ref. 5427]**. Relationships of the African killifish genus *Foerschichthys* (Teleostei: Cyprinodontiformes: Aplocheilidae). Proc. Biol. Soc. Wash. v. 95 (no. 3): 451-457.

———. 1984 (9 May) **[ref. 5359]**. A taxonomic revision of the Andean killifish genus *Orestias* (Cyprinodontiformes, Cyprinodontidae). Bull. Am. Mus. Nat. Hist. v. 178 (art. 2): 107-214.

———. 1984 (8 Feb.) **[ref. 5379]**. On the relationships of phallostethid fishes (Atherinomorpha), with notes on the anatomy of *Phallostethus dunckeri* Regan, 1913. Am. Mus. Novit. No. 2779: 1-12.

———. 1986 (6 May) **[ref. 5192]**. Bilateral asymmetry in phallostethid fishes (Atherinomorpha) with description of a new species from Sarawak. Proc. Calif. Acad. Sci. v. 44 (no. 10): 225-236.

———. 1989 (20 Dec.) **[ref. 13486]**. A phylogenetic revision of the phallostethid fishes (Atherinomorpha, Phallostethidae). Proc. Calif. Acad. Sci. v. 46 (no. 11): 243-277.

PARENTI, L. R., AND M. RAUCHENBERGER. 1989 **[ref. 13538]**. Systematic overview of the Poeciliines. Chapter 1. Pp. 1-14. In: Meffe, G. K., and F. F. Snelson, Jr. (eds.). Ecology and evolution of livebearing fishes (Poeciliidae). Prentice Hall. 453 pp.

PARIN, N. V. 1961 **[ref. 3362]**. [Principles of classification of flying fishes (Oxyporhamphidae and Exocoetidae).] Tr. Inst. Okeanol. v. 43: 92-183. [In Russian. English translation by Laurence Penny and John H. Slep.]

———. 1967 **[ref. 10272]**. Review of marine belonids [needlefishes] of the western Pacific and Indian oceans. Tr. Inst. Okeanol. v. 84: 3-83. [In Russian. English translation available.]

———. 1973 **[ref. 7191]**. Belonidae (pp. 258-260), Scomberesocidae (pp. 261-262), Exocoetidae (pp. 263-267), Hemiramphidae (pp. 268-269). In: Hureau & Monod 1973 [ref. 6590].

———. 1979 **[ref. 3363]**. *Melanostigma (Bandichthys) vitiazi* — a new deep-sea fish (Melanostigmatidae, Osteichthyes) from the Banda Sea. Voprosy Ikhtiol. v. 19 (no. 1): 167-170. [In Russian. English translation in J. Ichthyol. v. 19 (no. 1): 150-153.]

———. 1982 **[ref. 5305]**. New species of the genus *Draconetta* and a key for the family Draconettidae (Osteichthyes). Zool. J. Moscow v. 61 (no. 4): 554-563. [In Russian, English summ.]

———. 1983 **[ref. 5304]**. *Aphanopus mikhailini* sp. n. and *A. intermedius* sp. n. (Trichiuridae, Perciformes) two new scabbardfishes from the temperate waters of the Southern Hemisphere and the tropical Atlantic. Voprosy Ikhtiol. v. 23 (no. 3): 355-364. [In Russian. English translation in J. Ichthyol. v. 23 (no. 3): 1-12.]

———. 1983 **[ref. 14141]**. *Noemacheilus (Troglocobitis) starostini* sp. n. (Osteichthyes, Cobitidae), a new blind fish from subterraneous waters of Kugitangtau (Turkmenia). Zool. Zh. v. 62: 83-89. [In Russian, English summ.]

———. 1985 (20 Feb.) **[ref. 6722]**. A new hemerocoetine fish, *Osopsaron karlik* (Percophididae, Trachinoidei) from the Nazca Submarine Ridge. Jpn. J. Ichthyol. v. 31 (no. 4): 358-361.

———. 1989 **[ref. 12753]**. A review of the genus *Rexea* (Gempylidae) with descriptions of three new species. Voprosy Ikhtiol. v. 29 (no. 1): 3-23. [In Russian.]

———. 1989 **[ref. 14116]**. *Zenopsis oblongus* sp. n. (Zeidae, Osteichthyes) from the Nuska Ridge. Zool. Zh. v. 68 (no. 4): 150-153. [In Russian, English abst.]

PARIN, N. V., AND A. A. ABRAMOV. 1986 **[ref. 6006]**. Materials for a revision of the genus *Epigonus* Rafinesque (Perciformes, Epigonidae): species from the submarine ridges of the southern East Pacific and preliminary review of the "*Epigonus robustus* species-group." Trans. Shirshov Inst. Oceanol. v. 121: 173-194.

PARIN, N. V., AND D. A. ASTAKHOV. 1987 **[ref. 9146]**. *Rexichthys johnpaxtoni*—a new fish of the family Gempylidae from the Tasman Sea. Voprosy Ikhtiol. v. 27 (no. 1): 149-151. [In Russian. English translation in J. Ichthyol. v. 27 (no. 2): 154-157.]

PARIN, N. V., AND V. E. BEKKER. 1973 **[ref. 7206]**. Gempylidae (pp. 457-460), Scombrolabracidae (p. 461), Trichiuridae (pp. 462-464). In: Hureau & Monod 1973 [ref. 6590].

PARIN, N. V., AND O. D. BORODULINA. 1986 **[ref. 6005]**. Preliminary review of the bathypelagic fish genus *Antigonia* Lowe (Zeiformes, Caproidae). Trans. Shirshov Inst. Oceanol. v. 121: 141-172. [In Russian, English summ.]

PARIN, N. V., B. B. COLLETTE AND YU. N. SHCHERBACHEV. 1980 **[ref. 6895]**. Preliminary review of the marine halfbeaks (Hemiramphidae, Beloniformes) of the tropical Indo-West-Pacific. Trans. Shirshov Inst. Oceanol. v. 97: 7-173. [In Russian, English Summ.]

PARIN, N. V., AND A. W. EBELING. 1980 (1 Feb.) **[ref. 5523]**. A new western Pacific *Poromitra* (Pisces: Melamphaidae). Copeia 1980 (no. 1): 87-93.

PARIN, N. V., AND A. N. KOTLYAR. 1988 **[ref. 13518]**. A new armorhead species, *Pentaceros quinquespinis* (Pentacerotidae), from the southeast Pacific. Voprosy Ikhtiol. v. 28 (no. 3): 355-360. [In Russian. English translation in J. Ichthyol. v. 28 (no. 4): 79-84.]

———. 1989 (15 Mar.) **[ref. 12748]**. A new aulopodid species, *Hime microps*, from the eastern South Pacific, with comments on geographic variations of *H. japonica*. Jpn. J. Ichthyol. v. 35 (no. 4): 407-413.

PARIN, N. V., AND N. S. NOVIKOVA. 1974 **[ref. 7528]**. Taxonomy of viperfishes (Chauliodontidae, Osteichthyes) and their distribution in the world ocean. Tr. Inst. Okeanol. v. 96: 255-315. [In Russian, English summ.]

PARIN, N. V., AND YU. YE. PERMITIN. 1969 **[ref. 3365]**. Materials on the pelagic fish fauna of the Antarctic. A new genus of stromateoid fishes — *Pseudoicichthys* (Pisces, Centrolophidae). Voprosy Ikhtiol. v. 9 (no. 6): 981-987. [In Russian. English translation in Problems Ichthyol. v. 9 (no. 6): 789-794.]

PARIN, N. V., AND Y. N. SHCHERBACHEV. 1982 (27 Feb.) **[ref. 5344]**. Two new argentine fishes of the genus *Glossanodon* from the eastern South Pacific. Jpn. J. Ichthyol. v. 28 (no. 4): 381-384.

PARR, A. E. 1927 (20 Aug.) **[ref. 3366]**. Ceratioidae. Scientific results of the third oceanographic expedition of the "Pawnee" 1927. Bull. Bingham Oceanogr. Collect. Yale Univ. v. 3 (art. 1): 1-34.

———. 1927 (30 Dec.) **[ref. 3367]**. The Stomiatoid fishes of the suborder Gymnophotodermi (Astronesthidae, Melanostomiatidae, Idiacanthidae) with a complete review of the species. (Scientific Results of the third oceanographic expedition of the "Pawnee" 1927.) Bull. Bingham Oceanogr. Collect. Yale Univ. v. 3 (art. 2): 1-123.

———. 1928 (Dec.) **[ref. 3368]**. Deepsea fishes of the order Iniomi from the waters around the Bahama and Bermuda islands. With annotated keys to the Sudididae, Myctophidae, Scopelarchidae, Evermannellidae, Omosudidae, Cetomimidae and Rondeletidae of the world. Bull. Bingham Oceanogr. Collect. Yale Univ. v. 3 (art. 3): 1-193.

———. 1929 (Feb.) **[ref. 3369]**. A contribution to the osteology and classification of the orders Iniomi and Zenoberyces. With description of a new genus and species of the family Scopelarchidae, from the western coast of Mexico; and some notes on the visceral anatomy of *Rondeletia* Occas. Pap. Bingham Ocean. Coll. No. 2: 1-45.

———. 1930 (July) **[ref. 3370]**. Teleostean shore and shallow-water fishes from the Bahamas and Turks Island. (Scientific results of the third oceanographic expedition of the "Pawnee" 1927.) Bull. Bingham Oceanogr. Collect. Yale Univ. v. 3 (art. 4): 1-148.

———. 1931 (Oct.) **[ref. 3371]**. Deepsea fishes from off the western coast of North and Central America. With keys to the genera *Stomias*, *Diplophos*, *Melamphaes* and *Bregmaceros*, and a revision of the *Macropterus* group of the genus *Lampanyctus*. Bull. Bingham Oceanogr. Collect. Yale Univ. v. 2 (art. 4): 1-53.

———. 1931 (28 Dec.) **[ref. 3372]**. A substitute name for *Dolichodon* Parr, a genus of deep-sea fishes. Copeia 1931 (no. 4): 162.

———. 1933 (Dec.) **[ref. 3373]**. Deepsea Berycomorphi and Percomorphi from the waters around the Bahama and Bermuda islands. (Scientific results of the third oceanographic expedition of the "Pawnee" 1927.) Bull. Bingham Oceanogr. Collect. Yale Univ. v. 3 (art. 6): 1-51.

———. 1933 (27 Dec.) **[ref. 3374]**. Two new records of deep sea fishes from New England with description of a new genus and species. Copeia 1933 (no. 4): 176-179.

———. 1934 (Sept.) **[ref. 3375]**. Report on experimental use of a triangular trawl for bathypelagic collecting with an account of the fishes obtained and a revision of the family Cetomimidae. Bull. Bingham Oceanogr. Collect. Yale Univ. v. 4 (art. 6): 1-59.

———. 1937 (Aug.) **[ref. 3376]**. Concluding report on fishes. With species index for articles 1-7 (fishes of the third oceanographic expedition of the "Pawnee"). Bull. Bingham Oceanogr. Collect. Yale Univ. v. 3 (art. 7): 1-79.

———. 1945 (15 Oct.) **[ref. 3377]**. Barbourisidae, a new family of deep sea fishes. Copeia 1945 (no. 3): 127-129, Pl. 1.

———. 1946 (Nov.) **[ref. 3378]**. The Macrouridae of the western North Atlantic and Central American seas. Bull. Bingham Oceanogr. Collect. Yale Univ. v. 10 (art. 1): 1-99.

———. 1947 (20 Apr.) **[ref. 3379]**. A new genus of deepsea fish from

the Gulf of Panama. Copeia 1947 (no. 1): 59-61.
———. 1951 (24 July) **[ref. 3380]**. Preliminary revision of the Alepocephalidae, with the introduction of a new family, Searsidae. Am. Mus. Novit. No. 1531: 1-21.
———. 1952 (Sept.) **[ref. 3381]**. Revision of the species currently referred to *Alepocephalus*, *Halisauriceps*, *Bathytroctes* and *Bajacalifornia* with introduction of two new genera. Bull. Mus. Comp. Zool. v. 107 (no. 4): 255-269.
———. 1953 (4 Sept.) **[ref. 3382]**. A new genus of Searsidae from Japan. Am. Mus. Novit. No. 1628: 1-7.
———. 1954 (27 Apr.) **[ref. 3383]**. Review of the deep-sea fishes of the genus *Asquamiceps* Zugmayer, with descriptions of two new species. Am. Mus. Novit. No. 1655: 1-8.
———. 1960 (1 Sept.) **[ref. 3384]**. The fishes of the family Searsidae. Dana Rep. No. 51: 1-109.
PARRA, D. A. 1787 **[ref. 6840]**. Descripcion de differentes piezas de historia natural, las mas del ramo maritimo, representadas en setenta y cinco laminas. Havana. 1-195, Pls. 1-73.
PATTEN, J. M., AND W. IVANTSOFF. 1983 (10 Mar.) **[ref. 5424]**. A new genus and species of atherinid fish, *Dentatherina merceri* from the western Pacific. Jpn. J. Ichthyol. v. 29 (no. 4): 329-339.
PATTERSON, C., AND A. E. LONGBOTTOM. 1989 (27 Dec.) **[ref. 13507]**. An Eocene amiid fish from Mali, West Africa. Copeia 1989 (no. 4): 827-836.
PAUGY, D. 1984 (Feb.) **[ref. 6183]**. Characidae (pp. 140-184). In: Daget et al. 1984 [ref. 6168].
———. 1987 (30 Dec.) **[ref. 6738]**. Description de deux nouvelles espèce de *Synodontis* du bassin du Konkouré (Guinée), *S. dekimpei* et *S. levequei* (Pisces, Mochokidae). Cybium v. 11 (no. 4): 357-364.
PAULIN, C. D. 1979 **[ref. 6918]**. New Zealand roughies (Pisces: Berycomorphii: Trachichthyidae). N. Z. J. Zool. v. 6: 69-76.
———. 1983 (20 Jan.) **[ref. 5459]**. A revision of the family Moridae (Pisces: Anacanthini) within the New Zealand region. Natl. Mus. N. Z. Rec. v. 2 (no. 9): 81-126.
———. 1986 **[ref. 5326]**. A new genus and species of deepwater codfish (Pisces: Moridae) from New Zealand. N. Z. J. Zool. v. 12 (no. 3) [1985]: 357-361.
———. 1986 (30 May) **[ref. 5327]**. A new genus and species of morid fish from shallow coastal waters of southern Australia. Mem. Mus. Victoria v. 47 (no. 2): 201-206.
———. 1989 **[ref. 9297]**. Review of the morid genera *Gadella*, *Physiculus*, and *Salilota* (Teleostei: Gadiformes) with descriptions of seven new species. N. Z. J. Zool. v. 16: 93-133.
PAULIN, C. D., AND J. M. MORELAND. 1979 **[ref. 6915]**. *Congiopodus coriaceus*, a new species of pigfish, and a redescription of *C. leucopaecilus* (Richardson), from New Zealand (Pisces: Congiopodidae). N. Z. J. Zool. v. 6: 601-608.
PAULIN, C. D., AND C. D. ROBERTS. 1989 **[ref. 12435]**. A new genus and species of bythitid fish (Teleostei: Ophidiiformes) from New Zealand. J. Nat. Hist. v. 23: 355-361.
PAVLENKO, M. N. 1910 **[ref. 3393]**. Fishes of Peter the Great Bay. Tr. Obsc. Jest, Kazani v. 42 (no. 2): 1-95, pls. [In Russian.]
PAVLOV, A., W. IVANTSOFF, P. R. LAST AND L. E. L. M. CROWLEY. 1988 **[ref. 12285]**. *Kestratherina brevirostris*, a new genus and species of silverside (Pisces: Atherinidae) with a review of atherinid marine and estuarine genera of southern Australia. Aust. J. Mar. Freshwater Res. v. 39: 385-397.
PAXTON, J. R. 1972 (28 July) **[ref. 3394]**. Osteology and relationships of the lanternfishes (family Myctophidae). Nat. Hist. Mus. Los Ang. Cty. Sci. Bull. No. 13: 1-81.
———. 1973 **[ref. 7183]**. Mirapinnidae (p. 212), Eutaeniophoridae (p. 213), Cetomimidae (p. 214), Ateleopodidae (p. 215). In: Hureau & Monod 1973 [ref. 6590].
———. 1975 (3 Oct.) **[ref. 3395]**. *Heraldia nocturna*, a new genus and species of pipefish (family Syngnathidae) from eastern Australia, with comments on *Maroubra perserrata* Whitley. Proc. Calif. Acad. Sci. v. 40 (no. 15): 439-447.
———. 1979 (31 Dec.) **[ref. 6440]**. Nominal genera and species of lanternfishes (Family Myctophidae). Contrib. Sci. (Los Ang.) No. 322: 1-28.
———. 1989 **[ref. 13435]**. Synopsis of the whalefishes (family Cetomimidae) with descriptions of four new genera. Rec. Aust. Mus. v. 41: 135-206.
PAXTON, J. R., E. H. AHLSTROM AND H. G. MOSER. 1984 **[ref. 13625]**. Myctophidae: Relationships. Am. Soc. Ichthyol. Herpetol. Spec. Publ. No. 1: 239-244.
PAXTON, J. R., AND D. J. BRAY. 1986 **[ref. 5703]**. Order Cetomimiformes (pp. 433-434). In: Smiths' Sea Fishes (Smith & Heemstra 1986 [ref. 5715]).
PAXTON, J. R., D. F. HOESE, G. R. ALLEN AND J. E. HANLEY. 1989 **[ref. 12442]**. Zoological Catalogue of Australia. Volume 7. Pisces. Petromyzontidae to Carangidae. Australian Government Publishing Service, Canberra. i-xii + 1-665.
PEARSON, N. E. 1924 (Dec.) **[ref. 3396]**. The fishes of the eastern slope of the Andes. I. The fishes of the Rio Beni basin, Bolivia, collected by the Mulford expedition. Ind. Univ. Studies v. 11 (no. 64): 1-83, 12 pls.
PEDEN, A. E. 1978 **[ref. 5530]**. A systematic revision of the hemilepidotine fishes (Cottidae). Syesis v. 11: 11-49.
———. 1981 **[ref. 5512]**. Recognition of *Leuroglossus schmidti* and *L. stilbius* (Bathylagidae, Pisces) as distinct species in the North Pacific Ocean. Can. J. Zool. v. 59 (no. 12): 2396-2398.
———. 1984 **[ref. 5193]**. Redefinition of *Icelinus fimbriatus* and *I. oculatus* (Cottidae, Pisces), and their corrected geographic distributions, with a new key to the genus. Syesis v. 17: 67-80.
PEDEN, A. E., AND M. E. ANDERSON. 1981 **[ref. 5531]**. *Lycodapus* (Pisces: Zoarcidae) of eastern Bering Sea and nearby Pacific Ocean, with three new species and a revised key to the species. Can. J. Zool. v. 59 (no. 4): 667-678.
PEDEN, A. E., AND G. W. HUGHES. 1988 **[ref. 12855]**. Sympatry in four species of *Rhinichthys* (Pisces), including the first documented occurrences of *R. umatilla* in the Canadian drainages of the Columbia River. Can. J. Zool. v. 66 (no. 8): 1846-1856.
PELLEGRIN, J. 1900 **[ref. 3397]**. Poissons nouveaux ou rares du Congo Français. Bull. Mus. Natl. Hist. Nat. (Ser. 1) v. 6 (no. 4): 177-182.
———. 1900 **[ref. 3398]**. Poisson nouveau du lac Baïkal. Bull. Mus. Natl. Hist. Nat. (Ser. 1) v. 6: 354-356.
———. 1900 **[ref. 6253]**. Poissons nouveaux ou rares du Congo Français. Bull. Mus. Natl. Hist. Nat. (Ser. 1) v. 6 (no. 7): 348-354. [Possibly published in 1901.]
———. 1904 **[ref. 3419]**. Contribtution á l'étude anatomique, biologique et taxinomique des poissons de la famille des Cichlidés. Mem. Soc. Zool. Fr. v. 16 (nos. 3-4): 41-400, Pls. 4-7. [Although dated 1903, apparently published in 1904.]
———. 1905 **[ref. 3420]**. Poisson nouveau de Mozambique. Bull. Mus. Natl. Hist. Nat. (Ser. 1) v. 11 (no. 3): 145-146.
———. 1907 **[ref. 3422]**. Siluridé nouveau du Fouta-Djalon. Bull. Mus. Natl. Hist. Nat. (Ser. 1) v. 13 (no. 1): 23-25.
———. 1909 (Jan.) **[ref. 3423]**. Characinidés amëricains nouveaux de la collection du Muséum d'Histoire Naturelle. Bull. Mus. Natl. Hist. Nat. (Ser. 1) v. 14 (no. 7)[1908]: 342-347.
———. 1909 **[ref. 3424]**. Characinidés du Brésil, rapportés par M. Jobert Bull. Mus. Natl. Hist. Nat. (Ser. 1) v. 15 (no. 4): 147-153.
———. 1912 (26 Nov.) **[ref. 3426]**. Poissons des côtes de l'Angola. Mission de M. Gruvel. (4th note). Bull. Soc. Zool. Fr. v. 37: 290-296.
———. 1913 **[ref. 3427]**. Poisson des côtes de Mauritanie. Mission de M. Gruvel. Bull. Soc. Zool. Fr. v. 38: 116-118.
———. 1913 **[ref. 3401]**. Sur un nouveau genre de Centrarchidés du Gabon. C. R. Hebd. Seances Acad. Sci. v. 156 (no. 19): 1488-1489.
———. 1922 (27 Mar.) **[ref. 3402]**. Sur un nouveau poisson aveugle des eaux douces de l'Afrique occidentale. C. R. Hebd. Seances Acad. Sci. v. 174: 884-885.
———. 1922 **[ref. 5028]**. Poissons de l'Oubanghi-Chari recueillis par M. Baudon. Description d'un genre, de cinq espèces et d'une variété. Bull. Soc. Zool. Fr. v. 47: 64-76.

———. 1923 [**ref. 3403**]. Les poissons des eaux douces de l'Afrique occidentale (du Sénégal au Niger). Gouv. Gén. l'Afrique Occ. Fr., Pub. Com. d'Etud. Hist. Sci. Paris: 1-373.

———. 1926 (1 Apr.) [**ref. 3404**]. Description de Characinidés nouveaux récoltés au Congo Belge par le Dr. Schouteden. Rev. Zool. Afr. v. 13: 157-164.

———. 1927 (15 Sept.) [**ref. 3407**]. Mormyridés du Cameroun recueillis par M. Th. Monod. Description d'un genre, de quatre espèces et d'une varíté. Bull. Soc. Zool. Fr. v. 52 (for 1927): 294-300.

———. 1927 (1 Apr.) [**ref. 3408**]. Description de Cichlidés et d'un Mugilidé nouveaux du Congo Belge. Rev. Zool. Bot. Afr. v. 15 (no. 1): 52-57.

———. 1927 (30 Jan.) [**ref. 3405**]. Characinidé nouveaux du Cameroun recueilli par M. Th. Monod. Bull. Soc. Zool. Fr. v. 51 (for 1926): 390-392.

———. 1927 (30 Mar.) [**ref. 5042**]. Description d'un cyprinidé nouveau d'Asie Mineure. Bull. Soc. Zool. Fr. v. 52 (for 1927): 34-35.

———. 1928 (1 July) [**ref. 3409**]. Mutanda ichthyologica: *Clupeocharax* Pellegrin. Rev. Zool. Bot. Afr. v. 16 (no. 1): 82.

———. 1928 [**ref. 3410**]. Poisson du Kasai (Congo Belge). Description d'un genre nouveau et de quatre espèces nouvelles. Bull. Soc. Zool. Fr. v. 53: 103-113.

———. 1928 (Aug.) [**ref. 3411**]. Poissons du Chiloango et du Congo recueillis par l'expédition du Dr. H. Schouteden (1920-1922). Zool. - Ser. I. Matériaux pour la faune du Congo. Ann. Mus. Congo Belge v. 3 (fasc. 1): 1-49.

———. 1929 [**ref. 3412**]. Sur un poisson cavernicole africain microphthalme. C. R. Hebd. Seances Acad. Sci. v. 189 (no. 4): 204-205.

———. 1933 [**ref. 3413**]. Voyage de Ch. Alluaud et P. A. Chappuis en Afrique occidentale Française (Dec. 1930—Mars 1931). IV. Poissons. Arch. Hydrobiol. v. 26: 101-120.

———. 1934 (9 Jan.) [**ref. 3414**]. Description d'un poisson nouveau de la cote occidentale d'Afrique de la famille des Muraenesocidés. Bull. Soc. Zool. Fr. v. 59: 45-48.

———. 1935 (5 Dec.) [**ref. 5041**]. Poissons de la région du Kivu récoltés par M. Guy Babault. Rev. Zool. Bot. Afr. v. 27 (no. 3): 376-385.

———. 1936 (28 Apr.) [**ref. 3415**]. Poissons nouveaux du haut-Laos et de l'Annam. Bull. Soc. Zool. Fr. v. 61: 243-248.

PELLEGRIN, J., AND P. W. FANG. 1935 [**ref. 3416**]. A new homalopteroid, ***Paraprotomyzon multifasciatus***, from eastern Szechuan, China nov. gen. nov. sp. Sinensia v. 6 (no. 2): 99-106.

———. 1940 [**ref. 3418**]. Poissons du Laos recueillis par Mm. Delacour, Greenway, Ed. Blanc description d'un genre, de cinq espèce et d'une variété. Bull. Soc. Zool. Fr. v. 65: 111-123.

PENG, Y.-B., AND Z.-R. ZHAO. 1988 (Dec.) [**ref. 13758**]. A new genus and a new species of Chinese anchovies. J. Fish. China v. 12 (no. 4): 355-358. [In Chinese and English.]

PENRITH, M. J. 1972 (8 June) [**ref. 7140**]. Earliest description and name for the whale shark. Copeia 1972 (no. 2): 362.

———. 1973 (7 June) [**ref. 7143**]. A new species of *Parakneria* from Angola (Pisces: Kneriidae). Cimbebasia (Ser. A) v. 2 (no. 11): 131-135.

PEQUEÑO, G. 1980 (July) [**ref. 5422**]. *Mendosoma lineata* Guichenot 1848: Comentarios sobre su taxonomía y sequndo registro en Chile (Teleostomi, Latridae). Noticiario Mensuai Year 24 (no. 285): 3-7.

———. 1986 (15 Mar.) [**ref. 6718**]. Comments on fishes from the Diego Ramirez Islands, Chile. Jpn. J. Ichthyol. v. 32 (no. 4): 440-442.

———. 1989 [**ref. 14125**]. Peces de Chile. Lista sistematica revisada y comentada. Rev. Biol. Mar. Valparaiso v. 24 (no. 2): 1-132.

PEQUEÑO, G., R. NAVARRO AND J. OPORTO. 1988 [**ref. 12550**]. *Discopyge tschudii* Heckel 1845: aporte a su taxonomia con hincapie en su dimorfismo secual (Chondrichthyes, Narcinidae). Estud. Oceanol. v. 7: 41-50.

PEQUEÑO, G., AND R. PLAZA. 1987 (Dec.) [**ref. 6629**]. Descripcion de *Paralichthys delfini* n. sp., con notas sobre otros lenguados congenericos de Chile (Pleuronectiformes, Bothidae). Rev. Biol. Mar., Valparaiso v. 23 (no. 2): 159-172.

PERRY, G. 1811 (Feb.) [**ref. 12255**]. Ichthyology. In: Arcana; or The Museum of Natural History: containing the most recent discovered objects... London. 2 unnum. pp., 1 unnum. pl.

PERUGIA, A. 1891 (6-11 Apr.) [**ref. 3431**]. Appunti sopra alcuni pesci sud-americani conservati nel Museo Civico di Storia Naturale di Genova. Ann. Mus. Civ. Stor. Nat. Genova (Ser. 2) v. 10: 605-657.

———. 1892 (14 Dec.) [**ref. 3432**]. Descrizione di due nuove specie di pesci raccolti in Sarawak dai Sig. G. Doria ed O. Beccari. Ann. Mus. Civ. Stor. Nat. Genova (Ser. 2) v. 12: 1009-1010.

———. 1892 (27 June) [**ref. 3433**]. Intorno ad alcuni pesci raccolti al Congo dal Capitano Giacomo Bove. Ann. Mus. Civ. Stor. Nat. Genova (Ser. 2) v. 10: 967-977.

———. 1893 (6 May) [**ref. 3434**]. Di alcuni pesci raccolti in Sumatra dal Dott. Elio Modigliani. Ann. Mus. Civ. Stor. Nat. Genova (Ser. 2) v. 13: 241-247.

———. 1894 (30 Sept.) [**ref. 3435**]. Viaggio di Lamberto Loria nella Papuasia orientale. XIII. Pesci d'acqua dolce. Ann. Mus. Civ. Stor. Nat. Genova (Ser. 2) v. 14: 546-553.

———. 1897 (26 July) [**ref. 3436**]. Di alcuni pesci raccolti nell' alto Paraguay dal Cav. Guido Boggiani. Ann. Mus. Civ. Stor. Nat. Genova (Ser. 2) v. 18: 147-150.

PETERS, W. (C. H.). 1844 [**ref. 3447**]. Über einem den *Lepidosiren annectens* verwandten, mit Lungen und Kiemen zugleich versehenen Fisch aus den Sümpfen von Quellimane vor. Monatsb. Akad. Wiss. Berlin for 1844: 411-414. [Also in Ann. Mag. Nat. Hist. 16: 348-350 (1845); Arch. Anat. (Müller) 1845: 1-14, 3 pls.; L'Institut 13: 217-218.]

———. 1844 [**ref. 13442**]. Einige neue Fische und Amphibien aus Angola und Mossambique. Monatsb. Akad. Wiss. Berlin 1844: 32-37.

———. 1846 [**ref. 3448**]. Ueber eine neue Gattung von Labyrinthfischen aus Quellimane. Arch. Anat. (Müller) for 1846 (pt 4): 480-482, Pl. 10. [In English in Peters 1847, Ann. Mag. Nat. Hist. v. 19: 384-385, Pl. 11.]

———. 1847 [**ref. 6176**]. On a new genus of Labyrinthi-bronchial fish from Quellimane. Ann. Mag. Nat. Hist. v. 19 (no. 128): 384-385, Pl. 11. [A translation of Peters 1846 [ref. 3448].]

———. 1854 [**ref. 13481**]. Mittheilung über die Süsswasserfische von Mossambique. Monatsb. Akad. Wiss. Berlin for 1853: 783.

———. 1855 [**ref. 3449**]. Übersicht der in Mossambique beobachteten Seefische. Monatsb. Akad. Wiss. Berlin for 1855: 428-466. [Nearly the same in Arch. Naturgesch. v. 21 (pt 1): 234-282 [see ref. 13448]; and as a separate, Berlin 1855: 41 pp.]

———. 1855 [**ref. 13448**]. Uebersicht der in Mossambique beobachteten Fische. Arch. Naturgeschichte v. 21 (pt. 1): 234-282. [Nearly the same text as Peters 1855 [ref. 3449], but *Acanthopagrus* is in this one and not in ref. 3449.]

———. 1858 [**ref. 3450**]. [Neue Gattung von Chromiden.] Monatsb. Akad. Wiss. Berlin for 1857: 403. [From Aug. 1857 meeting, assumed published in 1858.]

———. 1861 [**ref. 3451**]. Über zwei neue Gattungen von Fischen aus dem Ganges. Monatsb. Akad. Wiss. Berlin for 1861: 712-713.

———. 1864 [**ref. 3437**]. Berichtete über einige neue Säugethiere ... Amphibien ... und Fische ... Monatsb. Akad. Wiss. Berlin for 1864: 381-399.

———. 1864 [**ref. 3438**]. Über eine neue Percoidengattung, *Plectroperca*, aus Japan und eine neue Art von Haifischen, *Crossorhinus tentaculatus*, aus Neuholland. Monatsb. Akad. Wiss. Berlin for 1864: 121-126.

———. 1866 (23 July) [**ref. 3439**]. Mittheilung über Fische (*Protopterus, Auliscops, Labrax, Labracoglossa, Nematocentris, Serranus, Scorpis, Opisthognathus, Scombresox, Acharnes, Anguilla, Gymnomuraena, Chilorhinus, Ophichthys, Helmichthys*). Monatsb. Akad. Wiss. Berlin for 1866: 509-526, 1 pl.

———. 1868 **[ref. 3440]**. Naturwissenschaftliche Reise nach Mossambique auf befehl Seiner Mäjestat des Königs Friedrich Wilhelm IV in den jahren 1842 bis 1848 Ausgeführt. Zoologie. IV. Flussfische. i-viii + 1-116, Pls. 1-20.

———. 1868 **[ref. 3442]**. Über die von Hrn. Dr. F. Jagor in dem ostindischen Archipel gesammelten und dem Königl. zoologischen Museum übergebenen Fische. Monatsb. Akad. Wiss. Berlin for 1868: 254-281. [Continued as pp. 460-461.]

———. 1868 **[ref. 3443]**. Ueber eine von dem Baron Carl von der Decken entdeckte neue Gattung von Welsen, *Chiloglanis deckenii*, und einige andere Süsswasserfische aus Ostafrika. Monatsb. Akad. Wiss. Berlin for 1868: 598-602, Pl. 2.

———. 1868 **[ref. 7935]**. Über eine neue Untergattung der Flederthiere, so wie über neue Gattungen und Arten von Fischen. Monatsb. Akad. Wiss. Berlin for 1868: 145-148, 454-460.

———. 1872 **[ref. 3452]**. Über eine neue Gattung von Fischen aus der Familie der Cataphracti Cuv., *Scombrocottus salmoneus*, von der Vancouvers-Insel. Monatsb. Akad. Wiss. Berlin for 1872: 568-570.

———. 1876 **[ref. 3453]**. Über eine neue, mit *Halieutaea verwandte* Fischgattung, *Dibranchus*, aus dem atlantischen Ocean. Monatsb. Akad. Wiss. Berlin for 1875: 736-742, 1 pl. [Read 25 Nov. 1975, evidently published in 1876.]

———. 1877 **[ref. 3454]**. Übersicht der während der von 1874 bis 1876 unter der Commando des Hrn. Capitän z. S. Freiherrn von Schleinitz ausgeführten Reise S. M. S. Gazelle gesammelten und von der Kaiserlichen Admiralität der Königlichen Akademie der Wissenschaften übersandten Fische. Monatsb. Akad. Wiss. Berlin for 1876: 831-854.

———. 1877 **[ref. 3445]**. Über eine merkwürdige von Hrn. Professor Dr. Buchholz entdeckte neue Gattung von Süsswasserfischen, *Pantodon buchholzi*, welche zugleich eine neue, den *Malacopterygii abdominales* angehörige Gruppe von Fischen, *Pantodontes*, repräsentirt. Monatsb. Akad. Wiss. Berlin for 1876: 195-200, 1 pl. [Read 13 Mar. 1876, apparently published in 1877.]

———. 1880 **[ref. 3455]**. Über die von der chinesischen Regierung zu der internationalen Fischerei-Austellung gesandte Fischsammlung aus Ningpo. Monatsb. Akad. Wiss. Berlin for 1880: 921-927. [Probably published in 1881.]

———. 1880 (13 Dec.) **[ref. 3456]**. Ueber eine Sammlung von Fischen, welche Dr. Gerlach in Hongkong gesandt hat. Monatsb. Akad. Wiss. Berlin for 1880: 1029-1037, 1 pl. [Possibly published in 1881.]

PETERSON, M. S., AND S. T. ROSS. 1987 (Dec.) **[ref. 6231]**. Morphometric and meristic characteristics of a peripheral population of *Enneacanthus*. Proc. Southeast Fish. Council No. 17: 1-4.

PETIT, G. 1933 **[ref. 3457]**. Un poisson cavernicole aveugle des eaux douces de Madagascar: *Typhleotris madagascariensis* gen. et sp. nov. C. R. Hebd. Seances Acad. Sci. v. 197 (no. 4): 347-348.

PEZOLD, F., AND C. R. GILBERT. 1987 (11 Feb.) **[ref. 6777]**. Two new species of the gobiid fish genus *Gobionellus* from the western Atlantic. Copeia 1987 (no. 1): 169-175.

PEZOLD, F., AND J. M. GRADY. 1989 **[ref. 13579]**. A morphological and allozymic analysis of species in the *Gobionellus oceanicus* complex (Pisces: Gobiidae). Bull. Mar. Sci. v. 45 (no. 3): 648-663.

PFAFF, J. R. 1942 (May) **[ref. 3459]**. Papers from Dr. Th. Mortensen's Pacific expedition 1914-16. LXXI. On a new genus and species of the family Gobiesocidae from the Indian Ocean, with observations on sexual dimorphism in the Gobiesocidae, and on the connection of certain gobiesocids with echinids. Vidensk. Medd. Dansk Naturh. Foren. Kjob. v. 105: 413-422.

PFEFFER, G. J. 1889 **[ref. 3460]**. Übersicht der von Herrn Dr. Franz Stuhlmann in Ägypten, auf Sanzibar und dem gegenüberliegenden Festlande gesammelten Reptilien, Amphibien, Fische, Mollusken und Krebse. Jahrb. Wiss. Anst. Hamburg v. 6 (art. 4): 1-36.

———. 1893 **[ref. 3461]**. Ostafrikanische Fische gesammelt von Herrn Dr. F. Stuhlmann in Jahre 1888 und 1889. Jahrb. Wiss. Anst. Hamburg v. 10: 131-177, 3 pls. [Also as a separate, pp. 1-49, Pls. 1-3. Proofed from separate.]

PHILIPPI, R. A. 1857 **[ref. 3462]**. Ueber einige Chilenische Vögel und Fische. Arch. Naturgeschichte v. 23 (no. 1): 262-272.

———. 1858 **[ref. 3463]**. Beschreibung neuer Wirbelthiere aus Chile. Arch. Naturgeschichte v. 24 (no. 1): 303-311.

———. 1887 **[ref. 3464]**. Historia natural.—Sobre los tiburones i algunos otros peces de Chile. [Plus:] Apendice sobre el peje-espada, peje-aguja, peje-perro i vieja negra. An. Univ. Santiago Chile Sec. 1, v. 71: 1-42, 535-574, Pls. 1-8. [Also as a separate, Santiago, 1887: 42 pp., 8 pls.]

———. 1896 **[ref. 3465]**. Peces nuevos de Chile. An. Univ. Chile, Mem. Cient. Lit. Santiago 93-95: 375-390.

PHILLIPPS, W. J. 1924 (July) **[ref. 3466]**. *Agrostichthys*, a new genus of ribbon fishes. Proc. Zool. Soc. Lond. 1924 (pt 2) (no. 24): 539-540.

———. 1926 **[ref. 6447]**. New or rare fishes of New Zealand. Trans. N. Z. Inst. v. 56: 529-537.

———. 1941 (Dec.) **[ref. 3467]**. New or rare fishes of New Zealand. Trans. Proc. R. Soc. N. Z. v. 71 (pt 3): 241-246, Pls. 40-41.

PIETSCH, T. W. 1969 (3 June) **[ref. 3471]**. A remarkable new genus and species of deep-sea angler-fish (family Oneirodidae) from off Guadalupe Island, Mexico. Copeia 1969 (no. 2): 365-369.

———. 1973 (22 May) **[ref. 3472]**. A new genus and species of deep-sea anglerfish (Pisces: Oneirodidae) from the northern Pacific Ocean. Copeia 1973 (no. 2): 193-199.

———. 1974 (22 May) **[ref. 5332]**. Systematics and distribution of ceratioid anglerfishes of the family Oneirodidae with a review of the genus *Oneirodes* Lütken. Sci. Bull. Nat. Hist. Mus., Los Angeles Co. No. 18: 1-113.

———. 1974 (28 June) **[ref. 7116]**. Systematics and distribution of ceratioid anglerfishes of the genus *Lophodolos* (family Oneirodidae). Breviora No. 425: 1-19.

———. 1975 (23 May) **[ref. 7120]**. Systematics and distribution of ceratioid anglerfishes of the genus *Chaenophryne* (family Oneirodidae). Bull. Mus. Comp. Zool. v. 147 (no. 2): 75-99.

———. 1978 (22 May) **[ref. 3473]**. A new genus and species of ceratioid anglerfish from the North Pacific Ocean with a review of allied genera *Ctenochirichthys*, *Chirophryne* and *Leptacanthichthys* (family Oneirodidae). Contrib. Sci. (Los Ang.) No. 297: 1-35.

———. 1978 (5 May) **[ref. 5322]**. The feeding mechanism of *Stylephorus chordatus* (Teleostei: Lampridiformes): functional and ecological implications. Copeia 1978 (no. 2): 255-262.

———. 1979 (16 Mar.) **[ref. 3474]**. Systematics and distribution of ceratioid anglerfishes of the family Caulophrynidae with the description of a new genus and species from the Banda Sea. Contrib. Sci. (Los Ang.) No. 310: 1-25.

———. 1981 **[ref. 5540]**. The osteology and relationships of the anglerfish genus *Tetrabrachium* with comments on lophiiform classification. U. S. Natl. Mar. Fish. Serv. Fish. Bull. v. 79 (no. 3): 387-419.

———. 1984 (23 Feb.) **[ref. 5378]**. A review of the frogfish genus *Rhycherus* with the description of a new species from Western and South Australia. Copeia 1984 (no. 1): 68-72.

———. 1984 (23 Feb.) **[ref. 5380]**. The genera of frogfishes (family Antennariidae). Copeia 1984 (no. 1): 27-44.

———. 1986 **[ref. 5704]**. Family No. 102: Antennariidae (pp. 366-369), No. 105: Ceratiidae (pp. 373-375), No. 106: Oneirodidae (p. 375), No. 107: Melanocetidae (pp. 375-376), No. 108: Himantolophidae (p. 376), No. 109: Diceratiidae (pp. 376-377). In: Smiths' Sea Fishes (Smith & Heemstra 1986 [ref. 5715]).

———. 1986 (10 Feb.) **[ref. 5950]**. The original manuscript sources for the Histoire Naturelle des Poissons, 1828-1849; keys to understanding the fishes described by Cuvier and Valenciennes. Copeia 1986 (no. 1): 216-219.

———. 1986 (9 May) **[ref. 5969]**. Systematics and distribution of bathypelagic anglerfishes of the family Ceratiidae (order: Lophiiformes). Copeia 1986 (no. 2): 479-493.

———. 1989 (23 May) **[ref. 12541]**. Phylogenetic relationships of trachinoid fishes of the family Uranoscopidae. Copeia 1989 (no. 2):

253-303.

Pietsch, T. W., M.-L. Bauchot and M. Desoutter. 1986 **[ref. 6339]**. Catalogue critique des types de poissons du Muséum national d'-Histoire naturelle. (Suite) Ordre des Lophiiformes. Bull. Mus. Natl. Hist. Nat. Sect. A Zool. Biol. Ecol. Anim. v. 8 (no. 4) suppl.: 131-156.

Pietsch, T. W., and R. H. Kuiter. 1984 (13 July) **[ref. 5194]**. A new species of frogfish of the genus *Echinophryne* (family Antennariidae) from southern Australia. Rev. Fr. Aquariol. v. 11 (no. 1): 23-26.

Pietsch, T. W., and R. J. Lavenberg. 1980 (5 Dec.) **[ref. 6913]**. A fossil ceratoid anglerfish from the Late Miocene of California. Copeia 1980 (no. 4): 906-908.

Pietsch, T. W., and J. P. Van Duzer. 1980 **[ref. 5333]**. Systematics and distribution of ceratioid anglerfishes of the family Melanocetidae with the description of a new species from the eastern North Pacific Ocean. U. S. Natl. Mar. Fish. Serv. Fish. Bull. v. 78 (no. 1): 59-87.

Pietschmann, V. 1926 **[ref. 3475]**. Ein neuer Tiefseefisch aus der Ordnung der Pediculati. Anz. Akad. Wiss. Wien v. 63 (no. 11): 88-89.

——. 1930 **[ref. 3476]**. *Phrynichthys wedli* Pietschm., nov. gen. et spec., ein Tiefsee-Piediculate. Ann. Naturf. Mus. Wien v. 44: 419-422.

——. 1935 **[ref. 3477]**. Eine neue Aalfamilie aus den hawaiischen Gewässern. Anz. Akad. Wiss. Wien v. 72 (no. 11): 93-94.

Pinna, M. C. C. de. 1989 (9 Aug.) **[ref. 12630]**. A new Sarcoglanidine catfish, phylogeny of its subfamily, and an appraisal of the phyletic status of the Trichomycterinae (Teleostei, Trichomycteridae). Am. Mus. Novit. No. 2950: 1-39.

——. 1989 (30 Nov.) **[ref. 13515]**. Redescription of *Glanapteryx anguilla*, with notes on the phylogeny of Glanapteryginae (Siluriformes, Trichomycteridae). Proc. Acad. Nat. Sci. Phila. v. 141: 361-374.

Pinto, S. Y. 1960 (2 Aug.) **[ref. 3479]**. Um nova Gobiidae do Estado da Bahia, Brasil (Acanthopterygii - Perciformes). Bol. Mus. Nac. Rio de J. Zool. (n. s.) No. 218: 1-9.

——. 1965 **[ref. 3480]**. Observações ictiológicas. I. Novo gênero e nova espécie de Clinidae (Actinopterygii). Atas Soc. Biol. Rio de J. v. 9 (no. 2): 15-17.

——. 1970 **[ref. 3481]**. *Jopaica* "nomen novum" para *Springeria* Carvalho & Pinto, 1965. (Actinoperygii, Perciformes, Dactyloscopidae). Atas Soc. Biol. Rio de J. v. 12 (Suppl.): 47.

——. 1970 **[ref. 3482]**. Observações ictiológicas. VI. *Antobrantia*, nôvo gênero de ofictídeo do Brasil (Actinopterygii, Anguilliformes, Ophichthyidae). Atas Soc. Biol. Rio de J. v. 14 (no. 1-2): 13-15.

Plate, L. H. 1897 **[ref. 3489]**. Ein neuer Cyclostom mit grossen, normal entwickelten Augen, *Macrophthalmia chilensis*, n. g. n. sp. Sitzungsber. Ges. Naturf. Freunde Berlin 1897: 137-141.

Playfair, R. L. 1866 **[ref. 3490]**. Acanthopterygii. In: R. L. Playfair & A. C. Günther, The fishes of Zanzibar, with a list of the fishes of the whole east coast of Africa. London. i-xix + 1-80, Pls. 1-21.

Poey, F. 1851-54 **[ref. 3497]**. Memorias sobre la historia natural de la Isla de Cuba, acompañadas de sumarios Latinos y extractos en Francés. La Habana. v. 1: 1-463, Pls. 1-34. [For dates of publication of parts see Norman 1938 [ref. 7314]; published Nov. 1851 - June 1854.]

——. 1858-61 **[ref. 3499]**. Memorias sobra la historia natural de la Isla de Cuba, acompañadas de sumarios Latinos y extractos en Francés. La Habana. [Sections have subtitles.] v. 2: 1-96 (1858), 97-336 (1860), 337-442, (1861), Pls. 1-19. [For dates see remarks under ref. 3497 above.]

——. 1865-66 **[ref. 3502]**. Various subtitles in: Repertorio fisico-natural de la Isla de Cuba. La Habana. v. 1: 1-420. [For dates of publication of sections see Norman 1938 [ref. 7314].]

——. 1866-68 **[ref. 3503]**. Various subtitles in: Repertorio fisico-natural de la isla de Cuba. La Habana. [Poey's "Synopsis piscium Cubensium" is pp. 279-484 of this work, but is listed separately as ref. 3505.] v. 2: 1-468 [484]. [For dates of sections see Norman 1938 [ref. 7314].]

——. 1868 **[ref. 3505]**. Synopsis piscium cubensium. Catalogo Razonado de los peces de la isla de Cuba. Repertor. Fisico-natural de la Isla de Cuba v. 2: 279-484. [For dates of sections see Norman 1938 [ref. 7314].]

——. 1871 **[ref. 3506]**. Genres de poissons de la fauna de Cuba, appartenant à la famille Percidae, avec une note d'introduction par J. Carson Brevoort. Ann. Lyc. Nat. Hist. N. Y. v. 10 (no. 1-3) (3): 27-79, Pl. 1.

——. 1872 (May) **[ref. 3508]**. Monographie des poissons de Cuba compris dans la sous-famille de Sparini. Ann. Lyc. Nat. Hist. N. Y. v. 10 (no. 6-7) (10): 170-184, Pls. 6-7.

——. 1873 **[ref. 3507]**. *Grammicolepis brachiusculus*, tipo de una nueva familia en la clase de los peces. An. Soc. Esp. Hist. Nat. Madrid v. 2: 403-406, Pl. 12.

——. 1875 (7 Apr.) **[ref. 3509]**. Enumeratio piscium cubensium. An. Soc. Esp. Hist. Nat. Madrid v. 4: 75-161, Pls. 1-3. [Continues as additional parts in same journal. Also as separate, pp. 1-87.]

——. 1876 (May/Oct.) **[ref. 3510]**. Enumeratio piscium cubensium (Parte Segunda). An. Soc. Esp. Hist. Nat. Madrid v. 5: 131-176 (3 May) 177-218 (4 Oct.), Pls. 4-9. [Part 3 continues in v. 5: 373-404 (Publ. 31 Dec. 1876); Part 4, Index in v. 6: 209-224 (1877).]

——. 1877 **[ref. 4937]**. Enumeratio piscium cubensium. An. Soc. Esp. Hist. Nat. Madrid v. 6: 139-154.

——. 1880 **[ref. 6524]**. Revisio piscium Cubensium. An. Soc. Esp. Hist. Nat. Madrid v. 9: 243-261, Pls. 6-10.

——. 1881 **[ref. 3511]**. Peces. Pp. 317-350, Pl. 6. In: J. Gundlach. Apuntes para la fauna puerto-riqueña. Tercera parte. An. Soc. Esp. Hist. Nat. Madrid v. 10. Pl. 6.

Poll, M. 1939 (Dec.) **[ref. 3513]**. Les poissons du Stanley-Pool. Ann. Mus. Congo Belge (Ser. 1) v. 4 (no. 1): 1-60.

——. 1942 (30 Apr.) **[ref. 3514]**. Description d'un genre nouveau de Bagridae du lac Tanganika. Rev. Zool. Bot. Afr. v. 35 (no. 3): 318-322.

——. 1942 (14 Aug.) **[ref. 3515]**. Description d'un genre nouveau de Clariidae du Congo belge. Rev. Zool. Bot. Afr. v. 36 (no. 1): 94-100.

——. 1942 **[ref. 3516]**. Cichlidae nouveaux du lac Tanganika appartenant aux collections du Musée du Congo. Rev. Zool. Bot. Afr. v. 36 (no. 4): 343-360.

——. 1943 (31 Aug.) **[ref. 3517]**. Description du *Tanganikallabes mortiauxi*, gen. nov., sp. n., de la famille des Clariidae. Rev. Zool. Bot. Afr. v. 37 (no. 1-2): 126-133.

——. 1943 (30 Dec.) **[ref. 3518]**. Descriptions de poissons nouveaux du lac Tanganika, appartenant aux familles des Clariidae et Cichlidae. Rev. Zool. Bot. Afr. v. 37 (No. 3-4): 305-318.

——. 1948 (3 July) **[ref. 3519]**. Descriptions de Cichlidae nouveaux recueillis par le Dr. J. Schwetz dans la rivière Fwa (Congo belge). Rev. Zool. Bot. Afr. v. 41 (no. 1): 91-104, Pl. 21.

——. 1950 (28 Oct.) **[ref. 3520]**. Description de deux Cichlidae pétricoles du lac Tanganika. Rev. Zool. Bot. Afr. v. 43 (no. 4): 292-302.

——. 1954 **[ref. 12591]**. Poissons Cichlidae. In: Exploration Hydrobiologique du Lac Tanganika (1946-1947). Résultats scientifiques. Inst. R. Sci. Nat. Belgique v. 3 (fasc. 5 B): 1-619, 10 Pls.

——. 1958 (12 July) **[ref. 3521]**. Description d'un poisson aveugle nouveau du Congo belge, appartenant à la famille des Mastacembelidae. Rev. Zool. Bot. Afr. v. 57 (no. 3-4): 388-392.

——. 1959 **[ref. 3522]**. Resultats scientifiques des missions zoologiques au Stanley Pool subsidiées par le Cemubac (Université Libre de Bruxelles) et la Musée Royal du Congo (1957-1958). III. Recherches sur la faune ichthyologique de la région du Stanley Pool. Ann. Mus. Congo Belge (Ser. 8) v. 71: 75-174, Pls. 12-26. [Also issued as a book.]

——. 1964 **[ref. 3523]**. Une famille dulcicole nouvelle de poissons africains: les Congothrissidae. Acad. R. Sci. Outre Mer, Cl. Sci. Nat. Méd. (n. s.) v. 15 (no. 2): 1-40, Pls. 1-8.

———. 1965 (30 Dec.) **[ref. 3525]**. Un genre nouveau de Clupeidae (Pellonulinae) du bassin central du Congo. Rev. Zool. Bot. Afr. v. 72 (pts 3-4): 309-315.

———. 1965 (3 July) **[ref. 3526]**. Contribution a l'étude des Kneriidae et description d'un nouveau genre, le genre *Parakneria* (Pisces, Kneriidae). Mem. Acad. R. Belg. Cl. Sci. (Ser. 8) v. 36 (fasc. 4): 1-28, Pls. 1-16.

———. 1966 (30 Dec.) **[ref. 3527]**. Genre et espèce nouveaux de Bagridae du fleuve Congo en région de Léopoldville. Rev. Zool. Bot. Afr. v. 74 (pts 3-4): 425-428.

———. 1967 **[ref. 3528]**. Contribution à la faune ichthyologique de l'Angola. Publ. Cult. Cia. Diamantes Angola No. 75: 11-381, Pls. 1-20.

———. 1967 (Dec.) **[ref. 3529]**. Revision des Characidae nains Africans. Ann. Mus. R. Afr. Cent. (Ser. 8) Zool. No. 162: 1-158.

———. 1971 **[ref. 3530]**. Un genre nouveau et une espèce nouvelle de Cyprinodontidae congolais. Rev. Zool. Bot. Afr. v. 83 (pts 3-4): 302-308.

———. 1971 (31 July) **[ref. 3531]**. Revision systématique des daurades du genre *Dentex* de la côte africaine tropicale occidentale et de la Méditerranée. Mem. Acad. R. Belg. Cl. Sci. (Ser. 2) v. 40 (no. 1): 1-51.

———. 1974 (29 Mar.) **[ref. 3532]**. Contribution à la faune ichthyologique du lac Tanganika, d'après les récoltes de P. Brichard. Rev. Zool. Afr. v. 88 (no. 1): 99-110.

———. 1977 **[ref. 3533]**. Les genres nouveaux *Platyallabes* et *Platyclarias* comparés au genre *Gymnallabes* Gthr. Synopsis nouveau des genres de Clariidae. Bull. Acad. R. Belg. Cl. Sci. (Ser. 5) v. 63 (no. 2): 122-149.

———. 1981 **[ref. 3534]**. Contribution a la faune ichthyologique du lac Tanganika. Révision du genre *Limnochromis* Regan, 1920. Description de trois genres nouveaux et d'une espèce nouvelle: *Cyprichromis brieni*. Ann. Soc. R. Zool. Belg. v. 111 (nos. 1-4): 163-179. [English summ.]

———. 1983 (31 Mar.) **[ref. 6498]**. Mutanda ichthyologica. *Greenwoodochromis* nom. nov. Cybium v. 7 (no. 1): 46.

———. 1984 (Feb.) **[ref. 6180]**. Kneriidae (pp. 129-133), Cromeriidae (p. 134), Grasseichthyidae (p. 135). In: Daget et al. 1984 [ref. 6168].

———. 1986 **[ref. 6136]**. Classification des Cichlidae du lac Tanganika. Tribus, genres et especes. Mem. Cl. Sci. Acad. R. Belg. (Ser. 2) v. 45 (no. 2): 1-163.

———. 1987 (30 June) **[ref. 6746]**. Un genre enédit pour une espèce nouvelle du lac Tanganyika: *Trematochromis schreyeni* gen. nov., sp. n. Statut de *Tilapia trematocephala* Blgr, 1901. Cybium v. 11 (no. 2): 167-172.

Poll, M., and J.-G. Lambert. 1965 **[ref. 3535]**. Contribution a l'étude systématique et zoogéographique des Procatopodinae de l'Afrique centrale (Pisces, Cyprinodontidae). Bull. Séanc. Acad. R. Sci. Outre Mer 1965: 615-631, 2 pls.

Poll, M., B. Lanza and A. Romoli Sassi. 1972 (15 Dec.) **[ref. 3536]**. Genre nouveau extraordinaire de Bagridae du fleuve Juba: *Pardiglanis tarabinii* gen. n. sp. n. (Pisces Siluriformes). Monit. Zool. Ital. Suppl. 4 (no. 15): 327-345, 3 pls. [In Italian, English summ.]

Poll, M., and N. LeLeup. 1965 **[ref. 3537]**. Un poisson aveugle nouveau de la famille des Brotulidae provenant des îles Galapagos. Bull. Acad. R. Belg. Cl. Sci. (Ser. 5) v. 51 (no. 4): 464-474, Pls. 1-2.

Poll, M., G. G. Teugels and P. J. P. Whitehead. 1984 (Feb.) **[ref. 6172]**. Clupeidae (pp. 41-55). In: Daget et al. 1984 [ref. 6168].

Poll, M., and D. F. E. Thys van den Audenaerde. 1974 (29 Mar.) **[ref. 3539]**. Genre nouveau *Triglachromis* proposé pour *Limnochromis otostigma* Regan, Cichlidae du lac Tanganika (Pisces Cichlidae). Rev. Zool. Afr. v. 88 (no. 1): 127-130.

Poll, M., P. J. P. Whitehead and A. J. Hopson. 1965 (6 Mar.) **[ref. 3524]**. A new genus and species of clupeoid fish from West Africa. Bull. Acad. R. Belg. Cl. Sci. (Ser. 5) v. 51: 277-292.

Polunin, N. V. C., and R. Lubbock. 1977 **[ref. 3540]**. Prawn-associated gobies (Teleostei: Gobiidae) from the Seychelles, western Indian Ocean: systematics and ecology. J. Zool. (Lond.) v. 183 (pt 1): 63-101.

Popov, A. M. 1930 (July) **[ref. 3545]**. A short review of the fishes of the family Cyclopteridae. Ann. Mag. Nat. Hist. (Ser. 10) v. 6 (no. 31): 69-76.

———. 1930 **[ref. 6576]**. Mullets of Europe (Mugilidae) with descriptions of a new species form the Pacific Ocean. Trudy Sevastopol. Biol. Sta. v. 2: 47-125, Pls. 1-4. [In Russian, English summ. (pp. 116-124).]

———. 1931 **[ref. 3543]**. Cyclopteridae (Pisces) recueillis par l'expédition hydrographique de l'océan Pacifique dans la mer d'Okhotsk. Bull. Acad. Sci. URSS, Leningrad (Ser. 7) 1931 (no. 1): 85-99. [In Russian, new taxa diagnoses in English.]

———. 1931 **[ref. 3544]**. Sur un nouveau genre de Poissons *Davidijordania* (Zoarcidae, Pisces) en Pacifique. C. R. Acad. Sci. Leningrad 1931: 210-215. [In Russian, English abst.]

———. 1931 **[ref. 5702]**. Contribution to the study of the ichthyofauna of the Okhotsk Sea. Issled. Morei SSSR v. 14: 121-154. [In Russian.]

———. 1931 **[ref. 12552]**. [The fish fauna of the Sea of Okhotsk.] Explor. Mers. URSS No. 14: 121-154, 2 pls. [In Russian, German summ.]

———. 1933 **[ref. 6535]**. Ichthyofauna of the Sea of Japan. Explor. Mers. URSS Inst. Hyd. No. 19: 139-155. [In Russian, German summ. Not seen.]

———. 1935 **[ref. 3546]**. A new genus and species, *Lycozoarces hubbsi*, gen. n. sp. n. (Pisces, Zoarcidae), of the Okhotsk Sea. C. R. (Doklady) Acad. Sci. U.R.S.S. (n. s.) v. 4 (no. 6-7): 303-304.

Popta, C. M. L. 1904 **[ref. 3547]**. Descriptions préliminaires des nouvelles espèces de poissons recueillies au Bornéo central par M. le Dr. A. W. Nieuwenhuis en 1898 et en 1900. Notes Leyden Mus. v. 24 (for 1902-04): 179-202.

———. 1905 **[ref. 3549]**. Descriptions préliminaires des nouvelles espèces de poissons recueillies au Bornéo central par M. le Dr. A. W. Nieuwenhuis en 1898 et en 1900. Notes Leyden Mus. v. 25 (note 15): 171-186.

———. 1922 **[ref. 3550]**. Vierte und letzte fortsetzung der Beschreibung von neuen Fischarten der Sunda-Expedition. Zool. Meded. (Leiden) v. 7: 27-39.

Posada, A. 1909 **[ref. 5005]**. Los peces. Pp. 285-322. In: Estudios cientificos del doctor Andres Posada con algunos otros escritos suyos sobre diversos temas. Medellin, Colombia. [Overall work is pp. 1-432.]

Poss, S. G. 1982 (27 Feb.) **[ref. 5474]**. A new aploactinid fish of the genus *Kanekonia* from Indonesia and redescription of *K. florida*. Jpn. J. Ichthyol. v. 28 (no. 4): 375-380.

———. 1986 **[ref. 6296]**. Family No. 150: Tetrarogidae (p. 479), Family No. 151: Aploactidae (pp. 479-480), Family No. 152: Congiopodidae (pp. 480-481). In: Smiths' Sea Fishes (Smith & Heemstra 1986 [ref. 5715]).

———. 1986 (30 May) **[ref. 6331]**. The systematic position of the scorpaenoid fish *Eschmeyer nexus* and the interrelationships of the *Cocotropus*-stem scorpaenoids [Abstract]. P. 955. In: Uyeno et al. (eds.) 1986 [ref. 6147].

Poss, S. G., and G. R. Allen. 1987 **[ref. 6616]**. New Australian fishes. Part 18. A new species of *Cocotropus* (Aploactinidae). Mem. Mus. Victoria v. 48 (no. 1): 79-82.

Poss, S. G., and W. N. Eschmeyer. 1975 **[ref. 6388]**. The Indo-West Pacific scorpionfish genus *Ocosia* Jordan and Starks (Scorpaenidae, Tetraroginae), with description of three new species. Matsya No. 1: 1-18.

———. 1978 (28 Dec.) **[ref. 6387]**. Two new Australian velvetfishes, genus *Paraploactis* (Scorpaeniformes: Aploactinidae), with a revision of the genus and comments on the genera and species of the Aploactinidae. Proc. Calif. Acad. Sci. v. 41 (no. 18): 401-426.

———. 1979 (15 June) **[ref. 3552]**. *Prosoproctus pataecus*, a new genus and species of velvetfish from the South China Sea (Aploactinidae: Scorpaeniformes). Jpn. J. Ichthyol. v. 26 (no. 1): 11-14.

———. 1980 (2 July) **[ref. 3553]**. *Xenaploactis*, a new genus for

Prosopodasys asperrimus Günther (Pisces: Aploactinidae), with descriptions of two new species. Proc. Calif. Acad. Sci. v. 42 (no. 8): 287-293.

Poss, S. G., and R. R. Miller. 1983 (10 Feb.) **[ref. 14470]**. Taxonomic status of the plains killifish, *Fundulus zebrinus*. Copeia 1983 (no. 1): 55-67.

Poss, S. G., and V. G. Springer. 1983 (7 July) **[ref. 5394]**. *Eschmeyer nexus*, a new genus and species of scorpaenid fish from Fiji. Proc. Biol. Soc. Wash. v. 96 (no. 2): 309-316.

Post, A. 1969 (July) **[ref. 3554]**. Ergebisse der Forschungsreisen des FFS "Walther Herwig" nach Südamerika. VIII. *Dolichosudis fuliginosa* gen. nov. spec. nov. (Osteichthyes, Iniomi, Paralepididae). Arch. FischereiWiss. v. 20 (no. 1): 15-21.

——. 1973 **[ref. 7182]**. Paralepididae (pp. 203-210). In: Hureau & Monod 1973 [ref. 6590].

——. 1976 (Feb.) **[ref. 5541]**. Ergebnisse der Forschungsreisen des FFS "Walther Herwig" nach Südamerika. XLII. *Diretmus* Johnson 1863 (Beryciformes, Berycoidei, Diretmidae). 2. Morphologie, Entwicklung, Verbreitung. Arch. FischereiWiss. v. 26 (no. 2/3): 87-114.

——. 1980 (Mar.) **[ref. 5577]**. Results of the research cruises of FRV "Walther Herwig" to South America. LIV. New records of extremely rare paralepidids from the South Atlantic (Osteichthyes, Myctophiformes, Alepisauroidei). Arch. FischereiWiss. v. 30 (no. 2/3): 121-124.

——. 1986 **[ref. 5705]**. Family No. 81: Paralepididae (pp. 274-278), Family No. 130: Diretmidae (pp. 414-415). In: Smiths' Sea Fishes (Smith & Heemstra 1986 [ref. 5715]).

——. 1987 (Dec.) **[ref. 6225]**. Results of the research cruises of FRV "Walther Herwig" to South America. LXVII. Revision of the subfamily Paralepidinae (Pisces, Aulopiformes, Alepisauroidei, Paralepididae). I. Taxonomy, morphology and geographical distribution. Arch. FischereiWiss. v. 38 (no. 1/2): 75-131.

Post, A., and J.-C. Quéro. 1981 **[ref. 3555]**. Révision des Diretmidae (Pisces, Trachichthyoidei) de l'Atlantique avec description d'un nouveau genre et d'une nouvelle espèce. Cybium (Ser. 3) v. 5 (no. 1): 33-60.

Postel, E. 1973 **[ref. 7208]**. Scombridae (pp. 465-466), Thunnidae (pp. 467-472), Scomberomoridae (pp. 473-475). In: Hureau & Monod 1973 [ref. 6590].

Prashad, B., and D. D. Mukerji. 1929 **[ref. 3558]**. The fish of the Indawgyi Lake and the streams of the Myitkyina District (Upper Burma). Rec. Indian Mus. (Calcutta) v. 31 (pt 3): 161-223, Pls. 7-10.

Prince, J. D., W. Ivantsoff and I. C. Potter. 1982 (June) **[ref. 5417]**. *Atherinosoma wallacei*, a new species of estuarine and inland water silverside (Teleostei: Atherinidae) from the Swan-Avon and Murray rivers, Western Australia. Aust. Zool. v. 21 (pt 1): 63-74.

Ptchelina, Z. M. 1939 **[ref. 3566]**. *Relictogobius kryzhanovskii* n. g. n. sp., un nouveau Gobiidé provenant d'un lac salé de la presqu'île Abraou (bassin de la Mer Noire). C. R. (Doklady) Acad. Sci. U.R.S.S. (n. s.) v. 23 (no. 6): 586-589.

Putnam, F. W. 1863 **[ref. 3567]**. List of the fishes sent by the museum to different institutions, in exchange for other specimens, with annotations. Bull. Mus. Comp. Zool. v. 1 (art. 1): 2-16. [Preface by Agassiz, but authorship is Putnam.]

Pylaie, M. de la. 1835 **[ref. 1086]**. Recherches en France, sur les poissons de l'océan, pendant les années 1832 et 1833. In: Mem. Congr. Sci. France, 2nd Sess., Poitiers, 1834. Rouen. 524-534. [Not seen.]

Pyle, R. L. 1988 (Sept.) **[ref. 6613]**. A new subspecies of butterflyfish (Chaetodontidae) of the genus *Roaops* from Christmas Island, Line Islands. Freshwater Mar. Aquar. v. 11 (no. 9): 56-59, 62, 123.

Quensel, C. 1806 **[ref. 3569]**. Försök att närmare bestämma och naturligare uppställa svenska arterna af flunderslägte. K. Sven. Vetenskapsakad. Handl. v. 27: 44-56 (continues on pp. 203-233).

Quéro, J.-C. 1973 **[ref. 7196]**. Grammicolepididae (p. 351). In: Hureau & Monod 1973 [ref. 6590].

——. 1976 **[ref. 9342]**. *Somniosus bauchotae* sp. nov. (Selachi, Squalidae, Scymnorhininae) espèce nouvelle de l'Atlantique N. O. Rev. Trav. Inst. Peches Marit. v. 39 (no. 4): 455-469.

Quéro, J.-C., D. A. Hensley and A. L. Maugé. 1988 (30 Dec.) **[ref. 12837]**. Pleuronectidae de l'île de la Réunion et de Madagascar. I. *Poecilopsetta*. Cybium v. 12 (no. 4): 321-330.

——. 1989 (30 June) **[ref. 12826]**. Pleuronectidae de l'île de la Réunion et de Madagascar. II. Genres *Samaris* et *Samariscus*. Cybium v. 13 (no. 2): 105-114.

Quoy, J. R. C., and J. P. Gaimard. 1824-25 **[ref. 3574]**. Description des Poissons. Chapter IX. In: Freycinet, L. de, Voyage autour du Monde...exécuté sur les corvettes de L. M. "L'Uranie" et "La Physicienne," pendant les années 1817, 1818, 1819 et 1820. Paris. 192-401 [1-328 in 1824; 329-616 in 1825], Atlas pls. 43-65. [See Whitley 1943:136-137 [ref. 4702] for route and localities; for dates see Sherborn & Woodward 1901:392 [ref. 13447].]

——. 1834 **[ref. 3573]**. Poissons. In: Voyage de découvertes de "l'Astrolabe," executeé par ordre du Roi, pendant les années 1826-29, sous le commandement de M. J. Dumont d'Urville. Paris. v. 3: 645-720, Poissons pls. 1-20.

Radcliffe, L. 1912 (31 Jan.) **[ref. 3576]**. Descriptions of fifteen new fishes of the family Cheilodipteridae, from the Philippine Islands and contiguous waters. Proc. U. S. Natl. Mus. v. 41 (no. 1868): 431-446, Pls. 34-38.

——. 1912 (30 Apr.) **[ref. 3577]**. New pediculate fishes from the Philippine Islands and contiguous waters. Proc. U. S. Natl. Mus. v. 42 (no. 1896): 199-214, Pls. 16-27.

——. 1912 (27 Sept.) **[ref. 3578]**. Descriptions of a new family, two new genera, and twenty-nine new species of anacanthine fishes from the Philippine Islands and contiguous waters. Proc. U. S. Natl. Mus. v. 43 (no. 1924): 105-140, Pls. 22-31.

——. 1913 (3 Apr.) **[ref. 3579]**. Descriptions of seven new genera and thirty-one new species of fishes of the families Brotulidae and Carapidae from the Philippine Islands and the Dutch East Indies. Proc. U. S. Natl. Mus. v. 44 (no. 1948): 135-176, Pls. 7-17.

Radda, A. C. 1969 **[ref. 6078]**. *Fundulosoma thierryi* und ihre Verwandten. Aquaria v. 3: 159-164. [Also as a separate, pp. 1-5.]

——. 1971 **[ref. 9343]**. Cyprinodontidenstudien im südliche Kamerun. 2. Das Tiefland der Küste. Aquaria v. 5: 109-121.

——. 1977 **[ref. 3580]**. Vorläufige Beschreibung von vier neuen subgenera der Gattung *Aphyosemion* Myers. Aquaria v. 24 (no. 12): 209-216.

Radda, A. C., and M. K. Meyer. 1981 **[ref. 5875]**. Revalidisierung der gattung *Xenophallus* Hubbs (Poeciliidae, Osteichthyes). Aquaria v. 28: 115-118.

Radda, A. C., and E. Pürzl. 1987 **[ref. 12592]**. *Episemion callipteron*, a new killifish from north Gabon. Dtsch. Killifisch Gemein J. v. 19 (no. 2): 17-22. [English translation by T. R. Griffin, as J. Amer. Killifish Assoc., v. 22 (no. 2): 61-65.]

——. 1987 **[ref. 14231]**. Colour atlas of cyprinodonts of the rain forests of tropical Africa. O. Hofmann. 1-160.

Rafinesque, C. S. 1809 **[ref. 13437]**. See Rafinesque 1810 [ref. 3594]; sometimes part one dated to 1809, but apparently entire article was published in 1810 [see under ref. 3594].

Rafinesque, C. S. [As Rafinesque Schmaltz, C. S.]. 1810 **[ref. 3594]**. Caratteri di alcuni nuovi generi e nuove specie di animali e piante della sicilia, con varie osservazioni sopra i medisimi. (Part 1 involves fishes, pp. [i-iv] 3-69 [70 blank], Part 2 with slightly different title, pp. ia-iva + 71-105 [106 blank]). Pls. 1-20. [Dates to 1810 (see Holthius & Boeseman 1977 [ref. 6877], Wheeler 1988 [ref. 6878]). Also see Boewe 1982 [ref. 6030].]

Rafinesque, C. S. 1810 (before 1 Sept.) **[ref. 3595]**. Indice d'ittiologia siciliana; ossia, catalogo metodico dei nomi latini, italiani, e siciliani dei pesci, che si rinvengono in Sicilia disposti secondo un metodo naturale e seguito da un appendice che contiene la descrizione de alcuni nuovi pesci sicilian. Messina. 1-70, Pls. 1-2. [Publication before 1 Sept. 1810, apparently predates Rafinesque 1810 [ref. 3594]; see Wheeler 1988 [ref. 6878].]

——. 1814 **[ref. 3581]**. Descrizione di un nuovo genere di pesce, *Leptopus peregrinus*. Pp. 16-17. In: Specchio delle scienze, o giornale enciclopedico de Sicilia, deposito letterario delle moderne cognizioni, scoperte ed osservazione sopra le scienze ed arte, etc. Palermo. v. 1: 1-216, 2 pls.

——. 1814 **[ref. 3582]**. Précis des découvertes et travaux somiologiques de Mr. C. S. Rafinesque-Schmaltz entre 1800 et 1814; ou choix raisonné de ses principales découvertes en zoologie et en botanique, pour servir d'introduction à ses ouvrages futurs. Palerme. 1-55.

——. 1815 **[ref. 3583]**. Descrizione di un nuovo genere di pesce siciliano, *Nemochirus*. Pp. 100-120. In: Specchio delle scienze, o giornale enciclopedico de Sicilia, deposito letterario delle moderne cognizioni, scoperte ed osservazione sopra le scienze ed arte, etc. Palermo. [See Rafinesque 1814, ref. 3581.]

——. 1815 **[ref. 3584]**. Analyse de la nature, ou tableau de l'univers et des corps organisés. Palerme. 1-224. [Fishes on pp. 79-94.]

——. 1818 (Jan.) **[ref. 3585]**. Description of two new genera of North American fishes, *Opsanus*, and *Notropis*. Amer. Monthly Mag. Crit. Rev. v. 2 (3) (Jan. 1918): 203-204.

——. 1818 (Sept.) **[ref. 3586]**. Discoveries in natural history, made during a journey through the western region of the United States. Amer. Monthly Mag. Crit. Rev. v. 3 (5)(Sept. 1818): 354-356.

——. 1818 **[ref. 3587]**. Further discoveries in natural history made during a journey through the western region of the United States. Amer. Monthly Mag. Crit. Rev. v. 3 (6) (Oct. 1818): 445-447.

——. 1818 (7 Nov.) **[ref. 3588]**. Description of three new genera of fluviatile fish, *Pomoxis*, *Sarchirus* and *Exoglossum*. J. Acad. Nat. Sci. Phila. v. 1: 417-422, Pl. 17.

——. 1818 (Nov.) **[ref. 3589]**. Further account of discoveries in natural history, in the western states, made during a journey through the western region of the United States. Amer. Monthly Mag. Crit. Rev. v. 4 (no. 1): 39-42.

——. 1818 **[ref. 5087]**. [Title uncertain.] Amer. Monthly Mag. Crit. Rev. v. 2: 274. [Not seen.]

——. 1819 (June) **[ref. 3590]**. Prodrome de 70 nouveaux genres d'animaux découverts dans l'intérieur des États-Unis d'Amérique, durant l'année 1818. J. Phys. Chim. Hist. Nat. v. 88: 417-429. [Fishes on pp. 418-422.]

——. 1819 **[ref. 4938]**. Description of a new genus of North American fresh-water fish, *Exoglossum*. Am. J. Sci. v. 1: 155-156. [Also in Isis (Oken) 1819, 10: 1038.]

——. 1819 (Dec.) **[ref. 14490]**. Ichthyologia Ohiensis [Part 1]. Western Rev. Misc. Mag. v. 1 (no. 5):305-313. [Same as pp. 1-13 in Rafinesque 1820 [ref. 3592].]

——. 1820 (Jan.) **[ref. 7308]**. Ichthyologia Ohiensis [Part 2]. Western Rev. Misc. Mag. v. 1 (no. 6): 361-377. [Same as pp. 13-29 in Rafinesque 1820 [ref. 3592].]

——. 1820 (Feb.) **[ref. 7305]**. Ichthyologia Ohiensis [Part 3]. Western Rev. Misc. Mag. v. 2 (no. 1): 49-57. [Same as pp. 29-37 in Rafinesque 1820 [ref. 3592].]

——. 1820 (Apr.) **[ref. 7309]**. Ichthyologia Ohiensis [Part 4]. Western Rev. Misc. Mag. v. 2 (no. 3): 169-177. [Same as pp. 37-45 in Rafinesque 1820 [ref. 3592].]

——. 1820 (May) **[ref. 7310]**. Ichthyologia Ohiensis [Part 5]. Western Rev. Misc. Mag. v. 2 (no. 4): 235-242. [Same as pp. 45-53 in Rafinesque 1820 [ref. 3592].]

——. 1820 (June) **[ref. 5006]**. Ichthyologia Ohiensis [Part 6]. Western Rev. Misc. Mag. v. 2 (no. 5): 299-307. [Same as pp. 53-60 in Rafinesque 1820 [ref. 3592].]

——. 1820 (July) **[ref. 7311]**. Ichthyologia Ohiensis [Part 7]. Western Rev. Misc. Mag. v. 6 (no. 6): 355-363. [Same as pp. 60-69 in Rafinesque 1820 [ref. 3592].]

——. 1820 (Oct.) **[ref. 7306]**. Ichthyologia Ohiensis [Part 8]. Western Rev. Misc. Mag. v. 3 (no. 3): 165-173. [Same as pp. 69-77 in Rafinesque 1820 [ref. 3592].]

——. 1820 (Nov.) **[ref. 5088]**. Ichthyologia Ohiensis [Part. 9]. Western Rev. Misc. Mag. v. 3 (no. 4): 244-252. [Same as pp. 77-84 in Rafinesque 1920 [ref. 3592].]

——. 1820 (Dec.) **[ref. 3592]**. Ichthyologia Ohiensis, or natural history of the fishes inhabiting the river Ohio and its tributary streams, preceded by a physical description of the Ohio and its branches. Lexington, Kentucky. 1-90. [Originally printed in the Western Rev. and Misc. Mag. 1819-20 (See Wheeler 1988 [ref. 6878]). Reprinted 1899 and 1960.]

——. 1820 **[ref. 3591]**. Annals of Nature, I. [Not seen.]

——. 1832 **[ref. 3593]**. Extracts from a second series of zoological letters written to Baron Cuvier of Paris, by Prof. Rafinesque in 1831. Atlantic J. Friend Knowl. v. 1 (no. 1): 19-22.

Rafinesque-Schmaltz, C. S. See Rafinesque.

Rainboth, W. J. 1983 (6 July) **[ref. 5429]**. *Psilorhynchus gracilis*, a new cyprinoid fish from the Gangetic lowlands. Proc. Calif. Acad. Sci. v. 43 (no. 6): 67-76.

——. 1985 (29 June) **[ref. 5968]**. *Neolissochilus*, a new genus of South Asian cyprinid fishes. Beaufortia v. 35 (no. 3): 25-35.

——. 1986 (20 Aug.) **[ref. 5849]**. Fishes of the Asian cyprinid genus *Chagunius*. Occas. Pap. Mus. Zool. Univ. Mich. No. 712: 1-17.

——. 1989 (18 Sept.) **[ref. 13537]**. *Discherodontus*, a new genus of cyprinid fishes from southeastern Asia. Occ. Pap. Mus. Zool. Univ. Mich. No. 718: 1-31.

Raj, B. S. 1941 (June) **[ref. 3596]**. A new genus of Schizothoracine fishes from Travancore, South India. Rec. Indian Mus. (Calcutta) v. 43 (pt 2): 209-214, Pl. 7.

Raj, U., and J. Seeto. 1983 (6 May) **[ref. 6817]**. A new species of *Paracesio* (Pisces: Lutjanidae) from the Fiji Islands. Copeia 1983 (no. 2): 450-453.

Raju, N. S. 1985 (Feb.) **[ref. 5287]**. Congrid eels of the eastern Pacific and key to their leptocephali. NOAA Tech. Rep. NMFS No. 22: i-iii + 1-19.

Rama-Rao, K. V. 1980 (24 Dec.) **[ref. 6797]**. New record of a scorpion fish *Pteroidichthys amboinensis* Bleeker (Pisces: Scorpaenidae) from inshore waters of Madras, India. Matsya No. 6 [for 1980]: 19-22.

Ramsay, E. P. 1883 **[ref. 6592]**. Catalogue of the exhibits in the New South Wales court [International Fisheries Exhibition]. London. 1-56. [Not seen.]

Ramsay, E. P., and J. D. Ogilby. 1887 (31 Aug.) **[ref. 3598]**. Notes on the genera of Australian fishes. Proc. Linn. Soc. N. S. W. (Ser. 2) v. 2 (pt 2): 181-184.

——. 1888 (21 Mar.) **[ref. 3597]**. On a new genus and species of labroid fish from Port Jackson. Proc. Linn. Soc. N. S. W. (Ser. 2) v. 2 (pt 4): 631-634.

Randall, J. E. 1955 (July) **[ref. 13648]**. An analysis of the genera of surgeon fishes (family Acanthuridae). Pac. Sci. v. 9 (no. 3): 359-367.

——. 1963 (28 May) **[ref. 3599]**. Review of the hawkfishes (family Cirrhitidae). Proc. U. S. Natl. Mus. v. 114 (no. 3472): 389-451, 16 pls.

——. 1964 **[ref. 3600]**. Notes on the groupers of Tahiti, with description of a new serranid fish genus. Pac. Sci. v. 18 (no. 3): 281-296.

——. 1964 (30 June) **[ref. 3148]**. A revision of the filefish genera *Amanses* and *Cantherhines*. Copeia 1964 (no. 2): 331-361.

——. 1975 (July) **[ref. 6490]**. A revision of the Indo-Pacific angelfish genus *Genicanthus*, with descriptions of three new species. Bull. Mar. Sci. v. 25 (no. 3): 393-421, 1 col. pl.

——. 1978 (20 Dec.) **[ref. 5545]**. *Pseudojulis* Bleeker, a probable invalid genus of labrid fishes (Perciformes: Labridae). Matsya No. 4 [for 1978]: 1-4.

——. 1978 **[ref. 7004]**. A revision of the Indo-Pacific labrid fish genus *Macropharyngodon*, with descriptions of five new species. Bull. Mar. Sci. v. 28 (no. 4): 742-770.

——. 1980 **[ref. 6717]**. Revision of the fish genus *Plectranthias* (Serranidae: Anthiinae) with descriptions of 13 new species. Micronesica v. 16 (no. 1): 101-187.

——. 1981 (15 Dec.) **[ref. 5447]**. Two new species and six new records of labrid fishes form the Red Sea. Senckenb. Marit. v. 13

(no. 1/3): 79-109, Pls. 1-3.

———. 1981 (Dec.) **[ref. 5493]**. Revision of the labrid fish genus *Labropsis* with descriptions of five new species. Micronesica v. 17 (no. 1-2): 125-155.

———. 1981 (Dec.) **[ref. 5495]**. A review of the Indo-Pacific sand tilefish genus *Hoplolatilus* (Perciformes: Malacanthidae). Freshwater Mar. Aquar. v. 4 (1981, no. 12): 39-46.

———. 1981 **[ref. 5542]**. Two new Indo-Pacific labrid fishes of the genus *Halichoeres*, with notes on other species of the genus. Pac. Sci. v. 34 (no. 4) [1980]: 415-432, 4 col pls.

———. 1981 (Sept.) **[ref. 5549]**. *Luzonichthys earlei* a new species of anthiine fish from the Hawaiian Islands. Freshwater Mar. Aquar. v. 4 (1981, no. 9): 13-18.

———. 1982 (26 May) **[ref. 5448]**. A review of the labrid fish genus *Hologymnosus*. Rev. Fr. Aquariol. v. 9 (no. 1): 13-20.

———. 1983 (14 Dec.) **[ref. 5360]**. Revision of the Indo-Pacific labrid fish genus *Wetmorella*. Copeia 1983 (no. 4): 875-883.

———. 1983 (30 Apr.) **[ref. 5361]**. A review of the fishes of the subgenus *Goniistius*, genus *Cheilodactylus*, with description of a new species from Easter Island and Rapa. Occas. Pap. Bernice P. Bishop Mus. v. 25 (no. 7): 1-24.

———. 1983 (Sept.) **[ref. 6022]**. A new fish of the genus *Anthias* (Perciformes: Serranidae) from the western Pacific, with notes on *A. luzonensis*. Aquarium v. 6 (no. 9): 27-37.

———. 1984 (Dec.) **[ref. 6067]**. Two new Indo-Pacific mugiloidid fishes of the genus *Parapercis*. Freshwater Mar. Aquar. v. 7 (no. 12): 41-49.

———. 1985 (28 Nov.) **[ref. 6719]**. On the validity of the tetraodontid fish *Arothron manilensis* (Procé). Jpn. J. Ichthyol. v. 32 (no. 3): 347-354.

———. 1986 **[ref. 5706]**. Family No. 167: Grammistidae (pp. 537-538), Family No. 214: Cirrhitidae (pp. 664-666), Family No. 220: Labridae (pp. 683-706), Family No. 221: Scaridae (pp. 706-714), Family No. 243: Acanthuridae (pp. 811-823). In: Smiths' Sea Fishes (Smith & Heemstra 1986 [ref. 5715]).

———. 1988 **[ref. 14250]**. Three new Indo-Pacific damselfishes of the genus *Chromis* (Pomacentridae). Mem. Mus. Victoria v. 49 (no. 1): 73-81.

———. 1988 (21 Nov.) **[ref. 14252]**. Three new damselfishes of the genus *Chromis* (Perciformes: Pomacentridae) from the Indian Ocean. Rev. Fr. Aquariol. v. 15 (no. 2): 49-56.

———. 1988 **[ref. 14253]**. Five new wrasses of the genera *Cirrhilabrus* and *Paracheilinus* (Perciformes: Labridae) from the Marshall Islands. Micronesia v. 21: 199-226, Col. pls. 1-3.

Randall, J. E., and T. A. Adamson. 1982 **[ref. 5445]**. A review of the monotypic Indo-Malayan labrid fish genus *Xenojulis*. Pac. Sci. v. 36 (no. 1): 119-126.

Randall, J. E., and G. R. Allen. 1973 **[ref. 7123]**. A revision of the gobiid fish genus *Nemateleotris*, with descriptions of two new species. Q. J. Taiwan Mus. (Taipei) v. 26 (nos. 3/4): 347-367.

———. 1977 (Dec.) **[ref. 6482]**. A revision of the damselfish genus *Dascyllus* (Pomacentridae) with the description of a new species. Rec. Aust. Mus. v. 31 (no. 9): 349-385.

———. 1987 **[ref. 6249]**. Four new serranid fishes of the genus *Epinephelus* (Perciformes: Epinephelinae) from Western Australia. Rec. West. Aust. Mus. v. 13 (no 3): 387-411.

———. 1989 (15 Feb.) **[ref. 13389]**. *Pseudanthias sheni*, a new serranid fish from Rowley Shoals and Scott Reef, Western Australia. Rev. Fr. Aquariol. v. 15 (no. 3): 73-78.

Randall, J. E., G. R. Allen and W. D. Anderson, Jr. 1987 (30 Apr.) **[ref. 6431]**. Revision of the Indo-Pacific lutjanid genus *Pinjalo*, with description of a new species. Indo-Pac. Fishes No. 14: 1-17, col. Pl. 1.

Randall, J. E., and R. W. Bruce. 1983 (Mar.) **[ref. 5412]**. The parrotfishes of the subfamily Scarinae of the western Indian Ocean with descriptions of three new species. Ichthyol. Bull. J. L. B. Smith Inst. Ichthyol. No. 47: 1-39, col. Pls. 1-6.

Randall, J. E., and D. K. Caldwell. 1966 **[ref. 9053]**. A review of the sparid fish genus *Calamus*, with descriptions of four new species. Nat. Hist. Mus. Los Ang. Cty. Sci. Bull. No. 2: 1-47.

Randall, J. E., and A. Cea Egaña. 1989 (15 Feb.) **[ref. 9295]**. *Canthigaster cyanetron* a new toby (Teleostei: Tetraodontidae) from Easter Island. Rev. Fr. Aquariol. v. 15 (no. 3): 93-96.

Randall, J. E., and J. R. Chess. 1979 **[ref. 6924]**. A new species of garden eel (Congridae: Heterocongrinae) of the genus *Gorgasia* from Hawaii. Pac. Sci. v. 33 (no. 1): 17-23.

Randall, J. E., and J. H. Choat. 1980 (Dec.) **[ref. 5543]**. Two new parrotfishes of the genus *Scarus* from the central and South Pacific, with further examples of sexual dichromatism. Zool. J. Linn. Soc. v. 70 (no. 4): 383-419, 8 col. pls.

Randall, J. E., and B. Condé. 1989 (15 Feb.) **[ref. 9294]**. *Frontilabrus caeruleus*, nouveaux genre et espèce de Labridé des Maldives. Rev. Fr. Aquariol. v. 15 (no. 3): 89-92.

Randall, J. E., and H. P. De Bruin. 1988 (30 June) **[ref. 6861]**. The butterflyfish *Prognathodes guyotensis* from the Maldive Islands, a first record for the Indian Ocean. Cybium v. 12 (no. 2): 145-149.

Randall, J. E., and J. K. Dooley. 1974 (13 June) **[ref. 5336]**. Revision of the Indo-Pacific branchiostegid fish genus *Hoplolatilus*, with descriptions of two new species. Copeia 1974 (no. 2): 457-471.

Randall, J. E., and M. Dor. 1980 **[ref. 3601]**. Description of a new genus and species of labrid fish from the Red Sea. Isr. J. Zool. v. 29: 153-162, 1 col. pl.

Randall, J. E., and C. J. Ferraris, Jr. 1981 (25 Nov.) **[ref. 5492]**. A revision of the Indo-Pacific labrid fish genus *Leptojulis* with descriptions of two new species. Rev. Fr. Aquariol. v. 8 (no. 3): 89-96.

Randall, J. E., and P. Guézé. 1981 (24 Apr.) **[ref. 6911]**. The holocentrid fishes of the genus *Miripristis* of the Red Sea, with clarification of the *muridjan* and *hexagonus* complexes. Contrib. Sci. (Los Ang.) No. 334: 1-16.

Randall, J. E., and L. Harmelin-Vivien. 1977 **[ref. 5323]**. A review of the labrid fishes of the genus *Paracheilinus* with description of two new species from the western Indian Ocean. Bull. Mus. Natl. Hist. Nat. Zool. No. 306: 329-342.

Randall, J. E., and P. C. Heemstra. 1978 (15 Dec.) **[ref. 6993]**. Reclassification of the Japanese cirrhitid fishes *Serranocirrhitus latus* and *Isobuna japonica* to the Anthiinae. Jpn. J. Ichthyol. v. 25 (no. 3): 165-172.

———. 1985 (Jan.) **[ref. 5144]**. A review of the squirrelfishes of the subfamily Holocentrinae from the western Indian Ocean and Red Sea. Ichthyol. Bull. J. L. B. Smith Inst. Ichthyol. No. 49: 1-27, 2 col. pls.

———. 1986 **[ref. 5707]**. Family No. 132: Holocentridae (pp. 415-427). In: Smiths' Sea Fishes (Smith & Heemstra 1986 [ref. 5715]).

Randall, J. E., and D. F. Hoese. 1985 (Sept.) **[ref. 5197]**. Revision of the Indo-Pacific dartfishes, genus *Ptereleotris* (Perciformes: Gobioidei). Indo-Pac. Fishes No. 7: 1-36, 4 col. pls.

———. 1986 (Dec.) **[ref. 6009]**. Revision of the groupers of the Indo-Pacific genus *Plectropomus* (Perciformes: Serranidae). Indo-Pac. Fishes No. 13: 1-31, col. Pls. 1-5.

Randall, J. E., and M. Hutomo. 1988 (3 Aug.) **[ref. 6679]**. Redescription of the Indo-Pacific serranid fish *Pseudanthias bimaculatus* (Smith). Copeia 1988 (no. 3): 669-673.

Randall, J. E., H. Ida and J. T. Moyer. 1981 (30 Nov.) **[ref. 5449]**. A review of the damselfishes of the genus *Chromis* from Japan & Taiwan, with description of a new species. Jpn. J. Ichthyol. v. 28 (no. 3): 203-242, 1 col. pl.

Randall, J. E., G. D. Johnson and G. R. Lowe. 1989 (15 Mar.) **[ref. 12737]**. *Triso*, a new generic name for the serranid fish previously known as *Trisotropis dermaterus*, with comments on its relationships. Jpn. J. Ichthyol. v. 35 (no. 4): 414-420.

Randall, J. E., and R. H. Kuiter. 1982 **[ref. 5446]**. Three new labrid fishes of the genus *Coris* from the western Pacific. Pac. Sci. v. 36 (no. 2): 159-173.

———. 1989 (30 Nov.) **[ref. 13502]**. *Cirrhilabrus punctatus*, a new species of labroid fish from the southwestern Pacific. Revue Fr. Aquariol. v. 16 (no. 2): 43-50.

RANDALL, J. E., E. A. LACHNER AND T. H. FRASER. 1985 (Sept.) **[ref. 9188]**. A revision of the Indo-Pacific apogonid fish genus *Pseudamia*, with descriptions of three new species. Indo-Pac. Fishes No. 6: 1-23, Pl. 1.

RANDALL, J. E., AND R. LUBBOCK. 1981 (25 May) **[ref. 5544]**. Labrid fishes of the genus *Paracheilinus*, with descriptions of three new species from the Philippines. Jpn. J. Ichthyol. v. 28 (no. 1): 19-30, 2 col. pls.

——. 1981 (24 Apr.) **[ref. 6912]**. A revision of the serranid fishes of the subgenus *Mirolabrichthys* (Anthiinae: *Anthias*), with description of five new species. Contrib. Sci. (Los Ang.) No. 333: 1-27.

RANDALL, J. E., K. MATSUURA AND A. ZAMA. 1978 **[ref. 5532]**. A revision of the triggerfish genus *Xanthichthys*, with description of a new species. Bull. Mar. Sci. v. 28 (no. 4): 688-706.

RANDALL, J. E., AND R. MELÉNDEZ C. 1987 (Feb.) **[ref. 9173]**. A new sole of the genus *Aseraggodes* from Easter Island and Lord Howe Island, with comments on the validity of *A. ramsaii*. Occas. Pap. Bernice P. Bishop Mus. v. 27: 97-105.

RANDALL, J. E., AND R. M. PYLE. 1989 (20 May) **[ref. 12854]**. *Cirrhilabrus scottorum*, a new labrid fish from the South Pacific Ocean. Rev. Fr. Aquariol. v. 15 (no. 4): 113-118.

——. 1989 (July) **[ref. 14121]**. A new species of anthiine fish of the genus *Rabaulichthys* (Perciformes: Serranidaie [sic]) from the Maldive Islands. J. L. B. Smith Inst. Ichthyol. Spec. Publ. No. 47: 1-7, 1 col. pl.

RANDALL, J. E., AND H. A. RANDALL. 1981 **[ref. 5494]**. A revision of the labrid fish genus *Pseudojuloides*, with descriptions of five new species. Pac. Sci. v. 35 (no. 1): 51-74, 3 col. pls.

RANDALL, J. E., AND S.-C. SHEN. 1978 **[ref. 7027]**. A review of the labrid fishes of the genus *Cirrhilabrus* from Taiwan, with description of a new species. Bull. Inst. Zool. Acad. Sin. (Taipei) v. 17 (no. 1): 13-24, col. Pls. 1-2.

RANDALL, J. E., T. SHIMIZU AND T. YAMAKAWA. 1982 (30 June) **[ref. 3602]**. A revision of the holocentrid fish genus *Ostichthys*, with descriptions of four new species and a related new genus. Jpn. J. Ichthyol. v. 29 (no. 1): 1-26, 2 col. pls.

RANDALL, J. E., AND C. L. SMITH. 1988 (5 Oct.) **[ref. 9278]**. Two new species and a new genus of cardinalfishes (Perciformes: Apogonidae) from Rapa, South Pacific Ocean. Am. Mus. Novit. No. 2926: 1-9.

RANDALL, J. E., M. M. SMITH AND K. AIDA. 1980 (Oct.) **[ref. 6923]**. Notes on the classification and distribution of the Indo-Pacific soapfish, *Belonoperca chabanaudi* (Perciformes: Grammistidae). J. L. B. Smith Inst. Ichthyol. Spec. Publ. No. 21: 1-8.

RANDALL, J. E., AND V. G. SPRINGER. 1973 (28 Sept.) **[ref. 3603]**. The monotypic Indo-Pacific labrid fish genera *Labrichthys* and *Diproctacanthus* with description of a new related genus, *Larabicus*. Proc. Biol. Soc. Wash. v. 86 (no. 23): 279-297.

RANDALL, J. E., AND B. E. STANALAND. 1989 (20 May) **[ref. 12853]**. A new dottyback of the genus *Pseudochromis* (Teleostei; Perciformes; Pseudochromidae) from the northwestern Indian Ocean. Rev. Fr. Aquariol. v. 15 (no. 4): 105-110.

RANDALL, J. E., AND R. C. STEENE. 1983 (July) **[ref. 6023]**. *Rhinecanthus lunula* a new species of triggerfish from the South Pacific. Aquarium v. 6 (no. 7): 45-51.

RANDALL, J. E., AND L. R. TAYLOR, JR. 1988 (May) **[ref. 6429]**. Review of the Indo-Pacific fishes of the serranid genus *Liopropoma*, with descriptions of seven new species. Indo-Pac. Fishes No. 16: 1-47, col. Pls. 1-4.

RANDALL, J. E., AND L. WROBEL. 1988 (15 Dec.) **[ref. 12743]**. A new species of soldierfish of the genus *Ostichthys* and records of *O. archiepiscopus* and *O. sandix* from Tahiti. Jpn. J. Ichthyol. v. 35 (no. 3): 243-246.

RANDALL, J. E., AND T. YAMAKAWA. 1988 (4 May) **[ref. 6410]**. A new species of the labrid fish of the genus *Hologymnosus* from the western Pacific, with notes on *H. longipes*. Rev. Fr. Aquariol. v. 15 (no. 1): 25-32.

RANZANI, C. 1818 **[ref. 3604]**. Descrizione di un pesce il quale ad un nuovo genere della famiglia dei Tenioidi del Signor G. Cuvier. Opuscoli scientifici, Bologna v. 2: 133-137, Pl. 6.

——. 1839 **[ref. 3605]**. Dispositio familiae Molarum in genera et in species. Novi Comment. Acad. Sci. Inst. Bonon. v. 3: 63-82, Pl. 6 + foldout table.

——. 1842 **[ref. 3606]**. De novis speciebus piscium. Dissertationes Secunda. Novi Comment. Acad. Sci. Inst. Bonon. v. 5: 1-21, Pls. 1-6.

——. 1842 **[ref. 9017]**. De novis speciebus piscium. Dissertationes IV. Novi. Ann. Sci. Nat. Bologna v. 5: 340-365, Pls. 29-38.

RAO, V. V. 1971 (Apr.) **[ref. 12496]**. *Incara multisquamatus* gen. et sp. nov. (family: Eleotridae) from Godavari Estuary. J. Mar. Biol. Assoc. India v. 11 (nos. 1 & 2): 329-332. [For the year 1969.]

——. 1971 (Dec.) **[ref. 12524]**. *Chiramenu fluviatilis* gen et. sp. nov. (Pisces: Gobiidae) from Godavari Estuary. J. Mar. Biol. Assoc. India v. 12 (nos. 1 & 2): 183-186. [For the year 1970, issue date on cover Dec. 1971; date possibly 1972.]

RAO, V. V., AND S. DUTT. 1966 (28 Apr.) **[ref. 3607]**. A new fish *Tentaculus waltairiensis* gen. et sp. nov. (family: Haliophidae) from Indian waters. Ann. Mag. Nat. Hist. (Ser. 13) v. 8 (nos. 91/92): 455-459.

RAPP, W. L. VON. 1854 **[ref. 3608]**. Die Fische des Bodensees. Jahresb. Ver. Vaterl. Nat. Wurttemberg v. 10 (no. 2): 137-175, Pls. 1-6.

RAPP PY-DANIEL, L. H. 1981 (16 Mar.) **[ref. 3568]**. *Furcodontichthys novaesi* n. gen., n. sp. (Osteichthyes, Siluriformes; Loricariidae) na bacia amazônia, Brasil. Bol. Mus. Para. Emilio Goeldi Nova Ser. Zool. No. 105: 1-17.

——. 1985 (June) **[ref. 6101]**. *Dekeyseria amazonica*, novo gênero e nova espécie na região amazonica, Brasil, e *Dekeyseria scaphirhyncha* (Kner, 1854) nova combinação (Loricariidae: Siluriformes). Amazoniana v. 9 (no. 2): 177-191.

——. 1989 (30 Sept.) **[ref. 13470]**. Redescription of *Parancistrus aurantiacus* (Castelnau, 1855) and preliminary establishment of two new genera: *Baryancistrus* and *Oligancistrus* (Siluriformes, Loricariidae). Cybium 1989, v. 13 (no. 3): 235-246.

RASCHI, W., J. A. MUSICK AND L. J. V. COMPAGNO. 1982 (23 Feb.) **[ref. 6823]**. *Hypoprion bigelowi*, a synonym of *Carcharhinus signatus* (Pisces: Carcharhinidae), with a description of ontognetic heterodonty in this species and notes on its natural history. Copeia 1988 (no. 1): 102-109.

RASS, T. S. 1954 **[ref. 3609]**. Contribution to the study of Pacific Ocean Moridae (Pisces, Gadiformes). Tr. Inst. Okeanol. v. 11: 56-61. [In Russian.]

——. 1955 **[ref. 3610]**. [Deepsea fishes of the Kurile-Kamchatka trench.] Tr. Inst. Okeanol. v. 12: 328-339. [In Russian.]

——. 1961 **[ref. 13630]**. *Prososcopa stilbia* Rass, gen. n., sp. n.—a new deep sea fish from the Indian Ocean. Zool. Zh. v. 40 (no. 12): 1858-1861.

——. 1962 **[ref. 13631]**. *Prososcopa stilbia* Rass, 1961, equals *Xenophthalmichthys danae* Regan, 1925 (Xenophthalmichthyidae, Pisces). Zool. Zh. v. 42 (no. 10): 1578-1579.

RAUCHENBERGER, M. 1988 (18 May) **[ref. 6411]**. A new species of *Allodontichthys* (Cyprinodontiformes: Goodeidae), with comparative morphometrics for the genus. Copeia 1988 (no. 2): 433-411.

REGAN, C. T. 1903 (Oct.) **[ref. 3615]**. On a collection of fishes made by Dr. Goeldi at Rio Janeiro. Proc. Zool. Soc. Lond. 1903 v. 2 (pt 1): 59-68, Pls. 7-8.

——. 1903 (Feb.) **[ref. 3616]**. A revision of the fishes of the family Lophiidae. Ann. Mag. Nat. Hist. (Ser. 7) v. 11 (no. 62): 277-285.

——. 1903 **[ref. 3617]**. On the systematic position and classification of the gadoid or anacanthine fishes. Ann. Mag. Nat. Hist. (Ser. 7) v. 11: 459-466.

——. 1903 (Sept.) **[ref. 3618]**. On the genus *Lichia* of Cuvier. Ann. Mag. Nat. Hist. (Ser. 7) v. 12 (no. 69): 348-350.

——. 1903 (Sept.) **[ref. 3619]**. On a collection of fishes from the Azores. Ann. Mag. Nat. Hist. (Ser. 7) v. 12 (no. 69): 344-348.

——. 1903 **[ref. 3620]**. Descriptions de poissons nouveaux faisant partie de la collection du Musée d'Histoire Naturelle de Genève. Rev. Suisse Zool. v. 11 (no. 2): 413-418, Pls. 13-14.

———. 1904 (Oct.) **[ref. 3621]**. III. A monograph of the fishes of the family Loricariidae. Trans. Zool. Soc. Lond. v. 17 (pt 3, no. 1): 191-350, Pls. 9-21.

———. 1904 **[ref. 12514]**. Descriptions of three new marine fishes from South Africa. Ann. Mag. Nat. Hist. (Ser. 7) v. 14: 128-130.

———. 1905 (Sept.) **[ref. 3622]**. A revision of the fishes of the American cichlid genus *Cichlasoma* and of the allied genera. Ann. Mag. Nat. Hist. (Ser. 7) v. 16 (no. 93): 316-340. [Article in 4 parts, (Ser. 7) v. 16: 60-77, 225-243, 316-340, 433-445; new subgenus in third part as above.]

———. 1905 (Apr.) **[ref. 3623]**. A revision of the fishes of the South-American cichlid genera *Acara, Nannacara, Acaropsis*, and *Astronotus*. Ann. Mag. Nat. Hist. (Ser. 7) v. 15 (no. 88): 329-347.

———. 1905 (Jan.) **[ref. 3624]**. On a collection of fishes from the inland sea of Japan made by Mr. R. Gordon Smith. Ann. Mag. Nat. Hist. (Ser. 7) v. 15 (no. 85): 17-26, Pls. 2-3.

———. 1905 (Feb.) **[ref. 3625]**. A synopsis of the species of the silurid genera *Parexostoma, Chimarrhichthys*, and *Exostoma*. Ann. Mag. Nat. Hist. (Ser. 7) v. 15 (no. 86): 182-185.

———. 1905 (10 Aug.) **[ref. 12256]**. A revision of the fishes of the South-American cichlid genera *Crenacara, Batrachops*, and *Crenicichla*. Proc. Zool. Soc. Lond. 1905, v. 1 (pt 2): 152-168, Pls. 14-15.

———. 1906 (Jan.) **[ref. 3626]**. Revision of the South American cichlid genera *Retroculus, Geophagus, Heterogramma*, and *Biotoecus*. Ann. Mag. Nat. Hist. (Ser. 7) v. 17 (no. 97): 49-66.

———. 1906 (Jan.) **[ref. 3627]**. Notes on some loricariid fishes, with descriptions of two new species. Ann. Mag. Nat. Hist. (Ser. 7) v. 17 (no. 97): 94-98.

———. 1906 (June) **[ref. 3628]**. Descriptions of new or little known fishes from the coast of Natal. Ann. Natal Govern. Mus. v. 1 (pt 1): 1-6, Pls. 1-5.

———. 1906 **[ref. 6552]**. A collection of fishes from the King River, Western Australia. Ann. Mag. Nat. Hist. (Ser. 7) v. 18 (no. 70): 450-453.

———. 1907 **[ref. 3629]**. Pisces. In: F. D. Gudman & O. Salvin. Biologia Central-America. Part 215: 33-160, Pls. 5-20. [First section is same title, 1906, Part 193: 1-32, Pls. 1-5.]

———. 1907 (Mar.) **[ref. 3630]**. Descriptions of two new characinid fishes from Argentina. Ann. Mag. Nat. Hist. (Ser. 7) v. 19 (no. 111): 261-262.

———. 1907 **[ref. 3631]**. Descriptions of two new characinid fishes from South America. Ann. Mag. Nat. Hist. (Ser. 7) v. 20: 402-403.

———. 1907 (9 Oct.) **[ref. 7317]**. On the anatomy, classification, and systematic position of the teleostean fishes of the suborder Allotriognathi. Proc. Zool. Soc. Lond. 1907 (pt 3): 634-643.

———. 1907 **[ref. 12987]**. Fishes. Pp. 157-158. In: Reports on a collection of Batrachia, reptiles and fish from Nepal and the western Himalayas. Rec. Indian Mus. (Calcutta) v. 1: 149-158, Pl. 6.

———. 1908 (Nov.) **[ref. 3632]**. A synopsis of the fishes of the subfamily Salanginae. Ann. Mag. Nat. Hist. (Ser. 8) v. 2 (no. 11): 444-446.

———. 1908 (Nov.) **[ref. 3633]**. A new generic name for an orectolobid shark. Ann. Mag. Nat. Hist. (Ser. 8) v. 2 (no. 11): 454-455.

———. 1908 (May) **[ref. 3634]**. Report on the marine fishes collected by Mr. J. Stanley Gardiner in the Indian Ocean. Trans. Linn. Soc. London (Ser. 2, Zool.) v. 12 (pt 3): 217-255, Pls. 23-32.

———. 1908 (Aug.) **[ref. 3635]**. A revision of the sharks of the family Orectolobidae. Proc. Zool. Soc. Lond. 1908 (pt 2): 347-364, Pls. 11-13.

———. 1908 (Oct.) **[ref. 3636]**. Description of new fishes from Lake Candidius, Formosa, collected by Dr. A. Moltrecht. Ann. Mag. Nat. Hist. (Ser. 8) v. 2 (no. 10): 356-360.

———. 1908 (Nov.) **[ref. 3637]**. A collection of freshwater fishes made by Mr. C. F. Underwood in Costa Rica. Ann. Mag. Nat. Hist. (Ser. 8) v. 2 (no. 11): 455-464.

———. 1911 (Jan.) **[ref. 3639]**. The anatomy and classification of the teleostean fishes of the order Iniomi. Ann. Mag. Nat. Hist. (Ser. 8) v. 7 (no. 37): 120-133.

———. 1911 (Feb.) **[ref. 3640]**. A synopsis of the marsipobranchs of the order Hyperoartii. Ann. Mag. Nat. Hist. (Ser. 8) v. 7 (no. 38): 193-204.

———. 1911 (Apr.) **[ref. 3641]**. The classification of the teleostean fishes of the order Synentognathi. Ann. Mag. Nat. Hist. (Ser. 8) v. 7 (no. 40): 327-335, Pl. 9.

———. 1911 (July) **[ref. 3642]**. The classification of the teleostean fishes of the order Ostariophysi.—I. Cyprinoidea. Ann. Mag. Nat. Hist. (Ser. 8) v. 8 (no. 43): 13-32, Pl. 2.

———. 1911 (Apr.) **[ref. 5761]**. The osteology and classification of the teleostean fishes of the order Microcyprini. Ann. Mag. Nat. Hist. (Ser. 8) v. 7 (no. 4): 320-327, Pl. 8.

———. 1911 (Sept.) **[ref. 5762]**. On some fishes of the family Poeciliidae. Ann. Mag. Nat. Hist. (Ser. 8) v. 8 (no. 45): 373-374.

———. 1912 (Sept.) **[ref. 3643]**. New fishes from Aldabra and Assumption, collected by Mr. J. C. F. Fryer. Trans. Linn. Soc. London (Ser. 2, Zool.) v. 15 (pt 2, no. 18): 301-302.

———. 1912 (Mar.) **[ref. 3644]**. The classification of the teleostean fishes of the order Pediculati. Ann. Mag. Nat. Hist. (Ser. 8) v. 9 (no. 51): 277-289.

———. 1912 (Apr.) **[ref. 3645]**. The anatomy and classification of the symbranchoid eels. Ann. Mag. Nat. Hist. (Ser. 8) v. 9 (no. 52): 387-390, Pl. 9.

———. 1912 (Sept.) **[ref. 3646]**. The classification of the blennioid fishes. Ann. Mag. Nat. Hist. (Ser. 8) v. 10 (no. 57): 265-280.

———. 1912 (Sept.) **[ref. 3647]**. Description of two new eels from West Africa, belonging to a new genus and family. Ann. Mag. Nat. Hist. (Ser. 8) v. 10 (no. 57): 323-324.

———. 1912 (Nov.) **[ref. 3648]**. A revision of the poeciliid fishes of the genera *Rivulus, Pterolebias* and *Cynolebias*. Ann. Mag. Nat. Hist. (Ser. 8) v. 10 (no. 59): 494-508.

———. 1912 (Dec.) **[ref. 3649]**. Sexual differences in the poeciliid fishes of the genus *Cynolebias*. Ann. Mag. Nat. Hist. (Ser. 8) v. 10 (no. 60): 641-642.

———. 1912 (19 July) **[ref. 3650]**. Philippine sharks. Science (n. s.) v. 36 (no. 916): 81.

———. 1912 **[ref. 12438]**. A synopsis of the myxinoids of the genus *Heptatretus* or *Bdellostoma*. Ann. Mag. Nat. Hist. (Ser. 8) v. 9 (no. 53): 534-536.

———. 1913 **[ref. 3651]**. The Antarctic fishes of the Scottish National Antarctic Expedition. Trans. R. Soc. Edinb. v. 49 (pt 2, no. 2): 229-292, Pls. 1-11.

———. 1913 (1 Sept.) **[ref. 3652]**. A collection of fishes made by Professor Francisco Fuentes at Easter Island. Proc. Zool. Soc. Lond. 1913 (pt 3): 368-374, Pls. 55-60.

———. 1913 (17 Dec.) **[ref. 3653]**. A revision of the cyprinodont fishes of the subfamily Poeciliinae. Proc. Zool. Soc. Lond. 1913 (pt 4): 977-1018, Pls. 99-101.

———. 1913 (July) **[ref. 3654]**. The classification of the percoid fishes. Ann. Mag. Nat. Hist. (Ser. 8) v. 12 (no. 67): 111-145.

———. 1913 (Sept.) **[ref. 3655]**. Fishes from the River Ucayali, Peru, collected by W. Mounsey. Ann. Mag. Nat. Hist. (Ser. 8) v. 12 (no. 69): 281-283.

———. 1913 (Nov.) **[ref. 3656]**. The fishes of the San Juan River, Colombia. Ann. Mag. Nat. Hist. (Ser. 8) v. 12 (no. 71): 462-473.

———. 1913 (Dec.) **[ref. 3657]**. *Phallostethus dunckeri*, a remarkable new cyprinodont fish from Johore. Ann. Mag. Nat. Hist. (Ser. 8) v. 12 (no. 72): 548-555.

———. 1914 (27 June) **[ref. 3659]**. Fishes. British Antarctic ('Terra Nova') expedition, 1910. Natural History Report. Zoology. v. 1 (no. 1): 1-54, Pls. 1-13.

———. 1914 (Mar.) **[ref. 3660]**. Report on the freshwater fishes collected by the British Ornithologists' Union expedition and the Wollaston expedition in Dutch New Guinea. Trans. Zool. Soc. Lond. v. 20 (pt 6, no. 1): 275-286, Pl. 1.

———. 1914 (Jan.) **[ref. 3661]**. Diagnoses of new marine fishes collected by the British Antarctic ('Terra Nova') expedition. Ann. Mag. Nat. Hist. (Ser. 8) v. 13 (no. 73): 11-17.

———. 1914 (Jan.) **[ref. 3662]**. A synopsis of the fishes of the family Macrorhamphosidae. Ann. Mag. Nat. Hist. (Ser. 8) v. 13 (no. 73): 17-21.

———. 1914 (Feb.) **[ref. 3663]**. Two new cyprinid fishes from Waziristan, collected by Major G. E. Bruce. Ann. Mag. Nat. Hist. (Ser. 8) v. 13 (no. 74): 261-263.

———. 1914 (July) **[ref. 3664]**. Descriptions of two new cyprinodont fishes from Mexico, presented to the British Museum by Herr A. Rachow. Ann. Mag. Nat. Hist. (Ser. 8) v. 14 (no. 79): 65-67.

———. 1916 (20 Apr.) **[ref. 3667]**. The morphology of the cyprinodont fishes of the subfamily Phallostethinae, with descriptions of a new genus and two new species. Proc. Zool. Soc. Lond. 1916 (pt 1) (no. 1): 1-26, Pls. 1-4.

———. 1916 (20 Apr.) **[ref. 12509]**. Fishes from Natal, collected by Mr. Romer Robinson. Ann. Durban Mus. v. 1 (pt 3): 167-170.

———. 1917 (Apr.) **[ref. 3665]**. A revision of the clupeoid fishes of the genera *Pomolobus*, *Brevoortia* and *Dorosoma* and their allies. Ann. Mag. Nat. Hist. (Ser. 8) v. 19 (no. 112): 297-316.

———. 1917 (Feb.) **[ref. 3668]**. A revision of the clupeid fishes of the genus *Pellonula* and of related genera in the rivers of Africa. Ann. Mag. Nat. Hist. (Ser. 8) v. 19 (no. 110): 198-207.

———. 1920 (Jan.) **[ref. 3669]**. The classification of the fishes of the family Cichlidae.—I. The Tanganyika genera. Ann. Mag. Nat. Hist. (Ser. 9) v. 5 (no. 25): 33-53.

———. 1920 (July) **[ref. 3670]**. Three new fishes from the Tanganyika Territory. Ann. Mag. Nat. Hist. (Ser. 9) v. 6 (no. 31): 104-105.

———. 1920 (25 Mar.) **[ref. 3671]**. A revision of the flat-fishes (Heterosomata) of Natal. Ann. Durban Mus. v. 2 (pt 5): 205-222.

———. 1921 (May) **[ref. 3672]**. New fishes from deep water off the coast of Natal. Ann. Mag. Nat. Hist. (Ser. 9) v. 7 (no. 41): 412-420.

———. 1922 (27 Jan.) **[ref. 3673]**. The cichlid fishes of Lake Nyassa. Proc. Zool. Soc. Lond. 1921 (pt 4) (no. 36): 675-727, Pls. 1-6.

———. 1922 (Sept.) **[ref. 3674]**. The classification of the fishes of the family Cichlidae.—II. On African and Syrian genera not restricted to the great lakes. Ann. Mag. Nat. Hist. (Ser. 9) v. 10 (no. 57): 249-264.

———. 1922 (11 Apr.) **[ref. 3675]**. The cichlid fishes of Lake Victoria. Proc. Zool. Soc. Lond. 1922 (pt 1) (no. 9): 157-191, Pls. 1-4.

———. 1925 (Jan.) **[ref. 3676]**. Description of a new salmonoid fish from the Caribbean Sea, obtained by the 'Dana' expeditions, 1920-22. Ann. Mag. Nat. Hist. (Ser. 9) v. 15 (no. 85): 59-60.

———. 1925 (May) **[ref. 3677]**. New ceratioid fishes from the N. Atlantic, the Caribbean Sea, and the Gulf of Panama, collected by the 'Dana.' Ann. Mag. Nat. Hist. (Ser. 9) v. 15 (no. 89): 561-567.

———. 1925 **[ref. 3678]**. Dwarfed males parasitic on the females in oceanic angler-fishes (Pediculati Ceratioidea). Proc. R. Soc. Lond. B. Biol. Sci. v. 97: 386-400, Pl. 20.

———. 1926 (24 Apr.) **[ref. 3679]**. The pediculate fishes of the suborder Ceratioidea. Danish Dana Exped. 1920-22 No. 2: 1-45, Pls. 1-13.

REGAN, C. T., AND E. TREWAVAS. 1929 (30 May) **[ref. 3680]**. The fishes of the families Astronesthidae and Chauliodontidae. Danish Dana Exped. 1920-22 No. 5: 1-39, Pls. 1-7.

———. 1930 (10 Mar.) **[ref. 3681]**. The fishes of the families Stomiatidae and Malacosteidae. Danish Dana Exped. 1920-22 No. 6: 1-143, Pls. 1-14.

———. 1932 **[ref. 3682]**. Deep-sea angler-fishes (Ceratioidea). Rep. Carlsberg Ocean. Exped. 1928-30 v. 2: 1-113, Pls. 1-10. [Printed 11 Oct. 1932.]

REID, E. D. 1935 (31 Dec.) **[ref. 3683]**. Two new fishes of the families Dactyloscopidae and Clinidae from Ecuador and the Galapagos. Copeia 1935 (no. 4): 163-166.

———. 1940 (11 Mar.) **[ref. 3684]**. A new genus and species of eel from the Puerto Rican deep. Reports on the collections obtained by the first Johnson-Smithsonian deep-sea expedition to the Puerto Rican deep. Smithson. Misc. Collect. v. 91 (no. 31): 1-5.

———. 1940 (24 Apr.) **[ref. 3685]**. A new genus and species of pearl fish, family Carapidae, from off Gorgona Island, Colombia. Rep. Allan Hancock Pacific Exped. 1932-1938 v. 9 (no. 2): 47-50, Pl. 6.

———. 1943 (15 Dec.) **[ref. 3686]**. Review of the genera of blennioid fishes related to *Ophioblennius*. J. Wash. Acad. Sci. v. 33 (no. 12): 373-384.

REID, J. 1849 (June) **[ref. 3687]**. An account of a specimen of the vaagmaer, or *Vogmarus islandicus* (*Trachypterus Bogmarus* of Cuvier and Valenciennes), thrown ashore in the Firth of Forth. Ann. Mag. Nat. Hist. (Ser. 2) v. 3 (no. 18): 456-477, Pl. 16.

REINHARDT, J. C. H. 1831 **[ref. 6533]**. [Bidrag til vor Kundskab om Grönlands Fiske.] Pp. 18-24. In: H. C. Örsted. Overs. Danske Vidensk. Selsk. Forhandl Kjobenhavn 1830-31: 1-40. [Not seen. Also in K. Danske Vidensk. Selsk. Naturvid. Math. Afhandl, 1832, v. 5: lxxiv-lxxvi (not seen).]

———. 1833 **[ref. 3690]**. Bemaerkninger til den Skandinaviske Ichtyologie. 1-37.

———. 1834 **[ref. 13469]**. [Om Gymnelus]. P. 4. In: H. C. Örsted. Overs. K. Dansk. Vidensk. Selsk. Forh. 1831-32: 1-40.

———. 1835 **[ref. 7155]**. [Untitled.] Overs. Danske Vidensk. Selsk. Forhandl. Kjobenhavn 1834-1835: 5-9.

———. 1837 **[ref. 3695]**. [Untitled report.] K. Dansk. Videnskab. Selsk. Nat. Math. Afh. v. 6: LXXV-LXXIX.

———. 1837 **[ref. 6587]**. [Untitled report.] K. Dansk. Videnskab. Selsk. Nat. Math. Afh. v. 6: CVII-CXI.

———. 1837 **[ref. 13398]**. Tillaeg til det første bidrag til den grönlandske fauna. Kobenhaven, pp. 115-122. Also in K. Dansk. Vidensk. Selsk. Naturvid. Math. Afhandl., 1838, v. 7:221-228. [Not seen.]

———. 1838 **[ref. 3691]**. Ichthyologiske bidrag til den Grönlandske fauna. Indledning, indeholdende tillaeg og forandringer i den fabriciske fortegnelse paa Grönlandske hvirveldyr. K. Danske Vidensk. Selsk. Naturvid. Math. Afhandl. v. 7: 83-196. [Also as separate (perhaps in 1837), pp. 1-114.]

REINHARDT, J. T. 1849 **[ref. 3692]**. Nye sydamerikanske Ferskvandsfiske. Vidensk. Medd. Naturh. Foren. Kjob. 1849 (nos. 3-5): 29-57. [Also as a separate, Copenhagen 1849, 32 pp.]

———. 1859 **[ref. 3693]**. *Stegophilus insidiosus*, en ny Mallefish fra Brasilien of dens Levemaade. Vidensk. Medd. Dansk Naturh. Foren. Kjob. Aaret 1858: 79-97, Pl. 2. [Date on cover is 1859.]

———. 1866 **[ref. 3694]**. Om trende, formeentligt ubeskrevne fisk af characinernes eller Karpelaxenes familie. Overs. Danske Vidensk. Selsk. Forhandl Kjobenhavn 1866: 49-68, Pls. 1-2.

REIS, R. E. 1983 (24 Mar.) **[ref. 12857]**. *Rhineloricaria longicauda* e *Rineloricaria quadrensis*, duas novas espéces de Loricariinae do sul do Brasil (Pisces, Siluriformes, Loricariidae). Iheringia, Ser. Zool. No. 62: 61-80.

———. 1987 (6 Oct.) **[ref. 6263]**. *Ancistrus cryptophthalmus* sp. n., a blind mailed catfish from the Tocantins River Basin, Brazil (Pisces, Siluriformes, Loricariidae). Rev. Fr. Aquariol. v. 14 (no. 3): 81-84.

———. 1989 **[ref. 14219]**. Systematic revision of the Neotropical characid subfamily Stethaprioninae (Pisces, Characiformes). Comun. Mus. Cienc. PUCRS, Ser. Zool. Porto Alegre v. 2 (no. 6): 3-86.

REIS, R. E., AND L. R. MALABARBA. 1988 (31 Mar.) **[ref. 6638]**. Revision of the neotropical cichlid genus *Gymnogeophagus* Ribeiro, 1918, with descriptions of two new species (Pisces, Perciformes). Rev. Bras. Zool. v. 4 (no. 4): 259-305.

RENDAHL, H. 1921 **[ref. 3700]**. Results of Dr. E. Mjöbergs Swedish scientific expeditions to Australia, 1910-13. XXVIII. Fische. K. Sven. Vetenskapsakad. Handl. v. 61 (no. 9): 1-24.

———. 1922 **[ref. 3701]**. A contribution to the ichthyology of north-west Australia. Nyt. Mag. Naturv. Kristiania (Medd. Zool. Mus. No. 5) v. 60: 163-197.

———. 1928 **[ref. 3702]**. Beiträge zur Kenntnis der Chinesischen Süsswasserfische. I. Systematischer Teil. Ark. Zool. v. 20 A (no.

1): 1-194.
——. 1930 **[ref. 6880]**. Pegasiden-studien. Ark. Zool. v. 21 A (no. 27): 1-56.
——. 1932 **[ref. 3703]**. Die Fischfauna der chinesischen Provinz Szetschwan. Ark. Zool. v. 24 A (pt 4): 1-134.
——. 1933 (ca. 23 Feb.) **[ref. 3704]**. Studien über innerasiatische Fische. Ark. Zool. v. 25 A (no. 11): 1-51.
——. 1944 **[ref. 3705]**. Einige Cobitiden von Annam und Tokin. Goteb. K. Veten. Vitt. Hets-Samh. Handl. Sja. Folj. (Ser. B) v. 3 (no. 3): 1-54.
Rennis, D. S., and D. F. Hoese. 1985 (19 Apr.) **[ref. 5859]**. A review of the genus *Parioglossus*, with descriptions of six new species (Pisces, Gobioidei). Rec. Aust. Mus. v. 36 (no. 3-4): 169-201.
——. 1987 **[ref. 6602]**. *Aioliops*, a new genus of ptereleotrine fish (Pisces: Gobioidei) from the tropical Indo-Pacific with descriptions of four new species. Rec. Aust. Mus. v. 39: 67-84.
Retzius, A. J. 1799 **[ref. 3706]**. *Lampris*, en ny fiskslaogt; beskriften af A. J. Retzius. Kongl. Vetensk. Acad. Handlingar v. 20 (for 1799): 91-100.
Ribbink, A. J., B. A. Marsh, A. C. Marsh, A. C. Ribbink, and B. J. Sharp. 1983 (Aug.) **[ref. 13555]**. A preliminary survey of the cichlid fishes of rocky habitats in Lake Malawi. So. African J. Zool. (Zool. Dierkunde) v. 18 (no. 3): 149-310.
Richards, W. J., and J. M. Leis. 1984 **[ref. 13668]**. Labroidei: development and relationships. Am. Soc. Ichthyol. Herpetol. Spec. Publ. No. 1: 542-547.
Richards, W. J., and V. P. Saksena. 1977 **[ref. 5285]**. Systematics of the gurnards, genus *Lepidotrigla* (Pisces, Triglidae), from the Indian Ocean. Bull. Mar. Sci. v. 27 (no. 2): 208-222.
Richardson, J. 1836 **[ref. 3730]**. Fishes. In: Back, G., Narrative of the Arctic land expedition to the mouth of the Great Fish River, and along the shores of the Arctic Ocean...1833-1835. London. i-x + 1-663, 14 pls. [Not seen.]
——. 1836 **[ref. 3731]**. The Fish. In: Fauna Boreali-Americana; or the zoology of the northern parts of British America: containing descriptions of the objects of natural history collected on the late northern land expeditions, under the command of Sir John Franklin, R.N. Part three: 1-xv + 1-327, Pls. 74-97.
——. 1839 (Nov.) **[ref. 3732]**. Account of an interesting collection of fish formed at Port Author in Van Diemen's Land, by T. J. Lempriere, Esq. Proc. Zool. Soc. Lond. Part 7 (1839): 95-100. [Also in Ann. Mag. Nat. Hist. 1840, v. 4: 450-457.]
——. 1840 (July) **[ref. 3733]**. [Description of a collection of fishes made at Port Arthur in Van Diemen's Land.] Proc. Zool. Soc. Lond. Part 8 (1840) (87): 25-30. [Also in Ann. Mag. Nat. Hist. 1841, v. 6: 306-310.]
——. 1842 **[ref. 3734]**. Catalogue of fish found at King George's Sound. In: Eyre, E. J., Journals of expeditions of discovery into central Australia. Vol. I. [Not seen.]
——. 1842 **[ref. 12568]**. Contributions to the ichthyology of Australia. Ann. Mag. Nat. Hist. (n. s.) v. 9: 120-131.
——. 1842-44 **[ref. 13097]**. Description of Australian fish. Trans. Zool. Soc. Lond. v. 3 (pts 1-2): 69-131, 133-185, 8 pls. [Date from Duncan 1937 [ref. 13606], 69-131 published 16 June 1842, 133-185 on 23 Jan. 1844. Not seen.]
——. 1843 (Sept.) **[ref. 3735]**. Description of the lurking machete (*Machaerium subduscens*) from the northern coast of New Holland. Ann. Mag. Nat. Hist. (n. s.) v. 12 (no. 76): 175-178, Pl. 6.
——. 1843 **[ref. 6537]**. Icones piscium, or plates of rare fishes. Part I. Richard and John E. Taylor, London. 1-8, col. Pls. 1-5.
——. 1843 **[ref. 12502]**. Report on the present state of the ichthyology of New Zealand. Rep. Brit. Assoc. Adv. Sci. (12th meeting) [1842]: 12-30.
——. 1843 **[ref. 13395]**. Contributions to the ichthyology of Australia. Ann. Mag. Nat. Hist. v. 2: 422-428.
——. 1844 (June) **[ref. 3736]**. Description of a genus of Chinese fish. Ann. Mag. Nat. Hist. (n. s.) v. 13 (no. 76): 462-464.
——. 1844 (June) **[ref. 3737]**. Description of a new genus of gobioid fish. Ann. Mag. Nat. Hist. (n. s.) v. 13 (no. 86): 461-462.
——. 1844 (Oct.) **[ref. 3738]**. Generic characters of an undescribed Australian fish. Ann. Mag. Nat. Hist. (n. s.) v. 14 (no. 91): 280.
——. 1844-45 **[ref. 3739]**. Ichthyology. In R. B. Hinds (ed.) The zoology of the voyage of H. M. S. Sulphur, under the command of Captain Sir Edward Belcher, R. N., C. B., F. R. G. S., etc., during the years 1836-42. London. v. 1: 51-150, Pls. 35-64. [Part 2: 51-86 published after June 1844, Part 3: 87-150 published fall 1845.]
——. 1844-48 **[ref. 3740]**. Ichthyology of the voyage of H. M. S. Erebus & Terror... In: J. Richardson & J. E. Gray. The zoology of the voyage of H. H. S. "Erebus & Terror," under the command of Captain Sir J. C. Ross ... during ... 1839-43. London v. 2 (2): i-viii + 1-139, Pls. 1-60. [1844: 1-16; 1845: 17-52; 1846: 53-74; 1848: i-viii + 75-139.]
——. 1845 (May) **[ref. 3741]**. Generic characters of *Gasteroschisma melampus*, a fish which inhabits Port Nicholson, New Zealand. Ann. Mag. Nat. Hist. (n. s.) v. 15 (no. 99): 346.
——. 1846 (June/July) **[ref. 3742]**. Report on the ichthyology of the seas of China and Japan. Rep. Brit. Assoc. Adv. Sci. (15th meeting) [1845]: 187-320.
——. 1846 **[ref. 3743]**. Descriptions of six fish. Pp. 484-497, Pls. 1-4. In: J. L. Stokes, vol. 1. Discoveries in Australia ... surveyed during the voyage of H. M. S. Beagle, between the years 1837 and 1843. Also a narrative ... islands of the Arafura Sea. London.
——. 1848 **[ref. 3744]**. Fishes. Pp. 1-28, Pls. 1-10. In: A. Adams. The zoology of the voyage of H. M. S. Samarang; under the command of Captain Sir Edward Belcher, during the years 1843-1846. London.
——. 1850 (12 Nov.) **[ref. 3745]**. Notices of Australian fish. Proc. Zool. Soc. Lond. Part 18 (1850): 58-77, 3 pls. [Also in Ann. Mag. Nat. Hist. (Ser 2) v. 7: 273-292.]
——. 1854 **[ref. 3746]**. Vertebrates, including fossil mammals. Fish. Pp. 156-171, Pls. 30-33. In: E. Forbes (ed.). The zoology of the voyage of H. M. S. Herald, under the command of Captain Henry Kellett, R. N., C. B., during the years 1845-51. London.
——. 1856 **[ref. 3747]**. Ichthyology. In: Encyclopaedia Britannica. London.
——. 1858 (12 Jan.) **[ref. 3748]**. On *Siphonognathus*, a new genus of Fistularidae. Proc. Zool. Soc. Lond. Part 25 (1857): 237-240, Pl. 6.
Richardson, J., and J. E. Gray. 1843 **[ref. 1885]**. List of fish hitherto detected on the coasts of New Zealand, by John Richardson, M. D., Inspector of Hospitals at Haslar; with the description, by J. E. Gray, Esq., and Dr. Richardson, of the new species brought home by Dr. Dieffenback. Pp. 206-228. In: E. Dieffenbach, Travels in New Zealand. London.
Richardson, L. R. 1953 (Dec.) **[ref. 3749]**. *Neomyxine* n. g. (Cyclostomata) based on *Myxine biniplicata* Richardson and Jowett 1951, and further data on the species. Trans. R. Soc. N. Z. v. 81 (pt 3): 379-383.
——. 1958 (May) **[ref. 3750]**. A new genus and species of Myxinidae (Cyclostomata). Trans. R. Soc. N. Z. v. 85 (pt 2): 283-287.
Richter, H. J. 1981 **[ref. 6578]**. Ein notwendiger Schritt — Einführung eines neuen Gattungsnamens für die maulbrütenden Kampffische unter besonderer Betrachtung von *Pseudobetta pugnax* (Cantor, 1849). Aquarien Terrarien v. 28 (no. 7): 272-275.
Ride, W. D. L., and T. Younès. 1986 **[ref. 13544]**. (eds.) Biological nomenclature today. A review of the present state and current issues of biological nomenclature of animals, plants, bacteria and viruses. Int. Union Biol. Sci. Monogr. Ser. No. 2: 1-70.
Ringuelet, R. A., and R. H. Aramburu. 1960 **[ref. 14229]**. Pesces Marinos de la Republica Argentina. AGRO Publicacion Tecnica, Min. Asuntos Agri. 1-141.
Risch, L. 1980 (31 Mar.) **[ref. 3754]**. Description of *Parasicydium bandama*, gen. nov., sp. nov., a new gobiid fish from the Bandama River, Ivory Coast (Pisces Gobiidae). Rev. Zool. Afr. v. 94 (no. 1): 126-132.

——. 1986 (Apr.) **[ref. 6190]**. Bagridae (pp. 2-35). In: Daget et al. 1986 [ref. 6189].

——. 1987 (31 Mar.) **[ref. 6751]**. Description of four new bagrid catfishes from Africa (Siluriformes: Bagridae). Cybium v. 11 (no. 1): 20-38.

——. 1988 (30 Mar.) **[ref. 6735]**. Description d'une espèce nouvelle de *Chrysichthys* (Pisces, Bagridae), provenant de la rivière Konkouré (République de Guinée). Cybium v. 12 (no. 1): 3-7.

Risso, A. 1810 **[ref. 3755]**. Ichthyologie de Nice, ou histoire naturelle des poissons du departement des Alpes Maritimes. F. Schoell, Paris. i-xxxvi + 1-388, Pls. 1-11.

——. 1820 **[ref. 3756]**. Mémoire sur un nouveau genre de poisson nommé Alépocéphale vivant dans les grandes profondeurs de la mer de Nice. Mem. Reale Accad. Sci. Torino v. 25: 270-272, Pl. 10. [Also in Bull. Sci. Nat. (Férussac), v. 2: 298-299 (not seen).]

——. 1826 **[ref. 3757]**. Histoire naturelle des principales productions de l'Europe méridionale, et particulièrement de celles des environs de Nice et des Alpes maritimes. F. G. Levrault, Paris & Strasbourg. v. 3: i-xvi + 1-480, Pls. 1-16. [Fishes in vol. 3 of 5.]

Risso, E. N. P. de, and M. I. Morra. 1964 **[ref. 5940]**. *Parapterodoras paranensis*: nuevo género, nueva especie de Doradidae (Pisces—Nematognathi). Not. Mus. Cienc. Nat. Chaco v. 1 (no. 2): 1-5, Pl. 1.

Risso, E. N. P. de, and F. J. J. Risso. 1953 **[ref. 5938]**. El "Cornalito" [*Sorgentinia incisa* (Jenyns) n. g.] y su ubicación sistemática (Atherinidae, Sorgentininae nueva subfamilia). Trabajo Museo Tres Arroyos, Caso Scouts "Santa Coloma." Año 1, no. 1: 5-25, Pls. 1-3.

Rita, S. D., P. Banarescu and T. T. Nalbant. 1978 **[ref. 3758]**. *Oreonectes (Indoreonectes) keralensis* a new subgenus and species of loach from Kerala, India (Pisces, Cobitidae). Trav. Mus. Hist. Nat. 'Grigore Antipa' v. 19: 185-188.

Rivas, L. R. 1963 (14 June) **[ref. 3761]**. Subgenera and species groups in the poeciliid fish genus *Gambusia* Poey. Copeia 1963 (no. 2): 331-347.

——. 1971 (1 Dec.) **[ref. 3762]**. A new genus and species of western Atlantic serranoid fishes, with anterior vent. Copeia 1971 (no. 4): 718-721.

——. 1980 (Sept.) **[ref. 3763]**. Eight new species of poeciliid fishes of the genus *Limia* from Hispaniola. Northeast Gulf Sci. v. 4 (no. 1): 28-38.

——. 1986 (4 Aug.) **[ref. 5210]**. Systematic review of the perciform fishes of the genus *Centropomus*. Copeia 1986 (no. 3): 579-611.

Rivas, L. R., and G. S. Myers. 1950 (12 Dec.) **[ref. 3764]**. A new genus of poeciliid fishes from Hispaniola, with notes on genera allied to *Poecila* and *Mollienesia*. Copeia 1950 (no. 4): 288-294, Pl. 1.

Roberts, C. D. 1989 **[ref. 12441]**. Reproductive mode in the percomorph fish genus *Polyprion* Oken. J. Fish Biol. v. 34: 1-9.

——. 1989 **[ref. 12486]**. A revision of New Zealand and Australian orange perches (Teleostei; Serranidae) previously referred to *Lepidoperca pulchella* (Waite) with description of a new species of *Lepidoperca* from New Zealand. J. Nat. Hist. v. 23 (no. 3): 513-524.

Roberts, T. R. 1966 (7 Oct.) **[ref. 3769]**. Description and osteology of *Lepidarchus adonis*, a remarkable new characid fish from West Africa. Stanford Ichthyol. Bull. v. 8 (no. 3): 209-227.

——. 1967 **[ref. 3770]**. *Rheoglanis dendrophorus* and *Zaireichthys zonatus*, bagrid catfishes from the lower rapids of the Congo River. Ichthyol. Aquarium J. v. 39: 119-131.

——. 1967 (5 Dec.) **[ref. 3771]**. *Virilia*, a new genus of sexually dimorphic characid fishes from West Africa, with remarks on characoids having an incomplete lateral line. Stanford Ichthyol. Bull. v. 8 (no. 4): 251-259.

——. 1971 (15 Jan.) **[ref. 3773]**. *Micromischodus sugillatus*, a new hemiodontid characin fish from Brazil, and its relationship to the Chilodontidae. Breviora No. 367: 1-25.

——. 1971 (29 Dec.) **[ref. 5528]**. Osteology of the Malaysian phallostethoid fish *Ceratostethus bicornis*, with a discussion of the evolution of remarkable structural novelties in its jaws and external genitalia. Bull. Mus. Comp. Zool. v. 142 (no. 4): 393-418.

——. 1972 (25 Feb.) **[ref. 3775]**. Osteology and description of *Thrattidion noctivagus*, a minute, new freshwater clupeid fish from Cameroon, with a discussion of pellonulin relationships. Breviora No. 382: 1-25.

——. 1972 (25 Feb.) **[ref. 12567]**. An attempt to determine the systematic position of *Ellopostoma megalomycter*, an enigmatic freshwater fish from Borneo. Breviora No. 384: 1-16.

——. 1973 (13 Mar.) **[ref. 3776]**. The glandulocaudine characid fishes of the Guayas Basin in western Ecuador. Bull. Mus. Comp. Zool. v. 144 (no. 8): 489-514.

——. 1973 (15 June) **[ref. 7051]**. Osteology and relationships of the Prochilodontidae, a South American family of characoid fishes. Bull. Mus. Comp. Zool. v. 145 (no. 4): 213-235.

——. 1974 (18 Dec.) **[ref. 6872]**. Osteology and classification of the noetropical characoid fishes of the families Hemiodontidae (including Anodontinae) and Parodontidae. Bull. Mus. Comp. Zool. v. 146 (no. 9): 411-472, Pl. 1.

——. 1981 (5 Mar.) **[ref. 6588]**. Sundasalangidae, a new family of minute freshwater salmoniform fishes from southeast Asia. Proc. Calif. Acad. Sci. v. 42 (no. 9): 295-302.

——. 1982 (13 Dec.) **[ref. 5460]**. *Gobiocichla ethelwynnae*, a new species of goby-like cichlid fish from the rapids in the Cross River, Cameroon. Proc. K. Ned. Akad. Wet. (Ser. C, Zool.) v. 85 (no. 4): 575-587.

——. 1982 (15 June) **[ref. 5513]**. The southeast Asian freshwater pufferfish genus *Chonerhinos* (Tetraodontidae), with descriptions of new species. Proc. Calif. Acad. Sci. v. 43 (no. 1): 1-16.

——. 1982 (14 May) **[ref. 6689]**. The Bornean gastromyzontine fish genera *Gastromyzon* and *Glaniopsis* (Cypriniformes, Homalopteridae), with descriptions of new species. Proc. Calif. Acad. Sci. v. 42 (no. 20): 497-524.

——. 1982 (21 Dec.) **[ref. 6807]**. A revision of the south and southeastern Asian angler-catfishes (Chacidae). Copeia 1982 (no. 4): 895-901.

——. 1982 (21 Dec.) **[ref. 6808]**. Systematics and geographical distribution of the Asian silurid catfish genus *Wallago*, with a key to the species. Copeia 1982 (no. 4): 890-894.

——. 1983 (6 May) **[ref. 6816]**. Revision of the south and southeast Asian sisorid catfish genus *Bagarius*, with description of a new species from the Mekong. Copeia 1983 (no. 2): 435-445.

——. 1984 (12 July) **[ref. 5318]**. Skeletal anatomy and classification of the neotenic Asian salmoniform superfamily Salangoidea (icefishes or noodlefishes). Proc. Calif. Acad. Sci. v. 43 (no. 13): 179-220.

——. 1984 (11 Dec.) **[ref. 5829]**. *Amazonsprattus scintilla*, new genus and species from the Rio Negro, Brazil, the smallest known clupeomorph fish. Proc. Calif. Acad. Sci. v. 43 (no. 20): 317-321.

——. 1984 (Feb.) **[ref. 6182]**. Hepsetidae (pp. 138-139). In: Daget et al. 1984 [ref. 6168].

——. 1986 (15 Aug.) **[ref. 5802]**. Systematic review of the Mastacembelidae or spiny eels of Burma and Thailand, with description of two new species of *Macrognathus*. Jpn. J. Ichthyol. v. 33 (no. 2): 95-109.

——. 1986 **[ref. 5942]**. *Danionella translucida*, a new genus and species of cyprinid fish form Burma, one of the smallest living vertebrates. Environ. Biol. Fishes v. 16 (no. 4): 231-241.

——. 1986 (Apr.) **[ref. 6223]**. Tetraodontidae (pp. 434-436). In: Daget et al. 1986 [ref. 6189].

——. 1989 **[ref. 6439]**. The freshwater fishes of western Borneo (Kalimantan Barat, Indonesia). Mem. Calif. Acad. Sci. No. 14: i-xii + 1-210.

——. 1989 (31 Mar.) **[ref. 12832]**. *Mormyrus subundulatus*, a new species of mormyrid fish with a tubular snout from West Africa. Cybium v. 13 (no. 1): 51-54.

——. 1989 (24 Aug.) **[ref. 13302]**. Systematic revision and description of new species of suckermouth catfishes (*Chiloglanis*, Mochokidae) from Cameroun. Proc. Calif. Acad. Sci. v. 46 (no. 6): 151-178.

ROBERTS, T. R., AND M. KOTTELAT. 1984 (17 Jan.) **[ref. 5352]**. Description and osteology of *Thryssocypris*, a new genus of anchovylike cyprinid fishes, based on two new species from southeast Asia. Proc. Calif. Acad. Sci. v. 43 (no. 11): 141-158.

ROBERTS, T. R., AND R. A. TRAVERS. 1986 (30 June) **[ref. 6759]**. *Afromastacembelus sexdecimspinus*, a new species of mastacembelid spiny-eel from rapids in the Cross River Basin, Cameroon. Cybium v. 10 (no. 2): 105-114.

ROBINS, C. H. 1989 **[ref. 13289]**. Family Derichthyidae (pp. 420-431). In: Böhlke, E. B. (ed.) 1989 [ref. 13282].

ROBINS, C. H., AND C. R. ROBINS. 1970 (31 Dec.) **[ref. 3783]**. The eel family Dysommidae (including the Dysomminidae and Nettodaridae), its osteology and composition, including a new genus and species. Proc. Acad. Nat. Sci. Phila. v. 122 (no. 6): 293-335.

———. 1971 (18 Oct.) **[ref. 7127]**. Osteology and relationships of the eel family Macrocephenchelyidae. Proc. Acad. Nat. Sci. Phila. v. 123 (no. 6): 127-150.

———. 1976 (15 Apr.) **[ref. 3784]**. New genera and species of dysommine and synaphobranchine eels (Synaphobranchidae) with an analysis of the Dysomminae. Proc. Acad. Nat. Sci. Phila. v. 127 (no. 18): 249-280.

———. 1989 **[ref. 13287]**. Family Synaphobranchidae (pp. 207-253). In: Böhlke, E. B. (ed.) 1989 [ref. 13282].

ROBINS, C. R. 1961 (19 June) **[ref. 3785]**. Studies on fishes of the family Ophidiidae—VI. Two new genera and a new species from American waters. Copeia 1961 (no. 2): 212-221.

———. 1967 (1 Sept.) **[ref. 3786]**. The status of the serranid fish *Liopropoma aberrans*, with the description of a new, apparently related genus. Copeia 1967 (no. 3): 591-595.

———. 1989 **[ref. 13483]**. The phylogenetic relationships of the anguilliform fishes (pp. 9-23). In: Böhlke, E. B. (ed.) 1989 [ref. 13282].

ROBINS, C. R., AND R. M. BAILEY. 1982 (23 Feb.) **[ref. 6548]**. The status of the generic names *Microgeophagus*, *Pseudoapistogramma*, *Pseudogeophagus* and *Papiliochromis* (Pisces: Cichlidae). Copeia 1982 (no. 1): 208-210.

ROBINS, C. R., R. M. BAILEY, C. E. BOND, J. R. BROOKER, E. A. LACHNER, R. N. LEA AND W. B. SCOTT. 1980 **[ref. 7111]**. A list of common and scientific names of fishes from the United States and Canada (Fourth Edition). Am. Fish. Soc. Spec. Publ. No. 12: 1-174.

———. In press **[ref. 14237]**. Common and scientific names of fishes from the United States and Canada (Fifth Edition). Am. Fish. Soc. Spec. Publ.

———. In press **[ref. 14238]**. World fishes important to North Americans exclusive of species from the continental waters of the United States and Canada. Am. Fish. Soc. Spec. Publ.

ROBINS, C. R., AND J. E. BÖHLKE. 1961 (17 Mar.) **[ref. 3787]**. A new gobioid fish from the Antilles and comments on *Ctenogobius fasciatus* and *C. curtisi*. Copeia 1961 (no. 1): 46-50.

ROBINS, C. R., AND P. L. COLIN. 1979 **[ref. 6986]**. Three new grammid fishes from the Caribbean Sea. Bull. Mar. Sci. v. 29 (no. 1): 41-52.

ROBINS, C. R., AND D. P. DE SYLVA. 1964 (10 Sept.) **[ref. 6550]**. *Mimocubiceps virginiae*, a supposed apogonid, a junior synonym of the sparid fish, *Stenotomus chrysops*. Copeia 1964 (no. 3): 589.

———. 1965 (Mar.) **[ref. 3788]**. The Kasidoroidae, a new family of mirapinniform fishes from the western Atlantic Ocean. Bull. Mar. Sci. v. 15 (no. 1): 189-201.

ROBINS, C. R., AND E. C. RANEY. 1956 (June) **[ref. 12222]**. Studies of the catostomid fishes of the genus *Moxostoma*, with descriptions of two new species. Mem. Cornell Univ. Agric. Exper. Sta. No. 343: 1-56, Pls. 1-5.

ROBINS, C. R., AND W. A. STARCK, II. 1961 (29 Dec.) **[ref. 3789]**. Materials for a revision of *Serranus* and related fish genera. Proc. Acad. Nat. Sci. Phila. v. 113 (no. 11): 259-314.

ROBISON, B. H., AND T. M. LANCRAFT. 1984 (1 May) **[ref. 6812]**. *Gorgasia barnesi* (Congridae: Heterocongrinae), a new garden eel from the Banda Sea. Copeia 1984 (no. 2): 404-409.

ROCHEBRUNE, A. T. DE. 1880 **[ref. 3790]**. Description de quelques nouvelles espèces de poissons propres à la Sénégambie. Bull. Soc. Philomath. Paris (Ser. 7) v. 4: 159-169.

———. 1885 **[ref. 3791]**. Vertebratorum novorum vel minus cognitorum orae Africae occidentalis incolarum. Diagnoses. Bull. Soc. Philomath. Paris (Ser. 7) v. 9: 86-99.

ROFEN, R. R. 1963 (15 July) **[ref. 3794]**. Diagnoses of new genera and species of alepisauroid fishes of the family Paralepididae. Aquatica No. 2: 1-7.

———. 1963 (22 July) **[ref. 3795]**. Diagnoses of new species and a new genus of alepisauroid fishes of the family Scopelarchidae. Aquatica No. 3: 1-4.

ROGERS, W. 1981 (15 May) **[ref. 5502]**. Taxonomic status of cichlid fishes of the Central American genus *Neetroplus*. Copeia 1981 (no. 2): 286-296.

ROHDE, F. C., AND R. G. ARNDT. 1987 (28 Dec.) **[ref. 13524]**. Two new species of pygmy sunfishes (Elassomatidae, *Elassoma*) from the Carolinas. Proc. Acad. Nat. Sci. Phila. v. 139: 65-85.

ROSA, I. L., AND R. S. ROSA. 1987 (9 Dec.) **[ref. 6066]**. *Pinguipes* Cuvier and Valenciennes and Pinguipedidae Günther, the valid names for the fish taxa usually known as *Mugilioides* and Mugiloididae. Copeia 1987 (no. 4): 1048-1051.

ROSA, R. S., H. P. CASTELLO AND T. B. THORSON. 1987 (13 May) **[ref. 5974]**. *Plesiotrygon iwamae*, a new genus and species of neotropical freshwater stingray (Chondrichthyes: Potamotrygonidae). Copeia 1987 (no. 2): 447-458.

RÖSE, A. F. 1793 **[ref. 3833]**. Petri Artedi Angermannia—Sueci synonymia nominum piscium fere omnium...Ichthyologiae, pars IV. Greifswald, Edition II. 1-140. [Supplement to Walbaum's Artedi Piscium; contains a few available generic names; see Jordan 1917:51-52 [ref. 2407].]

ROSEN, D. E. 1967 (20 Oct.) **[ref. 3808]**. New poeciliid fishes from Guatemala, with comments on the origins of some South and Central American forms. Am. Mus. Novit. No. 2303: 1-15.

———. 1979 (30 Mar.) **[ref. 7020]**. Fishes from the uplands and intermontane basins of Guatemala: revisionary studies and comparative geography. Bull. Am. Mus. Nat. Hist. v. 162 (art. 5): 267-376.

ROSEN, D. E., AND R. M. BAILEY. 1959 (31 Mar.) **[ref. 12020]**. Middle-American poeciliid fishes of the genera *Carlhubbsia* and *Phallichthys* with descriptions of two new species. Zoologica (N. Y.) v. 44: 1-44, Pls. 1-6.

———. 1963 (6 Dec.) **[ref. 7067]**. The poeciliid fishes (Cyprinodontiformes), their structure, zoogeography, and systematics. Bull. Am. Mus. Nat. Hist. v. 126 (art. 1): 1-176.

ROSEN, D. E., AND P. H. GREENWOOD. 1976 (9 June) **[ref. 7094]**. A fourth neotropical species of synbranchid eel and the phylogeny and systematics of synbranchiform fishes. Bull. Am. Mus. Nat. Hist. v. 157 (art. 1): 1-69.

ROSEN, D. E., AND L. R. PARENTI. 1981 (27 Nov.) **[ref. 5538]**. Relationships of *Oryzias*, and the groups of atherinomorph fishes. Am. Mus. Novit. No. 2719: 1-25.

ROSENBLATT, R. H., AND M. A. BELL. 1976 (7 July) **[ref. 7076]**. Osteology and relationships of the roosterfish, *Nematistius pectoralis* Gill. Contrib. Sci. (Los Ang.) No. 279: 1-23.

ROSENBLATT, R. H., AND D. M. COHEN. 1986 (24 Feb.) **[ref. 5198]**. Fishes living in deepsea thermal vents in the tropical eastern Pacific, with descriptions of a new genus and two new species of eelpouts (Zoarcidae). Trans. San Diego Soc. Nat. Hist. v. 21 (no. 4): 71-79.

ROSENBLATT, R. H., AND J. E. MCCOSKER. 1970 **[ref. 3809]**. A key to the genera of the ophichthid eels, with descriptions of two new genera and three new species from the eastern Pacific. Pac. Sci. v. 24 (no. 4): 494-505.

———. 1988 (5 Feb.) **[ref. 6383]**. A new species of *Acanthemblemaria* from Malpelo Island, with a key to the Pacific members of the genus (Pisces: Chaenopsidae). Proc. Calif. Acad. Sci. v. 45 (no. 7): 103-110.

ROSENBLATT, R. H., AND I. RUBINOFF. 1972 (June) **[ref. 7124]**. *Pythonichthys asodes*, a new heterenchelyid eel from the Gulf of Panama. Bull. Mar. Sci. v. 22 (no. 2): 355-364.

ROSENBLATT, R. H., AND J. S. STEPHENS, JR. 1978 (15 May) **[ref. 3810]**. *Mccoskerichthys sandae*, a new and unusual chaenopsid blenny from the Pacific coast of Panama and Costa Rica. Contrib. Sci. (Los Ang.) No. 293: 1-22.

ROSENBLATT, R. H., AND L. R. TAYLOR, JR. 1971 **[ref. 3811]**. The Pacific species of the clinid fish tribe Starksiini. Pac. Sci. v. 25 (no. 3): 436-463.

ROSENBLATT, R. H., AND R. R. WILSON, JR. 1987 (20 Feb.) **[ref. 6711]**. Cutlassfishes of the genus *Lepidopus* (Trichiuridae), with two new eastern Pacific species. Jpn. J. Ichthyol. v. 33 (no. 4): 342-351.

ROULE, L. 1911 **[ref. 3813]**. Sur quelques larves des poissons apodes. C. R. Hebd. Seances Acad. Sci. v. 153 (no. 16): 732-735.

———. 1913 **[ref. 3815]**. Deuxième expédition antarctique française. Poissons. Paris. 1-24, 4 pls.

———. 1913 (15 Apr.) **[ref. 3816]**. Notice préliminaire sur *Grimaldichthys profundissimus* nov. gen., nov. sp.. Poisson abyssal recueilli à 6.035 mètres de profondeur dans l'Océan Atlantique par S. A. S. le Prince de Monaco. Bull. Inst. Oceanogr. (Monaco) No. 261: 1-8.

———. 1914 **[ref. 3814]**. Description préliminaire d'un poisson abyssal nouveau (*Grimaldichthys profundissimus* nov. gen., nov. sp.). Recueilli dans l'Océan Atlantique, à 6.035 mètres de profondeur. Ninth Int. Congress Zool., Monaco 1914: 498-500.

———. 1915 **[ref. 3817]**. Sur un nouveau genre de poissons apodes, et sur quelques particularités de la biologie de ces êtres. C. R. Hebd. Seances Acad. Sci. v. 160 (no. 8): 283-284.

———. 1915 **[ref. 12566]**. Considérations sur les genres *Xenodermichthys* Gunth. et *Aleposomus* Gill dans la famille des Alépocéphalidés. Bull. Mus. Natl. Hist. Nat. (Ser. 1) v. 21 (no. 2) [1915]: 42-46. [Possibly published later than 1915.]

———. 1916 (20 May) **[ref. 3818]**. Notice préliminaire sur quelques espèces nouvelles ou rares des poissons provenant des croisières de S. A. S. le Prince de Monaco. Bull. Inst. Oceanogr. (Monaco) No. 320: 1-32.

———. 1921 **[ref. 3819]**. Sur un nouveau poisson abyssal (*Scombrolabrax heterolepis*, nov. gen. nov. sp.) pêché dans les eaux de l'île Madère. C. R. Hebd. Seances Acad. Sci. v. 172 (no. 24): 1534-1536.

———. 1922 (20 Mar.) **[ref. 3820]**. Description de *Scombrolabrax heterolepis* nov. gen. nov. sp., poisson abyssal nouveau de l'Ile Madère. Bull. Inst. Oceanogr. (Monaco) No. 408: 1-8.

———. 1923 **[ref. 3821]**. Un cas probable de mutation chez les poissons. C. R. Soc. Biol. Paris v. 89: 1027-1028.

———. 1925 **[ref. 5090]**. Les poissons des eaux douces de la France. Paris. i-xvi + 1-228, Pls. 1-37.

———. 1929 (25 Nov.) **[ref. 3822]**. Description de poissons abyssaux provenant de l'île Madère et des parages du Maroc. Bull. Inst. Oceanogr. (Monaco) No. 546: 1-18.

———. 1935 (22 May) **[ref. 3824]**. Nouvelles observations sur quelques espèces de poissons abyssaux provenant de Madère. Bull. Inst. Oceanogr. (Monaco) No. 674: 1-6.

ROULE, L., AND F. ANGEL. 1930 (10 Feb.) **[ref. 6884]**. Larves et alevins de poissons provenant des croisières du Prince Albert I de Monaco. Result. Campagnes Sci. Prince Albert I. Fasc. 79: 1-148, Pls. 1-6.

———. 1931 (20 Sept.) **[ref. 3825]**. Observations et rectifications concernant divers poissons recueillis par S. A. S. le Prince Albert Ier de Monaco au cours des compagnes 1911 à 1914. Bull. Inst. Oceanogr. (Monaco) No. 581: 1-8.

———. 1932 **[ref. 3826]**. Notice préliminaire sur un nouveau genre de poisson abyssal provenant des collections du Musée Océanographique de Monaco. Bull. Mus. Natl. Hist. Nat. (Ser. 2) v. 4 (no. 5): 500.

———. 1933 (25 Jan.) **[ref. 3827]**. Poissons provenant des campagnes du Prince Albert Ier de Monaco. Result. Campagnes Sci. Monaco Fasc. 86: 1-115 + 4, Pls. 1-4.

ROULE, L., AND L. BERTIN. 1924 **[ref. 3828]**. Notice préliminaire sur la collection des Nemichthydés recueillie par l'expedition du 'Dana' (1921-1922), suivie de considérations sur la classification de cette section des poissons apodes. Bull. Mus. Natl. Hist. Nat. (Ser. 1) v. 30 (no. 1): 61-67.

———. 1929 (1 Sept.) **[ref. 3829]**. Les poissons apodes appartenant au sous-ordre des Nemichthydiformes. Danish Dana Exped. 1920-22 No. 4: 1-113, Pls. 1-9.

ROUX, C. 1971 **[ref. 3830]**. Révision des poissons marins de la famille des Batrachoididae de la côte occidentale Africaine. Bull. Mus. Natl. Hist. Nat. (Ser. 2) v. 42 (no. 4): 626-643.

———. 1973 **[ref. 7200]**. Pomadasyidae (pp. 391-395). In: Hureau & Monod 1973 [ref. 6590].

———. 1976 **[ref. 6031]**. On the dating of the first edition of Cuvier's Régne Animal. J. Soc. Bibliogr. Nat. Hist. v. 8 (no. 1): 31.

———. 1986 (Apr.) **[ref. 6209]**. Gerridae (pp. 325-326), Pomadasyidae (pp. 327-330). In: Daget et al. 1986 [ref. 6189].

ROUX, C., AND G. P. WHITLEY. 1972 (25 Feb.) **[ref. 3832]**. *Perulibatrachus*, nouveau nom de genre de poissons téléostéens de la famille des Batrachoididae, en remplacement de *Parabatrachus* Roux, 1970. Bull. Mus. Natl. Hist. Nat. Zool. No. 6 [1971]: 349-350.

ROUX-ESTÈVE, R., AND P. FOURMANOIR. 1955 (5 Jan.) **[ref. 5324]**. Poissons capturés par la mission de la "Calypso" en Mer Rouge. Ann. Inst. Ocean. Monaco (n. s.) v. 30 (art. 7): 195-203.

RÜPPELL, W. P. E. S. 1828-30 **[ref. 3843]**. Atlas zu der Reise im nördlichen Africa. Fische des Rothen Meeres. Frankfurt-am-Main. 1-141 + 3 pp., col. Pls. 1-35. [Part 1 (1828): 1-26, Pls. 1-6; part 2 (1829): 27-94, Pls. 7-24; part 3 (1830): 95-141, Pls. 25-35.]

———. 1835-38 **[ref. 3844]**. Neue Wirbelthiere zu der Fauna von Abyssinien gehörig. Fische des Rothen Meeres. Frankfurt-am-Main. 1-148, Pls. 1-33. [1835:1-28, Pls. 1-7; 1836:29-52, Pls. 8-14; 1837:53-80, Pls. 15-21; 1838:81-148, Pls. 22-33.] [For dates see Sawyer 1952 [ref. 13582].]

———. 1836 **[ref. 3845]**. Neuer Nachtrag von Beschreibungen und Abbildungen neuer Fische, im Nil entdeckt. Mus. Senckenberg, Abhandl. Beschr. Naturg. v. 2 (no. 1): 1-28. [Date on cover is 1837, Heft. 1 (pp. 1-116) published Jan-Feb. 1836 [J. Soc. Nat. Hist., v. 1: 156].]

———. 1852 **[ref. 3846]**. Verzeichniss der in dem Museum der Senckenbergischen naturforschenden Gesellschaft aufgestellten Sammlungen. Vierte Abtheilung. Fische und deren Skelette. Frankfurt-am-Main. 1-40.

RUSSELL, B. C. 1983 (Jan.) **[ref. 5413]**. *Nelabrichthys*, a new genus of labrid fish (Perciformes: Labridae) from the southern Indian and Atlantic oceans. J. L. B. Smith Inst. Ichthyol. Spec. Publ. No. 27: 1-7.

———. 1985 (Jan.) **[ref. 5235]**. Revision of the Indo-Pacific labrid fish genus *Suezichthys*, with descriptions of four new species. Indo-Pac. Fishes No. 2: 1-21, col. Pls. 1-2.

———. 1986 **[ref. 5708]**. Family No. 186: Nemipteridae (pp. 600-601). In: Smiths' Sea Fishes (Smith & Heemstra 1986 [ref. 5715]).

———. 1986 **[ref. 5990]**. A new species of *Suezichthys* (Pisces: Labridae) from the Great Australian Bight. Trans. R. Soc. S. Aust. v. 110 (pt 2): 59-61.

———. 1986 (12 May) **[ref. 5991]**. Review of the western Indian Ocean species of *Nemipterus* Swainson 1839, with description of a new species. Senckenb. Biol. v. 67 (no. 1/3): 19-35.

———. 1986 **[ref. 5992]**. Two new species of *Parascolopsis* (Pisces: Nemipteridae) from north-western Australia, Indonesia and the Philippines. Occas. Pap. N. Terr. Mus. Arts Sci. v. 3 (no. 1): 137-142.

———. 1988 (15 July) **[ref. 12549]**. Revision of the labrid fish genus *Pseudolabrus* and allied genera. Rec. Aust. Mus. Suppl. 9: 1-72, col. Pls. 1-4.

RUSSELL, B. C., AND J. E. RANDALL. 1981 **[ref. 6392]**. The labrid fish genus *Pseudolabrus* from islands of the southeastern Pacific, with description of a new species from Rapa. Pac. Sci. v. 34 (no. 4): 433-440, 1 col. pl.

RUTTER, C. M. 1896 (22 June) **[ref. 3841]**. Notes on fresh water fishes of the Pacific slope of North America. II. The fishes of Rio Yaqui, Sonora, with the description of a new genus of Siluridae. Proc. Calif.

Acad. Sci. (Ser. 2) v. 6: 255-262.
———. 1904 (17 Aug.) **[ref. 3842]**. Notes on fishes from the Gulf of California, with the description of a new genus and species. Proc. Calif. Acad. Sci. (Ser. 3) v. 3 (No. 8): 251-254, Pl. 24.
RUTTY, J. 1772 **[ref. 7179]**. An essay towards a natural history of the county of Dublin, accommodated to the noble designs of the Dublin Society; affording a summary view. Dublin. v. 1: 1-392, Pls. 1-5. [Fishes on pp. 345-392.]
RYAN, P. A. 1986 (30 May) **[ref. 6318]**. A new species of *Stiphodon* (Gobiidae: Sicydiaphiinae) from Vanuatu. Pp. 655-662. In: Uyeno et al. (eds.) 1986 [ref. 6147].
S. D. W. 1837 **[ref. 12605]**. The fishes (Pisces) of Britain, systematically arranged. Analyst v. 18: 204-215. [See Whitley 1955: 52 [ref. 4724] for a discussion.]
SABATES, A., AND J. M. FORTUÑO. 1988 (30 Mar.) **[ref. 12842]**. Description de deux larves de *Cataetyx* Günther, 1887 (Pisces, Bythitidae) récoltées en mer catalane. Cybium v. 12 (no. 1): 67-71.
SABROSKY, C. W. 1974 (Dec.) **[ref. 12758]**. Article 50 and questions of authorship. Z.N.(S.) 1925. Bull. Zool. Nomencl. v. 31 (pt 4): 206-208.
SAEED, B., W. IVANTSOFF AND G. R. ALLEN. 1989 **[ref. 13533]**. Taxonomic revision of the family Pseudomugilidae (Order Atheriniformes). Aust. J. Mar. Freshwater Res. v. 40: 719-787.
SAKAIZUMI, M. 1985 (3 May) **[ref. 6790]**. Electrophoretic comparison of proteins in five species of *Oryzias* (Pisces: Oryziatidae). Copeia 1985 (no. 2): 521-522.
SAKAMOTO, K. 1931 (Mar.) **[ref. 3859]**. Type of a new family of mailed-cheek fish from the Japan Sea, *Marukawichthys ambulator*, n. g. n. sp. J. Imp. Fish. Inst. Tokyo v. 26 (no. 2): 53-56.
———. 1932 (Mar.) **[ref. 3860]**. Two new genera and species of cottoid fishes from Japan. J. Imp. Fish. Inst. Tokyo v. 27 (no. 1): 1-6.
———. 1984 (Dec.) **[ref. 5273]**. Interrelationships of the family Pleuronectidae (Pisces: Pleuronectiformes). Mem. Fac. Fish. Hokkaido Univ. v. 31 (no. 1-2): 95-215.
SANO, M., AND K. MOCHIZUKI. 1984 (1 Aug.) **[ref. 5216]**. A revision of the Japanese sillaginid fishes. Jpn. J. Ichthyol. v. 31 (no. 2): 136-149.
SANZO, L. 1915 **[ref. 12984]**. Notizie ittiologiche. iv. *Stylophthalmoides lobiancoi* e *S. mediterraneus* Mazzarelli sono rispettivamente le forme larvali di *Scopelus caninianus* e *Scopelus humboldti*. Monit. Zool. Ital. [Not seen.]
SARUWATARI, T., K. BETSUI AND M. OKIYAMA. 1987 (10 Dec.) **[ref. 6702]**. Occurrence of the grunt sculpin (*Rhamphocottus richardsoni*) larvae from northern central Japan. Jpn. J. Ichthyol. v. 34 (no. 3): 387-392.
SARUWATARI, T., AND K. MOCHIZUKI. 1985 (28 Nov.) **[ref. 5800]**. A new lophiid anglerfish, *Lophiodes fimbriatus* from the coastal waters of Japan. Jpn. J. Ichthyol. v. 32 (no. 3): 299-304.
SASAKI, K., AND K. AMAOKA. 1989 (15 Mar.) **[ref. 12749]**. *Johnius distinctus* (Tanaka, 1916), a senior synonym of *J. tingi* (Tang, 1937) (Perciformes, Sciaenidae). Jpn. J. Ichthyol. v. 35 (no. 4): 466-468.
SASAKI, K., AND P. J. KAILOLA. 1988 **[ref. 12553]**. Three new Indo-Australian species of the sciaenid genus *Atrobucca*, with a reevaluation of generic limit. Jpn. J. Ichthyol. v. 35 (no. 3): 261-277.
SASAKI, K., AND T. UYENO. 1987 (10 Dec.) **[ref. 6700]**. *Squaliolus aliae*, a dalatiid shark distinct from *S. laticaudus*. Jpn. J. Ichthyol. v. 34 (no. 3): 373-376.
SATO, T. 1978 **[ref. 8884]**. A synopsis of the sparoid fish genus *Lethrinus*, with the description of a new species. Bull. Univ. Mus. Tokyo No. 15: 1-70, Pls. 1-12.
———. 1986 (30 May) **[ref. 5152]**. A systematic review of the sparoid fishes of the subfamily Monotaxinae. Pp. 602-612. In: Uyeno et al. (eds.) 1986 [ref. 6147].
SAUTER, H. 1905 **[ref. 3867]**. Notes from the Owston collection. I. A new ateleopodid fish from the Sagami Sea (*Ijimaia dofleini*). Annot. Zool. Jpn. v. 5 (pt 4): 233-238.
SAUVAGE, H. E. 1873 **[ref. 3870]**. Note sur le *Sebastes minutus*. Ann. Sci. Nat. (Zool.) (Ser. 5) v. 17 (art. 5): 1 p.
———. 1874 **[ref. 3873]**. Notices ichthyologiques. [With subtitles I-VI.] Rev. Mag. Zool. (Ser. 3) v. 2 [1874]: 332-340.
———. 1874 **[ref. 3904]**. Révision des espèces du groupe des Épinoches. Nouv. Arch. Mus. Natl. Hist. Nat. Paris v. 10: 5-32, Pl. 1.
———. 1878 (26 Jan.) **[ref. 3878]**. Note sur quelques Cyprinidae et Cobitidae d'espèes inédites, provenant des eaux douces de la Chine. Bull. Soc. Philomath. Paris (Ser. 7) v. 2: 86-90. [Also as a separate, pp. 1-5 (proofed from separate).]
———. 1878 (13 July) **[ref. 3879]**. Note sur quelques poissons d'espèces nouvelles provenant des eaux douces de l'Indo-Chine. Bull. Soc. Philomath. Paris (Ser. 7) v. 2: 233-242.
———. 1878 **[ref. 3880]**. Description de poissons nouveaux ou imparfaitement connus de la collection du Muséum d'Histoire Naturelle. Famille des scorpénidées, des platycéphalidées et des triglidées. Nouv. Arch. Mus. Natl. Hist. Nat. Paris (Ser. 2) v. 1: 109-158, Pls. 1-2.
———. 1879 **[ref. 3881]**. Notice sur la faune ichthyologique de l'Ogôoué. Bull. Soc. Philomath. Paris (Ser. 7) v. 3: 90-103.
———. 1880 **[ref. 3887]**. Description des Gobioïdes nouveaux ou peu connus de la collection du Muséum d'Histoire Naturelle. Bull. Soc. Philomath. Paris (Ser. 7) v. 4: 40-58.
———. 1880 **[ref. 3888]**. Description de quelques poissons de la collection du Muséum d'Histoire Naturelle. Bull. Soc. Philomath. Paris (Ser. 7) v. 4: 220-228.
———. 1880 **[ref. 3889]**. Notice sur quelques poissons de l'île Campbell et de l'Indo-Chine. Bull. Soc. Philomath. Paris (Ser. 7) v. 4: 228-233.
———. 1882 **[ref. 3894]**. Descriptions de quelques poissons de la collection du Muséum d'Histoire Naturelle. Bull. Soc. Philomath. Paris (Ser. 7) v. 6: 168-176.
———. 1883 (7 July) **[ref. 3896]**. Sur une collection de poissons recuellie dans le lac Biwako (Japon) par M. F. Steenackers. Bull. Soc. Philomath. Paris (Ser. 7) v. 7: 144-150.
———. 1884 **[ref. 3886]**. Contribution a la faune ichthyologique du Tonkin. Bull. Soc. Zool. Fr. v. 9: 209-215, Pls. 7-8.
———. 1884 **[ref. 3898]**. Sur un siluroïde de la Réunion. Bull. Soc. Philomath. Paris (Ser. 7) v. 8: 147.
SAWADA, Y. 1977 (22 Sept.) **[ref. 6984]**. First record of the gobiid fish, *Kelloggella centralis*, from Japan. Bull. Natl. Sci. Mus. (Ser. A) (Zool.) v. 3 (no. 3): 193-197.
———. 1982 (Mar.) **[ref. 14111]**. Phylogeny and zoogeography of the superfamily Cobitoidea (Cyprinoidei, Cypriniformes). Mem. Fac. Fish. Hokkaido Univ. v. 28 (no. 2): 65-223.
SAWADA, Y., AND I. S. KIM. 1977 (15 Dec.) **[ref. 6985]**. Transfer of *Cobitis multifasciata* to the genus *Niwaella* (Cobitidae). Jpn. J. Ichthyol. v. 24 (no. 3): 155-160.
SAWYER, F. C. 1952 (Nov.) **[ref. 13582]**. The dates of publication of Wilhelm Peter Eduard Simon Rüppell's [1794-1884] "Neue Wirbelthiere zu der Fauna von Abyssinien gehörig" (fol., Frankfort a. M., 1835-1840). J. Soc. Bibliogr. Nat. Hist. v. 2 (pt 9): 369-411.
———. 1953 **[ref. 6842]**. The dates of issue of J. E. Gray's "Illustrations of Indian Zoology" (London, 1830-1835). J. Soc. Bibliogr. Nat. Hist. v. 3 (no. 1): 48-55.
SAZONOV, YU. I. 1977 **[ref. 3905]**. *Searsioides multispinus*, gen. et sp. n.—a new genus and species of Searsiidae (Salmoniformes, Alepocephaloidei) from the Indo-Pacific. Tr. Inst. Okeanol. v. 107: 55-58. [In Russian, English summ.]
———. 1981 **[ref. 3906]**. *Idiolophorhynchus andriashevi* gen. et sp. n. (Osteichthyes, Macrouridae) from the Australia-New Zealand region. Zool. Zh. v. 60 (no. 9): 1357-1363. [In Russian, English summ.]
———. 1986 **[ref. 6003]**. Morphology and classification of fishes of the family Platytroctidae (Salmoniformes, Alephcephaloidei). Trans. Shirshov Inst. Oceanol. v. 121: 51-96. [In Russian, English summ.]
———. 1988 **[ref. 14118]**. New species *Bajacalifornia* (Salmonifor-

mes, Alepocephalidae) from Indo-West-Pacific. Zool. Zh. v. 67 (no. 10): 1593-1596. [In Russian, English abst.]

SAZONOV, YU. I., AND N. V. PARIN. 1977 [**ref. 3907**]. Description of a new genus and species of slickheads, *Microphotolepis multipunctata* gen. et. sp. nov. (Alepocephalidae, Osteichthyes) from the Indonesian seas. Tr. Inst. Okeanol. v. 107: 49-54. [In Russian, English summ.]

SAZONOV, YU. I., AND YU. N. SHCHERBACHEV. 1982 [**ref. 3908**]. A preliminary review of grenadiers related to the genus *Cetonurus* Günther (Gadiformes, Macrouridae). Description of new taxa related to the genera *Cetonurus* Günther and *Kumba* Marshall. Voprosy Ikhtiol. v. 22 (no. 5): 707-721. [In Russian. English translation in J. Ichthyol. v. 22 (no. 5): 1-15.]

——. 1986 [**ref. 8047**]. A new species of the genus *Tripterophycis* (Gadiformes, Moridae) from the Thalassobathyal Zone of the Southern Hemisphere. Zool. Zh. v. 65 (no. 7): 1099-1103. [In Russian, English abst.]

SCHAEFER, S., R. K. JOHNSON AND J. BABCOCK. 1986 [**ref. 5709**]. Family No. 73: Photichthyidae (pp. 243-247), Family No. 74: Gonostomatidae (pp. 247-253). In: Smiths' Sea Fishes (Smith & Heemstra 1986 [ref. 5715]).

SCHAEFER, S. A. 1988 (5 Feb.) [**ref. 6236**]. A new species of the loricariid genus *Parotocinclus* from southern Venezuela (Pisces: Siluroidei). Copeia 1988 (no. 1): 182-188.

SCHAEFER, S. A., S. H. WEITZMAN AND H. A. BRITSKI. 1989 (30 Nov.) [**ref. 13514**]. Review of the neotropical catfish genus *Scoloplax* (Pisces: Loricarioidea: Scoloplacidae) with comments on reductive characters in phylogenetic analysis. Proc. Acad. Nat. Sci. Phila. v. 141: 181-211.

SCHÄFFER, J. C. 1760 [**ref. 4989**]. Epistola ad Regio-Borussicam Societatem litterariam Duisburgensem, de studii ichthyologici faciliori ac tutiori methodo, adiectis nonnullis speciminibus. Ratisbonae. 1-24, color pls. [Rejected work on Official List, Opinion 345. Not seen.]

——. 1761 [**ref. 3910**]. Piscium Bavarico-Ratisbonensium pentas; cum tab. iv aeri incisis icones coloribus suis distinctas exhibentibus. Ratisbonae. 1-82, 4 col. pls. [Not seen.]

SCHALLER, D., AND M. KOTTELAT. 1989 [**ref. 13604**]. *Betta strohi* sp. n., ein neuer Kampffisch aus Südborneo. Aquar. Terrar. Z. v. 43 (no. 1): 31, 33-37. [English summ.; also unpublished translation provided by authors, with date of 17 Dec. 1989 for Jan. 1990 issue.]

SCHEEL, J. J., AND R. ROMAND. 1981 (July) [**ref. 3923**]. A new genus of rivulin fish from tropical Africa (Pisces, Cyprinodontidae). Trop. Fish Hobby. v. 29 (no. 11, July): 22-30, 7 col. figs.

SCHENK, E. T., AND J. H. MCMASTERS. 1956 [**ref. 13545**]. Procedure in taxonomy. Third Edition. Enlarged and in part rewritten by A. Myra Keen and Siemon William Muller. Stanford Univ. Press. i-vii + 1-149.

SCHEUERMANN, H. 1977 [**ref. 3924**]. A partial revision of the genus *Limnochromis* Regan 1920. Cichlidae, Br. Cichlid Ass. v. 3 (no. 2): 69-73.

SCHILTHUIS, L. 1891 [**ref. 3925**]. On a collection of fishes from the Congo; with description of some new species. Tijdschr. Nederl. Dierk. Ver. (Ser. 2) v. 3: 83-92, Pl. 6.

SCHINZ, H. R. 1822 [**ref. 3926**]. Das Thierreich, II. Fische. [A translation, with emendations, of Cuvier's "Règne animal" [ref. 993].)

SCHIØDTE, J. C. 1868 [**ref. 3927**]. Om øiestillingens udvikling hos flynderfiskene. Naturhist. Tidsskr. Kjöbenhavn (Ser. 3) v. 5: 269-275, Pl. 11. [In English in Ann. Mag. Nat. Hist. (Ser. 4) v. 1: 378-383.]

SCHLEGEL, H. 1858 [**ref. 6605**]. Handleiding tot de beoefening der dierkunde. Nat. Leercurses Geb. Koninkl. Milit. Akad. Breda. v. 2: i-xx + 1-628 + 2 pp., Plates by chapter.

SCHMIDT, P. J. 1903 [**ref. 3945**]. Sur les conditions physicogéographiques et la faune de la mer du Japon et de la mer d'Okhotsk. Bull. Imp. Russ. Geog. Soc. St. Petersburg v. 38 (pt 5) 1902: 503-532. [Also as a separate, pp. 1-30, with original pagination in parentheses.]

——. 1904 [**ref. 3946**]. Pisces marium orientalium Imperii Rossici. St. Petersburg. i-xi + 1-466, Pls. 1-6. [In Russian.]

——. 1915 [**ref. 3935**]. Ichthyological notes. 1. On some new and little known Cottidae of North Pacific. 2. On a new cyclogasterid fish with a rudimentary ventral disk. Ann. Mus. Zool. Acad. Imp. Sci. St. Petersburg v. 20: 611-630. [Also as a separate, dated 1916.]

——. 1929 [**ref. 3936**]. On *Hoplosebastes armatus*, a new genus and new species of the family Scorpaenidae from Japan. C. R. Acad. Sci. Leningrad No. 8 (1929): 194-196.

——. 1930 [**ref. 3937**]. Fishes of the Riu-Kiu Islands. Trans. Pacif. Comm. Acad. Sci. U.S.S.R. v. 1: 19-156, Pls. 1-6.

——. 1931 [**ref. 3933**]. *Nessorhamphus*, a new cosmopolitan genus of oceanic eels. Vidensk. Medd. Dansk Naturh. Foren. Kjob. v. 90: 371-375, Pls. 4-5.

——. 1931 [**ref. 3938**]. An additional list of the fishes of the Riu-Kiu Islands with description of *Pseudochromichthys riukianus* n. g. n. sp. Trans. Pacif. Comm. Acad. Sci. U.S.S.R. v. 2: 177-185.

——. 1935 [**ref. 3939**]. On the genus *Icelus* Kröyer (Cottidae). Bull. Acad. Sci. URSS, Leningrad (Ser. 7) 1935 (no. 3): 413-418. [In Russian, English summ.]

——. 1936 [**ref. 3942**]. On the genera *Davidojordania* Popov and *Bilabria* n. (Pisces, Zoarcidae). C. R. (Doklady) Acad. Sci. U.R.S.S. (n. s.) v. 1 (no. 2) [1936]: 97-100.

——. 1938 [**ref. 3943**]. Three new deep-sea fishes from the Okhotsk Sea. C. R. (Doklady) Acad. Sci. U.R.S.S. (n. s.) v. 19 (no. 8) [1938]: 653-656.

——. 1940 [**ref. 3944**]. On the Pacific genera *Porocottus* Gill and *Crossias* Jordan and Starks (Pisces, Cottidae). Bull. Acad. Sci. U.R.S.S., Ser. Biol. v. 1940 (no. 3): 377-387. [Russian summ.]

SCHMIDT, P. J., AND G. U. LINDBERG. 1930 [**ref. 3940**]. On a new Japanese fish *Paracanthochaetodon modestus* n. gen. et sp. C. R. Acad. Sci. Leningrad 1930: 468-470.

SCHMIDT, R. E. 1987 (11 Feb.) [**ref. 6780**]. Redescription of *Vandellia beccarii* (Siluriformes: Trichomycteridae) from Guyana. Copeia 1987 (no. 1): 234-237.

SCHOMBURGK, R. H. 1843 [**ref. 3948**]. The natural history of the fishes of Guiana. 2 vols. Edinburgh, 1841-43 [not seen]. Also 1852 as: Ichthyology. Fishes of British Guinea.—Part II [pp. 17-214, Pls. 1-30]. In: The naturalist's library, vol. 40.

SCHRANK, F. VON P. 1798 [**ref. 6444**]. Fauna Boica. Durchgedachte Geschichte der in Baieren einhemischen und zahmen Thiere. Nürnberg. v. 1: i-xii + 1-720.

SCHULTZ, L. P. 1929 (July) [**ref. 3950**]. Description of a new type of mud-minnow from western Washington, with notes on related species. Univ. Wash. Publ. Fish. v. 2 (no. 6): 73-81, Pls. 1-2.

——. 1929 (Jan.) [**ref. 5039**]. Check-list of the fresh-water fishes of Oregon and Washington. Publ. Fish. Univ. Washington v. 2 (no. 4): 43-50.

——. 1938 (12 May) [**ref. 3951**]. A new genus and two new species of cottoid fishes from the Aleutian Islands. Proc. U. S. Natl. Mus. v. 85 (no. 3038): 187-191.

——. 1940 (26 Apr.) [**ref. 3952**]. Two new genera and three new species of cheilodipterid fishes, with notes on the other genera of the family. Proc. U. S. Natl. Mus. v. 88 (no. 3085): 403-423.

——. 1941 (25 Mar.) [**ref. 3953**]. The species of *Cirripectes* Swainson and a new genus of blennioid fishes from the tropical Pacific. Copeia 1941 (no. 1): 17-20.

——. 1941 (20 Sept.) [**ref. 3954**]. A new genus and species of cyprinid fish from the Cameroons, Africa. Proc. New England Zool. Club v. 18: 85-90, Pl. 13.

——. 1941 (15 May) [**ref. 3955**]. Notes on some fishes from the Gulf of California, with the description of a new genus and species of blennioid fish. J. Wash. Acad. Sci. v. 32 (no. 5): 153-156.

——. 1942 (13 Nov.) [**ref. 3956**]. The fresh-water fishes of Liberia. Proc. U. S. Natl. Mus. v. 92 (no. 3152): 301-348, Pls. 35-36.

——. 1943 (20 Jan.) [**ref. 3957**]. Fishes of the Phoenix and Samoan islands collected in 1939 during the expedition of the U. S. S.

"Bushnell." Bull. U. S. Natl. Mus. No. 180: i-x + 1-316, Pls. 1-9.

———. 1944 **[ref. 3958]**. A new genus and species of pimelodid catfish from Colombia. J. Wash. Acad. Sci. v. 34 (no. 3): 93-95.

———. 1944 (11 Feb.) **[ref. 3959]**. The catfishes of Venezuela, with descriptions of thirty-eight new forms. Proc. U. S. Natl. Mus. v. 94 (no. 3172): 173-338, Pls. 1-14.

———. 1944 (6 Sept.) **[ref. 3960]**. The fishes of the family Characinidae from Venezuela, with descriptions of seventeen new forms. Proc. U. S. Natl. Mus. v. 95 (no. 3181): 235-367.

———. 1944 (30 Dec.) **[ref. 3961]**. A revision of the American clingfishes, family Gobiesocidae, with descriptions of new genera and forms. Proc. U. S. Natl. Mus. v. 96 (no. 3187): 47-77, Pl. 1.

———. 1945 (6 Mar.) **[ref. 3962]**. A new genus and two new species of percoid fishes from New Guinea, family Centropomidae. Proc. U. S. Natl. Mus. v. 96 (no. 3191): 115-121.

———. 1945 (17 Apr.) **[ref. 3963]**. *Emmelichthyops atlanticus*, a new genus and species of fish (family Emmelichthyidae) from the Bahamas, with a key to related genera. J. Wash. Acad. Sci. v. 35 (no. 4): 132-136.

———. 1946 (5 Dec.) **[ref. 3965]**. A revision of the genera of mullets, fishes of the family Mugilidae, with descriptions of three new genera. Proc. U. S. Natl. Mus. v. 96 (no. 3204): 377-395.

———. 1948 (24 Mar.) **[ref. 3966]**. A revision of six subfamilies of Atherine fishes, with descriptions of new genera and species. Proc. U. S. Natl. Mus. v. 98 (no. 3220): 1-48, Pls. 1-2.

———. 1949 (10 May) **[ref. 3967]**. A further contribution to the ichthyology of Venezuela. Proc. U. S. Natl. Mus. v. 99 (no. 3235): 1-211, Pls. 1-3.

———. 1950 (30 June) **[ref. 3977]**. Correction for "A revision of six subfamilies of atherine fishes, with descriptions of new genera and species." Copeia 1950 (no. 2): 150.

———. 1951 (31 Aug.) **[ref. 3968]**. A nomenclatorial correction for "A revision of the American clingfishes, family Gobiesocidae, with descriptions of new genera and forms." Copeia 1951 (no. 3): 244.

———. 1957 (1 Nov.) **[ref. 3969]**. The frogfishes of the family Antennariidae. Proc. U. S. Natl. Mus. v. 107 (no. 3383): 47-105, Pls. 1-14.

———. 1958 **[ref. 3970]**. Review of the parrotfishes Family Scaridae. Bull. U. S. Natl. Mus. No. 214: i-v + 1-143, Pls. 1-27.

———. 1959 (May) **[ref. 3971]**. A new cyprinid fish from Siam. Trop. Fish Hobby. v. 7 (no. 9): 9-11, 36-37, 1 col. fig.

———. 1966 (Apr.) **[ref. 3973]**. *Pseudorhegma diagramma*, a new genus and species of grammistid fish, with a key to genera of the family and to the species of the subfamily Pseudogramminae. Ichthyol. Aquarium J. v. 37 (Apr.): 185-194.

———. 1967 (14 June) **[ref. 3974]**. A new genus and new species of zoarcid fish from the North Pacific Ocean. Proc. U. S. Natl. Mus. v. 122 (no. 3598): 1-5.

———. 1967 **[ref. 9645]**. A review of the fish genus *Labracinus* Schlegel, family Pseudochromidae, with notes on and illustrations of some related serranoid fishes. Ichthyol. Aquarium J. v. 39 (no. 1): 19-40.

SCHULTZ, L. P., W. M. CHAPMAN, E. A. LACHNER AND L. P. WOODS. 1960 **[ref. 3972]**. Fishes of the Marshall and Marianas islands. Vol. 2. Families from Mullidae through Stromateidae. Bull. U. S. Natl. Mus. No. 202, v. 2: i-ix + 1-438, Pls. 75-123.

SCHULTZ, L. P., E. S. HERALD, E. A. LACHNER, A. D. WELANDER AND L. P. WOODS. 1953 **[ref. 3975]**. Fishes of the Marshall and Marianas islands. Vol. I. Families from Asymmetrontidae through Siganidae. Bull. U. S. Natl. Mus. No. 202, v. 1: i-xxxii + 1-685, Pls. 1-74.

SCHULTZ, L. P., AND C. L. HUBBS. 1961 **[ref. 3949]**. Early nomenclatural history of the nominal cyprinid genus *Oregonichthys* and of the blennioid, *Pholis schultzi*, fishes of western North America. Copeia 1961 (no. 4): 477-478.

SCHULTZ, L. P., AND C. MILES. 1943 (15 Aug.) **[ref. 3976]**. Descriptions of a new genus and a new species of Parodontinae, characinid fishes from South America. J. Wash. Acad. Sci. v. 33 (no. 8): 251-255.

SCHULTZ, L. P., L. P. WOODS AND E. A. LACHNER. 1966 **[ref. 5366]**. Fishes of the Marshall and Marianas islands. Vol. 3. Families Kraemeriidae through Antennariidae. Bull. U. S. Natl. Mus. No. 202, v. 3: i-vii + 1-176, Pls. 124-148.

SCHULTZE, C. A. S. 1835 **[ref. 3978]**. Versammlung von Naturforschers in Bonn. [Not seen.]

SCHULZE, E. 1890 **[ref. 3984]**. Fauna piscium Germaniae. Verzeichnis der Fische der Stromgebiete der Donau, des Rheines, der Ems, Weser, Elbe, Oder, Weichsel, des Pregels und der Memel. Jahresb. Naturw. Ver. Magdeburg For 1889: 137-213. [Also an 1892 edition, pp. 1-24 + 1-94; proofed from 1892 separate (perhaps text of separate differs from original).]

SCHWASSMANN, H. O. 1984 (Apr.) **[ref. 5345]**. Species of *Steatogenys* Boulenger (Pisces, Gymnotiformes, Hypopomidae). Bol. Mus. Para. Emilio Goeldi Nova Ser. Zool. v. 1 (no. 1): 97-114.

———. 1989 **[ref. 13745]**. *Gymnorhamphichthys rosamariae*, a new species of knifefish (Rhamphichthyidae, Gymnotiformes) from the upper Rio Negro, Brazil. Stud. Neotrop. Fauna Environ. v. 24 (no. 3): 157-167.

SCOPOLI, G. A. 1777 **[ref. 3990]**. Introductio ad historiam naturalem, sistens genera lapidum, plantarum et animalium hactenus detecta, caracteribus essentialibus donata, in tribus divisa, subinde ad leges naturae. Prague. i-x + 1-506.

SCOTT, E. O. G. 1935 (1 Apr.) **[ref. 3991]**. On a new genus of fishes of the family Galaxiidae. Pap. Proc. R. Soc. Tasmania 1934: 41-46, Pl. 3.

———. 1935 (1 Apr.) **[ref. 3992]**. Notes on the gobies recorded from Tasmania, with description of a new genus. Pap. Proc. R. Soc. Tasmania 1934: 47-62, Pl. 4.

———. 1936 (17 Aug.) **[ref. 3993]**. Observations on some Tasmanian fishes. Part III. Pap. Proc. R. Soc. Tasmania 1935: 113-129.

———. 1936 (17 Aug.) **[ref. 3994]**. Observations on fishes of the family Galaxiidae. Part I. Pap. Proc. R. Soc. Tasmania 1935: 85-112.

———. 1967 (15 June) **[ref. 3995]**. Observations on some Tasmanian fishes: part XV. Pap. Proc. R. Soc. Tasmania v. 101: 189-220.

———. 1976 (Nov.) **[ref. 7055]**. Observations on some Tasmanian fishes: part XXII. Pap. Proc. R. Soc. Tasmania v. 110: 157-217.

———. 1979 (July) **[ref. 6995]**. Observations on some Tasmanian fishes: part XXV. Pap. Proc. R. Soc. Tasmania v. 113: 99-148.

———. 1981 (Sept.) **[ref. 5533]**. Observations on some Tasmanian fishes: part XXVII. Pap. Proc. R. Soc. Tasmania v. 115: 101-152.

———. 1982 (31 Aug.) **[ref. 5472]**. Observations on some Tasmanian fishes: part XXVIII. Pap. Proc. R. Soc. Tasmania v. 116: 181-217.

———. 1983 (31 Aug.) **[ref. 5346]**. Observations on some Tasmanian fishes: part XXIX. Pap. Proc. R. Soc. Tasmania v. 117: 167-202.

———. 1986 **[ref. 5807]**. Observations on some Tasmanian fishes: part XXXI—review of Gnathanacanthidae. Pap. Proc. R. Soc. Tasmania v. 120: 51-75.

SCOTT, J. K. 1976 (31 Dec.) **[ref. 3996]**. A review of the fish genus *Neoodax* (Odacidae) of Western Australia with description of a closely allied new genus and species. Rec. West. Aust. Mus. v. 4 (no. 4): 349-373.

SCOTT, T. D. 1957 **[ref. 3997]**. A new blenny (Tripterygiidae) and pipefish (Syngnathidae) from Kangaroo Island, South Australia. Trans. R. Soc. S. Aust. v. 80: 180-183.

———. 1962 (July) **[ref. 6608]**. The marine and fresh water fishes of South Australia. South Australian Branch of the British Science Guild. 1-338.

SCUDDER, S. H. 1882 **[ref. 6462]**. Nomenclator Zoologicus. An alphabetical list of all generic names that have been employed by naturalists for recent and fossil animals from the earliest times to the close of the year 1879. In two parts: I. Supplemental list. II. Universal Index. Bull. U. S. Natl. Mus. No. 19: i-xix + 1-376 (I.) and 1-340 (II.).

SEALE, A. 1896 (27 June) **[ref. 3998]**. Notes on *Deltistes*, a new genus of catostomoid fishes. Proc. Calif. Acad. Sci. (Ser. 2) v. 6: 269.

———. 1906 **[ref. 3999]**. Fishes of the South Pacific. Occas. Pap.

Bernice P. Bishop Mus. v. 4 (no. 1): 1-89, 1 pl.

———. 1910 (23 Feb.) **[ref. 4000]**. New species of Philippine fishes. Philipp. J. Sci. Sec. A v. 4 (no. 6): 491-543, Pls. 1-13. [Date on cover is 1909, date of issue of 23 Feb. given in 1969 reprint by T.F.H. Publications and the Smithsonian Press.]

———. 1917 (May) **[ref. 4001]**. New species of apodal fishes. Bull. Mus. Comp. Zool. v. 61 (no. 4): 79-94.

SEALE, A., AND B. A. BEAN. 1908 (21 Nov.) **[ref. 4002]**. On a collection of fishes from the Philippine Islands, made by Maj. Edgar A. Mearns, Surgeon, U. S. Army, with descriptions of seven new species. Proc. U. S. Natl. Mus. v. 33 (no. 1568): 229-248.

SEDOR, A. N., AND D. M. COHEN. 1987 (18 June) **[ref. 6041]**. New bythitid fish, *Dinematichthys minyomma*, from the Caribbean Sea. Contrib. Sci. (Los Ang.) No. 385: 5-10.

SEEGERS, L. 1985 **[ref. 14269]**. Prachtgrundkärpflinge. Die Gattung *Nothobranchius*: Systematik, Vorkommen, Pflege und Zucht. Deut. Killifish Gemeinschaften J.[DKG] Suppl. 1: 1-48. [Not seen.]

SEIGEL, J. A. 1978 (28 Dec.) **[ref. 6987]**. Revision of the dalatiid shark genus *Squaliolus*: anatomy, systematics, ecology. Copeia 1978 (no. 4): 602-614.

SENNA, A. 1924 **[ref. 4005]**. Sull'organo respiratorio soprabranchiale degli Ofiocefalidi e sua sempligicazione in *Parophiocephalus* subgen n. Monit. Zool. Ital. v. 35 (no. 8): 149-160, 8 pls.

SÉRET, B. 1986 (31 Dec.) **[ref. 6753]**. Deep water skates of Madagascar. Part I. Anacanthobatidae (Pisces, Chondrichthys, Batoidea), second record of the skate *Anacanthobatis ori* (Wallace, 1967) from off Madagascar. Cybium v. 10 (no. 4): 307-326.

———. 1987 (Aug.) **[ref. 6267]**. *Halaelurus clevai*, sp. n., a new species of catshark (Scylliorhinidae) from off Madagascar, with remarks on the taxonomic status of the genera *Halaelurus* Gill and *Galeus* Rafinesque. J. L. B. Smith Inst. Ichthyol. Spec. Publ. No. 44: 1-27.

———. 1988 (30 Dec.) **[ref. 12835]**. Captures nouvelles de *Penopus microphthalmus* (Vaillant, 1888), et statut de *Penopus macdonaldi* Goode & Bean, 1896 (Pisces, Ophidiidae). Cybium v. 12 (no. 4): 281-286.

———. 1989 (30 June) **[ref. 12827]**. Deep water skates of Madagascar. Part 3. Rajidae (Pisces, Chondrichthyes, Batoidea). *Raja (Dipturus) crosnieri* sp. n. Cybium v. 13 (no. 2): 115-130.

———. 1989 (31 Mar.) **[ref. 12833]**. Deep water skates of Madagascar. Part 2. Rajidae. *Gurgesiella (Fenestraja) maceachrani* sp. n. Cybium v. 13 (no. 1): 55-64.

SÉRET, B., AND J. D. MCEACHRAN. 1986 **[ref. 9312]**. Catalogue critique des types de Poissons du Muséum national d'Histoire naturelle. Bull. Mus. Natl. Hist. Nat. Sect. A Zool. Biol. Ecol. Anim. v. 8 (no. 4): 3-50.

SERVENTY, D. L. 1948 (27 Feb.) **[ref. 4008]**. *Allothunnus fallai* a new genus and species of tuna from New Zealand. Rec. Canterbury Mus. v. 5 (no. 3): 131-135, Pls. 28-29.

SETNA, S. B., AND P. N. SARANGDHAR. 1946 **[ref. 6848]**. Selachian fauna of the Bombay waters. (A classificatory representation with a key for their identification.) Proc. Natl. Inst. Sci. India v. 12 (no. 5): 243-259.

SEVASTIANOFF, A. 1802 **[ref. 4011]**. Description de l'*Acarauna longirostris*, nouveau genre de poisson, appartenant à l'ordre des torachiques, et qui se trouve dans le Musée de nôtre Academie des Sciences. Nova Acta Acad. Sci. Imp. Petropol. v. 13 (for 1796): 357.

SHAFFER, R. V., AND E. L. NAKAMURA. 1989 (Dec.) **[ref. 13517]**. Synopsis of biological data on the cobia *Rachycentron canadum* (Pisces: Rachycentridae). NOAA Tech. Rep. NMFS 82 FAO Fish. Synop. 153: i-iv + 1-21.

SHANDIKOV, G. A. 1987 **[ref. 6343]**. Review of the genus *Nototheniops* (Nototheniidae) from the Indian sector of the Southern Ocean. U.S.S.R. Acad. Sci., Proc. Zool. Inst. Leningrad v. 162: 115-140. [In Russian, English summ.]

SHAW, G. 1791 **[ref. 4012]**. Description of the *Stylephorus chordatus*, a new fish. Trans. Linn. Soc. London v. 1: 90-92, Pl. 6.

———. 1803 **[ref. 4014]**. General zoology or systematic natural history ... Pisces. G. Kearsley, London, 1800-1826. Pisces in vol. 4 (1803) and vol. 5 (1804). [Series is 14 vols., 1800-1826.] v. 4 (pt 1): i-v + 1-186, Pls. 1-25; v. 4 (pt 2): i-, xi + 187-632, Pls. 26-92.

———. 1804 **[ref. 4015]**. General zoology or systematic natural history ... [see Shaw 1803, ref. 4014]. v. 5 (pt 1): i-v + 1-25, Pls. 93-132, 43, *65*, 69, *74* and (pt 2): i-vi + 251-463, Pls. 132-182, 158.

SHAW, G., AND F. P. NODDER. 1789-1813 **[ref. 4013]**. The Naturalist's Miscellany, or coloured figures of natural objects; drawn and described from nature. London. v. 10 [yr. 1799]: unnumbered pages, Pls. 365-396. [For dates of publication of series see Sherborn 1895 [ref. 13425].]

SHAW, T.-H. 1929 (20 May) **[ref. 4016]**. A new fresh-water goby from Tientsin. Bull. Fan Memorial Inst. Biol. Peiping v. 1 (no. 1): 1-5, Pl. 1.

SHEIKO, V. A. 1988 **[ref. 13519]**. A new notacanthid fish, *Lipogenys plaxae* Sheiko, n. sp. (Notacanthidae, Halosauroidei) from the bathyal zone of the Pacific coast of Japan. Voprosy Ikhtiol. v. 28 (no. 3): 361-366. [In Russian. English translation in J. Ichthyol. v. 28 (no. 4): 85-90.]

SHEN, S.-C. 1971 (1 Dec.) **[ref. 4017]**. A new genus of clinid fishes from the Indo-West-Pacific, with a redescription of *Clinus nematopterus*. Copeia 1971 (no. 4): 697-707.

———. 1986 (Dec.) **[ref. 6381]**. A new species *Hexatrygon brevirostra* and a new record *Anacanthobatis borneensis* (Rajiformes) from Taiwan. J. Taiwan Mus. v. 39 (no. 2): 105-110.

———. 1986 **[ref. 8041]**. A new species of stingray *Hexatrygon taiwanensis* from Taiwan Strait. J. Taiwan Mus. v. 39 (no. 1): 175-179.

SHEN, S.-C., AND S.-K. CHAN. 1978 **[ref. 6945]**. Study on the demoiselles (Pomacentridae: Pomacentrinae) from Taiwan. Q. J. Taiwan Mus. (Taipei) v. 31 (nos. 3/4): 203-262.

———. 1979 **[ref. 6944]**. Study on the demoiselles (Pomacentridae: Pomacentrinae) from Taiwan (continued from v. 31 (nos. 3/4): 262 [ref. 1978]). Q. J. Taiwan Mus. (Taipei) v. 32 (nos. 1/2): 37-98.

SHEN, S.-C., AND C.-S. LIU. 1978 **[ref. 13598]**. Clarification of the genera of the angelfishes (Family Pomacanthidae). Taiwan Sci. Rept., Natl. Taiwan Univ. 57-77.

SHEN, S.-C., AND H.-S. YEH. 1987 (31 Dec.) **[ref. 6418]**. Study on pearlfishes (Ophiidiiformes [sic]: Carapidae) of Taiwan. J. Taiwan Mus. v. 40 (no. 2): 45-56.

———. 1987 (31 Dec.) **[ref. 6419]**. Study on the razorfishes genus *Xyrichtys* (Labridae) of Taiwan. J. Taiwan Mus. v. 40 (no. 2): 61-71.

SHERBORN, C. D. 1895 **[ref. 13425]**. On the dates of Shaw and Nodder's 'Naturalist's Miscellany.' Ann. Mag. Nat. Hist. (Ser. 6) v. 15: 375-376.

———. 1897 **[ref. 13554]**. Notes on the dates of "The Zoology of the 'Beagle.'" Ann. Mag. Nat. Hist. (Ser. 6) v. 20: 483.

———. 1937 (Feb.) **[ref. 13381]**. On the dates of publication of Costa (O. G.) and (A.) Fauna del Regno di Napoli, 1829-1886. J. Soc. Bibliogr. Nat. Hist. v. 1 (pt 2): 35-47.

SHERBORN, C. D., AND B. B. WOODWARD. 1901 **[ref. 13447]**. Notes on the dates of publication of the natural history portions of some French voyages.—Part I. 'Amerique méridionale'; 'Indes orientales'; 'ôle Sud' ('Astrolabe' and 'Zélée'); 'La Bonite'; 'La Coquile'; and 'L'-Uranie et Physicienne.' Ann. Mag. Nat. Hist. (Ser. 7) v. 3: 388-392.

———. 1907 **[ref. 13429]**. Dates of publication of the zoological and botanical portions of some French voyages. Ann. Mag. Nat. Hist. (Ser. 7) v. 8: 491-494.

SHIGANOVA, T. A. 1989 **[ref. 14115]**. A new species of the genus *Parataeniophorus* (Osteichthyes, Mirapinnidae) from the northern-eastern part of the Atlantic Ocean. Zool. Zh. v. 68 (no. 3): 147-150. [In Russian, English abst.]

SHIMADA, K., AND T. YOSHINO. 1984 (15 May) **[ref. 6733]**. A new trichonotid fish from the Yaeyama Islands, Okinawa Prefecture, Japan. Jpn. J. Ichthyol. v. 31 (no. 1): 15-19.

———. 1987 (10 Sept.) **[ref. 6703]**. A new creediid fish *Creedia bilineatus* from the Yaeyama Islands, Japan. Jpn. J. Ichthyol. v. 34 (no. 2): 123-127.

SHIOGAKI, M. 1984 (20 Nov.) **[ref. 5309]**. A review of the genera *Pholidapus* and *Opisthocentrus* (Stichaeidae). Jpn. J. Ichthyol. v. 31 (no. 3): 213-224.

———. 1985 (28 Nov.) **[ref. 5199]**. A new stichaeid fish of the genus *Alectrias* from Mutsu Bay, northern Japan. Jpn. J. Ichthyol. v. 32 (no. 3): 305-315.

———. 1987 (10 Sept.) **[ref. 6708]**. An additional record of the rare cottid fish *Ocynectes modestus* from Aomori Pref., Japan. Jpn. J. Ichthyol. v. 34 (no. 2): 222-226.

———. 1988 (20 Sept.) **[ref. 6854]**. A new gobiid fish of the genus *Clariger* from Mutsu Bay, northern Japan. Jpn. J. Ichthyol. v. 35 (no. 2): 127-132.

SHIOGAKI, M., AND Y. DOTSU. 1982 (15 Aug.) **[ref. 5396]**. Two new genera and two new species of clingfishes from Japan, with coments on head sensory canals of the Gobiesocidae. Jpn. J. Ichthyol. v. 30 (no. 2): 111-121.

SHIPP, R. L. 1974 (5 Mar.) **[ref. 7147]**. The pufferfishes (Tetraodontidae) of the Atlantic Ocean. Publ. Gulf Coast Res. Lab. Mus. No. 41: 1-162.

SIDELEVA, V. G. 1982 **[ref. 14469]**. Sismosensory systems and ecology of the Baikalian sculpins (Cottoidei). Isv. (Nauka), Novisibirsk., Akad. Sci. SSSR. 1-147. [In Russian.]

SIEBOLD, C. T. E. VON. 1863 **[ref. 4021]**. Die Süsswasserfische von Mitteleuropa. Leipzig. i-viii + 1-430, color Pls. 1-2.

SILAS, E. G. 1953 **[ref. 4024]**. Classification, zoogeography and evolution of the fishes of the cyprinoid families Homalopteridae and Gastromyzonidae. Rec. Indian Mus. (Calcutta) v. 50 (pt 2): 173-263, Pl. 5.

———. 1954 **[ref. 4025]**. New fishes from the western Ghats, with notes on *Puntius arulius* (Jerdon). Rec. Indian Mus. (Calcutta) v. 51 (pt 1): 27-37, Pl. 5.

———. 1957 (5 Apr.) **[ref. 11967]**. The Ceylonese cyprinid genus *Eustira* Günther considered a synonym of *Danio* Hamilton. Copeia 1957 (no. 1): 61-62.

———. 1958 **[ref. 4026]**. Studies on cyprinid fishes of the oriental genus *Chela* Hamilton. J. Bombay Nat. Hist. Soc. v. 55 (pt 1): 54-99, Pls. 1-2.

SILVESTER, C. F. 1915 **[ref. 4027]**. Fishes new to the fauna of Porto Rico. Carnegie Inst. Wash. Year Book No. 14: 214-217. [Possibly published in 1916.]

SILVESTER, C. F., AND H. W. FOWLER. 1926 (1 Nov.) **[ref. 4028]**. A new genus and species of phosphorescent fish, *Kryptophanaron alfredi*. Proc. Acad. Nat. Sci. Phila. v. 78: 245-247, Pls. 18-19.

SINGH, A., N. SEN, P. BANARESCU AND T. T. NALBANT. 1982 **[ref. 4030]**. New noemacheiline loaches from India (Pisces, Cobitidae). Trav. Mus. Hist. Nat. 'Grigore Antipa' v. 23 (for 1981): 201-212. [French & Romanian summs.]

SKELTON, P. H. 1988 (30 Mar.) **[ref. 6737]**. The taxonomic identity of the dwarf or blackspot *Ctenopoma* (Pisces, Anabantidae) in southern Africa. Cybium v. 12 (no. 1): 73-89.

———. 1988 (30 May) **[ref. 7302]**. A taxonomic revision of the redfin minnows (Pisces, Cyprinidae) from southern Africa. Ann. Cape Prov. Mus. Nat. Hist. v. 16 (pt 10): 201-307.

———. 1989 (Aug.) **[ref. 14123]**. Descriptions of two new species of West African amphiliid catfishes (Siluroidei: Amphiliidae). J. L. B. Smith Inst. Ichthyol. Spec. Publ. No. 48: 1-13.

SKELTON, P. H., L. RISCH AND L. DE VOS. 1984 (29 June) **[ref. 5835]**. On the generic identity of the *Gephyroglanis* catfishes from southern Africa (Pisces, Siluroidei, Bagridae). Rev. Zool. Afr. v. 98 (no. 2): 337-372.

SKELTON, P. H., AND G. G. TEUGELS. 1986 **[ref. 6192]**. Amphiliidae (pp. 54-65). In: Daget et al. 1986 [ref. 6189].

SMALL, G. J. 1981 (24 June) **[ref. 5546]**. A review of the bathyal fish genus *Antimora* (Moridae: Gadiformes). Proc. Calif. Acad. Sci. v. 42 (no. 13): 341-348.

SMITH, A. 1828 (Nov.) **[ref. 12603]**. Descriptions of new, or imperfectly known objects of the animal kingdom, found in the south of Africa. So. Afr. Commercial Advertiser v. 3 (no. 145): 2. [A transcript is provided by Penrith 1972: 362 [ref. 7140].]

———. 1829 **[ref. 4976]**. Contributions to the natural history of South Africa, &c. Zool. J. v. 4: 433-444.

———. 1838 (13 Feb.) **[ref. 4034]**. [On the necessity for a revision of the groups included in the Linnaean genus *Squalus*.] Proc. Zool. Soc. Lond. Part 5 (1837) (57): 85-86.

———. 1838-47 **[ref. 4035]**. Pisces. In: Illustrations of the zoology of South Africa; consisting chiefly of figures and descriptions of the objects of natural history collected during an expedition into the interior of South Africa in 1834-36. v. 4: 77 unnumb. pp, accompanying Pls. 1-31. [Published in parts; see Barnard 1950 [ref. 6080] for dates of individual parts; fishes from 1838-1847. Bound is 1849.]

SMITH, C. L. 1971 (12 Nov.) **[ref. 14102]**. A revision of the American groupers: *Epinehelus* and allied genera. Bull. Am. Mus. Nat. Hist. v. 146 (art. 2): 67-242.

SMITH, D. G. 1984 (1 Aug.) **[ref. 6810]**. A redescription of the rare eel *Myroconger compressus* (Pisces: Myrocongridae), with notes on its osteology, relationships and distribution. Copeia 1984 (no. 3): 585-594.

———. 1989 **[ref. 13285]**. [Various eel families; Leptocephali.] In: Böhlke, E. B. (ed.) [ref. 13282].

SMITH, D. G., J. E. BÖHLKE AND P. H. J. CASTLE. 1981 (20 July) **[ref. 6158]**. A revision of the nettastomatid eel genera *Nettastoma* and *Nettenchelys* (Pisces: Anguilliformes), with descriptions of six new species. Proc. Biol. Soc. Wash. v. 94 (no. 2): 533-560.

SMITH, D. G., AND P. H. J. CASTLE. 1982 **[ref. 5453]**. Larvae of the nettastomatid eels: systematics and distribution. Dana Rep. No. 90: 1-44.

SMITH, D. G., AND R. H. KANAZAWA. 1977 **[ref. 4036]**. Eight new species and a new genus of congrid eels from the western north Atlantic with redescriptions of *Ariosoma analis*, *Hildebrandia guppyi*, and *Rhechias vicinalis*. Bull. Mar. Sci. v. 27 (no. 3): 530-543.

SMITH, D. G., AND M. M. LEIBY. 1980 (28 Aug.) **[ref. 6930]**. The larva of the congrid eel *Acromycter alcocki* (Pisces: Anguilliformes), and the distinction between congrid and ophichthid larvae. Proc. Biol. Soc. Wash. v. 93 (no. 2): 388-394.

SMITH, D. G., AND J. G. NIELSEN. 1976 (20 May) **[ref. 7084]**. Preliminary note on sexual dimorphism in the Nemichthyidae and the identity of *Avocettinops* and *Paravocettinops* (Pisces, Anguilliformes). Steenstrupia v. 4 (no. 1): 1-5.

———. 1989 **[ref. 13290]**. Family Nemichthyidae (pp. 441-459). In: Böhlke, E. B. (ed.) 1989 [ref. 13282].

SMITH, H. M. 1902 (3 Jan.) **[ref. 4038]**. The smallest known vertebrate. Science (n. s.) v. 15 (no. 366): 30-31. [Also as: Le plus petit vertébré connu. Rev. Scient., 1902, (4) 17: 345-346.]

———. 1902 (28 Mar.) **[ref. 4039]**. Description of a new species of blenny from Japan. Bull. U. S. Fish Comm. v. 21 [1901]: 93-94.

———. 1904 (27 Dec.) **[ref. 4040]**. A new cottoid fish from Bering Sea. Proc. Biol. Soc. Wash. v. 17: 163-164.

———. 1912 (8 Feb.) **[ref. 4041]**. Description of a new notidanoid shark from the Philippine Islands representing a new family. Proc. U. S. Natl. Mus. v. 41 (no. 1872): 489-491.

———. 1912 (8 Feb.) **[ref. 4042]**. The squaloid sharks of the Philippine Archipelago, with descriptions of new genera and species. Proc. U. S. Natl. Mus. v. 41 (no. 1877): 677-685, Pls. 50-54.

———. 1913 (21 June) **[ref. 4043]**. The hemiscylliid sharks of the Philippine Archipelago, with description of a new genus from the China Sea. [Scientific results of the Philippine cruise of the Fisheries steamer "Albatross," 1907-1910.—No. 28.] Proc. U. S. Natl. Mus. v. 45 (no. 1997): 567-569, Pl. 45.

———. 1913 (21 June) **[ref. 4044]**. Description of a new carcharioid shark from the Sulu Archipelago. [Scientific results of the Philippine cruise of the fisheries steamer "Albatross," 1907-1910.—No. 29.] Proc. U. S. Natl. Mus. v. 45 (no. 2003): 599-601, Pl. 47.

———. 1917 (27 July) **[ref. 4045]**. New genera of deepwater gurnards (Peristediidae) from the Philippine Islands. Proc. Biol. Soc. Wash. v. 30: 145-146.

———. 1929 (Dec.) **[ref. 4046]**. Notes on some Siamese fishes. J.

Siam Soc. Nat. Hist. Suppl. v. 8 (no. 1): 11-14.

———. 1931 (26 Mar.) **[ref. 4047]**. Descriptions of new genera and species of Siamese fishes. Proc. U. S. Natl. Mus. v. 79 (no. 2873): 1-48, Pl. 1.

———. 1931 (Sept.) **[ref. 4048]**. Notes on Siamese fishes. J. Siam Soc. Nat. Hist. Suppl. v. 8 (no. 3): 177-190.

———. 1931 (30 Oct.) **[ref. 4049]**. *Sikukia stejnegeri*, a new genus and species of freshwater cyprinoid fishes from Siam. Copeia 1931 (no. 3): 138-139.

———. 1932 (30 June) **[ref. 4050]**. Contributions to the ichthyology of Siam. I. Descriptions of a new genus and three new species of Siamese gobies. J. Siam Soc. Nat. Hist. Suppl. v. 8 (no. 4): 255-262, Pl. 23.

———. 1933 (31 May) **[ref. 4051]**. Contributions to the ichthyology of Siam. II-VI. J. Siam Soc. Nat. Hist. Suppl. v. 9 (no. 1): 53-87, Pls. 1-3.

———. 1934 (10 Oct.) **[ref. 4052]**. Contributions to the ichthyology of Siam. IX-XIX. J. Siam Soc. Nat. Hist. Suppl. v. 9 (no. 3): 287-325, Pls. 10-14.

———. 1938 (15 Sept.) **[ref. 4053]**. Status of the Asiatic fish genus *Culter*. J. Wash. Acad. Sci. v. 28 (no. 9): 407-411.

———. 1938 (23 Aug.) **[ref. 4054]**. *Chagunius*, a new genus of Asiatic cyprinoid fishes. Proc. Biol. Soc. Wash. v. 51: 157-158.

———. 1939 (26 Dec.) **[ref. 4055]**. A new genus of clariid catfishes. Copeia 1939 (no. 4): 236.

———. 1945 (13 Nov.) **[ref. 4056]**. The fresh-water fishes of Siam, or Thailand. Bull. U. S. Natl. Mus. No. 188: i-xi + 1-622, Pls. 1-9.

SMITH, H. M., AND T. E. B. POPE. 1906 (24 Sept.) **[ref. 4058]**. List of fishes collected in Japan in 1903, with descriptions of new genera and species. Proc. U. S. Natl. Mus. v. 31 (no. 1489): 459-499.

SMITH, H. M., AND L. RADCLIFFE. 1912 (30 Aug.) **[ref. 4057]**. Description of a new family of pediculate fishes from Celebes. Proc. U. S. Natl. Mus. v. 42 (no. 1917): 579-581, Pl. 72.

SMITH, H. M., AND A. SEALE. 1906 (4 June) **[ref. 4059]**. Notes on a collection of fishes from the island of Mindanao, Philippine Archipelago, with descriptions of new genera and species. Proc. Biol. Soc. Wash. v. 19: 73-82.

SMITH, J. L. B. 1931 (Jan.) **[ref. 4062]**. New and little known fish from the south and east coasts of Africa. Rec. Albany Mus. Grahamstown v. 4 (no. 1): 145-160, Pl. 16.

———. 1933 **[ref. 4063]**. An interesting new myctophid fish from South Africa. Trans. R. Soc. S. Aust. v. 21 (pt 2): 125-127, Pl. 9.

———. 1934 **[ref. 4064]**. Marine fishes of seven genera new to South Africa. Trans. R. Soc. S. Aust. v. 22 (pt 1): 89-100, Pls. 5-6.

———. 1934 **[ref. 4065]**. The Triglidae of South Africa. Trans. R. Soc. S. Aust. v. 22 (pt 4): 321-336, Pls. 16-23.

———. 1935 **[ref. 4066]**. New and little known fishes from South Africa. Rec. Albany Mus. Grahamstown v. 4: 169-235, Pls. 18-23.

———. 1935 **[ref. 13662]**. The "Galjoen" fishes of South Africa. Trans. R. Soc. S. Aust. v. 23 (pt 3): 265-276, Pls. 13-17.

———. 1937 (May) **[ref. 6553]**. New records of South African fishes. Ann. Natal Mus. v. 8 (pt 2): 167-197, Pl. 11.

———. 1938 **[ref. 4067]**. The South African fishes of the families Sparidae and Denticidae. Trans. R. Soc. S. Aust. v. 26 (pt 3): 225-305, Pls. 18-29.

———. 1939 (18 Mar.) **[ref. 4068]**. A living fish of Mesozoic type. Nature (Lond.) v. 143: 455-456.

———. 1940 **[ref. 4069]**. Sparid fishes from Portuguese East Africa, with a note on the genus *Gymnocranius* Klunzinger. Trans. R. Soc. S. Aust. v. 28 (pt 2): 175-182, Pl. 50.

———. 1942 **[ref. 4070]**. The genus *Austrosparus* Smith. Trans. R. Soc. S. Aust. v. 29 (pt 4): 279-283.

———. 1943 **[ref. 4071]**. Interesting new fishes of three genera new to South Africa, with a note on *Mobula diabolus* (Shaw). Trans. R. Soc. S. Aust. v. 30 (pt 1): 67-77.

———. 1946 (1 May) **[ref. 4072]**. The fishes of the family Clinidae in South Africa. Ann. Mag. Nat. Hist. (Ser. 11) v. 12 (no. 92): 535-546. ["Published May 1, 1946" printed on cover of separate; was to have been published Aug. 1945.]

———. 1947 (31 Oct.) **[ref. 4073]**. New species and new records of fishes from South Africa. Ann. Mag. Nat. Hist. (Ser. 11) v. 13 (no. 108): 793-821. [Published October 31, 1947 printed on cover of separate; was to have been published Dec. 1946.]

———. 1948 (4 Feb.) **[ref. 4074]**. Brief revisions and new records of South African marine fishes. Ann. Mag. Nat. Hist. (Ser. 11) v. 14 (no. 113): 335-346. [Published February 4, 1948 printed on cover of separate; was to have been published May 1847.]

———. 1948 (18 June) **[ref. 4075]**. New clinid fishes from the south western Cape, with notes on other fishes. Ann. Mag. Nat. Hist. (Ser. 11) v. 14 (no. 118): 732-736. [Published 18 June, 1948 on cover of separate; was to have been published Oct. 1947.]

———. 1948 (3 Aug.) **[ref. 4076]**. A generic revision of the mugilid fishes of South Africa. Ann. Mag. Nat. Hist. (Ser. 11) v. 14 (no. 120): 833-843. [Published 3 August, 1948 on cover of separate; was to have been published Dec. 1847.]

———. 1949 (17 June) **[ref. 4077]**. Forty-two fishes new to South Africa, with notes on others. Ann. Mag. Nat. Hist. (Ser. 12) v. 2 (no. 14): 97-111. [Published 17 June, 1949 on cover of separate; was to have been published Feb. 1849.]

———. 1949 (19 Aug.) **[ref. 4078]**. A new aracanid fish from South Africa. Ann. Mag. Nat. Hist. (Ser. 12) v. 2 (no. 17): 354-359.

———. 1949 (19 Aug.) **[ref. 4079]**. Interesting fishes of three genera new to South Africa. Ann. Mag. Nat. Hist. (Ser. 12) v. 2 (no. 17): 367-374.

———. 1949 (11 Nov.) **[ref. 4080]**. The stromateid fishes of South Africa. Ann. Mag. Nat. Hist. (Ser. 12) v. 2 (no. 23): 839-851.

———. 1949 [-65] **[ref. 5846]**. The sea fishes of southern Africa. Central News Agency, Ltd., Cape Town. 1-550, 102 pls. [Also 1953 edition (564 pp., 107 pls.), 1961 edition (580 pp., 111 pls.) and 1965 edition (580 pp., 111 pls.).]

———. 1951 (July) **[ref. 4081]**. The fishes of the family Cirrhitidae of the western Indian Ocean. Ann. Mag. Nat. Hist. (Ser. 12) v. 4 (no. 43): 625-652.

———. 1952 (Jan.) **[ref. 4082]**. The fishes of the family Haliophidae. Ann. Mag. Nat. Hist. (Ser. 12) v. 5 (no. 49): 85-101, Pl. 6.

———. 1952 (Feb.) **[ref. 4083]**. Plesiopid fishes from South and East Africa. Ann. Mag. Nat. Hist. (Ser. 12) v. 5 (no. 50): 139-151, Pls. 9-10.

———. 1952 (Apr.) **[ref. 4084]**. The fishes of the family Batrachoididae from South and East Africa. Ann. Mag. Nat. Hist. (Ser. 12) v. 5 (no. 52): 313-339.

———. 1952 (July) **[ref. 4085]**. Preliminary notes on fishes of the family Plectorhynchidae from South and East Africa, with descriptions of two new species. Ann. Mag. Nat. Hist. (Ser. 12) v. 5 (no. 55): 711-716, Pl. 26.

———. 1953 (July) **[ref. 4086]**. The fishes of the family Pseudogrammidae from East Africa. Ann. Mag. Nat. Hist. (Ser. 12) v. 6 (no. 67): 548-560.

———. 1953 **[ref. 4087]**. Os peixes apanhados no canal de Mocambique pelo Sr. Mussolini P. Fajardo. [As separate: Fishes taken in the Moçambique Channel by Mussolini P. Fajardo.] Mem. Mus. Dr. Alvaro de Castro No. 2: 3-20, 1 pl.

———. 1953 (17 Jan.) **[ref. 4088]**. The second coelacanth. Nature (Lond.) v. 171 (no. 4342): 99-101.

———. 1954 (Jan.) **[ref. 4090]**. Two interesting new anthiid fishes from East Africa. Ann. Mag. Nat. Hist. (Ser. 12) v. 7 (no. 73): 1-6.

———. 1954 (Mar.) **[ref. 4091]**. Pseudoplesiopsine fishes from South and East Africa. Ann. Mag. Nat. Hist. (Ser. 12) v. 7 (no. 75): 195-208.

———. 1954 (Apr.) **[ref. 4092]**. The Anisochromidae, a new family of fishes from East Africa. Ann. Mag. Nat. Hist. (Ser. 12) v. 7 (no. 76): 298-302, Pl. 6.

———. 1954 (Oct.) **[ref. 4093]**. Apogonid fishes of the subfamily Pseudamiinae from south-east Africa. Ann. Mag. Nat. Hist. (Ser. 12) v. 7 (no. 82): 775-795, Pl. 23.

———. 1954 (Nov.) **[ref. 4094]**. Aberrant serraniform fishes from

East Africa. Ann. Mag. Nat. Hist. (Ser. 12) v. 7 (no. 83): 861-872, Pl. 27.

———. 1955 (Feb.) **[ref. 4095]**. An interesting new gobiiform fish from South Africa. Ann. Mag. Nat. Hist. (Ser. 12) v. 8 (no. 86): 106-110.

———. 1955 (May) **[ref. 4097]**. The fishes of the family Anthiidae of the western Indian Ocean. Ann. Mag. Nat. Hist. (Ser. 12) v. 8 (no. 89): 337-350.

———. 1955 (May) **[ref. 4098]**. The fishes of the family Pomacanthidae in the western Indian Ocean. Ann. Mag. Nat. Hist. (Ser. 12) v. 8 (no. 89): 378-384, Pls. 4-5.

———. 1955 (June) **[ref. 4099]**. The fishes of the family Carapidae in the western Indian Ocean. Ann. Mag. Nat. Hist. (Ser. 12) v. 8 (no. 90): 401-416.

———. 1955 (Jan.) **[ref. 4100]**. East African unicorn fishes from Mozambique. S. Afr. J. Sci. v. 51 (no. 6): 169-174, Pls. 1-2.

———. 1955 **[ref. 4101]**. New species and new records of fishes from Moçambique. Part I. Mem. Mus. Dr. Alvaro de Castro No. 3: 3-27, Pls. 1-3.

———. 1956 (Jan.) **[ref. 4102]**. An extraordinary fish from South Africa. Ann. Mag. Nat. Hist. (Ser. 12) v. 9 (no. 97): 54-57, Pl. 1.

———. 1956 (Aug.) **[ref. 4103]**. An interesting new gobioid fish from Madagascar, with a note on *Cryptocentrus oni* Tomiyama, 1936. Ann. Mag. Nat. Hist. (Ser. 12) v. 9 (no. 104): 553-556.

———. 1956 (Jan.) **[ref. 4104]**. The parrot fishes of the family Callyodontidae of the western Indian Ocean. Ichthyol. Bull. J. L. B. Smith Inst. Ichthyol. No. 1: 1-23, Pls. 41-45.

———. 1956 (July) **[ref. 4105]**. The fishes of the family Sphyraenidae in the western Indian Ocean. Ichthyol. Bull. J. L. B. Smith Inst. Ichthyol. No. 3: 37-46, 2 pls.

———. 1956 (14 Apr.) **[ref. 4106]**. Self-inflation of a gobioid fish. Nature (Lond.) v. 177 (no. 4511): 714.

———. 1956 (Apr.) **[ref. 4107]**. Swordfish, marlin and sailfish in South and East Africa. Ichthyol. Bull. J. L. B. Smith Inst. Ichthyol. No. 2: 25-34, 2 pls.

———. 1957 (15 Jan.) **[ref. 4108]**. A remarkable new unicorn fish from East Africa. Ann. Mag. Nat. Hist. (Ser. 12) v. 9 (no. 105): 686-688. [Published 15/1/1957 on cover of separate, was to have been published in Sept. 1956.]

———. 1957 (28 Jan.) **[ref. 4109]**. The fishes of Aldabra. Part V. Ann. Mag. Nat. Hist. (Ser. 12) v. 9 (no. 106): 721-729. [Published 28/1/1957 on cover of separate; was to have been published Oct. 1956.]

———. 1957 (5 Feb.) **[ref. 4110]**. The fishes of Aldabra. Part VI. Ann. Mag. Nat. Hist. (Ser. 12) v. 9 (no. 107): 817-829. [Published 5 Feb. 1957 on cover of separate; was to have been published Nov. 1956.]

———. 1957 (22 Mar.) **[ref. 4111]**. The fishes of Aldabra.—Part VII. Ann. Mag. Nat. Hist. (Ser. 12) v. 9 (no. 108): 888-892. [Published March 22, 1957 on cover of separate; was to have been published Dec. 1957.]

———. 1957 (July) **[ref. 4112]**. The fishes of the family Scorpaenidae in the western Indian Ocean. Part I. The sub-family Scorpaeninae. Ichthyol. Bull. J. L. B. Smith Inst. Ichthyol. No. 4: 49-72, 4 pls.

———. 1957 (Oct.) **[ref. 4113]**. List of the fishes of the family Labridae in the western Indian Ocean with new records and five new species. Ichthyol. Bull. J. L. B. Smith Inst. Ichthyol. No. 7: 99-114, 2 pls.

———. 1957 (May) **[ref. 4114]**. A new shark from South Africa. S. Afr. J. Sci. v. 53: 261-264.

———. 1957 (13 Nov.) **[ref. 4115]**. A new shark from Zanzibar, with notes on *Galeorhinus* Blainville. Ann. Mag. Nat. Hist. (Ser. 12) v. 10 (no. 116): 585-592, Pls. 18-19.

———. 1957 (20 Sept.) **[ref. 4116]**. Fishes of Aldabra. Part VIII. Ann. Mag. Nat. Hist. (Ser. 12) v. 10 (no. 113): 395-400, Pls. 13-14.

———. 1958 (Dec.) **[ref. 4117]**. Rare fishes from South Africa. S. Afr. J. Sci. v. 54: 319-323.

———. 1958 (July) **[ref. 4118]**. The fishes of the family Eleotridae in the western Indian Ocean. Ichthyol. Bull. J. L. B. Smith Inst. Ichthyol. No. 11: 137-163, 3 pls.

———. 1958 (Jan.) **[ref. 4119]**. The gunnellichthid fishes with description of two new species from East Africa and of *Gunnellichthys (Clarkichthys) bilineatus* (Clark), 1936. Ichthyol. Bull. J. L. B. Smith Inst. Ichthyol. No. 9: 123-129.

———. 1958 (Oct.) **[ref. 4120]**. Fishes of the families Tetrarogidae, Caracanthidae and Synanciidae, from the western Indian Ocean with further notes on scorpaenid fishes. Ichthyol. Bull. J. L. B. Smith Inst. Ichthyol. No. 12: 167-181, Pls. 7-8.

———. 1958 (17 Sept.) **[ref. 4121]**. Tetraodont fishes from South and East Africa. Ann. Mag. Nat. Hist. (Ser. 13) v. 1 (no. 2): 156-160, Pl. 2.

———. 1959 (Feb.) **[ref. 4122]**. Gobioid fishes of the families Gobiidae, Periophthalmidae, Trypauchenidae, Taenioididae and Kraemeriidae of the western Indian Ocean. Ichthyol. Bull. J. L. B. Smith Inst. Ichthyol. No. 13: 185-225, Pls. 9-13.

———. 1959 (May) **[ref. 4123]**. Fishes of the families Blenniidae and Salariidae of the western Indian Ocean. Ichthyol. Bull. J. L. B. Smith Inst. Ichthyol. No. 14: 229-252, Pls. 14-18.

———. 1959 (Aug.) **[ref. 4124]**. Serioline fishes (yellowtails: amberjacks) from the western Indian Ocean. Ichthyol. Bull. J. L. B. Smith Inst. Ichthyol. No. 15: 255-261.

———. 1960 (30 Dec.) **[ref. 4125]**. A new grammicolepid fish from South Africa. Ann. Mag. Nat. Hist. (Ser. 13) v. 3 (no. 28): 231-235, Pls. 3-4.

———. 1960 (May) **[ref. 4126]**. Fishes of the family Gobiidae in South Africa. Ichthyol. Bull. J. L. B. Smith Inst. Ichthyol. No. 18: 299-314.

———. 1961 (Feb.) **[ref. 4127]**. Fishes of the family Xenopoclinidae. Ichthyol. Bull. J. L. B. Smith Inst. Ichthyol. No. 20: 351-356.

———. 1961 (Sept.) **[ref. 4128]**. Fishes of the family Apogonidae of the western Indian Ocean and the Red Sea. Ichthyol. Bull. J. L. B. Smith Inst. Ichthyol. No. 22: 373-418, Pls. 46-52.

———. 1963 (Dec.) **[ref. 4129]**. Fishes of the families Draconettidae and Callionymidae from the Red Sea and the western Indian Ocean. Ichthyol. Bull. J. L. B. Smith Inst. Ichthyol. No. 28: 547-564, Pls. 83-86.

———. 1963 (Sept.) **[ref. 6516]**. Fishes of the family Syngnathidae from the Red Sea and the western Indian Ocean. Ichthyol. Bull. J. L. B. Smith Inst. Ichthyol. No. 27: 515-543.

———. 1964 (31 July) **[ref. 4130]**. A new apogonid fish from deeper water of the Gulf of Guinea. Ann. Mag. Nat. Hist. (Ser. 13) v. 6 (no. 70): 621-624.

———. 1964 (15 Nov.) **[ref. 4131]**. A new serranid fish from deep water off Cook Island, Pacific. Ann. Mag. Nat. Hist. (Ser. 13) v. 6 (no. 72): 719-720, Pl. 21.

———. 1965 (14 Dec.) **[ref. 4132]**. The discovery in Mozambique of the little known eel *Ophichthys tenuis* Günther, 1870, a redescription of the type of *Caecula pterygera* Vahl, 1794, notes on other species and on generic relationships. Ann. Mag. Nat. Hist. (Ser. 13) v. 7 (no. 84): 711-723, Pls. 15-16.

———. 1965 (1 Sept.) **[ref. 4133]**. A rare anthiid fish from Cook Island, Pacific, with a résumé of related species. Ann. Mag. Nat. Hist. (Ser. 13) v. 7 (no. 81): 533-537, Pl. 12.

———. 1965 (1 Sept.) **[ref. 4134]**. An interesting new fish of the family Chiasmodontidae from South Africa, with redescription of *Odontonema kerberti* Weber, 1913. Ann. Mag. Nat. Hist. (Ser. 13) v. 7 (no. 81): 567-574, Pl. 13.

———. 1965 (Aug.) **[ref. 4135]**. Fishes of the family Atherinidae of the Red Sea and the western Indian Ocean with a new freshwater genus and species from Madagascar. Ichthyol. Bull. J. L. B. Smith Inst. Ichthyol. No. 31: 601-632, Pls. 98-102.

———. 1966 (8 Mar.) **[ref. 4136]**. An interesting new eel of the family Xenocongridae from Cook Island, Pacific. Ann. Mag. Nat. Hist. (Ser. 13) v. 8 (nos. 89/90): 297-301, Pl. 10.

———. 1966 (8 Mar.) **[ref. 4137]**. An interesting new callionymid fish from Madagascar and the first record of a clingfish from there.

Ann. Mag. Nat. Hist. (Ser. 13) v. 8 (nos. 89/90): 321-324.

———. 1966 (6 July) **[ref. 4138]**. A new clingfish from southern Mozambique. Ann. Mag. Nat. Hist. (Ser. 13) v. 8 (nos. 95/96): 641-644, Pl. 19 [as "XVIV"].

———. 1966 (1 Sept.) **[ref. 4139]**. A new stromateid fish from South Africa with illustration of the unique rare *Centrolophus huttoni* Waite, 1910. Ann. Mag. Nat. Hist. (Ser. 13) v. 9 (nos. 97/99): 1-3, Pl. 1.

———. 1966 (Apr.) **[ref. 4140]**. Certain rare fishes from South Africa with other notes. Occas. Pap. Dep. Ichthyol. Rhodes Univ. No. 7: 65-80, Pls. 13-14.

———. 1967 (May) **[ref. 4141]**. A new squalid shark from South Africa with notes on the rare *Atractophorus armatus* Gilchrist. Occas. Pap. Dep. Ichthyol. Rhodes Univ. No. 11: 117-136, Pls. 24-29.

———. 1968 (5 June) **[ref. 4142]**. A new labrid fish from deep water of Mozambique. Copeia 1968 (no. 2): 343-345.

Smith, J. L. B., and M. M. Smith. 1986 **[ref. 5710]**. Family No. 183: Sparidae (pp. 580-594). In: Smiths' Sea Fishes (Smith & Heemstra 1986 [ref. 5715]).

Smith, M. L., and R. R. Miller. 1980 (6 Sept.) **[ref. 6906]**. *Allotoca maculata*, a new species of goodeid fish from western México, with comments on *Allotoca dugesi*. Copeia 1980 (no. 3): 408-417.

———. 1986 (30 June) **[ref. 5711]**. Mexican goodeid fishes of the genus *Characodon*, with description of a new species. Am. Mus. Novit. No. 2851: 1-14.

———. 1987 (5 Aug.) **[ref. 6773]**. *Allotoca goslini*, a new species of goodeid fish from Jalisco, Mexico. Copeia 1987 (no. 3): 610-616.

Smith, M. M. 1978 (6 Dec.) **[ref. 6936]**. A new *Polysteganus* (Pisces, Sparidae) from Mauritius. Proc. Biol. Soc. Wash. v. 91 (no. 3): 563-568.

———. 1979 (28 Nov.) **[ref. 6940]**. *Rhabdosargus trorpei*, a new sparid fish from South Africa, with a key to the species of *Rhabdosargus*. Copeia 1979 (no. 4): 702-709.

———. 1980 (11 Apr.) **[ref. 6907]**. A review of the South African cheilodactylid fishes (Pisces, Perciformes), with descriptions of two new species. Ichthyol. Bull. J. L. B. Smith Inst. Ichthyol. No. 42: 1-14, Pls. 1-2.

———. 1986 **[ref. 5712]**. [Various family accounts.] In Smiths' Sea Fishes (Smith & Heemstra 1986 [ref. 5715]).

Smith, M. M., and P. C. Heemstra. 1986 **[ref. 5714]**. Family No. 31: Hexatrygonidae (pp. 142-143), Family No. 204: Pomacentridae (pp. 623-626), Family No. 263: Balistidae (pp. 876-882), Family No. 268: Tetraodontidae (pp. 894-903). In: Smiths' Sea Fishes (Smith & Heemstra 1986 [ref. 5715]).

———. 1986 **[ref. 5715]**. (eds.) Smiths' Sea Fishes. Macmillan South Africa, Johannesburg. i-xx + 1-1047, Pls. 1-144. [Revision of J. L. B. Smith's, The Sea Fishes of Southern Africa, first published in 1949. Also a 1988 Edition.]

Smith, M. M., and R. J. McKay. 1986 **[ref. 5716]**. Family No. 179: Haemulidae (pp. 564-572). In: Smiths' Sea Fishes (Smith & Heemstra 1986 [ref. 5715]).

Smith, M. M., and J. L. B. Smith. 1986 **[ref. 5717]**. Family No. 178: Pomatomidae (p. 564), Family No. 222: Mugilidae (pp. 714-720). In Smiths' Sea Fishes (Smith & Heemstra 1986 [ref. 5715]).

Smith [Eigenmann], R. 1881 (22 Apr.) **[ref. 4143]**. Description of a new gobioid fish (*Othonops eos*), from San Diego, California. Proc. U. S. Natl. Mus. v. 4 [no. 187]: 19-21.

Smith-Vaniz, W. F. 1974 (28 Mar.) **[ref. 12815]**. A review of the jawfish genus *Stalix* (Opistognathidae). Copeia 1974 (no. 1): 280-283.

———. 1975 (15 Oct.) **[ref. 7074]**. Supplemental description of rare blenniid fish *Phenablennius heyligeri* (Bleeker). Proc. Acad. Nat. Sci. Phila. v. 127 (no. 6): 53-55.

———. 1976 (17 Dec.) **[ref. 4144]**. The saber-toothed blennies, tribe Nemophini (Pisces: Blenniidae). Monogr. Acad. Nat. Sci. Phila. No. 19: i-vii + 1-196, 18 unnum. plates.

———. 1980 (19 Dec.) **[ref. 5525]**. Revision of western Atlantic species of the blenniid fish genus *Hypsoblennius*. Proc. Acad. Nat. Sci. Phila. v. 132: 285-305.

———. 1984 **[ref. 13664]**. Carangidae: relationships. Am. Soc. Ichthyol. Herpetol. Spec. Publ. No. 1: 522-533.

———. 1986 **[ref. 5718]**. Family No. 210: Carangidae (pp. 638-661), Family No. 225: Opistognathidae (pp. 726-727), Family No. 226: Cepolidae (pp. 727-728). In: Smiths' Sea Fishes (Smith & Heemstra 1986 [ref. 5715]).

———. 1987 **[ref. 6404]**. The saber-toothed blennies, tribe Nemophini (Pisces: Blenniidae): an update. Proc. Acad. Nat. Sci. Phila. v. 139: 1-52.

———. 1989 **[ref. 13438]**. Revision of the jawfish genus *Stalix* (Pisces: Opistognathidae), with descriptions of four new species. Proc. Acad. Nat. Sci. Phila. v. 141: 375-407.

Smith-Vaniz, W. F., M.-L. Bauchot and M. Desoutter. 1979 **[ref. 12247]**. Catalogue critique des types de Poissons du Muséum national d'Histoire naturelle. (Suite) (Familles des Carangidae et des Nematistiidae). Bull. Mus. Natl. Hist. Nat. Sect. A Zool. Biol. Ecol. Anim. v. 1 (no. 2, suppl.): 1-66.

Smith-Vaniz, W. F., G. D. Johnson and J. E. Randall. 1988 **[ref. 9299]**. Redescription of *Gracila albomarginata* (Fowler and Bean) and *Cephalopholis polleni* (Bleeker) with comments on the generic limits of selected Indo-Pacific groupers (Pisces: Serranidae: Epinephelinae). Proc. Acad. Nat. Sci. Phila. v. 140 (no. 2): 1-23, 1 col. pl.

Smith-Vaniz, W. F., and F. J. Palacio. 1974 (4 Feb.) **[ref. 7151]**. Atlantic fishes of the genus *Acanthemblemaria*, with description of three new species and comments on Pacific species (Clinidae: Chaenopsinae). Proc. Acad. Nat. Sci. Phila. v. 125 (no. 11): 197-224.

Smith-Vaniz, W. F., and V. G. Springer. 1971 (30 Mar.) **[ref. 4145]**. Synopsis of the tribe Salariini, with description of five new genera and three new species (Pisces: Blenniidae). Smithson. Contrib. Zool. No. 73: 1-72.

Smith-Vaniz, W. F., and J. C. Staiger. 1973 (9 July) **[ref. 7106]**. Comparative revision of *Scomberoides, Oligoplites, Parona*, and *Hypacanthus* with comments on the phylogenetic position of *Campogramma* (Pisces: Carangidae). Proc. Calif. Acad. Sci. v. 39 (no. 13): 185-256.

Smith-Vaniz, W. F., and T. Yoshino. 1985 (30 May) **[ref. 6721]**. Review of Japanese jawfishes of the genus *Opistognathus* (Opistognathidae) with description of two new species. Jpn. J. Ichthyol. v. 32 (no. 1): 18-27.

Smitt, F. A. 1893-95 **[ref. 4146]**. A history of Scandinavian fishes, by B. Fries, C. U. Ekström, and C. Sundevall. 2nd edition, revised and completed by F. A. Smitt. Stockholm & London, 1893-95. v. 1 (1893): 1-566 + i-viii; v. 2 (1895):567-1240. Plates v. 1:1-27; v. 2: 27-53.

———. 1898 **[ref. 4147]**. Poissons de l'Expédition scientifique à la Terre de Feu. II. Bih. Svenska Vet. Akad. Handl. v. 24 (afd. 4) (no.5): 1-80, Pls. 1-6.

———. 1900 **[ref. 4148]**. Preliminary notes on the arrangement of the genus *Gobius*, with an enumeration of its European species. Öfv. Kongl. Vet. Akad. Förh. v. 56 (no. 6): 543-555. [For year 1889 but apparently published in 1900.]

Snoeks, J. 1988 (30 Sept.) **[ref. 6867]**. Redescription d'*Haplochromis paucidens* Regan, 1921 et description d'*Haplochromis occultidens* sp. n. (Pisces, Cichlidae) du lac Kivu en Afrique. Cybium v. 12 (no. 3): 203-218.

Snyder, J. O. 1904 (19 Jan.) **[ref. 4149]**. A catalogue of the shore fishes collected by the steamer "Albatross" about the Hawaiian Islands in 1902. Bull. U. S. Fish Comm. v. 22 [1902]: 513-538, Pls. 1-13.

———. 1908 (30 Oct.) **[ref. 4150]**. Descriptions of eighteen new species and two new genera of fishes from Japan and the Riu Kiu Islands. Proc. U. S. Natl. Mus. v. 35 (no. 1635): 93-111.

———. 1909 (18 June) **[ref. 4151]**. Descriptions of new genera and species of fishes from Japan and the Riu Kiu Islands. Proc. U. S. Natl. Mus. v. 36 (no. 1688): 597-610.

———. 1911 (26 May) **[ref. 4152]**. Descriptions of new genera and species of fishes from Japan and the Riu Kiu Islands. Proc. U. S. Natl. Mus. v. 40 (no. 1836): 525-549.

———. 1913 (24 July) **[ref. 4153]**. The fishes of streams tributary to Monterey Bay, California. Bull. Bur. Fish. v. 32 (for 1912): 47-72, Pls. 19-24.

———. 1917 (28 Sept.) **[ref. 4156]**. The fishes of the Lahontan system of Nevada and northeastern California. Bull. Bur. Fish. v. 35 (for 1915-16): 31-86, Pls. 3-5.

SOLDATOV, V. K. 1916 (Feb.) **[ref. 4158]**. A new genus of Blenniidae from Peter the Great Bay. Ann. Mus. Zool. Acad. Imp. Sci. St. Petersburg v. 20 (for 1915): 635-637.

———. 1922 **[ref. 4159]**. On a new genus and three new species of Zoarcidae. Ann. Mus. Zool. Russ. Petrograd v. 23 (no. 2): 160-163. [Date of 1917 on reprints, published 1922 (on cover).]

———. 1922 **[ref. 4160]**. A new genus and species of Cottidae (Pisces) from Peter the Great Bay. Ann. Mus. Zool. Russ. Petrograd v. 23: 352-354.

SOLDATOV, V. K., AND G. U. LINDBERG. 1929 **[ref. 4161]**. On a new genus and species of the family Zoarcidae (Pisces) from the Okhotsk Sea. Ann. Mus. Zool. Acad. Sci. U.R.S.S. 1929: 39-42.

———. 1930 **[ref. 4164]**. A review of the fishes of the seas of the Far East. Bull. Pacif. Sci. Fish. Inst. Vladivostock v. 5: 1-576, Pls. 1-15.

SOLDATOV, V. K., AND M. N. PAVLENKO. 1915 (May) **[ref. 4165]**. Two new genera of Cottidae from Tartar Strait and Okhotsk Sea. Ann. Mus. Zool. Acad. Imp. Sci. St. Petersburg v. 20: 149-154, Pl. 4.

———. 1916 **[ref. 4162]**. A new genus of family Blenniidae - *Kasatkia* gen. nov. Ann. Mus. Zool. Russ. Petrograd v. 20: 638-640.

SOLDATOV, V. K., AND A. M. POPOV. 1929 (22 Nov.) **[ref. 4163]**. On the new genus *Cyclopteropsis* (Pisces, Cyclopteridae) from the Okhotsk Sea. C. R. Acad. Sci. Leningrad 1929: 239-242.

SOUTH, J. F. 1845 **[ref. 4170]**. Encyclopedia Metropolitana; or, Universal Dictionary of Knowledge. Edition for 1845. [Description of *Thunnus* on pp. 620-622.]

SÖZER, F. 1942 **[ref. 4171]**. Türkiye Cyprinodontid'leri hakkinda. Contributions à la connaissance des Cyprinodontides de la Turquie. Rev. Fac. Sci. Univ. Istanbul (Ser. B) Sci. Nat. v. 7 (f. 4): 307-316.

SPEIRS, J. M. 1952 (26 June) **[ref. 14251]**. Nomenclature of the channel catfish and the burbot of North America. Copeia 1952 (no. 2): 99-103.

SPIX, J. B. VON, AND L. AGASSIZ. 1829-31 **[ref. 13]**. Selecta genera et species piscium quos in itinere per Brasiliam annos MDCCCXVII-MDCCCXX jussu et auspiciis Maximiliani Josephi I... colleget et pingendso curavit Dr J. B. de Spix... Monachii Part 1: i-xvi + i-ii + 1-82, Pls. 1-49; Part 2:, 83-138, Pls. 49-101. [Part 1 published in June 1829, part 2 in Jan. 1831; see Kottelat 1988 [ref. 13380], Whitehead & Myers 1971 [ref. 6584].]

SPRINGER, S. 1950 (9 Feb.) **[ref. 4172]**. A revision of north American sharks allied to the genus *Carcharhinus*. Am. Mus. Novit. No. 1451: 1-13.

———. 1951 (31 Aug.) **[ref. 4173]**. Correction for "A revision of North American sharks allied to the genus *Carcharhinus*." Copeia 1951 (no. 3): 244.

———. 1966 **[ref. 4174]**. A review of western Atlantic cat sharks, Scyliorhinidae, with descriptions of a new genus and five new species. U. S. Fish Wildl. Serv. Fish. Bull. v. 65 (no. 3): 581-624.

———. 1979 (Apr.) **[ref. 4175]**. A revision of the catsharks, family Scyliorhinidae. NOAA Tech. Rep. NMFS Circ. No. 422: 1-152.

SPRINGER, S., AND G. H. BURGESS. 1985 (5 Aug.) **[ref. 6785]**. Two new dwarf dogsharks (*Etmopterus*, Squalidae), found off the Caribbean coast of Colombia. Copeia 1985 (no. 3): 584-591.

SPRINGER, V. G. 1955 **[ref. 10208]**. The taxonomic status of the fishes of the genus *Stathmonotus*, including a review of the Atlantic species. Bull. Mar. Sci. Gulf Caribb. v. 5 (no. 1): 66-80.

———. 1958 **[ref. 10210]**. Systematics and zoogeography of the clinid fishes of a subtribe Labrisomini Hubbs. Inst. Mar. Sci. v. 5: 417-492.

———. 1966 (22 Mar.) **[ref. 4177]**. *Medusablennius chani*, a new genus and species of blennioid fish from the Tuamotu Archipelago: its implication on blennioid classification. Copeia 1966 (no. 1): 56-60.

———. 1972 (29 Nov.) **[ref. 4178]**. Synopsis of the tribe Omobranchini with descriptions of three new genera and two new species (Pisces: Blenniidae). Smithson. Contrib. Zool. No. 130: 1-31.

———. 1973 **[ref. 7162]**. Odontaspididae (p. 11), Mitsukurinidae (p. 12), Lamnidae (pp. 13-15), Cetorhinidae (p. 16), Alopiidae (p. 17), Orectolobidae (p. 18), Scyliorhinidae (pp. 19-21), Pseudotriakidae (p. 22). In: Hureau & Monod 1973 [ref. 6590].

———. 1976 (25 June) **[ref. 4179]**. *Cirrisalarias bunares*, new genus and species of blenniid fish from the Indian Ocean. Proc. Biol. Soc. Wash. v. 89 (no. 13): 199-203.

———. 1978 (4 Apr.) **[ref. 6955]**. Synonymization of the family Oxudercidae, with comments on the identity of *Apocryptes cantoris* Day (Pisces: Gobiidae). Smithson. Contrib. Zool. No. 270: i-iii + 1-14.

———. 1983 (21 Dec.) **[ref. 5365]**. *Tyson belos*, new genus and species of western Pacific fish (Gobiidae, Xenisthminae), with discussions of gobioid osteology and classification. Smithson. Contrib. Zool. No. 390: i-iii + 1-40.

———. 1985 (20 Mar.) **[ref. 6107]**. *Oman ypsilon*, a new genus and species of blenniid fish from the Indian Ocean. Proc. Biol. Soc. Wash. v. 98 (no. 1): 90-97.

———. 1986 **[ref. 5719]**. Family No. 235: Blenniidae (pp. 742-755). In: Smiths' Sea Fishes (Smith & Heemstra 1986 [ref. 5715]).

———. 1988 (13 Sept.) **[ref. 6683]**. *Rotuma lewisi*, new genus and species of fish from the southwest Pacific (Gobioidei, Xenisthmidae). Proc. Biol. Soc. Wash. v. 101 (no. 3): 530-539.

———. 1988 (14 Sept.) **[ref. 6804]**. The Indo-Pacific blenniid fish genus *Ecscenius*. Smithson. Contrib. Zool. No. 465: i-1v + 1-134, col. Pls. 1-14.

SPRINGER, V. G., AND T. H. FRASER. 1976 (13 Sept.) **[ref. 7086]**. Synonymy of the fish families Cheilobranchidae (=Alabetidae) and Gobiesocidae, with descriptions of two new species of *Alabes*. Smithson. Contrib. Zool. No. 234: i-iii + 1-23.

SPRINGER, V. G., AND W. C. FREIHOFER. 1976 (10 Feb.) **[ref. 7108]**. Study of the monotypic fish family Pholidichthyidae (Perciformes). Smithson. Contrib. Zool. No. 216: i-iii + 1-43.

SPRINGER, V. G., AND M. F. GOMON. 1975 (2 Apr.) **[ref. 6083]**. Revision of the blenniid fish genus *Omobranchus* with descriptions of three new species and notes on other species of the tribe Omobranchini. Smithson. Contrib. Zool. No. 177: i-iii + 1-135.

SPRINGER, V. G., C. L. SMITH AND T. H. FRASER. 1977 (25 Aug.) **[ref. 5510]**. *Anisochromis straussi*, a new species of protogynous hermaphroditic fish, and synonymy of Anisochromidae, Pseudoplesiopidae, and Pseudochromidae. Smithson. Contrib. Zool. No. 252: i-iii + 1-15.

SPRINGER, V. G., AND W. F. SMITH-VANIZ. 1972 (8 Mar.) **[ref. 4180]**. A new tribe (Phenablenniini) and genus (*Phenablennius*) of blenniid fishes based on *Petroscirtes heyligeri* Bleeker. Copeia 1972 (no. 1): 64-71.

SPRINGER, V. G., AND A. E. SPREITZER. 1978 (11 Apr.) **[ref. 4181]**. Five new species and a new genus of Indian Ocean blenniid fishes, tribe Salariini, with a key to genera of the tribe. Smithson. Contrib. Zool. No. 268: i-iii + 1-20.

STAINIER, F., M. CHARDON AND P. VANDEWALLE. 1986 (31 Dec.) **[ref. 6754]**. Os, muscles et ligaments de la région céphalique de *Ciliata mustela* (Linné, 1758) (Pisces, Gadidae). Cybium v. 10 (no. 4): 327-349.

STARCK, W. A., II. 1969 (12 Mar.) **[ref. 4192]**. *Ecsenius (Anthiiblennius) midas* a new subgenus and species of mimic blenny from the western Indian Ocean. Not. Nat. (Phila.) No. 419: 1-9.

STARK, J. 1828 **[ref. 4193]**. Elements of natural history, adapted to the present state of the science, containing the generic characters of nearly the whole animal kingdom, and descriptions of the principal species. 2 vols. Edinburgh & London. v. 1 (Vertebrata): i-vi + 1-527, Pls. 1-4. [Fishes are on pp. 371-493 of v. 1.]

STARKS, E. C. 1895 (5 Nov.) **[ref. 4194]**. Description of a new genus and species of cottoid fishes from Puget Sound. Proc. Acad. Nat. Sci. Phila. 1895 [v. 47]: 410-412.

———. 1896 **[ref. 4195]**. List of fishes collected at Port Ludlow, Washington. Proc. Calif. Acad. Sci. (Ser. 2) v. 6: 549-562, Pls. 74-75.

———. 1908 (30 Oct.) **[ref. 4196]**. On a communication between the air-bladder and the ear in certain spiny-rayed fishes. Science (n. s.) v. 28 (no. 722): 613-614.

———. 1913 (17 Mar.) **[ref. 4197]**. The fishes of the Stanford expedition to Brazil. Stanford Univ. Publ., Univ. Ser. 1-77, Pls. 1-15.

———. 1924 (29 Mar.) **[ref. 4198]**. *Hime*, a new genus of fishes related to *Aulopus*. Copeia No. 127: 30.

STARKS, E. C., AND W. M. MANN. 1911 (1 July) **[ref. 4199]**. New and rare fishes from southern California. Univ. Calif. Publ. Zool. v. 8 (no. 2): 9-19.

STARNES, W. C. 1988 **[ref. 6978]**. Revision, phylogeny and biogeographic comments on the circumtropical marine percoid fish family Priacanthidae. Bull. Mar. Sci. v. 43 (no. 2): 117-203.

STARNES, W. C., AND R. E. JENKINS. 1988 (13 Sept.) **[ref. 6686]**. A new cyprinid fish of the genus *Phoxinus* (Pisces: Cypriniformes) from the Tennessee River drainage with comments on relationships and biogeography. Proc. Biol. Soc. Wash. v. 101 (no. 3): 517-529.

STAUCH, A., AND J. BLACHE. 1964 **[ref. 6081]**. Contribution à la connaissance de genre *Ateliopus* Schlegel 1846 (Pisces, Teleostei, Ateleopoidei, Ateleopidae) dans l'Atlantique Oriental. Cah. O R S T O M Ser. Oceanogr. v. 2 (no. 1): 47-54.

STAUCH, A., AND M. BLANC. 1964 **[ref. 4200]**. *Dagetichthys lakdoensis* n. g., n. sp., téléostéen pleuronectiforme du bassin de la Haute-Bénoué. Bull. Mus. Natl. Hist. Nat. (Ser. 2) v. 36 (no. 2): 172-177.

STAUFFER, J. R., JR. 1988 (3 Aug.) **[ref. 6678]**. Three new rock-dwelling cichlids (Teleostei: Cichlidae) from Lake Malawi, Africa. Copeia 1988 (no. 3): 663-668.

STAUFFER, J. R., JR., AND K. R. MCKAYE. 1985 (5 Aug.) **[ref. 6786]**. *Cyrtocara macrocleithrum*, a deep-water cichlid (Teleostei: Cichlidae) from Lake Malawi, Africa. Copeia 1985 (no. 3): 591-596.

———. 1988 (18 May) **[ref. 6412]**. Description of a genus and three deep water species of fishes (Teleostei: Cichlidae) from Lake Malawi, Africa. Copeia 1988 (no. 2): 441-449.

STEBBING, T. R. R. 1910 **[ref. 13546]**. Genders in zoology. Knowledge 1910, v. 33 (July): 259-260.

STEHMANN, M. 1970 **[ref. 4202]**. Vergleichend morphologische und anatomische Untersuchungen zur Neuordnung der Systematik der nordostatlantischen Rajidae (Chondrichthyes, Batoidei). Arch. FischereiWiss. v. 21 (no. 2): 73-163, Pls. 1-27. [English summ.]

———. 1973 **[ref. 7168]**. Rajidae (pp. 58-69). In: Hureau & Monod 1973 [ref. 6590].

———. 1976 (30 June) **[ref. 7085]**. Revision der Rajoiden-Arten des nördlichen Indischen Ozean und Indopazifik (Elasmobranchii, Batoidea, Rajiformes). Beaufortia v. 24 (no. 315): 133-175.

———. 1977 (Dec.) **[ref. 6982]**. Ein neuer archibenthaler Roche aus dem Nordostatlantik, *Raja kreffti* spec. nov. (Elasmobranchii, Batoidea, Rajidae), die zweite Spezies im Subgenus *Malacoraja* Stehmann, 1970. Arch. FischereiWiss. v. 28 (no. 2/3): 77-93.

———. 1978 (June) **[ref. 6981]**. *Raja* "bathyphila", eine Doppelart des Subgenus *Rajella*: Wielderbeschreibung von *R. bathyphila* Holt & Byrne, 1908 und *Raja bigelowi* spec. nov. (Pisces, Rajiformes, Rajidae). Arch. FischereiWiss. v. 29 (no. 1/2): 23-58.

———. 1986 (30 May) **[ref. 6151]**. Notes on the systematics of the rajid genus *Bathyraja* and its distribution in the world oceans. Pp. 261-268. In: Uyeno et al. (eds.) 1986 [ref. 6147].

———. 1989 **[ref. 13266]**. Resurrection of *Notoraja* Ishiyama, 1958 and description of a new species of deep-water skate from the South China Sea *Notoraja subtilispinosa* sp. nov. (Pisces, Batoidea, Rajidae). Résultats des Campagnes Musorstom. Mem. Mus. Natl. Hist. Nat. Paris (A) v. 143: 247-260.

STEHMANN, M., AND G. KREFFT. 1988 (Dec.) **[ref. 13264]**. Results of the research cruises of FRV "Walther Herwig" to South America. LXVIII. Complimentary redescription of the dalatiine shark *Euprotomicroides zantedeschia* Hulley & Penrith, 1966 (Chondrichthys, Squalidae), based on a second record from the western South Atlantic. Arch. FischereiWiss. v. 39 (no. 1): 1-30.

STEIN, D. L. 1978 (8 Feb.) **[ref. 4203]**. A review of the deepwater Liparidae (Pisces) from the coast of Oregon and adjacent waters. Occas. Pap. Calif. Acad. Sci No. 127: 1-55.

———. 1979 (20 Dec.) **[ref. 6799]**. The genus *Psednos* a junior synonym of *Paraliparis*, with a redescription of *Paraliparis micrurus* (Barnard)(Scorpaeniformes: Liparidae). Matsya No. 4 [for 1978]: 5-10.

———. 1986 **[ref. 6297]**. Family No. 161: Liparididae (pp. 492-494). In: Smiths' Sea Fishes (Smith & Heemstra 1986 [ref. 5715]).

STEIN, D. L., AND L. S. TOMPKINS. 1989 (Feb.) **[ref. 12858]**. New species and new records of rare Antarctic *Paraliparis* fishes (Scorpaeniformes: Liparididae). Ichthyol. Bull. J. L. B. Smith Inst. Ichthyol. No. 53: 1-8.

STEINDACHNER, F. 1860 **[ref. 4205]**. Beiträge zur Kenntniss der Gobioiden. Sitzungsber. Math-naturw. Classe Wien v. 42: 283-292, 1 pl.

———. 1863 **[ref. 4206]**. Ichthyologische Mittheilungen (V). Verh. K.-K. Zool.-Bot. Ver. Ges. Wien v. 13: 1111-1114, Pl. 23.

———. 1863 **[ref. 4208]**. Beiträge zur Kenntniss der Sciaenoiden Brasiliens und der Cyprinodonten Mejicos. Sitzungsber. Akad. Wiss. Wien v. 48 (1. Abt.): 162-185, Pls. 1-4. [Also as a separate, Wien, 1864: 24 pp.]

———. 1866 **[ref. 4210]**. Zur Fischfauna von Port Jackson in Australien. Sitzungsber. Akad. Wiss. Wien v. 53 (pt 5): 424-481, Pls. 1-7.

———. 1866 **[ref. 5030]**. Ichthyologische Mittheilungen (VIII) and (IX). [With subtitled articles I-VI.] Verh. K.-K. Zool.-Bot. Ver. Ges. Wien v. 16: 475-484, 761-796, (IX) pls. 13-18.

———. 1867 **[ref. 4213]**. Über einige neue und seltene Meeresfische aus China. Sitzungsber. Akad. Wiss. Wien v. 55 (pts 4-5): 585-592.

———. 1867 **[ref. 4214]**. Über einige Fische aus dem Fitzroy-Flusse bei Rockhampton in Ost-Australien. Sitzungsber. Akad. Wiss. Wien v. 55 (1. Abt.): 9-16, 1 pl.

———. 1867 **[ref. 4215]**. Ichthyologische Notizen (IV). Sitzungsber. Akad. Wiss. Wien v. 55: 517-534, 6 pls. [Also as separate, pp. 1-18, Pls. 1-6.]

———. 1867 **[ref. 6393]**. Ichthyologische Notizen (V). [With subtitled articles I-V; new genus in V]. V. Über eine neue Labroiden(?) - Gattung. Sitzungsber. Akad. Wiss. Wien v. 55 (pts 4-5): 701-706.

———. 1869 **[ref. 4216]**. Ichthyologische Notizen (VIII). Beschreibungen einiger neuen Arten. Sitzungsber. Akad. Wiss. Wien v. 60 (1. Abt.): 120-139, Pls. 1-7. [Also as separate, pp. 1-20, pls. 1-7.]

———. 1869 **[ref. 4217]**. Ichthyologische Notizen (IX). Sitzungsber. Akad. Wiss. Wien v. 60 (1. Abt.): 290-318, Pls. 1-8. [Also as separate, pp. 1-29, Pls. 1-8.]

———. 1870 **[ref. 4218]**. Ichthyologische Notizen (X). Sitzungsber. Akad. Wiss. Wien v. 61 (1. Abt.): 623-642, Pls. 1-5. [Also as separate, pp. 1-20, Pls. 1-5.]

———. 1874 **[ref. 4219]**. Ichthyologische Beiträge. [I.] Sitzungsber. Akad. Wiss. Wien v. 69 (1. Abt.): 355-370, Pl. 1. [May have been published in 1875. Also as separate, pp. 1-16, Pl. 1.]

———. 1875 **[ref. 4220]**. Beiträge der Kenntniss der Chromiden des Amazonenstromes. Sitzungsber. Akad. Wiss. Wien v. 71 (1. Abt.): 61-137, Pls. 1-8. [Also as a separate, pp. 1-77, Pls. 1-8.]

———. 1875 **[ref. 4221]**. Über eine neue Gattung und Art aus der Familie der Pleuronectiden und über eine neue *Thymallus*-Art. Sitzungsber. Akad. Wiss. Wien v. 70 (1. Abt.): 363-371, Pls. 1-2. [Also as a separate, Wien, 1875, pp. 1-9, Pls. 1-2.]

———. 1875 **[ref. 4222]**. Ichthyologische Beiträge (II). I. Die Fische von Juan Fernandez in den Sammlungen des Wiener Museums. II. Über einige neue Fischarten von der Ost- und Westküste Süd-Amerikas. Sitzungsber. Akad. Wiss. Wien v. 71 (1. Abt.): 443-480,

1 pl. [Also as a separate, pp. 1-38, 1 pl.]

———. 1875 **[ref. 4223]**. Ichthyologische Beiträäge (III). Bemerkungen über *Serranus nebulifer* und *S. clathratus* sp. Gird. Sitzungsber. Akad. Wiss. Wien v. 72 (1. Abt.): 29-96, Pls. 1-8. [Also as a separate, pp. 1-68, Pls. 1-8.]

———. 1876 **[ref. 4224]**. Die Süsswasserfische des südöstlichen Brasilien (III). Sitzungsber. Akad. Wiss. Wien v. 74 (1. Abt.): 559-694, 13 pls. [Also as a separate, pp. 1-136, Pls. 1-13.]

———. 1876 **[ref. 4225]**. Ichthyologische Beiträge (V). [Subtitles I-V.] Sitzungsber. Akad. Wiss. Wien v. 74 (1. Abt.): 49-240, Pls. 1-15. [Also as a separate, pp. 1-192, Pls. 1-15.]

———. 1876 **[ref. 12584]**. Die Süsswasserfische des südöstlichen Brasilien (III). Anz. Akad. Wiss. Wien, Mathem.-Naturwiss. Cl. v. 13 (no. 4): 191.

———. 1878 **[ref. 4226]**. Ichthyologische Beiträge (VII). Sitzungsber. Akad. Wiss. Wien v. 78 (1. Abt.): 377-400. [Also as a separate, pp. 1-24.]

———. 1879 **[ref. 4227]**. Zur Fisch-fauna des Magdalenen-Stromes. Denkschr. Akad. Wiss. Wien v. 39: 19-78, Pls. 1-15. [Also as a separate, pp. 1-62, Pls. 1-15.]

———. 1879 **[ref. 4228]**. Über einige neue und seltene Fisch-Arten aus den k. k. zoologischen Museum zu Wien, Stuttgart, und Warschau. Denkschr. Akad. Wiss. Wien v. 41: 1-52, Pls. 1-9. [Pp. 1-52 may be from separate.]

———. 1879 **[ref. 4229]**. Ichthyologische Beiträge (VIII). Sitzungsber. Akad. Wiss. Wien v. 80 (1. Abt.): 119-191, Pls. 1-3. [Also as a separate, pp. 1-73, Pls. 1-3.]

———. 1881 **[ref. 4230]**. Ichthyologische Beiträge (IX). I. Über eine Sammlung von Flussfischen von Tohizona auf Madagascar. II. Über zwei neue *Agonus*-Arten aus Californien. III. Über einige Fischarten aus dem nördlichen Japan, gesammelt vom Professor Dybowski. Sitzungsber. Akad. Wiss. Wien v. 82 (1. Abt.): 238-266, Pls. 1-6. [For year 1880, probably published in 1881.]

———. 1881 **[ref. 4231]**. Ichthyologische Beiträge (X). Sitzungsber. Akad. Wiss. Wien v. 83 (1. Abt.): 179-219, Pls. 1-8. [Also as separate, pp. 1-39, Pls. 1-8.]

———. 1881 **[ref. 4232]**. Ichthyologische Beiträge (XI). Sitzungsber. Akad. Wiss. Wien v. 83 (1. Abt.): 393-408, Pl. 1. [Also as a separate, pp. 1-16, 1 pl.]

———. 1882 **[ref. 4233]**. Ichthyologische Beiträge (XII). Sitzungsber. Akad. Wiss. Wien v. 86 (1. Abt.): 61-82, Pls. 1-5. [Also as a separate, pp. 1-22, Pls. 1-5.]

———. 1884 **[ref. 4234]**. Ichthyologische Beiträge (XIII). I. Beiträge zur Kenntniss der Fische Australiens. II. *Caranx africanus* n. sp. III. *Macrones chinensis* n. sp. Sitzungsber. Akad. Wiss. Wien v. 88 (1. Abt.): 1065-1114, Pls. 1-8. [Also as a separate, pp. 1-50, Pls. 1-8.]

———. 1891 **[ref. 4236]**. Ichthyological Beiträge (XV). I. Über einige seltene und neue Fischarten aus dem canarischen Archipel. II. Über einige Characinin-Arten aus Südamerika. III. *Pomacentrus grandidieri*, n. sp. Sitzungsber. Akad. Wiss. Wien v. 100 (1. Abt.) (pt 5): 343-374, Pls. 1-3.

———. 1891 **[ref. 12571]**. Fische von dem canarischen Archipel, aus den Flüssen Südamerika's und von Madagascar unter dem Titel: 'Ichthyologische Beiträge' (XV). Anz. Akad. Wiss. Wien v. 28: 172-174.

———. 1894 **[ref. 4237]**. Die Fische Liberia's. Notes Leyden Mus. v. 16: 1-96, Pls. 1-4.

———. 1898 **[ref. 4238]**. Die Fische der Sammlung Plate. Pp. 281-338, Pls. 15-21. In: Fauna Chilensis. Abhandlungen zur Kenntniss der Zoologie Chiles. Zool. Jb.

———. 1902 **[ref. 4239]**. Über zwei neue Fischarten aus dem Rothen Meere. Anz. Akad. Wiss. Wien v. 39: 336-338.

———. 1903 **[ref. 4240]**. Über einige neue Reptilien- und Fischarten des Hofmuseums in Wien. Sitzungsber. Akad. Wiss. Wien v. 112 (1. Abt.): 15-22, 1 pl.

———. 1906 **[ref. 4241]**. Über eine neue Gattung und Art aus der Familie der Muraeniden, zunächst verwandt mit *Nettastoma*, und benennt dieselbe *Nettastomops barbatula*. Anz. Akad. Wiss. Wien 1906 (no. 17): 299-300.

———. 1906 **[ref. 4242]**. Zur Fischfauna der Samoa-Inseln. Sitzungsber. Akad. Wiss. Wien v. 115 (1. Abt.): 1369-1425.

———. 1908 **[ref. 4243]**. Über eine im Rio Juraguá bei Joinville im Staate S. Catharina (Brasilien) vorkommende noch unbeschriebene *Pseudochalceus*-Art, *Ch. affinis*, sowie über eine neue Characinengattung und -art, *Joinvillea rosae*, von gleichem Fundorte. Anz. Akad. Wiss. Wien v. 45: 28-31. [Also as a separate, pp. 28-30 [original not seen, pagination may differ from that of separate.]

———. 1908 **[ref. 13415]**. Ueber drei neue Characinen und drei Siluroiden aus dem Stromgebiete des Amazonas innerhalb Brasiliens. Anzeiger Kaiser. Akad. Wiss. Math. Nat. Klasse v. 45 (no. 6): 61-69.

———. 1915 **[ref. 4244]**. Beiträge zur Kenntniss der Flussfische Südamerikas. V. Denkschr. Akad. Wiss. Wien v. 93: 15-106. [Also as a separate, 1815, Wien.]

STEINDACHNER, F., AND L. DÖDERLEIN. 1883 **[ref. 4246]**. Beiträge zur Kenntniss der Fische Japan's. (I.) Denkschr. Akad. Wiss. Wien v. 47 (1. abt.): 211-242, Pls. 1-7. [Also separate, Wien, 1883.]

———. 1883 **[ref. 4247]**. Beiträge zur Kenntniss der Fische Japan's. (II.) Denkschr. Akad. Wiss. Wien v. 48 (1. abt.): 1-40, Pls. 1-7. [Also as a separate, Wien. Date on separate 1883.]

———. 1884 **[ref. 4248]**. Beiträge zur Kenntniss der Fische Japan's. (III.) Denkschr. Akad. Wiss. Wien v. 49 (1. abt.): 171-212, Pls. 1-7. [Also as separate, Wien, 1884.]

———. 1887 **[ref. 4249]**. Beiträge zur Kenntniss der Fische Japan's. (IV.) Denkschr. Akad. Wiss. Wien v. 53 (1. abt.): 257-296, Pls. 1-4. [Also as separate, Wien, 1887.]

STEINDACHNER, F., AND R. KNER. 1870 **[ref. 4250]**. Über einige Pleuronectiden, Salmoniden, Gadoiden und Blenniiden aus der Decastris-Bay und von Viti-Levu. Sitzungsber. Akad. Wiss. Wien v. 61 (1. abt.): 421-446, 1 pl. [Also as separate, pp. 1-26, 1 pl.]

STEPHANIDIS, A. 1974 **[ref. 4268]**. On some fish of the Ioniokorinthian region (W. Greece etc.) — a new genus of Cyprinidae: *Tropidophoxinellus* n. gen. Biol. Gallo-Hell. v. 5 (no. 2): 235-257.

STEPHENS, J. S., JR. 1961 (10 Nov.) **[ref. 4269]**. A description of a new genus and two new species of chaenopsid blennies from the western Atlantic. Not. Nat. (Phila.) No. 349: 1-8.

———. 1963 (31 Dec.) **[ref. 4270]**. A revised classification of the blennioid fishes of the American family Chaenopsidae. Univ. Calif. Publ. Zool. v. 68: 1-165, Pls. 1-15.

———. 1970 (1 June) **[ref. 6994]**. Seven new chaenopsid blennies from the western Atlantic. Copeia 1970 (no. 2): 280-309.

STEPHENS, J. S., JR., AND V. G. SPRINGER. 1974 (21 Jan.) **[ref. 7149]**. Clinid fishes of Chile and Peru, with description of a new species, *Myxodes ornatus*, from Chile. Smithson. Contrib. Zool. No. 159: 1-24.

STEPIEN, C. A., M. GLATTKE AND K. M. FINK. 1988 (5 Feb.) **[ref. 6384]**. Regulation and significance of color patterns of the spotted kelpfish, *Gibbonsia elegans* Cooper, 1864 (Blennioidei: Clinidae). Copeia 1988 (no. 1): 7-15.

STERN, W. T. 1937 (15 Feb.) **[ref. 13581]**. On the dates of publication of Webb and Berthelot's "Histoire Naturelle des Îles Canaries." J. Soc. Bibliogr. Nat. Hist. v. 1 (pt 2): 31-64.

STEVENS, E. G., A. C. MATARESE AND W. WATSON. 1984 **[ref. 13671]**. Ammodytoidei: development and relationships. Am. Soc. Ichthyol. Herpetol. Spec. Publ. No. 1: 574-575.

STEVENS, E. G., W. WATSON AND A. C. MATARESE. 1984 **[ref. 13633]**. Notothenioidea: development and relationships. Am. Soc. Ichthyol. Herpetol. Spec. Publ. No. 1: 561-564.

STEWART, D. J. 1985 (31 July) **[ref. 5239]**. A review of the South American catfish tribe Hoplomyzontini (Pisces, Aspredinidae), with descriptions of new species from Ecuador. Fieldiana Zool. (n. s.) No. 25: i-iii + 1-19.

———. 1985 (3 May) **[ref. 6788]**. A new species of *Cetopsorhamdia* (Pisces: Pimelodidae) from the Río Napo basin of eastern Ecuador. Copeia 1985 (no. 2): 339-344.

———. 1986 (4 Aug.) **[ref. 5211]**. Revision of *Pimelodina* and description of a new genus and species from the Peruvian Amazon (Pisces: Pimelodidae). Copeia 1986 (no. 3): 653-672.

——. 1986 (24 Dec.) **[ref. 5777]**. A new pimelodid catfish from the deep-river channel of the Río Napo, eastern Ecuador (Pisces: Pimelodidae). Proc. Acad. Nat. Sci. Phila. v. 138 (no. 1): 46-52.

Stewart, D. J., and M. J. Pavlik. 1985 (3 May) **[ref. 5240]**. Revision of *Cheirocerus* (Pisces: Pimelodidae) from tropical freshwaters of South America. Copeia 1985 (no. 2): 356-367.

Stewart, D. J., and T. R. Roberts. 1984 (23 Feb.) **[ref. 6480]**. A new species of dwarf cichlid fish with reversed sexual dichromatism from lac Mai-ndombe, Zaïre. Copeia 1984 (no. 1): 82-86.

Steyskal, G. C. 1980 **[ref. 14191]**. The grammar of family-group names as exemplified by those of fishes. Proc. Biol. Soc. Wash. v. 93 (no. 1): 168-177.

Storer, D. H. 1839 **[ref. 4278]**. Report upon the fishes of Massachusetts. Boston J. Nat. Hist. v. 2: 289-558. [Also as a separate (possibly published first), Boston, 1839: 1-202.]

——. 1855 **[ref. 4279]**. A history of the fishes of Massachusetts. Mem. Am. Acad. Arts Sci. v. 5 (pt 2): 257-296, Pls. 17-23. [Also pp. 49-92, 122-168 and continued in 1858, 1864, 1867; reprinted in book form, with a supplement, in 1867.]

Strand, E. 1928 (July) **[ref. 4285]**. Miscellanea nomenclatorica zoologica et palaeontologica. Arch. Naturgeschichte v. 92 (Abt. A) (no. 8): 30-75. [Volume for 1926.]

——. 1942 (15 Sept.) **[ref. 4289]**. Miscellanea nomenclatorica zoologica et palaeontologica. X. Folia Zool. Hydrobiol. Riga v. 11 (no. 2): 386-402.

Streets, T. H. 1877 **[ref. 4290]**. Ichthyology. In: Contributions to the natural history of the Hawaiian and Fanning islands and Lower California, made in connection with the United States North Pacific surveying expedition, 1873-75. Bull. U. S. Natl. Mus. No. 7: 43-102.

Strickland, H. E. and others. 1843 **[ref. 13534]**. Report of a committee appointed "to consider of the rules by which the Nomenclature of Zoology may by established on a uniform and permanent basis." Brit. Assoc. Adv. Sci., Rept. 12th Meeting, 1842: 105-121.

Strömman, H. 1895 **[ref. 4294]**. Leptocephalids in the University Zoological Museum at Upsala. Sitzungsber. K. Bohm. Ges. Wiss. Prag. v. 1895 (no. 33): 42 pp. [Also as separate, Upsala, 1896: 53 pp., 5 pls.]

Su, J.-X., G. S. Hardy and J. C. Tyler. 1986 (8 Sept.) **[ref. 12582]**. A new generic name for *Anchisomus multistriatus* Richardson 1854 (Tetraodontidae), with notes on its toxicity and pufferfish biting behavior. Rec. West. Aust. Mus. v. 13 (no. 1): 101-120.

Suckley, G. 1861 **[ref. 4298]**. Notices of certain new species of North American Salmonidae, chiefly in the collection of the N. W. Boundary Commission, in charge of Archibald Campbell, Esq., Commissioner of the United States, collected by Doctor C. B. R. Kennerly, naturalist to the Commission. Ann. Lyc. Nat. Hist. N. Y. v. 7 (art. 30): 306-313.

Suda, Y., and Y. Tominaga. 1983 (28 Nov.) **[ref. 5795]**. The percoid genus *Sphyraenops*, from the Pacific Ocean, with discussion on *Scombrosphyraena*. Jpn. J. Ichthyol. v. 30 (no. 3): 291-296.

Sufi, S. M. K. 1956 (Oct.) **[ref. 12498]**. Revision of the Oriental fishes of the family Mastacembelidae. Bull. Raffles Mus. No. 27: 93-146, Pls. 13-26.

Sulak, K. J. 1977 **[ref. 4299]**. The systematics and biology of *Bathypterois* (Pisces, Chlorophthalmidae) with a revised classification of benthic myctophiform fishes. Galathea Rep. v. 14: 49-108, Pls. 1-7.

——. 1986 **[ref. 5720]**. Family No. 52: Notacanthidae (pp. 195-196), Family No. 53: Halosauridae (pp. 196-197), Family No. 76: Chlorophthalmidae (pp. 261-265). In: Smiths' Sea Fishes (Smith & Heemstra 1986 [ref. 5715]).

Sulak, K. J., R. E. Crabtree and J.-C. Hureau. 1984 (31 Dec.) **[ref. 5143]**. Provisional review of the genus *Polyacanthonotus* (Pisces, Notacanthidae) with description of a new Atlantic species, *Polyacanthonotus merretti*. Cybium v. 8 (no. 4): 57-68.

Sulak, K. J., and Y. N. Shcherbachev. 1988 (3 Aug.) **[ref. 6677]**. A new species of tripodfish, *Bathypterois (Bathycygnus) andriashevi* (Chlorophthalmidae), from the western South Pacific Ocean. Copeia 1988 (no. 3): 653-659.

Sunobe, T. 1988 (15 Dec.) **[ref. 12744]**. A new gobiid fish of the genus *Eviota* from Cape Sata, Japan. Jpn. J. Ichthyol. v. 35 (no. 3): 278-282.

Suttkus, R. D. 1963 **[ref. 7110]**. Order Lepisostei. Pp. 61-88. In: Fishes of the Western North Atlantic. Mem. Sears Found. Mar. Res. No. 1 (pt 3).

Suvorov, E. 1935 **[ref. 4300]**. A new genus and two new species of fishes of the family Zoarcidae from the Okhotsk Sea. Bull. Acad. Sci. URSS, Classe Sci. Math. Nat. 1935: 435-440. [In Russian, English summ.]

Suzuki, A., and Y. Taki. 1988 (15 Dec.) **[ref. 12747]**. Karyotype and DNA content in the cyprinid *Catlocarpio siamensis*. Jpn. J. Ichthyol. v. 35 (no. 3): 389-391.

Suzuki, K. 1962 (15 Dec.) **[ref. 4301]**. Anatomical and taxonomical studies on the carangid fishes of Japan. Rep. Fac. Fish. Univ. Mie v. 4 (no. 2): 43-232. [Possibly not published until 1963.]

Svetovidov, A. N. 1958 **[ref. 6528]**. [The species composition of the Blenniidae of the Black Sea.] Zool. Zh. v. 37 (no. 4): 584-593. [English translation by Laurence Penny.]

——. 1973 **[ref. 7169]**. Acipenseridae (pp. 82-84), Clupeidae (pp. 99-109), Engraulidae (pp. 111-112), Merlucciidae (pp. 300-302), Gadidae (pp. 303-320). In: Hureau & Monod 1973 [ref. 6590].

——. 1978 **[ref. 6025]**. The types of the fish species described by P. S. Pallas in "Zoographia rosso-asiatica" (with a historical account of publication of this book). Nauka, Leningrad. 1-34, 84 figs. on 26 pls.

——. 1986 **[ref. 8033]**. Review of the three-bearded rocklings of the genus *Gaidropsarus* Rafinesque, 1810 (Gadidae) with description of a new species. Voprosy Ikhtiol. v. 26 (no. 1): 3-23. [In Russian. English translation in J. Ichthyol. v. 26 (no. 1): 114-135.]

Swain, J. 1883 (2 Jan.) **[ref. 5966]**. A review of Swainson's genera of fishes. Proc. Acad. Nat. Sci. Phila. 1882 [v. 34]: 272-284.

Swainson, W. 1838 **[ref. 4302]**. The natural history and classification of fishes, amphibians, & reptiles, or monocardian animals. London. v. 1: i-vi + 1-368.

——. 1839 **[ref. 4303]**. The natural history and classification of fishes, amphibians, & reptiles, or monocardian animals. London. v. 2: i-vi + 1-448.

Swinney, G. N. 1988 **[ref. 13445]**. Two species of *Bathophilus* (Stomiiformes, Stomiidae) new to the north-eastern Atlantic. J. Fish Biol. v. 32: 157-158.

Swinney, G. N., and T. W. Pietsch. 1988 (28 Dec.) **[ref. 9285]**. A new species of the ceratioid anglerfish genus *Oneirodes* (Pisces: Lophiiformes) from the eastern North Atlantic off Madeira. Copeia 1988 (no. 4): 1054-1056.

Sykes, W. H. 1839 (Sept.) **[ref. 4306]**. "An account of the fishes of Dukhun." In: Proceedings of Learned Societies. Zoological Society. Ann. Mag. Nat. Hist. (n. s.) v. 4 (no. 21): 54-62. [Also in Trans. Zool. Soc. London v. 2: 349-378, 8 pls. and as a separate, London, 1841.]

Szidat, L., and A. Nani. 1951 **[ref. 5955]**. Diplostomiasis cerebrales del pejerrey. Rev. Inst. Nac. Invest. Ciencias Nat. "Bernardino Riggi." v. 1 (no. 8): 324-384, Pls. 1-10.

Tachikawa, H., and T. Taniuchi. 1987 (20 Feb.) **[ref. 6712]**. *Galeus longirostris*, a new species of the sawtail catshark from Japan. Jpn. J. Ichthyol. v. 33 (no. 4): 352-359.

Takagi, K. 1951 **[ref. 4309]**. Sur la nouvelle raie torpille *Crassinarke dormitor* gen. et sp. nov., appartenant a la sous-famille narkinée. J. Tokyo Univ. Fish. v. 38 (no. 1): 27-34, Pl. 1.

——. 1957 **[ref. 4310]**. Descriptions of some new gobioid fishes of Japan, with a proposition on the sensory line system as a taxonomic appliance. J. Tokyo Univ. Fish. v. 43 (no. 1): 97-126.

——. 1966 **[ref. 4311]**. Taxonomic and nomenclatural status in chaos of the gobiid fish *Chaenogobius annularis* Gill, 1858—I and

II. J. Tokyo Univ. Fish. v. 52 (no. 1): 17-27, 29-45, 1 pl. [In Japanese, English summ.]

TAKATA, K., A. GOTO AND K. HAMADA. 1984 (20 Nov.) **[ref. 6727]**. Geographic distribution and variation of three species of ninespine sticklebacks (*Pungitius tymensis, P. pungitius* and *P. sinensis*) in Hokkaido. Jpn. J. Ichthyol. v. 31 (no. 3): 312-326.

TAKI, I. 1953 **[ref. 4314]**. On two new species of fishes from the Inland Sea of Japan. J. Sci. Hiroshima Univ. (Ser. B) Div. 1 (Zool.) v. 14: 201-212, Pl. 1.

TALIEV, D. N. 1946 **[ref. 4315]**. A new genus [of] Cottoidei from Lake Baikal. C. R. (Doklady) Acad. Sci. U.R.S.S. (n. s.) v. 54 (no. 1): 89-92.

———. 1955 **[ref. 4316]**. A study of the endemic fishes of Lake Baikal. Acad. Sci. USSR, Moscow & Leningrad. 1-603. [In Russian.]

TALWAR, P. K. 1970 **[ref. 5975]**. A new generic name for a sciaenid fish from India. Proc. Zool. Soc. (Calcutta) v. 23: 67-71.

———. 1970 **[ref. 12258]**. Taxonomic position of *Corvina albida* Cuvier, 1830 [Pisces: Sciaenidae]. Proc. Zool. Soc. (Calcutta) v. 23: 191-193.

———. 1971 **[ref. 4317]**. The taxonomic position of *Umbrina dussumieri* Valenciennes, 1833 and *Umbrina macroptera* Bleeker, 1853 (Pisces: Sciaenidae). J. Inl. Fish. Soc. India v. 3: 22-24.

———. 1975 (Aug.) **[ref. 4318]**. *Blythsciaena* in place of *Blythia* for a sciaenid genus of fishes. Newsl. Zool. Surv. India v. 1 (no. 2): 17.

———. 1977 **[ref. 6954]**. Identity of the deep-sea eel, *Sauromuraenesox vorax* Alcock (Anguilliformes: Muraenesocidae). Proc. Zool. Soc. (Calcutta) v. 30: 51-55.

TALWAR, P. K., AND A. JOGLEKAR. 1970 (July) **[ref. 4319]**. The taxonomic position of *Corvina axillaris* Cuvier, 1830 (Sciaenidae-Pisces). J. Mar. Biol. Assoc. India v. 10 (no. 2): 361-365. [Volume for Dec. 1968, issued July 1970.]

TALWAR, P. K., AND P. J. P. WHITEHEAD. 1971 (31 Dec.) **[ref. 4320]**. The clupeoid fish described by Francis Day. Bull. Br. Mus. (Nat. Hist.) Zool. v. 22 (no. 2): 59-85, Pls. 1-2.

TANAKA, S. 1908 **[ref. 4321]**. Notes on some rare fishes of Japan, with descriptions of two new genera and six new species. J. Coll. Sci. Imp. Univ. Tokyo v. 23 (art. 13): 1-24, Pls. 1-2.

———. 1908 **[ref. 6032]**. Notes on some Japanese fishes, with descriptions of fourteen new species. J. Coll. Sci. Imp. Univ. Tokyo v. 23 (art. 7): 1-54, Pls. 1-4.

———. 1909 (10 Oct.) **[ref. 4322]**. Descriptions of one new genus and ten new species of Japanese fishes. J. Coll. Sci. Imp. Univ. Tokyo v. 27 (art. 8): 1-27, Pl. 1.

———. 1912 (10 Mar.) **[ref. 4323]**. Figures and descriptions of the fishes of Japan, including the Riukiu Islands, Bonin Islands, Formosa, Kurile Islands, Korea and southern Sakhlin. v. 5: 71-86, Pls. 21-25. [In Japanese and English.]

———. 1912 (10 Apr.) **[ref. 6033]**. Figures and descriptions of the fishes of Japan, including Riukiu Islands, Bonin Islands, Formosa, Kurile Islands, Korea and southern Sakhalin. v. 6: 87-108, Pls. 26-30. [In Japanese and English.]

———. 1912 (26 Nov.) **[ref. 6034]**. Figures and descriptions of the fishes of Japan, including the Riukiu Islands, Bonin Islands, Formosa, Kurile Islands, Korea, and southern Sakhalin. v. 9: 145-164, Pls. 41-45. [In Japanese and English.]

———. 1912 (30 Dec.) **[ref. 6035]**. Figures and descriptions of the fishes of Japan including the Riukiu Islands, Bonin Islands, Formosa, Kurile Islands, Korea, and southern Sakhalin. v. 10: 165-186. [In Japanese and English.]

———. 1915 (15 Nov.) **[ref. 4324]**. Ten new species of Japanese fishes. Dobutsugaku Zasshi [Zool. Mag. Tokyo] v. 27 (no. 325): 565-568. [In Japanese.]

———. 1915 (10 Aug.) **[ref. 6036]**. Figures and descriptions of the fishes of Japan including the Riukiu Islands, Bonin Islands, Formosa, Kurile Islands, Korea, and southern Sakhalin. v. 20: 343-370, Pls. 96-100. [In Japanese and English.]

———. 1916 **[ref. 4326]**. Three new species of Japanese fishes. Dobutsugaku Zasshi [Zool. Mag. Tokyo] v. 27: 141-144. [In Japanese.]

———. 1916 **[ref. 4327]**. Two new species of Japanese fishes. Dobutsugaku Zasshi [Zool. Mag. Tokyo] v. 28: 102-103. [In Japanese.]

———. 1917 **[ref. 4329]**. Eleven new species of fish from Japan. Dobutsugaku Zasshi [Zool. Mag. Tokyo] v. 29: 7-12. [In Japanese.]

———. 1917 **[ref. 4330]**. Six new species of Japanese fishes. Dobutsugaku Zasshi [Zool. Mag. Tokyo] v. 29: 198-201. [In Japanese.]

———. 1917 **[ref. 4332]**. Three new species of Japanese fishes. Dobutsugaku Zasshi [Zool. Mag. Tokyo] v. 29: 268-269. [In Japanese.]

———. 1918 (28 Dec.) **[ref. 4331]**. Figures and descriptions of the fishes of Japan, including Riukiu Islands, Bonin Islands, Formosa, Kurile Islands, Korea, and southern Sakhalin. v. 29: 515-538, Pls. 138-139. [In Japanese and English.]

———. 1918 (28 Nov.) **[ref. 6037]**. Figures and descriptions of the fishes of Japan including the Riukiu Islands, Bonin Islands, Formosa, Kurile Islands, Korea, and southern Sakhalin. v. 28: 495-514, Pls. 136-147. [In Japanese and English.]

———. 1922 (1 July) **[ref. 4334]**. Figures and descriptions of fishes of Japan including Riukiu Islands, Bonin Islands, Formosa, Kurile Islands, Korea, and southern Sakhalin. v. 32: 583-606, Pls. 145-147. [In Japanese and English.]

TANG, D. S. 1942 (27 Aug.) **[ref. 4335]**. Fishes of Kweiyang, with descriptions of two new genera and five new species. Lingnan Sci. J. Canton v. 20 (nos. 2-4): 147-166.

TÅNING, A. V. 1918 **[ref. 12242]**. Mediterranean Scopelidae. Rep. Danish Oceanogr. Exped. Mediterr., 1908-1910 v. 2 (Biol.) (A. 7): 1-154. [Not seen.]

———. 1932 (July) **[ref. 5031]**. Notes on scopelids from the Dana Expeditions. I. Vidensk. Medd. Dansk Naturh. Foren. Kjob. v. 94: 125-146.

TANIUCHI, T., AND J. A. F. GARRICK. 1986 **[ref. 5721]**. A new species of *Scymnodalatias* from the southern oceans, and comments on other squaliform sharks. Jpn. J. Ichthyol. v. 33 (no. 2): 119-134.

TANIUCHI, T., H. KOBAYASHI AND T. OTAKE. 1984 (15 May) **[ref. 6732]**. Occurrence and reproductive mode of the false cat shark, *Pseudotriakis microdon*, in Japan. Jpn. J. Ichthyol. v. 31 (no. 1): 88-92.

TAPHORN, D. C., AND J. E. THOMERSON. 1978 (Oct.) **[ref. 4337]**. A revision of the South American cyprinodont fishes of the genera *Rachovia* and *Austrofundulus*, with the description of a new genus. Acta Biol. Venez. v. 9 (no. 4): 377-452.

TARANETZ, A. 1935 **[ref. 4339]**. Some changes in the classification of fishes of the Soviet Far East with notes on their distribution. Bull. Far Eastern Br. Acad. Sci. U.S.S.R. No. 13 (1935): 89-101. [In Russian, English summ. (pp. 99-101).]

———. 1936 **[ref. 6509]**. Description of three new species of the genus *Icelus* Kröyer (Pisces, Cottidae) from the Sea of Japan and from Okhotsk Sea. C. R. (Doklady) Acad. Sci. URSS v. 4 (13) No. 3: 149-152.

———. 1937 **[ref. 4340]**. A note on a new genus of gudgeons from the Amur Basin. Bull. Far Eastern Br. Acad. Sci. U.S.S.R. No. 23 (1937): 113-115. [In Russian, English summ. (p. 115).]

———. 1937 **[ref. 13384]**. Handbook for identification of fishes of Soviet Far East and adjacent waters. Izv. Tikhookean. Nauchno-Issled. Inst. Rybn. Khoz. Okeanogr. v. 11: 1-200 + map. [In Russian.]

———. 1941 **[ref. 5535]**. On the classification and origin of the family Cottidae. Izv. Akad. Nauk SSSR. Otd. Biol. No. 3: 427-447. [In Russian, English summ.; also translation by Wilimovsky & Lanz 1959, Inst. Fish. Univ. Br. Columbia, Mus. Contr. 5.]

TARANETZ, A., AND A. ANDRIASHEV. 1934 **[ref. 4338]**. On a new genus and species, *Petroschmidtia albonotata* (Zoarcidae, Pisces), from the Okhotsk Sea. C. R. (Doklady) Acad. Sci. U.R.S.S. (n. s.) v. 2 (no. 8): 506-512. [In Russian and English. Author's name as Taranec.]

———. 1935 (Jan.) **[ref. 4341]**. On a new fish of the family Zoarcidae from the littoral fauna of the Commanders' Islands. C. R. (Doklady) Acad. Sci. U.R.S.S. (n. s.) v. 1 (no. 4): 267-270. [In Russian and

English.]
TARP, F. H. 1952 (Oct.) **[ref. 12250]**. A revision of the family Embiotocidae (the surfperches). Fish Bull. Div. Fish Game Calif. No. 88: 1-99.
TAVERNE, L. 1971 (30 Sept.) **[ref. 4349]**. Note sur la systématique des poissons Mormyriformes. Le problème des genres *Gnathonemus* Gill, *Marcusenius* Gill, *Hippopotamyrus* Pappenheim, *Cyphomyrus* Myers et les nouveaux genres *Pollimyrus* et *Brienomyrus*. Rev. Zool. Bot. Afr. v. 84 (pts 1-2): 99-110.
———. 1972 (Dec.) **[ref. 6367]**. Ostéologie des genres *Mormyrus* Linné, *Mormyrops* Müller, *Hyperopisus* Gill, *Isichthys* Gill, *Myomyrus* Boulenger, *Stomatorhinus* Boulenger et *Gymnarchus* Cuvier. Considération générales sur la systématique des poissons de l'ordre des Mormyriformes. Ann. Mus. R. Afr. Cent. (Ser. 8) Zool. No. 200: 1-194, Pls. 1-2.
———. 1988 (30 June) **[ref. 6863]**. On the synonymy of the priacanthid genera *Pristigenys* Agassiz, 1835 and *Pseudopriacanthus* Bleeker 1869 (Teleostei, Percoidei). Cybium v. 12 (no. 2): 171-172.
TAVERNE, L., AND J. GÉRY. 1968 (30 Sept.) **[ref. 4360]**. Un nouveau genre de Mormyridae (Poissons Ostéoglossomorphes): *Boulengeromyrus knoepffleri* gen. sp. nov. Rev. Zool. Bot. Afr. v. 78 (pts 1-2): 98-106.
———. 1975 (30 Sept.) **[ref. 4348]**. Un nouveau genre de Mormyridae du Gabon: *Ivindomyrus opdenboschi* gen. nov., sp. nov. (Pisces Ostéoglossomorphes). Rev. Zool. Bot. Afr. v. 89 (no. 3): 555-563.
TAVERNE, L., D. F. E. THYS VAN DEN AUDENAERDE AND A. HEYMER. 1977 (30 Sept.) **[ref. 4363]**. *Paramormyrops gabonensis* nov. gen., nov. sp. du nord du Gabon (Pisces Mormyridae). Rev. Zool. Afr. v. 91 (no. 3): 634-640.
TAWIL, P., AND R. ALLGAYER. 1987 (30 June) **[ref. 6745]**. Description de *Aulonocara maylandi kandeensis* subsp. n. (Pisces, Cichlidae) du lac Malawi. Cybium v. 11 (no. 2): 159-166, 1 col. pl.
TAYLOR, J. 1831 **[ref. 6560]**. Art. IV.—On the respiratory organ and air-bladder of certain fishes of the Ganges. [Including:] On the anatomy of the *Cuchia*. Edin. J. Sci. (n. s.) v. 5 (no. 9): 42-50.
TAYLOR, L. R., JR., AND J. L. CASTRO-AGUIRRE. 1972 **[ref. 7158]**. *Heterodontus mexicanus*, a new horn shark from the Golfo de California. An. Esc. Nac. Cienc. Biol. Mex. v. 19: 123-143.
TAYLOR, L. R., JR., L. J. V. COMPAGNO AND P. J. STRUHSAKER. 1983 (6 July) **[ref. 5428]**. Megamouth—a new species, genus, and family of lamnoid shark (*Megachasma pelagios*, family Megachasmidae) from the Hawaiian Islands. Proc. Calif. Acad. Sci. v. 43 (no. 8): 87-110.
TAYLOR, W. R. 1964 **[ref. 12563]**. Comment on the proposed rejection of *Curimata* Walbaum, 1792. Bull. Zool. Nomencl. v. 21 (pt 4): 260.
———. 1969 **[ref. 6555]**. A revision of the catfish genus *Noturus* Rafinesque with an analysis of higher groups in the Ictaluridae. Bull. U. S. Natl. Mus. No. 282: i-vi +1-315, Pls. 1-21.
———. 1970 (Apr.) **[ref. 6162]**. Comment on the proposed validation of *Siganus* Forskål, 1775, and request that the name *Teuthis* Linnaeus (Pisces) be placed on the Official List of Generic Names in Zoology. Bull. Zool. Nomencl. v. 26 (pts 5/6): 178-179.
———. 1985 (Apr.) **[ref. 6640]**. Comment on the proposal concerning *Bagrus* Bosc, 1816, with requests to place *Bagre* Cloquet, 1816 on the Official List and to suppress *Porcus* Geoffroy Saint-Hilaire, 1808 Z.N.(S.) 2371. Bull. Zool. Nomencl. v. 42 (pt 1): 14-16.
———. 1986 (Apr.) **[ref. 6195]**. Ariidae (pp. 153-160). In: Daget et al. 1986 [ref. 6189].
———. 1986 **[ref. 6282]**. Family No. 59: Ariidae (pp. 211-213). In: Smiths' Sea Fishes (Smith & Heemstra 1986 [ref. 5715]).
TAYLOR, W. R., AND J. R. GOMON. 1986 **[ref. 6196]**. Plotosidae (pp. 160-162). In: Daget et al. 1986 [ref. 6189].
TCHANG, T.-L. 1930 **[ref. 4366]**. Nouveau genre et nouvelles espèces de cyprinidés de Chine. Bull. Soc. Zool. Fr. v. 55 (no. 1): 46-52.
———. 1935 (1 Jan.) **[ref. 4365]**. A new genus of loach from Yunnan. Bull. Fan Memorial Inst. Biol. Peiping (Zool. Ser.) v. 6 (no. 1): 17-19.
TCHANG, T.-L., T.-H. YUEH AND H.-C. HWANG. 1964 **[ref. 4364]**. Notes on fishes of southern Tibet, China, with proposal of one new genus, *Tetrostichodon*. Acta Zool. Sin. v. 16 (no. 2): 272-282. [In Chinese, English summ. (pp. 281-282).]
———. 1964 **[ref. 3501]**. Notes on fishes of the genus *Gymnocypris* of southern Tibet, China, with description of four new species and a new subspecies. Acta Zool. Sin. v. 16 (no. 1): 139-154.
TCHANG, T.-L., AND T.-H. YUEH. 1964 **[ref. 3504]**. Notes on fishes of the genus *Schizopygopsis* of southern Tibet, China, with description of a new species and a new subspecies. Acta Zool. Sin. v. 16 (no. 4): 661-673. [In Chinese, English summ. (pp. 672-673).]
TEAGUE, G. W., AND G. S. MYERS. 1945 **[ref. 13155]**. A new gurnard (*Prionotus alipionis*) from the coast of Brazil. Boll. Mus. Nac. Rio de Janeiro (n. s.) v. 31: 1-18.
TELLER, F. J. 1891 **[ref. 4369]**. Ueber den Schädel eines fossilen Dipnoërs, *Ceratodus sturii*, n. sp. aus den Schlichten den oberen Trias der Nordalpen. Abh. Geol. Reichsanstalt Wien v. 15 (pt. 3): 1-39, 4 pls. [Also as a separate, Wien, 1891.]
TEMMINCK, C. J., AND H. SCHLEGEL. 1842 **[ref. 4370]**. Pisces. In: Fauna Japonica, sive descriptio animalium quae in itinere per Japoniam suscepto annis 1823-30 collegit, notis observationibus et adumbrationibus illustravit P. F. de Siebold. Part 1: 1-20. [Dates for this series from Smith & Heemstra 1986: 983 [ref. 5715] and Hureau & Monod 1973: 149 [ref. 6590].]
———. 1843 **[ref. 4371]**. See Temminck & Schlegel 1842 [ref. 4370] Parts 2-4: 21-72.
———. 1844 **[ref. 4372]**. See Temminck & Schlegel 1842 [ref. 4370] Parts 5-6: 73-112.
———. 1845 **[ref. 4373]**. See Temminck & Schlegel 1842 [ref. 4370] Parts 7-9: 113-172, Pls. 1-196 + A.
———. 1846 **[ref. 4374]**. See Temminck & Schlegel 1842 [ref. 4370] Parts 10-14: 173-269.
———. 1850 **[ref. 4375]**. See Temminck & Schlegel 1842 [ref. 4370] Last part: 270-324.
TERASHIMA, A. 1984 (1 Aug.) **[ref. 6729]**. Three new species of the cyprinid genus *Schizothorax* from Lake Rara, northwestern Nepal. Jpn. J. Ichthyol. v. 31 (no. 2): 122-135.
TEUGELS, G. G. 1982 (31 Dec.) **[ref. 4377]**. Preliminary data of a systematic outline of the African species of the genus *Clarias* (Pisces, Clariidae). Rev. Zool. Afr. v. 96 (no. 4): 731-748.
———. 1982 **[ref. 6670]**. A systematic outline of the African species of the genus *Clarias* (Pisces; Clariidae), with an annotated bibliography. Ann. Mus. R. Afr. Cent. (Ser. 8) Zool. No. 236: 1-249.
———. 1983 (31 Mar.) **[ref. 12851]**. Notes on the status of *Clarias ngamensis* Castelnau 1861, *C. mellandi* Boulenger 1905, *C. prentissgrayi* (Fowler 1930) and *C. lamottei* Daget and Planquette 1967 (Pisces, Clariidae) with the rehabilitation of *Dinotopteroides* Fowler 1930 as a subgenus of *Clarias*. Cybium v. 7 (no. 1): 15-28.
———. 1986 (Apr.) **[ref. 6193]**. Clariidae (pp. 66-101). In: Daget et al. 1986 [ref. 6189].
———. 1986 **[ref. 12548]**. A systematic revision of the African species of the genus *Clarias* (Pisces; Clariidae). Ann. Mus. R. Afr. Cent. Tervuren No. 247: 1-199.
TEUGELS, G. G., J. J. BREINE AND D. F. E. THYS VAN DEN AUDENAERDE. 1986 (Apr.) **[ref. 6202]**. Channidae (= Ophicephalidae) (pp. 288-290). In: Daget et al. 1986 [ref. 6189].
TEUGELS, G. G., AND J. DAGET. 1984 (31 Dec.) **[ref. 5158]**. *Parachanna* nom. nov. for the African snake-heads and rehabilitation of *Parachanna insignis* (Sauvage, 1884) (Pisces, Channidae). Cybium v. 8 (no. 4): 1-7.
TEUGELS, G. G., L. DE VOS AND J. SNOEKS. 1986 (30 June) **[ref. 6761]**. *Botia macrolineata*, a new species of loach from India (Pisces; Cobitidae). Cybium v. 10 (no. 2): 187-192.
TEUGELS, G. G., B. DENAYER AND M. LEGENDRE. 1990 (Mar.) **[ref. 14142]**. A systematic revision of the African catfish genus *Heterobranchus* Geoffroy-Saint-Hilaire, 1809 (Pisces: Clariidae). Zool. J. Linn. Soc.
TEUGELS, G. G., AND T. R. ROBERTS. 1987 **[ref. 6479]**. *Silurus an-*

guilaris Linnaeus, 1758: designation as type species of *Clarias* Scopoli, 1777 and rediscovery of holotype (Pisces: Clariidae). Zool. J. Linn. Soc. v. 90: 95-98.

Teugels, G. G., P. H. Skelton and C. Leveque. 1987 **[ref. 6346]**. A new species of *Amphilius* (Pisces, Amphiliidae) from the Kankoure Basin, Guinea, West Africa. Cybium v. 11 (no. 1): 93-101.

Thienemann, F. A. L. 1828 **[ref. 4990]**. Lehrbuck der Zoologie. Berlin [Not seen.]

Thominot, A. 1880 (22 May) **[ref. 4383]**. Note sur un poisson de genre nouveau appartenant à la famille des scombéridés, voisin des sérioles. Bull. Soc. Philomath. Paris (Ser. 7) v. 4: 173-174. [Also as a separate, 2 pp. (proofed from separate).]

———. 1881 (11 June) **[ref. 4384]**. Sur deux genres nouveaux de poissons faisant partie de la famille des squammipennes et rapportés d'Australie par J. Verreaux. Bull. Soc. Philomath. Paris (Ser. 7) v. 8: 140-142.

———. 1883 **[ref. 4385]**. Notice sur un poisson de genre nouveau appartenant à la famille des Sparidées. Bull. Soc. Philomath. Paris (Ser. 7) v. 7: 140-141.

———. 1883 **[ref. 4386]**. Note sur le genre *Aplodon*, poisson de la famille des Sparidae, voisin des girelles. Bull. Soc. Philomath. Paris (Ser. 7) v. 7: 141-144.

———. 1884 **[ref. 4387]**. Note sur un poisson de la famille des Cyprinodontidae. Bull. Soc. Philomath. Paris (Ser. 7) v. 8: 149-150.

Thompson, W. 1837 (20 Dec.) **[ref. 4388]**. [Notes relating to the natural history of Ireland.] Proc. Zool. Soc. Lond. Part 5 (1837) (54): 52-63.

———. 1840 **[ref. 4389]**. On a new genus of fishes from India. Mag. Nat. Hist. (n. s.) v. 4: 184-187.

———. 1856 **[ref. 4390]**. Fishes of Ireland. Pp. 69-268. In: The natural history of Ireland. London. Vol. IV. Mammalia, reptiles, and fishes, also invertebrata.

Thompson, W. F. 1916 (20 May) **[ref. 4391]**. Fishes collected by the United States Bureau of Fisheries steamer "Albatross" during 1888, between Montevideo, Uruguay, and Tome, Chile, on the voyage through the Straits of Magellan. Proc. U. S. Natl. Mus. v. 50 (no. 2133): 401-476, Pls. 2-6.

Thompson, Z. 1850 (Jan.) **[ref. 4392]**. [Untitled.] Proc. Boston Soc. Nat. Hist. v. 3: 163-165.

Thomson, J. M. 1986 (Apr.) **[ref. 6215]**. Mugilidae (pp. 344-349). In: Daget et al. 1986 [ref. 6189].

Thys van den Audenaerde, D. F. E. 1963 (28 Sept.) [ref. 4404]. Description d'une espèce nouvelle d'*Haplochromis* (Pisces, Cichlidae) avec observations sur les *Haplochromis* rhéophiles du Congo oriental. Rev. Zool. Bot. Afr. v. 68 (pts 1-2): 140-152.

———. 1968 (28 June) **[ref. 4402]**. A preliminary contribution to a systematic revision of the genus *Pelmatochromis* Hubrecht sensu lato (Pisces, Cichlidae). Rev. Zool. Bot. Afr. v. 77 (pts 3-4): 349-391.

———. 1969 (31 Dec.) **[ref. 6582]**. Description of a new genus and species of clupeoïd fish from Sierra Leone. Rev. Zool. Bot. Afr. v. 80 (3-4): 385-390.

———. 1970 (30 Dec.) **[ref. 12518]**. The paternal mouthbrooding habit of *Tilapia (Coptodon) discolor* and its special significance. Rev. Zool. Bot. Afr. v. 82 (nos. 3-4): 285-300.

———. 1971 (15 Apr.) **[ref. 4403]**. Description of a new genus and species for a small cyprinid fish from southern Cameroon. Rev. Zool. Bot. Afr. v. 83 (pts 1-2): 132-140.

———. 1984 (Feb.) **[ref. 6181]**. Phractolaemidae (pp. 136-137). In: Daget et al. 1984 [ref. 6168].

Thys van den Audenaerde, D. F. E., and J. J. Breine. 1986 (Apr.) **[ref. 6214]**. Nandidae (pp. 342-343). In: Daget el al. 1986 [ref. 6189].

Tickell, S. R. 1865 **[ref. 4405]**. Description of a supposed new genus of the Gadidae, Arakan. J. Asiat. Soc. Bengal v. 34 (pt 2): 32-33, Pl. 1.

Tighe, K. A. 1989 **[ref. 13291]**. Family Serrivomeridae (pp. 613-627). In: Böhlke, E. B. (ed.) 1989 [ref. 13282].

Tilak, R. 1987 (25 Dec.) **[ref. 6794]**. Studies on the fish fauna of Uttar Pradesh Terai. I. On the extension of range of distribution of *Conta conta* (Hamilton) and *Chandramara chandramara* (Hamilton) (Sisoridae: Bagridae: Siluriformes). Matsya No. 12 & 13: 84-92.

Tilesius, W. G. von. 1809 **[ref. 4406]**. Description de quelques poissons observés pendant voyage autour du monde. Mem. Soc. Imp. Natural. Moscou v. 2: 212-249, Pls. 13-17.

———. 1810 **[ref. 12816]**. Piscium Camtschaticorum "Teerpuck" et "Wachnja." Descriptiones et icones. Mem. Acad. Imp. Sci. St. Petersb. v. 2: 335-372, Pl. 15.

———. 1811 **[ref. 4408]**. Piscium Camtschaticorum descriptiones et icones. Mem. Acad. Sci. St. Petersb. v. 3: 225-285, Pls. 8-13.

———. 1813 **[ref. 13413]**. Iconum et descriptionum piscium Camtschaticorum continuatio tertia tentamen monographiae generis Agoni blochiani sistens. Mem. Acad. Sci. St. Petersb. v. 4 (for 1811): 406-478, Pls. 11-16.

———. 1820 **[ref. 4407]**. De piscium Australium novo genere icone illustrato. Mem. Acad. Sci. St. Petersb. v. 7: 301-310, second Pl. 9.

Tollitt, M. E. 1986 (Apr.) **[ref. 6634]**. Dates and authorship of the text volumes of the Histoire Naturelle section of Savigny's Description de l'Egypte Z.N.(S.) 2515. Bull. Zool. Nomencl. v. 43 (pt 1): 107-111.

Tominaga, Y. 1986 (30 May) **[ref. 6315]**. The relationships of the families Glaucosomatidae and Pempheridae. Pp. 595-599. In: Uyeno et al. (eds.) 1986 [ref. 6147].

Tomiyama, I. 1936 **[ref. 4413]**. Gobiidae of Japan. Jpn. J. Zool. v. 7 (no. 1): 37-112.

———. 1955 (30 Sept.) **[ref. 4412]**. Notes on some fishes, including one new genus and three new species from Japan, the Ryukyus and Pescadores. Jpn. J. Ichthyol. v. 4 (nos. 1/2/3): 1-15.

Topp, R. W. 1973 **[ref. 7209]**. Luvaridae (p. 476). In: Hureau & Monod 1973 [ref. 6590].

Torchio, M. 1973 **[ref. 6892]**. Soleidae (pp. 628-634), Cynoglossidae (pp. 635-636). In: Hureau & Monod 1973 [ref. 6590].

Torres-Orozco, R., and J. L. Castro-Aguirre. 1982 **[ref. 5384]**. Nueva familia, género y especie nuevos del suborden Stromateoidei (Pisces: Perciformes), del Pacífico de México. An. Esc. Nac. Cienc. Biol. Mex. v. 26: 37-46.

Tortonese, E. 1937-38 **[ref. 10283]**. Viaggio del dott. Enrico Festa in Palestina e in Siria (1893). Pesci. Boll. Mus. Zool. Anat. Comp. Torino (Ser. 3) v. 46 (no. 85): 3-48, Pls. 1-2.

———. 1939 **[ref. 4414]**. Risultati ittiologici del viaggio di circumnavigazione del globo della R. N. "Magenta" (1865-68). Boll. Mus. Zool. Anat. Comp. Torino (Ser. 3) v. 47 (no. 100): 177-421, Pls. 1-9.

———. 1948 **[ref. 4415]**. Sulla nomenclatura di un Anacantino mediterraneo (*Rhynchogadus hepaticus*, nom. nov.). Bull. Zool. Torino v. 15 (nos. 1-3): 37-39.

———. 1954 **[ref. 4416]**. On *Ophidion vassali* Risso, type of a new genus of ophidiid fishes (*Parophidion*). Pubbl. Stn. Zool. Napoli v. 25 (fasc. 2): 372-379, Pl. 7.

———. 1959 (5 Dec.) **[ref. 4417]**. Un nuovo pesce Mediterraneo di profondità: *Eutelichthys leptochirus*, n. gen. e n. sp. (Fam. Eutelichthyidae, nov.). Ann. Mus. Civ. Stor. Nat. Genova v. 71: 226-232.

———. 1973 **[ref. 7192]**. [Various family accounts.] In: Hureau & Monod 1973 [ref. 6590].

Tortonese, E., T. Sertorio and M.-L. Bauchot. 1973 **[ref. 7202]**. Centracanthidae (pp. 417-419). In: Hureau & Monod 1973 [ref. 6590].

Townsend, C. H., and J. T. Nichols. 1925 (16 May) **[ref. 4420]**. Deep sea fishes of the 'Albatross' Lower California expedition. Bull. Am. Mus. Nat. Hist. v. 52 (art. 1): 1-20, Pls. 1-4, map.

Toyoshima, M. 1985 (Dec.) **[ref. 5722]**. Taxonomy of the subfamily Lycodontinae (family Zoarcidae) in Japan and adjacent waters. Mem. Fac. Fish. Hokkaido Univ. v. 32 (no. 2): 131-243.

Travassos, H. 1946 (Aug.) **[ref. 5009]**. Contribuições para o conhecimento da família Characidae Gill, 1893 III. Discussão sôbre os gêneros "Cynodon" Spix, 1929 e "Rhaphiodon" Agassiz, 1829, com novo nome de subfamilia. Summa Brasil. Biol. v. 1 (fasc. 9): 129-

141. [Also as Ano I, Vol. 1, pp. 1-9.]

———. 1951-52 **[ref. 4450]**. Catálogo dos gêneros a subgêneros da subordem Characoidei (Actinopterygii - Cypriniformes). Dusenia v. 2:205-224 [31 May 1951], 273-293 [31 July], 341-360 [30 Sept.], 419-434 [30 Nov.], v. 3:141-180 [31 Mar. 1952], 225-250 [31 May], 313-328 [31 July]. [Also as a separate, pp. 1-158.]

Travers, R. A. 1984 (26 July) **[ref. 5147]**. A review of the Mastacembeloidei, a suborder of synbranchiform teleost fishes. Part II: Phylogenetic analysis. Bull. Br. Mus. (Nat. Hist.) Zool. v. 47 (no. 2): 83-150.

———. 1988 (30 Sept.) **[ref. 6869]**. Diagnoses of a new African mastacembelid spiny-eel genus *Aethiomastacembelus* gen. nov. (Mastacembeloidei: Synbranchiformes). Cybium v. 12 (no. 3): 255-257.

———. 1989 (26 Oct.) **[ref. 13578]**. Systematic account of a collection of fishes from the Mongolian People's Republic: with a review of the hydrobiology of the major Mongolian drianage basins. Bull. Br. Mus. Nat. Hist. (Zool.) v. 55 (no. 2): 173-207.

Travers, R. A., G. Eynikel and D. F. E. Thys van den Audenaerde. 1986 (Apr.) **[ref. 6221]**. Mastacembelidae (pp. 415-427). In: Daget et al. 1986 [ref. 6189].

Trewavas, E. 1935 (July) **[ref. 4451]**. A synopsis of the cichlid fishes of Lake Nyasa. Ann. Mag. Nat. Hist. (Ser. 10) v. 16 (no. 91): 65-118.

———. 1942 (July) **[ref. 4452]**. The cichlid fishes of Syria and Palestine. Ann. Mag. Nat. Hist. (Ser. 11) v. 9 (no. 55): 526-536.

———. 1943 (Nov.) **[ref. 4453]**. New schilbeid fishes from the Gold Coast, with a synopsis of the African genera. Proc. Zool. Soc. Lond. (Ser. B) v. 113 (pt 3): 164-171.

———. 1955 (July) **[ref. 4454]**. A blind fish from Iraq, related to *Garra*. Ann. Mag. Nat. Hist. (Ser. 12) v. 8 (no. 91): 551-555.

———. 1961 **[ref. 9385]**. A new cichlid fish in the Limpopo basin. Ann. S. Afr. Mus. v. 46 (no. 5): 53-56.

———. 1962 (18 Nov.) **[ref. 4455]**. A basis for classifying the sciaenid fishes of tropical West Africa. Ann. Mag. Nat. Hist. (Ser. 13) v. 5 (no. 51): 167-176.

———. 1962 **[ref. 4456]**. Fishes of the crater lakes of the northwestern Cameroons. Bonn. Zool. Beitr. v. 13 (heft 1/3): 146-192.

———. 1964 (26 Mar.) **[ref. 4457]**. The sciaenid fishes with a single mental barbel. Copeia 1964 (no. 1): 107-117.

———. 1971 **[ref. 6577]**. The syntypes of the sciaenid *Corvina albida* Cuvier and the status of *Dendrophysa hooghliensis* Sinha and Rao and *Nibea coibor* (nec. Hamilton) of Chu, Lo & Wu. J. Fish Biol. v. 5: 453-461.

———. 1973 (25 June) **[ref. 4458]**. I. On the cichlid fishes of the genus *Pelmatochromis* with proposal of a new genus for *P. congicus*; on the relationship between *Pelmatochromis* and *Tilapia* and the recognition of *Sarotherodon* as a distinct genus. Bull. Br. Mus. (Nat. Hist.) Zool. v. 25 (no. 1): 1-26.

———. 1973 **[ref. 7201]**. Sciaenidae (pp. 396-401), Mugilidae (pp. 567-574). In: Hureau & Monod 1973 [ref. 6590].

———. 1977 (July) **[ref. 4459]**. The sciaenid fishes (croakers or drums) of the Indo-West-Pacific. Trans. Zool. Soc. Lond. v. 33 (pt 4): 253-541, Pls. 1-14.

———. 1983 **[ref. 6597]**. Tilapiine fishes of the genera *Sarotherodon, Oreochromis* and *Danakilia*. Publ. Brit. Mus. Nat. Hist. No. 878: 1-583.

———. 1984 (13 July) **[ref. 5302]**. Un nom et une description pour l'*Aulonocara* (Sulphur-head), Poisson cichlidé du lac Malawi. Rev. Fr. Aquariol. v. 11 (no. 1): 7-10.

———. 1984 (20 Mar.) **[ref. 5303]**. Nouvel examen des genres et sous-genres du complexe *Pseudotropheus-Melanochromis* du lac Malawi. Rev. Fr. Aquariol. v. 10 (no. 4): 97-106.

———. 1987 (Sept.) **[ref. 6377]**. *Sarotherodon melanotheron* Rüppell, 1852 (Osteichthyes, Perciformes): proposed conservation of the specific name. Case 2594. Bull. Zool. Nomencl. v. 44 (pt 3): 190-191.

Trewavas, E., J. Green and S. A. Corbet. 1972 (May) **[ref. 4460]**. Ecological studies on crater lakes in West Cameroon. Fishes of Barombi Mbo. J. Zool. (Lond.) v. 167 (pt 1): 41-95, Pl. 1.

Trewavas, E., and G. M. Yazdani. 1966 (20 Jan.) **[ref. 4461]**. *Chrysochir*, a new genus for the sciaenid fish *Otolithus aureus* Richardson, with consideration of its specific synonyms. Ann. Mag. Nat. Hist. (Ser. 13) v. 8 (nos. 87/88): 249-255, Pl. 6.

Troschel, F. H. 1856 **[ref. 12559]**. Bericht über die Leistungen in der Ichthyologie während des Jahres 1855. Arch. Naturgeschichte v. 22 (pt 2): 67-89.

———. 1860 **[ref. 4464]**. *Leptopterygius*, neue Gattung der Discoboli. Arch. Naturgeschichte v. 26 (no. 1): 205-209, Pl. 7.

———. 1866 **[ref. 4465]**. Ein Beitrag zur ichthyologischen Fauna der Inseln der Grünen Vorgebirges. Arch. Naturgeschichte v. 32 (no. 1): 190-239, Pl. 5.

Trott, L. B. 1981 **[ref. 14205]**. A general review of the pearlfishes (Pisces, Carapidae). Bull. Mar. Sci. v. 31 (no. 3): 623-629.

Trotter, E. S. 1926 (4 Nov.) **[ref. 4466]**. Brotulid fishes from the Arcturus oceanographic expedition. Zoologica (N. Y.) v. 8 (no. 3): 107-125, 1 pl.

Trunov, I. A. 1980 **[ref. 4467]**. *Haplomacrourus nudirostris* gen. et sp. n. (Osteichthyes, Macrouridae), a new genus and species of rat-tails from the south Atlantic. Voprosy Ikhtiol. v. 20 (no. 1): 3-11. [In Russian. English translation in J. Ichthyol. v. 20 (no. 1): 1-7.]

———. 1981 **[ref. 4468]**. *Paracumba maculisquama* gen. et sp. n. — a new macrourid fish (Macrouridae) from the South Atlantic. Voprosy Ikhtiol. v. 21 (no. 1): 28-36. [In Russian. English translation in J. Ichthyol. v. 21 (no. 1): 27-34.]

Tsao, W.-H. 1964 **[ref. 13501]**. Schizothoracinae. Pp. 137-197. In: Wu 1964 [ref. 4806]. [In Chinese.]

Tschudi, J. J. von. 1846 **[ref. 4469]**. Ichthyologie. Pp. ii-xxx + 1-35, Pls. 1-6. In: Untersuchungen über die Fauna Peruana. Scheitlin & Zollikofer, St. Gallen. 1844-46, in 12 parts. [Parts 1-2 issued in 1844, 3-5 in 1845, 6-12 in 1846. Overall pages 1-693.]

Tubbs, P. K. 1988 (June) **[ref. 13552]**. Note by P. K. Tubbs, Executive Secretary of the International Commission on Zoological Nomenclature. Bull. Zool. Nomencl. v. 45 (no. 2): 103.

Tucker, D. W. 1954 (Sept.) **[ref. 4470]**. Report on the fishes collected by S. Y. "Rosaura" in the North and Central Atlantic, 1937-38. Part I. Families Carcharhinidae, Torpedinidae, Rosauridae (nov.), Salmonidae, Alepocephalidae, Searsidae, Clupeidae. Bull. Br. Mus. (Nat. Hist.) Zool. v. 2 (no. 6): 163-214, Pls. 7-8.

Tuckey, J. K. 1818 **[ref. 5023]**. Narrative of an expedition to explore the river Zaire, usually called the Congo, in south Africa, in 1816. London. [Not seen.]

Turner, C. L. 1937 (5 Dec.) **[ref. 6400]**. The trophotaeniae of the Goodeidae, a family of viviparous cyprinodont fishes. J. Morphol. v. 61 (no. 3): 495-515, Pls. 1-4.

———. 1946 (12 June) **[ref. 4471]**. A contribution to the taxonomy and zoogeography of the goodeid fishes. Occas. Pap. Mus. Zool. Univ. Mich. No. 495: 1-13, Pl. 1.

Turton, W. 1807 **[ref. 12590]**. The British fauna, containing a compendium of the zoology; of the British Islands; arranged according to the Linnaean system. Swansea, London. 1-230. [Not seen.]

Tyler, J. C. 1966 (22 June) **[ref. 4474]**. A new genus and species of triacanthodid fish (Plectognathi) from the Indian Ocean. Not. Nat. (Phila.) No. 385: 1-5.

———. 1968 (26 Nov.) **[ref. 6438]**. A monograph on plectognath fishes of the superfamily Triacanthoidea. Monogr. Acad. Nat. Sci. Phila. No. 16: 1-364.

———. 1980 (Oct.) **[ref. 4477]**. Osteology, phylogeny, and higher classification of the fishes of the order Plectognathi (Tetraodontiformes). NOAA Tech. Rep. NMFS Circ. No. 434: 1-422.

———. 1983 (Dec.) **[ref. 5293]**. Records of fishes of the family Triacanthodidae (Tetraodontiformes) from the western Indian Ocean off East Africa. J. L. B. Smith Inst. Ichthyol. Spec. Publ. No. 31: 1-13.

———. 1986 **[ref. 5723]**. Family No. 265: Triacanthodidae (pp. 887-890). In: Smiths' Sea Fishes (Smith & Heemstra 1986 [ref. 5715]).

TYLER, J. C., G. D. JOHNSON, I. NAKAMURA AND B. B. COLLETTE. 1989 (4 Oct.) **[ref. 13460]**. Morphology of *Luvarus imperialis* (Luvaridae), with a phylogenetic analysis of the Acanthuroidei (Pisces). Smithson. Contrib. Zool. No. 485: i-vi + 1-78.

TYLER, J. C., AND M. D. LANGE. 1982 (12 May) **[ref. 5509]**. Redescription of the Indo-Australian filefish *Acreichthys radiatus* (Popta) (Monacanthidae, Tetraodontiformes). Am. Mus. Novit. No. 2727: 1-14.

TYLER, J. C., AND J. R. PAXTON. 1979 **[ref. 4478]**. New genus and species of pufferfish (Tetraodontidae) from Norfolk Island, southwest Pacific. Bull. Mar. Sci. v. 29 (no. 2): 202-215.

UWA, H. 1986 (30 May) **[ref. 6322]**. Karyotype evolution and geographic distribution in the ricefish, genus *Oryzias* (Oryziidae). Pp. 867-876. In: Uyeno et al. (eds.) 1986 [ref. 6147].

UWA, H., AND L. R. PARENTI. 1988 **[ref. 6852]**. Morphometric and meristic variation in ricefishes, genus *Oryzias*: a comparison with cytogenetic data. Jpn. J. Ichthyol. v. 35 (no. 2): 159-166.

UWATE, K. R. 1979 (20 Feb.) **[ref. 7015]**. Revision of the anglerfish Diceratiidae with description of two new species. Copeia 1979 (no. 1): 129-144.

UYENO, T. 1961 **[ref. 4479]**. Late Cenozoic cyprinid fishes from Idaho with notes on other fossil minnows in North America. Pap. Mich. Acad. Sci. Arts Lett. v. 46: 329-344.

UYENO, T., R. ARAI, T. TANIUCHI AND K. MATSUURA [EDS.]. 1986 (30 May) **[ref. 6147]**. Indo-Pacific Fish Biology. Proceedings of the Second International Conference on Indo-Pacific Fishes. Ichthyol. Soc. Japan 1986: i-xii + 1-985.

UYENO, T., AND S. KISHIDA. 1977 **[ref. 7016]**. The second specimen of the alepocephalid fish, *Rouleina tanakae*, collected off Kyushu, Japan. Jpn. J. Ichthyol. v. 24 (no. 2): 141-143.

UYENO, T., K. MATSUURA AND E. FUJII [EDS.]. 1983 **[ref. 14275]**. Fishes trawled off Surinam and French Guiana. Japan Marine Fishery Resource Research Center. 1-519, Many col. figs. [In Japanese and English.]

UYENO, T., R. R. MILLER AND J. M. FITZSIMONS. 1983 (6 May) **[ref. 6818]**. Karyology of the cyprinodontoid fishes of the Mexican family Goodeidae. Copeia 1983 (no. 2): 497-510.

VAHL, M. 1794 **[ref. 4482]**. Beskrivelse af en nye fiskeslaegt (*Caecula*). Skr. Naturh. Selsk. Kjobenhavn v. 3 (no. 2): 149-156. [Original not seen. A translation appeared in Smith 1965: 716-717 [ref. 4132].]

VAILLANT, L. L. 1873 **[ref. 4492]**. Recherches sur les poissons des eaux douces de l'Amérique septentrionale designés, par M. L. Agassiz sous le nom d'Etheostomatidae. Nouv. Arch. Mus. Natl. Hist. Nat. Paris v. 9: 5-154.

———. 1882 **[ref. 4493]**. Sur un poisson des grandes profondeurs de l'Atlantique, l'*Eurypharynx pelecanoides*. C. R. Hebd. Seances Acad. Sci. v. 95: 1226-1228. [Also in Ann. Mag. Nat. Hist. (Ser. 5) v. 11: 67-69. Also as a separate, pp. 1-3.]

———. 1886 **[ref. 4494]**. Considèrations sur les poissons des grandes profondeurs, en particulier sur ceux qui appartiennent au sous-ordre des Abdominales. C. R. Hebd. Seances Acad. Sci. v. 103: 1237-1239.

———. 1888 **[ref. 4495]**. Poissons. In: Mission scientifique du Cap Horn, 1882-83. VI. Zoologie. Paris. v. 6 (Zool.): 1-35, Pls. 1-4.

———. 1888 **[ref. 4496]**. Expéditions scientifiques du "Travailleur" et du "Talisman" pendant les années 1880, 1881, 1882, 1883. Poissons. Paris. 1-406, Pls. 1-28.

———. 1889 **[ref. 4483]**. Sur les poissons des eaux douces de Bornéo. C. R. Congr. Intern. Zool. Paris 1889: 81-82.

———. 1891 **[ref. 4497]**. Note sur un nouveau genre de Siluroïdes (*Diastatomycter*) de Bornéo. Bull. Soc. Philomath. Paris (Ser. 8) v. 3 (no. 4): 181-182.

———. 1893 (28 Feb.) **[ref. 4485]**. Sur une collection de poissons recueillie par M. Chaper, a Bornéo. Bull. Soc. Zool. Fr. v. 18: 55-62. [Also as separate, dated 28 Feb. 1893.]

———. 1893 **[ref. 4486]**. Sur les poissons provenant du voyage de M. Bonvalot et du Prince Henri d'Orléans. Bull. Soc. Philomath. Paris (Ser. 8) v. 5 (no. 4): 197-204.

———. 1893 **[ref. 4487]**. Sur un nouveaux genre de poissons voisin de *Fierasfer*. C. R. Hebd. Seances Acad. Sci. v. 117: 745-746. [Also as separate, Paris, pp. 1-2]

———. 1894 **[ref. 4488]**. Sur une collection de poissons recueillie en Basse-Californie et dans le Golf par M. Léon Diguet. Bull. Soc. Philomath. Paris (Ser. 8) v. 6: 69-75.

———. 1896 **[ref. 13482]**. Note sur l'oeuvre ichthyologique de C. A. LeSueur. Bull. Soc. Philomath. Paris (Ser. 8) v. 8 (no. 1): 15-33. [Also as a separate, 1896, pp. 1-19 (also 15-33) plus Pls. 1-35.]

———. 1897 **[ref. 4489]**. Siluroïde nouveau de l'Afrique orientale (*Chimarrhoglanis leroyi*). Bull. Mus. Natl. Hist. Nat. (Ser. 1) v. 3 (no. 3)[1897]: 81-84.

———. 1902 (Nov.) **[ref. 4490]**. Résultats zoologiques de l'expédition scientifique néerlandaise au Bornéo central. Poissons. Notes Leyden Mus. v. 24 (Note 1): 1-166, Pls. 1-2.

———. 1904 **[ref. 4491]**. Quelques reptiles, batraciens et poissons du Haut-Tonkin. Bull. Mus. Natl. Hist. Nat. (Ser. 1) v. 10 (no. 6)[1904]: 297-301.

VAILLANT, L. L., AND F. BOCOURT. 1874-1915 **[ref. 4498]**. Études sur les poissons. In: Mission scientifique au Mexique et dans l'Amérique centrale. Recherches zoologiques. Quatrième partie. Paris. Part 4: 1-265, 20 pls. (variously numbered). [Pp. 1-40 (1874), 41-120 (1878), 121-200 (1883), 201-265 (1915).]

VALENCIENNES, A. 1832 **[ref. 12986]**. Poissons. Pp. 337-399, Pls. 1-4. In: Voyage aux Indes-Orientales, publié par Charles Bélanger. Paris. [Published in 1832 (see Sherborn & Woodward 1907: 494 [ref. 13429]).]

———. 1837-44 **[ref. 4502]**. Ichthyologie des îles Canaries, ou histoire naturelle des poissons rapportés par Webb & Berthelot. In: P. B. Webb & S. Berthelot. Histoire naturelle des îles Canaries. Paris, 1835-1850. v. 2 (pt 2): 1-109, 26 pls. [For dates of individual pages and plates see Hureau & Monod 1973:v. 2: 157 [ref. 6590] and Stern 1937 [ref. 13581].]

———. 1846 **[ref. 6165]**. Table + Ichthyology Pls. 1-10. In: A. du Petit-Thouars. Atlas de Zoologie. Voyage autour du monde sur la frégate "Vénus," pendant les années 1836-1839. [Plates were published in 1846 (see Sherborn & Woodward 1907: 492 [ref. 13429]).]

———. 1847 **[ref. 5010]**. Poissons. Catalogue des principales espèces de poissons, rapportées de l'Amérique méridionale. In: A. d'-Orbigny. Voyage dans l'Amérique méridionale.

———. 1855 **[ref. 4504]**. Ichthyologie. Pp. ii-iii + 297-323. In: A. du Petit-Thouars. Voyage autour du monde sur la frégate la "Vénus," pendant les anées 1836-39. Zoology. Paris. [Ichthyology Pls. 1-10 published in Valenciennes 1846 [ref. 6165].]

———. 1861 **[ref. 4505]**. Rapport sur les collections des espèces de mamifères déterminées par leurs nombreaux ossements fossiles recueillis par M. Albert Gaudry, à Pikermi, près d'Athènes, pendant son voyage en Attique. C. R. Hebd. Seances Acad. Sci. v. 52: 1295-1300.

———. 1862 **[ref. 4506]**. Description de quelques espèces nouvelles de poissons envoyées de Bourbon par M. Morel, directeur du Muséum d'Histoire naturelle de cette île. C. R. Hebd. Seances Acad. Sci. v. 54: 1165-1170; (suite) 1201-1207.

VALMONT DE BOMARE, J. C. 1764 **[ref. 4507]**. Dictionnaire raisonné universel d'histoire naturelle, contenant l'histoire des animaux, des végétaux et des minéraux ... des météores, etc. 5 vols. Paris. [Subsequent editions in 1768, 1774 and 1791. All editions rejected nomenclaturally by ICZN (Direction 32, Opinion 89).]

———. 1791 **[ref. 4508]**. Dictionnaire raisonné d'histoire naturelle, contenant l'histoire des animaux, des végétaux et des minéraux ... des météores, etc. 4. éd. 8 vols. Paris. [Work rejected by ICZN (Direction 32, Opinion 89). Original not seen.]

VAN CLEAVE, H. J. 1943 **[ref. 13436]**. An index to the Opinions rendered by the International Commisson on Zoological Nomenclature. Amer. Midl. Natural. v. 30 (no. 1): 223-240.

VAN COUVERING, J. A. H. 1982 **[ref. 2042]**. Fossil cichlid fish of Africa. Spec. Pap. Palaeontol. No. 29: 1-103.

VAN DER HOEVEN, J. 1833 **[ref. 5061]**. Handboek der dierkunde. Amsterdam. A second edition in 1849-56. [Not seen.]

———. 1849 **[ref. 2182]**. Handboek der dierkunde; tweede verbeterde uitgave; met bijvoegsels en aanmerkingen door Leuckart. Amsterdam. 3 vols. Edition 2. [Fishes, vol. 2, pp. 188-419. Not seen.]

———. 1855 **[ref. 6527]**. Handbook of zoology. Vol. 2 (Vertebrate animals). [Original not seen; English translation by W. Clark (1858) examined.]

VAN HASSELT, J. C. 1823 **[ref. 4513]**. Uittreksel uit een' brief van Dr. J. C. van Hasselt, aan den Heer C. J. Temminck. Allg. Konst. Letter-Bode I Deel (no. 20): 315-317. [Also in French (1824). See Kottelat 1987 [ref. 5962].]

———. 1823 **[ref. 5105]**. Uittresel uit een' brief van Dr. J. C. van Hasselt, aan den Heer C. J. Temminck. Allg. Konst. Letter-Bode I Deel (no. 21): 329-331. [Also in French (1824); see also Kottelat 1987 [ref. 5962].]

———. 1823 **[ref. 5963]**. Uittreksel uit een' brief van Dr. J. C. van Hasselt, aan den Heer C. J. Temminck. Allg. Konst. Letter-Bode II Deel (no. 35): 130-133. [Also in French [ref. 5964].]

———. 1824 **[ref. 5104]**. Sur les poissons de Java. Extrait d'une première lettre du Dr. J.-P. van Hasselt à M. C. J. Temminck. Bull. Sci. Nat. Géol. (Férussac) v. 2 (Zool., 73): 89-92. [First published in Dutch, van Hasselt 1823 [ref. 5105].]

———. 1824 **[ref. 5964]**. Extrait d'une seconde lettre sur les poissons de Java, écrite par M. Van Hasselt à M. C.-J. Temminck, datée de Tjecande, résidence de Bantam, 29 décembre 1822. Bull. Sci. Nat. Geol. (Ser. 2) v. 2: 374-377.

VAN NEER, W. 1987 (30 Dec.) **[ref. 12843]**. A study of the variability of the skeleton of *Lates niloticus* (Linnaeus, 1758) in view of the validity of *Lates maliensis* Gayet, 1983. Cybium v. 11 (no. 4): 411-425.

VARI, R. P. 1977 (26 Jan.) **[ref. 7037]**. Notes on the characoid subfamily Iguanodectinae, with a description of a new species. Am. Mus. Novit. No. 2612: 1-6.

———. 1978 (17 Apr.) **[ref. 4514]**. The terapon perches (Percoidei, Teraponidae). A cladistic analysis and taxonomic revision. Bull. Am. Mus. Nat. Hist. v. 159 (art. 5): 175-340.

———. 1978 (3 May) **[ref. 7036]**. The genus *Leptagoniates* (Pisces: Characoidei) with a description of a new species from Bolivia. Proc. Biol. Soc. Wash. v. 91 (no. 1): 184-190.

———. 1979 (29 Nov.) **[ref. 5490]**. Anatomy, relationships and classification of the families Citharinidae and Distichodontidae (Pisces, Characoidea). Bull. Br. Mus. (Nat. Hist.) Zool. v. 36 (no. 5): 261-344.

———. 1982 (27 Aug.) **[ref. 5485]**. Systematics of the neotropical characoid genus *Curimatopsis* (Pisces: Characoidei). Smithson. Contrib. Zool. No. 373: i-iii + 1-28.

———. 1982 **[ref. 6765]**. The seahorses (subfamily Hippocampinae). Mem. Sears Found. Mar. Res. Mem. 1 (pt 8): 173-189.

———. 1983 (3 May) **[ref. 5419]**. Phylogenetic relationships of the families Curimatidae, Prochilodontidae, Anostomidae, and Chilodontidae (Pisces: Characiformes). Smithson. Contrib. Zool. No. 378: i-iii + 1-60.

———. 1984 (29 Aug.) **[ref. 5307]**. Systematics of the neotropical characiform genus *Potamorhina* (Pisces: Characiformes). Smithson. Contrib. Zool. No. 400: 1-36.

———. 1985 (16 May) **[ref. 5270]**. A new species of *Bivibranchia* (Pisces: Characiformes) from Surinam, with comments on the genus. Proc. Biol. Soc. Wash. v. 98 (no. 2): 511-522.

———. 1986 (4 June) **[ref. 5989]**. *Serrabrycon magoi*, a new genus and species of scale-eating characid (Pisces: Characiformes) from the Upper Río Negro. Proc. Biol. Soc. Wash. v. 99 (no. 2): 328-334.

———. 1986 (Apr.) **[ref. 6205]**. Teraponidae (pp. 304-305). In: Daget et al. 1986 [ref. 6189].

———. 1987 (14 Oct.) **[ref. 6059]**. Two new species of curimatid fishes (Ostariophysi: Characiformes) from Rio Grande do Sul, Brazil. Proc. Biol. Soc. Wash. v. 100 (no. 3): 603-609.

———. 1989 (13 Feb.) **[ref. 9189]**. A phylogenetic study of the neotropical characiform family Curimatidae (Pisces: Ostariophysi). Smithson. Contrib. Zool. No. 471: i-iv + 1-71.

———. 1989 **[ref. 13475]**. Systematics of the neotropical characiform genus *Pseudocurimata* Fernández-Yépez (Pisces: Ostariophysi). Smithson. Contrib. Zool. No. 490: i-iii + 1-26.

———. 1989 **[ref. 13506]**. Systematics of the neotropical characiform genus *Curimata* Bosc (Pisces: Characiformes). Smithson. Contrib. Zool. No. 474: i-iii + 1-63.

———. 1989 **[ref. 13548]**. Systematics of the neotropical characiform genus *Psectrogaster* Eigenmann and Eigenmann (Pisces: Characiformes). Smithson. Contrib. Zool. No. 481: i-iii + 1-43.

VARI, R. P., AND M. GOULDING. 1985 (4 Dec.) **[ref. 5200]**. A new species of *Bivibranchia* (Pisces: Characiformes) from the Amazon River basin. Proc. Biol. Soc. Wash. v. 98 (no. 4): 1054-1061.

VARI, R. P., S. L. JEWETT, D. C. TAPHORN AND C. R. GILBERT. 1984 (6 July) **[ref. 5261]**. A new catfish of the genus *Epapterus* (Siluriformes: Auchenipteridae) from the Orinoco River basin. Proc. Biol. Soc. Wash. v. 97 (no. 2): 462-472.

VARI, R. P., AND H. ORTEGA. 1986 (21 Nov.) **[ref. 5837]**. The catfishes of the neotropical family Helogenidae (Ostariophysi: Siluroidei). Smithson. Contrib. Zool. No. 442: i-iii + 1-20.

VARI, R. P., AND A. M. WILLIAMS. 1987 (25 Feb.) **[ref. 5980]**. Headstanders of the neotropical anostomid genus *Abramites* (Pisces: Characiformes: Anostomidae). Proc. Biol. Soc. Wash. v. 100 (no. 1): 89-103.

VARI, R. P., AND A. WILLIAMS VARI. 1989 (28 June) **[ref. 12508]**. Systematics of the *Steindachnerina hypostoma* complex (Pisces, Ostariophysi, Curimatidae), with the description of three new species. Proc. Biol. Soc. Wash. v. 102 (no. 2): 468-482.

VASIL'YEVA, E. D., AND M. S. KOZLOVA. 1988 **[ref. 13523]**. Taxonymy of the sawbelly genus *Hemiculter* in the Soviet Union. Voprosy Ikhtiol. v. 28 (no. 6): 883-895. [In Russian. English translation in J. Ichthyol. 1989, v. 29 (no. 1): 123-135.]

VASIL'YEVA, E. D., AND V. P. VASIL'EV. 1988 **[ref. 13477]**. Study of the intraspecific structure of *Sabanejewia aurata* (Cobitidae) with description of a new subspecies, *S. aurita kubanica*. Voprosy Ikhtiol. v. 28 (no. 2): 192-212. [In Russian. English translation in J. Ichthyol. v. 28 (no. 6): 15-35.]

VAZ-FERREIRA, R., AND B. SIERRA. 1974 (28 June (Impreso)) **[ref. 4517]**. *Campellolebias brucei* n. gen. n. sp., cyprinodontido con especializacion de la papila gentital y de los primeros radios de la aleta anal. Comun. Zool. Mus. Hist. Nat. Montev. v. 10 (no. 138): 1-17, Pls. 1-2.

VERGARA R., R. 1980 **[ref. 5201]**. Estudio filogenético de los peces ciegos del género *Lucifuga* (Pisces: Ophidiidae). I. Sistemática filogenética. Revista Cenic v. 11 (no. 2): 311-323.

VILLAMAR, A. 1980 (Dec.) **[ref. 6596]**. *Totoaba*, un nuevo género de la familia Sciaenidae del Golfo de California, México (Pisces: Teleostei). An. Esc. Nac. Cienc. Biol. Mex. v. 23 (nos. 1/4): 129-133.

VINCIGUERRA, D. 1890 (Apr.) **[ref. 4520]**. Viaggio di Leonardo Fea in Birmania e regioni vicine. XXIV. Pisci. Ann. Mus. Civ. Stor. Nat. Genova (Ser. 2) v. 9: 129-362, Pls. 7-11. [Also as a separate, Genova, 234 pp., 5 pls.]

———. 1895 **[ref. 4521]**. Esplorazione del Giuba e dei suoi affluenti compiuta dal Cap. V. Bottego durante gli anni 1892-93 sotto gli auspicii della Società geografica Italiana. III. Pesci. Ann. Mus. Civ. Stor. Nat. Genova (Ser. 2) v. 15: 19-60, Pl. 5.

———. 1898 (12 Sept.) **[ref. 4522]**. I pesci dell'ultima spedizione del Cap. Bottego. Ann. Mus. Civ. Stor. Nat. Genova (Ser. 2) v. 19: 240-261.

———. 1924 **[ref. 4523]**. Descrizione di un ciprinide cieco proveniente dalla Somalia Italiana. Ann. Mus. Civ. Stor. Nat. Genova v. 51: 239-243.

VISWESWARA RAO, V. 1968 **[ref. 4524]**. A new gobiid fish from Visakhapatnam. J. Nat. Hist. v. 2 (no. 1): 17-20.

VLADYKOV, V. D. 1929 **[ref. 4525]**. Sur un nouveau genre de Cobitides: *Sabanejewia*. Bull. Mus. Natl. Hist. Nat. (Ser. 2) v. 1 (no.

1): 85-90.
——. 1963 **[ref. 4526]**. A review of salmonid genera and their broad geographical distribution. Trans. R. Soc. Can. (Ser. 4) v. 1: 459-504.
——. 1973 **[ref. 7159]**. Petromyzonidae (pp. 2-5), Myxinidae (p. 6). In: Hureau & Monod 1973 [ref. 6590].
VLADYKOV, V. D., AND C. G. GRUCHY. 1972 **[ref. 4527]**. Comments on the nomenclature of some subgenera of Salmonidae. J. Fish. Res. Board Can. v. 29 (no. 11): 1631-1632.
VLADYKOV, V. D., AND E. KOTT. 1976 **[ref. 7095]**. Is *Okkelbergia* Creaser and Hubbs, 1922 (Petromyzonidae) a distinct taxon? Can. J. Zool. v. 54 (no. 3): 421-425.
——. 1978 (Apr.) **[ref. 7038]**. A new nonparasitic species of the Holarctic lamprey genus *Lethenteron* Creaser and Hubbs, 1922, (Petromyzonidae) from northwestern North America with notes on other species of the same genus. Biol. Pap. Univ. Alaska No. 19: 1-74.
VOGT, K. D. 1988 (June) **[ref. 6625]**. Liparidae Gill, [30 September] 1861 (Osteichthyes, Scorpaeniformes): proposed confirmation of spelling. Bull. Zool. Nomencl. v. 45 (pt 2): 130-131.
VOIGT, L. 1832 **[ref. 4948]**. Thier Cuvier. Vol. 2 [Not seen.]
VOLZ, W. 1903 (29 June) **[ref. 4531]**. Neue Fische aus Sumatra. (Reise von Dr. W. Volz.) (Vorläufige Mittheilung.) Zool. Anz. v. 26 (no. 703): 553-559.
VON BONDE, C. 1922 **[ref. 520]**. The Heterosomata (flat fishes) collected by the S. S. "Pickle." Rep. Fish. Mar. Biol. Surv. Union So. Afr. Rep. 2 (art. 1): 1-29, Pls. 1-6.
——. 1924 (25 Aug.) **[ref. 521]**. Shallow-water fishes procured by the S. S. "Pickle." Rep. Fish. Mar. Biol. Surv. Union So. Afr. Rep. 3 (art. 1): 1-40, Pls. 1-9.
VON BONDE, C., AND D. B. SWART. 1923 (25 Aug.) **[ref. 522]**. The Platosomia (skates and rays) collected by the S.S. "Pickle." Rep. Fish. Mar. Biol. Surv. Union So. Afr. Rep. 3 (art. 5): 1-22, Pls. 20-23.
VOSKOBOINIKOVA, O. S. 1988 **[ref. 12756]**. Comparative osteology of dragonfishes of the subfamily Gymnodraconinae (Bathydraconidae). Proc. Zool. Inst. Leningrad; Syst. Morph. Ecol. Fishes v. 181: 44-55. [In Russian, brief English Summ.]
VOSKOBOINIKOVA, O. S., AND A. V. BALUSHKIN. 1987 **[ref. 6342]**. On the taxonomical status of the *Gobionotothen angustifrons sandwichensis* (Nybelin, 1947) (Nototheniidae). USSR Acad. Sci., Proc. Zool. Inst. Leningrad v. 162: 100-107. [In Russian, English summ.]
WADE, C. B. 1946 (16 Dec.) **[ref. 4542]**. Two new genera and five new species of apodal fishes from the eastern Pacific. Allan Hancock Pac. Exped. v. 9 (no. 7): 181-213, Pls. 24-28.
WAITE, E. R. 1899 (23 Dec.) **[ref. 4557]**. Fishes. In: Scientific results of the trawling expedition of H. M. C. S. "Thetis." Mem. Aust. Mus. v. 4 (pt 1): 27-132, Pls. 1-31.
——. 1900 (15 June) **[ref. 4558]**. Additions to the fish-fauna of Lord Howe Island. Rec. Aust. Mus. v. 3 (no. 7): 193-209, Pls. 34-36.
——. 1902 (6 Jan.) **[ref. 4559]**. Notes on fishes from Western Australia, No. 2. Rec. Aust. Mus. v. 4 (no. 5): 179-194, Pls. 27-31.
——. 1903 (Apr.) **[ref. 4560]**. New records or recurrences of rare fishes from eastern Australia. No. 2. Rec. Aust. Mus. v. 5 (no. 1): 56-61, 1 pl. [Also as a reprint. Fowler (MS) dates to Apr. 1903.]
——. 1904 (11 Mar.) **[ref. 4561]**. Additions to the fish fauna of Lord Howe Island, No. 4. Rec. Aust. Mus. v. 5 (no. 3): 135-186, Pls. 17-24.
——. 1904 (16 June) **[ref. 13443]**. New records or recurrences of rare fishes from eastern Australia. Rec. Aust. Mus. v. 5 (pt 4): 231-244, Pls. 25-26.
——. 1905 **[ref. 4562]**. Notes on fishes from Western Australia.—No. 3. Rec. Aust. Mus. v. 6 (no. 2): 55-82, Pls. 8-17.
——. 1906 **[ref. 6937]**. Descriptions of and notes on some Australian and Tasmanian fishes. Rec. Aust. Mus. v. 6 (pt 3): 194-210, Pls. 34-36.
——. 1907 (23 Jan.) **[ref. 4563]**. The generic name *Crepidogaster*. Rec. Aust. Mus. v. 6: 315.
——. 1907 (25 Apr.) **[ref. 11968]**. A basic list of the fishes of New Zealand. Rec. Canterbury Mus. v. 1 (no. 1): 1-39.
——. 1909 (13 July) **[ref. 4564]**. Pisces. Part I. In: Scientific results of the New Zealand government trawling expedition, 1907. Rec. Canterbury Mus. v. 1 (no. 2): 131-155, Pls. 13-23.
——. 1910 **[ref. 4565]**. Additions to the fish fauna of New Zealand. Trans. N. Z. Inst. Part 1 (1910): 25-26.
——. 1910 **[ref. 4566]**. Notes on New Zealand fishes. Trans. N. Z. Inst. v. 42 [1909]: 384-391, Pl. 37.
——. 1911 (18 Jan.) **[ref. 4567]**. Additions to the fish-fauna of New Zealand: No. II. Trans. N. Z. Inst. Part 2 [1910]: 49-51.
——. 1916 (30 June) **[ref. 4568]**. Fishes. In: Australasian Antarctic expedition 1911-1914. Sci. Rept., Ser. C.—Zool. & Bot. Adelaide. v. 3 (pt 1): 1-92, Pls. 1-5, 2 maps.
WAITE, E. R., AND H. M. HALE. 1921 (29 Jan.) **[ref. 4569]**. Review of the Lophobranchiate fishes (pipe-fishes and sea-horses) of South Australia. Rec. Aust. Mus. v. 1 (no. 4): 293-324.
WAKIYA, Y. 1924 **[ref. 4570]**. The carangoid fishes of Japan. Ann. Carnegie Mus. v. 15 (nos. 2-3): 139-292, Pls. 15-38.
WAKIYA, Y., AND N. TAKAHASI. 1937 (Dec.) **[ref. 4571]**. Study on fishes of the family Salangidae. J. Coll. Agric. Imp. Univ. Tokyo v. 14 (no. 4): 265-296, Pls. 16-21.
WALBAUM, J. J. 1792 **[ref. 4572]**. Petri Artedi Sueci Genera piscium. In quibus systema totum ichthyologiae proponitur cum classibus, ordinibus, generum characteribus, specierum differentiis, observationibus plurimis. Redactis speciebus 242 ad genera 52. Ichthyologiae, pars iii. 1-723, Pls. 1-3. [Reprint 1966 by J. Cramer.]
——. 1793 **[ref. 12604]**. J. T. Kleinii ichthyologia enodata, sive index rerum ad historiam piscium naturalem synonymis recentissimorum systematicorum explicatus. Lipsiae. i-vi + 1-114.
WALKER, H. J., JR., AND R. H. ROSENBLATT. 1988 (28 Dec.) **[ref. 9284]**. Pacific toadfishes of the genus *Porichthys* (Batrachoididae) with descriptions of three new species. Copeia 1988 (no. 4): 887-904.
WALTERS, V. 1960 (26 Sept.) **[ref. 4577]**. Synopsis of the lampridiform suborder Veliferoidei. Copeia 1960 (no. 3): 245-247.
——. 1961 (Oct.) **[ref. 4578]**. A contribution to the biology of the Giganturidae, with description of a new genus and species. Bull. Mus. Comp. Zool. v. 125 (no. 10): 297-319.
WALTERS, V., AND J. E. FITCH. 1960 (Oct.) **[ref. 4580]**. The families and genera of the lampridiform (Allotriognath) suborder Trachipteroidei. Calif. Fish Game v. 46 (no. 4): 441-451.
WANG, K. F. 1935 **[ref. 4582]**. Preliminary notes on the fishes of Chekiang (Isospondyli, Apodes & Plectospondyli). Contrib. Biol. Lab. Sci. Soc. China Nanking (Zool. Ser.) v. 11 (no. 1): 1-65.
——. 1941 **[ref. 4583]**. The labroid fishes of Hainan. Contrib. Biol. Lab. Sci. Soc. China Nanking (Zool. Ser.) v. 15 (no. 6): 87-119.
WAPLES, R. S. 1981 **[ref. 5491]**. A biochemical and morphological review of the lizardfish genus *Saurida* in Hawaii, with the description of a new species. Pac. Sci. v. 35 (no. 3): 217-235.
WAPLES, R. S., AND J. E. RANDALL. 1988 **[ref. 9187]**. A revision of the Hawaiian lizardfishes of the genus *Synodus*, with descriptions of four new species. Pac. Sci. v. 42 (nos. 3-4): 177-213, Pls. 1-3.
WARPACHOWSKI, N. A. 1887 **[ref. 4516]**. Über die Gattung *Hemiculter* Bleek. und über eine neue Gattung *Hemiculterella*. Bull. Imp. Acad. Sci. St. Petersburg 1887: 14-24. [Fowler (MS) dates as 1888 [read 24 Mar. 1887] (not investigated).]
——. 1897 **[ref. 4515]**. Sur la faune ichthyologique du fleuve Obi. Ann. Mus. Zool. Acad. Imp. Sci. St. Petersburg v. 2 (1897): 241-271, Pls. 11-12. [In Russian.]
WASHINGTON, B. B. 1986 (6 Mar.) **[ref. 5202]**. Systematic relationships and ontogeny of the sculpins *Artedius, Clinocottus*, and *Oligocottus* (Cottidae: Scorpaeniformes). Proc. Calif. Acad. Sci. v. 44 (no. 9): 157-224.
WASHINGTON, B. B., W. N. ESCHMEYER AND K. M. HOWE. 1984 **[ref. 13660]**. Scorpaeniformes: relationships. Am. Soc. Ichthyol. Herpetol. Spec. Publ. No. 1: 438-447.
WATANABE, M. 1949 (1 May) **[ref. 6581]**. Studies on the fishes of the Ryukyo Islands. Bull. Biogeogr. Soc. Jpn. v. 14 (no. 4): 17-20.
WATSON, W., E. G. STEVENS AND A. C. MATARESE. 1984 **[ref. 13670]**.

Schindlerioidei: development and relationships. Am. Soc. Ichthyol. Herpetol. Spec. Publ. No. 1: 552-554.

WEBB, P. B., AND S. BERTHELOT. 1837-44 **[ref. 6471]**. Histoire naturelle des îles Canaries. See Valenciennes 1837-44 [ref. 4502].

WEBER, C. 1987 **[ref. 6241]**. *Hypostomus microstomus* sp. nov. et autres poissons-chats cuirassés du Rio Parana (Pisces, Siluriformes, Loricariidae). Arch. Sci. (Geneva) v. 40 (fasc. 3): 273-284.

WEBER, M. 1895 **[ref. 4607]**. Fische von Ambon, Java, Thursday Island, dem Burnett-Fluss und von der Süd-küste von Neu-Guinea. In: Zoologische Forschungsreisen in Australien und dem malayischen Archipel; mit Unterstützung des Herrn Dr. Paul von Ritter ausgeführt in den v. 5: 259-276. [Not seen.]

———. 1902 (3 Jan.) **[ref. 4608]**. Siboga-Expeditie. Uitkomsten op zoologisch, botanisch, ocenographisch en geologisch gebied verzameld in nederlandsch Oost-Indië, 1899-1900... Introduction et description de l'expédition. No. 1 (livr. 3): 1-159.

———. 1907 **[ref. 4599]**. Süsswasserfische von Neu-Guinea ein Beitrag zur Frage nach dem früheren Zusammenhang von Neu-Guinea und Australien. In: Nova Guinea. Résultats de l'expédition scientifique Néerlandaise à la Nouvelle-Guinée. v. 5 (Zool.): 201-267, Pls. 11-13. [Also as separate, E. J. Brill, Leiden.]

———. 1909 **[ref. 4600]**. Diagnosen neuer Fische der Siboga-Expedition. Notes Leyden Mus. v. 31 (note 4): 143-169.

———. 1913 **[ref. 4601]**. Neue Beiträge zur Kenntnis der Süsswasserfische von Celebes. Bijdr. Dierkd. 1913: 197-213.

———. 1913 **[ref. 4602]**. Die Fische der Siboga-Expedition. E. J. Brill, Leiden. i-xii + 1-710, Pls. 1-12.

———. 1913 **[ref. 4603]**. Süsswasserfische aus Niederländisch Süd- und Nord-Neu-Guinea. In: Nova Guinea. Résultats de l'expédition scientifique Néerlandaise à la Nouvelle-Guinée. Zoologie. Leiden. v. 9 (livr. 4): 513-613, Pls. 12-14.

WEBER, M., AND L. F. DE BEAUFORT. 1916 **[ref. 4604]**. The fishes of the Indo-Australian Archipelago. III. Ostariophysi: II Cyprinoidea, Apodes, Synbranchi. E. J. Brill, Leiden. v. 3: i-xv + 1-455.

———. 1922 **[ref. 4598]**. The fishes of the Indo-Australian Archipelago. IV. Heteromi, Solenichthyes, Synentognathi, Percesoces, Labyrinthici, Microcyprini. E. J. Brill, Leiden. v. 4: i-xiii + 1-410.

———. 1936 **[ref. 4606]**. The fishes of the Indo-Australian Archipelago. VII. Perciformes (continued). E. J. Brill, Leiden. v. 7: i-xvi + 1-607.

WEED, A. C. 1933 (11 Dec.) **[ref. 6557]**. Notes on fishes of the family Hemirhamphidae. Zool. Ser. Field Mus. Nat. Hist. v. 20: 41-66.

WEINLAND, D. F. 1858 (Oct.) **[ref. 4615]**. [A new division of the five species of flying fish found along the coast of North America, which have hitherto all been referred to the genus *Exocetus*.] Proc. Boston Soc. Nat. Hist. v. 6 (1856 to 1859): 385.

WEITZMAN, M. J., AND R. P. VARI. 1986 (12 Dec.) **[ref. 5979]**. *Astyanax scologaster*, a new characid (Pisces: Ostariophysi) from the Rio Negro, South America. Proc. Biol. Soc. Wash. v. 99 (no. 4): 709-716.

WEITZMAN, S. H. 1974 (26 July) **[ref. 5174]**. Osteology and evolutionary relationships of the Sternoptychidae with a new classification of stomiatoid families. Bull. Am. Mus. Nat. Hist. v. 153 (art. 3): 327-478.

———. 1978 (31 Mar.) **[ref. 7040]**. Three new species of fishes of the genus *Nannostomus* from the Brazilian states of Pará and Amazonas (Teleostei: Lebiasinidae). Smithson. Contrib. Zool. No. 263: 1-14.

———. 1986 (12 Dec.) **[ref. 5983]**. A new species of *Elachocharax* (Teleostei: Characidae) from the Río Negro region of Venezuela and Brazil. Proc. Biol. Soc. Wash. v. 99 (no. 4): 739-747.

———. 1986 **[ref. 6287]**. Family No. 75: Sternoptychidae (pp. 253-254). In: Smiths' Sea Fishes (Smith & Heemstra 1986 [ref. 5715]).

———. 1987 (25 Feb.) **[ref. 5982]**. A new species of *Xenurobrycon* (Teleostei: Characidae) from the Río Mamoré basin of Bolivia. Proc. Biol. Soc. Wash. v. 100 (no. 1): 112-120.

WEITZMAN, S. H., AND J. S. COBB. 1975 (5 Mar.) **[ref. 7134]**. A revision of the South American fishes of the genus *Nannostomus* Günther (family Lebiasinidae). Smithson. Contrib. Zool. No. 186: i-iii + 1-36.

WEITZMAN, S. H., AND S. V. FINK. 1985 (24 Dec.) **[ref. 5203]**. Xenurobryconin phylogeny and putative pheromone pumps in glandulocaudine fishes (Teleostei: Characidae). Smithson. Contrib. Zool. No. 421: i-iii + 1-121.

WEITZMAN, S. H., AND W. L. FINK. 1983 (22 Dec.) **[ref. 5383]**. Relationships of the neon tetras, a group of South American freshwater fishes (Teleostei, Characidae), with comments on the phylogeny of New World Characiformes. Bull. Mus. Comp. Zool. v. 150 (no. 6): 339-395.

WEITZMAN, S. H., AND J. GÉRY. 1981 (16 Jan.) **[ref. 14218]**. The relationships of the South American pygmy characoid fishes of the genus *Elachocharax*, with a redescription of *Elachocharax junki* (Teleostei: Characidae). Proc. Biol. Soc. Wash. v. 93 (no. 4): 887-913.

WEITZMAN, S. H., AND R. H. KANAZAWA. 1976 (12 Oct.) **[ref. 4619]**. *Ammocryptocharax elegans*, a new genus and species of riffle-inhabiting characoid fish (Teleostei: Characidae) from South America. Proc. Biol. Soc. Wash. v. 89 (no. 26): 325-346.

WEITZMAN, S. H., N. A. MENEZES AND H. A. BRITSKI. 1986 (4 June) **[ref. 5984]**. *Nematocharax venustus*, a new genus and species of fish from the Rio Jequitinhonha, Minas Gerais, Brazil. Proc. Biol. Soc. Wash. v. 99 (no. 2): 335-346.

WEITZMAN, S. H., N. A. MENEZES AND M. J. WEITZMAN. 1988 **[ref. 13557]**. Phylogenetic biogeography of the Glandulocaudini (Teleostei: Characiformes, Characidae) with comments on the distributions of other freshwater fishes in eastern and southeastern Brazil. Pp. 379-427. In: Heyer, W. R., and P. E. Vanzolini (eds.). Proc. Workshop Neotropical Distribution Patterns.

WEITZMAN, S. H., AND R. P. VARI. 1987 (14 Oct.) **[ref. 6055]**. Two new species and a new genus of miniature characid fishes (Teleostei: Characiformes) from northern South America. Proc. Biol. Soc. Wash. v. 100 (no. 3): 640-652.

WERNER, F. 1906 **[ref. 4625]**. Ergebnisse der mit Subvention aus der Erbschaft Treitl unternammenen zoologischen Forschungsreise Dr. Franz Werner's in den ägyptischen Sudan und nach Nord-Uganda. V. Beiträge zur kenntnis der Fischfauna des Nils. Anz. Akad. Wiss. Wien v. 43: 325-327, Pls. 1-4.

WERNER, U., AND R. STAWIKOWSKI. 1987 (Dec.) **[ref. 13492]**. Ein neuer Buntbarsch aus Südmexiko: *Paratheraps breidohri* gen. nov., spec. nov. Aquar. Terrar. Z. v. 41 (no. 1): 20-23. [Volume for 1988, distributed in Dec. 1987 (M. Kottelat, pers. comm.).]

———. 1989 (Dec.) **[ref. 14232]**. *Paratheraps breidohri*. Aquar. Terrar. Z. v. 43 (no. 1): 10. [Volume for 1990, distributed in Dec. 1989 (M. Kottelat, pers. comm.).]

WERTZ, P., AND H. BATH. 1989 (15 Jan.) **[ref. 9298]**. *Lipophrys caboverdensis* n. sp. from the Cape Verde Islands (Pisces: Blenniidae). Senckenb. Biol. v. 69 (no. 1/3): 15-27.

WEYMOUTH, F. W. 1910 (3 May) **[ref. 4632]**. Notes on a collection of fishes from Cameron, Louisiana. Proc. U. S. Natl. Mus. v. 38 (no. 1734): 135-145.

WHEELER, A. 1956 (Oct.) **[ref. 12499]**. The type species of *Mastacembelus* and the second edition of Russell's "Natural History of Aleppo." Bull. Raffles Mus. No. 26: 91-92.

———. 1958 (June) **[ref. 13434]**. The Gronovius fish collection: a catalog and historical account. Bull. Brit. Mus. (Nat. Hist.) Histor. Ser. v. 1 (no. 5): 185-249, Pls. 26-34.

———. 1969 **[ref. 6834]**. The fishes of the British Isles and North-west Europe. Michigan State Univ. Press. i-xvii + 1-613.

———. 1973 **[ref. 7190]**. [Various family accounts.] In: Hureau & Monod (eds.) 1973 [ref. 6590].

———. 1987 (May) **[ref. 12821]**. Peter Artedi, founder of modern ichthyology. Pp. 3-10. In: Kullander & Fernholm (eds.), Proceedings Fifth Congress of European Ichthyologists (1985). Stockholm.

———. 1988 (Mar.) **[ref. 6878]**. An appraisal of the zoology of C. S. Rafinesque. Bull. Zool. Nomencl. v. 45 (pt 1): 6-12.

———. 1990 **[ref. 14274]**. Family-group names in fishes: grammatical nicety of pragmatism? A plea for stability. Bull. Zool. Nomencl.

v. 47 (no. 2): 97-100.

WHITE, B. N. 1985 (15 Nov.) **[ref. 13551]**. Evolutionary relationships of the Atherinopsinae (Pisces: Atherinidae). Contr. Sci. (Los Angeles) No. 368: 1-20.

WHITE, B. N., R. J. LAVENBERG AND G. E. MCGOWEN. 1984 **[ref. 13655]**. Atheriniformes: development and relationships. Am. Soc. Ichthyol. Herpetol. Spec. Publ. No. 1: 355-362.

WHITE, E. I., AND J. A. MOY-THOMAS. 1940 (June) **[ref. 4650]**. Notes on the nomenclature of fossil fishes.—Part I. Homonyms A-C. Ann. Mag. Nat. Hist. (Ser. 11) v. 5 (no. 30): 502-507.

———. 1940 (July) **[ref. 4651]**. Notes on the nomenclature of fossil fishes.—Part II. Homonyms D-L. Ann. Mag. Nat. Hist. (Ser. 11) v. 6 (no. 31): 98-103.

———. 1941 (Apr.) **[ref. 4652]**. Notes on the nomenclature of fossil fishes.—Part III. Homonyms M-Z. Ann. Mag. Nat. Hist. (Ser. 11) v. 7 (no. 40): 395-400.

WHITE, J. 1790 **[ref. 4654]**. Journal of a voyage to New South Wales with sixty-five plates of non descript animals, birds, lizards, serpents, curious cones of trees and other natural productions. 1-297, Pls. 1-65. [See Paxton et al. 1989: 12 [ref. 12442] for remarks on authorship in this work.]

WHITEHEAD, P. J. P. 1965 (27 Apr.) **[ref. 4658]**. A new genus and subgenus of clupeid fishes and notes on the genera *Clupea*, *Sprattus* and *Clupeonella*. Ann. Mag. Nat. Hist. (Ser. 13) v. 7 (no. 78): 321-330.

———. 1967 **[ref. 6464]**. The clupeoid fishes described by Lacepède, Cuvier and Valenciennes. Bull. Br. Mus. (Nat. Hist.) Zool. Suppl. 2: 1-180.

———. 1967 **[ref. 13373]**. The dating of the 1st edition of Cuvier's 'Le Régne Animal distribué d'Après son organisation.' J. Soc. Bibliogr. Nat. Hist. v. 4 (pt 6): 300-301.

———. 1968 **[ref. 4659]**. A new genus for the South American clupeid fish, *Lile platana* Regan. J. Nat. Hist. v. 2: 477-486.

———. 1973 (14 Dec.) **[ref. 13755]**. The clupeoid fishes of the Guianas. Bull. Br. Mus. (Nat. Hist.) Zool. Suppl. no. 5: 1-227.

———. 1982 **[ref. 9738]**. Poland's Règne Animal. Newsl., Soc. Bibliogr. Nat. Hist. No. 14: 9-10.

———. 1985 **[ref. 5141]**. FAO species catalog. Clupeoid fishes of the world (suborder Clupeoidei). Part 1 - Chirocentridae, Clupeidae and Pristigasteridae. FAO Fish. Synop. No. 125, v. 7 (pt 1): i-x + 1-303.

———. 1986 (30 Sept.) **[ref. 5733]**. The synonymy of *Albula vulpes* (Linnaeus, 1758) (Teleostei, Albulidae). Cybium v. 10 (no. 3): 211-230.

———. 1986 **[ref. 6285]**. Family No. 58: Chirocentridae (p. 207). In: Smiths' Sea Fishes (Smith & Heemstra 1986 [ref. 5715]).

———. 1986 (30 Sept.) **[ref. 6756]**. A new species of *Microthrissa* in West African freshwaters (Pisces: Clupeidae). Cybium v. 10 (no. 3): 279-284.

WHITEHEAD, P. J. P., M.-L. BAUCHOT, J.-C. HUREAU, J. NIELSEN AND E. TORTONESE [EDS.]. 1984 **[ref. 13675]**. Fishes of the north-eastern Atlantic and the Mediterranean. Vol. 1. UNESCO. 1-510.

———. 1986 **[ref. 13676]**. Fishes of the north-eastern Atlantic and the Mediterranean. Vol. II. UNESCO. 517-1007.

———. 1986 **[ref. 13677]**. Fisahes of the north-eastern Atlantic and the Mediterranean. Vol. III. UNESCO. 1015-1473.

WHITEHEAD, P. J. P., AND A. BEN-TUVIA. 1973 **[ref. 7170]**. Dussumieriidae (p. 110). In: Hureau & Monod 1973 [ref. 6590].

WHITEHEAD, P. J. P., M. BOESEMAN AND A. C. WHEELER. 1966 **[ref. 6860]**. The types of Bleeker's Indo-Pacific elopoid and clupeoid fishes. Zool. Verh. (Leiden) No. 84: 1-152.

WHITEHEAD, P. J. P., AND W. IVANTSOFF. 1983 (10 Mar.) **[ref. 5418]**. *Atherina lacunosa* and the fishes described by J. R. Forster. Jpn. J. Ichthyol. v. 29 (no. 4): 355-364.

WHITEHEAD, P. J. P., AND G. S. MYERS. 1971 **[ref. 6584]**. Problems of nomenclature and dating of Spix and Agassiz's Brazilian fishes (1829-1831). J. Soc. Bibliogr. Nat. Hist. v. 5 (no. 6): 478-497.

WHITEHEAD, P. J. P., G. J. NELSON AND T. WONGRATANA. 1988 **[ref. 5725]**. FAO species catalogue. Clupeoid fishes of the world (Suborder Clupeoidei). An annotated and illustrated catalogue of the herrings, sardines, pilchards, sprats, anchovies and wolf-herrings. Part 2. Engraulididae. FAO Fish. Synop. No. 125, v. 7 (pt 2): 305-579.

WHITEHEAD, P. J. P., P. J. SMITH AND D. A. ROBERTSON. 1985 **[ref. 6542]**. The two species of sprat in New Zealand waters (*Sprattus antipodum* and *S. muelleri*). N. Z. J. Mar. Freshwater Res. v. 19: 261-271.

WHITEHEAD, P. J. P., AND G. G. TEUGELS. 1985 (12 Nov.) **[ref. 5726]**. The West African pygmy herring *Sierrathrissa leonensis*: general features, visceral anatomy, and osteology. Am. Mus. Novit. No. 2835: 1-44.

WHITEHEAD, P. J. P., AND A. C. WHEELER. 1966 **[ref. 14481]**. The generic names used for the sea basses of Europe and N. America (Pisces: Serranidae). Ann. Mus. Civ. Stor. Nat. Genova v. 76: 23-41.

WHITEHEAD, P. J. P., AND T. WONGRATANA. 1986 **[ref. 6284]**. Family No. 54: Clupeidae (pp. 199-204), Family No. 55: Engraulidae (pp. 204-207). In: Smiths' Sea Fishes (Smith & Heemstra 1986 [ref. 5715]).

WHITLEY, G. P. 1927 (6 Apr.) **[ref. 4662]**. Studies in ichthyology. No. 1. Rec. Aust. Mus. v. 15 (no. 5): 289-304, Pls. 24-25.

———. 1928 (28 Mar.) **[ref. 4661]**. Studies in ichthyology. No. 2. Rec. Aust. Mus. v. 16 (no. 4): 211-239, Pls. 16-18.

———. 1928 (11 June) **[ref. 4663]**. Fishes from the Great Barrier Reef collected by Mr. Melbourne Ward. Rec. Aust. Mus. v. 16 (no. 6): 294-304.

———. 1929 (11 Mar.) **[ref. 4664]**. R. M. Johnston's memoranda relating to the fishes of Tasmania. Pap. R. Soc. Tasmania 1928: 44-68, Pls. 2-4. [Jan. 16, 1929 on cover of reprints, but actual date of 11 Mar. given by Whitley in his unpublished bibliography.]

———. 1929 (27 June) **[ref. 4665]**. Studies in ichthyology. No. 3. Rec. Aust. Mus. v. 17 (no. 3): 101-143, Pls. 30-34.

———. 1929 (29 June) **[ref. 4666]**. Some fishes of the order Amphiprioniformes. Mem. Queensl. Mus. v. 9 (pt 3): 207-246, Pls. 27-28.

———. 1929 (15 May) **[ref. 4667]**. Fishes from Ongtong Java, Melanesia. Proc. Linn. Soc. N. S. W. v. 54 (pt 2): 91-95, Pl. 3.

———. 1929 (24 Mar.) **[ref. 4668]**. Additions to the check-list of the fishes of New South Wales. No. 2. Aust. Zool. v. 5 (pt 4): 353-357.

———. 1929 (28 Nov.) **[ref. 13468]**. Names of fishes in Meuschen's index to the "Zoophylacium Gronovianum." Rec. Aust. Mus. v. 17 (no. 6): 297-307.

———. 1930 (14 Jan.) **[ref. 4669]**. Additions to the check-list of the fishes of New South Wales. (No. 3). Aust. Zool. v. 6 (pt 2): 117-123, 1 pl.

———. 1930 (20 Aug.) **[ref. 4670]**. Five new generic names for Australian fishes. Aust. Zool. v. 6 (pt 3): 250-251.

———. 1930 (28 Aug.) **[ref. 4671]**. Ichthyological miscellanea. Mem. Queensl. Mus. v. 10 (pt 1): 8-31, Pl. 1.

———. 1930 (14 Jan.) **[ref. 5811]**. Leatherjacket genera. Aust. Zool. v. 6 (pt 2): 179.

———. 1931 (13 Feb.) **[ref. 4672]**. New names for Australian fishes. Aust. Zool. v. 6 (pt 4): 310-334, Pls. 25-27.

———. 1931 (25 Mar.) **[ref. 4673]**. Studies in ichthyology. No. 4. Rec. Aust. Mus. v. 18 (no. 3): 96-133, Pls. 9-16.

———. 1932 (20 Apr.) **[ref. 4674]**. Studies in ichthyology. No. 6. Rec. Aust. Mus. v. 18 (no. 6): 321-348, Pls. 36-39.

———. 1932 (30 Mar.) **[ref. 4675]**. Some fishes of the family Leiognathidae. Mem. Queensl. Mus. v. 10 (pt 2): 99-116, Pls. 13-14.

———. 1932 (27 Feb.) **[ref. 4676]**. Fishes. Sci. Rep. Great Barrier Reef Exped. v. 4 (no. 9): 267-316, Pls. 1-4.

———. 1933 (2 Aug.) **[ref. 4677]**. Studies in ichthyology. No. 7. Rec. Aust. Mus. v. 19 (no. 1): 60-112, Pls. 11-15.

———. 1933 (2 May) **[ref. 6595]**. George Tobin, a neglected naturalist. Aust. Mus. Mag. v. 2: 44-50. [Date of issue of 15 Apr. corrected to 2 May in Whitley's unpublished bibliography.]

———. 1934 (8 Feb.) **[ref. 4680]**. New fish from Victoria. Victorian

Nat. Melbourne v. 50: 241-242.
———. 1934 (26 Mar.) **[ref. 4681]**. Studies in ichthyology. No. 8. Rec. Aust. Mus. v. 19 (no. 2): 153-163.
———. 1934 (9 July) **[ref. 4682]**. Supplement to the check-list of the fishes of New South Wales by J. R. McCulloch. Fishes and fish-like animals of New South Wales. 3rd edition. 12 unpaginated pages.
———. 1934 (30 June) **[ref. 4949]**. Notes on some Australian sharks. Mem. Queensl. Mus. v. 10 (pt 4): 180-200, Pls. 27-29.
———. 1935 (19 Sept.) **[ref. 4683]**. Studies in ichthyology. No. 9. Rec. Aust. Mus. v. 19 (no. 4): 215-250, Pl. 18.
———. 1935 (30 Sept.) **[ref. 4684]**. Fishes from Princess Charlotte Bay, North Queensland. Rec. S. Aust. Mus. (Adelaide) v. 5 (no. 3): 345-365.
———. 1935 (30 Jan.) **[ref. 4685]**. The sunfish problem. Aust. Aquat. Life (Sydney) v. 1 (no. 1): 36-37. [Date of issue of 1 Feb. corrected to 30 Jan. in Whitley's unpublished bibliography.]
———. 1935 (9 July) **[ref. 4686]**. Whitebait. Victorian Nat. Melbourne v. 52: 41-51, Pl. 3.
———. 1935 (10 July) **[ref. 6396]**. Ichthyological genotypes. Aust. Zool. v. 8 (pt 2): 136-139. [Date of issue of 28 June corrected to 10 July in Whitley's unpublished bibliography.]
———. 1936 (17 Apr.) **[ref. 4687]**. More ichthyological miscellanea. Mem. Queensl. Mus. v. 11 (pt 1): 23-51, Pl. 4.
———. 1936 (21 Feb.) **[ref. 4688]**. Devil ray! Aust. Mus. Mag. v. 6 (no. 1): 4-12. [Date of issue of 21 Jan. corrected to 21 Feb. in Whitley's unpublished bibliography.]
———. 1936 (29 June) **[ref. 6075]**. The Australian devel ray, *Daemomanta alfredi* (Krefft), with remarks on the superfamily Mobuloidea (order Batoidei). Aust. Zool. v. 8 (pt 3): 164-188, Pl. 12.
———. 1936 (29 June) **[ref. 6397]**. Ichthyological genotypes: some supplementary remarks. Aust. Zool. v. 8 (pt 3): 189-192.
———. 1936 (25 Aug.) **[ref. 7315]**. A new fish from near Sydney. Proc. R. Zool. Soc. N. S. W. 1935-36: 19.
———. 1937 (24 June) **[ref. 4689]**. Further ichthyological miscellanea. Mem. Queensl. Mus. v. 11 (pt 2): 113-148, Pls. 11-13.
———. 1937 (12 Mar.) **[ref. 4690]**. The Middleton and Elizabeth reefs, South Pacific Ocean. Aust. Zool. v. 8 (pt 4): 199-273, Pls. 13-17. [Fishes on pp. 214-232, Pls. 13-14.]
———. 1937 (15 May) **[ref. 4691]**. Studies in ichthyology. No. 10. Rec. Aust. Mus. v. 20 (no. 1): 3-24, Pl. 2.
———. 1938 (31 Aug.) **[ref. 4692]**. Studies in ichthyology. No. 11. Rec. Aust. Mus. v. 20 (no. 3): 195-199, Pl. 21.
———. 1938 (31 Aug.) **[ref. 4693]**. Descriptions of some New Guinea fishes. Rec. Aust. Mus. v. 20 (no. 3): 223-233.
———. 1938 (24 Dec.) **[ref. 4694]**. A new stromateiform fish from South Australia. Rec. S. Aust. Mus. (Adelaide) v. 6 (no. 2): 159-161, Pl. 16.
———. 1939 (12 Dec.) **[ref. 4695]**. Taxonomic notes on sharks and rays. Aust. Zool. v. 9 (pt 3): 227-262, Pls. 20-22.
———. 1939 (23 June) **[ref. 4696]**. A new apogonid fish from Queensland. Occas. Pap. Mus. Zool. Univ. Mich. No. 405: 1-4, Pl. 1.
———. 1939 (17 Mar.) **[ref. 4697]**. A new fish, of the genus *Prionobutis*, from northern Australia. Mem. Queensl. Mus. v. 11 (pt 3): 296-298.
———. 1939 (31 Mar.) **[ref. 4698]**. Studies in ichthyology. No. 12. Rec. Aust. Mus. v. 20 (no. 4): 264-277.
———. 1940 (30 May) **[ref. 4660]**. The Nomenclator Zoologicus and some new fish names. Aust. Naturalist v. 10 (no. 7): 241-243.
———. 1940 (9 Dec.) **[ref. 4699]**. Illustrations of some Australian fishes. Aust. Zool. v. 9 (pt 4): 397-428, Pls. 30-31.
———. 1940 (20 July) **[ref. 4700]**. The fishes of Australia. Part I. The sharks, rays, devil-fish, and other primitive fishes of Australia and New Zealand. R. Zool. Soc. N. S. W., Austral. Zool. Handbook. 1-280.
———. 1941 (19 Dec.) **[ref. 4701]**. Ichthyological notes and illustrations. Aust. Zool. v. 10 (pt 1): 1-50, Pls. 1-2.
———. 1943 (15 Sept.) **[ref. 4702]**. Ichthyological descriptions and notes. Proc. Linn. Soc. N. S. W. v. 68 (pts 3-4): 114-144.
———. 1943 (30 Apr.) **[ref. 4703]**. Ichthyological notes and illustrations. (Part 2). Aust. Zool. v. 10 (pt 2): 167-187.
———. 1944 (31 Aug.) **[ref. 4704]**. Illustrations of some Western Australian fishes. Proc. R. Zool. Soc. N. S. W. v. for 1943-44: 25-29.
———. 1944 (10 May) **[ref. 4705]**. New sharks and fishes from Western Australia. Aust. Zool. v. 10 (pt 3): 252-273.
———. 1945 (27 July) **[ref. 4706]**. The Simpson desert expedition, 1939. Scientific reports: No. 5 Biology — Fishes. Trans. R. Soc. S. Aust. v. 69 (no. 1): 10-13.
———. 1945 (11 June) **[ref. 4707]**. New sharks and fishes from Western Australia. Part 2. Aust. Zool. v. 11 (pt 1): 1-42, Pl. 1.
———. 1946 (1 June) **[ref. 9300]**. Australian marine eels. Aust. Mus. Mag. v. 9 (no. 2): 60-65.
———. 1947 (20 June) **[ref. 4708]**. New sharks and fishes from Western Australia. Part 3. Aust. Zool. v. 11 (pt 2): 129-150, Pl. 11.
———. 1948 (11 Feb.) **[ref. 4709]**. New sharks and fishes from Western Australia. Part 4. Aust. Zool. v. 11 (pt 3): 259-276, Pls. 24-25.
———. 1948 (30 June) **[ref. 4710]**. Studies in ichthyology. No. 13. Rec. Aust. Mus. v. 22 (no. 1): 70-94.
———. 1950 (27 Jan.) **[ref. 4712]**. Studies in ichthyology. No. 14. Rec. Aust. Mus. v. 22 (no. 3): 234-245, Pl. 17.
———. 1950 (26 May) **[ref. 4713]**. New fish names. Proc. R. Zool. Soc. N. S. W. v. for 1948-49: 44.
———. 1951 (3 Aug.) **[ref. 4715]**. Studies in ichthyology. No. 15. Rec. Aust. Mus. v. 22 (no. 4): 389-408.
———. 1951 (2 Apr.) **[ref. 4711]**. New fish names and records. Proc. R. Zool. Soc. N. S. W. v. for 1949-50: 61-68.
———. 1952 (5 Mar.) **[ref. 4714]**. Some noteworthy fishes from eastern Australia. Proc. R. Zool. Soc. N. S. W. v. for 1950-51: 27-32.
———. 1952 (16 June) **[ref. 4716]**. Two new scorpion fishes from Queensland. Rec. Aust. Mus. v. 23 (no. 1): 25-28.
———. 1952 (5 Nov.) **[ref. 4717]**. Figures of some Australian fish types. Proc. R. Zool. Soc. N. S. W. v. for 1951-52: 23-31.
———. 1953 (21 Oct.) **[ref. 4718]**. Studies in ichthyology. No. 16. Rec. Aust. Mus. v. 23 (no. 3): 133-138.
———. 1954 (2 Apr.) **[ref. 4719]**. Some freshwater gudgeons mainly from tropical Australia. Aust. Mus. Mag. v. 11 (no. 5): 150-155. [Date published is from Whitley's bibliography.]
———. 1954 (24 May) **[ref. 4721]**. New locality records for some Australian fishes. Proc. R. Zool. Soc. N. S. W. v. for 1952-53: 23-30.
———. 1955 (18 July) **[ref. 4722]**. Sidelights on New Zealand ichthyology. Aust. Zool. v. 12 (pt 2): 110-119, Pl. 6.
———. 1955 (4 Mar.) **[ref. 4724]**. Taxonomic notes on fishes. Proc. R. Zool. Soc. N. S. W. v. for 1953-54: 44-57.
———. 1956 (10 Apr.) **[ref. 4726]**. New fishes from Australia and New Zealand. Proc. R. Zool. Soc. N. S. W. v. for 1954-55: 34-38.
———. 1957 (8 May) **[ref. 4727]**. Ichthyological illustrations. Proc. R. Zool. Soc. N. S. W. v. for 1955-56: 56-71.
———. 1958 (27 June) **[ref. 4728]**. Descriptions and records of fishes. Proc. R. Zool. Soc. N. S. W. v. for 1956-57: 28-51.
———. 1959 (10 Feb.) **[ref. 4729]**. Ichthyological snippets. Aust. Zool. v. 12 (pt 4): 310-323.
———. 1959 (18 Sept.) **[ref. 4730]**. More ichthyological snippets. Proc. R. Zool. Soc. N. S. W. v. for 1957-58: 11-26.
———. 1961 (28 Feb.) **[ref. 4731]**. Fishes from New Caledonia. Proc. R. Zool. Soc. N. S. W. v. for 1958-59: 60-65.
———. 1962 (Oct.) **[ref. 4732]**. A new goby from Sydney. Aust. Naturalist v. 12 (no. 3): 9-10.
———. 1965 **[ref. 4733]**. Some fish genera scrutinized. Proc. R. Zool. Soc. N. S. W. v. for 1964-65: 25-26.
———. 1966 (6 July) **[ref. 4734]**. Notes on some Queensland fishes. Aust. Zool. v. 13 (pt 3): 235-243, Pls. 13-14.
———. 1966 (6 July) **[ref. 12521]**. Genera Piscium: work in progress. Am. Zool. v. 13 (no. 3): 231-234.
———. 1970 **[ref. 6601]**. Ichthyological quiddities. Aust. Zool. v. 15

(no. 3): 242-247, Pl. 12.

———. 1976 (Sept.) **[ref. 4735]**. More fish genera scrutinized. Aust. Zool. v. 19 (pt 1): 45-50.

WHITLEY, G. P., AND A. N. COLEFAX. 1938 (15 Sept.) **[ref. 4736]**. Fishes from Nauru, Gilbert Islands, Oceania. Proc. Linn. Soc. N. S. W. v. 63 (pts 3-4): 282-304, Pl. 14.

WHITLEY, G. P., AND W. J. PHILLIPPS. 1939 (Sept.) **[ref. 4737]**. Descriptive notes on some New Zealand fishes. Trans. Proc. R. Soc. N. Z. v. 69 (no. 2): 228-236, 2 pls.

WICKLER, W. 1963 (28 Feb.) **[ref. 4738]**. Zur Klassifikation der Cichlidae, am Beispiel der Gattungen *Tropheus*, *Petrochromis*, *Haplochromis* und *Hemihaplochromis* n. gen. (Pisces, Perciformes). Senckenb. Biol. v. 44 (no. 2): 83-96.

WILDEKAMP, R. H. 1977 **[ref. 6449]**. *Nothobranchius lourensi* spec. nov. un *Nothobranchius janpapi* spec. nov., zwei neue Rivulinen aus Ostafrika. Aquarium Aqua Terra v. 11 (no. 98): 326-331.

———. 1986 (Apr.) **[ref. 6199]**. Pantanodontinae (pp. 169-170). In: Daget et al. 1986 [ref. 6189].

———. 1987 (25 Feb.) **[ref. 5994]**. Notes sur le poisson annuel *Nothobranchius jubbi* Wildekamp & Berkenkamp, 1979 (Cyprinodontiformes; Nothobranchiinae) du nord-est du Kenya et de Somalie du Sud. Rev. Fr. Aquariol. v. 13 (no. 4): 99-106.

WILDEKAMP, R. H., R. ROMAND AND J. J. SCHEEL. 1986 (Apr.) **[ref. 6198]**. Cyprinodontidae (pp. 165-276). In: Daget et al. 1986 [ref. 6189].

WILEY, E. O. 1976 (12 Nov.) **[ref. 7091]**. The phylogeny and biogeography of fossil and recent gars (Actinopterygii: Lepisosteidae. Misc. Publ. Univ. Kansas Mus. Nat. Hist. No. 64: 1-111.

WILLIAMS, J. D. 1975 **[ref. 7402]**. Systematics of the percid fishes of the subgenus *Ammocrypta*, genus *Ammocrypta*, with descriptions of two new species. Bull. Alabama Mus. Nat. Hist. No. 1: 1-56.

WILLIAMS, J. D., AND H. W. ROBISON. 1980 (Dec.) **[ref. 4743]**. *Ozarka*, a new subgenus of *Etheostoma*. Brimleyana No. 4: 149-156.

WILLIAMS, J. T. 1983 **[ref. 5367]**. Synopsis of the pearlfish subfamily Pyramodontinae (Pisces: Carapidae). Bull. Mar. Sci. v. 33 (no. 4): 846-854.

———. 1983 **[ref. 5370]**. Taxonomy and ecology of the genus *Chasmodes* (Pisces: Blenniidae) with a discussion of its zoogeography. Bull. Fla. State Mus. Biol. Sci. v. 29 (no. 2): 65-100.

———. 1984 **[ref. 5314]**. Synopsis and phylogenetic analysis of the pearlfish subfamily Carapinae (Pisces: Carapidae). Bull. Mar. Sci. v. 34 (no. 3): 386-397.

———. 1984 (1 May) **[ref. 6813]**. Studies on *Echiodon* (Pisces: Carapidae), with description of two new Indo-Pacific species. Copeia 1984 (no. 2): 410-422.

———. 1988 (Nov.) **[ref. 7000]**. Revision and phylogenetic relationships of the blenniid fish genus *Cirripectes*. Indo-Pac. Fishes No. 17: 1-78, col. Pls. 1-7.

———. 1989 (19 Jan.) **[ref. 13549]**. Phylogenetic relationships and revision of the blenniid fish genus *Scartichthys*. Smithson. Contrib. Zool. No. 492: i-iii + 1-30.

WILLIAMS, J. T., AND C. R. GILBERT. 1983 (15 Oct.) **[ref. 5369]**. Additional information on the gobiid fish *Varicus imswe*, with comments on the nominal species of *Varicus*. Northeast Gulf Sci. v. 6 (no. 2): 185-189.

WILSON, M. V. H., AND P. VEILLEUX. 1982 **[ref. 14203]**. Comparative osteology and relationships of the Umbridae (Pisces; Salmoniformes). Zool. J. Linn. Soc. London v. 76: 321-352.

WINANS, G. A. 1985 (10 Dec.) **[ref. 6784]**. Geographic variation in the milkfish *Chanos chanos*. II. Multivariate morphological evidence. Copeia 1985 (no. 4): 890-898.

WINTERBOTTOM, R. 1979 **[ref. 4754]**. A new genus and species of the family Congrogadidae (Pisces: Perciformes) from the western Indian Ocean. Bull. Mar. Sci. v. 29 (no. 3): 298-302.

———. 1980 (16 May) **[ref. 4755]**. Systematics, osteology and phylogenetic relationships of fishes of the ostariophysan subfamily Anostominae (Characoidei, Anostomidae). R. Ont. Mus. Life Sci. Contrib. No. 123: 1-112.

———. 1980 (Nov.) **[ref. 4756]**. A new genus and three new species of the family Congrogadidae (Pisces, Perciformes) from Natal, South Africa. Ann. S. Afr. Mus. v. 83 (pt 1): 1-12.

———. 1982 **[ref. 5436]**. A revision of the congrogadid fish genus *Halidesmus* (Pisces: Perciformes), with the description of a new species from Kenya and a list of the species included in the family. Can. J. Zool. v. 60 (no. 5): 754-763.

———. 1984 **[ref. 5321]**. A review of the gobiid fish genus *Trimma* from the Chagos Archipelago, central Indian Ocean, with the description of seven new species. Can. J. Zool. v. 62 (no. 4): 695-715, 1 col. pl.

———. 1985 **[ref. 5241]**. Revision of the congrogadid *Haliophis* (Pisces: Perciformes), with the description of a new species from Indonesia, and comments on the endemic fish fauna of the northern Red Sea. Can. J. Zool. v. 63 (no. 2): 209-217.

———. 1986 (24 Feb.) **[ref. 5727]**. Revision and vicariance biogeography of the subfamily Congrogadinae (Pisces: Perciformes: Pseudochromidae). Indo-Pac. Fishes No. 9: 1-34, 1 col pl. [Cover date Oct. 1985, issued 24 Feb. 1986 (stamped on original).]

———. 1986 **[ref. 5728]**. Family No. 227: Congrogadidae (pp. 729-730). In: Smiths' Sea Fishes (Smith & Heemstra 1986 [ref. 5715]).

———. 1987 (13 May) **[ref. 6776]**. Redescription of *Doryrhamphus* (*Dunkerocampus* [sic]) *pessuliferus* (Pisces: Syngnathidae). Copeia 1987 (no. 2): 519-521.

———. 1989 **[ref. 14487]**. A revision of the *Trimmatom nanus* species complex (Pisces, Gobiidae), with descriptions of three new species and redefinition of *Trimmatom*. Can. J. Zool. v. 67: 2403-2410.

WINTERBOTTOM, R., AND M. BURRIDGE. 1989 **[ref. 14486]**. A new species of *Priolepis* (Pisces; Gobiidae) from the Pacific plate, with biogeographic comments. Can. J. Zool. v. 67: 2398-2402.

WINTERBOTTOM, R., AND A. R. EMERY. 1981 **[ref. 4757]**. A new genus and two new species of gobiid fishes (Perciformes) from the Chagos Archipelago, central Indian Ocean. Environ. Biol. Fishes v. 6 (no. 2): 139-149.

WINTERBOTTOM, R., AND D. F. HOESE. 1988 (30 June) **[ref. 9274]**. A new genus and four new species of fishes from the Indo-West Pacific (Pisces; Perciformes; Gobiidae), with comments on relationships. R. Ont. Mus. Life Sci. Occas. Pap. No. 37: 1-17.

WINTERBOTTOM, R., J. D. REIST AND C. D. GOODCHILD. 1984 **[ref. 5140]**. Geographic variation in *Congrogadus subducens* (Teleostei, Perciformes, Congrogadidae). Can. J. Zool. v. 62 (no. 8): 1605-1617.

WINTERBOTTOM, R., AND J. C. TYLER. 1983 (14 Dec.) **[ref. 5320]**. Phylogenetic relationships of aracanin genera of boxfishes (Ostraciidae: Tetraodontiformes). Copeia 1983 (no. 4): 902-917.

WINTERS, G. H., AND E. L. DALLEY. 1988 (Mar.) **[ref. 12881]**. Meristic composition of sand lance (*Ammodytes* spp.) in Newfoundland waters with a review of species designations in the northwest Atlantic. Can. J. Fish. Aquat. Sci. v. 45 (no. 3): 516-529.

WINTHER, G. P. 1877 **[ref. 4758]**. Om de danske fiske af slaegten *Gobius*. Naturhist. Tidsskr. Kjöbenhavn (Ser. 3) v. 11: 41-56.

WIRTZ, P., AND H. BATH. 1982 (15 Sept.) **[ref. 5475]**. *Lipophrys bauchotae* n. sp. from the eastern tropical Atlantic. Senckenb. Biol. v. 62 (no. 4/6): 225-232.

WISNER, R. L. 1963 (30 Mar.) **[ref. 4759]**. A new genus and species of myctophid fish from the south-central Pacific Ocean, with notes on related genera and the designation of a new tribe, Electronini. Copeia 1963 (no. 1): 24-28.

———. 1976 (Aug.) **[ref. 6956]**. New data on the rare alepocephalid fish *Photostylus pycnopterus*. Bull. South. Calif. Acad. Sci. v. 75 (pt 2): 153-158.

WISNER, R. L., AND C. B. MCMILLAN. 1988 (24 Feb.) **[ref. 6335]**. A new species of hagfish, genus *Eptatretus* (Cyclostomata, Myxinidae), from the Pacific Ocean near Valparaiso, Chile, with new data on *E. bischoffii* and *E. polytrema*. Trans. San Diego Soc. Nat. Hist. v. 21 (no. 14): 227-244.

WITZELL, W. N. 1973 **[ref. 7172]**. Gonostomatidae (pp. 114-122). In: Hureau & Monod 1973 [ref. 6590].

——. 1978 (20 Dec.) **[ref. 6802]**. *Apolectus niger* (Family Apolectidae): synonymy and systematics. Matsya No. 3 [for 1977]: 72-82.

Wolfson, F. H. 1986 (30 May) **[ref. 6150]**. Occurrences of the whale shark, *Rhincodon typus* Smith. Pp. 208-226. In: Uyeno et al. (eds.) 1986 [ref. 6147].

Wood, W. 1846 (Sept.) **[ref. 4760]**. [Description of a species of shark.] Proc. Boston Soc. Nat. Hist. v. 2 (1845 to 1848): 174.

Woodland, D. J. 1972 (Dec.) **[ref. 6163]**. Proposal that the genus name *Teuthis* Linnaeus (Pisces) be suppressed. Bull. Zool. Nomencl. v. 29 (pt 4): 190-193.

——. 1973 (July) **[ref. 6164]**. Addendum to the porposal that the genus name *Teuthis* Linnaeus (Pisces) be suppressed. Bull. Zool. Nomencl. v. 30 (pt 1): 6-7.

——. 1986 **[ref. 6299]**. Family No. 194: Gerreidae (pp. 608-609). In: Smiths' Sea Fishes (Smith & Heemstra 1986 [ref. 5715]).

Woods, L. P. 1958 (29 Oct.) **[ref. 4761]**. A new genus and species of fish from the Gulf of Mexico (family Emmelichthyidae). Fieldiana Zool. v. 39 (no. 22): 249-252.

Woods, L. P., and P. M. Sonoda. 1973 **[ref. 6899]**. Order Berycomorphi (Beryciformes). Mem. Sears Found. Mar. Res. Mem. 1 (pt 6): 263-396.

Woolman, A. J. 1894 (3 May) **[ref. 4804]**. Report on a collection of fishes from the rivers of central and northern Mexico. Bull. U. S. Fish Comm. v. 14 (art. 8): 55-66, Pl. 2.

Wu, C.-K. 1964 **[ref. 13503]**. Acheilognathinae. Pp. 199-221. In: Wu 1964 [ref. 4806]. [In Chinese.]

Wu, H.-W. 1939 **[ref. 4805]**. On the fishes of Li-Kiang. Sinensia v. 10 (nos. 1-6): 92-142, Pls. 1-3.

——. 1964 **[ref. 4806]**. [The cyprinid fishes of China.] Shanghai. 1-228, Pls. 1-78. [In Chinese. Chapters with different authorships.]

Wu, H.-W. [ed.]. 1977 **[ref. 12558]**. [The cyprinid fishes of China.] Volume 2. Science Press, Peking. 229-598, Pls. 1-109. [In Chinese. Chapters with different authorships.]

Wu, H.-W., R.-D. Lin, Q.-X. Chen, X.-L. Chen and M.-Q. He. 1977 **[ref. 4807]**. Barbinae. Pp. 229-394. In: Wu 1977 [ref. 12558]. [In Chinese.]

Wu, X.-W., M. J. He and S.-L. Chu. 1981 (Jan.) **[ref. 4809]**. On the fishes of Sisoridae from the region of Xizang. Oceanol. Limnol. Sin. v. 12 (no. 1): 74-79. [In Chinese, English summ.]

Wu, X.-W., G.-R. Yang, P.-Q. Yue, and H.-J. Huang (eds.). 1963 **[ref. 12576]**. The economic fauna of China. Freshwater fishes. Science Press, Beijing 1-159, pls. [In Chinese.]

Wu, Y.-F. 1987 (May) **[ref. 12822]**. On the present status of cyprinid fish studies in China. Pp. 43-47. In: Kullander & Fernholm (eds.), Proceedings Fifth Congress Eureopean Ichthyologists (1985). Stockholm.

——. 1987 (May) **[ref. 12824]**. A survey of the fish fauna of the Mount Namjagbarwa region in Xizang (Tibet), China. Pp. 109-112. In: Kullander & Fernholm (eds.), Proceedings Fifth Congress European Ichthyologists (1985). Stockholm.

Yabe, M. 1981 (Nov.) **[ref. 5547]**. Osteological review of the family Icelidae Berg, 1940, (Pisces; Scorpaeniformes), with comment on the validity of this family. Bull. Fac. Fish. Hokkaido Univ. v. 32 (no. 4): 293-315.

——. 1985 **[ref. 11522]**. Comparative osteology and myology of the superfamily Cottoidea and its phylogenetic classification. Mem. Fac. Fish. Hokkaido Univ. v. 32 (no. 1): 1-130.

Yabe, M., S. Maruyama and K. Amaoka. 1983 (10 Mar.) **[ref. 5423]**. First records of five cottid fishes and a psychrolutid fish from Japan. Jpn. J. Ichthyol. v. 29 (no. 4): 456-464.

Yabumoto, Y., Y. Yogo and H. Tsukahara. 1984 (20 Nov.) **[ref. 6728]**. First record of the leiognathid fish, *Gazza minuta* from Japan. Jpn. J. Ichthyol. v. 31 (no. 3): 327-330.

Yamada, U., and T. Nakabo. 1986 (30 July) **[ref. 6373]**. Morphology and ecology of *Parastromateus niger* (Bloch) (family, Carangidae) from the East China Sea. Uo (Jpn. Soc. Ichthyol.) No. 36: 1-14.

Yamakawa, T. 1976 (20 Apr.) **[ref. 6969]**. The record of scorpaenoid fish, *Snyderina yamanokami*, collected from off Amami-Oshima, Kagoshima Prefecture, Japan. Jpn. J. Ichthyol. v. 23 (no. 1): 60-61.

Yamakawa, T., T. Taniuchi and Y. Nose. 1986 (30 May) **[ref. 5729]**. Review of the *Etmopterus lucifer* group (Squalidae) in Japan. Pp. 197-207. In: Uyeno et al. (eds.) 1986 [ref. 6147].

Yamaoka, K. 1983 (15 Aug.) **[ref. 5363]**. A revision of the cichlid fish genus *Petrochromis* from Lake Tanganyika, with description of a new species. Jpn. J. Ichthyol. v. 30 (no. 2): 129-141.

Yanagisawa, Y. 1976 (July) **[ref. 7088]**. Genus *Amblyeleotris* (Gobiidae) of Japan and geographical variations of *A. japonica* Takagi. Publ. Seto Mar. Biol. Lab. v. 23 (nos. 1/2): 145-168.

——. 1978 (Oct.) **[ref. 7028]**. Studies on the interspecific relationship between gobiid fishes and snapping shrimp. I. Gobiid fishes associated with snapping shrimps in Japan. Publ. Seto Mar. Biol. Lab. v. 24 (nos. 4/6): 269-325.

Yang, Y.-J. 1964 **[ref. 13500]**. Xenocyprininae = (Chondrostominae). Pp. 121-136. Hypophthalmichthyinae. Pp. 223-228. In: Wu 1964 [ref. 4806]. [In Chinese.]

Yang, Y.-J., and H.-C. Hwang. 1964 **[ref. 13497]**. Leuciscinae. Pp. 7-61. In: Wu 1964 [ref. 4806]. [In Chinese.]

Yang, Y.-R., B.-G. Zeng and J. R. Paxton. 1988 (18 Aug.) **[ref. 7301]**. Additional specimens of the deepsea fish *Hispidoberyx ambagiousus* [sic] (Hispidoberycidae, Berciformes [sic]) from the South China Sea, with comments on the family relationships. Uo (Jpn. Soc. Ichthyol.) No. 38: 3-8.

Yano, K. 1988 (25 Feb.) **[ref. 6695]**. A new laternshark *Etmopterus splendidus* from the East China Sea and Java Sea. Jpn. J. Ichthyol. v. 34 (no. 4): 421-425.

Yano, K., and M. Murofushi. 1985 (30 Aug.) **[ref. 5797]**. A new prickly dogfish, *Oxynotus japonicus*, from Japan. Jpn. J. Ichthyol. v. 32 (no. 2): 129-136.

Yasuda, F., and Y. Tominaga. 1976 (30 Dec.) **[ref. 5505]**. A new pomacanthid fish, *Chaetodontoplus caeruleopunctatus*, from the Philippines. Jpn. J. Ichthyol. v. 23 (no. 3): 130-132.

Yatsu, A. 1981 (22 Dec.) **[ref. 4814]**. A revision of the gunnel family Pholididae (Pisces, Blennioidei). Bull. Natl. Sci. Mus. (Ser. A) (Zool.) v. 7 (no. 4): 165-190.

——. 1985 (28 Nov.) **[ref. 5149]**. Phylogeny of the family Pholididae (Blennioidei) with a redescription of *Pholis* Scopoli. Jpn. J. Ichthyol. v. 32 (no. 3): 273-282.

——. 1986 (30 May) **[ref. 5150]**. Phylogeny and zoogeography of the subfamilies Xiphisterinae and Cebidichthyinae (Blennioidei, Stichaeidae). Pp. 663-678. In: Uyeno et al. (eds.) 1986 [ref. 6147].

Yatsu, A., and I. Nakamura. 1989 **[ref. 13449]**. *Xenobrama microlepis*, a new genus and species of bramid fish, from subantarctic waters of the South Pacific. Jpn. J. Ichthyol. v. 36 (no. 2): 190-195.

Yazdani, G. M. 1972 (18 Sept.) **[ref. 4815]**. A new genus and species of fish from India. J. Bombay Nat. Hist. Soc. v. 69 (pt 1, Apr.): 134-135.

Yazdani, G. M., and P. K. Talwar. 1981 (Dec.) **[ref. 4816]**. On the generic relationship of the eel-like fish *Pillaia khajuriai* Talwar, Yazdani & Kundu (Perciformes, Mastacembeloidei). Bull. Zool. Surv. India v. 4 (no. 3): 287-288.

Ye, M.-R., and T.-Y. Fu. 1983 (Oct.) **[ref. 6669]**. Description of a new genus and species of Danioninae from China (Cypriniformes: Cyprinidae). Acta Zootaxon. Sin. v. 8 (no. 4): 434-437. [In Chinese, English summ.]

Yen, M. D. 1978 **[ref. 13511]**. [Identification of the fresh-water fishes of North Viet Nam.] 1-340. [Reviewed by Kottelat, Copeia 1989 (no. 4):1102-1104.]

Yih, P.-L., and C.-K. Wu. 1964 **[ref. 13499]**. Abramidinae. Pp. 63-120. In: Wu 1964 [ref. 4806]. [In Chinese.]

Yoshino, T. 1982 (Mar.) **[ref. 5402]**. Damselfishes of the genus *Dischistodus* found in the Ryukyu Islands. Bull. Coll. Sci. Univ. Ryukyus No. 33: 69-74.

Yoshino, T., and T. Sata. 1981 (Mar.) **[ref. 5506]**. Records of a rare snapper, *Lipocheilus carnolabrum* (Chan), from the Ryukyu Islands. Bull. Coll. Sci. Univ. Ryukyus No. 31: 71-74.

Yoshino, T., and H. Senou. 1983 **[ref. 5395]**. A review of the gobiid fishes of the genus *Ctenogobiops* from Japan. Galaxea v. 2: 1-13.

YOSHINO, T., C. TOMINAGA AND K. OKAMOTO. 1983 (Sept.) **[ref. 5730]**. Damselfishes of the genus *Amblyglyphidodon* from Japan. Bull. Coll. Sci. Univ. Ryukyus No. 36: 105-114, Pl. 1.

YUEH, T.-H., AND H.-C. HWANG. 1964 **[ref. 12823]**. Description of a new genus and a new species of schizothoracid fish in China. Acta Hydrobiol. Sinica v. 5: 27-30. [In Chinese, English summ. Not seen.]

ZAISER, M. J., AND R. FRICKE. 1985 (20 Feb.) **[ref. 5267]**. *Synchiropus moyeri*, a new species of dragonet (Callionymidae) from Miyake-jima, Japan. Jpn. J. Ichthyol. v. 31 (no. 4): 389-397.

ZANDER, C. D., AND H. JELINEK. 1976 (Nov.) **[ref. 4828]**. Zur demersen Fischfauna im Bereich der Grotte von Banjole (Rovinj/YU) mit Beschreibung von *Speleogobius trigloides* n. gen. n. sp. (Gobiidae, Perciformes). Mitt. Hamb. Zool. Mus. Inst. v. 73: 265-280.

ZEHREN, S. J. 1987 (5 Aug.) **[ref. 6060]**. Osteology and evolutionary relationships of the boarfish genus *Antigonia* (Teleostei: Caproidae). Copeia 1987 (no. 3): 564-592.

ZHANG, Y.-L. 1985 (Jan.) **[ref. 12818]**. On the homonyms, synonyms and distribution of the type species of *Salanx*. Acta Zootaxon. Sinica v. 10 (no. 1): 111-112. [In Chinese.]

ZHENG, C.-Y., AND Y.-Y. CHEN. 1980 (Jan.) **[ref. 4838]**. The homalopterid fishes from Guangdong Province, China. Acta Zootaxon. Sin. v. 5 (no. 1): 89-101. [In Chinese, English summ. of new taxa.]

ZHENG, M., AND J. YAN. 1986 **[ref. 5852]**. A new species of the genus *Gobiobotia* (Pisces, Cyprinidae). Acta Zool. Sin. v. 32 (no. 1): 58-61.

ZHOU, C.-W., D.-L. CAI AND Y. QING. 1986 (30 May) **[ref. 6332]**. On the classification and distribution of the Sinipercine fishes (family Serranidae) of east Asia [Abstract]. Pp. 965-966. In: Uyeno et al. (eds.) 1986 [ref. 6147].

ZHU, S.-Q. 1981 **[ref. 4840]**. Notes on the scaleless loaches (Nemachilinae, Cobitidae) from Qinghai-Xizang Plateau and adjacent territories in China. Pp. 1061-1070. In: Proc. Sympos. Qinghai-Xizang (Tibet) Plateau. Vol. 2. Environment and ecology of Qinghai-Xizang Plateau. Science Press, Peking; Gordon & Breach Science Publ., N. Y. i-xiv + 975-2138.

———. 1983 (July) **[ref. 6667]**. A new genus and species of Nemachilinae (Pisces: Cobitidae) from China. Acta Zootaxon. Sin. v. 8 (no. 3): 311-313. [In Chinese, English summ.]

ZHU, S.-Q., AND W.-X. CAO. 1987 (July) **[ref. 14139]**. The noemacheiline fishes from Guangdong and Guangxi with descriptions of a new genus and three new species (Cypriniformes: Cobitidae). Acta Zool. Sin. v. 12 (no. 3): 321-331. [In Chinese; new taxa summarized in English.]

ZHU, S.-Q., AND Q.-Z. GUO. 1985 (July) **[ref. 6100]**. Descriptions of a new genus and a new species of noemacheiline loaches from Yunnan Province, China (Cypriniformes: Cobitidae). Acta Zootaxon. Sin. v. 10 (no. 3): 321-325.

ZHU, Y.-D., Q.-W MENG, A.-S. HU AND S. LI. 1981 (Mar.) **[ref. 4841]**. Description of four new species, a new genus and a new family of elasmobranchiate fishes from deep sea of the South China Sea. Oceanol. Limnol. Sin. v. 12 (no. 2): 103-116. [Chinese, with shortened version in English (pp. 115-116).]

ZHU, Y.-D., Y.-H. WANG AND N. YONG. 1982 **[ref. 6473]**. [*Carinozacco* gen. nov.] J. Fish. China v. 6 (no. 3): 267-272. [Not examined.]

ZUGMAYER, E. 1911 (30 Dec.) **[ref. 4846]**. Poissons provenant des campagnes du yacht *Princesse-Alice* (1901-1910). Result. Campagnes Sci. Monaco Fasc. 35: 1-174, Pls. 1-6.

———. 1911 (20 Jan.) **[ref. 6161]**. Diagnoses de poissons nouveaux provenant des campagnes du yacht "Princesse-Alice" (1901 à 1910). Bull. Inst. Oceanogr. (Monaco) No. 193: 1-14.

———. 1912 (June) **[ref. 4847]**. On a new genus of cyprinoid fishes from high Asia. Ann. Mag. Nat. Hist. (Ser. 8) v. 9 (no. 54): 682.

———. 1913 (1 Jan.) **[ref. 5032]**. Diagnoses de stomiatidés nouveaux provenant des campagnes du yacht "Hirondelle II" (1911 et 1912). Bull. Inst. Oceanogr. (Monaco) No. 253: 1-7.

———. 1914 (20 Mar.) **[ref. 4848]**. Diagnoses de quelques poissons nouveaux provenant des campagnes du yacht *Hirondelle II* (1911-1913). Bull. Inst. Oceanogr. (Monaco) No. 288: 1-4.

———. 1940 **[ref. 4849]**. Diagnosis des Stomiatidés nouveaux provenant des campagnes du yacht "Hirondelle II" (1911 et 1912). Result. Campagnes Sci. Monaco Fasc. 103: 201-205. [Reissue of Zugmayer 1913 [ref. 5032].]

———. 1940 **[ref. 4850]**. Diagnoses de quelques poissons nouveaux provenant des campagnes du yacht *Hirondelle II* (1911-1913). Result. Campagnes Sci. Monaco Fasc. 103: 209-211. [Reissue of Zugmayer 1914 [ref. 4848].]

GLOSSARY AND ABBREVIATIONS

Art. An Article of the Code of Zoological Nomenclature.

available. Admitted into zoological nomenclature— such as an available name or work; a name that can be used.

binominal nomenclature. Reference to a species by use of a combination of two names—a generic name plus a specific name. Used here mostly in the negative, nonbinominal and therefore not available, as for example, a name appearing in a work in which the author did not use binominal nomenclature.

Catalog. Short version to refer to the present *Catalog of the Genera of Recent Fishes.*

Code. The 1985 edition of *The International Code of Zoological Nomenclature.* See Appendix A.

conserved. Through action of ICZN, use of a name is preserved as the valid name (when it would not otherwise be valid); or a work is declared to be published (when it would not otherwise be available).

corrigendum (pl. **corrigenda**). Note published by author, editor, or publisher expressly to cite and correct one or more errors in the work.

description, original. The description of a nominal taxon when first established.

designation. Act of making a type fixation, e.g., type designated by Bleeker 1864.

original. Designation of a type of a nominal taxon when the taxon was established.

subsequent. Designation of a type subsequent to the date at which the taxon was established.

emendation. An intentional change in the spelling of a name.

justified. The correction of an incorrect original spelling.

unjustified. An emendation that is not justified.

fixed. See designation.

first reviser. The first person after the taxon was proposed to select one of the names over the other (or one nomenclatural act over another) when both names (or acts) were published at the same time. Also applies to first selection of multiple original spellings.

homonym. Each of two or more names that are identical in the meaning of the Code but apply to different taxa.

junior. The younger, or most recently established name.

primary. Identical species names first published in the same genus.

secondary. Identical species names later brought together in the same genus, thereby creating the homonymy.

senior. The older, or earliest established name.

homonymy. The condition of having homonyms.

ichnotaxon. A taxon based on the fossilized work of an animal, including fossilized trails, burrows, and tubes made by an animal.

ICZN. International Commission on Zoological Nomenclature; the judicial body empowered to enforce and interpret the Code.

Index, Official. See **Official Index**

indication. As used in the Catalog, a method of fixing the type species of a genus, e.g., type by indication.

invalid. A name or nomenclatural act that is not valid under the Code.

lectotype. A syntype later designated as the one name-bearing type specimen.

Linnaean tautonymy. See **tautonymy, Linnaean**

monotypy (monotypic). For genera, the generic group name when proposed was considered by the original author to contain a single valid species that was cited by an available name.

name, replacement. A new name expressly proposed for an already established one.

nomen dubium (pl. **nomina dubia**). Name(s) of unknown or doubtful application.

nomen oblitum. A forgotten name.

Official Index. One of four lists of names or works that have been rejected for use in rulings by the ICZN; Official Index of Generic Names, Specific Names, Family-Group Names, and Works.

Official List. One of four lists of names or works that have been approved (validated) by the ICZN; Official List of Generic Names, Specific Names, Family-Group Names, and Works.

opinion. A formal publication of an interpretation, ruling, or suspension of a provision of the Code (see Also Appendix B).

original description. See **description, original**

original designation. See **designation, original**

plenary power. Power of the International Commission to suspend articles of the Code to settle particular cases.

preoccupied. At the generic level, a name predated by use of the same generic or subgeneric name for another taxon in zoology at an earlier date.

priority. Seniority fixed by date of publication; the earliest published has priority.

replacement name. See **name, replacement**

subsequent designation. See **designation, subsequent**

suppressed. A name or work on which the Commission has ruled that the name or work is never to be used (totally suppressed) or only conditionally used (conditionally suppressed).

synonym. Each of two or more scientific names of the same rank used to denote the same taxon. Typically, two names for the same taxon—only one can be used; they are said to be synonyms.

junior. The younger name of two synonyms.

objective. Each of two or more synonyms that are based on the same name-bearing type. For genera, two or more different names based on the same type species.

subjective. Each of two or more synonyms that are based on different name-bearing types. For genera, two or more different names based on different type species which a specialist deems to represent the same taxon.

synonymy. The relationship between synonymous names, or a list of synonymous names. "Synonym of..." refers to the fact that a generic-group name is synonymous with another name.

systematics. The classification and study of organisms with regard to their natural relationships.

tautonymy. The use of the same word for the name of a genus-group taxon and for one of its included species or subspecies.

absolute. The identical spelling of a generic-group name and one of its included specific-group names. Such as *Brama brama.*

Linnaean. Identical spelling of a new genus-group name and a pre-Linnaean (i.e., before 1758) one-word name cited as a synonym of only one of the species or subspecies originally included in that genus (see Art. 68e(i) in Appendix A).

taxon (pl. **taxa**). A taxonomic unit, such as a species, genus, subgenus, family.

taxonomy. The study and practice of naming and classifying organisms, as done by taxonomists.

type species. The (nominal) species that is the name-bearing type of a genus or subgenus.

unavailable. Not available for use in zoological nomenclature. See Appendix A.

variety (var.). A category below the species level; interpretation varies on the basis of date of use (see the Code).

vernacular name. A name proposed in a language used for general purposes as opposed to a name proposed only for zoological nomenclature. In the Catalog one finds the expression, "Not available, appeared as a French vernacular."

work. Written zoological information, such as a manuscript or publication.

available. One that can be used in zoological nomenclature.

rejected. An unavailable work that has been rejected by the ICZN and placed on the Official Index of Works.

APPENDIX A

GENERA OF RECENT FISHES AND THE INTERNATIONAL CODE OF ZOOLOGICAL NOMENCLATURE

William N. Eschmeyer

Nomenclatural decisions in Part I of the Catalog were made on the basis of the provisions of the "International Code of Zoological Nomenclature," 1985 Edition (hereinafter called the Code, and begun with a capital C). In general, only provisions of the Code that apply to genera are discussed here; articles and subsections dealing with family-group names, species-group names, or other subjects are omitted, or are included only to the extent that they affect genus-group names or the treatment of type species in Part I of the Catalog. Below the articles of the Code are restated and summarized, and examples from fishes are given for many articles.

The Code is difficult to use because it has many interrelated articles and subsections; at the same time it is comprehensive. It is a code of law; items are stated precisely, but without explanation (although examples are given under some articles). It does not, however, have legal status in international law, and there is no "case law" as such; each case is settled primarily from the Code alone and not by precedent. The following references provide additional information: Mayr (1969 [ref. 13542]), Jeffrey (1973 [ref. 13543]), Ride and Younès (1985 [ref. 13544]), Schenk and McMasters (1956 [ref. 13545]. A concise summary of the Code in easy-to-read language is provided by Cogger 1987 [ref. 13912]. For a lighter treatment of some aspects of the Code, see Gould 1990 [ref. 14276].

The discussion and examples given here are intended to illustrate how the various applicable provisions of the Code were interpreted in preparing Part I of the Catalog and as an aid to understanding the terminology and reasoning used in Part I. My unofficial interpretation is intended to be used with the Code; the official interpretation can be made only by the International Commission on Zoological Nomenclature (ICZN).

For historical and interpretive purposes, I occasionally mention earlier editions of the Code, or the 1842 "Report of a Committee appointed 'to consider of the rules by which the Nomenclature of Zoology may be established on a uniform and permanent basis'" (see Strickland et al. 1843 [ref. 13534]), and subtitled, "Series of Propositions for Rendering the Nomenclature of Zoology Uniform and Permanent." This 1842 code (published in 1843; hereinafter termed the "the 1842 code") was widely circulated and was the primary basis for nomenclatural "rules" until 1905. In 1842, the principles of priority (at least of usage if not of publication), the concept of type species of genera, and binominal nomenclature were firmly established; homonymy was addressed; and such items as endings of family group names, a starting date for nomenclature (later changed), and nominotypical groups, were treated. Workers in the middle 1800s were operating under "rules" that were often much different than those that followed; for example, the 1842 code provided for more liberal replacement of names—e.g., "Names not clearly defined may be changed"; "A name whose meaning is glaringly false may be changed"; and "Latin orthography [is] to be adhered to." Also, "Specific names, when adopted as generic, must be changed." These propositions, as shown later, explain the many unneeded generic and specific replacement names proposed in the last half of the 19th century. In 1905, a new code appeared as the "Règles Internationales de la nomenclature Zoologique." This code, through a series of revisions and refinements led directly to the 1985 Code (see Ride in Ride and Younès 1986 [ref. 13544] for a brief history of zoological nomenclature). "The Code is complex, partly because of the interdependence of different parts of it, and partly because it must contain devices to validate actions and names in use but resulting from earlier, less satisfactory, standards of description and publication" (Ride 1986:29). Amendments to improve and modernize the 1985 Code are now being discussed, and the Code is continually evolving. Because it has articles and provisions that are interrelated, some subjects are mentioned in several different articles; this makes a summary of the provisions difficult and forces some repetition. A short index to the articles treated here is provided at the end of this appendix, and article numbers in the text below are in boldface to aid in finding them on any given page. Inquiries about purchasing the 1985 or future editions of the Code or to learn more about the International Commission may be made to the International Commission on Zoological Nomenclature, c/o The Natural History Museum, Cromwell Road, London SW7 5BD, England; or to the American Association for Zoological Nomenclature, c/o U. S. National Museum of Natural History, Washington D.C. 20560. The International Trust for Zoological Nomenclature, in which is vested the copyright of the *International Code of Zoological Nomenclature*, kindly gave permission to quote directly from the Code.

INTRODUCTORY CONSIDERATIONS

The Preamble of the 1985 Code clearly states the objectives of the Code (p. 3): "The object of the Code is to promote stability and universality in the scientific names of animals and to ensure that the name of each taxon is unique and distinct. All its provisions and recommendations are subservient to these ends and none restricts the freedom of taxonomic thought or action."

The Code consists of a series of provisions and recommendations that enable zoologists to name taxa or to determine the correct name to use in different taxonomic situations. Adherence is voluntary, but use of the Code by nearly all systematists is one of the few areas of total world cooperation.

A taxon name, such as that of a genus, must pass several nomenclatural hurdles before it may be used (is nomenclaturally available or is "legitimate," as the International Code of Botanical Nomenclature code calls it) in zoological nomenclature. It must meet the qualifying conditions for each hurdle. The major hurdles are (1) publication, (2) availability, (3) proper formation and authorship, and (4) typification. After these conditions have been met, it must be decided if the name is valid. Whether the name will be used as the valid name of a taxon (or be an unused synonym) depends **nomenclaturally** on priority of the name and of others in competition with it, and **taxonomically** on the limits of the taxon (i.e., on taxonomic decisions independent of nomenclature). For example, a zoologist may define a genus to contain four related species, only to find that two generic names are available for the taxon containing these four species. Which name to use as the valid one depends on which is the oldest (a nomenclatural decision), but bringing the species together (and creating the condition of two available generic names for the single taxon) is a taxonomic decision based on inferred relationships of the species.

ZOOLOGICAL NOMENCLATURE (ARTICLES 1–3)

The first chapter of the Code defines zoological nomenclature [**Art. 1a**] as "the system of scientific names applied to taxonomic units (taxa, singular: taxon) of animals known to occur in nature, whether extant [living] or extinct [usually meaning fossil]...." It also includes "substitutions" (such as fossil impressions, or casts of actual remains of animals), and taxa based on fossilized work of animals (ichnotaxa), such as fossilized worm tubes.

Exclusions, discussed in **Article 1b**, are such things as names proposed for hypothetical concepts, for teratological specimens (when the author knew it was a malformed specimen), for hybrids as such (meaning the original author knew he had a taxon of hybrid origin and not one later found to be based on a hybrid), and for taxa above the family-group name; as means of temporary reference and not for formal taxonomic use; and as modifications of available names throughout a taxonomic group by the addition of a standard prefix or suffix. Some generic examples from fishes follow.

Eigenmann and Allen 1942 [ref. 1246]) used the name *Protorestias* for the hypothetical ancestor of *Orestias* and allies; this name is used in a hypothetical way and is excluded [not available] on the basis of **Article 1b(1)**. (It is also not available for lack of a description [**Art. 13a**] and lack of type species fixation [**Art. 13b**].)

Leigh-Sharpe (1924, 1926 [refs. 5748, 5627]) proposed 12 "pseudogenera" for skates and rays that he defined by the morphology of the male clasper organ, but provided a type species for each pseudogenus. He formed these by adding Greek prefixes to an existing genus (Alpharaia, Betaraia... through Kapparaia, Alphascyllium, Betascyllium). Jordan (1925 [ref. 5077]) regarded them as subgenera, but Leigh-Sharpe (1928 [ref. 6152]) responded that he did not propose the names as subgenera, and defined his term "pseudogenus" as an "artificial assemblage of species (a) for the temporary convenience of treating a particular character or set of characters...." The use of "pseudogenera" in this case makes the names unavailable under **Article 1b(6)**, which states that names excluded from the Code are ones used "as means of temporary reference and not for formal taxonomic use as scientific names in zoological nomenclature."

Poey 1926 [ref. 5054] used "grupos" in a manner that suggested subgenera, but on his p. 11 defined "grupo" as "Para dar más vida al catálogo y señalar mejor afinidades entre géneros y especies, aceptamos *grupos*.... No tiene límites el concepto de grupo, lo empleo sólo como medio útil de señalar semejanzas y distanciar diferencias." I regard these as artificial assemblages and not available on the basis of **Article 1b(6)**. A different argument would be that the names are uninominal ones proposed for a genus-group division of a genus and are therefore available (**Art. 10e**).

A number of fish genera are based on deformed or abnormal specimens, but these names are available; they are not excluded on the basis of **Article 1b** because when they were proposed, the original authors did not know that they were based on malformed (teratological) specimens.

Zoological nomenclature is independent of other systems of nomenclature [**Art. 1c**] "in that the name of an animal taxon is not to be rejected merely because it is identical with the name of a taxon that does not belong in the animal kingdom."

As an example, a genus of plants and a genus of fishes may have the same name [although not true in the 1842 code], but within the animal kingdom a genus of fishes, for example, cannot have the same name as a genus of snakes. *Micropteryx* Agassiz 1829 was proposed as a replacement name for *Seriola* Cuvier 1816 and *Marcgravichthys* Miranda-Ribeiro 1915 was a replacement for *Marcgravia* Jordan 1887, both preoccupied in botany. But the use of the same name is now permitted in both botany and zoology; consequently, although Agassiz's and Miranda-Ribeiros's replacement names were unneeded, they were appropriate substitutions when they were proposed. The concept of having no two valid generic names spelled identically in zoology will become increasingly important as taxonomic information is computerized and electronic literature searches become widespread; such searches will be aided if the names are unique. Groups that are excluded from zoological nomenclature include plants and their allies and bacteria and viruses; these disciplines have separate codes.

Names based on organisms not thought to be animals but later classified as animals, or the reverse (being first thought to be animals but later not classified as animals) are addressed in **Article 2**. In the first instance, names of organisms later but not first classified as animals are eligible and come under the Code if, as first proposed, they met the certain provisions of the zoological Code with regard to availability (see **Art. 10f**) and at the same time were validly published as a non-animal—i.e., met the conditions of the code in the discipline under which they were described (e.g., an animal first described as a plant must have met the conditions of the International Code of Botanical Nomenclature when first proposed as a plant).

The reason for these restrictions is that, in the early days of classification, such groups as bryozoans might have been classified as plants; consequently, if the name was proposed under the rules governing the description of new taxa of plants, the name was fully available for use in zoology when bryozoans were classified as animals.

Article 3 defines the starting date for zoological nomenclature as 1 January 1758, and two important works are deemed published on that date (Linnaeus' *Systema Naturae, 10th Edi-*

tion, and Clerck's *Aranei Svecici*); all other works (entering into scientific nomenclature) are deemed to have been published after that date. Linnaeus' 1758 work, which was based primarily on the work of Artedi and other earlier workers, includes 157 genera of fishes. Clerck's *Aranei Svecici* (treating arachnids) has priority over Linnaeus' *Systema Naturae*, but any other work published in 1758 is deemed to have been published after Linnaeus' work.

The "Series of Propositions" in the 1842 code used Linnaeus' 12th Edition (rather than the 10th) as the starting date, but the reasons given on pp. 109–110 of that code provide the historical background:

> "As our subject matter is strictly confined to the *binomial system of nomenclature*, or that which indicates species by means of two Latin words, the one generic, the other specific, and as this invaluable method originated solely with Linnæus, it is clear that, as far as species are concerned, we ought not to attempt to carry back the principle of priority beyond the date of the 12th edition of the 'Systema Naturæ.' Previous to that period, naturalists were wont to indicate species not by a *name* comprised in one word, but by a *definition* which occupied a sentence, the extreme verbosity of which method was productive of great inconvenience. It is true that one word sometimes sufficed for the definition of a species, but these rare cases were only binomial by accident and not by principle, and ought not therefore in any instance to supersede the binomial designations imposed by Linnæus.
>
> "The same reasons apply also to generic names. Linnæus was the first to attach a definite value to genera, and to give them a systematic character by means of exact definitions; and therefore although the *names* used by previous authors may often be applied with propriety to modern genera, yet in such cases they acquire a new meaning, and should be quoted on the authority of the first person who used them in this secondary sense....
>
> "We therefore recommend the adoption of the following proposition:—
>
> "§ 2. The binomial nomenclature having originated with Linnæus, the law of priority, in respect of that nomenclature, is not to extend to the writings of antecedent authors."

In Part I of the Catalog, some genera can be traced to authors earlier than Linnaeus, especially to Artedi (see Wheeler 1987 [ref. 12821]), and current authors sometimes show these connections—e.g., Linnaeus (ex Artedi) or Linnaeus [Artedi]—but we do not do so in the Catalog.

Scientific Names (Articles 4–6)

The Code defines scientific names more precisely and discusses the use of subgeneric and subspecific names in **Articles 4–6**. The scientific name of a species is a combination of two names (a binomen), the first being the generic name and the second the specific name [**Art. 5**]; this then is the principle of binominal (or "two-name") nomenclature. Specific names must always begin with a lowercase letter. A taxon above the species level [**Art. 4a**], such as a subgenus or genus, or tribe, subfamily or family, must consist of one word (uninominal) and must begin with a capital letter. A subspecies [**Art. 5b**] is a combination of three names (a trinomen, i.e., a binomen [genus and species] followed by a subspecific name); the subspecific name also begins with a lowercase letter. A subgenus name [**Art. 6**], when cited with a genus and species, must also be one word, and it is to be placed in parentheses between the generic name and the specific name. Only two other interpolated names are permitted [**Art. 6b**]; they are single words begun with a lowercase letter and placed in parentheses; the first is a species-group name placed between a genus and species to refer to an aggregate of two or more species that form part of a larger genus, and the second is a subspecies-group name placed between a species and subspecies to refer to one or more subspecies that form part of several subspecies of one species; these are rarely used in fishes.

Publication (Articles 7–9)

To be available for use in zoological nomenclature, new names, nomenclatural acts, and information relevant in zoological nomenclature must meet certain requirements; Chapter III of the Code addresses these issues. **Article 7** states that the provisions of Chapter III apply not only to the publication of new names, and also to the publication of any nomenclatural act or information likely to affect nomenclature. A work either meets the criteria for publication [**Art. 8**] or it does not [**Art. 9**]. Before 1986, a work must have been produced in "ink on paper by conventional printing" [**Art. 8c**], but after 1985 [**Art. 8d**] a work published in a form other than conventional printing (e.g., photocopying, microcard) must contain a statement by the author that any new name or nomenclatural act in the work is intended for the permanent, public, scientific record [**Art. 8d(ii)**]. It also must have been produced in simultaneously obtainable copies. Other criteria are that the work must be issued publicly, and be obtainable free of charge or by purchase [**Art. 8a(2)**], etc. A work that contains a statement that it is not issued for permanent scientific record is not an available work [**Art. 8b**]. Some newsletters and printed abstracts for meetings are not issued for the permanent scientific record.

Works that do not meet the criteria of publication [**Art. 9**] include such ones as computer printouts, notes distributed only to colleagues or students, mention at a meeting, or placement of a document such as a thesis in a library. As printing technologies change, refinements can be expected.

For works in ichthyology there have been few problems in this area. A few works have been privately published. Ogilby 1910 [ref. 3289] is one work containing new genera that was privately circulated from reprints and regarded as available; the journal publication itself was canceled. One unavailable work that is often cited is Norman's, "A Draft Synopsis of the Orders, Families and Genera of Recent Fishes and Fish-Like Vertebrates" (Norman 1966 [ref. 13535]). The undated first printing contained the statement "(This Synopsis is *not* for public sale but for private circulation only)." It was reissued in 1966 (also with the disclaimer); neither edition is regarded as available for nomenclatural purposes (but it was a source used in proofing the database for genera).

AUTHORSHIP (ARTICLES 50–51)

The author of a name is the person who first publishes it (but it must of course meet the criteria for publication discussed above and must be an available name [see next section]). But one must be aware that the author of a name may not seem so obvious. First is the case where it is clear from the publication itself that some other person is responsible for both the name and for satisfying the criteria of availability (other than publication); that other person is then the author of the name [**Art. 50a**]. Also, if it is clear from the contents of the publication that only one of two or more joint authors, or some other person, is alone responsible, he or she is the author of the name [**Art. 50a**].

The Code goes to great lengths to give authorship to the person responsible for the entry of a new taxon into nomenclature. In the 1842 code, for example, this was the "person to whose labours we owe our first knowledge of the object," or the "authority" for the taxon. Problems arise when it is unclear from the original publication who was responsible for the description. One argument (e.g., Sabrosky 1974:206 [ref. 12758]), is that "for simplicity and objectivity we should recognize as 'the author' of a name that author who publishes the name **and** the qualifying conditions ..., except only in cases of direct quotation or equally clearcut attribution of *both* name and description (and of course the specific exception provided for names in minutes ...)." The Code specifically excludes publication as a criterion of authorship when it is clear from the contents that someone else is "alone responsible both for the name and for satisfying the criteria of availability other than publication ..." [**Art. 50a**]. In fact, in a few cases it is very difficult to determine authorship. In the Catalog I used the following guidelines (a–e), so that at least my interpretation of the Code is somewhat objective and consistent.

(a) The simplest cases are those where the author of the publication cites another author after the new taxon and places quotation marks around the description taken from a manuscript, or in other ways clearly indicates that he is taking the name and description from another person. In Part I of the Catalog these are shown as "manuscript author in publishing author," (e.g., Jones in Smith). (b) Less clear is the case where a manuscript author is cited and it can be seen from the text that no specimens were available to the author of the publication and that he or she could not have prepared the description; clearly the author of the new genera and species is then the manuscript author and not the author of the publication. (However, if a manuscript figure or drawing is involved, it is difficult to determine if the publishing author might not have made the description from the figure.) (c) The reverse of (b) is when an author (other than the publishing author) is cited for the new taxon, but from evidence presented it can be seen that the cited author of the taxon did not have specimens available or could not have participated in the description. But in the Catalog, in most of these cases, particularly when multiple authors are given, I simply accepted the authorship as given in the published work, for lack of other evidence. (d) In an even more confusing area, one must guess whether the author took the name and description from a manuscript. If it looks as if the author of the publication took only the name from the manuscript but the description is his own, this author is cited in the Catalog as the publishing author (ex manuscript author)—e.g., Jones (ex Smith). This is the case with many fossil genera in cases where names were taken from Agassiz publications (published as name only) and used by later workers. The author is not Agassiz, but the expression "(ex Agassiz)" provides some additional information; often the publishing author credits the species to Agassiz, though the species authorship goes to the author and not to Agassiz. (e) Finally, sometimes the published article contains informative comments. For example, if from the text it can be seen that someone merely suggested a name to the publishing author, or the name came from a museum label, or the publishing author is merely giving credit to a major professor or superior, etc., the author is the publishing author, and the "ex" convention is not used.

A paper published by Putnam (1863 [ref. 3567]) illustrates the complexity of authorship citation. In this work, some new taxa were credited to "Putnam, MS" and others to "Agassiz, MS" and most gave the year in which the manuscript was prepared, such as "Agassiz, MS. 1860." Descriptions of new taxa were very brief. I have no reason to doubt the authorships as given, and in Part I of the Catalog some authorships are Putnam and others are given as Agassiz in Putnam. I assume that the manuscripts were available to Putnam, such that he could take his descriptions from them. Clearly, the intended authorship was given. One can also look at contemporary use; Jordan and Evermann (1896–1898) credited new names to the listed author; e.g., authorship of *Microperca* goes to Putnam and *Nothonotus* goes to Agassiz in Putnam.

For the work by Bloch and Schneider (1801 [ref. 471]), Paxton et al. (1989:11 [ref. 12442]) are followed in attributing authorship to both Bloch and Schneider (see discussion in Paxton et al.). Schneider edited the book for publication after Bloch's death, and made additions; it is possible to attribute some names to one author or the other, but for other taxa this cannot be done with certainty. Fowler, in his *Fishes of the World*, credited all taxa in Bloch and Schneider to Schneider (except for those correctly attributable to Forster in Bloch and Schneider). For the various volumes of Cuvier and Valenciennes' *Histoire Naturelle des Poissons*, the authorship documented by Bailey (1951 [ref. 5587]) and confirmed in ICZN Opinion 580 is followed. Cuvier is the author of some taxa and Valenciennes is the author of others, based on volume number and page.

Sometimes the authorship is mentioned in the introduction or elsewhere in a work but not adjacent to the new taxon. In Eigenmann's (1912 [ref. 1227]) large synopsis of *The Freshwater Fishes of British Guiana*, a footnote on p. 422 states, "This account of the Gymnotidae was prepared by Dr. Max Mapes Ellis ...." Ellis is thus the author of the new gymnotid taxa.

An unusual case of authorship involves a species that was described without being placed in a genus, and a new genus name was later based on it. Poey (1868:305 [ref. 3505]) described a species *diapterus* but did not place it in a genus ("Genus...?"). Jordan (1886:586 [ref. 2388]) wrote, "*Amiichthys* Poey, genus novum. *Amiichthys diapterus* Poey. (P.)." In a footnote he said, "*Amiichthys* Poey, MSS., genus novum, for the fish described with the specific name of *diapterus* in the 'Synopsis Pisc. Cub.,' p. 305. It is regarded by Poey as belonging to the Cheilodipteridae." Without a genus, the species name in 1868 is apparently nonbinominal and not available; **Article 11h(iii)** states that a species, to be available, must be published in combination with a generic name, but the generic name need not be valid or even available. The species can date to the publication in Jordan, where it appeared in binomial form, and there is reference to an earlier description to validate the name. I treat the genus as *Amiichthys* Poey in Jordan 1886, and the species name seemingly should be cited as *Amiichthys diapterus* Poey in Jordan 1886.

What happens to authorship when an author provides a new genus name, and then in the same work withdraws the name and substitutes another earlier available name? Apparently the new name can be treated as available; however, some names may lend themselves to consideration as a name first published in synonymy or as a name not used in a valid sense (when withdrawn).

De Beaufort (1940: 50 [ref. 239]) described *Parabodianus* with one included species, but on a typeset "rectification" slip glued (but not bound) between pp. x and xi indicated that the genus was based on a specimen of *Pentapus carinus* and that it did not represent a new genus of labrids. I am unable to determine if the correction slip was added to all copies before distribution. There is no provision in the Code to cancel the publication of a new name (even by the original author) once it has appeared in an available way. *Parabodianus* is regarded as available as published.

Fleming (1828:183 [ref. 1339]) described the genus *Encrasicholus*, but withdrew the name in his Corrigenda following page 565 ("for *Encrasicholus* read *Engraulis*"). *Encrasicholus* is considered a name published in the synonymy of *Engraulis*. Vaillant (1888 [ref. 4496]) used the new name *Gyrinomene nummularis* on pp. 18 and 45, but identified it as the established *Diretmus argenteus* on p. 355. *Gyrinomene* is considered a name published first in synonymy. But based on the entire work, one might want to consider, in these cases, that the new name was not used for a valid taxon **[Art. 11d]**.

A more confusing example involves the new genus *Creolus* Jordan and Gilbert (1883 [ref. 2476]). This name appeared in the index (p. xxxvi) with a reference to the genus and one species on p. 916 (and on p. 972 [sic for 973]); on p. 916 the genus was given as *Brachyrhinus* Gill 1862; further in the addenda (p. 973), however, *Brachyrhinus* was stated to be preoccupied and the genus name *Paranthias* Guichenot 1868 was substituted. Apparently the genus name *Creolus* is available from the index, because of the reference to a description and an included species. It is not regarded as a replacement for *Brachyrhinus* (which would give it a different type, *creolus*) because it was not expressly proposed as such.

Then there are several cases, particularly involving Jordan and contemporaries in the late 1890s and early 1900s, where authors were sharing information or manuscripts before publication, and some names were changed or the same taxa were published with a different name in two works. In these cases, both names are typically available, often with confusing authorships.

The name *Escolar* Jordan and Evermann appeared first in Goode and Bean (1896:519 [ref. 1848]). Later in the same year the taxon was described as *Bipinnula* in Jordan and Evermann (1896:877 [ref. 2443]); according to Jordan (1920:474 [ref. 4905]), the name *Bipinnula* was left standing through a slip in proofreading. *Escolar* Jordan and Evermann in Goode and Bean is the senior objective synonym of *Bipinnula* Jordan and Evermann.

If the identity of an author cannot be determined from the contents of the publication, the author is deemed to be anonymous **[Art. 50a]**. **Article 14** states that a new name, act, or information that affects nomenclature published anonymously after 1950 is not available; before 1951 new taxa with anonymous authorship were acceptable.

The only cases of anonymous publication of genus-group names in Recent fishes are seemingly *Ovoides* and *Sphoeroides* [perhaps authored by Lacepède], and *Thinnis* attributed to "S.D.W." [probably S. D. Wood]; see generic accounts in Part I.

The author of a taxon made available by publication in the minutes of a meeting, or in an account of a meeting, is the person responsible for the name and description—not the secretary or other reporter of the meeting **[Art. 50b]**.

There are many examples in fishes of new genera reported in the activities of meetings, especially in the mid to late 1800s, for such scientific societies as the Philadelphia Academy of Sciences and the California Academy of Sciences. There is usually no confusion of authorships: the secretary or another reports on observations (typically from a submitted manuscript) made by another (the author).

In the report (published Jan. 1850) of the meeting of the Boston Society of Natural History on 18 July 1849, it is stated that, "Dr. Storer presented, in the name of Rev. Zadock Thompson, of Burlington, Vt., descriptions and drawings of a new species of *Esox*, to which he gives the name *E. nobilior*, and a fish for which he [Thompson] proposes to establish a new genus under the name of *Salmoperca*, unless it should be found to come under Prof. Agassiz's genus *Percopsis*. ... Mr. Ayres [an attendee] said, on examination of the drawing of the fish called *Salmoperca*, that it evidently belonged to the genus *Percopsis*." A complete species description from Thompson was presented under the name *Percopsis pellucida*. The author of *Salmoperca* is Thompson (not the presenter Storer) **[Art. 50b]**. Conditional proposals before 1961 are available **[Art. 15]**. This example is not regarded as a name first published in synonymy **[Art. 11e]**, since Thompson used *Salmoperca* validly but conditionally. The author of the species *pellucida* is also Thompson. It can be argued that the species was published first in the genus *Percopsis* and then in the conditionally proposed *Salmoperca* **[Art. 51c(ii)]**, so that the species, in its original combination, would be given as *Percopsis pellucida* Thompson and not *Salmoperca pellucida*.

Serving as a related example are letters from van Hasselt written to Temminck reporting on genera and species of fishes found by Kuhl and van Hasselt in the Dutch East Indies in the 1820s [refs. 5963, 5964, 4513, 5105]. Temminck, the Director of the Leiden Museum, published the letters (but he is not the author of the new taxa). Brief characterizations of genera and species were included, some of which remain unidentifiable; others are available and attributed generally to van Hasselt or to Kuhl and van Hasselt, but some authorships have still not been resolved satisfactorily (see Kottelat 1987 [ref. 5962]). Kuhl and van Hasselt died before their results could be published in detail.

Change in rank of a taxon (such as recognition at the generic and then downgrading to subgeneric level) does not affect the authorship of the taxon at the genus-group level **[Art. 50c (i)]**.

A justified emendation (an intentional and required change in the original spelling of a taxon) does not change the authorship; the taxon retains the original author, even though he or she may have misspelled the name **[Art. 50d]**. However, an unjustified emendation (an intentional change, but without a permissible reason) is equivalent to describing yet another taxon, and it takes the authorship (and date and spelling) of the author who published the unjustified emendation **[Art. 50e]**. This is an important distinction, currently overlooked by many workers (this subject is discussed more fully below under Art. 33).

When names are published simultaneously for the same taxon, the "first reviser," through selection of one name over the other, thereby determines precedence (and hence the authorship) **[Art. 50f]**. (The "first reviser" is discussed in more detail later, but in this case it is the first author to subsequently cite both names (of the same date and for the same taxon) and to select one of the names over the other.)

A special case exists for names first published in synonymy (as a secondary or other name for the taxon being described) **[Art. 50g]**. A name first published in synonymy, if before 1961 **[Art. 11e]**, can become available as a usable name, and in these cases the author is the one who first published the name in synonymy and not the person who later adopted the name as valid [and the taxon dates to its first publication in synonymy as well]. **Article 67(l)** states that the type species of a genus name first published in synonymy, and used validly before 1961 under the provisions of **Article 11e**, is the species first directly associated with it under an available species-group name; the type is not automatically the type species of the nominal taxon denoted by the senior synonym. In other words, if the genus *Alpha* is mentioned as a manuscript name in synonymy under two species in the genus *Beta*, both of these species are originally included in *Alpha*; one of them may or may not be the type species of *Beta*. If an unavailable species name is cited with the genus name in synonymy, it is not thereby available as the type species.

Pirarara bicolor was a manuscript genus and species name of Spix. Agassiz (in Spix and Agassiz 1829) cited Spix's manuscript names and used Spix's species name *bicolor* and his species description and attributed both to Spix, but instead of *Pirarara* he used his own new name *Phractocephalus* for the genus and provided a description. So the author of the genus *Phractocephalus* is Agassiz and the author of the species *bicolor* is Spix, and the name *Pirarara* is a name first published in synonymy. Bleeker (1862 and 1863) used the name *Pirarara* from Agassiz as a valid name, thereby making it available, and since it falls under **Article 11e**, the author of *Pirarara* is Agassiz (since he was the one who first published the name in synonymy) and not Bleeker or Spix (see **Art. 50g**). The type species of *Pirarara* is *bicolor* (see **Art. 67(l)**—an available species name first directly associated with *Pirarara*; Bleeker gave the type as *Silurus hemilopterus* Bloch, the species he associated with *Pirarara*. More examples of names first published in synonymy are given later.

Article 51 discusses the citation of authors' names, including the use of parentheses in changed combinations, i.e., if a species-group name is combined with a generic name other than the original one, the name of the author of the species-group name, if cited, is to be enclosed in parentheses. For example, "*Scorpaena alba* (Jones)," means that Jones originally described *alba* in a genus other than *Scorpaena*. A special case occurs when an author first publishes a new species in an established genus but at the same time conditionally proposes a new nominal genus for the new species in question [**Art. 51c (ii)**]. The specific name is to be considered as published in the old name first, and then combined with the conditionally proposed generic name. This applies only to names before 1961, because conditionally published names after 1960 are not available [**Art. 15**]. This priority determines the conditions under which the author name is placed in parentheses and determines the original genus of the type species.

As treated in Opinion 461 (see our Appendix B), Lowe (1843) described *gracilis* as a species of the fish genus *Seriola*, but conditionally established the new nominal genus *Cubiceps* for it in the same paper. The species *gracilis* was therefore first described in *Seriola* based on **Art. 51c**, and the correct citation of the type species is *Seriola gracilis*, not *Cubiceps gracilis*.

AVAILABILITY (ARTICLES 10–20)

If a work meets the criteria for publication, authorship was established, and it was published after 1757 [**Art. 11a**], the next consideration is that of whether names or nomenclatural acts in the work meet the criteria of availability. A distinction is made between available (or "legitimate") names that can be used in nomenclature or unavailable ("illegitimate") names that cannot be so used **versus** valid or invalid names (that normally concern the systematic status of the taxon represented by the name). An available name is one that has standing in nomenclature; it may or may not be used for a valid taxon, and it will be unusable if it is a homonym or objective synonym of an older name.)

A name must be spelled in Latin letters and be used as a scientific name [**Art. 11b**], and may be a Latin word or a latinized word. There are several technical issues regarding the formation of names and their gender and case [**Art. 11b**]. The author of the work must have used binominal nomenclature [**Art. 11c**]. A number of early works have been rejected because authors did not do so. For most of these, the ICZN has been requested to reject the works (see our Appendix B, Official Index of Works), but there are some additional technical considerations as well. In a work published before 1931, if an author used single-word genus names without associated species names, the work still meets the criteria of binominal nomenclature [**Art. 11c(i)**]. An index published before 1931 in a work that is not consistently binominal is acceptable itself if the Principle of Binominal Nomenclature is consistently applied to scientific names in the index.

To be available, names are to be treated as valid when proposed [**Art. 11d**], but there are exceptions. A name proposed conditionally after 1960 [**Art. 16**] is not available. It is available if published conditionally before 1961 [**Art. 11d**]. A name first published as a junior synonym is not available when first published [**Art. 11d**], but it can be made available later [**Art. 11e**].

Determination of whether a name was first published as a junior synonym is sometimes confusing. For example, Cuvier in Cuvier and Valenciennes (1829:174 [ref. 4879]) mentions the manuscript name *Ostichthys* Langsdorf and his species *O. aureus* under the new species *Myripristis japonicus* Cuvier. Obviously, the species *aureus* is published as a junior synonym of *japonicus*, but what about the genus? I interpret this to mean that *Ostichthys* was technically first published as a junior synonym of *Myripristis*. It is more clear when someone describes a new genus and includes in its synonymy a museum name or alternate name, in which case the name in synonymy was published literally in synonymy of a genus—for example if *Ostichthys* had been published under a treatment of *Myripristis* instead of under one of several species of *Myripristis*. In the case of *Ostichthys*, Jordan and Evermann (1896:846 [ref. 1443]) recognized the valid subgenus *Ostichthys* and credited it to Langsdorf and established a type species (*japonicus*). Current authors credit *Ostichthys* to Jordan and Evermann, but based on **Article 11e** and **Article 50b**, authorship and date should be Cuvier (ex Langsdorf) 1829.

Also, in Part I of the Catalog are statements such as, "Not available, a museum name mentioned in passing in synonymy of ...." [A museum name is typically one found in a bottle of specimens or in a catalog that a previous worker applied to the taxa, often as a manuscript name.] The name could have been made available by later use [**Art. 11e**] that causes authorship and date to revert to the first publication in synonymy, but only if that had been done prior to 1961; it cannot be made available by this method after that time [**Art. 11e**: "unless prior to 1961 ..."]. Correspondingly, if a name first published in synonymy has not been made available before 1961 [**Art. 11e**], and is used as a valid name after 1960, the name dates to the post-1960 author and date if the name met the conditions of other articles dealing with availability (such as having a description and a type established). In the case cited above, had Jordan and Evermann published *Ostichthys* after 1961, the genus would date to them. Further complications arise, however. What if Jordan and Evermann had made no mention of Langsdorf or to Cuvier and Valenciennes? Then **Article 11e** is less clear because one cannot know if Jordan and Evermann chose a name independently (clearly a homonym) and not "a name first published as a junior synonym," and one can only guess by the taxonomic placement of the genus, perhaps, that they were using Langsdorf's name. **Article 11e** is simply not precise enough (however, in fishes the number of genera coming under **Article 11e** is probably less than two dozen). Three more cases follow.

Myers (1951 [ref. 13464]) discussed the availability of manuscript names of Tickell published in Day (1888 [ref. 1082]). Day had available to him an unpublished manuscript by Tickell and used some of Tickell's generic and specific names and descriptions for valid taxa; these taxa date to Tickell in Day, 1888 (e.g., see *Acanthonotus*). However, Day also included three generic names and five species names from Tickell in the synonymy of other genera and species. For these Myers stated, "They are therefore validly published and available for use if Day's identifications prove to be wrong, if preoccupation makes older names unusable, or if generic, specific, or subspecific splitting occur." Myers was incorrect in stating that they were available names, since neither Myers nor any other author before 1961 used the names as valid before 1961.

A second case involves the genus *Salvelinus*. Richardson (1836:169 [ref. 3731]) provided under a description of *Salmo alipes* a short synonymy, including "Sub-genus, *Salvelinus*. Nilsson." Richardson did not formally use the name *Salvelinus* as valid, but stated under *alipes*, "This trout evidently belongs to the *Salvelini*, or Chars, a subgeneric group characterized by...." **Article 67(l)** states that the originally included species are those that were directly associated with it [genus or subgenus name in synonymy]; in the case of *Salvelinus*, *alipes* was directly associated with it (p. 169), but on p. 139 Richardson listed all the species in Nilsson's "Salvelini"; in addition, Richardson mentioned two more "chars" (pp. 171–173) but did not directly associate *Salvelinus* with them. One interpretation is that the species mentioned on p. 139 were "directly associated," so that the type of *Salvelinus* is the species *salvelinus* by tautonymy; the other view would be that only *alipes* was "directly" associated with *Salvelinus* so that it would be the type by monotypy. Subsequently, *Salvelinus* was used as a valid name, but who is the author? **Article 50g** states that, "If a scientific name (taken, for example, from a label or manuscript) is first published in the synonymy of an available name...its author is the person who first published it as a synonym, even if some other originator is cited...." [The Code does not clearly indicate who the author is if more than just a name is presented; in other words, What if Richardson had quoted an extensive description by Nilsson?] My interpretation is that if the name was published in synonymy, it could have been accompanied by a description, but it is still a name published first in synonymy. The name, with its description, was not treated as valid when proposed [**Art. 11d**] but as a synonym. Richardson provided a short description on p. 169; authorship is regarded as Richardson (ex Nilsson) 1836.

The third case of names first published in synonymy involves *Pacu* Agassiz, 1829 and *Pacu* Cuvier, 1829. Whitehead and Myers (1971 [ref. 6584]) and Kottelat (1988 [ref. 13380]) established that Cuvier (1829) predated Spix and Agassiz (1829), and Kottelat demonstrated that Agassiz is the author of most taxa in the latter work. Cuvier (1829:82 [ref. 995]) provided a description of "Les Curimates" and in a footnote listed several species and stated, "Ce sont les *Pacu* Spix." I regard *Pacu*, as used by Cuvier, as a name published in synonymy and definitely not intended as an available valid name for "Les Curimates" of Cuvier. *Pacu* Cuvier is therefore unavailable, and Kottelat's designation of the type species is illegal. Based on Kottelat's analysis, subsequent authors used only *Pacu* Agassiz, and apparently no one used *Pacu* Cuvier before 1961 as an available name or as a senior homonym [**Arts. 67(l)** and **11e**]. The two genera were proposed independently by Agassiz and by Cuvier, and subsequent use of *Pacu* Agassiz is not subsequent use of *Pacu* Cuvier. *Pacu* Agassiz is therefore not preoccupied, and it is potentially available for use. Kottelat stated that *Prochilodus* Agassiz, 1829 is a replacement name for *Pacu* Agassiz, but this appears incorrect. Agassiz adopted his name *Prochilodus* for the taxon, and included "Curimates" Cuvier and *Pacu* Spix in synonymy. The requirements for a name being a replacement name are explicit, and this use by Agassiz cannot be regarded as being a replacement name (*Pacu* Spix was not an available name at that time, and Agassiz did not state that it was a replacement name). It is also apparent that Agassiz did not intend to use Spix's name *Pacu* as valid (see also legend pages for plates), even though Spix's names appeared on the plates. In other words, I favor Kottelat's (p. 77) second interpretation "that names used in the text are available; names used on the plates are listed as synonyms in the text and, as synonyms, are only available if they have been treated as available names before 1961." But what Kottelat failed to note in some of his interpretations of genera from Spix and Agassiz is that later authors must treat names as available **and** [**Art. 11e**] "either adopted [the name] as the name of a taxon or treated [it] as a senior homonym...." For *Pacu* Cuvier, that apparently was not done before 1961; whereas in the case of *Pacu* Spix or Agassiz it was done (first by Müller and Troschel 1844, according to Kottelat). If one regards *Pacu* Spix in Spix and Agassiz as a name published in synonymy, then Müller and Troschel (1844) treated it as available and as the valid name (over *Prochilodus* Agassiz) for a taxon (so it is available from Agassiz, 1829). Kottelat's statement that, "As *Prochilodus* was intended as a replacement name for *Pacu* Agassiz, *P. argenteus* is also the type species of *Pacu* Agassiz" is erroneous. I found no subsequent type designation for *Pacu* Spix or Agassiz, although Kottelat's statement above is sufficient to establish a type ("for whatever reasons, right or wrong" [**Art. 69a(iv)**]). *Pacu* Agassiz, 1829 should be suppressed in favor of *Prochilodus* Agassiz. (For the same reasons, I feel that Kottelat's (1988:83) treatment of *Rhaphiodon* and *Cynodon* is in error; I regard *Cynodon* as a name published in synonymy of *Rhaphiodon*, but subsequently made available.) [However, this case brings up another problem; **Art. 11(e)** involves names "first published as a junior synonym..." but *Pacu* Cuvier was not published in the synonymy of a scientific name, only a vernacular name "Les Curimates"; and (as I interpret the Code) a synonym must be a scientific name (Code Glossary). Therefore, *Pacu* as it appears in Cuvier (1829) apparently does not meet the technical qualifications of a name published in synonymy.]

Article 11e(1) states that if a name is unavailable under any other provision of this chapter [**Arts. 10–20**], it cannot be made available by adoption from a citation as a junior synonym. In other words, it must have been published, in Latin or latinized, conform to binominal nomenclature, etc.

Girard (1859:57 [ref. 1821]) introduced *Pterognathus* as follows (also quoted in Jordan and Evermann 1898:2354 [ref. 2445], footnote to *Neoclinus blanchardi*): "It is more than probable that had we been acquainted with this second species of *Neoclinus* first, we would have been misled as to its real generical characters, and framed a name in allusion to the condition of the upper jaw, such as *Pterognathus* for example, which would have been more characteristic...." One could argue that this name in Girard (1859) is used in a hypothetical way and not intended as an available name. Jordan and Evermann adopted the name as a valid subgenus (p. 2355), so the name dates to 1898 if one regards the first use by Girard in 1859 as unavailable by being hypothetically used [**Art. 1b**]. On the other hand, if one regards Girard's 1859 use as a name published in synonymy of *Neoclinus*, Jordan and Evermann validate the name back to Girard, and the name *Pterognathus* belongs to Girard, 1859. I treat *Pterognathus* as available from Girard in Jordan and Evermann (1898).

The genus *Pseudogobius* is interesting nomenclaturally—illustrating problems of names first published in synonymy and of independently derived identical names. Popta (1922:36 [ref. 3550]) described *Pseudogobius penango* and included *P. javanicus* Bleeker [= *Gobius javanicus* Bleeker] (but did not fix a type species for it). Next, Koumans (1931:101 [ref. 5623]) mentioned Bleeker's museum name *Pseudogobius* in the synonymy of *Stigmatogobius* and directly associated (see **Article 67(l)**) several species names with it; he did not mention Popta. Aurich (1938:158 [ref. 152]) also described *Pseudogobius* (attributing it to himself but indicating that the name was Bleeker's museum name), and did not mention *Pseudogobius* Popta 1922. Current authors credit the genus to Aurich 1938. Although Aurich made reference to Koumans' papers, he apparently was not aware of Koumans' 1931 mention of *Pseudogobius*. However, since both Koumans' mention of the name and Aurich's treatment were based on Bleeker's museum name, one could consider that this meets the spirit of **Article 11e**, a name first published as a junior synonym [recognizing that in a strict sense the name was preoccupied by Popta's use]. Therefore, one interpretation is that Aurich's use makes available *Pseudogobius* from its appearance as a (Bleeker museum) name in synonymy in Koumans 1931, and that the author of a second *Pseudogobius* is Koumans' [**Art. 50g**], and that the originally included species are those mentioned by Koumans (p. 102) directly in association with *Pseudogobius*. The other view would be that the name was independently published by Aurich, and that Koumans' use is not involved—resulting in a *Pseudogobius* Popta and a *Pseudogobius* Aurich. The Code is not precise enough in this area: Is it the name alone that matters, or is it the "connections of use" that matters? In other words, if Aurich proceeded independently—describing his own genus—without mention of Koumans [or Popta], does Koumans' use have any bearing on use by Aurich, even though Aurich used the same Bleeker name first published in synonymy? We are left with two or three genera with the name *Pseudogobius*, based on a museum name coined by Bleeker, and the authors are Popta and Koumans or Popta and Aurich, or perhaps Popta, Koumans, and Aurich. The genus *Pseudogobius* Popta 1922 is the available, older name, but no one has yet designated a type for it. The best type [not designated here] would appear to be Bleeker's *G. javanicus*, resulting in a genus *Pseudogobius* Popta 1922, having as an objective synonym either *Pseudogobius* Koumans 1931 or Aurich 1938, or both.

Special conditions of availability apply to family-group names [**Art. 11f**], genus-group names [**Art. 11g**], and species-group names [**Art. 11h**]. To be available, genus-group names must have been treated as a noun in the nominative singular, or if proposed in Latin text but written otherwise than in the nominative singular, they are still available but must be corrected.

Apparently the only example of a fish genus-group name that was first written other than in the nominative singular and later corrected is *Ceratorhynchus* Agassiz. This name appeared as "Ceratorhynchi"; Kottelat (1988:78 [ref. 13380]) regarded this name as available from Agassiz with correction to *Ceratorhynchus* based on **Article 11g(i)**.

A special case of species-group name availability involves the "deliberate use of misidentification" [**Art. 11i**]. If an author establishes a new genus-group taxon but deliberately uses (designates) as its type-species an earlier misidentified species name, the author is considered to have created a new species-group name in the new genus. The new nominal species then has the same species-group name as was misidentified, but it is combined with the new genus-group name [**Art. 70c**].

Special availability considerations depend on whether the new scientific name was published before 1931 or after 1930; **Articles 12** and **13** address these issues. A name published before 1931 must be accompanied by a description or a definition of the taxon it denotes, or if not accompanied by such a description it must be accompanied by an "indication" in order to be available. Indications that are relevant here follow (1–8).

(1) There is a bibliographic reference to a previously published description or definition (and the previous work can predate 1758 or be in a work that is unavailable because it was nonbinominal).

(2) It is available with the inclusion of a name in an index to a work that is not consistently binominal but for which the index is available through **Article 11c(iii)**.

(3) The new name is a replacement name for a previously described available name.

(4) [Not applicable.]

(5) The name is available if it is a new genus-group name and one or more previously described species-group names is used in association with it or clearly included in it, or clearly referred to it by bibliographic reference. This situation proved to be common in fishes (several examples are given later).

(6) Also, before 1931, a combined description or definition of a new nominal genus and new nominal species provides an indication for both names and makes both available.

(7) Just as in item (1), the new genus-group or species-group name is available if proposed in association with an illustration of the taxon being named or by bibliographic reference to such an illustration (also even illustrations in works before 1758 or ones that are not consistently binominal).

(8) If before 1931, the new taxon is available if it is the description of the work [e.g., worm tube] of a living animal.

Exclusions are provided [**Art. 12c**]: "The mention of any of the following does not in itself constitute a description, definition, or indication: a vernacular name, locality, geological horizon, host, label, or specimen."

Names published after 1930, besides meeting the availability requirements above, have the following additional requirements [**Art. 13**]: Every new scientific name must (1) be accompanied by a description or definition that states in words the characters that are purported to differentiate the taxon, or (2) be accompanied by a bibliographic reference to such a published statement (even if contained in a work published before 1758 or that is not consistently binominal—but if an anonymous work it must have been published before 1950 [**Art. 14**]), or (3) be proposed expressly as a new replacement name. The purpose of **Article 13** is to make more precise the conditions that make a new scientific name available. Typically a new name will have a description; a reference to an earlier description is more vague but is still acceptable. A replacement name proposed expressly as such is available.

Because of **Article 13b**, some 50 genus-group names in

fishes are unavailable. This article added the restriction that every new genus name described after 1930 must also be accompanied by fixation of a type species for that nominal genus-group taxon by original designation [**Art. 68b**] or by indication [**Arts. 67h, 68c–e**]. Further, **Article 13b(i)** requires that a genus-group taxon established before 1931 and replaced after 1930 have a type species designated at that time if not done so previously [otherwise it is assumed that the name is unavailable although the Code does not specifically so state that in **Article 13b**].

In most instances where **Article 13b** applies in fishes, the original author apparently was unaware of requirements of the article, and later workers were also unaware of it, attributing the name to the original proposer and naming type species as if there were no **Article 13b**. Specifically, however, **Article 13** states that every new genus-group name published after 1930 must be accompanied by the fixation of a type species by (1) original designation or by (2) indication. Original designation [**Art. 67c, 68b**] involves explicit statements such as "Type:," "Type of the genus is...," "genotype is...," or "type species is ...." Three conditions qualify as type by indication [**Art. 67b**]: (a) one of the included species was named "*typicus, typica, typicum*, or *typus*" [**Art. 68c**], or (b) the genus-group name was established with only one originally included species, hence type by monotypy [**Art. 68d**], or (c) one included species is spelled exactly as the generic name such that there is absolute tautonymy [**Art. 68e**]. Names published after 1930 cannot involve type fixation by subsequent designation, and if the type species was not established by the remaining methods listed above, the name is unavailable [for certain technical exceptions, see **Arts. 67d, 68b, 68d(i)**]. In Part I of the Catalog these unavailable names are noted. Often, however, later authors have inadvertently made available some of the genera (a) by providing a description and designating a type or (b) by designating a type and citing the earlier unavailable description (see **Art. 13a**); the names end up being dated to and authored by these subsequent workers, even though they did not intend to be the authors. The consequence of having these unavailable names currently used as valid is that nomenclature is unstable. Any author finding one of these unavailable names can provide his own new name if the genus-group is recognized as a valid one, and there is no available junior synonym of the original name. Obviously, since in nearly all cases subsequent workers continue to attribute the name to the original author and accept type species fixation by such methods (unacceptable after 1930) as subsequent designation, it seems desirable to ask the ICZN to use its plenary powers to (a) make these names available from the first author and date and (b) confirm the type species as the one that has come into common use. On the other hand, if the pattern of acceptance of these **13b** names by later workers holds true for most or all disciplines, the ICZN should consider an amendment that would automatically allow for acceptance of these names and subsequent type designations unless there were special circumstances. All the names that were established as unavailable because of **13b** are so noted in Part I of the Catalog. The following examples illustrate **Article 13b**.

Fraser-Brunner (1933 [ref. 671]) described five new genus-group names of angelfishes: *Heteropyge* and *Pygoplites* as new genera and *Apolemichthys*, *Plitops*, and *Arusetta* as new subgenera. Because he designated a type, the two genera are available. *Arusetta* contained only one species and is therefore available with the type established by indication (only one species included, therefore type by monotypy). The other two names, however, contained more than one species and no included species was designated type for either taxon and none was named *typicus,-a,-um*, or *typus* and there was no absolute tautonymy; consequently, these are unavailable names from Fraser-Brunner, 1933, even though they are used in the current literature and attributed to Fraser-Brunner, 1933. Burton (1934), in the Zoological Record for 1933, reported the genera and subgenera of Fraser-Brunner and listed a type for each. For the two unavailable names, this would meet the requirements of **Article 13a (ii)** with regard to bibliographic reference to a previously published description. Since Fraser- Brunner had nothing to do with publication by Burton "in a way that satisfies the criteria of availability..." (see **Art. 50**), the two names would be credited to Burton 1934. Hypothetically, two other possibilities are possible. Shen and Liu (1978 [ref. 13598]) gave a description of *Apolomichthys*, attributed the name to Fraser-Brunner (1933), and illegally designated a type. Had Burton not made the name available in 1934, the genus would be cited as *Apolemichthys* Shen and Liu (ex Fraser-Brunner) 1978. If Shen and Liu had quoted the description from Fraser-Brunner, then I would regard the authorship as Fraser-Brunner in Shen and Liu 1978. These names can cause considerable instability, since a more thorough search might locate an earlier qualifying author, so that the authorship and date would change again. [In my opinion, a strong argument can be made that in the interests of stability, most if not all fish generic names with (currently unrecognized) later authorships resulting from strict application of Article 13b should be examined with the intent to submit all of them to the ICZN to validate them to their original authorship and date.]

A more complicated case involves the genus-group name *Pyrenophorus*. This name was described as a new subgenus of the genus *Chirolophius* by Le Danois 1974, but Le Danois included more than one species and did not designate a type. The name was referenced in Zoological Record for 1975 (Pisces, p. 509, published in 1980) and the type given as *Chirolophius caulinaris* Garman. The name could date to and be authored by the person compiling the Zoological Record, but authorship of the Pisces section is given as "Pisces compiled by the staff of the Zoological Society of London." Over forty persons are listed on the cover as the Zoological Record Staff employed during the compilation of volume 112. We therefore have a subgenus name with over forty authors or we have anonymous authorship. I regard authorship as anonymous; but if the authorship is anonymous (after 1950) then the name is not available (**Art. 14**). Pietsch et al. 1986:133 [ref. 6339] mention the name, treat is as valid on p. 135, provide a citation to the description by Le Danois, and state, "Espèce-type: *Chirolophius kempi* Norman, 1935, désigneée ici." Although Pietsch et al. attribute authorship to Le Danois, technically the correct authorship and date for this name is Pietsch, Bauchot and Desoutter, 1986 (unless the Commission is asked to establish authorship as Le Danois, 1974, or someone finds an earlier available treatment).

The subgenus *Parasalmo* appearing first in Vladykov (1963) was intentionally made available by Vladykov and Gruchy (1972), but in most cases ichthyologists apparently are unaware of **Article 13b**.

The care needed in analyzing the included species is shown by the genus *Lycozoarces*. This name appeared first in Popov 1933 without description and with one species *regani* as name only [neither name available]. Then *Lycozoarces* appeared in Popov 1935 with the species *hubbsi* described and the species *regani* included. Because neither species was designated type, it would appear that *Lycozoarces* would be unavailable (**Article 13b**—two included species after 1930, neither designated type), but the species name *regani* was still a nomen nudum and therefore unavailable; consequently there was only one **available** included species and this is type by monotypy (and the genus name is available from 1935).

There is a second, much smaller category of post-1930 genus-group names that are unavailable on the basis of **Article 13b**. For these names (which are not replacement names) a description of a genus is given but no species is mentioned by name. The description of the new taxon satisfies **Article 13a**, but if no species were mentioned, no fixation of a type species can occur by original designation or by indication; type designation would have to be subsequent to the original description of the genus. This differs from a bare name only (nomen nudum) that is unavailable. (A genus proposed with a description before 1931, but with no included species, is available so long as one or more nominal species were subsequently and expressly included in it [**Art. 69a(i)(1)**]).

If after 1930, the combined description of a new genus and new species [**Art. 13b**], if marked by "n. g., n. sp.," or an equivalent expression, is deemed to confer availability on each name; the type species is fixed by monotypy [**Art. 13c**] if it is not otherwise designated.

The genus and species *Tobinia paragaudata*, which appeared in a figure caption in Whitley (1933:47 [ref. 6595]) with a short combined description, does not meet the requirements of **Article 13c**; after 1930 it is unavailable from this reference.

The combined description of *Parupygus savannensis* by Hoedeman (1962:58 [ref. 13556]) made available both the genus and the species (with type by monotypy) by use of the expressions: n. gen. et sp., gen. et sp. nov., and new genus and species [**Art. 13c**].

On the other hand, Werner and Stawikowski (1987 [ref. 13432] described the new genus *Paratheraps* for *P. breidohri* "gen. nov., spec. nov." They also included the species *P. hartwegi* (Taylor and Miller 1980). Does this establish a type species?

The first part of **Art. 13c** states, "The combined description or definition of a new nominal genus and a single included new nominal species, if marked by..." What does the expression "single included new nominal species" mean? In the example of *Paratheraps*, the new taxon contains a single new nominal species (it also contains a second species that is not new). I interpret the Article to mean that there must be only one included species and it must be a new species (along with use of the appropriate expression). So, *Paratheraps* cannot date to 1987 but can date to the same authors in 1989 [ref. 14232] where a type was designated.

A combined description of a new family-group taxon and a single new genus [**Art. 13d**] (of which the genus name provides the basis for the new family-group name) if made after 1930, is deemed to confer availability on each name. The Code recommends [**13B**] that each new taxon be defined individually. Apparently no examples are found in Recent fishes.

Before 1931 the rules were more liberal, but after 1930 a name proposed only by an indication is not available [**Art. 13e**] for four of the eight conditions in **Article 12b**: A name is not made available by its inclusion in an index that is not consistently binominal, by the formation of a family-group name from the stem of a generic name, by the proposal of a new genus-group name or species-group name only in association with a previous illustration, or by the description of the work of an extant animal.

Whitley 1935 [ref. 4686] illustrated representatives of galaxiid genera on his Plate 3, including new generic names (*Lurogalaxias*, *Nesogalaxias*, and *Querigalaxias*), but he gave no description and mentioned no species. Before 1931, these names would have been available [**Art. 12b(7)**], but by being published after 1930 they are unavailable because they did not meet the more restrictive conditions of **Article 13e**.

In earlier times, anonymous authorship was acceptable for making a new taxon available, but after 1950 any new name or nomenclatural act published anonymously is not thereby available [**Art. 14**].

In earlier literature, authors sometimes proposed conditional names and these are available [**Art. 15**], but after 1960 any name proposed conditionally is not thereby available.

Some fish genera were proposed after 1960 with qualifying words that perhaps made them conditional proposals. For example, Rapp Py-Daniel in 1989 [ref. 13470] proposed two new genera and stated (p. 235) that they were "herein preliminary (sic) established," and in his title as "preliminary establishment of two new genera." Does this fall under conditional proposal? Without further clarification, I accept Rapp Py-Daniel's new genera as available. (It would appear in these cases that authors felt that their new genera were valid—and that they intended them to be used that way—but they simply did not do a thorough study, and their descriptions are imperfect.) I do not know of any later author who rejected a generic name in fishes because it was conditionally proposed after 1960.

On the other hand, a clear case of an unavailable name proposed conditionally after 1960 is that of *Igborichthys* Clausen (1959 [ref. 842]), suggested as an alternate name in the event his new genus *Denticeps* was found to be a homonym. [This alternate name is unavailable for another reason; it was first published in synonymy and not made available before 1961]. The genus *Teratichthys* Giglioli 1882 was published as an alternate name for *Paradoxichthys* "should that term be pre-occupied." This name is treated as a name published in synonymy.

Names found to denote more than one taxon are still available, as are names based on parts of animals, or on hybrids [**Art. 17**]. Nearly all the genus-group names included in the Catalog are based on species represented by whole specimens or drawings of whole specimens, but a few are based on parts (e.g., a dried skin). Many fossil genera on the other hand are based on incomplete material, such as a tooth or teeth, scales, or otoliths, or fragments of the skeleton. Hybrids are fairly rare in fishes, but there are genus-group names and species-group names based on hybrids. Most of these names are available, because the author did not know that they were based on a hybrid; but if the author knew it was a hybrid, the generic name is not available [**Art. 1b(3)**]. (For a species-group name established for an animal later found to be a hybrid, the name must not be used as the valid name for it or the parental species, but the name enters homonymy.)

Article 18 states that the "availability of a name is not affected by inappropriateness or tautonymy." But this was not true in earlier times, and many unneeded genus-group names were created in the 1800s because they were proposed as substitute names by an author who felt that the original name was inappropriate. The "permission" to do this comes from the 1842 code (p. 113):

"Our next proposition has no other claim for adoption than that of being a concession to human infirmity.... The attention is consequently liable in scientific studies to be diverted from the contemplation of the thing signified to the etymological meaning of the sign, and hence it is necessary to provide that the latter shall not be such as to propagate actual error.... But when we find a Batrachian reptile named in violation of its true affinities, *Mastodonsaurus*..., we feel justified in cancelling these names, and adopting that synonym which stands next in point of date. At the same time we think it right to remark that this privilege is very liable to abuse, and ought therefore to be applied only to extreme cases with great caution. With these limitations we may concede that

"§ 11. A name may be changed when it implies a false proposition which is likely to propagate important errors."

In fishes many (hundreds) unneeded replacement names were provided by such important authors as Agassiz, Rafinesque, Swainson, Günther, and Gill (also by Gistel). Their reasons were many: a name was felt to be barbarous, improperly formed, inappropriate with regard to characters of the taxon, etc. *Limnurgus* Günther 1866 was proposed to replace the "barbarous" *Girardinichthys* Bleeker 1860 [Günther and others felt that any genus name referring to a person was inappropriate]. In the Catalog we usually do not give the reason (such as presumed inappropriateness) for these replacement names, referring to them as "unneeded replacement for ..." without elaboration.

Article 19 concerns emendations, incorrect spellings, and mandatory changes. These are defined and treated in more detail later. For purposes of completeness under the heading "availability," we need to recognize only that an emendation (whether justified or unjustified) is an available name, but an incorrect original or subsequent spelling is not. A *corrected* original spelling [**Art. 19(i)**] is available and the author and date are as proposed incorrectly in the first instance; these are "technical" corrections. When an author spells the name in more than one way in the original description, a first reviser selects one of the spellings, so that any other spelling is an incorrect original spelling and unavailable. Mandatory changes do not affect availability of the name as first proposed.

Date of Publication (Articles 21–22)

A cornerstone of zoological nomenclature is date priority of names. If two available names are found to apply to the same taxon, the oldest name is the one used and the younger one is only a duplicate or junior synonym of the older name. This was recognized in the 1842 code (p. 109); a rather lengthy argument for the need for priority ended as follows:

"Now in zoology no one person can subsequently claim an authority equal to that possessed by the person who is the first to define a new genus or describe a new species; and hence it is that the name originally given, even though it may be inferior in point of elegance or expressiveness to those subsequently proposed, ought as a general principle to be permanently retained. To this consideration we ought to add the injustice of erasing the name originally selected by the person to whose labours we owe our first knowledge of the object...

"For these reasons, we have no hesitation in adopting as our fundamental maxim, the 'law of priority,' viz.

"§ 1. The name originally given by the founder of a group or the describer of a species should be permanently retained, to the exclusion of all subsequent synonyms (with the exceptions about to be noticed)."

The Code provides for setting aside priority under certain conditions (discussed later). Preparation of the Catalog did uncover some nomenclatural acts that might upset stability, particularly earlier type designations of species not currently regarded as the type; and remarks are provided in Part I of the Catalog where strict application of priority might upset current usage.

The date of a nomenclatural act is therefore very important. It is desirable to know the precise day on which the work was "in existence" (and available), as this would solve problems of priority about date of publication. But often the day or month of publication cannot be determined, or the year appearing on a work is wrong.

When it is impossible to determine, for example, which of two works was published first, the ICZN can be asked to select one over the other. In the ichthyological literature there continue to be problems about the dates of some works.

Except for Linnaeus' *Systema Naturae* and Clerck's *Aranei Svecici* of 1758, the date to be adopted is the date of publication [**Art. 21a**]. Normally a work has a date associated with it (usually a year), and this date is to be assumed to be correct in the absence of evidence to the contrary [**Art. 21b**]. Also, in the absence of information to the contrary, if month and year are given, but not a day, it is assumed that the work was published on the last day of the month [**Art. 21c (i)**], and if only a year is given it is assumed that it was published on the last day of the year given [**Art. 21c (ii)**]. If a date is found to be incorrect, the earliest day on which the work is demonstrated to be in existence as a published work is to be adopted [**Art. 21d**]. If parts of a work were published on different days, the date of publication of each part is to be separately determined [**Art. 21e**]. If the date of publication is given as a range of dates, the work is to be dated from the final day of the range, unless there is evidence to the contrary [**Art. 21f**]. If the date is not specified, the earliest day on which the work is demonstrated to have been in existence is to be adopted as the date of publication [**Art. 21g**]. Reprints or separates are sometimes provided to the author in advance of publication, and if it can be shown that the separates were distributed earlier, the date of that distribution is the publication date. The Code contains a number of recommendations to authors, editors, and librarians having to do with establishing, preserving, or correcting the date of publication. A discussion and examples follow.

Most scientific papers on systematics are published in journals or series associated with scientific societies or natural history museums, and most now are affixed with a precise date of publication—often with a day, month, and year, or with a month and year; sometimes dates for individual issues are given in the last issue for a year or in the following year. In reality, however, a systematist must question the publication date of each work (especially early works), and attempt to determine the most precise date possible. To solve particular priority problems, systematists may spend an inordinate amount of time researching the date of two or a few publications. In the Literature Cited section (Part

III), a month and day of publication are provided when available [much more work can be done on this subject]; often ichthyologists who spend considerable time researching a date state their conclusion in one paragraph buried in the body of the article.

Dates of publication may be determined in a number of ways; some examples may be helpful. In many early scientific societies, papers were read at meetings first, but published sometime later, and a common mistake is to interpret the date on which a paper was read as the publication date.

A second common wrong assumption is that all of a volume for a given year was published in that year. Frequently a journal has quarterly "parts" or issues; not infrequently, however, the last issue for a year is not published by the end of the year, but appears early in the succeeding year (carrying the date of the previous year on the cover).

Some journals periodically publish information on dates of publication, such as the U.S. National Museum Bulletin 193 (1947), which treats all U.S. National Museum publications through 1946. Each year, the annual report of the Smithsonian Institution includes dates of publication for articles published in that year by the Smithsonian. A number of important articles on dates of early works have been published in the Journal for the Bibliography of Natural History, and others have been published separately (e.g., Hays 1952 [ref. 9281] on Jordan). In the Literature Cited (Part III), one may find many of these date sources listed in brackets with individual references.

Methods useful in determining dates of publication include determining the date of receipt by organizations or libraries, searching information provided in abstracting services, finding bibliographies of individuals (often unpublished ones), and even searching records to find invoices or other evidence that will indicate approximately when the work was printed (and, it is to be hoped, distributed). For the Catalog the examination of the published activities of meetings of the Philadelphia Academy of Natural Sciences firmed up some dates of publication in the mid 1800s (especially through letters of acknowledgment of receipt by other organizations). Sometimes the examination of old works in natural history museums reveals dates added by hand and initialed by the original author, or receipt date notations are affixed to works.

VALIDITY OF TAXONOMIC NAMES (ARTICLE 23)

Validity differs from availability in that the latter refers to the legitimacy of the name for use in nomenclature, whereas validity involves taxonomic decisions on limits of taxa. Validity refers to the "rights" of a name in relation to homonyms and synonyms (Mayr 1969:349).

As an example, if Jones reviews a family and concludes that there are two genera (*Alpha* and *Beta*), each with two species, one says that he recognizes two valid genera (assuming that both names are technically available). If one further assumes that a second worker, Smith, later reviews the family and states that in his opinion all four species should be placed in one genus, his opinion involving relationships of the species and particularly the limits of genera differs from that of Jones (these are taxonomic decisions and not nomenclatural considerations). *Alpha* and *Beta* are synonyms in Smith's opinion, and one has "rights" over the other. In this case, if *Alpha* is the oldest name, it would be the valid name and *Beta* would be a junior subjective synonym of it.

First and foremost, the valid name for a taxon is the oldest available name applied to it [**Art. 23**], unless there is some other reason to invalidate the name. This "Principle of Priority" promotes stability, although there are some circumstances that warrant setting aside priority in determining the name to use for a taxon [**Art. 23b**]. **Article 23b** specifically deals with "unused" senior synonyms—most frequently involving the discovery of an old name not in current use that predates a younger synonymous name in common use. In these cases, the worker is to continue current usage and refer the case to the ICZN for a ruling [**Art. 79c**]. To be rejected by the ICZN, the unused name must meet certain criteria, and it must be shown that the use of the older name would disturb stability or universality, or cause confusion.

Article 23b has had a checkered history (see Declaration 43, Appendix B), but the major difference is that in the 1961 code a statute of limitations could be used, so that a forgotten name (nomen oblitum) was not to be used, but in the 1985 Code there is no statute of limitations and the ICZN is asked to make a ruling if the use of the old name would upset stability or cause confusion. In actual practice, in some poorly known fish groups, the use of a forgotten name generally causes no instability, and ichthyologists seem to adopt the old name rather quickly. For genera of Recent fishes, the few names in which **Article 23b** and **79c** might come into play are identified in Part I of the Catalog.

Priority is not affected by change in rank or any mandatory change in spelling that accompanies such a change in rank [**Art. 23c**]; for example, a taxon first described as a subgenus but later treated as a full genus retains the original date (and authorship) of publication as a subgenus.

If a supposedly valid name is found to be invalid or unavailable, it must be replaced with the next oldest name from among the contained taxa, of if there is not another available name for the taxon, a new name needs to be provided [**Art. 23e**].

Priority involving species-group names is addressed in **Articles 23f–g**, but **23g** includes exceptions involving genus-group names. A name established expressly for a collective group [an assemblage of species that cannot be placed with certainty in known genera] does not compete in priority with other genus-group names, and a name first established for a nominal genus-group taxon but later brought into use for a collective group no longer competes in priority with other genus-group names.... And a name established for an ichnotaxon does not compete in priority with one established for an animal, even for one that may have formed the ichnotaxon.

Changes in spelling of a name also do not change the fact that priority begins with the first proposal, but an unjustified emendation (an intentional change in a spelling that is not a mandatory change) has its own author and date—like a second taxon for the taxon that the author felt needed emending.

Priority is not affected by the placement of a name into or out of synonymy [**Art. 23(l)**]. In other words, once an authorship and date are established for a taxon, they remain fixed.

A valid name for a taxon cannot be rejected, even by the author of the taxon, for any reason such as inappropriateness or tautonymy [**Art. 23m**]. It remains available and under rules of priority. This was not true in the 1842 code.

PRINCIPLE OF THE FIRST REVISER (ARTICLE 24)

This concept covers situations where (1) the original author spelled a new taxon in more than one way, (2) two or more names of identical date are found to represent the same taxon and the question arises as to which of the two names should take precedence, and (3) there are two or more competing nomenclatural acts of the same date. Relative precedence is determined by the first reviser, and the first reviser is the one who recognizes the problem, mentions both names or nomenclatural acts, and selects one over the other. (Exceptions are [**Art. 56d**] two homonymous genus-group names of the same date where one was proposed for a genus (takes precedence) and one for a subgenus, and [**Art. 57g**] the same for species-group names when one was proposed for a species and the other for a subspecies.) This concept is best illustrated with examples.

For multiple original spellings, one must look closely for any published corrections (e.g., a corrigendum accompanying the work), and one must use judgment in looking for obvious misspellings. When two works are involved, it may be possible to determine more precise dates of publication that will resolve the problem.

When *Synanceia* was described by Bloch and Schneider (1801 [ref. 471]), on p. xxxvii it was spelled *Synanceia* and in the main text account (p. 194) as *Synanceja*, and on Pl. 45 as *Synanceia*, but in the published "Corrigenda" (p. 573) it is stated *"scr. [scribe] *Synanceia*"; in this case no first reviser is needed, although Briggs (1961 [ref. 13439]) overlooked the corrigenda and viewed himself as the first reviser.

If an author in the original description of a new genus-group name spells the name one way many times and a second way only once, a logical conclusion is that the unique spelling was a mistake, such as a typesetting error; I do not consider these cases as publication with two original spellings (and no first reviser is needed to make a selection). In Part I of the Catalog these are treated as misspellings, such as "misspelled once on p. 23 as ...." On the other hand, when an author mentions a new name only once, it is more difficult to determine typographical errors. For example, Parr (1951:8 [ref. 3380]) described the new genus *Brunichthys* in a key, and mentioned it only once. Later (1952: 255 [ref. 3381]) he mentioned the name only once and spelled it *Bruunichthys* without comment. One could assume from his second use that he named the genus after Anton Bruun and that the correct spelling should be *Bruunichthys*, but the Code does not accommodate corrections in these situations. Springer (1979:102 [ref. 4175]) described the subgenus *Campagnoia* (using that spelling twice), presumably for Leonard J. V. Compagno (which Springer spelled correctly on p. 99 and in his Literature Cited), but the derivation of the name was not given; the original spelling *Campagnoia* must stand, and might well have been the intent of the original author. The genus *Parabarossia* Kotthaus (1976:59 [ref. 2672]) was formed from the name *Barrossia* Smith, 1952 (with two r's); the spelling *Parabarossia* (with one r) is the correct original spelling. It is not in the purview of later authors to guess the intent of the original author.

A particularly problematic work in fishes is Swainson 1838–39 [refs. 4302, 4303], where he used one name in one section and another name in a later section; in addition, the work apparently suffered from poor editing or typesetting. Most of the problems have been solved and are mentioned under individual genera in Part I of the Catalog.

Another general condition is that where two taxa described on the same date are later considered to be synonymous. This may involve two taxa in one work, or two taxa in different works of the same date. When someone later treats the two taxa as synonyms, a first reviser is needed to select one name over the other [page precedence does not establish priority for two taxa appearing in one work].

Another instance needing a first reviser is the finding that two names of the same date are found to be homonyms (discussed later under Homonymy).

The last example involves nomenclatural acts other than new taxa. For example, a genus may not have a type species, and if two subsequent workers on the same date both select a different type species, then the first reviser serves to remove this conflict, the type species being the one the first reviser picks.

But there is another consideration involving first revisers that causes confusion and instability. Workers may accept one "first reviser" as solving the problem, but then someone finds an earlier first reviser. In these cases the earlier first reviser takes precedence (unless stability is so upset that the ICZN can be asked to intervene).

Action of first reviser should be based on what will best serve the stability and universality of nomenclature [Recommendation 24A].

Formation and Treatment of Names (Articles 25–34)

This subject is highly technical and difficult for current workers not schooled in classical languages. Chapter VII of the Code addresses these issues. Some considerations were previously discussed under "availability" (above), and the Code provides appendices to help scientists in the formation of names.

Most scientific names, particularly in earlier years, were taken from Greek and Latin words, written in Latin. If the spelling of a scientific name is the same as a Greek or Latin word, that name is to be treated as that word unless the author states otherwise when making the name available [**Art. 26**]. Some species names are compound words (two or more words joined together), and the above also applies to the last word in the compound. It is suggested (Recommendation 25B) that in forming a new scientific name, an author state its derivation because this is important for determining gender, determining the spelling of the family-group name based on the genus, etc.

Article 27 dictates that no diacritic mark, apostrophe, or dieresis is to be used in a scientific name; and a hyphen can be used in only one instance.

For example, a genus of basses was described as *Perca-Labrax*, and that genus is now to be written *Percalabrax*." The only time a hyphen can be used (and only for species) is when the first name of a compound species name is a Latin letter used to denote a character of a compound. The fish species *y-gricius* retains the hyphen. In the Catalog, we give genera and species in their corrected form, but often with amplifying remarks.

A family group name or genus-group name is to be printed with an initial capital letter and a species-group name with a lowercase letter [**Art. 28**]. If a species-group name was originally spelled with a capital letter (as many were in the early literature), this is to be corrected. To avoid any confusion between a genus and species name, the Code recommends [28A] that a species-group name should not begin a sentence (to avoid a capital first letter). When we cite type species in the Catalog we use lower case for the specific name regardless of how it was printed originally.

The gender of genus-group names is discussed in **Article 30**;

this subject is important in that species names under usual circumstances must agree in gender with the genus. (a) A genus-group name that is or ends in a Greek or Latin word takes the gender given for that word in standard Greek or Latin dictionaries, unless the ICZN rules otherwise. Numerous examples given in **Article 30** serve to fix the gender of a number of suffixes. But some words are variable in gender. The Code specifies that a genus-group name that is a noun or ends in a noun of variable gender is to be treated as masculine [**Art. 30a**], unless the author when establishing the genus-group name states that it is feminine or treats it as feminine (as judged by the combination with the species). A genus-group name ending in *-ops* (a common ending in fish genera) is to be treated as masculine. A genus-group name that ends in a latinized Greek word takes the gender normally appropriate to the Latin termination. A genus-group name that is or ends in a Latin word whose termination has been changed takes the gender normally appropriate to the new termination.

The following were typical steps used to determine the gender of a genus. Did the author give the derivation (usually not given in ichthyological literature until recent years)? If not, is the suffix a standard one, such is *-ichthys*? Does it have an ending addressed by the ICZN, especially in **Art. 30**? If gender is not given, how does the author treat included species, especially adjectival ones? In Part I of the Catalog we provide gender for most generic names.

A genus-group name ending in a Greek or Latin suffix, or in a letter or letters identical with such a suffix, takes the gender appropriate to its ending. Patronyms named after a man but with a feminine suffix (e.g., *–ia*, *–ella*) require that the genus be feminine (if the genus is named after a man, with a feminine ending, it does not matter that the man is ipso facto masculine).

Jeboehlkia was named for James E. Böhlke and stated by the author to be masculine, but the genus is feminine.

A genus-group name that reproduces exactly a noun in a modern Indo-European language having genders takes the gender of that noun.

Finally, genus-group names that are not Greek, Latin, or modern Indo-European [**Art. 30d**] take the gender attributed to them by the author (or implied by the gender of species associated with it when proposed), but if the gender cannot be determined, the word is to be considered masculine, except if the ending is clearly a natural Latin feminine or neuter one; the gender then is the one appropriate to the ending. In the genera accounts in Part I of the Catalog, we amplify genders with remarks as needed.

The formation and treatment of species-group names involve complicated issues, which are treated in **Articles 31–32**. Only a few items are relevant in the treatment of species names in the Catalog. First, we provide the original spelling of the species, except where mandatory changes are required. A major area of confusion at the present time involves species-group names formed from personal names [**Art. 31a**]. Typically [**Art. 31a (ii)**], a species-group name based on a person's name is the name plus one *i* (noun in the genitive case) if after a man and name plus *ae* if after a woman. A species named for a Mr. Smith would be *smithi* and after a Miss Smith would be *smithae*. Less used is name plus *orum* if of men or of man (men) and woman (women) together and name plus *arum* if of women. In early literature, names based on a man were often spelled with his name plus two i's (e.g. *smithii*). In these cases, it means the author latinized the name first and then correctly modified the name with a terminal *i*: cuvier = cuvierius = *cuvierii*. Bailey and Robins (1988 [ref. 6610]) discussed this issue in detail, and provided examples from fishes for several subsections of **Article 31**.

However, Bailey and Robins raised one subject of controversy, which involves the double *ii* ending of species-group patronyms. Bailey and Robins argued that the way the Code is written requires that patronyms ending in *ii* be corrected to one *i* unless the stem of the name ended in i (e.g., *bellotti* becomes *bellottii*). Their argument is complicated and involves the interaction of two articles and several subsections of the Code, but see Tubbs 1988 [ref. 13352]. **Article 31a(i)** seems very clear: "A species-group name, if a noun in the genitive case formed from a personal name that is Latin, or from a modern personal name that is or has been latinized, is to be formed in accordance with the rules of Latin grammar." Obviously, early authors latinized the names—that is how they came to use an *ii* termination. An author under the Code was free to latinize the name to *cuvierius* and correctly use the name *cuvierii*. This seems to conflict with **Article 31a(ii)**, "A species-group name, if a noun in the genitive case formed directly from a modern personal name is to be formed by adding to the stem of that name *-i* if the personal name is that of a man...." I believe the key word is "directly," i.e., without previous latinization. Often, especially until recent years, authors did not indicate who they were naming the species after; this places a later worker in the position of having to guess for whom the species was named, and to surmise the process of latinization that the author did or did not go through in forming the ending. "Guesswork" is contrary to the operation of the Code; and it would appear to be contrary to **Article 32a**, which states that the original spelling of a name is to be preserved unaltered unless it is "demonstrably incorrect." How is it possible to demonstrate that the author did not latinize the name first? Without going into more detail, suffice it to say that the ICZN must address this problem, one that perhaps results from poor editing or writing of this section of the Code or obvious confusion among the Commissioners. The evidence from the expression "directly from" in **Article 31a(ii)** and the fact that a name may be latinized first [**Art. 31a(i)**] and if so "is to be formed in accordance with the rules of Latin grammar" indicate to me that Bailey and Robins incorrectly interpreted this section of the Code. [Also in legal matters (I am told), if a specific issue is addressed (e.g., **Art. 31a(i)**), it normally takes precedence over a more general treatment, such as tying together **Article 31a(iii)** and **Article 32c(i)**.] In Part I of the Catalog, these species names are spelled as originally proposed.

A second item involving spelling of species-group names used in the Catalog involves **Articles 31b** and **32d(ii)**. A species-group name (if it is a Latin adjective or participle in the nominative singular, or is latinized) must agree in gender with the generic name with which it is at any time combined, and its termination must be changed according to Latin inflection. In other words, if a species-group name is an adjective and is first described in a masculine genus, the species name will be, for example, *marmoratus*. If this species is then classified in a feminine genus, the name changes to *marmorata*, and if it is put into a neuter genus, the name becomes *marmoratum*. If the species-group name is not a Latin or latinized word, it is to be treated as undeclinable and the original spelling is to be preserved regardless of the gender of the genus. In the Catalog, if an author used the wrong termination for a species (not counting the *i* or *ii* discussed above) on the basis of wrong interpretation of gender, we have made that correction. We have also made, usually without comment, corrections in the spelling of species names that are mandatory; this involves such items as beginning the species name with a lowercase letter [**Art. 5**]; removing of a diacritic mark, apostrophe, diaeresis, or hyphen; and making other mandatory changes in species-group names required by the Code [see **Art. 32c(vi), 32d(i), 32c(ii), 32c(iii), 31d(iii), 34(b)**].

It has been suggested, for example, that genders of species moved to taxa of different genders should not be declined, or that all generic names should be treated as masculine. With computerization, each new combination of genus and species spelling is another "species" insofar as a computer is concerned; this outdated convention of having genders of adjectival species agree with the gender of the genus causes confusion and prevents the effective maintenance of computerized information about taxa. In my opinion, serious consideration should be given to the retention of the original spelling for all species-group names (except for mandatory changes), regardless of the gender of the genera in which they may later be placed.

Article 32 involves original spelling of names, and consists mostly of restatements of subjects treated elsewhere in the Code. The following portions of this article affect genera. The original spelling is that used in the work in which the name was established [**Art. 32a**]. If the name was spelled in more than one way originally, the "correct original spelling" is the one chosen by the first reviser [**Art. 24c**]. The "correct original spelling" is to be preserved unaltered unless it is demonstrably incorrect (as provided for in **Article 32c**). Among genera, demonstrably incorrect spellings involve (a) diacritic and other marks [**Art. 27**], (b) names not starting with a capital letter [**Art. 28**], or (c) gender problems [**Art. 30**]. These are mandatory corrections, are normally clear-cut, and have been made in Part I of the Catalog.

However, there is a separate category of incorrect original spellings [**Art. 32c(ii)**] that causes confusion and sometimes poses problems of interpretation. If, in the original publication (without considering other works, dictionaries, or other sources of information), there is clear evidence of an inadvertent error, such as a copyist's or printer's error, the name is considered an incorrect original spelling. The error must have been unintentional or inadvertent (incorrect transliteration or latinization are not considered inadvertent errors).

The following example serves to illustrate the finer points between an inadvertent error, an intentional act, and an error in transliteration. Gill 1862 [ref. 1659] described two genera, *Orycnopsis* and *Grammatorycnus*, and mentioned the genus name *"Orycnus"* of Cuvier. Cuvier spelled the genus as *Orcynus*. Based on the original work, it is clear that Gill intended the spelling to be "orycnus" and that it was not an inadvertent error that arose in printing, for example. If Gill incorrectly transliterated the name, that does not make the original spelling incorrect. In the absence of action by the ICZN, strict interpretation of the Code requires that the "oryc" spellings be used for Gill's names.

An incorrect original spelling is to be corrected [**Art. 32d**]. In its original form, the name has no separate availability and cannot (in that original form) enter into homonymy or be used as a replacement name. A name published with a diacritic mark, apostrophe, diaeresis, or hyphen, or a species-group name published as separate words of which any is an abbreviation, is to be corrected.

The German umlaut is a special case. If in a name published before 1985, the umlaut is deleted and an "e" is inserted after the vowel, and if there is any doubt that the name is based on a German word, it is to be so treated. The following are examples: ***güntheri*** to ***guentheri***, ***rüppelli*** to ***rueppelli***. When the word is of German origin and the umlaut normally would have been used but the author did not use it, the change would not be made. Unfortunately, this procedure often yields two spellings for different species named after the same person (e.g., ***guentheri*** and ***guntheri***).

Subsequent spellings are treated in **Article 33**. In ichthyology, this subject is one of the most confused because many workers fail to make the proper distinctions between justified emendations and incorrect subsequent spellings. A subsequent spelling of a name (differing from the original spelling) is one of the following: (1) an emendation, (2) an incorrect subsequent spelling, or (3) a mandatory change. Each has different nomenclatural consequences, and distinguishing between them is important.

An emendation is a "demonstrably intentional change" other than a mandatory change. The key to understanding the difference between an emendation and an incorrect subsequent spelling hinges on the phrase "demonstrably intentional change." **Article 33b(i)** states that "A change in the original spelling of a name may only be interpreted as 'demonstrably intentional' when in the work itself, or in an author's (or publisher's) corrigenda [in the same work], the original and the changed spelling are cited and the latter is adopted in place of the former, or when two or more names in the same work are treated in a similar way."

The latter half of the 1800s was a period when many unjustified emendations were introduced in fishes, and these resulted from the proposition in the 1842 code (p. 114) that "Latin orthography [is] to be adhered to." (In addition, other modifications in names were based on the 1842 code in which, "Names not clearly defined may be changed" and "A name whose meaning is glaringly false may be changed.") For example, Günther in his monumental *Catalogue of the Fishes in the British Museum* (1859–1870) introduced many such names, most seemingly with the intent of correcting improper latinization. If Günther spelled the genus (or species) in the main heading one way but included the original spelling (which one assumes he regarded as not properly latinized or in some cases inappropriate) in synonymy, then I regard this as evidence that the change was intentional and therefore an emendation.

Gill (in many works, circa 1860–65) made similar changes in spelling, as did Agassiz in his *Nomenclatoris Zoologici* [refs. 64, 4889].

Frequently one does not know if a change was intentional—even though it probably was but cannot be demonstrated. Rafinesque and Swainson, for example, both created apparent shortened versions of existing genera.

A problem often involves deciding if a name was proposed technically as a replacement name, or was merely an unjustified emendation, or was an incorrect subsequent spelling.

Kaup 1858 [ref. 2580] changed the spelling *Peristedion* Lacepède to *Peristethus* because he felt that Lacepède's name was wrongly formed. I regard these as replacement names. Fortunately, nomenclaturally, there are no significant differences between unjustified emendations and replacement names.

Demonstrably intentional changes are either (1) justified emendations or (2) unjustified emendations. A justified emendation is the correction of an incorrect original spelling in accordance with **Article 32d** (discussed above). The corrected name retains the author of the original spelling. One might confuse the correction of incorrect original spellings with mandatory changes; the Code distinguishes between them. Mandatory changes are only two. The first involves family-group names, the suffix of which must be changed when there is a change in rank from family to subfamily or vice versa [standard endings for superfamily and tribe are recommended (29A) but not required]. The second involves species-group names: the termination of a Latin or latinized adjectival or participial species-group name "must agree in gender with the generic name with which it is at any time combined" [**Art. 31b**]. If the termination is incorrect it must be changed. For both mandatory changes, the author and date remain unchanged, being attributed to the original author and date.

If a change was not a mandatory one, and it was not a justified emendation (a needed correction), it is an unjustified emendation as long as it was a demonstrably intentional change.

It is important to note that a justified emendation retains the original authorship and date; it is as if a later author were making a needed change in the original spelling, but he or she does not receive authorship for such action. The original incorrect spelling (the word as such) has no standing. On the other hand, unjustified emendations are available with their own author and date (as if the later author described another new taxon). To complicate matters further, an incorrect subsequent spelling is not available and has no standing.

If a change in spelling from the original is not one of the two mandatory changes or is not an intentional emendation, it is an incorrect subsequent spelling. In the current literature in ichthyology, many workers are not making the correct distinction between justified and unjustified emendations and incorrect subsequent spellings.

The new fish genus name *Cheimarrichthys* was published by Haast 1874, and evidently later in 1874 Sauvage published the new fish genus name with the nearly identical spelling *Chimarrichthys* in another family. Regan 1907 proposed the replacement name *Euchiloglanis* for Sauvage's genus (p. 158): "For one of these I revived the name *Chimarrhichthys* [sic], Sauv. 1874, but as was pointed out by O'Shaughnessy (Zool. Record, 1874) this is preoccupied, and I therefore propose to substitute for it the new generic name *Euchiloglanis*." Haast's name has priority and the genera are spelled differently, so there is no preoccupation, and Sauvage's name is also available for use. But there can be preoccupation if Haast's name was unjustifiably emended, so that the emended name was spelled exactly like Sauvage's spelling. One must remember that an unjustified emendation takes the date and authorship of the person making the emendation, and enters into homonymy. O'Shaughnessy, in Zoological Record for 1874, recorded (p. 95) "*Cheimarrichthys* [*Chi-*], g. n." of Haast and (p. 104) for Sauvage, "*Chimarrichthys* [//, Haast, suprà Trachinidae]...." In this way, O'Shaughnessy indicated that Haast's name should be emended as *Chi-* rather than *Chei-*; perhaps technically it is not an emendation since he did not use it in a valid sense, but the point here is that one must look for emendations that might cause preoccupation. But because both genera were proposed in 1874, the emendation would have had to have been made after the publication of Haast's name and before the publication of Sauvage's name. Since Zoological Record for the year 1874 was published after 1874, and no other emendations matching Sauvage's spelling are found during 1874, Sauvage's name *Chimarrichthys* is available (and should replace *Euchiloglanis* in current literature). The availability of Sauvage's name is not affected by later emendations of Haast's name to the same spelling as Sauvage's spelling, since an unjustified emendation has its own date and author.

A family-group name based on an unjustified emendation of a generic name is an unjustified original spelling and must be corrected [**Art. 35d(ii)**], but if an unjustifiably emended genus name becomes a valid replacement name because the original name could not be used, the family-group name changes to agree with the stem of the replacement name [**Art. 39a**]. The aim of the Code is to make it impossible for a family of fishes, for example, to have the same name as a family of birds.

The genus *Phosichthys* was described by Hutton in 1872, but in 1873 Hutton emended the spelling to *Photichthys* at the suggestion of Dr. Günther; the family name Photichthyidae is in current use. The correct family name should be Phosichthyidae. Clearly there is no evidence to suggest an inadvertent error when the genus was proposed. [Note that **Article 39a** provides that if *Phosichthys* were preoccupied, *Photichthys* and Photichthyidae could be used.]

A further problem involves misidentified type genera and overlooked type fixations; these cases are to be referred to the ICZN for a ruling [**Art. 41**].

GENUS-GROUP TAXA AND NAMES (ARTICLES 42–44).

In general, information treated in other articles is restated here. Genus-group names are subject to the same provisions and recommendations of the Code, except those that apply explicitly to names at only one rank [genus or subgenus]. Treatment of collective group names and ichnotaxa [**Art. 10**] are restated. The application of a genus-group name is determined by reference to its type species [**Arts. 61, 66, 70**]. A genus-group name is to be formed and treated in accordance with **Articles 10d, 10e, 11g,** and relevant provisions of **Articles 25 to 33**. The Principle of Coordination [**Art. 43**] states that a name established for a taxon at either rank in the genus-group [genus or subgenus] is deemed to be simultaneously established with the same author and date for a taxon based on the same name-bearing type (type species) at the other rank in the group, whether the type was fixed originally or subsequently. **Article 44** reviews nominotypical taxa.

HOMONYMY (ARTICLES 52–60) AND REPLACEMENT NAMES.

Homonyms can be defined as two names representing different taxa that are spelled identically. Note that they must be spelled exactly the same—a one-letter difference between genus-group names is sufficient to make them non-homonyms (except for the suffix of family-group names; species taxa have special considerations) (see **Art. 55c** and **Art. 56b**). Each level (family-, genus-, and species-group names) has slightly different considerations: (1) In the family group, homonyms are each of two or more available names having the same spelling or differing only in suffix and denoting different taxa; (2) in the genus group they are each of two or more available names having the same spelling, and denoting different nominal taxa; and (3) in the species group, primary homonyms are two or more available specific names having the same spelling that were described in the same genus-group name, and secondary homonyms are two or more specific names that were spelled the same but were later classified in the same genus (e.g., one cannot have two species with the identical specific name in the same genus). It is obvious that confusion would result, for example, if two identical generic names were in use, or if two species within one genus had the same name. Articles in this chapter tell what to do in these circumstances.

The Principle of Homonymy states that: "An available name that is a junior [younger] homonym of another available name must not be used as a valid name." This principle traces its roots back to the 1842 code (pp. 112–113):

> "It being essential to the binomial method to indicate objects in natural history by means of *two words* only, without the aid of any further designation, it follows that a generic name should only have one meaning, in other words, that two genera should never bear the same name. For a similar reason, no two species in the same genus should bear the same name. When these cases occur, the later of the two duplicate names should be canceled, and a new term, or the earliest synonym, if there be any, substituted.... It is, we conceive, the bounden duty of an author when naming a new genus, to ascertain by careful search that the name which he proposes to employ has not been previously adopted in other departments of natural history .... We submit therefore, that
>
> "§ 10. A name should be changed which has before been proposed for some other genus in zoology or botany, or for some other species in the same genus, when still retained for such genus or species."

Homonyms in the family group (**Art. 55**) do not concern us here, but homonyms in generic groups do. Two or more available names established independently with the same spelling are homonyms. It is dictated that there cannot be two valid names in use in the animal kingdom with the same spelling; consequently one (the younger) must not be used. Occasionally, different authors may select the same name for taxa having the same type species; these are homonyms and also objective synonyms (discussed later).

The selection of unused, unique generic names is a difficult task. Typically, this means making a search of "nomenclators" (such as those by Neave 1939 et seq.) and recording publications (such as the Zoological Record). An eventual solution will be on-line databases of all genera. Ways to minimize the chances of homonymy include formation of new names by adding a prefix to an existing genus (especially a compound name), using the suffix *ichthys* for fish genera, or using long compounds.

Some authors (especially Whitley in fishes) provided replacement names for genera with near-identical spellings; the "near-homonyms" were regarded by them as homonymous even though they differed slightly. The remnant of this point of view is Recommendation D I.3. in the Code, "A zoologist should not publish a new genus-group name that differs from other such names only in its termination or in small differences in spelling ...."

At the same time, there are many other unneeded genus-group replacement names in fishes, especially in the early literature. These names may have been proposed because of supposed homonymy, but also may have been proposed only because the author felt the existing name was inappropriate, formed incorrectly, etc. Which of these are available and which are not?

As an example, consider Rafinesque 1815 [ref. 3584]. In this work he classified the universe, and in animal groups defined all families and higher categories known at the time and included the known genera. On page 36 he stated: "La Nomenclature adoptée pour ces Groupes consiste en un nom singulier substantif pour les Genres, et adjectif pour les Espèces...." Many of the generic names he included are apparently changes in existing names because (according to Jordan 1917:87 [ref. 2407]) they were too long, too short, or involved termination changes. Some appear to be new replacement names because the existing name was preoccupied, but most are not. In others, it appears that Rafinesque merely wanted to provide a new name. The style used by Rafinesque enables one to sort the names into several categories. It also points out the importance of examining the whole work to look for patterns and to understand the style of the author, especially in the early literature where rules of nomenclature were not applicable, not yet defined, or not as precise. The following is from Rafinesque 1815:82:

> "1. Famille. BLENNIDIA. Les *Blennidiens*. Corps allongé, nageoires jugulaires formées....
>
> "1. S.F. MONACTYLIA. Les *Monactyles*. *Un seul rayon aux nageoires jugulaires. G.1. Dactyleptus* R. *Murenoide* Lac. 2. *Pteraclidus* Gr. *Oligopodus* Lac.
>
> "2. S.F. POLACTYLIA. Les Polactyles. Deux ou plusieurs soudes aux nageoires jugulaires. G.3. *Blennius* L. 4. *Phycis* R. sp. do. 5. *Pholidus* R. sp. do. 6. *Enchelyopus* Gr. 7. *Pacamus* R. 8. *Ictias* R. sp. do. 9. *Dropsarus* R."

The interpretation of the above is as follows, based in part on examination of other sections of the same work. Rafinesque included two subfamilies (S.F.) in one family Blennidia. In the first subfamily he includes two genera (G.1 and 2). The second subfamily contains seven genera (nos. 3–9). In genus 1 Rafinesque was apparently proposing a new replacement name *Dactyleptus* for *Murenoide* Lacepède [actually *Muraenoides* Lacepède 1800]. *Dactyleptus* is regarded as an available replacement or substitute name for *Muraenoides* and takes the same type. In genus 2 Rafinesque was equating (synonymizing) *Pteraclis* Gronow and *Oligopodus* Lacepède. In this case, Rafinsque's "*Pteraclidus*" is an incorrect subsequent spelling of *Pteraclis* Gronow, and is an unavailable name (**Art. 19**). The second subfamily is more complicated. *Blennius* was a well-known Linnaean genus. *Phycis* is a name predating Lacepède [the "sp. do." means "based on a species of the preceding" [genus] according to Jordan 1917:88 [ref. 2407]]; in this case one cannot be sure if Rafinesque was taking credit for *Phycis* or including it from earlier sources; if he was calling it his new genus, it was a nomen nudum and not available. *Pholidus* R. sp. do. must refer to *Pholis* of earlier authors (since Rafinesque's work was a summary of all genera, and *Pholis* of earlier authors would have been placed in this area of his classification). Since Rafinesque did not give both names (see below) we can assume that this was a change in termination and can be considered an unavailable incorrect subsequent spelling. *Enchelyopus* refers to Gronow's genus. *Pacamus* cannot be traced to an earlier name and is an unavailable nomen nudum [**Art. 12**]. *Ictias* is also a nomen nudum and unavailable. *Dropsarus* was evidently substituted for *Gaidropsarus* Rafinesque 1810, an earlier name that would be placed here in the classification. Since Rafinesque gave only the one name, it is assumed that this was an intentional modification of the name and therefore an unavailable incorrect subsequent spelling (or it could be considered as a nomen nudum).

On page 83 of the same work he wrote, "*Nasonus* R. *Naso* Lac." and when he gave a new name and an old name, the new name is considered to be a replacement name.

Article 67h states that a replacement name must be "expressly" proposed as such; this means, for example, that *Dactyleptus* was a new name for *Muraenoides* and *Nasonus* for *Naso*. It must be remembered that in 1815 there was no standard code, and giving both a new name and the old name is about as "expressly proposed" as one can expect—or at least there is no reason to suspect that it was not intended as a replacement name. But where there was no direct tie of Rafinesque's new names to older generic names, these names can be regarded as unavailable (either as nomina nuda, or if there might be a tie, as incorrect subsequent spellings). A search of names that were in the literature but not treated by Rafinesque might allow more ties to be made, but these names are unavailable anyway. In Part I we include the unavailable names for completeness.

Two technical details involve homonyms in genus-group names. (1) In paleontology, a genus-group name applied for fossils by substituting *-ites*, *-ytes*, or *-ithes* for the original termination of a genus-group name, and applied only to fossils, enters into homonymy [**Art. 56c**]. (2) Of two homonymous genus-group names of **identical** date, one established for a genus and one for a subgenus, the former is deemed to be the senior homonym [**Art. 56d**]. The latter means that if the same genus-group name was proposed, for example, in fishes as a genus and in birds as a subgenus, and they are of the same date, the senior homonym is the fish name because it was used at the generic level, and the junior homonym is the bird name because it was used as a subgenus; the bird name might need to be replaced.

Homonymy is more complicated in species-group names [**Art. 57**] than in family- or genus-group names, but is not of concern here except that there is a special case [**Art. 57h(i)**] where two genus-group names are homonyms and include species with the same spelling; in this case identical species-group names included in them are not themselves homonyms—it is as if the two homonymous genera were actually two different generic group names for purposes of the availability of the species names. For example, if there were an *Alba beta* in fishes and *Alba beta* in birds, the two genera would be homonyms, but the species are not (and both species names would be available).

One unusual example of homonymy involves the name *Gymnochanda*. The genus was described by Fraser-Brunner 1955 for his new species *Gymnochanda filamentosa*. Boeseman in 1957 used the same genus and species names for his new genus and species in the same family. He circulated a correction slip with his publication indicating that by chance both Fraser-Brunner and he independently picked the same names for both the genus and the species. The species are regarded as subjective synonyms (different type specimens), but they are also homonyms; the genera are homonyms and subjective synonyms.

The normal replacement of homonyms [**Art. 60**] proceeds as follows. Typically, a junior (more recent, younger) homonym must be rejected (so that the first, older) name may be used without confusion, and the younger name must be replaced either by an existing available name or, for lack of such a name, by a new replacement name. If the junior homonym has an available junior synonym then it is used, and a new replacement name is unnecessary [**Art. 60b**]. If the rejected junior homonym has no known available synonym, it must be replaced by a new name (nomen novum), with its own author and date. This name then competes in priority with any synonym recognized later [**Art. 60c**].

In the Code of Ethics (Appendix A of the Code) it is suggested that a zoologist should not publish a new replacement name for a junior homonym during the lifetime of its author without informing that person of the homonymy and allowing him a reasonable interval (at least a year) in which to publish a replacement name. In the 1842 code, it was stated as, "though such cases [preoccupations] would be less frequent if the detectors of these errors would, as an act of courtesy, point them out to the author himself, if living, and leave it to him to correct his own inadvertencies." This is why many replacement names (especially recent ones) and the names they replaced have the same author.

THE CONCEPT OF TYPES (ARTICLE 61).

The concept of types in the system of nomenclature is fundamental. A type is the "name carrier" or voucher. For example, one might assume that an author described a new genus and included in it three new species; then a later author decided that the three species should be placed in three different genera. Because a genus has a type species (or single representative species), the genus name remains with the type species, and the later worker is free to describe new genera for the two species that he removed from the original genus, if there are not already generic names available for them. Similarly, an author may describe a species from several specimens, but a later worker may determine that the specimens the first author used actually belonged to more than one species; the type concept solves the problem: the first author's name applies to the species represented by the type specimen, and the later author may name other specimens as a new species or refer them to existing species.

The principle of name-bearing types is addressed in **Article 61**. This article merely states that each taxon has (actually or potentially) its name-bearing type. The name-bearing type for a family-group taxon is a single nominal genus, that of a genus-group taxon is a single nominal species, and that of a species is a type (one or more specimens—and ultimately, if needed, one specimen). The name-bearing type once fixed (established) cannot be changed except by special action of the ICZN (using plenary powers), with the exception that under certain circumstances the type of a species-group name can be changed. The name-bearing type then provides the objective standard of reference, and the application of the name it represents is determined from it, no matter how the boundaries of the taxon may change.

The name-bearing type of a nominal taxon [**Art. 61b**] is also the name-bearing type of its nominotypical taxon, and fixation of a name-bearing type for one entails fixation for the other. In other words, if a nominal genus-group taxon is split into subgenera, the genus has a type species and each subgenus has a type species, but one of the subgenera (the nominotypical one) must be spelled the same as the genus and automatically has the same type species.

If different name-bearing types are fixed simultaneously for a nominal taxon as well as its nominotypical taxon [**Art. 61b(i)**], the fixation of the former takes precedence. This can occur when an author made a mistake (for example an author might have named a type species for the genus and by mistake named another type species to represent the nominotypical subgenus), or when types were designated in two separate works on the same date.

When a taxon name is lowered or raised in rank, or is used in more than one rank simultaneously [**Art. 61b(ii)**], the name-bearing type remains the same. For example, a generic group name retains the same type species regardless of whether it is later recognized as a genus or subgenus.

The synonymy of name-bearing types follows in **Article 61c** (discussed more fully later). With regard to types, if nominal taxa with different name-bearing types are united within a single taxonomic unit (taxon) at the same rank, their names are subjective synonyms [**Art. 61c (i)**]. [If two taxa of equal rank have the same type, they are objective and not subjective synonyms.] If two or more nominal genus-group taxa have the same type species, they are objective synonyms; if two or more nominal genus-group taxa have type species with different species-group names but are based on the same name-bearing type [specimen], they are also objective synonyms [**Art. 61c(iii)**]. It is easiest to remember that "objective" ones are automatic and subjective ones involve the discretion of a later worker.

For technical reasons, **Article 61d** states that, if a nominal subspecies (rather than a species) is designated as the type species of a nominal genus-group taxon, it is deemed to have been first raised to the rank of species. If a nominal subgenus (rather than a genus) is designated as type genus of a nominal family-group taxon, it is deemed to have been first raised to the rank of genus. This article is necessitated, for example, by the fact that the name-bearing type of a genus is a species and not a subspecies. Examples follow.

McCulloch (1914:114–115 [ref. 2940]), in describing a new genus *Allocyttus* and a new variety *propinquus*, designated the type of *Allocyttus* as follows: "Type—*Cyttosoma verrucosum*, Gilchrist, var. *propinquus*, var. nov." [**Article 45** states that if a name is published as a "variety" before 1961, it is to be considered subspecific.] **Article 61d** indicates that the type is to be cited as *Allocyttus propinquus* McCulloch 1914, and not as *Cyttosoma verrucosum* Gilchrist. In other words, the subspecies *propinquus* is a different entity [and potentially a different species] than the nominate subspecies *verrucosum* and since the type of a genus is a species, the subspecies *propinquus* is raised to species rank for purposes of establishing a type species for the new genus. On the other hand, Whitley (1943:183 [ref. 4703]), in describing the genus *Amniataba*, stated: "Orthotype: *Therapon percoides* Günther...." Whitley added a new subspecies *burnettensis*, differing from the "typical *percoides*." In this case the type is *percoides*.

TYPES IN THE GENUS GROUP (ARTICLES 66–70).

Types in the family group (**Articles 62–65**) are not concerned here, but of special concern is the method of type designation used to establish the type species for each genus-group name. The subject is not simple, especially because the method for establishing type species is based on a prioritized system.

General considerations are given first in **Article 66**. The provisions and recommendations of the Code apply equally to nominal genera and subgenera [**Art. 66**] (including genus-group divisions deemed to be subgenera, and further subdivisions of genera such as sections or divisions but not aggregates of species such as superspecies). But the provisions do not apply to collective groups [name used for convenience for more than one species] or ichnotaxa [taxa based on the fossilized work of an animal] at the genus-group level, because collective groups and ichnotaxa have no type species.

No ichnotaxa (an earlier name is a "trace fossil") are included in Part I of the Catalog. An example from fishes was published recently by Feibel (1987:130 [ref. 6113]), who described *Piscichnus* as an "ichnogenus" for fossil fish nests from Kenya, with a diagnosis as "A shallow, circular, dishshaped structure...." He provided the "ichnospecies" name *P. brownii*. [Note that this is a taxon based on the fossilized work of an animal—it can be a species that is still living.] Feibel proposed that the nests were excavated by mouth, and that cichlid fishes were the likely trace makers.

The name-bearing type of a nominal genus or subgenus is a single nominal species known as the "type species" [**Art. 67a**]. A nominal genus and its nominotypical subgenus have the same type species.

The type species of a genus may be established (fixed) [**Art. 67b–c**] in two primary ways—either (1) in the original publication at the time the genus was first described, or (2) sometime after the initial publication of the genus.

The type may be fixed in the original publication of the genus in two ways [**Arts. 67** and **68**]: (1) type by original designation or (2) type by indication. The most desirable and explicit method of type designation is **by original designation**. To qualify in this category, the designation must be "rigidly construed" [**Art. 67c**]. The author must state that a given species is the type species. Several expressions may be used, but they must be very precise. Usually the type is designated at or near the genus description, but it can be done anywhere in the article.

For example, the author in his or her introduction may state that species so-and-so is the type of a new genus, or in describing another species, he or she may say something like "differs from the type species so-and-so of the genus...." For at least one genus, the type species was designated only in the title of the article.

Parr 1927, in describing *Trachinostomias* (subgenus of *Photonectes*), stated that *P. marginata*...and *P. flagellatus*... "may be regarded as the type species"; but the type species is a single species, so this does not establish the type species.

Examples that do not qualify as type by original designation [**Art. 67c**] include statements such as "this species is typical of the genus" or "this species is an example of the genus" or a designation made in a conditional way, such as "type might be...." (Also, in looking for the type designation, one must be aware that an author may use the word "type" many times but only in reference to the type specimen and not to the type species.)

Goode and Bean (1896:537 [ref. 1848]) stated, "We propose the generic name *Lophiodes* for this type of Lophiidae...." This is not an original designation.

If a species is specified as the type of the genus but the species is misspelled, it is still deemed to have been cited in its correct original spelling [**Art. 67d**]. In citing a type species the author also may misspell the original author's name or not cite the original author, have the wrong date, the wrong original genus for the species, etc. [**Art. 67f**]; but if the nominal species is otherwise eligible (and traceable), the author is considered to have validly designated the type species. In the early literature, there were relatively few species known and few authors; consequently authorship and date did not have the significance they do under present rules, and therefore **Article 67** accommodates type designations made in earlier times under different conditions.

Gill (1861 [ref. 1766]), in his *Catalog of the fishes of the eastern coast of North America* presented a number of new genera without descriptions, but under some new genera included available species names, so these genera date to this work [**Art. 12b(5)**]. Gill often merely referred to species treatments by Storer. For example (p. 30), one account is "Genus *Triloburus* Gill/*Triloburus trifurcus* Gill./*Centropristis nigricans* Storer. Synopsis Fishes N. A., p. 35." Gill wrote (p. 29), "As we could not conveniently, except in very few cases, refer to more than one author in the synonymy, we have used the work of Dr. Storer; on the Fishes of North America. In that compilation will be found references to other authors." This is, of course, a very unsatisfactory way to establish type species, and lends itself to new genera being based on misidentified type species. In the case of *Triloburus*, one finds "*Perca trifurca* L." included in Storer's synonymy. That species can be traced to Linnaeus 1766. In the Catalog one may find under the type species: *Centropristis trifurca* of Storer = *Perca trifurca* Linnaeus 1766. More typically in Part I of the Catalog, we merely give the earliest and true author of the type species. Based on **Article 67f**, Gill's names are available even though he did not provide the correct original author and date for many of the type species. [If Gill knowingly based a new genus on a misidentified type species, the type, for example, would be *Triloburus trifurcus* Gill based on **Art. 11i**; there is no species *trifurcus* Storer.]

Only the published statements or other nomenclatural acts of the author made at the time of establishing a nominal genus or subgenus are relevant [**Art. 67e**] in deciding whether the type species has been fixed in conformity with the Code [**Art. 67–68**] and which are the originally included nominal species in the meaning of **Article 69a(i)**.

Type by original designation can also be made by designating a synonym, although the Code does not clearly address this issue. For example, an author may have specimens of a species available to him for study and base his genus description on that species, yet he or she, feeling that it is likely that the species is a junior synonym of another species, includes the species studied (and familiar to him) in the synonymy of another species, but names the junior synonym as the type species. This is an excellent example of why original designation takes precedence over other methods of type designation.

For example, Hubbs 1926, in describing *Poecilistes*, treated it as monotypic but designated a junior synonym as the type. The same applies to *Epigeichthys* Hubbs 1927, in which *Xiphister rupestris* is designated type but placed in the synonymy of *Ophidium atropurpureum*.

A replacement name is one proposed to replace an earlier name that is invalid or thought to be invalid. If an author publishes a new scientific name expressly as a replacement name, or replaces a previously established genus-group name by an unjustified emendation (an intentional change in the spelling of the original name), both the prior and the new replacement have the same type species, and type fixation for one applies also to the other, despite any statement to the contrary [**Art. 67h**]. The type species must be a nominal species eligible for fixation as the type species of the initial taxon (e.g., it must have been one of the species included in the initial taxon).

The subgenus *Ulaula* Jordan and Thompson 1911 was proposed as, "new subgenus; type, *Bowersia ulaula* Jordan and Evermann; substitute for *Chaetopterus*, preoccupied" and "*Ulaula* = *Chaetopterus*, preoccupied." The type of *Chaetopterus* is *sieboldi*, and since *Ulaula* is undoubtedly a replacement name, it's type is *sieboldi*, "despite any statement to the contrary...."

On the other hand, there are cases where a presumed replacement name was not "expressly" proposed as such, particularly in the early literature. But a problem arises for several genera named by Whitley: the names appear to be replacement names, but Whitley sometimes provided a description and designated a type that was different from that of the preoccupied name. **Article 67h** states that if it is expressly proposed as a replacement, the type is then that of the original genus, "regardless of any statement to the contrary"; this exclusion obviously is valuable when, for example, an old genus with several included species had a type fixed by subsequent designation, but an author replacing the preoccupied name cited another species as type. Three examples follow.

(a) Whitley (1927), in describing *Ellerkeldia*, wrote (p. 298 [ref. 4662]), "This name is proposed for the Australian fish *Gilbertia annulata* (Günther), originally described as a *Plectropoma* (Cat. Fish. Brit. Mus., i, 1859, p. 158)." He continued by stating that *Gilbertia* was preoccupied, and concluded, "and *Ellerkeldia* should be used in its stead." But the type of *Gilbertia* is *Plectropoma semicinctum*. Whitley clearly based *Ellerkeldia* on *annulata*, and also specifically cited *annulata* as its type species [orthotype]. Based on subjective synonymy (since both are treated by Whitley in the same genus), *Ellerkeldia* would be used in *Gilbertia's* stead as the next available name. It can perhaps be argued that Whitley did not "expressly" propose *Ellerkeldia* as a replacement name, as required by **Article 72e**. At the same time, **Article 67h** states that if it is a replacement name, it and the prior nominal taxon must have the same type species, "despite any statement to the contrary." Anderson and Heemstra (1989 [ref. 13526]) regarded *Ellerkeldia* as a replacement name [based on Art. 67 and the expression "used in its stead"]. Earlier authors and Fowler (MS), with whom I agree, did not. Whitley, in the same paper, proposed three other genus-group replacement names, and "expressly" did so, using such expressions as, "I propose the new name *Zev* for..." "I accordingly propose the new subgeneric name *Usa* as a substitute..." and "so I have renamed it...."

(b) Whitley (1933 [ref. 4677]) described *Scopelapogon* as a subgenus of *Adenapogon* McCulloch 1921 and designated *Adenapogon woodi* McCulloch as type. He clearly described *Scopelapogon* as a new subgenus, but in a comment stated, "*Scopelapogon* also replaces *Neoscopelus* Castelnau, preocc." The type of *Neoscopelus* Castelnau 1875 is *Scopelus cephalotes* Castelnau by monotypy. Whitley (p. 74, above the new subgenus account) remarked that Castelnau's genus *Neoscopelus* is an "Apogonid fish closely allied to *Adenapogon woodi* McCulloch." He included both *woodi* and *cephalotes* in the subgenus *Scopelapogon*. (On p. 73, Whitley used *Adenapogon* as the valid genus name, and considered *Neoscopelus* Castelnau as a preoccupied senior synonym.) Is *Scopelapogon* an intentional new subgenus with type as *woodi*, and a "subjective" rather than an intentional "objective" replacement name?

(c) In 1937 [ref. 4690] Whitley named the genus *Wanderer* as a replacement for *Thynnichthys* Giglioli 1880, preoccupied, "hence the new nomination [*Wanderer*] proposed here." But Whitley went on to say that "Since the European species, *Wanderer allitteratus* (Rafinesque), differs at sight from its Australian representative, I name the latter as a new species and designate it as the orthotype of my new genus."

Whitley provided more replacement names (over 125) for fish genera than anyone else in the 1900s, and certainly was well aware of the Code; usually his new names were expressly proposed as replacements. However, when it was clearly Whitley's intention to describe a new genus [and indicate preoccupation at the same time], I believe that most authors would regard the type as the one designated by Whitley, and that two conflicting nomenclatural acts occurred in each case: (a) establishment of a new genus-group name and (b) replacement of a preoccupied name. I prefer to give preference to the establishment of the new name; but the cases are apparently few, and if conflicts arise, the ICZN can be asked to interpret each one as needed.

On the other hand, some "replacement names" may not technically be replacement names. Cohen (1973 [ref. 6589]) proposed *Svetovidovia* as a replacement for the preoccupied name *Gargilius* Jensen 1953 (see account of *Gargilius* in Part I of the Catalog), which, however, was unavailable on the basis of **Art. 13b** (no type established for a name published after 1930). Consequently this is a case of a technical replacement name that cannot technically be a replacement name since the name for which it was proposed was unavailable. Since Cohen gave a description and named a type, his genus name stands on its own with Cohen as author and with the type by original designation (and not the type by being a replacement name).

There is an example where an author proposed one replacement name for two preoccupied names at the same time. Whitley 1950 proposed the name *Didymophysa* as a replacement for *Diplophysa* Kessler 1874 and for *Deuterophysa* Rendahl 1933, objective synonyms of each other and preoccupied. (Fowler in 1958 independently proposed the name *Diplophysoides* for the same two preoccupied names.) The Code is not equipped to handle this matter definitively. Does one assume that Whitley provided a new name for both genera individually, thus creating two homonymous names, or that he just replaced the younger or the older preoccupied name?

Occasionally, a validly established type species is later found to have been misidentified [**Art. 67i**]; these cases are to be submitted to the ICZN [**Art. 70**]. A few instances of apparent misidentified type species are noted in remarks under genera in Part I.

If two or more genera or subgenera are united, the respective type species remain unchanged [**Art. 67j**]. In other words, once the type species is fixed for a genus-group name, it remains with that genus-group name and is unaffected by changes in the status of that name. Also, the fact that a nominal species is already the type species of a nominal genus or subgenus does not prevent it from being fixed as the type species of another genus or subgenus [**Art. 67k**]. A special case involves type species of nominal generic names first published as junior synonyms [**Art. 67(l)**]. If a genus-group name was first published as a junior synonym and later made available before 1961 under the provisions of **Article 11e**, the type species is the nominal species first associated with it; it is not automatically the type species of the nominal taxon denoted by its senior synonym. And if more than one nominal species is associated with the name, these nominal species are the originally included species.

Article 67m states that if a name of a nominal genus-group taxon is later applied to a collective group, the type species of that taxon is disregarded while the name is used as a collective group; in other words, collective groups do not have type species. Collective groups are rarely used in Recent fishes—some uses of *Leptocephalus* (to contain eel species described from larvae and of uncertain generic placement) qualify.

The first priority (and clearest) is type by original designation. The only other way for a type species to be by original designation (and only up to 1931) is by the inclusion by the original author of *two* or more *new* species, but use of the formula "n. gen., n. sp." or its equivalent (gen. and sp. n.; gen. new, sp. new, etc.) for only one of the included new species [**Art. 68b(i)**].

Under *Neostethus*, Regan 1916 used the expression "Gen. et sp. n." for one of two included new species, and that is noted in Part I of the Catalog as type by original designation, "use of...for one of two included new species before 1931." Miranda-Ribeiro (1903:41 [ref. 3709]) described the genus *Pseudopercis* and included three species—two established ones and one new species; he noted the latter as "g. & sp. n." on p. 14; since not all species are new, the type was not established under this article. It is assumed that the purpose of the article is to reflect a conscious choice made by the author; for example, if Jones described two new species and for one says "n. gen. n. sp." and for the other "n. sp.," this should mean that he made a choice—i.e., he intended one of the species to represent the genus. As **Article 68b(i)** is written, if Jones also had included one or more available previously described species in his new genus, **68b(i)** would not apply. Type designation under this article is rare in fishes.

The second way in which a type can be established or fixed in the original publication is by "indication." Forms of indication follow:

When (and only when) no species was specifically designated but (1) one of the included species was named *typus*, *typicus*, *typica*, or *typicum* [**Art. 68c**]. In the Catalog this is shown with statements like, "Type species by use of *typicus* for one included species." Or (2) there was only one valid [and available] species specifically included in the genus when originally proposed. The type fixation is then by monotypy [meaning one-type], which is the second form of type by "indication." But monotypy needs further comment and amplification. The use of the formula "gen. n., sp. n." (see above) when there is only one included species is not type by original designation but type by indication—specifically type by monotypy. This point seems to confuse many ichthyologists.

Specifically, **Article 68d** states, "A nominal genus-group taxon established with only one originally included species takes that nominal species as its type species by indication (type by monotypy), regardless of whether the author considered the taxon to contain other species that he or she did not name and regardless of any cited synonyms, subspecies, or unavailable names, and regardless of nominal species-group taxa doubtfully included or identified." This article—and especially the various conditions stated in the last half of it—needs amplification.

In some new generic descriptions in fishes, an author mentioned only one species, although it is clear from the text that in his or her opinion the genus contained additional species not mentioned by name. In other words, the author did not regard the genus as monotypic, but for purposes of type designation it is by monotypy (only one available species mentioned by name).

Based on **Article 68d**, if one or more species is conditionally referred to the genus, and there is only one species definitely included in the genus, that still qualifies as type by monotypy. In Part I of the Catalog are statements such as, "Type by monotypy, second species questionably included."

On the other hand, *Myoglanis* is a genus name that appeared first in Eigenmann 1910 (p. 384 [ref. 1224]) without a description but with a stated type as *Myoglanis potaroensis* Eigenmann and a second species *Myoglanis collettii* (Steindachner) included, but with a footnote stating "I am not sure of the generic position of this species." The species *potaroensis* (at this time) was a nomen nudum (and not available) and the available species was referred to the genus with question; therefore the genus is unavailable from Eigenmann 1910 since there was no description and no definitely included available species [The name was made available by Eigenmann in 1912].

The citation of junior synonyms under a single included valid species can still involve type designation by monotypy. But note that synonyms are available and can be designated as type by original designation, but in the absence of original designation, if the author recognized only one valid species, that is the type by monotypy even if he or she included junior synonyms.

But what if the author includes or recognizes subspecies for a single included species? A subspecies can be originally designated, and, as discussed above, when a subspecies (other than the nominate one) is designated, then for purposes of the type species, the subspecies is raised to species level. For example, the type of *Micropoecilia* Hubbs 1926 was designated as *P. vivipara parae* Eigenmann 1894, and the type is *P. parae*. If the author did not designate a type and included several valid subspecies for one species, then **Article 68d** states that type is by monotypy regardless of any cited subspecies. In other words, the type is the single species recognized as valid, and the cited subspecies do not enter into the type species decision. If the author mentions only subspecies (without placing them under a single species heading), one does not raise the subspecies to species level for purposes of type designation, but the nominate species is the type by monotypy.

Le Danois (1954:1358 [ref. 6451]), under the new name *Atinga*, included four subspecies of *A. atinga*: *atinga* (sic for *atringa*), *mauretanicus*, *spinosus*, and *schoepfi*. Since only one species was included and no original designation was present, the type is the nominate *A. atringa* Linnaeus by monotypy [**Art. 68d**]. (Note that if another subspecies was designated as type, that designation is acceptable [**Art. 61d**], the subspecies being raised to species for purposes of the type.) If Le Danois had designated the subspecies *A. a. spinosus* as type, the type would be listed as *A. spinosus* by original designation.

If subgenera are described at the same time that the new genus is described, and if the nominotypical subgenus contains only one valid species, this is the type of the new genus by monotypy [**Art. 68d(i)**]. In another condition the author establishes a new subgenus, including in it one species (at the same time the author may describe or treat other species in the genus but not in the subgenus). This condition is covered in **Article 68d** by the expression, "A new nominal genus-group taxon..."; meaning that the conditions of **68d** apply to both a genus and a subgenus). We refer to this in the Catalog as "Type by monotypy in subgenus."

Finally, the type species can be indicated in the original publication if the spelling of one of the included species names (or one of its stated synonyms) is "identical" with that of the genus. Note that this applies only if there were two or more included available and valid species. This is type by *absolute tautonymy*. Most cases are clear-cut, and in the Catalog statement "type by absolute tautonymy" is used frequently.

Rafinesque (1810:18 [ref. 3594]) described the genus *Tiphle*, and in the synonymy of one species included *typhle* Linnaeus. Because the genus and species are not spelled exactly alike, this is not regarded as absolute tautonymy. [**Article 58** indicates that variant spellings of species where *y* and *i* are interposed are deemed to be identical; however, since **Article 58** requires that the species-group names be established for different taxa, and does not apply to a comparison of species name with a genus name.] But **Article 69a(i)** states that an originally included nominal species can be an incorrect spelling. If the author of the new genus-group name misspells the name of an available species (incorrect subsequent spelling), but the spelling of his or her genus is the same as that of the misspelled species, then this apparently qualifies as absolute tautonymy.

There is one more type of tautonymy, where a pre-1758 name is cited in synonymy of one of the included available species, and the new genus-group name is spelled exactly like that pre-Linnaean name [**Art. 68e(i)**]. **Article 68e(i)** states: "If in the synonymy of only one of the originally included nominal species [**Art. 69a(i)**] in a nominal genus-group taxon established before 1931, there is cited a pre-1758 name of one word identical with the new genus-group name, that nominal species is the type species by indication (type by Linnaean tautonymy)." The Code is imprecise on the term "one word," but in the example in the Code is stated a one-word name or "name of one word." Interesting cases are found in Linnaeus (1758), although it should be pointed out that "Linnaean tautonymy" can apply to any pre-1931 author. The conflict over the term "one word" should become clear in the examples that follow.

Linnaeus (1758:236) described the genus *Chimaera*, with two species: *monstrosa* and *callorynchus*. Under *monstrosa* he cited, "Mus. Ad. Fr. I. p. 53. t. 25. *Chimaera*." "Chimaera" is a one-word pre-Linnaean name. This is type by Linnaean tautonymy—more than one species, and a one-word name mentioned under only one of the species that is spelled exactly as the genus.

Linnaeus (1758:237) described *Acipenser*, with four species. Under the first species, *sturio*, he included the citation: "It. Scan. 187. *Acipenser*"; under the second species he cited, "Fn. Svec. 272. *Acipenser ordinibus*..."; and under the third species "Art. Gen. 65. Syn. 92. *Acipenser tuberculis carens*." If **Article 68e(i)** meant one-word, then all three have *Acipenser* as one word *Acipenser*, but the Code, based on the example given therein, means a "one-word name." Clearly, *Acipenser tuberculis carens* is not a one-word name but a three-word name, i.e. a polynomial of pre-Linnaean authors. In this case, the type of *Acipenser* is regarded as *sturio*, by Linnaean tautonymy, since it is the only one identified with the one-word name "*Acipenser*."

In a more complicated case, consider Linnaeus' (1758:327) description of *Mormyrus*. He included two species, *M. cyprinoides* and *M. anguilloides*. Under *anguilloides* he cited a pre-Linnaean work as "Hasselqu. iter 398. *Mormyrus caschive*." Since *Mormyrus caschive* is not a one-word name, *anguilloides* cannot be the type by Linnaean tautonymy. At one time or another an author has cited each of Linnaeus' valid species and *M. caschive* as type. If type designation was not established in the original description, all the nominal species are available for later designation, but here *M. caschive* is not available because it was published as a name in synonymy. But Bloch and Schneider 1801 used *caschive* as a valid name, thereby making *caschive* available back to Linnaeus 1758 [**Art. 11e**]. If the type had been designated before 1801, it would have had to be either of the two available species (and not *caschive*). The first type designation seems to be Gill (1862:139 [ref. 1661, and Gill's style of type in parentheses in key]) as *M. caschive*, and that would be the correct type of *Mormyrus*, as *M. caschive* Linnaeus 1758, as made available by Bloch and Schneider 1801 and as designated by Gill 1862. However, one more relevant Article [**69a(i)**] states that the originally included species are only those actually cited by available names in the newly established nominal genus or subgenus (i.e., I interpret this to mean **when** the new genus or subgenus was described). Because *M. caschive* was not an available name when it was cited by Linnaeus, it cannot be the type species. This means that the type designation of Gill 1862 is invalid. The next type designation apparently was by Jordan 1917 as *M. cyprinoides*, preceding the designation of *M. anguilloides* by Jordan 1919. The ICZN (Opinion 77, Direction 56) accepts *M. cyprinoides* as the type.

The following genera described by Linnaeus (1758) have type by Linnaean tautonymy: *Gymnotus*, *Stromateus*, and *Cyclopterus*. Other fish genera of Linnaeus 1758 have the type by monotypy or by subsequent designation, although several have a pre-Linnaean one-word name in synonymy; however, this name is **repeated** under more than one included species and therefore does not isolate or distinguish one of the included species.

One must remember that the method of type fixation is in order of precedence. If a type was designated originally, that action takes precedence, even if the taxon was monotypic when proposed. In the Catalog and where appropriate, we tend to give more than one condition of type fixation. For example we write, "Type by original designation (also monotypic)." The phrase "also monotypic" has no importance for type designation but does convey the additional information that the author included only one valid species (and adds a measure of certainty, for if the type was not technically designated, the type must still remain the same). However, Recommendation 68A states, "If a type species is fixed under more than one of the means of fixation provided in this article, only the provision first in order of precedence need be cited."

If the type was not fixed in the original publication, **Article 69** becomes significant. After 1930, a new genus or subgenus must have a type species definitely fixed at the time the name was first proposed (e.g., original designation, monotypy) [**Arts. 69a, 13b**]; otherwise the name is not available. In preparation of the Catalog, we encountered many such names (perhaps 50). The names can be subsequently made available, and in fact many of them have already been subsequently made available inadvertently because authors were unfamiliar with the Code; these are discussed under the context of **Article 13** (in an earlier section).

We are now concerned with genera proposed before 1931, where subsequent designation comes into play in cases where the type species was not fixed in the original publication (i.e., no original designation, no monotypy). If the original author did not fix the type species, the first author who subsequently designates (fixes) the type species takes precedence, and no later designation is valid. This frequently involves much searching to find the first subsequent designator. Also, the originally included species must have been available ones as noted above.

If someone finds an earlier subsequent type designation, a change in the type species may occur, and this may result in a change in status for several taxa. When confusion develops, a case can be referred to the ICZN. But typically, one merely finds an earlier work in which the type species designated there is the same one that current workers recognize as the type species, and dating to a more recent subsequent designation. In the Catalog some "first" designations are pushed back earlier in time, e.g., to Bleeker's 1850s–1870s publications on Indo-Pacific fishes, particularly his general reviews of a family, where, for example, type species are designated for American genera, and these have been overlooked.

The first issue to determine is the originally included species [**Art. 69a(i)**]. The originally included nominal species comprise only those actually cited by available names (including misspelled ones) when the new genus or subgenus was described. They include both species and subspecies (and before 1961, varieties and forms with subspecific rank). Also, the article continues, these available names are originally included ones, whether as valid names or junior synonyms, or as stated misidentifications of a previously established species. [This last statement is in apparent conflict with **Article 68d**, which states that, "A nominal genus-group taxon established with only one originally included species takes that nominal species as its type by indication (type by monotypy),...regardless of any cited synonyms, subspecies...."] Thus, in the first instance [**Art. 69a(i)**] it appears that cited junior synonyms are originally included species, but on the other hand [**Art. 68d**] if there is only one originally included species, its synonyms are apparently not originally included species. Actually, in monotypy, what **Article 68d** probably should say is that if the author treats only one "valid" species, that is the type by monotypy, even if the author included other nominal species in its synonymy.

An example illustrates problems of establishment of included species and availability of generic names. Giglioli 1882 [ref. 1618] mentioned in passing that, "While there [Straits of Messina] last November I secured a fine *Malacocephalus laevis*, and ...." In 1883 [possibly late 1882, ref. 1620] Giglioli stated, "I must correct my assertion as to the occurrence of *Malacocephalus laevis* in the Mediterranean .... I have now not the slightest doubt that they [specimens] are quite distinct. They are an undescribed and most interesting form of Macrouridae, which I propose calling *Hymenocephalus italicus*." In 1884 [ref. 5325] Giglioli in Giglioli and Issel gave a description of the genus and species. The synonymy of the species *italicus* includes three entries based on the three treatments by Giglioli: (1) *Malacocephalus laevis* (not of Lowe, name only) Giglioli 1882, a misidentification, (2) *Hymenocephalus italicus* (name only) Giglioli 1883, and then (3) *Hymenocephalus italicus* Giglioli in Giglioli and Issel 1884. Because there was no description of the specimens in 1882, the species *italicus* is not available from 1883 nor is the genus available from its first mention in 1883 because there was no description in 1882 or 1883. [**Had** there been a description of the specimens in 1882, the first mention of the genus in 1883 as name only would be available from 1883 by indication, **Article 12b(1)** [new genus name in association with an available species], since the species would have been available—new name *italicus* 1883 going back to description of *laevis* not of Lowe in 1882]. In 1883 the genus did not have an available species associated with it and no generic description was provided; consequently, publication must wait for the 1884 treatment where both the genus and the species were first published in an available way.

If no [available] nominal species was or were included at the time the genus or subgenus was first described [meaning description of its properties were given], the name can still date to (and have authorship of) this first proposal, but in these cases [**Art. 69a(i)(1)**], the nominal species "that were first subsequently and expressly included in it in any of the ways referred to in this Subsection are deemed to be the only originally included nominal species." A few hundred genus-group names of fishes fit this category.

Kner in 1866:545 [ref. 2636] described *Choeroplotosus* as a new genus and included in it "*Plotosus limbatus*? C.V." In 1867:300 [ref. 2638] Kner again described the genus as new and described a new species *C. decemfilis*, with *P. limbatus* questionably in synonymy of his new species. Although there was no definitely included species in 1866, the genus can still date to 1866 (since there was a description), but the type is *decemfilis* by subsequent monotypy.

"Mere reference to a publication containing the name of a species does not by itself constitute an express reference of a nominal species to a nominal genus" [**Art. 69a(i)(2)**]. For example, an author Jones may give a description of a new genus and state something like "Based on the species described by Bloch and Schneider 1801." If the species described by Bloch and Schneider was not specifically mentioned by Jones, there is no express reference of that species to the new genus, and one must look for a later inclusion of a named species in Jones' genus; the genus dates to Jones, but the first technical addition of one or more species occurs later, and if only one is added later it does not have to be the species described by Bloch and Schneider.

"Mere citation of an available genus-group name as a synonym of another does not constitute inclusion of the nominal species of the former in the latter" [**Art. 69a(i)(3)**]. If Jones (above) had said that the genus *Alpha* should be included as a synonym of his new genus *Beta*, the species of *Alpha* would not be specifically included in his new genus because they were not mentioned by name. [But note that if he proposed *Beta* specifically as a **replacement name** for *Alpha*, the type of *Beta* would be the same as the type of *Alpha* and he would not have to specifically mention a species [**Art. 67h**].]

A special case concerning included species involves generic names proposed by Cuvier (1816 [ref. 993]). Here, Cuvier latinized most generic names, sometimes only in footnotes (which is satisfactory), but provided some names only in the French vernacular spelling (e.g., "Les Bagres," "Les Crénilabres"). In a few cases he latinized the name in a footnote, but gave only the first letter or first few letters of the name as it would occur in Latin, but did not spell out the entire word in Latin—which is not acceptable). The French vernacular names are not available as new generic names [**Art. 11b**]; these names were latinized by (and date to) later workers. In "latinizing" a vernacular name, the latinized name is not technically a replacement name, since replacement names can replace only available scientific names; the Code Glossary defines a replacement name as "Any available name used to replace an older available name." Vernacular names are not available names, and there is no provision in the Code that makes the species mentioned by Cuvier the originally included species. This is most problematical for the French vernacular names latinized first by Oken (1817 [ref. 3303]) in which Oken gave just a list of the genera and higher taxa compiled from Cuvier, comparing them to his system of classification. If Cuvier included only one species, some current authors date the genus to Oken 1817 and state that the type is by monotypy, but that is incorrect. As I interpret the Code, Oken's latinized names are available because he was clearly summarizing the taxa appearing in Cuvier 1816; i.e., Oken's names are available because they were latinized names clearly tied to descriptions appearing in Cuvier 1816. But one should note that Oken did not mention species; consequently at the time Oken's names appeared, the taxa did not have included species—the species are not necessarily the ones mentioned by Cuvier. One must trace the first inclusion of species (frequently in later publications by Cuvier and Valenciennes) and determine the method of type designation, such as subsequent monotypy. Some of Cuvier's vernacular names were first latinized by Bosc in 1816–19 [ref. 5126] and by Cloquet in 1816–30 [ref. 852] in "science dictionaries," but Bosc and Cloquet sometimes gave a description and mentioned species, so the species mentioned become the originally included species in those cases. For Cuvier's "Les Bagres," Bosc, Cloquet, and Oken all latinized the name; the history was summarized by Bailey and Stewart (1983 [ref. 5242]). As a further complication, some genera appeared in Bosc or Cloquet **before** publication of Cuvier's vernacular accounts, and Bailey and Stewart (p. 168) indicated that apparently Bosc and Cloquet had access to Cuvier's manuscript or to proof sheets; consequently, when Bosc or Cloquet provided a description the name dates to one of them (preceding Cuvier); if they gave only a name in Latin form and no description, the genus cannot date to them (no description or included species or reference to a previous publication) or to Cuvier (not latinized). Furthermore, some names were later made available (latinized) from Cuvier by other authors (in the case of "Les Bagres" by Fleming 1822:387 [ref. 5063] and later by Rüppell 1829:5 [not examined]), and it is usually assumed that these authors based their account directly on Cuvier's treatment, and not on (for example) Oken's latinization; one must therefore regard these proposals as independent of Oken, with their own author and included species. A final complication is that when "latinizers" quoted directly the earlier author's description, authorship could be regarded, for example, as Cuvier in Cloquet. Suffice it to say, these cases are very complicated with regard to date and authorship of publication, "originally included" species, and to subsequent type designation. In the Catalog one must regard the information provided for names based on Cuvier's vernacular names as preliminary.

An originally included nominal species is not rendered ineligible for later designation as type species by reason of its being the type species of another genus or by its having been included in another genus [**Art. 69a(ii)**]. In other words, if genus A contained three species originally, all are available for later designation as the sole type species for genus A, even if one or more had been a type of or became a type of another genus or were placed in another genus at any time.

"If an author subsequently designates a type species by using an unjustified emendation or an incorrect spelling of the name of one of the originally included nominal species, he or she is deemed to have designated the type species under its correct name..." [**Art. 69a(iii)**]. In other words, the subsequent author may misspell the species or modify the species spelling, but if the species taxon in question is clear (perhaps by inclusion of the author, a citation, or the emendation or misspelling is clearly of an existing species), the type designation is acceptable. "In the absence of a prior type species fixation for a nominal genus or subgenus, an author is considered to have designated one of the originally included nominal species as type species, if he or she states that it is the type or type species (for whatever reason, right or wrong), or uses an equivalent term, and if it is clear that that author accepts it as the type species" [**Art. 69a(iv)**].

There are many examples in the Catalog where **Article 69** applies. For example, a subsequent author may say that the type is so-and-so species by monotypy (when in fact there were several originally included species). Others might say that the type is so-and-so, first species treated, or type by page preference, or type by tautonymy (when there was no absolute tautonymy). As long as the subsequent author states that a species is the type (and as long as it was an originally included available species and there was no previous type fixation), that is a valid subsequent type designation. In the Catalog, for example, we merely state that the type is *alpha* by subsequent designation of Smith 1945, and are not concerned with Smith's reasons for selecting the type.

Some confusion has been caused by special methods used to designate types in fish genera in the late 1800s and early 1900s, especially by Jordan, Gill, and their colleagues, but also by others. This involves the use of a convention or system for designating the type, such as first species listed, type in parentheses, etc. The method is usually explained in their introduction.

Bonaparte (1838:196 [ref. 4979]), who summarized elasmobranch genera known to that time, stated in his introduction: "iconumque addita speciebus typicis indicatione...." He gave only one species name with each genus, and I regard that as type designation.

Jordan and Copeland (1876 [ref. 5961]), who provided a *Check list of the fishes of the fresh waters of North America* stated (p. 134) that, "The type of a genus is the species first mentioned, unless otherwise expressed." Under many genera, they listed several species, and for some North American genera, this work serves (through the method indicated by them in their introduction) as the first subsequent designation of a type species.

Gill (several publications) established a style of consistently placing one species in parentheses, usually in a key, to indicate the type species, and generally these have been accepted as type designations (and in the Catalog they are often given as "type in parentheses in key"). Problems arise when authors are inconsistent: Jordan and Davis (1891 [ref. 2437]) seemingly used species in parentheses to indicate the type; they normally included only one species in parentheses, but occasionally more than one—for example under *Dalophis* on p. 622 they gave "(*serpa*; *bimaculata*)."

"If an author designates as the type species a nominal species that was not originally included (or accepts another author's such designation) and if, but only if, at the same time he or she places that nominal species in synonymy with one of the originally included nominal species...that act constitutes fixation of the latter as type species of the nominal genus or subgenus" [**Art. 69a(v)**].

Bleeker designated the type of *Micropogon* as *M. costatus* DeKay = *M. lineatus* Cuvier and Valenciennes; *M. costatus* was not an originally included species but *lineatus* was; consequently the latter was established as the subsequently designated type. For *Scorpaenopsis* Heckel 1837, Bleeker designated the type as *Scorpaena gibbosa* Bloch, but synonymized *gibbosa* with *nesogalica* (an included species). Consequently, *S. nesogalica* is the type; both *gibbosa* and *nesogalica* are now treated as valid, but Bleeker's treatment was sufficient to establish the type as *nesogalica*. Although the Code does not define the expression "at the same time," I regard it to be "in the same work." For example, an author may designate the (non-included-species) type on one page and show the synonymy on another page or in another section of the same publication—it need not be in the same sentence or paragraph.

"A subsequent designation first made in a literature- recording publication is to be accepted, if valid in all other respects" [**Art. 69a(vi)**].

The type for *Neosteus* Norman 1923 was established by Norman in the *Zoological Record* for 1923. Günther, Norman, Burton, and others, for example, as authors of the Pisces section of the *Zoological Record*, established the type species for several genera.

"If only one [available] species was first subsequently included in a nominal genus or subgenus established [first] without included species, that nominal species is automatically the type species, by subsequent monotypy" [**Art. 69a(vii)**]. This situation was the most common one for genera established without available included species. In the Catalog are statements such as, "Type by subsequent monotypy; appeared first without included species, one species added by Jones 1880."

Article 69b states that "Elimination of all but one of the originally included nominal species from a nominal genus or subgenus **does not** in itself constitute type fixation" [emphasis added].

In earlier literature, and in Jordan's *Genera of Fishes* one finds such statements as "type restricted by Gill." Typically, this means that Gill redefined the genera involved, but often did not specifically designate a type, and the designation of the type dates to a later author (frequently to Jordan himself). Unfortunately, even where a previous genus contained two species and Gill left one in that genus and treated the second species in another genus, the type of the original genus still has not been designated. Note that this is **not** subsequent monotypy, which refers [**Art. 69a(vii)**] only to the condition where a genus was proposed without originally included species, and then only one species was first subsequently associated with it.

The Code provides recommendations (69A, 69B) to guide systematists in the selection of type species when no type species was established at the time of the initial description of the genus. It is in these recommendations that the terms "virtual tautonymy" and "page" or "position precedence" are mentioned; they are included here because these terms appear in literature of the early 1900s as methods of type designation, although they are not valid methods of type designation under the 1985 Code. As discussed above, authors may have based their type selection on "page preference" (i.e., statements such as, "first species is type") and that species is the type, but the stated reason has no bearing on the type selection.

Identification of the type species is treated in **Article 70**. "If an author either (1) includes an already established nominal species in a new nominal genus or subgenus when he or she establishes it, or (2) designates such a species as type species of a new or previously established nominal genus or subgenus, it is to be assumed that the author has identified the species correctly" [**Art. 70a**]. An author may include established species in his or her new genus, or may select a type species for the new genus, or make a type designation for an established genus. We assume that the author correctly identified the species involved—i.e., that his or her concept of these species corresponds to the actual species described by the original authors of those species.

Occasionally, however, it can be shown that the author of a genus name misidentified the species in question. If his or her new genus-group name is based on a misidentification, his or her new taxon does not "represent" the true features of the named type species. In the fixation of a type species (that is misidentified) for a previously established genus, the same confusion arises.

Article 70b states that if "a type species is considered to have been misidentified, the case is to be referred to the Commission to designate as the type species whichever nominal species will in its judgment best serve stability and universality of nomenclature, either the nominal species named in the fixation, regardless of misidentification; or, by the use of the plenary power...." To designate another species, the Commission uses its plenary power (see below) and can fix as the type species (1) the species actually involved, which was wrongly named in the type fixation, or (2) if the identity of the misidentified species is doubtful, it can choose a nominal species that best fits the concept of the genus or subgenus in use at the time the misidentification was noted, or (3) if neither 1 or 2 is appropriate, the Commission may designate any nominal species to be the type species. We identify in the Catalog about a dozen examples that have not come before the ICZN but where the type species apparently was based on a misidentification. Usually the best type species can be indicated; frequently the misidentified specimens have been subsequently renamed as another species, and this species makes the appropriate type (agreeing with the genus description), rather than the misidentified species.

"If an author fixes [deliberately] as the type species of a new nominal genus or subgenus a previously described nominal species, but states that its name is used in the sense of the misidentification or misapplication of a previous author, the type species fixed by that action is deemed to be a new nominal species, not the nominal species cited..." [**Art. 70c**]. That new nominal species will then have a new author and date, as if the author had described a new species with an old specific name and new genus or subgenus name. It is a new nominal species, and it will have its own type specimen(s)—not the type specimen(s) of the original species. Apparently no genera in fishes come under this Article. A more typical case in fishes, however, involves description of a new genus-group taxon based on a misidentified species, but in these cases the author provides a new name for the misidentified species. For example, Jones recognizes that the treatment of *Alpha beta* by Smith is not the true *Alpha beta* of Linnaeus, so in describing the new genus, Jones renames Smith's misidentification as a new species (or refers Smith's misidentification to yet another established species); this does not then constitute the basing of a genus on a misidentified type species.

Two complicated cases involving type species are given here.

Case 1: The genus *Wallago* was described by Bleeker (1851:295 [ref. 325]) in a footnote; two available included species (*walagoo* and *muelleri*) were mentioned in the text. Later in the same journal (1851:198, 202 [ref. 329]), Bleeker described *Wallago dinema*. Myers was unaware of Bleeker's 1851:295 description, and he erred twice (1938 [ref. 3116] and 1948 [ref. 12606]) in attempting to determine the type species, first as *dinema* and then *attu*. Bleeker in 1862:394 [ref. 391] designated *attu* as type, but that is invalid because *attu* was not an originally included species. In 1862:17 [ref. 393], Bleeker again designated *attu* as type and on page 79 [ref. 393] included *muelleri* in the synonymy of *attu*. Therefore, this conforms to **Art. 69a(v)**—designation as type species a nominal species that was not originally included but at the same time synonymizing it with an included species, thereby constituting designation of the included species as type. This would be true except for one minute technical detail: the first part of reference 393 (pp. 1–32) was published on 26 Nov. 1862 and the later part (pp. 65–96) on 3 Apr. 1863. Thus, the type was not designated "at the same time" as the synonymization was made, so this does not meet completely the requirements of **69a(v)**. Although we made no thorough search, we believe that the person who first validly designated the type (*muelleri*) was Haig 1952 [ref. 12607].

Case 2: Giorna 1809 [ref. 1808] proposed three generic names, two for macrourids and one for a lophotid (all in current use) and described a new species in each. On p. 179 he listed the three genera and their characters: "Je nommerai le premier (fig. 1.re) le Trachyrinque-Trachyrincus, à cause de la rudesse de son bec." "Le second est (fig. 2.e) le Lophote-Lophotus, ainsi nommé par sa crete." and "Le troisième sera (fig. 3.e) le Cœlorinque- Cœlorinchus, qui signifie bec échancré." On p. 180 he listed the species as "Le Trachyrinque-Anonyme," "Le Lophote-Lacepede," and "Le Cœlorinque-La-Ville."

Authors vary in their evaluation of the availability of Giorna's names. [Also, see the comment on the original spelling **Coelorinchus** in Part I of the Catalog.] Palmer (1973:334 [ref. 7195]) credited both the genus and species *Lacepedi* (sic) to Giorna, but macrourid workers have not recognized the species "anonyme" and "la-Ville" as latinized names. In my opinion, Giorna's generic names are available, but all three species are not available (not latinized). The genera can date to Giorna, but they still do not have available species associated with them. One must now [**Art. 69a(i)(1)**] look for the first available species to determine those that are "deemed to be the originally included" nominal species." Risso in 1810 referred to Giorna's accounts and provided the generic name *Lepidolepris* to include both generic names *Trachyrincus* and *Cœlorinchus*. He stated (p. 197) "1. L. Trachyrinque. *L. [species] Trachyrincus*." and (p. 200), "2. L. Cœlorinque. *L. [species] Cœlorhincus*." and provided descriptions. Risso thus provided latinized species names for Giorna's vernacular species, and Risso is the author of these species; however, Risso did not treat Giorna's genera as valid, including them instead in his *Lepidolepris*. Thus we are still left with no included species for Giorna's genera, nor with any technical fixation of type. (Probably because of the so-called Stickland tautonymy of the 1842 code, Risso would not have used either of Giorna's names as valid, because the names of the two species would be the same as the genera.) To my knowledge, the first use of Giorna's generic names as valid was by Günther 1887 [ref. 2013]. He included three species (pp. 152–153) in *Trachyrincus* (credited to Giorna but spelled by Günther as *Trachyrhynchus*), including Risso's species (but spelled by Günther as *trachyrhynchus*). Günther recognized *Cœlorhincus* as a subgenus of *Macrurus* (p. 125) but spelled it *Cœlorhynchus* and included five species (pp. 127–130)), one of which was Risso's, but spelled *cœlorhynchus*. Günther's treatment thus established the "originally included" species for Giorna's genera, and the type must come from among them. Günther did not designate types. His spelling of both the genera and the species differed from their original form; since Günther did not cite the original spelling, there is no direct evidence that the change was intentional, and his spellings would have to be regarded as incorrect subsequent spellings (although Günther did make intentional changes to conform to better Latin). Because of the spelling differences, however, it does not appear that we can regard the type species as established by subsequent absolute tautonymy, and we must look for subsequent designation from among Günther's included species. For *Trachyrincus*, Jordan (1917 [ref. 2407]) designated the type as *Lepidoleprus trachyrincus* Risso, and unless an earlier designation is found, this is the first fixation of a type. Jordan did not designate the type for *Cœlorhyncus*, stating only, "type *Cœlorhynchus la ville* Giorna." One could argue that this latinizes Giorna's species, but since it was not mentioned by Günther, it is not an "originally included" species and cannot be the type. To my knowledge (without a thorough search) the earliest valid designation was by Fowler (1936 [ref. 6546]), with type as *Cœlorhynchus cœlorhynchus*.

Determining the type of *Lophotus* Giorna is easier (Risso 1910 did not treat this genus). Cuvier (Nov. 1816:243 [ref. 993]) described "Les Lophotes" but did not include in latinized form either the genus or species, only "Le Lophote Lacépède." In 1816, Bosc [ref. 5126] treated the genus "LOPHOTE, *Lophotes*..." and species "Le Lophote cépédien." So, Bosc apparently provided an alternate generic name but not a latinized species name. In 1823, Cloquet [ref. 852], drawing from Giorna and other authors, treated "LOPHOTE, *Lophotus*. (Ichthyol.)..." but latinized the single species (p. 195) as "*Lophotus cepedianus*, Giorna." That appears to be the first inclusion of an available species in the genus, and the type is by subsequent monotypy.

Finally, in some unusual cases of genera no type has been established, yet the names are apparently still available.

Pagetodes sp. Richardson 1844 was described and figured, but no species name was provided, because "a cat carried it [the specimen] away...and ate it." No provision of the Code excludes this genus, and one or more species can still be added to the genus and a type designated; it has, "actually or potentially, its name-bearing [neotype] type" [**Art. 61**]. Beebe (1932 [ref. 5015], 1934 [ref.247]) described *Bathysphaera, Bathyceratias, Bathyembryx,* and *Bathysidus* and four corresponding new species from observations made from a window of a bathysphere. These genera and species are still of uncertain status, and I know of no provision in the Code that will exclude them.

The Code still does not, insofar as I can tell, specifically require that a new species be based on an actual specimen (or part of a specimen or impression), and (given the importance of the type concept) it seems desirable that such a provision be considered for the future. Technology today even permits collection of specimens by deep-diving submersibles at the greatest ocean depths, and since examination of specimens is crucial to understanding the characters and relationships of a species (and therefore its genus), it would seem that having a specimen or part of a specimen (or impression) would be a requirement. The Code also does not require that a specimen (if there is one) be placed in a museum. Peer pressure in ichthyology seems to work well, as current authors base taxa on specimens and place those specimens in museums. In ichthyology there are no significant personal specimen collections, but this is not true in some other branches of zoology.

Articles 71-75 treat in detail the types in the species group; this subject does not concern us here.

THE INTERNATIONAL COMMISSION ON ZOOLOGICAL NOMENCLATURE (ARTICLES 76-82)

This section of the Code addresses such items as the authority of the ICZN, its constitution, powers, and duties. **Article 78** treats Declarations, Opinions, Directions, and the Offical Lists and Indexes. "A Declaration published by the Commission...shall have the force of a provisional amendment to the Code, and shall remain in force until the next succeeding Congress ratifies or rejects it. If the Declaration is ratified, the Code shall be deemed to have been amended from the date of the Declaration." "A ruling in an Opinion may be completed or corrected by a Direction, which shall have the same status as the Opinion." An Opinion involves the application of the Code to a particular situation relating to an individual work, name, or nomenclatural act. A case is brought before the ICZN, and the ICZN rules on that case by giving an Opinion. In the Opinion, the ICZN determines how the Code is to be applied or interpreted, or the ICZN may use its plenary power [**Art. 79**] in a particular case to set aside the code and state the course to be followed. In Part I of the Catalog we cite Opinion numbers and sometimes Direction numbers, and these are summarized in Appendix B.

Opinions and Directions result in names and works being placed on Official Lists or Official Indexes; these also are given in Appendix B. If a name or act is placed on a "List" it is available and legitimate, but if it is placed on an "Index" it has only the status attributed to it in the relevant Opinion or Direction; in general, however, it means that the work is not available or the names are unavailable or invalid—although a name, for example, may be placed on an index only for purposes of priority and not for homonymy.

Article 79 discusses the plenary power of the ICZN, whereby the ICZN may suspend parts of the Code to solve particular problems. **Article 80** instructs that "when a case is under consideration by the ICZN, existing usage is to be maintained until the ruling of the ICZN is published." The remaining articles do not involve genera directly, and they deal with technical issues, regulations governing the Code, application of the Code, interpretation of the Code, and amendments to the Code.

The Code also includes six appendices: (A) Code of Ethics, (B) Transliteration and Latinization of Greek Words, (C) Latinization of Geographical and Proper Names, (D) Recommendations on the Formation of Names, (E) General Recommendations, and (F) The Constitution of the International Commission on Zoological Nomenclature. These are of interest to the working taxonomist, but are not relevant to decisions made in the Catalog. A Glossary completes the Code, and "In interpreting the Code, the meaning attributed in the Glossary to a word or expression is to be taken as its meaning for the purposes of the Code" [**Art. 87a**]; however, "recommendations, examples,...all titles, footnotes, and appendices [appearing in the Code] do not form part of the legislative text of the Code."

Index to Appendix A

GENERA:

APPENDIX B

OPINIONS AND OTHER ACTIONS OF THE INTERNATIONAL COMMISSION INVOLVING FISHES

William N. Eschmeyer, Barbara Weitbrecht, and William F. Smith-Vaniz

The International Commission on Zoological Nomenclature (ICZN) was founded in 1895. Its role is to stabilize and promote uniformity in the nomenclature of animals without interfering with taxonomic freedom (see Arts. 76-82 in the Code). Among its duties (see Appendix A), the Commission is empowered to suspend the "Rules" when their strict application will cause confusion or act against the stability or universality of nomenclature. Typically (and currently) a scientist makes a petition to the Commission; the petition is assigned a case number and published in *The Bulletin of Zoological Nomenclature.* A period of time is allowed for other zoologists to offer comments on the proposal, and these are also published in the *Bulletin.* The Commission must then vote on the matter, and the Commission's rulings, normally "Opinions," are published in the *Bulletin.* To pass, a proposal requires approval by simple majority of the votes validly cast by mail, except that a two-thirds majority is needed for cases involving use of plenary powers. The Commission also may issue a "Direction" if the ruling completes or corrects an earlier Opinion. On its own initiative, the Commission may also take up issues involving interpretation of the Code and issue Opinions or Directions. (Minor amendments to the Code also may be decided by the Commission and rendered as Declarations.)

Most Opinions or Directions affect taxonomic names (family-group, generic-group, or species-group) or the status of works (available or unavailable)—such as the rejection of a work for nomenclatural purposes because the author did not consistently use binominal nomenclature. Names or works that have been the subject of rulings by the Commission in its Opinions and Directions are entered in the "Official Lists of Names in Zoology" and "Works Approved as Available for Zoological Nomenclature" and the "Official Indexes of Rejected and Invalid Names and Works." A compilation of names on the Official Lists and Official Indexes was published in 1987 (Melville & Smith (eds.) [ref. 13620]) and is available from the ICZN. There are eight lists: an Official List for each of the three categories of names (family-group, genus-group, and species-group) and one for works, along with four corresponding "Indexes" which show rejected names and works that may not enter zoological nomenclature.

Except for the Official Lists and Indexes that treat affected names and works, there is no recent summary of Opinions and Declarations. We have gone through the Opinions and Declarations and noted those involving both Recent and fossil fishes. Below we summarize each pertinent Opinion or Direction (occasionally providing additional commentary), and then present the summaries of Official Lists and Official Indexes, and conclude with a list of fish taxa that are mentioned in Opinions and Directions, but were not subject to placement on the Official Lists or Indexes (also includes taxa that were once on an Official List or Index but were later removed, and taxa mentioned in pending cases—as of July 1990). This Appendix is to be used as a supplement to information in Part I of the Catalog, where, for example, an Opinion is cited or placement on an Official List or Index is mentioned with regard to availability, type species, or other matter involving generic-group names of fishes.

Works helpful in preparation of this compilation and articles that provide historical information include the following: Van Cleave (1943 [ref. 13436]), Schenk & McMasters (1956 [ref. 13545]), Follett & Dempster (1965 [ref. 13619]), and Melville & Smith, editors (1987 [ref. 13620]).

The publication of early Opinions has a complicated history (see Van Cleave 1943 [ref. 13436]). The first five opinions were published in *Science* in 1907 and reprinted and distributed by the Smithsonian Institution in 1910, along with additional opinions. The special Smithsonian publication no. 1938, covering opinions 1-25, was published in 1910; the Smithsonian continued to publish opinions in separate publications, and later in the *Smithsonian Miscellaneous Collections*, ending with opinion 133. In 1943 the International Trust for Zoological Nomenclature began publishing a series, "Opinions and Declarations rendered by the International Commission on Zoological Nomenclature." In this series, earlier opinions and declarations were repeated and new ones added—as volume 1 (with sections A-F) and volume 2 (with sections A-B) and volumes 3-20 (ending in 1959). The Trust began *The Bulletin of Zoological Nomenclature* concurrently in 1943, where proposals to the Commission were published; after volume 20 of the "Opinions and Declarations...," proposals and the opinions and declarations were published together in the *Bulletin.*

Consequently, our literature citations below are somewhat difficult to follow.

Various abbreviations and terminology are used in this section: BZN—*The Bulletin of Zoological Nomenclature*; ICZN—International Commission on Zoological Nomenclature; O/D—the publication *Opinions and Declarations...*; Smithson. Inst. Publ.—*Smithsonian Institution Publications*, or Smithson. Misc. Coll.—*Smithsonian Miscellaneous Collections.* The publication site has a complicated system of identification, for example "O/D (1957) 1D(D.19): 389-470" means the publication appeared in "Opinions and Declarations..." in 1957 in volume 1, Section D, as part D 19 on pages

389-470.

For each Opinion or Direction, we typically provide three citations: (1) to the original "Proposal" where applicable; (2) to "Comments" on the proposal that were published in the BZN, if any; and (3) to the "Ruling" of the Commission. These are sometimes amplified with "See also" citations.

OPINIONS AND DIRECTIONS

Opinion 13. Catesby's (1743) pre-Linnaean name *Cancer arenarius* is not available under the code, although reprinted in 1771. This does not deal directly with any fish names, but concerns the validity of names in the 1771 edition of Catesby's *Natural History of Carolina.* This work was rejected for nomenclatural purposes in Opinion 89, except for the Linnaean names listed in the concordance by Edwards. Ruling: Smithson. Inst. Publ. (1910) 1938:22-24; O/D (1947) 1A(22):207-234, 2 pls. See also: O/D (1955) 1A(Appendix 3):351-352 (clarification); O/D (1955) 1C(C.7.):xiv-xv (summary of history of case).

Opinion 14. Agassiz's designation of *Etheostoma blennioides* as type species of *Etheostoma* Rafinesque is upheld. The portion of Opinion 14 containing an interpretation of the "Règles," and not concerned with the question of the type species of *Etheostoma* was repealed for all except historical purposes during the 13th International Congress, Paris, 1948. Ruling: Smithson. Inst. Publ. (1910) 1938:25-27; O/D (1947) 1B(23):235-244. See also: BZN (1950) 4:165-166 (parts of Opinion 14 repealed); O/D (1955) 1A(Appendix 1):325-326 (action of 13th International Congress).

Opinion 16. Involves the status of prebinominal specific names (published before 1758) under Art. 30d. Citation of a tautonymous prebinominal specific name in synonymy is an adequate designation of type species. No fish names involved in ruling, but the following are mentioned as examples: *Chimaera, Acipenser, Gymnotus, Stromateus, Cyclopterus, Echeneis.* Ruling, other than parts relating to specific names cited as examples, repealed for all except historical purposes by 13th International Congress, Paris, 1948. Ruling: Smithson. Inst. Publ. (1910) 1938:31-39; O/D (1947) 1B(25):255-304. See also: BZN (1950) 4: 165-166 (partial repeal); O/D (1955) 1A-(Appendix 1):329-330 (action by 13th Congress); Case 276 (follow-up); O/D 1C(C.7.):xv-xvi (history).

Opinion 19. *Plesiops* Cuvier 1817 [= 1816] vs. *Pharopteryx* Rüppell 1828 — *Plesiops* provisionally is accepted as the senior synonym of *Pharopteryx*, in accordance with Rüppell's point of view. Ruling: Smithson. Inst. Publ. (1910) 1938:45-47.

Opinion 20. Rules that the genera of Gronow 1763 (*Zoophylacium*) are available under the Code. This ruling was reversed by Opinion 89 (1925), in which the *Zoophylacium* was provisionally rejected under suspension of the rules, and Opinion 261 (1954) in which the *Zoophylacium* and its *Index* were placed on the Official Index of rejected works. The 13th International Congress canceled Opinion 20 (1948). Ruling: Smithson. Inst. Publ. (1910) 1938:48-50. See also: BZN (1950) 4:63-66 (cancellation of Opinion); O/D (1955) 1C(C.7.):xvii (history of case); Opinions 89 & 261 (reversal of ruling on *Zoophylacium*).

Opinion 21. The genera of Klein 1774 are not available by reason of being reprinted in condensed form in Walbaum 1792. Ruling: Smithson. Inst. Publ. (1910) 1938:51-52.

Opinion 22. *Ceraticthys* Baird & Girard 1853 and *Ceratichthys* Baird MS, Girard 1856 vs. *Cliola* Girard 1856. *Ceraticthys* Baird & Girard 1853 was published as a monotypic genus of which the type is *C. vigilax. Ceratichthys* Baird MS, Girard 1856 is considered to be a separate genus, with type *Ceratichthys biguttatus.* It is regarded as a synonym of *Nocomis* Girard 1856. The status of *Cliola* is uncertain until its type species can be determined. Ruling: Smithson. Inst. Publ. (1910) 1938:53-54.

Opinion 23. *Aspro* (Commerson) Lacepède 1802 vs. *Cheilodipterus* Lacepède 1802, or *Ambassis* Cuvier 1829. *Centropomus macrodon* is ruled to be the type of *Aspro. Aspro* is suppressed as a synonym of *Cheilodipterus*, thus safeguarding *Ambassis.* Since Commerson's names cited in footnotes in Lacepède were provisionally rejected for nomenclatural purposes in Opinion 89 (1925), Opinion 23 was canceled "except for historical purposes" by the 13th International Congress, Paris, 1948. Ruling: Smithson. Inst. Publ. (1910) 1938:55-56. See also: Opinion 89 (rejection of Commerson names); BZN (1950) 3(4/6):126-127 (proposed cancellation); BZN (1950) 4:335-337 (Opinion 23 canceled).

Opinion 24. *Antennarius* (Commerson) Lacepède 1798, and Cuvier 1817 [= 1816], vs. *Histrio* Fischer 1813. *Antennarius* Commerson receives nomenclatural status by virtue of Lacepède 1798, predating Cuvier 1817 [= 1816]; thus *Histrio* is a junior synonym of *Antennarius.* Since Commerson's names cited in footnotes in Lacepède were provisionally rejected for nomenclatural purposes in Opinion 89, Opinion 24 was canceled for all but historical purposes by the 13th International Congress, Paris, 1948. Ruling: Smithson. Inst. Publ. (1910) 1938:57-58. See also: Opinion 89 (rejection of Commerson names); BZN (1950) 3(4/6):126-127 (proposed cancellation); BZN (1950) 4:335-337 (Opinion 24 canceled).

Opinion 26. *Cypsilurus* vs. *Cypselurus* Swainson 1839. Rules that *Cypsilurus* is an evident typographical error and should be corrected to *Cypselurus.* The portions of this Opinion containing interpretations of the Rules were repealed for all but historical purposes by the 13th International Congress, Paris, 1948. Ruling: Smithson. Inst. Publ. (1910) 1989:63-64. See also: BZN (1950) 4:165-166 (partial repeal).

Opinion 27. *Ruppelia* and *Rupellia* vs. *Rüppellia.* Many typographical errors are evident in Swainson 1839. The correct spelling is ruled to be *Rüppellia.* The portions of this Opinion containing interpretations of the Rules were repealed for all but historical purposes by the 13th International Congress, Paris, 1948. Ruling: Smithson. Inst. Publ. (1910) 1989:65. See also: BZN (1950) 4:165-166 (partial repeal).

Opinion 29. *Pachynathus* vs. *Pachygnathus.* Suppresses the fish name *Pachynathus* Swainson 1839 (ruled to be a typographical error for *Pachygnathus*) in favor of *Pachygnathus* Dugès 1834 in arachnids. The portions of this Opinion which contained interpretations of the Rules were repealed for all but historical purposes by the 13th International Congress, Paris, 1948. Ruling: Smithson. Inst. Publ. (1910) 1989:68. See also: BZN (1950) 4:165-166 (partial repeal).

Direction 30. Gender is assigned to 57 names placed on the Official List; includes 46 fish names placed on the Official List in Opinions 75, 77, 92 & 93. Ruling: O/D (1955) 1C(C.19.): 287-298.

Direction 32. Adds to the Official List and Official Index several works dealt with in earlier Opinions. Ruling: O/D (1956) 1C(C.21.):307-328.

Direction 33. Nomenclature of *Pleuronectes* Linnaeus 1758 is stabilized; *Pleuronectes* is added to the Official List; other affected taxa are placed on the Official List and Official Index. (Supplement to Opinion 68.) Proposal: BZN (1950) 4(10/12): 337-338; BZN (1952) 7(7/8): 202-203. Ruling: O/D (1956) 1C(C.22.):329-340. See also: Opinion 68.

Opinion 33. *Cyprinus rutilus* is ruled to be the type of *Rutilus* Rafinesque 1820. *Rutilus plargyrus* is ruled to be the type of *Plargyrus* Rafinesque 1820. Ruling: Smithson. Inst. Publ. (1911) 2013:78.

Direction 34 [Case 607]. *Sparus* Linnaeus 1758 is added to Official List; other affected names are placed on the Official List and Official Index. (Supplement to Opinion 69.) Proposal: BZN (1950) 3(4/6):127-128; BZN (1950) 4(10/12):337-338; BZN (1952) 7(7/8):203. Ruling: O/D (1956) 1C(C23):341-352.

Direction 37 [Case 987]. Completion of entries of decapod Crustacea on the Official List of Generic Names. Fish involved: *Acanthopus* Oken 1816, *Bathynectes* Günther 1878 and *Homalaspis* Kaier 1932 placed on the Official Index. This Opinion was canceled by the 13th International Congress (Paris, 1948) because the interpretation of the Rules contained in it was incorrect. Ruling: O/D (1956) 1D(D.2.):47-82. See also: BZN (1950) 4:63-66 (cancellation of Opinion).

Opinion 39. The Latin names in the systematic tables given in Cuvier 1800, *Leçons d'anatomie comparée*, are available insofar as they are identifiable through the bibliographic references given in the introduction. Ruling: Smithson. Inst. Publ. (1912) 2060:91. See also: Direction 32.

Opinion 40. 1) *Salmo eriox* vs. *S. trutta* and *S. fario*, all of Linnaeus 1758. It is not necessary to substitute *S. eriox* (which has page priority) for *S. fario*, the name most commonly used. 2) *Heniochus acuminatus* vs. *H. macrolepidotus*, both of Linnaeus 1758. Cuvier's (1817 [= 1816]) selection of *macrolepidotus* has precedence over the adoption of *acuminatus* by Jordan & Seale 1908 as the valid name for this taxon. Ruling: Smithson. Inst. Publ. (1912) 2060:92-93.

Direction 41 [Case 1048]. Addition to the Official List and Official Index of the family-group names involved in Opinions and Declarations, vol. 11, other than family-group names already placed on the Official List and Index. Ruling: O/D (1956) 11(30):431-452.

Opinion 41. *Athlennes* Jordan & Fordice 1886 is ruled to be a lapsus calami for *Ablennes*. The name is emended to *Ablennes*. The portions of this Opinion which contain interpretations of the Rules were repealed for all but historical purposes by the 13th International Congress, Paris, 1948. Ruling: Smithson. Inst. Publ. (1912) 2060:94-95. See also: BZN (1950) 4:165-166 (partial repeal).

Opinion 42. *Carapus* Rafinesque 1810 is monotypic, with type species *Gymnotus acus* Linnaeus. Ruling: Smithson. Inst. Publ. (1912) 2060:96.

Direction 44 [Case 994]. Correction of entries for genera on the Official List and for genera and species on the Official Indexes (Aves). Fish involved: *Alauda* Daudin 1816, *Cephalopterus* Risso 1810, *Cephalopterus* Powrie 1870 and *Psittacus* Catesby 1777 placed on the Official Index. Ruling: O/D (1956) 1D(D.8.):211-232.

Opinion 44. *Leptocephalus* Gronovius 1763, and Gmelin 1789, type *Leptocephalus morrisii*, takes precedence over any later generic name for which the adult stage of this animal has been designated as type. By this ruling, *Leptocephalus* would have replaced *Conger* Cuvier. Opinion 44 was effectively canceled by Opinion 89, in which Gronovius (1763) was rejected for nomenclatural purposes. Opinion 44 was canceled for all except historical purposes by the 13th International Congress, Paris, 1948. Ruling: Smithson. Inst. Publ. (1912) 2060:99-100. See also: Opinion 89 (Gronovius 1763 rejected); BZN (1950) 3(4/6):126-127 (proposed cancellation); BZN (1950) 4:335-337 (Opinion 44 canceled).

Opinion 45. The type of *Syngnathus* Linnaeus 1758 has apparently never been designated. *Syngnathus acus* Linnaeus is here designated the type, in accordance with general custom and convenience. Ruling: Smithson. Inst. Publ. (1912) 2060:101-103.

Opinion 47. *Carcharias* Rafinesque 1810 is determined to be monotypic, with type *Carcharias taurus* Rafinesque 1810. The portions of this Opinion which contained interpretations of the Rules were repealed for all but historical purposes by the 13th International Congress, Paris, 1948. Opinion 47 was fully repealed in Opinion 723. Ruling: Smithson. Inst. Publ. (1912) 2060:108-109. See also: BZN (1950) 4:165-166 (partial repeal); Opinion 723 (Opinion 47 repealed).

Opinion 52. *Cyprinus corporalis* and *C. cornutus* Mitchill, Aug. 1817 vs. *C. bullaris* and *C. megalops* Rafinesque, Dec. 1817. Mitchill's names have priority, since the preliminary notice given was judged to constitute adequate description. The portions of this Opinion which contain interpretations of the Rules were repealed for all but historical purposes by the 13th International Congress, Paris, 1948. Ruling: Smithson. Inst. Publ. (1913) 2169:119-121. See also: BZN (1950) 4:165-166 (partial repeal).

Opinion 53. The specific name *grayi* Kaup 1856 takes priority over *koilomatodon* Bleeker, "about 1865." Kaup 1856 published *Halicampus grayi* Kaup in synonymy with *Syngnathus conspicullatus* Jenyns 1842. Günther 1870 recognized *Syngnathus koilomatodon* Bleeker as identical with the form misidentified as *S. conspicullatus* by Kaup, and declared *H. grayi* to be the senior synonym. Günther's decision is accepted by the Commission. Ruling: Smithson. Inst. Publ. (1913) 2169:122-123.

Opinion 54. The genera *Dobula*, *Phoxinus* and *Alburnus* date from Rafinesque 1820. The claim is made by Jordan & Evermann 1896 that *Phoxinus* Agassiz 1835 is identical with *Phoxinus* Rafinesque 1820. This claim is considered correct until proven otherwise. *Cyprinus phoxinus* Linnaeus is thus the type of both genera. Similarly, if it is accepted that *Alburnus* Rafinesque 1820 is identical to *Alburnus* Heckel 1840 then *Cyprinus alburnus* is the type of both genera. Ruling: Smithson. Inst. Publ. (1913) 2169:124-125.

Direction 56 [Case 1015]. Correction and completion of entries for several genera, including fishes placed on the Official List in Opinions 77, 92 and 93. Correction of method of type designation in the Official List for 24 genera of fishes; 16 fish genera placed on the Official Index. One fish genus added to the

Official Index in Supplement to Direction 56. Ruling: O/D (1956) 1D(D.17.):337-364; O/D (1957) 1D(D.19.):389-470. (Supplement to Direction 56).

Direction 57 [Case 1014]. Addition to the Official List of 48 species, 40 of which are fishes. Ruling: O/D (1956) 1D(D.18): 365-388.

Opinion 58. "Rigidly construed," neither Rafinesque (1810) nor Cuvier (1817 [= 1816]) designated the type of *Esox* Linnaeus 1758. Jordan & Gilbert 1883 selected *Esox lucius* Linnaeus 1758 as type species of *Esox*. (The type species of *Belone* Cuvier 1817 [= 1816] is discussed but no type is selected. The type of *Belone* was later established in Opinion 225.) Ruling: Smithson. Inst. Publ. (1914) 2256:135-139. See also: Opinion 225 (*Belone* Cuvier 1817 [= 1816] stabilized); O/D (1955) 1C(C.7.):xix (history of case).

Opinion 60. *Salmo iridia* Gibbons 1855 is evidently a lapsus calami or a typographical error and may be corrected to *Salmo irideus*. The portions of this Opinion which contain interpretations of the Rules were repealed for all but historical purposes by the 13th International Congress, Paris, 1948. Ruling: Smithson. Inst. Publ. (1914) 2256:144. See also: BZN (1950) 4:165-166 (partial repeal).

Opinion 63. *Leuciscus hakuensis* Günther 1880 is to be corrected to *Leuciscus hakonensis* on the basis either of a lapsus calami or a typographic error. Ruling: Smithson. Inst. Publ. (1914) 2256:150.

Opinion 68. Rules that the type species of *Pleuronectes* Linnaeus 1758 was not designated by Fleming 1828. This Opinion was supplemented by Direction 33, in which the type species was specified. Ruling: Smithson. Misc. Coll. (1922) 73(1):1-8. See also: BZN (1950) 3(4/6):127-128 (recommends action by ICZN); BZN (1950) 4(10/12):337-338 (resolves to fix types); Direction 33 (types fixed).

Direction 69 [Case 564]. Validation under the plenary powers of the generic name *Osmerus* as of subgeneric status as from Linnaeus 1758; validation of an error in the ruling given in Opinion 77. Proposal: BZN (1955) 11(9):281-282; BZN (1956) 12(1):14-15. Ruling: O/D (1957) 1E(E.9.):137-150. See also: Opinion 77.

Opinion 69. Rules that the type species of *Sparus* Linnaeus 1758 was not designated by Fleming 1828. This Opinion was supplemented by Direction 34, in which the type species was specified. Ruling: Smithson. Misc. Coll. (1922) 73(1):9-12. See also: BZN (1950) 3(4/6):127-128 (recommends action by ICZN); BZN (1950) 4(10/12):337-338 (resolves to fix types); Direction 34 (types fixed).

Direction 72 [Case 1123]. Completion and in certain cases correction of entries relating to the names of genera of Mollusca, Brachiopoda, Echinodermata and Chordata in the Official List of Generic Names. The fish genus *Limax* Pallas 1774 was placed on the Official Index. Ruling: O/D (1957) 1E(E.11.): 161-192.

Opinion 75. Twenty-five generic names, including nine fish genera, placed on the Official List and type species established. Ruling: Smithson. Misc. Coll. (1922) 73(1):35-37.

Opinion 77. Thirty-five generic names, including 24 fish genera, placed on the Official List. *Diodon* and *Muraena* were temporarily withdrawn from the Official List when the First Installment was printed in 1958 because of "major defects" in their entries. The Official List entries for 20 fish genera were completed and corrected in Direction 56 (1956), and the entry for *Cottus* was completed in Direction 87 (1958). An erroneous entry for *Osmerus* was validated in Direction 69 (1957). Ruling: Smithson. Misc. Coll. (1922) 73(1):71-73. See also: O/D (1955) 1C(C.7.):xx (history of case); Directions 56 and 87 (entries completed and corrected); Direction 69 (erroneous entry validated). See also case pending no. 1173 for *Muraena*.

Direction 87 [Case 1171]. Completion and correction of Official List entries for *Cottus* Linnaeus 1758 (placed on the Official List in Opinion 77) and *Conger* Oken 1817 (placed on the Official List in Opinion 93 as "*Conger* Cuvier 1817 [= 1816]."). Ruling: O/D (1958) 1F(F.1.):1-16. See also: Opinion 77; Opinion 93.

Opinion 89. Under suspension of the Rules, the following works are eliminated from consideration for nomenclatural matters in any case where such suspension may be considered necessary: Gronow 1763, Commerson 1803, Gesellschaft Schauplatz 1775 to 1781, Catesby 1771, Browne 1789, Valmont de Bomare 1768 to 1775. The decision on Catesby does not include the concordance published in Volume 2 of the 1771 edition. (This Opinion is clarified in Opinion 259.) Ruling: Smithson. Misc. Coll. (1925) 73(3):27-33. See also: Opinion 13 (status of Catesby names); BZN (1950) 4(19/21):568-571 (clarification); Opinion 259 (clarification).

Remarks: In the initial request of Opinion 89, Jordan asked that Commerson and Plumier names mentioned in footnotes in Lacepède's *Histoire Naturelle des Poissons* be regarded as ineligible. When the opinion was rendered, there was no mention of Plumier, and Commerson's names in footnotes were restricted to 1803; or (p. 28) "1803 mostly." Direction 32 caused Commerson footnotes in Lacepède to be placed on the "Official Index of Rejected Works," but only Commerson 1803. That date refers to Lacepède's volume 5, and not to the first four volumes of 1798-1802. Unfortunately, no citation was given, and volume 4 of this work has sometimes been dated to 1803. In fact, generic names mentioned in the discussion in Opinion 89 (p. 29) include, for example, *Alticus* which was from volume 2 (1800). Unless the Commission reconsiders this case, the Commerson footnotes in Lacepède's first four volumes (and Plumier manuscript names in all 5 volumes) appear to be potentially available nomenclaturally. [In Opinion 24 a Commerson name in a footnote in Lacepède 1798 (v. 1) was accepted as available.] On the other hand, many of the names in footnotes appear to be nonbinominal, lack a description, or are otherwise unavailable. Some names could be regarded as names first published in synonymy. About 25-30 generic names are involved, and this case deserves more investigation and clarification.

Opinion 92. Sixteen generic names are placed on the Official List. Fishes involved are *Blennius*, *Echeneis*, *Esox* and *Ophidion*. In this Opinion the type of *Echeneis* was indicated to be *Echeneis remora* Linnaeus 1758. The type published in the Official List was *Echeneis naucrates* Linnaeus 1758. The type of *Echeneis* was stabilized in Opinion 242 (1954). The Official List entries for the remaining genera were completed in Direction 56 (1956). Ruling: Smithson. Misc. Coll. (1926) 73(4):3-4. See also: Opinion 242 (*Echeneis* stabilized); O/D (1955) 1A(Appendix 3):356-357; O/D (1955) 1C(C.7.):xxi-xxiii (history of case); Direction 56.

Opinion 93. Twelve generic names of fishes are placed on the Official List. *Sciaena, Stolephorus* and *Teuthis* were temporarily withdrawn from the First Installment of the Official List because of "major defects" in their entries. The entry for *Eleotris* was corrected in Direction 56 (1956) by the substitution of the correct type species. The entry for *Conger* Cuvier 1816 was deleted from the Official List in Direction 87 (1958). Ruling: Smithson. Misc. Coll. (1926) 73(4):5-11. See also: Direction 56 (correction of *Eleotris*); Direction 87 (deletion of *Conger* Cuvier 1816).

Direction 100 [Case 1278]. The genders of the 11 generic names on the Official List which end in *-gnathus* or *-rhynchus* are determined to be masculine. The fish taxon affected is *Syngnathus* Linnaeus 1758. (This Direction is supplemental to Declaration 39, a general ruling that all such latinized generic names must take the gender of their Latin suffix, rather than their original non-Latin root.) Proposal: BZN (1955) 11(8):260-262. Comments: BZN (1955) 11(9):302. Ruling: O/D (1958) 1F(F.11.):175-190.

Direction 102 [Case 553]. Validation of *Dracunculus* Reichard 1759 (Nematoda). Direction supplementary to Opinion 66, in which *Dracunculus* was placed on the Official List. The fish genus *Dracunculus* Krøyer [1838-1840] is placed on the Official Index. Proposal: BZN (1957) 13(5):154-159. Ruling: O/D (1958) 1F(F.13.):201-216.

Direction 114 [Case 2133]. Herrera's (1899) *Sinonimia vulgar y cientifica de los principales vertebrados mexicanos*, is rejected for nomenclatural purposes. The designations used for animals are ruled to be formulae, not names, and consequently have no status in zoological nomenclature. Supplementary to Direction 32. Proposal: BZN (1980) 36(4):246-248. Ruling: BZN (1984) 41(1):39-40.

Opinion 123. Gmelin's (1758-77) *Onomatologia Historiae Naturalis Completa*, a work partly binominal and partly polynominal, is rejected for nomenclatural purposes. Ruling: Smithson. Misc. Coll. (1931) 73(7):34-36.

Opinion 212 [Case 25]. Designates dates of publication for Pallas, *Zoographia Rosso-Asiatica*. Volumes 1 and 2 date to 1811, Volume 3 dates to 1814. Proposal: BZN (1947) 1(9):198-199; BZN (1947) 1(9):199-200. Ruling: O/D (1954) 4(2):15-24.

Opinion 222 [Case 123]. Designates *Tremataspis schmidti* Rohon 1892, as the type species of *Tremataspis* Schmidt 1866 (Cephalaspidomorphi). Proposal: BZN (1947) 1(10):237-238. Comments: BZN (1950) 4(13/15):433-435. Ruling: O/D (1954) 4(12):125-138.

Opinion 223 [Case 132]. Suppression of *Teleosteus* Volger 1860 and its type species *Teleosteus primaevus* Volger 1860, described as a fossil fish but later shown to be an anthozoan. Proposal: BZN (1947) 1(10):228-229. Ruling: O/D (1954) 4(13):139-148.

Opinion 225 [Case 145]. Validation of *Belone* Cuvier 1816 and suppression of *Raphistoma*, Rafinesque 1815. Proposal: BZN (1947) 1(10):225-228. Ruling: O/D (1954) 4(15):161-176. See also: BZN (1950) 4(13/15):426-428 (decision by Commission at it's 14th Meeting, Paris, 1948).

Opinion 230 [Case 146]. The work by J. Gesner (1758), *Tractatus physicus de Petrificatis* is suppressed for nomenclatural purposes by use of plenary powers, and is placed on the Official Index. Proposal: BZN (1947) 1(9):222. Ruling: O/D (1954) 4(20):231-238. [Not examined, may include no fish taxa.]

Opinion 242 [Case 156]. *Echeneis naucrates* (emendation of *neucrates*) Linnaeus 1758 is designated as the type species of *Echeneis* Linnaeus 1758 in harmony with accustomed nomenclatural usage (correction of Opinion 92). Taxa affected placed on the Official Lists and Official Indexes. Proposal: BZN (1950) 4(16/18):536-539. Ruling: O/D (1954) 5(3):23-44.

Opinion 259 [Case 269]. Clarification of Opinion 89. The rejection of Catesby (1771), *The Natural History of Carolina* does not apply to the concordance inserted by Edwards in volume 2 of the 1771 edition, "A Catalogue of the Animals and Plants represented in Catesby's *Natural History of Carolina*. With the Linnaean Names." This was not made sufficiently clear in Opinion 89. The works affected are placed on the Official List and Official Index. Ruling: O/D (1954) 5(20):253-264. See also: Opinion 89.

Opinion 260 [Case 270]. The work by F.C. Meuschen (1778), *Museum Gronovianum*, is not available for nomenclatural purposes because it is not "published" in the sense of Article 25, and because Meuschen did not apply the principles of binominal nomenclature. Ruling: O/D (1954) 5(21):265-280. [Not examined; may include no fish taxa.]

Opinion 261 [Case 311]. Rejection for nomenclatural purposes of the Index to the *Zoophylacium Gronovianum* of Gronovius prepared by Meuschen (F.C.) and published in 1781. Ruling: O/D (1954) 5(22):281-296, 1 facsimile.

Opinion 279 [Case 394]. Rules that in any zoological work where either Linnaeus or J. C. Fabricius placed a term between the generic name and the specific name of a species, the intermediate term is not a subgeneric name and has not acquired the status of a subgeneric name from having been published in this manner. Ruling: O/D (1954) 6(11):179-188.

Opinion 296 [Case 418]. Suppression under the plenary powers, for nomenclatural purposes, of Volume 3 (*Regnum Lapideum*) of the twelfth edition of the *Systema Naturae* of Linnaeus published in 1768, and of the corresponding volume in the Houttuyn (1785), Gmelin (1793) and Turton (1806) editions of the same work. Ruling: O/D (1954) 8(13):167-178.

Opinion 326 [Case 340]. Validation of *Hexarthra* Schmarda 1854 (Rotifera) and related matters. The fish genus *Pedalion* Swainson 1838 is placed on the Official Index. Proposal: BZN (1951) 6(3):73-78. Ruling: O/D (1955) 9(17):267-282.

Opinion 329 [Case 587]. Scopoli's (1777) *Introductio ad Historiam Naturalem* is accepted for nomenclatural purposes and placed on the Official List. Proposal: BZN (1951) 6(4):122-125. Comments: BZN (1952) 6(8):255. Ruling: O/D (1955) 9(23):309-320.

Opinion 332 [Case 543]. The work of W. Borlase (1758), *The Natural History of Cornwall*, is rejected for nomenclatural purposes because the author did not apply the principles of binominal nomenclature. This work and the work by L. T. Gronovius (1762), "Animalium belgicorum observatorum Centuria Quinta," published in the journal *Acta Helvetica physico-mathematico-botanico-medica*, are placed on the Official Index of rejected works. Proposal: BZN (1945) 1(5):115-118. Ruling: O/D (1955) 9(26):355-368. [Not examined; may include no fish taxa.]

Opinion 345 [Case 202]. Refusal to use plenary powers to validate *Rhina* Latreille [1802-1803] in Insecta. Validation of *Rhina* Schneider [Bloch & Schneider] 1801 in fishes. *Platyrhina* Müller & Henle 1838 is placed on the Official List. Five fish genera are placed on the Official Index. Proposal: BZN (1951) 2(2):47-55. Ruling: O/D (1955) 10(12):353-388.

Opinion 353 [Case 533]. Validation of *Hoplites* Neumayr 1875 (Cephalopoda). The fish genus *Hoplites* Agassiz 1846 is placed on the Official Index. Proposal: BZN (1951) 6(4):110-114. Comments: BZN (1952) 6(8):241. Ruling: O/D (1955) 11(3): 47-78.

Opinion 375 [Case 382]. *Heterandria formosa* Agassiz 1855 is designated the type species of *Heterandria* Agassiz 1853. Three genera and three species of fishes are placed on the Official Lists. Proposal: BZN (1952) 6:263-365. Ruling: O/D (1955) 11(25):379-390.

Opinion 380 [Case 293]. The catalog of animals by Houttuyn 1787, *Animalium Musaei Houttuiniani Index*, is placed on the Official Index of Rejected Works. The 19 fish species published in this work are placed on the Official Index. Proposal: BZN (1952) 6:292-303. Ruling: O/D (1956) 12(1):1-32.

Opinion 417 [Case 153]. The work by L. Oken (1815-1816), *Okens Lehrbuch der Naturgeschichte*, Volume 3 (Zoology), is rejected for nomenclatural purposes because the author did not apply the principles of binominal nomenclature, and the work is placed on the Official Index. Ruling: O/D (1956) 14(1):1-42. See also: BZN (1945) 1(5):112-113 (preliminary mention of the case).

Opinion 438 [Case 863]. *Rhinopteraspis* Jaekel 1919 is validated. *Archaeoteuthis* Roemer 1855 is suppressed under the plenary powers. Affected names are placed on the Official List and Official Index. Proposal: BZN (1955) 11(2):66-67. Comments: BZN (1955) 11(8):266. Ruling: O/D (1957) 15(3):41-50.

Opinion 445 [Case 721]. The work by J. P. Eberhard (1768), *Versuch eines neuen Entwurfs der Thiergeschichte*, is rejected for nomenclatural purposes because the author did not apply the principles of binominal nomenclature. Proposal: BZN (1955) 11(3):95-96. Ruling: O/D (1957) 15(10):191-198. [Not examined; may contain no fish taxa.]

Opinion 447 [Case 256]. Rejection for nomenclatural purposes of the 1791 and 1792 editions of Bartram's *Travels through North and South Carolina, Georgia, East and West Florida, the Cherokee Country, the extensive territories of the Muscogulges or Creek Confederacy, and the country of the Chactaws*; the work is a non-binominal one. Ruling: O/D (1957) 15(12):211-224.

Opinion 461 [Case 905]. Addition to the Official List of *Cubiceps* Lowe 1843 and *Seriola gracilis* Lowe 1843. Lowe described *gracilis* as a species of *Seriola*, but conditionally established the new nominal genus *Cubiceps* for it in the same paper. The species *gracilis* is ruled to have been described in the genus *Seriola*. *Seriola gracilis* is the type species of *Cubiceps*. This Opinion supplements Declaration 30, which addresses the general issue involved. Proposal: BZN (1955) 11(6):170-180; BZN (1955) 11(6):181-182. Ruling: O/D (1957) 15(28):475-484.

Opinion 485 [Case 1082]. Determination of relative priority of names *Cheirodon axelrodi* Schultz and *Hyphessobrycon cardinalis* Myers & Weitzman, both published in February 1956. Supplementary resolution emphasizes that only dates of publication were considered material to the case. Proposal: BZN (1956) 12(6):184; BZN (1956) 12(6):185-190. Comments: BZN (1956) 12(11):317. Ruling: O/D (1957) 17(7):87-104. See also: O/D (1958) 17(23):104A-104J (Supplementary Resolution).

Opinion 487 [Case 923]. Validation of *Gempylus* Cuvier 1829 (Pisces) and *Acinaces* Gerstaecker 1858 (Coleoptera). Affected names are placed on the Official List and Official Index. Proposal: BZN (1955) 11(9):285-288; BZN (1956) 12(6):181-182. Comments: BZN (1956) 12(11):315-316. Ruling: O/D (1957) 17(9):119-142.

Opinion 494 [Case 332]. Validation of *Diloba* Boisduval 1840 and establishment of the type species of *Episema* Ochsenheimer 1816 (Insecta: Lepidoptera). The fish genus *Episema* Cope & Jordan 1877 is placed on the Official Index. Proposal: BZN (1952) 6(10):315-317. Ruling: O/D (1957) 17(16):265-268.

Opinion 502 [Case 1020]. Validation of *Lepidurus* Leach 1819 (Crustacea) and other rulings on Crustacea and Aves. The fish genera *Micropus* Gray 1831 and *Micropus* Kner 1868 are placed on the Official Index. Proposal: BZN (1956) 12(3):67-85. Ruling: O/D (1958) 18(3):65-120.

Opinion 513 [Case 273]. Determined the type species for *Culter* and *Nasus*, both of Basilewsky 1855. Affected names are placed on the Official List. Proposal: BZN (1956) 12(5):136-138. Comments: BZN (1956) 12(10):274. Ruling: O/D (1958) 18(17):291-302.

Opinion 519 [Case 1039]. Addition to the Official List of 23 genera of Crustacea. The fish genus *Palinurus* De Kay 1842 was placed on the Official Index. Proposal: BZN (1956) 12(4):107-119. Ruling: O/D (1958) 19(6):133-168.

Opinion 529 [Case 1121]. The work by J.E.I. Walch (1768-1774), *Die Naturgeschichte der Versteinerungen zur Erläuterung der Knorrischen Sammlung von Merkwürdigkeiten der Natur*, Nürnberg, is rejected for nomenclatural purposes because the author did not apply the principles of binominal nomenclature. Proposal: BZN (1956) 12(6):191-192. Ruling: O/D (1958) 19(18):325-332. [Not examined; may contain no fish taxa.]

Opinion 569 [Case 952]. First reviser selections for relative precedence are set aside for *Selene* and *Argyreiosus* (both of Lacepède 1803) and for four pairs of specific names in fishes. Each pair of names was published in the same work. The plenary powers are invoked to establish relative precedence for each pair of names. The senior synonyms so determined are placed on the Official List. Proposal: BZN (1957) 13(10/11): 303-308. Ruling: BZN (1959) 17(3-5):92-94.

Opinion 572 [Case 255]. *Calandra* Clairville & Schellenberg 1798 suppressed and *Curculio abbreviatus* Fabricius validated (Coleoptera). The fossil fish genus *Sphenophorus* Newberry 1890 is placed on the Official Index. Proposal: BZN (1957) 16(1):5-47. Ruling: BZN (1959) 17(3/5):112-116.

Opinion 580 [Case 1228]. Determination of authorship and date of the parts of the *Histoire Naturelle des Poissons* by Cuvier & Valenciennes 1828-1850. Attribution is to be "Cuvier in Cuvier & Valenciennes" or "Valenciennes in Cuvier & Valenciennes" except as otherwise noted in the original descriptions. Proposal: BZN (1957) 13(10/11):309-312. Ruling: BZN (1959) 17(3-5):148-152.

Opinion 592 [Case 1185]. Bertrand's (1763) *Dictionnaire Universel des Fossiles Propres et des Fossiles Accidentels* is rejected for nomenclatural purposes; the work and names proposed in it are placed on the Official Index. The names listed here are those which Bertrand stated to be fossil fish parts. Most of those described only as tongue stones (*les glossopètres*) are omitted, although many are probably fossil shark teeth. The tongue stone *Ornitoglossum* is synonymous with *Odontaspis* Agassiz 1835 (BZN 17:50). Proposal: BZN (1959) 17(1/2):49-53. Ruling: BZN (1961) 18(2):114-120.

Opinion 638 [Case 1330]. *Lepidogaster [sic] couchii* Kent 1883 is suppressed under plenary powers. Affected names are placed on the Official List and Index. Proposal: BZN (1960) 18(1):79-80. Ruling: BZN (1962) 19(5):268-269.

Opinion 660 [Case 1459]. Suppression of seven specific names of turtles. Affected names are placed on the Official List and Official Index. The work by Fermin (1765), *Histoire naturelle de la Hollande équinoxiale*, is rejected for nomenclatural purposes because the author did not apply the principles of binominal nomenclature. Proposal: BZN (1961) 18(3):211-213. Comments: BZN (1961) 18(5):348; BZN (1962) 19(1):50. Ruling: BZN (1963) 20(3):187-190. [Not examined; may contain no fish taxa.]

Opinion 701 [Case 1496]. Various rulings on the nomenclature of porcelain crabs (Crustacea). Works of Linck (1783-1787) and Müller (1766) are suppressed under the plenary powers and placed on the Official Index. Proposal: BZN (1962) 19(3):177-181. Ruling: BZN (1964) 21(2):108-110.

Opinion 712 [Case 1499]. Forty-seven genera of decapod Crustacea are placed on the Official List. The fish genus *Plagusia* Jarocki 1822 is placed on the Official Index. Proposal: BZN (1962) 19(4):232-253. Ruling: BZN (1964) 21(5):336-351.

Opinion 723 [Case 920]. Opinion 47 repealed. *Carcharias* Rafinesque 1809, and *Triglochis* Müller & Henle 1837 are suppressed under the plenary powers. *Carcharhinus* Blainville 1816, *Carcharodon* A. Smith 1838, and *Odontaspis* Agassiz 1838, are stabilized in their accustomed senses by use of the plenary powers. Affected names are placed on Official List and Official Index. Proposal: BZN (1961) 18(4):273-280; BZN (1962) 19(2):100-102. Comments: BZN (1962) 19(2):66-67; BZN (1962) 19(3):139. Ruling: BZN (1965) 22(1): 32-36. See also: Opinion 47.

Opinion 749 [Case 569]. *Atherina japonica* Houttuyn 1782 suppressed under the plenary powers. Affected names are placed on the Official List and Official Index. Proposal: BZN (1963) 20(4):281-284. Comments: BZN (1964) 21(3):186-188. Ruling: BZN (1965) 22(4):218-219.

Opinion 764 [Case 1250]. *Chaetoderma* Lovén 1844 (Mollusca), and *Chaetodermis* Swainson 1839 (Pisces) added to Official List. Proposal: BZN (1963) 20(6):429-431. Ruling: BZN (1966) 23(1):22-24.

Opinion 772 [Case 1590]. *Curimata* Bosc 1817 supersedes *Curimata* Walbaum 1792, which is judged not to be a generic name. Proposal: BZN (1963) 20(5):390. Comments: BZN (1964) 21(4):260. Ruling: BZN (1966) 23(1):41-45.

Opinion 796 [Case 1633]. *Ambalodus* Branson & Mehl 1933 (conodonts) is added to Official List. Proposal: BZN (1964) 21(4):310-314. Ruling: BZN (1960) 23(6):271-272.

Opinion 799 [Case 1614]. *Sardina pilchardus* (Walbaum 1792) is added to Official List as the name of the European Sardine. Proposal: BZN (1964) 21(5):360. Comments: BZN (1965) 22(2):133-134. Ruling: BZN (1966) 23(6):277-278.

Opinion 809 [Case 1652]. *Thinnus* S. D. W. [?S. D. Wood] 1837 suppressed under the plenary powers; *Thunnus* South 1845 validated. Affected names are placed on the Official List and Official Index. Proposal: BZN (1964) 21(6):442-443. Comments: BZN (1965) 22(1):31. Ruling: BZN (1967) 24(2):85-86.

Opinion 846 [Case 1714]. *Mullus auriflamma* Forsskål 1775 is suppressed under the plenary powers. Affected names are placed on the Official List and Official Index. Proposal: BZN (1965) 22(4):263. Ruling: BZN (1968) 25(1):14-15.

Opinion 859 [Case 1736]. *Alosa fallax* (Lacepède 1803) is preserved as the name for the Twaite Shad and placed on the Official List. The work by Monceau, 1769-1782, *Traité général des Pêches...* is placed on the Official Index. Proposal: BZN (1966) 23(1):52-54. Ruling: BZN (1968) 25(2/3):92-93.

Opinion 860 [Case 1737]. *Gobius lenkoranicus* Kessler 1877 is suppressed under the plenary powers in favor of *Pomatoschistus caucasicus* Berg 1916. Affected names are placed on the Official List and Index. Proposal: BZN (1966) 23(1):55-56. Ruling: BZN (1969) 25(2/3):94-95.

Opinion 870 [Case 1753]. Refusal to use plenary powers to suppress *Hippocampus erectus* Perry 1810. Proposal: BZN (1966) 23(4):178. Comments: BZN (1967) 24(2):80. Ruling: BZN (1969) 25(6):212-213.

Opinion 880 [Case 1655]. Refusal to set aside a first reviser selection of *Gobius scorpioides* Collett 1874, as opposed to *Gobius orca* Collett 1874, as the type species of *Lebetus*. Proposal: BZN (1964) 21(5):388-391. Ruling: BZN (1969) 26(1):22-23.

Opinion 888 [Case 1651]. Several measures to stabilize tunicate nomenclature. *Salpa* Forsskål 1775 (Tunicata) is conserved by the suppression of *Salpa* G. Edwards 1771 (Pisces). Proposal: BZN (1966) 23(5):232-234. Ruling: BZN (1969) 26(3):136-138.

Opinion 900 [Case 1723]. Three specific names in the family Belonidae are suppressed under the plenary powers. Affected names are placed on the Official List and Official Index. Proposal: BZN (1966) 22(5/6):325-329. Comments: BZN (1966) 23(4):149-154; BZN (1967) 24(1):2; BZN (1967) 24(4):196-201. Ruling: BZN (1970) 26(5/6):213-216.

Opinion 901 [Case 1740]. The names of five species of Clupeidae published by Richardson (1844, 1846) are suppressed for the purposes of the priority but not for homonymy. Affected names are placed on the Official List and Official Index. Proposal: BZN (1966) 23(1):62-64. Comments: BZN (1966) 23(4):146-148. Ruling: BZN (1970) 26(5/6):217-220.

Opinion 903 [Case 1657]. Designates *Xiphias platypterus* Shaw & Nodder 1792 as the type-species of *Istiophorus* Lacepède 1802; all earlier designations are set aside. Affected names are placed on the Official List and Official Index. The holotype of *Xiphias platypterus* is officially designated the lectotype of *Scomber gladius* Bloch 1793, making the latter name a junior objective synonym of the former. Proposal: BZN (1964) 21(6):444-445, pl. 5. Comments: BZN (1965) 22(3):148-152. Ruling: BZN (1970) 26(5/6):223-224.

Opinion 921 [Case 1803]. Removes homonymy of Plethodontidae in fossil fishes (based on *Plethodus* Dixon 1850) and

Amphibia (based on *Plethodon* Tschudi 1838). Plethodidae is declared to be the official name in fishes, with Plethodontidae retained for Amphibia. Proposal: BZN (1967) 24(4):252-254. Ruling: BZN (1970) 27(2):79-80.

Opinion 930 [Case 1690]. Preserves in accustomed usage the fossil fish genera *Megalichthys* Agassiz 1835 and *Rhizodus* Owen 1840 through neotype designation under the plenary powers. *Megalichthys hibberti* Agassiz in Hibbert 1835 is ruled under the plenary powers to be a name distinct from *Rhizodus hibberti* Owen 1840. Affected names and their type species are placed on the Official List and Official Index. Proposal: BZN (1966) 23(2/3):117-120. Comments: BZN (1967) 24(5):262. Ruling: BZN (1970) 27(2):97-98.

Opinion 960 [Case 1821]. Conserves the family name Centracanthidae Fowler 1925 (1829), given precedence over Maenidae Cuvier 1829. Affected names are placed on the Official List and Official Index. "The adopted family-group name Centracanthidae is to be considered the senior synonym of the rejected name, Maenidae [Art. 40b], with its own author and date, followed by the date of the replaced name in parentheses..." Proposal: BZN (1969) 26(1):32-36. Ruling: BZN (1971) 28(1/2):36-38.

Opinion 962 [Case 1556]. Removes homonymy in family Gerridae in fishes (based on *Gerres*) and Hemiptera (based on *Gerris*). The stem of *Gerres* Quoy & Gaimard 1824 for the purposes of forming family-group names is ruled to be *Gerre-*, making the official name of the fish family Gerreidae. Affected names are placed on the Official List and Official Index. Proposal: BZN (1963) 20(4):307-308. Ruling: BZN (1971) 28(1/2):41-43.

Opinion 971 [Case 1874]. *Pseudoscaphirhynchus* Nikolski 1900 and *Scaphirhynchus hermanni* Kessler 1877 are placed on the Official List. Proposal: BZN (1969) 26(2):93-94. Ruling: BZN (1971) 28(5/6):145-146.

Opinion 988 [Case 850]. *Sciaena umbra* Linnaeus 1758 is designated type-species of *Sciaena* Linnaeus 1758. Affected names are placed on the Official List. Proposal: BZN (1963) 20(5):349-360. Comments: BZN (1964) 21(5):362; BZN (1966) 23(1):2-5. Ruling: BZN (1972) 29(3):123-124.

Opinion 1010 [Case 1910]. Designation under the plenary powers of a type species for *Callopanchax* Myers 1933. Affected taxa are placed on Official List and Official Index. Proposal: BZN (1971) 27(5/6):246-249. Comments: BZN (1971) 28(5/6):139; BZN (1972) 29(3):105; BZN (1972) 29(4):193. Ruling: BZN (1974) 30(3/4):164-166.

Opinion 1021 [Case 1941]. Suppresses *Clinus aculeatus* Reinhardt 1837 in favor of *Clinus maculatus* Fries 1838. Affected names are placed on Official List and Official Index. Proposal: BZN (1971) 28(1/2):64. Comments:BZN (1972) 29(3):110. Ruling: BZN (1974) 31(3):123-124.

Opinion 1031 [Case 1964]. *Eostomias eximius* Jordan & Gilbert 1925 is placed on the Official List. Proposal: BZN (1971) 28(5/6):164-165. Comments: BZN (1972) 29(3):111. Ruling: BZN (1974) 31(4):192-193.

Opinion 1033 [Case 1967]. *Echeneis sexdecimlamellata* Eydoux & Gervais 1838 and *Echeneis quatuordecimlaminatus* Storer 1839 are suppressed for purposes of priority but not homonymy, thereby validating *Echeneis brachyptera* Lowe 1839. Affected names are placed on the Official List and Official Index. Proposal: BZN (1971) 28(5/6):168-170. Comments: BZN (1972) 29(3):112; BZN (1973) 30(2):76. Ruling: BZN (1975) 32(1):31-32.

Opinion 1046 [Case 1958]. Removes homonymy of family-group names in Pisces, Aves, and Lepidoptera. The stem of *Drepane* is ruled to by Drepane- for family name formation. Drepaneidae Gill 1847 is the official name in fishes; Drepanididae Cabanas 1847 is the official name in Aves. (Drepanidae Boiduval [Nov. 1828] was established as the official name in Lepidoptera in Opinion 610.) Affected names are placed on the Official List and Official Index. Proposal: BZN (1971) 28(3/4):119-120; BZN (1973) 30(1):35-36. Comments: BZN (1972) 29(3):111; BZN (1974) 30(3/4):138-139. Ruling: BZN (1976) 32(4):222-229.

Opinion 1082 [Case 1981]. Gives the specific name *Etmopterus kleinenbergi* Giglioli 1889, precedence over *Pharopteryx benoit* Rüppell 1852 if both names are considered to represent the same taxon. *Pharopteryx* Rüppell 1828 is the correct spelling for the genus. Affected names are placed on the Official List and Official Index. Proposal: BZN (1972) 29(1):37-38; BZN (1974) 31(4):172-173; BZN (1976) 33(1):9. Ruling: BZN (1977) 34(1): 27-29.

Opinion 1121 [Case 1946]. Designates *Chanda nama* Hamilton 1822, the type species of *Chanda* Hamilton 1822. [The author of the proposal, Dr. P. K. Talwar, used the name Hamilton-Buchanan, as do many authors, for this 1822 work, but other authors use Hamilton and some Buchanan. The title page of the work states that the author is "Hamilton (formerly Buchanan)"; we feel that authorship clearly must be "Hamilton".] Proposal: BZN (1971) 28(3/4):104-105. Comments: BZN (1973) 30(2): 69; BZN (1974) 31(3):107-111. Ruling: BZN (1979) 35(4): 223-226.

Opinion 1123 [Case 2052]. Plesiadapidae Trouessart 1897 is given nomenclatural precedence over Platychoeropidae Lydekker 1887 (Mammalia). The fish genus *Platychoerops* Klunzinger 1879 is placed on the Official Index. Proposal: BZN (1974) 30(3/4):207-209. Comments: BZN (1974) 31(4):177. Ruling: BZN (1979) 35(4):229-232.

Opinion 1124 [Case 2058]. *Lichia* Cuvier 1817 [= 1816] conserved. *Hypacantus* Rafinesque 1810 is suppressed for the purposes of priority, but not homonymy. Affected names are placed on the Official List and Official Index. Proposal: BZN (1974) 31(1):27-28. Comments: BZN (1975) 32(2):99-100. Ruling: BZN (1979) 35(4):233-235.

Opinion 1132 [Case 1807]. Two works by Hemprich & Ehrenberg (1828) are suppressed. *Heterotis* Rüppell 1829 (ex Ehrenberg MS) is validated. *Heterotis* and *Arapaima* Müller 1843 are placed on the Official List. Proposal: BZN (1967) 24(5):291-293; (1975) 32(1):56-59. Comments: BZN (1968) 25(1):64; BZN (1969) 25(6):194-195; BZN (1970) 26(5/6):180-182; BZN (1970) 27(1):2; BZN (1976) 32(4):200. Ruling: BZN (1979) 36(2):85-90.

Opinion 1150 [Case 1502]. *Chilodus* Müller & Troschel 1844 and *Caenotropus* Günther 1864 and their type species are placed on the Official List. Proposal: BZN (1962) 19(3):191-192. Comments: BZN (1963) 20(2):147. Ruling: BZN (1980) 37(2): 72-74.

Opinion 1153 [Case 1877]. *Galaxias platei* Steindachner 1898 is to be given precedence over *Galaxias delfini* Philippi 1895 whenever the two names are regarded as synonyms. Both names are placed on the Official List. Proposal: BZN (1973) 30(2):88-89; BZN (1977) 34(2):80. Comments: BZN (1974) 31(1):8. Ruling: BZN (1980) 37(2):81-84.

Opinion 1169 [Case 1950]. The neotype of *Cataphractus punctatus* Bloch 1794 designated by Nijssen and Isbrücker in 1967 is set aside. A rediscovered syntype, designated in the proposal as the lectotype, is accepted as the basis of the species. The species is placed on the Official List. Proposal: BZN (1975) 32(1):63-64, pl. 1. Comments: BZN (1979) 35(4):198. Ruling: BZN (1981) 38(1):72-73.

Opinion 1171 [Case 2045]. Establishes the stem of the generic name *Petromyzon* Linnaeus 1758 as Petromyzont-. The correct family name is thus Petromyzontidae Bonaparte 1832. Affected names are placed on the Official List. Proposal: BZN (1974) 30(3/4):198-199; BZN (1975) 32(3):154-155. Comments: BZN (1975) 32(1): 18-21; BZN (1976) 32(4): 200; BZN (1977) 33(3/4):142-143. Ruling: BZN (1981) 38(2):98-99.

Opinion 1190 [Case 2113]. *Pterois zebra* Cuvier in Cuvier & Valenciennes 1829 is conserved. *Pterois zebra* Quoy & Gaimard 1825 is suppressed for the purposes of both priority and homonymy. Affected names are placed on the Official List and Official Index. Proposal: BZN (1976) 32(4):250-251. Ruling: BZN (1981) 38(4):247-248.

Opinion 1200 [Case 2126]. *Genypterus* Philippi 1857 is conserved. *Xiphiurus* Smith 1847 is suppressed. Affected names are placed on the Official List and Official Index. Proposal: BZN (1976) 33(2):90-93. Ruling: BZN (1982) 39(1):19-20.

Opinion 1206 [Case 2154]. Designates the lectotype for *Alburnops plumbeolus* Cope 1865 and *Hypsilepis cornutus cerasinus* Cope 1868. Affected names are placed on the Official List. Proposal: BZN (1977) 33(3/4):245-247. Ruling: BZN (1982) 39(2):104-105.

Opinion 1217 [Case 1578]. *Liparis koefoedi* Parr 1932 is conserved. *Ophidium parrii* Ross 1826 is suppressed. Affected names are placed on the Official List and Official Index. Proposal: BZN (1977) 34(1):58-60. Ruling: BZN (1982) 39(2):130-131.

Opinion 1230 [Case 663]. The gender of *Notropis* Rafinesque 1818 is ruled to be masculine by use of plenary powers. Affected names are placed on the Official List. Proposal: BZN (1954) 9(9):272-274; BZN (1954) 9(9):274-275; BZN (1978) 34(4):240-242. Comments: BZN (1954) 9(9):276-277; BZN (1955) 11(6):188. Ruling: BZN (1982) 39(4):241-242. See also: BZN (1953) 10(7):228 (letter from R. M. Bailey, 1949, on problem.)

Opinion 1235 [Case 2183]. *Sebastichthys hubbsi* Matsubara 1937 is designated as the type species of *Sebastocles* Jordan & Hubbs 1925. Affected names are placed on the Official List. Proposal: BZN (1977) 34(2):88-89. Ruling: BZN (1982) 39(4):255-257.

Opinion 1237 [Case 2167]. *Otolithus macrophthalmus* Bleeker 1850 is designated as the type species of *Pennahia* Fowler 1926. Affected names are placed on Official List. Proposal: BZN (1977) 34(3):185-186. Ruling: BZN (1982) 39(4):260-261.

Opinion 1272 [Case 2226]. *Sciaena nibe* Jordan & Thompson 1911 is conserved by suppression of *Pseudotolithus brunneolus* Richardson 1909. Affected names are placed on the Official List and Official Index. Proposal: BZN (1979) 36(3):155-157. Ruling: BZN (1984) 41(1):26-27.

Opinion 1278 [Case 2090]. *Rhincodon* Smith 1829 is conserved; *Rhiniodon* Smith 1828 is suppressed. Affected names are placed on the Official List and Official Index. Proposal: BZN (1975) 32(3):163-167. Comments: BZN (1976) 33(1):4-5; BZN (1976) 33(2):70-71; BZN (1977) 34(2):67-68; BZN (1982) 39(1):6. Ruling: BZN (1984) 41(4):215-217.

Opinion 1285 [Case 2164]. *Barbus altianalis* Boulenger 1900 and *Barbus rueppelli* Boulenger 1902 are conserved. *Labeo rueppellii* Pfeffer 1896 is suppressed. Affected names are placed on the Official List and Official Index. Proposal: BZN (1980) 36(4):249-251. Ruling: BZN (1984) 41(4):233-234.

Opinion 1333 [Case 1393]. *Ipnops murrayi* Günther 1878 is conserved. *Lychnoculus* and *Lychnoculus mirabilis* Murray 1877 are suppressed. Affected names are placed on the Official List and Official Index. Proposal: BZN (1962) 19(5):295-296; BZN (1982) 39(1):27-28. Ruling: BZN (1985) 42(3):236-237.

Opinion 1388 [Case 2435]. Designates a neotype for *Callionymus sagitta* Pallas 1770. The species is to be determined by reference to this neotype, which differs from Pallas' original species but is consistent with current usage. *Callionymus sagitta* and *Callionymus filamentosus* Valenciennes in Cuvier & Valenciennes 1837 are placed on the Official List. Proposal: BZN (1984) 41(1):58-61. Ruling: BZN (1986) 43(2):132-133.

Opinion 1390 [Case 2445]. Designates a replacement lectotype for *Pellonula bahiensis* Steindachner 1879, and that species is placed on the Official List. Proposal: BZN (1984) 41(1):65-66. Ruling: BZN (1986) 43(2):136-137.

Opinion 1402 [Case 2371]. *Bagrus* Bosc 1816 is conserved and placed on the Official List. *Porcus* Etienne Geoffroy Saint-Hilaire 1808 is suppressed. *Silurus bajad* Forsskål 1775 is designated type species of *Bagrus* in the proposal (BZN 40:170). Affected names are placed on the Official List and Official Index. Proposal: BZN (1983) 40(3):167-172. Comments: BZN (1985) 42(1):14-16. Ruling: BZN (1986) 43(3):233-234.

Opinion 1415 [Case 2279]. *Polygnathus bilineatus* Roundy 1926 designated as type species of *Gnathodus* Pander 1856. Both names are placed on the Official List. (Conodonts.) Proposal: BZN (1979) 36(1):57-62; BZN (1984) 41(4):205-207. Comments: BZN (1980) 36(4):201-202; BZN (1980) 37(2):67; BZN (1981) 38(2):83-93; BZN (1982) 39(1):7-13. Ruling: BZN (1986) 43(3):262-263.

Opinion 1417 [Case 2329]. *Chromis* Cuvier in Desmarest 1814 is placed on the Official List, and its gender is ruled to be feminine. The application requested that the gender be ruled masculine and all generic names ending in *-chromis* be ruled to be masculine; this was refused. This decision does not fix the gender for other genera ending in *-chromis*. *Sparus chromis* Linnaeus 1758 is placed on the Official List as type species of *Chromis* Cuvier. Proposal: BZN (1980) 37(4):247-255. Comments: BZN (1985) 42(3):215-218. Ruling: BZN 43(3):267-268.

Opinion 1438 [Case 2434]. *Semionotus bergeri* Agassiz 1833 is designated as the type species of the fossil fish genus *Semionotus* Agassiz 1832 using plenary powers, and the affected names are placed on the Official List. Proposal: BZN (1985) 42(4):371-373. Ruling: BZN (1987) 44(2):141.

Opinion 1439 [Case 2470]. *Cephalopholis argus* Schneider

[Bloch & Schneider] 1801 is conserved by suppression of *Anthias argus* Bloch 1792 for both priority and homonymy. *Serranus sexmaculatus* Rüppell 1830 is conserved by suppression of *Serranus zanana* Valenciennes 1828 for priority only. Affected names are placed on the Official List and Official Index. *Bodianus guttatus* Bloch 1790 is noted to be a junior homonym of *Perca guttata* Linnaeus 1758 when both species are included in *Serranus* or *Epinephelus*. Proposal: BZN (1985) 42(4):374-378. Comments: BZN (1986) 43(3):227-228. Ruling: BZN (1987) 44(2):142-143.

Opinion 1459 [Case 2414]. *Carcharias* Rafinesque is conserved. This is a partial repeal of Opinion 723. *Carcharias* is removed from the Official Index and placed on the Official List. *Odontaspis* Agassiz 1838 is to be given precedence over *Carcharias* when they are considered synonyms. The specific name *taurus* Rafinesque, type species of *Carcharias* is placed on the Official List. The family name Carchariidae is placed on the Official List; it is not to be given precedence over Odontaspididae Müller & Henle when the two are conidered synonyms. Proposal: BZN (1986) 43(1):89-92. Ruling: BZN (1987) 44(3) :216-217.

Opinion 1481 [Case 2517]. *Siphamia* Weber 1909 and *Siphamia permutata* Klausewitz 1966 are conserved by suppression (for the purpose of priority but not homonymy) of *Beanea* Steindachner 1902 and *Beanea trivittata* Steindachner 1902. *Siphamia* Weber 1909, *Siphamia tubifer* Weber 1909, and *Siphamia permutata* Klausewitz 1966 are placed on the Official List. *Beanea* Steindachner 1902 and *Beanea trivittata* Steindachner 1902 are placed on the Official Index. Proposal: BZN (1986) 43(2):193-195. Ruling: BZN (1988) 45(1):82-83.

Opinion 1500 [Case 2566]. *Cobitis taenia* Linnaeus 1758 is designated the type species of *Cobitis* Linnaeus 1758. The spelling of the family-group name as Cobitidae, dating to Swainson 1839, is confirmed. Affected names are placed on the Official List. *Acantophthalmus* van Hasselt 1823 is a junior objective synonym of *Cobitis* and placed on the Official Index. Proposal: BZN (1986) 43(4):360-362. Ruling: BZN (1988) 45(2):178-179.

Opinion 1547 [Case 2533]. Under plenary powers, a neotype is designated for *Silurus felis* Linnaeus 1766, and the species is placed on the Official List. The species *marinus* described by Mitchill 1815 in the binomen *Silurus marinus* is placed on the Official List. Proposal: BZN (1987) 44(1):31-35. Comments: BZN (1988) 45(3):219-221. Ruling: BZN (1989) 46(2):151.

Opinion 1548 [Case 2594]. The species *Sarotherodon melanotheron* Rüppell 1852 is conserved by using plenary powers to suppress *Labrus melagaster* Bloch 1792. Names are placed on the Official List and Official Index. Proposal: BZN (1987) 44(3):190-191. Ruling: BZN (1989) 46(2):152.

Opinion 1562 [Case 2595.] It is confirmed that the principle of priority would apply to the specific names *Ctenopoma oxyrhynchum* Boulenger 1902 and *Ctenopoma weeksii* Boulenger 1896, thereby not conserving the former. *C. weeksii* is placed on the Official List. Proposal: BZN (1987) 44(3):192-193. Comments: BZN (1988) 45(2):143-144. Ruling: BZN (1989) 46(3):212.

Opinion 1563 [Case 2516]. Under plenary powers, the specific names *caeruleus* Cuvier 1830, *lepisurus* Cuvier 1830, and *frenatus* Cuvier 1830 (all first published in the genus *Heliases*) are suppressed for the purposes of priority but not homonymy in order to conserve the species *Heliases ternatensis* Bleeker 1856. Affected names are placed on the Official List and Official Index; the species *Pomacentrus viridis* Cuvier 1830 also is placed on the Official List. Proposal: BZN (1987) 44(4):248-250. Ruling: BZN (1989) 46(3):213-214.

Opinion 1564 [Case 2541]. *Neamia octospina* Smith & Radcliffe 1912 is conserved by use of plenary powers through the suppression of *Apogon sphenurus* for the purposes of priority. Affected names are placed on the Official List and Official Index. Proposal: BZN (1987) 44(4):251-252. Ruling: BZN (1989) 46(3):215-216.

Opinion 1581 [Case 2556]. *Hydrolycus* Müller & Troschel 1844 is placed on the Official List and its type species is confirmed as *Hydrocyon scomberoides* Cuvier 1819. Proposal: BZN (1988) 45(1):38-40. Ruling: BZN (1990) 47(1):76.

Opinion 1582 [Case 2598]. *Ictiobus* Rafinesque 1820 is conserved by use of plenary powers to suppress *Amblodon* Rafinesque 1820 for the purposes of priority but not homonymy. Plenary powers are also used to rule that *Ictiobus* is the correct original spelling, thereby rejecting *Ictiorus* Rafinesque 1820. These names and *Catostomus bubalus*, type species of *Ictiobus*, are placed on the appropriate Official List and Official Index. Proposal: BZN (1988) 45(1):36-37. Ruling: BZN (1990) 47(1):77-78.

Opinion 1583 [Case 2619]. *Hemitripteras* [sic] *marmoratus* Ayres 1854 is ruled to have priority over *Scorpaenichthys marmoratus* Girard 1854, and the former is ruled the type species of *Scorpaenichthys* Girard 1854. Names are placed on the Official List. Proposal: BZN (1988) 45(2):132-134. Ruling: BZN (1990) 47(1):79-80.

Opinion 1584 [Case 2631]. *Silurus lividus* Rafinesque 1820 is, by use of plenary powers, designated type species of *Ameiurus* Rafinesque 1820 to conserve the use of *Ameiurus* and avoid its falling as a junior synonym of *Pylodictis*. The genera *Ameiurus* and *Pylodictis* and the species *Pimelodus natalis* and *Silurus olivaris* are placed on the Official List. Proposal: BZN (1988) 45(2):135-137. Ruling: BZN (1990) 47(1):81-81.

Opinion 1603 [Case 2625]. Under plenary powers it is ruled that *Saccopharynx* Mitchill 1824 is deemed to be a new nominal genus and not a replacement for *Stylephorus* Shaw 1791, and *Saccopharynx flagellum* Cuvier is designated the type species of *Saccopharynx*. Affected names are placed on the Official List. Proposal: BZN 45(4):204-206. Ruling: BZN 47(2):164-165.

Cases Pending

Case 276. Follow-up to Opinion 16. A request was made to specialists for information on the status of the 27 names from Opinion 16 which had not already been placed on the Official List. Fish genera involved: *Gymnotus* Linnaeus 1758, and *Stromateus* Linnaeus 1758. Proposal: BZN (1950) 4(19/20):580-583; BZN (1952) 7(7/8) 202.

Case 1173. The Commission is requested to conserve *Muraena* Linnaeus 1758 in its accustomed usage by using plenary powers to establish *M. helena* Linnaeus 1758 as its type species. This also would allow *Anguilla* Shaw 1803 to be conserved in its present use. Affected names would be placed on the Official

List. Proposal: BZN (1989) 46(4):259-261 and reopened as BZN (1990) 47(2):138.

Case 1279. The Commission is requested to determine whether Jordan & Evermann validly designated type species in *Fishes of North and Middle America* (1896-1900) or *Check list of the Fishes and Fish-Like Vertebrates of North & Middle America* (1896), particularly in the case of *Bathylagus* Günther 1878. Proposal: BZN (1958) 16(2):73-78; (1962) 19(4):200-229. *Bathylagus antarcticus* Günther 1878, *Argentina* Linnaeus 1758, Argentininae Bonaparte 1846 (correction of Argentinini), *Bathylagus* Günther 1878, Bathylagidae Gill 1884, and *Argentina sphyraena* Linnaeus 1758 are proposed for placement on respective Official Lists. Argentinini Bonaparte 1846 proposed for placement on the Official Index. Proposal: BZN (1958) 16(2):73-78; BZN (1962) 19(4):200-229.

Case 1308. The Commission is requested to place *Puntius* Hamilton 1822 on the Official List in order to stabilize the designation of the type species. *Cyprinus sophore* is proposed for placement on Official List of species. Proposal: BZN (1961) 18(3):199-200.

Case 1579. The Commission is requested to suppress *Pleuronectes grohmanni* Bonaparte 1837 as a nomen dubium and place it on the Official Index; *Arnoglossus kessleri* Schmidt 1915 and *Arnoglossus thori* Kyle 1913 are proposed for placement on the Official List. Proposal: BZN (1963) 20(5):372.

Case 1721. The Commission is requested to validate *Siganus* Forsskål 1775 and to suppress *Teuthis* Linnaeus 1766. *Scarus psittacus* Forsskål 1775, *Scarus rivulatus* Forsskål 1775, *Scarus* Forsskål 1775, Siganidae Rutter 1897, and *iganus* Forsskål 1775 are proposed for placement on the Official Lists. *Teuthis* Linnaeus 1766 is proposed for placement on the Official Index. Proposal: BZN (1968) 25(1):26-28; BZN (1972) 29(4):190-193; BZN (1973) 30(1):6-7. Comments: BZN (1970) 26(5/6):178-179.

Case 1743. The Commission is requested to add *Chromis aureus* Steindachner 1864 to the Official List. Proposal: BZN (1966) 23(4):157.

Case 1744. The Commission is requested to add *Otolithus aureus* Richardson 1846 to the Official List. Proposal: BZN (1966) 23(4):158-159.

Case 1825. The Commission is requested to suppress *Elipesurus* Schomburgk 1843 in order to conserve *Potamotrygon* Garman 1878. *Trygon hystrix* Garman 1878, *Potamotrygon* Garman 1878, and Potamotrygonidae Garman 1878 are proposed for placement on the Official List. *Elipesurus* Schomburgk 1843, *Ellipesurus* Günther 1870, and *Elipesurus spinicauda* Schomburgk 1843 are proposed for placement on the Official Index. Proposal: BZN (1968) 24(6):353-355. Comment: BZN (1969) 25(4/5):133-134.

Case 1951. The Commission is requested to suppress *Cestracion phillipi* var. *japonica* Duméril 1865 in order to preserve *Heterodontus japonicus* Maclay & Macleay 1884. *Heterodontus japonicus* Maclay & Macleay 1884 is proposed for placement on the Official List. *Cestracion japonica* Duméril 1865 is proposed for placement on the Official Index. Proposal: BZN (1971) 28(3/4):107-108.

Case 2440. The Commission is requested to confirm the spelling of the family name Liparidae although it is grammatically incorrect. The ruling desired would fix the stem of the generic name is Lipar-. The family, type genus, and type species would be placed on the Official List. Proposal: BZN (1988) 45(2):130-131. Comments: BZN (1988) 45(4):292, BZN (1989) 46(1):45.

Case 2515. The Commission is requested to stabilize the dates and authorship of *Histoire naturelle* section of M.J.C.L. de Savigny's *Description de l'Egypte*. Fishes are treated in 2 sections, both by Geoffroy Saint-Hilaire, 1827 ('...Poissons du Nil' [pp. 265-310], and '...Poissons de la Mer Rouge et de la Méditerranée' [pp. 311-343]. Proposal: BZN (1986) 43(1):107-111.

Case 2594. The Commission is requested to conserve the cichlid specific name *melanotheron* Rüppell 1852 by the suppression of the senior subjective synonym *Labrus melagaster* Bloch 1792. Affected names would be placed on the appropriate lists and indexes.

Case 2595. The Commission is requested to conserve the specific name of the climbing perch, *Ctenopoma oxyrhynchum* Boulenger 1902 by suppression of the senior synonym *C. weeksii* Boulenger 1896. Affected names would be placed on the appropriate lists and indexes. Proposal: BZN (1987) 44(3):192-193.

Case 2659. The Commission is requested to conserve the species *Osteoglossum bicirrhosum* Cuvier 1829 and to suppress *Osteoglossum vandellii*. Affected taxa would be placed on the appropriate lists and indexes. Proposal: BZN (1989) 46(2):130-131.

Case 2681. The Commission is requested to conserve the species *Chromis ovalis* Steindachner 1900 by using plenary powers to rule that it is not invalid because it was replaced before 1961 as a junior secondary homonym; the taxon would be placed on the Official List. Proposal: BZN (1989) 46(1):35-37.

Case 2688. The Commission is requested to conserve *Callionymus pusillus* Delaroche 1809, a species name threatened by the unused *C. dracunculus* Linnaeus 1758. Proposal: BZN (1989) 46(4):255-258.

Case 2738. The Commission is asked to designate *Cobitis kuhlii* Valenciennes as the type species of *Acathophthamus* van Hasselt in Temminck 1824 and to suppress the original spelling *Acantophthalmus*. Proposal: BZN (1990) 47(2):118-121.

NAMES PLACED ON THE OFFICIAL LIST OF SPECIFIC NAMES IN ZOOLOGY

aculeatus, Gasterosteus, Linnaeus 1758. Syst. Nat. (ed. 10) v. 1:295. Type species of *Gasterosteus* Linnaeus 1758. Dir. 57.

acus, Syngnathus, Linnaeus 1758. Syst. Nat. (ed. 10) v. 1:337. Type species of *Syngnathus* Linnaeus 1758. Dir. 57.

acuta, Dussumieria, Valenciennes 1847. In: Cuvier & Valenciennes, Hist. Nat. Poiss. v. 20:467. Op. 901.

alburnus, Culter, Basilewsky 1855. Nouv. Mém. Soc. Imp. Nat. Moscou v. 10:236. Type species of *Culter* Basilewsky 1855. Op. 513.

altianalis, Barbus, Boulenger 1902. Ann. Mag. Nat. Hist. (Ser. 7) v. 6:159. Op. 1285.

amia, Scomber, Linnaeus 1758. Syst. Nat. (ed. 10) v. 1:299. Type species of *Lichia* Cuvier 1817 [= 1816]. Op. 1124.

ampullaceus, Ophiognathus Harwood 1827. Philoso. Trans. R. Soc. London 1827:51. Op. 1603.

ancyclostomus, Rhina, Schneider [Bloch & Schneider] 1801. In: Bloch, Syst. Ichthyol.:352. Type species of *Rhina* Schneider [Bloch & Schneider] 1801. Op. 345.

argenteus, Prochilodus, Agassiz 1829. Sel. Gen. Spec. Pisc. Brasil.:63, pl. 38. Type species of *Prochilodus* Agassiz 1829. Op. 772.

argus, Cephalopholis, Schneider [Bloch & Schneider] 1801. In: Bloch, Syst. Ichthyol.:311. Conserved by suppression of *Anthias argus* Bloch 1792. Op. 1439.

atherinoides, Notropis, Rafinesque 1818. Amer. Mon. Mag. Crit. Rev. v. 2:204. Type species of *Notropis* Rafinesque 1818. Op. 1230.

aurata, Sparus, Linnaeus 1758. Syst. Nat. (ed. 10) v. 1:277. Type species of *Sparus* Linnaeus 1758. Dir. 34.

aurita, Sardinella, Valenciennes 1847. In: Cuvier & Valenciennes, Hist. Nat. Poiss. v. 20:263. Op. 901.

axelrodi, Cheirodon, Schultz 1956. Tropical Fish Hobbyist v. 4 (no. 4):42. Ruled to have been published Feb. 20, 1956; *Hyphessobrycon cardinalis* was ruled to have been published on Feb. 21, 1956. Op. 485.

bagre, Silurus, Linnaeus 1766. Syst. Nat. (ed. 12) v. 1:505. Type species of *Bagre* Cloquet 1816. Op. 1402.

bahiensis, Pellonula, Steindachner 1879. Sitzungsber. Akad. Wiss. Wien v. 80:181, pl. 3, fig. 2. Ruled to be interpreted by reference to the lectotype designated in Opinion 1390. Op. 1390.

bajad, Silurus, Forsskål 1775. Descript. Animal. Itin. Orient. Observ.:66. Type species of *Bagrus* Bosc 1816. Op. 1402.

barbatum, Ophidion, Linnaeus 1758. Syst. Nat. (ed. 10) v. 1:259. Type species of *Ophidion* Linnaeus 1758. Dir. 57.

barbatus, Mullus, Linnaeus 1758. Syst. Nat. (ed. 10) v. 1:299. Type species of *Mullus* Linnaeus 1758. Dir. 57.

barberinus, Mullus, Lacepède 1802. Hist. Nat. Poiss. v. 3:406. Op. 846.

belone, Esox, Linnaeus 1761. Faun. Svec. (ed. 2):126. Type species of *Belone* Cuvier 1817 [= 1816]. Op. 225.

benoit, Pharopteryx, Rüppell 1852. Verz. Mus. Senck. Naturf. Gesell. Aufges. Samml., v. 4:16. Not to be given priority over *Eretmophorus kleinenbergi* Giglioli 1889, if regarded as same taxon. Op. 1082.

bergeri, Semionotus, Agassiz 1833. Rech. Poiss. Foss. v. 2 (1):8. Type species of *Semionotus* Agassiz 1832. Op. 1438.

bifasciatus, Mullus, Lacepède 1802. Hist. Nat. Poiss. v. 3:383. Type species of *Parupeneus* Bleeker 1863. Op. 846.

bilineatus, Polygnathus, Roundy 1926. U.S. Geol. Surv. Prof. Paper No. 146:13. Declared to be the type of *Gnathodus* Pander 1856. (Conodonts) Op. 1415.

brachyptera, Echeneis, Lowe 1839. Proc. Zool. Soc. London v. 7:89. Op. 1033.

cabrilla, Perca, Linnaeus 1758. Syst. Nat. (ed. 10) v. 1:294. Type species of *Serranus* Cuvier 1817 [= 1816]. Dir. 57.

bubalus, Catostomus, Rafinesque 1818. J. Phys. Chim. Hist. Nat. Arts. Paris v. 88:421. Type species of *Ictiobus* Rafinesque 1820. Op. 1582.

carcharias, Squalus, Linnaeus 1758. Syst. Nat. (ed. 10) v. 1:235. As interpreted by Bigelow & Schroeder 1948. Type species of *Carcharodon* Smith 1838. Op. 723.

carpio, Cyprinus, Linnaeus 1758. Syst. Nat. (ed. 10) v. 1:320. Type species of *Cyprinus* Linnaeus 1758. Dir. 57.

caucasicus, Pomatoschistus, Berg 1916. Les poissons des eaux douces de la Russie:409. Op. 860.

cephalus, Mugil, Linnaeus 1758. Syst. Nat. (ed. 10) v. 1:316. Type species of *Mugil* Linnaeus 1758. Dir. 57.

cerasinus, Hypsilepis cornutus, Cope 1868. Proc. Acad. Nat. Sci. Phila. 1867:159. Ruled under the plenary powers to be interpreted by the lectotype designated by Gilbert 1964. Op. 1206.

chilensis, Conger, Guichenot 1849. In: Gay, Hist. Fis. Polit. Chile, Zoologia v. 2:339. Valid name at the date of Opinion 1200 of the type species of *Genypterus* Philippi 1857. Op. 1200.

chordatus, Stylephorus, Shaw 1791. Op. 1603.

chromis, Sparus, Linnaeus 1758. Syst. Nat. (ed. 10) v. 1:280. Type species of *Chromis* Cuvier in Desmarest 1814. Op. 1417.

cirrosa, Sciaena, Linnaeus 1758. Syst. Nat. (ed. 10) v. 1:289. Type species of *Umbrina* Cuvier 1817 [= 1816]. Op. 988.

cirrus, Centracantus (sic), Rafinesque 1810. Caratt. Nuovi Gen. Nuove Spec. Anim. Piante Sicilia:43. (April 1910) Type species of *Centracanthus* Rafinesque 1810. Op. 960.

commersonii, Stolephorus, Lacepède 1803. Hist. Nat. Poiss. v. 5:381. Type species of *Stolephorus* Lacepède 1803. Op. 749.

conger, Muraena, Linnaeus 1758. Syst. Nat. (ed. 10) v. 1:245. Type species of *Conger* Oken 1817. Dir. 87.

chordatus, Stylephorus Shaw 1791. Philoso. Trans. R. Soc. London, v. 1:90. Op. 1603.

crocodila, Belona, Peron & Lesueur 1821. J. Acad. Nat. Sci. Phila. v. 2:129. Op. 900.

cyprinoides, Mormyrus, Linnaeus 1758. Syst. Nat. (ed. 10) v. 1:327. Type species of *Mormyrus* Linnaeus 1758. Dir. 57.

delfini, Galaxias, Philippi 1895. Verh. Deutsch. Wiss. Ver. Santiago Chile v. 3:17-22. Must not be given precedence over *G. platei* Steindachner 1898 when they are considered synonyms. Op. 1153.

draco, Trachinus, Linnaeus 1758. Syst. Nat. (ed. 10) v. 1:250. Type species of *Trachinus* Linnaeus 1758. Dir. 57.

dumerili, Caranx, Risso 1810. Ichth. Nice:175, pl. 6, fig. 20. Type species of *Seriola* Cuvier 1817 [= 1816]. Op. 461.

dunensis, Palaeoteuthis, Roemer 1855. Palaeontographica v. 4:72. Type species of *Rhinopteraspis* Jaekel 1919. Op. 438.

edentulus, Salmo, Bloch 1794. Naturg. Ausl. Fische v. 8:pl. 380. Type species of *Curimata* Bosc 1817. Op. 772.

electricus, Silurus, Gmelin in Linnaeus [1789]. Syst. Nat. (ed. 13) v. 1:1354. Type species of *Malapterurus* Lacepède 1803. Dir. 57.

eperlanus, Salmo, Linnaeus 1758. Syst. Nat. (ed. 10) v. 1:310. Type species of *Osmerus* Linnaeus 1758. Dir. 69.

eximius, Eostomias, Jordan & Gilbert 1925. Stanford Univ. Publs. (Biol. Sci.) v. 4 (1):13. Op. 1031.

expansus, Plethodus, Dixon 1850. Geol. Foss. Tertiary & Cretaceous Sussex:394. Type species of *Plethodus* Dixon 1950. Op. 921.

faber, Zeus, Linnaeus 1758. Syst. Nat. (ed. 10) v. 1:267. Type species of *Zeus* Linnaeus 1758. Dir. 57.

fallax, Clupea, Lacepède 1803. Hist. Nat. Poiss. v. 5:424 or 10:188, depending on edition. Op. 859.

felis, Silurus, Linnaeus 1766. Syst. Nat. (ed. 10) v. 1:501. Op. 1547.

ferox, Carcharias, Risso 1826. Hist. Nat. Princip. Prod. Europ. Mérid. v. 3:122. Type species of *Odontaspis* Agassiz 1838. Op.

723.

filamentosus, Callionymus, Valenciennes 1837. In: Cuvier & Valenciennes, Hist. Nat. Poiss. v. 12:303. Op. 1388.

fimbriata, Spratella, Valenciennes 1847. In: Cuvier & Valenciennes, Hist. Nat. Poiss. v. 20:359. Op. 901.

flavolineatus, Mullus, Lacepède 1802. Hist. Nat. Poiss. v. 3:406. Type species of *Mulloidichthys* Whitley 1929. Op. 846.

fluviatilis, Perca, Linnaeus 1758. Syst. Nat. (ed. 10) v. 1:289. Type species of *Perca* Linnaeus 1758. Dir. 57.

formosa, Heterandria, Agassiz 1855. Amer. J. Sci. Arts (2) v. 19:136. Type species of *Heterandria* Agassiz 1853. Op. 375.

fuscus, Syngnathus, Storer 1839. Fishes of Massachusetts:162, in Repts. Ichthy. Herp. Mass. This name given precedence under plenary powers over *Syngnathus peckianus* Storer 1839. Op. 569.

gigas, Sudis, Schinz 1822. In: Cuvier, Thierreich französischen frey übersetzt...v. 2:305. Type species of *Arapaima* Müller 1843. Op. 1132.

gladius, Xiphias, Linnaeus 1758. Syst. Nat. (ed. 10) v. 1:248. Type species of *Xiphias* Linnaeus 1758. Dir. 57.

glanis, Silurus, Linnaeus 1758. Syst. Nat. (ed. 10) v. 1:304. Type species of *Silurus* Linnaeus 1758. Dir. 57.

glaucus, Squalus, Linnaeus 1758. Syst. Nat. (ed. 10) v. 1:235. Type species of *Prionace* Cantor 1850. Op. 723.

glutinosa, Myxine, Linnaeus 1758. Syst. Nat. (ed. 10) v. 1:650. Type species of *Myxine* Linnaeus 1758. Dir. 57.

gobio, Cottus, Linnaeus 1758. Syst. Nat. (ed. 10) v. 1:265. Type species of *Cottus* Linnaeus 1758. Dir. 87.

gracilis, Seriola, Lowe 1843. Proc. Zool. Soc. London v. 11:82. Type species of *Cubiceps* Lowe 1843. Op. 461.

gracilis, Clupea, Schlegel 1846. In: Siebold, Fauna Japon. (Pisces) (10-14):238, pl. 108, fig. 2. Op. 749.

harengus, Clupea, Linnaeus 1758. Syst. Nat. (ed. 10) v. 1:317. Type species of *Clupea* Linnaeus 1758. Dir. 57.

hepsetus, Atherina, Linnaeus 1758. Syst. Nat. (ed. 10) v. 1:315. Type species of *Atherina* Linnaeus 1758. Dir. 57.

hermanni, Scaphirhynchus, Kessler 1877. Ryby Aralo-Kaspo-Ponticheskoi Oblasti:190, Tab. 8, fig. 25. Op. 971.

hibberti, Megalichthys, Agassiz 1835. In: Hibbert, Trans. Roy. Soc. Edinb. v. 13:202. Type species of *Megalichthys* Agassiz 1835, as defined by neotype designated under the plenary powers. Op. 930.

hibberti, Rhizodus, Owen 1840. Odontography, Expl. pls.:12. Type species of *Rhizodus* Owen 1849, as defined by neotype designated by Thomson 1966. Op. 930.

hippurus, Coryphaena, Linnaeus 1758. Syst. Nat. (ed. 10) v. 1:261. Type species of *Coryphaena* Linnaeus 1758. Dir. 57.

hubbsi, Sebastichthys, Matsubara 1937. Copeia 1937 (no. 1):57. Type species of *Sebastocles* Jordan & Hubbs 1925. Op. 1235.

imperialis, Esox, Rafinesque 1810. Caratt. Nuovi Gen. Nuove Spec. Anim. Piante Sicilia:59. Op. 900.

japonica, Anguilla, Temminck & Schlegel 1846. In: Siebold, Fauna Japon. (Pisces):258. Op. 901.

japonicus, Engraulis, Schlegel 1846. In: Siebold, Fauna Japon. (Pisces) (10-14):239, pl. 108, fig. 3. Op. 749.

kleinenbergi, Eretmophorus, Giglioli 1889. Proc. Zool. Soc. London 1889:328. Ruled under plenary powers to take precedence over *Pharopteryx benoit* when regarded as synonymous. Op. 1082.

koefoedi, Liparis, Parr 1932. Bergens Mus., Årbok No. 6:39, fig. 6. Op. 1217.

labyrinthicus, Microdus, Kner 1858. Sitzungsber. Akad. Wiss. Wien v. 30 (13):77. Type species of *Caenotropus* Günther 1864. Op. 1150.

latipinna, Mollienesia, Lesueur 1821. J. Acad. Nat. Sci. Phila. v.2 (1):3, 4. Ruled to take precedence over *Poecilia multilineata* Lesueur 1821, published in the same work. Op. 569.

lavaretus, Salmo, Linnaeus 1758. Syst. Nat. (ed. 10) v. 1:310. Type species of *Coregonus* Linnaeus 1758. Dir. 57.

leiogaster, Sardinella, Valenciennes 1847. In: Cuvier & Valenciennes, Hist. Nat. Poiss. v. 20:270. Op. 901.

longimanus, Squalus (Carcharias), Poey 1861. Mém. Hist. Nat. Cuba v. 2:338. Type species of *Pterolamiops* Springer 1951. Op. 723.

lucius, Esox, Linnaeus 1758. Syst. Nat. (ed. 10) v. 1:314. Type species of *Esox* Linnaeus 1758. Dir. 57.

lumpus, Cyclopterus, Linnaeus 1758. Syst. Nat. (ed. 10) v. 1:260. Type species of *Cyclopterus* Linnaeus 1758. Dir. 57.

lupus, Anarhichas, Linnaeus 1758. Syst. Nat. (ed. 10) v. 1:247. Type species of *Anarhichas* Linnaeus 1758. Dir. 57.

lyra, Callionymus, Linnaeus 1758. Syst. Nat. (ed. 10) v. 1:249. Type species of *Callionymus* Linnaeus 1758. Dir. 57.

macrophthalmus, Otolithus, Bleeker 1850. Verh. Batav. Genootsch. v. 23:16. Type species of *Pennahia* Fowler 1926. Op. 1237.

maculatus, Clinus, Fries 1838. K. Svenska VetenskAkad. Handl. 1837:51. Op. 1021.

maena, Sparus, Linnaeus 1758. Syst. Nat. (ed. 10) v. 1:278. Op. 960.

marginalis, Epinephelus, Bloch 1793. Naturg. Ausl. Fische v. 7:14. Type species of *Epinephelus* Bloch 1793. Dir. 57.

marinus, Petromyzon, Linnaeus 1758. Syst. Nat. (ed. 10) v. 1:230. Type species of *Petromyzon* Linnaeus 1758. Op. 1171.

marinus, Esox, Walbaum 1792. Artedi Ichthyol. v. 3:88. Op. 900.

marinus, Silurus, Mitchill 1815. Trans. Liter. Philos. Soc. New York v. 1:433. Op. 1457.

marmoratus, Hemitripteras Ayres 1854. The Pacific, San Francisco, v.3 (44):174. Op. 1583.

melanopterus, Carcharias, Quoy & Gaimard 1824. In: Freycinet, Voy. "Uranie" et "la Physicienne" (Zool.):194. Op. 723.

melanotheron, Sarotherodon Rüppell 1852. Verz. Mus. Senkenb. Naturf. Ges. Aufg. Sammlung., part 4:21. Op. 1548.

microcephalus, Lepadogaster, Brook 1889. Proc. Roy. Phys. Soc. Edinb. v. 10:166, pl. 7, figs. 1-4. Type species of *Apletodon* Briggs 1955. Op. 638.

monstrosa, Chimaera, Linnaeus 1758. Syst. Nat. (ed. 10) v. 1:236. Type species of *Chimaera* Linnaeus 1758. Dir. 57.

morhua, Gadus, Linnaeus 1758. Syst. Nat. (ed. 10) v. 1:252. Type species of *Gadus* Linnaeus 1758. Dir. 57.

murrayi, Ipnops, Günther 1878. Ann. Mag. Nat. Hist. (Ser. 5) v. 2:187. Type species of *Ipnops* Günther 1878. Op. 1333.

mustelus, Squalus, Linnaeus 1758. Syst. Nat. (ed. 10) v. 1:235. Type species of *Mustelus* Linck 1790. Dir. 57.

nama, Chanda, Hamilton 1822. An account of the fishes of the Ganges:109. Type species of *Chanda* Hamilton-Buchanan [= Hamilton] 1822. Op. 1121.

nasus, Cyprinus, Linnaeus 1758. Syst. Nat. (ed. 10) v. 1:325.

Type species of *Nasus* Basilewsky 1855. Op. 513.

natalis, Pimelodus Lesueur 1819. Mem. Mus. Hist. Nat. Paris v. 5:154. Op. 1584.

naucrates, Echeneis, Linnaeus 1758. Syst. Nat. (ed. 10) v. 1:261. Emendation of *neucrates,* an invalid original spelling. Op. 242.

nibe, Sciaena, Jordan & Thompson 1911. Proc. U.S. Natl. Mus. v. 39:258. Op. 1272.

niger, Gobius, Linnaeus 1758. Syst. Nat. (ed. 10) v. 1:262. Type species of *Gobius* Linnaeus 1758. Dir. 57.

niloticus, Sudis, Cuvier 1829, ex Ehrenberg MS. Règne Anim. (ed. 2) v. 2:328. Type species of *Heterotis* Rüppell 1829, ex Ehrenberg MS. Op. 1132.

nobilissimus, Holoptychius, Agassiz 1839. In: Murchison, Silurian System:599-601, pl. 2 bis, figs. 1, 2. Type species of *Holoptychius* Agassiz 1839. Op. 930.

occidentale, Aphyosemion, Stenholt Clausen 1966. Rev. Zool. Bot. Afr. v. 73:331. Type species of *Callopanchax* Myers 1933. Op. 1010.

ocellaris, Blennius, Linnaeus 1758. Syst. Nat. (ed. 10) v. 1:256. Type species of *Blennius* Linnaeus 1758. Dir. 57.

octospina, Neamia, Smith & Radcliffe 1912. Proc. U.S. Natl. Mus. v. 41:441. Type species of *Neamia* Smith & Radcliffe 1912. Op. 1564.

olivaris, Silurus, Rafinesque 1818. Amer. Monthly Mag. Crit. Rev. New York v.3 (5):355. Op. 1584.

paradiseus, Polynemus, Linnaeus 1758. Syst. Nat. (ed. 10) v. 1:317. Type species of *Polynemus* Linnaeus 1758. Dir. 57.

penicilligerus, Balistes, Cuvier 1817 [= 1816]. Règne Anim. v. 4:185, pl. 9, fig. 3. Type species of *Chaetodermis* Swainson 1839. Op. 764.

permutata, Siphamia, Klausewitz 1966. Senckenberg. Biol. v. 47: 217.

pilchardus, Clupea, Walbaum 1792. Artedi Ichthyol. v. 3:38. Valid name at the date of Opinion 799 of the type species of *Sardina* Antipa 1940. Op. 799.

piscatorius, Lophius, Linnaeus 1758. Syst. Nat. (ed. 10) v. 1:236. Type species of *Lophius* Linnaeus 1758. Dir. 57.

pisonis, Gobius, Gmelin [1789]. In: Linnaeus, Syst. Nat. (ed. 13) v.1 (3):1206. Type species of *Eleotris* Schneider [Bloch & Schneider] 1801. Dir. 57.

platei, Galaxias, Steindachner 1898. Zool. Jahrb., Suppl., v. 4:329. Given precedence over *G. delfini* Philippi 1895 whenever the two names are considered synonyms. Op. 1153.

platessa, Pleuronectes, Linnaeus 1758. Syst. Nat. (ed. 10) v. 1:269. Type species of *Pleuronectes* Linnaeus 1758. Dir. 33.

platypterus, Xiphias, Shaw & Nodder 1792. Naturalist's Miscellany 28:pl. 88. Type species of *Istiophorus* Lacepède 1802. Op. 903.

plumbeolus, Alburnops, Cope 1865. Proc. Acad. Nat. Sci. Phila. 1864:276-285. Ruled under the plenary powers to be interpreted by the lectotype designated by Gilbert 1964. Op. 1206.

porcus, Scorpaena, Linnaeus 1758. Syst. Nat. (ed. 10) v. 1:266. Type species of *Scorpaena* Linnaeus 1758. Dir. 57.

presidionis, Poecilia, Jordan & Culver 1895. Proc. Calif. Acad. Sci. (Ser.2) v. 5:413. Type species of *Poeciliopsis* Regan 1913. Op. 375.

punctata, Gambusia, Poey 1854. Mém. Hist. Nat. Cuba v. 1:384. Type species of *Gambusia* Poey 1854. Op. 375.

punctatus, Cataphractus, Bloch 1794. Naturg. Ausl. Fische v. 8:90, pl. 377, fig. 2. Op. 1169.

punctatus, Chaetodon, Linnaeus 1758. Syst. Nat. (ed. 10) v. 1:273. Type species of *Drepane* Cuvier 1831. Op. 1046.

punctatus, Chilodus, Müller & Troschel 1844. Arch. Naturg., Jahrg. v.10 (1):85. Type species of *Chilodus* Müller & Troschel 1844. Op. 1150.

regia, Perca, Asso 1801. An. Cienc. Nat. Madrid v. 4:42. As interpreted by the neotype designated by Trewavas. Type of *Argyrosomus* de la Pylaie 1835. Op. 988.

remora, Echeneis, Linnaeus 1758. Syst. Nat. (ed. 10) v. 1:260. Type species of *Remora* Gill 1862. Op. 242.

reticularis, Gymnothorax, Bloch 1795. Naturg. Ausl. Fische v. 9:85. Type species of *Gymnothorax* Bloch 1795. Dir. 57.

rostrata, Muraena, Lesueur 1817. J. Acad. Nat. Sci. Phila. v.1 (5):81. Given precedence over *Muraena bostoniensis* Lesueur 1817 published in the same work. Op. 569.

rueppelli, Barbus, Boulenger 1902. Ann. Mag. Nat. Hist. (Ser. 7) v. 10:423, 427, 428. Op. 1285.

sagitta, Callionymus, Pallas 1770. Spicil. Zool. v. 1 (8):29. Ruled to be interpreted by reference to the neotype designated in Opinion 1388. Op. 1388.

salar, Salmo, Linnaeus 1758. Syst. Nat. (ed. 10) v. 1:308. Type species of *Salmo* Linnaeus 1758. Dir. 57.

scaber, Uranoscopus, Linnaeus 1758. Syst. Nat. (ed. 10) v. 1:250. Type species of *Uranoscopus* Linnaeus 1758. Dir. 57.

schmidti, Tremataspis, Rohon 1892. Mém. Acad. Imp. Sci. St. Pétersbourg (7) v. 38 (13):61. Type species of *Tremataspis* Schmidt 1866. Op. 222.

scomberoides, Hydrocyon, Cuvier 1819. Mem. Mus. Hist. Nat. Paris v. 5:357. Type species of *Hydrolycus* Müller & Troschel 1844. Op. 1581.

scombrus, Scomber, Linnaeus 1758. Syst. Nat. (ed. 10) v. 1:297. Type species of *Scomber* Linnaeus 1758. Dir. 57.

scorpius, Cottus, Linnaeus 1758. Syst. Nat. (ed. 10) v. 1:265. Dir. 87.

serpens, Gempylus, Cuvier 1829. Règne Anim. (ed. 2):200. Type species of *Gempylus* Cuvier 1829. Op. 487.

sexmaculata, Cephalopholis, Rüppell 1830. Atlas Reise nord. Afrika. Fische des rothen Meeres:107. Conserved by suppression of *Serranus zanana* Valenciennes 1828. Op. 1439.

sinensis, Rhina, Schneider [Bloch & Schneider] 1801. In: Bloch, Syst. Ichthyol.:352. Type species of *Platyrhina* Müller & Henle 1838. Op. 345.

sjoestedti, Fundulus, Lönnberg 1895. Öfvers. K. Vetensk.-Akad. Forh. Stockh. v. 52:191. Valid name at the date of Opinion 1010 of the type species of *Fundulopanchax* Myers 1924. Op. 1010.

smaris, Sparus, Linnaeus 1758. Syst. Nat. (ed. 10) v. 1:278. Op. 960.

sturio, Acipenser, Linnaeus 1758. Syst. Nat. (ed. 10) v. 1:237. Type species of *Acipenser* Linnaeus 1758. Dir. 57.

tabacaria, Fistularia, Linnaeus 1758. Syst. Nat. (ed. 10) v. 1:312. Type species of *Fistularia* Linnaeus 1758. Dir. 57.

taenia, Cobitis, Linnaeus 1758. Syst. Nat. (ed. 10) v. 1:303. Type species of *Cobitis* Linnaeus 1758. Op. 1500.

taurus, Carcharias, Rafinesque 1810. Carat. Nuovi Gen. Nuove Spec. Anim. Piante Sicilia:10. Op. 1459.

ternatensis, Heliases, Bleeker 1856. Nat. Tijds. Neder.-Indië v. 10:377. Op. 1563.

thynnus, Scomber, Linnaeus 1758. Syst. Nat. (ed. 10) v. 1:297,

298. Type species of *Thunnus* South 1845. Op. 809.

tobianus, Ammodytes, Linnaeus 1758. Syst. Nat. (ed. 10) v. 1:247. Type species of *Ammodytes* Linnaeus 1758. Dir. 57.

triangularis, Ambalodus, Branson & Mehl 1933. Univ. Missouri Studies v.8 (2):128, pl. 10, figs. 35-37. Type species of *Ambalodus* Branson & Mehl 1933. (Conodonts) Op. 796.

tubifer, Siphamia, Weber 1909. Notes Leyden Mus. No. 31:168. Type species of *Siphamia* Weber 1909. Op. 1481.

typus, Rhiniodon, Smith 1828. South African Commercial Advertiser 3(145):2. Type species of *Rhincodon* Smith 1829. Op. 1278.

umbra, Sciaena, Linnaeus 1758. Syst. Nat. (ed. 10) v. 1:289. Ruled to be interpreted by neotype designated by Trewavas (1966). Type of *Sciaena* Linnaeus 1758. Op. 988.

vaigiensis, Gerres, Quoy & Gaimard 1824. Voy. "Uranie" et "la Physicienne" 1817-1820 (Zool.):292. Type species of *Gerres* Quoy & Gaimard 1824. Op. 962.

viridis, Pomacentrus, Cuvier [in Cuvier & Valenciennes] 1830. Hist. Nat. Poiss. v. 5:420. Op. 1563.

vomer, Zeus, Linnaeus 1758. Syst. Nat. (ed. 10) v. 1:266. Op. 569.

weeksi, Ctenopoma, Boulenger 1902. Ann. Mag. Nat. Hist. Ser. 6, v. 17:310. Op. 1562.

zebra, Pterois, Cuvier 1829. In: Cuvier & Valenciennes, Hist. Nat. Poiss. v. 4:269. Op. 1190.

Names Placed on the Official Index of Rejected and Invalid Specific Names in Zoology

aculeatus, Clinus, Reinhardt 1837. Ichthyol. Bidr. grønlandske Fauna. Köbenhavn.:114, 122. Suppressed under the plenary powers for the purposes of priority but not for those of homonymy. Op. 1021.

acus, Sphyraena, Lacepède 1803. Hist. Nat. Poiss. v. 5:325. Suppressed under the plenary powers for the purposes of priority but not for those of homonymy. Op. 900.

alatus, Cottus, Houttuyn [1787]. Anim. Mus. Houtt. Index:39. Published in a work rejected for nomenclatural purposes. Op. 380.

argus, Anthias, Bloch 1792. Naturg. Ausl. Fische v. 6:111. Suppressed under the plenary powers for the purposes of both priority and homonymy. Op. 1439.

auriflamma, Mullus, Forsskål 1775. Descript. Animal. Itin. Orient. Observ.:X, 30. Suppressed under the plenary powers for the purposes of priority but not for those of homonymy. Op. 846.

brunneolus, Pseudotolithus, Jordan & Richardson 1909. Mem. Carnegie Mus. v. 4:191. Suppressed under the plenary powers for the purposes of priority but not for those of homonymy. Op. 1272.

caeruleovittata, Clupea, Richardson 1846. 15th. Rept. Brit. Assoc. (Cambridge, 1845):305. Suppressed under the plenary powers for the purposes of priority but not for those of homonymy. Op. 901.

caeruleus, Heliases Cuvier [in Cuvier & Valenciennes] 1830. Hist. Nat. Poiss. v. 5:497. Suppressed under the plenary powers for the purposes of priority but not for homonymy. Op. 1563.

clathrata, Anguilla, Richardson 1844. Zool. Voy. "Sulphur" v. 1:104. Suppressed under the plenary powers for the purposes of priority but not for those of homonymy. Op. 901.

commersonianus, Stolephorus, [Lacepède 1803]. Smithson. Misc. Coll. v. 73 (4):1, 2. A cheironym created by accident in Opinion 93, in error for *commersonii*. Op. 749.

cornutus, Callionymus, Houttuyn [1787]. Anim. Mus. Houtt. Index:37. Published in a work rejected for nomenclatural purposes. Op. 380.

couchii, Lepidogaster [sic], Kent 1883. Handb. Marine Freshw. Fishes Brit. Is.:55, 56. Suppressed under the plenary powers for the purposes of priority but not for those of homonymy. Op. 638.

curimata, Salmo, Walbaum 1792. Artedi Genera Piscium, Ichth. (ed. 2) v. 3:80. Suppressed under the plenary powers for the purposes of priority but not those of homonymy. Op. 772.

falcata, Perca, Houttuyn [1787]. Anim. Mus. Houtt. Index:43. Published in a work rejected for nomenclatural purposes. Op. 380.

fasciatus, Chaetodon, Houttuyn [1787]. Anim. Mus. Houtt. Index:40. Published in a work rejected for nomenclatural purposes. Op. 380.

fasciatus, Tetrodon, Houttuyn [1787]. Anim. Mus. Houtt. Index:32. Published in a work rejected for nomenclatural purposes. Op. 380.

flos-maris, Clupea, Richardson 1846. 15th. Rept. Brit. Assoc. (Cambridge, 1845):305. Suppressed under the plenary powers for the purpose of priority but not homonymy. Op. 901.

frenatus, Heliases, Cuvier [in Cuvier & Valenciennes] 1830. Hist. Nat. Poiss. v. 5:420. Suppressed under the plenary powers for the purposes of priority but not homonymy. Op. 1563.

fuscatus, Sparus, Houttuyn [1787]. Anim. Mus. Houtt. Index:40. Published in a work rejected for nomenclatural purposes. Op. 380.

giganteus, Gyrolepis, Agassiz 1835. Rech. Poiss. Foss. v. 2 (1):175, pl. 19, fig. 13. Suppressed under the plenary powers for the purposes of priority but not for those of homonymy. Op. 930.

gladius, Scomber, erroneously attributed to Boussonet 1786. Mém. Acad. Sci. (1786):454. A cheironym; not made available in the work cited. *Scomber gladius* was first used by Bloch 1793. Op. 903.

grammistes, Perca, Houttuyn [1787]. Anim. Mus. Houtt. Index:43. Published in a work rejected for nomenclatural purposes. Op. 380.

guttata, Perca, Houttuyn [1787]. Anim. Mus. Houtt. Index:43. Published in a work rejected for nomenclatural purposes. Op. 380.

guttatus, Bodianus, Bloch 1790. Naturg. Ausl. Fische v. 4:36. Suppressed as a junior homonym of *Perca guttata* Linnaeus 1758, since both species have been placed in *Serranus* and *Epinephelus*. Op. 1439.

houttuyni, Esox, Walbaum 1792. Artedi Ichthyol. v. 3:88. Suppressed under the plenary powers for the purposes of priority but not for those of homonymy. Op. 900.

immaculatus, Salmo, Linnaeus 1758. Syst. Nat. (ed. 10) v. 1:312. Suppressed under the plenary powers for the purposes of priority but not for those of homonymy. Op. 772.

isingleena, Clupea, Richardson 1846. 15th. Rept. Brit. Assoc. (Cambridge, 1845):304. Suppressed under plenary powers for the purposes of priority but not for those of homonymy. Op. 901.

japonica, Atherina, Houttuyn 1782. Verh. Holland. Maatsch. Haarlem v. 20:340. Suppressed under the plenary powers for the purposes of priority but not for those of homonymy. Op. 749.

lamia, Carcharias, Rafinesque 1810. Indice Ittiol. Sicil.:44. A junior objective synonym of *Squalus carcharias* Linnaeus 1758. Op. 723.

lenkoranicus, Gobius, Kessler 1877. Tr. Aralo-Casp. Exp. v. 4:34. Suppressed under the plenary powers for the purposes of priority but not for those of homonymy. Op. 860.

lepisurus, Heliases, Cuvier [in Cuvier & Valenciennes] 1830. Hist. Nat. Poiss. v. 5:498. Suppressed under the plenary powers for the purposes of priority but not homonymy. Op. 1563.

littoralis, Scopula, Bertrand 1763. Dict. Univ. Foss. Propres Foss. Accid. v. 2:176. Published in a work rejected for nomenclatural purposes. Op. 592.

maculatus, Sparus, Houttuyn [1787]. Anim. Mus. Houtt. Index:42. Published in a work rejected for nomenclatural purposes. Op. 380.

Marggravii (=marcgravi), Salmo (Curimata), [Walbaum 1792]. Artedi Genera Piscium, Ichth. (ed. 2) v. 3:80. A cheironym; not made available in the work cited. Op. 772.

marisrubri, Esox belone, Schneider [Bloch & Schneider] 1801. In: Bloch, Syst. Ichthyol.:391. Suppressed under the plenary powers for the purposes of priority but not for those of homonymy. Op. 900.

melagastes, Labrus, Bloch 1792. Naturg. Ausl. Fische, v. 6:27. Suppressed under the plenary powers for purposes of priority but not homonymy.

minor, Arengus, Cornide 1788. Hist. Peces Galicia:91. Published in a work rejected for nomenclatural purposes. Op. 799.

mirabilis, Lychnoculus, Murray 1877. Science Lectures for the People (9) v. 4:132. Suppressed under the plenary powers for the purposes of priority but not for those of homonymy. Op. 1333.

neucrates, Echeneis, Linnaeus 1758. Syst. Nat. (ed. 10) v. 1:261. An invalid original spelling; emended to *naucrates*. Op. 242.

notha, Acinacea, Bory de St. Vincent 1804. Voy. Isles Afrique v. 1:93. Suppressed under the plenary powers for the purposes of priority but not for those of homonymy. Op. 487.

nymphaea, Clupea, Richardson 1846. 15th. Rept. Brit. Assoc. (Cambridge, 1845):304. Suppressed under the plenary powers for the purposes of priority but not for homonymy. Op. 901.

ornatus, Tetrodon, Houttuyn [1787]. Anim. Mus. Houtt. Index:32. Published in a work rejected for nomenclatural purposes. Op. 380.

ovata, Hamiltonia, Swainson 1839. Nat. Hist. Class. Fishes Amph. Rept. v. 2:176, 250. A junior objective synonym of *Chanda nama* Hamilton 1822. Op. 1121.

parrii, Ophidium, Ross 1826. In: Parry, J. Third Voyage Discovery North-West Passage:109. Suppressed under the plenary powers for the purposes of priority but not for those of homonymy. Op. 1217.

pennicilligerus, Balistes, Cuvier 1817 [= 1816]. Règne Anim. v. 4:185, pl. 9, fig. 3. An incorrect original spelling for *Balistes penicilligerus* Cuvier 1817 [= 1816]. Op. 764.

primaevus, Teleosteus, Volger 1860. Ber. Offenbach. Ber. Naturk. 1:37. Suppressed under the plenary powers for the purposes of priority but not for those of homonymy. Op. 223.

punctata, Perca, Houttuyn [1787]. Anim. Mus. Houtt. Index:43. Published in a work rejected for nomenclatural purposes. Op. 380.

quatuordecimlaminatus, Echeneis, Storer 1839. Fishes of Massachusetts:155, In: Repts. Ichthy. Herp. Mass. Suppressed under the plenary powers for the purposes of priority but not for those of homonymy. Op. 1033.

reticulatus, Chaetodon, Houttuyn [1787]. Anim. Mus. Houtt. Index:40. Published in a work rejected for nomenclatural purposes. Op. 380.

ruepellii, Labeo, Pfeffer 1896. Fische:Thierwelt Deutsch-ost-Afrikas u.d. Nachbargebiete (3):51, 52. Suppressed under the plenary powers for the purposes of both priority and homonymy. Op. 1285.

sexdecimlamellata, Echeneis, Eydoux & Gervais 1838. Poissons. Voy. Favorite. Cl. IV. In: Magasin de Zoologie v. 7:1. Suppressed under the plenary powers for the purposes of priority but not for those of homonymy. Op. 1033.

specularis, Cyprinus, Houttuyn [1787]. Anim. Mus. Houtt. Index:47. Published in a work rejected for nomenclatural purposes. Op. 380.

sphenurus, Apogon, Klunzinger 1884. Fische Rothen Meeres:20. Suppressed for the purposes of priority but not for homonymy. Op. 1564.

spinosus, Ostracion, Houttuyn [1787]. Anim. Mus. Houtt. Index:35. Published in a work rejected for nomenclatural purposes. Op. 380.

trivittata, Beanea, Steindachner 1902. Anz. Akad. Wiss. Wien v. 39:337. Suppressed under the plenary powers for the purpose of priority but not homonymy. Op. 1481.

varius, Gymnotus, Houttuyn [1787]. Anim. Mus. Houtt. Index:37. Published in a work rejected for nomenclatural purposes. Op. 380.

verrucosus, Silurus, Houttuyn [1787]. Anim. Mus. Houtt. Index:46. Published in a work rejected for nomenclatural purposes. Op. 380.

vexillifera, Coryphaena, Houttuyn [1787]. Anim. Mus. Houtt. Index:39. Published in a work rejected for nomenclatural purposes. Op. 380.

vittatus, Sparus, Houttuyn [1787]. Anim. Mus. Houtt. Index:42. Published in a work rejected for nomenclatural purposes. Op. 380.

vittatus, Chaetodon, Houttuyn [1787]. Anim. Mus. Houtt. Index:40. Published in a work rejected for nomenclatural purposes. Op. 380.

zanana, Serranus, Valenciennes 1828. In: Cuvier & Valenciennes, Hist. Nat. Poiss. v. 2:339. Suppressed under the plenary powers for the purposes of priority but not for homonymy. Op. 1439.

zebra, Pterois, Quoy & Gaimard 1825. Voy. "Uranie" et "la Physicienne" 1817-1820, Zool. 4:329. Suppressed under the plenary powers for the purposes of both priority and homonymy. Op. 1190.

Names Placed on the Official List of Generic Names in Zoology

Acipenser Linnaeus 1758. Syst. Nat. (ed. 10) v. 1:237. Masc. Op.

77.

Ambalodus Branson & Mehl 1933. Univ. Missouri Studies v. 8 (2):127. Masc. (Conodonts) Op. 796.

Ameiurus Rafinesque 1820. West. Rev. Misc. Mag. v. 2 (6):359. Masc. Type species *Silurus lividus* Rafinesque 1820. Op. 1584.

Ammodytes Linnaeus 1758. Syst. Nat. (ed. 10) v. 1:247. Masc. Op. 75.

Anarhichas Linnaeus 1758. Syst. Nat. (ed. 10) v. 1:247. Masc. Op. 75.

Apletodon Briggs 1955. Stanford Ichth. Bull. v. 6:22, 25. Masc. Op. 638.

Arapaima Müller 1843. Arch. Naturg., Jahrg. v. 9 (1):192. Fem. Op. 1132.

Argyrosomus de la Pylaie 1835. C. R. Congrès Sci. France, Poitiers:532. Masc. Op. 988.

Atherina Linnaeus 1758. Syst. Nat. (ed. 10) v. 1:315. Fem. Op. 75.

Bagre Cloquet 1816. Dict. Sci. Nat. v. 4:52, 53. Masc. Op. 1402.

Bagrus Bosc 1816. Nouv. Dict. Hist. Nat. v. 3:147. Masc. Op. 1402.

Belone Cuvier 1817 [= 1816]. Règne Anim. (ed. 1) v. 2:185. Masc. Validated under the plenary powers. Op. 225.

Blennius Linnaeus 1758. Syst. Nat. (ed. 10) v. 1:256. Masc. Op. 92.

Caenotropus Günther 1864. Cat. Fishes Brit. Mus. v. 5:297. Masc. Op. 1150.

Callionymus Linnaeus 1758. Syst. Nat. (ed. 10) v. 1:249. Masc. Op. 77.

Callopanchax Myers 1933. Copeia 1933 (no. 4):184. Masc. Op. 1010.

Carcharias Rafinesque 1810. Caratt. Nuovi Gen. Nuove Spec. Anim. Piante Sicilia:10. Masc. Op. 1459.

Carcharhinus Blainville 1816. Bull. Sci. Soc. Philomat. Paris 1816:121. Masc. Op. 723.

Carcharodon Smith 1838. In: Müller & Henle, Mag. Nat. Hist. (n.s.) v. 2:37. Masc. Op. 723.

Centracanthus Rafinesque 1810. Caratt. Nuovi Gen. Nuove Spec. Anim. Piante Sicilia:42. (April 1810) Masc.; emendation under plenary powers of *Centracantus* Rafinesque, 1810. Op. 960.

Chaetodermis Swainson 1839. Nat. Hist. Fishes Amphib. Rept. Monocardian Animals v. 2:194, 327, 441. Masc. Op. 764.

Chanda Hamilton 1822. An account of the fishes of the Ganges:103, 370. Fem. Op. 1121.

Chilodus Müller & Troschel 1844. Arch. Naturg., Jahrg. v. 10 (1):85. Masc. Op. 1150.

Chimaera Linnaeus 1758. Syst. Nat. (ed. 10) v. 1:236. Fem. Op. 77.

Chromis Cuvier 1814. In: Desmarest. Bull. Sci. Soc. Philom. Paris (3) v. 1:88. Fem. Op. 1417.

Clupea Linnaeus 1758. Syst. Nat. (ed. 10) v. 1:317. Fem. Op. 77.

Cobitis Linnaeus 1758. Syst. Nat. (ed. 10) v. 1:303. Fem. Op. 1500.

Conger Oken 1817. Isis (Oken) 1817:1181. Masc. Replaces non-existent *Conger* Cuvier 1817 placed on the Official List in Opinion 93. Dir. 87.

Coregonus Linnaeus 1758. Syst. Nat. (ed. 10) v. 1:310. Masc. Validated under the plenary powers. Op. 93.

Coryphaena Linnaeus 1758. Syst. Nat. (ed. 10) v. 1:261. Fem. Op. 77.

Cottus Linnaeus 1758. Syst. Nat. (ed. 10) v. 1:265. Masc. Op. 77.

Cubiceps Lowe 1843. Proc. Zool. Soc. London v. 11:82. Masc. Op. 461.

Culter Basilewsky 1855. Nouv. Mém. Soc. Imp. Nat. Moscou v. 10:236. Masc. Op. 513.

Curimata Bosc 1817. Nouv. Dict. Hist. Nat. (nouv. ed.) v. 9:9. Fem. Op. 772.

Cyclopterus Linnaeus 1758. Syst. Nat. (ed. 10) v. 1:260. Masc. Op. 77.

Cyprinus Linnaeus 1758. Syst. Nat. (ed. 10) v. 1:320. Masc. Op. 77.

Drepane Cuvier 1831. In: Cuvier & Valenciennes, Hist. Nat. Poiss. v. 7:132. Fem. Op. 1046.

Echeneis Linnaeus 1758. Syst. Nat. (ed. 10) v. 1:260. Fem. Op. 92.

Eleotris Schneider [Bloch & Schneider] 1801. In: Bloch, Syst. Ichthyol.:65. Fem. Op. 93.

Epinephelus Bloch 1793. Naturg. Ausl. Fische v. 7:11. Masc. Op. 93.

Esox Linnaeus 1758. Syst. Nat. (ed. 10) v. 1:313. Masc. Op. 92.

Fistularia Linnaeus 1758. Syst. Nat. (ed. 10) v. 1:312. Fem. Op. 75.

Fundulopanchax Myers 1924. Amer. Mus. Novit. No. 116:1-11. Masc. Op. 1010.

Gadus Linnaeus 1758. Syst. Nat. (ed. 10) v. 1:252. Masc. Op. 77.

Gambusia Poey 1854. Mém. Hist. Nat. Cuba v. 1:382. Fem. Op. 375.

Gasterosteus Linnaeus 1758. Syst. Nat. (ed. 10) v. 1:295. Masc. Op. 77.

Gempylus Cuvier 1829. Règne Anim. (ed. 2):200. Masc. Op. 487.

Genypterus Philippi 1857. Arch. Naturg., Jahrg. v. 23 (1):268. Masc. Op. 1200.

Gerres Quoy & Gaimard 1824. Voy. "Uranie" et "la Physicienne" 1817-1820 (Zool.):292. Masc. Op. 962.

Gnathodus Pander 1856. Monogr. Foss. Fische Silur. Syst. Russ.-Balt. Gouvern.:33. Type established as *Polygnathus bilineatus* Roundy, 1926. (Conodonts) Op. 1415.

Gobius Linnaeus 1758. Syst. Nat. (ed. 10) v. 1:262. Masc. Op. 77.

Gymnothorax Bloch 1795. Naturg. Ausl. Fische v. 9:83. Masc. Op. 93.

Heterandria Agassiz 1853. Amer. J. Sci. Arts (2) v. 16:135. Fem. Op. 375.

Heterotis Rüppell 1829, ex Ehrenberg MS. Beschreibung und Abbildung mehrerer neuer Fische im Nil entdeckt:10. Masc. Ruled under plenary powers to be available from publication in synonymy by Rüppell 1829. Op. 1132.

Holoptychius Agassiz 1839. In: Murchison, Silurian System:599. Masc. Op. 930.

Hydrolycus Müller & Troschel 1844. Arch. Naturgesch. Berlin v. 10 (1):93. Masc. Op. 1581.

Ictiobus Rafinesque 1820. West. Rev. Misc. Mag. v. 2 (5):299 as *Ictiorus* and Ichthyol. Ohiensis, pp. 55, 89 as *Ictiobus*. Masc. *Ictiobus* ruled to be the correct original spelling. Op. 1582.

Ipnops Günther 1878. Ann. Mag. Nat. Hist. (Ser. 5) v. 2:187. Masc. Op. 1333.

Istiophorus Lacepède 1802. Hist. Nat. Poiss. v. 3:374. Masc. Op. 903.

Lichia Cuvier 1817 [= 1816]. Règne Anim. v. 2:321. Fem. Op. 1124.
Lophius Linnaeus 1758. Syst. Nat. (ed. 10) v. 1:236. Masc. Op. 77.
Malapterurus Lacepède 1803. Hist. Nat. Poiss. v. 5:90. Masc. Op. 93.
Megalichthys Agassiz 1835. In: Hibbert, Trans. Roy. Soc. Edinb. v. 13:202. Masc. Op. 930.
Merolepis Rafinesque 1810. Indice Ittiol. Sicil.:25. (May 1810) Fem. Op. 960.
Mormyrus Linnaeus 1758. Syst. Nat. (ed. 10) v. 1:327. Masc. Op. 77.
Mugil Linnaeus 1758. Syst. Nat. (ed. 10) v. 1:316. Masc. Op. 75.
Mulloidichthys Whitley 1929. Rec. Austral. Mus. v. 17:123. Masc. Op. 846.
Mullus Linnaeus 1758. Syst. Nat. (ed. 10) v. 1:299. Masc. Op. 77.
Mustelus Linck 1790. Mag. Phys. Naturg. v. 6 (3):31. Masc. Op. 93.
Myxine Linnaeus 1758. Syst. Nat. (ed. 10) v. 1:650. Fem. Op. 75.
Nasus Basilewsky 1855. Nouv. Mém. Soc. Imp. Nat. Moscou v. 10:234. Masc. Op. 513.
Neamia Smith & Radcliffe in Radcliffe 1912. Proc. U.S. Natl. Mus. v. 41:441. Fem. Op. 1564.
Notropis Rafinesque 1818. Amer. Mon. Mag. Crit. Rev. v. 2:204. Masc. by ruling under the plenary powers. Op. 1230.
Odontaspis Agassiz 1838. Rech. Poiss. Foss. v. 3:87. Fem. Op. 723 (Confirmed in Op. 1459).
Ophidion Linnaeus 1758. Syst. Nat. (ed. 10) v. 1:259. Neut. Op. 92.
Osmerus Linnaeus 1758. Syst. Nat. (ed. 10) v. 1:310. Masc. Validated under the plenary powers in Direction 69. Op. 77.
Parupeneus Bleeker 1863. Ned. Tijdschr. Dierk. v. 1:234. Masc. Op. 846.
Pennahia Fowler 1926. J. Bombay Nat. Hist. Soc. v. 31:776. Fem. Op. 1237.
Perca Linnaeus 1758. Syst. Nat. (ed. 10) v. 1:289. Fem. Op. 77.
Petromyzon Linnaeus 1758. Syst. Nat. (ed. 10) v. 1:230. Masc. Op. 1171.
Platyrhina Müller & Henle 1838. Arch. Naturg. v. 4 (1):85. Fem. Op. 345.
Plethodus Dixon 1850. Geol. Foss. Tertiary & Cretaceous Sussex:394. Masc. Op. 921.
Pleuronectes Linnaeus 1758. Syst. Nat. (ed. 10) v. 1:268. Masc. Dir. 33.
Poeciliopsis Regan 1913. Proc. Zool. Soc. London 1913:996. Fem. Op. 375.
Polynemus Linnaeus 1758. Syst. Nat. (ed. 10) v. 1:317. Masc. Op. 93.
Prionace Cantor 1850. J. Roy. Asiat. Soc. Bengal v. 18 (2):1381. Fem. Op. 723.
Prochilodus Agassiz 1829. Sel. Gen. Spec. Pisc. Brasil.:62. Masc. Op. 772.
Pseudoscaphirhynchus Nikolski 1900. Ann. Mus. Zool. Acad. Sci. Pétersb. v. 5 (no. 1/2):257. Masc. Op. 971.
Pterolamiops Springer 1951. Copeia 1951 (no. 3):244. Masc. Op. 723.
Pylodictis Rafinesque 1819. J. Phy. Chim. Hist. Nat. Arts v. 88:422. Masc. Op. 1584.
Remora Gill 1862. Proc. Acad. Nat. Sci. Phila. 1862:239. Fem. Op. 242.
Rhina Schneider [Bloch & Schneider] 1801. In: Bloch, Syst. Ichthyol.:352. Fem. Op. 345.
Rhincodon Smith 1829. Zool. Journ. v. 4:433, 434. Masc. Op. 1278.
Rhinopteraspis Jaekel 1919. SitzBer. Ges. Naturf. Freunde Berlin 1919:74. Fem. Validated under the plenary powers. Op. 438.
Rhizodus Owen 1840. Odontography:75. Masc. Op. 930.
Saccopharynx Mitchill 1824. Ann. Lyc. Nat. Hist. N. Y. v. 1 (no. 1):86. Masc. Op. 1603.
Salmo Linnaeus 1758. Syst. Nat. (ed. 10) v. 1:308. Masc. Op. 77.
Sardina Antipa 1904. Anz. Akad. Wiss. Wien v. 41:302. Fem. Op. 799.
Sarotherodon Rüppell 1852. Verz. Mus. Senkenb. Nat. Fors. Ges. Aufg. Samml. Part 4:21. Masc. Op. 1548.
Sciaena Linnaeus 1758. Syst. Nat. (ed. 10) v. 1:288. Fem. Op. 988.
Scomber Linnaeus 1758. Syst. Nat. (ed. 10) v. 1:297. Masc. Op. 77.
Scorpaena Linnaeus 1758. Syst. Nat. (ed. 10) v. 1:266. Fem. Op. 77.
Scorpaenichthys Girard 1854. Proc. Acad. Nat. Sci. Philad. v. 7:131. Op. 1583.
Sebastocles Jordan & Hubbs 1925. Mem. Carnegie Mus. v. 10 (2):260. Masc. Op. 1235.
Selene Lacepède 1803. Hist. Nat. Poiss. v. 4:560. Fem.; given precedence over *Argyreiosus* Lacepède, 1803. Op. 569.
Semionotus Agassiz 1832. Jahrb. Mineral. Geogn. Geol. Petrefaktenk. 1832(3):144. Type established as *Semionotus bergeri* Agassiz 1833. Op. 1438.
Seriola Cuvier 1817 [= 1816]. Règne Anim. (ed. 1) v. 2:315. Fem. Op. 461.
Serranus Cuvier 1817 [= 1816]. Règne Anim. (ed. 1) v. 2:276. Masc. Op. 93.
Silurus Linnaeus 1758. Syst. Nat. (ed. 10) v. 1:304. Masc. Op. 77.
Siphamia Weber 1909. Notes Leyden Mus. No. 31:168. Fem. Op. 1481.
Sparus Linnaeus 1758. Syst. Nat. (ed. 10) v. 1:277. Masc. Dir. 34.
Spicara Rafinesque 1810. Caratt. Nuovi Gen. Nuove Spec. Anim. Piante Sicilia:51. (April 1810) Fem. Op. 960.
Stolephorus Lacepède 1803. Hist. Nat. Poiss. v. 4:381. Masc. Defects in the Official List entry corrected in Opinion 749. Op. 93.
Stylephorus Shaw 1791. Philoso. Trans. R. Soc. London v. 1:90. Masc. Op. 1603.
Syngnathus Linnaeus 1758. Syst. Nat. (ed. 10) v. 1:336. Masc. Op. 77.
Thunnus South 1845. Encycl. Metrop. 25:620. Op. 809.
Trachinus Linnaeus 1758. Syst. Nat. (ed. 10) v. 1:250. Masc. Op. 75.
Tremataspis Schmidt 1866. Verh. Russ. Min. Ges. St. Pétersburg (2) v. 1:233. Fem. Op. 222.
Umbrina Cuvier 1817 [= 1816]. Règne Anim. v. 2:297. Fem. Op. 988.
Uranoscopus Linnaeus 1758. Syst. Nat. (ed. 10) v. 1:250. Masc. Op. 75.
Xiphias Linnaeus 1758. Syst. Nat. (ed. 10) v. 1:248. Masc. Op.

75.

Zeus Linnaeus 1758. Syst. Nat. (ed. 10) v. 1:266. Masc. Op. 77.

Names Placed on the Official Index of Rejected and Invalid Generic Names in Zoology

Acanthiodos Bertrand 1763. Dict. Univ. Foss. Propres Foss. Accid. v. 1:1. Published in a work rejected for nomenclatural purposes. Op. 592.

Acanthopus Oken 1816. Lehrb. Naturg. v. 3 (Zool.) (2):iii, 122. A junior homonym of *Acanthopus* Klug 1807, and published in a rejected work. Dir. 37.

Acantophthalmus van Hasselt 1823. Algem. Konst-en Letter-Bode, II deel, no. 35:133. A junior objective synonym of *Cobitis* Linnaeus 1758. Op. 1500. See Case pending 2738 which seeks to amend this entry.

Acinacea Bory de St. Vincent 1804. Voy. Isles Afrique v. 1:93. Suppressed under the plenary powers for the purposes of priority but not for those of homonymy. Op. 487.

Acinaces Agassiz 1846. Nomencl. Zool. Index Univ.:4. Suppressed under the plenary powers for the purposes of both priority and homonymy. Op. 487.

Acipenses Linck 1790. Mag. Neuste Phys. Naturgesch. Gotha v. 6 (no. 3):37. An incorrect subsequent spelling for *Acipenser* Linnaeus 1758. Dir. 56.

Alauda Daudin 1816. Dict. Sci. Nat. (Levrault) v. 1:513. A junior homonym of *Alauda* Linnaeus 1758. Dir. 44.

Amblodon Rafinesque 1819. J. Phy. Chim. Hist. Nat. Arts Paris v. 88:421. Suppressed under the plenary powers for the purposes of priority but not homonymy. Op. 1582.

Ambolodus Branson & Mehl 1934. Univ. Missouri Studies v. 8 (no. 4):errata. Unjustified emendation of *Ambalodus* Branson & Mehl 1933. (Conodonts.) Op. 796.

Analithis Gistl 1848. Nat. Thierr.:x. A junior objective synonym of *Platyrhina* Müller & Henle 1838. Op. 345.

Anarhicas Latreille 1804. Nouv. Dict. Hist. Nat. v. 24 (Tab.):103. An incorrect subsequent spelling for *Anarhichas* Linnaeus 1758. Dir. 56.

Archaeoteuthis Roemer 1855. In: Bronn, Lethaea Geogn. (ed. 3) v. 1:520. Suppressed under the plenary powers for the purposes of priority but not for those of homonymy. Op. 438.

Arengus Cornide 1788. Hist. Peces Galicia:91. Published in a work rejected for nomenclatural purposes. Op. 799.

Bathynectes Günther 1878. Ann. Mag. Nat. Hist. (Ser. 5) v. 2:20. A junior homonym of *Bathynectes* Stimpson [1871]. Dir. 37.

Beanea Steindachner 1902. Anz. Akad. Wiss. Wien v. 39:337. Suppressed under the plenary powers for the purpose of priority but not homonymy. Op. 1481.

Belone Oken 1816. Lehrb. Naturg. v. 3 (Zool.) (2):102. Suppressed under the plenary powers for the purposes of both priority and homonymy. Op. 225.

Bufonites Bertrand 1763. Dict. Univ. Foss. Propres Foss. Accid. v. 1:105. Published in a work rejected for nomenclatural purposes. Op. 592.

Buglossa Bertrand 1763. Dict. Univ. Foss. Propres Foss. Accid. v. 1:106. Published in a work rejected for nomenclatural purposes. Op. 592.

Calliongmus Linck 1790. Mag. Neuste. Phys. Naturgesch. Gotha v. 6 (no. 3):34. An incorrect subsequent spelling for *Callionymus* Linnaeus 1758. Dir. 56.

Callionimus Gouan 1770. Hist. Pisc.:121. An incorrect subsequent spelling for *Callionymus* Linnaeus 1758. Dir. 56.

Carcharias Cuvier 1817 [= 1816]. Règne Anim. v. 2:125. A junior homonym of *Carcharias* Rafinesque 1809. Op. 723.

Carcharias Müller & Henle [1839]. Syst. Beschr. Plagiost.:37. A junior homonym of *Carcharias* Rafinesque 1809 [1810]. Op. 723.

Carcharias Risso 1826. Hist. Nat. Princip. Prod. Europ. Mérid. v. 3:119. A junior homonym of *Carcharias* Rafinesque 1809. Op. 723.

Carcharinus Cloquet 1817. Dict. Sci. Nat. v. 7:7. An incorrect subsequent spelling for *Carcharhinus* Blainville 1816. Op. 723.

Carcharorhinus Agassiz 1846. Nomencl. Zool. Index Univ.:65. Unjustified emendation of *Carcharhinus* Blainville 1816. Op. 723.

Centracantha Rafinesque 1810. Indice Ittiol. Sicil.:67. (May 1810). An unjustified emendation of *Centracanthus* Rafinesque 1810. Op. 960.

Centracantus Rafinesque 1810. Caratt. Nuovi Gen. Nuove Spec. Anim. Piante Sicilia:42 (April 1810). Ruled under the plenary powers to be an incorrect original spelling for *Centracanthus* Rafinesque 1810. Op. 960.

Cephalopterus Powrie 1870. Trans. Edinb. Geol. Soc. v. 1:298. A junior homonym of *Cephalopterus* Geoffroy Saint-Hilaire 1809. Dir. 44.

Cephalopterus Risso 1810. Ichth. Nice:14. A junior homonym of *Cephalopterus* Geoffroy Saint-Hilaire 1809. Dir. 44.

Chaetoderma Swainson 1839. Nat. Hist. Fishes Amphib. Rept. Monocardian Animals v. 2:194, 327, 441. An incorrect original spelling for *Chaetodermis* Swainson 1839. Op. 764.

Chimaira Duméril 1856. Mém. Acad. Sci. Inst. France v. 27:155. An incorrect subsequent spelling for *Chimaera* Linnaeus 1758. Dir. 56.

Choetoderma Swainson 1839. Nat. Hist. Fishes Amphib. Rept. Monocardian Animals v. 2:194, 327, 441. An incorrect original spelling for *Chaetodermis* Swainson 1839. Op. 764.

Conger Cuvier 1817 [= 1816]. Règne Anim. (ed. 1) v. 2:231. A cheironym; deleted from the Official List. Dir. 87.

Conger Houttuyn 1764. Natuurl. Hist. (Deel 1) 7:103. A cheironym; not made available in the work cited. Dir. 87.

Conger Schaeffer 1760. Epistola Stud. Ichthyol. Meth.:20. Published in a work rejected for nomenclatural purposes in Opinion 345. Dir. 87.

Conger Walbaum 1792. Artedi Ichthyol. (ed. 2) v. 3:580. Published in a work rejected for nomenclatural purposes in Opinion 21. Dir. 87.

Coregonus Jarocki 1822. Zoologiia v. 4:35. A junior homonym of *Coregonus* Linnaeus 1758. Dir. 56.

Coregonus Lacepède 1803. Hist. Nat. Poiss. v. 5:239. A junior homonym of *Coregonus* Linnaeus 1758. Dir. 56.

Coryhaena Stiles 1922. Smithson. Misc. Coll. v. 73 (no. 1):73. An incorrect subsequent spelling for *Coryphaena* Linnaeus 1758. Dir. 56.

Curimata Walbaum 1792. Artedi Genera Piscium, Ichth. (ed. 2) v. 3:80. Published in the binomen *Salmo (Curimata) Marggravii* as a specific name, but mistakenly considered to be a generic name by some authors. Op. 772.

Discobatus Garman 1880. Proc. U.S. Natl. Mus. v. 3:523. A junior objective synonym of *Platyrhina* Müller & Henle 1838. Op. 345.

Draco Gouan 1770. Hist. Pisc.:117. A nomen nudum. Dir. 56.

Dracunculus Krøyer [1838-1840]. Danmarks Fiske v.1 (no. 8):1. A junior homonym of *Dracunculus* Reichard 1759. Dir. 102.

Drepanichthys Bonaparte 1831. Giorn. Acad. Sci. Lett. Arti. v. 52:172. A junior objective synonym of *Drepane* Cuvier 1831. Op. 1046.

Eleotris Gronovius 1763. Zoolphylac. Gronov. v. 1:83. Published in a work rejected for nomenclatural purposes in Opinion 417. Dir. 56.

Enixe Gistl 1848. Naturg. Thierr. hohere Schulen:ix. A junior objective synonym of *Drepane* Cuvier 1831. Op. 1046.

Episema Cope & Jordan 1877. Proc. Acad. Nat. Sci. Phila. 1877:77. A junior homonym of *Episema* Ochsenheimer 1816. Op. 494.

Falcatula Bertrand 1763. Dict. Univ. Foss. Propres Foss. Accid. v. 1:210. Published in a work rejected for nomenclatural purposes. Op. 592.

Gobio Bertrand 1763. Dict. Univ. Foss. Propres Foss. Accid. 1:250. Published in a work rejected for nomenclatural purposes. Op. 592.

Gymnothorax Cuvier [1800]. Leçons Anat. Comp. v. 1:tab 4. A nomen nudum. Dir. 56.

Hamiltonia Swainson 1839. Nat. Hist. Class. Fishes Amph. Rept. v. 2:176, 250. A junior objective synonym of *Chanda* Hamilton 1822. Op. 1121.

Harpochris Cantor 1849. J. Roy. Asiat. Soc. Bengal v. 18:1144. A junior objective synonym of *Drepane* Cuvier 1831. Op. 1046.

Holoptychius Egerton 1837. System. Stratig. Cat. Foss. Fish. Cab. Cole & Egerton:275, pl. 27. Suppressed under the plenary powers for the purposes of both priority and homonymy. Op. 930.

Holoptychus Buckland 1837. Geol. Min. Ref. Nat. Theology v. 2:43. Suppressed under the plenary powers for the purposes of both priority and homonymy. Op. 930.

Homalaspis Kaier 1932. Skr. Svalbard Ishavet, Oslo v. 52:14. A junior homonym of *Homalaspis* Milne Edwards 1863. Dir. 37.

Hoplites Agassiz 1846. Nomencl. Zool. Index Univ.:185. An invalid emendation of *Aplites* Rafinesque 1820. Suppressed under the plenary powers for the purposes of both priority and homonymy. Op. 353.

Hypacantha Rafinesque 1810. Indice Ittiol. Sicil.:67. An incorrect subsequent spelling for *Hypacantus* Rafinesque 1809. Op. 1124.

Hypacanthus Rafinesque 1810. Indice Ittiol. Sicil.:19. An incorrect subsequent spelling for *Hypacantus* Rafinesque 1809. Op. 1124.

Hypacantus Rafinesque 1809. Caratt. Nuovi Gen. Nuove Spec. Anim. Piante Sicilia:43. Suppressed under the plenary powers for the purposes of priority but not for those of homonymy. Op. 1124.

Ictiobus Rafinesque 1820. West. Rev. Misc. Mag. v. 2 (no. 5):299, 301. Ruled by plenary powers that the correct original spelling is *Ictiobus*. Op. 1582.

Lepidogaster Kent 1883. Handb. Marine Freshw. Fishes Brit. Is.:55, 56. An incorrect subsequent spelling for *Lepadogaster* Gouan 1770. Op. 638.

Leptocephalus Basilewsky 1855. Nouv. Mém. Soc. Imp. Nat. Moscou v. 10:234. A junior homonym of *Leptocephalus* Scopoli 1777. Dir. 87.

Leptocephalus Cuvier [1797]. Tabl. Élém. Hist. Nat. Anim.:329. A junior homonym of *Leptocephalus* Scopoli 1777. Dir. 87.

Leptocephalus Gmelin [1789]. In: Linnaeus, Syst. Nat. (ed. 13) v. 1 (3):1130. A junior homonym of *Leptocephalus* Scopoli 1777. Dir. 87.

Leptocephalus Gronovius 1763. Zoolphylac. Gronov. v. 1:135. Published in a work rejected for nomenclatural purposes in Opinion 261. Dir. 87.

Leptocephalus Scopoli 1777. Introd. Hist. Nat.:453. Suppressed under the plenary powers for the purposes of priority but not for those of homonymy in Opinion 93; placed on the Official Index in Direction 87. Dir. 87.

Limax Pallas 1774. Spicil. Zool. v. 10:19. A junior homonym of *Limax* Linnaeus 1758. Dir. 72.

Lucoscombrus Van der Hoeven 1855. Handb. Zool. (ed. 2) v. 2:367. A junior objective synonym of *Gempylus* Cuvier 1829. Op. 487.

Lychnoculus Murray 1877. Science Lectures for the People (9)4:132. Suppressed under the plenary powers for the purposes of priority but not for those of homonymy. Op. 1333.

Malapterus Jarocki 1822. Zoologiia v. 4:87. An incorrect subsequent spelling for *Malapterurus* Lacepède 1803. Dir. 56.

Malapturus Swainson 1838. Nat. Hist. Class. Fishes Amph. Rept. v. 1:348, 353. An incorrect subsequent spelling for *Malapterurus* Lacepède 1803. Dir. 56.

Micropus Gray 1831. Zool. Miscell. (1):20. A junior homonym of *Micropus* Wolf 1810. Op. 502.

Micropus Kner 1868. Sitz. Akad. Wiss. Wien (Math.-Nat. Cl.) v. 58 (no. 1):29, 322. A junior homonym of *Micropus* Wolf 1810. Op. 502.

Mugie Macklot 1830. Bijd. Natuurk. Wetensch. v. 5:177. An incorrect subsequent spelling for *Mugil* Linnaeus 1758. Dir. 56.

Mustellus Fischer von Waldheim 1813. Zoognosia (ed. 3) v. 1:78. An incorrect subsequent spelling for *Mustelus* Linck 1790. Dir. 56.

Ophidium Linnaeus 1766. Syst. Nat. (ed. 12) 1:431. An unjustified emendation of *Ophidion* Linnaeus 1758. Dir. 56.

Ornitoglossum Bertrand 1763. Dict. Univ. Foss. Propres. Foss. Accid. v. 2:87. Published in a work rejected for nomenclatural purposes. Op. 592.

Palaeoteuthis Roemer 1855. Palaeontographica v. 4:72. A junior homonym of *Palaeoteuthis* d'Orbigny [1850]. Op. 438.

Palinurus De Kay 1842. Zool. New York v. 4:118. A junior homonym of *Palinurus* Weber 1795. Op. 519.

Pedalion Swainson 1838. Nat. Hist. Class. Fishes Amph. Rept. v. 1:199. A junior homonym of *Pedalion* Dillwyn 1817. Op. 326.

Pharopterix Rüppell 1828. Atlas Reise nord. Afrika Ruppell (Senck. Nat. Ges.) v. 4 Fische (10):15. An incorrect original spelling of *Pharopteryx* Rüppell 1828. Op. 1082.

Pharopteryx Rüppell 1852. Verz. Mus. Senck. Naturf. Gesell. Aufges. Samml. v. 4:16. A junior homonym of *Pharopteryx* Rüppell 1828. Op. 1082.

Pinnularia Bertrand 1763. Dict. Univ. Foss. Propres Foss. Accid. v. 2:128. Published in a work rejected for nomenclatural purposes. Op. 592.

Plagusia Jarocki 1822. Zoologiia v. 4:295. A junior homonym of

Plagusia Latreille 1804. Op. 712.

Platessa Cuvier 1817 [= 1816]. Règne Anim. v. 2:220. A junior objective synonym of *Pleuronectes* Linnaeus 1758. Dir. 33.

Platychoerops Klunzinger 1879. Anz. Akad. Wiss. Wien v. 16:255. A junior homonym of *Platychoerops* Charlesworth 1855. Op. 1123.

Platyrrhynchus Bertrand 1763. Dict. Univ. Foss. Propres Foss. Accid. v. 2:130. Published in a work rejected for nomenclatural purposes. Op. 592.

Plectronita Bertrand 1763. Dict. Univ. Foss. Propres Foss. Accid. v. 2:130. Published in a work rejected for nomenclatural purposes. Op. 592.

Plectronites Bertrand 1763. Dict. Univ. Foss. Propres Foss. Accid. v. 2:130. Published in a work rejected for nomenclatural purposes. Op. 592.

Porcus Etienne Geoffroy Saint-Hilaire 1808. Description de l'-Egypte, ... Histoire Naturelle, Planches v. 1:15. Suppressed under the plenary powers for the purposes of priority but not for those of homonymy. Op. 1402.

Portellaria Bertrand 1763. Dict. Univ. Foss. Propres Foss. Accid. v. 2:137. Published in a work rejected for nomenclatural purposes. Op. 592.

Prionodon Müller & Henle [1839]. Syst. Beschr. Plagiost.:35. A junior homonym of *Prionodon* Horsfield 1822. Op. 723.

Psetites Bertrand 1763. Dict. Univ. Foss. Propres Foss. Accid. v. 2:147. Published in a work rejected for nomenclatural purposes. Op. 592.

Psittacus Catesby 1777. Pisc. Serp. Ins. Imagines:29. A junior homonym of *Psittacus* Linnaeus 1758. Dir. 44.

Pterolamia Springer 1950. Amer. Mus. Novit. No. 1451:7. A junior homonym of *Pterolamia* Breuning 1942. Op. 723.

Raphistoma Rafinesque 1815. Analyse Nature:89. Suppressed under the plenary powers for the purposes of both priority and homonymy. Op. 225.

Remora Forster 1771. Cat. Anim. N. Amer.:20. A cheironym; not made available in the work cited. Op. 242.

Remora Gouan 1770. Hist. Pisc.:10, [107], 183. A cheironym; not made available in the work cited. Op. 242.

Rhina Rafinesque 1810. Caratt. Nuovi Gen. Nuove Spec. Anim. Piante Sicilia:14. A junior homonym of *Rhina* Schneider [Bloch & Schneider] 1801. Op. 345.

Rhina Schaeffer 1760. Epistola Stud. Ichthyol. Meth.:20. Published in a work rejected for nomenclatural purposes. Op. 345.

Rhina Walbaum 1792. Artedi Ichthyol. (ed. 2) v. 3:580. Published in a work rejected for nomenclatural purposes in Opinion 21. Op. 345.

Rhiniodon Smith 1828. South African Commercial Advertiser v. 3 (145):2. Suppressed under the plenary powers for the purposes of priority but not for those of homonymy. Op. 1278.

Rhombiscus Bertrand 1763. Dict. Univ. Foss. Propres Foss. Accid. v. 2:157. Published in a work rejected for nomenclatural purposes. Op. 592.

Rhombites Bertrand 1763. Dict. Univ. Foss. Propres Foss. Accid. v. 2:157. Published in a work rejected for nomenclatural purposes. Op. 592.

Roloffia Stenholt Clausen 1966. Rev. Zool. Bot. Afr. v. 73:338. A junior objective synonym of *Callopanchax* Myers 1933. Op. 1010.

Rostrago Bertrand 1763. Dict. Univ. Foss. Propres Foss. Accid. v. 2:159. Published in a work rejected for nomenclatural purposes. Op. 592.

Salpa G. Edwards 1771. In: Catesby, Nat. Hist. Carolina (ed. 3) v. 2:17. Suppressed under the plenary powers for the purposes of both priority and homonymy. Op. 888.

Scopula Bertrand 1763. Dict. Univ. Foss. Propres Foss. Accid. v. 2:176. Published in a work rejected for nomenclatural purposes. Op. 592.

Serella Bertrand 1763. Dict. Univ. Foss. Propres Foss. Accid. v. 2:185. Published in a work rejected for nomenclatural purposes. Op. 592.

Siliquastrum Bertrand 1763. Dict. Univ. Foss. Propres Foss. Accid. v. 2:185. Published in a work rejected for nomenclatural purposes. Op. 592.

Smaris Cuvier 1814. Bull. Soc. Philomat. Paris, 1814:2. A junior homonym of *Smaris* Latreille 1796. Op. 960.

Sphenophorus Newberry 1890. Monogr. U.S. Geol. Surv. No. 16:91. A junior homonym of *Sphenophorus* Schoenherr 1838. Op. 572.

Syngnathus Rafinesque 1810. Indice Ittiol. Sicil.:57. A junior homonym of *Syngnathus* Linnaeus 1758. Dir. 56.

Teleosteus Volger 1860. Ber. Offenbach. Ber. Naturk. v. 1:37. Suppressed under the plenary powers for the purposes of priority but not for those of homonymy. Op. 223.

Teuthys Linck 1790. Mag. Neuste. Phys. Naturgesch. Gotha v. 6 (no. 3):32. An incorrect subsequent spelling for *Teuthis* Linnaeus, 1766. (Placed on the Official Index in Supplement to Direction 56.) Dir. 56.

Thinnus S. D. W. [? S. D. Wood] 1837. Analyst v. 18:108. Suppressed under the plenary powers for the purposes of priority but not for those of homonymy. Op. 809.

Thynnus Cuvier 1817 [= 1816]. Règne Anim. v. 2:313. A junior homonym of *Thynnus* Fabricius 1775. Op. 809.

Triglochis Müller & Henle 1837. Arch. Naturg. v. 3 (no. 1):396; Ber. Verh. preuss. Akad. Wiss. 1837:113. Suppressed under the plenary powers for the purposes of priority but not for those of homonymy. Op. 723.

Xiphiurus Smith 1847. Illustrations of the Zoology of South Africa, Pisces:pl. xxxi. Suppressed under the plenary powers for the purposes of priority but not for those of homonymy. Op. 1200.

NAMES PLACED ON THE OFFICIAL LIST OF FAMILY-GROUP NAMES IN ZOOLOGY

Bagridae Bleeker 1858. Act. Soc. Sci. Indo-Neerl. v. 4:42. Op. 1402.

Carcharhinidae Garman 1913. The Plagiostoma:106. Op. 723.

Carchariidae Müller & Henle 1839. Syst. Besch. Plagiost.:xvii. Op. 1459.

Centracanthidae Fowler 1925 (1829). Amer. Mus. Novit. No. 162:4. Given precedence over Maenidae Cuvier 1829. Author and date followed by those of the replaced name in parentheses. Op. 960.

Cobitidae Swainson 1839 in Lardner, D., The Cabinet Cyclopedia, v. 2:190. Op. 1500.

Cottidae Bonaparte [1832]. Saggio Distrib. Met. Anim. Vert.:90, 103. Correction of Cottini. Dir. 87.

Curimatinae Eigenmann & Eigenmann 1889. Ann. N. Y. Acad. Sci. v. 4:409. Op. 772.

Drepaneidae Gill 1872. Smithson. Misc. Coll. v. 11 (no. 247):8. Op. 1046.

Gambusiinae Gill 1893. Mem. Natl. Acad. Sci. v. 6:133. Dir. 41.

Gempylinae Goode & Bean 1895. Oceanic Ichth.:193. Op. 487.

Gerreidae Bleeker 1859. Act. Soc. Sci. Indo-Neerl. v. 6:xx. Correction of Gerreiformes. Op. 962.

Heterandriini Hubbs 1924. Misc. Publ. Mus. Zool. Univ. Mich. No. 13:7. Published as a name for a taxon below subfamily rank, so it does not require a standardized ending. Dir. 41.

Ipnopidae Jordan 1923. Stanford Univ. Publs. (Biol. Sci.) v. 3:155. Op. 1333.

Odontaspididae Müller & Henle [1839]. Syst. Beschr. Plagiost.: xvii. Correction of Odontaspides Müller & Henle [1839]. Op. 723. Also Op. 1459.

Osmeridae Regan 1913. Trans. Roy. Soc. Edinb. v. 49:290. Dir. 69.

Petromyzontidae Bonaparte 1832. Giorn. Arcadia 52:165, 189. Op. 1171.

Plethodidae Loomis 1900. Palaeontographica v. 46:229. Op. 921.

Pleuronectidae Rafinesque 1815. Analyse Nature:83. Correction by Bonaparte [1832], Saggio Distrib. Met. Anim. Vert.:96, 117, of Pleuronectia Rafinesque, 1815. Dir. 33.

Poeciliopsinae Hubbs 1924. Misc. Publ. Mus. Zool. Univ. Mich. No. 13:9. Dir. 41.

Prochilodinae Eigenmann 1910. Rept. Princeton Univ. Exped. Patag. v. 3 (no. 4):424. Op. 772.

Rhincodontidae Müller & Henle 1841. Syst. Beschr. Plagiost. v. 2:77. Originally as Rhinodontes, invalid under Article 32c (iii). Op. 1278.

Saccopharyngidae Bleeker 1859. Acta Soc. Sci. Indo-Neerl. v. 6:xxxiii. Op. 1603.

Sparidae Bonaparte [1832]. Saggio Distrib. Met. Anim. Vert.:91, 105. Dir. 34.

Stylephoridae Swainson 1839. Nat. Hist. Classif. v. 2:47. Op. 1603.

Thunninae Starks 1910. J. Morph. v. 21 (no. 1):79-80. Op. 809.

Names Placed on the Official Index of Rejected and Invalid Family-Group Names in Zoology

Acinaceidae McCulloch 1929. Mem. Aust. Mus. v. 5:258. Invalid because the name of type genus was suppressed under the plenary powers. Op. 487.

Centracantidae Fowler 1936. Mar. Fish. W. Africa v. 2:860. An incorrect subsequent spelling for Centracanthidae Fowler 1925 (1829). Op. 960.

Cottini Bonaparte [1832]. Saggio Distrib. Met. Anim. Vert.:90, 103. An incorrect original spelling for Cottidae Bonaparte [1832], but available for a category not having a prescribed ending. Dir. 87.

Drepanidae Gill 1872. Smithson. Misc. Coll. v. 11 (no. 247):8. Ruled to be an incorrect original spelling of Drepaneidae Gill 1872; a junior homonym of Drepanidae Boisduval [Nov. 1828]. Op. 1046.

Gerreiformes Bleeker 1859. Act. Soc. Sci. Indo-Neerl. v. 6:xx. An incorrect original spelling for Gerreidae Bleeker 1859. Op. 962.

Gerridae Günther 1862. Cat. Fish. Brit. Mus. v. 4:252. Ruled to be an incorrect subsequent spelling for Gerreidae Bleeker 1859. Op. 962.

Odontaspides Müller & Henle [1839]. Syst. Beschr. Plagiost.:xvii. An incorrect original spelling for Odontaspididae Müller & Henle [1839]. Op. 723.

Plethodontidae Hay 1929. 2nd. Bibliography & Cat. Foss. Verts. N. Amer. v. 1:736. An incorrect subsequent spelling for Plethodidae Loomis 1900. Op. 921.

Pleuronectia Rafinesque 1815. Analyse Nature:83. An incorrect original spelling for Pleuronectidae Rafinesque 1815. Dir. 33.

Pleuronectides Risso 1826. Hist. Nat. Princip. Prod. Europ. Mérid. v. 3:245. An incorrect subsequent spelling for Pleuronectidae (correction of Pleuronectia) Rafinesque 1815. Dir. 33.

Sparoides Cuvier 1817 [= 1816]. Règne Anim. (ed. 1) v. 2:269. Invalid because a vernacular (French) name. Dir. 34.

Thinninae Whitley 1955. Proc. Roy. Zool. Soc. N.S. Wales 1953-1954:51, 52. Invalid because the name of the type genus has been suppressed under the plenary powers. Op. 809.

Partial List of Names Not Placed on Any List, but Mentioned in Rulings or Proposals

Ablennes Jordan & Fordice 1886. Proc. U.S. Natl. Mus. 1886:342 etc. *Athlennes* ruled a lapsus calami, and emended to *Ablennes*. Op. 41.

Acanthophthalmus van Hasselt in Temminck 1824. Proposed to designate a type species and place on Official List. Case pending (no. 2738).

Acantophthalmus van Hasselt in Temminck 1824. Proposed to suppress this spelling and emend its listing on the Official Index. Case pending (no. 2738).

Acantopsis van Hasselt in Temminck 1824. Mentioned. Case pending (no. 2738).

Acipenser Linnaeus 1758. Type designation changed to "by Linnaean tautonymy." Dir. 56.

Acipenser Linnaeus 1758. Gender determined as masculine. Dir. 30.

acuminatus, Heniochus, (Linnaeus 1758). Has page priority over *Heniochus macrolepidotus*, but the latter is accepted and is the valid name. Op. 40.

Alburnus Heckel 1840. *Alburnus* dates from Rafinesque 1820; *Cyprinus alburnus* is type species for both genera. Op. 54.

Alburnus Rafinesque 1820. *Alburnus* dates from Rafinesque 1820, not Heckel 1840; *Cyprinus alburnus* is type for both. Op. 54.

Ambassis Cuvier 1829. Conserved by making *Centropomus macrodon* the type of *Aspro*, and thus a junior synonym of *Cheilodipterus*. Op. 23.

Ammodytes Linnaeus 1758. Gender determined as masculine. Dir. 30.

Anarhichas Linnaeus 1758. Gender determined as masculine. Dir. 30.

antarcticus, Bathylagus, Günther 1878. Proposal to place name on the Official List. Case pending (no. 1279).

Antennarius (Commerson) Lacepède 1798. *Antennarius* receives status from Lacepède's republication, thus predates *Histrio.* Op. 24.

Antennarius Cuvier 1817 [= 1816]. *Antennarius* receives status from Lacepède's republication in 1798, thus predates *Histrio* (1813). See also Opinion 89. Op. 24.

Argentina Linnaeus 1758. Proposal to place name on the Official List. Case pending (no. 1279).

Argentininae Bonaparte 1846. Proposal to place name on the Official List. (Correction of Argentinini) Case pending (no. 1279).

Argentinini Bonaparte 1846. Proposal to place name on Official Index. (Corrected to Argentininae.) Case pending (no. 1279).

Argyreiosus Lacepède 1803. Hist. Nat. Poiss. 4:566. Declared to be a junior synonym of *Selene* Lacepède 1803, published in the same work. Op. 569.

Aspro (Commerson) Lacepède 1802. Type established as *Centropomus macrodon. Aspro* declared to be a junior objective synonym of *Cheilodipterus* Lacepède 1802. Op. 23.

Atherina Linnaeus 1758. Gender determined as feminine. Dir. 30.

Athlennes Jordan & Fordice 1886. Proc. U.S. Natl. Mus. 1886:342 etc. Ruled to be a *lapsus calami* for *Ablennes*, to which it is emended. Op. 41.

aureus, Otolithus, Richardson 1846. Proposal to place name on the Official List. Case pending (no. 1744).

aureus, Chromis, Steindachner 1864. Proposal to place name on the Official List. Case pending (no. 1743).

Bathylagidae Gill 1884. Proposal to place name on the Official List. Case pending (no. 1279).

Bathylagus Günther 1878. Proposal to place name on the Official List. Case pending (no. 1279).

bicirrhosum Cuvier 1829. Proposal to conserve and to place on the Official List; also to confirm as type species of *Osteoglossum.* Case pending (no. 2659).

blennioides, Etheostoma, Rafinesque 1819. Agassiz's designation as type species of *Etheostoma* is upheld. Op. 14.

Blennius Linnaeus 1758. Official List entry updated. Dir. 56.

Blennius Linnaeus 1758. Gender determined as masculine. Dir. 30.

bostoniensis, Muraena, Lesueur 1817. J. Acad. Nat. Sci. Phila. 1(5). Declared a junior synonym of *M. rostrata* Lesueur 1817, in the same work. Op. 569.

bullaris, Cyprinus, Rafinesque 1817 (Dec.). *Cyprinus corporalis* Mitchill 1817 (Aug.) judged to have priority, despite its short description. Op. 52.

Callionymus Linnaeus 1758. Official List entry updated. Dir. 56.

Callionymus Linnaeus 1758. Gender determined as masculine. Dir. 30.

Carapus Rafinesque 1810. Declared to be a monotypic genus, with type species *Gymnotus acus* Linnaeus. Op. 42.

Carcharias Rafinesque 1810. Determined to be monotypic, with type *Carcharias taurus* Rafinesque. *Carcharias* May thus replace *Odontaspis* Agassiz. Op. 47. (See also Op. 723, Op. 1459.)

Ceratichthys Baird MS. Girard 1856. Proc. Acad. Nat. Sci. Phila. 1856:212. Type established as *Ceratichthys biguttatus*; *Ceratichthys* is declared to be a junior synonym of *Nocomis* Girard 1856. Op. 22.

Ceraticthys Baird & Girard 1853. Proc. Acad. Nat. Sci. Phila. 1853:390. Type established as *Ceratichthys vigilax* Baird & Girard 1853. Op. 22.

Chimaera Linnaeus 1758. Type designation changed to "by Linnaean tautonymy." Dir. 56.

Chimaera Linnaeus 1758. Gender determined as feminine. Dir. 30.

cinnamomea, Cobitis McClelland 1839. Mentioned. Case pending (no. 2738).

Cliola Girard 1856. Status uncertain until type species determined; if type is *Ceraticthys vigilax*, it is a junior synonym of *Ceraticthys* Baird & Girard 1853. Op. 22.

Clupea Linnaeus 1758. Official List entry updated. Dir. 56.

Clupea Linnaeus 1758. Gender determined as feminine. Dir. 30.

Conger Oken 1817. Gender determined as masculine. Dir. 30.

Coregonus Linnaeus 1758. Gender determined as masculine. Dir. 30.

cornutus, Cyprinus, Mitchill 1817 (Aug.). Judged to have priority over *Cyprinus megalops* Rafinesque 1817 (Dec.) despite short description. Op. 52.

corporalis, Cyprinus, Mitchill 1817 (Aug.). Judged to have priority over *Cyprinus bullaris* Rafinesque 1817 (Dec.) despite short description. Op. 52.

Coryphaena Linnaeus 1758. Official List entry updated. Dir. 56.

Coryphaena Linnaeus 1758. Gender determined as feminine. Dir. 30.

Cottus Linnaeus 1758. Official List entry completed. Dir. 87.

Cottus Linnaeus 1758. Gender determined as masculine. Dir. 30.

Cyclopterus Linnaeus 1758. Type designation changed to "by Linnaean tautonymy." Dir. 56.

Cyclopterus Linnaeus 1758. Gender determined as masculine. Dir. 30.

Cyprinus Linnaeus 1758. Official List entry updated. Dir. 56.

Cyprinus Linnaeus 1758. Gender determined as masculine. Dir. 30.

Cypselurus Swainson 1838. Ruled to be correct spelling of genus, and *Cypsilurus* a misprint. Op. 26.

Cypsilurus Swainson 1838. Ruled to be a misprint for *Cypselurus.* Op. 26.

Diodon Linnaeus 1758. Syst. Nat. (ed. 10) v. 1:334. *Diodon* was placed on the Official List with name number 257, but was later withdrawn. Op. 77.

Diodon Linnaeus 1758. Gender determined as masculine. Dir. 30.

Dobula Rafinesque 1820. *Dobula* is shown to date from Rafinesque 1820 despite the absence of a designated type species. Op. 54.

dracunculus, Callionymus Linnaeus 1758. Proposal to suppress and place on the Official Index. Case pending (no. 2688).

Echeneis Linnaeus 1758. Entry on the Official List emended; *Echeneis naucrates* (emendation of *neucrates*) declared to be the type species. Op. 242.

Echeneis Linnaeus 1758. Gender determined as feminine. Dir. 30.

Eleotris Schneider [Bloch & Schneider] 1801. Gender determined as feminine. Dir. 30.

Elipesurus Schomburgk 1843. Proposal to place name on the Official Index. Case pending (no. 1825).

Ellipesurus Günther 1870. Proposal to place name on the Official Index. Case pending (no. 1825).

Epinephelus Bloch 1793. Gender determined as masculine. Dir. 30.

erectus, Hippocampus, Perry 1810. Refusal to use the plenary powers to suppress the species. Op. 870.

eriox, Salmo, Linnaeus 1758. *Salmo eriox* has page priority over *Salmo fario* and *Salmo trutta,* but *Salmo fario* is the accepted and valid name for this taxon. Op. 40.

Esox Linnaeus 1758. Official List entry updated. Dir. 56.

Esox Linnaeus 1758. Gender determined as masculine. Dir. 30.

Esox Linnaeus 1758. Type is *Esox lucius* Linnaeus, designated by Jordan & Gilbert 1882. Op. 58.

Etheostoma Rafinesque 1819. Agassiz's designation of *Etheostoma blennioides* as type species is upheld. Op. 14.

fario, Salmo, Linnaeus 1758. *Salmo eriox* has page priority over *Salmo trutta* and *Salmo fario,* but the latter is the accepted name for this taxon, and is thus the valid name. Op. 40.

fasciatus, Noemacheilus van Hasselt in Temminck 1824. Mentioned. Case pending (no. 2738).

Fistularia Linnaeus 1758. Gender determined as feminine. Dir. 30.

flagellum, Saccopharynx Cuvier 1829. Proposal to rule that Cuvier's designation of this species as type of *Saccopharynx* is valid, and to place *flagellum* on the Official List. Case pending (no. 2625).

Gadus Linnaeus 1758. Official List entry updated. Dir. 56.

Gadus Linnaeus 1758. Gender determined as masculine. Dir. 30.

Gasterosteus Linnaeus 1758. Official List entry updated. Dir. 56.

Gasterosteus Linnaeus 1758. Gender determined as masculine. Dir. 30.

Gobius Linnaeus 1758. Official List entry updated. Dir. 56.

Gobius Linnaeus 1758. Gender determined as masculine. Dir. 30.

grayi, Halicampus, Kaup 1856. Declared to take priority over *Syngnathus koilomatodon* Bleeker, though described in synonymy. Op. 53.

grohmanni, Pleuronectes, Bonaparte 1837. Proposal to suppress name and place on the Official Index. Case pending (no. 1579).

Gymnothorax Bloch 1795. Gender determined as masculine. Dir. 30.

Gymnotus Linnaeus 1758. Follow-up to Opinion 16. Request to specialists for information on status of this name. Case pending (no. 276).

gyrinus, Eleotris, Cuvier & Valenciennes 1837. Replaced as type of *Eleotris* Schneider [Bloch & Schneider] 1801. Dir. 56.

hakonensis, Leuciscus, Günther 1880. Shore Fishes, Challenger:72. *Leuciscus hakuensis* judged to be a lapsus calami or typographic error for this name. Op. 63.

hakuensis, Leuciscus, Günther 1880. Shore Fishes, Challenger:72. Judged to be a lapsus calami or typographic error for *Leuciscus hakonensis.* Op. 63.

Histrio Fischer 1813. *Antennarius* receives status from Lacepède's republication in 1798, thus predates *Histrio* (1813). Op. 24.

hystrix, Trygon, Garman 1878. Proposal to place name on the Official List. Case pending (no 1825).

Ischnosoma Spix in Spix & Agassiz. A manuscript name mentioned in a case pending (no. 2659).

irideus, Salmo, Gibbons 1855. Proc. Calif. Acad. Nat. Sci. 1855:36. *Salmo iridia* ruled to be a lapsus calami for *Salmo irideus.* Op. 60.

iridia, Salmo, Gibbons 1855. Proc. Calif. Acad. Nat. Sci. 1855:36. Ruled to be a lapsus calami for *irideus.* Op. 60.

japonica, Cestracion, Duméril 1865. Proposal to suppress name and place on the Official Index. Case pending (no. 1951).

japonicus, Heterodontus, Maclay & Macleay 1884. Proposal to place name on the Official List. Case pending (no. 1951).

kessleri, Arnoglossus, Schmidt 1915. Proposal to place name on the Official List. Case pending (no. 1579).

koilomatodon, Syngnathus, Bleeker "about 1865". *Halicampus grayi* Kaup declared to take priority despite being described in synonymy. Op. 53.

kuhlii, Cobitis, Valenciennes in Cuvier & Valenciennes 1846. Proposal to make this species the type species of *Acanthophthalmus* van Hasselt 1824 and to place on Official List. Case pending (no. 2738).

Leptocephalus Gronovius 1763. This name given priority over any subsequent genus with same type species, in this case *Conger.* Op. 44.

Lophius Linnaeus 1758. Official List entry updated. Dir. 56.

Lophius Linnaeus 1758. Gender determined as masculine. Dir. 30.

macrodon, Centropomus, (?) (Commerson) Lacepède 1802. Declared to be the type of *Aspro,* making it a junior objective synonym of *Cheilodipterus* and protecting *Ambassis.* Op. 23.

macrolepidotus, Heniochus, (Linnaeus 1758). *Heniochus accuminatus* has page priority, but this is the accepted name for this taxon, and thus valid. Op. 40.

Malapterurus Lacepède 1803. Gender determined as masculine. Dir. 30.

megalops, Cyprinus, Rafinesque 1817 (Dec.). *Cyprinus cornutus* Mitchill 1817 (Aug.) is judged to have priority, despite its short description. Op. 52.

melagaster, Labrus, Bloch 1792. Request to suppress for purposes of priority and place on Official List. Case pending (no. 2594).

melanotheron, Sarotherodon, Rüppell 1852. Request to conserve. Case pending (no. 2594).

Mormyrus Linnaeus 1758. Official List entry updated. Dir. 56.

Mormyrus Linnaeus 1758. Gender determined as masculine. Dir. 30.

Mugil Linnaeus 1758. Gender determined as masculine. Dir. 30.

Mullus Linnaeus 1758. Official List entry updated. Dir. 56.

Mullus Linnaeus 1758. Gender determined as masculine. Dir. 30.

multilineata, Poecilia, Lesueur 1821. J. Acad. Nat. Sci. Phila. v. 2 (no. 1). Declared a junior synonym of *Mollienesia latipinna* Lesueur 1821 in the same work. Op. 569.

Muraena Linnaeus 1758. Syst. Nat. (ed. 10) v. 1:244. *Muraena* was placed on the Official List with name number 264, but was later removed. Op. 77.

Muraena Linnaeus 1758. Gender determined as feminine. Dir. 30.

Mustelus Linck 1790. Gender determined as masculine. Dir. 30.

Myxine Linnaeus 1758. Gender determined as feminine. Dir. 30.

Ophidion Linnaeus 1758. Official List entry updated. Dir. 56.

Ophidion Linnaeus 1758. Gender determined as neuter. Dir. 30.

Osmerus Linnaeus 1758. Official List entry emended and extended, type species designated and subgeneric status validated. Dir. 69.

Osmerus Linnaeus 1758. Gender determined as masculine. Dir. 30.

Osteoglossum Cuvier 1829. Request to fix its type species and to place on the Official List. Case pending (no. 2659).

oxyrhynchus, Anabas, Boulenger 1902. Ann. Mus. R. Congo Belge (Zool.), ser. 1, v. 2 (no. 2):52. Proposed to place on the Official List. Case pending (no. 2595).

ovalis, Heliastes Steindachner 1900. Request to conserve and place on the Official List. Case pending (no. 2681).

ovalis, Chromis Steindachner 1866. Mentioned as a senior secondary homonym of *Heliastes ovalis* Steindachner 1900. Case pending (no. 2681).

Pachygnathus Swainson 1839. Ruled to be correct spelling of "Pachynathus," and thus preoccupied by *Pachygnathus* in arachnids. Op. 29.

Pachynathus Swainson 1839. Ruled to be misprint for *Pachygnathus*, and thus preoccupied by *Pachygnathus* in arachnids. Op. 29.

Pangio Blyth 1860. Mention. Case pending (no. 2738).

pangio, Cobitis Hamilton 1822. Mention. Case pending (no. 2738).

peckianus, Syngnathus, Storer 1839. Fishes of Massachusetts:163, In: Repts. Ichthy. Herp. Mass. Declared a junior synonym of *S. fuscus* Storer 1839 in the same work. Op. 569.

Perca Linnaeus 1758. Official List entry updated. Dir. 56.

Perca Linnaeus 1758. Gender determined as feminine. Dir. 30.

Pharopteryx Rüppell 1828. *Plesiops* Cuvier 1817 [= 1816] is provisionally accepted as the senior synonym. Op. 19.

Phoxinus Agassiz 1835. *Phoxinus* dates from Rafinesque 1820; *Cyprinus phoxinus* is type species for both *Phoxinus* Rafinesque and *Phoxinus* Agassiz. Op. 54.

Phoxinus Rafinesque 1820. *Phoxinus* dates from Rafinesque, preceding *Phoxinus* Agassiz; *Cyprinus phoxinus* is type species. Op. 54.

pisonis, Gobius, Gmelin [1789]. Established as type of *Eleotris* Schneider [Bloch & Schneider] 1801. Dir. 56.

Plagyrus Rafinesque 1820. Ichth. Ohiensis:48-50. Established *Rutilus plagyrus* Rafinesque as type of genus. Op. 33.

Plesiops Cuvier 1817 [= 1816]. Provisionally accepted as senior synonym of *Pharopteryx* Rüppell 1828. Op. 19.

Pleuronectes Linnaeus 1758. Rules that the type species was not designated by Flemming (1822). Actual type not determined. Op. 68.

Polynemus Linnaeus 1758. Gender determined as masculine. Dir. 30.

Potamotrygon Garman 1878. Proposal to place name on the Official List. Case pending (no. 1825).

Potamotrygonidae Garman 1878. Proposal to place name on the Official List. Case pending (no. 1825).

psittacus, Scarus, Forsskål 1775. Proposal to place name on the Official List. Case pending (no. 1721).

Puntius Hamilton 1822. Proposal to place name on the Official List. Case pending (no. 1308).

pusillus, Callionymus Delaroche 1809. Proposal to conserve and place name on the Official List. Case pending (no. 2688).

rivulatus, Scarus, Forsskål 1775. Proposal to place name on the Official List. Case pending (no. 1721).

Ruppelia Swainson 1839. Ruled to be a typographical error for *Rüppellia*. Op. 27.

Rutilus Rafinesque 1820. Ichth. Ohiensis:48-50. Established *Cyprinus rutilus* Linnaeus as the type of the genus. Op. 33.

Rüppellia Swainson 1839. Ruled to be correct spelling of genus in question. Op. 27.

Salmo Linnaeus 1758. Official List entry updated. Dir. 56.

Salmo Linnaeus 1758. Gender determined as masculine. Dir. 30.

Sarotherodon Ruüppell 1852. Proposal to place name on the Official List. Case pending (no. 2594).

Scarus Forsskål 1775. Proposal to place name on the Official List. Case pending (no. 1721).

Sciaena Linnaeus 1758. *Sciaena* was placed on the Official List in Opinion 93, but was later temporarily removed from the list because of "major defects" corrected in Opinion 988. Op. 93.

Sciaena Linnaeus 1758. Gender determined as feminine. Dir. 30.

Scomber Linnaeus 1758. Official List entry updated. Dir. 56.

Scomber Linnaeus 1758. Gender determined as masculine. Dir. 30.

Scorpaena Linnaeus 1758. Official List entry updated. Dir. 56.

Scorpaena Linnaeus 1758. Gender determined as feminine. Dir. 30.

scorpioides, Gobius, Collett 1874. Refusal to use plenary powers to set aside a first reviser selection as type of *Lebetus* Op. 880.

Serranus Cuvier 1817 [= 1816]. Gender determined as masculine. Dir. 30.

Siganidae Rutter 1897. Proposal to place name on the Official List. Case pending (no. 1721).

Siganus Forsskål 1775. Proposal to place name on the Official List. Case pending (no. 1721).

Silurus Linnaeus 1758. Type designation changed to "by Linnaean tautonymy." Dir. 56.

Silurus Linnaeus 1758. Gender determined as masculine. Dir. 30.

sophore, Cyprinus, Hamilton 1822. Proposal to place name on the Official List. Case pending (no. 1308).

Sparus Linnaeus 1758. Rules that Fleming (1828) did not designate the type species. The actual type is not determined here. Op. 69.

sphyraena, Argentina, Linnaeus 1758. Proposal to place name on the Official List. Case pending (no. 1279).

spinicauda, Elipesurus, Schomburgk 1843. Proposal to place name on the Official Index. Case pending (no. 1825).

Stromateus Linnaeus 1758. Follow-up to Opinion 16. Request to specialists for information on status of this name. Case pending (no. 276).

Syngnathus Linnaeus 1758. Official List entry updated. Dir. 56.

Syngnathus Linnaeus 1758. Rules that the type species has never been designated. *Syngnathus acus* Linnaeus 1758 is designated here. Op. 45.

Syngnathus Linnaeus 1758. Gender of name declared to be masculine. Dir. 100.

taenia, Cobitis Linnaeus 1758. Mention. Case pending (no. 2738).

Teuthis Linnaeus 1758. Gender determined as feminine. Dir. 30.

Teuthis Linnaeus 1766. *Teuthis* was placed on the Official List with name number 447, but was temporarily removed because of "major defects" in the entry. Op. 93.

Teuthis Linnaeus 1766. Proposal to suppress name and place on the Official Index. Case pending (no. 1721).

thori, Arnoglossus, Kyle 1913. Proposal to place name on the Official List. Case pending (no. 1579).

Trachinus Linnaeus 1758. Gender determined as masculine. Dir. 30.

trutta, Salmo, Linnaeus 1758. *Salmo eriox* has page priority among the three names discussed, but *Salmo fario* is the accepted and thus the valid name. Op. 40.

Uranoscopus Linnaeus 1758. Gender determined as masculine. Dir. 30.

vandellii, Osteoglossum Cuvier 1829. Proposal to suppress and place on the Official Index. Case pending (no. 2659).

velox, Chromis Jenkins 1901. Mentioned. Case pending (no. 2681).

vigilax, Ceratichthys, Baird & Girard 1853. Proc. Acad. Nat. Sci. Phila. 1853:390. Declared to be type species of *Ceratichthys* Baird & Girard 1853. Op. 22.

Xiphias Linnaeus 1758. Gender determined as masculine. Dir. 30.

Zeus Linnaeus 1758. Official List entry updated. Dir. 56.

Zeus Linnaeus 1758. Gender determined as masculine. Dir. 30.

Titles Placed on the Official List of Works in Zoology

Brookes, J. 1828. *A catalogue of the anatomical and zoological museum of Joshua Brookes, Esq., F.R.S. F.L.S. etc.* (Part 1, London.) Approved as available for zoological nomenclature. Op. 1080.

Cuvier, G. [1800]-1805. *Leçons d'Anatomie Comparée ... Recueilles et publiées sous ses yeux par C. Duméril.* (5 volumes.) Latin names in systematic tables in Volume 1 are available provided they are provided with "indications" through the citation of bibliographical references on page xix of the Introduction. Dir. 32.

Cuvier, G. and A. Valenciennes 1828-1850. *Histoire Naturelle des Poissons.* (Paris.) The authorship and dates of publication are to be cited as specified in the tables published in Opinion 580. Op. 580.

Edwards, G. 1771. *A Catalogue of the Animals and Plants represented in Catesby's "Natural History of Carolina." With the Linnaean Names.* (Appended to Edwards's (1771) edition of Catesby's *Natural History of Carolina.*). The names used by Edwards in the first column of this concordance, but not those used by Catesby in the original (1743) edition and given in the second column, are available from 1771. Op. 259.

Fabricius, J. C. all works. Any intermediate term placed between a generic and a specific name is not to be treated as having acquired the status of a subgeneric name from having been published in this manner. Op. 279.

Linnaeus, C. all works. Any intermediate term placed between a generic and a specific name is not to be treated as having acquired the status of a subgeneric name from having been published in this manner. Op. 279.

Pallas, P. S. 1811-[1814]. *Zoographia Rosso-asiatica.* (3 volumes. Vols. 1 & 2, 1811; Vol. 3 [1814].) Op. 212.

Scopoli, G. A. 1777. *Introductio ad Historiam Naturalem.* The author is ruled to have applied the principles of binominal nomenclature, confirming a provisional ruling in Opinion 160. Op. 329.

Titles Placed on the Official Index of Rejected and Invalid Works in Zoology

Bartram, W. 1791. *Travels through North and South Carolina, Georgia, East and West Florida, the Cherokee Country, the extensive territories of the Muscogulges or Creek Confederacy, and the Country of the Chactaws.* (Philadelphia edition) Rejected for nomenclatural purposes because the author did not apply the principles of binominal nomenclature. Op. 447.

Bartram, W. 1792. *Travels through North and South Carolina, Georgia, East and West Florida, the Cherokee Country, the extensive territories of the Muscogulges or Creek Confederacy, and the Country of the Chactaws.* (London edition) Rejected for nomenclatural purposes because the author did not apply the principles of binominal nomenclature. Op. 447.

Bartram, W. 1792. *Travels through North and South Carolina, Georgia, East and West Florida, the Cherokee Country, the extensive territories of the Muscogulges or Creek Confederacy, and the Country of the Chactaws.* (Dublin edition) Rejected for nomenclatural purposes because the author did not apply the principles of binominal nomenclature. Op. 447.

Bertrand, E. 1763. *Dictionnaire Universel des Fossiles Propres et des Fossiles Accidentels.* Rejected for nomenclatural purposes because the author did not apply the principles of binominal nomenclature. Op. 592.

Borlase, W. 1758. *The Natural History of Cornwall.* Rejected for nomenclatural purposes because the author did not apply the principles of binominal nomenclature. Op. 332.

Browne, P. 1789. *Civil and Natural History of Jamaica.* (2nd edition) First published in 1756, before the starting-point of zoological nomenclature. Suppressed under the plenary powers for nomenclatural purposes in Opinion 89. Dir. 32.

Catesby, M. 1771. *The Natural History of Carolina.* (edition published by G. Edwards. 2 volumes) Suppressed under the plenary powers in Opinion 89. This suppression does not apply to names employed by Edwards in his appended concordance. Op. 259.

Commerson, F. (footnotes in Lacepède) 1803. *Histoire Naturelle des Poissons.* Suppressed under the plenary powers for nomenclatural purposes in Opinion 89. Dir. 32.

Cornide, J. 1788. *Ensayo de una historia de los Peces y otras producciones marinas de la Costa de Galicia, arreglado al sistema del caballero Carlos Linneo.* [Corruna.] Rejected for nomenclatural purposes because the author did not apply the principles of binominal nomenclature. Op. 799.

Duhamel du Monceau, H. L. 1769-1782. *Traité général des Pêches, et Histoire des Poissons qu'elles fournissent, tant pour la substance des Hommes, que pour plusiers autres usages qui on rapport aux Arts et Commerce.* (Paris.) Rejected for nomenclatural purposes because the author did not apply the principles of binominal nomenclature. Op. 859.

Eberhard, J. P. 1768. *Versuch eines neuen entwurfs der Thiergeschichte.* Rejected for nomenclatural purposes because the author did not apply the principles of binominal nomenclature. Op. 445.

Fabricius, J. C. all works. Any intermediate term placed between a generic and a specific name is not to be treated has having acquired the status of a subgeneric name from having been published in this manner. Op. 279.

Fermin, P. 1765. *Histoire naturelle de la Hollande équinoxiale.* Rejected for nomenclatural purposes because the author did not apply the principles of binominal nomenclature. Op. 660.

Gesner, J. 1758. *Tractatus physicus de Petrifactis.* Suppressed under the plenary powers for nomenclatural purposes. Op. 230.

Gmelin, J. F. 1793. Linnaeus' *Systema Naturae.* (13th edition. Volume 3.) Suppressed under the plenary powers for nomenclatural purposes. Op. 296.

Gmelin, P. F. 1758-1777. *Onomatologia medica completa seu Onomatologia Historiae naturalis.* (7 volumes.) Suppressed under the plenary powers for nomenclatural purposes in Opinion 123. Dir. 32.

Gronovius, L. T. 1762. Animalium belgicorum observatorum Centuria Quinta. *Acta Helv. Phys.-Math.-Botan.-Med.* 5.. Rejected for nomenclatural purposes because the author did not apply the principles of binominal nomenclature. Op. 332.

Gronovius, L. T. 1763-1781. *Zoophylacium Gronovianum.* (3 parts.) Rejected for nomenclatural purposes because the author did not apply the principles of binominal nomenclature. The status of this work was also discussed in Opinions 20 and 89. Op. 261.

Hasselquist, F. 1757. *Iter Palaestinum.* A work rejected in Opinion 57 because published before the starting point of zoological nomenclature. Dir. 32.

Hasselquist, F. 1762. *D. F. Hasselquists ... Reise nach Palästina.* A German translation by T. H. Gadebusch of the *Iter Palaestinum* of 1757. Rejected for nomenclatural purposes in Opinion 57 because the names therein were not reinforced by adoption or acceptance. Dir. 32.

Hemprich, F. G. & C. G. Ehrenberg 1828. *Symbolae Physicae seu Icones et Descriptiones Piscium.* (Mittler, Berlin.) Suppressed under the plenary powers for nomenclatural purposes. Op. 1132.

Herrera, A. L. 1901-1904. *Nouvelle Nomenclature des Etres organisés et des Minéraux.* 88 pp. Issued in installments with the *Memorias* of the Sociedad Cientifica 'Antonio Alizate.' The designations used for animals in this paper were declared in Opinion 72 to be formulae, not names, and accordingly to possess no status in zoological nomenclature. Dir. 32.

Houttuyn, M. 1780-1785. *Natuurlyke Historie.* (Volume 3, 5 parts.) Suppressed under the plenary powers for nomenclatural purposes. Op. 296.

Houttuyn, M. 1787. *Animalium Musaei Houttuiniani Index.* Suppressed under the plenary powers for nomenclatural purposes. Op. 380.

Linck, J. H. 1783-1787. *Index Musaei Linckiani, oder kurzes systematisches Verzeichnis der vornehmsten Stücke der Linckischen Naturaliensammlung zu Leipzig.* (3 vols. v. 1, 1783; v. 2, 1786; Vol. 3, 1787.) Suppressed for nomenclatural purposes under the plenary powers. Op. 701.

Linnaeus, C. 1768. *Systema Naturae,* Volume 3 (Regnum Lapideum.) (12th edition.) Suppressed under the plenary powers for nomenclatural purposes. Op. 296.

Linnaeus, C. all works. Any intermediate term placed between a generic and a specific name is not to be treated as having acquired the status of a subgeneric name from having been published in this manner. Op. 279.

Meuschen, F. C. 1778. *Museum Gronovianum.* Rejected for nomenclatural purposes because it was not properly published, and because the author did not apply the principles of binominal nomenclature. Op. 260.

Meuschen, F. C. 1781. Index to Gronovius, *Zoophylacium Gronovianum.* Rejected for nomenclatural purposes because the author did not apply the principles of binominal nomenclature. Op. 261.

Müller, P. L. S., of Erlangen (?), 1775-1781. *Neuer Schauplatz der Natur, nach den richtigsten Beobachtungen und Versuchen, in alphabetischer Ordnung; durch eine Gesellschaft der Gelehrten.* (10 volumes.) Suppressed under the plenary powers for nomenclatural purposes in Opinion 89. Dir. 32.

Müller, P. L. S. 1766. *Deliciae Naturae selectae; oder auslerlesenes Naturalien-Cabinet, welches aus den drey Reichen der Natur zeiget, was von curiosen Liebhabern aufbehalten und gesammelt zu werden verdient. Ehemals herausgegeben von Georg Wolfgang Knorr; fortgesetzt von.* 3 vols. (ed. 1, 1766; ed. 2, 1778; Dutch trans., 1771). Suppressed under the plenary powers for nomenclatural purposes. Op. 701.

Oken, L. 1815-1816. *Okens Lehrbuch der Naturgeschichte.* (Volume 3, Zoology.) Rejected for nomenclatural purposes because the author did not apply the principles of binominal nomenclature. Op. 417.

Schaeffer, J. C. 1760. *Epistola ad Regio-Borussican Societatem Litterariam Duisbergensem de Studi ichthyologici facilior ac tutiori Methodo.* Rejected for nomenclatural purposes because the author did not apply the principles of binominal nomenclature. Op. 345.

Turton, W. 1806. *A General System of Nature,* Volume 7. [2nd edition.] Suppressed under the plenary powers for nomenclatural purposes. Op. 296.

Valmont de Bomare, J. C. 1764. *Dictionnaire Raisonée Universelle d'Histoire Naturelle.* Also suppressed editions of 1768, 1775 and 1791. Suppressed under the plenary powers for nomenclatural purposes in Opinion 89. Dir. 32.

Walch, J.E.I. 1768-1774. *Die Naturgeschichte der Versteinerungen zur Erläuterung der Knorrischen Sammlung von Merkwürdigkeiten der Natur.* (Nürnberg.) Rejected for nomenclatural purposes because the author did not apply the principles of binominal nomenclature. Op. 529.